VARIETY

WHO'S WHO
IN SHOW BUSINESS

Revised Edition

WHO'S WHO
IN SHOW BUSINESS

Revised Edition

Mike Kaplan
Editor

Garland Publishing, Inc.
New York & London
1985

Distribution to bookstores by Kampmann and Co., Inc., New York

Library of Congress Cataloging-in-Publication Data

Main entry under title:

Variety's who's who in show business.

1. Performing arts—Biography—Dictionaries.
I. Kaplan, Mike, 1918–   II. Daily Variety.
PN1583.V37   1985   790.2′092′2 [B]   85-20578
ISBN 0-8240-9806-4
ISBN 0-8240-4191-7 (pbk. paper)

Manufactured in the United States of America

ABBREVIATIONS

AADA American Academy of Dramatic Art

AAMDA American Academy of Music and Dramatic Art

ABT American Ballet Theatre

Act actor, actress

ACT American Conservatory Theatre

ADMN administration, administrator

ADV advertising

ADVR advisor

AFF affairs

AK Alaska

AL Alabama

ANI Animation, animator

AR Arkansas

ARR arrangements

AS American Samoa

ASSO associate

ASST assistant

AZ Arizona

b. born

B of brother of

BCST broadcast

BCSTNG broadcasting

BD CHMN board chairman

BR branch

CA California

CAM camera

CEO Chief Executive Officer

CHF chief

CHG charge

CHMN chairman

CIN cinematographer, cinematography

CLASS classical

CM Northern Mariana Islands

CNSL counsel

CNSLTS consultants

CO Colorado

COLLAB collaborator, collaborating

COMP Composer

COMPS Compositions

CONT controller

COO chief operating officer

CORP corporation

CORR Correspondent

COS costume

CREA creative, creator

CT Connecticut

CZ Canal Zone

D of daughter of

DC District of Columbia

DE Delaware

DEL delegate

DIR director

DIST district

DIV division

DOM domestic

DSGN design, designer

DVLP Development

e. education

E East, Eastern

EDTR editor

ENG engineer, engineering

ENT entertainment, entertainer

ENTS Enterprises

EQPT Equipment

EXEC executive

EXP export

F of father of

FIN Finance, financing, financial

FL Florida

GA Georgia

GEN General

GU Guam

H of Husband of

HD head

HI Hawaii

IA Iowa

ID Idaho

IDHEC Institute des Hautes Etude Cinematographiques

IL Illinois

IMP import

IN Indiana

INC include, including

IND industry

INST Instrumental

INTL international

KS Kansas

KY Kentucky

LA Louisiana

LAMDA London Academy of Musical and Dramatic Art

LCL local

LIC licensing

M of mother of

M-DIR managing director

MA Massachusetts

MAN ED managing editor

MAT Material

MD Maryland

MDSNG Merchandising

ME Maine

MGR manager

MI Michigan

MIN miniatures

MINS minutes

MKTG Marketing

MN Minnesota

MO Missouri

MS Mississippi

MT Montana

MUS music, musical, musician

MUSICOMEDY musical comedy

N North, Northern

NC North Carolina

ND North Dakota

NE Nebraska

NET network

NH New Hampshire

NJ New Jersey

NM New Mexico

NRE Northeast

NV Nevada

NW Northwest

NY New York

O&O owned and operated

OFC office

OH Ohio

OK Oklahoma

OPS operations

OR Oregon

OWN owner

P Pres

PA Pennsylvania

PERF performer

PERS personality

PGM program

PGMG programming

PHO photographer, photography

PLYWRI playwright

PPV Pay Per View TV

PR Puerto Rico

PRCTS practices

PROD producer

PRODN production

PROJ projects

PROJST projectionist

PUB Publicity

PUBL publisher, publishing

RADA Royal Academy of Dramatic Art

REG regulatory

REGL regional

REL releasing

RES research

RESD resigned

RET retired

RETD returned

RI Rhode Island

S South, Southern

S of son of

Sis of sister of

SC South Carolina

SCH scheduling

SD South Dakota

SE Southeast

SEC secretary

SLS sales

SNGWRI songwriter

SP Screenplay

SPEC Special

STA station

STNDS standards

STV Subscription television

SUPV supervisor, supervising, supervisory

SVS service

SW Southwest

SYN syndication

TECH technical

TN Tennessee

TREAS treasurer

TT Trust Territories

TV television

TX Texas

UT Utah

VA Virginia

VAUDE vaudeville

VI Virgin Islands

VOC vocal, vocalist

VP vice president

VT Vermont

W West, Western

w of wife of

WA Washington

WI Wisconsin

WLD world

WLDWDE worldwide

WRI writer

WV West Virginia

WY Wyoming

BIOGRAPHIES

These career profiles reflect credits through June 30, 1985. Personalities who died between Jan. 1, 1983, and June 30, 1985, are included.

AALBERG, John O.: Sound Eng. b. Chicago, Apr 3, 1897. e. IL Institute of Technology, EE. Head of sound department RKO Studios, 1932-57. During this period RKO sound dept. won 3 Oscars; *(Academy "Medal of Commendation", 1980; Gordon E. Sawyer Award 1982).*
(Died Aug. 30, 1984).

AAMES, Willie: Act. (nee Upton)b. CA, Jul 15, 1960. TV inc: We'll Get By; Courtship of Eddie's Father; The Odd Couple; Swiss Family Robinson; Wait Til Your Father Gets Home; Eight Is Enough; Paradise; The Tom Swift & Linda Craig Mystery Hour; Charles in Charge.
Films inc: Hog Wild; Scavenger Hunt; Zapped!

AARON, Paul: Dir. Bway inc: Salvation; Paris is Out; '70 Girls '70; That's Entertainment; Love Me, Love My Children; The Burnt Flowerbed; A Talent for Murder.
Films inc: A Different Story; A Force of One; Deadly Force.
TV inc: The Miracle Worker; Thin Ice; Maid In America; When She Says No.

AARON, Roy H.: Exec. b. Los Angeles, Apr 8, 1929. e. UCLA, BA; USC, LLB. Specialist in exhibition law, handled acquisition and disposition of major theatres and circuits while with LA firm of Pacht, Ross, Warne, Bernhard & Sears; joined Plitt Companies 1978 as sr vp, genl counsel; 1980 P & CEO Plitt Theatres and related companies.

ABBA: Swedish Rock Group. Members inc: Bjorn Ulvaeus, Agnetha Faltskog, Anni-Frid Lyngstad, Benny Andersson.
Albums inc: Waterloo; ABBA; Greatest Hits; Arrival; The Album. Films inc: ABBA, the Movie; P & B. TV inc: Entertainer of the Year Awards.

ABBOTT, George: Wri-Prod-Dir. b. Forestville, NY, Jun 25, 1887. e. Rochester U, BA; Harvard. Began on Bway (1913) as act in Misleading Lady; Queen's Enemies; Daddies; The Broken Wing; Hell-Bent Fer Heaven; Lazybones; Processional; 1926 co-wrote The Fall Guy with James Gleason and thereafter appeared only in A Holy Terror (& co-wri); Cowboy Crazy; Those We Love (& co-wri); John Brown (& prod-dir); revival of The Skin of Our Teeth.
As co-wri-dir: Broadway; Four Walls; Coquette; Ringside; Lilly Turner (& co-prod); Heat Lightning; Page Miss Glory; Three Men on a Horse; On Your Toes; The Boys from Syracuse (solo wri); Best Foot Forward; Where's Charley?; A Tree Grows in Brooklyn; The Pajama Game *(Tony-author-1955)*; Damn Yankees *(Tony-author-1956)*; New Girl In Town; Fiorello *(Tonys-author & dir-1960; also Pulitzer Prize)*; Tenderloin; Flora, The Red Menace; Anya.
As dir: Chicago, Jarnegan; The Great Magoo; Twentieth Century (& co-prod); Small Miracle; Jumbo; Boy Meets Girl (& prod); Brother Rat (& prod); Room Service (& prod); Brown Sugar (& prod); Too Many Girls (& prod); Barefoot Boy with Cheek (& wri); High Button Shoes (& prod); Call Me Madam; Wonderful Town; Me and Juliet; Once Upon a Mattress; Take Her, She's Mine; A Funny Thing Happened on the Way to the Forum *(Tony-dir-1963)*; Fade Out-Fade In; How Now, Dow Jones; The Education of H*Y*M*A*N* K*A*P*L*A*N; Norman, Is That You?; On Your Toes (rev).
(Lawrence Langner Award-1976).
Films inc: (As wri-dir) Half-Way To Heaven; Why Bring That Up; All Quiet on the Western Front (sp only); Manslaughter; Secrets of a Secretary; My Sin; The Cheat; (As dir) Too Many Girls; The Pajama Game; Damn Yankees.
TV inc: The Kennedy Center Honors (honoree).

ABBOTT, John: Act. b. London, Jun 5, 1905. Films inc: Mademoiselle Docteur; The Return of the Scarlet Pimpernel; The Saint in London; Mrs Miniver; They Got Me Covered; Jane Eyre; Secret Motive; The Woman in White; The Merry Widow; Gigi; Who's Minding the Store; Greatest Story Ever Told; Gambit; Two Thousand Years Later; Slapstick of Another Kind.
TV inc: The Harmfulness of Tobacco; Tender is the Night; Child of Virtue; The Glorious Gift of Mollie Malone; The Song of David; The Suicide Club; The Waltz of the Toreadors; The Cat Creature.

ABBOTT, L.B. (Lenwood Ballard Abbott): Cin. b. Pasadena, CA, Jun 13, 1908. Specializing in visual effects. Films inc: Three Faces of Eve; Peyton Place; Some Like It Hot; South Pacific; Journey to the Center of the Earth; The Longest Day; Cleopatra; The Agony and the Ecstacy; The Sound of Music; Von Ryans Express; Sand Pebbles; Fantastic Voyage; Dr Doolittle *(Oscar-1967)*; Planet of the Apes; The Prime of Miss Jean Brodie; Hello Dolly; Butch Cassidy and the Sundance Kid; Mash; The Great White Hope; Patton; Tora, Tora, Tora *(Oscar-1970)*; The Poseidon Adventure *(Oscar-1972)*; Logan's Run *(Oscar-1976)*.
TV inc: Voyage to the Bottom of the Sea *(Emmys-(2)-1965 & 1966)*; Time Tunnel *(Emmy-1967)*; City Beneath the Sea *(Emmy-1971)*.

ABBOTT, Philip (nee Alexander): Act. b. Lincoln, NE, Mar 21, 1923. e. Fordham U. Bway inc: Harvest of Years; Detective Story; Springtime Folly; Square Root of Wonderful; Two for the Seesaw; Robert Frost (adapt & dir): Promises to Keep; O Socrates.
Films inc: The Bachelor Party; The Invisible Boy; The Miracle of the White Stallions; Those Calloways; Sweet Bird of Youth; The Spiral Road; Hangar 18; Savannah Smiles.
TV inc: The House on High Street; The FBI; Tailgunner Joe; Rich Man, Poor Man; The Fantastic World of D.C. Collins.

ABDUL-JABBAR, Kareem (Lew Alcindor): Act. b. NYC, Apr 16, 1947. e. UCLA. Pro basketball player with Milwaukee Bucks, LA Lakers. Films inc: Game of Death; The Fish That Saved Pittsburgh; Airplane.

ABEL, Walter: Act. b. St Paul, Jun 6, 1898. e. AADA. In vaudeville, summer stock, Bway stage. Screen debut, 1936, The Three Musketeers. Films inc: The Witness Chair; Fury; Portia on Trial; Racket Busters; King of the Turf; Miracle on Main Street; Arise My Love; Hold Back the Dawn; Beyond the Blue Horizon; Star Spangled Rhythm; Holiday Inn; Wake
Bway inc: Saturday, Sunday, Monday; Trelawney of the Wells.

ABELES, Arthur: Exec. b. 1914. e. Duke, U; Columbia. Began with WB 1941 as gm West Indies; 1942 asst gm U, Brazil; 1945 supv WB various South American countries; 1968 m-dir WB, vp Warner Intl; 1970 M-dir U, vp U Int'l in chg U.K., Europe, Middle East; when U and Par former Cinema International Corp in 1970 he became co-chmn with Henri Michaud; 1977 formed, with Michaud, A-M Film Consultants Ltd.

ABRAHAM, F. Murray: Act. b. Oct. 24. e. U TX El Paso. Studied at Herbert Berghof Studio with Uta Hagen. Off-Bway inc: Fantasticks; To-Nite In Living Color; Little Murders; Last Chance Saloon; The Survival of Joan; Antigone; Caretaker; Uncle Vanya. Bway inc: The Man In the Glass Booth; Bad Habits; The Ritz; Legend; Teibele and Her Demon; The Seagull.
Films inc: Serpico; The Sunshine Boys; The Ritz; All the President's Men; The Big Fix; Scarface; Amadeus *(Oscar-1984)*.
TV inc: Love Of Life; Marco Polo; Sex and the Married Woman.

ABRAHAMS, Doris Cole: Prod. b. NYC, Jan 29, 1925. e. Ohio U; Leland Powers School of Theatre. Briefly an actress and agent, turned to prodn 1945 with Blue Holiday.
Bway inc: Equus *(Tony-1975)*; Travesties *(Tony-1976)*; Once a Catholic. (London) Enter A Free Man; Out of the Question; Enemy; Child's Play; Lovers Dancing.

ABRAHAMS, Mort: Prod. b. NYC, Mar 26, 1916. e. NYU, BA; Columbia U, MA. TV inc: Tales of Tomorrow; GE Theatre; Producer's Showcase; Suspicion; Target: The Corrupters; Route 66; Kraft Suspense Theatre; Man from U.N.C.L.E; The House on Garibaldi Street; The Deadly Game (cable) (exec prod); Separate Tables (exec prod); Laurence Olivier and Jackie Gleason as Mr. Halpern and Mr. Johnson (cable) (exec prod).
Films inc: Dr Doolittle; Planet of the Apes; Goodbye Mr Chips; The Chairman; Beneath the Planet of the Apes (& sp); Luther (exec prod); Man in the Glass Booth; Homecoming; Lost in the Stars; Rhinocerous; The Greek Tycoon (exec prod).

ABRAMS, Gerald W.: Exec prod. b. West Chester, PA, Sep 26, 1939. e. Penn State U. TV inc: Red Alert; Ski Lift to Death; James Dean-Portrait of a Friend; The Defection of Simas Kudirka; Flesh and Blood; Steeltown; Letters From Frank; The Gift; Act of Love; Berlin Tunnel 21; Marion Rose White; Running Out; Cutter to Houston; Found Money; Scorned And Swindled; Florence Nightingale.

ABRAVANEL, Maurice: Cond-mus dir. b. Salonica, Greece, Jan. 6, 1903. e. U of Lausanne; studied with Kurt Weill. Made debut as mus dir at Metropolitan Opera, 1936. Bway inc: Knickerbocker Holiday; Lady In The Dark; One Touch Of Venus; The Seven Lively Arts; The Firebrand Of Florence; Street Scene; Regina *(Tony-Cond & Mus Dir-1950).*

ABULADZE, Tengiz: Dir-Wri. b. Russia, Jan 31, 1924. e. Moscow Film Institute. Films inc: (doc) Dmitry Arakishvili; Our Palace; The Georgian State Dancing Company; An Open Air Museum. (Features) Magdan's Donkey; Someone Else's Children; Me, Grandma, Iliko and Hillarion; The Entreaty; A Necklace for My Beloved; A Tree of Wishes.

ACHTERNBUSCH, Herbert: Prod-Dir-Wri-Act. b. Munich, 1938. e. Academy of Arts, Nuremberg. A painter for 10 years before turning to films.
Films inc: The Adechser Feeling; The Comanche; The Atlantic Swimmer; Beer Chase; Servus Bayern (Bye Bye Bavaria); Der Neger Erwin (Black Erwin); Der Jonge Moench (The Young Monk); Das Letzte Loch (The Last Hole); Der Depp (The Blockhead); Das Gespenst (The Ghost); Wanderkrebs (Itinerant Cancer); Rita Ritter; Die Olympiasiegerin (The Woman Olympic Winner.); Blaue Baumen (Blue Flowers).

ACKER, Sharon: Act. b. Toronto, Canada, Apr 2, 1935.
Films inc: Lucky Jim; Off Your Rocker; Threshold; Point Blank; Happy Birthday To Me.
TV inc: Executive Suite; Star Trek; A Cry for Justice; Dallas; Stone; Battles--The Murder That Wouldn't Die; Simon & Simon; Texas.

ACKERMAN, Bettye: Act. b. Cottageville, SC, Feb 28, 1928. e. Columbia U. W of Sam Jaffe. Bway inc: No Count Boy; Tartuffe; Sophocles; Antigone; Oedipus at Colonus.
Films inc: Face of Fire; Companions in Nightmare; Rascal.
TV inc: Heat of Anger; Ben Casey; Medical Center; Trouble In High Timber Country; A Day For Thanks on Walton's Mountain; Confessions Of A Married Man; Me And Mom.

ACKERMAN, Forrest J.: Act-Wri-Prod. b. Los Angeles, Nov 24, 1916. Films inc: The Time Travelers (cameo); Queen (aka Planet) of Blood; Dracula vs. Frankenstein; Schlock; Hollywood Boulevard; Kentucky Fried Movie; Aftermath; Scalps.

ACKERMAN, Harry S.: Prod. b. Albany, NY, Nov 17, 1912. e. Dartmouth Coll. Began as writer, actor. Joined Young & Rubicam adv. agency, 1936; exec prod. CBS, 1948; VP chge network programs CBS-TV. 1950; formed ind co, 1957; VP and exec prod. Screen Gems Inc., 1958-77; pres. Harry Ackerman Prods. TV inc: Gunsmoke (also radio); Dennis the Menace; The Farmer's Daughter; Bewitched; The Flying Nun; Hazel; The Sky's the Limit (supv prod); Welcome Home, Jellybean (exec prod); Gidget's Summer Reunion (exec prod).

ACKLAND, Joss: Act. b. London, England, Feb 29, 1928. Appeared in rep; member of Old Vic with whom he toured Russia, US; spent some time in Central Africa as tea planter; in thea and deejay, South Africa. Thea inc: (London) The Hasty Heart; The Rising Sun; Arms and the Man; Lock Up Your Daughters; The Life of Galileo; The Possessed; The Bacccbae; The Professor; Hotel in Amsterdam; Come As You Are; A Streetcar Named Desire; A Little Night Music.
Films inc: Seven Days to Noon; Royal Flash; Crescendo; The House That Dripped Blood; Villain; England Made Me; Penny Gold; The Black Windmill; Great Expectations; The Little Prince; Seven Men At Daybreak; Silver Bears; Who Is Killing the Great Chefs of Europe?; Watership Down (voice); Saint Jack; The Apple; Rough Cut; Dangerous Davies--The Last Detective.
TV Inc: Coriolanus.

ACKROYD, David: Act. b. Orange, NJ, May 30, 1940. e. Bucknell, BA; Yale, MFA. TV inc: Secret Storm; The Great American Dream Machine; Another World; Harvest Home; Joanne and Tom; The Word; And I Alone Survived; Women in White; Mind Over Murder; The Yeagers; The Sound of Murder (cable); Cocaine--One Man's Seduction; Deadly Lesson; When Your Lover Leaves; The Sky's the Limit.
Films inc: The Mountain Men.
Bway inc: Hamlet; Unlikely Heroes; Full Circle; Hide and Seek.

ACUFF, Roy: Mus. b. Maynardsville, TN, Sep 15, 1903. Joined Grand Ole Opry, 1940; shortly after organized his band, the Smokey Mountain Boys; entered mus publishing business in the 50s; elected to Country Mus Hall of Fame, 1962. TV inc: Merry Christmas From the Grand Ole Opry House; The Concrete Cowboys; Country Comes Home; Roy Acuff--50 Years the King of Country Music; Country Comes Home (1982); Barbara Mandrell-Something Special.

ADAM, Ken: Art dir. b. Berlin, Feb 5, 1921. Films inc: Around the World in 80 Days; Trials of Oscar Wilde; Dr. No; Sodom and Gomorrah; Dr. Strangelove; Ipcress File; Goldfinger; You Only Live Twice; Funeral in Berlin; Chitty Chitty Bang Bang; Goodbye Mr. Chips; The Owl and the Pussycat; Thunderball; Diamonds are Forever; Barry Lyndon *(Oscar-1975)*; The Spy Who Loved Me; Moonraker; King David.

ADAMS, Berle: Exec. b. Chicago, Jan 11, 1917. e. Northwestern U, BA. Started with GAC, Chicago, 1940; formed Mutual Entertainment Agency, 1942; formed (with Irving Green) Mercury Records, 1945; served as p; sold Mercury Records in 1948, joined MCA 1950; became vp of MCA TV, 1952; created MCA mus publ co; elected vp of MCA Inc in Jan 1965; named exec vp, 1968; left MCA to head WM Sports; p, BAC, Inc. Films inc: (prod) Brass Target.

ADAMS, Brooke: Act. b. NYC, Feb 8, 1949. e. NY High School for Performing Arts. Off-Bway inc: Split; Key Exchange; The Petrified Forest.
Films inc: Days of Heaven; Invasion of the Body Snatchers; A Man, A Woman, and a Bank; Cuba; Shock Waves; Tell Me A Riddle; Utilities; The Dead Zone; Almost You; Key Exchange.
TV inc: East Side/West Side; O.K. Crackerby; Last of the Belles; James Dean. . .Portrait of A Friend; Black Bart; The Daughters of Joshua Cabe; The Lords of Flatbush; Murder on Flight 502; Rex Stout's Nero Wolfe; Family; The Innocents Abroad; Lace; Haunted; Special People --Based on a True Story; Lace II.

ADAMS, Casey: See SHOWALTER, Max.

ADAMS, Catlin (nee Barab): Act. b. Los Angeles, Oct 11, 1950. Thea inc: Safe House; Scandalous Memories; Dream of a Blacklisted Actor; The Candy Store.
Films inc: Katherine; Panic in Needle Park; The Jerk; The Jazz Singer.
TV inc: How to Survive the 70's and Maybe Even Bump Into A Little Happiness; She Loves Me, She Loves Me Not.

ADAMS, Don (ne Yarmy): Act. b. NYC, Apr 13, 1926. Nitery impressionist, won Arthur Godfrey talent contest, began guesting on tv shows.
TV inc: The Bill Dana Show; Get Smart *(Emmy-1967, 1968,1969)*; The Partners; Hooray for Hollywood; Don Adams Screen Test; Three Times Daley; Billy.
Films inc: The Nude Bomb; Jimmy the Kid.

ADAMS, Edie (nee Enke): Act-Singer. b. Kingston, PA, Apr 16, 1931. e. Juilliard; Columbia U. Thea inc: Wonderful Town; Li'l Abner *(Tony*-supp-1957); Anything Goes.
Films inc: The Apartment; It's A Mad, Mad, Mad, Mad World; Call Me Bwana; Under the Yum Yum Tree; Love With The Proper Stranger; Lover Come Back; The Best Man; Maid in Paris; The Honey Pot; The Happy Hooker Goes to Washington; Cheech & Chong's Up in Smoke; The Happy Hooker Goes To Hollywood; Boxoffice.
TV inc: The Ernie Kovacs Show; Cinderella; Here's Edie; The Edie Adams Show; Fast Friends; The Seekers; Make Me An Offer; Portrait of an Escort; A Cry For Love; Bosom Buddies; The Haunting of Harrington House; Ernie Kovacs--Television's Original Genius (exec prod) (cable); Shooting Stars; Ernie Kovacs. . .Between the Laughter (& tech advsr).

ADAMS, Joey: Wri-Comedian. b. NYC, Jan 6, 1911. e. CCNY. Syndicated humor columnist; host daily radio show WEVD, NY. Toastmaster, emcee niteries, concerts.
Bway inc: Guys and Dolls; The Gazebo.
Films inc: (prod-act) Ringside; Singing in the Dark.

ADAMS, Julie (Betty May Adams): Act. b. Waterloo, IA, Oct 17,

1928. Films inc: Bright Victory; Bend of the River; Mississippi Gambler; The Creature from the Black Lagoon; One Desire; Away all Boats; Slaughter on Tenth Avenue; Valley of Mystery; The Private War of Major Benson; The Last Movie; McQ; The Wild McCulloughs; Killer Force; The Killer Inside Me; The Fifth Floor.

TV inc: The Jimmy Stewart Show; Go Ask Alice; The Trackers; Six Characters In Search of An Author; Greatest Heroes of the Bible; Code Red; Capitol.

ADAMS, Mason: Act. b. NYC, Feb 26, 1919. e. U of WI. Started on radio 1946; spent nearly two decades in Pepper Young's Family. Bway inc: Get Away Old Man; Inquest; The Sign in Sidney Brustein's Window; Tall Story; You Know I Can't Hear You When the Water's Running; The Trial of the Catonsville Nine; The Shortchanged Review; Checking Out.

TV inc: Another World; The Deadliest Season; Lou Grant; And Baby Makes Six; A Shining Season; Flamingo Road; Murder Can Hurt You!; Revenge of the Stepford Wives; The Kid with the Broken Halo; The Grinch Grinches The Cat-In-The-Hat (voice); Peking Encounter; Great Day; Passions; The Night They Saved Christmas; Solomon Northrup's Odyssey.

Films inc: The Final Conflict.

ADAMS, Maud (nee Wikstrum): Act. b. Lulea, Sweden, Feb 12, 1945. Former model. Films inc: The Christian Licorice Store; U-Turn; Mahoney's Estate; The Man With the Golden Gun; Rollerball; Killer Force; The Merciless Man; Tattoo; Octopussy; Target Eagle.

TV inc: Laura--Shades of Summer; The Hostage Tower; Playing for Time; Chicago Story; Emerald Point, N.A.S.; Nairobi Affair.

ADAMS, Neile: Act. b. Jul 10, 1936. Films inc: This Could Be the Night.

Bway inc: Kismet; Me and Juliet; Best Foot Forward; Pajama Game.

TV inc: Women in Chains; Fuzz.

ADAMS, Peter: Act. b. Los Angeles, Sep 22, 1917. e. Williams Coll, BA. Films inc: Turnabout; Fountainhead; Battle Zone; Flat Top; Dragonfly; Ruby Gentry; Courtmartial of Billy Mitchell; Brigadoon; Bullwhip; The Big Fisherman; Midnight Lace; How to Murder Your Wife; Funny Girl.

ADAMS, Phillip: Prod-Columnist-Broadcaster. b. Victoria, Australia, Jul 12, 1939. Films inc: Jack and Jill: A Postscript; The Naked Bunyip; The Adventures of Barry McKenzie; Don's Party; The Getting of Wisdom; Grendel, Grendel, Grendel; Lonely Hearts (exec prod).

Sept 1983 became Chmn Australian Film Commission.

ADAMS, Stanley: Lyr. b. NYC, Aug 14, 1907. e. NYU; NYU Law School. Began with songs for Connie's Inn Revue. Bway inc: The Show Is On; The Lady Says Yes; Shoestring Revue.

Films inc: Everyday's a Holiday; Duel in the Sun; My Reputation; The Great Lie; Road Show; Viva Villa!; Strategic Air Command.

Songs inc: Little Old Lady; My Shawl; What A Diff'rence A Day Made; La Cucaracha; My Silent Mood; Rollin' Down the River; You Stole My Heart.

ADAMS, Tony: Prod. b. Dublin, Ireland, Feb 15, 1953. Films inc: (assoc prod) Return of the Pink Panther; The Pink Panther Strikes Again. Revenge of the Pink Panther; 10; S.O.B; Victor/Victoria; Trail of the Pink Panther; The Man Who Loved Women; Micki & Maude (prod).

TV inc: Julie Andrews in Japan.

ADATO, Perry Miller: Prod-Dir. TV inc: Dylan Thomas--The World I Breathe (Emmy-prod-1968); Gertrude Stein--When You See This, Remember Me; An Eames Celebration; Frankenthaler--Toward a New Climate; Mary Cassatt--Impressionist from Philadelphia; Georgia O'-Keefe; Carl Sandburg--Echoes and Silences; Picasso--A Painter's Diary.

ADDAMS, Dawn: Act. b. Felixstowe, Suffolk, England, Sep 21, 1930. e. RADA. In repertory in Europe, on British stage. Moved to Hollywood, 1950. Films inc: Night into Morning; Singin' in the Rain; The Robe; The Silent Enemy; The Two Faces of Dr. Jekyll; Come Fly With Me; The Vault of Horror.

Thea inc: Peter Pan; The Coming Out Party; The Wild Duck. TV inc: Romans and Friends; Star Maidens.

(Died May 7, 1985)

ADDISON, John: Comp. b. Chobham, Surrey, England, Mar 16, 1920. e. Wellington Coll; Royal Coll of Music. Film scores inc: The Guinea Pig; Seven Days to Noon; Private's Progress; I Reach for the Sky; I Was Monty's Double; Look Back in Anger; The Entertainer; A Taste of Honey; The Loneliness of the Long Distance Runner; Tom Jones (Oscar-1963); Guns at Batasi; Torn Curtain; The Honey Pot; Mr Forbush and the Penguin; Sleuth; Dead Cert; A Bridge Too Far; The Charge of the Light Brigade; The 7% Solution; Joseph Andrews; Strange Invaders; The Ultimate Solution of Grace Quigley; Highpoint.

TV inc: Hamlet; Centennial; Pearl; T.J. Hooker; Eleanor, First Lady of the World; I Was A Mail Order Bride; Murder, She Wrote; Ellis Island.

Thea inc: The Entertainer; The Chairs; Luther; Bloomsbury.

(Grammy-Soundtrack-1963).

ADDISON, Nancy: Act. b. NYC, Mar 21. e. Fisher Coll; NYU. TV inc: The Guiding Light; Ryan's Hope; The Dain Curse.

Thea inc: The Impossible Years; Talent For Murder.

Films inc: Roll Over.

ADDY, Wesley: Act. b. Omaha, NE, Aug 4, 1913. Films inc: The First Legion; The Big Knife; Whatever Happened to Baby Jane?; Hush, Hush, Sweet Charlotte; Seconds; Tora! Tora! Tora!; The Grissom Gang; Network; The Europeans; The Bostonians.

Bway inc: Hamlet; Twelfth Night; Romeo and Juliet; Antigone; Candida; Invitation to a March; A Month in the Country.

TV inc: The Edge of Night; Days of Our Lives; The Private History of a Campaign That Failed; Rage of Angels; Loving.

ADELMAN, Joseph A.: Exec. b.Winnipeg, Man, Canada, Dec 27, 1933. e. NYU, BA; Harvard Law School, JD. 1957, Attorney, UA, NY; 1958, West Coast Counsel; 1964, exec asst to VP in chg prodn; 1968, VP West Coast business, legal affairs; 1972, exec VP AMPTP; 1977, admitted to NY, CA, Supreme Court bars; 1979 VP in chg of bus aff, Par; resd. Sept 1982.

ADELSON, Gary: Prod. b. 1954. e. UCLA, BA. S of Merv Adelson. TV inc: Helter Skelter (prodn asst); Sybil (asso prod); Eight Is Enough (prod); The Blue Knight (prod); Too Good To Be True (exec prod); Our Family Business (exec prod); Cass Malloy (exec prod); John Steinbeck's The Winter Of Our Discontent (exec prod); Lace (exec prod); Detective In The House (exec prod); Lace II (exec prod).

Films inc: The Last Starfighter (prod).

ADELSON, Merv: Prod. b. Los Angeles, Oct 23, 1929. e. UCLA. Chmn Board Lorimar Prodns, Inc. Films inc: Twilight's Last Gleaming; The Choirboys; Who's Killing the Great Chefs of Europe; Avalanche Express; The Big Red One.

TV inc: The Waltons; Eight is Enough; Dallas; Kaz; The Waverly Wonders; Knots Landing; Sybil; A Man Called Intrepid; The Blue Knight; Helter-Skelter.

ADJANI, Isabelle: Act. b. Germany, Jun 27, 1955. Films inc: The Slap; The Story of Adele H; The Tenant; Faustine; Barocco; Violette et Francois; The Driver; NOSFERATU--The Vampire; The Bronte Sisters; Clara and the Swell Guys; Possession; Quartet; L'Annee Prochaine si tout Va Bien (Next Year if All Goes Well); Tout Feu, Tout Flamme (All Fired Up); Antonieta; Mortelle Randonne (Deadly Circuit); L'ete Meurtrier (One Deadly Summer); Subway.

ADLER, Allen: Exec-prod. b. NYC, 1946. e. Princeton, AB; Harvard Business School, MBA. After law school, with Standard & Poor's Inter- Capital, later joined Alan Hirschfield at American Diversified Enterprises, private investment firm associated with Allen & Co.; when Allen & Co. became major stockholder in Columbia Pictures 1973, Hirschfield and Adler went to film company, former as P, latter as corporate officer; 1979, became sr. vp; resd after Hirschfield was forced out of company over handling of David Begelman situation; 1981 teamed with Daniel Melnick in IndieProd Company.

Films inc: Making Love.

ADLER, Gerald L.: Exec. b. Pittsburgh, PA, Jan 30, 1931. e. Carnegie Mellon U, BFA; Syracuse U, MS. VP U-TV 1956-68; VP Cinema Center 100, 1968-71; Exec VP WB-TV 1971; Prod Sandy Howard Prodns 1975-76; Prod-Dir Teens World Intl 1977-1979; VP in chg tv prodn Melvin Simon Prodns Jan 1980.

ADLER, Jerry: Mus. b. Baltimore, MD, Oct 30, 1918. e. Baltimore City Coll. Command perf before King George V & Queen Mary and King George VI & Queen Elizabeth. Toured as solo perf. Recorded over 150 Film and TV sound tracks.

ADLER, Jerry: Dir. b. NYC, Feb 4, 1929. e. Syracuse U. Bway inc: Fun City; We Interrupt This Program; Words And Music; Good Evening; Checking Out; My Fair Lady (revival); Play Me A Country Song.

ADLER, Larry: Mus. b. NYC, Feb 10, 1914. Virtuoso who raised what the Musicians Union considered a toy to the level of a musical instrument. Started in showbusiness in 1928 when Rudy Vallee gave him a brief job at the Heigh-Ho Club; Bway inc: Smiles, Clowns in Clover; Flying Colors; and the English revues Streamline and Time Inn; during World War II teamed with dancer Paul Draper for USO tours that led to post-war concert engagements around the world.
Films inc: Many Happy Returns; The Singing Marine; St. Martin's Lane; Sidewalks of London; The Big Broadcast of 1937; Music for Millions.
TV inc: The Monte Carlo Show.

ADLER, Lou: Prod. b. Los Angeles. Began wri, prod records 1958 with Herb Alpert. In 1963 formed Dunhill Records, sold to ABC; started Ode Records, joined Alpert in A&M Records.
(Grammys-Record of the Year-Album of the Year-1971).
Films inc: Monterey Pop (doc); Brewster McCloud; The Rocky Horror Picture Show; Cheech and Chong's Up In Smoke; Shock Treatment (exec prod); Ladies and Gentlemen--The Fabulous Stains (dir).

ADLER, Luther: Act. b. NYC, May 4, 1903. Studied under his father, Jacob P Adler and appeared with Adler Yiddish Theatre Company from 1908 through 1921. Bway inc: Humoresque; The Monkey Talks; Money Business; We Americans; Is Zat So?; Street Scene; Night Over Taos; Success Story; Alien Corn; Men In White; Golden Boy; Rocket to the Moon; Thunder Rock; Two On An Island; Dunnigan's Daughter; A Flag Is Born (& prod); The Passion of Joseph D.; Three Sisters; toured in Fiddler on the Roof.
Films inc: Lancer Spy; Cornered; Saigon; Loves of Carmen; Wake of the Red Witch; House of Strangers; D.O.A.; South Sea Sinner; Under My Skin; Kiss Tomorrow Goodbye; M; The Desert Fox; The Hoodlum Empire; The Last Angry Man; Cast A Giant Shadow; Crazy Joe; Murph The Surf; The Man In the Glass Booth; Voyage of the Damned; Absence of Malice.
TV inc: Hedda Gabler; Billy Budd; The Plot to Kill Stalin; The Lincoln Murder Case; The Brotherhood.
(Died Dec. 8, 1984).

ADLER, Richard: Comp-Lyr-Prod. b. NYC, Aug 3, 1921. Bway inc: (mus-lyr) John Murray Anderson's Almanac; Pajama Game *(Tony*-comp-1955); Damn Yankees *(Tony*-comp-1956); Kwamina; A Mother's Kisses; Rex (prod only); Music Is (prod only).
TV inc: (scores) The Gift of the Magi (& co-prod); Little Women (& co-prod).

ADLER, Stella: Act-Dir-Teacher. b. NYC, Feb 10, 1902. Sis of Luther Adler. Studied with her father, Jacob Adler; Maria Ouspenskaya; Constantin Stanislavsky. Thea: debut at age 4 with father's company in Yiddish Theatre and appeared with him for many years; in vaude for year; starred in repertory of plays all over the world; joined Group Theatre 1931; directs and teaches at Stella Adler Conservatory, NY.
Bway inc: The House of Connelly; 1931; Night Over Taos; Success Story; Big Night; Hilda Cassidy; Gentlewoman; Gold-Eagle Guy; Awake and Sing!; Paradise Lost; Sons and Soldiers; Manhattan Nocturne (dir); Pretty Little Parlor; Polonaise (dir); He Who Gets Slapped; Sunday Breakfast (dir); Johnny Johnson (dir).
Films inc: Love On Toast; The Thin Man; My Girl Tisa.

ADORF, Mario: Act. b. Zurich, Switzerland, Sep 8, 1930. Films inc: The Devil Strikes At Night; Rosemary; Das Totenschiff; Brainwashed; The Royal Game; Lulu; Station Six Sahara; Apache Gold; Major Dundee; Ten Little Indians; Treasure of San Gennaro; A Rose for Every-

one; The Bird With the Crystal Plumage; The Red Tent; The Italian Connection; Bomber and Paganini; The Main Actor; On A Silver Platter; Fedora; The Tin Drum; King, Queen, Knave; La Cote D'Amour (The Coast of Love); Klassenverhaltnisse (Class Relations).
TV inc: Smiley's People; Marco Polo.

ADRIAN, Iris (nee Hostetter): Act. b. Los Angeles, May 29, 1913. In Ziegfeld Follies, 1931. Films inc: Paramount on Parade; Rumba; Our Relations; Professional Bride; The G-String Murders; I'm From Arkansas; The Paleface; G.I. Jane; The Buccaneer; That Darn Cat; The Odd Couple; Scandalous John; Freaky Friday.
TV inc: Murder Can Hurt You!

AGAR, John: Act. b. Chicago, Jan 31, 1921. Films inc: Fort Apache; Sands of Iwo Jima; The Magic Carpet; Joe Butterfly; Journey to the Seventh Planet; Of Love and Desire; Waco; The St. Valentine's Day Massacre; The Curse of the Swamp Creature; The Undefeated; Big Jake; King Kong.

AGHAYAN, Ray: Cos dsgn. b. Jul 29, 1934. e. LA City Coll, BA; UCLA. Films inc: The Art of Love; Do Not Disturb; Our Man Flint; The Glass Bottom Boat; In Like Flint; Caprice; Dr Doolittle; Gaily, Gaily; Hannie Caulder; Lady Sings the Blues; The Four Musketeers; Funny Lady.
TV inc: The Judy Garland Show; The Dick Van Dyke Show; Wonderful World of Burlesque; Robin Hood; Alice Through the Looking Glass *(Emmy*-1966); Carol Channing & 101 Men; Carol Channing & Pearl Bailey on Broadway; Leslie Uggams Show; Jim Nabors Show; Diahann Carroll Variety Show (prod); The Tenth Month; 55th Annual Academy Awards; Burnett Discovers Domingo; Consenting Adult (prod).
Bway inc: Catch My Soul; Applause; On the Town; Lorelei.

AGUTTER, Jenny: Act. b. London, Dec 20, 1952. Film debut age 11, East of Sudan. Films inc: Gates To Paradise; Star !; Walkabout; The Railway Children; Logan's Run; The Eagle Has Landed; Equus; China 9, Liberty 37; Riddle of the Sands; Sweet William; Amy; An American Werewolf in London; The Survivor; Secret Places; Dominique (made in 1977).
TV inc: Ballerina; The Wild Duck; The Snow Goose *(Emmy*-supp-1972). Shelley; War of Children; School Play; Mayflower: The Pilgrim's Adventure; Beulah Land; Love's Labour's Lost.
Thea: School For Scandal; Rooted; Arms and the Man; The Ride Across Lake Constance; The Tempest; Spring Awakening; Breaking The Silence.

AHERNE, Brian: Act. b. Worcestershire, Eng., May 2, 1902. A child actor from age 8 on London stage; silent films. To Bway 1933 as star Barretts of Wimpole Street. Films inc: The Eleventh Commandment; Safety First; The Constant Nymph; Song of Songs; Sylvia Scarlett; Beloved Enemy; The Great Garrick; Merrily We Live; Juarez; Captain Fury; Hired Wife; My Son My Son; Smilin' Through; Skylark; My Sister Eileen; A Night To Remember; Forever and a Day; The Locket; Smart Woman; I Confess; Titanic; Prince Valiant; The Swan; The Best of Everything; Susan Slade; Rosie.

AIDMAN, Charles: Act-Dir-Wri. b. Frankfort, IN, Jan 31, 1925. e. IN U. Films inc: Pork Chop Hill; War Hunt; Count Down; Hour of the Gun; Dirty Little Billy; Kotch; Twilight's Last Gleaming; Zoot Suit.
TV inc: Spoon River Anthology (dir); The Picture of Dorian Gray; The Red Badge of Courage; Amelia Earhart; The Last Song; Alcatraz-The Whole Shocking Story; Prime Suspect; Marion Rose White.
Bway inc: Spoon River Anthology (conceived-dir-lyr); Julius Caesar; The Cretan Woman; Macbeth; Career; After the Fall; Zoot Suit.

AIELLO, Danny: Act. b. Jun 20, 1933. Films inc: Blood Brothers; Fingers; Defiance; Hide in Plain Sight; Fort Apache, The Bronx; Chu Chu and the Philly Flash; Once Upon A Time in America; Old Enough; The Purple Rose Of Cairo; The Protector; Key Exchange.
Bway inc: Lampost Reunion; Wheelbarrow Closers; Knockout; The Floating Light Bulb.
TV inc: Family of Strangers *(Emmy*-1981); The Unforgivable Secret; A Question of Honor; Blood Feud; Lady Blue.

AILES, Roger: Prod-Dir. b. Warren, OH, May 15, 1940. e. OH U, BFA. TV inc: The Last Frontier (& dir); Fellini--Wizards, Clowns and

Honest Liars (& dir); 1981, exec prod Tomorrow Coast-to-Coast; Television and the Presidency; Television--Our Life And Times.

Bway inc: Mother Earth; Hot L Baltimore.

AILEY, Alvin: Chor-Dir. b. Rogers, TX, Jan 5, 1931. Began as a member of Lester Horton Dance Troupe in LA; chor Mourning Morning; According to St Francis; Darius Milhaud's Creation of the World; formed Alvin Ailey Dancers; chor Revelations; Knoxville Summer of 1915; Been Here and Gone; Feast of Ashes; Labrynth; Ariadne.

Films inc: Carmen Jones (dancer).

Bway inc: The Carefree Tree; The House of Flowers; Sing, Man, Sing; Jamaica; Tiger, Tiger Burning Bright (act).

AIMEE, Anouk (Francoise Sorya): Act. b. Paris, Apr 27, 1934. Films inc: Les Amants de Verone (The Lovers of Verona); The Golden Salamander; The Man Who Watched the Trains Go By; Paris Express; Pot Bouille; La Dolce Vita; Sodom and Gomorrah; Eight and a Half; Of Flesh and Blood; The Journey; A Man and a Woman; Un Soir Un Train; The Appointment; The Model Shop; Justine; If It Were to Do Over Again; My First Love; Leap Into The Void; La Tragedia Di Un Uomo Ridicolo (Tragedy of a Ridiculous Man); Qu-est-ce Qui Fait Courir David? (What Makes David Run?); Le General de l'Armee Morte (The General of the Dead Army); Success Is the Best Revenge; Viva la Vie! (Long Live Life!)

AJAYE, Franklyn: Act. b. Brooklyn, May 13, 1949. Nightclubs, TV, records. Films inc: The All-American Girl; Car Wash; Convoy; Sweet Revenge; The Jazz Singer; Hysterical; Get Crazy.

TV inc: The Cheap Detective; National Lampoon's Hot Flashes.

AKINS, Claude: Act. b. Nelson, GA, May 25, 1918. e. Northwestern U. Films inc: From Here to Eternity; The Caine Mutiny; The Sea Chase; Johnny Concho; The Defiant Ones; Porgy and Bess; Inherit The Wind; How the West Was Won; The Killers; Return of the Seven; Skyjacked; Waterhole Three; The Devil's Brigade; The Great Bank Robbery; Flap; Battle for the Planet of the Apes; Timber Tramps; Tentacles.

TV inc: Movin' On; Nashville 99; Murder In Music City; Ebony, Ivory and Jade; The Misadventures of Sheriff Lobo; The Concrete Cowboys; Lobo; The Way They Were; Bus Stop (cable); Desperate Intruder; The Master; Celebrity; Legmen; Murder, She Wrote; The Baron and the Kid.

ALBECK, Andy: Exec. b. Russia, Sep 25, 1921. Entered film industry 1939 with Columbia Pictures Int'l, worked for Central Motion Picture Exchange and Eagle Lion Classics before joining UA Int'l dept 1951; named VP UA & UA Broadcasting 1972; became P UA Broadcasting following year; became UA sr vp ops 1976; P, CEO 1978; Dec 1980, ChmnB; Ret Feb, 1981.

ALBEE, Denny: Act. b. Oklahoma City, OK, Mar 19, 1949. e. TN State U, BA; FL State U, MFA. Thea inc: An American Dream; Halloween. TV inc: The Edge of Night.

ALBEE, Edward: Wri-Dir-Prod. b. Washington, DC, May 12, 1928. e. Trinity Coll. Plays inc: The Zoo Story; The Death of Bessie Smith; The American Dream; Who's Afraid of Virginia Woolf? (Tony-1963); The Ballad of the Sad Cafe; Tiny Alice; A Delicate Balance; All Over; Seascape (& dir) (Pulitzer Prize-1975); Lady From Dubuque; Lolita; The Man Who Had Three Arms (& dir); Faustus In Hell (segment). Dir: The Sandbox; The Palace at 4 a.m. (Prod) Corruption in the Palace of Justice; Two Executioners; The Dutchman; The Butter and Egg Man; Night of the Dunce; The Front Page.

(Grammy-Drama Recording-1963).

ALBERG, Mildred Freed: Prod. b. Montreal. TV inc: Playhouse 90; Our American Heritage series; The Story of Jacob and Joseph; The Story of David; The Royal Archives of Elba; Archeological Dig in Syria.

ALBERGHETTI, Anna Marie: Act. b. Pesaro, Italy, May 15, 1936. US debut Carnegie Hall, 1950. Films inc: The Medium; Here Comes the Groom; The Stars Are Singing; The Last Command; Ten Thousand Bedrooms; Cinderfella.

TV inc: Forever and a Day; Smart Woman; The Locket; Titanic; The Swan; Lancelot and Guinevere; The Waltz King; Duel At Apache Wells; Rosie.

Bway inc: Carnival (Tony-1962).

ALBERT, Chris: Mus. b. Gottingen, W Germany, Jun 17, 1963. See Blood, Sweat & Tears.

ALBERT, Eddie (nee Heimberger): Act. b. Rock Island, IL, Apr 22, 1908. e. U of MN. H of Margo. F of Edward Albert. On radio in Minneapolis; vaude and radio career before Bway debut in O Evening Star. Bway inc: Brother Rat; Room Service; The Boys From Syracuse; Miss Liberty; Say Darling; The Music Man; No Hard Feelings.

Films inc: Brother Rat; Four Wives; A Dispatch From Reuters; Four Mothers; Bombardier; Smash-Up; Actors and Sin; Carrie; Roman Holiday; Oklahoma!; I'll Cry Tomorrow; Attack; Teahouse of the August Moon; The Sun Also Rises; The Longest Day; Captain Newman; M.D.; Seven Women; The Heartbreak Kid; The Longest Yard; Escape To Witch Mountain; Birch Interval; Airport '79, Concorde; Yesterday; Foolin' Around; How To Beat The High Cost Of Living; Take This Job and Shove It; Yes, Giorgio; Dreamscape; The Act.

TV inc: Miracle of the White Stallion; Green Acres; Evening in Byzantium; Switch; Trouble in High Timber Country; Beulah Land; The Oklahoma City Dolls; Peter and Paul; The Fall Guy; Goliath Awaits; Beyond Witch Mountain; Rooster; The Demon Murder Case; The Television Academy Hall of Fame; Burning Rage.

ALBERT, Edward: Act. b. Los Angeles, Feb 20, 1951. S of Margo and Eddie Albert. Films inc: Butterflies are Free; Forty Carats; Midway; The Purple Taxi; The Domino Principle; The Greek Tycoon; When Time Ran Out; The Squeeze; Butterfly; Galaxy of Terror; The House Where Evil Dwells; A Time To Die; Ellie.

TV inc: The Word; Silent Victory - The Kitty O'Neil Story; The Last Convertible; Blood Feud; The Yellow Rose.

ALBRIGHT, Lola: Act. b. Akron, OH, Jul 20, 1925. Screen debut, 1948, The Pirate. Films inc: Easter Parade; Champion; The Good Humor Man; Arctic Flight; The Tender Trap; Seven Guns to Mesa; A Cold Wind in August; Kid Galahad; The Love Cage; Lord Love a Duck; The Way West; Where Were You When the Lights Went Out?; The Impossible Years; The Money Jungle.

TV inc: Peter Gunn.

ALCOTT, John: Cin. b. England. Films inc: A Clockwork Orange; Barry Lyndon (Oscar-1975); March or Die; Disappearance; Who is Killing the Great Chefs of Europe; Terror Train; Fort Apache, The Bronx; Vice Squad; The Beastmaster; Greystoke: The Legend of Tarzan, Lord of the Apes; Triumphs of a Man Called Horse; Baby.

ALDA, Alan: Act. b. NYC, Jan 28, 1936. e. Fordham U. S of Robert Alda. Studied at Cleveland Playhouse; performed with Second City. Bway inc: The Owl and the Pussycat; Purlie Victorious; Fair Game for Lovers; The Apple Tree.

Films inc: Gone Are the Days; The Moonshine War; Jenny; The Mephisto Waltz; Paper Lion; To Kill a Clown; California Suite; Same Time, Next Year; The Seduction of Joe Tynan (& sp); The Four Seasons (& dir-sp).

TV inc: That Was the Week That Was; M*A*S*H (Emmys-act, 1974, 1982; dir, 1977; wri, 1979 also actor of the year 1974;); The Glass House; Kill Me If You Can; 6 Rms Riv Vu (& dir); Greatest Heroes of the Bible; Entertainer of the Year Awards; The Four Seasons (& exec prod-crea).

ALDA, Robert (Alphonso D'Abruzzo): Act. b. NYC, Feb 26, 1914. e. NYU. Radio; dramatic stock; signed by WB 1943. Films inc: Cinderella Jones; Rhapsody in Blue; Cloak and Dagger; The Man I Love; Nora Prentiss; The Beast with Five Fingers; Beautiful but Dangerous; Musketeers of the Sea; Revenge of the Barbarians; Cleopatra's Daughter; A Soldier and One Half; Imitation of Life; I Will, I Will . . . For Now; Bittersweet Love; The Squeeze.

Bway inc: Guys and Dolls (Tony-1951); Harbor Lights; What Makes Sammy Run; My Daughter, Your Son; Front Page.

TV inc: Police Story; The Invisible Man; Rhoda; Fame; Supertain; Lucy Moves to NBC; Perfect Gentlemen; Code Red.

ALDEN, Norman: Act. b. Fort Worth, TX, Sep 13, 1924. e. TCU. Films inc: The Walking Target; Portrait of a Mobster; Operation Bottleneck; Bedtime Story; The Wild Angels; Tora Tora Tora; The Great Bank Robbery; I Never Promised You a Rose Garden; Hindenburg;

Where Does It Hurt; Semi-Tough; Cloud Dancer; Borderline.

TV inc: No Other Love; Flamingo Road; Desperate Lives; Snow Job; California Girls; The Heart Of A Champion--The Ray Mancini Story.

ALDERTON, John: Act. b. Gainsborough, Lincs, England, Nov 27, 1940. Thea inc: Spring and Port Wine; Dutch Uncle; The Night I Chased the Women With an Eel; Punch and Judy Stories; Birthday Party; Confusions; Rattle of a Simple Man.

Films inc: The System; Duffy; Hannibal Brooks; Please Sir; Zardoz; It Shouldn't Happen to a Vet; All Things Bright and Beautiful.

TV inc: Emergency Ward 10; Please Sir; My Wife Next Door.

ALDREDGE, Theoni V. (nee Vachlioti): Costume Des. b. Salonika, Greece, Aug. 22, 1932. Bway inc: The Distaff Side; Subject to Fits; Underground; The Basic Training of Pavlo Hummel; Timon of Athens; Two Gentlemen of Verona; Much Ado About Nothing; Sticks and Stones; Voices; The Hunter; The Wedding Band; The Three Sisters; The Dance of Death; Music! Music!; An American Millionaire; In Praise of Love; Little Black Sheep; A Chorus Line; The Au Pair Man; Annie (Tony-1977); Three Penny Opera; Clothes For A Summer Hotel; Break A Leg; I Remember Mama; Ballroom; Barnum (Tony-1980); 42d Street; Woman of the Year; Dreamgirls; A Little Family Business; Merlin; Private Lives; La Cage Aux Folles (Tony-1984); The Corn Is Green; The Rink.

Films inc: Girl of the Night; You're a Big Boy Now; No Way to Treat a Lady; Uptight; Last Summer; I Never Sang for My Father; Promise at Dawn; The Great Gatsby (Oscar-1974); The Fury; The Cheap Detective; Eyes of Laura Mars; The Champ; Semi-Tough; The Rose; Rich and Famous; Annie; Monsignor; Ghostbusters.

TV inc: Much Ado About Nothing; Sarah In America (Kennedy Center Tonight); Alice at the Palace.

ALDREDGE, Tom: Act. b. Dayton, OH, Feb 28, 1928. e. U of Dayton. Bway inc: Electra; The Nervous Set; The Tempest; Between Two Thieves; Love's Labour's Lost; Troilus and Cressida; The Mutilated; The Butter and Egg Man; Romeo and Juliet; Twelfth Night; The Boys in the Band; The Happiness Cage (dir only); How the Other Half Loves; Sticks and Bones; The Leaf People; Rex; Where's Charley?; Vieux Carre; Stages; Saint Joan; On Golden Pond; The Little Foxes; Strange Interlude.

Films inc: The Mouse on the Moon; The Troublemaker; The Rain People.

TV inc: The Blue Hotel; Nurse; Henry Winkler Meets William Shakespeare (Emmy-1978); The Gentleman Bandit; Robbers, Rooftops and Witches; Pudd'nhead Wilson.

ALDRICH, Adell: Dir. b. Los Angeles, Jun 11, 1943. e. USC. D of the late Robert Aldrich. TV inc: Daddy, I Don't Like It Like This; The Kid from Left Field.

ALDRICH, Robert: Dir. b. Cranston, RI, Aug 9, 1918. e. U of VA. Films inc: The Big Leaguer; World for Ransom (& prod); Apache; Vera Cruz; Kiss Me Deadly (& prod); The Big Knife (& prod); Attack (& prod); Autumn Leaves; The Ride Back (& exec prod); Ten Seconds to Hell; The Angry Hills; The Last Sunset; Sodom and Gomorrah; Whatever Happened to Baby Jane? (& prod); Four For Texas (& prod); Hush, Hush Sweet Charlotte (& prod); Flight of the Phoenix (& prod); The Dirty Dozen; The Legend of Lylah Claire (& prod); The Killing of Sister George (& prod); Whatever Happened to Aunt Alice (prod only); Too Late the Hero (& prod); The Grissom Gang (& prod); Ulzana's Raid; Emperor of the North; The Longest Yard; Hustle (& prod); Twilight's Last Gleaming; Choirboys; Sundance Kid; The Frisco Kid; All the Marbles.

TV inc: China Smith; The Doctor; Adventures in Paradise;
(Died Dec 5, 1983).

ALDRICH, William McLaughry: Prod. b. Los Angeles, Oct 17, 1944. e. USC. S of the late Robert Aldrich. P Aldrich Co, Inc. Films inc: Who's Killing the Great Chefs of Europe; The Choirboys; All the Marbles.

ALDRIDGE, Michael: Act. b. Glastonbury, Somerset, England, Sep 9, 1920. Thea inc: With Old Vic in various Shakespearean roles; Escapade; Salad Days; Free As Air; A Moon for the Misbegotten; State of Emergency; Vanity Fair; The Fighting Cock; The Farmer's Wife;

Heartbreak House; The Unknown Soldier and His Wife; The Tempest; The Cocktail Party; Caucasian Chalk Circle; The Magistrate; A Bequest to the Nation; Reunion in Vienna; Absurd Person Singular; Jeeves; Lies!; The Last of Mrs. Cheyney; Noises Off.

TV inc: Love In A Cold Climate; A Voyage Round My Father; Charters & Caldicott.

ALEXANDER, Denise: Act. b. Long Island, NY, Nov 11, 1939. Performed in 5,000 radio programs inc A Tree Grows in Brooklyn; I Remember Mama; Perry Mason; Martin Kane, Private Eye.

Bway inc: Children's Hour; A Member of the Wedding.

TV inc: Days of Our Lives; General Hospital; The Lindbergh Kidnapping Case.

ALEXANDER, Jane (nee Quigley): Act. b. Boston, Oct 28, 1939. e. Sarah Lawrence Coll; U of Edinburgh. Films inc: The Great White Hope; A Gun Fight; The New Centurions; All the President's Men; The Betsy; Kramer vs Kramer; Brubaker; Night Crossing; Testament; City Heat.

TV inc: Eleanor and Franklin; Death Be Not Proud; A Question of Love. Mourning Becomes Electra; The Time of Your Life; Find Your Way Home; Hamlet; Playing For Time (Emmy-supp-1981); Dear Liar; In The Custody of Strangers; When She Says No; Calamity Jane (& prod); National Science Test 1984; Malice In Wonderland.

Bway inc: The Great White Hope (Tony-supp-1969); 6 Rms Riv Vu; The Merry Wives of Windsor; Find Your Way Home; Hamlet; The Heiress; First Monday in October; Goodbye Fidel; Monday After the Miracle; Other thea inc: Old Times (Off Bway).

ALEXANDER, Jeff: Comp-Cond. b. Seattle, WA, Jul 2, 1910. e. Becker Cons. Film scores inc: The Tender Trap; Escape From Fort Bravo; The Mating Game; The Gazebo; It Started with a Kiss; Kid Galahad; The George Raft Story; The Rounders; The Sea Gypsies.

TV inc: Sam Benedict; The Lieutenant; The Greatest Show on Earth; Valentine's Day; More Wild Wild West.

ALEXANDER, Shana: Wri-TV pers. b. NYC, Oct 6, 1925. D of Cecelia Ager and the late Milton Ager. With PM (NYC newspaper) 1944-46; Harper's Bazaar, 1946-47; reporter Life Mag 1951-1961; staff wri 1961-64; edtr McCall's Mag 1969-71.

TV inc: 60 Minutes.

ALEXANDER, Van: Cond-Arr-Comp. b. NYC, May 2, 1915. e. Columbia U. Formed own orch, played in theatres, radio; arr for Benny Goodman, Paul Whiteman. Film scores inc: Baby-Face Nelson; Straight-Jacket; Big Operation; Andy Hardy Comes Home.

TV inc: Hazel; Gene Kelly's Wonderful World of Girls with 50 Girls, Count 'Em, 50; Dean Martin's Xmas In California; The Golddiggers Chevrolet Show (mus dir); The Wacky World of Jonathan Winters (mus dir).

Songs: A Tisket a Tasket (collab. w. Ella Fitzgerald); I'll Close My Eyes; Where, O Where Has My Little Dog Gone?.

ALFIERI, Richard (aka Richard J Anthony): Act. b. FL. e. Yale. Thea inc: Awake and Sing; The Justice Box; People of the Empire; Vieux Carre.

Films inc: The Rivals; Children of Rage (& wri); In Search of Historic Jesus; Echoes (& wri).

TV inc: Stories From the Bible; Macbeth; I Love Liberty (wri only).

ALGAR, James Nelson: Prod-Wri-Dir. b. Modesto, CA, Jun 11, 1912. e. Stanford U, BA, MA Journalism. With Walt Disney Prods. since 1934. Animator: Snow White. Directed: Fantasia; Bambi; Ichabod & Mr. Toad. Films inc: Ten Who Dared; The Incredible Journey; The Jungle Cat; Run, Cougar, Run.

TV inc: Run Light Buck, Run; The Not So Lonely Lighthouse Keeper; Two Against The Arctic; Wild Geese Calling.

ALI, Muhammad (Cassius Clay): Act. b. Louisville, KY, Jan 18, 1942. Former champion fighter. Films inc: Requiem for a Heavyweight; The Greatest; Body and Soul.

TV inc: Freedom Road.

ALICIA, Ana: Act. (nee Ortiz)b. Mexico City, Dec. 12, 1956. e. Wellesley; U of TX, BA.

TV inc: Ryan's Hope; The Sacketts; Roughnecks; Condominium;

Coward of the County; The Ordeal of Bill Carney; Happy Endings; Falcon Crest.
Films inc: Halloween II.

ALJIAN, James D.: Exec. b. Oakland, CA, Nov 5, 1932. Senior v.p.-finance, MGM; April 1982 same post for MGM/UA Entertainment Co.

ALLAN, Ted: Wri. b. Montreal, Canada, Jan 25, 1916. Plays inc: The Money Makers; The Ghost Writers; Oh, What A Lovely War; I've Seen You Cut Lemons; Love Streams.
Films inc: Fuse; Lies My Father Told Me; Them Damned Canadians; Falling In Love Again.

ALLAN, Ted: Cin. b. Clifton, AZ. Portrait pho for MGM, FOX; Selznick. Featurettes for the following films: Von Ryan's Express; Fantastic Voyage; Sand Pebbles; Dr Doolittle; Lady in Cement; Tora! Tora! Tora!; The Hindenburg; The 7% Solution; Rollercoaster; Two Minute Warning; House Calls; Dracula; Same Time Next Year; Love Streams; "I'm Almost Not Crazy. . ." John Cassavetes, The Man And His Work.

ALLAND, William: Prod. b. Delmar, DE, Mar 4, 1916. Originally with Orson Welles' Mercury Theatre; acted in Citizen Kane; later staff producer for U-I. Films inc: It Came from Outer Space; This Island Earth; The Lady Takes a Flyer; The Rare Breed; Look in Any Window (& dir).

ALLEGRET, Yves: Dir. b. Asnieres, France, Oct 13, 1907. Films inc: Les Deux Timides; Dedee (& sp); Riptide; The Cheat; Les Orgueilleux; Oasis; Mam'zelle Nitouche (& sp); La Meilleure Part (& sp); Young Girls Beware; L'Ambitieuse; Germinal; Johnny Banco; L'Invasion; Mords pas--on t'aime (& sp).

ALLEN, Byron: TV pers. b. Detroit, MI, Apr 22, 1961. e. USC. Started writing comedy material as teen-ager for Jimmie Walker, the late Freddie Prinze. TV inc: Mel Tillis, Joey Bishop specials; Real People (co-host); Animals Are the Funniest People; Salute to Lady Liberty.

ALLEN, Corey: Dir. b. Cleveland, OH, Jun 29, 1934. e. UCLA, BA. On stage dir. Death of a Salesman; Who's Afraid of Virginia Woolf?; The Time of Your Life.
TV inc: Dr. Kildare; Stone; The Return of Frank Cannon; Lobo; Simon & Simon; Capitol; Whiz Kids; Hill Street Blues (Emmy-1984); Murder, She Wrote; Codename Foxfire.
Films inc: Thunder and Lightning; Avalanche (& wri).

ALLEN, Debbie: Act. b. Houston, TX, Jan 16. e. Howard U, BA. Thea inc: Purlie; Raisin; West Side Story (rev). (London) The Kids From Fame (& prod-dir-chor).
TV inc: Roots--The Next Generation; Ben Vereen--His Roots; 3 Girls 3; Fame (& chor) (Emmys-chor-1982, 1983); Loretta Lynn in Big Apple Country; Texaco Star Theater--Opening Night. The Kids From Fame; Women of San Quentin; John Schneider's Christmas Holiday; A Tribute to Martin Luther King Jr.--A Celebration of Life; Celebrity; Disneyland's 30th Anniversary Celebration; Night Of 100 Stars II; Motown Returns To Whe Apollo.
Films inc: Ragtime.

ALLEN, Dede: Flm Ed. b. Cleveland, OH, 1924. Films inc: Odds Against Tomorrow; The Hustler; America, America; Bonnie and Clyde; Rachel, Rachel; Alice's Restaurant; Little Big Man; Slaughterhouse 5; Serpico; Night Moves; Dog Day Afternoon; The Missouri Breaks; Slap Shot; The Wiz; Reds (& exec prod); Mike's Murder; The Breakfast Club.

ALLEN, Duane: Singer-Sngwri. b. Taylortown, TX, Apr 29, 1943. e. U of TX, BS. Deejay KPLT (Paris, TX) before joining Oak Ridge Boys (see group listing for Grammys). Songs inc: Here's A Song for The Man; How Much Further Can We Go; I Will Follow The Sun; He Did It All For Me.

ALLEN, Elizabeth (nee Gillease): Act. b. Jersey City, NJ, Jan 25 1934. Films inc: From the Terrace; Diamond Head; Donovan's Reef; Cheyenne Autumn; The Carey Treatment; Star Spangled Girl.
Thea inc: Romanoff & Juliet; Lend An Ear; The Gay Life; Do I Hear

a Waltz?; Sherry; Cactus Flower; California Suite.
TV inc: Jackie Gleason Show; The Jimmy Walker Story; Bracken's World; The Paul Lynde Show; No Other Love.

ALLEN, Irving: Dir-Prod. b. Poland, Nov 24, 1905. e. Georgetown, PhD. Film editor U, PAR, REP, 1929-40. Shorts Prod-dir RKO, WB. 1941-42. Shorts inc: Forty Boys and A Song; Climbing the Matterhorn (Oscar-shorts-1947). WW II, 1942-45. Debut as director Strange Voyage, 1945. Films inc: Avalanche; Fire Down Below; No Time To Die; Trials of Oscar Wilde; Hammerhead; The Wrecking Crew; The Desperados; Run Wild, Run Free; Cromwell.

ALLEN, Irwin: Prod. b. NYC, 1916. e. Columbia U; CCNY. Films inc: The Sea Around Us (Oscar-short-1952); The Animal World; The Story of Mankind (& dir); The Big Circus; The Lost World; A Voyage to the Bottom of the Sea (& dir); Five Weeks in a Balloon (& dir); The Poseidon Adventure; The Towering Inferno (& co dir); The Swarm (& dir); Beyond The Poseidon Adventure (& dir); When Time Ran Out.
TV inc: Voyage to the Bottom of the Sea; Lost in Space; Time Tunnel; Land of the Giants; The Swiss Family Robinson; The Time Travelers; The Memory of Eva Ryker; Code Red; The Night The Bridge Fell Down; Cave-In! (exec prod).

ALLEN, Jay Presson: Wri. b. Fort Worth, TX, Mar 3, 1922. W of Lewis Allen. Films inc: Marnie; Prime of Miss Jean Brodie; Travels with My Aunt; Cabaret; Funny Lady; Just Tell Me What You Want; It's My Turn (exec prod); Prince of the City (& exec prod); Deathtrap (& exec prod).
Plays inc: Prime of Miss Jean Brodie; Forty Carats; A Little Family Business.
TV inc: Prime of Miss Jean Brodie.

ALLEN, Karen: Act. b. MD, Oct 5, 1951. Films inc: A Small Circle of Enemies; Cruising; The Wanderers; National Lampoon's Animal House; Raiders of the Lost Ark; Shoot the Moon; Split Image; Until September; Starman.
TV inc: John Steinbeck's East of Eden; Fridays.
Bway inc: Monday After the Miracle.

ALLEN, Lewis M.: Prod. b. Berryville, VA, 1922. e. U of VA, BA. H of Jay Presson Allen. Bway inc: Ballad of the Sad Cafe; Big Fish, Little Fish; The Physicists; Half a Sixpence; Annie (Tony-1977); Billy Bishop Goes To Washington.
Films inc: The Connection; The Balcony; Lord of the Flies; Fahrenheit 451; Fortune and Men's Eyes; Never Cry Wolf; 1918.

ALLEN, Marty: Comedian. b. Pittsburgh, PA, Mar 23, 1922. Began working niteries while USC student after WW2 service; appeared as opening act with Nat "King" Cole; Eydie Gorme; teamed with Steve Rossi for several years in niteries; solo since 1968, niteries, tv guestings. Other TV inc: Mr. Jericho; The Ballad of Billie Blue; Comedy Is Not Pretty; Murder Will Kill You.

ALLEN, Mel: Sportscaster. b. Birmingham, AL, Feb 14, 1913. e. U of AL, AB; AL Law School, LLB. Staff announcer CBS, early 30s. Commentator NY Yankees three decades. Also sports commentator Fox Movietone Newsreel (1946-64).

ALLEN, Nancy: Act. b. NYC, Jun 24. Films inc: The Last Victim; The Last Detail; Carrie; I Wanna Hold Your Hand; Home Movies; 1941; Dressed To Kill; Blow Out; Strange Invaders; The Buddy System; Forced Entry; Not For Publication; The Philadelphia Experiment; Terror In The Aisles.

ALLEN, Patrick: Act. b. Malawi, Mar 17, 1927. Thea inc: The Desperate Hours; The Rough and Ready Lot; Ondine; The Devils; Troilus and Cressida; The Flip Side; The Sandboy; The Island of the Mighty; Present Laughter.
Films inc: 1984; High Tide At Noon; The Long Haul; Dunkirk; I Was Monty's Double; The Traitors; Captain Clegg; Night of the Big Heat; When Dinosaurs Ruled the Earth; Persecution.
TV inc: Churchill and the Generals; Pericles, Prince of Tyre.

ALLEN, Philip: Act. b. Pittsburgh, PA, Mar 26, 1939. e. Neighborhood Playhouse. Bway inc: Sticks and Bones. Films inc: The Onion Field; Special Delivery; Midway.

TV inc: Helter Skelter; Washington--Behind Closed Doors; Trapped Beneath the Sea; Mary Jane Harper Cried Last Night; Bad News Bears; A Family Upside Down; Friendly Fire.

ALLEN, Rex: Act. b. Wilcox, AZ, Dec 31, 1922. Started in radio, vaudeville, rodeo perf, rec artist. Films inc: Arizona Cowboy; Hills of Oklahoma; I Dream of Jeanie; Phantom Stallion; For the Love of Mike; Tomboy and the Champ; Charlotte's Web (voice).

TV inc: Frontier Doctor; Town Hall Party; Music City News' Top Country Hits of the Year.

ALLEN, Sian Barbara: Act. b. Reading, PA, Jul 12, 1946. e. Pasadena Playhouse. Films inc: You'll Like My Mother; Billy Two Hats.

TV inc: The Waltons; The Lindbergh Kidnapping Case; Captains and the Kings; Scream, Pretty Peggy; The Family Rico; Eric.

ALLEN, Steve: Act-Comp. b. NYC, Dec 26, 1921. Started career as announcer-writer-pianist at KOY, Phoenix. On TV in N.Y. in '50. TV inc: What's My Line; Tonight; Steve Allen Show. Stone; The Big Show; The Gossip Columnist; 32d Annual Emmy Awards (host); Steve Allen Comedy Hour; A Funny Thing Happened On The Way to the White House (cable); Meeting of the Minds (& wri); TV's Censored Bloopers; I've Had It Up To Here (host); Wait Till We're 65; Texaco Star Theatre--Opening Night; The Great American Sing-A-Long (host); Ernie Kovacs--Television's Original Genius (cable); Here's Television Entertainment (host); In the Swing (host); New Year's Eve with Bill Lombardo & his Orchestra-- An American Tradition Renewed; Comedy Zone (host); The Ratings Game (PC); The Start Of Something Big.

Films inc: Down Memory Lane; I'll Get By; The Benny Goodman Story; The Big Circus; College Confidential; Warning Shot; Where Were You When the Lights Went Out?; The Comic;

Songs inc: This Could Be the Start of Something Big; South Rampart Street Parade; Picnic; Houseboat; On The Beach.

(Grammy-original Jazz comp-1963).

ALLEN, Woody (Allen Stewart Konigesberg): Act-Dir-Wri. b. NYC, Dec 1, 1935. Began writing comedy at age 17, contributing to various magazines and top comics. Started career as stand-up comic 1961, in niteries. On screen from 1963. Films inc: What's New Pussycat? (wri-act); Casino Royale (act); What's Up Tiger Lily? (dubbed scr, act); Take the Money and Run; Bananas; Play It Again, Sam (wri-act); Everything You Always Wanted to Know About Sex But Were Afraid To Ask; Sleeper; Love and Death (wri-act) The Front (act); Annie Hall *(Oscars*-1977 for dir-wri); Interiors (wri-dir); Manhattan; Stardust Memories; A Midsummer Night's Sex Comedy; Zelig; Broadway Danny Rose; The Purple Rose Of Cairo.

Plays inc: Play It Again, Sam; Don't Drink the Water; The Floating Light Bulb.

TV inc: The Television Academy Hall Of Fame.

ALLEY, Kirstie: Act. b. Wichita, KS., Jan. 12, 1955. e. KS State U, U KS. Films inc: One More Chance; Star Trek II--The Wrath of Khan; Blind Date; Champions; Runaway.

TV inc: Tow Heads; Highway Honeys; Masquerade; A Midsummer Night's Dream; A Bunny's Tale.

ALLIO, Rene: Dir. b. Marseilles, France, 1924. Films inc: Les Ames Mortes; La Meule; The Shameless Old Lady; Skin Deep; L'Une et L'Autre; Pierre et Paul; Les Camisards; Rude Journee pour la Reine; Return to Marseilles (& wri).

ALLISON, Charles Gary: Wri-Prod. b. Newport, RI, Jul 12, 1940. e. USC. TV inc: Fraternity Row (& prod): C.C. Julian; In Country The Hanoi Hilton (co-prod); The 33rd of August. The First Olympics-Athens 1896. VP, Troystar Prodns.

ALLISON, Fran: Act. b. LaPorte City, IA, Nov. 20, 1907. e. Coe Coll. Started as radio singer, 1934; moved to Chicago 1937 where for many years portrayed Aunt Fanny on Don McNeill's Breakfast Club; best known as the live member of the puppet TV series, Kukla, Fran & Ollie (1947-57 and since revived). TV inc: Happy Birthday, Beulah Witch.

ALLMAN, Sheldon: Act. b. Chicago, Jun 8, 1924. Films inc: Hud; Good Neighbor Sam; Pattern for Murder; The Sons of Katie Elder; Nevada Smith; In Cold Blood.

ALLYSON, June (Ella Geisman): Act. b. Westchester, NY, Oct 7, 1917. Started as chorus girl. Screen debut Best Foot Forward, 1943. Films inc: Girl Crazy; Thousands Cheer; Two Girls and A Sailor; Meet the People; Two Sisters From Boston; Till The Clouds Roll By; High Barbaree; Good News; The Three Musketeers; Words and Music; Little Women; The Stratton Story; The Reformer and the Redhead; Battle Circus; Remains To Be Seen; The Glenn Miller Story; Executive Suite; Strategic Air Command; The Shrike; My Man Godfrey; They Only Kill Their Masters; That's Entertainment; Blackout.

TV inc: The Kid With The Broken Halo.

ALMEIDA, Laurindo: Comp-Mus. b. Sao Paulo, Brazil, Sep 2, 1917. To US 1947. Guitarist in Stan Kenton orch; left Kenton 1950 to record, compose, tour US.

Film scores inc: Maracaibo; Cry Tough; The Naked Sea.

Comps inc: Naked Sea; Johnny Peddler; Sighs; Gold Brazilian Sun; The Gypsy with Fire in His Shoes; Sunset in Copacabana; Pancho's Guitar; Guitar Tristesse.

(Grammys-(5)-Class Perf Vocal/Inst-1960; Class Perf Inst 1960, 1961; Class Comp 1961; Inst Jazz 1964).

ALMENDROS, Nestor: Cin. b. Barcelona, Spain, 1930. Films inc: La Collectionneuse; My Night At Maud's; Clare's Knee; Wild Child; Chloe in the Afternoon; The Gentleman Tramp; The Marquise of O; Bed and Board; Story of Adele H; General Idi Amin (doc); The Man Who Loved Women; Days of Heaven *(Oscar*-1978); Goin' South; Madame Rosa; Days of Heaven; Perceval; Kramer vs Kramer; The Green Room; Love On The Run; The Valley; The Blue Lagoon; The Last Metro; Still of the Night; Sophie's Choice; Pauline a la plage (Pauline at the Seaside); Vivement Dimanche (Let It Be Sunday); Mauvaise Conduite (Improper Conduct) (co-wri & co-dir); Places in the Heart.

ALMOND, Paul: Prod-Dir-Wri. b. Montreal, Apr 26, 1931. e. McGill U; Balliol Coll; Oxford. Toured British Isles with Shakespearean company. Joined CBS as a prod-dir, 1954. Prod, dir over 100 TV dramas in Canada, England, U.S. Films inc: Isabel; Act of the Heart; Journey; Ups & Downs.

ALONSO, Alicia: Dancer. b. Havana, Cuba, Dec 21, 1921. Debut 1938, Musicomedy, Great Lady; also appeared in Stars In Your Eyes; joined American Ballet Caravan 1939 as soloist; moved to American Ballet Theatre following year; career interrupted 1942 when she suffered detached retina; replaced ailing Alicia Markova in Giselle 1943, thereafter a star member of American Ballet Theatre with Markova, Anton Dolin, Andre Eglevsky, Igor Youskevitch; promoted to principal dancer 1964 danced Fall River Legend; Undertow; Romeo and Juliet; Billy The Kid; founded Ballet Alicia Alonso, Havana, 1948, company disbanded mid-fifties after Batista government cut its susbsidies; joined Ballet Russe de Monte Carlo 1955; 1957 first Western dancer invited to dance in USSR; 1959, with help from Castro goverment, founded Ballet Nacional de Cuba of which she, despite growing blindness, continues as prima ballerina.

Films inc: Alicia (doc).

ALONZO, John A.: Cin-Dir. b. Dallas, TX, 1934. Films inc: (as cin) Bloody Mama; Vanishing Point; Chinatown; Harold and Maude; Lady Sings the Blues; The Bad News Bears; Black Sunday; Sounder; Pete 'n' Tillie; Conrack; Casey's Shadow; The Cheap Detective; Norma Rae; Tom Horn; FM; Blue Thunder; Cross Creek; Scarface; Terror In The Aisles; Runaway; Beyond Reason. (Dir) Back Roads; Zorro, The Gay Blade.

TV inc: Champions, A Love Story; Belle Starr (dir-cin); Blinded By The Light (dir-cin); The Kid From Nowhere (cin).

ALOV, Alexander: Dir. b. Kharkov, Russia, Sept 26, 1923. e. Moscow Film Institute. Always co-directs with Vladimir Naumov. Both worked as asst dirs on Igor Savchenko's Taras Shevchenko which they completed after Savchenko's death.

Films inc: Turbulent Youth; Pavel Korchagin; The Wind (& wri); Peace to the Newcomer (& wri); The Flight (& wri); The Legend of Thyl Uylenspiegel (& wri); Bereg (River Bank) (& wri).

TV inc: The Coin (& wri).

ALPERT, Herb: Mus. b. Los Angeles, Mar 31, 1935. Leader, trumpeter of Tijuana Brass. Formed A&M Records 1962.

Recordings inc: The Lonely Bull, Tijuana Taxi; Spanish Flea; A

Taste of Honey (Grammys-(3)-record of year, non-jazz inst, inst arr-1965); Zorba the Greek; What Now, My Love (Grammys-non-jazz inst, inst arr-1966); This Guy's In Love With You; Solid Brass; Summertime; Rise (Grammy-pop inst-1979); You Smile-the Song Begins; Main Event; Beyond.

ALSTON, Howard P.: Exec. b. Glendale, CA, Jan 26, 1921. Joined CBS TV as prodn asst 1951; dir of ops Television City, 1956; later prodn mgr. Filmaster Prodns, CBS Films, Goodson-Todman, QM Prodns; joined U 1977 as prod; Oct 1981, prodn VP Marble Arch Prodns; resd Dec 19, 1983.
    TV inc: Centennial; The Return of Marcus Welby, M.D. Films inc: Mask.

ALTMAN, Robert: Dir-Wri-Prod. b. Kansas City, MO, Feb 20, 1922. e. U of MO. Films inc: The Delinquents; The James Dean Story (co-dir & prod); Countdown; That Cold Day in the Park; M*A*S*H; Brewster McCloud; McCabe and Mrs. Miller; Images; The Long Goodbye; Thieves Like Us; California Split; Nashville; Buffalo Bill and the Indians; The Late Show; 3 Women (wri-prod); Welcome to LA (prod); Remember My Name (prod); A Wedding; A Perfect Couple; Quintet; Rich Kids (prod); Health; Popeye (dir); Before The Nickelodeon--The Early Cinema of Edwin S Porter (doc) (voice); Streamers; Secret Honor (prod-dir).
    TV inc: Bonanza; The Roaring Twenties; Bus Stop; Combat; The Laundromat.
    Bway inc: Come Back to The 5 & Dime, Jimmy Dean, Jimmy Dean (dir).

ALVES, Joe: Dsgn-Prod. b. San Leandro, CA, May 21, 1938. e. San Jose State; USC. Films inc: Sugarland Express; Jaws; Close Encounters; Jaws II (assoc prod & 2nd unit dir); Jaws 3-D (dir); Starman (visual cnslt).
    TV inc: Night Gallery.

ALVIN, John (ne Hoffstadt): Act. b. Chicago, Oct 24, 1917. Screen debut, 1944, Destination Tokyo. Films inc: Missing Women; Two Guys from Texas; Train to Alcatraz; Shanghai Chest; Carrie; April in Paris; Torpedo Alley; Somewhere In Time.
    TV inc: Police Woman; MASH; Mannix; All in the Family; Visions; Passions.

ALWYN, William: Comp. b. Northampton, England, 1905. e. Royal Academy of Music. Films inc: Odd Man Out; Fallen Idol; Svengali; Cure for Love; The Ship that Died of Shame; Manuela; I Accuse; Silent Enemy; Swiss Family Robinson; The Running Man.

AMATEAU, Rod: Dir-Wri. b. NYC, Dec 20, 1923. Films inc: Pussy Cat, I Love You; The Statue; Where Does It Hurt?; The Wild Conspiracy; Drive-In; Seniors; Hitler's Son; Lovelines.
    TV inc: Private Secretary; Dobie Gillis; Lassie; Dennis Day Show; Dukes of Hazzard; Enos (& supv prod); Border Pals (exec prod-wri); Uncommon Valor; Highway Honeys (& exec prod); Six Pack (& supv prod); High School U.S.A. (dir).

AMBLER, Eric: Wri. b. England, Jun 29, 1909. Films inc: The Way Ahead; The October Man; Encore; The Magic Box; The Card; The Cruel Sea; Lease of Life; Battle Hell; A Night to Remember; The Wreck of the Mary Deare.

AMECHE, Don: Act. b. Kenosha, WI, May 31, 1908. In stock, on radio before screen debut 1936. Films inc: Sins of Man; Ramona; One In A Million; Love Is News; You Can't Have Everything; In Old Chicago; Alexander's Ragtime Band; The Three Musketeers; The Story of Alexander Graham Bell; Swanee River; Lillian Russell; Four Sons; Down Argentine Way; That Night In Rio; Kiss the Boys Goodbye; Wing And A Prayer; Greenwich Village; Sleep My Love; A Fever in the Blood; Picture Mommy Dead; Suppose They Gave A War and Nobody Came; The Boatniks; Trading Places; Cocoon.
    TV inc: Not in Front of the Kids.

AMES, Ed: Singer-Act. b. Jul 9. Originally a member of the Ames Brothers singing act, went solo and studied acting under Herbert Berghof. Bway inc: One Flew Over the Cuckoo's Nest. TV inc: Daniel Boone.
    Recordings inc: Try to Remember; My Cup Runneth Over; Who

Will Answer.

AMES, Leon (ne Wycoff): Act. b. Portland, IN, Jan 20, 1903. Screen debut, 1932, Murders in the Rue Morgue. Films inc: The Count of Monte Cristo; Charlie Chan on Broadway; Ellery Queen and the Murder Ring; Meet Me in St. Louis; Thirty Seconds Over Tokyo; Little Women; On Moonlight Bay; Peyton Place; From the Terrace; The Absent-Minded Professor; On a Clear Day You Can See Forever; Hammersmith Is Out; Just You And Me Kid; Testament.
    TV inc: Life with Father; Father of the Bride; Mister Ed; The Best Place To Be.

AMES, Rachel: Act. b. Portland, OR, Nov 2. Films inc: When Worlds Collide.
    TV inc: General Hospital.

AMFITHEATROF, Daniele: Comp-Cond. b. St Petersburg, Russia, Oct 29, 1901. e. Royal Conservatory of Music, Rome. Guest cond symphony orchs Paris, Rome, Budapest, Vienna, Boston. Film scores inc: La Signora di tutti; Lassie Come Home; Cry Havoc; Days of Glory; Song of the South; O.S.S.; I'll Be Seeing You; Suspense; Smash-Up; The Senator Was Indiscreet; Letter From an Unknown Woman; Another Part of the Forest; Desert Fox; Human Desire; The Mountain; Unholy Wife; Heller in Pink Tights; Edge of Eternity; Major Dundee.
    (Died June 7, 1983).

AMLEN, Seymour: Exec. b. April 28, 1928. e. U of MO, BA; OH State U, MA. With Kenyon & Eckhardt Agency; joined ABC 1955 as senior ratings analyst; 1969, dir of Program & Primary Research; 1972, VP; 1973, VP in chg Research; 1975, VP & Asst to P, AP, ABC Entertainment; 1979, responsibilities expanded to inc Daytime, Early-Morning and Childrens programming.

AMOS, John: Act-Wri-Prod. b. Dec 27, 1941. Films inc: The World's Greatest Athlete; Vanishing Point; Let's Do It Again; Touched By Love; The Beastmaster.
    TV inc: Tim Conway Hour; Mary Tyler Moore; Good Times; Roots; Willa; Alcatraz--The Whole Shocking Story; Hang Tight, Willy Bill; Brother Tough.

AMRAN, Robert: Prod-Dir-Wri. b. Budapest, Hungary, Jun 12, 1938. e. London School of Economics, BS. Films inc: The Mini Affair; Sentinels of Silence (Oscar-1972); Sky High!; Pacific Challenge; The Late Great Planet Earth.

AMSTERDAM, Morey: Act-Wri-Comp. b. Chicago, Dec 14, 1914. Radio, 1922. Nightclub performer. Films inc: Don't Worry. . .We'll Think Of A Title; Machine Gun Kelly; Murder, Inc.
    TV inc: Stop Me If You've Heard This One; Morey Amsterdam Silver Swan Show; Dick Van Dyke Show; Can You Top This; Sooner or Later; Believe You Can--And You Can.
    Songs inc: Rum and Coca Cola; Why Oh Why Did I Ever Leave Wyoming, Yak A Puk.

ANDERMAN, Maureen: Act. b. Oct 26, 1946. Bway inc: Othello; Moonchildren; The Last of Mrs. Lincoln; Hamlet; An Evening With Richard Nixon; The History of American Film; Seascape; Who's Afraid of Virginia Woolf; The Lady from Dubuque; Macbeth; Einstein and the Polar Bear; You Can't Take It With You.
    TV inc: King Crab; Out of Our Father's House; Once Upon A Family; Search for Tomorrow; The Adams Chronicles; The Best of Families; Every Stray Dog and Kid; Cocaine and Blue Eyes.
    Films inc: The Seduction of Joe Tynan; Man, Woman and Child.

ANDERS, Luana: Act. b. 1940. Films inc: Life Begins at Seventeen; The Pit and the Pendulum; The Young Racers; Dementia; B.J. Presents; When the Legends Die; The Last Detail; The Killing Kind; Shampoo; The Missouri Breaks; Goin' South; Harper Valley PTA; One From The Heart; Movers & Shakers.

ANDERS, Merry: Act. b. 1932. Films inc: Les Miserables; Phfft; The Desk Set; The Dalton Girls; Violent Road; The Hypnotic Eye; Young Jesse James; 20,000 Eyes; Tickle Me; Legacy of Blood; Women of the Prehistoric Planet.
    TV inc: How to Marry a Millionaire.

ANDERSEN, Carl: Act. b. Lynchburg, VA, Feb 27, 1945. Started career with rock group in Washington, D.C. Joined road tour as Judas in Jesus Christ Superstar. Repeated role in film version.

ANDERSON, Daphne (nee Scrutton): Act. b. London, Apr 27, 1922. London stage debut, 1938. Thea inc: Three Penny Opera; Blithe Spirit; Cat on a Hot Tin Roof; Spring and Port Wine; A Woman Named Anne; Sadler's Wells; Lord Arthur Savile's Crime; Alice Through the Looking Glass; Jane Eyre; The Sleeping Beauty; Lloyd George Knew My Father.
Films inc: Trottie True; The Beggar's Opera; Hobson's Choice; A Kid for Two Farthings; The Prince and the Showgirl; Snowball; Captain Clegg; The Launching; I Want What I Want.
TV inc: Silas Marner; Gideon's Way; The Imposter; The Whitehall Worrier; The Suede Jacket; Casanova; Justice Is A Woman; The Scarlet Pimpernel.

ANDERSON, Daryl: Act. b. Seattle, WA, Jul 11, 1951. e. U of WA, BFA. Films inc: Sweet Revenge; Butch and Sundance - The Early Days.
TV inc: Lou Grant; The Phoenix.

ANDERSON, Don: Prod. b. Hobart, Tasmania, Australia, Jul 29, 1929. Dir or prod over 200 doc inc Challenge; For Better - For Worse; Hard to Windward; I Hate Holidays; Noise Annoys; Olives Don't Float; Tasmanian Wild Life; The Big Catch; Winter.

ANDERSON, Howard A.: Cin. b. Los Angeles, Mar 31, 1920. e. UCLA. Specialist in special effects. Films inc: Jack the Giant Killer; Tobruk; Superman.
TV inc: Star Trek; My World and Welcome to It.

ANDERSON, Jack: Syndicated columnist-TV report b. Long Beach, CA, Oct 19, 1922. Pulitzer Prize 1972, nat'l reporting. TV inc: Good Morning America; Jack Anderson Confidential; Break Away.

ANDERSON, John: Act. b. Clayton, IL, Oct 20, 1922. e. U of IA, MA. Films inc: Psycho; Ride the High Country; Cotton Comes to Harlem; Soldier Blue; Executive Action; The Lincoln Conspiracy; In Search of Historic Jesus; Zoot Suit; Lone Wolf McQuade.
TV inc: The Deerslayer; Shadow of Fear; Backstairs At The White House; Mark Twain's America--Young Will Rogers; The First Time; Missing Children--A Mother's Story; Insight/The Hit Man; Sins of the Past.

ANDERSON, Judith, Dame: Act. b. Adelaide, Australia, Feb 10, 1898. Stage debut (Sydney) in Royal Divorce, 1915. Bway, stock, 1918. Screen debut Blood Money, 1933. Films inc: Rebecca; Forty Little Mothers; Free and Easy; Lady Scarface; All Through The Night; King's Row; Edge of Darkness; Stage Door Canteen; Laura; And Then There Were None; Diary of A Chambermaid; The Strange Love of Martha Ivers; Specter of the Rose; Pursued; The Red House; Tycoon; The Furies; Salome; The Ten Commandments; Cat on a Hot Tin Roof; Cinderfella; Don't Bother To Knock; Inn of the Damned; Star Trek III-- The Search for Spock.
TV inc: Macbeth (Emmy-1954), Macbeth (Emmy-1961).
Bway inc: Dear Brutus; Cobra; Strange Interlude; Mourning Becomes Electra; Macbeth; Medea(Tony-1948); Medea (1982 rev); Toured in Dame Judith Anderson as Hamlet.

ANDERSON, Lindsay: Dir. b. Bangalore, India, Apr 17, 1923. e. Cheltenham Coll; Wadham Coll; Oxford. Started as film critic, doc dir. Films inc: O Dreamland; Thursday's Children; Every Day Except Christmas; This Sporting Life; If...; O Lucky Man!; In Celebration; Britannia Hospital.
Thea inc: The Long and the Short and the Tall; Billy Liar; The Fire Raisers; Diary of a Madman; The Cherry Orchard; Inadmissible Evidence; The Changing Room; What the Butler Saw; The Sea Gull; The Bed Before Yesterday; Kingfisher; Alice's Boys; Early Days.
TV inc: Robin Hood.
Thea inc: In Celebration (London & Off Bway).

ANDERSON, Loni: Act. b. St Paul, MN, Aug 5, 1945. Taught school briefly.
TV inc: WKRP in Cincinnati; Three on A Date; The Fantastic Fun-nies; 4th Annual Circus of the Stars; Christmas in Opryland; Shaun Cassidy Special; Bob Hope's Bob Hope's Spring Fling of Glamour and Comedy; A Shaun Cassidy Special; Christmas, A Time For Cheer and A Time for Hope; Country Gold; The Merriest of the Merry--Bob Hope's Christmas Show--A Bagful of Comedy; The Sunday Funnies (host); My Mother's Secret Life; Bob Hope's Wicky-Wacky Special From Waikiki; Partners In Crime.
Films inc: Stroker Ace.

ANDERSON, Marian: Singer. b. South Philadelphia, PA, Feb 27, 1902. Appeared on concert stages throughout the world. Received Presidential Medal of Freedom, 1963.

ANDERSON, Melissa Sue: Act. b. Berkeley, CA, Sep 26, 1962. TV inc: The Brady Bunch; Shaft; Very Good Friends; James at 15; The Loneliest Runner; Little House on the Prairie; The Survival of Dana; Which Mother Is Mine? (Emmy-1980); Midnight Offerings; Advice To The Lovelorn; An Innocent Love; First Affair; Finder of Lost Loves.
Films inc: Happy Birthday To Me.

ANDERSON, Melody: Act. b. Edmonton, Canada., Dec. 3 Worked as radio reporter for Canadian Broadcasting Corp; later in Australia; to Hollywood as model before act. TV inc: Pleasure Cove; Elvis; Battlestar Galactica; The A Team; Manimal; Policewoman Centerfold; Ernie Kovacs--Between the Laughter; High School USA.
Films inc: Flash Gordon; Dead and Buried.

ANDERSON, Michael: Dir. b. London, Jan 3, 1920. Debuted in films as actor, 1936, asst. dir. on In Which We Serve, Pygmalion, French Without Tears. (Dir) The Dam Busters; Hell Is Sold Out; 1984; Around the World in 80 Days; Shake Hands With the Devil; The Wreck of the Mary Deare; All The Fine Young Cannibals; The Naked Edge; Flight From Ashiya; Operation Cross Bow; The Quiller Memorandum; Shoes of the Fisherman; Pope Joan; Conduct Unbecoming; Logan's Run; Orca; Dominique; Murder by Phone; Second Time Lucky.
TV inc: The Martian Chronicles.

ANDERSON, Michael, Jr.: Act. b. London, 1943. Started as child actor. Films inc: Tiger Bay; The Sundowners; Greatest Story Ever Told; Major Dundee; The Sons of Katie Elder; Logan's Run; A .Different Image.
TV inc: Queen's Champion; Ivanhoe; The Monroes; The Martian Chronicles; The Million Dollar Face; Love Leads The Way.

ANDERSON, Richard: Wri. b. Long Branch, NJ, Aug 8, 1926. Films inc: 12 O'Clock High; The People Against O'Hara; Across the Wide Missouri; Escape from Fort Bravo; The Student Prince; Forbidden Planet; The Long Hot Summer; Compulsion; Paths of Glory; A Gathering of Eagles; Seven Days In May; Tora! Tora! Tora!; Doctors Wives; Play It As It Lays; The Honkers; Black Eye.
TV inc: Perry Mason; Dan August; Six Million Dollar Man; Bionic Woman; Pearl; The Immigrants; The French Atlantic Affair; Lobo; Condominium; Darkroom; Cover Up.

ANDERSON, Robert: Wri. b. NYC, Apr 28, 1917. e. Harvard U, AB, MA. Films inc: Tea and Sympathy; Until They Sail; The Nun's Story; The Sand Pebbles; I Never Sang for My Father.
Plays inc: All Summer Long; Tea and Sympathy; Silent Night, Lonely Night; The Days Between; You Know I Can't Hear You When the Water's Running; I Never Sang for My Father; Solitaire, Double Solitaire.
TV inc: Biography; The Old Lady Shows Her Medals; The Patricia Neal Story.

ANDERSON, William H.: Prod. b. Smithfield, UT, Oct 12, 1911. e. Compton Coll. Films inc: Old Yeller; Third Man on the Mountain; Swiss Family Robinson; Moon Pilot; Savage Sam; A Tiger Walks; The Happiest Millionaire; The One and Only, Genuine, Original Family Band; The Barefoot Executive; The Biscuit Eater; Superdad; The Strongest Man in the World; The Apple Dumpling Gang; The Treasure of Matecumbe; The Shaggy D.A.
TV inc: Zorro; The Wonderful World of Disney; Daniel Boone; The Swamp Fox; Pop Warner Football; The Scarecrow of Romney Marsh; The Legend of Young Dick Turpin; Willie and the Yank; A Boy Called Nuthin'; The Young Loner; The Mystery of Dracula's Castle; The Bull

from the Sky; Adventure in Satan's Canyon; Three on the Run.

ANDERSSON, Bibi (Berit Elisabet Andersson): Act. b. Stockholm, Nov 11, 1935. e. Royal Dramatic Theatre School. Films inc: Smiles of a Summer Night; The Seventh Seal; Wild Strawberries; Brink of Life; The Face; So Close to Life; The Mistress; The Devil's Eye; My Sister My Love; Duel at Diablo; A Question of Rape; The Story of a Woman; The Kremlin Letter; The Passion of Anna; The Touch; I Never Promised You a Rose Garden; Quintette; The Concorde - Airport '79; Tree Vrouwen; Not For Children; Enemy of the People; The Marmalade Revolution; Jag Rodnar (I'm Blushing); Exposed; Ett Berg Pa Manen's Baksida (A Hill On the Dark Side of the Moon); Sorte Fuger (Black Crows); Sista Leken (The Last Summer);

Thea inc: Who's Afraid of Virginia Woolf?; Dollhouse; After the Fall; The Night of the Tribades.

TV inc: Wallenberg--A Hero's Story.

ANDERSSON, Harriet: Prod. b. Stockholm, Jan 14, 1932. Films inc: Medan Staden Sover; Anderssonskans Kalle; Biffen Och Bananen; Sabotage; Summer With Monika; Ubat 39; Trots; Sawdust and Tinsel; A Lesson in Love; Journey Into Autumn; Smiles of a Summer Night; Kvinna i leopard; Britt i paradiset; Through a Glass Darkly; Siska; Now About These Women; To Love; Loving Couples; The Deadly Affair; The Girls; Anna; Cries and Whispers; Linus; Monismanien; La Sabina; Fanny and Alexander; Raskenstam.

ANDES, Keith: Act. b. Ocean City, NJ, Jul 12, 1920. e. Temple U; Oxford. Films inc: The Farmer's Daughter; Clash by Night; Blackbeard the Pirate; Split Second; Back From Eternity; Damn Citizen; Surrender Hell!; Tora! Tora! Tora!; And Justice For All.

TV inc: Glynis; This Man Dawson; The Ultimate Impostor; Blinded By The Light.

Thea inc: Wildcat; Winged Victory; Kiss Me Kate; Maggie.

ANDRESS, Ursula: Act. b. Berne, Switzerland, Mar 19, 1936. Films inc: The Loves of Casanova; Dr. No; Four For Texas; Fun in Acapulco; She; Nightmare in the Sun; What's New Pussycat?; Once Before I Die; The Blue Max; Casino Royale; The Southern Star; Perfect Friday; Red Sun; Five Against Capricorn; The Fifth Musketeer; Clash of the Titans; Mexico In Flames; Letti Selvaggi (Tigers In Lipstick); Liberte, Egalite, Choucroute (Liberty, Equality, Sauerkraut).

TV inc: Manimal; I Love Men.

ANDREWS, Anthony: Act. b. England, 1948. TV inc: A Beast With Two Backs; Romeo and Juliet; A War of Children; QB VII; Upstairs, Downstairs; Danger UXB; Love Boat Special; Mistress of Paradise; Brideshead Revisited; Ivanhoe; The Scarlet Pimpernel; Sparkling Cyanide; A.D.

Films inc: Operation Daybreak; Under the Volcano; Observations Under the Volcano (doc); Notes from Under the Volcano (doc).

Thea inc: Forty Years On.

ANDREWS, Dana: Act. b. Collins, MS, Jan 1, 1909. e. Pasadena Playhouse. Film debut 1940, The Westerner; Films inc: Lucky Cisco Kid; Kit Carson; Tobacco Road; Belle Starr; Swamp Water; Ball of Fire; Berlin Correspondent; Crash Dive; The Ox-Bow Incident; December 7 (Doc; narr); The North Star; The Purple Heart; Wing and a Prayer; Up In Arms; Laura; State Fair; A Walk in the Sun; Canyon Passage; The Best Years of Our Lives; Boomerang; Night Song; Daisy Kenyon; The Iron Curtain; Deep Waters; Sword in the Desert; My Foolish Heart; Where the Sidewalk Ends; The Frogmen; Assignment-Paris; Elephant Walk; Comanche; While the City Sleeps; Beyond a Reasonable Doubt; Zero Hour; The Fearmakers; The Crowded Sky; Madison Avenue; The Satan Bug; In Harm's Way; Battle of the Bulge; Johnny Reno; Devil's Brigade; Innocent Bystanders; Airport '75; Take A Hard Ride; The Last Tycoon; Born Again; Good Guys Wear Black; Prince Jack.

TV inc: The Right Hand Man; One Small Step Forward; A Wind of Hurricane Force; The Town That Died; Last of the Big Spenders; Ike.

ANDREWS, Eamonn: TV pers-Wri. b. Dublin, Dec 19, 1922. Radio Eireann bcaster 1941-1950; BBC 1950, switched to BBC-TV 1951. Host of British versions of What's My Line; This Is Your Life; host Eamonn Andrews Show; World of Sport; Today; Time for Business. Served 1960-66 as chmn Radio Telefis Eireann, statutory authority charged with establishment of TV in Ireland. Author play The Moon is

Black.

ANDREWS, Edward: Act. b. Griffin, GA, Oct 9, 1915. e. U of VA. Bway debut 1935, How Beautiful with Shoes. Films inc: The Phenix City Story; The Tattered Dress; Tea and Sympathy; The Fiend Who Walked the West; Elmer Gantry; Advise and Consent; Kisses for My President; Youngblood Hawke; Send Me No Flowers; The Glass Bottom Boat; Birds Do It; Tora! Tora! Tora!; Avanti; Charley and the Angel; Seniors; Gremlins.

TV inc: Supertrain; Undercover With The KKK; Insight/Little Miseries.

Bway inc: So Proudly We Hail; Of Mice and Men; The Time of Your Life; The Knew What They Wanted; I Am a Camera; A Visit to a Small Planet; The Gazebo.

(Died March 8, 1985)

ANDREWS, Harry Act. b. Tonbridge, Kent, England. Nov. 10, 1911. e. Wrekin College. Thea inc: Worse Things Happen At Sea; Snow In Summer; Hamlet; He Was Born Gay; School For Scandal; Three Sisters; Hundreds And Thousands; The Critic; An Inspector Calls; The Cherry Orchard; Caesar And Cleopatra; Antony And Cleopatra; Camino Real; Coriolanus; The Lizard On The Rock; Baal; You Never Can Tell.

Films inc: The Red Beret; A Hill In Korea; Moby Dick; Ice Cold In Alex; The Devil's Disciple; Solomon And Sheba; The Best Of Enemies; Lisa; 55 Days At Peking; The Informers; The Hill; The Deadly Affair; The Charge Of The Light Brigade; The Night They Raided Minsky's; The Seagull; A Nice Girl Like Me; Wuthering Heights; Nicholas And Alexandra; Man Of La Mancha; The Mackintosh Man; Man At The Top; The Bluebeard; The Big Sleep; Crossed Swords; Equus; Death On The Nile; Medusa; Superman; Watership Down; Hawk The Slayer.

TV inc: S.O.S. Titanic; The Four Feathers; The Curse Of King Tut's Tomb; The Seven Dials Mystery.

ANDREWS, Julie (Julia Wells) Act. b. Walton-On-Thames, England, Oct. 1, 1935. W of Blake Edwards. Films inc: Mary Poppins *(Oscar-1964)*; The Americamization Of Emily; The Sound Of Music; Torn Curtain; Hawaii; Thoroughly Modern Millie; Star!; Darling Lili; The Tamarind Seed; 10; Little Miss Marker; S.O.B.; Victor/Victoria; The Man Who Loved Women.

Bway inc: The Boy Friend; My Fair Lady; Camelot.

TV inc: High Tor; Julie And Carol At Carnegie Hall; The Julie Andrews Hour *(Emmy-1973)*; An Evening With Julie Andrews And Harry Belafonte; Julie Andrews' Invitation To The Dance With Rudolf Nureyev.

(Grammy-children's recording-1964).

ANDREWS, Peter: Dir. TV inc: How to Survive a Marriage; The Guiding Light; Search for Tomorrow; The Doctors; One Life to Live; All My Children; Gold Coast; Take Five.

ANDREWS, Ralph: Prod. b. Chicago, 1928. e. Tulane U; U of MI; LA City Coll. TV inc: Wedding Party; Mickie Finn; Mickie Finn's Happy Time Hour; Liars Club; Celebrity Sweepstakes; Divorce Hearing; You Don't Say.

ANDREWS SISTERS: Singing Trio. Patty (1918), Maxine (1916), Laverne (1913-67). Popular singing trio of the forties. Films inc: Argentine Nights; In the Navy; Buck Privates; Hold that Ghost; Give Out Sisters; Private Buckaroo; What's Cookin'?; Always a Bridesmaid; Follow the Boys; Hollywood Canteen; Moonlight and Cactus; Her Lucky Night; Make Mine Music (voices); Road to Rio; Melody Time (voices).

Bway inc: Over Here.

ANDREWS, Tige: Act. b. Brooklyn, Mar 19. e. U of Beirut; AADA. Films inc: Mr. Roberts; Imitation General; China Doll; Until They Sail; Onion Head; The Last Tycoon.

TV inc: Sgt. Bilko; Detectives; Mod Squad; Werewolf of Woodstock; Skyway to Death; Raid on Entebbe; Return of the Mod Squad.

Thea inc: Threepenny Opera; Mr. Roberts; Hidden Horizons; Guys and Dolls; Hasty Heart; My Sister Eileen.

ANDREWS, Tina: c Act. b. Chicago, Apr 23. Films inc: Hit; Conrack; Shoot It; Crawly; Carny.

TV inc: McNaughton's Daughter; Born Innocent; The Weekend Nun; The Girls of Huntington House; Billy; Days of Our Lives; Roots,

Part II; The Contender; The Atlanta Child Murders.

ANGEL, Heather: c Act. b. Oxford, England, Feb 9, 1909. On stage 1926-30. US screen debut, 1932, Pilgrimage. Films inc: Berkeley Square; The Informer; The Mystery of Edwin Drood; Last of the Mohicans; Army Girl; Pride and Prejudice; Time to Kill; Lifeboat; In the Meantime, Darling; The Saxon Charm; Alice In Wonderland; Peter Pan; The Premature Burial.

TV inc: Peyton Place; Family Affair; Backstairs at the White House.

ANGELOU, Maya (Marguerite Johnson): Wri-Dir-Act. b. St Louis, MO, Apr 4, 1928. Studied dance with Pearl Primus; worked as singer-dancer in niteries; toured Europe and Africa for two years in State Department sponsored production Porgy and Bess; wrote, produced (with Godfrey Cambridge) performed in Cabaret for Freedom; act in The Blacks, off-Broadway. Thea inc: Look Away (act); Ajax (wri).

Films inc: Georgia, Georgia, (wri).

TV inc: The Slave Coast (narr); Circles (dir); Tapestry (dir); I Know Why The Caged Bird Sings (wri); Sister, Sister (co-prod & wri).

ANGLIM, Philip: Act. b. Feb 11, 1953. e. Yale.

Films inc: All American Boy; Mohammed--Messenger of God; Testament.

TV inc: The Adams Chronicles; Tomorrow's Families; Elephant Man; Elephant Tintypes (prod); The Thorn Birds.

Bway inc: The Elephant Man; Macbeth.

ANHALT, Edna: Wri. b. NYC, Apr 10, 1914. Films inc: Panic in the Streets (Oscar-1950); The Sniper; Not As A Stranger; Pride and the Passion; Girls, Girls, Girls; Decision at Delphi; Becket (Oscar-1964).

ANHALT, Edward: Wri. b. NYC, 1914. Films inc: Avalanche; Bulldog Drummond Strikes Back; Panic in the Streets (Oscar-1950); The Sniper; The Member of the Wedding; Not as a Stranger; The Pride and the Passion; The Young Lions; A Girl Named Tamiko; Becket (Oscar-1964); The Satan Bug; Hour of the Gun; The Boston Strangler; The Mad Woman of Chaillot; The Salzburg Connection; Jeremiah Johnson; Luther; The Man in the Glass Booth; Escape to Athena; Green Ice.

TV inc: Q.B. VII; The Day Christ Died; Madame X (& act).

Plays inc: Thomas and the King.

ANKA, Paul: Singer-Sngwri. b. Ottawa, Canada, Jul 30, 1941. At age 16, launched career with recording of Diana, which he wrote. Since then has written more than 400 songs, inc My Way; You Are My Destiny; Puppy Love; Lonely Boy. Appears in niteries, TV specials.

Films inc: Girls' Town; Look in Any Window; The Longest Day; Atlantic City, USA (song).

TV inc: Sinatra--The First 40 Years; Anka.

ANNABELLA (Suzanne Charpentier): Act. b. France, 1909. Films inc: Napoleon; Le Million; Veille d'Armes; Under the Red Robe; Dinner at the Ritz; Wings of the Morning; Suez; Hotel du Nord; Bridal Suite; Bomber's Moon; Tonight We Raid Calais; 13 Rue Madeleine; Don Juan (sp).

ANNAKIN, Ken: Singer-Sngwri. b. Yorkshire, England, Aug 10, 1914. Film inc: Holiday Camp; Miranda; Quartet (part); Trio (part); Hotel Sahara; Robin Hood; The Sword and the Rose; Three Men in a Boat; Loser Take All; Across the Bridge; The Swiss Family Robinson; Third Man on the Mountain; Very Important Person; The Longest Day; The Fast Lady; Those Magnificent Men in Their Flying Machines; Battle of the Bulge; Monte Carlo or Bust; Call of the Wild; White Fang; Paper Tiger; Behind the Iron Mask; The Fifth Musketeer; Cheaper To Keep Her; The Pirate Movie.

TV inc: The Pirate; Institute for Revenge; Hunter's Moon.

ANNAUD, Jean-Jacques: Dir-Wri. b. Draveil, France, Oct 1,1943. e. IDHEC. Started as film dir French army, making edu film; later dir commercials. Films inc: Black and White In Color; Coup de Tete (dir only); Quest for Fire.

ANNIS, Francesca b. England, 1944. Films inc: Act. The Cat Gang; Cleopatra; Flipper and the Pirates; Saturday Night Out; Murder Most Foul; The Pleasure Girls; The Sky Pirate; The Walking Stick; Macbeth;

Stronger than the Sun; Krull; Dune.

TV inc: Lillie/Emilie; Why Didn't They Ask Evans?; Coming Out of the Ice; The House of Lurking Death.

Thea inc: A Month In The Country.

ANN-MARGRET (Ann-Margret Olsson): Act. b. Stockholm, Sweden, Apr 28, 1941. Toured with bands. Worked with George Burns in Las Vegas. Made TV debut with Jack Benny. Films inc: Pocketful of Miracles; State Fair; Bye, Bye Birdie; Carnal Knowledge; The Pleasure Seekers; Once A Thief; Joseph Andrews; The Twist (Folies Bourgeoises); The Last Remake of Beau Geste; The Cheap Detective; Magic; The Villain; Middle Age Crazy; I Ought To Be In Pictures; The Return of the Soldier; Lookin' To Get Out.

TV inc: Ann-Margret Olsson; Ann-Margret Smith; Ann-Margret-Rhinestone Cowgirl; A Holiday Tribute to the Radio City Music Hall; Hollywood Movie Girls; The Way They Were; George Burns' Early, Early, Early Christmas Special; Who Will Love My Children?; A Streetcar Named Desire; Perry Como's Christmas In England.

ANOUILH, Jean: Plywri. b. Bordeaux, France, Jun 23, 1907. e. College Chaptal; U of Paris. Plays inc: The Ermine; Thieves' Carnival; Mandarin; Y Avait un Prisonnier; Traveller Without Luggage; La Sauvage; Cavalcade D'Amour; Time Remembered; Point of Departure; Antigone; Oreste; Jezabel; Ring Around the Moon; The Rehearsal; Colombe; Waltz of the Toreadors; The Lark; The Fighting Cock; Becket (Tony-1961); Catch As Catch Can; The Cavern; Dear Antoine; Ne Reveillez pas Madame; Le Directeur de L'Opera; The Arrest; The Scenario; Number One.

Films inc: Monsieur Vincent; Pattes Blanches.

ANSARA, Michael: Act. b. Lowell, MA, Apr 15, 1922. Early training Pasadena Playhouse. Films inc: The Robe; Magnificent Seven; The Greatest Story Ever Told; Mohammad-Messenger of God; Day of the Julius Caesar; Soldiers Three; Only the Valiant; New Orleans, Uncensored; Guns of the Animals; The Manitou; Target - Harry; Gas.

TV inc: Ordeal; Broken Arrow; Law of the Plainsman; Deadly Target; Shootout in a One-Dog Town; Centennial; The Fantastic World of D.C. Collins.

ANSPACH, Susan: Act. b. NYC, Nov. 23, 1939. e. Catholic U of America. Films inc: The Landlord; Five Easy Pieces; Play It Again, Sam; Blume in Love; Nashville; The Big Fix; Running; The Devil and Max Devlin; Montenegro (Pigs and Pearls); Gas; Musunderstood.

TV inc: The Last Giraffe; Portrait of an Escort; The First Time; Deadly Encounter; The Yellow Rose; Space.

Bway inc: A View From the Bridge; Journey to the Fifth House.

ANSTEY, Edgar: Prod. b. Watford, England, 1907. Films inc: (doc) Uncharted Waters; Eskimo Village; German Trawler; Housing Problems; Enough to Eat?; Journey Into Spring; The England of Elizabeth; Terminus; Snow; Wild Wings.

ANTHONY, Joseph (ne Deuster): Dir-Act. b. Milwaukee, WI, May 24, 1912. e. U of WI. Bway inc: (act) Mary of Scotland; Professor Mamlock; On the Rocks; Liberty Jones; The Country Girl; Flight Into Egypt; Anastasia. (Dir) Celebration; Bullfight; The Rainmaker; Once Upon a Tailor; The Lark; The Most Happy Fella; Rhinocerous; Mary, Mary; Happily Never After; Finishing Touches.

Films inc: (act) Hat, Coat and Glove; She; Joe Smith, American; Shadow of the Thin Man. (Dir): The Rainmaker; The Matchmaker; Career; All in a Night's Work; Captive City; Tomorrow.

TV inc: (dir) Brenner; Profiles in Courage; Return at Night.

ANTHONY, Ray: Orch Ldr. b. Bentleville, PA, Jan 20, 1922. Recorded for Capitol Records 19 years; Ranwood Records, 9 years. Films inc: Daddy Long Legs; Five Pennies; High School Confidential; This Could Be the Night.

TV inc: Variety shows; summer replacement for Perry Como on CBS, ABC.

ANTHONY, Richard: See ALFIERI, Richard

ANTON, Susan: Act-Singer. b. Oak Glen, CA, Oct 12. Recording artist; niteries. Films inc: Golden Girl; Spring Fever; Cannonball Run II.

TV inc: The Cliffhangers; Susan Anton--and 10,000 GI's; Presenting Susan Anton; Bob Hope's Stand Up and Cheer For The NFL's

60th Year; The Boy Who Loved Trolls; Placido Domingo Steppin' Out With The Ladies; The 39th Annual Tony Awards; How To Be A Man.

ANTONELLI, Laura: Act. Films inc: Lovers and Other Relatives; The Divine Nymph; Wifemistress; Till Marriage Do Us Part; The Innocent; The Hypochondriac; Mi Faccio La Barca (I'm Getting A Yacht); Passione D'Amore (Passion of Love); Letti Selvaggi (Tigers In Lipstick); Tranches de Vie (Slices Of Life).

ANTONIO, Lou: Act-Wri-Dir. b. Oklahoma City, OK, Jan 23, 1934. e. U of OK, BA. Films inc: The Strange One; Splendor in the Grass; America, America; Hawaii; Cool Hand Luke; The Phynx, Mission Batangas (wri); Micki & Maude (exec prod).

Bway inc: The Girls of Summer; The Good Soup; The Garden of Sweets; Andorra; The Lady of the Camellias; The Ballad of the Sad Cafe; Ready When You Are, C.B.

TV inc: (act) Piece of Blue Sky; The Power and the Glory; Danny Thomas Hour; Partners in Crime; Sole Survivor; Where The Ladies Go; Snoop Sisters; Dog and Cat; Making It. (Dir) Gentle Ben (& wri); Flying Nun; McCloud; Rockford Files; Delvecchio; Three for the Road; Rich Man, Poor Man; Lannigan's Rabbi; The Young Rebels (& wri); Someone I Touched; The Girl in the Empty Grave; Something for Joey; The Critical List; Silent Victory--The Kitty O'Neil Story; Breaking Up Is Hard To Do; The Contender; We're Fight Back; The Star Maker; Gabe & Walker; The Steeler and the Pittsburgh Kid; Something So Right; A Good Sport; Threesome; Rearview Mirror.

ANTONIONI, Michelangelo: Dir. b. Ferrara, Italy, Sep 29, 1912. e. Bologna U. Films inc: Le Amiche; Il Grido; L'Avventura; La Notte; L'Eclisse; The Red Desert; Blow-Up; Zabriskie Point; Chung Kuo; The Passenger; Story of a Love Affair; The Mystery of Oberwald; Identificazione D'Una Donna (Identification of a Woman) (&sp); Room 666 (doc-int).

ANTONOWSKY, Marvin: Exec. b. NYC, Jan 31, 1929. e. CCNY, BA, MBA. With adv agencies Kenyon & Eckhardt; Norman Craig & Kummel; J. Walter Thompson before joining ABC 1969 as vp research svs; 1972 VP-asso dir planning, Mktg Dvlpmt, Research; July 1973, NBC VP pgm dvlpmnt; Sept 1973, VP Pgms East Coast; 1975, VP Pgms NBC-TV net; 1977 sr vp U-TV; 1979, Sr vp, asst to pres Col; 1980 exec vp mktg; April 1981, pres mktg & research; resd, Oct. 1983, month later became, sr. exec vp Universal Theatrical Motion Picture Group & P Universal marketing division.

ANTOON, A.J.: Dir. b. Lawrence, MA, Dec 7, 1944. e. Boston Coll. Bway inc: Subject to Fits; The Tale of Cumbeline; That Championship Season (*Tony*-1973); Much Ado About Nothing; The Good Doctor; The Dance of Death; Trelawney of the Wells; The Effect of Gamma Rays on Man-In-the-Moon Marigolds; The Rink.

TV inc: Much Ado About Nothing.

ANZARUT, Raymond: Exec Prod. b. Lebanon, 1912. Films inc: (prod mgr) Flight From Folly; Caesar and Cleopatra; Meet Me at Dawn; Scott of the Antartic. (Prod): Sea Devils; Man Between; An Inspector Calls; The Man Who Loved Readheads; Summer Madness; Storm Over the Nile. (Asso prod): The Silent Enemy; Room at the Top; Our Man in Havana; The Hill; The Dirty Dozen.

APTED, Michael: Dir. b. Aylesbury, England, Feb 10, 1941. e. Cambridge. Began in tv in England. TV inc: Coronation Street; The Lovers; Folly Foot; The Collection; Another Sunday and Sweet F.A.; Poor Girl; Mosedale Horshoe; Jack Point.

Films inc: Triple Echo; Stardust; The Squeeze; Agatha; Coal Miner's Daughter; Continental Divide; Gorky Park; Kipperbang; The River Rat (exec prod); Firstborn; 28 Up (& prod).

ARBUS, Allan: Act. b. NYC, Feb 15, 1918. Films inc: Putney Swope; The Christian Licorice Store; Cisco Pike; Coffy; The Young Nurses; Cinderella Liberty; Law and Disorder; W C Fields and Me; Damien-Omen II; Americathon; The Electric Horseman; The Last Married Couple in America.

TV inc: The Trial of Ethel and Julius Rosenberg; The Gangster Chronicles; The Four Seasons.

Bway inc: Dreyfus in Rehearsal.

ARCHARD, Bernard b. England, 1922. Films inc: Act. Village of the

Damned; The List of Adrian Messenger; Face of a Stranger; The Song of Norway; The Horror of Frankenstein; The Sea Wolves; Krull.

Thea inc: (London) The Case of the Oily Levantine.

TV inc: A Tale of Two Cities; Separate Tables (cable-HBO).

ARCHER, Anne: Act. b. Aug 25, 1947. Films inc: Cancel My Reservations; Paradise Alley; Good Guys Wear Black; Hero at Large; Raise The Titanic; Green Ice; Waltz Across Texas; The Naked Face; Too Scared To Scream.

TV inc: The Pirate; The Wedding; The Sky's the Limit; Falcon Crest.

ARCHER, Ronald Graham: Exec. b. Brisbane, Australia, Oct 25, 1933. GM Channel O, commercial TV.

ARCHERD, Army (Armand Archerd): Columnist. b. NYC, Jan 13. e. UCLA, BA. Joined AP Hollywood Bureau 1945; Herald-Express; Daily Variety columnist since 1953. MC Hollywood premieres; Pre-show MC Academy Awards Since 1958. P, founder Hollywood Press Club. Films inc: California Suite.

TV inc: Movie Game; People's Choice Awards TV Show; The Star Maker; Jacqueline Susann's Valley of the Dolls 1981; The Ratings Game (PC).

ARCHINAL, Harry: Exec. b. NYC, Jun 3, 1928. e. Wagner Coll, BA; Georgetown U, MH. Began working for Buena Vista 1954 as part-time clerk in foreign dept while at Georgetown; became Latin American sales supv, later gen sls mgr BV's foreign division; vp Buena Vista Int'l; named P BVI 1972.

ARDANT, Fanny: Act. b. France.Films inc: Les Chiens (The Dogs); Les uns et les Autres (The Ins and the Outs); La Femme d'a cota (The Woman Next Door); La vie est un roman (Life Is a Novel); Vivament Dimanche (Let it be Sunday); Benevenuta; Desiderio (Desire); Un Amour de Swann (Swann in Love); L'Amour A'Mort (Love Unto Death); Les Enrages (The Rabid Ones); L'Ete Prochain (Next Summer).

TV inc: Les Dames de la cote; Memoiras de deux jeune marines; La chute de la Maison Usher; le Chef de famille.

Thea inc: Les bons Bourgeois.

ARDEN, Eve (Eunice Quedens): Act. b. Mill Valley, CA, Apr 12, 1912. Appeared with Alcazar stock co., Bandbox Repertory Theatre. B'way debut, Ziegfeld Follies of 1936. On Screen from 1937. Films inc: Oh, Doctor; Stage Door; Having A Wonderful Time; A Letter of Introduction; Eternally Yours; Comrade X; That Uncertain Feeling; Ziegfeld Girl; She Knew all the Answers; Manpower; Cover Girl; The Doughgirls; Mildred Pierce; The Kid from Brooklyn; Night and Day; Voice of the Turtle; Tea for Two; Goodbye My Fancy; Our Miss Brooks; Anatomy of a Murder; The Dark at the Top of the Stairs; Sgt. Deadhead, The Astronaut; The Strongest Man in the World; Grease; Under the Rainbow; Grease 2.

Bway inc: Mame; Hello Dolly; Butterflies Are Free.

TV inc: Our Miss Brooks; The Eve Arden Show; The Mothers-in-Law (*Emmy*-female personality-1953); The Dream Merchants; Nuts and Bolts; A Gift of Music (host); Alice In Wonderland.

ARDOLINO, Emile: Prod-Dir. TV inc: Dance in America--Live From Lincoln Center; Balanchine IV--Dance in America; Great Performances (*Emmy*-series coord prod-1979); Alice At the Palace (dir); A Lincoln Center Special - - NYC Ballet Tribute to George Balanchine (dir); He Makes Me Feel Like Dancin' (*Emmys*-Prod & dir-1984).

Films inc: He Makes Me Feel Like Dancin' (prod) (*Oscar*-doc-1983).

ARGENTO, Dario: Wri-Dir. b. Italy, 1943. Films inc: The Bird With The Crystal Plumage; Metti; Una Sera a Cena(One Night, At Dinner) (sp only); Cat O'Nine Tails; Four Flies on Grey Velvet; Le Cinque Giornate; Deep Red; Suspiria; Inferno; Phenomena.

ARGO, Allison: Act. b. Richmond, VA, Dec 23. Bway inc: Grease; Night of the Iguana; Lady From the Sea.

TV inc: Search for Tomorrow; The Gift; High Ice; Casino; The Return of Frank Cannon; Ladies' Man; An Uncommon Love.

ARKIN, Adam: Act. b. NYC, Aug 19, 1956. S of Alan Arkin. Debuted,

1969, in Short People Soup, prod by his father. Films inc: Made for Each Other; Baby Blue Marine; Improper Channels (sp); Under the Rainbow; Chu Chu and the Philly Flash.

TV inc: We'll Get By; All Together Now; It Couldn't Happen to a Nicer Guy; Busting Loose; Pearl; Mark Twains's America-Tom Edison; Teachers Only; The Fourth Wise Man.

ARKIN, Alan: Act-Dir. b. NYC, Mar 26, 1934. e. LA City Coll; LA State Coll; Bennington Coll. Professional debut, 1959, St Louis in improvisations; later joined Second City Group, Chicago. NY debut, 1961, revue, From the Second City; Bway inc: Man Out Loud; Girl Quiet; Enter Laughing (*Tony*-supp-1963); Luv; The Opening; (dir): Hail Scrawdyke!; Little Murders; The White House Murder Case; The Sunshine Boys; Molly; Joan of Lorraine.

Films inc: The Russians Are Coming, The Russians Are Coming; Woman Times Seven; Wait Until Dark; Inspector Clouseau; The Heart Is a Lonely Hunter; Popi; the Monitors; Catch 22; Little Murders (& dir); Last of the Red Hot Lovers; Freebie and the Bean; Rafferty and the Gold Dust Twins; Hearts of the West; The Seven Per Cent Solution; Fire Sale (& dir); The In-Laws; The Magician of Lublin; Simon; Improper Channels; Chu Chu and the Philly Flash; Deadhead Miles; The Last Unicorn (voice); The Return of Captain Invincible; Joshua Then And Now.

TV inc: (dir) Twigs; Fay; A Matter of Principle; The Fourth Wise Man.

ARKOFF, Louis S.: Exec. b. Los Angeles, Jan 4, 1950. e. USC, BA. S of Samuel Z Arkoff. Prodn Asst 1967, Wild in the Streets; Asst to VP Prodn (part time), 1967-69; Legal Admin & Asst to VP bus aff AIP, 1973-74; Prodn super 1975, Return to Macon County; Exec Prod 1976, Small Town in Texas; VP Prodn AIP, 1977; Exec in charge Prodn 1978, Our Winning Season; California Dreaming; Gorp. Other films inc: Up the Creek (exec prod); Going For The Gold--The Bill Johnson Story (prod).

ARKOFF, Samuel Z.: Exec. b. Fort Dodge, IA, Jun 12, 1918. e. U of CO; U of IA; Loyola U School of Law, JD. Prod; ChmnB & P, AIP until Dec 1979; May 1981 formed Arkoff International Pictures; Prod more than 150 films inc: The House of Usher; The Pit and the Pendulum; The Raven; Comedy of Terrors; Wild in the Streets; Scream and Scream Again; Cry of the Banshee; Bloody Mama; Wuthering Heights; Frogs; Blacula; Dillinger; The Great Scout and Cathouse Thursday; A Matter of Time; The Island of Dr Moreau; Force 10 From Navarone; Our Winning Season; The Amityville Horror; California Dreaming; C.H.O.M.P.S.; How To Beat The High Cost Of Living; Dressed To Kill; The Winged Serpent; Up the Creek (exec prod); The Final Terror (presenter).

ARKUSH, Allan: Dir. b. NYC, Apr 30, 1948. e. Franklin & Marshall; NYU Film School. Worked as flm ed, trailer prod for New World. Films inc: Hollywood Boulevard (Co-Dir); Grand Theft Auto (Asst dir); Deathsport; Rock "n" Roll High School; Heartbeeps; Get Crazy.

TV inc: Summer.

ARLEDGE, Roone: Exec. b. NYC, Jul 8, 1931. e. Columbia U. Leading figure in TV sports since 1960 when as vp ABC-Sports he developed programs such as Wide World of Sports and The American Sportsman. Named p ABC Sports, 1968; developed Monday Night Football; acquired Olympics for ABC 1968, 1972, 1976. In Spring of 1977, also named p ABC-News.

(22 Emmys-9 as prod Wide World of Sports-1966, 1968, 1970, 1971, 1972, 1973, 1974, 1976, 1983; 19th Summer Olympics, 1969; 20th Summer Olympics 1973; Munich Olympic Tragedy, 1973; NFL Monday Night Football, 1976; XII Winter Olympics 1976; NCAA Football, 1980; Wide World of Sports 20th Anniversary Show; Kentucky Derby 1981; American Sportsman 1981, 1982, 1983; NATAS Founders Award, 1981; 1982 Indianapolis 500).

ARLEN, Harold (Hyman Arluck): Comp. b. Buffalo, NY, Feb 15, 1905. Films inc: The Big Broadcast; Strike Me Pink; Let's Fall in Love; Stage Struck; Artists and Models; Love Affair; Babes In Arms; The Wizard of Oz; A Day at the Circus; The Sky's the Limit; Rio Rita; Star Spangled Rhythm; Cabin in the Sky; Here Come the Waves; Casbah; My Blue Heaven; The Farmer Takes a Wife; A Star is Born; Country Girl; Gay Purr-ee; I Could Go On Singin'.

Bway inc: You Said It; Earl Carroll's Vanities; Americana; Life Begins at 8:40; Bloomer Girl.

Songs inc: Over the Rainbow (*Oscar*-1939); Stormy Weather; I've Got the World on a String; Let's Fall in Love; Blues in the Night; Happiness is a Thing Called Joe; My Shining Hour; Black Magic; Accentuate the Positive; The Man That Got Away.

ARLETTY (Arlette-Leonie Bathiat): Act. b. Courbevoie, France, 1898. Films inc: Un Chien Qui Rapporte; La Guerre des Valses; Aloha; Hotel du Nord; Le Jour Se Leve; Les Enfants du Paradis; L'Air de Paris; Les Petits Matins; La Gamberge.

ARLING, Arthur: Cin. b. MO, Sep 2, 1906. e. NY Institute of Photography. Joined Fox Studio 1927 as asst cameraman; op cameraman on Gone with the Wind, 1939. Films inc: The Yearling (*Oscar*-1946); Homestretch; Mother Was A Freshman; My Blue Heaven; I'll Cry Tomorrow; Story of Ruth; Pillow Talk; Notorious Landlady; Boys Night Out; My Six Loves.

ARLISS, Dimitra: Act. b. Oct 23, 1932. Films inc: The Sting; A Perfect Couple; Xanadu; Firefox.

TV inc: The Pirate; Guyana Tragedy--The Story of Jim Jones; Murder In Texas; The Fall of the House of Usher.

Bway inc: Arms And The Man.

ARLT, Lewis: Act. b. Kingston, NY, Dec 5, 1949. e. Carnegie Tech, BFA. Started in repertory. Thea inc: Murder Among Friends. TV inc: As the World Turns.

ARMATRADING, Joan: Singer-Comp. b. St Kitts, West Indies, Dec 9, 1950. Singer; recording artist. Films inc: Wild Geese (Title Song).

ARMER, Alan A.: Prod. b. Los Angeles, Jul 7, 1922. e. Stanford, BA. TV inc: My Friend Flicka; Broken Arrow; Man Without a Gun; The Untouchables; The Dick Powell Theatre; The Fugitive (*Emmy*-1966); The Invaders; Lancer; Name of the Game; Cannon; Westside Medical; Along Came a Spider; Birds of Prey; The Stranger.

ARMSTRONG, Bess: Act. b. Baltimore, MD, Dec 11, 1953. e. Brown U. TV inc: On Our Own; Getting Married; Walking Through Fire; The 11th Victim; How To Pick Up Girls; This Girl For Hire; Lace.

Films inc: The Four Seasons; Jekyll and Hyde--Together Again; High Road To China; Jaws 3-D; The House of God.

ARMSTRONG, Gillian: Dir. b. Melbourne, Australia, 1950. e. Swinbourne Coll. Films inc: (Shorts) Storytime; Four Walls; Old Man and Dog; The Roof Needs Mowing; One Hundred A Day; Satdee Night; The Singer and the Dancer. (Doc) Smokes and Lollies; A Time and a Place; A Busy Kind of Bloke; Tassie Wood. (Features) My Brilliant Career; Starstruck; Mrs. Soffel.

ARMSTRONG, R.G.: Act. b. Apr 7, 1917. Films inc: Garden of Eden; From Hell to Texas; Never Love a Stranger; The Fugitive Kind; Ride the High Country; Major Dundee; El Dorado; The Great White Hope; J.W. Coop; The Great Northfield Minnesota Raid; Pat Garrett and Billy the Kid; My Name is Nobody; Who Fears the Devil; White Line Fever; Stay Hungry; The Car; Mr. Billion; Going South; Fast Charlie, the Moonbeam Rider; Heaven Can Wait; Good Luck, Miss Wyckoff; Where the Buffalo Roam; Steel; Raggedy Man; The Pursuit of D.B. Cooper; Evilspeak; The Beast Within; Hammett; Lone Wolf McQuade; Children of the Corn.

TV inc: Last Ride of the Dalton Gang; The Shadow Riders.

ARNALL, Ellis G.: Exec. b. Newman, GA, Mar 20, 1907. Former gov of GA. P Society Independent Motion Picture Producers (SIMPP) 1948-1960, P Independent Producers Export Corp 1953-60.

ARNAUD, Leo: Comp. b. Lyons, France, Jul 24, 1904. Music dir & arr in France and England, 1927-30; to U.S. 1931; music dir MGM, 1936-44. Film scores inc: One Touch of Venus; Easter Parade; Date with Judy; Three Little Words; Lovely to Look At; Stars & Stripes Forever; Rose Marie; Seven Brides for Seven Brothers; The Unsinkable Molly Brown.

ARNAZ, Desi: Act-Mus. b. Santiago, Cuba, Mar 2, 1917. Began as vocalist with a band at age 17. Later with own rhumba band. N.Y. nightclubs, on Bway in Too Many Girls. Screen debut in Too Many

Girls, 1940. Films inc: Father Takes A Wife; Four Jacks and a Jill; Bataan; Holiday in Havana; Forever Darling.

TV inc: Bob Hope Show (mus dir); I Love Lucy (act-exec prod); The Lucille Ball-Desi Arnaz Show (act-exec prod).

ARNAZ, Desi, Jr: Act-Singer. b. Los Angeles, Jan 19, 1953. S of Lucille Ball and Desi Arnaz. Began appearing on I Love Lucy show on TV in infancy. Gained own status as rock singer and musician with the Dino, Desi and Billy group. Film debut in Red Sky at Morning, 1972. Films inc: Marco; She Lives; Joyride; A Wedding; Fakeout; The House of Long Shadows.

TV inc: The Great American Traffic Jam; Advice to the Lovelorn; The Night The Bridge Fell Down; Automan; All-Star Party for Lucille Ball; The Coronation.

ARNAZ, Lucie: Act. b. Los Angeles, Jul 17, 1951. D of Lucille Ball and Desi Arnaz. Bway inc: Cabaret; Once Upon A Mattress; Bye, Bye Birdie; Mack and Mabel; Goodbye Charlie; Lil Abner; They're Playing Our Song.

TV inc: Here's Lucy; The Black Dahlia; The Mating Season; Washington Mistress; One More Try; All-Star Party For Lucille Ball; Night Of 100 Stars II; The Lucie Arnaz Show.

Films inc: Billy Jack Goes To Washington; The Jazz Singer; Second Thoughts.

ARNE, Peter: Act. b. British Malaya, 1922. Films inc: Time Slip; The Purple Plain; The Cockleshell Heroes; The Moonraker; Danger Within; Ice Cold In Alex; The Hellfire Club; The Victors; Khartoum; Battle Beneath the Earth; Chitty Chitty Bang Bang; Murders in the Rue Morgue; Straw Dogs; Antony and Cleopatra; Return of the Pink Panther; Providence; Agatha; The Passage; Trail of the Pink Panther.

TV inc: The Mask of Janus; The Third Man; The Champions; The Shattered Eye; The Stallion; Rivals of Sherlock Holmes; Task Force; The Fox; The Venturers; Quiller; The Expert; The Far Pavilions (PC). (Died Aug. 1, 1983).

ARNER, Gwen: Dir. Films inc: Ritoru Chanpion (My Champion).

TV inc: Please Don't Hit Me, Mom; Nurse; Mother's Day on Walton Mountain.

ARNESS, James (ne Aurness): Act. b. Minneapolis, MN, May 26, 1923. B of Peter Graves. Films inc: Farmer's Daughter; Battleground; The Thing; The People Against O'Hara; Hell Gate; Carbine Williams; Big Jim McLain; Horizons West; Man from Texas; Island in the Sky; Hondo; Them; Her 12 Men; Flame of the Islands; Sea Chase.

TV inc: Gunsmoke; How the West Was Won; McClain's Law; An NBC Family Christmas.

ARNOLD, Danny (Arnold Rothman): Wri-Act. b. NYC, Jan 23, 1925. Appeared in summer stock, nightclubs, vaudeville. Started in films as sound effects ed., Columbia, 1944-46. Films inc: (act) Breakthrough; Inside the Walls of Folsom Prison; Sailor Beware; Scared Stiff; Stars Are Singing. (Wri): The Caddy; Desert Sands; Fort Yuma; Rebel in Town; Outside the Law.

TV inc: My World and Welcome To It *(Emmy*-prod-1970); The Real McCoys; Bewitched; That Girl; Barney Miller *(Emmy*-prod-1982). Live From Studio 8H; 100 Years of America's Popular Music (exec prod); Don't Look Back (exec prod).

ARNOLD, Eddy: Singer. b. Henderson, TN, May 15, 1918. Country singer, recording artist since 1946. Nicknamed The Tennessee Plowboy. TV inc: The Eddy Arnold Show; Eddy Arnold Time; Country Comes Home. Elected to Country Mus Hall of Fame, 1966.

ARNOLD, Jack: Prod-Dir. b. New Haven, CT, Oct 14, 1916. e. OH State U; AADA. US Air Force 1942-45; prod docs for State Dept., Army and private industry before features. Films inc: Girls in the Night; It Came From Outer Space; The Glass Web; Creature From the Black Lagoon; Revenge of the Creature; Tarantula; Red Sundown; The Incredible Shrinking Man; The Tattered Dress; Man in the Shadow; High School Confidential; Monster on the Campus; No Name on the Bullet; The Mouse That Roared; Bachelor in Paradise; A Global Affair; The Lively Set; Red Sundown; Black Eye; Boss Nigger; Games Girls Play; The Swiss Conspiracy.

TV inc: Sid Caesar, Imogene Coca, Carl Reiner, Howard Morris Special *(Emmy*-prod); It Takes A Thief (exec prod); Marilyn--The Untold Story (dir).

ARNOLD, Malcolm: Comp. b. England, Oct 12, 1921. Films inc: The Sound Barrier; The Captain's Paradise; Hobson's Choice; I Am A Camera; Trapeze; Island in the Sun; The Bridge on the River Kwai; *(Oscar*-1957); The Key; The Roots of Heaven; Inn of the Sixth Happiness; The Angry Silence; Tunes of Glory; The Lion; The Chalk Garden; The Heroes of Telemark; The Reckoning; David Copperfield.

ARNOUL, Francoise (nee Gautsch): Act. b. Constantine, Algeria, Jun 3, 1931. Films inc: Forbidden Fruit; Companions of the Night; The Sheep Has Five Legs; French Can-Can; The Face of the Cat; The Devil and the Ten Commandments; Le Dimanche de la Vie; Violette and Francois; Derniere Sortie Avant Roissy (Last Exit Before Roissy); Ronde de nuit (Night Patrol).

ARNSTEIN, Eugene: Exec. b. Milwaukee, WI, Aug 13, 1907. e. Marquette U. Exhibitor, 1926-44; Sec-Treas, Film Classics; controller, Eagle Lion Classics; exec Pathe Lab; left NY for LA, 1951, to be Studio M, Monogram; 1962-64, Exec VP Society of Independent Producers; 1964-74, VP AMPTV. Since 1974 motion picture industrial labor relations consultant.

ARQUETTE, Rosanna: Act. b. NYC, Aug 10, 1959. Grand d of the late Cliff Arquette. TV inc: The Dark Secret Of Harvest Home; Having Babies Part II; James at 15; Mom and Dad Can't Hear Me; Class of '65; Get Patty Hearst; Zuma Beach; Shirley; The Wall; A Long Way Home; The Executioner's Song; Johnny Belinda; The Parade; Insight/ Butterfly.

Films inc: Gorp; S.O.B.; Baby It's You; Off the Wall; The Aviator; Desperately Seeking Susan.

ARRANTS, Rod: Act. b. LA; Sept 5, 1944. e. U of Pacific. TV inc: The Young and the Restless; McCoy; Helter Skelter; The Lives of Jenny Dolan; Cross Current; Lisa Bright and Dark; Lovers and Friends; Search for Tomorrow.

Films inc: Vamping.

ARTHUR, Beatrice: Act. b. NYC, May 13, 1926. Films inc: That Kind of Woman; Lovers and Other Strangers; Mame; History of the World--Part I.

TV inc: Caesar's Hour; Maude *(Emmy*-1977); The Beatrice Arthur Special; Hope, Women & Song; 30 Years of TV Comedy's Greatest Hits (co-host); Omnibus; Kennedy Center Tonight--Broadway to Washington; Amanda's; Dean Martin's Celebrity Roast; P.O.P.

Bway inc: Dog Beneath The Skin; Gas; Yerma; No Exit; Six Characters in Search of an Author; The Owl and the Pussycat; Ulysses in Nighttown; Chic; Mame *(Tony*-supp-1966); Fiddler on the Roof; The Floating Light Bulb.

ARTHUR, Jean (Gladys Greene): Act. b. NYC, Oct 17, 1905. Made more than 70 films inc: Cameo Kirby; Fast and Fearless; Bringin' Home the Bacon; Thundering Romance; Drug Store Cowboy; A Man of Nerve; Hurricane Horseman; Under Fire; Born to Battle; The Fighting Cheat; Lightning Bill; The Cowboy Cop; Twisted Triggers; The College Boob; Husband Hunters; Horseshoes; The Poor Nut; Wallflowers; Brotherly Love; Sins of the Fathers; The Canary Murder Case; The Greene Murder Case; The Mysterious Dr. Fu Manchu; The Saturday Night Kid; Half-Way to Heaven; Young Eagles; Paramount on Parade; The Return of Dr. Fu Manchu; The Gang Buster; Virtuous Husbands; Get That Venus; The Past of Mary Holmes; Whirlpool; The Defense Rests; The Whole Town's Talking; Public Hero No. 1; Diamond Jim; The Public Menace; If You Could Only Cook; Mr. Deeds Goes to Town; The Ex-Mrs. Bradford; Adventure in Manhattan; More Than a Secretary; The Plainsman; History Is Made at Night; Easy Living; You Can't Take It With You; Only Angels Have Wings; Mr. Smith Goes to Washington; Too Many Husbands; Arizona; The Devil and Miss Jones; The Talk of the Town; The More The Merrier; A Lady Takes a Chance; A Foreign Affair; Shane; George Stevens . . . A Filmmaker's Journey (doc).

ARTHUR, Karen (nee Jensen): Dir. b. Omaha, NE, Aug 24, 1941. Started as perf, chor; then dir. Films inc: Legacy; The Mafu Cage (& prod).

TV inc: Charleston; Cagney & Lacey; Victims For Victims-The Theresa Saldana Story; A Bunny's Tale; Return To Eden; The Rape Of

Richard Beck.

ARTHUR, Robert (ne Feder): Prod. b. NYC, Nov 1, 1909. Joined MGM as writer, 1937. Films inc: Buck Private Come Home; For The Love of Mary; Mexican Hayride; Abbott And Costello in the Foreign Legion; Abbott And Costello Meet Frankenstein; Bedtime Story; Father Goose; Shenandoah; A Man Could Get Killed; Sweet Charity.

ASHBY, Hal: Dir. b. Ogden, UT, 1936. e. UT State U. Started as flm ed. Films inc: The Loved One; The Cincinnati Kid; The Russians Are Coming, The Russians Are Coming; In The Heat of the Night (& asso prod); (Oscar-ed-1967); The Thomas Crown Affair. (Dir) The Landlord; Harold and Maude; The Last Detail; Shampoo; Bound for Glory; Coming Home; Being There; Second-Hand Hearts; Time Is On Our Side; Lookin' To Get Out; The Slugger's Wife.

ASHCROFT, Peggy, Dame: Act. b. Croydon, England, Dec 22, 1907. London debut 1927, One Day More. Thea inc: When Adam Delved; The Way of the World; The Land of Heart's Desire; A Hundred Years Old; Requital; Jew Suss; Othello; The Breadwinner; various Shakespearean roles for Old Vic and Sadlers Wells Companies; She Stoops to Conquer; School for Scandal; The Importance of Being Earnest; Rebecca; Edward My Son; The Deep Blue Sea; Hedda Gabler; The Good Woman of Setzuan; Ghosts; The Hollow Crown; A Delicate Balance; Lloyd George Knew My Father; Happy Days; Hullabaloo Over George and Bonnie's Pictures; Watch On The Rhine (rev).
    Films inc: The Wandering Jew; The 39 Steps; Rhodes of Africa; The Nun's Story; Secret Ceremony; Sunday, Bloody Sunday; Joseph Andrews; Hullabaloo Over George & Bonnie's Pictures; A Passage To India (Oscar-supp-1984).
    TV inc: Shadow of Heroes; The Cherry Orchard; The Wars of the Roses; Days in the Trees; Edward and Mrs Simpson; Cream In My Coffee; The Jewel In The Crown.

ASHER, Irving: Prod-exec. b. San Francisco, CA., Sep. 16, 1903. H of Laura La Plante. M-Dir WB England; 1938, exec prod Columbia Britain; 1945, P Rainbow Prodns; with 20th-Fox tv before retirement. Films inc: Prison Without Bars; The Four Feathers; Billy the Kid; Blossoms in the Dust; Mr. and Mrs. North; Nazi Agent; The War Against Mrs. Hadley; Here Comes the Groom; Turning Point; The Stars are Singing; Elephant Walk.
    (Died March 17, 1985)

ASHER, Jane: Act. b. London, England, Apr 5, 1946. Thea inc: (London) Will You Walk A Little Faster?; Peter Pan; Level Crossing; Summer; Look Back In Anger; The Philanthropist; Treats; Whose Life Is It Anyway? (Bway) Measure for Measure; The Philanthropist.
    Films inc: The Greengage Summer; The Girl in the Headlines; The Masque of Red Death; Alfie; Deep End; The Buttercup Chain; Henry VIII and his 6 Wives; Runners.
    TV inc: Brideshead Revisited; A Voyage Round My Father.

ASHER, William: Dir. b. 1919. Films inc: Leather Gloves (& co-prod); The Shadow on the Window; The 27th Day; Beach Party; Johnny Cool (& prod); Muscle Beach Party; Bikini Beach (& wri); Beach Blanket Bingo (& wri); How To Stuff A Wild Bikini (& wri); Fireball 500; Night Warning; Movers & Shakers (& prod).
    TV inc: Bewitched (& prod) (Emmy-dir-1966); A Christmas For Boomer; Charley's Aunt (cable).

ASHERSON, Renee: Act. b. London, England, 1921. Thea inc: Within Seven Hours; Wuthering Heights; with repertory groups and Old Vic in London and on tour; Lottie Dundass; The Cure for Love; Much Ado About Nothing; The Animal Kingdom; The Taming of the Shrew; The Government Inspector; A Streetcar Named Desire; Spring at Marino; Three Sisters; The Big Knife; The Dazzling Hour; Kill Two Birds; Portrait of Murder; The Magistrate; Dear Antoine; All Over.
    Films inc: Henry V; The Way Ahead; The Way to the Stars; The Small Back Room; The Cure for Love; The Day The Earth Caught Fire; Rasputin The Mad Monk; The Smashing Bird I Used to Know.
    TV inc: Romance On The Orient Express.

ASHKENAZY, Vladimir: Pianist. b. Russia, Jul 6, 1927. e. Moscow Conservatory. London debut 1962. Recs inc: Rachmaninoff Concerto #3 in D Minor; Mozart/Schumann Recital; Chopin Ballades; Prokofiev Sonatas for Violin and Piano; Beethoven Concerti for Piano and Orchestra (Grammy-Class Inst Solo-1973); Chopin Etudes; Beethoven--The Five Piano Concertos (Grammy-Class Inst Solo-1976); Rachmaninoff--23 Preludes; Beethoven Sonatas for Violin and Piano (Grammy-Chamber Music-1978); Tschaikovsky Piano Trio In A Minor (Grammy-Chamber Music-1981).

ASHLEY, Elizabeth (nee Cole): Act. b. Ocala, FL, Aug 20, 1939. Bway inc: The Highest Tree; Take Her, She's Mine (Tony-supp-1962); Barefoot in the Park; Cat on a Hot Tin Roof; The Skin of Our Teeth; Caesar and Cleopatra; Agnes of God.
    Films inc: The Carpetbaggers; Ship of Fools; The Third Day; Marriage of a Young Stockbroker; The Paperback Hero; 92 in the Shade; Great Scout and Cathouse Thursday; Coma; Windows; Paternity; Split Image.
    TV inc: When Michael Calls; The Face of Fear; Second Chance; Sad Figure Laughing; One of My Wives Is Missing; A Fire in the Sky; The Ambassadors; Svengali; He's Fired, She's Hired.

ASHLEY, Ted: Exec. b. NYC, Aug 3, 1922. e. CCNY. With William Morris Agency, 1939-46; formed Ted Ashley Assoc, 1946; pres Ashley Famous Agency, 1954; dir & chmn of exec committee of Warner Communications 1967-74; bd chmn-CEO WB, 1969 to Nov 1980 when became consultant; rejoined as Vice Chmn Oct 1982.

ASHMAN, Chuck: Exec. b. NYC, Jun 7, 1936. e. U FL., Cumberland U. TV inc: On and Off Camera (prod); Heroes (prod); The Jesters; Metronews (host); The Ashman File (host); became mktg cnslt; 1983, P 20th-Fox wldwde licensing, merchandising and special projects div; resd Dec. 1984 to head new McGregor/Faberge Licensing Co.

ASKIN, Leon: Act. b. Vienna, Sep 18, 1907. e. Max Reinhardt School of Acting. Performed in Europe, stage, cabarets. To US, 1940. In stock as actor, dir. Films inc: Road to Bali; South Sea Woman; The Robe; Secret of the Incas; Valley of the Kings; One Two Three; What Did You Do in the War Daddy?; Guns for San Sebastian; Frightmare.
    TV inc: Hogans Heroes; Insight/The Game Room.

ASNER, Edward: Act. b. Kansas City, MO, Nov 15, 1929. Films inc: Peter Gunn; The Slender Thread; The Satan Bug; Kid Galahad; The Wrestler; Fort Apache, The Bronx; O'Hara's Wife; Daniel.
    TV inc: The Doomsday Flight; Mary Tyler Moore Show (Emmys-supp-1971, 1972, 1975); Hey, I'm Alive; Rich Man, Poor Man (Emmy-1976); Roots Part I (Emmy-supp-1977); Lou Grant (Emmys-1978, 1980); Insight--This Side of Eden; The Family Man; Combat In The Classroom (host); Narco (narr); Passover (narr); Lights! Action! Africa! (narr); A Small Killing; A Case of Libel; Auschwitz and the Allies (narr); Auschwitz and America (narr); Anatomy of an Illness; Donald Duck's 50th Birthday; Off The Rack.

ASPINALL, David Roy: Exec. b. New South Wales, Australia, May 19, 1947. Sr exec m, TV Channel 9, Perth.

ASSANTE, Armand: Act. b. NYC, Oct 4, 1949. e. AADA. Appeared off-Bway, with regional theatre groups. Bway inc: Why I Went Crazy; Boccaccio; Comedians; Romeo and Juliet; Kingdoms.
    TV inc: Human Feelings; Lady of the House; The Pirate; Sophia Loren--Her Own Story; Rage of Angels; Why Me?; Evergreen.
    Films inc: Lords of Flatbush; Paradise Alley; Prophecy; Little Darlings; Love and Money; Private Benjamin; I, The Jury; Unfaithfully Yours.

ASSAYEV, Tamara: Prod. b. 1942. Started in films as asst to Roger Corman on Targets; Pit Stop; Saint Valentine's Day Massacre; Devil's Angels; The Trip; The Pit and the Pendulum. Became ind prod 1967: The Wild Racers, Paddy; The Arousers; teamed with Alex Rose on Drive In; I Wanna Hold Your Hand; Big Wednesday; Norma Rae.
    TV inc: Norma Rae (exec prod).

ASSELIN, Diane (nee Dailey): Prod. b. Detroit, MI, Mar 11, 1941. e. Miami U of OH, BA. Reporter-researcher Time Inc; asso prod David Wolper Prodns; asso prod PBS before indie. TV inc: Journey Together; I Can; Dinky Hocker; Once Upon a Midnight Dreary (Emmy-1980); Animal Talk (Emmy-1980); The Treasure of Alpheus T Winterborn; The Haunting of Harrington House; Have You Ever Been Ashamed of Your Parents?; The Zertigo Diamond Caper; Daisy (asso prod).

ASSELIN, Paul: Prod. b. Lynn, MA, Dec 23, 1935. e. Yale, BA. H of Diane Asselin. With ABC News; CBS News; Wolper Prodns before forming Asselin Prodns. TV inc: An American Portrait; The National Disaster Survival Test; CBS Mystery Theatre; CBS Television Library; Dinky Hocker; Once Upon a Midnight Dreary (Emmy-1980); Animal Talk (Emmy-1980); The Treasure of Alpheus T Winterborn; The Haunting of Harrington House; The Zertigo Diamond Caper (& dir).

ASTAIRE, Fred (ne Austerlitz): Perf. b. Omaha, NE, May 10, 1899. Formed dance team with sister, Adele. Vaudeville debut 1908. On screen from 1933 in Dancing Lady. (Oscar-Special-1949, "for his unique artistry and his contribution to the technique of musical pictures.") Films inc: Flying Down to Rio; The Gay Divorcee; Roberta; Top Hat; Follow the Fleet; Swing Time; Shall We Dance; A Damsel In Distress; Carefree; The Story of Vernon and Irene Castle; Broadway Melody of 1940; Second Chorus; You'll Never Get Rich; You Were Never Lovelier; Holiday Inn; The Sky's the Limit; Ziegfeld Follies; Blue Skies; Easter Parade; The Barkleys of Broadway; Let's Dance; Three Little Words; Royal Wedding; The Band Wagon; Daddy Long Legs; Funny Face; Silk Stockings; On the Beach; The Pleasure of His Company; The Notorious Landlady; Finian's Rainbow; Midas Run; The Towering Inferno; That's Entertainment, Part Two; The Amazing Dobermans; The Purple Taxi; Ghost Story; George Stevens. . .A Filmmaker's Journey (doc-int).

Bway inc: Over the Top; Passing Show of 1918; Apple Blossoms; Lady Be Good; Smiles; Funny Face; Gay Divorcee; The Bandwagon.

TV inc: An Evening with Fred Astaire (Emmy-1959); Astaire Time (Emmy-1961); Alcoa Premiere; The Fred Astaire Show; It Takes a Thief; A Family Upside Down (Emmy-1978); The Man in the Santa Claus Suit; AFI Salute to Fred Astaire; AFI Salute To Gene Kelly.

ASTIN, John: Act. b. Baltimore, Mar 30, 1930. e. John Hopkins U, BA. First prof. job off-Broadway in Threepenny Opera. Broadway debut, Major Barbara. Did voices in cartoon. Films inc: West Side Story; That Touch of Mink; The Wheeler Dealers; Candy; Viva Max!; Every Little Crook and Nanny; The Brothers O'Toole; Freaky Friday.

TV inc: (dir) Getting There; Ethel Is An Elephant; Mr Merlin; Scared Silly; CHiPS; Just Our Luck.

ASTIN, Patty Duke: (See DUKE, Patty):

ASTOR, Mary (Lucile V Langhanke): Act. b. Quincy, IL, May 3, 1906. Beauty contest winner, 1920. Screen debut in Beggar's Maid, 1920. On stage in Among the Married; Tonight at 8:30; Male Animal. Films inc: (silent) Bright Shawl; Beau Brummel; Don Juan; (sound) Lost Squadron; Red Dust; The Kennel Murder Case; Man of Iron; Dodsworth; The Prisoner of Zenda; Midnight; The Great Lie; (Oscar-supp-1941); Maltese Falcon; Thousands Cheer; Meet Me in St. Louis; Claudia and David; Cass Timberlane; Act of Violence; Any Number Can Play; A Kiss Before Dying; Return to Peyton Place; Youngblood Hawke; Hush, Hush Sweet Charlotte.

ASTRUC, Alexandre: Dir. b. Paris, 1923. Originally a critic and novelist, started in films as asst to Marc Allegret on Blanche Fury.

Films inc: Aller-Retour; Ulysses et les Amauvaise Recontres; The Crimson Curtain (short); Une Vie; La Proie pour l'ombre; Education Sentimentale; Le Puits et Le Pendule (short); La Longue Marche; Flammes sur l'Adriatique.

ATHERTON, William: Act. (nee Knight):b. New Haven, CT, Jul 30, 1947. Films inc: Class of '44; The New Centurions; The Sugarland Express; The Day of the Locust; The Hindenberg; Looking for Mr. Goodbar; Ghostbusters.

Bway inc: The House of Blue Leaves; The Basic Training of Pavlo Hummel; The Sign in Sidney Brustein's Window; The American Clock; The Caine Mutiny Court Martial.

TV inc: Centennial; The House of Mirth; Tomorrow's Child; Malibu.

ATKINS, Chet: Guitarist-Comp. b. Luttrell, TN, Jun 20, 1924. Started as mus on WRBL, Columbus GA; worked several other stations before joining Grand Ole Opry 1950; later worked with Carter Sisters; recorded with Hank Williams; Elvis Presley; Dolly Parton, others; finally solo. Albums inc: Chet Atkins Plays Guitar; Chet Atkins in Three Dimensions; Chet Atkins Picks the Best (Grammy-inst-1967);

Chet Atkins Picks on the Beatles; Me and Jerry (Grammy-country inst-1970); Snowbird (Grammy-country inst-1971); The Atkins-Travis Traveling Show (Grammy-country inst-1974); The Entertainer (Grammy-country inst-1975); Chester and Lester (Grammy-country inst-1976); Country--After All These Years (Grammy-country inst-1981).

Songs inc: Country Gentleman; Midnight; How's The World Treating You?; Heartbreak Avenue.

TV inc: Music City News' Top Country Hits of the Year; An Evening With The Statler Bros-A Salute to the Good Times; Louise Mandrell--Diamonds, Gold & Platinum.

ATKINS, Christopher: Act. b. Feb. 21, 1961. Films inc: Blue Lagoon; The Pirate Movie.

TV inc: Child Bride at Short Creek; Dallas; Secret Weapons.

ATKINS, Eileen: Act. b. London, Jun 16, 1934. First professional appearance in Love's Labours Lost. Thea inc: Semi-Detached; Exit the King; The Promise; She Fell Among Thieves; Passion Play.

Films inc: Inadmissable Evidence; Equus; Nelly's Version; The Dresser.

TV inc: The Lady's Not for Burning; Party Games; Major Barbara; Oliver Twist; Sons and Lovers; Titus Andronicus.

ATKINSON, J. Brooks: Critic. b. Melrose, MA, Nov 28, 1894. e. Harvard. English instructor at Dartmouth for one year before joining Springfield Daily News, 1917, as reporter; 1918, asst drama critic Boston Transcript; 1922, literary editor NY Times; 1926, drama critic; 1941, foreign corr; 1946 retd as drama critic; 1960, critic at large; retired, 1970.

(Special Tony-1962).

(Died Jan. 13, 1984.

ATTENBOROUGH, David, Sir: Prod-Bcast exec. b. London, May 8, 1926. e. Cambridge. B of Richard Attenborough. Knighted, June 1985. Started as exec in British publishing firm; joined BBC 1952 as a prodn trainee; 1968 controller BBC-2; 1969-72 dir pgms for tv. TV inc: Zoological and Ethnographic docs all over the world; Zoo Quest; Travellers Tales; Eastward with Attenborough; Tribal Eye; Life on Earth; The Living Planet--A Portrait Of Earth.

ATTENBOROUGH, Richard, Sir: Prod-Dir-Act. b. Cambridge, England, Aug 29, 1923. e. RADA. Made London stage debut Awake and Sing, 1942. Film debut In Which We Serve, 1942.

Thea inc: The Little Foxes; Brighton Rock; The Way Back Home (Home of the Brave); To Dorothy, A Son; Sweet Madness; The Mousetrap; Double Image; Rape of the Belt.

Films inc: (as act) School for Secrets; The Man Within; Brighton Rock; London Belongs to Me; The Magic Box; Gift Horse; Eight O'-Clock Walk; The Ship That Died of Shame; Private's Progress; Dunkirk; The Man Upstairs; I'm All Right Jack; SOS Pacific; The Angry Silence (& co-prod); League of Gentlemen; Whistle Down the Wind (prod); Only Two Can Play; The L-Shaped Room (prod only); The Great Escape; Seance on a Wet Afternoon (& prod); The Third Secret; Guns at Batasi; Flight of the Phoenix; The Sand Pebbles; The Bliss Of Miss Blossom; Only When I Larf; Dr. Dolittle; David Copperfield; 10 Rillington Place; Ten Little Indians; Rosebud; Brannigan; Conduct Unbecoming; The Chess Players; The Human Factor. (Dir) Oh! What A Lovely War; Young Winston; A Bridge Too Far; Magic; Gandhi (& prod) (Oscars-Prod & dir-1982) .

ATTERBURY, Malcolm: Act. b. Philadelphia, PA, Feb 20, 1907. In vaude. Bway inc various Shubert musicals; One Flew Over the Cuckoo's Nest.

Films inc: Dragnet; Storm Center; Crime in the Streets; Toward The Unknown; No Time for Sergeants; Rio Bravo; North By Northwest; From the Terrace; Summer and Smoke; Advise and Consent; The Birds; The Chase; Hawaii.

AUBERJONOIS, Rene: Act. b. NYC, Jun 1, 1940. Bway inc: Dark of the Moon; The Hostage; Beyond the Fringe; Tartuffe; Charley's Aunt; King Lear; A Cry of Players; Chemin de Fer; Coco (Tony-supp-1970); Tricks;The Good Doctor; The Ruling Class; Break A Leg; Every Good Boy Deserves Favor; Big River.

Films inc: Lilith; Petulia; M*A*S*H; Brewster McCloud; McCabe and Mrs Miller; Pete 'n Tillie; Hindenberg; King Kong; The Big Bus;

Eyes of Laura Mars; Where the Buffalo Roam; The Last Unicorn (voice).

TV inc: Shirts/Skins; The Wild Wild West Revisited; More Wild Wild West; Benson; The Kid From Nowhere; The Smurfs Christmas Special (voice).

AUBREY, James T.: Exec Prod. b. LaSalle, IL, Dec 14, 1918. e. Princeton. Started as account exec KNX (radio) LA; M KNXT (TV) 1952; vp creative svcs CBS 1955-56. VP pgms & talent ABC-TV 1957; exec vp CBS-TV 1958-59. P CEO MGM 1969-1973; ind prodn. Films inc: (prod) Futureworld; The Hunger.

TV inc: Dallas Cowboys Cheerleaders I & II; When Hell Was in Session; Fugitive Family; Mark, I Love You; Shannon.

AUCLAIR, Michel (Vladimir Vujovic): Act. b. Germany, Sep 14, 1922. Films inc: Beauty and the Beast; The Damned; Manon; Eternal Conflict; Justice Is Done; Holiday for Henrietta; One Step to Eternity; Andrea Chenier; Funny Face; A Mistress for the Summer; The Day of the Jackal; Impossible Object; Black Thursday; French Provincial; Le Juge Fayard dit le Sheriff (Judge Fayard Called the Sheriff); L'Amour en Question (Love In Question); Trois Hommes a abattre (Three Men to Destroy); Mille Milliards de Dollars (A Thousands Billion Dollars); Deux heures moint le quart avant Jesus Christ (A Quarter To Two Before Jesus Christ); Le Bon Plaisir.

AUDLEY, Maxine: Act. b. London, Apr 29, 1923. Thea inc: Old Vic Co; Carissima; Celestina; Thieves Carnival; The Constant Couple; A Letter from Paris; Angels in Love; Love Affair; Speaking of Murder; Present Laughter; Conduct Unbecoming; All My Sons; A Touch of Purple; Private Lives; A Streetcar Named Desire; Saratoga; After The Ball Is Over.

Films inc: Anna Karenina; The Sleeping Tiger; The Barretts of Wimpole Street; The Prince and the Showgirl; A King in New York; The Vikings; Our Man in Havana; The Trials of Oscar Wilde; A Jolly Bad Fellow; The Agony and the Ecstasy; Here We Go Round The Mulberry Bush; Frankenstein Must Be Destroyed; The Looking Glass War.

AUDRAN, Stephane: Act. b. Versailles, France, 1936. W of Claude Chabrol. Films inc: Kill or Cure; The Cousins; The Sign of Leo; Bluebeard; The Champagne Murders; Les Biches; La Femme Infidele; The Beast Must Die; Le Boucher; Dead Pigeon on Beethoven Street; And Then There Were None; The Black Bird; The Twist (Folies Bourgeoises); Silver Bears; Violette; The Eagle's Wing; Face to the Sun; The Big Red One; Le Coeur L'envers (My Heart is Upside Down); Coup De Torchon (Pop 1280) (Clean Slate); Le Choc (The Shock); Paradis par tout (Paradise for All); Mortelle Randonee (Deadly Circuit); Les Voleurs de la nuit (Thieves After Dark); Le Sang des Autres (The Blood of Others); Bay Boy; La Scarlantine (Scarlet Fever); Poulet au Vinaigre; Night Magic.

TV inc: Brideshead Revisited; Mistral's Daughter; The Sun Also Rises.

AUERBACH, Norbert: Exec. b. Vienna, Nov 4, 1922. e. UCLA. Entered film industry in 1946. Held numerous managerial posts in foreign depts of COL, Seven Arts, WB, Cinema Center Films & UA. In 1977, named UA sales m for Europe and the Middle East; named senior vp Int'l Dept UA in 1978; Dec. 1980, P & COO, UA; Jan. 1981, CEO; Oct 1981, P of United International Pictures, dist firm formed by U, Par, MGM & UA; resd Oct 1982; Cnsltnt to Samuel Goldwyn Co., Aurora Prodns; Sept. 1983, P & CEO Almi Distribution Corp.

AUGER, Claudine: Act. b. France, Apr 26, 1942. Films inc: Testament of Orpheus; Terrain Vague; A Certain Desire; Thunderball; Our Man From Marrakesh; Operation San Genero; The Killing Game; Triple Cross; The Devil in Love; Love Birds; Equinoxe; A Bay of Blood; The Eiger Sanction; Flic Story; Paris Mon amour; A Butterfly On The Shoulder; Travels With Anita; L'Associe; Fantastica; Lovers and Liars; Secret Places.

TV inc: The Girls In Their Summer Dresses and other stories by Irwin Shaw.

AUMONT, Jean-Pierre: Act. b. Paris, Jan 5, 1909. e. Conservatoire of Drama. Films inc: The Cross of Lorraine; Scheherazade; Blindman's Buff; Castle Keep; Lili; The Horse Without a Head; Day for

Night; Two Solitudes; Blackout; Cat and Mouse; Something Short of Paradise; Allons Z'Enfants (The Boy Soldier); Nana; La Java des Ombres (Shadow Dance); Le Sang des Autres (The Blood of Others.)

TV inc: The French Atlantic Affair; Beggarman, Thief; The Memory of Eva Ryker; A Time For Miracles.

Bway inc: A Talent for Murder. Other Thea inc: Coup de Soleil (Paris); Pense A L' Afrique (Paris)

AUREL, Jean: Dir-wri. b. Romania (aboard the Orient Express), Nov. 6, 1925. Film critic, began making short films on art. Films inc: (shorts) Joan Miro; Kandinski; L'Affaire Manet; Fetes Galantes; Les aventures extraordinaires; L'Embarquement pour le ciel. (Features): Over There 1914-1918 (doc); The Battle Of France (doc); De l'amour; Lamiel; Manon; Les Femmes; Etes-vous Fiancee a un Marin Grec ou a un Pilot de Ligne ? (Are You Engaged To A Greek Sailor Or An Airline Pilot?); Comme un pot de Fraises (Like A Pot Of Strawberries!); La femme d'a cote (The Woman Next Door); Vivement Dimanche (Let It Be Sunday) (wri); Staline.

AURENCHE, Jean: Wri. b. France, Sep 11, 1904. Started as gag writer on adfilms. Films inc: The Courier of Lyons; Hotel du Nord; Hotel Sans-Gene; Le Mariage de Chifon; Douce; La Symphonie Pastorale; Sylvie and the Phantom; Devil in the Flesh; The Walls of Malapaga; God Needs Men; The Red Inn; Forbidden Games; Seven Deadly Sins; Mademoiselle Nitouche; The Proud and the Beautiful; Le Ble en Herbe; The Red and the Black; Gervaise; The Hunchback of Notre Dame; La Traversee de Paris; En Cas de Malheur; Crime Does Not Pay; Enough Rope; Is Paris Burning?; The Oldest Profession; The Clockmaker; The Judge and the Assassin; Let Joy Reign Supreme; L'Etoile du nord (The North Star); Coup de Torchon (Pop. 1280) (Clean Slate).

AUSTIN, Bud (Harold M Austin): Exec. b. NYC. e. U of NC; NYU. Initially with Official Films and NTA in the early 50s; then Goodson-Todman, 1956-65; Filmways, 1965-71, as exec VP; joined PAR 1973; head PAR TV, 1974-76; P, Bud Austin Prodns. TV inc: Still The Beaver (exec prod).

Films inc: Johnny Dangerously (exec prod).

AUSTIN, Ronald: Prod-Wri-Dir. b. Los Angeles, Apr 9, 1934. e. UCLA, BA. TV inc: Death Squad; Jigsaw John; Charlie's Angels; The Return of Frank Cannon (wri).

Films inc: (sp) Harry in Your Pocket; Beach Patrol.

AUTANT-LARA, Claude: Dir. b. Luzarches, France, 1903. Film inc: Ciboulette; Fric Frac; Lettres de l'Amour; Le Diable au Corps; The Red Inn; Ripening Seed; Le Rouge et le Noir; En Cas de Malheur; The Green Mare's Nest; The Count of Monte Cristo; The Seven Deadly Sins; Oh Amelia; Game of Love.

AUTEUIL, Daniel: Act. b. Algeria, Jan. 24, 1950. Films inc: L'Agression/Sombres Vacances; Attention Les Yeaux; La Nuit de Saint-Germain des Pres; Monsieur Papa; L'Amour Viole (Violated Love); Les Heroes n'ont pas froid aux oreilles (Heroes Are Not Wet Behind the Ears); A Nous Deux (Us Two); Bete Mais Discipline (Dumb but Disciplined); Les Sous-Doues (The Under-Gifted); La Banquiere (The Woman Banker); Clara et les chic types (Clara and the Swell Guys); Les hommes preferent les grosses (Men Prefer Fat Girls); Les sous-doues en Vacance (The Under-gifted on Holiday); Pour 100 briques t'as plus rien maintenant (For 200 Grand You Get Nothing Now); Que les gros salaires levent le doigt !!! (Will the High-Salaried Workers Please Raise Their Hands); L'Indic (The Informer); P'tit Con (Little Jerk); Les Fauvres (The Beasts); L'Arbalete (The Syringe); Palace; L'Amour en Douce (Love On The Quiet).

AUTRY, Gene: Act-Exec. b. Tioga, TX, Sep 29, 1907. Started as unpaid radio singer (KVOO, Tulsa) while working as railroad telegrapher. Co-wrote "That Silver-Haired Daddy Of Mine," which became one of all-time top-selling records. Began working on WLS, Chicago, 1930, appearing on such programs as National Barn Dance; became network performer when station was sold; signed by Republic as film's first singing cowboy after appearing in serial The Phantom Empire. Between films and radio he was the top western personality through early 1942, when he enlisted in the Army. Returning after the war, he made five more films for Republic and then formed own company which produced films and several tv series. Owner of radio and tv stations and the California Angels Baseball Team; April 1983, sold TV interests.

TV inc: Gene Autry--An American Hero.

Songs inc: You're the Only Star in My Blue Heaven; Be Honest With Me; Back in the Saddle Again.

AVAKIAN, Aram: Dir. b. NYC. Still photog and editor before dir The End of the Road. Films inc: Cops and Robbers; 11 Harrowhouse.

AVALON, Frankie (nee Avallone): Act. b. Philadelphia, Sep 18, 1940. Trumpet prodigy at age 9. TV variety shows; niteries; recording artist. Films inc: Jamboree; Guns of the Timberland; The Alamo; Voyage to the Bottom of the Sea; Sail a Crooked Ship; Panic in the Year Zero; Bikini Beach; Beach Blanket Bingo; Jet Set; I'll Take Sweden; Fireball 500; How to Stuff a Wild Bikini; The Take; Grease.

TV inc: Ed Sullivan; Perry Como; Pat Boone; Dick Clark Shows; Milton Berle; Golden Circle Spectacular; Dinah Shore Show; Frankie and Annette--The Second Time Around; Beach Girls; The Roots of Rock 'n Roll (The Early Years) (host); The Sound of Philadelphia (host).

AVALON, Phillip: Prod-Wri-Act. b. Australia, Feb 24, 1945. Films inc: Backstreet General (sp-dir-prod); Double Dealer (sp-prod-act); Summer City (sp-prod-act); Little Boy Lost (prod).

AVERBACK, Hy: Dir. b. 1925. Films inc: Chamber of Horrors; Where Were You When The Lights Went Out; I Love You Alice B. Toklas; The Great Bank Robbery; Suppose They Gave a War and Nobody Came; Where the Boys Are '84.

TV inc: The Brothers; The Real McCoys; Donna Reed Show; Richie Brockelman; Quark; M*A*S*H; Friends; The New Maverick; Anna and the King; Needles and Pins; Movin' On; Look Out World; Friends; Pearl; The Night Rider; The Girl, The Gold Watch and Dynamite; She's In The Army Now; At Ease (& prod); Venice Medical; The Four Seasons.

AVERY, Margaret: Act. b. Mangum, OK. Films inc: Magnum Force; Which Way Is Up?; The Fish that Saved Pittsburgh.

TV inc: Hudson Street; Louis Armstrong, Chicago Style; Scott Joplin; For Us, The Living.

Thea inc: Sistuhs; Revolution; Does a Tiger Wear a Necktie; Baby, I'm Back.

AVERY, Val: Act. Films inc: The Harder They Fall; Edge of the City; The Long Hot Summer; Requiem for a Heavyweight; Hud; The Hallelujah Trail; Hombre; A Dream of Kings; The Anderson Tapes; The Laughing Policeman; Lucky Lady; Harry and Walter Go To New York; Heroes; Cheech and Chong's Up In Smoke; The Amityville Horror; Love and Bullets; Choices; The Chosen; Continental Divide; Jinxed!; The Pope of Greenwich Village.

TV inc: The Streets.

AVIAN, Bob: Chor-prod. b. NYC, Dec 26, 1937. e. Boston U, BFA. Started as dancer in West Side Story; Funny Girl. Bway chor inc: Henry Sweet Henry; Promises, Promises; Coco; Company; Follies; Twigs; Seesaw; God's Favorite; A Chorus Line (Tony-chor-1976); Ballroom (Tony-chor-1979).

AVIDAN, David: Dir-Wri-Prod. b. Tel Aviv, Feb 21, 1934. Films inc: You Name It; Split; Sex; Telepathic Codes (anim); Stress.

TV inc: Multivista (series of talkshows in Israel).

AVILDSEN, John G.: Dir. b. Oak Park, IL. e. NYU. Films inc: Turn on to Love; Out of It (& cin); Sweet Dreams (& cin); Guess What We Learned in School Today? (& cin); Joe (& cin); Cry Uncle (& cin); Save the Tiger; W W and the Dixie Dancekings; The President's Women; Rocky (Oscar-1976); Slow Dancing in the Big City (& prod-edtr); The Formula (& edtr); Neighbors; A Night in Heaven (& edtr); The Karate Kid (& edtr).

TV inc: Murder Ink.

AVNET, Jon: Prod-Dir. b. Brooklyn, NY. e. U of PA; Sarah Lawrence; dir fellowship at AFI. Films inc: Confusion's Circle; Thursday Night Woman. (Asso prod) It's Showtime; Checkered Flag or Crash; Trial By Combat; Outlaw Blues. (Prod) Coast to Coast; Risky Business; Deal of the Century (exec prod).

TV inc: No Other Love; Homeward Bound; Prime Suspect; Something So Right (exec prod); Call To Glory (exec prod); The Burning Bed (exec prod); Silence of the Heart (exec prod).

AXELROD, George: Wri. b. NYC, Jun 9, 1922. Films inc: Phffft; The Seven Year Itch; Bus Stop; Will Success Spoil Rock Hunter; Breakfast at Tiffany's; The Manchurian Candidate (& prod); Paris When It Sizzles (& prod); How to Murder Your Wife (& prod); Goodbye Charlie; Lord Love a Duck (& prod-dir); The Secret Life of an American Wife (& prod); The Lady Vanishes.

Plays inc: The Seven Year Itch; Will Success Spoil Rock Hunter; Visit to a Small Planet; Once More with Feeling; Goodbye Charlie.

AXELROD, Jonathan: Exec. b. NYC, Jul 9, 1949. Stepson of George Axelrod. Started as screenwri. Films inc: The Dirty Movie; Every Little Crook and Nanny.

Agent with Ufland Agency; 1978, Exec Prod Movies for TV, ABC; 1979, VP Dramatic Dvlpmt ABC; 1980, VP-Sr Exec Primetime Dvlpmt, ABC; Aug 1981, Sr VP Columbia Pictures TV; Sept 1982, exec VP in chg prodn; resd Aug. 1983 to become P of Motion Picture & TV Prodn New World Pictures.

AXTON, Hoyt: Singer-Comp. b. OK, Mar 25, 1938. Films inc: Smoky; The Black Stallion; Cloud Dancer; The Junkman; Endangered Species; Liar's Moon; Heart Like A Wheel; Gremlins.

TV inc: Skinflint; The Hoyt Axton Show; The Rousters; Diff'rent Strokes; Cocaine Blues (narr-singer).

Songs inc: Greenback Dollar; Joy to the World; The No No Song.

AYCKBOURN, Alan: Wri-Dir. b. London, Apr 12, 1939. e. Haileybury Coll. Plays inc: Mr Whatnot; Relatively Speaking; How The Other Half Loves; Ernie's Incredible Illucinations; Family Circles; Time and Again; Absurd Person Singular; The Norman Conquests; Absent Friends; Confusions; Jeeves; Bedroom Farce (& co-dir) (Tony-dir-1979); Just Between Ourselves; Ten Times Table (& dir); Joking Apart (& dir); Sisterly Feelings; Taking Steps; Men on Women on Men; Season's Greetings (& dir); Way Upstream; Intimate Exchanges (& dir).

TV inc: Relatively Speaking; Service Not Included.

AYKROYD, Dan: Wri-Act. b. Ottawa, Can, Jul 1. TV inc: Coming Up Rosie (Canadian TV series); Beach Boys Special; All You Need is Cash; Saturday Night Live (Emmy-wri-1977); Steve Martin's Best Show Ever; E.T. & Friends--Magical Movie Visitors; Sweet Home Chicage.

Performed and recorded with the late John Belushi as Blues Brothers. Albums inc: Briefcase Full of Blues.

Films inc: Mr Mike's Mondo Video; Love At First Sight; 1941; The Blues Brothers; Neighbors; It Came From Hollywood; Doctor Detroit; Trading Places; Twilight Zone--The Movie; The Coneheads (voice); Ghostbusters; Nothing Lasts Forever; Into The Night.

AYRES, Lew: Act. b. Minneapolis, MN, Dec 28, 1908. Originally musician, toured Mexico with own band, sideman with Henry Halstead Orch before films; during WW2 served as medic, asst chaplin. Screen debut 1929 The Sophomore.

Films inc: The Kiss; All Quiet on the Western Front; Common Clay; Doorway to Hell; State Fair; Servants Entrance; Dr. Kildare Series; Hearts In Bondage (dir); Dark Mirror; Unfaithful; Johnny Belinda; The Capture; Donovan's Brain; The Carpetbaggers; Altars to The East (& prod-dir-narr); Advise and Consent; The Last Generation; The Biscuit Eater; The Man; Planet of the Apes; Damien--Omen II; Battlestar Galactica.

TV inc: Greatest Heroes of the Bible; Suddenly Love; Salem's Lot; Letters From Frank; Reunion; Of Mice and Men; Savage: In The Orient.

AZENBERG, Emanuel: Prod. b. Bronx, NY, Jan 22, 1934. e. NYU, BA. Bway inc: The Lion in Winter; Mark Twain Tonight; The Investigation; Something Different; Ain't Supposed to Die a Natural Death; The Sunshine Boys; The Poison Tree; The Good Doctor; Scapino; God's Favorite; California Suite; Something Afoot; Chapter Two; They're Playing Our Song; Ain't Misbehavin' (Tony-1978); Whose Life is it Anyway?; Devour the Snow; Last Licks; Children of a Lesser God; (Tony-1980) I Ought to Be in Pictures; Division Street; Fools; Einstein and the Polar Bear; Grownups; Duet For One; Little Me; Master

Harold. . .and the Boys; Brighton Beach Memoirs; The Real Thing *(Tony-*1984); A Moon For the Misbegotten; Sunday in the Park with George; Whoopi Goldberg; Joe Egg *(Tony-reproduction-1985)*; Biloxi Blues *(Tony-1985)*; The Odd Couple.

AZNAVOUR, Charles: Act. b. Paris, May 22, 1924. Films inc: Shoot The Pianist; Passage du Rhin; Candy; The Adventurers; The Games; Un Beau Monstre; And Then There Were None; The Twist (Folies Bourgeoises); Sky Riders; Ciao, Les Mecs; The Tin Drum; Der Zauberberg (The Magic Mountain); Les Fantomes Du Chapelier (The Hatter's Ghosts); Qu-est-ce Qui Fait Courir David? (What Makes David Run?); Edith et Marcel (lyrics); Viva la Vie! (Long Live Life!)

AZZARA, Candy: Act. b. Brooklyn, May 18, 1947. Films inc: Made For Each Other; They Might Be Giants; Hearts of the West; World's Greatest Lover; House Calls; Fatso; Easy Money.
TV inc: Secret Storm; Calucci's Department; The Girl Who Couldn't Lose; Rhoda; The Cop and the Kids; Soap; The Two of Us; Million Dollar Infield; Divorce Wars--A Love Story; The Rainbow Girl; Bway inc: Engagement Baby; Lovers and Other Strangers.

BABBIN, Jacqueline: Prod. Started as prodn sec to agent Audrey Wood; worked with Irene Selznick on A Streetcar Named Desire; worked for David Susskind as story edtr, later asso prod, prod; VP limited series ABC; resd Mar 1982 to become prod All My Children.
TV inc: DuPont Theatre; Armstrong Circle Theatre; Beacon Hill; Sybil *(Emmy-*1977); Friendships, Secrets and Lies; Once Upon a Family; Brave New World; All My Children.

BABCOCK, Barbara: Act. b. Feb 27, 1937. e. U of Milan, Italy; U of Lausanne, Switzerland; Wellesley; Neighborhood Playhouse; Actors Studio. Thea inc: Nature of the Crime; Pleasure of His Company; Auntie Mame; The Torchbearers.
Films inc: Heaven With a Gun; Gypsy Moths; Day of the Evil Gun; Chosen Survivors; Bang the Drum Slowly; The Black Marble; Back Roads; Lords of Discipline.
TV inc: The Last Child; Delancey Street; The Christmas Caulfield Mine Disaster; Salem's Lot; The Light on Synanon; Stranger in the House; Hill Street Blues *(Emmy-*1981); The Big Easy; Memories Never Die; Quarterback Princess; The Four Seasons; Bliss; Attack On Fear.

BACALL, Lauren (Betty Perske): Act. b. NYC, Sep 16, 1924. e. AADA. Screen debut in: To Have and Have Not, 1944. Films inc: The Big Sleep; Key Largo; Young Man with a Horn; How To Marry a Millionaire; Written on the Wind; Designing Woman; Sex and the Single Girl; Murder on the Orient Express; The Shootist; Health; The Fan.
Bway inc: Cactus Flower; Goodbye Charlie; Applause *(Tony-*1970); Woman Of The Year *(Tony-*1980).
TV inc: Applause; Perfect Gentlemen; The Wayne Newton Special--Coast To Coast. Natalie--A Tribute To A Very Special Lady; Eye On the Media--Private Lives, Public Press; Parade of Stars.

BACH, Barbara: Act. b. NYC, Aug 27, 1947. Films inc: The Odyssey; Il Mio Monsignore; Masculi Ruspanti; Paolo Il Caldo; The Sea Wolf; Last Chance; The Spy Who Loved Me; Force 10 From Navarone; The Sensual Man; Jaguar Lives!; Up The Academy; Caveman; The Unseen; Screamers; Give My Regards to Broad Street.
TV inc: Princess Daisy.

BACH, Catherine: Act. b. Warren, OH, Mar 1, 1954. Films inc: The Widow; The Midnight Man; Thunderbolt and Lightfoot; Hustle; Cannonball Run II.
TV inc: Strange New World; The Dukes of Hazzard; Enos; The Magic of David Copperfield; White Water Rebels; I Love TV Test; George Burns' How To Live To Be 100 or More.

BACH, Steven: Prod-Exec. b. Pocatello, ID, Apr 29, 1940. Former teacher, became asst to Gordon Davidson at Mark Taper Theatre, LA, 1967; story ed for Gabriel Katzka; 1970 prodn exec with Palomar; 1974 formed Palladium Productions with Katzka; May 1978 named sr. vp prodn East Coast for UA; Jan 1980 named Sr vp worldwide prodn UA; fired May 1981; Feb 1982, P & CEO of MMA.
Films inc: The Taking of Pelham 1-2-3; The Parallax View; Mr. Billion; Butch and Sundance--The Early Days.

BACHARACH, Burt: Comp-Cond-Arr. b. Kansas City, MO, May 12, 1928. e. McGraw U; Mannes School of Music; Music Academy of the West. H of Carole Bayer Sager. Cond. for Vic Damone, Ames Bros., Marlene Dietrich. Films inc: What's New Pussycat; Butch Cassidy and the Sundance Kid *(Oscars-*(2)-1969-score & best song, Raindrops Keep Fallin' on My Head); Bob & Carol & Ted & Alice; The Boys In The Band; Lost Horizon; Arthur; *(Oscar-*song-1981); Night Shift.
Songs inc: It's Great to be Young; Any Day Now; Baby, It's You; Only Love Can Break a Heart; I Wake Up Crying; A Lifetime of Loneliness; What the World Needs Now. Film title songs inc: The Sad Sack; Wives and Lovers; A House Is Not a Home; Send Me No Flowers; What's New Pussycat; Alfie; Promise Her Anything.
TV inc: Burt Bacharach Special *(Emmy-*1971); Here's Television Entertainment (host).
(Grammys-(3)-Arr-1967; Film Score & Orig cast album-1969).

BACKE, John D.: Exec. b. Akron, OH, Jul 5, 1932. e. Miami of OH, BS; Xavier, MBA. With General Electric; General Learning Corp; joined CBS 1973 as P of Publishing Group; 1976, VP CBS Inc; 1978, P & CEO; 1980, P Tomorrow Entertainment. TV inc: Kudzu; The Body Human-- The Journey Within; Backwards--The Riddle of Dyslexia; Attack On Fear (exec prod); Lots Of Luck (exec prod).

BACKER, Brian: Act. b. Brooklyn. e. High School for Performing Arts; Neighborhood Playhouse. Studied with Lee Strasberg, Herbert Berghof. Thea inc: The Life of the Male Calico; The Matchmaker; Dark At the Top of the Stairs. Bway inc: The Floating Light Bulb *(Tony-*supp-1981).
Films inc: The Burning; The West Orange Cowboy; Fast Times at Ridgemont High; Moving Violations.
TV inc: Hal Linden's Big Apple.

BACKES, Alice: Act. b. Salt Lake City, UT, May 17. e. U of UT. Films inc: I Want to Live; It Started with a Kiss; Touch of Mink; Glory Guys; The Boatniks; Snowball Express; Gable and Lombard; The Cat from Outer Space.
TV inc: Young and the Restless; Vicky; Bachelor Father; Mayberry RFD; Hazel; Rich Man, Poor Man; Fear on Trial; Maude; Man from Independence.

BACKUS, Jim: Act. b. Cleveland, OH, Feb 25, 1913. e. AADA. Began in stock & vaudeville; voice of Oscar winning cartoon Mr Magoo. Films inc: The Great Lover; Hollywood Story; His Kind of Woman; Pat and Mike; Rebel Without a Cause; The Great Man; Ice Palace; Boys' Night Out; It's Mad, Mad, Mad, Mad World; Advance to the Rear; Where Were You When the Lights Went Out?; Now You See Him, Now You Don't; Good Guys Wear Black; C.H.O.M.P.S.; There Goes The Bride; Slapstick of Another Kind; Prince Jack.
TV inc: I Married Joan; Hot Off the Wire; Gilligan's Island; Blondie; The Jim Backus Show. The Gift of the Magi; The Castaways on Gilligan's Island; The Rebels; The Gossip Columnist; The Harlem Globetrotters On Gilligan's Island; Natalie--A Tribute To A Very Special Lady.
Bway inc: Our Town.

BACSO, Peter: Wri-dir. b. Hungary, 1928. e. Budapest film school. Films inc: No Problems in Summer; Cyclists in Love; Summer on the Hill; Shot in the Head; Present Times; The Agony of Mr. Boroca; A Piano in Mid-Air; Warning Shot; A Very Moral Night (dir only); The Man Who Went Up in Smoke (dir only); The Witness; The Day Before Yesterday; A Sertes (The Insult); Te Rongyos Elet!...(Oh, Bloody Life! ...); Hany Az Ora, Vekker Ur? (What's The Time, Mr. Clock?).

BADDELEY, Hermione: Act. b. Shropshire, England, Nov 13, 1908. Films inc: Passport to Pimlico; Quartet; Christmas Carol; The Pickwick Papers; Mr Prohack; Room at the Top; Let's Get Married; Midnight Lace; Rag Doll; Mary Poppins; The Unsinkable Molly Brown; C.H.O.M.P.S.; There Goes The Bride; The Secret of NIMH (voice).
TV inc: Richard of Bordeaux; Drink Doggie Drink; The Gambler; Airmail from Cyprus; The Castaway; Maude; I Take These Men; This Girl For Hire.
Thea inc: The Milk Train Doesn't Stop Here Anymore; Canterbury Tales; Whodunnit.

BADHAM, John: Dir. b. England, 1939. e. Yale. Started Universal mail room clerk. TV credits inc: The Impatient Heart; Isn't It Shocking; Diabolique; The Gun; The Law.

Films inc: The Bingo Long Traveling All-Stars and Motor Kings; Dracula; Saturday Night Fever; Whose Life Is It Anyway?; Blue Thunder; WarGames.

BADHAM, Mary: Act. b. 1952. Sis of John Badham. Films inc: To Kill a Mockingbird; This Propery is Condemned; Let's Kill Uncle.

BADIYI, Reza: Dir. b. Iran, Apr 17, 1936. e. U of Tehran. Cin for 15 years in Iran, Europe, US; then dir. TV inc: Hawaii Five-O; The Doris Day Show; Cades County; The Eyes of Charles Sand; Switch; Incredible Hulk; Quincy; Rockford Files; Baretta; Starsky & Hutch; W.E.B.; Million Dollar Man; Bionic Woman; The Hardy Boys; Joe Dancer; Of Mice and Men; Modesty Blaise; White Water Rebels; Murder One-Dancer 0; Policewoman Centerfold; Peyton Place--The Next Generation.

Films inc: Death of A Stranger; Trader Horn.

BAER, Art: Wri-Prod. b. NYC, Sep 17, 1925. e. Washington Square Coll, BA. TV inc: Dick Van Dyke; Good Times; The Jeffersons; Hogan's Heros; Gomer Pyle; Get Smart; Victor Borge Show; Perry Como Show; Jim Nabors Hour; Jonathan Winters Show; Carol Burnett Show (Emmy-wri-1972); The Cop & the Kid (prod); The Love Boat (& prod); Glitter (& supv prod).

BAER, Hanania: Cin. b. Israel, Sept. 24, 1943. e. London Film School. Films inc: Jerusalem, Image and Art (doc); Northern Frontier (doc); Fyre; Echoes; Alligator (2d unit); Choices; The Being (addl photog); Fellow Travelers; The Unknown Comic; Ninja II--The Domination (addl photog); Maria's Lovers (addl photog); Breaking; Electric Boogaloo/Breaking II; Always.

TV inc: A Special Gift; What Are Friends For; Schoolboy Father; Bloomers; Daddy, I'm Their Mother Now; She Drinks A Little; Invisible Thread; The Wave; Echoes; Between Two Loves; Andrea--A Hitchhiker's Tragedy; A Killer In the Family; The Cartier Affair; Obsessed With A Married Woman.

BAER, Max: Prod-Dir. b. Oakland, CA, Dec 4, 1937. e. U of Santa Clara. TV inc: (act) The Beverly Hillbillies; The Circle Family. Films inc: (prod) The McCullochs; Ode to Billie Joe; Hometown, USA (dir); The Asphalt Cowboy (act).

BAEZ, Joan: Singer. b. NYC, Jan 9, 1941. e. Boston U. Films inc: Sacco and Vanzetti (sang and wrote lyrics for theme ballad); Don't Look Back (doc); Carry It On (doc); Woodstock; Celebration at Big Sur; Banjo Man; Renaldo & Clara; Sag Nein! (Say No!); In Our Hands (doc).

TV inc: A Tribute to Martin Luther King Jr.--A Celebration of Life.

BAGGETTA, Vincent: Act. b. Paterson, NJ, Dec 7. e. LA City Coll. Films inc: Embryo; Two Minute Warning; The Man Who Wasn't There.

TV inc: Love Is A Many Splendored Thing; Mary Hartman, Mary Hartman; Family; The Rhinemann Exchange; In the Matter of Karen Ann Quinlan; Murder on Flight 502; The Eddie Capra Mysteries; Eischeid-Only the Pretty Girls Die; The Chicago Story; The Ordeal of Bill Carney; MacGruder & Loud.

BAIL, Chuck: Dir. Started as 2d unit dir. Films inc: Cleopatra Jones and the Casino of Gold; Gumball Rally (& prod); Black Sampson; The Stunt Man (act); Rainy Day Friends (act).

BAILEY, Pearl: Singer-Act. b. Newport News, VA, Mar 29, 1918. Started show business age 15 as singer and dancer in vaudeville, NY clubs. Stage debut, St. Louis Woman, 1946. Other Bway appearances inc: Arms and the Girl; Bless You All; House of Flowers; Hello, Dolly. (Special Tony-1968).

Films inc: Variety Girl; Carmen Jones; Isn't it Romantic; That Certain Feeling; Porgy and Bess; All the Fine Young Cannibals; Norman Is That You?; The Fox and The Hound.

TV inc: The Pearl Bailey Show; Disney Animation-The Illusion of Life; Over Easy; Bob Hope's All-Star Celebration opening the Gerald R Ford Museum; Kennedy Center Tonight--Broadway to Washington; The Member of the Wedding; Silver Spoons.

BAILEY, Robin: Act. b. Hucknall, Nottingham, England, Oct 5, 1919. Films inc: School for Secrets; Private Angelo; For Better for Worse;

The Spy with a Cold Nose; The Whisperers; You Only Live Twice; The Eliminator; Blind Terror; Nightmare Rally; The Four Feathers.

TV inc: Seven Deadly Sins; The Power Game; Person to Person; The Newcomers; Murder Must Advertise; Upstairs, Downstairs; I Didn't Know You Cared; The Velvet Glove; Crown Court; Charters & Caldicott; Bleak House.

Thea inc: Barretts of Wimpole Street; You'll Never be Michael Angelo; Quartermaine's Terms; Camelot; Beethoven's Tenth.

BAIN, Barbara: Act. b. Sep 13, 1931. e. U of IL, BA. W of Martin Landau. Former fashion model. TV inc: Mission Impossible (Emmys-1967, 1968, 1969); Goodnight My Love; Murder Once Removed; Savage; A Summer Without Boys; Space 1999; The Harlem Globetrotters On Gilligan's Island.

BAIN, Conrad: Act. b. Alberta, Canada, Feb 4, 1923. e. AADA. Thea inc: The Iceman Cometh; Sixth Finger in a Five Finger Glove; Candide; Dark of the Moon; Lost in the Stars; The Family Reunion.

Films inc: Who Killed Mary What's Her Name?; Up the Sandbox; A Fan's Notes; I Never Sang for My Father; A Pleasure Doing Business; C.H.O.M.P.S.

TV inc: The Defenders; Look Up and Live; Grandpa Goes to Washington; Maude; The Waverly Wonders; Diff'rent Strokes; Child Bride At Short Creek; The TV Funnies (host).

BAIO, Jimmy: Act. b. Brooklyn, NY, Mar 15. Bway inc: All God's Chillun Got Wings. TV inc: Joe and Sons; Soap.

BAIO, Scott Vincent: Act. b. NYC, Sep 22, 1961. Films inc: Bugsy Malone; Skatetown USA; Foxes; Zapped!.

TV inc: Luke Was There; Muggsy; Happy Days; Blansky's Beauties; Who's Watching the Kids; The Boy Who Drank Too Much; Stoned; Run, Don't Walk; Senior Trip; Joanie Loves Chachi; Lily For President?; Dom DeLuise and Friends Part II; Charles in Charge; How To Be A Man.

BAIRD, Roy: Prod. b. London. Films inc: Our Mother's House; Women in Love; The Devils; If. . .; Spring and Port Wine; The Music Lovers; That'll Be the Day; Stardust; The Final Program; Henry VIII and His Six Wives; Mahler; Quadrophenia; McVicar.

TV inc: The Who--The Final Concert (exec prod) (PPV).

BAKER, Benny (nee Zifkin): Act. b. St Joseph, MO, May 5, 1907. Started in George Cukor's stock co in Rochester, NY; later in vaude with Lou Holtz; began in films in shorts; made 57 features inc: The Hell Cat; Belle of the Nineties; Big Broadcast of 1936; Thanks A Million; Rose Bowl; Champagne Waltz; Up In Arms; My Girl Tisa; The Inspector General; Public Pigeon No. 1; Thunder Birds; Boy Did I Get a Wrong Number; Papa's Delicate Condition; Paint Your Wagon; Car Wash.

Bway inc: The Tempest; Front Page; DuBarry Was a Lady; Let's Face It; Jackpot; No, No Nanette (rev).

TV inc: The Jerk, Too.

BAKER, Blanche: Act. b. Dec 20, 1956. d. of Carroll Baker. Films inc: French Postcards; The Seduction of Joe Tynan; Cold Feet.

TV inc: Holocaust (Emmy-supp-1978); Mary and Joseph-A Story of Faith; The Day The Bubble Burst.

Bway inc: Lolita.

BAKER, Buddy (Norman Dale Baker): Comp-Cond. b. Springfield, MO, Jan 4, 1918. Prior to 1954 did arranging for Stan Kenton; Harry James; Bob Crosby; Glen Gray; for radio: Bob Hope; Jack Benny; Kay Kyser Shows. TV inc: Pearl Bailey Show. 1954, composer for Walt Disney Productions.

Films inc: Napoleon and Samantha; The Apple Dumpling Gang; The Shaggy D.A.; The Treasure of Matacumbe; Hot Lead and Cold Feet; The Apple Dumpling Gang Rides Again; The Devil and Max Devlin; The Fox and The Hound.

BAKER, Carroll: Act. b. Johnstown, PA, May 28, 1931. Films inc: Easy to Love; Giant; Baby Doll; The Miracle; Something Wild; Bridge to the Sun; How the West Was Won; The Carpetbaggers; Station Six Sahara; The Greatest Story Ever Told; Sylvia; Harlow; Jack of Diamonds; The Sweet Body of Deborah; Paranoia; Captain Apache; Andy Warhol's Bad; The World is Full of Married Men; The Watcher in the

Woods; Red Monarch; Star 80; The Secret Diary of Sigmund Freud.
TV inc: Coast of Dreams; Hitler's SS--Portrait In Evil.

BAKER, Diane: Act. b. Hollywood, 1938. Films inc: The Diary of Anne Frank; Journey to the Centre of the Earth; Hemingway's Adventures of a Young Man; Strait Jacket; Nine Hours to Rama; The Prize; Marnie; Mirage; The Horse in the Grey Flannel Suit; East of Java; Baker's Hawk.
TV inc: Can I Save My Children; The Killers; Arrowsmith; The Badge or the Cross; Do You Take This Stranger; Congratulations, It's a Boy; One of A Kind; Here We Go Again; Fugitive Family; The Blue and the Gray; Impact '84--Miracles in the Making (prod); A Woman of Substance (& prod).

BAKER, George: Act-dir. b. Bulgaria, Apr 1, 1931. Thea inc: Aren't We All; Restless Heart; Look After Lulu; joined Old Vic appearing in Richard II; Saint Joan; What Every Woman Knows; toured Great Britain and Russia; The Glad and Sorry Season; Vanity Fair; A Shot in the Dark; Portrait of Murder; The Sleeping Prince (& dir); I Never Sang For My Father; The Lady's Not For Burning (dir).
Films inc: The Intruder; The Ship That Died of Shame; The Dambusters; No Time For Tears; Moonraker; Lancelot and Guinevere; Curse of the Fly; Goodbye Mr. Chips; On Her Majesty's Secret Service; The Executioner; A Warm December; The Spy Who Loved Me.
TV inc: Death of a Salesman; Medea; Candida; I, Claudius; Print Out; A Woman of Substance.

BAKER, Herbert (nee Abrahams): Wri. b. Dec 25, 1920. e. Yale U, BA. S of late Belle Baker, and late Maurice Abrahams. Films inc: So This Is New York; Jumping Jacks; Scared Stiff; Loving You; The Silencers; King Creole; Murderers Row; Sextette; The Jazz Singer.
TV inc: An Evening With Fred Astaire (Emmy-1959); John Denver and the Muppets; Danny Kaye Show; Perry Como Show; Danny Kaye's Lock-in At the Met; Ted Knight Special; Gladys Knight and the Pips; Mac Davis Show; Flip Wilson Show (Emmy-1971); Norman Rockwell's America; Some of Manie's Friends; Specials for Perry Como; Frank Sinatra; Danny Kaye; Dean Martin; John Denver and the Muppets--A Christmas Get Together;
Bway: lyr for Helen Goes to Troy. Special material for Belle Baker; Danny Kaye; Lena Horne. The World of Entertainment; The Wayne Newton Special--Coast to Coast.
(Died Jun 30, 1983).

BAKER, Jim B.: Act. b. Great Falls, MT, Jul 12. e. U of MT. Worked with ACT, various repertory groups. Films inc: Manny's Orphans. TV inc: In Memory Of; Flo.

BAKER, Joe Don: Act. b. Groesbeck, TX, Feb 12, 1936. Films inc: Adam at 6 A.M.; Wishbone Cutter; Charley Varrick; Walking Tall; Golden Needles; Cool Hand Luke; Mitchell; Wild Rovers; The Pack; Checkered Flag or Crash; Speedtrap; Wacko; Joysticks; The Natural; Fletch.
TV inc: Mongo's Back in Town; That Certain Summer; To Kill a Cop; Power; Eischeid.

BAKER, Richard A. (Rick): Makeup. b. Binghamton, NY, 1950. Films inc: (frequently plays monster characters he creates) The Octoman; Schlock; Black Caesar; The Thing With Two Heads; Live and Let Die; It's Alive; Death Race 2000; Squirm; King Kong (& act); Kentucky Fried Movie (& act); Star Wars; Up the Academy; The Incredible Shrinking Woman (& act); An American Werewolf in London (Oscar-makeup-1981); Greystoke--The Legend of Tarzan, Lord of the Apes; Starman.
TV inc: numerous commercials; The Autobiography of Miss Jane Pittman (Emmy-makeup-1974).

BAKER, Roy Ward: Dir. b. England, 1916. With Gainsborough studios prior to WW2. Films inc: The October Man; The Weaker Sex; Morning Departure; I'll Never Forget You; Inferno; Don't Bother To Knock; Passage Home; Tiger in the Smoke; That One That Got Away; A Night to Remember; The Singer not the Song; Flame in the Streets; Quatermass and the Pit; The Anniversary; Moon Zero Two; The Vampire Lovers; Dr. Jekyll and Sister Hyde; Asylum; Vault of Horror; Legend of the Seven Golden Vampires; The Seven Brothers Meet Dracula; The Monster Club.
TV inc: The Flame Trees of Thika.

BAKER, Suzanne: Prod. b. London, 1942. Freelance interviewer/researcher, wri Australian TV & radio, 1962-64, prod-dir-wri Australia network, 1964-68; dir BBC-TV, 1968; Women's Edtr, Sydney Morning Herald, 1971-73; prod, Film Australia, 1974-78. Films inc: Leisure (Oscar-ss-1976).

BAKEWELL, William: Act. b. Los Angeles, May 2, 1908. Films inc: The Iron Mask; All Quiet on the Western Front; Dance, Fools, Dance; The Spirit of Notre Dame; Back Street; Quality Street; Three Cornered Moon; Seven Sinners; Come, Fill the Cup; Davy Crockett; The Strongest Man in the World.

BAKSHI, Ralph: Prod-dir-wri-ani. b. NYC, 1939. Films inc: Fritz the Cat; Heavy Traffic; Coonskin; Wizards; The Lord of the Rings; American Pop; Hey, Good Lookin'; Fire and Ice; Cannonball Run II (ani only).

BALABAN, A.J.: Thea Exec. b. Chicago, Aug 18, 1889. Began as operator of nickelodeon in Chicago, 1907. Co-founder Balaban & Katz Corp, 1917. Affiliated with Paramount, named director of entertainment, then VP. Abroad 9 years, returned to U.S. as circuit exhibitor, 1935. General manager Roxy Theatre, NY, 1942-52.

BALABAN, Bob (Robert Elmer Balaban): Act. b. Chicago, Aug. 16, 1945. e. NYU. Grand S of Sam Katz. Thea inc: You're a Good Man, Charlie Brown (off Bway); Plaza Suite; The Basic Training of Pavlo Hummel; The Inspector General; Marie and Bruce; Girls, Girls, Girls (dir); The Children; The White House Murder Case.
Films inc: Midnight Cowboy; Me Natalie; Catch-22; The Strawberry Statement; Making It; Bank Shot; Report to the Commissioner; Close Encounters of the Third Kind; Girlfriends; Altered States; Whose Life Is It Anyway?; Absence of Malice; Prince of the City; In Our Hands (doc); 2010.
TV inc: Marriage--Year One; Tales From the Darkside (dir).

BALANCHINE, George (Georges Malitonovitch Balanchivadze): Chor. b. St Petersburg, Russia, Jan 22, 1904. e. Imperial School of Ballet in St Petersburg. Began as a dancer, 1923-24; appointed ballet master and chor to Les Ballets Russes de Diaghilev; ballet master to the Royal Danish Ballet, 1931; formed the School of American Ballet, NY, which later became the American Ballet Co, 1934; chor to Metropolitan Opera, NY, 1935-38; founded Ballet Society, 1946, renamed the NY City Ballet, 1948, toured US & abroad.
Bway inc: (chor) Wake Up and Dream; Cochran's 1931 Revue; The Ziegfeld Follies; On Your Toes; Babes in Arms; The Boys from Syracuse; Louisiana Purchase; Cabin in the Sky; The Song of Norway; Where's Charley?.
Films inc: Goldwyn Follies; On Your Toes; I Was an Adventuress.
TV inc: (chor) Stravinsky's The Flood; Ringling Bros Barnum & Bailey Circus.
(Died Apr 30, 1983).

BALIN, Ina: Act. (nee Rosenberg).b. NYC, Nov 12, 1937. Films inc: The Black Orchid; From the Terrace; The Young Doctors; The Greatest Story Ever Told; The Patsy; Act of Reprisal; Run Like a Thief; Charro; The Projectionist; The Comeback Trail; The Don Is Dead.
TV inc: The Lonely Profession; Desperate Mission; The Immigrants; The Children of An Lac.

BALL, Lucille: Act-Prod. b. Celeron, NY, Aug 11, 1911. Worked as model in NY. To Hollywood as a Goldwyn Girl in Roman Scandals. Under contract to Columbia, later to RKO in number of un-billed parts, including two-reelers with Leon Errol and The Three Stooges. First credit in Carnival.
Films inc: Roberta; The Three Musketeers; I Dream Too Much; That Girl From Paris; Stage Door; Affairs of Annabel; Annabel Takes a Tour; Five Came Back; Dance, Girl, Dance; Too Many Girls; The Big Street; Best Foot Forward; Thousands Cheer; DuBarry Was A Lady; Meet the People; Lured; Her Husband's Affairs; Sorrowful Jones; Fancy Pants; Easy Living; Miss Grant Takes Richmond: Fuller Brush Girls; Facts of Life; Critic's Choice; Yours, Mine And Ours; Mame.
Radio inc: Phil Baker Show; Jack Haley's Wonder Bread Show; Screen Guild Playhouse; My Favorite Husband.
TV inc: I Love Lucy (with former husband Desi Arnaz) (Emmys-1952, 1955); The Lucy Show (Emmys-1967, 1968): Here's Lucy; Happy Anniversary and Goodbye; What Now, Catherine Curtis; The

Lucille Ball Specials; Lucy Moves to NBC; The Steve Allen Comedy Hour; Bob Hope 30th Anniversay Special; High Hopes--The Capra Years (host); An All-Star Party for Carol Burnett; The 4th Annual TV Guide Special; Bob Hope's Road To Hollywood; Happy Birthday, Bob. The Television Academy Hall of Fame (honoree); Bob Hope's Who Makes the World Laugh--Part II; The Hilarious Unrehearsed Antics of the Stars; All-Star Party For Lucille Ball; Night Of 100 Stars II; On Top All Over The World; The Television Academy Hall of Fame.

Bway: Wildcat.

BALL, William: Act-dir. b. Apr 29, 1931. e. Fordham U; Carnegie Tech. Founder of American Conservatory Theatre in Pittsburgh 1965, moved to permanent quarters in San Francisco in 1967. Started as actor with Margaret Webster Shakespeare troupe, worked with various Shakespearean groups. Bway inc: (act) The Misanthrope; Hamlet; The Lady's Not For Burning; The Country Wife. (Dir) Six Characters In Search of an Author; Cosi Fan Tutte; The Inspector General; Under Milkwood; Porgy and Bess; Don Giovanni; Tartuffe.

TV inc: Cyrano; Tartuffe.

BALLARD, Carroll: Dir. b. Los Angeles, Oct 14, 1937. e. UCLA. Films inc: The Black Stallion; Never Cry Wolf.

BALLARD, Kaye (Catherine Gloria Balota): Act-Singer. b. Cleveland, OH, Nov 20, 1926. Began show business 1946 at The Bowery, Detroit, as impressionist. Toured vaudeville houses with Spike Jones, Vaughn Monroe, Stan Kenton. Films inc: The Girl Most Likely; A House is Not a Home; The Ritz; Freaky Friday; Falling In Love Again.

TV inc: Red Skelton Show; Ed Sullivan; Perry Como Show; Laugh-In; The Mothers-in-Law; The Dream Merchants; Irene; Alice In Wonderland.

Bway inc: Three To Make Ready; Carnival!; Molly; The Beast in Me; Reuben, Reuben; The Pirates of Penzance; She Stoops To Conquer (off Bway).

BALLARD, Lucien: Cin. b. Miami, OK, May 6, 1908. e. U of OK; U of PA. Films inc: Crime and Punishment; Craig's Wife; Blind Alley; Wild Geese Calling; The Lodger; Laura; Inferno; The Killing; Al Capone; Pay or Die; The Caretakers; Nevada Smith; Hour of the Guns; Will Penny; The Wild Bunch; True Grit; The Ballad of Cable Hogue; What's the Matter with Helen; Junior Bonner; The Getaway; Breakout; Rabbit Test.

BALLARD, Lucinda: Dsgn. b. Apr 13, 1908. W of the late Howard Dietz. Bway inc: Happy Birthday; Another Part of the Forest (Tony-1947); John Loves Mary; Chocolate Soldier (& sets); I Remember Mama; Annie Get Your Gun; Show Boat; Fourposter; A Streetcar Named Desire; The Gay Life (Tony-1962). Silk Stockings.

Opera inc: Peter and the Wolfe; Giselle.

BALLHAUS, Michael: Cin. b. Berlin, Germany, Aug. 5, 1935. TV inc: Der Klassenaufsatz (The Classroom Essay); The Martyrdom of Peter O'Hey; The Great Wildenberg; Great Love; Abscheid (Farewell); House of Pure Love; Whole Days in the Trees; Gold for Montevasal; The Kidnapper; The Trojan Chair; I Am a Citizen of the German Democratic Republic (doc); The Marquis of Keith; The Hero; Adele Spitzeder; World on the Wire; Dead People Don't Need Apartments; Aus der familie der Panzerechsen die Insil (From the Family of Saurian); The Piggy Bank; Dorothea Merz; The Election; I Only Want You To Love Me; On the Chimborazzo; Bolwieser (Stationmaster's Wife); Big and Small; The Release.

Films inc: Deine Zartlichkeiten (Your Tenderness); Two of Us; Whity; Beware of a Holy Whore; Tschetan, The Indian Boy; The Bitter Tears of Petra von Kant; Fox and his Friends; Mother Kusters Goes to Heaven; Summerfolks; Satan's Brew; Chinese Roulette; Adolf and Marlene; Once Upon a Time; Women in New York; Despair; Just for the Fun of It; The Marriage of Maria Braun; Germany in Autumn; Venice--Island of Happiness (doc); The First Polka; Bourbon Street Blues; The Uprising; Looping; Malou; Wo geht's denn hier zum film? (How to Make it in the Movies); The Magic Mountain; The Release; Stadttraume (Dear Mr. Wonderful); Baby It's You; Heller Wahn (Bright Madness); Edith's Diary; Reckless; Das Autogram (The Autograph); Old Enough; Heartbreakers.

BALNAVES, Neil Richard: Prod. b. Adelaide, S Australia, May 5, 1944. M dir Hanna-Barbera Pty, Ltd. Films inc: (exec prod) Last of

the Mohicans; Five Weeks in a Balloon; Black Beauty. TV inc: Clue Club; The Robonic Stooges; Undercover Elephant; The Popeye Show.

BALSAM, Martin: Act. b. NYC, Nov 4, 1919. TV inc: Playhouse 90; Studio One; Philco Playhouse; Doctor Kildare; Naked City; The Defenders; The Millionaire; Rainbow; The Seeding of Sarah Burns; The House on Garibaldi Street; Archie Bunkers Place; Aunt Mary; The Love Tapes; Raid on Entebbe. People vs. Jean Harris; Little Gloria--Happy At Last; I Want To Live; Space.

Bway inc: You Know I Can't Hear You When the Water's Running (Tony-1968); Cold Storage.

Films inc: On the Waterfront; Twelve Angry Men; Psycho; Breakfast at Tiffanys; The Carpetbaggers; Seven Days in May; Harlow; A Thousand Clowns (Oscar-supp-1965); 2001-A Space Odyssey; Tora! Tora! Tora!; Little Big Man; Summer Wishes-Winter Dreams; Catch 22; The Taking of Pelham 1-2-3; Murder On the Orient Express; All the President's Men; Two Minute Warning; The Sentinel; Silver Bears; Cuba; There Goes The Bride; The Salamander; Innocent Prey; The Goodbye People; St. Elmo's Fire.

BANAS, Robert Joseph: Dir-Chor. b. NYC, Sep 20, 1933. TV inc: Judy Garland Show; Tony Martin Special; Tennessee Ernie Ford Special; Jonathan Winters Show; Frank Sinatra Special II; Eleanor and Franklin; Lindsey Wagner Special; Bud and Lou; Kaz; Quincy.

BANCROFT, Anne (nee Italiano): Act. b. NYC, Sep 17, 1931. e. AADA. W of Mel Brooks. On screen from 1952 in Don't Bother to Knock. Films inc: Tonight We Sing; The Kid From Left Field; Demitrius and the Gladiators; Gorilla at Large; The Raid; New York Confidential; The Brass Ring; Naked Street; The Miracle Worker (Oscar-1962); The Pumpkin Eater; The Slender Thread; The Graduate; Young Winston; The Prisoner of Second Avenue; The Hindenburg; The Turning Point; Fatso (& dir-sp); The Elephant Man; To Be Or Not To Be; Garbo Talks.

Bway inc: Two for the Seasaw (Tony-1958); The Miracle Worker (Tony-1960); The Devils; A Cry of Players; Golda; Duet For One.

TV inc: Torrents of Spring; Annie, the Woman in the Life of Men (Emmy-1970); Annie and the Seven Hoods; Marco Polo; That Was The Week That Was.

BAND, Albert: Prod-Wri-Dir. b. Paris, May 7, 1924. e. Lyceum Louis le Grand. Started as film cutter Pathe Lab; Prodn Asst MGM. Films inc: The Young Guns (dir); I Bury the Living (prod-dir); Face of Fire (prod-dir); The Avenger (dir); The Tramplers (prod-dir); The Hellbenders (prod); A Minute to Pray, A Second to Die (prod-dir); Little Cigars (prod); Dracula's Dog (prod); She Came to the Valley (prod-dir); Metalstorm--The Destruction of Jared-Syn (exec prod); Swordkill (exec prod).

BAND, Charles: Prod-dir. b. Los Angeles, 1952. S of Albert Band. Films inc: Crash (prod); End of the World (prod); Laserblast (prod); Tourist Trap (prod); The Alchemist; Parasite; Metalstorm-The Destruction of Jared-Syn; Swordkill (prod); Ghoulies (exec prod); The Dungeonmaster; Future Cop.

BANGERT, Charles A.: Prod-Dir. b. Kansas City, MO, Oct 14, 1943. e. Hofstra. TV inc: Lifeline; The Body Human--The Sexes; The Body Human--The Magic Sense (Emmy-co-prod-1980); The Body Human--The Body Beautiful; The Body Human--The Sexes II; The Body Human--The Bionic Breakthrough (Emmy-prod-1981); The Body Human--The Loving Process, Men; The Body Human--The Living Code (Emmys-dir & prod-1983).

BANKY, Vilma (nee Lonchit): Act. b. Budapest, Hungary, Jan 9, 1903. Silent screen star. Films inc: The Dark Angel; The Eagle; Son of the Sheik; The Winning of Barbara Worth; A Lady to Love; The Rebel.

BANNEN, Ian: Act. b. Airdrie, Scotland, Jun 29, 1928. e. Ratcliffe Coll. Films inc: Private's Progress; The Birthday Present; Macbeth; A French Mistress; Suspect; Station Six Sahara; Rotten to the Core; The Hill; The Flight of he Phoenix; Penelope; Lock Up Your Daughters; Too Late the Hero; Fright; Doomwatch; The Offence; The Mackintosh Man; Bite the Bullet; Sweeney; Inglorious Bastards; The Watcher in the Woods; Eye of the Needle; Night Crossing; Gandhi; Gorky Park.

Bway inc: A View From the Bridge; The Iceman Cometh; Long

Day's Journey Into Night; Hedda Gabler; Toys in the Attic; Sergeant Musgrave's Dance; A Moon for the Misbegotten.

TV inc: Johnny Belinda; Tinker, Tailor, Soldier, Spy; Dr. Jekyll and Mr. Hyde.

BANNER, Bob: Prod-Dir. b. Ennis, TX, Aug 15, 1921. e. SMU, BA; Northwestern U, MA. Staff dir, NBC-TV Chicago-1949-50; TV inc: The Dinah Shore Chevy Show (*Emmy*-dir-1957); The Garry Moore Show; Garroway at Large; Candid Camera. His co, Bob Banner Assoc, prod specials inc Carnegie Hall Salutes Jack Benny; Julie and Carol at Carnegie Hall; Here's Peggy Fleming; The John Davidson Shows; Love! Love! Love!; To Europe with Love; Perry Como's Early American Christmas; The Darker Side of Terror; If Things Were Different; Perry Como's Bahama Holiday; Perry Como's Spring In San Francisco; The Way They Were; A Gift Of Music; Countdown '81--A Solid Gold Special; Andy Williams' Early New England Christmas; Perry Como's Christmas In Paris; The Music Of Your Life (exec prod).

BANNON, Jack: Act. b. Los Angeles, Jun 14, 1940. e. UCSB, BA. S of the late Bea Benadaret. TV inc: Petticoat Junction; Quincy; Tail Gunner Joe; Amelia Earhart; Lou Grant; Insight/Unfinished Business; Take Your Best Shot.

BARAKA, Imamu Amiri (Everett LeRoi Jones): Plywri. b. Newark, NJ, Oct 7, 1934. Plays inc: Dante; Dutchman; The Slave; The Baptism; The Toilet; Jello; Experimental Death Unit 1; Black Mass; Mad Heart; Slave Ship; Great Goodness of Life; Junkies are Full of Sh. . .; Bloodrites; Baraka; A Recent Killing; Sidnee Poet Historical (& dir); The Motion of History (& dir).

BARANSKI, Christine: Act. b. May 2, 1952. e. Juilliard, BA. Bway inc: Hide and Seek; The Real Thing. Other thea inc: The Undefeated Rumba Champ; Sally and Marsha; A Midsummer Night's Dream; Otherwise Engaged.

Films inc: Soup For One; Crackers; Lovesick.

TV inc: The Adams Chronicles; Playing For Time; Murder Ink; All My Children; Texas; Another World; Bigshots In America.

BARASH, Olivia: Act. b. Miami, FL, Jan 11, 1965. Films inc: Who Is Harry Kellerman...?; American Hot Wax; Repo Man; Tuff Turf.

TV inc: A World Apart; Big Blue Marble; Code R; The Secret Storm; Michel's Bird; The Ghost Belongs to Me; In the Beginning; Zack and the Magic Factory; Through the Magic Pyramid.

Bway inc: Gypsy; Panama Hattie.

BARBEAU, Adrienne: Act. b. Sacramento, CA, Jun 11. Bway inc: Fiddler on the Roof; Grease; The Owl and the Pussycat.

TV inc: Maude; Houdini; Having Babies; Red Alert; Someone is Watching Me; The Darker Side of Terror; The Top of the Hill; Valentine Magic On Love Island; Tourist; Charlie and the Great Balloon Chase; The Next One (feevee); Seduced.

Films inc: The Fog; Escape From New York; The Cannonball Run; Swamp Thing; Creepshow.

BARBER, Red (Walter L Barber): Sportscaster. b. Columbus, MS, 1908. Chiefly assoc with baseball. Play-by-play Cincinnati Reds, 1934-39; Brooklyn Dodgers, 1939-54; NY Yankees, 1954-66. Ret. Bway inc: The First.

BARBERA, Joseph R.: Exec Prod. b. NYC, Mar 24, 1911. e. NYU; American Institute of Banking. Started submitting cartoons to leading magazines; joined Van Buren Associates as a sketch artist; later worked in the animation department of MGM where he met William Hanna in 1937; they were teamed to produce a single animated short and developed Tom & Jerry, the first of seven Academy Award winning cartoons. Left MGM in 1957 to form Hanna-Barbera Prods to make cartoons for TV. Cartoon series inc: Yogi Bear; Huckleberry Hound; The Flintstones. Company entered theatrical prod with Charlotte's Web in 1973.

TV inc: The Curlews (*Emmy*-1973); The Runaways (*Emmy*-1974); The Gathering (*Emmy*-exec prod-1978); The Popeye Valentine Special - Sweethearts At Sea; Beach Girls; The Gathering, Part II; Scooby Goes Hollywood; Belle Starr; The Flintstone's New Neighbors; Smurfs (Emmys-Exec Prod-1983, 1984); The Smurfs Springtime Special; The Jokebook (& dir); The Smurfs Christmas Special; Yogi Bear's All-Star Comedy Christmas Caper; Christmas Comes To Pac-land; The Smurfic Games; Smurfily Ever After.

Films inc: C.H.O.M.P.S.; Heidi's Song; Les Dalton en cavale (Escape from Grumble Gulch).

BARBOUR, John: Comedian-TV pers. b. Toronto, Canada, Apr 24. Started as nitery comic. Hosted 4 LA area tv shows. TV inc: The Tonight Show; The Dean Martin Show; The Marty Feldman Show; Gomer Pyle USMC (wri); My Mother, The Car (wri); Real People (Co-host & prod); Ernie Kovacs--Television's Original Genius (exec prod-prod-wri-host); John Barbour's World (wri-dir-prod); On Stage, America (act).

BARDEM, Juan-Antonio: Dir-Wri. b. Madrid, Jun 2, 1922. Films inc: Welcome, Mr Marshall; Death of a Cyclist; Calle/Mayor; La Venganza; Los Innocentes; The Uninhibited; El Puente; 7 dias de Enero.

Thea inc: (Dir) The House of Bernarda Alba.

BARDOT, Brigitte: Act. b. Paris, Sept 28, 1934. Began as model. Films inc: Le Trou Normand; Helen of Troy; Doctor at Sea; The Bride Is Much Too Beautiful; Will You Dance With Me; And God Created Woman; Love Is My Profession; Babette Goes To War; A Very Private Affair; Two Weeks in September; Spirits of the Dead; Les Femmes.

BARE, Richard L.: Prod-Dir. b. Turlock, CA, 1909. e. USC. Films inc: This Rebel Breed; Girl on the Run; Return of the Frontiersman; Shootout at Medicine Bend; This Side of the Law; Smart Girls Don't Talk; Flaxy Martin; House Across the Street; Wicked, Wicked. June, 1985, named to head film production for American Entertainment Venture Corp.

TV inc: Green Acres; 77 Sunset Strip; Cheyenne; The Islanders; Man Against Crime; Gangbusters; So This Is Hollywood; Walt Disney Presents; You're Only Young Once; Run for Your Life; Bus Stop; Gallant Men; Casablanca; Nanny and the Professor; Petticoat Junction; Donna Reed Show; Topper; Behind the Eightball; Alias Smith and Jones; The Virginian; Maverick; Lawman; Sugarfoot.

BARENBOIM, Daniel: Pianist-cond. b. Buenos Aires, Nov. 15, 1942. e. Mozarteum; Accademia Chigiana; Santa Cecilia Academy. Debuted as pianist at age seven; debuted with Israel Philharmonic, 1953; appeared with Royal Philharmonic, Berlin Philharmonic, NY Philharmonic; Carnegie Hall Debut 1957; first solo U.S. recital, 1958; debut as conductor 1962 with English Chamber Orchestra; has conducted London Symphony; Israel Philharmonic; NY Philharmonic; Philadelphia Symphony; Boston Symphony.

Recs inc: Brahms Sonatas in E Minor and F Major for Cello and Piano; Beethoven Five Concertos (*Grammys*-class album of year & class inst solo - 1976); Beethoven Sonatas for Cello; Berg Chamber Concerto for Piano & Violin/Four Pieces for Clarinet & Piano); Messiaen Quartet for the End of Time; Elgar concerto for Violin in B Minor (*Grammy*-inst solo with orch - 1982).

BARI, Lynn (Marjorie Bitzer): Act. b. Roanoke, VA, 1917. First appeared on screen as dancing girl in Dancing Lady. Films inc: Shock; Home Sweet Homicide; Sunny Side of the Street; I Dream of Jeanie; Damn Citizen; Trauma.

BARISH, Keith: Prod. b. Los Angeles. Films inc: Endless Love; Sophie's Choice; Kiss Me Goodbye; Misunderstood (exec prod).

TV inc: A Streetcar Named Desire (exec prod).

BARKER, Bob: TV Host. b. Darrington, WA, Dec 12, 1923. e. Drury Coll. Started as news wri, announcer, disc jockey. MC Truth or Consequences, 1956. Formed Bob Barker Prods, Inc. Since 1967, MC for both the Miss Universe Beauty Pageant and the Miss USA Beauty Pageant; also created Lucky Pair; prod the Pillsbury Bake-Off Special; host of the Indianapolis 500 Parade; The Price is Right (*Emmys*-host-1982, 1984); That's My Line.

BARKER, Howard: Plywri. b. London, Jun 28, 1946. e. Sussex U. Plays inc: Cheek; No One Was Saved; Alpha, Alpha; Edward, The Final Days; Private Parts; Rule Britannia; Skipper; My Sister and I; Claw; Stripwell; No End of Blame; Victory.

BARKIN, Ellen: Act. b. Bronx, NY, 1958. e. High School of the Performing Arts; Hunter College. Thea inc: Tobacco Road; Irish Coffee; Shout Across the River; Killings on the Fast Lane; Eden Court. P0ilms inc: Diner; Tender Mercies; Eddie and the Cruisers; Daniel; Enormous Changes at the Last Moment; Harry & Son; The Adventures of Buckaroo Banzai--Across the 8th Dimension; Terminal Choice.

TV inc: Search for Tomorrow; Kent State; We're Fighting Back; Parole; Ordinary Lives; Murder Ink; Terrible Joe Moran.

BARKLEY, Deanne: Exec Prod. b. New Orleans, LA, 1930. e. Northwestern U. Began in public affairs at WDSU-TV, New Orleans; to NYC as headwriter for Dick Cavett A.M. Shows; prod Virginia Graham Show; Helen Gurley Brown Show; network staff writer; joined Robert Stigwood Organization as vp crea aff, exec prod Virginia Hill Story; All Together Now; Death Scream; 1975 to NBC as vp pgm dev West Coast; 1976 vp Dramatic Problems; 1977, vp motion pictures for tv and miniseries; joined Paul Klein in indie prodn as part of Osmond Group Productions, Oct 1979.

TV inc: Valentine Magic on Love Island; The Day The Women Got Even; The Ordeal of Bill Carney; Side By Side--The True Story of the Osmond Family; Emergency Room; Desperate Intruder; Private Sessions; This Wife For Hire.

BARNES, Binnie: Act. b. London, May 25, 1905. W of Mike Frankovich. On screen from 1931. Films inc: Love Lies; Murder at Covent Gardens; The Private Life of Henry VIII; The Private Life of Don Juan; Diamond Jim; Three Smart Girls; The Adventures of Marco Polo; The Three Musketeers; Tight Shoes; Three Girls About Town; Up in Mabel's Room; It's in the Bag; The Trouble with Angels; Forty Carats.

BARNES, Joanna: Act. b. Nov 15, 1934. e. Smith Coll. Films inc: Auntie Mame; Spartacus; The Parent Trap; Goodbye Charlie; The War Wagon; I Wonder Who's Killing Her Now.

TV inc: Beacon Street; Trial of O'Brien; Dateline, Hollywood; Terror Among Us (wri); Secrets of a Mother and Daughter.

BARNETT, Jack: Prod-Wri. b. NYC, Jul 5, 1920. Writer and producer for the late Jimmy Durante for 20 years; also wrote special material for Al Jolson; Bob Hope; Eddie Cantor; Don Rickles; has produced more than 100 tv specs, scores of cable specials and Las Vegas shows.

BARNETT, Joan: Prod. b. NYC, Nov. 19, 1945. Started on staff of Bway producer Alexander H. Cohen, serving as company manager, later associate producer for annual Tony Awards TV shows from 1969 to 1974 and Your Money or Your Wife; Marlene Dietrich; I'm a Fan. Casting director from 1975 to 1980, handling some 50 series, miniseries and MOWs as well as feature films; ind prod 1978-1980; named VP, movies for Television, NBC, 1980; became VP crea aff Alan Landsburg Prodns 1983.

TV inc: Torn Between Two Lovers; Marathon; Jayne Mansfield; Adam (exec prod); Kennedy (supv prod).

BARNETT, John: Prod. b. Auckland, New Zealand, Aug 17, 1945. e. Auckland U, Victoria U. Films inc: Prisoners; Wild Horses; Strange Behaviour; Race to the Yankee Zephyr; Beyond Reasonable Doubt; Nutcase; Middle Age Spread; Dead Kids.

BARON, Allen: Dir-Wri. b. NYC, 1935. Films inc: Blast of Silence (wri-dir-act); Pie in the Sky (prod-dir).

BARR, Anthony (Morris Yaffe): Prod-Dir. b. St Louis, MO, Mar 14, 1921. e. WA U, BS. VP primetime dramatic series, ABC; 1976, exec prod CBS-TV pgm dept; 1979, VP and dir current dramatic pgmmg. TV inc: (dir) Art Linkletter's Houseparty; About Faces; Climax; Shower of Stars; Playhouse 90; The Law and Mr. Jones.

Films inc: Dime with A Halo (co-prod).

BARR, Julia: Act. b. Fort Wayne, IN, Feb 8, 1949. e. Purdue. TV inc: Gathering of One; The Adams Chronicles; Ryan's Hope; All My Children.

Films inc: I, The Jury.

BARR, Richard (nee Baer): Prod. b. Washington, DC, Sep 6, 1917. e. Princeton U. Began as an actor with Orson Welles' Mercury Theatre Co, 1938. Later moved to dir & prod. Bway inc: Who's Afraid of Virginia Woolf? (Tony-prod-1963); Tiny Alice; A Delicate Balance; Everything in the Garden; Johnny-No-Trump; The Front Page; All Over; Seascape; The Grass Harp; The Last of Mrs Lincoln; Noel Cow-

ard in Two Keys; PS Your Cat is Dead; Sweeney Todd (Tony-prod-1979); The Lady From Dubuque; Home Front.

BARRAULT, Jean-Louis: Act. b. France, Sept. 8, 1910. Active on French stage as actor-director since 1931. Films inc: Les Beaux Jours; Razumov; Life and Loves of Beethoven; Helene; Mademoiselle Docteur; The Pearls of the Crown; Bizarre Bizarre; Orage; Le Puritain; Symphonie Fantastique; Mlle. Desiree; Les Enfants du Paradis; Blind Desire; Man to Man; La Ronde; Le Dialogue des Carmelites; Le Testament du Docteur Cordelier; The Longest Day; Chappaqua; La Nuit de Varennes; Jean-Louis Barrault - A Man of the Theatre (doc).

BARRAULT, Marie-Christine: Act. b. Paris, Mar 21, 1944. Films inc: My Night at Maud's; The Daydreamer; Lancelot of the Lake; The Aspern Papers; Les Intrus; La Famille Grossfelder; John Gluckstadt; Cousin Cousine; By The Tennis Courts; L'Etat Sauvage; Perceval; The Medusa Touch; Tout est a nous; Femme Entre Chien et Loup; Ma Cherie; Stardust Memories; Table For Five; Josephs Tochter (Joseph's Daughter); Eine Liebe in Deutschland (A Love In Germany); Les Mots Pour le Dire (Words To Say It); Un Amour de Swann (Swann in Love); Pianoforte (Grand Piano).

BARRETT, James Lee: Wri-Prod. b. Charlotte, NC, Nov 19, 1929. e. Furman U; Penn State U. Films inc: The D.I.; The Greatest Story Ever Told; The Truth About Spring; Shenandoah; Bandolero; The Green Berets; The Cheyenne Social Club (& prod); Fools' Parade; Smokey and the Bandit.

Plays inc: The Wiz (Tony-book-1975).

TV inc: (wri) The Awakening Land; Mayflower - The Pilgrims' Adventure; The Day Christ Died; Belle Starr; Angel City; Big John; You Are the Jury.

BARRETT, Rona: Journalist. b. NYC, Oct 8, 1936. e. NYU. Syndicated Hollywood gossip columnist. Created first daily syndicated TV news segment for Metromedia; Hollywood corr ABC's Good Morning, America; 1980, Tomorrow Show; 1985, columnist on Mutual Radio Network. TV inc: Television--Inside and Out; People to People with Rona Barrett. Films inc: Sextette.

BARRIE, Barbara: Act. b. Chicago, IL, May 23, 1931. e. U TX Austin. Bway inc: The Wooden Dish; The Selling of the President; Company; Killdeer; The Prisoner of Second Avenue; California Suite.

Films inc: One Potato, Two Potato; The Caretakers; Giant; Breaking Away; Private Benjamin.

TV inc: Barney Miller; Diana; Tell Me My Name; 79 Park Avenue; The Summer of My German Soldier; Breaking Away; The Children Nobody Wanted; Barefoot In The Park (cable); Working; Not Just Another Affair; Tucker's Witch; Two of a Kind; Reggie; All Together Now; Double Trouble; The Execution.

BARRIE, George: Exec-Sngwri. b. NYC, Feb 9, 1918. Chmn & CEO, Faberge, Inc; p Brut Prods. Films inc: A Touch of Class; Night Watch; Welcome to Arrow Beach; Book of Numbers; Hang-Up; Miracles Still Happen; I Will, I Will. . .for Now; Hugo the Hippo (ani); Whiffs; Thieves; Nasty Habits; Hedda; Fingers; The Class of Miss MacMichael.

Songs inc: All That Love Went to Waste; Now That We're in Love; What Becomes of Love.

BARRIE, Mona (nee Smith): Act. b. London, Dec 18, 1909. Films inc: Sleepers East; One Night of Love; Charlie Chan in London; King of Burlesque; Message to Garcia; Love on the Run; I Met Him in Paris; Say It In French; I Take This Woman; When Ladies Meet; Never Give A Sucker an Even Break; Skylark; Cairo; One Dangerous Night; Storm Over Lisbon; Just Before Dawn; I Cover the Big Town; When A Girl's Beautiful; The First Time; Cass Timberlane; Strange Fascination; Plunder of the Sun.

BARRIS, Chuck: Prod-TV Host. b. Philadelphia, Jun 3. e. U of Miami; Drexel Institute of Technology. TV shows inc: Dream Girl; Operation: Entertainment; The Newlywed Game; The Dating Game; How's Your Mother-In-Law?; The Family Game; The Etiquette Game; The Game Game; The Cass Elliott Special; The New Treasure Hunt; Your Hit Parade; The Bobby Vinton Show; The Gong Show.

Films inc: The Gong Show Movie.

BARRON, William A, Jr: Dir-Prod. b. St Louis, MO, Sep 8, 1927. e. Hobart Coll, BA. Staff dir WABC-TV, 1962-63. Freelance next 12 years; many Gemini (space probe) missions; first live Gemini telecast from ship at sea; many Apollo Missions; now Mellow Prods, children's programming.

BARROW, Bernard: Act. b. NYC, Dec 30. Films inc: Serpico; Rachel, Rachel; Glass Houses; Claudine.
TV inc: The Edge of Night; The Secret Storm; Where the Heart Is; Senior Trip; Ryan's Hope.

BARRY, Dave: Comedian. b. NYC, Aug 26, 1918. Started on radio, vaudeville. Later in big band shows, niteries; with Wayne Newton Show, Las Vegas.

BARRY, Gene (Eugene Klass): Act. b. NYC, Jun 14, 1921. Films inc: Atomic City; War of the Worlds; Those Redheads from Seattle; Soldier of Fortune; Back from Eternity; Maroc 7; Red Garters; Naked Alibi; China Gate; Thunder Road; Subterfuge; The Second Coming of Suzanne (& exec prod); Guyana, Cult of the Damned.
TV inc: Bat Masterson; Burke's Law (Emmy-1965); The Name of the Game; The Adventurer; Istanbul Express; Prescription Murder; The Devil and Miss Sarah; Aspen; A Cry For Love. The Girl, The Gold Watch and Dynamite; The Adventures of Nellie Bly.
Thea inc: Rosalinda; Catherine Was Great; The Would Be Gentleman; Glad to See You; Happy Is Larry; Bless You All; The Merry Widow; La Cage Aux Folles.

BARRY, Jack: TV Prod-Act. b. Lindenhurst, NY, Mar 20, 1918. e. U of PA. TV shows inc: The Jokers Wild; Blank Check; Break the Bank; Juvenile Jury; Life Begins at 80; Tic Tac Dough; 21; Television--Inside and Out; A Concert of the World.
Films inc: Search and Destroy (prod); Private Lessons (exec prod).
(Died May 2, 1984).

BARRY, Jeff: Comp. b. Brooklyn, Apr 3, 1939. Staff writer for various mus pubs before starting career. Films inc: The Idolmaker. TV inc: The Jeffersons; One Day At A Time; Baby Sister.
Bway inc: Leader Of The Pack (songs).

BARRY, John (J B Prendergast): Comp-Arr-Cond. b. York, England, 1933. Films inc: Beat Girl; Amorous Prawn; From Russia with Love; Zulu; Goldfinger; The Ipcress File; Thunderball; King Rat; The Chase; Born Free (Oscars-(2)-Best Score, Title Song-1966); The Wrong Box; The Quiller Memorandum; Petulia; Boom; Deadfall; The Lion in Winter (Oscar-1968); Midnight Cowboy; Murphy's War; The Might Be Giants; Diamonds Are Forever; Robin and Marian; King Kong; The Deep; The Betsy; The White Buffalo; Hanover Street; Moonraker; Starcrash; The Black Hole; Night Games; Touched by Love; Raise The Titanic; Somewhere In Time; Inside Moves; The Legend of The Lone Ranger; Body Heat; Hammett; Frances; Murder By Phone; High Road To China; The Golden Seal; Octopussy; Mike's Murder; Until September; The Cotton Club; A View To A Kill.
TV inc: Elizabeth Taylor in London; Sophia Loren in Rome; Eleanor and Franklin; Eleanor and Franklin-The White House Years; Love Among The Ruins; Svengali.
(Grammy-inst theme-1969).

BARRY, Philip: Prod. b. NYC. e. Yale U. S of late Philip Barry. Films inc: The Mating Game; Sail a Crooked Ship.
TV inc: The Elgin Hour; The Motorola Playhouse; The Alcoa Hour; The Goodyear Playhouse; Just an Old Sweet Song; Kinfolks; The Animals; First You Cry. Friendly Fire (Emmy-1979); Father Brown, Detective; Bogie; Kent State; The Steeler and the Pittsburgh Kid (supv prod); Evergreen.

BARRY, W. Russell: Exec. b. Brooklyn, Mar 7, 1936. e. Dartmouth; Harvard Grad School of Business. Joined WBBM TV, Chicago, as acct exec 1960; vp CBS radio div 1969; vp TV stations div & gen mgr KNXT 1973; named network sales vp 20th Fox 1976; vp sals & syndication 1977; named prexy 20th Fox TV 1979; P Playboy Productions, July 1980 resd Aug 1982 to become P of Taft Entertainment Television.

BARRYMORE, Drew: Act. b. 1976. D of John Barrymore Jr. Films inc: Altered States; E.T. The ExtraTerrestrial; Firestarter; Irreconcilable Differences; Cat's Eye.
TV inc: Suddenly Love; Bogey; Disneyland's 30th Anniversary Celebration; Night Of 100 Stars II.

BART, Lionel: Comp-Lyr-Plywri. b. Aug 1, 1930. Thea inc: Fings Ain't Wot They Used T' Be (mus-lyr); Lock Up Your Daughters (lyr); Oliver! (book-lyr-mus) (Tony-1963); Blitz (co-book-lyr-mus-dir); Merry Roosters panto (contributed mus-lyr); Maggie May (mus-lyr); Twang! (book-mus-lyr); Lock Up Your Daughters (mus-lyr); La Strada (mus-lyr); The Londoners (songs); Costa Packet (songs); So You Want To Be In Pictures (mus supv).
Films inc: The Tommy Steele Story; The Duke Wore Jeans; Tommy The Toreador; Oliver!.
Title songs inc: From Russia With Love; Man in the Middle.

BART, Peter: Exec. b. Jul 24, 1932. e. Swarthmore Coll; London School of Economics. Joined Paramount Pictures 1965; exec asst to Robert Evans, exec in charge world wide prod; VP prod; resigned 1973; pres Lorimar Films April '78-June '79; March 1983, Sr VP Theatrical film prodn MGM. Films inc: (co-prod) Islands in the Stream; Fun with Dick and Jane; Revenge of the Nerds (co-exec prod).

BARTEL, Paul: Dir. b. NYC, Aug 6, 1938. e. UCLA, BA. Films inc: The Secret Cinema; Naughty Nurse; Private Parts; Death Race 2000; Cannonball; Piranha (act); Rock 'n' Roll High School (act); Eating Raoul (& wri-act); Trick or Treats; Heart Like A Wheel (act); Get Crazy; Not For Publication (& wri); Lust In The Dust; Into The Night (act).

BARTH, Eddie: Act. (nee Bartholetti):b. Philadelphia, PA., Sep. 29, 1931
Thea inc: Guys and Dolls; A View from the Bridge; A Streetcar Named Desire.
Films inc: Supercops; How To Save A Marriage; The Amityville Horror; Boardwalk; Fame.
TV inc: Shaft; Husbands, Wives and Lovers; Mary Tyler Moore Special; Rich Man, Poor Man; Amelia Earhart; The Man in the Santa Claus Suit; Jimmy B and Andre; Simon & Simon; The Red-Light Sting; Murder, She Wrote.

BARTHOLOMEW, Freddie: Act. b. London, Mar 28, 1924. Stage debut, 1927. Screen debut, David Copperfield, 1935. Films inc: Anna Karenina; Lloyds of London; Little Lord Fauntleroy; Kidnapped; Swiss Family Robinson; Yank at Eton; The Town Went Wild; St. Benny the Dip.

BARTKOWIAK, Andrzej: Cin. b. Lodz, Poland. e. Polish Film School. Emigrated to U.S. in 1972. Films inc: Deadly Hero; Prince of the City; Deathtrap; The Verdict; Daniel; Terms of Endearment; Garbo Talks; Prizzi's Honor.
TV inc: 5:48.

BARTLETT, Hall: Prod-Dir-Wri. b. Kansas City, MO, Nov 27, 1924. e. Yale U, BA. Films inc: Navajo; Crazy-Legs; Unchained; Drango; Zero Hour; All the Young Men; The Caretakers; A Global Affair; Changes; The Sandpit Generals; Jonathan Livingston Seagull; The Children of Sanchez; Comeback.
TV inc: Cleo Laine Special; The Search of Zubin Mehta.

BARTLETT, Juanita: Wri-prod. b. San Francisco, CA., Nov. 8. TV inc: (wri) Nichols; Bonanza; Alias Smith and Jones; Little House on the Prairie; Paper Moon; Cool Million; Toma; Planet Earth; The New Maverick (pilot); The Rockford Files (& prod); Tenspeed and Brownshoe (& prod); Greatest American Hero (& exec prod); Midnight Offerings (& exec prod); The Quest (& exec prod); No Man's Land (& crea).

BARTOK, Eva (nee Szoke): Act-Wri-Prod. b. Hungary, Jun 18, 1926. In films since 1933 in Crimson Pirate; Tale of Five Cities; The Venetian Bird; Spaceways; Park Plaza; Front Page Story; The Gamma People; Carnival Story; Operation Amsterdam; S.O.S. Pacific; Beyond the Curtain; 10,000 Bedrooms; Blood and Back Lace.

BARTON, Gary: Exec. b. Boston, MA., Sept. 1, 1949. e. NYU. Started as an actor, later casting dir for Universal Pictures, CBS Motion Pictures for TV; Sept. 1983, vp dvlpt Disney TV; Aug. 1984, vp motion picture prodn. Disney.

BARTY, Billy: Act. b. Millsboro, PA, Oct 25 (circa 1919). Films inc: Footlight Parade: Golddiggers of 1933; A Midsummer Night's Dream; The Day of the Locust; The Happy Hooker Goes to Washington; W C Fields and Me; Rabbit Test; Foul Play; Firepower; Skatetown USA; Hardly Working; Under the Rainbow; Being Different (doc); Night Patrol.
TV inc: Concrete Cowboys; Ace Crawford, Private Eye.

BARUCH, Andre: Radio-TV pers. b. Paris. e. Pratt Institute of Fine Arts; Columbia U; Ecole de Beaux Arts. H of Bea Wain. Started as radio announcer, became voice of some of top-rated radio programs of era: Your Hit Parade; The United States Steel Hour; The Kate Smith Show; The Shadow; Exploring the Unknown. Did play-by-play broadcasts for Brooklyn Dodgers Baseball team; was voice of Pathe News (newsreel); news commentator on CBS and ABC networks. With wife conducted Mr and Mrs Music Show, later did the Bea and Andre show on WPBR, Palm Beach. TV and radio commercials for top sponsors. Inducted into National Broadcasters Hall of Fame 1979.

BARWOOD, Hal: Wri. b. Hanover, NH, Apr 16. e. Brown U; USC. Made prize-winning A Child's Introduction to the Cosmos while at USC; teamed with Matthew Robbins. Films inc: Sugarland Express; The Bingo Long Traveling All-Stars and Motor Kings; MacArthur; Corvette Summer (& prod); Dragonslayer (& prod).

BARYSHNIKOV, Mikhail: Dancer-Act. b. Riga, Latvia, Jun 1947. Joined Korov ballet, Leningrad; then American Ballet Theatre in US; New York City Ballet Company. Films inc: The Turning Point; That's Dancing!.
TV inc: Baryshnikov at the White House (Emmy-1979); Bob Hope on the Road to China; Baryshnikov on Broadway; AFI Salute to Fred Astaire; Baryshnikov In Hollywood; AFI SAlute To Gene Kelly.

BASEHART, Richard: Act. b. Zanesville, OH, Aug 31, 1914. Debuted with local stock company age 13. Joined Hedgerow Theatre, Moylan, PA, played in repertory there, 1938-42. Broadway debut in Counterattack, 1943. Film debut, Cry Wolf, 1945. Films inc: Roseanna McCoy; Tension; Outside the Wall; Fourteen Hours; The House on Telegraph Hill; Titanic; Rage; Time Limit; Four Days in November; The Satan Bug; Island of Dr. Moreau; Shenanigans; Being There.
TV inc: Voyage to the Bottom of the Sea; Let My People Go (Emmy-narr-1965); The Andersonville Trial; The Critical List; The Girl Who Saved Our America; The Rebels; Eric Hoffer--The Crowded Life; Marilyn--The Untold Story; The Ten Thousand Day War; Masada (narr); The Mysterious Powers of Man (narr); Life On Earth; Egypt--Quest For Eternity (narr); Knight Rider (pilot); Vietnam--The Ten Thousand Day War (narr); Save The Panda (narr); Olympic Finale (narr); Egypt--Quest For Eternity (narr).
Bway inc: Land of Fame; Othello; Hickory Stick; The Hasty Heart. (Died Sept. 17, 1984).

BASIE, Count (William Basie): Comp-Pianist. b. Red Bank, NJ, Aug 21, 1906. Accompanist to vaude acts; later organized own orch; appeared in hotels, theatres, niteries. Songs inc: One O'Clock Jump; Good Morning Blues; Basie Boogie; Gone with the Wind; I Left My Baby.
(Grammys-(8)-Dance Band-1958, 1960, 1963; Jazz Large Group-1958; Jazz solo-1976; Jazz Big Band-1977, 1980, 1982.)
TV inc: Grammy Hall of Fame; To The Count Of Basie; Sinatra: The Man and His Music; Bennett and Basie Together. (Died April 26, 1984).

BASINGER, Kim: Act. b. Athens, GA, Dec 8, 1953. Former model. TV inc: The Ghost of Flight 401; Katie--Portrait of a Centerfold; From Here to Eternity; Killjoy.
Films inc: Hard Country; Mother Lode; Never Say Never Again; The Man Who Loved Women; The Natural.

BASS, Alfie (Alfred Bass): Act. b. London, Apr 8, 1921. Thea inc: Those Were The Days; He Who Gets Slapped; Headlights; Finian's Rainbow; The Golden Door; The Gentle People; Trelawney of the Wells; Starched Aprons; The Bespoke Overcoat; The World of Sholem Aleichem; The Punch Revue; The Silver Whistle; Fiddler on the Roof.
Films inc: Holiday Camp; It Always Rains on Sunday; Lavender Hill Mob; The Hasty Heart; The Bespoke Overcoat; A Kid for Two Farthings; A Tale of Two Cities; I Only Arsked; The Millionairess; Alfie; The Fearless Vampire Killers; The Magnificent Seven Deadly Sins; Up the Junction; Moonraker.
TV inc: Robin Hood; The Army Game; Bootsie and Snudge; Till Death Do Us Part.

BASS, Saul: Title Dsgn-Prod-Dir. b. NYC, May 8, 1920. e. Arts Students League. Films inc: (shorts) The Searching Eye; From Here to There; Why Man Creates; (titles): Carmen Jones; The Man With the Golden Arm; Around the World in Eighty Days; Vertigo; Bonjour Tristesse; North by Northwest; Psycho; A Walk on the Wild Side; It's a Mad, Mad, Mad, Mad World; Bunny Lake is Missing. Directorial debut, 1974, Phase IV.

BASSEY, Shirley: Singer. b. England, 1937. Nitery and concert performer, recording artist.

BATES, Alan: Act. b. Derbyshire, England, Feb 17, 1934. e. RADA. London Stage debut 1956 in The Mulberry Bush; Bway 1958 in Look Back in Anger. Thea inc: Hamlet; The Taming of the Shrew; The Seagull; Life Class; Butley (Tony-1973); Otherwise Engaged; Stage Struck.
Films inc: The Entertainer; The Caretaker; Zorba the Greek; Georgy Girl; Three Sisters; Far From the Madding Crowd; The Fixer; Royal Flash; An Unmarried Woman; The Shout; The Rose; Nijinsky; Quartet; Rece do Gory (Hands Up!); The Return of the Soldier; The Wicked Lady; Dr. Fischer Of Geneva.
TV inc: The Thug; A Memory of Two Mondays; The Square Ring; Look Back in Anger; A Hero for Our Time; The Mayor of Casterbridge; Separate Tables (cable); A Voyage Round My Father; An Englishman Abroad.

BATES, Michael: Act. b. Jhansi, India, Dec 4, 1920. e. Cambridge. Films inc: I'm All Right Jack; Bedazzled; Here We Go Round the Mulberry Bush; Salt and Pepper; Don't Raise the Bridge, Lower the River; Hammerhead; Patton; The Rise and Rise of Michael Rimmer; A Clockwork Orange; No Sex Please, We're British.
Thea inc: HMS Pinafore; The Birdwatcher; Forget-Me-Not Lane; Made in Heaven.
TV inc: The Navy Lark; Last of the Summer Wine; It Ain't Half Hot, Mum.

BATTLE, Hinton: Act. b. Germany. Bway inc; The Wiz; Dance Theater of Harlem; Dancin'; Sophisticated Ladies (Tony-featured-1980); The Tap Dance Kid (Tony-featured-1984).
TV inc: Sophisticated Ladies (PPV); Night Of 100 Stars II; 39th Annual Tony Awards.

BAUER, Jaime Lyn: Act. b. Phoenix, AZ, Mar 9, 1949. Former fashion model. TV inc: The Young and the Restless (since Dec 1973); The Girl Who Came Gift-Wrapped; The Mysterious Island of Beautiful Women; Bare Essence.

BAUER, Steven: Act. b. Cuba, 1957. To the U.S. at age three. e. U of Miami. H of Melanie Griffith. TV inc: Que Pasa U.S.A.; From Here to Eternity; She's In the Army Now; Nichols & Dymes; An Innocent Love; Alfred Hitchcock Presents.
Films inc: Scarface; Thief of Hearts.

BAUGHN, David: Exec. b. Los Angeles, May 3, 1939. e. Santa Monica City Coll. P Scope III, Inc.; exec VP Intercontinental Releasing Corp; Films inc: Beyond Evil; Graduation Day.

BAUM, Martin: Exec. b. NYC, Mar 2, 1924. Formed Baum & Newborn Thea Agency; sold agency to GAC; head of West Coast office, GAC; sr exec vp Creative Management Corp; left 1968 to become p ABC Pictures; returned to agency work and in 1973 became sr exec vp, Creative Management Corp.

BAVA, Mario: Dir. b. San Remo, Italy, July 31, 1914. Cin for almost 20 years.
Films inc: (cin) Il Tacchino Prepotente; Uomini e Cieli; Cose da Pazzi; Terza Liceo; Mio Figlio Nerone; Il Diavolo Bianco; Esther and

the King; The Giant of Marathon (& asst dir). (Dir): Black Sunday (& sp-cin); Hercules in the Center of the Earth (& sp-cin); Erik the Conqueror (& sp); La Ragazza che Sapeva Troppo; Black Sabbath (& sp); The Evil Eye (& sp-cin); Blood and Black Lace (& sp-cin); Planet of Blood; Dr Goldfoot and the Girl Bombs; Curse of the Dead (& sp); Five Dolls for An August Moon; The Antecedent; Quella Notte; Il Diavolo et il Morto.

BAXLEY, Barbara: Act. b. Stockton, CA, Jan 1, 1927. e. Coll of the Pacific; Neighborhood Playhouse; Actors Studio. Bway inc: Private Lives; Peter Pan; Out West of Eighth; I Am A Camera; Camino Real; Frogs of Spring; The Flowering Peach; Bus Stop; The Dark at the Top of the Stairs; Period of Adjustment; Brecht on Brecht; Plaza Suite; To Be Young, Gifted and Black; Are You Now Or Have You Ever Been?; Oh, Pioneers; Whodunnit.
Films inc: East of Eden; All Fall Down; The Savage Eye: Nashville; Norma Rae; A Stranger Is Watching.
TV inc: Come Along With Me; Last Resort; All That Glitters.

BAXTER, Anne: Act. b. Michigan City, IN, May 7, 1923. e. Theodora Ervine School of Drama. Summer stock Cape Cod. Bway in Madam Carpet, 1938. Screen debut, Twenty Mule Team, 1940. Films inc: The Great Profile; Charley's Aunt; Magnificent Ambersons; The Razor's Edge (Oscar-supp-1946); All About Eve; The Spoilers; Cimarron; The Ten Commandments; The Late Liz; Jane Austen In Manhattan; The Architecture Of Frank Lloyd Wright (narr).
Bway inc: Applause; Noel Coward in Two Keys.
TV inc: The Moneychangers; Rex Stout's Nero Wolfe; John Steinbeck's East of Eden; Arthur Hailey's "Hotel"; Dean Martin's Celebrity Roast.

BAXTER, Les: Comp-Cond-Arr. b. Mexia, TX, Mar 14, 1922. e. Pepperdine. Comp scores for more than 100 films inc: The Yellow Tomahawk; A Woman's Devotion; Untamed Youth; Hot Blood; The Invisible Boy; The Keyman; The Vicious Breed; What's In It For Harry; Monika; All the Loving Couples; Fall of the House of Usher; The Pit and the Pendulum; Tales of Terror; Panic in the Year Zero; Marco Polo; House of Sand; Comedy of Terrors; Bikini Beach; How To Stuff A Wild Bikini; Dr. Goldfoot and the Bikini Machine; Dr. Goldfoot and the Girl Bombs; Mondo Sadismo; Wild in the Streets; The Dunwich Horror; Battle Beyond the Sun; The Girl in the Black Silk Stockings; The Lost Battalion; Escape From Red Rock; Black Sunday; Escape From Devil's Island; The Dalton Girls; Born Again; Target--Harry; Macabre; The Beast Within.
TV inc: The Bob Hope Show (cond-choral arr); Music of the Sixties (The Les Baxter Show); Halls of Ivy; The Milton Berle Show; Hollywood Palace; An Evening With Vincent Price; Dean Martin's Christmas At Sea World; Dean Martin at the Wild Animal Park.
Recs inc: (Singles) Quiet Village; Poor People of Paris; Unchained Melody; April in Portugal; Shrimp Boats; Sparrow in the Treetops; Wake the Town and Tell the People. (Albums) Music Out of the Moon; Perfume Set to Music; Voices of Xtabay; African Jazz; Exotica Suite; Wild Guitars; Le Sacre du Sauvage; Midnight on the Cliffs.
Comps inc: Quiet Village; Exotica Suite; Metamorphosis; Tamboo; Ports of Pleasure.

THE BAY CITY ROLLERS: Group. Originally formed in Scotland in 1967 as The Saxons; name changed 1969. Members are Stuart (Woody) Wood; Leslie McKeown, Alan Longmuir; Derek Longmuir; Eric Faulkner. Concerts, several world tours. TV inc: The Krofft Superstar Hour (hosts).
Albums inc: Bay City Rollers; Rock and Roll Love Letter; Dedication.

BAYE, Nathalie: Act. b. France, Jul 6, 1948. Films inc: Two People; La Nuit Americaine (Day for Night); La Geule Ouverte; Un jour de fete; La gifle; Le voyage de noces (The Honeymoon Trip); Le plein de super (Fill 'er up With Super); L'ultima donna (La derniere femme) (The Last Woman); La Jalousie; Mado; L'homme qui aimait les femmes (The Man Who Loved Women); Monsieur Papa; La Communion solennelle (Solemn Communion); La chambre vert (The Green Room); Mon premier amour (My First Love); La memoire courte (Short Memory); Je vais craquer! (The Rat Race); Sauve qui peut la vie (Everyone for Himself in Life); Une Semaine de vacances (A Week's Vacation); La provinciale (The Provincial); Beau-Pere (Stepfather); L'ombre rouge (The Red Shadow); Une Etrange affaire (A

Strange Affair); La retour de Martin Guerre (The Return of Martin Guerre); La balance (The Nark); J'ai epouse une ombre (I Married a Dead Man); Notre Histoire (Our Story); Rive Droit, Rive Gauche (Right Bank, Left Bank); Detective.

BAYNES, Andrea L: Exec. b. Sep 27, 1946. e. USC, BA. Started with NBC-TV; 1974 west coast mgr pgm dvlpt; 1977, vp Columbia Pictures-TV; 1979, sr vp; Sept. 1980, exec vp chg prodn Fox-TV; resd. Aug. 1984; Nov. 1984, formed Andrea Baynes Prodns with exclusive tie to Col.

THE BEACH BOYS: Group. Organized 1960. Members are Brian Wilson (Died Dec 28, 1983), Carl Wilson, Dennis Wilson, Al Jardine, Mike Love. Albums inc: Surfin' Safari; Surfin' USA; Surfer Girl; Little Deuce Coupe; Pet Sounds; All Summer Long; Beach Boys in Concert; Wild Honey; Sunflower; Surfs Up; Endless Summer; Good Vibrations; Spirit of America; Love You; Light Album.
TV inc: D.C. Beach Party ... A Musical Celebration (feevee).

BEACHAM, Stephanie: Act. b. Feb 28, 1947. e. RADA. Thea inc: The Basement; On Approval; The London Cuckolds; Can You Hear Me At the Back?
Films inc: The Games; Tam Lin; The Nightcomers; Schizo; The Confessional; Horror Planet.
TV inc: Marked Personal; Jane Eyre; A Sentimental Education; Call My Bluff.

BEAL, John (Alexander Bliedung): Act. b. Joplin, MO, Aug 13, 1909. e. U of PA. Bway inc: Another Language; She Loves Me Not; Petrified Forest. Screen debut, 1933, Another Language. Films inc: The Little Minister; Les Miserables; Laddie; The Man Who Found Himself; I Am the Law; The Cat and the Canary; The Great Commandment; Edge of Darkness; Alimony; My Six Convicts; Remains to be Seen; That Night; The Vampire; Ten Who Dared; Amityville 3-D.
TV inc: The Legend of Lizzie Borden; Jennifer--A Woman's Story.

BEALS, Jennifer: Act. b. Chicago, Dec. 19, 1963. E. Yale. Films inc: My Bodyguard (bit); Flashdance; The Bride.

BEAN, Orson (Dallas Frederick Burroughs): Act. b. Burlington, VT, Jul 22, 1928. Performed in niteries. Bway inc: Men of Distinction; The School for Scandal; Almanac; Will Success Spoil Rock Hunter; Mr Roberts (rev); Nature's Way; Subways Are for Sleeping; Never Too Late; Warm Heart, Cold Feet; The Roar of the Grease Paint-The Smell of the Crowd; Ilya Darling.
Films inc: Lola; Skateboard; Forty Deuce.
TV inc: Return of the King (voice); Garfield In The Rough (voice).

BEATLES, The Group. British pop group whose unprecedented popularity in the early sixties sparked a musical revolution before they split up to go their separate ways. (See HARRISON, George; McCARTNEY, Paul; STARR, Ringo). (John Lennon was murdered Dec. 8, 1980).
Films inc: A Hard Day's Night; Help!; Yellow Submarine; Let It Be (Oscar-Song Score-1970).
(Grammys-(4)-vocal Group and new artist-1964; Album of Year and Contemporary Album-1967).

BEATON, Alex: Prod-Dir. TV inc: Centennial; The Duke; The Night Rider (Exec prod); Stone (supv prod); 10 Speed and Brownshoe (prod); Nightside (prod); The Greatest American Hero (prod); Moonlight (prod); Nightmares (exec prod); Legmen (prod); Codename Foxfire (supv prod); Otherworld (supv prod).

BEATTS, Anne: Wri. b. Buffalo, NY. e. McGill U (Canada), BA. TV inc: Saturday Night Live (Emmys-wri-1976, 1977, 1980); Gilda Radner Live From New York (cable); Square Pegs (& prod). Bway inc: Leader Of The Pack (book).

BEATTY, John Lee: Dsgn. b. Palo Alto, CA., Apr. 4, 1948. e. Brown U., BA; Yale School of Drama, MFA. Thea inc: Knock, Knock; Ashes; A Life in the Theatre; The Water Engine; Ain't Misbehavin; Talley's Folly (Tony-1980); Fifth of July; Crimes of the Heart; Livin Dolls; Whoopee; Alice in Wonderland; Angel's Fall; Baby; Fools; Monday After the Miracle; Passion; Other Places (off Bway); In Celebration (off Bway); The Octette Bridge Club.

BEATTY, Ned: Act. b. Lexington, KY, Jul 6, 1937. Films inc: Deliverance; The Thief Who Came to Dinner; White Lightning; W W and the Dixie Dancekings; Nashville; All the President's Men; Silver Streak; Mickey and Nicky; Network; Exorcist II-The Heretic; Shenanigans; Gray Lady Down; Superman; Promises in the Dark; The America Success Company; Wise Blood; 1941; Hopscotch; Superman II; The Incredible Shrinking Woman; The Toy; Touched; Stroker Ace; Restless Natives.

TV inc: The Execution of Private Slovik; Attack on Terror; The Marcus-Nelson Murders; A Question of Love; Friendly Fire; Guyana Tragedy-The Story of Jim Jones; All God's Children; The Violation of Sarah McDavid; Splendor In The Grass; All The Way Home; Pray TV; Denmark Vesey's Rebellion; A Woman Called Golda; The Ballad of Gregorio Cortez; Kentucky Woman; Celebrity; The Last Days of Pompeii; Murder, She Wrote; Charlotte Forten's Mission--Experiment In Freedom; Robert Kennedy & His Times; Alfred Hitchcock Presents.

BEATTY, Roger: Wri-Dir. b. Los Angeles, Jan 24, 1933. TV inc: The Carol Burnett Show (Emmy-wri-1972, 1973, 1974, 1975, 1978); I Do, I Don't; Tim Conway Show; Dolly and Carol in Nashville; The Grass is Always Greener Over the Septic Tank; Carol Burnett and Co; Eunice; Mama's Family.

Films inc: Billion Dollar Hobo (wri).

BEATTY, Warren: Act. b. Richmond, VA, Mar 30, 1938. e. Northwestern U. B of Shirley MacLaine. Films inc: Splendor in the Grass; Roman Spring of Mrs. Stone; All Fall Down; Lilith; Mickey One; Promise Her Anything; Kaleidoscope; Bonnie and Clyde (& prod); The Only Game in Town; McCabe and Mrs. Miller; Year of the Woman (doc); The Parallax View; Shampoo (& prod-wri); The Fortune; Heaven Can Wait (& prod-dir-wri); Reds (& prod-dir-wri) (Oscar-dir-1981); George Stevens ... A Filmmaker's Journey (doc-int).

Bway inc: A Loss of Roses.

BEAUDINE, William, Jr: Prod-Dir. b. Hollywood, Apr 28, 1921. e. USC, BS. TV inc: Prod Lassie, 1968-72; Prod-Dir two shows for Disney's Wonderful World of Color, 1973; (Assoc Prod), Sandburg's Lincoln; Roots. Prod TV pilot Lassie, the New Beginning; Escape; Baby Sister (exec prod); On Our Way.

Film inc: The Magic of Lassie (prod).

BECK, John: Act. b. Chicago, Jan 28. Films inc: Three in the Attic; The Unexpected Mrs Pollifax; The Lawman; Deadly Honeymoon; The Paper Back Hero; Pat Garrett and Billy the Kid; Sleepers; Only God Knows; Rollerball; Sky Riders; The Big Bus; Call of the Wild; Audrey Rose; Nightmare Honeymoon; The Other Side of Midnight.

TV inc: Nichols; Nourish the Beast; Greatest Heroes of the Bible; The Buffalo Soldiers; Flamingo Road; The Great American Traffic Jam; Peyton Place--The Next Generation.

BECK, Kimberly: Act. b. 1956. Films inc: Torpedo Run; The F.B.I. Story; Marnie; Yours, Mine and Ours; Friday The 13th--The Final Chapter.

TV inc: Peyton Place; Rich Man, Poor Man Book II; Westwind To Hawaii; Murder In Peyton Place; Zuma Beach; Roller Boogie; Capitol; That Was The Week That Was; Deadly Intentions.

BECK, Michael: Act. b. Memphis, TN, Feb 4, 1949. Films inc: The Warrior; Xanadu; Battletruck; Megaforce; The Golden Seal; Triumphs of a Man Called Horse; Blackout.

TV inc: Holocaust; Mayflower--the Pilgrims' Adventure; Alcatraz--The Whole Shocking Story; Fly Away Home; The Last Ninja; Celebrity; The Streets; Rearview Mirror; Chiller.

BECKER, Harold: Dir. Films inc: The Ragman's Daughter; The Onion Field; The Black Marble; Taps; Vision Quest.

BECKER, Ivan Lawrence: Wri-Prod. b. Harrison Co, NE, Aug 13, 1911. e. Columbia U. Plays inc: Etched in Granite; The King's Darling; Ruby; The Vapor Trail; This Kiss for this Kingdom; After the Rocks, the Martini.

BECKETT, Samuel: Plywri. b. Dublin, Apr 13, 1906. e. Trinity Coll. Plays inc: Waiting for Godot; Endgame; Krapp's Last Tape; Happy Days; and one-acters The Old Tune; That Time; Footfalls. (Awarded Nobel Prize Literature 1969).

BEDELIA, Bonnie: Act. b. 1946. Films inc: The Gypsy Moths; They Shoot Horses Don't They?; Lovers and Other Strangers; The Strange Vengeance of Rosalie; The Big Fix; Heart Like A Wheel; Death Of An Angel.

TV inc: Hawkins on Murder; A Question of Love; Salem's Lot; Fighting Back; Million Dollar Infield; The Lady from Yesterday.

BEDFORD, Brian: Act. b. England, Feb 16, 1935. e. RADA. Thea inc: (London) The Young and the Beautiful; A View From the Bridge; Five Finger Exercise; Write Me A Murder; The Doctors Dilemma; The Knack. (Bway) Five Finger Exercise; Lord Pengo; The Private Ear; The Astrakhan Coat; The Unknown Solider and His Wife; The Cocktail Party; Private Lives; School For Wives (Tony-1971); Jumpers; Measure for Measure; Twelfth Night; The Misanthrope.

Films inc: The Angry Silence; The Pad and How to Use It; Grand Prix.

TV inc: Winterset; The Judge and His Hangman; The Secret Thread; Tartuffe.

BEE, Molly: Act-Singer. b. Oklahoma City, OK, Aug 18, 1939. TV inc: Hometown Jamboree; Swingin' Country. Films inc: Chartroose Caboose. Appearances in niteries, fairs, club circuit. Records inc: I Saw Mommy Kissing Santa Claus:

BEE GEES: Group. Group consisting of the Gibb Brothers, Andy, Barry, Robin and Maurice. Films inc: Staying Alive (Songs). Albums inc: Children of the World; Here At Last--Bee Gees Live; Main Course; Saturday Night Fever; Spirits Having Flown; Too Much Heaven; Tragedy; Bee Gees Greatest.

(Grammys-(6)-group vocal-1977; Album of the year (2 awards, one as artists one as prods), group vocal, arr for voices, prod of year-1978).

BEERY, Noah, Jr: Act. b. NYC, Aug 10, 1916. Travelled with parents in stock company. Appeared as child in Mark of Zorro, 1920. Films inc: Father and Son; Only Angels Have Wings; Two Flags West; Cimarron Kid; Wagons West; Story of Will Rogers; Jubal; Fastest Gun Alive; Walking Tall; The Spikes Gang; The Asphalt Cowboy; The Best Little Whorehouse In Texas; Waltz Across Texas.

TV inc: Rockford Files; Revenge of the Red Chief; The Bastard; The Great American Traffic Jam; The Big Stuffed Dog; Revenge of the Gray Gang; Beyond Witch Mountain; The Capture of Grizzly Adams; Mysterious Two; The Quest; The Yellow Rose.

BEGELMAN, David: Exec. b. NYC, 1922. Started as agent with MCA 1949; resigned as vp - special projects 1960 to form agency with Freddie Fields; firm acquired General Artists Agency 1968, merger resulting in formation of Creative Management Associates, of which he was vice-chmn; resigned 1973 to become pres Columbia Pictures; in 1977 took added duties as pres tv divison; forced to leave Columbia 1978 following charges of fiscal irregularities; re-united with Fields in Begelman-Fields prodn co, releasing through Columbia; named P-CEO MGM Film Div Jan 1980; prod doc short Angel Dust as part of legal arrangement leading to probation on charges growing out of Columbia resignation; became P & CEO of UA after MGM acquired it in July 1981; ousted July 1982; named P of indie Sherwood Prodns, Aug 1982; May, 1984 formed Gladden Entertainment Corp. Films inc: (exec prod) Wholly Moses.

BEGLEY, Ed Jr: Act. b. Sept 16, 1949. Films inc: Blue Collar; Goin' South; The One and Only; Hardcore; Battlestar Galactica; The Concorde--Airport '79; The In-Laws; Private Lessons; Eating Raoul; Cat People; Get Crazy; Spinal Tap; Protocol.

TV inc: My Three Sons; Room 222; Roll Out; Amateur Night at the Dixie Bar and Grill; A Shining Season; Riker; Rascals and Robbers--The Secret Adventures of Tom Sawyer and Huck Finn; Tales of the Apple Dumpling Gang; Voyagers; St. Elsewhere; Not Just Another Affair; Still The Beaver; An Uncommon Love; Insight/The Clearing House.

BEICH, Albert: Wri. b. Bloomington, IL, Jun 25, 1919. e. McGill U. Wrote for radio. Films inc: Girls in Chains; The Perils of Pauline; The Bride Goes Wild; Key to the City; The Lieutenant Wore Skirts; Dead Ringer.

BELAFONTE Harry: Act-Singer. b. NYC, Mar 1, 1927. Started professionally as singer in NY clubs. Films inc: Bright Road; Carmen Jones; Island in the Sun; The World, The FLesh & The Devil; Odds Against Tomorrow; The Angel Levine; Buck and the Preacher; Uptown Saturday Night (& prod); Sometimes I Look At My Life (doc); Sag Nein (Say No!) Beat Street (prod); First Look (doc) (narr).

TV inc: Tonight With Belafonte (*Emmy*-1960); The Strollin' Twenties; A Time For Laughter; Grambling's White Tiger; Parade of Stars; Belafonte Sings.

Bway inc: Three For Tonight; John Murray Anderson's Almanac (*Tony*-supp-1954); A Night With Belafonte.

(*Grammys*-(3)-Folk perf-1960; Folk recording-1961, 1965).

BELAFONTE-HARPER, Shari: Act. b. NYC, Sept. 22, 1954. e. Carnegie Tech (Mellon) U., BFA. D of Harry Belafonte. Films inc: If You Could See What I Hear; Time Walker.

TV inc: The Night the City Screamed; Hotel; Velvet.

BELASCO, Leon (Leonid Simeonovich Berladsky): Act. b. Odessa, Russia, Oct 11, 1902. e. St Josephs Coll, Yokohama, Japan. Began as violinist, orch. leader. Performed in niteries, hotels; in 1936, added the Andrews Sisters to orchestra in Kansas City. On screen from 1939 in Topper Takes a Trip. Films inc: Broadway Serenade; Comrade X; Design for Scandal; Road to Morocco; Over My Dead Body; Holiday Inn; Yankee Doodle Dandy; Earl Carroll Vanities; Suspense; Bagdad; Ma and Pa Kettle Go to Town; Abbott & Costello in the Foreign Legion; Son of Ali Baba; Call Me Madam; Geraldine; Jalopy; Art of Love; The Woman of the Year.

BELFER, Hal B: Chor-Dir. b. Los Angeles, Feb 16. Head of dance department U, 20th Century Fox, 1949-54. Dir of entertainment Riviera Hotel, Flamingo Hotel, Las Vegas, 1955-mid-60s. Exec prod Premore Prodns since 1970.

BELFORD, Christine: Act. b. Amityville, NY, Jan 14, 1949. TV inc: Vanished; Ironside; World Premier; Banacek; Cool Million; High Midnight; Kenny Rogers as the Gambler; Desperate Voyage; Insight/ Missing Persons Bureau; The Neighborhood; Insight/The Fiddler; Personal and Confidential (host); It's Not Easy; Sparkling Cyanide; Empire.

Films inc: Pocket Money; The Groundstar Conspiracy; Christine.

BEL GEDDES, Barbara: Act. b. NYC, Oct 31, 1922. NY stage debut 1941, Out of the Frying Pan. Films inc: The Gangster; The Long Night; I Remember Mama; Blood on the Moon; Caught; Panic in the Streets; Fourteen Hours; Vertigo; The Five Pennies; Five Branded Women; By Love Possessed; The Todd Killings; Summertree.

Bway inc: Deep Are the Roots; The Moon Is Blue; The Living Room; Cat on a Hot Tin Roof; The Sleeping Prince; Silent Night, Lonely Night; Mary, Mary; LUV; Finishing Touches; Ah, Wilderness; Everything in the Garden.

TV inc: Lamb to the Slaughter; Our Town; Dallas (*Emmy*-1980).

BELKIN, Alan Prod. b. Cleveland, OH, Jul 14, 1934. e. UCLA, BS. Exec vp The Petersen Co., 1960; P American Communications Industries, 1979; P Alan Belkin prodns 1980. Films inc: Five on the Black Hand Side (exec in chg prodn); The Late Great Planet Earth (prod); A Different Story (prod); A Force of One (prod); The Octagon (exec prod); Charlie Chan and the Curse of the Dragon Queen (exec prod).

TV inc: This Far By Faith.

BELL, Steve: TV newsman. b. Oskaloosa, IA, Dec 9, 1935. e. Central Coll, Pella IA, BA; Northwestern U, MSJ. Started 1955 as anncr KBOE, Oskaloosa; 1959, reporter WOI-TV, Ames, IA; 1960, wri WGN-TV Chicago; 1962, anchor WOW-TV, Omaha; 1965, anchor WNEW (radio), NYC; 1967 corr ABC; 1970, combat corr Vietnam; 1972 ABC Bureau chief Hong Kong; 1974 White House Corr; 1975, anchor news segs Good Morning America. TV doc inc: The People of People's China.

BELLAMY, Earl: Prod-Dir. b. Minneapolis, MI, Mar 13, 1917. e. LA City Coll. Films inc: (Dir) Seminole Uprising; Blackjack Ketchum; Toughest Gun In Tombstone; Stagecoach To Dancers Rock (& prod); Fluffy; Gunpoint; Incident at Phantom Hill; Seven Alone; Munsters Go Home; Part Two Walking Tall; Sidewinder; Speedtrap .

TV inc: Bachelor Father; Wells Fargo; Lone Ranger; Rawhide; The

Donna Reed Show; Andy Griffith Show; Wagon Train; Laramie; Laredo; I Spy; Mod Squad; Medical Center; Fantasy Island; Castaways on Gilligan's Island; Valentine Magic on Love Island (dir); Trapper John, M.D.

BELLAMY, Madge (Margaret Derden Philpott): Act. b. Hillsboro, TX, Jun 30, 1902. Silent screen star. Films inc: The Riddle Woman; Hail the Woman; Lorna Doone; The Hottentot; Love's Whirlpool; Love and Glory; The Iron Horse; The Parasite; Lightnin'; Summer Bachelors; Bertha, the Sewing Machine Girl; The Telephone Girl; Silk Legs; The Play Girl; White Zombie; Charlie Chan in London; the Daring Young Man; Northwest Mounted.

Bway inc: The Love Mill; Dear Brutus; Pollyanna; Peg O'My Heart; Intermission; Holiday Lady; See My Lawyer.

BELLAMY, Ralph: Act. b. Chicago, Jun 17, 1905. In stock, repertory, 1922-30. Films inc: Secret Six; The Awful Truth; Forbidden Company; Flying Devils; Spitfire; Hands Across the Table; The Man Who Lived Twice; The Court-Martial of Billy Mitchell; Sunrise at Campobello; Rosemary's Baby; Cancel My Reservation; Oh, God!; Trading Places.

Bway inc: Town Boy; Roadside; Tomorrow the World; State of the Union; Detective Story; Sunrise at Campobello (*Tony*-supp-1958).

TV inc: The Eleventh Hour; The Survivors; The Immortal; The Most Deadly Game; The Clone Master; The Millionaire; The Billion Dollar Threat; Power; The Memory of Eva Ryker; Condominium; The Winds of War; Love Leads The Way; The Fourth Wise Man; Space.

BELLAVER, Harry: Act. b. Feb 12, 1905. Films inc: Another Thin Man; The House on 92d St; No Way Out; The Lemon Drop Kid; From Here to Eternity; Miss Sadie Thompson; Love Me or Leave Me; Slaughter on Tenth Avenue; The Birds and the Bees; The Old Man and The Sea; One Potato, Two Potato; Madigan; Blue Collar; Hero at Large.

TV inc: Naked City; Murder in Music City; Rivkin--Bounty Hunter.

BELLE, Barbara (nee Einhorn): Sngwri. b. NYC, Nov 22, 1922. e. NYU. Wrote special material for Louis Armstrong; Louis Prima; pers mgr for Jose Ferrer; Penny Singleton; Keely Smith. Songs inc: A Sunday Kind of Love; You Broke the Only Heart That Ever Loved You; Early Autumn.

BELLER, Kathleen: Act. b. Westchester, NY, Feb 10, 1956. TV inc: Search for Tomorrow; Something for Joey; Mary White; Are You in the House Alone?; Mother and Daughter--The Loving War; No Place To Hide; The Manions of America; The Blue and The Gray; Dynasty; Deadly Messages.

Films inc: The Godfather, Part II; The Betsy; Promises in the Dark; Movie, Movie; Fort Apache, The Bronx; Surfacing; The Sword and the Sorceror; Touched.

BELLOCCHIO, Marco: Dir-Wri. b. Italy, 1939. Films inc: Fists in the Pocket; China Is Near; Leap Into the Void; Vacations in Val Trebbia; Gli Occhi la Bocca (The Eyes, The Mouth); Enrico IV (Henry IV).

BELLSON, Louis: Drummer. b. Rock Falls, IL, Jul 6, 1924. e. Augustana Coll. H of Pearl Bailey. With Ted Fio Rito orch 1942; Benny Goodman, 1943-44; Tommy Dorsey 1947-1950; Duke Ellington, 1951-54; Jazz At Philharmonic; formed own orch; backs Pearl Bailey in nitery, concert dates.

BELLWOOD, Pamela: Act. b. NYC, Jun 26. Films inc: Two Minute Warning; Airport '77; Serial; Hangar 18; The Incredible Shrinking Woman.

TV inc: The War Widow; Emily, Emily; W.E.B.; The Girl Who Saved Our America; Dynasty; The Wild Women of Chastity Gulch; Cocaine--One Man's Seduction; Baby Sister; Sparkling Cyanide; Choices of the Heart; Breakaway.

Bway inc: Butterflies are Free; Finishing Touches; Philadelphia, Here I Come; The Tenth Man; The Effect of Gamma Rays on Man-in-the-Moon Marigolds.

BELMONDO, Jean-Paul: Act. b. Neuilly-sur-Seine, France, Apr 9, 1933. e. Conservatoire d'Art Dramatique. Films inc: A Double Tour; A Bout de Souffle; Moderato Cantabile; La Viaccia; Two Women; Cartouche; Un Singe en Hiver; That Man from Rio; Weekend in Dunkirk;

Is Paris Burning?; The Brain; Ho!; The Mississippi Mermaid; A Man I Like; Borsalino; Scoundrel; Le Magnifique; Stavisky; L'Incorrigible; Le Corps de Mon Ennemi; Flic ou Voyou; Le Guignolo; Le Professional; L'As des As (Ace of Aces); Le Marginal (The Outsider); Les Morfalous (The Vultures); Joyeuses Paques (Happy Easter).

Thea inc: Caesar and Cleopatra; Treasure Party.

BELUSHI, James (Jim): Act. b. Chicago, Jun 15, 1954. e. DuPage Coll; Southern IL U. B of late John Belushi. Worked with Chicago's Second City Revue. Films inc: Thief. TV inc: Working Stiffs; Who's Watching the Kids?; The Joseph Jefferson Awards (host); The Best Legs In The 8th Grade; Saturday Night Live.

BEN AMMAR, Tarak: Prod. b. Tunis, Jun. 12, 1949. e. Georgetown U. Films inc: The Thief; Io e Caterina (Catherine and I); Tais-toi quand tu parles! (Shut Up When You Speak!); Deux Heures moint le quart avant Jesus Christ (A Quarter to Two Before Jesus Christ); La Ballade de Mamlouk; LaTraviata; Le Grand Carnaval (The Big Carnival); Misunderstood; Les Cavaliers de l'Orage (The Horsemen of the Storm); Par Ou t'Es Rentre ? On T'A Pas Vue Sortir (How'd You Get In ? We Didn't See You Leave).

BENCHLEY, Peter: Wri. b. NYC, May 8, 1940. e. Harvard, BA. S of Nathaniel Benchley, Grandson Robert Benchley. Films inc: Jaws; The Deep; The Island.

TV inc: Sharks (narr).

BENEDEK, Laslo: Dir. b. Budapest, Mar 5, 1907. e. U of Vienna. Films inc: The Kissing Bandit; Port of New York; Storm Over the Tiber; Death of a Salesman; The Wild One; Affair in Havana; Moment of Danger; Namu the Killer Whale (& prod.); The Daring Game; The Night Visitor; King Kongs Faust (act).

TV inc: Dupont Theatre; Loretta Young Show; Perry Mason; Naked City; Untouchables; Outer Limits; etc.

Thea inc: Belial; Twelfth Night.

BENEDICT, Dirk (nee Niewoehner): Act. b. Helena, MT, Mar 1. e. Whitman Coll, BFA. Started in repertory. Films inc: Georgia, Georgia; Sssssss; Battlestar Galactica; Scavenger Hunt.

Thea inc: Abelard and Heloise; Butterflies Are Free.

TV inc: Chopper One; Battlestar Galactica; Georgia Peaches; Scruples; Family In Blue; The A Team.

BENEDICT, Nick: Act. b. Los Angeles, Jul 14. TV inc: Medical Center; Emergency; All My Children.

Thea inc: Of Mice and Men; Hello Out There; The Glass Menagerie; Lovers and Other Strangers.

BENEDICT, Paul: Act. b. Silver City, NM, Sep 17, 1938. Started with Boston's Image Theatre; Theatre Company of Boston. Bway inc: Little Murders; The White House Murder Case; Bad Habits.

Films inc: Taking Off; Up the Sandbox; Jeremiah Johnson; The Front Page; The Goodbye Girl; Spinal Tap.

TV inc: Sesame Street; The Jeffersons; The Electric Grandmother; The Blue and The Gray; The Jeffersons (retd).

BENENSON, Bill: Prod. e. Hobart Coll; Ecole Nationale de Beaux Arts, Paris; Columbia. Films inc: (doc) Easter Island Raises; The Marginal Way; Diamond Rivers. (Fea) Boulevard Nights.

BENJAMIN, Richard: Act. b. NYC, May 22, 1939. e. Northwestern U. Thea: toured in Tchin Tchin; A Thousand Clowns; Barefoot in the Park; The Odd Couple. Bway debut, The Star Spangled Girl. Directed London prodn Barefoot in the Park.

Films inc: Thunder Over the Plains; Crime Wave; Diary of a Mad Housewife; Catch 22; Goodbye, Columbus; Westworld; Sunshine Boys; House Calls; Love at First Bite; Scavenger Hunt; The Last Married Couple in America; How To Beat The High Cost Of Living; First Family; Saturday, The 14th; My Favorite Year (dir); Racing With the Moon (dir); City Heat; Witches' Brew.

TV inc: He and She; Fame; Quark; Insight/Goodbye; The Way They Were; Natalie--A Tribute To A Very Special Lady; Packin' It In.

BENNENT, Heinz: Act. b. Aachen, Germany, Jul 23, 1921. Films inc: Katharina Blum; Wild Ducks; The Net; NEA; Ich Will Leben; Special Section; Femme Fatale; Rendezvous; Serpent's Egg; Hitler's Son; The

Tin Drum; Lulu; From the Life of the Marionettes; Clair de Femme; The Last Metro; Possession; L'Amour Des Femmes (Women's Love); Espion Leve-Toi (Rise Up, Spy); Krieg Und Frieden (War and Peace); Via Degli Specchi (Street of Mirrors); Le Lit (The Bed); La Mort de Mario Ricci (The Death of Mario Ricci); Sarah; Le Rapt (The Kidnapping).

BENNET, Spencer G: Dir. b. NYC, Jan 5, 1893. Started as stunt man, then dir from 1925-64. Films inc: numerous serials; Submarines Seahawk; Atomic Submarine; Bounty Killer; Requiem for a Gunfighter.

BENNETT, Alan: Act-Wri. b. Leeds, England, May 9, 1934. e. Oxford. Thea inc: (London) Beyond the Fringe (& co-wri); Blood of the Bambergs; A Cuckoo in the Nest; Forty Years On (& wri); Getting On (wri); Habeas Corpus (& wri); The Old Country (wri).

(Bway): Beyond the Fringe. (Special Tony 1963); Enjoy (wri).

TV inc: A Day Out; Sunset Across the Bay; On the Margin (& wri); An Englishman Abroad.

Films inc: A Private Function (wri).

BENNETT, Bruce (Herman Brix): Act. b. Tacoma, WA, 1909. e. U of WA. Films inc: Student Tour; The New Adventures of Tarzan; Before I Hang; Atlantic Convoy; The More the Merrier; Sahara; Mildred Pierce; The Treasure of Sierra Madre; Task Force; Without Honor; Sudden Fear; Dream Wife; Strategic Air Commmand; Three Violent People; The Outsider; Deadhead Miles.

BENNETT, Charles: Wri. b. Shoreham, England, 1899. Films inc: Blackmail; The Man Who Knew Too Much; The Thirty-nine Steps; Secret Agent; Sabotage; King Solomon's Mines; Balalaika; Foreign Correspondent; Reap the Wild Wind; The Story of Dr. Wassell; Ivy; Madness of the Heart (& dir); Black Magic; Where Danger Lives; No Escape (& dir.); The Story of Mankind; The Lost World; Five Weeks in a Balloon; War Gods of the Deep.

Plays inc: Blackmail; The Last Hour; Sensation; The Danger Line; Page from a Diary; After Midnight.

TV inc: Cavalcade of America; The Christophers.

BENNETT, Harve (nee Fischman): Prod. b. Chicago, IL, Aug 17, 1930. e. UCLA. Member Quiz Kids radio show as child; special events prod CBS-TV; vp pgms ABC-TV; 1977-1980 partnered with Harris Katleman.

TV inc: Mod Squad (& wri); Six Million Dollar Man; Bionic Woman; Rich Man, Poor Man; The Gemini Man; American Girls; Salvage; From Here To Eternity; Legend of the Golden Gun; From Here to Eternity--The War Years; Alex and the Doberman Gang; Nick and the Dobermans; A Woman Called Golda (Emmy-exec prod-1982); The Powers of Matthew Star (exec prod); The Jesse Owens Story (exec prod).

Films inc: Star Trek II--The Wrath of Khan;

BENNETT, Hywel: Act. b. South Wales, Apr 8, 1944. e. RADA. Thea inc: In repertory, appeared with Young Vic; Dear Wormwood; A Smashing Day; Henry IV; Bakke's Night of Fame; The Birthday Party; Night Must Fall; Look Back in Anger; Toad of Toad Hall; I Must Have Been Here Before; Rosencrantz and Guildenstern are Dead; A Man For All Seasons; The Case of the Oily Levantine.

TV inc: Romeo and Juliet; The Idiot; Three's One; Tinker, Tailor, Soldier, Spy.

Films inc: The Virgin Soldiers; Loot; Alice in Wonderland.

BENNETT, Jill: Act. b. Penang, Federated Malay States, Dec 24, 1931. Thea inc: Captain Cavallo; Antony and Cleopatra; Caesar and Cleopatra; The Seagull; The Seagull; The Bald Prima Donna; Dinner with the Family; Castle in Sweden; Time Present; Hedda Gabler; The End of Me Old Cigar; Loot; Watch It Come Down.

Films inc: Moulin Rouge; Hell Below Zero; The Criminal; Lust for Life; The Skull; The Nanny; The Charge of the Light Brigade; Inadmissible Evidence; I Want What I Want; Quilp; Full Circle; For Your Eyes Only; Brittania Hospital.

TV inc: The Heiress; Trilby; Jealousy; The Three Sisters; Intent Is Murder; Almost a Vision; Hello Lola; The Aerodrome.

BENNETT, Joan: Act. b. Palisades, NJ, Feb 27, 1910. On stage with father, Richard Bennett. Screen debut in Bulldog Drummond, 1929. Films inc: Three Live Ghosts; Disraeli; Moby Dick; Reckless Moment;

Little Women; Woman in the Window; Father of the Bride; Father's Little Dividend; There's Always Tomorrow; Navy Wife; Desire in the Dust; Suspiria.
TV inc: Dark Shadows; Suddenly Love; Divorce Wars--A Love Story.

BENNETT, Julie: Act. b. Beverly Hills, CA, Jan 24, 1943. Films inc: Hey There, It's Yogi Bear; What's Up, Tiger Lily; On a Clear Day You Can See Forever; Westworld.
TV inc: Goliath Awaits.

BENNETT, Meg: Act. b. Los Angeles, Oct 4. e. Northwestern U, BA. Bway inc: Grease. TV inc: Search for Tomorrow; After Hours; Camera Three; The Young and the Restless.

BENNETT, Michael: Dir-Chor. (nee diFiglia):b. Buffalo, NY, Apr 8, 1943. Bway: (Chor) A Joyful Noise; Henry, Sweet Henry; Promises, Promises (& dir); Coco (& dir); (Company (& co-dir); Follies (& co-dir) (2 Tonys-dir, chor-1972); Twigs (dir); God's Favorite (dir); Seesaw (& dir) (Tony-chor-1974); A Chorus Line (& conceived-dir) (Pulitzer Prize; 2 Tonys-dir-chor-1976); Ballroom (Tony-chor-1979); Dreamgirls (& prod); (Tony-chor-1982).

BENNETT, Richard Charles: Dir. b. Milwaukee, WI, Apr 24, 1923. e. UCLA. TV inc: Girl from UNCLE; The Bold Ones; Alias Smith & Jones; Insight; Toma; Barnaby Jones; Emergency; Lucas Tanner; Apples Way; Waltons; Gibbsville; This Is the Life; Insight/Goodbye; Insight/The Sixth Day.
Films inc: Harper Valley PTA.

BENNETT, Richard Rodney: Comp. b. England, 1936. Films inc: Interpol; Indiscreet; Only Two Can Play; One Way Pendulum; The Nanny; Far from the Madding Crowd; Nicholas and Alexandra; Murder on the Orient Express; The Brinks Job; Equus; Permission To Kill; Yanks; The Return of the Soldier.

BENNETT, Tony: Singer. (nee Benedetto):b. NYC, Aug 3, 1926. Recording artist, niteries. (Grammys-(2)-solo vocal & record of year-1962). TV inc: King; Bennett and Basie Together; On The Town With Tony Bennett.

BENNINGTON, William A. (Bill): Dir. TV inc: Hawaii Calls; 19th Summer Olympics (Emmy-1969); Wide World of Sports; Macy Thanksgiving Day Parade; NCAA Football; Tournament of Roses Parade; The Pet Set.

BENSLEY, Russ: Prod. b. Chicago, IL., June 12, 1930. e. Northwestern U Medill School of Journalism, BS, MS. With WBBM-TV, Chicago, before joining CBS News, 1960 as wri; 1963, mgr CBS Chicago bureau; 1971, dir Special Events. TV inc: Eyewitness (& dir); CBS Evening News With Walter Cronkite (& exec prod); CBS Evening News (exec prod); The World of Charlie Company (Emmy-prod-1971); The U.S.-Soviet Wheat Deal--Is There A Scandal? (Emmy-exec prod-1973); Coverage of the Shooting of Gov. Wallace; Jackie Robinson; Watergate--The White House Transcripts (Emmy-exec prod-1974); On the Road With Charles Kuralt; The American Parade; Crossroads.

BENSON, George: Singer-Guitarist. b. Pittsburgh, PA, Mar 22, 1943. Recordings inc: This Masquerade; Body Talk; White Rabbit. Albums inc: Breezin'; In Flight; Weekend In LA; Give Me the Night.
(Grammys-(8)-Record of Year-1976; Pop inst-1976; R&B inst-1976, 1980; R&B vocal-1978, 1980; inst arr-1979; Jazz vocal-1980).

BENSON, Hugh: Prod. b. NYC, Sep 7, 1917. During WW II was master sergeant in charge of Special Service units under Joshua Logan. Asst to prods of Ed Sullivan Show 1947. Joined WB 1955 as head of radio-TV promotion. In 1956 exec. asst. to William T. Orr, Warner Production VP; Exec. prod. Screen Gems; prod. MGM.
TV inc: Shirts/Skins; Contract on Cherry Street; A Fire in the Sky; The Child Stealer; Goldie and the Boxer; Confessions of a Lady Cop; The Dream Merchants. Goldie and the Boxer Go to Hollywood; Goliath Awaits; The Shadow Riders (supv prod); The Blue and The Gray; The Master of Ballantrae; Anna Karenina (supv prod).
Films inc: Nightmare Honeymoon.

BENSON, Lucille: Act. b. AL, Jul 17, 1922. Films inc: Little Fauss and Big Halsey; Slaughterhouse Five; Mame; Tom Sawyer; Huck Finn; The Greatest; Silver Streak.
TV inc: Women in Chains; Duel; Petrocelli; Murder in Music City; The Adventures of Pollyanna; When Your Lover Leaves.
(Died Feb. 17, 1984).

BENSON, Ray (ne Seifert): Mus-Act. b. Philadelphia, PA, Mar 16, 1951. Founder of group Asleep at the Wheel, 1970. Leader, lead singer of band. (Grammy-country instrumental-1978).

BENSON, Robby (ne Segal): Act. b. Dallas, Jan 21, 1956. Appeared Bway at age of 5, The King and I. Films inc: Ode to Billy Joe; Jeremy; Joey; The Godfather Part II; Lucky Lady; One On One (& wri); The End; Ice Castles; Walk Proud (& comp); Die Laughing (& prod-wri-comp); Tribute; The Chosen; Running Brave; National Lampoon Goes to the Movies; Harry & Son; City Limits. POV inc: Death Be Not Proud; Search For Tomorrow; All the Kind Strangers; Virginia Hill; Remember When; The Death of Richie; Two of A Kind; California Girls.
Bway inc: The Pirates of Penzance.

BENTON, Barbi: Act-Sing. b. Sacramento, CA, Jan 28, 1950. e. UCLA. TV inc: Laugh-In; Playboy After Dark (host); Hee Haw; Love on the Run; The Great American Beauty Pageant; Murder at the Mardi Gras; Sugartime; A Barbi Doll for Christmas; A Country Christmas; For the Love of It; Dean Martin at the Wild Animal Park; Gary Owen's All Nonsense News Network Special; I Love Men; Celebrity Fun Cruise.
Films inc: Hospital Massacre; Deathstalker.

BENTON, Doug: Prod. b. Hollis, OK, Sep 24, 1925. e. Northwestern U. TV inc: Thriller; Wide Country; Dr Kildare; The Girl from UNCLE; Cimmaron Strip; Name of the Game; Columbo (Emmy-1974); Ironside; Hec Ramsey; The Rookies; Police Woman; A Last Cry for Help; Transplant; Undercover with the KKK; Skag; Gauguin the Savage; Victims; Codename Foxfire (supv prod).

BENTON, Robert: Wri-Dir. b. Waxahachie, TX, 1933. e. U of TX, BA. Films inc: Bonnie and Clyde; There Was A Crooked Man; What's Up Doc?; Bad Company (& dir); The Late Show (& dir); Superman; Money's Tight; Kramer vs Kramer (& dir) (Oscars-dir-wri-1979); Still of the Night; Places In The Heart (Oscar-screenplay-1984).
Bway inc: It's a Bird. . .It's a Plane. . .It's Superman (libretto); Oh, Calcutta (one sketch).

BERADINO, John: Act. b. Los Angeles, May 1, 1917. In "Our Gang" comedies as child; former pro baseball player. TV inc: The New Breed; I Led Three Lives; Do Not Fold, Spindle or Mutilate; Moon of the Wolf; General Hospital (since 1963); Don't Look Back.

BERCOVICI, Eric: Wri-Prod. b. NYC, Feb 27, 1933. e. St John's Coll; Yale Drama School; April 1982 formed Bercovici-St Johns Prodns with Richard St. Johns. Films inc: The Culpepper Cattle Company; Hell in the Pacific.
TV inc: Police Story; Strange Homecoming; Washington Behind Closed Doors; Flesh and Blood; The Top of the Hill; Shogun (Emmy-prod-1981); The Chicago Story; McClain's Law (& crea); Cowboy (exec prod).

BERCOVICI, Leonardo: Wri. b. NYC, Jan 4. Films inc: Puccini; Under Ten Flags; The Bishop's Wife; The Lost Moment; The Unafraid; Kiss the Blood Off My Hands; Portrait of Jennie; Dark City; Monsoon; Square of Violence (& prod-dir); Story of a Woman (& prod-dir).

BERCOVITCH, Reuben: Wri-Prod. Films inc: Hell in the Pacific; What's Up, Tiger Lilly? (prod only); Out of Season.
TV inc: (wri) Bonanza; Virginian; Bold Ones; Richard Boone Theatre.

BERENGER, Tom: Act. b. May 31, 1950. Films inc: Looking for Mr. Goodbar; The Sentinel; Butch and Sundance--The Early Days; In Praise of Older Women; The Dogs of War; Oltre la porta (Beyond the Door); Eddie and the Cruisers; The Big Chill; Fear City; Rustler's Rhapsody.
TV inc: Flesh and Blood.

BERENSON, Marisa: Act. b. Feb 15, 1947. Fashion model. Films inc: Death in Venice; Cabaret; Barry Lyndon; Killer Fish; S.O.B.; The Secret Diary of Sigmund Freud; La Tete Dans Le Sac (Led By The Nose); L'Arbalete (The Syringe).
    TV inc: Tourist; Playing For Time.

BERESFORD, Bruce: Dir. b. Australia, 1940. Films inc: King Size Woman (short); Rene Magritte (doc); The Adventures of Barry McKenzie; Barry McKenzie Holds His Own; The Getting of Wisdom; Side By Side; Don's Party; Money Movers; Breaker Morant; The Club; Puberty Blues; Tender Mercies; King David.
    TV inc: Poor Fella Me; Wreck of the Batavia; It Droppeth As the Gentle Rain.

BERG, Dick: Exec Prod. TV inc: Are You in the House Alone?; The Word; The Martian Chronicles; A Rumor of War; Rape and Marriage--The Rideout Case; Johnny Belinda; An Invasion of Privacy; Wallenberg--A Hero's Story; Space (& wri).

BERGEN, Candice: Act. b. Beverly Hills, May 9, 1946. e. U of PA. D of the late Edgar Bergen. Model, freelance photographer. Films inc: The Group; The Sand Pebbles; The Day The Fish Came Out; Carnal Knowledge; T.R. Baskin; 11 Harrowhouse; The Wind And The Lion; The Domino Principle; The End of the World in Our Usual Bed in a Night Full of Rain; Oliver's Story; Starting Over; Rich and Famous; Gandhi; Stick.
    TV inc: The Way They Were; Hollywood Wives; Arthur The King.
    Bway inc: Hurlyburly.

BERGEN, Polly: Singer-Act. b. Knoxville, TN, Jul 4, 1930. Started on radio at age 14; in light opera, summer stock, niteries. Films inc: At War with the Army; That's My Boy; Warpath; The Stooge; Escape from Fort Bravo; Cape Fear; Move Over Darling; Kisses for My President; A Guide for the Married Man.
    TV inc: Belle Sommers; The Life of Helen Morgan (Emmy-1957); Death Cruise; The Million Dollar Face; Born Beautiful; The Winds of War; Velvet.

BERGER, Helmut: Act. b. Salzburg, Austria, May 29, 1944. e. Feld-kirk Coll; U of Perugia. Films inc: The Damned; Un Beau Monstre; The Garden of the Finzi, Continis; Dorian Gray; Ash Wednesday; Ludwig; Conversation Piece; The Romantic Englishwoman; Madam Kitty; The Roses of Danzig; Heroin; Fluechtige Bekanntschafen (Fleeting Acquaintances); Die Jaeger (Deadly Game); Femmes (women); Victoria (Victory).

BERGER, Richard L.: Exec. b. Oct 25, 1939. e. UCLA, BA. Joined 20th Century-Fox in 1966; vp in charge of programs, 1972; asst vp, Feature Films Prodn, 1975-76; vp dramatic development, CBS, 1976-78; Retd to Fox 1978 vp, World Wide Prodn; March, 1983, P Touchstone, new Disney subsid formed to handle film and tv mktg; ousted Oct. 1984 when new management team of Michael Eisner and Frank Wells announced Jeffrey Katzenberg as new P of film and tv; Feb. 1985, sr prodn VP, UA; March, 1985 upped to P.

BERGER, Robert: Prod. b. Feb. 9, 1914. TV inc: Holocaust (Emmy-1978); Hollow Image; Doctor Franken; Death Penalty; FDR-The Last Year; The Henderson Monster; King Crab; Skokie; My Body, My Child (supv prod); Benny's Place (supv prod); The Firm.
    Films inc: Sakharov.

BERGER, Senta: Act. b. Austria, May 13, 1941. Films inc: The Secret Ways; The Good Soldier Schweik; The Victors; Major Dundee; The Glory Guys; Cast a Giant Shadow; The Quiller Memorandum; Our Man in Marrakesh; The Ambushers; Treasure of San Gennaro; De Sade; Percy; The Swiss Conspiracy; Cross of Iron; Killing Me Softly; The Chinese Miracle; Goodnight Ladies and Gentlemen; Nest of Vipers; La Giacla Berger.

BERGERAC, Jacques: Act. b. Biarritz, France, May 26, 1927. Films inc: Twist of Fate; Strange Intruder; Les Girls; Gigi; Thunder in The Sun; The Hypnotic Eye; A Global Affair; Taffy and the Jungle Hunter; The Emergency Operation; Lady Chaplin; The Last Party; One Plus One.

BERGHOF, Herbert: Act-Dir. b. Vienna, Sep 13, 1909. Stage debut Vienna, 1927. Appeared in more than 120 plays during the next 12 years. In 1939 to Bway to dir From Vienna; appeared in Reunion in New York; The Innocent Voyage; Jacobowski and the Colonel; The Man Who Had All the Luck; The Key and Rip Van Winkle; Waiting for Godot (dir); The Infernal Machine (dir); The Queen and the Rebels (dir); The Andersonville Trial; Do You Know the Milky Way (dir); In the Matter of J Robert Openheimer; The Unknown Soldier; Marius; The Doctor's Dilemma; The Sponsor (dir); Poor Murderer (dir); Charlotte (dir).
    Films inc: (Act) Five Fingers; Red Planet Mars; Cleopatra; Voices; Those Lips, Those Eyes; Times Square.
    TV inc: Kojak--The Belarus File.

BERGMAN, Alan: Lyr. b. NYC, Sep 11, 1925. e. U of NC, BA; UCLA. Films inc: In the Heat of the Night; The Thomas Crown Affair (Oscar-song, The Windmills of Your Mind-1968); Happy Ending; Gaily, Gaily; Pieces of Dreams; Sometimes A Great Notion; The Way We Were (Oscar-title song-1974); A Star Is Born; John and Mary; Life and Times of Judge Roy Bean; The One and Only; Same Time Next Year; And Justice For All; The Promise; A Change of Seasons; Yentl (Oscar-Song Score-1983); Micki & Maude.
    TV inc: Queen of the Stardust Ballroom (Emmy-1975); Sybil (Emmy-1977); themes for: Maude; Good Times; Alice; Nancy Walker Show; Sandy Duncan Show.
    Bway inc: Something More.
    Chief Collaborators: Marilyn Bergman (wife); Lew Spence; Norman Luboff; Paul Weston; Sammy Fain; Alex North. Songs inc: Yellow Bird; Nice 'n' Easy; Cheatin' Billy; Outta My Mind; Sentimental Baby; Pieces of Dreams; All His Children; The Last Time I Felt Like This; Sleep Warm.
    (Grammys-(2)-film score & song of the year-1974).

BERGMAN, Ingmar: Wri-Dir. b. Uppsala, Sweden, Jul 14, 1918. e. Stockholm U. Directed University plays. First theatrical success as director, Macbeth, 1940. Wri-Dir Svensk Film-Industri, 1942. First screenplay, Frenzy, 1943. First directorial assignment, Crisis, 1946.
    Films inc: Night Is My Future; Port of Call; The Devil's Wanton; Three Strange Loves; Wild Strawberries; Brink of Life; The Magician; The Virgin Spring; Through a Glass Darkly; Shame; Face to Face; The Serpent's Egg; Autumn Sonata; Summer Paradise (Prod); From The Life of the Marionettes (dir-wri); Faro Document; Sally och Friheden (Sally and Freedom); Fanny And Alexander.
    TV inc: The Magic Flute; Efter Repetitionen (After the Rehearsal).
    (Irving Thalberg Award 1969).

BERGMAN, Jules: TV News. b. NYC, Mar 21, 1929. e. CCNY; Columbia. Started 1947 on news desk, CBS; 1948 to Time Mag; 1950 asst news dir WFDR; 1951 prod-wri ABC news; 1955 science wri; 1959 science edtr; covered space program for ABC.
    TV inc: Closeup on Fire (Emmy-narr-1973); Closeup on Oil--The Policy Crisis; Closeup on the Danger in Sports--Paying the Price; Closeup on Crashes--The Illusion of Safety; Union in Space; Closeup on Automobiles; Closeup--the Weekend Athlete; Asbestos--the Way to a Dusty Death; National Science Test 1984.

BERGMAN, Marilyn (nee Keith): Lyr. b. NYC, Nov 10, 1929. e. NYU, BA. W of Alan Bergman. Films inc: In the Heat of the Night; The Thomas Crown Affair (Oscar-song, The Windmills of Your Mind, 1968); Happy Ending; Gaily, Gaily; Pieces of Dreams; Sometimes A Great Notion; The Way We Were (Oscar-title song-1974); A Star Is Born; John and Mary; Life and Times of Judge Roy Bean; The One and Only; Same Time Next Year; And Justice For All; The Promise; A Change of Seasons; Yentl (Oscar-Song Score-1983); Micki & Maude.
    TV inc: Queen of the Stardust Ballroom (Emmy-1975); Sybil (Emmy-1977); Women In Song (host); themes for: Maude; Good Times; Alice; Nancy Walker Show; Sandy Duncan Show.
    Bway inc: Something More.
    Chief Collaborators: Alan Bergman (husband); Lew Spence; Norman Luboff; Sammy Fain; Alex North. Songs inc: Yellow Bird; Nice 'n' Easy; Outta My Mind; Sentimental Baby; Sleep Warm; Pieces of Dreams; All His Children; The Last Time I Felt Like This. (Grammys-(2)-film score & song of the year-1974).

BERGMAN, Peter: Act. b. Guantanamo Bay, Cuba, June 11. e. AADA. TV inc: Pity The Poor Soldier; The Guiding Light; Love Of Life; Fantasies; All My Children.

BERGMAN, Sandahl: Act. b. KS. Nov. 14, 1951. Films inc: All That Jazz; Conan The Barbarian; Airplane II The Sequel. TV inc: Getting Physical.

BERGMANN, Alan: Act-Dir. b. Brooklyn, NY. e. Syracuse U, BS. Bway inc: Danton's Death; Gideon; Night Life; Lorenzo; Luther.

TV inc: (Dir) Operation Petticoat; Flying High.

BERGNER, Elisabeth: Act. b. Vienna, Aug 22, 1900. e. Vienna Conservatory. On stage since 1919. Recent plays inc: The Gay Invalid; Long Day's Journey Into Night; First Love; The Madwoman of Chaillot; Catsplay.

Films inc: Der Evangelimann; Der Traumende Mund; Ariane; Catherine the Great; Escape Me Never; As You Like It; Dreaming Lips; Stolen Life; Paris Calling; Cry of the Banshee; Courier to the Tsar; Der Fussganger; Michael Strogoff; Der Pfingstausflug; Feine Gesellschaft Beschraenkte Haftung (Society Limited).

BERKOWSKY, Paul B.: Thea prod-Gen mgr. b. Cornwall, NY, Sep 8, 1932. e. Hobart Coll, BA; Yale U, MFA. GM for NY's Phoenix Theatre; VP League of Off-Bway Theatres and Producers. Bway inc: (GM) Yentl; Molly; Les Blancs; The Enemy Is Dead; Dear Oscar; You Know I Can't Hear You When the Water's Running; The Club; What the Wine-Sellers Buy; Showdown; The Fabulous Miss Marie; The Prodigal Sister. (Prod) Medal of Honor Rag.

BERLE, Milton (nee Berlinger): Perf. b. NYC, Jul 12, 1908. Film debut at age 5 in Tillie's Punctured Romance. Stage debut 1920 revival of Floradora, Atlantic City. Played Palace, starred in Ziegfeld Follies, headlined top night clubs.

TV inc: Star of own NBC show; (Emmy-Kinescoped Personality-1950); Texaco Star Theatre; Kraft Music Hall; The Milton Berle Show (Special Emmy-to "Mr. Television"); Bob Hope Anniversary Special; TV's Censored Bloopers; An NBC Family Christmas; Bob Hope's Women I Love--Beautiful and Funny; Family Business; Parade of Stars; Live--And in Person; Dean Martin's Celebrity Roast; The Television Academy Hall of Fame (honoree); The Cracker Brothers; The Hilarious Unrehearsed Antics Of The Stars.

Films inc: Tall, Dark and Handsome; Sun Valley Serenade; Margin for Error; It's A Mad Mad Mad World; The Happening; Who's Minding The Mint; Lepke; The Muppet Movie; Smorgasbord; Broadway Danny Rose.

BERLIN, Irving (Israel Baline): Comp-Sngwri. b. Russia, May 11, 1888. Began as singing waiter. Started writing songs in 1907 (Marie From Sunny Italy).

Bway scores inc: Watch Your Step; Stop! Look! Listen!; The Century Girl; Cohan Revue of 1918; Yip Yap Yaphank (all soldier show); Music Box Revue; The Cocoanuts; Ziegfeld Follies of 1927; Face the Music; As Thousands Cheer; Louisiana Purchase; This Is the Army (all-soldier show); Annie Get Your Gun; Miss Liberty; Call Me Madam; Mr President.

Film scores inc: Top Hat; Follow The Fleet; On the Avenue; Alexander's Ragtime Band; Carefree; Second Fiddle; Holiday Inn; Blue Skies; Easter Parade; White Christmas; There's No Business Like Show Business.

Also wrote songs for films: Puttin' on the Ritz; Hallelujah; Reaching for the Moon; Sayonara.

Songs inc: My Wife's Gone to the Country, Hurrah, Hurrah; Alexander's Ragtime Band; Everybody's Doin' It; Call Me Up Some Rainy Afternoon; When the Midnight Choochoo Leaves for Alabam; Play A Simple Melody; Oh, How I Hate to Get Up in the Morning; Mandy; A Pretty Girl Is Like a Melody; All By Myself; Say It With Music; Crinoline Days; All Alone; What'll I Do; Always; How Many Times; Remember; Blue Skies; Russian Lullaby; The Song Is Ended; Coquette; Marie; Puttin' On The Ritz; Reachin' for the Moon; Soft Lights and Sweet Music; How Deep Is the Ocean?; Let's Have Another Cup o' Coffee; Easter Parade; Heat Wave; I Never Had A Chance; Cheek to Cheek; Isn't This a Lovely Day; The Piccolino; Top Hat, White Tie and Tails; I'm Putting All My Eggs in One Basket; Let's Face the Music and Dance; I've Got My Love To Keep Me Warm; This Year's Kisses; Change Partners; God Bless America (received Congressional Medal of Honor--all proceeds from song to God Bless America Fund); It's A Lovely Day Tomorrow; Happy Holiday; White Christmas (Oscar-1942); This is the Army, Mr Jones; You Keep Coming Back Like a Song; Doin' What Comes Natur'lly; The Girl That I Marry; There's No

Business Like Showbusiness; You Can't Get a Guy With a Gun'; A Couple of Swells; It's A Lovely Day Today; You're Just In Love; Count Your Blessings.

(Special Tony-Award 1963). (Special Grammy-Award 1968).

BERLIN, Jeannie: Act. b. 1949. D of Elaine May. Films inc: On a Clear Day You Can See Forever; Getting Straight; Move; The Strawberry Statement; The Baby Maker; Bone; Why; Portnoy's Complaint; The Heartbreak Kid; Sheila Levine.

BERLIND, Roger S.: Prod. b. NYC, Jun 27, 1930. e. Princeton, AB. Former stockbroker. Bway inc: Rex; Music Is; Diversions and Delights; The Merchant; The 1940's Radio Hour; The Lady from Dubuque; Passione; Amadeus (Tony-1980); Sophisticated Ladies; Nine (Tony-1982); All's Well That Ends Well; The Real Thing (Tony-1984); The Rink; Joe Egg (Tony-reproduction-1985).

BERLINGER, Warren: Act. b. Brooklyn, Aug 31, 1937. e. Columbia U. Films inc: Teenage Rebel; Three Brave Men; Blue Denim; The Wackiest Ship in the Army; All Hands on Deck; Thunder Alley; Lepke; I Will. . .I Will. . .For Now; Harry and Walter Go to New York; The Shaggy D.A; The Magician of Lublin; The Cannonball Run.

TV inc: The Funny Side; Touch of Grace; The Most Wanted Woman; Sex and the Single Parent; Holy Moses; Crash Island; Quick and Quiet; Strike Force; Lily for President?; Small & Frye; The Other Woman.

Bway inc: Annie Get Your Gun; The Happy Time; Bernardine; Come Blow Your Horn; Take a Giant Step; Anniversary Waltz; Who's Happy Now; California Suite (tour).

BERMAN, Monty: Prod. b. London, 1913. Films inc: Jack the Ripper (& dir); The Flesh and the Fiends; Sea of Sand; Blood of the Vampire; The Hellfire Club; What a Carve Up.

TV inc: The Saint; Gideon's Way; The Adventurer.

BERMAN, Monty M.: Cost. b. London, 1912. Films inc: Doctor Zhivago; Tom Jones; Chitty Chitty Bang Bang; The Longest Day; My Fair Lady; Oliver; Battle of Britain; Where Eagles Dare; Cromwell; Patton; The Devils; Fiddler on the Roof; A Bridge Too Far; The Other Side of Midnight; Julia; The Seven Per Cent Solution; The Slipper and the Rose.

BERMAN, Pandro S.: Prod. b. Pittsburgh, Mar 28, 1905. Started as Asst Film Ed FBO (later RKO) 1923; asst to prod heads William Le Baron & David Selznick; became prod 1931; head of prodn RKO 1937-1940. Joined MGM 1940. Films inc: What Price Hollywood; Symphony of Six Million; Bachelor Mother; The Gay Divorcee; Of Human Bondage; Morning Glory; Roberta; Alice Adams; Top Hat; Winterset; Stage Door; Vivacious Lady; Gunga Din; Hunchback of Notre Dame; Ziegfeld Girl; Honky Tonk; Seventh Cross; National Velvet; Dragon Seed; Portrait of Dorian Grey; Love Affair; Undercurrent; Sea of Grass; The Three Musketeers; Madame Bovary; Father of the Bride; Father's Little Dividend; The Prisoner of Zenda; Ivanhoe; All the Brothers Were Valiant; Knights of the Round Table; Long, Long Trailer; Blackboard Jungle; Bhowani Junction; Something of Value; Tea and Sympathy; Brothers Karamazov; Reluctant Debutante; Butterfield 8; Sweet Bird of Youth; The Prize; A Patch of Blue; Justine; Move; George Stevens--A Filmmaker's Journey (Doc-int).

(Irving Thalberg Award 1976).

BERMAN, Shelley: Act. b. Chicago, Feb 3, 1926. Appears mostly in niteries. Films inc: The Best Man; The Wheeler Dealer; Divorce American Style; Every Home Should Have One.

TV inc: Brenda Starr; On Stage, America; Second City--25 Years In Revue.

(Grammy-Comedy Performance-1959).

BERNARD, Ed: Act. b. Philadelphia, Jul 4. e. Temple U. Films inc: Across 110th Street; The Hot Rock; Shaft; Julia; Blue Thunder.

TV inc: The Doctors; As the World Turns; Somerset; One Life to Live; Police Woman; The Last Song; Two Marriages.

Bway inc: Ceremonies in Dark Old Men; A Man's Man; Oedipus Rex; The Blacks.

BERNARD, Judd (Sherman Bernard Goldberg): Wri-Prod. b. Chicago, Jun 20, 1927. Films inc: Double Trouble; Point Blank; Blue; Fade In;

Negatives; The Man Who Had Power Over Women; Deep End; And Now for Something Completely Different; Glad All Over; The Marseilles Contract; Inside Out; The Class of Miss MacMichael; Enter the Ninja.

BERNARDI, Herschel: Act. b. NYC, Oct 20, 1923. Films inc: Green Fields; Miss Susie Slagle's; Stakeout on Dope Street; Irma La Douce; Murder by Contract; A Cold Wind in August; The George Raft Story; Love with the Proper Stranger; The Honey Pot; Almonds and Raisins (doc).

TV inc: A Hatful of Rain; Arnie; But I Don't Want to Get Married; No Place To Run; Sandcastles; The Miracle of Hannukah; The Million Dollar Face; Hail To The Chief.

Bway inc: The Goodbye People; Fiddler on the Roof (rev).

BERNAU, Christopher: Act. b. Santa Barbara, CA, Jun 2, 1940. e. UCSB. Bway inc: Lloyd George Knew My Father; The Jockey Club Stakes; The Boys in the Band; The Real Inspector Hound; Sweet Bird of Youth; The Passion of Dracula (off-Bway).

TV inc: Dark Shadows; Guiding Light; The Passion of Dracula (cable).

BERNHARD, Harvey: Prod. b. Seattle, WA, Mar 5, 1924. e. Stanford U. Films inc: Thomasine & Bushrod; The Mack; The Omen; Damien-Omen II; The Final Conflict; The Beast Within; Ladyhawke (exec prod); The Goonies (prod).

BERNHARDT, Melvin: Dir. b. Buffalo, NY, Feb 26. e. U of Buffalo; Yale U. Thea inc: Conerico Was Here To Stay; 110 in the Shade; Father Uxbridge Wants to Marry; A View From the Bridge; Who's Happy Now?; Honour & Offer; Homecoming; Cop-Out; The Effects of Gamma Rays On Man-In-The-Moon Marigolds; Early Morning; And Miss Reardon Drinks A Little; Other Voices, Other Rooms; The Killdeer; Da (Tony-1978); Crimes of the Heart; Dancing In The End Zone.

TV inc: Another World; Mr. Roberts.

BERNHEIM, Alain: Exec prod. b. Paris, Oct 5, 1922. Films inc: The Good Leviathan; Fun & Games; Yes, Giorgio; Racing With the Moon (prod).

BERNS, Seymour: Dir. Started as Radio Dir. Shows inc: Art Linkletter's House Party; Double or Nothing; Hollywood Barn Dance; Free for All.

TV inc: Art Linkletter's House Party; Meet Millie; The Red Skelton Show; Shower of Stars; My Friend Irma; Jack Benny Show; Gunsmoke; Lineup; Jan. 1981 named VP Polygram Television.

(Died May 16, 1982).

BERNSEN, Randy: Mus. b. Needham, MA, Jul 15, 1954. See Blood, Sweat & Tears.

BERNSTEIN, Alex: Exec. b. Mar 15, 1936. S of Cecil Bernstein. With Granada TV rental 1964; dir Granada TV Ltd 1970; m-dir 1971; chmn, 1975; deputy chmn Granada Group Ltd 1974; chmn since 1979.

BERNSTEIN, Charles: Comp. b. NYC. e. Juilliard School of Music; UCLA, BA. Films inc: The Honey Factor; Grasslands; Daddy's Deadly Darlings (The Pigs); White Lightning; Mr. Majestik; A Small Town in Texas; Viva Knievel!; Outlaw Blues; Love at First Bite; Foolin' Around; Coast to Coast; The Entity; Independence Day; Cujo; A Nightmare On Elm Street.

TV inc: Kate McShane; Look What's Happened To Rosemary's Baby; Leonard; Cops and Robin; Wild & Wooly; Thaddeus Rose and Eddy; Bogie; Scruples; Sadat; Generation; Secret Weapons; Malice In Wonderland.

Documentaries: The New Indians; Last Jews from Poland; Helen Keller Story; Soutine; Czechoslovakia.

BERNSTEIN, Elmer: Comp-Cond. b. NYC, Apr 4, 1922. e. NYU; Juilliard. Concert career 1939 to 1950, except for WW 2 service in Air Force; wrote scores for Army radio shows; two United Nations shows; debut as film composer 1950, Saturday's Hero.

Films inc: Sudden Fear; Man With the Golden Arm; To Kill a Mockingbird; Summer and Smoke; The Magnificent Seven; Walk on the Wild Side; Hud; Love with a Proper Stranger; Return of the Seven; Hawaii; Thoroughly Modern Millie (Oscar-1967); The Great Escape; The Carpetbaggers; True Grit; The Shootist; Bloodbrothers; Casey's Shadow; National Lampoon's Animal House; Saturn 3; Airplane; Going Ape!; Stripes; Heavy Metal; An American Werewolf in London; Honky Tonk Freeway; The Chosen; Genocide (doc); Five Days One Summer; Airplane II--The Sequel; Spacehunter--Adventures in the Forbidden Zone; Trading Places; Class; Prince Jack; Ghostbusters.

TV inc: Hollywood-The Golden Years; The Race for Space; D-Day; The Making of the President (Emmy-1963); Four Days in November; Julia; Owen Marshall; The Rookies; Little Women; Guyana Tragedy--The Story of Jim Jones; Moviola; Today's FBI (theme); Gulag.

Bway inc: Merlin.

Songs inc: Wherever Love Takes Me; Baby the Rain Must Fall; Walk on the Wild Side; My Wishing Doll; True Grit.

BERNSTEIN, Jack B.: Prod-exec. b. Brooklyn. e. Brooklyn College. Started as shipping clerk TV Graphics, later prodn mgr, studio mgr; East Coast prodn mgr Paramount commercial div; vp CPI Prodns; Aug. 1983, vp wldwde prodn Walt Disney Pictures. Films inc: (prodn mgr) American Dreamer; Silver Streak. (Asst dir) Hearts of the West. (Asso prod) The Fury; Butch and Sundance--the Early Years; The Other Side of Midnight; Six Pack; Unfaithfully Yours. (Exec prod) The Beast Within.

BERNSTEIN, Jay: Prod. b. Oklahoma City, OK, Jun 7, 1937. Films inc: Sunburn; Nothing Personal.

TV inc: Wild Wild West Revisited; More Wild Wild West; Mickey Spillane's Margin For Murder; Bring 'em Back Alive (exec prod); Mickey Spillane's Murder Me, Murder You (exec prod); More Than Murder (exec prod & act).

BERNSTEIN, Leonard: Cond-Comp. b. Lawrence, MA, Aug 25, 1918. e. Harvard, BA. Asst cond NY Philharmonic 1943-44; cond NY Symphony 1945-48; prof of music Brandeis U, 1951-56. Film scores inc: On the Waterfront.

Bway inc: On the Town; Fancy Free (ballet); Facsimile (ballet); Wonderful Town (Tony-1953); The Age of Anxiety (Ballet); Candide; West Side Story; Peter Pan; The Lark; The Firstborn; By Bernstein; 1600 Pennsylvania Avenue; (Special Tony-1969).

TV inc: Omnibus (Emmys-1956, 1957); Leonard Bernstein and the New York Philharmonic (Emmys-1960, 1961, 1976); New York Philharmonic Young People's Concerts (Emmy-1965); Beethoven's Birthday-A Celebration in Vienna (Emmy-1972); A Time There Was; The Kennedy Center Honors 1980; Bernstein/Beethoven; Leonard Bernstein's West Side Story.

Songs inc: New York, New York; Lonely Town; It's Love; Maria; Tonight; America.

(Grammys-(8)-Spoken Word-1961; Children's Recording, 1961-1962-1963); Classical Album of the year, 1964, 1977; Classical choral performance 1967; opera recording 1973).

BERNSTEIN, Sidney, Lord: Exec. b. Jan 30, 1899. Founder member of British Film Society 1924; founder of the Granada entertainment group, entertainment industry complex which started with theatres and now includes television, publising; originator (1927) of Saturday Morning film matinees for children; served as film adviser to British Ministry of Information during WW2; Chief of Film Section, Allied Forces in North Africa 1942-43, Allied Forces in Europe 1943-45.

Films inc: (as prod) Rope; Under Capricorn; I Confess.

Life peerage created 1969.

BERNSTEIN, Walter: Wri. b. NYC, Aug. 20, 1919. Films inc: Kiss the Blood Off My Hands; Heller in Pink Tights; Fail-Safe; The Money Trap; Paris Blues; The Molly Maguires; Semi-Tough; The Front (drawn from experience as blacklisted writer); The Betsy; An Almost Perfect Affair; Yanks; Little Miss Marker (& dir).

TV inc: Rich Boy.

BERRI, Claude (ne Langmann): Act-Dir-Prod. b. Paris, Jul 1, 1934. Began in films in 1966 prod & dir Le Poulet which won an Oscar for short subjects.

Films inc: The Two Of Us (dir); Marry Me, Marry Me (dir-act); Le Pistonne (dir); Le Cinema de Papa (prod-dir); Sex Shop (dir-sp); Male of the Century (dir-sp-act); The First Time (dir-sp); Tess (prod); Inspecteur la Bavure (Inspector Blunder) (prod); Je Vous Aime (prod-wri); Le Maitre d'Ecole (The Schoolmaster) (prod-dir-wri); Deux heures moins le quart avant Jesus Christ (A Quarter to Two Before Jesus Chirst) (prod); L'Africain (The African) (prod); Banzai (prod); L'Homme Blesse (The Wounded Man) (prod); Garcon!; Tchao Pantin (So Long, Stooge) (prod-dir); Scemo Di Guerra (Madman At War).

BERRY, Chuck: Mus-Singer-Sngwri. b. San Jose, CA, Jan 15, 1926. Creator of rock 'n' roll classics Roll Over Beethoven; Rock 'n' Roll Music; Johnny B. Goode. Credited with being the most influential figure in the development of rock music in the '50s and 60s.
Films inc: Rock, Rock, Rock; American Hot Wax.

BERRY, John: Dir. b. NYC, 1917. Films inc: Cross My Heart; From This Day Forward; Miss Susie Slagle's; Casbah; Tension; He Ran All The Way; The Great Lover; Je Suis un Sentimental; Tamango; Maya; Claudine; The Bad News Bears Go to Japan; Thieves.
TV inc: One Drink at a Time; Farewell Party; Mr. Broadway; Angel on my Shoulder; Sister, Sister (& prod).

BERRY, Ken: Act. b. Moline, IL, Nov 3. Films inc: Two for the Seesaw; Hello Down There; Herbie Rides Again; The Cat from Outer Space.
TV inc: Soldier Parade; Every Man Needs One; The Reluctant Heroes; Wake Me When the War is Over; The Ken Berry WOW Show; Mayberry RFD; F Troop; Texaco Star Theatre. . .Opening Night; Mama's Family.

BERRY, Richard: Act. b. France. e. Conservatoire National d'Art Dramatique. With the Comedie Francaise from 1972 to 1980. Films inc: La Gifle; Mon premier Amour (My First Love); Premier voyage; Vive la Mariee; L'Homme fragile (The Weak Man); Un assassin qui passe (A Passing Killer); Le crime d'amour; Le grand pardon (The Big Pardon); Une chambre en ville (A Room in Town); La balance (The Nark); La jeune Marie (The Young Bridegroom); Le Grand Carnaval (The Big Carnival); L'Addition (The Bill); Sauvage et Beau (Wild And Beautiful)(narr); Urgence (Emergency).

BERTINELLI, Valerie: Act. b. Wilmington, DE, Apr 23, 1960. TV inc: The Secret of Charles Dickens; One Day at a Time; Young Love, First Love; The Promise of Love; The Princess and the Cabbie; I Was A Mail Order Bride; The Seduction of Gina; Shattered Vows.
Films inc: C.H.O.M.P.S.

BERTOLUCCI, Bernardo: Dir. b. Parma, Italy, Mar 16, 1941. Films inc: The Grime Reaper; Before the Revolution; Once Upon A Time in the West (sp only); The Spider's Stratagem; The Conformist; Last Tango in Paris; 1900; Luna; La Tragedia Di Un Uomo Ridicolo (Tragedy of A Ridiculous Man); Sconcerto Rock (Rock Disconcert) (prod).

BERTOLUCCI, Giovanni: Prod. b. Parma, Italy, Jun 24, 1940. e. U of Parma. Films inc: Partner; The Spider's Stratagem; The Conformist; Conversation Piece; The Intruder; One Evening at Dinner; The Bishop's Room; Nene; Just As You Are; Theresa The Thief; The Innocent; Cose Come Sei; Luna; La Tragedia Di Un Uomo Ridicolo (Tragedy of A Ridiculous Man); La Chiave (The Key).
TV inc: Marco Polo (Venice & Middle East Sequences).

BERTOLUCCI, Giuseppe: Wri-Dir. b. Parma, Italy, Feb 27, 1947. B of Bernardo Bertolucci. Films inc: 1900; Luna; Berlinguer, I Love You; Lost and Found; Tu Mi Turbi (You Disturb Me) (wri); Non Ci Resta Che Piangere (Nothing Left To Do But Cry); Segreti Segreti (Secrets Secrets).
TV inc: Going, Coming.

BERUH, Joseph: Prod. b. Pittsburgh, PA, Sep 27, 1924. e. Carnegie Institute; Mellon U. Bway inc: Kittiwake Island; Promenade; Long Day's Journey Into Night; Godspell; Nourish the Beast; American Buffalo; Gypsy (London); Blasts and Bravos; An Evening with H L Mencken; Night that Made America Famous; Broadway Follies.
Films inc: The Wild Party; Blue Sunshine; He Knows You're Alone.

BESCH, Bibi: Act. b. Vienna, Feb 1, 1940. e. Studied with Herbert Berghof. D of Gusti Huber. Bway inc: Fame; The Chinese Prime Minister; Here Lies Jeremy Troy; Once For the Asking.
Films inc: The Pack; Hardcore; Meteor; The Promise; The Beast Within; Star Trek II--The Wrath of Khan; The Lonely Lady.

TV inc: The Secret Storm; Love Is A Many Splendored Thing; Somerset; Three Times Daley; Victory at Entebbe; Peter Lundy and the Medicine Hat Stallion; Backstairs at the White House; Transplant; Secret of Midland Heights; Tough Girl; Death of a Centerfold--The Dorothy Stratten Story; McClain's Law; Skyward Christmas; Insight/God's Guerrillas; The Hamptons; Secrets of a Mother And Daughter; The Day After; Hear Me Cry; Lady Blue.

BESSELL, Ted: Act. b. Flushing, NY, Mar 20, 1935. Studied with Sanford Meisner at Neighborhood Playhouse, NY. Films inc: The Outsider; Lover, Come Back; Captain Newman, M.D.; Don't Drink the Water.
TV inc: Your Money or Your Wife; That Girl; It's A Man's World; The Ted Bessell Show; Breaking Up Is Hard to Do; Good Time Harry; The Acorn People; Hail To The Chief.

BESSIE, Alvah: Wri. b. NYC, 1904. e. Columbia. Films inc: Northern Pursuit; The Very Thought of You; Hotel Berlin, Objective, Burma!; Smart Woman. Career halted when he was imprisoned for contempt of Congress after refusing to testify before the House Committee on Un-American Activities.

BEST, James: Act. b. Corydon, IN, Jul 26, 1926. Films inc: Winchester 73; Commanche Territory; The Cimarron Kid; Apache Drums; The Caine Mutiny; Come Next Spring; The Naked and the Dead; Shenandoah; First to Fight; Gaby; The Rack; Sounder; Ode to Billy Joe; The End (& prod); Hooper; Rolling Thunder.
TV inc: The Runaway Barge; Savages; The Dukes of Hazzard.

BETHUNE, Zina: Act. b. NYC, Feb 17, 1950. Films inc: Sunrise at Campobello; Who's That Knocking At My Door?; Tuesday's Child; August, September.
TV inc: The Nurses; The Guiding Light; Young Dr Malone; Love of Life.
Thea inc: Most Happy Fella; Nutcracker Suite.

BETTGER, Lyle: Act. b. Philadelphia, Feb 13, 1915. e. AADA. Films inc: No Man of Her Own; Union Station; All I Desire; The Greatest Show on Earth; Gunfight at OK Corral; Nevada Smith; The Fastest Guitar Alive; The Seven Minutes.
TV inc: Grand Jury; Court of Last Resort.
Bway inc: John Loves Mary; Love Life; Eve of St. Mark; M Station-Hawaii.

BEY, Turhan: Act. b. Vienna, Mar 30, 1920. US screen debut, 1941. Films inc: Footsteps in the Dark; Drums of the Congo; The Mummy's Tomb; Arabian Nights; Ali Baba and the Forty Thieves; Dragon Seed; The Climax; A Night in Paradise; Out of the Blue; Adventures of Casanova; Song of India; Prisoners of the Casbah; Stolen Identity (prod).

BEYMER, Richard: Act-Cin. b. Avoca, IA, Feb 21, 1939. Films inc: (Act) Indiscretions of an American Wife; So Big; Diary of Anne Frank; High Time; West Side Story; Bachelor Flat; Five Finger Exercise; Hemingway's Adventures of a Young Man; The Longest Day; The Stripper; Innerview (& dir); Cross Country.
TV inc: God in the Dock (act); Insight/Resurrection (act); The Soup Man (cin); Who Loves Amy Tonight (cin); Girl On The Edge Of Town (cin); A Step Too Slow (cin-ed); To Climb A Mountain (cin); The Trouble With Grandpa (cin); Insight/When Heroes Fall (cin); Leadfoot (cin); Hang Tight, Willy Bill (cin); Clay Feet (cin); Paper Dolls (act); Generation (act).

BEZZERIDES, A.I.: Wri. Films inc: Juke Girl; Northern Pursuit; Thieves Highway; Sirocco; On Dangerous Ground; Holiday for Sinners; Beneath the 12-Mile Reef; Track of the Cat; A Bullet for Joey; Kiss Me Deadly; The Angry Hills; The Jayhawkers.
TV inc: Bonanza; Rawhide; Great Adventures; Destry; The Virginian; Big Valley; William Faulkner--A Life On Paper.

BICK, Jerry: Prod. b. NYC, Apr 26, 1923. e. U of GA; OH State U; Columbia U; Sorbonne. Films inc: Michael Kohlhaas (1969 in Czechoslovakia); The Long Goodbye; Thieves Like Us; Russian Roulette; Farewell My Lovely; The Big Sleep; Against All Odds (exec prod); Swing Shift.

BIKEL, Theodore: Act-Singer. b. Vienna, May 2, 1924. e. RADA. Stage debut 1943, Habimah Theatre, Israel. On London stage 1948, You Can't Take It With You. Films inc: The African Queen; Never Let Me Go; The Little Kidnappers; A Day to Remember; The Pride and the Passion; The Enemy Below; The Defiant Ones; I Want to Live; A Dog of Flanders; My Fair Lady; Sands of Kalahari; The Russians Are Coming, The Russians Are Coming; My Side of the Mountain; Nobody Loves a Drunken Indian; The Little Ark; Two Hundred Motels; Prince Jack.

Bway: Tonight In Samarkand; The Lark; The Rope Dancers; The Sound of Music; Cafe Crown; Pousse-Cafe; Fiddler on the Roof.

TV inc: The Eternal Light; Look Up and Live; Who Has Seen the Wind?; Diary of Anne Frank; Hallmark Hall of Fame; Killer by Night; The Return of the King (voice).

BILL, Tony: Prod-Act. b. San Diego, CA, Aug 23, 1940. e. Notre Dame, BA, MA. Films inc: (act) Come Blow Your Horn; None But the Brave; You're a Big Boy Now; Never a Dull Moment; Ice Station Zebra; Castle Keep; Shampoo; Las Vegas Lady; Heart Beat. (Prod): Deadhead Miles; The Sting *(Oscar*-1973); Hearts of the West; Harry & Walter Go to New York (exec prod); Boulevard Nights (exec prod); The Little Dragons (exec prod); Going in Style; My Bodyguard (dir only); Six Weeks (dir only); Love Thy Neighbor (dir only).

TV inc: (act) Are You in the House Alone?; Portrait of an Escort; Freedom; Washington Mistress; Running Out; Full House (dir).

BILLINGSLEY, Peter: Act. b. NYC, 1972. TV inc: Real People; Massarati and the Brain; Memories Never Die; The Hoboken Chicken Emergency.

Films inc: If I Ever See You Again; Paternity; Honky Tonk Freeway; Death Valley; A Christmas Story.

BILLINGTON, Ken: Light dsgn. b. White Plains, NY., Dec. 29, 1946. Bway inc: Don't Bother Me I Can't Cope; The Visit; Chemin de Fer; Holiday; Bad Habits; Hosanna; Love For Love; The Rules of the Game; The Skin Of Our Teeth; Sweet Bird Of Youth; Checking Out; Fiddler On The Roof; She Loves Me; Side By Side By Sondheim; Knickerbocker Holiday; Ethel Merman and Mary Martin Together On Broadway; Some Of My Best Friends; Do You Turn Somersaults; On The Twentieth Century; Working; Sweeney Todd; Lerner and Loewe, A Very Special Evening; The Madwoman Of Central Park West; But Never Jam Today; Happy New Year; Perfectly Frank; Copperfield; Wally's Cafe; My Fair Lady; A Talent For Murder; Blues In The Night; A Doll's Life; Foxfire; Shirley MacLaine on Broadway; Play Memory; End Of The World; Home Front; Grind.

Operas inc: Ashmedai; L'Histoire d'un Soldat; The Pearl Fishers; Silverlake; Ernani; Candide; Madame Butterfly; Lucia di Lammermoor; Turandotte (Vienna); Cosi Fan Tutte.

BILLINGTON, Kevin: Dir. b. England, Jun 12, 1934. e. Cambridge. Thea inc: The Birthday Party; Bloody Neighbors; The Caretakers; Emigres; The Homecoming.

Films inc: Interlude; The Rise and Rise of Michael Rimmer; Light At the Edge of the World; Reflections (& prod).

TV inc: Tonight; And No One Could Save Her; Echoes of the Sixties; Once Upon A Time is Now -- The Story of Princess Grace; Henry VIII; The Jail Diary of Albie Sachs; The Good Soldier.

BILSON, Bruce: Dir. b. NYC, May 19, 1928. e. UCLA, BA. TV inc: Hawaii 5-0; Barney Miller; Get Smart *(Emmy*-1968); BJ and the Bear; Pleasure Cove; The Dallas Cowboys Cheerleaders; The Halloween That Almost Wasn't; The Ghosts of Buxley Hall; Harper Valley PTA; The Fall Guy; Finder Of Lost Loves; Half Nelson; Gidget's Summer Reunion.

Films inc: The North Avenue Irregulars.

BINDER, Steve: Prod-Dir-Wri. b. Los Angeles. e. USC. TV inc: Soupy Sales; A Funny Thing Happened on the Way to the White House; Hulabaloo; America; Liza Minelli Special; Elvis Presley Special; Mac Davis Show; Shields & Yarnell; Barry Manilow Special *(Emmy*-1977); Olivia Newton-John; Star Wars Holiday Special; Dorothy Hamill Special; Diana; Legends of The West--Truth and Tall Tales; An Innocent Love (exec prod); Ringling Bros and Barnum & Bailey Circus; Debby Boone's One Step Closer; Stanley The Ugly Duckling (exec prod); The 113th Edition Ringling Bros And Barnum & Bailey Circus; A Special Eddie Rabbitt; Blondes Vs. Brunettes (exec prod-co-dir); Elvis--One

Night With You (prod-dir)(cable); Ringling Bros. And Barnum & Bailey Cirucs (1985).

Films inc: Give 'em Hell Harry!

BING, Rudolph, Sir: Opera Mgr. b. Vienna, Austria, Jan 9, 1902. Opera and concert agent in Germany, 1921-1933; became GM Glyndebourne Festival, England, 1934 to 1939; artistic dir Edinburgh Int'l Festival 1947-1949; GM Metropolitan Opera NY, 1950-1972.

TV inc: A Time There Was.

BINNS, Edward: Act. b. PA. Films inc: Fail-Safe; Twelve Angry Men; Compulsion; Patton; The Americanization of Emily; Judgement at Nuremberg; Lovin' Molly; Night Moves; Oliver's Story; The Man You Love To Hate (narr); The Verdict.

Bway inc: Command Decision; Detective Story; Caligula; The Caine Mutiny Court Martial; A Touch of the Poet; Ghosts.

TV inc: The Power Within; Battles - The Murder That Wouldn't Die; FDR - The Last Year.

BIRCH, Patricia: Chor. Originally dancer with Martha Graham Dance Company, later with NYC Light Opera Company. Thea inc: Up Eden; Fireworks; The Me Nobody Knows; F. Jasmine Addams; The Real Inspector Hound; After Magritte; A Little Night Music; Candide; Diamond Studs; Grease; Over Here!; Pacific Overtures; Music Is.

Films inc: Zoot Suit; Grease 2 (& dir).

BIRKIN, Jane: Act. b. England, Dec 12, 1946. On stage in London in bit parts in Carving A Statue; Passion Flower Hotel. Films inc: The Knack; Blow-Up; Don Juan; Slogan; Swimming Pool; Je t'aime moi non plus; Le Diable au Coeur; The Wild Goose Chase; Projection Privee; Love at the Top; Death on the Nile; Melancholy Baby; A Bout du Bout de Banc; La Miel (Honey); Egon Schiele--Excess and Punishment; La Fille Prodigue (The Prodigal Daughter); Evil Under the Sun; Nestor Burma, Detective de Choc; (Nestor Burma, Shock Detective); Circulez Y'a Rien a Voir (Move Along, There's Nothing to See); L'Ami de Vincent (A Friend of Vincent); Le garde du corps (The Bodyguard); La Pirate; L'Amour Par Terre (Love On The Ground); Dust; Leave All Fair.

BIRNBAUM, Bob: Dir-Prod. b. NYC, Dec. 2, 1938. TV inc: (Dir) Love American Style; The Odd Couple; Shirley (& Prod); Visions of Christmas Past. (Prod) You Gotta Start Somewhere; Better Late Than Never; The Phoenix (Supv Prod).

BIRNEY, David: Act. b. Washington, DC, Apr 23, 1939. e. Dartmouth, AB; UCLA, MA. On stage Lincoln Center Repertory Theatre; NY Shakespeare Festival; The American Shakespeare Festival. Bway inc: Amadeus.

Films inc: Caravan to Vaccares; Trialby Combat; Au Revoir. . .A Lundi; Oh, God! Book II.

TV inc: Bridget Loves Bernie; Serpico; The Adams' Chronicles; Greatest Heroes of the Bible; High Midnight; Ohms; Mom, the Wolfman and Me; I Think I'm Having A Baby; The Five Of Me; Jacqueline Susann's Valley of the Dolls 1981; St. Elsewhere; Master of the Game; Glitter; Missing--Have You Seen This Person?

BIRNEY, Meredith Baxter: Act. b. Los Angeles, Jun 21, 1947. Films inc: Ben; Bittersweet Love; All the President's Men.

TV inc: The Interns; Bridget Loves Bernie; The Imposter; The Night That Panicked America; Target Risk; The Stranger Who Looks Like Me; Family; Little Women; The Family Man; Beulah Land; The Two Lives of Carol Leitner; Family Ties; Take Your Best Shot; Missing--Have You Seen This Person?; The Rape Of Richard Beck.

Bway inc: Guys and Dolls.

BIROC, Joseph: Cin. b. NYC, Feb 12, 1903. Films inc: Bwana Devil; The Tall Texan; The Ride Back; Home Before Dark; Hitler; The Devil at Four O'Clock; Bullet for a Badman; Hush, Hush Sweet Charlotte; The Flight of the Phoenix; The Russians Are Coming, The Russians Are Coming; The Killing of Sister George; Whatever Happened to Aunt Alice?; Too Late the Hero; The Grissom Gang; The Organization; Blazing Saddles; The Longest Yard; The Towering Inferno *(Oscar*-1974); Hustle; The Dutchess and the Dirtwater Fox; The Choirboys; Beyond The Poseidon Adventure; Airplane; All the Marbles; Hammett; Airplane II--The Sequel.

TV inc: Wonder Woman; Honky Tonk; The Moneychangers; Washington D C; Scruples; Kenny Rogers as the Gambler; Desperate Lives; Casablanca (Emmy-1983); The Jerk, Too; Hell Town; A Death In California.

BISHOP, Joey (Joseph Abraham Gottlieb): Act. b. NYC, 1918. Films inc: The Naked and the Dead; Ocean's Eleven; Sergeants Three; Texas Across the River; A Guide for the Married Man; Who's Minding the Mint?; Valley of the Dolls.

TV inc: The Joey Bishop Show. Bway inc: Sugar Babies.

BISHOP, Julie: Act. b. Denver, CO, Aug 30, 1914. On screen as Jacqueline Wells from 1923 in Maytime; Tarzan the Fearless; Happy Landing; Paid to Dance; Coronado; Torture Ship; The Girl in 313. Since 1941 billed as Julie Bishop. Films inc: Northern Passage; Rhapsody in Blue; Sands of Iwo Jima; Westward the Women; The High and the Mighty; The Big Land.

BISHOP, Kelly (Carole Bishop): Act. b. Colorado Springs, CO, Feb 28, 1944. e. American Ballet Theatre School. Started as dancer in Radio City corps de ballet. Bway inc: Golden Rainbow; Promises, Promises; On the Town (dancer only); Rachel Lily Rosenblum; A Chorus Line (Tony-featured-1976); Vanities.

Films inc: An Unmarried Woman; O'Hara's Wife.

BISHOP, Stephen: Singer-Comp. b. San Diego, CA, Nov 14, 1951. Films inc: Phantom of the Paradise; Kentucky Fried Movie; Sgt Pepper's Lonely Hearts Club Band; National Lampoon's Animal House; The China Syndrome (comp).

BISOGLIO, Val: Act. b. NYC, May 7, 1926. Films inc: Saturday Night Fever; The Frisco Kid.

TV inc: The Mary Tyler Moore Show; All in the Family; The Marcus-Nelson Murders; Quincy; Johnny Garage.

Bway inc: Wait Until Dark.

BISSELL, Whit: Act. b. NYC, Oct 25, 1909. e. U of NC, BA. Films inc: (more than 85) Destination Tokyo; Another Part of the Forest; It Should Happen to You; The Young Stranger; I Was A Teenage Frankenstein; The Time Machine; Hud; Seven Days in May; Covenant with Death; Airport; Pete and Tillie; Soylent Green; Psychic Killer; Casey's Shadow; Conspiracy to Kill Lincoln.

More than 350 TV roles inc: Andersonville Trial; A Tattered Web; Cry Rape; Mark Twain's America - Abe Lincoln: Freedom Fighter; Walking Tall.

BISSET, Jacqueline: Act. b. Weybridge, England, Sep 13, 1944. Model. Film debut in The Knack. Films inc: Arriverdci Baby; The Capetown Affair; Cul de Sac; Casino Royale; Two for the Road; The Sweet Ride; The Detective; Bullitt; Airport; The Grasshopper; The Thief Who Came To Dinner; Day for Night; End of the Game; The Life And Times of Judge Roy Bean; The Thief Who Came To Dinner; Murder on the Orient Express; St. Ives; The Deep; The Greek Tycoon; Sunday Woman; Secrets; Who's Killing The Great Chefs of Europe; Together; When Time Ran Out; Amo Non Amo; Inchon; Rich and Famous; Class; Under the Volcano; Observations Under the Volcano (doc); Notes From Under the Volcano (doc).

TV inc: Pavarotti and Friends; John Ritter, Mr. T and Jacqueline Bisset--Going Back Home; Anna Karenina; Forbidden.

BIXBY, Bill: Act. b. San Francisco, Jan 29, 1934. Stage debut Detroit Civic Theatre production The Boy Friend. TV inc: Dobbie Gillis; Joey Bishop Show; My Favorite Martian; The Courtship of Eddie's Father; The Magician; Shirts/Skins; The Incredible Hulk; How To Survive The 70's and Maybe Bump Into A Little Happiness; Bill Bixby And The Adventures of a Young Magician; Murder Is Easy; Book of Lists (host); I've Had It Up To Here; Against The Odds (cable); Wizards and Warriors (dir); Goodnight Beantown (& exec prod); The Best of Times (dir); Walter (dir); Dreams (dir); Detective In The House (dir); International Airport.

Films inc: Lonely Are The Brave; Irma La Douce; Yum Yum Tree; The Apple Dumpling Gang; Kentucky Fried Movie.

Bway inc: The Paisley Convertible; Sunday in New York.

BLACK, David: Prod-Dir. b. NYC, Nov 20, 1931. e. Harvard U, BA. Performed in operetta, opera, musical comedy, 1951-61. (Dir):As You Like It; The Killing of Sister George; The Typists; The Children's

Hour; Girl in My Soup; Two for the Seasaw; The Advertisement; Eros in Exile; Augusta; Rosewood; The Last Minstrel Show; Spotlight; Cabaret; The Guys in the Truck. (Prod): Look We've Come Through; The Aspen Papers; Semi-Detached; Cambridge Circus; Ready When You Are C.B.; The Knack; The Ides of March; The Impossible Years; Those That Play the Clowns; The Natural Look; To Clothe the Naked; George M!; Fire!; Paris Is Out; Salvation; W.C.; A Funny Thing Happened On The Way to the Forum; Lysistrata; Fearless Frank.

BLACK, Karen: Act. b. Park Ridge, IL, Jul 1, 1942. Bway: We're Civilized; The Uncommon Denominator; Happily Never After; On a Clear Day You Can See Forever; After the Fall; Come Back To The 5 & Dime, Jimmy Dean, Jimmy Dean.

Films inc: Five Easy Pieces; Easy Rider; A Gunfight; Born to Win; Portnoy's Complaint; You're A Big Boy Now; Law and Disorder; Airport 1975; Family Plot; Capricorn One; In Praise of Older Women; Killer Fish; The Last Word; The Squeeze; Graset Stunger (The Grass Is Singing); Chanel Solitaire; Can She Bake A Cherry Pie (& mus); Separate Ways; Growing Pains; Martin's Day; Savage Dawn.

TV inc: Power; Where The Lady's Go; Confessions of a Lady Cop.

BLACK, Noel: Dir. b. Jun 30, 1940. Films inc: Skaterdater (The American Boy) (short); Pretty Poison; Mirrors (Marianne); A Man, A Woman and A Bank (A Very Big Withdrawal); The Golden Honeymoon; Private School; Mischief (wri-exec prod); Deadly Intentions.

TV inc: The Other Victim; The Electric Grandmother; Prime Suspect; Happy Endings; Quarterback Princess.

BLACKMAN, Honor: Act. b. London, 1926. Films inc: Fame Is the Spur; Diamond City; The Rainbow Jacket; Breakaway; A Night to Remember; The Square Peg; Goldfinger; The Secret of My Success; Life at the Top; Moment to Moment; A Twist of Sand; Shalako; The Last Grenade; The Virgin and the Gypsy; Fright; To the Devil a Daughter; The Cat and the Canary.

Thea inc: The Exorcism; The Sound of Music; On Your Toes.

TV inc: Lace; The First Olympics-Athens 1896.

BLACKSTONE, Milton Wri-Prod. b. NYC, May 5, 1924. e. U of Miami; NYU. Thea Agent & personal mgr 1948-66. Prod-wri Guy Lombardo New Years Eve Specials 1960-65; Arthur Murray Show 1955-64; prod Comedians' Golf Classic since 1961; Andy Williams Golf Special 1977.

(Died Oct. 29, 1983).

BLACKTON, Jay S.: Comp-Arr. (Jacob Schwartzdorf):b. NYC, Mar 25, 1909. e. Juilliard. Musical dir for Bway prodns inc: Oklahoma!; Annie Get Your Gun; Miss Liberty; Call Me Madam; New Faces of 1956; Redhead; Mr President; Sherry; George M; Two By Two; Rex; Revivals of Oklahoma!; Finian's Rainbow; Showboat.

Films inc: Oklahoma (Oscar-1955); Guys and Dolls. Named to recording Academy Hall of Fame for dir orig cast album of Oklahoma!.

BLAIN, Gerard: Act-Dir. b. Paris, Oct 23, 1930. Films inc: (act) Avant le deluge; Escalier de service; Le Temps des Assassins; Crime et Chatiment; Desire Takes the Men; Les Mistons; Le Beau Serge; Charlotte et son Jules; Les Cousins; Les Dauphins; Hatari!; La Frenesie; Les Vierges; La Bonne Soupe;Via Veneto; Il Generale; Joe Caligula; Un Homme de Trop; Ripley S'Amuse; La Guepe. (Dir): Les Amis (& co-sp); Le Pelican (& sp-act); un enfant dans la foule (& co-sp); A Second Wind (& sp); The Rebel (& sp).

BLAINE, Vivian (nee Stapleton): Act. b. Newark, NJ, Nov 21, 1924. Singer with various bands, 1937-39, then nightclubs; 20th-Fox contract, 1942. Appeared in Guys and Dolls, Broadway, London stage. Films inc: He Married His Boss; Guys and Dolls; Greenwich Village; Nob Hill; State Fair; Skirts Ahoy; Public Pigeon No. 1; The Dark; Parasite; I'm Going To Be Famous.

TV inc: The Cracker Factory; Fast Friends; Sooner or Later.

BLAIR, Betsy (nee Boger): Act. b. NYC, Dec 11, 1923. Films inc: The Guilt of Janet Ames; A Double Life; Another Part of the Forest; The Snake Pit; Kind Lady; Marty; The Halliday Brand; All Night Long; A Delicate Balance.

TV inc: Steel Hour; Ford Theatre; Kraft; Philco.

Bway inc: Beautiful People; Richard II.

BLAIR, Janet (Martha Lafferty): Act. b. Blair, PA, Apr 23, 1921. Films inc: Three Girls About Town; Two Yanks in Trinidad; Broadway; My Sister Eileen; Something to Shout About; Tonight and Every Night; Gallant Journey; The Fabulous Dorseys; The Fuller Brush Man; Public Pigeon Number One; Boys' Night Out; Night of the Eagle; The One and Only Genuine Original Family Band.

TV inc: The Smith Family.

BLAIR, Linda: Act. b. Westport, CT, 1959. Model for children's apparel and TV commercials. Films inc: The Exorcist; Airport 1975; The Heretic; Wild Horse Hank; Roller Boogie; Hell Night; Chained Heat; Savage Streets; Night Patrol; Red Heat.

TV inc: Born Innocent.

BLAKE, Amanda (Beverly Neill): Act. b. Buffalo, NY, Feb 20, 1929. Films inc: Duchess of Idaho; Stars in My Crown; Lili; Sabre Jet; A Star Is Born; About Mrs. Leslie; High Society.

TV inc: Exposure; Cavalcade of America; Gunsmoke.

BLAKE, Eubie (James Hubert Blake): Comp. b. Baltimore, MD, Feb 7, 1883. Began career at 15 playing pianos in Baltimore bordellos; joined traveling medicine show at 17; following year made NY debut in cast of musical In Old Kentucky; teamed with Noble Sissle, first as songwriting team with Sissle handling lyrics, later as vaudeville act touring U.S., Europe; later teamed with Andy Razaf as songwriting team; in 1946 began studying Schillinger system of Composition at NYU, completing four year course in 30 months; career was basis of Broadway musical Eubie, 1979.

Bway inc: Shuffle Along; Blackbirds of 1929; Singing the Blues (cond only); Swing It; C.B. Cochran's Revue; Will Morrisey's Folies Bergere; Brown Skin Models of 1954; Eubie.

Songs inc: Love Will Find a Way; Memories of You; You Were Meant For Me; Strange What Love Will Do; Baby Mine; I'm Just Wild About Harry; You're Lucky To Me; Lindy Hop; Green Pastures; Lovin You the Way I Do.

(Died Feb 12, 1983).

BLAKE, Robert (Michael Gubitosi): Act. b. Nutley, NJ, Sep 18, 1934. Child actor in Our Gang comedies, also Little Beaver in Red Ryder series. Later films inc: Andy Hardy's Double Life; The Horn Blows at Midnight; Treasure of Sierra Madre; Revolt in the Big House; The Purple Gang; Town Without Pity; The Greatest Story Ever Told; In Cold Blood; Tell Them Willie Boy Is Here; Corky; Electra Glide in Blue; Second Hand Hearts; Coast to Coast.

TV inc: Baretta (Emmy-1975); Joe Dancer; The Youngest Victim--America's Sexually-Exploited Child (host-narr); Of Mice and Men (& exec prod); Blood Feud; Murder One - Dancer 0 (& exec prod); Hell Town (& wri); The Heart Of A Champion--The Ray Mancini Story.

BLAKE, Yvonne: Cost desgn. Films inc: Nicholas and Alexandra (Oscar-1971); The Four Musketeers; The Eagle Has Landed; Superman; Escape to Athena; Flesh & Blood.

BLAKELY, Colin: Act. b. Bangor, County Down, Northern Ireland, Sep 23, 1930. Stage debut Ulster Group, Belfast. London debut 1959. Joined Royal Shakespeare Co. Stratford-on-Avon, 1961. Thea inc: Enjoy; All My Sons; Royal Hunt of the Sun; The Crucible; Judgement; Lovers Dancing; Other Places.

Films inc: Murder on the Orient Express; A Man For All Seasons; The Pink Panther Strikes Again; Saturday Night and Sunday Morning; The Informers; Young Winston; Equus; All Things Bright and Beautiful; The Big Sleep; Nijinsky; Meetings With Remarkable Men; The Dogs of War; Loophole; Evil Under the Sun; Red Monarch.

TV inc: The Day Christ Died; Vikings; Anthony and Cleopatra; Laurence Olivier Presents King Lear.

BLAKELY, Susan: Act. b. Germany, Sep 7, 1948. e. U of TX. Started as commercial model. Screen debut 1972, Savages. Films inc: The Lords of Flatbush; The Towering Inferno; Report to the Commissioner; Shampoo; Capone; Dreamer; The Concorde - Airport '79.

TV inc: Rich Man, Poor Man; Secrets; Make Me An Offer; A Cry For Love; The Oklahoma City Dolls; The Bunker; Will There Really Be A Morning?; International Airport.

BLAKEMORE, Michael: Dir. b. Sydney, Australia, Jun 18, 1928. e. Sydney U; RADA. Former actor. Thea inc: (London) A Day in the Death of Joe Egg (& Bway); The Strange Case of Martin Richter; The Resistible Rise of Arturo Ui; The National Health; Widowers' Houses; Forget-me-not-Lane; Long Day's Journey Into Night (prod); The Front Page (prod); Macbeth (prod); Design for Living; Grand Manoeuvres; Knuckle; Don's Party; Engaged (prod); Plunder (prod); Noises Off (Bway); Benefactors.

Films inc: Privates on Parade.

TV inc: The Last Bastion (act).

BLAKLEY, Ronee: Act. b. Caldwell, ID, 1946. e. Stanford U; Juilliard. Recording artist, niteries. Films inc: Nashville; Renaldo & Clara; The Driver; Good Luck Miss Wyckoff; The Baltimore Bullet; Lightning Over Water (Nick's movie) (& mus); Nightmare On Elm Street.

TV inc: The Oklahoma City Dolls.

BLALACK, Robert C: SFX Dir. b. Panama Canal Zone, Dec 12, 1948. e. Pomona Coll, BA; Cal Arts, MFA. Films inc: Star Wars (Oscar-1977); China Syndrome; Meteor; Blues Brothers; Airplane!; 9 to 5; Altered States; Wolfen; Zapped!; Get Crazy.

TV inc: Fantasy Island; Cosmos; The Day After (Emmy-1094)

BLANC, Mel: Voice specialist. b. San Francisco, May 30, 1908. Voice of Warner Bros cartoon characters, Bugs Bunny, Porky Pig, Daffy Duck, since 1937. TV inc: (voice) The Bugs Bunny Show; The Porky Pig Show; The Munsters; Flintstones; The Bugs Bunny Mothers Day Special; Daffy Duck's Easter Show; Murder Can Hurt You! (act); Bugs Bunny's Bustin' Out All Over; Daffy Duck's Thanks-For-Giving Special; Bugs Bunny Mystery Special; Bugs Bunny-- All American Hero; Bugs Bunny's Mad World of Television; Yogi Bear's All-Star Comedy Christmas Caper.

Occasional cameo appearance in films inc: Neptune's Daughter; Kiss Me Stupid; Buck Rogers in the 25th Century; Looney, Looney Looney Bugs Bunny Movie (voice); Bugs Bunny's 3rd Movie--1001 Rabbit Tales (voice); Daffy Duck's Movie: Fantastic Island (voice).

BLANCO, Ray: Dist-Prod. b. Havana, Cuba, Oct 31, 1955. e. CCNY; NYU. Exec dir, Independent Film Critics Assn, 1973-75; Chmn/Admin. Bauer Int'l, Art Film Distributors USA, 1975; 1977, co-prod, The Red Dress; 1978, prod, The Lonely Road.

BLANE, Sally (Elizabeth Jung): Act. b. Salt Lake City, UT, 1910. Sis of Loretta Young. Films inc: Sirens of the Sea; Rolled Stockings; The Vagabond Lover; Once a Sinner; Ten Cents a Dance; I Am a Fugitive from a Chain Gang; Advice to the Lovelorn; The Silver Streak; One Mile from Heaven; Charlie Chan at Treasure Island; A Bullet for Joey.

BLANK, Tom: Dir. b. Minneapolis, MN, Dec 29, 1938. e. Northwestern U. TV inc: Bionic Woman; American Girls; Spiderman; Dinky Hockey; Harris & Company-Choices.

BLATT, Daniel H: Prod. Resident counsel ABC Pictures; exec vp Palomar Pictures; partnered with Edgar J Scherick; ind prod since 1978. Films inc: I Never Promised You A Rose Garden; The American Success Company; The Howling; Independence Day; Cujo.

TV inc: Raid on Entebbe; Circle of Children; Zuma Beach; Thou Shalt Not Commit Adultery; The Children Nobody Wanted; Thou Shalt Not Kill; Three Eyes; Night Eyes; Sadat; V--The Final Battle (exec prod); V (Series).

BLATTY, William Peter: Wri-Prod. b. NYC, Jan 7, 1928. Films inc: The Man from the Diners' Club; A Shot in the Dark; John Goldfarb, Please Come Home; What Did You Do in the War, Daddy?; Gunn; The Great Bank Robbery; Darling Lili; The Exorcist (& prod) (Oscar-1973-wri); The Ninth Configuration (prod-dir-wri).

BLAUSTEIN, Julian: Prod. b. NYC, May 30, 1913. e. Harvard. Reader, Universal, 1935; story ed. 1936-38; headed story dept. MCA, 1938-39; story ed. Paramount, 1939-41; U.S. Signal Corps, 1941-46; edit. supv Selznick, 1946-48; 20th-Fox as prod., 1949; exec. prod. 1951-52. Films inc: Broken Arrow; Mister 880; Day the Earth Stood Still; Don't Bother to Knock; Desiree; The Racers; The Wreck of the Mary Deare; The Four Horsemen of the Apocalypse, Khartoum.

BLECKNER, Jeffrey: Dir. b. Brooklyn, NY. e. Amherst, BA; Yale, MFA. Dir at the Long Wharf; Yale. Bway inc: The Basic Training of Pavlo

Hummel; Sticks and Bones. Other thea inc: Secret Affairs of Mildred West; Death and Life of Jesse James.

Films inc: A Sunday Dinner.

TV inc: Sticks and Bones; Another World; Doc; Guilding Light; The Stockard Channing Show; Willow B--Women in Prison; Knots Landing; King's Crossing; Daddy, I'm Their Mama Now; Hill Street Blues *(Emmy-1983)*; Ryan's Four; When Your Lover Leaves; Concealed Enemies *(Emmy-1984)*; Things Are Looking Up. RTCA DBF

BLEES, Robert: Wri-Prod. b. Lathrop, MO, Jun 9, 1922. e. Dartmouth. Films inc: Paid in Full; The Glass Web; Slightly Scarlet; Magnificent Obsession; Autumn Leaves; Night Games; Savage Harvest.

TV inc: Climax; Westinghouse Playhouse; Alfred Hitchcock Presents; Zane Grey Theater; Bonanza; Bus Stop; Combat!; Harry O; The Class of '65; Quincy; Columbo.

BLEIFER, John: Act. b. Zawiercie, Poland, Jul 26, 1901. Films inc: We Americans; Captured; Black Fury; Les Miserables; Charlie Chan at Monte Carlo; Mr. Moto Takes A Vacation; The Mark of Zorro; In Our Town; The Juggler; The Hook; F.I.S.T.; The Frisco Kid.

TV inc: Highway To Heaven.

BLESSED, Brian: Act. b. Yorkshire, England. e. Bristol Old Vic. Thea inc: Incident at Vichy; Oedipus; Cats. TV inc: Z Cars; The Three Musketeers; Son of a Man; I Claudius; The Master of Ballantrae; The Last Days of Pompeii.

Films inc: Barry Lyndon; Man of La Mancha; The Trojan Women; A Last Valley; Henry VIII; Flash Gordon; High Road To China; The Hound of the Baskervilles.

BLIER, Bernard: Act. b. France, 1916. Films inc: Hotel du Nord; Quai des Orfevres; Dedee d'Anvers; L'Ecole Buissoniere; The Wanton; Souvenirs Perdus; Les Grandes Familles; A Question of Honor; Breakdown; Catch Me a Spy; Cher Victor; Daydreamer; Serie Noire; Cold Cuts; The Hypochondriac; Passione D'Amore (Passion of Love); Petrole, Petrole; Ca N'Arrive Qu'a Moi (It Only Happens To Me); Cuore (Heart); La Due Vite di Mattia Pascal (The Two Lives Of Mattia Pascal); Scemo di Guerra (Madman At War).

BLIER, Bertrand: Prod-Dir. b. Paris, Mar 14, 1939. S of Bernard Blier. Researched contemporary cinema verite film project for prod Andre Michelin and launched directorial career with the film, Hitler, Connais Pas which featured on-camera interviews with 11 French teenagers.

Films inc: La Grimace (short); Breakdown; Going Places; Femmes Fatales; Calmos; The Body of My Enemy; Get Out Your Handkerchiefs; Buffet Froid (& sp); Beau-Pere (Stepfather) (& sp); La Femme de mon pote (My Buddy's Girl) (& sp); Notre Histoire (Our Story) (dir-sp).

BLOCH, Charles B: Exec Prod. b. NYC, Mar 31, 1915. e. Columbia U; CCNY. Pres Globe Photos until 1972 when formed Charles Publishing Co, Inc; West Coast editorial rep Bantam books. Films inc: (exec prod) The Fog. TV inc: (exec prod) The House on Garibaldi Street.

BLOCH, Richard L: Exec. b. Pontiac, MI, Jun 12, 1929. e. U of Chicago, BS. On boards of Center Theatre Group; American Ballet Theatre; American Film Institute; became director Filmways 1969, elected chmn, CEO 1971.

BLOCH, Robert: Wri. b. Chicago, Apr 5, 1917. Films inc: Psycho; The Cabinet of Caligari; Strait Jacket; The Night Walker; The Psychopath; The Deadly Bees; The Torture Garden; The House That Dripped Blood.

TV inc: The Cat Creature; The Dead Don't Die; A Man Called Satan.

BLOCK, David Greenberg: Exec. b. Johannesburg, S Africa, Mar 21, 1936. To Australia, 1964. Investment banker; part time commissioner, Australian Film Commission.

BLOOM, Arthur: Dir-Prod. b. NYC, Apr 19, 1940. e. NYU, BS. TV inc: 60 Minutes; Democratic & Republican National Conventions; Carter-Ford Presidential Debate from San Francisco; Tricia Nixon tour of White House; CBS Election Night, 1974-76-78; CBS Reports; The

American Assassins (series); Walter Cronkite's Universe; 60 Minutes.

BLOOM, Claire: Act. b. London, Feb 15, 1931. Stage debut at Playhouse, Oxford, 1947. Screen debut in Limelight, 1951. Films inc: Innocents in Paris; Richard III; Alexander The Great; The Brothers Karamazov; Look Back in Anger; The Chapman Report; The Spy Who Came In From The Cold; The Illustrated Man; A Doll's House; Islands in the Stream; Clash of the Titans; Deja Vu.

TV inc: Anna Karenina; Wuthering Heights; An Imaginative Woman; In Praise of Love; Backstairs At The White House; Hamlet; Misunderstood Monsters (voice); Brideshead Revisited; Cymbeline; Separate Tables (cable); The Ghost Writer; Ellis Island; The Life And Death Of King John; Florence Nightingale.

Thea inc: A Streetcar Named Desire; The Innocents.

BLOOM, John: Flm Ed. b. England, 1935. Script reader for Rank before becoming ed. Films inc: The Party's Over; Funeral in Berlin; The Last Safari; The Lion In Winter; The Last Valley; Travels With My Aunt; The Six Wives of Henry VIII; The Ritz; Who'll Stop the Rain; The French Lieutenant's Woman; Gandhi *(Oscar-1982)*; Betrayal.

TV inc: The Glass Menagerie; Masada; Mistral's Daughter.

BLOOM, Verna: Act. b. Lynn, MA, Aug 7, 1939. e. Boston U. Films inc: Medium Cool; The Hired Hand; High Plains Drifter; Badge 373. National Lampoon's Animal House; Honkytonk Man.

Bway inc: Marat/Sade.

TV inc: Playing For Time.

BLOOMFIELD, George: Dir. b. Montreal, Canada. e. McGill U. Started as act; later dir for Nat'l Film Board, Canada and CBC. TV inc: Riel; Hedda Gabler; Love on the Nose; Saturday, Sunday, Monday; Paradise Lost; Second City.

Films inc: Jenny (& co-sp); To Kill A Clown; Child Under A Leaf (& sp); Nothing Personal; Double Negative.

BLOSSOM, Roberts: Act. Bway inc: The Physicists. Films inc: Deranged; Slaughterhouse Five; Handle With Care; Hospital; The Great Gatsby; Close Encounters of the Third Kind; Escape From Alcatraz; Resurrection; Reuben, Reuben; Christine; Flashpoint.

TV inc: Mourning Becomes Electra; Another World; Strangers in the Homeland; Family Reunion; Johnny Belinda; Noon Wine.

BLOUNT, Lisa: Act. b. AR. e. U of AR. Films inc: 9/30/55; Dead and Buried; An Officer and a Gentleman.

TV inc: Mickey Spillane's Murder Me, Murder You; Stormin' Home.

BLUES BROTHERS, THE: (See BELUSHI, John and AYKROYD, Dan).

BLUHDORN, Charles G: Exec. b. Sep 20, 1926. e. CCNY; Columbia. After Air Force Service, entered export import business, launched his own firm in 1949; 1956 acquired Michigan Plating and Stamping Co.; 1958 merged it with a Houston automotive parts distribution company to form Gulf & Western Industries; merged with Paramount Oct 19, 1966, With G&W as the surviving corporation and Bluhdorn as Chmn and CEO.

(Died Feb 19, 1983).

BLUHDORN, Paul: Exec. S of the late Charles G. Bluhdorn. Joined Paramount Aug. 1980 as director film acquisition; June, 1983, VP prodn/acquisition; Oct. 1983, Sr VP Prodn, Par Motion Picture division.

BLUM, Harry N: Prod. b. Cleveland, OH, Oct 3, 1932. e. U of MI, BA, LLB. Films inc: The Bluebird; Diamonds; At The Earth's Core; Obsession; Skateboard; The Magician of Lublin.

BLUM, Stanford: Prod-Dir. b. Baltimore, MD, Jul 8, 1940. e. U of MD. Film inc: (shorts) The Thrill of Victory, the Agony of the Feet; Kathy Rigby; Joan Baez; Burton Cummings; Foreigner; Circle of Sound.

BLUMENTHAL, Ann (nee Jacobs): Prod. b. St Louis, MO, Apr 24, 1942. TV inc: (Asso prod) The Patriots; Uncommon Women and Others; mus specials for PBS. Series prod for WNET int'l co-prodns inc the plays of Shakespeare. Also prod Tartuffe; Mourning Becomes

Electra; The Sorrows of Gin; O Youth and Beauty!; Big Blonde; The Shady Hill Kidnapping; The File On Jill Hatch; Alice In Wonderland.

BLUMOFE, Robert F: Prod. b. NYC. e. Columbia Coll, AB; Columbia U, JD. Director, The American Film Institute, West; resd Jan '82 to return to indie prodn. Films inc: Yours, Mine & Ours; Pieces of Dreams; Bound for Glory.

BLYE, Allan: Wri-Prod. b. Winnipeg, Canada, Jul 19, 1937. Worked in Canadian TV as singer, wri, act; to Hollywood 1967 as wri for Smothers Brothers Comedy Hour (Emmy-1969); also wri for Glen Campbell Summer Series, Elvis Presley's 1st TV special, two Andy Williams specials, Petula Clark's 1st TV special. From 1967-70, joined with Chris Beard to prod: The Sonny and Cher Show; The Sonny Comedy Review; Lil' Abner; Wow; The American Bag; Ray Stevens (summer series); That's My Mama. In 1975, partnered with Bob Einstein and produced Van Dyke and Company (Emmy-1977); Lola Falana specials; Redd Foxx Show.

BLYTH, Ann: Act. b. Mt Kisco, NY, Aug 16, 1928. Films inc: Chip off the Old Block; The Merry Monahans; Mildred Pierce; Brute Force; Killer McCoy; Another Part of the Forest; Mr. Peabody and the Mermaid; Once More My Darling; The Great Caruso; I'll Never Forget You; The World in His Arms; One Minute to Zero; Rose Marie; The Student Prince; Kismet; Slander; The Buster Keaton Story; The Helen Morgan Story.

BOARDMAN, True: Wri-Act-Dir. b. Seattle, WA, Oct 25, 1909. e. UCLA, AB; Occidental Coll, MA. Started as child actor; later wrote for radio, screen. Films inc: (as wri) Son of the Navy; Ride 'em Cowboy; Keep 'em Flying; Pardon My Sarong; Between Us Girls; Arabian Nights; The Painted Hills.
TV inc: Colgate Theatre; Revlon Playhouse; Donna Reed Show; Perry Mason; My Three Sons; Ironside; The Virginian; Bonanza.

BOASBERG, Charles: Exec. b. Buffalo, NY, Aug 20, 1906. e. Cornell U. Started with MGM in 1927; then salesman for RKO, 1930; named gen sales mgr, dir, RKO, 1952; joined Par, 1955, in charge of worldwide sales of The Ten Commandments; gen sales mgr, p WB Dist Corp, 1958; domestic gen sales mgr & vp Par Dist Corp, 1962; p, Par Film Dist Corp, 1963; vp Par Pictures, Inc, 1967; vp National General Corp, 1968; P, 1969. In 1974 formed Boasberg-Goldstein, consultants to film producers, now Charles Boasberg, Inc.

BOBKER, Lee R: Dir. b. NYC, Jul 19, 1925. e. NYU, BA. Over 600 docus. TV inc: I, Leonardo--A Journey of the Mind (& prod).

BOCHCO, Steven: Prod-Wri. b. NYC, 1945. e. Carnegie Tech, MFA. Won MCA fellowship while in college, joined U-TV as apprentice. TV inc: (wri & story ed) Name of the Game; Columbo; McMillan and Wife; Delvecchio (wri-prod); Paris (Exec prod); Richie Brockelman (co-crea); Turnabout (wri); Invisible Man (wri); Vampire (wri); Hill St. Blues (crea-prod-wri) (Emmys-prod & wri-1981, 1982; prod-1983, 1984); ; Every Stray Dog and Kid (exec prod); Bay City Blues (exec prod-wri-crea). (March, 1985, asked to leave Hill Street Blues, moved to 20th Fox TV on exclusive three-year-deal).
Films inc: Silent Running (co-wri).

BOCHNER, Hart: Act. b. LA, CA.,1956. e. UC San Diego. S of Lloyd Bochner. Films inc: Islands in the Stream; Breaking Away; Terror Train; Rich and Famous; The Wild Life; Supergirl.
TV inc: Haywire; John Steinbeck's East of Eden; Having It All; Callahan; The Sun Also Rises.

BOCHNER, Lloyd: Act. b. Canada, Jul 29, 1924. Films inc: Drums of Africa; The Night Walker; Sylvia; Tony Rome; Point Blank; The Detective; The Horse in the Gray Flannel Suit; Tiger By the Tail; Ulzana's Raid; The Man in the Glass Booth; Hot Touch; The Lonely Lady; Louisiane.
TV inc: A Fire in the Sky; Greatest Heroes of the Bible; The Immigrants; The Best Place To Be; The Golden Gate Murders; Mary and Joseph--A Story of Faith; Dynasty; Rona Jaffe's Mazes & Monsters; Hotel; Manimal.

BOCK, Jerry: Comp. b. New Haven, CT, Nov 23, 1928. e. U of WI. Bway inc: Catch A Star (songs); Mr Wonderful; The Ziegfeld Follies;

The Body Beautiful; Fiorello!; She Loves Me; Fiddler on the Roof (Tony-1965); The Apple Tree; The Rothschilds.
TV inc: The Admiral Broadway Revue; The Show of Shows; The Mel Torme Show; The Kate Smith Hour.
(Grammy-cast album-1963).

BODARD, Mag: Prod. b. Sweden, 1927. Films inc: The Umbrellas of Cherbourg; The Young Girls of Rochefors; Le Bonheur; Mouchette; Benjamin; Le Viol; La Chinoise; Peau d'Ane; The Best Way.

BOEHM, Karl: Act. b. Germany, 1928. Films inc: Peeping Tom; Too Hot to Handle; The Magnificent Rebel; The Four Horsemen of the Apocalypse; The Wonderful World of the Brothers Grimm; Come Fly with Me; The Venetian Affair.

BOEHM, Sydney: Wri. b. Philadelphia, Apr 4, 1908. e. Lehigh U. Films inc: High Wall; The Undercover Man; Side Street; Mystery Street; Union Station; When Worlds Collide; The Savage; The Big Heat; The Atomic City; The Secret of the Incas; Rogue Cop; Black Tuesday; Violent Saturday; The Tall Men; Hell on Frisco Bay; The Revolt of Mamie Stover; Harry Black; A Woman Obsessed (& prod.); Seven Thieves (& prod.); Shock Treatment; Sylvia; Rough Night in Jericho.

BOETTICHER, Budd (Oscar Boetticher): Prod-Dir-Wri. b. Chicago, Jul 29, 1916. e. OH State U. Former Bullfighter, served as tech dir, Blood and Sand, 1941; became feature dir, 1944. Films inc: The Missing Juror; Assigned to Danger; Sword of D'Artagnan; The Bullfighter and the Lady (& sp-prod); Red Ball Express; Horizons West; City Beneath The Sea; East of Sumatra; The Magnificent Matador (& sp); Decision at Sundown; Buchanan Rides Alone; Ride Lonesome; The Rise and Fall of Legs Diamond; Arruza; A Time for Dying.

BOFFETY, Jean: Cin. b. France. Films inc: Act of the Heart; Journey; Cesar and Rosalie; Thieves Like Us; A Simple Story; Un Mauvais Fils (A Bad Son); Les Uns et les Autres (The Ins and The Outs); Espion Leve-Toi (Rise Up, Spy); Edith et Marcel; Garcon!; Canicule (Dog Day).

BOGARDE, Dirk (Derek van den Bogaerde): Act. b. London, Mar 28, 1921. Films inc: Quartet (Alien Corn episode); So Long at the Fair; Penny Princess; Doctor in the House; The Sea Shall Not Have Them; The Spanish Gardener; A Tale of Two Cities; The Doctor's Dilemma; Libel; Song Without End; Victim; I Could Go On Singing; The Servant; Doctor in Distress; The High Bright Sun; King and Country; Darling; Accident; Our Mother's House; Sebastion; The Fixer; Justine; Oh What a Lovely War; The Damned; Death in Venice; Le Serpent; The Night Porter; Permission to Kill; Providence; A Bridge Too Far; Despair.
TV inc: The Little Moon of Alban; Blythe Spirit; Upon This Rock; The Patricia Neal Story; Schindler (narr).

BOGART, Paul: Dir. b. NYC, Nov 21, 1919. Films inc: Marlowe, Halls of Anger; Skin Game; Cancel My Reservations; Class of '44; Mr Ricco; The Three Sisters; Oh, God! You Devil.
TV inc: Ages of Man; The Defenders (Emmy-1965); Mark Twain Tonight; The Final War of Ollie Winter; Dear Friends (Emmy-1968); The House Without a Christmas Tree; Look Homeward Angel; The Country Girl; Double Solitaire; Tell Me Where It Hurts; Shadow Game (Emmy-1970); All in the Family (Emmy-1978); The Adams Chronicles; The Shady Hill Kidnapping; Weekend; Mama Malone (& exec prod).

BOGDANOV, Michael: Dir. b. London, Dec 15, 1938. e. Trinity College, Dublin; Sorbonne. Asso dir Royal Shakespeare Company 1970; dir The Young Vic 1978; asso dir The National Theatre, 1980. Thea inc: (London) The Bootleg Gentleman; A Comedy of the Changing Years; Taming of the Shrew; Bartholomew Fair; The Canterbury Tales; Faust; Shadow of a Gunman; The Romans In Britain; The Mayor of Zalamea; Uncle Vanya.
TV inc: Focus on Britain (panelist).

BOGDANOVICH, Peter: Prod-Dir. b. Kingston, NY, Jul 30, 1939. Actor summer stock 1955-58. Prod off-Bway plays, The Big Knife; Once in a Lifetime.
Films inc: Targets (dir-act-sp); The Last Picture Show (dir-sp); What's Up Doc? (dir-prod-sp); Paper Moon (dir-prod); Daisy Miller

(dir-prod); At Long Last Love (dir-prod-sp); Nickelodeon (dir-prod-wri); Saint Jack (dir-act-sp); They All Laughed (dir-wri); Bonjour Monsieur Lewis (doc); The City Girl (exec prod); Mask (dir).

Books inc: Orson Welles; Howard Hawks; Alfred Hitchcock; John Ford; Fritz Lang in America; Allan Dwan--The Last Pioneer; Pieces of Time--Peter Bogdanovich on the Movies.

BOHEM, Endre: Wri. b. Hungary. e. U of Vienna. Films inc: Night Has a Thousand Eyes; The Redhead and the Cowboy; Alias Nick Beal; Streets of Laredo; Thirst; House with a Thousand Candles; Two Wise Maids; Little Orphan Annie; Lord Jeff; Crime of the Century; Twin Stars; Bengazi.

TV inc: Revlon Mirror; Ford Theatre; Rawhide.

BOISSETT, Yves: Dir. b. Paris, Mar 14, 1939. Worked as an assistant to Jean-Pierre Melville, Vittorio De Sica and Rene Clement; location scout for James Bond films; made directorial debut with Coplan Saves His Skin.

Films inc: Cran D'Arret (& co-sp); Angel's Leap (& co-sp); The French Conspiracy; R.A.S.; Rape of Innocence; The Purple Taxi; La Cle Sur La Porte; La Femme Flic (& co-sp); Allons Z'Enfants (The Boy Soldier) (& sp); Espion Leve-Toi (Rise Up, Spy) (& sp); Le Prix Du Danger (The Prize Of Peril) (& sp); Canicule (Dog Day) (& sp).

BOLEN, Lin L: Prod. b. Benton, IL, Mar 23, 1941. e. CCNY. Began as prodn asst, 1961, working on several hundred commercials, docs in various capacities; exec in chg prodn for ABC 1968; NBC vp daytime programs, 1971-1976 then formed indie prodn company; Nov 1981, VP Crea Aff Intermedia.

TV inc: Twiggy in New York; Twiggy in Los Angeles; Twiggy in London; Stravinsky's Requiem to Martin Luther King with NY City Ballet; Living With the Lennon Sisters; Crisis in America on Welfare (asso prod-wri); Good Against Evil; Christmas Miracle in Caulfield, USA; Stumpers; Back Talk; W.E.B.; Golden Gate; Farrell For The People.

BOLGER, Ray: Act. b. Dorchester, MA, Jan 10, 1906. Stage debut with a musicomedy repertory company touring New England. Screen debut in The Great Ziegfeld, 1936; own TV show, ABC, 1954-55. Films inc: Rosalie; Wizard of Oz; Where's Charley?; April in Paris; Babes in Toyland; Four Jacks and a Jill; Look For The Silver Lining; The Entertainer; Just You And Me Kid; The Runner Stumbles; That's Danc ing!

Bway inc: Scandals of 1931; Life Begins at 8:40; On Your Toes; By Jupiter; All American; Come Summer; Where's Charley? (Tony-1949); Three to Make Ready.

BOLKAN, Florinda: Act. b. 1945. Films inc: Candy; The Damned; Investigation of a Citizen; The Last Valley; Romance; The Island; A Man to Respect; Hearts and Minds; Royal Flash; Assassination in Sarajevo; Manaos; Acqua e Sapone (Soap and Water).

TV inc: The Word.

BOLLINGER, Henri: Pub-prod. b. Aug 9, 1929. e. Columbia U; UCLA. With Loew's Theatres as pub; 1953 switched to film and tv prodn pub; prod since 1970. Films inc: (prod) Fools; Mary, Mary, Bloody Mary.

TV inc: Imus, Plus; Circus Spectacular; World Series of Poker; Ernie Kovacs--Television's Original Genius (Asso prod).

BOLOGNA, Joseph: Act-Plywri. b. Dec 30, 1936. H of Renee Taylor. (Writes in collaboration with wife).

Bway inc: Lovers and Other Strangers (& wri); It Had To Be You (& wri).

Films inc: Honor Thy Father; Cops and Robbers; Lovers and Other Strangers (& wri); Made for Each Other (& wri); Mixed Company; The Big Bus; Torn Between Two Lovers; Chapter Two; My Favorite Year; Blame it on Rio; The Woman In Red.

TV inc: (wri): Acts of Love and Other Comedies (Emmy-1973); Paradise; Calucci's Department (created); The American Dream Machine; Drink, Drank, Drunk; A Cry For Love; Lovers and Other Strangers (& prod); One Cooks, The Other Doesn't; The Joe Piscopo Special (cable).

BOLOGNINI, Mauro: Dir. b. Italy, 1923. Worked as asst to Yves Allegret, Mario Zampi, Luigi Zampi; directed films for tv.

Feature films inc: I Cavalieri della Regina; Gli Inamorati; Marisa la Civetta; Giovanni Mariti; La Viaccia; La Corruzione; Madamigella di Maupin; Un Bellissimo Novembre; Metello; Down the Ancient Staircase; Libera, Amore mio; The Inheritance; Dove Va In Vacanza (When Are You Going on Vacation?); The True Story of Camille.

TV inc: The Charterhouse of Parma (cable).

BOLT, Robert: Wri. b. Manchester, England, Aug 15, 1924. e. Manchester U. Films inc: Lawrence of Arabia; Doctor Zhivago (Oscar-1965); A Man For All Seasons (Oscar-1966); Ryan's Daughter; Lady Caroline Lamb (& dir); The Bounty.

Plays inc: The Critic and the Heart; Flowering Cherry; The Tiger and the Horse; A Man for All Seasons (Tony-1962); Brother and Sister; State of Revolution.

BOMBECK, Erma: Wri-TV pers. b. Dayton, OH, Feb 21, 1927. e. U Dayton, BA. Syndicated columnist. TV inc: Good Morning, America; Maggie (wri-exec prod); Texaco Star Theatre Presents Bob Hope in "Who Makes The World Laugh'; S.O.S..Secrets of Surviving.

BOND, C(hristopher) G(odfrey): Plywri. b. Sussex, England, 1945. e. Central School for Speech and Drama; Drama Center. Plays inc: Sweeney Todd, The Demon Barber of Fleet Street; Downright Hooligan; Tarzan's Last Stand; Judge Jeffrys; Under New Management; Scum; Death, Destruction and Dirty Washing.

BOND, Edward: Wri. b. London, Jul 18, 1934. Plays inc: The Pope's Wedding; Saved; Narrow Road to the Deep North; Early Morning; Black Mass; Passion; The Sea; Bingo; Scenes on Bread and Love; Stone; The Woman; The Worlds.

Films inc: Blow-Up; Laughter in the Dark.

BOND, Sudie: Act. b. Louisville, KY, Jul 13, 1928. e. Intermont Coll; NYU. Studied dance with Jose Limon, Martha Graham, Merce Cunningham. Bway inc: Waltz of the Toreadors; Grease; A Piece of Blue Sky; The Sandbox; The American Dream; Come Back to the 5 & Dime, Jimmy Dean, Jimmy Dean.

Films inc: Cold Turkey; Where Lilies Bloom; A Thousand Clowns; They Might Be Giants; Enormous Changes at the Last Minute; I Am the Cheese; Silkwood; Swing Shift; Johnny Dangerously.

TV inc: Philco Playhouse; Mary Hartman, Mary Hartman; The Greatest Man in the World; Jolly Corner; Flo.

(Died Nov. 10, 1984)

BONDARCHUK, Sergei: Act-Dir. b. Russia, Sep 25, 1920. Films inc: (act) The Young Guard; Taras Shevchenko; A Night of The Gold Star; The Grasshopper; An Unfinished Story; Othello; The Soldiers Marched On; It Was Night in Rome; The Battle of the Neretva; Uncle Vanya; Dr. Evans' Silence; Such High Mountains; The Choice of a Goal; The Fate of a Man (& dir); War and Peace; Waterloo (& dir); They Fought for Their Motherland (& dir; co-sp); The Steppe (& dir-sp); Mexico In Flames (dir-sp); Red Bells--I've Seen the Birth of the New World (dir-sp).

BONDELLI, Phil: Dir. b. Chicago, Dec 10, 1927. e. Crane Coll. TV inc: The Mikado; First Nixon-Kennedy Debates; Something Special; Jack Carter Special; Mod Squad; The Rookies; Six Million Dollar Man; The Bionic Boy; The Bionic Woman; SWAT; Charlie's Angels; Switch; CHiPS.

BONERZ, Peter: Act-Dir. b. Portsmouth, NH, Aug 6, 1938. e. Marquette U. Films inc: Funnyman; Medium Cool; Catch-22; Jennifer on My Mind; Fuzz; The Committee; Nobody's Perfekt.

TV inc: (act): Mirror, Mirror; Bob Newhart Show; The Bastard; 9 to 5; Your Place Or Mine. (Dir) Sysznyk (all episodes); Love, Natalie; G.I.'s; Park Place; The Two Of Us; In Security (cable); High Five; Back Together; Suzanne Pleshette is Maggie Briggs; E.R.; It's Your Move.

Thea inc: The White Murder Case.

BONNER, Frank Act. (Frank Woodrow Boers, Jr.).b. Little Rock, AR, Feb 28, 1942. Films inc: Hearts of the West; Las Vegas Lady; The Equinox; The Hoax; Stop Me.

TV inc: The Lives of Jenny Dolan; Fer-de-Lance; The Amazing Howard Hughes; WKRP in Cincinnati; The Facts of Life Goes To Paris; Sutters Bay; No Man's Land.

BONO, Sonny (Salvatore Bono): Singer-Act. b. Detroit, Feb 16, 1935. Started writing songs at age 16. Entered record business with Specialty Records as apprentice prod Became asst to Phil Spector, rock music prod and did background singing. Recorded albums with then wife Cher and formed nightclub act with her.

Films inc: Good Times; Chastity; Escape To Athena; Airplane II--The Sequel.

TV: Sonny & Cher Comedy Hour; Sonny Comedy Revue; Murder in Music City; The Top of the Hill; Rockin' & Rollin' With Phil Spector.

BONSALL, Joe (See Oakridge Boys).

BOOKE, Sorrell: Act. b. Buffalo, NY, Jan 4, 1930. e. Columbia U; Yale U. Bway inc: The White Devil; Moby Dick; A Month in the Country; The Sleeping Prince; Nature's Way; Heartbreak House; Finian's Rainbow; Fiorello!; The White House; Come Live With Me; Night.

Films inc: Gone Are the Days; Fail Safe; Black Like Me; Lady in a Cage; Up the Down Staircase; Slaughterhouse Five; The Take; The Iceman Cometh; What's Up Doc?; Bank Shot; The Other Side of Midnight; Freaky Friday; Special Delivery; Devil Times Five.

TV inc: Greatest Heroes of the Bible; The Dukes of Hazzard.

BOOKMAN, Robert: Exec. b. Los Angeles, Jan 29, 1947. e. UC Berkeley; Yale Law School. VP in charge of worldwide prodns, ABC Motion Pictures; Dec 1983, exec vp in chg wldwde prodn Columbia Pictures.

BOONE, Ashley: Exec. b. Springfield, MA, Dec 8, 1938. e. Brandeis U, BA. Dir of Foreign Adv & pub, UA, 1963-68; dir Foreign Adv & Pub, Cinema Center Films, 1968-69; asst to ChmnB, Motown Records, 1970; moved to 20th Century-Fox Film Corp in 1972; named sr vp domestic mktg & dist, 1979; resigned Jan. 1980 to form own marketing firm, ABJ Enterprises; also vp mktg The Ladd Co; Dec. 1983, resd to become P Columbia Pictures Distribution & Marketing Group.

BOONE, Debby: Singer. b. Hackensack, NJ, Sep 22, 1956. D of Pat Boone. TV inc: The Gift of the Magi; Pat Boone and Family Christmas Special; Hope, Women and Song; Debby Boone--The Same Old Brand New Me; The Magic of David Copperfield; A Country Christmas; Opryland: Night of Stars and Future Stars; Bob Hope's All-Star Celebration Opening the Gerald R. Ford Museum; Perry Como's French-Canadian Christmas; Debbie Boone's One Step Closer; Christmas In Washington; Sins of the Past.

Bway inc: Seven Brides For Seven Brothers.

(Grammys-new artist-1977; Inspirational-1980).

BOONE, Pat: Singer-Act. b. Jacksonville, FL, Jun 1, 1934. e. Columbia U, Magna Cum Laude with a BS. Winner of Ted Mack's TV Amateur Show, joined Arthur Godfrey TV Show, 1955. Recordings inc: Ain't That A Shame; I Almost Lost My Mind; Friendly Persuasion; Love Letters in the Sand; April Love; Tutti Frutti; Speedy Gonzalez; Days of Wine & Roses; Moody River. Films inc: Bernadine; April Love; Mardi Gras; Journey to the Center of the Earth; All Hands on Deck; State Fair; The Main Attraction; The Yellow Canary; The Horror of it All; The Perils of Pauline; The Cross and the Switchblade. Author: Twixt Twelve and Twenty; Between You & Me and the Gatepost.

TV inc: The Miracle of America; Pat Boone and Family Christmas Special; Bob Hope Laughs With The Movie Awards; The Christmas Legend of Nashville (host).

BOORMAN, John: Dir. b. London, 1933. Films inc: Catch Us If You Can; Point Blank; Hell In the Pacific; Leo the Last; Deliverance; Zardoz (& sp); Exorcist II - The Heretic; The Long Shot (act); Excalibur (& prod-wri); Angel (exec prod); Dream One (Nemo) (prod); The Emerald Forest (& prod).

TV inc: The Hard Way (exec prod).

BOOTH, James (nee Geeves-Booth): Act. b. London, Dec 19, 1933. e. RADA. Member of Old Vic Company 1956-57. Thea inc: King Lear; Comedy of Errors; A Thousand Clowns; The Entertainer; The Tempest.

Films inc: The Trials of Oscar Wilde; The Hellions; Sparrows Can't Sing; Zulu; Robbery; The Bliss of Mrs. Blossom; Macho Callahan; Revenge; Brannigan; Airport '77; It's Not The Size That Counts; The Jazz Singer; Zorro, The Gay Blade.

TV inc: The Ruffians; The Great Gold Bullion Robbery; Stray Cats and Empty Bottles; Hotline; The Cowboy And The Ballerina.

BOOTH, Margaret: Film ed. b. Los Angeles, 1898. Films inc: Why Men Leave Home; Husbands and Lovers; The Gay Deceiver; Bringing Up Father; Mysterious Lady; Bridge of San Luis Rey; Redemption; The Lady of Scandal; A Lady's Morals; New Moon; The Southerner; Susan Lenox; Strange Interlude; Smilin' Through; Peg O' My Heart; Riptide; The Barretts of Wimpole Street; Mutiny on the Bounty; Romeo and Juliet; Camille; A Yank at Oxford; supv film ed: The Owl and the Pussycat; To Find a Man; Fat City; The Way We Were; Funny Lady; The Sunshine Boys; Murder by Death; The Goodbye Girl; California Suite; The Cheap Detective (assoc prod); Chapter Two (& prod); The Toy (asso prod); The Slugger's Wife (exec prod).

(Honorary Oscar-1977).

BOOTH, Shirley: Act. b. NYC, Aug 20, 1907. Stage debut 1919 with Poli Stock Co., Hartford, CT.; starred on radio in Duffy's Tavern for several years.

Bway inc: Hell's Bells; Laff That Off; The Mask and the Face; After Such Pleasures; Three Men on a Horse; Philadelphia Story; My Sister Eileen; Tomorrow The World; Goodbye, My Fancy *(Tony-*supp-1949); Come Back Little Sheba *(Tony-*1950); A Tree Grows in Brooklyn; Time of the Cuckoo *(Tony-*1953); Desk Set; Loot to The Lilies; Hay Fever (rev); toured in Harvey; Mourning in a Funny Hat.

Films inc: Come Back Little Sheba *(Oscar-*1952); About Mrs. Leslie; Hot Spell; The Matchmaker. Starred on radio in Duffy's Tavern for several years.

TV inc: Perle Mesta Story; Hazel (from 1961-68) *(Emmys-*1962 & 1963).

BOOTHE, Powers: Act. b. Snyder, TX, 1949. Bway inc: Richard III; Lone Star. TV inc: Skag; The Plutonium Incident; Guyana Tragedy--The Story of Jim Jones *(Emmy-*1980); A Cry For Love; Philip Marlowe-Private Eye (cable).

Films inc: Southern Comfort; A Breed Apart; Red Dawn; The Emerald Forest.

BORCHERS, Cornell (Cornelia Bruch): Act. b. Heydekrug, Germany, Mar 16, 1925. Films inc: The Big Lift; The Divided Heart; Never Say Goodbye; Istanbul; Oasis; Alone Together.

BORETZ, Alvin: Wri. Films inc: My Pleasure Is My Business; Brass Target.

TV inc: Follow the North Star; Young Dr. Kildare; Medical Center; Murder By Proxy; The Rookies; Swiss Family Robinson; Kojak; ADA; Spider Man; Stedman; Crisis At Sun Valley; The Night The Bridge Fell Down; Master of the Game.

BORGE, Victor: Perf. b. Copenhagen, Denmark, Jan 3, 1909. Child piano prodigy at age 10. Later became humorous concert artist. Wrote and starred in musical plays and films in Denmark. Fled Nazis in 1941, came to U.S. Concert and nightclub tours. One-man Broadway show. TV variety shows. TV inc: Tonight Scandinavia.

BORGNINE, Ernest: Act. b. Hamden, CT, Jan 24, 1918. In stock companies; on Bway in Harvey; Mrs. McThing. Film debut in Whistle at Eaton Falls. Films inc: Vera Cruz; Bad Day at Black Rock; Marty *(Oscar-*1955); Run For Cover; Catered Affair; Dirty Dozen; Bunny O'-Hare; The Revengers; Convoy; Crossed Swords; Ravagers; The Greatest; The Double McGuffin; The Black Hole; When Time Ran Out; High Risk; Escape From New York; Deadly Blessing; Super Fuzz; Young Warriors.

TV inc: Wagon Train; Laramie; Zane Grey Theater; McHale's Navy; All Quiet on the Western Front; Take One; Blood Feud; Carpool; Masquerade; Airwolf; The Last Days of Pompeii; Love Leads The Way; The Dirty Dozen--The Next Mission.

BOROWCZYK, Walerian: Wri-Dir. b. Poland, 1923. Films inc: (Shorts) Photographies Vivantes; Striptease; Dom; Szkola; Terra Incognita; Le Magicien; Solitude; Le Concert de Monsieur et Madame Kabal; Les Jeux des Anges; Rosalie; Gavotte; Le Theatre de Monsieur et Madame Kabal; Le Phonographe. (Features): Goto, the Island of Love; Blanche; Interior of a Convent; Private Collections; Lulu; L'Art d'Aimer (The Art of Love) (& edtr).

BOSLEY, Tom: Act. b. Chicago, Oct 1, 1927. e. De Paul U. Films inc: The Street with No Name; Call Northside 777; The World of Henry Orient; Love with the Proper Stranger; Divorce American Style; The Secret War of Harry Frigg; Yours, Mine and Ours; To Find a Man; O'Hara's Wife.

Bway inc: Golden Boy; Fiorello! (Tony-1960); Nowhere to Go But Up; Natural Affection; The Education of H*Y*M*A*N K*A*P*L*A*N.

TV inc: Arsenic and Old Lace; Debbie Reynolds Show; Happy Days; Return of the Mod Squad; Stingiest Man In Town; Doug Hennings World of Magic; Triangle Factory Fire Scandal; The Bastard; With This Ring; Death Trap; Castaways of Gilligan's Island; The Rebels; Pat Boone and Family Christmas Special; The California Earthquake Test; For The Love Of It; That's Hollywood (narr); Joanie Loves Chachi; Natalie--A Tribute To A Very Special Lady; The Jesse Owens Story; Murder, She Wrote; Private Sessions.

BOSSON, Barbara: Act. b. Charleroi, PA, Nov 1, 1939. e. Carnegie Tech. W of Steven Bochco. Worked with San Francisco improv group the Committee. Films inc: The Committee; The Last Starfighter.

TV inc: Richie Brockelman; Sunshine; Hill Street Blues; The Calendar Girl Murders.

BOSTWICK, Barry: Act. b. San Mateo, CA., Feb 24, 1945. Bway inc: Grease; They Knew What They Wanted; The Robber Bridegroom (Tony-1977).

TV inc: Once Upon a Family; Scruples; Moviola-The Silent Lovers; Foul Play; Red Flag--The Ultimate Game; Kennedy Center Tonight--Broadway to Washington; Working; The Kennedy Center Honors; Summer Girl; An Uncommon Love; George Washington; A Woman Of Substance; Deceptions.

Films inc: Movie Movie; Megaforce.

BOSUSTOW, Nick: Prod. b. Los Angeles, Mar 28, 1940. e. Menlo Coll, BS. S of the late Stephen R Bosustow. P. Bosustow Entertainment Inc. Prod more than 100 short ani films inc Is It Always Right To Be Right? (Oscar-1970); The Legend of John Henry.

TV inc: The Running Condition; Segs of Sesame Street, The Electric Company; The Incredible Book Escape; Misunderstood Monsters; A Tale of Four Wishes.

BOTKIN, Perry, Jr: Comp-Arr-Mus. b. NYC, Apr 16, 1933. Films scores inc: R.P.M.; Bless the Beasts and the Children; Sky Terror; They Only Kill Their Masters; Lady Ice; Your Three Minutes Are Up; Tarzan, The Ape Man; Silent Night, Deadly Night.

Provided mus arrs for Andy Williams; Barbra Streisand; Herb Alpert; George Burns; Sammy Davis.

TV inc: Co-author of Nadia's Theme (Grammy-1977); When She Was Bad; The Golden Moment--An Olympic Love Story; Landon, Landon and Landon; The Wonderful World of Philip Malley; The Circle Family; Ziggy's Gift.

BOTTOMS, Joseph: Act. b. Santa Barbara, CA, Apr 22, 1954. Films inc: The Dove; Crime and Passion; The Black Hole; Cloud Dancer; King of the Mountain; Surfacing; Blind Date.

TV inc: Winesburg, Ohio; Adventures of Major Effects; The Intruder Within; Side By Side--The True Story of the Osmond Family; The Sins of Dorian Gray; Wishman; Celebrity; Time Bomb.

Bway inc: Fifth of July.

BOTTOMS, Sam: Act. b. Santa Barbara, CA, Oct 17, 1955. B of Timothy, Joseph Bottoms. Films inc: The Last Picture Show; Class of '44; Zandy's Bride; The Outlaw Josey Wales; Apocalypse Now; Up From the Depths; Bronco Billy.

TV inc: Savages; Greatest Heroes of the Bible; John Steinbeck's East of Eden; Desperate Lives.

BOTTOMS, Timothy: Act. b. Santa Barbara, CA, Aug 30, 1951. Film debut in Johnny Got His Gun. Films inc: Rollercoaster; The Last Picture Show; Love and Pain and the Whole Damn Thing; The Paper Chase; The Moneychangers; Operation Daybreak; A Small Town in Texas; The Other Side of the Mountain, Part II; Hurricane; The High Country; Tin Man; Hambone and Hillie; The Census Taker.

TV inc: Cage Without a Key; The Gift of Love; A Shining Season; Escape; John Steinbeck's East of Eden; Love Leads The Way.

Bway inc: Fifth of July.

BOULEZ, Pierre: Comp-Cond. b. Montbrison, France, Mar 26, 1925. e. Paris Conservatory of Music. Named mus dir Jean-Louis Barrault's Theatre co 1948, toured world with Barrault; principal guest cond Cleveland Symphony 1970-71; mus dir NY Philharmonic 1971-77; guest cond major orchs, Bayreuth Festival, Edinburgh Festival.

Films inc: Jean-Louis Barrault--A Man Of The Theatre (doc).

(Grammys-(11)-class alb of year-1967, 1973, 1980; opera rec-1967, 1980, 1982; class perf-1968, 1969, 1970, 1973, 1975).

BOULTING, John: Prod-Dir-Wri. b. Bray, Buchinghamshire, England, Nov 21, 1913. With twin brother Roy, formed Charter Film Productions, 1937. Films listed are joint efforts unless otherwise noted: Consider Your Verdict; Inquest; True Crime; Pastor Hall; Thunder Rock; Journey Together (John); Fame Is the Spur; Brighton Rock; The Guinea Pig; Seven Days to Noon; The Magic Box; Seagulls Over Sorrento; Josephine and Men; Private's Progress; Brothers in Law; Lucky Jim; Happy Is the Bride; I'm All Right Jack; Suspect; A French Mistress; Heavens Above; Rotten to the Core; Twisted Nerve; There's a Girl in My Soup (John); Endless Night.

(Died June 17, 1985)

BOULTING, Roy: Prod-Dir. b. Bray, Buckinghamshire, England, Nov 21, 1913. See films listed under twin brother John Boulting. Solo film credits inc: Desert Victory; Sailor of the King; Run for the Sun; Soft Beds and Hard Battles; The Last Word.

BOUQUET, Michel: Act. b. Paris, Nov 1926. Films inc: Monsieur Vincent; Brigade Criminelle; Manon; Trois Femmes; La Tour de Nesle; Le Piege; Katia; Lamiel; La Femme Infidele; La Sirene du Mississippi; Borsalino; Un Conde; La Raison d'Etat; The Order and Security of the World; The Toy; Les Miserables; Poulet au Vinaigre.

Thea inc: La Danse de la Mort (The Dance Of Death).

BOURGIGNON, Serge: Wri-Dir. b. France, 1928. Films inc: Sundays and Cybele (Oscar-wri-1963); The Reward; Two Weeks in September; The Picasso Summer.

BOURKE, Terry: Wri-Prod-Dir. b. Bairnsdale, Australia, Apr 19, 1940. Films inc: Sampan; Noon Sunday; Night of Fear; Inn of the Damned; Plugg; Little Boy Lost; Lady, Stay Dead; Brothers.

TV inc: Spyforce; Catch Kandy; Murcheson Creek.

BOVASSO, Julie: Wri-dir-act. b. Brooklyn, Aug. 1, 1930. e. CCNY. Founder of Tempo Playhouse; teacher at Sarah Lawrence Coll. With the Davenport Theatre at age 13, later in rep and toured. Thea inc: (act) The Importance of Being Earnest; Salome; Hedda Gabler; Naked; Earth Spirit; Ivanov; The Typewriter; Amedee; The Lesson (& prod-dir); Monique; Dinny and the Witches; Victims of Duty; Gallows Humor; Minor Miracle; The Moondreamers (& dir); Gloria and Esperanza (& dir); The Maids; Down By the River Where the Water Lilies Are Disfigured Every Day; The Screens; The Nothing Kid; Standard Safety.

Plays inc: The Moondreamers; Gloria and Esperanza; Schubert's Last Serenade; Monday on the Way to Mercury Island; Down By the River Where the Water Lilies are Disfigured Every day; The Nothing Kid; Standard Safety; Super Lover; The Final Analysis.

Films inc: Saturday Night Fever; The Verdict; Staying Alive; Daniel.

TV inc: From These Roots; The Iceman Cometh; Nurse; The Gentleman Bandit.

BOWDEN, Charles: Prod-Dir. b. Somerville, MA, Aug 7, 1913. e. Harvard U. Began career as actor, Wharf Players, Provincetown, MA, 1929. Thea inc: (act) Ah, Wilderness; Meet the Prince; Hedda Gabler; Dr. Knock; The Three Sisters; Ten Million Ghosts; Antony and Cleopatra; Hamlet; The Taming of the Shrew. US Army, 1941-45. On return to civilian life was tech dir for the Lunts' prod of O Mistress Mine; tech dir, 1949, I Know My Love, also starring the Lunts; M Dir Westport, CT, Country Playhouse, 1948-53; owned, operated New Parsons Theatre, Hartford, CT, Bahama Playhouse, Nassau, 1950-54.

Bway inc: (prod or co-prod) Seagulls Over Sorrento (& dir); At Home with Ethel Waters; Ruth Draper; Ruth Draper and Paul Draper; All in One; Twenty-Seven Wagons Full of Cotton; Fallen Angels (& dir); Hotel Paradiso; Auntie Mame (road shows, & dir); Romanoff and Juliet (& dir); Caligula; The Night of the Iguana (& dir); Slapstick

Tragedy; A Streetcar Named Desire (road show); The Changing Room. In 1974 joined NY Telephone Co. as creative consultant.

BOWEN, Bill: Exec. b. Amsterdam, Aug 19, 1936. Chmn, Council for Childrens Film and TV; member of West Australian Film Council.

BOWER, Dallas: Prod-Dir. b. London, 1907. Originally snd recorder, edtr, wri; then dir of BBC-TV, 1939; supv of Ministry of Information film prodn, 1940-42. Asso prod: As You Like It; Henry V; prod: Sir Lancelot, TV series; dir: Alice in Wonderland; The Second Mrs. Tanqueray; Doorway to Suspicion.

BOWERS, Lally (Kathleen Bowers): Act. b. England, Jan 21, 1917. With Old Vic Co. Thea inc: Lady Precious Stream; Drama at Inish; The Comedy of Errors; Camino Real; Dinner With the Family (& Bway); The Honor of the Family; Call It Love; The Pleasure Garden; Castle in Sweden; The Empire Builders; Difference of Opinion; The Killing of Sister George (& Bway); Dear Octopus; Council of Love; The Watched Pot; The Beastly Beatitudes of Balthazar B.
　　TV inc: Pygmalion; The Importance of Being Earnest; Fallen Angels.
　　(Died July 18, 1984)

BOWERS, William: Wri-Prod. b. Las Cruces, NM, Jan 17, 1916. e. U of MO. Plays inc: Where Do We Go from Here; Back to Eden. Films inc: My Favorite Spy; Night and Day; The Web; Black Bart; Larceny; The Gunfighter; Cry Danger; The Mob; Split Second; Five Against the House; The Best Things in Life Are Free; The Sheepman; Alias Jesse James; The Last Time I Saw Archie; Advance to the Rear; Support Your Local Sheriff.
　　TV inc: The Wild Wild West Revisited; More Wild Wild West.

BOWIE, David: Singer-Act. b. London, Jan 8, 1947. Films inc: The Man who Fell to Earth; Just a Gigolo; Wir Kinder von Bahnof Zoo (We Children From Bahnof Zoo); The Hunger; Merry Christmas, Mr. Lawrence; Hero. Ziggy Stardust and the Spiders from Mars (mus); Into The Night.
　　TV inc: Star Chart; Omnibus; David Bowie--Serious Moonlight (cable).

BOX, Betty E: Prod. b. Beckenham, Kent, England, 1920. Films inc: Miranda; Here Come the Huggetts; Doctor in the House; The Iron Petticoat; A Tale of Two Cities; The Thirty-nine Steps; No Love for Johnnie; A Pair of Briefs; No My Darling Daughters; Deadlier Than the Male; The High Commissioner; The Love Ban; Percy's Progress; It's Not the Size that Counts!.

BOX, John: Art dir. b. Kent, England, Jan. 27, 1920. Films inc: The Million Pound Note; The Black Knight; The Cockleshell Heroes; Zarak; Fire Down Below; Inn of the Sixth Happiness; Our Man in Havana; The World of Suzie Wong; Lawrence of Arabia *(Oscar-1962)*; Of Human Bondage; Doctor Zhivago *(Oscar-1965)*; A Man for All Seasons; Oliver! *(Oscar-1968)*; *The Looking Glass War (prod)*; *Nicholas and Alexander (Oscar-1971)*; Travels With My Aunt; The Great Gatsby; Rollerball; Sorcerer; The Keep; A Passage To India.

BOX, Muriel: Wri-Prod-Dir. b. Surrey, England, 1905. W of the late Sydney Box. Films inc: The Seventh Veil *(Oscar-sp-1946)*; The Man Within (sp); The Brothers (sp); A Girl in a Million (sp & prod); The Happy Family (& dir); The Beachcomber (& dir); Cash On Delivery (dir); Simon and Laura (dir); Eyewitness (dir); To Dorothy A Son (dir); The Truth About Women (prod-dir); Subway in the Sky (dir); This Other Eden (dir); Rattle of a Simple Man (dir).

BOX, Sydney: Prod-Dir-Wri. b. Kent, England, Apr 29, 1907. Films inc: The Seventh Veil; The Years Between; Holiday Camp; Jassy; The Brothers; Dear Murderer; Quartet; Don't Take It To Heart; Broken Journey; Daybreak; A Girl in a Million; So Long at the Fair; The Prisoner.
　　(Died May 25, 1983).

BOXLEITNER, Bruce: Act. b. Elgin, IL, May 12. TV inc: How the West Was Won; Jack and the Princess; The Last Convertible; Wild Times; Kenny Rogers As The Gambler; John Steinbeck's East of Eden; Fly Away Home; Bring 'em Back Alive; Bare Essence; I Married Wyatt Earp; Scarecrow and Mrs. King; I Love Men; Kenny Rogers as the

Gambler--The Adventure Continues.
　　Films inc: The Baltimore Bullet; Tron.

BOYAR, Sully: Act. b. NYC, Dec 14, 1923. Films inc: Car Wash; King of Marvin Gardens; The Gambler; Panic in Needle Park; Made for Each Other; Last of the Red Hot Lovers; Dog Day Afternoon; Oliver's Story; The Jazz Singer; The Entity.
　　TV inc: The Deadliest Season.

BOYD, Don: Prod. b. Scotland, 1950. Started career as dir of tv commercials; dir films Intimate Reflections; East of Elephant Rock before becoming prod. Films inc: Scum; Black Suede Shoes; Hussy; The Tempest; The Great Rock 'n Roll Swindle (doc); Sweet William; Honky Tonk Freeway; Scrubbers.

BOYETT, Bob: Prod. (Robert L Boyett) TV inc: Happy Days (crea cons); Laverne & Shirley (crea cons); Angie (supv prod); Out of the Blue (supv prod); Goodtime Girls (exec prod); Bosom Buddies (exec prod-crea); Foul Play (supv prod); Joannie Loves Chachi (exec prod).
　　Films inc: The Best Little Whorehouse In Texas.

BOYLE, Peter: Act. b. Philadelphia, Oct 18, 1935. e. La Salle U, BA. Stage debut road company The Odd Couple. Performed in Chicago's Second City Improvisational Repertory Co. Bway inc: The Roast.
　　Films inc: Joe; T.R. Baskin; Steelyard Blues; Kid Blue; Slither; The Candidate; Taxi Driver; Swashbuckler; The Brink's Job; F.I.S.T.; Hardcore; Beyond The Poseidon Adventure; Where The Buffalo Roam; In God We Trust; Outland; Hammett; Yellowbeard; Ghost in the Noonday Sun (made in 1973); Johnny Dangerously; Morons From Outer Space; Turk 182.
　　TV inc: From Here To Eternity.

BOYLE, Robert: Prod dsgn. e. USC. Films inc: Saboteur; Buchnanan Rides Alone; Cape Fear; The Birds; Marnie; The Russians Are Coming, The Russians Are Coming; How To Succeed in Business Without Really Trying; In Cold Blood; The Thomas Crown Affair; Gaily Gaily; The Landlord; Fiddler on the Roof; Portnoy's Complaint; Bite the Bullet; W.C. Fields and Me; The Shootist; The Big Fix; Magic; Winter Kills; Brinks; Lookin' To Get Out; The King Of Comedy; Staying Alive; Rhinestone; No Small Affair.

BOZZETTO, Bruno: Prod-Dir. b. Milan, 1939. Prod, Tampu! A History of Weapons, 1958 (short). Started own studio 1960. Films inc: (shorts) An Oscar for Mr Rossi; Mr Rossi Buys a Car; Alpha Omega; The Two Castles; Pickles; Opera; Self-Service. (Features) West and Soda; VIP - My Brother Superman; Allegro Non Troppo.

BRABOURNE, John, Lord: Prod. b. London, Nov 9, 1924. Films inc: Harry Black; Sink the Bismarck; HMS Defiant; The Mikado; Romeo and Juliet; Tales of Beatrix Potter; Murder on the Orient Express; Death on the Nile; Stories From A Flying Trunk; The Mirror Crack'd; Evil Under the Sun; A Passage To India.

BRACH, Gerard: Wri-Dir. b. Montrouge, France. Films inc: (Wri) The Beautiful Swindlers; Repulsion; The Tenant; Tess; Chere Inconnu (I Sent A Letter To My Love); Chariots of Fire; L'Africain (The African); La Femme de mon Pote (My Buddy's Girl); Maria's Lovers; Les Favoris de la Lune (Minions Of The Moon); Le Bon Roi Dagobert (Good King Dagobert); Le Meilleur de la Vie (The Best In Life); Les Enrages (The Rabid Ones); Gazl El Banat (The Adolescent Sugar Of Love). (Dir) Les Bleuets dans la Tete; La Maison; Le Bateau sur L'Herbe.

BRACHMAN, Leon S: Exec. b. NYC, Nov 28, 1929. e. U of OK; Brooklyn Law School, LLB. With UA as an atty; 1965 legal dept Col; 1978, bus aff vp UA; 1980 sr vp wldwde bus aff Fox thea films; Aug, 1981, exec vp 20th-Fox Prodns.

BRACKEN, Eddie: Act. b. NYC, Feb 7, 1920. Stage debut, Lottery, 1930. Screen debut in, Life With Henry, 1940. Films inc: Fleet's In; Sweater Girl; Miracle of Morgan's Creek; About Face; We're Not Married; Slight Case of Larceny.
　　Bway inc: The Lady Refuses; So Proudly We Hail; Brother Rat; Seven Year Itch; You Know I Can't Hear You When the Water's Running; The Odd Couple; Sunshine Boys; Hello, Dolly! (London): Hello, Dolly!.
　　TV inc: Masquerade Party.

BRADBURY, Ray: Wri. b. Waukegan, IL, Aug 22, 1920. Films inc: It Came from Outer Space; The Beast from 20,000 Fathoms; Moby Dick; Fahrenheit 451; The Illustrated Man; Something Wicked This Way Comes; Mirrors (Mar ianne) (crea cnslt).
TV inc: Infinite Horizons-Space Beyond Apollo; The Electric Grandmother.

BRADEMAN, Bill: Prod-Exec. b. Minneapolis, MN. e. U of MN. Talent VP Universal Studios; Development VP, ABC; Development VP 20th-Fox TV; VP Programs and Development, Universal; Sr VP Crea Aff & Mktg, QM Prodns; Partnered with Ed Self in Brademan-Self Prodns; July 1983, P Walt Disney TV Division; resd. May 1985. TV inc: (Exec prod) Two the Hard Way; Quick and Quiet; Help Wanted--Male; Uncommon Valor.

BRADLEY, Ed: Newscaster. b. Philadelphia, June 22, 1941. e. Cheyney State Coll, BS. Joined CBS as stringer in the Paris Bureau, 1971; transferred to the Saigon Bureau; named CBS News Corr, 1973; named CBS News White House Corr and anchorman of CBS Sunday Night News, 1976; 1981, co-editor 60 Minutes.
TV inc: What's Happened To Cambodia?; The Boat People; The Boston Goes To China; Blacks in America--with all Deliberate Speed; Return of the CIA; Miami. . .The Trial That Sparked the Riot (Emmy-corr-1980); The Saudis; Embassy; Too Little, Too Late (Emmy-corr-1980); Murder--Teenage Style (Emmy-corr-1981); Eye On The Media--Private Lives, Public Press; Best in the West; In the Belly of the Beast (Emmy-corr-1982); Lena (Emmy-corr-1982).

BRADY, Scott (Jerry Tierney): Act. b. NYC, Sep 13, 1924. e. Bliss-Hayden Drama School, Beverly Hills. Films inc: Born to Fight; He Walked by Night; Perilous Journey; Johnny Guitar; Vanishing American; Fort Utah; The Loners; Wicked, Wicked; The China Syndrome; Dead Kids; Gremlins.
TV inc: The Last Ride of the Dalton Gang; Power; American Dream; McClain's Law; The Winds Of War; This Girl For Hire.
(Died April 16, 1985)

BRAEDEN, Eric (Hans Gudegast): Act. b. Kiel, Germany. Films inc: Colossus: The Forbin Project; The Law and Jake Wade; The Ultimate Thrill; Morituri; Escape from the Planet of the Apes; Lady Ice; A Hundred Rifles; Herbie Goes to Monte Carlo.
TV inc: Jack and the Princess; The Power Within; The Aliens Are Coming; The Young and the Restless.

BRAMBELL, Wilfrid: Act. b. Dublin, Ireland, 1912. Thea inc: Blind Man's Bluff; Stop It, Whoever You Are; The Ghost Train.
Films inc: Dry Rot; Serious Charge; What a Whopper; In Search of the Castaways; Thomasina; A Hard Day's Night; Crooks in Cloisters; Where the Bullets Fly; Witchfinder General; The Adventures of Picasso; The Terence Davies Trilogy; Sword Of The Valiant.
Radio & TV: Steptoe and Son.
(Died Jan. 18, 1985).

BRAND, Harry: Pub exec. b. NYC, Oct 20, 1895. e. USC. Originally newspaperman; sports ed LA Express three years; sec to former LA Mayor Snyder; handled pub for Buster Keaton; Norma and Constance Talmadge; later with WB; Goldwyn; joined Darryl Zanuck as pub dir Twentieth Century Pictures, when that firm merged with Fox 1935 became pub dir 20th-Fox.

BRAND, Neville: Act. b. Kewanee, IL, Aug 13, 1921. Studied acting in NY. Screen debut in D.O.A. Films inc: Halls of Montezuma; Stalag 17; Riot in Cell Block 11; Prince Valiant; The Prodigal; The Adventures of Huckleberry Finn; Birdman of Alcatraz; Psychic Killer; Eaten Alive; The Mouse and His Child; Five Days From Home; The Ninth Configuration; Without Warning.
TV inc: Laredo; The Captain and the Kings; The Seekers; Evils Of The Night.

BRANDO, Jocelyn: Act. b. San Francisco, 1919. e. Lake Forest Coll. Sis of Marlon Brando. Films inc: The Big Heat; China Venture; Nightfall; The Explosive Generation; The Ugly American; Bus Riley's Back in Town; The Chase; The Appaloosa; Movie Movie; Good Luck, Miss Wyckoff; Why Would I Lie?; Mommie Dearest.
Bway inc: Mr. Roberts; Desire Under the Elms; Golden State.
TV inc: A Question of Love; Dark Night of the Scarecrow;

Starflight--The Plane That Couldn't Land.

BRANDO, Marlon: Act. b. Omaha, NE, Apr 3, 1924. e. Dramatic Workshop, NY. Played stock. Bway in I Remember Mama; Truckline Cafe; Candida; A Flag Is Born; Streetcar Named Desire. Films inc: The Men; Streetcar Named Desire; Viva Zapata; Julius Caesar; On The Waterfront (Oscar-1954); Sayonara; Teahouse of the August Moon; The Young Lions; Mutiny on the Bounty; Reflections in a Golden Eye; Last Tango In Paris; The Missouri Breaks; The Godfather (Oscar-1972); Superman; Apocalypse Now; The Formula.
TV inc: Roots-The Next Generation (Emmy-supp-1979).

BRANDON, Clark: Act. b. NYC, Dec 30, 1958. Films inc: Chicken Chronicles; My Tutor. TV inc: When, Jenny, When; Like Mother, Like Me; Teenage Millionaire; The Fitzpatricks; Out of the Blue; Mr. Merlin.

BRANDON, Henry (nee Kleinbach): Act. b. 1912. Films inc: Babes in Toyland; Killer at Large; Black Legion; Jungle Jim (serial); Buck Rogers (serial); Drums of Fu Manchu (serial); Beau Geste; Nurse Edith Cavell; Son of Monte Cristo; Underground; Joan of Arc; The Paleface; The Fighting O'Flynn; Hurricane Smith; The War of the Worlds; Vera Cruz; The Searchers; Auntie Mame; The Buccaneer; The Big Fisherman; Two Rode Together; The Manhandlers; Assault on Precinct 13.
TV inc: Evita Person; Look Back to Yesterday.

BRANDON, Michael: Act. b. Brooklyn, NY. e. AADA. Bway inc: Does a Tiger Wear a Necktie?
Films inc: Lovers and Other Strangers; Jennifer on My Mind; FM; Promises in the Dark; A Change of Seasons.
TV inc: Third Girl From the Left; The Red Badge of Courage; The Queen of the Stardust Ballroom; James Dean, Portrait of a Friend; Red Alert; Scot Free; Hitchhike; Vacation in Hell; Comedy Company; A Perfect Match; Between Two Brothers; Venice Medical; The Seduction of Gina; Deadly Messages.

BRANDT, Victor: Act. b. Los Angeles, Sep 19. e. UCLA; AADA. Films inc: Battle of the Bulge; Point Blank; Three the Hard Way; Wacko.
TV inc: Assignment Vienna; Cry Rape; Strange Homecoming; Nobody's Perfect.

BRANDT, Yanna Kroyt: Prod. b. Bonn, Germany, Sept. 6, 1933. e. Vassar, BA; Columbia, MS. TV inc: Vibrations--Boulez; High Feathers (Exec prod & crea); Vegetable Soup (exec prod); The Nutcracker (& wri); A House Divided; FYI (Emmys-prod-1980, 1981, 1982); Solomon Northrup's Odyssey; Charlotte Forten's Mission--Experiment in Freedom.

BRASSEUR, Claude: Act. b. Paris, 1936. Youngest of an acting family famous in France since 1820. Films inc: Rue Des Prairies; Green Harvest; The Soft-Hearted Guy; Dr. Faustus' Horror Chamber; Les Menteurs; Les Distractions; The Elusive Corporal; Les Ennemis; The Seven Deadly Sins; Banana Peel; Lucky Jo; Du Rififi a Paname; Such A Gorgeous Kid Like Me; Act of Aggression; An Elephant Can Be Extremely Deceptive; Barocco; The Big Operator; Pardon Mon Affaire; Pardon Mon Affaire, Too; Other People's Money; Au Revoir---a Lundi; A Simple Story; La Guerre des Policiers; These Kids are Grown Ups; La Banquiere (The Woman Banker); The Party; A Black Gown For A Killer; Une Affaire D'Hommes (A Man's Affair); L'Ombre Rouge (The Red Shadow); Josepha; Guy de Maupassant; Legitime Violence (Lawful Violence); La Boum 2 (The Party--2); La Crime (Coverup); Signes Exterieurs de Richesse (Outer Signs of Wealth); Le Leopard; Souvenirs, Souvenirs (Memories, Memories); Palace; Detective.

BRAUDY, Susan: Exec. b. Jul 8, 1941. e. Bryn Mawr, BA; U PA; Yale. Wri-edtr Newsweek; wri-edtr, MS Magazine; dvlpmt exec for Alberto Grimaldi; Dec 1980 named East Coast prodn vp, WB; axed March 1982.

BRAUN, Zev: Prod. b. Chicago, Oct 19, 1928. e. U of Chicago. Films inc: Goldstein; The Pedestrian; Angela (exec prod); The Little Girl Who Lives Down the Lane; The Fiendish Plot of Dr. Fu Manchu.
TV inc: Freedom Road.

BRAUS, Mort: Wri. b. NYC, Nov 21, 1908. e. Cornell U, AB, DL. Films inc: Women in Prison; The Other One Am I; Three Loves Has Nancy; The Postman Didn't Ring; Wing and a Prayer; Strange Triangle; Let's Make it Legal; Hannibal.

TV inc: Loretta Young Show; Lassie; Lux Theatre; G E Theatre; Kraft Theatre.

BRAVERMAN, Bart: Act. b. Los Angeles, Feb 1. e. Carnegie Tech, MFA. B of Charles Braverman. TV inc: Started as child actor on Bob Hope Show; Red Skelton Show; I Love Lucy; Magic Mongo; Vega$; Fast Lane Blues; The Best of the Big Laff Off (dir). Films inc: Alligator; Hit and Run.

Thea inc: Godspell; The Rocky Horror Show.

BRAVERMAN, Charles: Prod-Dir. b. Los Angeles, Mar 3, 1944. e. USC, BA. Films inc: Dillinger; Soylent Green (titles and montages); Hit and Run.

TV inc: An American Time Capsule; The World of '68; Moon Journey; The Smothers Brothers; How to Stay Alive; David Hartman. . .Birth and Babies; Breathe a Sigh of Relief; Getting Married; The Making of a Live TV Show; Televisionland; The Best of the Big Laff Off.

BRAXTON, Anthony: Mus-Comp. b. Chicago, Jun 4, 1945. e. Roosevelt U; Chicago Musical Coll. Multi-instrumentalist of int'l stature; recording artist.

BRAZZI, Rossano: Act. b. Bologna, Italy, 1916. e. U of Florence. Started career on Italian stage. Films inc: (U.S.) Three Coins in the Fountain; Barefoot Contessa; Summertime; South Pacific; Light in the Piazza; Rome Adventure; Woman Times Seven; The Adventurers; The Great Waltz; A Time For Miracles; Catherine and I; The Final Conflict; Il Paramedico (The Orderly); La Voce (The Voice); Fear City.

TV inc: The Far Pavilions (PC); Christopher Columbus.

BREALEY, Gil: Prod. b. Australia, Apr 9, 1932. Chmn, Tasmanian Film Corp. TV inc: After the Miracle; Two Trumpets for St Andrew; The Lad that Waited; Legend of Damien Parer.

Films inc: My Brother Jack; The Stranger; Three to Go; The Gallery; Sunday Too Far Away; Annie's Coming Out (dir).

BREAM, Julian: Classical guitarist. b. London, Jul 15, 1933. e. Royal Coll of Music. London debut 1950. Formed Julian Bream Consort 1960; expert in Elizabethan lute music; Malcolm Arnold Guitar Concerto written for him.

Albums inc: The Art of Julian Bream; An Evening of Elizabethan Music (Grammy-Chamber Music-1963); Popular Classics for Spanish Guitar; Julian Bream in Concert; Baroque Guitar (Grammy-class inst-1966); 20th Century Guitar; Julian Bream and His Friends; Dances of Dowland; Bach and Vivaldi Sonatas for Lute and Harpsichord; Villa Lobos Concerto for Guitar (Grammy-class inst with orch-1971); Julian and John (Grammy-chamber music-1972); Concerto for Guitar and Chamber Ensemble; Julian and John Vol. 2; Berkeley Guitar Concerto/Rodrigo concierto de Aranjuez for Guitar. TV inc: A Time There Was.

BRECHER, Irving: Wri. b. NYC, Jan 17, 1914. Radio writer for Milton Berle; Willie Howard; Al Jolson. Films inc: New Faces of 1937; At the Circus; Go West; Shadow of the Thin Man; Dubarry Was a Lady; Meet Me in St. Louis; Yolanda and the Thief; Summer Holiday; The Life of Riley (& dir-prod); Somebody Loves Me (& dir); Cry for Happy; Sail a Crooked Ship ((& dir); Bye Bye Birdie.

TV inc: People's Choice; The Life of Riley.

BREGMAN, Buddy: Dir-Prod. b. Chicago, Jul 9, 1940. e. UCLA. Started as an arranger, composer, conductor for such artists as: Judy Garland; Ella Fitzgerald; Sammy Davis Jr; Joel Grey; Debbie Reynolds; Jerry Lewis. Films scores inc: The Delicate Delinquent; Secret of the Purple Reef; The Wild Party; Five Guns West; Born Reckless; Pajama Game.

TV inc: (prod-dir) Richard Rodgers Special; Chicago in the Roaring Twenties; Saga of the Wild West; The American Civil War; Miriam Makeba; George Gershwin Special; Cole Porter Special; An Evening with Ethel Merman; Juliet Prowse Special; Diahann Carroll Special; Bing Crosby in Dublin; Superkid; Great American Music Celebration; Circus of the Stars; Pure Gold; The Danny Thomas Special; Sunpower; The Force Is With Us; Ain't Misbehavin' (prod).

BREGMAN, Martin: Prod. b. NYC. May 18, 1926. e. IN U; NYU. Business rep 1960 for Barbra Streisand; Elliott Gould; Joel Gray; Can-

dice Bergen; Alan Alda; formed Artists Entertainment Complex in 1971, functioning as career counselor, prod. Films inc: Serpico; Dog Day Afternoon; The Next Man; The Seduction of Joe Tynan; Simon; The Four Seasons; Venom; Eddie Macon's Run; Scarface.

TV inc: S*H*E; The Four Seasons (exec prod).

BRENNAN, Eileen: Act. b. Los Angeles, Sep 3, 1937. e. Georgetown U; AADA. Summer stock. Off-Broadway: Little Mary Sunshine. Films inc: Divorce, American Style; The Last Picture Show; The Sting; At Long Last Love; Hustle; Murder By Death; The Cheap Detective; FM; The Great Smokey Roadblock; Private Benjamin; The Funny Farm.

Bway inc: The Miracle Worker; Hello, Dolly!; revivals of The King And I; Guys and Dolls; Camelot.

TV inc: All That Glitters; 13 Queens Boulevard; A New Kind of Family; When She Was Bad; My Old Man; Black Beauty; When The Circus Came To Town; Private Benjamin (Emmy-supp-1981); Incident at Crestridge; Kraft Salutes Walt Disney World's 10th Anniversary; Working; Lily For President?; Off The Rack; The Fourth Wise Man.

BRENNAN, Richard: Prod. b. Sydney, Australia, Jun 24, 1945. e. U of Sydney. Films inc: Lend Me Your Stable; Or Forever Hold Your Peace; The Adventures of Barry McKenzie; The Great McCarthy; The Trespassers; Death Cheaters; News Front; Starstruck.

BRENNER, David: Act. b. Philadelphia, Feb. 4, 1945. e. Temple U. Prod at WBBM-TV, WRCV-TV, KYW-TV, WNEW-TV. TV inc: Tonight Show (guest host); Ebony, Ivory and Jade; Entertainer of the Year Awards; Live--and in Person; The Young At Heart Comedians Special (feevee).

BRENTON, Howard: Plywri. b. Portsmouth, England, Dec 13, 1942. e. St Catherine's Coll; Cambridge. Plays inc: Ladder of Fools; It's My Criminal (one-act); Christie in Love; Fruit; Winter; Daddykins; Revenge; Wesley; Scott of the Antarctic; A Sky-Blue Life; Hitler Dances; Brass Neck; The Churchill Play; Weapons of Happiness; The Romans in Britain; The Genius; Pravda.

Films inc: Skinflicker.

TV inc: Lushly; The Saliva Milkshake; The Paradise Run.

BRESLER, Jerry: Prod. b. CO, 1912. Films inc: (Shorts): Heavenly Music (Oscar-1943); Main Street Today; Luckiest Guy In The World; Stairway To Light (Oscar-1944). (Fea): Main Street after Dark; Dr Kildare series; Bewitched; The Web; Another Part of the Forest; Shop Around The Corner; Ziegfeld Girl; The Flying Missile; The Mob; Assignment Paris; Lizzie; The Vikings; Gidget Goes Hawaiian; Diamond Head; Major Dundee; Pussycat Pussycat I Love You.

TV inc: Ray Bolger Show.

BRESSLAW, Bernard: Act. b. England, 1933. Films inc: I Only Arsked; Too Many Crooks; The Ugly Duckling; Morgan; Carry on Screaming; Up Pompeii; Vampire; One of our Dinosaurs Is Missing; The Fifth Musketeer; Jabberwocky; Hawk, the Slayer; Krull.

TV inc: The Army Game. Thea inc: (London) Lancelot and Guinevere.

BRESSON, Robert: Wri-Dir. b. France, Sep 25, 1907. Films inc: Les Anges du Peche; Les Dames du Bois de Boulogne; Le Journal d'un Cure de b. France, Sep 25, 1907. Films inc: Les Anges du Peche; Les Dames du Bois de Boulogne; Le Journal d'un Cure de Campagne; Pickpocket; The Trial of Joan of Arc; Au Hazard Balthasar; Mouchette; Une Femme Douce; Lancelot du Lac; Le Diable Probablement; De Weg Naar Bresson (The Way To Bresson) (doc) (int).

BREST, Martin: Dir-Wri. b. NYC, 1951. e. NYU; AFI. Films inc: Hot Dogs for Gauguin (short made at NYU); Hot Tomorrows; Going In Style; Beverly Hills Cop (dir).

BRETT, Jeremy (nee Huggins): Act. b. Berkswell, England, Nov 3, 1935. e. Eton Coll. Thea inc: Richard II; Troilus and Cressida; Meet Me by Moonlight; Variations on a Theme; Mr. Fox of Venice; Hamlet; Saint Joan; A Measure of Cruelty; Hedda Gabler; A Voyage Round My Father; The Way of the World; Aren't We All? (Bway).

Films inc: War and Peace; The Wild and the Willing; The Very Edge; My Fair Lady; The Medusa Touch.

TV inc: The Picture of Dorian Gray; Dinner with the Family; The

Merry Widow; School for Scandal; Madame X; The Good Soldier; The Adventures Of Sherlock Holmes; Florence Nightingale; Deceptions.

BREWER, Teresa: Singer. b. Toledo, OH, May 7, 1931. Recording artist; on radio, TV and in niteries. Films inc: Three Red Heads from Seattle.

BRIALY, Jean-Claude: Act-Dir. b. Algeria, Mar 30, 1933. Films inc: Elena et les Hommes; Lift to the Scaffold; Le Beau Serge; The Four Hundred Blows; Tire au Flane; La Chambre Ardente; The Devil and Ten Commandments; La Ronde; Un Homme de Trop; King of Hearts; Le Rouge et le Noir; Claire's Knee; Le Fantome de la Liberte; Catherine et Cie; The Accuser; L'Annee Sainte; Robert and Robert. Eglantine; Les Volets Clos; L'oiseau Rare; Un Amour De Pluie; Bobo Jacco; L'oeil Du Maitre; La Banquiere (The Woman Banker); La Nuit de Varennes (The Night of Varennes); Cap Canaille; Le Demon Dans L'Isle (The Demon of The Isle); Edith et Marcel; Sarah; Stella; La Crime (Coverup); Papy Fait de la Resistance (Gramps is in the Resistance); Pinot, Simple Flic (Pinot, Just A Cop).
Thea inc: Desire.

BRIAN, David: Act. b. NYC, Aug 5, 1914. Films inc: Flamingo Road; Beyond the Forest; Intruder in the Dust; The Damned Don't Cry; This Woman Is Dangerous; The High and the Mighty; The First Travelling Saleslady; The Rabbit Trap; A Pocketful of Miracles; How the West Was Won; The Rare Breed; The Destructors; The Seven Minutes.
Bway inc: New Moon; Bittersweet; Let 'Em Eat Cake; Beat the Band; Candle in the Wind.
TV inc: Mr. District Attorney.

BRICKMAN, Marshall: Wri-Dir. b. Rio de Janeiro. e. U of WI. With folk groups The Tarriers, The Journeymen, began writing for tv.
TV inc: Candid Camera; The Tonight Show.
Films inc: Sleeper; Annie Hall (Oscar-1977); Manhattan; Simon (& dir); Lovesick.

BRICUSSE, Leslie: Wri-Comp-Lyr-Prod. b. London, Jan 29, 1931. e. Cambridge, MA. Thea inc: book mus & lyr (with Anthony Newley) for: Stop the World--I Want to Get Off. The Roar of the Grease Paint--the Smell of the Crowd; The Good Old Bad Old Days; Kings and Clowns; The Traveling Music Show.
Films inc: Sp, mus & lyrics: Pickwick; Goodbye Mr Chips; Scrooge; Doctor Doolittle; Sammy Stops The World. Film scores inc: Willy Wonka and the Chocolate Factory; Revenge of the Pink Panther; Superman (lyr only); Sunday Lovers (sp only); Victor/Victoria (Oscar-Orig score & adaptation--1982).
Songs inc: Goldfinger; You Only Live Twice; If I Ruled The World; What Kind of Fool Am I (Grammy-1962); We Were Lovers; Talk to the Animals (Oscar-1967). TV inc: I'm a Big Girl Now (lyr).

BRIDGES, Alan: Dir. b. England, Sept 28, 1927. Films inc: Act of Murder; Invasion; The Hireling; Out of Season; The Age of Innocence; Phobia; The Little Girl In Blue Velvet; The Return of the Soldier; The Shooting Party.
TV inc: Brief Encounter; Rain on the Roof; Puddinhead Wilson.

BRIDGES, Beau: Act. b. Hollywood, 1941. S of Lloyd Bridges. Began film career age 4, The Red Pony. On stage 1947, in All My Sons. Films inc: The Incident; For Love of Ivy; Gaily, Gaily; The Landlord; Hammersmith Is Out; The Other Side of the Mountain; Two-Minute Warning; The Fifth Musketeer; Greased Lightning; Norma Rae; The Runner Stumbles; Silver Dream Racer; Honky Tonk Freeway; Night Crossing; Love Child; Heart Like A Wheel; The Hotel New Hampshire.
TV inc: Sea Hunt; Ensign O'Toole; Man Without A Country; The Stranger Who Looks Like Me; The Four Feathers; The Child Stealer; United States; Mom, I Want To Come Home (host); The Kid From Nowhere (& dir); Dangerous Company; Witness For the Prosecution; The Red-Light Sting; Space.

BRIDGES, James: Wri-Dir. b. Paris, AR, Feb 3, 1936. Originally actor in Johnny Trouble; Faces; numerous tv segs. Films inc: (wri) Appaloosa; Colossus: The Forbin Project; Limbo. (Wri-dir): The Baby Maker; The Paper Chase; 9/30/55; The China Syndrome; Urban Cowboy; Mike's Murder; Perfect (& prod).
TV inc: (wri) 18 Alfred Hitchcock Presents; The Paper Chase.

BRIDGES, Jeff: Act. b. Los Angeles, Dec 4, 1949. S of Lloyd Bridges. Appeared in TV series Sea Hunt at age 8. On stage, NY, Hollywood. Films inc: Halls of Anger; The Last Picture Show; The Iceman Cometh; Thunderbolt and Lightfoot; Rancho Deluxe; Hearts of the West; Somebody Killed Her Husband; Winter Kills; The American Success Company; Heaven's Gate; Cutter and Bone; Tron; The Last Unicorn (voice); Kiss Me Goodbye; Against All Odds; Starman.
TV inc: Heroes of Rock N Roll; The Girls In Their Summer Dresses and Other Stories by Irwin Shaw.

BRIDGES, Lloyd: Act. b. San Leandro, CA, Jan 15, 1913. e. UCLA. Films inc: High Noon; The Master Race; A Walk in the Sun; Home of the Brave; White Tower; The Rainmaker; The Goddess; Around the World Under the Sea; The Fifth Musketeer; Bear Island; Airplane; Airplane II--The Sequel.
Thea inc: Oh, Men! Oh, Women!; The Dead Pigeon.
TV inc: Sea Hunt; The Loner; The Critical List; Disaster On The Coastline; Moviola-This Year's Blonde; John Steinbeck's East of Eden; Life of the Party--The Story of BeAtrice; The Blue and The Gray; Grace Kelly; Grandpa, Will You Run With Me?; George Washington; Paper Dolls.

BRIDGES, Todd: Act. b. San Francisco, CA., May 27, 1965. TV inc: Fish; Diff'rent Strokes; Good Evening, Captain; Hang Tight, Willy Bill; High School, USA.

BRIGHT, Richard S: Prod. b. New Rochelle, NY, Feb 28, 1936. e. Hotchkiss School; Wharton School of Finance; U PA. Partner in Persky-Bright Org arr film financing before turning prod. Films inc: Tribute. TV inc: The President's Mistress.
Bway inc: A History of the American Film.

BRILEY, John: Wri. b. Kalamazoo, MI., Jun. 25, 1925. e. U MI, BA, MA. Staff writer at MGM studios Britain from 1960 to 1964, then freelance. Films inc: Invasion Quartet; Postman's Knock; Children of the Damned; Pope Joan; That Lucky Touch; The Medusa Touch; Eagle's Wing; Gandhi (Oscar-1982).
Plays inc: Seven Bob a Buck; So Who Needs Men.
TV inc: Hits and Misses; The Airbase.

BRIMLEY, Wilford: Act. b. UT. Films inc: Electric Horseman; Brubaker; The China Syndrome; Borderline; Death Valley; Absence of Malice; The Thing; Tender Mercies; Tough Enough; High Road to China; 10 To Midnight; Country; Cocoon.
TV inc: Joe Dancer; The Firm.

BRINCKERHOFF, Burt: Dir. b. Oct 25, 1936. Films inc: Dogs.
TV inc: The Cracker Factory; The Funny Side of Love; Can You Hear The Laughter?-The Story of Freddie Prinze; Mother and Daughter-The Loving War; Rollergirls; Brave New World; The Day The Women Got Even; Stephanie; Born to Be Sold; Lovers and Other Strangers; The Hamptons; Just A Little More Love; 9 to 5; You Are the Jury. (& co-prod); Steambath (cable).

BRINKLEY, David: News Commentator. b. Wilmington, NC, Jul 20, 1920. Started writing for hometown newspaper. Joined United Press before serving in Army, WW II. After discharge in 1943, joined NBC News in Washington as White House corr. Co-anchored NBC Nightly News with late Chet Huntley; resd Sept 1981, after 38 years with net, joined ABC.
TV inc: David Brinkley's Journal; The American Presidency; NBC Reports--Gambling (wri-corr); NBC Magazine with David Brinkley; This Week; FDR.

BRISEBOIS, Danielle: Act. b. NYC, Jun 28, 1969. Films inc: The Premonition; If Ever I See You Again; King of the Gypsies; Slow Dancing In The Big City.
TV inc: All My Children; As the World Turns; All in the Family; Archie Bunker's Place; Mom, the Wolfman and Me; Knots Landing; Rich Little And Friends In New Orleans.
Bway inc: The Saint of Bleecker Street; Annie.

BRISKIN, Mort: Prod-Wri. b. Oak Park, IL, 1919. e. USC; Harvard and Northwestern Law Schools. Films inc: The River; The Magic Face; No Time for Flowers; The Second Woman; Quicksand, The Big Wheel; The Jackie Robinson Story; Ben; Willard; You'll Like My Mother; Walking Tall; Framed.

TV inc: Sheriff of Cochise; U S Marshall; The Texan; Grand Jury; The Walter Winchell File; Official Detective; Whirlybirds.

BRISSON, Frederick: Prod. b. Copenhagen, Denmark, Mar 17, 1913. e. Rossall Coll, England. H of the late Rosalind Russell. Formerly actor's agent. First stage production at the Hippodrome, London, Sep, 1933. Came to U.S. in 1939. Bway inc: The Pajama Game *(Tony*-1955); Damn Yankees *(Tony*-1956); The Pleasure of His Company; The Gazebo; Five Finger Exercise; Under the Yum-Yum Tree; Jumpers; So Long 174th St; Mixed Couples; Dance A Little Closer.

Founded Independent Artists Pictures 1948; Films inc: The Velvet Touch; Never Wave at a WAC; The Pajama Game; Damn Yankees; Five Finger Exercise; Under the Yum-Yum Tree; Generation; Mrs. Pollifax-Spy.

(Died Oct. 8, 1984)

BRITT, Elton: Singer. b. Marshall, AR, Jul 7, 1917. Country and western perf during the 40s and 50s. Films inc: Laramie; The Prodigal Son.

BRITT, Mai (Maybritt Wilkens): Act. b. Sweden, 1933. Films inc: Affairs of a Model; La Lupa; The Young Lions; The Hunters; The Blue Angel; Murder Inc.; Secrets of a Woman; The Ship of Condemned Women; Haunts.

BRITTANY, Morgan (Suzanne Cupito): Act. b. Hollywood, Dec 5, 1951. Films inc: Marnie; The Birds; Gypsy; Gable and Lombard. TV inc: Amazing Howard Hughes; Delta County; Initiation of Sarah; Samurai; Fantastic Seven; Going Home Again; The Dream Merchants; Moviola; Faeries (voice); The Wild Women of Chastity Gulch; Dallas; Glitter; Half Nelson; Bob Hope's Comedy Salute To The Soaps; On Top All Over The World.

BRITTEN, Benjamin: Comp. b. Lowestoft, England, Nov 22, 1913. Operas inc: Peter Grimes; The Rape of Lucretia; Albert Herring; The Beggar's Opera (new version); Billy Budd; The Turn of the Screw; A Midsummer Night's Dream; Death in Venice. Numerous choral works inc War Requiem *(Grammys*-class album of year, class perf choral, class comp-1963).

Films inc: Doktor Faustus. TV inc: A Time There Was.

BRITTON, Tony: Act. b. Birmingham, England, Jun 9, 1924. Performed in repertory; first London stage appearance 1952, The Firstborn. Films inc: Salute the Toff; Loser Take All; The Rough and the Smooth; Suspect; Stork Talk; The Break; There's a Girl in My Soup; Sunday, Bloody Sunday; The Day of the Jackal; The People That Time Forgot; Night Watch; Agatha.

TV inc: Melissa; Romeo and Juliet; The Nearly Man.

Thea inc: Move Over Mrs. Markham; No, No, Nanette; The Dame of Sark; The Chairman; The Bells of Hell; My Fair Lady (rev); Murder Among Friends.

BROCCOLI, Albert R: Prod. b. NYC, Apr 5, 1909. Began as asst dir, Fox, 1938; exec. prod., Warwick Films. Films inc: Cockleshell Heroes; No Time to Die; The Black Knight; Red Beret; Hell Below Zero; Fire Down Below; The Trials of Oscar Wilde; Dr. No; From Russia With Love; Goldfinger; Thunderball; You Only Live Twice; On Her Majesty's Secret Service; Chitty Chitty Bang Bang; Diamonds Are Forever; Live and Let Die; Man With The Golden Gun; The Spy Who Loved Me; Moonraker; For Your Eyes Only; Octopussy; A View To A Kill.

(Irving G Thalberg Award-1981).

BROCKMAN, Michael: Exec. e. Ithaca Coll. With ABC 1974 as vp, daytime programming, ABC Entertainment, later vp, tape prod ops and admin. Joined NBC Nov 1977 as vp, daytime programs, NBC Entertainment.

BROCKWAY, Merrill: Prod. b. New Carlisle, IN., Feb. 28, 1923. e. IN U, BA; MA Musicology. Originally a concert pianist. Joined CBS 1953 as prod-dir in arts, later exec prod-dir Camera Three; series producer Dance In America *(Emmy*-1979); exec prod CBS Cable. Shows inc: An Evening With Alan Jay Lerner; A Song For Dead Warriors (San Francisco Ballet-Dance In America) *(Emmy-dir-1984)*; Balanchine (dir).

BRODERICK, Matthew: Act. b. NYC, Aug. 21, 1962. Studied with Uta Hagen. S of the late James Broderick. Thea inc: (Off-Bway) Valentine's Day. (Bway) Torch Song Trilogy; Brighton Beach Memoirs *(Tony*-featured-1983); Biloxi Blues.

Films inc: Max Dugan Returns; WarGames; Ladyhawke; 1918.

BRODKIN, Herbert: Prod. b. NYC, Nov 9, 1912. e. MI U; Yale Drama School. TV inc: The Defenders; The Nurses; Shane; Coronet Blue; Holocaust *(Emmy*-exec prod-1978); Hollow Image; Doctor Franken; Death Penalty; FDR - The Last Year; The Henderson Monster; Pueblo; The Missiles of October; F Scott Fitzgerald; Last of the Belles; King Crab; Skokie (exec prod); My Body, My Child (exec prod); Benny's Place (exec prod); Ghost Dancing (exec prod); The Firm (exec prod).

Films inc: Sakharov (exec prod). *(NATAS Founders Award*-1983).

BRODNEY, Oscar: Wri-Prod. b. Boston, 1905. e. Boston U, LLB; Harvard, LLM. Films inc: When Johnny Comes Marching Home; Are You With It?; Yes Sir, That's My Baby; Francis; Little Egypt; The Glenn Miller Story; Lady Godiva; Tammy and the Bachelor; The Bobbikins; Tammy and the Doctor; The Brass Bottle; I'd Rather be Rich.

BRODZIAK, Kenn: Prod. b. Sydney, Australia, May 31, 1913. Joint Man Dir Playbox Theatres Pty, Ltd; Chmn, Man Dir, J C Williamson Prods Ltd.

BROGLIATTI, Barbara: Pub exec. (nee Spencer):b. Los Angeles, Jan 8, 1946. e. UCLA, BA. Handled publicity on many top tv shows inc: Mission Impossible; Mannix; All in The Family; The Jeffersons; Mary Hartman, Mary Hartman; Eleanor, First Lady of the World; I Love Liberty. Aug 1981, Sr VP Wldwde ad-pub-prom Embassy Communications.

BROIDY, Steve: Exec. b. Malden, MA, Jun 14, 1905. b. Boston U. Started in sls, Franklin Film Co, then U & WB, before joining Monogram as sls m, 1933; in 1940, elected to bd of dir; in 1945, vp-oper; then p until 1964. P Associated Films Ents.

Jean Hersholt Humanitarian Award, 1962.

BROKAW, Norman R.: Exec. b. NYC, Apr 21, 1927. e. UCLA. Joined William Morris Agency as trainee, 1943. Sr agent, exec. in m.p., TV, 1951; 1974, VP William Morris Agency, World Wide, all areas.

BROKAW, Tom: TV News. b. Yankton, SD, Feb 6, 1940. e. U of SD. Former NBC anchor, LA; NBC White House corr, 1973-76; Aug 1976 Host of Today; April, 1982, co-anchor NBC Nightly News; Sept, 1983 became sole anchor. TV inc: To Be A Doctor; The Changing West--Reflections on the Stillwater (& wri); An American Profile--The Narcs; Reagan at Midterm; Journey to the Heart of China; Iacocca--An American Profile; D-Day Plus 40 Years (wri-corr).

BROLIN, James: Act. b. Los Angeles, Jul 18, 1940. TV inc: The Monroes; Marcus Welby, M.D. *(Emmy*-supp-1970); A Short Walk To Daylight; Trapped; The Ambush Murders; Mae West; White Water Rebels; Cowboy; Arthur Hailey's "Hotel".

Films inc: Take Her, She's Mine; Von Ryan's Express; Morituri; Fantastic Voyage; The Capetown Affair; Our Man Flint; The Car; Gable and Lombard; Capricorn One; The Amityville Horror; Night of the Juggler; High Risk.

BROMFIELD, John: Act. b. South Bend, IN, Jun 11, 1922. e. St Mary's Coll. Films inc: Harpoon; Rope of Sand; Paid in Full; The Furies; Flat Top; Easy to Love; Ring of Fear; Crime Against Joe; Manfish; Hot Cars.

TV inc: Sheriff of Cochise; U.S. Marshall.

BRON, Eleanor: Act. b. Stanmore, Middlesex, England, 1934. Films inc: Help; Alfie; Two for the Road; Bedazzled; Women in Love; The Millstone.

TV inc: Not So Much a Programme, More a Way of Life.

Thea inc: The Doctor's Dilemma; Howard's End; The Prime of Miss Jean Brodie; Two for the Seesaw; The Prince of Darkness.

BRONFMAN, Edgar Jr.: Prod. b. NYC, May 16, 1955. Films inc: The Blockhouse; The Border. TV inc: The All-Star Jazz Show.

Bway inc: Ladies of the Alamo.

BRONSON, Charles (nee Buchinsky): Act. b. Ehrenfeld, PA, 1921. Stock companies, off-Broadway. Films inc: You're in the Navy Now; Red Skies of Montana; Pat and Mike; House of Wax; The Magnificent Seven; The Dirty Dozen; The Great Escape; The Sandpiper; Rider In The Rain; You Can't Win 'em All; The Valachi Papers; The Stone Killer; Mr Majestyk; Death Wish; Breakout; Hard Times; Break Heart Pass; From Noon Till Three; St. Ives; The White Buffalo; Telefon; Love and Bullets; Borderline; Caboblanco; Death Hunt; Death Wish II; 10 To Midnight; The Evil That Men Do.

TV inc: The Lineup; The Legend of Jesse James; Raid On Entebbe.

BRONSON, Lillian: Act. b. Lockport, NY, Oct 21, 1902. e. U of MI. Films inc: Happy Land; What a Man; A Tree Grows in Brooklyn; Junior Miss; Sentimental Journey; The Hucksters; Sleep My Love; No Room for the Groom; Walk on the Wild Side; Spencer's Mountain; Fail Safe; The Americanization of Emily.

TV inc: Playhouse 90; Studio One; Playhouse of Stars.

Bway inc: Five Star Final; Camille; The Druid Circle.

BRONSTON, Samuel: Prod. b. Bessarabia, Russia, Mar 26, 1908. e. Sorbonne. Films inc: Martin Eden; City Without Men; Jack London; Ten Little Indians; A Walk in the Sun; The Count of Monte Cristo; John Paul Jones; King of Kings; El Cid; 55 Days at Peking; Fall of the Roman Empire; Circus World.

BROOK, Peter: Dir. b. London, Mar 21, 1925. e. Magdalen Coll; Oxford. Films inc: The Beggar's Opera; Moderato Cantabile; Lord of the Flies; Marat/Sade; Tell Me Lies; King Lear; Meetings With Remarkable Men; La Tragedie de Carmen.

Thea inc: Pygmalion; Man and Superman; King John; The Lady from the Sea; The Brothers Karamazov; The Little Hut; Faust; The Dark is Light Enough; Both Ends Meet; The House of Flowers; Irma La Douce; The Visit; The Fighting Cock; Marat/Sade *(Tony*-1966); The Physician; The Investigation; A Midsummer Night's Dream *(Tony*-1971); La Tragedie de Carmen (& wri); Un Amour de Swann (Swann in Love) (wri); Jean-Louis Barrault--A Man Of The Theatre (doc-int).

TV inc: (wri) The Birthday Present; Box for One.

BROOKS, Albert (nee Einstein): Dir-Wri-Act. b. Los Angeles, Jul 22, 1947. e. Carnegie Tech. S of late comedian Harry Einstein (Parkyakarkus); B of Bob Einstein. TV inc: (Act) Steve Allen Show; Gold-Diggers of 1969; Tonight Show; Saturday Night Live (& wri). Films inc: Taxi Driver (actonly); Real Life; Private Benjamin (act only); Modern Romance;Twilight Zone--The Movie (act only); Unfaithfully Yours (act only); The Newcomers.

Recordings inc: Comedy Minus One; A Star is Bought.

BROOKS, Bob: Dir. b. Philadelphia, PA, 1927. e. PA State Coll, BA. With Benton & Bowles Ad Agency, NY & London; opened own photo studio, later started firm specializing in tv commercials. TV inc: Space 1999; The Knowledge.

Films inc: Tattoo.

BROOKS, Dick: Pub exec. b. NYC, 1930. e. U of GA. 1951, reporter Atlanta Journal; 1952, sports ed Gainesville Times; 1953, war correspondent Pacific Stars & Stripes; 1957, joined 20th-Fox as staff writer NY pub dept; 1958, NY press rep Embassy Pictures; 1960, NY press rep 20th-Fox; 1962, natl pub dir Seven Arts; 1965, pub mgr Paramount; 1967, natl pub dir 20th-Fox; 1970, pub-ad dir Rastar Productions; 1972, formed Dick Brooks Organization, indie pubbery; 1977, dir film mktg division Rogers & Cowan; 1978, pub dir WB; 1980, launched Dick Brooks Unlimited, indie pubbery.

BROOKS, Donald: Cos dsgn. b. NYC, Jan 10, 1928. e. Fine Arts School, Syracuse; Parsons School of Design. Films inc: The Cardinal; Star!; Darling Lili; The Bell Jar.

Bway inc: No Strings; Barefoot in the Park; Fade Out, Fade In; The Third Day; Flora, The Red Menace; On A Clear Day You Can See Forever; Promises, Promises; Dance A Little Closer.

TV inc: The Letter *(Emmy*-1982).

BROOKS, Foster: Act-Singer. b. Louisville, KY, May 11, 1912. In baseball's Hall of Fame for writing Riley on the Mound. Films inc: Tammy; The Great Race; Yours, Mine and Ours; The Villain; Smorgasbord; Cannonball Run II.

TV inc: Love on a Rooftop; Dean Martin Roasts; Bobby Vinton Show; Bob Hope's All-Star Celebration Opening the Gerald R. Ford Museum; The Great American Sing-A-Long; All-Star Party for Frank Sinatra.

BROOKS, James L.: Prod-Wri. b. Brooklyn, NY, May 9, 1940. With CBS News as wri, 1964-1966; to David Wolper Prodns 1966 as wri-prod of docs.

TV inc: Room 222 (crea-exec story ed); Mary Tyler Moore *(Emmys*-wri-1971,1977; exec prod 1975, 1976, 1977); Thursday's Game (wri-prod); The End (prod); Paul Sand in Friends and Lovers (Exec Prod); Rhoda (co-crea-exec prod); Lou Grant; Cindy (wri); Taxi (co-crea-exec prod) *(Emmys*-1979, 1980, 1981); The Associates.

Films inc: Starting Over; Modern Romance (act); Terms of Endearment (& dir) *(Oscars-prod-dir-wri-1983)*.

BROOKS, Joseph: Sngwri-Prod-Dir. With ad agency. Wrote jingles inc the Pepsi Generation. You Light Up My Life (sp-prod-dir-mus score); *(Oscar*–1977) Films inc: Marjoe (score); Jeremy (score); Lords of Flatbush (score); If Ever I See You Again (sp-act-comp); Heading For Broadway (prod-dir-sp-comp); Eddie and the Cruisers (prod); Invitation To The Wedding (prod-dir-comp).

(Grammy-song-1977).

BROOKS, Louise: Act. b. Cherryvale, KS, Nov 14, 1905. Originally a dancer with Ruth St. Denis, later on Bway.

Films inc: (silent) The Street of Forgotten Men; The American Venus; A Social Celebrity; It's the Old Army Game; The Show-Off; Just Another Blonde; Love 'em and Leave 'em; Rolled Stockings; The City Gone Wild; A Girl in Every Port; Beggars of Life; went to Europe to make Pandora's Box (snd); Diary of a Lost Girl; Prix de Beaute; returned to Hollywood and made It Pays To Advertise; God's Gift to Women; Empty Saddles; When You're In Love; King of the Gamblers; Overland Stage Riders before retiring in 1938.

BROOKS, Mel (nee Kaminsky): Act-Wri-Dir. b. NYC, 1926. H of Anne Bancroft. First appeared as actor in Golden Boy, Red Bank, NJ; also dir and social dir, Catskills. Became wri for Sid Caesar on TV's Broadway Revue & Your Show of Shows; teamed with Carl Reiner for comedy record album, 2000 Year Old Man & The 2000 and 13 Year Old Man.

Films inc: The Critic (short-sp-narr); The Producers *(Oscar*-sp-1968); The Twelve Chairs (sp); Blazing Saddles (sp-prod-co-dir); Young Frankenstein; High Anxiety (prod-sp-dir-act); The Muppet Movie; History of the World--Part I (prod-dir-sp-act); Bonjour Monsieur Lewis (doc); To Be Or Not To Be (prod-act).

TV inc: Sid Caesar, Imogene Coca, Carl Reiner, Howard Morris Special *(Emmy*-wri-1967); Get Smart (wri); When Things Were Rotten (creator); The Television Academy Hall Of Fame 1985.

Thea inc: (wri) Shinbone Alley; All American; Dom DeLuise And Friends.

BROOKS, Richard: Wri-Dir. b. Philadelphia, May 18, 1912. e. Temple U. Films inc: White Savage; The Killers; Brute Force; Crossfire; Key Largo; Any Number Can Play; Crisis; Storm Warning; Deadline; The Last Time I Saw Paris (dir only); Take the High Ground (dir only); The Blackboard Jungle; The Last Hunt; The Catered Affair (dir only); Something of Value; The Brothers Karamazov; Cat on a Hot Tin Roof (dir only); Elmer Gantry *(Oscar*-sp-1960); Lord Jim (& prod); The Professionals (& prod); In Cold Blood (& prod); The Happy Ending (& prod.); Dollars (& prod); Bite the Bullet (& prod); Looking for Mr Goodbar; Wrong Is Right (& prod).

BROOKS, Stan: Exec. b. Los Angeles, Aug. 23, 1958. e. Brandeis U (BA), AFI (MA). Joined Centerpoint Prodns. 1981; dir of dvlpmt 1982; vp 1983; Oct. 1984, sr. vp Guber-Peters Co. TV inc: (prodn supv) Dreams; Oceanquest.

BROOKSHIER, Tom: Sportscaster. b. Roswell, NM, 1931. e. U of CO. Former pro football player. TV inc: (Host) This Is The NFL; Sports Illustrated; CBS Sports Spectacular.

BROOME, Peter J.: Sls Exec. b. Sydney, Australia, Feb 22, 1930. VP 20th Century Fox Int'l, Inc.

BROSNAN, Pierce: Act. b. Ireland, May 16, 1953. Thea inc: (London) Wait Until Dark; The Red Devil Battery Sign; Filumena.

TV inc: Murphy's Stroke; The Manions of America; Nancy Astor; Remington Steele.

Films inc: The Mirror Crack'd; The Long Good Friday; Nomads.

BROSTEN, Harve: Wri-Dir-Prod. b. May 15, 1943. e. Goodman Memorial Theatre-Art Institute, BA. TV inc: All in the Family *(Emmy*-wri-1978); The Jeffersons; The Guiding Light (dir). Prod various industrial shows and Bway revues at St. Regis Hotel, NY.

BROTHERS, Joyce, Dr: Bcst personality. (nee Bauer):b. NYC, Sep 20, 1928. e. Cornell U, BS; Columbia U, PHD. TV inc: Dr Joyce Brothers; Consult Dr Brothers; Ask Dr Brothers; An Appointment with Dr Joyce Brothers; Beggarman, Thief; Daytime Star; More Wild Wild West; Desperate Lives; National Snoop; I Love Men; The Great Survivors.

Films inc: Oh God! Book II; The Lonely Guy.

BROTHERS JOHNSON: Group. Band featuring Louis Johnson, bass; George Johnson, guitar and voc. Albums inc: Look Out For #1; Right On Time; Blam!; Light Up the Night.

(Grammy-R&B inst-1977).

BROUGH, Walter: Prod-Wri. b. Philadelphia, Dec 19, 1935. e. La Salle Coll; USC. Films inc: (as wri) The Desperados; Run Wild, Run Free; A New Life; No Place to Hide; Jed & Sonny (& prod); Funeral for An Assassin (& prod); On a Dead Man's Chest (& prod).

TV inc: (as wri) Doctor Kildare; The Fugitive; Branded; Name of the Game; Mannix; Mission: Impossible; The Magician; Man from Atlantis; Police Story; Lucan.

BROUMAS, John G.: Exec. b. Youngstown, OH, Oct 12, 1917. GM, Pitts & Roth Theatres 1946-54; P, Broumas Theatres; P, Showcase Theatres; secy & treas Tenley Circle Twin Theatre Corp; P, Cinema Mgt Corp.

BROWN, Arvin: Dir. b. Los Angeles, May 24, 1940. e. Stanford, BA; U of Bristol (England) on Fulbright Scholarship; Harvard (Woodrow Wilson Scholar), MA; Yale School of Drama; Artistic dir Long Wharf Theatre, New Haven, since 1967. Bway inc: Solitaire/Double Solitaire; The National Health; Ah Wilderness; Strangers; Watch on the Rhine; A View From The Bridge; Requiem For A Heavyweight. Off-Bway inc: A Long Day's Journey Into Night; Memory of Two Mondays and 27 Wagons Full of Cotton (double bill); American Buffalo (& revival). Also dir (at Long Wharf) American premieres A Whistle in the Dark; Country People; Forget-Me-Not-Lane; The Widowing of Mrs Holroyd; On the Outside/On the Inside; Privates on Parade; Mary Barnes; World premieres You're Too Tall But Come Back in Two Weeks; Artichoke; The Lunch Girls; I Sent A Letter To My Love.

TV inc: The Widowing of Mrs Holroyd; Forget-Me-Not-Lane; Ah Wilderness; Blessings.

BROWN, Blair: Act. b. Washington, DC. e. National Theatre School of Canada. Thea inc: Love and Maple Syrup; School for Scandal; The Merchant of Venice; King Lear; Comedy of Errors; What Every Woman Knows; Three Penny Opera.

Films inc: Paper Chase; One Trick Pony; Altered States; Continental Divide; A Flash Of Green.

TV inc: White Oaks of Jalna; School for Scandal; Oregon Trail (pilot); Captains and the Kings; Wheels; And I Alone Survived; The Child Stealer; Kennedy; The Bad Seed; Space.

BROWN, Bryan: Act. b. Australia 1950. Films inc: Cathy's Child; Newsfront; Money Movers; The Odd Angry Shot; Palm Beach; Blood Money; Stir; Breaker Morant; The Last Wave; My Brilliant Career; Kangaroo; The Winter of Our Dreams; Far East; Give Ny Regards To Broad Street; Parker.

TV inc: Against the Wind; A Town Like Alice; The Thorn Birds; Eureka Stockade; Kim.

BROWN, Charlotte: Wri-Dir. b. Cleveland, OH, Oct 20, 1943. e. UCLA, BA. TV inc: (wri) Mary Tyler Moore Show; Bob Newhart Show; Doris Day Show; Mitzi Gaynor Tribute To American Housewife; Rhoda (& dir, exec prod); The Associates (dir); Letting Go.

BROWN, Clarence: Dir. b. Clinton, MA, May 10, 1890. e. U of TN. Dir debut 1920, The Great Redeemer. Joined MGM 1924. Launched

Greta Garbo as star U.S. 1926, Flesh and the Devil. Films inc: The Last of the Mohicans; The Eagles; The Goose Woman; A Woman of Affairs; Anna Christie; Romance; Inspiration; A Free Soul; Possessed; Chained; Anna Karenina; Ah Wilderness; Conquest; Idiot's Delight; The Rains Came; Edison, the Man; Come Live with Me (& prod); The Human Comedy (& prod); The White Cliffs of Dover; National Velvet; The Yearling; Song of Love (& prod); Intruder in the Dust (& prod); To Please a Lady (& prod); Angels in the Outfield (& prod); When in Rome (& prod); Plymouth Adventure; Never Let Me Go (prod. only).

BROWN, David: Prod. b. NYC, Jul 28, 1916. e. Stanford U, AB; Columbia, MS. Reporter, edtr, drama critic. Story ed, head of scenario dept. 20th-Fox; apptd member of exec staff, Darryl F Zanuck; exec VP Warner Bros. Partnered with Richard D. Zanuck in Zanuck-Brown Prods. Films inc: Sssssss; Willie Dynamite; The Sugarland Express; Black Windmill; The Eiger Sanction; The Girl from Petrovka; The Sting *(Oscar*-1973); Jaws; MacArthur; Jaws 2; The Island; Neighbors; The Verdict; Cocoon.

BROWN, Denys E.: Prod. b. England, Aug 8, 1915. e. Oxford U, BA, MA. From 1948 to 1966, prod more than 100 docs, travelogues, educ films before becoming prod-in-chief at Film Australia.

BROWN, Georg Sanford: Act. b. Havana, Jun 24. Films inc: The Comedians; Dayton's Devils; Bullitt; Colossus; The Forbin Project; The Man; God Bless You, Uncle Sam.

TV inc: The Rookies; Barefoot in Athens; The Young Lawyers; Next Time; My Love; Dawn; Portrait of a Teenage Runaway; Roots; The Night the City Screamed; Grambling's White Tiger (dir); The Greatest American Hero (dir); Cagney & Lacey (dir); The Kid With the Broken Halo; In Defense Of Kids; The Jesse Owens Story.

Thea inc: All's Well That Ends Well; Measure for Measure; Macbeth; Murderous Angels; Hamlet; Detective Story.

BROWN, George H.: Prod. b. London, 1913. Films inc: Sleeping Car to Trieste; The Chiltern Hundreds; The Seekers; Jacqueline; Dangerous Exile; Tommy the Toreador; Murder at the Gallop; Guns at Batasi; The Trap; Finders Keepers; Assault; Revenge; Innocent Bystander; Open Season.

BROWN, Georgia (nee Klot): Act. b. London, Oct 21, 1933. Stage debut, 1956, The Threepenny Opera, London. Films inc: Running Scared; The Fixer; The Raging Moon; Lock Up Your Daughters; Nothing But the Night; The Seven-Per-Cent Solution.

TV inc: Upstairs, Downstairs; Shoulder to Shoulder; The Roads to Freedom.

Thea inc: Oliver!; Maggie May.

BROWN, Harry: Wri. b. Portland, ME, Apr 30, 1917. e. Harvard. Films inc: The True Glory; A Walk in the Sun; Arch of Triumph; Sands of Iwo Jima; A Place in the Sun *(Oscar*-sp-1951); Bugles in the Afternoon; The Sniper; Eight Iron Men; All the Brothers Were Valiant; D-Day the Sixth of June; Between Heaven and Hell; Ocean's II; El Dorado.

BROWN, James H.: Prod-Dir. b. Berkeley, CA, Jul 26. e. Stanford U; UCLA. TV inc: (dir) Wagon Train; Honey West. (Prod) Gibbsville; The First 36 Hours of Dr Durant; Joe Forrester; Magnificent Magical Magnet of Santa Mesa; The Quest; Alcatraz--The Whole Shocking Story; Terror Among Us; This Is Kate Bennett; Seven Brides For Seven Brothers; For Love and Honor.

BROWN, Jim: Act. b. St Simons Island, GA, Feb 17, 1936. e. Syracuse U. Played pro football, Cleveland Browns. Won Hickock Belt as Professional Athlete of year, 1964; P of Richard Pryor's Indigo Prodns; ousted Dec. 1983. Films inc: Rio Conchos; The Dirty Dozen; 100 Rifles; Slaughter; The Slams; Three the Hard Way; Take A Hard Ride; Superbug; The Wild Ones; Fingers; One Down, Two To Go. Richard Pryor Here and Now (exec prod); Pacific Inferno.

TV inc: Lady Blue.

BROWN, Johnny: Perf. b. St Petersburg, FL, Jun 11, 1937. TV inc: The Leslie Uggams Show; Laugh-In; Sammy & Company; Hang Tight, Willy Bill. Thea inc: Golden Boy.

BROWN, Les: Comp-Cond. b. Reinerton, PA, Mar 14, 1912. e. Duke

U. Started own band while in college; worked as arr, freelance mus. formed Band of Reknown for recs, tours; cond for Steve Allen; Bob Hope.

TV inc: Bob Hope Shows; Book of Lists.

Songs inc: Trylon Stomp; Duckfoot Waddle; Bill's Well; Bill's Ill; We Wish You the Merriest; Sentimental Journey.

BROWN, Lisa: Act. b. Kansas City, MO, Aug 2, 1954. Thea inc: Seesaw; Hello, Dolly!; Pal Joey; Hit the Deck. Bway inc: The Best Little Whorehouse in Texas.

TV inc: The Guiding Light.

BROWN, Peter: Act. Films inc: Darby's Rangers; Merrill's Marauders; Ride The Wind; Surf; Kitten With a Whip; Three Guns from Texas; Backtrack; Chrome and Hot Leather; The Concrete Jungle.

TV inc: Lawman; Laredo; Salvage; The Top of the Hill; Days of Our Lives; The Girl, The Gold Watch and Everything; Three Eyes; Cover Up.

BROWN, Reb: Act. b. Los Angeles, Apr. 29, 1948. e. Cal State LA, BA. Films inc: Sssssss; Big Wednesday; The One and Only; Hardcore; Fast Break; the Sword and the Sorcerer; Yor -- The Hunter from the Future; Uncommon Valor; Howling II--Your Sister Is A Werewolf.

TV inc: Brave New World; Goldie and the Boxer Go to Hollywood; Captain America; Centennial.

BROWN, Ruth: Singer-Act. Thea inc: Living Fat; Selma; Guys and Dolls; Amen Corner.

TV inc: Hello, Larry.

BROWN, Tom: Act. b. NYC, Jan 6, 1913. On radio, then stage. Screen debut in A Lady Lies, 1929. Films inc: Buck Privates Come Home; Duke of Chicago; Operation Haylift; Fireman Save My Child.

TV inc: General Hospital.

BROWN, Vanessa (Smylla Brind): Act. b. Vienna, 1928. e. UCLA. W of Mark Sandrich, Jr. One of original Quiz Kids on radio. Bway inc: Watch on the Rhine; Seven Year Itch. Films inc: Margie; The Late George Apley; Mother Wore Tights; The Foxes of Harrow; The Heiress; Tarzan and the Slave Girl; The Bad and the Beautiful; Rosie; Bless the Beasts and the Children.

BROWNE, Coral: Act. b. Melbourne, Australia, Jul 23, 1913. W of Vincent Price. Thea inc: Lover's Leap; Mated; Basalik; This Desirable Residence; The Golden Gander; Heroes Don't Care; Death Asks a Verdict; The Great Romancer; The Man Who Came to Dinner; Bonne Soupe; The Rehearsal; Lady Windermere's Fan; What the Butler Saw; My Darling Daisy; The Waltz of the Toreadors.

Films inc: The Amateur Gentlemen; Pygmalion; The Prime Minister; Quartet; Madeleine; All at Sea; Rooney; The Ruling Class; Theatre of Blood; The Drowning Pool; American Dreamer.

TV inc: Time Express; Eleanor, First Lady of the World; An Englishman Abroad.

BROWNE, Jackson: Songwri-Act. b. Heidelberg, Germany, Oct 9, 1948. Songs inc: Fountain of Sorrow; Before the Deluge; Doctor My Eyes; Here Comes Those Tears; The Pretender.

Albums inc: The Pretender; Running On Empty; Hold Out. Films inc: No Nukes.

BROWNE, Leslie Act. b. NYC, 1958. e. School of American Ballet, NY. Debut in the corps de ballet of Balanchine's Symphony in C, Lincoln Center, 1974; Union Jack, 1976. Hired by Dir Herbert Ross for minor parts in film The Turning Point. When girl originally chosen for key role became ill, Browne replaced her and received Oscar nomination; Nijinsky.

BROWNE, Roscoe Lee: Act-Dir-Wri. b. Woodbury, NJ, 1925. e. Lincoln U; Middlebury Coll; Columbia U. International track star, 1946-56; published poet, short story writer. Films inc: The Comedians; Uptight; The Liberation of L.B. Jones; The Cowboys; World's Greatest Athlete; Superfly T.N.T.; Logan's Run; Twilight's Last Gleaming; Nothing Personal.

Bway inc: The Ballad of the Sad Cafe; The Cool World; Tiger, Tiger Burning Bright!; The Old Glory; A Hand Is On the Gate (& dir); My One and Only.

TV inc: King; The Haunting of Harrington House; High Five; For Us, The Living; Space.

BROWNING, Kirk: Dir. b. NYC, Mar 28, 1921. e. Cornell. Worked as reporter; with American Field Services; as ad writer before joining NBC-TV 1949 as floor mgr. TV inc: Trial of Mary Lincoln; Jascha Heifetz Special; Harry and Lena; NBC Opera Theatre (40 programs); Producers Showcase; Evening with Toscanini; Bell Telephone; The Flood; Beauty and the Beast; Lizzie Borden; World of Carl Sandburg; La Gioconda (Emmy-1980); Big Blonde; Working: Ian McKellen Acting Shakespeare; Fifth Of July; Alice in Wonderland; Live From the Met--The Metropolitan Opera Centennial parts I and II.

BRUBECK, Dave: Comp-Mus. b. Concord, CA, Dec 6, 1920. e. U Pacific, BA. Studied under Darius Milhaud. One of the pioneers of modern jazz, formed own trio 1950, quartet following year; played niteries; several Carnegie Hall appearances; disbanded quartet 1967. TV inc: Jazz Comes Home To Newport.

Compositions inc: The Light in the Wilderness; Beloved Son; Gates of Justice.

BRUCE, Brenda: Act. b. Manchester, England, 1918. Stage debut, 1934, Babes in the Wood. Films inc: Night Boat to Dublin; Millions Like Us; Piccadilly Incident; My Brother's Keeper; Marry Me; The Final Test; Law and Disorder; Nightmare; The Uncle; Steaming.

Thea inc: Gently Does It; Woman in a Dressing Gown; Merry Wives of Windsor; Little Murders; Winters Tale; Pericles; Hamlet; Romeo and Juliet.

TV inc: Nearer to Heaven; Wrong Side of the Park; The Lodger; Love Story; Give the Clown His Supper; Knock on Any Door; Death of a Teddy Bear; Family at War; Henry IV; Macbeth.

BRUCE, Carol (Shirley Levy): Act-Singer. b. NYC, Nov 15, 1919. Professional debut as bandsinger. As single, headlined top U.S. niteries. Bway inc: George White's Scandals of 1939; Nice Goin'; Louisiana Purchase; New Priorities of 1943; Show Boat; Along Fifth Avenue; Pal Joey; A Family Affair; Do I Hear a Waltz; Henry, Sweet Henry.

Films inc: This Woman Is Mine; Keep 'Em Flying; Behind the Eight Ball; The Messenger; American Gigolo.

TV inc: Ed Sullivan show; Studio One; Armstrong Circle Theatre; Love Of Life; WKRP in Cincinnati.

BRUCE, Lydia (nee Slubowski): Act. b. Detroit, MI, Jan 8. Thea inc: Twelfth Night; A Call on Kuprin.

TV inc: The Doctors (since 1967); The War and Mary Kate.

BRUCKHEIMER, Jerry: Prod. Started as ad agency exec. Films inc: Farewell, My Lovely (co-prod); March Or Die (co-prod); Defiance; American Gigolo; Thief; Cat People; Young Doctors In Love; Flashdance; Thief Of Hearts; Beverly Hills Cop.

BRUNDIN, Bo: Act. b. Stockholm, Apr 25, 1937. Arrived U.S. in 1958. Worked in summer stock and off-Broadway. Since 1964 has alternated time between U.S. and Sweden. Films inc: The Great Waldo Pepper; Russian Roulette; The Day The Clown Cried; Meteor; Raise The Titanic; The Headless Eyes.

TV inc: The Word; Centennial; Swan Song; Masquerade.

BRUNING, Robert: Prod. b. Western Australia. TV inc: The Godfathers; The Spoilers; Crisis; The People Next Door; The True Blue Show; Paradise; Is There Anybody There; Mama's Gone A-Hunting; The Alternative; Gone to Ground; The Night Nurse; Plunge Into Darkness; Image of Death; The Death Train; Roses Bloom Twice; Demolition.

BRUNNER, Robert F.: Comp-Cond-Arr. b. Pasadena, CA, Jan 9, 1938. Comp., arr., Walt Disney Studios. Scores inc: That Darn Cat; The Computer Wore Tennis Shoes; The Barefoot Executive; Snowball Express; The Castaway Cowboy; The Strongest Man in the World; The North Avenue Irregulars.

TV inc: Gallegher Goes West; Salute to Alaska; The Owl That Didn't Give a Hoot; Hamad and the Pirates; Cavalcade of Songs; Mustang; Adventure in Satan's Canyon; Coomba, Dingo of the Outback; The Young Runaways; The Wonderful World of Disney Special.

BRUNS, George: Comp. b. Sandy, OR, Jul. 3, 1914. Film scores inc:

Sleeping Beauty; Babes in Toyland; The Sword in the Stone; Jungle Book; 101 Dalmatians; Aristocats; Robin Hood; The Absent-Minded Professor; The Love Bug.

TV inc: Wonderful World of Disney.

Songs inc: Ballad of Davy Crockett; Zorro; Love. (Died May 23, 1983)

BRYAN, Dora (nee Broadbent): Act. b. Southport, England, Feb 7, 1924. Stage debut, 1935; screen debut, 1948, Fallen Idol. Films inc: The Cure for Love; The Blue Lamp; High Treason; Lady Godiva Rides Again; Fast and Loose; See How They Run; Cockleshell Heroes; The Green Man; The Night We Got the Bird; A Taste of Honey; The Great St. Trinian's Train Robbery; The Sandwich Man; Two a Penny; Hands of the Ripper; Up the Front.

BRYANT, Anita: Act. b. Barnsdall, OK, Mar 25, 1940. Former Miss Oklahoma. Recording artist. Does promo work for Florida Citrus Commission.

BRYANT, Michael: Act. b. London, Apr 5, 1928. Thea inc: The New Tenant; The Iceman Cometh; Five Finger Exercise (& Bway); Ross; Next Time I'll Sing To You; Trap for a Lonely Man; Victor; The Jew of Malta; Henry V; The Homecoming; The Duel; The Siege; The Return of A J Raffles; The Family Dance; Man and Superman; Jean Seberg.

Films inc: Life for Ruth; The Mindbenders; Goodbye, Mr. Chips; Nicholas and Alexandra; The Ruling Class; Sakharov.

TV inc: The Merry Wives of Windsor.

BRYDEN, Bill (William Campbell Bryden): Plywri-Dir. b. Scotland, Apr 12, 1942. Plays inc: Willie Rough; Benny Lynch. Thea inc: (dir) Backbone; Passion; The Baby Elephant; The Iceman Cometh; Watch It Come Down; The Crucible; Don Quixote; Glengarry Glen Ross.

BRYGGMAN, Larry: Act. b. Concord, CA, Dec 21, 1938. e. City College San Francisco. Bway inc: Ulysses in Nighttown; The Lincoln Mask; Checking Out; The Basic Training of Pavlo Hummel; Richard III. Other thea inc: The Winter Dancers; Marco Polo Sang A Solo; Waiting for Godot; Madonna; The Long Grass; Dearly Beloved; Two Small Bodies; Irma La Douce; Death of a Salesman; The Ballad Of Sopay Smith (off-Bway).

TV inc: Trail of the Panther 13; The Witches of Salem; A Celebration for William Jennings Bryan; Love Is A Many Splendored Thing; As The World Turns (since 1969) (Emmy-1984).

BRYNNER, Yul: Act. b. Sakhalin Island, Japan, Jul 11, 1920. Started singing in night clubs in Paris at age 12. Later joined circus as trapeze artist. Performed with repertory co. in Paris, made American stage debut in Twelfth Night. Bway inc: Lute Song; Dark Eyes; The King and I (Tony-supp-1952); Home, Sweet Homer; The King and I (Rev). (London) The King and I.

Films inc: Port of New York; The King and I (Oscar-1956); Ten Commandments; Anastasia; Solomon and Sheba; The Magnificent Seven; Taras Bulba; Invitation to a Gunfighter; Return of the Seven; Madwoman of Chaillot; Romance of a Horsethief; Fuzz; Futureworld.

TV inc: Anna and the King of Siam; The 39th Annual Tony Awards.

BUCHANAN, James D: Wri-Prod. b. Detroit, MI, Dec 17, 1929. e. MI State. TV inc: Death Squad (wri); Paperman (wri); Jigsaw John (wriprod); Charlie's Angels (prod); Beach Patrol (wri); The Return of Frank Cannon (wri).

Films inc: Harry in Your Pocket (wri).

BUCHHOLZ, Horst: Act. b. Berlin, Dec 4, 1933. In radio, stage plays. Screen debut in Marianne (French), 1955. Films inc: Robinson Must Not Die; The Confessions of Felix Krull; Tiger Bay; Fanny; One, Two, Three; Nine Hours to Rama; The Empty Canvas; The Great Waltz; Cervantes; From Hell to Victory; Avalanche Express; Aphrodite; Sahara; Wenn Ich Mich Furchte (Fear Of Falling).

TV inc: Raid on Entebbe; The French Atlantic Affair; Berlin Tunnel 21.

Thea inc: Arms And The Man.

BUCK, Jules: Prod. b. St Louis, MO, Jul 30, 1917. Films inc: Love Nest; Fixed Bayonets; Treasure of the Golden Condor; The Day They Robbed the Bank of England; Great Catherine. Under Milkwood; The Ruling Class; Man Friday; The Great Scout and Cathouse Thursday.

TV inc: O.S.S.

BUCKLEY, Anthony: Prod. b. Sydney, Australia, Jul 27, 1937. Films inc: Caddie; The Irishman; The Night of the Prowler; The Killing of Angel Street; Bliss.

BUCKLEY, Betty: Act. b. Big Springs, TX, Jul 3, 1947. Films inc: Carrie; Tender Mercies. TV inc: Eight is Enough; The Ordeal of Bill Carney; Bobby and Sarah (Special Treat); Salute to Lady Liberty; The Three Wishes Of Billy Grier; Evergreen.

Bway inc: 1776; Promises, Promises; Pippin; Cats (Tony-featured--1983).

BUCKLEY, William F, Jr: Wri-Tv personality. b. NYC, Nov 24, 1925. e. Yale, BA; Seton Hall, LHD; St Peters, LLD. Editor in chief of the National Review. TV host of Firing Line since 1966. Other TV inc: Eye On The Media--Private Lives, Public Press; Citizen--The Political Life Of Allard K Lowenstein.

BUFMAN, Zev: Act-Prod. b. Tel Aviv, Israel, Oct 11, 1931. e. LA City Coll, MA. Films inc: Bengal Rifles; Flight to Tangiers; The Prodigal; The Ten Commandments; Buccaneer.

Thea inc: (act) See How They Run; Lady in the Dark; Brigadoon; Caesar and Cleopatra; Merton of the Movies. (Prod): A Hole in the Head; Laffcapades; Fair Game; Murder in the Red Barn; The Barber of Seville; Our Town; Pajama Tops. (Bway) (prod) The Egg; Fair Game for Lovers; Minor Miracle; Marat/Sade; Spofford; Your Own Thing; Jimmy Shine; Big Time Buck White; Oklahoma! (rev); West Side Story (rev); Peter Pan (rev); Brigadoon (rev); The First; Oh, Brother!; Joseph and the Amazing Technicolor Dreamcoat; A View From The Bridge; Private Lives; The Corn Is Green; Peg; Requiem For A Heavyweight.

BUJOLD, Genevieve: Act. b. Montreal, Jul 1, 1942. e. Montreal Conservatory of Drama. On screen from 1967. Films inc: La Guerre est Finie; La Fleur de L'age; King of Hearts; The Thief; Isabel; Anne of The Thousand Days; The Act of the Heart; The Journey; Earthquake; Swashbuckler; Obsession; Alex and the Gypsy; Another Man, Another Chance; Coma; Murder By Decree; The Last Flight of Noah's Ark; Final Assignment; Monsignor; Tightrope; Choose Me.

TV inc: St. Joan; Anthony and Cleopatra; Mistress of Paradise.

Thea inc: The Barber of Seville; A Midsummer Night's Dream; A House. . .A Day.

BUKTENICA, Raymond: Act. b. NYC, Aug 6, 1943. e. UCLA. TV inc: Rhoda; The Amazing Mr. Hughes; Circle of Children; Mary Jane Harper Cried Last Night; The Amazing Nellie Bly; House Calls; The Jayne Mansfield Story; The Adventures of Nellie Bly; Wait Till Your Mother Gets Home; Walter; For Love Or Money; Goodbye, Charlie.

Films inc: King Kong; Annie Hall.

BULAJIC, Veljko: Dir. b. Montenegro, Yugoslavia, Mar 23, 1928. Originally a newspaperman, studied at Rome's Centro Sperimentale film school, worked as assistant to several Italian directors. Films inc: Train Without A Timetable; War; Boom Town; Hill of Death; Skopje (doc); Battle of Neretva; Assassination in Sarajevo; High Voltage.

BULIFANT, Joyce: Act. b. Newport News, VA, Dec 16. e. AADA. Bway inc: Tall Story; Whisper to Me; The Paisley Convertible.

TV inc: 90 Bristol Court; Love Thy Neighbor; Big John, Little John; Darn You, Harry Landers; Hanging By A Thread; Flo; Charley's Aunt (cable).

Films inc: The Happiest Millionaire; Airplane.

BULOFF, Joseph: Act-Dir. b. Wilno, Lithuania, Dec 12, 1899. To US in 1928. Joined Yiddish Art Theatre, NY, in 1930; Bway inc: Don't Look Now; Morning Star; Oklahoma!; Mrs McThing (dir); The Fifth Season; Once More with Feeling; Moonbirds; Slow Dance on a Killing Ground; The Price.

Films inc: Let's Make Music; Somebody Up There Likes Me; Silk Stockings.

(Died Feb. 27, 1985)

BUMSTEAD, Henry: Art dir. Films inc: To Kill a Mockingbird (Oscar-1962); The Sting (Oscar-1973); Rollercoaster; Slap Shot; House

Calls; Same Time Next Year; A Little Romance; The Concorde--Airport 79; Smokey and The Bandit II; The Little Drummer Girl.

BUNIM, Mary-Ellis: Prod. b. Northampton, MA, Jul 9, 1946. e. Fordham U. TV inc: Search for Tomorrow, exec prod, since 1975; Santa Barbara (co-exec prod)

BUNUEL, Luis (Jean-Louis Bunuel): Wri-Dir. b. Calanda, Spain, 1900. Films inc: Un Chien Andalou; L'Age d'Or; Land Without Bread; Los Olvidados; The Brute; Wuthering Heights; Robinson Crusoe; Una Mujer Sin Amor (A Woman Without Love); La Ilusion Viaja en Tranvia; La Mort en ce Jardin; The Young One; Viridiana; The Exterminating Angel; Diary of a Chambermaid; Belle de Jour; The Milky Way; Tristana; The Discreet Charm of the Bourgeoisie; The Phantom of Liberty; That Obscure Object of Desire.
(Died July 29, 1983).

BURCH, Shelly: Act. b. Tucson, AZ., Mar. 19. Bway inc: Stop the World, I Want to Get Off; Annie; Nine.
Films inc: Stop the World, I Want to Get Off.
TV inc: One Life to Live.

BURGE, Stuart, CBE: Dir. b. Essex, England, Jan 15, 1918. Originally act with Old Vic. Thea inc: (Dir) Let's Make an Opera; Hook, Line and Sinker; Henry V (& overseas tour); Public and Confidential (Bway); Serjeant Musgrave's Dance (Bway); The Judge; Two Gentlemen of Verona; The Ruling Class; The Demonstration; The Daughter-in-law; The Rivals; A Close Shave; See How They Run; The White Raven; The Devil Is An Ass; The London Cuckolds; The Seagull; Another Country.
Films inc: There Was a Crooked Man; Othello; The Mikado; Julius Caesar.
TV inc: The Power and the Glory; The Devil and John Brown; Luther; School for Scandal; Sons and Lovers; Much Ado About Nothing.

BURGESS, Wilma: Act. b. Orlando, FL, Jun 11, 1939. e. Stetson Coll. Country mus perf, recording artist.

BURGHOFF, Gary: Act. b. Bristol, CT, May 24, 1943. Films inc: M*A*S*H; B S I Love You.
TV inc: An Evening's Journey to Conway, Mass; M*A*S*H *(Emmy-*1977); The Man In The Santa Claus Suit; Casino; Walter.
Thea inc: You're a Good Man, Charlie Brown; Finian's Rainbow; Look Homeward, Angel; Bells Are Ringing; Sound of Music; The Boy Friend; Romanoff and Juliet.

BURKE, Alfred: Act. b. London, Feb 28, 1918. e. RADA. Films inc: The Angry Silence; Moment of Danger; The Man Inside; The Man Upstairs; No Time to Die; Law and Disorder; Yangtse Incident; Interpol; Bitter Victory.
TV inc: The Crucible; Mock Auction; Parole; The Big Knife; Parnell; The Strong are Lonely; Home of the Brave; The Birthday Party; The Watching Eye; The House on Garabaldi Street; Pope John Paul II; Kim; The Glory Boys.
Thea inc: The Universal Legacy; Henry VI; The MacRoary Whirl; The Father; Pictures in a Bath of Acid; Murder in the Cathedral; Dr. Knock.

BURKE, David: Act. b. Liverpool, England, May 25, 1934. e. RADA. Thea inc: (London) War and Peace; Hotel in Amsterdam; several seasons with Royal Lyceum Company Edinburgh; A Pagan Place; Absurd Person Singular; Watch on the Rhine.
TV inc: King Henry VI; The Adventures Of Sherlock Holmes.

BURKE, Delta: Act. b. Orlando, FL, Jul 30, 1956. e. LAMDA. TV inc: The Seekers; Charleston; A Last Cry for Help; The Chisholms; Filthy Rich; Rooster; Mickey Spillane's Murder Me, Murder You; A Bunny's Tale.

BURKE, Graham William: Exec. b. Australia, Jun 10, 1942. Member, Australian Film Commission.

BURKE, Patricia: Act. b. Milan, Italy, Mar 23, 1917. London stage debut 1933, I Hate Men. Films inc: The Lisbon Story; The Trojan Brothers; Love Story; While I Live; Forbidden; The Happiness of Three

Women; Spider's Web; The Day the Fish Came Out.
TV inc: Robin Hood; For Dear Life; Sword of Freedom.

BURKE, Paul: Act. b. New Orleans, Jan 21, 1929. Films inc: South Sea Woman; Screaming Eagles; Valley of the Dolls; The Thomas Crown Affair; Once You Kiss A Stranger; Daddy's Gone A-Hunting.
TV inc: Noah's Ark; Five Fingers; Harbor Master; Naked City; Killing At Hell's Gate; Advice to the Lovelorn; The Red-Light Sting.

BURLEIGH, Stephen: Act. b. Wheeling, WV, Jul 29, 1949. e. UC Berkeley, AB; Neighborhood Playhouse. Thea inc: Translations; Crimes of the Heart; Scenes and Revelations. Thea inc: A Talent for Murder (Bway); Sand Dancing (Off Bway).
TV inc: For Richer, For Poorer; Search For Tomorrow; Texas; Enola Gay; The Kidnapping At Shady Hill; The Doctors.

BURMESTER, Leo: Act. b. Louisville, KY, Feb 1. e. Western KY Coll, BA; U Denver, MA. Films inc: Cruising. Bway inc: Lone Star.
TV inc: All My Children; The Caretaker; Flo; A Fine Romance; Chiefs; George Washington.

BURNETT, Carol: Act. b. San Antonio, TX, Apr 26, 1933. e. UCLA. W of Joe Hamilton. Summer stock and nitery experience prior to appearance on Jack Paar show and subsequent Garry Moore daytime tv show. Bway debut in Once Upon a Mattress.
TV inc: Garry Moore Show *(Emmy-*1962); Julie and Carol at Carnegie Hall *(Emmy-*1963); Carol & Company; Calamity Jane; Once Upon a Mattress; Carol Burnett Show *(Emmys-*1972, 1974, 1975); Julie and Carol at Lincoln Center; 6 Rms Riv Vu; Twigs; Sills and Burnett at the Met; Dolly and Carol in Nashville; The Grass is Always Greener Over the Septic Tank; Friendly Fire; The Tenth Month; This Side Of Eden; Entertainer of the Year Awards; Get High On Yourself; Jim Nabor's Christmas in Hawaii; Eunice; Cheryl Ladd--Scenes from A Special; Hollywood--The Gift of Laughter; Texaco Star Theatre--Opening Night; Life of the Party--The Story of BeAtrice; An All-Star Party For Carol Burnett; The 4th Annual TV Guide Special; Between Friends (cable); Here's Television Entertainment (host); Burnett "Discovers" Domingo; The Laundromat (PC); On Top All Over The World.
Films inc: Who's Been Sleeping in My Bed; Pete'n Tillie; The Front Page; A Wedding; Health; The Four Seasons; Chu Chu and the Philly Flash; Annie.
*(Special Tony-*1969). *(Television Academy Hall Of Fame 1985)*

BURNS, Allan: Wri-Prod. b. Baltimore. Films inc: (Wri) A Little Romance; Butch and Sundance, The Early Years; Just The Way You Are.
TV inc: He and She *(Emmy-*1968); Mary Tyler Moore Show *(Emmys-*(5)-wri-1971 & 1977; exec prod-1975, 1976, 1977); Rhoda; Lou Grant; The Duck Factory.

BURNS, Bonnie: Prod. b. Seattle, May 28, 1949. e. U of WA, BA. TV inc: (prod): Don Kirshners Rock Concert; The Jacksons; Rock Music Awards; The World's Most Spectacular Stuntman; Sweeney Todd (cable).

BURNS, Catherine: Act. b. NYC, Sep 25, 1945. e. AADA. Thea inc: The Crucible; The Prime of Miss Jean Brodie.
Films inc: Last Summer; Red Sky At Morning.

BURNS, George (Nathan Birnbaum): Act. b. NYC, 1896. In show business from age of seven. Vaudeville song and dance man. Teamed with Gracie Allen, 1925 for long career on radio, TV.
Films inc: The Big Broadcast; We're Not Dressing; Many Happy Returns; International House; Love in Bloom; College Swing; Honolulu; Two Girls and A Sailor; The Sunshine Boys *(Oscar-*supp-1975); Oh, God!; Sgt. Pepper's Lonely Hearts Club Band; Just You and Me Kid; Going in Style; Oh, God! Book II; Oh, God! You Devil.
TV inc: Wendy and Me; Ann-Margret - Hollywood Movie Girls; George Burns In Nashville???; Bob Hope Anniversary Special; A Love Letter To Jack Benny; Two Of A Kind; Live From Studio 8H--100 Years of American Popular Music (Emcee); George Burns' Early, Early, Early Christmas Special; Bob Hope Laughs with the Movie Awards; Two of A Kind; George Burns & Other Sex Symbols; The 4th Annual TV Guide Special; Bob Hope's Road To Hollywood; The Kids From Fame; Grandpa, Will You Run With Me? Happy Birthday, Bob; Parade of Stars; George Burns Celebrates 80 Years in Show Busi-

ness; Bob Hope's Who Makes the World Laugh--Part II; George Burns' How To Live To Be 100 Or More; Bob Hope Lampoons Television 1985; Night Of 100 Stars II.

BURNS, Ralph J: Comp-Cond. b. Newton, MA., June 29, 1922. e. New England Conservatory. Films inc: Cabaret (Oscar-adapt-1972); Movie Movie; All That Jazz (Oscar-adapt-1979); Urban Cowboy; First Family (adapt-cond); Annie; My Favorite Year; Kiss Me Goodbye; National Lampoon's Vacation; The Muppets Take Manhattan; Perfect.

TV inc: IBM Presents Baryshnikov on Broadway (Emmy-arr-1980); Side Show; Golden Gate; Ernie Kovacs--Between the Laughter.

BURR, Raymond: Act. b. New Westminister, BC, Canada, May 21, 1917. e. Stanford U; U CA; Columbia U; U Chungking. Appeared on stage in many countries in Night Must Fall; Mandarin; Crazy With The Heat; Duke in Darkness; Underground. Dir, Pasadena Community Playhouse, 1943.

Films inc: Pitfall; Raw Deal; Place in the Sun; Rear Window; A Man Alone; Count Three and Pray; Great Day in the Morning; Cry in the Night; P.J.; Out of the Blue; Airplane II--The Sequel.

TV inc: Perry Mason (Emmys-1959, 1961); Ironside; Love's Savage Fury; The Bastard (narr); The Jordan Chance; Centennial; Only The Pretty Girls Die; Disaster on the Coastline; The 13th Day - The Story of Esther; The Curse of King Tut's Tomb (narr); The Night the City Screamed; Peter and Paul.

BURROWS, Abe: Comp-Wri-Dir. b. NYC, Dec 18, 1910. e. CCNY; NYU. Began as radio script writer: Duffy's Tavern; Rudy Vallee; Joan Davis Show; Dinah Shore Show; Texaco Star Theatre; Abe Burrows Show. Performed in nighteries, TV. Bway librettist, Guys and Dolls (Tony-1951). (Dir): Happy Hunting; Silk Stockings; Can-Can; Say, Darling; How to Succeed in Business Without Really Trying (dir-co-wri) (Tony & Pulitzer Prize-1962); Two on the Aisle; The Golden Fleecing; What Makes Sammy Run?; Cactus Flower (& wri); Three Wishes For Jamie (& co-wri); Can Can (& wri).

Films inc: Reclining Figure; Say Darling; Forty Carats; The Solid Gold Cadillac.

Songs inc: The Girl With the Three Blue Eyes; Leave Us Face It, We're in Love.

(Died May 17, 1985.)

BURROWS, James: Dir. b. Los Angeles, Dec 30, 1940. e. Oberlin, BA; Yale, MFA. S of Abe Burrows. Dir for off-Bway dinner theatres.

TV inc: Mary Tyler Moore; Bob Newhart; Laverne & Shirley; Phyllis; Rhoda; Fay; Bustin Loose; More Than Friends; Like Father Like Daughter; Taxi (Emmys-dir-1980, 1981) Lou Grant; The Associates; The Best Of the West; Every Stray Dog and Kid; Goodbye Doesn't Mean Forever; Cheers (& exec prod-crea) (Emmys-prod & dir-1983, 1984); Night Court; P.O.P.; At Your Service; Bigshots In America.

Films inc: Partners.

BURRUD, Bill: Prod. b. Hollywood, Jan 12, 1925. e. USC; Harvard; Notre Dame. Started as child actor; formed Bill Burrud Prods, 1952. TV inc: Vagabond; Holiday; Wanderlust; Islands in the Sun; True Adventure; Challenging Sea; Animal World; Safari to Adventure; World of the Sea; Wildlife Adventure; Wonderful World of Travel.

Open Heart Surgery; This Nation Israel; Is There an Ark?; Centerfold Pets; Where Did All the Animals Go?; Baja; Secret World of Reptiles; Vanishing Africa; The Great American Wilderness; Predators of the Sea; The Amazing Apes; Curse of the Mayan Temple; Montezuma's Lost Gold; Animals Are the Funniest People (& co-host).

BURSTALL, Tim: Prod-Dir. b. Australia. Films inc: Stork; Libido (episode dir); Alvin Purple; Petersen; Alvin Rides Again; The Love Epidemic; End Play (& wri); Eliza Fraser; High Rolling; The Last of the Knucklemen (& wri); Attack Force Z; Partners; The Naked Country (Dir-wri).

TV inc: Descant for Gossips.

BURSTYN, Ellen (Edna Rae Gilhooley): Act. b. Detroit, Dec 7, 1932. Worked as fashion model, dancer, bit player under names of Keri Flynn, Erica Dean, Edna Rae, Ellen McRae. Films inc: Goodbye Charlie; For Those Who Think Young; Tropic of Cancer; Alex in Wonderland; King of Marvin Gardens; The Last Picture Show; Exorcist; Alice Doesn't Live Here any More (Oscar-1974); Harry and Tonto;

Providence; A Dream of Passion; Same Time Next Year; Resurrection; Acting--Lee Strasberg and the Actors Studio (doc); Silence of the North; In Our Hands (doc); The Ambassador.

Bway inc: Fair Game; Same Time Next Year (Tony-1975); 84 Charing Cross Road.

TV inc: The Doctors; Thursday's Game; People vs. Jean Harris; Tony Awards (host); Kennedy Center Tonight--Broadway to Washington!; Surviving.

BURTON, Al: Prod-Wri-Dir-Exec. b. Chicago, IL, Apr 4, 1928. e. Northwestern U, BS. TV consultant to Edgar Bergen, 1948; prod-dir-act Al Burton Productions, 1948-1972; wri Oscar Levant Show 1958-59; dev dir TAT Communications 1974, sr vp-exec vp Tandem/TAT. TV inc: All in the Family (Emmy-exec prod-1979); Charles In Charge (exec prod-mus).

BURTON, Gary: Mus. b. Anderson, IN, Jan 23, 1943. e. Boston Conservatory of Music.

(Grammys-(3)-jazz solo-1972; jazz duet-1979); jazz group-1981).

BURTON, Kate: Act. b. England, 1958. e. Yale Drama School. D. of the late Richard Burton. Bway inc: Present Laughter; Alice in Wonderland; Doonesbury. Off-Bway inc: Winners.

TV inc: Alice in Wonderland; Ellis Island; Evergreen.

BURTON, LeVar: Act. b. Landsthul, Germany, Feb 16, 1957. e. USC. Films inc: Looking for Mr. Goodbar.

TV inc: Roots; Almos' a Man; Billy: Portrait of a Street Kid; Battered; One in a Million--The Ron Leflore Story; Dummy; Guyana Tragedy - The Story of Jim Jones; The Hunter; The Acorn People; Barney (host); Grambling's White Tiger; Emergency Room; A Tribute to Martin Luther King Jr. . .A Celebration of Life; The Jesse Owens Story; Booker; And The Children Shall Lead.

BURTON, Richard (Richard Jenkins): Act. b. Pontrhydyfen, So Wales, Nov 10, 1925. Thea inc: (London) The Lady's Not For Burning; Montserrat; Dark Summer; A Phoenix Too Frequent. Bway inc: The Lady's Not For Burning; Camelot (Tony-1961); Hamlet; Legend of Lovers; Time Remembered; Camelot (rev); Private Lives.

TV inc: Anna Christie; Wuthering Heights; The Fifth Column; The Broadway of Lerner and Loewe; I, Leonardo--A Journey of the Mind (narr); 1983 Tony Awards (host); Alice in Wonderland; To The End Of The Earth (host-narr); Ellis Island.

Films inc: The Last Days of Dolwyn; Now Barabbas; Waterfront; The Woman With No Name; My Cousin Rachel; The Robe; Alexander The Great; Look Back in Anger; The Spy Who Came In From The Cold; Becket; Night of The Iguana; The Sandpiper; Who's Afraid of Virginia Woolf?; Anne of the Thousand Days; Doctor Faustus; Where Eagles Dare; The Voyage; Exorcist II - The Heretic; Equus; The Medusa Touch; The Wild Geese; Breathrough; Circle of Two; Absolution; Wagner; 1984.

(Died Aug. 5, 1984). Name; My Cousin Rachel; The Robe; Alexander The Great; Look Back in Anger; The Spy Who Came In From The Cold; Becket; Night of The Iguana; The Sandpiper; Who's Afraid of Virginia Woolf?; Anne of the Thousand Days; Doctor Faustus; Where Eagles Dare; The Voyage; Exorcist II - The Heretic; Equus; The Medusa Touch; The Wild Geese; Breathrough; Circle of Two; Absolution; Wagner.

(Died Aug. 5, 1984).

BURTON, Val: Wri-Prod. b. Kent, England, Feb 22, 1900. Films inc: The Ghost Steps Out; Everything But The Truth; Two Years Before the Mast; Henry Aldrich (series); The Time of Their Lives; Bedtime for Bonzo; So This is Harris (short); The Preferred List (short); Passport to Destiny; Lord Jeff; Girl Without A Room; Melody Cruise; Carnival.

BURTON, Warren: Act. b. Chicago, IL, Oct 23, 1944. e. Northwestern U. Bway inc: Hair; A Patriot for Me; P.S. Your Cat is Dead.

Films inc: Rabbit Test; The World's Greatest Lover; Baby Blue Marine.

TV inc: One Day at a Time; All My Children (Emmy-supp-1980); Another World.

BURY, John: Set dsgn. b. Wales, Jan 27, 1925. e. University Coll,

London. Thea inc: The Cruel Daughters; The Chimes; Richard III; Volpone; The Quare Fellow; Love and Lectures/Man of Destiny (& dir); A Taste of Honey; A Christmas Carol; Fings aint Wot They Used To Be; Ned Kelly; Sparrers Can't Sing; Oh, What A Lovely War!; numerous plays as head of design for Royal Shakespeare Company; Indians; A Delicate Balance; Dutch Uncle; The Homecoming; The Government Inspector; Old Times; The Silver Tassie; The Blood Knot; The Lionel Touch; several plays as head of design The National Theatre; The Hypochondriac; The Importance of Being Earnest; Uncle Vanya. (Bway) The Homecoming; The Rothchilds; Hedda Gabler; A Doll's House; Via Galactica; Old Times; Amadeus (Tonys-set desgn & light dsgn-1980).

BUSCH, Niven: Wri. b. NYC, Apr 26, 1903. e. Princeton U. Films inc: Babbitt; In Old Chicago; The Westerner; Duel in the Sun; Pursued; The Furies; The Moonlighter; Treasure of Pancho Villa.

BUSEY, Gary: Act-Mus. b. Goose Creek, TX, Jun 29, 1944. Films inc: Angels Hard As They Come; Dirty Little Billy; Last American Hero; Lolly Madonna; Gumball Rally; Alex and the Gypsy; A Star is Born; The Buddy Holly Story; Straight Time; Big Wednesday; Foolin' Around; Carny; Barbarosa; D.C. Cab; The Bear; Insignificance.
TV inc: Bloodsport; The Execution of Private Slovik.

BUSSERT, Meg: Act-sing. b. Chicago, Dec. 21, 1949. e. U IL; studied at Herbert Berghof Studio. Bway inc: The Music Man; Brigadoon; Camelot; Irene; Gorey Stories; Lorelei; Something's Afoot.
TV inc: Camelot (cable).

BUTLER, Bill: Cin. b. Colorado, Apr 7, 1921. e. IA Wesleyan; State U of IA. Films inc: The Rain People; The Conversation; Jaws; One Flew Over the Cuckoo's Nest; Bingo Long; Lipstick; Demon Seed; Capricorn One; Grease; Omen II; Ice Castles; Uncle Joe Shannon; Rocky II; Discoland; It's My Turn; The Night The Lights Went Out In Georgia; Stripes; The Sting II.
TV inc: Sunshine; The Execution of Pvt Slovak; Hustling; Fear on Trial; Raid on Entebbe (Emmy-1977); Death Ray 2000; Killing At Hell's Gate; Hollywood--The Gift of Laughter; The Thorn Birds; A Streetcar Named Desire (Emmy-1984).

BUTLER, Daws (Charles Dawson Butler): Act. b. Toledo, OH, Nov 16, 1916. Voice of many cartoon characters inc Yogi Bear; Huckleberry Hound; Peter Potamus, etc. TV inc: Raggedy Ann & Andy in the Pumpkin Who Couldn't Smile (voice); Deck the Halls with Wacky Walls (voice).

BUTLER, Michael: Cin. b. 1944. Films inc: Charley Varrick; Harry and Tonto; The Missouri Breaks; Telefon; Jaws 2; Wanda Nevada; A Small Circle of Friends; Smokey and The Bandit II; The Cannonball Run; Megaforce.

BUTLER, Robert: Dir. b. Los Angeles, Nov 16, 1927. TV inc: Gunsmoke; Cimarron Strip; Hennessey; Star Trek (pilot); Hogan's Heroes (pilot); Batman (pilot); Death Takes A Holiday; Strange New World; The Blue Knight (Emmy-1974 & dir of year 1974); Dark Victory; Mayday at 40,000 Feet; The Andros Targets (pilot); In the Glitter Palace; James Dean, Portrait of a Friend; A Question of Guilt; Lacy and the Mississippi Queen; Hill Street Blues; (Emmy-1981); Insight/ The Needle's Eye; Remington Steele (& crea); One Night Band (& prod).
Films inc: The Secret of Boyne Castle; The Computer Wore Tennis Shoes; The Barefoot Executive; Scandalous John; Now You See Him, Now You Don't; Hot Lead and Cold Feet; Night of the Juggler; Up the Creek; Concrete Beat; Moonlighting.

BUTTOLPH, David: Comp-Cond. b. NYC, Aug 3, 1902. e. Juilliard. Films inc: Show Them No Mercy; Nancy Steele is Missing; Four Sons; The Mark of Zorro; Tobacco Road; This Gun for Hire; Wake Island; Moontide; My Favorite Blonde; Crash Dive; The Hitler Gang; The House on 92nd Street; Somewhere in the Night; Kiss of Death; Rope; Roseanna McCoy; Three Secrets; The Enforcer; My Man and I; House of Wax; Secret of the Incas; The Lone Ranger; The Big Land; The Horse Soldiers; Guns of the Timberland; Steel Jungle; Santiago; The Burning Hills; Cry in the Night.
TV inc: Maverick.

BUTTON, Dick: TV pers. b. Englewood, NJ. World Champion Skater; Olympic Skating Champ. TV inc: The Superstars (prod); Battle of the Network Stars (prod).
(Emmy-sports analyst-1981).

BUTTONS, Red (Aaron Chwatt): Act. b. Bronx, NY, Feb 5, 1919. Began singing for pennies on street corners as a teenager. Comic, Minsky's Burlesque Shows. After WW 2 appeared on Broadway in Barefoot Boy With Cheek. TV inc: The Red Buttons Show; The Secret Life of Henry Phyfe; Rudolph and Frosty's Christmas in July (voice); Power; The Dream Merchants; Leave'em Laughing; Side Show; Dean Martin's Celebrity Roast; Reunion At Fairborough.
Films inc: Sayonara (Oscar-supp-1957); Imitation General; The Big Circus; Five Weeks in a Balloon; Stagecoach; Harlow; They Shoot Horses Don't They?; Who Killed Mary What's Her Name?; Pete's Dragon; The Poseidon Adventure; Gable and Lombard; Viva Knievel; Movie Movie; C.H.O.M.P.S.; When Time Ran Out.

BUTTS, R Dale: Comp-Arr-Cond. b. Lamasco, KY, Mar 12, 1910. e. Louisville Conservatory of Music. Pianist, arr with dance orchs; also in radio. Film scores inc: My Buddy; The Catman of Paris; My Pal Trigger; Gay Blades; One Exciting Week; Flame of Barbary Coast; Night Train to Memphis.
TV inc: Laramie; Wagon Train; The Virginian; Whispering Smith.
Songs inc: I'm in Love with a Guy Who Flies in the Sky; Please Take Me Home This Moment; I Get to Feeling Like This; Lilacs in the Spring; Will You Marry Me, Mr. Larramie; Welcome to My Heart.

BUXTON, Frank: Wri-Dir. b. Wellesley, MA, Feb 13. e. Northwestern U, BS; Syracuse U, MS. TV inc: (wri) Discovery; The Wonder of it all; The Second Bill Cosby Special; Me and the Chimp; Children's Letters to God (dir); Hot Dog (& prod-dir); This Is Your Life; No Man's Valley (wri & voice); The Romance Of Betty Boop (voice).

BUYSE, Emile: Exec. b. Brussels, Belgium, Apr 16, 1927. e. College Ecole Normale Charles Buls, Brussels. Pub-ad Mgr, 1952, Col; transferred to Paris, 1957 pub-ad Mgr for France, Belgium, Col; 1962, pub-ad-pro dir for continental Europe, UA; 1966, Fox, Paris, pub-ad-pro dir for continental Europe; 1969, VP of Fox Int'l Corp, Paris; 1973, VP, mktg mgr, Paris; 1975, VP, GM for Europe & Middle East, Paris; 1976, appointed VP Fox Int'l Dist in LA and P, Fox Int'l Corp; Dec 1980 resd to form ind prods rep-mktg firm.

BUZZELL, Edward: Dir. b. NYC, Nov 13, 1905. 60 films inc: Best Foot Forward; Youngest Profession; Keep Your Powder Dry; Three Wise Fools; Song of Thin Man; Neptune's Daughter; At the Circus; Women of Distinction; Emergency Wedding; Easy to Wed; Confidentially Connie; Ain't Misbehavin'; My Favorite Husband.
(Died Jan. 11, 1985)

BUZZI, Ruth: Act. b. Westerly, RI, Jul 24, 1936. Studied at Pasadena Playhouse. Stage debut San Francisco with Rudy Vallee in Jenny Kissed Me. Played summer stock, off-Bway. Bway inc: Sweet Charity. Films inc: Freaky Friday; The North Avenue Irregulars; The Apple Dumpling Gang Rides Again; The Villain; Skatetown, USA; Chu Chu and the Philly Flash; The Being; Surf II.
TV inc: Laugh-In; Almost Anything Goes; Medical Center; The Lost Saucer; Linus the Lionhearted; That Girl; The Incredible Book Escape (voice); A Gift of Music; Book of Lists; Janie Fricke--You Ought to be in Pictures; Celebrity Fun Cruise; Dom DeLuise and Friends Part II; The Magic of David Copperfield II.

BYERS, Billy: Mus-Comp-Arr. b. May 1, 1927. Bway inc: (orchs) A Chorus Line; Perfectly Frank.
TV inc: (Arr) America Salutes Richard Rodgers--The Sound of His Music; Ben Vereen--His Roots; IBM Presents Baryshnikov on Broadway (Emmy-mus dir-1980); Linda In Wonderland (Emmy-arr-1981); Andy Williams' Early New England Christmas (mus dir); The Screen Actors Guild 50th Anniversary Celebration (Emmy-arr-1984)

BYGRAVES, Max: Act. b. London, Oct 16, 1922. Films inc: Skimpy in the Navy; Tom Brown's Schooldays; Charley Moon; A Cry from the Streets; Bobbikins; Spare the Rod. TV inc: Roamin Holiday.

BYRNE, Anne: Act. Films inc: Papillon; The End of the World in Our Usual Bed in a Night Full of Rain; Manhattan; Why Would I Lie?.

BYRNE, Eddie: Act. b. Dublin, 1911. Films inc: Odd Man Out; The Gentle Gunman; Time, Gentlemen Please; A Kid for Two Farthings; The Mummy; The Bulldog Breed; Devils of Darkness; Island of Terror; Never Mind the Quality, Feel the Width; The MacIntosh Man; Stardust.

TV inc: Strumpet City (cable).

BYRNE, Patsy: Act. b. Ashford, England, Jul 13, 1933. Thea inc: Chicken Soup With Barley; Roots; Serjeant Musgrave's Dance; One Way Pendulum; joined Royal Shakespeare Company for numerous Shakespearean roles 1960-62; again in 1964; Caucasian Chalk Circle; Virtue In Danger; Endgame; Eh?; The Government Inspector; Equus; The Streets of London.

BYRNES, Edd (nee Breitenberger): Act. b. NYC, Jul 30, 1933. Films inc: Girl On The Run; Darby's Rangers; Up Periscope; Marjorie Morningstar; Yellowstone Kelly; Secret Invasion; Wicked, Wicked; Payment in Blood; Tunisia; Any Gun Can Play; Star Wars; Grease.

TV inc: 77 Sunset Strip; Crossroads; Wire Service; Where The Action Is; Twirl.

BYRON, Kathleen: Act. b. London, Jan 11, 1922. e. London U. Screen debut 1943, Young Mr. Pitt. Films inc: The Silver Fleet; A Matter of Life and Death; Black Narcissus; The Small Back Room; Madness of the Heart; The Reluctant Widow; Four Days; The Gambler and the Lady; Hand in Hand; Night of the Eagle; Private Road; Twins of Evil; One of Our Dinosaurs Is Missing.

TV inc: Emergency Ward 10; Design for Murder; Breaking Point; Young Bess; Secret Venture; Heidi.

BYRUM, John: Wri-Dir. b. Evanston, IL, Mar 14, 1947. Films inc: (wri) Mahogany; Harry and Walter Go to New York; Scandalous. (Wri-dir) Inserts; Heart Beat; Sphinx; The Razor's Edge.

CAAN, James: Act. b. NYC, Mar 26, 1939. Appeared off-Broadway in La Ronde, 1961. Films inc: Lady in a Cage; Games; Journey to Shiloh; Rain People; Rabbit; The Godfather; Slither; Godfather II; Funny Lady; Silent Movie; Another Man, Another Chance; A Bridge Too Far; Comes A Horseman; Chapter Two; Hide In Plain Sight (& dir); Thief; Les Uns et Les Autres (The Ins and The Outs); Kiss Me Goodbye.

TV inc: Ben Casey; Wagon Train; Combat; Naked City; Brian's Song; Playboy's 25th Anniversary Celebration.

CACAVAS, John: Comp-Cond-Arr. b. Aberdeen, SD, Aug 13, 1930. e. Northwestern U, BM. Films inc: Blade; Horror Express; Satanic Rites of Dracula; Redneck; Airport 75; Airport 77; Once Upon A Spy; Mortuary; Separate Ways; They're Playing With Fire.

TV inc: She Cried Murder; Linda; Elevator; Hazard's People; Kate McShane; Murder at the World Series; SST Death Flight; Human Feelings; Kojak; Hawaii Five-0; segments of Quincy; Bionic Woman; The Contest Kid Strikes Again; California Gold Rush; Border Pals; The Notorious Jumping Frog of Calaveras County; Today's FBI; Shannon; Child Bride at Short Creek; The Joke's On Mr Little; My Palikari; The Shooting; The Executioner's Song; Cry For the Strangers; Still The Beaver; The Four Seasons; Her Life as a Man; Jessie; Lady Blue; A Death In California.

CACOYANNIS, Michael: Prod-Dir-Wri. b. Cyprus, Jun 11, 1922. e. Admitted to bar, London. Producer of BBC's wartime Greek programs. Films inc: Windfall; Stella; A Girl in Black; A Matter of Dignity; One Last Spring; The Wastrel; Electra; Zorba the Greek; The Day the Fish Came Out; The Trojan Women; Iphigenia; Attila, '74. Bway inc: The Bacchae (dir-translator); Zorba (dir).

CAESAR, Adolph: Act. e. NYU. Thea inc: Sty of the Blind Pig; The Perry's Mission; Waiting For Mongo; The River Niger; The Great McDaddy; Square Root of a Soul (one-man show); The Brownsville Raid; A Season To Unravel; A Soldier's Play.

Films inc: A Soldier's Story.

TV inc: Men of Bronze (narr); I Remember Harlem (narr).

CAESAR, Irving: Lyr-Comp-Act. b. NYC, Jul 4, 1895. Toured in vaudeville. First lyric for the theater was Swanee, with George Gershwin as composer, for Al Jolson in Sinbad. Songs inc: Tea for Two; Sometimes I'm Happy; I Want to be Happy; Lady Play Your Mandolin; Songs of Safety; Songs of Friendship; Songs of Health; Pledge of Allegiance to the Flag.

Films scores inc: George White's Scandals. Bway scores inc: Greenwich Village Follies; Betty Lee; Sweetheart Time; No, No, Nanette; Ziegfeld Revue; Yes, Yes, Yvette; Here's How; Americana; The Wonder Bar; George White's Scandals of 1928; Hit the Deck; White Horse Inn; My Dear Public.

CAESAR, Sid: Act. b. Yonkers, NY, Sep 8, 1922. Band musician. Film debut Tars and Spars. Worked nightclubs, Bway. Films inc: The Guilt of Janet Ames; It's A Mad, Mad, Mad World; Guide For The Married Man; The Busy Body; Airport '75; Silent Movie; Fire Sale; The Cheap Detective; Grease; The Fiendish Plot of Dr. Fu Manchu; History Of The World-Part I; Grease 2; Over the Brooklyn Bridge; Cannonball Run II.

TV inc: Your Show of Shows (Emmy-1952); Caesar's Hour (Emmy-1956); Thanksgiving In The Land of Oz (narr); The Munster's Revenge; A Gift of Music; It Only Hurts When You Laugh; Found Money; All Star Party For Lucille Ball.

(Television Academy Hall Of Fame 1985).

CAGE, Nicolas (ne Coppola): Act. b. 1964. Studied at ACT. Films inc: Valley Girl; Rumble Fish; Racing With the Moon; Cotton Club; Birdy.

CAGNEY, James: Act. b. NYC, July 17, 1899. e. Columbia U. In vaude, 1924, later on Bway as dancer. On screen from 1930. Films inc: Sinners Holiday; Doorway To Hell; The Steel Highway; The Millionaire; Other Men's Women; The Public Enemy; Illicit; Smart Money; Blonde Crazy; Taxi; The Crowd Roars; Winner Take All; Hard To Handle; The Picture Snatcher; Mayor of Hell; Footlight Parade; Lady Killer; Jimmy the Gent; He Was Her Man; Here Comes the Navy; The St. Louis Kid; Devil Dogs of the Air; G-Men; The Irish In Us; Midsummer Night's Dream; The Frisco Kid; Ceiling Zero; Great Guy; Something To Sing About; Boy Meets Girl; Angels With Dirty Faces; The Oklahoma Kid; Each Dawn I Die; The Roaring Twenties; The Fighting 69th; Torrid Zone; City For Conquest; Strawberry Blonde; The Bride Came C.O.D.; Captains of the Clouds; Yankee Doodle Dandy (Oscar-1942); Johnny Come Lately; Blood on the Sun; 13 Rue Madeleine; The Time of Your Life; White Heat; West Point Story; Kiss Tomorrow Goodbye; Come Fill the Cup; Starlift; What Price Glory; A Lion Is in the Streets; Run For Cover; Love Me Or Leave Me; The Seven Little Foys; Mister Roberts; Tribute To a Bad Man; These Wilder Years; Man Of a Thousand Faces; Short Cut To Hell (dir); Shake Hands With the Devil; The Gallant Hours; One Two Three; Ragtime.

TV inc: AFI Salute to James Cagney; AFI Salute to Fred Astaire; Terrible Joe Moran.

(Kennedy Center Honoree 1984).

CAGNEY, Jeanne: Act. b. NYC, Mar 25, 1919. e. Hunter. Sis of James Cagney. Films inc: All Women Have Secrets; Golden Gloves; Queen of the Mob; Yankee Doodle Dandy; Time of Your Life; Don't Bother to Knock; A Lion Is in the Streets; Man of a Thousand Faces; Town Tamer.

TV inc: Big Hello; Legal Tender; Mr. and Mrs. North; Big Town; Wild Bill Hickok.

(Died Dec. 7, 1984)

CAGNEY, William: Prod. b. NYC, 1902. B of James Cagney. Films inc: (asso prod): Strawberry Blonde; Bride Came C.O.D.; Captains of the Clouds; Yankee Doodle Dandy. (Prod): Johnny Come Lately; Blood on the Sun; The Time of Your Life; Kiss Tomorrow Goodbye; A Lion is in the Streets.

CAHN, Sammy: Lyr. b. NYC, Jun 18, 1913. Organized band with Saul Chaplin, duo also wrote songs for niteries; Vitaphone shorts before Hollywood.

Films inc: Anchors Aweigh; Three Coins in a Fountain; Romance on the High Seas; The Kid from Brooklyn; Two Guys from Texas; West Point Story, April in Paris; Three Sailors and a Girl; Love Me or Leave Me; The Court Jester; Meet Me in Las Vegas; Road to Hong Kong; Robin and the Seven Hoods; The Tender Trap; Pocketful of Miracles; Thoroughly Modern Millie.

Bway inc: High Button Shoes; Two's Company; Skyscraper; Walking Happy; Words and Music (& act); Falling In Love Again.

Songs (chief collaborators Chaplin, Jule Styne, James Van Heusen)inc: Rhythm Is Our Business; Shoe Shine Boy; Until the Real Thing Comes Along; Bei Mir Bist du Schon; Joseph Joseph; Please Be Kind; Saturday Night is the Loneliest Night in the Week; Let It Snow; Let It Snow; I Should Care; It's Been A Long, Long Time; It Seems to Me I've Heard That Song Before; I'll Walk Alone; It's Magic; Be My Love; Teach Me Tonight; Three Coins in a Fountain *(Oscar*-1954); Love and Marriage *(Emmy*-1955); The Tender Trap; All the Way *(Oscar*-1957); High Hopes *(Oscar*-1959); Second Time Around; Pocketful of Miracles; Call Me Irresponsible *(Oscar*-1962) My Kind of Town; Thoroughly Modern Millie; Star; All That Love Went to Waste; What Becomes of Love.

CAIN, Christopher (Bruce Doggett): Prod-Dir-Wri. b. Sioux Falls, SD, Oct 29, 1943. e. Dakota Wesleyan U, BA. Films inc: Brother, My Son; Elmer; Buzzard; Grand Jury; Sixth & Main; Key West Crossing (dir only); The Stone Boy (dir only).

CAINE, Howard (nee Cohen): Act. b. Nashville, TN, Jan 2, 1928. e. Columbia U, BS. Films inc: Pay or Die; From the Terrace; Judgment at Nuremberg; Pressure Point; The Man from the Diners' Club; Alvarez Kelly; Watermelon Man; 1776; Helter Skelter; Forced Vengeance.

Thea inc: Wonderful Town; Inherit the Wind; Lunatics and Lovers; Tiger at the Gates; Damn Yankees. TV inc: Marilyn--The Untold Story; apptd member of exec staff, Darryl F Zanuck; exec VP Warner Bros.

CAINE, Michael (Maurice Joseph Micklewhite): Act. b. London, March 14, 1933. Asst. stage mgr. Acted with repertory group. Films inc: Zulu; The Ipcress File; Alfie; The Wrong Box; Gambit; Funeral in Berlin; Hurry Sundown; Deadfall; The Magus; The Battle of Britain; Play Dirty; Too Late The Hero; Get Carter; Kidnapped; X, Y and Zee; Pulp; The Destructors; The Wilby Conspiracy; Peeper; The Romantic Englishwoman; Harry and Walter Go To New York; A Bridge Too Far; The Eagle Has Landed; The Man Who Would Be King; California Suite; Silver Bears; The Swarm; Beyond The Poseidon Adventure; Ashanti; The Island; Dressed to Kill; The Hand; Victory; Deathtrap; The Jigsaw Man; Sleuth; ; Educating Rita; Beyond the Limit; Blame It on Rio; The Jigsaw Man; Water.

TV inc: The Compartment; The Playmates; Hobson's Choice; Hamlet; Luck of the Draw; The Royal London Gala For Bob Hope's Happy Birthday Homecoming.

CALABRESE, Peter B: Exec. b. NJ

TV inc: Treasure Isle (dir); The Mike Douglas Show (dir); The Smothers Brothers Show (dir); Ben Vereen Comin' At Ya (dir); Tony Orlando and Dawn (dir); Roberta Flack In Mexico (prod); Barry White In Mexico (prod); A Joke's A Joke (prod-dir); Farewell to the Smothers Brothers (prod-dir); Photoplay Awards; with Viacom, later 20th-Fox in pgm dvlpt; June 1980, Dir, Specials & Late Night Pgms NBC; Feb 1981, VP Specials; Nov. 1983, VP Variety pgmg Alan Landsburg Prodns.

CALDER-MARSHALL, Anna: Act. b. Kensington, England, Jan 11, 1947. Thea inc: Uncle Vanya; The Lady's Not for Burning; The Country Wife; Absurd Person Singular; Objections to Sex and Violence; Dear Janet Rosenberg; Too True to be Good.

Films inc: Pussycat, Pussycat I Love You; Wuthering Heights; Zulu Dawn.

TV inc: The Male of the Species *(Emmy*-supp-1969); King Lear; Titus Andronicus.

CALDICOT, Richard: Act. b. London, Oct 7, 1908. e. RADA. Thea inc: Major Barbara; The Critic; Journey's End; She Stoops to Conquer; Caravan; Within the Gates; Floodlight; Edward My Son; Six Months Grace; The Kidder; A Shred of Evidence; No Sex Please, We're British; My Fair Lady (rev).

Films inc: The Card; The VIPs; The Spy Who Came in from the Cold.

CALDWELL, Sarah: Opera prod-Dir-Cond. b. Maryville, MO, Mar 6, 1924. Dir Boston U Opera Workshop, 1953-1957; founder Boston Opera Group; cond-dir at Metropolitan Opera; Dallas Civic Opera; Houston Opera; NYC Opera. Bway inc: Macbeth (dir).

CALDWELL, Zoe, OBE: Act. b. Australia, Sept. 14, 1933. Bway inc: The Mad Woman of Chaillot; The Way of the World; The Caucasian Chalk Circle; Slapstick Tragedy *(Tony*-supp-1966); The Prime of Miss Jean Brodie *(Tony*-1968); A Bequest to the Nation; The Creation of the World and Other Business; Love and Master Will; An Almost Perfect Person; Medea (rev) *(Tony*-1982).

TV inc: The Apple Cart; Macbeth; The Lady's Not for Burning; Medea.

CALHOUN, Rory (Francis Timothy Durgin): Act. b. Los Angeles, Aug 8, 1923. Screen debut, 1944, Something for the Boys. Films inc: The Red House; Miraculous Journey; I'd Climb the Highest Mountain; With a Song in My Heart; Powder River; How to Marry a Millionaire; Dawn at Socorro; Treasure of Pancho Villa; The Spoilers; Domino Kid (& prod-dir-sp); Hired Gun (& prod-dir); The Colossus of Rhodes; Marco Polo; A Face in the Rain; Apache Uprising; Night of the Lepus; Koo Lau (doc: prod-dir); Operation Crosseagles; Mule Feathers; Bitter Heritage; Just Not the Same Without You; Midnight Auto Supply; The Main Event; Motel Hell; Angel; Avenging Angel.

TV inc: The Road Ahead; Bet the Wild Queen; Suspicion; The Texan (prod-dir-sp many segments). Flatbed Annie & Sweetipie, Lady Truckers; The Rebels; Harris & Co, Pottsville; Capitol; The Blue and The Gray; Half Nelson.

Thea inc: (London) Belle Star.

CALLAN, Michael: Act. b. Philadelphia, Nov 22, 1935. Bway inc: The Boy Friend. Films inc: They Came to Cordura; Pepe; Mysterious Island; The Victors; The Magnificent Seven Ride Again; Lepke; The Cat and the Canary; Chained Heat.

TV inc: Blind Ambition; Mark Twain's America - Tom Edison; Scruples; The Great Survivors; My Wicked, Wicked Ways.

CALLAS, Charlie: Act. b. NYC, Dec 20. Started as a drummer with various bands; later became night club comedian. Films inc: The Big Mouth; High Anxiety; Pete's Dragon; History Of The World--Part I; Hysterical.

TV inc: The Andy Williams Show; The Flip Wilson Show; Switch; Take One. Dean Martin's Christmas at Sea World; Rooster; The Jerry Lewis Show.

CALLEY, John: Exec. b. NJ, 1930. Dir nighttime prog NBC, 1951-57; prod exec Henry Jaffee Enterprises, 1957; joined Filmways, Inc, 1960; exec vp and prod to 1969; exec vp - world-wide prod Warner Bros; p WB; Nov 1980 became cnsltnt. Films inc: (Prod): Wheeler Dealer; The Americanization of Emily; Topkapi; The Cincinnati Kid; Loved One; Don't Make Waves; Ice Station Zebra; Catch-22.

CALLOW, Simon: Act. b. London, Jun 13, 1949. e. Queens, U, Belfast; The Drama Centre. Thea inc: Plumber's Progress; The Doctor's Dilemma; Soul of the White Ant; Blood Sports; The Resistible Rise of Arturo Ui; Amadeus (& Bway); Restoration; The Beastly Beatitudes of Balthazar B.

TV inc: Wings of Song; The Dybbuk; Instant Enlightenment.

Films inc: Amadeus.

CALLOWAY, Cab: Orch leader-Singer-Act. b. Dec 24, 1907. In vaudeville, playing top theatres inc The Palace; band was one of the top attractions during the big band era. Bway inc: Porgy and Bess; Cotton Club Revue of 1957; Hello Dolly!; Pajama Game. Films inc: The Big Broadcast; International House; The Singing Kid; Manhattan Merry-Go-Round; Stormy Weather; Sensations of 1945; St. Louis Blues; The Cincinnati Kid; A Man Called Adam; The Blues Brothers.

TV inc: A Gift of Music; Love Boat (spec); Eubie Blake--A Century of Music.

CALVERT, Phyllis (nee Bickle): Act. b. London, Feb 18, 1915. On stage at age 10. Most recent thea inc: A Woman of no Importance; Blithe Spirit; The Cherry Orchard; Hay Fever; The Reluctant Debutante; Dear Daddy; Before The Party.

Films inc: Two Days to Live; They Came by Night; Kipp; The Young Mr. Pitt; The Man in Grey; Fanny by Gaslight; Madonna of the Seven Moons; My Own True Love; Appointment with Danger; Mandy; It's Never Too Late; Indiscreet; Oscar Wilde; Twisted Nerve; Oh! What a Lovely War; The Walking Stick.

TV inc: Kate.

CALVET, Corinne (nee D'ibos): Act. b. Paris, Apr 30, 1925. e. U of

Paris School of Fine Arts. Screen debut 1945, La Part de l'Ombre. Hollywood debut 1949, Rope of Sand. Films inc: When Willie Comes Marching Home; My Friend Irma Goes West; On the Riviera; What Price Glory?; Powder River; The Far Country; So This is Paris; The Plunderers; Painted Flats; Bluebeard's Ten Honeymoons; Hemingway's Adventures of a Young Man; Apache Uprising; Quebec; On the Riviera; Too Hot To Handle; Dr. Heckyl and Mr. Hype.

TV inc: She's Dressed To Kill.

CAMERON, John: Comp. b. England. Films inc: Every Home Should Have One; Kes; Night Watch; A Touch of Class; Scalawag; Nasty Habits; Made; The Bermuda Triangle; Lost and Found; Sunburn; The Mirror Crack'd; The Jigsaw Man; The Young Visiters.

TV inc: She Fell Among Thieves; Philip Marlowe-Private Eye.

CAMERON, Rod (nee Cox): Act. b. Calgary, Alberta, Canada, Dec 7, 1912. Films inc: Christmas in July; North West Mounted Police; Henry Aldrich for President; Panhandle; Plunderers; Wagons West; Santa Fe Passage; The Bounty Killer; Evel Knievel; Psychic Killer; Midnight Auto Supply.

(Died Dec 21, 1983).

CAMP, Colleen: Act. b. San Francisco, CA. Films inc: Battle for the Planet of the Apes; Funny Lady; Smile; Death Game; The Game of Death; Apocalypse Now; Cloud Dancer; The Seduction; They All Laughed; Smokey and the Bandit Part 3; Valley Girl; Deadly Game; The City Girl (& asso prod); Joy of Sex; Police Academy 2--Their First Assignment; The Rosebud Beach Hotel; D.A.R.Y.L.

TV inc: Amelia Earhart; Rich Man, Poor Man; Dallas.

CAMP, Joe: Prod-Dir-Wri. b. St Louis, Apr 20, 1939. e. U of MS, BA. Films inc: Benji; Hawmps; For the Love of Benji; The Double McGuffin; Oh, Heavenly Dog.

TV inc: The Phenomenon of Benji; Benji's Very Own Christmas Story; Benji at Cannes; Benji at Work; Benji (Takes A Dive) at Marineland.

CAMPANELLA, Joseph: Act. b. 1927. Films inc: Murder Inc; The Young Lovers; The St. Valentine's Day Massacre; Ben; Meteor; Hangar 18; Earthbound.

TV inc: Mannix; The Bold Ones; Greatest Heroes of the Bible; One Day At A Time; Rex Stout's Nero Wolfe; The Plutonium Incident; My Body, My Child; Computers Are People Too (voice); This is Your Life (host); Cousteau/Amazon--Journey to a Thousand Rivers (narr); The New El Dorado-Invaders and Exiles (narr); The Coronation.

CAMPBELL, Glen: Singer-Act. b. Billstown, AR, Apr 22, 1935. Films inc: Baby, the Rain Must Fall; The Cool Ones; True Grit; Norwood.

TV Inc: Solid Gold '79; A Country Christmas; Bob Hope 30th Anniversary Special; Country Comes Home (host: 1981-1982-1983); Bob Hope's All Star Birthday Party at West Point; 100 Years of Golden Hits; Bob Hope's All-Star Celebration Opening the Gerald R. Ford Museum; The Glen Campbell Music Show; Johnny Cash--Cowboy Heroes; Jerry Reed and Special Friends; The Glen Campbell Music Show; Anne Murray's Winter Carnival--From Quebec. (Grammys-(5)-vocal-contemp vocal-c & w, rec-c & w, vocal-1967; album of year-1968).

CAMPBELL, Judy (nee Gamble): Act. b. Grantham, Lincs, England, May 31, 1916. On stage since 1935. Screen debut 1940, Saloon Bar. Films inc: Breach of Promise; The World Owes Me a Living; Green for Danger; Bonnie Prince Charlie; There's a Girl in My Soup; Forbush and the Penguins.

Thea inc: You Never Can Tell; Mourning Becomes Electra; Relatively Speaking; Hay Fever; Death on Demand.

TV inc: The Chinese Prime Minister; Anna Karenina.

CAMPBELL, Nicholas: Act. b. Toronto, Canada, 1952. e. Queen's U; RADA. Films inc: The Omen; The Spy Who Loved Me; A Bridge Too Far; The Eagle Has Landed; Fast Company; The Brood; Love; The Amateur; The Dead Zone; Certain Fury; Terminal Choice; Killing 'Em Softly.

TV inc: Come Back Little Sheba; Bless This House; The July Group.

CAMPBELL, William: Act. b. Newark, NJ, 1926. Films inc: The

Breaking Point; The People Against O'Hara; Escape from Port Bravo; The High and the Mighty; Man Without a Star; Cell 2455 Death Row; Backlash; The Naked and the Dead; Hush, Hush Sweet Charlotte; Dementia; Blood Bath; Black Gunn; Dirty Mary, Crazy Larry.

CAMPOS, Rafael: Act. b. Santiago, Dominican Republic, May 13, 1936. Films inc: Blackboard Jungle; Trial; This Could Be the Night; Tonka; The Light in the Forest; Mister Buddwing; Lady in a Cage; The Appaloosa; The Doll Squad; Oklahoma Crude; Let the Good Times Roll; Slumber Party '57; Where The Buffalo Roam; Heartbreaker.

TV inc: Centennial; Return of the Mod Squad; The Return of Frank Cannon; V; A Streetcar Named Desire; V--The Final Battle.

Thea inc: Infidel Caesar; The Oxcart; Ten Years of Love; Ceremony for an Assassinated Black Man.

CANALE, Gianna Maria: Act. b. Reggio Calabria, Italy, Sep 12, 1927. Films inc: Rigoletto; Go for Broke; The Man from Cairo; The Silent Enemy; The Whole Truth; Queen of the Pirates; Scaramouche.

CANBY, Vincent: Critic. b. Chicago, Jul 27, 1924. e. Dartmouth. Worked in Paris after WW II; retd to Chicago 1951, joining Motion Picture Herald staff; 1959, Variety; 1965, reporter NY Times; 1969, film critic.

CANDOLI, Pete: Trumpeter-Act. b. Mishawaka, IN. e. Purdue U. H of Edie Adams. Films inc: Bell, Book and Candle (& score); Meet Me After the Show; Presenting Lily Mars; Dubarry was a Lady.

TV inc: Al Hirt Special; One Step Beyond; Peter Gunn; Johnny Staccato.

CANDY, John: Act-Wri. b. Canada, Oct. 31, 1950. TV inc: SCTV (Emmy-wri-1983); Welcome to the Fun Zone; The Last Polka (& exec prod-act).

Films inc: It Came From Hollywood; National Lampoon's Vacation; Going Berserk; Splash (act); Brewster's Millions (act)..

CANNELL, Stephen J.: Wri-Prod. b. Los Angeles, Feb 5, 1942. TV inc: The Rockford Files (Emmy-supv prod-1978); The Jordan Chance; The Duke; The Night Rider; Stone (Exec prod-co-crea); 10 Speed and Brownshoe; Nightside; Midnight Offerings (exec prod); The Greatest American Hero (exec prod-crea-wri); The Quest (co-exec prod); The A-Team (exec prod-crea-wri); Hardcastle and McCormick; (exec prod-creator-wri); The Rousters; Riptide (exec prod-crea-wri); Hunter (exec prod); Brothers-In-Law (exec prod-wri); On Top All Over The World (act).

CANNON, Dyan (Samille Diane Friesen): Act. b. Tacoma, WA, Jan 4, 1937. Acting debut TV's Playhouse 90 in Ding-A-Ling Girl. Bway debut The Fun Couple. Films inc: The Last of Sheila; The Love Machine; Bob and Carol and Ted and Alice; Number One (doc: prod-dir-ed); Such Good Friends; The Burglars; Shamus; Doctors' Wives; Heaven Can Wait; Revenge of the Pink Panther; Honeysuckle Rose; Coast To Coast; Deathtrap; Author! Author!

TV inc: Matinee Theatre; 77 Sunset Strip; Full Circle; Lady of the House; Natalie--A Tribute To A Very Special Lady; Having It All; Master of the Game; Arthur The King.

CANNON, J D: Act. b. Apr 24, 1922. e. AADA. Started with Joe Papp's NY Shakespeare Festival. Other thea inc: Peer Gynt; Great God Brown; Great Day in the Morning; The Little Foxes (London).

Films inc: An American Dream; Cool Hand Luke; Cotton Comes to Harlem; The Lawman; Scorpio; Raise The Titanic; Death Wish II.

TV inc: The Defenders; Profiles in Courage; Wedding Band; McCloud; Testimony of Two Men; Ike; The Top of the Hill; Pleasure Palace; My Kidnapper, My Love; The Adventures Of Nellie Bly; Beyond Witch Mountain; Rooster.

CANNON, Katherine: Act. b. Sept. 6, 1953. e. Pasadena Playhouse. Films inc: Fool's Parade.

TV inc: Survivors; Baa Baa Black Sheep. High Noon Part II--The Return of Will Kane; Gabe and Walker; High Ice; The Contender; Will-G. Gordon Liddy; Father Murphy; The Red-Light Sting.

CANOVA, Diana: Act. b. West Palm Beach, FL, Jun 1, 1953. D of Judy Canova. Films inc: The First Nudie Musical. TV inc: Happy Days; Mel & Susan Together; Love Boat; Fantasy Island; Soap; With This

Ring; Perry Como's Early American Christmas; The Death of Ocean View Park; I'm A Big Girl Now; Peking Encounter; Foot In The Door; Night Partners.

CANOVA, Judy: Act-Singer. b. Jacksonville, FL, Nov 20, 1916. On radio with Paul Whiteman for 10 Years; Woodbury Soap Hour; Judy Canova Show; Colgate Show. TV inc: Colgate Comedy Hour; Love American Style; numerous guest star shots.

Films inc: In Caliente; Broadway Gondolier; Going High Brow; Artists and Models; Thrill of a Lifetime; Scatter Brain; Sis Hopkins; Puddinhead; Sleepy Time Gal; True to the Army; Joan of the Ozarks; Chatter Box; Sleepy Lagoon; Louisiana Hayride; Hit the Hay; Singin' in the Corn; Honey Chile; Oklahoma Annie; The WAC from Walla Walla; Untamed Heiress; Carolina Cannonball; Lay That Rifle Down; Adventures of Huckleberry Finn; Cannonball.

Bway inc: Calling All Stars; Ziegfeld Follies, Yokel Boy.
(Died Aug. 5, 1983).

CANTAMESSA, Gene S: Sound. b. NYC, Feb 17, 1931. Films inc: The Candidate; Blazing Saddles; Nickel Ride; Young Frankenstein; Leadbelly; Smile; Bad News Bears; Black Sunday; Close Encounters of the Third Kind; Citizen Band; Sextette; High Anxiety; Bad New Bears Go to Japan; Same Time Next Year; Prophecy; 1941; Stripes; Wrong Is Right; Annie; E.T. The ExtraTerrestrial (Oscar-1982); The Toy; The Big Chill; To Be Or Not To Be; Ghostbusters; Star Trek III--The Search For Spock; Terror In The Aisles; Fast Forward.

CANTINFLAS (Mario Moreno): Act. b. Mexico, Aug 12, 1911. Clown, acrobat, bullfighter in Mexican comedies for years. Films inc: Neither Blood Nor Sand; Romeo and Juliet; Around the World in Eighty Days; Pepe; The Minister and Me.

TV inc: Olympic Gala.

CANTON, Mark C: Exec. b. NYC, Jun 19, 1949. e. UCLA. 1978, VP Motion Picture Development, MGM; 1979, exec vp JP Organization; 1980 vp prodn WB.; 1983, sr vp. Films inc: Die Laughing (prod).

CANTOR, Arthur: Prod. b. Boston, Mar 12, 1920. e. Harvard, BA. Started as press rep in 1945; entered prod Nov 1959, The Tenth Man. Bway inc: All the Way Home; Gideon; A Thousand Clowns; Man in the Moon; Put it in Writing; The Golden Age; The Passion of Josef D; The Committee; The Trigon (& dir); The World of Gunter Grass; The Concept; The Wizard of Oz; Tango; Winnie the Pooh; Golden Bat; In London, 1970-71, (co-prod): Vivat! Vivat!; A Bequest to the Nation; The Winslow Boy; Butterflies Are Free; The Patrick Pearse Motel. (Bway) Old Times; Promenade, All!; Captain Brassbound's Conversion; The Little Black Book; 42 Seconds from Broadway; In Praise of Love; Private Lives; The Constant Wife; A Party With Betty Comden and Adolph Green; Emlyn Williams as Charles Dickens; The Hothouse; A Little Family Business; Ian McKellen Acting Shakespeare; Pack Of Lies.

Films inc: Here Are Ladies.

CANTRELL, Lana: Singer-Act. b. Sydney, Australia, Aug 7, 1943. Nitery singer Australia 1958. To US 1962, debut on Tonight Show. Nitery, recording star. U.S. rep Int'l Song Festival Poland 1966.

CANUTT, Yakima: Dir. b. Colfax, WA, Nov 29, 1895. World's champion All-around Rodeo, 1917-24. In 1924 became stunt man, double for such stars as Clark Gable, Errol Flynn, John Wayne. Received special Oscar 1966. Films inc: (dir) The Angel and the Badmen; Oklahoma Badlands; Carson City Raiders; Sons of Adventure; G-Men Never Forget; Dangers of the Canadian Mounted; Adventures of Frank and Jesse James; Lawless Rider.

CAPERS, Virginia: Act. b. Sumter, SC, Sep 22. Films inc: House of Women; Ride the Hangman Tree; The World's Greatest Athlete; Five on the Black Hand Side; Trouble Man; Lady Sings the Blues; The Lost Man; The North Avenue Irregulars; The Toy; Da Capo.

TV inc: Mannix; Breaking Point; Ben Casey; Class of '65; White Mama; Willow B-Women in Prison; Inmates--A Love Story.

Bway inc: Saratoga; Jamaica; Raisin (Tony-1974).

CAPICE, Philip: Prod. b. Bernardsville, NJ, Jun 24, 1931. e. Dickinson, BA; Columbia, MFA. 1965 vp pgm dvlp Benton & Bowles; 1969 dir special pgms CBS-TV; 1974, Sr VP Crea aff Lorimar Prodns;

1978 P Lorimar; 1979 resd to enter indie prodn.

TV inc: Sybil (Emmy-exec prod-1977); Long Journey Back; Some Kind of Miracle; Studs Lonigan; A Man Called Intrepid; A Matter of Life and Death; Two Marriages.

CAPLAN, Harry: Exec. b. New Haven, CT, Jun 2, 1908. e. UCLA; Southwestern U. With Paramount 1940-60 as asst dir and unit prod m; assoc prod UA, 1960; prod m Filmways, 1962; unit prod m and 2d unit dir, 20th Century Fox, 1963-66; exec prod m National General Productions Inc, 1966-69. Prod: Charro.

CAPOTE, Truman: Wri. b. New Orleans, LA, Sep 30, 1924. Films inc: Breakfast at Tiffany's; In Cold Blood; Other Voices, Other Rooms. Murder by Death (act); CS Blues (act).

TV inc: A Christmas Memory (Emmy-adapt-1967).
(Died Aug. 25, 1984).

CAPRA, Frank: Dir. b. Palermo, Sicily, May 18, 1897. e. CalTech. Wrote 26 Mack Sennett comedies, Two Harry Langdon features. Films inc: (as dir) Platinum Blonde; American Madness; Bitter Tea of General Yen; Lady for a Day; Broadway Bill; It Happened One Night (Oscar-1934); Mr. Deeds Goes to Town (Oscar-1936); Lost Horizon; You Can't Take it With You (Oscar-1938); Mr. Smith Goes to Washington; Meet John Doe; Prelude to War (Doc); Why We Fight (war doc series 1942-44); Arsenic and Old Lace; It's a Wonderful Life; State of the Union; Riding High; Here Comes the Groom; A Hole in the Head; A Pocketful of Miracles; George Stevens--A Filmmaker's Journey (doc-int).

TV inc: Four one-hour science films for AT&T; AFI Salute to Frank Capra; A Walk Through the 20th Century With Bill Moyers (WW II--The Propaganda Battle).

CAPRA, Frank, Jr: Prod-Exec. b. Los Angeles, March 20,1934. Films inc: Marooned; Born Again; The Black Marble; An Eye for an Eye; The Seduction; Vice Squad; Firestarter. March 1981, VP in chg wldwde prodn Avco Embassy; June 1981, P & CEO; resd April 1982; May, 1985, partnered in Pinehurst Industries, will head company's production at new studios in Reidsville, NC., in Sept.

TV Inc: High Hopes--The Capra Years.

CAPSHAW, Kate: Act. b. Ft. Worth, TX. e. U MO, BA, MA. Schoolteacher for two years before act. TV inc: Edge Of Night; Love of Life; Missing Children.

Films inc: A Little Sex; Indiana Jones and the Temple of Doom; Dreamscape; Windy City.

CAPTAIN AND TENNILLE: Husband and wife singing duo. See DRAGON, Daryl and TENNILLE, Toni.

CAPUCINE (Germaine Lefebvre): Act. b. Toulon, France, Jan 6, 1933. Model. Films inc: Song Without End; A Walk on the Wild Side; The Pink Panther; The Seventh Dawn; What's New Pussycat?; The Honey Pot; The Queens; Fellini's Satyricon; Red Sun; Jaguar Lives!; Arabian Adventure; From Hell To Victory; Aphrodite; Trail of the Pink Panther; Balles Perdues (Stray Bullets); Curse of the Pink Panther.

CARA, Irene: Singer-act. b. Bronx, NY., Mar. 18, 1959. Bway inc: Maggie Flynn; The Me Nobody Knows (Off-Bway); Via Galactica; Ain't Misbehavin'; Lotta (Off-Bway).

TV inc: Over 70; The Electric Company; Roots - The Next Generation; Guyana Tragedy - The Story of Jim Jones; Sister, Sister; Irene; For Us the Living; Bob Hope Goes to College; A Tribute to Martin Luther King Jr. . .A Celebration of Life.

Films inc: Aaron Loves Angela; Sparkle; Fame (Oscar-song-1983); D.C. Cab; City Heat; Certain Fury; Killing 'Em Softly.
(Grammys (3)-score-pop vocal-rock vocal-1983).

CARD, Lamar: Prod-Dir. b. TN, Sep 8, 1942. e. Tulane U, BS; UCLA grad program. Films inc: The Clones; Super Van (dir); Disco Fever; Terror Train (prod); Savage Harvest (co-prod); Le Sang des Autres (The Blood of Others) (exec prod).

CARDEA, Frank: Prod. b. Norwalk, CT, Aug 17, 1947. e. La Salle Coll, BS, Accounting. Originally an accountant for Aramco in Saudi Arabia, Middle East, Europe, joined Gulf & Western, Paramount parent company, moved to Par in 1974 as head of finance for features

& tv on West Coast. TV inc: Busting Loose (exec in chg prodn); Washington--Behind Closed Doors (asso prod); Shogun (exec in chg prodn); Sawyer and Finn (co-exec prod); Bring 'em Back Alive; It Came Upon A Midnight Clear (& wri); Crazy Like A Fox (exec prod-wri).

CARDIFF, Jack: Dir-Cin. b. Yarmouth, England, Sep 18, 1914. Films inc: (cin) Wings of the Morning; The Four Feathers; Caesar and Cleopatra; A Matter of Life and Death; Black Narcissus (Oscar-1947); The Red Shoes; Pandora and the Flying Dutchman; The Barefoot Contessa; War and Peace; The Vikings; Crossed Swords; Death on the Nile; The Fifth Musketeer; The Prince and the Pauper; A Man, A Woman and a Bank; Avalanche Express; The Awakening; The Dogs of War; The Wicked Lady; Scandalous; Conan the Destroyer; Cat's Eye; Rambo--First Blood Part II. (Dir): Intent to Kill; Beyond this Place; Scent of Mystery; Sons and Lovers; My Geisha; The Lion; The Long Ships; Young Cassidy; The Liquidator; Dark of the Sun; Girl on a Motorcycle (& prod-cin); The Mutations; Penny Gold; Ghost Story.

TV inc: The Far Pavilions (PC); The Last Days of Pompeii.

CARDINALE, Claudia: Act. b. Italy, Apr 15, 1939. Films inc: Persons Unknown; Upstairs and Downstairs; Il Bell'Antonio; Rocco and his Brothers; Cartouche; The Leopard; The Pink Panther; Blindfold; Lost Command; The Professionals; Don't Make Waves; Day of the Owl; The Hell with Heroes; A Fine Pair; Adventures of Brigadier Gerard; Popsy Pop; The Red Tent; Papal Audience; Days of Fury; The Gun; The Little Girl In Blue Velvet; Escape To Athena; Corleone; La Pelle (The Skin); Le Cadeau (The Gift); Fitzcarraldo; Le Ruffian; Stelle Emigranti (Wandering Stars); The Salamander; Enrico IV (Henry IV); Claretta; L'Ete Prochain (Next Summer).

TV inc: Princess Daisy.

CARELLI, Joann: Prod. b. NYC. Films inc: The Deer Hunter (asso prod); Heaven's Gate.

CAREW, Alyce S.: Exec prod. b. Fredericksburg, VA., Nov. 7, 1945. e. Hampton Institute (BA); Catholic U (MA); Union Graduate School (PhD Urban Ed.) W. of Topper Carew. TV inc: Rainbow Movies Of The Week; Tales In a Golden Groove; The Righteous Apples; And The Children Shall Lead.

CAREW, Topper (Colin A. Carew): Prod. b. Boston, MA., July 16, 1943. e. Yale (BA, MA Architecture), Union Graduate School (PhD Communications). H of Alyce S. Carew. TV inc: The Righteous Apples; Rainbow Movies Of The Week (& wri); Tales In A Golden Groove (& wri); And The Children Shall Lead.

Films inc:DC Cab.

CAREY, Harry, Jr: Act. b. Saugus, CA, May 16, 1921. Performed in summer stock with father, silent screen western star. Screen debut in Pursued. Films inc: Three Godfathers; She Wore A Yellow Ribbon; Rio Grande; Warpath; Wild Blue Yonder; Monkey Busines; Beneath the 12-Mile Reef; The Long Gray Line; Mister Roberts; House of Bamboo; The Undefeated; One More Train To Rob; The Long Riders; Endangered Species.

TV inc: Wild Times; The Shadow Riders.

CAREY, MacDonald: Act. b. Sioux City, IA, Mar 15, 1913. e. U of IA, MA. Performed in summer stock, radio. On Bway in Lady In The Dark; Anniversary Waltz. Screen debut in 1942. Films inc: Dr. Broadway; Take a Letter Darling; Wake Island; Shadow of a Doubt; Suddenly It's Spring; Hazzard; Excuse My Dust; Let's Make It Legal; My Wife's Best Friend; Fire Over Africa; Stranger at My Door; American Gigolo; End of the World.

TV inc: Days of Our Lives (since 1965) (Emmys-1974, 1975); Roots; The Rebels; The Top of the Hill; The Girl, The Gold Watch and Everything; Condominium.

CAREY, Philip: Act. b. Hackensack, NJ, Jul 15, 1925. Films inc: Operation Pacific; Pushover; Mister Roberts; Afrique; Wicked as they Come; Screaming Mimi; Tonka; The Great Sioux Massacre; The Seven Minutes.

TV inc: 77th Bengal Lancers; Philip Marlowe; Laredo; The Untamed World; One Life To Live.

CAREY, Ron: Act. b. Newark, NJ, Dec 11, 1935. Films inc: The Out-of-Towners; Silent Movie; High Anxiety; Fatso.

TV inc: The Corner Bar; The Montefuscos; Barney Miller; History Of The World--Part I; Johnny Garage; Pump Boys & Dinettes on Television.

CARFAGNO, Edward: Prodn Dsgn. Films inc: Quo Vadis; The Bad and The Beautiful (Oscar-1952); Julius Caesar (Oscar-1953); Executive Suite; Ben Hur (Oscar-1959); Period of Adjustment; The Wonderful World of the Brothers Grimm; The Cincinnati Kid; The Shoes of the Fisherman; Skyjacked; The Man Who Loved Cat Dancing; The Hindenburg; Gable and Lombard; Time After Time; Meteor; Honky Tonk Man; The Sting II; Sudden Impact; All of Me; Tightrope; City Heat; Pale Rider.

CARIOU, Len: Act-Dir. b. St Boniface, Manitoba, Canada, Sep 30, 1939. e. St Paul's Coll. NY debut, 1968, The House of Atreus. Thea inc: Much Ado about Nothing; The Three Sisters; Henry V; Applause; Cyrano de Bergerac; The Taming of the Shrew; became assoc dir of The Tyrone Guthrie in 1972; Of Mice and Men (dir); Sondheim: A Musical Tribute; The Petrified Forest (dir); King Lear; The Crucible; Don't Call Back (dir); One Man; A Little Night Music; Cold Storage; Sweeney Todd (Tony-1979); Dance A Little Closer.

TV inc: The Master Builder; Juno and the Paycock; Don't Forget; Drying up The Streets; Madame X; Just a Little Special; An Ounce Of Cure.

Films inc: A Little Night Music; The Four Seasons; Louisiane.

CARLIN, George: Act. b. NYC, May 12, 1937. Deejay, nightclub comedian. TV debut 1965 on Merv Griffin Show. Films inc: Car Wash; Americathon. TV inc: 100 Years of Golden Hits.

(Grammy-comedy-1972).

CARLIN, Lynn: Act. b. Los Angeles, Jan 31, 1930. Films inc: Faces; Tick...Tick...Tick; Taking Off; Wild Rovers; Baxter; Superstition.

TV inc: Silent Night, Lonely Night; The Morning After; The Honorable Sam Houston; The Tenth Level; The Waltons; James at 16; French Postcards; Battle Beyond The Stars; Girl On The Edge Of Town (Reflections); The Kid From Nowhere; Forbidden Love; A Killer in the Family.

CARLINO, Lewis John: Wri. b. NYC, Jan 1, 1932. e. El Camino Coll, BA; USC MA. Films inc: Seconds; The Fox; The Brotherhood; The Mechanic; A Reflection of Fear; Crazy Joe; The Sailor Who Fell From Grace With the Sea (& dir); I Never Promised You a Rose Garden; The Great Santini (& dir); Resurrection; Class (dir).

TV inc: The Brick and The Rose; Where Have All the People Gone?; Doc Elliot; In Search of America; Honor Thy Father.

Plays inc: The Brick and the Rose; Cages (2 plays); Telemachus Clay; Double Talk (2 plays); The Exercise.

CARLISLE, Kitty (Catherine Conn): TV Pers. b. New Orleans, Sep 3, 1914. Widow of Moss Hart. Former opera singer. Films inc: Murder at the Vanities; She Loves Me Not; Here Is My Heart; A Night at the Opera; Hollywood Canteen.

TV inc: What's My Line?; To Tell the Truth; Just a Little Special.

CARLSEN, Henning: Dir-Wri. b. Aalborg, Denmark, Jun 4, 1927. Made more than 30 shorts before turning to features. Films inc: Dilemma; Epilogue (dir); The Cats (dir); Hunger; Two People Meet and Sweet Music Fills The Heart; We Are All Demons; Are You Afraid?; Oh, to Be On the Bandwagon; A Happy Divorce (dir); Da Svante Forsvandt; Did Somebody Laugh?; Pengene Eller Livet (Your Money or Your Life).

CARLSON, Linda: Act. b. Knoxville, TN, May 12. e. IA U; NYU. TV inc: Westside Medical; Kaz; Pals; Sutters Bay; Victims For Victims--The Theresa Saldana Story.

Thea inc: Full Circle.

CARMEL, Roger C: Act. b. Sept, 27, 1932. Bway inc: A Man For All Seasons; Purlie Victorious; Half A Sixpence; Rhinoceros.

Films inc: The Greatest Show on Earth; The Silencers; Alvarez Kelly; A House Is Not A Home; Goodbye Charlie; Hardly Working.

TV inc: Naked City; Star Trek; Stump the Stars; The Mothers-in-Law; Fitz and Bones.

CARMEN, Julie: Act. b. Millburn, NJ, 1955. e. State U NY, BFA; studied with Sanford Meisner at Neighborhood Playhouse and with Uta Hagen. Bway inc: Zoot Suit. TV inc: The Guiding Light; Love of Life; As The World Turns; Can You Hear the Laughter--The Story of Freddie Prinze; Three Hundred Miles for Stephanie; She's In The Army Now; Fire On The Mountain; Condo.
Films inc: Night of the Juggler; Gloria; Die Mann Auf Der Mauer (The Man on the Wall); Last Plane Out.

CARMET, Jean: Act. b. France. Films inc: The Tall Blond Man With One Black Shoe; La Raison du plus Fou; Don't Cry With Your Mouth Full; Le Concierge; Les Gaspards; Bons Baisers a Lundi; Return of the Tall Blond Man; Rape of Innocence; Black and White in Color; Alice ou la Derniere Fugue; Plus Ca Va, Moins Ca Va, The Sugar; Violette; Such a Lovely Town; Allons Z'Enfants (The Boy Soldier); Die Faelschung (Circle of Deceit); Une Affaire D'Hommes (A Man's Affair); Guy de Maupassant; Les Miserables; Un Chien dans un Jeu de Quilles (A Dog in a Game of Nine-Pins); Papy Fait de la Resistance (Gramps is in the Resistance); Canicule (Dog Day); Tir a vue (Fire On Sight); Sac de Noeuds (All Mixed Up).; Night Magic.

CARMICHAEL, Ian: Act. b. Hull, England, Jun 18, 1920. Films inc: Meet Mr. Lucifer; The Colditz Story; Storm Over the Nile; Simon and Laura; Private's Progress; Brothers in Law; Lucky Jim; Left, Right and Centre; School for Scoundrels; I'm All Right Jack; Light Up the Sky; The Amorous Prawn; Heavens Above; Smashing Time; The Magnificent Seven Deadly Sins.
TV inc: Twice Upon a Time; Lady Luck; The Importance of Being Earnest; Simon and Laura; The Last of the Big Spenders; The Coward Revue.
Thea inc: Overheard.

CARMICHAEL, Ralph R: Comp-Arr-Cond. b. Quincy, IL, May 27, 1927. TV inc: (Arr) Campus Christian Hour; I Love Lucy (& comp); Nat King Cole (& cond).
Films inc: (Comp): Series of films for Billy Graham inc Mr Texas; Joni.
Songs inc: He's Everything To Me; Tell It Like It Is; The Saviour Is Waiting.

CARNE, Judy: Act. b. Southampton, England, 1939. Films inc: A Pair of Briefs; The Americanization of Emily; All the Right Noises.
TV inc: Love on a Rooftop; Laugh-In; I Love Men.

CARNE, Marcel: Dir. b. Paris, 1909. Films inc: Jenny; Drole de Drame; Quai des Brumes; Le Jour Se Leve; Les Visiteurs du Soir; Les Enfants du Paradis; L'Air de Paris; Terrain Vague; Three Rooms in Manhattan; The Young Wolves; Les Assassins de L'Ordre; La Merveilleuse Visit.

CARNEY, Art: Act. b. Mt Vernon, NY, Nov 4, 1918. In vaudeville and on Broadway prior to radio and tv. TV inc: Cavalcade of Stars; The Jackie Gleason Show *(Emmy*-supp-1953 & 1954); Harvey; The Honeymooners *(Emmy*-1955); Art Carney Meets Peter and the Wolf; Our Town; Very Important People; You Can't Take It With You; Letters From Frank; Alcatraz--The Whole Shocking Story; Fighting Back; Bitter Harvest; The Leprechaun's Christmas Gold (narr); Terrible Joe Moran *(Emmy-supp-1984)*; A Doctor's Story; The Night They Saved Christmas; The Undergrads (feevee).
(Special Emmys-1967 & 1968).
Films inc: A Guide for the Married Man; The Yellow Rolls Royce; Harry and Tonto *(Oscar*-1974); Scott Joplin; The Late Show; House Calls; Movie Movie; Sunburn; Ravagers; Going In Style; Defiance; Roadie; Steel; Take This Job and Shove It; St. Helens; Better Late Than Never; Firestarter; The Naked Face; The Muppets Take Manhattan.
Bway inc: The Rope Dancers; The Odd Couple; Lovers; The Prisoner of Second Avenue.

CARNOVSKY, Morris: Act-Dir. b. St Louis, MO, Sep 5, 1897. First NY stage appearance 1922 in The God of Vengeance. Joined the Group Theatre, 1931. Has appeared regularly with the American Shakespeare Festival Company of Stratford, CT. Thea inc: Saint Joan; Doctors Dilemma; View From The Bridge.
Films inc: The Life of Emile Zola; Rhapsody in Blue; Address Unknown; Our Vines Have Tender Grapes; Cornered; Miss Susie Slagle's; Cyrano de Bergerac; Tovarich.

TV inc: Medea; The World of Sholom Aleichem; The Cafeteria.

CARON, Leslie: Act. b. Paris, Jul 1, 1931. e. Nat'l Conservatory of Dance. Joined Ballet des Champs Elysees. Screen debut 1951 as star An American in Paris. Films inc: The Story of Three Loves; Lili; Daddy Longlegs; Gaby; Gigi; The Doctor's Dilemma; The Subterraneans; Fanny; The L-Shaped Room; Father Goose; A Very Special Favour; Promise Her Anything; Is Paris Burning?; Head of the Family; Madron; Chandler; The Man Who Loved Women; Serail; Valentino; Goldengirl; Tous Vedettes; Kontrakt; Die Unerreichbare (The Unapproachable); Imperativ; La Diagonale du Fou (Dangerous Moves).
TV inc: QB VII; Pavlova (Canadian paycable); Master of the Game; AFI Salute To Gene Kelly.

CAROTHERS, A J: Wri. b. Houston, TX, Oct 22, 1931. e. UCLA. Films inc: Miracle of the White Stallions; Emil and the Detectives; The Happiest Millionaire; Never a Dull Moment; Hero at Large.
TV inc: Goldilocks and the Crosby Family; Nanny and the Professor; Topper Returns; Shakespeare Loves Rembrandt; Forever; Goodnight, Beantown (& exec prod-crea); Summer Girl; The Making of a Male Model.

CARPENTER, Carleton: Act. b. Bennington, VT, Jul 10, 1926. Thea inc: Bright Boy; Career Angel; Three to Make Ready; The Magic Touch; The Big People; Art of Dust; Almanac.
Films inc: Summer Stock; Father of the Bride; Two Weeks with Love; Whistle at Eaton Falls; Fearless Fagan; Sky Full of Moon; Take the High Ground; Some of My Best Friends Are. . .

CARPENTER, Freddie: Dir. b. Melbourne, Australia, Feb 15, 1908. Appeared on stage as dancer in Australia, New York, London. Thea (dance dir) inc: Tulip Time; Life Begins at Oxford Circus; The Town Talks; Mother Goose; And On We Go; Maritza; The Dancing Years; Lady Behave; Irene. (Dir): The Sleeping Beauty; Dear Miss Phoebe; One Fair Daughter; Never Too Late; The World of Jamie; Let's Get Swinging; Cinderella; Hans Andersen.
Films inc: (arr dances) Carnival; London Town; The Winslow Boy.
TV (dance numbers) inc: Tribute to Sir Winston Churchill; Noel Coward Revue; Tarbuck's Luck.

CARPENTER, John: Dir-Wri. b. Carthage, NY, Jan 16, 1948. e. USC. H of Adrienne Barbeau. Films inc: Dark Star; Assault on Precinct 13 (& mus & ed); Halloween (& mus); Eyes of Laura Mars (wri); The Fog (& mus); Escape From New York (& mus); Halloween II (prod-wri-music); The Thing (dir); Halloween III--Season of the Witch (prod); Christine (dir-mus); The Philadelphia Experiment (exec prod); Starman.
TV inc: Someone Is Watching Me; Better Late Than Never (wri); Elvis.

CARPENTER, Robert L: Exec. b. Memphis, TN, Mar 20, 1927. Joined U Memphis exchange 1949 as booker; named branch mgr 1958; moved to LA as branch mgr 1963; to NY 1971 as asst gen sls mgr; became gen sls mgr 1973 when H.H. Martin moved up to president of company; resd Jan 1981.

CARPENTERS: Singers. b. New Haven, CT, Richard, 1945, Karen b. 1950, died Feb 4, 1983. Brother and sister recording duo. TV inc: Christmas Portrait (1978); Music, Music, Music. *(Grammys*-(3)-New Artist & Group Vocal-1970; Group Vocal-1971).

CARR, Allan: Prod. b. Highland Park, IL, 1939. e. Lake Forest Coll; Northwestern U. Entered showbusiness on production staff of Playboy Penthouse TV series. Produced plays at Chicago Civic Theatre; Asst to Nicholas Ray on film King of Kings; became personal mgr; Prod West Coast version of Sunday in New York, introducing Marlo Thomas; Creative consultant on Tommy for Robert Stigwood Organization; presented Survive! in assoc with Stigwood; Films inc: The First Time; C.C. and Company; Grease (co-prod & wri); Can't Stop the Music (& wri); Grease 2; Where the Boys Are '84; Cloak And Dagger.
TV inc: Ann-Margret Olsson (exec prod).
Bway inc: La Cage Aux Folles; *(Tony-1984); Cyrano de Bergerac; Much Ado About Nothing.*

CARR, Darleen (nee Farnon): Act. b. Chicago, 1950. Films inc: The Sound of Music (voice only); Monkeys Go Home; Death of a Gunfighter; The Impossible Years; The Beguiled.

TV inc: The Smith Family; Streets of San Francisco; Once an Eagle; Young Joe Kennedy; Miss Winslow and Son; Rage; Bret Maverick.

CARR, Martin: Prod-Dir-Wri. b. NYC, Jan 20, 1932. e. Williams Coll. TV inc: Dublin Through Different Eyes; The Search for Ulysses; CBS Reports - Gauguin in Tahiti (Emmy-1968); Hunger in America (Emmy-1969); The Search For Ulysses; Five Faces of Tokyo; NBC White Paper-Migrant; This Child is Rated X; Leaving Home Blues; ABC Closeup - The Culture Thieves.

CARR, Richard: Wri. b. Cambridge, OH, Feb 24, 1929. e. Pasadena City Coll. Films inc: The Man from Del Rio; Hell Is for Heroes; Too Late Blues; Heaven with a Gun; Americana.

TV inc: Four Star Playhouse; Richard Diamond (pilot); Maverick; Zane Grey Theatre; G.E. Theatre; Guns of Will Sonnett (created); The Waltons; Charlie's Angels; Vegas.

CARR, Vikki Singer. (Florencia Bisenta de Casillas Martinez Cardona):b. El Paso, TX, 1942. Sang with bands and in night clubs. Appeared on TV as guest star with Dean Martin, Ed Sullivan, Jack Gleason, Bob Hope, Red Skelton, Carol Burnett. Hosted the Tonight Show; A Gift of Music.

CARRADINE, David: Act. b. Hollywood, Oct 8, 1940. S of John Carradine. TV inc: Shane; Kung Fu; Mr Horn; Gauguin The Savage; High Noon Part II--The Return of Will Kane; Jealousy; The Bad Seed.

Thea inc: The Deputy; Royal Hunt of the Sun.

Films inc: Taggart; The Violent Ones; Heaven With A Gun; McCabe and Mrs. Miller; Boxcar Bertha; Bound for Glory; The Serpent's Egg; Thunder and Lightning; Deathsport; Gray Lady Down; Circle of Iron; Fast Charlie The Moonbeam Rider; The Long Riders; Cloud Dancer; Americana (& prod-dir); The Winged Serpent; Trick Or Treats; Lone Wolf McQuade; The Warrior and the Sorceress; Rio Abajo (On The Line); Safari 3000.

CARRADINE, John: Act. b. NYC, Feb 5, 1906. Originally on Bway in Shakespearean roles. On screen from 1936. Films inc: Fallen Angel; House of Dracula; House of Frankenstein; Johnny Guitar; The Egyptian; Stranger on Horseback; Desert Sands; The Kentuckian; Dark Venture; Black Sheep; Everything You Always Wanted to Know About Sex; Boxcar Bertha; The Shootist; The Killer Inside Me; The Last Tycoon; The Sentinel; Crash; Journey Into Beyond (narr); Satan's Cheerleaders; Shock Waves; The White Buffalo; The Bees; The Mouse and His Child; The Boogey Man; The Howling; The Nesting; The Monster Club; The Secret of NIMH (voice); Satan-Mistress; The House of Long Shadows; Boogeyman III; Nocturna; The Ice Pirates; Evils Of The Night.

TV inc: The Seekers; Misunderstood Monsters (voice); Goliath Awaits; Umbrella Jack.

Bway inc: Frankenstein.

CARRADINE, Keith: Act. b. San Mateo, CA, Aug 8, 1950. S of John Carradine. Bway inc: Hair; Foxfire. Films inc: A Gunfight; McCabe and Mrs. Miller; Idaho Transfer; Emperor of the North; Thieves Like Us; Nashville (Oscar-best song-1975); Lumiere; Welcome to L.A.; The Duellists; Pretty Baby; An Almost Perfect Affair; Old Boyfriends; The Long Riders; Southern Comfort; Maria's Lovers; Choose Me; Blackout.

TV inc: A Rumor of War; Chiefs; Scorned And Swindled.

CARRADINE, Robert: Act. b. Mar 24, 1954. S of John Carradine. Films inc: Joyride; Orca; Blackout; Coming Home; The Long Riders; The Big Red One; Heartaches; Tag; Wavelength; Revenge of the Nerds; Just The Way You Are.

TV inc: The Sun Also Rises.

CARRERA, Barbara: Act. b. Nicaragua. Was top model. Films inc: The Master Gun Fighter; Embryo; The Island of Dr. Moreau; When Time Ran Out; Condorman; I, The Jury; Lone Wolf McQuade; Never Say Never Again; Wild Geese II.

TV inc: Centennial; Masada; Sins of the Past.

CARRERAS, James, Sir: Exec. b. England, 1910. British prod. exec; former exhibitor; chmn. Hammer Films.

CARRERAS, Michael: Prod. b. England, 1927. S of James Carreras. M-dir. Hammer Films since 1971. Films inc: Blackout; The Snorkel; Ten Seconds to Hell; Passport to China; What a Crazy World; She; One Million Years BC; The Lost Continent; The 7 Brothers Meet Dracula; The Lady Vanishes.

CARRIERE, Jean-Claude: Wri-Prod. b. France, 1931. Films inc: Viva Maria; Heureux Anniversaire (Happy Anniversary) (Oscar-short co-prod-1962); Borsalino; Taking Off; The Discreet Charm of the Bourgeoisie; That Obscure Object of Desire; Leonor; L'Associe; The Tin Drum (wri); Die Faelschung (Circle of Deceit); Le Retour de Martin Guerre (The Return of Martin Guerre) (sp); L'Indiscretion (The Indiscretion) (sp); Antoinieta (sp); Danton; Le General de l'Armee Mort (The General of the Dead Army) (sp); Un Amour de Swann (Swann in Love) (sp).

Plays inc: La Tragedie de Carmen.

CARROLL, Carroll: Wri. b. NYC, Apr 11, 1902. Started as newspaperman; film critic NY Sunday World; joined J Walter Thompson Agency 1932 as head wri, edit supv radio shows inc Bing Crosby; Rudy Vallee; Al Jolson; Eddie Cantor; Burns & Allen; Joe Penner; Kraft Music Hall; Frank Sinatra; ghosted bios of Henny Youngman; Ed McMahon; Liberace; Mike Douglas; Bob Hope; columnist (And Now A Word From. . .) Variety.

TV inc: Bob Crosby Show; Fred Allen; General Electric Hour.

CARROLL, Diahann: Act-Singer. b. NYC, Jul 17, 1935. Films inc: Carmen Jones; Porgy and Bess; Goodbye Again; Paris Blues; Hurry Sundown; The Split; Claudine.

TV inc: Julia; A Holiday Tribute To Radio City Music Hall; I Know Why The Caged Bird Sings; Hope Women & Song; Sister, Sister; Christmas In Washington; Dynasty; George Burns' How To Live To Be 100 Or More; Bob Hope's Comedy Salute To The Soaps.

Bway inc: No Strings (Tony-1962); Agnes of God.

CARROLL, J. Larry: Wri-prod. b. Oct. 7, 1946. e. U TX, BA. Films inc: The Texas Chainsaw Massacre (film editor); Tourist Trap; The Day Time Ended (wri only); Parasite (prodn supv); Swordkill (dir).

TV inc: The Future Is Now; Nobody Knows.

CARROLL, Madeleine: Act. b. West Bromwich, England, Feb 26, 1906. e. Birmingham U, BA. Films inc: The Guns of Loos; The American Prisoner; Atlantic; Young Woodley; French Leave; School for Scandal; Madame Guillotine; I Was a Spy; Thirty-Nine Steps; Case Against Mrs. Ames; Secret Agent; The General Died at Dawn; Lloyds of London; On The Avenue; Prisoner of Zenda; It's All Yours; Blockade; Honeymoon in Bali; Cafe Society; Safari; Northwest Mounted Police; One Night in Lisbon; Bahama Passage; Lady in Distress; My Favorite Blonde; Don't Trust Your Husband; The Fan.

CARROLL, Matt: Prod. b. Sydney, Australia, Jun 6, 1944. e. Sydney U. Films inc: Shirley Thompson Versus the Aliens; Private Collection; Sunday Too Far Away; Fourth Wish; Storm Boy; Money Movers; Weekend of Shadows; Blue Fin; The Plumber; Breaker Morant; The Club; Freedom.

TV inc: Stacey's Jim; Harvest of Hate.

CARROLL, Pat: Act. b. Shreveport, LA, May 5, 1927. e. Immaculate Heart Coll; Catholic U. Films inc: With Six You Get Egg Roll. TV inc: Cinderella; Caesar's Hour (Emmy-supp-1956); The Danny Thomas Show; Busting Loose; Getting Together; Gertrude Stein, Gertrude Stein, Gertrude Stein.

Bway inc: Catch A Star!; On the Town (rev); Dancing In The End Zone.

(Grammy-spoken word-1980).

CARROLL, Vinnette: Act-Dir. b. NYC, Mar 11, 1922. e. Long Island U, BA; NYU, MA. In stock, repertory, toured in one-woman variety show; artistic dir Urban Arts Corps; teacher at NYC High School for Performing Arts. Bway inc: (act) A Streetcar Named Desire; Small War on Murray Hill; The Crucible; Jolly's Progress; Moon On A Rainbow Shawl (off-Bway); The Octoroon; Your Arms Too Short To Box With God (& co-wri & dir). (Dir) Don't Bother Me I Can't Cope (& conceived); Bury The Dead; Croesus and the Witch; Step Lively Boy; But Never Jam Today; I'm Laughin' But I Ain't Tickled (& conceived). London inc: Moon On A Rainbow Shawl (act); Black Nativity (dir).

Films inc: A Morning for Jimmy; One Potato, Two Potato; Up The Down Staircase; Alice's Restaurant.

THE CARS: Group. Members inc: Ric Ocasek, Elliot Easton, David Robinson, Benjamin Orr, Greg Hawkes. Began as regional group in New England.
Albums inc: The Cars; Candy-O; Panorama.

CARSEY, Marcia: Exec. b. South Weymouth, MA, Nov 21, 1944. e. U of NH. Joined ABC July 1974 as general program exec in comedy programming; May 1976 named VP Prime Time Comedy Development; Oct. 1976 VP Prime Time Comedy Programs-VP Comedy and Variety Programs; June 1978 Sr VP Comedy & Variety Programs; June 1979 SR VP all Prime Time Series; Dec 1980, resd to go into indie prodn. TV inc: Callahan (exec prod); I Do, I Don't (prod); Oh Madeline (exec prod); The Cosby Show (exec prod); Single Bars, Single Women (exec prod).

CARSON, Dick: Dir. TV inc: Merv Griffin Show *(Emmys*-1974, 1982); The Don Rickles Show; Tonight Show; Wheel of Fortune.

CARSON, Jeannie (Jean Shufflebottom): Act. b. Yorkshire, England, 1928. Films inc: Love in Pawn; As Long as They're Happy; An Alligator Named Daisy; Rockets Galore; Seven Keys.
TV inc: Hey Jeannie!; Best Foot Forward; Jeannie Carson Show.
Thea inc: (tour) Sound of Music; Camelot; 110 in the Shade.

CARSON, Johnny: TV Pers. b. Corning, IA, Oct 23, 1925. e. U of NE. Started on radio station KFAB, Lincoln, NE. Then to WOW, WOW-TV, Omaha, 1948; announcer, KNXT, LA, 1950; then Carson's Cellar; quizmaster; Earn Your Vacation, 1954; writer for Red Skelton; Johnny Carson Show, Who Do You Trust, Host of Oscar Telecasts (1979-1980-1981-1982-1984). The Tonight Show. *(Emmys*-1976, 1977, 1978, 1979); Lucy Moves To NBC; A Love Letter to Jack Benny; Johnny Goes Home (& wri); Johnny Carson's Greatest Practical Jokes (& wri); Johnny Carson Presents The Tonight Show Comedians.
Films inc: Looking For Love; Cancel My Reservation.
(ATAS Governors Award-1980).

CARSON, Robert: Wri. b. Clayton, WA, Oct 6, 1909. Wri-prod CBS 1954-55. Films inc: Men With Wings; The Light That Failed; Bundle of Joy; Action of the Tiger; Beau Geste; Western Union; The Desperadoes; A Star Is Born *(Oscar*-1937).
(Died Jan 19, 1983).

CARSON, Sunset (Kit)(Michael Harrison): Act. b. Plainview, TX, Nov 12, 1927. Films inc: Stage Door Canteen; Janie; Call of the Rockies; Code of the Prairie; The Oregon Trail; Days of Buffalo Bill; Alias Billy the Kid; The El Paso Kid Deadline; Rio Grande; Outlaw Grizzly; Buckstone County Prison; Marshall of Windy Hollow.
TV inc: Six Gun Heroes; Dukes of Hazard.

CARTER, Bennett Lester (Benny): Comp-Saxophonist-Arr-Act. b. NYC, Aug 7, 1907. e. Wilberforce U. To Paris 1935, joined Willie Lewis orch; staff arr, BBC, Eng. Formed own band in NY, Hollywood. Films inc: A Man Called Adam (score); The View From Pompey's Head (act); Snows of Kilimanjaro (act). TV background score: M Squad.
Songs inc: Because of You; When Lights Are Low; Manhattan Mood; Cow Cow Boogie.

CARTER, Dixie: Act. b. McLemoresville, TN, May 25. Thea inc: (Bway) Pal Joey; Sextet. (Off-Bway) Jesse and the Bandit Queen; Fathers and Sons; Taken In Marriage.
TV inc: On Our Own; The Andros Targets; The Edge of Night; Out of the Blue; The Killing of Randy Webster; Cassie & Co; The Greatest American Hero; Filthy Rich; Diff'rent Strokes.
Films inc: Going Berserk.

CARTER, Jack (nee Chakrin): Act. b. NYC, Jun 24, 1923. e. Brooklyn Coll. Stage debut, 1947, Call Me Mister. Films inc: The Horizontal Lieutenant; Viva Las Vegas; The Extraordinary Seaman; The Resurrection of Zachary Wheeler; The Happy Hooker Goes To Washington; The Octagon; Alligator; The Glove; History of the World--Part I; Heartbeeps; The Funny Farm; Separate Ways; Hambone and Hillie.

TV inc: Kraft 75th Anniversary Show; Rainbow; The Gossip Columnist; The Hustler of Muscle Beach; For The Love Of It; Bunnicula The Vampire Rabbit (voice).
Bway inc: Top Banana; Mr. Wonderful.

CARTER, June: Singer. b. Maces Spring, VA, Jun 23, 1929. W of Johnny Cash. Member of Carter Family Singing Group; member Grand Ole Opry; co-wri song Ring of Fire. TV inc: A Johnny Cash Christmas (1979); A Johnny Cash Christmas (1980); Johnny Cash and the Country Girls; 100 Years of Golden Hits; Johnny Cash--Christmas In Scotland; Johnny Cash--Cowboy Heroes; Johnny Cash--A Merry Memphis Christmas; Murder In Coweta County; Johnny Cash Christmas, 1983; The Baron And The Kid; Johnny Cash--Christmas On The Road. *(Grammys*-(2)-Group country voc/inst-1967; Country Group-1970).

CARTER, Lynda: Act. b. Phoenix, AZ, Jul 24. Named Miss World-USA 1973. TV inc: The New Adventures of Wonder Woman; Lynda Carter's Special; Lynda Carter Encore!; The Last Song; Lynda Carter Celebration; Born To Be Sold; Lynda Carter--Street Life; Hotline; Happy Birthday, Bob; Rita Hayworth--The Love Goddess; Linda Carter Body and Soul; Partners In Crime.

CARTER, Nell: Act. b. Birmingham, AL, Sept 13, 1948. Bway inc: Dude; Don't Bother Me, I Can't Cope; Jesus Christ Superstar; Bury The Dead; Ain't Misbehavin' *(Tony*-Supp-1978); Hair.
TV inc: Baryshnikov on Broadway; The Big Show; Lobo; An NBC Family Christmas; Ain't Misbehavin'; Gimme A Break; Christmas In Washington.
Films inc: Hair; Quartet; Back Roads; Modern Problems.

CARTER, Ralph: Act. b. NYC, May 30, 1961. TV inc: Sesame Street; I'm a Fan; Good Times. Thea inc: Tough to Get Help; Dude; Via Galactica; Raisin.

CARTER, T. K.: Act. b. NYC, Dec 18. Films inc: Abby; Foxy Brown; Benji. TV inc: Dr Kildare; Mannix; Six Million Dollar Man; Sgt Bilko; Julia; Mc Cloud; Battlestar Galactica.
Thea inc: The Hostage; Mrs Patterson; Kwamina.

CARTER, Terry: Act. b. Los Angeles, Dec. 14, 1956. Started as stand-up comic. TV inc: Billy, Portrait of a Street Kid; Just Our Luck; Border Pals; Adams House.
Films inc: Southern Comfort; The Thing; Seems Like Old Times; Doctor Detroit.

CARTWRIGHT, Angela: Act. b. Cheshire, England, Sep 9, 1952. Films inc: The Sound of Music; Lad: A Dog; Somebody Up There Likes Me; Something of Value; Beyond The Poseidon Adventure.
TV inc: The Danny Thomas Show; Lost in Space; Make Room for Granddaddy; Room 222; My Three Sons; Adam 12; Logan's Run; Scout's Honor; High School U.S.A. F0030
Thea inc: Forty Carats.

CARTWRIGHT, Veronica: Act. b. Bristol, England, 1950. Sis of Angela Cartwright. Films inc: Love and War; The Children's Hour; The Birds; One Man's Way; Spencer's Mountain; Inserts; Goin' South; Invasion of the Body Snatchers; Alien; Nightmares; The Right Stuff.
TV inc: Leave It to Beaver; Guyana Tragedy--the Story of Jim Jones; Joe Dancer; Prime Suspect; Robert Kennedy & His Times.

CARVER, Mary: Act. b. LA, May 3, 1924. e. UCLA. Studied with Lee Strasberg; Stella Adler. Bway inc: Out West of 8th; The Shadow Box; The Fifth of July; Other thea inc: Bury the Dead; Lo and Behold; A View From the Bridge; The Chairs; Between Two Thieves; A Touch of the Poet; Rhinoceros; The Last of the Red Hot Lovers.
Films inc: Goodbye, My Fancy; Invitation to a Gunfigher; Pay or Die; I Never Promised You A Rose Garden; Golden Girl; Protocol.
TV inc:Danger; Armstrong Circle Theatre; Simon & Simon.

CARVER, Randall: Act. b. Fort Worth, TX, May 25. Films inc: Midnight Cowboy; Time to Run. TV inc: Forever Fernwood; The Waltons; The Daughters of Joshua Cabe; Taxi.

CARVER, Steve: Dir. b. Brooklyn, NY, Apr 5, 1945. e. U of Buffalo; WA U. Films inc: Big Bad Mama; Capone; Drum; Moonbeam Rider; Steel; Lone Wolf McQuade (& prod).

CASARES, Maria (nee Quiroga): Act. b. France, 1922. Films inc: Les Enfants du Paradis; Les Dames du Bois de Boulogne; Orphee; Le Testament d'Orphee; The Rebel Nun.

CASEY, Bernie: Act. b. WV. e. Bowling Green U, MFA. Pro football player with San Francisco 49ers, LA Rams. Studied with Jeff Corey. Films inc: Guns of the Magnificent Seven; Box Car Bertha; Tick, Tick, Tick, Black Gun; Hit Man; Cleopatra Jones; Maurie; Cornbread Earl and Me; Brothers; The Watts Monster; Sharky's Machine; Never Say Never Again; Revenge of Nerds.

TV inc: Mary Jane Harper Cried Last Night; Brian's Song; Gargoyles; Ring of Passion; Love Is Not Enough; Harris and Company; The Martian Chronicles; The Sophisticated Gents; Denmark Vesey's Rebellion; Hear No Evil; Bay City Blues; The Fantastic World of D.C. Collins.

CASH, Johnny: Act-Folk singer. b. Kingsland, AR, Feb 26, 1932. Films inc: Hootenanny Hoot; Five Minutes to Live; Festival; A Gunfight; The Gospel Road.

TV inc: The Johnny Cash Show; The Unbroken Circle - A Tribute to Mother Maybelle Carter; A Johnny Cash Christmas 1979; Johnny Cash - The First 25 Years; A Johnny Cash Christmas 1980; The Pride of Jesse Hallam; Country Comes Home; Johnny Cash and the Country Girls; 100 Years of Golden Hits; Johnny Cash-Christmas In Scotland; Country Comes Home; Johnny Cash--Cowboy Heroes; Johnny Cash--A Merry Memphis Christmas. Murder In Coweta County; Johnny Cash Christmas, 1983; The Baron And The Kid; Johnny Cash--Christmas On The Road.

(Grammys-(6)-country vocal group-1967, 1970; country vocal-1968, 1969; Album Notes-1968, 1969.)

CASH, June Carter: (See CARTER, June).

CASH, Rosalind: Act. b. Atlantic City, NJ, Dec 31, 1938. e. CCNY. Films inc: Klute; The Omega Man; The New Centurions; Hickey and Boggs; Melinda; Uptown Saturday Night; Amazing Grace; Hit the Open Man; The Class of Miss McMichael; The Watts Monster; Wrong Is Right; Go Tell It On The Mountain; The Adventures of Buckaroo Banzai - Across the 8th Dimension.

Thea inc: The Wayward Stork; Junebug Graduates Tonight!; Fiorello!; God Is a (Guess What?); Ceremonies in Dark Old Men;

TV inc: Ceremonies in Dark Old Men; Angel Dust - The Wack Attack; Guyana Tragedy - The Story of Jim Jones; The Sophisticated Gents; Denmark Vesey's Rebellion; Sister, Sister; Keeping On; Hang Tight, Willy Bill; Special Bulletin; Go Tell It On The Mountain; The Joy That Kills.

CASON, Barbara: Act. b. Memphis, TN, Nov 15. e. U of MS, BA, MA. Bway inc: Oh, Coward; Marat/Sade.

TV inc: Carter Country; A Matter Of Life and Death; The Adventures of Pollyanna; Memories Never Die.

CASS, Peggy: Act. b. Boston, May 21, 1924. Bway inc: Burlesque; The Live Wire; Bernardine; Othello; Oh Men! Oh Women!; Auntie Mame (Tony-supp-1957); A Thurber Carnival; Don't Drink the Water; The Front Page; Plaza Suite; Last of the Red Hot Lovers; Once A Catholic; The Octette Bridge Club.

Films inc: The Marrying Kind; Auntie Mame; Gidget Goes Hawaiian; The Age of Consent; If It's Tuesday, This Must be Belgium; Paddy.

TV inc: The Hathaways; The Garry Moore Show; To Tell the Truth; The Jack Paar Show; The Leprechaun's Christmas Gold (voice).

CASSAVETES, John: Act-Dir. b. NYC, 1929. H of Gena Rowlands. Film debut in The Night Holds Terror, 1953. Films inc: (act) Crime in The Streets; Rosemary's Baby; Edge of the City; Affair in Havana; Saddle the Wind; The Dirty Dozen; Two Minute Warning; Brass Target; The Fury. (Dir): Shadows; Too Late Blues; A Child Is Waiting; Faces; Husbands; Minnie and Moskowitz (& sp); A Woman Under The Influence (& sp); Killing of a Chinese Bookie (& sp); Mikey and Nicky; Opening Night (& sp-act); Gloria (& sp); Whose Life Is It Anyway?; Tempest; The Incubus; Marvin and Tige; Love Streams (& sp-act);

"I'm Almost Not Crazy..." John Cassavetes - The Man and His Work (doc-int).

TV inc: Flesh and Blood.

CASSEL, Jean-Pierre: Act. b. France, Oct 27, 1932. Films inc: Les Jeux de l'Amour; L'Amant de Cinq Jours; The Vanishing Corporal; La Ronde; Those Magnificent Men in Their Flying Machines; Is Paris Burning?; Baxter; The Discreet Charm of the Bourgeoisie; The Three Musketeers; Murder on the Orient Express; That Lucky Touch; No Time For Breakfast; Who's Killing The Great Chefs of Europe?; From Hell To Victory; Le Soleil en Face; 5% Risk; Je Me Tiens, Tu Me Tiens par La Barbichette; La Vie Continue (Life Goes On); Ehrengard; La Truite (The Trout); Vive La Sociale!; Les Temps Difficiles (Times Have Changed).

CASSEL, Seymour: Act. b. Jan 22, 1935. Films inc: Murder Inc; Too Late Blues; Juke Box Racket; Coogan's Bluff; The Revolutionary; Faces; Minnie and Moskowitz; Black Oak Conspiracy; Valentino; Killing of a Chinese Bookie; Convoy; Sunburn; Ravagers; California Dreaming; The Mountain Men; King of the Mountain; Love Streams; "I'm Almost Not Crazy. . . " John Cassavetes - The Man and His Work (doc-int).

TV inc: Angel on My Shoulder; I Want To Live.

CASSIDY, David: Act. b. Apr 12, 1950. S of Shirley Jones and the late Jack Cassidy. TV inc: The Partridge Family; Man Undercover; The Night the City Screamed; Frank Mills Christmas Special.

CASSIDY, Joanna: Act. b. Camden, NY, Aug. 2, 1944. e. Syracuse U. Films inc: Bullitt; Fools; The Laughing Policeman; The Outfit; Bank Shot; The Stepford Wives; Stay Hungry; Prime Time; The Late Show; Night Child; Stunts; Our Winning Season; Night Games; The Glove; Blade Runner; Under Fire.

TV inc: 240-Robert; Dallas; Reunion; Insight/Resurrection; Buffalo Bill; Invitation to Hell; Codename Foxfire; Hollywood Wives.

CASSIDY, Shaun: Singer-Act. b. LA, Sep 27, 1958. S of Shirley Jones and the late Jack Cassidy. Films inc: Born of Water. TV inc: Hardy Boys Mysteries; Like Normal People; Breaking Away; A Shaun Cassidy Special; Breakfast With Les and Bess.

Thea inc: On a Clear Day; The Sound of Music; High Button Shoes.

Recordings inc: Da Doo Ron Ron; That's Rock n' Roll; Hey Deanie. Albums inc: Shaun Cassidy; Born Late; Under Wraps; Wasp.

CASTELLANO, Richard S: Act. b. NYC, Sep 4, 1933. e. Columbia U. Films inc: A Fine Madness; Lovers and Other Strangers; The Godfather; Night of the Juggler.

Thea inc: A View from the Bridge; The Investigation; That Summer, That Fall; Sheep on the Runway; Lovers and other Strangers; Night of the Juggler.

TV inc: The Gangster Chronicles.

CASTLE, Nick, Jr.: Wri-dir. b. Los Angeles, Sept. 21, 1947. e. Santa Monica College, USC. Films inc: Skatetown U.S.A.(wri); Escape From New York (wri); Tag; The Last Starfighter (dir).

CATES, Gilbert: Prod-Dir. b. NYC, Jun 6, 1934. e. Syracuse U, BS, MA. Films inc: The Painting (short); Rings Around the World; I Never Sang for My Father; Summer Wishes, Winter Dreams; Dragonfly; The Promise; The Last Married Couple in America (& exec prod); Oh, God! Book II.

TV inc: International Showtime (exec prod-dir); To All My Friends on Shore (dir-prod); The Affair (dir); After the Fall (dir-prod); Johnny We Hardly Knew Ye (dir-prod); Have I Got a Christmas for You (dir-prod); Fame; The Berenstain Bears - Xmas Tree (exec prod); Skinflint (exec prod); Elvis Remembered - Nashville to Hollywood (exec prod); Tony Randall's Royal All Star Circus (dir); The Kid from Nowhere (prod); Country Gold (Supv prod & dir); Johnny Cash--A Merry Memphis Christmas; Johnny Cash Christmas 1983; Hobson's Choice (dir); Burning Rage; Johnny Cash--Christmas On The Road; Consenting Adult (dir); Kraft All-Star Salute To Ford's Theatre (dir).

Bway inc: (Dir): Voices; The Price. (Prod) You Know I Can't Hear You When the Water's Running; I Never Sang for My Father; The Chinese and Dr. Fish; Tricks of the Trade (& dir).

CATES, Joseph: Prod-Dir. b. 1924. e. NYU. B of Gilbert Cates. One of the first producers of live tv with Bess Myerson's Wish Upon a Star, 1947; asso prod Jackie Gleason Show.

(Prod) Stop the Music; $64,000 Question; Johnny Carson All Star Comedy Hour; Ethel Merman Chevy Special; Annie The Women in The Life of A Man (Emmy-exec prod-1970). 'S Wonderful, 'S Marvelous, 'S Gershwin (Emmy-exec prod-1972); George M; Monte Carlo International Circus Special; Circus Lions, Tigers and Melissas Too; Fame; Spoon River; Dames at Sea; Berenstain Bears' Christmas Tree; Johnny Cash Christmas (1979); Skinflint; Fame; Elvis Remembered--Nashville to Hollywood; Comedy is Not Pretty; All Commercials; The Berenstain Bears Meet Bigpaw (exec prod); Daredevils (exec prod); A Johnny Cash Christmas (1980); Command Peformance--The Stars Salute The President; The Berenstain Bears Easter Surprise (exec prod); Johnny Cash and the Country Girls (exec prod); The Robert Klein Show (prod); Tony Randall's Royal All Star Circus (exec prod); The Magic of David Copperfield (exec prod 1981-1983); Johnny Cash-Christmas In Scotland; Magic With The Stars; The Berenstain Bears' Valentine Special; Country Comes Home (exec prod 1981-1982-1983); The Berenstain Bears' Littlest Leaguer; The Cradle Will Fall; Johnny Cash Christmas 1983; The Magic of David Copperfield VI (exec prod); Comedy Zone; Special People; Johnny Cash--Christmas On The Road; Mr. T. and Emmanuel Lewis In A Christmas Dream.

Bway inc: Spoon River Anthology; Joe Egg.

Films inc: The Last Married Couple in America.

CATES, Phoebe: Act. b. NYC, 1964. e. Professional Childrens School. D of Joseph Cates. Films inc: Paradise; Fast Times at Ridgemont High; Private School; Gremlins

TV inc: Mr. and Mrs. Dracula; Baby Sister; Lace; Lace II.

CATTRALL, Kim: Act. b. Liverpool, Eng. Aug 21, 1956. TV inc: The Bastard; The Night Rider; The Rebels; Scruples; The Gossip Columnist; Sins of the Past.

Films inc: Rosebud; The Other Side of the Mountain Part--Part II; Tribute; Ticket to Heaven; Porky's; Police Academy; Turk 182; City Limits.

CAULFIELD, Joan: Act. b. Orange, NJ, Jun 1, 1922. e. Columbia U. Screen debut 1945, Miss Susie Slagle's. Films inc: Dear Ruth; Variety Girl; Unsuspected; Sainted Sisters; Larceny; Dear Wife; The Petty Girl; The Rains of Ranchipur; Cattle King; Red Tomahawk; Buckskin;

TV inc: My Favorite Husband.

CAVALIER, Alain (nee Fraisse): Dir-wri. b. France, Sep 14, 1931. e. IDHEC. Films inc: Un Americain (short); Le combat dans l'ile; L'Insoumis; Mise a sac; La Chamade; Le Plein de super (Fill 'er up with Super); Martin et Lea.

CAVANI, Liliana: Dir-wri. b. Italy, Jan 12, 1936. e. U of Bologna, Italy, Centro Sperimentale Film School, Rome. Films inc: Galileo; The Cannibals; L'Ospite; The Night Porter; Oltre il Bene e il Male (Beyond Evil); La Pelle (The Skin); Oltre La Porta (Beyond the Door).

TV inc: Francis of Assisi.

CAVEN, Ingrid: Act. Films inc: Fear of Fear; Satan's Brew; Nea; In Einem Jahr Mit 13 Monden (In A Year of 13 Months); Malou; Looping; Wo Geht's Denn Hier Zum Film (How To Make It In the Movies); Die Hure under der Hurensohn (Dirty Daughters); Tag der Idioten (Day of the Idiots); Die Wilden Fuenfziger (The Roarin' Fifties).

CAVETT, Dick: Act-Wri. b. Kearny, NE, Nov 19, 1936. e. Yale U. Writer for Jack Parr and his successors on the Tonight Show and had comedy writing assignments with Merv Griffin, Jerry Lewis, Johnny Carson. In 1967 wrote for self and appeared in night clubs. Performed in TV specials for ABC-TV. TV inc: The Dick Cavett Show, PBS. (Emmys-1972, 1974); Time Was (cable) (host); Yesteryear-1917 (cable) (host); The Year That Was: 1982 (cable).

Films inc: Annie Hall; CS Blues; Power Play; Health; Acting--Lee Strasberg and the Actors Studio (doc).

CAVILL, Joy: Prod-Wri. b. Sydney, Australia, Feb 2. Films inc: King of the Coral Sea; Walk into Paradise; Dust in the Sun; The Stowaway; The Dispossessed; Nickel Queen.

TV inc: Adventure Unlimited; Seaway; Skippy; Barrier Reef; Boney; Shannon's Mob.

CAYATTE, Andre: Wri-Dir. b. Carcassonne, France, Feb. 3, 1909. Films inc: Justice est Faite; Nous Sommes Tous les Assassins; An Eye for an Eye; The Mirror Has Two Faces; The Crossing of the Rhine; La Vie Conjugale; A Trap for Cinderella; Die of Loving.

CAZENOVE, Christopher: Act. b. Winchester, England, Dec 17, 1945. e. Bristol Old Vic Theatre School. Thea inc: The Lionel Touch; My Darling Daisy; The Winslow Boy; Joking Apart; Goodbye Fidel (Bway).

Films inc: The Girl in Blue Velvet; Royal Flash; Zulu Dawn; Eye of the Needle; From A Far Country--Pope John Paul II; Heat and Dust; Until September; Mata Hari.

TV inc: The Regiment; Jennie; The Duchess of Duke Street; The Letter; Lace II.

CECIL, Jonathan: Act. b. England, 1939. Films inc: The Yellow Rolls Royce; Otley; The Private Life of Sherlock Holmes; Barry Lyndon; Joseph Andrews.

CELI, Adolfo: Act. b. Italy, July 27, 1922. Films inc: Escape into Dreams; The Man from Rio; Von Ryan's Express; Thunderball; El Greco; Grand Prix; The Honey Pot; Grand Slam; Fragment of Fear; Murders in the Rue Morgue; Hitler-The Last Ten Days; And Then There Were None; The Big Operator; Goodnight Ladies and Gentlemen; Cafe Express; Innamorato Pazzo (Madly In Love); Monsignor; Amici, Miei, Atto 2 (All My Friends 2); Cenerentola '80 (Cinderella '80).

TV inc: The Borgias.

CELLAN-JONES, James: Dir. b. Swansea, Wales, Jul 13, 1931. e. St. John's College, Cambridge. Films inc: The Nelson Affair; Sleeps Six (& prod).TV inc: The Scarlet and the Black; The Forsyte Saga; Portrait of A Lady; The Way We Live Now; Sold; The Roads To Freedom; Eyeless In Gaza; The Golden Bowl; Jennie; Caesar and Cleopatra; The Adams Chronicles; The Day Christ Died; The Ambassadors; Unity Mitford; The Comedy of Errors.

CHABROL, Claude: Dir. b. Sardent, France, June 24, 1930. H of Stephane Audran. Films inc: Le Beau Serge (& sp); Les Cousins (& sp); A Double Tour; Ophelia (& sp); The Third Lover; The Seven Deadly Sins; Landru; Marie Chantal; Line of Demarcation; The Champagne Murders; The Road to Corinth; Les Biches (& sp); La Femme Infidele (& sp); The Beast Must Die; The Butcher (& sp); Just Before Night (& sp); Blood Wedding; Ten Days Wonder; The Wolf Trap; Scoundrel in White; Une Partie de Plaisie; Les Magiciens; Folies Bourgeoises; Alice Ou La Derniere Fugue (& sp); Violette Noziere; Dirty Hands (& sp); Rascals (act); Le Cheval D'orgeuil (& sp); Les Fantomes Du Chapelier (The Hatter's Ghosts) (& sp); Les voleurs de la nuit (Thieves After Dark) (act); Le Sang des Autres (The Blood of Others): Polar (act); Poulet au Vinaigre.

Thea inc: La Danse de la mort (The Dance Of Death) (adapt-dir).

CHAFFEY, Don: Dir. b. England, Aug. 5, 1917. Films inc: Time is My Enemy; The Girl in the Picture; The Flesh is Weak; A Question of Adultery; The Man Upstairs; Dentist in the Chair; Nearly a Nasty Accident; A Matter of Who; The Prince and the Pauper; Jason and the Argonauts; A Jolly Bad Fellow; One Million Years B.C.; The Viking Queen; A Twist of Sand; Creatures the World Forgot; Persecution; Pete's Dragon; The Magic of Lassie; C.H.O.M.P.S.

TV inc: The Gift of Love; Casino; Riding For the Pony Express; International Airport.

CHAIKIN, Joseph: Act-Dir-Prod. b. Brooklyn, Sep 16, 1935. e. Drake U. Studied with Herbert Berghof. Joined Living Theatre, 1959-1963; Thea inc: Many Loves; The Cave at Machpelah; Tonight We Improvise; The Connection; Jungle of the Cities; Man is Man; Two by Ionescu; Sing to Me Through Open Windows; founded Open Theatre (1964); Terminal; Serpent; Endgame; Nighwalk; Woyzeck; The Tempest.

CHAIKIN, William E: Exec. b. Cleveland, OH, Apr 7, 1919. e. OH State U, BS, MS. Newspaper reporter, columnist before joining Fox publicity dept, 1945. Also in pub. depts of Republic, Eagle Lion. Later p of Chaikin-Perrett, p.r. firm. Became vp-treas of Standard Capital, investment banking firm which financed over 60 films. In 1963 named p, board chairman of Charter Title Ins. Co, LA. From

1968-74 was vp in charge of West Coast operation of Avco Embassy Pictures Corp. In July, 1974, p Avco Embassy. Ret 1980.

CHAKIRIS, George: Act-Dancer. b. Norwood, OH, Sep 16, 1934. Films inc: Brigadoon; Two and Two Make Six; West Side Story (Oscar-supp-1961); Diamond Head; King of the Sun; Flight from Ashiya; Squadron; The High Bright Sun; Is Paris Burning?; The Young Girls of Rochefort; The Big Cube.
TV inc: Natalie--A Tribute To A Very Special Lady.

CHALLIS, Christopher: Cin. b. England, March 18, 1919. Films inc: Theirs is the Glory; The Small Back Room; Tales of Hoffman; The Elusive Pimpernel; Genevieve; The Story of Gilbert and Sullivan; Malaga; The Flame and the Flesh; Footsteps in the Fog; Miracle in Soho; Sink the Bismark; The Grass is Greener; The Captain's Table; The Long Ships; Those Magnificent Men in Their Flying Machines; The Victors; The Americanization of Emily; Arabesque; Chitty Chitty Bang Bang; Villain; Catch Me a Spy; Mary Queen of Scots; The Boy who Turned Yellow; The Little Prince; Quilp; The Incredible Sarah; The Deep; Force 10 From Navarone; Riddle of the Sands; The Mirror Crack'd; Evil Under the Sun; Top Secret; Secrets; Steaming.
TV inc: The Visitation Mystery.

CHAMBERLAIN, Richard: Act. b. LA, Mar 31, 1935. Films inc: A Thunder of Drums; Twilight of Honor; Joy in the Morning; Petulia; The Madwoman of Chaillot; Julius Caesar; The Music Lovers; The Three Musketeers; The Towering Inferno; The Slipper and the Rose; The Swarm; The Last Wave; Murder By Phone.
TV inc: Dr. Kildare series (1961-65); Hamlet; F. Scott Fitzgerald and the Last of the Belles; The Lady's Not For Burning; The Man in the Iron Mask; The Count of Monte Cristo; The Woman I Love; Centennial; Shogun; Tony Awards (host); Entertainment Tonight; The Thorn Birds; Cook and Peary--The Race to the Pole; Raymond Massey--Actor of the Century; Wallenberg--A Hero's Story.
Thea inc: Hamlet (London & Bway); The Lady's Not For Burning.

CHAMBERLIN, Lee: Act. b. NYC, Feb 14, 1938. e. NYU; Sorbonne. Originally dancer with Pearl Primus and Alvin Ailey companies, then studied with Herbert Berghof and Uta Hagen. Thea inc: Your Own Thing; Slave Ship; King Lear.
TV inc: The Electric Company (Grammy-childrens rec-1972); All's Fair; Roots--The Next Generation; Paris; Ryan's Four.
Films inc: Uptown Saturday Night; Let's Do It Again.

CHAMBERS, Ernest: Prod-Wri. b. Philadelphia, Dec 28, 1928. e. Columbia, AB. TV inc: (Co-prod) Smothers Brothers Comedy Hour; Tony Orlando and Dawn; The Second Barry Manilow Special; The Third Barry Manilow Special; Barry Manilow--One Voice. (Prod) The Captain and Tennille Songbook; Donna Summers Special; John Schneider--Back Home; Barbara Mandrell and the Mandrell Sisters; The Rainbow Girl (prod); Love, Sidney (supv prod); Pump Girls & Dinettes On Television; America's Funniest Foul-Ups; 99 Ways To Attract The Right Man.

CHAMBERS, Everett: Prod-Dir-Wri. b. Montrose, CA, Aug 19, 1926. e. New School for Social Research; Dramatic Workshop, NY. TV inc: Target - The Corruptors; The Lollipop Cover; Peyton Place; Nightslaves; Monty Nash; Moon of the Wolf; Trouble Comes to Town; Can Ellen be Saved?; The Girl Must Live; They Only Come Out at Night; Variety '77-The Year In Entertainment; Rex Stout's Nero Wolfe; B.A.D. Cats; Turnover Smith; Berlin Tunnel 21 (supv prod); Will There Really Be A Morning?; A Matter of Sex (exec prod).
Films inc: Tess of the Storm Country.

CHAMCHOUM, Georges Farouk N: Prod-Dir. b. Niamey, Niger, Jul 16, 1946. Founder Cam 9 - Group 4 Prodns. Films inc: Inside Out; Salam, After Death; Lebanon. . .Why? (doc).

CHAMIE, Alfred P: Atty. b. NYC, Jun 1, 1910. e. UCLA, AB; Harvard, LLB. Legal counsel Assn. Motion Picture Prods Inc.; sec. Central Casting Corp; VP, sec, gen counsel Assn Motion Pictures and TV; bd dirs Motion Picture and TV Relief Fund; pres. LA Film Development Committee; chmn. Motion Picture & TV Fund Investment Committee.

CHAMPION, John: Prod-Dir. b. Denver, CO, Oct 13, 1923. Films inc: Panhandle; Stampede; Hellgate; Dragonfly Squadron; Zero Hour; The Last Escape; Mustang Country.

CHAMPION, Marge: Dancer-Chor. (nee Belcher)b. Los Angeles, Sep 2, 1923. W of the late Boris Sagal. Appeared in Blossom Time, Student Prince for LA Civic Opera. Made debut with then husband Gower Champion as nightclub dance team, Bway, films. TV inc: Queen of the Stardust Ballroom (Emmy-chor-1975); Night Of 100 Stars II.

CHAMPLIN, Charles: Critic-Editor. b. Hammondsport, NY, Mar 23, 1926. e. Harvard, AB. Joined Time-Life 1948 as wri-corr; 1965, entertainment ed-columnist LA Times; 1967, film critic; 1981 arts editor-book critic. Author The Flicks (1977, revised four years later as The Movies Grow Up, 1940-1980); TV inc: Stanley Kramer On Film.

CHANCELLOR, John: TV Anchorman. b. Chicago, 1927. e. U. of IL. Joined Chicago Sun Times, 1948. To NBC News as Midwest corr. 1950. Subsequently Vienna Bureau, Chief of Moscow Bureau before returning to US. Host Today program for one year, 1961. Served as dir. of Voice of America, 1965-67. Then anchorman, principal reporter on NBC TV News, commentator on NBC Radio. TV inc: America In Search of Itself; A Portrait Of The Press, Warts And All (& prod-wri).

CHANDLER, George: Act. b. Waukegan, IL, Jun 30, 1898. In vaudeville as The Musical Nut. On screen from 1927. Films inc: Tenderfoot Thrillers; Pretty Baby; This Woman Is Dangerous; Meet Me at the Fair; Hans Christian Anderson; Island in the Sky; Only Saps Work; In Gay Madrid; Too Many Cooks; The Country Doctor; Libeled Lady; Second Fiddle; The Return of Frank James; The Great Man's Lady; Since You Went Away; Lover Come Back; Perfect Strangers; Across the Wide Missouri; Apache Uprising; The Ghost and Mr. Chicken; One More Train to Rob; Every Which Way But Loose; The Apple Dumpling Gang Rides Again.
TV inc: Waterfront; Lassie.
(Died June 10, 1985)

CHANDLER, John Davis: Act. b. 1937. Films inc: The Young Savages; Mad Dog Coll; Major Dundee; Once a Thief; The Good Guys and the Bad Guys; Barquero; Shootout; Capone; The Jaws of Death; Scorchy; Chesty Anderson - U.S. Navy.

CHANNING, Carol: Act. b. Seattle, WA, Jan 30, 1923. Starred in West Coast revue, Lend an Ear. On Broadway 1950, Gentlemen Prefer Blondes; Hello, Dolly! (Tony-1964); Lorelei; Hello, Dolly! (rev). (London) Hello, Dolly!. (Special Tony-1968).
Films inc: Thoroughly Modern Millie.
TV inc: An Evening With Carol Channing; Love Boat (special); Parade of Stars; Night Of 100 Stars II.

CHANNING, Stockard (Susan Stockard): Act. b. NYC, Feb 13, 1944. Films inc: The Fortune; The Big Bus; Sweet Revenge; The Cheap Detective; Grease; The Fish That Saved Pittsburgh; Without A Trace; Safari 3000.
TV inc: The Girl Most Likely To...; The Stockard Channing Show; Not My Kid.
Thea inc: Absurd Person Singular; No Hard Feelings; The Golden Age (Bway); The Rink (Bway); Joe Egg (Bway) (Tony-1985).

CHAPIN, Miles: Act. b. NYC. e. National Theatre Institute. Studied with Herbert Berghof. Films inc: Ladybug, Ladybug; The Silence; To Find A Man; Bless the Beasts and Children; Hair; French Postcards; The Funhouse; Buddy Buddy; The Funny Farm; Get Crazy.
Bway inc: Summer Brave.
Tv inc: Our Man In Oklatown.

CHAPLIN, Geraldine: Act. b. Santa Monica, CA, Jul 31, 1944. D of late Charles Chaplin. Films inc: Limelight; The Countess From Hong Kong; Doctor Zhivago; Stranger in the House; I Killed Rasputin; The Hawaiians; Zero Population Growth; Innocent Bystanders; The Three Musketeers; Nashville; Buffalo Bill and the Indians; Cria!; Roseland; Welcome to L.A.; Northwest Wind; Remember My Name; Elisa My Love; A Wedding; Blindfolded Eyes; Mama Cumple 100 Anos; L'A-doption; Travels on the Sly; La Viuda De Monteil; The Mirror Crack'd; Les Uns et Les Autres (The Ins and the Outs); La vie est un roman

(Life Is A Novel); L'Amour Par Terre (Love On The Ground).

TV inc: The House of Mirth; My Cousin Rachel; The Corsican Brothers.

CHAPLIN, Saul: Prod-Sngwri. b. NYC, Feb 19, 1912. e. NYU. Sgwri at Vitaphone Corp. NY, 1937-39; to Hollywood 1940.

Films inc: (Mus dir) Cover Girl; The Jolson Story; Down To Earth; Jolson Sings Again; On The Town; An American in Paris *(Oscar*-scoring-1951); Lovely To Look At; Kiss Me Kate; Seven Brides for Seven Brothers *(Oscar*-scoring-1954); High Society. (Asso prod) Les Girls; Merry Andrew; Can Can; West Side Story *(Oscar*-scoring-1961) also *(Grammy*-for soundtrack album); I Could Go On Singing; The Sound of Music; Man of La Mancha. (Prod) Star!; That's Entertainment II.

Songs inc: Bei Mir Bist Du Schoen; Shoe Shine Boy; Please Be Kind; Until The Real Thing Comes Along; Anniversary Song.

CHAPLIN, Sydney: Act. b. Beverly Hills, CA, 1926. S of Charles Chaplin. Films inc: Limelight; Confession; Land of the Pharaohs; Four Girls in Town; Quantez; Follow that Man; A Countess from Hong Kong; The Sicilian Clan; Satan's Cheerleaders; Unknown Chaplin.

Bway inc: Bells Are Ringing *(Tony*-supp-1957).

CHAPMAN, Graham: Act-Wri. b. Leicester, England, 1940. e. Cambridge. Member Monty Python's Flying Circus. Thea inc: Footlights Revue; Cambridge Revue (& Bway); Python Live at Drury Lane; Python Live at City Center (NY).

Films inc: The Magic Christian; Rise and Rise of Michael Rimmer; And Now For Something Completely Different; Monty Python and the Holy Grail; Doctor in Trouble; The Odd Job (prod-act); Monty Python's Life of Brian; Monty Python's The Meaning of Life (& mus); Yellowbeard.

TV inc: Frost Report; Ronnie Corbett TV; At Last, the 1948 Show; No, That's Me Over Here; Doctor series; Pythons in Deutschland; Out of the Trees.

CHAPMAN, Marguerite: Act. b. Chatham, NY, Mar 9, 1918. Films inc: Charlie Chan at the Wax Museum; The Body Disappears; Parachute Nurse; Destroyer; Pardon My Past; The Walls Came Tumbling Down; Mr. District Attorney; Kansas Raiders; Man Bait; Flight to Mars; The Seven Year Itch; The Amazing Transparent Man.

CHAPMAN, Michael: Cin. b. MA, Nov 21, 1935. Films inc: The Last Detail; White Dawn; Taxi Driver; The Front; The Next Man; The Last Waltz; Invasion of the Body Snatchers; Hardcore; The Wanderers; Raging Bull; Personal Best.

TV inc: Death Be Not Proud; King.

CHARISSE, Cyd (Tula Ellice Finklea): Act. b. Amarillo, TX, Mar 8, 1923. W of Tony Martin. Toured U.S. & Europe with Ballet Russe. Screen debut in Something to Shout About, 1943. Films inc: Mission to Moscow; Till The Clouds Roll By; Words and Music; Kissing Bandit; East Side, West Side; Bandwagon; Brigadoon; Silk Stockings; Two Weeks in Another Town; The Silencers; Maroc 7; Warlords of Atlantis. TV inc: Portrait of an Escort; AFI Salute To Fred Astaire; The Kennedy Center Honors; AFI Salute To Gene Kelly.

CHARLAP, Morris (Moose): Comp. b. Philadelphia, PA., Dec. 19, 1928. e. U PA; U WI; Philadelphia Conservatory. Musicals inc: Peter Pan; Whoop-Up; The Conquering Hero. TV inc: The King and Mrs. Candle.

Songs inc: You Only You; Mademoiselle; Great Day in the Morning; Young Ideas.

CHARLES, Glen: Wri-Prod. b. Henderson, NV. e. U of Redlands, CA. B of Les Charles. Former Adwriter. TV inc: M*A*S*H (wri); Mary Tyler Moore Show (wri); Phyllis (wri-prod 1976-77); Bob Newhart Show (prod); Like Father, Like Daughter; Taxi (wri-prod) *(Emmys*-Prod-1979, 1980, 1981); Cheers *(Emmys*-prod & wri-1983; prod-1984).

CHARLES, Les: Wri-Prod. b. Henderson, NV. e. U of Redlands, CA. B of Glen Charles. Former Teacher. TV inc: M*A*S*H (wri); Mary Tyler Moore Show (wri); Phyllis (Wri-prod 1976-77); Bob Newhart Show (prod); Like Father, Like Daughter; Taxi (wri-prod) *(Emmys*-prod-1979,1980, 1981); Cheers *ys*-prod & wri-1983; prod-1984).

CHARLES, Lewis (nee Cholost): Act. b. NYC, Nov 2, 1920. e. St Johns U. Films inc: Panic in the Streets; To Catch a Thief; Jodie; Sweet Smell of Success; A House is Not a Home; Barney Ross Story; Soldier in the Rain; Al Capone; Island in the Sun; Penelope; Who's Got the Action; Topaz; The Midnight Oil; The Rose Tattoo; Our Man Flint; Now You See Her, Now You Don't; Maurie; I Love A Mystery.

CHARLES, Ray (nee Robinson): Mus-Singer-Comp. b. Albany, GA, Sep 23, 1930. Blind since childhood. Formed own band 1954. Now recording artist, does concerts, tv specials. Recs inc: Georgia On My Mind *(Grammys*-male vocal & pop singer artist-1960); Let The Good Times Roll *(Grammy*-R&B Perf-1960); Hit The Road Jack *(Grammy*-R&B-1961); I Can't Stop Loving You *(Grammy*-R&B Perf-1962); Busted; Crying Time *(Grammys*-R&B Rec & R&B solo-1966); Yesterday; Doing His Thing; What Have They Done To My Song Ma; Living for the City *(Grammy*-R&B Vocal-1975); I Can See Clearly Now; True To Life; Some Enchanted Evening.

Albums inc: Genius of Ray Charles *(Grammy*-Male Vocal-1960); Genius Plus Soul Jazz; Modern Sounds in Country and Western Music; I Can't Stop Loving You *(Grammy*-Male Vocal-1962); Porgy and Bess.

Ray Charles Singers recs inc: Deep Night; Love Me With All Your Heart; MacArthur Park; Slices of Life.

Films inc: Blues Brothers. TV inc: Country Comes Home; Ray Charles--A Man and His Soul, A 40th Anniversary Celebration; A Tribute to Martin Luther King Jr.--A Celebration of Life; Salute to Lady Liberty.

CHARLES, Ray (Charles Raymond Offenberg): Comp-lyr-arr-choral dir. b. Chicago, IL, Sep 13, 1918. On Bway conducted original prodn and cast album Finian's Rainbow; Peg (voc arr). Films inc: Funny Lady. Songs inc: Letters, We Get Letters; Dear Perry; Sing To Me Mr. C; Fifty Nifty United States; Christ is Born.

TV inc: All Perry Como Shows 1950-1958; Your Hit Parade; Hollywood Palace; Glen Campbell Show, The First Nine Months Are the Hardest *(Emmy*-spec material-1971); The Funny Side of Marriage *(Emmy*-spec material-1972); Julie Andrews Special; Mac Davis Specials (3); John Denver specials (2); The Carpenters Specials (2); Dorothy Hamill Specials (2); Gene Kelly Special; Academy Awards; Grammy Awards; 100 Years of Recorded Sound; A Gift of Music--L.A. Bicentennial; Ray Charles' World of Music (BBC); Val Doonican Show (BBC); Rocky Mountain Holiday with John Denver and the Muppets; Perry Como's Christmas in New York; Perry Como's Christmas In England. Sings theme on Three's Company.

CHARLESON, Ian: Act. b. Edinburgh, Scotland, Aug 11, 1949. e. Edinburgh U, MA; LAMDA. Thea inc; With Young Vic Company in Joseph and the Amazing Technicolor Dreamcoat; Look Back in Anger; Rosencrantz and Guildenstern are Dead; The Taming of the Shrew (NY); Scapino (NY); French Without Tears (NY); Hamlet; Otherwise Engaged; with National Theatre Company in Julius Caesar; Volpone; joined Royal Shakespeare Company 1978; Piaf; Once In A Lifetime; The Innocent; Guys and Dolls.

Films inc: Jubilee; Chariots of Fire; Gandhi; Ascendancy; Louisiane; Greystoke. . .BThe Legend of Tarzan, Lord of the Apes.

TV inc: Rock Follies; Churchill's People; The Paradise Run; Antony and Cleopatra; All's Well That Ends Well; Master of the Game; Reilly-Ace of Spies; The Sun Also Rises.

CHARLESON, Leslie: Act. b. Feb 22, 1945. Films inc: Day of the Dolphin.

Bway inc: One Night Stand.

TV inc: A Flame in the Wind (later called a Time for Us); Love Is a Many Splendored Thing; General Hospital.

CHARMOLI, Tony: Chor-Dir. b. MN. e. Coll of St Thomas. TV inc: Hit Parade *(Emmy*-chor-1955); Dinah Shore Show; Mitzi--A Tribute To The American Housewife *(Emmy*-chor-1974); Gypsy in My Soul *(Emmy*-chor-1976); The Nutcracker; John Denver and the Muppets; John Davidson Christmas Show; Third Annual Circus of the Stars; John Denver and The Muppets - A Christmas Get Together; From Raquel With Love (chor); Julie Andrews' Invitation to the Dance with Rudolf Nureyev (dir); Lily--Sold Out; Musical Comedy Tonight; Bob Hope's All-Star Celebration Opening the Gerald R Ford Museum (dir); Bonnie and the Franklins; The Wayne Newton Special--Coast To Coast (dir); Olympic Gala (dir).

Bway inc: Woman of the Year.

CHARNIN, Martin: Dir-Lyr. b. NYC, Nov 24, 1934. e. Cooper Union, BFA. Bway inc: Hot Spot (lyr); Mata Hari (lyr); Two by Two (lyr); Nash at Nine (dir); Music! Music! (dir); Annie (Tony-lyr-1977); I Remember Mama; The Bar Mitzvah Boy; The First; A Little Family Business (dir).
Films inc: Annie (lyr).
TV inc: Anne Bancroft Special; Jackie Gleason Show; Annie, The Women in the Life of a Man (Emmy-prod-1970); 'S Wonderful, 'S Marvelous, 'S Gershwin (Emmys-prod & dir-1972).
(Grammy-Cast Album-1977.)

CHARO (Maria Rosario Pilar Martinez): Singer-Act. b. Murcia, Spain, Jan 15, 1951. Recording artist. Numerous TV and nitery appearances. Films inc: Don Juan Teniorio (in Spain); The Concorde - Airport '79.
TV inc: Perry Como's Easter in Guadalajara.

CHARTERIS, Leslie: Wri-Prod. b. Singapore, 1907. e. Cambridge, England. Novelist. Creator The Saint, series of mystery novels on which several films, TV series based.

CHARTOFF, Robert: Prod. b. NYC, Aug 26, 1933. e. Columbia U, LLB. Films inc: Double Trouble; Point Blank; The Split; They Shoot Horses, Don't They?; The Strawberry Statement; Believe in Me; The Gang that Couldn't Shoot Straight; The Mechanic; The New Centurions; Up the Sandbox; Busting; S.P.Y.S.; Fat Chance; Breakout; Nickelodeon; Rocky (Oscar-1976); New York, New York; Valentino; Comes a Horseman; Uncle Joe Shannon; Rocky II; Raging Bull; True Confessions; Rocky III; The Right Stuff.

CHASE, Chevy (Cornelius Crane Chase): Act-Wri. b. NYC, Oct 8, 1943. e. Bard Coll, BA; Columbia, MA; MIT, MA. TV inc: Great American Dream Machine; Saturday Night Live (Emmys-supp act & wri-1976); Chevy Chase Special; Paul Simon Special (Emmy-wri-1978); Ernie Kovacs--Television's Original Genius (cable).
Films inc: Foul Play; Oh Heavenly Dog; Caddyshack; Seems Like Old Times; Under the Rainbow; Modern Problems; National Lampoon's Vacation; Deal of the Century; Fletch.

CHASE, David: Wri-Prod. b. Aug 22, 1945. e. Stanford, MFA. TV inc: The Magician (wri); The Nightstalker (story ed); The Rockford Files (prod-wri) (Emmy-prod-1978); Off The Minnesota Strip (Emmy-wri-1980); Palms; (exec prod-wri) Moonlight (exec prod-wri); Exploding Gas Tanks (Emmy-corr-1979); VW Beetle--The Hidden Danger (Emmy-corr-1980); Throwaway Kids.

CHASE, Sylvia: TV news. b. St Paul, MN, Feb 23, 1938. e. UCLA, BA. Action reporter KNX, LA, 1969; 1971 CBS News corr; 1977, ABC Weekend News co-anchor, corr.
TV inc: Magazine; Caution--Drinking Water May Be Hazardous to your Health; The American Woman; 20/20; (ATAS broadcast journalism award-1978).

CHASMAN, David: Prod-Exec. b. NYC, Sep 28, 1925. With various film cos inc UA; Fox; Col; Samuel Goldwyn; City Film. In 1974, p Convivium Prod, Inc; 1979 exec vp chg prodn Col; June 1980 exec vp film prodn MGM; Dec 1980 exec vp in chg wldwde theatrical prodn; Oct 1982-July 1983, Exec VP in chg prodn UA.
TV inc: Murder on Flight 502.

CHECCO, Al: Act. b. Pittsburgh, Jul 21, 1925. e. Carnegie Mellon U, BA. Films inc: Skipping; Super Dad; Pete's Dragon; Move Over Darling; Hotel; The Ghost and Mr. Chicken; Bullitt; Movie Maker; Daddy's Gone A Hunting; There Was a Crooked Man; I Love My Wife; How to Frame a Fig; Get to Know Your Rabbit; Skin Game; Repo; How To Beat The High Cost of Living.
TV inc: The Blue Knight; Helter Skelter; 79 Park Ave; Some Kind of Miracle; Tales of the Apple Dumpling Gang; Jerry Reed and Special Friends; Sins Of The Father.
Thea inc: An Inspector Calls; Lend an Ear; Two on the Aisle; The Gazebo; Damn Yankees; Leave It To Jane; Reuben-Reuben.

CHECKER, Chubby (Ernest Evans): Singer. b. Philadelphia, 1941. Films inc: Twist Around the Clock; Don't Knock the Twist. (Grammy-Rock & Roll-1961).

CHEECH AND CHONG: (See MARIN, Richard and CHONG, Tommy).

CHENAULT, Robert: Prod-Dir. TV inc: The Big Hex of Little Lulu: The Contest Kid Strikes Again; The Girl with ESP; The Ghost of Thomas Kempe; Where Do Teen Agers Come From?; Arthur The Kid (prod); Zack and the Magic Factory (prod); The Notorious Jumping Frog of Calaveras County; The Joke's On Mr Little (prod).

CHER (Cherilyn Sarkisian): Singer-Act. b. El Centro, CA., May 20, 1946. Began singing 1965 with Sonny Bono to whom she was then married. First hit record, I Got You Babe, sold 3 million; nitery performer. Films inc: Good Times; Chastity; Silkwood; Mask.
TV inc: Sonny & Cher Hour; Cher.
Bway inc: Come Back to the 5 & Dime, Jimmy Dean, Jimmy Dean.

CHERMAK, Cy: Wri-Prod. b. Bayonne, NJ, Sep 20, 1929. e. Brooklyn Coll; Ithaca Coll. TV inc: (wri) Rocky King; Detective; Philco Playhouse. (Prod): The Virginian; Convoy; Ironside; The New Doctors; Amy Prentiss; The Night Stalker; CHiPS; Murder at the World Series; The Circle Family.

CHERRY, Helen: Act. b. England, 1915. W of Trevor Howard. Films inc: The Courtneys of Curzon Street; Adam and Evelyn; Morning Departure; Young Wives' Tale; Castle in the Air; Three Cases of Murder; High Flight; The Naked Edge; Flipper's New Adventure; Hard Contract; Harrowhouse; Die Rebellen (Flashpoint Africa).
Thea inc: The Streets of London; Ladies In Retirement.

CHERTOK, Jack: Prod. b. Atlanta, GA, Jul 13, 1906. Worked as script clerk, asst dir, head of music dept, shorts prod at MGM; features prod inc The Penalty; Joe Smith, American; Kid Glove Killer; The Omaha Trail; Eyes in the Night; The Corn is Green; Northern Pursuit.
TV inc: Private Secretary; The Lawless Years; Johnny Midnight; My Favorite Martian.

CHESTER, Hal E: Prod. b. Brooklyn, NY, Mar 6, 1921. Child actor (Little Tough Guys, etc).
Films inc: (prod) Joe Palooka series; Underworld Story; The Highwayman; Triple Cross; Models, Inc; Beast from 20,000 Fathoms; Crashout; The Bold and the Brave; The Weapon; The Haunted; School for Scoundrels; Two-Headed Spy; Hide and Seek; The Secret War of Harry Frigg; The Double Man; The Comedy Man.

CHETWYN, Robert: Dir. b. London, Sep 7, 1933. Worked briefly as act. Dir of prodns at various provincial repertory groups; asso dir Mermaid Theatre, London. Thea inc: The Beaver Coat; There's A Girl In My Soup (& Bway); The Importance of Being Earnest; The Real Inspector Hound; What the Butler Saw; The Bandwagon; When We Are Married; Who's Who; Chez Nous; The Doctor's Dilemma; Kidnapped at Christmas; Getting Away With Murder; Moving; Eastward Ho; Beethoven's Tenth (& Bway); Number One; Why Me?
TV inc: Beyond a Joke; Making Faces; Private Shultz.

CHETWYND, Lionel: Wri. b. London, 1940. e. Sir George Williams U; McGill U; Trinity Coll; Oxford. Joined Col Pictures Int'l, NY, 1968; transferred to Col, London, 1968; asst man dir, 1969; asst man dir Columbia-Warner UK, 1971; freelance wri. Films inc: The Apprenticeship of Duddy Kravitz; It Happened One Christmas; Hanoi Hilton; Two Solitudes (& dir); Johnny We Hardly Knew Ye; Goldenrod; Quintet.
TV inc: The Adams Chronicles; The Guest Room; Please, Remember Me; Quintet; A Whale For the Killing; Miracle On Ice; Escape from Iran--The Canadian Caper; Sadat; Children In The Crossfire.
Plays inc: Bleeding Great Orchids.

CHEW, Richard: Flm Ed. b. LA, Jun 28, 1940. e. UCLA, AB. Films inc: The Conversation; One Flew Over the Cuckoo's Nest; Star Wars (Oscar-1977); Goin' South; When You Comin' Back, Red Ryder; Saint Jack; My Favorite Year; Risky Business.

CHIARI, Walter (nee Annichiarico): Act. b. Italy, 1924. Films inc: Bellissima; OK Nero; The Moment of Truth; Nana; The Little Hut; Bonjour Tristesse; Pepote; Chimes at Midnight; They're a Weird Mob; Squeeze a Flower; The Valachi Papers.

CHIHARA, Paul: Comp. b. Seattle, WA, Jul 9, 1938. e. U WA, BA; Cornell, MA, DMA. Fulbright Fellow 1965; Asso prof music UCLA 1966; Teacher of comp California Institute of Arts 1975; composer in residence for San Francisco Ballet 1981.

Films inc: Prince of the City; The Survivors; Crackers; Impulse.

TV inc: The Children of An Lac; The Promise of Love; Divorce Wars--A Love Story; The Ambush Murders; The Rules of Marriage; The Tempest--Live With the San Francisco Ballet; A Bunny's Tale; Miss All American Beauty; Whiz Kids; Noon Wine;Legmen; With Intent To Kill; The Bad Seed; Victims For Victims--The Theresa Saldana Story; MacGruder & Loud; Right To Kill?

CHILD, Julia: TV pers. b. Pasadena, CA, Aug 15, 1912. e. Smith Coll, BA. With adv dept W & J Sloane; served with OSS in Washington and Ceylon during WW2.

TV inc: The French Chef *(Emmy*-1966); Julia Child and Co; Julia Child and More Company.

CHILES, Lois: Act. b. Alice, TX., 1950. Former model. Films inc: The Way We Were; The Great Gatsby; Coma; Death on the Nile; Moonraker; Courage.

Thea inc: The Incredibly Famous Willy Rivers (Off-Bway).

CHISHOLM, Samuel Hewlings: TV Exec. b. Auckland, New Zealand, Oct 8, 1939. GM TCN Channel Nine Pty Ltd Willoughby NSW.

CHODOROV, Edward: Wri-Prod. b. NYC, Apr 17, 1904. Films inc: The World Changes; Kind Lady; The Story of Louis Pasteur; Yellow Jack; Undercurrent; The Hucksters; Roadhouse; Craig's Wife.

Plays inc: Wonder Boy; Kind Lady; Cue for Passion; Those Endearing Young Charms; Decision; Common Ground; Signor Chicago; Oh Men, Oh Women, Listen to the Mocking Bird.

CHODOROV, Jerome: Wri-Dir. b. NYC, Aug 10, 1911. Films inc: Louisiana Purchase; My Sister Eileen; Junior Miss; Happy Anniversary.

Plays inc: My Sister Eileen; Pretty Penny; Wonderful Town *(Tony*-1953); The Girl in Pink Tights; The Tunnel of Love; Three Bags Full; The Student Prince; Make a Million (& dir); The Gazebo (& dir); Blood Sweat and Stanley Poole (dir only); A Talent For Murder.

CHOMSKY, Marvin J: Dir. b. NYC, May 23, 1929. e. Syracuse U, BS; Stanford U, MA. Films inc: Maya; Evel Knievel; Murph the Surf; Mackintosh and TJ; Good Luck Miss Wyckoff; Tank.

TV inc: The Wild, Wild West; Gunsmoke; Star Trek; Then Came Bronson; Victory at Entebbe; Roots; Holocaust *(Emmy*-1978); Hollow Image; Doctor Franken; Attica *(Emmy*-1980); King Crab; Evita (& prod); My Body, My Child; Inside The Third Reich *(Emmy*-1982); I Was A Mail Order Bride; Nairobi Affair; Robert Kennedy & His Times. subtotal? (Y/N):

CHONG, Tommy: Singer-Act-Wri. b. Edmonton, Alta, Canada, May 24, 1938. Guitar player with various Canadian R&B combos, teamed with Richard Marin (Cheech) in improvisational group; spotted by Lou Adler at Hollywood's Troubadour club began comedy recordings *(Grammy*-1973).

Films inc: Cheech and Chong's Up in Smoke, Cheech and Chong's Next Movie; Cheech and Chong's Nice Dreams; Things Are Tough All Over; It Came From Hollywood; Cheech and Chong's Still Smokin' (& dir); Yellowbeard (act); Cheech & Chong's The Corsican Brothers (wri-dir-act).

TV inc: It Only Hurts When You Laugh.

CHOOLUCK, Leon: Prod-Dir. b. NYC, Mar 19, 1920. Worked as Asst Dir, apprentice cutter, projectionist, film examiner, cin. Films inc: (prod): Hell on Devil's Island; Plunder Road; Murder by Contract; City of Fear; Take A Hard Ride. (Assoc prod): The Fearmakers; Day of the Outlaw; The Bramble Bush; The Rise and Fall of Legs Diamond; Studs Lonigan; Three the Hard Way. Dir: Three Blondes in His Life. (Prodn supv): God's Little Acre; Anna Lucasta; El Cid; Battle of the Bulge; The Midas Run; The Grissom Gang; The Phynx; Kotch; Slaughter; Apocalypse Now.

TV inc: The Pinky Lee Show; The Outer Limits; I Spy; Highway Patrol; Lockup; Stoney Burke; Dynasty; Judge Horton and the Scottsboro Boys.

Thea inc: Boy Meets Girl.

CHOW, Raymond: Prod-Exec. b. Hong Kong, May 17, 1927. e. St John's U, Shanghai, BAJ. Journalist with US Information Service; pub dir Shaw Brothers. Formed Golden Harvest group of companies in 1970; has produced more than 100 films inc: Fists of Fury; Chinese Connection; Enter The Dragon; The Contract; Return Of the Dragon; Game of Death; Night Games; The Big Brawl; Encounter of the Spooky Kind; Security Unlimited; Dreadnaught; Death Hunt (exec prod); The Cannonball Run (exec prod); Super Fool; To Hell With The Devil; Megaforce; The Miracle Fighters; Plain Jane To the Rescue; Zu (Warriors From The Magic Mountain); Duel To The Death; High Road to China (exec prod); The Trail; Winners & Sinners (exec prod); Better Late Than Never (exec prod); The Champions; The Body is Willing (exec prod); Project A (exec prod); Lassiter (exec prod); Teppanyaki (exec prod); Cannonball Run II (exec prod); Wheels On Meals (exec prod); And Now, What's Your Name?; The Protector (exec prod).

CHRISTIAN, Linda (Blanca Rosa Welter): Act. b. Tampico, Mexico, Nov 13, 1924. Screen debut 1946, Holiday in Mexico. Films inc: Green Dolphin Street; Tarzan and the Mermaid; The Happy Time; Athena; Thunderstorm; The House of Seven Hawks; The VIPs; How to Seduce a Playboy.

CHRISTIAN, Robert: Act. b. Dec 27. Bway inc: We Bombed in New Haven; Does the Tiger Wear a Necktie?; An Evening With Richard Nixon and--; All God's Chillum Got Wings; Piaf. Other thea inc: Coriolanus; Blood Knot.

Films inc: The Seduction of Joe Tynan; Bustin' Loose; Prince of the City.

TV inc: Roll of Thunder, Hear My Cry; King; Muggable Mary; The Neighborhood; Another World.

(Died Jan 27, 1983).

CHRISTIAN, Roger: Art dir-Dir. b. England. Films inc: (Art) Oliver; Akenfield; Landscape; Vampira; Lucky Lady; Star Wars (Oscar-set dec-1977); Last Remake of Beau Geste; Alien; The Life of Brian. (Dir) Black Angel (short); The Dollar Bottom (short); The Sender; Lorca And The Outlaws.

TV inc: (Art) Randall and Hopkirk; Jason King. (Dir) Duxe De Luxe (& prod).

CHRISTIAN-JAQUE (Christian Maudet): Dir. b. Paris, Sep 4, 1904. Les Disparus de Saint-Agil; La Symphonie Fantastique; Sortileges; Un Revenant; D'Homme a Hommes; Bluebeard; Fanfan la Tulipe; Lucrezia Borgia; Nana; Race for Life; Babette Goes to War; The Black Tulip; The Secret Agents; Two Tickets to Mexico; Doctor Justice; La Vie Parisienne; The Making of a Lady (& sp).

CHRISTIANSEN, Robert: Prod. b. Porterville, CA. Prod asst Monte Walsh; Hail Hero.

Films inc: (prod) Adam at Six A.M.; Hide in Plain Sight.

TV inc: Suddenly Single; The Glass House; A Brand New Life; The Autobiography of Miss Jane Pittman *(Emmy*-1974); I Love You..- .Goodbye; Queen of the Stardust Ballroom; Born Innocent; A Death in Canaan; Strangers; Wishman; Robert Kennedy & His Times.

CHRISTIE, Audrey: Act. b. Chicago, Jun 27, 1912. NY stage debut 1928, Palace Theatre, in a dancing act. Bway inc: Good News; Follow Thru; Sweet and Low; Of Thee I Sing; Shady Lady; Sailor Beware; No, No, Nanette; A Connecticut Yankee; The Red Mill; I Married an Angel; My Sister Eileen; The Voice of the Turtle; Light Up the Sky; Holiday for Lovers; Mame.

Films inc: Deadline; Carousel; Splendour in the Grass; The Unsinkable Molly Brown; The Ballad of Josie; Harlow; Mame; Harper Valley PTA.

TV inc: Shirts/Skins: Fair Exchange; The Streets of L.A.

CHRISTIE, Howard J: Prod. b. San Francisco, Sep 16, 1912. e. UC Berkeley, BA. Began career as actor, 1934; Asst dir 1936-40; Assoc prod 1942-44, Deanna Durbin pictures. Films inc: Lady on a Train; Because of Him; Abbott and Costello Meet the Invisible Man (7 other A&C pictures); Comin' Round the Mountain; Lost in Alaska; Against All Flags; Yankee Buccaneer; Seminole; Back to God's Country; Yankee Pasha; Smoke Signal; The Looters; Price of Fear; Congo Crossing; Showdown at Abilene; Toy Tiger; Away All Boats; I've Lived Before; Wagon Train; The Raiders; Sword of Ali Baba; Laredo; Ride to Hangman's Tree; Journey to Shiloh; Nobody's Perfect; A Man Called Gan-

non.
TV inc: Wagon Train; Laredo; The Virginian.

CHRISTIE, Julie: Act. b. Assam, India, Apr 14, 1941. Joined a repertory company at Sussex, England. Performed in TV. Films inc: Billy Liar; Young Cassidy; Darling (Oscar-1965); Doctor Zhivago; Fahrenheit 451; Far From the Madding Crowd; Petulia; In Search of Gregory; The Go-Between; McCabe and Mrs Miller; Don't Look Now; Shampoo; Demon Seed; Heaven Can Wait; Memoirs of a Survivor; The Return of the Soldier; Les Quarantiemes Rugissants (The Roaring Forties); Heat and Dust; The Gold Diggers
TV inc: Separate Tables (cable).

CHRISTINE, Virginia (nee Kraft): Act. b. Stanton, IA, Mar 5, 1920. e. UCLA. W of Fritz Feld. In addition to appearing for 15 years as Mrs. Olson in Folger's coffee commercials, film and TV credits number more than 400. Films inc: Edge of Darkness; Mission to Moscow; Counter Attack; The Killers; Cover Up; The Men; Cyrano De Bergerac; Cobweb; High Noon; Not as a Stranger; The Spirit of St. Louis; Three Brave Men; Judgment at Nuremberg; The Prize; Four For Texas; A Rage to Live; Guess Who's Coming to Dinner; Hail Hero; Daughter of the Mind.
Thea inc: Hedda Gabler; Mary, Queen of Scots; Miss Julie; Desdemona.

CHRISTOPHER, Dennis: Act. b. Philadelphia, PA, 1954. Films inc: Breaking Away; The Last Word; Fade To Black; Chariots of Fire; Don't Cry, It's Only Thunder.
Bway inc: The Little Foxes; Brothers.

CHRISTOPHER, Jordan: Mus-Act. b. Youngstown, OH, Oct 23, 1942. Formed band, The Wild Ones which played Peppermint Lounge; became mus dir Arthur, NYC discotheque. Films inc: Return of the Seven; The Fat Spy; The Tree; Pigeons; Angel, Angel Down We Go; Brainstorm.
Bway inc: Black Comedy; Sleuth.
TV inc: Heart in Hiding; The Secret of Midland Heights; Paper Dolls; Seduced.

CHRISTOPHER, William: Act. b. Evanston, IL, Oct 20, 1932. e. Wesleyan U. Films inc: The Fortune Cookie; With Six You Get Eggroll; The Shakiest Gun in the West; The Private Navy of Sgt. O'Farrell; Hearts of the West.
TV inc: Gomer Pyle, USMC; Hogan's Heroes; The Andy Griffith Show; M*A*S*H; For The Love Of It; AfterMASH.

CHUA, Robert (Robert Chua Wah Peng): Prod. b. Singapore, May 20, 1946. M-dir, Robert Chua Productions; Robert Chua TV Academy. Created & prod Hong Kong's longest running variety show, 90 min. strip, Enjoy Yourself Tonight. TV inc: Miss Hong Kong Contest; Popular Song Contest; Amateur Song Contest.

CHUKHRAI, Grigori: Wri-dir. b. Ukraine, Russia, May 23, 1921. e. Moscow Film Institute. Films inc: Nazar Stodolya (dir only); The Forty-First (dir only); The Ballad of a Soldier (& co-sp); There Lived an Old Man and an Old Woman (dir only); Memory; An Untypical Story; La Vita e Bella (Life is Wonderful).

CHUNG, Connie (Constance Yu-Hwa Chung): TV News. b. Washington, DC., Aug. 20, 1946. e. U MD, BA. Entered field 1969 as reporter WTTG-TV, Washington; 1971, Washington correspondent CBS; 1976, anchor KNXT, Los Angeles; Aug. 1983 anchor NBC News at Sunrise; Summer Sunday U.S.A.

CHURIKOVA, Inna: Act. b. Russia, Oct 5, 1943. e. Schchepkin Drama School. W of Gleb Panfilov. Films inc: Clouds Over Borsk; Where Are You Now, Maxim?; Morozko; 33; The Cook; The Elder Sister; No Ford in the Fire; The Beginning; I Wish to Speak; Valentina, Valentina; Tema; Vassa.

CILENTO, Diane: Act. b. Rabaul, New Guinea, Apr 2, 1934. e. Studied ballet. Attended AADA; RADA. Films inc: Moulin Rouge; Angel Who Pawned Her Harp; Passing Stranger; Passage Home; Admirable Crichton; Hombre; Tom Jones; The Wicker Man; Duet for Four; The Boy Who Had Everything.
London Thea inc: The Big Knife; Arms and The Man; Tiger at the

Gates; I Thank a Fool; The Third Secret; Tom Jones; The Streets of London (dir).
TV inc: La Belle France; Court Martial; Blackmail; Dial M for Murder; Big Toys; For The Term of His Natural Life.

CIMINO, Michael: Wri-Dir. b. 1943. e. Yale, BFA, MFA. Films inc: Silent Running (sp only); Magnum Force (sp only); Thunderbolt and Lightfoot; Deer Hunter (& co-prod), (Oscars-picture, dir-1978); Heaven's Gate.

CIOFFI, Lou: TV newsman. b. NYC, Apr 30, 1926. e. CCNY; Muhlenberg. Joined CBS 1947 as copyboy; 1948 wri; 1950 Washington News Bureau edtr; 1952 Korean War corr; 1954 NY Bureau CBS; 1956, Paris corr; 1961, CBS Washington corr; 1961 joined ABC News; corr Viet Nam; 1968, headed Tokyo Bureau; 1970, Bonn Bureau; 1973, Paris Bureau; 1977 named UN corr ABC; March 1982, head of Washington Bureau, Satellite News Channel.

CLAIRE, Ina (nee Fagan): Act. b. Washington, DC, Oct 15, 1892. In vaude as child, noted for imitation of Sir Harry Lauder. Legit debut at age 16, Jumping Jupiter.
Bway inc: Quaker Girl; Lady Luxury; Ziegfeld Follies of 1915; Polly With A Past (first straight comedy role); The Gold Diggers; Bluebeard's Eighth Wife; The Awful Truth; Grounds for Divorce; The Last of Mrs. Cheyney; Biography; Ode to Liberty; End of Summer; Once is Enough; Ninotchka; The Talley Method; The Fatal Weakness; The Confidential Clerk (1954, last Bway appearance).
Films inc: Polly With Past (1915); The Awful Truth; The Royal Family of Broadway; Rebound; The Greeks Had a Word for Them; Ninotchka; Claudia (1943, last film).
(Died Feb. 21, 1985)

CLAMPETT, Bob: Ani-Wri-Prod-Dir. b. San Diego, CA, May 8. e. Otis Art School. Creator of cartoon characters. Ani cartoons inc: Bugs Bunny; Porky Pig; Daffy Duck; Tweety; Beany and Cecil; Thunderbolt the Wonder Colt; Time for Beany; Lone Stranger and Porky; Bugs Bunny Superstar (host); Uncensored Cartoons.
(Died May 2, 1984).

CLAPTON, Eric: Singer-Sngwri. b. Ripley, Surrey, England, Mar 30, 1945. With various groups inc Casey Jones and the Engineers; Yardbirds; Joe Mayall's Bluesbreakers; Cream; Blind Faith; Delaney and Bonnie and Friends; Derek and the Dominoes before going solo.
Recordings inc: Concert for Bangladesh (Grammy-Album of Year-1972); 461 Ocean Boulevard; There's One In Every Crowd; E.C. Was Here; No Reason to Cry; Slowhand; Backless.
Films inc: Concert for Bangladesh; Tommy; The Last Waltz; Eric Clapton and His Rolling Hotel (doc); The Secret Policeman's Other Ball (doc); The Hit (mus).
Songs inc: Let It Rain; Layla.

CLARK, Bob: Dir. b. New Orleans, LA, Aug. 5, 1941. e. Hillsdale Coll, MI. Films inc: The Emperor's New Clothes; Children Shouldn't Play With Dead Things; Dead of Night; Black Christmas; Breaking Point; Murder By Decree; Tribute; Porky's (& prod-wri); Porky's II--The Next Day (& prod-wri); A Christmas Story (& prod-wri); Rhinestone; Turk 182.

CLARK, Brian: Wri. b. Bristol, England. Plays inc: Whose Life Is It, Anyway?; Can You Hear Me At The Back?; Kipling.
TV inc: Achilles Heel; Magic Carpet; Parole; Easy Go; The Saturday Party; The Country Party; All Creatures Great and Small; Telford's Change.
Films inc: Whose Life Is It Anyway?

CLARK, Candy: Act. b. Oklahoma, Jun 20, 1947. Model. Films inc: Fat City; American Graffiti; The Man Who Fell to Earth; Citizens Band; The Big Sleep; When You Comin' Back, Red Ryder; More American Graffiti; The Winged Serpent; Blue Thunder; National Lampoon Goes to the Movies; Amityville 3-D; Hambone and Hillie; Cat's Eye.
TV inc: Amateur Night at the Dixie Bar and Grill; Where The Ladies Go; Rodeo Girl; Twilight Theatre; Johnny Belinda; Cocaine and Blue Eyes; I Gave at the Office.

CLARK, Dane: Act. b. NYC, Feb 18, 1915. e. Cornell U; John Hopkins U. Started in radio. Bway inc: Of Mice and Men; Dead End. Films inc: The Glass Key; Pride of the Yankees; Destination Tokyo; God Is My Co-Pilot; Whiplash; Go Man Go; Blackout; Thunder Pass; Toughest Man Alive; The Woman Inside.

TV inc: No Exit; The Closing Door; Bold Venture; The French Atlantic Affair; Riker; Condominium.

CLARK, Dick: TV Pers. b. Mt Vernon, NY, Nov 30, 1929. e. Syracuse U. Started as radio announcer. Host of American Bandstand since 1956 (Emmy-exec prod-1983); Dick Clark Beechnut Show; Dick Clark's World of Talent; The Object Is; Missing Links. Formed Dick Clark Productions, 1956 to produce films, TV.

Films inc: Because They're Young; The Young Doctor; Psychout; The Savage Seven; Killers Three; The Dark.

TV inc: Dick Clark's Live Wednesday; Dick Clark's Rockin' New Year's Eve; Elvis; Birth of the Beatles; The Man in the Santa Claus Suit; The Sensational Shocking Wonderful Wacky 70's; $20,000 Pyramid (Emmy-host-1979); Valentine Magic on Love Island; 32d Annual Emmy Awards (host); Murder In Texas (exec prod); TV's Censored Bloopers (& exec prod); Opryland--Night of Stars and Future Stars (exec prod); The Krypton Factor (host); Whatever Became Of. . .?(exec prod); The First All American Ultra Quiz (exec prod); Inside America (exec prod); I've Had It Up To Here (exec prod); An All-Star Tribute To Ernest Tubb--An American Original (exec prod); Conway Twitty On the Mississippi; The Woman Who Willed A Miracle (exec prod) (Emmy-1983); The Demon Murder Case (co-exec prod); Hollywood's Private Home Movies (exec prod); The 1/2 Hour Comedy Hour (exec prod); Ray Charles - A Man and His Soul, A 40th Anniversary Celebration (emcee); I Love Men (exec prod); Animals Are the Funniest People; Here's Television Entertainment (host).; Super Stars and Classic Cars (exec prod); TV Bloopers and Practical Jokes (exec prod-host); Celebrity Fun Cruise (exec prod); Black Gold Awards (exec prod); You Are the Jury (exec prod); Celebrities! Where Are They Now? (exec prod); Puttin' On The Ritz (exec prod); Hollywood Stars' Screen Tests.

CLARK, John Richard: Dir. b. Hobart, Tasmania, Oct 30, 1932. e. U of Tasmania, BA; UCLA, MA. School teacher in London and Hobart before joining Hobart Repertory Theatre; since 1960 dir National Institute of Dramatic Art, Sydney Australia. Thea inc: Don's Party; The Bald Prima Donna; Entertaining Mr. Sloane; The Merchant of Venice; The Country Wife; A Midsummer Night's Dream; Saint Joan.

Films inc: Lagged, The Story of a Convict; Running On Empty.

CLARK, Marilyn: Act. b. Spokane, WA, Sep 28, 1929. e. UCLA, BA. W of Philip Langner. Films inc: Shadows; Husbands; Too Late Blues; A Child Is Waiting; Slaves.

Thea inc: Seven Year Itch; Middle of the Night; Dinner at Eight.

CLARK, Oliver: Act. b. Buffalo, NY, Jan 4. e. U of Buffalo. Films inc: The Landlord; End of the Road; They Might Be Giants; A Star is Born; Another Man, Another Chance; Fire Sale. TV inc: We've Got Each Other; Fame; The Two of Us.

CLARK, Petula: Singer-Act. b. Ewell, Surrey, England, Nov 15, 1932. Films inc: The Huggets; Dance Hall; Made in Heaven; Runaway Bus; Finian's Rainbow; Goodbye Mr. Chips.

Thea inc: (London) The Sound Of Music.

TV inc: Night Of 100 Stars II.

(Grammys-(2)-Rock & Roll-1964; Contemporary R & R-1965).

CLARK, Roy Linwood: Singer. b. Meherrin, VA, Apr 15, 1933. C&W recording artist. TV inc: The Sensational, Shocking, Wonderful, Wacky 70's; Country Comes Home. The Nashville Palace (host); A Country Christmas; Country Comes Home.

(Grammy-Country inst-1982).

CLARK, Susan: Act. b. Sarnia, Ont, Canada, Mar 8, 1940. e. RADA. Films inc: Ganning; Madigan; Coogan's Bluff; The Forbin Project; Tell Them Willie Boy is Here; Skullduggery; Valdez is Coming; The Skin Game; Showdown; Airport 75; The Midnight Man; The Apple Dumpling Gang; Murder By Decree; The North Avenue Irregulars; Real Life; City on Fire; Promises in the Dark; Double Negative; Nobody's Perfekt; Porky's.

TV inc: Trapped; Amelia Earhart; Babe (Emmy-1976); Jimmy B and Andre (& prod); Word of Honor (exec prod); Maid In America (& exec prod); Webster.

CLARKE, Mae (Mary Klotz): Act. b. Philadelphia, Aug. 16, 1910. On stage as dancer before Hollywood. Films inc: Big Time; Nix On Dames; The Fall Guy; The Dancers; The Front Page; The Public Enemy; Waterloo Bridge; Frankenstein; Reckless Living; Three Wise Girls; The Final Edition; Night World; Fast Workers; Parole Girl; Turn Back The Clock; Penthouse; Made On Broadway; Lady Killer; Nana; This Side of Heaven; The Man With Two Faces; The Daring Young Man; The House Of a Thousand Candles; Hearts In Bondage; Trouble In Morocco; Women In War; Flying Tigers; Here Come The Waves; And Now Tomorrow; Kitty; Daredevils In The Clouds; Annie Get Your Gun; The Great Caruso; Singin' In The Rain; Magnificent Obsession; Not As A Stranger; Ask Any Girl; Big Hand For The Little Lady; Thoroughly Modern Millie; The Watermelon Man.

CLARKE, T.E.B: Wri. b. England, 1907. Films inc: Johnny Frenchman; Hue and Cry; Passport to Pimlico; The Blue Lamp; The Lavender Hill Mob (Oscar-1952-story & sp); The Titfield Thunderbolt; Barnacle Bill; Law and Disorder; Sons and Lovers; The Horse Without a Head; A Man Could Get Killed.

CLARY, Robert (nee Widerman): Act-Singer. b. Paris, Mar 1, 1926. Films inc: Ten Tall Men; Thief of Damascus; New Faces; A New Kind of Love; The Hindenburg.

Thea inc: New Faces of 1952; Seventh Heaven; La Plume de ma Tante; Around the World in 80 Days; Sugar.

TV inc: Hogan's Heroes; The Young and the Restless; Days of Our Lives; Remembrance of Love.

CLAVELL, James: Dir-Wri. b. Australia, 1922. Film inc: (sp only) The Fly; Watusi; The Great Escape; 633 Squadron; The Satan Bug. (Prod-dir-sp) Five Gates to Hell; Walk Like a Dragon; To Sir with Love; Where's Jack?; Last Valley.

Plays inc: Countdown to Armageddon. TV inc: Shogun (author & exec prod) (Emmy-prod-1981); James Clavell's The Children's Story (& prod).

CLAXTON, William: Dir-Prod. b. CA, Oct 22, 1914. Films inc: God Is My Partner; Young and Dangerous; Desire in the Dust.

TV inc: Twilight Zone; Bonanza; High Chaparral; Little House on the Prairie.

CLAYBURGH, Jill: Act. b. NYC, Apr 30, 1944. Films inc: The Wedding Party; Portnoy's Complaint; the Thief Who Came to Dinner; The Terminal Man; Gable and Lombard; Griffin and Phoenix; Silver Streak; Semi-Tough; An Unmarried Woman; Luna; Starting Over; It's My Turn; First Monday In October; I'm Dancing As Fast As I Can; Hannah K.; In Our Hards (doc).

TV inc: Search for Tomorrow; The Choice; Hustling.

Bway inc: The Rothschilds; Pippin; Jumpers; Design For Living.

CLAYTON, Jack: Prod-Dir. b. England, 1921. Films inc: The Bespoke Overcoat; Three Men in a Boat (prod); Room at the Top (dir); The Innocents (dir); The Pumpkin Eater (dir); Our Mother's House (dir); The Great Gatsby (dir); Something Wicked This Way Comes (dir).

CLAYTON, Jan: Act. b. Tularosa, NM, Aug 26, 1917. Films inc: Flight Angels; several Hopalong Cassidy westerns; This Man's Navy; The Snake Pit.

TV inc: Lassie; Scruples.

Bway inc: Show Boat; Carousel.

(Died Aug. 28, 1983).

CLEESE, John: Act. b. Weston-Super-Mare, England, Oct 27, 1939. e. Clifton College; Cambridge. Member Monty Python's Flying Circus. Films inc: Interlude; The Best House in London; The Magic Christian; The Rise and Rise of Michael Rimmer; The Love Ban; And Now For Something Completely Different; Monty Python and the Holy Grail; Life of Brian (& sp); The Tom Machine; The Great Muppet Caper; Time Bandits; The Strange Case of the End of Civilization As We Know It; Romance with A Double Bass; The Secret Policeman's Other Ball (doc); Monty Python Live at the Hollywood Bowl; Privates On Parade; Monty Python's The Meaning of Life (& mus); Yellowbeard.

TV inc: At Last The 1948 Show; The Taming of the Shrew; Doctor In the House; Fawlty Towers. Thea inc: Footlights Revue; Cambridge Revue (& Bway); Half A Sixpence (& Bway); Monty Python at City Center (NY).

CLEMENS, Brian: Wri-Prod-Dir. b. Croydon, England, 1931. Films inc: Station Six Sahara; The Corrupt Ones; And Soon the Darkness; See No Evil; Dr. Jekyll and Sister Hyde; Captain Kronos - Vampire Hunter; The Golden Voyage of Sinbad; The Watcher in the Woods (sp).

TV inc: Danger Man; Scene of the Crime; The Avengers.

CLEMENT, Dick: Wri-Dir. b. England, 1937. Films inc: The Jokers; Otley; A Severed Head (dir); Villain; Catch Me a Spy; The Likely Lads; The Prisoner of Zenda; Bullshot; Water.

Thea inc: Billy (wri); Anyone For Denis? (dir).

TV inc: (wri) My Wife Next Door; Sunset Limousine.

CLEMENT, Rene: Dir. b. France, 1913. Films inc: Bataille du Rail; Les Maudits; Knave of Hearts; Gervaise; The Sea Wall; The Day and the Hour; The Love Cage; Is Paris Burning?; Rider on the Rain; The House under the Trees; And Hope to Die.

CLIBURN, Van (Harvey Lavan Cliburn Jr): Concert pianist. b. Shreveport, LA, Jul 12, 1934. e. Juilliard. Debut 1947 with Houston Symphony; guest soloist NY Philharmonic 1954; winner Moscow International Tschaikowsky Piano Competition 1958; guest with major world orchestras.

(Grammys-(2)-class inst solo-1958, 1959).

CLIFTON, Peter: Prod-Dir. b. Sydney, Australia, Apr 1, 1943. e. Sydney U. Films inc: Popcorn; The London Rock & Roll Show; The Song Remains the Same; Sound of the City--London 1964-73.

CLOONEY, Rosemary: Singer. b. Maysville, KY, 1928. Niteries; recording artist. Films inc: The Stars Are Singing; Here Come the Girls; Red Garters; White Christmas; Deep in My Heart.

TV inc: Pat Boone and Family Christmas Special; Mitch Miller's Singalong Sampler; A Gift of Music; Twilight Theatre; Rosie--The Rosemary Clooney Story (vocals); Bob Hope's Road to Hollywood.

CLOSE, Glenn: Act. b. Greenwich, CT, 1947. e. William & Mary College. Thea inc: Love for Love; The Member of the Wedding; Rex (Bway); The Crucifer of Blood (Bway); Rules Of The Game; The Singular Life Of Albert Nobbs; Uncommon Women and Others; The Crazy Locomotive; The Wine Untouched; Barnum (Bway); The Real Thing (Bway) (Tony-1984).

TV inc: Too Far To Go; The Orphan Train; The Elephant Man; Something About Amelia.

Films inc: The World According to Garp; The Big Chill; The Stone Boy; The Natural.

CLOTHIER, William H: Cin. b. 1903. Films inc: Sofia; Track of the Cat; Blood Alley; The Horse Soldiers; The Alamo; The Deadly Companions; The Man Who Shot Liberty Valance; A Distant Trumpet; Cheyenne Autumn; Shenandoah; The War Wagon; Firecreek; The Devil's Brigade; The Cheyenne Social Club; Big Jake.

CLOUSE, Robert: Dir. Started making shorts inc: The Cadillac; The Legend of Jimmy Blue Eyes.

Films inc: Happy Mothers Day; Love George (wri); Darker Than Amber; Enter the Dragon; Golden Needles; The Ultimate Warrior; The Amsterdam Kill; The Pack; Game of Death; The Big Brawl (& wri); Force Five (& wri); The Rats; Gymkata.

TV inc: The Omega Connection; The Kids Who Knew Too Much.

COBE, Sandy: Exec. b. NYC, Nov 30, 1928. e. Columbia U; Tulane U. P Intercontinental Releasing Corp, P Sandy Cobe Productions, P Sandon Companies, Inc: Films inc: Terror on Tour; To All A Good Night.

COBLENZ, Walter: Prod. Films inc: The Candidate; All the President's Men; The Onion Field; The Legend of the Lone Ranger; Strange Invaders. May 1983 named Sr vp to supv physical prodn Tri-Star Pictures.

TV inc: The Blue Knight.

COBURN, D.L. (Donald Lee Coburn): Plywri. b. Baltimore, MD, Aug 4, 1938. Ad salesman, later ad agcy exec. Plays inc: The Gin Game (Pulitzer Prize-1978); Bluewater Cottage; The Corporation Man; Currents Turned Away.

COBURN, James: Act. b. Laurel, MD, Aug 31, 1928. e. LA City Coll. Films inc: Ride Lonesome; The Magnificent Seven; Hell is for Heroes; The Great Escape; Charade; The Americanization of Emily; Major Dundee; A High Wind in Jamaica; Our Man Flint; What Did You Do in the War Daddy?; Dead Heat on a Merry-Go-Round; In Like Flint; The President's Analyst; Duffy; Candy; A Fistful of Dynamite; The Honkers; A Reason to Live, A Reason to Die; Pat Garrett and Billy the Kid; The Intercine Project; Hard Times; Sky Riders; Cross of Iron; The Last Hard Man; Firepower; Circle of Iron (wri); The Muppet Movie; Goldengirl; The Baltimore Bullet; Mr Patman; Loving Couples; High Rise; Looker; Digital Dreams; Martin's Day.

TV inc: Klondike; Acapulco; The Dain Curse; Escape (narr); All Hands On Deck For Bob Hope's All-Star Birthday Party At Annapolis; Malibu; Draw! (PC); Sins Of The Father.

COCA, Imogene: Act. b. Philadelphia, Nov 18, 1908. Debut as tap dancer in vaudeville at age 11. Solo dancer in Broadway musicals then comedienne on Broadway in New Faces, 1934. Night clubs.

TV inc: Your Show of Shows (Emmy-1952); Imogene Coca Show; Sid Caesar Invites You; A Gift of Music; Return of the Beverly Hillibillies; Kennedy Center Tonight--Broadway to Washington?; TV Academy Hall Of Fame 1985.

Films inc: Under the Yum Yum Tree; Rabbit Test; National Lampoon's Vacation; Nothing Lasts Forever.

Bway inc: On The 20th Century.

COCHRAN, Hank: Singer-Comp. b. Greenville, MS, Aug 2, 1935. Comp C & W songs for such artists as Patsy Cline; Eddy Arnold; Burl Ives; Ray Price. Also appeared on radio, TV; recorded for RCA Victor.

COCKER, Joe (John Robert Cocker): Singer-Mus. b. Sheffield, England, May 21, 1944. With groups the Cavaliers; Vance Arnold and the Avengers before starting The Grease Band; hit single With A Little Help from My Friends.

Albums inc: Mad Dogs and Englishmen; Cocker Happy; Something to Say; I Can Stand a Little Rain; Jamaica Say You Will; Stingray.

Films inc: Sound of the City--London 1964-73. TV inc: Motown Returns To The Apollo.

(Grammy-Pop duo-1982).

COCO, James: Act. b. NYC, Mar 21, 1929. Films inc: A New Leaf; The Strawberry Statement; Tell Me That You Love Me, Junie Moon; Such Good Friends; Man of La Mancha; The Wild Party; Murder by Death; Bye Bye Monkey; Charleson; The Cheap Detective; Scavenger Hunt; Wholly Moses! Only When I Laugh; The Muppets Take Manhattan.

Bway inc: Hotel Paradiso; Last of the Red Hot Lovers; The Devils; Passage to India; Man of La Mancha; Everybody Loves Opal; Next; Wally's Cafe; Little Me; You Can't Take It With You.

TV inc: The Flip Wilson Show; The Trouble with People; Calucci's Dept; The Dumplings; The French Atlantic Affair; The Diary of Anne Frank; From Raquel With Love; Debbie Boone's One Step Closer; Lily For President?; St. Elsewhere (Emmy-supp-1983); Alice In Wonderland; Mr. Success.

CODRON, Michael: Prod. b. London, Jun 8, 1930. e. Oxford. Thea inc: (London) Ring for Catty; A Month of Sundays; Share My Lettuce; The Birthday Party; Fool's Paradise; Pieces of Eight; Stop It, Whoever You Are; Everything in the Garden; A Cheap Bunch of Nice Flowers; The Cloud; Hedda Gabler; A Scent of Flowers; The Killing of Sister George; Ride a Cock Horse; Entertaining Mr Sloane; There's a Girl in My Soup; The Flip Side; Not Now, Darling; The Philanthropist; Butley; Absurd Person Singular; Crown Matrimonial; My Fat Friend; The Golden Pathway Annual; John, Paul, George, Ringo. . .and Bert; A Family and a Fortune; Otherwise Engaged; The Old Country; The Homecoming; Alice's Boys; Night and Day; The Unvarnished Truth; Ten Times Table; The Rear Column; Joking Apart; Stage Struck; Taking Steps; Enjoy; Make and Break; Hinge & Brackett; The Dresser (& Bway); House Guest; Quartermaine's Terms; Noises Off (& Bway); Funny Turns; The Real Thing (& Bway) (Tony-1984); The Hard Shoulder; Benefactors; Why Me?

CODUN, Sergio (Bruno Blumer): Dir. b. St Galen, Switzerland, Dec 29, 1949. Dir of Swiss docs, industrial, adv films.

COE, Peter: Dir. b. London, Apr 18, 1929. e. London Academy of

Music and Dramatic Art. Thea inc: (London) Lock Up Your Daughters; The World of Suzie Wong; Treasure Island; Oliver!; The Miracle Worker; Caligula; In White America; In the Matter of J Robert Oppenheimer; The Silence of Lee Harvey Oswald; World War 2 1/2; Kiss Me Kate; Fish Out of Water; Black Macbeth; Games; Poets to the People; The Exorcism; Ride, Ride, Lucy Crown; Cages (& wri); Barnum. (Bway) Oliver! (& revival); On a Clear Day You Can See Forever; Next Time I'll Sing To You; Golden Boy; Pickwick; Six; Woman of the Dunes (& wri); A Life; Othello.
Films inc: Lock Up Your Daughters.
TV inc: Mr. Lincoln.

COEN, Franklin: Wri. b. NYC, Apr 25, 1912. e. U of VA. Films inc: Till We Meet Again; We're On the Jury; Exposed; Glory Brigade; Four Guns to the Border; Johnny Dark; Chief Crazy Horse; The Island Earth; Kiss of Fire; Interlude; Night of the Quarter Moon; The Train; Alvarez Kelly; Black Gunn; The Take.

COHEN, Alexander H.: Prod. b. NYC, Jul 24, 1920. e. NYU. Bway inc: Angel Street; The Duke in Darkness; King Lear; The First Gentleman; At the Drop of a Hat; An Evening with Mike Nichols and Elaine May; Beyond the Fringe; Maurice Chevalier at 77; The School for Scandal; Ages of Man; Man and Boy; Victor Borge's Comedy in Music; A Time for Singing; At the Drop of Another Hat; The Homecoming (Tony-1967); Little Murders; The Unknown Soldier and His Wife; Marlene Dietrich; Halfway Up the Tree; Dear World; Home; Good Evening; Ulysses in Nighttown; Words and Music; Who's Who in Hell; Comedians; Anna Christie; I Remember Mama; A Day in Hollywood and a Night in the Ukraine; Edmund Kean; La Tragedie de Carmen; Play Memory; Accidental Death Of An Anarchist. London inc: The Doctor's Dilemma; Man and Boy; Ivanov; You Never Can Tell; Season of Goodwill; The Merchant of Venice; The Rivals; Plaza Suite; The Price; Come As You Are; 1776; The Happy Apple; Who Killed Santa Claus?; Applause; Harvey; Overheard; Beethoven's Tenth.
TV inc: Since 1967 has produced the annual TV coverage of the Tony Awards (Emmy-1980); On the Air (50th anniversary celebration of seven special programs, 1978); Night of 100 Stars (Emmy-1982); Parade of Stars; The Best of Everything (exec prod); Night Of 100 Stars II; Placido Domingo Steppin' Out With The Ladies (Exec prod).
Films inc: Purple Rose Of Cairo (act).

COHEN, Herman: Prod-Wri. b. Detroit, MI, Aug 27, 1928. Films inc: Two Dollar Bettor; The Basketball Fix; Bela Lugosi Meets the Brooklyn Gorilla; River Beat; Crime of Passion; I Was a Teenage Werewolf; How to Make a Monster; The Traitors; Berserk; Crooks and Coronets; Trog; Today We Kill--Tomorrow We Die; Craze; The Dragon Lives.

COHEN, Larry: Wri. b. Chicago, Apr 20, 1947. e. U of WI, BA. Films inc: Alice Doesn't Live Here Anymore (prodn exec); Carrie; God Told Me To; The American Success Company (sp); The Winged Serpent (& prod-dir); I, The Jury; Special Effects (& dir); Perfect Strangers (& dir).
Plays inc: Trick (& dir).
TV inc: Momma The Detective (prod-dir-wri).

COHEN, Rob: Prod. b. Cornwall-on-the-Hudson, NY, Mar 12, 1949. e. Harvard, BA. Films inc: Mahogany; Bingo Long; Scott Joplin; The Wiz; Almost Summer; Thank God It's Friday; A Small Circle of Friends (dir); Scandalous (dir); The Razor's Edge (exec prod). April 1985, P Keith Barish Prodns.

COHEN, Stuart: Prod. b. Salt Lake City, UT. With U TV as head of children's prgmmg. TV inc: The Bold Ones (asst prod); Senior Year; The Gangster Chronicles; Sins of the Past; Single Bars, Single Women; Obsessed With A Married Woman (supv prod).
Films inc: Chandler; The Thing.

COHN, Bruce: Prod. b. San Francisco, Apr 8, 1931. e. UC Berkeley, BA, MJ. News dir KNBC-TV 1962; West Coast prod ABC News 1966; exec prod National Public Affairs Center for TV 1972.
Films inc: Dogs; Acapulco Gold; Good Guys Wear Black (wri only); The Seduction.
TV inc: 1968-A Crack In Time (& wri); Remember When--Wheels, Wines and Whistles (& dir); (cable) Yesteryear-1917 (& dir) (cable).

COHN, Robert: Prod. b. Avon, NJ, Sep 6, 1920. e. U of MI, BA. Joined Columbia as asst dir; later headed Robert Cohn prodn unit at Columbia; formed Robert Cohn Productions. Film inc: Black Eagle; Rusty Leads the Way; Palomino; Kazan; Killer that Stalked New York; The Barefoot Mailman; Mission Over Korea; The Interns; The New Interns; The Young Americans.

COLASANTO, Nicholas: Dir-Act. b. Providence, RI, Jan 19, 1924. Films inc: (act) Fat City; Family Plot; Raging Bull.
TV inc: (dir) Name of the Game; Felony Squad; Hawaii 5-0; Police Story; Streets of San Francisco; SWAT.
Bway inc: (act) A Hatful of Rain.
(Died Feb. 12, 1985)

COLBERT, Claudette (Lily Chauchoin): Act. b. Paris, Sep 13, 1905. Films inc: For the Love of Mike; The Sign of the Cross; I Cover the Waterfront; Three Cornered Moon; It Happened One Night (Oscar-1934); Cleopatra; Private Worlds; Imitation of Life; Under Two Flags; Maid of Salem; I Met Him in Paris; Bluebeard's Eighth Wife; Midnight; Drums Along the Mohawk; Boom Town; Arise My Love; The Palm Beach Story; Since You Went Away; Tomorrow is Forever; The Egg and I; Three Came Home; Let's Make It Legal; The Planter's Wife; Si Versailles M'Etait Conte; Texas Lady; Parrish.
Bway inc: See Naples and Die; Marriage-Go-Round; Jake, Julia and Uncle Joe; The Irregular Verb to Love; Diplomatic Relations; A Community of Two; Kingfisher; A Talent for Murder; Aren't We All. (London) Aren't We All.
TV inc: The Royal Family; The Guardsman; Blithe Spirit; The American Film Institute Salute to Frank Capra; The Kennedy Center Honors.

COLE, Dennis: Act. b. Detroit, MI, Jul 19, 1940. e. U of Detroit. TV inc: Paradise Bay; Bracken's World; Bearcats!; Felony Squad; Barbary Coast; Cave-In; Big Shamus, Little Shamus; The Young and the Restless; Cave-In!

COLE, George: Act. b. London, Apr 22, 1925. Films inc: Cottage to Let; Quartet; Lady Godiva Rides Again; Top Secret; The Belles of St. Trinian's; The Green Man; Too Many Crooks; The Bridal Path; Cleopatra; The Legend of Young Dick Turpin; The Great St. Trinian's Train Robbery; Fright; Take Me High; The Bluebird.
TV inc: Life of Bliss; A Man of Our Times; Don't Forget to Write.

COLE, Lester: Wri. b. NYC, Jun 19, 1904. Began writing career 1930 with co-sp credit If I had A Million. Films inc: Charlie Chan's Greatest Case; Pursued; Follow Your Heart; The President's Mystery; Affairs of Cappy Ricks; Some Blondes Are Dangerous; Crime of Dr. Hallet; Midnight Intruder; Winter Carnival; I Stole a Million; Invisible Man Returns; House of Seven Gables; Hostages; None Shall Escape; Objective Burma; Blood On the Sun; Fiesta; Romance of Rosy Ridge; High Wall; one of "Hollywood Ten" who declined (Oct. 1947) to testify before House of Un-American Activities Committee, imprisoned for contempt of Congress. While blacklisted wrote (under pseudonyms) Operation Eichman; Born Free.
TV inc: (under pseudonyms) Time-Life TV plays; Pied Piper.
Plays inc: Love Technique; Still Life; Honorable Johnson; Potiphar's House; My Uncle's Dream (adapt from Dostoievski); Say Uncle.

COLE, Maria: Singer. b. Boston, MA, Aug 1, (circa 1920). Widow of Nat King Cole. Singer with Duke Ellington Band, 1945-46. TV inc: Tempo (hosted 1968-69).

COLE, Natalie: Singer. b. LA, Feb 6, 1950. e. U MA. D of Maria and the late Nat "King" Cole. TV inc: Uptown--A Tribute to the Apollo Theatre; Grammy Hall of Fame; Yearbook--Class Of 1967.
Albums inc: Unpredictable; Thankful.
(Grammys-(3)-new artist-1975; R&B vocal-1975, 1976).

COLE, Olivia: Act. b. Memphis, TN, Nov 26, 1942. e. RADA. Bway inc: NY Shakespeare Festival; Skin of Our Teeth; Three-Penny Opera; Black Comedy; The National Health.
TV inc: Guiding Light; Roots (Emmy-Supp-1977); Szysznk; Backstairs at the White House; Children of Divorce; Fly Away Home; Mistress of Paradise; Report to Murphy; Something About Amelia.
Films inc: Heroes; Coming Home; Some Kind of Hero; Go Tell It

On the Mountain.

COLEMAN, Cy: Comp. b. NYC, Jun 14, 1929. e. NY Coll of Music. Piano debut at age 7, Town Hall & Steinway Hall. Played bars, niteries; then formed trio, performed in hotels. Songs inc: Witchcraft; The Best Is Yet to Come; Hey, Look Me Over; I'm Gonna Laugh You Out of My Life; Real Live Girl; Big Spender.

Film scores inc: Father Goose; The Art of Love; Garbo Talks.

Bway inc: Wildcat; Little Me; Sweet Charity; Compulsion (background music); On the 20th Century (Tony-1978); Barnum (& prod).

TV inc: Shirley MacLaine-If They Could See Me Now (Emmy-wri-1975); Gypsy In My Soul (Emmy-prod-1976).

COLEMAN, Dabney: Act. b. Austin, TX, Jan 3, 1932. Films inc: This Property is Condemned; The Slender Thread; The Scalp Hunters; The Other Side of the Mountain; The Black Streetfighter; Rolling Thunder; Viva Knievel!; North Dallas Forty; Nothing Personal; How To Beat The High Cost of Living; Melvin and Howard; Nine To Five; On Golden Pond; Modern Problems; Young Doctors In Love; Tootsie; WarGames; The Muppets Take Manhattan; Cloak And Dagger.

TV inc: Mary Hartman; Forever Fernwood; Fernwood 2 Night; Apple Pie; When She Was Bad; Callie & Son; Buffalo Bill.

COLEMAN, Gary: Act. b. Zion, IL, Feb 8, 1968. TV inc: The Little Rascals; America 2-Night; Good Times; The Jeffersons; Diff'rent Strokes; The Kid From Left Field; Lucy Moves to NBC; The Big Show (host); Scout's Honor; TV's Censored Bloopers; Anson 'N' Lorrie; The Kid With The Broken Halo; The Kid With the 200 I.Q; The Fantastic World of D.C. Collins; Playing With Fire.

Films inc: On The Right Track; Jimmy the Kid.

COLEMAN, Nancy: Act. b. Everett, WA, Dec. 30, 1917. e. U of WA. In radio serials; NY stage; repertory. Films inc: Kings' Row; Dangerously They Live; The Gay Sisters; Desperate Journey; Edge of Darkness; In Our Time; Devotion; Her Sister's Secret; Mourning Becomes Electra; That Man from Tangier; Slaves.

COLEMAN, Ornette: Mus. b. Fort Worth, TX, Mar 19, 1930. Rec artist; band ldr; Films inc (mus) Boxoffice; Ornette-Made In America; Detective.

COLICOS, John: Act. b. Toronto, Canada, Dec 10, 1928. NY stage debut 1956, City Center in King Lear. Joined American Shakespeare Festival Theatre 1957, Stratford, CT. Films inc: Anne of the Thousand Days; Raid on Rommel; Red Sky at Morning; Doctor's Wives; The Wrath of God; Scorpio; Drum; Breaking Point; Battlestar Galactica; The Changeling; Phobia; The Postman Always Rings Twice.

TV inc: Beaverbrook--The Life and Times of Max Aitken; The Bastard; The Girl Who Saved Our America; American Caesar.

COLLA, Richard: Dir. b. Milwaukee, WI, Apr 18, 1918. e. Marquette U, BA, MA. Films inc: Zig Zag; Sometimes A Great Notion; Fuzz; Battlestar Galactica. TV inc: Live Again, Die Again; Jake's Way; Don't Look Back.

COLLINGWOOD, Charles: TV news. b. Three Rivers, MI, Jun 4, 1917. e. Cornell, AB; Oxford. Started with United Press, 1939, joined CBS two years later as corr; 1946, UN corr; 1948, White House corr; 1952, Commentator; 1957, London Bureau chief and also commentator; 1966-75, chief foreign corr. Retd July 1982. TV inc: Hanoi--A Report by Charles Collingwood (& prod); CBS Reports--A Timetable for Vietnam.

COLLINS, Gary: Act. b. Boston, MA, 1938. Films inc: Cleopatra; The Pigeon That Took Rome; The Longest Day; Airport; Angel in My Pocket; Killer Fish; Hangar 18.

TV inc: The Secret of Lost Valley; Hour Magazine (host) (Emmy-1984); Daredevils; Jacqueline Susann's Valley of the Dolls 1981.

COLLINS, Joan: Act. b. London, May 23, 1933. Films inc: I Believe in You; Judgement Deferred; Decameron Nights; The Square Ring; The Good Die Young; Warning Shot; Land of the Pharaohs; Sea Wife; Virgin Queen; Island in the Sun; Rally Round The Flag Boys; Wayward Bus; The Bravados; The Bawdy Adventures of Tom Jones; Empire of the Ants; The Big Sleep; Sunburn; The Stud; The Bitch; Homework;

Nutcracker.

Thea inc: The Last of Mrs. Cheyney.

TV inc: Barry Norman's London Season; The Man Who Came To Dinner; The Moneychangers; Dynasty; Paper Dolls; The Wild Women of Chastity Gulch; The 4th Annual TV Guide Special; The 1/2 Hour Comedy Hour; The Making of a Male Model; Dean Martin's Celebrity Roast; Her Life as a Man; Blondes vs. Brunettes; The Cartier Affair; All-Star Party For Lucille Ball; On Top All Over The World.

COLLINS, Judy: Folksinger-Sngwri. b. Denver, CO, May 1, 1939. Albums inc: A Maid of Constant Sorrow; Who Knows Where the Time Goes; Whalers and Nightingales; Living; Judith; Colors of the Day; The Best of Judy Collins.

TV inc: The Special Magic of Herself the Elf (voice); Yearbook--Class Of 1967.

(Grammy-folk rec-1968).

COLLINS, Pat (nee Allan): Hypnotist. b. Detroit, May 7, 1935. Works niteries, tv guestints.

COLLINS, Richard: Wri-Prod. b. NYC, Jul 20, 1914. e. Stanford U. Films inc: Rulers of the Sea; One Crowded Night; Lady Scarface; Thousands Cheer; Little Giant; China Venture; Riot in Cell Block 11; The Adventures of Hajji Baba; The Bob Mathias Story; Kiss of Fire; My Gun Is Quick; Spanish Affair; The Badlanders; Edge of Eternity; Pay or Die.

TV inc: Clown; Shadow On the Heart; That's the Man; The Great Alberti; The Breaking Point; Sarah; Chrysler Theatre; The Family Holvak; The Godchild; Breaking Point; The Immigrants.

COLLINS, Stephen: Act. b. Des Moines, IA, Oct 1, 1949. e. Amherst. Thea inc: Twelfth Night; Moonchildren; Macbeth; The Ritz; Beyond Therapy; The Loves Of Anatol.

Films inc: All the President's Men; Fedora; The Promise; Star Trek--The Motion Picture; Loving Couples; Brewster's Millions.

TV inc: Brinks--The Great Robbery; The Rhinemann Exchange; Summer Solstice; The Henderson Monster; Edith Wharton--Looking Back; Inside the Third Reich; Tales of the Gold Monkey; Chiefs; Dark Mirror; Threesome.

COLON, Miriam: Act-Prod. b. Puerto Rico 1945. e. Actors Studio. Founder Puerto Rican Traveling Theatre. Bway inc: The Summer House; The Innkeepers; Me, Candido, The Ox Chart; The Wrong Way Light Bulb; prod and dir various Puerto Rican plays and stories for tours.

Films inc: The Appaloosa; One-Eyed Jacks; The Possession of Joel Delaney; Back Roads; Scarface.

TV inc: Starstruck; Best Kept Secrets.

COLONNA, Jerry: Act. b. Boston, Aug 17, 1904. Films inc: College Swing; Little Miss Broadway; Sis Hopkins; True to the Army; Star Spangled Rhythm; Ice Capades; Atlantic City; It's in the Bag; Road to Rio; Kentucky Jubilee; Meet Me in Las Vegas; Andy Hardy Comes Home.

COMDEN, Betty (Elizabeth Cohen): Wri. b. NYC, May 3, 1918. e. NYU. Films inc: Good News; The Barkleys of Broadway; On the Town; Singin' in the Rain; Band Wagon; It's Always Fair Weather; Auntie Mame; What a Way to Go; Garbo Talks (act).

Bway inc: Wonderful Town (Tony-1953); Peter Pan; Do Re Mi; On the Town; Billion Dollar Baby; Two on the Aisle; Bells Are Ringing; Subways Are for Sleeping; Hallelujah Baby (Tonys-best musical & lyr-1968); Fade Out - Fade In; Applause (Tony-best musical-1970); On the 20th Century (Tonys-book & lyr-1978); A Party With Betty Comden and Adolph Green; Peter Pan; A Doll's Life; Singin' In the Rain (London).

Songs: New York, New York; Lonely Town; Ohio; Give a Little, Get A Little; The Party's Over; Just in Time; Make Someone Happy.

TV inc: The Kennedy Center Honors, 1980, 1982; AFI Salute To Gene Kelly.

COMENCINI, Luigi: Dir-wri. b. Italy, Jun 8, 1916. Co-founder of Cineteca Italiana. Films inc: Bambini in Citta (doc); Guaglio; The Emperor of Capri; Behind Closed Shutters; Heidi; Bread, Love and Dreams; La Valigia dei Sogni; La Bella di Roma; Everybody Go Home; Il Commissario; Bebo's Girl; Six Days a Week; Italian Secret Service;

Senza Sapere nulla di Lei; The Sunday Woman; Tra Mogli e Marito; Il Gatto; Bottleneck; L'Ingorgo; Eugenio; Cercasi Geso (Looking For Jesus); Cuore (Heart).

COMER, Anjanette: Act. b. 1942. Films inc: Quick Before it Melts; The Loved One; The Appaloosa; Banning; Rabbit, Run; The Baby; Lepke; Fire Sale.
TV inc: The Firechasers; The Long Summer of George Adams.

COMO, Perry (Nick Perido): Act. b. Canonsburg, PA, May 18, 1912. Barber at age 15; joined Carlone Band, then Ted Weems, 1936; performed in niteries. Screen debut, Something for the Boys, 1944. Films inc: Doll Face; If I'm Lucky; Words and Music.
TV inc: The Chesterfield Supper Club; The Perry Como Show; The Kraft Music Hall. (Emmy-male singer-1954 & 55); (Emmy-host-1955); (Emmy-male personality-1957); (Emmy-act-mus-1959); Perry Como's Early American Christmas; Perry Como's Christmas in New Mexico; Perry Como's Bahama Holiday; Perry Como's Spring In San Francisco; Perry Como's French-Canadian Christmas; Perry Como's Easter in Guadalajara; Perry Como's Christmas In Paris; Perry Como's Christmas in New York (& exec prod).
(Grammy-vocal-1958).

COMPTON, Forrest: Act. b. Reading, PA, Sep 15. Films inc: Inherit the Wind; The Children's Hour; The Outsider; Kings Go Forth.
TV inc: Gomer Pyle, USMC; Hogan's Heroes; That Girl; Mayberry RFD; Bright Promise; The Brighter Day; The Edge of Night.
Thea inc: Look Homeward, Angel; An Evening with Oscar Wilde; Under The Yum Yum Tree; Detective Story; The Happy Time; Othello.

COMPTON, Richard B: Dir. Films inc: Angels Die Hard; Welcome Home Soldier Boys; Macon County Line; Return to Macon County; Maniac; Ravagers; Wild Times.
TV inc: The California Kid.

CONAWAY, Jeff: Act. b. NYC, Oct 5. Films inc: Jennifer On My Mind; The Eagle Has Landed; Pete's Dragon; I Never Promised You a Rose Garden; Grease; Covergirl.
TV inc: The Mary Tyler Moore Show; Happy Days; Movin' On; Having Babies; Delta County, U S A; Taxi; Breaking Up Is Hard to Do; For The Love Of It;The Nashville Grab; Wizards and Warriors; Movie Blockbusters! The 15 Greatest Hits of all Time; The Making of a Male Model; I Love Men; Berrenger's.
Bway inc: All The Way Home; Grease.

CONLEY, Renie: Cost Dsgn. b. Republic, WA, Jul 31, 1919. e. UCLA; Chouinard School of Art. Under contract RKO 10 years, Fox 6 years using first name only on credits.
Films inc: The Model and the Marriage Broker; The President's Lady; The Big Fisherman; Cleopatra (Oscar-1953); The Legend of Lylah Clare; The Killing of Sister George; Whatever Happened to Aunt Alice; Great Scout and Cathouse Thursday; Caravans; Body Heat.
TV inc: Haywire; Woman's Room.
Desgd all costumes for Disneyland when park opened; dsgnr for Shipstad and Johnson's Ice Follies 7 years.

CONN, Didi (nee Bernstein): Act. b. Brooklyn, Jul 13, 1951. e. Brooklyn College; Brooklyn Acad of Music; American Musical Dramatic Academy. Films inc: You Light Up My Life; Almost Summer; Grease.
TV inc: Keep On Truckin'; Happy Days; The Practice; Three On a Date; Murder at the Mardi Gras; Benson; Working.

CONNERY, Sean: Act. b. Edinburgh, Scotland, Aug 25, 1930. Stage debut chorus of London company South Pacific. On screen from 1955. Films inc: No Road Back; Another Time, Another Place; Tarzan's Greatest Adventure; Dr. No; From Russia With Love; Goldfinger; Thunderball; A Fine Madness; You Only Live Twice; The Anderson Tapes; Diamonds Are Forever; The Offence; Ransom; Murder on the Orient Express; The Wind and the Lion; The Man Who Would Be King; Robin and Marian; The Last Man; A Bridge Too Far; The Great Train Robbery; Meteor; Cuba; Outland; Time Bandits; Wrong Is Right; Five Days One Summer; G'Ole (doc) (narr); Never Say Never Again; Sword oOf The Valiant.
TV inc: Requiem for a Heavyweight; Anna Karenina; Age of Kings.

Thea inc: (London) I've Seen You Cut Lemons (dir).

CONNIFF, Ray: Comp-Cond. b. Attleboro, MA, Nov 6, 1916. Played trombone and arranged for Bunny Berigan; Bob Crosby; Artie Shaw; Glen Gray; Mitch Miller; arr for Col Records; formed own orch and chorus; recorded 63 albums. (Grammy-Chorus-1966).

CONNOR, Kevin: Dir. b. England, 1939. Originally flm edtr on Oh, What A Lovely War; Young Winston; Hitler, The Last 10 Days. Films inc: (dir) The Land That Time Forgot; From Beyond the Grave; At the Earth's Core; A Choice of Weapons; The People That Time Forgot; Warlords of Atlantis; Arabian Adventure; Motel Hell; Savanna Smiles.
TV inc: Goliath Awaits; Master of the Game; Mistral's Daughter.

CONNORS, Carol: Songwri. Films inc: (Lyr) Rocky; Orca; The Other Side of Midnight; Looking for Mr. Goodbar; Heroes; Matilda (mus); Fast Break; Golden Girl; Mountain Family Robinson; The Onion Field; Scavenger Hunt; Cheaper To Keep Her; Resurrection; Falling in Love Again; Dressed to Kill; Fade to Black.
TV inc: American Gothic; Dallas Cowboy Cheerleaders I & II; Next Step Beyond (& mus); Archie's Prime Time (& mus); San Pedro Beach Bums (& mus); A Sensitive Passionate Man (& mus); Zuma Beach; The Million Dollar Face; Bare Essence; Getting Physical.
Songs inc: Gonna Fly Now; Someone's Waiting for You.

CONNORS, Chuck (Kevin Joseph Connors): Act. b. NYC, Apr 10, 1924. e. Seton Hall Coll. Former professional baseball player. Films inc: Pat and Mike; Dragonfly Squadron; Target Zero; Hold Back The Night; Geronimo; Kill Them All And Come Back Alive; The Deserter; Support Your Local Gunfighter; 99 and 44/100ths % Dead; Tourist Trap; Virus; Airplane II --The Sequel; Target Eagle.
TV inc: Dennis Day Show; Gunsmoke; West Point; Rifleman; Roots; The Capture of Grizzly Adams; Lone Star; The Yellow Rose.

CONNORS, Mike (Kregor Ohanian): Act. (early billing as Touch Connors).b. Fresno, CA, Apr 15, 1925. e. UCLA. Films inc: Sudden Fear; The Ten Commandments; Day of Triumph; Five Guns West; Seed of Violence; Where Love Has Gone; Good Neighbor Sam; Situation Hopeless But Not Serious; Harlow; Stagecoach; Kiss the Girls and Make Them Die; Avalanche Express; Too Scared To Scream (& prod).
TV inc: The Killer Who Wouldn't Die; Tightrope; Mannix; Long Journey Back; Death of Ocean View Park; High Midnight; Casino; Nightkill; Today's FBI; Earthlings; Glitter.

CONRAD, Michael: Act. b. NYC, Oct 16, 1925. TV inc: The Edge of Night; Donovan's Kid; Delvecchio; Hill Street Blues (Emmys-supp-1981, 1982); Bob Hope's Stand Up and Cheer for the NFL's 60th Year; Fire On the Mountain.
Films inc: Castle Keep; They Shoot Horses, Don't They?; The Longest Yard.
(Died Nov. 22, 1983).

CONRAD, Robert (nee Falk): Act. b. Chicago, Mar 1, 1935. e. Northwestern U. Films inc: Thundering Jets; Palm Springs Weekend; Young Dillinger; Murph the Surf; Sudden Death; Hotel Madrid; You Can't Steal Love; The Lady in Red; Wrong Is Right.
TV inc: Hawaiian Eye; Wild, Wild West; The D A; Baa, Baa, Black Sheep; Weekend of Terror; Five Desperate Men; The Adventures of Nick Carter; The Last Day; Centennial; The Duke; Wild Wild West Revisited; Breaking Up is Hard to Do; A Man Called Sloane; More Wild Wild West; Daredevils (host); Coach of the Year; The Way They Were; Will, G. Gordon Liddy; Confessions of a Married Man; Victory! (narr); Hard Knox (& story); Two Fathers Justice.

CONRAD, Scott: Film ed. Films inc: Rocky (Oscar-1976); Outlaw Blues; Cheech and Chong's Up in Smoke; Wanda Nevada; Spacehunter--Adventures In the Forbidden Zone; Cat's Eye.
TV inc: Ernie Kovacs--Between the Laughter.

CONRAD, William: Act. b. Louisville, KY, Sep 27, 1920. e. Fullerton Coll. Radio station KMPC, LA, wri, anncr, dir. WW 2 fighter pilot. Returned to radio drama as original Matt Dillon of Gunsmoke series. Films inc: The Killers; Body and Soul; Arch of Triumph; Sorry, Wrong Number; Joan of Arc; Any Number Can Play; East Side, West Side; Cry Danger; The Naked Jungle; 30; Five Against the House; Johnny Concho; The Man From Galveston (dir); Two on A Guillotine (prod-dir); My Blood Runs Cold (prod-dir); Brainstorm (prod-dir); Moonshine County Express.

TV inc: This Man Dawson; The Brotherhood of the Bell; The D A; Conspiracy to Kill; O'Hara, U.S. Treasury; Cannon; The Rebels; The Lost Treasure of the Conception (narr); The Murder That Wouldn't Die; Return of the King (voice); Turnover Smith (& prod); The Return of Frank Cannon; Nero Wolfe; Side Show (dir).

CONSTANTINE, Eddie: Act. b. Oct 29, 1915. Films inc: SOS Pacific; Treasure of San Teresa; Riff Raff Girls; Alphaville; The Lemmy Caution series; The Third Generation; It Lives Again; Portrait of a Female Drunkard; The Long Good Friday; Panische Zeiten (Panic Times); Exit...But No Panic; Tango Through Germany; Freak Orlando; Rote Liebe (Red Love); Boxoffice; La Bete Noire; Flight to Berlin; Der Schnuffler (Sniffing Around).

CONSTANTINE, Michael (Constantine Joanides): Act. b. Reading, PA, May 22, 1927. Films inc: Hustler; Quick Before It Melts; Hawaii; Fat Chance; Skidoo; Justine; Don't Drink the Water; If It's Tuesday, This Must be Belgium; Voyage of the Damned; The North Avenue Irregulars; Pray For Death.

TV inc: Hey Landlord; Room 222 *(Emmy*-1970); Conspiracy of Terror; Sirota's Court; The Pirate; The Love Tapes; Evita Peron; My Palikari; Amanda's; Finder Of Lost Loves.

Bway inc: Inherit the Wind; Compulsion; The Miracle Worker; The Egg; Arturo Ui.

CONTE, John: Act. b. MA. Former actor now P KMIR-TV, Channel 36, Desert Empire TV Corp, Palm Springs. TV inc: John Conte's Little Show; Matinee Theatre (host); Mantovani Welcomes You.

Thea inc: Windy City; Allegro; Carousel; Arms and the Girl.

CONTI, Bill: Comp. b. Providence, RI, Apr 13, 1942. e. LSU, BM; Juilliard School of Music. Film scores inc: Blume in Love; Harry & Tonto; Next Stop Greenwich Village; Rocky; Citizen Band; Pacific Challenge; Slow Dancing in the Big City; An Unmarried Woman; F.I.S.T.; The Big Fix; Paradise Alley; Uncle Joe Shannon; Dreamer; Five Days From home; Rocky II; Goldengirl; A Man, A Woman and a Bank; The Seduction of Joe Tynan; Gloria; Private Benjamin; The Formula; Victory; Carbon Copy; Neighbors; Rocky III; I, The Jury; Split Image; That Championship Season; Bad Boys; The Terry Fox Story; The Right Stuff *Oscar*-1983); Unfaithfully Yours; The Karate Kid; The Bear; The Coolangatta Gold; Mass Appeal; Gotcha; Nomads.

TV inc: Executive Suite; The Andros Targets; Pappa and Me; Smashup On Interstate 5; A Sensitive, Passionate Man; Kill Me If You Can; In the Matter of Karen Ann Quinlan; Ring of Passion; The Pirate; Dynasty; Falcon Crest; Farrell For the People; 55th Academy Awards (mus dir); Emerald Point, N.A.S; The Master (theme); Cagney & Lacey; Stark.

CONTI, Tom: Act. b. Scotland, Nov 22, 1941. Films inc: Full Circle; The Duelists; Reuben, Reuben; American Dreamer.

Bway inc: Whose Life Is It Anyway? *(Tony*-1979); Last Licks (dir); Before the Party (dir). (London) They're Playing Our Song; Whose Life Is It Anyway?; The Housekeeper (dir); Romantic Comedy.

TV inc: The Norman Conquests; Glittering Prizes; Blade on the Feather; Lester (narr); The Wall.

CONVERSE, Frank: Act. b. St Louis, MO, May 22, 1938. e. Carnegie Tech. Films inc: Hurry Sundown; Hour of the Gun; The Rowdyman; The Bushido Blade; Spring Fever.

TV inc: Movin' On; Marilyn--The Untold Story; Momma The Detective; Guests of the Nation; Gabe & Walker; The Miracle of Kathy Miller; Mystery At Fire Island; The Wedding.

Thea inc: The Seagull; Death of a Salesman; Night of the Iguana; A Man for All Seasons; The House of Blue Leaves; First One Asleep Whistle; Arturo Ui; The Philadelphia Story; Brothers.

CONVERSE, Tony: Prod-Exec. b. 1936. e. Yale, BA. Worked as asst dir CBS-TV prior to Army service as pgm dir AFRN Europe; 1971 joined CBS as pgm exec; 1974 vp special pgms; 1977 vp-exec prod EMI Televison Programs Inc.

TV inc: (Prod) Secret Storm; Love of Life. (Exec Prod) Forever; Deadman's Curve; Special Olympics; Just Me and You; Steel Cowboy; One In a Million; Betrayal; The Cracker Factory; Survival of Dana; Can You Hear The Laughter--The Story of Freddie Prinze; Orphan Train;

My Kidnapper, My Love; The Killing of Randy Webster; Broken Promise; The Manions of America; A Piano for Mrs Cimino; A Question of Honor; The Legend of Walks Far Woman; Deadly Encounter; Packin' It In; Sessions (exec prod); Aurora (exec prod).

CONVY, Bert: Act. b. St Louis, Jul 23, 1933. e. UCLA, BA. Former professional baseball player. Bway inc: The Matchmaker; Billy Barnes Revue; Fiddler On The Roof; Cabaret; The Fantasticks; Nine.Films inc: Gunman's Walk; Susan Slade; Act One; Semi-Tough; Jennifer; Hero at Large; The Cannonball Run.

TV inc: Tattletales *(Emmy*-host-1977); Dallas Cowboys Cheerleaders; Ebony, Ivory and Jade; Man in the Santa Claus Suit; Jacqueline Susann's Valley of the Dolls 1981; Help Wanted Male; It's Not Easy; The Snoop Sisters; Love Thy Neighbor; Super Password (host); People Do The Craziest Things (host); Murder, She Wrote.

CONWAY, Gary (Gareth Monello Carmody): Act. b. Boston, Feb 4, 1936. e. UCLA. Films inc: Young Guns of Texas; Once Is Not Enough; The Farmer (& prod.). TV inc: Burke's Law; Land of the Giants.

CONWAY, James L.: Wri-Prod-Dir. b. NYC, Oct 27, 1950. e. U of Denver, BA. TV inc: (Dir) Grizzly Adams; Last of the Mohicans; The Incredible Rocky Mountain Race; Greatest Heroes of the Bible; House of Usher (& prod); The Legend of Sleepy Hollow (prod); The Adventures of Nellie Bly (prod); California Gold Rush (prod); The Nashville Grab (dir); The Capture of Grizzly Adams (prod); The Fall of the House of Usher (prod-dir).

Films inc: Beyond and Back; In Search of Historic Jesus (prod); Hangar 18 (dir); Earthbound (prod-dir); The Boogens

CONWAY, Kevin: Act. b. NYC, May 29, 1942. Bway inc: When You Comin Back, Red Ryder; One Flew Over the Cuckoo's Nest; Moonchildern; The Plough and the Stars; Indians; Saved; Muzeeka; Long Day's Journey Into Night; The Elephant Man.

Films inc: Slaughterhouse Five; Shamus; Portn oy's Complaint; F.I.S.T.; Paradise Alley; The Funhouse; Flashpoint.

TV inc: Johnny We Hardly Know You; The Deadliest Season; Lathe of Heaven; The Elephant Man; Flashback (The Great Plague) (Narr); Rage Of Angels; The Firm; Something About Amelia; Attack On Fear.

CONWAY, Russ (nee Zink): Act. b. Brandon, Manitoba, Canada, Apr 25, 1913. e. UCLA. Films inc: The Heiress; War of the Worlds; Fort Dobbs; Bramble Bush; Tomahawk; The Lively Set; Our Man Flint.

TV inc: Wagon Train; Mission Impossible; Bonanza; Sea Hunt; The Hardy Boys.

Thea inc: Prologue To Glory; The American Way; Johnny 2 by 4; The Land Is Bright.

CONWAY, Tim: Act. b. Willoughby, OH, Dec 15, 1933. e. Bowling Green State U. Joined KWY-TV, Cleveland as wri, dir and occasional performer. Films inc: McHale's Navy; The World's Greatest Athlete; The Apple Dumpling Gang; Gus; The Shaggy D.A.; Billion Dollar Hobo (& wri); They Went Thataway and Thataway (& wri); The Apple Dumpling Gang Rides Again; The Prizefighter (& wri); Private Eyes (& wri); Cannonball Run II.

TV inc: Carol Burnett Show *(4 Emmys*-supp-1973, 1977, 1978; wri-1978); Steve Allen Show; McHale's Navy; Red Skelton; Danny Kaye; Dean Martin; Cher; Doris Day Shows; The Tim Conway Show; An All-Star Party For Carol Burnett; Ace Crawford, Private Eye (& wri); Great Day; Johnny Carson's Greatest Practical Jokes; TV Academy Hall Of Fame 1985.

COOGAN, Jackie: Act. b. LA, Oct 26, 1914. e. Villanova Coll. Film debut in The Kid at age 4. Films inc: Peck's Bad Boy; My Boy Trouble; Daddy; Oliver Twist; Circus Days; Long Live the King; Boy of Flanders; Rag Man; Johnny Get Your Gun; Buttons; Tom Sawyer; Huckleberry Finn; Million Dollar Legs; Kilroy Was Here; Lost Women; Marlowe; Human Experiments; Dr. Heckyl and Mr. Hype; The Prey; The Escape Artist.

TV inc: The Kids Who Knew Too Much.

(Died March 1, 1984)

COOK, Elisha, Jr: Act. b. San Francisco, Dec 26, 1902. Films inc: Sergeant York; The Maltese Falcon; I Wake Up Screaming; Casanova Brown; Up in Arms; Dillinger; The Big Sleep; The Fall Guy; The Gangster; Shane; The Killing; Welcome to Hard Times; El Condor; The

Outfit; The Black Bird; Messiah of Evil; Winterhawk; St. Ives; The Champ; Carny; 1941; Harry's War; Hammett; National Lampoon Goes to the Movies.

TV inc: Salem's Lot; Leave 'Em Laughing; The Trouble with Grandpa; Insight/White Star Garage; This Girl for Hire; Off Sides.

COOK, Fielder: Prod-Dir. b. Atlanta, GA, Mar 9, 1923. Films inc: Patterns of Power; Home Is the Hero; Big Hand for a Little Lady; How to Save a Marriage; Prudence and the Pill; Eagle in a Cage; From the Mixed Up Files of Mrs. Basil E. Frankenweiler; Too Far To Go.

TV inc: Studio One; Theatre Guild of the Air; Playhouse 90; Brigadoon (Emmys-prod & dir-1967); The Price (Emmy-dir-1971); The Fifty-Minute Hour; Ben Casey; The Eleventh Hour; The Waltons; Beacon Hill; Gauguin the Savage; Family Reunion; Will There Really Be A Morning?; Evergreen.

Bway inc: A Cook for Mr General.

COOK, Peter: Act-Wri. b. Torquay, England, Nov 17, 1937. e. Cambridge. Thea inc: Beyond the Fringe; Behind the Fringe; Good Evening. (Special Tonys-1963 & 1974).

Films inc: (act) A Dandy in Aspic; The Wrong Box; Bedazzled; The Bed Sitting Room; The Rise and Rise of Michael Rimmer; Hound of the Baskervilles; Derek and Clive Get the Horn (& prod); Yellowbeard; Haunted (exec prod); Supergirl.

TV inc: The Two of Us; The Ghost Writer (prod).

(Grammy-spoken word-1974).

COOK, Robin, Dr: Wri. b. NYC, 1940. e. Columbia U; Coll of Physicians and Surgeons. MD, Ophthalmic surgeon, clinical instructor at Harvard Medical School.

Films inc: Coma.

COOK, Roderick: Act. b. London, 1932. e. Cambridge, BA. Thea inc: (London) Twelfth Night; Listen to the Wind; Waiting For Godot; Waltz of the Toreadors; Zuleika; Present Laughter (dir). Bway inc: Kean; The Girl Who Came To Supper; Roar Like a Dove; Hadrian VII; A Scent of Flowers; Oh, Coward (& prod-dir); The Man Who Came To Dinner; Woman Of the Year.

Films inc: The Great Waldo Pepper; Girl Friends; Silent Madness.

TV inc: The Guiding Light; Search For Tomorrow; One Life To Live.

COOK, T S (Thomas S Cook): Wri. b. Cleveland, OH, Aug 25, 1947. e. Denison U, BA; U of TX, MFA. Films inc: China Syndrome.

TV inc: Baretta; Paper Chase; Project UFO; Scared Straight!--Another Story; Red Flag--The Ultimate Game; Attack On Fear.

COOK, Tommy: Act-Wri-Prod. b. Duluth, MN, Jul 5, 1930. e. UCLA. On screen from 1942. Films inc: The Tuttles of Tahiti; Hi, Buddy; Wanderer of the Wasteland; Gallant Journey; Panic in the Streets; Mohawk; Alaska Passage; Rollercoaster (asso prod); Players (prod).

TV inc: (co-creator) The Challenge of the Sexes; Celebrity challenge of the Sexes.

COOKE, Alan: Prod-Wri-Dir. b. England, Mar 29, 1935. e. Merton Coll Oxford. TV inc: (England) Armchair Theatre; BBC Play of the Month; Play for Today; A Picture of Katherine Mansfield; Shades of Green; Devil's Crown; Cover; Brack Report. (US) NBC Matinee Theatre; Dear Detective; Lou Grant; Quincy; Hart to Hart.

Films inc: Mind of Mr. Soames; Nadia (dir only).

COOKE, Alistair: Journalist-TV Commentator. b. England, Nov 20, 1908. e. Jesus Coll; Cambridge; Yale; Harvard. Film critic, BBC, 1934-37. London corr NBC, 1936-37. BBC commentator in U.S. since 1933. Chief Amer corr Manchester Guardian since 1948.

TV inc: (emcee) Omnibus; America (2 Emmys-narr & wri-1973); Masterpiece Theatre (Emmy-1974); Pride and Prejudice; Testament of Youth; Danger UXB; I Remember Nelson; Flickers (host); The Good Soldier (host).

Films inc: Unknown Chaplin.

COOLIDGE, Martha: Dir. b. New Haven, CT., 1946. e. RI School of Design; School of Visual Arts; Columbia U; NYU Institute of Film and TV. Films inc: (shorts) Passing Quietly Through (prod-edtr); David: Off and On (doc)(& prod-wri-edtr); More Than A School (doc)(& prod-edtr); Old Fashioned Woman (doc)(& prod-wri-edtr); Employment Discriminations; The Trouble Shooters; Bimbo (& coprod-edtr);

Go Ahead and Rain (rock video). Features inc: Not A Pretty Picture (& prod-wri-coedtr); The City Girl (& prod); Valley Girl; Joy Of Sex.

TV inc: Magic Tom (prod-wri); Strawberries and Gold.

COOLIDGE, Rita: Singer. b. Nashville, TN. May 1, 1944. Singer with Delaney and Bonnie Bramlett; Joe Cocker; Leon Russell; Kris Kristofferson before going solo.

Records inc: Rita Coolidge; Nice Feelin' The Lady's Not for Sale; Love Me Again; Satisfied; Anytime, Anywhere.

(Grammys-(2)-country vocal duo-1973, 1975).

Films inc: Pat Garrett and Billy the Kid; Octopussy (sang theme).

TV inc: The Christmas Raccoons (mus).

COONEY, Dennis: Act. b. NYC. e. Fordham. Thea inc: (Off-Bway) Whisper To Me; Every Other Evil; Young Jefferson; In The Summer House. (Bway) Ross; Love and Kisses; The Last of Mrs Lincoln; Sherlock Holmes.

TV inc: Love of Life; The Magnificent Yankee; The Secret Storm; As The World Turns.

COONEY, Joan Ganz: Exec. b. Phoenix, AZ., Nov. 30, 1929. e. U AZ. Worked as reporter and publicist, produced docs before founding Childrens Television Workshop of which she is Executive Director. TV inc: Poverty, Anti-Poverty and the Poor; Sesame Street. (Grammy-Childrens Rec-1970).

COONEY, Ray: Prod-Act-Dir-Wri. b. London, May 30, 1932. Thea inc: (act) Simple Spymen; One for the Pot (& wri); The Mousetrap; Doctor at Sea; Uproar in the House. (Dir): Thark; In at the Death; Press Cuttings; Not Now, Darling; Move Over, Mrs. Markham; The Mating Game; Why Not Stay for Breakfast; Birds of Paradise (& prod); Run For Your Wife (& wri). Prod: Lloyd George Knew My Father; Two and Two Make Sex; Say Goodnight to Grandma; At the End of the Day; The Dame of Sark; The Bedwinner; Jack the Ripper; A Ghost on Tiptoe; The Sack Race; Murder at the Vicarage; A Ghost on Tiptoe; Hello Dolly; Beatlemania; They're Playing Our Song; Duet For One (also Bway); Her Royal Highness (& dir-wri); Andy Capp.

Films inc: There Goes The Bride (prod); Whose Life Is It Anyway (exec prod).

COOPER, Alice (Vincent Damon Furnier): Singer-Songwri. b. Detroit, MI., Feb. 4, 1948. Pioneer of Shockrock; concert tours featuring bizarre and elaborate equipment.

Films inc: Welcome to My Nightmare (doc); Sgt. Pepper's Lonely Hearts Club Band; Sextette; Roadie.

COOPER, Ben: Act. b. Hartford, CT, Sep 30, 1930. e. Columbia U. Films inc: The Woman They Almost Lynched; Perilous Journey; Johnny Guitar; Jubilee Trail; The Eternal Sea; The Rose Tattoo; Red Tomahawk; The Fastest Gun Alive; One More Train to Rob; Support Your Local Gunfighter.

Thea inc: Life With Father.

COOPER, Hal: Dir. b. NYC, Feb 23, 1923. e. U MI, BA. TV inc: TV Babysitter; Magic Cottage; Search for Tomorrow; Valiant Lady; Portia Faces Life; Kitty Foyle; Death Valley Days; Dick Van Dyke Show; I Spy; Courtship of Eddie's Father; Mary Tyler Moore Show; Odd Couple; All in the Family; Maude (exec prod); Insight/Holy Moses; Pottsville; Mr. & Mrs. . .and Mr.; Did You Hear About Josh and Kelly (& prod-song); The Long Road Home; And They Lived Happily Ever After (& mus); Two the Hard Way; Million Dollar Infield; The Astronauts (& exec prod); A Fine Romance; Never Again.

COOPER, Jackie: Act-Dir-Prod. b. LA, Sep 15, 1922. e. Notre Dame, BA. On screen at age 3, Our Gang Comedies. First starring role 1930, Skippy. Films inc: (Act) Sunny Side Up; Sooky; The Champ; When a Fellow Needs a Friend; Lumpy; Lost; The Bowery; Treasure Island; The Devil Is a Sissy; Gangster's Boy; Seventeen; Her First Beau; Stork Bites Man; Kilroy Was Here; Everything's Ducky; The Love Machine; Chosen Survivors; Superman; Superman II; Superman III. (Dir): Stand Up and Be Counted.

TV inc: People's Choice (act & dir 71 segments); Hennessy (act & dir 91 segments); Mobile Two (act). VP in chg. of TV Prodn, Screen Gems, 1964-69; resd to return to acting, dir, prod. TV inc: (dir) M*A*S*H (Emmy-dir-1974); White Shadow (Emmy-dir-1979); Sex and the Single Parent; Trapper John; Paris; White Mama; Rodeo Girl;

Leave 'Em Laughing (dir); Family In Blue (dir); Rosie--The Rosemary Clooney Story (prod-dir); Glitter (dir); The Night They Saved Christmas (dir).

COOPER, Lester: Prod. b. NYC, Jan 20, 1919. e. NYU. Freelance screenwriter, joined CBS News 1953 as wri; 1956 wri Today Show, NBC; 1961, head-wri, supv prod PM; 1967 exec prod ABC News doc unit; 1969 exec prod ABC Summer Focus Series.

TV inc: (exec prod-wri) Heart Attack; This Land is Mine; Can You Hear Me; The Right to Live; Hemingway's Spain--A Love Affair; Make A Wish (*Emmy*-prod-children's series-1974); Animals, Animals, Animals (& crea) (*Emmy*-1978).

(Died June 6, 1985)

COOPER, Marilyn: Act. b. NYC, Dec 14, 1939. e. NYU. Bway inc: West Side Story; Gypsy; I Can Get It For You Wholesale; Hallelujah Baby; Golden Rainbow; Two By Two; On the Town (rev); Ballroom; Woman of the Year (*Tony*-supp-1981); The Odd Couple.

COOPER, Robert: Prod-Bdcstr. b. Montreal, Dec 3, 1944. TV inc: Ombudsman (host); Between Friends (cable); The Guardian (cable).

Films inc: Power Play (exec prod); Running (prod); Middle Age Crazy (prod); Murder By Phone (prod); The Terry Fox Story (prod); Utilities; Breaking All The Rules (exec prod).

COOPERMAN, Alvin: Prod. b. NYC, Jul 24, 1923. e. NYU. Served with NBC-TV on three separate occasions as program exec. Also exec dir of the Shubert Theaters; P of Madison Square Garden Prodns; chmn, Athena Communications Corp (a cable TV co).

TV inc: The Bolshoi Ballet; Romeo and Juliet; Producers Showcase; Wide Wide World; 1972 Republican National Convention in Miami Beach (conceived format & prod); Live from Studio 8H--A Tribute to Toscanini (*Emmy*-1980); Live From Studio 8H--An Evening of Jerome Robbin's Ballets with Members of the N.Y. City Ballet (*Emmy*-1981); Ain't Misbehavin' (exec prod); Pope John Paul II (exec prod).

COPELAND, Joan (nee Miller): Act. b. NYC, Jun 1, 1922. e. AADA; Actors Studio. Sis of Arthur Miller. Bway inc: Othello; Sundown Beach; Detective Story; Not For Children; The Grass Is Always Greener; The Miser; Handful of Fire; Tovarich; My Fair Lady (tour); Something More!; The Price; Two By Two; The American Clock.

Films inc: The Goddess; Middle of the Night; It's My Turn; A Little Sex.

TV inc: Search For Tomorrow; The Iceman Cometh; How To Survive A Marriage; Cagney and Lacey; The Kennedy Center Honors 1984.

COPLAND, Aaron: Comp-Cond. b. NYC, Nov 14, 1900. Film scores inc: The City; Of Mice and Men; Our Town; North Star; The Red Pony; The Heiress (*Oscar*-1949); Something Wild. TV inc: Kennedy Center Honors-A Celebration of the Performing Arts.

Works: Dance Symphony; Piano Variations; El Salon Mexico; Outdoor Adventure.

(*Grammy*-classical comp-1960); Presidential Medal of Freedom 1964.

COPPERFIELD, David: Illusionist-Act. b. 1957. Admitted to American Society Magicians at age 12, youngest member ever admitted. In musicomedy Magic Man; Chicago. Films inc: Terror Train.

TV inc: The Magic of ABC; The Magic of David Copperfield; The Magic of David Copperfield II; Entertainer of the Year Awards; The Magic of David Copperfield (1981); Magic With the Stars (co prod); The World of Entertainment; The Magic World of David Copperfield (& dir); The President's Command Performance; The Magic World of David Copperfield VI; Mr. T. and Emmanuel Lewis In A Christmas Dream; The Magic Of David Copperfield VI (& dir); Kraft All-Star Salute To Ford's Theatre.

COPPOLA, Carmine: Comp-Cond. b. NYC, Jun 11, 1910. e. Manhattan School of Music, BA, MA; Juilliard, MM. F of Francis Ford Coppola. Chief arr Radio City Music Hall; 1st flutist, Detroit Symphony & Toscanini Symphony; cond David Merrick Productions. Films inc: Tonight For Sure; Wide Open Places; Once Upon a Mattress; Kismet; La Plume de Ma Tante; Godfather Part II (*Oscar*-1974); Apocalypse Now; The Black Stallion; One From the Heart; The Outsiders.

TV inc: The People.

Works: Flute Fling; Phantom Cavalry; Woodwind Quintet; Oboe Fantasie.

COPPOLA, Francis Ford: Dir-Wri-Prod. b. Detroit, MI, Apr 7, 1939. e. Hofstra, BA; UCLA, MFA. Owns Omni Zoetrope Prodn facility San Francisco; 1980 purchased Hollywood General Studios; Sold at Auction, Feb. 1984.

Films inc: (dir) Tonight For Sure (& prod-wri); Dementia 13; You're A Big Boy Now; Finian's Rainbow; The Rain People (& wri); The Godfather (& wri) (*Oscar*-sp-1972); The Conversation (& wri-prod); The Godfather, Part 2 (& wri-prod) (*Oscars*-picture-dir-sp-1974); Apocalypse Now (& wri-prod-mus); One From the Heart (& wri); The Outsiders; Rumble Fish (& exec prod-wri); The Cotton Club (& wri). Wri: Is Paris Burning?; This Property is Condemned; Reflections In a Golden Eye; Patton (*Oscar*-sp-1970). (Prod): American Graffiti; THX 1138; The Black Stallion (exec prod); The Escape Artist (exec prod); Hammett (exec prod); The Black Stallion Returns (exec prod); Mishima (exec prod).

CORBETT, Gretchen: Act. b. Camp Sherman, OR, Aug 13, 1947. Films inc: The Other Side of the Mountain, Part II; Jaws Of Satan (King Cobra).

TV inc: The Rockford Files; Mandrake; She's Dressed to Kill; High Ice; Million Dollar Infield; Things Are Looking Up; Otherworld.

Thea inc: Forty Carats.

CORBY, Ellen (nee Hansen): Act. b. Racine, WI, 1913. Films inc: The Dark Corner; The Spiral Staircase; I Remember Mama; Fighting Father Dunne; Madame Bovary; On Moonlight Bay; About Mrs. Leslie; The Seventh Sin; Macabre; Visit to a Small Planet; The Strangler; The Gnome Mobile.

TV inc: The Waltons (*Emmys*-supp-1973-1975-1976); All the Way Home; A Wedding on Walton's Mountain; A Day Of Thanks On Walton's Mountain.

CORD, Alex (nee Viespi): Act. b. Floral Park, NY, Aug 3, 1935. Films inc: Synanon; Stagecoach; The Brotherhood; Stiletto; Dead or Alive. The Last Grenade; The Dead Are Alive; Chosen Survivors; Sidewinder 1; Grayeagle; Jungle Warriors.

TV inc: Genesis II; The Girl Who Saved Our America; Beggarman, Thief; Hunter's Moon; Goliath Awaits; Airwolf.

CORDAY, Barbara Prod-wri-exec. b. NYC., Oct. 15, 1944. VP Comedy series dvlpt ABC TV; indie prod; June, 1984 P Columbia Pictures TV. TV inc: writer various segs; co-creator American Dream; co-creator Cagney & Lacey; exec prod Reggie.

CORDAY, Mara (Marilyn Watts): Act. b. Santa Monica, CA, Jan 3, 1932. Films inc: Drums Across the River; Playgirl; Dawn at Socorro; Francis Joins the WACS; So This Is Paris; Man Without a Star; Man from Bitter Ridge; Tarantula; A Day of Fury; Girl on Death Row; The Gauntlet.

COREA, Chick (Armando Corea): Pianist-Comp. b. Chelsea, MA, Jun 12, 1941. e. Juilliard. With Blue Mitchell, Stan Getz, Miles Davis, Sarah Vaughan before starting own group Return to Forever.

Recordings inc: No Mystery; Leprechaun; My Special Heart; Mad Hatter; Light as a Feather.

(*Grammys*-(6)-group jazz-1975, 1976, 1978, 1979, 1981; inst arr-1976).

COREA, Nicholas: Wri. b. St Louis, MO, Apr 7, 1943. TV inc: Police Woman, The Blue Knight; Kingston Confidential (story ed); Oregon Trail (exec story ed); Starsky & Hutch; Black Sheep Squadron; The Incredible Hulk (prod-dir); The Archer--Fugitive From The Empire (& prod-dir); The Renegades (supv prod-dir).

COREY, Irwin: Act. b. NYC, Jan 29, 1912. Stage debut in musical, Pins and Needles. Developed into double-talking comedian. Bway inc: Mrs. McThing; Happy as Heaven.

Films inc: Thieves; Car Wash; How to Commit Marriage; The Comeback Trail; Stuck On You; Crackers.

COREY, Jeff: Act. b. NYC, Aug 10, 1914. e. UCLA, BA. On stage 1936, Hamlet. Screen debut 1940, All That Money Can Buy. Films inc: The Killers; Ramrod; Joan of Arc; In Cold Blood; The Boston Strangler; True Grit; Butch Cassidy and the Sundance Kid; Beneath the Planet of the Apes; They Call Me Mr. Tibbs; A Clear and Present Danger; Catlow; Something Evil; Premonition; Moonshine County Express; The Last Tycoon; Oh, God!; Jennifer; Butch and Sundance-The Early Years; Battle Beyond The Stars; The Sword and the Sorcerer; Conan the Destroyer.

TV inc: Sixth Sense; Sons and Daughters; Greatest Heroes of the Bible; The Pirate; Homeward Bound; Cry For the Strangers; Hell Town.

CORMAN, Gene: Prod. b. Detroit, Sep 24, 1927. e. Stanford U. Partner with brother Roger in Corman Co. and New World Distrib. Films inc: Secret of the Purple Reef; Beast from Haunted Cave; The Intruder; Secret Invasion; Ski Party; Blood and Steel; Girls on the Beach; Tobruk; What's in it for Harry?; You Can't Win 'Em All; Cool Breeze; Hit Man; Private Parts; I Escaped From Devil's Island; Vigilante Force; F.I.S.T.; Target Harry; The Big Red One; If You Could See What I Hear (exec prod).

TV inc: Mary and Joseph-A Story of Faith; A Woman Called Golda *(Emmy-*1982).

CORMAN, Roger William: Exec-Prod-Dir. b. Detroit, Apr 5, 1926. e. Stanford U; Oxford U. Joined Fox prod dept 1948; then story analyst, literary agent; formed Roger Corman Prod. and Filmgroup, prod over 200 feature films & dir over 60 of them; 1970, formed New World Pictures, Inc, production-releasing co; sold company Jan 1983, remaining as consultant for two years.

Films inc: Five Guns West; Apache Woman; The Day the World Ended; Swamp Woman; The Gunslinger; Naked Paradise; Not of this Earth; War of the Satellites; Machine Gun Kelly; A Bucket of Blood; House of Usher; The Last Woman on Earth; The Pit and the Pendulum; The Intruder; The Raven; The Man with X-ray Eyes; The Masque of the Red Death; The St. Valentine's Day Massacre. (Prod): Boxcar Bertha; I Escaped From Devil's Island (co-prod); Big Bad Mama; Cockfighter; Grand Theft Auto; I Never Promised You A Rose Garden; Thunder and Lightning; Avalanche; Deathsport; Piranha; Rock 'n' Roll High School; Saint Jack; Fast Charlie the Moonbeam Rider; Humanoids From the Deep; Battle Beyond The Stars; Georgia Peaches; Galaxy of Terror; Smokey Bites the Dust; Der Stand der dinge (The State of Things) (act); My Love Letters; Space Raiders; The Wild Side; The Warrior and the Sorceress (presenter).

TV inc: Forbidden World (prod).

CORNEAU, Alain: Wri-Dir. b. Meung-sur-Loire, France, 1943. e. IDHEC. Films inc: France Societe Anonyme; Police Python 357; La Menace; Serie Noire; Les Choix Des Armes (Choice of Weapons); Fort Saganne.

CORNFIELD, Hubert: Dir-Wri. b. Istanbul, Turkey, 1929. e. U of PA. Films inc: Sudden Danger; Lure of the Swamp; Plunder Road; The Third Voice; Angel Baby; Pressure Point; Night of the Following Day; Les Grand Moyens; Short and Sweet.

CORSARO, Frank: Act-Dir. b. NYC, Dec 22, 1924. e. Yale Drama School; Actors Studio. Thea inc: dir numerous off-Bway prodns inc No Exit; Family Reunion; Heartbreak House; The Scarecrows; A Hatful of Rain; Fitz and Biscuit; Baby Want a Kiss; The Sweet Enemy. (Bway) The Night of the Iguana; Treemonisha; Knockout; It's So Nice To Be Civilized. (Opera) La Traviata; Mme Butterfly; Prince Igor; Rigoletto; Don Giovanni; Manon Lescaut.

Bway (act); The Taming of the Shrew; Mrs. McThing; The Merchant of Venice.

TV inc: A Piece of Blue Sky (dir-wri).

CORSAUT, Aneta: Act. b. Hutchinson, KS, Nov 3, 1933. e. Northwestern U; studied with Lee Strasberg. TV inc: Philco Playhouse; Studio One; Kraft Theatre; Andy Griffith Show; Mrs G Goes to College; Bad Ronald; The Runaways; House Calls.

CORT, Bud (Walter Edward Cox): Act. b. New Rochelle, NY, Mar 29, 1950. Started as standup comic in NY niteries. Films inc: M*A*S*H; Brewster McCloud; Harold and Maude; Why Shoot The Teacher; Die Laughing; She Dances Alone; My Love Letters; Hysterical; Maria's Lovers; The Secret Diary of Sigmund Freud; Electric Dreams.

TV inc: Brave New World; Insight/Teddy.

CORTESE, Valentina: Act. b. Milan, Italy, Jan 1, 1925. Started career at 15 in Rome. Screen debut in La Cens Delle Beffe, 1941. Films inc: A Yank in Rome; Cagliostro; Glass Mountain; House on Telegraph Hill; The Dinner of Jests; No One Turns Back; Barefoot Contessa; Legend of Lylah Clare; Day for Night; Widow's Nest; The Big Operator; When Time Ran Out; La Ferdinanda.

CORTEZ, Stanley (nee Kranz): Cin. b. NYC, 1908. Films inc: Four Days Wonder; The Black Doll; Lady in the Morgue; The Last Express; Risky Business; Alias the Deacon; The Leatherpushers; San Antonio Rose; The Magnificent Ambersons; The Secret Beyond the Door; The Man on the Eiffel Tower; Abbott and Costello Meet Captain Kidd; The Night of the Hunter; The Three Faces of Eve; Back Street; The Candidate; The Naked Kiss; The Bridge at Remagen; The Date; Another Man, Another Chance.

TV inc: Do Not Fold, Spindle or Mutilate.

CORWIN, Bruce C: Exec. b. LA, Jun 11, 1940. e. Wesleyan U. S of late Sherrill Corwin. P Metropolitan Theatres Corp.

CORWIN, Norman: Wri-Dir-Prod. b. Boston, May 3, 1910. Films inc: Once Upon a Time; Blue Veil; The Grand Design; Scandal in Scourie; Lust for Life; The Story of Ruth.

TV inc: Inside the Movie Kingdom; The FDR series; The Plot to Overthrow Christmas; Norman Corwin Presents; The Court Martial of General Yamashita.

Plays inc: The Rivalry; The World of Carl Sandburg; The Hyphen; Together Tonight- Jefferson, Hamilton and Burr.

Radio inc: Words Without Music series; Ballad for Americans; Pursuit of Happiness; 26 by Corwin; We Hold These Truths; Bill of Rights Show; On a Note of Triumph; The Lonesome Train; One World Flight; Word from the People.

COSBY, Bill: Act. b. Philadelphia, Jul 12, 1938. e. Temple U. Night club, TV comedian. Recorded comedy and musical albums. Films inc: Uptown Saturday Night; Man and Boy; Hickey and Boggs; Let's Do It Again; A Piece of the Action; California Suite; The Devil and Max Devlin.

TV inc: I Spy *(Emmy-*1966-1967-1968); Bill Cosby Special *(Emmy-*1969); The Fat Albert Easter Special (voice). Bill Cosby Show; Fat Albert; The New Fat Albert Show *(Emmy-*1981); The Fat Albert Easter Special (voice); Bill Cosby--Himself (& exec prod-dir-wri); Hollywood's Private Home Movies (host); Super Stars and Classic Cars; The Cosby Show (& co-crea-exec cnslt); Johnny Carson Presents The Tonight Show Comedians; S.O.S.--Secrets of Surviving; Motown Returns To The Apollo.

(Grammys-(8)-comedy 1964-65-66-67-68-69; rec for children (2) 1971-1972).

COSCARELLI, Don: Wri-Dir. b. Tripoli, Libya, Feb 17, 1954. Films inc: Jim the World's Greatest; Kenny and Company; Phantasm; The Beastmaster.

COSELL, Howard: TV Pers. b. Winston-Salem, NC, Mar 21, 1920. Hosted own TV show; commentator on ABC's Monday Night Football & Monday Night Baseball. TV inc: Fighting Back; ABC Sportsbeat *(Emmy-*prod-1983); Bob's Hope's Stand Up and Cheer for the National Football League's 60th Year; Night Of 100 Stars II.

Films inc: Bananas; Sleeper; The World's Greatest Athlete.

COSMATOS, George Pan: Dir-Wri-Prod. b. Jan 4, 1941. e. London Film School; London U. Prod-dir of TV commercials in Europe. Asst dir Zorba the Greek; Exodus.

Films inc: Massacre in Rome; The Cassandra Crossing; Escape to Athena; Of Unknown Origin; Rambo--First Blood Part II

COSSETTE, Pierre: Prod. b. LA, Dec 15, 1928. e. USC. Personal manager, Ann-Margret. Founder Dunhill Records. TV inc: Andy Williams Show; Sammy Davis Jr. Show; Sammy & Co; Sha Na Na; Hollywood Diamond Jubilee; Grammy Awards; Super Night at Super Bowl; New Adventures of Heidi; Alcatraz--The Whole Shocking Story; The Promise of Love; Grammy Hall of Fame (exec prod); 100 Years of Golden Hits (exec prod); The Glen Campbell Show (exec prod); The Glen Campbell Music Show (exec prod).

COSTA-GAVRAS, Henri: Dir. b. Athens, 1933. Studied at the Sorbonne. Worked as asst to Rene Clair, Rene Clement, Jacques Demy. Directorial debut, The Sleeping Car Murders. Films inc: The Thieves; Un Homme De Trop; The Vow; Z; State of Siege; Special Section; Clair de Femme; Madame Rosa (act); Missing (& wri) (Oscar-sp adaptation-1982); Hannah K (& wri).

COSTELLO, Elvis (Declan Patrick McManus): Singer. b. London, 1954. Recordings inc: My Aim Is True; This Year's Model; Armed Forces.
Films inc: Americathon; If It Ain't Stiff It Ain't Worth A. . .

COSTELLO, Mariclare: Act. b. Peoria, IL, Feb 3. Films inc: Tiger Makes Out; Let's Scare Jessica to Death; Ordinary People; Nightmares.
TV inc: The Waltons; The Execution of Pvt Slovak; Raid on Entebbe; A Sensitive Passionate Man; The Fitzpatricks; A Family of Winners; All God's Children; Coward of the County; Skeezer; Victims For Victims--The Theresa Saldana Story; The Heart Of A Champion--The Ray Mancini Story.
Thea inc: The Hostage; Lovers and Other Strangers.

COSTELLO, Robert E: Prod. b. Chicago, IL, Apr 26, 1921. e. Dartmouth, BA; Yale Drama School, MFA. Began 1952 as NBC unit mgr. TV inc: Mr. Peepers; Family Classics; Armstrong Circle Theatre; Patty Duke Show; Dark Shadows; Strange Paradise; Secret Strom; Adams Chronicles; Ryan's Hope (Emmys-1977, 1979); Another World.

COSTER, Nicolas: Act. b. London, England. e. RADA; Neighborhood Playhouse, NY; studied with Lee Strasberg. Films inc: My Blood Runs Cold; The Sporting Club; All the President's Men; MacArthur; Slow Dancing in the Big City; The Big Fix; Concorde--Airport '79; Just You and Me Kid; The Electric Horseman; Goldengirl; Little Darlings; Why Would I Lie?; Stir Crazy; The Pursuit of D.B. Cooper; Reds.
TV inc: Elizabeth the First; Another World; The Word; A Fire in the Sky; Bender; The Women's Room; Lobo; The Day The Bubble Burst; M.A.D.D.--Mothers Against Drunk Drivers; Ryan's Four; Princess Daisy; Santa Barbara.

COSTIGAN, James: Wri. TV inc: The Turn of the Screw; The Little Moon of Alban (Emmy-1959); War of Children; Last of the Belles; In This House of Brede; Love Among the Ruins (Emmy-1975); Eleanor and Franklin (Emmy-1976); F Scott Fitzgerald in Hollywood; Eleanor and Franklin--The White House Years; Titanic.
Films inc: King David.

COTLER, Kami: Act. b. Long Beach, CA, Jun 17, 1965. TV inc: The Waltons; A Wedding on Walton's Mountain; Mother's Day on Walton's Mountain; A Day Of Thanks On Walton's Mountain.

COTTEN, Joseph: Act. b. Petersburg, VA, May 15, 1905. H of Patricia Medina. Bway inc: Absent Father; Jezebel; Accent on Youth; The Postman Always Rings Twice. 1936 joined Orson Welles Federal Theatre project, remained with him through Mercury Players productions; Horse Eats Hat; Dr. Faustus; Julius Caesar; Shoemaker's Holiday; Danton's Death; Philadelphia Story; Sabrina Fair; Once More With Feeling; Calculated Risk.
Films inc: Citizen Kane; The Magnificent Ambersons; Journey Into Fear; Shadow of a Doubt; Gaslight; Since You Went Away; Love Letters; I'll Be Seeing You; Duel in the Sun; Farmer's Daughter; Portrait of Jennie; Under Capricorn; The Third Man; September Affair; Man With a Cloak; Peking Express; Steel Trap; Niagara; Blue Print for Murder; The Angel Wore Red; The Last Sunset; Hush, Hush Sweet Charlotte; Petulia; Days of Fire; Doomsday Voyage; Tora, Tora, Tora; Soylent Green; A Delicate Balance; Twilight's Last Gleaming; Airport 77; F For Fake; The Order and Security of the World; Caravans; Guyana - Cult of the Damned; The Hearse; Heaven's Gate; The Survivor; Screamers; Rambo Sfida la Citta (Syndicate Sadists); The House Where Death Lives.
Numerous radio shows inc: War of the Worlds.
TV inc: Hollywood and the Stars (Narr); Casino; Churchill and the Generals.

COULOURIS, George: Act. b. Manchester, England, Oct 1, 1903. Stage debut Manchester 1926, Outward Bound. On screen from 1933. Films inc: Christopher Bean; All This and Heaven Too; Citizen Kane; Watch on the Rhine; Hotel Berlin; Sleep My Love; A Southern Yankee; An Outcast of the Islands; Doctor in the House; The Runaway Bus; I Accuse; King of Kings; The Skull; Arabesque; Papillon; Mahler; Murder on the Orient Express; The Antichrist; The Tempter; It's Not the Size That Counts.
Thea inc: The Alchemist; The Moon of the Caribbees; The Insect Comedy; The Admirable Crichton; The Provok'd Wife.

COURTENAY, Tom: Act. b. Hull, England, Feb 25, 1937. e. University Coll, London; RADA. Films inc: Billy Liar; The Loneliness of the Long Distance Runner; King and Country; Operation Crossbow; King Rat; Doctor Zhivago; The Day the Fish Came Out; A Dandy in Aspic; Otley; One Day in the Life of Ivan Denisovitch; The Dresser.
Thea inc: The Seagull; Peer Gynt; Charley's Aunt; Time and Time Again; Arms and the Man; The Prince of Homburg; The Rivals; The Norman Conquest; The Fool; Otherwise Engaged; The Dresser; Andy Capp.
TV inc: Private Potter; The Lads.

COURTLAND, Jerome (Courtland Jourolmon): Act-Prod-Dir. b. Knoxville, TN, Dec 27, 1926. Film debut in Together Again, 1944. Films inc: (act) Tonka; Bamboo Prison; Take The High Ground; Tokyo Joe; Battleground. (Prod): Pete's Dragon; Ride A Wild Pony; Escape to Witch Mountain; Return From Witch Mountain; The Devil and Max Devlin; Amy.
TV inc: (dir) Flying Nun; Nancy; The Wonderful World of Disney; The Partridge Family; The Sky Trap; The Sultan and the Rock Star; The Ghosts of Buxley Hall (prod).
Bway inc: Flahooley.

COURTNEY, Jacqueline: Act. b. East Orange, NJ, Sep 24, 1946. Former child act. TV inc: The Edge of Night; Our Five Daughters; Secret Storm; Another World (11 years); One Life To Live.

COUSTEAU, Jacques-Yves: Prod. b. France, 1910. Films inc: The Silent World; The Golden Fish (Oscar-ss-1959); World Without Sun; Voyage To The Edge of the World.
TV inc: Blind Prophets of Easter Island; Time Bomb at 50 Fathoms; The Nile (narr); The Undersea World of Jacques Cousteau; Clipperton--The Island Time Forgot; The Warm-Blooded Sea--Mammals of the Deep; Jacques Cousteau--Cries From the Deep; The Mississippi--Reluctant Ally; Cousteau/Amazon--Journey to a Thousand Rivers (& narr); The New El Dorado--Invaders and Exiles; Snowstorm In The Jungle (exec prod).

COUTARD, Raoul: Cin. b. France, 1924. Films inc: Ranuntcho; A Bout de Souffle; Shoot the Pianist; Lola; Jules et Jim; Bay of Angels; Les Carabiniers; Silken Skin; Sailor from Gibraltar; The Bride Wore Black; Z; L'Aveu; L'Explosion; Du Sel Sur la Peau (Salt On The Skin); Le Diagonale du Fou (Dangerous Moves).

COVER, Franklin: Act. b. Cleveland, OH, Nov 20, 1928. e. Denison U, BA; Western Reserve U, MA, MFA. Bway inc: Applause; Forty Carats; A Warm Body; The Investigation; Any Wednesday; Calculated Risk.
Films inc: The Stepford Wives; The Great Gatsby; Such Good Friends; Mirage; What's So Bad About Feeling Good?
TV inc: The Connection; The Investigation; What Makes Sammy Run?; The Jeffersons; The Day the Bubble Burst; A Woman Called Golda.

COWAN, Warren J.: Pub exec. b. NYC, Mar 13, 1921. e. UCLA, BA. Pub with Alan Gordon Associates before WW II; 1946, joined Henry Rogers pubbery; 1949, became partner, firm name changed to Rogers & Cowan; since 1964, P Rogers & Cowan Inc. Prod (Bway) A Woman of Independent Means.

COWITT, Ben L: Exec. b. Los Angeles, Nov 23, 1934. e. Claremont Men's Coll; USC. Studio mgr MGM 1958; studio mgr Hollywood Zoetrope, 1980; 1982, asso vp admn Los Angeles Olympic Organizing Committee; June, 1985, dir studio ops Walt Disney Pictures.

COX, Richard: Act. b. NYC, May 6, 1948. e. Yale. Thea inc: Moonchildren (Off-Bway); Grease (tour). Bway inc: Captain Brassbound's Conversion; Platinum.
Films inc: Maidstone; Between the Lines; Cruising; King of Mountain; The Oasis.

TV inc: Love of Life; Executive Suite; Doonesbury Special (voice).

COX, Ronny: Act. b. Aug 23, 1938. Films inc: The Happiness Cage; Deliverance; Hugo the Hippo (voice only); Gray Lady Down; Harper Valley PTA; The Oni on Field; Taps; The Beast Within; Some Kind of Hero; Courage (& prod-wri); Beverly Hills Cop; Vision Quest.

TV inc: Apple's Way; Transplant; When Hell Was in Session; Kavik the Wolf Dog; One Last Ride; Fugitive Family; The Last Song; First Time, Second Time--For Better or Worse; Alcatraz--The Whole Shocking Story; Fallen Angel; The Jesse Owens Story; Spencer; Reckless Disregard.

COYOTE, Peter: Act. With San Francisco Actors Workshop; San Francisco Mime Troupe; Magic Theatre. Thea inc: The Minstrel Show (dir); Olive Pits (& co-author); The Red Snake; True West; Autobiography of a Pearl Diver; Charles, The Irrelevant.

TV inc: The People Vs Jean Harris; In the Child's Best Interest; Up and Coming; Isabelle's Choice; Golden Gate; Best Kept Secrets; Scorned and Swindled.

Films inc: Die Laughing; Tell Me A Riddle; The Pursuit of D.B. Cooper; Southern Comfort; E.T. The Extraterrestrial; Endangered Species; Timerider; Cross Creek; Stranger's Kiss; Slayground; Heartbreakers.

CRABBE, Larry (Buster): Act. b. Oakland, CA, Feb 7, 1907. e. USC. A 1932 Olympic swimming champ, on screen since 1933. Films inc: Tarzan series; Sweetheart of Sigma Chi; The Thundering Herd; Million Dollar Legs; Flash Gordon (serial); Pirates of the High Seas (serial); Billy the Kid; Badman's Country; Comeback Trail.

TV inc: The Foreign Legion.

(Died Apr 23, 1983).

CRAIG, Diane: Act. b. Ireland. e. Australian National Institute of Dramatic Art. Worked with Old Tote Theatre Company, Tasmanian Theatre Company. Thea inc: Hobson's Choice; Marginal Farm.

Films inc: Ned Kelly; The Mango Tree; Double Deal; Stress (doc) Minami Jujisei (Southern Cross).

TV inc: Dead Men Running; Homicide; And Big Men Fly; Young Ramsay; Roses Bloom Twice; Skyways; Young Doctors; Taurus Rising; All the Rivers Run.

CRAIG, Helen: Act. b. San Antonio, TX, May 13, 1912. W of John Beal. With Hedgerow Repertory Theatre 1929-1934; various stock cos. Bway inc: Russet Mantle; New Faces; Julius Caesar; Soliloquoy; Family Portrait; The Unconquered; Johnny Belinda; As You Like It; Lute Song; Land's End; The House of Bernarda Alba; Medea; More Stately Mansions.

Films inc: They Live By Night; The Keys of the Kingdom; The Snake Pit; The Sporting Club; Heroes.

CRAIG, James (nee Meador): Act. b. Nashville, TN., Feb. 4, 1912. e. Rice Inst. Films inc: Thunder Trail; The Big Broadcast of 1938; The Buccaneer; The Man They Could Not Hang; Zanzibar; Flying G-Men (serial); Winners of the West (serial); South to Karanga; Seven Sinners; Kitty Foyle; All That Money Can Buy; Valley of the Sun; Friendly Enemies; The Omaha Trail; The Human Comedy; Swing Shift Maisie; The Heavenly Body; Kismet; Marriage Is a Private Affair; Our Vines Have Tender Grapes; Dangerous Partners; She Went to the Races; Dark Delusion; Northwest Stampede; Side Street; Drums in the Deep South; Hurricane Smith; Fort Vengeance; Massacre; While the City Sleeps; Cyclops; Four Fast Guns; Fort Utah; Arizona Bushwhackers; Bigfoot; The Doomsday Machine.

CRAIG, Michael (nee Gregson): Act. b. Poona, India, Jan 27, 1928. e. Upper Canada Coll, Toronto. London stage debut, 1949, The Merchant of Venice. Bway inc: Homecoming. Films inc: Malta Story; The Love Lottery; High Tide at Noon; The Silent Enemy; Sea of Sand; Sapphire; Upstairs and Downstairs; The Angry Silence (& sp); Cone of Silence; Mysterious Island; Payroll; Stolen Hours; Life at the Top; Sandra; Star!; The Royal Hunt of the Sun; Twinky; Brotherly Love; A Town Called Bastard; Vault of Horror; The Irishman; The Killing of Angel Street (wri); Turkey Shoot; Stanley.

TV inc: Saint Joan; Spoiled; The Hotel in Amsterdam; The Timeless Land.

CRAIG, Tony (nee Kulasa): Act. b. Pittsburgh, PA, Dec 23, 1946. e.

Mansfield, OH, State Coll; OH U. High school English and drama teacher before turning pro. TV inc: Love Is A Many Splendored Thing; Search for Tomorrow; The Edge of Night.

Films inc: Reaching Out.

CRAIG, Wendy: Act. b. England, Jun 20, 1934. e. Central School Dramatic Art. Thea inc: (London) Soho So What; Mr Kettle and Mrs Moon; Man Alive!; A Resounding Tinkle; Epitaph for George Dillon; The Ginger Man; Three (triple bill); Something from Collette; Ride a Cock Horse; Happy Family; Finishing Touches; Hobson's Choice.

Films inc: The Mind Benders; The Servant; The Nanny; Just Like A Woman; I'll Never Forget Whatshisname; Joseph Andrews.

TV inc: Not in Front of the Children; And Mother Makes Five.

CRAIN, Jeanne: Act. b. Barstow, CA, May 25, 1925. Model; Miss Long Beach of 1941. Films inc: Home in Indiana; Winged Victory; State Fair; Leave Her to Heaven; Margie; Centennial Summer; Apartment for Peggy; Letter To Three Wives; Vicki; Gentlemen Marry Brunettes; Fastest Gun Alive; The Joker; Skyjacked.

CRAIN, William: Dir. b. Jun 20, 1943. Films inc: Blacula; The Watts Monster. TV inc: Mod Squad; Rookies; S.W.A.T.; Starsky & Hutch; Roots-The Next Generation.

CRAMER, Douglas S(choolfield): Prod. b. Louisville, KY, Aug 22, 1931. e. Columbia U; Sorbonne, Paris. Exec VP Development ABC-TV & Fox; Exec VP Paramount TV; P Douglas S. Cramer Co; 1978, exec VP Aaron Spelling Productions. TV inc: Bridget Loves Bernie; QB VII; The Cat Creature; The Dead Don't Die; The Black Dahlia; Nightmare in Badham County; Dawn-Portrait of a Teenage Runaway; Alexander--The Other Side of Dawn; Cage Without A Key; San Pedro Bums; Snowbeast; Love Boat; Wonder Woman; Love's Savage Fury; Friends-Going Out; The Power Within; The French Atlantic Affair; B.A.D. Cats; Waikiki; Murder Can Hurt You; Casino; Aloha Paradise; The Best Little Girl In The World; Dynasty; Strike Force; Sizzle; Massarati and the Brain; Scared Silly; Matt Houston; The Wild Women of Chastity Gulch; Don't Go To Sleep; At Ease; Shooting Stars; Venice Medical; Arthur Hailey's "Hotel" (exec prod); The Making of A Male Model; Dark Mirror; Velvet; Glitter; Finder Of Lost Loves; MacGruder & Loud; Hollywood Wives; International Airport.

CRAMER, Floyd: Mus. b. Shreveport, LA, Oct 27, 1933. Recording artist; between 1952-55, toured country with such performers as Hank Williams and Elvis Presley; became regular perf on the Grand Ole Opry in mid-50s.

CRAMPHORN, Rex: Dir. b. Brisbane, Australia, Jan 10, 1945. Thea inc: Jesus Christ Superstar; The Tempest; Measure for Measure; Interplay.

CRAVEN, Gemma: Act. b. Dublin, Jun 1, 1950. e. Loretto Coll. Thea inc: Fiddler on the Roof; Audrey; Saturnalia; Sabrina Fair; Trelawny; The Confederacy; A Month in the Country; Underground; The Threepenny Opera; Black Comedy; Songbook; They're Playing Our Song.

Films inc: The Slipper and the Rose; Wagner. TV inc: Pennies From Heaven.

CRAWFORD, Broderick: Act. b. Philadelphia, Dec 9, 1911. Films inc: Submarine D-1; Ambush; Undercover Doctor; Slightly Honorable; Butch Minds The Baby; Anna Lucasta; All The King's Men *(Oscar-1949)*; Born Yesterday; New York Confidential; Not as a Stranger; The Oscar; The Private Files of J. Edgar Hoover; A Little Romance; Harlequin; There Goes The Bride; Den Tuechtigen Gehort (The Upper Crust); Liar's Moon.

TV inc: Highway Patrol; The Interns; True Position.

Thea inc: That Championship Season.

CRAWFORD, Cheryl: Prod. b. Akron, OH, Sep 24, 1902. e. Buchtel Coll; Smith Coll. Thea inc: All the Living; Porgy and Bess (revival 1941); The Flowers of Virtue; A Kiss for Cinderella; One Touch of Venus; The Perfect Marriage; The Tempest; founded the American Repertory Theatre, as m-dir co-prod Henry VIII; What Every Woman Knows; John Gabriel Borkman; Androcles and the Lion; A Pound on Demand; Alice in Wonderland; Through the Looking Glass; appointed joint-gen dir of the ANTA play series 1950.

Plays at ANTA Playhouse inc: The Tower Beyond Tragedy; Peer

Gynt; The Rose Tattoo (Tony-1951); Paint Your Wagon; Camino Real; Oh, Men! Oh, Women!; The Honeys; Girls of Summer; The Shadow of a Gunman; Sweet Bird of Youth; Period of Adjustment; Brecht on Brecht; Jennie; Doubletalk; Celebration; Colette; The Love Suicide at Schofield Barracks; The Web and the Rock; Yentl; Do You Turn Somersaults?

CRAWFORD, Henry James: Prod. b. Woodend, Victoria, Australia, Feb 8, 1947. TV inc: Homicide; Mattlock Police; Young Ramsay; Solo One; (& creator); The Sullivans; Against the Wind; A Town Like Alice; Five Mile Creek; Eureka Stockade.
Films inc: No Nukes.

CRAWFORD, Joanna Jane: Wri. b. Jan 14, 1943. Films inc: My Side of the Mountain; The Little Ark; Birch Interval.
TV inc: Betrayal; Friendships, Secrets and Lies; Sophia Loren--Her Own Story.

CRAWFORD, John: Act. b. Los Angeles, Mar 26, 1946. On stage at age 5 in Mr. Belvedere. At 9 title role in film Little Boy Lost. Films inc: Village of the Giants; Indian Paint; Outlaw Blues; Dreamer; The Apple Dumpling Gang Rides Again.
TV inc: The Rifleman; The Other Victim; McClain's Law; The Powers of Matthew Star; Gun Shy; Kenny Rogers as the Gambler--The Adventure Continues.

CRAWFORD, Michael: Act. b. Salisbury, England, Jan 19, 1942. Thea inc: (London) Striplings; Travelling Light; The Anniversary; Come Blow Your Horn; No Sex Please, We're British; Billy; Same Time, Next Year; Flowers for Algernon; Barnum. (Bway) White Lies & Black Comedy (double bill).
Films inc: Two Left Feet; The War Lover; Two Living, One Dead; The Knack; A Funny Thing Happened on the Way to the Forum; How I Won the War; The Jokers; Hello, Dolly!; The Games; Hello and Goodbye; Alice in Wonderland; Condorman.
TV inc: Not Such Much a Programme, More a Way of Life; Some Mothers Do 'Ave 'Em; Private View; Audience; Chalk and Cheese.

CREMER, Bruno: Act. b. Paris, 1929. Appeared in plays on French stage. Films inc: Marco Polo; Is Paris Burning?; One Man Too Many; Breakdown; Special Section; The Good and the Bad; Sorcerer; The Order and Security of the World; On Efface Tout (We Forget Everything); A Simple Story; Cet Age Sans Pitie; A Black Gown For A Killer; La Puce et le Prive (The Cute Chick and the Private Eye); Espion Leve-Toi (Rise Up, Spy); Josepha; Le prix du danger (The Prize of Peril); Effraction (Break-In); Fanny Pelopaja (Fanny Strawhair); Derborence.

CRENNA, Richard: Act. b. Los Angeles, Nov 30, 1927. e. USC. On radio in Boyscout Jamboree; A Date With Judy; The Great Gildersleeve; Our Miss Brooks. Films inc: Red Skies Of Montana; Pride of St. Louis; It Grows On Trees; Over Exposed: John Goldfarb, Please Come Home; Made In Paris; Wait Until Dark; The Sand Pebbles; Star!; Marooned: The Deserter; Doctor's Wives; The Man Called Noon; Catlow; Dirty Money; The Evil; Stone Cold Dead; Death Ship; Body Heat; First Blood; Table for Five; The Flamingo Kid; Rambo--First Blood Part II.
TV inc: Our Miss Brooks; The Real McCoys; Slattery's People; All's Fair; Thief; Double Indemnity; Nightmare; First You Cry; A Fire in the Sky; Better Late Than Never; Turnabout (dir); Joshua's World; Fugitive Family; Musical Comedy Tonight; Look At Us (host); The Hoyt Axton Show (dir); The Ordeal of Bill Carney; The Day The Bubble Burst; It Takes Two; Allison Sidney Harrison (dir);London and Davis in New York; Passions; The Rape Of Richard Beck.

CRESPIN, Regine: Dramatic soprano. b. Marseilles, France, Feb 23, 1927. Operatic debut 1951, Mulhouse, France; to Paris Opera later same year; debut La Scala 1958. Has starred at Chicago Opera; Metropolitan Opera; Covent Garden.
Recs inc: Les Dialogues des Carmelites; Carmen; La Grande Duchesse de Gerolstein; La Perichole; Nuits D'Ete (Song Cycle) (Grammy-class solo-1964); La Vie Parisienne.

CRIBBINS, Bernard: Act. b. England, Dec. 29, 1928. Thea inc: The Comedy of Errors; Salad Days; The Chicken Play; Harmony Close; Lady at the Wheel; The Big Tickle; Hook, Line and Sinker; New

Cranks; And Another Thing; The Fire of London; Not Now, Darling; Run For Your Wife.
Films inc: Two Way Stretch; The Girl on the Boat; The Wrong Arm of the Law; Carry on Jack; Crooks in Cloisters; She; The Sandwich Man; Daleks Invasion; The Railway Children; Frenzy; Dangerous Davies--The Last Detective.
TV inc: Cribbins.

CRICHTON, Dr. Michael Wri-Dir. b. Chicago, Oct 23, 1942. e. Harvard Medical School. While there completed 1st novel, Easy God. Has written 15 books under four different names, inc A Case of Need (filmed as The Carey Treatment); The Andromeda Strain; Dealing; The Terminal Man, all filmed. Films inc: Westworld; Coma; The Great Train Robbery; Looker; Runaway.
TV inc: Pursuit (dir).

CRINKLEY, Richmond: Prod. b. Blackstone, VA, Jan 20, 1940. e. U VA; Oxford. 1967 joined faculty of U NC; 1969, dir of pgms and prod Folger Shakespeare Library; 1973, asst to chmn Kennedy Center; 1979, exec dir Vivian Beaumont Theatre, Lincoln Centre; resd. Oct. 15, 1984. Thea inc: Summer Brave; Skin of Our Teeth; Sweet Bird of Youth; Royal Family; Out of Our Father's House; Ladybury Blues; The Philadelphia Story; The Elephant Man (Tony-1979); Tintypes; Passion.
TV inc: The Elephant Man.

CRIST, Judith (nee Klein): Critic. b. NYC, May 22, 1922. e. Hunter College, BA; Columbia Grad School of Journalism, MSC. Asso drama critic NY Herald-Tribune, 1958-1968; film critic 1963-1966; arts editor 1960-1963; film & drama critic NBC-TV Today Show 1963-1966; film critic TV Guide since 1966; film critic NY Magazine 1968-1975; Saturday Review 1975-1977, retd 1980; adjunct prof Columbia Graduate School of Journalism, since 1958.

CRISTALDI, Franco: Prod. b. Turin, Italy, Oct 3, 1924. Films inc: White Nights; The Strawman; The Challenge; Big Deal On Madonna Street; Kapo; The Dauphins; The Assassin; Divorce Italian Style; The Organizer; Seduced and Abandoned; Time of Indifference; Sandra; A Rose for Every-One; China Is Near; A Quiet Couple; The Red Tent; Christ Stopped at Eboli; Wife-Mistress; Ogro; Ratataplan; The Persian Lamb Coat; Cafe Express; Domani si balla (Tomorrow we Dance).

CRISTOFER, Michael (nee Procaccino): Plywri-Act. b. Jan 22, 1945. Plays inc: The Shadow Box (Pulitzer Prize & Tony-1977); Ice; Black Angel; The Lady and the Clarinet.
Bway inc: (act) Cherry Orchard; Candida (dir).
Films inc: (act) Enemy of the People; The Little Drummer Girl; Falling In Love (wri).
TV inc: (act) Family; Sad Figure Laughing; Crime Club; The Shadow Box (wri); Candida (dir) (cable).

CROFTS, Dash: Mus-Singer. b. Cisco, TX. With The Champs, The Dawnbreakers before teaming with James Seals. Albums inc: Seals and Crofts I and II; Year of Sunday; Summer Breeze; Diamond Girl; Unborn Child; I'll Play For You; Greatest Hits; Get Closer; Sudan Village; Takin It Easy.

CROMBIE, Donald: Dir. b. Australia. Films inc: Caddie; The Irishman (& wri); Cathy's Child; The Killing of Angel Street; Kitty and the Bagman; Robbery Under Arms.
TV inc: Who Killed Jenny Langby?; Do I Have to Kill My Child? (& wri).

CRONENBERG, David: Wri-Dir. b. Toronto, Canada, 1944. e. U of Toronto. Films inc: Stereo; Crimes Of The Future; Shivers (wri); Rabid; Fast Company; The Brood; Scanners; Videodrome; The Dead Zone (dir); Into The Night (act).

CRONENWETH, Jordan: Cin. Films inc: Play It As It Lays; Zandy's Bride; The Nickel Ride; Gable and Lombard; The Front Page; Cutter and Bone; Blade Runner; Best Friends; Stop Making Sense (doc).

CRONKITE, Walter: TV Newsman. b. St Joseph, MO, Nov 4, 1916. e. U of TX. Joined CBS as Washington news correspondent 1950; mng ed-anchorman CBS Evening News 1963-1981.
TV inc: You Are There; Twentieth Century; Eyewitness to History;

CBS Reports; Universe (narr); Man on the Moon--The Epic Journey of Apollo XI (Emmy-1970); Space Coverage (Emmy-1971); U S Soviet Wheat Deal--Is There a Scandal? (Emmy-exec prod-1973); The Watergate Affair (Emmy-1973); The Shooting of Gov Wallace (Emmy-1973); The Agnew Resignation (Emmy-1974); Watergate--The White House Transcripts (Emmy-1974); The Key Biscayne Bank Charter Struggle; The Rockefellers (Emmy-1974); Solzhenitsyn (Emmy-1974); Sadat's Eternal Egypt; A Private Battle (act); Walter Cronkite's Universe; The Kennedy Center Honors 1982 (host); I, Leonardo--A Journey of the Mind (host); 1984 Revisited (host); D-Day & Eisenhower; JFK--A One Man Show (host); Salute to Lady Liberty; The Legacy of Harry S. Truman; High Tech--Dream Or Nightmare?; Night Of 100 Stars II; Honor, Duty And A War Called Vietnam; Terrorism--War In The Shadows.

(ATAS-second annual Governors Award) (NATAS-Trustees Award 1982) (TV Academy Hall Of Fame 1985).

CRONYN, Hume: Act-Dir. b. London, Ontario, Canada, Jul 18, 1911. e. AADA; Mozarteum. Worked at Barter Theatre. Bway inc: (Act) Hipper's Holiday; Boy Meet Girl; Room Service; High Tor; Escape This Night; There's Always a Breeze; Off to Buffalo; The Weak Link; The Survivors; Now I Lay Me Down To Sleep (dir only); Hilda Crane (Dir only); The Fourposter; Madame Will You Walk (& dir); The Egghead (dir only); Triple Play (& dir); Hamlet (Tony-supp-1964); The Physicists; Slow Dance on a Killing Ground (prod only); Promenade All; Act Without Words; Krapp's Last Tape; Noel Coward in Two Keys; The Many Faces of Love; The Gin Game; Foxfire (& wri).

Films inc: Cross of Lorraine; Lifeboat; The Seventh Cross; Main Street After Dark; The Sailor Takes a Wife; A Letter for Evie; The Green Years; Brute Force; The Bride Goes Wild; The Postman Always Rings Twice; Top O' The Morning; People Will Talk; Crowded Paradise; Sunrise at Campobello; Cleopatra; Gaily, Gaily; The Arrangement; There Was a Crooked Man; Conrack; The Parallax View; Honky Tonk Freeway; Rollover; The World According to Garp; Impulse; Brewster's Millions; Cocoon.

TV inc: The Bridge of San Luis Rey; The Fourposter; The Moon and Sixpence; The Marriage (also on radio); The Dollmaker (wri).

CROSBY, Bob: Orch Ldr. b. Spokane, WA, Aug 23, 1913. e. Gonzaga U. B of late Bing Crosby. Began as singer; featured vocalist with Jimmie & Tommy Dorsey band. Org own band, the Bobcats. Films inc: Sis Hopkins; Reveille With Beverly; As Thousands Cheer; Kansas City Kitty; Pardon My Rhythm; Singing Sheriff; Two Tickets to Broadway.

TV inc: The Bob Crosby Show.

CROSBY, Cathy Lee: Act. b. Los Angeles. e. USC. Films inc: Call Me by my Rightful Name; The Laughing Policeman; Trackdown; The Coach; The Dark.

TV inc: Third Annual Circus of the Stars; The Funny Side of Love; That's Incredible! (host); Roughnecks; The World's Most Spectacular Stuntmen (host); Get High on Yourself (host-exec prod); Bob Hope's All-Star Comedy Look at the New Season; World War III; Life's Most Embarrassing Moments; Bob Hope's USO Christmas in Beirut.

CROSBY, David: Sngwri-Singer-Mus. b. Los Angeles, Aug, 1941. Member of Les Baxter's Balladeers before going solo; With Roger McGuinn and Gene Clark formed The Byrds; 1967 teamed with Graham Nash and Stephen Sills to form Crosby, Stills & Nash (Grammy-new artist-1969).

Songs inc: Everybody's Been Burned; Renaissance Fair; What's Happening.

CROSBY, Floyd Delafield: Cine (ret). b. NYC, Dec 12, 1899. Lensed 80 films inc: Tabu (Oscar-1930-31); High Noon; Wonderful Country; Cold Wind in August; The Explosive Generation; Tales of Terror; The Firebrand; The Raven; The Comedy of Terrors; Pajama Party; Beach Blanket Bingo; Sallah; Fireball 500; The Cool Ones.

Docs inc: The River; Power and the Land; The Fight for Life.

CROSBY, Kathryn: Act. b. Houston, TX, Nov 25, 1933. e. U of TX; UCLA. W of late Bing Crosby. Films inc: Forever Female; Rear Window; Cassanova's Big Night; Unchained; Five Against the House; Phoenix City Story; The Night the World Exploded; The Big Circus; Operation Mad Ball.

TV inc: The Bing Crosby Christmas Specials; Suspense Theatre; Ben Casey; The Kathryn Crosby Show.

CROSBY, Mary: Act. b. Los Angeles, Sep 14, 1959. e. U TX, Austin. D of Kathryn Grant and the late Bing Crosby. TV inc: various specials with parents; With This Ring; Guide for the Married Women; Brothers and Sisters; Pearl; Dallas; Midnight Lace; Grammy Hall of Fame; Golden Gate; The Big Easy; Confessions of a Married Man; Cover Up; Charters & Caldicott.

Films inc: Last Plane Out; The Ice Pirates.

CROSBY, Norm: Comedian. b. Boston, MA, Sep 15, 1927. Nitery and concert perf; opening act for Robert Goulet for three years.

TV inc: Norm Crosby's Comedy Shop; A Funny Thing Happened on the Way to the White House (cable TV).

CROSS, Beverley: Wri. b. London, Apr 13, 1931. e. Nautical Coll, Oxford. H of Maggie Smith. Former actor. Plays inc: The Singing Dolphin; The Three Cavaliers; Boeing-Boeing (adapted from the French of Marc Camoletti); Half-a-Sixpence (book of musical); The Mines of Sulphur (libretto); The Rising of the Moon (libretto); Victory (libretto); Spook; The Great Society; Hans Andersen (book).

Films inc: Jason and the Argonauts; The Long Ships; Ghenghis Khan; Half-a-Sixpence; Sinbad and The Eye of the Tiger; Clash of the Titans.

TV inc: The Dark Pits of War; Catherine Howard.

CROSS, Irv: Sportscaster. b. Hammond, IN, Jul 27, 1939. e. Northwestern U. Former pro football player. Joined CBS sports 1971. Commentator for The NFL Today.

CROTHERS, Joel: Act. b. Cincinnati, OH, Jan 28, 1941. e. Harvard, BA. Bway debut age 12, The Remarkable Mr. Pennypacker. TV inc: Studio One; Playhouse 90; Goodyear Playhouse; Dark Shadows; The Secret Storm; Somerset Five; The Edge of Night.

CROTHERS, Scatman (Sherman Crothers): Act. b. Terre Haute, IN, May 23, 1910. Started own band; made recordings; on TV with Dixie Showboat, 1949. Films inc: Bloody Mama; Black Belt Jones; Truck Turner; Coonskin; One Flew Over the Cuckoo's Nest; Friday Foster; The Cheap Detective; Scavenger Hunt; The Shining; The Rats; Zapped!; Twilight Zone--The Movie; Two of a Kind; Chesty Anderson--U.S. Navy.

TV inc: The Puppy's Great Adventure (voice); The Harlem Globetrotters On Gilligan's Island; Revenge of the Gray Gang (& song); One of the Boys; Banjo the Woodpile Cat (voice); Missing Children--A Mother's Story; Grandpa, Will You Run With Me; Casablanca.

CROUCH, Andrae: Singer-Mus-Comp. b. Los Angeles, Jul 1, 1942. Organizer and leader of The Disciples. TV inc: A Gift of Music; The Mac Davis Christmas Special--Christmas Is A Song.

Recordings inc: Live at Carnegie Hall; Just Andrae; Take Me Back. (Grammy-soul gospel-1975); This is Another Day; Crouch in London (Grammy-soul gospel-1978); Crouch Alone (Grammy-soul Gospel-1979); The Lord's Prayer (Grammy-contemporary or inspirational gospel-1980); Don't Give Up (Grammy-soul gospel Contemporary-1981).

CROUSE, Lindsay: Act. b. NYC. e. Radcliffe. D of the late Russel Crouse. Films inc: All the President's Men; Between the Lines; Slap Shot; Prince of the City; The Verdict; Daniel; Iceman; Places In The Heart.

TV inc: Eleanor and Franklin; The Tenth Level; Summer Solstice.

CROWLEY, Mart: Plywri. b. Vicksburg, MS. Aug. 21, 1935. Plays inc: The Boys in the Band; Remote Asylum; A Breeze from the Gulf.

CROWLEY, Pat: Act. b. Olyphant, PA, Sep 17, 1933. Films inc: Forever Female; Money From Home; Red Garters; There's Always Tomorrow; Hollywood or Bust; Key Witness; To Trap a Spy.

TV inc: Please Don't Eat the Daisies; The Millionaire; The Sky Trap; Confessions of a Lady Cop; The World of Entertainment (guest host); It's My Tomorrow, Too; International Airport.

CRUISE, Tom: Act. b. Syracuse, NY., 1962. Films inc: Endless Love (bit); Taps; Losin' It; The Outsiders; Risky Business; All the Right Moves.

CRYSTAL, Billy: Act. b. Long Beach, NY, Mar 14, 1948. Films inc: Rabbit Test; Spinal Tap. TV inc: That Was The Year That Was; Death Flight; The Love Boat; Soap; Breaking Up Is Hard to Do; Enola Gay--The Men, The Mission, The Atomic Bomb; An NBC Family Christmas; The Billy Crystal Comedy Hour; Doug Henning's World of Magic; Saturday Night Live.

CRYSTAL, Lester M.: Exec. b. Duluth, MI, Sep 13, 1934. e. Northwestern U. P, NBC News Oct 5, 1977-April, 1983. Prior to that served as exec prod, NBC Nightly News; vp, special programming, NBC News: exec vp, NBC TV News; April 1983, resd to become exec prod McNeil/Lehrer report on PBS. TV inc: An Investigation of Teenage Drug Addiction *(Emmy*-prod-1970); Reports on World Hunger *(Emmy*-exec prod-1974); The Presidency and the Nation; Ask NBC News; America In Search of Itself (sr exec prod).

CUGAT, Xavier: Orch Ldr. b. Barcelona, Spain, Jan 1, 1900. Films inc: You Were Never Lovelier; Two Girls and a Sailor; Holiday in Mexico; This Time for Keeps; A Date with Judy; Neptune's Daughter; Chicago Syndicate.

CUKOR, George: Dir. b. NYC, Jul 7, 1899. Started as asst Stage M, Chicago, NY. In 1926 dir first Bway play, The Great Gatsby. Bway inc: The Dark; The Furies; A Free Soul; Young Love; Gypsy. To Hollywood in 1929 as dialogue dir for River of Romance; All Quiet on the Western Front; then co-dir Grumpy; The Virtuous Sin; The Royal Family of Broadway.
   Solo dir debut 1931, Tarnished Lady. Films inc: One Hour With You; What Price Hollywood?; A Bill of Divorcement; Dinner at Eight; Little Women; Susan and God; The Philadelphia Story; Two-Faced Woman; Her Cardboard Lover; A Double Life; Keeper of the Flame; Gaslight; Winged Victory; Adam's Rib; Edward My Son; A Life of Her Own; Born Yesterday; The Marrying Kind; Pat and Mike; The Actress; A Star Is Born; Les Girls; Wild Is the Wind; Song Without End; The Chapman Report; My Fair Lady *(Oscar-*1964); Justine; Travels With My Aunt; The Bluebird; Rich and Famous.
   TV inc: Love Among the Ruins *(Emmy-*1975); The Corn Is Green. (Died Jan 24, 1983).

CULLEN, Bill: Act. b. Pittsburgh, PA, Feb 18, 1920. e. U of Pittsburgh, BA. Started as radio announcer, Pittsburgh, then staff announcer for CBS, 1944. Game show host since the 50's. Shows inc: Where Was 1?; Place the Face; Hit the Jackpot; Give and Take; The Price is Right; I've Got a Secret; To Tell the Truth; $25,000 Pyramid; Blockbusters; Child's Play; Joker's Wild.

CULLEN, William Kirby: Act. b. Santa Ana, CA, Mar 9, 1952. TV inc: General Hospital; Portrait of a Teen-Age Alcoholic; The Force of Evil; How the West Was Won; Fugitive Family.

CULLUM, John: Act-Singer. b. Knoxville, TN, Mar 2, 1930. e. U of TN. Bway inc: NY Shakespeare Festival Theatre in various roles; Camelot; Infidel Caesar; Hamlet; On a Clear Day You Can See Forever; The Man of La Mancha (matinees); 1776; Vivat! Vivat Regina!; Shenandoah *(Tony-*1975); The Elizabethans; On the 20th Century *(Tony-*1978); Private Lives; The Loves Of Anatol.
   Films inc: 1776; The Act.
   TV inc: Summer; Looking Back; Carl Sandburg--Echoes and Silences; Kennedy Center Tonight--Broadway To Washington; The Day After.

CULP, Robert: Act. b. Berkeley, CA, Aug 16, 1930. Films inc: P.T. 109; The Raiders; Sunday in New York; Rhino; The Hanged Man; Bob & Carol & Ted & Alice; Hickey and Boggs; Sky Riders; The Great Scout & Cathouse Thursday; Goldengirl; National Lampoon Goes to the Movies; Turk 182.
   TV inc: Trackdown; I Spy; Greatest Heroes of the Bible; Women in White; A Cry for Justice; The Dream Merchants; The Night the City Screamed; The Greatest American Hero; Killjoy; Thou Shalt Not Kill; Her Life as a Man; The Calendar Girl Murders; Brothers-In-Law; The Key To Rebecca.
   Thea inc: The Prescott Proposals; A Clearing in the Woods.

CULVER, Roland: Act. b. London, Aug 31, 1900. e. RADA. London stage debut 1925 with the Greater London Players. Thea inc: Gentlemen Prefer Blondes; The Stranger Within; Dance With No Music; An

Ideal Husband; Who Is Sylvia?; The Deep Blue Sea; The Little Hut; Five Finger Exercise; Sergeant Dower Must Die; His, Hers, and Theirs; The Bedwinner; Hamlet.
   Films inc: French Without Tears; To Each His Own; The Greek Tycoon.
   TV inc: The Pallisers; The Word; The Hunchback of Notre Dame. (Died Feb. 29, 1984).

CUMBUKA, Ji-Tu: Act. b. Montgomery County, AL, Mar 4. e. Columbia Coll, MA. Films inc: Uptight; Bound for Glory; Mandingo; Fun With Dick and Jane; Walk Proud.
   TV inc: Roots; Young Dan'l Boone; A Man Called Sloane; Night of the Wizard; Flesh and Blood; Death Ray 2000; The Cracker Brothers.

CUMMINGS, Constance (nee Halverstadt): Act. b. Seattle, WA, May 15, 1910. NY stage debut, 1928, in chorus of Treasure Girl. On screen from 1931. Films inc: The Criminal Code; The Guilty Generation; Movie Crazy; Channel Crossing; Glamour; Looking for Trouble; Remember Last Night?; Blithe Spirit; John and Julie; In the Cool of the Day; Battle of the Sexes; A Boy 10 Feet Tall.
   TV inc: Touch of the Sun; The Last Tycoon; Ruth; Late Summer; Wings.
   Bway inc: This Man's Town; June Moon; Accent on Youth; Young Madame Conti; Madame Bovary; If I Were You; Goodbye Mr. Chips; The Jealous God; Saint Joan; The Petrified Forest; The Shrike; Trial and Error; Lysistrata; Fallen Angels, Hamlet; The Milk Train Doesn't Stop Here Any More; The Visit; Children; Stripwell; The Cherry Orchard; Wings *(Tony-*1979).

CUMMINGS, Jack: Prod. b. New Bedford, Canada, Feb 16, 1905. Films inc: The Winning; Born to Dance; Go West; Ship Ahoy; Bathing Beauty; Neptune's Daughter; Three Little Words; The Last Time I Saw Paris; Romance of Rosy Ridge; The Stratton Story; Lovely to Look At; Kiss Me Kate; Seven Brides for Seven Brothers; Interrupted Melody; Many Rivers to Cross; The Teahouse of the August Moon; The Blue Angel; Can Can; Bachelor Flat; Viva Las Vegas.

CUMMINGS, Quinn: Act. b. Los Angeles, Aug 13, 1967. Discovered by cin. James Wong Howe, first work in TV commercials. TV inc: Big Eddie; Intimate Stranger; Night Terror; The Dancing Bear; Family; The Incredible Book Escape; The Baby Sitter; Grandpa, Will You Run With Me; Hail To The Chief.
   Films inc: The Goodbye Girl.

CUMMINGS, Robert: Act. b. Joplin, MO, Jun 9, 1910. e. Drury Coll; Carnegie Tech; AADA. Films inc: The Virginia Judge; Last Train from Madrid; Three Smart Girls Grow Up; The Devil and Mrs. Jones; It Started with Eve; King's Row; Saboteur; The Bride Wore Boots; Heaven Only Knows; The Accused; Paid in Full; Dial M for Murder; My Geisha; What a Way to Go; The Carpetbaggers; Promise Her Anything; Stagecoach; Five Golden Dragons.
   TV inc: The Bob Cummings Show; My Hero; Twelve Angry Men *(Emmy-*1954).

CUNNINGHAM, Sean S.: Dir. Films inc: Together; The Case of the Smiling Stiffs; Sex on the Groove Tube; Here Come the Tigers; Friday the 13th; A Stranger Is Watching; Spring Break (& prod); The New Kids (& prod).

CURB, Mike: Exec. b. Savannah, GA, Dec 24, 1944. Began as jingle wri; formed Sidewalk Prodns, handling mus dir, prodn for records and films inc Mondo Hollywood; 1968 sold Sidewalk Prodns to Transcontinental Investing for $2,000,000, became P MGM Records; created Mike Curb Congregation; 1974 formed Mike Curb Prodns, organized Warner-Curb Records; 1979 elected Lt-Gov CA; formed Elektra/Curb Records and Mike Curb Records.

CURBISHLEY, Bill (William George Curbishley): Prod. b. London, Mar 13, 1942. Trinifold Ltd., William Tell Music Publishing Ltd.; Manager of 'The Who' for seven years; became film prod 1979.
   Films inc: Quadrophenia; The Kids Are Alright (doc); McVicar.
   TV inc: The Who--The Final Concert (exec prod) (PPV).

CURRLIN, Lee: Exec. b. NY. e. CCNY; Hofstra U. Started with Benton & Bowles advertising agency; joined CBS-TV in 1968 as dir of mktg; subsequently vp, sales admn; joined NBC in July, 1978 as vp, broadcast planning; appointed vp, program planning, NBC Entertainment, March 1979.

CURTIN, Jane: Act. b. Cambridge, MA, Sep 6, 1947. e. Northeastern U. Thea inc: Proposition (improvisational group); Last of the Red Hot Lovers (tour); Pretzels (off-Bway); Bway inc: Candida.

TV inc: Saturday Night Live; 30 Years of TV Comedy's Greatest Hits; Divorce Wars--A Love Story; Candida (cable); The Coneheads (voice); Kate & Allie *(Emmy-1984)*.

Films inc: Mr. Mike's Mondo Video; How To Beat the High Cost of Living.

CURTIN, Valerie: Act. Films inc: Alice Doesn't Live Here Anymore; All The President's Men; Silver Streak; Silent Movie; And Justice For All (wri); Why Would I Lie?; Inside Moves (wri); Best Friends (wri); Unfaithfully Yours (wri).

TV inc: A Christmas Without Snow (wri); 9 to 5.

CURTIS, Dan: Prod-Dir. b. Bridgeport, CT, Aug 12, 1928. e. Syracuse U, BA. Started as sales exec with NBC, later with MCA; formed Dan Curtis Productions. Films inc: House of Dark Shadows; Night of Dark Shadows; Burnt Offerings (& wri).

TV inc: (Prod) CBS Golf Classic from 1963-1973 (& owner); Dark Shadows; The Night Strangler; The Norliss Tapes; Dracula; Kolchak--The Night Stalker; When Every Day Was the Fourth of July; Melvin Purvis, G-Man; The Kansas City Massacre; The Great Ice Rip-Off; The Turn of the Screw; The Strange Case of Dr Jekyll and Mr Hyde; Trilogy of Terror; Mrs R's Daughter; Last Ride of the Dalton Gang; The Long Days of Summer; The Big Easy; The Winds of War.

CURTIS, Jamie Lee: Act. b. LA Nov 22, 1958. D of Janet Leigh and Tony Curtis. Films inc: Halloween; The Fog; Terror Train; Road Games; Halloween II; My Love Letters; Trading Places; Grandview, U.S.A.; Perfect.

TV inc: Operation Petticoat; She's In The Army Now; Death of A Centerfold--The Dorothy Stratten Story; Inside America; Callahan; Money On the Side; Coming Soon (host) (pay TV).

CURTIS, Keene: Act. b. Salt Lake City, UT, Feb 15, 1923. e. U of UT, MS. Stage mgr for Martha Graham Dance troupe; various plays; Alvin Ailey-Carmen DeLavallade Dance troupe; joined Association of Producing Artists, appearing in several plays over a 12 year period. Bway inc: Man and Superman; War and Peace; You Can't Take It With You; The Cherry Orchard; Cock-A-Doodle Dandy; Collision Course; A Patriot For Me; Indians; Colette; The Rothschilds *(Tony-supp-1971)*; Keene Curtis in A Ride Across Lake Constance; Annie (road); Division Street.

Films inc: Macbeth; Blade; American Hot Wax; Heaven Can Wait; Rabbit Test; The Buddy System.

TV inc: Unit 4; Private Benjamin; The Smurf Springtime Special (voice); Modesty Blaise; There Goes the Neighborhood.

CURTIS, Ken (Curtis Gates): Act. b. Bent County, CO., Jul. 2, 1916. e. CO U. Staff singer on NBC Radio, later with Shep Fields, Tommy Dorsey orchs; after WW II worked with Sons of Pioneers group while launching act career. Films inc: Song of the Prairie; Rhythm Roundup; Singing on the Trail; Cowboy Blues; Lone Star Moonlight; Over the Santa Fe Trail; The Quiet Man; Call of the Forest; Rio Grande; Mister Roberts; The Searchers; Wings of Eagles; The Last Hurrah; The Horse Soldiers; Escort West; My Dog Buddy; How the West Was Won; The Alamo; Two Rode Together; Cheyenne Autumn; Pony Express Rider.

TV inc: Gunsmoke (11 years); Ripcord; The Yellow Rose.

CURTIS, Tony (Bernard Schwartz): Act. b. NYC, Jun 3, 1926. Films inc: Criss Cross; Winchester 73; Son of Ali Baba; Houdini; Six Bridges to Cross; The Square Jungle; Trapeze; Sweet Smell of Success; The Defiant Ones; Some Like It Hot; Spartacus; Taras Bulba; Captain Newman, M.D.; The Boston Strangler; Lepke; The Last Tycoon; The Bad News Bears Go to Japan; The Manitou; Sextette; Title Shot; Little Miss Marker; The Mirror Crack'd; Othello (Black Commando); Brain-Waves; Where Is Parsifal?; Insignificance; King Of The City.

TV inc: The Persuaders; Second Girl on the Right; Vega$; Centerfold-Playboy's 25th Anniversary Celebration; Moviola-The Scarlett O'Hara War; Inmates--A Love Story; The Million Dollar Face; Portrait of A Showgirl; Half Nelson.

CUSACK, Cyril: Act. b. Durban, S Africa, Nov 26, 1910. e. University Coll Dublin. Joined Abbey Theatre, Dublin 1932, appearing in approximately 75 prodns; London debut Ah, Wilderness.

Thea inc: Playboy of the Western World; The Plough and the Stars; Les Parents Terribles; The Doctors Dilemma; Pommy; formed own company presenting several classics and premiere of O'Casey's The Bishop's Bonfire. Bway inc: A Moon for the Misbegotten.

Films inc: Odd Man Out; The Blue Lagoon; The Blue Veil; Soldiers Three; The Man Who Never Was; Jacqueline; Shake Hands with the Devil; Waltz of the Toreadors; The Spy Who Came in From the Cold; Fahrenheit 451; Oedipus the King; Galileo; David Copperfield; The Day of the Jackal; The Homecoming; True Confessions; 1984; Dr. Fischer Of Geneva.

TV inc: The Big Toe; Moon in the Yellow River; Deirdre; The Golden Bowl; Cry of the Innocent; Strumpet City (cable); The Comedy of Errors; Two By Forsyth.

CUSACK, Sinead: Act. b. Ireland, Feb 18, 1948. e. Dublin U. D of Cyril Cusack. Thea debut at age 12 in The Importance of Mr. O. Other thea inc: The Changeling; The Silence of St. Just; Romeo and Juliet; London Assurance; The Glass Menagerie; Othello; Arms and the Man; Wild Oats; Children of the Sun; As You Like It; The Maid's Tragedy; Twelfth Night. Bway inc: Cyrano de Bergerac; Much Ado About Nothing.

Films inc: Alfred the Great; Hoffman; The Last Remake of Beau Geste.

TV inc: The Shadow of a Gunman; Trilby; Twelfth Night.

CUSHING, Peter: Act. b. Kenley, Surrey, England, May 26, 1913. Films inc: Vigil in the Night; Moulin Rouge; The Black Knight; Hamlet; Alexander the Great; The Curse of Frankenstein; The Abominable Snowman; Dracula; John Paul Jones; The Hound of the Baskervilles; The Revenge of Frankenstein; Cone of Silence; The Naked Edge; Cash on Demand; The Man Who Finally Died; The Frightened Island; Torture Garden; Some May Live; Scream and Scream Again; The House That Dripped Blood; Tales From the Crypt; Fear in the Night; Horror Express; Frankenstein and the Monster from Hell; The Revenge of Dr. Death; Golden Vampires; The Ghoul; Legend of the Werewolf; The Devil's People; Trial by Combat; At the Earth's Core; Land of the Minotaur; Shock Waves; Star Wars; Battleflag; The Uncanny; Count Dracula and His Vampire Bride; The 7 Brothers Meet Dracula; Arabian Adventure; Shock Waves; Monster Island; The House of Long Shadows; Top Secret; Sword Of The Valiant.

TV inc: Asmodee; Anastasia; 1984; Gaslight; Home at Seven; Tovarich; Beau Brummell; Epitaph for a Spy; Pride and Prejudice; The Moment of Truth; The Browning Version; The Winslow Boy; Julius Caesar; Monica; Sherlock Holmes; Orson Welles Great Mysteries; Space 1999; The New Avengers; The Great Houdini; A Tale of Two Cities; Helen Keller--The Miracle Continues.

DABNEY, Augusta: Act. b. Berkeley, CA., Oct. 23. e. U CA Berkeley (BA); AADA. W of William Prince. Thea inc: Abe Lincoln In Illinois; Dear Ruth; Another Love Story; Return Engagement; Everything In The Garden; Seascape; Children Of A Lesser God.

TV inc: Young Doctor Malone; A World Apart; The Guiding Light; As The World Turns; Another World; One Life To Live; General Hospital; The Doctors; Loving; Love Is A Many Splendored Thing; The Best Of Families; F.D.R., The Last Years.

Films inc: That Night; Plaza Suite; Heartbreak Kid; Cold River; Montgomery Clift.

Da COSTA, Morton (nee Tecosky): Dir-Act. b. Philadelphia, Mar 7, 1914. e. Temple U, BS. Bway inc: (act) The Skin of Our Teeth; War President; It's a Gift; Hamlet; Man and Superman (dir): Captain Brassbound's Conversion; Dream Girl; The Wild Duck; Dark Legend; The Grey-Eyed People; Plain and Fancy; No Time for Sergeants; Auntie Mame; The Music Man; Saratoga; The Wall; Hot Spot; To Broadway with Love; The Coffee Lover; Maggie Flynn; Show Me where the Good Times Are; The Women; Musical Jubilee; Doubles (dir).

Films inc: (dir) Auntie Mame; The Music Man; Island of Love.

DAHL, Arlene: Act. b. Minneapolis, MN, Aug 11, 1928. On radio at age 8. Broadway debut in Mr. Strauss Goes to Boston, 1946. On Screen from 1947. Films inc: My Wild Irish Rose; Reign of Terror; Three Little Words; Journey to the Center of the Earth; Kisses for My President; Land Raiders.

Bway inc: Applause; The King and I; Pal Joey; One Touch of Venus; Liliom; Blithe Spirit.

DAHL, Roald: Wri. b. Norway, 1916. Films inc: Chitty Chitty Bang Bang; You Only Live Twice; Willy Wonka and the Chocolate Factory; Hair.

DAILEY, Irene: Act-Teacher. b. NYC, Sep 12, 1920. e. Actors Studio. Sis of late Dan Dailey. Founder, artistic dir School of the Actors Company. Bway inc: Nine Cards; Truckline Cafe; Idiot's Delight; Good Woman of Setzuan; Miss Lonely hearts; Andorra; The Subject Was Roses; Rooms; The Effect Gamma Rays on Man-In-the Moon Marigolds; You Know I Can't Hear You When the Water's Running. Other thea inc: Tomorrow--With Pictures (London); Laughing Water (tour); Skylark (tour); various stock appearances. Films inc: Five Easy Pieces; The Grissom Gang; No Way To Treat A Lady; Daring Game; The Amityville Horror. TV inc: Robert Montgomery Presents; Another World *(Emmy-*1979).

DAKIN, A Douglas: Exec. b. Gloucester, England, Apr 20, 1913. 1932 extra casting dir Fox; 1943-1960 chief casting dir Central Casting; 1960-1975 gm Central Casting. Ret. 1975.

DALE, Jim (nee Smith): Act. b. Rothwell, Northants, England, Aug 15, 1935. Made debut as solo comedian, 1951, at the Savoy. Joined National Theatre Company at the Old Vic. Appeared in numerous plays, touring Europe and appearing in NY in The Taming of the Shrew; Scapino (& co-dir & mus); Barnum *(Tony-*1980).

Films inc: Raising the Wind; Carry On Spying; Carry On Cleo; The Big Job; Carry On Cowboy; Carry on Screaming; Lock Up Your Daughter; The National Health; Digby; Joseph Andrews; Pete's Dragon; Unidentified Flying Oddball; Scandalous.

TV inc: 39th Annual Tony Awards.

DALEY, Robert H: Prod. Films inc: Dirty Harry; Play Misty For Me; Joe Kidd; High Plains Drifter; Breezy; Magnum Force; Thunderbolt and Lightfoot; The Eiger Sanction; The Outlaw Josey Wales; The Enforcer; The Gauntlet; Every Which Way But Loose; Escape from Alcatraz; Bronco Billy; Any Which Way You Can; Stick (exec prod).

DALIO, Marcel: Act. b. Paris, 1900. Films inc: La Grande Illusion; Pepe le Moko; La Regle du Jeu; Unholy Partners; Casablanca; The Song of Bernadette; Wilson; A Bell for Adano; To Have and Have Not; On the Riviera; The Happy Time; The Snows of Kilimanjaro; Sabrina Fair; Miracle in the Rain; Pillow Talk; Can Can; Jessica; Wild and Wonderful; Lady L; The 25th Hour; How Sweet It is; Catch 22; The Great White Hope; The Mad Adventures of Rabbi Jacob.

(Died Nov. 20, 1983).

DALRYMPLE, Ian Murray: Wri-Prod. b. England, Aug 26, 1903. e. Cambridge. Films inc: The Citadel; Pygmalion *(Oscar-*1938); The Lion Had Wings; Once a Jolly Swagman; The Woman in the Hall; The Wooden Horse; The Heart of the Matter; Three Cases of Murder; The Admirable Crichton; A Cry from the Streets.

DALRYMPLE, Jean: Prod. b. Morristown, NJ, Sep 2, 1910. Former act. Started play prodn 1945, Hope for the Best. Subsequently prod: Harvey; The Voice of the Turtle; The Second Man. In 1953 became Gen Dir, NY City Center Drama Company and the City Center Light Opera Company;

Thea inc: Cyrano de Bergerac; The Shrike; King Lear; The Teahouse of the August Moon; The Glass Menagerie; The Beggar's Opera; Brigadoon; The Pajama Game; South Pacific; Porgy and Bess; Oklahoma; Pal Joey; The King and I; My Fair Lady; West Side Story; Kiss Me Kate.

Films inc: The Children of Theatre Street (doc).

DALTON, Abby: Act. b. Las Vegas, NV, Aug 15, 1932. TV inc: Belle Starr; Hennesey; The Jonathan Winters Show; The New Joey Bishop Show; Hollywood Squares; Storybook Squares; Falcon Crest.

Films inc: Viking Women; Cole Younger, Gunfighter; Rock All Night; Plainsman.

DALTON, Timothy: Act. b. Colwyn Bay, Wales, Mar 21, 1946. Films inc: The Lion in Winter; Cromwell; The Voyeur; Wuthering Heights; Mary, Queen of Scots; Permission to Kill; Sextette; Agatha; Flash Gor-

don; Chanel Solitaire.

TV inc: Five Finger Exercise; Candida; Centennial; The Flame is Love; The Master of Ballantrae; Mistral's Daughter; Florence Nightingale.

Thea inc: (London) Shakespeare's Rome.

DALTREY, Roger: Singer-Act. b. London, Mar 1, 1944. Lead Voc with The Who.

Films inc: Woodstock; Tommy; Lisztomania; The Legacy; The Kids Are Alright; McVicar (& prod); The Beggar's Opera;

TV inc: The Comedy of Errors.

DALY, John: Prod. b. England 1937. Former journalist, became David Hemmings manager 1966, formed Hemdale Company, 1967, with Hemmings. P. Hemdale Film Company. Films inc: Sunburn; The Passage; Going Ape; Cattle Annie and Little Britches; High Risk; Dead Kids; Carbon Copy; Race to the Yankee Zephyr; Turkey Shoot; Yellowbeard; A Breed Apart; Deadly Force; The Terminator (exec prod); The Falcon And The Snowman (exec prod); The Return Of The Living Dead (exec prod).

DALY, John C: Newscaster-TV pers. b. Johannesburg, S Africa, 1914. Newsman and panel-show personality during the 50's and 60's; What's My Line? (moderator); VP in charge of news, special events and public affairs for ABC (1953-60). *(Emmy-*Commentator-1954). TV inc: We Take Your Word; News of the World; Critique.

DALY, Robert A.: Exec. b. NYC, Dec 8, 1936. e. Brooklyn Coll. Joined CBS TV in 1955; served successively as dir of program accounting; dir of research and cost planning; dir of business affairs, NY; vp, business affairs, NY; exec vp of the network on Apr 1976; named p, CBS Entertainment in Oct 1977; Nov 1980, co-chmn, co-CEO, WB.

DALY, Tyne: Act. b. Madison, WI, Feb 21. W of Georg Stanford Brown. D of late James Daly. Films inc: John and Mary; Angel Unchained; Play It as It Lays; The Entertainer; The Enforcer; Telefon; Speedtrap; Zoot Suit; The Aviator; Movers & Shakers.

Thea inc: Butter & Egg Man; The Summer, The Fall; Ashes; Three Sisters.

TV inc: Larry; Greatest Heroes of the Bible; Better Late Than Never; The Women's Room; A Matter of Life and Death; Cagney and Lacey *(Emmys-*1983, 1984); Your Place Or Mine.

DAMITA, Lili (nee Liliane Carre): Act. b. Bordeaux, France, Jan 10, 1904. Films inc: Le Prince Charmant (billed as Damita del Maillo Rojo); Maman Pierre; L'Empereur des Pauvres (billed as Lily Deslys); La Fille Sauvage; La Voyante (billed as Lily Damita); Das Speilzug von Paris; Fiaker Number 13; Der Goldene Schmetterling; Man Spielt Nicht Mit Der Liebe; The Rescue; the Bridge of San Luis Rey; The Cock Eyed World; Fighting Caravans; The Woman Between; Friends and Lovers; This is the Night; The Match King; Goldie Gets Along; Brewster's Millions; The Frisco Kid; The Devil on Horseback; L'Escadrille de le Chance.

DAMON, Cathryn: Act. b. Seattle, WA, Sep 11. TV inc: The Love Boat; Soap *(Emmy-*1980); The Hal Linden Special; Friendship, Secrets and Lies; Midnight Offerings; Not in Front of the Children; Who Will Love My Children?

Thea inc: The Secret Life of Walter Mitty; LA Under Siege; Siame; The Prodigal; L'Histoire Du Soldat; Criss-Crossing; Show Me Where the Good Times Are; Your Own Thing; The Effect of Gamma Rays on Man-in-the Moon Marigolds; Passion.

Films inc: How To Beat the High Cost of Living; The First Time.

DAMON, Mark: Exec. b. Chicago, April 22, 1933. e. UCLA (BA, BS, MA). Studied with Sanford Meisner at Neighborhood Playhouse. Originally an actor in several Hollywood films, moved to Italy 1961, appearing in more than 40 films; directed, wrote and prod several films with PAC, Italian distribution company before founding Producers Sales Organization; Nov. 1984, PSO and Delphi Comnpanies merged with Damon becoming chmn & CEO of PSO Delphi. Films inc: (act) Between Heaven and Hell; Fall Of The House Of Usher; The Young Racers; Son Of El Cid; Anzio; The Longest Day. (Exec prod): Das Boot (The Boat); The Neverending Story; The Clan Of The Cave Bear.

DAMON, Stuart: Act. (nee Zonis):b. NYC, Feb 5, 1937. e. Brandeis U. Thea inc: Irma La Douce; Entertain a Ghost; The Boys from Syracuse; Do I Hear a Waltz?; Houdini-Man of Magic; Macbeth; Cadenza; The Sunshine Boys.
TV inc: The Champions; Fantasies; General Hospital; I Love Men.

DAMONE, Vic (Vito Farinola): Act. b. NYC, Jun 12, 1928. Winner Arthur Godfrey talent show, 1945. Nightclubs, radio, theatres, hotels. Screen debut in Rich, Young and Pretty. Films inc: The Strip; Athena; Deep in My Heart; Hit the Deck; Kismet; From Hell to Eternity.
TV inc: The Vic Damone Show; The Lively Ones; All-Star Party For Frank Sinatra; Bob Hope's USO Christmas in Beirut.

DAMSKI, Mel: Dir. b. NYC, July 21, 1946. e. Colgate; AFI. Worked as reporter, journalism prof. TV inc: M*A*S*H; Lou Grant; Long Journey Back; The Child Stealer; A Perfect Match; Word of Honor; An American Dream; The Legend of Walks Far Woman; For Ladies Only; Making the Grade; An Invasion of Privacy; Attack on Fear.
Films inc: Yellowbeard; Mischief.

DANA, Bill: Act-Wri. b. Quincy, MA, 1924. Niteries, TV. Films inc: The Barefoot Executive; The Nude Bomb (& wri); Murder In Texas. TV inc: No Soap, Radio; I've Had It Up To Here; Zorro and Son.

DANA, Leora: Act. b. NYC, Apr 1, 1923. e. RADA. Stage debut London, 1947, Chiltern Hundreds. Returned to U.S. 1948. Bway inc: The Madwoman of Chaillot; Point of No Return; Sabrina Fair; The Milktrain Doesn't Stop Here Anymore; The Trojan Woman; A Place Without Mornings; The Last of Mrs Lincoln (Tony-supp-1973); Mourning Pictures.
Films inc: The 3:10 to Yuma; Kings Go Forth; Some Came Running; A Gathering of Eagles; The Norman Vincent Peale Story; Shoot the Moon; Baby It's You; Amityville 3-D.
TV inc: The Barretts of Wimpole Street; Rip Van Winkle; Nurse; Another World.
(Died Dec. 13, 1983).

DANA, Viola: Act. b. Brooklyn, Jun 26, 1897. Sis of Shirley Mason. On Bway in The Poor Little Rich Girl. Film debut in A Christmas Carol.
Films inc: The Flower of No Man's Land; Blue Jeans; The Winding Trail; A Weaver of Dreams; The Willow Tree; Merton of the Movies.
Briefly in vaudeville in a skit, The Ink Well, written by Anita Loos, after retiring from films with advent of sound.

DANDREA, Ron: Exec. b. Montreal, Feb 27, 1930. e. Loyola U. Former Bank of America vp; Chief financial officer Golden Harvest Group; May 1982, Sr VP Finance.

DANELIA, Georgi: Dir. b. Russia, Aug 25, 1930. e. Moscow Architectural Institute. Films inc: Seryozha; The Way to the Harbour; Walking the Streets of Moscow; 33; Don't Grieve; Hopelessly Lost; Afonya; Mimino; Autumn Marathon; Sliozy Kapali (Tears Are Flowing) (& wri).

DANGERFIELD, Rodney: Act. b. Babylon, NY, Nov. 22, 1921. Films inc: The Projectionist; Caddyshack; Easy Money (& wri). TV inc: Entertainer of the Year Awards; It's Not Easy Being Me, The Rodney Dangerfield Show (& wri); The Rodney Dangerfield Special-- I Can't Take It No More (& writing supv); Johnny Carson Presents The Tonight Show Comedians; Rodney Dangerfield Exposed (& wri).
Recs inc: No Respect (Grammy-comedy-1980).

DANIEL, Eliot: Comp-Lyr-Cond. b. Jan 7, 1910. Radio during 30s and 40s for Rudy Vallee Fleischmann Hour; Frank Morgan Show; Danny Thomas Show; Fibber McGee. TV inc: I Love Lucy (theme and all original music); September Bride; The Whiting Girls; Willy; Angel; various Bob Hope specials.
Films inc: with Disney in the 40s; then to 20th Century-Fox in 50s; later freelanced at Paramount, Columbia, RKO.
Songs for films inc: Lavender Blue; So Dear to My Heart; Never.

DANIELS, Billy: Act. b. Jacksonville, FL, Sep 12, 1915. Started as singing waiter; then band singer; niteries. Films inc: Cruising Down the River; Sunny Side of the Street; Rainbow Round My Shoulder. TV inc: The Big Operator; Night of the Quarter Moon; Beat Generation; All God's Children Got Rhythm.

Thea inc: Memphis Bound; Golden Boy; Norman, Is That You?; Hello, Dolly!; Bubbling Brown Sugar.

DANIELS, Charlie: Mus-Sngwri. b. NC, Oct 28, 1936. Began professional career in teens as guitarist in smalltown bars; organized the Jaquars; went to Nashville, began working as recording session musician for Bob Dylan, Flatt & Scruggs, Marty Robbins, Claude King, Pete Seeger, Ringo Starr before forming Charlie Daniels Band, 1971.
TV inc: Crystal; The Robert Klein Show.
Films inc: Heartworn Highways.
Recordings inc: Grease and Wolfman; Honey in Rock; Orange Blossom Special; Long Haired Country Boy; Night Rider; Saddle Tramp; High Lonesome; The South's Gonna Do It; Midnight Wind; Million Mile Reflection; Full Moon.
(Grammy-country vocal-1979).

DANIELS, Jeff: Act. b. GA, 1955. e. Central MI U. Thea inc: Brontosaurus; The Short-Changed Review; Minnesota Moon; The Farm; My Life; Fifth of July (Bway); Three Sisters; Johnnie Got His Gun; The Golden Age (Bway).
TV inc: A Rumor of War; Asking for it; Breaking Away; Catalina C-Lab; Invasion of Privacy; Fifth of July (cable).
Films inc: Ragtime; Terms of Endearment; The Purple Rose Of Cairo.

DANIELS, William: Act. b. Brooklyn, NY, Mar 31, 1927. e. Northwestern U, BS. Bway inc: The Zoo Story; Dear Me The Sky Is Falling; One Flew Over the Cuckoo's Nest; A Thousand Clowns; On A Clear Day You Can See Forever; Daphne in Cottage D.
Films inc: The Graduate; Two For the Road; The President's Analyst; 1776; A Thousand Clowns; Black Sunday; Oh, God!; The One and Only; Sunburn; The Blue Lagoon; All Night Long.
TV inc: A Case of Rape; One of Our Own; Sarah T--Portrait of a Teenage Alcoholic; The Adams Chronicles; Francis Gary Powers; The Bastard; Blind Ambition; The Rebels; City in Fear; Damien...The Leper Priest; Freebie and the Bean; The Million Dollar Face; The Wonderful World of Philip Malley; Rooster; Drop Out Father; St. Elsewhere.

DANKWORTH, John: Mus-Comp. b. England. H of Cleo Laine. Organized Johnny Dankworth Seven, debut London Palladium 1950; John Dankworth Band 1953; mus dir Nat "King" Cole; Buddy Greco; Mel Torme; Ella Fitzgerald; guest cond London Symphony, London Philharmonia; London Philharmonic; Los Angeles Philharmonic.
Films inc: (comp) We Are The Lambeth Boys; Saturday Night and Sunday Morning; The Servant; Darling; Morgan; The Idol; Perfect Friday; The Engagement; 10 Rillington Place; Modesty Blaise.
Thea inc: Midsummer Night's Dream; Twelfth Night; Colette.

DANN, Michael H (Mike): Exec. Began as comedy wri late 40's; moved to pub dept, later pgm dept CBS; 1958, vp NY pgms CBS; 1963, head of pgms; 1966, sr vp pgms; 1970, vp & asst to P of Childrens Television Workshop; 1979 consltnt to Disney on planned experimental prototype community; 1980 sr pgm advsr ABC Video Enterprises.

DANNER, Blythe: Act. b. Philadelphia, Feb 3, 1943. e. Bard Coll. Films inc: 1776; To Kill a Clown; Lovin' Molly; Hearts of the West; Futureworld; The Great Santini; Too Far To Go; Man, Woman and Child.
TV inc: Dr Cook's Garden; To Confuse the Angel; George M; To Be Young Gifted and Black; The Scarecrow; Adam's Rib; F Scott Fitzgerald and the Last of the Belles; Eccentricities of a Nightingale; Too Far to Go; You Can't Take It With You; Are You in the House Alone?; Inside the Third Reich; In Defense of Kids; Helen Keller--The Miracle Continues; Guilty Conscience.
Bway inc: Cyrano de Bergerac; Up Eden; The Miser; Butterflies Are Free (Tony-supp-1970); Major Barbara; The Seagull; Ring Around the Moon; Betrayal; The Philadelphia Story.

DANNING, Sybil: Act. b. Austria. Films inc: Bluebeard; The Three Musketeers; The Four Musketeers; Meteor; Operation Thunderbolt; The Man With Bogart's Face; Airport '79; Battle Beyond the Stars; Julie Darling; Chained Heat; The Salamander; Hercules; They're Playing With Fire; Jungle Warriors; The Day Of The Cobra; Private Passions; Young Lady Chatterley II; Howling II--Your Sister Is A Werewolf.
TV inc: Nightkill; A Man Called Sloan.

DANO, Royal: Act. b. NYC, Nov 16, 1922. Films inc: Undercover Girl; Red Badge of Courage; Bend of the River; The Far Country; Moby Dick; Never Steal Anything Small; The Adventures of Huckleberry Finn; Welcome to Hard Times; Death of a Gunfighter; The Undefeated; The Wild Party; The Outlaw Josey Wales; The Killer Inside Me; In Search of Historic Jesus; Hammett; Something Wicked This Way Comes; The Right Stuff; Teachers.

TV inc: Lights Out; Lost in Space; Death Valley Days; Planet of the Apes; How the West Was Won; Heroes of the Bible; The Raid on Coffeyville; Murder In Peyton Place; Greatest Heroes of the Bible; The Last Ride of the Dalton Gang; From Here to Eternity-The War Years; Will There Really Be A Morning?; Murder One--Dancer 0.

Thea inc: Finian's Rainbow; Three Wishes for Jaimey; Stalag 17; White Cargo.

DANOVA, Cesare: Act. b. Rome, Mar 1. Films inc: The Captain's Son; King of Kings; Tender Is the Night; Cleopatra; Gidget Goes to Rome; Boy, Did I Get a Wrong Number!; Che!; Mean Streets; Scorchy; Tentacles; National Lampoon's Animal House; Invisible Strangler (made in 1977 as The Astral Factor).

TV inc: The Magician; Police Story; The Manhunters; A Matter of Wife. . .and Death.

DANSON, Ted: Act. b. San Diego, Ca., Dec. 29, 1947. e. Stanford U.; Carnegie Tech. Thea inc: The Real Inspector Hound; Status Quo Vadis.

TV inc: The Doctors; Somerset; The Women's Room; Once Upon a Spy; Cheers; Cowboy; Allison Sidney Harrison; Something About Amelia.

Films inc: Body Heat; Creepshow; Little Treasure.

DANTE, Nicholas: Plywri. b. NYC, Nov 22, 1941. Originally a dancer, worked summer stock. Bway inc: I'm Solomon; Applause.

Plays inc: A Chorus Line *(Pulitzer Prize & Tony-1976).*

DANTON, Ray: Act. b. NYC, Sep 19, 1931. Began as radio actor; in summer stock. Films inc: Chief Crazy Horse; The Looters; The Spoilers; The Night Runner; Onionhead; Legs Diamond; Majority of One; The George Raft Story; The Chapman Report; The Longest Day.

TV inc: (dir) Psychic Killer; Bender; Feel the Heat.

D'ANTONI, Philip: Prod-Dir. b. NYC, Feb 19, 1929. e. Fordham U. Films inc: Bullitt; The French Connection *(Oscar-1971);* The Seven Ups.

TV inc: Elizabeth Taylor in London; Sophia Loren in Rome; Melina Mercouri in Greece; This Proud Land; Movin' On; Mr Inside/Mr Outside; Strike Force; The Connection.

DANZA, Tony: Act. b. Brooklyn, NY, Apr 21, 1951. e. U Dubuque. TV inc: Fast Lane Blues; Taxi; Just Men; Who's The Boss?; Single Bars, Single Women; The Real Trivial Pursuit; 99 Ways To Attract The Right Man.

Films inc: The Hollywood Knights; Going Ape!

DANZIGER, Maia: Act. b. NYC, Apr 12. e. NYU. Thea inc: Milk of Paradise; Total Eclipse; The Little Foxes; Waltz of the Toreadors (Bway).

TV inc: My Body, My Child; Sooner or Later; Another World; Love Is A Many Splendored Thing; The Late Great Me--Story of a Teenage Alcoholic *(Emmy-1980);* The Doctors.

Films inc: The Magician of Lublin.

DARBY, Ken: Comp-Lyr-Cond-Arr. b. Hebron, NE, May 13, 1909. e. Chapman Coll. Originated the King's Men, male quartet, 1929, appearing on radio, TV, films, records; leader arr. Ken Darby Singers; asso mus supv, cond. for films inc: The Wizard of Oz; Elmer Gantry; The King and I *(Oscar-1956);* South Pacific; Porgy and Bess *(Oscar-1959);* Camelot *(Oscar-1967);* Finian's Rainbow; The Great Bank Robbery; Airport.

Songs inc: Barbie; This Friendly World; Forever Hold Me; The Story of Christmas; Whispering Wind; How the West Was Won; No Goodbye; Come Share My Life; Daniel Boone Theme for TV.

(Grammy-soundtrack-1959).

DARBY, Kim (Deborah Zerby): Act. b. Los Angeles, Jul 8, 1948. Films inc: Bus Riley's Back in Town; True Grit; Generation; Norwood;

The Strawberry Statement; The Grissom Gang; The One and Only.

TV inc: Eleventh Hour; Gunsmoke; Flesh and Blood; Flatbed Annie & Sweetiepie-Lady Truckers; The Last Convertible; Enola Gay--The Men, The Mission, The Atomic Bomb; The Capture of Grizzly Adams; Summer Girl; First Steps.

DARC, Mireille: Act. b. Toulon, France, May 15, 1940. Films inc: Galia; Du Rififi a Paname; Weekend; Jeff; The Blonde from Peking; There Was Once a Cop; Return of the Big Blonde; Le Telephone Rose; Man In A Hurry; Les Passagers; Mort d'un Pourri (Death Of A Corrupt Man); Reveillon Chez Bob (New Year's Eve At Bob's).

Thea inc: Chapitre II (Chapter 2).

DARCEL, Denise (nee Billecard): Act. b. Paris, 1925. Films inc: To the Victor; Battleground; Tarzan and the Slave Girl; Westward the Women; Dangerous When Wet; Flame of Calcutta; Vera Cruz; Seven Women from Hell.

DARDEN, Severn: Act. b. Nov 9, 1929. Films inc: Dead Heat on a Merry-Go-Round; The President's Analyst; Luv; Pussycat, Pussycat I Love You; Vanishing Point; The Hired Hand; Cisco Pike; The War Between Men and Women; Who Fears the Devil; Wanda Nevada; Why Would I Lie?; In God We Trust; Saturday the 14th.

TV inc: Love for Rent; Orphan Train; A Cry For Love; Evita Peron; Homeroom; Quarterback Princess; The Cowboy And The Ballerina; Half Nelson.

DARION, Joe: Lyr. b. NYC Jan. 30, 1917. e. CCNY. Plays inc: Shinbone Alley; Man of La Mancha *(Tony-*1966); Ilya Darling.

Songs inc: Ricochet Romance; Changing Partners; Midnight Train; The Impossible Dream.

DARLING, Joan (nee Kugell): Dir-Act. b. Apr 14, 1935. TV inc: (dir) Mary Hartman, Mary Hartman; Chuckles Bites the Dust; Phyllis; Doc; Rhoda; Rich Man, Poor Man; M*A*S*H; The Nurses; Mom's On Strike. (Perf): Frieda; Owen Marshal; Margret; Viola; The Two Worlds of Jenny Logan; The Wedding; a.k.a. Pablo.

Films inc: (perf) The Troublemaker; The President's Analyst; Fearless Frank; Kansas City Bomber; Sunnyside; First Love (dir).

DARREN, James: Act. b. Philadelphia, Jun 8, 1936. Films inc: Rumble on the Docks; The Brothers Rico; The Guns of Navarone; Gidget Goes Hawaiian; The Lively Set; Venus in Furs.

TV inc: Turnover Smith; Scruples; T.J. Hooker.

DARRIEUX, Danielle: Act. b. Bordeaux, France, May 1, 1917. Film debut age 14 in Le Bal. Films inc: Chateau de Reve; Volga en Flammes; Dede; Le Domino Vert; Mademoiselle Mozart; Mayerling; Club des Femmes; I Give My Life; Tarass Boulba; Abused Confidence; Mademoiselle Ma Mere; The Rage of Paris; Katia; Battements de Coeur; Premier Rendezvous; Caprices; Ruy Blas; Oh, Amelia; La Ronde; Rich, Young and Pretty; Le Plaisir; Five Fingers; Adorable Creatures; The Earrings of Madame De...; Le Rouge et le Noir; Alexander the Great; Lady Chatterley's Lover; Typhon sur Nagasaki; Night Affair; Marie-Octobre; The Greengage Summer; Bluebeard; 24 Hours in a Woman's Life; Friend of the Family; Le Coup de Grace; The Young Girls of Rochefort; Birds of Peru; A House in the Country; The Lonely Woman; Divine; Une Chambre en Ville (A Room in Town); En Haut des Marches (At the Top of the Stairs).

Bway inc: Coco; Ambassador. Other thea inc: Gigi (Paris).

Da SILVA, Howard (nee Silverblatt): Act. b. Cleveland, OH, May 4, 1909. e. Carnegie Tech. Steel worker prior to joining Civic Repertory Theatre, NY 1929. Remained with CRT five years appearing in The Would Be Gentleman; The Green Cockatoo; The Three Sisters; The Cherry Orchard.

Bway inc: Ten Million Ghosts; Golden Boy; The Cradle Will Rock; Casey Jones; Abe Lincoln in Illinois; Two on an Island; Oklahoma!; Burning Bright; The World of Sholem Aleichem (& dir-coprod); The Adding Machine; Volpone; Fiorello!; Compulsion; Purlie Victorious (dir); Dear Me, The Sky is Falling; The Zulu and the Zayda (co-auth); My Sweet Charlie (dir); 1776.

Films inc: I'm Still Alive; Abe Lincoln in Illinois; Sea Wolf; Big Shot; Omaha Trail; Tonight We Raid Calais; Lost Weekend; Two Years Before the Mast; Duffy's Tavern; Unconquered; Blaze of Noon; They Live By Night; Tripoli; Underworld Story; Three Husbands; 14 Hours;

M; David and Lisa; 1776; The Great Gatsby; Mommie Dearest; Garbo Talks.

TV inc: Walter Fortune; For the People; Missiles of October; Stop, Thief; Smile Jenny, You're Dead; Hollywood on Trial; Verna--USO Girl (Emmy-supp-1978); When the Boat Comes In (host); Power; Masquerade; The Cafeteria.

DASSIN, Jules: Dir-Wri. b. Middletown, CT, Dec 18, 1911. H of Melina Mercouri. Started as actor on stage. Joined MGM 1941 as dir. Films inc: Nazi Agent; The Affairs of Martha; The Canterville Ghost; A Letter for Evie; Brute Force; Naked City; Thieves Highway; Rififi (& sp-act); He Who Must Die (& sp); Where the Hot Wind Blows (& sp); Never on Sunday (& sp-act); Phaedra (& sp); Topkapi; 10:30 P M Summer (& sp); Survival; Uptight (& sp); Promise at Dawn (& sp-act); A Dream of Passion (& prod-sp); Circle of Two; Keine Zufallige Geschichte (Not By Coincidence) (doc) (act).

Bway: Magdalena (dir); Ilya, Darling (wri-dir).

DAVENPORT, Nigel: Act. b. Cambridge, England, May 23, 1928. e. Trinity Coll, Oxford. Thea inc: Relative Values; The Country Wife; The Mulberry Bush; The Crucible; The Death of Satan; Cards of Identity; Good Woman of Setzuan; Epitaph for George Dillon; A Resounding Tinkle; A Taste of Honey; Bonne Soupe; Incident at Vichy; Notes on a Love Affair; Three Sisters; Cowardice.

Films inc: Peeping Tom; A High Wind in Jamaica; Where the Spies Are; A Man For All Seasons; Royal Hunt of the Sun; The Virgin Soldiers; A Last Valley; No Blade of Grass; Villain; Living Free; Mary, Queen of Scots; The Island of Dr. Moreau; Zulu Dawn; Nighthawks; Chariots of Fire; Den Tuechtigen Gehort die Welt (The Uppercrust); Strata; Greystoke--The Legend of Tarzan, Lord of the Apes.

TV inc: South Riding; Dracula; Oil Strike North; Phase IV; The Ordeal of Dr. Mudd; Cry of the Innocent; Masada; A Midsummer Night's Dream; A Christmas Carol.

DAVID, Hal: Lyr. b. May 25, 1921. e. NYU. B of Mack David. Songs inc: American Beauty Rose; My Heart is an Open Book; Magic Moments; Blue on Blue; Walk On By; Any Old Time of Day; The First Night of the Full Moon; There's Always Something To Remind Me; Trains and Boats and Planes; What The World Needs Now Is Love; The Look of Love; Raindrops Keep Fallin on My Head (Oscar-1969). Film title songs inc: Wives and Lovers; A House is Not a Home; Send Me No Flowers; Alfie; What's New Pussycat; Promise Her Anything; Moonraker.

(Grammy-cast album-1969).

DAVID, Mack: Comp. b. NYC, Jul 5, 1912. e. Cornell U; St Johns U Law School. Film scores inc: Cinderella; At War with the Army; Sailor Beware; Jumping Jacks.

Songs inc: Falling Leaves; A Sinner Kissed an Angel; Lili Marlene; Spellbound; Chi-Baba Chi-Baba; La Vie en Rose; Bibbidi Bobbidi Boo; I Don't Care if the Sun Don't Shine; It Only Hurts for a Little While; My Wishing Doll; To Me.

Film title songs inc: The Hanging Tree; Walk on the Wild Side; To Kill a Mockingbird; It's a Mad Mad Mad Mad World; Cat Ballou.

DAVID, Pierre: Exec prod. b. Montreal. e. U of Montreal. Taught in Rwanda, served in that country's communications dept. Joined radio station CJMS 1966 as pub relations & special events dir; 1968, formed CJMS Productions which became Mutual Productions, prodn-dist firm which is part owner of Filmplan Int'l; May 1983, P of Film Packages International; May, 1985, exec vp Larry A. Thompson Organization and P of motion picture division. Films inc: The Brood; Hog Wild; Scanners; Dirty Tricks; Gas; Visiting Hours; Videodrome; Going Berserk; Au nom de tous les Miens (For Those I Loved); Of Unknown Origin; Covergirl; Breaking All The Rules (coprod).

DAVID, Saul: Prod. b. NYC, Jun 27, 1921. Radio, newspaper work, editorial dir Bantam Books. With Col, 1960-62; WB, 1962-62; Fox, 1963-67; U, 1968-69; Exec story edtr MGM, 1972. Films inc: Von Ryan's Express; Our Man Flint; Fantastic Voyage; In Like Flint; Skullduggery; Logan's Run; Ravagers.

DAVIDSON, Boaz: Dir-wri. b. Tel Aviv, Aug 11, 1943. e. London Film School. 1979, VP Crea Aff Cannon Films. Films inc: Erostratus (short); It's A Funny, Funny World; Lupo Goes to New York; The Tzanani Family; Lemon Popsicle; Going Steady (Lemon Popsicle 2);

Hot Bubblegum (Lemon Popsicle 3); Seed of Innocence; Hospital Massacre (dir only); Last American Virgin; Hot Resort (wri only).

DAVIDSON, Gordon: Dir-Prod. b. NYC, May 7, 1933. e. Cornell U, BA; Case Western Reserve U, MA. Artistic dir Mark Taper Forum. Thea inc: Savages; In the Matter of J Robert Oppenheimer; Leonard Bernstein's Mass; Who's Happy Now?; Murderous Angels; Rosebloom; The Trial of the Catonsville Nine; The Shadow Box (Tony-1977); And Where She Stops Nobody Knows; Black Angel; Children of a Lesser God; Zoot Suit.

Films inc: The Trial of the Catonsville Nine; Zoot Suit (exec prod).

TV inc: Who's Happy Now?; Right To Kill? (coprod).

DAVIDSON, John: Act. b. Pittsburgh, Dec 13, 1941. Films inc: The Happiest Millionaire; The Concorde-Airport '79. TV inc: The Entertainer; The Fantasticks; The Interns; The Girl With Something Extra; The John Davidson Christmas Show; Dallas Cowboys Cheerleaders; That's Incredible! (host); The Carpenters-Music, Music, Music; 100 Years of Golden Hits (host); Goodbye, Charlie.

Bway inc: Foxy.

DAVIDSON, Martin: Dir. b. NYC, Nov 7, 1939. Films inc: The Lords of Flatbush (co-dir); Almost Summer (& sp); If Ever I See You Again (sp); Hero at Large; Eddie and the Cruisers (& sp).

DAVIS, Allan: Prod-Dir. b. London, Aug 30, 1913. e. Sydney U, Australia. Started as act; after WW2 service became asst-dir, later dir Bristol Old Vic. Thea inc: (London) Arabian Nightmare; The Shadow of Doubt; Breath of Spring; Joshua Tree; Fool's Paradise (& co-prod); A Shred of Evidence; The Bird of Time (& co-prod); The Big Killing; The Apricot Season; Honey, I'm Home; Did You Feel It Move?; The Sacred Flame (co-prod); The Night I Chased the Women With an Eel; Come As You Are (& co-prod); No Sex Please--We're British; Friends, Romans, and Lovers; Signs of the Times (& co-prod); A Touch of Spring (& co-prod); In The Red (& prod).

DAVIS, Ann B.: Act. b. Schenectady, NY, May 5, 1926. e. U MI, BA. With stock and repertory companies. Bway inc: Once Upon a Mattress.

TV inc: The Bob Cummings Show (Emmy-supp-1957, 1958, 1959); Keefe Brasselle Show; John Forsythe Show; The Brady Bunch; The Brady Brides.

DAVIS, Bette (Ruth Elizabeth Davis): Act. b. Lowell, MA, Apr 5, 1908. Performed in stock and repertory. Bway debut 1929, Broken Dishes. Film debut 1931, Bad Sister. Films inc: Seed; Waterloo Bridge; Way Back Home; The Man Who Played God; So Big; The Rich Are Always With Us; Three on a Match; 20,000 Years in Sing Sing; Bureau of Missing Persons; The Shakedown; Jimmy the Gent; Fog Over Frisco; Of Human Bondage; Bordertown; The Girl From Tenth Avenue; Front Page Woman; Dangerous (Oscar-1935); The Petrified Forest; The Golden Arrow; Satan Met A Lady; Kid Galahad; That Certain Woman; It's Love I'm After; Jezebel (Oscar-1938); The Sisters; Dark Victory; Juarez; The Old Maid; The Private Lives of Elizabeth and Essex; All This and Heaven Too; The Letter; The Bride Came C.O.D.; The Little Foxes; The Man Who Came to Dinner; Now Voyager; Watch on the Rhine; Thank Your Lucky Stars; Old Acquaintance; Mr. Skeffington; Hollywood Canteen; The Corn is Green; A Stolen Life; Deception; Winter Meeting; June Bride; Beyond the Forest; All About Eve; Payment on Demand; Phone Call from a Stranger; The Star; The Virgin Queen; The Catered Affair; Storm Center; A Pocketful of Miracles; What Ever Happened to Baby Jane?; Dead Ringer; Hush, Hush. . .Sweet Charlotte; The Nanny; The Anniversary; Bunny O'Hare; Madame Sin; Burnt Offerings; Return from Witch Mountain; Death on the Nile; The Watcher in the Woods; Right of Way.

TV inc: The Dark Secret of Harvest Home; Strangers-- The Story of a Mother and Daughter (Emmy-1979); White Mama; Skyward; Family Reunion; A Piano For Mrs. Cimino; American Film Institute Salute to Frank Capra; Natalie--Tribute To A Very Special Lady; Little Gloria--Happy At Last; An All-Star Party For Carol Burnett; Arthur Hailey's "Hotel"; Murder With Mirrors.

Toured U.S., Australia and New Zealand with "Bette Davis In Person and on Film".

DAVIS, Bill: Dir. b. Belleville, Ontario, Canada, Aug 13, 1931. e. Ryerson Inst of Tech. TV inc: Hullabaloo; Smothers Brothers; Hee Haw;

Jonathan Winters; Lennon Sisters; Julie Andrews Special (Emmy-1973); Herb Alpert; Lily Tomlin; Frank Sinatra; John Denver (Emmy-1975); Gabe Kaplan; Marlo Thomas; Omnibus; Opryland--Night of Stars and Future Stars; The Nashville Palace; Johnny Cash--A Merry Memphis Christmas; Anka; National Snoop; Super Stars and Classic Cars; TV's Bloopers and Practical Jokes.

DAVIS, Brad: Act. b. Nov 6, 1949. e. AADA. Films inc: Midnight Express; A Small Circle of Friends; Chariots of Fire; The Wizard of Babylon (doc); Querelle.
TV inc: How To Survive A Marriage; Sybil; A Rumor of War; Roots; Mrs Reinhardt; Chiefs; Robert Kennedy & His Times.

DAVIS, Clifton: Act. b. Chicago, Oct 4, 1945. Films inc: Scott Joplin.
TV inc: Little Ladies of the Night; The Clifton Davis Show; That's My Mama; The Night The City Screamed; Don't Look Back.

DAVIS, Jimmie: Act. b. Quitman, LA, Sep 11, 1902. e. LA Coll, BA. Co-author western song standard You Are My Sunshine. Toured country as singer and guitarist. Twice elected governor of Louisiana.

DAVIS, Judy: Act. b. Australia, 1956. With Australian State Repertory Group. Thea inc: Piaf; Inside the Island; Insignificance; Lulu.
Films inc: High Rolling; My Brilliant Career; Heatwave; Hoodwink; The Winter of Our Dreams; Who Dares Wins; A Passage To India.
TV inc: Water Under the Bridge (Australia); A Woman Called Golda; The Merry Wives of Windsor.

DAVIS, Luther: Prod-Wri. b. NYC, Aug 29, 1921. e. Yale U. Films inc: (sp); The Hucksters; B.F.'s Daughter; Black Hand; A Lion Is in the Streets; The Gift of Love; Holiday for Lovers; The Wonders of Alladin; Across 110th St. (prod) Lady in the Cage.
Plays inc: Kismet (Tony-prod & co-author-1954); Timbuktu (prod & author). Other thea inc: Eden Court (prod).
TV inc: Arsenic and Old Lace; Bus Stop series; Daughters of the Mind; The Old Man Who Cried Wolf.

DAVIS, Mac: Act-Lyr. b. Lubbock, TX, Jan 21, 1942. Began as country-western sngwri; has written for Elvis Presley, Kenny Rogers, Andy Williams, Sammy Davis Jr, Dolly Parton.
Songs inc: In the Ghetto; Baby Don't Get Hooked On Me; One Hell of a Woman; I Believe in Music; Stop and Smell the Roses; Watching Scotty Grow; You're Good For Me; Friend, Lover, Woman, Wife; Daddy's Little Man; Something's Burning; I'll Paint You A Song; Everything a Man Could Ever Need; A Little Less Conversation; Memories; Don't Cry Daddy.
TV inc: Mac Davis Special--Christmas Odyssey; Kenny Rogers--The American Cowboy; Mac Davis--A Christmas Special With Love; The Mac Davis Show; The Monte Carlo Show; A Johnny Cash Christmas (1980); I'll Be Home For Christmas; The Mac Davis Christmas Special - Christmas Is A Song; The Merriest of the Merry--Bob Hope's Christmas Show--A Bagful of Comedy; Grandpa, Will You Run With Me? Country Comes Home (1983 host); Live--And in Person; The Mac Davis Special--The Music of Christmas; Brothers-In-Law.
Films inc: North Dallas Forty; Cheaper to Keep Her; The Sting II.

DAVIS, Madelyn Pugh: Wri. b. Indianapolis, IN. e. IN U. TV inc: I Love Lucy; Lucy; Here's Lucy; Mothers-in-Law; Lucille Ball Special; Alice (prod); Private Benjamin (exec prod).

DAVIS, Martin S.: Exec. b. NYC, Feb. 5, 1927. e. CCNY. Joined Samuel Goldwyn Prodns 1946; Allied Artist, 1955; moved to Paramount publicity dept. 1958; became Par ad-pub-exploitation dir 1960; became vp 1963; exec vp 1966; exec vp Gulf & Western 1967 after firm took over Paramount; March 1983, vice chmn, CEO of Gulf & Western.

DAVIS, Marvin: Exec. b. Newark, NJ, Aug 8, 1925. e. NYU. In family garment mfg. business; into oil business in 40's with Ray Ryan; first venture in film business in Jan 1981, formed Neufeld-Davis Productions with Mace Neufeld; June, 1981 acquired 20th Century-Fox, paying $724,681,000 for control of firm in partnership with Richco, commodities trading firm subsidiary of Marc Rich & Co.; March, 1982 formed Rifkin-Fox Communications in partnership with Monroe Rifkin; Oct. 1984, became sole owner of 20th Fox; April, 1985 sold 50% interest to Rupert Murdoch.

DAVIS, Miles: Mus-Comp. b. Alton, IL, May 25, 1926. e. Juilliard. With Charlie Parker and Benny Carter bands before solo.
Films inc: (scores) Elevator to the Gallows; Jack Johnson; Die Ruckseite des Mondes (The Other Side Of The Moon).
(Grammys-(3)-original comp-1960; jazz group-1970; jazz inst solo-1982).

DAVIS, Nancy: Act. b. NYC, Jul 6, 1921. W of Ronald Reagan. Films inc: Shadow on the Wall; The Doctor and the Girl; Night and Morning; It's a Big Country; Donovan's Brain; Crash Landing; Hellcats of the Navy.
TV inc: Diff'rent Strokes.

DAVIS, Ossie: Act-Wri-Dir. b. Cogdell, GA, 1917. e. Howard U. H of Ruby Dee. Stage debut with Rose McClendon Players in Harlem, 1941; Bway debut 1946, Jeb. Thea inc: (act) Anna Lucasta; The Washington Years; The Leading Lady; The Smile of the World; The Royal Family; Touchstone; Green Pastures; A Raisin in the Sun; Purlie Victorious (& wri).
Films inc: (act) The Scalphunters; The Slaves; The Hill; The Cardinal; Purlie Victorious; Avenging Angel. (Dir): Cotton Comes to Harlem; Kongi's Harvest; Black Girl; Gordon's War; Countdown at Kusini; Hot Stuff; Harry & Son.
TV inc: Teacher, Teacher; The Defenders; The Sheriff; The Tenth Level; King; Roots-The Next Generation; Freedom Road (narr); All God's Children; With Ossie and Ruby; Don't Look Back; For Us, The Living (wri); Blacks--Present and Accounted For (host).

DAVIS, Phyllis: Act. b. Nederland, TX, Jul 17, 1940. Films inc: Day of the Dolphin; The Choirboys.
TV inc: Love American Style; Vega$; Knight Rider (pilot); The Wild Women of Chastity Gulch; Mr. Mom.

DAVIS, Sammy, Jr: Perf. b. NYC, Dec 8, 1925. On stage at age 2 in act with father, uncle, Will Mastin. Bdwy inc: Mr. Wonderful; Golden Boy. Niteries.
Films inc: Anna Lucasta; Porgy & Bess; Ocean's 11; Robin and the Seven Hoods; Salt and Pepper; A Man Called Adam; Sweet Charity; One More Time; Sammy Stops The World; The Cannonball Run; Bonjour Monsieur Lewis (doc); Heidi's Song (voice); Cannonball Run II; That's Dancing!
TV inc: The Sammy Davis Jr. Show; Sammy and Company; Mod Squad; Name of the Game; The Trackers; One Life To Live; Funtastic World of Hanna-Barbera Arena Show (voice); Entertainer of the Year Awards; Bob Hope's All-Star Celebration Opening the Gerald R. Ford Museum; All Hands On Deck For Bob Hope's All-Star Birthday Party At Annapolis; Texaco Star Theatre--Opening Night; An All-Star Party for Carol Burnett; All-Star Party For Lucille Ball.

DAVIS, Skeeter (Mary Frances Penick): Act. b. Dry Ridge, KY, Dec 30, 1931. C & W rec artist. Started as teenager; formed duo, The Davis Sisters; went solo in 1955; regular on Nashville's Grand Ole Opry; performed at Carnegie Hall, 1950.

DAWBER, Pam: Act. b. Detroit, MI, Oct 18, 1951. Films inc: A Wedding. TV inc: Sister Terri; Mork & Mindy; The Girl, The Gold Watch and Everything; Twilight Theatre; Texaco Star Theatre--Opening Night; Remembrance of Love; Through Naked Eyes; The Great Survivors; This Wife For Hire.

DAWSON, Richard: Act. b. Gosport, Hampshire, England, Nov 20, 1932. Films inc: The Devil's Brigade; King Rat; Munsters Go Home; Promises, Promises.
TV inc: The New Dick Van Dyke Show; Hogan's Heroes; I've Got a Secret; Match Game; Masquerade Party; Laugh-In; Family Feud. (Emmy-host-1978).

DAY, Dennis (Eugene Denis McNulty): Sing-Act. b. NYC, May 21, 1917. e. Manhattan Coll. Debut on Jack Benny radio show. Films inc: Buck Benny Rides Again; Music in Manhattan; One Sunday Afternoon; I'll Get By; Golden Girl; The Girl Next Door.

DAY, Doris (nee Kappelhoff): Act. b. Cincinnati, Apr 3, 1924. Toured as dancer, radio, band singer. Screen debut, Romance on the High Seas, 1948. Films inc: Young Man With a Horn; Tea for Two; On Moonlight Bay; I'll See You in My Dreams; By the Light of the Silvery

Moon; Calamity Jane; With Six You Get Eggroll; Where Were You When the Lights Went Out?; Glass Bottom Boat; Young at Heart; Love Me or Leave Me; Man Who Knew Too Much; Pajama Game; That Touch of Mink; Teacher's Pet; Pillow Talk; Please Don't Eat the Daisies; Midnight Lace; Lover Come Back; Jumbo; The Thrill of It All.

TV inc: The Doris Day Show.

DAY, Laraine (nee Johnson): Act. b. Roosevelt, UT, Oct 13, 1920. Screen debut Border G-Men, 1938. Films inc: Story of Dr. Wassell; Those Endearing Young Charms; Tycoon; My Son, My Son; The High and the Mighty; Mr. Lucky; Bride By Mistake; My Dear Secretary.

TV inc: Playhouse 90; Let Freedom Ring; The Name of the Game; Medical Center; Murder on Flight #504; Love Boat.

DAY, Linda: Dir. b. Los Angeles, Aug 12, 1938. TV inc: WKRP; Too Close for Comfort; Archie's Place; Benson; Insight; Alice; Insight/Missing Persons Bureau; After George.

DAY, Robert F.: Dir. b. England, Sep 11, 1922. Started as cin. Films (as dir) inc: The Haunted Strangler; The Green Man; First Man Into Space; Corridors of Blood; Bobbikins; Two-Way Stretch; The Rebel; Operation Snatch; Tarzan's Three Challenges; She; Tarzan and the Valley of Gold; Tarzan and the Great River; Tarzan, The Magnificent; The Man With Bogart's Face.

TV inc: The House on Greenapple Road; Ritual of Evil; In Broad Daylight; Mr. And Mrs. Bo Bo Jones; Reluctant Heroes; Banyon (pilot); Kodiak (pilot); Dan August (pilot); The Great American Beauty Contest; Sunshine (pilot); Death Stalk; Switch (pilot); Having Babies; Kingston (pilot); Logan's Run; Black Market Baby; The Grass is Always Greener Over the Septic Tank; Murder by Natural Causes; Dallas (pilot); Scruples; Marian Rose White; Pollyanna; Beyond Witch Mountain; Your Place Or Mine; China Rose; Cook and Peary--The Race to the Pole; London And Davis In New York; Hollywood Wives; The Lady From Yesterday.

DAYAN, Assaf: Act. b. Israel, 1945. Films inc: The Day the Fish Came Out; A Walk With Love and Death; Promise at Dawn; Fifty-Fifty (& Co-prod-sp); Saint Cohen (co-prod-dir-wri); The Sellout; Each Other; Operation Thunderbolt; The Uranium Conspiracy; Moments; Schlager (Hit Song) (wri-dir); Melech L'Yom Echad (King For A Day) (wri-dir); Bekhinath Bagruth (Finals) (wri-dir); Ad Sof Halayla (When Night Falls).

DEAN, Isabel (nee Hodgkinson): Act. b. England, May 29, 1918. London stage debut 1940, Peril at End House. Thea inc: All's Well that Ends Well; Witch Errant; Night of the Fourth; The Centaur; What the Butler Saw; Claw; The Fool; Half-Life; Dear Daddy; Ladies In Retirement.

Films inc: The Light in the Piazza; A High Wind in Jamaica; Inadmissible Evidence; Catch Me a Spy; Rough Cut; Five Days One Summer; The Weather in the Streets.

TV inc: The Quatermass Experiment; The Parachute; Sense and Sensibility.

DEAN, Jimmy: Sing. b. Plainview, TX, Aug 10, 1928. Hosted Morning Show, CBS-TV Washington; had own show NYC, later on ABC. TV inc: Texas and Tennessee--A Musical Affair.

Recs inc: Big Bad John (Grammy-C&W rec-1961); P.T. 109.

DEAN, Morton: TV news. b. Fall River, MA, Aug 22, 1935. e. Emerson Coll, BA. News for NY Herald Tribune radio net 1957; corr WBZ 1960; 1964 corr WCBS-TV; 1967 anchor WCBS-TV News; joined CBS News 1967 as corr; 1975 anchor CBS Sunday Night News; 1976 anchor Sunday edition CBS Evening News; also anchored Newsbreak; Jan. 1985 to Independent Network News as co-anchor.

TV inc: The Case of Plastic Peril; Vietnam--A War That is Finished; Energy--The Facts, The Fears, The Future; Pope John Paul II--The American Journey; Iran--A Week of Tumult; Space Shuttle--$14 Billion Question Mark; Louis is 13 (Emmy-corr-1981).

DEAS, Justin: Act. b. Connellsville, PA, Mar 30, 1948. e. William and Mary Coll; Juilliard. Thea inc: Julius Caesar; The November People (Bway); Grease (tour); Porno Stars at Home; Crimes of the Heart.

TV inc: Ryan's Hope; As the World Turns (Emmy-Supp-1984).

De BONT, Jan: Cin. b. Netherlands, Oct 22, 1943. e. Amsterdam Film Academy. Films inc: Turkish Delight; Keetje Tippel; Last Train; Joao; Paranoia; White Slave; The Family; Max Havelaar; Expresse; Dakota; What Do I See; Private Lessons; Roar; Cujo; All The Right Moves; Growing Pains; American Dreamer (addl photog); Flesh & Blood.

TV inc: Sadat; The Heart Of A Champion--The Ray Mancini Story.

De BROCA, Philippe: Dir. b. France, 1933. Films inc: Playing at Love; Infidelity; That Man From Rio (sp); Un Monsieur de Compagnie; Tribulations Chinoise en Chine; King of Hearts; Devil by the Tail; Give Her the Moon; Chere Louise; Le Magnifique; Dear Inspector (& sp); Le Cavaleur; Premier Voyage; Psy; L'Africain (& wri).

DECAE, Henri: Cin. b. France, 1915. Films inc: Le Silence de la Mer; Les Enfants Terribles; Lift to the Scaffold; Le Beau Serge; A Double Tour; Les Quatre Cents Coup; Les Cousins; Les Bonnes Femmes; Sundays and Cybele; Viva Maria; Weekend at Dunkirk; Night of the Generals; La Voleur; The Comedians; Castle Keep; The Sicilian Clan; The Light at the Edge of the World; Bobby Deerfield; The Wild Goose Chase; The Boys From Brazil; An Almost Perfect Affair; The Island; Le Guignol; Le Coup du Parapluie (The Umbrella Coup); Inspector la Bavure (Inspector Blunder); Est-ce bien Raisonnable? (Is This Really Reasonable?); Le Professionel; Exposed; Le Vengeance du Serpent a Plumes (The Vengeance Of The Plumed Serpent).

De CAMP, Rosemary: Act. b. Prescott, AZ, Nov 14, 1910. Films inc: Hold Back the Dawn; Cheers for Miss Bishop; The Jungle Book; Yankee Doodle Dandy; Practically Yours; Weekend at the Waldorf; Many Rivers to Cross; Tora! Tora! Tora!; Saturday the 14th.

TV inc: Robert Cummings Show; That Girl; Life of Riley; Death Valley Days; Partridge Family; Blind Ambition; Mark Twain's America-Thomas Edison.

De CARLO, Yvonne (Peggy Middleton): Act. b. Vancouver, BC, Sep 1, 1924. Began as dancer. Screen debut This Gun For Hire, 1942. Films inc: The Story of Dr. Wassell; Salome; Frontier Gal; Brute Force; Casbah; Criss Cross; Calamity Jane; The Ten Commandments; McClintock; A Global Affair; Blazing Stewardesses; Satan's Cheerleader; It Seemed Like a Good Idea At the Time; Guyana-Cult of The Damned; Silent Scream; The Man With Bogart's Face; Liar's Moon; Nocturna; Flesh And Bullets.

TV inc: The Munster's Revenge.

De CORDOVA, Frederick: Dir. b. NYC, Oct 27, 1910. e. Northwestern U, BS. Gen stage dir, Shubert enterprises, 1938-41; prod Louisville (KY) Amphitheatre, 1942-43. Films inc: Too Young to Know; Her Kind of Man; Wallflower; For the Love of Mary; Peggy; Desert Hawk; Yankee Buccaneer; Columns South.

TV inc: (prod-dir) Burns and Allen; Jack Benny Program; Smothers Bros Show; My Three Sons (dir). Tonight Show (prod) (Emmys-1976-1977-1978-1979); A Love Letter To Jack Benny (exec prod).

De CUIR, John: Art dir. b. San Francisco, 1918. Films inc: The Naked City; Snows of Kilimanjaro; My Cousin Rachel; Call Me Madam; Three Coins in the Fountain; Daddy Long Legs; The King and I (Oscar-1956); Island in the Sun; South Pacific; The Big Fisherman; Cleopatra (Oscar-1963); The Agony and the Ecstacy; The Honey Pot; Hello, Dolly! (Oscar-1969); The Great White Hope; Once Is Not Enough; That's Entertainment!; Ziegfeld-The Man and His Women; Love and Bullets; Raise The Titanic; Monsignor; Ghostbusters.

DEE, Frances: Act. b. Los Angeles, Nov 26, 1907. e. Chicago U. W of Joel McCrea.

Films inc: Follow Through; Playboy of Paris; American Tragedy; Rich Man's Folly; King of the Jungle; This Reckless Age; If I Had a Million; Silver Cord; Little Women; Of Human Bondage; Becky Sharp; Meet the Stewarts; If I Were King; So Ends Our Night; Happy Land; Patrick the Great; Private Affairs of Bel Ami; Four Faces West; Payment on Demand; Reunion in Reno; Because of You; Mr. Scoutmaster; Gypsy Colt. Ret 1955.

DEE, Ruby (nee Wallace): Act. b. Cleveland, OH, Oct 27, 1923. e. Hunter Coll. W of Ossie Davis. Bway debut 1943, South Pacific. Thea inc: Walk Hard; Jeb; Anna Lucasta; Purlie Victorious; King Lear; The Imaginary Invalid; Boesman And Lena; Wedding Band; Hamlet; A

Raisin In The Sun.

Films inc: No Way Out; The Jackie Robinson Story; St Louis Blues; Take a Giant Step; A Raisin in the Sun; The Balcony; Buck and the Preacher; Black Girl; Countdown at Kusini; Cat People.

TV inc: Actor's Choice; Seven Times Monday; Go Down Moses; Twin-Bit Gardens; I Know Why the Caged Bird Sings; All God's Children; Roots--The Next Generations; Wedding Band; With Ossie and Ruby; Blacks--Present and Accounted For (host); Go Tell It On The Mountain; The Atlanta Child Murders.

DEE, Sandra: Act. b. Bayonne, NJ, Apr 23, 1942. Began as model. Films inc: Until They Sail; The Restless Years; The Reluctant Debutante; Gidget; Imitation of Life; Romanoff and Juliet; Tammy Tell Me True; Tammy and the Doctor; The Dunwich Horror.

DEELEY, Michael: Prod. b. London, Aug 6, 1932. Started as film editor. Ind. prod 1961-63; Gen M Woodfall Films, 1964-67; Ind Prod 1967-72; M-dir EMI Films, 1976-77; Chief Exec EMI Films, 1978. Films inc: Robbery; Italian Job; The Knack; Murphy's War; Conduct Unbecoming; The Man Who Fell to Earth; The Deer Hunter (Oscar-1978); Convoy; Blade Runner.

De FARIA, Walt: Prod-Dir-Wri. b. Sep 3, 1929. e. St Mary's Coll. Film inc: The Mouse and His Child; Winds of Change; Nutcracker Fantasy.

TV inc: The Wonderful World of Pizzazz; Children's Letters to God; The Unexplained; Travels With Charley (& dir); Snoopy at the Ice Follies; Snoopy Directs the Ice Follies; The Borrowers; Wild Science; The Wild Places; The Rivalry; The Yellow Bus; Beach Girls; Hanna-Barbera Happy Hour.

Named VP & dir Sanrio Communications, Sept 1980.

De FELITTA, Frank: Wri. b. NYC, Aug 3, 1921. Films inc: The First of January; The Savage Is Loose; Trapped; Audrey Rose (& prod); The Entity.

TV inc: Chosen Child (doc); Odyssey; The Two Worlds of Jenny Logan (& dir); Dark Night Of the Scarecrow (dir).

De FORE, Don: Act. b. Cedar Rapids, IA, Aug 25, 1917. e. Pasadena Community Theatre. Bway inc: Where Do We Go From Here; Steel; The Male Animal.

Films inc: We Go Fast; The Male Animal; City Without Men; The Human Comedy; A Guy Named Joe; Thirty Seconds Over Tokyo; Affairs of Susan; You Came Along; Stork Club; It Happened On Fifth Avenue; Romance on the High Seas; One Sunday Afternoon; My Friend Irma; Southside 1-1000; Girl In Every Port; She's Working Her Way Through College; No Room for the Groom; Jumping Jacks; Battle Hymn; A Rare Breed.

TV inc: Lux Theatre; Philco Playhouse; Mr and Mrs Detective; Ozzie and Harriet; Hazel; A Punt, A Pass and a Prayer.

De FUNES, Louis: Act. b. Paris, Jul 31, 1914. Films inc: The Seven Deadly Sins; No Exit; The Sheep Has Five Legs; Lock Up the Spoons; Femmes de Paris; Taxi; A Pied a Chevel et en Spoutnik; The Sucker; Fantomas; Fantomas vs Scotland Yard; Don't Look Now; Jo; The Mad Adventures of Rabbi Jacob; L'aile ou la Cuisse; La Zizanie; The Miser; The Gendarme and the Creatures from Outer Space.

(Died Jan 27, 1983).

DEGERMARK, Pia: Act. b. Sweden. Films inc: Elvira Madigan; The Looking Glass War.

DE HARTOG, Jan: Plywri. b. Haarlem, Netherlands, Apr 22, 1914. Plays inc: Skipper Next To God; This Time Tomorrow; The Fourposter (Tony-1952); William and Mary; I Do, I Do (mus version of Fourposter).

De HAVEN, Carter, III: Prod. b. Los Angeles, Feb 16, 1932. e. UCLA, BS. Films inc: Dead Heat On a Merry-Go-Round; The Kremlin Letter; A Walk With Love and Death; The Last Run; Ulzana's Raid; The Outfit; Seven Men At Daybreak; The Seniors; Carbon Copy; Yellowbeard; Scandalous (exec prod); Special Effects; Perfect Strangers (exec prod).

TV inc: Make Me An Offer.

De HAVEN, Gloria: Act. b. Los Angeles, Jul 23, 1925. Films inc: Susan and God; Thousands Cheer; Two Girls and a Sailor; The Thin Man Goes Home; Summer Holiday; Three Little Words; Two Tickets to Broadway; So This Is Paris; The Girl Rush; Bog.

TV inc: As The World Turns; Call Her Mom; Who Is the Black Dahlia?; Lucy Moves to NBC; Ryan's Hope; Off Sides.

de HAVILLAND, Olivia: Act. b. Tokyo, Jul 1, 1916. Sis of Joan Fontaine. Film debut, A Midsummer's Night Dream. Films inc: Captain Blood; The Charge of The Light Brigade; The Adventures of Robin Hood; To Each His Own (Oscar-1946); The Snake Pit; The Heiress (Oscar-1949); Airport '77; The Swarm; The Fifth Musketeer.

TV inc: Murder Is Easy; The Royal Romance of Charles and Diana; Movie Blockbusters! The 15 Greatest Hits of All Time.

DEHNER, John (nee Forkum): Act. b. NYC, Nov 23, 1915. e. UC Berkeley. Films inc: Thirty Seconds Over Tokyo; The Corn is Green; Ten Tall Men; Scaramouche; Man on a Tightrope; The Prodigal; Carousel; Fastest Gun Alive; Left Handed Gun; The Chapman Report; Critics Choice; Youngblood Hawke; Cheyenne Social Club; Dirty Dingus McGee; Day of the Dolphin; The Killer Inside Me; Fun with Dick and Jane; The Lincoln Conspiracy; The Boys from Brazil; Airplane II--The Sequel.

TV inc: The Roaring Twenties; The Baileys of Balboa; The Westerner; Doris Day Show; The Virginian; Missiles of October; Big Hawaii; Greatest Heroes of the Bible; Young Maverick; Enos; California Gold Rush; Bare Essence; The Winds of War.

DELAIR, Suzy: Act. b. Paris, Dec 31, 1931. Films inc: Le Dernier des Six; Defense D'Aimer; Quai des Orfevres; Lady Paname; Robinson Crusoe Land; Gervaise; Rocco and his Brother; Is Paris Burning?; The Mad Adventures of Rabbi Jacob.

De LAURENTIIS, Dino: Prod. b. Torre Annunziata, Italy, Aug 8, 1919. Films inc: The Bandit Mussolino; Bitter Rice; War and Peace; Ulysses; Mambo; La Strada; The Bible; Anzio; Barbarella; Waterloo; The Vilachi Papers; Serpico; The Stone Killer; Three Days of the Condor; Death Wish; The Shootist; King Kong. Orca; The Serpent's Egg; Hurricane; Mean Frank, Crazy Tony; Flash Gordon; Ragtime; Fighting Back; The Dead Zone; Amityville 3-D; The Bounty (presenter); Firestarter (presenter). Conan the Destroyer (presenter); Dune (presenter); Cat's Eye (presenter).

De LAURENTIIS, Raffaella: Prod. b. Italy, June 28, 1954. D. of Silvana Mangano and Dino De Laurentiis. Films inc: Hurricane (prod asst); Beyond The Reef; Dune; Conan The Destroyer.

DELERUE, Georges: Comp-cond. b. Roubaix, France, Mar. 12, 1925. e. Paris Conservatory; studied under Darius Milhaud. Stage scores inc: Danton's Death; The Hostage; Macbeth.

Films inc: Hiroshima Mon Amour; The Day of the Dolphin; A Walk With Love and Death; Anne of a Thousand Days; Women in Love; Day of the Jackal; A Man For All Seasons; Viva Maria; King of Hearts; Cartouche; That Man From Rio; L'Amour a Vingt Ans; Jules et Jim; Tirez sur le Pianiste (Shoot the Piano Player); La Nuit Americaine (Day for Night); Julia; L'Incorrigible; Tendre Poulet; Preparez vos mouchoirs (Get Out Your Handkerchiefs); Simone de Beauvoir; A Little Romance (Oscar-1979); Your Turn, My Turn; Richard's Things; The Last Metro; The Escape Artist; True Confessions; La Femme d'a cote (The Woman Next Door); Rich and Famous; Documenteur--an Emotion Picture; Garde a vue (The Grilling); La Vie Continue (Life Goes On); Broken English; A Little Sex; Josepha; Partners; Guy de Maupassant; Exposed; The Black Stallion Returns; Man, Woman and Child; L'Africain; Vivement Dimanche (Let It Be Sunday); Liberty Belle; Silkwood; Le Bon Plaisir; Femmes de personne (Nobody's Women); Les Morfalous (The Vultures); Love Thy Neighbor; Silence Of The Heart.

TV inc: Le Chandelier; Photo Souvenir; A Smile for the Crocodile; Our World (Emmy-1968); Easter Island; The Nile; Borgia; Deadly Intentions; Arch Of Triumph.

Thea inc: Un Otage (The Hostage).

DELFONT, Bernard, Lord: Exec. b. Tomak, Russia, Sep 5, 1909. B of Lord Lew Grade. Entered thea mgt in Great Britain, 1941; first London prodn 1942; presenter with Louis Benjamin annual Royal Variety Performance; chmn and chief exec EMI film & Theatre Corp, 1969; chmn EMI Cinemas Ltd; EMI Leisure Enterprises; EMI Films; EMI-Elstree Studios; dir Bernard Delfont Organisation, Blackpool

Tower Co; vice chmn Associated Film Distrib Corp, USA.

Thea inc: Henry IV; Stop The World, I Want To Get Off; Ulysses in Nighttown; The Good Companions; Harvey; Dad's Army; It's Alright If I Do It; An Evening with Tommy Steele; Mardi Gras; Sizwe Banze Is Dead & The Island; The Best Little Whorehouse In Texas; Underneath the Arches; Singin' In the Rain.

De LIAGRE, Alfred, Jr: Prod-Dir. b. NYC, Oct 6, 1904. e. Yale U. Bway inc: Three Cornered Moon; By Your Leave; Pure in Heart (co-prod); Petticoat Fever; Fresh Fields; Yes, My Darling Daughter; I am My Youth; No Code to Guide Her; Mr and Mrs North; The Walrus and the Carpenter; Ask My Friend Sandy; The Voice of the Turtle (prod); The Madwoman of Chaillot; The Golden Apple; The Caine Mutiny Court Martial (tour); Photo Finish; The Irregular Verb to Love; J B *(Tony*-1959); Deathtrap; as exec prod for ANTA presented The American Conservatory Theatre in The Three Sisters; Tiny Alice; A Flea in Her Ear.

DELL, Gabriel (nee del Vecchio): Act. b. Barbados, BWI, Oct 7, 1919. Studied with Lee Strasberg. Bway debut age 9 in The Good Earth; in orig co Dead End; went to Hwd for film version.
Bway inc: Tickets Please; Ankles Aweigh; Can-Can; Wonderful Town; Marathon; Anyone Can Whistle; The Sign in Sidney Brustein's Window; Luv; Something Diff'rent; Fun City; The Prisoner of Second Avenue; Lamppost Reunion.
Films inc: Dead End; Angels With Dirty Faces; Crime School; Little Tough Guy; They Made Me A Criminal; Angels Wash Their Faces; Tough as They Come; Bowery Champs; Million Dollar Kid; Hard-Boiled Ma honey; Jinx Money; Fighting Fools; Blonde Dynamite; Triple Trouble; Who is Harry Kellerman; Framed; Earthquake; The Escape Artist.
TV inc: Broadway Open House; The Corner Bar; Risko.

DELL, Wanda: Prod. b. Miami, FL, 1941. Partner, co-founder TriStar Pictures Inc. Films inc: The Billion Dollar Hobo (asso prod); They Went That-A-Way and That-A-Way (asso prod); Prize Fighter (co-prod); The Private Eyes (co-prod); Marvin and Tige (& exec prod-wri).

DELON, Alain: Act. b. Paris, Nov 8, 1935. Films inc: Plein Soleil; The Eclipse; The Big Snatch; The Yellow Rolls Royce; The Love Cage; Once a Thief; Lost Command; Is Paris Burning; Texas Across the River; Histoires Extraordinaires; Diabolically Yours; Girl on a Motorcycle; Borsalino; The Sicilian Clan; Red Sun; The Assassination of Trotsky; Scorpio; Borsalino and Co; Shock; Mr Klein; Like A Boomerang; Le Gang; L'Homme Presse; Mort d'un Pourri; The Concorde-Airport '79; Le Toubib; Trois Hommes a Abattre (Three Men To Destroy); Teheran '43; Pour La Peau d'un Flic (For A Cop's Hide) (& wri-prod-dir); Le Choc (The Shock) (& wri); Le Battant (The Cache) (& prod-dir-wri); Un Amour de Swann (Swann in Love); Notre Histoire (Our Story).

DELORME, Daniele (Gabrielle Girard): Act. B. France, Oct. 9, 1926. Films inc: Gigi; La Cage aux filles; Minne; Souvenirs perdus; Olivia; Sans laisser d'Adresse; Desperate Decision; Royal Affairs in Versailles; No Exit; House of Ricordi; Le dossier noir; Deadlier Than the Male; Les Miserables; Prisons de Femmes; La Guerre des Boutons (prod); The Seventh Juror; Marie Soleil (& prod); The Crook; Absences repetees; Belle; An Elephant Can Be Extremely Deceptive; Pardon Mon Affaire; Nous irons tous au Paradis; Un Etrange Voyage (On the Track) (prod); La fille prodigue (The Prodigal Daughter) (prod); Qu-est-ce Qui fait Courir David (What Makes David Run?) (prod); La Cote D'Amour (The Coast of Love); Le Jumeau (The Twin) (prod); Novembermond (November Moon).

Del RIO, Dolores (nee Ansunsolo): Act. b. Durango, Mexico, Aug 3, 1905. Studied voice in Madrid, Paris. Screen debut in Joanna, 1925. Films inc: What Price Glory?; Resurrection; Ramona; Flying Down to Rio; Wonderbar; Madame DuBarry; Journey Into Fear; Portrait of Maria; The Fugitive; Cheyenne Autumn; The Children of Sanchez.
(Died Apr 11, 1983).

De LUISE, Dom: Act. b. NYC, Aug 1, 1933. Launched TV career as bumbling magician on Gary Moore Show. Films inc: Fail Safe; The Busybody; The Glass Bottom Boat; Who Is Harry Kellerman?; Every Little Crook and Nanny; The Adventures of Sherlock Holmes' Smarter Brother; The World's Greatest Lover; Silent Movie; The Cheap Detec-

tive; The End; Sextette; Hot Stuff (& dir); The Muppet Movie; The Last Married Couple in America; Fatso; Wholly Moses!; Smokey and the Bandit II; History of the World--Part I; The Cannonball Run; The Secret of NIMH (voice); The Best Little Whorehouse In Texas; Cannonball Run II; Johnny Dangerously.
TV inc: The Entertainers; The Dean Martin Summer Show; The Dom DeLuise Variety Show; Lotsa Luck; Ann-Margret-Hollywood Movie Girls; Dean Martin At the Wild Animal Park; Baryshnikov In Hollywood; Hollywood--The Gift of Laughter; Dom DeLuise and Friends; Happy (& exec prod); Dean Martin's Celebrity Roast; Dom DeLuise and Friends Part II.

DELVAUX, Andre: Dir. b. Belgium, 1926. Originally a teacher. Made docs before turning to features.
Film inc: The Man Who Had His Hair Cut Short; Un soir--Un Train; Rendezvous at Bray; Belle; Femme Entre Chien et Loup; To Woody Allen, From Europe With Love (& wri); Benvenuta (& wri).

DEMAREST, William: Act. b. St Paul, MN, Feb 27, 1894. Films inc: When the Wife's Away; The Jazz Singer; The Gracie Allen Murder Case; Mr Smith Goes to Washington; The Farmer's Daughter; The Miracle of Morgan's Creek; Duffy's Tavern; Along Came Jones; The Jolson Story; When Willie Comes Marching Home; What Price Glory?; The Private War of Major Benson; Lucy Gallant; Pepe; Son of Flubber; It's a Mad, Mad, Mad, Mad World; That Darn Cat; The Wild McCullochs; Won Ton Ton, the Dog Who Saved Hollywood.
TV inc: Wells Fargo; Love and Marriage; My Three Sons; The Millionaire.
(Died Dec. 28, 1983).

De MILLE, Agnes: Chor-Act. b. NYC, 1905. D of late William C DeMille. First appeared as a dancer in NY, 1927, in La Finta Giardiniera; danced in US, England, France, Denmark, 1928-41. Thea inc: The American Legend: Oklahoma!; One Touch of Venus; Bloomer Girl; Carousel; Brigadoon *(Tony*-1947); Allegro; Gentlemen Prefer Blondes (& dir); Paint Your Wagon; The Girl in Pink Tights; Goldilocks; Juno; Bitter Weird; Kwamina *(Tony*-1962); 110 in the Shade; The Wind in the Mountains; Carousel.
TV inc: Narrator for the TV programs of the Bolshoi Ballet; The Kennedy Center Honors, 1980; Ready When You Are, Mr DeMille.

DEMME, Jonathan: Wri-Dir. Films inc: Caged Heat; Crazy Mama (dir only); Fighting Mad; Citizens Band; Murder in Aspic; The Incredible Melting Man (act); Last Embrace; Melvin and Howard; Swing Shift; Stop Making Sense (doc); Into The Night (act).
TV inc: Who Am I This Time?

DEMY, Jacques: Dir. b. Pont-Chateau, France, 1931. Films inc: Lola; la Baie des Anges; The Umbrellas of Cherbourg (& sp); The Young Girls of Rochefort (& mus); The Model Shop; Donkey-Skin; The Pied Piper of Hamelin; The Most Important Event Since Man Walked on the Moon; Lady Oscar; Une Chambre En Ville (A Room In Town) (& wri).
Songs inc: I Will Wait for You.

DENCH, Judi: Act. b. York, England, Dec 9, 1934. Thea inc: Hamlet; Twelfth Night; Henry V; Midsummer Night's Dream; Importance of Being Earnest; Romeo and Juliet; A Shot in the Dark; The Promise; Cabaret; The Merchant of Venice; Macbeth; King Lear; Juno and the Paycock; The Importance of Being Earnest; Pack of Lies.
Films inc: He Who Rides a Tiger; Study in Terror; The Third Secret; A Midsummer Night's Dream; Dead Cert; Brannigan; Angelic Conversations (voice); Wetherby.
TV inc: Major Barbara; Pink String and Sealing Wax; Age of Kings; Neighbours; Emilie; A Village Wooing; On Giant's Shoulders; The Mechanical Paradise; Love In A Cold Climate; Saigon--Year of the Cat.

DENEUVE, Catherine (nee Dorleac): Act. b. France, Oct 22, 1943. Films inc: The Doors Slam; Vice and Virtue; Satan Leads the Dance; Umbrellas of Cherbourg; Repulsion; Le Chant du Monde; La Vie de Chateau; Les Creatures; The Young Girls of Rochefort; Belle de Jour; Benjamin; Manon; Mayerling; The April Fools; The Mississippi Mermaid; Tristana; Hustle; La Grande Bourgeoise; Le Sauvage; March or Die; If It Were To Do Over Again; The Forbidden Room; L'argent des Autres (Other People's Money); Ils Sont Grand Ces Petits; Courage Fuyons; A Nous Deux; The Last Metro; I Love You; Le Choix des

Armes (Choice of Weapons); Hotel Des Ameriques (Hotel of the Americas); Le Choc (The Shock); L'Africain; The Hunger; Le Bon Plaisir; Fort Saganne; Paroles et Musiques (Words And Music).

DENHAM, Maurice: Act. b. Beckenham, Kent, England, Dec 23, 1909. Originally an engineer, turned to act in 1934; with various British rep groups before London debut 1936 in Rain Before Seven. Other thea inc: Busman's Holiday; Flying Blind; Fumed Oak; Satellite Story; Shadow of Fear; Who's Your Father; The Andersonville Trial; with Old Vic company 1961-63; Do You Know the Milky Way; Nathan the Wise; The Apple Cart; The Lovers of Viorne.

Films inc: Blanche Fury; No Highway in the Sky; The Net; Time Bomb; Man With a Million; 23 Paces to Baker Street; Checkpoint; Doctor at Sea; The Captain's Table; Our Man in Havana; Sink the Bismarck; Greengage Summer; Invasion; Quartette; The Mark; Operation Crossbow; Those Magnificent Men In Their Flying Machines; Heroes of Telemark; After the Fox; Sunday, Bloody Sunday; Nicholas and Alexandra; The Day of the Jackal; Luther; Shout at the Devil; Julia; From A Far Country--Pope John Paul II; Mr. Love; The Chain.

TV inc: Uncle Harry; Soldier Soldier; Maigret; Somerset Maugham; Sherlock Holmes series; Talking To A Stranger; From Chekhov with Love; Saint Joan; The Lotus Eaters; A Chink in the Wall; Secret Army.

DENHAM, Reginald: Dir. b. London, Jan 10, 1894. Thea inc: Rope; Jew Suss; An Object of Virtue; Cold Blood; Jupiter Laughs; Ladies in Retirement; Play with Fire; The Devil Also Dreams; Dial M for Murder; Be Your Age; A Date with April; Sherlock Holmes; The Bad Seed; Hostile Witness; Minor Murder; Grass Widows; The Last Straw; Wallflower; The Man They Acquitted; Sweet Peril; A Dash of Bitters; Stars in My Hair.

(Died Feb 4, 1983).

De NIRO, Robert: Act. b. NYC, Aug 17, 1943. Films inc: The Wedding Party; Greetings; Hi, Mom; Bloody Mama; The Gang That Couldn't Shoot Straight; Bang the Drum Slowly; Mean Streets; The Last Tycoon; 1900; The Godfather, Part II (Oscar-supp-1974); Taxi Driver; New York, New York; The Deer Hunter; Raging Bull (Oscar-1980); True Confessions; Elia Kazan, Outsider (doc); The King of Comedy; Once Upon A Time In America; Falling In Love; Brazil.

DENISON, Michael: Act. b. England, Nov 1, 1915. e. Oxford. Stage debut 1938, Charlie's Aunt. Thea inc: Ever Since Paradise; Let Them Eat Cake; Candida; Where Angels Fear to Tread; Hostile Witness; At The End of the Day; The Sack Race; The Black Mikado; The First Mrs Fraser; Robert and Elizabeth; The Cabinet Minister; A Coat of Varnish.

Films inc: Hungry Hill; The Blind Goddess; The Glass Mountain; Angels One Five; Tall Headlines; Importance of Being Earnest; The Truth About Women; Faces in the Dark.

TV inc: Funeral Games; Tale of Piccadilly; The Provincial Lady.

DENKER, Henry: Wri. b. NYC, Nov 25, 1912. e. NY Law School, LLB. Lawyer and tax consultant before turning to writing. Wrote, prod-dir radio series The Greatest Story Ever Told.

Plays inc: Time Limit; Venus at Large; A Case of Libel; What Did We Do Wrong?; Something Old, Something New; Horowitz and Mrs. Washington; The Name of the Game; A Sound of Distant Thunder; A Far Country.

Films inc: The Heartfarm; The Hook; Twilight of Honor; Time Limit.

TV inc: Give Us Barabbas; The Court Martial of Lt. Calley; Neither Are We Enemies; The Choice; A Time For Miracles; A Case of Libel; Love Leads The Way.

DENNEHY, Brian: Act. b. Bridgeport, CT, Jul 9. e. Columbia U, BA. Thea inc: Shadow of a Gunman; Julius Caesar; Sez I, Sez He; Streamers (Bway).

Films inc: Looking for Mr Goodbar; Semi-Tough; Foul Play; F.I.S.T.; Butch and Sundance--The Early Days; 10; Little Miss Marker; Split Image; First Blood; Never Cry Wolf; Gorky Park; Finders Keepers; The River Rat; Cocoon.

TV inc: A Real American Hero; Dummy; Silent Victory--The Kitty O'Neil Story; Pearl; Big Shamus, Little Shamus; The Seduction of Miss Leona; The Girls In Their Summer Dresses and Other Stories by Irwin Shaw; Fly Away Home; Skokie; Star of the Family; I Take These Men; Blood Feud; Off Sides; Hunter; Evergreen.

DENNING, Richard: Act. b. Poughkeepsie, NY, 1914. Films inc: Hold 'Em Navy; Buccaneer; Illegal Traffic; Adam Had Four Sons; Glass Key; Black Beauty; The Fabulous Suzanne; Caged Fury; No Man of Her Own; Hangman's Knot; The Glass Web; Creature of the Black Lagoon; The Gun That Won the West; An Affair to Remember; Twice Told Tales.

TV inc: Mr and Mrs North; Flying Doctor; Hawaii Five-O; The Asphalt Cowboy.

DENNIS, Sandy: Act. b. Hastings, NE, Sep 27, 1937. Films inc: Splendor in the Grass; Who's Afraid of Virginia Woolf? (Oscar-supp-1966); Up the Down Staircase; The Fox; Sweet November; That Cold Day in the Park; A Touch of Love; The Out-of-Towners; The Only Way Out is Dead; Nasty Habits; God Told Me To; The Four Seasons.

Bway inc: A Thousand Clowns (Tony-supp-1963); Any Wednesday (Tony-1964); Absurd Person Singular; The Supporting Cast; Come back To The 5 & Dime, Jimmy Dean, Jimmy Dean; My One And Only.

TV inc: Perfect Gentlemen; The Execution.

DENOFF, Sam: Wri-Prod. b. Brooklyn, July 1, 1928. Partnered with Bill Persky for 21 years, originally writing nitery acts.

TV inc: Steve Allen Show; Andy Williams Show; Dick Van Dyke Show (& prod) (Emmy-wri-1964, 1966); Sid Caesar-Imogene Coca-Carl Reiner-Howard Morris Special (Emmy-1967); McHale's Navy; Dick Van Dyke and the Other Woman (& prod); The First Nine Months are the Hardest; Pure Goldie (& prod); Confessions of Dick Van Dyke (prod); The Funny Side (crea-exec prod); Don Rickles Show (crea-exec prod); Lotsa Luck (crea-exec prod); That Girl (crea-exec prod); Bill Cosby Special; The Man Who Came to Dinner.

Since splitting with Persky: Turnabout (exec prod); On Our Own (prod); Harper Valley PTA (exec prod); Wait Till Your Mother Gets Home; The Lucie Arnaz Show (exec prod). and the Other Woman (& prod); The First Nine Months are the Hardest (crea-prod); Pure Goldie (& prod); Confessions of Dick Van Dyke (prod); The Funny Side (crea-exec prod); Don Rickles Show (

DENVER, Bob: Act. b. New Rochelle, NY, 1935. Films inc: Take Her She's Mine; For Those Who Think Young; Who's Minding the Mint?; The Sweet Ride; Do You Know the One About the Travelling Saleslady?

TV inc: Dobie Gillis; Gilligan's Island; Dusty's Trail; The Castaways on Gilligan's Island; The Harlem Globetrotters on Gilligan's Island; Scamps; The Invisible Woman; High School U.S.A.

DENVER, John (Henry John Deutschendorf): Singer-Act. b. Roswell, NM, Dec 31, 1943. Recording artist; concerts; niteries. Films inc: Oh, God!; America Censored.

TV inc: An Evening with John Denver (Emmy-1975); Rocky Mountain Christmas; John Denver and the Muppets, A Christmas Get Together; The Higher We Fly (host); Two Of A Kind; John Denver--Music and the Mountains (& prod); Rocky Mountain Holiday with John Denver and the Muppets (& prod); Bob Hope's Salute to NASA--25 Years of Reaching for the Stars; Salute to Lady Liberty; How To Be A Man; Jacques Cousteau--The First 75 Years.

Albums inc: Spirit; I Want to Live; A Christmas Together.

De PALMA, Brian: Dir. b. Newark, NJ, Sep 11, 1940. e. Columbia Coll, BA; Sarah Lawrence Coll, MA. Films inc: Murder a la Mod; Greetings; Hi Mom; Get to Know Your Rabbit; Sisters; Phantom of the Paradise; Obsession; Carrie; The Fury; The Wedding Party; Home Movies (& prod); Dressed To Kill; Blow Out (& wri); The First Time (creative cnslt); Scarface; Body Double (& prod-wri).

DEPARDIEU, Gerard: Act. b. Chateauroux, France, Dec 27, 1948. Films inc: Le Cormoran le soir au-dessus des Jonques; Le Tueur; L'Affaire Dominici; Un peu de Soleil dans l'eau froide; Au rendez-vous de la mort Joyeuse; La Scoumoune; Deux Hommes dans la Ville; 1900; The Wonderful Crook; Bye Bye Monkey; Sugar; The Last Woman; Get Out Your Handkerchiefs; L'Ingorgo; Cold Cuts; Mistress; My American Uncle; Les Chiens; The Last Metro; Inspector la Bavure (Inspector Blunder); I Love You; Les Choix des Armes (Choice of Weapons); La Femme D'a Cote (The Woman Next Door); La Chevre (The Goat); Le Retour de Martin Guerre. (The Return of Martin Guerre); The Big Brother; Danton; Wajda's Danton (doc); La Lune dans le Caniveau (The Moon in the Gutter); Les Comperes (The Co-fathers); Fort Saganne; Le Tartuffe (& adap-dir); Rive Droite, Rive Gauche (Right Bank, Left Bank).

Thea inc: Tartuffe.

de PASSE, Suzanne: exec. b. July 19. e. Manhattan Community College; Syracuse U; New Lincoln School. W of Paul Le Mat. Joined Motown Records 1968 as crea asst to P; dir West Coast Creative Div; VP Creative Div; VP Motown Industries; 1981, P Motown Prodns.

Films inc: Lady Sings The Blues (wri). TV inc: Git On Broadway--Diana Ross & Supremes & Temptations (crea cnslt); Diana (wri); Jackson 5 Goin' Back To Indiana (wri); Happy Endings (exec prod); Motown 25:Yesterday, Today, Forever (exec prod) *(Emmy-1983)*; Motown Returns To The Apollo (exec prod).

De PATIE, David H.: Prod. b. Los Angeles, Dec 24, 1930. e. UC Berkeley, AB. Partner DePatie-Freleng Ent, 1963-80. Films inc: Pink Panther; Return to the Planet of the Apes. Shorts inc: The Pink Phink *(Oscar-1964)*; Super President; Super Six; The Inspector; Roland & Rattfink; The Ant and the Aardvark; The Tijuana Toads; Here Comes the Grump; The Adventures of Dr. Dolittle; My World and Welcome To It; The Blue Racer; The Houndcats; The Barkleys; Bailey's Comets; Sheriff Hoot Kloot; The Oddball Couple; Baggy Pants & The Nitwits; What's New Mr. Magoo?

TV inc: My Mom's Having a Baby *(Emmy-1974)*; Halloween Is Grinch Night *(Emmy-1978)*; The Bear Who Slept Through Christmas; Pink Panther in Olympinks; Where Do Teen Agers Come From?; Dr Seuss' Pontoffel Pock Where Are You?; Pink At First Sight; Dennis The Menace; The Grinch Grinches The Cat-In-The-Hat (exec prod); *(Emmy-1982)*.

De PAUL, Gene: Comp-Arr-Pianist. b. NYC, Jun 17, 1919. Songs inc: Pig Foot Pete; I'll Remember April; Mister Five by Five; He's My Guy; Cow Cow Boogie; Irresistible You; Sobbin' Women; Namely You; Cornpone; Your Red Wagon; A Song Was Born; Teach Me Tonight; You Can't Run Away From It;

Film Scores inc: Seven Brides for Seven Brothers; You Can't Run Away From It.

Bway inc: Seven Brides for Seven Brothers.

DEREK, Bo (Mary Cathleen Collins): Act. b. Long Beach, CA, Nov 20, 1956. W of John Derek. Films inc: Once Upon A Time (Fantasies); Orca; 10; A Change of Seasons; Tarzan, The Ape Man (& prod); Bolero (& prod).

DEREK, John (Derek Harris): Act. b. Aug 12, 1926. Films inc: I'll Be Seeing You; Knock on Any Door; All the King's Men; Rogues of Sherwood Forest; Mask of the Avenger; Scandal Sheet; Mission Over Korea; Prince of Players; Run for Cover; The Ten Commandments; Omar Khayyam; Exodus; Nightmare in the Sun; Once Before I Die (& dir); Childish Things (& dir); Once Upon A Time (Fantasies) (wri-dir-cin); Tarzan, The Ape Man (dir-cin); Bolero (wri-dir-cin).

DERN, Bruce: Act. b. Chicago, Jun 4, 1936. e. U of PA. On screen from 1960, Wild River. Films inc: Marnie; Hush, Hush Sweet Charlotte; The Wild Angels; The St. Valentine's Day Massacre; Waterhole #3; Psyche-Out; The War Wagon; Will Penny; Castle Keep; They Shoot Horses, Don't They?; Bloody Mama; The Incredible Two-Headed Transplant; Drive, He Said; Suport Your Local Sheriff; The Cowboys; Silent Running; King of Marvin Gardens; The Laughing Policeman; The Great Gatsby; Posse; Smile; Family Plot; Won Ton Ton, the Dog Who Saved Hollywood; The Twist (Folies Bourgeoises); Black Sunday; Coming Home; Driver; Middle Age Crazy; Tattoo; Harry Tracy-Desperado; That Championship Season; On The Edge.

TV inc: Space.

Bway inc: Strangers.

DESCHANEL, Caleb: Cin. b. Philadelphia, PA, Sep 21, 1944. e. Johns Hopkins U; USC. Films inc: The Black Stallion; More American Graffiti; Being There; The Escape Artist (dir); Time Is On Our Side; The Right Stuff; The Natural; The Slugger's Wife.

De SHIELDS, Andre: Act-Dir-Chor. b. Baltimore, MD, Jan 12, 1946. e. U WI, BA. Chor Bette Midler's Harlettes, 1973-1977. Bway inc: (act) Warp; The Wiz; Ain't Misbehavin' (& London).

TV inc: Ain't Misbehavin' *(Emmy-Ind Achievement-1982)*; Alice in Wonderland.

DESMOND, John J: Dir. b. Freeport, IL, Dec 28, 1931. e. U of IL, BA; Neighborhood Playhouse; Actors Studio. Started on radio; with Voice of America; programs inc: Picnic; Ethan Frome; various nighttime serials.

TV inc: Studio One; Odyssey; Omnibus; Camera Three; Accent; Beacon Hill; Feeling Good; Visions; The Widowing of Mrs. Holroyd; All Over; The Seagull; Theatre in America; My Mother's House; Dinner with the President; The President; The First Lady; A Dickens Chronicle; First Ladies Diaries--Martha Washington; Suzy Visits; Barbara Walters Special; Castle Rock; Guests of the Nation.

DESNY, Ivan: Act. b. 1922. Films inc: Madeleine; The Respectful Prostitute; Lola Montes; The Mirror Has Two Faces; The Magnificent Rebel; I Killed Rasputin; Mayerling; Adventures of Gerard; Paper Tiger; The Conquest of the Citadel; Fifty-Fifty; Sidney Sheldon's Bloodline; The Marriage of Maria Braun; Berlin Alexanderplatz; Fabian; Malou; Odio Le Blonde (I Hate Blondes); Lola; Who?; Die Wilden Fuenfziger (The Roarin' Fifties); Flugel und Fesseln (The Future Of Emily).

De TOTH, Andre (Andreas Toth): Dir. b. Mako, Hungary, 1913. Worked for Alexander Korda as edtr, asst dir, in Eng. In 1943, dir in Hollywood. Films inc: Passport to Suez; None Shall Escape; Since You Went Away; Pitfall; Springfield Rifle; The Gunfighter (co-sp); House of Wax; Bounty Hunter; Monkey on My Back; Two-Headed Spy; Man on a String; The Mongols; Gold for the Caesars; Billion Dollar Brain; Play Dirty; El Condor; The Dangerous Game.

DEUBEL, Robert E: Dir-Prod. b. Cleveland, Oct 12, 1933. e. Cleveland Inst of Art; Western Reserve U. TV inc: Norman Rockwell's World. . .An American Dream; The American Woman; Portraits of Courage.

DEUTSCH, Armand: Prod. b. Chicago, IL, Jan 25, 1913. e. U Chicago, BA. Films inc: Ambush; Right Cross; Magnificent Yankee; Three Guys Named Mike; Kind Lady; Girl in White; Carbine Williams; The Girl Who Had Everything; Slander.

DEUTSCH, Helen: Wri. b. NYC, Mar 21, 1912. e. Barnard Coll, BA. Films inc: Seventh Cross; Golden Earrings; National Velvet; King Solomon's Mines; Kim; Plymouth Adventure; Lili; I'll Cry Tomorrow; The Unsinkable Molly Brown; Valley of the Dolls.

TV inc: Jack & the Beanstalk; GM's 50th Anniversary Show; Hallmark Christmas Show.

Plays inc; Love on an Island; Carnival.

DEUTSCH, Stephen: Prod. b. Los Angeles, Jun 30, 1946. e. UCLA, BA; Loyola Law School. S of the late S Sylvan Simon. Stepson of Armand Deutsch. Was adm asst John Tunney's senatorial campaign 1968-70; in private law practice until joined Rastar 1976 as asst to Ray Stark; 1977, sr vp Rastar Films; resd 1978 to enter indie prodn. Films inc: Somewhere In Time; All the Right Moves.

DEVANE, William: Act. b. Albany, NY, Sep 5, 1939. e. AADA. Appeared in Othello, Coriolanus, Hamlet during NY Shakespeare Festival. Bway inc: G. R. Point (dir).

Films inc: Lady Liberty; Report to the Commissioner; McCabe and Mrs. Miller; Family Plot; Marathon Man; Bad News Bears in Breaking Training; Rolling Thunder; The Dark; Yanks; Honky Tonk Freeway; Testament; Hadley's Rebellion.

TV inc: Missiles of October; Fear on Trial; From Here to Eternity; From Here to Eternity-The War Years; Red Flag--The Ultimate Game; The Other Victim; Jack London--A Personal Perspective; Ireland--A Television History (host). The Big Easy; The World's Greatest Escape Artist (narr); Jane Doe; Knots Landing; Wilderness Journal (host).

DEVILLE, Michel: Dir. b. Boulogne-sur-Seine, France, Apr 13, 1931. Films inc: Une Balle Dans le Canon; Ce Soir ou Jamais; L'Apartment de Filles; Tricky Jo; Benjamin; Bye Bye Barbara; The Bear and the Doll; La Femme en Bleu; Love at the Top; L'Apprenti Salaud; Dossier 51; Travels on the Sly; Eaux Profondes (Deep Water) (& wri); Le Petit Bande (The Little Bunch) (& wri); Peril en la Demeure (Danger In The House) (& wri).

De VITO, Danny: Act. b. Neptune, NJ, Nov 17, 1944. Films inc: One Flew Over the Cuckoo's Nest; The Van; The World's Greatest Lover; Goin' South; Going Ape!; Terms of Endearment; Romancing the Stone.

TV inc: Taxi (Emmy-supp-1981); Like Father, Like Daughter; Valentine; Ann-Margaret-Hollywood Movie Girls; Saturday Night Live; The Ratings Game (& dir) (PC).

De VOL, Frank: Comp-Cond-Arr. b. Moundsville, WV, Sep 20, 1911. e. Miama U. Film scores inc: The Big Knife; Good Neighbor Sam; Send Me No Flowers; Pillow Talk; Cat Ballou; Hush, Hush, Sweet Charlotte; The Flight of the Phoenix; Guess Who's Coming to Dinner; The Glass Bottom Boat; The Choirboys; Herbie Goes to Monte Carlo; The Frisco Kid (& act); Herbie Goes Bananas; All the Marbles. (Act): Boys Night Out; Parent Trap; W C Fields and Me.

TV inc: Family Affair; GE Theatre; The Colgate Hour; The George Gobel Show; My Three Sons; The Brady Bunch; The Ghosts of Buxley Hall; The Brady Brides; Tales of the Apple Dumpling Gang; Herbie, The Love Bug; The Wild Women of Chastity Gulch.

DEVON, Richard: Act. b. Glendale, CA, Dec 11, 1931. Films inc: The Prodigal; The Undead; Viking Women; Gunfighters of Abilene; Machine Gun Kelly; 3:10 to Yuma; The Bandlanders; The Comancheros; Kid Galahad; Cattle King; The Silencers; Magnum Force.

Thea inc: It Pays to Advertise; A Light From Saint Agnes; Maisie; The Same Old Thing.

De VORZON, Barry: Comp. b. NYC, Jul 31, 1934. e. Pasadena City Coll. Films inc: Dillinger; Bless the Beasts and Children; The Warriors; The Ninth Configuration; Xanadu; Tattoo; Looker; Jekyll and Hyde--Together Again; Mischief (supv); Stick.

TV inc: The Young and the Restless; S.W.A.T.; Stunts Unlimited; The Comeback Kid; Reward; Simon & Simon; The Children Nobody Wanted; The Renegades; High Performance; Lone Star; Just Our Luck; V--The Final Battle; Kojak--The Belarus File.

Songs inc: Nadia's Theme (Grammy-inst arr-1977); Treasure of Your Love; Dreamin'; Hey Little One; I Wonder What She's Doin' Tonight; Bless the Beasts and Children; Theme from S.W.A.T.; In the City.

DEWELL, Michael: Prod. b. Woodbridge, CT, 1931. e. Yale, BA; RADA. Thea inc: Elizabeth the Queen; Mary Stuart; Hedda Gabler; Liliom; The Crucible; The Seagull; Ring Round the Moon; Madwoman of Chaillot; The Trojan Women; The Imaginary Invalid; As You Like It; Macbeth; The Comedy of Errors.

TV inc: Mary Stuart; Inaugural Night at Ford's.

DEWHURST, Colleen: Act. b. Montreal, Jun 3, 1926. Bway inc: Desire Under the Elms (rev); The Ballad of the Sad Cafe; Hello and Goodbye; The Good Woman of Setzuan; All the Way Home (Tony-supp-1961); The Big Coca Cola Swamp in the Sky; Mourning Becomes Electra; A Moon for the Misbegotten (Tony-1973); Who's Afraid of Virginia Woolf? Ned and Jack; The Queen and the Rebels; You Can't Take It With You.

Films inc: The Nun's Story; McQ; Annie Hall; Ice Castles; When a Stranger Calls; Arthur Miller on Home Ground; Final Assignment; Tribute; The Dead Zone; The Good Fight (doc).

TV inc: No Exit; Antony and Cleopatra; Medea; Focus; Silent Victory-The Kitty O'Neil Story; Studs Lonigan; And Baby Makes Six; Mary and Joseph-A Story of Faith; Death Penalty; Escape; Guyana Tragedy-The Jim Jones Story; The Women's Room; A Perfect Match; Baby Comes Home; A Few Days In Weasel Creek; It Happens Next Door (host); The Blue and the Gray; Alice in Wonderland; One Man's Fight For Life (narr); The Glitter Dome (PC); A.D.

De WITT, Joyce: Act. b. Wheeling WV, Apr 23, 1949. e. Ball State U, BA. TV inc: The Osmond Family Hour; Susan Anton Show; With This Ring; Three's Company; John Ritter, Being of Sound Mind and Body; The Real Trivial Pursuit.

DEXTER, Alan (nee Dreeben): Act. b. Seychelles Island, Africa, Oct 21, 1925. e. Hammadryad U, Zanzibar. Films inc: It Came from Outer Space; Time Limit; The Enemy Below; Paint Your Wagon; Kiss Me Stupid; Gable and Lombard.

TV inc: Helter Skelter.

Thea inc: Call Me Mister; The G.I. Hamlet; The Music Man.

(Died Dec. 19, 1983).

DEXTER, John: Dir. b. England, 1935. Thea inc: Each in His Own Wilderness; Chicken Soup with Barley; Toys in the Attic; The Sponge Room; Saint Joan; Hobson's Choice; Othello; A Woman Killed with Kindness; The Misanthrope; Equus (Tony-1975); The Party; Phaedra Britannica; Black Comedy and White Lies; The Unknown Soldier and His Wife; In Praise of Love; The Merchant; The Portage to San Cristobal of A.H.; Heartbreak House.

Films inc: The Virgin Soldiers; Sidelong Glances of a Pigeon Kicker; I Want What I Want.

De YOUNG, Cliff: Act. b. Inglewood, CA, Feb 12, 1946. e. CA State Coll, BA; IL State U. Films inc: Sunshine; A Perfect Couple; Shock Treatment; Independence Day; The Hunger; Reckless; Protocol; Secret Admirer.

TV inc: Sticks and Bones; Centennial; The Seeding of Sarah Burns; Hunter's Moon; King; Fun and Games; Scared Straight; An Invasion of Privacy; This Girl For Hire; Master of the Game; Robert Kennedy & His Times; Deadly Intentions.

Thea inc: Hair.

DIAMOND, I.A.L.: Wri. b. Unghani, Rumania, Jun 27, 1920. e. Columbia U, BA. Films inc: Murder in the Blue Room; Never Say Goodbye; Love and Learn; Always Together; The Girl from Jones Beach; Monkey Business; Something for the Birds; That Certain Feeling; Love in the Afternoon; Merry Andrew; Some Like It Hot; The Apartment (Oscar-1960); One, Two, Three; Irma la Douce; Kiss Me, Stupid; The Fortune Cookie; Cactus Flower; The Private Life of Sherlock Holmes; The Front Page; Avanti; Fedora (& prod); Buddy Buddy.

DIAMOND, Neil: Singer-Sngwri. b. Brooklyn, NY, Jan 24, 1941. Recording artist; concerts.

Films inc: Jonathan Livingston Seagull (mus) (Grammy-score-1973); Every Which Way But Loose (mus); The Last Waltz (act); The Jazz Singer (act & mus).

Bway inc: Dancin'.

TV inc: Live--And in Person; Olympic Gala.

Songs inc: Kentucky Woman; Sweet Caroline; I'm A Believer; Cherry, Cherry, Cherry: Solitary Man; You'll Be a Woman Now; Song Sung Blue; Play Me; Walk on Water.

Albums inc: Beautiful Noise; Love At the Greek; I'm Glad You're Here Tonight; You Don't Bring Me Flowers; September Morn.

DICKINSON, Angie: Act. b. Kulm, ND, Sep 30, 1932. Films inc: Sins of Rachel Cade; Rio Bravo; Oceans 11; The Killers; Point Blank; The Outside Man; Klondike Fever; Dressed To Kill; Charlie Chan and the Curse of the Dragon Queen; Death Hunt.

TV inc: Police Woman; Overboard; Pearl; The Suicide's Wife; Alan King's Thanksgiving Special--What Do We Have To Be Thankful For; Dial "M" For Murder; Sixty Years Of Seduction (host); Cassie & Co; One Shoe Makes It Murder; Perry Como's Christmas In Paris; Dom DeLuise and Friends; Candid Camera--Now and Then (co-host); The Rodney Dangerfield Special--I Can't Take it No More; Jealousy; Dean Martin's Celebrity Roast; The Hilarious Unrehearsed Antics Of The Stars; A Touch Of Scandal; The Magic Of David Copperfield VII; Hollywood Wives.

DICKINSON, Thorold: Dir. b. Bristol, England, 1903. Films inc: The High Command; Spanish ABC; The Arsenal Stadium Mystery; Gaslight; The Prime Minister; Next of Kin; Men of Two Worlds; The Queen of Spades; Secret People; Hill 24 Doesn't Answer.

Ret. 1956 to teach film at Slade School, London.

(Died April 14, 1984).

DIDION, Joan: Wri. b. Sacramento, CA, Dec 5, 1934. e. UC Berkeley. Winner of Vogue mag contest for young writers, began with mag writing promotional copy; later asso feature ed; film reviewer. Films inc: (in collab with husband John Gregory Dunne) Panic in Needle Park; Play It As It Lays (from her novel); A Star Is Born (Remake); True Confessions.

DIEHL, Walter: Union Exec. b. Revere, MA, Apr 13, 1907. e. Northeastern U. Started as proj 1927; 1946; bus agt Local 182 1953 Int'l Rep IATSE; 1957 Int'l asst p; 1974, IATSE p; (Tony-special-1979).

DIENER, Joan: Act. b. Cleveland, OH, Feb 24. e. Sarah Lawrence Coll. NY stage debut, 1948, Small Wonder. Bway inc: Season in the Sun; Kiss Me Kate; Kismet; Ziegfeld Follies; At the Grand; Destry Rides Again; La Belle; Man of La Mancha; Cry for us All; Odyssey; Home Sweet Homer.
TV inc: Androcles and the Lion.

DIERKOP, Charles: Act. b. LaCrosse, WI, Sep 11, 1936. Films inc: Butch Cassidy and the Sundance Kid; Pound; The Pawnbroker; The Sting.
TV inc: Police Woman; The Deerslayer; Revenge of the Gray Gang.

DIETRICH, Dena: Act. Bway inc: The Prisoner of Second Avenue; Here's Where I Belong; The Freaking out of Stephanie Blake; Cindy; The Rimers of Eldritch.
TV inc: Adam's Rib; Karen; Friends and Lovers; The Practice; Trouble With People; Turnabout; Baby Comes Home; Scamps.
Films inc: The Wild Party; Crazy World of Julius Vrooder; North Avenue Irregulars; Captain Midnight.

DIETRICH, Marlene (Maria Magdalene von Losch): Act. b. Berlin, Dec 27, 1901. Attended Max Reinhardt's School of Drama. Debut in Viennese version of play, Broadway. Films inc: (in Germany) Blue Angel. (In Hollywood): Morocco; Blonde Venus; Desire; Destry Rides Again; Manpower; Pittsburgh; The Spoilers; Golden Earrings; Witness for the Prosecution; Judgment at Nuremberg; Just A Gigolo.
(Special Tony 1968).

DIETZ, Howard M: Lyr-Wri. b. NYC, Sep 8, 1896. H of Lucinda Ballard. Publicist, became Dir Pub MGM 1924, remained that position until 1957. Named VP Loew's Inc, 1957. Began writing for Broadway 1924, Dear Sir, in collab with Jerome Kern.
Shows inc: Poppy; Ziegfeld Follies; Merry-Go-Round; Keep Off the Grass; Inside USA; The Gay Life; Jennie; Three's A Crowd; The Band Wagon; Flying Colors; Revenge With Music; At Home Abroad.
Films inc: The Band Wagon, That's Entertainment; That's Entertainment II.
Opera inc: English versions of Die Fledermaus; La Boheme.
Songs inc: Moanin' Low; I Guess I'll Have To Change My Plans; I Love Louisa; Dancing in the Dark; A Shine On Your Shoes; You and The Night and the Music; That's Entertainment.
(Died July 30, 1983)

DIFFRING, Anton: Act. b. Koblenz, Germany, Oct 20, 1918. e. Berlin Acad of Drama. Films inc: State Secret; Albert RN; The Sea Shall Not Have Them; The Colditz Story; I Am a Camera; The Man Who Could Cheat Death; Circus of Horrors; The Heroes of Telemark; Fahrenheit 451; Counterpoint; Where Eagles Dare; Zeppelin; Operation Daybreak; Valentino; The Accuser; The Swiss Conspiracy; Tusk; Victory; S.A.S. a San Salvador (S.A.S.--Terminate With Extreme Prejudice); Der Schnuffler (Sniffing Around).
TV inc: The Last Hours; A Small Revolution; The Fourposter; The Million Pound Note; A Place in the Sun; The Winds of War.

DIGHTON, John: Wri. b. London, Dec 8, 1909. e. Cambridge. Films inc: Champagne Charlie; Nicholas Nickleby; Saraband for Dead Lovers; Kind Hearts & Coronets; The Happiest Days of Your Life; The Man in the White Suit; Who Goes There!; Roman Holiday; The Swan; The Devil's Disicple.

DILLER, Barry: Exec. b. Feb 2, 1942. Joined ABC 1966. In 1968, made exec asst to vp in chg pgmng and dir of feature films; 1971, made vp feature films and Circle Entertainment, responsible for, The Tuesday Movie of the Week, The Wednesday Movie of the Week and Circle Film original features for airing on ABC-TV; also acquired and scheduled theatrical features for TV on ABC Sunday Night Movie and ABC Monday Night Movie. In 1974 joined Par Pictures, ChmnB and CEO; March 1983, in corporate reorganization, also P of all Gulf & Western leisure-time enterprises; resd. Sept. 1984 to become bd chmn and CEO of 20th Century Fox and an associate in TCF Holdings Inc., the parent company.

DILLER, Phyllis: Act. b. Lima, OH, Jul 17, 1917. On stage for 1st time at age 37, stand-up comedienne, San Francisco's Purple Onion. Bway inc: Hello, Dolly. Films inc: Boy, Did I Get a Wrong Number!; Eight on the Lam; Did You Hear the One About the Traveling Sales-

lady?; The Private Navy of Sgt. O'Farrell; The Adding Machine; Pink Motel.
TV inc: The Phylis Diller Show; The Beautiful Phyllis Diller Show; The Monte Carlo Show; Take One; Gary Owens' All Nonsense News Network Special; The Merriest of the Merry--Bob Hope's Christmas Show--A Bagful of Comedy; I Love Men; Dean Martin's Celebrity Roast.

DILLMAN, Bradford: Act. b. San Francisco, Apr 14, 1930. e. Yale. Films inc: A Certain Smile; In Love and War; Compulsion; Francis of Assisi; A Rage to Live; Jigsaw; Escape from the Planet of the Apes; The Iceman Cometh; The Enforcer; The Lincoln Conspiracy; The Amsterdan Kill; Piranha; The Swarm; Love & Bullets; Guyana-Cult of the Damned; Sudden Impact; El Tesoro del Amazones (The Treasure Of The Amazon).
TV inc: Last Bride of Salem *(Emmy-*1975); Jennifer-A Woman's Story; Before and After; The Memory of Eva Ryker; Tourist; King's Crossing; The Legend of Walks Far Woman; Hot Pursuit.

DILLON, Matt: Act. b. Westchester, NY, Feb 18, 1964. Films inc: Over The Edge; Little Darlings; My Bodyguard; Tex; Liar's Moon; The Outsiders; Rumble Fish; The Flamingo Kid.
TV inc: The Great American Fourth of July and Other Disasters.

DILLON, Melinda: Act. b. Hope, AR. Films inc: Bound for Glory; Slap Shot; Close Encounters of the Third Kind; F.I.S.T.; Absence of Malice; Right Of Way; A Christmas Story; Songwriter.
Thea inc: Who's Afraid of Virginia Woolf?; You Know I Can't Hear You When the Water's Running; A Way of Life.
TV inc: The Critical List; Transplant; Marriage Is Alive and Well; The Shadow Box; Fallen Angel; Hellinger's Law; Insight/Decision To Love; Insight/Rendezvous; The Juggler of Notre Dame; Insight/The Fiddler; Insight/The Game Room; Space.

DIMMOCK, Peter: Exec. b. England, Dec 6, 1920. e. Dulwich Coll. Prod and Commentator BBC-TV. Head of BBC Outside Broadcasts, 1954-72; Head of BBC Enterprises, 1973; joined ABC Sports as an exec, 1977.

DISHY, Bob: Act. Bway inc: Chic; From A to Z; Second City; Flora, The Red Menace; By Jupiter; Something Different; The Goodbye People; A Way of Life; The Creation of the World and Other Business; An American Millionaire; The Good Doctor; Murder at Howard Johnsons; Sly Fox.
Films inc: Lovers and Other Strangers; The Big Bus; The Last Married Couple in America; First Family; Author! Author!
TV inc: The Cafeteria; The Comedy Zone.

DIXON, Ivan: Act-Dir. b. NYC, Apr 6, 1931. e. Western Reserve U. Began as extra in Edge of the City. Films inc: Car Wash (act); Trouble Man (dir); The Spook Who Sat By The Door (dir). Palmerstown (dir); Palms (dir); Frederick Douglass--Slave and Statesman (dir).
TV inc: Studio One;Plamerstown (dir); Palms (dir).

DIZON, Jesse: Act. b. Oceanside, CA, Jun 16, 1950. e. UC Santa Barbara. Films inc: Cambodian; Prisoners; Midway; MacArthur.
TV inc: Lady of the House; Critical List; Operation Petticoat; Gold Watch; Dinky Hocker; Court Martial of General Yamashita.

DMYTRYK, Edward: Dir. b. Grand Forks, BC, Canada, Sep 4, 1908. Films inc: The Hawk; The Devil Commands; Seven Miles from Alcatraz; Hitler's Children; Murder My Sweet; Back to Bataan; Cornered; Till the End of Time; Crossfire; So Well Remembered; Obsession; (career interrupted when, as one of so-called Unfriendly 10, went to prison for contempt of Congress for refusal to testify before House Un-American Activities Committee; after serving term he testified and resumed career); Mutiny; The Sniper; Eight Iron Men; The Juggler; The Caine Mutiny; Broken Lance; The End of the Affair; Soldier of Fortune; The Left Hand of God; The Mountain; Raintree County; The Young Lions; Warlock; The Blue Angel; A Walk on the Wild Side; The Carpetbaggers; Where Love Has Gone; Mirage; Alvarez Kelly; Anzio; Shalako; Bluebeard; Hollywood on Trial (act) (Doc).

DOBSON, Kevin: Act. b. NYC, Mar 18, 1943. Films inc: Love Story; Bananas; Klute; The Anderson Tapes; The French Connection; Carnal Knowledge; Midway; All Night Long.

TV inc: The Nurses; The Doctors; Kojack; Stranded; Greatest Heroes of the Bible; The Immigrants; Transplant; Orphan Train; Hardhat and Legs; Reunion; Mark, I Love You; Mickey Spillane's Margin For Murder; Shannon; Knots Landing; Sweet Revenge.

DOBSON, Kevin: Dir. b. Australia. Films inc: The Mango Tree.

TV inc: Gone to Ground; Image of Death; Demolition; The Last Outlaw; I Can Jump Puddles; Winner Take All; Squizzy Taylor; The Dean Case; The Keepers.

DOBSON, Tamara: Act. b. Baltimore, MD, May 14. e. MD Inst of Art, BA. Films inc: Fuzz; Cleopatra Jones; Cleopatra Jones and the Casino of Gold; Norman, Is That You?; Chained Heat.

TV inc: Murder at the World Series; Jason of Star Command; Amazons.

DOBYNS, Lloyd: TV News. b. Newport News, VA., Mar, 12, 1946. e. Washington and Lee University. Began as newsman WDBJ-TV, later with WCUM, WAVY-TV, WNEW-TV before joining NBC, 1969; 1972, Paris corr; 1974, wri-anchor Weekend; co-anchor NBC News Overnight; Monitor. TV inc: Gambling; If Japan Can, Why Can't We?; America Works When America Works; An American Adventure--The Rocket Pilots; Bataan - The Forgotten Hell; First Camera; The Falklands/Oh, What A Sorry War.

DOCKRY, Nancy: Exec. b. Niagara Falls, NY, Mar 24. e. Syracuse U, BS chem eng; Columbia, PhD, Math. Started as wri on soaps; joined ABC 1960 in corporate training program; 1962 dir pgm dept Dancer-Fitzgerald-Sample; 1964 media dir Procter and Gamble; 1967, account exec Procter & Gamble; 1969 account supv Procter & Gamble; 1970 vp-adv American Home Products; 1975 vp, sr agent William Morris NY office; 1976 moved to Coast office; 1978 vp for pgm devlpt & prodn Nephi Productions; 1979, vp Universal TV; 1980 vp of network tv for Time-Life TV; Dec. 1983, VP film & TV Dvlpmnt Jay Bernstein Prodns.

TV inc: (Supv prod) The Wall.

DOCTOROW, E(dgar) L(awrence): Wri. b. NYC, Jan. 6, 1931. Author of novels Welcome to Hard Times and Ragtime which were made into films. Plays inc: Drinks Before Dinner. Films inc: Daniel.

DR. SEUSS: (See GEISEL, Ted).

DODERER, Joop: Act. b. Velsen, Holland, Aug 28, 1921. Early career with Amsterdam City Theatre interrupted by WW2; resumed stage career; in 1958 began children's TV series Swiebertga which ran 17 years becoming most popular tv show in Holland before he decided to end it; continued local theatre career while on TV.

TV inc: Mother Makes Five (Britain); Wuthering Heights; Professor Stranger.

Films inc: The Human Factor; Moord in Extase (Murder in Ecstasy); De Prooi (The Prey).

DOLIN, Anton: Dancer-Chor. (Sydney Patrick Healey-Kay):b. Sussex, England, 1904. First English dancer in 20th century to achieve world recognition. Joined Diaghilev's Ballet Russe as soloist. 1924-25, again 1928-29, Train Bleu created for him; 1934, Principal dancer with Old Vic Sadler Wells ballet, dancing Giselle with Markova; 1935 formed Markova-Dolin Company; 1939 joined American Ballet Theatre; during WW2 toured extensively again with Markova; 1949 formed group which became London Festival Ballet; 1962-64, dir Rome Opera Ballet; art advisor Les Grands Ballets Canadiens.Knight ed 1981. Thea inc: (London) The Mitford Girls.

Died Nov. 25, 1983.

DOMBASLE, Arielle: Act. b. Norwich, CT., 1955. Films inc: Perceval; Tess; Fruits of Passion; Le Beau Mariage (A Perfect Marriage); Pauline at the Beach; Los Motivos de Berta (Berta's Motives).

TV inc: Lace; Lace II.

DOMERGUE, Faith: Act. b. New Orleans, Jun 16, 1925. Films inc: Vendetta; Where Danger Lives; This Island Earth; California; One on Top of the Other; Legacy of Blood; The House of the Seven Corpses.

DOMINGO, Placido: Tenor. b. Madrid, Spain, Jan. 21, 1941. e. Conservatory Mexico City. Made operatic debut 1961. Star tenor with Metropolitan Opera (debut 1968), La Scala, Covent Garden, Hamburg State Opera; Vienna State Opera; NYC Opera; San Francisco Opera; National Hebrew Opera.

Films inc: La Traviata; Carmen.

TV inc: Texaco Star Theatre--Opening Night;; Burnett 'Discovers' Domingo; International OTI Song Festival; Olympic Gala; Placido Domingo Celebrates Seville (Great Performances) *(Emmy-host-1984)*; Night Of 100 Stars II; Placido Domingo Steppin' Out With The Ladies.

Recs inc: La Voce D'Oro; Verdi and Puccini duets; Le Villi.

DOMINO, Fats (Antoine Domino): Pianist-Singer-Sngwri. b. New Orleans, Feb 26, 1928. Albums inc: Here Comes Fats Domino; Fats On Fire; Getaway With Fats Domino; Stompin' Fats Domino; Trouble in Mind; Fats Is Back.

DONAHUE, Elinor: Act. b. Tacoma, WA, Apr 19,1937. W of Harry Ackerman. Films inc: Mr Big; Tenth Avenue Angel; Unfinished Dance; Three Daring Daughters; Girls Town; Love Is Better Than Ever.

TV inc: Father Knows Best; The Odd Couple; Sign-On; The Grady Nutt Show; High School U.S.A.; Days Of Our Lives; Hear Me Cry.

DONAHUE, Phil: TV pers. b. Cleveland, OH, Dec 21, 1935. e. Notre Dame, BBA. H of Marlo Thomas. Began working as anncr at KYW-TV & AM, Cleveland, news dir WABJ, Adrian, MI, moved to WHIO-TV & AM, Dayton, to do morning newscasts; interviews with Teamster Boss Jimmy Hoffa and Billy Sol Estes were picked up nationally by CBS; became host of Conversation Piece, phone-in talk show; debuted the Phil Donahue Show Nov 6, 1967 on WLWD-TV, Dayton; show syndicated two years later; moved to Chicago 1974 where program, now called Donahue, rated as reaching more households than any other syndicated talk show *(Emmys-host-1977, 1978, 1979, 1980, 1981, 1982, 1983)*; Love, Sex--and Marriage (narr); does tri-weekly segments for Today Show.

DONAHUE, Troy (Merle Johnson, Jr): Act. b. NYC, Jan 17, 1937. Summer stock, Bucks County Playhouse, Sayville Playhouse. Films inc: A Summer Place; The Crowded Sky; Rome Adventure; A Distant Trumpet; Sweet Savior; Godfather, Part II; Tin Man; Grandview, U.S.A.

TV inc: Surfside 6; Hawaiian Eye; CHiPS; Malibu.

DONALDSON, Roger: Dir-Prod. b. Ballarat, Australia, Nov 15, 1945. Films inc: The Adventure World of Sir Edmund Hillary; Winners & Losers; Sleeping Dogs; Smash Palace (& wri); The Bounty (dir only).

DONALDSON, Sam (Samuel Andrew Donaldson Jr): TV News. b. El Paso, TX, Mar 11, 1934. e. U of TX El Paso, BA; USC. Started 1961 as radio-tv reporter WTOP, Washington; joined ABC 1967 as Capitol Hill reporter; 1977, White House Correspondent; 1979 also became anchor ABC World News Tonight Sunday.

DONAT, Peter: Act. b. Kentville, Nova Scotia, Jan 20. Films inc: Russian Roulette; The Godfather II; The Hindenburg; A Different Story; F.I.S.T.; The China Syndrome; City on Fire; Highpoint; Bay Boy; Mirrors (Marianne); Massive Retaliation.

TV inc: Cyrano de Bergerac; The Missiles of October; The Suicide's Wife; Fun and Games; A Matter of Life and Death; Golden Gate; The Princess and the Cabbie; Flamingo Road; Rona Jaffee's Mazes & Monsters.

Thea inc: The Chinese Prime Minister; A Touch of Spring.

DONATI, Danilo: Cos dsgn. b. Luzzara, Italy. dsgn for Luchino Visconti stage prodns, Italy; supervising art dir RAI, Italian tv net. Films inc: La Mandragola; The Gospel According to St. Matthew; The Taming of the Shrew; Romeo and Juliet *(Oscar-1968)*; Oedipus Rex; Medea; The Clowns; Decameron; Fellini's Satyricon; Brother Sun, Sister Moon; Fellini's Amarcord; Fellini's Casanova *(Oscar-1976)*; Hurricane; Flash Gordon.

DONEN, Stanley: Prod-Dir. b. Columbia, SC, Apr 13, 1924. On Broadway as dancer in Pal Joey; Best Foot Forward; Beat The Band. (Dance dir) Cover Girl; Anchors Aweigh. Films inc: (dir) Kiss Them For Me; Seven Brides For Seven Brothers; Funny Face; On The Town; Damn Yankees; Indiscreet (& co-prod). (Prod-dir) Once More, With Feeling; Surprise Package; Arabesque; Staircase; Two for the Road;

Bedazzled; The Little Prince; Lucky Lady; Movie, Movie; Saturn 3; Blame It On Rio.

DONFELD (Donald Lee Feld): Cos dsgn. b. Los Angeles, Jul 3, 1934. e. Chouinard Art Institute; LA Trade Tech Jr Coll. Films inc: Hemingway's Adventures of a Young Man; The Second Time Around; Under the Yum Yum Tree; Hombre; The Chase; The Outrage; The Cincinnati Kid; Days of Wine and Roses; The Great Race; The April Fools; They Shoot Horses, Don't They?; Fun With Dick and Jane; Who'll Stop The Rain (Tuesday Weld cos only); Le Magnifique; Diamonds Are Forever; One on One; Who Is Killing the Great Chefs of Europe?; The China Syndrome; Class; Brainstorm; Prizzi's Honor.

TV inc: The Pirate; Wonder Woman; Herb Alpert and the Tijuana Brass Specials; Dinah Shore in Las Vegas.

DONIGER, Walter: Dir-Wri-Prod. b. NYC, 1917. e. Duke U; Harvard Grad School of Business. Films inc: Rope of Sand (sp); Duffy of San Quentin (prod-dir-sp); Along the Great Divide (sp); The Steel Cage (prod-dir-sp); Safe at Home Cease Fire (sp); The Steel Jungle (dir-sp); Unwed Mother (dir); Tokyo Joe (adapt); Alaska Seas (sp); Hold Back the Night (sp); Guns of Fort Petticoat (sp).

TV inc: Peyton Place; The Survivors (exec prod); Jigsaw; The Bold Ones; Bracken's World; Maverick; The Man Who Never Was; Checkmate; Bat Masterson; Men Into Space; MacKenzie's Raiders; 77 Sunset Strip; Bourbon Street; Cheyenne; Movin' On; Switch; McCloud; Delvecchio; Roots (sp); Kentucky Woman.

DONLAN, Yolande: Act. b. Jersey City, NJ, Jun 2, 1920. Thea inc: School for Brides; Kiss and Tell; Three's a Family; Born Yesterday.

Films inc: Turnabout; Miss Pilgrim's Progress; Mr Drake's Duck; Penny Princess; They Can't Hang Me; Expresso Bongo; Jigsaw; Eighty Thousand Suspects; Seven Nights in Japan.

DONLEAVY, J P (James Patrick Donleavy): Wri. b. NYC, Apr 23, 1926. e. Trinity Coll. Plays inc: Fairy Tales of New York; What They Did in Dublin with the Ginger Man; A Singular Man; The Onion Eaters; The Plays of J P Donleavy; The Beastly Beatitudes of Balthazar B. Novels inc: The Ginger Man.

DONNELL, Jeff: Act. b. S Windham, ME, Jul 10, 1921. Films inc: A Night to Remember; He's My Guy; In a Lonely Place; Sweet Smell of Success; Gidget Goes Hawaiian; The Iron Maiden; Stand Up and Be Counted.

TV inc: Portrait of a Stripper; General Hospital.

DONNELLY, Donal: Act. b. Bradford, Yorks, England, Jul 6, 1931. Thea inc: Serjeant Musgrave's Dance; The Playboy of the Western World; The Scatterin'; Red Roses for Me; Philadelphia, Here I Come; The Mundy Scheme (dir); Sleuth; My Astonishing Self; Faith Healer (Bway).

Films inc: Shake Hands With The Devil; The Knack; The Mind of Mr Soames; Waterloo.

TV inc: Juno and the Paycock; The Plough and the Stars; Yes Honestly; The Statesman-Benjamin Franklin; Omnibus.

DONNELLY, Ralph E: Exec. b. Lynbrook, NY, Jan 20, 1932. Started at Variety 1949; 1951 to Long Island Press; gm, Associated Independent Theatres, 1953-65; film buyer, AIT, 1965-73; Independent film buyer, 1973-76; head film buyer, RKO Stanley Warner, 1976-79; dir of ops & film buying, Cinema Five, 1979.

DONNENFELD, Bernard: Exec. b. NYC, Oct 28, 1926. e. NYU; NYU School of Law, LLB. Supv corp affairs, Legal Dept Par Pictures, 1957-61; exec asst, asst secy Par Hollywood studio, 1961-64; asst to p 1964-65; vp, World Wide prod & admin 1965-69; p, The Filmmakers group, 1970.

DONNER, Clive: Dir. b. London, Jan 21, 1926. Films inc: The Secret Place; Heart of a Child; A Marriage of Convenience; Here We Go Round the Mulberry Bush; Alfred the Great; Vampire; The Nude Bomb; Charle Chan and the Curse of the Dragon Queen.

TV inc: Danger Man; Sir Francis Drake; Mighty and Mystical; British Institutions; Tempo; Rogue Male; The Thief of Baghdad; She Fell Among Thieves; Oliver Twist; The Scarlet Pimpernel; To Catch A King; A Christmas Carol; Arthur The King.

Thea inc: Kennedy's Children.

DONNER, Jorn: Wri-Dir. b. Helsinki, Feb 5, 1933. e. Helsinki U. Dir at Swedish Film Institute, 1972-75; then prod of feature films; dir, prod Jorn Donner Prodns. Films inc: (in Sweden & Finland) A Sunday in September; To Love; Rooftree; Black and White (& prod); Portraits of Women (& prod); Three Scenes with Ingmar Bergman (& prod); The Bergman File (& prod); Home and Refuge; Black Sun (A Necessary Action); Yhdeksan Tapaa Lahestya Helsinkia (Nine Ways To Approach Helsinki) (& prod-edtr-commentator); Fanny and Alexander (exec prod); Eishockey-Fieber (Hockey Fever); Angelan Sota (Angela's War) (exec prod-act); Dirty Story (& prod).

TV inc: Efter Repetitionen (After the Rehearsal) (prod).

DONNER, Richard: Dir. Films inc: X-15; Salt and Pepper; Twink; The Omen; Superman; Inside Moves; The Toy; Ladyhawke (& prod); The Goonies (& prod).

DOOHAN, James Montgomery: Act. b. Vancouver, BC, Mar 3, 1920. Films inc: The Wheeler Dealers; The Satan Bug; Bus Riley's Back in Town; Pretty Maids All in a Row; Star Trek-the Movie; Star Trek II--The Wrath of Khan; Star Trek III--The Search For Spock.

TV inc: Star Trek.

DORAN, Ann: Act. b. Amarillo, TX, Jul 28, 1911. On screen from 1934 in numerous two-reelers with Three Stooges, Harry Langdon, Andy Clyde; Films inc: Zoo in Budapest; Way Down East; Penny Serenade; Air Force; I Love a Soldier; Pride of the Marines; Roughly Speaking; The Strange Love of Martha Ivers; Magic Town; No Sad Songs for Me; The High and the Mighty; Rebel Without a Cause; The Female Animal; Where Love Has Gone; Topaz; There Was a Crooked Man; The Hired Hand.

TV inc: National Velvet; Jesse James; Hey, Landlord; Longstreet; How the West Was Won; Peter Lundy and the Medicine Hat Stallion; Little Mo; Greatest Heroes of the Bible; Backstairs at the White House; Shirley; Crazy Times; Advice to the Lovelorn; All the Way Home.

DORATI, Antal: Comp-Cond. b. Budapest, 1906. e. Budapest Academy of Music, becoming at 18 youngest person ever to receive degree. On graduation appointed coach, later cond of Budapest Royal Opera House; 1928-33 permanent First Cond Munster Opera House; 1934-41 mus dir Ballet Russe de Monte Carlo; US debut as cond with National Symphony Orch, Washington, 1937; 1941-42 dir NY Opera Co; 1942-45 Mus Dir American Ballet Theatre; org Dallas Symphony Orch 1945. Remained as mus dir until 1949 when he was named mus dir Minneapolis Symphony; 1963-1967 Chief Cond BBC Symphony; 1967-74 Chief Cond Stockholm Symphony; since Sep 1977 Mus Dir Detroit Symphony; made more than 500 recordings.

DORS, Diana (nee Fluck): Act. b. Swindon, England, Oct 23, 1931. e. London Academy of Music and Dramatic Art. Films inc: Lady Godiva Rides Again; The Weak and the Wicked; Is Your Honeymoon Really Necessary?; Miss Tulip Stays the Night; Yield to the Night; I Married a Woman; The Unholy Wife; The Long Haul; On the Double; The Sandwich Man; Berserk; There's a Girl in My Soup; The Amazing Mr Blunden; The Amorous Milkman; Confessions of a Driving Instructor; Steaming.

TV inc: The Innocent; Dr. Jekyll and Mr. Hyde; Timon of Athens.

(Died May 4, 1984).

D'ORSAY, Fifi (Yvonne Lussier): Act. b. Montreal, Canada, Apr 16, 1904. In vaude before Hollywood. Films inc: They Had To See Paris; Hot For Paris; Women Everywhere; On the Level; Those Three French Girls; Mr. Lemon Of Orange; Young As You Feel; Going Hollywood; Wonder Bar; Accent on Youth; Three Legionnaires; The Gangster; What A Way To Go; The Art of Love; Assignment to Kill.

Bway inc: Follies.

(Died Dec. 2, 1983).

DORTORT, David: Wri-Prod. b. NYC, Oct 23, 1920. e. CCNY, BA. Films inc: The Lusty Men; Cry in The Night; The Big Land; Reprisal; Clash By Night; TV inc: (wri) Cavalcade of America; Panic; Waterfront; Public Defender; An Error in Chemistry; The Ox Bow Incident. (Prod) The Cowboys; The Restless Gun; Hunter's Moon (& wri). (Crea-exec prod) Bonanza; High Chaparral.

DOTRICE, Roy: Act. b. Guernsey, Channel Islands, May 26, 1925. Began acting in revue by ex-POW's; in rep groups; joined Royal Shakespeare Company. Thea inc: A Midsummer Night's Dream; King Lear; The Cherry Orchard; Richard II; Henry IV; Brief Lives (& Bway); The Latent Heterosexual; The Hero; One at Night; Mother Adam; Lucy Crown; The Apple Cart; The Passion of Dracula; Oliver!; Mr. Lincoln (Bway); A Life (Bway); Murder in Mind; Kingdoms (Bway).
TV inc: Brief Lives; The Caretaker; Imperial Palace; Dickens of London.
Films inc: Cheech and Chong's The Corsican Brothers; Amadeus.

DOTY, Dennis E.: Exec. b. Newhall, CA, Jul 20, 1941. e. USC, BA. VP primetime variety programs, ABC-TV; vp TV crea aff, Marble Arch Prodns; 1980 sr vp crea aff; resd, Jan 1983. TV inc: (exec prod) Jane Doe; Sunset Limousine; The Return of Marcus Welby, M.D. (prod); Consenting Adult (supv prod).

DOUGLAS, Gordon: Dir. b. NYC, Dec 15, 1907. Small roles in Eastern studios. To Hollywood 1932. Hal Roach Co. Writer; collab. Topper series; The Housekeeper's Daughter. Dir 30 Our Gang Shorts. Films inc: Saps at Sea; Broadway Limited; The Devil with Hitler; First Yank into Tokyo; Walk a Crooked Mile; Mr. Soft Touch; Between Midnight and Dawn; Kiss Tomorrow Goodbye; The Great Missouri Raid; Only the Valiant; I Was a Communist for the FBI; Come Fill the Cup; Mara Maru; Them; So This Is Love; The Charge at Feather River; The McConnell Story; Sincerely Yours; Santiago; The Big Land; Bombers B-52; Fort Dobbs; Yellowstone Kelly; Follow That Dream; Rio Conchos; Robin and the Seven Hoods; Sylvia; Harlow; Stagecoach (remake); In Like Flint; Chuka; Tony Rome; The Detective; The Lady in Cement; Barquero; They Call Me Mr. Tibbs; Slaughter's Big Rip Off; Viva Knievel.
TV inc: Nevada Smith.

DOUGLAS, Kirk (Issur Danielovich): Act. b. Amsterdam, NY, Dec 9, 1916. e. St Lawrence U, BA. Bway inc: Spring Again; The Sisters; Kiss and Tell; The Wind Is Ninety; One Flew Over The Cuckoo's Nest.
On screen from 1946. Films inc: Out of the Past; I Walk Alone; Mourning Becomes Electra; The Walls of Jericho; A Letter to Three Wives; Champion; Young Man With a Horn; The Glass Menagerie; Along the Great Divide; Detective Story; The Big Sky; The Juggler; Ulysses; 20,000 Leagues Under the Sea; Lust for Life; Gunfight at the OK Corral; Paths of Glory; The Vikings (& prod); Spartacus (& prod); Town Without Pity; Lonely Are the Brave (& prod); Two Weeks in Another Town; The List of Adrian Messenger (& prod); Seven Days in May (& prod); Cast a Giant Shadow; The War Wagon; There Was a Crooked Man; Catch Me a Spy; A Man to Respect; The Fury; Indian Fighter; The Brotherhood (& prod); Summertree (& prod); Scalawag (& dir); Once Is Not Enough (& prod-dir); Posse (& prod-dir); Holocaust 2000 (& prod-dir); The Chosen; Home Movies; The Villain; Saturn 3; The Final Countdown; The Man From Snowy River; Eddie Macon's Run.
TV inc: Mousey; The Money Changers; Remembrance of Love; Draw! (PC); Salute to Lady Liberty.

DOUGLAS, Michael Kirk: Act-Prod. b. New Brunswick, NJ, Sep 25, 1944. e. U of CA at Santa Barbara, BA. S of Kirk Douglas. Films inc: (act) Hail Hero!; Adam at 6 A.M.; Summertree; Napoleon & Samantha; Coma; The China Syndrome (& prod); Running (& prod); It's My Turn; The Star Chamber. (Prod): One Flew Over the Cuckoo's Nest (Oscar-1975); Romancing the Stone (& act); Starman (exec prod).
TV inc: (act) When Michael Calls; The Streets of San Francisco.

DOUGLAS, Mike: TV Pers. b. Chicago, Aug. 11, 1925. Syndicated host of daily talk-variety program, The Mike Douglas Show. Originally a singer; hosted a celebrity talk-show on radio in Chicago before moving to TV in the Early 60s. TV show started in Cleveland, then Philadephia; moved to Hollywood in 1978; (Emmy-1967); TV inc: A Gift of Music.

DOUGLAS, Robert (nee Finlayson): Act-Dir. b. Bletchley, England, Nov 9, 1909. e. Bickley Hall Coll; RADA. Films inc: (act) The Decision of Christopher Blake; The Adventures of Don Juan; The Fountainhead; The Buccaneer's Girl; The Flame and the Arrow; Kim; Thunder on the Hill; At Sword's Point; The Prisoner of Zenda; The Desert Rats; Saskatchewan; The Virgin Queen; Good Morning, Miss Dove; Helen of Troy.

TV inc: (dir) 12 O'Clock High; Fugitive; Cannon; Streets of San Francisco; Barnaby Jones; Medical Center; Baretta; Columbo; Big Hawaii; Hunter; Man from Atlantis; Quincy; Centennial; Hart to Hart.

DOUGLAS, Sarah: Act. b. Stratford-on-Avon, England, Dec. 12, 1952. Thea inc: Gnomes.
Films inc: Final Program; The Brute; The People That Time Forgot; Superman; Superman II; Conan The Destroyer.
TV inc: Harlequinade; The Inheritors; Falcon Crest; On Top All Over The World.

DOUGLAS, Wallace: Dir. b. Winnipeg, Canada, Aug 15, 1911. Former actor. Thea inc: Zoo in Silesia; Love Goes to Press; Twice Upon a Time; Collector's Item; A Month of Sundays; Let Them Eat Cake; Let Sleeping Wives Lie; She's Done It Again; Don't Just Lie There, Say Something; A Bit Between the Teeth; Fringe Benefits.

DOUGLASS, Robyn: Act. b. Japan. e. UC San Francisco; ACT. With improv groups The Committee and Story Theatre before joining Second City in Chicago. Films inc: Breaking Away; Partners; Romantic Comedy.
TV inc: Golden Gate; Girls in the Office; The Clone Master; Ten Speed and Brownshoe; Nightingale; Her Life as a Man.

DOURIF, Brad: Act. b. Huntington, WV. Thea inc: The Ghost Sonata; The Doctor In Spite of Himself; Three Sisters; Future is the Eggs; Time Shadows; When You Comin Back, Red Ryder?.
Films inc: Split; W W and the Dixie Dancekings; One Flew Over the Cuckoos's Nest; Group Portrait With Lady; Eyes of Laura Mars; Wise Blood; Heaven's Gate; Ragtime; Dune.
TV inc: The Mound Builders; The Gardener's Son; Studs Lonigan; Guyana Tragedy--The Story of Jim Jones; I, Desire.

DOVE, Billie (Lilian Bohny): Act. b. May 14, 1900. Originally a model. Joined Ziegfeld Follies 1917. Films inc: Beyond the Rainbow; Polly of the Follies; Wanderer of the Wasteland; The Black Pirate; All the Brothers Were Valiant; The Marriage Clause; The Yellow Lily; The Night Watch; One Night at Susie's; Painted Angel; Blondie of the Follies; Diamond Head; The Age of Love.

DOWD, Nancy: Wri. b. Framingham, MA. e. Smith Coll. Films inc: Slap Shot; Coming Home (Oscar-story-1978); Love (& dir).

DOWELL, Anthony J: Dancer. b. London, Feb 16, 1943. e. Royal Ballet School. Principal dancer the Royal Ballet since 1963; principal dancer American Ballet Theatre since 1978.

DOWLING, Doris: Act. b. 1921. Films inc: The Lost Weekend; The Blue Dahlia; Bitter Rice; Othello; Running Target; The Car.
TV inc: Scruples.

DOWN, Lesley-Anne: Act. b. London, Mar 17, 1954. Child model for TV and film commercials. Film debut at age 14 in All the Right Noises. Films inc: Pope Joan; Scalawag; Brannigan; The Pink Panther Strikes Again; A Little Night Music; The Betsy; Hanover Street; The Great Train Robbery; Rough Cut; Sphinx; Nomads.
TV inc: Upstairs, Downstairs; Heartbreak House; The One and Only Phyllis Dixie; Unity Mitford; Murder Is Easy; The Hunchback of Notre Dame; The Last Days of Pompeii; Arch Of Triumph.
Thea inc: Great Expectations; Hamlet.

DOWNS, Hugh: Bcaster-Act. b. Akron, OH, Feb 14, 1921. e. Columbia U. Supv of Science Programming, NBC's Science Dept. TV inc: Hawkins Falls; Kukla, Fran & Ollie; American Inventory; Home; Sid Caesar Show; Tonight (Jack Paar Show); Concentration; Today. Radio inc: NBC's Monitor. Films inc: Oh, God! Book II.

DOWNS, Johnny: Act. b. Brooklyn, NY, Oct. 10, 1913. Started in silent short films; member "Our Gang" for two years; toured in vaude with Our Gang revue, later as a single. Bway inc: Strike Me Pink; Growing Pains; The Ragged Army; Are You With It.
Films inc: Outlaw of the Red River; Valley of the Giants; The Crowd; Babes in Toyland; College Scandal; The Virginia Judge; Coronado; The First Baby; Pigskin Parade; College Holiday; Blonde Trouble; Thrill of a Lifetime; Hunted Men; Algiers; Swing Sister Swing; Laugh It Off; A Child is Born; I Can't Give You Anything But Love,

Baby; Melody and Moonlight; Honeymoon for Three; Adam Had Four Sons; Redhead; All American Co-Ed; Campus Rhythm; Trocadero; Forever Yours; Rhapsody in Blue; The Kid From Brooklyn; Square Dance Jubilee; The Girls of Pleasure Island; Cruisin' Down The River.

DOYLE, David: Act. b. Omaha, NE, Dec 1. Films inc: Paper Lion; A New Leaf; April Fools; Loving; Six Gates to Hell; Capricorn One; The Comeback.

TV inc: 200 Years of American Humor;The New Dick Van Dyke Show; The Confessions of Dick Van Dyke; Bridget Loves Bernie; A Very Special Love. Charlie's Angels; John Ritter-Being of Sound Mind and Body; The Blue and The Gray; Wait Till Your Mother Gets Home; The Invisible Woman.

Bway inc: Will Success Spoil Rock Hunter?; Promises, Promises; The Beauty Part; I Was Dancing.

DOZIER, William: Exec (ret). b. Omaha, NE, Feb 13, 1908. e. Creighton U, AB. Literary agent for: Sinclair Lewis; Kathleen Norris; Erle Stanley Gardner; F. Scott Fitgerald. Head of story & writing dept Paramount, 1941-45; exec asst to vp in chg. prod RKO, 1945-48; asso head of prod, Universal, 1948-51; CBS-TV, vp chg. programs, 1951-59; vp chg. production & member bd of dir, Screen Gems (Col) 1959-64; p of own co. Greenway Prods, 1964-72. Films inc: Harriet Craig; Two of a Kind; Batman.

TV inc: Batman; The Green Hornet; The Donna Reed Show; Bewitched; The Farmer's Daughter; Not Just Another Affair (act).

DRABINSKY, Garth H: Prod-Exec. b. Toronto, Canada, 1950. e. U Toronto, LLD. Co-founder Pan-Canadian Film Distributors; P Cineplex Corp., Canadian multi-screen circuit; dir CFMT-TV, Toronto; former publ Canadian Film Digest. Films inc: The Disappearance; The Silent Partner; The Changeling; Tribute; The Amateur; Losin' It (exec prod).

Bway inc: A Broadway Musical.

DRAGON, Carmen: Comp-Cond. b. Antioch, CA, Jul 28, 1914. e. San Jose State Coll, MA. F of Daryl Dragon. Cond Hollywood Bowl Symphony; Capitol Symph; Royal Philharmonic, BBC Symphony. Films inc: Cover Girl (Oscar-1944).

(Died March 28, 1984).

DRAGON, Daryl: Mus. b. Pasadena, CA, Aug 27, 1942. S of the late Carmen Dragon. With The Beach Boys before teaming with wife Toni Tennille as The Captain and Tennille. TV inc: The Toni Tennille Show; The Great American Sing-A-Long.

(Grammy-Record of the Year-1975).

DRAGOTI, Stan: Dir. b. NYC Oct. 4, 1932. Films inc: Dirty Little Billy; Love At First Bite; Mr. Mom.

DRAKE, Alfred (nee Capurro): Act-Dir. b. NYC, Oct 7, 1914. e. Brooklyn Coll, BA. Bway inc: (act) Oklahoma!; Sing Out, Sweet Land; Beggar's Holiday; Kiss Me Kate; succeeded Yul Brunner in The King and I; Kismet (Tony-1954); Much Ado About Nothing. (Dir): The Liar; Courtin' Time; Salt of the Earth; Millicent's Castle; Love Me Little; Lock Up Your Daughter; The Skin of Our Teeth.

Films inc: (act) Tars and Spars.

DRAKE, Betsy: Act. b. Paris, 1923. Films inc: Every Girl Should be Married; Room for One More; Pretty Baby; The Second Woman; Clarence the Cross-Eyed Lion.

DRAKE, Jim: Dir. e. Columbia U. TV inc: Mary Hartman, Mary Hartman (150 episodes); Fernwood 2Night; Alice; Ball Four; The Supreme Court and Civil Liberties; Young and Restless; Love of Life; Where the Heart Is; Sanford; Double Trouble.

DREIFUSS, Arthur: Dir-Wri-Prod. b. Frankfurt, Germany, Mar 25, 1908. e. U of Frankfurt; NYU; Columbia. Former child cond and chor. Films inc: (dir) Mystery in Swing; Baby Face Morgan; The Payoff; Campus Rhythm; Ever Since Venus; Eadie Was a Lady; Boston Blackie's Rendezvous; Two Blondes and a Redhead; Manhattan Angel; The Quare Fellow; The Love-Ins; For Singles Only; The Young Runaways. TV inc: Wildlife in Crisis.

Thea inc: Allure; Baby Pompadour.

Feb 1981 quit directing to become agent.

DREYFUSS, Richard: Act. b. NYC, 1948. Films inc: Dillinger; American Graffiti; The Apprenticeship of Duddy Kravitz; The Second Coming of Suzanne; Jaws; Inserts; Close Encounters of the Third Kind; The Goodbye Girl (Oscar-1977); The Big Fix (& prod); The Competition; Whose Life Is It Anyway? Sept 1982, formed indie company with Andrew Fogelson.

Thea inc: Journey to the Day; Incident at Vichy; People Need People; Major Barbara; Line; But Seriously; Whose Little Boy Are You?; The Time of Your Life; Total Abandon; The Buddy System.

DRIVAS, Robert (nee Choromokos): Act-Dir. b. Chicago, Nov 21, 1938. e. U of Chicago; U of Miami. Bway inc: (act) The Firstborn; One More River; The Wall; Diff'rent; Mrs Daly Has a Lover; The Irregular Verb to Love; And Things That Go Bump in the Night. (Dir): Bad Habits; The Ritz; Legend; Cheaters; It Had To Be You; The Man Who Had Three Arms; Peg.

Films inc: (act) Where It's At; Janice; God Told Me To; Road Movie.

TV inc: (dir) The Ugily Family.

DRIVER, Donald: Act-Dir-Plywri. Bway inc: (act) Buttrio Square; Show Boat; Hit the Trail; Status Quo Vadis. (Dir) Marat/Sade; Broadway Follies.

Plays inc: From Paris With Love (& dir); Your Own Thing (& dir); Oh, Brother (& dir-chor).

DROMGOOLE, Patrick: Dir. b. Chile, Aug 30, 1930. e. Dulwich Coll; University Coll, Oxford. Thea inc: Periphery (& act); Cockade; Entertaining Mr. Sloane; The Love Game; Little Malcolm and His Struggle Against the Eunuchs; The Anniversary; Say Goodnight to Grandma; The Case of the Oily Levantine; Man and Superman.

TV inc: (Prod) Armchair Theatre; Sunday Night Theatre; The Curse of King Tut's Tomb; Arch Of Triumph (exec prod); Jamaica Inn (supv exec prod).

DRU, Joanne (nee La Cock): Act. b. Logan, WV, Jan 31, 1923. On screen from 1946, Abie's Irish Rose. Films inc: Red River; She Wore a Yellow Ribbon; All the King's Men; Wagonmaster; 711 Ocean Drive; Vengeance Valley; Mr Belvedere Rings the Bell; Return of the Texan; The Pride of St Louis; Hell on Frisco Bay; Sincerely Yours; The Light in the Forest; September Storm; The Wild and the Innocent; Sylvia; Super Fuzz.

TV inc: Guestward Ho.

DRURY, James: Act. b. NYC, 1934. Films inc: Forbidden Planet; Love Me Tender; Bernardine; Pollyanna; Ride the High Country; The Young Warriors.

TV inc: The Virginian; Firehouse.

DRYSDALE, Don: Sports Commentator. b. Van Nuys, CA, Jul 23, 1936. Former pitcher LA Dodgers. TV inc: ABC's Monday Night Baseball; World Championship Tennis.

DUART, Louise: Act. b. Quincy, MA, Oct 30, 1950. TV inc: Kapt Kool and the Kongs; Ace's Diner; Krofft Superstars. Various voices for cartoons.

DUBIN, Charles S: Dir. b. NYC, Feb 1, 1919. e. Brooklyn Coll. TV inc: Kojak; Baretta; Movin' On; Toma; Kung Fu; Sanford and Son; The New Dr Kildare; Room 222; Hawaii Five-0; Bracken's World; Omnibus; M*A*S*H; Roots; Rodgers and Hammerstein's Cinderella; Bolshoi Ballet; Never Say Never; Topper; The Gathering, Part II; Landon, Landon and Landon; Nightengales; Man's Greatest Sports--Dribble; The Manions of America; Herbie, The Love Bug; My Palikari; Born To The Wind (Night Eyes); Ace Crawford, Private Eye; Jennifer Slept Here.

Du BOIS, Ja'net: Act. b. Philadelphia, Aug 5. Films inc: Diary of a Mad Housewife; Five on the Black Hand Side; A Piece of the Action; The Pawnbroker; Love With the Proper Stranger.

TV inc: Love of Life; Sammy Davis Special; On Being Black; Another World; As the World Turns; J.T.; Good Times; Hellinger's Law; Good Evening, Captain; The Sophisticated Gents; The Big Easy; The Tom Swift & Linda Craig Mystery Hour; Spencer.

Thea inc: Golden Boy; A Raisin in the Sun; Nobody Loves an Albatross.

DUBOIS, Marie: Act. b. Paris, Jan 12, 1937. e. Conservatoire of Dramatic Arts. Films inc: Le Signe de Lion; Une Femme est une Femme; Jules et Jim; La Ronde; Les Fetes Galantes; Le Voleur; Gonfles a Bloc; La Maison des Bories; The Innocent; My American Uncle; Garcon!

Du BREY, Claire: Act. b. Bonner's Ferry, ID, Aug 31, 1892. Silent screen star. Films inc: Reward of the Faithless; Heart of a Child; Two Sisters; Broadway to Hollywood; The Sin of Nora Moran; The Devil Doll; Ramona; Wife, Doctor and Nurse; Nothing Sacred; The Baroness and the Butler; Everybody's Baby; Alexander Graham Bell; The Blue Bird; Charlie Chan's Murder Cruise; Brigham Young; Black Diamonds; Juke Box Jenny. Ret May 1962.

DUBS, Arthur R.: Prod. Films inc: Adventures of the Wilderness Family; The Great Adventure; Across the Great Divide; Mountain Family Robinson (& wri); Wilderness Family Part 2 (& wri); Windwalker; Sacred Ground; Mystery Mansion.

DUFF, Howard: Act. b. Bremerton, WA, Nov 24, 1917. Repertory Playhouse, Seattle. With KOMO radio. In Army, 1941-45. Radio's original Sam Spade. Films inc: Brute Force; All My Sons; Private Hell 36; Broken Star; Naked City; While the City Sleeps; Boy's Night Out; Panic in the City; The Late Show; A Wedding; Kramer vs Kramer; Double Negative; Oh God! Book II.

TV inc: Mr Adams and Eve; Dante; Felony Squad; The D.A.; Battered; The Heist; Valentine Magic on Love Island; Flamingo Road; The Dream Merchants; Flamingo Road; John Steinbeck's East of Eden; Lily for President?; The Wild Women of Chastity Gulch; This Girl For Hire.

DUFFY, James E: Exec. b. Decatur, IL. Joined ABC in Chicago, 1949. Moved to ABC TV, 1955. Returned to radio as dir of sls, ABC Central Div; named exec vp, national dir of sls for ABC Radio, 1962. In 1963, named vp in charge of sls for ABC TV; 1970 P ABC-TV Network; June 1984 added duties as sr vp ABC Broadcast Group.

DUFFY, Patrick: Act. b. Townsend, MT, Mar 17, 1949. e. U of WA. TV inc: The Stranger Who Looks Like Me; Hurricane; The Last of Mrs Lincoln; Man From Atlantis; Dallas; Knot's Landing; Enola Gay--The Men, The Mission, The Atomic Bomb; Don't Go To Sleep; A Tribute to Martin Luther King Jr.--A Celebration of Life; Yearbook--Class Of 1967.

Films inc: Vamping (& exec prod).

DUFOUR, Val: Act. b. New Orleans, Feb 5, 1927. e. LA State U, BA; Catholic U of America, MA. Films inc: The Lonely Night; Ben Hur; LA Confidential; King of Kings; Land of Plenty.

TV inc: The Edge of Night; Another World; Search for Tomorrow (Emmy-1977).

Thea inc: High Button Shoes; South Pacific; Picnic; Mister Roberts; Stalag 17.

DUGGAN, Andrew: Act. b. Dec 28, 1923. Films inc: Patterns; The Bravados, The Chapman Report; FBI Code; Westbound; Merrill's Marauders; Seven Days in May; Secret War of Harry Frigg; The Glory Guys; The Skin Game; It's Alive; The Bears and I; Doctor Detroit.

TV inc: Jigsaw; Bourbon Street Beat; Room for One More; Lancer; Overboard; A Fire in the Sky; The Incredible Journey of Dr. Meg Laurel; Backstairs at the White House; One Last Ride; The Long Days of Summer; M-Station-Hawaii; Jake's Way; Momma The Detective; The Winds of War.

DUKE, Daryl: Dir. TV inc: The Senator (Emmy-The Day the Lion Died-1971); I Heard the Owl Call My Name (& prod); The Thorn Birds; Florence Nightinga le.

Films inc: Payday; Griffin & Phoenix; The Silent Partner; Hard Feelings.

DUKE, Patty: Act. b. NYC, Dec 14, 1947. W of John Astin (since marriage billed as Patty Duke Astin). Bway inc: The Miracle Worker; Isle of Children. Films inc: The Miracle Worker (Oscar-supp-1962); Billie; The Valley of the Dolls; My Sweet Charlie; Me, Natalie; You'll Like My Mother; The Swarm; By Design.

TV inc: Armstrong Circle Theatre; The Prince and the Pauper; Wuthering Heights; US Steel Hour; Meet Me in St. Louis; Swiss Family Robinson; My Sweet Charlie (Emmy-1970); The Power and the Glory; The Patty Duke Show; Captains and Kings (Emmy-1977); Before and After; Women in White; The Miracle Worker (Emmy-1980); The Women's Room; Mom, The Wolfman and Me; Girl On The Edge of Town (Reflections); The Violation of Sarah McDavid; Please Don't Hit Me, Mom. Insight/God's Guerrillas; It Takes Two; Something So Right; September Gun; Insight/The Hit Man; Best Kept Secrets; George Washington; Hail To The Chief.

DUKES, David: Act. b. San Francisco. Bway inc: School for Wives; The Great God Brown; Don Juan; The Visit; Holiday; Love for Love; Rules of the Game; Travesties; Rebel Women; Dracula; Bent; Frankenstein.

Films inc: The Wild Party; A Little Romance; The First Deadly Sin; Only When I Laugh; Without A Trace.

TV inc: Glory Hallelujah; Beacon Hill; 79 Park Avenue; Family; A Fire In the Sky; Go West, Young Girl; Some Kind of Miracle; The Triangle Factory Fire Scandal; Mayflower--The Pilgrim Adventure; Portrait of a Rebel--Margaret Sanger; Miss All-American Beauty; The Winds of War; George Washington; Cat On A Hot Tin Roof (Broadway On Showtime); Sentimental Journey; Space.

DULLEA, Keir: Act. b. Cleveland, OH, May 30, 1936. Films inc: The Hoodlum Priest; David and Lisa; Mail Order Bride; The Thin Red Line; Bunny Lake is Missing; Madame X; The Fox; 2001, A Space Odyssey; Last of the Big Guns; Paperback Hero; Paul and Michelle; Black Christmas; Because He's My Friend; BrainWaves; Blind Date; 2010.

TV inc: Brave New World; The Legend of John Hammer; Starlost; Legend of the Golden Gun; Brave New World; The Hostage Tower; No Place To Hide; The Next One (feevee).

Bway inc: Cat on a Hot Tin Roof; Bus Stop.

DUNAWAY, Faye: Act. b. Bascom, FL, Jan 14, 1941. e. Boston U. Films inc: Doc; Puzzle of A Downfall Child; The Arrangement; The Happening; Hurry Sundown; Bonnie and Clyde; The Thomas Crown Affair; Oklahoma Crude; Little Big Man; The Three Musketeers; Chinatown; The Towering Inferno; Network (Oscar-1976); The Champ; Arthur Miller on Home Ground; The First Deadly Sin; Mommie Dearest; The Wicked Lady; Ordeal By Innocence; Supergirl.

TV inc: Trials of O'Brien; On the Seaway; After the Fall; Hogan's Goat; The Woman I Love; Evita Peron; Ellis Island; Christopher Columbus.

Bway inc: A Man for All Seasons; After the Fall; But for Whom Charlie?; Hogan's Goat; Candida; Old Times; Streetcar Named Desire; The Curse of An Aching Heart.

DUNCAN, Sandy: Act. b. Henderson, TX, Feb 20, 1946. Bway inc: Music Man; Carousel; The Sound of Music; Finian's Rainbow; Life with Father; Canterbury Tales; The Boy Friend; Peter Pan.

Films inc: Million Dollar Duck; Star Spangled Girl; The Cat From Outer Space; The Fox and the Hound.

TV inc: Funny Face; Sandy in Disneyland; The Sandy Duncan Special; Christmas at Disneyland; Pinocchio; Roots; 100 Years of Golden Hits.

DUNHAM, Katherine: Dancer-Chor. b. Joliet, IL, 1910. e. U Chicago. Formed own dance school, created idea of Negro Ballet; formed Katherine Dunham Dancers, debut with Chicago Opera Co at Chicago World's Fair; chor Aida for Metropolian Opera 1963.

Bway inc: Cabin In the Sky; Windy City; Bal Negre; Bamboche.

Films inc: Cabin In the Sky; Carnival of Rhythm (short); Star Spangled Rhythm; Stormy Weather; Pardon My Sarong (chor only); Casbah.

DUNING, George: Comp-Arr-Cond. b. Richmond, IN, Feb 25, 1908. e. Cincinnati Conservatory of Music. Arr. for Kay Kyser orch; dir. radio program Kollege of Musical Knowledge. Film scores inc: From Here to Eternity; Salome; The Jolson Story; All Ashore; My Sister Eileen; Pal Joey; Picnic; The Eddie Duchin Story; Cowboy; Houseboat; Bell, Book and Candle; The World of Suzy Wong; That Touch of Mink; Toys in the Attic; The Man With Bogart's Face.

TV inc: The Naked City; Tightrope; The Big Valley; The Farmer's Daughter; Glynis; No Time for Sergeants; The Silent Force; The Partridge Family; The Top of the Hill; The Dream Merchants; Goliath Awaits; Beyond Witch Mountain; Zorro and Son.

Songs inc: Cry for Happy; My Kind of Guy; Picnic; Song Without End; Strangers When We Met; You Are My Dream.

DUNLAP, Richard D: Dir-Prod. b. Pomona, CA, Jan 30, 1923. e. Yale, BA, MFA. TV inc: Kraft Theatre; Omnibus; Bell Telephone Hour; Frank Sinatra & Mitzi Gaynor Specials; The Young and the Restless (*Emmys*-dir-1975-1978).

DUNLOP, Frank: Dir. b. Leeds, England, Feb 15, 1927. e. University Coll. Thea inc: The Bishop's Bonfire; Schweik in the Second World War; Son of Oblomov; The Taming of the Shrew; Any Wednesday; Too True to be Good; Saturday Night and Sunday Morning; The Trojan Women; Edward H; Home and Beauty; The White Devil; The Captain of Kopenick; The Maids; Deathwatch; The Alchemist; Bible One; French Without Tears; Scapino; Macbeth; Habeas Corpus; Antony and Cleopatra; Camelot; Lolita (Bway).

DUNNE, Griffin: Act-prod. b. NYC, Jun 8, 1955. Studied at Neighborhood Playhouse; with Uta Hagen. Thea inc: (act) Album; Marie and Bruce; Coming Attractions; Hotel Play.
   Films inc: American Werewolf in London (act); Head Over Heels (prod & act); The Fan (act); Baby It's You (prod); Almost You (act); Johnny Dangerously (act).
   TV inc: The Wall (act).

DUNNE, Irene: Act. b. Louisville, KY, Dec 20, 1904. e. Chicago Coll of Music. Screen debut 1931. Films inc: Cimarron; Back Street; The Age of Innocence; Sweet Adeline; Roberta; The Magnificent Obsession; Showboat; The Awful Truth; Love Affair; Anna and the King of Siam; Life With Father; I Remember Mama; The Mudlark; Theodora Goes Wild.

DUNNE, John Gregory: Wri. b. Hartford, CT., May 25, 1932. e. Princeton, BA. H of Joan Didion. Films inc: Panic in Needle Park; Play It As It Lays; True Confessions.

DUNNE, Philip: Wri-Dir-Prod. b. NYC, Feb 11, 1908. e. Harvard U. Films inc: The Count of Monte Cristo; The Rains Came; Stanley and Livingston; Johnny Apollo; How Green Was My Valley; The Late George Apley; The Ghost and Mrs. Muir; Pinky; David and Bathsheba; Prince of Players (prod-dir); The View from Pompey's Head (& Prod-dir); Three Brave Men (& dir); Ten North Frederick (& dir); Blue Denim (& dir); Blindfold (& dir). Plays inc: Mr. Dooley's America.

DUNNING, John: Prod. b. Montreal, Canada, May 27, 1927. Films inc: The House By the Lake; Rabid; Blackout (& wri); Meatballs; Happy Birthday to Me; My Bloody Valentine; Spacehunter--Adventures in the Forbidden Zone; The Surrogate; Hot Water (exec prod).

DUNNOCK, Mildred: Act. b. Baltimore, MD, Jan 25, 1904. Films inc: The Corn Is Green; Kiss of Death; Death of a Salesman; Viva Zapata; The Jazz Singer; The Trouble with Harry; Love Me Tender; Peyton Place; Baby Doll; The Nun's Story; Sweet Bird of Youth; Behold a Pale Horse; Seven Women; Whatever Happened to Aunt Alice; The Spiral Staircase; Arthur Miller on Home Ground.
   TV inc: Death of a Salesman; The Best Place to Be; And Baby Makes Six; Baby Comes Home; The Big Stuffed Dog; The Patricia Neal Story; Isabel's Choice; James Clavell's Children's Story.
   Bway inc: The Corn is Green; Foolish Notion; Lute Song; Another Part of the Forest; Death of a Salesman; Cat on a Hot Tin Roof; The Milk Train Doesn't Stop Here Anymore; The Chinese; Colette; Days in the Trees; Tartuffe.

DURANG, Christopher: Plywri. b. Montclair, NJ., Jan. 2, 1949. e. Harvard (BA); Yale School of Drama (MFA). Plays inc: The Nature Of The Universe; 'dentity Crisis; Better Dead Than Sorry; I Don't Generally Like Poetry But Have You Read 'Trees?'; The Life Story of Mitzi Gaynor, or Gyp; The Marriage Of Betty and Boo; The Idiots Karamazov; Das Lusitania Songspiel; A History Of American Film; Sister Mary Ignatius Explains It All To You; Beyond Therapy; Baby With The Bath Water. Acted in: I Don't Generally Like Poetry But Have You Read 'Trees?'; Das Lusitania Songspiel; Hotel Play; The Birthday Present.

DURAS, Marguerite: Wri. b. Indo-China, 1914. e. Sorbonne, Paris. Plays inc: The Square; La Musica; The Viaduct; Days in the Trees; The Truck; A Place Without Doors; The Lovers of Viorne.
   Films inc: Hiroshima Mon Amour; Nathalie Granger; India Song (dir); Les Enfants (The Children).

DURBIN, Deanna: Act. b. Winnipeg, Canada, Dec 4, 1922. Films inc: Three Smart Girls: One Hundred Men and a Girl; Mad About Music; That Certain Age; Three Smart Girls Grow Up; First Love; It Started with Eve; The Amazing Mrs Holliday; Christmas Holiday; Can't Help Singing; Because of Him; I'll Be Yours; Something in the Wind; Up in Central Park; For the Love of Mary (last film 1948).
   (*Honorary Oscar*-1938).

DURNING, Charles: Act. b. Highland Falls, NY. Bway inc: The Andersonville Trial; The Championship Season; The Au Pair Man.
   Films inc: Harvey Middleman, Fireman; I Walk the Line; The Pursuit of Happiness; Hi, Mom!; The Fury; Sisters; The Sting; Twilight's Last Gleaming; Dog Day Afternoon; The Hindenburg; Harry and Walter Go To New York; The Choir Boys; Tilt; When a Stranger Calls; The Greek Tycoon; The Muppet Movie; Starting Over; Enemy of the People; North Dallas 40; Die Laughing; The Final Countdown; True Confessions; Sharky's Machine; The Best Little Whorehouse In Texas; Deadhead Miles; Tootsie; To Be or Not to Be; Two of a Kind; Hadley's Rebellion; Mass Appeal; Stick.
   TV inc: The Connection; Queen of the Stardust Ballroom; Studs Lonigan; Attica; A Perfect Match; Crisis At Central High; The Best Little Girl In The World; Casey Stengel; The Girls In Their Summer Dresses and Other Stories by Irwin Shaw (The Monument); Dark Night of the Scarecrow; Working; Mr. Roberts; P.O.P.; Side By Side; Eye To Eye.

DURRELL, Michael: Act. b. Brooklyn, Oct 6, 1943. Bway inc: Phedre; Hamlet; Murder Among Friends: Death of a Salesman (rev.); Emperor Henry IV; Cock-A-Doodle Dandy; The Sunshine Boys.
   TV inc: The Guiding Light; Search for Tomorrow; The Class of '65; When Every Day Was the 4th of July; A Killing Affair; Harvest Home; The Immigrants; The Sunshine Boys; V; Chiefs; V--The Final Battle; V (The Series).
   Films inc: Thank God It's Friday.

DURRENMATT, Friedrich: Wri. b. Berne, Switzerland, Jan 5, 1921. e. U of Zurich; U of Berne. Plays inc: Es Steht Geschrieben; Der Blinde; Romulus Der Grosse; The Marriage of Mr Mississippi; An Angel Comes to Babylon; The Visit; The Physicists; Portrait of a Planet; Der Mitmacher; Achterloo.
   Films inc: Es Gesachah am Hellichten Tage; The Marriage of Mr Mississippi; The Visit.
   TV inc: Breakdown; The Physicists.

DUSAY, Marj (nee Mahoney): Act. b. Russell, KS, Feb 20, 1936. Films inc: Sweet November; Pendulum; Breezy; Clam Bake; 30 Dangerous Seconds; MacArthur.
   TV inc: Peace in the Family; Climb An Angry Mountain; Most Wanted; Murder in Peyton Place; A Fire in the Sky; Paradise Connection; Battles - The Murder That Wouldn't Die; Capitol.

DUSSAULT, Nancy: Act. b. Pensacola, FL, Jun 30, 1936. e. Northwestern U. Bway inc: Street Scene; Dr Willy Nilly; The Mikado; The Cradle Will Rock; Do Re Mi; The Sound of Music; Bajour; Carousel; Half a Sixpence; Fiorello!; Detective Story; The Gershwin Years.
   TV inc: The Beggar's Opera; Love Is; Good Morning America (co-host); Too Close For Comfort; Musical Comedy Tonight; The Way They Were; A Gift of Music; Singin (Love Songs) (& crea) (cable); I Love TV Test; Night Of 100 Stars II.
   Films Inc: The In-Laws.

d'USSEAU, Loring: Prod-Dir. b. Los Angeles, Dec 19, 1930. In prodn dept KTLA, LA, 1959; pgm dir 1964; exec prod NBC/KNBC 1971; sr pgm exec KCET 1975; entered indie prodn 1979.
   TV inc: (Prod) Steve Allen Show; Korean Legacy; Harkness Ballet; Up Through the Ranks; And the Children Die; Steve Allen's Meeting of the Minds (*Emmy*-prod-1981); Nancy Wilson Show; James Wong Howe--The Man and His Movies; Handle With Care and Dignity; Number Our Days; The Good Old Days of Radio; Agnes DeMille and the Joffrey Ballet.

DUVALL, Robert: Act. b. San Diego, CA, Jan. 5, 1931. e. Principia Coll. Neighborhood Playhouse, NY. Broadway, off-Broadway prodns. Films inc: To Kill A Mockingbird; Captain Newman, M.D.; The Chase; The Detective; M*A*S*H; Bullitt; The Godfather; The Godfather Part II; The Conversation; The 7 1/2% Solution; Network; The Eagle Has

Landed; The Greatest; The Betsy; Apocalypse Now; The Great Santini; True Confessions; The Pursuit of D.B. Cooper; Tender Mercies (& asso prod) (*Oscar*-act-1983); Angelo, My Love (wri-dir); The Terry Fox Story; The Stone Boy; The Natural; 1918 (singer).

TV inc: Ike.

DUVALL, Shelley: Act. b. Houston, TX, 1949. Films inc: Brewster McCloud; McCabe and Mrs Miller; Thieves Like Us; Nashville; Three Women; Annie Hall; The Shining; Popeye; Time Bandits.

TV inc: Twilight Theatre; The Secret World Of The Very Young; Booker; Faerie Time Theatre (cable) (prod).

DYER-BENNET, Richard: Singer-Comp. b. Leicester, England, Oct 6, 1913. e. UC Berkeley. Recognized as a major innovator in folk mus.

DYKSTRA, John: Cin. b. Long Beach, CA, Jun 3, 1947. Films inc: Silent Running; Star Wars (*Oscar*-visual effects-1977; also Class II Academy Technical Award 1977); Battlestar Galactica; Star Trek - The Movie; Firefox (prod special visual effects).

TV inc: Battlestar Galactica (*Emmy*-1979) (prod first five hours and theatrical); Starflight--The Plane That Couldn't Land (sfx); Lifeforce (special visual effects).

DYLAN, Bob (nee Zimmerman): Act-Comp. b. Duluth, MN, May 24, 1941. Recording artist; concert tours in US, Europe. Films inc: Don't Look Back; The Last Waltz; Renaldo and Clara (prod-dir-wri-act-edtr).

Albums inc: Desire; Slow Train Coming.

(*Grammys*-album of the year-1972; rock vocal-1979).

DYSART, Richard A.: Act. Bway inc: The Quare Fellow; Six Characters in Search of an Author; A Man for All Seasons; All In Good Time; The Little Foxes; The Ruffian on the Stair; A Place Without Doors; That Championship Season.

Films inc: The Crazy World of Julius Vrooder; The Terminal Man; Meteor; Enemy of the People; Prophecy; Being There; The Thing; The Falcon And The Snowman; Mask; Pale Rider.

TV inc: First You Cry; Bogie; The Ordeal of Dr. Mudd; Churchill and the Generals; People vs. Jean Harris; Bitter Harvest; The Seal; Missing Children--A Mother's Story; Concealed Enemies; Insight/The Game Room; Malice In Wonderland.

DZUNDZA, George: Act. b. Rosenheim, Germany. e. St John's U; studied with Stella Adler. Thea inc: King Lear; That Championship Season; Legend; A Streetcar Named Desire; The Ritz.

Films inc: The Deer Hunter; Honky Tonk Freeway; Brubaker; Streamers; Best Defense.

TV inc: Salem's Lot; The New Maverick; Skokie; A Long Way Home; Open All Night; The Face of Rage; The Lost Honor of Kathryn Beck; When She Says No; Brotherly Love; The Rape Of Richard Beck.

EARLEY, Candice: Act. b. Ft Hood, TX, Aug 18, 1950. e. Trinity U. Bway inc: Hair; Jesus Christ, Superstar; Grease. TV inc: All My Children.

EASDALE, Brian: Comp. b. England, 1909. Film scores inc: Ferry Pilot; Black Narcissus; The Red Shoes (*Oscar*-1948); An Outcast of the Islands; The Battle of the River Plate.

EASTHAM, Richard (Dickinson Swift Eastham): Act-Singer. b. Opelousas, LA, Jun 22, 1918. Films inc: There's No Business Like Show Business; Man on Fire; Toby Tyler; That Darned Cat; Not With My Wife You Don't; Murderers Row; Tom Sawyer; Battle for the Planet of the Apes; McQ.

Bway inc: A Flag is Born; Medea; South Pacific; Call Me Madam.

TV inc: Tombstone Teritory; Wonder Woman; Silent Night, Lonely Night; The President's Plane Is Missing; Missiles of October; Attack on Terror; Rich Man, Poor Man; Salvage; Condominium; A Wedding on Walton's Mountain.

EASTON, Robert (nee Burke): Act. b. Milwaukee, WI, Nov 23, 1930. Quiz Kid on radio 1945. Dialect Coach for many top stars. Films inc: The Red Badge of Courage; Belles on Their Toes; Comin' Round the Mountain; The Warlover; The Loved One; Paint Your Wagon; Pete's Dragon; When You Comin' Back, Red Ryder.

TV inc: Burns and Allen; Playhouse 90; Climax; Hallmark Hall of Fame; Profiles in Courage; Centennial; The Oklahoma City Dolls;

Jacqueline Bouvier Kennedy.

EASTON, Sheena Singer b. Glasgow, Scotland, April 27, 1959. e. Royal Scottish Academy Of Music And Drama. Worked local clubs; picked for BBC doc on beginning artists, which led to EMI recording contract. Films inc: For Your Eyes Only (title song). TV inc: The Glen Campbell Music Show; Sheena Easton--Act One; Live At The Palace (cable); Album Flash (cable).

Albums inc: Sheena Easton; You Could Have Been With Me; Madness, Money And Music; Best Kept Secret; A Private Heaven.

(*Grammys*-New Artist, 1981; Mexican-American Performance, 1984).

EASTWOOD, Clint: Act. b. San Francisco, May 31, 1930. In TV series Rawhide for seven and one-half years. Formed Malpaso Productions, 1969. Films inc: A Fistful of Dollars; The Good, The Bad and The Ugly; The Beguiled; Paint Your Wagon; Where Eagles Dare; Two Mules for Sister Sara; Dirty Harry; Magnum Force; Play Misty For Me (& dir); High Plains Drifter (& dir); Joe Kidd; The Outlaw Josey Wales (& dir); The Eiger Sanction (& dir); The Gauntlet (& dir); Thunderbolt & Lightfoot; The Enforcer; Every Which Way But Loose; Escape From Alcatraz; Bronco Billy (& dir); Any Which Way You Can; Firefox (& prod-dir); Honkytonk Man (& prod-dir); Sudden Impact (& prod-dir); Tightrope (& prod); City Heat; Pale Rider (& prod-dir).

EBB, Fred: Lyr. b. NYC, Apr 8, 1933. Bway inc: Flora, The Red Menace; Cabaret (*Tony*-lyr-1967); The Happy Time; Zorba; 70, Girls, 70; Liza (& prod-dir); Chicago; The Act; Woman Of the Year (*Tony*-1980); The Rink.

Films inc: Funny Lady; Lucky Lady; Cabaret ; A Matter of Time; New York, New York; French Postcards.

TV inc: Liza; Liza with a Z (*Emmys*-prod & special material-1973); Ole Blue Eyes Is Back; Gypsy in My Soul; (*Emmy*-prod-1976) Goldie and Liza Together (wri-prod).

(*Grammy*-cast album-1973).

EBERT, Roger: Critic-Wri-Tv pers. b. Urbana, IL., Jun 18, 1942. e. U of IL (BS); grad work at U of Cape Town, South Africa, U of IL., U of Chicago. Film critic Chicago Sun-Times since 1967 (Pulitzer Prize for criticism 1975).

Films inc: Beyond the Valley of the Dolls; Beneath the Valley of the Ultra Vixens.

TV inc: Sneak Previews (co-host); At the Movies (co-host); Stanley Kramer on Film; Siskel & Ebert--If We Picked The Oscars; Saturday Night Live; Carnival in Cannes.

EBSEN, Buddy: Act. b. Belleville, IL, Apr 2, 1908. Bway debut dancer in Ziegfeld's Whoopee, 1928. Dance team with sister, Vilma; played nightclubs. Films inc: Broadway Melody of 1936; Captain January; Banjo On My Knee; Red Garters; Davy Crockett; Attack; Breakfast at Tiffany's; Mail Order Bride; The Family Band.

TV inc: The Beverly Hillbillies; Davy Crockett; Barnaby Jones; The Bastard; The Critical List; Paradise Connection (& prod); Fire On The Mountain; Matt Houston.

Thea inc: Take Her, She's Mine; Our Town.

ECKSTEIN, George: Prod-Wri. b. LA, May 3, 1928. e. Stanford, BA; USC, LLB. TV inc: (Wri) The Untouchables; Gunsmoke; The Fugitive; Dr. Kildare; House on Greenapple Road. (Prod) The Fugitive; Name of the Game; Sunshine; Sara; Duel; Banacek; Tailgunner Joe; Amelia Earhart; 79 Park Avenue; Christmas Sunshine; Where the Ladies Go; Masada; Heaven on Earth (& wri); Sidney Shorr; Love, Sidney; Victims (exec prod); The Letter (exec prod); The Mississippi (exec prod); Travis McGee; The Bad Seed (exec prod-wri); Murder With Mirrors (exec prod-wri).

ECKSTINE, Billy: Singer. (William Clarence Eckstine):b. Pittsburgh, PA, Jul 8, 1914. Band singer with Earl 'Fatha' Hines then solo as headliner niteries, vaude.

Films inc: Skirts Ahoy!; Let's Do It Again. TV inc: Motown Returns To The Apollo.

Recs inc: Prime of My Life; For the Love of Ivy; My Way; Senior Soul; Feel the Warm; Stormy; If She Walked Into My Life; Soul Session.

EDELMAN, Herb: Act. b. NYC, 1930. Films inc: In Like Flint; Barefoot in the Park; The Odd Couple; The Front Page; The Yakuza; California Suite; Goin' Coconuts; On The Right Track; Smorgasbord.

TV inc: Marathon; A Cry For Love; Strike Force; 9 to 5; Shooting Stars; Murder, She Wrote.

EDEN, Barbara (nee Huffman): Act. b. Tucson, AZ, Aug 23, 1934. Films inc: Back from Eternity; Twelve Hours to Kill; Flaming Star; Voyage to the Bottom of the Sea; Five Weeks in a Balloon; The Wonderful World of the Brothers Grimm; The Brass Bottle; Seven Faces of Dr Lao; Harper Valley PTA.

TV inc: The Feminist and the Fuzz; A Howling in the Woods; How to Marry a Millionaire; I Dream of Jeannie; Harper Valley PTA; Condominium; Bob Hope's All-Star Comedy Look at the New Season; Return of the Rebels; Allen Funt's It's Only Human (Host); An NBC Family Christmas; The Best of Everything (host); Frank Mills Christmas Special.

EDGLEY, Michael Christopher: Prod. b. Melbourne, Australia, Dec 17, 1940. e. Christian Brothers Coll. Chmn of Directors of Michael Edgley International Pty, Ltd. Films inc: The Man From Snowy River; The Coolangatta Gold (exec prod); An Indecent Obsession (exec prod).

EDLUND, Richard: Cin. b. Fargo, ND, Dec 6, 1940. e. USC; US Naval Photographic School. Films inc: Star Wars (Oscar-visual effects-1977); The Empire Strikes Back (Oscar-visual effects-1980); Raiders of the Lost Ark (Oscar-visual effects-1981) (scientific Oscars (2) for concept and engineering of a beam splitter optical printer and for engineering of the Empire Motion Picture Camera System-1981); Return of The Jedi; Oscar-visual effects-1983); Ghostbusters; 2010.

TV inc: Battlestar Galactica (Emmy-1979).

EDWARDS, Blake: Prod-Dir-Wri. b. Tulsa, OK, Jul 26, 1922. H of Julie Andrews. Films inc: Panhandle; Stampede; Rainbow Round My Shoulder; Drive A Crooked Road; Notorious Landlady; Breakfast at Tiffany's; Experiment in Terror; Days of Wine and Roses; Soldier in the Rain; The Pink Panther; A Shot in the Dark; The Great Race; The Tamarind Seed; The Return of the Pink Panther; The Pink Panther Strikes Again; Revenge of the Pink Panther; 10; S.O.B; Victor/Victoria; Trail of the Pink Panther; Curse of the Pink Panther; The Man Who Loved Women; Micki & Maude (dir); City Heat (wri--as 'Sam O. Brown')

TV inc: (crea) Dante's Inferno; Peter Gunn; Mr. Lucky.

EDWARDS, Douglas: Newscaster. b. Ada, OK., July 14, 1917. e. U of AL; Emory U; U of GA Evening Coll. Joined CBS Radio News, 1942; served as chief of CBS News' Paris Bureau; has anchored a daily CBS tv news broadcast since 1949.

EDWARDS, Geoff: Act. b. Westfield, NJ, Feb 15. e. Duke U, BA. Daily morning radio show KMPC, LA. TV host of Jackpot, The New Treasure Hunt; Shoot for the Stars. Films inc: W.U.S.A.; The Comic.

EDWARDS, Ralph: Prod-TV Pers. b. Merino, CO, Jun 13, 1913. e. U of CA Berkeley, AB. Started in radio, 1929, as wri-act-prod-anncr station KROW, Oakland. Later joined CBS & NBC Radio, New York, as announcer. 1940, orig, prod, emceed Truth or Consequences for both radio & TV (Emmy-1950). Other shows inc: This Is Your Life (crea-prod-MC) (Emmys-1953,-1954); The Ralph Edwards Show (crea-prod-MC); Place the Face; Funnyboners; It Could Be You; End of the Rainbow; About Faces; Wide Country; Who in the World; The Woody Woodbury Show; Name That Tune; The Cross Wits; Knockout; This Is Your Life (exec prod); The People's Court (exec prod).

EDWARDS, Vince: Act. b. NYC, Jul 9, 1928. e. OH State U; U of HI; AADA. Films inc: Sailor Beware; Rogue Cop; The Night Holds Terror; The Killing; The Three Faces of Eve; Devil's Brigade; The Desperados; Las Vegas. The Seduction; Space Raiders; Deal of the Century.

TV inc: Studio One; Ben Casey; The Untouchables; The Deputy; The Rhinemann Exchange; Knight Rider (pilot).

EFRAIM, R. Ben: Prod. b. Afula, Israel, Jan. 19, 1938. e. Hebrew U. Exec vp Barry & Enright Films Inc; P, Unity Pictures Corp.; P, Fulton Enterprises Ltd. Films inc: The Jerusalem File; Mitchell; Shoot; Search and Destroy; Private Lessons; Private School.

EGAN, Eddie: Act. b. NYC, Jan 3, 1930. Former NYC Detective. Films inc: The French Connection; Prime Cut; Badge 272.

TV inc: Joe Forrester; Eischied; Police Story; Mickey Spillane's Murder Me, Murder You.

EGAN, Richard: Act. b. San Francisco, Jul 29, 1923. e. U of SF, BA; Stanford U, MA. Films inc: The Damned Don't Cry; Split Second; Demetrius and the Gladiators; Wicked Woman; Gog; Untamed; Violent Saturday; The View from Pompey's Head; Love Me Tender; Tension at Table Rock; These Thousand Hills; A Summer Place; Pollyanna; Esther and the King; The 300 Spartans; The Destructors; Chubasco; The Big Cube; The Amsterdam Kill.

TV inc: The Day of the Wolves; Empire; Redigo; Capitol.

Thea inc: (London) Arms and the Man.

EGGAR, Samantha: Act. b. London, Mar 5, 1939. Films inc: The Wild and the Willing; Dr. Crippen; Doctor in Distress; Psyche; The Collector; Walk Don't Run; Doctor Doolittle; The Walking Stick; The Lady in the Car; The Light at the End of the World; The Sellout; The Seven Per Cent Solution; Why Shoot The Teacher?; The Brood; The Exterminator; Demonoid; Hot Touch; Curtains.

TV inc: Anna and the King; For the Term of His Natural Life.

EGGLESTON, Colin Richard Francis: Prod-Dir-Wri. b. Melbourne, Australia, Sep 23, 1941. Films inc: Long Weekend; Innocent Prey. TV inc: Matlock Police; Rush; The Sullivans; Cop Shop; Lap Dog; Lion's Share.

EICHHORN, Lisa: Act. b. NY, Feb 4, 1952. e. Oxford; RADA. Films inc: Yanks; The Europeans; Why Would I Lie?; Cutter and Bone; The Weather in the Streets; Wildrose.

TV inc: The Wall; Feel the Heat.

Thea inc: (London) Golden Boy.

EIKENBERRY, Jill: Act. b. New Haven, CT, Jan 21, 1947. e. Yale Drama School. Bway inc: All Over Town; The Primary English Class; Just Spokes; Watch on the Rhine (rev); Onward Victoria.

Films inc: Between The Lines; The End of the World In Our Usual Bed In a Night Full of Rain; An Unmarried Woman; Butch and Sundance--The Early Days; Orphan Train; Rich Kids; Hide in Plain Sight; Arthur; The Ultimate Solution of Grace Quigley.

TV inc: Orphan Train; The Deadliest Season; Swan Song; Sessions.

EILBACHER, Cynthia (Cindy): Act. b. Saudi Arabia, Jul 7. TV inc: My Mother, the Car; Crowhaven Farm; The Senator; The Great Man's Whiskers; A Fire in the Sky; Donner Pass; The Road to Survival; Blind Sunday; Shirley; City In Fear.

Films inc: The Big Bounce; Golden Girl; Thunder Alley.

EILBACHER, Lisa: Act. b. Saudi Arabia. Sis of Cindy Eilbacher. Films inc: The Thoroughbreds; The War Between Men and Women; On the Right Track; An Officer and A Gentleman; 10 to Midnight; Beverly Hills Cop.

TV inc: The Patty Hearst Story; To Race the Wind; Love for Rent; Hardy Boys Mysteries; Going Home Again; Wheels; The Winds of War; Ryan's Four; Me & Mom.

EINHORN, Lawrence C: Prod-Dir. b. Chicago, IL, Jan 18, 1936. e. U MI. TV inc: Warner Brothers--a 50 Year Salute; Paramount Presents; Mrs America Pageant; Victor Awards; Rona Barrett Specials; That's Hollywood; Kids are People Too (Emmy-exec prod-1979); That's My Line; Television - Inside and Out.

EINSTEIN, Bob: Wri-Prod. b. Los Angeles, Nov 20, 1940. e. Chapman Coll. S of late Harry (Parkyakarkus) Einstein; B of Albert Brooks. TV inc: (wri) Smothers Brothers Show (Emmy-1969); Andy Williams Show; Love Concert; Just Friends; Pat Paulsen Show; Three for Tahiti; Sonny and Cher Show; Sonny Comedy Revue. (Prod) Van Dyke and Company (Emmy-1977); Lola Falana Specials; Redd Foxx Show.

Films inc: Another Nice Mess (wri-dir); Modern Romance (act).

EISNER, Michael: Exec. b. NYC, March 7, 1942. e. Denison U, BA. Started with programming dept, CBS-TV; joined ABC, 1966, as asst to vp & nat'l pgm dir; 1968, became dir of pgm dev, east coast; 1971, named vp daytime pgmng, ABC-TV; May, 1976, named sr vp, prime time prod and dev; Nov, 1976, left ABC to join Par as p &

CEO; Sept. 1984, resd. to go to Walt Disney Prodns. as chmn & CEO.

EKBERG, Anita: Act. b. Malmo, Sweden, Sep 29, 1931. Model. Films inc: Man in the Vault; Blood Alley; Artists and Models; War and Peace; Sheba and the Gladiator; La Dolce Vita; Boccaccio '70; The Cobra; Fellini's Clowns.
TV inc: Gold of the Amazon Women; S*H*E*.

EKLAND, Britt: Act. b. Stockholm, Sep 29, 1931. Films inc: After the Fox; The Bobo; The Double Man; The Night They Raided Minsky's; Stiletto; Percy; A Time for Loving; Baxter; Endless Night; Asylum; The Man with the Golden Gun; Royal Flash; Slaves; The Wicker Man; The Monster Club; Satan--Mistress; Dead Wrong; Fraternity Vacation.
TV inc: A Cold Peace; Trials of O'Brien; The Hostage Tower; Jacqueline Susann's Valley of the Dolls 1981.

ELAM, Jack: Act. b. Miami, AZ, Nov 13, 1916. Films inc: The Sundowners; Rawhide; Ride Vaquero; Kansas City Confidential; Jubilee Trail; Kiss Me Deadly; The Man from Laramie; Kismet; Jubal; Night Passage; Gunfight at the O.K. Corral; Baby Face Nelson; Day of the Gun; The Rare Breed; Firecreek; Support Your Local Sheriff; Cock-eyed Cowboys of Calico County; Support Your Local Gunfighter; Dirty Dingus Magee; Rio Lobo; Daughters of Joshua Cabe; Sidekicks; Huckleberry Finn; The Winds of Autumn; Grayeagle; The Norseman; Hot Lead and Cold Feet; The Apple Dumpling Gang Rides Again; The Villain; The Cannonball Run; Jinxed!; Cannonball Run II.
TV inc: The Dakotas; Temple Houston; The Texas Wheelers; Daughters of Joshua Cabe; How the West Was Won; Black Beauty; Lacy & the Mississippi Queen; Struck By Lightning; Revenge of the Red Chief; Mark Twain's America--Young Will Rogers; Legends of the West--Truth and Tall Tales; The Girl, The Gold Watch and Dynamite; Here's Boomer; Skyward Christmas; Sawyer & Finn; Detective In The House.

ELCAR, Dana: Act. b. Ferndale, MI, Oct 10. Films inc: Report to the Commissioner; The Sting; The Northfield; Minnesota Raid; A Gunfight; Soldier Blue; The Amazing Mrs Pollifax; W.C. Fields and Me; The Champ; Good Luck Miss Wyckoff; The Nude Bomb; The Last Flight of Noah's Ark; Condorman; Buddy Buddy; Blue Skies Again; All of Me; 2010; Jungle Warriors.
TV inc: St Joan; Elizabeth the Queen; Centennial; Samurai; Death Penalty; Mark, I Love You; Wendy Hooper, U.S. Army; Flamingo Road; The Long Summer of George Adams; The Day The Bubble Burst; Seven Brides For Seven Brothers; Forbidden Love; Inspector Perez; I Want To Live; Quarterback Princess; Insight/Dutton's Choice; Sweet Revenge.
Bway inc: The Pinter Plays; Summer of the 17th Doll; As Good As Gold.

ELDER, Ann: Wri. TV inc: Mitzi Gaynor Special; Perry Como Special; Flip Wilson Show; Lily Tomlin (Emmy-1974); Paul Lynde Comedy Hour; 3 Girls 3; Lily Tomlin Show (Emmy-1976); Osmond Specials; Marilyn Monroe; Collegiate Cheerleaders Championships; Carol Burnett & Co; Playboy Pajama Party; The Big Hex of Little Lulu; The Girl With ESP; Zack and the Magic Factory; That's My Line (prod); An NBC Family Christmas; Lily for President?; Texaco Star Theatre--Opening Night; Live--And in Person; Disneyland's 30th Anniversary Celebration.

ELDER, Lonne, III: Wri. b. Dec 26, 1931. e. Yale School of Drama. Films inc: Melinda; Sounder; Sounder Part 2.
TV inc: The Terrible Veil; N.Y.P.D.; Toma; Ceremonies in Dark Old Men; A Woman Called Moses; Thou Shalt Not Kill.
Plays inc: Kissin' Rattle Snakes Can Be Fun; Seven Comes Up & Seven Comes Down (Two one act plays prod off Bdway); Charades On East Fourth Street; Ceremonies in Dark Old Men.

ELDRIDGE, Florence: Act. b. NYC, 1901. Widow of Fredric March. Films inc: The Greene Murder Case; The Divorcee; The Matrimonial Bed; The Great Jasper; The Story of Temple Drake; Les Miserables; Mary of Scotland; Another Part of the Forest; An Act of Murder; Christopher Columbus; Inherit the Wind.
TV inc: First You Cry.

ELFAND, Martin: Prod. b. 1937. Started as agent, with William Morris; Chasin-Park-Citron; CMA; joined Artists Entertainment Complex

as prod; 1976 exec vp chg wldwde prodn WB; resd 1977.
Films inc: Kansas City Bomber; Dog Day Afternoon; It's My Turn; An Officer and a Gentleman; King David.

ELG, Taina: Act. b. Helsinki, Finland, Mar 9, 1931. With Sadler Wells Ballet. Films inc: The Prodigal; Diane; Gaby; Les Girls; Imitation General; The 39 Steps; The Bacchantes; The Great Experiment
Bway inc: Where's Charley; The Utter Glory of Morrissey Hall.
TV inc: Blood and Honor--Youth Under Hitler (narr).

ELIAS, Hal: Exec. b. NYC, Dec 23. Western exploitation m MGM, 1926-34; exec asst to Fred Quimby, MGM Studios, 1935-55; head MGM cartoon studio, 1955-58; VP & studio m UPA, 1959-62. Honorary Oscar 1979.

ELIKANN, Larry: Dir. b. NYC, Jul 4, 1923. e. Brooklyn Coll; Walter Hervey Coll. TV inc: James at 16; Westside Medical; Weekend Specials; After School Specials; The Great Wallendas; Charlie and the Great Balloon Chase; Supertrain; Grandpa Goes to Washington; Paper Chase; The Seven Wishes of a Rich Kid; The Revenge of the Red Chief; Where Do Teenagers Come From?; Here's Boomer; Charlie And the Great Balloon Chase; Spraggue; Berrenger's; Peyton Place--The Next Generation.

EL INDIO: See FERNANDEZ, Emilio.

ELINSON, Jack: Prod-Wri. Began as radio wri on Jimmy Durante Show; Ed Wynn Show; Garry Moore Show. TV inc: The Danny Thomas Show; Gomer Pyle, USMC; Andy Griffith (wri); The Real McCoys (wri); That Girl; The Doris Day Show; One Day at a Time; Good Times; Joe's World; Facts of Life; a.k.a. Pablo (supv prod); P.O.P. (supv prod).

ELIZONDO, Hector: Act. b. NYC, Dec 22, 1936. Films inc: Valdez is Coming; Pocket Money; Stand Up and Be Counted; Born To Win. The Taking of Pelham One Two Three; Report to the Commissioner; Thieves; Cuba; The Eves; American Gigolo; The Fan; Young Doctors In Love; Deadhead Miles; T he Flamingo Kid.
Bway inc: Mr. Roberts; Great White Hope; So Proudly We Hail; The Prisoner of Second Avenue; The Dance of Death.
TV inc: Popi; The Impatient Heart; Freebie and the Bean; Insight/Missing Persons Bureau; Medal of Honor Rag; Honeyboy; Casablanca; Feel the Heat; Women of San Quentin; a.k.a. Pablo.

ELKINS, Hillard: Prod. b. NYC, Oct 18, 1929. e. Brooklyn Coll; NYU. Bway inc: Come on Strong; Golden Boy; Oh, Calcutta!; The Rothschilds; A Doll's House; An Evening with Richard Nixon and...; Sizwe Banzi is Dead.
Films inc: Alice's Restaurant; A New Leaf; A Doll's House.
TV inc: The Importance of Being Earnest; The Deadly Game (cable); Princess Daisy.

ELKINS, Saul: Prod-Dir-Wri. b. NYC, Jun 22, 1907. e. CCNY. Started in radio as wri-dir-prod. To Hollywood 1934 as dialogue dir-wri Fox; contract wri Fox, Col, RKO, Rep; 1947 became prod WB. Films inc: Younger Brothers; One Last Fling; Homicide; House Across the Street; Flaxy Martin; Barricade; Return of the Frontiersman; This Side of the Law; Colt .45; Sugarfoot; Raton Pass; The Big Punch; Smart Girls Don't Talk; Embraceable You.

ELLIMAN, Yvonne: Singer. b. HI, 1953. Singer with Eric Clapton before solo. Recordings inc: I Don't Know How to Love Him; Food of Love; Rising Sun; Night Flight; If I Can't Have You.
Bway inc: Jesus Christ Superstar.
Films inc: Jesus Christ Superstar; Saturday Night Fever.
(Grammy-album of year-1978).

ELLINGTON, Mercer: Mus. b. Washington, D.C., Mar 11, 1919. e. Juilliard. S of late Duke Ellington. Formed own band after graduation from Juilliard; 1949, road mgr & trumpeter with Cootie Williams; 1954, gen asst to Duke Ellington; 1965, leader; mus dir Sophisticated Ladies (Bway & PPV).

ELLIOTT, Denholm: Act. b. London, May 31, 1922. e. RADA. Stage debut 1945, The Drunkard. Films inc: The Sound Barrier; The Cruel Sea; The Heart of the Matter; They Who Dare; The Night My Number Came Up; Station Six Sahara; Nothing But the Best; King Rat; Alfie;

The Spy with a Cold Nose; Here We Go Round the Mulberry Bush; The Night They Raided Minsky's; The Rise and Rise of Michael Rimmer; A Doll's House; Madame Sin; Robin and Marian; The Little Girl In Blue Velvet; Russian Roulette; Hound of the Baskervilles; The Boys From Brazil; Partners; Watership Down; It's Not The Size That Counts; Saint Jack; Zulu Dawn; Cuba; Bad Timing; Rising Damp; Sunday Lovers; Raiders of the Lost Ark; Brimstone and Treacle; The Missionary; The Wicked Lady; Trading Places; The Hound of the Baskervilles; The Razor's Edge; A Private Function.

TV inc: Sextet; Clayhanger; Blade On The Feather; Marco Polo; Camille.

Thea inc: King Of Hearts; Traveller Without Luggage; Write Me a Murder; The Crucible; The Imaginary Invalid; Chez Nous; The Return of A J Raffles.

ELLIOTT, Lang: Prod. b. Los Angeles, 1950. Co-founder The International Picture Show; co-founder, P, TriStar Pictures Inc. Films inc: They Went That-A-Way and That-A-Way; The Billion Dollar Hobo; Prize Fighter; The Private Eyes.

TV inc: Experiment in Love (doc).

ELLIOTT, Paul: Prod. b. Bournemouth, England, Dec 9, 1941. Former actor. Has presented over 100 touring shows. Thea inc: (London) When We Are Married; The Chalk Garden; Big Bad Mouse; Grease; The King and I; Her Royal Highness; Underground. (Bway) Brief Lives; I Do, I Do; 13 Rue de l'Amour; Bus Stop; Hello, Dolly!; Beatlemania.

ELLIOTT, Sam: Act. b. Sacramento, CA, Aug 9, 1944. Films inc: Butch Cassidy and the Sundance Kid; Lifeguard; The Games; Frogs; Molly and Lawless John; The Legacy; The Mask.

TV inc: Mission Impossible; Once an Eagle; Wild Times; Murder In Texas; The Shadow Riders; Travis McGee; The Yellow Rose; A Death In California.

ELLIOTT, Stephen: Act. b. NYC, Nov 27. Bway inc: Command Decision; Livin' the Life; Roman Candle; Traveller Without Luggage; Marat/Sade; A Cry of Players; In the Matter of J Robert Oppenheimer; The Miser; A Whistle in the Dark; Georgy; The Good Woman of Setzuan; The Playboy of the Western World; An Enemy of the People; A Ride Across Lake Constance; The Crucible; The Creation of the World and Other Business.

Films inc: The Hospital; Death Wish; Report to the Commissioner; The Hindenburg; Cutter and Bone; Arthur; Kiss Me Goodbye; Roadhouse 66; Beverly Hills Cop.

TV inc: Beacon Hill; Son Rise: A Miracle of Love; The Golden Honeymoon; Jacqueline Bouvier Kennedy; My Body, My Child; Hardcase; Not in Front of the Children; Winston Churchill--The Wilderness Years; Prototype; Maximum Security.

ELLIS, Brian James: Prod. b. Cheyenne, WY, Apr 3, 1953. e. USC. Films inc: Whitewater Sam; Time for the Arrow; Avalanche. TV inc: Walter Cronkite's Universe (sr prod); Honor, Duty And A War Called Vietnam.

ELY, Ron (Ronald Pierce): Act. b. Hereford, TX, Jun 21, 1938. Films inc: The Night of the Grizzly; Once Before I Die; Tarzan's Deadly Silence; Tarzan's Jungle Rebellion; Doc Savage, The Man of Bronze; Killing Me Softly; Slavers.

TV inc: Tarzan; The Seal.

EMERSON, Faye: Act. b. Elizabeth, LA, Jul 7, 1917. Films inc: Between Two Worlds; The Mask of Dimitrios; Hotel Berlin; Danger Signal; Nobody Lives Forever; Guilty Bystander; A Face in the Crowd. (Died Mar 9, 1983).

EMHARDT, Robert: Act. b. Jul 24, 1914. Films inc; The Iron Mistress; 3.10 to Yuma; Underworld USA; The Stranger; Kid Galahad; The Group; Where Were You When the Lights Went Out; Seniors; Forced Vengeance.

TV inc: Greatest Heroes of the Bible; Institute for Revenge; Aunt Mary; One Last Ride.

ENBERG, Dick: Sportscaster. e. Central MI U; IN U, PhD. Asso prof & asst baseball coach CA State Northridge before becoming voice of CA Angels baseball team; became NBC sportscaster 1975. TV inc:

Sports Challenge; Three For The Money; Sportsworld; The Way It Was (Emmy-prod-1978).

(Other Emmys-Play By Play Personality - 1981; Host, 1983).

ENDELSON, Robert Allen: Prod-Dir. b. NYC, Dec 9, 1947. e. Adelphi U, BS. Films inc: The Filthiest Show in Town; Fight for Your Life.

ENDERS, Howard: Wri-Prod-Dir. b. Philadelphia, Jul 31, 1926. e. Johns Hopkins U. TV inc: How Life Begins; The Other Walls; Black Fiddler; Rape: The Unspeakable Crime; Americans All (21 episodes); The Religions of Asia; Gerim Means Strangers; Television in America.

ENDERS, Robert J: Prod-Wri. Films inc: A Thunder of Drums (prod); The Maltese Bippy (prod); How Do I Love Thee (prod); Voices; The Maids (sp); Winter Rules (exec prod); Conduct Unbecoming (sp); Hedda (prod); Nasty Habits; Stevie (prod & dir).

TV inc: The Best of the Post; Ben Franklin; Acad Awards Show, 1968 (co-prod).

ENFIELD, Cy: Prod-Dir-Wri. b. Nov 1914. Films inc: Gentleman Joe Palooka; Stork Bites Man; The Argyle Secrets; Underworld Story; The Sound of Fury; The Search; Child in the House; Hell Drivers; Sea Fury; Jet Storm; Mysterious Island; Zulu; Sands of Kalahari; De Sade; Universal Soldier; Zulu Dawn.

ENGEL, Charles F: Exec. b. Los Angeles, Aug 30, 1937. e. MI State U, BA; UCLA. S of Samuel G Engel. In pgm development dept ABC-TV 1964-1968; 1969 exec prod Run a Crooked Mile; The Aquarians; 1972, named vp U TV; 1977, sr vp; 1980, exec vp; Sept 1981, P MCA Pay Television New Programming.

ENGEL, Georgia: Act. b. Washington, DC, Jul 28, 1948. e. HI U, BA. Bway inc: Hello, Dolly!; My One And Only. Films inc: Taking Off; The Care Bears Mov ie.

TV inc: Mary Tyler Moore Show; Betty White Show; Good Time Girls; The Day The Women Got Even; Misunderstood Monsters (voice); The Special Magic of Herself, The Elf (voice); Jennifer Slept Here; Night Of 100 Stars II.

ENGEL, Samuel G: Prod. b. Woodbridge, NY, Dec 29, 1904. e. Union U. Films inc: Wrote and produced several of the Charlie Chan & Cisco Kid films for Fox; My Darling Clementine (& sp); Sitting Pretty; Daddy Long Legs; The Jackpot; Come to the Stable; The Frogmen; A Man Called Peter; The Story of Ruth; Boy on a Dolphin; The Lion; Belles on Their Toes.

(Died April 7, 1984).

ENGEL, Susan: Act. b. Vienna, Mar 25, 1935. e. Sorbonne; Bristol U; Bristol Old Vic School. Thea inc: The Happy Haven; Wakefield Mystery Circle; Arden of Faversham; With Royal Shakespeare Company 1963-66; Julius Caesar; War of Roses; Henry IV; The Comedy of Errors; Macbeth; The Hotel in Amsterdam; The Friends; Ballad of the Sad Cafe; The Old Ones; Spring Awakening; Three Sisters; Watch on the Rhine.

Films inc: Charlie Bubbles; Ascendancy.

ENGELBERG, Mort: Prod. b. Memphis, TN, Aug 20, 1937. e. U of IL; U of MO. Films inc: Smokey and the Bandit; Hot Stuff; The Villain; The Hunter; Nobody's Perfekt; Smokey & the Bandit Part 3.

ENGLANDER, Roger: Prod-Dir. b. Cleveland, OH, Nov 23, 1926. e. U of Chicago, PhB. TV inc: (dir) Omnibus; Odyssey; Let's Take a Trip; Twentieth Century; Great American Dream Machine; 60 Minutes; The Performing Arts. (Prod) Young People's Concerts; What Is Sonata Form? (Emmy-1965); Vladimir Horowitz at Carnegie Hall; S Hurok Presents; The Bell Telephone Hour; Candid Camera.

Feb, 1981 named sr prod music, CBS Cable.

ENGLUND, George H: Prod-Dir. b. Washington, DC, Jun 22, 1926. Films inc: The World, The Flesh and the Devil (prod); The Ugly American; Signpost to Murder (dir); Dark of the Sun (prod); Zachariah (dir); Snowjob (dir).

TV inc: A Christmas To Remember; The Streets of L.A. (prod); Dixie--Changing Habits; Las Vegas Strip War (Exec prod-dir-wri).

ENGLUND, Ken: Wri. b. Chicago, May 6, 1914. Films inc: Big Broadcast of 1928; Artists and Models; No, No Nanette; Sweet Rosie O'-Grady; Secret Life of Walter Mitty; A Millionaire for Christy; The Wicked Dream of Paula Schultz; Surviving the Savage Sea.

TV inc: Jackie Gleason Show; Ray Milland Show; Loretta Young Show; My Three Sons; Bewitched; Dr. Joyce Brothers.

ENRIGHT, Dan (nee Ehrenreich): Prod. e. CCNY; RCA Institute. TV inc: Juvenile Jury; Life Begins at 80; The Joe DiMaggio Show; You're On Your Own; Tic Tac Dough; Twenty One; Concentration; Dough Re Mi; Magistrate's Court; Family Court; Line 'Em Up; Hi-Do; Oh Baby!; Break the Bank; The Hollywood Connection; Crossfire; Meet the McGees; It's the Barrys; Marriage Confidential; The James Beard Show; Junior Celebrities; The Fred Davis Show; Winky Dink; Make a Face; A Concert of the World.

Films inc: Search and Destroy (prod-wri); Private Lessons (exec prod); Private School.

ENRIGHT, Don: Wri-prod. b. NYC, Mar. 5, 1950. e. UCLA. S of Dan Enright. Films inc: Acapulco Gold (co-sp); Search & Destroy (wri); Hit and Run (wri); Private School (co-prod); Spasms (wri).

ENRIQUEZ, Rene: Act. b. San Francisco, CA, Nov 25, 1933. e. San Francisco State Coll; AADA. Thea inc: Camino Real; Marco Millions; Truckload; organized Artists Repertory Theater.

Films inc: Bananas; Midnight Cowboy; Popi; Harry and Tonto; Under Fire; The Evil That Men Do.

TV inc: Hallmark Hall of Fame; The Defenders; Hill Street Blues; Choices of the Heart.

ENTWISTLE, John: Comp-Mus. b. London, Oct 9, 1944. Member of The Who rock group for 15 years.

Films inc: (as mus dir) Quadrophenia; The Kids Are Alright (doc).

EPHRON, Amy: Exec. b. Beverly Hills, CA, Oct 21, 1952. D of Phoebe and Henry Ephron. With Sidney Beckerman Prodns; Marty Ehrlichman Prodns; joined Martin Bregman Prodns as vp Acquisition & Dvlpment; 1980 VP prodn, Col.

EPHRON, Henry: Wri. b. 1912. Collaborated with wife, Phoebe, until her death in 1971. Films inc: Bride by Mistake; Always Together; John Loves Mary; The Jackpot; On the Riviera; Belles on Their Toes; There's No Business Like Show Business; Daddy Long Legs; Carousel (& prod); The Best Things in Life are Free (prod only); Desk Set; Take Her She's Mine; Captain Newman, MD.

EPHRON, Nora: Wri. b. NYC, May 19, 1941. e. Wellesley. D of Phoebe and Henry Ephron. Sis of Amy Ephron. Films inc: Silkwood. TV inc: Perfect Gentlemen.

EPSTEIN, Alvin: Act-Dir. b. NYC, May 14, 1925. e. Queens Coll. Bway inc: Clerambard; No Strings; Waiting for Godot; King Lear; Passion of Josef D.; The Tempest; The Government Inspector; The Bacchae; The Merchant of Venice; Enrico IV; Ivanov; Don Juan; A Kurt Weill Cabaret (off-Bway).

TV inc: Waiting for Godot; Prayers from the Ark; Terezin Requiem; Histoire Du Soldat; Grimm's Fairy Tales.

EPSTEIN, Julius: Wri. b. NYC, Aug 22, 1909. e. Penn State Coll. Collab. with twin brother Philip until latter's death, 1952. Films inc: Four Daughters; Four Wives; No Time for Comedy; Strawberry Blonde; The Man Who Came to Dinner; Casablanca (Oscar-1942); Mr Skeffington (& prod); Romance on the High Seas; My Foolish Heart; Forever Female; The Last Time I Saw Paris; (solo): The Tender Trap; Tall Story; Take a Giant Step (& prod); Fanny; Send Me No Flowers; Any Wednesday (& prod); Pete 'n Tillie (& prod); House Calls; Reuben, Reuben (& co-prod)

TV inc: The Pirate.

ERDMAN, Richard: Act-Dir. b. Enid, OK, Jun 1, 1925. Films inc: Janie; The Very Thought of You; Danger Signal; Too Young to Know; Nobody Lives Forever; The Time of Your Life; Easy Living; Jumping Jacks; The Stooge; Stalag 17; The Brass Bottle; A Delicate Balance; Heidi's Song (voice); Tomboy. (Dir): Bleep; The Brothers O'Toole.

TV inc: The Great Mans Whiskers; The Dick Van Dyke Show; The Tab Hunter Show; Murder, She Wrote.

ERICKSON, C.O.(Doc): Prod. Started as prodn mgr at Paramount, worked on five Alfred Hitchcock films inc Rear Window, To Catch A Thief, The Trouble With Harry, The Man Who Knew Too Much; 1960, joined John Huston as asso prod on The Misfits, Freud, Reflections in a Golden Eye. prod mgr on Cleopatra; exec prod on There Was a Crooked Man. Exec prod: Chinatown; Players; Urban Cowboy; Popeye; The Lonely Guy; Cloak and Dagger; The Wild Life.

ERICKSON, Leif: Act. b. Alameda, CA, Oct 27, 1911. On stage in A Midsummer Night's Dream. Joined Olsen & Johnson comedy team. Screen debut, Wanderer of the Wasteland, 1935. On Broadway in Tea and Sympathy, 1953-55. Films inc: Sorry, Wrong Number; Joan of Arc; Snake Pit; Perilous Journey; On the Waterfront; Fastest Gun Alive; Twilight's Last Gleaming.

TV inc: High Chapparal; Hunter's Moon; Wild Times; Savage: In the Orient.

ERICSON, Devon: Act. b. Salt Lake City, UT, Dec 21. e. USIU. Films inc: Return to Macon County. TV inc: The Waltons; Eleanor and Franklin; The Dream Makers; The Skating Rink; Testimony of Two Men; The Bluegrass Special; Young Dan'l Boone; Baby Comes Home; The Mystic Warrior.

ERICSON, John: Act. b. Dusseldorf, Germany, Sep 25, 1926. e. AADA. On stage Stalag 17. Films inc: Teresa; Rhapsody; Green Fire; Bad Day at Black Rock; The Return of Jack Slade; Forty Guns; Pretty Boy Floyd; Under Ten Flags; The Seven Faces of Dr Lao; The Destructors; Operation Bluebook; Bedknobs and Broomsticks; Hustler Squad.

TV inc: Honey West; Robert Kennedy & His Times; Detective In The House.

ERMAN, John: Dir. b. Chicago. e. UCLA, BA. Films inc: (as act) Blackboard Jungle; Anything Goes; The Benny Goodman Story; (as dir): Making It; Ace Eli and Rodger of the Skies.

TV inc: (dir) Stoney Burke; My Favorite Martian; Please Don't Eat the Daisies; That Girl; The Fugitive; Ben Casey; Peyton Place; Gomer Pyle; Star Trek; The Flying Nun; Letters From Three Lovers; Green Eyes; Child of Glass; Just Me and You; Moviola; The Letter; Eleanor, The First Lady of the World; Another Woman's Child; Who Will Love My Children? (Emmy-1983); A Streetcar Named Desire; The Atlanta Child Murders; Right To Kill?

ERSKINE, Howard: Prod-Dir. b. Bronxville, NY, Jun 29, 1926. e. Williams Coll. Act in stock before prodn. Bway inc: (Prod) Late Love; The Desperate Hours (Tony-prod-1955); The Happiest Millionaire (& dir); The Midnight Sun; Calculated Risk; Any Wednesday (& dir); Minor Miracle.

ESMOND, Carl (Willy Eichberger): Act. b. Vienna, Jun 14, 1908. e. Academy of Dramatic Arts. On stage in many European cities. On screen in Germany, then USA. Films inc: Evensong; Invitation to the Waltz; Dawn Patrol; Thunder Afloat; The Story of Dr. Wassell; Ministry of Fear; Address Unknown; Catman of Paris; Smash-Up; Walk a Crooked Mile; From the Earth to the Moon; Thunder in the Sun; Agent for HARM; Morituri; Kiss of Evil.

TV inc: Climax; Playhouse 90; Four Star Playhouse.

ESSERT, Gary: Film Fest Exec. b. Oakland, CA, Oct 15, 1938. e. UCLA, BA. Between 1964-67 coordinated and supervised the design and planning of UCLA Motion Pictures Center; designed the m.p. exhibition facilities at the U of CA, Berkeley; 1965-67 San Francisco Int'l Film Festival; 1968-1970 Tech coordinator for the American Film Institute's Center for Advanced Film Studies; Co-founded (1971) Los Angeles Film Exposition (Filmex); demoted to artistic director June, 1983, after long battle with the board; resd, Aug. 24, 1983.

ESSEX, Harry: Wri-Dir. b. NYC, Nov 29, 1915. e. St Johns U, BA. Films inc: He Walked By Night; Man and Boy; The Amigos; The Sons of Katie Elder; It Came From Outer Space; The Creature From the Black Lagoon.

TV inc: The Untouchables; The Racers; The Corrupters; Bewitched.

Thea inc: Something for Nothing; One for the Dame.

ESTEVEZ, Emilio: Act. b. Los Angeles, 1963. S of Martin Sheen. TV inc: Making the Grade; To Climb a Mountain; 17 Going on Nowhere; In the Custody of Strangers; Insight/When Heroes Fall.

Films inc: Tex; The Outsiders; Nightmares; Repo Man; The Breakfast Club; St. Elmo's Fire.

ESTRADA, Erik: Act. b. NYC, Mar 16, 1949. Films inc: The Cross and the Switchblade; The New Centurions; Airport '75; Midway; Trackdown; Where is Parsifal?; A Colpi Di Luce (Light Blast).

TV inc: CHiPs; Donnie and Marie Christmas Special; Dean Martin Christmas Special 1980; Women Who Rate A 10; Entertainment Tonight; Honeyboy; Doug Henning's Magic On Broadway; Grandpa, Will You Run With Me?

ETAIX, Pierre: Act. b. Roanne, France, 1928. Films inc: Rupture (short); Heureux Anniversaire (Happy Anniversary) (Oscar-short, co-prod-1962); The Suitor; Yo Yo; As Long As You Have Your Health; Le Grand Amour; Pays de Cocagne.

ETKES, Raphael: Exec. b. Paris, May 6, 1930. e. USC. 1961 joined MCA as exec in int'l sales dept; In London as prodn exec; retd to studio, sr vp U and vp MCA; Feb 1980, named p, CEO Filmways Pictures; fired Dec, 1980; sr wwide prodn vp UA June-Nov, 1981; April 1983, Prodn P Embassy Pictures; resd. April, 1985.

EUBANKS, Bob: TV host. b. Flint, MI., Jan. 8 e. CA State Northridge. Worked as deejay, KRLA, LA; launched string of young adult niteries called The Cinnamon Cinder; promoter first West Coast concert of Beatles at Hollywood Bowl; formed Concert Express which books acts around the country.

TV inc: Rhyme and Reason; The Diamond Head Game; The Newlywed Game; All Star Secrets; The Toni Tennille Show (exec prod); You Bet Your Life (exec prod); Life's Most Embarrassing Moments; Dream House; Martin Mull Presents The History Of White People In America--Part 1 (feevee).

EVANS, Clifford: Act. b. Cardiff, Wales, Feb 17, 1912. e. RADA. London stage debut 1930 in The Witch; Bway debut in The Distaff Side, 1934. Films inc: The Mutiny of the Elsinore; Love on the Dole; Stryker of the Yard; Passport to Treason; The Curse of the Werewolf; Kiss of the Vampire; Twist of Sand; One Brief Summer.

TV inc: The Accused; Treason; The Quiet Man; War and Peace; Who's for Tennis.

(Died June 9, 1985)

EVANS, Dale (Frances O Smith): Act. b. Uvalde, TX, Oct 31, 1912. W of Roy Rogers. Started as band singer. Films inc: Orchestra Wives; Swing Your Partner; Casanova in Burlesque; The Yellow Rose of Texas; Utah; My Pal Trigger; Apache Rose; Susanna Pass; Twilight in the Sierras; Trigger Jr; Pals of the Golden West.

EVANS, Gene: Act. b. Holbrooke, AZ, Jul 11, 1924. Films inc: Under Colorado Skies; Berlin Express; Park Row; Donovan's Brain; Hell and High Water; The Sad Sack; Operation Petticoat; Apache Uprising; Support Your Local Sheriff; The Ballad of Cable Hogue; Walking Tall; The Magic of Lassie; Devil Times Five.

TV inc: My Friend Flicka; Matt Helm; The Last Day; Spencer's Pilots; The Concrete Cowboys; Wild Times; Casino; Mark Twain's America--The Young Will Rogers; California Gold Rush; The Shadow Riders; Travis McGee.

EVANS, Jerry: Dir. b. Santa Monica, CA, June 14, 1935. e. UC Berkeley, BA; Yale U School of Drama, MFA. TV inc: Another World; Search for Tomorrow; Somerset; Secret Storm; Love of Life; Ryan's Hope (Emmys-1979, 1980).

EVANS, Linda: Act. b. Hartford, CT, Nov 18, 1942. Films inc: Twilight of Honor; Those Callaways; The Klansman;Mitchell; Avalanche Express; Tom Horn.

TV inc: The Big Valley; Hunter; Nowhere to Run; Standing Tall; Dynasty; Bob Hope's All-Star Comedy Look at the New Season; Bare Essence; George Burns & Other Sex Symbols; The 4th Annual TV Guide Special; Kenny Rogers as the Gambler--The Adventure Continues; Night Of 100 Stars II; Kraft All-Star Salute To Ford's Theatre.

EVANS, Maurice: Act. b. Dorchester, England, Jun 3, 1901. On stage since 1926. London theatrical career inc: Justice; Loyalties; Diversion; Journey's End. To U.S. in 1935, appeared in Romeo and Juliet; Hamlet; Richard II; Macbeth; Man and Superman; The Devil's Disciple; Dial M for Murder; Tenderloin; The Aspern Papers; Program for Two Players; Teahouse of the August Moon (co-prod) (Tony-1954). Honorary Tony, 1950.

Films inc: Kind Lady; Androcles and the Lion; Gilbert and Sullivan; Macbeth; Planet of the Apes; Rosemary's Baby; The Body Stealers; The Jerk.

TV inc: Hamlet; Richard II; Macbeth (Emmy-1961); Devil's Disciple; Bewitched; Taming of the Shrew; St. John (series of 7 plays for Hallmark, NBC); Caesar & Cleopatra; The Girl, The Gold Watch and Everything; A Caribbean Mystery.

EVANS, Mike: Act-Wri. b. Salisbury, NC, Nov 3. e. LACC. TV inc: All in the Family; Call Her Mom; Now You See Him, Now You Don't; The Voyage of the Yes; Rich Man, Poor Man, Book I; The Jeffersons; Good Times (crea).

EVANS, Ray: Comp. b. Salamanca, NY, Feb 4, 1915. e. Wharton School; U of PA. Wrote special material for Olsen & Johnson; Betty Hutton; Joel Gray; Mitzi Gaynor; Cyd Charisse; Polly Bergen. Film scores inc: My Friend Irma; Red Garter; All Hands on Deck; Monsieur Beaucaire; The Paleface; Sorrowful Jones; The Lemon Drop Kid; Fancy Pants.

Songs: Buttons and Bows (Oscar-1948); A Thousand Violins; Mona Lisa (Oscar-1950); Silver Bells; Misto Cristofo Columbo; My Beloved; Never Let Me Go; Que Sera Sera (Oscar-1956); Almost in Your Arms; Dear Heart.

Film title songs: To Each His Own; Golden Earrings; Another Time, Another Place; Tammy; Saddle the Wind. TV title songs: Bonanza; Mr. Lucky; Mr. Ed; To Rome with Love.

Thea inc: Oh Captain; Let It Ride.

EVANS, Robert: Prod. b. NYC, Jun 29, 1930. Former actor, later business exec, became Paramount head of prod, 1966. After 10 years resigned to become indie prod. Films inc: (act) Lydia Bailey; The Man of a Thousand Faces; The Sun Also Rises; The Fiend Who Walked the West; The Best of Everything. (Prod): Chinatown; Marathon Man; Black Sunday; Players; Urban Cowboy; Popeye; The Cotton Club.

TV inc: Get High on Yourself.

EVE, Trevor: Act. b. Birmingham, England, July 1, 1951. e. RADA. Thea inc: John, Paul, George, Ringo and Bert; Children of a Lesser God; Filumena; The Genius.

TV inc: Hindle Wakes; Shoestring; Jamaica Inn; A Brother's Tale; Lace; The Corsican Brothers; Jamaica Inn.

Films inc: Dracula.

EVERETT, Chad (Ray Canton): Act. b. South Bend, IN, Jun 11, 1936. Films inc: Claudelle Inglish; The Chapman Report; The Singing Nun; The Last Challenge; Made in Paris; Return of the Gunfighter; The Impossible Years; Airplane II--The Sequel.

TV inc: Hawaiian Eye; 77 Sunset Strip; Lawman; The Dakotas; Redigo; Route 66; Ironside; Medical Center; Centennial; The French Atlantic Affair; Hagen; The Intruder Within; Mistress of Paradise; Malibu; The Rousters.

EVERLY BROTHERS: Mus. b. Brownie, KY, Don, Feb 1, 1937, Phil, Jan 19, 1939. Country mus recording artists.

EVIGAN, Greg: Act. b. South Amboy, NJ, Oct 14. Thea inc: Jesus Christ, Superstar; Grease.

TV inc: A Year at the Top; Operation Runaway; BJ and the Bear; Debby Boone--The Same Old Brand New Me; The Osmond Family Christmas Show; Masquerade; Scene Of The Crime; Private Sessions.

EWELL, Tom (Yewell Tompkins): Act. b. Owensboro, KY, Apr 29, 1909. e. U of WI. Bway debut, They Shall Not Die, 1934. In Navy, 1942-46. Returned to Bway in John Loves Mary; The Seven-Year Itch (Tony-1953); Tunnel of Love.

Films inc: Adam's Rib; A Life of Her Own; Up Front; Finders Keepers; The Seven-Year Itch; Tender Is the Night; State Fair; They Only Kill Their Masters; The Great Gatsby; Easy Money.

TV inc: Only the Pretty Girls Die; The Best of the West.

EYEN, Tom: Wri. b. Cambridge, OH., Aug. 14, 1941. e. OH State U. Plays inc: Tour de Four; The White Whore and the Bit Player; My Next Husband Will Be A Beauty; The Demented World of Tom Eyen; Miss Nefertiti Regrets; Sinderella Revisited; Give My Regards To Off-Off-Broadway; Grand Tenement; Why Johnny Comes Dancing Home; Alice Through the Looking Glass Lightly;The Four No Plays; Areatha in the Ice Palace; What Is Making Gilda So Gray ?; Gertrude Stein and Other Great Men; The Dirtiest Show in Town; 2008 1/2 A Space Oddity; Women Behind Bars; The Dirtiest Musical; The Neon Woman; Dreamgirls *(Tony-book-1982) (Grammy-cast album-1982)*.

TV inc: Mary Hartman, Mary Hartman; The Bette Midler Special.

EYRE, Ronald: Dir-Plywri. b. Yorkshire, England, Apr 13, 1929. e. Oxford. Former teacher. Dir in rep. Thea inc (London) Widowers Houses; Events While Guarding the Bofors Gun; Enemy; Three Months Gone; London Assurance; Mrs Warren's Profession; Much Ado About Nothing; A Voyage Round My Father; Veterans; A Pagan Place; Habeas Corpus; Saratoga; Tishoo; Enjoy; Hobson's Choice.

Plays inc: Something's Burning; The Marquis of Keith (adapt).

TV inc: A Crack in the Ice; The Long Search.

FABARES, Shelley: Act. b. Jan 19, 1944. Films inc: Never Say Goodbye; Rock Pretty Baby; Summer Love; Ride the Wild Surf; Girl Happy; Hold On; Spin Out; Clambake; A Time to Sing; UMC.

TV inc: Pleasure Cove; Donovan's Kid; Friendships, Secrets and Lies; The Great American Traffic Jam; Mork and Mindy; One Day At A Time; His & Hers.

FABER, Robert: Prod-Dir-Wri. b. NYC, Jun 6, 1908. e. CCNY. Started with Paramount in adv dept 1928; National Screen Service, 1933; Universal 1938 until retirement in 1979, when formed own firm. Prod features, featurettes, trailers.

Features inc: Easy To Look At; The Crimson Canary; (short) The World's Most Beautiful Girls. Doc featurettes: The Far Country; 1954 Hollywood Spotlight Series; Focus on Airport; Gambit; The Changing Image of the Western Hero; The Andromeda Strain; From Then Till Now; Swashbuckler; Thoroughly Modern Millie; The Hindenburg; Midway; Same Time Next Year; The Island.

FABIAN (Fabian Forte Bonaparte): Act. b. Philadelphia, Feb. 6, 1943. Teenage singer, guitarist. Films inc: The Hound Dog Man; North to Alaska; Mr Hobbs Takes a Vacation; Dear Brigitte; Ten Little Indians; Fireball 500; The Devil's Eight; A Bullet for Pretty Boy; Lovin' Man; Get Crazy.

FABIAN, Francoise (Michele Cortes de Leon): Act. b. Algiers, May 10, 1935. Films inc: Le Feu Aux Poudres; Les Fanatiques; Les Violents; La Brune Que Voila; Maigret Voit Rouge; Le Voleur; Ma Nuit Chez Maud; Deux Heures Mont le quart avant Jesus Christ (A Quarter to Two Before Jesus Christ); Benvenuta; L'Ami de Vincent (A Friend of Vincent); Partir Revenir (Departure, Return).

FABRAY, Nanette (nee Fabares): Act. b. San Diego, CA, Oct 27, 1920. e. Juillard. First appeared as Baby Nanette in vaudeville. On screen in Our Gang Comedies. Films inc: Elizabeth and Essex; A Child is Born; The Happy Ending; Cockeyed Cowboys; Wonderful Town; Last of the Red Hot Lovers; Never Too Late; Amy.

Bway inc: Meet the People; By Jupiter; Jackpot; Bloomer Girl; High Button Shoes; Love Life *(Tony-1949)*; Mr President; No Hard Feelings; Wonderful Town.

TV inc: Yes, Yes Nanette; Caesar's Hour *(Emmys-*(3)-supp & comedienne of year-1955; comedienne of year-1956); Man in the Santa Claus Suit; One Day At A Time; Night Of 100 Stars II.

FABRIZI, Aldo: Act. b. Italy, 1905. Films inc: Go Ahead Passengers; Square of Rome; Open City; My Son, the Professor; To Live in Peace; Christmas at Camp; Emigrants; Father's Dilemma; Mishappy Family; Cops and Robbers; Times Gone By; Lucky Five; The Angel Wore Red; Three Bites of the Apple; Those Were The Days; We All Loved Each Other So Much.

FADIMAN, Clifton: Ed-TV pers. b. NYC, May. 15, 1904. e. Columbia U. Contributor to magazines since 1924. Asst. editor Simon & Schuster, 1927-29, ed. 1929-35; Book Editor The New Yorker, 1933-43; MC on Information Please radio program, 1938-48, TV '52; MC This Is Show Business, TV; MC Conversation, 1954; MC Quiz Kids, 1956; Board of Editors, Encyclopaedia Britannica; Edit. consultant Encyclopaedia Britannica Educational Corp; Senior Editor, Cricket: The Magazine for Children.

FAIN, Sammy: Comp. b. NYC, Jun 17, 1902. Self-taught pianist; worked as staff comp-pianist for various mus pubs; in vaude.

Bway inc: Everybody's Welcome; Hellzapoppin'; Sons o' Fun; George White's Scandals of 1939; Toplitzky of Notre Dame; Flahooley; Ankles Aweigh; Christine; Around the World in 80 Days.

Films inc: Young Man of Manhattan; Footlight Parade; Sweet Music; New Faces of 1937; No Leave, No Love; Alice in Wonderland; George White's Scandals; Call Me Mister; Peter Pan; Weekend at the Waldorf; Anchors Aweigh; Calamity Jane; Marjorie Morningstar; Love Is a Many-Splendored Thing; Tender is the Night.

Songs inc: I Left My Sugar Standing in the Rain; Let A Smile Be Your Umbrella; Wedding Bells Are Breaking Up That Old Gang of Mine; You Brought a New Kind of Love to Me; When I Take My Sugar To Tea; Was That the Human Thing To Do; By A Waterfall; That Old Feeling; I Can Dream, Can't I; I'll Be Seeing You; Secret Love *(Oscar-*1953); Dear Heats and Gentle People; April Love; A Certain Smile; Love Is A Many-Splendored Thing *(Oscar-*1955); Tender Is the Night; Strange Are The Ways of Love; A World That Never Was.

FAIRBANKS, Douglas, Jr (nee Ullman): Act. b. NYC, Dec. 9, 1909. Son of silent screen star. Began screen career 1923 in Stephen Steps Out. On stage in NY, England. In US Navy during WW II. Films inc: Dawn Patrol; Little Caesar; Union Depot; Catherine the Great; Accused; The Prisoner of Zenda; Gunga Din; The Corsican Brothers; Sinbad the Sailor; State Secret; Ghost Story. Prod: Another Man's Poison; Chase a Crooked Shadow.

TV inc: (prod) Douglas Fairbanks Presents; The Hostage Tower (act); From Raquel With Love; The Bob Hope 30th Anniversary Special; Sarah In America (Kennedy Center Tonight); AFI Salute to Lillian Gish (mc); George Stevens--A Filmmaker's Journey (doc-int).

Thea inc: The Pleasure of His Company.

FAIRBANKS, Jerry: Exec prod. b. San Francisco, Nov 1, 1904. Started as projectionist, cameraman; indep shorts prod. Formed Jerry Fairbanks Productions, 1944. Prod shorts for Par; films for TV; developed Zoomar Lens. Films inc: Who's Who In Animal Land *(Os-*car-short subj-1944); Moon Rockets; Lost Wilderness; Down Liberty Road; With This Ring; Counterattack; Collision Course; Land of the Sea; Brink of Disaster; The Legend of Amaluk; North of the Yukon; Damage Report.

TV inc: Front Page Detective; Crusader Rabbit.

FAIRCHILD, Morgan: Act. b. Dallas, TX, Feb 3, 1950. e. SMU. Films inc: Bullet for Pretty Boy; The Seduction.

TV inc: Search for Tomorrow; Murder in Music City; The Memory of Eva Ryker; Flamingo Road; The Dream Merchants; Women Who Rate A 10 (host); Bob Hope's Spring Fling of Glamour and Comedy; The Girl, The Gold Watch and Dynamite; Shape of Things; Bob Hope's Stars Over Texas; Honeyboy; The Magic of David Copperfield; Bob Hope Goes to College; Time Bomb; Blondes Vs. Brunettes; The Zany Adventures of Robin Hood; Paper Dolls; Bob Hope Lampoons Television 1985; Rodney Dangerfield Exposed.

FAIRCHILD, William: Wri. b. Cornwall, England, 1918. Films inc: Morning Departure; An Outcast of the Islands; The Gift Horse; The Net; The Malta Story; Front Page Story; John and Julie (& dir); Value for Money; The Silent Enemy (& dir); Star!; Embassy; Invitation To The Wedding.

Plays inc: Sound of Murder; The Pay-Off; The Flight of the Bumble B.

TV inc: The Man with the Gun; No Man's Land; Four Just Men; Some Other Love; The Zoo Gang; The Sound of Murder (cable);

FAISON, George: Dir-Chor. Bway inc: 1600 Pennsylvania Ave; The Wiz *(Tony-*chor-1975); The Moony Shapiro Songbook; Porgy & Bess (chor).

FALANA, Lola: Singer-Act. b. Camden, NJ, Sept 11, 1939. Started as dancer-singer in niteries. Films inc: The Liberation of Lord Byron Jones; The Klansman; Lady Coco.

TV inc: Ben Vereen NBC Summer Variety Show; Eubie Blake--A Century of Music; Capitol.

Thea inc: Golden Boy; Dr Jazz.

FALK, Harry: Dir. TV inc: Three's A Crowd; The Death Squad; Men of the Dragon; The Abduction of St. Anne; Mandrake; Centennial; Beulah Land; The Night the City Screamed; The Contender; The Wonderful World of Philip Malley; The Sophisticated Gents; Advice to the Lovelorn; Hear No Evil.

FALK, Peter: Act. b. NYC, Sep 16, 1927. Off-Bway, The Iceman Cometh; The Lady's Not For Burning; St. Joan; Diary of a Scoundrel; The Prisoner of Second Avenue.
Films inc: Murder; Pocketful of Miracles; Robin and the Seven Hoods; It's A Mad, Mad, Mad, Mad World; Griffin and Phoenix; Mikey and Nicky; Murder by Death; The In-Laws; The Brink's Job; All the Marbles.
TV inc: The Price of Tomatoes (Emmy-1962); Brenner; The Untouchables; Sacco-Vanzetti Story; Columbo (Emmys-1972,1975,1976); AFI Salute To Frank Capra; Shoot/Don't Shoot (Host); Natalie--A Tribute To A Very Special Lady; The Television Academy Hall of Fame.

FAPP, Daniel: Cin. b. Kansas City, KS, Apr 4, 1921. Films inc: Five Card Stud; Double Trouble; The Pleasure Seekers; Send Me No Flowers; The Unsinkable Molly Brown; Move Over Darling; The Great Escape; One, Two, Three; Kings Go Forth; Desire Under the Elms; Joker is Wild; West Side Story (Oscar-1961); Let's Make Love; I'll Take Sweden; Our Man Flint; Lord Love a Duck; Sweet November; Ice Station Zebra; Marooned.

FARBER, Sandy: Thea prod. b. NYC, May 16, 1931. Thea inc: Student Gypsy; Riverside Drive; Babes in the Wood; Family Way; Summer Tree; Frank Merriwell; Tough to Get Help.

FARENTINO, James: Act. b. NYC, Feb 24, 1938. Films inc: Psychomania; Ensign Pulver; The War Lord; The Pad; Banning; Rosie; Me Natalie; The Story of a Woman; The Final Countdown; Dead and Buried.
TV inc: Death of a Salesman; The Bold Ones; Cool Million; Silent Victory - The Kitty O'Neil Story; Son Rise - A Miracle of Love; The Family Rico; Vanished; Jesus of Nazareth; Evita Peron; Insight/Resurrection; Dynasty; Insight/Rendezvous; Insight/God's Guerrillas; Something So Right; The Cradle Will Fall; The Changing Family (host); Blue Thunder; License to Kill; A Summer To Remember.
Thea inc: The Night of the Iguana; One Flew over the Cucko's Nest: Desire (rev); Death of a Salesman (rev).

FARGAS, Antonio: Act. b. NYC, Aug 14, 1946. Films inc: Putney Swope; Shaft; Pound; Across 110th Street; Cleopatra Jones; Bustin'; Car Wash; Pretty Baby; Up the Academy; Model Behavior; Streetwalkin'.
TV inc: Starsky & Hutch; Hereafter; Huckleberry Finn; Escape; Nurse; All Commercials. Huckleberry Finn; The Roast; The Ambush Murders; Denmark Vesey's Rebellion; Paper Dolls; A Good Sport; P.O.P.
Thea inc: The Great White Hope; The Slave; The Toilet; The Amen Corner.

FARGO, Donna: Singer-Sngwri. b. Mt Airy, NC, 1945. C & W Recording artist. (Grammy-1972). TV inc: A Gift of Music; The Great American Sing-A-Long.

FARGO, James: Dir. b. Republic, WA, Aug 14,1938. e. U of WA, BA. Films inc: The Enforcer; Caravans; Every Which Way But Loose; Game for Vultures; Forced Vengeance.

FARLEIGH, Lynn: Act. b. Bristol, England, May 3, 1942. Joined Royal Shakespeare Co, 1966. Thea inc: The Homecoming; All's Well that Ends Well; The Relapse; Julius Caesar; Exiles; Suzanne Andler; Ashes; The Doctor's Dilemma; Sex and Kinship in a Savage Society; Twelfth Night; Close of Play; The Crucible; Harvest.
Films inc: Three Into Two Won't Go; A Phoenix Too Frequent; Watership Down (voice only).
TV inc: The Rivals; Force of Circumstance; Eyeless in Gaza; The Word; Anthony and Cleopatra.

FARMER, Mimsy: Act. b. 1945. Films inc: Spencer's Mountain; Bus

Riley's Back in Town; Hot Rods to Hell; The Devil's Angels; Move; The Road to Salina; Four Flies on Gray Velvet; Autopsy; L'amant de Poche (The Pocket Lover); La Mort de Mario Ricci (The Death of Mario Ricci); Un Foro nel Parabrezza (A Hole In the Windshield); The Black Cat.

FARNSWORTH, Richard: Act. b. Los Angeles, Sept. 1, 1920. Spent 40 years as stuntman. Films inc: (act) Comes a Horseman; Tom Horn; Resurrection; The Legend of the Lone Ranger; The Grey Fox; Independence Day; Waltz Across Texas; The Natural; Rhinestone; Into The Night; Sylvester.
TV inc; A Few Days In Weasel Creek; Louis L'Amour's The Cherokee Trail; Travis McGee; Ghost Dancing.

FARR, Derek: Act. b. London, Feb 7, 1912. On screen From 1940. Films inc: The Outsider; Spellbound; Quiet Wedding; Wanted for Murder; Teheran; Noose; Silent Dust; Man on the Run; Reluctant Heroes; The Dam Busters; Town on Trial; Doctor at Large; The Truth About Women; The Projected Man; Thirty Is a Dangerous Age; Cynthia; Pope Joan.
TV inc: The Saint; The Human Jungle; King Henry VI.

FARR, Felicia: Act. b. Westchester, NY, Oct 4, 1932. e. Penn State Coll. W of Jack Lemmon. Films inc: Timetable; Jubal; 3:10 to Yuma; The Last Wagon; Hell Bent for Leather; Kiss Me Stupid; The Venetian Affair; Charley Varrick.

FARR, Jamie (Jameel Joseph Farah): Act. b. Toledo, OH, Jul 1, 1934. Films inc: The Blackboard Jungle; No Time for Sergeants; The Greatest Story Ever Told; Who's Minding the Mint?; With Six You Get Egg Roll; The Cannonball Run; Cannonball Run II.
TV inc: The Red Skelton Show; The Danny Kaye Show; The Chicago Teddy Bears; M*A*S*H; Amateur Night at the Dixie Bar & Grill; Murder Can Hurt You; Return of the Rebels; I Love TV Test; AfterMASH; For Love Or Money.

FARRAR, David: Act. b. Forest Gate, England, 1908. Films inc: Return of the Stranger; Danny Boy; The Night Invader; The Dark Tower; The World Owes Me a Living; Meet Sexton Blake; The Lisbon Story; Black Narcissus; Mr Perrin and Mr Traill; The Small Back Room; Night Without Stars; The Golden Horde; Duel in the Jungle; Lilacs in the Spring; The Sea Chase; I Accuse; Solomon and Sheba; John Paul Jones; Best Girl; The 300 Spartans.

FARRELL, Charles: Act. b. Onset Bay, MA, Aug 9, 1901. e. Boston U. Started in silent films. Films inc: Seventh Heaven; Sandy; Street Angel; Lucky Star; Sunny Side Up; Tess of the Storm Country; The First Year; Change of Heart; Moonlight Sonata; Just Around the Corner; Tailspin.
TV inc: My Little Margie; The Charles Farrell Show.

FARRELL, Mike: Act. b. St Paul, MN, Feb 6, 1939. Films inc: Capt Newman, MD; The Graduate; The Americanization of Emily; Targets. TV inc: The Interns; The Man and the City; M*A*S*H; The Longest Night; The Questor Tapes; Battered; Ladies of the Corridor; Sex and the Single Parent; Letters From Rank; Damien...The Leper Priest; Streets of Anger--Streets of Hope; Good Evening, Captain; El Salvador--Another Viet Nam (narr); In A New Light (narr); The Body Human--Becoming A Man (host); Prime Suspect; Choices of the Heart; JFK--A One Man Show; Private Sessions.

FARRELL, Sharon: Act. b. Dec 24, 1946. Films inc: The Spy With My Face, A Lovely Way to Die; The Reivers; The Love Machine; The Premonition; The Fifth Floor; Out of the Blue; The Stunt Man; Lone Wolf McQuade; Sweet Sixteen; Separate Ways; Night Of The Comet.
TV inc: The Last Ride of the Dalton Gang; Rage; Born To Be Sold.

FARROW, Mia: Act. b. Los Angeles, Feb 9, 1947. D of Maureen O'Sullivan and John Farrow. Summer stock, off-Bway. NY debut 1963, The Importance of Being Earnest. Screen debut, 1964, Guns at Batasi. Films inc: A Dandy in Aspic; Rosemary's Baby; Secret Ceremony; John and Mary; See No Evil; The Public Eye; The Great Gatsby; Full Circle; A Wedding; Death on the Nile; Avalanche; Hurricane; A Midsummer Night's Sex Comedy; Sarah (The Seventh Match); The Last Unicorn (voice); Zelig; Broadway Danny Rose; Supergirl; The Purple Rose Of Cairo.

TV inc: Peyton Place; Johnny Belinda.

Thea inc: Mary Rose; The House of Bernarda Alba; The Three Sisters; The Marrying of Anne Leete; Zykovs; Ivanov; Romantic Comedy.

FARROW, Tisa: Act. b. Jul 22, 1951. D of Maureen O'Sullivan, Sis of Mia Farrow. Films inc: Homer; Strange Shadows in an Empty Room; Fingers; Manhattan; Winter Kills; Zombie; Search and Destroy; The Grim Reaper; The Last Hunter.

FAST, Howard: Wri. b. NYC, Nov 11, 1914. Foreign corr, mag wri; author several historical novels which have been filmed.

Plays inc: The Crossing; The Hill.

TV inc: The Ambassador (Ben Franklin) (Emmy-1975); The Immigrants.

FATHER GUIDO SARDUCCI: (See NOVELLO, Don).

FAWCETT, Farrah: Act. b. Corpus Christi, TX, Feb 2, 1947. Made TV commercials. (Billed as Fawcett-Majors while married to Lee Majors). Films inc: Love Is a Funny Thing; Myra Breckenridge; Logan's Run; Somebody Killed Her Husband; Sunburn (dropped Majors from name); Saturn 3; The Cannonball Run.

TV inc: Owen Marshall, Counselor at Law; The Six Million Dollar Man; The Feminist and the Fuzz; Harry O.; Charley's Angels; Murder In Texas; The Fall Guy; The Red-Light Sting; The Burning Bed.

Bway inc: Extremities.

FAYE, Alice: Act-Singer. b. May 5, 1915. W of Phil Harris. On screen From 1934. Films inc: George White's Scandals; The King of Burlesque; Poor Little Rich Girl; Wake Up and Live; In Old Chicago; Alexander's Ragtime Band; Sally, Irene and Mary; Rose of Washington Square; Lillian Russell; Tin Pan Alley; The Great American Broadcast; State Fair.

Bway inc: Good News (rev).

TV inc: The Magic of Lassie.

FAYE, Joey (Joseph Antony Palladino): Act-Comedian. b. NYC, Jul 12, 1909. In vaudeville, burlesque in the early 30's. Bway inc: Room Service; The Milky Way; Boy Meets Girl; High Button Shoes; Top Banana; Strip for Action; DuBarry Was a Lady; Waiting for Godot; Guys and Dolls; Anatomy of Burlesque (& wri-dri); Man of La Mancha; Grind.

Began in films in 30's in WB shorts. Features inc: Top Banana; The Tender Trap; Ten North Frederick; North to Alaska; The Grissom Gang; The War Between Men and Women.

FAYLEN, Frank: Act. b. 1907. Films inc: Bullets or Ballets; The Grapes of Wrath; Top Sergeant Mulligan; The Lost Weekend; Blue Skies; Road to Rio; Detective Story; Riot in Cell Block Eleven; Killer Dino; The Monkey's Uncle; Funny Girl.

TV inc: The Doby Gillis Show; That Girl.

FEDDERSON, Don: Prod. b. Beresford, SD, Apr 16. Created and prod: Liberace Show, 1950; Life with Elizabeth; Betty White Show; The Millionaire; consultant Lawrence Welk Show, 1954-70; 1971, began syndication Welk Show. Other TV Shows inc: Date with Angels; Do You Trust Your Wife?; Who Do You Trust?; Charley Weaver Show; My Three Sons; Family Affair; To Rome with Love; Smith Family.

FEHMIU, Bekim: Act. b. Yugoslavia, Jun 1, 1936. Films inc: Cagliostro; Black Sunday; Madam Kitty; Special Education; Permission to Kill; Siroko Je Lisce (The Leaves Are Wide); La Voce (The Voice).

FEIFFER, Jules: Wri. b. NYC, Jan 26, 1929. Syndicated cartoonist. Films inc: Little Murders; Carnal Knowledge; Popeye.

Plays inc: Little Murders; The White House Murder Case; Knock Knock; Grownups.

TV inc: The Comedy Zone.

FEINSTEIN, Alan: Act. b. NYC, Sep 8. Films inc: Looking For Mr Goodbar. TV inc: Edge of Night; Love of Life; Search for Tomorrow; Jigsaw John; Alexander; The Other Side of Dawn; The Users; Visions; The Runaways; The Two Worlds of Jenny Logan; Masada; Insight/ Thea; Insight/Missing Persons Bureau; The Wedding; Berrenger's.

Thea inc: Malcolm; Zelda; A View From the Bridge.

FEITSHANS, Buzz: Prod. b. Los Angeles. e. USC. Started as film editor at ABC; film editor American-International Pictures, later head of editorial dept; 1975, formed A-Team Prodns with John Milius. Films inc: Boxcar Bertha (supv); Dillinger; Big Wednesday; Hardcore; 1941; Conan the Barbarian; First Blood; Uncommon Valor; Red Dawn; Rambo-First Blood Part II.

FELD, Donald Lee (See DONFELD).

FELD, Fritz: Act. b. Berlin, Oct 15, 1900. e. Berlin U; Max Reinhardt School of Drama. H of Virginia Christine. On screen From 1918, The Golem. In more than 400 films inc: Wives and Lovers; Promises, Promises; Who's Minding the Store?; Four for Texas; The Patsy; Harlow; The Comic; Barefoot in the Park; Hello, Dolly!; The Phynx; Which Way to the Front?; The Strongest Man in the World; Only with Married Men; The Sunshine Boys; Won Ton Ton, the Dog Who Saved Hollywood; Broadway Rose; Silent Movie; Pennsylvania Lynch; Freaky Friday; The World's Greatest Lover; Herbie Goes Bananas; History of the World--Part I; Heidi's Song (voice).

TV inc: Please Don't Eat the Daises; The Smothers Bros.; Bewitched; The Beverly Hillbillies; Land of the Giants; Arnie; Love, American Style; The New Bill Cosby Show; The Julie Andrews Hour; The Odd Couple; The Night Stalker; The Mike Douglas Show; The Great Survivors.

Thea inc: Once More with Feeling; Would Be Gentleman; Midsummer Night's Dream; Arsenic and Old Lace.

FELD, Irvin: Prod. b. Hagerstown, MD, May 9, 1918. Pres, prod and CEO Ringling Bros-Barnum & Bailey Combined Shows; March 1982, bought circus back from Mattel in deal that included Ice Follies, Holiday on Ice, Disney on Ice, Beyond Belief, became Bdchmn.

TV inc: (exec prod): Klowns; Highlights of Ringling Bros and Barnum and Bailey Circus; Gunther Gebel Williams-Lord of the Rings; International Circus Festival of Monte Carlo; Circus Super Heroes; Siegfried and Roy--Superstars of Magic; Highlights of Ringling Bros and Barnum & Bailey Circus, 111th Edition; Ringling Bros & Barnum and Bailey Circus 1982; The 113th Edition Ringling Bros & Barnum and Bailey Circus.

Bway inc: Barnum; The Three Musketeers.

(Died Sept. 6, 1984)

FELDMAN, Edward S.: Prod. b. NYC, Sep 5, 1929. e. MI State U. Publicist Fox; Paramount; Embassy; Seven Arts. Vp-Exec Asst to head of Prod WB-Seven Arts, 1967; P mp dept, Filmways, 1970.

Films inc: (exec prod) What's the Matter with Helen?; Fuzz; Save The Tiger; The Other Side of the Mountain; Two-Minute Warning; The Other Side of The Mountain, Part II; The Last Married Couple in America; Six Pack; The Sender; Hot Dog--The Movie; Witness.

TV inc: King (Exec Prod); Valentine; Pioneer Woman; The Stranger Who Looks Like Me; My Father's House; Smashup on Interstate 5; Three Hundred Miles For Stephanie; Flamingo Road; Charles and Diana-A Royal Love Story; Not in Front of the Children; Obsessed With A Married Woman (Exec prod).

FELDMAN, Philip: Exec. b. Boston, MA, Jan 22, 1922. e. Harvard; Georgetown; Harvard Law School; Harvard Business School. Entered ind as legal counsel for Famous Artists; 1953 asso dir bus aff CBS; 1954, dir bus aff; 1957, vp talent CBS; 1960 exec vp Broadcast Management Inc; 1962 prodn vp Seven Arts Corp; formed Phil Feldman Prodns; 1972 vp Rastar Prodns; 1975, P First Artists Prodns; 1980 exec vp Rastar Films.

Films inc: The Wild Bunch; The Ballad of Cable Hogue; You're A Big Boy Now; Posse; The Toy; Blue Thunder (exec prod).

FELDON, Barbara: Act. b. Pittsburgh, Mar 12, 1941. Fashion model. TV commercials. TV inc: East Side, West Side; Get Smart; Man From U.N.C.L.E.; Profiles in Courage; Children of Divorce; Sooner or Later; A Vacation in Hell; Before and After; The Bear Who Slept Through Christmas (voice); The Unforgivable Secret.

Films inc: Fitzwilly; Smile; No Deposit, No Return.

Bway inc: Past Tense.

FELDSHUH, Tovah: Act. b. NYC, Dec 27, 1953. e. Sarah Lawrence Coll, BA; U of MN, MA. TV inc: The Amazing Howard Hughes; Holocaust; Connecticut Yankee in King Arthur's Court; Terror in the Sky; The Great Triangle Factory Fire; Beggarman, Thief; The Women's

Room; Murder Ink; Hot Properties.

Bway inc: Cyrano; Brainchild; Straws in the Wind; Three Sisters; Dreyfus in Rehearsal; Rodgers and Hart; Yentl; Sarava; She Stoops To Conquer (off-Bway).

Films inc: Cheaper to Keep Her; The Idolmaker; Nunzio; Daniel.

FELICIANO, Jose: Singer-Comp. b. Lares, Puerto Rico, Sep 10, 1945. Recording artist. Film scores inc: Aaron Loves Angels; TV theme songs: Chico and the Man; Love at First Sight. TV inc: Sound Festival. *(Grammys-(2)-new artist, contemporay pop voc-1968).*

FELL, Norman: Act. b. Philadelphia, Mar 24, 1924. e. Temple U, BA. Films inc: Inherit the Wind; Catch 22; The Graduate; Oceans 11; Pork Chop Hill; Bullitt; If It's Tuesday This Must Be Belgium; The Stone Killer; The End; Rabbit Test; On The Right Track; Paternity; The Kinky Coaches and the Pom-Pom Pussycats.

TV inc: Twelve Angry Men; 87th Precinct; Dan August; Needles and Pins; Joe and Mabel; Rich Man, Poor Man (Part 1); Three's Company; The Ropers; Roots--The Next Generations; Pat Boone and Family Christmas Special; Moviola (This Year's Blonde); For The Love Of It; Teachers Only; Uncommon Valor; The Jesse Owens Story.

FELLINI, Federico: Dir-Wri. b. Rimini, Italy, Jan 8, 1920. Cartoonist, caricaturist, writer. Wrote scripts for films Open City; Paisan. Dir debut, Variety Lights 1950. Films inc: La Dolce Vita; The Clowns; Juliet of the Spirits; Fellini's Rome; The Wastrels; La Strada; Vitelloni; Fellini's 8-1/2; Fellini's Satyricon; Amarcord; Fellini's Casanova; Orchestra Rehearsal; City of Woman; E La Nave Va (And the Ship Sails On); Il Tassinaro (The Cabbie) (act).

FELTON, Norman: Prod. b. London, England, Apr 29. e. U of IA; BFA, MA. TV inc: (Wri-dir) Dave Garroway Show; Robert Montgomery Presents; US Steel Hour; Studs Place; Alcoa Playhouse; Studio One. (Prod) Studio One; Playhouse 90; Dr. Kildare; The 11th Hour; The Man From UNCLE; The Psychiatrist; Mr. Novak; Babe.

FENADY, Andrew J: Prod-Wri. b. Toledo, OH, Oct 4, 1928. e. U of Toledo, BA. Films inc: Stakeout on Dope Street; The Young Captives; Ride Beyond Vengeance; Chisum; Terror in the Wax Museum; Arnold; The Man With Bogart's Face.

TV inc: Black Noon; The Woman Hunter; The Stranger; The Mask of Alexander; The Hostage Heart.

FENADY, George J: Dir. b. Toledo, OH, Jul 2, 1930. e. U of Toledo. Films inc: Arnold; Terror In the Wax Museum.

TV inc: Mission Impossible; Sarge; Emergency; Chase; Code R; Hanging by a Thread; Firehouse; CHiPs; Sierra; The Texas Rangers; Quincy; Cave-In!; The Night the Bridge Fell Down.

FENDER, Freddy (Baldemar Huerta): Mus. b. San Benito, TX, Jun 4, 1937. Country mus recording artist.

FENNELL, Albert: Prod. b. England, 1920. Films inc: The Green Scarf; Next to No Time; Tunes of Glory; The Innocents; Night of the Eagle; And Soon the Darkness; Dr. Jekyll and Sister Hyde; The Legend of Hell House.

TV inc: The Avengers.

FERBER, Mel: Prod-Dir. b. NYC, Oct 2, 1922. TV inc: Adventure; Seven Lively Arts; That Was the Week That Was; Alias Smith and Jones; Mary Tyler Moore; The Odd Couple; CPO Sharkey; From Here to the Seventies; Polynesian Adventure; A Bell for Adano; Comedy in Music; Wonderful Town; (prod pilot) Sixty Minutes; Calendar; exec prod: Democratic National Committee Convention 1972; Good Morning America; Clonemaster; Sarah In America (Kennedy Center Tonight); Alice.

FERDIN, Pamelyn: Act. b. Feb 4, 1959. Films inc: What a Way To Go!; Never Too Late; Beguiled; The Mephisto Waltz; Happy Birthday, Wanda June; The Tool Box Murders; Heidi's Song (voice).

TV inc: A Tree Grow In Brooklyn; Miles to Go Before I Sleep.

FERGUSON, Allyn M. Jr: Comp-Cond-Arr. b. San Jose, CA, Oct 18, 1924. e. San Jose State U, AB, MA; Stanford U, PhD; studied with Nadia Boulanger, Ernest Toch, Aaron Copland. Films inc: Avalanche Express.

TV inc: Johnny Mathis Show; Andy Williams Show; Fast Freight; The Count of Monte Cristo; Captains Courageous; Man in The Iron Mask; All Quiet on the Western Front; Big Island; The Gossip Colum-

nist; Cry of the Innocent; A Country Christmas--1979; Beulah Land; Love Boat; Pleasure Palace; House Calls; Little Lord Fauntleroy; A Tale of Two Cities; Terror Among Us; Peter and Paul; 100 Years of Golden Hits; Big Bend Country; Red Flag--The Ultimate Game; Ivanhoe; Computercide; The Adventures of Little Lord Fauntleroy; Master of the Game; Camille; The Corsican Brothers; The Royal London Gala For Bob Hope's Happy Birthday Homecoming.

FERGUSON, Graeme: Dir. b. Toronto, Can, Oct 7, 1929. e. U of Toronto, BA. P IMAX Systems Corp since 1967. Films inc: The Love Goddesses; The Virgin President. TV inc: The Legend of Rudolph Valentino.

FERGUSON, Jay: Mus. b. Los Angeles, May 10, 1943. Pianist with two groups, Spirit and Jo Jo Gunne, before launching solo career in 1975. Films inc: Deadly Passion.

FERGUSON, Maynard: Mus. b. Montreal, Canada, May 4, 1928. Briefly with Boyd Rayburn orch, then Jimmy Dorsey. To the US permanently 1949 with Charlie Barnet; worked with Stan Kenton 1950-1953 then freelance as studio musician before becoming charter member all-star Birdland Dream Band; formed sextet 1965.

Albums inc: Maynard Ferguson; Maynard Ferguson Horn 1-2-3-4-5; Live at Jimmy's; Primal Scream; Montreaux Summit 1 & 2; New Vintage; Carnival; Hot; It's My Time;

TV inc: Jazz Alive.

FERNANDEZ, Emilio: Dir-act. (El Indio)b. Mexico, Mar. 26, 1904. Came to Hollywood around 1923 to escape prison term for taking part in revolutions. Worked as extra, bit player until he was able to return to Mexico in 1933 as a result of a general amnesty. Began writing and directing in 1941. Films inc: Passion Island; Soy puro Mexico; Flor Sylvestre (& act); Maria Candelaria; Las Abandonadas; Pepita Jimenez; The Pearl; Enamorada; Hidden River; Salon Mexico; Pueblerina; La Malquerida; Duelo en las Montanas; The Torch (remake of Enamorada); Un Dia de Vida; Victimas del Pecado; La Bienamada; Acapulco; Siempre tuya; Tu y el Mar; The Net; El Reportage; El Rapto; La Rosa Blanca; La Rebellion de los Colgados; Nostros Dos; La Tierra del Fuego se Apaga; Una Cita de Amor; El Impostor; Pueblito; The Night of the Iguana (asst dir); The Reward (act); A Loyal Soldier of Pancho Villa; The Appaloosa (act); Return of the Seven (act); The War Wagon (act); Pat Garrett and Billy the Kid (act); Bring Me the Head of Alfredo Garcia (act & dir opening sequence); Lucky Lady (act); Zona Roja; Las Amantes del Senor de la Noche (The Lovers of the Lord of the Night (act); Under the Volcano (act); Observations Under the Volcano (doc-int); El Tesoro del Amazones (The Treasure Of The Amazon).

FERRELL, Conchata: Act. b. WV. Bway inc: Hot L Baltimore. TV inc: Hot L Baltimore; Network; A Death in Canaan; Hatter Fox; The Seduction of Miss Leona; Reunion; Rape and Marriage--The Rideout Case; McClain's Law; Life of the Party--The Story of BeAtrice; Miss Lonelyhearts; Emergency Room; The Three Wishes Of Billy Grier.

FERREOL, Andrea: Act. Films inc: La scoumoune; Les gants blancs du diable; La raison du plus fou; The Day of the Jackal; La grand bouffe; Le trio infernal; La Femme c'est beau; Serieux comme le plaisir; Parlez moi d'amour; Peppino e la vergine Maria; L'Incorrigible; Les barons; Mesdames et Messieurs, bonsoir; Marie Poupee; Servante et Maitresse; Casanova and Company; L'amante Latino; L'amant de poche (The Pocket Lover); Despair; Mysteries; Voyage avec Anita; The Tin Drum; Return to Marseilles; Milo Milo; The Last Metro; Tre Fratelli (Three Brothers); L'ombre rouge (The Red Shadow); La nuit de Varennes (The Night of Varennes); Y'a-t'il une Francais dans la salle? (Is There a Frenchman in the House?); La Ragazza di Trieste; Gli innocenti vanno all'estero; Le prix du danger (The Prize of Peril); Le battant; Stelle sulla citta; Balles perdue (Stray Bullets); Louisiane; Aldo et Junior; Le Juge (The Judge); Cuore (Heart); Sogni e Bisogni (Needs and Dreams); Le Jumeau (The Twin); Le Due Vite di Mattia Pascal (The Two Lives Of Mattia Pascal).

FERRER, Jose: Act-Prod-Dir. b. Santurce, Puerto Rico, Jan 8, 1912. e. Princeton U. Dir, act Bway prior to film career. Films inc: Joan of Arc; Whirlpool; Cyrano de Bergerac (Oscar-1950); Moulin Rouge; Lawrence of Arabia; Enter Laughing; Forever Young, Forever Free; The Sentinel; The Swarm; Fedora; Dracula's Dog; Natural Enemies;

The Big Brawl; A Midsummer Night's Sex Comedy; Blood Tide; The Being; To Be or Not to Be; The Evil That Men Do; Dune.

TV inc: Fame; The French Atlantic Affair; Battles-The Murder That Wouldn't Die; Gideon's Trumpet; The Dream Merchants; Debbie Boone--The Same Old Brand New Me; Pleasure Palace; Evita Peron; Berlin Tunnel 21; Peter and Paul; The Hunter and the Hunted (Narr); Blood Feud; Impact '83--East of the L.A. River (host; This Girl for Hire; Samson and Delilah; George Washington; Hitler's SS--Portrait In Evil; Seduced; Jacques Cousteau--The First 75 Years.

Bway inc: Cyrano de Bergerac (Tony-1947); The Shrike (prod-dir-act) (Tonys-dir-act-1952); The Chase (prod-dir); Stalag 17.

FERRER, Mel: Prod-Dir-Act. b. Elberon, NJ, Aug 25, 1917. e. Princeton U. Spent early career in summer stock, Cape Cod Playhouse. Bway as dancer, You'll Never Know; Everywhere I Roam. Later prod-dir NBC. Started in films, 1945, as dial dir. Films inc: The Secret Fury; The Brave Bulls; Scaramouche; Lili; War and Peace; The Flesh and the Devil; Blood and Roses; The Net; The Black Pirate; Lili Marleen; Mille Milliards de Dollars (A Thousand Billion Dollars); Screamers; Die Jaeger (Deadly Game); City of the Walking Dead. (Prod) Wait Until Dark; "W"; The Norseman; The Tempter; The Fifth Floor; The Visitor.

Bway inc: Lost Boundaries; Born To Be Bad; Ondine.

TV inc: (act) The Top of the Hill; The Memory of Eva Ryker; Fugitive Family; Behind the Screen; Falcon Crest; One Shoe Makes It Murder (& prod); Seduced.

FERRERI, Marco: Dir. b. Italy, 1928. Films inc: El Pisito; The Wheelchair; Queen Bee; The Bearded Lady; Wedding March; Dillinger is Dead; Blowout; Tales of Ordinary Madness (& wri); Storia di Piera; Il Futuro E 'Donna (The Future Is Woman))& wri).

FERRIGNO, Lou: Act. b. NYC, Nov 9, 1951. Won Mr America contest, 1973; won Mr Universe contest, 1974 & 1975. TV inc: The Incredible Hulk; Trauma Center. Films inc: Pumping Iron; Hercules.

FERTIK, Bill: Dir. b. NYC, Nov 28, 1942. e. Syracuse U, BA; NYU, MA. Films inc: Ga Guerre; Forty-One North, Sixty-One West; The Bolero (Oscar-ss-1973); Relations; The 1812 Overture; Ernest Bloch, A Portrait; Ned Williams Dance Theatre.

FERZETTI, Gabrielle: Act. b. Italy, 1925. Films inc: William Tell; Puccini; L'Avventura; Torpedo Bay; Once Upon a Time in the West; On Her Majesty's Secret Service; Hitler-The Last 10 Days; Night Porter; The Order and Security of the World; The Psychic; Gli anni Struggenti (The Burning Years); Grog; Morte in Vaticano (Death In the Vatican).

FETCHIT, Stepin (Lincoln Theodore Perry): Act-Comedian. b. Key West, FL, 1892. On screen From 1927. Films inc: In Old Kentucky; Showboat; The Galloping Ghost; Stand Up and Cheer; David Harum; Miracle in Harlem; Bend of the River; Won Ton Ton, The Dog Who Saved Hollywood; Amazing Grace.

TV inc: Cutter.

FEUER, Cy: Prod-Dir. b. NYC, Jan 15, 1911. e. Juilliard. Bway (Prodns) (in assoc with Ernest N Martin): Where's Charley?; Guys and Dolls (Tony-1951); Can-Can; The Boy Friend; Silk Stockings; How to Succeed in Business Without Really Trying (Tony-1962); Little Me; Skyscraper; Walking Happy; The Goodbye People; The Act. Also prod-co-wri Whoop-up; On the 20th Century; I Remember Mama (rev).

Films inc: (with Martin); Cabaret; Piaf.

FEUILLERE, Edwige: Act. b. France, 1907. Films inc: Topaze; I Was An Adventuress; Lucrezia Borgia; The Idiot; Blind Desire; The Eagle With Two Heads; Woman Hater; Olivia; Adorable Creatures; The Fruits of Summer; Love is My Profession; Crime Doesn't Pay;

Thea inc: Leocadia.

FICKETT, Mary: Act. b. Bronxville, NY, May 23. Films inc: Man in Fire; Kathy O.

TV inc: Edge of Night; The Nurses; Pueblo; All My Children (Emmy-1973).

Bway inc: Sunrise at Campobello; I Know My Love; Tea and Sympathy; Love and Kisses.

FIEDEL, Brad: Comp-Wri-Singer. b. NYC, Mar 10, 1951. Films inc: Deadly Hero; Night School; Hit and Run; Right of Way; Eyes of Fire; The Terminator; Fraternity Vacation.

TV inc: Mayflower--The Pilgrim Adventure; Hardhat and Legs; Seven Wishes of a Rich Kid; A Movie Star's Daughter; Playing for Time; The Day The Women Got Even; The Bunker; My Mother Was Never A Kid; Dream House; Mae West; Dreams Don't Die; Tucker's Witch; Murder In Coweta County; Cocaine--One Man's Seduction. Jacobo Timerman--Prisoner Without A Name, Cell Without A Number; Girls of the White Orchid; Heart of Steel; When She Says No; My Mother's Secret Life; The Calendar Girl Murders; Anatomy of an Illness; High School USA; The Three Wishes Of Billy Grier; The Baron And The Kid; Children In The Crossfire.

Songs inc: I Don't Want To Be Your Fool Anymore; The Love That I Give You.

FIEDLER, John: Act. b. Platville, WI, Feb. 3, 1925. Bway inc: The Sea Gull; The Odd Couple; Raisin in the Sun.

Films inc: Twelve Angry Men; Stage Struck; That Touch of Mink; The World of Henry Orient; Kiss Me Stupid; Fitzwilly; The Odd Couple; Raisin in the Sun; True Grit; Making It; Boulevard Nights; Sharky's Machine; Savannah Smiles; I Am the Cheese.

TV inc: The Aldrich Family; Studio One; Buffalo Bill.

FIELD, Fern: Prod. b. Milan, Italy, Jun 28, 1934. e. Columbia; Hunter Coll; UCLA. Films inc: (short) A Different Approach. TV inc: Please Don't Hit Me, Mom; The Wave (Emmy-Childrens Pgm-1982); Eleanor, First Lady of the World; Heartsounds.

FIELD, Leonard S: Prod. b. St Paul, MN, Jul 10, 1908. e. U of MN. Bway inc: Good Hunting; Pretty Penny; Bell, Book and Candle (GM); Porgy and Bess (GM); The Hostage; The Birthday Party; The Au Pair Man; Susanna Andler; Passion of Dracula.

FIELD, Sally: Act. b. Pasadena, CA, Nov 6, 1946. Films inc: The Way West; Stay Hungry; Smokey and the Bandit; Heroes; The End; Norma Rae (Oscar-1979); Beyond the Poseidon Adventure; Smokey and The Bandit II; Back Roads; Absence of Malice; Kiss Me Goodbye; Places In The Heart)Oscar-1984)

TV inc: Gidget; The Flying Nun; The Girl With Something Extra; Home for the Holidays; Maybe I'll Come Home in the Spring; Marriage Year One; Sybil (Emmy-1977); All the Way Home; Lily for President?

FIELD, Shirley Ann: Act. b. London, 1938. Films inc: Dry Rot; Once More With Feeling; The Entertainer; Saturday Night and Sunday Morning; The Man in the Moon; The Damned; The War Lover; Lunch Hour; Kings of the Sun; Doctor in Clover; Hell is Empty; Risking It.

TV inc: Two By Forsyth.

FIELDING, Harold: Prod. b. England. Originally concert violinist, later concert impresario. Thea inc: (London) Cinderella; Aladdin; The Gazebo; The Billy Barnes Revue; The Music Man; Progress to the Park; The Bird of Time; Critic's Choice; A Thurber Carnival; How Are You Johnny?; Half A Sixpence; Looking For the Action; Fielding's Music Hall; Charlie Girl; Man of Magic; Sweet Charity; You're a Good Man Charlie Brown; Mame; Phil the Fluter; The Great Waltz; Show Boat; Gone With the Wind; Finishing Touches; Let My People Come; The Charles Pierce Show; The Biograph Girl; Barnum; Singin' In the Rain.

FIELDS, Freddie: Prod. b. Ferndale, NY, Jul 12, 1923. VP, member of bd of dir, MCA Corp; P Freddie Fields Assoc Ltd, 1961; P, chief exec ofcr Creative Management Assoc Ltd Agency; resigned CMC (now Int'l Creative Mgt), 1975; became indy prod; Oct 1981, P MGM Films theatrical prodn; Sept 1982, named head all film prodn MGM/UA, Oct 1982 given title of P of all prodn; Feb 1983, P & COO MGM Film Co; July, 1984 retd to indie prodn. Films inc: Handle With Care; Looking for Mr Goodbar; American Gigolo; Wholly Moses!; Victory.

FIELDS, Kim: Act. b. Los Angeles, May 12, 1969. Films inc: The Taking of Pelham 1-2-3; Come Back Charleston Blue.

TV inc: Roots--The Next Generation; Facts of Life; Baby I'm Back; The Kid With the Broken Halo; Two of Hearts (cable); Have I Got a Christmas For You.

FIERSTEIN, Harvey: Plywri-act. b. NYC, Jun. 6, 1954. e. Pratt Institute. Plays inc: Torch Song Trilogy *(Tonys*-play & act-1983); La Cage Aux Folles; *(Tony*-play-1984); Spookhouse.
Films inc: The Times Of Harvey Milk (doc-narr); Garbo Talks (act).

FIGUEROA, Gabriel: Cin. b. Mexico, 1907. Films inc: The Fugitive; Maclovia; Night of the Iguana; Kelly's Heroes; The Children of Sanchez; Under the Volcano; Observations Under the Volcano (doc-int).

FINCH, Jon: Act. b. England, 1941. Films inc: The Vampire Lovers; Horror of Frankenstein; Macbeth; Sunday Bloody Sunday; Frenzy; Lady Caroline Lamb; The Final Program; A Faithful Woman; The Second Power; Battleflag; Death on the Nile; La Sabina; Breaking Glass; Gary Cooper Who Art In Heaven; Doktor Faustus; Giro City.
TV inc: Henry IV; Peter and Paul; The Seven Last Words (Family Theatre); Much Ado About Nothing.

FINE, Sylvia: Wri. b. NYC, Aug 29. e. Brooklyn Coll. Wrote special material for husband, Danny Kaye. Stage scores inc: Straw Hat Review; Films inc: The Court Jester (score); Up in Arms (songs).
TV inc: Danny Kaye's Look-In At The Metropolitan Opera *(Emmy*-exec prod-1976); Musical Comedy Tonight; Musical Comedy Tonight II.
Songs inc: The Moon Is Blue; The Five Pennies.

FINKEL, Robert S (Bob): Prod-Dir-Wri. b. Pittsburgh, PA, Mar 25, 1918. TV inc: (prod) Andy Williams Show *(Emmys*-1966, 1967); Elvis Presley Special; Bing Crosby Christmas Special; Julie Andrews Hour; Circus of the Stars. (Dir): Bob Newhart; Barney Miller; McMillan & Wife; The John Davidson Christmas Show; Third Annual Circus of the Stars; John Denver and the Muppets, A Christmas Get Together; Two Of A Kind; All Star Salute to Mother's Day; The World of Entertainment (exec prod); The Wayne Newton Special--Coast To Coast (wri-prod); Olympic Gala (wri-prod).

FINLAY, Frank: Act. b. Farnworth, Lancs, England, Aug 6, 1926. e. RADA. Appeared with Guildford Repertory Theatre Co, 1957. Thea inc: The Telescope; The Queen and the Welshman; Chicken Soup with Barley; The Happy Haven; The Workhouse Donkey; Hamlet; The Crucible; Othello; Filumena. The Return of the Soldier.
Films inc: The Informer; Othello; Inspector Clouseau; Twisted Nerve; Cromwell; Gumshoe; Danny Jones; Sitting Target; Shaft in Africa; The Three Musketeers; The Four Musketeers; Murder by Decree; The Return of the Soldier; Enigma; The Ploughman's Lunch; Sakharov; 1919; Lifeforce.
TV inc: The Thief Of Baghdad; Casanova; The Adventures of Don Quixote; The Death of Adolph Hitler; A Christmas Carol; The Spanish Civil War (narr); Arch Of Triumph.

FINNERMAN, Gerald Perry: Cin. b. Los Angeles, Dec 17, 1931. e. Loyola U of LA. TV inc: Night Gallery (& dir); Star Trek; Kojak; Planet of the Apes; Police Woman; Joe Forrester; Salvage I (& dir); The Last Hurrah; Ziegfeld--The Man and His Woman *(Emmy*-1978); The Dream Merchants; From Here To Eternity; To Find My Son; The Gangster Chronicles; The Ordeal of Bill Carney; Dangerous Company; The Gift of Life; Drop Out Father; September Gun; Bay City Blues; Eye To Eye.
Films inc: Smorgasbord; Nightmares.

FINNEY, Albert: Act. b. Salford, England, May 9, 1936. e. RADA. Stage debut, 1956, Birmingham Repertory Theatre. Screen debut, 1960, The Entertainer. Films inc: Saturday Night and Sunday Morning; Tom Jones; Night Must Fall; Two for the Road; Charlie Bubbles; Scrooge; Gumshoe; Alpha Beta; Murder on the Orient Express; The Duelists; Loophole; Wolfen; Looker; Shoot the Moon; Annie; The Dresser; Under the Volcano; Observations Under the Volcano (doc-int); Notes From Under the Volcano (doc-int).
Thea inc: The Party; Coriolanus; The Lily White Boys; Billy Liar; Luther; Much Ado About Nothing; Love for Love; Miss Julie; A Flea in Her Ear; Joe Egg; Alpha Beta; Krapp's Last Tape; Cromwell; Chez Nous; Hamlet; Loot; Tamburlaine; The Country Wife; Uncle Vanya; The Cherry Orchard; Present Laughter; Sgt. Musgrave's Dance (& dir).
TV inc: View Friendship and Marriage; The Claverdon Road Job; The Miser; Pope John Paul II.

FINNEY, Edward F: Exec. b. NYC, Apr 18, 1913. e. CCNY. In 1941 org Edward Finney Productions. Discovered the late Tex Ritter and made his first 40 features. TV inc: Things that Make America Great; Baron Munchhausen; Seven Wonders of Arkansas; Journey to Freedom; Call of the Forest.

FIRESTONE, Eddie: Act. b. San Francisco, Dec 11, 1920. Films inc: Jackpot; With a Song in My Heart; One Minute to Zero; The Revolt of Mamie Stover; Bail Out at 40,000; Two for the Seesaw; A Man Called Cannon; Suppose They Gave a War and Nobody Came?; Play It As It Lays.
TV inc: The Big Slide; Revenge of the Red Chief; I Take These Men.

FIRKUSNY, Rudolf: Pianist. b. Czechoslovakia, Feb 11, 1912. Debut 1922, Prague; fled Czechoslovakia after German occupation; has performed all over the world.

FIRSTENBERG, Jean (nee Picker): Exec. b. NYC, Mar 13, 1936. e. Boston U, BS. D of Eugene Picker. With WRC-TV, Washington as asst prod pub aff tv shows; J. Walter Thompson Agcy; 1972 Princeton U, dir publications; in chg of grants for Markle Foundation; Jan 1980 dir AFI.

FIRSTENBERG, Sam: Dir. b. Israel, 1950. e. Columbia College, BA; Loyola Marymount, MA. Films inc: One More Chance (& wri); Revenge Of The Ninja; Ninja III--The Domination; Breakin 2 Electric Boogaloo.
TV inc: For The Sake Of A Dog.

FIRTH, Peter: Act. b. Bradford, Yorkshire, England, 1955. First appeared in TV series, The Flaxton Boys, at age 15; Other TV inc: The Aerodrome. Films inc: Here Come the Double Deckers; Brother Sun and Sister Moon; Equus; When You Comin' Back, Red Ryder; Tess; White Elephant; Lifeforce.
Thea inc: Spring Awakening; Equus; Romeo and Juliet; Amadeus (Bwy).

FISHER, Art: Dir-Prod-Wri. b. NYC, Feb 2, 1934. TV inc: Andy Williams Special; Sunny & Cher Comedy Hour *(Emmy*-dir-1972); Chevy Chase Show; Neil Diamond; Ann-Margret; Bing Crosby; Elton John; Tom and Dick Smothers Brothers Special I; Siegfried and Roy--Superstars of Magic (dir); A Shaun Cassidy Special; The Suzanne Somers Special; Suzanne Somers--and 10,000 GI's.
(Died Feb. 22, 1984).

FISHER, Carrie: Act. b. Beverly Hills, CA, Oct 21, 1956. e. London Central School of Speech and Drama. D of Debbie Reynolds and Eddie Fisher. Films inc: Shampoo; Star Wars; Mr. Mike's Mondo Video; The Empire Strikes Back; The Blues Brothers; Under the Rainbow; Return of the Jedi; Garbo Talks.
Bway inc: Irene (rev); Censored Scenes from King Kong.
TV inc: Come Back, Little Sheba; Saturday Night Live (guest host).

FISHER, Eddie: Act. b. Philadelphia, Aug 10, 1928. Niteries, Radio, TV performer. Discovered by Eddie Cantor, 1949. Films inc: All About Eve; Bundle of Joy; Butterfield 8; Nothing Lasts Forever.

FISHER, Jules: Light dsgn. b. Norristown, PA, Nov 12, 1937. e. PA State U, Carnegie Tech, BFA. Bway inc: All The Kings Men; Here Come the Clowns; All in Love; Red Roses for Me; The Subject Was Roses; A Girl Could Get Lucky; The Sign in Sidney Brustein's Window; Do I Hear A Waltz; Serjeant Musgrave's Dance; The Three Penny Opera; You're A Good Man Charlie Brown; You Know I Can't Hear You When the Water's Running; Little Murders; The Unknown Soldier and his Wife; A Moon for the Misbegotten; The Man in the Glass Booth; Butterflies Are Free; Gantry; Minnie's Boys; No, No Nanette; Lenny (& co-prod); Jesus Christ Superstar; Fun City; Pippin *(Tony*-1973); Seesaw; The Iceman Cometh; Ulysses in Nighttown *(Tony*-1974); Tommy; David Bowie Concert Tour; Liza at the Wintergarden; Chicago; Dancin (& prod) *(Tony*-1978); La Cage Aux Folles.

FISHER, Lucy: Exec. b. Oct 2, 1949. e. Harvard U, BA. Story ed, Samuel Goldwyn Jr Prodns; exec story ed, MGM; exec in charge of creative affairs, MGM; vp creative affairs, Fox; vp prodn, Fox. Feb 1980, prodn vp Zoetrope Studios; Aug, 1981 vp-sr prodn exec WB; July 1983, sr vp prodn.

FISK, Jack: Dir. b. Ipava, IL, Dec 19, 1945. e. Cooper Union. H of Sissy Spacek. Started as dsgn. Films inc: Badlands; Phantom of the Paradise; Carrie; Movie Movie; Days of Heaven; Heart Beat (dir).

FITZGERALD, Ella: Singer. b. Newport News, VA, April 25, 1918. Films inc: Ride Em Cowboy; Pete Kelly's Blues; St Louis Blues; Let No Man Write My Epitaph.
TV inc: The Kennedy Center Honors - A Celebration of the Performing Arts; The Carpenters - Music, Music, Music. *(Grammys-*(11)-vocal-1958, 1959, 1960, 1962; jazz-vocal-1958, 1959, 1976, 1979, 1980, 1981, 1983; vocal album 1960).

FITZGERALD, Geraldine: Act. b. Dublin, Ireland, Nov 24, 1914. e. Dublin Art School. M of Michael Lindsay-Hogg. On stage Gate Theatre, Dublin. British films inc: Turn of the Tide; Mill on the Floss. To Hollywood 1939. Films inc: Wuthering Heights; Dark Victory; Till We Meet Again; Flight From Destiny; Watch on the Rhine; Wilson; Obsessed; Ten North Frederick; The Pawnbroker; Rachel, Rachel; The Last American Hero; Harry and Tonto; Echoes of a Summer; Bye Bye Monkey; Arthur; Easy Money; The Link.
Bway inc: A Long Day's Journey Into Night; Ah, Wilderness!; A Touch of the Poet; The Shadow Box; Mass Appeal (dir).
TV inc: The Best of Everything; Dixie--Changing Habits; Kennedy; Do You Remember Love.

FITZSIMMONS, Tom: Act. b. San Francisco, Oct 28, 1947. e. Yale, BA; Yale School of Drama, MFA. Films inc: Swashbuckler. TV inc: June Moon; The Last of the Belles; The Paper Chase.

FIX, Paul: Act. b. Dobbs Ferry, NY, Mar 13, 1901. Films inc: The First Kiss; The Last Mile; Back Street; The Prisoner of Shark Island; The Ex-Mrs Bradford; The Buccaneer; Dr. Cyclops; Back to Bataan; Wake of the Red Witch; The Plunderers; Red River; Island in the Sky; The High and the Mighty; The Bad Seed; Giant; Santiago; To Kill a Mockingbird; The Sons of Katie Elder; Shenandoah; Welcome to Hard Times; The Ballad of Josie; Day of the Evil Gun; Dirty Dingus Magee; Zabriskie Point; Shoot Out; Night of the Lepus; Pat Garrett & Billy the Kid; Cahill, United States Marshal; Grayeagle; Wanda Nevada.
TV inc: The Rifleman; The Rebels.
(Died Oct 14, 1983).

FLACK, Roberta: Singer-Comp. b. Black Mountain, NC, Feb 10, 1940. e. Howard U. Recording artist *(Grammys-*(4)-record of year-1972, 1973; pop vocal-1972, 1973).
TV inc: The Bill Cosby Show; The First Time Ever.
Films inc: Renaldo and Clara; Bustin' Loose (mus).

FLAGG, Fannie (Patricia Neal): Act. b. Birmingham, AL, Sep 21. 1944. e. U of AL. Films inc: Five Easy Pieces; Stay Hungry; Rabbit Test; Grease.
TV inc: Fernwood 2Night; Match Game; Sex and the Married Woman; Candid Camera; The New Dick Van Dyke Show; The New Wonder Woman; Harper Valley PTA.
Thea inc: Here Today; Gingerbread Lady; Little Mary Sunshine; Come Back to the Five and Dime, Jimmy Dean, Jimmy Dean.

FLAHERTY, Joe: Wri-act. b. Pittsburgh, PA., Jun. 21, 1940. Studied at Pittsburgh Playhouse. Joined Second City group in Chicago, went to Toronto to start group there, later started another in Pasadena, CA. Films inc: 1941; Used Cars; Double Negative; Nothing Personal; Stripes; By Design; Going Berserk.
TV inc; SCTV Network *(Emmys-*wri-1982, 1983); From Cleveland.

FLAMM, Donald J: Exec. b. Pittsburgh, PA, Dec 11, 1899. Started as publicist for the Shuberts, 1918; a pioneer in radio, he owned and operated WMCA, NYC, 1925-1941; WPCH NYC 1927-1932 and co-owned WPAT, Paterson, NJ, 1942-1948. Founded Intercity Network, one of first regional networks in US, 1927; with OWI during World War II conceived and executed plan for American Broadcasting Station in England which became basis for Voice of America; co-prod of plays in London and NY through directorship in Oscar Lewenstein Plays Ltd.

FLANAGAN, Fionnula: Act. b. Dublin, Dec 10, 1941. e. Universite de Fribourg, Switzerland; Abbey Theatre School. Films inc: Ulysses; Sinful Davey; Mr. Patman; Reflections; James Joyce's Women (& prod-wri).
TV inc: How The West Was Won; The Legend of Lizzie Borden; Rich Man, Poor Man *(Emmy-*supp-1976); Young Love, First Love; Through Naked Eyes; Scorned And Swindled; The Ewok Adventure.
Bway inc: Ulysses In Nighttown.

FLANDERS, Ed: Act. b. Minneapolis, MN, Dec. 29, 1934. Bway inc: The Birthday Party; The Trial of the Catonsville Nine; A Moon for the Misbegotten *(Tony-*supp-1974).
TV inc: The Legend of Lizzie Borden; A Moon for the Misbegotten *(Emmy-*supp-1976); Harry S Truman - Plain Speaking *(Emmy-*1977); Backstairs at the White House; Blind Ambition; Eleanor and Franklin; Meeting at Potsdam; Howard, The Amazing Mr. Hughes; Salem's Lot; Last Licks; Skokie; Tomorrow's Child; St. Elsewhere *(Emmy-*1983); Special Bulletin.
Films inc: MacArthur; The Grasshopper; The Ninth Configuration; True Confessions; Twinkle, Twinkle Killer Kane; The Pursuit of B.D. Cooper.

FLANNERY, Susan: Act. b. NYC, Jul 31, 1943. Films inc: The Towering Inferno; The Gumball Rally.
TV inc: Voyage to the Bottom of the Sea; The Time Tunnel; Days of Our Lives *(Emmy-*1975); The Moneychangers; Women in White; Anatomy of a Seduction; Dallas; Money On the Side.

FLATT, Ernest O: Chor. b. Oct 30, 1928. Bway inc: Fade Out, Fade In; It's A Bird, It's A Plane, It's Superman; Sugar Babies (& dir). Films inc: Anything Goes.
TV inc: Your Hit Parade (1955-1958); Garry Moore Show (1958-1963); Julie and Carol at Carnegie Hall; Julie and Carol at Lincoln Center; Carol Burnett Show *(Emmy-*1971); Bubbles and Burnett at the Met; Annie Get Your Gun; Damn Yankees; Kiss Me Kate; Calamity Jane.

FLAUM, Marshall: Prod-Wri-Dir. b. NYC, Sep 13, 1930. e. U of IA, BA; U of S IL, DFA. TV inc: The Twentieth Century (series CBS-TV); Let My People Go; The Yanks Are Coming; Day of Infamy; Battle of Britain; Berlin: Kaiser to Khruschev; Hollywood--The Great Stars; Bogart; Hollywood: The Selznick Years; The Time of Man; Jane Goodall and the World of Animal Behaviour *(Emmy-*1973); Killy Le Champion; Bing Crosby - His Life and Legend; You Asked For It (prod). Exec prod & co-wri 25 Jacques Cousteau Specials; Playboy's 25th Anniversary Celebration; Ripley's Believe It Or Not (Supv prod); Bob Hope's Who Makes the World Laugh--Part II (prod-wri).

FLEETWOOD, Susan: Act. b. Scotland, Sep 21, 1944. e. RADA. With various stock and rep groups before joining Royal Shakespeare Company, later with National Theatre Company. Thea inc: The Relapse; The Criminals; Under Milk Wood; Murder In the Cathedral; Comrades; Playboy of the Western World; Watch It Come Down; Tamburlaine the Great; The Plough and the Stars; The Cherry Orchard; The Women; Way Upstream.
TV inc: The Watercress Girl; Playboy of the Western World; Don't Be Silly; Hamlet (cable); The Good Soldier.
Films inc: Clash of the Titans; Heat and Dust.

FLEISCHER, Richard: Dir. b. NYC, Dec 8, 1916. e. Brown U, BA; Yale, MFA. Films inc: Design for Death *(Oscar-*short-co-prod-1947); Child of Divorce; Banjo; So This Is New York; Bodyguard; Follow Me Quietly; The Clay Pigeon; Trapped; The Narrow Margin; The Happy Time; Arena; 20,000 Leagues Under the Sea; Violent Saturday; The Girl in the Red Velvet Swing; Bandido; Between Heaven and Hell; The Vikings; These Thousand Hills; Compulsion; Crack in the Mirror; The Big Gamble; Barabbas; Fantastic Voyage; Doctor Dolittle; The Boston Strangler; Che; Tora, Tora, Tora; 10 Rillington Place; See No Evil; The Last Run; The New Centurians; Soylent Green; The Don Is Dead; The Spikes Gang; Mr. Majestyk; Mandingo; The Incredible Sarah; Ashanti; Crossed Swords; The Jazz Singer; Tough Enough; Amityville 3-D; Conan the Destroyer.

FLEISCHMAN, Stephen: Prod-Wri. b. NYC, Feb 19, 1919. e. Haverford Coll, BA. H of Dede Allen. TV inc: The Search series; Let's Take a Trip (prod); The Twentieth Century; CBS Reports; joined ABC News 1964 as prod doc unit; Close Up series; Life, Liberty and the Pursuit of Oil; Assault on Privacy; The Long Childhood of Timmy; Anatomy of

Pop--The Music Explosion; Oil; Nobody's Children; Death In A Southwest Prison; The Gene Merchants; Swords, Plowshares and Politics (& dir); The Cocaine Cartel (prod).

FLEMING, Art: Act-TV Personality. b. NYC. TV inc: The Californians; International Detective; Jeopardy (host); National Science Test 1984. Films inc: The Moneychanger; Conspiracy to Assassinate President Lincoln; MacArthur.

FLEMING, Rhonda (Marilyn Lewis): Act. b. Los Angeles, Aug. 10, 1923. Films inc: Spellbound; Spiral Staircase; A Connecticut Yankee in King Arthur's Court; The Redhead and the Cowboy; Crosswinds; Inferno; While the City Sleeps; Gunfight at the OK Corral; The Buster Keaton Story; The Crowded Sky; Won Ton Ton, The Dog Who Saved Hollywood; The Nude Bomb.
Bway: The Women (rev).
TV inc: Love For Rent; Bob Hope's Road to Hollywood.

FLETCHER, Bramwell: Act. b. Bradford, England, Feb 20, 1904. London stage debut, 1927, Paul I. Films inc: Chick; To What Red Hell; Raffles; Svengali; The Mummy; The Scarlet Pimpernel; Random Harvest; White Cargo; The Immortal Sergeant.
Thea inc: Tonight at 8:30; Margin for Error; The Doctor's Dilemma; The Bernard Shaw Story; Pygmalion.

FLETCHER, Louise: Act. b. Birmingham, AL, 1938. Appeared in Playhouse 90, other TV shows. Retired for 10 years to raise family. Returned in Thieves Like Us; One Flew Over The Cuckoo's Nest, (Oscar-1975); Russian Roulette; Exorcist II: The Heretic; The Cheap Detective; The Lady In Red; Natural Enemies; Magician of Lublin; The Lucky Star; Dead Kids; Talk To Me; Strange Invaders; Brainstorm; Firestarter.
TV inc: Islands (WonderWorks); A Summer To Remember.

FLICKER, Theodore J: Wri-Dir-Prod-Act. b. Freehold, NJ, Jun 6, 1930. e. Bard Coll; RADA. Plays inc: The Nervous Set (& dir); The Premise (& prod-dir-act).
Films inc: The Trouble Maker (dir); The President's Analyst (sp-dir); Jacob Two-Two Meets The Hooded Fang (sp-dir).
TV inc: (dir) Andy Griffith; Dick Van Dyke; Man From UNCLE; Barney Miller (co-creator & dir, pilot); Just a Little Inconvenience (wri-dir); Last of the Good Guys (wri-dir); Where The Ladies Go; The Legend of the Lone Ranger (act).

FLINN, John C, Jr: Publicist. b. Yonkers, NY, May 4, 1917. e. UCLA. Publicist, Warner Bros 1936-46; joined Monogram 1946; Allied Artists 1951; dir of adv & pub Columbia 1959; joined MGM 1973; rejoined Columbia Pictures 1974, studio pub dir; 1979 named dir Industry Relations.

FLINT-SHIPMAN, Veronica: Prod. b. England, 1931. Owner of the Phoenix Theatre London since 1967. Productions inc: Winnie the Pooh (& dir-chor); I Do! I Do!; 13 Rue de l'amour; Bus Stop.

FLON, Suzanne: Act. b. Paris, Jan. 28, 1918. Former sec. to Edith Piaf, began career in Paris musichalls. Thea inc: Romeo et Jeannette; L'Alouette; Le Mal Court; La Petite Hutte; Taming Of The Shrew; The Cherry Orchard; Gigi.
Films inc: Capitaine Blomet; Dernier Amour; Suzanne et ses Brigands; La Cage aux Filles; La Belle Image; Proces au Vatican (Miracle of Ste. Therese); Moulin Rouge; Mr. Arkadin; Tu ne tuera point (Thou Shalt Not Kill); Un singe en Hiver (A Monkey in Winter); Le Proces (The Trial); Chateau en Suede (Nutty Naughty Chateau); The Train; Le Soleil des Voyous (Action Man); Zita; Teresa; Les Silencieux (Escape To Nowhere); Les violets clos; Un amour de Pluie; Mr. Klein; Comme Une Boomerang (Like A Boomerang); Blackout; Quartet; Pablo Picasso (voice); L'Ete Meurtrier (One Deadly Summer).

FLOOD, Ann: Act. b. Jamaica, NY, Nov 12, 1934. Bway inc: Kismet; Holiday for Lovers.
TV inc: West Point; Annapolis; Matinee Theatre; From These Roots; The Edge of Night (since 1962).

FLOREA, John: Dir-Wri-Prod. b. Alliance, OH, May 28, 1920. Films inc: A Time to Every Purpose; The Astral Factor (Invisible Strangler).
TV inc: The Island of the Lost; The Americans; Wide Country;

Daniel Boone; Sea Hunt; Everglades; Primus; Convoy; Firehouse; Bonanza; The Virginian; High Chapparral; Destry Rides Again; Mission Impossible; Not for Hire; Highway Patrol; Target; CHiPs; Daktari; Gentle Ben; Flipper; The Runaways.

FLOREN, Myron: Comp-Mus-Singer. b. Webster, SD, Nov 5, 1919. With USO during WW 2, touring front lines. On radio, St Louis, postwar while head accordion dept St Louis Coll of Music. Soloist with various orchs; featured perf with Lawrence Welk orch.
Comps inc: Skating Waltz in Swing; Swingin' in Vienna; Kavallo's Kapers; Windy River; Dakota Polka; Long Long Ago in Swing; Minute Waltz in Swing.

FLUELLEN, Joel: Act. b. Dec 1, 1910. Films inc: The Burning Cross; The Jackie Robinson Story; Miss Lucy Gallant; The Decks Ran Red; Friendly Persuasion; Porgy and Bess; A Raisin in the Sun; Sitting Bull; Imitation of Life; Run Silent, Run Deep; He Rides Tall; Good Neighbor Sam; The Chase; The Learning Tree; The Great White Hope; The Skin Game; Man Friday; Casey's Shadow; Butch and Sundance Kid-The Early Days.
TV inc: Roots 2; Freedom Road.

FLYNN, John: Dir. Films inc: The Sergeant; The Jerusalem File; The Outfit (& sp); Rolling Thunder; Defiance; Touched.
TV inc: Marilyn--The Untold Story; Lone Star (& wri).

FOCH, Nina: Act. b. Leyden, Holland, Apr 20, 1924. On screen since 1943. Films inc: Return of the Vampire; Strange Affair; My Name Is Julia Ross; Ten Commandments; The Guilt of Janet Ames; An American in Paris; Spartacus; Prescription: Murder; Executive Suite; Such Good Friends; Jennifer.
TV inc: Ebony, Ivory and Jade; Pottsville; Natalie--A Tribute To A Very Special Lady.

FOGEL, Ira: Dir. TV inc (flr mgr): One Life to Live; All My Children; Sammy & Co. (Asso dir) Inside Pro Football; Stiller and Meara Take Five; AM America; Good Night America; Good Morning America. (Dir) Rona Barrett segs of Good Morning America.

FOGELBERG, Dan (Daniel Grayling Fogelberg): Sngwi-Mus. b. Peoria, IL, Aug 13, 1951. e. U IL. Albums inc: Home Free; Souvenirs; Captured Angel; Nether Lands; Twin Sons of Different Mothers; Phoenix.

FOGELMAN, Ted: Exec. b. Minneapolis, Feb 5, 1913. Bd member, Sec-Treas, then chmn local section SMPTE. Bd member, local chmn, SMPTE International. Assoc member ASC, ACE.

FOGELSON, Andrew M.: Exec. b. New Rochelle, NY, Aug 5, 1942. e. Union Coll. 1968, ad coypwriter WB; 1971 vp mktg svs; 1973 vp pub-ad Col; 1975, vp & exec asst to P; 1977, exec vp wldwde pub-ad WB; 1979 P Rastar Pictures; Sept 1982 formed indie company with Richard Dreyfuss. Films inc: Wrong Is Right (exec prod); Blue Thunder (exec prod); The New Kids (prod); Just One Of The Guys (prod).

FOGERTY, John C Sngwri-Singer b. Berkeley, CA, May 28, 1945. With Creedence Clearwater Revival 1968-1972 as writer-performer; later with Blue Ridge Rangers before solo.
Songs inc: Proud Mary; Have You Ever Seen the Rain; Who'll Stop the Rain; Bad Moon Rising; Fortunate Son; Travelin' Band; Look Out My Back Door; Down on the Corner; Green River; Run Through The Jungle; Hey Tonight; Up Around the Bend; It Came Out of The Sky; Commotion; Born on the Bayou; Rockin' All Over The World.

FOLSEY, George: Cin. b. 1898. Films inc: The Fear Market; Born Rich; Applause; Reunion in Vienna; The Smiling Lieutenant; Reckless; The Gorgeous Hussy; The Great Ziegfeld; Meet Me in St. Louis; White Cliffs of Dover; A Guy Named Joe; Under The Clock; The Green Years; Green Dolphin Street; State of the Union; Take Me Out to the Ballgame; The Great Sinner; Adam's Rib; Million Dollar Mermaid; Executive Suite; Seven Brides for Seven Brothers; All the Brothers Were Valiant; The Fastest Gun Alive; Imitation General; The Balcony.
TV inc: Here's Peggy Fleming (Emmy-1969).

FONDA, Jane: Act. b. NYC, Dec 21, 1937. D of the late Henry Fonda. Screen debut 1960 Tall Story. Films inc: Walk on the Wild

Side; The Chapman Report; Period of Adjustment; In the Cool of the Day; Sunday in New York; La Ronde; Cat Ballou; Hurry Sundown; Barefoot in the Park; Barbarella; They Shoot Horses Don't They?; Klute *(Oscar*-1971); Steelyard Blues; A Doll's House; Fun with Dick and Jane; Julia; Coming Home *(Oscar*-1978); California Suite; Comes A Horseman; The China Syndrome; The Electric Horseman; Nine To Five; Acting--Lee Strasberg and the Actors Studio (doc); On Golden Pond; Rollover; Montgomery Clift.

TV inc: Lily--Sold Out; 9 to 5 (exec prod); Lily For President?; Stanley Kramer on Film (narr); Tell Them I'm a Mermaid; The Doll-maker *(Emmy*-*1984)*; Olympic Gala (host); USA For Africa--The Story Of 'We Are The World.'

FONDA, Peter: Act. b. NYC, Feb 23, 1939. e. NE U. S of the late Henry Fonda. Acting debut at Lincoln (NE) Playhouse, where his father had made pro bow 35 years earlier. Bway: Blood, Sweat and Stanley Poole. On screen from 1963, Tammy and the Doctor. Films inc: The Victors; Lilith; The Wild Angels; The Trip; Easy Rider (& prod); The Last Movie; The Hired Hand (& dir); Two People; Dirty Mary, Crazy Larry; Open Season; Race with the Devil; Fighting Mad; Outlaw Blues; High Ballin'; Wanda Nevada (& dir); The Cannonball Run; Split Image; Peppermint Frieden (Peppermint Peace); Daijoobu Mai Furendo (All Right, My Friend); Spasms; Certain Fury.

TV inc: The Hostage Tower; A Reason To Live.

FONG, Benson: Act. b. Sacramento, CA, Oct 10, 1916. Appeared in more than 200 films inc Charlie Chan Series; Behind the Rising Sun; The Purple Heart; Thirty Seconds Over Tokyo; Keys of the Kingdom; Calcutta; Boston Blackie's Chinese Adventure; His Majesty O'Keefe; The Flower Drum Song; Our Man Flint; The Love Bug; The Strongest Man in the World; Oliver's Story; Jinxed.

TV inc: Family In Blue; Moonlight; The Glitter Dome (PC).

FONG, Kam: Act. b. Honolulu, May 27. Films inc: Gidget Goes Hawaiian; Ghost of the China Sea; Seven Women From Hell; Diamond Head.

TV inc: Hawaii Five-O.

FONTAINE, Joan: Act. b. Tokyo, Oct 22, 1917. Sis of Olivia de Havilland. On Broadway in Tea and Sympathy. Screen debut, Quality Street, 1937. Films inc: Rebecca; Suspicion *(Oscar*-1941); Women; The Constant Nymph; Gunga Din; This Above All; Jane Eyre; Frenchman's Creek; Affairs of Susan; Emperor Waltz; September Affair; Ivanhoe; Casanova's Big Night; Island in the Sun; Until They Sail; A Certain Smile; Tender is the Night; The Devil's Own. TV inc: Ryan's Hope.

FONTANNE, Lynn: Act. b. Woodford, England, Dec 6, 1897. Widow of Alfred Lunt. London stage debut 1905, in pantomine, Cinderella. Bway debut 1910, Mr Preedy and the Countess.

Bway inc: The Guardsman; Pygmalion; Strange Interlude; Reunion in Vienna; Point Valaine; The Seagull; The Taming of the Shrew; There Shall Be No Night; O Mistress Mine; Quadrille; The Visit.

(Special Tony-1974). Received the Peace Medal From Pres Johnson, 1964.

Films inc: Second Youth; The Guardsman; Stage Door Canteen.

TV inc: The Great Sebastians; The Magnificent Yankee *(Emmy*-1965); The Bunny Raasch Special; The Kennedy Center Honors, 1980.

(Died July 30, 1983).

FONTEYN, Margot, Dame (Margaret Hookham): Ballerina. b. Surrey, England, May 18, 1919. Prima Ballerina of Britain's Royal Ballet, Dame Margot made her professional debut, 1934. Starred with Royal Ballet until 1970, then guest starring appearances with the Stuttgart Ballet, The National Ballet in Washington, DC, and other companies.

FOOTE, Horton: Wri. b. Wharton, TX, Mar 14. Former act. Plays inc: Out of My House; Only the Heart; Celebration; The Chase; The Trip to Bountiful; The Traveling Lady; book for the musical Gone With the Wind.

Films inc: To Kill a Mockingbird *(Oscar*-1962); Tender Mercies (& asso prod) *(Oscar*-wri-1983); 1918.

TV inc: The Trip to Bountiful; Young Lady of Property; Death of the Old Man; The Dancers; Flight; Tomorrow; the Night of the Storm;

Keeping On.

FORAY, June: Act. b. Springfield, MA. Voice specialist; on radio for several years; to Hollywood to do voice characterizations for Capital Records

Films inc: Looney Looney Looney Bugs Bunny Movie; Daffy Duck's Movie--Fantastic Island.

TV inc: The Bugs Bunny Mother's Day Special; Rikki Tikki Tavi; Raggedy Childrens Albums; voice of many cartoon characters. Ann and Andy in the Pumpkin Who Couldn't Smile; Yankee Doodle Cricket; The White Seal; Mowgli's Brothers; The Incredible Book Escape; Scruffy; Faeries; Smurfs; A Chipmunk Christmas; Miss Switch To The Rescue; The Smurf Springtime Special; The Smurfs' Christmas Special; The Smurfic Games; Smurfily Ever After; A Chipmunk Reunion.

FORBES, Bryan (John Theobald Clarke): Act-Wri-Prod-Dir. b. London, Jul 22, 1926. e. RADA. Head of Prodn EMI Films, 1969-1971. London Stage debut, 1942, The Corn Is Green. Screen debut, 1948, The Small Back Room. Films inc: (Act) The Wooden Horse; The Million Pound Note; The Colditz Story; The World in His Arms; The Black Night; The Cockleshell Heroes (& sp); The Black Tent; The Body and the Battleship (& sp); The Key; I Was Monty's Double (& sp); Only Two Can Play; Of Human Bondage; Station Six Sahara; The League of Gentlemen (& wri), The Angry Silence; Restless Natives. (Dir): Whistle Down the Wind; Seance on a Wet Afternoon; The L-Shaped Room; King Rat (& sp); The Wrong Box (& prod); The Whisperers (& sp-prod); Deadfall (& sp); Madwoman of Chaillot; The Stepford Wives; The Slipper and the Rose (& co-sp): International Velvet (& sp-prod): Hopscotch (wri); Sunday Lovers; Better Late than Never (& sp); The Naked Face (& sp).

TV inc: (prod-dir): I Caught Acting Like the Measles; Goodbye, Norma Jean; Elton John.

Thea inc: Macbeth (dir).

FORBES, David: Exec. b. Omaha, NE, Nov 9, 1945. e. U NE. Started with MGM, 1968 as field man in Detroit; later asst natl field coordinator at studio; 1973, dir Metrovision; 1974, dir special projects Fox; 1976 natl dir mktg svs Fox; 1977, mktg dir Rastar Prodns; 1980, vp & asst to pres, Columbia Pictures; resd Aug 1982; Dec 1982, Vice Chmn Almi Distribution Corp; Film inc: The Big Score (exec prod).

FORBES, Lou: Comp-Cond. b. St Louis, MO, Aug 12, 1902. Film scores inc: Intermezzo; Up in Arms; Wonder Man; This is Cinerama. Mus dir Intermezzo; Gone With the Wind.

FORD, Cecil: Prod. b. Dublin, 1911. e. Trinity Coll. Began career as an actor. Films inc: (Asst dir): Odd Man Out. (Prodn Mgr): Moby Dick; Around the World in 80 Days; The Bridge on the River Kwai; The Inn of the Sixth Happiness; Young Winston. (Prod): The Guns of Navarone; Squadron 64; All Things Bright and Beautiful.

FORD, Constance: Act. b. NYC 1928. Thea inc; Death of a Salesman; Say, Darling; Nobody Loves an Albatross.

Films inc: The Last Hunt; Bailout at 43,000; A Summer Place; Home From the Hill; Claudelle Inglish; Rome Adventure; House of Women; All Fall Down; The Cabinet of Dr. Caligari; The Caretakers.

TV inc: Anna Christie; Burlesque; Another World.

FORD, Glenn: Act. b. Quebec, May 1, 1916. Bway inc: Groom for a Bride; Soliloquy. Screen debut, 1940, Heaven With a Barbed Wire Fence. U.S. Marine Corps, 1942-45. Films inc: So Ends Our Night; Desperadoes; Gilda; Framed; The Mating of Millie; Loves of Carmen; The Redhead and the Cowboy; Follow the Sun; The Secret of Convict Lake; Affair in Trinidad; Man From the Alamo; Appointment in Honduras; The Americano; Violent Men; Blackboard Jungle; Ransom; Fastest Gun Alive; Jubal; Teahouse of the August Moon; Don't Go Near the Water; The Sheepman; Imitation General; Torpedo Run; It Started With a Kiss; The Gazebo; Cimarron; The Four Horsemen of the Apocalypse; Experiment in Terror; The Courtship of Eddie's Father; The Rounders; The Money Trap; Fate Is the Hunter; Dear Heart; Time for Killing; Heaven With a Gun; Santee; Midway; Superman; The Visitor; Virus; Happy Birthday To Me.

TV inc: The Brotherhood of The Bell; Cade's Country; Jarret; The Holvak Family; When The West Was Fun; Once An Eagle; Beggarman,

Thief; The Gift.

FORD, Harrison: Act. b. Chicago, Jul 13, 1942. e. Ripon Coll. Films inc: Dead Heat on a Merry-Go-Round; Luv; Getting Straight; The Long Ride Home; Journey To Shiloh; Zabriskie Point; The Conversation; American Graffiti; Star Wars; Heroes; Force 10 From Navarone; Hanover Street; Apocalypse Now; The Frisco Kid; The Empire Strikes Back; Raiders of the Lost Ark; Blade Runner; Return of the Jedi; Indiana Jones and the Temple of Doom; Witness.

TV inc: Dynasty; The Trial of Lt. Calley; The Possessed; Great Movie Stunts--Raiders of the Lost Ark (host).

FORD, Tennessee Ernie: Singer. b. Bristol, TN, Feb 13, 1919. e. Cincinnati Conserv. of Music. Radio announcer, 1939-41; U.S. Air Force, 1942-45; hillbilly disc jockey, Pasadena; Capital Recording artist. TV inc: Tennessee Ernie Show; I Love Lucy; Red Skelton Show; Perry Como Show; George Gobel Show.

(Grammy-Gospel-1964).

FORD, Tony: Exec. b. NYC, Aug 6, 1925. e. St Johns U. Agent with MCA, 1949-53; Indy prod tv specials for Ringling Bros Circus, Victor Borge; reentered agency business, General Artists Corp, vp, tv dept. Headed own agency, Tony Ford Mgt, Inc, which was acquired by William Morris Agency; headed creative services division WMA; left Morris Agency 1977; to re-open own agency; Oct 1979 named sr vp crea aff Metromedia Producers Corp; Aug. 1984, exec VP Gaylord Television Prodns.

FOREMAN, Carl: Wri-Prod-Dir. b. Chicago, Jul 23, 1914. e. U of IL; Northwestern U. Films inc: So This Is New York (sp); The Clay Pigeon (sp); Home of the Brave (sp); Champion (sp); The Men (sp); Cyrano de Bergerac (sp); High Noon (sp); The Key (sp & prod); The Mouse That Roared (exec prod); The Guns of Navarone (sp & prod); The Victors (sp, dir & prod); Born Free (prod); MacKenna's Gold (prod); Otley (prod); The Virgin Soldiers (prod); Living Free (prod); Young Winston (sp & prod); Force 10 From Navarone (sp); When Time Ran Out (sp).

TV inc: The Golden Gate Murders.

(Died June 26, 1984).

FOREMAN, John: Prod. b. Idaho Falls, ID. Co-founder of CMA Agency. Resigned 1968 to found Newman-Foreman Co; Oct 1982, VP in chg wldwide theatrical prodn MGM/UA; Feb 1983, retd to indie prodn. Films inc: Winning; Butch Cassidy and the Sundance Kid; WUSA; Puzzle of a Downfall Child; They May Be Giants; Pocket Money; The Effect of Gamma Rays on Man-in-the-Moon Marigolds; The Macintosh Man; The Man Who Would Be King; The Great Train Robbery; The Ice Pirates; Prizzi's Honor.

FORMAN, Sir Denis: Exec. b. Scotland, Oct 13, 1917. e. Cambridge. Joined prodn staff Central Office of Information, London, 1946; became chief prodn officer 1947; 1948, dir British Film Institute; 1971, chmn of Board of Governors; Joint M-Dir Granada TV 1965; became chmn 1974.

FORMAN, Milos: Dir. b. Caslaz, Czechoslovakia, Feb 18, 1932. e. Academy of Music and Dramatic Arts, Prague. Wrote scripts, radio commentator. First directorial job, Magic Lantern. Films inc: Black Peter; Loves of A Blonde; Talent Competition; Fireman's Ball; One Flew Over the Cuckoo's Nest *(Oscar*-1975); Hair; Ragtime; Before The Nickelodeon--The Early Cinema of Edwin S Porter (voice); Chytilova vs. Forman; Amadeus *(Oscar-1984)*

FORREST, Frederic: Act. b. Dec 23, 1936. Films inc: The Don is Dead; The Conversation; The Missouri Breaks; Apocalypse Now; The Rose; One From the Heart; Hammett; Valley Girl; The Stone Boy.

TV inc: Who Will Love My Children; Saigon--The Year of the Cat; The Parade; Calamity Jane; Best Kept Secrets; Right To Kill?

FORREST, George (Chet): Lyr-Comp. b. NYC, Jul 31, 1915. At 13 became partner of Robert Wright; as team, under contract to MGM Studios; wrote songs for films inc: Maytime; Sweethearts; Firefly; Balalaika; The New Moon; I Married an Angel.

Bway scores inc: Song of Norway; Kismet *(Tony*-1954); Magdalena.

Songs inc: Always and Always; It's a Blue World; Elena; Donkey Serenade; Stranger in Paradise; Baubles, Bangles and Beads; And This is My Beloved.

FORREST, Steve (William Forrest Andrews): Act. b. Huntsville, TX, Sep 29, 1924. B of Dana Andrews. Films inc: The Bad and the Beautiful; Phantom of the Rue Morgue; Prisoner of War; Bedevilled; The Living Idol; Heller in Pink Tights; The Yellow Canary; Rascal; The Wild Country; The Late Liz; North Dallas Forty; Mommie Dearest; Sahara.

TV inc: The Baron; S.W.A.T.; Wanted, the Sundance Woman; The Deerslayer; Roughnecks; A Rumor of War; Condominium; The Manions of America; Hotline; Malibu; Finder Of Lost Loves.

FORSTER, Robert: Act. b. Rochester, NY, Jul 13, 1941. e. Heidelberg Coll; Alfred U; Rochester U, BS. Thea inc: Mrs. Dally; A Streetcar Named Desire (tour).

Films inc: Reflections in a Golden Eye; Medium Cool; Justine; Journey Through Rosebud; The Don Is Dead; Avalanche; The Black Hole; Alligator; The Kinky Coaches and the Pom Pom Pussycats; Vigilante; Walking The Edge; Hollywood Harry (& prod-dir).

TV inc: Judd for the Defense; Banyon; The Darker Side of Terror; Goliath Awaits.

FORSYTH, Bruce: Act. b. London, Feb 22, 1928. Started in vaudeville, worked as comic at Windmill Theatre, London, 1949-1951. Thea inc: Little Me; Birds on the Wing; Bruce Forsyth (one-man show); The Travelling Music Show.

Films inc: Star!; Hieronymus Merkin; Bedknobs and Broomsticks; The Magnificent Seven Deadly Sins; Pavlova.

TV inc: Sunday Night at the London Palladium (host for three years); The Generation Game.

FORSYTHE, Henderson: Act. b. Macon, MO, Sep 11, 1917. e. U of IA, MFA. In various rep companies. Bway inc: The Cellar and the Well (& dir); Romeo and Juliet; The Iceman Cometh; An Enemy of the People; Who's Afraid of Virginia Woolf?; The Right Honourable Gentleman; Malcolm; A Delicate Balance; The Birthday Party; Harvey; The Engagement Baby; The Happiness Cage; Freedom of the City; The Last Meeting of the Knights of the White Magnolia; The Oldest Living Graduate; Best Little Whorehouse in Texas *(Tony*-supp-1979) (also London); Other Places (off-Bway); Cliffhanger (Off-Bway).

TV inc: As the World Turns (since 1960); Sessions; Concealed Enemies.

Films inc: Dead of Night; Silkwood.

FORSYTHE, John (John Lincoln Freund): Act. b. Carney's Point, NJ, Jan 29, 1918. Early career as sports announcer, radio. Bway debut, 1942, Vickie. On screen From 1944, Destination Tokyo. Films inc: The Captive City; It Happens Every Thursday; The Glass Web; Escape From Fort Bravo; The Trouble With Harry; The Ambassador's Daughter; See How They Run; Madame X; In Cold Blood; The Happy Ending; Topaz; And Justice For All.

TV inc: Studio One; Kraft Theatre; Robert Montgomery Presents; Bachelor Father; To Rome with Love; Charlie's Angels (voice); A Time For Miracles; Dynasty; Sizzle; Mysterious Two; Dom DeLuise and Friends; The 4th Annual TV Guide Special; George Burns Celebrates 80 Years in Show Business (host); Dean Martin's Celebrity Roast; Disneyland's 30th Anniversary Celebration; Night Of 100 Stars II; Kraft All-Star Salute To Ford's Theatre.

Thea inc: Mr. Roberts; All My Sons; Yellow Jack; Teahouse of the August Moon; Detective Story; Weekend.

FORTE, Chet: Prod-Dir. b. Hackensack, NJ, Aug 7, 1935. e. Columbia Coll. TV inc: (Dir) Monday Night Football; Monday Night Baseball; World Series; Wide World of Sports; Kentucky Derby; Indianapolis 500; Preakness; Prime Time Fights. (Prod) Wide World of Sports *(Emmy*-1976); Olympic Games 1968 through 1980 *(Emmy*-1976); Kentucky Derby *(Emmy*-1981).

FOSSE, Bob: Dir-Chor-Act. b. Chicago, 1927. On stage as dancer at age 13. Toured in Call Me Mister. Signed by MGM, 1953. Films inc: (act): Give a Girl A Break; The Affairs of Dobie Gillis; Kiss Me Kate; The Little Prince. (Chor): My Sister Eileen. (Dir-chor): Sweet Charity; Cabaret *(Oscar*-dir-1972); All That Jazz, (Dir): Lenny; Star 80 (dir-wri)

Bway inc: (chor): Pajama Game *(Tony*-chor-1955); How to Succeed in Business Without Really Trying. (Dir-chor): Redhead *(Tony*-chor-1959); Damn Yankees *(Tony*-chor-1956); New Girl In Town; Little Me *(Tony*-chor-1963); Sweet Charity *(Tony*-chor-1966); Pippin *(Tonys*-dir-chor-1973); Chicago; Dancin' *(Tony*-chor-1978).

TV inc: Liza With A Z *(Emmys*-(3)-Prod-Dir-Chor-1973); Pippin (cable).

FOSSEY, Brigitte: Act. b. France, 1945. Films inc: Jeux Inderdits; Le Grand Meaulnes; Adieu l'ami; M Comme Matthieu; The Man Who Loved Women; The Good and the Bad; The Swiss Affair; Blue Country; Quintet; Mais ou et donc Orincar; The Triple Death of the Third Character; A Bad Son; The Party; Chanel Solitaire; Croque La Vie (A Bite of Living); Imperativ; La Boum 2 (The Party--2); Enigma; Le Jeune Marie (The Young Bridegroom); Le Batard (The Bastard); Au nom de tous les Miens (For Those I Loved); La Scarlatine (Scarlet Fever); Una Strana Passione (Nicole 'Ou L'Enfant Trouve) (A Strange Passion); Un Casa di Inconscienza (A Case Of Irresponsibility); Flugel und Fesseln (The Future Of Emily); Les Fausses Confidences (The False Confidences).

FOSTER, David: Prod. b. NYC, Nov 25, 1929. Entered ind as pub, became prod, 1968. Films inc: McCabe and Mrs. Miller; The Getaway; The Nickel Ride (exec prod); The Drowning Pool; First Love; Heroes; The Legacy; Tribute (exec prod); Caveman; The Thing; Second Thoughts; Mass Appeal; The Mean Season.

TV inc: Between Two Brothers; The Gift of Life.

FOSTER, Desmond Lionel: Exec. b. Wellington, Australia, Jan 14, 1924. Broadcast industry association dir.

FOSTER, Jodie: Act. b. LA, Nov 19, 1962. Made TV commercials starting at age 3. Screen debut in Disney's Napoleon and Samantha, 1972. Films inc: Tom Sawyer; One Little Indian; Alice Doesn't Live Here Anymore; Echoes of Summer; Bugsy Malone; Taxi Driver; Freaky Friday; The Little Girl Who Lives Down The Lane; Candleshoe; Foxes; Carny; Cassotto; O'Hara's Wife; The Hotel New Hampshire; Le Sang des Autres (The Blood of Others).

TV inc: The Courtship of Eddie's Father; My Three Sons; Paper Moon; Smile Jenny, You're Dead; Rookie of the Year; Svengali.

Bway inc: Agnes of God.

FOSTER, Julia: Act. b. Lewes, Sussex, England, 1942. Films inc: The Small World of Sammy Lee; Two Left Feet; The System; The Bargee; One-Way Pendulum; Alfie; Half a Sixpence; All Coppers Are.

TV inc: Crime and Punishment; Good Girl; Moll Flanders; Richard III; King Henry VI.

Thea inc: Travelling Light; What the Butler Saw; Notes on a Love Affair; Saint Joan.

FOSTER, Meg: Act. b. May 14, 1948. e. NY Neighborhood Playhouse. Films inc: Adam at 6 A.M.; Promise Her Anything; A Different Story; Once In Paris; Carny; Ticket To Heaven; The Osterman Weekend; The Emerald Forest.

TV inc: Sunshine Christmas; Things In Their Season; James Dean, Portrait of a Friend; Washington Behind Closed Doors; Scarlet Letter; Guyana Tragedy--the Story of Jim Jones; The Legend of Sleepy Hollow; Cagney and Lacey; Desperate Intruder; Best Kept Secrets.

FOSTER, Paul: Wri. b. Penn's Grove, NJ, 1931. e. Rutgers U; St John's U. Plays inc: Hurrah for the Bridge; The Recluse; The Madonna in the Orchard; The Hessian Corporal; Tom Paine Satyricon; Silver Queen Saloon.

FOSTER, Phil: Act. b. NYC, Mar 29, 1914. Nitery Comic. Films inc: Conquest of Space. TV inc: Laverne & Shirley; The Great American Traffic Jam.

FOWLEY, Douglas: Act. b. NYC, May 30, 1911. Films inc: Let's Talk it Over; Crash Donovan; Charlie Chan on Broadway; Mr Moto's Gamble; Dodge City; Tanks a Million; The Kansan; The Hucksters; Battleground; Edge of Doom; Singin' in the Rain; The High and the Mighty; Desire in the Dust; Barabbas; The Good Guys and the Bad Guys; Homebodies; Black Oak Conspiracy; The White Buffalo; The North Avenue Irregulars.

TV inc: Pistols and Petticoats.

FOX, Charles: Comp-Cond. b. NYC, Oct 30, 1940. e. Fontainbleu Conservatory of Music and with Nadia Boulanger. Films inc: Barbarella; Goodbye, Columbus; A Separate Peace; Pufnstuf; The Laughing Policeman; The Last American Hero; The Other Side of The Mountain; The Duchess and the Dirtwater Fox; Two Minute Warning; Victory at Entebbe; Foul Play; Our Winning Season; One on One; Little Darlings; Why Would I Lie?; Oh, God! Book II; Nine To Five; Six Pack; Zapped!; Trenchcoat; Strange Brew.

TV inc: Love American Style *(Emmys*-1970, 1973); Shirley; Foul Play; Aloha Paradise; Family Secrets; He's Not Your Son; A Summer To Remember; Goodbye, Charlie.

FOX, Edward: Act. b. England, Apr 13, 1937. Films inc: The Naked Runner; The Long Duel; Oh! What a Lovely War; Skullduggery; The Go-Between; The Day of the Jackal; Doll's House; The Squeeze; A Bridge Too Far; The Cat and the Canary; The Big Sleep; The Duellists; Force 10 From Navarone; Soldier of Orange; The Mirror Crack'd; Gandhi; Never Say Never Again; The Dresser; The Bounty; The Shooting Party; Wild Geese II.

TV inc: Edward and Mrs Simpson; Glittering Crowns (narr).

Thea inc: Anyone for Denis?; Quartermaine's Terms.

FOX, James: Act. b. England, May 19, 1939. Film debut as child actor 1950, The Magnet. Films inc: The Loneliness of the Long-Distance Runner; The Servant; Tamahine; Those Magnificent Men in Their Flying Machines; King Rat; The Chase; Thoroughly Modern Millie; Duffy; Isadora; Arabella; Performance; Runners; Greystoke--The Legend Of Tarzan, Lord of the Apes; Pavlova; A Passage To India.

TV inc: The Door; Espionage.

FOX, Maxine: Prod. b. Baltimore, MD, Dec 26, 1946. e. Boston U. Plays inc: Grease; Over Here!; And Miss Reardon Drinks a Little; Fortune and Men's Eyes.

FOX, Michael J.: Act. b. Edmonton, Canada, Jun. 9, 1961. TV inc: Leo and Me (Canada); Letters from Frank; Palmerstown; Family Ties; High School, USA; Po ison Ivy.

Films inc: Midnight Madness; The Class of 1984; Back To The Future.

FOX, Ray Errol: Lyr. b. Jul 13, 1941. Films inc: La Guerre Est Finie; The Clowns. Plays inc: The Sign in Sidney Brustein's Window.

FOXWELL, Ivan: Prod-wri. b. London, Feb 22, 1914. Originally a technician with various British firms; became prod-wri in asso with Curtis Bernhard. Films inc: Carefour; Train To Venice; Sarajevo; No Room at the Inn; Guilt Is My Shadow; 24 Hours In A Woman's Life (prod only); The Intruder; The Colditz Story; A Touch of Larceny; The Quiller Memorandum; Decline and Fall.

FOXWORTH, Robert: Act. b. Houston, TX, Nov 1, 1941. e. Mellon U. Films inc: Treasure of Matecumbe; The Astral Factor (Invisible Strangler); Airport '77; Damien-Omen II; Prophecy; The Black Marble.

TV inc: The Storefront Lawyers; Mrs Sundance; Hogan's Goat; The Memory of Eva Ryker; Act of Love; Peter and Paul; Falcon Crest.

FOXX, Redd: Act. b. St Louis, MO, Dec 9, 1922. Nightclub performer; recording artist. TV inc: Soul; Green Acres; Sanford and Son; Motown Returns To The Apollo.

Films inc: Norman...Is That You?

FOY, Eddie, Jr: Act. b. New Rochelle, NY, Feb 4, 1905. Films inc: Fugitive From Justice; The Farmer Takes a Wife; Lucky Me; The Pajama Game; Bells are Ringing; Thirty is a Dangerous Age; Cynthia.

TV inc: Fair Exchange.

(Died Jul 15, 1983).

FRADY, Marshall: Wri. b. Augusta, GA., 1942. e. Furman U. TV inc: The Apocalypse Game; Soldiers of the Twilight; When Crime Pays; The Monastery; The Gene Merchants; Wounds From Within; Fortress Israel; J. Edgar Hoover; Swords, Plowshares and Politics; Adapt or Die; The American Inquisition; Vanishing America; To Save Our Schools, To Save Our Children (& corr); The Supreme Court Of The United States; The Fire Unleashed (& corr).

FRAKER, William A: Cin. b. Los Angeles, 1923. e. USC. Films inc:

Games; The President's Analyst; Rosemary's Baby; Bullitt; Paint Your Wagon; Dusty and Sweets McGee; Day of the Dolphin; The Killer Inside Me; Bobby and Rose; Gator; Close Encounters of the Third Kind; The Exorcist; Looking for Mr. Goodbar; American Hot Wax; Heaven Can Wait; Old Boyfriends; 1941; The Hollywood Knights; Divine Madness; The Best Little Whorehouse In Texas; WarGames; Irreconcilable Differences; Protocol; (Dir): Monte Walsh; Reflection of Fear; The Legend of the Lone Ranger; Sharky's Machine.

FRAMPTON, Peter: Singer-Mus. b. Beckenham, Kent, England, Apr 22, 1950. With groups The Herd, Humble Pie, Frampton's Camel before solo.
Albums inc: Winds of Change; Something's Happening; Frampton; Frampton Comes Alive; I'm in You; Where I Should Be.
Films inc: Sgt Pepper's Lonely Hearts Club Band.

FRANCIOSA, Anthony: Act. b. NYC, Oct 25, 1928. Films inc: A Face in the Crowd; This Could Be the Night; A Hatful of Rain; Wild Is the Wind; The Long Hot Summer; The Naked Maja; The Story on Page One; Period of Adjustment; Rio Conchos; The Pleasure Seekers; A Man Could Get Killed; Assault on a Queen; The Swinger; In Enemy Country; A Man Called Gannon; Across 110th Street; The Drowning Pool; Firepower; Help Me Dream; Death Wish II; Julie Darling; Ghost in the Noonday Sun (made in 1973).
TV inc: Valentine's Day; Name of the Game; Search; Matt Helm; Earth II; Hide and Go Seek; The Deadly Hunt; Ryan's the Name; The Black Widow; Side Show; The World is Full of Married Men; Side Show; Finder Of Lost Loves.
Bway inc: End as a Man; Wedding Breakfast; A Hatful of Rain.

FRANCIS, Anne: Act. b. Ossining, NY, Sep 16, 1932. Radio, TV shows as child. Films inc: Summer Holiday; So Young So Bad; Elopement; Lydia Bailey; Susan Slept Here; Bad Day at Black Rock; The Blackboard Jungle; Forbidden Planet; Don't Go Near the Water; Girl of the Night; The Satan Bug; Funny Girl; The Love God; More Dead than Alive; Pancho Villa; Born Again.
TV inc: Haunts of the Very Rich; Honey West; Greatest Heroes of the Bible; The Rebels; Beggarman, Thief; Detour to Terror; Rona Jaffe's Mazes & Monsters; O'Malley; Charley's Aunt (cable); Riptide; Murder She Wrote.

FRANCIS, Arlene (nee Kazanjian): Act. b. Boston, MA, 1908. W of Martin Gabel. Films inc: All My Sons; One, Two, Three; The Thrill of it All.
Thea inc: All That Glitters; Once More With Feeling; Dinner at Eight; Pal Joey; Who Killed Santa Claus?; Gigi.
TV inc: Regular panelist What's My Line; Arlene Francis Show; Talent Patrol.

FRANCIS, Connie (Constance Franconero): Act. b. Newark, NJ, Dec 12, 1938. Won Arthur Godfrey's Talent Scout Show at age 12. Films inc: Where The Boys Are; Follow The Boys; Looking For Love.

FRANCIS, Freddie: Cin-Dir. b. London, 1917. Films inc: (Cin) Mine Own Executioner; Time Without Pity; Room at the Top; Sons and Lovers (Oscar-cin-1960); The Innocents; The Elephant Man; The French Lieutenant's Woman; The Jigsaw Man; Memed, My Hawk; Dune. (Dir): Two and Two Make Six; Vengeance; Paranoiac; Nightmare; The Evil of Frankenstein; The Skull; They Came From Beyond Space; The Torture Garden; Dracula Has Risen From the Grave; Tales From the Crypt; Asylum; Tales that Witness Madness; Legend of the Werewolf.
TV inc: The Executioner's Song.

FRANCIS, Genie: Act. b. Los Angeles, May 26, 1962. TV inc: Family; General Hospital; Bare Essence.

FRANCIS, Kevin: Prod. b. London, 1948. Co-founder, M-Dir Tyburn Prodns Ltd. Started as prod mgr, asso prod. Films inc: (prod) It's A Life; Passport; The Flesh; Persecution; The Ghoul; Legend of the Werewolf.

FRANCIS, Missy: Act. b. Los Angeles, Dec. 12, 1972. TV inc: Son-Rise--A Miracle of Love; Midnight Lace; A Gun in the House; Joe's World; The Ghost of Flight 401; When the Whistle Blows; Little House on the Prairie.

Films inc: Man, Woman and Child.

FRANCISCUS, James: Act. b. Clayton, MO, Jan 31, 1934. e. Yale U. Films inc: Four Boys and a Gun; I Passed for White; The Outsider; The Miracle of the White Stallions; Youngblood Hawke; The Valley of Gwangi; Marooned; Beneath the Planet of the Apes; Cat O'Nine Tails; City on Fire; Killer Fish; When Time Ran Out; Butterfly; The Great White.
TV inc: Mr Novak; Longstreet; Hunter; The Dream Makers; The 500 Pound Jerk; The Pirate; Nightkill; Jacqueline Bouvier Kennedy; Secret Weapons.

FRANJU, Georges: Dir. b. Fougeres, France, 1912. Films inc: (doc) Le Sange des Betes; Hotel des Invalides; Le Grand Melies; (features): La Tete Contre les Murs; Eyes Without a Face; Spotlight on a Murderer; Jude; Thomas the Impostor; Les Rideaux Blancs; The Last Melodrama.

FRANK, Gary: Act. b. Spokane, WA, Oct 9. TV inc: General Hospital; Senior Year; Family (Emmy-supp-1977); The Gift; Enola Gay--The Men, The Mission, The Atomic Bomb; The Night the City Screamed; Midnight Lace; Norma Rae; Emergency Room.

FRANK, Harriet: Wri. W of Irving Ravetch. Films inc: Silver River; Whiplash; The Long Hot Summer; The Sound and the Fury; Home from the Hill; The Dark at the Top of the Stairs; Hud; Hombre; The Reivers; Conrack; Norma Rae.

FRANK, Melvin: Wri. b. 1917. Films inc: (collab) My Favorite Blonde; Thank Your Lucky Stars; Road to Utopia; Monsieur Beaucaire; Mr Blanding Builds His Dream House; The Reformer and the Redhead; Above and Beyond; White Christmas; That Certain Feeling; Lil Abner; The Facts of Life; The Road to Hong Kong; Strange Bedfellows; (solo): A Funny Thing Happened on the Way to the Forum (& prod); Buona Sera Mrs. Campbell (& prod-dir); A Touch of Class (& prod-dir); The Dutchess and the Dirtwater Fox (& prod-dir); Lost and Found (& prod-dir).

FRANK, Reuven: Prod-Exec. b. Montreal, Canada, Dec 7, 1920. e. CCYN, BS; Columbia, MSJ. On staff ABC News, 1950-1967; named exec vp 1967; P 1968-1972; sr exec prod 1972; prod political convention news coverage; P NBC News March 1982; resd May, 1984, to serve as editorial advisor.
TV inc: (prod) Huntley-Brinkley Reports; Berlin - Window on Fear (& wri); The Road To Spandau; Outlook; Time Present; The S-Bahn Stops at Freedom; The Big Ear; Our Man in the Mediterranean; Our Man in Hong Kong; Our Man in Vienna; The Problem With Water Is People; Weekend; America Works When America Works (exec prod).

FRANK, Sandy: Exec. b. Mt Kisco, NY, Jul 11, 1929. e. Columbia U; NYU. P Sandy Frank tv prodn & dist company. TV inc: The New You Asked For It.

FRANKEL, Gene: Dir. b. NYC, Dec 23, 1923. e. NYU. Thea inc: Salem Story; They Shall Not Die; All My Sons; Stalag 17; Country Girl; Volpone; An Enemy of the People; Brecht on Brecht; Split Lip; The Night That Made America Famous.

FRANKEN, Al: Wri. TV inc: Saturday Night Live (Emmys-1976, 1977); Paul Simon Special (Emmy-1978); Steve Martin's Best Show Ever; The New Show.

FRANKEN, Steve: Act. b. Brooklyn. Bway inc: Inherit the Wind.
TV inc: Dobie Gillis; The Ghosts of Buxley Hall; Scared Silly; Not Just Another Affair; Ryan's Four; High School U.S.A.; The Sheriff and the Astronaut.
Films inc: Follow Me Boys; Westworld; The Party; Which Way To The Front?; The Americanization of Emily; Avalanche; The Missouri Breaks; 10; The Fiendish Plot of Dr. Fu Manchu; There Goes The Bride; Hardly Working.

FRANKENHEIMER, John: Dir. b. Malba, NY, Feb 19, 1930. e. Williams Coll. Act-dir summer stock. Joined CBS. TV inc: Mama; You Are There; Danger; Climax; Studio One; Ford Startime; Sunday Showcase; The Rainmaker (cable).
Films inc: The Young Stranger; The Young Savages; Birdman of

Alcatraz; The Manchurian Candidate; Seven Days in May; The Iceman Cometh; 99 and 44/100% Dead; The French Connection II; Black Sunday; Prophecy; The Challenge.

FRANKLIN, Aretha: Singer. b. Memphis, TN, Mar 25, 1942. Recording artist. *(Grammys-(11)-R&B-1967; R&B vocal-1967, 1968, 1969, 1970, 1971, 1972, 1973, 1974, 1981; Gospel-1972).*
Films inc: The Blues Brothers. TV inc: It's Not Easy Being Me--The Rodney Dangerfield Show; A Concert of the World.

FRANKLIN, Bonnie: Act. b. Santa Monica, CA, Jan 6, 1944. e. UCLA, BA. TV inc: Broadway; The Law; One Day at a Time; Breaking Up Is Hard To Do; Portrait Of A Rebel-Margaret Sanger; Musical Comedy Tonight II; Laugh Trax; Your Place Or Mine; Night Of 100 Stars II.
Bway inc: Dames at Sea; Your Own Thing; Applause.

FRANKLIN, Michael H.: Exec. b. Los Angeles, Dec 25, 1923. e. UCLA, AB; USC, LLB. Pvt. practice 1951-52; CBS, 1952-54, atty; 1954-58, Paramount, atty; 1958-78, Exec Dir, Writers Guild of America; 1978, National Exec Sec, Directors Guild of America.

FRANKLIN, Pamela: Act. b. Tokyo, Feb 4, 1950. Films inc: The Innocents; The Lion; Flipper's New Adventure; The Prime of Miss Jean Brodie; The Night of the Following Day; And Soon the Darkness; The Legend of Hell House; Food of the Gods.

FRANKLIN, Richard: Dir. b. Melbourne, Australia, Jul 15, 1948. Films inc: The True Story of Eskimo Nell; Fantasm; Patrick (& co-prod); The Blue Lagoon (co-prod); Road Games (& prod); Psycho II; Cloak And Dagger; Into The Night (act).
TV inc: Homicide.

FRANKOVICH, M.J.: Exec. b. Bisbee, AZ, Sep 29,1910. e. UCLA, BA. Started in radio, 1934, as prod, commentator. Wrote screen plays for Universal, Republic. In Army during WW II. In Europe, 1949, to make Fugitive Lady; Decameron Nights; Lucky Nick Kane; Thief of Venice; 1955 appointed man. dir. Columbia in U.K., Eire; 1958, VP Columbia Pics Int.; 1959, VP Col. Pics. Corp.; first VP chg wldwde prodn Columbia; resd 1967 to return to ind prodn.
Films inc: Footsteps In The Dark; Marooned; Bob & Carol & Ted & Alice; Cactus Flower; There's A Girl in My Soup; The Love Machine; Butterflies Are Free; Stand Up And Be Counted; From Noon Till Three; The Shootist.
(Jean Hersholt Humanitarian Award-1984).

FRANN, Mary: Act. b. St. Louis, MO, Feb 27. e. Northwestern U. Thea inc: Story Theatre (& Bway); Line.
TV inc: My Friend Tony; Return to Peyton Place; The Nashville Rebel; Days of Our Lives; Portrait of an Escort; Kings Crossing; Newhart; Gidget's Summer Reunion.

FRANZ, Arthur: Act. b. Perth Amboy, NJ, Feb 29, 1920. Films inc: Jungle Patrol; Sands of Iwo Jima; Abbott and Costello Meet the Invisible Man; The Sniper; Eight Iron Men; The Caine Mutiny; The Unholy Wife; Running Target; Hellcats of the Navy; Alvarez Kelly; Anzio; The Human Factor; That Championship Season.
Thea inc: Streetcar Named Desire; Second Threshold.
TV inc: Bogie.

FRANZ, Eduard: Act. b. Milwaukee, WI, Oct 31, 1902. Thea inc: Miss Swan Expects; The Brown Danube; Farm of Three Echoes; First Stop to Heaven; Cafe Crown; The Russian People; Outrageous Fortune; The Cherry Orchard; Embezzled Heaven; The Stranger; Home of the Brave; The Egghead; Conversation at Midnight; In the Matter of J Robert Oppenheimer.
Films inc: The Iron Curtain; The Magnificent Yankee; The Ten Commandments; Johnny Got His Gun; Twilight Zone--The Movie.
TV inc: The Breaking Point.
(Died Feb 10, 1983).

FRASER, Fil: Prod-Broadcaster. b. Montreal, Canada, Aug 19, 1932. Films inc: Why Shoot the Teacher?; Marie Anne; Back to Beulah; The Hounds of Notre Dame; Latitude 55 (exec prod).

FRASER, Ian: Comp-Con-Arr. b. Hove, England, Aug 23, 1933. Arr-Cond for: Liza Minnelli; Sammy Davis Jr.; Anthony Newley; Petula Clark; Paul Anka. Films inc: Doctor Doolittle; Goodbye Mr. Chips; Scrooge; Hopscotch; Zorro, The Gay Blade; First Monday in October.
TV inc: (mus dir) Julie Andrews Specials; Bing Crosby Christmas Shows, 1975/77; America Salutes Richard Rodgers *(Emmy-1977)*; Sentry collection presents Ben Vereen--His Roots *(Emmy-1978)*; IBM presents Baryshnikov on Broadway *(Emmy-1980)*; Linda In Wonderland *(Emmy-1981)*; Walt Disney--One Man's Dream; Goldie and the Kids--Listen To Us; Life of the Party--The Story of BeAtrice; Christmas In Washington; Here's Television Entertainment; 56th Oscar Show (1984); The Screen Actors Guild 50th Anniversary Celebration *(Emmy-1984)*; Christmas In Washington; The Television Academy Hall Of Fame 1985.

FRASER, Ronald: Act. b. Ashton-under-Lynn, England, 1930. Films inc: The Sundowners; The Pot Carriers; The Punch and Judy Man; Crooks in Cloisters; The Beauty Jungle; The Flight of the Phoenix; The Killing of Sister George; Sinful Davey; Too Late the Hero; The Rise and Rise of Michael Rimmer; The Magnificent Seven Deadly Sins; Swallows and Amazons; Paper Tiger; Trail of the Pink Panther.
TV inc: Sealed with a Loving Kiss; Stray Cats and Empty Bottles; All the Walls Came Tumbling Down; The Corn Is Green; The Brahmin Widow.

FRAYN, Michael: Wri. b. London, Sep 8, 1933. e. Cambridge. Plays inc: The Sandboy; Alphabetical Order; Donkey's Years; Clouds; Make and Break; Noises Off; Benefactors; Number One (adapt).
TV inc: Jamie; Birthday.

FRAZER, Dan: Act. b. NYC, Nov 20. Films inc: Lilies of the Field; Requiem for a Heavyweight; Counterpoint; Bananas; Take the Money and Run; Fuzz; Cleopatra Jones; Super Cops.
TV inc: Kojak; Greatest Heroes of the Bible; A Good Sport; Kojak--The Belarus File.
Thea inc: Once More With Feeling; Who Was That Lady I Saw You With?; Golden Boy; Goodbye Charlie; Christopher Blake; Play It Again, Sam; Conflict of Interest; Animals.

FRAZIER, Dallas: Singer. b. Spiro, OK, 1939. C & W recording artist.

FRAZIER, Sheila E: Act. b. NYC, Nov 13, 1948. Former fashion model. Studied drama with NY Negro Ensemble Co; NY Federal Theatre. Films inc: Super Fly; Super Fly T.N.T.; The Super Cops; California Suite.

FREBERG, Stan: Act. b. Los Angeles, Aug 7, 1926. Developed TV puppet series: Time for Beany, 1949-54; did voice for UPA cartoon characters, Walt Disney films; had own radio show; wrote commercials. P Freberg, Ltd, adv firm. Films inc: Calloway Went Thataway; Looney Looney Looney Bugs Bunny Movie (voice).
(Grammy-Spoken Word-1958).

FREDERICKSON, H. Gray, Jr: Prod. b. Oklahoma City, OK, Jul 21, 1937. e. U of Lausanne, Switzerland; U of OK, BA. Films inc: Candy; Inspector Sterling; An Italian in America; The Man Who Wouldn't Die; The Good, Bad & Ugly; Intrigue in Suez; Wedding March; An American Wife; Echoes in the Village; Little Fauss & Big Halsey; Making It; The Godfather; The Godfather Part II *(Oscar-1974)*; Hit (exec prod); Big Wednesday; Apocalypse Now; One From the Heart; The Outsiders.
TV inc: Thunder Guys.

FREDRIK, Burry (nee Gerber): Dir-Prod. b. Staten Island, NY, Aug 9, 1925. e. Sarah Lawrence Coll, BA. Off-Bway inc: Thieves Carnival; Exiles; Buried Child; Pretzels. Bway inc: Too True to be Good; The Royal Family; Summer Brave; Travesties *(Tony-1976)*; An Almost Perfect Person; Night of the Tribades; To Grandmother's House We Go.

FREED, Bert: Act. b. NYC, Nov 3, 1919. Films inc: Where the Sidewalk Ends; No Way Out; Detective Story; Desperate Hours; Paths of Glory; The Swinger; Wild in the Streets; There Was a Crooked Man; Evel Knievel; Billy Jack; La Devoradora des Hombres (Venezuela); Barracuda; Norma Rae.
TV inc: Shane; Skag; Charlie and the Great Balloon Chase.
Thea inc: One Touch of Venus; Joy to the World; Annie Get Your Gun; A Stone for Danny Fisher; Romanoff and Juliet; Rope Dancers;

Time of Your Life.

FREEDMAN, Gerald: Dir-Prod-Wri. b. Lorain, OH, Jun 25, 1927. e. Northwestern U. London directorial debut 1957, Bells Are Ringing; NY debut 1959, On the Town (revival). Thea inc: The Taming of the Shrew; Rosemary; The Alligators; The Gay Life; The Tempest; West Side Story; Electra; The Day the Whores Came Out to Play Tennis; A Time For Singing; artistic dir of the New York Shakespeare Festival prodn of All's Well That Ends Well; The Comedy of Errors; Hair; Hamlet; Titus Adronicus; Sambo; No Place to be Somebody; Colette; The Incomparable Max; The Au Pair Man; The Robber Bridegroom; Mrs Warren's Profession; The Grand Tour.
    TV inc: Antigone; Ford Theatre; Du Pont Show of the Week.

FREEDMAN, Jerrold: Wri-dir. TV inc: A Cold Night's Death; Blood Sport; The Last Angry Man; Betrayal; Some Kind of Miracle; This Man Stands Alone; The Streets of L.A. (dir); The Boy Who Drank Too Much (dir); Victims (dir); Legs; The Seduction of Gina (dir); Best Kept Secrets (dir); Seduced (dir).
    Films inc: Kansas City Bomber; Borderline.

FREEMAN, Al, Jr: Act. b. San Antonio, TX, Mar 21, 1934. e. LA City Coll. Bway inc: The Long Dream; Kicks and Co; Tiger Tiger Burning Bright; Trumpets of the Lord; Blues for Mister Charlie; Conversation at Midnight; Look to the Lilies; Are You Now or Have You Ever Been?; The Poison Tree.
    Films inc: Torpedo Run; Dutchman; Finian's Rainbow; Sweet Charlie; Castle Keep; The Lost Man; The Detective; A Fable (& dir).
    TV inc: My Sweet Charlie; Roots; King; One Life To Live (Emmy-1979).

FREEMAN, Devery: Wri. b. NYC, Feb 13, 1913. e. Brooklyn Coll, BA. Films inc: Main Street Lawyer; Guilt of Janet Ames; Dear Brat; The Fuller Brush Man; Tell It To the Judge; Miss Grant Takes Richmond; Three Sailors and a Girl; Francis in the WACS; Francis Joins the Navy; Dance With Me, Henry; Three Bad Sisters; The Girl Most Likely.
    TV inc: Ford Theatre; Climax; Loretta Young Show; Sugarfoot; Beledevere; Dear Midge; The Thin Man; Pete and Gladys; Happily Ever After; Harris Against the World.

FREEMAN, Everett: Wri. b. NYC, 1912. Films inc: George Washington Slept Here; Larceny Inc; Thank Your Lucky Stars; The Princess and the Pirate; It Happened on Fifth Avenue; The Secret Life of Walter Mitty; Jim Thorpe--All American; Million Dollar Mermaid; Destination Gobi; My Man Godfrey; Marjorie Morningstar; Sunday in New York; The Glass Bottomed Boat; Where Were You When the Lights Went Out? The Maltese Bippy; Zig Zag.

FREEMAN, Joel: Prod. b. Newark, NJ, Jun 12, 1922. e. Upsala Coll. Films inc: The Farmer's Daughter; The Setup; Battleground; Bad Day at Black Rock; Blackboard Jungle; Music Man; Finian's Rainbow; Camelot; The Heart Is a Lonely Hunter; Trouble Man; Shaft; Love At First Bite; The Octagon.

FREEMAN, Kathleen: Act. b. Circa 1919. Films inc: Naked City; Lonely Heart Bandits; Athena; The Fly; The Ladies' Man; The Disorderly Orderly; Three on Couch; Support Your Local Gunfighter; Stand Up and Be Counted; The Norseman; The Blues Brothers.
    Thea inc: 13 Rue de l'amour (Bway); Annie (road); An Uncommon Love ($ prod).
    TV inc: Hogan's Heroes; Sutters Bay.

FREEMAN, Seth: Wri. TV inc: The Waltons; Fish; The Blue Knight; Doc; Rhoda; Phyllis; The New Zoo Revue; Lou Grant (& prod) (Emmy-prod-1979, 1980; wri 1980); In Defense of Kids (prod); An Uncommon Love (& prod); Things Are Looking Up (exec prod); The Best Times (& exec prod); Dirty Work (exec prod-wri).

FREES, Paul: Act. b. Chicago, Jun 22, 1920. In vaude as child. Later host of radio shows, Suspense; Escape. Films inc: Red Light; A Place in the Sun; The Big Sky; War of the Worlds; Riot in Cellblock II; Suddenly; The Raven; Wild in the Streets; The Last Unicorn (voice); Twice Upon A Time (voice); The Milpitas Monster (narr).
    TV inc: Jack Benny Show; My Friend Irma; voice for TV cartoons inc Rudolph and Frosty's Christmas in July; The Case of Dashiell Hammett (narr).

FREGONESE, Hugo: Dir. b. Argentina, 1908. Films inc: Pampa Barbara; Donde Mueren las Palabras; Saddle Tramp; One Way Street; Apache Drums; Mark of the Renegade; My Six Convicts; Untamed Frontier; Decameron Nights; Blowing Wild; The Man in Attic; Black Tuesday; Live in Fear; Marco Polo; Apaches Last Battle; Savage Pampas; Beyond the Sun.

FREIBERGER, Fred: Wri-Prod. b. NYC, Feb 19, 1915. e. Pace Inst. Films inc: (wri) Garden of Evil; Beast From 40,000 Fathoms; Crash Landing; The Weapon.
    TV inc: (wri) Climax; Fireside Theatre; Zane Grey Theatre; Ben Casey; Slattery's People; The Senator; Trackdown; Rawhide; Starsky and Hutch. (Wri-prod) Ben Casey; Star Trek; Wild Wild West; Space 1999; Iron Horse; Big Shamus, Little Shamus.

FRELENG, Friz: Prod-Dir. b. Kansas City, MO, Aug 21, 1906. Animator, Walt Disney Studio, 1928-29; animator, Charles Mintz Studio, NY, 1929-30; prod-dir., Warner Bros., 1930-63; partner DePatie-Freleng Ent., 1963-1980. Cartoons inc: Tweetie Pie; Speedy Gonzales; Birds Anonymous; Knighty Knight Bugs; Halloween is Grinch Night (Emmy-1978); The Bear Who Slept Through Christmas; Pink Panther In Olympinks; Where Do Teenagers Come From?;; Dr Seuss' Pontoffel Pock, Where Are You? Bugs Bunny Mystery Special; Bugs Bunny--All American Hero (& wri); Dennis the Menace--Mayday For Mother; Loóney Looney Looney Bugs Bunny Movie (prod-dir-wri); Bugs Bunny's Mad World of Television; The Grinch Grinches The Cat-In-The-Hat (prod) (Emmy-1982).
    Films inc: Uncensored Cartoons (dir); Bugs Bunny's 3d Movie--1001 Rabbit Tales (prod-wri); Daffy Duck's Movie--Fantastic Island (Prod-dir-wri).

FRENCH, Robin: Exec. b. London, Nov 20, 1936. e. Cal Institute of Technology. 1956, VP & Partner Hugh French Agency; 1968, exec VP & partner Chartwell Artists Ltd.; 1971, conslt International Famous Artists; 1973, prodn VP Par; 1976, P synd div TAT; 1982, P Embassy Tele Communications; Jan 1983, Sr exec VP Embassy Communications.

FRENCH, Valerie (nee Harrison): Act. b. London, Mar 11, 1932. London stage debut 1954, Cockles and Champagne. NY stage debut 1965, Inadmissible Evidence. Films inc: Jubal; Garment Center; Decision at Sundown; The Four Skulls of Jonathan Drake; Shalako.
    TV inc: The Nurses.

FRENCH, Victor: Act. b. Santa Barbara, CA, Dec 4, 1934. e. LA (CA) State Coll. Studied With Herbert Berghoff. TV inc: Gunsmoke; It's A Great Life; TV Readers Digest; Little House On The Prairie; Carter Country; Amateur Night at the Dixie Bar and Grill; Riding for the Pony Express; The Ghosts of Buxley Hall; Louis L'Amour's the Cherokee Trail; Little House--A New Beginning; Look Back to Yesterday (& dir); Little House--The Last Farewell; Highway To Heaven; Bless All The Dear Children (& dir).
    Films inc: Choices; An Officer and A Gentleman.

FRENKE, Eugene: Prod. b. Russia, Jan 1, 1907. e. Moscow U. H of Anna Sten. Films inc: Life Returns (& dir); Two Who Dared (& dir); Three Russian Girls (& dir); Let's Live a Little; Lady in the Iron Mask; Miss Robinson Crusoe (& dir); Heaven Knows, Mr. Allison; Barbarian and the Geisha; The Last Sunset.

FRESSON, Bernard: Act. b. France, 1933. Films inc: Hiroshima Mon Amour; Please Not Now; La Guerre est Fini; Is Paris Burning?; Je t'aime, Je t'aime; Belle de Jour; Triple Cross; Zita; The Prisoner; Z; The Lady in the Car with the Glasses and the Gun; The Cop; Where There's Smoke; French Connection; Le Locataire (The Tenant); Marie Poupee; Le Dernier Baiser; The Passengers; Mado; Le Guepiot; Madame Claude 2 (Intimate Moments); Garcon!; Rive Droite, Rive Gauche (Right Bank, Left Bank).
    Thea inc: La Dixieme de Beethoven (Beethoven's Tenth).
    TV inc: Los Desastres de la Guerra (Guerilla); Reveillon Chez Bob (New Year's Eve At Bob's); Zielscheiben (Moving Targets).

FREY, Leonard: Act. b. Brooklyn, Sept. 4, 1938. Bway inc: The Boys in the Band; Fiddler On the Roof; Beggar on Horseback; The National Health; Knock Knock.
    Films inc: The Boys in the Band; Fiddler on the Roof; Where The

Buffalo Roam; Tattoo.

TV inc: Leonard; Testimony of Two Men; The Best of the West; Fit For A King; The Sound of Murder (cable); Mr. Smith; Earthlings.

FRIDELL, Squire: Act. b. Oakland, CA, Feb 9, 1943. e. U of Pacific, BA; Occidental Coll, MA. TV inc: Adam 12; Ironside; Police Story; Bold Ones; Love Story; The Heist; Rossetti and Ryan; For Love Or Money.

Films inc: Pink Motel.

FRIED, Gerald: Comp. b. NYC, Feb 13, 1928. e. Juilliard. Film scores inc: Killer's Kiss; Terror in a Texas Town; A Cold Wind in August; The Cabinet of Caligari; One Potato, Two Potato; The Killing of Sister George; Too Late the Hero; The Grissom Gang; Soylent Green; Birds Do It, Bees Do It; Vigilante Force; Survive; The Bell Jar.

TV inc: Francis Gary Powers; Roots *(Emmy*-1977); Sex and the Married Woman; Testimony of Two Men; Son Rise; The Ordeal of Dr. Mudd; Gauguin The Savage; Flamingo Road; Moviola (The Silent Lovers); The Wild and The Free; Number 96; Condominium; Murder Is Easy; Australia's Animal Mysteries; For Us, The Living; Return of the Man from UNCLE; A Killer in the Family; The Mystic Warrior.

FRIEDBERG, A Alan: Exec. b. NYC, Apr 13, 1932. e. Columbia Coll, BA; Harvard Law School. Pres. Sack Theatres; P, Theatre Owners of New England; Board of Dir, NATO.

FRIEDKIN, Johnny: Exec. b. NYC, Dec 9, 1926. e. Columbia U. Publicist Col, NY, 1946-48; Young & Rubicam, 1948-57; Partner, Sumner & Friedkin, 1957-60; VP, Rogers & Cowan, 1960-67; to Fox, 1967; 1978, VP, World Wide Publicity & Promotion; 1979, vp Intl ad-pub WB.

FRIEDKIN, William: Dir. b. Chicago, 1939. Joined NBC-TV, 1957. Worked for National Educational TV. Films inc: Good Times; The Night They Raided Minsky's; The French Connection *(Oscar*-1971); The Birthday Party; The Exorcist; Sorcerer (& prod); The Brink's Job; Cruising (& sp); Deal of the Century.

Bway inc: Duet For One.

FRIEDLAND, Louis N: Exec. b. NYC, Apr 18, 1913. e. NYU, BS, MA. ChmnB, MCA-TV & vp MCA Inc.

FRIEDMAN, Bruce Jay: Wri. b. Bronx, NY., Apr. 26, 1930. e. U MO. Plays inc: Scuba Duba; Steambath. Films inc: The Heartbreak Kid (orig story); Stir Crazy; Doctor Detroit; Splash.

FRIEDMAN, Seymour Mark: Dir. b. Detroit, Aug 17, 1917. e. Cambridge, BS. Films inc: To the Ends of the Earth; Rusty's Birthday; Prison Warden; Her First Romance; Son of Dr Jekyll; Loan Shark; Flame of Calcutta; I'll Get You; Saint's Girl Friday; African Manhunt; Secret of Treasure Mountain.

FRIEDMAN, Stephen: Prod-Wri. b. NYC. e. U of PA; Harvard Law School. Film inc: The Last Picture Show; Lovin' Molly (& sp); Slap Shot; Fast Break; Bloodbrothers; Little Darlings; Hero At Large; Eye of the Needle; The Incubus (exec prod); All of Me (prod).

FRIEDMAN, Stephen R: Prod. b. NYC, Apr 10, 1936. e. CCNY Bway inc: Annie *(Tony*-1977); Working.

FRIEDMAN, Steve: Prod. b. Chicago, Jul 22, 1946. e. U of IL, BSJ. Started as newswriter WBBM (radio) Chicago; 1969, to KNBC as newswriter; special projects prod; 1975, prod early evening news; 1977, asso prod Today Show, based in LA; 1979, to NY as prod Today Show; 1980, exec prod; 1984, exec prod Summer Sunday, U.S.A.

FRIENDLY, Andy: Prod-wri. b. Nov. 6, 1951. e. USC Film School. S of Ed Friendly. Started as wri-prod-reporter WNBC (NY) news. TV inc: Tomorrow Show; I'll See You in Court; News Magazine; Tom Snyder Specials; Speak Up America (prod); 30th Anniversary This Is Your Life Special; Entertainment Tonight; World of Entertainment (prod); All New This Is Your Life Series; Being Your Best; Circus of the Stars (Cnslt prod).

FRIENDLY, Ed: Exec-Prod. b. NYC. Indy tv prod since 1967. Prev-

iously with BBD&O and vp - special pgms at NBC-TV. Teamed with George Schlatter to produce Laugh-In. Formed own prod co.

TV inc: Little House on the Prairie; Peter Lund and the Medicine Hat Stallion; Backstairs at the White House; The Flame Is Love.

FRIES, Charles: Prod. b. Cincinnati, OH, Sep 30, 1928. e. OH State U, BS. Exec Prod Ziv TV; VP, Prodn Screen Gems; VP, Prodn Columbia; Exec VP, Prodn & Exec Prod Metromedia Producers Corp, 1970-74; formed own co.

TV inc: Are You In The House Alone?; The Word; Winds of Kitty Hawk; The Martian Chronicles; Bogie; A Rumor of War; Rage; For the Love Of It; The Home Front; The Children of An Lac; High Noon, Part II--The Return of Will Kane; A Cry For Love; Leave 'Em Laughing; Bitter Harvest; Twirl; The Ambush Murders; In Love With An Older Woman; Rosie--The Rosemary Clooney Story; Cocaine--One Man's Seduction; For Us, The Living; Murder Ink; Dempsey; Carpool; Through Naked Eyes; Jealousy; The Zany Adventures of Robin Hood; Sins Of The Father; Starcrossed.

Films inc: Cat People.

FRIESEN, Gil: Exec. (Gilbert Brian):b. Pasadena, CA, Mar 10, 1937. e. UCLA, BA. Promotion man, Capitol Records; Promotion man Kapp Records; personal manager in England; GM, A&M Records; Sr VP A&M Records; July 1981, P & CEO A&M Films. Films inc: The Breakfast Club (exec prod).

FRISBY, Terence: Act-Dir-Wri. b. London, Nov 28, 1932. Perf & dir 1957-66 under the name of Terence Holland. London stage debut 1958, Gentlemen's Pastime. Plays inc: The Subtopians; There's a Girl in My Soup; The Bandwagon; It's All Right If I Do It.

TV (wri) inc: Take Care of Madam; Don't Forget the Basics.

FROEBE, Gert: Act. b. Germany, 1912. Films inc: The Heroes Are Tired; He Who Must Die; Goldfinger; Those Magnificent Men in Their Flying Machines; Is Paris Burning?; Rocket to the Moon; Monte Carlo or Bust; Dollars; And Then There Were None; The Serpent's Egg; Sidney Sheldon's Bloodline; The Umbrella Coup; Banovic Strahinja (The Falcon).

FRONTIERE, Dominic: Comp. b. New Haven, CT, Jun 17, 1931. e. Yale School of Mus. Films inc: Giant; The Marriage Go Round; Hero's Island; Billie; Hang 'Em High; Popi; Chisum; Cancel My Reservation; Hammersmith is Out; Defiance; The Stunt Man; Roar; Modern Problems; The Aviator.

TV inc: The New Breed; Stoney Burke; Outer Limits; Branded; Iron Horse; Rat Patrol; Twelve O'Clock High; Zig Zag; The Love War; Swing Out Sweet Land *(Emmy*-1971); Funtastic World Of Hanna-Barbera Arena Show; Strike Force; Matt Houston; Don't Go To Sleep; Shooting Stars; Dark Mirror; Velvet.

Bway inc: Peg (orchs).

FROST, David: TV Pers. b. Tenterdon, England, Apr 7, 1939. e. Cambridge U. TV inc: That Was the Week That Was; The David Frost Show *(Emmys*-1970, 1971); The Nixon Interviews; This Is Your Life (& exec prod); That Was The Week That Was (1985).

FRY, Christopher: Plywri. b. Bristol, England, Dec 18, 1907. originally a teacher, later act & dir with various rep groups before turning to writing. Plays inc: The Boy With a Cart; The Tower; A Phoenix Too Frequent; The Lady's Not For Burning; Thor With Angels; The Firstborn; Venus Observed; Ring Round the Moon (adapt); A Sleep of Prisoners; The Dark is Light Enough; The Lark (trans); Tiger at the Gates (trans).

Films inc: The Beggar's Opera; A Queen is Crowned; Ben Hur; Barrabas; The Bible.

FRYE, Dwight: Prod. b. Spokane, WA, Dec 26, 1930. e. U of ME, BS, MS. Thea inc: Man of La Mancha (prod-dir London & Paris companies); Chu Chem; Halloween; Cry For Us All; Odyssey (Home Sweet Homer); So Long 174th Street.

FRYE, William: Prod. Started as talent agent; entered prodn 1953 as assoc prod of the Four Star Playhouse TV series. Films inc: The Trouble With Angels; Where Angels Go, Trouble Follows; Airport 1975; Airport 1977; Raise The Titanic.

TV inc: General Electric Theatre; The Alfred Hitchcock Hour; The

Deputy; Thriller; The Elevator; Linda; The Other Man; the Longest Night; The Screaming Woman.

FRYER, Robert: Prod. b. Washington, DC, Dec 18, 1920. e. Western Reserve U, BA. Films inc: The Boston Strangler; The Prime of Miss Jean Brodie; Myra Breckenridge; The Salzburg Connection; Travels with My Aunt; Mame; The Abdication; Great Expectations; Voyage of the Damned; The Boys From Brazil.

Bway inc: A Tree Grows in Brooklyn; Wonderful Town *(Tony-*1953); By the Beautiful Sea; The Desk Set; Shangri-La; Auntie Mame; Redhead *(Tony-*1959); Saratoga; Hot Spot; There Was A Little Girl; Advise and Consent; A Passage to India; Roar Like a Dove; A Dream of Swallows; Sweet Charity; Mame; Chicago; California Suite; On The 20th Century; Sweeney Todd *(Tony-*1979); Merrily We Roll Along; A Doll's Life; Noises Off.

TV inc: Wonderful Town.

FUCHS, Daniel: Wri. b. NYC, Jun 1909. e. CCNY, BA. Films inc: The Day the Bookies Wept; The Hard Way; Love Me or Leave Me *(Oscar-*1955); Jeanne Eagels.

FUCHS, Leo: Prod. b. Vienna, Jun 14, 1929. Films inc: Gambit; Secret War of Harry Frigg; A Fine Pair; Jo; La Mandarine; La Femme en Bleu; Le Moutun Enrage; Les Passagers; Sunday Lovers; Le Guepiot; Just The Way You Are.

FUCHS, Michael: Pay TV Exec. b. NYC, Mar 9, 1946. e. Union Coll; NYU. VP & exec. prod. Home Box Office; March 1984, P.; Oct. 1984, chmn.

FUDGE, Alan: Act. b. Wichita, KS, Feb 27, 1944. e. U of AZ. Films inc: Two People; Family Plot; Airport '75; Capricorn One; Brainstorm; The Natural.

TV inc: Sunshine; The Marcus-Nelson Murders; Man From Atlantis; Eischeid; Golden Gate Murders; The Children of An Lac; Every Stray Dog and Kid; Goliath Awaits; Thursday's Child; M.A.D.D.--Mothers Against Drunk Drivers; Attack On Fear; Chiller; Space.

FUEST, Robert: Dir. b. London, 1927. Joined ABC-TV as designer, 1958. Dir docs, commercials, 1962. TV (as dir) inc: Just Like A Woman; The Avengers; And Soon the Darkness; Wuthering Heights; Doctor Phibes; Doctor Phibes Rises Again; The Final Programme; The Devils Rain; A Movie Star's Daughter; The Gold Bug; Family of Strangers; Revenge of the Stepford Wives; The Big Stuffed Dog; My Mother Was Never A Kid; Mystery at Fire Island.

FUGARD, Athol: Wri-Dir-Act. b. South Africa, 1932. e. U of Cape Town. Plays inc: No-Good Friday; Blood-Knot (& act-dir); People Are Living There; Hello and Goodbye; Boesman and Lena; Sizwe Bansi is Dead (& dir); The Island; Statements After an Arrest under the Immorality Act (& dir); Dimetos; A Lesson From Aloes (& dir); Master Harold...and the Boys (& dir); The Road To Mecca (& dir).

Films inc: Marigolds In August (Sp & act); Gandhi (act); The Guest (wri-act).

FUISZ, Robert E, Dr Wri-Prod. b. Pennsylvania, Oct 15, 1934. e. Georgetown School of Medicine. TV inc: The Body Human--The Sexes; Lifeline *(Emmy-*1979); The Body Human--The Magic Sense *(Emmy-*1980); The Body Human--The Body Beautiful; The Body Human--The Sexes II; The Body Human--The Facts for Boys; The Body Human--Facts for Girls *(Emmy-*1981); The Body Human--The Bionic Breakthrough (& dir); *(Emmy-*1981); The Body Human-Becoming A Man; The Body Human--Becoming A Woman; The Body Human--The Loving Process, Men; The Body Human--The Loving Process, Women; The Body Human--The Living Code (Emmys-prod & individual achievement-1983); To Catch A King; The Body Human--The Journey Within; A Christmas Carol (exec prod).

FULLER, Charles: Plywri. b. Philadelphia, PA., Mar. 5, 1939. Plays inc: The Perfect Party; The Brownsville Raid; Sparrows in Flight; Zooman and the Sign; A Soldier's Play *(Pulitzer Prize-*1982).

Films inc: A Soldier's Story.

FULLER, Robert: Act. b. Troy, NY, Jul 29, 1934. Films inc: Teenage Thunder; Return of the Seven; Whatever Happened to Aunt Alice?; King Gun; The Hard Ride; The Gatling Gun; Separate Ways.

TV inc: Laramie; Wagon Train; Emergency; Disaster on the Coastliner; Jake's Way.

FULLER, Samuel: Wri-Dir-Prod. b. NYC, 1911. Films inc: I Shot Jesse James; The Baron of Arizona; Fixed Bayonets; The Steel Helmet; Park Row; Pickup On South Street; Hell and High Water; House of Bamboo; Forty Guns; The Crimson Kimona; Underworld USA; Merrill's Marauders; The Naked Kiss; Shark; Dead Pigeon on Beethoven Street; The American Friend (act); The Big Red One; White Dog (& act); Hammett; Der stand der dinge (The State of Things) (act); Les Voleurs de la nuit (Thieves After Dark) (Dir-wri-act); Slapstick of Another Kind (act).

FUNICELLO, Annette: Act. b. Los Angeles, Oct 22, 1942. Films inc; Johnny Tremaine; The Shaggy Dog; Babes in Toyland; Misadventures of Merlin Jones; Bikini Beach; Beach Party; Pajama Party; How to Stuff A Wild Bikini; The Monkey's Uncle; Fireball 500.

TV inc: Easy Does It; Frankie and Annette--The Second Time Around; The Mouseketeer Reunion; Lots Of Luck; Disneyland's 30th Anniversary Celebration.

FUNT, Allen: Act. b. NYC, 1914. Host of Candid Camera TV show; Candid Camera--Now and Then (exec prod-dir); Candid Kids. Films inc: What Do You Say to a Naked Lady? (act & prod); Candid Camera Special.

FURIA, John: Wri. TV inc: The FBI; The Name of the Game; Hawaii Five-O; Kung Fu; The Waltons; The Healers; Death of Ocean View Park; 240-Robert; The Hustler of Muscle Beach; The Intruder Within (exec prod); Rage of Angels (prod); Arthur Hailey's "Hotel"; My Mother's Secret Life (& exec prod); The Sun Also Rises (exec prod).

Films inc: The Singing Nun.

FURIE, Sidney J: Dir-Wri-Prod. b. Toronto, Canada, Feb 28, 1933. Films inc: Dangerous Age; A Cool Sound From Hell; The Ipcress File; The Appaloosa; The Naked Runner; Hit!; Gable and Lombard; The Boys In Company C; The Entity; Purple Hearts (& wri).

FURNEAUX, Yvonne: Act. b. France, 1928. Films inc: Meet Me Tonight; The Dark Avenger; Lisbon; The Mummy; La Dolce Vita; Repulsion; The Scandal; The Man Who Never Was; Frankenstein's Great-Aunt Tillie.

TV inc: Tigress on the Hearth; Danger Man; The Baron; The Survivors.

FURNESS, Betty: Act. b. NYC, Jan 3, 1916. On screen From 1933. Films inc: Professional Sweetheart; Emergency Call; Lucky Devils; Beggars in Ermine; Keeper of the Bees; Magnificent Obsession; Swing Time; The President's Mystery; Mama Steps Out; North of Shanghai. Consumer Advocate for NBC-TV.

FURTH, George: Wri-Act. b. Dec 14, 1932. e. Northwestern U, BS. Stage debut 1961, A Cook for Mr. General. Films inc: (Act) Butch Cassidy and the Sundance Kid; Myra Breckenridge; Blazing Saddles; Hooper; The Cannonball Run; Megaforce; Doctor Detroit. Plays inc: Company *(Tony-*1971); Twigs; The Act; The Supporting Cast; Merrily We Roll Along.

GABEL, Martin: Act-Prod-Dir. b. Philadelphia, Jun 19, 1912. e. AADA. H of Arlene Francis. Bway debut 1933, Man Bites Dog. Films inc: The Lost Moment (dir only); Fourteen Hours; The Thief; Tip on a Dead Jockey; Marnie; Lord Love a Duck; Divorce American Style; Lady in Cement; There Was a Crooked Man; The Front Page; The First Deadly Sin.

Bway inc: Will Success Spoil Rock Hunter?; The Hidden River (co-prod); Once More with Feeling (co-prod); Big Fish, Little Fish *(Tony-*Supp-1961); Children From Their Games; Baker Street; Sheep on the Runway; In Praise of Love.

TV inc: The Making of the President, 1964 (narr).

GABOR, Eva: Act. b. Budapest, Feb 11, 1921. Films inc: The Wife of Monte Cristo; The Last Time I Saw Paris; Artists and Models; My Man Godfrey; Don't Go Near the Water; Gigi; The Trouble with Woman; New Kind of Love; It Started with a Kiss; The Rescuers; Nutcracker Fantasy.

TV inc: Green Acres; The Eva Gabor Show; Almost Heaven.

Thea inc: The Happy Time; Present Laughter; Blithe Spirit; Strike a Match; Oh Men, Oh Women; Her Cardboard Lover; Uncle Vanya; A Shot in the Dark; Private Lives.

GABOR, Zsa Zsa: Act. b. Hungary, Feb 6, 1919. Stage debut in Europe. Films inc: Lovely to Look At; We're Not Married; Lili; Moulin Rouge; Boys' Night Out; Picture Mommy Dead; Jack of Diamonds; Frankenstein's Great-Aunt Tillie.

TV inc: Texaco Star Theatre--Opening Night; I Love Men; Dean Martin's Celebrity Roast; Dom DeLuise and Friends Part II; California Girls.

GABRIEL, John: Act. b. Niagara Falls, NY, May 25, 1931. e. UCLA, BA. Bway inc: the Happy Time; Applause.

Films inc: Redline 7000; El Dorado; Network; Just Tell Me What You Want.

TV inc: Mary Tyler Moore Show; Ryan's Hope; Fantasies.

GAFFNEY, Robert: Prod-Dir. b. NYC, Oct 8, 1931. e. Iona Coll. Films inc: Rooftops of New York (Short); Man on a String; Light Fantastic; Troublemaker; Frankenstein Meets the Space Monster.

GAIDAI, Leonid: Wri-Dir. b. Russia, Jan 30, 1923. e. Moscow Film Institute. Films inc: Lyana (act); The Long Path (co-dir); A Fiancee from the Other world (dir); Barbos, the Dog and a Cross-Country Run; Bootleggers; Business People; Operation "Y" and Shurik's Other Adventures; Prisoner of the Caucasus: The Diamond Hand; The Twelve Chairs; Ivan Vasillievich Changes His Profession; It Can't Be!.

GAIL, Max: Act. b. Detroit, MI, Apr 5. e. U of MI. Films inc: The Organization; Dirty Harry; D.C. Cab; The Secret Agent (doc-narr); Heartbreakers.

TV inc: Like Mom, Like Me; Pearl; Desperate Women; Barney Miller; The 11th Victim; The Aliens Are Coming; Fun & Games; Insight/The Game Room; Letting Go.

Bway inc: The Babe.

GALABRU, Michel: Act. b. Safi, Morocco, Oct. 27, 1924. Films inc: The Groper; Group Portrait With Lady; The Gendarme and the Creature from Outer Space; Surprise Sock; The Pawn; Confidences for Confidences; Cop or Hood; The Bit Between the Teeth; La Cage Aux Folles; A Week's Vacation; Le Guignolo; It All Depends on Girls; Les Sous-Doues (The Under Gifted); La Cage Aux Folles II; The Trickeries of Scapin; Est-ce Bien Raisonnable? (Is This Really Reasonable?); Les Choix des Armes (Choice of Weapons); Le Bourgeois Gentilhomme; Y'at-il Un Francois Dans La Salle?. (Is There A Frenchman In the House?); Les Diplomes du dernier ranc (The Graduates of the Last Row); L'ete Meurtrier (One Deadly Summer); Papy Fait de la Resistance (Gramps is in the Resistance); Notre Histoire (Our Story); La Triche (The Cheat); Les Fausses Confidences (The False Confidences); Reveillon Chez Bob (New Year's Eve At Bob's); Partenaires (Partners); Tranches de Vie (Slices Of Life); Les Telephone Sonne Toujours Deux Fois!! (The Telephone Always Rings Twice); Du Sel Sur la Peau (Salt On The Skin); Subway; Monsieur de Pourceaugnac.

GALE, John: Prod. b. England, Aug 2, 1929. Former act. Thea inc (as prod): Inherit The Wind; Candida; On the Brighter Side; Caesar and Cleopatra; Boeing Boeing (& Bway); Big Fish, Little Fish; Windfall; Where Angels Fear to Tread; Amber for Anna; The Easter Man; Present Laughter; Maigret and the Lady; Platinum Cat; Sacred Flame; An Evening with GBS; The Secretary Bird; Dear Charles; Highly Confidential; Abelard and Heloise; No Sex Please, We're British; Lloyd George Knew My Father; The Mating Game; Parents Day; Signs of the Times; Birds of Paradise; Murder Among Friends; Under the Greenwood Tree; Can You Hear Me at the Back?; Middle Age Spread; The Mitford Girls; A Personal Affair.

GALLAGHER, Helen: Act. b. NYC, Jul 19, 1926. Bway debut 1945, The Seven Lively Arts. Bway inc: Mr. Strauss Goes to Boston; Billion Dollar Baby; Brigadoon; High Button Shoes; Make a Wish; Pal Joey (Tony-Supp-1952); Hazel Flagg; Guys and Dolls; Finian's Rainbow; The Pajama Game; Sweet Charity; No, No, Nanette (Tony-1971); Tallulah (Off Bway).

TV inc: Ryan's Hope (Emmys-1976 & 1977). Films inc: Roseland.

GALLERY, Michele: Wri. TV inc: Lou Grant (Emmy-1979); In Defense of Kids; Things Are Looking Up (& prod); The Best Times (& prod); Dirty Work (prod).

GALLO, Fred T.: Exec. Originally an asst dir-prodn mgr in tv, later asst dir or prodn mgr various Mel Brooks and Woody Allen films; Aug. 1980, vp-wldwde prodn mgr Warner Bros. Films inc: (assoc prod) Love and Death; The Bad News Bears; Annie Hall; American Hot Wax; Hide in Plain Sight. (Prod) Going in Style; Body Heat.

GALLO, Lew: Prod. b. Mt Kisco, NY, Jun 12, 1928. e. Ithaca Coll; Columbia U. TV inc: The Ghost and Mrs. Muir; That Girl; Love American Style; Lucan; Having Babies; Don Rickles Show; Aloha Paradise; Mickey Spillane's "Murder Me, Murder You"; More Than Murder.

GALLO, Lillian B: Prod. b. Springfield, MA, Apr 12. e. U of MI, BA. TV inc: The Natural Look; Hustling; The Stranger Who Looks Like Me; What Are Best Friends For?; Playmates; The Haunts of the Very Rich; Fun & Games; I Take These Men; Princess Daisy.

GALLOWAY, Don: Act. b. Brooksville, KY, Jul 27, 1937. e. KY U, AB. Films inc: The Rare Breed; Gunfight in Abilene; The Ride To Hangman's Tree; Rough Night in Jericho; Satan-Mistress; The Big Chill.

TV inc: Tom, Dick And Mary; Arrest And Trial; The Virginian; Boot Hill; Ironside; The Life and Times of Grizzly Adams; Condominium; Automan; With God On Their Side (narr); Rearview Mirror.

GAM, Rita: Act. b. Pittsburgh, Apr 2, 1928. Films inc: The Thief; Sign of the Pagan; Night People; Magic Fire; Mohawk; King of Kings; Klute; Such Good Friends; Seeds of Evil.

TV inc: Greatest Heroes of the Bible.

GANG, Martin: Atty. b. Passaic, NJ, Mar 12, 1901. e. Harvard U, BA; Heidelberg, PhD; U CA, JurD. Film Business Atty.

GANIS, Sidney M: Exec. b. NYC, Jan 8, 1940. e. Brooklyn College. 1961, joined pub staff 20th-Fox; 1963, Columbia; 1965, pub mgr Seven Arts; 1967, prodn pub mgr Warner-Seven Arts; 1970, Studio pub dir Cinema Center Films; 1973 retd to WB as pub-ad dir on "Mame"; 1974, ad dir WB; 1977, vp wldwde ad-pub; Nov, 1978, exec vp Lucasfilm.

TV inc: The Making of "Raiders of the Lost Ark" (Emmy-exec prod-1982).

GANS, Sharon: Act. b. NY, Jul 29, 1942. Films inc: Zabriskie Point; Tell Me Lies; Slaughterhouse Five.

GARAGIOLA, Joe: TV Pers. b. St Louis, MO, 1926. Former Pro baseball player. TV inc: NBC's Today Show; Baseball Game of the Week; The Baseball World of Joe Garagiola; He Said, She Said (host).

GARAS, Kaz: Act-Wri. b. Kaunas, Lithuania, Mar 4, 1940. e. U CT, BA. Films inc: The Last Safari; Ben; Love Is a Funny Thing.

TV inc: Separate Lives; Strange Report; Riker; Massarati and the Brain; Bay City Blues.

GARBO, Greta (nee Gustafson): Act (ret). b. Stockholm, Sep 18, 1906. On screen in Sweden in Peter The Tramp; Atonement of Gosta Berlibg; Joyless Street; brought to Hollywood 1926 by Swedish dir Mauritz Stiller and made Hollywood debut in Torrent.

Films inc: The Temptress; Flesh and the Devil; Love; Mysterious Lady; The Divine Woman; The Kiss; A Woman of Affairs; Wild Orchids; The Single Standard; Anna Christie; Romance; Inspiration; Susan Lennox; Mata Hari; Grand Hotel; As You Desire Me; Queen Christina; The Painted Veil; Anna Karenina; Camille; Conquest; Ninotchka; Two-Faced Woman.

(Honorary Oscar 1954 "for her unforgettable film performances.")

GARCI, Jose Luis: Dir. b. Madrid, 1944. Films inc: My Marilyn (short); El Crack; Volver A Empezar (Begin the Beguine/Starting Over Again); Sesion Continua (Double Feature).

GARCIA, Jerry: Mus. b. Aug 1, 1942. Founder-member Grateful Dead; occasionally records with other musicians. Albums inc: Garcia; Cats Under the Stars; Garcia/Reflections.

Films inc: Hells Angels Forever (exec prod & act).
(See The Grateful Dead for group credits).

GARDENIA, Vincent: Act. b. Naples, Jan 7, 1922. Bway inc: The Visit; The Prisoner of Second Ave (Tony-Supp-1971); God's Favorite.
Films inc: Cop Haters; Little Murders; Murder, Inc.; Jenny; Cold Turkey; Hickey and Boggs; Death Wish; Bang The Drum Slowly; The Front Page; Heaven Can Wait; Firepower; Home Movies; The Last Flight of Noah's Ark; Death Wish II; Movers & Shakers.
TV inc: All in the Family; The Untouchables; The Rookies; Marciano; Goldie and the Boxer; Insight/Holy Moses; The Dream Merchants; Breaking Away; Thornwell; Muggable Mary--Street Cop; Charley's Aunt (cable); Kennedy; Dark Mirror; Night Of 100 Stars II.

GARDINER, Frank Reid: Atty. b. Australia, Nov 26, 1938. Member Australian Film Commission. Films inc: Final Cut (exec prod).

GARDNER, Arthur (nee Goldberg): Prod. b. Marinette, WI. Started as screen actor, 1929; asst dir 1941; then asst prod; formed Allart Pictures Corp; then VP Levy-Gardner-Laven Productions. Films inc: Without Warning; Vice Squad; Geronimo; The Glory Guys; Scalphunters; The Honkers; Hunting Party; Kansas City Bomber; White Lightning; McQ; Brannigan; Gator; Safari 3000 (& story).
TV inc: Rifleman; Law of the Plainsman; The Big Valley.

GARDNER, Ava: Act. b. Smithfield, NC, Dec 24, 1922. Films inc: We Were Dancing; Joe Smith; American; Whistle Stop; The Killers; The Hucksters; One Touch of Venus; Show Boat; Pandora and the Flying Dutchman; Snows of Kilimanjaro; Mogambo; Barefoot Contessa; The Naked Maja; Bhowani Junction; On the Beach; Night of the Iguana; 55 Days at Peking; Mayerling; Life and Times of Judge Roy Bean; Earthquake; Permission to Kill; The Bluebird; The Cassandra Crossing; The Sentinel; City on Fire; The Kidnapping of the President; Priest of Love.
TV inc: Knots Landing; A.D.

GARDNER, Herb: Wri. Originally a commercial artist, drew comic strip, The Nebbishes, for eight years before devoting time to writing. Plays inc: A Thousand Clowns; Thieves.
Films inc: A Thousand Clowns; Who is Harry Kellerman? (& prod); Thieves; The Goodbye People (& dir).
TV inc: Happy Endings; Word of Mouth.

GARFEIN, Jack: Dir-Teacher. b. Mukacevo, Czechoslovakia, Jul 2, 1930. e. New School for Social Research. Act on Bway in The Burning Bush. Bway directorial debut 1953, End as A Man. Other Bway inc: Girls of Summer; The Sin of Pat Muldoon; Shadow of a Gunman; The Lesson. other thea inc: Anna Christie; Don't Go Gentle; How Tall is Toscanini?; prod first revival of The Price; The American Clock; Avner The Eccentric; A Kurt Weill Cabaret. Artistic dir Harold Clurman Theatre; founder Actors Studio West; prof USC, Actors and Directors Lab NYC.
Films inc: The Strange One; Something Wild (& sp).

GARFIELD, Allen (See GOORWITZ, Allen).

GARFINKLE, Louis: Wri. b. Seattle, WA, Feb 11, 1928. e. UC Berkeley; U of WA; USC. Films inc: The Young Guns; I Bury the Living; Face of Fire; The Hellbenders; A Minute to Pray, A Second to Die; The Love Doctors; Beautiful People; The Doberman Gang; Little Cigars; The Deer Hunter.
Plays inc: Molly; I Shall Return.

GARFUNKEL, Art: Act. b. NYC, Oct 13, 1942. e. COL U. Formed vocal and instrumental duo with Paul Simon, dissolved in 1970 to go their separate ways. Garfunkel continued as a recording artist; also turned actor. Films inc: Catch-22; Carnal Knowledge; Bad Timing. (Grammys-(4)-Record of year-1968; Record of year-album of year-best arr-1970.)

GARGIULO, Mike: Prod-Dir. b. Sep 23, 1926. e. U of MO, BA. TV inc: Jackpot (Emmy-dir-1974); $20,000 Pyramid (Emmys-dir-1976, 1978, 1981); Thanksgiving Day Parade; Cotton Bowl Parade; Leningrad Ice Show; Rose Parade; Happy New Year America; Loretta Lynn--The Lady, The Legend; FYI; Farber.
(Emmy-Trustees citation-1960)

GARLAND, Beverly (nee Fessenden): Act. b. Santa Cruz, CA, Oct 17, 1930. Films inc: The Mad Room; Where the Red Fern Grows; Airport, 1975; Roller Boogie; It's My Turn.
TV inc: Decoy; Scarecrow and Mrs. King; This Girl for Hire; Insight/The Day Everything Went Wrong.

GARLAND, Patrick: Dir-Wri. b. England. e. Oxford. Thea (dir) inc: Brief Lives; Forty Years On; The Stiffkey Scandals of 1932; A Doll's House; Hedda Gabler; Getting On; Kilvert and His Diary; Mad Dog; Billy; Enemy of the People; Signed and Sealed; Chichester; Beecham; My Fair Lady (Bway rev); The Mitford Girls; Underneath the Arches (wri); Kipling (Bway).
TV inc: On the Margin; The Snow Goose.

GARNER, Erroll: Comp-pianist. b. Pittsburgh, PA, Jun 15, 1923. In niteries; concerts; European tours. Film scores inc: A New Kind of Love.

GARNER, James: Act. b. Norman, OK, Apr 7, 1928. Films inc: Toward the Unknown; The Jolly Pink Jungle; Hour of the Guns; Sayonara; Cash McCall; Children's Hour; Duel at Diablo; Grand Prix; The Great Escape; The Americanization of Emily; A Man Could Get Killed; Mister Buddwing; Support Your Local Sheriff; Marlowe; Skin Game; They Only Kill Their Masters; One Little Indian; Hawaiian Cowboy; Health; The Fan; Victor/Victoria; Tank.
TV inc: Cheyenne; Maverick; Rockford Files (Emmy-1977); Young Maverick; Sixty Years of Seduction (Host); Bret Maverick; The Long Summer of George Adams; Lily For President?; Heartsounds; The Glitter Dome (PC); Space.

GARNER, Peggy Ann: Act. b. Canton, OH, Feb 8, 1933. Screen debut 1938, Little Miss Thoroughbred. Honorary oscar 1945, as "outstanding child actress." Films inc: Blondie Brings Up Baby; Abe Lincoln in Illinois; The Pied Piper; Jane Eyre; A Tree Grows in Brooklyn; The Keys of the Kingdom; Nob Hill; Home Sweet Homicide; Daisy Kenyon; The Sign of the Ram; Bomba the Jungle Boy; The Big Cat; Teresa; The Black Widow; Eight Witnesses; The Black Forest; The Cat; A Wedding.
TV inc: Studio One; Lux Playhouse; Betrayal.
(Died Oct. 16, 1984)

GARNETT, Gale: Singer-Songwri-Act. b. Auckland, New Zealand. Thea inc: Stratford Shakespeare Festival; Factory Theatre Lab. (Bway) Ulysses in Nighttown; Ladyhouse Blues; Crack; Jesse and the Bandit Queen.
Films inc: The Children; Tribute.
Songs inc: We'll Sing in the Sunshine (Grammy-Folk Recording-1964); Down Here on the Ground; Street Tattoo.

GARR, Teri: Act. b. 1949 With San Francisco Ballet at age 13. Films inc: Head; The Conversation; Young Frankenstein; Won Ton Ton, The Dog That Saved Hollywood; Oh, God!; Close Encounters of the Third Kind; Mr. Mike's Mondo Video; Black Stallion; Honky Tonk Freeway; One From the Heart; The Escape Artist; Tootsie; The Sting II; The Black Stallion Returns; Mr. Mom; Firstborn; Witches' Brew
TV inc: Sonny Comedy Hour; McCloud; Law and Order; Prime Suspect; John Steinbeck's The Winter of our Discontent; To Catch A King; Martin Mull Presents The History Of White People In America--Part 1 (feevee).

GARRETT, Betty: Act. b. St Joseph, MO, May 23, 1919. Bway debut 1938, Danton's Death. Films inc: Big City; Words and Music; Take Me Out to the Ball Game; Neptune's Daughter; On the Town; My Sister Eileen; The Shadow on the Window.
TV inc: All in the Family; Laverne and Shirley; All The Way Home; AFI Salute To Gene Kelly.
Bway inc: Jackpot; Laffing Room Only; Call Me Mister; Beg, Borrow, or Steal; A Girl Could Get Lucky; Bells Are Ringing; Who's Happy Now?; Plaza Suite; And Miss Reardon Drinks a Little; The Supporting Cast.

GARRETT, Lila: Prod-Wri-Dir. b. NYC., Nov 21, 1925. TV inc: Mother of the Bride (2 Emmys-Writing & Daytime Wri of Year-1974); The Girl Who Couldn't Lose (prod) (Emmy-1975); Another April (wri); Dick Van Dyke pilot; MacLeish (wri & prod); Newman's Drugstore pilot (wri); This Better Be It (prod-wri); Instant Family (exec prod);

Terraces (prod-wri & dir); Baby I'm Back (prod-wri); Getting There (exec prod-wri); The Other Woman (prod-wri).

GARSON, Greer: Act. b. County Down, Northern Ireland, Sep 29, 1908. e. London U, BA cum laude; Grenoble U. Stage debut Birmingham Rep. theatre 1932; London debut 1935, Golden Arrow. Screen debut 1939, Goodbye, Mr. Chips. Films inc: Pride and Prejudice; When Ladies Meet; Mrs. Miniver (Oscar-1942); Random Harvest; Mme. Curie; Mrs. Parkington; Valley of Decision; Adventure; Desire Me; That Forsythe Woman; The Miniver Story; Scandal at Scourie; Julius Caesar; Strange Lady in Town; Sunrise at Campobello; The Singing Nun; The Happiest Millionaire.

TV inc: Crown Matrimonial; My Father Gave Me America; Little Women; Holiday Tribute to Radio City; Perry Como's Christmas in New Mexico; A Gift of Music (host).

Bway inc: The Madwoman of Chaillot; On Golden Pond (prod).

GARY, Lorraine (nee Gottfried): Act. b. NYC, Aug 16, 1937. e. Columbia U. W of Sidney J Sheinberg. Films inc: Jaws; Car Wash; Jaws 2; Just You and Me Kid; 1941.

GASSMAN, Vittorio: Act. b. Genoa, Italy, Sep 1, 1922. e. Academy Dramatic Art, Rome. Screen deubt, 1946. Films inc: Daniele Cortis; Mysterious Rider; Bitter Rice; The Outlaws; Cry of the Hunted; Sombrero; The Glass Wall; Mambo; War and Peace; The Tiger; Woman Time Seven; Ghosts-Italian Style; Scent of a Woman; Desert of the Tartars; Goodnight Ladies and Gentlemen; The Forbidden Room; Due Pezzi Di Pane; Viva Italia; A Wedding; Quintet; Caro Papa; La Terrazza (The Terrace); The Nude Bomb; Sharky's Machine; Tempest; Il Conte Tacchia (Count Tacchia); La Vie est un roman (Life is a Novel); Benvenuta.

GASTONI, Lisa: Act. b. Italy, 1935. Films inc: The Runaway Bus; Man of the Moment; The Baby and the Battleship; Intent to Kill; Hello London; Passport to China; Maddalena; The Last Days of Mussolini.

GATELY, Frederick: Cin. b. Oct 5, 1909. Films inc: Harpoon; Four Seasons.

TV inc: Operation Petticoat; Nancy Drew; Executive Suite; Medical Center; Nanny and the Professor; Lancer; Hazel; My Sister Eileen; Father Knows Best; Ozzie and Harriet; Dragnet; Trapper John, M.D.

GATES, Larry: Act. b. St Paul, MN, Sep 24, 1915. Films inc: Has Anybody Seen My Gal?; The Girl Rush; Invasion of the Body Snatchers; Jeanne Eagels; Cat on a Hot Tin Roof; One Foot in Hell; The Hoodlum Priest; Some Came Running; Toys in the Attic; The Sand Pebbles; Airport.

Bway inc: Shakespeare repertory; Teahouse of the August Moon; Bell, Book and Candle; Love of Four Colonels; Hamlet; Poor Murderer; First Monday in October.

TV inc: Backstairs at the White House; FDR-The Last Year; The Henderson Monster; Playboy of the Western World.

GATLIN, Larry: Singer-Songwri. b. Seminole, TX, May 2, 1948. Leader Gatlin Bros Band. Songs inc: Broken Lady (Grammy-country song-1976); I Don' Wanna Cry; All the Gold in California; Take Me To Your Lovin' Place.

TV inc: Merry Christmas from the Grand Ole Opry; Johnny Cash Christmas; Bob Hope All Star Comedy Christmas; Country Comes Home; Perry Como's Spring in San Francisco; Larry Gatlin and the Gatlin Bros Band; Kraft Salutes Walt Disney World's 10th Anniversary; Bob Hope's Stars Over Texas; The President's Command Performance; John Schneider's Christmas Holiday; Night Of 100 Stars II.

GAUTIER, Dick: Act. b. 1939. Films inc: Wild in the Sky; The Manchu Eagle Murder Caper Mystery; Fun with Dick and Jane.

TV inc: Here We Go Again; Marathon; This Wife For Hire.

GAVIN, Bill: Exec. b. Wellington, New Zealand, Oct 8, 1936. Man-dir GTO Films, London, 1973-78; GM (Films and Mktg) Hoyts Theatres Ltd, Sydney, 1978.

GAVIN, John: Act. b. Los Angeles, Apr 8, 1928. e. Stanford. Brief job as a press agent. On screen From 1956. Films inc: Behind the High Wall; Four Girls in Town; Quantez; A Time to Love and a Time to Die;

Imitation of Life; Spartacus; A Breath of Scandal; Psycho; Midnight Lace; Romanoff and Juliet; Tammy and the Professor; Back Street; Thoroughly Modern Millie; The Madwoman of Chaillot; Jennifer; History Of The World--Part I.

TV inc: Convoy; Destry; Cutter's Trail; Doris Day Show; New Adventures of Heidi.

Bway inc: Seesaw; Equus; Heaven Can Wait.

Named Ambassador to Mexico by Pres Reagan, May 1981.

GAY, John: Wri. b. Whittier, CA, Apr 1, 1924. e. LA City Coll. Films inc: Run Silent, Run Deep; Separate Tables; The Happy Thieves; Four Horsemen; The Courtship of Eddie's Father; The Hallelujah Trail; The Last Safari; The Power; No Way to Treat a Lady; Soldier Blue; Sometimes a Great Notion; Hennessey; Matter of Time.

TV inc: Amazing Howard Hughes; Kill Me If You Can; Captains Courageous; Red Badge of Courage; All My Darling Daughters; Les Miserables; Transplant; A Private Battle; A Tale of Two Cities; The Bunker; Berlin Tunnel 21; Stand By Your Man; Dial "M" For Murder; The Long Summer of George Adams; A Piano for Mrs Cimino; The Hunchback of Notre Dame; Ivanhoe; Witness for the Prosecution; Samson and Delilah; Fatal Vision. eat a Lady; Soldier Blue; Sometimes a Great Notion; Hennessey; Matter of Time.

TV inc: Amazing Howard Hughes; Kill Me If You Can; Captains Courageous; Red Badge of Courage; All My Darling Daughters; Les Miserables; Transplant; A Private Battle; A Tale of Two Cities; T

GAYE, Marvin: Singer-Sngwri. b. Washington, DC, Apr 2, 1939. With the Rainbows; co-founder The Marquees (later the Moonglows) before going solo 1962.

Recordings inc: What's Going On?; Trouble, Man; Let's Get It On; Marvin Gaye Live; Live at the London Palladium; I Want You; Sexual Healing (Grammys-R&B vocal, R&B inst-1982).

Songs inc: What's Going On?; Mercy, Mercy Me; Inner City Blues. (Died April 1, 1984).

GAYLE, Crystal: Singer. b. Paintsville, KY. Sis of Loretta Lynn. Albums inc: Crystal Gayle; Somebody Loves You; We Must Believe in Magic; When I Dream. Singles inc: Somebody Loves You; Don't It Make My Brown Eyes Blue (Grammy-c&w vocal-1977); Ready for the Times to Get Better.

TV inc: Midnight Special; Dean Martin Christmas Special; Wayne Newton Special; Merry Christmas from Grand Ole Opry; Crystal Gayle Special; Crystal; Country Comes Home; Loretta Lynn--The Lady, The Legend; Country Comes Home; Johnny Cash--A Merry Memphis Christmas; Masquerade (sings title song).

GAYNES, George (nee Jongejans): Act-Sing. b. Helsinki, Finland. e. College Classique, Switzerland; Scuola Musicale di Milan. Started in Opera, appearing with Mulhouse and Strasbourg Operas in France and NY City Opera. Bway inc: The Consul; Out of This World; Wonderful Town; Beggar's Opera; Bells Are Ringing; Brecht on Brecht; Can Can; Lady of the Camellias; Any Wednesday; Of Love Remembered; Gigi.

Films inc: The Group; The Way We Were; Doctors Wives; Nickelodeon; Harry and Walter Go To New York; Altered States; Dead Men Don't Wear Plaid; Tootsie; To Be Or Not To Be; Police Academy; Micki & Maude; Police Academy 2--Their First Assignment.

TV inc: Le Bourgeois Gentilhomme; Mary Hartman, Mary Hartman; Rich Man, Poor Man; Washington Behind Closed Doors; Breaking Up Is Hard To Do; Scruples II; Evita Peron; General Hospital; Punky Brewster; Mom's On Strike; It Came Upon A Midnight Clear.

GAYNOR, Janet (Laura Gainer): Act. b. Philadelphia, 1906. Films inc: The Johnstown Flood; Seventh Heaven, Sunrise, Street Angel (Oscar-1927-28); Sunny Side Up; High Society Blues; Daddy Longlegs; Merely Mary Ann; Tess of the Storm Country; State Fair; Carolina; The Farmer Takes a Wife; Ladies in Love; A Star is Born; Three Loves has Nancy; The Young in Heart; Bernardine.

Bway inc: Harold and Maude.

(Died Sept. 14, 1984)

GAYNOR, Mitzi (nee von Gerber): Act. b. Chicago, 1931. Studied ballet From age 4. Appeared in light opera. Screen debut, 1950, My Blue Heaven. Films inc: The I Don't Care Girl; We're Not Married; There's No Business Like Show Business; Anything Goes; Les Girls; South Pacific; Happy Anniversary; For Love or Money. Opera: The

Fortune Teller; Song of Norway; Louisiana Purchase; Naughty Marietta; The Great Waltz.

TV: Mitzi Gaynor Specials.

GAZZARA, Ben: Act. b. NYC, Aug. 28, 1930. Won scholarship to study with Erwin Piscator. Joined Actor's Studio, performing in improvised play, End As A Man. Screen debut 1957 in film version of that play retitled The Strange One. Films inc: Anatomy of a Murder; The Passionate Thief; The Young Doctors; Convicts Four; A Rage to Live; The Bridge at Remagen; Husbands; Capone; Killing of a Chinese Bookie; Voyage of the Damned; Saint Jack; Sidney Sheldon's Bloodline; Inchon;

Thea inc: Cat on a Hot Tin Roof; A Hatful of Rain; Who's Afraid of Virginia Woolf? They All Laughed;; Tales of Ordinary Madness; Uno Scandalo Perbene (A Proper Scandal).

TV inc: Arrest and Trial; Run For Your Life; A Question of Honor; Hollywood's Most Sensational Mysteries (host).

GAZZO, Michael V: Act-Wri. b. 1923. Bway (act) inc: Arsenic and Old Lace; The Petrified Forest; Shadow of a Gunman; The Little Foxes; The Aristocrats; Juno and the Paycock; A Hatful of Rain (wri).

Films inc: On the Waterfront; (act) The Godfather, Part II; Fingers; King of the Gypsies; Love and Bullets; The Fish that Saved Pittsburgh (sp); King Creole; Cuba Crossing; Alligator; Back Roads; Fear City; Cannonball Run II.

TV inc: Sizzle; Blood Feud; John Steinbeck's The Winter of our Discontent.

GEARY, Anthony: Act. b. Coalville, UT, May 29. e. U of UT. TV inc: Bright Promise; The Young and the Restless; Osmond Family Holiday Special; General Hospital (Emmy-1982); Intimate Agony; Sins of the Past; The Imposter; Kicks.

Films inc: Johnny Got His Gun.

GEBEL-WILLIAMS, Gunther: Animal Trainer. b. Germany, Sept 12, 1934. With Circus Williams in Europe; joined Ringling Brothers Barnum & Bailey in 1968.

TV inc: Gunther Williams, Lord of The Ring; Highlights of Ringling Bros & Bailey Circus; 113th Edition Ringling Bros and Barnum & Bailey Circus; Ringling Bros. and Barnum & Bailey Circus (1985).

GEESON, Judy: Act. b. Arundel, Sussex, England, Sep 10, 1948. W of Kristoffer Tabori. Films inc: To Sir With Love; Here We Go Round The Mulberry Bush; Three Into Two Won't Go; The Executioner; Brannigan; The Eagle Has Landed; Carry On England; It's Not the Size That Counts; The Plague Dogs (voice); Horror Planet; Dominique (Made in 1977).

TV inc: Dance of Death; Lady Windermere's Fan; The Skin Game; She; A Room With a View; The Seven Last Words; The Coronation.

Thea inc: Othello; Two Gentlemen of Verona; An Ideal Husband; Caught In the Act.

GEFFEN, David: Exec. b. 1944. Started as agent with William Morris; opened own agcy with Elliott Roberts; founded Asylum Records, 1970. 1973, sold to Warners, merged with Elektra with Geffen as P; 1975 vice chmn Warner Brothers Pictures; 1977 exec asst to Warner Communications chmn Steven J Ross; resd 1978 to teach music at Yale; 1980 P new diskery bankrolled by WCI.

Films inc: (exec prod) Personal Best. Bway inc: Master Harold. . .and the Boys; Cats; Good.

GEISEL, Ted (Dr Seuss): Prod-Wri-Ani. b. Springfield, MA, Mar 2, 1904. e. Dartmouth; Oxford. Started as adv artist; cartoons inc: "Quick Henry the Flit" campaign, wri of children's books. Films inc: Oscar-winning shorts If Hitler Lives; Design for Death; Gerald McBoing-Boing.

TV inc: (prod-wri) How the Grinch Stole Christmas; Horton Hears A Who; The Cat in the Hat; The Lorax; Dr. Seuss on the Loose; The Hoober Blood Highway; Hallowe'en is Grinch Night (Emmy-1978); Dr. Seuss' Pontoffel Pock, Where Are You?; The Grinch Grinches The Cat-In-The-Hat (& lyr) (Emmy-prod-1982).

GEISINGER, Elliot: Wri-Dir-Prod. b. NYC, Feb 8, 1930. e. Columbia U, BS. Films inc: The Prince and the Pauper (sp-prod-dir); The Great Adventure (sp-prod); The Amityville Horror (prod); The Night The Lights Went Out In Georgia (prod).

TV inc: Meteor-Messenger From Space.

GELBART, Larry: Wri. b. Chicago, Feb 25, 1928. Films inc: The Notorious Landlady; The Wrong Box; Oh, God!; Movie, Movie; Neighbors; Tootsie; Blame It On Rio (exec prod).

TV inc: M*A*S*H (Emmy-prod-1974); United States (exec prod-wri); AfterMASH.

Plays inc: A Funny Thing Happened on the Way to the Forum (Tony-1963); Sly Fox.

GELIN, Daniel: Act. b. Angers, France, 1921. Films inc: Rendezvous de Juillet; Edouard et Caroline; La Ronde; Les Mains Sales; Rue de l'Estrapade; The Lovers of Lisbon; The Man Who Knew Too Much; Charmants Garcons; There's Always a Price Tag; Carthage in Flames; The Season for Love; Black Sun; Le Souffle au Coeur; Pardon Mon Affaire, Too; L'Oeil du Maitre (His Master's Eye); Sezona Mira U Parizu (Season of Peace In Paris); La Nuit de Varennes (The Night of Varennes); Guy de Maupassant; Un Delitto (A Crime); Les Enfants (The Children).

Thea inc: Le Scenario.

GENET, Jean: Wri. b. France, Dec 19, 1910. Plays inc: Haute Surveillance (Deathwatch); Le Balcon (The Balcony); Les Negres (The Blacks); Les Paravents (The Screens). Films inc: Un Chant d'Amour (Love Song); Black Mirror.

GENTRY, Bobbie: Comp-Singer. b. Chickasaw Co, MS, 1944. Recording artist. (Grammys-(3)-new artist-vocal-contemporary solo-1967).

TV inc: All-Star Salute To Mother's Day.

GEORGE, Christopher: Act. b. Royal Oak, MN, Feb 25, 1929. e. U of Miami. Thea inc: Mr Roberts; Petrified Forest; Streetcar Named Desire.

TV inc: Rat Patrol; The Immortal; Last Survivors; Voyage into Evil.

Films inc: El Dorado; In Harms Way; The Delta Factor; Chisum; Day of the Animals; Grizzly; Tiger by the Tail; The Exterminator; Graduation Day; Enter the Ninja; Paura nella citta dei morti viventi (The Gates of Hell); Mortuary; Pieces.

(Died Nov. 29, 1983).

GEORGE, Linda Day: Act. b. San Marcos, TX, Dec 11. W of the late Christopher George. Films inc: Chisum; Day of the Animals; Gentle Rain; Racquet; Beyond Evil; The Junkman; Mortuary; Pieces; Young Warriors.

TV inc: Mission Impossible; Once an Eagle; Roots; Rich Man, Poor Man; Murder at the World Series; Trial of Capt Jensen; Casino; Quick & Quiet.

Thea inc: The Devils; The Crucible.

GEORGE, Phyllis: TV Pers. b. Denton, TX. Former Miss America (1971). Joined CBS, 1975. Co-Host of The NFL Today. Co-host, with Bert Parks, The Miss America Pageant TV Broadcast. Macy's Thanksgiving Day Parade telecast; People; Jan. 1985, co-anchor CBS Morning News.

GEORGE, Susan: Act. b. England, 1950. W of Simon MacCorkindale. Former child actress. Films inc: Billion Dollar Brain; The Strange Affair; Twinky; Spring and Port Wine; The Looking Glass War; Die Screaming, Marianne; Eye Witness; Fright; The Straw Dogs; Dirty Mary, Crazy Larry; Sonny and Jed; Mandingo; Out of Season; Tintorera; Venom; Enter the Ninja; The House Where Evil Dwells; The Jigsaw Man.

TV inc: Computercide; Pajama Tops (cable).

Thea inc: The Importance Of Being Oscar (prod).

GERAGHTY, Maurice: Wri-Dir-Prod. b. Rushville, IN, Sep 29, 1908. e. Princeton U. Films inc: Red Canyon; Dakota Lil; Calamity Jane and Sam Bass; Tomahawk; Sword of Monte Cristo; Rose of Cimarron; Mohawk; Love Me Tender.

TV inc: Virginian; Bonanza; Daniel Boone; 87th Precinct; Beacon St; Cavalcade of America; No Warning; Flight; Laramie; Lassie.

GERARD, Gil: Act. b. Little Rock, AR, Jan 23, 1943. TV inc: The Doctors; Killing Stone; Buck Rogers in the 25th Century; Help Wanted Male; Not Just Another Affair; Hear No Evil; Johnny Blue; For Love Or

Money.

Films inc: Airport '77; Buck Rogers in the 25th Century; Stormin' Home; International Airport.

Thea inc: I Do! I Do!

GERASIMOV, Sergei: Dir-Wri. b. May 21, 1906. Started as actor, films inc: The Bears Versus Yudenich; The Devil's Wheel; The Overcoat; Buddy; S.V.D.; The New Babylon; Alone; Three Soldiers; The Deserter; The Boarder; The Vyborg Side. (Dir-wri): Twenty-Two Mishaps; (co-dir) Solomon's Heart; If I Love You; The Brave Seven; Komsomolsk; The Teacher; Masquerade (& act); The Mainland; The Young Guard; Nadezhda; Men and Beasts; The Journalist; At the Lake; For The Love of Man. (Dir only): The Old Guard; The Village Doctor; Lev Tolstoy (& act). (Sp only) The The Road of Truth; And Quiet Flows the Don; Memory of the Heart.

GERBER, David: Exec. b. NYC. e. U of Pacific. Before joining 20th Century-Fox as vp-TV sales, 1965, was packaging agent with GAC and Famous Artists Corp; became ind prod 1972; June 1985, P MGM/UA TV Broadcast Group, in chg wldwde prodn. TV inc: (Exec prod) Nanny and the Professor; The Ghost and Mrs. Muir; Cade's County; Police Story (Emmy-1976); Police Woman; Needles and Pins; Born Free; Joe Forrester; The Quest; Bibbsville; Man Undercover; Doctor's Private Lives; The Billion Dollar Threat; Only the Pretty Girls Die; Power; Once Upon A Spy; Beulah Land; The Night the City Screamed; Terror Among Us; Walking Tall; Elvis and the Beauty Queen; Riker; The Wonderful World of Philip Malley; Nuts and Bolts; Revenge of the Gray Gang; Today's FBI; The Neighborhood; Seven Brides for Seven Brothers; Cry For The Strangers; For Love and Honor; Women of San Quentin; George Washington; The Last Days of Pompeii; The Boys In Blue; Jessie; Lady Blue.

GERE, Richard: Act. b. Philadelphia, PA, Aug 31, 1949. Films inc: Report to the Commissioner; Baby Blue Marine; Days of Heaven; Looking for Mr Goodbar; Bloodbrothers; Yanks; American Gigolo; An Officer and A Gentleman; Breathless; Beyond the Limit (The Honorary Consul); The Cotton Club; King David.

Bway inc: Grease; Bent. (London): Grease; Habeus Corpus; The Taming of the Shrew.

GERSHENSON, Joseph: Comp-Cond. b. Russia, Jan 12, 1904. Cond orch B F Keith Theatres 1920-28; music dir RKO Theatres, 1928-33; joined Universal 1933; 1941 appted exec prod, head of music dept Ul. Film scores inc: Glenn Miller Story; Magnificent Obsession; There's Always Tomorrow; Written in the Wind; My Man Godfrey; Imitation of Life; Pillow Talk; Operation Petticoat; Father Goose; Shenandoah; Blindfold; Thoroughly Modern Millie; Sweet Charity.

GERSHWIN, Ira: Lyr. b. NYC, Dec 6, 1896. e. CCNY. B of late George Gershwin. Bway inc: Two Little Girls in Blue (under name of Arthur Francis); Lady Be Good; Tell Me More; Tip-Toes; Oh, Kay; Funny Face; Rosalie; Treasure Girl; Show Girl; Strike Up The Band; Girl Crazy; of Thee I Sing (Pulitzer Prize-1932); Let 'Em Eat Cake; Life Begins at 8:40; Ziegfeld Follies of 1936; Porgy and Bess; Lady in the Dark; Park Avenue; My One and Only (compilation); Singin' In The Rain (London) (compilation).

Films inc: Delicious; Shall We Dance; A Damsel in Distress; The Goldwyn Follies; Cover Girl; The Shocking Miss Pilgrim; The Barkleys of Broadway; An American In Paris; A Star is Born; Country Girl; Kiss Me Stupid.

Songs inc: Fascinatin' Rhythm; Oh, Lady Be Good; The Man I Love; Do Do Do; Someone to Watch Over Me; Strike Up the Band; Funny Face; 'S Wonderful; Liza; Bidin' My Time; Embraceable You; I Got Rhythm; But Not For Me; Cheerful Little Earful; Wintergreen for President; Of Thee I Sing; Who Cares; I Got Plenty of Nuttin; It Aint Necessarily So; Let's Call The Whole Thing Off; Shall We Dance; They Can't Take That Away From Me; A Foggy Day; Nice Work If You Can Get It; Love Walked In; Saga of Jenny; My Ship; Long Ago; The Man That Got Away.

(Died Aug. 17, 1983).

GERTZ, Irving: Comp-Mus dir. b. Providence, RI, May 19, 1915. e. Providence Coll of Music. US Army, 1941-46; then comp, arranger, Mus Dir for Col, 1946-49; NBC, 1949-51; U Pictures, 1951-60; Fox, 1960-70. Films inc: Bandits of Corsica; Gun Belt; Long Wait;

The Fiercest Heart; First Travelling Saleslady.

TV inc: America; The Golden Voyage; Across the Seven Seas; The Legend of Jesse James; Daniel Boone; Voyage to the Bottom of the Sea; Peyton Place; Land of the Giants; Lancer; Medical Center.

GETHERS, Steven: Wri-Dir-Prod. b. Jun 8, 1922. e. AADA. Plays inc: A Cook for Mr. General.

TV inc: (Wri) It's Good To Be Alive; A Circle of Children (& prod); Billy--Portrait of a Street Kid (& dir); Silent Victory; Damien. . .The Leper Priest (& dir); Jacqueline Bouvier Kennedy (& dir); A Woman Called Golda; Confessions of a Married Man (& dir).

GETZ, John: Act. TV inc: Another World; Kent State; Rafferty; Three's Company; Loose Change; A Woman Called Moses; Rivkin--Bounty Hunter; Muggable Mary--Street Cop; Concrete Beat; The Execution; MacGruder & Loud.

Films inc: Tattoo; Blood Simple; Thief Of Hearts.

GETZ, Stan: Mus. b. Philadelphia, Feb 2, 1927. Sideman with Jack Teagarden; Stan Kenton; Jimmy Dorsey; Benny Goodman; Woody Herman bands before forming own group in 1949. Films inc: The Benny Goodman Story; Get Yourself a College Girl; The Hanged Man; Mickey One; Een Pak Slaag (Mr. Slotter's Jubilee).

TV inc: Jazz Comes Home To Newport.

(Grammy-(4)-jazz solo-1962; record of year-1964; album of year-1964; small group jazz-1964).

GEWALD, Robert M: Prod. b. NYC, Mar 8, 1934. Prod first appearance at Lincoln Center of an American Symphony Orchestra, 1963; prod First Children's Folk Festival at Lincoln Center, 1965; prod An Evening of Rodgers and Hammerstein; mgr: Jose Iturbi; Eleanor Steber; Pittsburgh Ballet Theatre; Rochester Philharmonic.

GHIA, Fernando: Prod. b. Rome, Jul 22, 1935. e. U of Rome. Thea (Rome). inc: Miracle Worker; Requiem for a Man; Becket.

Films inc: China Is Near; The Red Tent; The Audience; A Fine Pair; The Mattei Affair; Lady Caroline Lamb.

GHOSTLEY, Alice: Act. b. Eve, MO, Aug 16, 1926. e. U of OK. Films inc: New Faces; To Kill a Mockingbird; My Six Loves; Ace Eli and Rodger of the Skies; Rabbit Test; Grease; Not For Publication.

Bway inc: New Faces of 1952; Sandhog; Trouble in Tahiti; Maybe Tuesday; A Thurber Carnival; Gentlemen Be Seated; The Sign in Sidney Brustein's Window (Tony-supp-1965); Stop, Thief, Stop.

TV inc: Sutter's Bay.

GIAMBALVO, Louis: Act. b. Brooklyn, NY., Feb. 8. e. NY State U. Cofounder of Colonnades Theatre rep group. Thea inc: Moliere in Spite of Himself; The Ballroom in St. Patrick's Cathedral; A Flea in Her Ear; Reflections.

TV inc: The Gangster Chronicles; Mae West; The Chicago Story; Fly Away Home; Jessica Novak; The Ambush Murders; Marion Rose White; The Devlin Connection; Oh, Madeline; The Ratings Game (PC); Dirty Work.

Films inc: Death Wish; Godfather II; Next Stop Greenwich Village; Just Tell Me What You Want; Second Thoughts.

GIANNINI, Giancarlo: Act. b. Spezia, Italy, Aug 1, 1942. Films inc: Love and Anarchy; The Seduction of Mimi; How Funny Can Sex Be?; Seven Beauties; The End of the World In Our Usual Bed In A Night Full of Rain; The Innocent; Buone Notizie (& prod); Revenge; Travels with Anita; Lili Marleen; Lovers and Liars; La Vita e Bella (Life Is Wonderful); Mi Manda Picone (Picone Sent Me); American Dreamer.

Thea inc: Two Plus Two No Longer Make Four.

GIBB, Andy: Mus-Prod. b. March 5, 1958. TV inc: Dean Martin Christmas Special 1980; Grammy Hall of Fame; Grandpa, Will You Run With Me?; I Love Men; Celebrity Fun Cruise; Music Of Your Life.

Albums inc: Shadow Dancing; Shadow Gibb; Flowing Rivers.

See also BEEGEES.

GIBB, Barry: Mus-Prod. b. Sep 1, 1946. Films inc: Saturday Night Fever; Sgt. Pepper's Lonely Hearts Club Band.

(Grammy-pop vocal duo-1980).

See also BEEGEES.

GIBB, Maurice: Mus-Prod. b. Dec 22, 1949. Films inc: Saturday Night Fever; Sgt. Pepper's Lonely Hearts Club Band; A Breed Apart.
See also BEEGEES.

GIBB, Robin: Mus-Prod. b. Dec 22, 1949. Films inc: Saturday Night Fever; Sgt. Pepper's Lonely Hearts Club Band.
See also BEEGEES.

GIBBONS, Peter (Walter Peter Gibbons-Fly): Cin. b. Philadelphia, Jan 15, 1913. e. NYU, BS; USC, MFA. Tech advisor on: Seven Wonders of the World; Search for Paradise; South Seas Adventure; Wonderful World of the Brothers Grimm; How the West Was Won. Personal tech advisor to George Stevens on The Greatest Story Ever Told; (Cin) Fraternity Row.
(Died May 27, 1983).

GIBBS, Marla: Act. b. Chicago, IL, Jun 14, 1946. Films inc: Black Belt Jones; Sweet Jesus, Preacher Man.
TV inc: The Moneychanger; Tell Me Where It Hurts; You Can't Take It With You; The Jeffersons; Checking In; Fade Out--The Erosion of Black Images in the Media (int).

GIBNEY, Sheridan: Wri. b. NYC, Jun 11, 1903. e. Exeter, Amherst, AB, MA. Films inc: I Am A Fugitive From a Chain Gang; The Story of Louis Pasteur (Oscar-1936); Anthony Adverse; Letter of Introduction; Cheers For Miss Bishop; Once Upon a Honeymoon; The Locket; Our Hearts Were Young and Gay.
Plays inc: The Wiser They Are; Encore; Merry Madness.

GIBSON, Henry: Act. b. Germantown, PA, 1935. e. Catholic U. Broadway, My Mother, My Father and Me. Film debut in The Long Goodbye. Films inc: Kiss Me Stupid; The Nutty Professor; The Gunslingers; Evil Roy Slade; The Last Remake of Beau Geste; A Perfect Couple; The Blues Brothers; Health; The Incredible Shrinking Woman; Tulips.
TV inc: Mister Roberts; F-Troop; Laugh-In; The Halloween That Almost Wasn't; For the Love of It; The Nashville Grab; High School USA.

GIBSON, Mel: Act. b. NY, 1956. Moved to Australia when he was 12. Films inc: Mad Max; Tim; Attack Force Z; Gallipoli; Mad Max II (Road Warrior); The Year of Living Dangerously; The Bounty; The River; Mrs. Soffel; Mad Max Beyond Thunderdrome.

GIBSON, William: Wri. b. NYC, Nov 13, 1914. e. CCNY. Plays inc: I Lay in Zion; A Cry of Players; The Miracle Worker (Tony-1960); Dinny and the Witches; John and Abigail; The Butterfingers Angel; A Season in Heaven; Golda; Monday After the Miracle; Handy Dandy.
Films Inc: Two for the Seesaw; The Miracle Worker; The Cobweb.
TV inc: The Miracle Worker.

GIDDING, Nelson: Wri. b. 1915. Films inc: I Want to Live; Odds Against Tomorrow; Nine Hours to Rama; The Inspector; The Haunting; Lost Command; Skullduggery; The Andromeda Strain; Beyond the Poseidon Adventure.

GIELGUD, John, Sir: Act. b. London, Apr 14, 1904. e. RADA. Knighted, 1953. Began stage career in Shakespearean roles London stage; also in The Constant Nymph; The Good Companions; The Importance of Being Earnest; Half-Life. (Bway): various Shakespearean roles; Bingo; No Man's Land; also dir Big Fish, Little Fish (Tony-1961); Private Lives; The Constant Wife; No Man's Land; The Gay Lord Quex (Special Tony-1959).
Films inc: Secret Agent; Julius Caesar; Richard III; Around the World in 80 Days; The Barretts of Wimpole Street; Becket; The Loved One; St. Joan; The Charge of the Light Brigade; The Shoes of the Fisherman; Oh What a Lovely War; Lost Horizon; Murder on the Orient Express; Portrait of the Artist As A Young Man; Joseph Andrews; Providence; Murder By Decree; Caligula; The Human Factor; Drygent (The Orchestra Conductor); The Elephant Man; The Formula; Lion of the Desert; Sphinx; Chariots of Fire; Arthur (Oscar-supp-1981); Priest of Love; Gandhi; The Wicked Lady; Wagner; Scandalous; The Shooting Party.
TV inc: A Day by the Sea; The Browning Version; Mayfly and the Frog; The Cherry Orchard; From Chekov With Love; St. Joan; Deliver Us From Evil; Heartbreak House; To Be An Actor; Les Miserables; The

Seven Dials Mystery; Why Didn't They Ask Evans?; Brideshead Revisited; The Hunchback of Notre Dame; Inside The Third Reich; Marco Polo; The Scarlet and the Black; The Master of Ballantrae; The Far Pavilions (PC); Buddenbrooks (host-narr); Camille.
(Grammy-spoken word-1979).

GIFFORD, Alan: Act. b. Boston, Mar 11, 1911. Films inc: The Iron Petticoat; The Flying Scot; Screaming Mimi; Onionhead; Mouse That Roared; The Royal Game; The Road to Hong Kong; Town Without Pity; One Spy Too Many; 2001: A Space Odyssey; Isadora.
TV inc: High Tension; Philadelphia Story; A Quiet Game of Cards; Portrait of a Lady; The Male Animal; As The World Turns.

GIFFORD, Frank: Sports Commentator. b. Santa Monica, CA, Aug 16, 1930. e. USC. Former football great (Hall of Fame 1977). ABC sportscaster. TV inc: Monday Night Football; Olympic Games 1972 and 1976; Superstar series (host); (Emmy-outstanding sports personality-1977).

GIL, David: Prod. b. Tel Aviv, Israel, Jan 24, 1930. e. U of Jerusalem. Headed Gilart Productions, 1962-68; Foreign sls dir, Commonwealth United, 1968. Films inc: Guess What We Learned in School Today; Joe; A Journey Through Rosebud; A Change in the Wind; Gas Pump Girls.
TV inc: Nightkill.

GILARDI, Jack Leo: Agent. b. Chicago, Oct 5, 1930. e. Loras Coll. H of Annette Funicello. Started as agent at GAC; then sr vp ICM.

GILBERT, Bruce: Prod. b. Los Angeles, Mar 28, 1947. e. UC Berkeley. Partnered with Jane Fonda in IPC Films; story ed CineArtists. Films inc: Coming Home (asso prod); The China Syndrome (exec prod); Nine To Five; On Golden Pond; Rollover.
TV inc: 9 to 5; The Dollmaker (exec prod).

GILBERT, Lewis: Dir. b. London, Mar 6, 1920. Films inc: Little Ballerina; Bismarck; The Sea Shall Not Have Them; The Admirable Crichton; Carve Her Name With Pride; Alfie; You Only Live Twice; H.M.S. Defiant; Loss of Innocence; The Spy Who Loved Me; Moonraker; Educating Rita (& prod); Not Quite Jerusalem (& prod).

GILBERT, Melissa: Act. b. Los Angeles, May 8, 1964. TV inc: Gunsmoke; Tenafly; The Hanna-Barbera Happy Hour; Christmas Miracle; Little House on the Prairie; The Miracle Worker; The Diary of Anne Frank; Like Magic; Splendor In The Grass; Choices of the Heart; Look Back to Yesterday; Little House-- The Last Farewell; Family Secrets; Bless All The Dear Children.
Films inc: Nutcracker Fantasy; Sylvester.

GILBERT, Ray: Lyr-Comp. b. Hartford, CT, Sep 15, 1912. Wrote special material for Sophie Tucker; Harry Richman; Buddy Rogers. To Hollywood 1939. Films scores inc: The Three Caballeros; Make Mine Music; Song of the South; A Date with Judy.
Songs inc: You Belong to My Heart; Two Silhouettes; Zip-a-Dee-Doo-Dah (Oscar-1947); My Fickle Eye; Bahia; Muskrat Ramble; Casey at the Bat; Bonita; If You Went Away.

GILBRIDE, Andrew D: Mus. b. Seattle, WA, Jul 5, 1953. Performs on 5-string banjo. On tour with the Bunk Hokum travelling Bluegrass Show.

GILFORD, Jack (nee Gellman): Act. b. NYC, Jul 25, 1907. Started in vaudeville, niteries. Films inc: Hey Rookie; A Funny Thing Happened on the Way to the Forum; Mister Buddwing; Enter Laughing; The Happening; Who's Minding the Mint? They Might be Giants; Catch 22; Save the Tiger; Wholly Moses!; Cheaper to Keep Her; Caveman; Cocoon.
TV inc: Once Upon a Mattress; Of Thee I Sing; Friends and Lovers; The World of Sholem Aleichem; The Diary of Anne Frank; The Tenth Man; Apple Pie; Goldie and the Boxer Go to Hollywood; Heaven On Earth; Happy.
Bway inc: The Sunshine Boys; No, No Nanette; Cabaret; Sly Fox; The Supporting Cast; The World of Sholom Aleichem.

GILKYSON, Terry: Act-Comp. b. Phoenixville, PA, circa 1919. One of the pioneers of the pop folk movement of the 50s and 60s.

GILLESPIE, Dizzy (John Birks Gillespie): Mus-Comp. b. Cheraw, SC, Oct 21, 1917. e. Laurinburg Inst. Trumpet player with Teddy Hill; Cab Calloway; Earl "Fatha" Hines before forming own group 1944; world tours for State Dept; concerts; later rec artist with Charlie Parker; Miles Davis; Stan Getz; Oscar Peterson.

Songs inc: A Night in Tunisia; Groovin' High; Tour de Force; Con Alma; This Is The Way; Manteca; Lorraine; Cool World; Something Old, Something New; Swing Low Sweet Cadillac.

TV inc: A Family Circus Easter (voice); Jazz Comes Home To Newport.

(Grammy-jazz solo-1975).

GILLIAM, Terry: Wri-Dir-Ani. b. Minneapolis, MN, Nov 22, 1940. e. Occidental College. Member Monty Python's Flying Circus. Freelance wri, illustrator for various magazines, ad agencies, moved to London. TV inc: Do Not Adjust Your Set; We Have Ways of Making You Laugh; The Marty Feldman Comedy Machine; William (title sequence dsgn).

Films inc: Monty Python and the Holy Grail (co-dir); Jabberwocky (dir); Life of Brian (dsgn-ani-sp); Time Bandits (dir); Monty Python's The Meaning of Life (wri-act); Brazil (wri-dir).

GILLIAT, Sidney: Wri-Dir-Prod. b. England, 1908. Wrote several films before collabing with Frank Launder on Seven Sinners; they subsequently formed Launder and Gilliat Productions, in which they worked together on script and prodn but usually directed individually. Films inc: Orders is Orders; Friday the 13th; Chu Chin Chow; Where There's A Will; Seven Sinners; A Yank At Oxford; The Lady Vanishes; The Gaunt Stranger; Jamaica Inn; Ask A Policeman; Night Train; Kipps; The Young Mr Pitt; began dir on Millions Like Us; Waterloo Road; The Rake's Progress; Green For Danger; State Secret; The Story of Gilbert & Sullivan; Only Two Can Play; The Great St. Trinian's Train Robbery; Get Charlie Tully.

GILLIATT, Penelope: Wri. b. England, 1933. Films inc: Sunday, Bloody Sunday.

GILLING, John: Wri-Dir-Prod. b. England, 1912. Films inc: Interpol; The Man Inside; Odongo; High Flight; The Flesh and the Fields; The Challenge; The Pirates of Blood River; The Shadow of the Cat; Scarlet Blade; Plague of the Zombies; The Reptile; The Night Caller.

(Died Nov. 22, 1984)

GILMAN, Sam: Act. b. Lynn, MA. Films inc: Shadow of the Window; Somebody Up There Likes Me; Away All Boats; Desiree; PT 109; One-Eyed Jacks; Burn; Gator Bait; Fluffy; Wild Rovers; Macon County Line; Missouri Breaks; Sometimes a Great Notion; Every Which Way But Loose; Gatorbait; National Lampoon Goes to the Movies.

TV inc: Insight/Teddy.

GILMORE, William S: Prod. b. Los Angeles, Mar 10, 1934. e. UC Berkeley. Films inc: The Last Remake of Beau Geste; Defiance; Deadly Blessing (exec prod); Tough Enough; Against All Odds.

TV inc: S O S Titanic; The Legend of Walks Far Woman; Another Woman's Child (supv prod).

GILROY, Frank D: Wri. b. NYC, Oct 13, 1925. e. Dartmouth. Films inc: The Fastest Gun Alive; The Subject Was Roses; The Gallant Hours; The Only Game in Town; Desperate Characters (& dir); From Noon Till Three (& dir); Once in Paris (& dir).

TV inc: Studio One; Playhouse 90; Kraft Theatre; Rex Stout's Nero Wolfe.

Plays inc: Who'll Save the Plowboy (& prod); The Subject Was Roses (& prod); *(Pulitzer Prize & Tony*-1965) That Summer--That Fall; The Only Game in Town; Present Tense; Last Licks; The Housekeeper.

GIMBEL, Norman: Lyr. b. Brooklyn, Nov 16, 1927. e. Baruch Coll, BBA. Bway inc: Whoop Up; The Conquering Hero. TV inc: Don't Look Back.

Songs inc: Ready To Take A Chance Again; Canadian Sunset; Girl From Ipanema; Watch What Happens; Live for Life; I Got a Name; I Will Wait For You; Richard's Window; Killing Me Softly With His Song *(Grammy*-song of year-1973); Love Is; Sail On; Love Theme from Five Days From Home; Are You Ready for the Summer; Meatballs; Good Friend; Moondust; It Goes Like It Goes *(Oscar*-1979); Here Is Where The Love Is.

GIMBEL, Peter: Wri-Dir-Prod. b. NYC, Feb 14, 1928. e. Yale. Films inc: Blue Water, White Death; Mystery of the Andrea Doria; Andrea Doria--The Final Chapter.

GIMBEL, Roger: Exec prod. b. Philadelphia, Mar 11, 1925. e. Yale. Copy and creative chief of RCA Victor TV; Became assoc prod, Tonight Show; made head of pgm dvlpt of NBC daytime programming; later named prod of Tonight specials, including the Jack Paar, Ernie Kovacs shows; also responsible for the Bing Crosby/Mary Martin Special; the Dean Martin Special; in 1969 prod, co-packager The Glen Campbell Goodtime Hour; 1971, named prodn vp, Tomorrow Entertainment, Inc; June 1976, merged company with EMI, became the first P of EMI TV, Inc.

TV inc: The Autobiography of Miss Jane Pittman; Born Innocent; Glass House; A War of Children *(Emmy*-1973); Gargoyles; I Heard the Owl Call My Name; I Love You, Goodbye; Tell Me Where It Hurts; Things in Their Season; Minstrel Man; Miles to Go Before I Sleep; Queen of the Stardust Ballroom; A Piano for Mrs Cimino; The Amazing Howard Hughes; TVTV; Hatter Fox; Lawman Without a Gun; Forever; Deadman's Curve; Deathmoon; Just Me and You; Peterbilt; The Ron Le Flore Story-One in a Million; Betrayal; Steel Cowboy; The Cracker Factory; This Man Stands Alone; The Survival of Dana; Can You Hear the Laughter-The Story of Freddie Prinze; S.O.S. Titanic; Orphan Train; Sophia Loren--Her Own Story; My Kidnapper, My Love; The Killing of Randy Webster; Broken Promise; The Manions of America; Report to Murphy; A Question of Honor; The Legend of Walks Far Woman; Deadly Encounter; Packin' It In; Sessions; Aurora.

Films inc: Blackout (exec prod).

GINGOLD, Dan: Prod-Dir. b. Los Angeles, Jan 1, 1928. Started 1951 as staff dir KNXT (CBS); 1959, staff prod-dir; 1972, exec news prod; 1976, exec prod pgms; 1979 field prod Real People. TV inc: Combat in the Classroom; Hard Time; Whatever Happened to Lori Jean Lloyd? (& wri).

GINGOLD, Hermione: Act. b. London, Dec 9, 1897. Thea inc: (London) Pinkie and the Fairies; The Merry Wives of Windsor; The Merchant of Venice; Little Lord Fauntleroy.

Films inc: Around the World in 80 Days; Bell, Book and Candle; Gigi; The Naked Edge; The Music Man; Promise Her Anything; Those Fantastic Flying Fools; Garbo Talks.

TV inc: Amy And The Angel.

(Grammy-childrens record-1976).

GINN, Robert: Prod. b. Melbourne, Australia, Jun 6, 1943. Exec Dir J C Williamson Productions Ltd. Plays prod inc: (Australia) A Chorus Line; Funny Peculiar; Boeing-Boeing; Dracula; Annie.

GINNANE, Antony I: Prod. b. Melbourne, Australia, Jun 11, 1949. e. U of Melbourne, LLD. Dir-chmn FGH Group, Australia, dir-partner Film & General Holdings, USA.

Films inc: Sympathy in Summer; Fantasm; Fantasm Comes Again; Blue Fire Lady; Patrick; Snapshot (The Day After Halloween); Thirst; Harlequin, The Survivor; Race for the Yankee Zephyr; Dead Kids; Turkey Shoot; Prisoners; Second Time Lucky.

GINSBERG, Sidney: Exec. b. NYC, Oct 26, 1920. e. CCNY. Started as asst mgr Loew's Theatres; joined Trans-Lux, 1943, as thea mgr; film booker; helped form Trans-Lux Dist. Corp, 1956; vp in charge of world wide sls, 1969; Haven Int'l Pictures, Inc, 1970; vp-sls, Scotia Int'l. Films Inc, 1971; exec vp, Scotia American Prods; 1977, p, Rob-Rich Films Inc.

GINTY, Robert: Act. b. NYC, Nov 14, 1948. Films inc: Bound for Glory; Two Minute Warning; Incident of October 20th; Coming Home; The Act; Exterminator 2; Vivre Pour Survivre (White Fire); Mission Kids; Warrior Of The Lost World.

TV inc: Police Story; The Rockford Files; Baa Baa Black Sheep; The Big Stuffed Dog; I Want To Live; Hawaiian Heat.

Thea inc: My Three Angels; Once in a Lifetime; The Lion in Winter; The Indian Wants the Bronx.

GIRARDOT, Annie: Act. b. France, Oct 25, 1931. Films inc: Rocco and His Brothers; Maigret Sets a Trap; Vice and Virtue; Dillinger Is Dead; A Man I Like; The Novices; Story of a Woman; Love Is a Funny Thing; The Slap; Love and Cool Water; To Each His Hell; Dear Inspector; No Time for Breakfast; Go On, Mama; The Last Kiss; The Key Is in the Door; L'ingorgo; Bobo, Jacco; Le Coeur a L'envers (My Heart Is Upside Down); All Night Long; A Black Gown For A Killer; La Vie Continue (Life Goes On); Souvenirs, Souvenirs (Memories, Memories); Liste Noir (Black List); Partir Revenir (Departure, Return); Io E Il Duce (Mussolini And I).

GIRAUDEAU, Bernard: Act. b. La Rochelle, France, Jun. 18, 1947. Thea inc: Pauve France; La camisole; La Reine de Cesaree; Attention Fragile. Films inc: Du ciel plein de coeur; Deux hommes dans la ville; Revolver; Le gitan; Jamais plus toujours (Never Again Always); La petite gare; Le Juge Fayard, dit le sheriff (Judge Fayard Called the Sheriff); Bilitis; Moi, fleur bleue (Stop Calling Me Baby); Et la tendresse. . .? Bordel! (Tenderness, My Fanny); Le toubib (The Medic); Le cri du silence (short- & dir); La boum; Viens chez moi, j'habite chez une copine; Passione d'amore; Croque la vie (A Bite of Living); Hecate; Meurtres a domicile (Home Murders); Marc Lobet; Le Ruffian; Rue Barbare (Barbarous Street); L'Annee des Meduses (Year Of Medusa); Les Specialistes (The Specialists).

GISH, Lillian (Lillian de Guiche): Act. b. Springfield, OH., Oct. 14, 1893. Sis of the late Dorothy Gish. On stage as child, appeared on Broadway 1913 with Marion Davies. Began film career for D.W. Griffith for whom she made 40 films inc: Birth Of A Nation; Intolerance; Broken Blossoms; Way Down East; Orphans Of The Storm; The Scarlet Letter; Annie Laurie. Other films inc: His Double Life; The Commandos Strike At Dawn; Miss Susie Slagle's; Duel In The Sun; Portrait Of Jennie; Night Of The Hunter; Orders To Kill; The Unforgiven; Follow Me Boys; The Comedians; A Wedding; Hambone and Hillie; Lillian Gish (doc).

Bway inc: Camille; Nine Pine Street; Hamlet; The Star Wagon; Dear Octopus; Crime And Punishment; The Curious Savage; All The Way Home; A Passage To India; Anya; I Never Sang For My Father; Uncle Vanya; A Musical Jubilee. One-woman international tour in Lillian Gish and the Movies; international lecture tour on the art of film and tv.

TV inc: Birth Of The Movies (narr); Ladies In Retirement; Detour; The Joyous Season; The Trip To Bountiful; Grandma Moses; The Quality Of Mercy; The Corner Drugstore; The Sound And The Fury; The Day Lincoln Was Shot; Morning's At Seven; The Grass Harp; The Spiral Staircase; Arsenic And Old Lace; The Silent Years (host); Sparrow; Thin Ice; A Gift Of Music; Kennedy Center Honors 1982 (honoree); Hobson's Choice; AFI Salute To Lillian Gish.

(Honorary Oscar-1971)

GIULINI, Carlo Maria: Cond. b. Barletta, Italy, May 9, 1914. Debuted 1944 as cond Rome; asst cond Rome Radio Orchestra; 1946, principal cond; founder-principal cond orchestra of Radio Milan; 1951 debuted as opera cond at Bergamo; 1954-58 principal cond La Scala; guest cond principal orchestras of the world; mus dir L.A. Philharmonic 1968-1984. Recs inc: Marriage of Figaro; Verdi Requiem Mass; Berlioz Romeo & Juliet; Mahler Symphony One in D Major *(Grammy-*classical orch-1971); Verdi Don Carlo; Missa Solemnis; Mahler Smphony #9 in D Major *(Grammy-*classical orch-1977); Brahms Concerto for Violin in D-Major *(Grammy-*Class album of year-1978); Bruckner Symphony #9 in D Minor; Dvorak New World Symphony; Mozart Requiem *(Grammy-*choral-1980).

GLASER, Paul Michael: Act. b. Cambridge, MA, Apr 25. Films inc: Fiddler on the Roof; Butterflies Are Free; Phobia.

TV inc: Trapped Beneath the Sea; The Great Houdini; Starsky & Hutch; Wait Till Your Mother Gets Home; Princess Daisy; Jealousy; Amazons (dir); Single Bars, Single Women; Attack On Fear.

GLASS, George: Prod. b. Los Angeles, Aug 19, 1910. Former publicist. Founder member Publicists Guild, founder member Producers Guild of America. Films inc: (asso prod) The Men; Cyrano de Bergerac; Death of a Salesman; Guess Who's Coming to Dinner; The Secret of Santa Victoria; Bless the Beasts and the Children. (Co-prod) Shake Hands with the Devil; The Naked Edge; Paris Blues. (Exec prod): One Eyed Jacks.

(Died April 1, 1984).

GLASS, Ned: Act. b. Poland, Apr 1, 1906. e. CCNY. Films inc: The Bad and Beautiful; Julius Caesar; West Side Story; Experiment in Terror; Lady Sings the Blues; Charade; Save the Tiger; Street Music.

TV inc: The Phil Silvers Shows; Julia *(Emmy-*supp-1969); Bridget Loves Bernie; Goldie and the Boxer; The Soup Man.

(Died June 15, 1984)

GLASS, Ron: Act. b. Evansville, IN, Jul 10, 1945. e. U of Evansville, BA. TV inc: Beg, Borrow or Steal; Shirts and Skins; Change at 125th Street; Crash; Barney Miller; The New Odd Couple; Gus Brown & Midnight Brewster.

GLAZER, Tom: Act-Comp. b. Philadelphia, Sep 3, 1914. e. CCNY. Folk singer; NY debut, 1948, Town Hall. Film scores inc: A Face in the Crowd.

GLAZIER, Sidney: Prod. b. Philadelphia, May 29, 1918. Films inc: The Eleanor Roosevelt Story *(Oscar-*doc-1965); Take the Money and Run; The Gamblers; Quackser Fortune Has a Cousin in the Bronx; The 12 Chairs; Glen and Panda; The Night Visitor; The Only Way.

GLEASON, Jackie: Act. b. NYC, Feb 26, 1916. Started as nitery entertainer. Films inc: The Hustler; Requiem For A Heavyweight; Gigot; Soldier in the Rain; Smokey and the Bandit; Smokey and the Bandit II; The Toy; The Sting II; Smokey & the Bandit Part 3.

TV inc: The Life of Riley; The Laugh Maker; Peacock City; Cavalcade of Stars; The Jackie Gleason Show; Best of Broadway; The Honeymooners; Uncle Ed and Circumstance; The Million Dollar Incident; Laurence Olivier and Jackie Gleason as Mr. Halpern and Mr. Johnson (cable); 39th Annual Tony Awards.

Bway inc: Take Me Along *(Tony-*1960); Hellzapoppin'; Artists and Models.

GLEASON, Joanna: Act. b. Toronto, Canada, Jun 2. e. Occidental Coll. D of Monty Hall. Thea inc: I Love My Wife; As You Like It; A Midsummer Night's Dream; Hamlet.

TV inc: Hello, Larry; Why Us?; Great Day.

GLEASON, Michael: Wri-prod. b. Brooklyn, NY., Jan. 4. 1938. e. AADA. TV inc: (wri) Maverick; Laramie; It's A Man's World; My Favorite Martian; Mr. Novak; Peyton Place; Insight; Big Valley; The Survivors (& prod-co-crea); Bracken's World; Paris 7,000 (& prod-co-crea); Marcus Welby; Owen Marshall; Cade's County; Cannon; The Man and the City; McCloud (& prod); Fools, Females and Fun (& prod); Six Million Dollar Man (& prod); Force Five (& prod); The Oregon Trail (& prod); Sarah (& crea); Yesterday's Child; Rich Man, Poor Man--Book II (& exec prod); Sword of Justice (& co-crea); The Gossip Columnist; Crazy Times; Remington Steele (& exec prod-co-crea).

Films inc: (wri) Fast Charlie, The Moon Beam Rider.

GLENN, Christopher: TV news. b. NYC, Mar. 23, 1938. e. U CO. Began career with Armed Forces Broadcasting in Korea; later with WICC radio; WNEW radio; 1970, man ed Metromedia News Network; 1970, to CBS News as producer radio special events; 1976 became CBS news correspondent; 1978, co-editor 30 Minutes.

GLENN, Scott: Act. b. Pittsburgh, PA. Thea inc: Fortune and Men's Eyes; Long Day's Journey Into Night; Collision Course.

Films inc: The Baby Maker; Nashville; Cattle Annie and Little Britches; Urban Cowboy; Personal Best; More American Graffiti; Apocalypse Now; The Challenge; The Right Stuff; The Keep; The River; Wild Geese II.

TV inc: The Edge of Night; Countdown To Looking Glass (cable).

GLENVILLE, Peter: Act-Dir. b. London, England, Oct 28, 1913. e. Oxford U. Professional debut with Manchester Repertory Co, 1934; act in various prodns before dir the following plays; Point Valaine; Major Barbara; The Giaconda Smile; Crime Passionnel; The Browning Verson; Summer and Smoke; Under the Sycamore Tree; The Innocents; Letter From Paris; The Living Room; Separate Tables; Rashomon; Take Me Along; Silent Night, Lonely Night; Becket; Tovarich; Dylan; A Patriot for Me; A Bequest to the Nation; Outcry.

Films inc: (dir) The Prisoner; Term of Trial; Becket; Summer and Smoke; The Comedians; Hotel Paradiso.

GLESS, Sharon: Act. b. Los Angeles, May 31, 1943. TV inc: The Longest Night; All My Darling Daughters; My Darling Daughters' Anniversary; Switch; The Immigrants; The Scream of Eagles; The Last Convertible; Hardhat and Legs; The Kids Who Knew Too Much; Turnabout; Moviola (The Scarlett O'Hara War); Revenge of the Stepford Wives; The Miracle of Kathy Miller; House Calls; Palms; Cagney and Lacey; Hobson's Choice; The Sky's the Limit; Letting Go.

Films inc: The Star Chamber.

GLICK, Michael Schaffer: Prod-Exec. b. Brooklyn, Apr 3, 1934. e. UC Berkeley, BS. Film inc: (Prod mgr) Paradise Alley; Other Side of the Mountain II; Which Way Is Up; Domino Principle; Battle for the Planet of the Apes; Godfather Two. Other films inc: Embryo (asso prod); Devil's Rain (prod); Busting Loose (prod). Sept. 1981, sr vp prodn mgt Filmways; April 1982, VP-prodn Embassy Pictures.

GLICKMAN, Fred: Comp. b. Chicago, Sep 22, 1903. Violinist in dance bands, symph orchs; also cond own orch; has own recording, publ cos.

Songs inc: Mule Train; Little Old Band of Gold; Angel of Mine.

GLICKMAN, Joel: Prod. b. Los Angeles, Jul 29, 1930. e. UCLA, BA. Early TV work on series, documentaries, commercials. Prodn assoc, Wedding and Babies, 1958.

Films inc: Terror in the City; The Balcony; All the Way Home; Last Summer; Hamlet; Brother John; Buck and the Preacher; Trial of the Catonsville Nine.

TV inc: East Side, West Side; Mr. Broadway; N.Y.P.D.; Among the Paths to Eden; Night Terror; Angel on Horseback; Blood Feud.

GLICKSMAN, Frank: Prod-Wri. b. NYC, Jun 29, 1921. e. UCLA, BA. Story ed CBS-TV 1956-60; 20th-Fox TV, 1960-64. TV inc: (prod) 12 O'Clock High; Long Hot Summer; Custer; Medical Center (Exec prod & co-crea); Trapper John, M.D.; Hagen; Family In Blue.

(Died Jan. 19, 1984)

GLOBUS, Yoram: Prod. Films inc: Margo; Lupo; Diamonds; Operation Thunderbolt; Lemon Popsicle; The Magician of Lublin; Lemon Popsicle 2; The Apple; Schizoid; The Godsend; Dr. Heckyl and Mr Hype; The Happy Hooker Goes to Hollywood; Lemon Popsicle 3; Lady's Chatterley's Lover; Death Wish 2; Enter the Ninja; Last American Virgin; That Championship Season; Treasure of the Four Crowns (exec prod). Sapiches (Private Popsicle); Nana; The Wicked Lady; The House of Long Shadows; Hercules; Revenge of the Ninja; Hospital Massacre; Sahara; Over the Brooklyn Bridge; Love Streams; Breakin' (exec prod); making the Grade (exec prod); The Ultimate Solution of Grace Quigley; The Ambassador (exec prod); Maria's Lovers (exec prod); The Naked Face; Ordeal By Innocence (exec prod); Ninja III--The Domination (exec prod); 'I'm Almost Not Crazy'..John Cassavetes, The Man And His Work (doc-int); Bolero (exec prod); Exterminator 2 (exec prod); Edut Me' Oness (Forced Witness);Missing In Action; Sword Of The Valiant; Breakin' 2 Electric Bugaloo; Missing In Action 2--The Beginning; Mata Hari (exec prod); Thunder Alley (exec prod); Deja Vu; Rappin'; Hot Resort; Up Your Anchor; Lifeforce.

GLOUNER, Richard C: Cin. b. Los Angeles, Aug 12, 1931. e. LA City Coll; Glendale Coll. Films inc: Payday; Gumball Rally.

TV inc: Cry for Help; Louis Armstrong; Bloodsport; Savage Swarm; Sweet Hostage; Columbo (Emmy-1974, 1975); Bud and Lou; A Cry For Love; Peter and Paul; Scruples; Marion Rose White; Farrell For the People; Cocaine and Blue Eyes; Wizards and Warriors; Goodnight, Beantown; Special Athletes; The Best of Times; Summer.

GLOVER, John: Act. b. Kingston, NY. Aug. 7, 1944. e. Towson State College. Thea inc: A Scent of Flowers; Subject to Fits; The House of Blue Leaves; The Selling of the President; The Great God Brown; Don Juan; The Visit; Chemin de Fer; Holiday; The Importance of Being Earnest; Hamlet; Frankenstein; Whodunnit; Digby.

Films inc: Julia; Annie Hall; Somebody Killed Her Husband; The Last Embrace; Melvin and Howard; Mountain Men; The Incredible Shrinking Woman; A Little Sex; The Evil That Men Do; A Flash Of Green.

TV inc: Rage of Angels; George Washington; Ernie Kovacs--Between the Laughter.

GLOVER, Julian: Act. b. London, Mar. 27, 1935. e. RADA. Thea inc: The Lower Depths; Naked; The Ides of March; The Constant Couple; The Man of Mode; Subject to Fits; We Bombed in New Haven; Antony and Cleopatra; Gaslight; Sherlock's Last Case; The Way of the World; Otherwise Engaged; Jumpers; Henry VI.

Films inc: Tom Jones; The Alphabet Murders; Time Lost and Time Remembered; The Magus; Nicholas and Alexandra; The Internecine Project; Juggernaut; For Your Eyes Only; Heat and Dust.

TV inc: An Age of Kings; Ivanhoe; Q.E.D.; Kim.

GLYNN, Carlin: Act. b. Feb. 19, 1940. Studied with Stella Adler and Lee Strasberg. Thea inc: Waltz of the Toreadors; The Best Little Whorehouse in Texas (& London)(Tony-featured-1979);Winterplay; Alterations.

Films inc: Three Days Of the Condor; Continental Divide; Sixteen Candles.

GOBEL, George: Act. b. Chicago, May 20, 1919. Played with country western group on radio. Appeared in niteries.

TV inc: The George Gobel Show (Emmy-1954); Better Late Than Never; A Country Christmas; The Incredible Book Escape (voice); Harper Valley PTA; Bob Hope's Stand Up and Cheer for the National Football League's 60th Year; The Invisible Woman; The Fantastic World of D.C. Collins.

Bway, Three Men on a Horse (musical).

Films inc: Rabbit Test; Ellie.

GODARD, Jean-Luc: Wri-Dir. b. Paris, Dec 3, 1930. Films inc: A Bout de Souffle; Une Femme Est Une Femme; Vivre Sa Vie; Le Petit Soldat; Les Carabiniera; Bande a Part; Une Femme Mariee; A Little Godard; Pierrot Le Fou; Made in USA; Weekend; Tout va Bien; Passion; Prenom Carmen (First Name Carmen) (& Prod); Room 666 (doc-int).

GODDARD, Paulette: Act. b. Great Neck, NY, Jun 3, 1911. Bway inc: Rio Rita. On screen from 1931.

Films inc: City Lights; Roman Scandals; Modern Times; The Cat and the Canary; Northwest Mounted Police; The Great Dictator; So Proudly We Hail; Hold Back the Dawn; Reap the Wild Wind; I Love a Soldier; Standing Room Only; Kitty; Unconquered; Anna Lucasta; Sins of Jezebel; Time of Indifference.

GODFREY, Arthur: Act. b. NYC, Aug 31, 1903. News commentator; act-wri-narr-on radio, TV.

Films inc: The Glass Bottom Boat; Where Angels Go. . .Trouble Follows; Four for Texas; Shenanigans.

TV inc: The Arthur Godfrey Show (also radio); The Arthur Godfrey Talent Show; Flatbed Annie and Sweetie Pie-Lady Truckers.

(Died Mar 16, 1983).

GODFREY, Bob: Prod. b. England, 1921. Animated shorts inc: The Do It Yourself Cartoon Kit; The Plain Man's Guide to Advertising; Kama Sutra Rides Again; Great (Oscar-1975).

GOETZ, Ruth Goodman: Wri. b. Philadelphia, Jan 11, 1918. Formerly a story edtr. Plays (with late husband Augustus Goetz) inc: Franklin Street; One Man Show; The Heiress The Immoralist; The Hidden River; also Here Today (with George Oppenheimer); adapted Madly in Love from the French of Andre Broussin.

Films inc: (with husband) The Heiress; Sister Carrie; Rhapsody; Trapeze; Stage Struck.

GOFF, Ivan: Wri. b. Australia, 1910. Usually in collab with Ben Roberts. Films inc: My Love Came Back; White Heat; Captain Horatio Hornblower; Come Fill the Cup; King of the Khyber Rifles; Green Fire; Serenade; Man of a Thousand Faces; Shake Hands with the Devil; Portrait in Black; The Legend of the Lone Ranger.

TV inc: The Rogues; Charlie's Angels; Time Express; Nero Wolfe (exec prod).

GOLAN, Menahem: Prod-Dir. b. Palestine (now Israel) 1929. e. NYU. Worked with Roger Corman before returning to Israel to launch career. Films inc: El Dorado (dir only); Eight Against One; Dalia and the Sailors; Sallah (prod only); Trunk to Cairo (dir only); Tevye and His Seven Daughters; What's Good for the Goose (dir only); Eagles Attack At Dawn; Margo; Lupo; Highway Queen; I Love You Rosa (prod only); Escape to the Sun; Kazablan; The House on Chelouche Street (prod only); Lepke; Diamonds; Operation Thunderbolt; The Uranium Conspiracy; Lemon Popsicle (prod); The Magician of Lublin (dir); The Apple (& wri); Lemon Popsicle 2 (prod); The Godsend (prod); Schizoid (prod); Dr. Heckyl and Mr. Hype (prod); The Happy Hooker Goes to Hollywood (prod); Body and Soul (prod); Lemon Popsicle 3 (prod); Lady Chatterley's Lover (prod); Death Wish 2 (prod); Enter the Ninja (dir); Last American Virgin (prod); That Championship Season; Treasure of the Four Crowns (exec prod); Sapiches (Private Popsicle) (prod); Nana (prod); The Wicked Lady (prod); The House of Long Shadows (prod); Hercules (prod); Revenge of the Ninja (prod); Hospital Massacre (prod); Sahara (prod); Over the Brooklyn Bridge; Love Streams (prod); Breakin' (exec prod); Making the Grade (exec prod); The Ultimate Solution of Grace Quigley (prod); The Ambassador (exec prod); Maria's Lovers (exec prod); The Naked Face (prod); Ordeal By Innocence (exec prod); Ninja III--The Domination (exec prod); 'I'm Almost Not Crazy..' John Cassavetes, The Man And His Work (Doc-int); Bolero (exec prod); Exterminator 2 (exec prod); Edut Me' Oress (Forced Witness) (prod); Missing In Action (prod); Sword Of The Valiant (prod); Breakin' 2 Electric Bugaloo; Missing In Action 2--The Beginning; Mata Hari (exec prod); Thunder Alley (exec prod); Deja Vu; Rappin'; Hot Resort; Up Your Anchor; Lifeforce.

GOLD, Ernest: Comp-Cond. b. Vienna, Jul 13, 1921. Film scores inc: Too Much, Too Soon; On the Beach; Inherit the Wind; Exodus (Oscar-1960); Judgment at Nuremberg; A Child Is Waiting; It's a Mad, Mad, Mad, Mad World; Ship of Fools; The Secret of Santa Vittoria; Fun With Dick and Jane; Cross of Iron; Good Luck, Miss Wyckoff; Tom Horn; Safari 3000.
    TV inc: Wallenberg--A Hero's Story.
    Songs inc: On the Beach; It's a Mad, Mad, Mad, Mad World. (Grammys-(2)-song of year & soundtrack-1960).

GOLD, Missy: Act. b. Great Falls, MT, Jul 14, 1970.
    TV inc: How The West Was Won, Captains and Kings; Nancy Drew; Benson; Twirl.

GOLD, Tracey: Act. b. May 16, 1969. TV inc: Jennifer-A Woman's Story; The Dark Secrets of Harvest Home; The Child Stealers; Shirley; I Think I'm Having A Baby; A Few Days In Weasel Creek; Goliath Awaits; Beyond Witch Mountain; Another Woman's Child; Thursday's Child; Who Will Love My Children?; Goodnight, Beantown; A Reason To Live; Lots Of Luck.
    Films inc: Shoot the Moon.

GOLDBERG, Fred: Exec. b. NYC, Aug 26, 1921. e. Pace Coll. Exec asst to dir pub, adv, UA, 1958; exec dir pub, adv, exp 1961; named vp, 1962; sr vp, 1972; sr vp, dir of mktg, 1977; 1978, sr vp ad-pub-prom, Col; 1981 resd but continued as consultant; Sept 1981, Ad VP Orion Pictures; Oct 1982, resd but continued as consultant.

GOLDBERG, Gary David: Prod. b. Brooklyn, NY, Jun 25, 1944. TV inc: Bob Newhart Show (wri); Tony Randall Show (1976 story ed; 1978 co-prod); Lou Grant (co-prod) (Emmy-1979); The Last Resort (prod-crea-wri); Making the Grade (exec prod-wri-crea); Family Ties (exec prod-crea); Sara (exec prod).

GOLDBERG, Leonard: Prod. b. NYC, Jan 24, 1934. e. U PA, BS. Joined research dept CBS 1956; to NBC research 1957 as supv special proj; 1961 BBD&O agcy in chg daytime tv; 1963 mgr pgm dvlpt ABC; 1964 vp daytime pgm & dir pgm dvlpt; 1965 vp network pgms; 1966 vp chg prodn Screen Gems; 1969 teamed with Aaron Spelling in Spelling- Goldberg Prodns; 1972 Leonard Goldberg Prodns; 1978 Goldberg-Weintraub Prodns.
    TV inc: The Rookies; People's Choice; Charley's Angels; Starsky and Hutch; Beach Patrol; Hart to Hart; When the Whistle Blows; Blue Jeans; Fantasies; T.J. Hooker; Paper Dolls; Gavilan; Deadly Lesson; Something About Amelia (Emmy-Exec prod-1984); Sins of the Past; Paper Dolls.
    Films inc: All Night Long; WarGames.

GOLDBLUM, Jeff: Act. b. Pittsburgh, PA. e. Neighborhood Playhouse. Bway inc: Two Gentlemen of Verona; El Grande de Coca Cola; The Moony Shapiro Songbook.
    Films inc: Death Wish; Nashville; Next Stop, Greenwich Village; Annie Hall; Between the Lines; Thank God It's Friday; Invasion of the Body Snatchers; Threshold; The Big Chill; The Right Stuff; The Adventures Of Buckaroo Banzai--Across The 8th Dimension; Into The Night.
    TV inc: Ten Speed and Brownshoe; The Legend of Sleepy Hollow; Rehearsal for Murder; The New Show; Popular Neurotics; Ernie

Kovacs--Between the Laughter.

GOLDEMBERG, Rose Leiman: Wri. b. NYC. e. Brooklyn College, BA; OH State U, MA; Plays inc: Gandhiji; The Merry War; The Rabinowitz Gambit; Love One Another; Letters Home.
    TV inc: Out Of Wedlock; Classified Love; Born Beautiful; Victory Of the Heart; Mother and Daughter--The Loving War; Memoirs Of an Ex-Prom Queen; Life In the Fast Lane; The Burning Bed; Growing Pains; The Medicine Men; Land Of Hope; A Celebration of Women; Florence Nightingale.
    Films inc: Doubles.

GOLDENBERG, Billy: Comp. b. NYC, Feb 10, 1936. e. Columbia Coll, BA. Films inc: Red Sky At Morning; Play It Again, Sam; Up The Sandbox; The Grasshopper; The Domino Principle; Scavenger Hunt; The Last of Sheila; Reuben, Reuben.
    TV inc: Queen of the Stardust Ballroom; The Rebel--Benjamin Franklin (Emmy-1975); Duel; The Neon Ceiling; The Miracle Worker; The Glass House; The Incredible Machine; Helter Skelter; An Evening with Diana Ross (Emmy-spec mat-1977); King (Emmy-1978); All God's Children; The Love Tapes; Haywire; The Women's Room; Act of Love; A Perfect Match; Father Figure; The Diary of Anne Frank. Crisis At Central High; Dial "M" For Murder; The Best Little Girl In The World; Sidney Shorr; Callie and Son; Jacqueline Bouvier Kennedy; The Ordeal of Bill Carney; Washington Mistress; Marion Rose White; The Gift of Life; A Question of Honor; Rehearsal For Murder; Massarati and the Brain; Country Gold; Another Woman's Child; Confessions of A Married Man; Bare Essence (song); Rage of Angels (Emmy-1983); Will There Really Be A Morning?; Intimate Agony; Prototype; Why Me?; Sentimental Journey; His Mistress; For Love Or Money; The Sun Also Rises; Obsessed With A Married Woman; The Atlanta Child Murders; Guilty Conscience.
    TV themes inc: Kojak; Rhoda; Alias Smith and Jones; Banacek; Columbo; Harry-O; The Sixth Sense; Delvecchio; Crisis At Central High.

GOLDENSON, Leonard: Exec. b. Scottdale, PA, Dec 7, 1905. e. Harvard Coll, BA; Harvard Law School, LLB. Counsel in reorg. Paramount theatres in New England, 1933-37. Appointed asst to vp Paramount in charge theatre operations, 1937. Became head of theatre operations, 1938; elected pres. Paramount Theatre Service Corp., vp Paramount Theatres Inc., 1938. Then pres, CEO, director United Paramount Theatres, Inc. and American Broadcasting Companies which merged into American Broadcasting Companies, Inc. Chairman of the Board and CEO of ABC since 1972.

GOLDING, David: Pub. b. Oct. 20, 1915. e. U of WI, BA. Entered industry as publicist Samuel Goldwyn; later with Sir Alexander Korda; pub dir 20th-Fox, NY; Hecht-Hill- Lancaster; Otto Preminger; Universal; April 1985, cnslt CBS Prodns.

GOLDMAN, Bo: Wri. Films inc: One Flew Over the Cuckoo's Nest (Oscar-1975); The Rose; Melvin and Howard (Oscar-1980); Shoot the Moon.

GOLDMAN, James: Wri. Plays inc: Blood, Sweat and Stanley Poole; They Might Be Giants; The Lion in Winter; Family Affair; Follies; Waldorf; Myself as Witness.
    Films inc: The Lion in Winter (Oscar-1968); They Might Be Giants; Nicholas and Alexandra; Robin and Marian.
    TV inc: Evening Primrose; Oliver Twist; Anna Karenina.

GOLDMAN, William: Wri. b. Chicago, 1931. e. Oberlin Coll, BA; Columbia U, MA. Films inc: Soldier in the Rain; Masquerade; Harper; No Way to Treat a Lady; Butch Cassidy and the Sundance Kid (Oscar-story-sp-1969); The Hot Rock; The Great Waldo Pepper; All the President's Men (Oscar-sp-1976); A Bridge Too Far; Magic; Butch and Sundance-The Early Days.
    TV inc: Mr Horn.

GOLDONI, Lelia: Act. b. NYC. Films inc: Shadows; Day of the Locust; Alice Doesn't Live Here Anymore; Baby Blue Marine; Bloodbrothers; Invasion Of The Body Snatchers; Choices; The Unseen; Rainy Day Friends.
    TV inc: Espionage; Secret Agent; Attorneys At Law; The Spider's Web; Blackmail; The Dream Divided; Scott and Zelda Fitzgerald; A

Kiss is Just a Kiss; Sister Aimee; Scruples; Mistress of Paradise; Anatomy of an Illness; Victims For Victims--The Theresa Saldana Story.

GOLDSBORO, Bobby: Mus. b. Marianne, FL. Jan. 18, 1941. Recording artist. TV inc: The Bobby Goldsboro Show.

GOLDSMITH, Clio: Act. b. France, 1957. Films inc: La Cicala; Plein Sud (Heading South); Le Grand Arrow; Le Cadeau (The Gift); L'Etincelle (Tug of Love); E La Vita Continua (And Life Goes On).

GOLDSMITH, David: Prod. b. Los Angeles, Jul 22, 1948. e. USC, BS; Southwestern U School of Law. Member The Thomas Group (rock band) while in college; 1970 prodn asst T&L Prodns, Paramount TV; 1972, mgr pgm dvlpmt Screen Gems; 1974, dir films for tv & pgm dvlpmt MGM TV; 1977 vp pgm devlpmt Bennett-Katleman Prodns; 1978, vp dramatic pgms, Paramount TV; 1980 joined Charles Fries Prodns to develop projects under David Goldsmith Prodns banner in ass'n with Fries.
TV inc: (Exec prod) Mind Over Murder; Comedy Company; Deadly Tower; The Ambush Murders; Cocaine--One Man's Seduction.

GOLDSMITH, Jerry: Comp. b. Los Angeles, 1930. e. LA City Coll. Film scores inc: Lonely Are The Brave; Freud; Lilies of the Field; The Blue Max; Seven Days in May; Von Ryan's Express; A Patch of Blue; The Sand Pebbles; Planet of the Apes; Patton; Papillon; Mephisto Waltz; The Wild Rovers; Chinatown; The Wind and the Lion; Logan's Run; Islands in the Stream; MacArthur; The Omen *(Oscar-1976)*; The Cassandra Crossing; The Boys From Brazil; Coma; Damien-Omen II; Capricorn One; Magic; The Swarm; The Great Train Robbery; Alien; Players; Star Trek-The Motion Picture; Caboblanco; The Final Conflict; Inchon; Outland; Raggedy Man; The Challenge; Poltergeist; The Secret of NIMH; First Blood; The Salamander; Psycho II; Twilight Zone--The Movie; The Lonely Guy; Gremlins; Supergirl; Runaway; Baby; Rambo--First Blood Part II.
TV inc: Climax; Playhouse 90; The Man From UNCLE; Dr. Kildare; Gunsmoke; The Red Pony *(Emmy-1973)*; QB-VII *(Emmy-1975)*; The Waltons; Babe *(Emmy-1976)*; Masada *(Emmy-1981)*.

GOLDSMITH, Lester: Prod. b. Chicago, IL, Mar 2, 1934. e. U of IL, BSJ; Northwestern U, MA. VP Radio-TV Edward Weiss Adv Agency; VP Paramount; Prod UPA Pictures.
TV inc: Watch Mr Wizard.
Films inc: Happy Birthday, Wanda June; The Passage.
Bway inc: Happy Birthday, Wanda June.

GOLDSMITH, Martin M: Wri. b. NYC, Nov 6, 1913. Films inc: Detour; Blind Spot; The Narrow Margin; Mission Over Korea; Overland Pacific; Hell's Island.

GOLDSTEIN, Milton: Exec. b. NYC, Aug 1, 1926. e. NYU. Started as Slsmn, Par; later Sls VP Samuel Bronston Prodns; Foreign Sls Mgr, Par; Exec vp worldwide dist Cinerama, 1967-68,; Cinema Center Films, 1969-73, exec vp, then P; 1973-74 vp theatrical dist worldwide, Metromedia; 1974-75 p Boasberg-Goldstein; 1975-77, exec vp Avco Embassy Pictures; 1977, exec vp Mel Simon Productions; 1981, Chmn & COO Simon-Reeves-Landsburg Productions. Films inc: Porky's Revenge (exec prod).

GOLDSTONE, James: Dir. b. Los Angeles, Jun 8, 1931. e. Dartmouth, BA TV inc: Star Trek; Ironside; Studs Lonigan; Kent State *(Emmy-1981)*; Charles and Diana--A Royal Love Story; Rita Hayworth--the Love Goddess; Sentimental Journey; The Sun Also Rises.
Films inc: Jigsaw; Man Called Gannon; The Gang That Couldn't Shoot Straight; Swashbuckler; Rollercoaster; When Time Ran Out.

GOLDSTONE, Richard: Prod. b. NYC, Jul 14, 1912. e. UCLA, BA. Films inc: The Outsider; Inside Straight; The Tall Target; The Devil Makes Three; Cinerama's South Seas Adventure; No Man Is an Island (& sp-dir); Rage; The Sergeant; The Babymaker.
TV inc: Adventures in Paradise; Combat; Peyton Place.

GOLDWURM, Jean: Exec. b. Bucharest, Romania, Feb 21, 1893. e. U of Vienna. Founder-pres of Times Film Corp., which has been importing European films to the U.S. since 1945. Ownr-opr of the Little

Carnegie and World Theatres. Began import business with To Live In Peace; has since imported Two Cents Worth of Hope; Forbidden Games; One Summmer of Happiness and some 200 other films. Founder of the International Film Importers and Distributors Association of America.

GOLDWYN, Samuel, Jr: Prod-Dir. b. Los Angeles, Sep 7, 1926. e. U of VA. U.S. Army, 1944. After war, writer, assoc. prod. J. Arthur Rank Org. Prod. Gathering Storm London stage. Returned to US, 1948; prod. Adventure TV series for CBS; The Unexpected. Formed Formosa Prod. Inc., 1955.
Films inc: Man With the Gun; The Sharkfighters; The Proud Rebel; The Adventures of Huckleberry Finn; The Young Lovers; Cotton Comes to Harlem; Come Back Charleston Blue; The Golden Seal.

GOLITZEN, Alexander: Art Dir (ret). b. Moscow, Russia, Feb 28, 1907. Films inc: Phantom of the Opera; Spartacus *(Oscar-1960)*; To Kill a Mockingbird *(Oscar-1962)*.

GOLOD, Jerry: Exec. b. NY. e. CCNY. Joined CBS in 1975 as an exec in the children's programming area; Jan. 1979, moved to NBC; April 1979, National Program Dir, NBC Entertainment; 1980, vp QM Prodns. TV inc: Tales from the Darkside (exec prod).

GOMBERG, Sy: Wri-Prod. b. NYC, Aug 19, 1918. e. USC, BA. Films inc: When Willie Comes Marching Home; Summer Stock; Toast of New Orleans; Because You're Mine; Bloodhounds of Broadway; Joe Butterfly; The Wild and the Innocent; Three Warriors.
TV inc: The Law and Mr. Jones; Accidental Family; Good Heavens; Margaret Jean; Bender; High Ice; The Ghosts of Buxley Hall. World Premiere Theatre; The Wonderful World of Disney; The Snatching of Little Freddie and

GONZALEZ-GONZALEZ, Pedro: Act. b. Aguilares, TX, Dec 21, 1926. Films inc: Wings of the Hawk; Ring of Fear; The High and the Mighty; Strange Lady in Town; The Sheepman; Rio Bravo; The Adventures of Bullwhip Griffin; The Love Bug; Support Your Local Gunfighter; Dreamer; There Goes The Bride; Lust In The Dust.
TV inc: O'Henry Stories; Hostile Guns.

GOODEVE, Grant: Act. b. Middlebury, CT, Jul 6, 1952.
Films inc: All the King's Horses.
TV inc: Eight Is Enough; Hot Rod; A Last Cry for Help; Aloha Paradise; High Powder; Insight/Leave Me Alone, God; Off Sides.

GOODFRIED, Bob: Pub. b. NYC, Apr 8, 1913. Started with Skouras Theatres. To west coast 1945 as PA mgr Columbia Pictures; vp in charge of studio and West Coast publicity, Paramount pictures, 1971; became PR Consultant for Paramount 1980.
(Died Feb 2, 1983).

GOODMAN, Benny: Mus. b. Chicago, May 30, 1909. Played in Broadway theater orchestras. Organized own band 1933. Appeared in hotels, ballrooms, night clubs.
Films inc: Hollywood Hotel; The Big Broadcast of 1937; Stage Door Canteen; The Powers Girl; Sweet and Low Down; A Song Is Born; Fantasma D'Amore (Fantasy of Love) (cond).
TV inc: Grammy Hall Of Fame; The Kennedy Center Honors 1982 (honoree).

GOODMAN, David Zelag: Wri. Films inc: Monte Walsh; Lovers and Other Strangers; The Straw Dogs; Man on the Swing; Farewell My Lovely; Logan's Run; March Or Die; The Eyes of Laura Mars; Fighting Back; Man, Woman and Child.
TV inc: Freedom Road.

GOODMAN, Dody: Act. b. Columbus, OH, 1929. Joined ballet companies of the Radio City Music Hall, the Metropolitan Opera. Danced on Broadway in High Button Shoes, Call Me Madam, Wonderful Town. Started career as comic on TV, nightclubs, off-Broadway revues.
Films inc: Bedtime Story; Women, Women, Women!; Grease; Grease 2; Max Dugan Returns; Splash.
TV inc: Jack Paar Show; Mary Hartman, Mary Hartman; Search for Tomorrow; Fernwood Tonight; The Treasure of Alpheus T. Winterborn.
Bway inc: Period of Adjustment; My Daughter, Your Son; Rainy

Day in Newark; Valentine Magic on Love Island.

GOODMAN, Julian: Exec. b. Glasgow, KY, May 2, 1922. e. Western KY U, BA. Joined NBC as a news wri for WRC, Washington 1945. Appointed M, News, Special Events, NBC TV, 1951; in 1959, assigned to NBC News, NY, as dir News Public Affairs; appointed vp, NBC News, Jan 1961, and exec vp, Oct 1965. Became chief admin officer NBC with title sr exec vp, Dec 1965. Elected to NBC Board of Dir, Jan 1966; P, NBC March 1, 1966. ChmnB, April 1974.

Retired May 31, 1979.

GOODRICH, Frances: Wri. b. 1901. Usually in collab with husband, Albert Hackett.

Films inc: The Thin Man; After the Thin Man; Naughty Marietta; Another Thin Man; The Hitler Gang; It's A Wonderful Life; Summer Holiday; Father of the Bride; Seven Brides for Seven Brothers; The Diary of Anne Frank.

Bway: The Diary of Anne Frank (Tony-1956).

TV inc: The Diary of Anne Frank.

(Died Jan. 29, 1984)

GOODSON, Mark: TV Prod. b. Sacramento, CA, Jan 24, 1915. e. U of CA, AB. Anncer, newscaster, dir. radio, KFRC, San Francisco, 1938-41. Anncer dir. NY, 1941-43. Dir. for ABC, 1943. Formed Goodson-Todman Prodns., 1946.

Originated radio shows: Winner Take All; Stop the Music; Hit the Jackpot. Creator-prod of TV game shows: What's My Line (Emmy-1952); News to Me; The Name's the Same; I've Got a Secret; To Tell the Truth; The Price Is Right; Password; Match Game;Family Feud.

TV films: The Web; The Rebel; Branded.

GOODWIN, Ron: Comp-Arr-Cond. b. Plymouth, England, 1930. Films inc: I'm All Right, Jack; The Trials of Oscar Wilde; Murder She Said; 633 Squadron; Operation Crossbow; Those Magnificent Men in Their Flying Machines; The Alphabet Murders; Where Eagles Dare; Battle of Britain; Frenzy; The Happy Prince; One of Our Dinosaurs is Missing; Escape From the Dark; Force 10 From Navarone.

GOORWITZ, Allen (sometimes billed as Allen Garfield): Act. b. Newark, NJ, Nov 22, 1939. Films inc: (as Garfield) Orgy Girls; Greetings; Putney Swope; The Owl and the Pussycat; Roommates; The Commitment; Bananas; Cry Uncle; Deadhead Miles; The Organization; The Candidate; Slither; Busting; The Conversation; The Front Page; Nashville; Paco; Gable and Lombard; Skateboard; Irreconcilable Differences; Teachers; Nev er Again; The Cotton Club. (As Goorwitz) The Brink's Job; The Stunt Man; One Trick Pony; Continental Divide; One From the Heart; Der Stand der dinge (The State of Things); The Black Stallion Returns; Get Crazy.

TV inc: Leave 'Em Laughing; Lottery!

GORDON, Alex: Prod. b. London, Sep 8, 1922. Films inc: Lawless Rider; Bride of the Monster; Apache Woman; The Day the World Ended; Oklahoma Woman; Shake, Rattle and Rock; Flesh and the Spur; Voodoo Woman; Dragstrip Girl; Submarine Seahawk; Atomic Submarine; The Underwater City; The Bounty Killer; Requiem for a Gunfighter.

TV inc: Movie of the Year; Golden Century; Great Moments in Motion Pictures.

GORDON, Bert: Prod-Dir-Wri. b. Kenosha, WI, 1922. e. U of WI. Films inc: The Beginning of the End; The Amazing Colossal Man; Cyclops; The Boy and the Pirates; The Magic Sword; Picture Mommy Dead; Necromancy; The Mad Bomber; The Police Connection; The Food of the Gods; Empire of the Ants.

GORDON, Don: Act. b. Los Angeles, Nov 23, 1926. Films inc: Bullitt; WUSA; Cannon for Cordoba; The Gamblers; The Last Movie; Fuzz; Slaughter; ZPG; The Mack; Papillon; The Education of Sonny Carson; Out of The Blue; The Final Conflict; The Beast Within.

TV inc: Street Killing; The Sparrow; The Contender; Confessions of A Married Man.

GORDON, Gale (Charles T Aldrich Jr): Act. b. NYC, Feb 2, 1906. Films inc: The Pilgrimage Play; Rally 'Round The Flag, Boys; All in a Night's Work; Don't Give up the Ship; Visit To a Small Planet; All Hands on Deck.

TV inc: Dennis the Menace; Our Miss Brooks; Here's Lucy; The Lucy Show; Lucy Moves to NBC.

GORDON, Gerald: Act. b. Chicago, Jul 12. e. Northwestern U. TV inc: The Doctors; First Ladies Diaries--Rachel Jackson (Emmy-1976); General Hospital; Force Five; High Cliff Manor; 1982 retd to General Hospital.

Thea inc: Compulsion (Bway); Three Penny Opera; Nature of the Crime; Me Candido; Independence Night; Don't Get Married, We Need You; Big Time Boogy.

Films inc: Mirage; Forty Pounds of Trouble; One Man's Way.

GORDON, Hayes: Act-Dir-Prod. b. Boston, MA, Feb 25, 1920. Studied for stage under Lee Strasberg, Sandy Meisner.

Bway (act) inc: Oklahoma!; Winged Victory; Show Boat; Brigadoon; Sleepy Hollow; Small Wonder; Along Fifth Avenue; went to Australia 1952 to star in Kiss Me Kate; Annie Get Your Gun; Kismet; founded Ensemble Theatre, Sydney, 1958, has since prod more than 30 plays.

TV (US) inc: Hayes Gordon Presents; Potted Musicals; The Fashion Story. (Australia) Medico; The Late Show; The Dawn Lake Show.

Films inc: (Act) Winged Victory; Stage Door Canteen; The Return of Captain Invincible.

GORDON, Jack: Exec. b. NYC, Mar. 13, 1929. e. UCLA. S of the late Mack Gordon. Worked as tv prodn asst before Army service in Korea. Joined MGM in sales div, 1953; dir non-thea div 1956; VP MGM Int'l, 1973; exec VP MGM Int'l, 1979; named sr vp MGM/UA Int'l Motion Picture Distribution; July, 1983, P MGM/UA Int'l Motion Picture Distribution.

GORDON, Keith: Act. b. Bronx, NY., 1961. Thea inc: A Traveling Companion; Gimme Shelter; Richard III (Bway); Sunday Runner in the Rain; Album; Back to Back; The Buddy System; Third Street.

Films inc: Jaws 2; All That Jazz; Home Movies; Dressed to Kill; Christine.

TV inc: Studs Lonigan; Kent State; My Palikari; Single Bars, Single Woman.

GORDON, Lawrence: Prod. b. Belzoni, MS. e. Tulane. Exec with Bob Banner Associates; joined ABC TV as head West Coast Talent Dvlpmnt; vp Screen Gems; vp chg wldwde prodn AIP; left to form own company; July, 1984, P 20th Century Fox Prodns; Sept. 1984, P & COO after resignation of Norman Levy.

TV inc: Burke's Law (asso prod-wri); Nightengales; Stunts Unlimited; The Renegades (exec prod); Matt Houston (exec prod); Lone Star (exec prod); Just Our Luck (crea & exec prod).

Films inc: Dillinger (exec prod); Heavy Traffic; Hard Times; Rolling Thunder; The Driver; The End; Hooper; Xanadu; Paternity; Jekyll and Hyde--Together Again; 48 Hours; Streets of Fire; The Streets (exec prod); Brewster's Millions.

GORDON, Leo: Act-Wri. b. Dec 2, 1922. Films inc: China Venture; Riot in Cell Block 11; Seven Angry Men; The Man Who Knew Too Much; Cry Baby Killer (& sp); The Big Operator; The Stranger; The Terror (& sp); The Haunted Palace; Beau Geste; Tobruk (& sp); The St. Valentine's Day Massacre; You Can't Win 'Em All; Savage Dawn.

TV inc: (Act) Directors Playhouse; Playhouse 90; The Untouchables; Rage. (Wri) Adam 12, Bonanza; Maverick; Black Sheep Squadron; Little House on the Prairie.

GORDON, Michael: Dir. b. Baltimore, Sep, 1909. e. Johns Hopkins U, BA; Yale, MFA. Films inc: Boston Blackie Goes Hollywood; Underground Agent; One Dangerous Night; Texas Across The River; Pillow Talk; Move Over Darling.

Bway inc: The Tender Trap; Deadfall; The Lovers.

GORDON, Richard: Prod. b. London, England, Dec. 14, 1925. e. U of London. b of Alex Gordon. Originally magazine wri-publicist, formed indie prodn company 1949. Films inc: The Counterfeit Plan; The Haunted Strangler; Fiend Without a Face; The Secret Man; First Man into Space; Corridors of Blood; Devil Doll; Curse of Simba; The Projected Man; Naked Evil; Island of Terror; Tales of the Bizarre; Tower of Evil; Horror Hospital; The Cat and the Canary; Inseminoid (Horror Planet).

GORDON, Ruth (nee Jones): Act-Wri. b. Wollaston, MA, Oct 30, 1896. e. AADA. W of Garson Kanin. Stage debut, 1915, Peter Pan. Films inc: (act) Abe Lincoln in Illinois; Two Faced Woman; Edge of Darkness; Inside Daisy Clover; Whatever Happened to Aunt Alice?; Rosemary's Baby (Oscar-supp-1968); Where's Poppa?; Harold and Maude; The Big Bus; Every Which Way But Loose; Boardwalk; My Bodyguard; Any Which Way You Can; Jimmy The Kid. (Wri): A Double Life; Adam's Rib; Pat and Mike; The Marrying Kind; Delta Pi.

Bway: A Doll's House; Ethan Frome; Three Cornered Moon; Saturday's Children; The Matchmaker; (also London, Berlin); My Mother, My Father and Me; Mrs Warren's Profession; Over 21 (& wri); Years Ago (& wri); Leading Lady (& wri).

TV inc: Taxi (Emmy-1979); Hardhat and Legs (wri); Perfect Gentlemen; Natalie--A Tribute To A Very Special Lady; Don't Go To Sleep; The Secret World Of The Very Young.

GORDY, Berry: Exec. b. Nov. 28, 1929. Founded Motown record co in 1961; expanded into mus publishing, personal mgt, recording studios, film, TV; now bd chmn Motown Industries. Films inc: Lady Sings the Blues (prod); Mahogony (dir); Almost Summer; The Last Dragon (exec prod).

TV inc: Scott Joplin, King of Ragtime.

GORETTA, Claude: Dir. b. Geneva, Italy, Jun 23, 1929. e. U of Geneva; British Film Inst. Films inc: The Madman; The Wedding Day; The Invitation; The Wonderful Crook; The Lace Maker; The Provincial (& sp); La mort de Mario Ricci (The Death of Mario Ricci) (& wri).

GORING, Marius: Act. b. Newport, Isle of Wight, May 23, 1912. e. Cambridge. Films inc: Consider Your Verdict; Rembrandt; The Case of the Frightened Lady; A Matter of Life and Death; The Red Shoes; Mr Perrin and Mr Traill; So Little Time; Ill Met by Moonlight; Exodus; Up From the Beach; Girl on a Motorcycle; Subterfuge; First Love; Zeppelin; The Little Girl in Blue Velvet.

TV inc: Man in a Suitcase; The Scarlet Pimpernel; The Expert; Edward and Mrs Simpson; Levkas Man; Cymbeline.

GORMAN, Cliff: Act. b. NYC, Oct 13. e. UCLA; U of NM; NYU. Stage debut 1965, Hogan's Goat. Films inc: Justine; Boys in the Band; Cops and Robbers; Rosebud; An Unmarried Woman; Night of the Juggler; Angel.

TV inc: Paradise Lost; Class of '63; The Bunker; Cocaine and Blue Eyes.

Bway inc: Ergo; Lenny (Tony-1971).

GORME, Eydie: Act. b. NYC, Aug 16, 1931. In niteries, TV. Usually performs with husband, Steve Lawrence. TV inc: Steve and Eydie Celebrate Irving Berlin (Emmy-1979); The Bob Hope 30th Anniversary Special; Live From Studio 8H--100 Years of America's Popular Music.

(Grammys-vocal group-1960; Vocal, female-1966).

GOROG, Laszlo: Wri. b. Hungary, Sep 30, 1903. Films inc: Tales of Manhattan; The Affairs of Susan; She Wouldn't Say Yes; The Land Unknown.

TV inc: The Roaring Twenties; 77 Sunset Strip; Maverick.

GORSHIN, Frank: Act. b. Pittsburgh, PA, 1935. Films inc: The True Story of Jesse James; Warlock; Studs Lonigan; Ring of Fire; The George Raft Story; Batman; Den Tuechtigen Gehort Die Welt (The Uppercrust); Hot Resort.

TV inc: Batman; Greatest Heroes of the Bible; Death Car on the Freeway; Goliath Awaits.

GORTNER, Marjoe: Act. b. Long Beach, CA, Jan 14, 1944. Former child evangelist. Screen debut, 1972, Marjoe, full-length autobiographical documentary.

Films inc: Earthquake; Bobbie Jo and the Outlaws; The Food of the Gods; Viva Knievel!; Starcrash; When You Comin Back, Red Ryder (& prod); Mausoleum; Jungle Warriors; Hellhole.

TV inc: The Marcus Nelson Murders; The Gun and the Pulpit; Pray for the Wildcats; Speak Up America.

GOSSETT, Louis, Jr: Act. b. May 27, 1937. e. NYU, BS. Films inc: The Landlord; River Niger; Choirboys; The Deep; It Rained All Night the Day I Left; An Officer and A Gentleman; (Oscar-supp-1982);

Jaws 3-D; Finders Keepers.

TV inc: Roots-Part I (Emmy-1977); To Kill a Cop; Backstairs at the White House; Critical List; Africans; This Man Stands Alone; The Lazarus Syndrome; Don't Look Back; Benny's Place; The Powers of Matthew Star; Sadat; A Tribute to Martin Luther King Jr.-- A Celebration of Life; The Guardian (cable).

Thea inc: Take a Giant Step; The Desk Set; Lost in the Stars; A Raisin in the Sun; Golden Boy; The Zula and the Zayda; The Blacks; My Sweet Charley; Blood Knot; Murderous Angels.

GOTTLIEB, Alex: Wri-Prod. b. Russia, Dec 21, 1906. e. U of WI, BA. Plays inc: Wake Up Darling; Separate Rooms; Susan Slept Here; Stud; Your Place or Mine?; Divorce Me, Darling; September Song.

Films inc: I'll Take Sweden; Frankie and Johnny; Arizona Ranger; The Pigeon; Blue Gardenia; Macao; Susan Slept Here.

TV (wri-prod) inc: Dear Phoebe; The Gale Storm Show; The Tab Hunter Show; Bob Hope Chrysler Theatre Show; Donna Reed Show; The Smothers Brothers.

GOTTLIEB, Carl: Wri. b. Mar 18, 1938. Films inc: Jaws; Which Way Is Up?; The Committee (act); Jaws 2; The Jerk (& act); Caveman (& dir); Doctor Detroit; Jaws 3-D; Into The Night (act).

TV inc: Smothers Brothers Show (Emmy-1969); The Odd Couple; Flip Wilson; Bob Newhart Show; The Super; Crisis at Sun Valley.

GOTTLIEB, Linda (nee Salzman): Prod. b. NJ, 1939. e. Wellesley, BA; Columbia U; Russian Institute, MA. Films inc: Limbo.

TV inc: Big Henry and The Polka Dot Kid (Emmy-1977); Snowbound; Summer of My German Soldier; The Tap Dance Kid (Emmy-exec prod-1979); Seven Wishes of a Rich Kid; A Movie Star's Daughter; Make-Believe Marriage; The Gold Bug; A Family of Strangers; Stoned; The Mating Season; My Mother Was Never A Kid; We're Fighting Back; The Gentleman Bandit; The Electric Grandmother.

GOTTLIEB, Morton: Prod-Mgr. b. NYC, May 2, 1921. e. Yale U, BA. Made pro stage debut 1941, Liberty Jones. Turned to press rep then business Mgr 1946 for Dream Girl; Joan of Lorraine; prod first show 1953, tour of Arms and the Man.

Bway inc: His and Hers; Waiting for Gillian; The Stronger Sex; The Last Tycoon; The Facts of Life; A Palm Tree in a Rose Garden; The Better Mousetrap; The Amazing Adele; An Adventure; Enter Laughing; The Killing of Sister George; The Promise; Lovers; We Bombed in New Haven; The White House; The Mundy Scheme; Sleuth (Tony-1970); Veronica's Room; Same Time Next Year; Romantic Comedy; Special Occasions; Dancing In The End Zone.

Films inc: Same Time, Next Year; Romantic Comedy.

GOUDAL, Jetta: Act. b. France, 1898. Silent star in The Bright Shawl; The Green Goddess; Open All Night; Salome of the Tenements; Road To Yesterday; Three Faces East; White Gold; Forbidden Woman; Her Cardboard Lover; Lady of the Pavements; made three sound films--Plutocrat; Business and Pleasure; Tarnished Youth. Ret. 1935.

(Died Jan. 14, 1985)

GOUGH, Lloyd: Act. b. Sept. 21, 1907. H of Karen Morley. Films inc: Black Bart; All My Sons; A Southern Yankee; Roseanna McCoy; Tulsa; Sunset Boulevard; Storm Warning; Valentino, Rancho Notorious; Tony Rome; Madigan; Earthquake; House Calls.

(Died July 23, 1984).

GOUGH, Michael: Act. b. Malaya, Nov 23, 1917. e. Old Vic School. Films inc: Blanche Fury; The Small Back Room; The Man in the White Suit; Dracula; The Horse's Mouth; Konga; Circus of Blood; The Corpse; The Go-Between; Henry VIII and His Six Wives; The Boys From Brazil; Horror Hospital; Venom; The Dresser; Memed, My Hawk; Top Secret; Oxford Blues.

Bway inc: Love of Women; The Hollow Crown; Maigret and the Lady; The Prime of Miss Jean Brodie; Free for All; King Lear; Events in an Upper Room; Phaedra Brittanica; Counting the Ways; Bedroom Farce (Tony-supp-1979); Before the Party. (London) A Month In the Country.

TV inc: The Gift of Friendship (cable); The Visitation Mystery; Brideshead Revisited; Witness For the Prosecution; Cymbeline; Mistral's Daughter; To The Lighthouse; A Christmas Carol; Lace II; Arthur The King.

GOULD, Elliott: Act. b. NYC, Aug 29, 1938. Films inc: The Night They Raided Minsky's; Bob & Carol & Ted & Alice; M*A*S*H; I Will. . .I Will. . .For Now; Harry and Walter Go To New York; A Bridge Too Far; Capricorn One; Escape to Athena; The Muppet Movie; The Lady Vanishes; The Silent Partner; The Last Flight of Noah's Ark; Falling In Love Again; The Devil and Max Devlin; Dirty Tricks; Who?; Over the Brooklyn Bridge; Strawanzer (The Bums); The Naked Face; The Muppets Take Manhattan.

TV inc: Once Upon A Mattress; Saturday Night Live; The Rules of Marriage; E.R.

Thea inc: Rumple; Say Darling; Irma La Douce; I Can Get It For You Wholesale.

GOULD, Harold: Act. b. Schenectady, NY, Dec 10, 1923. e. Cornell U, MA, PhD. Films inc: Two for the Seesaw; Harper; Inside Daisy Clover; Marnie; The Arrangement; The Lawyer; Where Does It Hurt?; The Sting; Love and Death; The Front Page; The Silent Movie; The One and Only;-Seems Like Old Times.

TV inc: Washington--Behind Closed Doors; Soap; Love Boat; Feather and Father; Rhoda; Gunsmoke; Petrocelli; Double Solitaire; Streets of San Francisco; Mary Tyler Moore Show; The 11th Victim; Aunt Mary; Man in the Santa Claus Suit; Insight/Holy Moses; Kenny Rogers as the Gambler; Moviola (The Scarlett O'Hara Wars & The Silent Lovers); King Crab; The Long Road Home; Park Place; Born To Be Sold; Help Wanted Male; Foot In The Door; Kenny Rogers as the Gambler--the Adventure Continues; The Red-Light Sting; Under One Roof; The Fourth Wise Man.

Thea inc: Once in a Lifetime; The Miser; The Devils; The Birthday Party; The House of Blue Leaves; The Price; The World of Ray Bradbury; Rhinocerous; Seidman and Son; Fools; Grownups.

GOULET, Robert: Singer-Act. b. Lawrence, MA, Nov 26, 1933. Made concert debut in Edmonton, Canada, 1951, Handel's Messiah. Other stage appearances in Canada inc: The Beggar's Opera; South Pacific; Finian's Rainbow; Gentlemen Prefer Blondes.

Bway inc: Camelot; The Happy Time *(Tony*-1968); prod the US tour of Gene Kelly's Salute to Broadway, 1975.

Films inc: Honeymoon Hotel; I'd Rather Be Right; I Deal in Danger; Underground; Atlantic City, USA.

TV inc: The Broadway of Lerner and Loewe; The Robert Goulet Show; Brigadoon; Carousel; Kiss Me Kate; The Dream Merchants; All Hands On Deck For Bob Hope's All-Star Birthday Party At Annapolis. *(Grammy-*new artist-1962).

GOWDY, Curt: Sportscaster. b. Green River, WY, 1919. Basketball star, U. of Wyoming. In Air Force, WW II, then became sportscaster. Voted Sportscaster of the Year, 1967.

TV inc: American Sportsman *(Emmys*-1981, 1982); The Way It Was (host).

GOWERS, Bruce: Dir. b. West Kilbride, Scotland, Dec 21, 1940. e. BBC College. TV inc: Hello Dali; Finnan Games; Headliners with David Frost; Juke Box; Toni Tennille Show; This Is Your Life Anniversary Special; Show Business; All Star Salute to Mothers Day; We Dare You; The World of Entertainment; Double Platinum; Greater Tuna (PC)(& prod); That Was The Week That Was.

GRACE, Nickolas: Act. b. Cheshire, England, Nov. 21, 1949. Began acting career at age 11; as teenager dir British entries for Interdrama Festival Berlin, 1965 & 1968. Thea inc: Erb; The Sport of My Mad Mother; Lower Depths; Murder in the Cathedral; Richard II (& Bway); Taming of the Shew; Schweyk; A Winter's Tale; The Comedy of Errors; Cabaret; Dracula; What the Butler Saw; Next Time I'll Sing To You.

Films inc: City of the Dead; Europe after the Rain; Heat and Dust.

TV inc: The Loveschool; The Professionals; All's Well That Ends Well; Brideshead Revisited; The Master of Ballantrae; Lace.

GRADE, Lew, Lord: Exec. b. Russia, 1907. B of Lord Delfont. Started in showbiz as dancer; founded theatrical agency 1933; moved into prodn in 60's; Chmn & M-Dir, Associated Communications Corp; Chmn & M-Dir Incorporated TeleVision Co, Ltd; Chmn Assoc Television Corp Ltd; Chmn, Marble Arch Productions; ACC taken over April 1982 by Australian publishing-TV tycoon Robert Holmes a'Court; resd June 1982, became chmn & CEO of Embassy Communications Int'l; Knighted 1969; Life Peerage created 1976.

Thea inc: Sly Fox; Merrily We Roll Along. Films inc: From the Life of the Marionettes. TV inc: Jesus of Nazareth; Edward the King; The Muppet Show.

(NATAS Directorate Award, 1981).

GRADINGER, Edward Barry: Exec. b. Brooklyn, Jun 1, 1940. e. NYU, BA; Brooklyn Law School, LLB/JD. Named group exec vp 20th-Fox TV May 1980; CEO & group Exec VP, April 1982;

GRAF, William N: Prod. b. NYC, Oct 11, 1912. Films inc: A Man for All Seasons (exec prod); Sinful Davey; The African Elephant. VP Columbia Pictures Intl Corp; head of prodn for Europe, 1952-65; asst to head wldwde prodn, 1962-65.

GRAFF, Richard B: Exec. b. Milwaukee, WI, Nov 9, 1924. Joined U branch Chicago 1946 as film booker, advancing to sales mgr before moving, 1956, to Detroit as branch mgr; 1961, Chicago branch mgr; 1963, asst to GSM; in chg of sls & mktg first closed circuit telecast Indianapolis 500; 1964 asst to exec VP National General Corp.; 1965, asst vp; 1967 vp-GSM National General Pictures; 1968, exec VP chg mktg-dist; 1969, vp of parent company, exec asst to Pres; 1971, VP-GSM AIP; 1977, P Cine Artists Pictures; 1977 formed Richard Graff Company, specializing in producer representation; May 1983, P MGM/UA domestic dist.

GRAFTON, Sue: Wri. b. Louisville, KY., Apr. 24, 1940. e. U of Louisville, BA. TV inc: Walking Through Fire; Sex and the Single Parent; Nurse; Mark, I Love You; Seven Brides for Seven Brothers; Svengali (story).

Films inc: The Lolly-Madonna War.

GRAHAM, Martha: Dancer-Cho. b. Pittsburgh, PA, May 11, 1894. Studied with Ruth St. Denis. Soloist 1920 with Denishawn Dancers; Greenwich Village Follies 1923. debut as chor-dancer 1926; founded Martha Graham Dancers, Martha Graham School of Contemporary Dance; guest soloist with leading orchs in Judith; Triumph of St. Joan. Has made eight world tours, some under sponsorship of US State Dept.

Chor more than 150 ballets inc: Appalachian Spring; Clytemestra; Tragic Pattern; A Time of Snow; Holy Jungle; Dream; Scarlet Letter; Point of Crossing. TV inc: The Kennedy Center Honors--A Celebration of the Performing Arts.

GRAHAM, Ronny: Act-Dir-Comp-Wri. b. Philadelphia, PA, Aug 26, 1919. Started as comedian in niteries. Wrote songs for Bway revues.

Bway inc: (dir) Free Fall; Grin and Bare It!; Postcards; A Place for Polly.

Films inc: New Faces (& sp); Dirty Little Billy; History of the World--Part I; To Be Or Not To Be (& sp); Finders Keepers (sp).

TV inc: Omnibus; Toast of the Town; The Osmond Family Holiday Special (wri); The Ratings Game (PC).

GRAHAM, Sheilah: Wri. b. England, 1905. Hollywood columnist since 1936. Had own radio & TV shows. Books inc: Beloved Infidel; The Rest of the Story; The Garden of Allah; Confessions of a Hollywood Columnist; How to Marry Super Rich; The Real Scott Fitzgerald.

GRAHAM, Virginia: Act. b. Chicago, IL, Jul 4, 1913. e. U of Chicago, BA; Northwestern MJ. Originally on radio, At Home With Virginia Graham; Week Day.

TV inc: Week Day; Girl Talk; Virginia Graham Show. Films inc: The Carpetbaggers; Face in the Crowd.

Thea inc: Any Wednesday; Butterflies Are Free; Barefoot in the Park.

GRAHAM SCOTT, Peter: Wri-prod-dir. b. London, England, Oct. 27, 1923. Started as film editor; 1952, prod BBC-TV; 1955, prod Associated Rediffusion; 1958, exec prod school pgms; 1959, sr. drama prod; 1965, prod drama series BBC-TV; 1976, drama prod Harlech TV. TV inc: (wri) The Last Enemy; The Quare Fellow; The Citadel; Memory of October. (Prod) The Troubleshooters; The Onedin Line; The Curse of Tutankhamen's Tomb; Kidnapped; Children of the Stones; Follow Me; Into the Labrynth (& dir); Jamaica Inn; Quiller; The Master of Ballantrae. (Dir) The Avengers; Danger Man; The Prisoner.

Films inc: (dir) Capt. Clegg; The Pot Carriers; The Cracksman; The Promise.

GRALNICK, Jeff: Prod-Exec. b. NYC, Apr 3, 1939. e. NYU, BS Mktg. Joined CBS news 1959, corr in Vietnam, prod spec events; 1970, press sec Sen. George McGovern; 1972, asso prod ABC Evening News; 1975, prod Special Events Unit; 1977, exec prod Special Events; 1978, vp. TV inc: Post Election Special Edition Nightline (Emmy-prod-1980)

GRAND, Robert: Exec. Originally an asst dir, then prodn mgr; exec in chg prodn Tomorrow Entertainment; March 1983, vp-exec prodn mgr Warner Bros. Films inc: (assoc prod) Body Heat; National Lampoon's Vacation.

GRANDY, Fred: Act. b. Sioux City, IA, Jun 29, 1948. e. Harvard U. Films inc: Death Race 2000; The Lincoln Conspiracy.
   TV inc: Fernwood 2Night; Love Boat; Blind Ambition.
   Bwy inc: The Proposition; Green Julia; In the Boom Boom Room.

GRANET, Bert: Wri-Prod. b. NYC, Jul 10, 1910. e. Yale U, School of Fine Arts. Films inc: Quick Money; The Affairs of Annabel; Mr. Doodle Kicks Off; Laddie; My Favorite Wife; Bride by Mistake; Those Endearing Young Charms; Do You Love Me?; The Marrying Kind; Berlin Express; The Torch; Scarface.
   TV inc: Desilu; Twilight Zone; The Mob; The Untouchables; Loretta Young Show; Walter Winchell File; Lucille Ball-Desi Arnaz Show; The Great Adventure.

GRANGER, Farley: Act. b. San Jose, CA, Jul 1, 1925. Screen debut, 1943, North Star. In Army, 1944-46. Films inc: They Live By Night; Side Street; Edge of Doom; Strangers on a Train; Three Loves; Arrowsmith; The Heiress; The Prisoner of Zenda; Call Me Trinity; Arnold; A Crime for a Crime; The Prowler.
   TV inc: One Life to Live; Wagon Train; Masquerade Party; The Royal Romance of Charles and Diana.

GRANGER, Stewart (nee James Stewart): b. London, May 6, 1913. On stage From 1935 with Hull Repertory, Birmingham Repertory. Screen debut in So This Is London, 1940.
   Films inc: Convoy; Secret Mission; Thursday's Child; Madonna of the Seven Moons; Caesar and Cleopatra; King Solomon's Mines; Scaramouche; The Prisoner of Zenda; Salome; Beau Brummel; Green Fire; Flaming Frontier; The Trygon Factor; The Last Safari; The Wild Geese.

GRANT, B. Donald (Bud): Exec. b. Baltimore, MD, 1934. e. John Hopkins U, BS. Joined NBC 1958 on Today show; subsequently mgr nightime pgms, later daytime pgms; 1967, nat'l dir daytime pgms; 1972 to CBS as vp daytime pgms; 1976 vp-pgms; 1977 vp-pgms for CBS Entertainment; Nov 1980, P CBS Entertainment; March 1982 Sr Entertainment VP CBS Broadcast Group.

GRANT, Cary (Archibald Alexander Leach): Act. b. Bristol, England, Jan 18, 1904. On stage in England, then to US, appearing for a season with St. Louis Municipal Opera Co. Screen debut, 1932, This Is The Night. Films inc: Blonde Venus; The Devil and the Deep; She Done Him Wrong; Gambling Ship; Alice in Wonderland; Sylvia Scarlett; Suzy; Topper; Bringing Up Baby; Gunga Din; His Girl Friday; The Philadelphia Story; Penny Serenade; Suspicion; Mr Lucky; Destination Tokyo; None But The Lonely Heart; Arsenic and Old Lace; The Bachelor and the Bobby Soxer; The Bishop's Wife; Mr Blandings Builds His Dream House; I Was a Male War Bride; Room for One More; Dream Wife; Monkey Business; To Catch a Thief; The Pride and the Passion; An Affair to Remember; Houseboat; North by Northwest; Operation Petticoat; The Grass Is Greener; That Touch of Mink; Charade; Father Goose; Walk Don't Run; George Stevens--A Filmmaker's Journey (doc-int).
   TV inc: All-Star Party For Lucille Ball.
   (Special Academy Award, 1969).

GRANT, Lee: Act. b. NYC, Oct 31, 1927. e. Julliard School of Music. Debut age 4 on stage of Metropolitan Opera; member American Ballet at age 11. Bway inc: Joy to the World; Detective Story; Arms and the Man; A Hole in the Head; Wedding Breakfast; Plaza Suite; Prisoner of Second Avenue.
   Films inc: Detective Story; Terror in the Streets; Portnoy's Complaint; The Landlord; In the Heat of the Night; Buona Sera, Mrs. Campbell; Plaza Suite; Marooned; Shampoo (Oscar-supp-1975);

Voyage of the Damned; Airport 77; The Swarm; The Mafu Cage; Damien--Omen 2; When You Comin' Back, Red Ryder; Little Miss Marker; Charlie Chan and the Curse of the Dragon Queen; The Willmar 8 (dir); Visiting Hours; Teachers; What Sex Am I? (& dir) (also on TV).
   TV inc: Peyton Place (Emmy-1966); The Neon Ceiling (Emmy-1971); Why Me (doc); Fay; Rape-The Hidden Crime (doc); The Spell; Princess Grace, Once Upon a Time is Now; For the Use of the Hall (dir); The Shape of Things (dir); You Can't Go Home Again; Tell Me A Riddle (dir); The Million Dollar Face; For Ladies Only; Thou Shalt Not Kill; Bare Essence; Will There Really Be A Morning?; When Women Kill (& dir) (cable); A Matter of Sex (dir).

GRANT, Merrill: Prod. b. NYC, Jul 9, 1932. Joined Benton & Bowles ad agency 1957, becoming vp & dir pgmg; 1970 sr vp & dir radio-tv, Grey Ad agency; 1972 vp Viacom; 1974 P Don Kirshner Prodns; left to go into indie prodn.
   TV inc: The Triangle Factory Fire Scandal; She's Dressed to Kill; OHMS; That's Incredible!; Those Amazing Animals; The World's Most Spectacular Stuntman; 30 Years of TV Comedy's Greatest Hits; The Krypton Factor (exec prod); The Future...What's Next? (exec prod); Search (exec prod); The World's Funniest Commercial Goofs (exec prod); People to People with Rona Barrett (exec prod); Kate & Allie (exec prod); Getting The Last Laugh (exec prod).

GRANVILLE, Bonita: Act. b. NYC, Feb 2, 1923. W of the late Jack Wrather. On screen as child.
   Films inc: Westward Passage; Cradle Song; Ah Wilderness; These Three; Merrily We Live; Maid of Salem; Call it a Day; Nancy Drew Detective (and subsequent series); Angels With Dirty Faces; H M Pulham, Esq; The Glass Key; Hitler's Children; Love Laughs at Andy Hardy; The Guilty; Treason; The Lone Ranger. (Prod): Lassie's Greatest Adventure; The Magic of Lassie.
   TV inc: Lassie (prod).
   Became chmn Wrather Corp. after death of her husband, Nov. 1984.

GRAPPELLI, Stephane: Violinist. b. Paris, Jan 27, 1908. Founder with Django Reinhardt of Hot Club of Paris. Recording artist, concerts.

GRASSHOFF, Alex: Prod-Dir. b. Boston, MA, Dec 10, 1930. e. USC, BA. Films inc: Young Americans; The Jailbreakers.
   TV inc: Future Shock; Frank Sinatra-Family and Friends; Journey to the Outer Limits (Emmy-1974); Rockford Files; Night Stalker; Toma; Barbary Coast; Movin' On; CHiPs; The Wave; The Unforgivable Secret; Counterattack--Crime In America; Sometimes I Don't Love My Mother; Backwards--The Riddle of Dyslexia.

GRASSLE, Karen: Act. b. Berkeley, CA, Feb 25, 1944. e. UC Berkeley; LAMDA. TV inc: Little House on the Prairie; Battered (& wri); Cocaine--One Man's Seduction; Little House--the Last Farewell.
   Thea inc: The Gingham Dog; Butterflies Are Free; Cymbeline.
   Films inc: Harry's War.

GRAUMAN, Walter: Dir. b. Milwaukee, WI, Mar 17, 1922. Films inc: Lady in a Cage; 633 Squadron; A Rage to Live; I Deal in Danger; The Last Escape.
   TV inc: The Untouchables; Naked City; Route 66; The Felony Squad; Are You in the House Alone?; The Golden Gate Murders; The Top of the Hill; To Race the Wind (& prod); Crisis In Mid-Air; The Memory of Eva Ryker; Pleasure Palace; Jacqueline Susann's Valley of the Dolls 1981; Bare Essence (& prod); Illusions (& exec prod); Scene Of The Crime.

GRAVES, Peter: Act. (nee Aurness).b. Minneapolis, MN, Mar 18, 1936. e. U of MN. B of James Arness. Appeared in summer stock. Screen debut Rogue River.
   Films inc: Fort Defiance; Stalag 17; Beneath The 12-Mile Reef; Black Tuesday; The Long Gray Line; Night of the Hunter; Court Martial of Billy Mitchell; The Five Man Army; Sidecar Racers. Clonus Horror; Survival Run; Airplane; Savannah Smiles; Airplane II--The Sequel; Aces Go Places III (Our Man from Bond Street).
   TV inc: Fury; Mission Impossible; The Gift of the Magi; The Rebels; Death Car on the Freeway; Comedy Is Not Pretty; The Memory of Eva Ryker; Three Hundred Miles For Stephanie; Discover--The World of

Science (host); The Winds of War.

GRAY, Coleen (Doris Jensen): Act. b. Staplehurst, NE, Oct 23, 1922. e. Hamline U, BA, summa cum laude. Screen debut, 1945, State Fair. Films inc: Kiss of Death; Nightmare Alley; Fury at Furnace Creek; Father Is A Bachelor; The Killing; Copper Sky; The Phantom Planet; The Late Liz.

TV inc: Days of Our Lives; Family Affair; Name of the Game; The Best Place to Be.

GRAY, Dolores: Act. b. Chicago, Jun 7, 1924. Started as singer in niteries. NY stage debut 1944, Seven Lively Arts.

Bway inc: Are You With It; Sweet Bye and Bye; Annie Get Your Gun; Two on the Aisle; Carnival in Flanders *(Tony-*1954).

Films inc: It's Always Fair Weather; Kismet; The Opposite Sex; Designing Woman.

GRAY, Dulcie: Act-Wri. b. Kuala Lumpur, Federated Malay States, Nov 20, 1919. London stage debut 1939 in Hay Fever. Thea inc: The Little Foxes; Rain on the Just; Candida; An Ideal Husband; Where Angels Fear to Tread; Out of the Question; At the End of the Day; A Murder has been Announced; The Sack Race; The Pay Off; A Coat of Varnish.

Films inc: Two Thousand Women; Mine Own Executioner; The Glass Mountain; Wanted for Murder; Angels One Five; A Man Could Get Killed.

TV inc: Milestones; The Will; Lesson in Love; Winter Cruise; Unexpectedly Vacant; The Importance of Being Earnest; Crown Court; Making Faces; Life After Death.

GRAY, Erin: Act. b. Honolulu, HI., Jan 7, 1952. Former model. TV inc: Police Story; Gibbsville; Evening in Byzantium; Buck Rogers in the 25th Century; Coach of the Year; Silver Spoons; Born Beautiful; Code Of Vengeance.

Films inc: Winter Kills; Six Pack.

GRAY, Linda: Act. b. Santa Monica, CA, Sep 12, 1940. Films inc: Fun With Dick and Jane; The World Between; Under the Yum Yum Tree; Palm Springs Weekend; Dogs.

TV inc: Murder in Peyton Place; All That Glitters; The Grass Is Greener Over the Septic Tank; The Two Worlds of Jenny Logan; The Starmakers; Haywire; Dallas; The Wild and the Free; I'll Be Home For Christmas; The Puppy Saves the Circus (voice); Get High on Yourself; Not in Front of the Children; Salute to Lady Liberty; On Top All Over The World.

GRAY, Simon: Wri. b. Hayling Island, Hants, England, Oct 21, 1936. e. Cambridge. Plays inc: Wise Child; Dutch Uncle; The Idiot (adapt); Spoiled; Butley; Otherwise Engaged; Stage Struck; Close Of Play; Quartermaine's Terms; The Common Pursuit.

TV inc: Death of a Teddy Bear; Defendants; Two Sundays.

GRAY, Tom (Thomas Robert Gray Jr V): Exec. b. Jasper, AL, Mar 19, 1939. e. U MO; Southern IL U. After service as Army Public Information Officer, joined Atlanta Constitution 1965 as ent edtr; 1966 MGM fieldman, Chicago & Washington; 1967 asst to pub dir Par; 1969 pub for new talent program U; dir corp pub Lion Country Safari; 1976 LA press contact, U; 1978 unit pub Hurricane; The Villain; Health; 1979 natl pub dir U; 1980 VP & studio pub dir UA; 1981 pub vp Polygram Pictures; resd. 1982.

GRAYSON, Kathryn (Zelma Hedrick): Act. b. Winston-Salem, NC, Feb 9, 1923. Films inc: The Vanishing Virginian; Rio Rita; Seven Sweethearts; Thousands Cheer; Ziegfeld Follies; Anchors Aweigh; Two Sisters From Boston; Till the Clouds Roll By; The Kissing Bandit; Showboat; The Grace Moore Story (So This Is Love); Kiss Me Kate; The Vagabond King; That's Entertainment; That's Entertainment, Part 2; The Amazing World of Psychic Phenomena; Now I Lay Me Down to Sleep.

TV inc: GE Theatre; Die Fledermaus; AFI Salute To Gene Kelly.

Thea inc: Rosalinda; Merry Widow; Kiss Me Kate; Showboat.

GRAZER, Brian: Prod. b. LA, CA., July 12, 1951. e. USC. Started as legal intern at WB, became script reader, talent agent; joined Edgar J. Scherick-Daniel Blatt indie; later partnered with Ron Howard. TV inc: Zuma Beach; Thou Shalt Not Commit Adultery.

Films inc: Night Shift; Splash.

GREAVES, William: Prod-Dir. b. NYC, Oct 8, 1926. e. CCNY; McGill U. TV inc: Black Journal *(Emmy-*1970); From These Roots; In the Company of Men; Voice of La Raza.

Films inc: (act) Lost Boundaries; Miracle in Harlem; Sand of Sin; (Prod-dir) Ali The Fighter (& wri); The Marijuana Affair (& wri); Take One (& wri); Bustin' Loose (exec prod).

Bway inc: (act) Finian's Rainbow; Lost in the Stars; John Loves Mary.

GRECO, Jose: Dancer. b. Abruzzi, Italy, 1918. Flamenco dancer. Final U.S. performance 1975, retired to Marbella, Spain, to operate dance school. On screen From the '50s.

Films inc: Sombrero; Around the World in 80 Days; Holiday for Lovers; Ship of Fools.

GREEN, Adolph: Wri-Act. b. NYC, Dec 2, 1915. e. CCNY. Usually collab with Betty Comden on books, lyr for shows, musical films. Bway scores inc: Wonderful Town *(Tony-*1952); Peter Pan; Do Re Mi; On the Town; Two on the Aisle; Bells Are Ringing; Subways Are For Sleeping; Fade Out-Fade In; Hallelujah, Baby *(Tony-*1968); Applause *(Tony-*1970); On the 20th Century *(Tony-*1978); A Party With Betty Comden and Adolph Green (& act); Peter Pan; A Doll's Life; Singin' In the Rain (London).

Films inc: The Band Wagon; It's Always Fair Weather; On the Town; Good News; The Barkleys of Broadway; Singin' In the Rain; Auntie Mame; Bells Are Ringing; What a Way to Go; Simon (act); My Favorite Year (act); Garbo Talks (act); Jatszani Kell (Lily In Love) (act).

Songs inc: New York, New York; Lonely Town; Ohio; Give a Little, Get a Little; The Party's Over; Just in Time; Make Someone Happy; Get Acquainted.

TV inc: The Kennedy Center Honors, 1980, 1982; AFI Salute To Gene Kelly.

GREEN, Gerald: Wri. b. Brooklyn, NY, 1922. e. Columbia. Novelist, writer of tv docs.

TV inc: Today Show With Dave Garroway; Wide Wide World; Chet Huntley Reporting; Holocaust *(Emmy-*1978); Kent State;

Films inc: High Risk (prod).

GREEN, Guy: Dir. b. Frome, Somerset, England, 1913. Started as cin. Films inc: (cin) In Which We Serve; The Way Ahead; Great Expectations *(Oscar-*1947); Take My Life; Oliver Twist; Captain Horatio Hornblower; The Beggar's Opera; Rob Roy. (Dir): River Beat; Portrait of Alison; Postmark for Danger; House of Secrets; Sea of Sand; SOS Pacific; The Mark; The Angry Silence; Diamond Head; A Patch of Blue; The Magus; A Walk in the Spring Rain; Luther; Once Is Not Enough; The Devil's Advocate.

TV inc: (dir) The Incredible Journey of Dr Meg Laurel; Jennifer: A Woman's Story; Jimmy B and Andre; Inmates--A Love Story; Isabel's Choice.

GREEN, John: Mus Dir-Cond-Comp. b. NYC, Oct 10, 1908. e. Harvard U, AB. Started as rehearsal pianist. Comp-cond 1930-32, Paramount Astoria, NY; accompanist to: Ethel Merman; Gertrude Lawrence; James Melton; led own orch., Bway shows, niteries. Radio inc: Jack Benny; Philip Morris Shows. Comp, cond, arr 1942-46, MGM; WB and U, 1947-48; Gen Mus Dir & Exec-in-charge-of-Mus, MGM 1949-58; Prod, TV Desilu, 1959-60. Guest cond major symphony orchestras since 1959.

Songs inc: Coquette; I'm Yours; Out of Nowhere; The Waterfront; I Wanna Be Loved; Body and Soul.

Films inc: Easter Parade *(Oscar-*1951); Fiesta; Bathing Beauty; The Toast of New Orleans; An American in Paris *(Oscar-*1953); Merry Wives of Windsor Overture *(Oscar-*short-1953); Royal Wedding; High Society; Meet Me in Las Vegas; Raintree County; Pepe; West Side Story *(Oscar-*1961); Bye Bye Birdie; Oliver! *(Oscar-*1968); They Shoot Horses, Don't They?;

*(Grammy-*soundtrack-1961).

GREEN, Walon: Prod-Dir-Wri. b. Baltimore, Dec 15, 1936. e. U of Barcelona; U of Gottingin. Films inc: The Wild Bunch (sp); Hellstrom Chronicles *(Oscar-*doc-1971) (prod); Sorcerer (sp); Brink's Job (sp); Secret Life of Plants (doc) (dir-sp).

TV inc: Mysteries of the Sea (wri); Robert Kennedy & His Times (wri).

GREENBAUM, Everett: Wri. b. Buffalo, NY, Dec 20, 1919. e. MIT; Sorbonne. TV inc: Mr Peepers; The George Gobel Show; The Real McCoys; The Andy Griffith Show; M*A*S*H; Lou Grant; Semi-Tough; Walter.
Films inc: Good Neighbor Sam; The Ghost and Mr. Chicken; The Shakiest Gun in the West; The Reluctant Astronaut; Angel in My Pocket.

GREENBERG, Stanley R.: Wri. b. Chicago, IL, Sep 3. e. Brown U. TV inc: The Defenders; East Side, West Side; Route 66; Nurses; A Day Like Today; Welcome Home Johnny; Pueblo; The Missiles of October; The Silence; Blind Ambition; FDR--The Last Year; The Day the Bubble Burst (& co-prod).
Films inc: Skyjacked; Soylent Green.
Play: Pueblo.

GREENBURG, Earl David: Exec. b. 1946. e. U of PA, BA, JD. Dep Federal Atty Gen, PA; publisher Metropolitan Magazine, Philadelphia; atty with Atlantic Richfield; 1978, dir Compliance & Practices NBC; 1980, VP Compliance & Practices; Jan. 1981, VP Daytime Pgmmg West Coast, NBC Entertainment. TV inc: Life's Most Embarrassing Moments.

GREENE, Clarence: Wri. b. 1918. Films inc: The Town Went Wild; D O A; The Well; New York Confidential; Pillow Talk (Oscar-story & sp-1959); A House Is Not a Home; The Oscar; Caper of the Golden Bulls.
TV inc: Tightrope.

GREENE, David: Dir. b. Manchester, England, Feb 22, 1921. Films inc: The Shuttered Room; Sebastian; The Strange Affair; I Start Counting; Madame Sin; Godspell; Gray Lady Down; Hard Country (& prod); The Act (prod).
TV inc: The Defenders; The Count of Monte Cristo; The People Next Door (Emmy-1969); Rich Man, Poor Man (Emmy-1976); Roots Part 1 (Emmy-1977); The Trial of Lee Harvey Oswald; Friendly Fire (Emmy-1979); A Vacation in Hell (& exec prod); World War III; Rehearsal For Murder; Take Your Best Shot; A Marriage; Ghost Dancing; Prototype; The Guardian (cable); Sweet Revenge (& exec prod); Fatal Vision; Guilty Conscience.

GREENE, Graham: Wri. b. England, 1904. Author of books that provided material for the screen. Novels which became films inc: This Gun for Hire; The Ministry of Fear; Confidential Agent; The Fugitive; The Fallen Idol; The Third Man; The Stranger's Hand; The End of the Affair; The Quiet American; Our Man in Havana; The Comedians; Travels with My Aunt; Dr. Fischer of Geneva.
Plays inc: The Power and the Glory; The Living Room; The Potting Shed; The Complaisant Lover; The Return of A.J. Raffles.

GREENE, Lorne: Act. b. Ottawa, Canada, Feb 12, 1915. e. Queen's U; New York's Neighborhood Playhouse. Films inc: The Silver Chalice; Tight Spot; The Hard Man; The Buccaneer; Peyton Place; Battlestar Galactica; Klondike Fever; Heidi's Song (voice).
TV inc: Bonanza; Big Brother; The Bastard; Battlestar Galactica; A Time For Miracles; Aloha Paradise; A Journey of Love (narr); A Gift of Music (host); Code Red; Police Squad; Lorne Greene's New Wilderness (exec prod-narr); The Nutcracker; A Fantasy On Ice (host); Empire.
Bway: Speaking of Murder; Edwin Booth.

GREENE, Mort: Lyr. b. Cleveland, OH, Oct 3, 1912. e. U of PA. Wri-dir night club acts; then wrote songs for films inc; The Big Street; Call Out the Marines; Beyond the Blue Horizon; Tulsa.
TV theme songs inc: Leave It to Beaver; Restless Gun; Tales of Wells Fargo; Lawrence Welk Champagne Time.

GREENE, Shecky (Sheldon Greenfield): Act. b. Chicago, 1925. Films inc: Tony Rome; The Love Machine; History of the World--Part I; Splash.
TV inc: The Colgate Comedy Hour; Combat; Hal Linden's Big Apple; Midnight Lace; All-Star Salute To Mother's Day.b. Malden, MA, Feb 27, 1934. e. U of MI; Columbia U. Films inc: Harry and Tonto.

GREENFELD, Josh: Wri. b. Malden, MA, Feb 27, 1934. e. U of MI; Columbia U. Film inc: Harry and Tonto.
TV inc: Lovey; A Circle of Children Part II.

GREENFIELD, Leo: Exec. b. NYC, Apr 25, 1916. e. St John's U. Joined Buena Vista 1956, mgr east sls div; 1961 west div mgr; 1966 domestic sls mgr; 1966 vp, gm-sls Cinerama Release Corp; 1969 vp, gm-sls Warners; 1975 sr vp, worldwide dist, MGM.

GREENLAW, Charles F: Exec. b. CA, Jan 18, 1914. Prodn dept, WB, 1933-42; asst prodn m, 1942-56; studio prodn m, 1956-65; vp, prod exec U, 1965-69; vp prod & studio ops, WB, 1969-73; exec vp worldwide prod mgt. WB, 1973; Ret. Dec 31, 1980.
Films inc: Superman, The Movie (asso prod).

GREENWALD, Robert: Prod-Dir. b. NYC, Aug 28, 1943. e. NYC High School of Performing Arts; Antioch Coll. Dir off-Bway; teacher NYU; New School for Social Research; ran experimental theatre program Mark Taper Forum, LA. Thea inc: Soon; The Amazing Flight of the Goonie Bird; Me and Bessie; A Sense Of Humor. Bway inc: I Have A Dream.
TV inc: (prod) The Desperate Miles; 21 Hours at Munich; Delta County, USA; Escape From Bogen County; Getting Married; Portrait of a Stripper; Miracle On Ice; The Texas Rangers; Lois Gibbs and the Love Canal; The First Time; Challenge Of A Lifetime (exec prod). (Dir) Sharon--Portrait of a Mistress; Katie--Portrait of a Centerfold; Flatbed Annie and Sweetiepie--Lady Truckers; In The Custody of Strangers; The Burning Bed.
Films inc: Xanadu (dir).

GREENWOOD, Joan: Act. b. London, Mar 4, 1921. e. RADA. Thea inc: (London) The Robust Invalid; Little Ladyship; The Women; Rise Above It; Peter Pan; Striplings; Damaged Goods; It Happened in New York; Frenzy; Young Wives Tale; Bell, Book and Candle; Cards of Identity; Lysistrata; The Grass is Greener; Hedda Gabler; Fallen Angels; The Au Pair Man; The Chalk Garden; The Understanding. (Bway) The Confidential Clerk; Those That Play the Clowns. Films inc: My Wife's Family; He Found a Star; The Gentle Sex; The Man Within; The October Man; The White Unicorn; Saraband for Dead Lovers; Whiskey Galore; Kind Hearts and Coronets; The Man in the White Suit; The Importance of Being Earnest; Father Brown; Moonfleet; Mysterious Island; The Amorous Prawn; Tom Jones; Moon Spinners; Girl Stroke Boy; Hound of The Baskervilles; The Water Babies.
TV inc: Ellis Island.

GREER, Dabbs: Act. b. Fairview, MO, Apr 2, 1917. e. Drury Coll, AB. On screen From 1948. Films inc: The Black Book; House of Wax; Affair with a Stranger; Riot in Cell Block 11; Bitter Creek; Invasion of the Body Snatchers; The Vampire; Baby Face Nelson; I Want to Live; The Lone Texan; Roustabout; Shenandoah; Cheyenne Social Club; Rage; White Lightning.
TV inc: Big Town; Gunsmoke; Hank; The Ghost and Mrs. Muir; Little House on the Prairie; The Winds of Kitty Hawk; Look Back to Yesterday; Little House--The Last Farewell.

GREER, Jane: Act. b. Washington, DC, Sep 9, 1924. Films inc: Pan Americana; Two O'Clock Courage; George White's Scandals; Dick Tracy; Bamboo Blonde; Sunset Pass; Sinbad the Sailor; They Won't Believe Me; Out of the Past; Station West; The Big Steal; The Prisoner of Zenda; Desperate Search; The Clown; Down Among the Sheltering Palms; Run for the Sun; Man of a Thousand Faces; Where Love Has Gone; Billie; The Outfit; Against All Odds.
TV inc: A Christmas for Boomer; The Shadow Riders.

GREFE, William: Dir-Prod. b. Miami, May 17. e. U of Miami. Films inc: The Checkered Flag; Racing Fever; Devil Sisters; Sting of Death; Tartu; Wild Rebels; Hooked Generation; The Grove; Electric Shades of Grey; Stanley; Impulse; Jaws of Death; Godmothers; Whiskey Mountain; Live and Let Die. P Ivan Tors Studios, Miami.

GREGG, Virginia: Act. On screen From 1947. Films inc: Body and Soul; Dragnet; I'll Cry Tomorrow; The D.I.; Twilight for the Gods; Operation Petticoat; Spencer's Mountain; A Big Hand for a Little Lady; Madigan; A Walk in the Spring Rain.
TV inc: Little Women; Evita Peron; The 25th Man; Forbidden Love.

GREGORY, James: Act. b. NYC, Dec 23, 1911. Films inc: The Naked City; The Young Stranger; Onionhead; Al Capone; The Manchurian Candidate; Twilight of Horror; The Great Escape; PT-109; Captain Newman, M.D.; Quick, Before It Melts; The Sons of Katie Elder; The Ambushers; The Secret War of Harry Frigg; Beneath the Planet of the Apes; The Late Liz; The Strongest Man in the World; The Main Event; The In-Laws.

TV inc: Studio One; Climax!; Suspense; The Lawless Years; Big Valley; The Bastard; Detective School; The Comeback Kid; The Great American Traffic Jam; Goldie and the Boxer Go to Hollywood; Wait Till Your Mother Gets Home.

Bway inc: Death of a Salesman; The Desperate Hours; Fragile Fox; All My Sons; Dream Girl; Key Largo; Dead Pigeon.

GREGORY, Paul (nee Lenhart): Prod. b. Waukee, IA, Aug 27, 1920. H of Janet Gaynor. Began as agent; 1947 headed MCA Concert Div, launched Charles Laughton reading tours; became prod 1951.

Thea inc: Don Juan in Hell; John Brown's Body; Caine Mutiny Court Martial; Elsa Lanchester's Private Music Hall; Three for To-night; Rivalry; The Pink Jungle; Captains and Kings; Prescription for Murder; Lord Pengo; Dame Judith Anderson as Hamlet; Camelot (London).

Films inc: Night of the Hunter; The Naked and the Dead.

TV inc: Caine Mutiny Court Martial (Emmy-adapt-1955).

GREY, Joel (nee Katz): Act. b. Cleveland, OH, Apr 11, 1932. S of Mickey Katz. Worked in father's stage revues, niteries. Bway inc: Cabaret (Tony-supp-1967); George M!; Goodtime Charley; Marco Polo Sings a Solo; The Grand Tour.

Films inc: Cabaret (Oscar-supp-1972); The Seven-Per-Cent Solution; Man on a Swing; Buffalo Bill and the Indians.

TV inc: Colgate Comedy Hour; Jack and the Beanstalk; Live From Wolf Trap (host); Evening at Pops '79; To Hear (host).

GREY, Nan (Eschal Miller): Act. b. 1918. W of Frankie Laine. Films inc: Dracula's Daughter; Three Smart Girls; Three Smart Girls Grow Up; Tower of London; The Invisible Man Returns; Sandy Is a Lady; Under Age.

TV inc: Rawhide.

GREY, Virginia: Act. b. Los Angeles, Mar 22, 1917. On screen From 1927, Uncle Tom's Cabin.

Films inc: Secrets; Dames; The Firebird; The Great Ziegfeld; Ros-alie; Test Pilot; The Hardys Ride High; Hullaballoo; Idaho; Strangers in the Night; Unconquered; Who Killed Doc Robbin?; Jungle Jim; The Last Command; Crime of Passion; The Restless Years; Back Street; Love Has Many Faces; Madame X; Rosie; Airport.

TV inc: General Hospital.

GRIER, Pam: Act. b. Winston-Salem, NC. Films inc: Beyond the Valley of the Dolls; Twilight People; Blacula; Hit Man; Coffy; Black Mama, White Mama; The Arena; The Big Doll House; Greased Lightning; Fort Apache, The Bronx; Tough Enough; Something Wicked This Way Comes; On The Edge.

GRIFFETH, Simone: Act. b. Savannah, GA, Apr 14. e. U of SC. Films inc: Death Race; Slap Shot; The House Where Death Lives. TV inc: Mandrake; Ladies Man; Fighting Back; Amanda's.

GRIFFIN, Merv: TV Pers. b. San Mateo, CA, Jul 6, 1925. Sang on local radio station, San Francisco. Joined Freddy Martin band.

Films inc: This Is Love; The Boy From Oklahoma; By The Light of the Silvery Moon; The Phantom of the Rue Morgue; The Seduction of Joe Tynan; The Lonely Guy; Slapstick of Another Kind.

TV inc: The Merv Griffin Show (Emmy-wri-1974); The Merv Show (Emmys-Host-1982, 1984); Keep Talking; The Jack Paar Show; The Robert Q Lewis Show.

GRIFFITH, Andy: Act. b. Mount Airy, NC, Jun 1, 1926. e. NC U. Per-formed on TV, Niteries. Starred in outdoor pageant, The Lost Colony. Screen debut, 1957, A Face in the Crowd.

Films inc: No Time for Sergeants; Onionhead; The Second Time Around; Angel in My Pocket; Hearts of the West; Rustler's Rhapsody.

TV inc: The Andy Griffith Show; Andy of Mayberry; No Time for Sergeants; The Headmaster; Go Ask Alice. Salvage; Centennial; From Here to Eternity; The Yeagers; Murder In Texas; For Lovers Only;

Murder In Coweta County; The Demon Murder Case; Fatal Vision.

Thea inc: No Time for Sergeants; Destry Rides Again.

GRIFFITH, Melanie: Act. b. NYC., Aug. 9, 1957. W of Steven Bauer. D of Tippi Hedren. Films inc: Night Moves; The Drowning Pool; Smile; Roar; One on One; Joyride; Fear City; Body Double.

TV inc: Steel Cowboy; She's In the Army Now; Golden Gate; Carter Country; Starmaker; Alfred Hitchcock Presents.

GRILLO, Basil: Exec (ret). b. Antel's Camp, CA, Oct 8, 1910. e. U of CA, Berkeley. Dir Seven League Ent, Inc; dir Electrovision Prodns; CEO, Bing Crosby Enterprises.

GRIMALDI, Alberto: Prod. b. Naples, 1927. Pres of PEA (Produzioni Europee Assoc, S.A.S.). Films inc: For a Few Dollars More; The Good, The Bad, and The Ugly; Three Steps in Delirium; Satyricon; Burn!; The Decameron; The Canterbury Tales; 1001 Nights; Salo, or the 100 Days of Sodom; Bawdy Tales; Man of La Mancha; Last Tango in Paris; Avanti; Fellini's Casanova; 1900; The True Story of General Custer; Lovers and Liars.

GRIMES, Gary: Act. b. San Francisco, 1955. Films inc: Summer of 42; The Culpepper Cattle Co; Class of 44; Cahill; The Spikes Gang; Gus.

GRIMES, Tammy: Act. b. Lynn, MA, Jan 30, 1934. e. Stephens Coll. Bway inc: Bus Stop (replaced Kim Stanley). The Amazing Adele; The Lark; Look After Lulu; The Unsinkable Molly Brown (Tony-supp-1961); Rattle of a Simple Man; High Spirits; Finian's Rainbow; The Decline and Fall of the Whole World as Seen Through the Eyes of Cole Porter; The Only Game in Town; Private Lives (Tony-1970); In Praise of Love; Trick; A Musical Jubilee; California Suite; Tartuffe; Father's Day; 42d Street.

Films inc: Three Bites of an Apple; Play It As It Lays; Somebody Killed Her Husband; The Runner Stumbles; Can't Stop the Music; Just Crazy About Horses (narr); The Last Unicorn (voice).

TV inc: Holiday; You Can't Go Home Again; The Incredible Book Escape (voice); An Invasion of Privacy.

GRIZZARD, George: Act. b. Roanoke Rapids, NC, Apr 1, 1928.

Films inc: From The Terrace; Advise and Consent; Warning Shot; Happy Birthday, Wanda June; Comes a Horseman; Fire Power; Seems Like Old Times; Wrong Is Right; Bachelor Party.

Bway inc: The Desperate Hours; The Happiest Millionaire; The Country Girl; The Royal Family; Who's Afraid of Virginia Woolf?; You Know I Can't Hear You When the Water's Running; The Gingham Dog; Inquest; California Suite.

TV inc: My Three Angels; Notorious; A Case of Libel; The Front Page; Travis Logan, D.A.; The Night Rider; Attica; The Oldest Living Graduate (Emmy-supp-1980); The Shady Hill Kidnapping; Not in Front of the Children; Robert Kennedy & His Times; International Airport.

GRODIN, Charles: Act-Dir-Wri. b. Pittsburgh, Apr 21, 1935. e. U of Miami. NY stage debut 1962 in Tchin-Tchin. Plays inc: Absence of a Cello; wrote the book and lyr for Hooray! It's a Beautiful Day. . .And All That (also dir); Lovers and Other Strangers (dir); Steambath; Thieves (prod); Same Time, Next Year; Unexpected Guests (prod-dir).

Films inc: (act) Rosemary's Baby; Catch 22; The Heartbreak Kid; 11 Harrowhouse; King Kong; Heaven Can Wait; Real Life; Sunburn; It's My Turn; Seems Like Old Times; The Incredible Shrinking Woman; The Great Muppet Caper; The Lonely Guy; The Woman In Red; Movers & Shakers (& prod-wri).

TV inc: Simon and Garfunkel Special (wri-dir); Paradise (prod-dir); The Paul Simon Special (Emmy-wri-1978); Charley's Aunt (act) (cable); Love, Sex--& Marriage?

GROH, David: Act. b. Brooklyn, May 21, 1939. e. Brown U; London Academy of Music and Fine Arts on Fulbright Scholarship. Films inc: Change in the Wind; A Hero Ain't Nothin' But a Sandwich; Two-Minute Warning.

TV inc: Love Is A Many-Splendored Thing; Edge of Night; Rhoda; The Child Stealer; Power; The Dream Merchants; Tourist; Victory At Entebbe; Murder at the Mardi Gras; This Is Kate Bennett; The Zertigo

Diamond Caper; General Hospital.

Bway inc: Antony and Cleopatra; Elizabeth The Queen; Hot L Baltimore; Chapter Two.

GROOM, Sam: Act. TV inc: Police Surgeon; Sharon - Portrait of a Mistress; Beyond the Bermuda Triangle; Institute for Revenge; The Day the Loving Stopped; Blood Feud; More Than Murder; Otherworld.

Films inc: The Babymaker; Act One; Run for the Roses; The Rats.

Bway inc: Paradise Lost; Diplomatic Relations.

GROSBARD, Ulu: Dir. b. Antwerp, Belgium, Jan 9, 1929. e. U of Chicago, BA; Yale Drama School. Bway inc: The Days and Nights of Beebee Fenstermaker; The Subject Was Roses; A View from the Bridge; The Investigation; That Summer-That Fall; American Buffalo; The Floating Light Bulb; The Wake of Jamey Foster (& prod).

Films inc: Splendor in the Grass (asst dir); West Side Story (asst dir): The Subject Was Roses; Who Is Harry Kellerman and Why Is He Saying Those Terrible Things About Me?; Straight Time; True Confessions; Falling In Love.

GROSS, Michael: Act. b. Chicago, IL., Jun. 21, 1947. e. U IL, BA; Yale, MFA. Bway inc: Bent; The Philadelphia Story.

TV inc: FDR-The Last Year; A Girl Named Sooner; Little Gloria, Happy at Last; Family Ties; Cook and Peary--The Race to the Pole; Summer Fantasies; Assault On Freedom (host).

GROSS, Shelly: Thea Prod. b. Philadelphia, May 20, 1921. e. U of PA, AB; Northwestern U, MSJ. Bway inc: Catch Me If You Can; Sherry; Inquest; Grand Music Hall of Israel; Lorelei; The King and I; Bring Back Birdie.

GROSS, Yoram Jerzy: Prod-Dir. b. Poland. Film inc: Joseph the Dreamer; Chansons sans Paroles; One Pound Only; Dot and the Kangaroo (anim); The Little Convict (anim); Dot and Santa Claus (anim); Sarah (The Seventh Match) (anim); Save the Lady (sp); Dot and the Bunny; The Camel Boy (& sp); Epic (& edtr).

GROSSBERG, Jack: Prod. b. NYC, Jun 5, 1927. Films inc: Requiem for a Heavyweight; Pretty Poison; The Producers; Take the Money and Run; Don't Drink the Water; They Might Be Giants; Bananas; Everything You Always Wanted to Know About Sex; The Betsy; Fast Break.

GROSSMAN, Kenneth Lewis: Exec (ret 1976). b. Minneapolis, MN, Apr 11, 1905. e. USC. Prod TV sports programs; business mgr, MGM Radio; asso to Louis K Sidney, exec vp MGM Studios, 1948-55; asso to Edward J. Mannix, vp, gm, MGM, 1955-57; Universal City Studios prodn mgr, 1960-76.

GROTTA, Kare J: Exec. b. Andalsnes, Norway, Jan 21, 1943. Dir PR Norwegian Cinema and Film Foundation; M-dir, founder Royal Film AS; Grotta Invest AS; founder Norwegian Film Festival.

GROUT, James: Act. b. London, Oct, 22, 1927. e. RADA. Thea inc: Old Vic Co; Stratford Memorial Theatre Co (now Royal Shakespeare Co); Lysistrata; The Mousetrap; Ross; Half-A-Sixpence (also Bway); Volpone; Rafferty's Chant; Sometime Never; Flint; Straight Up; Lloyd George Knew My Father; The Provoked Wife; Hollow Crown; A Murder Is Announced; Make and Break; Quartermaine's Terms; Man and Superman.

GROVENOR, Linda: Act. b. Baltimore, MD, Feb 6, 1956. e. Villa Julie Coll, BS. TV inc: The Tenth Month; The Terrible Secret; Valentine; Secret of Midland Heights.

Films inc: Die Laughing.

GRUENBERG, Leonard: Exec. b. Minneapolis, MN, Sep 10, 1913. e. U of MN. Began as salesman Republic Pictures, 1935; with RKO in same capacity, 1936; then branch thea mgr, 1941; later that year apptd dist mgr; vp NTA; vp Cinemiracle Prodn; p, ChmnB, Sigma III Corp, 1962; ChmnB Filmways, 1967; ChmnB Gamma III Dist Co & ChmnB and p Gamma III Group Ltd, 1976.

GRUNDY, Reg: Prod. b. Sydney, Australia, Aug 4, 1923. TV inc: Pass Word; Junior Money Makers; Price is Right; Penthouse Club; Gambit; Emergency Line.

Films inc: Barry McKenzie Holds His Own; Abba--The Movie.

GRUSIN, Dave: Comp-Cond. b. Littleton, CO., 1934. Films inc: Divorce American Style; The Graduate; Candy; Winning; Tell Them Willie Boy Is Here; The Pursuit of Happiness; The Great Northfield Minnesota Raid; The Front; Murder By Death; The Yakuza; Three Days of the Condor; Bobby Deerfield; Fire Sale; The Goodbye Girl; Mr. Billion; Heaven Can Wait; And Justice For All; The Champ; The Electric Horseman; My Bodyguard; On Golden Pond; Absence of Malice; Reds; Author! Author!; Tootsie; Scandalous; Racing With the Moon; The Pope Of Greenwich Village; The Little Drummer Girl; Falling In Love; The Goonies.

TV inc: St. Elsewhere.

(Grammy-inst arr-1983)

GUARDINO, Harry: Act. b. NYC, Dec 22, 1925. Films inc: Houseboat; The Five Pennies; Five Branded Women; The Pigeon That Took Rome; Madigan; The Hell With Heroes; The Enforcer; Goldengirl; Any Which Way You Can.

Bway inc: End As A Man; A Hatful of Rain; Anyone Can Whistle; One More River; Natural Affection; Seven Descents of Myrtle; Woman Of the Year.

TV inc: Studio One; Playhouse 90; The Reporter; Pleasure Cove; Bender; The Sophisticated Gents; Lovers and Other Strangers.

GUARE, John: Plywri. b. NYC, Feb 5, 1938. e. Georgetown; Yale School of Drama, MFA. Plays inc: Universe; To Wally Pantoni, We Leave A Credenza; Day for Surprises; Loveliest Afternoon of the Year; Muzeeka; Cop Out; Home Fires; The House of Blue Leaves; Two Gentlemen of Verona (adapt & lyr) (Tony-book-1972); Marco Polo Sings a Solo; Rich and Famous; Landscape of the Body; Bosoms and Neglect; Woman And Water; Gardenia; Lydie Breeze; Faustus In Hell (segment).

Films inc: Taking Off; Atlantic City.

GUBER, Lee: Thea Prod. b. Philadelphia, Nov 20, 1920. e. Temple U, MA. With partners, Shelly Gross & Frank Ford, owns, operates and produces musicals at six summer theatres.

Bway inc: The Happiest Girl in the World; Catch Me If You Can; Inquest; Grand Music Hall of Israel; Lorelei; The King and I; Bring Back Birdie; The World of Sholom Aleichem.

GUBER, Peter: Prod-Exec. b. 1939. e. Syracuse U, BA; NYU Law School, JD, LLM. Recruited by Col as mgt trainee while working to MBA degree at NYU; 1973 exec vp chg wldwide prodn; 1975 formed Peter Guber Filmworks; 1976 merged with Neil Bogart's Casablanca Records to form Casablanca Record & Filmworks Inc; March 1980, firm bought by Polygram, Guber remaining as bd chmn; May 1980 formed Boardwalk with Bogart, Jon Peters but retained connection with Polygram Pictures of which he was 50% owner; June, 1981 Boardwalk partnership dissolved; Jan 1982, Sold interest in Polygram.

Films inc: The Deep; Midnight Express; An American Werewolf In London (exec prod); Missing; Six Weeks; Flashdance (exec prod); D.C. Cab (exec prod); Vision Quest (prod).

TV inc: Mysteries of the Sea (doc); Television and the Presidency (exec prod); Double Platinum (exec prod); Dreams (exec prod); The Toughest Man In The World (Exec prod).

GUENETTE, Robert: Prod-Dir-Wri. b. Holyoke, MA, Jan 12, 1935. TV inc: William Faulkner's Mississippi; Our War In Vietnam; The Hungry Americans; The Defector; They've Killed President Lincoln (Emmy-wri-1971); The Tree; The Plot to Murder Hitler; The Crucifixion of Jesus; Peary's Race to the North Pole; Monsters! Mysteries or Myths?; The World Turned Upside Down; Bigfoot; The Amazing World of Psychic Phenomena; The National Disaster Survival Test; I Can; Journey Together; Dinky Hocker Shoots Smack; The Making of Star Wars; SPFX--The Empire Strikes Back; Roots--One Year Later; Do You Know How to Talk To Your Kids About Sex?; Women Who Rate A 10 (prod); Ripley's Believe It Or Not; Great Movie Stunts--Raiders of the Lost Ark; Counterattack--Crime In America.

Films inc: The Man Who Saw Tomorrow (doc).

GUEST, Christopher: Act-Wri-Comp. b. NYC, Feb 5, 1948. Wrote mus & act in National Lampoon's Lemmings off-Bway. Bway inc: Room Service; Moonchildren.

Films inc: The Long Riders; The Fortune; Death Wish; The Hot Rock; Heartbeeps; Spinal Tap.

TV inc: The TV Show; The Chevy Chase Special (& wri); The Billion Dollar Bubble; Lily Tomlin (& wri) *(Emmy*-wri-1976); A Nice Place to Visit (wri only); A Piano For Mrs. Cimino; The Million Dollar Infield; Haywire; Blind Ambition; Saturday Night Live.

GUEST, Lance: Act. b. Saratoga, CA., July 21, 1960. e. UCLA. Films inc: I Ought To Be In Pictures; Halloween II; The Last Starfighter.

TV inc: Between Two Loves; Why Us ?; Please Don't Hit Me, Mom; Lou Grant; Confessions of a Married Man; St. Elsewhere; One Too Many; My Father, My Rival.

GUEST, Val: Wri-Prod-Dir. b. London, 1911. Films inc: Miss Pilgrim's Progress; The Body Said No; Happy Go Lovely; Another Man's Poison; Men of Sherwood Forest; Lyons in Paris; It's a Great Life; They Can't Hang Me; The Abominable Snowman; Carry on Admiral; Up the Creek; Further Up the Creek; Hell is a City; The Day the Earth Caught Fire; Jigsaw; Where the Spies Are; Casino Royale; When Dinosaurs Ruled the Earth; The Adventurers; Confessions of a Window Cleaner; Killer Force; Diamond Mercenaries; The Shillingbury Blowers; Dangerous Davies--The Last Detective.

TV inc: Space 1999; Return of the Saint; And The Band Played On.

GUETTEL, Henry: Prod-Exec. b. Kansas City, MO, Jan 8, 1928. e. U of PA; U of Kansas City. Act and stg mgr in stock and Bway; Mgr Royal Winnipeg Ballet; Gen Mgr Sacramento Music Circus; Sombrero Theatre; gen mgr Music Theatre of Lincoln Center.

Bway inc: Romulus (asso prod); The Merry Widow; The King and I; Kismet; Carousel; Show Boat; Annie Get Your Gun.

Thea prodns inc: The Best Man; The Sound of Music; Camelot; Oliver. Originated Music Theatre Concerts at Philharmonic Hall. VP Cinema 5 Ltd.; VP crea aff Col; 1980, Sr. VP Prodn Fox (NY).

GUFFEY, Burnett: Cin. b. Del Rio, TN, May 26, 1905. Films inc: The Informer; Foreign Correspondent; All the King's Men; The Sniper; From Here to Eternity *(Oscar*-1953); The Harder They Fall; Birdman of Alcatraz; King Rat; Bonnie and Clyde *(Oscar*-1967); The Split; The Madwoman of Chaillot; The Great White Hope.

(Died May 30, 1983).

GUILLAUME, Robert (Robert Williams): Act. b. St Louis, MO, Nov 30. e. WA U. Bway inc: Finian's Rainbow; Carousel; Guys and Dolls; Purlie; Golden Boy; Othello; Porgy and Bess; Jacques Brel.

TV inc: Mel and Susan Together; Rich Little's Washington Follies; S'Wonderful, S'Marvelous, S'Gershwin; Soap *(Emmy*-197); Benson; The Kid From Left Field; The Starmakers; Hal Linden's Big Apple; The Kid With The Broken Halo; Texaco Star Theatre--Opening Night; Sophisticated Ladies (PPV) (host); It Only Hurts When You Laugh (host); The Kid With The 200 IQ (& exec prod); The World's Funniest Commercial Goofs (host); A Tribute to Martin Luther King Jr--A Celebration of Life; The Fantastic World of D.C. Collins (exec prod); Kraft All-Star Salute To Ford's Theatre.

Films inc: Seems Like Old Times; Prince Jack.

GUILLERMIN, John: Dir. b. London, 1925. Films inc: Torment; Smart Alec; Miss Robin Hood; Adventures in the Hopfields; The Crowded Day; Town on Trial; I Was Monty's Double; Tarzan's Greatest Adventure; The Day They Robbed the Bank of England; Waltz of the Toreadors; Tarzan Goes to India; Guns at Batasi; Rapture; The Blue Max; P.J.; House of Cards; The Bridge at Remagen; El Condor; Skyjacked; Shaft in Africa; The Towering Inferno; King Kong; Death on the Nile; Mr. Patman; Sheena.

GUINNESS, Alec, Sir: Act. b. London, Apr 2, 1914. Knighted, 1959. Stage debut London, 1934. Also on stage in NY, Europe. On screen From 1934, Evensong.

Films inc: Great Expectations; Oliver Twist; Kind Hearts and Coronets; The Lavender Hill Mob; The Man in the White Suit; The Promoter; The Malta Story; Captain's Paradise; The Detective; To Paris With Love; The Prisoner; The Lady Killers; The Swan; The Bridge on the River Kwai *(Oscar*-1957); The Horse's Mouth; The Scapegoat; Our Man in Havana; Tunes of Glory; A Majority of One; H.M.S. Defiant; Lawrence of Arabia; Dr. Zhivago; The Comedian; Cromwell; Scrooge; Brother Sun and Sister Moon; Hitler; The Last Ten Days;

Murder by Death; Star Wars; The Empire Strikes Back; Raise The Titanic; Lovesick; Return of the Jedi; A Passage To India.

Honorary Oscar (April 1980) for advancing the art of screen acting through a host of memorable performances.

TV inc: The Wicked Scheme of Jebel Deeks; Twelfth Night; Conversation at Night; Solo; E.E. Cummings; Little Gidding; The Gift of Friendship; Caesar & Cleopatra; Tinker, Tailor, Soldier, Spy; Little Lord Fauntleroy; The Gift of Friendship (cable); Smiley's People.

Bway inc: Dylan *(Tony*-1964); The Cocktail Party (prod-act); Time Out of Mind; A Voyage Round My Father; Macbeth; Yahoo; The Old Country.

GULAGER, Clu: Act. b. Holdenville, OK, Nov 16, 1928. e. Baylor U. Studied with Jean Louis Barrault and Etienne Decroix in Paris.

Films inc: The Killers; Winning; The Last Picture Show; Company of Killers; McQ; The Other Side of Midnight; A Force of One; Touched by Love; The Initiation; Into The Night; Prime Risk; The Return Of The Living Dead.

TV inc: A Different Drummer; The Virginian; SFX; A Question of Love; Willa; Once An Eagle; This Man Stands Alone; Sticking Together; King; MacKenzies of Paradise Cove; Kenny Rogers as the Gambler; Skyward; Living Proof--The Hank Williams Jr Story; The Master; Space.

GULKIN, Harry: Prod. b. Montreal, Nov 14, 1927. Films inc: Two Solitudes; Jacob Two-Two Meets the Hooded Fang; Lies My Father Told Me; Bayo.

GUMBEL, Bryant: Sportscaster. b. New Orleans, LA., Sept. 29, 1949. e. Bates Coll. Sports dir KNBC, LA since 1976. Network tv inc: (host) NCAA Basketball Championships; Super Bowl XI; Super Bowl XII; Games People Play; Different as Night and Day; Fourth Annual TV Guide Special; Macy's Thanksgiving Day Parade; The TV Academy Hall Of Fame 1985.

GUNEY, Yilmaz: Prod-Dir-Wri-Act. b. Turkey, 1937. Originally an actor, career interrupted when Turkish govt imprisoned him on Communist propaganda charges; released after 18 months, resumed acting becoming one of country's top stars; formed own prodn company, later began directing own films. Imprisoned again in 1972 for harboring student activists, released 1974 in general amnesty but six months later (Sept 1974) sentenced to 18 years for murder; completed the film Endise (Anxiety) in prison and made five others from behind bars (writing, directing and editing by memo) before escaping from prison Oct 1981.

Films inc: At Avrat Silah (The Horse, The Woman, The Gun); Seyyit Iran (Bride of Earth); Ac Kurtlar (Hungry Wolves); Umut (Hope); Agit (Elegy); Yarin Son Dundur (Tomorrow Is the Last Day); Arkadas (The Friend); Endise (Anxiety); Izin; Bir Gun Mutlaka; Suru (The Herd); Dusman (The Enemy); Yol; Le Mur (The Wall); Autour du Mur (About "The Wall") (doc).

(Died Sept. 9, 1984)

GUNN, Moses: Act. b. St Louis, MO, Oct 2, 1929. e. TN State U. Films inc: The Great White Hope; The Wild Rovers; Shaft; The Hot Rock; Amazing Grace. Rollerball; Aaron Loves Angela; Remember My Name; The Ninth Configuration; Ragtime; Amityville II--The Possession; Firestarter; The Neverending Story; Certain Fury.

TV inc: Mr Carter's Army; Of Mice and Men; Haunts of the Very Rich; If You Give a Dance, You Gotta Pay the Band; The Cowboys; Roots; The Contender; Father Murphy; The Killing Floor; The House Of Dies Drear (WonderWorks); Charlotte Forten's Mission--Experiment In Freedom.

Thea inc: In White America; Song of the Lusitanian Bogey; Measure for Measure; Romeo and Juliet; As You Like It; Macbeth; Othello; A Hand Is on the Gate.

GURLEY, Randy: Mus. b. Salem, MA, Nov 29, 1952. Recording artist. TV inc: Hee Haw; Good Old Nashville Music.

GUTHRIE, Arlo: Act. b. NYC, Jul 10, 1947. S of Woody Guthrie. Films inc: Alice's Restaurant; Renaldo and Clara.

GUTTENBERG, Steve: Act. b. Brooklyn, NY., Aug. 24, 1958. e. High School for the Performing Arts; Juilliard; studied with Lee Strasberg, Uta Hagen. Films inc: The Chicken Chronicles; The Boys From Brazil;

Players; Can't Stop the Music; Diner; The Man Who Wasn't There; Police Academy; Police Academy 2--Their First Assignment; Cocoon.

TV inc: Something for Joey; To Race the Wind; Miracle on Ice; Billy; No Soap, Radio.

GWYNNE, Anne (Marguerite Gwynne Trice): Act. b. Waco, TX, Dec 10, 1918. e. Stephens Coll. Films inc: Framed; Unexpected Father; Honeymoon Deferred; House of Frankenstein; Fear; The Ghost Goes West; Dick Tracy Meets Gruesome; Call of the Klondike; Breakdown; Teenage Monster.

Thea inc: Stage Door; Inside Story; The Colonel's Lady.

GWYNNE, Fred: Act. b. NYC, Jul 10, 1926. e. Harvard U. Thea inc: Mrs McThing; Love's Labour's Lost; Irma la Douce; The Lincoln Mask; More Than You Deserve; Cat On a Hot Tin Roof; The Winter's Tale; Angel; Whodunit.

Films inc: Luna; Simon; So Fine; The Cotton Club; Water.

TV inc: The Munsters; The Munster's Revenge; Any Friend of Nicholas Nickleby Is A Friend of Mine; The Mysterious Stranger.

GYLLENHAAL, Stephen: Dir. b. Cleveland, OH, Oct 4, 1949. e. Trinity Coll, BA. TV inc: Exit 10; What Are Friends For?; The House That Half-Jack Built; Lost In Death Valley (& wri); Help Wanted (& prod).

Films inc: Certain Fury (dir); The New Kids (wri).

HAACK, Morton R: Cos Dsgn. b. Los Angeles, Jun 26, 1924. Films inc: Games; Walk Don't Run; The Unsinkable Molly Brown; Jumbo; Come September; Please Don't Eat the Daisies; Planet of the Apes.

Bway inc: Make Mine Manhattan. Has also des prima donna costumes for LaScala.

HACK, Shelley: Act. b. CT, Jul 6. e. Smith Coll. Former model. TV inc: Death Car; Charlie's Angels; Cutter to Houston; Trackdown--Finding the Goodbar Killer; Found Money; Single Bars, Single Women; Kicks.

Films inc: Annie Hall; If I Ever See You Again; The King of Comedy.

HACKETT, Albert: Wri. b. 1900. Usually in collab with late wife, Frances Goodrich. Films inc: The Thin Man; After the Thin Man; Naughty Marietta; Another Thin Man; The Hitler Gang; It's A Wonderful Life; Summer Holiday; Father of the Bride; Seven Brides for Seven Brothers; The Diary of Anne Frank.

Bway inc: The Diary of Anne Frank (Tony-1956).

TV inc: The Diary of Anne Frank.

HACKETT, Buddy: Comedian-Act. b. NYC, Aug 31, 1924. Began professional career in the Catskills.

Bway inc: Lunatics and Lovers; I Had a Ball.

Films inc: Walking My Baby Back Home; Fireman, Save My Child; God's Little Acre; All Hands on Deck; The Music Man; The Wonderful World of the Brothers Grimm; It's A Mad, Mad, Mad, Mad World; The Love Bug; The Good Guys and the Bad Guys; Loose Shoes; Hey Babe!

TV inc: Jack Frost (voice); You Bet Your Life; There Goes the Neighborhood; On Location--Buddy Hackett Live and Uncensored (& exec prod) (cable).

HACKETT, Joan: Act. b. NYC, 1942. Films inc: The Group; Will Penny; Support Your Local Sheriff; Assignment to Kill; The Rivals; The Last of Sheila; Mr Mike's Mondo Video; One-Trick Pony; Only When I Laugh; The Escape Artist.

TV inc: The Young Country; Class of '63; Reflections of Murder; Pleasure Cove; Long Days of Summer; The Long Summer of George Adams; Paper Dolls; A Girl's Life.

Thea inc: Laurette; She Didn't Say Yes.

(Died Oct. 8, 1983).

HACKFORD, Taylor: Dir. b. 1945. H of Lynne Littman. Started with KCET (LA) as prod-dir. Films inc: Teenage Father (Oscar-short-1978); The Idolmaker; An Officer and A Gentleman; Against All Odds (& prod).

HACKMAN, Gene: Act. b. San Bernardino, CA, Jan 30, 1931. Films inc: Lilith; Hawaii; First To Fight; A Covenant With Death; Banning; Bonnie And Clyde; The French Connection (Oscar-1971); The Split; Riot; Downhill Racer; I Never Sang For My Father; Gypsy Moths; Marooned; Doctors Wives; Hunting Party; Cisco Pike; Prime Cuts; The

Poseidon Adventure; Conversation; Scarecrow; Zandy's Bride; Young Frankenstein; Bite The Bullet; French Connection 2; Lucky Lady; Night Moves; The Domino Principle; A Bridge Too Far; March Or Die; Superman; Superman II; All Night Long; Eureka; Under Fire; Uncommon Valor; Misunderstood.

HADJIDAKIS, Manos: Comp. b. Greece, 1925. Films inc: Stella; A Matter of Dignity; Never On Sunday (Oscar-song-1959); America, America; Blue; Topkapi; Memed, My Hawk.

Bway inc: Ilya, Darling.

HAEBERLE, Horatius: Wri-Prod. b. Berlin, Feb 24, 1940. Films inc: Fort Travis; Anaconda Run.

HAGEN, Jean (nee Verhagen): Act. b. Chicago, 1924. Films inc: Side Street; Adam's Rib; The Asphalt Jungle; Singin' in the Rain; Carbine Williams; Latin Lovers; Half a Hero; Spring Reunion; The Shaggy Dog; Sunrise at Campobello; Panic in Year Zero; Dead Ringer.

TV inc: Make Room for Daddy.

HAGEN, Uta: Act. b. Gottingen, Germany, Jun 12, 1919. e. RADA. Stage debut 1937, with Eva Le Gallienne's Civic Repertory Co.

Bway inc: The Seagull; Happiest Days; Key Largo; Othello; Faust; A Streetcar Named Desire; The Country Girl (Tony-1950); The Affairs of Anatol; Island of Goats; One Touch of Venus; Show Boat; Pandora and the Flying Dutchman; Snows of Kilimanjaro; Mogambo;

TV inc: Macbeth; Out of the Dust; A Month in the Country; A Doctor's Story.

Films inc: The Other; The Boys From Brazil.

HAGGARD, Merle: Singer. b. Bakersfield, CA, Apr 6, 1937. C & W recording artist. TV inc: Huck Finn; Movin' On (score); Centennial; Johnny Cash Christmas 1983.

(Grammy-country vocal-1984).

HAGGARD, Piers: Dir. b. Scotland, 1939. e. U of Edinburgh. Worked in various Scottish theatrical prodns before joining Britain's National Theatre where he spent two years as asst to Franco Zeffirelli and Laurence Olivier. Asst to Michaelangelo Antonioni on Blow Up.

Films inc: Wedding Night; Satan's Skin; Quatermass Conclusion; The Fiendish Plot of Dr. Fu Manchu; Venom.

TV inc: A Divorce; The Chester Mystery Plays; Poor Cherry; Pennies from Heaven; Mrs. Reinhardt.

HAGGERTY, Dan: Act. b. Hollywood, CA, Nov 19. Films inc: Where the North Wind Blows; Wild Country; Grasslands; Easy Rider; King of the Mountain.

TV inc: The Life and Times of Grizzly Adams; Terror Out of the Sky; Condominium; California Gold Rush; The Capture of Grizzly Adams.

HAGMAN, Larry: Act. b. Ft Worth, TX, Sep 21, 1931. S of Mary Martin. Films inc: Fail Safe; Ensign Pulver and the Captain; The Cavern; Stardust; 3 in the Cellar; Mother, Jugs and Speed; Harry and Tonto; The Eagle Has Landed; Checkered Flag or Crash; Superman; S.O.B.; Jag Rodnar (I'm Blushing).

TV inc: Edge of Night; The President's Mistress; Last of the Good Guys; Battered; I Dream of Jeannie; The Good Life; Here We Go Again; Dallas; A Cry for Justice; Diana; Omnibus; Deadly Encounter; On Top All Over The World.

Thea inc: Once Around the Block; Career; Comes a Day; A Priest in the House.

HAGMANN, Stuart: Dir. b. Sturgeon Bay, WI, Sep 2, 1942. Films inc: The Strawberry Statement; Believe In Me; Good Night, Socrates (short).

TV inc: Mission Impossible; Mannix; Code Three; Sparrow; She Lives; Tarantula.

HAGUE, Albert: Comp. b. Berlin, Germany, Oct 13, 1920. e. Royal Conservatory, Rome; College of Music U of Cincinnati, B Mus. Stage scores inc: The Madwoman of Chaillot; Dance Me A Song (songs); Plain and Fancy; Redhead (Tony-1944); Cafe Crown; The Fig Leaves Are Falling; Miss Moffat.

Films inc: Coney Island USA; The Funniest Man in the World; Fame (act); Nightmares (act).

TV inc: The Mercer Girls; How the Grinch Stole Christmas; Fame (act); Not Just Another Affair; Passions.

HAID, Charles: Act. b. San Francisco, Jun 2, 1943. e. Carnegie Tech, BFA. Bway inc: Elizabeth The First; Godspell (co-prod). Films inc: The Choirboys; Oliver's Story; Who'll Stop the Rain; Altered States; The House of God.

TV inc: Grandpa Goes to Washington; Sweepstakes; A Death In Canaan; The Execution of Private Slovik; Foster & Laurie; Things In Their Season; Death Moon; Kate McShane; Delvecchio; The Bastard; Hill Street Blues; Twirl; Divorce Wars--A Love Story; Working; Children In The Crossfire (& prod); Code Of Vengeance.

HAILEY, Arthur: Wri. b. Luton, England, Apr 4, 1920. Wrote for TV before turning to novels. Authored Airport. Other novels made into films inc: Hotel; The Young Doctors; Zero Hour.

HAILEY, Oliver: Wri. b. Pampa, TX, Jul 7, 1932. e. U of TX; Yale School of Drama, MFA. Plays inc: Hey You, Light Man!; First One Asleep; Father's Day; Continental Divide; And Where She Stops Nobody Knows; Tryptich; I Won't Dance.

TV inc: McMillan & Wife (ed); Mary Hartman, Mary Hartman (cnsltnt); Another Day (co-prod); Sidney Shorr; Isabel's Choice.

Films inc: Just You and Me Kid.

HAINES, Larry: Act. b. Mt Vernon, NY, Aug 3. Bway inc: Twigs; Last of the Red Hot Lovers; Promises, Promises; A Thousand Clowns; Generation; Paris Is Out.

TV inc: Search for Tomorrow (Emmys-1976; Supp-1981); Doc; Maude; Sunshine Boys; Phil & Mikky.

Films inc: The Odd Couple; The Seven-Ups.

HAKIM, Robert: Prod. b. Egypt, 1907. Partnered for years with late brother Raymond in Paris Film Prodns. Films inc: Pepe le Moko; La Bete Humaine; Le Jour se leve; The Southerner; Her Husband's Affairs; The Long Night; The Blue Veil; Belle de Jour; Isadora; La Marge.

HALAS, John: Prod-Dir. b. Budapest, Hungary, Apr 16, 1912. Prod over 500 docs, educational shorts & cartoons.

Films inc: Animal Farm; Ruddigore; The Kid From Outer Space; Parkinson's Law.

HALE, Alan, Jr: Act. b. Los Angeles, 1918. Films inc: I Wanted Wings; Spirit of West Point; It Happens Every Spring; Lady in the Iron Mask; Springfield Rifle; Destry; Many Rivers to Cross; The Sea Chase; The True Story of Jesse James; Bullet for a Bad Man; Hang 'Em High; Dead Heat; There Was a Crooked Man; The Fifth Musketeer; The North Avenue Irregulars; Hambone and Hillie.

TV inc: Wagon Train; Cheyenne; Maverick; Biff Baker, USA; Casey Jones; Gilligan's Island; The Castaways on Gilligan's Island; Revenge of the Red Chief; The Harlem Globetrotters On Gilligan's Island.

HALE, Barbara: Act. b. DeKalb, IL, Apr 18, 1922. Films inc: Higher and Higher; The Falcon in Hollywood; First Yank into Tokyo; Lady Luck; The Boy with Green Hair; The Window; Jolson Sings Again; The Jackpot; Lorna Doone; A Lion is in the Streets; Unchained; The Far Horizons; The Oklahoman; Airport; Big Wednesday.

TV inc: Perry Mason (Emmy-supp-1959).

HALEY, Alex: Autobiography of Malcolm X; Roots (Special Pulitzer Prize citation, 1977). TV inc: Palmerstown USA (exec prod).

HALEY, Jack, Jr: Prod-Dir-Wri. b. Los Angeles, Oct 25, 1933. e. Loyola U, BS. Joined David L Wolper Prodns 1959; named sr vp 1967; in 1973 moved to MGM as dir of creative arts; in 1975 became p, Fox TV; indie prod in 1976.

TV inc: The Incredible World of James Bond; The General; The Legend of Marilyn Monroe; The Supremes; The Hidden World; Movin' with Nancy (Emmy-dir-1968); With Love, Sophia; Monte Carlo, C'est La Rose; The Best of the Brass; Academy Award Show dir, 1970, prod, 1974; Life Goes to War: Hollywood and the Homefront; Heroes of Rock n' Roll (exec prod); 51st Annual Academy Awards (Emmy-1979); Ripley's Believe It or Not; Hollywood--The Gift of Laughter; 56th Annual Academy Awards (prod). The Night They Saved Christmas (exec prod).

Films inc: Norwood; The Love Machine; That's Entertainment; Bet-

ter Late Than Never (prod).

HALEY, Jackie Earle: Act. b. Northridge, CA, Jul 14, 1961. Films inc: The Outside Man; The Day of the Locust; Damnation Alley; Bad News Bears; The Bad News Bears Break Training; The Bad News Bears in Japan; Breaking Away; Losin' It; The Zoo Gang.

TV inc: Breaking Away; Every Stray Dog and Kid; Miss Lonely Hearts.

Bway inc: Slab Boys.

HALL, Conrad: Cin. b. Tahiti, 1927. Films inc: Morituri; Harper; The Professionals; Cool Hand Luke; In Cold Blood; Hell in the Pacific; Butch Cassidy and the Sundance Kid (Oscar-1969); Tell Them Willie Boy is Here; The Happy Ending; Fat City; The Day of the Locust; Smile; Marathon Man.

HALL, Huntz (Henry): Act. b. NYC, 1920. e. Professional Children's School. On Bway in Dead End prior to films. Films inc: Dead End; Crime School; Angels with Dirty Faces; They Made Me A Criminal; Hell's Kitchen; Angels Wash Their Faces; The Return of Dr X; You're Not So Tough; Give Us Wings; Hit The Road; Bowery Blitzkrieg; Mob Town; Mr. Wise Guy; Private Buckaroo; Kid Dynamite; Bowery Champs; Wonder Man; Bowery Bombshell; A Walk In The Sun; Angels in Disguise; Lucky Losers; Loose in London; Paris Playboys; High Society; Bowery To Bagdad; Spook Chasers; The Gentle Giant; The Love Bug Rides Again; Gas Pump Girls; Valentino.

TV inc: Chicago Teddy Bears; The Ratings Game (PC).

HALL, Ken G.: Prod-Dir. b. Sydney, Australia, Feb 22, 1901. Films inc: On Our Selections; Squatter's Daughter; Tall Timbers; Lovers and Luggers; Mr Chedworth Steps Out; Vengeance of the Deep; Pacific Adventure (ret).

HALL, Monty: Act. b. Winnipeg, Canada, 1923. e. U of Manitoba, BS. Teenage radio actor, 1940. TV since 1952.

TV inc: (host) Let's Make a Deal; Strike It Rich; Video Village; Your First Impression; An All-Star Party For Carol Burnett; All-Star Party For Lucille Ball.

Films inc: Courage and the Passion.

HALL, Peter, Sir: Prod-Dir. b. Suffolk, England, Nov 22, 1930. e. Cambridge. Dir Oxford Playhouse 1954-55; Arts Theatre 1955-57; M-Dir Royal Shakespeare Company 1960-68, creating RSC as permanent ensemble; succeeded Lord Olivier as dir National Theatre Company of Great Britain 1973.

Thea inc; The Lesson; Waiting for Godot; Waltz of the Toreadors; Becket; The Collection; The Homecoming (Tony-1967); A Delicate Balance; Old Times; Tristan und Isolde; Via Galactica; Happy Days; John Gabriel Borkman; No Man's Land; Judgement; Tamburlaine the Great; Bedroom Farce; Betrayal; Amadeus (London & Bway) (Tony-dir-1980); 84 Charing Cross Road; The Importance of Being Earnest; numerous Shakespearean prodns for RSC; Jean Seberg; Martine.

Films inc: A Midsummer Night's Dream; Three Into Two Won't Go; Perfect Friday; Landscape; The Homecoming; Akenfield.

TV inc: The Wars of the Roses (adaptation of four Shakespeare plays).

HALL, Tom T.: Singer-Sngwri. b. Olive Hill, KY, May 25, 1936. Worked as deejay, WMOR; with groups Tom Hall and the Kentucky Travelers; The Technicians; The Story Tellers. Albums inc: In Search of Song; We All Got Together and--; The Story Teller; Songs of Fox Hollow; Magnificent Music Machine; Tom T Hall's Greatest Hits.

TV inc: Harper Valley PTA; Music City News' Top Country Hits of the Year.

Film inc: Deadhead Miles (mus).

HALLER, Daniel: Dir. b. Glendale, CA, 1928. Films inc: Die Monster Die; The Devil's Angels; The Wild Racers; Paddy; The Dunwich Horror; Pieces of Dreams; Buck Rogers in the 25th Century.

TV inc: Sword of Justice; Kojak; Owen Marshall; Black Beauty; Little Mo; High Midnight; Georgia Peaches; Mickey Spillane's Margin for Murder; The 25th Man; Knight Rider; The Fall Guy; Welcome to Paradise.

HALLIWELL, Leslie: Exec-Wri. b. Bolton, England, Feb 23, 1929. e.

Cambridge. Film buyer for Granada TV. Author of film books The Filmgoers Companion; The Filmgoers Book of Quotes; The Clapperboard Book of the Cinema (with Graham Murray); Halliwell's Movie Quiz; Halliwell's Film Guide; Halliwell's Television Companion; Mountains of Dreams; Halliwell's Hundred. Plays inc: Make Your Own Bed; A Night on the Island.

HALMI, Robert: Prod. b. Budapest, Hungary, Jan 22, 1924. Originally wri-photog, under contract to Life Magazine. TV inc: Bold Journey (dir-cin); American Sportsman; The Oriental Sportsman; The Flying Doctor; The Outdoorsman; Julius Boros Series; Rexford; Who Needs Elephants; Calloway's Climb; Oberndorf Revisited; True Position; Wilson's Reward; Nurse; Buckley Sails; A Private Battle; My Old Man; Mr. Griffin and Me; When the Circus Came to Town; Best of Friends; Bush Doctor; Peking Encounter; Svengali; China Rose; Cook and Peary--The Race to the Pole; Terrible Joe Moran; Nairobi Affair; The Night They Saved Christmas.
Films inc dox for UN. Features inc: Hugo the Hippo; Visit To a Chief's Son; One and Only; Brady's Escape.

HALSEY, Richard: Flm Ed. Started as apprentice ed, later ed on TV. Series inc: Maverick; Cheyenne; 77 Sunset Strip; Peyton Place (more than 500 episodes).
Films inc: Payday; Harry and Tonto; W.W. and the Dixie Dance Kings; Next Stop Greenwich Village; Rocky (Oscar-1976); Thank God It's Friday; Boulevard Nights; American Gigolo; Tribute; The Amateur; That Championship Season; Losin' It; Moscow on the Hudson; Dreamscape; Body Rock; Heated Vengeance.

HAMBLEN, Stuart: Act-Comp. b. Kellyville, TX, Oct 20, 1908. One of the major C&W recording artists; also performed on radio. Ran for P of the U S in 1952 on the Prohibition Party ticket.

HAMBLETON, Thomas Edward: Prod. b. Towson, MD, Feb 12, 1911. e. Yale U, BA. Founder (1953) and M-dir Phoenix Theatre, NY. Prodns inc: Robin Landing; I Know What I Like; The First Crocus; The Great Campaign; Galileo; Temporary Island; Ballet Ballads; Pride's Crossing; The American Bell; Once Upon a Mattress; Saint Joan; Diary of a Scoundrel; The Power and the Glory; The Matchmaker; Man and Superman; War and Peace; Judith; You Can't Take It With You; Cock-A-Doodle-Dandy; Harvey; The Criminals; The Persians; The School for Wives; The Trial of the Catonsville 9; Murderous Angels.

HAMEL, Veronica: Act. b. Philadelphia, PA, Nov 20, 1943. e. Temple U. Films inc: Cannonball; Beyond the Poseidon Adventure; When Time Ran Out.
TV inc: Ski Lift; 79 Park Avenue; The Gathering; Gathering II; Hill Street Blues; Jacqueline Susann's Valley of the Dolls 1981; Sessions.

HAMILL, Mark: Act. b. San Francisco, Sep 25, 1951. TV inc: General Hospital; Texas Wheelers; Sarah: Portrait of a Teenage Alcoholic; Erick; Mallory; SPFX--The Empire Strikes Back (host).
Films inc: Star Wars; Corvette Summer; The Empire Strikes Back; The Big Red One; The Night The Lights Went Out In Georgia; Return of the Jedi.
Thea inc: The Elephant Man. (Bway) Amadeus; Harrigan 'n Hart.

HAMILL, Pete (William Hamill): Wri. b. Brooklyn, NY, Jun 24, 1935. Columnist, NY newspapers.
Films inc: Doc; Badge 373.

HAMILTON, Arthur: Comp-Lyr. b. Seattle. TV inc: I Love Lucy.
Thea inc: What A Day.
Songs inc: He Needs Me; Sing a Rainbow; Cry Me a River; You'll Remember Me; Till Love Touches Your Life.

HAMILTON, Bernie: Act. b. Los Angeles, Jun 12. Films inc: The Jackie Robinson Story; Let No Man Write My Epitaph; The Devil at 4 O' Clock; One Potato, Two Potato; Synanon; The Swimmer; The Losers; The Organization.
TV inc: That's My Mama; Hec Ramsey; The Bold Ones; Starsky & Hutch.
Thea inc: Take a Giant Step; The Petrified Forest; Othello; Waiting for Lefty; No Time for Sergeants.

HAMILTON, Dirk: Sngwri-Singer. b. IN, Aug 31, 1949. Recording

artist.

HAMILTON, George: Act. b. Memphis, TN, Aug 12, 1939. Films inc: Crime and Punishment U.S.A; Home From The Hill; Where the Boys Are; All the Fine Young Cannibals; Light in the Piazza; Two Weeks in Another Town; Act One; Your Cheatin' Heart; Viva Maria!; The Power; Evel Knievel; Once Is Not Enough; Sextette; Love at First Bite (& prod); From Hell to Victory; Zorro, the Gay Blade (& prod).
TV inc: Institute for Revenge; Death Car on the Freeway; The Seekers; The Great Cash Giveaway; The Fantastic Miss Piggy Show; Malibu; Poor Richard; Two Fathers' Justice.

HAMILTON, Guy: Dir. b. Paris, Sep 1922. Former asst to Carol Reed. Films inc: The Ringer; The Intruder; An Inspector Calls; The Colditz Story; Charley Moon; The Devil's Disciple; A Touch of Larceny; The Best of Enemies; Live and Let Die; The Man with the Golden Gun; The Man in the Middle; Goldfinger; The Battle of Britain; Diamonds are Forever; Force 10 From Navarone; The Mirror Crack'd; Evil Under The Sun.

HAMILTON, Joe: Prod. b. Los Angeles, Jan 6. H of Carol Burnett. Orig singer with the Skylarks.
TV inc: The Gary Moore Show; exec prod Carol Burnett Show (3 Emmys-1972, 1974, 1975); Julie and Carol at Carnegie Hall; Calamity Jane; Once Upon A Mattress; 6 Rms Riv Vu; Twigs; Sills and Burnett at the Met; The Grass Is Always Greener Over the Septic Tank; The Tenth Month; Eunice; Mama's Family (exec prod).

HAMILTON, Linda: Act. b. Salisbury, MD, Sep 26. Studied with Lee Strasberg. TV inc: Rape and Marriage--The Rideout Case; Reunion; Secrets of Midland Heights; King's Crossing; Country Gold; Wishman; Secrets of a Mother and Daughter; Secret Weapons.
Films inc: Tag; Children of the Corn; The Terminator.

HAMILTON, Margaret: Act. b. Cleveland, OH, Dec 9, 1902. Films inc: Another Language; These Three; Nothing Sacred; The Wizard of Oz; Invisible Woman; Guest in the House; Mad Wednesday; State of the Union; The Great Plane Robbery; Thirteen Ghosts; The Daydreamer; Rosie; The Anderson Tapes; Brewster McCloud.
TV inc: Letters From Frank.
(Died May 16, 1985.)

HAMILTON, Murray: Act. b. 1923. Films inc: Bright Victory; No Time for Sergeants; The FBI Story; Seconds; The Graduate; No Way to Treat a Lady; The Boston Strangler; If It's Tuesday This Must Be Belgium; The Way We Were; Jaws; Jaws II; Casey's Shadow; The Amityville Horror; 1941; Brubaker; Hysterical; Too Scared To Scream.
TV inc: Donovan's Kid; Swan Song; All the Way Home; Rona Jaffee's Mazes & Monsters; Summer Girl; The Boys In Blue; Hail To The Chief.

HAMILTON, Neil: Act. b. Lynn, MA, Sep 9, 1899. Films inc: White Rose; America; Isn't Life Wonderful; Beau Geste; The Great Gatsby; Keeper of the Bees; The Dawn Patrol; The Animal Kingdom; Tarzan the Ape Man; One Sunday Afternoon; Tarzan and His Mate; The Little Shepherd of Kingdom Come; Madame X.
TV inc: Batman.
(Died Sept. 24, 1984)

HAMLIN, Harry: Act. b. CA, Oct 30, 1951. e. UC Berkeley; ACT. Films inc: Movie Movie; King of the Mountain; Clash of the Titans; Making Love; Blue Skies Again.
TV inc: Studs Lonigan; Master of the Game; Space.
Bway inc: Awake and Sing.

HAMLISCH, Marvin: Comp-Cond. b. NYC, Jun 2, 1944. e. Juilliard. Films inc: Flap; The Sting (Oscar-adapt-score-1973); The Way We Were (Oscar-score-1973), (Oscar-best song-1973); The Spy Who Loved Me; Same Time, Next Year; Ice Castles; Starting Over; Ordinary People; Seems Like Old Times; The Devil and Max Devlin; I Ought To Be In Pictures; Sophie's Choice; Romantic Comedy; D.A.R.Y.L.
Bway inc: A Chorus Line (Pulitzer Prize & Tony-1976); They're Playing Our Song; Jean Seberg (London); Shirley MacLaine on Broadway.
TV inc: The Entertainer (prod); Omnibus (theme); A Streetcar

Named Desire; Shirley MacLaine.

(Grammys-(4)-New Artist, Song of Year, Film Score, Pop Instrumental-1974).

HAMMOND, Peter: Act-Wri-Dir. b. London, Nov 15, 1923. Films inc: They Knew Mr Knight; Holiday Camp; Fly Away Peter; Morning Departure; Vote for Huggett; The Adventurers; Spring and Port Wine (dir only).

TV inc: William Tell; Robin Hood; The Buccaneers; Three Musketeers; Treasure Island; Our Mutual Friend; The House that Jack Built; The Black Knight.

HAMNER, Earl: Prod-Wri. b. Schuyler, VA, Jul 10, 1923. With WLW, Cincinnati as radio-wri-prod; joined NBC 1949 as wri; 1960 freelance.

TV inc: The Waltons (crea-co-prod); Joshua's World; Falcon Crest (exec prod); A Wedding On Walton's Mountain (exec prod); Mother's Day On Walton's Mountain (exec prod-act); A Day of Thanks On Walton's Mountain (exec prod-act); Boone (exec prod); The Gift of Love--A Christmas Story (exec prod-wri).

Films inc: Spencers Mountain; You Can't Get There From Here; The Homecoming.

HAMPSHIRE, Susan: Act. b. London, May 12, 1942. Films inc: Upstairs and Downstairs; During One Night; The Long Shadow; The Three Lives of Thomasina; Night Must Fall; Wonderful Life; The Fighting Prince of Donegal; The Trygon Factor; Monte Carlo or Bust; A Time for Loving; Living Free.

TV inc: David Copperfield; Baffled; (series): The Forsyte Saga (Emmy-1970); The First Churchills (Emmy-1971); The Pallisers; Vanity Fair (Emmy-1973); The Barchester Chronicles.

Thea inc: Expresso Bongo; Follow That Girl; Fairy Tales of New York; Ginger Man; Past Imperfect; She Stoops to Conquer; Peter Pan; Romeo & Jeanette; The Circle; Arms and the Man; Man and Superman; The Crucifer of Blood; House Guest.

HAMPTON, Christopher: Wri. b. Azores, Jan. 26, 1946. Plays inc: When Did You Last See My Mother?; Total Eclipse; The Philanthropist; Savages; Treats; Tidbits; The Portage to San Cristobal of A.H.

TV inc: Abel's Will; The History Man; Tales from Hollywood.

Films inc: A Doll's House; Tales From the Vienna Woods; Beyond the Limit.

HAMPTON, James: Act. b. Oklahoma City, OK, Jul 9, 1936. e. North TX State U. Films inc: Fade In; Soldier Blue; The Man Who Loved Cat Dancing; The Longest Yard; W.W. and the Dixie Dance Kings; Hustle; The Cat From Outer Space; The China Syndrome; Champs; McIntosh and TJ; Eyewitness; Hangar 18; Condorman.

TV inc: F Troop; Doris Day Show; Stand By Your Man; Maggie; World War III; Kudzu; The Burning Bed.

HAMPTON, Lionel: Mus. b. Birmingham, AL, Apr 12, 1913. Virtually self-taught on drums, vibraharp; worked with Les Hite and Eddie Elkins Bands while attending USC; guest drummer with Louis Armstrong on recording dates; with Benny Goodman Quartet 1936 to 1940; organized own band; a top attraction during big band era, band toured the world.

TV inc: No Maps On My Taps (doc); (Emmy-music-1980); The Kennedy Center Honors 1982.

HANCOCK, John: Dir. b. Kansas City, MO, Feb 12, 1939. e. Harvard U. Films inc: Let's Scare Jessica to Death; Bang the Drum Slowly; Baby Blue Marine; Foul Play; California Dreaming; The In-Laws.

HANCOCK, Sheila, OBE: Act. b. Isle of Wight. e. RADA. Thea inc: (London) Breath of Spring; One to Another; Make Me an Offer; One Over the Eight; Rattle of a Simple Man; The Anniversary; The Soldier's Fortune; Fill The Stage With Happy Hours; A Delicate Balance; So What About Love; All Over; Absurd Person Singular; Deja Revue; Annie.

Films inc: Light Up Sky; A Girl in a Boat; Night Must Fall; The Anniversary; Take A Girl Like You.

TV inc: Mr. Digby Darling; Now Take My Wife; But Seriously, It's Sheila Hancock.

HANDEL, Leo A: Dir-Prod-Wri. b. Vienna. P Handel Film Corp. Films

inc: The Case of Patty Smith (prod-dir-wri); Phantom Planet (prod).

TV inc: Everyday Adventures; Magic of the Atom; The American Indian; Police Dog.

HANDELMAN, Stanley Myron: Comedian. Worked top niteries as single, opening act for Frank Sinatra, Bobbie Gentry. TV inc: Dean Martin Show; Golddiggers; Merv Griffin Show; Hollywood Squares; Make Room for Granddaddy; A Cry For Love; It's Not Easy Being Me--The Rodney Dangerfield Show (wri).

HANKS, Tom: Act. b. Oakland, CA., July 9, 1956. e. CA State U Sacramento. Started with Great Lakes Shakespeare Festival, Cleveland. TV inc: Bosom Buddies; Rona Jaffe's Mazes & Monsters.

Films inc: He Knows You're Alone; Splash; Bachelor Party.

HANLEY, William: Wri. b. Lorain, OH., Oct. 22, 1931. e. Cornell; AADA. TV inc: Flesh and Blood; Too Far To Go; The Family Man; The Scarlett O'Hara War (Movieola); The Silent Lovers (Movieola); Father Figure; Something About Amelia; Celebrity.

Films inc: The Gypsy Moths.

Plays inc: Whisper Into My Good Ear; Mrs. Dally Has a Lover; Conversations in the Dark; Today is Independence Day; Slow Dance on the Killing Ground; No Answer.

HANNA, William: Prod-Exec. b. Melrose, NM, Jul 14, 1911. e. Compton Coll. Worked briefly as a structural engineer; turned to cartooning with Leon Schlessinger's company in Hollywood; in 1937 hired by MGM as dir and story man in cartoon dept; met Joseph R Barbera and created Tom & Jerry, the first of seven Academy Award winning cartoons; left MGM in 1957 to form Hanna-Barbera Prodns (of which Hanna is VP) to make cartoons for TV.

TV inc: Jack and the Beanstalk; The Last of the Curlews (Emmy-1973); The Runaways (Emmy-1974); The Popeye Valentine Special; Sweethearts at Sea; Scooby Goes to Hollywood; The Flintstone's New Neighbors; Smurfs (Emmys-prod-1983, exec prod 1984); The Smurf Springtime Special; The Jokebook (& dir); The Smurf's Christmas Special; Yogi Bear's All-Star Comedy Christmas Caper; Christmas Comes to Pacland; The Smurfic Games; Smurfily Ever After.

Films inc: Charlotte's Web; Heidi's Song; Les Dalton en cavale (Escape From Grumble Gulch) (dir).

HANNAH, Daryl: Act. b. Chicago. Studied at Goodman Theater; USC; with Stella Adler. TV inc: Paper Dolls.

Films inc: The Fury; Hard Country; Blade Runner; Summer Lovers; Reckless; Splash; The Pope Of Greenwich Village.

HANNAY, David: Wri-Prod. b. Wellington, New Zealand, Jun 23, 1939. e. Scots Coll; Auckland U. Films inc: The Set; Stone; The Man From Hong Kong; Solo; Alison's Birthday.

TV inc: Crisis; Spoiler; Polly My Love; Paradise; Is There Anybody There; Mama's Gone A-Hunting; The Alternative; The Godfathers; The Spoiler; The People Next Door; The Unisexers; Kung Fu Killers.

HANNEMANN, Walter: Film edtr. b. Atlanta, GA, May 2, 1914. e. USC; Pomona Coll. Films inc: Hell's Five Hours; Getting Gertie's Garter; Guest in the House; Fabulous Dorseys; Blood on the Sun; Johnny Come Lately; A Lion Is In The Streets; Only the Valiant; Kiss Tomorrow Goodbye; Search for Paradise; Wagons Westward; Jet Pilot; Fort Vengeance; The Rose Bowl Story; The Bob Mathias Story; Pay or Die; Al Capone; A Cannon for Cordova; Guns of the Magnificent Seven; El Condor; A Dream of Kings; Lost in the Stars; Maurie; Two Minute Warning; Smokey and the Bandit; The Other Side of the Mountain Part II; The Villain; The Nude Bomb.

TV inc: Gene Autry; Annie Oakley; Range Riders; Death Valley Days; Dr Christian; June Allyson Show; Wagons West; The Rifleman; The Fugitive; 12 O'Clock High; The Invaders; Streets of San Francisco; Barnaby Jones; Storefront Lawyers; Hawaii Five-O.

HANSEN, Peter: Act. b. Oakland, CA, Dec 5, 1921. e. U MI; Pasadena Playhouse. Films inc: Branded; The Savage; When Worlds Collide; The Goldbergs; Darling, How Could You.

Bway inc: Berkeley Square; The Bat.

TV inc: Matinee Theatre; News Dir KCOP-TV; Day in Court; General Hospital (since 1965) (Emmy-supp-1979).

HANSON, Barry Anthony: Prod. b. England, Aug 10, 1943. TV inc:

Gangsters; The Naked Civil Servant; Plays for Britain; ITV Playhouse.
Films inc: The Long Good Friday; Morons From Outer Space.

HARBACH, William O: Prod. b. NYC, Oct 12, 1919. e. Brown U. S of late Otto Harbach. TV inc: Tonight Show (Steve Allen); Steve Allen Show; Bing Crosby Specials (& dir); Hollywood Palace; Julie Andrews Show *(Emmy*-1973); Gypsy in My Soul *(Emmy*-Exec prod-1976); Steve Allen Comedy Hour; The Kennedy Center Honors, 1980 (cnsltnt); Bob Hope's All-Star Celebration Opening the Gerald R. Ford Museum.

HARDIN, Ty (Orson Hungerford II): Act. b. NYC 1930. Films inc: (as Ty Hungerford) I Married A Monster From Outer Space; (as Hardin) Merrill's Marauders; The Chapman Report; PT 109; Wall of Noise; Palm Springs Weekend; Battle of the Bulge; Berserk; Custer of the West; One Step to Hell; The Last Rebel.
TV inc: Bronco; Riptide; Hunter's Moon.

HARDY, Joseph: Dir-Prod. b. Carlsbad, NM, Mar 8, 1929. e. NM Highland U, BA, MA, DFA; Yale U School of Drama, MFA. Bway inc: (as dir) You're a Good Man, Charlie Brown; Play It Again, Sam; Child's Play *(Tony*1970); What the Butler Saw; Bob and Ray; The Two and Only; Children! Children!; The Crucible; Romantic Comedy.
TV inc: (as prod) Love of Life; The Secret Storm; Time for Us; Love Is a Many Splendored Thing; James at 15 (& dir); The Paper Chase; Love's Savage Fury; The Seduction of Miss Leona; Dream House (dir); The Day The Bubble Burst (dir); Not in Front of the Children (dir); Two Marriages (dir).

HAREWOOD, Dorian: Act. b. Dayton, OH., Aug. 6. Thea inc: Jesus Christ, Superstar (road); Tribute To Oscar Hammerstein; Two Gentlemen Of Verona (Bway); Brainchild; Miss Moffat; Don't Call Back (Bway); Streamers (Bway); The Mighty Gents.
TV inc: Roots-The Next Generations; An American Christmas Carol; High Ice; Beulah Land; Strike Force; The Ambush Murders; I, Desire; Trauma Center; Medstar; The Jesse Owens Story; Dirty Work.
Films inc: Foster & Laurie; Gray Lady Down; Looker; Tank; Against All Odds; The Falcon And The Snowman.

HARGREAVES, John: Act. b. Australia. e. Australian National Institute of Dramatic Art. Worked with Old Tote Theatre; State Theatre Company of South Australia; Sydney Theatre Company. Thea inc: A Month in the Country; Arturo Ui; The National Health; The Government Inspector; The Importance of Being Earnest; Measure for Measure; The Au Pair Man; Cat on a Hot Tin Roof; Present Laughter.
Films inc: The Removalists; Mad Dog Morgan; Don's Party; Long Weekend; The Odd Angry Shot; Beyond Reasonable Doubt; Hoodwink; Killing of Angel Street; Careful, He Might Hear You; The Great Gold Swindle; My First Wife.
TV inc: The Dismissal.

HARGROVE, Dean: Wri-Prod-Dir. b. Iola, KS, Jul 27, 1938. TV inc: wrote Bob Newhart Show, 1961-62; Man From Uncle series; Ransom for a Dead Man (wri-prod); Columbo (wri-prod) *(Emmy*-exec prod-1974); McCloud; Name of the Game; McCoy; The Family Holvak; Madigan (exec prod); Alias Sherlock Holmes (dir); Manchu Eagle Murder Caper Mystery (co-wrote & dir); Me & Mom (supv prod); Goldie And The Bears (exec prod).

HARMAN, Barry: Wri. TV inc: Carol Burnett Show *(Emmy*-1974); Joe and Sons; All in the Family *(Emmy*-1978); The Jeffersons; The Secret World Of The Very Young (lyr).

HARMON, Mark: Act. b. Burbank, CA, Sep 2, 1951. e. UCLA. S of Tom Harmon. Films inc: Comes A Horseman; Beyond the Poseidon Adventure.
TV inc: Eleanor and Franklin; The White House Years; Sam; Centennial; Little Moe; Getting Married; 240-Robert; Flamingo Road; The Dream Merchants; Goliath Awaits; Intimate Agony; St. Elsewhere.

HARMON, Tom: Sportscaster. b. Rensselaer, IN, Sep 28, 1919. e. U of MI, BS. All-American Football player, 1939-40. U.S. Air Force, 1941-46. After service became sportscaster, joined Columbia Pacific Radio Network as sports dir, 1948-61; Tom Harmon Sports Show, ABC, 19621-70; Golden West Broadcasters, 1970-74; Hughes TV Network sports dir, 1974. Editor-Publisher Tom Har-

mon's Football Today. TV inc: Off Sides.

HARNICK, Sheldon M: Lyr. b. Chicago, Apr 30, 1924. e. Northwestern U. Bway inc: New Faces of 1932; Two's Company; John Murray Anderson's Almanac; Shoestring Revue; The Littlest Revue; Body Beautiful; Fiorello *(Pulitzer Prize & Tony*-1960); Tenderloin; She Loves Me; Fiddler on the Roof *(Tony*-1965); Apple Tree; The Rothschilds; Smiling the Boy Fell Dead; Rex; Capt. Jinks of the Horse Marines; Dr Heidegger's Fountain of Youth.
TV inc: The Way They Were.
(Grammy-cast album-1963).

HARPER, Gregory W.: Prod. b. Bethesda, MD, May 4, 1952. e. Amherst Coll, BA. TV inc: 1971-74 CBS News Paris freelance; 1975-76 WGBY TV/WGBH Educational Foundation; 1976-78 $128,000 Question; World Chess Championship.

HARPER, Ron: Act. b. Turtle Creek, PA, Jan 12. e. Princeton U. TV inc: 87th Precinct; Wendy and Me; Garrison's Gorillas; Planet of the Apes; Land of the Lost; Love of Life; Where the Heart Is.
Thea inc: A Palm Tree in a Rose Garden; Night Circus; Sweet Bird of Youth; 6 Rms Riv Vu.
Films inc: Splendor in the Grass; The Savage Season.

HARPER, Valerie: Act. b. Suffern, NY, Aug 22, 1940. TV inc: The Mary Tyler Moore Show *(3 Emmys*-supp-1971, 1972, 1973); Rhoda *(Emmy*-1975); The Shadow Box; The Day The Loving Stopped; Farrell For the People; Don't Go To Sleep; An Invasion of Privacy; The Execution.
Bway inc: Story Theater; Second City; Take Me Along; Wildcat; Subways Are for Sleeping.
Films inc: Chapter Two; The Last Married Couple in America; Fun and Games; Blame It On Rio.

HARPER, William A.: Prod. b. Port Jervis, NY, Sep 3, 1915. e. USC, BS. Prod/dir commercial & industrial films, 1945-51. Films inc: The Silken Affair; S O S Ecuador; The Last Blitzkreig. 1964, organized American-European Film Service, Paris, as prod rep.

HARRINGTON, Curtis: Dir. b. Los Angeles, Sep 17, 1928. Films inc: Night Tide; Queen of Blood; Games; What's the Matter with Helen?; Who Slew Auntie Roo?; Mata Hari.
TV inc: The Dead Don't Die; The Deadly Bees.

HARRINGTON, Pat: Act. b. NYC, Aug 13, 1929. Launched career on Jack Paar Show. Later joined Steve Allen's show, then became a regular on the Danny Thomas Show. Also worked niteries.
Films inc: The President's Analyst.
TV inc: One Day At A Time *(Emmy*-supp-1984); Mr. Deeds Goes To Town; The Critical List; Counsellor-at-Law; Benny and Barney; Between Two Brothers.

HARRIS, Barbara: Act. b. Evanston, IL, Jul 25, 1935. Bway inc: Oh Dad, Poor Dad, Mamma's Hung You in the Closet and I'm Feelin' So Sad; On a Clear Day You Can See Forever; The Apple Tree *(Tony*-1967).
Films inc: A Thousand Clowns; Who Is Harry Kellerman?; The War Between Men and Women; Nashville; Family Plot; Movie Movie; The North Avenue Irregulars; The Seduction of Joe Tynan; Second Hand Hearts; Night Magic.

HARRIS, Ed: Act. b. Tenafly, NJ., 1952. e. CA Institute of the Arts, BA. Films inc: Coma; Borderline; Knightriders; Creepshow; Under Fire; The Right Stuff; Swing Shift; Places In The Heart; A Flash Of Green; Alamo Bay. or in CREATE REPORT state machine.

HARRIS, Emmylou: Singer. b. NC, 1947. Recording artist. *(Grammys*-(4)-country vocal-1976, 1979,1984-country vocal duo-1980).
Films inc: The Last Waltz; Honeysuckle Rose.
TV inc: The Unbroken Circle-A Tribute to Mother Maybelle Carter; Johnny Cash and the Country Girls; Sylvia Tyson's Country Classic.

HARRIS, Harry: Dir. b. Kansas City, MO, Sep 8, 1922. Started as flm edtr. TV inc: (dir) The Texan; Death Valley Days; Wanted Dead or Alive; The Islanders; Gunsmoke; Voyage to the Bottom of the Sea; Lost in Space; Time Tunnel; High Chaparral; Bonanza; Shenandoah;

The Waltons; Blue Knight; Spencer's Pilots; Naked City; Swiss Family Robinson; Love American Style; Kung Fu; The Runaways; The Home Front; Fame *(Emmy-*1982); Have You Ever Been Ashamed Of Your Parents?

HARRIS, James B.: Prod-Dir. b. NYC, Aug 3, 1928. e. Juilliard School of Music. Films inc: The Killing; Paths of Glory; Lolita; The Bedford Incident; Some Call It Loving (& sp); Telefon; Fast-Walking (& sp).

Thea inc: Make A Million; Tovarich; Sweet Charity; Mame.

HARRIS, Julie: Act. b. Grosse Pointe, MI, Dec 2, 1925. e. Yale Drama School. Films inc: Member of the Wedding; East of Eden; I Am a Camera; The Truth About Women; Requiem for a Heavyweight; The Haunting; Reflections in a Golden Eye; The Hiding Place; The Voyage of the Damned; The Bell Jar; Bronte.

Bway inc: Sundown Beach; The Young and The Fair; Magnolia Alley; The Member of the Wedding; I Am a Camera *(Tony-*1952); Mlle Colombe; The Lark *(Tony-*1956); The Country Wife; Little Moon of Alban; Skyscraper; A Streetcar Named Desire; Forty Carats *(Tony-*1969); And Miss Reardon Drinks a Little; The Last of Mrs Lincoln *(Tony-*1973); The Au Pair Man; In Praise of Love; The Belle of Amherst *(Tony-*1976); Break A Leg; Mixed Couples.

TV inc: Little Moon of Alban *(Emmy-*1959); Victoria Regina *(Emmy-*1962); The Belle of Amherst; The Family Holvak; The Last of Mrs. Lincoln. Backstairs at the White House; The Gift; Knot's Landing; TV Academy Hall Of Fame; The 39th Annual Tony Awards.

*(Grammy-*spoken word-1977).

HARRIS, Louis: Prod-Dir (ret). b. NYC, Jan 18, 1906. Assoc prod C B Demille, 1941-42; assoc prod & prod Par short subjects, 1943-46. Prod trailers for Par and National Screen Service to 1970.

Film shorts inc: Mardi Gras; Bombalera; Caribbean Romance; Lucky Cowboy; Bonnie Lassie.

HARRIS, Pat (Patricia): Casting dir. b. NYC, Mar 17. e. Feagin School of Dramatic Arts; NYU. W of Frank Liberman. Started as agent in NY with Olga Lee, later partnered in Harris & Draper Agency; to coast to work in casting with Ruth Birch; established own company, specializing in tv. Shows cast inc: Life of Riley; You Are There; Loretta Young Show; Get Smart; McMillan and Wife; Lizzie Borden; Happy Days; Laverne and Shirley; Top of the Hill; Serpico; Nero Wolfe; Terraces; Moviola; Too Close for Comfort; Foot In the Door.

(Died Oct. 3, 1984)

HARRIS, Phil: Orch Ldr. b. Linton, IN, Jun 24, 1904. H of Alice Faye. Appeared on TV, radio. On screen From 1933.

Films inc: Turn Off the Moon; Buck Benny Rides Again; Dreaming Out Loud; I Love a Bandleader; Wabash Avenue; The High and the Mighty; The Patsy; King Gun.

TV inc: The Concrete Cowboys.

HARRIS, Richard, Sir: Act. b. Limerick, Ireland, Oct 1, 1930. On screen since 1958.

Films inc: Alive and Kicking; Shake Hands with the Devil; The Long, The Short and The Tall; The Guns of Navarone; Mutiny on the Bounty; This Sporting Life; The Heroes of Telemark; The Bible; Hawaii; A Man Called Horse; Robin and Marian; The Cassandra Crossing; Orca; Return of a Man Called Horse; Echoes of a Summer; Golden Rendezvous; The Ravagers; The Last Word; Highpoint; Tarzan, the Ape Man; Triumphs of a Man Called Horse; Martin's Day.

Bway inc: Camelot (also London).

TV inc: Camelot (cable).

*(Grammy-*spoken word-1973).

(Knighted June 1981).

HARRIS, Rosemary: Act. b. Ashby, Suffolk, England, Sep 19, 1930. Films inc: Beau Brummel; The Shiralee; A Flea in Her Ear; The Boys From Brazil; The Ploughman's Lunch.

TV inc: Othello; The Prince and the Pauper; Wuthering Heights; Dial M for Murder; Notorious Woman *(Emmy-*1976); Blithe Spirit; The Chisholms; To The Lighthouse.

Bway inc: Climate of Eden; Seven Year Itch; The Crucible; Much Ado About Nothing; The Lion in Winter *(Tony-*1966); Heartbreak House; Pack Of Lies. (London) All My Sons; Heartbreak House.

HARRIS, Stan: Prod-Dir. b. Toronto, Feb 3, 1932. e. Ryerson Institute of Technology. TV inc: Nat King Cole Special; Perry Como Presents; Bing Crosby Special; Jim Nabors Special; Milton Berle Show; The Smothers Brothers Comedy Hour; Bob Hope Specials (1968 & 69); The Dick Van Dyke Show; Jack Benny Special; John Wayne Special; The Mancini Generation; Duke Ellington Special; George Burns' One Man Show; The Phenomenon of Benji; George Burns 100th Birthday; Rich Littles' Washington Follies; Pat Boone's Thanksgiving; The Muppets Go Hollywood; The Magic of David Copperfield; Kenny Rogers and The American Cowboy; Lynda Carter's Special; Lynda Carter Encore; Country Gold--The First Fifty Years; The Nashville Palace; Command Performance--The Stars Salute the President; Two of a Kind; Live From Studio 8H--100 Years of America's Popular Music; Lynda Carter--Celebration; Johnny Cash--Christmas In Scotland; Lynda Carter--Street Life; Johnny Cash--Cowboy Heroes; Yearbook--Class Of 1967.

HARRISON, Cathryn: Act. b. England, 1960. Grand D of Rex Harrison. Thea inc: Nicholas Nickleby. TV inc: The Intruders; The Witches of Pendle; Moths; Joe and Mary; Lisa; Wuthering Heights; Nicholas Nickleby; New Gods for Old; A Christmas Carol.

Films inc: The Pied Piper; Images; Black Moon; Blue Fire Lady; The Dresser.

HARRISON, George: Singer-Mus-Comp. b. Liverpool, England, Feb 25, 1943. Member of The Beatles (see group listing).

Individual film credits inc: Let It Be (score); Life of Brian (exec prod); Eric Clapton and His Rolling Hotel; Time Bandits (exec prod); Monty Python Live At the Hollywood Bowl (exec prod); The Missionary (exec prod); Privates On Parade (exec prod); Scrubbers (exec prod); Bullshot (exec prod); A Private Function (exec prod); Water (exec prod).

(Grammys-(2)-(in addition to group awards): Film Soundtrack-1970; album of year-1972).

HARRISON, Gregory: Act. b. Avalon, Catalina Island, CA, May 31, 1950. Films inc: Jim, the World's Greatest; Fraternity Row; Razorback.

TV inc: Logan's Run; Trilogy In Terror; The Best Place to Be; The Gathering; Centennial; Trapper John; The Women's Room; Enola Gay--The Men, The Mission, The Atomic Bomb; For Ladies Only (& prod); Thursday's Child (exec prod); The Fighter; Legs (exec prod); The Hasty Heart (& exec prod) (cable); Samson and Delilah (exec prod); Seduced (& exec prod).

HARRISON, Joan: Wri-Prod. b. Guildford, Eng, 1911. Films inc: (wri) Jamaica Inn; Rebecca; Foreign Correspondent; Saboteur; Dark Waters. (Prod) Phantom Lady; Uncle Harry; Ride the Pink Horse; Circle of Danger.

TV inc: Alfred Hitchcock Presents.

HARRISON, Rex: Act. b. Derry House, Huyton, Lancashire, England, Mar 5, 1908. Stage debut, Thirty Minutes in a Street, Liverpool Repertory theatre, 1924. London debut, Getting George Married, 1930. To NY in Sweet Aloes, 1936. Screen debut 1929.

Films inc: Cleopatra; The School for Scandal; Storm in a Teacup; The Citadel; Night Train; Blithe Spirit; Anna and the King of Siam; Notorious Gentleman; The Ghost and Mrs. Muir; The Foxes of Harrow; The Four Poster; The Reluctant Debutante; Midnight Lace; My Fair Lady *(Oscar-*1964); The Yellow Rolls-Royce; The Agony and the Ecstasy; Doctor Doolittle; A Flea in Her Ear; Staircase; The Prince and the Pauper; Crossed Swords; Ashanti; The Fifth Musketeer; A Time to Die.

Bway inc: Anne of 1000 Days *(Tony-*1949); Cocktail Party; Bell, Book and Candle; Venus Observed; My Fair Lady *(Tony-*1957); Henry IV; In Praise of Love *(Special Tony-*1969); My Fair Lady (rev). (London) Heartbreak House (& Bway); Aren't We All (& Bway).

TV inc: The 39th Annual Tony Awards.

HARRISON, Robert A: Exec. b. Aurelia, IA, Sep 10, 1926. e. USC, BS. Joined MGM as asst. Studio Controller 1959. Named Controller of MGM, 1973.

HARROLD, Kathryn: Act. b.Tazewell, VA, Aug 2, 1950. e. Mills Coll. Studied with Sanford Meisner; Uta Hagen; Stella Adler. TV inc: The Doctors; Woman in White; The Rockford Files; Son Rise--a Miracle of

Love; Vampire; Bogie; The Women's Room; An Uncommon Love; The Best Legs In The 8th Grade (PC); MacGruder & Loud.

Films inc: Nightwing; The Hunter; Modern Romance; The Pursuit of D.B. Cooper; Yes, Giorgio; The Sender; Heartbreakers; Into The Night.

HARRY, Deborah: Singer-songwri-act. b. Miami, Jul. 11, 1945. One of founders of rock group Blondie. Albums inc: Blondie; Plastic Letters; Parallel Lines; Eat to the Beat; Autoamerican. Songs inc: Call Me; The Tide Is High; Heart of Glass.

Films inc: Union City; Roadie; Videodrome.

Bway inc: Teaneck Tanzi, the Venus Flytrap.

HART, Bruce: Prod-Wri-Sngwri. TV inc: Sesame Street (wri & title song); Free To Be. . .You and Me; Sooner Or Later (dir-lyr); Hot Hero Sandwich (Emmy-exec prod-1980); Oh, Boy! Babies!

Songs inc: You Take My Breath Away; Bang the Drum Slowly; Who Are You Now?; One Way Ticket.

HART, Carole: Prod-Wri. TV inc: Sesame Street (wri); Free to Be.-.You and Me (Emmy-prod-1974); It Happened One Christmas; Sooner or Later; Hot Hero Sandwich (Emmy-exec prod-1980); Oh, Boy! Babies.

HART, Dolores (nee Hicks): Act. b. 1938. Gave up film career after 1963 to enter convent of Regina Laudis in Bethlehem, CT. She remains there as Mother Dolores. On screen From 1957.

Films inc: Loving You; Wild in the Wind; Lonely Hearts; Where the Boys Are; Francis of Assisi; Sail a Crooked Ship; Come with Me; Lisa.

In 1971 subject of David Wolper TV doc.

HART, Harvey: Dir. b. Canada, 1928. Films inc: Dark Intruder; Bus Riley's Back in Town; Sullivan's Empire; The Sweet Ride; Fortune and Men's Eyes; The Pyx; The Aliens Are Coming; The High Country; Utilities.

TV inc: John Steinbeck's East of Eden; This Is Kate Bennett; Massarati and the Brain; Born Beautiful; The Yellow Rose; Master of the Game; Reckless Disregard.

HARTFORD-DAVIS, Robert: Prod-Dir. b. England, 1923. Films inc: That Kind of Girl; The Yellow Teddybears; Saturday Night Out; Black Torment; The Sandwich Man; Corruption; The Smashing Bird I Used to Know; The Field; Black Gunn; The Take.

HARTLEY, Mariette: Act. b. NYC, Jun 21, 1940. Films inc: Ride the High Country; Marooned; Skyjacked; Marnie; Improper Channels; O'-Hara's Wife.

TV inc: Peyton Place; Stone; The African Queen; The Incredible Hulk (Emmy-1979); The Second Time Around; The Halloween That Almost Wasn't; The Love Tapes; The Secret War of Jackie's Girls; No Place To Hide; TV's Censored Bloopers (co-host); Drop Out Father; M.A.D.D.--Mothers Against Drunk Drivers; Goodnight, Beantown; Small World (guest host); Silence Of The Heart.

HARTMAN, David: Act-TV Personality. b. Pawtucket, RI, May 19, 1935. e. Duke U; AADA. Off-Broadway, summer stock; toured with Belafonte Singers. Bway debut, Hello, Dolly.

Films inc: The Ballad of Josie; Nobody's Perfect; Ice Station Zebra; The Island at the Top of the World.

TV inc: The Virginian; The Bold Ones; Lucas Tanner; host of Good Morning, America; The Shooters (wri-exec prod-narr); David Hartman--The Future Is Now (& exec prod-wri).

HARTMAN, Elizabeth: Act. b. Youngstown, OH, Dec 23, 1941. Cleveland Playhouse. Thea inc: The Madwoman of Chaillot; Becket; Everyone Out the Castle is Sinking.

Films inc: A Patch of Blue; The Group; The Fixer; Beguiled; You're a Big Boy Now; Walking Tall; The Secret of NIMH (voice).

TV inc: Willow B-Women in Prison.

HARTMANN, Edmund: Wri-Prod. b. St Louis, MO, Sep 24, 1911. Films inc: The Feminine Touch; Ali Baba and the 40 Thieves; The Naughty Nineties; The Paleface; Sorrowful Jones; Lemon Drop Kid; Fancy Pants; Mr. Casanova; Sherlock Holmes and the Scarlet Claw.

TV inc: My Three Sons; Family Affair; To Rome With Love; The Smith Family.

HARTZ, Jim: TV pers. b. Tulsa, OK., Feb. 3, 1940. Started on KTOV, KRMG, Tulsa; 1964 joined NBC News; 1974, co-host Today Show; 1979, co-host Over Easy.

HARVEY, Anthony: Dir. b. London, Jun 5, 1931. e. RADA. Films inc: Dutchman; The Lion in Winter; They Might Be Giants; The Abdication; Players; The Eagle's Wing; Richard's Things; The Ultimate Solution of Grace Quigley.

TV inc: The Glass Menagerie; The Disappearance of Aimee; The Patricia Neal Story; Svengali.

HARWOOD, Richard S: Dir. b. Nashville, TN, Jun 3, 1941. e. U of WA. TV inc: Sanford Arms; Szysznyk; Baby I'm Back; Cliffhangers; Misadventures of Sheriff Lobo; The Incredible Hulk; Bob Hope's Stand Up and Cheer for the NFL's 60th Year.

Film inc: Secret Empire II.

HARWOOD, Ronald (nee Horwitz): Plywri. b. Capetown, South Africa, Nov 9, 1934. e. RADA. Actor in stock and rep. Plays inc: Country Matters; A Family; The Dresser; The Good Companions.

TV inc: The Barber of Stamford Hill; Private Potter; A Sense of Loss; Evita Peron.

Films inc: High Wind in Jamaica; One Day in the Life of Ivan Denisovich; The Dresser.

HASKELL, Jimmie: Comp-Cond-Arr. b. Brooklyn, NY. e. LA City Coll. Started as prod-arr for Rick Nelson. Owner Horn Records. TV inc: (Comp) See How She Runs (Emmy-1978); The Jericho Mile; Silent Victory--The Kitty O'Neill Story; One Last Ride; The Jayne Mansfield Story; Mark, I Love You; A Cry For Love; Goldie and the Boxer Go to Hollywood; Crash Island; Leave 'Em Laughing; The Star Maker; Twirl; High Hopes--The Capra Years; Portrait of a Showgirl; Dixie--Changing Habits; Carpool; Jealousy; Hear Me Cry; Eye To Eye.

Films inc: Hard Country; Rainy Day Friends.

(Grammys-(3)-arr accomp voc-1967, 1970, 1976).

HASKELL, Peter: Act. b. Oct 15, 1934. Films inc: Passages from Finnegan's Wake; Christina.

TV inc: Bracken's World; The Jordan Chance; Mandrake; Shadow of Fear; Rich Man, Poor Man Book II; Shirley; The Cracker Factory; Stunt Seven; Love, Hate, Love; The Ballad of Andy Crocker; God In The Dock; Ryan's Hope.

HASSANEIN, Salah M: Exec. b. Egypt, May 31, 1921. e. British School, Alexandria. Exec vp United Artists Theatre Circuit, Inc; P, United Artists Eastern Theatres, Inc; P, Todd AO Corp; Bd of dir, NATO. Films inc: (exec prod) Knightriders; Creepshow.

HASSELHOFF, David: Act. b. Baltimore, MD., Jul. 17, 1952. TV inc: Griffin and Phoenix; Semi Tough; After Hours--Getting to Know Us; The Young and the Restless; Knight Rider; The Cartier Affair; Disneyland's 30th Anniversary Celebration; On Top All Over The World.

Films inc: Starcrash.

HASSETT, Marilyn: Act. b. Los Angeles, Dec 17, 1947. Films inc: They Shoot Horses, Don't They?; Shadow of the Hawk; The Other Side of the Mountain; Two-Minute Warning; The Other Side of the Mountain--Part 2; The Bell Jar; Massive Retaliation.

HASSO, Signe: Act. b. Stockholm, Aug 15, 1915. Films inc: Assignment in Brittany; The Seventh Cross; The House on 92nd Street; Johnny Angel; A Scandal in Paris; Where There's Life; To the Ends of the Earth; A Double Life; Outside the Wall; Crisis; Picture Mommy Dead; Reflection of Fear; The Black Bird.

TV inc: Evita Peron.

HASTINGS, Don: Act-Wri. b. Brooklyn, NY, Apr 1, 1934. On radio at age six; toured in Life With Father three years. Bway inc: I Remember Mama; On Whitman Avenue; A Young Man's Fancy; Summer and Smoke.

TV inc: (Act) Captain Video; Studio One; Crunch and Des; The Edge of Night; As The World Turns (since 1960). (Wri) As The World Turns; Guiding Light.

HATCH, Richard: Act. b. Santa Monica, CA, May 21, 1946. TV inc: All My Children; Addy and the King of Hearts; The Last of the Belles;

Streets of San Francisco; Battlestar Galactica; The Hustler of Muscle Beach.

Films inc: Charlie Chan and the Curse of the Dragon Queen; Prisoners Of The Lost Universe; Heated Vengeance.

HATFIELD, Hurd: Act. b. NYC, 1918. Films inc: Dragon Seed; The Picture of Dorian Gray; The Diary of a Chambermaid; The Beginning or the End; The Unsuspected; The Checkered Coat; Joan of Arc; Tarzan and the Slave Girl; The Left Handed Gun; King of Kings; El Cid; Mickey One; The Boston Strangler; Von Richthofen and Brown; King David.

TV inc: You Can't Go Home Again; The Manions of America.

HATHAWAY, Henry (Henri Leopold de Fiennes): Dir. b. Sacramento, CA, Mar 13, 1898. More than 60 films inc: Wild Horse Mesa; Sunset Pass; Now and Forever; Lives of a Bengal Lancer; Peter Ibbetson; Trail of the Lonesome Pine; Spawn of the North; Shepherd of the Hills; The Real Glory; Brigham Young; Johnny Apollo; China Girl; Wing and a Prayer; Nob Hill; House on 92nd Street; 13 Rue Madeleine; Kiss of Death; Call Northside 777; Down to the Sea in Ships; The Black Rose; The Desert Fox; 14 Hours; Rawhide; Prince Valiant; Garden of Evil; 23 Paces to Baker Street; Legend of the Lost; How the West Was Won; Circus World; Nevada Smith; The Sons of Katie Elder; The Last Safari; 5 Card Stud; True Grit; Raid on Rommel; Shoot Out.

(Died Feb. 11, 1985)

HATLEY, Marvin T.: Comp-Cond. b. Reed, OK, Apr 3, 1905. e. UCLA. Head of mus dept Hal Roach Studios; comp-cond-arr for Our Gang; Charlie Chase; Laurel & Hardy films. Films inc: Way Out West; Captain Fury; Merrily We Live; Broadway Limited: Topper Takes a Trip; There Goes My Heart; Blockheads.

HAUBEN, Lawrence: Wri. b. Mar 3, 1931. e. UC Santa Barbara, BFA. Films inc: One Flew Over the Cuckoo's Nest *(Oscar-1975)*.

HAUER, Rutger: Act. b. Breukelen, Netherlands, Jan 23, 1944. On stage in Amsterdam for six years. Films inc: Turkish Delight; Repelstweltje; Pusten Blume; Konter Bande; The Wilby Conspiracy; Keetje Tipple; Max Havelaar; Soldier of Orange; Pastorale 1943; Femme Entre Chien et Loup; Mysteries; Nighthawks; Chanel Solitaire; Blade Runner; Grijpstra & DeGier (Outsider In Amsterdam); Eureka; The Osterman Weekend; A Breed Apart; Ladyhawke; Flesh & Blood.

TV inc: Inside The Third Reich.

HAUFF, Reinhard: Dir. b. Marburg/Lahn, Germany, May 23, 1939. Films inc: Mathias Kneissl; The Brutalization of Franz Blum; Fuses; Paule Paulander; The Main Actor (& sp); 10 Days In Calcutta (doc).

HAUSER, Rick (Richard A. Hauser): Prod-dir-wri. b. Wichita, KS., Nov. 18, 1939. e. Yale, BA; Ohio U, MFA; Universite du Theatre des Nations; Sorbonne. TV inc: Godspell Goes to Plimoth Plantation for Thanksgiving with Henry Steele Commager; The Fight to Be Remembered; Eye to Eye; Nine Heroes; the Scarlet Letter; Tzaddik; Beyond the Horizon; From Here to Eternity; Feasting with Panthers.

HAUSER, Robert B.: Cin. b. Spokane WA, Mar 25, 1919. Films inc: The Odd Couple; The Riot; Willard; A Man Called Horse; Soldier Blue; Le Mans; Twilight's Last Gleaming; The Frisco Kid; Walking Tall--Final Chapter.

TV inc: Peyton Place (3 Yrs); The Legend of Lizzie Borden; Combat; When Hell Was In Session; Roll of Thunder Hear My Cry; Fugitive Family; Alcatraz--The Whole Shocking Story; Terror Among Us; The Day the Loving Stopped; Killjoy.

HAVELOCK-ALLEN, Anthony, Sir: Prod. b. Durham County, England, 1905. Films inc: This Man is News; In Which We Serve; Blithe Spirit; Brief Encounter (co-sp); Great Expectations (co-sp); Oliver Twist; The Small Voice; Never Take No for an Answer; The Young Lovers; Orders to Kill; The Quare Fellow; An Evening with the Royal Ballet; Othello; The Mikado.

HAVER, June (nee Stovenour): Act. b. Rock Island, IL, Jun 10, 1926. W of Fred McMurray. Films inc: The Gang's All Here; Home in Indiana; The Dolly Sisters; Three Little Girls in Blue; I Wonder Who's Kissing Her Now; Scudda Hoo, Scudda Hay; Oh You Beautiful Doll; Look for the Silver Lining; The Daughter of Rosie O'Grady; Love Nest;

The Girl Next Door.

HAVOC, June (nee Hovick): Act. b. Seattle, WA, Oct 8, 1916. Sis of the late Gypsy Rose Lee. Film debut at age 2 in Hal Roach comedy. Danced with Anna Pavlova troupe, then entered vaudeville in own act. To Hollywood in 1942.

Films inc: Hello Frisco, Hello; No Time for Love; Sweet and Low Down; Intrigue; Gentleman's Agreement; Once a Thief; Follow the Sun; Lady Possessed; Can't Stop The Music.

Thea inc: Pal Joey; Sadie Thompson; Mexican Hayride; The Infernal Machine; The Beaux Strategem; Habeas Corpus.

TV inc: Anna Christie; The Bear; Cakes and Ale; The Untouchables.

HAWES, Bess Lomax: Act-Comp. b. Austin, TX, Jan 21, 1921. Folklore authority. An accomplished guitarist; performs at concerts, festivals.

HAWES, Stanley Gilbert: Prod. b. London, Jan 19, 1905. Prod or dir 10 documentary films for Strand Films, London; 100 for National Film Board of Canada; 400 for the Australian Commonwealth Film Unit (now Film Australia).

HAWKINS, Rick: Wri. TV inc: Dorothy; Welcome Back, Kotter; Carol Burnett Show *(Emmy*-1978); Love Boat; The Rodney Dangerfield Special--I Can't Take It No More; Punky Brewster (prod); Rodney Dangerfield Exposed.

HAWKINS, Robert F.: Journalist. b. Genoa, Italy, Jun 18, 1924. e. Princeton. Became Variety stringer, Rome, 1948; freelance photographer, regular contributor NY Times 1948-1960; became Rome bureau chief Variety 1954; London bureau chief & European mgr 1966; exec vp & int'l editor 1977, based in NY; April 1984 added duties as dir of mktg.

HAWN, Goldie: Act. b. Washington, DC, Nov 21, 1945. Began professionally as dancer in Can-Can, NY Worlds Fair, 1964.

Films inc: The One and Only Genuine Original Family Band; Cactus Flower *(Oscar*-supp-1969); There's a Girl in My Soup; Dollars; Butterflies Are Free; The Sugarland Express; The Girl From Petrovka; Shampoo; The Dutchess and the Dirtwater Fox; Travels With Anita; Foul Play; Private Benjamin (& exec prod); Seems Like Old Times; Lovers and Liars; Best Friends; Swing Shift; Protocol (& exec prod).

TV inc: Good Morning World; Laugh-In; Goldie & Liza Together; Goldie and Kids--Listen To Us (& exec prod).

HAWORTH, Ted: Art Dir. b. Willoughby, OH, 1917. Films inc: Strangers on a Train; The Body Snatcher; Sayonara *(Oscar*-1957); Some Like It Hot; The Getaway; Jeremiah Johnson; The Professionals; The Longest Day; Claudine; Harry and Tonto; Bloodline; I Want to Live; Marty; Half a Sixpence; The Bachelor Party; Beguiled; What a Way to Go; Somebody Killed Her Husband; When You Comin' Back, Red Ryder; Sidney Sheldon's Bloodline; Jinxed!

TV inc: Honeyboy; Confessions of a Married Man.

HAYDEN, Jeffrey: Dir. b. NYC, Oct 15, 1926. e. U of NC. H of Eva Marie Saint. TV inc: Omnibus; The Big Payoff; The Bert Parks Show; Lassie; Leave it to Beaver; Dennis the Menace; 77 Sunset Strip; Peyton Place; The Bold Ones; Batman; Mannix; Ironsides; The Incredible Hulk; Cliff Hangers; The Mississippi; Santa Barbara exec prod).

HAYDEN, Sterling: Act. b. Montclair, NJ, Mar 26, 1916. Films inc: Virginia; Bahama Passage; The Asphalt Jungle; Hellgate; Flat Top; So Big; Johnny Guitar; Shotgun; The Killing; The Godfather; The Long Goodbye; King of the Gypsies; Winter Kills; The Outsider; Nine to Five; Gas; Venom; Leuchtturm des Chaos (Lighthouse of Chaos).

TV inc: The Blue and The Gray.

HAYDN, Richard: Act. b. England, 1905. Films inc: Ball of Fire; Charley's Aunt; Forever and a Day; And Then There Were None; Cluny Brown; Sitting Pretty; Jupiter's Darling; Please Don't Eat the Daisies; The Lost World; Mutiny on the Bounty; Five Weeks in a Balloon; The Sound of Music; Clarence the Cross-Eyed Lion; Bullwhip Griffin; Young Frankenstein.

(Died April 25, 1985)

HAYERS, Sidney: Dir. b. Edinburgh, Aug. 24, 1922. e. Cambridge. Started as editor. Films inc: (editor) Brief Encounter (asst.); Warning To Wantons; Stop Press Girl; Never Take No For An Answer; Romeo and Juliet; A Town Like Alice; A Night To Remember (& 2d unit dir); Tiger Bay; House Of Secrets; Passage Home; Blanche Fury; A Matter Of Life and Death; Operation Amsterdam (& 2d unit dir). (Dir): Violent Moment; The White Trap; Circus Of Horrors; The Malpas Mystery; Echo Of Barbara; Burn, Witch, Burn; Payroll; This Is My Street; Three Hats For Liza; The Trap; Finders Keepers; The Southern Star; Assault; Inn Of The Frightened People; Deadly Strangers (& co-prod); What Changed Charley Farthing (& co-prod); Diagnosis Murder (& co-prod); One Way (& co-prod).

TV inc: Mister Jerico; The Seekers; The Last Convertible (co-dir); Condominium; Phlip Marlowe--Private Eye.

HAYES, Helen (nee Brown): Act. b. Washington, DC, Oct 10, 1900. Pro debut age 5 in stock company; Bway debut 1909, Old Dutch. Film debut 1931, The Sin of Madelon Claudet (Oscar-1931/32).

Bway inc: The Prodigal Husband; Penrod; To the Ladies; We Moderns; She Stoops to Conquer; Dancing Mothers; Caesar and Cleopatra; What Every Woman Knows; Coquette; Mr. Gilhooley; Petticoat Influence; The Good Fairy; Mary of Scotland; Victoria Regina; The Merchant of Venice; Candle in the Wind; Harriet; Happy Birthday (Tony-1947); Mrs. McThing; Glass Menagerie; The Show-Off; Time Remembered (Tony-1958); The Front Page. (Special Tony-Lawrence Langner Award-1980).

Films Inc: Arrowsmith; A Farewell To Arms; The Son Daughter; The White Sister; Another Language; Night Flight; What Every Woman Knows; Vanessa; Stage Door Canteen; My Son John; Anastasia; Airport (Oscar-supp-1970); Herbie Rides Again; One Of Our Dinosaurs is Missing; Candleshoe; Hopper's Silence (voice).

TV inc: The Twelve Pound Look (Emmy-1952); Mary of Scotland; Dear Brutus; The Skin of Our Teeth; Do Not Fold, Spindle or Mutilate; The Snoop Sisters; Christmas Tie; Drugstore on a Sunday Afternoon; Omnibus; Murder Is Easy; Kennedy Center Tonight--Broadway to Washington!; A Caribbean Mystery; Highway To Heaven; Murder With Mirrors.

Radio inc: The Best Years.

(Grammy-spoken word-1976).

HAYES, Isaac: Comp-Singer. b. Covington, KY, Aug 20, 1942. Recordings inc: Hot Buttered Soul; B-A-B-Y; Soul Man; Chocolate Chip; Juicy Fruit; A Man and a Woman; Tough Guys; Shaft (Grammy-inst arr-1971); Black Moses (Grammy-pop inst-1972).

Films inc: Shaft (Oscar-song-1971) (Grammy-film score-1972); Escape From New York.

HAYES, John Michael: Wri. b. Worcester, MA, May 11, 1919. e. U of MA. Films inc: Rear Window; To Catch a Thief; The Trouble with Harry; Peyton Place; The Carpetbaggers; Where Love Has Gone; Harlow; Judith; Nevada Smith.

HAYES, Joseph: Wri. b. Aug. 2, 1918. e. IN U (BA). Plays inc: Leaf And Bough; The Desperate Hours (Tonys-Author & Prod-1955).

Films inc: The Desperate Hours; The Young Doctors; Stolen Hours; The Third Day.

HAYES, Peter Lind: Act. b. San Francisco, Jun 25, 1915. On radio as singer. Also performed in vaudeville, niteries.

Films inc: Million Dollar Legs; Seventeen; Dancing on a Dime; Playmates; Seven Days Leave; Lookin' To Get Out.

HAYES, Raphael: Wri. b. Mar 2, 1915. Films inc: One Potato, Two Potato.

TV inc: The Defenders; Lamp Unto My Feet.

Thea inc: Man Most Likely.

HAYS, Robert: Act. b. Bethesda, MD, Jul 24, 1947. Films inc: Airplane; Take This Job and Shove It; Airplane II--The Sequel; Trenchcoat; Utilities; Touched; Scandalous; Cat's Eye.

TV inc: Will Rogers-Champion of the People; California Gold Rush; The Girl, The Gold Watch and Everything; Angie; Mark Twain's America--The Young Will Rogers; California Gold Rush; The Day The Bubble Burst; The Fall of the House of Usher; Mr. Roberts.

HAYWARD, Louis: Act. b. Johannesburg, So Africa, Mar 19, 1909.

On London stage in Dracula; Vinegar Tree; Conversation Piece. To Bway in 1935. In Point Valaine. Screen debut in Self-Made Lady.

Films inc: Anthony Adverse; Man in the Iron Mask; My Son, My Son; And Then There Were None; Walk A Crooked Mile; Camelot; Search for Bridey Murphy; Chuka.

TV inc: The Lone Wolf; Climax; Pursuers; The Survivors.

(Died Feb. 21, 1985)

HAYWORTH, Rita (Margarita Carmen Cansino): Act. b. NYC, Oct 17, 1918. On stage as dancer From age 6.

Films inc: Dante's Inferno; Charlie Chan in Egypt; Human Cargo; A Message to Garcia; Only Angels Have Wings; The Lady in Question; The Strawberry Blonde; Blood and Sand; You'll Never Get Rich; Tales of Manhattan; Cover Girl; Gilda; Affair in Trinidad; Tonight and Every Night; The Lady From Shanghai; Salome; Miss Sadie Thompson; Fire Down Below; Pal Joey; Separate Tables; They Came to Cordura; Circus World; The Money Trap; The Poppy is also a Flower; The Rover; Sons of Satan; The Road to Salina; The Wrath of God.

HEARD, John: Act. b. Mar 7, 1946. Thea inc: Streamers; Hamlet; Macbeth; The Wager; The Pokey; The Creditors; Warp; Total Abandon; The Glass Menagerie.

Films inc: First Love; Heart Beat; Head Over Heels; Between The Lines; On the Yard; Cat People; C.H.U.D.; Too Scared To Scream; Heaven Help Us.

TV inc: Valley Forge; The Silencers; The Scarlet Letter; Will There Really Be A Morning?; Legs.

HEATHERTON, Joey: Act. b. Rockville Centre, NY, Sep 14, 1944. Films inc: Twilight of Honor; Where Love has Gone; My Blood Runs Cold; Bluebeard; The Happy Hooker Goes to Washington.

HEATTER, Merrill: Prod-Wri. b. NYC, Dec 16, 1926. e. Bates Coll; NYU; OH State. H of Elaine Stewart. Wri-prod of numerous tv game shows inc Hollywood Squares (Emmys-1975, 1978, 1979, 1980); Gambit; High Rollers; Fantasy (exec prod).

HECHT, Harold: Prod. b. NYC, Jun 1, 1907. Former dance dir, literary agent. From 1947 prod jointly with Burt Lancaster and later James Hill.

Films inc: Vera Cruz; Marty (Oscar-1955); Trapeze; Separate Tables; Taras Bulba; Cat Ballou; The Way West.

(Died May 26, 1985)

HECKART, Eileen: Act. b. Columbia, OH, Mar 29, 1919. e. OH State U. Films inc: Miracle in the Rain; The Bad Seed; Somebody Up There Likes Me; Hot Spell; Heller in Pink Tights; No Way to Treat a Lady; Butterflies Are Free (Oscar-supp-1972); Zandy's Bride; The Hiding Place; Burnt Offerings.

Bway inc: The Time of the Cuckoo; And Things That Go Bump in the Night; A View From the Bridge; The Dark at the Top of the Stairs; Barefoot in the Park; Butterflies Are Free; Picnic; Ladies at the Alamo.

TV inc: Save Me a Place at Forest Lawn; Mary Tyler Moore Show; Suddenly Love; Backstairs at the WHite House; White Mama; FDR-The Last Year; Joe Dancer; Games Mother Never Taught You; Trauma Center.

HECKERLING, Amy: Dir. b. Bronx, NY., May 7, 1954. e. Art & Design High School, NYU, AFI. Films inc: (Shorts) Modern Times; High Finance; Getting It Over With. (Features) Fast Times at Ridgemont High; Johnny Dangerously; Into The Night (act).

HEDISON, David (ne Heditsian): Act. b. Providence, RI, May 20, 1929. Films inc: The Enemy Below; The Fly; Son of Robin Hood; The Lost World; Marines Let's Go; The Greatest Story Ever Told; Live and Let Die; Ffolkes; The Naked Face.

TV inc: Five Fingers; Voyage to the Bottom of the Sea; The Power Within; Amanda's; Kenny Rogers as the Gambler--the Adventure Continues; A.D.

HEDREN, Tippi: Act. b. 1935. M of Melanie Griffith. Films inc: The Birds; Marnie; A Countess From Hong Kong; The Man with the Albatross; Tiger by the Tail; Satan's Harvest; Mr Kingstreet's War; The Harrad Experiment; Roar.

TV inc: Alfred Hitchcock Presents.

HEELEY, David E: Dir-Prod. b. England, Dec 26, 1940. e. Oxford, BA. With BBC London, 1961-69 as dir Late Night Line Up; How It Is; Music Now; then to WNET, NY 1969.
TV inc: (dir) Free Time; How Do Your Children Grow; Behind the Lines; The Arc of Civilization; We Interrupt This Week; (prod & dir): Skyline (series); Fred Astaire-Puttin' On His Top Hat *(Emmy-Prod-1980)*; Nature.

HEFFLEY, Wayne: Act. b. Bakersfield, CA, Jul 15, 1927. TV inc: Highway Patrol; Voyage to the Bottom of the Sea; Nichols; Little House on the Prairie; Roots; A Matter of Time; Fly Away Home; Johnny Belinda.
Films inc: Tora, Tora, Tora; Lonely Are the Brave; The Outsider; Johnny Got His Gun.

HEFFRON, Richard: Dir. b. Chicago, Oct 6, 1930. e. Harvard. Started as dir documentaries, political films.
TV inc: The Bold Ones; Banacek; Toma; A Rumor of War; A Killer in the Family; V--The Final Battle; Anatomy of an Illness; The Mystic Warrior.
Films inc: Newman's Law; Foolin' Around; I, The Jury.

HEFNER, Hugh M: Exec. b. Chicago, IL, Apr 9, 1926. e. U of KS. In promotion dept Esquire Magazine; Childrens Activities Magazine; started Playboy Magazine 1953; P Playboy Enterprises which inc film activities, tv.
Films inc: (prod) Saint Jack; The Fiendish Plot of Dr. Fu Manchu; History of the World--Part I (act); The Comeback Trail.

HEFTI, Neal: Comp-Cond. b. Hastings, NE, Oct 29, 1922. Trumpeter with Woody Herman and Harry James Orchs before starting own orch 1950. Cond on TV for Arthur Godfrey Show; Kate Smith Show; American Bandstand.
Films inc: Sex and the Single Girl; How To Murder Your Wife; Synanon; Harlow; Boeing-Boeing; Lord Love a Duck; Duel at Diablo; Oh Dad, Poor Dad; Barefoot in the Park; PJ; Odd Couple.
TV inc: Fred Astaire Show; Odd Couple; Batman *(Grammy-inst theme-1966)*.
Songs inc: Lil Darlin'; Don't Dream of Anyone But Me; Girl Talk; Batman Theme; The New Odd Couple.

HEIDT, Horace: Band Ldr (ret). b. Oakland, CA, 1901. e. U CA Berkeley. Formed own orch, Horace Heidt and his Musical Knights. On radio, TV. Radio inc: Pot O'Gold. TV inc: Youth Opportunity Program.

HEIFETZ, Jascha: Violinist. b. Vilna, Russia, Feb 2, 1901. Child prodigy; became int'l concert artist. *(Grammys-(3)-classical-1961, 1962, 1964).*

HEIFITS, Iossif: Wri-Dir. b. Russia, Dec 17, 1905. Began as a writer, collaborating with Alexander Zarkhi while both students at the Leningrad Film Factory; after two films, The Moon On Your Left and The Fiery Transport, they began directing in tandem and turned out a dozen films inc: Wind in The Face; Midday; My Homeland; Those Were the Days!; The Baltic Deputy; Member of the Government; His Name is Sukhe-Bator; Precious Grains; The Lights of Baku. Solo dir inc: The Big Family; The Rumyantsev Case (& co-sp); My Dear Man (& co-sp); The Lady With a Dog (& sp); The Horizon; A Day of Happiness(& co-sp); Salute, Maria (& co-sp); A Bad Goody (& sp); The Only One (& sp); Asya (& sp); Married for the First Time.

HEIM, Alan: Film edtr. Films inc: Twelve Chairs; Godspell; Hair; Network; All That Jazz *(Oscar-1979)*; The Fan; So Fine; Star 80; Goodbye, New York.
TV inc: Liza With a Z; Lenny; Holocaust *(Emmy-1978)*.

HEINEMAN, Laurie: Act. TV inc: Almost Heaven; Terror on the 40th Floor; Mad Bull; Another World *(Emmy-1978)*; An Apple and An Orange; Loose Change; Holier Than Thou; Studs Lonigan; Ryan's Four.
Films inc: Inaugural Ball; Save The Tiger; The Lady in Red.

HELDFOND, Susan: Act. b. Los Angeles. TV inc: Kingston Confidential; C O P; The Trial of Lee Harvey Oswald; Fast Friends. Films inc: Why Would I Lie?; Love & Money.

HELLER, Lukas: Wri. b. Germany, 1930. Films inc: Sapphire; Candidate for Murder; What Ever Happened to Baby Jane?; Agent 8 3/4; Hush Hush Sweet Charlotte; The Flight of the Phoenix; The Dirty Dozen; The Killing of Sister George; Too Late the Hero; Monte Walsh; The Deadly Trackers; Damnation Alley.
TV inc: Hitler's SS--Portrait In Evil.

HELLER, Paul M: Prod. b. NYC, Sep 25, 1927. Films inc: David & Lisa; The Eavesdropper; Once Upon a Tractor; Red Over Red; Secret Ceremony; Enter the Dragon; Black Belt Jones; Golden Needles; Hot Potato; Dirty Knight's Work; Crash; Those Cuckoo Crazy Animals; Outlaw Blues; Checkered Flag or Crash; The Pack; The Promise (& sp); First Monday In October; Robbers of the Sacred Mountain (Falcons Gold) (exec prod).

HELLER, Randee: Act. b. Brooklyn, NY, Jun 10. e. Adelphi U. Bway inc: Grease; Godspell; Hurry Harry.
TV inc: Husbands, Wives & Lovers; Soap; And Your Name is Jonah; Can You Hear the Laughter--The Story of Freddie Prinze; Mama Malone; Obsessed With A Married Woman.
Films inc: Honky Tonk Freeway; Fast Break; The Karate Kid.

HELLMAN, Jerome: Prod. b. NYC, Sep 4, 1928. e. NYU. With William Morris and Jaffee Agencies before forming own agency, Ziegler, Hellman, and Ross. Switched to feature prod with The World of Henry Orient, 1964.
Films inc: A Fine Madness; Midnight Cowboy *(Oscar-1969)*; The Day of the Locust; Coming Home; Promises in the Dark (& dir).

HELLMAN, Lillian: Plywri. b. New Orleans, LA, Jun 20, 1905. e. NYU; Columbia U. Plays inc: The Children's Hour; Days to Come; The Little Foxes; Watch on the Rhine; The Searching Wind; Another Part of the Forest (& dir); Montserrat (& dir); Autumn Garden; Toys in the Attic; My Mother, My Father and Me.
Films inc: These Three; Dead End; The Little Foxes; The North Star; The Searching Wind; The Chase.
TV inc: The Case of Dashiell Hammett (doc) (interviewee).
(Died June 30, 1984)

HELLMAN, Monte: Dir-Wri-Prod. b. NYC, Jul 12, 1932. e. Stanford U, BA. Films inc: Beast From Haunted Cave; Back to Hell; Flight to Fury; The Shooting (& prod); Ride in the Whirlwind (& prod); Two-Lane Blacktop; Cockfighter; China 9-Liberty 37 (& prod).

HELLMAN, Richard: Prod. b. Bucharest, Oct 8, 1936. e. Oxford U; London Polytechnic. P, Dasar Film Inc, Montreal, exec vp Canafox Films Inc & Prospec Films Inc.
Films inc: Secret War (asso prod); Surcouf; Killer Likes Candy; Montreal; Tiens Toi Bien; Le Petit Vient Vite; Les Corps Celestes; Il Etait Une Fois Dans L'est; Sweet Movie; Les Beaux Dimanches.
TV inc: Nightkill.

HELLWIG, Klaus: Dist-Prod. b. Frankfurt, Germany, Jul 20, 1941. P Janus Film, 1965; P Action Films, Paris.
Films inc: Your Turn, My Turn; Lillian Gish (doc) (asso prod).

HELMOND, Katherine: Act. b. Galveston, TX, Jul 5. Films inc: Baby Blue Marine; The Hindenberg; Family Plot; Time Bandits; Brazil.
TV inc: Wanted-The Sundance Woman; The Legend of Lizzie Borden; Cage Without a Key; Liza's Pioneer Diary; Little Ladies of the Night; Meeting of the Minds; Getting Married: Soap; Scout's Honor. Pearl; Diary of a Teenage Hitchhiker; World War III; Fit For A King; For Lovers Only; Rosie--The Rosemary Clooney Story; Not in Front of the Kids; Side By Side; Who's The Boss ?
Thea inc: Great God Brown; House of Blue Leaves.

HELPMANN, Robert, Sir: Act-Dancer. b. Mount Gambler, Australia, Apr 9, 1909. e. Prince Alfred's Coll. Films inc: One of Our Aircraft is Missing; Henry V; The Red Shoes; Tales of Hoffman; 55 Days in Peking; The Quiller Memorandum; Chitty Chitty Bang Bang; Alice's Adventures in Wonderland; Don Quixote; Patrick; Second Time Lucky; He Who Gets Slapped; Camelot (dir); Duel of Angels; La Contessa.
Thea inc: Hamlet; The Fairy Queen; Conduct Unbecoming (dir); Peter Pan (dir); The Cobra.
Chor numerous ballets; dir Dame Margot Fonteyn's World Tour.

TV inc: Sarah In America (Kennedy Center Tonight).

HEMINGWAY, Margaux: Act. b. Portland, OR, Feb 1955. Grand D of the late Ernest Hemingway. Model. Films inc: Lipstick; Killer Fish; A Fistful of Chopsticks; Over the Brooklyn Bridge.

HEMINGWAY, Mariel: Act. Sis of Margaux Hemingway. Films inc: Lipstick; Manhattan; Personal Best; Star 80; The Mean Season.
TV inc: I Want To Keep My Baby.

HEMION, Dwight A.: Dir-Prod. b. New Haven, CT, Mar 14, 1926. Asso dir ABC-TV. 1946-49; dir Tonight Show, NBC-TV, 1950-60; Perry Como Show, 1960-67; prod-dir Yorkshire Prods, 1967-70; prod-dir TV specials with ATV, London 1971-75; prod-dir Smith-Hemion Prods, 1975-present.
TV inc: My Name Is Barbra (dir); Frank Sinatra: A Man and His Music (Emmy-prod-1966); The Sound of Burt Bacharach (Emmy-dir-1970); Singer presents Burt Bacharach (Emmy-prod-1971); Barbra Streisand and Other Musical Instruments (Emmy-dir-1974 & dir of year); Steve and Eydie-Our Love Is Here to Stay (Emmy-dir-1976); American Salutes Richard Rodgers-The Sound of His Music (Emmy-Dir-1977); Bette Midler-Ol Red Hair is Back (Emmy-prod-1978); Ben Vereen-His Roots (Emmy-dir-1978); Merry Christmas From the Grand Ole Opry House (1978); A Holiday Tribute to Radio City Music Hall (dir); Cheryl Ladd Special; Steve and Eydie Celebrate Irving Berlin (Emmy-exec prod-1979); Merry Christmas From the Grand Ole Opry House (1979); Kraft Salutes Disneyland's 25th Anniversary; Baryshnikov on Broadway (dir) (Emmy-1980); Ann Margret-Hollywood Movie Girls; Shirley MacLaine-Every Little Movement; Uptown-A Tribute to the Apollo Theatre; Linda In Wonderland; Larry Gatlin and the Gatlin Bros. Band; A Special Anne Murray Christmas; Walt Disney--One Man's Dream; Kraft Salutes Walt Disney World's 10th Anniversary; Pavarotti and Friends; Goldie and Kids--Listen to Us (Emmy-1982); EPCOT Center--The Opening Celebration; Christmas In Washington; Anne Murray's Caribbean Cruise; Sheena Easton-Act One (Emmy-dir-1983); Romeo and Juliet On Ice; Here's Television Entertainment (Emmy-dir-1984); The Television Academy Hall of Fame; Anne Murray's Winter Carnival--From Quebec; On Stage America; Screen Actors Guild 50th Anniversary Celebration; Christmas In Washington; Anne Murray--The Sounds Of London; The Television Academy Hall Of Fame; The Royal London Gala For Bob Hope's Happy Birthday Homecoming (dir).

HEMMINGS, David: Act. b. Guildford, England, 1941. Films inc: No Trees in the Street; The Wind of Change; Live It Up; Dateline Diamonds; Eye of the Devil; Blow Up; Camelot; The Charge of the Light Brigade; A Long Day's Dying; Only When I Larf; Barbarella; Alfred the Great; The Walking Stick; Fragment of Fear; The Love Machine; Running Scared; The Squeeze; Dripping Deep Red; Islands in the Stream; Disappearance (& prod); Crossed Swords; Power Play (& co-prod); Murder by Decree; Just a Gigolo (dir); Thirst; Harlequin; Beyond Reasonable Doubt; Dead Kids (exec prod); The Survivor (dir); Man, Woman and Child; Turkey Shoot (exec prod).
Thea inc: Dylan Thomas in Adventures in the Skin Trade.
TV inc: Auto Stop; The Big Toe; Out of the Unknown; Dr. Jekyll and Mr. Hyde; Charlie Muffin; Airwolf; Calamity Jane; The Key To Rebecca (& dir). lines/page:

HEMMINGS, Peter Williams: Exec. b. London, Apr 10, 1934. e. Cambridge U. 1959-65, Repertory & Planning Mgr Sadlers Wells Opera; gen administrator Scottish Opera, 1962-77; The Australian Opera, 1977; M-Dir London Symphony 1979; exec dir Music Center Opera Assn (Los Angeles), 1984.

HEMPHILL, Shirley: Act. b. Asheville, NC, Jul 1. TV inc: Rich Man, Poor Man, Book II; Richard Pryor Special; What's Happening; One in a Million.

HEMSLEY, Sherman: Act. b. Philadelphia, Feb 1, 1938. Films inc: Love at First Bite.
TV inc: All in the Family; The Jeffersons; The Sensational, Shocking, Wonderful, Wacky 70's; Pink Lady; E.R.
Thea inc: Purlie.

HENDERSON, Florence: Singer-Act.
Thea inc: Purlie.b. Dale, IN, Feb 14, 1934. e. AADA. Bway inc:

Wish You Were Here; Oklahoma!; The Great Waltz; Fanny; The Sound of Music; The Girl Who Came to Supper; South Pacific (rev); Annie Get Your Gun (tour).
TV inc: Rodgers and Hammerstein Anniversary Show; The Gershwin Years; Huckleberry Finn; Little Women; The Brady Bunch; The Brady Brides; Live--And in Person.
Films inc: Song of Norway.

HENDERSON, Skitch (Lyle Henderson): Orch Ldr. b. Halstad, MN, 1918. e. U of CA. TV inc: Steve Allen Show; Tonight Show.

HENDLER, Lauri: Act. b. Ft Belvoir, VA, Apr 22, 1965. Appeared on juvenile news program KRON-TV, San Francisco. TV inc: It Isn't Easy Being a Teenage Millionaire; The Grass is Always Greener Over the Septic Tank; Little Lulu Goes to Camp; The Big Hex of Little Lulu; Three's Company; The Child Stealer; You Can't Keep A Horse In The Garage (host); A New Kind of Family; The Promise of Love; Why Us?; Gimme A Break; High School U.S.A.

HENDRICKS, Bill (William L. Hendricks): Pub-Prod. b. Grand Prairie, TX, May 3. e. St John's Coll. Thea mgr and prod of stageshows WB Theatres in midwest; pub at WB Studios, later pub dir; special asst to Jack L. Warner; exec dir WB Cartoons; headed WB ind film division, producing hundreds of commercials, industrial and doc films; founder-owner Bill Hendricks Films.
Films inc: A Force in Readiness (Oscar-special-1961); The John Glenn Story; The FBI; The Land We Love; Scenes To Remember; An American Legend; Busby Berkeley and the Golddiggers; One Giant Leap; Drug Alert; Great Comedies; Great Westerns; Great Adventures; Great Love Scenes; Best of Bogart; series on Cinematographer, Director, Film Editor, Makeup Artist, Sound Man; Welcome to the Movies; Your FBI.
TV inc: The Bugs Bunny Road Runner Hour (1970, 1975, 1976); The Merrie Melodies Show; The Bugs Bunny Show.

HENEKER, David: Comp-Lyr. b. Southsea, England, Mar 31, 1906. e. Wellington Coll; Royal Military Coll. Thea inc: Expresso Bongo; Make Me An Offer; Irma La Douce (adapt); The Art of Living; Half a Sixpence; Charlie Girl; Jorrock; Phil the Fluter; Popkiss; Peg.
Films inc: Half a Sixpence; The Two Faces of Dr Jekyll; I've Got a Horse.

HENLEY, Beth (Elizabeth Becker Henley): Plywri. b. Jackson, MS., May 8, 1952. e Southern Methodist U, BFA. Plays inc: Am I Blue (one-act); Crimes of the Heart (Pulitzer Prize-1981); The Miss Firecracker Contest; The Wake of Jamey Foster; The Debutante Ball.

HENNER, Marilu: Act. b. Chicago, Apr 6, 1952. e. U of Chicago. Films inc: Between the Lines; Blood Brothers; Hammett; The Man Who Loved Women; Cannonball Run II; Johnny Dangerously; Rustlers Rhapsody; Perfect.
TV inc: The Paper Chase; Off-Campus; Seventh Avenue; Leonard; Like Father, Like Daughter; Taxi; Dream House; Fridays; Stark.
Thea inc: Grease; Over Here; Pal Joey (rev).

HENNING, Doug: Act-wri. b. Winnipeg, Canada, May 3, 1947. Toured colleges with lectures, demos entitled Illusion and Reality; also toured major US cities with magic show. Bway inc: The Magic Show; Merlin; created stage illusions for rock band Earth, Wind and Fire's 1978 touring show.
TV inc: Doug Henning's World of Magic (Emmy-1976); The Crystal Gayle Special; The Osmond Family Christmas Show; Doug Hennings World of Magic (1981); Doug Henning's World of Magic (1982); Doug Henning's Magic On Broadway; Night Of 100 Stars II.

HENNING, Paul: Prod-Wri. b. Independence, MO, Sep 16, 1911. e. Kansas City School of Law. Started as radio wri for Rudy Vallee, Fibber McGee and Molly, Joe E Brown, Burns and Allen.
TV inc: (created, wrote & prod) The Beverly Hillbillies; Petticoat Junction; Bob Cummings Show; exec prod Green Acres; Return of the Hillbillies (& theme).
Films inc: Lover Come Back; Bedtime Story.

HENREID, Paul: Act-Dir. b. Trieste, Italy, 1908. On stage, in films Vienna, London, before U.S.
Films inc: Joan of Paris; Now Voyager; Casablanca; Of Human

Bondage; Devotion; Deception; Between Two Worlds; Song of Love; Stolen Face; Man in Hiding; Pirates of Tripoli; Holiday for Lovers; Madwoman of Chaillot; Colors of Love; Exorcist II;

TV inc: (dir) Bracken's World; The Man And The City.

HENRIKSEN, Lance: Act. b. NYC. Bway inc: The Basic Training of Pavlo Hummel; Richard III; Saved; Cat on a Hot Tin Roof.

Films inc: Dog Day Afternoon; Network; Omen II; Close Encounters of the Third Kind; Prince of the City; The Dark End of the Street; The Spawning; Nightmares; The Right Stuff; The Terminator; Savage Dawn.

TV inc: Blood Feud.

HENRY, Buck (nee Zuckerman): Wri. b. 1930. Films inc: Troublemaker; The Graduate; Candy; Catch 22; The Owl and the Pussycat; What's Up Doc?; The Day of the Dolphin; The Man Who Fell To Earth; Heaven Can Wait (Act, Co-Sp, Co-Dir) Old Boyfriends (act); Gloria (act); First Family (& dir-act); Eating Raoul (act); Protocol.

TV inc: Get Smart (Emmy-wri-1967); The New Show.

HENRY, Justin: Act. b. Rye, NY., May 25, 1971. Films inc: Kramer vs. Kramer; Sixteen Candles; Martin's Day.

TV inc: Tiger Town (cable).

HENSHAW, Jere C: Exec. b. Kansas City, MO, Sep 7, 1932. e. UCLA, BA. Started with Col 1954 in mail room; successively wardrobe dept stock clerk, casting clerk, asst casting dir; in 1956 exec in chg casting, 1959 vp-exec in chg talent & casting, Revue Prodns; 1962 vp-exec in chg talent & casting U-TV; 1964, vp-exec in chg talent & casting U; 1966, vp-exec in chg crea aff for World Premiere films for tv U-TV; 1967, vp chg crea aff Cinema Center Films; 1968, vp in chg wldwide prodn theatrical and tv film; 1972 vp crea aff Fox; 1973, vp chg wldwde prodn Fox; 1975, vp for prodn, U; 1977 sr vp chg wldwde theatrical prodn; 1980, exec vp in chg wldwde prodn Polygram Group.

HENSLEY, Pamela: Act. b. Los Angeles, Oct 3, 1950. e. RADA. TV inc: Owen Marshall, Counselor at Law; Toma; Marcus Welby, M.D.; Ironsides; The Rebels; Buck Rogers In the 25th Century; Condominium; Rooster; Matt Houston.

Films inc: Doc Savage; Rollerball; The Nude Bomb.

HENSON, Jim: Puppeter-Prod. b. Greenville, MS, Sep 24, 1936. e. U MD, BA. Created the Muppetts, 1954.

TV inc: Sesame Street (Emmys-childrens pgm-1974, 1976); The Muppet Show (Emmys-prod & perf-1978; wri-1981); Emmet Otter's Jug Band Christmas (& dir); The Muppets Go To The Movies; The Fantastic Miss Piggy Show (& dir); Fraggle Rock "Wembley and The Grogs" (& dir) (cable); Rocky Mountain Holiday With John Denver and the Muppets (& dir); Big Bird In China.

Films inc: The Time Piece (short); The Muppet Movie; The Great Muppet Caper (& dir); The Dark Crystal (& dir-act-wri); The Muppets Take Manhattan; Into The Night (act only).

(NATAS Founders Award, 1981) (Grammy-childrens-1981).

HEPBURN, Audrey: Act. b. Brussels, May 4, 1929. On London stage. Screen debut, Laughter in Paradise.

Bway inc: Ondine (Tony-1954); Gigi. Special Tony 1968.

Films inc: Laughter in Paradise; Roman Holiday (Oscar-1958); One Wild Oat; Lavender Hill Mob; Sabrina; War and Peace; Funny Face; Love in the Afternoon; The Nun's Story; Breakfast at Tiffany's; Charade; My Fair Lady; Wait Until Dark; Robin and Marian; Sidney Sheldon's Bloodline; They All Laughed.

TV inc: Producers Showcase; Mayerling; AFI Salute To Fred Astaire.

HEPBURN, Katharine: Act. b. Hartford, CT, Nov 9, 1909. e. Bryn Mawr Coll. Films inc: A Bill of Divorcement; Morning Glory (Oscar-1932-33); Little Women; Spitfire; The Little Minister; Mary of Scotland; Stage Door; Bringing Up Baby; Holiday; The Philadelphia Story; Woman of the Year; Keeper of the Flame; Dragon Seed; Sea of Grass; State of the Union; Adam's Rib; The African Queen; Pat and Mike; Summertime; The Rainmaker; Desk Set; Suddenly Last Summer; Long Day's Journey Into Night; Guess Who's Coming to Dinner (Oscar-1967); The Lion in Winter (Oscar-1968); The Madwoman of Chaillot; A Delicate Balance; Rooster Cogburn; Olly, Olly, Oxen Free;

On Golden Pond (Oscar-1981); The Ultimate Solution of Grace Quigley; George Stevens--A Filmmakers Journey (doc-int).

Bway inc: Night Hostess; The Lake; Jane Eyre; The Philadelphia Story; Without Love; The Millionairess; Antony and Cleopatra; Coco; A Matter of Gravity; The West Side Waltz.

TV inc: Love Among the Ruins (Emmy-1975); The Corn Is Green; Stanley Kramer on Film.

HEREFORD, Kathryn: Act-Prod. b. Campbell, VA. W of Pandro Berman. Films inc: (prod or asso prod) Something of Value; Jailhouse Rock; Brothers Karamzov; The Reluctant Debutante; All the Fine Young Cannibals; Key Witness; Butterfield 8; Sweet Bird of Youth; The Prize; Honeymoon Hotel; Patch of Blue; Justine.

HERLIE, Eileen (nee Herlihy): Act. b. Glasgow, Scotland, Mar 8, 1920. Films inc: Hungry Hill; Hamlet; The Angel with the Trumpet; The Story of Gilbert and Sullivan; Isn't Life Wonderful; For Better, For Worse; She Didn't Say No; Freud; The Seagull.

Thea inc: Take Me Along; All American; Hamlet; Halfway Up the Tree; Who's Afraid of Virginia Woolf?; Crown Matrimonial; The Great Sebastians.

HERMAN, George: TV pers. b. NYC, 1919. e. Dartmouth, BA; Columbia. Started as newsman WQXR (radio), NYC; joined CBS News, 1944; night news editor CBS Radio 1945; switched to TV 1948; toured Asia 1949 as CBS stringer; 1951, Far Eastern Bureau Mgr CBS; 1953, White House Correspondent; 1969, moderator Face the Nation.

HERMAN, Jerry: Comp-Lyr. b. NYC, Jul 10, 1933. e. Parsons School of Design; U of Miami, AB. Bway inc: I Feel Wonderful; Nightcap; Parade; Milk and Honey; Madame Aphrodite; Hello, Dolly! (Tony-comp-1964); Mame; Dear World; Mack and Mabel; Grand Tour; La Cage Aux Folles (Tony-1984).

(Grammys-(2)-song of the year-1964; cast album-1966).

HERMAN, Kenn R.: Dir. b. Detroit, Jul 2, 1930. e. MI State U. TV inc: General Hospital (1961-1978); Days of Our Lives.

HERMAN, Norman T.: Prod-Dir. b. Newark, NJ, Feb 10, 1924. e. Rutgers U, BA. (Prod), Sierra Stranger; Crime Beneath the Seas; Hot Rod Rumble; Hot Rod Girl; Rolling Thunder; Dirty Mary, Crazy Larry; Legend of Hill House. (Prod-dir), Tokyo After Dark; Mondo Teeno (Co-prod); Killers Three; Bunny O'Hare; Angel Unchained; Bloody Mama; Dillinger (Wri only); In God We Trust (exec prod).

TV inc: (wri) Lancer; Adam 12; Invaders; You Are the Judge; Hannibal Cobb; Iron Horse.

HERMAN, Pinky: Sngwri. b. NYC, Dec 23, 1905. Songs inc: Boom Ta Ra Ra; It Must Be LUV; Manhattan Merry Go Round; If I Had A Million Dollars.

HERMAN, Woody: Band Ldr. b. Milwaukee, WI, May 16, 1913. e. Marquette U. Played clarinet, sax with dance bands; formed own orch appearing in hotels, theatres, ballrooms, toured Europe. TV inc: A Gift of Music; The Nashville Palace; Jazz Alive; Night Of 100 Stars II.

Films inc: What's Cookin'?; Winter Time; Sensations of 1945; Earl Carroll's Vanities.

(Grammys-(3)-jazz perf large group-1963; jazz perf-big band-1973, 1974).

HEROUX, Claude: Prod. b. Montreal, Jan 26, 1942. e. U of Montreal. Films inc: Valerie; L'Initiation; L'Amour Humain; Un enfant comme les autres; J'ai mon voyage; Je t'aime; Echoes of a Summer; Jacques Brel Is Alive and Well and Living in Paris; Breaking Point; Born for Hell; Angela; The Uncanny; In Praise of Older Women; The Brood; City on Fire; Hog Wild; Scanners; Dirty Tricks; Gas; Visiting Hours; Videodrome; The Funny Farm; Going Berserk; Au nom de tous Miens (For Those I Loved); Of Unknown Origin; Covergirl. Named Prod VP Film Plan International, Montreal, 1979.

HEROUX, Denis: Exec prod. b. Montreal, Canada, Jul 1941. e. U of Montreal, MA. Entered film industry while a history prof at U of Quebec, dir Seul Ou Avec D'Autres; 1969, formed own company, International Cinema Corp. Films inc: (Dir) Jusqu'au Cou; Pas des Vacances pour les Idoles; Valerie; L'Initiation; L'Amour Humain; Sept

Fois--Par Jour (Seven Times--A Day); Un Enfant Comme Les Autres; Quelques Arpents de Neige; J'Ai Mon Voyage; Jacques Brel is Alive and Well and Living in Paris; Pousse Mais Pousse Egal; Ne Pour L'Enfer; The Uncanny. (Prod) The Little Girl Who Lives Down the Lane; Blood Relatives; Tomorrow Never Comes; Violette Noziere (Violette); L'Homme En Colere (Jigsaw); A Nous Deux (An Adventure for Two); Atlantic City, USA (exec prod); Les Plouffe (The Plouffe Family) (Exec prod); Quest For Fire; Louisiane; Le sang des Autres (The Blood of Others); Bay Boy.

HERRMANN, Edward: Act. b. Washington, DC, Jul 31, 1943. e. Bucknell U. Films inc: The Paper Chase; The Day of the Dolphin; The Great Gatsby; The Great Waldo Pepper; The Betsy; The North Avenue Irregulars; Brass Target; Take Down; Harry's War; Reds; Death Valley; A Little Sex; Annie; Mrs. Soffel; The Purple Rose Of Cairo.

TV inc: Beacon Hill; Eleanor and Franklin; Eleanor and Franklin-The White House Years; The Lou Gehrig Story; Portrait of a Stripper; The Sorrows of Gin; Freedom Road; The Private History of a Campaign That Failed; Dear Liar; The Electric Grandmother; The Gift of Life; Concealed Enemies.

Bway inc: Mrs. Warren's Profession *(Tony*-1976); The Philadelphia Story; Plenty; Tom And Viv (Off-Bway).

HERSEY, David: Light dsgn. b. Rochester, NY., Nov. 30, 1939. e. Oberlin Coll. Started as act, stage mgr in NY, moved to England 1968 founded David Hersey Associates; lighting supv National Theatre since 1974. Thea inc: She Stoops to Conquer; The Architect and the Emperor of Assyria; Danton's Death; Hamlet; Too True to Be Good; The Marrying of Ann Leete; Elvis; Evita (& Bway) *(Tony*-1980); The Crucifer of Blood; Cats (& Bway) *(Tony*-1982); Guys and Dolls; Marilyn!; Starlight Express; Corpse!; Rough Crossing.

Films inc: Nijinsky (ballet sequences).

HERSHEY, Barbara (nee Hertzstein; also known as Barbara Seagull): Act. b. Los Angeles, Feb 5, 1948. Films inc: With Six You Get Eggroll; Last Summer; The Liberation of L B Jones; The Pursuit of Happiness; The Baby Maker; Boxcar Bertha; Diamonds; The Last Hard Men; The Stunt Man; Take This Job and Shove It; Americana; The Entity; The Right Stuff; The Natural.

TV inc: The Monroes; From Here To Eternity-The War Years; A Man Called Intrepid; Angel on My Shoulder; Working; Weekend; My Wicked, Wicked Ways.

HERSKOVITZ, Arthur M.: Exec. b. Mukden, China, Nov 28, 1920. e. CCNY. Joined RKO scenario dept, 1939; m RKO Radio Pictures of Peru, 1955; Warner Bros. Peru, 1958-64; MGM, Panama, 1965-67; MGM rep in Japan, 1968; Far East Supv, 1970; joined National General Pictures, 1973, as foreign sls m; in 1974 appt dir of sls, JAD Films International.

HERTZ, William F.: Exec. b. Wishek, ND, Dec 5, 1923. e. U of MN. Thea Mgr, Fox West Coast Theatres, 1946; LA 1st-run district Mgr, National General Corp, 1965; Pacific Coast Div Mgr NGC, 1967; vp & So Pac Div M, NGC, 1971; now dir thea ops, Mann Theatres.

HERZOG, Werner: Dir. b. Germany, 1942. Films inc: Signs of Life; Even Dwarfs Started Small; Fata Morgana; The Land of Silence Darkness; Aguirre-Wrath of God; Soufriere; Heart of Glass; Stroszek; Kaspar Hauser; Nosferatu; Woyzeck (& sp); Burden of Dreams (prod) (doc); Fitzcarraldo (& wri-prod); Man of Flowers (act); Wo Die Grunen Ameisen Traumen (Where The Green Ants Dream) (& wri); Room 666 (doc-int); Tokyo-Ga (act).

HESSEMAN, Howard: Act. b. Salem, OR, Feb 27, 1940. With the San Francisco group The Committee. Films inc: Petulia; Billy Jack; Steelyard Blues; Shampoo; The Sunshine Boys; Jackson County Jail; The Big Bus; The Other Side of Midnight; Silent Movie; Honky Tonk Freeway; Private Lessons; Loose Shoes; Doctor Detroit; Spinal Tap; Police Academy 2--Their First Assignment.

TV inc: Mary Hartman, Mary Hartman; Fernwood 2night; Hustling; The Life and Times of Sen. Joseph McCarthy; The Amazing Howard Hughes; The TV TV Show; Tarantulas--The Deadly Cargo; The Ghost on Flight 401; WKRP in Cincinnati; John Ritter, Being of Sound Mind and Body; The Great American Traffic Jam; Skyward; 30 Years of TV Comedy's Greatest Hits; Women Who Rate A 10 (host); Loretta Lynn-The Lady, The Legend; Victims; One Shoe Makes It Murder; Mr. Rob-

erts; Best Kept Secrets; One Day At a Time; Silence Of The Heart; How To Be A Man.

HESSLER, Gordon: Prod-Dir. b. Berlin, 1930. Films inc: The Last Shot You Hear; The Oblong Box (& prod); Scream and Scream Again; Cry of the Banshee (& prod); Murders in the Rue Morgue (& prod); Embassy; Sinbad's Golden Voyage; Medusa; Next Week Rio; Puzzle; Pray For Death.

TV inc: Alfred Hitchcock Presents; Alfred Hitchcock Hour; Run For Your Life; Bob Hope Chrysler Show; Lucas Tanner; Night Stalker; Switch; Kung Fu; Hawaii Five-O; The Secret War of Jackie's Girls.

HESTON, Charlton: Act. b. Evanston, IL, Oct 4, 1924. e. Northwestern U. Films inc: Dark City; The Greatest Show on Earth; The Savage; Ruby Gentry; The President's Lady; Arrowhead; The Naked Jungle; Far Horizons; Private War of Major Benson; Lucy Gallant; The Ten Commandments; Three Violent People; Touch of Evil; The Big Country; Ben Hur *(Oscar*-1959); The Wreck of the Mary Deare; El Cid; The Pigeon That Took Rome; 55 Days at Peking; The Greatest Story Ever Told; The Agony and the Ecstasy; The War Lord; Khartoum; Will Penny; Planet of the Apes; Beneath the Planet of the Apes; Julius Caesar; The Omega Man; Antony and Cleopatra; Skyjacked; Call of the Wild; Soylent Green; Airport 1975; Earthquake; The Four Musketeers; The Last Hard Men; Midway; Two Minute Warning; Crossed Swords; Gray Lady Down; The Mountain Men; The Awakening; Mother Lode (& dir).

Bway inc: Antony and Cleopatra; Leaf and Bough; Cockadoodle Doo; Design for a Stained Glass Window. London inc: The Caine Mutiny Court Martial (& dir).

TV inc: Macbeth; The Taming of the Shrew; Of Human Bondage; Julius Caesar; A Man For All Seasons; This Is Your Life; AFI Tribute To Fred Astaire; The Way They Were; Ready When You Are, Mr. De Mille; All Hands On Deck For Bob Hope's All-Star Birthday Party At Annapolis; Chiefs; Nairobi Affair.

(Jean Hersholt Humanitarian Award-1977).

HEYES, Doug: Act. b. Los Angeles, May 22, 1956. TV inc: The Barbary Coast; City of Angels; Captains and the Kings; Aspen; The Hardy Boys; The French Atlantic Affair (dir-wri).

HEYMAN, John: Prod. b. Leipzig, Germany, 1933. Publicist, later pers mgr for stars. Films inc: Boom; Privilege; Jesus; Daniel; A Passage To India; D.A.R.Y.L.

HEYWARD, Louis M.: Exec. b. NYC, Jun 29, 1920. e. NYU; Brooklyn Law School. Radio writer, CBS: Garry Moore Show; Ernie Kovacs Show; co-owner Heyward-Wilkes Industrial Film Co.; vp prodn AIP; m-dir AIP, London; Hanna-Barbera Prods. 1973, vp live prodn, asst to pres; 1981 joined Barry-Enright to develop new programs.

Films inc: Chomps; Dr. Phibes; Dr. Phibes Rises Again; Wuthering Heights (remake); Scream and Scream Again.

TV inc: (prod over 5000 shows): Bell Telephone Hour; Dick Clark Show; The Gathering; Beasts Are in the Street; Kiss Meets Phantom of the Park.

HEYWOOD, Anne (Violet Pretty): Act. b. England, 1931. W of Raymond Stross. Films inc: Find the Lady; Checkpoint; Dangerous Exile; The Depraved; Violent Playground; Floods of Fear; Upstairs and Downstairs; A Terrible Beauty; Petticoat Pirates; Stork Talk; Vengeance; Ninety Degrees in the Shade; The Fox; The Chairman; The Midas Run; I Want What I Want; Trader Horn; The Nun and the Devil; The Most Dangerous Man in the World; And Presumed Dead. Good Luck Miss Wyckoff.

TV inc: Sadat.

HIBBLER, Al: Act. b. Little Rock, AR, Aug 16, 1915. Born blind. Vocalist with Duke Ellington, 1943-51. Left Ellington for career as solo recording artist.

HICKMAN, Darryl: Act-TV Prod. b. Hollywood, Jul 28, 1931. On screen since 1939. Films inc: The Star Maker; The Grapes of Wrath; Joe Smith, American; Keeper of the Flame; Captain Eddie; Leave Her to Heaven; Destination Gobi; Tea and Sympathy; Network; Looker; Sharky's Machine.

TV inc: Love of Life (Exec prod).

HICKMAN, Dwayne B.: Act-Exec. b. Los Angeles, May 18, 1934. e. Loyola U, BS econ. B of Darryl Hickman. To CBS 1979 as exec prod handling comedy series after act career. Films inc: Captain Eddie; Return of Rusty; The Boy With Green Hair; Rally Round The Flag Boys; Cat Ballou; How To Stuff a Wild Bikini; Ski Party; Dr. Goldfoot and the Bikini Machine; Doctor, You've Got To Be Kidding.
TV inc: Bob Cummings Show; The Many Loves of Dobie Gillis; High School U.S.A.

HICKS, Catherine: Act. b. Scottsdale, AZ, Aug 6, 1951. e. Notre Dame, BA Bway inc: Tribute. Films inc: Death Valley; Better Late Than Never; Garbo Talks; The Razor's Edge.
TV inc: Ryan's Hope; Sparrow; The Bad News Bears; Marilyn--the Untold Story; Jacqueline Susann's Valley of the Dolls 1981; Tucker's Witch; Happy Endings.

HICKSON, Joan: Act. b. Northampton, England, Aug 5, 1906. e. RADA. Thea inc: (London) A Damsel in Distress; Baa Baa Black Sheep; The Middle Watch; Leave it to Psmith; Crime at the Blossoms; Crime on the Hill; Distinguished Gathering; Murder Gang; Festival Time; The Gusher; It's A Wise Child; The Proposal; See How They Run; Appointment With Death; The Guinea Pig; Foxhole in the Parlor; Rain Before Seven; The Gay Dog; Man Alive!; A Day in the Death of Joe Egg; The Card; The Freeway; Blithe Spirit. (Bway) A Day in the Death of Joe Egg; Bedroom Farce (Tony-supp-1979).
Films inc: Widow's Might; Love From a Stranger; I See a Dark Stranger; The Guinea Pig; Seven Days to Noon; The Card; The Man Who Never Was; Happy Is The Bride; The 39 Steps; A Day in the Death of Joe Egg; Theatre of Blood; Yanks; The Wicked Lady.
TV inc: Sinister Street; Bachelor Father; Why Didn't They Ask Evans?

HIELSCHER, Leo Arthur: Exec. b. Eumundi, Queensland, Australia, Oct 1, 1926. Commissioner, Queensland Film Corp.

HIFT, Fred: Pub. b. Vienna, Nov 27, 1924. Reporter, Chicago Sun; 1941 CBS News; 1946, Boxoffice; 1947, Quigley Publications; 1948, NY Times; 1950, Variety; 1960, dir pub Otto Preminger Prodns; 1961, Darryl F. Zanuck Prodns; 1962, European ad-pub dir 20th-Fox; 1970, set up indie pub office London; 1979, dir East Coast pub Columbia; 1980, intl ad-pub vp UA; Mar 1982, reopened Fred Hift Associates as int'l mktg org; Oct. 1983, wldwde mktg VP Almi Distribution.

HIGGINS, Colin: Wri-Dir. b. New Caledonia, July 28, 1941. Former actor. Films inc: Harold and Maude (wri); Silver Streak (wri); Foul Play; Nine to Five; The Best Little Whorehouse in Texas; Into The Night (act).
TV inc: Brideshead Revisited.

HIGGINS, Joel: Act. b. Bloomington, IL., Sep. 28, 1946. e. MI State U, BA. Bway inc: Shenandoah; Music Is; Oklahoma!. Other thea inc: Grease (tour); Camp Meeting (off Bway).
TV inc: Search for Tomorrow; Salvage 1; Best of the West; Silver Spoons; Threesome.

HIKEN, Gerald: Act-Dir. b. Milwaukee, WI, May 23, 1927. e. U of WI. Bway inc: The Lovers; Good Woman of Szetzuan; The Cave Dwellers; The Nervous Set; The Fighting Cock; The 49th Cousin; Gideon; Brecht on Brecht; Strider; Fools.
Films inc: Uncle Vanya; The Goddess; Invitation to a Gunfighter; Funnyman.
TV inc: The Wall; Love Leads The Way; Space.

HILDYARD, Jack: Cin. b. England, 1915. Films inc: Secret Flight; Breaking the Sound Barrier; Hobson's Choice; Summertime; Anastasia; The Bridge on the River Kwai (Oscar-1957); Another Time, Another Place; The Journey; The Devil's Disciple; Suddenly Last Summer; The Millionairess; The Sundowners; The Road to Hong Kong; Cleopatra (part); 55 Days at Peking; The V.I.P's; Circus World; The Yellow Rolls Royce; Battle of the Bulge; Casino Royale; Hard Contract; Topaz; Puppet on a Chain; The Beast Must Die; The Message; Omar Mukhtar, Lion of the Desert; Mohammed, Messenger of God; The Wild Geese.
TV inc: The Zany Adventures of Robin Hood; Ellis Island; Florence Nightingale.

HILL, Arthur: Act. b. Melfort, Saskatchewan, Canada, Aug 1, 1922. Bway: The Matchmaker; The Gang's All Here; A Death in the Family; All The Way Home; Who's Afraid of Virginia Woolf? (Tony-1963).
Films inc: The Deep Blue Sea; Harper; The Ugly American; Petulia; Don't Let The Angels Fall; The Chairman; Killer Elite; Futureworld; The Andromeda Strain; A Bridge Too Far; The Champ; The Glacier Fox; A Little Romance; Butch and Sundance-The Early Years; Dirty Tricks; Making Love; The Amateur; Something Wicked This Way Comes.
TV inc: Owen Marshall; Death Be Not Proud; Hagen; The Ordeal of Dr. Mudd; Revenge of the Stepford Wives; The Return of Frank Cannon; Angel Dusted; Churchill and the Generals; Tomorrow's Child; Miss Lonelyhearts; Intimate Agony; Prototype; Glitter; Murder She Wrote; Love Leads The Way; The Guardian (cable).

HILL, Benny (Alfred Hawthorn Hill): Act. b. Southampton, England, Jan. 21, 1925. TV inc: The Service Show; Showcase; The Benny Hill Show; Midsummer Night's Dream.
Films inc: Who Done It?; Light Up the Sky; Those Magnificent Men in Their Flying Machines; Chitty Chitty Bang Bang.

HILL, Dana (nee Goetz): Act. b. Los Angeles, May, 1964. TV inc: The Paul Williams Show; Fallen Angel; What Are Friends For?; The $5.20 an Hour Dream; The French Atlantic Affair; The Two of Us; Member of the Wedding; Branagan & Mapes; Welcome Home, Jellybean; Silence Of The Heart.
Films inc: The Kids Who Knew Too Much; Shoot the Moon; Cross Creek.

HILL, Debra: Prod. Films inc: Halloween (& wri); The Fog (& co-wri); Escape From New York; Halloween II (& wri); Halloween III--Season of the Witch; The Dead Zone.

HILL, George Roy: Prod-Dir. b. Minneapolis, MS, Dec 20, 1922. e. Yale U, BA; Trinity Coll, Dublin. Films inc: Period of Adjustment; Toys in the Attic; The World of Henry Orient; Hawaii; Thoroughly Modern Millie; Butch Cassidy and the Sundance Kid; Slaughterhouse Five; The Sting (Oscar-1973); The Great Waldo Pepper; Slap Shot; A Little Romance; The World According to Garp; The Little Drummer Girl (dir).
Bway inc: Look Homeward Angel; The Gang's All Here; Greenwillow; Period of Adjustment; Moon on a Rainbow Shawl; Henry, Sweet, Henry.
TV inc: A Night to Remember; Helen Morgan; Child of Our Time; Judgment at Nuremberg.

HILL, Leonard F.: Prod. b. Los Angeles, CA., Oct. 11, 1947. e. Yale, BA; Stanford, MA. ABC Entertainment vp in chg of vidpix 1976-1980; Aug. 1980 formed Hill-Mandelker Productions with Phillip Mandelker. TV inc: (exec prod) Freedom; Dream House; Mae West; Dreams Don't Die; Tucker's Witch; Having it All; Girls of the White Orchid; Parade; High School USA; The Cartier Affair.

HILL, Pamela: Exec prod. (nee Abel):b. Winchester, IN, Aug 18, 1938. e. Bennington Coll. Researcher, asso prod, dir NBC News, 1965-1973; dir White Paper Series, 1969-1972; prod, Edwin Newman's Comment, 1972; prod ABC News Closeup doc series, 1973-1978; vp ABC News, 1979. TV inc: Fire! (Emmys-prod & dir-1974); Nobody's Children; Escape From Justice-Nazi War Criminals in the U.S.; This Shattered Land; To Die For Ireland; Lights, Camera; Can't It Be Anyone Else; Death In A Southwest Prison; The Apocalypse Game; The Shattered Badge; A Matter of Survival; Invasion; Soldiers of the Twilight; Near Armageddon--The Spread of Nuclear Weapons In The Middle East; When Crime Pays; The Monastery; The Gene Merchants; Hooray For Hollywood; Wounds From Within; Rain of Terror; Japan--Myths Behind the Miracles; FDR; Fortress Israel; The Oil Game; J. Edgar Hoover; Vietnam Requiem; Mexico--Times of Crisis; Swords, Plowshares and Politics; Asbestos--The Way to Dusty Death; Adapt or Die; The American Inquisition; The Money Masters; Vanishing America; Alias A John Blake; Water--A Clear and Present Danger; The Cocaine Cartel; JFK (wri).; To Save Our Schools, To Save Our Children; The Supreme Court Of The United States; The Fire Unleashed.

HILL, Sandy: Newscaster. b. Centralia, WA. e. U of WA. One of first women to co-anchor early evening news in the country (Channel 7,

LA). In April 1977, joined ABC TV's Good Morning America; Sep 1982, anchor KNXT. Other TV inc: Show Business (host).

HILL, Steven (Solomon Berg): Act. b. Seattle, WA. Studied with Lee Strasberg; Elia Kazan; Joshua Logan. Bway inc: Mister Roberts; The Lady from the Sea; The Country Girl.
Films inc: Lady Without a Passport; The Goddess; A Child Is Waiting; The Slender Thread; It's My Turn; Eyewitness; Rich and Famous; Yentl; Garbo Talks.
TV inc: Mission Impossible; King.

HILL, Terence (Mario Girotti): Act. b. Venice, Italy, Mar 1941. Screen debut age 12, Holiday for Gangsters.
Films inc: My Name is Nobody; They Call Me Trinity; Trinity Is Still My Name; Boot Hill; Ace High; Mr Billion; March or Die; Super Fuzz.

HILL, Walter: Wri. b. Long Beach, CA, Jan 10, 1942. e. MI State U. Films inc: Hickey & Boggs; The Getaway; The Thief Who Came to Dinner; The Mackintosh Man; The Drowning Pool; Hard Times (& dir); The Driver (& dir); The Warriors (& dir); Alien (prod); The Long Riders (dir); Southern Comfort (& dir); 48 Hours (& dir); Streets of Fire (& dir); Brewster's Millions.

HILLAIRE, Marcel: Act. b. Cologne, Germany, Apr 23, 1908. Films inc: Sabrina; Seven Thieves; The Honeymoon Machine; The Wheeler Dealers; A Very Special Favor; Made in Paris.
TV inc: Adventures in Paradise; Beggerman, Thief.

HILLER, Arthur: Dir. b. Edmonton, Canada, Nov 22, 1923. Films inc: The Careless Years; The Americanization of Emily; Tobruk; The Tiger Makes Out; Poppi; The Out of Towners; Love Story; Plaza Suite; Hospital; Man of La Mancha; WC Fields and Me; Man in the Glass Booth; Silver Streak; Nightwing; The In-Laws; Making Love; Author!, Author!; Romantic Comedy; The Lonely Guy (& prod); Teachers.
TV inc: Matinee Theatre; Climax; Playhouse 90; Alfred Hitchcock Presents; Naked City; Massacre at Sand Creek.

HILLER, Wendy: Act. b. Bramhall, Cheshire, England, Aug 15, 1912. Performed with Manchester Repertory Theatre. London debut, Love on the Dole, 1935. Screen debut, Lancashire Luck, 1937.
Films inc: Pygmalion; Major Barbara; Something of Value; Separate Tables (Oscar-supp-1958); Sons and Lovers; Toys in the Attic; A Man for All Seasons; Murder on the Orient Express; Voyage of the Damned; The Cat and The Canary; The Elephant Man; Making Love.
Thea inc: Wings of the Dove; Sacred Flame; Crown Matrimonial; John Gabriel Borkman; Lies; Waters of the Moon; The Aspern Papers.
TV inc: The Curse of King Tut's Tomb; Mrs. Morrison's Ghosts; Witness For the Prosecution; The Comedy of Errors.

HILLERMAN, John: Act. b. Denison, TX, Dec 30, 1932. e. U of TX. Films inc: Paper Moon; The Day of the Locust; Chinatown; Audrey Rose; Sunburn; History of the World--Part I; Up the Creek.
TV inc: Ellery Queen; The Law; The Betty White Show; Beane's of Boston; Kill Me If You Can; Betrayal; Marathon; Battles-The Murder That Wouldn't Die; Don't Eat the Snow In Hawaii (Magnum P.I. pilot); Magnum P.I. Tales of the Gold Monkey (pilot); Little Gloria--Happy At Last.

HINCK, Jon W: Dist. b. CA, Jan 1954. e. U of PA, BA. Northwest Diversified Entertainment, 1977; Cinemaworld Releasing, 1978.

HINES, Earl Kenneth (Fatha): Comp-Cond. b. Duquesne, PA, Dec 28, 1905. Formed own band, 1928; recorded with Louis Armstrong; toured Europe; performed at White House 1969, 1976,1977.
(Died Apr 22, 1983).

HINES, Gregory: Act-Dancer. b. Feb 14, 1946. Had dance act with brother and father; later had own jazz-rock band, Severance. Bway inc: Eubie; Coming Uptown; Sophisticated Ladies.
Films inc: History of the World Part I; Wolfen; Deal of the Century; The Muppets Take Manhattan; The Cotton Club.
TV inc: Live From Studio 8H--100 Years of America's Popular Music; Steve Martin's Best Show Ever; Shirley MacLaine--Illusions; I Love Liberty; The Kennedy Center Honors 1982; Night Of 100 Stars II; Motown Returns To The Apollo; The AFI Salute To Gene Kelly.

HINGLE, Pat: Act. b. Denver, CO, Jul 19, 1923. e. U of TX. Stage debut, 1950, Johnny Belinda.
Films inc: On the Waterfront; The Strange One; No Down Payment; Splendor in the Grass; The Ugly American; Invitation to a Gunfighter; Nevada Smith; Hang 'Em High; Bloody Mama; Norwood; The Carey Treatment; One Little Indian; Run Wild; Norma Rae; When You Comin' Back Red Ryder; Running Brave; Going Berserk; Sudden Impact; The Act; The Falcon And The Snowman; Brewster's Millions.
Bway inc: A Man for All Seasons; A Girl Could Get Lucky; The Odd Couple; Johnny No-Trump; A Grave Undertaking; A Life.
TV Inc: Elvis; Stone; Disaster on the Coastliner; Wild Times; The Private History of a Campaign That Failed; Of Mice and Men; Washington Mistress; Bus Stop (cable); The Fighter; Noon Wine; The Lady From Yesterday; The Rape Of Richard Beck.

HINKLE, Robert: Act-Dir-Prod. b. Brownfield, TX, Jul 25, 1930. Rodeo performer. Films inc: The First Texan; Dakota Incident; Gun The Man Down; Ole Rex; Stuntman; Texas Long Horns; Country Music (prod-dir); Guns of a Stranger (prod-dir).
TV inc: Test Pilot; Dial 111; Juvenile Squad; Giant; Opposite Sex.

HIRSCH, Judd: Act. b. NYC, Mar 15, 1935. e. CCNY; Cooper Union Coll; AADA. Films inc: Serpico; King of the Gypsies; Ordinary People; Without A Trace; In Our Hands (doc); The Goodbye People; Teachers.
TV inc: The Law; Delvecchio; Valentino; Fear on Trial; Like Father, Like Daughter; Taxi (Emmys-1981, 1983); Sooner or Later; The Halloween That Almost Wasn't; Marriage is Alive and Well; The Robert Klein Show; I Love Liberty; Loretta Lynn In Big Apple Country; Detective In The House; First Steps; Brotherly Love.
Bway inc: The Hot L Baltimore; Knock Knock; Chapter Two; Talley's Folly.

HIRSCHFELD, Gerald: Cin. b. NYC, Apr 25, 1921. e. Columbia U. Films inc: Fail Safe; The Incident; Goodbye Columbus; Last Summer; Cotton Comes to Harlem; Diary of a Mad Housewife; Child's Play; Summer Wishes, Winter Dreams; Young Frankenstein; Two-Minute Warning; The Car; The World's Greatest Lover; The Bell Jar; Americathon; Why Would I Lie?; Neighbors; My Favorite Year; To Be Or Not To Be; The House of God.
TV inc: Country Gold; Love Lives On.

HIRSCHFIELD, Alan J.: Exec. b. Oklahoma City, OK, Oct 10, 1935. e. U of OK; Harvard Business School, MA. 1959 joined Allen & Co., investment bankers, later becoming vp; 1966 financial vp WB-Seven Arts; 1970, vp American Diversified Enterprises, investment firm; 1973 p, CEO Columbia Pictures Industries; July 1978, fired in furore over his handling of David Begelman situation; 1979 consultant to Warner Communications; Oct 1979 vice chmn, COO Fox; Aug 1981, chmn & chief exec.; resd. Sept. 1984.

HIRSCHHORN, Joel: Sngwri. Writes in collaboration with Al Kasha.
Songs inc: My Empty Arms; I'm Comin' On Back To You; Let's Start All Over Again; Wake Up; Your Time Hasn't Come Yet Baby; Will You Be Staying After Sunday?; One More Mountain To Climb; The Subject Was Roses; Living Is Dying Without You; The Morning After (Oscar-1972); We May Never Love Like This Again (Oscar-1974); Candle on the Water; I'd Like To Be You For a Day; May the Best Man Win; Mississippi Magic; Pass A Little Love Around.
Bway inc: Copperfield; Seven Brides For Seven Brothers (add'l songs). TV inc: Goodbye, Charlie.To You; Let's Start All Over Again; Wake Up; Your Time Hasn't Come Yet Baby; Will You Be Staying After Sunday?; One More Mountain To Climb; The Subject Was Roses; Living Is Dying Without You; The Morning After (Oscar-1972); We May Never Love Like This Again (Oscar-1974); Candle on the Water; I'd Like To Be You For a Day; May the Best Man Win; Mississippi Magic; Pass A Little Love Around.
Bway inc:

HIRSCHMAN, Herbert: Prod-Dir. b. NYC, Apr 13. e. U of MI, BA; Yale U, MFA. Films inc: (prod.): Halls of Anger; They Call Me Mr. Tibbs.
Thea inc: (London) (dir) A Thousand Clowns.
TV inc: (dir) Omnibus; Starlight Theatre; Mr. I-Magination; Steve Allen Show; Celebrity Time; What's My Line; The Defenders; For the People; Iron Horse; Felony Squad. (Prod-dir.): The Web; Alcoa Hour; Goodyear Playhouse; Studio One; Playhouse 90; Perry Mason; Dr. Kildare; Twilight Zone; Wackiest Ship in the Army; Men From Shiloh;

Young Lawyers; The Bold Ones; Tell Me Where It Hurts; Returning Home; Eric; The Zoo Gang; The Amazing Howard Hughes; Morris Bird III; Flesh and Blood; And Baby Makes Six; The Scarlet Letter; Calamity Jane (prod only); Mistral's Daughter (prod only); Attack On Fear (prod only). (Exec prod): Iron Horse; Planet of the Apes.

HIRT, Al: Mus. b. New Orleans, LA, Nov 7, 1922. e. Cincinnati Conservatory of Music. Played with Tommy and Jimmy Dorsey bands, Ray McKinley, Horace Heidt; worked niteries, TV.
   Films inc: World By Night; Rome Adventure.
   (Grammy-orch perf-1963).

HITZIG, Rupert: Prod. e. Harvard. Joined CBS as doc wri-prod-dir, later moved into dramas. Partnered with Alan King in King-Hitzig Prodns. TV inc: Much Ado About Nothing; The Wonderful World of Jonathan Winters; Playboy After Dark; How To Pick Up Girls; Return to Earth.
   Films inc: Electra Glide in Blue; Happy Birthday, Gemini; Cattle Annie and Little Britches; Jaws 3-d (& 2d unit dir); Wolfen; The Last Dragon.

HO, Don: Singer-Act. b. Oahu, HI, Aug 13, 1930. Nightclubs. TV inc: The Don Ho Show.

HOBERMAN, Ben: Exec. b. 1923. Started as anncr-slsm WMFG, Hibbing, MN. Enlisted as private in WW2, won field commission as lieutenant, in chg American Forces Network stations France, England. 1946, asst gm WELI, New Haven, CT; 1948, gm WDET (FM), Detroit, MI; 1950 joined WXYZ-TV Detroit (ABC O&O) as first fulltime slsmn; 1958 gm WABC (AM) (ABC flagship NY); 1960 gm KABC-AM (ABC O&O); 1961, vp ABC; 1980, P ABC Radio net.

HOBIN, Bill: Prod-Dir. b. Evanston, IL, Nov 12, 1923. e. USC. TV inc: Garroway at Large; Assignment Manhattan; Fred Waring Show; Andy Williams Show; Pat Boone; The Bell Telephone Hour; Sing Along with Mitch; Meredith Wilson Special; Red Skelton Hour; The Bill Cosby Special; The Tim Conway Comedy Hour; The CBS Newcomers series; An Evening with My Three Sons; Fred Astaire Special; A Touch of Grace; Bobby Goldsboro Show; Welcome Back Kotter; Bert Convy Show; George Burns Special; Three's Company.

HODGES, Mike: Dir. b. Jul 29, 1932. TV inc: Sunday Break; World in Action; Tempo; Suspect; Rumour; Missing Pieces (& wri).
   Films inc: Suspect (& wri-prod); Rumor (& wri-prod); Get Carter; Pulp (& wri); The Terminal Man; Flash Gordon.

HOFFMAN, Dustin: Act. b. Los Angeles, Aug 8, 1934. e. Santa Monica City Coll; Pasadena Playhouse. Films inc: The Graduate; Midnight Cowboy; John and Mary; Little Big Man; Who is Harry Kellerman and Why Is He Saying those Terrible Things about Me?; Straw Dogs; Alfredo, Alfredo; Papillon; Lenny; All the President's Men; Marathon Man; Straight Time; Agatha; Kramer vs Kramer *(Oscar*-1979); Tootsie.
   Bway inc: A Cook for Mr General; Harry, Noon and Night; Journey of the Fifth Horse; Eh?; Jimmie Shine; All Over Town (dir); Death of a Salesman.
   TV inc: To Be An Actor.

HOFFMAN, Joseph: Wri-Prod. b. NYC, Feb 20, 1909. e. UCLA. Started as newspaperman, radio wri. TV prod. for Screen Gems, Warner Bros., Four Star; later TV and screen freelance wri.
   Films inc: China Sky; Don't Trust Your Husband; Gung Ho; And Baby Makes Three; At Sword's Point; Against All Flags; No Room for the Groom; Yankee Pasha; Tall Man Riding; Live a Little; How to Make Love and Like It; Sex and the Single Girl.
   TV (prod) inc: Ford Theatre; Celebrity Theatre; Damon Runyon Theatre; Colt 45.

HOFFMAN, Ross A.: Cin (ret). b. Mar 30, 1905. Specialized in special photography. Films inc: Island Earth; Incredible Shrinking Man; The Brass Bottle; Pillow Talk; Earthquake. With U 50 years.

HOFSISS, Jack: Dir. b. Brooklyn, NY, Sep 28, 1950. e. Georgetown. Dir for NY Shakespeare Festival 1976; ANTA.
   Bway inc: The Elephant Man *(Tony*-1979); Total Abandon.
   TV inc: For Richer for Poorer; The Sorrows of Gin; The Oldest

Living Graduate; The Elephant Man; Family Secrets; Cat On A Hot Tin Roof (cable).
   Films inc: I'm Dancing As Fast As I Can.

HOLBROOK, Hal: Act. b. Cleveland, OH, Feb 17, 1925. Bway debut 1959, one-man show, Mark Twain Tonight!; then toured US, Europe, Saudi Arabia. Screen debut, 1966, The Group.
   Films inc: Wild in the Streets; The People Next Door; The Great White Hope; They Only Kill Their Masters; Magnum Force; The Girl from Petrovka; All the President's Men; Midway; Julia; Capricorn One; Natural Enemies; The Fog; Creepshow; The Star Chamber; Girls Nite Out.
   TV inc: Mark Twain Tonight!; A Clear and Present Danger; The Glass Menagerie; The Senator *(Emmy*-1970); Pueblo *(Emmy*-1974); Legend of the Golden Gun; Sandburg's Lincoln *(Emmy*-1976); When Hell Was In Session; Off The Minnesota Strip; Omnibus (host); The Kidnapping of the President; The Killing of Randy Webster; America Remembers John F. Kennedy (narr); Celebrity; George Washington; The Three Wishes Of Billy Grier; Four Americans In China.
   Bway inc: The Apple Tree; I Never Sang For My Father; Man of La Mancha; Mark Twain Tonight *(Tony*-1966); Does a Tiger Wear a Necktie?;Country Girl (Off Bway).

HOLDEN, Gloria: Act. b. London, Sep 5, 1911. e. AADA. Films inc: Dracula's Daughter; The Life of Emile Zola; Test Pilot; A Child Is Born; The Corsican Brothers; Behind the Rising Sun; The Hucksters; Dream Wife; The Eddie Duchin Story; This Happy Feeling.

HOLDER, Geoffrey: Chor-Act-Dir. b. Trinidad, West Indies, Aug 1, 1930. e. Queens Royal Coll. Made US debut with own dance co in 1953; perf as solo dancer Metropolitan Opera in Aida & La Perichole, 1956-57 season; dramatic debut 1957, Waiting for Godot; toured with own dance co. Bway inc: I Got a Song (chor); The Wiz (chor & cos dsgn) *(2 Tonys*-1975); Timbuktu, (chor & cos dsgn) 1977.
   Films inc: All Night Long; Everything You've Ever Wanted to Know About Sex but Were Afraid to Ask; Live and Let Die; The Gold Bug; Annie; Dance Black America.
   TV inc: Alice in Wonderland.

HOLDRIDGE, Lee: Comp. b. Port-au-Prince, Haiti, March 3, 1944. e. Manhattan School of Music. Arr for Neil Diamond. Films inc: Mustang Country; Jonathan Livingston Seagull; Moment By Moment; The Other Side of the Mountain Part II; Oliver's Story; The Pack; French Postcards; American Pop; The Beastmaster; Splash; Micki and Maude; Sylvester.
   TV inc: McCloud; Hec Ramsey; John Steinbeck's East of Eden; Fly Away Home; The Day The Loving Stopped; For Ladies Only; Skyward Christmas; The Sharks; Thou Shalt Not Kill; This Is Kate Bennett; In Love With an Older Woman; Running Out; Thursday's Child; Wizards and Warriors; The Mississippi; Legs; I Want To Live; Moonlighting; He's Fired, She's Hired; Letting Go.

HOLLAND, Anthony: Act. b. NYC, 1946. e. U Chicago, studied at Actors Studio. Joined Second City Troupe. Thea inc: My Mother, My Father and Me; The White House Murder Case.
   Films inc: Goldstein; The Last Mohican; Bye, Bye Braverman; The Out of Towners; Midnight Cowboy; Lovers and Other Strangers; The Anderson Tapes; Klute; Lucky Lady; House Calls; King of the Gypsies; All That Jazz; The Tempest; Lonely Lady.
   TV inc: M*A*S*H; Mary Tyler Moore Show; And They All Lived Happily Ever After; P.O.P.; Paper Dolls.

HOLLAND, Anthony: Dsgn. b. England, Jun 3, 1912. e. Manchester School of Art. Thea inc: The King and Mistress Shore; The Eagle Has Two Heads; Edward My Son; The Sleeping Clergyman; Life With Father; The Indifferent Shepherd; Traveller's Joy; People Like Us; The Philadelphia Story; The Cocktail Party; The Four Poster; The Seventh Veil; The Three Sisters; The Amorous Prawn; A Visit to a Small Planet; Miss Pell is Missing; Menage a Trois; Reluctant Peer; Hostile Witness; Wait Until Dark; Let's All Go Down to the Strand; The Jockey Club Stakes; Birds of Paradise; The Dame of Sark; The Last of Mrs Cheyney; Cards On The Table.
   Films inc: Tempest.
   Ice shows inc: Robinson Crusoe; The Sleeping Beauty; Aladdin; The Babes in the Wood; Cinderella; Snow White; Around the World in

80 Days; Ali Baba and the 40 Thieves.

HOLLIDAY, Jennifer: Singer-act. b. Riverside, TX, Oct. 19, 1960. Thea inc: Don't Bother Me, I Can't Cope; Your Arms Too Short to Box With God (tour & Bway revival); Dreamgirls *(Tony*-1982).

(Grammy-R&B vocal-1982).

TV inc: 56th Oscar Show (1984); Night Of 100 Stars II; Motown Returns To The Apollo.

HOLLIDAY, Kene: Act. b. NYC, Jun 25. e. U of MD. TV inc: Burglar-Proofing; Carter Country; Momma the Detective; The Chicago Story; The Two Lives of Carol Letner; Dangerous Company; Farrell for the People; The Best of Times; Clay Feet; The Sheriff and the Astronaut.

Thea inc: Streamers; Films inc: The Philadelphia Experiment.

HOLLIDAY, Polly: Act. b. Jasper, AL, Jul 2. Films inc: All the President's Men; W W and the Dixie Dance Kings; Distance; The One and Only; Gremlins.

TV inc: The Silence; The 34th Star; Bernice Bobs Her Hair; Alice; You Can't Take It With You; Flo; All the Way Home; The Shady Hill Kidnapping; Missing Children--A Mother's Story; A Gift of Love--A Christmas Story; Lots Of Luck.

HOLLIMAN, Earl: Act. b. Delhi, LA, 1928. On stage in Camino Real; Streetcar Named Desire.

Films inc: Bridges of Toko-Ri; Giant; Gunfight at the OK Corral; Summer and Smoke; Good Luck Miss Wyckoff; Sharky's Machine.

TV inc: The Dark Side of the Earth; Alexander; The Other Side of Dawn; Police Woman; The Solitary Man; Where The Ladies Go; The Real Rookies (narr); Country Gold; The Thorn Birds.

HOLLOWAY, Julian: Act. b. Oxford, England, Jun. 24, 1944. e RADA. Thea inc: All Square; When Did You Last See My Mother; Spitting Image; The Norman Conquest; Pygmalion; Arsenic and Old Lace.

Films inc: (Shorts) The Spy's Wife (& Wri-prod); The Chairman's Wife (& Wri-prod). (Features) Nothing But the Best; Rough Cut; The Brute (asso prod); Loophole (prod).

TV inc: Our Man at St. Marks; Rebecca; The Sweeney; Helen, Woman of Today; An Adventure in Bed; The Punch Review; The Scarlet and the Black.

HOLLOWAY, Sterling: Act. b. Cedartown, GA, Jan 4, 1905. Films inc: Casey at the Bat; Alice in Wonderland; Life Begins at Forty; The Bluebird; A Walk in the Sun; The Beautiful Blonde from Bashful Bend; Shake, Rattle and Roll; Live a Little, Love a Little; The Aristocrats; Won Ton Ton, The Dog Who Saved Hollywood; Super Seal; Thunder and Lightning.

TV inc: The Life of Riley; Willy; The Baileys of Balboa.

(Grammy-childrens recording-1974).

HOLLY, Edwin E.: Exec. b. Elizabethtown, TN, Oct 3, 1926. e. U of TN. P First Artists Production Co.

HOLM, Celeste: Act. b. NYC, Apr 29, 1919. On screen from 1946. Films inc: Three Little Girls in Blue; Gentlemen's Agreement *(Oscar-*supp-1947); Snake Pit; Chicken Every Sunday; All About Eve; Come to the Stable; Tom Sawyer; Bittersweet Love.

Bway inc: Time of Your Life; Return of the Vagabond; Oklahoma; Bloomer Girl; Candida; Habeas Corpus; Utter Glory of Morrissey Hall.

TV inc: Clearing House in the Wood; Play of the Week; Cinderella; Backstairs at the White House; Midnight Lace; Grammy Hall of Fame; The Shady Hill Kidnapping; Trapper John, M.D.; This Girl For Hire; Jessie; Dynasty.

HOLM, Hanya: Chor-Dancer. b. Wurms-am-Rheim, Germany, circa 1900. e. Hoch Conservatory, Frankfurt; Dalcroze Institute; Wigman School of Dance, Dresden. Appeared in Max Reinhardt's The Miracle before joining Wigman company where she was a member of the original company and later chief instructor; formed own dance company, toured Europe; to U.S. 1931, founded the NY Wigman School which later became the Hanya Holm School; prodns include Trend; Metropolitan Daily; Tragic Exodus.

Bway inc: Ballet Ballads; Kiss Me, Kate (received first copyright for choreographic composition); The Insect Comedy; Blood Wedding; Out of This World; My Darlin' Aida; The Golden Apple; My Fair Lady; Anya.

Films inc: The Vagabond King.

TV inc: Pinocchio; Dinner With the President.

HOLM, Ian (nee Cuthbert): Act. b. Ilford, Essex, England, Sep 12, 1931. e. RADA. Thea inc: (London) Love Affair; Titus Andronicus; various roles with Royal Shakespeare Company; Ondine; Becket; The Cherry Orchard; The Homecoming; The Friends; A Bequest to the Nation; The Sea. (Bway) The Homecoming *(Tony*-supp-1967).

Films inc: A Midsummer Night's Dream; The Fixer; The Homecoming; Juggernaut; Shout at the Devil; Alien; Chariots of Fire; Time Bandits; The Return of the Soldier; Greystoke--The Legend of Tarzan, Lord of the Apes; Laughterhouse; Brazil; Wetherby; Dance With A Stranger.

TV inc: Les Miserables; S.O.S. Titanic; All Quiet on the Western Front; Inside The Third Reich; Television.

HOLT, Charlene: Act. TV inc: Faith For Today; The Hero. Films inc: Zig Zag; Eldorado; Man's Favorite Sport; Redline 7000; Melvin and Howard.

HOLZER, Adela: Prod. Bway inc: (Voices) Dude; Bad Habits; Sherlock Holmes; All Over Town; Hair; The Ritz; Treemonisha (opera); Something Old, Something New.

HOME, William Douglas: Wri. b. Edinburgh, Scotland, Jun 3, 1912. e. Oxford. Plays inc: Great Possessions; Passing By; Now Barabbas; The Chiltern Hundreds; Up a Gum Tree; The Cigarette Girl; The Reluctant Peer; The Secretary Bird; A Friend In Need; The Grouse Moor Image; The Jockey Club Stakes; Lloyd George Knew My Father; The Dame of Sark; The Lord's Lieutenant; In The Red; Rolls Hyphen Royce; The Kingfisher; The Perch; The Eleventh Hour; After The Ball Is Over.

Films inc: Now Barrabas; The Chiltern Hundreds; The Colditz Story; The Reluctant Debutante.

HOMEIER, Skip: Act. b. Chicago, IL, Oct 5, 1930. e. UCLA. On radio as child actor; Bway in Tomorrow the World.

Films inc: Tomorrow The World; Boy's Ranch; Mickey; Arthur Takes Over; The Big Cat; The Gunfighter; Halls of Montezuma; The Black Widow; Cry Vengeance; The Captives; No Road Back; Decision at Durango; The Greatest.

TV inc: Playhouse 90; Kraft Theatre; Studio One; Overboard; Helter Skelter; The Wild Wild West Revisited.

HONEY, John: Prod-Dir-Wri. b. Tasmania, Australia, Jul 10, 1944. TV reporter, 1968-72; prod-wri-dir short films, 1972; exec prod TV series; 1978, prod-wri-dir Tasmanian Film Corp. TV inc: Writers Playhouse (dir).

HOOKS, Kevin: Act. b. Philadephia, PA, Sep 19, 1958. S of Robert Hooks. TV inc: Just an Old Sweet Song; The Greatest Thing That Almost Happened; Friendly Fire; Backstairs at the White House; White Shadow; Can You Hear The Laughter?--The Story of Freddie Prinze; For Members Only.

Films inc: Sounder; Aaron and the Angels; A Hero Ain't Nothin' But A Sandwich; Take Down.

HOOKS, Robert: Act. b. Washington, DC, Apr 18, 1937. Films inc: Sweet Love, Bitter; Hurry Sundown; Fast-Walking; Star Trek III--The Search for Spock.

TV inc: N Y P D; Crosscurrent; Trapped; Ceremonies In Dark Old Men; Backstairs at the White House; Hollow Image; The Oklahoma City Dolls; Madame X; The Sophisticated Gents; Cassie & Co; Sister, Sister; Starflight--The Plane That Couldn't Land; Feel the Heat; A Tribute to Martin Luther King Jr--A Celebration of Life; Fade Out--The Erosion of Black Images in the Media (host); The Execution.

HOOL, Lance: Prod. b. Mexico City, May 11, 1948. Exec dir, Mexico Film International, 1977-78; ChmnB, Azteca Films, 1978-79.

Films inc: Survival Run; Wolf Lake; Caboblanco; 10 to Midnight; The Evil That Men Do (exec prod); Missing In Action (exec prod); Missing In Action 2--The Beginning (dir).

HOOPER, Tobe: Dir. b. TX. Started as dir of tv commercials, later into dox before features. Films inc: The Heiress (short); The Texas Chainsaw Massacre; Eaten Alive; The Funhouse; Poltergeist; Life-

force.
TV inc: Salem's Lot.

HOPE, Bob: Perf. b. Eltham, England, May 29, 1903. Started in vaudeville.

Bway inc: Ballyhoo; Roberta; Ziegfeld Follies; Red Hot and Blue.

On screen from 1938 (after shorts made in 1934). Films inc: The Big Broadcast of 1938; College Swing; Thanks for the Memory; The Road to Singapore (and 6 other "Road" pictures); My Favorite Blonde; Lets Face It; Nothing But The Truth; Monsieur Beaucaire; The Paleface; Sorrowful Jones; Fancy Pants; The Lemon Drop Kid; Seven Little Foys; That Certain Feeling; Beau James; Critic's Choice; Alias Jesse James; Boy Did I Get a Wrong Number; The Private Navy of Sergeant O'Farrell; A Global Affair; I'll Take Sweden; Eight on the Lam; How to Commit Marriage; Cancel My Reservation. The Muppet Movie.

Many times MC of Oscar presentations, (4 Special Oscar citations).

TV inc: Bob Hope Shows;(Emmy-Trustees Award-1959); Chrysler Presents The Bob Hope Christmas Specials (Emmys-1966-exec prod & star); On the Road to China; Kenny Rogers and the American Cowboy; Hope, Women and Song; Lucy Moves to NBC; The Starmakers; Bob Hope's Birthday Party; Debbie Boone--The Same Old Brand New Me; Hope For President; The Bob Hope 30th Anniversary Special; A Love Letter To Jack Benny (host); Bob Hope's Spring Fling of Glamor and Comedy; Bob Hope's All Star Birthday Party at West Point; Get High On Yourself; Bob Hope's All-Star Comedy Look at the New Season (& prod); Bob Hope's All-Star Celebration Opening the Gerald R. Ford Museum (& exec prod); George Burns' Early, Early, Early, Christmas Special; Bob Hope's Stand up and Cheer For the National Football League's 60th Year (& exec prod); Christmas, A Time of Cheer and A Time For Hope (& prod); Bob Hope's Women I Love--Beautiful and Funny (& prod); AFI Salute to Frank Capra; Bob Hope Laughs With the Movie Awards; Bob Hope's Stars Over Texas; All Hands On Deck For Bob Hope's All-Star Birthday Party At Annapolis; The Merriest of the Merry--Bob Hope's Christmas Show--A Bagful of Comedy (& exec prod); On The Town With Tony Bennett; Bob Hope's Road To Hollywood; Texaco Star Theatre presents Bob Hope in "Who Makes The World Laugh" (host-narr-exec prod); Happy Birthday, Bob; Bob Hope's Salute to NASA--25 Years of Reaching for the Stars; Bob Hope Goes to College (& exec prod); Here's Television Entertainment (host); Bob Hope's USO Christmas in Beirut (& exec prod); Bob Hope's Wicky-Wacky Special from Waikiki; Bob Hope's Who Makes the World Laugh--Part II; George Burns' How To Live To Be 100 Or More; The Hilarious, Unrehearsed Antics Of The Stars (& exec prod); It's Ho-Ho Hope's 35th Jolly Christmas Hour (& exec prod); Bob Hope Lampoons Television 1985 (& exec prod); Bob Hope's Comedy Salute To The Soaps (& exec prod).

(Emmy-Governors Award-1984).

HOPE, Harry: Prod-Wri. b. May 26, 1926. e. UCLA. Films inc: Arch of Virtue; #13 Sin Alley; The Mad Butcher; The War of the Tongs; The Wild Girl; Doomsday Machine; Thunderfist; Sunset Cove; Save Our Beach; Death Dimension.

HOPKINS, Anthony: Act. b. Port Talbot, S Wales, England, Dec 31, 1941. e. RADA. Films inc: The Lion in Winter; A Bridge Too Far; A Doll's House; Young Winston; Dark Victory; Audrey Rose; International Velvet; Magic; The Elephant Man; A Change of Seasons; The Bounty; Io E Il Duce (Mussolini And I).

TV inc: All Creatures Great and Small; The Lindbergh Kidnapping Case (Emmy-1976); Kean; Mayflower-The Pilgrims' Adventure; The Bunker (Emmy-1981); Peter and Paul; Othello; The Hunchback of Notre Dame; A Married Man; Hollywood Wives; Guilty Conscience; Arch Of Triumph.

Bway inc: Equus. London inc: Old Times; Pravda.

HOPKINS, Bo: Act. b. Greenville, SC, Feb 2, 1942. Films inc: White Lightning; The Moonshine War; Macho Callahan; Culpepper Cattle Co; Killer Elite; A Small Town in Texas; The Wild Bunch; The Bridge at Remagen; The Getaway; American Graffiti; The Day of the Locust; Posse; Tentacles; Midnight Express; More American Graffiti; The Fifth Floor; Sweet Sixteen; Night Shadows (Mutant).

TV inc: Kansas City Massacre; The Courtmartial of Lt William Calley; Aspen; Dawn: Portrait of a Teen-Age Runaway; The Last Ride of the Dalton Gang; Beggarman, Thief; The Plutonium Incident; Casino;

Rodeo Girl; Dynasty; Ghost Dancing.

HOPKINS, Linda: Singer-Act. Bway inc: Purlie; Inner City (Tony-supp-1972); Me and Bessie; An Evening with Linda Hopkins.

TV inc: Mitzi--Roarin' Into the 20's. Films inc: Go Tell It on the Mountain.

HOPPER, Dennis: Act. b. Dodge City, KS, May 17, 1936. Films inc: Johnny Guitar; Rebel Without a Cause; From Hell to Texas; The Young Land; Giant; Cool Hand Luke; Panic in the City; Hang 'Em High; Easy Rider (& sp-dir); True Grit; The Last Movie; The American Friend; The Order and Security of the World; The Apprentice Soldiers; Apocalypse Now; Out of the Blue (& dir); King Of The Mountain; Reborn; Human Highway; The Osterman Weekend; Rumble Fish; The Inside Man.

TV inc: Medic; Loretta Young Show; Wild Times; Stark.

HOPPER, Jerry: Dir. b. Guthrie, OK, Jul 29, 1907. Films inc: The Atomic City; Hurricane Smith; The Secret of the Incas; Naked Alibi; The Private War of Major Benson; One Desire; The Square Jungle; Toy Tiger; The Sharkfighters; Everything But the Truth; The Missouri Traveller; Blueprint for Robbery; Madron.

TV inc: Kung Fu.

HORDERN, Michael: Act. b. Berkhampstead, England, 1911. e. Brighton Coll. On Screen from 1939, The Girl in the News. Films inc: Mine Own Executioner; Passport to Pimlico; The Heart of the Matter; Sink the Bismark; El Cid; Genghis Khan; The Spy Who Came in From the Cold; Khartoum; A Funny Thing Happened on the Way to the Forum; Where Eagles Dare; The Bed-Sitting Room; Anne of the Thousand Days; Alice's Adventures in Wonderland; The Mackintosh Man; Mister Quilp; Royal Flash; Lucky Lady; The Slipper and the Rose; The Medusa Touch; Watership Down; The Missionary; Gandhi; Yellowbeard.

TV inc: Tartuffe; Don Juan in Hell; The Magistrate; King Lear; Cakes and Ale; Gauguin The Savage; The Tempest; Shogun; All's Well That Ends Well; Ivanhoe; Oliver Twist; King Lear; Cymbeline; The Zany Adventures of Robin Hood. (Knighted Jan 1, 1983).

HORN, Alan: Exec. b. NYC, Feb 28, 1943. e. Union Coll; Harvard Business School. Joined Tandem Productions, 1972; became vp of business affairs, 1973, of Tandem and its sister company T A T Communications Co; named exec vp and COO in 1977; 1978, named p with complete creat control; Jan 1982 named chmn & CEO of new parent company Embassy Communications.

HORNBECK, William: Exec-Film ed. b. Los Angeles, Aug 23, 1901. Began in motion pictures in 1916 in film lab., Keystone Comedies. Then editor. 1964 named VP Universal Pictures; retired 1976.

Films inc: The Scarlet Pimpernel; Ghost Goes West; Things To Come; (Supv Ed) It's A Wonderful Life; State of the Union; Heiress; Shane; A Place in the Sun (Oscar-1951); Act of Love; Barefoot Contessa; Giant; The Quiet American; I Want To Live.

(Died Oct. 11, 1983).

HORNE, Lena: Act. b. NYC, Jun 30, 1917. Performed in supper clubs. Screen debut, Panama Hattie. Films inc: Death of a Gunfighter; Meet Me in Las Vegas; Words and Music; Ziegfeld Follies; Till The Clouds Roll By; Patch; The Wiz.

TV inc: 1983 Tony Awards (host); The Kennedy Center Honors 1984 (honoree); Night Of 100 Stars II.

Bway inc: Blackbirds; Dance With Your Gods; Jamaica; Lena Horne--The Lady and Her Music.

(Special Tony-1980); (Grammy-pop vocal-1981).

HORNE, Marilyn: Mezzo-soprano. b. Bradford, PA, Jan 16, 1934. e. USC. As child teamed with sis Gloria as Horne Sisters, playing dates around LA. Operatic debut at LA Guild Opera; soloist with LA Philharmonic; member Roger Wagner Chorale; concerts and opera in Europe; first major US opera appearance with San Francisco Opera 1960; soloist with NY Philharmonic; with Metropolitan Opera; La Scala; Covent Garden. TV inc: 100 Years of Golden Hits.

Recordings inc: The Age of Bel Canto; Presenting Marilyn Horne; Souvenir of a Golden Era.

(Grammys-most promising new artist-1964; Classical vocal solo-1981).

HORNER, Harry: Art Dir-Dir. b. Holitsch, Czechoslovakia, Jul 24, 1910. Films inc: (art dir) Our Town; The Little Foxes; A Double Life; The Heiress *(Oscar*-1949); Born Yesterday; The Hustler *(Oscar*-1961); They Shoot Horses Don't They?; Who is Harry Kellerman?; Sandbox; The Black Bird; Harry and Walter Go to New York; Audrey Rose; The Driver; Moment By Moment; The Jazz Singer. (Dir): The Wild Party; Beware My Lovely.

TV inc: (dir) Omnibus; Four Star Theatre; Gunsmoke; Dupont Theatre.

HOROVITZ, Israel: Wri. b. Wakefield, MA, Mar 31, 1939. e. RADA., City U. of NY. Plays inc: The Comeback; This Play Is About Me; The Hanging of Emanuel; The Death of Bernard the Believer; The Simon Street Harvest; Hop, Skip and Jump; It's Called the Sugar Plum; The Indian Wants the Bronx; Line; Rats; Chiaroscuro; The Honest-to-God Schnozzola; The World's Greatest Play; Morning; Acrobats; Shooting Gallery; Hero; The Wakefield Plays; Hopscotch; The 75th; Alfred the Great; Our Father's Failing; Alfred Dies; Stage Directions; The Reason We Eat; The Bottom; Mackerel; Sunday Runners in the Rain; The Widow's Blind Date; Park Your Car In Harvard Yard.

Films inc: Speed is of the Essence; Camerian Climbing; The Sad-Eyed Girls in the Park; The Strawberry Statement; Author! Author!

TV inc: VD Blues; A Day with Conrad Green; Bartleby, the Scrivener; Today I Am a Fountain Pen; Play for Trees; Funny Books; Happy; A Rosen by any Other Name; The Chopin Playoffs Full House.

HOROWITZ, Norman: Exec. Started with Col in shipping dept, 1956; with Col in various sls & exec positions for 24 years except for two year period, 1968-70 as dir int'l sls CBS Enterprises; became sr vp worldwide dist Col TV syndication 1976; became P 1978; 1980, P & CEO Polygram Television; resd. Sept. 1984, formed Norman Horowitz Co. Sept. 1984.

HOROWITZ, Vladimir: Pianist. b. Kiev, Russia, Oct 1, 1904. Launched career in Berlin, 1926. *(Grammys*-(18)-album of year-1962, 1965, 1971 1977; classical perf-1962, 1963, 1964, 1965, 1967, 1968, 1971, 1972, 1973, 1976, 1978 (2), 1979, 1981).

TV inc: Horowitz In London--A Royal Concert.

HORSFORD, Anna Maria: Act. b. NYC, 1945. e. NY High School For Performing Arts. Thea inc: Coriolanus; In the Well Of the House; Perfection in Black; Les Femmes Noires; Sweet Talk; For Colored Girls Who Have Considerd Suicide/When The Rainbow Is Enuf; Peep.

TV inc: The Doctors; The Tap Dance Kid; Hollow Image; The Guiding Light; Murder Ink; Star Struck; Bill; Muggable Mary; Benny's Place; A Doctor's Story; The Firm.

Films inc: An Almost Perfect Affair; Times Square; The Love Child; The Fan; Class; Crackers.

HORSLEY, Lee: Act. b. Muleshoe, TX, May 15, 1955. e. U of Northern CO. TV inc: Nero Wolfe; The Wild Women of Chastity Gulch; Matt Houston; When Dreams Come True.

Films inc: The Sword and the Sorcerer.

HORTON, Robert: Act. b. Los Angeles, Jul 29, 1924. e. Miami U; UCLA. Films inc: The Tanks are Coming; Bright Road; Prisoner of War; This Man is Armed; The Dangerous Days of Kiowa Jones; The Green Slime.

TV inc: Wagon Train; A Man Called Shenandoah; As The World Turns.

Bway inc: 110 In The Shade.

HOSKINS, Bob: Act. b. Suffolk, England, Oct. 26, 1942. On stage with Royal Shakespeare Company, National Theatre Company. Thea inc: Antony and Cleopatra; Pygmalion; As You Like It; Happy End; The Iceman Cometh; Ivanov; Guys and Dolls.

TV inc: New Scotland Yard; Crown Court; Her Majesty's Pleasure; Thick As Thieves; The Villains; Othello; Pennies From Heaven; Flickers.

Films inc: The National Health; Royal Flash; Inserts; Zulu Dawn; The Long Good Friday; Beyond the Limit; Lassiter; The Cotton Club; Brazil; Io E Il Duce (Mussolini And I). r:

HOSSEIN, Robert: Act. b. France, 1927. Films inc: Rififi; Crime and Punishment; The Wicked Go To Hell (& dir); Nude in a White Car;

Paris Pickup; Love on a Pillow; Enough Rope; Marco the Magnificent; I Killed Rasputin (& dir); The Burglars (& dir); Les Uns et Les Autres (The Ins and The Outs); Le Professionel; Les Miserables (& dir).

Thea inc: (Dir) Notre Dame de Paris; Les Miserables; Surprise Party.

HOUGH, John: Dir. b. London, Nov 21, 1941. Films inc: Wolfshead; Eye Witness; Twins of Evil; Treasure Island; The Legend of Hell House; Dirty Mary, Crazy Larry; Escape to Witch Mountain; Return to Witch Mountain; Brass Target; The Watcher In The Woods; The Incubus; Triumphs of a Man Called Horse.

TV inc: The Avengers; The Zoo Gang.

HOUGHTON, James: Act. b. Los Angeles, Nov 7. e. UC Berkeley. S of Buck Houghton. Films inc: Sweet Sugar; The Carey Treatment; One On One; I Wanna Hold Your Hand; More American Graffiti; Superstition.

TV inc: Dynasty; Aspen; The Young and the Restless; Code R; Knots Landing.

HOUSEMAN, John (Jean Haussmann): Prod-Dir-Wri-Act. b. Rumania, Sep 22, 1902. Came to U.S. 1925. In 1932 prod Four Saints in Three Acts on Broadway; later dir Valley Forge; Panic. Helped Orson Welles launch Mercury Theatre, 1927. Wrote radio scripts for Helen Hayes. Exec, Selznick Prods, 1941-42. Chief of overseas radio div OWI, 1942-43.

Films inc: Jane Eyre (sp); (prod) The Blue Dahlia; Julius Caesar; Letters from An Unknown Woman; The Bad and the Beautiful; Executive Suite; The Cobweb; Lust for Life. Acting debut 1964, Seven Days In May. Films (as act) inc: The Paper Chase *(Oscar*-supp-1973); Rollerball; Three Days of the Condor; St. Ives; The Cheap Detective; Old Boyfriends; The Fog; My Bodyguard; Wholly Moses; Ghost Story; Murder By Phone.

TV inc: The Paper Chase; The Last Convertible; The French Atlantic Affair; Gideon's Trumpet (& exec prod); Justice--A Matter of Balance; The Baby Sitter; A Christmas Without Snow; The Joseph Jefferson Awards (host); Marco Polo; Roses In December--The Story of Jean Donovan (narr); The Winds of War; Silver Spoons; Choices of the Heart (exec prod); Olympic Gala; A.D.

Bway inc: (Dir) Lute Song; King Lear; Coriolanus; Measure For Measure; Clarence Darrow.

HOUSER, John: Act. b. Los Angeles, Jul 14, 1952. Films inc: Summer of '42; Bad Company; Class of '44; Slap Shot.

TV inc: Maude; Phyllis; Barnaby Jones; Three Times Daley.

HOUSTON, David: Act. b. Shreveport, LA, Dec 9, 1938. Country mus recording artist. Films inc: Cottonpickin' Chickenpickers. *(Grammys*-C&W rec, C&W vocal-1966).

HOUWER, Rob: Prod. b. Holland. e. German Institute for Film. Films inc: A Degree of Murder; Business is Business; Turkish Delight; Keetje Tippel; Soldier of Orange; Al je beerijpt wat ik bedoel (If You Know What I Mean); De vierde man (The Fourth Man); Grijpstra & de Gier (Outsider in Amsterdam); Brandende Liefde (Burning Love) (& sp); Het bittere kruid (Bitter Sweet).

HOWAR, Barbara: TV pers. b. Nashville, TN, Sep 27, 1934. Wri for Washington Post; New Yorker mag; TV inc: Panorama (host); CBS-TV corr; Who's Who (host).

HOWARD, Chuck (Charles Wooster Howard Jr): Prod-Exec. b. Pittsburgh, PA, Jul 7, 1933. e. Duke U. Joined ABC Sports 1960. Now VP in chg pgm prodn ABC Sports. TV inc: U.S-Russian Track Meet; 10th Winter Olympics; NCAA College Football *(Emmy*-1980); Bobby Riggs vs Billie Jean King--Tennis Battle of the Sexes; ABC Championship Golf; 12th Winter Olympics *(Emmy*-1976); 1976 Olympic Games *(Emmy*-1977); A Special Preview of the 1976 Olympic Games from Montreal *(Emmy*-1977); ABC's Wide World of Sports; Indianapolis 500 *(Emmys*-1979, 1982); 1980 Winter Olympic Games *(Emmy*-1980); 1979 World Series; 1980 American League Championship Series; 1980 Kentucky Derby *(Emmy*-1981); 1981 Sugar Bowl; 1981 U.S. Open.

HOWARD, Cy: Prod-Dir. b. Milwaukee, WI, Sep 27, 1915. Radio Wri for Jack Benny; Milton Berle; Danny Thomas; Bert Lahr; Jerry Lewis;

created My Friend Irma; Life with Luigi (radio & TV); exec prod Desilu Studios, created and prod Harrigan & Son; Westward Ho; Fair Exchange; My Friend Irma Goes West.

Films inc: Lovers and Other Strangers; Won Ton Ton, The Dog Who Saved Hollywood; Every Little Crook and Nanny.

HOWARD, John C.: Film Edtr. b. Los Angeles, Jul 1, 1930. Films inc: Butch Cassidy and the Sundance Kid; Blazing Saddles; Young Frankenstein; W C Fields and Me; Silent Movie; High Anxiety; Sgt Pepper's Lonely Hearts Club Band; Nightwing; Why Would I Lie; History of the World--Part I.
(Died May 28, 1983).

HOWARD, Ken: Act. b. El Centro, CA, Mar 28, 1944. Films inc: Tell Me That You Love Me Junie Moon; Such Good Friends; The Strange Vengeance of Rosalie; 1776; Second Thoughts.

TV inc: Adam's Rib; Manhunter; The White Shadow; A Real American Hero; Damien...The Leper Priest; The Body Human--The Facts for Boys (host) *(Emmy*-1981); Victims; The Power Pinch (host); Rage of Angels; The Thorn Birds; It's Not Easy; Pudd'nhead Wilson; Glitter; He's Not Your Son; Citizen Soldier--The U.S. Army Story.

Bway inc: Child's Play *(Tony*-supp-1970); The Norman Conquests; 1600 Pennsylvania Ave.

HOWARD, Ron: Act. b. Duncan, OK, Mar 1, 1954. Films inc: The Journey; Mother's Day; Five Minutes to Live; Music Man; Eat My Dust; The Courtship of Eddie's Father; Village of the Giants; Wild Country; American Graffiti; Run, Stranger, Run; The Shootist; Grand Theft Auto (& co-wri, dir); More American Graffiti; Leo and Loree; Night Shift (dir); Splash (dir); Cocoon (dir).

TV inc: Migrants; Locust; Smith Family; Huck Finn; Happy Days; Cotton Candy (co-wrote, dir, exec-prod); Act of Love; Skyward (dir); Bitter Harvest; Anson 'N' Lorrie; Insight/The Needle's Eye; Fire on the Mountain; Skyward Christmas (exec prod); Through the Magic Pyramid (exec prod-dir); Little Shots (exec prod-dir); When Your Lover Leaves; Maximum Security (exec prod).

HOWARD, Sandy: Prod. b. NYC, Aug 1, 1927. Films inc: A Man Called Horse; Man in the Wilderness; The Neptune Factor; Together Brothers; Embryo; Return of a Man Called Horse; Sky Riders; The Island of Dr. Moreau; The Silent Flute; Circle of Iron; Jaguar Lives; Meteor; City on Fire; Death Ship; Savage Harvest; Vice Squad (exec prod & wri); Deadly Force; Triumphs of a Man Called Horse (exec prod); Hambone and Hillie; Courage; Avenging Angel; The Boys Next Door.

HOWARD, Susan: Act. b. Marshall, TX, Jan 28, 1943. e. U TX Austin. TV inc: Petrocelli; Dallas; Special Athletes (host). Films inc: Moonshine County Express; Sidewinder One.

HOWARD, Trevor: Act. b. Clifton, England, Sep 29, 1916. e. RADA. Stage debut, 1933, Revolt in a Reformatory. Screen debut, The Way Ahead.

Films inc: Brief Encounter; So Well Remembered; The Third Man; Sons and Lovers; Heart of the Matter; Cockleshell Heroes; Around the World in 80 Days; Mutiny On The Bounty; Father Goose; Von Ryan's Express; Morituri; The Lion; The Battle of Britain; Ryan's Daughter; Pope Joan; 11 Harrowhouse; Hennessy; Conduct Unbecoming; The Bawdy Adventures of Tom Jones; The Last Remake of Beau Geste; Slaves; Stevie; Superman; Hurricane; Meteor; The Shillingbury Blowers; The Sea Wolves; Sir Henry At Rawlinson End; Windwalker; Les Annees Lumiere (Light Years Away); Who?; The Missionary; Gandhi; Sword Of The Valiant; Die Rebellen (Flashpoint Africa); Dust.

TV inc: The Invincible Mr. Disraeli *(Emmy*-1963); Catholics; The Count of Monte Cristo; Night Flight; Staying On; And The Band Played On; Inside The Third Reich; The Deadly Game (cable); George Washington.

HOWELL, C. Thomas: Act. b. Van Nuys, CA., Dec. 7, 1966. Films inc: The Outsiders; E.T. The ExtraTerrestrial; Tank; Grandview, U.S.A.; Red Dawn Secret Admirer.

TV inc: Little People; Thunder; It Happened One Christmas; Two Marriages.

HOWELLS, Ursula: Act. b. London, Sep 17, 1922. Films inc: Flesh

and Blood; The Constant Husband; They Can't Hang Me; The Long Arm; Dr Terror's House of Horrors; Mumsy, Nanny, Sonny and Girly; Crossplot; The Cold Room.

TV inc: The Small Back Room; A Woman Comes Home; For Services Rendered; Mine Own Executioner; The Cocktail Party.

Thea inc: The Gimmick; Doctors of Philosophy; Return Ticket; Dear Octopus; The Lion in Winter; Two and Two Make Sex.

HOWERD, Frankie: Act. b. York, England, Mar 6, 1921. Films inc: The Runaway Bus; Jumping for Joy; The Ladykillers; A Touch of the Sun; Further Up the Creek; The Cool Mikado; The Great St Trinian's Train Robbery; Carry on Doctor; Up Pompeii; Up the Chastity Belt; Up the Front; The House in Nightmare Park.

TV inc: Frankie Howerd Show; Comedy Playhouse.

Thea inc: A Funny Thing Happened on the Way to the Forum; Way Out in Picadilly; Wind in the Sassafras Trees.

HOWES, Sally Ann: Act. b. London, 1934. Films inc: Thursday's Child; Halfway House; Dead of Night; Pink String and Sealing Wax; My Sister and I; Anna Karenina; The History of Mr Polly; Fool Rush In; Honeymoon Deferred; The Admirable Crichton; Chitty Chitty Bang Bang; Death Ship.

TV inc: The Hounds of the Baskervilles.

HOWLAND, Beth: Act. b. Boston, May 28, 1942. Films inc: Bye Bye Birdie.

TV inc: The Ted Bessel Show; Bronk; Cannon; Little House on the Prairie; You Can't Take It With You; Alice; Working; A Caribbean Mystery; Night Of 100 Stars II.

Bway inc: George M; Company (& London); A Tribute to Stephen Sondheim.

HOYT, John (nee Hoysradt): Act. b. 1905. Films inc: OSS; The Unfaithful; Brute Force; Winter Meeting; The Great Dan Patch; The Desert Fox; When Worlds Collide; Androcles and the Lion; Julius Caesar; The Girl in the Red Velvet Swing; Baby Face Nelson; The Blackboard Jungle; Never So Few; Spartacus; Cleopatra; Duel at Diablo.

TV inc: Greatest Heroes of the Bible; The Winds of Kitty Hawk; Rex Stout's Nero Wolfe.

HU, King (Hu Chin-Ch'uan): Dir. b. Peking, 1931. e. Peking National Art Coll. Began as journalist, artist, act. Films inc: The Love Eterne; Sons of the Good Earth; Come Drink With Me; Dragon Inn; A Touch of Zen; Four Moods; The Fate of Lee Khan; The Valiant Ones; Legend of the Mountain; Tien Shia de Yi (The World's Best Men); Anger.

HUBBARD, Elizabeth: Act. b. NYC, Dec 22. e. Lee Strasberg Institute; RADA. Bway inc: A Day in the Life of Joe Egg; The Passion of Josef D; John Gabriel Borkman; I Remember Mama; The Physicists; Present Laughter.

TV inc: The Doctors, 1964-1977, retd 1981 *(Emmy*-1974); First Ladies Diaries--Elizabeth Bolling Wilson *(Emmy*-Daytime Actress of Year-1976); ABC Mystery Theatre; I Remember Mama.

Films inc: I Never Sang For My Father; The Bell Jar; Ordinary People.

HUBLEY, Faith: Prod-Dir. b. NYC, Sep 16, 1924. W of John Hubley. Worked as mus edtr Spectre of the Rose; script supv 12 Angry Men; became prod ani films after marrying Hubley.

Films inc: Women of the World; Second Chance; The Hole *(Oscar*-cartoon-1962); Herb Alpert and the Tijuana Brass Double Feature *(Oscar*-cartoon-1966); Windy Day; Of Men and Demons; Everybody Rides the Carousel; Voyage to Next; The Doonesbury Special.

HUBLEY, John: Ani-Prod-Dir. b. Marinette, WI, 1914. With Disney; art dir Pinocchio; Bambi; Rite of Spring; Fantasia (section).

Films inc: (Dir) Robin Hoodlum; Magic Fluke; Ragtime Bear. (Prod) Moonbird *(Oscar*-cartoon-1959); The Hole *(Oscar*-cartoon-1962); Herb Alpert and the Tijuana Brass Double Feature *(Oscar*-cartoon-1966); Windy Day; Of Men and Demons; Everybody Rides the Carousel (& Dir); Voyage to Next; The Doonesbury Special.

HUBLEY, Season: Act. b. NYC, May 14, 1951. Studied with Herbert Berghoff. Films inc: Lolly Madonna War; Catch My Soul; Hardcore; Escape From New York; Vice Squad.

TV inc: She Lives; The Healers; Family; Elvis; Mrs. R's Daughter; A

Caribbean Mystery; London And Davis In New York; The Three Wishes Of Billy Grier; The Key To Rebecca.

HUDDLESTON, David: Act-Prod. b. Vinton, VA, Sep 17, 1930. e. AADA. Films inc: All the Way Home; A Lovely Way to Die; Slaves; Norwood; Rio Lobo; Fools Parade; Country Blue; Bad Company; Billy Two-Hats; Blazing Saddles; McQ; The Klansman; Capricorn I; I Superpiedi Quasipiatti; The World's Greatest Lover; Gorp; Smokey and the Bandit II; The Act.

TV inc: Gunsmoke; Brian's Song; Suddenly Last Summer; The Homecoming; The Waltons; Heat Wave; Dirty Sally; Hizzonner (prod & act); The Kallikaks; The Oklahoma City Dolls; Family Reunion; Computercide; Amy and the Angel; M.A.D.D. Mothers Against Drunk Drivers; Finnegan Begin Again.

Thea inc: Woman Is My Idea; A Man for all Seasons; My Three Angels; Front Page; Everybody Loves Opal; Ten Little Indians; Silk Stockings; Can-Can; Fanny; Guys and Dolls; The Music Man; Desert Song; Mame; The Roast; The First (Bway); Death of A Salesman (Bway).

HUDSON, Rock (Roy Fitzgerald): Act. b. Winnetka, IL, Nov 17, 1925. Films inc: Fighter Squadron; Double Crossbones; Undertow; I Was A Shoplifter; One Way Street; Winchester 73; Peggy; The Desert Hawk; Shakedown; Air Cadet; Tomahawk; Iron Man; Bright Victory; Bend Of The River; Here Come The Nelsons; Scarlet Angel; Has Anybody Seen My Gal?; Horizons West; The Lawless Breed; Gun Fury; Seminole; The Golden Blade; Son Of Cochise; Magnificent Obsession; Bengal Brigade; Captain Lightfoot; One Desire; All That Heaven Allows; Never Say Goodbye; Giant; Battle Hymn; Written On The Wind; Four Girls In Town; Something Of Value; The Tarnished Angels; A Farewell To Arms; Twilight For The Gods; This Earth Is Mine; Pillow Talk; The Last Sunset; Come September; Lover Come Back; The Spiral Road; A Gathering of Eagles; Marilyn (narr); Man's Favorite Sport; Send Me No Flowers; Blindfold; Seconds; Tobruk; Ice Station Zebra; A Fine Pair; The Undefeated; Showdown; Embryo; Darling Lili; Hornet's Nest; Pretty Maids All In A Row; Avalanche; The Mirror Crack'd; The Ambassador; George Stevens--A Filmmaker's Journey (doc-int).

TV inc: McMillan & Wife; Wheels; The Martian Chronicles; The Star Maker; World War III; The Devlin Connection; Las Vegas Strip War; Dynasty.

Thea inc: I Do! I Do!; John Brown's Body; Camelot; On the 20th Century.

HUEBING, Craig: Act. b. Reedsburg, WI, Mar 4. TV inc: From These Roots; The Doctors; General Hospital.

Thea inc: The Thurber Carnival; Time of the Cuckoo.

HUGGINS, Roy: Wri-Dir. b. Litelle, WA, Jul 18, 1914. Films inc: I Love Trouble; Too Late for Tears; Lady Gambler; Fuller Brush Man; Good Humor Man; Woman in Hiding; Sealed Cargo; Hangman's Knot; Three Hours to Kill; Pushover; A Fever in the Blood.

TV inc: Cheyenne; Conflict; Colt 45; 77 Sunset Strip; Maverick; The Fugitive; Run for Your Life (exec prod); The Outsiders; The Bold Ones; Alias Smith and Jones; Toma; The Rockford Files; Captains and the Kings (exec prod); Aspen; Wheels (exec prod); The Jordan Chance (exec prod); The Last Convertible; Blue Thunder (exec prod); Hunter (exec prod).

HUGHES, Barnard: Act. b. Bedford Hills, NY, Jul 16, 1915. Thea inc: Please, Mrs. Garibaldi; A Majority of One; All Over Town; Hamlet; Advise and Consent; How Now, Dow Jones; Sheep on the Runway; Abelard and Heloise; The Good Doctor; Da (Tony-1978); End of the World.

Films inc: Midnight Cowboy; Oh, God!; Where's Poppa; The Hospital; Rage; Sisters; Cold Turkey; Pursuit of Happiness; Deadhead Miles; First Monday In October; Tron; Best Friends; Under The Biltmore Clock.

TV inc: Doc; See How She Runs; The Caryl Chessman Story; Tell Me My Name; Look Homeward, Angel; Judge (Lou Grant Series) (Emmy-1978); Father Brown, Detective; Nova--The Wizard Who Spat on the Floor (host); Homeward Bound; Mr. Merlin; Little Gloria--Happy At Last; A Caribbean Mystery; Tales From the Darkside (Trick or Treat); The Sky's the Limit.

HUGHES, Del: Dir-Act. b. Detroit, Sep 4, 1909. Thea inc: Vickie; Open House; Rip Van Winkle; Command Decision; Death of a Sales-

man; Legend of Sarah; The Autumn Garden; The Crucible.

TV inc: (act) The Brighter Day; (dir) One Life to Live; All My Children.

Films inc: (act) A Face in the Crowd.

(Died May 18, 1985.)

HUGHES, Finola: Act-dancer. b. England, 1950. e. Arts Educational School. Thea inc: A Day in the Death of Joe Egg; Cats; Nutcracker.

TV inc: The Prime of Miss Jean Brodie; Starburst; Grace Kennedy; The Monte Carlo Show; The Master of Ballantrae.

Films inc: Nutcracker; The Apple; Staying Alive.

HUGHES, Kathleen (Betty von Gerkan): Act. b. Los Angeles, Nov 14, 1928. Films inc: Mother is a Freshman; For Men Only; The Golden Blade; It Came From Outer Space; The Glass Web; Dawn at Socorro; Cult of the Cobra; Promise Her Anything; The President's Analyst; The Take.

TV inc: The Ghost and Mrs Muir; Bracken's World; Babe; Forbidden Love.

HUGHES, Ken: Dir. b. Liverpool, England, 1922. Films inc: Wide Boy; Black Thirteen; Joe Macbeth; Wicked as They Come (& sp); The Long Haul; In the Nick; The Trials of Oscar Wilde (& sp); Of Human Bondage; Drop Dead Darling (& sp); Casino Royale; Chitty Chitty Bang Bang (& sp); Cromwell (& sp); The Internecine Project; Alfie Darling; Sextette; Night School.

TV inc: Solo for Canary; Eddie (Emmy-wri-1959); An Enemy of the State; Sammy; The Haunting; The Voice.

HUGH-KELLY, Daniel: Act. b. Elizabeth, NJ, Aug. 10. e. St. Vincent College. TV inc: Ryan's Hope; Thin Ice; Chicago Story; Hardcastle & McCormick; Murder Ink.

Thea inc: The Hunchback of Notre Dame; Fishing.

Films inc: Cujo.

HULCE, Tom: Act. b. White Water, WI. Thea inc: Equus (Bway); Memory Of Two Mondays; Julius Caesar; Candida; The Sea Gull; Sleep Around Town (dir); The Rise and Rise Of Daniel Rocket.

Films inc: Sept. 30, 1955; National Lampoon's Animal House; Those Lips, Those Eyes; Amadeus.

TV inc: Emily, Emily.

HUMBERSTONE, Bruce: Dir. b. Buffalo, NY, Nov 18, 1903. e. OH State U. Films inc: If I Had a Million; Crooked Circle; Pack Up Your Troubles; Tall, Dark and Handsome; I Wake Up Screaming; Sun Valley Serenade; To the Shores of Tripoli; Iceland; Hello, Frisco, Hello; Pin-Up Girl; Wonder Man; Three Little Girls in Blue; The Homestretch; Fury at Furnace Creek; Happy Go Lovely; Desert Song; Ten Wanted Men; Purple Mask.

(Died Oct. 11, 1984)

HUME, Alan: Cin. b. England, 1924. Worked as camera assistant on several films including Great Expectations, Oliver Twist. Films as cin inc: The Legend of Hell House; Carry on Girls (and 15 others in Carry On series); The Land That Time Forgot; Trial by Combat; Warlords of Atlantis; Captain Nemo and the Underwater City; Bear Island; Birth of the Beatles; The Legacy; Eye of the Needle; Caveman; For Your Eyes Only; Return of the Jedi; Octopussy; Supergirl; A View To A Kill; Lifeforce.

TV inc: The Hunchback of Notre Dame; The Adventures of Little Lord Fauntleroy.

HUMPERDINCK, Engelbert (Arnold George Dorsey): Singer. b. India, May 3, 1936. TV inc: The Engelbert Humperdinck Show; Celebrity Fun Cruise.

Albums inc: Release Me; A Man Without Love; Last Waltz; We Made It Happen; Miracles; Last of the Romantics; After the Lovin'.

HUNNICUT, Gayle: Act. b. Ft Worth, TX, Feb 6, 1943. Films inc: The Wild Angels; P.J.; Marlowe; Eye of the Cat; Fragment of Fear; Running Scared; The Legend of Hell House; The Sellout; The Ambassadors; Return of the Saint; Once In Paris.

TV inc: Man and Boy; The Golden Bowl; The Ripening Seed; Fall of Eagles; The Switch; Humboldt Girl; Strange Shadows In An Empty Room; A Man Called Intrepid; The Martian Chronicles; The Million Dollar Face; The Ambassadors; Return of the Man From U.N.C.L.E.;

Savage--In the Orient; Two By Forsyth; The First Olympics--Athens 1896; A Woman Of Substance.

Thea inc: The Ride Across Lake Constance; Twelfth Night; The Tempest; Dog Days; The Admirable Crichton.

HUNT, Helen: Act. b. Los Angeles, Jun 15, 1963. TV inc: All Together Now; Swiss Family Robinson; The Fitzpatricks; Angel Dusted; Weekend; Amy Prentiss; The Miracle of Kathy Miller; Child Bride at Short Creek; Desperate Lives; The Two of Us; Bill--On His Own; Quarterback Princess; Choices of the Heart; Sweet Revenge.

Films inc: Rollercoaster; Girls Just Want To Have Fun; Future Cop.

HUNT, Linda: Act. b. 1946. e. Goodman School of Drama. Thea inc: Ah, Wilderness; The Dance of Death; Trelawney of the Wells; Hamlet; Five Finger Exercise; Elizabeth Dead; Tennis Game; A Metamorphosis in Miniature; Little Victories; Top Girls; End of the World.

Films inc: Popeye; The Year of Living Dangerously (Oscar-supp-1983); The Bostonians; Dune.

TV inc: Ah, Wilderness; Fame (Hallmark Hall of Fame).

HUNT, Marsha: Act. b. Chicago, Oct 17, 1917. Films inc: The Virginia Judge; Gentle Julia; Pride and Prejudice; Cheers for Miss Bishop; Joe Smith, American; Cry Havoc; Blue Denim; The Plunderers; Johnny Got His Gun.

TV inc: Twelfth Night; The Breaking Point; Profiles in Courage; Accidental Family; The Young Lawyers; Terror Among Us.

Thea inc: Joy to the World; The Devil's Disciple; Banned in Texas; Legend of Sarah; The Tunnel of Love; The Paisley Convertible.

HUNT, Peter (Peter Edward Roger Hunt): Dir-Wri. b. London, Mar 11, 1928. e. Rome U. Started as film ed. Films inc: (ed) The Man Who Watched The Trains Go By; The Admirable Crichton; Ferry to Hong Kong; Sink the Bismarck; Loss of Innocence; The Ipcress File; There Was a Crooked Man. (Ed & 2d unit dir) Dr. No; From Russia With Love; Goldfinger; Thunderball; Chitty Chitty Bang Bang (& asso prod); You Only Live Twice. (Dir); On Her Majesty's Secret Service; Gold; Shout at the Devil; Gulliver's Travels; Death Hunt; Wild Geese II.

TV inc: Beasts in the Streets; The Last Days of Pompeii.

HUNT, Peter H.: Dir. b. Pasadena, CA, Dec 16, 1938. Bway inc: Arturo Ui; Georgy; Bully; The Three Penny Opera; Scratch; 1776 (Tony-1969) Goodtime Charley; Give 'Em Hell Harry.

Films inc: 1776; Bully; Give 'Em Hell Harry.

TV inc: Ivan the Terrible; Quark; Mixed Nuts; Adam's Rib; Rendezvous Hotel; Hello Mother, Goodbye; Karen Valentine Show; When Things Were Rotten; Life on the Mississippi (& prod); Bus Stop (cable) (& prod); Tucker's Witch; The Mysterious Stranger; Skeezer; Masquerade; The Parade; Sins of the Past; It Came Upon A Midnight Clear.

HUNT, Willie (Willett Hunt): Exec. b. Los Angeles, Oct 1, 1941. e. UT State, BA. Named VP-dvlpt, MGM, June 1979; Jan 1982, prodn vp UA; Jan 1983, sr vp prodn Ray Stark Production; Fired, with entire prod staff, when Howard Koch, Jr., became P of company; 1985, launched indie production.

HUNTER, Evan: Wri. b. 1926. Films inc: The Blackboard Jungle; Strangers When We Meet; The Young Savages; The Birds; Mister Buddwing; Walk Proud.

TV inc: 87th Precinct; The Legend of Walks Far Woman.

HUNTER, Kim (Janet Cole): Act. b. Detroit, Nov 12, 1922. Started in summer stock. Films inc: The Seventh Victim; Stairway to Heaven; A Streetcar Named Desire (Oscar-supp-1951); Anything Can Happen; Deadline: U.S.A.; Lilith; Planet of the Apes; The Swimmer; Escape From the Planet of the Apes. Blacklisted during the 50s she later testified for radio personality John Henry Faulk who sued after he was similarly blacklisted. Her testimony paved the way for clearance of many performers unjustly accused of Communist connections.

Bway inc: A Streetcar Named Desire; Darkness at Noon; The Children's Hour; The Tender Trap; Write Me a Murder; The Women; And Miss Reardon Drinks a Little.

TV inc: Requiem for a Heavyweight; The Comedian; Give Us Barabbas; Lamp at Midnight; The Prodigal; Bad Ronald; This Side of Innocence; Backstairs at the Whitehouse; Golden Gate Murders; FDR-The Last Year; Edge of Night; Skokie; Private Sessions; Three Sove-

reigns For Sarah.

HUNTER, Ronald: Act. b. Boston, Jun 14, e. U of PA, AB; NYU, MFA. Bway inc: The Basic Training of Pavlo Hummel; Hamlet; Richard III.

Films inc: The Sentinel; The Seduction of Joe Tynan.

TV inc: The Edelin Conviction; One Life to Live ; The Lazarus Syndrome; Cagney and Lacey; Rage of Angels; Three Sovereigns For Sarah.

HUNTER, Ross (Martin Fuss): Prod. b. Cleveland, May 6, 1916. e. Western Reserve U, MA. School teacher, 1938-43; actor, under contract at Columbia 1944-46; returned to teaching; Dial Director-Assoc Prod U, 1950-51; Prod U, 1951; to Col, 1971; to Par 1974.

Films inc: Louisiana Hayride; Ever Since Venus; The Bandit of Sherwood Forest; The Groom Wore Spurs; Son of Cochise; Magnificent Obsession; Naked Alibi; Yellow Mountain; Captain Lightfoot; One Desire; The Spoilers; All That Heaven Allows; There's Always Tomorrow; Battle Hymn; Tammy and the Bachelor; Interlude; My Man Godfrey; The Wonderful Years; Stranger in My Arms; Imitation of Life; Pillow Talk; Portrait in Black; Midnight Lace; Back Street; Flower Drum Song; Tammy and the Doctor; The Thrill of It All; The Chalk Garden; I'd Rather Be Rich; The Art of Love; Madame X; The Pad; Thoroughly Modern Millie; Rosie; Airport; Lost Horizon.

TV inc: Suddenly Love; The Best Place To Be.

HUNTER, Tab: Act. b. NYC, Jul 11, 1931. Screen debut, 1950, The Lawless.

Films inc: Island of Desire; Track of the Cat; Battle Cry; Lafayette Escadrille; Damn Yankees; That Kind of Woman; Pleasure of his Company; They Came to Cordura; Ride the Wild Surf; The Life and Times of Judge Roy Bean; Polyester; Grease 2; Lust In The Dust (& prod).

TV inc: The Kid From Left Field; Just Our Luck.

HUPPERT, Isabelle: Act. b. Paris, Mar 16, 1955. Films inc: Faustine et le Bel Ete; Cesar and Rosalie; Going Places; Rosebud; Aloise; Serieux Comme le Plaisir; The Rape of Innocence; No Time for Breakfast; Silence...on Tourne; The Lacemaker; The Indians Are Still Far Away; Violette; The Bronte Sisters; Loulou; Sauve Qui Peut la Vie; Orokseg; Heaven's Gate; The True Story of Camille; Les Ailes de la Colombe (Wings of the Dove); Coup de Torchon (Pop 1280); Eaux Profondes (Deep Water); Passion, La Truite (The Trout); Coup de Foudre; Storia di Piera; La Femme de Mon Pote (My Buddy's Girl); Signe Charlotte (Signed Charlotte); Sac de Noeuds (All Mixed Up).

HURKOS, Peter (Pieter Van der Hurk): Act-Psychic. b. Dordrecht, Holland, May 21, 1911. Films inc: The Peter Hurkos Story; Sixth Sense; New World; Boston Strangler; The Mysterious Monsters; The Amazing World of Psychic Phenomena; Now I Lay Me Down to Sleep; Boxoffice.

HURST, Rick: Act. b. Houston, TX, Jan 1. e. Tulane. Worked niteries. Films inc: W W and the Dixie Dance Kings; The Cat From Outer Space; Going Ape!

TV inc: On the Rocks; Amateur Night at the Dixie Bar and Grill; The Dukes of Hazzard; Enos.

HURT, John: Act. b. Lincolnshire, England, Jan 22, 1940. e. RADA. Films inc: The Wild and the Willing; A Man for All Seasons; Before Winter Comes; Spectre; Sinful Davey; In Search of Gregory; 10 Rillington Place; Little Malcolm; East of Elephant Rock; The Shout; The Disappearance; Midnight Express; The Lord of the Rings; Watership Down; Alien; The Elephant Man; Heaven's Gate; History of the World-Part I; Night Crossing; Partners; The Plague Dogs (voice); The Osterman Weekend; Champions; Success Is The Best Revenge; The Hit; Observations Under the Volcano (doc-narr); 1984; After Darkness.

TV inc: The Stone Dance; The Playboy of the Western World; The Naked Civil Servant; Nijinsky; I, Claudius; Crime and Punishment; Laurence Olivier Presents King Lear.

Thea inc: The Dwarfs; Man and Superman; Ride a Cock-Horse; The Caretaker; The Only Secret; The Dumb Waiter; Travesties; Chips with Everything; Inadmissible Evidence.

HURT, Mary Beth: Act. b. Marshalltown, IA, Sep 26. Thea inc: More Than You Deserve; Boy Meets Girl; Love for Love; Trelawney of the Wells; Crimes of the Heart; The Misanthrope.

Films inc: Interiors; Change of Seasons; The World According to

Garp; D.A.R.Y.L.

TV inc: Head Over Heels; The 5:48.

HURT, William: Act. b. Washington, D.C., March 20, 1950. e. Tufts U; Juilliard. Thea inc: Hamlet; Henry V; My Life; Ulysses in Traction; Lulu; Fifth of July; The Runner Stumbles; Hurlyburly.

TV inc: The Best of Families; Verna--USO Girl; All the Way Home.

Films inc: Altered States; Eyewitness; Body Heat; The Big Chill; Gorky Park; Kiss Of The Spider Woman. lines/page:

HUSKY, Ferlin: Singer. b. Flat River, MO, Dec 3, 1927. Also sang under the name of Simon Crum. Country & Pop Mus recording artist. On radio, TV. Film inc: Country Music Holiday.

HUSSEIN, Waris: Dir. b. India, 1938. Films inc: A Touch of Love; Quackser Fortune; Melody; The Possession of Joel Delaney; The Six Wives of Henry VIII.

TV inc: Shoulder to Shoulder; Notorious Woman; Sleeping Dogs; St. Joan; A Casual Affair; A Passage To India; Chips With Everything; And Baby Makes Six; Edward and Mrs. Simpson; Death Penalty; The Henderson Monster; Callie and Son; Coming Out of The Ice; Little Gloria--Happy At Last; Princess Daisy; John Steinbeck's The Winter Of Our Discontent; Surviving; Arch Of Triumph.

Thea inc: Half-Life; The Queen and the Rebels.

HUSSEY, Olivia: Act. b. Buenos Aires, Apr 17, 1951. Films inc: The Battle of the Villa Florita; Cup Fever; Romeo and Juliet; All the Right Noises; Summertime Killer; Lost Horizon; Black Christmas; Death On The Nile; The Cat and the Canary; Virus; The Man With Bogart's Face; Turkey Shoot.

TV inc: Jesus of Nazareth; The Pirate; The Bastard; The Thirteenth Day-The Story of Esther; Ivanhoe; The Last Days of Pompeii; The Corsican Brothers.

HUSSEY, Ruth: Act. b. Providence, RI, Oct 30, 1917. Films inc: Madame X; Judge Hardy's Children; Marie Antoinette; Time Out for Murder; Spring Madness; Maisie; The Women; Another Thin Man; Fast and Furious; Northwest Passage; Susan and God; The Philadelphia Story; Married Bachelor; H M Pulham Esq.; The Uninvited; Marine Raiders; Jane Doe; The Great Gatsby; Louisa; Stars and Stripes Forever; The Lady Wants Mink; The Facts of Life.

HUSTON, Anjelica: Act. b. 1952. D of John Huston. Films inc: Sinful Davey; A Walk with Love and Death; The Last Tycoon; The Postman Always Rings Twice; The Ice Pirates; Prizzi's Honor.

TV inc: The Cowboy And The Ballerina.

HUSTON, John: Dir-Wri-Act. b. Nevada, MO, Aug 5, 1906. S of late Walter Huston. In vaude as child, with father; on stage briefly in youth. Appeared in a few films inc: The Shakedown; Hell's Heroes; The Storm, before becoming writer. Films inc: Law and Order; Murders in the Rue Morgue (dialog); Jezebel; The Amazing Dr. Clitterhouse; Juarez; Dr. Ehrlich's Magic Bullet; High Sierra; Sergeant York; Three Strangers; made dir debut on The Maltese Falcon (& wri). Other films as dir inc: In This Our Life; Across The Pacific; Report From the Aleutians (doc) (&wri-narr); The Battle Of San Pietro (doc)(& wri-narr); Let There Be Light (doc) (& wri-narr); The Treasure Of The Sierra Madre (& wri-act) (Oscars-dir & sp-1948); Key Largo (& co-wri); We Were Strangers (& co-wri); The Asphalt Jungle (& prod-co-wri); The Red Badge Of Courage (& wri); The African Queen (& co-wri); Moulin Rouge (& co-wri); Beat The Devil (& prod-co-wri); Moby Dick (& prod-co-wri); Heaven Knows Mr. Allyson (& co-wri); The Barbarian and the Geisha; The Roots Of Heaven; The Unforgiven; The Misfits; Freud; The List Of Adrian Messenger (& act); The Cardinal (act); The Night Of The Iguana (& co-wri); The Bible--In The Beginning (& act); Casino Royale (& act); Reflections In A Golden Eye; Sinful Davey; A Walk With Love and Death (& act); The Kremlin Letter (& co-wri-act); De Sade (act); Fat City; Myra Breckenridge (act); The Life and Times of Judge Roy Bean; The Mackintosh Man; Battle For The Planet Of The Apes (act); Chinatown (act); The Man Who Would Be King (& co-wri); Jaguar Lives!; Wise Blood; Breakout (act); The Wind And The Lion (act); Winter Kills (act); Il Visitatore (The Visitor); The Return Of The King (ani-voice only); Phobia; Agee (act); Victory; Cannery Row (narr); Annie; Lovesick; Angela (act); Under The Volcano; Observations Under The Volcano (doc); Notes From Under The Volcano (doc-int); Prizzi's Honor.

TV inc: Money and Medicine (narr); American Caesar (narr); Alfred Hitchcock Presents (act); John Huston's Dublin (narr).

HUTCHINS, Will (Marshall Lowell Hutchason): Act. b. Los Angeles, May 5, 1932. e. Pomona Coll, BA. TV inc: Sugarfoot; Hey Landlord!; Blondie; then toured for two years with circus (clown & ringmaster). Films inc: Teenage Slumber Party; No Time for Sergeants; Claudelle Inglish; Merrill's Marauders; The Shooting; Spin-Out; Clambake; Roar!

HUTCHINSON, Josephine: Act. b. Seattle, WA, Oct 12, 1903. Film debut as extra in The Little Princess. Films inc: Happiness Ahead; The Right To Live; Oil For the Lamps of China; The Melody Lingers On; The Story of Louis Pasteur; I Married A Doctor; The Women Men Marry; The Crime of Dr. Hallet; Son of Frankenstein; My Son My Son; Tom Brown's School Days; Somewhere in the Night; Cass Timberlane; The Tender Years; Adventure in Baltimore; Love Is Better Than Ever; Ruby Gentry; Many Rivers to Cross; Miracle in the Rain; Sing Boy Sing; North By Northwest; The Adventures of Huckleberry Finn; Walk Like a Dragon; Baby The Rain Must Fall; Nevada Smith; Rabbit, Run.

Bway inc: The Hairy Ape; A Man's Man; Hedda Gabler; Peter Pan; Twelfth Night; The Cradle Song; The Seagull; Alice in Wonderland.

HUTTON, Betty: Act. b. Battle Creek, MI, Feb 26, 1921. Screen debut, 1942, The Fleet's In. Last seen on screen in Spring Reunion, 1957.

Films inc: Star-Spangled Rhythm; The Miracle of Morgan's Creek; Incendiary Blonde; The Perils of Pauline; Annie Get Your Gun; Let's Dance; The Greatest Show on Earth; Somebody Loves Me.

HUTTON, Brian: Dir. b. NYC, 1935. Films inc: The Wild Seed; The Pad; Sol Madrid; Where Eagles Dare; Kelly's Heroes; X Y and Z; Night Watch; The First Deadly Sin; High Road to China.

TV inc: Someone Is Watching Me; Institute For Revenge.

HUTTON, Lauren (Mary Hutton): Act. b. Charleston, SC, Nov 17, 1943. Films inc: Little Fauss and Big Halsy; The Gambler; Welcome to LA; A Wedding; American Gigolo; Zorba, the Gay Blade; Paternity; Tout Feu, Tout Flamme (All Fired Up); Hecate; Burroughs; Lassiter.

TV inc: Starflight--The Plane That Couldn't Land; The Cradle Will Fall; Scandal Sheet.

HUTTON, Robert (nee Winne): Act. b. Kingston, NY, Jun 11, 1920. Films inc: Destination Tokyo; Janie; Too Young To Know; Always Together; The Steel Helmet; Cassanova's Big Night; Cinderfella; The Slime People; The Secret Man; Finders Keepers; Torture Garden; Tales from the Crypt.

HUTTON, Tim: Act. b. Los Angeles, Aug 16, 1960. S of the late Jim Hutton. TV inc: Zuma Beach; The Best Place To Be; Friendly Fire; And Baby Makes Six; Young Love, First Love; The Sultan and the Rock Star; Father Figure; A Long Way Home; Teenage Suicide--Don't Try It! (narr).

Films inc: Ordinary People. (Oscar-supp-1980); Taps; Daniel; Iceman.

HUYCK, Wiliard: Wri. e. USC. H of Gloria Katz. Started as reader at AIP, later worked as wri various scenes AIP films; teamed with Katz writing six unproduced screenplays for Francis Ford Coppola's Zoetrope Productions. Films inc: The Devil's Eight (sp with John Milius); American Graffiti; Lucky Lady; French Postcards (& dir); Indiana Jones and the Temple of Doom; Best Defense (& dir).

HYAMS, Nessa: Dir. b. NYC, Nov 21, 1941. e. Syracuse U. W of David Picker. TV inc: Mary Hartman, Mary Hartman.

HYAMS, Peter: Wri-Dir. b. NYC, Jul 26, 1943. e. Hunter Coll; Syracuse U. With CBS News, NY before going to Par as writer. Films inc: T.R. Baskin (wri-prod); Busting; Our Time (dir); Peeper (dir); Telefon (wri); Capricorn One; Hanover Street; The Hunter (wri); Outland; The Star Chamber; 2010 (& prod-cin).

TV inc: The Rolling Man; Goodnight My Love.

HYDE-WHITE, Wilfrid: Act. b. Bourton-on-the Water, England, May 12, 1903. Films inc: Murder by Rope; Rembrandt; The Third Man; The Story of Gilbert and Sullivan; See How They Run; North-West Frontier; Carry on Nurse; Two-Way Stretch; My Fair Lady; John Goldfarb Please Come Home; Ten Little Indians; The Liquidator; Our Man in Marrakesh; Chamber of Horrors; Skullduggery; Gaily Gaily; Fragment of Fear; The Cat and the Canary; Battlestar Galactica; In God We Trust; Oh, God! Book II; The Toy; Fanny Hill.

Thea inc: The Philadelphia Story; Caesar and Cleopatra; Antony and Cleopatra; The Reluctant Debutante; The Happiest Millionaire; Not in the Book; The Pleasure of His Company; Rolls Hyphen Royce.

TV inc: The Rebels; The Associates; The Cat and the Canary; Scout's Honor; Damien...The Leper Priest; The Letter.

HYER, Martha: Act. b. Fort Worth, TX, Aug 10, 1924. e. Northwestern U; Pasadena Playhouse. W of Hal Wallis. Screen debut 1946. Films inc: The Locket; The Judge Steps Out; Sabrina; Cry Vengeance; Battle Hymn; The Big Fisherman; Some Came Running; The Carpetbaggers; The Sons of Katie Elder; House of a Thousand Dolls; Once You Kiss A Stranger.

TV inc: The Way They Were; Bob Hope's Road To Hollywood.

HYLTON, Jane: Act. b. London, Jul 16, 1927. Films inc: The Upturned Glass (as Gwen Clark); My Brother's Keeper; Passport to Pimlico; Here Comes the Huggetts; Secret Venture; Circus of Horrors; One Man's Navy.

TV inc: Sir Lancelot; The Four Seasons of Rosie Carr; Nightmare on Installments.

HYMAN, Kenneth: Prod. b. NYC, 1928. e. Columbia U. S of the late Eliot Hyman. Entered films as packager; exec vp Associated Artists; exec VP Seven Arts Prodns; Exec vp world-wide prodn WB-Seven Arts 1967-69; Films inc: (exec prod) Hound of the Baskervilles; Small Sad World of Sammy Lee; Whatever Happened to Baby Jane?; Emperor of the North Pole. (Prod) The Hill; The Dirty Dozen.

IAN, Janis: Singer. b. NJ, Apr 7, 1951. Films inc: Virus (theme song); Freedom (mus). TV inc: Star Chart. (Grammy-pop vocal-1975).

IBBETSON, Arthur: Cin. b. England, 1922. Films inc: The Horse's Mouth; The Angry Silence; The League of Gentlemen; Tunes of Glory; Whistle Down the Wind; The Inspector; Nine Hours to Rama; The Chalk Garden; The Countess from Hong Kong; Inspector Clouseau; Where Eagles Dare; Anne of the Thousand Days; The Railway Children; Willie Wonka and the Chocolate Factory; A Doll's House; Harrowhouse 11; All Things Bright and Beautiful; The Medusa Touch; The Prisoner of Zenda; Hopscotch; The Bounty.

TV inc: Frankenstein--The True Story; Little Lord Fauntleroy (Emmy-1981); Witness For the Prosecution; Master of the Game.

ICHIKAWA, Kon: Dir. b. Japan, Nov 20, 1915. Films inc: A Flower Blooms; 365 Nights; Design of a Human Being; Endless Passion; Pursuit at Dawn; Nightshade Flower; The Lover; Stolen Love; River Solo Flows; Wedding March; The Young Generation; This Way--That Way; The Blue Revolution; The Youth of Heiji Senigata; The Lovers; All of Myself; A Billionaire; The Heart; The Burmese Harp; Punishment Room; Bridge of Japan; The Crowded Train; The Hole; Conflagration; Money and Three Bad Men; Odd Obsession; Fires on the Plain; A Ginza Veteran; Her Brother; Ten Black Women; The Sin; An Actor's Revenge; My Enemy the Sea (Alone On the Pacific); Money Talks; To Love Again; I Am A Cat; The Inugami Family; Queen Bee; The Devil's Island; The Phoenix; Hinotori; Bonchi; Kofuku (Lonely Hearts); Sasame Yuki (The Makioka Sisters) (& sp); Biruma No Tategoto (The Burmese Harp) (remake);Ohan (& prod-wri).

TV inc: Tokio Olympiad; The Tale of Genji; Kyoto; Tournament.

IDLE, Eric: Act-Wri. b. England, Mar 29, 1943. e. Cambridge. Member Monty Python Flying Circus. Thea inc: My Girl Herbert; Oh, What A Lovely War; One For the Pot; Python Live at Drury Lane; Pass the Butler.

TV inc: Frost Report; Ronnie Corbett Show; Do Not Adjust Your Set; Rutland Weekend Television; Saturday Night Live.

Films inc: Monty Python and the Holy Grail; Crackerbox Palace (short); True Love (short); Body Language (short); Pirates of Penzance (sp only); Life of Brian; Yellowbeard (act).

ILLES, Robert: Wri. Works with James R Stein. TV inc: Lily (Emmy-1974); Van Dyke and Co; What's Happening; One Day at a Time; Love Boat (Pilot); Fernwood 2Night; Carol Burnett Show (Emmy-

1978); Lou Rawls Special; America 2night; Mary Tyler Moore Show; Helen Reddy Special; New Kind of Family; Dick Clark Specials; Flo; Steve Allen Comedy Hour; Private Benjamin (prod); The Cracker Brothers.

ILSON, Saul: Wri-Prod. Writer for Canadian TV, to Hollywood in late 50's; from 1967 to 1978 partnered with Ernie Chambers in indie firm producing variety shows; April 1980 named vp pgms & talent NBC Entertainment; Oct 1980, vp comedy and variety; resd Nov 1981 to return to Indie prodn.

TV inc: Dinah Shore; Smothers Brothers; Tony Orlando and Dawn; Lynda Carter Special; Beatrice Arthur Special; The Billy Crystal Comedy Hour; The TV Funnies; Washington Follies; Rich Little's Christmas Carol; There Goes The Neighborhood (exec prod); For Members Only (exec prod).

IMMEL, Jerrold: Comp-Cond. b. Los Angeles. TV inc: Gunsmoke; Hawaii Five-O; The Macahans; How The West Was Won; The Fitzpatricks; Harry-O; Dallas; The American Girls; Married, The First Year; Alcatraz--The Whole Shocking Story; Secret of Midland Heights; The Oklahoma City Dolls; The Texas Rangers; Knots Landing; Louis L'Amour's The Cherokee Trail; King's Crossing; The Adventures of Pollyanna; The Shadow Riders; Voyagers!; Travis McGee; The Yellow Rose; The Outlaws; Berrenger's; Peyton Place--The Next Generation.

Films inc: Death Hunt; Silence of the North; Megaforce.

IMMERMAN, William J.: Exec. b. NYC, Dec 29, 1937. e. U of WI, BS; Stanford U, JD. VP, AIP, 1965-72; sr vp Twentieth Fox, 1972-77; pres Scoric Prodns, Inc, 1977; 1980, P & Bd Chmn Cinema Group. Films inc: (Exec prod) Highpoint; Take This Job and Shove It; Southern Comfort; Hysterical.

INGELS, Marty: Act. b. NYC, Mar 9, 1936. H of Shirley Jones. Arranges star commercials for various firms. Films inc: Armored Command; The Horizontal Lieutenant; The Ladies Man; Irving's Root Canal; For Singles Only; Monsieur Bouquet; If It's Tuesday This Must Be Belgium.

TV inc: Dickens and Fenster; Burke's Law; Pat Boone and Family Christmas Special; Christmas Comes to Pacland (voice).

IONESCU, Eugene: Plywri. b. Romania, Nov 13, 1912. Plays inc: The Lesson; The Chairs; The Bald Prima Donna; Amedee; Victims of Duty; The New Tenant; Rhinocerous; The Killer; The Man With the Suitcases; Pedestrian in the Air; Ce Formidable Bordel.

IRELAND, Jill: Act. b. London, Apr 24, 1936. Began career in music halls age 12, played Palladium, toured continent. Film contract with J. Arthur Rank. Screen debut as a ballet dancer in Oh, Rosalinda.

Films inc: Three Men in a Boat; Carry On, Nurse; The Mechanic; The Valachi Papers; Hard Times; From Noon Till Three; Love and Bullets; Death Wish II; The Evil That Men Do (asso prod).

TV inc: Shane; Night Gallery; Ben Casey; Daniel Boone; Mannix; Star Trek; The Girl, The Gold Watch and Everything.

IRELAND, John: Act. b. Vancouver, BC, Jan 30, 1915. Films inc: A Walk in the Sun; All the King's Men; My Darling Clementine; Red River; I Shot Jesse James; Little Big Horn; Gunfight at the O.K. Corral; Spartacus; 55 Days at Peking; The Fall of the Roman Empire; Farewell, My Lovely; The Adventurers; Madam Kitty; Maniac; Midnight Auto Supply; The Swiss Conspiracy; Guyana, Cult of the Damned; Incubus; The Delta Fox; Martin's Day; El Tesoro del Amazones (The Treasure Of The Amazon).

TV inc: The Millionaire; Kavik The Wolf Dog; Crossbar; Tourist; Marilyn--The Untold Story; Cassie & Co; Takeover.

IRONS, Jeremy: Act. b. Isle of Wight, Eng, 1950. e. Bristol Old Vic Theatre School. Joined Bristol Old Vic Group appearing in Winter's Tale; What the Butler Saw; Hayfever. Other Thea inc: Godspell; Much Ado About Nothing; The Caretaker; The Taming of the Shrew; Wild Oats; Rear Column; An Audience Called Edouard; The Real Thing (Bway) (Tony-1984).

TV inc: The Pallisers; Notorious Woman; Love for Lydia; Langrishe Go Down; Brideshead Revisited; The Captain's Doll; Night Of 100 Stars II.

Films inc: Nijinsky; The French Lieutenant's Woman; Moonlighting; Betrayal; The Wild Duck; Un Amour de Swann (Swann in Love).

IRVIN, John: Dir. b. England, May 7, 1940. Worked in cutting rooms of Rank Organization. First film, doc, Gala Day, made on grant from British Film Institute. Made several documentaries before turning to TV and features. TV inc: Hard Times; Tinker, Tailor, Soldier, Spy.

Films inc: Dogs of War; Ghost Story; Champions.

IRVING, Amy: Act. b. Palo Alto, CA, Sep 10, 1953. e. American Conservatory Theatre; London Academy of Dramatic Art. D of the late Jules Irving. Films inc: Carrie; The Fury; Honeysuckle Rose; The Competition; Yentl; Micki & Maude.

TV inc: I'm A Fool; Dynasty; Voices; Once an Eagle; The Far Pavilions (PC).

Bway inc: Amadeus; Heartbreak House.

IRVING, George S. (nee Shelasky): Act-Singer. b. Springfield, MA, Nov 1, 1922. In stock and touring companies before Bway debut in chorus of Oklahoma!

Bway inc: Lady in the Dark; Call Me Mister; Along Fifth Avenue; Gentlemen Prefer Blondes; Two's Company; Me and Juliet; Can-Can; Bells Are Ringing; The Beggar's Opera; Oh Kay; Irma La Douce; Seidman and Son; Tovarich; A Murderer Among Us; An Evening With Richard Nixon and...; Irene *(Tony-*supp-1972); Who's Who in Hell; Copperfield; On Your Toes.

Opera inc: The Telephone and The Medium (London); Boris Godunov (Montreal).

TV inc: Omnibus; Barry Wood's Variety Show; I Remember Mama; Getting There; Pinocchio's Christmas (voice).

IRVING, Richard: Prod-Dir. b. NYC, Feb 13, 1917. e. NYU. TV inc: Biff Baker, USA; State Trooper; The Virginian; Court Martial; Laredo; Columbo; Name of the Game; Six Million Dollar Man; Seventh Avenue; Class of '65; Quincy; Johnny Blue; The Last Days of Pompeii (prod); The Jesse Owens Story (dir); Wallenberg--A Hero's Story.

ISAACS, Phil: Exec. b. NYC, May 22, 1922. e. CCNY. Joined Par 1946 as booker's asst; worked up to asst eastern sls mgr; 1966 natl sls mgr Ten Commandments; 1967 vp dom dist Cinema Center Films; 1972 mktg vp Tomorrow Entertainment; 1975, vp gen sls mgr Avco Embassy; 1978 vp General Cinema Corp; 1980 vp gen sls mgr Orion Pictures; resd April, 1983 to set up producers rep firm.

ISCOVE, Rob: Dir-Chor. b. Toronto, Canada, Jul 4, 1947. e. Juilliard School of Music. TV inc: (Chor); Dorothy Hamill Special; Rock Awards 1976; Super Night at the Super Bowl; three Burt Bacharach specials; Steve and Eydie Celebrate Irving Berlin; 50th Academy Awards; 100 Years of Golden Hits. (Dir) Mary; Pontiac Special with Raquel Welch; Welcome to My Nightmare; Rock Awards; Roller Revolution; Jack; Clowns; Pajama Tops (& prod) (cable); Chautauqua Girl; Romeo and Juliet On Ice (& prod) *(Emmy-*dir-1984).

Films inc; (chor) Jesus Christ Superstar; Duchess and the Dirtwater Fox; Silent Movie.

Thea inc: Peter Pan (dir-chor); Copperfield (dir-chor).

ISENBERG, Gerald I.: Prod. b. Cambridge, MA, May 13, 1940. e. Bowdoin Coll, BA; Harvard Business School, MBA. TV inc: The People; Go Ask Alice; Great American Tragedy; Sandcastles; It's Good to be Alive; Where Have All the People Gone; The Last Angry Man; Betrayal; It Couldn't Happen to a Nicer Guy; Winner Take All; Katherine. (Exec prod); James Dean; Portrait of a Friend; The Bureau; Having Babies; Secrets; The Secret Life of John Chapman; Red Alert; The Defection of Simas Kudirka; Having Babies II; Having Babies III; Seizure-The Story of Kathy Morris (& dir); Fame (exec prod); When She Says No; The Three Wishes Of Billy Grier (exec prod); When Dreams Come True (exec prod); Forbidden (exec prod).

Thea inc: Let the Good Times Roll.

ISHERWOOD, Christopher: Wri. b. Aug 26, 1904. Plays inc: Dog Beneath the Skin, or Where is Francis; Ascent of F 1; On the Frontier. His short stories, Goodbye to Berlin, formed the basis of the play I Am a Camera, subsequently musicalized as Cabaret; both versions subsequently filmed.

Films inc: The Loved One.

Bway inc: A Meeting by the River.

ISRAEL, Neil: Wri-Dir. TV inc: (wri) Lola Falana Special; Mac Davis Show; Ringo; Marie (prod); Twilight Theatre (wri-prod).

Films inc: Tunnelvision (exec prod-wri); Americathon; Police Academy (wri); Bachelor Party.

ITO, Robert: Act. b. Vancouver, BC, Jul 2. Films inc: Midway; Rollerball; Special Delivery; The Adventures Of Buckaroo Banzai--Across The 8th Dimension.

TV inc: Men of the Dragon; Helter Skelter; Kung Fu; Quincy.

Thea inc: Flower Drum Song; What Makes Sammy Run.

IVANEK, Zeljko: Act. b. Yugoslavia, 1957. e. Yale; LAMDA. Bway inc: The Survivor; Cloud 9; Master Harold...And the Boys; Brighton Beach Memoirs.

Films inc: Tex; The Sender; Mass Appeal.

TV inc: The Edge of Night; Alice in Wonderland; The Sun Also Rises.

IVERS, Irving N.: Exec. b. Montreal, Canada, Feb. 23, 1939. e. Sir George Williams U. Station mgr KHJ (AM) Los Angeles, 1972; GM KIQQ/FM, 1973; joined Columbia Pictures 1973 as dir of adv; 1977, GM Columbia Pictures Canada; 1978, VP pub-ad-promo, Columbia; 1980, exec vp wldwde pub-adv-promo, 20th-Fox; April 1983, P wldwde mktg MGM/UA.

IVES, Burl: Act-Singer. b. Hunt Township, IL, Jun 14, 1909. On screen from 1946. Films inc: The Big Country *(Oscar-*supp-1958); Smoky; East of Eden; Cat on a Hot Tin Roof; Desire Under the Elms; Let No Man Write My Epitaph; Ensign Pulver; Those Fantastic Flying Fools; The Only Way Out Is Dead; Baker's Hawk; Hugo The Hippo (voice); Just You and Me, Kid; Earthbound; White Dog.

TV inc: The Bold Ones; The New Adventures of Heidi; The Ewok Adventure (narr).

IVEY, Judith: Act. b. El Paso, TX., Sept. 4, 1951. e. IL State U. Bway inc; Bedroom Farce; Piaf; Steaming *(Tony-*featured-1983); Hurlyburly *(Tony-featured-1985)*.

TV inc: The Shady Hill Kidnapping; Dixie--Changing Habits.

Films inc: The Lonely Guy; Harry & Son; The Woman In Red.

IVORY, James: Dir. b. Jun 7, 1928. e. U of OR, BA; USC, MA. Films inc: The Householder; Shakespeare Wallah; The Guru; Bombay Talkie; Savages; The Wild Party; Roseland; The Europeans (& prod); Jane Austen In Manhattan; Quartet; Heat and Dust; The Courtesans of Bombay (& prod-wri); The Bostonians.

TV inc: Autobiography of a Princess; The Five Forty Eight; Noon Wine.

JABARA, Paul: Act-Sngwri. b. Jan 31, 1948. Thea inc: Hair (Bway); Jesus Christ Superstar (London).

Films inc: Midnight Cowboy; Day of the Locust; Thank God It's Friday (& song, Last Dance - *Oscar* 1978; *Grammy-*1979); Main Event (song); Honky Tonk Freeway; Chanel Solitaire.

JACKS, Robert L.: Prod. b. Oxnard, CA, Jun 14, 1927. e. USC. Films inc: Man on a Tightrope; Prince Valiant; Gambler from Natchez; White Feather; Black Tuesday; Stranger on Horseback; A Kiss Before Dying; Man in the Middle; Guns at Batasi; Zorba The Greek; Bandolero; The Undefeated.

TV inc: Honeymoon with a Stranger; Victor Borge Show; Three Coins in the Fountain; Arnie; The Homecoming; Pomeroy's People; The Waltons *(Emmy-*1973); Crunch; State Fair; Eight Is Enough; Mr. Horn; The Wild, Wild West Revisited; Young Love, First Love; The Young Pioneers; Murder Can Hurt You; A Matter of Life and Death; The Day the Loving Stopped; A Few Days In Weasel Creek; The Dukes of Hazzard (exec prod).

JACKSON, Anne: Act. b. Allegheny, PA, Sep 3, 1926. Studied at Neighborhood Playhouse and with Sanford Meisner, Herbert Berghof, Lee Strasberg. W of Eli Wallach. Films inc: So Young So Bad; The Journey; Tall Story; The Tiger Makes Out; How to Save a Marriage; The Secret Life of an American Wife; Lovers and Other Strangers; Zigzag; Dirty Dingus Magee; Nasty Habits; The Bell Jar; The Shining; Sam's Son.

TV inc: The Family Man; A Private Battle; Leave 'Em Laughing; A Woman Called Golda.

Bway inc: Signature; The Last Dance; Summer and Smoke; Oh, Men! Oh, Women; Rhinoceros; The Tiger and the Typist (& London);

The Waltz of the Toreadors; Twice Around the Park.

JACKSON, Calvin: Pianist-Comp. b. Philadelphia, PA, May 26, 1919. Films inc: Blood and Steel; The Unsinkable Molly Brown. TV inc: Asphalt Jungle; Rehearsal With Calvin.

JACKSON, Freda: Act. b. Nottingham, England, Dec 29, 1909. Films inc: Henry V; Great Expectations; No Room at the Inn; Bhowani Junction; The Flesh Is Weak; A Tale of Two Cities; The Shadow of the Cat; Tom Jones; House at the End of the World.
    TV inc: Macadam and Eve; Sorry Wrong Number; Release; Maigret in Montmartre; Knock on Any Door; Midland Profile.
    Thea inc: Tell Tale Murder; Starched Aprons; The Lady of the Camellias; Camino Real; The Man on the Stairs; Error of Judgement; The Devil's Disciple; The White Devil.

JACKSON, Glenda: Act. b. Cheshire, England, May 9, 1936. Films inc: Marat-Sade; Negatives; Women in Love (Oscar-1970); The Music Lovers; Sunday Bloody Sunday; Mary Queen of Scots; A Touch of Class (Oscar-1973); The Triple Echo; A Bequest to the Nation; Hedda; The Incredible Sarah; Nasty Habits; House Calls; Stevie; Lost & Found; Class of Miss MacMichael; Hopscotch; Health; The Return of the Soldier; Giro City; Sakharov.
    TV inc: Elizabeth R (Emmy-1972); Shadow In The Sun (Emmy-1972); The Patricia Neal Story; The Thames (narr).
    Thea inc: Hedda Gabler; The White Devil; Stevie; Rose; Summit Conference. (Bway) Rose; Strange Interlude.

JACKSON, Gordon: Act. b. Glasgow, Dec 19, 1923. Films inc: The Foreman Went to France; Millions Like Us; Pink String and Sealing Wax; Tight Little Island; Tunes of Glory; The Great Escape; The Ipcress File; Cast a Giant Shadow; The Prime of Miss Jean Brodie; Kidnapped; Russian Roulette; A Medusa Touch; The Shooting Party.
    TV inc: Upstairs, Downstairs (Emmy-supp-1976); A Town Like Alice.
    Thea inc: What Every Woman Knows; Macbeth; Noah; Cards on The Table.

JACKSON, Kate: Act. b. Birmingham, AL, Oct 29, 1948. e. AADA. Thea inc: Night Must Fall; Constant Wife; Little Moon of Alban. Films inc: Limbo; Night of Dark Shadows; Thunder and Lightning; Dirty Tricks; Making Love.
    TV inc: Dark Shadows; The Rookies; Charlie's Angels; Homicide; Killer Bees; Topper (& exec prod); Inmates--A Love Story; Thin Ice; Listen To Your Heart; Scarecrow and Mrs. King.

JACKSON, Keith: Sportscaster. b. GA. TV inc: Monday Night Baseball; NCAA Football; Wide World of Sports; The Superstars; The Woman Superstars; Superteams.

JACKSON, Michael: Sing-mus-sngwri. b. Gary, IN, Aug. 29, 1958. Leader of the group The Jackson Five, later called the Jacksons, before going solo. Films inc: The Wiz. TV inc: Diana Ross Presents the Jacksons; Going Back to Indiana.
    Albums inc: Diana Ross Presents the Jackson Five; Got To Be There; Ben; Music and Me; Forever Michael; Triumph; The Best of Michael Jackson; Get It Together; Dancing Machine; Moving Violation; Off the Wall; E.T. The ExtraTerrestrial (Grammy-childrens-1983; Thriller (Grammys-album of the year & pop vocal-1983).
    Recs inc: Ease On Down the Road; Don't Stop 'Till You Get Enough (Grammy-R&B vocal-1979); Working Day and Night; Heartbreak Hotel; Lovely One; Muscles; Wanna Be Startin' Somethin'; Billie Jean (Grammy-R&B vocal-1983); Beat It (Grammys-record of the year & rock vocal-1983); The Girl Is Mine (Grammy-prod of the year-1983).

JACKSON, Michael: Radio-TV Pers. b. London, England, Apr 16, 1934. H of Alana Ladd. TV inc: The Big Question; The Michael Jackson Show. Radio inc The Michael Jackson Show (since 1966).

JACKSON, Sherry: Act. Films inc: The Breaking Point; The Miracle of Our Lady of Fatima; The Lion and the Horse; Trouble Along the Way; Come Next Spring; Wild on the Beach; Gunn; The Silent Treatment; The Mini-Skirt Mob; Bare Knuckes; Stingray.
    TV inc: Brenda Starr.

JACKSONS, THE: Musical group. Members of the group (all brothers) are: Sigmund (Jackie) b. May 4, 1951; Toriano Aldryll (Tito) b. Oct 15, 1953; Marlon David b. Mar 12, 1957; Michael Joe, b. Aug 29, 1958; Steven Randall (Randy) b. Oct 29, 1961. Recording artists, concert tours.
    Films inc: The Wiz.
    Albums inc: Destiny; Shake Your Body; Triumph.
    See also JACKSON, Michael.

JACOBI, Derek: Act. b. London, Oct 22, 1938. e. Cambridge. Films inc: Othello; The Day of the Jackal; Blue Blood; The Odessa File; The Medusa Touch; The Human Factor; Charlotte; The Secret of NIMH (voice); Enigma.
    TV inc: The Strauss Family; She Stoops to Conquer; Man of Straw; The Pallisers; I Claudius; Philby, Burgess and MacLean; Hamlet; The Hunchback of Notre Dame; Inside The Third Reich.
    Thea inc: Pericles; A Month in the Country; The Hollow Crown; Hamlet; Hay Fever; Royal Hunt of the Sun; Black Comedy; Pleasure and Repentance; Hobson's Choice; The Suicide; Cyrano de Bergerac (& Bway); Much Ado About Nothing (Bway) (Tony-1985).

JACOBI, Lou: Act. b. Toronto, Ont, Canada, Dec 28, 1913. Stage experience in Canada before debuting London. Thea inc: (London) Remains to Be Seen; Pal Joey; Bontche Schweig; Embassy. (Bway) The Diary of Anne Frank; The Tenth Man; Come Blow Your Horn; Fade Out-Fade In; Don't Drink The Water; A Way of Life; Norman, Is That You?; Cheaters.
    Films inc: The Diary of Anne Frank; Song Without End; Irma La-Douce; Everything You've Ever Wanted To Know About Sex But Were Afraid To Ask; Penelope; Roseland; Magician of Lublin; The Lucky Star; Chu Chu and the Philly Flash; My Favorite Year; Isaac Littlefeathers.
    TV inc: Rheingold Theatre; Better Late Than Never; Joanna.

JACOBS, Lawrence-Hilton: Act. b. NYC, Sep 4. Films inc: Claudine; Cooley High; Young Blood.
    TV inc: Roots; Welcome Back, Kotter; For the Love of It.

JACOBS, Ronald: Prod. e. UCLA. B of Danny Thomas. Started as prodn asst on Danny Thomas Show, later becoming asso prod, prod exec for Danny Thomas Productions, Sheldon Leonard Productions; Thomas-Spelling Productions; Mirisch-Rich Productions; Calvada Productions, Daisy Productions. TV inc (prod): City Versus Country; Young and Foolish; Yesterday, Today and Tomorrow; The Unbroken Circle; The Over-the-Hill Gang; Three on a Date; Satan's Triangle; Samurai.
    Films inc: On the Right Track; Jimmy The Kid.

JACOBS, Seaman: Wri. b. Kingston, NY. Films inc: It Happened at the World's Fair; Oh, God! Book II.
    TV inc: Ed Wynn; Bing Crosby; Johnny Carson; Edgar Bergen; My Favorite Martian; Petticoat Junction; My Three Sons; F Troop; Adams Family; Bachelor Father; Family Affair; The Lucy Show; Tony Orlando & Dawn; The Jeffersons; Maude; Alice; Love Boat; George Burns In Nashville?; Bob Hope 30th Anniversary Special; Bob Hope's Spring Fling of Glamour and Comedy; Bob Hope's All-Star Comedy Look at the New Season; Bob Hope's All-Star Celebration Opening the Gerald R. Ford Museum; George Burns' Early, Early, Early Christmas Special; Bob Hope's Stand Up and Cheer for the National Football League's 60th Year; Christmas, A Time of Cheer and A Time For Hope; Bob Hope's Women I Love--Beautiful and Funny; Bob Hope Laughs with the Movie Awards; George Burns & Other Sex Symbols; Bob Hope's Road to Hollywood; Texaco Star Theatre Presents Bob Hope in "Who Makes The World Laugh"; Happy Birthday, Bob; George Burns Celebrates 80 Years in Show Business; Bob Hope Goes to College; Bob Hope's USO Christmas in Beirut; Bob Hope's Wicky-Wacky Special from Waikiki; Bob Hope's Who Makes the World Laugh--Part II; George Burns' How To Live To Be 100 Or More; The Hilarious Unrehearsed Antics Of The Stars; It's Ho-Ho Hope's 35th Jolly Christmas Hour; Bob Hope Lampoons Television 1985; Bob Hope's Comedy Salute To The Soaps.

JACOBY, Billy: Act. b. Flushing, NY, Apr. 10, 1969. TV inc: That Certain Summer; Horrible Honchos; The Bad News Bears; Maggie; The Notorious Jumping Frog of Calaveras County; The Red Room; Little Lulu; How Do You Eat Like A Child; Working; Feathers, Furs and Tails;

Angel on my Shoulder; Murder in Texas; Crazy Times; Nightmares; It's Not Easy; The New Man (Tales From The Darkness).

Films inc: The Runner Stumbles; The Beastmaster; Man, Woman and Child; Cujo; Reckless; Superstition; Just One Of The Guys.

JACOBY, Coleman: Wri. TV inc: Phil Silvers Show *(Emmys*-1955, 1956, 1957); Dick Cavett Show; Alan King Specials; The Hallowe'en That Almost Wasn't; Strippers (cable).

JACOBY, Joseph: Prod-dir-wri. b. Brooklyn, Sept. 22, 1942. e. NYU. Wrote and developed tv game shows while in college; worked with Bil Baird Marionettes making commercials; produced and directed industrial, commercial films. Adjunct Prof. of Film at New School for Social Research.

TV inc: Let's Make A Deal (wri); The Michael Jackson Show (prod); Magistrate's Court (wri).

Films inc: Hurry Up Or I'll Be 30; Shenanigans (The Great Bank Hoax).

JACOBY, Scott: Act. Films inc: The Little Girl Who Lives Down the Lane; Midnight Auto Supply; Our Winning Season.

TV inc: That Certain Summer *(Emmy*-supp-1973); No Other Love; The Diary of Anne Frank.

JADE, Claude: Act. b. Dijon, France. Films inc: Stolen Kisses; Topaz; Le Temoin; Domicile Conjugal; Le Miroir Ecarlate; Home Sweet Home; Number One; Le Malin Plaisir; Trop, C'est Trop; The Pawn; Le Choix; Cap Du Nord; Lenin U Parize (Lenin In Paris); L'honneur d'un Capitaine (A Captain's Honor).

TV inc: Les Oiseaux Rares.

JAE, Jana: Singer. b. Great Falls, MT, Aug 30, 1946. e. CO Women's Coll. C&W recording artist.

JAECKEL, Richard: Act. b. Long Beach, NY, Oct 10, 1926. Films inc: Guadalcanal Diary; A Wing and a Prayer; Battleground; Sands of Iwo Jima; Come Back, Little Sheba; The Naked and the Dead; The Gallant Hours; The Dirty Dozen; Sometimes a Great Notion; The Devil's Brigade; Chisum; Ulzana's Raid; The Drowning Pool; Walking Tall, Part II; Twilight's Last Gleaming; Speedtrap; The Dark; Herbie Goes Bananas; All the Marbles; Cold River; The Delta Fox; Starman; Pacific Inferno.

TV inc: U.S. Steel Hour; Elgin Hour; Goodyear Playhouse; Firehouse; The Last Day; Champions-A Love Story; Salvage; The $5.20 An Hour Dream; Princess; Reward; Hot WACS; At Ease; The Dirty Dozen--The Next Mission.

JAECKIN, Just: Dir. b. 1940. Originally a Fashion photographer. Films inc: Emmanuelle; Story of O; Madame Claude; Le Dernier Amant Romantique; Private Collections; Lady Chatterley's Lover (& wri); Gwendoline (& wri).

JAFFE, Henry: Exec Prod. b. Jan 19, 1907. e. Columbia U; Columbia Law School. TV inc: The Chevy Mystery Theatre; The Chevy Show; The Dinah Shore Chevy Show; Bell Telephone Hour; Producers Showcase; Jubilee; TV-- The Fabulous 50's; Emily, Emily; Death of Ritchie; Dinah's Place *(Emmy*-1973); Battered; Dinah! *(Emmy*-1976) A Woman Called Moses; Aunt Mary; When She Was Bad; Escape; Dinah And Friends; Cheryl Ladd Souvenirs; Cheryl Ladd--Scenes From A Special.

JAFFE, Herb: Prod. b. NYC. e. Brooklyn Coll; Columbia U. Started as press agent, then talent agent. Joined UA in 1965 as vp in charge of worldwide prod; left in 1973 and for short time served as p of Rastar Pictures; then entered indy prod.

Films inc: The Wind and the Lion; Demon Seed; Who'll Stop the Rain; Time after Time; Those Lips, Those Eyes; Motel Hell; Jinxed!; The Lords of Discipline; Little Treasure.

JAFFE, Leo: Exec. b. NYC, Apr 23, 1909. e. NYU. Joined accounting dept of Columbia 1930. Became vp, Columbia, 1954; 1st vp, treas, member of the board; 1958; exec vp, 1962; pres, 1968; pres Columbia Pictures Industries, Inc, 1970; pres & CEO, 1973; chm, 1973; became consultant July 1981.

(Jean Hersholt Humanitarian Award-1978).

JAFFE, Michael: Prod. b. NYC, Jan 9, 1945. e. Yankton Coll, BA; U of Chicago; Cornell. S of Jean Muir and Henry Jaffe. TV inc: Alexander; Death of Richie; Emily, Emily; A Woman Called Moses; Battered; When She Was Bad; Aunt Mary; Escape; Incident At Crestridge (exec prod); I Was A Mail Order Bride.

JAFFE, Sam: Act. b. NYC, Mar 10, 1891. e. CCNY, BS. Bway inc: The Clod; Samson and Delilah; The Jazz Singer; The Eternal Road; A Doll's House; The Merchant of Venice; Cafe Crown; Mademoiselle Columbo; The Seagull; The Lark; A Meeting By the River.

Films inc: The Scarlet Empress; Lost Horizon; Gunga Din; Gentleman's Agreement; The Asphalt Jungle; The Barbarian and the Geisha; Ben Hur; Guns for San Sebastian; The Kremlin Letter; Bedknobs and Broomsticks; Battle Beyond The Stars; Nothing Lasts Forever; George Stevens--A Filmmaker's Journey (doc-int).

TV inc: Ben Casey; Gideon's Trumpet.

(Died March 24, 1984).

JAFFE, Stanley R.: Prod. b. New Rochelle, NY, Jul 31, 1940. e. U of PA. S of Leo Jaffe. Joined Seven Arts Associated Corp 1962; named exec asst to P 1964; dir pgmg 1965; 1969 exec vp Par; 1970 P Par Pictures Corp and Par TV; 1971 P Jafilms, Inc; 1975 exec vp Col; 1976 P Stanley Jaffe Prodns; Jan 1983 formed Jaffe-Lansing Prodns with Sherry Lansing.

Films inc: Goodbye, Columbus; A New Leaf (exec prod); Bad Company; The Bad News Bears; Kramer Vs. Kramer *(Oscar*-1979); Taps; Without A Trace (& dir); Firstborn (exec prod).

JAGGER, Dean: Act. b. Lima, OH, Nov 7, 1903. Vaudeville, Bway prior to screen debut, 1929, Woman from Hell.

Films inc: Star for a Night; Western Union; Valley of the Sun; Sister Kenny; 12 O'Clock High *(Oscar*-supp-1949); Driftwood; Executive Suite; White Christmas; Elmer Gantry; Jumbo; The Kremlin Letter; Vanishing Point; Game of Death; Alligator.

TV inc: Gideon's Trumpet; Haywire; Independence and 76 *(Emmy*-1980).

JAGGER, Mick: Singer-Sngwri-Act. b. Dartford, Kent, England, Jul 26, 1943. Lead Singer with Rolling Stones; Films inc: Performance; Ned Kelly; Gimme Shelter; Sympathy for the Devil; Ladies and Gentlemen, The Rolling Stones; Time Is On Our Side; Ziggy Stardust and the Spiders From Mars (made in 1973, released 1983).

Songs inc: Satisfaction; Get Off My Cloud; Paint It Black; Let's Spend the Night Together; Ruby Tuesday; Stray Cat Blues.

JAGLOM, Henry: Wri-Dir. b. London, Jan 26, 1941. e. U of PA. Films inc: A Safe Place; Tracks; Hearts and Minds (presenter only); Sitting Ducks (& act); Can She Bake A Cherry Pie; National Lampoon Goes to the Movies; Always (& prod-act).

JAMAL, Ahmad: Pianist-Comp. b. Pittsburgh, PA, Jul 2, 1930. Albums inc: One For Miles; Minor Moods; Extension; Jamal Plays Jamal; Jamalca; The Awakening; Poinciana Revisited; Tranquility; Cry Young; Heatwave.

JAMES, Dennis: Act-TV host. b. Jersey City, NJ, Aug 24,1917. TV Shows inc: Price Is Right; Name That Tune.

Films inc: The One and Only.

JAMES, Emrys: Act. b. England, Sep 1, 1930. With Old Vic; Royal Shakespeare Co. Thea inc: The Long and the Short and the Tall; Macbeth; Indians; Relapse; The Plebeians Rehearse the Uprising; Othello; The Merchant of Venice; The Island of Mighty; Dr Faustus; King John; Merry Wives of Windsor.

Films inc: Darling.

TV inc: Pygmalion; Twelfth Night; Testament of Youth; Anthony and Cleopatra.

JAMES, Francesca: Act. b. Montebello, CA, Jan 23. e. Carnegie-Mellon U. With various stock companies before Bway in The Rothschilds. TV inc: One Life to Live; All My Children *(Emmy*-supp-1980).

JAMES, Harry: Orch Ldr. b. Albany, GA, May 15, 1916. As a child performed as contortionist with circus. Played trumpet with Benny Goodman band. Formed own orchestra 1939. On screen from 1942.

Films inc: Private Buckaroo; Springtime in the Rockis; Two Girls and a Sailor; Young Man with a Horn; To Catch a Thief; Anything Goes.

(Died July 5, 1983).

JAMES, Monique: Exec. b. Paris, France, Apr 2, 1926. e. Vassar, BA. Started 1949 in cast dept CBS NY; 1950 in partnership with Eleanor Kilgallen in Casting Consultants; 1952, MCA, NY; 1958, MCA West Coast; 1962 vp talent dept U; 1980 formed K-S Productions with Eleanor Kilgallen.

JAMES, Sonny (Jimmie Loden): Singer. b. Hackleburg, AL, May 1, 1929. Recording artist; Grand Ole Opry perf.
Films inc: Second Fiddle to a Steel Guitar; Las Vegas Hillbillies; Nashville Rebel; Hillbilly in a Haunted House.

JAMESON, Jerry: Dir. b. Hollywood. Began as editorial asst, later edtr, supv edtr Danny Thomas prodns, before dir. TV inc: Mod Squad; Dan August; Ironside; Hawaii Five-O; Cannon; Streets of San Francisco; The Elevator; Heat Wave; Hurricane; Terror on the Fortieth Floor; The Secret Night Caller; The Lives of Jenny Dolan; The Deadly Tower; Call of the Wild; Brahman; A Fire in the Sky; High Noon Part II--The Return of Will Kane; Stand By Your Man; Killing At Hell's Gate; Hotline; Starflight--The Plane That Couldn't Land; Cowboy; This Girl for Hire; The Great Survivors; The Cowboy And The Ballerina; Stormin' Home (& prod-wri).
Films inc: Dirt Gang; The Bat People; Brute Core; Airport 77; Raise the Titanic.

JAMPOLIS, Neil Peter: Lght Dsgn. b. Mar 14, 1943. Bway inc: Borstal Boy; One Flew Over the Cuckoo's Nest; Sherlock Holmes (Tony-1975); The Innocents; Kipling; Rap Master Ronnie (Off-Bway); also lght dsn for Pilobolus Dance Theatre, many operas.

JANIS, Conrad: Act. b. NYC, Feb 11, 1928. Films inc: Snafu; Margie; That Hagen Girl; Airport 75; The Duchess and the Dirtwater Fox; Roseland; The Buddy Holly Story; Oh, God! Book II.
TV inc: Mork and Mindy; Quark; Insight/Every Ninety Seconds; The Red-Light Sting.
Bway inc: Junior Miss; Dark of the Moon; The Next Half Hour; The Brass Ring; Time Out for Ginger; Visit to a Small Planet; Make a Million; Sunday in New York; Marathon 33; The Front Page; Same Time Next Year.

JANKOWSKI, Gene F.: Exec. b. Buffalo, NY, May 21, 1934. e. Canisius, BS; MI State U, MA. Joined CBS Radio Network Sales 1961 as account exec; eastern sls mgr 1966; moved to CBS TV network as account exec 1969; gen sls mgr WCBS-TV 1970; dir sales 1970; vp sales, CBS TV 1973; vp finance & planning 1974; vp, controller 1976; vp adm/Jan 1977; exec vp CBS Broadcast Group July 1977; named pres Oct 1977.

JANNI, Joseph: Prod. b. Milan, Italy, May 21, 1916. e. Milan U; Rome Film School. Films inc: The Glass Mountain; White Corridors; Something Money Can't Buy; Romeo and Juliet; A Town Like Alice; Savage Innocents; Billy Liar; Darling; Modesty Blaise; Far From the Madding Crowd; Poor Cow; Sunday, Bloody Sunday; Made; Yanks.

JANSSEN, Werner: Comp-Cond. b. NYC, Jun 1, 1900. e. Dartmouth Coll. Cond symph orchs throughout world.
Film scores inc: The General Died at Dawn; Blockade; Eternally Yours, Captain Kidd; Guest in the House; The Southerner; Acting--Lee Strasberg and the Actors Studio (doc).
Bway inc: Ziegfeld Follies of 1925-26.
TV inc: Ghost of Canterville.

JARMAN, Claude, Jr: Act. b. Nashville, TN, Sep 27, 1934. e. Vanderbilt U. Started as child actor. Dir San Francisco Int'l Film Festival, 1967-1979.
Films inc: The Yearling (Honorary Oscar-1946); High Barbaree; Intruder in the Dust; Rio Grande; Hangman's Knot; Fair Wind to Java; The Great Locomotive Chase.
TV inc: Centennial.

JARRE, Maurice: Comp. b.Lyon, France, 1924. Films inc: Hotel des Invalides; La Tetre Contre les Murs; Eyes Without a Face; Crack in the Mirror; The Longest Day; Lawrence of Arabia (Oscar-1962); Sundays

and Cybele; Weekend at Dunkirk; Dr Zhivago (Oscar-1965); Is Paris Burning?; The Professionals; Five Card Stud; Isadora; The Damned; Ryan's Daughter; Mohammad, Messenger of God; Two Solitudes; Crossed Swords; Winter Kills; The Black Marble; The Last Flight of Noah's Ark; Resurrection; Lion of the Desert; Taps; Don't Cry, It's Only Thunder; Firefox; Young Doctors In Love; The Year of Living Dangerously; Au nom de tous Miens (For Those I Loved); Dreamscape; A Passage To India (Oscar-1984); Witness; Mad Max Beyond Thunderdrome.
TV inc: Shogun; Enola Gay--The Men, The Mission, The Atomic Bomb; Coming Out of the Ice; The Sky's the Limit; Samson and Delilah.

JARREAU, Al: Singer. b. Mar 12, 1940. Recording artist. (Grammys-(4)-jazz vocal-1977, 1979, 1981; Pop vocal 1981.) TV inc: Sheena Easton--Act One; Night Of 100 Stars II.

JARRICO, Paul: Wri. b. Los Angeles, Jan 12, 1915. Films inc: Salt of the Earth; Tom, Dick and Harry; Thousands Cheer; The White Tower; Not Wanted; The Girl Most Likely; Assassination in Sarajevo.

JARRIEL, Tom: TV News. b. LaGrange, GA. e. U of Houston. Started at KPRC, Houston, as copyboy, became news editor before moving to Atlanta 1965 as ABC corr; 1968, Washington corr; 1978, senior regional corr; anchor World News Tonight-- The Weekend Report; contributor to 20/20. TV inc: Death in a Southwest Prison; The Uranium Factor; Moment of Crisis--Hyatt Disaster (Emmy-corr-1981); Moment of Crisis--Berlin Wall (Emmy-corr-1981); Moment of Crisis--Vietnam Withdrawal (Emmy-corr-1981); Crime and Punishment; Under the Israeli Thumb; Life After Doomsday; Apache--The Tank Chopper; Moment of Crisis--The Munich Massacre; Watergate--An Untold Story.

JARROTT, Charles: Dir. b. London, Jun 16, 1927. Films inc: Anne of the Thousand Days; Mary, Queen of Scots; Lost Horizon; The Dove; The Littlest Horse Thieves; The Other Side of Midnight; The Last Flight of Noah's Ark; Condorman; The Amateur.
TV inc: The Hot Potato Boys; Roll On; Girls in a Birdcage; The Picture of Dorian Gray; Rain; The Young Elizabeth; A Case of Libel; Dr. Jekyll and Mr. Hyde; A Married Man.
Thea inc: The Duel; Galileo; The Basement; Tea Party; The Dutchman.

JARVIS, Graham: Act. b. Toronto, Canada, Aug 25, 1930. e. Williams Coll. Bway inc: The Best Man; The Investigation; Halfway Up a Tree; The Rocky Horror Show.
Films inc: The Out of Towners; Cold Turkey; The Organization; What's Up, Doc?; Prophecy; Middle Age Crazy; The Amateur; Mr. Mom; Deal of the Century; Silkwood; Mischief.
TV inc: Mary Hartman, Mary Hartman; Forever Fernwood; Arthur the Kid; Border Pals; The Two Lives of Carol Letner; A Piano for Mrs Cimino; Making the Grade; Cass Malloy; There Goes The Neighborhood; Carpool; Off Sides; Draw! (PC).

JASON, Rick: Act. b. NYC, May 21, 1926. e. AADA. Bway debut, 1949, Now I Lay Me Down to Sleep.
Films inc: Sombrero; Saracen Blade; This Is My Love; The Lieutenant Wore Skirts;The Wayward Bus; Partners.
TV inc: The Case of the Dangerous Robin; Combat; The Best Place To Be.

JAYSTON, Michael: Act. b. Nottingham, England, Oct 28, 1935. With Old Vic Theatre Co., Bristol Old Vic. Thea inc: The Sound of Music.
Films inc: Cromwell; The Nelson Affair; Nicholas and Alexandra; A Midsummer Night's Dream; The Public Eye; Dominique (made in 1977).
TV inc: She Fell Among Thieves; Tinker, Tailor, Soldier, Spy; Jane Eyre.

JEAKINS, Dorothy: Dsgn. b. San Diego, CA, Jan 11, 1914. Films inc: Joan of Arc (Oscar-1948); Samson and Delilah (Oscar-1950); My Cousin Rachel; The Greatest Show on Earth; The Ten Commandments; The Childrens Hour; The Music Man; The Night of the Iguana (Oscar-1964); The Sound of Music; Hawaii; The Way We Were; The Betsy; North Dallas Forty; Audrey Rose; The Postman Always Rings

Twice; On Golden Pond.

Bway inc: Major Barbara; Too Late The Phalarope; The World of Suzie Wong.

JEAN, Gloria (nee Schoonover): Act. b. Buffalo, NY, Apr 14, 1928. Films inc: The Underpup; Pardon My Rhythm; If I Had My Way; Moonlight in Vermont; She's My Lovely; I'll Remember April; Fairy Tale Murder; Copacabana; I Surrender, Dear; There's a Girl in My Heart; The Ladies' Man.

JEAN, Norma: Singer. b. Wellston, OK, Jan 30, 1938. C&W recording artist. Joined Porter Wagner Show on national TV in the Mid 60's; later joined the Grand Ole Opry.

JEANMAIRE, Renee (Zizi): Act-Ballet star. b. Paris, 1924. Films inc: Hans Christian Andersen; Anything Goes; Folies Bergere; Charmante Garcons; Black Tights.

Bway inc: Can-Can (revival).

JEFFERSON, Herb, Jr: Act. b. Jersey City, NJ, Sep 28. TV inc: The Silent Force; Battlestar Galactica.

Thea inc: The Great White Hope; Murderous Angels; The Blacks; Dream on Monkey Mountain.

JEFFREY, Tom M.: Prod-Dir. b. Sydney, Australia, Sep 26, 1938. Films inc: The Removalists; Weekend of Shadows; The Odd Angry Shot.

TV inc: Pastures of the Blue Crane; Devlin; The Best of Friends.

JEFFREYS, Anne: Act. b. Goldsboro, NC, Jan 26, 1923. Powers model. On screen from 1943.

Films inc: X Marks the Spot; I Married an Angel; Step Lively; Sing Your Way Home; Riffraff; Return of the Bad Men.

Bway inc: Street Scene; Kiss Me Kate; Three Wishers for Jamie; Kismet.

TV inc: Topper; Love That Jill; Delphi Bureau; Beggarman, Thief; Finder Of Lost Loves.

JEFFRIES, Lionel: Act. b. London, England. Films inc: High Terrace; Bhowani Junction; Lust for Life; The Nun's Story; Two-Way Stretch; The Trials of Oscar Wilde; Fanny; The Notorious Landlady; Wrong Arm of the Law; The First Men in the Moon; Call Me Bwana; You Must Be Joking; The Crimson Blade; Arriverderci Baby; Spy With the Cold Nose; Camelot; Chitty Chitty Bang Bang; Who Slew Auntie Roo?; Eye Witness; Railway Children (& dir-sp); Gingerbread House; Baxter (& dir); The Amazing Mr. Blundern; Water Babies (dir); Better Late Than Never.

TV inc: Cream in My Coffee.

Thea inc: Two Into One.

JENKINS, George: Dsgn. b. Baltimore, MD, 1908. e. U PA. Started as asst to Jo Mielziner. Bway inc: Early to Bed; Mexican Hayride; I Remember Mama; Dark of the Moon; Common Ground; Strange Fruit; Are You With It?; Lost In the Stars; Bell, Book and Candle; Three Wishes for Jamie; Gently Does It; The Immoralist; The Bad Seed; Ankles Aweigh; The Desk Set; Too Late the Phalarope; The Happiest Millionaire; The Merry Widow; Two for the Seesaw; Tall Story; The Miracle Worker; 13 Daughters; One More River; Critic's Choice; A Thousand Clowns; Jennie; Everybody Out, The Castle Is Sinking; Catch Me If You Can; Generation; Wait Until Dark (& London); The Only Game In Town; Night Watch.

Films inc: The Best Years of Our Lives; The Secret Life of Walter Mitty; A Song Is Born; The Miracle Worker; Klute; 1776; The Paper Chase; The Parallax View; Funny Lady; All the President's Men (Oscar-1976); Comes a Horesman; The China Syndrome; Starting Over; The Postman Always Rings Twice; Sophie's Choice.

TV inc: Out of the Dark; The Royal Family; Annie Get Your Gun; Mary Martin Specials; The Dollmaker.

JENNER, Bruce: Act. b. Mt Kisco, NY, Oct 28, 1949. Former Olympic decathlon champ. TV inc: America Alive! (co-host); Bob Hope's All-Star Comedy Look at the New Season; Grambling's White Tiger; Doug Henning's World of Magic (1982); Grandpa, Will You Run With Me?; John Schneider's Christmas Holiday; CHiPS; Olympic Gala; Donald Duck's 50th Birthda y.

JENNINGS, Peter: TV news. b. Toronto, Canada, Jul. 29, 1938. e. Carleton U; Rider College, L1D. Began as newsman CFJR (radio), Ottawa, later with CJOH-TV and CBC before becoming co-anchor of first national news program on Canadian commercial network, CTV; joined ABC, 1964 as correspondent in NY; 1965, anchor Peter Jennings with the News; 1967, National correspondent ABC News; 1969, moved to overseas assignments; 1975, Washington correspondent and anchor for AM America; 1977, chief Foregin correspondent; 1978, Foreign Desk Anchor, World News Tonight; Aug. 1983, Anchor, Sr Editor World News Tonight. TV inc: Report on Slaughter of Baby Seals; Personal Note/Beirut (Emmy-corr-1982) The Arab World; FDR; JFK; War and Power--the Rise of Syria; To Save Our Schools, To Save Our Children; Ask The Media; The Fire Unleashed.

JENNINGS, Talbot: Wri. b. Shoshone, ID. e. Harvard, MA. Films inc: Mutiny on the Bounty; The Good Earth; Romeo and Juliet; Northwest Passage; Frenchman's Creek; Anna and the King of Siam; Across the Wide Missouri; Escape to Burma; Pearl of the South Pacific; Untamed; The Naked Maja; The Sons of Katy Elder.Died May F030, 1985) T

JENNINGS, Waylon: Singer. b. Littlefield, TX, Jun 15, 1937. C&W recording artist. Featured on Grand Ole Opry TV shows. Films inc: Nashville Rebel. TV inc: Anatomy of Pop; American Swing-Around; Carl Smith's Country Music Hall; The Dukes of Hazzard (title song); The Unbroken Circle-A Tribute To Mother Maybelle Carter; Waylon-Starring Waylon Jennings; The Oklahoma City Dolls; The Executioner's Song (songs); My Heroes Have Always Been Cowboys (cable); Johnny Cash--Christmas On The Road.

Albums inc: The Outlaws; Ol' Waylon; Waylon & Willie; Greatest Hits.

(Grammy-country vocal duo-1969).

JENS, Salome: Act. b. Milwaukee, WI, May 8, 1935. e. Northwestern U. Thea inc: Sixth Finger in a Five Finger Glove; The Bald Soprano; The Disenchanted; Deirdre of the Sorrows; USA; Freud in A Far Country; Night Life; The Winter's Tale; First One Asleep; I'm Solomon; A Patriot for Me; Mary Stuart; The Ride Across Lake Constance; Antony and Cleopatra; A Break in the Skin.

Films inc: Angel Baby; The Fool Killer; Seconds; Me, Natalie; Cloud Dancer; Harry's War.

TV inc: From Here To Eternity; From Here To Eternity-The War Years; The Golden Moment-An Olympic Love Story; The Two Lives of Carol Letner; Tomorrow's Child; Uncommon Valor; Grace Kelly; A Killer in the Family; Playing With Fire.

JENSEN, Maren: Act. b. Arcadia, CA, Sep 23. TV inc: Hardy Boys/ Nancy Drew Mysteries; Battlestar Galactica. Films inc: Beyond The Reef; Deadly Blessing.

JENSON, Roy Cameron: Act. b. Calgary, Canada, Feb 1935. e. UCLA, BA. Films inc: Harper; Will Penny; Water Hole 3; Paint Your Wagon; Fools; Big Jake; Sometimes a Great Notion; Judge Roy Bean; The Glass House; The Getaway; Deadly Honeymoon; Dillinger; Chinatown; Breakout; The Wind and the Lion; Breakout Pass; The Dutchess and the Dirt Water Fox; The Car.

TV inc: The Wish; Bonanza.

JERGENS, Adele: Act. b. NYC, Nov 26, 1917. W of Glenn Langan. Films inc: Edge of Doom; Side Street; Sugarfoot; Show Boat; Somebody Loves Me; Overland Pacific; Miami Story; Fireman Save My Child; Strange Lady in Town; The Cobweb.

JEWISON, Norman: Prod-Dir. b. Toronto, Canada, Jul 21, 1926. e. U of Toronto, BA. Act, wri for BBC. Prod, dir TV for CBC.

Films inc: Forty Pounds of Trouble; The Thrill of it All; Send Me No Flowers; The Cincinnati Kid; In The Heat of the Night; The Russians Are Coming, The Russians Are Coming; Fiddler On The Roof; Jesus Christ, Superstar; Rollerball; F.I.S.T.; And Justice For All; The Dogs of War (exec prod); Best Friends; Iceman (prod); A Soldier's Story.

TV inc: Judy Garland; Harry Belafonte; Danny Kaye; Andy Williams specials; Wayne and Shuster; Showtime; Barris Beat.

JHABVALA, Ruth Prawer: Wri. b. Cologne, Germany, 1927. Films inc: The Householder; Shakespeare Wallah; Roseland; Quartet; Hullabaloo Over Georgie and Bonnie's Pictures; Jane Austen in Manhattan; Heat and Dust; The Courtesans of Bombay (& prod-dir); The Bostonians.

JILLIAN, Ann (Ann Jura Nauseda): Act. b. Cambridge, MA, Jan 29, 1951. e. Pierce Jr. College; LA; AA. Grad of LA Civic Light Opera courses. Films inc: Babes In Toyland; Gypsy; Mr. Mom. Bway inc: Sugar Babies.
TV inc: Hazel; Sammy The Way Out Seal; Blue Eyed Horse (Chrysler Theatre); Partridge Family; Odd Fathers; It's A Living; Doug Henning's World of Magic; America at Play; Women Who Rate at 10; Perry Como's Easter in Guadalajara; The Rainbow Girl; Mae West; Texaco Star Theatre--Opening Night; Malibu; The Magic Planet; Jennifer Slept Here; Girls of the White Orchid; It's the Real Thing--Television's Greatest Commercials IV (host); Bob Hope's USO Christmas in Beirut; Ellis Island; This Wife For Hire.

JOBERT, Marlene: Act. b. Algiers, 1943. Films inc: Masculin Feminin; Le Voleur; L'Astragale; Rider on the Rain; Last Known Address; Catch Me a Spy; Ten Days' Wonder; The Good and the Bad; The Wonderful Crook; The Accuser; Your Turn, My Turn; La Guerre Des Policiers; Une Sale Affaire (A Filthy Business); L'Amour Nu (Naked Love); Effraction (Break-In); Les Cavaliers de l'Orage (The Horsemen of the Storm); Souvenirs, Souvenirs (Memories, Memories).
TV inc: Mademoiselle Pygmalion; Les Quatre Chemins.

JOBIM, Antonio Carlos: Comp-Mus. b. Rio de Janeiro, 1927. Mus dir with Odeon Records, credited with introducing bossa nova with Joao Gilberto recording. Comps inc: Desafinado; One Note Samba; The Girl From Ipanema; Quiet Nights; Meditation.
Films inc: Black Orpheus; The Adventurers; Gabriela.

JOEL, Billy: Singer. b. NYC, May 9, 1949. Singer, songwriter, musician. Recording artist. (Grammys-(5)-record of year, song of year-1978; album of year, pop vocal-1979; rock vocal-1980).
Albums inc: The Stranger; 52d Street; Glass Houses.

JOFFE, Charles H.: Exec Prod. b. NYC. Films inc: Don't Drink the Water; Take the Money and Run; Everything You Always Wanted to Know About Sex But Were Afraid to Ask; Love and Death; Annie Hall (Oscar-1977); Play It Again, Sam; Bananas; Sleeper; Interiors; Manhattan; Stardust Memories; Arthur; A Midsummer Night's Sex Comedy; Zelig; The House of God; The Purple Rose Of Cairo.
TV inc: Woody Allen Specials; Good Time Harry; The Acorn People; Star of the Family.

JOFFREY, Robert: Dancer-Chor. b. Seattle, WA, Dec 24, 1930. On faculty of High School for the Performing Arts, NYC, 1950-55; faculty American Ballet Theatre school; resident chor NY City Center Opera 1955-1961; founded City Center Joffrey Ballet 1956; chor NBC-TV operas 1955, 1957, 1958.
Ballets inc: Persephone; Scaramouche; Bal Masque, Pierot Lunaire; Harpsichord; Astarte; Remembrances.

JOHAR, I.S.: Act. b. India. Films inc: Harry Black and the Tiger; North West Frontier; Lawrence of Arabia; Death on the Nile.
(Died March 10, 1984).

JOHN, Elton (Reginald Kenneth Dwight): Act-Sngwri. b. Pinner, Mx, England, Mar 25, 1947. Played (as Reg Dwight) with nondescript rock groups around London; In 1967 met Berni Taupin, changed his name, they began collaborating, in 1969 first hit album Elton John led to p.a.'s which established him as a leading rock star, retired in 1975 having split with Taupin; resumed career 1979.
Songs inc: (with Taupin) The Bitch Is Back; Someone Saved My Life Tonight; Country Comfort.
Albums include Honky Chateau; Don't Shoot Me I'm Only the Piano Player; Yellow Brick Road; Blue Moves; Elton John's Greatest; A Single Man.
Films inc: Friends (score); Tommy (act); Oh Heavenly Dog (songs); Eric Clapton and His Rolling Hotel.

JOHNS, Glynis: Act. b. Pretoria, South Africa, Oct 5, 1923. In ballet, London stage, films as child. Thea debut 1935, Buckie's Bears; film debut 1936 South Riding.
Thea inc: (London) St Helena; The Children's Hour; The Melody

That Got Lost; Quiet Weekend; The Way Things Go; The King's Mare; Come As You Are; 13 rue de l'Amour. (Bway) Gertie; Major Barbara; Too True to be Good; A Little Night Music (Tony-1973).
Films inc: Prison Without Bars; 49th Parallel; Perfect Strangers; Frieda; Miranda; An Ideal Husband; State Secret; The Card; Rob Roy; The Beachcomber; The Court Jester; The Day They Gave Babies Away; The Sundowners; The Spider's Web; The Chapman Report; Mary Poppins; Dear Brigitte; Don't Just Stand There; Lock Up Your Daughters; Under Milkwood; Vault of Horror.
TV inc: Glynis; Noel Coward's Star Quality; Mrs Amworth; All You Need is Love; Across a Crowded Room; Little Gloria--Happy At Last; Spraggue.

JOHNSON, Alan: Chor. Originally a dancer on Bway in New Girl in Town; West Side Story; No Strings; Anyone Can Whistle; Hallelujah Baby; later worked as chor in Europe. Bway (chor) inc: The First; Ann Reinking--Music Moves Me (& dir)(Off-Bway).
TV inc: George M!; Jack Lemmon in 'S Wonderful, 'S Marvelous, 'S Gershwin (Emmy-1972); Shirley MacLaine--If They Could See Me Now; The Shirley MacLaine Special--Where Do We Go From Here; Shirley MacLaine--Every Little Movement (Emmy-1980); Texaco Star Theatre--Opening Night; Shirley MacLaine.
Films inc: The Producers; Blazing Saddles; Young Frankenstein; High Anxiety; History of the World--Part One (asso prod); To Be Or Not To Be (dir).

JOHNSON, Arte: Act. b. Chicago, Jan 20. Films inc: Miracle in the Rain; The Subterraneans; The Third Day; The President's Analyst; Love At First Bite.
TV inc: Laugh-In (Emmy-1969); Knockout; Baggy Pants and the Nitwits (voice); The Bear Who Slept Through Christmas (voice); Detour To Terror; The Love Tapes; The Incredible Book Escape (voice); Misunderstood Monsters (voice); Condominium; Tales of the Apple Dumpling Gang; The Making of a Male Model; Glitter.

JOHNSON, Ben: Act. b. Foreacre, OK, Jun 13, 1918. Began film career as a wrangler, stuntman. Competed in rodeos. Acting debut, Mighty Joe Young.
Films inc: The Sugarland Express; Dillinger; The Getaway; The Train Robbers; The Last Picture Show (Oscar-supp-1971); The Wild Bunch; Grayeagle; The Swarm; The Hunter; Terror Train; Tex; Champions; Red Dawn.
TV inc: Wild Times; The Shadow Riders.

JOHNSON, Bruce: Prod-Wri. b. Oakland, CA, Jul 7, 1939. e. USC, BA. TV inc: Gomer Pyle; Jim Nabors Hour; Arnie; The Little People; The New Temperatures Rising Show; Sierra; Excuse My Friend; Alice; Blansky's Beauties; Quark; Mork and Mindy; Angie; Hot WACS (supv prod); The New Odd Couple (prod); Littleshots (prod).

JOHNSON, Charles F.: Prod. b. Feb 12. e. Howard U, BA; Howard U Law School, JD; U DE. TV inc: The Rockford Files (asso prod 1974-1976; prod 1976- 1980) (Emmy-1978); Baa Baa Black Sheep; The Black Filmmakers Hall of Fame; Hellinger's Law; Simon and Simon; Voices of Our People; Bret Maverick; Magnum, P.I; Fade Out--The Erosion of Black Images in the Media (int).

JOHNSON, Don: Act. b. Flatt Creek, MO, Dec 15. Worked with ACT, San Francisco. Films inc: The Magic Garden of Stanley Sweetheart; The Harrad Experiment; A Boy and His Dog.
TV inc: Amateur Night; The Rebels; From Here To Eternity--The War Years; Beulah Land; Revenge of the Stepford Wives; Elvis and the Beauty Queen; The Two Lives of Carol Letner; Six Pack.

JOHNSON, Kenneth A.: Dir-Wri-Prod. b. Pine Bluff, AR, Oct 26, 1942. e. Carnegie Tech. TV inc: The Mike Douglas Show (prod); An Evening of Edgar Allan Poe (prod-wri); The Last Bride of Salem (wri-prod); The Bionic Woman (exec prod); The Incredible Hulk (wri-prod); A Death in the Family (wri-prod); Senior Trip; V; Hot Pursuit.

JOHNSON, Lamont: Dir-Prod. b. Stockton, CA, Sep 30, 1922. Films inc: Covenant with Death; The Mackenzie Break; A Gunfight; The Groundstar Conspiracy; You'll Like My Mother; The Last American Hero; Lipstick; One on One; Somebody Killed Her Husband; Cattle Annie and Little Britches; Spacehunter--Adventures in the Forbidden Zone.

TV inc: The Defenders; Profiles in Courage; Twilight Zone; My Sweet Charlie; That Certain Summer; The Execution of Private Slovik; Fear on Trial; Sunnyside; Off The Minnesota Strip; Crisis at Central High; Escape From Iran--The Canadian Caper; Dangerous Company; Life of the Party--The Story of BeAtrice; Ernie Kovacs--Between the Laughter; Wallenberg--A Hero's Story (& co-prod).

Thea inc: The Egg; Yes is for a Very Young Man.

JOHNSON, Lynn-Holly: Act. b. Chicago, 1959. Former iceskater with Ice Capades. Films inc: Ice Castles; The Watcher in the Woods; For Your Eyes Only. TV inc: More Than Murder.

JOHNSON, Mary Lea: Prod. W of Martin Richards. Bway inc: Sweeney Todd (Tony-1979); Goodbye, Fidel; Crimes of the Heart; A Doll's Life; Foxfire; Grind. Off-Bway inc: Mayor.

Films inc: Fort Apache, The Bronx.

JOHNSON, Richard: Act. b. Upminster, England, Jul 30, 1927. e. RADA. Films inc: Captain Horatio Hornblower; Never So Few; Cairo; The Haunting; The Pumpkin Eater; Operation Crossbow; Khartoum; Deadlier Than the Male; Oedipus the King; A Twist of Sand; Lady Hamilton; Some Girls Do; Julius Caesar; Hennessy; Aces High; The Making of a Lady; Zombie; Screamers; The Comeback.

Thea inc: The Complaisant Lover; The Devils; Thomas and the King; Blithe Spirit; The Guardsman.

TV inc: A Marriage; Murder on Your Mind; Portrait of a Rebel-Margaret Sanger; Haywire; The Monster Club; Cymbeline; The Aerodrome.

JOHNSON, Van: Act. b. Newport, RI, Aug 28, 1916. In vaudeville, on Bway, New Faces of 1937. On screen in 1941 in Murder in the Big House.

Films inc: The War Against Mrs. Hadley; Thirty Seconds Over Tokyo; Romance of Rosy Ridge; State of the Union; Command Decision; Remains to be Seen; The Caine Mutiny; Brigadoon; Miracle in the Rain; Battle Squadron; Spider on the Wall; Eagles Over London; The Kidnapping of the President; The Purple Rose Of Cairo.

TV inc: The Girl on the Late Late Show; McMillan & Wife; Aloha Paradise; Love Boat (spec); The Kennedy Center Honors 1982; John Schneider's Christmas Holiday; Glitter; Night Of 100 Stars II; The 39th Annual Tony Awards.

Thea inc: The Bells Are Ringing; I Do! I Do!; The Music Man; La Cage aux Folles.

JOHNSTONE, Anna Hill: Cos dsgn. b. Greenville, SC., April 7, 1913. e. Barnard, BA. Bway inc: Temper the Wind; For Love Or Money; Lost In the Stars; The Country Girl; Bell, Book and Candle; The Autumn Garden; Flight Into Egypt; The Children's Hour; Tea And Sympathy; The Tender Trap; The Chalk Garden (supv); The Egghead; The Man In the Dog Suit; Sweet Bird of Youth; Triple Play; After the Fall; The Investigation.

Films inc: Portrait of Jennie; East of Eden; Baby Doll; Edge of the City; A Face In the Crowd; Splendor In the Grass; David and Lisa; America, America; Ladybug, Ladybug; The Pawnbroker; FailSafe; The Group; Bye, Bye Braverman; The Night They Raided Minsky's; The Godfather; Play It Again, Sam; Come Back Charleston Blue; The Effect of Gamma Rays On Man-In-The-Moon-Marigolds; Summer Wishes, Winter Dreams; The Taking of Pelham 1-2-3; Stepford Wives; Dog Day Afternoon; The Last Tycoon; The Next Man; King Of the Gypsies; Going In Style; Prince Of the City; The Verdict; Ragtime; Daniel; Heaven; Garbo Talks.

JOLLEY, Stan: Art Dir. b. NYC, May 17, 1926. e. USC, BA. Films inc: The Good Guys and The Bad Guys; The Phynx; City Beneath the Sea; The War Between Men and Women; Walking Tall; Framed; Drum; Swarm; Superman; Americathon; Witness.

TV inc: The Strangers; Punch and Jody; Eagle One; Swiss Family Robinson; Flood; Howard, The Amazing Mr Hughes; Rescue from Gilligan's Island; Happily Ever After; A Very Special Love; The Great Survivors; No Man's Land.

JONES, Allan: Singer-Act. b. Scranton, PA, 1907. Films inc: A Night at the Opera; Rose Marie; Showboat; A Day at the Races; The Firefly; Honeymoon in Bali; The Great Victor Herbert; The Boys from Syracuse; One Night in the Tropics; Moonlight in Havana; Crazy House; The Singing Sheriff; The Senorita From the West; Stage to Thunder Rock; A Swingin' Summer.

JONES, Carolyn: Act. b. Amarillo, TX, Apr 28, 1932. On screen from 1952 in The Turning Point.

Films inc: Road to Bali; Desiree; Baby Face Nelson; House of Wax; Seven Year Itch; The Tender Trap; The Bachelor Party; A Hole in the Head; Ice Palace; Sail a Crooked Ship; A Ticklish Affair; Good Luck, Miss Wyckoff.

TV inc: Addams Family; Roots; The French Atlantic Affair; The Dream Merchants; Midnight Lace; Capitol.

Thea inc: Summer and Smoke; Live

(Died Aug. 3, 1983).

JONES, Chuck: Prod-Dir. b. Spokane, WA, Sep 21, 1912. e. Chouinard Art Institute. Dir, Warner Bros Animation until 1962 where he created and dir Roadrunner & Coyote; Pepe le Pew; dir and helped create Bugs Bunny; Porky Pig; Daffy Duck.

Cartoons inc: Nelly's Folly; Ersatz; (Oscar-1961); Beep Prepared; The Dot and the Line (Oscar-1965).

Films inc: Gay Purree; The Phantom Tollbooth.

TV inc: Raggedy Ann and Andy in the Pumpkin Who Couldn't Smile; Bugs Bunny's Bustin' Out All Over; Daffy Duck's Thanks-For-Giving Special; The Bugs Bunny Mystery Special; Uncensored Cartoons.

JONES, Clark: Dir. b. Clearfield, PA, Apr 10, 1920. TV inc: Your Hit Parade; Ford 50th Anniversary Show; Sleeping Beauty; Cinderella; Romeo and Juliet; The Fourposter; Peter Pan; Sid Caesar Show; Patrice Munsel Series; Bell Telephone Hour; Perry Como Specials; Carol Burnett Show; Dinah Shore Special; Carol Channing Specials; Twigs; 6 Rms Rv Vu; Tony Awards; 1981 Tony Awards; The Way They Were; Night of 100 Stars; Sophisticated Ladies (PPV); Parade of Stars; Night Of 100 Stars II; The 39th Annual Tony Awards.

JONES, Dean: Act. b. Decatur, AL, Jan 25, 1931. e. Asbury Coll; UCLA. Films inc: The Great American Pastime; Jailhouse Rock; Under the Yum Yum Tree; That Darn Cat; Any Wednesday; The Horse in the Gray Flannel Suit; The Love Bug; Snowball Express; The Shaggy D.A.; Herbie Goes to Monte Carlo.

TV inc: Ensign O'Toole; The Teddy Bears; The Long Days of Summer; Aloha Paradise; I Love Her Anyway; Kraft Salutes Walt Disney World's 10th Anniversary; Herbie, The Love Bug.

Thea inc: There Was a Little Girl; Company.

JONES, Gemma: Act. b. London, Dec 4, 1942. e. RADA. Thea inc: Baal; Alfie; The Cavern; The Pastime of M Robert; Portrait of a Queen; Next of Kin; The Marriage of Figaro; And A Nightingale; Breaking The Silence.

Films inc: The Devils.

TV inc: The Lie; The Way of the World; The Duchess of Duke Street; The Merchant of Venice.

JONES, Grace: Singer-act. b. Jamaica, May 19. e. Syracuse U. Worked as model, appeared in several Italian films before career as a singer. Films inc: Conan the Destroyer; A View To A Kill.

JONES, Henry: Act. b. Philadelphia, Aug 1, 1912. e. St Joseph's Coll, AB. Films inc: Never Too Late; Stay Away Joe; Support Your Local Sheriff; Rascal; Angel in My Pocket; Butch Cassidy & the Sundance Kid; Rabbit Run; Cock-eyed Cowboys of Calico County; Dirty Dingus Magee; Support Your Local Gunman; Skin Game; Napoleon & Samantha; Tom Sawyer; Pete n Tillie; The Outfit; Nine to Five; Deathtrap.

Bway inc: Hamlet; The Time of your Life; Village Green; My Sister Eileen; This Is the Army; The Solid Gold Cadillac; The Bad Seed; Sunrise at Campobello (Tony-supp-1958) Advise and Consent; Comedians.

TV inc: California Gold Rush; Quick and Quiet; Tales of the Apple Dumpling Gang; Gun Shy; Scene Of the Crime; Codename Foxfire.

JONES, Jack: Singer-Act. b. Los Angeles, Jan 14, 1942. S of Irene Hervey and Allan Jones. Professional debut with parents act, Las Vegas; works niteries, concerts. Films inc: (Act) Juke Box Rhythm; The Comeback. (Title Song) Love With the Proper Stranger; Where Love Has Gone; A Ticklish Affair; A Battle For Anzio Kotch.

TV inc: (act) The Palace; Holiday Tribute to Radio City. (Title song) Funny Face; Love Boat; Condominium; The Comeback.

Recs inc: Lollipops and Roses (Grammy-voc-1961); Wive and Lovers (Grammy-voc-1963).

JONES, James Earl: Act. b. Arkabutla, MS, Jan 17, 1931. e. U of MI, BA. S of Robert Earl Jones. Films inc: Dr. Strangelove; The Comedians; The End of the Road; The Great White Hope; The Man; Malcolm X (doc); Claudine; The Swashbuckler; The Bingo Long Traveling All-Stars and Motor Kings; The River Niger; The Heretic; The Greatest; The Last Remake of Beau Geste; A Piece of the Action; The Bushido Blade; Conan the Barbarian; Blood Tide; Return of the Jedi; City Limits.

TV inc: Trumpets of the Lord; Black Omnibus (host-narrator); King Lear; The Cay; Interrupted Journey; A Day Without Sunshine; Jesus of Nazareth; The Greatest Thing that Almost Happened; Roots; Paris; Paul Robeson; Guyana Tragedy--The Story of Jim Jones; Golden Moment-An Olympic Love Story; Philby, Burgess and MacLean; The Knowledge; Misunderstood Monsters (voice); Amy and the Angel; The Lions Of Etosha--King Of The Beasts (narr); Las Vegas Strip War; The Atlanta Child Murders; Night Of 100 Stars II; Me & Mom.

Bway inc: Sunrise at Campobello; The Cool World; Infidel Caesar; A Hand is on the Gate; The Great White Hope (Tony-1969); Les Blancs; The Iceman Cometh; Of Mice and Men; Paul Robeson; A Lesson From Aloes; Othello; Master Howard...And the Boys.

(Grammy-spoken word-1976).

JONES, Jennifer (Phyllis Isley): Act. b. Tulsa, OK, 1919. e. AADA. Toured with parents' stock company as a child. On screen in 1939 under real name in New Frontier; Dick Tracy's G-Men. On screen from 1942 as Jennifer Jones.

Films inc: The Song of Bernadette (Oscar-1944); Since You Went Away; Love Letters; Duel in the Sun; Love is a Many Splendored Thing; Portrait of Jennie; Ruby Gentry; The Barretts of Wimpole Street; A Farewell to Arms; Tender is the Night; The Towering Inferno; Eagles Over London.

JONES, Quincy: Comp-Arr-Cond-Prod. b. Chicago, Mar 14, 1933. e. Seattle U; Berklee School of Mus; Boston Cons. Trumpeter, arr for Lionel Hampton orch, 1950-53; arr for orchs, singers, inc: Ray Anthony; Count Basie; Sarah Vaughn; Peggy Lee; prod 10 gold records for pop songstress Lesley Gore in the 60s; also introduced and prod The Brothers Johnson.

Films inc: Pawnbroker; Mirage; The Slender Thread; For The Love Of Ivy; In Cold Blood; In the Heat of the Night; The Wiz; Fast Forward; The Slugger's Wife.

TV inc: Roots (Emmy-1977).

Songs inc: Evening in Paris; The Boy in the Tree Theme; Je ne sais pas; Jasmin.

(Grammys-(14)-inst arr-1963, 1973, 1978, 1980, 1981, 1984; group jazz-1969; pop inst-1971); cast show album prod-1981; R & B Duo-1981; Arr accomp vocal-1981; Producer of year-1981, 1983; Prod-record of year & album of year, 1983).

JONES, Robert C.: Wri-Flm Ed. b. Los Angeles, Mar 30, 1930. S of Harmon Jones. Films inc: (ed) I Love You Alice B Toklas; Tobruk; Mad, Mad, Mad, Mad, World; A Child is Waiting; Ship of Fools; Guess Who's Coming to Dinner; Love Story; Man of La Mancha; The Last Detail; Shampoo; Bound for Glory; Heaven Can Wait (& mus); Coming Home (sp) (Oscar-1978); Lookin' To Get Out.

JONES, Sam J.: Act. b. Chicago, IL, Aug 12, 1954. TV inc: Stunts Unlimited; Code Red; No Man's Land. Films inc: 10; Flash Gordon.

JONES, Shirley: Act. b. Smithton, PA, Mar 31, 1934. Thea inc: Lady in the Dark; Call Me Madam; South Pacific.

Films inc: Elmer Gantry (Oscar-supp-1960); Oklahoma; Carousel; A Ticklish Affair; The Music Man; Bedtime Story; The Cheyenne Social Club; Beyond The Poseidon Adventure; Tank.

TV inc: Silent Night, Lonely Night; The Partridge Family; Shirley; Hope, Women & Song; The Children of An Lac; Inmates--A Love Story; The Adventures of Pollyanna; Frank Mills Christmas Special; It's Ho-Ho Hope's 35th Jolly Christmas Hour.

JONES, Terry: Wri-Act. b. Wales, 1942. Member Monty Python's Flying Circus. With various rep groups before joining BBC script dept. TV inc: Late Night Lineup; The Late Show; A Series of Birds; Do Not

Adjust Your Set; The Complete and Utter History of Britain; Monty Python's Flying Circus; Secrets.

Films inc: And Now For Something Completely Different; Monty Python and the Holy Grail (& co-dir); Monty Python's Life of Brian (& dir); Monty Python's The Meaning of Life (dir-mus).

JONES, Tom: Playwri-Lyr. b. Littlefield, TX, Feb 17, 1928. e. U of TX, BFA, MFA. Plays inc: Kaleidoscope; Shoestring '57; Four Below; Demi-Dozen; Anatol; The Fantasticks; 110 in the Shade; I Do! I Do!; Celebration; Colette (four songs); Philemon; Portfolio Revue; The Bone Room; Colette Collage.

Films inc: Texas Romance 1909 (& dir).

TV inc: New York Scrapbook; The Fantasticks; Philemon; I Do! I Do!.

JONES, Tom (ne Woodward): Singer. b. Pontypridd, Wales, Jun 7, 1940. Began singing in village stores at age 3. Organized group the Playboys 1964 for recordings, London nitery dates. U.S. tours in 1965 and 1968.

Recordings inc: It's Not Unusual (Grammy-new artist-1965).

TV inc: This is Tom Jones; Pleasure Cove; Lynda Carter Encore!

JONES, Tommy Lee: Act. b. San Saba, TX, Sep 15, 1946. e. Harvard. Bway inc: A Patriot For Me; Four on a Garden; Ulysses in Nighttown.

Films inc: Love Story; Jackson County Jail; Rolling Thunder; The Betsy; Eyes of Laura Mars; Coal Miner's Daughter; Back Roads; Nate and Hayes; The River Rat.

TV inc: Charlie's Angels (pilot); The Amazing Howard Hughes; The Rainmaker (cable); The Executioner's Song; (Emmy-1983); Cat On A Hot Tin Roof (cable).

JONSSON, Linda: Prod. b. Woburn, MA, 1950. e. U of CO, BA. Joined NBC 1974 as sec; became prodn asst 1975; Jan 1978, asst to prod of Sportsworld; 1979, coord prod, Sportsworld. TV inc: Olympic Trials; The Arlberg Kandahar Downhill from St. Anton (Emmy-coord prod-1981).

JORDAN, Glenn: Dir-Prod. b. San Antonio, TX, Apr 5, 1936. e. Harvard Coll, BA; Yale Drama School. TV inc: Hogan's Goat; Paradise Lost; Eccentricities of a Nightingale; Benjamin Franklin (Emmy-prod-1975); Les Miserables; The Oath; Shell Game; Family; In the Matter of Karen Ann Quinlan; Sunshine Christmas; The Court Martial of Gen George Armstrong Custer; Delta County; Son-Rise; The Family Man; The Women's Room (& prod); The Princess and the Cabbie; Lois Gibbs and the Love Canal; Heartsounds.

Films inc: Only When I Laugh (dir); The Buddy System (dir); Mass Appeal (dir).

Thea inc: Another Evening with Harry Stoones (off-Bway); A Taste of Honey (tour); A Delicate Balance (tour).

JORDAN, Richard: Act. b. 1938. Films inc: The Yakuza; Kamouraska; Rooster Cogburn; Old Boyfriends; Interiors; Raise The Titanic; A Flash Of Green (& prod); Dune; The Mean Season.

TV inc: Captains and the Kings; Les Miserables; The French Atlantic Affair; The Bunker; Washington Mistress; Insight/Leave Me Alone, God.

JORDAN, Will: Act. b. Jul 27. e. AADA. Comedian and impressionist; over 400 major TV credits including 22 appearances on the Ed Sullivan Show where he created imitation of Sullivan.

Bway inc: Bye Bye Birdie.

Films inc: The Buddy Holly Story; I Wanna Hold Your Hand; Broadway Danny Rose.

JOSEFSBERG, Milt: Wri-Prod. b. NYC, Jun 29, 1911. Wri for Bob Hope; Jack Benny; Joey Bishop; Lucille Ball; Here's Lucy (created format); All in the Family (prod-wri-script supv) (Emmy-prod-1978); Hot WACS (exec prod).

JOSEPHSON, Erland: Act-dir-wri. b. Stockholm, Jun. 15, 1923. In Swedish theatre most of his career; joined Sweden's Royal Dramatic Theatre 1956; replaced Ingmar Bergman as head of the theater in 1966, remaining in that position for ten years. Films inc: (act) It Rains on Our Love; To Joy; Brink of Life; The Magician; Hour of the Wolf; The Passion of Anna; Cries and Whispers; Scenes from a Marriage; Face to Face; Beyond Good and Evil; I'm Afraid; Autumn Sonata; To Forget Venice; One and One (& dir); The Marmaldade Revolution (& dir-wri); Montenegro (Pigs and Pearls); Sezona Mira u Parizu (Season of Peace in Paris); Fanny and Alexander; Bella Donna; Nostalgia; La Casa del tappeto gialla (House of the Yellow Carpet);-Angela Sota (Angela's War); Bakom Jalusin (Behind The Shutters);Un Caso Di Incoscienza (A Case Of Irresponsibility); Dirty Story.

TV inc: Efter Repetitionen (After the Rehearsal).

JOSEPHSON, Marvin A.: Agt. b. NYC, Jun 5, 1935. e. Long Island U, BA. Liebling-Wood Agency; Music Corp of America; General Artists Corp; Agency for the Performing Arts; ChmnB Marvin Josephson Associates, Parent Company of International Creative Mgt.

JOURDAN, Louis: Act. b. Marseilles, France, Jun 19, 1921. On stage prior to screen debut 1939.

Films inc: Her First Affair; The Paradine Case; Letter from an Unknown Woman; Madame Bovary; Three Coins in the Fountain; Gigi; Can-Can; A Flea in Her Ear; To Commit a Murder; The More It Goes, The Less It Goes; Silver Bears; Swamp Thing; Octopussy; Double Deal.

TV inc: The French Atlantic Affair; Aloha Paradise; The First Olympics--Athens 1896; Salute to Lady Liberty; Cover Up.

Bway inc: 13 Rue de l'Amour.

JOUVE, Nicole: Dist exec. b. Paris, 1928. M-dir, Interama.

JOY, Leatrice (nee Zeidler): Act. b. New Orleans, LA, Nov 7 1899. Started as extra at Fort Lee Studios in A Girl's Folly; worked in stock company in San Diego to gain experience; worked in Roscoe "Fatty" Arbuckle two-reeler, appeared in comedy series before achieving feature, later starring billing. Made more than 50 films inc: One Dollar Bid; The City of Tears; Three X Gordon; The Man Hunter; Blind Youth; Bunty Pulls the Strings; A Tale of Two Worlds; Down Home; Ladies Must Live; Voices of the City; The Poverty of Riches; The Bachelor Daddy; Manslaughter; The Man Who Saw Tomorrow; Java Head; The Ten Commandments; The Marriage Cheat; Changing Husbands; Made for Love; The Clinging Vine; For Alimony Only; Nobody's Widow; Vanity; The Angel of Broadway; The Blue Danube; The Bellamy Trial; First Love; The Old Swimmin' Hole; Red Stallion in the Rockies; Air Hostess; Love Nest.

(Died May 13, 1985.)

JOYCE, Elaine: Act. b. Cleveland, OH, Dec 19. W of the late Bobby Van. Bway inc: Sugar; Julis Caesar; Black Sheep.

Films inc: West Side Story; The Music Man; Bye Bye Birdie; The Lost Flight; Funny Girl; Christine; How To Frame a Figg; Such Good Friends; A Guide for the Married Woman.

TV inc: Here Come the Brides; The Don Knotts Show; The Carol Burnett Show; The Tony Awards; Circus of the Stars; The Bobby Van and Elaine Joyce Special; Mrs. America Pageant (co-host) City of Angels; Mr. Merlin; Computers Are People Too (host); Allison Sidney Harrison; Night Of 100 Stars II.

JULIA, Raul: Act. b. San Juan, Puerto Rico, Mar 9, 1940. e. U of Puerto Rico. Bway inc: The Marriage Proposal; Mobile; Macbeth; Titus Andronicus; No Exit; Your Own Thing; The Cuban Thing; Indians; Two Gentlemen of Verona; Via Galactica; As You Like It; King Lear; Where's Charley; Three Penny Opera; 'Nine'; Design for Living; Arms And The Man.

Films inc: Panic In Needle Park; The Organization; The Eyes of Laura Mars; One From The Heart; The Escape Artist; Tempest; Kiss Of The Spider Woman.

TV inc: Overdrawn At The Memory Bank; The 39th Annual Tony Awards.

JULIEN, Jay: Prod. b. NYC, Aug 11, 1924. e. CCNY, BSS; Georgetown, LLB. Bway inc: A Hatful of Rain; The Night Circus; The Fun Couple; Hostile Witness; Hughie/Duet; It's So Nice to Be Civilized.

JUMP, Gordon: Act. b. Dayton, OH, Apr 1, 1932. e. KS State U. Started as prodn dir WIBW-TV, Topeka, KS, wri-prod WLWD, Dayton.

Films inc: Conquest of the Planet of the Apes; Trouble Man; Adam at 6 A.M; Making the Grade.

TV inc: Goldie and the Boxer; Hamlet; Archie; Fawn Story; McDuff the Talking Dog; WKRP in Cincinnati; The Big Stuffed Dog; Midnight

Offerings; Take My Word For It; For Lovers Only; Just a Little More Love; Great Day; Second Edition; Gus Brown & Midnight Brewster.

JURADO, Katy (Maria Christina Jurado): Act. b. Guadalajara, Mexico, Jan 16, 1924. In Mexican films, Hollywood debut 1951. Films inc: The Bullfighter and the Lady; High Noon; Broken Lance; Trapeze; One-Eyed Jacks; Barabbas; A Covenant with Death; The Bridge in the Jungle; The Children of Sanchez; La Viuda De Montiel; El Recurso Del Metedo; La Seduccion (The Seduction); Under the Volcano.

TV inc: Evita Peron; a.k.a Pablo; Lady Blue.

JUROW, Martin: Prod. b. NYC, Dec 14, 1911. e. Harvard Law, BA, JD. Agent with MCA, William Morris, Famous Artists before becoming prod.

Films inc: The Hanging Tree; The Fugitive Kind; Breakfast at Tiffanys; Soldier in the Rain; The Pink Panther; The Great Race; Waltz Across Texas; Terms of Endearment; Sylvester.

JUSTIN, John: Act. b. London, Nov 23, 1917. Films inc: Thief of Bagdad; The Sound Barrier; The Village; Melba; Crest of the Wave; King of the Khyber Rifles; Untamed; Safari; Island in the Sun; The Savage Messiah; Barcelona Kill; Lisztomania; Valentino; The Big Sleep.

TV inc: Timon of Athens.

KACZENDER, George: Dir. b. Budapest, Apr 19, 1933. e. Film Academy. Films inc: Don't Let the Angels Fall; U-Turn; In Praise of Older Women; Agency; Chanel Solitaire.

KAGAN, Jeremy Paul: Dir-Wri. b. Mt Vernon, NY, Dec 14, 1945. e. Harvard; NYU, MFA. TV inc: Columbo; The Bold Ones; Unwed Father; Judge Dee; My Dad Lives in a Downtown Hotel; Katherine (& wri); Scott Joplin.

Films inc: Heroes; The Big Fix; The Chosen; The Sting II.

KAHN, Madeline: Act. b. Boston, MA., Sept 29, 1942. Films inc: What's Up Doc?; Paper Moon; Blazing Saddles; Young Frankenstein; The Adventures of Sherlock Holmes' Smarter Brother; At Long Last Love; Won Ton Ton, The Dog Who Saved Hollywood; The Cheap Detective; The Muppet Movie; Simon; Happy Birthday, Gemini; Wholly Moses; First Family; History of the World--Part I; Yellowbeard; Slapstick of Another Kind; City Heat.

Bway inc: La Boheme; Showboat; Two by Two; Candide; In the Boom Boom Room; On the 20th Century.

TV inc: Oh Madeline.

KAHN, Michael: Dir. b. NYC. e. Columbia U, BA. Prod-dir McCarter Theatre, Princeton; dir NY Shakespeare Festival. Thea inc: The Love Nest; Funnyhouse of a Negro; Victims of Duty; America Hurrah; Here's Where I Belong; As You Like It; The Crucible; Winter's Tale; Our Town; Cat on a Hot Tin Roof; Romeo and Juliet; Macbeth; Julius Caesar; Mourning Becomes Electra; All's Well That Ends Well; Show Boat; Whodunnit.

KAHN, Richard: Exec. b. New Rochelle, NY, Aug 19, 1929. e. U of PA, BS. Joined MGM 1974 from Columbia Pictures, where he was vp in charge of Worldwide special marketing projects; 1975, MGM's vp worldwide advertising, publicity and exploitation; 1978, Sr VP Worldwide Mktg; 1979, P MGM Int'l; Nov 1981 same position with merged MGM-UA; Apr 1982, Exec VP Motion Picture & Mktg div MGM-UA, in chg wldwde ad-pub-prom MGM-UA Entertainment; resd Aug. 1983.

KAHN, Sheldon: Film Edtr. b. Mar 21, 1940. e. USC, BA. Films inc: One Flew Over The Cuckoo's Nest; Great Scout and Cathouse Thursday; Mikey and Nicky; Enemy of the People; Blood Brothers; Same Time Next Year; The Electric Horseman; Private Benjamin; Kiss Me Goodbye; Ghostbusters.

TV inc: Bring 'em Back Alive.

KALBER, Floyd: TV Newsman. b. Omaha, NE, Dec 23, 1924. e. Creighton U. Joined NBC News in 1960 after 11 years as news dir KMTV, Omaha; anchorman for NBC Sunday News; newscaster on Today.

KALSER, Konstantin: Act. b. Munich, Germany, Sep 4, 1920. Founded Marathon International Prodns, Inc, p, exec prod; p, Kleiner-

man-Kalser Asso, Ltd.
Films inc: Crashing the Water Barrier *(Oscar*-1956-ss); Give and Take; Right Hand of Plenty; The Carmakers; I'm Takin' the Time; Each Day at Dawn; In Spite of Walls; The One for the Road (dir).

KAMM, Larry: Dir-Prod. b. Long Branch, NJ, Oct 10, 1939. e. Northwestern U, BS. TV inc: 1972 Winter Olympics; 1976 Winter Olympics *(Emmy*-dir); Indianapolis 500; Grand Prix of Monaco; NCAA Football; Frankie Valli On Stage; Friday Night at the Kentucky Derby; Wide World of Sports 20th Anniversary Show *(Emmy*-1981). Wide World of Sports (Great American Bike Race) *(Emmys-prod & dir-*1983).

KANALY, Steve: Act. b. Burbank, CA, Mar 14. Films inc: The Life and Times of Judge Roy Bean; Dillinger; The Sugarland Express; Terminal Man; The Wind and the Lion; Midway; Fleshburn.

KANDER, John: Comp. b. Kansas City, MO, Mar 18, 1927. e. Columbia, MA. Bway inc: Gypsy (arr); Irma la Douce (arr); A Family Affair; Never Too Late; Flora, The Red Menace; Cabaret *(Tony-*1967); The Happy Time; Zorba; Chicago; 70 Girls 70; The Act Woman of the Year; *(Tony-*1980); The Rink.
Films inc: Cabaret; Funny Lady; Lucky Lady; New York, New York; Still of the Night; Blue Skies Again; Places In The Heart.
TV inc: Liza with a Z *(Emmy-*1973).
*(Grammy-*cast album-1967).

KANE, Carol: Act. b. OH, Jun 18, 1952. Bway inc: The Prime of Miss Jean Brodie; The Effect of Gamma Rays on Man-in-the-Moon Marigolds.
Films inc: Carnal Knowledge; Wedding in White; Desperate Characters; The Last Detail; Hester Street; Dog Day Afternoon; Harry and Walter Go To New York; Valentino; The Mafu Cage; When A Stranger Calls; The Muppet Movie; La Sabina; Les Jeux de la Contessa Dolingen de Gratz (The Games of the Countess Dolingen of Gratz); Norman Loves Rose; Over the Brooklyn Bridge; The Secret Diary of Sigmund Freud.
TV inc: The Greatest Man In the World; The Girls In Their Summer Dresses and Other Stories by Irwin Shaw; Taxi *(Emmy-*1982; Emmy-supp-1983); An Invasion of Privacy; Keeping On; Burning Rage.

KANE, Josh: Exec. b. NYC. e. Brooklyn Coll, BA. Joined NBC in 1965 as a page; In pub dept 1969-1976; to program dept 1976; named vp, programs, East Coast, Nov 1977; named vp for theatrical features and asst to Brandon Tartikoff, Feb 1981; Aug 1982, VP pgm dvlpt CBS Entertainment; Nov. 1984, VP Pgms.

KANE, Thomas J.: Story Ed. b. Chicago, Mar 24, 1920. e. Northwestern U, BA. With Batjac Prods; worked on all John Wayne films since 1952. Sec, asst treas Batjac Prods.

KANIN, Fay (nee Mitchell): Wri. b. NYC. e. Elmira Coll; USC. W of Michael Kanin. Films inc: Blondie for Victory; Sunday Punch; My Pal Gus; Rhapsody; The Opposite Sex; Teacher's Pet; Swordsman of Siena; The Right Approach; The Outrage.
Plays inc: Goodbye My Fancy; His and Hers; Rashomon; The Gay Life; Grind.
TV inc: Heat of Anger; Tell Me Where It Hurts *(Emmy-*1974-also wri of the year); Hustling; Friendly Fire *(Emmy-*co-prod-1979); Fun & Games (co-prod); Heartsounds (& prod).

KANIN, Garson: Prod-Dir-Wri. b. Rochester, NY, Nov 24, 1912. e. AADA. H of Ruth Gordon. Briefly Bway actor then prod asst to George Abbott. Dir, Hitch Your Wagon; Too Many Heroes. Joined Samuel Goldwyn's prod staff, 1937. To RKO, 1938 as prod-dir. Films inc: Adam's Rib; Born Yesterday; Pat and Mike; Tom, Dick and Harry; The Rat Race; Woman of the Year; The More the Merrier.
Plays inc: Born Yesterday; The Diary of Anne Frank; Hole in the Head; Sunday in New York; Funny Girl; Idiot's Delight. Bway (dir) Dreyfus In Rehearsal.
TV inc: Hardhat & Legs.

KANIN, Michael: Wri-Prod. b. Rochester, NY, Feb 1, 1910. Worked as commercial and scenic artist, musician and entertainer before turning to writing.
Films inc: They Made Her a Spy; Panama Lady; Anne of Windy

Poplars; Woman of the Year *(Co-Oscar-*1942); The Cross of Lorraine; Centennial Summer; Honeymoon; Sunday Punch; My Pal Gus; Rhapsody; The Swordsman of Siena; The Opposite Sex; Teacher's Pet; The Outrage; How to Commit Marriage. When I Grow Up (& dir); prod A Double Life.
Bway inc: (prod) Goodbye My Fancy; Seidman and Son. Wrote (with wife Fay Kanin) His and Hers; Rashomon; The Gay Life.

KANTER, Hal: Wri-Dir-Prod. b. Savannah, GA, Dec 18, 1918. Wri: Danny Kaye Show; Amos 'n Andy; Bing Crosby Show; Ed Wynn TV Show, 1949. Paramount, 1951-54; dir RKO Radio, 1956; prod, dir, wri, Kraft Music Hall, 1958-59.
TV inc: Chrysler Theatre; George Gobel Show *(Emmy-*1954); Julia; Jimmy Stewart; All in the Family; Chico & The Man; Lucy Moves To NBC (prod-wri); For the Love of It (dir); joined Walt Disney prodns March 1981 to develop episodic series.
Films inc: My Favorite Spy; Road to Bali; Artists and Models; Rose Tattoo; Pocketful of Miracles; Move Over, Darling; Brigitte.

KANTER, Jay: Exec. b. 1927. Started as agent with MCA, when agency dissolved became European prodn head for U, which MCA had acquired; resd to enter indie prodn with Elliott Kastner; 1972, P First Artists Prodns; 1975 to Fox as prodn vp; 1976 sr vp; 1978 sr vp wldwde prodn; resd 1979 with Alan Ladd Jr, Gareth Wigan, joining them in new indie The Ladd Co; resd July 1984 to become P Wldwide prodn motion picture div MGM/UA Entertainment; Jan. 1985, P wldwide film prodn UA; March 1985, P Metro-Goldwyn-Mayer Film Co.

KAPER, Bronislau: Comp. b. Warsaw, Poland, Feb 5, 1902. Film scores inc: Gaslight; Without Love; Green Dolphin Street; The Forsyte Saga; The Red Badge of Courage; Lili *(Oscar-*1953); Them; The Swan; The Brothers Karamazov; Butterfield 8; Mutiny on the Bounty; Kisses for My President; Lord Jim; Tobruk; A Flea in Her Ear.
(Died April 25, 1983).

KAPLAN, Gabe: Act. b. NYC, Mar 31, 1946. Nitery comic.
TV inc: Welcome Back Kotter; Lewis and Clark (& wri); The Hoboken Chicken Emergency.
Films inc: Fast Break; Nobody's Perfekt; Tulips.

KAPLAN, Jonathan: Dir-Wri. b. Paris, Nov 25, 1947. e. U of Chicago, BA; NYU, MFA. Films inc: The Slams; Truck Turner; White Line Fever; Mr Billion; Over the Edge; Heart Like A Wheel (dir).
TV inc: The 11th Victim; The Hustler of Muscle Beach; The Gentleman Bandit; Girls of the White Orchid.

KAPLAN, Marvin: Act. b. NYC, Jan 24, 1927. e. Brooklyn College. Films inc: Adam's Rib; The Reformer and the Redhead; Criminal Lawyer; Angels in the Outfield; The Fabulous Senorita; The Nutty Professor; Wake Me When It's Over; The Great Race.
TV inc: Meet Millie; Maggie Brown; Out of the Blue; Chicago Teddy Bears; Top Cat; Alice; Arthur the Kid; Deck the Halls with Wacky Walls (voice).

KAPLAN, Mike: Newspaperman. b. Salem, MA, May 7, 1918. Reporter Playhouse (thea tradepaper) 1933, asso edtr 1934; 1936 city edtr Boston Bureau Transradio Press; 1939 man edtr Boston City News Bureau; 1942 night newscast edtr NY Daily News; 1947 West Coast edtr Variety (weekly) and legit, nitery critic for Daily Variety; 1958-1961 freelance film publicist, Europe; 1961-1964 with Stanley Kramer Prodns; 1964 pub dir Robert Wise Prodns; 1966 exec asst to Wise; 1973 organized National News Service for U; 1978 returned to Variety to create, edit Variety Reference Books.

KAPLAN, Nelly: Wri-Dir. b. Argentina, Apr 11, 1931. Worked with Abel Gance; began directing shorts & docs inc: Gustave Moreau; Rodolphe Bresdin; Abel Gance, Today and Tomorrow; A la Source, la Femme Aimee; Dernier et Merveilles; Les Annees 25; La Nouvelle Orangerie; Le Regard Picasso. Feature films inc: la Fiancee du Pirate; Papa les Petits Bateaux; Nea; Charles et Lucie (& act); Abel Gance et Son Napoleon (& prod-edtr).

KAPRISKY, Valerie: Act. b. France, 1963. Films inc: Breathless; Aphrodite; Lawful Violence; La Femme Publique (The Public Woman); L'Annee des Meduses (Year Of The Medusa).

KAPROFF, Dana: Comp-Cond. b. Los Angeles, Apr 24, 1954. e. UCLA. TV inc: Once An Eagle; Ellery Queen; The Bionic Woman; Hawaii 5-0; Belle Starr; Scared Straight; Inmates--A Love Story; Berlin Tunnel 21; Every Stray Dog and Kid; Boone; Second Sight--A Love Story; The Bounder; Chiller.

Films inc: The Late Great Planet Earth; When A Stranger Calls; The Big Red One; Death Valley; The Golden Seal.

KARINA, Anna (Hanne Karin Beyer): Act. b. Copenhagen, 1940. Films inc: She'll Have To Go; Une Femme Est Une Femme; Vivre Sa Vie; Le Petit Soldat; Bande a Part; Alphaville; The Magus; Before Winter Comes; Laughter in the Dark; Justine; Rendezvous At Bray; The Salzburg Connection; Surprise Sock; Bread and Chocolate; Also es war so (Willie and the Chinese Cat); Vivre Ensemble (& dir); Story of a Mother; L'Ami de Vincent (A Friend of Vincent); Ave Maria.

KARLAN, Richard: Act. b. NYC, Apr 24, 1919. e. Brooklyn Coll. Films inc: Union Station; The Lemon Drop Kid; Sailor Beware; The Racket; Wait Till The Sun Shines Nellie; Blowing Wild; All the Brothers Were Valiant; I Died a Thousand Times; While the City Sleeps; Inside the Mafia; Star!

TV inc: Betrayal; Missiles of October; The Blue Knight; The Partners.

KARLIN, Fred: Comp-Cond. b. Chicago, Jun 16, 1936. e. Amherst Coll, BA. Comp, arr for orchs inc: Benny Goodman; Harry James.

Films inc: Up the Down Staircase; Yours, Mine and Ours; The Sterile Cuckoo; Lovers and Other Strangers (Co-Oscar-song, For All We Know-1970); Westworld; Gravy Train; Mixed Company; Leadbelly; Minstrel Man; California Dreaming; Ravagers; Cloud Dancer; Loving Couples.

TV inc: Autobiography of Miss Jane Pittman (Emmy-1974); Once Upon A Family; Marriage Is Alive and Well; The Plutonium Incident; Baby Comes Home; Sophia Loren--Her Own Story; Homeward Bound; The Secret War of Jackie's Girls; Fighting Back; My Kidnaper, My Love; Mom, The Wolfman and Me; A Time For Marriage; Thornwell; Miracle On Ice; We're Fighting Back; Broken Promise; The Five of Me; Bitter Harvest; Jacqueline Susann's Valley of the Dolls 1981; Jessica Novak; The Marva Collins Story; Catalina C-Lab; Inside The Third Reich; Hollywood--The Gift of Laughter; Not in Front of the Children; Missing Children--A Mother's Story; Deadly Encounter; Inspector Perez; Baby Sister; In Defense of Kids; Wishman; Lovers and Other Strangers; Full House; Night Partners; Policewoman Centerfold; The Gift of Love--A Christmas Story; Cougar!; Love Leads The Way; Off The Rack; Robert Kennedy & His Times.

Songs: Come Saturday Morning; Come Follow, Follow Me; Early in the Morning.

KARLSON, Phil (ne Karlstein): Dir. b. Chicago, 1980. Films inc: A WAVE, a WAC and a Marine; Swing Parade; Dark Alibi; The Missing Lady; Black Gold; Kilroy was Here; Thunderhoof; The Big Cat; Down Memory Lane; Lorna Doone; The Texas Rangers; Scandal Sheet; Kansas City Confidential; Hell's Island; Five Against the House; The Phenix City Story; The Brothers Rico; Key Witness; The Young Doctors; Kid Galahad; Rampage; The Silencers; A Time for Killing; Hornet's Nest; Ben; Walking Tall; Framed.

KARP, David: Wri. Films inc: Sol Madrid; Cervantes; Che!.

TV inc: The Defenders (Emmy-1965); Garrison's Gorillas; The Storefront Lawyers (& crea); The Family Rico; Hawkins (& crea); Archer (developed); W.E.B. (crea).

KARRAS, Alex: Act. b. Gary, IN, Jul 15, 1935. e. IA U. Former pro football player.

Films inc: Blazing Saddles; Another Day at the Races; Jacob Two-Two Meets The Hooded Fang; Mad Bull; When Time Ran Out; Nobody's Perfekt; Porky's; Victor/Victoria; Against All Odds.

TV inc: The Paper Lion; Hardcase; The 500 Lb Jerk; Babe; For As Long As the Water Flows; The Longhorns; The Big Event; The Storm; The Crime; The Winds of Change; The Winds of Death; Jimmy B & Andre; Alcatraz--The Whole Shocking Story; Word of Honor (exec prod); Maid in America (& exec prod); Webster.

KASDAN, Lawrence: Wri. b. Miami Beach, FL, Jan 14, 1949. e. U of MI, BA, MA. Films inc: The Empire Strikes Back; Raiders of the Lost Ark; Body Heat (& dir); Continental Divide; Return of the Jedi; The Big Chill (& exec prod-dir); Into The Night (act).

KASHA, Al: Sngwri. b. NYC, Jan 22, 1937. e. NYU, BS; Juilliard. Writes in collaboration with Joel Hirschhorn.

Songs inc: My Empty Arms; I'm Comin' On Back To You; Let's Start All Over Again; Wake Up; Your Time Hasn't Come Yet, Baby; Will You Be Staying After Sunday?; One More Mountan to Climb; The Subject Was Roses; Living is Dying Without You; The Morning After (Oscar-1972); We May Never Love Like This Again (Oscar-1974); Candle on the Water; I'd Like To Be You for a Day; May the Best Man Win; Mississippi Magic; Pass A Little Love Around.

Bway inc: Copperfield; Seven Brides For Seven Brothers (add'l songs). TV inc: Goodbye, Charlie.

KASHA, Lawrence N.: Prod-Dir-Plywri. b. NYC, Dec 3, 1932. e. NYU, BA, MA. Dir nat'l companies L'il Abner; Camelot; Funny Girl; Cactus Flower; Star Spangled Girl; Bway prodn Bajour; Lovely Ladies, Kind Gentlemen before becoming prod. Bway inc: She Loves Me; Hadrian VII; Applause (Tony-1970); Father's Day; Inner City; Seesaw; No Hard Feelings; Seven Brides for Seven Brothers; Woman of the Year.

TV inc: Applause; Another April; Rosenthal and Jones; Busting Loose; Komedy Tonite; Willow B--Women in Prison.

Plays inc: The Pirate; Where Have You Been, Billy Boy?; Heaven Sent; Seven Brides for Seven Brothers.

KASTNER, Elliott: Prod. b. NYC, Jan 7, 1933. e. U of Miami; Columbia U. Started as agent with MCA, named vp 1960; became prod when MCA took over Universal; became ind prod with Harper.

Films inc: Kaleidoscope; The Bobo; Sweet November; Sol Madrid; Laughter In the Dark; The Night of the Following Day; Where Eagles Dare; A Severed Head; When Eight Bells Toll; Tam Lin; X Y and Zee; The Nightcomers; Big Truck and Poor Clare; Fear is the Key; The Long Goodbye; Cops and Robbers; 11 Harrowhouse; Rancho Deluxe; 92 in the Shade; Farewell, My Lovely; Russian Roulette; Breakheart Pass; The Missouri Breaks; Swashbuckler; Black Joy; A Little Night Music; Equus; The Stick Up; The Medusa Touch; The Big Sleep; Goldengirl; Yesterday's Hero; Ffolkes; The First Deadly Sin; Absolution; Death Valley; Man, Woman and Child; Oxford Blues; Garbo Talks; Nomads.

Thea inc: Marilyn (London).

KATLEMAN, Harris L.: Exec. b. Omaha, NE, Aug 19, 1928. e. UCLA, BA. Joined MCA in 1949; joined Goodson-Todman Prodns in 1955; named vp in 1956; exec vp in 1958; sr exec vp in 1968; joined MGM in 1972 as vp MGM-TV; 1973, P MGM-TV, sr vp MGM Inc; resd 1977 to enter indie prod with Harve Bennett; partnership dissolved, became chmn Fox-TV May 1, 1980.

TV inc: Salvage; From Here to Eternity; The Golden Gun; From Here To Eternity-The War Years; Alex and the Doberman Gang; Nick and the Dobermans.

KATSELAS, Milton: Dir. b. Pittsburgh, PA, Feb 22, 1933. e. Carnegie Institute of Technology. Thea inc: The Zoo Story; Call Me By My Rightful Name; The Garden of Sweets; On an Open Roof (& co-prod); The Rose Tattoo (rev); Butterflies Are Free; Camino Real; Private Lives.

Films inc: Butterflies Are Free; 40 Carats; Report to the Commissioner; When You Coming Back, Red Ryder.

TV inc: The Rules of Marriage.

KATT, William: Act. b. Los Angeles, Feb. 16, 1951. S of Barbara Hale and Bill Williams. Films inc: First Love; Big Wednesday; Carrie; Butch And Sundance--The Early Days; Baby.

TV inc: The Greatest American Hero; Pippin (Cable); The Rainmaker (cable).

KATZ, Gloria: Wri. e. UCLA Film School. W of Willard Huyck. Started with U as flm edtr on edu films; teamed with Huyck to write six unproduced screenplays for Francis Ford Coppola's Zoetrope Productions. Films inc: American Graffiti; Lucky Lady; French Postcards (& prod); Indiana Jones and the Temple of Doom; Best Defense (& prod).

KATZ, Norman B.: Exec. b. Scranton, PA, Aug 23, 1919. Exec asst to head of prodn, Discina-Speva Films (Paris), 1948-49; 1950-53, vp, exec vp, Discina International Films; 1954-57, foreign Mgr, Asso

Artists Prodns; 1958-59, dir of foreign operations, UA Prodns; 1959-61, dir of foreign operations, UA; 1961-64, vp in charge, foreign operations, Seven Arts Associates Corp; 1964-67, exec vp, Seven Arts Prodns Intl; 1967-69, exec vp, WB-Seven Arts Intl; 1969-72, exec vp, chief exec ofcr, WB Intl, board member WB, Inc; 1975, P, Cinema Arts Assoc Corp; 1979 exec vp American Communications Industries; 1980 p American Communications Intl; 1981 Bd Chmn; 1983 formed Consolidated Entertainment Group when ACI folded; 1984 formed Norkat Company Inc., for foreign sales; June, 1985 named chmn American Film Marketing Association.

KATZENBERG, Jeff: Exec. Joined Par NY 1975 as asst to chmn of board; 1976, exec dir mktg & adm; 1977 to Hollywood as vp film div; 1978, prodn vp in chg acquisitions, pickups; 1980 sr vp prodn; June 1982 named P of Wldwde prodn; resd. Sept. 1984, effective Feb. 1985, to become P of motion picture & TV operations at Walt Disney Prodns.

KATZIN, Lee H.: Dir. b. Detroit, Apr 12, 1935. e. Harvard Coll, AB. Films inc: Heaven with a Gun; Whatever Happened to Aunt Alice?; The Phynx; Le Mans; The Salzburg Connection.
   TV inc; The Rat Patrol; Wild, Wild West; Hondo; Felony Squad; Mission Impossible; It Takes a Thief; The Mod Squad; Mannix; Along Came a Spider; Visions; Strange Homecoming; Savages; Space 1999; McMillan & Wife; Sky Heist; The Last Survivor; Firebird; Police Story; Relentless; McLaren's Riders; Man from Atlantis; The Quest; The Bastard; Broken Badge; River of Promises; Terror Out Of The Sky; Samurai; Zuma Beach; T. R. Sloane; Death Ray 2000; The Neighborhood; Hardcase; The Mississippi; Emergency Room; Automan.

KATZKA, Gabriel: Prod. b. NYC, Jan 25, 1931. e. Kenyon Coll. Films inc: Marlowe; Kelly's Heroes; Soldier Blue; The Parallax View; The Taking of Pelham 1-2-3; The Heartbreak Kid; Sleuth; A Bridge Too Far; Who'll Stop the Rain; Meteor; Butch and Sundance--The Early Days; The Beast Within; The Lords of Discipline; The Falcon And The Snowman.
   Bway inc: Pal Joey; Hamlet; The Little Foxes; Anna Christie; Same Time Next Year; The Comedians; Hughie; A View From the Bridge.
   TV inc: Kavik-the Wolf Dog; Isabel's Choice; Ellis Island.

KATZMAN, Leonard: Prod-wri. b. NYC, Sep 2. Asst dir on various live tv shows; later asso prod Route 66; Wild Wild West. TV inc: (prod) Gunsmoke (& wri-dir); Hawaii Five-O; Dirty Sally; Petrocelli; The Fantastic Journey; Logan's Run; Dallas.

KAUFER, Jonathan: Wri. b. Los Angeles, Mar 14, 1955. TV inc: The Practice; Alice; Destination: Uranus; Quark (story ed). Films inc: Soup For One (wri-dir); Into The Night (act); Always (act).

KAUFMAN, Andy: Act. b. NYC, Jan 17, 1949. TV inc: Saturday Night Live; The New Dick Van Dyke Show; Taxi; Johnny Cash Christmas; Fridays; The Fantastic Miss Piggy Show; The Rodney Dangerfield Special--I Can't Take It No More.
   Films inc: In God We Trust; Heartbeeps; My Breakfast With Blassie.
   Bway inc: Teaneck Tanzi, The Venus Flytrap.
   (Died May 16, 1984).

KAUFMAN, Leonard: Prod-Wri. b. Newark, NJ, Aug 31, 1927. e. NYU. Films inc: Clarence, the Cross-eyed Lion (prod); Birds Do It (sp only).
   TV inc: (prod) Daktari; Jambo; O'Hara, US Treasury; Escape;- Archer; Grizzly Adams; Sam; Hawaii Five-O; (wri): Hawaii Five-O; Baretta; Grizzly Adams; Policewoman; Harry-O; Chase; Adam 12; Maude; Daktari; Barbary Coast; The Danger Game; Archer; Flipper; King Family; (dir-wri-crea): Jambo; (wri-prod): Keeper of the Wild (pilot); African Queen (pilot); Mr. & Mrs. Cop (pilot); Time Express (prod); Scruples (prod); Private Benjamin (prod).

KAUFMAN, Millard: Wri. b. NYC, Mar 12, 1917. e. Johns Hopkins U, BA. Films inc: To the Center of the Earth; Take the High Ground; Bad Day at Black Rock; Raintree County; Never So Few; Reprieve (& dir); War Lord; John Collier; Living Free; The Klansman.
   TV inc: The Nativity; Enola Gay--The Men, The Mission, The Atomic Bomb.

KAUFMAN, Philip: Dir. b. Chicago, Oct 23, 1936. e. Chicago U. Films inc: Goldstein; Fearless Frank; The Great Northfield; Minnesota Raid; Invasion Of The Body Snatchers; The Wanderers (& sp); The Right Stuff.

KAUFMAN, Robert: Wri-Prod. b. NYC. e. Columbia U. Films inc: (wri) Ski Party; Dr. Goldfoot and the Bikini Machine; Divorce American Style; I Love My Wife; Freebie and the Bean; Harry and Walter Go To New York; Love at First Bite (& co-exec prod); How to Beat the High Cost of Living; Split Image.
   TV inc: Ben Casey; Get Smart; McHale's Navy; Alfred Hitchcock Presents; The Bob Newhart Show; The Zany Adventures of Robin Hood.

KAVNER, Julie: Act. b. Los Angeles, Sep 7. e. CSU San Diego. TV inc: Rhoda (Emmy-supp-1978); No Other Love; Revenge of the Stepford Wives; A Fine Romance.
   Films inc: National Lampoon Goes to the Movies.

KAYDEN, William: Prod. b. NYC. TV inc: I Heard the Owl Call My Name; The Family Nobody Wanted; Yesterday's Child; Final Eye; Cops and Robin; Lady of the House; To Race The Wind; Crazy Times; Computercide; Missing Children--A Mother's Story.

KAYE, Buddy: Sngwri-Mus. b. NYC, Jan 3, 1918. Began career as saxophonist; wrote special material for Mills Bros; Ted Lewis; McGuire Sisters; wrote songs for Walt Disney Films; also for Popeye the Sailor cartoons; Bouncing Ball series.
   Films inc: The Trouble with Girls; Change of Habit; Not as a Stranger; Treasure of Sierra Madre; Twist Around the Clock.
   TV inc: I Dream of Jeannie; Cross Wits.
   Songs: Till the End of Time; Full Moon and Empty Arms; A-You're Adorable; Quiet Nights; What You See Is Who I Am.

KAYE, Caren: Act. b. NYC, Mar 12. e. Carnegie Tech. TV inc: The Betty White Show; Blansky's Beauties; Who's Watching the Kids; The Future--What's Next? (host); Help Wanted--Male; Side By Side; It's Your Move; Poison Ivy.
   Films inc: My Tutor.
   Thea inc: USA; Barefoot in the Park (road co).

KAYE, Danny: Act. b. NYC, Jan 18, 1913. Performed on stage, night clubs. Screen debut, 1944, Up In Arms. Films inc: The Secret Life of Walter Mitty; A Song Is Born; Hans Christian Andersen; White Christmas; The Court Jester; The Madwoman of Chaillot (retired from screen after this film, 1969).
   TV inc: The Danny Kaye Show (Emmy-1964); Kraft Salutes Disneyland's 25th Anniversary (host); Skokie; Live From Lincoln Center--An Evening with Danny Kaye and the New York Philharmonic; EPCOT Center--The Opening Celebration (host); Kennedy Center Honors 1984 (honoree); (Oscar-special-1954); (Jean Hersholt Humanitarian Award-1981).
   (Tony-special-1953).

KAYE, Lila: Act. b. England, Nov 7. Thea inc: (with Royal Shakespeare Company); The Merry Wives of Windsor; The Suicide; The Revengers Tragedy; Romeo and Juliet; The Life and Adventures of Nicholas Nickleby (& Bway).
   Films inc: An American Werewolf in Paris.
   TV inc: The Warrior's Return; David Copperfield; Vile Bodies; Nicholas Nickleby; Mama Malone; Pericles, Prince of Tyre; Ellis Island; Camille.

KAYE, Nora: Dancer-Prod. b. NYC, 1920. e. NY Metropolitan Opera Ballet School. W of Herbert Ross. As a child performed with Met Opera Ballet and at Radio City. Joined American Ballet Theatre at its inception; hailed as leading drama dancer of her time after appearance in Hagar; also danced classic roles; 1951-54 with NYC Ballet where Jerome Robbins created Cage for her; 1954-1960 returned to ABT where Kenneth MacMillan created ballets Winters Eve and Journey for her; married Herbert Ross and with him formed Ballet of Two worlds with which she toured extensively as prima ballerina. Retired from dancing 1961 to work with Ross.
   Films inc: (prod) Turning Point; Nijinsky; Pennies From Heaven.

KAYE, Sammy: Orch ldr-Comp. b. Rocky River, OH, Mar 13, 1910. e. OH U. Organized own band while in college; played niteries, radio. Started radio pgm So You Want To Lead a Band.

Films inc: Iceland; Song of the Open Road.

Songs inc: Until Tomorrow; Hawaiian Sunset; Tell Me That You Love Me; Wanderin'.

KAYE, Stubby: Act. b. NYC, Nov 11, 1918. Toured as a comedian in vaudeville, 1939-42.

Thea inc: Guys and Dolls; Li'l Abner; Everybody Loves Opal; Good News; The Ritz; Dear Anyone (London); Grind.

Films inc: Guys and Dolls; Li'l Abner; The Dirt   Girl I Ever Met; 40 Pounds of Trouble; Cat Ballou; Sweet C'   tv.

TV inc: Goldie and the Boxer Go To '   e Wonderful World of Philip Malley; Ellis Island.

KAZAN, Elia: Dir. b. Constantinople, Sep   Williams Coll; Yale Drama School. Stage, films as actor bel   g dir.

Films inc: Gentleman's Agreement (Oscar- ___, Boomerang; A Streetcar Named Desire; On the Waterfront (Oscar-1954); Man on a Tightrope; East of Eden; Splendor in the Grass; America, America (& sp); The Arrangement (& sp); The Last Tycoon; Elia Kazan, Outsider (doc) (act).

Thea inc: (as act) Waiting for Lefty; Golden Boy; Gentle People; Liliom. (Dir) The Skin of Our Teeth; A Streetcar Named Desire; All My Sons (Tony-1947); Death of a Salesman (Tony-1949); Cat On a Hot Tin Roof; One Touch Of Venus; Jacobowsky and the Colonel; Tea and Sympathy; JB (Tony-1959); Sweet Bird of Youth.

Author of The Arrangement; The Assassins; The Understudy.

KAZAN, Lainie (nee Levine): Singer. b. NY, May 15, 1943. e. Hofstra U. On stage, niteries, TV.

Films inc: Romance of a Horse Thief; Lady in Cement; Dayton's Devils; One From The Heart; My Favorite Year; Lust In The Dust.

TV inc: A Cry For Love; Sunset Limousine; The Jerk, Too; Obsessive Love.

KAZANJIAN, Howard: Prod. b. Pasadena, CA, circa 1943. e. USC Film School; DGA Training Program. Films inc: (Asst dir) Camelot; Finian's Rainbow; The Wild Bunch; The Arrangement; The Front Page; The Hindenberg; Family Plot. (Asso prod) Rollercoaster. (Prod) More American Graffiti; Raiders of the Lost Ark; The Making of Raiders of the Lost Ark (doc) (Emmy-Informational Special-1982); Return of the Jedi.

KEACH, Stacy: Act. b. Savannah, GA, Jun 2, 1941. Films inc: The Heart is a Lonely Hunter; End of the Road; The Travelling Executioner; Brewster McCloud; Judge Roy Bean; The New Centurions; Fat City; The Gravy Train; The Killer Inside Me; Conduct Unbecoming; The Squeeze; Cheech & Chong's Up In Smoke; Gray Lady Down; Big Wednesday; Street People; The Search For Solutions (narr); The Ninth Configuration; Road Games; Cheech and Chong's Nice Dreams; Butterfly; That Championship Season.

TV inc: Caribe; Odyssey-Seeking The First Americans; A Rumor of War; The Blue and The Gray; Mickey Spillane's "Murder Me, Murder You"; Princess Daisy; More Than Murder; Mistral's Daughter.

KEANE, James: Act. b. Buffalo, NY, Sep 26, 1952. Films inc: Three Days of the Condor; Close Encounters of the Third Kind; The Ninth Configuration; Uncle Joe Shannon; Apocalypse Now; 48 Hours.

TV inc: Intimate Strangers; Night Cries; The Paper Chase; Life On The Mississippi; Pray TV; In Security (cable); The Sound of Murder (cable).

KEATON, Diane: Act. b. Santa Ana, CA, Jan 5, 1949. Performed in summer stock. Bway debut 1968, Hair.

Bway inc: Play It Again, Sam; The Primary English Class. Screen debut 1970, Lovers and Other Strangers.

Films inc: The Godfather; Play It Again, Sam; Sleeper; The Godfather, Part II; Love and Death; I Will, I Will...For Now...; Harry and Walter Go to New York; Annie Hall (Oscar-1977); Looking for Mr. Goodbar; Interiors; Manhattan; Reds; Shoot the Moon; The Little Drummer Girl; Mrs. Soffel.

TV inc: Love American Style; The FBI; Mannix.

KEATON, Michael: Act. b. Pittsburgh, PA, Sep. 9, 1951. Started as stand-up comic. TV inc: All's Fair; Working Stiffs; Mary; Mary Tyler Moore Hour; Studs Lonigan; Report to Murphy.

Films inc: Night Shift; Mr. Mom; Johnny Dangerously.

KEDROVA, Lila: Act. b. Russia, 1918. Films inc: Zorba the Greek (Oscar-supp-1964); A High Wind in Jamaica; Torn Curtain; Penelope; The Kremlin Letter; Soft Beds, Hard Battles; The Tenant; Widow's Nest; March or Die; Le Cavaleur; Claire De Femme; The Sewers of Paradise; Tell Me A Riddle; Blood Tide; Sword Of The Valiant.

Bway inc: Zorba (Tony-Featured-1984).

KEEFER, Don: Act. b. High Spire, PA. e. AADA. Films inc: Death of a Salesman; Riot in Cell Block II; Away All Boats; Six Bridges to Cross; Caine Mutiny; The Russians Are Coming! The Russians Are Coming!; Butch Cassidy and the Sundance Kid; The Way We Were; Sleeper; The Car; Firesale; Not So Big; Mirrors (Marianne); Marathon.

Thea inc: Junior Miss; Harriet; Othello; Death of a Salesman; Flight Into Egypt.

TV inc: Moviola (The Scarlett O'Hara War); The Five of Me.

KEEL, Howard: Act. b. Gillespie, IL, Apr 13, 1919. Stage debut, 1945, Carousel. Screen debut, 1948, The Small Voice.

Films inc: Annie Get Your Gun; Rose Marie; Showboat; Seven Brides For Seven Brothers; Kismet; Three Guys Named Mike; Ride Vaquero; Desperate Search; Calamity Jane; The Big Fisherman; Day of the Tiffids; War Wagon; Red Tomahawk.

Bway inc: Oklahoma; South Pacific; The Rainmaker; Mr. Roberts; Sunrise at Campobello; I Do, I Do; Ambassador.

TV inc: Dallas.

KEELER, Ruby: Act. b. Halifax, NS, Aug 25, 1909. Films inc: 42nd Street; Gold Diggers of 1933; Footlight Parade; Dames; Flirtation Walk; Go Into Your Dance; Shipmates Forever; Colleen; Ready Willing and Able; Mother Carey's Chickens; Sweetheart of the Campus; The Phynx.

Bway inc: The Rise Of Rosie O'Reilly; Bye, Bye Bonnie; Sidewalks of New York; Whoopee; Show Girl. Retired 1941. Retd to Bway 1971 revival No, No Nanette.

KEEP, Stephen: Act. b. Camden, SC, Aug 24. e. Columbia U; Yale School of Drama. Bway inc: Metamorphosis; Story Theatre; The Shadow Box.

Films inc: The Front; Love and Money.

TV inc: A Rumor of War; Bogie; Moviola; When Hell Was In Session; Panic On Page One; Billion Dollar Threat; Terror Among Us; Thursday's Child; Insight/The Fiddler; Mom's On Strike.

KEESHAN, Bob: Act. b. Lynbrook, NY, Jun 27, 1927. Hosted from its inception (1955) the children's program, Captain Kangaroo, on CBS-TV; (Emmys-star & prod-1982; Exec Prod-1983, 1984). Prior to that he was Clarabelle the Clown on Howdy Doody. Also created Tinker the Toymaker and prod and performed in the program Tinker's Workshop. TV inc: Good Evening, Captain (& exec prod); Revenge of the Nerd (exec prod); CBS Storybreak (host); How To Be A Man (& exec prod).

KEHOE, Jack: Act. b. NYC, Nov 21, 1938. Films inc: Panic in Needle Park; The Gang That Couldn't Shoot Straight; Law and Disorder; Serpico; The Sting; The Fish That Saved Pittsburgh; On The Nickel; Melvin and Howard; The Star Chamber; Two of a Kind; The Pope of Greenwich Village; The Killers; The Little Sister.

TV inc: Shell Game; Most Wanted; The Chicago Story; The Ballad of Gregorio Cortez.

KEIGHLEY, William: Dir. b. Philadelphia, PA, Aug. 4, 1889. Asst dir and dir Bway before turning to Hollywood in 1932.

Films inc: The Match King (co-dir); Ladies They Talk About (co-dir); Easy to Love; Big Hearted Herbert; Kansas City Priness; Babbitt; G-Men; Mary Jane's Pa; Special Agent; Stars Over Broadway; Green Pastures (co-dir); Bullets or Ballots; Prince and the Pauper; Adventures of Robin Hood (co-dir); Brother Rat; Yes, My Darling Daughter; Each Dawn I Die; The Fighting 69th; Torrid Zone; No Time for Comedy; The Bride Came C.O.D.; The Man Who Came to Dinner; George Washington Slept Here; The Street With No Name; Close to My Heart; The Master of Ballantrae.

(Died June 24, 1984).

KEIR, Andrew: Act. b. Scotland, 1926. Films inc: Scotch on the Rocks; High and Dry; Cleopatra; Lord Jim; The Long Duel; Five Million Years to Earth; Attack on the Iron Coast; Zeppelin; Blood from the Mummy's Tomb; Absolution.

KEITEL, Harvey: Act. b. NYC, May 13, 1939. Films inc: Who's that Knocking at My Door?; Mean Streets; Alice Doesn't Live Here Anymore; Taxi Driver; Mother, Jugs and Speed; Welcome to LA; Blue Collar; The Duellists; Fingers; The Eagle's Wing; Deathwatch; Bad Timing; The Border; La Nuit de Varennes (The Night of Varennes); Exposed; Order of Death; Une Pierre dans le Bouche (A Stone in the Mouth); Falling In Love; Dream One (Nemo).

Thea inc: Hurlyburly.

KEITH, Brian: Act. b. Bayonne, NJ, Nov 14, 1921. Bway inc: Mister Roberts; Darkness at Noon. Screen debut 1953, Arrowhead.

Films inc: Jivaro; Tight Spot; Storm Center; Chicago Confidential; The Parent Trap; The Pleasure Seekers; Moon Pilot; The Russians Are Coming, The Russians Are Coming; Reflections in a Golden Eye; Gaily, Gaily; Suppose They Gave a War And Nobody Came; With Six You Get Eggroll; The Wind and the Lion; Nickelodeon; Hooper; Meteor; Moonraker; The Mountain Men; Charlie Chan and the Curse of the Dragon Queen; Sharky's Machine.

TV inc: Studio One; Suspense; Philco Playhouse; The Crusader; The Westerner; Family Affair; Little People; Centennial; The Seekers; Power; Moviola (The Silent Lovers); World War III; Cry For the Strangers; Hardcastle and McCormick; Murder She Wrote; The Sun Also Rises.

KEITH, David: Act. b. Knoxville, TN, 1954. e. U of TN. TV inc: Co-Ed Fever; Golden Moment; Friendly Fire. Films inc: The Rose; Take This Job and Shove It; The Great Santini; Brubaker; Back Roads; An Officer and a Gentleman; Independence Day; The Lords of Discipline; Firestarter.

TV inc: Gulag.

KELLER, Harry: Dir. b. Los Angeles, Feb 22, 1913. Former film editor. Dir debut 1949, The Blonde Bandit.

Films inc: The Unguarded Moment; The Brass Bottle; Send Me No Flowers; That Funny Feeling; Voice in the Mirror; Tammy Tell Me True; Mirage; Texas Across the River; In Enemy Country; The Skin Game (& prod); Stir Crazy (edit); Stripes (edit).

TV inc: The Loretta Young Show; Schlitz Playhouse; Four Star Theatre; The Swamp Fox (pilot); Texas John Slaughter.

KELLER, Marthe: Act. b. Switzerland. e. Stanislavsky School, Munich; Brecht Theatre, East Berlin. Films inc: The Devil By the Tail; Les Caprices de Marie; And Now My Love; Down the Ancient Stairs; The Hornet's Nest; Marathon Man; Black Sunday; Bobby Deerfield; Fedora; The Formula; The Amateur; Wagner; Femmes de Personne (Nobody's Women).

TV inc: (France) Arsene Lupin; Le Demoiselle d'Avignon; The Charterhouse of Parma (cable).

Thea inc: (Paris) A Day In the Death of Joe Egg; Exiles. (Salzburg) Jedermann.

KELLERMAN, Sally: Act. b. Long Beach, CA, Jun 2, 1936. Films inc: The Boston Strangler; The April Fools; M*A*S*H; Brewster McCloud; Last of the Red Hot Lovers; Lost Horizon; Slither; Rafferty and the Gold Dust Twins; The Big Bus; Welcome to LA; The Mouse and his Child (voice); A Little Romance; Foxes; Serial; Loving Couples; Head On; Moving Violations.

TV inc: Centennial; Verna--USO Girl; Big Blonde; For Lovers Only; Dempsey; September Gun; Secret Weapons.

KELLEY, DeForest: Act. b. Atlanta, GA, Jan 20, 1920. Films inc: Fear in the Night; Canon City; The Men; House of Bamboo; Man in the Gray Flannel Suit; Tension at Tablerock; Gunfight at the OK Corral; Raintree County; The Law and Jake Wade; Warlock; Where Love Has Gone; Marriage on the Rocks; Star Trek-The Motion Picture; Star Trek II--The Wrath of Khan; Star Trek III--The Search For Spock.

TV inc: Star Trek.

KELLEY, William: Wri. b. NYC, May 27, 1929. e. Brown U, AB; Harvard U, AM. TV inc: Route 66; Gunsmoke; Kung Fu; Serpico; Petrocelli; How the West Was Won; The Winds of Kitty Hawk; Key Tor-

tuga (& prod); The Demon Murder Case.

Films inc: Witness.

KELLIN, Mike: Act. Films inc: So Young, So Bad; At War With the Army; Lonely Hearts; The Great Imposter; The Wackiest Ship In the Army; Invitation To A Gunfighter; Banning; The Boston Strangler; The Maltese Bippie; Fool's Parade; Freebie and the Bean; Girl Friends; Midnight Express; On the Yard; The Jazz Singer; So Fine; Paternity; Sleepaway Camp; Echoes.

TV inc: Battles--The Murder That Wouldn't Die; FDR--The Last Year; Fitz and Bones.

Bway inc: Pipe Dream; The Ritz.

(Died Aug. 26, 1983).

KELLY, Gene: Act-Dir. b. Pittsburgh, Aug 23, 1912. e. U of Pittsburgh, BA. Bway debut, 1938, Leave It To Me. Film debut, 1942, For Me and My Gal.

Films inc: Du Barry Was A Lady; Thousands Cheer; Cross of Lorraine; Cover Girl; Christmas Holiday; Anchors Aweigh (chor); Ziegfeld Follies; The Three Musketeers; The Pirate; Words and Music; Take Me Out to the Ball Game (chor); On The Town; An American in Paris (chor); Singin' in the Rain (chor & co-dir); Brigadoon (chor); Invitation to the Dance (dir & chor); Marjorie Morningstar; Les Girls; Inherit the Wind; Gigot (dir); What a Way to Go!; A Guide for the Married Man; Hello, Dolly (dir); The Cheyenne Social Club (dir); 40 Carats; That's Entertainment (narr); That's Entertainment Part 2 (narr-dir new sequences); That's Dancing!

(Oscar-special-1951).

Bway inc: Pal Joey; The Time of Your Life; One for the Money.

TV inc: Jack and the Beanstalk (Emmy-prod-1967); Julie Andrews Show; New York, New York (host, chor); Gene Kelly and 50, Count 'Em Girls; The Funny Side; Lucy Moves To NBC; Debby Boone--The Same Old Brand New Me (prod); AFI Salute To Fred Astaire; Opryland--Night of Stars and Future Stars (host); The World of Entertainment (host); The Kennedy Center Honors 1982 (honoree); Dom DeLuise and Friends; Olympic Gala; AFI Salute To Gene Kelly.

Sep 1980 signed with Francis Ford Coppola to create musical prodn unit at Zoetrope Studio.

KELLY, Jack: Act. b. NYC, 1927. Films inc: Where Danger Lives; Drive a Crooked Road; To Hell and Back; Hong Kong Affair; Love and Kisses; Young Billy Young.

TV inc: King's Row; Maverick.

KELLY, Nancy: Act. b. Lowell, MA, Mar 25, 1921. On Bway as child in Give Me Yesterday.

Bway inc: Susan and God; The Big Knife; Bad Seed (Tony-1955); Season In The Sun; The Gingerbread Lady.

Films inc: (silent) Untamed Lady; Great Gatsby. (Sound) Stanley and Livingston; Tailspin; To The Shores of Tripoli; Murder in the Music Hall; Jesse James; Friendly Enemies.

KELLY, Paula: Act-sing. b. Jacksonville, FL, Oct 21, 1943. e. Juilliard. With Harry Belafonte's touring company while at Juilliard. Bway inc: Something More; Sweet Charity; The Dozens.

Films inc: Sweet Charity; The Andromeda Strain.

TV inc: Al Hirt Show; Harry Belafonte Special; Gene Kelly Special; Sammy Davis Jr, Special; A Step Too Slow; Komedy Tonite; The Cheap Detective; Sophisticated Ladies (PPV); Feel the Heat; Chiefs.

KELMAN, Alfred R.: Prod. b. NYC, May 17, 1936. e. Boston U, MJ. TV inc: Agassiz the Man; Martin Luther King in Boston; The Face of Genius; This Week; The Government; Scopitone; The Transplanter; Drug of Choice; The Body Human (Emmy-1978); Lifeline (Emmy-1979); The Body Human--The Sexes; The Body Human--The Magic Sense (Emmy-1980); The Body Human--The Body Beautiful; The Body Human--The Sexes II; The Body Human--Facts for Boys (& prod); The Body Human--The Bionic Breakthrough (& dir) (Emmy-1981); The Body Human--Becoming A Man (& dir); The Body Human--Becoming A Woman (& dir); The Body Human--The Loving Process--Men (& dir); The Body Human--The Loving Process--Women (& dir) (Emmy-dir-1982); The Body Human--The Living Code (& dir) (Emmys-prod & dir-1983); To Catch A King; The Body Human--The Journey Within (& dir); A Christmas Carol.

KELSEY, Linda: Act. b. Minneapolis, MN, Jul 28, 1946. e. U of MI,

BA.

TV inc: Picture of Dorian Gray; Something for Joey; Eleanor and Franklin; The Last of Mrs. Lincoln; Lou Grant; A Perfect Match; Attack On Fear; His Mistress.

Thea inc: The Tempest; Summer and Smoke; The Crucible; A Pagan Place.

KEMENY, John: Prod. b. Budapest, Hungary, Apr 17, 1925. Films inc: Don't Let the Angels Fall; Sept Fois Par Jour; Un Enfant Comme Les Autres; The Apprenticeship of Duddy Kravitz; White Line Fever; Shadow of the Hawk; Ice Castles; Les Plouffe; La Guerre de Feu (Quest For Fire); Louisiane; Le Sang des Autres (The Blood of Others); Bay Boy.

KEMP, Jeremy: Act. b. Chesterfield, England, Feb 3, 1935. Films inc: Cast a Giant Shadow; Operation Crossbow; The Blue Max; Twist of Sand; Strange Affair; Darling Lili; The Games; The Salzburg Connection; The Seven-Per-Cent Solution; Caravans; Prisoner of Zenda; The Return of the Soldier; Top Secret.

TV inc: Z Cars; Colditz; The Rainmaker; The Lovers of Florence; School Play; The Last Roundup; Vikings; Evita Peron; Unity Mitford; The Winds of War; Laurence Olivier Presents King Lear; Sadat; George Washington.

KEMPSON, Rachel: Act. b. Dartmouth, Devon, England, May 28, 1910. e. RADA. W of the late Sir Michael Redgrave. M of Corin, Lynn & Vanessa Redgrave. London stage debut 1933 in the Lady from Alfaqueque.

Thea inc: Twelfth Night; Love's Labour's Lost; Venus Observed; Hedda Gabler; Not for Children; Romeo and Juliet; Teresa of Avila; Saint Joan of the Stockyards; The Freeway; A Family and a Fortune; The Old Country.

Films inc: The Captive Heart; Georgy Girl; The Jokers; Charge of the Light Brigade; The Virgin Soldiers; Jane Eyre.

TV inc: Little Lord Fauntleroy; Camille; The Jewel In The Crown. chael Redgrave. M of Lynn & Vanessa Redgrave. London stage debut 1933 in the Lady from Alfaqueque.

Thea inc: Twelfth Night; Love's Labour's Lost; Venus Observed; Hedda Gabler; Not for Children; Romeo and Juliet; Teresa of Avila; Saint Joan of the Stockyards; The Freeway; A Family and a Fortune; The Old Country.

Films inc: The Captive Heart; Georgy Girl; The Jokers; Charge of the Light Brigade; The Virgin Soldiers; Jane E

KEMP-WELCH, Joan: Act-Dir. b. Wimbledon, England, 1906. Thea inc: (Act) John Gabriel Borkman; Silent Witness; Glory Be; Nina; The Melody That Got Lost; Nora; Lady Fanny; Ladies in Retirement; It Happened In September. (Dir) Desire Under The Elms; Dead On Nine; dir various repertory and festival prodns.

Films inc: (Act) Once A Thief; The Girl in the Taxi; Busman's Honeymoon; Pimpernel Smith; They Flew Alone; Goodbye Mr. Chips; The Citadel; Jeanie.

TV inc: (Dir) A Birthday Party; A View From the Bridge; A Midsummer Night's Dream; Elektra.

KENDAL, Felicity: Act. b. Birmingham, England, 1946. Stage debut age 9 months in parents' Shakespearean productions. Toured with them in India, Far East through childhood. London debut 1967 in Minor Murder.

Thea inc: Various Shakespearean roles, The Norman Conquest; Clouds; Amadeus; Othello; On The Razzle. The Second Mrs Tanqueray; The Real Thing; Jumpers.

Films inc: Shakespeare Wallah; Valentino.

TV inc: The Good Life; Edward the Seventh; The Mayfly And The Frog.

KENDALL, Suzy (Frieda Harrison): Act. b. Belper, England, 1943. Film inc: Circus of Fear; To Sir with Love; Penthouse; Up the Junction; Thirty is a Dangerous Age; Cynthia; Fraulein Doktor; The Betrayal; Darker than Amber; The Bird with the Crystal Plumage; Assault; Craze; Fear is the Key.

KENDALL, William: Act. b. London, Aug 26, 1903. Thea inc: The Royal Visitor; Old Heidelberg; March Hares; The Command Performance; This'll Make You Whistle; Between the Devil; The Lady Asks for Help; Primrose and the Peanuts; Castle in the Air; Night Call; The

Nest Egg; It's Different for Men; Star Maker; Towards Zero; The Brides of March; August for the People; The Circle; Highly Confidential.

KENNEDY, Arthur: Act. b. Worcester, MA, Feb 17, 1914. On screen from 1940 in City for Conquest.

Films inc: Champion; Bright Victory; Trial; Peyton Place; Some Came Running; High Sierra; They Died With Their Boots On; The Glass Menagerie; The Desperate Hours; Elmer Gantry; Lawrence of Arabia; The Sentinel; The Tempter; Covert Action.

Bway inc: Merrily We Roll Along; Life and Death of an American; All My Sons; Death of a Salesman (Tony-supp-1949); See The Jaguar; The Crucible; Time Limit.

KENNEDY, Betty: Act. b. Roswell, NM, Oct 2. Films inc: Cheech and Chong's Next Movie. TV inc: Rockford Files; Ladies Man.

KENNEDY, Burt: Wri-Dir. b. Muskegon, MI, Sep 3, 1922. Films inc: Rounders (sp-dir); War Wagon (dir); Support Your Local Sheriff (dir); Mail Order Bride (sp-dir); Welcome to Hard Times (sp-dir); Return of the Seven (dir); Good Guys Bad Guys (dir); Dirty Dingus Magee (sp-prod-dir); Train Robbers (sp-dir); Wolf Lake (sp-dir). TV inc: (dir) The Wild, Wild West Revisited; The Concrete Cowboys; More Wild Wild West.

KENNEDY, Byron Eric: Prod. b. Melbourne, Aug 18, 1949. Films inc: Mad Max; Mad Max 2; (Road Warrior); The Cowra Breakout.

(Died July 17, 1983).

KENNEDY, George: Act. b. NYC, Feb 18, 1927. Started career at age 2 in touring company of Bringing Up Father.

Films inc: Lonely Are The Brave; Strait Jacket; Charade; Shenandoah; The Dirty Dozen; Cool Hand Luke (Oscar-supp-1967); Airport; Airport '75; The Eiger Sanction; Airport '77; Brass Target; Death on the Nile; Concorde-Airport '79; The Double McGuffin; Death Ship; Virus; Steel; Modern Romance; Search and Destroy; Wacko; A Rare Breed; The Jupiter Menace; Bolero; Savage Dawn; Rigged.

TV inc: Sarge; The Blue Knight; Backstairs At The White House; Never Say Never; Hard Times (host); Steve Allen Comedy Hour; The Archer--Fugitive From The Empire; Deathwatch (cable tv) (narr); Decoys (narr); Counterattack--Crime In America (host); Going Straight (host); Bliss; The Jesse Owens Story; Half Nelson; International Airport.

KENNEDY, Jayne: Act-TV pers. b. Washington, DC, Oct 27, 1951. TV inc: The NFL Today; Speak Up America (Co-host); All-Star Salute To Mother's Day (host); The First All-American Ultra Quiz (host).

Films inc: Big Time; Death Force; The Muthers; Group Marriage; Lady Sings The Blues; Let's Do It Again; Body and Soul.

KENNEDY, Madge: Act. b. Chicago, IL, 1892. Bway inc: Little Miss Brown; Twin Beds; Fair and Warmer; Cornered; Poppy; Paris Bound; Bridal Wise.

Films inc: Baby Mine; The Danger Game; The Fair Pretender; Friendly Husband; A Perfect Lady; A Kingdom of Youth; Leave It to Susan; Three Miles Out; Bad Company; Lying Wives; Oh, Baby!; The Marrying Kind; The Rains of Ranchipur; Catered Affair; Lust For Life; A Nice Little Bank That Should Be Robbed; Let's Make Love; They Shoot Horses, Don't They?; The Baby Maker; Day of the Locust.

KENNEY, H. Wesley: Dir. TV inc: All in the Family; Days of Our Lives (& exec prod); (Emmys-(4) dir drama, dir special pgm, dir of year-1974; exec prod-1978); Filthy Rich; The Young & the Restless (Emmy-Exec Prod-1983).

KENWITH, Herbert: Prod-Dir. TV inc: Daktari; Star Trek; Temperatures Rising; The Partridge Family; Love American Style; Mary Tyler Moore; Marcus Welby; All That Glitters; Good Times; One Day at a Time; Different Strokes; Me and Maxx; The Rainbow Girl.

KENYON, Curtis: Wri. Films inc: Woman Who Dared; Lloyds of London; Wake Up and Live; Love and Hisses; She Knew All the Answers; Seven Days Leave; Thanks for Everything; Princess and the Pirate; Bathing Beauty; Fabulous Dorseys; Tulsa; Two Flags West.

TV inc: Cavalcade of America; Fireside Theatre; U.S. Steel Hour; Waikiki.

KERCHEVAL, Ken: Act. b. Wolcottville, IN, Jul 15. e. U of IN; Pacific U. Bway inc: Who's Afraid of Virginia Woolf?; Fiddler on the Roof; Cabaret; The Apple Tree; Who's Happy Now?; Father's Day.

Films inc: Pretty Poison; The Seven-Ups; Network; F.I.S.T; Too Far To Go.

TV inc: The Coming Asunder of Jimmy Bright; The Scottsboro Boys; Separating; Something in the Air; Dallas; The Patricia Neal Story; The Demon Murder Case; Calamity Jane.

KERKORIAN, Kirk: Exec. b. Fresno, CA, Jun 6, 1917. A captain in the RAF Transport Command during WW2, he opened flight training school after war, branched into non-sked airline field, later charter; subsequently sold 58% interest in Trans International Airlines to Transamerica Corp for $104 million; bought Flamingo Hotel, Las Vegas, began acquiring land Las Vegas, built International Hotel; began acquiring MGM stock, became majority owner 1974, served as vice chmn, CEO until Nov 1978 when, having acquired large interest in Columbia Pictures, he stepped down from executive positions while retaining financial interest; with split of MGM into two companies (films and hotels) is biggest stockholder in each.

KERR, Anita (nee Grilli): Comp-Arr-Vocalist. b. Memphis, TN, Oct 13. Founder of the Anita Kerr Singers; co-founder of the San Sebastian Strings. Films scores inc: Limbo. (Grammys-(3)-vocal group-1965, 1966; Gospel-1965).

KERR, Deborah (nee Kerr-Trimmer): Act. b. Helensburgh, Scotland, Sep 30, 1921. London stage debut, 1938, Sadler's Wells ballet. Screen debut, 1940, Major Barbara. Bway debut 1953, Tea and Sympathy.

Films inc: Love on the Dole; The Life and Death of Colonel Blimp; Perfect Strangers; I See a Dark Stranger; Black Narcissus; The Hucksters; Edward, My Son; Quo Vadis; Julius Caesar; From Here to Eternity; The King and I; Tea and Sympathy; Heaven Knows, Mr. Allison; An Affair to Remember; Separate Tables; Bonjour Tristesse; The Sundowners; The Journey; The Grass Is Greener; The Innocents; The Chalk Garden; The Night of the Iguana; Casino Royale; Prudence and the Pill; The Gypsy Moths; The Arrangement.

Bway inc: The Day After the Fair; Seascape; Souvenir; Long Day's Journey Into Night; Last of Mrs. Cheyney; Candida. London thea inc: Overheard.

TV inc; Witness For the Prosecution; A Woman Of Substance; Reunion At Fairborough.

KERR, Elizabeth: Act. b. Kansas City, MO, Aug 12. e. Northwestern U. Became actress 1944 after her sons were grown. Bway inc: Angel in the Pawnshop; The Righteous Are Bold; Conquering Hero; Redhead. (Tours) Music Man; The Front Page; Joe Egg; Anything Goes; Harvey.

Films inc: Coma; Matilda; Spree; Dogs; Going Berserk.

TV inc: Hitch Hike; Mork and Mindy; Double Trouble; Punky Brewster; Highway To Heaven.

KERR, Jean (nee Collins): Plywri. b. Scranton, PA, Jul 10, 1923. e. Marywood Coll; Catholic U. W of Walter Kerr. Plays inc: Song of Bernardette (with husband); Jenny Kissed Me; Touch and Go (with husband); sketches for John Murray's Almanac; King of Hearts (with Eleanor Brooke); Goldilocks (with husband); Mary, Mary; Poor Richard; Finishing Touches; Penny Candy; Lunch Hour.

TV inc: The Good Fairy. (Book: Please Don't Eat the Daisies was adapted as a tv series).

KERR, John: Act. b. NYC, Nov 15, 1931. Films inc: The Cobweb; Gaby; Tea and Sympathy; South Pacific; The Pit and the Pendulum; Seven Women From Hell.

TV inc: Peyton Place.

Thea inc: Tea and Sympathy (Tony-supp-1954).

KERR, Walter: Wri-Dir. b. Evanston, IL, Jul 8, 1913. e. Northwestern U. H of Jean Kerr. Drama Critic For Commonweal; NY Herald Tribune; NY Times.

Plays inc: Song of Bernardette (with wife); Count Me In (co-author); Swing Out Sweet Land (& dir); Touch and Go (with wife); King of Hearts (dir); Goldilocks (with wife).

TV inc: Esso Repertory Theatre (host).

(Pulitzer Prize-for criticism-1978).

KERSHNER, Irvin: Dir. b. Philadelphia, Apr 29, 1923. e. Temple U; USC. Films inc: Stakeout on Dope Street; The Young Captives; The Hoodlum Priest; Face in the Rain; The Luck of Ginger Coffey; A Fine Madness; The Flim Flam Man; Loving; Up the Sandbox; S P Y S; The Return of a Man Called Horse; Eyes of Laura Mars; The Empire Strikes Back; Never Say Never Again.

TV inc: Raid on Entebbe.

KERWIN, Brian: Act. b. Chicago, Oct 25, 1949. e. USC. TV inc: The Young and Restless; American Girls; The Chisholms; A Real American Hero; Power; The Misadventures of Sheriff Lobo; Lobo; The Blue and The Gray; Miss All-American Beauty; Intimate Agony; Wet Gold.

Films inc: Hometown U.S.A.; Soft Explosion.

KERWIN, Lance: Act. b. Newport Beach, CA, Nov 6, 1960. Films inc: Escape to Witch Mountain.

TV inc: Reflections of Terror; Pssst, Hammerman's After You; The Healers; The Cloning of Richard Swimmer; The Family Holvak; Amelia Earhart; The Death of Richie; Me And Dad's New Wife; The Loneliest Runner; James at 16; Salem's Lot; The Boy Who Drank Too Much; Animal Talk; Children of Divorce; Side Show; Advice to the Lovelorn; The Shooting; The Mysterious Stranger; Insight/A Gun For Mandy; A Killer in the Family; The Fourth Wise Man.

KESSLER, Bruce: Dir. b. CA, Mar 23, 1936. Films inc: Angels From Hell; Killers Three; Gay Deceivers; Simon. TV inc: Border Pals.

KESSLER, Ralph: Comp-Cond. b. NYC, Aug 1, 1919. e. Juilliard School of Music, BS, MS. Trumpeter with dance bands, Bway pit orchs inc: This Is The Army; created original music treatments and sketches for Man of La Mancha. P Ralph Kessler Prodns, specializing in music for commercials.

TV inc: arr-comp for Arthur Godfrey Show, 1951-1959; scores inc Barnaby Jones; Police Story.

KEYES, Evelyn: Act. b. Port Arthur, TX, 1919. Began career as a dancer in niteries.

Films inc: Gone With The Wind; Union Pacific; The Jolson Story; The Prowler; The Killer That Stalked New York; The Iron Man; 99 River Street; Seven-Year Itch; Around the World in 80 Days; Artie Shaw--Time Is All You've Got (doc-int).

Thea inc: No, No, Nanette.

KEYES, Paul W.: Prod-wri. b. Boston, MA. Started as anncr on New England radio stations, began writing comedy material for Kaye Ballard. TV inc: Tonight Show (wri); Dean Martin Show (wri); Laugh In (wri); AFI Salutes (James Cagney; Orson Welles; William Wyler); The Grammy Awards; The People's Choice Awards; The Emmy Awards; Swing Out Sweet Land; All Star Party for Ingrid Bergman; Take One; All Star Party for Burt Reynolds; Sinatra and His Friends; Sinatra - The First 40 Years; Sinatra-The Man and His Music; All Star Party for Carol Burnett; All Star Party for Frank Sinatra; All Star Party For Lucille Ball.

KIBBEE, Lois: Act. b. Wheeling, WV, Jul 13. Member of theatrical family, on stage from age five in stock, repertory; on radio. Bway inc: A Man For All Seasons; Venus Is.

TV inc; The Edge of Night (since 1970) (& assoc-wri since 1981).

KIBBEE, Roland: Wri. b. Monongahela, PA, Feb 15, 1914. Writer for Fred Allen Show; Fanny Brice; Groucho Marx.

Films inc: A Night in Casablanca; Angel on my Shoulder; The Crimson Pirate.

TV inc: (wri-prod) The Ford Show; The Deputy; The Bob Cummings Show; The Bob Newhart Show; Columbo (Emmy-exec prod-1974); Barney Miller (exec prod) (Emmy-1982).

(Died Aug. 5, 1984)

KIBLER, William Stephan (Steve): Prod. b. St Louis, MO, Sep 8, 1941. e. Eastern KY U, BA. Started as agent with William Morris; exec dir development Aaron Spelling Prodns & Spelling-Goldberg Prodns; became m-dir Seven Keys TV, Sydney, Australia; exec prod Gemini Prodns, Sydney; exec prod Reg Grundy Prodns, Sydney.

KIDD, Michael (Milton Greenwald): Dir-Chor-Act. b. NYC, Aug 12, 1919. e. CCNY; School of the American Ballet. On stage as dancer from 1938.

Films inc: (chor) Where's Charley?; The Band Wagon; Seven Brides for Seven Brothers; Guys and Dolls; Merry Andrew (dir only); Star!; Hello, Dolly!; Smile (perf); Movie Movie (chor & perf). Bway inc: (chor) Finian's Rainbow (Tony-1947); Hold It; Love Life; Arms and the Girl; Guys and Dolls (Tony-1951); Can-Can (Tony-1954); Skyscraper; Li'l Abner (Tony-1957); Wildcat (& prod); Destry Rides Again (Tony-1960); Subways Are for Sleeping; Ben Franklin in Paris; The Rothschilds; Cyrano; Good News; The Music Man (rev).

TV inc: Baryshnikov in Hollywood (conceived & supv).

Ballets inc: Pillar of Fire; Dim Lustre; Fancy Free; Romeo & Juliet; Giselle; Copellia.

KIDDER, Margot: Act. b. Yellowknife, Canada, Oct 17, 1948. Films inc: Gaily, Gaily; Quackser Fortune Has A Cousin in the Bronx, Sisters; The Great Waldo Pepper; Superman; Mr. Mike's Mondo Video; The Amityville Horror; Willy & Phil; Superman II; Heartaches; Some Kind of Hero; Trenchcoat; Superman III; Louisiane; Little Treasure.

TV inc: Bus Stop (cable); The Glitter Dome (PC).

KIEL, Richard: Act. b. Detroit, Sep 13, 1939. Films inc: Eegah; The Human Duplicators; Skidoo; The Longest Yard; The Spy Who Loved Me; Force 10 From Navarone; They Went Thataway & Thataway; Flash and the Firecat; Moonraker; So Fine; Hysterical; War of the Wizards; Aces Go Places II (Our Man From Bond Street); Cannonball Run II; Pale Rider.

TV inc: Klondike; The Riflemen; I Spy; The Barbary Coast.

KIERNAN, Laurence James: Exec. b. Perth, Western Australia, Jun 1, 1927. Exec dir Swan Television Ltd, 1969; m-dir, 1971.

KIESER, Father Ellwood E. C.S.P.: Prod. b. Philadelphia, PA, Mar 27, 1929. e. LaSalle Coll, BA; St. Paul's College, MA; Graduate Theological Union Berkeley, PhD. Creator-producer of Insight tv series (Emmys-1981, 1983, 1984); exec producer Capital Cities Family Specials; Reflections; The Soup Man; Who Loves Amy Tonight; The Juggler of Notre Dame (Emmy-exec prod-1983); Leadfoot; Hang Tight, Willy Bill; Insight/The Fiddler (wri); Clay Feet.

KILEY, Richard: Act. b. Chicago, Mar 31, 1922. e. Loyola U. Began in radio. Films inc: The Mob; The Sniper; Pick-up on South Street; The Blackboard Jungle; Pendulum; The Little Prince; Looking for Mr. Goodbar; Endless Love.

Bway inc: A Streetcar Named Desire; A Month of Sundays; Kismet; Redhead (Tony-1959); Advise and Consent; Man of LaMancha (Tony-1966); The Heiress (rev); Knickerbocker Holiday (rev); The Incomparable Max; Absurd Person Singular.

TV inc: Patterns; Arrowsmith; POW; Close Quarters; Angel On My Shoulder; Golden Gate; Isabel's Choice; Pray TV; Come Along With Me; Rain Forest; The Thorn Birds (Emmy-supp-1983); Parade of Stars; George Washington; The Bad Seed; Land Of The Tiger (narr); Ballad Of The Irish Horse (narr); A.D.; Do You Remember Love.

KILTY, Jerome: Act-Dir-Plywri. b. Pala Indian Reservation, CA, Jun 24, 1922. e. Harvard, BA. Co-founder of Brattle Theatre, Cambridge, MA. Bway inc: (Act) The Relapse; Love's Labour's Lost; Mesalliance; A Pin to See The Peep Show; Frogs of Spring; Quadrille; Othello; Henry IV; A Moon For the Misbegotten; Enter A Free Man (Off-Bway). (Dir) Dear Liar (& adapt). Also dir Dear Liar London, Paris & Berlin prodns; asso dir ACT, visiting act-dir Goodman Theatre, Chicago; Alley Theatre, Houston.

Plays inc: the Ides of March; Nymphs & Satires; Don't Shoot Mabel, It's Your Husband; Long Live Life; Dear Love; The Laffing Man; Look Away.

KINBERG, Judy: Prod. b. Freeport, NY., Sept. 15, 1948. e. Hofstra U (BA). Started with CBS Camera Three program. Became prod at PBS l977. TV inc: (co-prod) Pilobolus Dance Theatre; Trailblazers Of Modern Dance; San Francisco Ballet--Romeo and Juliet; Choreography By Balanchine, Part III; Choreography By Balanchine, Part IV (Emmy-classical-1979); The Spellbound Child; Nureyev and the Joffrey Ballet In Tribute To Nijinsky; The Tempest; Paul Taylor--Three Modern Classics; Paul Taylor--Two Landmark Dances; Bournelville Dances; He Makes Me Feel Like Dancin' (Emmy-1984). (Prod) Out Of Our Father's House; The Feld Ballet; The Green Table, With The Joffrey Ballet; The Magic Flute With the NYC Ballet; San Francisco Ballet--A Song For Dead Warriors; A Choreographer's Notebook--Stravinsky Piano Ballets by Peter Martins; Balanchine, Parts I and II; San Francisco Ballet in Cinderella.

KING, Alan: Act. b. NYC, Dec. 26, 1926. Performs on stage, TV. Films inc: Hit the Deck; Miracle in the Rain; The Helen Morgan Story; Operation Snafu; Bye Bye Braverman; The Anderson Tapes; Just Tell Me What You Want; Happy Birthday, Gemini (exec prod); Cattle Annie and Little Britches (prod); Wolfen (exec prod); I, The Jury; Author! Author!; Lovesick; Cat's Eye.

TV inc: Alan King's Energy Crisis; Alan King's Third Annual Final Warning; Seventh Avenue; Alan King's Thanksgiving Special--What Do We Have To Be Thankful For; Pinocchio's Christmas (voice); The 4th Annual TV Guide Special; America's Funniest Foul-Ups (host); Reunion At Fairborough; The Television Academy Hall Of Fame 1985.

Bway inc: The Impossible Years; Dinner at Eight; The Lion in Winter.

KING, Allan Winton: Prod-Dir-Wri. b. Vancouver, Canada, 1930. e. U of BC. Joined Canadian Broadcasting Corp 1954, became dir 1956; opened indie firm in England 1962, specializing in documentaries. Films inc: (Doc) Skid Row; Portrait of a Harbor; Morocco; Bull Fight; Rickshaw; Portrait of a Ballerina; A Matter of Pride; The Pursuit of Happiness; The Peacemakers; Bjorn's Inferno; Coming of Age in Ibiza; Running Away Backwards; Warrendale (originally made for CBC which refused to show it); The New Woman; A Married Couple; Come on Children; Six Years War. (Features) A Bird in the House; Who Has Seen the Wind; One Night Stand; Silence of the North.

TV inc: Who's In Charge (prod).

KING, Andrea: Act. b. Paris, Feb 7, 1915. Films inc: Mr. Skeffington; The Very Thought of You; My Wild Irish Rose; Ride the Pink Horse; Hollywood Canteen; God Is My Co-Pilot; Hotel Berlin; Roughly Speaking; The Man I Love; Shadow of a Woman; Mr. Peabody and the Mermaid; Dial 1119; The World In His Arms; The Lemon Drop Kid; Red Planet Mars; Band of Angels; Darby's Rangers; Daddy's Gone A Hunting; Prescription Murder.

TV inc: The Days of Our Lives.

KING, Bob: Wri-Exec. b. Cincinnati, OH, Aug 1, 1928. Dir Mktg Svs, Disney; 1980, VP Mktg. Films inc: Now You See Him, Now You Don't (orig story); The Illusion of Life (prod).

TV inc: 50 Happy Years; Disney's Greatest Villains.

KING, Carole: Singer-Sngwri. b. Brooklyn, NY, Feb 9, 1942. Songs inc: Will You Love Me Tomorrow; He's A Rebel; Go Away, Little Girl; Up on the Roof; Natural Woman; Take Good Care of My Baby; You've Got a Friend (Grammy-song of year-1971); It's Too Late.

(Grammys-(3)-album of year-record of year-pop vocal-1971).

KING, Frank (PeeWee): Comp-Mus. b. Milwaukee, WI, Feb 18, 1914. Country mus recording artist; TV inc Grand Ole Opry. Films inc: Gold Mine in the Sky; Riding the Outlaw Trail.

Songs inc: Tennessee Waltz.

KING, Larry L.: Wri-Act. b. Putnam, TX, Jan 1, 1929. e. TX Tech; Nieman Fellow at Harvard. Bway inc: Co-author Best Little Whorehouse in Texas (& act); The Kingfish. Films inc: The Best Little Whorehouse in Texas. TV inc: The Best Little Statehouse in Texas.

KING, Mabel: Act. b. Charlestown, SC, Dec 25. Films inc: Blood Couple; The Bingo Long Traveling All-Stars and Motor Kings; The Wiz; Getting Over.

Bway inc: Hello Dolly; Don't Play Us Cheap; The Wiz.

TV inc: What's Happening!; The Jerk, Too.

KING, Paul: Exec. b. Los Angeles. e. Loyola U; USC. Started as a wri. Films inc: Operation Petticoat; Wild Heritage; Canyons of Jade; The Iron Horse.

With CBS from 1966 to 1976, rising to vp of development, then vp, program prodns. Moved to WB; then Quinn Martin Prodns; joined NBC; appointed vp, Prime Time Series, NBC Entertainment, Oct 1978; VP Drama Programs, Feb 1980; June 1983, exec prod NBC Productions.

KING, Perry: Act. Films inc: Slaughterhouse Five; The Possession of Joel Delaney; The Lords of Flatbush; Mandingo; The Wild Party; Lipstick; Andy Warhol's Bad; The Choirboys; A Different Story; Search and Destroy; Class of 1984.

TV inc: The Cracker Factory; Love's Savage Fury; The Last Convertible; City in Fear; Foster and Laurie; Inmates--A Love Story; Golden Gate; The Quest; The Hasty Heart (cable); Riptide; Helen Keller--The Miracle Continues.

KINGI, Henry: Act. b. Los Angeles, Dec 2, 1943. Films inc: R.P.M.; Buck and the Preacher; Cleopatra Jones; Uptown Saturday Night; Smoke in the Wind; Swashbuckler; Car Wash.

TV inc: Search for the Gods.

KINGSLEY, Ben: Act. b. Yorkshire, England, Dec 31, 1943. In repertory, several seasons with Royal Shakespeare Company. Thea inc: The Relapse; Troilus and Cressida; Much Ado About Nothing; Midsummer Night's Dream (& U.S. Tour); Enemies; Occupations; Hello and Goodbye; A Lesson in Blood and Roses; Volpone; Julius Caesar; Baal; Nicholas Nickleby. Bway: Edmund Kean.

TV inc: The Love School; Every Good Boy Deserves Favour; The Merry Wives of Windsor; A Tribute to Martin Luther King Jr.--A Celebration of Life; Camille.

Films inc: Fear Is the Key; Gandhi; (Oscar-1982); Betrayal; Sleeps Six.

KINGSLEY, Dorothy: Wri. b. NYC, Oct 14, 1909. Radio wri for Bob Hope; Edgar Bergen.

Films inc: Date With Judy; Neptune's Daughter; When in Rome; It's A Big Country; Kiss Me Kate; Seven Brides for Seven Brothers; Pal Joey; Can Can; Pepe; Half a Sixpence; Valley of the Dolls.

TV inc: created series Bracken's World.

KINGSLEY, Sidney (nee Kirchner): Wri-Prod-Dir. b. NYC, Oct 22, 1906. e. Cornell U. H of Madge Evans. Plays inc: Men in White (Pulitzer Prize-1934); Dead End; Ten Million Ghosts (& dir); The World We Make (& dir); The Patriots; Detective Story; Lunatics and Lovers; Darkness At Noon; Night Life (& prod).

TV inc: The Patriots (prod).

THE KINGSTON TRIO: Group. Members are Bob Shane, Roger Gambill; George Grove. Rec inc: Tom Dooley (Grammy-C&W-1958); Kingston Trio At Large (Grammy-Folk-1959); Here We Go Again; Close Up; Something Special.

KINSKI, Klaus: Act. b. Berlin, 1926. Films inc: For A Few Dollars More; Dr. Zhivago; Circus of Fear; Aguirre-Wrath of God; The Bloody Hands of the Law; Nuit D'or; Mort D'un Pourri; L'importance C'est D'aimer; The Net; Madame Claude; Woyzeck; Nosferatu The Vampire; Haine; La Femme Enfant; Schizoid; Les Fruits de la Passion (The Fruits of Passion); Buddy Buddy; Venom; Love & Money; Burden of Dreams (doc); The Soldier; Fitzcarraldo; Android; The Secret Diary of Sigmund Freud; The Little Drummer Girl; Sylvia.

KINSKI, Nastassia: Act. b. Berlin, Jan 24, 1960. D of Klaus Kinski. Films inc: False Moments; To The Devil A Daughter; Passion Flower Hotel; Cosi Come Sei (Stay As You Are); Tess; One From the Heart; Cat People; Exposed; Fruehlingssinfonie (Symphony of Love); La lune dans le caniveau (The Moon In the Gutter); Unfaithfully Yours; The Hotel New Hampshire; Maria's Lovers; Paris, Texas.

TV inc: Reifezeugnis (For Your Love Only); Walter Halfbetsgnets.

KIRGO, George: Wri-Prod. b. Hartford, CT, Mar 26, 1926. e. Wesleyan U. Films inc: Red Line 7000; Spinout; Don't Make Waves; Voices; No Room to Run; Shimmering Light.

TV inc: Norby; Home; Young Dr. Kildare; Adam's Rib; Get Christie Love (created); Another Day (prod); Topper; The Man In The Santa Claus Suit; Angel On My Shoulder; Side Show; The Kid With the Broken Halo (wri); My Palikari (wri); Massarati and the Brain (wri).

KIRK, Lisa: Singer-Act. b. Brownsville, PA, Sep 18, 1925. Bway inc: Good Night, Ladies; Allegro; Kiss Me Kate; Here's Love; Applause; Mack and Mabel; An Evening with Jerry Herman; Me Jack, You Jill; Design For Living.

TV inc: A Toast to Jerome Kern; The Man in the Moon; Shubert Alley; The Taming of the Shrew.

KIRK, Phyllis (nee Kirkegaard): Act. b. Syracuse, NY, Sep 18, 1926. Films inc: Our Very Own; The Iron Mistress; House of Wax; Canyon Crossroads; The Sad Sack; The Woman Opposite; City After Midnight.

Bway inc: My Name is Aquilon; Point of No Return.

TV inc: The Thin Man.

KIRKLAND, Sally: Act. b. NYC, Oct 31, 1944. e. Actors Studio. Thea inc: The Love Nest; Fitz; Tom Paine; Futz!; Sweet Eros; Witness; The Noisy Passenger; The Justice Box; Delicate Champion; Felix; Chicken Coop Chinaman; Has Tommy Flowers Gone?; Canadian Gothic.

Films inc: Blue; Futz!; Comin' Apart; The Way We Were; Cinderella Liberty; Big Bad Mama; Bite The Bullet; Pipe Dreams; Human Highway; My Love Letters; Fatal Games.

TV inc: Willow B--Women in Prison; Georgia Peaches; Summer.

KIRKWOOD, Gene: Prod. Films inc: New York, New York (asso prod); Comes A Horseman; Uncle Joe Shannon; The Idolmaker; .. A Night in Heaven; Gorky Park; The Keep; The Pope of Greenwich Village.

KIRKWOOD, James: Wri-act. b. Los Angeles, Aug. 22, 1930. Studied with Sanford Meisner; Neighborhood Playhouse. On Bway in Small Wonder; toured in Joan of Lorraine.

Plays inc: There Must Be a Pony; UTBU (Unhealthy to be Unpleasant); P.S. Your Cat Is Dead; A Chorus Line (Tony & Pulitzer Prize-1976).

KIRSTEN, Dorothy: Soprano. b. 1917. Diva with the Metropolitan Opera for more than 30 years until her retirement in 1975.

Films inc: Mr. Music; The Great Caruso.

KIRTLAND, Louise: Act. b. Lynn, MA, Aug 4, 1905. Has appeared in more than 300 plays, inc Night Hostess; Light Wines and Beer; Murder at the Vanities; The Only Girl; Few Are Chosen; No, No Nanette; Little Women; Alive and Kicking; Gigi; Tea and Sympathy; Waltz of the Toreadors; Church Mouse; The Tunnel of Love; Tovarich; Music Man; Take Me Along; Forty Carats; The Torch Bearers; Mame (and revival).

TV inc: Search for Tomorrow; Love of Life.

KITT, Eartha: Singer. b. Columbia, SC, 1928. Began career as a dancer, touring US, Mexico, Europe with Katherine Dunham group. Opened nitery in Paris. Returned to US, appearing in niteries, stage. Screen debut, 1954, New Faces.

Films inc: St. Louis Blues; Anna Lucasta; Synanon; Friday Foster; All By Myself (doc).

Bway inc: Timbuktu.

KIVLER, Steve: Exec prod. b. St Louis, MO, Sep 8, 1941. e. Eastern KY U, BA. Agent with William Morris Agency; then exec dir of dev for Aaron Spelling Prodns & Spelling-Goldberg Prodns; M-dir Seven Keys Television, Sydney, Australia; exec prod, Gemini Prodns, Sydney; exec prod, Reg Grundy Prodns, Sydney.

KJELLIN, Alf: Act-Dir. b. Sweden, 1920. Films inc: (act) Frenzy; My Six Convicts; The Iron Mistress; The Juggler; Ship of Fools; Assault on a Queen. (Dir) The Midas Run; The McMasters.

TV inc: (dir) Walking Tall.

KLEBAN, Edward L.: Comp-lyr. b. NYC Apr. 30, 1939. e. Columbia Coll, BA. Prod for CBS Records Hollywood, 1961, moved to NY office 1965. Plays inc: A Chorus Line (Tony & Pulitzer-1976).

KLEIN, Allen: Prod. b. Dec 18, 1931. Pres ABKCO Industries Inc. Films inc: Force of Impulse; Pity Me Not; Strangers in Town; The Stranger Returns; Samurai on a Horse; El Topo; The Silent Stranger; Pete, Pearl & the Pole; The Grand Boufe; The Greek Tycoon; Concert For Bangladesh.

Bway inc: It Had To Be You; The Man Who Had Three Arms.

KLEIN, Eugene V.: Exec. b. NYC, Jan 29, 1921. Automobile dealer, later chmn bd Columbia Savings & Loan, entered ind with National Theatres; P National Theatres 1955; P & chmn bd National General Theatres 1961; owner San Diego Chargers football team.

KLEIN, Paul L.: Prod-Exec. b. Brooklyn, Nov 6, 1928. e. Brooklyn

Coll, BA. Originally in audience research with Doyle Dane Bernbach ad agency, joined NBC audience research dept 1961, helped reshape daytime tv sales patterns; 1963 planned all color tv net; founded Computer Television, pioneering pay tv for hotels; prod Pop-Up, childrens educational tv spots; sold CT to Time, Inc., 1976 and retd to NBC as vp pgmmg; originator of so-called "Least Objectional Program" theory; 1979 became ind prod; Aug 1982, P Playboy Cable Network; June, 1984 contract not renewed.

TV inc: Valentine Magic on Love Island; Owner of Mr. Mike's Mondo Video; Hitler; The Day the Women Got Even; People Vs Jean Harris.

KLEIN, Robert: Act-Wri-Comedian. b. NYC, Feb 8, 1942. e. Alfred U, BA; Yale Drama School. Worked with Chicago's Second City group, on Bway with Second City Revue; The Apple Tree; They're Playing Our Song.

Films inc: The Landlord; The Owl and the Pussycat; The Pursuit of Happiness; Rivals; The Bell Jar; Hooper; Nobody's Perfekt; The Last Unicorn (voice).

TV inc: Tonight Show (guest host); Saturday Night Live; A Secret Space; All Commercials; Entertainer of the Year Awards; Your Place or Mine; Pajama Tops (cable); Poison Ivy; Second City--25 Years In Revue (act); Night Of 100 Stars II (act); This Wife For Hire (act).

Recordings inc: Child of the Fifties; Mind Over Matter; The Robert Klein Show.

KLEINER, Harry: Wri. b. Philadelphia, 1916. e. Temple U, BS; Yale U, MFA. Films inc: Fallen Angel; The Street With No Name; Red Skies of Montana; Salome; Miss Sadie Thompson; Carmen Jones; The Garment Jungle (& prod); Ice Palace; Fantastic Voyage; Bullitt; Le Mans.

TV inc: The Virginian; Bus Stop; The Rosenberg Trial.

KLEINERMAN, Isaac (Ike): Prod. b. NYC, Jul 21, 1916. Has prod more than 400 network docs. Began at NBC 1951 as film edtr Victory at Sea series; became prod in NBC's Project 20 unit; between 1952-57 prod The Great War; The Twisted Cross; The Jazz Age; Nightmare in Red; Wisdom; 1957 to CBS to organize Twentieth Century unit; also prod CBS Reports; The 21st Century (Emmy-1968); The Trail of the Feathered Serpent; Hitler and His Henchmen; Lure of the Tall Ships; Mr. Justice Dogulas; The Great Depression; Gandhi; Revolt in Hungary; The Violent World of Sam Huff; The Age of Anxiety; Who Killed Anne Frank?; The Dissenter--Norman Thomas; The Majestic Polluted Hudson; resd 1976 to enter indie prodn.

KLEINSCHMITT, Carl: Wri-Prod. b. Los Angeles, Aug 28. TV inc: (as wri) Gomer Pyle; That Girl; The Dick Van Dyke Show; My World and Welcome To It; Odd Couple; M*A*S*H; Funny Face (created & prod); Karen (prod); Pete N'Tillie (wri & prod).

KLEISER, Randal: Dir. b. Jul 20, 1946. e. USC. Films inc: Grease; Street People; The Blue Lagoon; Summer Lovers (& prod-wri); Grandview, U.S.A.

TV inc: Marcus Welby, M D; The Rookies; Starsky & Hutch; Family; All Together Now; Dawn; Portrait of a Teenage Runaway; Boy in the Plastic Bubble; Portait of Grandpa Doc; The Gathering.

KLEMPERER, Werner: Act. b. Cologne, Germany, 1920. S of late Otto Klemperer. Films inc: Death of a Scoundrel; Five Steps to Danger; The Goddess; Operation Eichmann; Judgment at Nuremberg; Escape from East Berlin; Youngblood Hawke; Ship of Fools; The Wicked Dreams of Paula Schultz.

TV inc: Hogan's Heroes (Emmys-1968 & 1969); Return of the Beverly Hillbillies.

KLINE, Herbert: Dir. b. Chicago, Mar 13, 1909. Former editor New Theatre Magazine. Films inc: (doc) Heart of Spain (Cin); Return to Life; Crisis; Lights Out in Europe; The Forgotten Village; My Father's House (& prod); The Kid From Cleveland (& wri); The Challenge; Acting-- Lee Strasberg and the Actors Studio.

KLINE, Kevin: Act. b. St. Louis, Oct 24, 1947. e. Juilliard. With NY Shakespeare Festival Co; founding member The Acting Company. Bway inc: Three Sisters; The Beggar's Opera; Measure for Measure; Scapin; The Robber Bridegroom; The Time of Your Life; On the Twentieth Century (Tony-Featured-1978); Loose Ends; The Pirates of Penzance (Tony-1981); Henry V (off Bway); Arms And The Man.

Films inc: Sophie's Choice; The Pirates of Penzance; The Big Chill.

KLINE, Richard: Act. b. NYC, Apr 29. e. Queens College, BA; Northwestern U, MA. Started with Jules Irving's rep company at Lincoln Center. Other thea inc The Rothchilds; Troilus and Cressida; Child's Play; Chemin de Fer; Henry V; Death of a Salesman; Come Blow Your Horn; The Sunshine Boys.

TV inc: Seventh Avenue; Three's Company; Take My Word For It; Not Just Another Affair; Insight/The Clearing House; His & Hers.

KLINE, Richard H.: Cin. b. Nov 15, 1926. Films inc: Camelot; The Boston Strangler; Gaily Gaily; A Dream of Kings; The Moonshine War; The Andromeda Strain; Kotch; Hammersmith Is Out; When The Legends Die; The Mechanic; Soylent Green; Black Gunn; Battle For The Planet Of The Apes; The Don Is Dead; The Terminal Man; Mr. Majestyk; The Harrad Experiment; Mandingo; King Kong; The Fury; Who'll Stop The Rain; Tilt; Star Trek-The Motion Picture; Touched By Love; The Competition; Body Heat; Death Wish III; Man, Woman and Child; Breathless; Deal of the Century; Hard to Hold; All Of Me.

TV inc: Coming Out of The Ice.

KLING, Woody: Wri-Prod. b. NYC. e. Wesleyan Coll. TV inc: Milton Berle Show; Jackie Gleason Show; Carol Burnett Show (Emmys-wri-1972, 1973); A Year at the Top (crea-wri); All in the Family (co-exec prod); Sanford Arms (prod); Hot L Baltimore (prod); Hello, Larry (prod).

Films inc: Here Come The Littles (wri).

KLINGER, Michael: Prod. b. England, Nov 2, 1920. Managing dir Avton Films; Tonav Films; Three Michaels Films.

Films inc: That Kind of Girl; Saturday Night Out; Repulsion; Cul de Sac; The Yellow Teddy Bears; Penthouse; A Study in Terror; Baby Love; Something To Hide; Get Carter; Pulp; Gold; Shout at the Devil; Blood Relatives.

KLOTZ, Florence: Cos Dsgn. b. NYC. Bway inc: A Call on Kuprin; Take Her, She's Mine; Never Too Late; On an Open Roof; Nobody Loves an Albatross; Everybody Out, The Castle Is Sinking; The Owl and the Pussycat; The Mating Dance; Best Laid Plans; This Winter's Hobby; It's A Bird...It's A Plane...It's Superman; Norman, Is That You?; Paris Is Out; Follies (Tony-1972); A Little Night Music (Tony-1973); Sondheim--A Musical Tribute; Dreyfus In Rehearsal; Pacific Overtures (Tony-1976); Legend; Little Foxes; A Doll's Life; Peg.

Films inc: Something for Everyone; A Little Night Music.

KLUGE, Alexander: Prod-Dir-Wri. b. Germany, 1932. Former attorney; served as asst to late Fritz Lang on latter's return to Germany 1958. Films inc: Yesterday Girl; Disoriented; Ein Arzt aus Halberstadt; Der grosse Verhau; Willy Tobler; Part Time World of a Domestic Slave; Augen aus einem anderen Lande; Ferdinand the Strongman; Die Patriotin (The Patriot); Die Macht der Gefuehle (The Power of Emotion).

KLUGMAN, Jack: Act. b. Philadelphia, PA, Apr 27, 1922. Bway inc: Saint John; Stevedore; Gypsy; other thea inc: Lyndon (One Man Show). Films inc: Timetable; Twelve Angry Men; The Days of Wine and Roses; Act One; The Detective; Goodbye Columbus; Two-Minute Warning.

TV inc: The Defenders (Blacklist) (Emmy-1964); The Odd Couple (Emmys-1971, 1973); Quincy; Packy; Lucy Moves To NBC; The Magic of David Copperfield; Command Performance--The Stars Salute the President.

KNEF, Hildegarde (aka NEFF): Act. b. Ulm, Germany, Dec 18, 1925. e. Art Academy, Berlin. Film cartoonist for UFA, Berlin. Films inc: Between Yesterday and Tomorrow; The Sinner; Decision Before Dawn; Diplomatic Courier; The Snows of Kilimanjaro; Sunderlin; Svengali; Catherine of Russia; Valley of the Doomed; The Threepenny Opera; Escape From Sahara; Subway in the Sky; Mozambique; Everyone Dies In His Own Time; Fedora; Warum die UFOs Unsere Salat Klauen (Why the UFOs Steal Our Lettuce); Flugel und Fessen (The Future Of Emily).

KNIEVEL, Evel: Stuntman. b. Butte, MT, Oct 17, 1939. Films inc: Viva Knievel.

TV inc: The Sensational Shocking Wonderful Wacky 70's.

KNIGHT, David (ne Mintz): Act. b. Niagara Falls, NY, Jan 16, 1927. e. Syracuse U; RADA. Films inc: The Young Lovers; Lost; Across the Bridge; Nightmare.

London thea inc: The Caine Mutiny Court Martial; The Iceman Cometh; The Tenth Man; A Present for the Past; Out of the Question.

TV inc: Abe Lincoln in Illinois; Strange Interlude; Berkeley Square; Kate.

KNIGHT, Gladys: Singer-Lyr. b. Atlanta, GA, May 28, 1944. Winner Ted Mack Amateur Hour 1952; toured with Morris Brown Choir; with Terry Lloyd Jazz Ltd, before organizing Gladys Knight and the Pips.

Songs inc: I Don't Want to do Wrong; Do You Love Me Just A Little Honey; Me and My Family; Way Back Home.

(Grammys-(2)-pop vocal group & R&B vocal group-1973).

TV inc: Uptown--A Tribute to the Apollo Theatre; 100 Years of Golden Hits; The Suzanne Somers Special; The Mac Davis Special--The Music of Christmas; Black Gold Awards (co-host).

KNIGHT, Shirley: Act. b. Gossell, KS, Jul 5, 1936. e. Lake Forrest Coll. Films inc: Five Gates to Hell; Ice Palace; The Dark at the Top of the Stairs; The Couch; Sweet Bird of Youth; House of Women; Flight from Ashiya; The Group; The Counterfeit Killer; The Rain People; Juggernaut; Beyond The Poseidon Adventure; Endless Love; The Sender.

TV inc: The Lie; The Country Girl; Champion-A Love Story; Playing For Time; With Intent To Kill.

Bway inc: Journey to the Day; The Three Sisters; We Have Always Lived in the Castle; The Watering Place; Kennedy's Children (Tony-supp-1976). Other thea inc: Come Back Little Sheba (Off-Bway).

KNIGHT, Ted: Act. (Tadeus Wladyslaw Konopka):b. Terryville, CT, Dec 7. TV inc: Mary Tyler Moore Show (2 Emmys-supp-1973 & 1976); Mac Davis Special; The Sensational, Shocking, Wonderful Wacky 70's; Too Close For Comfort; The Real Trivial Pursuit.

Films inc: Caddyshack.

KNOTTS, Don: Act. b. Morgantown, WV, Jul 21, 1924. e. WV U, BA. In Army Special Services during WW2. On radio after war; on Bway in No Time for Sergeants.

Films inc: No Time for Sergeants; Wake Me When It's Over; It's A Mad, Mad, Mad, Mad World; Move Over Darling; The Incredible Mr Limpet; The Ghost and Mr Chicken; The Reluctant Astronaut; The Shakiest Gun in The West; How to Frame a Figg; The Apple Dumpling Gang; No Deposit, No Return; Gus; Herbie Goes to Monte Carlo; Hot Lead and Cold Feet; The Apple Dumpling Gang Rides Again; The Prize Fighter; The Private Eyes; Cannonball Run II.

TV inc: The Garry Moore Show; The Steve Allen Show; The Mouse Factory; The Andy Griffith Show (Emmys-supp-1961, 1962, 1963, 1966, 1967); The Don Knotts Show; Bob Hope's Stand Up and Cheer For the National League's 60th Year; Three's Company.

KNOWLES, Patric: Act. b. Leeds, England, Nov 11, 1911. Films inc: Irish Hearts; Charge of the Light Brigade; Honour's Easy; Mister Hobo; Give Me Your Heart; It's Love I'm After; Adventures of Robin Hood; How Green Was My Valley; Forever and a Day; Of Human Bondage; The Bride Wore Boots; Kitty; Monsieur Beaucaire; Three Came Home; Mutiny; Jamaica Run; Flame of Calcutta; Khyber Patrol; No Man's Woman; Auntie Mame; The Devil's Brigade; In Enemy Country; Chisum: Terror in The Wax Museum.

KNOX, Alexander: Act. b. Strathroy, Ont, Jan 16, 1907. On screen in England from 1938 in Four Feathers; in U.S. from 1941 in The Sea Wolf.

Films inc: Khartoum; Puppet on a Chain; Nicholas and Alexandra; You Only Live Twice; Oscar Wilde; Wilson; Sister Kenny; The Longest Day; Wreck of the Mary Deere; Mr Moses; Villa Rides; Shalako; Skullduggery; Khartoum; Nicholas and Alexander; Potsdam; The Chosen; Gorky Park; Joshua Then And Now.

TV inc: Cry of the Innocent; Tinker, Tailor, Soldier, Spy; Churchill and the Generals; Oppenheimer; Empire, Inc; Helen Keller--The Miracle Continues; Empire.

KOBAYASHI, Masaki: Dir. b. Otaru, Japan, Jan 14, 1916. e. Waseda U. Served as apprentice (asst dir) to Keisuke Kinoshita, 1946-52. Films inc: My Son's Youth; Room with Thick Walls; Three Loves; Beneath the Wide Sky; Beautiful Days; Fountain Head; I'll Buy You;

Black River; The Human Condition; The Inheritance; Harakiri; The Black Hair; In A Cup of Tea; Hymn to a Tired Man; Inn of Evil; Kaseki; Glowing Autumn; Tokyo Saiban (The Tokyo Trial). heading:

KOCH, Howard: Wri. b. NYC, Dec 12, 1902. e. Bard Coll; Columbia U. Films inc: The Sea Hawk; The Letter; Sergeant York; Casablanca (Oscar-1943); Three Strangers; No Sad Songs For Me; Letter From An Unknown Woman; The Thirteenth Letter; The War Lover; The Fox.

Plays inc: In Time To Come; Straitjacket.

Radio plays inc: War of the Worlds.

KOCH, Howard W.: Prod-Dir. b. NYC, Apr 11, 1916. Asst dir, 20th-Fox; Eagle Lion; MGM. Exec prod Frank Sinatra Enterprises; vp chg prod Paramount, 1965.

Films inc: Beachhead; The Manchurian Candidate; Four For Texas; None But The Brave; The Odd Couple; Plaza Suite; Once Is Not Enough; Dragonslayer (exec prod); Airplane II--The Sequel (prod); Beyond Reason (prod).

TV inc: (prod) The Untouchables; Maverick; Cheyenne; Hawaiian Eye; The Pirate; Who Loves Ya Baby; 50th Annual Academy Awards (Emmy-prod-1978); Oscar's Best Movies; Hollywood Wives.

KOCH, Howard W. Jr.: Prod. b. Los Angeles, Dec 14, 1945. e. UCLA. Worked various positions in industry inc asst dir before becoming prod; Aug. 1983, P Ray Stark Prodns. Films inc: Heaven Can Wait; The Other Side of Midnight; The Frisco Kid; The Idolmaker; Honky Tonk Freeway; Some Kind of Hero; A Night in Heaven; Gorky Park; The Keep.

KOENEKAMP, Fred J.: Cin. b. Los Angeles, Nov 11, 1922. Films inc: Heaven with a Gun; The Great Bank Robbery; Patton; Billy Jack; Skin Game; Rage; Kansas City Bomber; Papillon; Doc Savage; Towering Inferno (Oscar-1974); Posse; Embryo; Islands in the Stream; Fun with Dick and Jane; Domino Principle; The Other Side of Midnight; Swarm; The Champ; Amityville Horror; The Day the World Ended; Love and Bullets; When Time Ran Out; The Hunter; First Family; First Monday In October; Carbon Copy; Wrong Is Right; Yes Giorgio; It Came From Hollywood; Two of a Kind; The Adventures Of Buckaroo Banzai--Acxross The 8th Dimension.

TV inc: Disaster on the Coastline; Tales of the Gold Monkey; Money on the Side; Return of The Man From U.N.C.L.E.; Summer Girl; Whiz Kids; Flight 90--Disaster on the Potomac; Summer Fantasies; Obsessive Love; City Killer; Las Vegas Strip War; A Touch Of Scandal; Not My Kid.

KOHAN, Buz (Alan W Kohan): Wri-Comp-Prod. b. NYC, Aug 9, 1933. e. Eastman School of Music, BM, MM. TV inc: Perry Como Specials, 1963-1967 (wri); Carol Burnett Show, 1967-1973 (wri-prod) (Emmy-wri-1973); Ann-Marget Smith (wri); Ann-Margret--Rhinestone Cowgirl (wri); America Salutes Richard Rodgers--The Sound of His Music (Emmy-wri-1977); 50th Annual Academy Awards (Emmy-mus-1978); Kraft 75th Anniversary Special (wri); A Country Christmas--1979 (prod-wri); Merry Christmas From Grand Ole Opry House (wri); Kraft Salutes Disneyland's 25th Anniversary (prod); Debby Boone--The Same Old Brand New Me; Shirley MacLaine...Every Little Movement (Emmy-wri-1980); 30 Years of TV Comedy's Greatest Hits (wri); A Country Christmas--1980 (prod-wri); Julie Andrews' Invitation to the Dance with Rudolf Nureyev (wri); Doug Henning's World of Magic (wri); Diana (wri); Two of A Kind (wri); 100 Years of Golden Hits (prod-wri); Good Evening, Captain (wri); A Country Christmas (wri); Kraft Salutes Walt Disney World's 10th Anniversary; Doug Henning's World of Magic (1982); Pavarotti and Friends; Baryshnikov In Hollywood (wri). Goldie and Kids--Listen To Us (wri); Shirley MacLaine--Illusions (Emmy-Song-1982); The Fantastic Miss Piggy Show (wri); EPCOT Center--The Opening Celebration (wri); Christmas In Washington (wri); Sheena Easton-Act One (wri); Motown 25-Yesterday, Today, Forever (Emmy-prod-1983); It's the Real Thing--Television's Greatest Commercials IV (wri); Here's Television Entertainment (wri)(Emmy-lyrics-1984);Schneider's Christmas Holiday (wri); On Stage America (wri); Blondes vs. Brunettes; Screen Actors Guild 50th Anniversary Celebration; Kenny & Dolly--A Christmas To Remember (wri); Christmas In Washington (wri); Night Of 100 Stars II (spec mus & lyr); TV Academy Hall Of Fame (wri); Motown Returns To The Apollo (wri).

Bway inc; Shirley MacLaine on Broadway.

KOHLER, Estelle: Act. b. South Africa, Mar 28, 1940. e. RADA. Thea in South Africa before joining Royal Shakespeare Company. Thea inc: Hamlet; Twelfth Night; All's Well That Ends Well; Two Gentlemen of Verona; The Exiles; Occupations; The Balcony; The Island of the Mighty; Romeo and Juliet; Summerfolk; The Marrying of Anne Leete; The Devil's Disciple; Ivanov; Tonight at 8:30.

KOHNER, Pancho: Prod. b. Los Angeles, Jan 7, 1939. e. USC; U of Mexico; Sorbonne. Films inc: The Bridge in the Jungle (& dir-wri); The Lie; Mr Sycamore; St Ives; The White Buffalo; Love and Bullets; Why Would I Lie?; 10 To Midnight; The Evil That Men Do.

KOHNER, Susan: Act. b. Los Angeles, Nov 11, 1936. Films inc: To Hell and Back; The Last Wagon; Dino; Imitation of Life; The Big Fisherman; The Gene Krupa Story; All the Fine Young Cannibals; By Love Possessed; Freud.
Bway inc: Love Me Little; He Who Gets Slapped; Rose Tattoo; Bus Stop; St Joan; Sunday in New York; Take Her, She's Mine; Hiawatha.

KOKUBO, Christina: Act. b. Detroit, Jul 27, 1950. In ballet, on stage, US, Europe.
Films inc: The Yakuza, Midway.

KOLTAI, Ralph: Dsgn. b. Berlin, Jul 31, 1924. Has designed 100 opera, play and ballet prodns around the world. Thea inc: (London) Caucasian Chalk Circle; The Representative; The Birthday Party; End Game; The Merchant of Venice; Major Barbara; Too True to Be Good; The General's Tea Party; Little Murders; Soldiers (& Bway); Back to Methuselah; Hullabaloo; The Highwayman; Man and Superman (prod); The Love Girl and the Innocent; Bugsy Malone; Cyrano de Bergerac (& Bway); Pack of Lies (& Bway); Dear Anyone; Much Ado About Nothing (Bway).

KOMACK, James: Wri-Prod-Dir-Act. b. NYC, Aug 3, 1930. Films inc: (act) Damn Yankees; Hole in the Head; Senior Prom; Bell Boy; Contessa Azura; Porky's Revenge (dir).
TV inc: Hennessey (& wri); My Favorite Martian (wri); Mr. Roberts (prod & dir); Courtship of Eddie's Father (crea, wri, act & dir); Chico and the Man (dir & crea); Welcome Back Kotter (dir & crea); Sugar Time (dir & crea); Another Day (dir & crea); Rollergirls (dir & crea); Me and Maxx (wri-crea-exec prod). Bway inc: (act) Damn Yankees.

KONCHALOVSKY, Andrei: Dir. (See MIKHALKOV-KONCHALOVSKY, Andrei)

KONIGSBERG, Frank: Prod. Started ind prodn co with Stirling Silliphant in 1975; 1979 exec prod Fox TV. TV inc: Bing Crosby Christmas Shows; Bing Crosby--Life and Legend; Gene Kelly--An American In Pasadena; Pearl; Before and After; Dummy; It's Not Easy; Breaking Away; Dorothy; Guyana Tragedy-The Story of Jim Jones (exec prod); A Christmas Without Snow (exec prod); The Pride of Jesse Hallam (exec prod); Divorce Wars--A Love Story (exec prod); Coming Out of The Ice (exec prod); Hardcase (exec prod); His & Hers; Rituals (exec prod); Wet Gold (exec prod); Ellis Island (exec prod); The Glitter Dome (PC) (exec prod); Surviving (exec prod); Right To Kill? (exec prod).
Films inc: Joy Of Sex.

KONVITZ, Jeffrey Steven: Wri-Prod. b. NYC, Jul 22, 1944. e. Cornell U, BA; Columbia U School of Law, JD. Films inc: Silent Night, Bloody Night; The Sentinel; Gorp.

KOPELL, Bernie: Act. b. NYC, Jun 21, 1933. Films inc: The Loved One. TV inc: Jack Benny Show; Steve Allen; Danny Kaye; My Favorite Martian; The Farmer's Daughter; Get Smart; That Girl; Doris Day Show; Mr. Deeds Goes to Washington; Bewitched; Needles and Pins; When Things Were Rotten; Love Boat; Greatest Heroes of the Bible; Half Nelson.

KOPELSON, Arnold: Prod. b. NYC, Feb 14, 1935. e. NY Law School, LLB. Films inc: Lost and Found; The Legacy; Night of the Juggler; Foolin' Around; Final Assignment; Dirty Tricks; Model Behavior (presenter); Jungle Warriors (presenter); Gimme An ıF' (exec prod); Red Heat (presenter).

KOPIT, Arthur: Wri. b. NYC, May 10, 1937. e. Harvard U, BA. Plays

inc: Gemini; On the Runway of Life; You Never Know What's Coming Off Next; Across the River and into the Jungle; Sing to Me Through Open Windows; To Dwell in a Palace of Strangers; Oh Dad, Poor Dad, Mama's Hung You in the Closet and I'm Feelin' So Sad; Indians; The Day the Whores Came Out to Play Tennis; What the Gentlemen Are Up To, and As for the Ladies; Wings; "Nine" (book); Ghosts (adapt); End of the World.
TV inc: The Conquest of Everest; Starstruck.

KOPPEL, Ted: TV newsman. b. Lancashire, England, 1940. e. Syracuse U, BA; Stanford U, MA. Started as news corr WMCA radio; 1963 joined ABC News NYC as youngest news reporter ever to join a tv net; 1965, anchor ABC Radio News; 1966, Vietnam corr for ABC; 1968, Miami Bureau Chief; 1969, Hong Kong Bureau Chief; 1971, Diplomatic Corr; 1980, anchor ABC News Nightline. TV inc: The People of People's China; Kissinger--Action Biography; Post Election Special Edition Nightline (Emmy-prod-1980); Disaster on the Potomac (Emmy-anchor-1982); The Palestinians' Viewpoint (Emmy-int-1982); The War in Lebanon; What's Ailing Medical News?; Racism, New Times..New Questions.

KORDA, David: Prod. b. England. Films inc: (asso prod) A Day in the Death of Joe Egg; The Ruling Class; Cattle Annie and Little Britches. (Prod) Great Scout and Cathouse Thursday; Man Friday; Loophole.

KORMAN, Harvey: Act. b. Chicago, IL, Feb 15, 1927. TV inc: Danny Kaye Show; Carol Burnett Show (Emmys-1969, 1971, 1972, 1974); How To Survive The 70's and Maybe Even Bump Into A Little Happiness; The John Davidson Christmas Show; Eunice (& dir); Mama's Family (& dir); The Invisible Woman; Carpool; The Cracker Brothers (dir); Rodney Dangerfield Exposed; The TV Academy Hall Of Fame.
Films inc: Three Bites of an Apple; Lord Love a Duck; The April Fools; Blazing Saddles; Huckleberry Finn; Americathon; Herbie Goes Bananas; First Family; History of the World--Part I; Trail of the Pink Panther; Curse of the Pink Panther.

KORTY, John: Dir-Wri-Ani. b. Lafayette, IN, Jun 22, 1936. e. Antioch Coll. Animator of Breaking the Habit; A Scrap of Paper and a Piece of String; The Owl and the Pussycat.
Films inc: The Crazy Quilt; Funnyman; Riverrun; Silence; Alex & the Gypsy; Who Are the DeBolts? And Where Did They Get Nineteen Kids? (Oscar-doc fea-1977); Oliver's Story (dir & sp); Twice Upon A Time (dir-wri).
TV inc: The Autobiography of Miss Jane Pittman (Emmy-dir-1974); Farewell to Manzanar; The Music School; Who Are The DeBolts? And Where Did They Get 19 Kids? (Emmy-dir-1978); Can't It Be Anyone Else? (exec prod); A Christmas Without Snow (wri-dir-prod); Vietnam Requiem (exec prod); The Haunting Passion (dir); Second Sight--A Love Story (dir); The Ewok Adventure (dir-cin); The Kennedy Center Honors 1984 (wri).

KOSCINA, Sylva: Act. b. Yugoslavia, Aug 22, 1933. Films inc: Hercules Unchained; Jessica; Hot Enough for June; Juliet of the Spirits; Three Bites of the Apple; Deadlier Than the Male; A Lovely Way to Die; The Battle for Neretva; The Secret War of Harry Frigg; Hornet's Nest; Sunday Lovers; Asso (Ace); Stelle Emigranti (Wandering Stars); Cenerentola '80 (Cinderella '80).
TV inc: E La Vita Continua (And Life Goes On).

KOSLECK, Martin: Act. b. Barketzen, Germany, Mar 24, 1907. Films inc: Confessions of a Nazi Spy; Foreign Correspondent; The Mad Doctor; Nazi Agent; Manila Calling; The Hitler Gang; Crime of the Century; House of Horrors; Assigned to Danger; Smuggler's Cove; Hitler; 36 Hours; The Flesh Eaters; Which Way to the Front; A Day at the White House.

KOSSOFF, David: Act. b. London, Nov 24, 1919. Stage debut with Unity Theatre, later joined BBC repertory group.
Thea inc: The Love of Four Colonels; The Shrike; The Bespoke Overcoat; The World of Sholem Aleichem; Stars in Your Eyes; The Tenth Man; Come Blow Your Horn; Seidman and Son; Enter Solly Gold. On Such a Night (& wri).
TV inc: The Larkins; Little Big Business; Storytime; The Visitation Mystery.
Films inc: The Good Beginning; The Young Lovers; A Kid for Two

Farthings; The Bespoke Overcoat; The Journey; Freud; Ring of Spies.

KOSTAL, Irwin: Mus Dir. b. Chicago, Oct 1, 1911. Films inc: West Side Story *(Oscar*-1961) *(Grammy*-soundtrack-1961); Mary Poppins; The Sound of Music *(Oscar*-scoring adapt-1965); Bedknobs and Broomsticks; Chitty Chitty Bang Bang; Pete's Dragon; The Magic of Lassie.

TV inc: Your Show of Shows; Julie Andrews Specials; Brigadoon.

Bway inc: West Side Story; Fiorello; A Funny Thing Happened on the Way to the Forum; Sail Away; Copperfield; Seven Brides for Seven Brothers.

KOSTER, Henry: Dir. b. Berlin, May 1, 1905. Films inc: 100 Men and a Girl; Rage of Paris; It Started With Eve; Music for Millions; Two Sisters from Boston; The Bishop's Wife; Come to the Stable; My Blue Heaven; Harvey; Mr Belvedere Rings the Bell; Stars and Stripes Forever; The Robe; Desiree; A Man Called Peter; D-Day, the Sixth of June; My Man Godfrey; The Naked Maja; The Story of Ruth; Flower Drum Song; Mr Hobbs Takes a Vacation; Take Her She's Mine; Dear Brigitte; The Singing Nun.

KOTCHEFF, Ted: Dir. b. Toronto, Canada, 1931. Films inc: Life at the Top; Two Gentlemen Sharing; Outback; Billy Two Hats; The Apprenticeship of Duddy Kravitz; Fun with Dick and Jane; Who Is Killing The Great Chefs of Europe?; North Dallas 40 (& sp); Split Image (& prod); First Blood; Uncommon Valor (& exec prod); Joshua Then And Now.

Thea inc: Play with a Tiger; Luv; Have You Any Dirty Washing, Mother Dear?

KOTTO, Yaphet: Act. b. Nov 15, 1937. Films inc: The Thomas Crown Affair; Across 110th Street; Live and Let Die; Truck Turner; Friday Foster; Report to the Commissioner; Drums; The Shootist; Blue Collar Alien; Brubaker; Fighting Back; The Star Chamber.

Thea inc: The Great White Hope; The Zulu and the Zayda; Black Monday; In White America.

TV inc: Rage; Denmark Vesey's Rebellion; For Love and Honor; Women of San Quentin; Playing With Fire.

KOVACS, Laszlo: Cin. Films inc: Targets; Easy Rider; Five Easy Pieces; Alex in Wonderland; The Last Movie; What's Up Doc?; Freebie and the Bean; Shampoo; At Long Last Love; Nickelodeon; Harry and Walter Go to New York; New York, New York; F.I.S.T.; The Last Waltz; Paradise Alley; Butch and Sundance-The Early Days; The Runner Stumbles; Inside Moves; The Legend of the Lone Ranger; The Toy; Frances; Crackers; Ghostbusters; Mask.

KOWAL, Stefanie: Exec. b. Chicago, Dec 18, 1941. e. U of IL; Webster Coll. Wri-prod Ann Landers Radio Show, 1970-72; asso prod Kennedy & Co, 1972-74; prod A M Chicago, 1975-77; Development exec, Universal TV, 1977-79; VP movies & mini series, Universal TV, 1979.

TV inc: Story of Esther; The Thirteenth Day-The Story of Ruth; Codename Foxfire.

KOWALSKI, Bernard L.: Dir. b. Brownsville, TX, Aug 2, 1929. Act as a child before becoming dir. TV inc: The Nativity; Marciano; B.A.D. Cats; Nick and the Dobermans; Baretta (& exec prod); Turnover Smith; Nightside; Johnny Blue.

Films inc: Hot Car Girl; Attack of the Giant Leeches; Night of the Blood Beast; Blood and Steel; Krakatoa--East of Eden; Stiletto; Macho Callahan.

KOZLENKO, William: Wri. b. Philadelphia, PA. Plays inc: Jacob Comes Home; This Earth is Ours; A Fearful Madness.

Films inc: Stranger In Town: Holiday in Mexico; The Man Who Loved Children; Stone Wall; The Raw Edge.

TV inc: Pulitzer Prize Playhouse; Lux Video Theatre; Climax; G.E. Theatre; Playhouse of the Stars; also served as story consltnt G.E. Theatre; Alfred Hitchcock; Hubbell Robinson Prodns.

KOZOLL, Michael: Wri-prod. b. WI, Aug 16, 1940. TV inc: (wri) Night Stalker; Switch; Kojak; Vampire. Story ed McCloud; Quincy; Delvecchio. Crea-wri-exec prod Hill Street Blues *(Emmys*-wri & exec prod-1981; wri-1982).

Films inc: First Blood.

KRAMER, Anne Pearce: Exec. b. Saginaw, MI. e. USC (BA, PhD). D of the late Perce Pearce. Former W of Stanley Kramer. Originally under contract at U as act. Served as story edtr, casting dir, dialog dir, later asso prod on 10 Kramer films. VP Dvlpmnt Castle Hill Films; 1981, story edtr Columbia Pictures; 1983, exec story edtr.

KRAMER, Jerry: Prod-Dir. b. Los Angeles, Sep 3, 1945. e. USC. Films inc: Paradise Garage; opening prolog for re-release of Hard Day's Night; Once Upon a Mouse--60 Years of Disney Animation.

KRAMER, Lee: Prod. b. England, Nov 3, 1951. Personal mgr of Olivia Newton-John. TV inc: The Silver Surfer. Films inc: Xanadu; The Man Who Saw Tomorrow.

KRAMER, Stanley: Prod-Dir. b. NYC, Sep 29, 1913. e. NYU. Films inc: The Moon and Sixpence; Home of the Brave; The Men; Death of a Saleman; High Noon; My Six Convicts; The Member of the Wedding; The Fourposter; The Juggler; The Wild One; The Caine Mutiny; Not as a Stranger (& dir); The Pride and Passion (& dir); The Defiant Ones (& dir); On the Beach (& dir); Inherit the Wind (& dir); Judgment at Nurenberg (& dir); Pressure Point; A Child Is Waiting; It's a Mad, Mad, Mad, Mad, World (& dir); Invitation to a Gunfighter; Ship of Fools (& dir); Guess Who's Coming to Dinner (& dir); The Secret of Santa Vittoria (& dir); R P M (& dir); Bless the Beasts and Children (& dir); Oklahoma Crude (& dir); The Domino Principle (& dir); The Runner Stumbles (& dir).

Irving Thalberg Award 1961.

TV inc: The Trial of Julius and Ethel Rosenberg; The Court Martial of the Tiger of Malaya - Gen Tomobumi Yamashita; The Court Martial of Lt. William Calley; Stanley Kramer On Film.

KRAMM, Joseph: Wri-Dir-Act. b. Philadelphia, Sep 30, 1907. e. U of PA, BA. Bway debut as act 1928, Lilac Time.

Bway inc: L'Aiglon; Bury the Dead; Golden Boy; Liliom; Journey to Jerusalem; Uncle Harry; Hope Is The Thing with Feathers (dir).

Plays inc: The Shrike *(Pulitzer Prize*-1952); Build With One Hand; Giants, Sons of Giants; The Gypsies Wore High Hats; All Honourable Men.

KRANTZ, Steve: Prod. b. NYC, May 20, 1923. e. Columbia, BA. TV dir with NBC 1953; dir pgm dvlpt Screen Gems; formed Steve Krantz Films 1964.

TV inc: (wri) Steve Allen Show; Kate Smith Show; Winston Churchill-The Valiant Years; Princess Daisy (exec prod); Mistral's Daughter (exec prod).

Films inc: (Prod) Fritz the Cat; Heavy Traffic; Ruby (& wri); Which Way Is Up?; Jennifer (& wri); Swap Meet (& wri).

KRASNA, Norman: Wri-Prod. b. NYC, Nov 7, 1909. e. NYU; Columbia U; Brooklyn Law School. N.Y. drama edtr before joining Warner publicity dept, began writing for films 1932.

Films inc: Fury; It Started With Eve; Princess O'Rourke *(Oscar*-sp-1943); White Christmas; Indiscreet; My Geisha; I'd Rather Be Rich.

Plays inc: Louder, Please; John Loves Mary; Sunday In New York; Lady Harry.

(Died Nov. 1, 1984)

KRASNY, Paul: Dir. b. Cleveland, OH, Aug 8, 1935. TV inc: Mission Impossible *(Emmy*-ed-1967); Mannix; Police Story; Born Free; Blue Knight; Quincy; Chips; Islander; Centennial; Christina; Joe Panther; 240 Robert; When Hell Was In Session; Fugitive Family; Alcatraz--The Whole Shocking Story; Terror Among Us; Fly Away Home; Catalina C-Lab; Time Bomb; V (The Series).

KRAUSS, Marvin A: Prod. b. NYC, Oct 11, 1928. GM many Bway shows inc Rocky Horror Show; American Buffalo; Minnie's Boys; Frankenstein; Godspell; Beatlemania; Dancin'; Woman of the Year. Bway as prod inc: Teibele and Her Demon; Poison Tree; La Cage Aux Folles; *(Tony*-1984).

KRESKIN (legal single name; nee Kresge): Mentalist. b. Montclair, NJ, Jan 12, 1935. e. Seton Hall U. TV inc: Amazing World of Kreskin; Misadventures of Ichabod Crane.

KRESS, Carl: Film Edtr. b. Los Angeles, Feb 3, 1937. S of Harold

Kress. Films inc: The Liberation of L Q Jones; Doctor's Wives; Watermelon Man; Towering Inferno (Oscar-1974); Audrey Rose; Meteor; Hopscotch; Looker; Stroker Ace; Cannonball Run II.
TV inc: Airwolf; Generation.

KRESS, Harold F: Flm Ed. b. Pittsburgh, PA, Jun 26, 1913. e. UCLA. Films inc: Command Decision; Madame Curie; Mrs Miniver; The Yearling; How the West was Won (Oscar-1963); Poseidon Adventure; The Iceman Cometh; 99-44/100ths % Dead; The Towering Inferno (Oscar-1974); The Other Side of Midnight; Viva Knievel!; Swarm.

KREUGER, Kurt: Act. b. Switzerland, Jul 23, 1919. e. U of Lausanne. Films inc: Mademoiselle Fifi; Hotel Berlin; Paris Underground; Dark Corner; Unfaithfully Yours; Fear; The St. Valentine's Day Massacre; What Did You Do in the War Daddy?

KRIGE, Alice: Act. b. South Africa, 1955. TV inc: A Tale of Two Cities; The Professionals; Ellis Island; Wallenberg--A Hero's Story.
Films inc: Chariots of Fire; Ghost Story; King David.
Thea inc: (London) Arms and the Man; Cyrano de Bergerac.

KRIM, Arthur B.: Atty. b. NYC, 1910. e. Columbia U. Became member of law firm, Philips, Nizer, Benjamin & Krim, NY. P, Eagle Lion Films 1946-49; elected P, United Artists, 1951; ChmnB, 1969. Co-founder Orion Pictures Corp, 1978.
Jean Hersholt Humanitarian Award 1974.

KRIMS, Milton: Wri. b. NYC, Feb 7, 1904. e. OR Inst Tech; OR U; U of Rome. Films inc: Strangers All; Dude Ranch; West of the Pecos; Harmony Lane; The Great O'Malley; Confessions of a Nazi Spy; We Are Not Alone; Prince of Foxes; Iron Curtain; Crossed Swords; One Minute To Zero.
TV inc: Perry Mason; Wagon Train; Hotel deParis.

KRISTEL, Sylvia: Act. b. Sep 28, 1952. Films inc: Because of the Cats; Living Apart Together; Naakt over de Schutting; Emmanuelle; Un Lincoln n'a pas de poches; Le Jeu avec le Feu; Julia; Eswar die nachtigall und Night die Lerche; Emmanuelle 2; La Marge; Alice ou la Derniere Fugue; Une Femme Fidele; Fene La Canne; Behind the Iron Mask; Good-bye Emmanuelle; Mysteries; The Fifth Musketeer; Concorde--Airport 79; Lady Chatterley's Lover; Private Lessons; Private School; Emmanuelle 4; Letti Selvaggi (Tigers In Lipstick); Mata Hari; Red Heat.
TV inc: The Million Dollar Face.

KRISTOFFERSON, Kris: Act. b. Brownsville, TX, Jun 22, 1936. Rock mus comp, singer. Songs inc: Me and Bobby McGee; Why Me, Lord; Sunday Mornin' Comin' Down; Help Me Make It Through The Night (Grammy-1971).
Films inc: Cisco Pike; Pat Garrett And Billy The Kid; Bring Me The Head of Alfredo Garcia; Blume In Love; Alice Doesn't Live Here Anymore; Vigilante Force; The Sailor Who Fell From Grace with the Sea; A Star Is Born; Semi-Tough; Convoy; Heaven's Gate; Rollover; Flashpoint; Songwriter (& songs).
TV inc: Freedom Road; The Unbroken Circle-A Tribute to Mother Maybelle Carter; A Special Anne Murray Christmas: Country Comes Home; Texas & Tennessee--A Musical Affair; The Hawk; The Lost Honor of Kathryn Beck; Johnny Cash--Christmas On The Road.
(Other Grammys-(2)-C&W perf-1973, 1975).

KROFFT, Marty: Puppeteer-Prod. b. Montreal, Canada. Member of family that has operated puppet theatre in Athens since 18th century. TV inc: H R Pufnstuf; Land of the Lost; Sigmund and the Sea Monsters; Lost Saucer; Far Out Space Nuts; Donny and Marie Series; Brady Bunch Variety Hour; Really Raquel; Kaptain Kool and the Kongs Present ABC All-Star Saturday; Jimmy Osmond Special; Krofft Comedy Hour; Krofft Superstars Hour; Pink Lady; Barbara Mandrell and the Mandrell Sisters; Side Show (exec prod); Anson ıN' Lorrie (exec prod); The Cracker Brothers; Pryor's Place.
Films inc: Middle Age Crazy.

KROFFT, Sid: Puppeteer-Prod. b. Athens, Greece. B of Marty Krofft. Created Les Poupees de Paris. For other credits see KROFFT, Marty.

KROLL, Nathan: Prod-Dir. b. NYC, Nov 5, 1911. e. Juilliard. TV inc: A Dancer's World; Appalachian Spring; Night Journey; The World of

Carl Sandburg; Who's Afraid of Opera?; Portrait of an American Actress; Prado Museum - Masterpieces and Music; Casals at Marlboro; Impact.
Films inc: The Guns of August (doc).

KRUGER, Hardy: Act. b. Berlin, Apr 12, 1928. On screen since 1943.
Films inc: As Long As You're Near Me; Taxi For Tobruk; Sundays and Cybele; The Flight of the Phoenix; The Defector; The Battle on the Neretva; The Secret of Santa Vittoria; The Red Tent; Paper Tiger; Barry Lyndon; A Bridge Too Far; The Wild Geese; Blue Fin; Feine Gesellschaft Beschraentke Haftung (Society Limited); Wrong Is Right; The Inside Man.

KRUGER, Jeffrey S.: Prod. b. London, England, Apr 19, 1931. Prod numerous concerts with top US, British stars. Pres Ember Enterprises which includes mus pub, concert promotion, film dist & prodn.
Films inc: Sweetbeat; Rock You Sinners; The Amorous Sex.

KRUGMAN, Lou: Act. b. Chicago, Jul 19, 1914. Started as radio actor, 1929.
Films inc: To the Ends of the Earth; The Lady of Fatima; Kim; Caper of the Golden Bulls; I Want to Live; Irma La Douce.
Thea inc: Yoshe Kalb; Midsummer Night's Dream; Cafe Crown; Cotton Candy; Diary of Anne Frank.

KRUMGOLD, Joseph: Wri. b. Jersey City, NJ, 1908. e. NYU. Films inc: And Now Miguel; Dream No More; Magic Town; Seven Miles From Alcatraz; The Crooked Road; The Phantom Submarine; Main Street Lawyer; Speed to Burn; Blackmailer; Adventure in Manhattan; Lady from Nowhere; Join the Marines.

KRUSCHEN, Jack: Act. b. Winnipeg, Canada, Mar 20, 1922. Films inc: Red Hot and Blue; The Last Voyage; The Apartment; Lover Come Back; The Unsinkable Molly Brown; Harlow; Caprice; McClintock; Cry Terror; Freebie and the Bean; Satan's Cheerleader; Sunburn.
TV inc: Deadly Harvest; Busting Loose; The Life and Times of Grizzly Adams; Adventures of Huckleberry Finn; No Soap, Radio; The Devlin Connection; Zorro and Son; Dark Mirror; Deadly Intentions.
Thea inc: I Can Get it For You Wholesale (Bway); Promises, Promises (London).

KUBRICK, Stanley: Dir-Prod-Wri. b. NYC, Jul 26, 1928. Films inc: (doc) Day of the Fight; Flying Padre. (Features) Fear and Desire; Killer's Kiss; The Killing; Paths of Glory; Spartacus; Lolita; Dr Strangelove; 2001: A Space Odyssey; A Clockwork Orange; Barry Lyndon; The Shining.

KULIDJANOV, Lev: Dir. b. Russia, Mar. 19, 1924. e. Moscow Film Institute. Films inc: Ladies (co-dir, co-sp); This is how it Began (co-dir, co-sp); The House Where I Live (co-dir); The Paternal Home; When the Trees were Big; The Blue Notebook (& sp); Crime and Punishment (& co-sp); The Moment in the Stars (& co-sp).

KULIK, Seymour (Buzz): Prod-Dir. b. NYC, 1923. Films inc: The Explosive Generation; The Yellow Canary; Warning Shot (& prod); Villa Rides; Riot; To Find a Man; The Hunter.
TV inc: Brian's Song; Vanished; The Lindbergh Kidnapping Case; From Here To Eternity; Insight/Decision To Love; Rage of Angels; George Washington (supv prod-dir).

KULUKUNDIS, Eddie: Prod. b. London, Apr 20, 1932. e. Yale. Thea inc: (London) Enemy; Happy Apple; Poor Alice; How the Other Half Loves; The Disorderly Woman; Skyvers; The Plotters of Cabbage Patch Corner; Straight Up; Small Craft Warnings; A Private Matter; Cromwell; The Waltz of the Toreadors; A Little Night Music; The Gay Lord Quex; What the Butler Saw; A Room With a View; Dimetos; Outside Edge; Once A Catholic; Born In the Gardens; Beecham; Censored Scenes from King Kong; Tonight At 8:30 (rev); Steaming; Arms and the Man; Steafel Variations; Pack of Lies. (Bway): How the Other Half Loves; Sherlock Holmes; London Assurance; Travesties; Steaming; Pack Of Lies.
TV inc: Hamlet (cable).

KUPCINET, Irv: Columnist-TV host. b. Jul 31. e. U of ND, BA.

KURALT, Charles: TV newsman. b. Wilmington, NC, Sep 10, 1934. e. U NC, BA. Reporter Charlotte News 1955; reporter CBS 1957-1959, then spec assignments.

TV inc: On the Road with Charles Kuralt (*Emmys*-1969, 1980; ATAS Broadcast Journalism Award 1978.); Inside Hollywood--The Movie Business; Picasso--A Retrospective--Once In A Lifetime; Juilliard And Beyond--A Life In Music; After the Dream Comes True; Cicada Invasion; Eye On The Media--Private Lives, Public Press; The American Parade; What's A Nice Guy Like You Doing in TV News?; Crossroads.

KUROSAWA, Akiro: Dir. b. Japan, Mar 23, 1910. Films inc: Rashomon; Scandal; The Idiot; Red Beard; I Live in Fear; Doomed; The Hidden Fortress; The Cobweb Castle; Stray Dog; Seven Samurai; High and Low; The Man Who Tread on A Tiger's Tail; Sanjuro; The Bad Sleep Well; Drunken Angels; Lower Depths; No Regret for Our Youth; A Quiet Duel; Dodes'ka-den; Yojimbo; The Double; Ran.

KURTZ, Gary: Prod. b. 1941. e. USC. Worked with Roger Corman, Monte Hellman, other dirs as cin, soundman, edtr. Became asst prod on Two Lane Blacktop. Films inc: Chandler (asst prod); American Graffiti (co-prod); Star Wars (prod); The Empire Strikes Back (prod); Return To Oz (exec prod).

KURTZ, Swoozie: Act. b. Omaha, NE, Sep 6, 1944. Bway inc: Enter A Free Man; Tartuffe; A History of The American Film; Fifth of July (*Tony*-1980).

TV inc: Uncommon Women; Ah, Wilderness; Marriage Is Alive and Well; The Mating Season; Love, Sidney; Fifth of July; A Caribbean Mystery.

Films inc: Slap Shot; First Love; Oliver's Story; The World According To Garp; Against All Odds.

KURTZMAN, Katy: Act. b. Washington, DC, Sep 16, 1965. TV inc: Child of Class; When Every Day Was the 4th of July; Little House on the Prairie; The New Adventures of Heidi; Long Journey Back; Donovan's Kid; Dynasty; Allison Sidney Harrison.

KWAN, Nancy: Act. b. Hong Kong, 1939. Films inc: The World of Suzie Wong; Flower Drum Song; The Main Attraction; Honeymoon Hotel; Fate Is the Hunter; The House of Seven Joys; The Wrecking Crew; Fortress in the Sun; Night Creature; Walking The Edge.

TV inc: The Last Ninja; Blade In Hong Kong.

KWIT, Nathaniel Troy Jr.: Exec. b. NYC 1941. e. Cornell, BA; NYU, MBA. Joined ABC 1964, exec asst to P ABC Films; 1968 br mgr National Screen Service NY; 1971 founded Audience Marketing Inc., later sold to Viacom; 1974, VP Marketing Services WB; 1975 switched to Warner Cable Co.; 1979, VP Video & Special Markets, UA; Jan 1981, Sr VP, launched UA Classics; July 1981, P Domestic and Mktg Div MGM/UA; April 1982, removed as P but remained as head of UA Classics; July 1982 ousted from company; Dec 1982, P United Satellite Television.

KYSER, Kay: Orch Ldr. b. Rocky Mt, NC, 1905. Retired in 1947. Now lives in Boston where he is manager of the film and broadcasting departments of the Christian Science church.

LA BONTE, C. Joseph: Exec. b. Salem, MA, Sep 23, 1939. e. Northeastern U, BS; Harvard, MBA. Exec with H. P. Hood & Sons, 1958-1963; mktg coord Market Forge Co., 1963; vp food svs ARA 1969; exec vp 1971; Aug. 1979 P 20th-Fox Enterprises & sr vp 20th Century-Fox; Sept 1979 named P 20th Century-Fox; Aug 1981, COO; Nov 1982, resd to form the Vantage Group, venture capital firm.

LABORTEAUX, Matthew: Act. b. Los Angeles, Dec 1965. Films inc: Woman Under the Influence.

TV inc: Poppa and Me; Little House on the Prairie; Legends of the West--Truth and Tall Tales; Kids n' Booze--A Minor Problem (co-host); Whiz Kids; Look Back to Yesterday.

LABRO, Philippe: Dir-Wri. b. France, Aug 27, 1936. Films inc: Don't Be Blue; Without Apparent Motive; The Inheritor; Le Hasard et la Violence; L'Aplaguer; La Crime (Coverup) (dir); Rive Droite, Rive Gauche (Right Bank, Left Bank).

LACHMAN, Mort: Wri-Dir-Prod. b. Seattle, WA, Mar 20, 1918. e. U WA, BA. TV inc: Bob Hope TV Specials; Flip Wilson Specials; Oscar Shows; Emmy Shows; The Girl Who Couldn't Lose (*Emmy*-dir-1975); All in the Family (*Emmy*-exec prod-1978); One Day at a Time (exec prod); No Soap, Radio; Book of Lists; She's With Me; Madame's Place; It Only Hurts When You Laugh (exec prod); Baby Makes Five (exec prod); Sutters Bay; Kate & Allie (exec prod); Not In Front of the Kids (exec prod-wri); Spencer (exec prod); Under One Roof (exec prod).

Films inc: Yours, Mine and Ours (wri); Mixed Company (wri).

LADD, Alan Walbridge, Jr.: Exec. b. Los Angeles, Oct 22, 1937. e. USC. S of late Alan Ladd. Agent, CMA, 1962-68; prod, 1969-73. Films inc: Walking Stick; A Severed Head; Tam Lin; Nightcomers; Fear Is the Key; with 20th Century-Fox Film Corp 1973; Sr vp Worldwide Prod, 1974-76; appointed pres 20th Century-Fox, Aug 30, 1976; resigned June 1979; formed The Ladd Company, Oct 1979; Jan. 1985, P-CEO UA Corp. and vice chmn MGM/UA; March 1985, P & COO MGM/UA Entertainment.

LADD, Cheryl (nee Stoppelmoor): Act. b. Huron, SD, Jul 2. TV inc: Charlie's Angels; Ben Vereen. . .His Roots; General Electric's All-Star Anniversary; John Denver and the Ladies; The Cheryl Ladd Special; When She Was Bad; Cheryl Ladd Special-Souvenirs; Perry Como's Spring In San Francisco; Cheryl Ladd--Scenes From A Special; Kentucky Woman; Grace Kelly; The Hasty Heart (cable); Romance On The Orient Express; A Death In California.

Films inc: Now and Forever; Purple Hearts.

LADD, David Alan: Act-Exec. b. Los Angeles, Feb 5, 1947. e. USC, BA. S of late Alan Ladd. Films inc: The Lone Ranger (at age 9); The Big Land; Raymie; Misty; R.P.M.; Catlow; Deathline; Jamaica Reef; Jonathan Livingston Seagull; Day of the Locusts; Kansan; Wild Geese.

TV inc: Zane Gray Theatre; Wagon Train; Playhouse 90; Pursuit; Ben Casey; Gunsmoke; Love American Style; Kojak; When She Was Bad (prod).

Thea inc: The Glass Menagerie; Alpha Beta.

May 1983 joined John Veitch's prodn firm as vp of prodn & dvlpmt of projects.

LADD, Diane (nee Ladnier): Act. b. Nov 29, 1932. Films inc: White Lightning; Chinatown; Alice Doesn't Live Here Any More; All Night Long; Something Wicked This Way Comes.

TV inc: Willa; Guyana Tragedy-The Story of Jim Jones; Desperate Lives; Grace Kelly; I Married A Centerfold.

Bway inc: Lu Ann Hampton Laverty Oberlander.

LAFFERTY, Perry: Exec. b. Oct 3, 1920. Former vp, pgms, Hollywood, for the CBS TV Network from 1965-1976. In 1976 with Filmways as an exec prod; June 1979 named sr vp pgms and talent, West Coast, NBC Entertainment; resd. Feb. 1985 to enter indie prodn.

TV inc: The Danny Kaye Show; Robert Montgomery Presents; U S Steel Hour; Studio One; Twilight Zone; Mary Tyler Moore Show; The Funny Side of Love.

LAFONT, Bernadette: Act. b. Nimes, France, Oct 28. Films inc: Le Beau Serge; Bal De Nuit; A Double Tour; Les Bonnes Femmes; Les Mordus; Tire Au Flanc; Un Clair De Lune A Maubeuge; La Chasse A L'Homme; Le Bons Vivante; Le Voleur; Le Trouble-Fesses; Noroit; La Tortue sur le dos; Violette Noziere; Chaussette Surprise; Nous Maigrirons Ensemble; La Guele de l'autre; Retour En Force; Il Ladrone; The King of Jerks; La Bete Noire; Canicule (Dog Day); Gwendoline; Le Pactole (The Boodle).

Thea inc: Desire.

LAHTI, Christine: Act. b. Detroit, MI., Apr. 4, 1950. e. U MI, BA. Studied with Uta Hagen; Neighborhood Playhouse. Bway inc: Loose Ends; Division Street; The Woods; Scenes and Revelations; Present Laughter; Hooters (off-Bway).

Films inc: And Justice for All; Whose Life is it Anyway?; Ladies and Gentlemen, The Fabulous Stains; Swing Shift.

TV inc: The Last Tenant; The Henderson Monster; The Executioner's Song; All Washed Up; Single Bars, Single Women; Love Lives On.

LAI, Francis: Comp. b. France, 1933. Film scores inc: A Man and a Woman; Mayerling; House of Cards; Rider on the Rain; Love Story *(Oscar-1970)*; Le Petit Matin; Another Man, Another Chance; Bilitis; The Good and the Bad; Widow's Nest; Cat and Mouse; International Velvet; Oliver's Story *(Oscar-1970)*; Beyond the Reef;; Les Uns et Les Autres (The Ins and The Outs); Edith et Marcel; Canicule (Dog Day); Les Ripoux; J'Ai Recontre le Pere Noel (Here Comes Santa Claus).

LAINE, Cleo (Clementina Dinah Campbell): Singer-Act. b. Southall, Middlesex, England, 1934. W of John Dankworth. Singing debut 1952 with Dankworth Seven, later John Dankworth Orch. U S debut Lincoln Center 1972; appeared Carnegie Hall; world tours. Albums inc: I Am A Song; Cleo Laine Live at Carnegie Hall; A Beautiful Thing; Born on a Friday; Porgy and Bess; Best Friends.
Thea inc: (London) The Seven Deadly Sins; Show Boat; Valmouth; Flesh to a Tiger; Hedda Gabler; A Time to Laugh; A Midsummer Night's Dream; Colette.
TV inc: The Monte Carlo Show.

LAINE, Frankie: Act. b. Chicago, Mar 30, 1913. Recording, nitery star. Films inc: When You're Smiling; Make Believe Ballroom; The Sunny Side of the Street; Rainbow Round My Shoulder; Bring Your Smile Along; He Laughed Last; Viva Las Vegas.

LAIRD, Jack: Prod-Wri-Dir. b. Bombay, India, May 8, 1923. Prod with Bing Crosby Prodns 1961; U, 1963. Films inc: Dark Intruder; Destiny of a Spy; Intrigue at Monte Carlo; Perilous Voyage.
TV inc: Ben Casey; Kraft Suspense Theatre; The Bold Ones; Night Gallery; Kojak; Doctors Hospital; Whatever Happened to the Class of '65?; Testimony of Two Men; Beggarman, Thief; The Dark Secret of Harvest Home; The Gangster Chronicles (exec prod); Hellinger's Law (wri-exec prod).

LAIRD, Marlene: Dir. b. London, Mar 21, 1949. TV inc: The Miss World Beauty Pageant; All That Glitters; A Year at the Top; The Baxters; General Hospital *(Emmys-1981, 1982)*; All in the Family; Friendships, Secrets and Lies; Laverne and Shirley; Archie Bunker's Place; The Righteous Apples; Applause (& asso-prod); Double Trouble.

LAKE, Arthur (nee Silverlake): Act. b. Corbin, KY, 1905. On screen since 1924.
Films inc: Skinner's Dress Suit; The Irresistible Lover; Harold Teen; On with the Show; Indiscreet; Midshipman Jack; Orchids to You; Topper; Blondie series; Three is a Family; Sixteen Fathoms Deep.

LAKIN, Rita: Wri. b. NYC. e. Hunter Coll, BA. TV inc: The Doctors; Peyton Place; Mod Squad; Death Takes a Holiday; Women in Chains; A Summer Without Boys; Message to My Daughter; Last Bride of Salem; Medical Center; Hey, I'm Alive; A Sensitive; Passionate Man; Executive Suite; Flamingo Road; The Home Front (& supv prod); Peyton Place--The Next Generation.

LAMARR, Hedy: Act. b. Vienna, Nov 9, 1915. On screen in Europe from 1929.
Films inc: One Doesn't Need Money; Storm in a Water Glass; Ecstasy. In US from 1938 in: Algiers; I Take This Woman; Boom Town; Comrade X; H.M. Pulham, Esq.; Tortilla Flat; Crossroads; White Cargo; Samson and Delilah; Lady Without A Passport; Dishonored Lady; Experiment Perilous; My Favorite Spy; The Female Animal.

LAMAS, Lorenzo: Act. b. Los Angeles, Jan 20, 1958. S of Arlene Dahl and the late Fernando Lamas. Films inc: Grease; Tilt; Take Down; Body Rock.
TV inc: California Fever; Detour to Terror; Secret of Midland Heights; Falcon Crest; On Top All Over The World.

LAMB, Gil: Dancer-Act. b. Minneapolis, MN, Jun 14, 1906. In Vaude, on Bway. Films inc: The Fleet's In; Ridin' High; Rainbow Island; Practically Yours; Hit Parade of 1947; Make Mine Laughs; Humphrey Takes a Chance; Bye, Bye Birdie; The Gnomemobile; Blackbeard's Ghost; The Love Bug.
TV inc: For The Love of It.

LAMBERT, Gavin: Wri. b. England, 1924. Films inc: Bitter Victory; Sons and Lovers; The Roman Spring of Mrs Stone; Inside Daisy Clover; I Never Promised You a Rose Garden.

LAMOUR, Dorothy (Dorothy Raumeyer): Act. b. New Orleans, LA, Dec 10, 1914. Screen debut, 1938, Jungle Princess.
Films inc: Hurricane; Johnny Apollo; Typhoon; The Road to Singapore (and 4 other "Road" pix); Star Spangled Rhythm; The Fleet's In; Beyond the Blue Horizon; A Medal for Benny; Duffy's Tavern; My Favorite Brunette; Lulu Belle; The Greatest Show on Earth; Donovan's Reef; The Phynx.
TV inc: Bob Hope's Road to Hollywood.

LAMPELL, Millard: Wri. b. Paterson, NJ, Jan 10, 1919. e. WV U. Films inc: The Hero; Chance Meeting; Escape from East Berlin; The Idol.
TV inc: No Hiding Place; Eagle In a Cage *(Emmy-1966)*; The Deadly Visitor; Grand Ole Opry at 50; Rich Man, Poor Man; Wheels; Orphan Train; The Wall (& co-prod).

LAMPERT, Zohra: Act. b. May 13, 1937. Films inc: Odds Against Tomorrow; Posse from Hell; Splendor in the Grass; A Fine Madness; Bye, Bye Braverman; Let's Scare Jessica To Death; Opening Night; Alphabet City; Teachers.
TV inc: Queen of the Gypsies (Kojak) *(Emmy-1975)*;The Nurses; Lady of the House; The Suicide's Wife; The Girl, The Gold Watch and Everything; Children of Divorce; The Girl, The Gold Watch and Dynamite; The Cafeteria.
Bway inc: Look, We've Come Throught; Mother Courage and Her Children; Unexpected Guests.

LANCASTER, Burt: Act. b. NYC, Nov 2, 1913. Screen debut, 1946, The Killers.
Films inc: Desert Fury; Brute Force; All My Sons; The Flame and the Arrow; Jim Thorpe-All American; Crimson Pirate; Come Back, Little Sheba; From Here To Eternity; His Majesty O'Keefe; Apache; Vera Cruz; The Rose Tattoo; Trapeze; The Rainmaker; Gunfight at The OK Corral; Sweet Smell of Success; Separate Tables; Elmer Gantry *(Oscar-1960)*; Judgment at Nuremberg; Bird Man of Alcatraz; Seven Days in May; The Swimmer; The Gypsy Moths; Airport; Scorpio; Executive Action; Conversation Piece; Buffalo Bill and the Indians; The Cassandra Crossing; Twilight's Last Gleaming; The Island of Dr. Moreau; Go Tell The Spartans; Zulu Dawn; Arthur Miller On Home Ground; Atlantic City, USA; Cattle Annie and Little Britches; La Pelle (The Skin); Local Hero; The Osterman Weekend; Little Treasure.
TV inc: Marco Polo; The Making of a Local Hero--With A Little Help from his Friends; Scandal Sheet.

LANCHESTER, Elsa: Act. b. London, Oct 28, 1902. W of late Charles Laughton. Performed on stage with husband in London, NY. On screen in England from 1938. On screen in US from 1935.
Films inc: David Copperfield; Naughty Marietta; The Razor's Edge; Bell, Book and Candle; Come To The Stable; Witness for the Prosecution; Mary Poppins; Murder by Death; Die Laughing.
TV inc: Where's Poppa?

LANDAU, Ely: Prod. b. NYC, Jan 20, 1920.
In the 50's he founded and headed NTA (National Telefilm Associates). During this period he created and developed Play of the Week series, inc such plays as Medea; The World of Sholem Aleichem, No Exit; Tiger at the Gates.
Films inc: Long Day's Journey Into Night; The Pawnbroker; The Madwoman of Chaillot; A Filmed Record. . .Montgomery to Memphis (doc); A Face of War (doc); The Iceman Cometh; Rhinoceros; Lost in the Stars; The Homecoming; A Delicate Balance; Luther; In Celebration; Butley; Galileo; The Man in the Glass Booth (all under the banner of the American Film Theatre Subscription series); The Greek Tycoon; Hopscotch; Beatlemania; The Chosen.
TV inc: The Deadly Game (cable); Laurence Olivier and Jackie Gleason as Mr. Halpern and Mr. Johnson (cable).

LANDAU, Martin: Act. b. NYC, Jun 20, 1928. H of Barbara Bain. Films inc: Pork Chop Hill; North by Northwest; The Gazebo; Cleopatra; The Hallelujah Trail; Nevada Smith; They Call Me Mr Tibbs; Strange Shadows in an Empty Room; Meteor; The Last Word; Without

Warning; Alone In the Dark; The Being.

TV inc: Mission Impossible; Space 1999; The Death of Ocean View Park; The Harlem Globetrotters on Gilligan's Island; The Fall of the House of Usher.

Bway inc: Middle of the Night; Uncle Vanya; Stalag 17; First Love; The Goat Song.

LANDAU, Richard: Wri. b. NYC, Feb 21, 1914. e. U of AZ; Yale. Started as agent; became wri with MGM Shorts Dept. Films inc: Gun In His Hand; Strange Confession; Back To Bataan; Christmas Eve; Crooked Way; Johnny One Eye; The Lost Continent; FBI Girl; Stolen Face; Bad Blonde; The Sins of Jezebel; Blackout; Pearl of the Pacific; Creeping Unknown; Fort Courageous; The Black Hole.

TV inc: The FBI; Manhunter; Run, Joe, Run; Cannon; Switch; The $6 Million Man; The Incredible Hulk; American Girls; Misadventures of Sheriff Lobo; One Last Ride.

LANDER, David L.: Act. b. Brooklyn, NY, Jun 22. e. NYC High School for Performing Arts; Carnegie Tech. Teamed with Michael McKean in comedy group The Credibility Gap, toured US for four years. TV inc: Viva Valdez; The Bob Newhart Show; The Hollywood Squares; Kids Are People Too; Laverne & Shirley.

LANDERS, Audrey: Act-Sing-Sngwri. b. Philadelphia, PA, Jul 18. e. Columbia U, BA; Juilliard. TV inc: The Secret Storm; Somerset; Archie Musical Comedy Variety Show; Highcliffe Manor; The Waverly Wonders; The Magic of David Copperfield; Fit For a King; Singles Magazine; Dallas.

Rec inc: The Apple Don't Fall Far From the Tree; You Thrill Me.

LANDERS, Hal (ne Waxlander): Prod. b. Chicago, Jun 26, 1928. Films inc: Joy Ride; Damnation Alley; Gypsy Moths; Monte Walsh; The Hot Rock; Back Shot; Death Wish; Death Wish II (exec prod).

TV inc: Money On the Side.

LANDESBERG, Steve: Act. b. NYC, Nov 3. TV inc: Johnny Carson Show; Paul Sand Show; Barney Miller; The Steve Allen Comedy Hour; Stephanie; Insight/For Love Or Money; The Steve Landesberg Television Show (& crea-wri); Comedy Zone.

Films inc: Loose Shoes.

LANDIS, John: Dir. b. Chicago, IL, 1951. Films inc: Schlock; Kentucky Fried Movie; National Lampoon's Animal House; The Blues Brothers (& wri); An American Werewolf in London (& wri); Bonjour Monsieur Lewis (doc); Trading Places; Twilight Zone--The Movie (& wri); The Muppets Take Manhattan (act); Into The Night (& act).

TV inc: Coming Soon! (& wri) (Feevee).

LANDON, Michael (ne Eugene Orowitz): Act-Wri-Dir. b. Forest Hills, NY, Oct 31, 1937. e. USC. Films inc: (act) I Was a Teenage Werewolf; God's Little Acre; The Legend of Tom Dooley; Comeback; Sam's Son (& wri-dir).

TV inc: (as actor) Restless Gun; Bonanza; Little House on the Prairie (& co-prod). Love Came Laughing (wri-dir); The Loneliest Runner; Killing Stone (wri-dir-prod); The Roy Campanella Story (dir); Highlights of Ringling Bros and Barnum & Bailey Circus (host); The Funtastic World Of Hanna-Barbera Arena Show (host); Father Murphy (exec prod-crea-wri-dir); Fourth Annual TV Guide Special (co-host); Love Is Forever (exec prod-act); Here's Television Entertainment (host); Look Back to Yesterday (exec prod-act); Little House--The Last Farewell (& exec prod); Highway To Heaven (& exec prod-wri-di r); Bless All The Dear Children.

(NATAS Founders Award 1982).

LANDRES, Paul: Dir. b. NYC, Aug 21, 1912. Films inc: Miracle of the Hills: Johnny Rocco; Vampire; Flame Barrier; Oregon Passage; Last of the Badmen; Son of a Gunfighter.

TV approximately 400 segments of various shows inc: The Outcasts; Bonanza; Daktari; The Rifleman; 77 Sunset Strip; Maverick; Hawaiian Eye.

LANDRY, Robert J.: Edtr. b. East Haddon, CT, Jun 14, 1903. Manager of Variety offices in Chicago and Los Angeles before becoming original radio editor of Variety in 1932; dir division of program writing CBS, 1942-1948; dir NYU Radio-tv workshop for 13 yrs; sec Authors Guild 14 years; retd to Variety 1952 as managing editor;

Sept. 1983, became editor emeritus.

LANDSBURG, Alan W.: Exec prod. b. NYC, May 10, 1933. e. NYU. Prod NBC News, 1951-59; prod-wri CBS, 1959-60; exec prod, Wolper Prodns/Metromedia Prods Corp, 1961-70; p Alan Landsburg Prodn 1970; sold company to Reeves Communications, 1978, remaining with firm until April, 1985 when he resd. to form The Landsburg Co.

TV inc: A Storm In Summer (Emmy-prod-1970); Terror Out Of The Sky; The Triangle Factory Fire Scandal; And Baby Makes Six; Mysterious Island of Beautiful Women; Marathon; The Chisholms; That's Incredible; Those Amazing Animals; No Holds Barred; Baby Comes Home; The World's Most Spectacular Stuntman; 30 Years of TV Comedy's Greatest Hits; Me and Mr. Stenner; The Krypton Factor; The Future--What's Next?; A Long Way Home; Bill; Mysterious Two; It Only Hurts When You Laugh; Search (& wri-dir); Life's Most Embarrassing Moments; Personal & Confidential; Sutters Bay; Adam; Bill--On His Own; The World's Funniest Commercial Goofs; People to People With Rona Barrett; The Glory Boys; Getting The Last Laugh; People Do The Craziest Things,

Films inc: Porky's II--The Next Day; The White Lions; Jaws 3-D.

LANDSBURG, Valerie: Act. b. NYC, Aug 12. D of Alan Landsburg. Bway inc: I Ought To Be In Pictures; The Floating Lightbulb. Films inc: Thank God It's Friday.

TV inc: Marathon; The Triangle Shirtwaist Factory Fire Scandal; Fame; The Kids From Fame.

LANE, Abbe: Singer. b. NYC, 1932. Appeared with bands, in niteries. Films inc: Wings of the Hawk; Ride Clear of Diablo; The Americano; Twilight Zone--The Movie.

LANE, Burton (nee Levy): Comp. b. NYC.b. Feb 2, 1912. Bway scores inc: Hold On to Your Hats; Laffing Room Only; Finian's Rainbow; On a Clear Day You Can See Forever.

Songs inc: Everything I Have Is Yours; The Lady's in Love with You; I Hear Music; How Are Things in Glocca Morra; That Old Devil Moon; When I'm Not Near The Girl I Love; On a Clear Day You Can See Forever.

Film scores inc: Dancing Lady; College Swing; St. Louis Blues; Babes on Broadway; Ship Ahoy; Royal Wedding.

(Grammy-cast album-1965).

LANE, Diane: Act. b. NYC, Jan 22, 1965. Films inc: A Little Romance; Touched By Love; Cattle Annie and Little Britches; Six Pack; The Outsiders; Rumble Fish; National Lampoon Goes to the Movies; Streets of Fire; The Cotton Club.

Thea inc: The Cherry Orchard; Agamemnon; Runaways.

TV inc: Summer; Child Bride at Short Creek; Miss All-American Beauty.

LANG, Charles B. Jr.: Cin. b. Bluff, UT, Mar 27, 1902. Began in film laboratory, then asst cameraman; dir of photography, Paramount, 1929-52, then freelance.

Films inc: The Right To Love; A Farewell to Arms (Oscar-1933); The Ghost and Mrs. Muir; Ace In The Hole; Sundown; Sabrina; Sudden Fear; The Uninvited; The Rainmaker; So Proudly We Hail; Some Like It Hot; Separate Tables; How The West Was Won; The Magnificent Seven; Charade; The Love Machine; Doctor's Wives; Bob and Carol & Ted & Alice; Butterflies Are Free.

LANG, Jennings: Exec. b. NYC, May 28, 1915. e. St Johns U, BS, JD. H of Monica Lewis. Law practice, 1937. Opened own office as actor's agent, Hollywood. In 1940 joined Jaffee Agency; made partner and vp in 1942; pres from 1948-50; resigned to join MCA; in 1952 made vp of MCA-TV Ltd and bd member; exec prod, MCA (Universal). Creator and developer of the Sensurround System which won (Oscar-1974); Nov 1981 formed own indie firm.

Films inc: Winning; Puzzle of a Downfall Child; Coogan's Bluff; Joe Kidd; High Plains Drifter; Play Misty For Me; Charley Varrick; Pete 'N Tillie; Slaughterhouse Five; Breezy; The Great Waldo Pepper; Airport 75; The Eiger Sanction; Airport 77; The Front Page; The Hindenburg; Rollercoaster; House Calls; Nunzio; The Concorde-Airport '79; Real Life (act); Little Miss Marker; The Nude Bomb; The Sting II; Stick.

TV inc: Wagon Train; The Robert Cummings Show; Bachelor Father; Wells Fargo; Mike Hammer.

LANG, Otto: Prod-Dir. b. Austria, Jan 21, 1908. Films inc: (docs) New Guinea; New Zealand; Australia; Philippines; Thailand; Singapore; Turkey. (Features) Five Fingers; Call Northside 777; White Witch Doctor; Lowell Thomas' Search for Paradise; Tora! Tora! Tora! (asso prod).

TV inc: Beethoven - Ordeal and Triumph; Man from UNCLE; Daktari; Iron Horse; Cheyenne; Bat Masterson; Rifleman; Sea Hunt.

LANG, Richard (W. Richard Lang Jr): Dir. Films inc: Wind River; Rough Mix; The Mountain Men; A Change of Seasons.

TV inc: Fantasy Island; Vega$ (pilot); The Word; Strike Force; Matt Houston (& prod); Don't Go to Sleep (& prod); Shooting Stars (& prod); Dark Mirror (& prod); Velvet (& prod); Obsessed With A Married Woman.

LANGAN, Glenn: Act. b. Denver, CO, Jul. 8, 1917. H of Adele Jergens. Films inc: The Return of Dr. X; Riding High; Something for the Boys; Four Jills in a Jeep; A Wing and a Prayer; In the Meantime, Darling; A Bell for Adano; Hangover Square; Sentimental Journey; Margie; Dragonwyck; Forever Amber; Fury At Furnace Creek; The Snake Pit; The Treasure of Monte Cristo; 99 River Street; Jungle Heat; The Big Chase; The Amazing Colossal Man; Mutiny in Outer Space.

LANGDON, Sue Ane: Act. b. Mar 8, 1936. Films inc: The Outsider; The Rounders; A Fine Madness; A Guide For The Married Man; Cheyenne Social Club; The Evictors; Without Warning; Zapped!

TV inc: Arnie.

LANGE, Hope: Act. b. Redding Ridge, CT, Nov 28, 1933. Bway debut age 12, The Patriots. Screen debut, 1956, Bus Stop.

Films inc: Peyton Place; The Young Lions; In Love and War; A Pocketful of Miracles; How the West Was Won; Jigsaw; Death Wish; I Am the Cheese.

TV inc: The Ghost and Mrs. Muir (Emmys-1969, 1970); That Certain Summer; The Day Christ Died; Beulah Land; Pleasure Palace; Natalie--A Tribute To A Very Special Lady (host); Finder Of Lost Loves; Private Sessions.

Bway inc: The Supporting Cast.

LANGE, Jessica: Act. b. Apr 20, 1949. Films inc: King Kong; All That Jazz; How to Beat the High Cost of Living; The Postman Always Rings Twice; Frances; Tootsie; (Oscar-support-1982); Country (& prod).

TV inc: Cat On A Hot Tin Roof (cable).

LANGE, Ted: Perf. b. Oakland, CA, Jan 5. Films inc: Love Gift; Trick Baby; Wattstax; Black Belt Jones; Friday Foster; Record City.

TV inc: The Last Detail; A.F.I. Salute to James Cagney; That's My Mama; Mr. T. and Tina; The Love Boat; Good Evening, Captain; The Fall Guy (dir); Hollywood--A Legacy In Silhouette (host).

Thea inc: Hair; Ain't Supposed to Die a Natural Death.

LANGELLA, Frank: Act. b. Bayonne, NJ, Jan 1, 1940. e. Syracuse U. Bway inc: The Immoralist; Benito Cereno; A Cry of Players; The Relapse; Seascape (Tony-1975); Ring Around the Moon; Dracula; Passione (dir); Passion; Design For Living.

Films inc: The Twelve Chairs; Diary of a Mad Housewife; The House Under the Trees; The Deadly Trap; The Wrath of God; Dracula; Those Lips, Those Eyes; Sphinx.

TV inc: I, Leonardo--A Journey of the Mind; Balanchine (narr).

LANGFORD, Francis: Act. b. Lakeland, FL, Apr 4, 1913. Stage, vaudeville, niteries prior to screen debut Broadway Melody of 1936.

Films inc: Born to Dance; The Hit Parade; This Is the Army; Follow the Band; Radio Stars on Parade; The Purple Heart Diary; The Glenn Miller Story.

LANGLOIS, Lisa: Act. b. North Bay, Ontario, Canada. Films inc: Blood Relatives; Violette; Phobia; Happy Birthday to Me; Class of 1984; Rats; Hard Feelings; The Man Who Wasn't There; Joy Of Sex; The Slugger's Wife.

LANGNER, Philip: Prod. b. NYC, Aug 24, 1926. e. Yale U, BS. S of Armina Marshall and late Lawrence Langner. Films inc: Judgment at Nuremburg; A Child is Waiting; The Pawnbroker; Slaves; Born to Win.

Bway inc: Seagulls Over Sorrento; The Tunnel of Love; The Sum-

mer of the Seventeenth Doll; Sunrise at Campobello (Tony-1957); Third Best Sport; The 49th Cousin; Help Stamp Out Marriage; The Homecoming; Absurd Person Singular. Ownr Westport Country Playhouse, Westport CT.

LANKFORD, Kim: Act. b. Montebello, CA., June 14 Films inc: Harry and Walter Go To New York; Malibu Beach; Convoy; The Octagon.

TV inc: Terror Among Us; Three Eyes; Knots Landing.

LANNING, Jerry: Act. b. Miami, FL, May 17, 1943. H of Sherry Mathis. Bway inc: Mame; Where's Charley; My Fair Lady (20th anni prodn); 1776; Camelot.

TV inc: Search for Tomorrow; Texas.

LANOUX, Victor: Act. b. France, 1936. Films inc: La vieille dame indigne; La vie normale; Tu seras terriblement gentille; L'affaire domenici; Trois milliards dans un ascenseur; Elle court, elle court la banlieue; Deux hommes dans la ville; Dupont la joie; Mort d'un guide; Folle a tuer; Cousin, Cousine; Adieu Poulet; Un elephant ca trompe enormement; Un femme a sa fenetre; Servant et maitresse; Le passe simple; Nous irons tous au Paradis (We Will All Go To Heaven); Un moment d'egarement (In a Wild Moment); La carapate (Out of It); Les chiens (The Dogs); Un si joli village (Such a Lovely Town); Au bout du bout du banc (At the Brink of the Brink of the Bench); Retour en force (Return in Bond); Une sale affaire (A Filthy Business); La revanche; Boulevard des assassins; Y'a-t'il un Francais dans le salle? (Is There A Frenchman in the House?); Un Dimanche de flics (A Cop's Sunday); Les voleurs de la nuit; Stella; Canicule (Dog Day); Louisiane; Les Voleurs de la nuit (Thieves After Dark); La Triche (The Cheat); La Smala (The Tribe).

LANSBURY, Angela: Act. b. London, Oct 16, 1925. Sis of Bruce and Edgar Lansbury. Screen debut, 1943, Gaslight.

Films inc: National Velvet; The Picture of Dorian Gray; The Hoodlum Saint; Till the Clouds Roll By; If Winter Comes; State of the Union; The Three Musketeers; Samson and Delilah; Kind Lady; Mutiny; Remains to be Seen; A Life at Stake; Please Murder Me; The Court Jester; The Long Hot Summer; The Dark at the Top of the Stairs; A Breath of Scandal; All Fall Down; The Manchurian Candidate; Dear Heart; The Greatest Story Ever Told; Harlow; Mister Buddwing; Something for Everyone; Bedknobs and Broomsticks; Death on the Nile; The Lady Vanishes; The Mirror Crack'd; The Last Unicorn (voice); The Pirates of Penzance; The Company of Wolves.

Bway inc: Hotel Paradiso; Mame (Tony-1966); Dear World (Tony-1979); Hamlet; Gypsy (Tony-1975); Sweeney Todd (Tony-1979); A Little Family Business; Mame (rev).

TV inc: Little Gloria--Happy At Last; The Gift of Love--A Christmas Story; Lace; The First Olympics--Athens 1896; Murder, She Wrote.

LANSBURY, Bruce: Prod. b. London, Jan 12, 1930. e. UCLA, BA. B of Angela and Edgar Lansbury. Wri, prod KABC-TV, LA, 1957-59; joined CBS-TV 1959, supervised daytime and nighttime programming; promoted to vp 1964; joined Paramount TV 1969 as prod; appointed vp 1972; joined Columbia TV as indie prod, 1975.

TV inc: Wild, Wild West; Mission Impossible; Silent Gun; Assault on the Wayne; Escape; Banjo Hackett; Bell, Book and Candle; The Fantastic Journey (exec prod); Mobile Medics (exec prod); The Aeromeds (exec prod; New Adventures of Wonder Woman (supv prod); Buck Rogers (supv prod); World War III; Summer Girl (exec prod).

Films inc: The Initiation.

LANSBURY, Edgar: Prod-Desgn. b. London, Jan 12, 1930. e. UCLA. B of Angela and Bruce Lansbury. Began career as scenic dsgn and art dir. First designs in NY were for The Wise Have Not Spoken, 1954, Cherry Lane Theatre. Art dir CBS, 1955-60; exec art dir, prod for WNDT educational TV, NY, 1962-63; art dir for award winning TV series The Defenders.

Films inc: (prod) The Subject Was Roses; Godspell; The Wild Party; Squirm; Blue Sunshine; He Knows You're Alone.

Bway inc: (prod) The Subject Was Roses (Tony-1964); The Only Game in Town; That Summer-That Fall; Promenade; Waiting for Godot; Long Day's Journey Into Night; Nourish the Beast; The Enclave; Gypsy; The Night that Made America Famous; The Magic Show; Godspell; American Buffalo; Broadway Follies.

TV inc: Summer Girl (exec prod).

LANSING, Robert (ne Broom): Act. b. San Diego, 1929. Films inc: The 4-D Man; A Gathering of Eagles; Under the Yum, Yum Tree; The Grissom Gang; Wild in the Sky; Bittersweet Love; Scalpel.
TV inc: 87th Precinct; 12 O'Clock High; S*H*E*; Life On The Mississippi; Automan.
Bway inc: Stalag 17; Suddenly Last Summer; Great God Brown; (London) The Little Foxes.

LANSING, Sherry Lee: Exec. b. Chicago, Jul 31, 1944. e. Northwestern, BS. Films (as act) Loving; Rio Lobo; Then Story Ed Talent Associates; exec story ed, MGM 1975-77; vp, Creative Affairs, MGM; vp, prod, Col; sr vp prodn, Col, 1978; Resd to become P 20th Fox Jan 1980; resd Dec 1982; Jan 1983 formed Jaffe-Lansing Prodns with Stanley Jaffe. Films inc: (exec prod) Firstborn.

LANTEAU, William (nee Lanctot): Act. b. St Johnsbury, VT, Nov 17, 1922. e. Yale School of Drama. Films inc: Li'l Abner; The Honeymoon Machine; The Facts of Life; Hotel; That Touch of Mink; From Noon Till Three.
TV inc: Our Town; All in the Family; Bronk; Sanford and Son; First You Cry; Sutters Bay; This Girl for Hire.
Bway inc: At War With the Army; Mrs. McThing; The Remarkable Mr. Pennypacker; What Every Woman Knows; The Matchmaker; Li'l Abner.

LANTOS, Robert: Prod. b. Budapest, Hungary, Apr 3, 1949. e. McGill U, BA, MA. Pres R.S.L. Films, Ltd, pres Viva Film. Films inc: L'Ange et la Femme; In Praise of Older Women; Suzanne; Agency; Paradise; Bedroom Eyes; Heavenly Bodies; Joshua Then And Now; Night Magic.
TV inc: Night Heat (supv prod).

LANTZ, Walter: Prod. b. New Rochelle, NY, Apr 27, 1900. Cartoonist for Hearst, 1916-20; prod cartoons for J. R. Bray Studios, 1922-27; then for Universal; became independent prod, 1937; pres Walter Lantz Prods. Created Woody Woodpecker; Chilly Willy; Oswald Rabbit; Katzenjammer Kids; Happy Hooligan; Krazy Kat. Also prod educational & commercial pictures for non-theatrical release & TV; prod, the Woody Woodpecker Show (TV). (Honorary Oscar-1978).

LANVIN, Gerard: Act. b. Boulogne-Billancourt, France, 1950. Films inc: Vous n' aurez pas L'Alsace et la Lorraine (You Won't Have Alsace-Lorraine); Les heros n'ont pas froid aux oreilles (Heroes Are Not Wet Behind the Ears); Bete mais discipline (Dumb But Disciplined); Tapage nocturne (Nocturnal Uproar); Exterieur Nuit (Exterior Night); L'entourloupe (The Swindle); Une semaine de vacances (A Week's Vacation); Le Choix des armes (Choice of Weapons); Est-ce bien raisonnable? (Is This Really Reasonable?); Tir groupe (Shot Pattern); Le prix du danger (The Prize of Peril); Ronde de nuit (Night Patrol); Marche a l'Ombre (Walk In The Shadow); Les Specialistes (The Specialists).

La PLANTE, Laura: Act. b. St Louis, MO, Nov 1, 1904. On screen from 1921. Films inc: The Old Swimming Hole; Perils of the Yukon; Sporting Youth; The Cat and the Canary; Show Boat; Spring Reunion.

LAPOTAIRE, Jane: Act. b. Ipswich, Suffolk, England, Dec 26, 1944. e. Bristol Old Vic. Debuted with Bristol Old Vic 1965; joined Old Vic 1967. Thea inc: (London) The Dance of Death; A Flea In Her Ear; Covent Garden Tragedy; The Way of the World; Guevara; The White Devil; the Merchant of Venice; Scapino; Taming of the Shrew; Oedipus; Measure for Measure; As You Like It; A Month in the Country; A Room With A View; Piaf; Dear Anyone. (Bway) Piaf (Tony-1981).
Films inc: Anthony and Cleopatra; Eureka.
TV inc: Stockers Copper; Love and Mr. Lewisham; Edward VII; Anthony and Cleopatra; The Other Woman; Marie Curie; Macbeth; To Catch A King.

LARDNER, Ring W. Jr.: Wri. b. Chicago, IL, Aug 19, 1915. e. Princeton. Originally a reporter then pub for Selznick Int'l before writing. Films inc: Woman of the Year (Oscar-1942); The Cross of Lorraine; Forever Amber; Forbidden Street; Four Days Leave; Cloak and Dagger; (career interrupted when, as member of so-called Unfriendly 10, he served year in prison for refusing to testify before House Committee on UnAmerican Activities); The Cincinnati Kid; M*A*S*H (Oscar-

1970); The Greatest; Hollywood on Trial (act).

LARNER, Jeremy: Wri. Films inc: Drive, He Said; The Candidate (Oscar-1972).

La ROSA, Julius: Singer. b. NYC, 1930. Pop singer of the 50's. TV inc: Arthur Godfrey and His Friends; Another World.

LARSON, Glen: Prod-Wri. Member of the Four Preps singing group in the 1950's, moved to tv 1960.
TV inc: It Takes a Thief; McCloud; The Virginian; Get Christie Love; Six Million Dollar Man; Sword of Justice; Battlestar Galactica; BJ and the Bear; Evening in Byzantium; Quincy; The Misadventures of Sheriff Lobo; Buck Rogers in the 25th Century; Battles--The Murder That Wouldn't Die; Nightside; Magnum P.I; Lobo; Fitz and Bones (crea-exec prod); The Fall Guy (exec prod-wri); Rooster (exec prod-wri); Knight Rider (exec prod-wri); Trauma Center (exec prod-wri); Manimal (exec prod-wri); Automan (exec prod-wri); Masquerade (exec prod-wri); Cover Up (exec prod-crea-wri); Half Nelson (exec prod-wri).

LARSON, Jack: Act. b. Feb 8, 1933. Films inc: Fighter Squadron; Star Lift; Three Sailors and a Girl; Kid Monk Baroni; Battle Zone; Man Crazy; Johnny Trouble; Montgomery Clift (doc); Mike's Murder (asso prod); Perfect (co-prod).
Thea inc: The Great Man; Androcles and the Lion.
TV inc: Superman.

La RUE, Jack: Act. b. NYC, 1900. Screen debut, 1932, When Paris Sleeps. On stage in Diamond Lil.
Films inc: Three on a Match; A Farewell to Arms; Valley of the Giants; Charlie Chan in Panama; Murder in the Music Hall; Robin and the Seven Hoods; A Voice in the Night.
(Died Jan. 11, 1984).

LASKY, Jesse, Jr.: Wri. b. NYC, Sep 19, 1910. Worked in foreign dept, Paramount, Spain. Asst to Sol Wurtzel, Fox.
Films inc: Secret Agent; The Redhead; Union Pacific; Northwest Mounted Police; Reap The Wild Wind; Samson and Delilah; Ten Commandments; John Paul Jones.
TV inc: Naked City; Avengers; The Saint; The Baron; The Protectors; Danger Man; The World of Lowell Thomas; Ready When You Are, Mr. De Mille; Philip Marlowe, Private Eye.

LASSER, Louise: Act. b. NYC, Apr 11, 1939. Films inc: What's New Pussycat?; Take the Money and Run; Bananas; Everything You Always Wanted to Know About Sex and Were Afraid to Ask; Slither; In God We Trust; Stardust Memories; Crimewave.
TV inc: Mary Hartman, Mary Hartman; Making A Living; The Lie; Isn't It Shocking; Just You and Me (& wri); For Ladies Only.

LASTFOGEL, Abe: Agt. b. May 20, 1898. Ret p of William Morris Agency.
(Died Aug. 25, 1984)

LASZLO, Andrew: Cin. b. Hungary, Jan. 12, 1926. Films inc: One Potato, Two Potato; You're a Big Boy Now; The Night They Raided Minsky's; Popi; The Out of Towners; Lovers and Other Strangers; The Owl and the Pussycat; Class of 44; The Warriors; The Funhouse; Southern Comfort; I, The Jury; First Blood; Comeback; Streets of Fire; Thief Of Hearts; That's Dancing! (addl photog).
TV inc: The Naked City; Ed Sullivan Specials; The Beatles At Shea Stadium; Top of the Hill; Washington Behind Closed Doors; Spinner's Key; Give Me Your Poor; The Man Without a Country; The Dain Curse; Teacher, Teacher; Shogun; Thin Ice; Love Is Forever.

LASZLO, Ernest: Cin. b. Yugoslavia, Apr 23, 1905. Films inc: The Hitler Gang; Two Years Before the Mast; The Steel Trap; Stalag 17; Vera Cruz; Inherit the Wind; Judgment at Nuremberg; It's a Mad, Mad, Mad, Mad World; Ship of Fools (Oscar-1965); Fantastic Voyage; Star!; Airport; Logan's Run; The Domino Principle.
(Died Jan. 6, 1984)

LATHAM, Louise: Act. Films inc: Marnie; Firecreek; Adam at 6 A.M.; 92 in the Shade; Mass Appeal.
TV inc: Amateur Night at the Dixie Bar and Grill; Backstairs at the

White House; Scruples; The Contender; The Ghost of Buxley Hall; Thin Ice; Pray TV; Lois Gibbs and the Love Canal; Obsessive Love; Love Lives On.

LATHROP, Philip: Cin. b. 1916. Films inc: The Monster of Piedras Blancas; Experiment in Terror; Lonely are the Brave; Days of Wine and Roses; The Pink Panther; The Americanization of Emily; The Cincinnati Kid; What Did You Do in the War, Daddy?; The Russians are Coming; The Happening; Point Blank; Finian's Rainbow; The Gypsy Moths; The Illustrated Man; They Shoot Horses Don't They?; Von Richthofen and Brown; Airport '77; Earthquake; A Different Story; The Driver; The Concorde-Airport '79; Little Miss Marker; Foolin' Around; Loving Couples; A Change of Seasons; All Night Long; Hammett; Jekyll and Hyde--Together Again;. National Lampoon's Class Reunion.

TV inc: Malice In Wonderland.

LATIMORE, Frank (nee Kline): Act. b. Darien, CT, Sep 28, 1925. Films inc: In The Meantime, Darling; The Dolly Sisters; Shock; Three Little Girls In Blue; The Razor's Edge; 13 Rue Madeleine; Black Magic; Yvonne la Nuit; Three Forbidden Stories; Napoletani a Milano; Capitan Fantasma; La Figlia de Mata Hari; Plein Soleil; Then There Were Three; La Venganza del Zorro; Cast a Giant Shadow; It Comes Up Murder; The Sergeant; If It's Tuesday, This Must Be Belgium; Patton; All the President's Men.

LAUGHLIN, Tom: Dir-Prod-Act. b. Minneapolis, MN, 1938. P Billy Jack Enterprises.

Films inc: Tea and Sympathy (act); South Pacific (act); Gidget (act); Tall Story (act); The Young Sinners; Born Losers; Billy Jack; The Trial of Billy Jack; The Master Gunfighter; Billy Jack Goes to Washington.

LAUNDER, Frank: Wri-Dir-Prod. b. England, 1907. Act briefly before becoming wri; wrote several films before collabing with Sidney Gilliat on Seven Sinners; they subsequently formed Launder and Gilliat Productions, in which they worked together on script and prodn but usually directed individually. Films inc: Under the Greenwood Tree; Children of Chance; After Office Hours; Josser in the Army; Facing the Music; Those Were the Days; Emil and the Detectives; Seven Sinners; Educated Evans; Oh, Mr. Porter; The Lady Vanishes; A Girl Must Live; Night Train; The Young Mr. Pitt; began dir on Millions Like Us; 2,000 Women; I See a Dark Stranger; Captain Boycott; The Blue Lagoon; The Happiest Days of Your Life; The Belles of St. Trinian's; Wee Geordie; Blue Murder at St. Trinian's; The Bridal Path; The Pure Hell of St. Trinian's; Get Charlie Tully.

LAURE, Carole: Act. b. Quebec, Canada. Films inc: L'ange et la femme (The Angel and the Woman); Get Out Your Handkerchiefs; Au Revoir a Lundi (Goodbye, See You Monday); Fantastica; Asphalte; Uun Assassin qui passe (A Passing Killer); Victory; Croque la vie (A Bite of Living); Maria Chapdelaine; A Mort l'Arbitre (Kill the Referee); Stress; Heartbreakers; The Surrogate; Night Magic.

LAUREN, Tammy: Act. b. San Diego, CA, Nov 16, 1969. TV inc: Who's Watching the Kids; Angie; Out of the Blue; M.A.D.D.--Mothers Against Drunk Drivers; Things Are Looking Up; The Best Times; Playing With Fire.

LAURENCE, Douglas: Prod. b. Totowa, NJ, Dec 16, 1922. Films inc: Quick Before It Melts; Mister Buddwing; Dr. You've Got to be Kidding; Speedway; Stay Away Joe; Live a Little, Love a Little.

TV inc: Strange Wills; Some of the Pioneers; All Star Hit Parade; John Gunther's High Road.

Industrial, Trade Shows inc: LA Auto Show; LA Home Show; California State Fair; Wisconsin State Fair; Texas State Fair; Miami Auto Show.

LAURENCE, John: TV News. b. Bridgeport, CT, 1939. e. Rensselaer Polytechnic Institute; U of PA. Worked as news editor WICC, Bridgeport, CT., WWDC, Washington before joining WNEW radio (NY) 1962 as writer-reporter; joined CBS Radio 1965; switched to tv, covering war in Southeast Asia; 1971, London corr; 1978, joined ABC News London. TV inc: First Cavalry *(Emmy*-1968); The Ordeal of Con Thien; Police After Chicago *(Emmy*-1969); The Cities; The World of Charlie Company *(Emmy*-1971); **Coverage of the October War From**

Israel's Northern Front *(Emmy*-1974); Generations Apart; A Tale of Two Irelands.

LAURENTS, Arthur: Wri-Dir. b. NYC, Jul 14, 1918. e. Cornell U. Plays inc: Home of the Brave; The Bird Cage; The Time of the Cuckoo; A Clearing in the Woods; West Side Story; Gypsy; Invitation to March (& dir); Anyone Can Whistle (& dir); Do I Hear a Waltz; Hallelujah, Baby *(Tony*-1968); dir musical I Can Get It for You Wholesale; The Enclave (& dir); The Madwoman of Central Park West (& dir); La Cage Aux Folles *(Tony*-1984).

Films inc: The Snake Pit; Rope; Anna Lucasta; Caught; Anastasia; Bonjour Tristesse; The Way We Were; The Turning Point.

LAURIE, Piper (Rosetta Jacobs): Act. b. Detroit, Jan 22, 1932. Screen debut 1950, Louisa.

Films inc: The Milkman; The Prince Who Was a Thief; Mississippi Gambler; Smoke Signal; Kelly and Me; Until They Sail; The Hustler; Carrie; Tim; Return To Oz.

TV inc: Quality Town; The Road that Led Afar; The Days of Wine and Roses; The Lee Wiley Story; The Woman Rebel; In The Matter Of Kathleen Ann Quinlan; Rainbow; Skag; The Bunker; Mae West; The Thorn Birds.

Bway inc: The Glass Menagerie.

LAUTER, Ed: Act. b. Long Beach, NY, Oct 30, 1940. Films inc: The Last American Hero; Executive Action; Lolly Madonna; The Longest Yard; The French Connection II; Breakheart Pass; Family Plot; King Kong; Magic; Death Hunt; Loose Shoes; The Amateur; Timerider; Eureka; Cujo; The Big Score; Lassiter; Finders Keepers; Girls Just Want To Have Fun.

TV inc: Last Hours Before Morning; Love's Savage Fury; The Clone Master; The Greatest Heroes of the Bible; The Jericho Mile; Undercover With The KKK; The Boy Who Drank Too Much; Guyana Tragedy-The Story of Jim Jones; Alcatraz--The Whole Shocking Story; In The Custody of Strangers; Rooster; Hardcastle and McCormick; Manimal; The Seduction of Gina; The Three Wishes Of Billy Grier; The Cartier Affair; Crazy Like A Fox.

LAUTNER, Georges: Dir. b. France, Jan 24, 1926. Started as shorts director. Films inc: La Mome aux Boutons; Women in War; Le Monocle Noir; The Seventh Juror; L'Oeil du Monocle; The Great Spy Chase; Sauterelle; Le Pacha; Road to Salina; Il etait un fois un Flic; La Valise (The Girl in the Trunk); Les Seines de Glace (Icy Breasts); On aura tout vu; Mort d'un Pourri; Il sont Fous ces Sorciers; The Bottom Line; Est-ce Bien Raisonnable (Is This Really Reasonable?); Le Professionel (The Professional); Joyeuses Paques (Happy Easter); Le Cowboy. Hungary, Apr 3, 1949. e. McGill U, BA, MA. Pres R.S.L. Films, Ltd, pres Viva Film. Films inc: L'Ange et la Femme; In Praise of Older Women; Suzanne; Agency; Paradise; Bedroom Eyes.

LAVEN, Arnold: Dir. b. Chicago, Feb 23, 1922. Films inc: Without Warning; Vice Squad; Down Three Dark Streets; The Rack; Slaughter on 10th Avenue; Anna Lucasta; The Glory Guys; Rough Night In Jericho; Sam Whiskey.

TV inc: The Rifleman; The Detective; The Plainsman; Friends; Time Express; Two of Hearts (cable).

LAVERY, Emmet: Wri. b. Poughkeepsie, NY, Nov 2, 1902. e. Fordham U, LLB. Research dir of Hallie Flanagan's History of Federal Theatre. Plays inc: The First Legion; Monsignor's Hour; Second Spring; The Magnificent Yankee; Tarquin; Fenelon; Hail to the Chief; Dawn's Early Light; Ladies of Soissons.

Films inc: Hitler's Children; Behind the Rising Sun; The First Legion; Guilty of Treason; The Magnificent Yankee; Bright Road; The Court Martial of Billy Mitchell.

TV inc: The Magnificent Yankee; Gideon's Trumpet.

LAVERY, Emmet, Jr: Prod. b. Poughkeepsie, NY, Aug 10, 1927. e. UCLA, AB, LLB. In law practice; 1965, dir bus aff Fox; 1967 vp buss aff Par-TV; 1967 exec vp Par-TV; became prod 1974.

TV inc: Serpico; Rex Stout's Nero Wolfe; Ghost of Flight 401.

LAVIN, Linda: Act. b. Portland, ME, Oct 15, 1937. e. William and Mary Coll. Bway inc: A Family Affair; Cop Out; On a Clear Day; Last of the Red Hot Lovers; Superman; Something Different.

TV inc: Phyllis; Rhoda; Barney Miller; Like Mother, Like Me; Sad

Bird; Alice; The John Davidson Christmas Show; The $5.20 An Hour Dream; Linda in Wonderland; A Matter of Life and Death; Lily For President?; Another Woman's Child (& prod); Night Of 100 Stars II.
Films inc: The Muppets Take Manhattan.

LAW, John Philip: Act. b. Los Angeles, 1937. e. U of HI. Films inc: The Russians Are Coming, The Russians Are Coming; Hurry Sundown; Barbarella; Skidoo; The Sergeant; Danger: Diabolik; The Hawaiians; Von Richthofen and Brown; The Love Machine; The Last Movie; The Golden Voyage of Sinbad; The Cassandra Crossing; The Pioneers; Attack Force Z; Tarzan, the Ape Man; Tin Man; Rainy Day Friends; Night Train To Terror.

LAWFORD, Peter: Act. b. London, Sep 7, 1923. On screen at 7 in Britain. U.S. screen debut 1938, Lord Jeff.
Films inc: Mrs. Miniver; Good News; Mrs. Parkinton; Little Women; Easter Parade; A Yank at Eton; White Cliffs of Dover; Canterville Ghost; Never So Few; Royal Wedding; The Picture of Dorian Gray; Advise and Consent; Harlow; Exodus; The Longest Day; Sergeants Three; Salt and Pepper; They Only Kill Their Masters; Seven From Heaven; That's Entertainment; Rosebud; Body and Soul; Where Is Parsifal?
TV inc: Phoebe; The Thin Man; A Step Out of Line; The Doris Day Show; How I Spent My Summer Vacation; Island Of Beautiful Women.
(Died Dec. 24, 1984)

LAWRENCE, Barbara: Act. b. Carnegie, OK, Feb 24, 1930. e. UCLA. Films inc: Billy Rose's Diamond Horse Shoe; Margie; Captain from Castile; Give My Regards to Broadway; Street With No Name; Unfaithfully Yours; Letter to Three Wives; Mother is a Freshman; Thieves' Highway; Two Tickets to Broadway; Jessie James Versus the Daltons; Oklahoma; Joe Dakota.

LAWRENCE, Carol: Act. b. Melrose Park, IL, Sept. 15, 1932. Bway inc: Me and Juliet; Guys and Dolls; Finian's Rainbow; Plain and Fancy; South Pacific; West Side Story; Funny Girl.
TV inc: Indiscriminate Woman; Rashomon; The Dybbuk; Run For Your Life; Kraft Theatre; Medical Center; Greatest Heroes of the Bible; Mr. and Mrs. Dracula; The Girl, The Gold Watch and Dynamite; The Way They Were; A Gift of Music; Jacqueline Susann's Valley of the Dolls 1981.

LAWRENCE, Elliot (ne Broza): Comp-Cond. b. Philadelphia, PA, Feb 14, 1925. Had own orch. Bway inc: (mus dir) How To Succeed in Business Without Really Trying (Tony-1962); Golden Boy; Sugar.
TV inc: (mus dir) The Berenstain Bear's Christmas Tree; Command Performance--The Stars Salute The President; The Berenstain Bears' Easter Surprise; The Berenstain Bears' Valentine Special; Baker's Dozen; The Unforgiveable Secret (Emmy-comp-1982); Night of 100 Stars (Emmy-mus dir-1982); Johnny Garage; The Berenstain Bears' Littlest Leaguer; Sometimes I Don't Love My Mother (Emmy-mus comp/dir-1983); The Cradle Will Fall; The Best of Everything; Deck the Halls With Wacky Walls (mus comp/dir); Zack of All Trades; Mr. T. and Emmanuel Lewis In A Christmas Dream; Night Of 100 Stars II; Placido Domingo Steppin' Out With The Ladies; The 39th Annual Tony Awards.
Songs inc: Heart to Heart; Sugartown Road; Once Upon a Moon.

LAWRENCE, Jerome: Wri. b. Cleveland, OH, Jul 14, 1915. e. OH State U. Plays inc: (with Robert E Lee) Look, Ma. I'm Dancin'!; Inherit the Wind; Auntie Mame; Shangri La (based on Lost Horizon); Only in America; A Call on Kuprin; Turn on the Night; Sparks Fly Upward; The Incomparable Max; The Night Thoreau Spent in Jail; Jabberwock; First Monday In October. Films inc: First Monday In October.

LAWRENCE, Marc (Max Goldsmith): Act-Dir-Prod. b. NYC, Feb 17, 1914. Films inc: White Woman; Shepherd of the Hills; Ox Bow Incident; Key Largo; Cloak and Dagger; Asphalt Jungle; Nightmare in the Sun (prod only); Daddy's Deadly Darlings (The Pigs) (& prod-dir-wri); The Marathon Man; Man with the Golden Gun; Foul Play; Goin' Coconuts; Hot Stuff; Super Fuzz; Night Train To Terror.
TV inc: Border Pals.

LAWRENCE, Steve (Sidney Liebowitz): Act. b. NYC, Jul 8, 1935. In niteries, TV.
Films inc: Stand Up and Be Counted; The Blues Brothers; The

Lonely Guy.
TV inc: Steve and Eydie Celebrate Irving Berlin (Emmys-exec prod & star-1979); The Bob Hope 30th Anniversary Special; Live From Studio 8H--100 Years of America's Popular Music; All-Star Party for Frank Sinatra; Foul-Ups, Bleeps and Blunders (host).
(Grammy-vocal group-1960).

LAWRENCE, Vicki: Act. b. Los Angeles, Mar 26, 1949. e. UCLA. Recording artist. Appeared with Young Americans singing group for three years. TV inc: The Carol Burnett Show (Emmy-supp-1976); Eunice; Jerry Reed and Special Friends; Mama's Family; TV Academy Hall Of Fame 1985.

LAYE, Dilys: Act. b. London, Mar 11, 1934. Thea inc: (London) And So To Bed; High Spirits; Intimacy at 8:30; For Amusement Only; The Boy Friend; The Purging and The Singer. (Bway): Tunnel of Love; Make Me An Offer; Say Who You Are; Children's Day The Bewitched; The Purging and the Singer; Beethoven's Tenth; Top People.
Films inc: Doctor at Large; The Carry On series.

LAYE, Evelyn, CBE: Act-Singer. b. London, Jul 10, 1900. Thea inc: (London) The Beauty Spot; Going Up; The Kiss Call; The Shop Girl; Nighty Night; The Merry Widow; Madame Pompadour; The Dollar Princess; Cleopatra; Mayfair; Princess Charming; Lilac Time; The New Moon; Bitter Sweet; Paganini; The Sleeping Beauty; Lights Up; Sunny River; School for Scandal; Two Dozen Red Roses; The Amorous Prawn; Never Too Late; The Circle; Let's All Go Down to the Strand; Charlie Girl; No Sex Please-We're British; Ladies in Retirement. (Bway) The New Moon; Sweet Aloes; Between the Devil. Films inc: Luck of the Navy; One Heavenly Night; Waltz Time; Princess Charming; Evensong; The Night is Young; Make Mine a Million; Theatre of Death; Say Hello to Yesterday.

LAYTON, Joe: Chor. b. NYC, May 3, 1931. Bway inc: (dancer) Oklahoma!; High Button Shoes; Gentlemen Prefer Blondes; Wonderful Town. (Chor) Once Upon a Mattress; The Sound of Music; Sail Away; No Strings (Tony-1962); The Girl Who Came to Supper (& dir); Peter Pan (& dir); Drat the Cat (& dir); Sherry!; George M! (Tony-1969); Carol Channing and Her Ten Stout-Hearted Men (London); Two by Two; The Grand Tour (ballet); Gone With the Wind (& dir); Clams on the Half Shell Revue (& dir); Barnum; Bring Back Birdie (& dir); Rock 'n Roll! The First 5,000 Years; The Three Musketeers (dir); Harrigan 'n Hart (dir).
TV inc: The Gershwin Years; Once Upon a Mattress; My Name is Barbra (Emmy-1965); Color Me Barbra (& dir).
Films inc: Thoroughly Modern Millie; Richard Pryor Live on the Sunset Strip (dir); Annie (exec prod).

LAZARUS, John T.: Exec. b. NYC, Dec 27, 1940. e. U of VT, BA. NBC-TV Sales; Foote Cone & Belding; ABC Sports, acct exec; dir radio/TV, Major League Baseball; vp Sports sales, ABC-TV.

LAZARUS, Paul N.: Exec (ret). b. NYC, Mar 31, 1913. e. Cornell U, BA. Joined Warner Bros, 1933, ad-pub dept; became ad mgr; 1942, ad-pub dir, UA; then exec asst to pres Gradwell Sears; 1950-62, vp Columbia Pictures; 1962-64, exec vp Samuel Bronson Prods, Madrid; 1964, vp Subscription TV, LA; 1964-65, exec vp Landau Releasing Org; 1965-75, exec vp and dir, National Screen Service Corp, NY.

LAZARUS, Paul N. III: Prod. b. NYC, May 25, 1938. e. Williams Coll, BA; Yale Law School, LLB. Exec vp Palomar Pictures, 1967-69; joined ABC Pictures, 1969-71; then P, CRM Prods., 1970-74; Film VP Marble Arch 1979-1980; Resd to become ind prod with ties to Marble Arch.
Films inc: Extreme Close-up; Westworld; Futureworld; Capricorn One; Hanover Street; Barbarosa.

LAZARUS, Thomas: Wri. b. NYC, Nov 5, 1942. TV inc: The President's Mistress; Uncle Bill and the Queen of Hollywood; Revenge or Justice; Columbo; The Ordeal of Bill Carney; Side By Side--The True Story of the Osmond Family; Hear No Evil; Rona Jaffe's Mazes & Monsters.
Film inc: Just You and Me Kid.

LAZENBY, George: Act. b. Goulburn, Australia, Sep 5, 1939. Films inc: On Her Majesty's Secret Service; Universal Soldier; Stoner; The Man From Hong Kong; Operation Regina; Saint Jack.

TV inc: Jack of Hearts; Return of the Man From U.N.C.L.E.; Rituals.

LEACH, Wilford: Plywri-dir. b. Petersburg, VA, Aug. 26, 1932. e. William & Mary. Prof theatre & film at Sarah Lawrence College. Principal director NY Shakespeare Festival; artistic dir La Mama. Thea inc: Othello; The Taming of the Shrew; All's Well That Ends Well; Marie and Bruce; Mandrake; Mother Courage; Summer Evening; Pirates of Penzance (Tony-1981); The Human Comedy; Henry V; La Boheme.

Films inc: The Pirates of Penzance.

Plays inc: Gertrude; In 3 Zones; Carmilla; C.O.R.F.A.X. (Don't Ask); Ondine.

LEACHMAN, Cloris: Act. b. Des Moines, IA, Apr 30, 1930. Films inc: Kiss Me Deadly; The Rack; The Chapman Report; Butch Cassidy and the Sundance Kid; The Last Picture Show (Oscar-supp-1971); Dillinger; Charley and the Angel; Daisy Miller; Crazy Mama; The North Avenue Irregulars; High Anxiety; The Mouse and His Child (voice); The North Avenue Irregulars; The Muppet Movie; Scavenger Hunt; Foolin' Around; Herbie Goes Bananas; History of the World--Part I.

TV inc: The Migrants; A Brand New Life (Emmy-1973); Phyllis; Mary Tyler Moore Show (Emmy-supp-1974 & 1975); Cher (Emmy-supp-1975); A Girl Named Sooner; Death Sentence; Long Journey Back; Backstairs At The White House; Willa; Mrs R's Daughter; SOS Titanic; The Oldest Living Graduate; The Acorn People; The Way They Were; Advice to the Lovelorn; Miss All-American Beauty; The Woman Who Willed A Miracle (Emmy-1983); Dixie--Changing Habits; The Demon Murder Case; Screen Actors Guild 50th Anniversary Celebration (Emmy-Ind Perf-1984); Ernie Kovacs...Between the Laughter; Donald Duck's 50th Birthday; Breakfast With Les & Bess; Deadly Intentions.

Bway inc: Come Back Little Sheba; As You Like It; South Pacific.

LEACOCK, Philip: Dir. b. London, Oct 8, 1917. Films inc: The Brave Don't Cry; Appointment in London; The Kidnappers; Escapade; The Spanish Gardener; High Tide at Noon; Innocent Sinners; The Rabbit Trap; Let No Man Write My Epitaph; Hand in Hand; Take a Giant Step; The War Lover; Tamahine; Adam's Woman.

TV inc: The Birdmen; The Great Man's Whiskers; When Michael Calls; Key West; The Daughters of Joshua Cabe; Baffled; Killer Aboard; Wild and Wooly; Gunsmoke (series prod); Cimarron Strip (exec prod); Hawaii 5-0 (supv prod); The Curse of King Tut's Tomb; Angel City; Heaven On Earth; The Two Lives of Carol Letner; The Wild Women of Chastity Gulch; Three Sovereigns For Sarah.

LEADER, Anton M.: Dir-Prod. b. Boston, Dec 23, 1913. Films inc: It Happened Every Thursday; Sally and St Anne; Go Man Go!; Children of the Damned; The Cockeyed Cowboys of Calico County.

TV inc: The Virginian; Rawhide; Tarzan; Daniel Boone; Father of the Bride; It Takes a Thief; Ironside; Star Trek; Lost in Space; I Spy; Get Smart; Hawaii Five-O; Movin' On; This Is the Life.

LEAF, Paul: Wri-Dir-Prod. b. NYC, May 2, 1929. e. CCNY, BA. TV inc: Top Secret (dir); Sergeant Matlovich vs. The Air Force (prod-dir); Every Man a King; Sister Aimee (prod); Judge Horton and the Scottsboro Boys (prod).

LEAN, David, Sir: Dir. b. Croydon, England, Mar 25, 1908. Entered industry 1919 as tea boy, later clapper boy, worked in cutting rooms, as asst. cameraman, asst edtr, edtr before directing. Films inc:Pygmalion (edtr); The Invaders (edtr); Major Barbara (edtr-co-dir); One Of Our Aircraft Is Missing (edtr); In Which We Serve (co-dir); This Happy Breed (& co-wri); Blithe Spirit (& co-wri); Brief Encounter (& co-wri); Great Expectations (& co-wri); Escape Me Never (co-dir);Oliver Twist (& co-wri); The Passionate Friends; Madeleine; Breaking The Sound Barrier; Hobson's Choice (& co-prod-wri); Summertime (& co-wri); The Bridge on the River Kwai (Oscar-1957); Lawrence of Arabia (Oscar-1962); Dr Zhivago; Ryan's Daughter; A Passage To India (& wri-edtr).

LEAR, Norman: Prod-Dir-Wri. b. New Haven, CT, Jul 27, 1922. Began in TV as co-wri of weekly variety show, The Ford Star Revue in 1950; then wrote for Dean Martin & Jerry Lewis, Martha Raya, George Gobel, Carol Channing, Don Rickles; formed Tandem Prodns

and TAT with Alan Yorkin; Nov 1981, bought control of Avco Embassy with Jerry Perenchio.

Films inc: (prod-wri) Come Blow Your Horn; Never Too Late; Divorce-American Style; The Night They Raided Minsky's; Start the Revolution Without Me; Cold Turkey.

TV inc: All in the Family (Emmys-(4)-comedy series-1971; 1972; 1973; New Series-1971); Maude; Good Times; Sanford and Son; The Jeffersons; Mary Hartman, Mary Hartman; The Dumplings; One Day at a Time; All's Fair; A Year At The Top; All That Glitters; Fernwood 2Night; America 2Night; The Baxters; Palmerstown, USA; I Love Liberty (wri-creator); a.k.a. Pablo (exec prod-creator); P.O.P (exec prod-wri); Heartsounds (exec prod).

(Television Academy Hall Of Fame--1984).

LEARNED, Michael: Act. b. Washington, DC, Apr 9, 1939. TV inc: Gunsmoke; Hurricane Hunters; Widow; Little Mo; The Waltons (Emmy-(3)-1973, 1974 & 1976); Politics of Poison; Off The Minnesota Strip; Widow; A Christmas Without Snow; Moe; Nurse (Emmy-1982); Mother's Day On Walton's Mountain; The Parade.

Films inc: Touched By Love.

Bway inc: The Loves Of Anatol.

LEAUD, Jean-Pierre: Act. b. Paris, 1944. Films inc: Les Quatre Cent Coups (The 400 Blows); Le Testament d'Orphee (Testament of Orpheus); L'Amour a Vingt Ans (Love At 20); Made In USA; Le Chinoise; The Oldest Profession; Bed and Board; Last Tango in Paris; Day for Night; Love On the Run; Rebelote; Paris vu par...Vingt Ans Apres (Paris Seen By...20 Years After).

LEAVITT, Sam: Cin. b. 1917. Films inc: The Thief; A Star is Born; Carmen Jones; The Man with the Golden Arm; The Defiant Ones (Oscar-1958); Anatomy of a Murder; Exodus; Advise and Consent; Two on a Guillotine; Major Dundee; Brainstorm; An American Dream; Guess Who's Coming to Dinner; The Desperados; The Grasshopper; Star Spangled Girl; The Man in the Glass Booth.

(Died March 21, 1984)

LEBER, Steven E.: Agt-Prod. b. NYC, Dec 12, 1941. e. Northeastern U. Former head of music dept, William Morris Agency. Partner with David Krebs in agency. Bway inc: Beatlemania; Wally's Cafe; Little Me; Little Johnny Jones.

LEBER, Titus, Dr: Dir-Prod-Wri. b. Zellam See, Austria, Mar 2, 1951. e. Lycee Francais de Vienna; U of Vienna. Films inc: On Plato's Banquet; Sisyphus; Ophelia; Melancolie D'Un Fou; Hyperhidrosis; Neue Coelome; Kindertotenlieder; A Stranger I Came; Anima.

Le BORG, Reginald (nee Grobel): Dir. b. Vienna, Dec 11, 1902. Films inc: She's for Me; The Mummy's Ghost; Jungle Woman; Destiny; Honeymoon Ahead; Philo Vance's Secret Mission; The Squared Circle; G I Jane; Great Jesse James Raid; Sins of Jezebel; Joe Palooka; Port Said; Fall Guy; Black Sheep; Voodoo Island; War Drums; The Dalton Girls.

TV inc: Wire Service; Navy Log; Maverick; Court of Last Resort; The Flight That Disappeared; Deadly Duo; The Diary of a Madman; The Eyes of Annie Jones; So Evil My Sister.

LECONTE, Patrice: Dir-wri. b. France, 1947. Films inc: Les Bronzes (The Suntanned Ones); Les bronzes font du ski; Viens chez moi, j'habite chez une copine (Come to My Place, I'm Living at My Girlfriend's); Ma femme s'appelle Reviens (Singles); Circulez y'a rien a voir (Move Along, There's Nothing to See); Les Specialistes (The Specialists).

LEDERER, Francis: Act. b. Prague, Nov 6, 1902. On screen in Europe from 1929. Hollywood debut 1934, Man of Two Worlds. Films inc: The Pursuit of Happiness; The Gay Deception; Confessions of a Nazi Spy; The Man I Married; One Rainy Afternoon; The Lone Wolf in Paris; A Voice in the Wind; Diary of a Chambermaid; Million Dollar Weekend; Captain Carey USA; Stolen Identity; Lisbon; Terror Is A Man; The Bridge of San Luis Rey; The Curse of Dracula; A Breath of Scandal.

LEDERER, Richard: Exec. b. NYC, Sep 22, 1916. e. U of VA, BS. Adv copywriter, Columbia, 1946-50; to Warners, adv copywriter, 1950-53; copy chief, 1953-57; asst Nat'l Adv Mgr, 1957-59; prod, theatrical TV Warner Bros. Studios, 1959-60; adv-pub dir, Warner, 1960; vp Warner, 1963; vp prod, Warner, 1969-70; ind prod, to May, 1971; returned Warners as ad-pub vp; 1981 vp wldwde mktg. American Cinema; Nov 1982, Sr VP ad Orion Pictures. Films inc: The Hollywood Knights.

LEDERER, Suzanne: Act. b. Great Neck, NY, Sep 29. e. Hofstra U. Thea inc: The National Health; Days in the Trees; Ah, Wilderness.
TV inc: The Best of Families; Judge Horton and the Scottsboro Boys; Eischied; Power; Obsessed With A Married Woman.

LEDNER, Caryl: Wri. TV inc: The Waltons; Apple's Way; Gibbsville; Winner Take All; The Great American Tragedy; Mary White (Emmy-1978); A Gift of Love; Eleanor, First Lady of the World.
(Died March 31, 1984).

LEE, Anna (Joanna Winnifrith): Act. b. England, 1914. Films inc: Ebb Tide; The Camels Are Coming; King Solomon's Mines; The Four Just Men; My Life with Caroline; Summer Storm; Fort Apache; Whatever Happened to Baby Jane?; The Sound of Music; Seven Women; In Like Flint.
TV inc: Scruples; General Hospital.

LEE, Brenda: Singer-Act. Began singing professionally at age six. Films inc: Two Little Bears; Smokey and The Bandit II.
TV inc: An Evening with the Statler Bros.--A Salute to the Good Old Times; Jerry Reed and Special Friends.

LEE, Christopher: Act. b. London, May 27, 1922. On screen since 1947 in more than 50 films inc: Corridor of Mirrors; Hamlet; Moulin Rouge; The Crimson Pirate; Moby Dick; Curse of Frankenstein; Tale of Two Cities; Dracula; The Hound of the Baskervilles; The Man Who Could Cheat Death; The Mummy; Hands of Orlac; Sherlock Holmes and the Deadly Necklace; The Face of Fu Manchu; Rasputin the Mad Monk; Julius Caesar; The Three Musketeers; The Man With The Golden Gun; To The Devil A Daughter; Killer Force; Dracula, Father and Son; Airport 77; Alien Encounter; Return from Witch Mountain; Caravans; Count Dracula and His Vampire Bride; Starship Invasions; Circle of Iron; The Passage; The Wicker Man; The Nutcracker Fantasy; Jaguar Lives; Count Dracula and His Vampire Bride; Arabian Adventure; 1941; Bear Island; Serial; An Eye For An Eye; The Last Unicorn (voice); The Salamander; The House of Long Shadows; The Return of Captain Invincible; Safari 3000; The Rosebud Beach Hotel; Howling II--Your Sister Is A Werewolf.
TV inc: Once Upon A Spy; Goliath Awaits; Massarati and the Brain; Charles and Diana--A Royal Love Story; The Far Pavilions (PC).

LEE, Jack: Dir. b. England, 1913. Films inc: Close Quarters; Children on Trial; The Woman in the Hall; Once a Jolly Swagman; The Wooden Horse; Turn the Key Softly; A Town Like Alice; Robbery Under Arms; The Captain's Table; Circle of Deception.

LEE, Joanna: Wri-Prod-Dir. TV inc: Babe; Cage Without a Key; I Want to Keep My Baby; Mary Jane Harper Died Last Night; Tell Me My Name; The Thanksgiving Story (Emmy-wri-1974); Mulligan's Stew; Mirror, Mirror; Like Normal People; The Love Tapes; Children of Divorce; Hear Me Cry.
Films inc: Making the Grade (act).

LEE, Michele (nee Dusiak): Act. b. Jun 24, 1942. Films inc: How to Succeed in Business Without Really Trying; The Love Bug; The Comic.
TV inc: Knots Landing; The Tim Conway Show; All-Star Salute To Mother's Day; Bonnie and the Franklins; Kraft Salutes Walt Disney World's 10th Anniversary; The Magic of David Copperfield; All-Star Party for Frank Sinatra; Perry Como's Christmas in New York; John Ritter, Mr T and Jacqueline Bisset--Going Back Home (host-int); Night Of 100 Stars II.
Bway inc: How To Succeed in Business Without Really Trying; Seesaw.

LEE, Ming Cho: Dsgn. b. Shanghai, China, Oct. 3, 1930. e. Occidental Coll, BA; UCLA. Apprenticed to Jo Mielziner; principal dsgn NY Shakespeare Festival since 1962; principal dsgn Juilliard Opera Theatre since 1964. Bway inc: The Crucible; The Moon Besieged; Walk in Darkness; Mother Courage; Conversations in the Dark;

Gandhi; All God's Children Got Wings; Billy; The Glass Menagerie; Angel; K2 (Tony-1983).

LEE, Peggy (Norma Egstrom): Singer-Act. b. Jamestown, ND, May 26, 1920. In niteries, on radio, with Will Osborne, Benny Goodman Bands. Screen debut, 1950, Mr. Music. Films inc: The Jazz Singer; Pete Kelly's Blues; Lady and the Tramp (score).
TV inc: A Gift of Music; The Kennedy Center Honors 1982.
Bway inc: Peg (act & songs).
(Grammy-pop vocalist-1969).

LEE, Robert E.: Wri. b. Elyria, OH, Oct 15, 1918. e. Northwestern U; OH Wesleyan; Drake U. Plays inc: (with Jerome Lawrence) Look Ma, I'm Dancin'!; Inherit the Wind; Auntie Mame; Shangri La (based on Lost Horizon); The Gang's All Here; Only in America; A Call on Kuprin; Turn on the Night; Sparks Fly Upward; The Night Thoreau Spent in Jail; The Incomparable Max; Jabberwock; First Monday in October.
Films inc: First Monday In October. TV inc: Lincoln.

LEE, Ruta: Act. b. May 30, 1936. Films inc: Twinkle in God's Eye; Funny Face; Marjorie Morningstar; Operation Eichman; Sergeants 3; Bullet for a Badman.
TV inc: Lucy Moves to NBC; The Ghosts of Buxley Hall; Elvis and the Beauty Queen.

LEEDS, Andrea: Act. b. 1914. Films inc: Come and Get It; Stage Door; It Could Happen To You; The Goldwyn Follies; Letter of Introduction; Swanee River; Earthbound. Ret 1941.
(Died May 21, 1984).

LEETCH, Tom: Prod. b. Grand Island, NE, Apr 16, 1933. Started as asst dir, later dir. TV inc: The Magic or Walt Disney World; The Sky's The Limit; The Year of the Big Cat; Whiz Kids; Tales of the Apple Dumpling Gang.
Films inc: (prod) The Apple Dumpling Gang Rides Again; North Avenue Irregulars; Night Crossing.

LEEWOOD, Jack: Prod. b. NYC, May 20, 1913. e. Upsala Coll. Films inc: Holiday Rhythm; Gunfire; Hijacked; Roaring City; Lost Continent; F B I Girl; Train to Tombstone; I Shot Billy the Kid; Motor Patrol; Three Desperate Men; Thundering Jets; Little Savage; Alligator People; 13 Fighting Men; Young Jesse James; We'll Bury You; 20,000 Eyes; Thunder Island; The Plainsman; Longest 100 Miles; Escape to Mindanao.

LEFKOWITZ, Nat: Exec. b. NYC, Jul 24, 1905. e. CCNY; Brooklyn Law School. Co-Chmn, William Morris Agency, Inc.
(Died Sept. 4, 1983).

LeFRAK, Francine: Prod. b. Oct 18, 1948. e. L'Ecole Superior de Neufchatel, Switzerland; Sarah Lawrence College in Florence and Greece; Finch College, BA; Institute of Fine Arts. P The Whole Picture Company Ltd. Bway inc: Children of a Lesser God (asso prod); Ain't Misbehavin' (asso prod); March of the Falsettos; Crimes of the Heart; Nine (Tony-1982); My One and Only; Leader Of The Pack. London inc: They're Playing Our Song.

Le GALLIENNE, Eva: Act. b. London, Jan 11, 1899. Stage debut London as page in Monna Vanna; appeared briefly on London stage before going to U.S; Founder Civic Repertory Theatre which she operated between 1926 and 1933; founder (with Cheryl Crawford and Margaret Webster), the American Repertory Theatre 1946.
Bway inc: Mrs. Boltay's Daughters; Melody of Youth; Saturday to Monday; The Off-Chance; Elsie Janis and Her Gang; Not So Long Ago; Liliom; The Rivals (& dir); Hannele; The Three Sisters; Cradle Song; Hedda Gabler; Peter Pan; The Seagull; The Master Builder; John Gabriel Borkman; Alison's House; Camille; The Rivals; Uncle Harry; The Cherry Orchard (& dir); All's Well That Ends Well; Exit the King; Alice in Wonderland (& dir-adapt). (Tony-special-1964).
Films inc: Prince of Players; The Devil's Disciple; Resurrection.
TV inc: Alice In Wonderland; The Corn Is Green; The Bridge of San Luis Rey; Mary Stuart; The Royal Family (Emmy-supp-1978); Alice in Wonderland.

LEGRAND, Michel Jean: Comp-Cond. b. Paris, 1932. e. Paris Conservatory. Film scores inc: Lola; Eva; The Umbrellas of Cherbourg; Un

Femme Mariee; Les Demoiselles de Rochefort; Ice Station Zebra; The Thomas Crown Affair, (*Oscar*-song-The Windmills of Your Mind-1968); Summer of '42 (*Oscar*-1971); A Time for Loving; One Is a Lonely Number; Portnoy's Complaint; Cops and Robbers; The Three Musketeers; The Hunter; Atlantic City, USA; Falling In Love Again; Le Cadeau (The Gift); Qu-est-ce Qui Fait Courir David? (What Makes David Run?); Best Friends; Eine Liebe in Deutschland (A Love in Germany); Never Say Never Again; Yentl (*Oscar*-Song Score-1983); The Smurfs and the Magic Flute; Secret Places; Micki & Maude; Paroles et Musiques (Words And Music); Train d'Enfer (Hell Train); Palace; Partir Revenir (Departure, Return).

TV inc: Brian's Song; A Woman Called Golda; The Jesse Owens Story.

(*Grammys*-(5)-inst comp-1971, 1972, 1975; arr accomp voc-1972; Jazz Big Band-1975).

LEHMAN, Ernest: Wri-Prod-Dir. b. NYC, 1920. Films inc: The King and I; Somebody Up There Likes Me; Inside Story; Executive Suite; Sabrina; The Sweet Smell of Success; North by Northwest; From The Terrace; West Side Story; The Prize; The Sound of Music; Who's Afraid of Virginia Woolf? (& prod); Hello Dolly (& prod); Portnoy's Complaint (& prod-dir); Family Plot; Black Sunday.

LEHRER, Jim: TV newsman. b. 1935. e. U of MO. Reporter Dallas Morning News, Dallas Times Herald 1959-1966; became city ed 1968; moved to public tv 1969, exec dir pub aff KERA-TV; edtr Newsroom; joined Nat'l Public Affairs Center for TV 1973.

TV inc: Senate Watergate Hearings (*Emmy*-1974); MacNeil-Lehrer Report; House Impeachment Inquiry; Washington Straight Talk; Washington Connection; The Power and the Glory.

LEHRER, Tom: Act. b. NYC, Apr 9, 1928. e. Harvard U, BA, MA. Comp-perf. Wrote special material for films, TV; recording artist, singer-pianist niteries, concerts. Wrote songs for A Gathering of Eagles (film); The Electric Company (TV).

LEIBMAN, Ron: Act. b. NYC, Oct 11, 1938. Films inc: Where's Poppa?; Hot Rock; Slaughterhouse Five; Super Cops; Won-Ton-Won, The Dog Who Saved Hollywood; Your Three Minutes Are Up; Norma Rae; Up The Academy; Zorro, the Gay Blade; Phar Lap; Romantic Comedy; Door To Door; Rhinestone.

TV inc: A Question of Guilt; Kaz (*Emmy*-1979); Linda In Wonderland; Rivkin--Bounty Hunter; Side By Side.

Bway inc: Dear Me, the Sky is Falling; Bicycle Ride to Nevada; The Deputy; We Bombed in New Haven; I Ought To Be In Pictures; Doubles.

LEIDER, Jerry (Gerald J Leider): Prod. b. Camden, NJ, May 28, 1931. e. Syracuse U, BA. Fulbright Fellow U of Bristol, Eng, 1954. Thea prod NYC & London 1956-1959; prod John Gielgud's Ages of Man; dir spec pgms CB TV 1960-61; dir pgm sls 1961-62; vp tv operations Ashley Famous Agency 1962-69; pres WB TV 1969-74; exec vp foreign prodn WB 1975-76; launched indie GJL prods 1977; Sep 1982, P & CEO ITC Prodns.

TV inc: And I Alone Survived; Willa; The Hostage Tower.

Films inc: The Jazz Singer; Trenchcoat.

LEIGH, Janet (nee Jeanette Helen Morrison): Act. b. Merced, CA, Jul 6, 1927. e. Coll of the Pacific. Films inc: Romance of Rosy Ridge; If Winter Comes; Hills of Home; Words and Music; Act of Violence; Little Women; That Forsythe Woman; Jet Pilot; It's A Big Country; Two Tickets to Broadway; Strictly Dishonorable; Angels in the Outfield; Night of the Lepus; Harper; The Naked Spur; Houdini; Walking My Baby Back Home; Prince Valiant; The Black Shield of Falworth; Rogue Cop; My Sister Eileen; Pete Kelly's Blues; Touch of Evil; The Vikings; Psycho; The Manchurian Candidate; Bye Bye Birdie; Wives and Lovers; Grand Slam; One is a Lonely Number.

TV inc: Death's Head; The Monk; Honeymoon With a Stranger; House on Green Apple Road; Deadly Dreams; Mirror Mirror; The Chairman; World Series Murders; All Star Salute To Mother's Day; Inside America; On Our Way.

LEIGH, Jennifer Jason: Act. b. Hollywood, 1958. e. AADA. D of the late Vic Morrow. Studied with Lee Strasberg; Stella Adler. Films inc: Eyes of a Stranger; Wrong Is Right; Fast Times at Ridgemont High; Easy Money; Grandview, U.S.A.; Flesh & Blood.

TV inc: Angel City; I Think I'm Having A Baby; The Killing of Randy Webster; The Best Little Girl in the World; The First Time; Girls of the White Orchid.

LEIGH, Mitch: Comp. b. Brooklyn, NY, Jan 30, 1928. e. Yale, BA, MA. Studied with Hindemith.

Bway inc: Too True to Be Good; Never Live Over a Pretzel Factory; Man of La Mancha (*Tony*-score-1966); Home Sweet Homer; Sarava; The King And I (dir 1985 rev).

LEIGH-HUNT, Barbara: Act. b. Bath, Somerset, England, Dec 14, 1935. Films inc: Frenzy; Henry VIII and his Six Wives; The Nelson Affair; A Bequest to the Nation; Oh Heavenly Dog; The Plague Dogs (voice).

Thea inc: Measure for Measure; Hamlet; La Ronde; Pack of Lies.

LEINSDORF, Erich: Cond. b. Vienna, Feb 4, 1912. Asst cond Salzburg Festival 1934; to US 1937 cond Metropolitan Opera; 1943 Cleveland Orchestra; 1947 Rochester Philharmonic; 1956 dir NY Center Opera; 1957-1962 Metropolitan Opera; guest cond major orchs inc Philadelphia, Los Angeles; St. Louis; Minneapolis; Concertgebouw, Amsterdam; Israel Philharmonic.

(*Grammys*-(8)-class perf-1959, 1960, 1963, 1964, 1966; opera-1963, 1968, 1971).

LELOUCH, Claude: Dir. b. Paris, Oct 30, 1937. Formed Films 13, prod, dir shorts; Dec. 1981 formed Double 13 with Georges Alain Vuille and Alain Siritzky to import films to U.S. Films inc: A Man and A Woman (*Oscar*-foreign film-1966); Live for Life; To Be A Crook; Love, Life, Death; A Man I Like; Smic Smac Smoc; Adventure Is Adventure; La Bonne Annee; Marriage; Another Man, Another Chance; The Good and the Bad; Robert et Robert; And Now My Love; A Nous Deux (& sp); Les Uns et Les Autres (The Ins and The Outs) (& sp); Edith et Marcel (& prod-wri); Viva la Vie! (Long Live Life!) (& prod-wri); Partir Revenir (Departure, Return) (& prod-wri).

Le MAIRE, George: Prod. b. Los Angeles, Aug 6, 1935. exec MGM-TV, 1958-68; left to form Chamberlain-LeMaire Prods, 1972-76, pgm exec Par-TV; formed George LeMaire Prods, 1977; Aug 1980, Sr vp feature prodn COL.

TV inc: Hamlet; The Family Rico; The Legend of Lizzie Borden; Some Kind of Miracle.

Le MAT, Paul: Act. b. NJ. Studied with Milton Katselas; Herbert Berghof; ACT. Films inc: American Graffiti; Aloha, Bobby and Rose; Citizen's Band; More American Graffiti; Melvin and Howard; Death Valley; Jimmy the Kid; Rock & Rule (voice); Strange Invaders.

TV inc: Firehouse; The Gift of Life; The Burning Bed; The Night They Saved Christmas.

LEMBECK, Michael Roberts: Act. b. Brooklyn, Jun 25, 1948. e. LACC; Cal State LA. S of Harvey Lembeck. Films inc: Hang 'Em High; Boys in Company C; The In-Laws; G.O.R.P; On the Right Track.

TV inc: Gidget Grows Up; Mary Hartman, Mary Hartman; Summer Without Boys; The Funny Side; Bloodsport; Having Babies; Krofft Supershow; One Day at a Time; Goodbye Doesn't Mean Forever; Insight/For Love Or Money.

Le MESURIER, John: Act. b. England, 1912. Films inc: Death in the Hand; Beautiful Stranger; Private's Progress; Happy Is the Bride; I Was Monty's Double; School for Scoundrels; Only Two Can Play; The Pink Panther; Masquerade; Where the Spies Are; The Midas Run; The Magic Christian; The Garnett Saga; Confessions of a Window Cleaner; Stand Up Virgin Soldiers; Who Is Killing The Great Chefs of Europe?; Unidentified Flying Oddballs; The Shillingbury Blowers; The Fiendish Plot of Dr. Fu Manchu.

TV inc: Dad's Army; And The Band Played On; Brideshead Revisited; A Married Man.

Thea inc: Dad's Army.

(Died Nov 15, 1983).

LEMMON, Jack: Act. b. Boston, Feb 8, 1925. e. Harvard U. Started in stock, then radio. Bway inc: Room Service; Face of a Hero; Tribute.

Films inc: It Should Happen to You; Three For The Show; My Sister Eileen; Mister Roberts (*Oscar*-supp-1955); Operation Mad Ball; Bell, Book and Candle; Some Like It Hot; The Apartment; The Notorious

Landlady; Days of Wine and Roses; Irma La Douce; How To Murder Your Wife; The Great Race; The Fortune Cookie; The Out-of-Towners; The Odd Couple; The April Fools; Kotch (dir only); The War Between Men and Women; Avanti; Save the Tiger (Oscar-1973); The Front Page; The Prisoner of Second Avenue; Alex and the Gypsy; Airport '77; The Gentleman Tramp (& narr); The China Syndrome; Portrait of a 60% Perfect Man (doc); Tribute; Buddy Buddy; Missing; Mass Appeal.

TV inc: The Entertainer; 'S Wonderful, 'S Marvelous, 'S Gershwin (Emmy-1972); An All-Star Party for Jack Lemmon; Bob Hope's Stars Over Texas; Hollywood--The Gift of Laughter; Ernie Kovacs--Television's Original Genius (cable); 1983 Tony Awards (host); The Gentleman Tramp; Jacques Cousteau--The First 75 Years.

LEMON, Meadowlark: Act. b. Wilmington, NC, Apr 25. Former trick shot basketball player with the Harlem Globetrotters.
Films inc: Sweepstakes; The Fish That Saved Pittsburgh; Modern Romance.
TV inc: Hello, Larry; Crash Island; The World's Funniest Commercial Goofs.

LENZ, Kay: Act. b. Los Angeles, Mar 4, 1953. W of David Cassidy. Films inc: American Graffiti; Breezy; White Line Fever; The Great Scout and Cathouse Thursday; The Passage; Fast-Walking; Prisoners Of the Lost Universe.
TV inc: Playmates; Weekend Nun; Lisa Bright and Dark; Heart in Hiding (Emmy-1975); The Seeding of Sarah Burns; Escape; The Hustler of Muscle Beach; Insight/Matchpoint.

LENZ, Rick: Act. b. 1939. Films inc: Cactus Flower; Where Does It Hurt?; The Little Dragons; Melvin and Howard.
TV inc: Reunion; Elvis and the Beauty Queen; Aloha Paradise (wri); Advice to the Lovelorn; Insight/The Fiddler; Malice In Wonderland.

LEO, Malcolm: Prod-Dir-Wri. b. Los Angeles, Oct 9, 1944. e. UC at Santa Barbara. Films inc: (doc) Up Here Looking Down; Search for the Vampire Bat; Flight; The Sky's the Limit; Banapple Gas; Majacat, Cat Stevens in Concert; Birds Do It, Bees Do It; This Is Elvis; It Came From Hollywood.
TV inc: (doc) Life Goes to the Movies; Life Goes to War; Hollywood and the Homefront; Heroes of Rock 'N Roll; E.T. & Friends--Magical Movie Visitors; Prime Time (exec prod); The Beach Boys--An American Band.

LEONARD, Bill (William Augustus Leonard): Exec. b. NYC, Apr 9, 1916. Started in radio in 1946, with CBS station in NY; shifted to WCBS-TV; moved to the CBS News division in 1959 as prod-correspondent of CBS Reports; in 1965 became an exec responsible for editorial policies, prodn planning and special events coverage; in 1975, named Washington, DC vp and chief liaison between CBS Inc and Capital Hill; named CBS p of News, Mar 30, 1979.

LEONARD, Herbert B.: Prod. b. NYC, Oct 8, 1922. e. NYU. Began as ind prod 1945; vp Allied Artists TV 1974-1977; 1980 signed with Playboy to develop films and TV.
TV inc: Tallahasee 7000; Rin Tin Tin; Circus Boy; Naked City; Route 66; Starstruck; Breaking Away.

LEONARD, Hugh (John Keyes Byrne): Playwri. b. Dublin, Eire, Nov 9, 1926. Plays inc: The Big Birthday; A Leap in the Dark; Madigan's Lock; A Walk on the Water; The Passion of Peter Ginty; Stephen D; Dublin One; The Poker Session; The Family Way; When the Saints Go Cycling In; Mick and Mick; The Quick and the Dead; The Au Pair Man; The Barracks; The Patrick Pearse Motel; Da (Tony-1977); Summer; A Suburb of Babylon; A Life.
TV inc: Me Mammy; Tales from the Lazy Acre; Country Matters; Father Brown.

LEONARD, Sheldon: Act-Dir-Prod. b. NYC, Feb 22, 1907. e. Syracuse U, BA. Films inc: Another Thin Man; Tall, Dark and Handsome; Tortilla Flat; Somewhere in the Night; Her Kind of Man; If You Knew Susie; Sinbad the Sailor; Here Come the Nelsons; Stop You're Killing Me; Money From Home; Guys and Dolls. (Dir): The Real McCoys; Pocketful of Miracles; The Brink's Job.
TV inc: (dir) Make Room for Daddy; Damon Runyon; Jimmy Du-

rante Show; prod & dir Danny Thomas Show (Emmys-dir-1956 & 1961); exec prod Gomer Pyle, USMC; I Spy; My World and Welcome to It (Emmy-exec prod-1970); Big Eddie (act).

LEONE, Sergio: Wri-Dir. b. Rome, Italy, 1922. Worked as asst to various Italian and American directors; co-wrote Sign of the Gladiator; Last Days of Pompeii before solo debut. Films inc: The Colossus of Rhodes; A Fistful of Dollars; For A Few Dollars More; The Good, The Bad and the Ugly; Once Upon A Time In The West; Il Gatto; Once Upon A Time In America.

LEONTOVICH, Eugenie: Act. b. Moscow, Mar 21, 1900. e. Imperial School of Dramatic Art. Member of Moscow Art Theatre, left Moscow after Revolution, worked in Europe before arriving U.S., 1922; appeared as showgirl in Topics of 1923; Artists and Models while learning English, in later years operated own theatre, LA; on faculty Goodman School of Drama, Chicago.
Bway inc: Revue Russe; Candlelight; Grand Hotel; Twentieth Century; Blood Wedding; Antony and Cleopatra; Dark Eyes; Obsession; Anastasia; The Cave Dwellers (& dir); A Call on Kuprin.
Films inc: Anything Can Happen; Four Sons; The Man In Her Arms.

LERNER, Alan Jay: Wri. b. NYC, Aug 31, 1918. e. Harvard, BS. Bway inc: What's Up; The Day Before Spring; Brigadoon; My Fair Lady; (Tony-1956); Camelot; Coco; On A Clear Day You Can See Forever; Gigi (Tony-1974); 1600 Pennsylvania Ave; Dance A Little Closer (& dir).
Films inc: Royal Wedding; An American in Paris (Oscar-story & sp-1951); Gigi (Oscars-sp & best song-1958); Camelot; Paint Your Wagon; On A Clear Day You Can See Forever; The Little Prince; Tribute.
TV inc: An Evening With Alan Jay Lerner.
(Grammy-best score-1965).

LeROY, Mervyn: Prod-Dir. b. San Francisco, Oct 15, 1900. In vaudeville prior to films. Dir debut, 1928, No Place To Go. Films inc: Little Caesar; I Am A Fugitive From A Chain Gang; Five Star Final; Three On A Match; Two Seconds; Golddiggers of 1938; Tugboat Annie; Oil For The Lamps of China; Sweet Adeline; Anthony Adverse; The Wizard of Oz; Waterloo Bridge; Blossoms in the Dust; Johnny Eager; Random Harvest; Madame Curie; Thirty Seconds Over Tokyo; Homecoming; Any Number Can Play; Little Women; Quo Vadis; Mister Roberts; Strange Lady in Town; No Time For Sergeants; The FBI Story; Gypsy; Devil At Four O'Clock; Majority of One; Moment to Moment.
(Oscar-special-1945). (Irving Thalberg Award, 1975).

LESH, Phil: Mus. b. Mar 15, 1940. Founder-member of The Grateful Dead. Solo albums inc: Seastones.
(See The Grateful Dead for group credits).

LESLIE, Bethel: Act. Films inc: The Rabbit Trap; Captain Newman, M.D.; A Rage To Live; The Molly Maguires; Old Boyfriends.
TV inc: The Richard Boone Show; White Shadow; The Gift of Love; A Christmas for Boomer; Reflections (Girl on the Edge of Town).

LESLIE, Joan (nee Brodell): Act. b. Detroit, Jan 26, 1925. Films inc: Camille; Men with Wings; Foreign Correspondent; High Sierra; Sergeant York; The Male Animal; Yankee Doodle Dandy; This is the Army; Thank Your Lucky Stars; Hollywood Canteen; Rhapsody in Blue; Too Young to Know; Cinderella Jones; Royal Flush; Repeat Performance; Born to be Bad; The Woman They Almost Lynched; The Revolt of Mami Stover;
TV inc: The Keegans.

LESTER, Mark: Act. b. Oxford, England, 1958. Films inc: Our Mother's House; Oliver; Run Wild, Run Free; The Boy Who Stole the Elephant; Eye Witness; Black Beauty; Whoever Slew Auntie Roo?; Redneck; Crossed Swords.
TV inc: Scalawag; Graduation Trip; Seen Dimly Before Dawn.
Thea inc: The Murder Game; The Prince and the Pauper.

LESTER, Mark Leslie: Dir. b. Cleveland, OH, Nov 26, 1946. e. U CA Northridge, BA. Films inc: Steel Arena; Truck Stop Women; Bobbie Jo and the Outlaw; Stunts; Roller Boogie; The Funhouse (exec prod only); Class of 1984; Firestarter.

TV inc: Gold of the Amazon Women.

LESTER, Richard: Dir. b. Philadelphia, 1932. Films inc: It's Trad Dad; The Mouse on the Moon; A Hard Day's Night; The Knack; A Funny Thing Happened on the Way to the Forum; How I Won the War; Petulia; The Three Musketeers; Juggernaut; The Four Musketeers; Royal Flash; Robin and Marian; The Ritz; Butch and Sundance-The Early Days; Cuba; Superman II; Superman III; Finders Keepers (& exec prod).

LETERRIER, Francois: Dir-wri. b. France, May 26, 1929. e. Sorbonne. Entered film industry as act in A Man Escaped. Later asst dir for Louis Malle. Films inc: Naked Autumn; Un Roi sans divertissement; La chasse royale; Projection Prive; Milady; Va Voir Maman--Papa Travaille (Go See Mother--Father Is Working); Goodbye Emmanuelle; Le garde du Corps (The Bodyguard); Tranches de Vie (Slices Of Life).

LETTERMAN, David: Wri-Act. b. Indianapolis, IN, Apr 12, 1947. e. Ball State U, IN. Started as weatherman, talk show host on Indianapolis tv before going to Hollywood.
TV inc: (wri) Good Times; Paul Lynde Comedy Hour; John Denver Special; Bob Hope Special. (Act) Mary; Good Friends; guesthost Tonight Show; David Letterman Show (Emmys-wri-1981, 1984); An NBC Family Christmas.

LEVATHES, Peter G.: Exec. b. Pittsburgh, PA, Jul 28, 1911. e. George Washington U; Georgetown U, AB, MA, Law. Exec VP charge of prodn, 20th Century-Fox Films; VP TV Young & Rubicam Adv; Currently dir pgm development, Corp for Public Broadcasting.

LEVEN, Boris: Art Dir. b. Moscow. Films inc: Alexander's Ragtime Band; Second Chorus; The Shanghai Gesture; Tales of Manhattan; Hello, Frisco, Hello; Mr Peabody and the Mermaid; I Wonder Who's Kissing Her Now; Criss Cross; The Prowler; Sudden Fear; Giant; Anatomy of a Murder; West Side Story (Oscar-1961); Two For The Seesaw; The Sound of Music; The Sand Pebbles; Star!; A Dream of Kings; The Andromeda Strain; Jonathan Livingston Seagull; Mandingo; New York, New York; The Last Waltz; Matilda; Fletch.

LEVEY, William A.: Prod-Dir. Films inc: To Be A Rose (& wri); A Make Believe Mind (dir); Blackenstein (dir); Wham, Bam, Thank You Spaceman; Slumber Party '57; The Happy Hooker Goes to Washington; Skatetown, USA.

LEVI, Alan J.: Dir. TV inc: ABC Wide World of Sports; Gemini Man; The Invisible Man; Oregon Trail; Class of '65; $6 Million Man; The Bionic Woman; The Incredible Hulk; Battlestar Galactica; The Immigrants; Legend of the Golden Gun; A Man Called Sloan; Scruples; The Last Song; The Invisible Woman (& prod).

Le VIEN, Jack: Prod. b. NYC July 18, 1918. Started as film ed, reporter with Pathe News, later dir of prodn Hearst Metrotone News. Formed LeVien Films Ltd. Films inc: Black Fox; The Finest Hours; A King's Story.
TV inc: The Valiant Years; The Other World of Winston Churchill; The Gathering Storm; Walk With Destiny; The Amazing Voyage of Daffodil and Daisy; The Queens Drum Horse; Where the Lotus Fell; Churchill and the Generals.

LEVIN, Alan M.: Exec. b. NYC, 1943. e. Brooklyn Coll; Brooklyn Law School. In law practice before joining CBS News Bus Affairs Dept 1969 as asst dir; 1970, talent & pgm negotiator for network bus affairs; 1971, asso dir bus affairs; 1974, dir talent & pgm contracts; 1975, dir talent & pgm negotiations; 1976, vp bus affairs CBS NY; 1977, vp bus affairs CBS Entertainment; April 1978, vp & asst to pres; Sept 1978, vp bus affairs; 1980, bus affairs & administration; Sep 1982, exec VP; Dec. 1984, head of newly created CBS Prodns. to include film, homevideo, cable.

LEVIN, Herman: Prod. b. Philadelphia, Dec 1, 1907. e. U of PA; St Johns U Law School. Admitted to NY Bar, 1935, practiced until 1946.
Bway inc: Call Me Mister; No Exit; Bonanza Bound; Richard III; Gentlemen Prefer Blondes; Bless You All; My Fair Lady (Tony-1957); The Girl Who Came to Supper; The Great White Hope; Lovely Ladies,

Kind Gentlemen.

LEVIN, Ira: Wri. b. NYC, Aug 27, 1929. e. Drake U, BA. Films inc: A Kiss Before Dying; Rosemary's Baby; This Perfect Day; The Stepford Wives; The Boys From Brazil.
Plays inc: No Time for Sergeants; Interlock; Critic's Choice; General Seeger; Drat! The Cat; Dr. Cook's Garden; Veronica's Room; Deathtrap; Break A Leg.

LEVIN, Irving H.: Exec. b. Chicago, Sep 8, 1921. e. U of IL. Entered film industry as partner of Kranz-Levin Pictures and Realart Pictures, 1948; formed Mutual Prodns, 1952; p, Filmakers Releasing Org, 1953; p AB-PT Picture Corp, 1956; p, exec prod Oakhurst TV Prod Inc; p, exec prod Atlas Enterprises; p Atlantic Pictures, 1959; exec vp, member of bd of dir National General Corp, 1961; p National General, 1966; p & COO NGC; formed Levin-Schulman Prodns, 1975; formed Group L Prodns, 1978; acquired ownership of Royal Theatres, Hawaii, 1979.

LEVIN, Michael: Act. b. Minneapolis, MN, Dec 8. e. U of MN. TV inc: Adams Chronicles; Two Faces West; Ryan's Hope.
Thea inc: The Royal Hunt of the Sun.

LEVIN, Peter: Dir. TV inc: James at 15; James at 16; Family; Kaz; Lou Grant; Starsky and Hutch; Beacon Hill; The Best of Families; Married; Rape and Marriage--The Rideout Case; The Marva Collins Story; Washington Mistress; The Royal Romance of Charles and Diana; Two Marriages; A Doctor's Story.

LEVINE, Irving R.: TV news. b. Pawtucket, RI, 1923. e. Brown U, BA; Columbia U, MA. Began career with Providence (RI) Journal-Bulletin; Vienna Bureau Chief for International News Service; joined NBC 1950, based in Rome for 10 years, then four years in Moscow, two years in Tokyo and one year in London; NBC economic affairs corr since 1971. Author Main Street USSR; Main Street Italy; The New Worker in Soviet Russia.

LEVINE, James: Cond. b. Cincinnati, OH, 1943. e. Juilliard. Studied with Rudolf Serkin, Rosina Lhevinne. Debuted as piano soloist at age 10 with Cincinnati Symphony. Joined Cleveland Orch 1964 as asst conductor; soloist, conductor with every major U.S. and European orch; since 1976, music dir Metropolitan Opera; Cond Chicago Symphony (Grammy-Class orch-1982); TV inc: Live From the Met--Centennial Gala Part I (& mus dir) (Emmys-class pgm & perf. arts 1984).

LEVINE, Joseph E.: Exec. b. Boston, MA, Sep 9, 1905. Former theatre owner. Formed Embassy Pictures in late 50's; financed foreign films Eight and a Half; Divorce Italian Style; Boccaccio.
Films inc: (prod) The Carpetbaggers; Darling; Woman Times Seven; Carnal Knowledge; Where Love Has Gone; Harlow; The Graduate; The Producers; The Lion In Winter; A Bridge Too Far; Magic; Tattoo.

LEVINSON, Barry: Prod. b. NYC, 1932. Films inc: The Only Way; First Love; The Night Visitor; The Amazing Mr. Blunden; Catholics; The Internecine Project (& wri); And Justice for All (wri); Inside Moves (wri); Love; Who?; Best Friends (wri); Diner (exec prod-dir-wri); Unfaithfully Yours (wri); The Natural (dir).

LEVINSON, Richard L.: Wri-Prod. b. Philadelphia, PA, Aug 7, 1934. e. U of PA, BS. Partnered with William Link in TV-film prod. Plays inc: Prescription Murder; Merlin.
TV inc: Mannix (& crea); Ellery Queen (& crea); Tenafly (& crea); That Certain Summer; My Sweet Charlie (Emmy-wri-1970); Columbo (& crea) (Emmy-wri-1972); The Execution of Private Slovik; The Gun; Stone; Crisis at Central High; Rehearsal For Murder; Take Your Best Shot; Prototype (exec prod-wri); Murder, She Wrote (exec prod); The Guardian (cable)(exec prod-wri); Guilty Conscience (exec prod-wri).

LEVITT, Gene: Wri-Dir-Prod. b. NYC, May 28, 1920. e. U of WY, BA. Started writing for radio, then TV (over 100 hour shows).
TV inc: (prod) Adventures In Paradise; Combat; The Outsider; Any Second Now; (as dir): Run a Crooked Mile; Alias Smith and Jones (pilot); Cool Million (pilot); Phantom of Back Lot; Maggie and the

Lady; Fantasy Island (crea).

LEVY, Edmond A.: Dir-Wri. b. Toronto, Canada, Sep 26, 1929. e. Harvard. Has made more than 100 documentary and entertainment shorts inc A Year Toward Tomorrow *(Oscar*-1967); Beyond Silence; Trouble In the Family; After the Applause.

TV inc: The Farmer's Daughter.

LEVY, Eugene: Wri-act. b. Toronto, Canada, Dec. 17, 1946. e. McMaster U. Thea inc: (Toronto) Godspell; Second City Company; The Owl and the Pussycat; Love Times Four.

Films inc: (Act) Cannibal Girls; Running; Going Berserk; Splash.

TV inc: King of Kensington; The Sunshine Hour; Stay Tuned; SCTV Network 90 *(Emmys*-wri-1982, 1983); From Cleveland; The Last Polka (& exec prod).

LEVY, Jules V.: Prod. b. Los Angeles, Feb 12, 1923. e. USC. P, Levy-Gardner-Laven Prodns. Films inc: Without Warning; Vice Squad; Down Three Dark Streets; Geronimo; The Glory Guys; Sam Whiskey; Scalphunters; The McKenzie Break; The Honkers; Kansas City Bomber; White Lightning; McQ; Brannigan; Gator; Safari 3000 (& story);

TV inc: The Rifleman; The Detectives; The Plainsman; The Big Valley.

LEVY, Norman: Exec. b. NYC, Jan 3, 1935. e. CCNY, BA. Joined U 1957, various sales positions; moved to Nat'l General Pictures 1967-74; moved to Col 1974, vp & gm-sls; exec vp marketing 1975-77; p, domestic distrib 1978; became P 20th-Fox Entertainment Feb 19, 1980; Aug 1981, vice chmn; resd. Sept. 1984, effective early 1985.

LEWIN, Albert E.: Wri-Story Edtr. b. Chicago, Jul 29, 1916. e. Art Institute of Chicago. Wrote for radio: Scattergood Baines; Eddie Cantor Comedy Hour; Edgar Bergen.

Films inc: Alice in Wonderland; Call Me Mister; Down Among the Sheltering Palms; Boy, Did I Get a Wrong Number; Eight on the Lamb; I Will, I Will. . .For Now.

TV inc: My Friend Irma; Life with Luigi; The Dennis Day Show; The West Point Story; Alfred Hitchcock Presents; the Ray Milland Show; The Hathaways; Margie; The Farmer's Daughter; McHales Navy; The Donna Reed Show; Bob Hope Special; My Favorite Martian. Plays inc: A Gift Horse; Trashman.

LEWIN, Dennis: Prod-exec. b. Forest Hills, NY, 1944. e. MI State U. Joined ABC Sports 1966 as dir Rights Acquisitions, asst to coord prod Wide World of Sports; 1969, asso prod; 1971, coord prod & co-prod Monday Night Football. TV inc: Monday Night Football *(Emmy*-1979); Wide World of Sports *(Emmys*-1974, 1975, 1976); 1976 Olympic Games *(Emmy*-1977); Special Preview of the Olympic Games From Montreal *(Emmy*-1977); 15th Annual Wide World of Sports; Winter Olympic Games *(Emmy*-1980); 1980 American and National League Championships; Wide World of Sports 20th Anniversary Show *(Emmy*-1981).

LEWINE, Richard b. NYC., July 28, 1910. e. Columbia U. Bway inc: Prod-comp-wri. (comp) Make Mine Manhattan; The Girls Against The Boys; Naughty-Naught; The Fireman's Flame; The Girl from Wyoming; The Ziegfeld Follies (songs); Fools Rush In (songs).

TV inc: (Prod) Wonderful Town; The Fabulous Fifties; New York Philharmonic Young People's Concerts; Hootenanny; Blithe Spirit; Aladdin; Noel Coward-Mary Martin Special; Cinderella; My Name Is Barbra *(Emmy-1963(.*

LEWIS, Arthur: Prod-Dir-Wri. b. NYC, Sep 15, 1916. e. USC; Yale U. Started film career as a writer, 1941. Films inc: Oh, You Beautiful Doll (wri); Golden Girl (wri); Conquest of Cochise (wri); Loot (prod); Brass Target (prod).

Thea inc: Three Wishes for Jamie; dir first London prodn Guys and Dolls, 1953; returned to Bway as asso prod of Can Can; The Boy Friend; Silk Stockings; in 1963 returned to London to take over operation of the Shaftsbury Theatre where he prod or presented How to Succeed in Business Without Really Trying; A Thousand Clowns; The Brig; Little Me (also dir); The Solid Gold Cadillac (also dir); Barefoot in the Park; The Owl and the Pussycat; Funny Girl; The Odd Couple; Golden Boy. Bway 1968, Rockefeller and the Red Indian.

TV inc: Brenner; The Asphalt Jungle; The Nurses; The Diary of Anne Frank; Splendor In the Grass.

LEWIS, David: Act-Dir. b. Pittsburgh, Oct 19, 1916. Thea inc: Goodbye Again; Take It As It Comes; The Three Sisters; The King of Hearts; Anastasia.

TV inc: The John Forsythe Show; The Farmer's Daughter; General Hospital *(Emmy*-supp-1982).

Films inc: That Certain Feeling; The Apartment; Honeymoon Hotel; John Goldfarb, Please Come Home; Generation.

LEWIS, Emmanuel: Act. b. Brooklyn, NY, Mar. 9, 1971. Thea inc: A Midsummer Night's Dream. TV inc: Samurai in New York (Japanese tv); Webster; A Tribute to Martin Luther King Jr.--A Celebration of Life; Salute to Lady Liberty; The Secret World Of The Very Young; Mr. T. and Emmanuel Lewis in A Christmas Dream

LEWIS, Fiona: Act. b. England, Sep 28, 1946. Films inc: The Fearless Vampire Killers; Joanna; Otley; Where's Jack; Villain; Dr. Phibes Rises Again; Lisztomania; Drum; Stunts; The Fury; Wanda Nevada; Dead Kids; Strange Invaders.

LEWIS, Geoffrey: Act. b. San Diego, CA, Jan 1, 1935. Films inc: The Wind and the Lion; Dillinger; Return of a Man Called Horse; Lucky Lady; The Great Waldo Pepper; The Culpepper Cattle Company; Macon County Line; Every Which Way But Loose; Human Experiments; Bronco Billy; Any Which Way You Can; I, The Jury; 10 to Midnight; Night Of the Comet; Lust In The Dust

TV inc: The Jericho Mile; Samurai; Salem's Lot; Flo; Belle Starr; Skyward Christmas; The Shadow Riders; Life of the Party--The Story of BeAtrice; Gun Shy; Return of the Man From U.N.C.L.E.; Travis McGee; September Gun; Poor Richard; Maximum Security; Stormin' Home.

LEWIS, Jerry: Act-dir. b. Newark, NJ, Mar. 16, 1925. Formed comedy team with Dean Martin, Atlantic City, 1946. Appeared in niteries, films, on tv until 1956 when team split. Film debut as team, My Friend Irma, 1949.

Films inc: (as team) My Friend Irma Goes West; At War With the Army (& wri); That's My Boy; Sailor Beware (& wri); Jumping Jacks; Scared Stiff; The Caddy (& wri); The Stooge; Money From Home; Living It Up; Three Ring Circus (& wri); You're Never Too Young; Artists and Models; Partners; Hollywood or Bust.

Solo films inc: (act) The Delicate Delinquent (& prod-wri); The Sad Sack (& wri); The Geisha Boy (& prod-wri); Rockabye Baby (& prod-wri); Don't Give Up the Ship (& wri); Visit to a Small Planet; The Bellboy (& prod-dir-wri); Cinderfella (& prod-wri); The Ladies Man (& prod-dir-wri); The Nutty Professor (& prod-dir-wri); Who's Minding The Store?; The Patsy (& prod-dir-wri); The Disorderly Orderly (& wri); The Family Jewels (& prod-dir-wri); Boeing-Boeing; Three on a Couch (& prod-dir-wri); Way. . .Way...Out (& wri); The Big Mouth (& prod-dir-wri); Don't Raise the Bridge, Lower the Water (& prod); Hook, Line and Sinker (& prod); One More Time (dir only); Which Way to the Front (& prod-dir-wri); Hardly Working (& dir-wri); Bonjour Monsieur Lewis (doc); The King of Comedy; Smorgasbord; Retenez Mois--Ou je fais un Malheur (To Catch A Cop); Slapstick of Another Kind; Par ou t'Es Rentre ? On T'A Pas vue sortir (How'd You Get In ? We Didn't See You Leave).

TV inc: Colgate Comedy Hour; Jerry Lewis Show; The Jazz Singer; National Snoop; The Jerry Lewis Show (1984).

LEWIS, Jerry Lee: Mus-Singer. b. Ferriday, LA, Sep 29, 1935. Films inc: Disc Jockey Jamboree; High School Confidential; American Hot Wax.

Recordings inc: Crazy Arms; Whole Lotta Shakin' Goin' On; Great Balls of Fire; Original Golden Hits; Rare Jerry Lee Lewis; Rockin' Up A Storm; The Greatest Live Show on Earth; Best of Jerry Lee Lewis; The Killer Rocks On.

LEWIS, Joseph H.: Dir. b. NYC, Apr 6, 1900. Films inc: Two-Fisted Rangers; The Mad Doctor of Market Street; Bombs Over Burma; Minstrel Man; My Name is Julia Ross; So Dark the Night; The Jolson Story (musical numbers only); The Swordsman; The Return of October; The Undercover Man; Gun Crazy; Retreat Hell; The Big Combo; A Lawless Street; Seventh Cavalry; The Halliday Brand; Terror in a Texas Town.

LEWIS, Monica: Act. b. Chicago, May 5, 1925. e. Hunter Coll. W of Jennings Lang. Radio, band singer. Films inc: Inside Straight; Excuse My Dust; The Strip; Everything I Have is Yours; Affair with a Stranger; D.I.; Charlie Varrick; Earthquake; Roller Coaster; Airport '77; Nunzio; Concorde-Airport '79; Boxoffice.
TV inc: The Immigrants.

LEWIS, Morton M.: Prod-Dir. b. NYC, Oct 25, 1917. Started at B.I.P. Elstree, 1931; with Warner Bros., Hollywood, 1937-42; currently chmn, Meadway Prodns Ltd, Overseas Prodn Services Ltd, E.P.A. International Programmers Ltd.
TV inc: World Cup Mexico, 1970; The World at Their Feet; Suburban Wives; Secret Rights; Commuter Husbands; Heading for Glory; TV series of World Cup 1974 Munich games; Diary of a Space Virgin; Sexplorer; Secrets of a Super Stud; Golfing with Jacklin; Sex Is No Alibi.

LEWIS, Richard: Prod. b. NYC, Jan 2, 1920. e. Yale, BA. Radio producer Take It or Leave It; Crime Doctor, Philip Morris Playhouse.
TV inc: Blind Date; Mr. & Mrs. North; Quick as a Flash; Mike Hammer; Jake's Way (exec prod); Mama Malone (exec prod).
Films inc: The Borgia Stick; A Lovely Way To Die.

LEWIS, Robert Michael: Dir. TV inc: The Alpha Caper (pilot); The Invisible Man (pilot); Married (pilot); The Astronaut; Money to Burn; Message to My Daughter; The Day The Earth Moved; Guilty or Innocent--The Sam Sheppard Murder Case; The Night They Took Miss Beautiful; Ring of Passion; If Things Were Different; Escape; S*H*E*; A Private Battle; Secret of Midland Heights; Fallen Angel; The Miracle of Kathy Miller; Child Bride At Short Creek; Desperate Lives; Between Two Brothers; Computercide; Summer Girl; A Caribbean Mystery; Sparkling Cyanide;Flight 90--Disaster On The Potomac; City Killer; A Summer To Remember. The Astronaut; Money to Burn; Message to My Daughter; The Day The Earth Moved; Guilty or Innocent--The Sam Sheppard Murder Case; The Night They Took Miss Beautiful; Ring of Passion; If Things Were Different; Escape; S*H*E*; A Private Battle; Secret of Midland Heights; Fallen Angel; The Miracle of Kathy Miller; Child Bride At Short Creek; Desperate Lives; Between Two Brothers; Computercide; Summer Girl; A Caribbean

LEWIS, Robert Q.: TV Pers. b. NYC, 1924. Hosted or was a panelist on numerous game shows, conducted Robert Q. Lewis Show.
Films inc: An Affair to Remember; Good Neighbor Sam; How to Succeed in Business Without Really Trying; CHOMPS.

LEWIS, Roger H.: Exec. b. NYC, Mar 14, 1918. e. Lafayette Coll; UCLA; Columbia. Joined WB 1939 as apprentice pub dept; after WW II service, to Fox as spec asst to dir pub-ad-exploit; vp Monroe Greenthal agcy; 1952, adv mgr UA; 1956 natl dir pub-ad-exploit; 1959, vp; resd 1961 to enter prodn, exec vp Garrick Prodns; prodn exec National General; prodn exec, WB; vp Max Youngstein Enterprises.
Films inc: The Pawnbroker; The Swimmer; Shaft; Shaft's Big Score; Shaft in Africa; Night Games.
(Died July 26, 1984).

LEWIS, Shari (nee Hurwitz): Puppeteer-Ventriloquist. b. NYC, Jan 17, 1934. TV inc: Shari Lewis Show (both U.S. and Britain); A Picture of Us; Magic. Recordings inc: Fun in Shariland; The Kids; Shari in Storyland.

LEYTES, Josef: Wri-Dir-Prod. b. Warsaw, Poland, Nov 22, 1901. Dir 23 features, many docs in Poland where he lectured at State Drama School.
Films inc: The Young Fores; The Day of the Great Adventure; Les Hommes Maudits; during WW 2 made several docs for British Government inc From Homes to Tobruk; made The Great Promise (doc) and features Ein Breira and The Faithful City in Israel before coming to US in 1958.
Films in Hollywood inc: Valley of Mystery; The Movie Maker; The Counterfeit Killers. TV inc: Sugarfoot; Adventures in Paradise; June Allyson Show; Target-The Corruptors; Dick Powell Theatre; The Outlaws; Alfred Hitchcock Presents; 12 O'Clock High; Voyage to the Bottom of the Sea; Bonanza; Marcus Welby MD.

(Died May 27, 1983).

LHERMITTE, Thierry: Act. b. Paris, Nov. 24, 1957. Films inc: Que la fete commence (Let Joy Reign Supreme); Des enfant gates (Spoiled Children); Vous n'aurez pas l'Alsace et la Lorraine (You Won't Have Alsace-Lorraine); Les Bronzes (The Suntanned Ones); Les heros n'ont pas froid aux oreilles (Heroes Are Not Wet Behind the Ears); Le dernier amant romantique (The Last Romantic Lover); Les Bronzes font du ski; Alors--heureux?; Tout depend des filles (It All Depends on the Girls); La Banquiere (The Woman Banker); Clara et les chics types (Clara and the Swell Guys); L'annee prochaine si tout va bien (Next Year if All Goes Well); Les hommes preferent les grosses (Men Prefer Fat Girls); La pere Noel est une ordure (Santa Claus is a Louse); Legitime Violence (Lawful Violence); L'indic (The Informer); Le prefere (Rock and Torah) (The Favorite/Rock & Torah); Stella; Un homme a ma taille (A Man of My Measure); La femme de Mon Pote (My Buddy's Girl); La fiancee qui venait du froid (The Fiancee Who Came in from the Cold); Pappy Fait de la Resistance (Gramps is in the Resistance); Until September; Les Ripoux; La Smala (The Tribe); Un Ete d'Enfer (A Summer In Hell); Les Rois du Gag (The Gag Kings).

LIBERACE (Wladziu Valentino Liberace): Mus. b. Milwaukee, WI, May 29, 1917. e. WI Coll of Music. Guest soloist with the Chicago Symphony age 16. Performed in niteries, TV.
Films inc: South Sea Sinner; Footlight Varieties; Sincerely Yours; When the Boys Meet the Girls; The Loved One.
TV inc: The Liberace Show (Emmy-male personality-1953); A Gift of Music; Live--And in Person; Special People; Another World.

LIBERACE, George J.: Mus. b. Menasha, WI, Jul 31, 1911. e. Chicago Conservatory of Music. B of Liberace. Violinist in orchs inc: Anson Weeks; Orrin Tucker; musical dir for brother; founded Geo Liberace Enterprises, 1957; cond of symph orchs inc Kansas City, Dallas, St Louis, Phila., Denver, LA Philh. Films inc: Girl in the Convertible; Sincerely Yours.
(Died Oct. 16, 1983).

LIBERMAN, Frank P. Pub. b. White Plains, NY, May 29, 1917. e. Lafayette Coll, BA. H of Patricia Harris. Started with WB in homeoffice; tsfd to Chicago as field man prior to Army service; after WW II joined WB studio staff; 1947 opened own agency.

LIBOV, Mort: Prod. b. Baltimore, MD, Apr 20, 1935. e. U MD. P, Mort Libov Prodns, indie tv commercials firm. TV inc: Del Mar State Fair; State Fair-USA/Peoria; Frank Zappa Special; It's Your Business.

LIEBER, Perry W.: Pub Exec. b. Pleasant Prairie, WI, Jun 1, 1905. e. U of IL. Started career with adv dept J.P. Seeburg Co., Chicago; entered film industry with RKO 1930 in studio pub dept.; named pub dir 1939; 1953, natl pub-ad-expl dir; 1956 to Fox on special pub projects; 1962 natl pub ad dir; 1966 relinquished ad duties; 1970 became pub relations mgr Summa Corp (Howard Hughes company); became firm's consultant 1977.

LIEBERSON, Sanford (Sandy): Exec. b. 1936. Started as agent. Became ind film prod; joined CMA as exec in chg European activities; 1979 named P 20th Century Fox Prodns; resgd 1980 to join The Ladd Co. as Int'l vp; Resgd Dec. 1983 to become prodn head at Goldcrest Film & Television.
Films inc: Jabberwocky; Swastika; All This and World War II.

LIGHT, Judith: Act. b. Trenton, NJ, Feb 9, 1949. e. Carnegie-Mellon U, BFA. Bway inc: A Doll's House; Last of the Red Hot Lovers; Our Town; Measure for Measure; Herzl.
TV inc: One Life to Live (Emmys-1980, 1981); Intimate Agony; You Are the Jury; Who's The Boss ?

LIGHTFOOT, Gordon: Singer-Sngwri. b. Orillia, Ont, Canada, Nov 17, 1938. Songs inc: Early Morning Rain; Canadian Railroad Trilogy; If You Could Read My Mind; Sundown; Carefree Highway; Wreck of the Edmund Fitzgerald; Race Among the Ruins. TV inc: Live 'n Kickin.

LIGON, Tom: Act. b. New Orleans, LA, Sep 10. e. Yale, BA. Bway inc: Angela; Love Is A Time of Day; Have I Got a Girl For You.
Films inc: Nothing But A Man; Joyride; Paint Your Wagon; Bang the Drum Slowly; Young Doctors in Love; Fury on Wheels; Last Ameri-

can Hero.

TV inc: The Adams Chronicles; The Demon Murder Case; Judge Horton and the Scottsboro Boys; The Young and the Restless; The Execution of Private Slovik; F. Scott Fitzgerald in Hollywood.

LILLIE, Beatrice: Act. b. Toronto, Canada, May 29, 1898. London stage debut age 16, The Daring of Diane. Screen debut, 1926, Exit Smiling.

Films inc: Around The World In 80 Days; Thoroughly Modern Millie; On Approval; Dr. Rhythm.

Bway inc: A Late Evening With Beatrice Lillie; High Spirits; Ziegfeld Follies; Seven Lively Arts. (Tony-special-1953).

THE LIMELITERS: Folk trio. Members are Alex Hassilev, Lou Gottlieb, Glenn Yarbrough. Formed in the 60's, became top recording and concert attraction before breaking up in 1977. Re-grouped in 1980.

LINDEN, Hal (nee Lipshitz): Act. b. NYC, Mar 20, 1931. e. CCNY, BA. Sax player, perf with Sammy Kaye Band. Bway inc: Bells are Ringing; On a Clear Day; Wildcat; Subways Are for Sleeping; On a Clear Day; Pajama Game; The Love Match; The Rothschilds (Tony-1971); Wildcat; Ilya Darling; The Apple Tree; Education of H*Y*M*A*N K*A*P*L*A*N; The Sign in Sidney Brustein's Window.

Films inc: When You Comin' Back Red Ryder.

TV inc: Barney Miller; Animals, Animals, Animals (Host); Hal Linden Special; Hal Linden's Big Apple; Father Figure; FYI (Emmys-Host-1983, 1984); The Kennedy Center Honors 1982; Starflight--The Plane That Couldn't Land; The Other Woman; The Best of Everything (host); Second Edition; Christmas In Washington; My Wicked, Wicked Ways; Bob Hope Lampoons Television 1985; Night Of 100 Stars II; The Real Trivial Pursuit; How To Be A Man.

LINDFORS, Viveca: Act. b. Uppsala, Sweden, Dec 29, 1920. e. Royal Dramatic School. On screen, Sweden 1941, The Crazy Family; If I Should Marry the Minister. Hollywood debut 1948, Night Unto Night.

Films inc: Adventures of Don Juan; Dark City; Flying Missile; Gypsy Fury; No Sad Songs For Me; Journey Into Light; Four in a Jeep; The Raiders; No Time for Flowers; Run for Cover; Captain Dreyfus; Coming Apart; Puzzle of a Downfall Child; The Way We Were; Welcome to L.A.; Girlfriends; A Wedding; Voices; Linus; Natural Enemies; The Hand; Creepshow; Dies rigorose leben (Nothing Left to Lose); Silent Madness; The Sure Thing.

TV inc: The Diary of Anne Frank; Medical Center; FBI; Interns; Marilyn--The Untold Story; Playing For Time; Mom, The Wolfman and Me; The Best Little Girl In The World; For Ladies Only; Divorce Wars--A Love Story; Inside The Third Reich; A Doctor's Story; Passions; The Three Wishes Of Billy Grier; Secret Weapons.

LINDGREN, Goran: Exec. b. Stockholm, Oct 5, 1927. Pres Sandrew Films & Theater, AB, since 1969.

LINDLEY, Audra: Act. b. Los Angeles, Sep 24. Films inc: Taking Off; The Heartbreak Kid; When You Comin' Back, Red Ryder?; Cannery Row; Best Friends.

TV inc: Bridget Loves Bernie; Fay; Doc; Another World; Three's Company; Getting Married; Pearl; The Ropers; Pat Boone and Family Christmas Special; Moviola (The Silent Lovers); Revenge of the Stepford Wives; Skyward Christmas; The Day the Bubble Burst; Insight/Little Miseries.

Bway inc: The Young and the Fair; Spofford; Take Her, She's Mine; A Case of Libel.

LINDSAY-HOGG, Michael: Dir. b. NYC, May 5, 1940. S of Geraldine Fitzgerald. Films inc: Stop The World--I Want To Get Off; Let It Be (doc); Nasty Habits; Dr. Fischer Of Geneva.

TV inc: Brideshead Revisited; The Sound of Murder (Cable).

Bway inc: Whose Life Is It Anyway?

LINK, Andre: Prod. b. Hungary, Jul 25, 1932. Films inc: Shivers; Rabid; The House By the Lake; Meatballs; Happy Birthday to Me; Merlin. My Bloody Valentine; Spacehunter--Adventures in the Forbidden Zone; The Surrogate (exec prod); Hot Water (exec prod).

LINK, William: Wri-Prod. Partnered with Richard L Levinson in TV-film prod. Plays inc: Prescription Murder; Merlin.

TV inc: Mannix (& crea); Ellery Queen (& crea); Tenafly (& crea); That Certain Summer; My Sweet Charlie (Emmy-wri-1970); Columbo (& crea) (Emmy-wri-1972); The Execution of Private Slovik; The Gun; Stone; Crisis At Central High; Rehearsal For Murder; Take Your Best Shot; Prototype (exec prod-wri); Murder, She Wrote (exec prod); The Guardian (cable)(exec prod-wri); Guilty Conscience (exec prod-wri).

LINKLETTER, Art: TV Pers. b. Moose Jaw, Sask, Canada, Jul 17, 1912. Radio pgm mgr San Diego Exposition, 1935; radio pgm mgr S.F. World's Fair, 1937-39; freelance radio anncer, 1939-42.

TV inc: MC People Are Funny; Inside Beverly Hills; Art Linkletter's Secret World of Kids; Art Linkletter's House Party; The Linkletter Show. (Grammy-spoken word-1969).

LINKLETTER, Jack: TV Pers. b. San Francisco, Nov 20, 1937. e. USC, BA. S of Art Linkletter. TV inc: America Alive! (Co-host).

LINSK, Lester: Prod. b. Philadelphia, Jan 19, 1919. e. U of MI; Columbia U. Films inc: The Games; Run Shadow Run; Mr & Mrs Bo Jo Jones.

LINSON, Art: Prod. b. Chicago. Films inc: Rafferty and the Gold Dust Twins; Car Wash; American Hot Wax; Where The Buffalo Roam; Melvin and Howard; Fast Times At Ridgemont High; The Wild Life (& dir).

LINVILLE, Larry: Act. b. Ojai, CA, Sep 29, 1939. e. RADA. Bway inc: More Stately Mansions. Films inc: Kotch.

TV inc: M*A*S*H; Grandpa Goes to Washington; A Christmas for Boomer; Checking In; The Girl, The Gold Watch and Dynamite; Herbie, the Love Bug.

LIPPERT, Robert L. Jr: Exec. b. Alameda, CA, Feb 28, 1928. e. St Mary's Coll. S of exhib-prod. Operated d.i. theatre San Francisco; film edtr on 65 films his father prod; now P Robert L. Lippert Theatres.

Films inc: (prod) The Tall Texan; Great Jesse James Raid; Sins of Jezebel; Fangs of the Wild; The Big Chase; Black Pirates; Bandit Island; The Charge of the Rurales; Massacre.

LIPSTONE, Howard: Exec Prod. b. Chicago, Sep 28, 1928. e. USC, BA. 1950-55, asst to GM KTLA; 1955-64, Film/pgm dir, KABC-TV; 1964-69, exec asst to p, exec prod, Selmur Prodns, Inc; 1969-70, exec vp, Ivan Tors Films & studios; 1970-present, P Alan Landsburg Prodns, Inc.

Films inc: The Outer Space Connection; The Bermuda Triangle Mysteries; The White Lions; Jaws 3-D.

TV inc: Shindig; In Search of Ancient Astronauts; The American Idea; The Small Miracle; The Savage Bees; Ruby and Oswald; The Triangle Factory Fire Scandal.

LIPTON, David A.: Exec. b. Chicago, Nov 6, 1906. Started 1921 as office boy for Balaban and Katz Theatres, in Chicago, later pub dept; 1933 pub for Sally Rand; 1938 NY pub dir U; later studio pub dir; 1941 COL as pub-ad-exp dir; retd to Universal after war as exec/coordinator of advertising and promotion; 1949, nat'l pub-ad dir; 1951, VP; 1974 in charge of pub-ad, MCA Discovision; 1979 Consultant.

LISI, Virna: Act. b. Ancona, Italy, Nov 8, 1937. Films inc: How To Murder Your Wife; Casanova 70; The Birds, The Bees and the Italians; Not With My Wife You Don't; Assault On A Queen; The Lady And The General; Arabella; Better A Widow; Ernesto; The Secret Of Santa Vittoria; The Statue; The Serpent; Beyond Good and Evil; Sapore di mare (A Taste of Sea); Stelle Emigranti (Wandering Stars).

TV inc: E La Vita Continua (And Life Goes On); Christopher Columbus.

LISTER, Moira: Act. b. Cape Town, S Africa, Aug 6, 1923. On stage as a child. Thea inc: Felicity Jasmine; Juliet; Desdemona; Twelfth Night; Anthony and Cleopatra; Don't Listen, Ladies!; French Without Tears; The Gazebo; Any Wednesday; Move Over Mrs Markham; Bird of Paradise; Great Expectations; Murder Among Friends; Key For Two.

Films inc: The Shipbuilders; The Deep Blue Sea; The Yellow Rolls Royce; The Double Man.

TV inc: Major Barbara; Simon and Laura; The Very Merry Widow.

LITHGOW, John: Act. b. Rochester, NY. June 6, 1945. e. Harvard; LAMDA under Fulbright Scholarship. Act-dir with Royal Shakespeare Company, Royal Court Theatre before returning to US. Bway inc: The Changing Room (Tony-supp-1973); My Fat Friend; The Comedians; A Memory of Two Mondays; Secret Service; Anna Christie; Once In A Lifetime; Spokesong; Division Street; Requiem For A Heavyweight. Off-Bway inc: Hamlet; Trelawny of the Wells; Salt Lake City Skyline.

Films inc: Blow Out; Obsession; All That Jazz; Rich Kids; I'm Dancing As Fast As I Can; The World According to Garp; Twilight Zone--The Movie; Terms of Endearment; Footloose; The Adventures of Buckaroo Banzai--Across the 8th Dimension; 2010.

TV inc: The Oldest Living Graduate; Big Blonde; Mom, The Wolfman and Me; The Day After; The Glitter Dome (PC)

LITTLE, Cleavon: Act. b. Chickasha, OK, Jun 1, 1939. e. AADA. Bway inc: Macbeth; Scuba Duba; Hamlet; Jimmy Shine; Someone's Comin' Hungry; Purlie (Tony-1970); All Over Town; The Poison Tree.

Films inc: Cotton Comes To Harlem; Greased Lightning; John and Mary; Vanishing Point; Blazing Saddles; FM; Scavenger Hunt; High Risk; Jimmy the Kid; The Salamander; Surf II; Toy Soldiers.

TV inc: Don't Look Back; The Day the Earth Moved; Homecoming; Denmark Vesey's Rebellion; Now We're Cookin'.

LITTLE, Rich: Act. b. Ottawa, Canada, 1938. Impersonator in niteries; Films inc: Dirty Tricks. TV inc: Rich Little's Christmas Carol; Rich Little's Washington Follies; The Christmas Raccoons (narr); Take One; Nuts and Bolts; You Asked For It (host); The World of Entertainment; Parade of Stars; The Raccoons and the Lost Star (narr); The Christmas Raccoons (narr); Dean Martin's Celebrity Roast; Dom Deluise and Friends--Part II; Rich Little And Friends In New Orleans.

LITTMAN, Lynne: Dir-prod. W of Taylor Hackford. Researcher for National Educational Television; exec vp movies-for-television ABC, 1979-1980. Films inc: (Doc) In the Matter of Kenneth; Wanted--Operadoras; Till Death Do Us Part; Once a Daughter; Number Our Days (Oscar-doc short-1976). (Feature) Testament.

LITTO, George: Prod. b. Philadelphia, PA, Dec 9, 1930. e. Temple U. Started as agent with William Morris; later had own literary agcy; Feb 1981 became Bd Chmn, CEO Filmways; departed Filmways after takeover by Orion.

Films inc: Thieves Like Us; Drive-In; Over The Edge; Dressed to Kill; Blow Out.

LIVINGSTON, Alan W.: Exec. b. McDonald, PA. e. Wharton School of Finance and Commerce, BS. Wri-prod, VP-A&R Capitol Records, Inc., 1946-55; VP-TV programming NBC, 1955-60; then P and ChmnB, Capitol Records and P, Capitol Industries, Inc., 1960-68; from 1968-76, P and ChmnB, Mediarts, Inc. and Investment Fund M; 1976 to present, P Entertainment Group, Twentieth Century-Fox Film Corp; 1980 P Atlanta Investment Co.

TV inc: One In A Million (wri).

LIVINGSTON, Bob (nee Randell): Act. b. Quincy, IL, Dec 8, 1904. Studied at Pasadena Playhouse, signed by MGM as a contract player. Later under contract to Republic, became western star in studio's Three Mesquiteer series.

Films inc: Mutiny on the Bounty; The Vigilantes Are Coming; Lone Ranger Rides Again; Bold Caballero; later starred in PRC's Lone Ranger Series.

Ret 1955.

LIVINGSTON, Harold: Wri. b. Haverhill, MA, Sep 4, 1924. e. Brandeis U. Films inc: The Hell With Heroes; The Street is My Beat; Star Trek--The Motion Picture.

TV inc: Mission Impossible; Barbary Coast; Mannix; Banacek; Mannix; Star Trek; Destination Mindanao.

LIVINGSTON, Jay: Comp. b. McDonald, PA, Mar 28, 1915. e. U of PA, BA. Film scores inc: My Friend Irma; Red Garters; All Hands on Deck; The Paleface; Fancy Pants; Captain Carey, USA; The Lemon-Drop Kid; Houseboat; Tammy and the Bachelor; The Man Who Knew Too Much; Dear Heart; This Property is Condemned; The Oscar; Harlow; What Did You Do in the War, Daddy?; Wait Until Dark.

Songs inc: To Each His Own; Golden Earrings; Silver Bells; Button and Bows (Oscar-1948); Mona Lisa (Oscar-1950); Tammy; Dear Heart; Wish Me a Rainbow; Que Sera Sera (Oscar-1956); Almost in Your Arms.

TV title songs inc: Bonanza; Mr. Lucky; Mr. Ed.

LIVINGSTON, Jerry: Comp-Arr. b. Denver, CO, Mar 25, 1909. e. U of AZ. Films scores inc: Cinderella; At War with the Army; Sailor Beware; Jumping Jacks. TV scores inc: Shirley Temple Storybook; Jack and the Beanstalk.

Songs inc: Under a Blanket of Blue; What's the Good Word, Mr Bluebird?; Mairzy Doats; Promises; Chi-Baba Chi-Baba; Wake the Town and Tell the People; The Hanging Tree; The Ballad of Cat Ballou.

TV title songs inc: 77 Sunset Strip; Bourbon Street Beat; Hawaiian Eye; The Roaring Twenties; Lawman.

LIZZANI, Carlo: Dir. b. Italy, 1922. Films inc: Bitter Rice (co-sp only); Achtung Banditi; The Great Wall; Hunchback of Rome; The Hills Run Red; The Violent Four; Crazy Joe; The Last Days of Mussolini; Fontamara (& wri); La Casa Del Tappeto Giallo (House of the Yellow Carpet); Nucleo Zero.

LLOYD, Christopher: Act. b. Stamford, CT, Oct 22, 1938. Started with Neighborhood Playhouse, NY. Bway inc: Happy End; Red, White and Maddox.

Films inc: The Onion Field; Butch and Sundance--The Early Days; One Flew Over the Cuckoo's Nest; Another Man, Another Chance; The Black Marble; Three Warriors; The Legend of the Lone Ranger; Mr. Mom; National Lampoon Goes to the Movies; To Be or Not to Be; Star Trek III--The Search For Spock; Joy Of Sex; The Adventures of Buckaroo Banzai--Across the 8th Dimension; Back To The Future.

TV inc: The Word; Lacy and the Mississippi Queen; Visions; Stunt Seven; Taxi (Emmys-supp-1982, 1983); The Best of the West; Pilgrim, Farewell; Money On The Side; September Gun; Old Friends; The Cowboy and the Ballerina; Street Hawk.

LLOYD, Euan: Prod. b. Rugby, England, Dec 6, 1923. Films inc: April in Portugal; Invitation to Monte Carlo; The Secret Ways; Genghis Khan; Murderer's Row; Shalako; Catlow; The Man Called Noon; Paper Tiger; The Wild Geese; The Sea Wolves; Who Dares Wins; Wild Geese II.

LLOYD, Kathleen: Act. Winner of UCLA Hugh O'Brian Best Actress Award 1969. Films inc: Missouri Breaks; The Car; Take Down; Skateboard.

TV inc: Incident on a Dark Street; Sorority Kill; Lacy and the Mississippi Queen; House Hunting; High Midnight; Make Me an Offer; The Jayne Mansfield Story; The Gangster Chronicles; Shooting Stars; Call To Glory; Obsessed With A Married Woman; Sins Of The Father.

LLOYD, Norman: Prod. b. Jersey City, NJ, Nov 8, 1914. e. NYU. Former act.

Films inc: (act) Spellbound; The Southerner; The Green Years; Limelight; Jaws Of Satan (King Cobra); The Nude Bomb. (Prod) Arch of Triumph; The Red Pony.

TV inc: The Alfred Hitchcock Show; Beggarman, Thief (act); The Dark Secret of Harvest Home (act); St. Elsewhere (act); Insight/The Hit Man (dir). Bway inc: (act) Noah; Liberty Jones; Everywhere I Roam; The Cocktail Party; The Lady's Not for Burning; The Golden Apple.

LLOYD WEBBER, Andrew: Comp. b. London, England, Mar 22, 1948. Had first comp published at age eight. Thea inc: Jesus Christ, Superstar; Evita (Tony-score-1979); Cats (Tony-score-1983); Joseph and the Amazing Technicolor Dream Coat; Song and Dance; Daisy Pulls It Off; Starlight Express; The Hired Man (prod).

Films inc: Gumshoe; The Odessa File; Jesus Christ, Superstar.

TV inc: Tell Me On Sunday (wri).

(Grammy-cast album-1980).

LOBELL, Michael: Prod. b. NYC, May 7, 1941. e. MI State U. Films inc: Dreamer; Windows; So Fine.

LoBIANCO, Tony: Act. b. NYC. Oct. 19. Films inc: The Honeymoon Killers; The Merciless Man; The Roots of the Mafia; The Seven-Ups; The French Connection; God Told Me To; F.I.S.T.; Bloodbrothers; Separate Ways; City Heat; Too Scared To Scream (dir).

Thea inc: The Office; The Royal Hunt of the Sun; The Rose Tattoo; The 90 Day Mistress; The Goodbye People; The Threepenny Opera; The Nature of the Crime; A View From the Bridge; Hizzoner - The Mayor (one-man show).

TV inc: Mr Inside, Mr Outside; Shadow in the Streets; Jesus of Nazareth; Third Annual Circus of the Stars; The Last Tenant; Champions (A Love Story); The Last Cry For Help; Marciano; Pals; Today's FBI (pilot); Marco Polo; Another Woman's Child; Jessie; Lady Blue.

LOCKE, Sondra: Act. b. Shelbyville, TN, May 28, 1947. Films inc: The Heart Is a Lonely Hunter; Willard; A Reflection of Fear; The Second Coming of Suzanne; The Outlaw Josey Wales; The Gauntlet; Every Which Way but Loose; Any Which Way You Can; Sudden Impact.

TV inc: Friendships, Secrets and Lies; Rosie--The Rosemary Clooney Story.

LOCKHART, June: Act. b. NYC, Jun 25, 1925. D of the late Gene and Kathleen Lockhart. Professional debut at eight in Metropolitan Opera production of Peter Ibbetson. Film debut 1938, A Christmas Carol. Films inc: All This and Heaven Too; Sergeant York; Adam Had Four Sons; The White Cliffs of Dover; Meet Me in St Louis; The Yearling; Son of Lassie; Keep Your Powder Dry; Bury Me Dead; Time Limit; Butterfly; Strange Invaders; Deadly Games.

TV inc: Lassie; Lost in Space; Petticoat Junction; Dinky Hocker; The Gift of Love; The Capture of Grizzly Adams; Peking Encounter; Insight/Teddy; Take My Word For It; The Night They Saved Christmas.

Bway inc: For Love or Money (Special Tony 1948).

LOCKLEAR, Heather: Act. b. LA.,CA.,Sept. 25, 1962. TV inc: The Beverly Hillbillies Special; Twirl; T.J.Hooker; Dynasty; City Killer; The Real Trivial Pursuit.

Films inc: Firestarter.

LOCKWOOD, Gary (John Gary Yusolfsky): Act. b. 1937. Films inc: Tall Story; Splendor in the Grass; Wild in the Country; The Magic Sword; It Happened at The World's Fair; Firecreek; 2001--A Space Odyssey; They Came to Rob Las Vegas; Model Shop; RPM; Stand Up and Be Counted.

TV inc: Follow the Sun; The Incredible Journey of Dr. Meg Laurel; The Top of the Hill; The Girl, The Gold Watch and Dynamite; Emergency Room; Half Nelson.

LOCKWOOD, Margaret, CBE (nee Day): Act. b. Karachi, Pakistan, Sep 15, 1916. e. RADA. Thea inc: Subway in the Sky; Suddenly It's Spring; Signpost to Murder; An Ideal Husband; On a Foggy Day; Lady Frederick; Relative Values; Double Edge; Mother Dear.

Films inc: Lorna Doone; Some Day; Honours Easy; Jury's Evidence; The Amateur Gentleman; The Lady Vanishes; The Stars Look Down; Rulers of the Sea; Night Train to Munich; Alibi; The Man in Grey; Dear Octopus; Love Story; The Wicked Lady; Hungry Hill; Jassy; Cardboard Cavalier; Trent's Last Case; Trouble in the Glen; Cast a Dark Shadow; The Slipper and the Rose.

LOEWE, Frederick: Comp. b. Vienna, Jun 10, 1901. Usually collab with Alan Jay Lerner.

Films inc: Brigadoon; Paint Your Wagon; My Fair Lady; Gigi (Oscar-song-1958); Camelot; The Little Prince.

Bway inc: Petticoat Fever; Salute to Spring; The Day Before Spring; Brigadoon; Paint Your Wagon; My Fair Lady; Camelot; Gigi (Tony-1973).

TV inc: Salute to Lerner and Loewe; The Lerner and Loewe Songbook.

LOGAN, Joshua: Dir-Wri-Prod. b. Texarkana, TX, Oct 5, 1908. e. Princeton U; Moscow Art Theatre. Films inc: I Met My Love Again; Picnic; Bus Stop; Sayonara; South Pacific; Tall Story; Fanny; Ensign Pulver; Camelot; Paint Your Wagon.

Bway inc: To See Ourselves; Stars In Your Eyes; Charley's Aunt; Mister Roberts (Tony-co-author-1948); South Pacific (3 Tonys-wri, prod, & dir-1950; also Pulitzer Prize); The Wisteria Trees; Picnic (Tony-dir-1953); Fanny; Bus Stop; The World of Suzie Wong; All American; Tiger, Tiger Burning Bright; Look at the Lilies; Miss Moffat; Rip Van Winkle; Lysistrata (new adaptation); Joshua Logan (act); Trick (prod); Horowitz and Mrs. Washington.

TV inc: Mr. Roberts (prodn cnslt).

LOGGIA, Robert: Act. b. NYC, Jan 3, 1930. e. U MO. Films inc: Somebody Up There Likes Me; Cop Hater; The Nine Lives of Elfego Baca; Cattle King; The Greatest Story Ever Told; Che; First Love; Revenge of the Pink Panther; The Sea Gypsies; The Ninth Configuration; S.O.B.; An Officer and A Gentleman; Trail of the Pink Panther; Psycho II; Curse of the Pink Panther; Scarface; Prizzi's Honor.

TV inc: T.H.E. Cat; No Other Love; Casino; A Woman Called Golda; A Touch Of Scandal.

Thea inc: Toys in the Attic; Three Sisters; Boom Boom Room; Wedding Band.

LOGGINS, Kenny: Singer-Comp. b. Jan 7, 1947. With groups Second Helping, Loggins and Messina, Electric Prunes before going solo.

Songs inc: Danny's Songs; Love Song; House at Pooh Corner; Your Mama Don't Dance; Celebrate Me Home; Whenever I Call You Friend; This Is It; What A Fool Believes, (Grammy-song of year-1979).

Albums inc: Nightwatch; Celebrate Me Home; Alive (Grammy-pop vocal for track This Is It-1980).

Films inc: Caddyshack (songs). TV inc: Fridays.

LOLLOBRIGIDA, Gina: Act. b. Auviaco, Italy, Jul 4, 1928. e. Academy Fine Arts, Rome. Films inc: Love of a Clown; Fanfan The Tulip; Pagliacci; Beat the Devil; Crossed Swords; Trapeze; Woman of Rome; Bread, Love and Dreams; Bread, Love and Jealousy; Solomon and Sheba; Go Naked in the World; Come September; Strange Bedfellows; Assassination Bureau; Hotel Paradiso; Buena Sera Mrs. Campbell; Bambole; Plucked; Stelle Emigranti (Wandering Stars).

TV inc: Bob Hope's Women I Love--Beautiful and Funny; Falcon Crest; Deceptions.

LOM, Herbert (Herbert Kuchacevich ze Schluderpacheru): Act. b. Prague, 1917. Films inc: Mein Kampf; The Young Mr Pitt; The Dark Tower; The Seventh Veil; Dual Alibi; State Secret; The Ladykillers; War and Peace; I Aim at the Stars; Mysterious Island; El Cid; Phantom of the Opera; Return from the Ashes; Uncle Tom's Cabin (Ger); Gambit; Assignment to Kill; Murders in the Rue Morgue; Asylum; The Return of the Pink Panther; And Then There Were None; The Pink Panther Strikes Again; Revenge of the Pink Panther; Charleston; The Lady Vanishes; The Man With Bogart's Face; Hopscotch; Trail of the Pink Panther; Curse of the Pink Panther; The Dead Zone; Memed, My Hawk.

TV inc: The Human Jungle; Peter and Paul; Lace.

LOMAX, Alan: Act-Author. b. Austin, TX, Jan 15, 1915. e. Harvard; U of TX. Folk music collector. With father, the late John Avery Lomax, helped make the Archive of American Folk Song of the Library of Congress one of the most comprehensive in the world. Author of many books on folk music.

LONDON, Jerry: Dir. b. Los Angeles, Jan 21, 1937. TV inc: Mary Tyler Moore Show; Hogans Heroes; Kojack; Police Story; Swan Song; Women In White; Evening in Byzantium; Wheels; Swan Song; Shogun; Father Figure; The Chicago Story; The Ordeal of Bill Carney (& prod); The Gift of Life (& prod); The Scarlet and the Black; Arthur Hailey's "Hotel" (& prod); Chiefs (& supv prod); With Intent To Kill (exec prod); Ellis Island (& supv prod); MacGruder & Loud (& prod).

LONDON, Julie: Act. b. Santa Rosa, CA, Sep 26, 1926. Began as singer in niteries. Screen debut, 1944, Jungle Woman.

Films inc: A Night in Paradise; The Red House; Tap Roots; Task Force; Drango; Saddle the Wind; A Question of Adultery; The George Raft Story.

TV inc: Emergency.

LONG, Avon: Sing-act-dancer. b. Baltimore, MD., Jun. 18, 1910. Appeared in Cotton Club revues and vaude. Bway inc: Black Rhythm; Porgy and Bess; Memphis Bound; Carib Song; Beggar's Holiday; Green Pastures; Shuffle Along; Mrs. Patterson; The Ballad of Jazz Street; Don't Play Us Cheap; Bubbling Brown Sugar.

Films inc: Manhattan Merry-Go-Round; Finian's Rainbow; Ziegfeld Follies; Centennial Summer; Harry and Tonto; The Sting.

LONG, Shelley: Act. b. Fort Wayne, IN, Aug 23, 1949. e. Northwestern U. Films inc: A Small Circle of Friends; Caveman; Night Shift; Losin' It; Irreconcilable Differences.

TV inc: That Thing on ABC; The Cracker Factory; Promise of Love; The Princess and the Cabbie; Cheers *(Emmy-*1983); All Star Party For Lucille Ball.

LONGET, Claudine: Act. b. France, Jan 29, 1942. Films inc: McHale's Navy; The Party; The Scavengers.

LONGSTREET, Stephen: Wri. b. NYC, Apr 18, 1907. e. Rutgers U. Films inc: The Jolson Story; The Greatest Show on Earth; The First Travelling Saleslady; The Helen Morgan Story; Untamed Youth; Duel in the Sun; The Crime. TV inc: Casey Jones; Clipper Ship; Agent of Scotland Yard. Plays inc: High Button Shoes.

LONSDALE, Michel: Act. b. Paris, 1931. On stage in Paris. Films inc: C'est Arrive a Aden; Adorable Menteuse; The Immoral Moment; The Trial; Behold a Pale Horse; Hail, Mafia; The Bride Wore Black; Stolen Kisses; Murmur of the Heart; Le Printemps; Il etait une fois un Flic; The Day of the Jackal; Stavisky; Le Fantome de la Liberte; Les Suspects; Special Section; Galileo; The Romantic Englishwoman; The Pink Telephone; The Left Handed Woman; The Passage; Moonraker; Les Jeux de la Comtesse Dolingen de Gratz (The Games of the Countess Dolingen of Graz); Seuls (Loners); Douce Enquete sur la Violence (Sweet Inquest on Violence); Chronopolis (narr); Enigma; Erendira; Le Juge (The Judge); Le Bon Roi Dagobert (Good King Dagobert).

TV inc: Smiley's People.

LOO, Richard: Act. b. HI, 1903. Films inc: Thank You, Mr Moto; The Good Earth; Bombs Over Burma; China; Jack London; The Keys to the Kingdom; The Story of Dr Wassell; God is My Co-Pilot; Back to Bataan; Tokyo Rose; The Clay Pigeon; I Was an American Spy; Hell and High Water; Soldier of Fortune; Around the World in 80 Days; The Quiet American; Confessions of a Opium Eater; A Girl Named Tamiko; The Sand Pebbles; One More Train to Rob; Chandler; The Man with the Golden Gun.

(Died Nov. 20, 1983).

LOPEZ, Priscilla: Act. b. Brooklyn, Feb 26, 1948. e. High School for Performing Arts. Bway inc: Breakfast At Tiffany's; Henry, Sweet Henry; Company; A Chorus Line; A Day in Hollywood, A Night in the Ukraine *(Tony-*supp-1980).

TV inc: Feeling Good; In The Beginning.

LOPEZ, Trini: Act. b. Dallas, TX, May 15, 1937. Bandleader, recording artist.

Films inc: Marriage on the Rocks; The Poppy is Also a Flower; The Dirty Dozen. TV inc: A Gift of Music.

LOQUASTO, Santo: Dsgn. e. Yale School of Drama Repertory Theatre. Set and costume dsgn for repertory companies. Bway inc: Sticks and Bones; That Championship Season; The Secret Affairs of Mildred Wild; Siamese Connections; The Orphans; As You Like It; King Lear; The Tempest; The Dance of Death; Mert and Phil; Kennedy's Children; Murder Among Friends; American Buffalo; The Three Penny Opera; The Cherry Orchard *(Tony-*costumes-1977); The Floating Light Bulb; The Wake Of Jamey Foster; Virginia (Off-Bway).

Films inc: Sammy Stops The World; The Fan; So Fine; A Midsummer Night's Sex Comedy; Zelig; Falling In Love; Desperately Seeking Susan.

LORD, Jack (John Joseph Ryan): Act. b. NYC, Dec 30, 1930. e. NYU, BS in Fine Arts. Thea inc: Traveling Lady; Cat on a Hot Tin Roof.

Films inc: Court Martial of Billy Mitchell; Tip on a Dead Jockey; God's Little Acre; Walk Like A Dragon; Dr. No; Doomsday Flight; Ride to Hangman's Tree; Counterfeit Killer.

TV inc: Omnibus; Studio One; Playhouse 90; Stoney Burke; Hawaii Five-O; M Station--Hawaii.

LORD, Marjorie: Act. b. San Francisco, Jul 26, 1922. Films inc: Border Cafe; Escape From Hong Kong; Moonlight in Havanna; Sherlock Holmes in Washington; Johnny Come Lately; Flesh and Fantasy; New Orleans; The Argyle Secrets; The Strange Mrs. Crane; Riding High; Chain Gang; Port of Hell; Boy Did I Get a Wrong Number.

TV inc: The Pirate.

LORD, Stephen: Wri-Dir. b. New Orleans, LA, Dec 14, 1933. e. Notre Dame; Tulane; Loyola. TV inc: Loretta Young Show; Johnny Ringo; Zane Grey Theatre; Death Valley Days; Outer Limits; Virginian; Ironside; Banacek; Madigan; McCloud; Hawaii 5-0; Fantasy Island; CHiPS; Widow's Peak; Last of the Mohicans; Heroes of the Bible; Fall of the House of Usher; California Beat; Earthbound.

Films inc: From Hell to Eternity; Bourbon Street Beat; Blood Hunt; The Devil's Hand; Tarzan and the Jungle Boy; The Fur and Feather Cops; Beyond and Back; The Bermuda Triangle.

LORD, William E.: Exec. b. ME, 1938. e. Boston U, BA; U of PA, MA. Started as anncr-eng on Maine radio station, later in news depts Massachusetts radio stations while in college. Joined ABC News 1961 as wri-reporter; 1964, Washington prod; 1966, sr prod in Washington of ABC Evening News; 1974, VP Washington bureau; 1976, VP in chg TV news; 1978, VP-exec prod of news on Good Morning America; 1980, VP-exec prod ABC News Nightline *(Emmy-*prod-1980); Washington Monument Siege; Disaster on the Potomac *(Emmy-*exec prod-1982); Brezhnev Death; Cuban Missile Crisis 1962; May 1984, exec prod World News Tonight.

LOREN, Sophia (nee Scicoloni): Act. b. Rome, Italy, Sep 20, 1934. W of Carlo Ponti. On screen from 1950 (as extra).

Films inc: The Sign of Venus; Attila; The Gold of Naples; The Miller's Wife; The Pride and the Passion; Boy on a Dolphin; Desire Under the Elms; The Key; Houseboat; Black Orchid; That Kind of Woman; Heller in Pink Tights; A Breath of Scandal; Two Women *(Oscar-*1961); The Millionairess; El Cid; Boccaccio '70; The Condemned of Altona; Five Miles to Midnight; Yesterday, Today and Tomorrow; The Fall of the Roman Empire; Lady L; Marriage Italian Style; Judith; Arabesque; A Countess from Hong Kong; More Than a Miracle; Sunflower; Cinderella Italian Style; Ghosts Italian Style; Man of La Mancha; Lady Liberty; The Voyage; The Cassandra Crossing; Revenge; A Special Day; Brass Target; Firepower; Angela.

TV inc: Brief Encounter; Sophia Loren--Her Own Story; Aurora.

LORENTZ, Pare: Dir-Wri. b. Clarksburg, WV, Dec 11, 1905. Documentarist. Advisor to the US Resettlement Administration in 1935; organizer of U.S. Film Service. Films inc: The Plow That Broke the Plains; The River; The City (treatment); The Fight for Life.

LOSEY, Joseph: Dir. b. La Crosse, WI, Jan 14, 1909. e. Dartmouth U, BA. Stage mgr in NY, inc opening of Radio City Music Hall.

Films inc: The Boy With Green Hair; The Prowler; The Lawless; The Big Night; The Servant; King and Country; The Damned; Accident; Boom!; The Go-Between; Assassination of Trotsky; A Doll's House; Mr. Klein; Don Giovanni; La truite (The Trout) (& wri); Steaming.

(Died June 22, 1984).

LOUDON, Dorothy: Act. b. Boston, MA, Sep 17, 1933. Worked niteries before Bway debut in Nowhere to Go But Up, 1962. Other Bway inc: Sweet Potato; The Fig Leaves Are Falling; Three Men on a Horse (rev); The Women (rev); Annie *(Tony-*1977); Ballroom; Sweeney Todd; The West Side Waltz; Noises Off.

TV inc: Kraft Music Hall; Dean Martin Show; Dupont Project 20; Dorothy; Parade of Stars; The Best of Everything (host).

Films inc: Garbo Talks.

LOUIS, Jean: Des. b. Paris, Oct 5, 1907. Head designer for Hattie Carnegie before accepting post as chief designer Columbia Pictures. Later Universal Studios. Then freelance in motion pictures, TV. President Jean-Louis Inc.

Films inc: Born Yesterday; Affair in Trinidad; From Here To Eternity; It Should Happen To You; A Star Is Born; Queen Bee; The Solid Gold Cadillac *(Oscar-*1956); Pal Joey; Bell, Book and Candle; Judgement at Nuremberg; Back Street; Ship of Fools; Gambit; Thoroughly Modern Millie.

LOUISE, Tina: Act. b. NYC, 1934. e. Miami U. Films inc: God's Little Acre; Day of the Outlaw; Armored Command; For Those Who Think Young; Wrecking Crew; The Good Guys and the Bad Guys; How to Commit Marriage; The Stepford Wives; Canicule (Dog Day); Hell Riders.

TV inc: Gilligan's Island; Friendships, Secrets and Lies; The Day the Women Got Even; Advice to the Lovelorn; Rituals; Evils Of The Night.

LOURIE, Eugene: Dsgn-Dir. b. France, 1908. Prodn dsgn many films in France inc: Las Bas Fonds; La Grande Illusion; La Regle du Jeu. In Hollywood dsgd This Land Is Mine; The Southerner; The River; Battle of the Bulge; Krakatoa--East of Java. (Dir) The Beast from 20,000 Fathoms; Behemoth (& wri); Gorgo (& wri); Breathless (act).

LOVE, Bessie (Juanita Horton): Act. b. Midland, TX, 1898. On screen from childhood. Films inc: Intolerance; The Aryan; A Sister of Six; The Song and Dance Man; Has Anybody Here Seen Kelly?; Broadway Melody; Conspiracy; Touch and Go; The Wild Affair; Isadora; Sunday, Bloody Sunday.
TV inc: Mousey; S.O.S. Titanic; Edward and Mrs. Simpson.
Thea inc: (London) Gone With the Wind.

LOVE, Cecil D.: Cin. b. Roseland, LA, Feb 7, 1898. Special Academy Award for design of Acme-Dunn optical printer (1980).

LOVELL, Dyson: Prod. b. Salisbury, Rhodesia, Aug 8, 1939. Films inc: Brother Sun, Sister Moon; Murder on the Orient Express; Galileo; Death on the Nile; Jesus of Nazareth; The Champ; Endless Love; The Cotton Club (exec prod).

LOVELL, Patricia: Prod. b. Sydney, Australia. Films inc: Picnic at Hanging Rock; Break of Day; Summerfield; Gallipoli; Monkey Grip.

LOWE, Rob: Act. b. 1963. TV inc: Schoolboy Father; A Matter Of Time; A New Kind Of Family; Thursday's Child.
Films inc: The Outsider; Class; Hotel New Hampshire; Oxford Blues; Youngblood; St. Elmo's Fire.

LOWRY, Dick: Dir. b. Bartlesville, OK. e. U OK; AFI. Originally a commercial photographer before being accepted at AFI. Films inc: The Drought (short); Smokey and the Bandit--Part 3.
TV inc: OHMS; Kenny Rogers as The Gambler; The Jayne Mansfield Story; Angel Dusted; Coward of the County; A Few Days in Weasel Creek; Missing Children - A Mother's Story; Rascals and Robbers--The Secret Adventures of Tom Sawyer and Huck Finn; Kenny Rogers as the Gambler--the Adventure Continues (& prod); Wet Gold; The Toughest Man In the World; Murder With Mirrors.

LOWTISCH, Klaus: Act. b. Berlin, Germany, Feb 8, 1936. On stage in Germany before films and tv. Films inc: Madchen Mit Gewalt; Pioneers in Ingolstadt; The Merchant of Four Seasons; Disaster; The Odessa File; Rosebud; Schatten der Engel; Cross Of Iron; Despair; The Marriage of Maria Braun; The Wizard of Babylon (doc) (narr).

LOY, Myrna (nee Williams): Act. Act. b. Helena, MT., Aug. 2, 1905. Dancer in ballet chorus of Grauman's Chinese Theatre before film career. Started as bit player in Pretty Ladies; Ben Hur. Films inc: The Cave Man; The Gilded Highway; Across the Pacific; Don Juan; The Exquisite Sinner; So This Is Paris; Finger Prints; The Jazz Singer; If I Were Single; The Girl From Chicago; What Price Beauty; Turn Back the Hours; The Crimson City; Pay As You Enter; The Midnight Taxi; Noah's Ark; The Desert Song; The Black Watch; Hardboiled Rose; Evidence; The Show of Shows; The Great Divide; Cameo Kirby; Isle of Escape; Bride of the Regiment; Last of the Duanes; Renegades; The Jazz Cinderella; The Truth About Youth; The Devil To Pay; Body and Soul; A Connecticut Yankee; Transatlantic; Rebound; Skyline; Arrowsmith; Vanity Fair; The Woman in Room 13; Thirteen Women; The Mask of Fu Manchu; The Animal Kingdom; Topaze; The Barbarian; When Ladies Meet; Penthouse; Night Flight; The Prizefighter and the Lady; Men In White; Manhattan Melodrama; The Thin Man; Stamboul Quest; Evelyn Prentice; Broadway Bill; Whipsaw; Petticoat Fever; The Great Ziegfeld; To Mary--With Love; Libeled Lady; After the Thin Man; Parnell; Double Wedding; Man-Proof; Test Pilot; Too Hot to Handle; Lucky Night; The Rains Came; Another Thin Man; I Love You Again; Third Finger, Left Hand; Love Crazy; Shadow of the Thin Man; The Thin Man Goes Home; So Goes My Love; The Best Years of Our Lives; The Bachelor and the Bobby Soxer; The Senator Was Indiscreet; Song of the Thin Man; Mr. Blandings Builds His Dream House; The Red Pony; Cheaper By the Dozen; Belles On Their Toes; The Ambassador's Daughter; Lonelyhearts; From the Terrace; Midnight Lace;

The April Fools; Airport '75; The End; Just Tell Me What You Want.
Thea inc: The Women; Marriage-Go-Round; There Must Be A Pony; Barefoot In the Park; Dear Love.
TV inc: Summer Solstice.

LOY, Nanni: Dir. b. Italy, 1925. Films inc: Parola di Ladra; The Four Days of Naples; Made in Italy; Cafe Express; Testa o Croce (Heads or Tails) (& wri); Mi manda Picone (Picone Sent Me) (& wri).

LUBOFF, Norman: Comp-Cond. b. Chicago, IL, May 14, 1917. e. Chicago U. Arr and coach for shows in early days of Chicago radio. After WW2 service, to Hollywood to work on Railroad Hour; under contract WB, formed choral group for concerts, recordings.
Songs inc: Yellow Bird; Warm; It's Some Spring.
(Grammy-chorus-1960).

LUCAS, George: Prod-Dir-Wri. b. Modesto, CA, May 14, 1944. e. USC. Made short film, THX and won National Student Film Festival Grand Prize, 1967. Joined WB; asst to Francis Ford Coppola on the Rain People; made 2-hr documentary on filming of that feature. Debut as dir. with THX 1138.
Films inc: American Graffiti (dir, co-sp); Star Wars (dir-sp); More American Graffiti (prod); The Empire Strikes Back (exec prod); Raiders of the Lost Ark (exec prod-wri); Return of the Jedi (exec prod-wri); Twice Upon A Time (exec prod); Indiana Jones and the Temple of Doom (exec prod & story); Mishima (exec prod).
TV inc: The Ewok Adventure (exec prod & story).

LUCAS, Marcia (nee Griffin): Film edtr. b. Modesto, CA, Oct 4, 1945. e. LA City Coll; USC. Films inc: American Graffiti; Alice Doesn't Live Here Anymore; Taxi Driver; Star Wars (Oscar-1977); New York, New York; Return of the Jedi.

LUCE, Claire: Act. b. Syracuse, NY, Oct 15, 1901. On stage from 1921 in Little Jessie James; Dear Sir; in 1924 appeared for a time as a dancer with Texas Guinan's troupe; made first appearance in London 1928 in Burlesque;
Bway inc: Atlantic City; Society Girl; The Taming of the Shrew; A Doll's House; Rain; Mary Stuart, Queen of Scots; And So, Farewell; The Wedding and the Funeral; The Cave Dwellers. On screen in 1930 in Up the River.
TV inc: Peer Gynt; Becky Sharp.

LUCE, Clare Boothe: Wri. b. NYC, Apr 10, 1903. Plays inc: Abide With Me; The Women; Kiss The Boys Goodbye; Margin for Error; Child of the Morning; Slam the Door Softly.
Films inc: Come to the Stable.

LUCKINBILL, Laurence George: Act. b. Fort Smith, AR, Nov 21, 1934. e. U of AR; Catholic U of America. Bway inc: Oedipus Rex; There Is a Play Tonight; A Man for All Seasons; Arms and the Man; The Boys in the Band; What the Butler Saw; Alpha Beta; The Shadow Box; Poor Murderer; Past Tense; Dancing In The End Zone.
Films inc: The Boys in the Band; Such Good Friends; The Money; The Promise; Not For Publication.
TV inc: As I Lay Dying; The Secret Storm; The Boston Massacre; The Senator; Ike; Delphi Bureau; The Mating Season; Our Brother's Keeper; Momma The Detective; One More Try; Space.

LUDWIG, Jerry: Wri-Prod. b. NYC, Jan 23, 1934. e. CCNY, BA. Films inc: Fade In (sp); Three the Hard Way (sp); Take A Hard Ride (sp).
TV inc: I Spy; Run For Your Life; The Virginian; Mission Impossible; Hawaii Five-0; Police Story; (wri-prod) Assignment: Munich; Assignment: Vienna; Wheeler & Murdoch; Strange Homecoming; Bunco; In the Glitter Palace; Samurai; Riker (crea); Today's FBI (crea-wri); Jessica Novak.

LUFT, Lorna: Act. b. Los Angeles, Nov 21, 1952. D of late Judy Garland. Vaude and concert appearances with mother inc: London Palladium. Also played niteries. Bway debut Promises, Promises; Films inc: Where the Boys Are '84.

LUISI, James: Act. b. NYC., Nov. 2. e. St. Francis College, BA; AADA. Films inc: The Tiger Makes Out; Ben; Moment By Moment; Norma Rae.
TV inc: First Ladies Diaries--Martha Washington (Emmy-1976);

The Asphalt Cowboy; Our Family Business; The Rockford Files; Beyond Witch Mountain; The Renegades; Sunset Limousine; The Red-Light Sting.

Bway inc: Detective Story; Three Penny Opera; Alfie; Sweet Charity; Zorba the Greek.

LUKE, Keye: Act. b. Canton, China, 1904. Began as artist for Fox West Coast Theatres & RKO Studios. Also technical advisor on Chinese Films Screen debut, 1935, Painted Veil.

Films inc: Oil for the Lamps of China; The Good Earth; First Yank in Tokyo; Tokyo Rose; Love Is A Many Splendored Thing; Ten Charlie Chan Films; The Chairman, Won Ton Ton, The Dog That Saved Hollywood; The Amsterdam Kill; Just You and Me Kid; Gremlins.

TV inc: Anna and the King of Siam; Follow the Sun; Kung Fu; Fly Away Home; Unit 4; Cocaine and Blue Eyes; Blade In Hong Kong.

LUKE, Peter: Plywri. b. England, Aug. 12, 1919. Plays inc: Hadrian VII; Bloomsbury; Prospera; Rings For a Spanish Lady (translation);

TV inc: Small Fish Are Sweet; Devil A Monk Would Be; Black Sound and Deco Song.

LULU BELLE (Myrtle Wiseman): Act. b. Boone, NC, Dec 24, 1913. Country music singer-guitarist; teamed with husband, Scotty Wiseman. They performed on radio, TV, Grand Ole Opry, National Barn Dance.

LUMET, Sidney: Dir. b. Philadelphia, PA, Jun. 15, 1924. On stage at age 9 in The Eternal Road. Also appeared Bway in Dead End; George Washington Slept Here; My Heart's in the Highlands. In 1947 began directing off-Broadway and summer stock prodns. Became staff dir CBS-TV 1950. TV inc: Mama; Danger; You Are There; Twelve Angry Men; All the King's Men; The Sacco-Vanzetti Story.

Films inc: Twelve Angry Men; Stage Struck; That Kind of Woman; The Fugitive Kind; A View from the Bridge; Long Day's Journey Into Night; Failsafe; The Pawnbroker; The Hill; The Group; The Deadly Affair; Bye, Bye Braverman; The Seagull; The Appointment; The Last of the Mobile Hotshots; King--A Filmed Record, Montgomery to Memphis (doc); The Anderson Tapes; Child's Play; The Offense; Serpico; Lovin' Molly; Murder on the Orient Express; Dog Day Afternoon; Network; Equus; The Wiz; Just Tell Me What You Want; Prince of the City; Deathtrap; The Verdict; Daniel; Garbo Talks.

LUNA, Barbara: Act. b. NYC, 1939. Bway inc: South Pacific; The King and I; Teahouse of the August Moon.

Films inc: Tank Battalion; Cry Tough; The Devil at 4 O'Clock; Five Weeks in a Balloon; Dime With A Halo; Mail Order Bride; Synanon; Ship of Fools; Firecreek; Che!; The Gatling Gun; Woman in the Rain; The Concrete Jungle.

LUND, Art: Act-Sing. b. Salt Lake City, UT, Apr 1, 1920. nitery singer before thea. Bway inc: Most Happy Fella (& London); Of Mice and Men; Destry Rides Again; Donnybrook; Fiorello!; Sophie; No Strings; The Wayward Stork; Breakfast at Tiffany's.

Films inc: The Molly Maguires.

TV inc: The Contender; The Oklahoma City Dolls; The Gift of Life; The Winds of War.

LUND, Deanna: Act. b. Oak Park, IL. Started as weather girl on Miami TV. TV inc: Land of the Giants; Stump the Stars; Hanging By A Thread; Revenge for Rape; General Hospital.

Films inc: Johnny Tiger; Tony Rome; Hardly Working; Stick.

LUND, John: Act. b. Rochester, NY, Feb. 6, 1913. Bway inc: As You Like It; The Hasty Heart. Films inc: To Each His Own; The Perils of Pauline; Variety Girl; The Night Has A Thousand Eyes; Miss Tatlock's Millions; Bride of Vengeance; My Friend Irma; No Man of Her Own; Duchess of Idaho; My Friend Irma Goes West; The Mating Season; Darling, How Could You!; Steel Town; Battle at Apache Pass; Latin Lovers; Chief Crazy Horse; Five Guns West; Battle Stations; High Society; The Dakota Incident; The Wackiest Ship in the Army; If a Man Answers.

LUNDEN, Joan: TV pers. b. 1951. TV inc: anchor KCRA-TV; 1975, anchor WABC-TV; Feb. 1980, feature reporter Good Morning, America; Aug. 1980, int Good Morning, America; The Secret World Of The Very Young.

LUNGHI, Cherie: Act. b. London. With English repertory companies, Royal Shakespeare Company. Thea inc: Teeth 'n Smiles; Twelfth Night.

TV inc: Bill Brand; Edward And Mrs. SImpson; Kean; Prince Regent; The Misanthrope; 'Tis Pity She's A Whore; Strangers and Brothers; Desert Of Lies; Praying Mantis.

Films inc: The Sign Of Four; Excalibur; King David; Parker.

LUPINO, Ida: Act. b. London, Feb 4, 1918. e. RADA. D of Stanley Lupino. Screen debut, 1932, Her First Affair. To Hollywood, 1934, Money for Speed.

Films inc: Peter Ibbetson; Artists and Models; The Light that Failed; The Adventures of Sherlock Holmes; High Sierra; Ladies in Retirement; In Our Time; Escape Me Never; Road House; Outrage (dir); Beware My Lovely; The Hitch-Hiker (& dir); The Bigamist (& dir); Private Hell 36; The Big Knife; While the City Sleeps; The Devil's Rain; The Food of the Gods; Deadhead Miles.

TV inc: Mr Adams & Eve; The Trial of Mary Surrat; The Bill Cosby Show. Dir many TV segs.

LuPONE, Patti: Act. b. Northport, NY; April 21, 1949. e. Juilliard. Thea inc: The School for Scandal; The Three Sisters; The Beggers Opera; The Robber Bridegroom; Measure for Measure; Edward II; The Water Engine; Working; The Time of Your Life; Evita (Tony-1980); Oliver!

Films inc: Fighting Back; Witness.

LuPONE, Robert: Act. b. Northport, NY., Jul. 29. e. Juilliard, BFA. b. of Patti LuPone. Bway inc: Nefertiti; St. Joan; Swing; A Chorus Line.

TV inc: Ryan's Hope, Rich Man, Poor Man; Search for Tomorrow.

LYLES, A.C.: Prod. b. Jacksonville, FL, May 17, 1912. Started as mailboy Paramount Studios; 1938 to pub dept; 1940 ad-pub head for Pine-Thomas unit; became asso prod, then prod. Films inc: The Mountain; Short Cut to Hell; Raymie; The Young and the Brave; The Law of the Lawless; Stage to Thunder Rock; Young Fury; Black Spur; Hostile Guns; Arizona Bushwackers; Town Tamer; Apache Uprising; Johnny Reno; Waco; Red Tomahawk; Fort Utah; Buckskin; Rogue's Gallery; Night of the Lepus.

TV inc: The Last Day; A Christmas for Boomer; Here's Boomer; Dear Mr. President.

LYMAN, Dorothy: Act. b. Minneapolis, MN, Apr 18, 1947. e. Sarah Lawrence College; studied with Uta Hagen. Thea inc: Later; Fefu and Her Friends; Action; A Coupla White Chicks Sitting Around Talking (& prod-dir); Dancing In The End Zone.

TV inc: Another World; Search For Tomorrow; The Edge of Night; A World Apart; All My Children (Emmys-1982, 1983); Mama's Family; Summer Fantasies.

LYNCH, David: Pro-Dir-Wri. b. Missoula, MT, Jan. 20, 1946. e. PA Academy of Fine Arts. Began career with grant from AFI. Films inc: The Grandmother (16m); Eraserhead; The Elephant Man; Dune.

LYNCH, Richard: Act. b. Apr 29, 1936. Bway inc: The Devils; The Lion in Winter. London thea inc: King Richard.

Films inc: Scarecrow; Steel; Formula; The Sword And The Sorcerer; The Delta Fox; Savage Dawn.

TV inc: Vampire; Buck Rogers in the 25th Century; Alcatraz--The Whole Shocking Story; Sizzle; The Phoenix; White Water Rebels; The Last Ninja; Blue Thunder.

LYNLEY, Carol: Act. b. NYC, Feb 13, 1942. Films inc: The Light in the Forest; Holiday for Lovers; Blue Denim; The Hound Dog Man; Return to Peyton Place; The Last Sunset; The Stripper; Under the Yum Yum Tree; The Cardinal; Shock Treatment; The Pleasure Seekers; Bunny Lake is Missing; The Shuttered Room; Danger Route; The Maltese Bippy; Norwood; Once You Kiss a Stranger; The Poseidon Adventure; Cotter; The Cat and the Canary; The Shape of Things to Come; Vigilante.

TV inc: Harlow; Weekend of Terror; Crosscurrent; The Night Stalker; Death Stalk; Willow B-Women in Prison.

LYNN, Ann: Act. b. London, 1934. Films inc: Piccadilly Third Stop; The Wind of Change; Strongroom; Flame in the Streets; Black Torment; Four in the Morning; Baby Love; Hitler - The Last Ten Days.

TV inc: The Cheaters; After the Show; All Summer Long; Trump Card; The Zoo Gang.

LYNN, Jeffrey (Ragnar Godfrey Lind): Act. b. Auburn, MA, Feb 16, 1909. e. Bates Coll, BA. High school teacher before appearing in stock. Bway inc: Cyrano de Bergerac; Brother Rat; The Moon is Blue; Teahouse of The August Moon; Dinner at Eight (rev).

Films inc: Four Daughters; Cowboy From Brooklyn; Yes My Darling Daughter; Daughters Courageous; Espionage Agent; The Roaring Twenties; Four Wives; A Child is Born; The Fighting 69th; It All Came True; All This and Heaven Too; Four Mothers; Million Dollar Baby; The Body Disappears; Underground; For the Love of Mary; Whiplash; A Letter to Three Wives; Strange Bargain; Captain China; Up Front; Come Thursday; Lost Lagoon; Butterfield 8; Tony Rome.

TV inc: Secret Storm.

LYNN, Judy: Act. b. Boise, ID, Apr 12, 1936. C&W recording artist; appeared with Grand Ole Opry.

TV inc: Judy Lynn Show.

LYNN, Loretta (nee Webb): Act. b. Butchers Hollow, KY, Apr 14, 1935. C&W recording artist. Toured US, Europe; joined Grand Ole Opry.

TV inc: A Country Christmas, 1979; George Burns In Nashville?; A Country Christmas, 1980; Loretta Lynn-The Lady, The Legend; Country Comes Home; Loretta Lynn in Big Apple Country; Conway Twitty on the Mississippi; Happy Birthday, Bob. (Grammy-country vocal-1971).

LYNNE, Gillian: Chor-dir. b. England, 1951. Stage debut as dancer with Sadler's Wells Ballet; remained with the company seven years. Appeared as act-dancer in Can Can; Becky Sharp; Queen of Catland before becoming chor & dir. Thea inc: Round Lester Square; Collages; The Matchgirls; The Roar of the Greasepaint (Bway-Chor); Pickwick (Bway-Chor); Bluebeard; Love on the Dole; Tonight At Eight; Lilywhite Lies; Ambassador; Once Upon A Time; Liberty Ranch; The Papertown Chase; The Card (chor); Hans Christian Anderson; Once In A Lifetime; Jeeves Takes Charge; Cats; (asso dir-chor) (& Bway).

Films inc: (chor) Half A Sixpence; Man of La Mancha; Quilp.

LYNTON-WILLIAMS, David Bruce: Exec. b. Sydney, Australia, Nov 23, 1925. e. Sydney U. M dir, Greater Union Organisation, Pty, Ltd.

LYON, Francis D.: Dir. b. Bowbells, ND, Jul 29, 1905. e. UCLA. Started as edtr. Films inc: Shape of Things to Come; Knight Without Armor; Intermezzo; Adam Had Four Sons; The Great Profile; Daytime Wife; Body and Soul (Oscar-1947); He Ran All the Way. (Dir) Crazylegs; The Bob Mathias Story; Cult of the Cobra; The Great Locomotive Chase; The Oklahoman; Gunsight Ridge; Bail out at 43,000; Escort West; Cinerama South Seas Adventure; The Tomboy and the Champ; Destination Inner Space; The Destructors; The Money Jungle; The Girl Who Knew Too Much; Tiger By the Tail.

TV inc: Laramie; Zane Grey Theatre; Perry Mason; Bus Stop; M Squad; Wells Fargo.

LYON, Ron: Prod-Exec. Asso prod at MGM 1970-1973; formed Ronald Lyon Prodns 1973; joined with Jim Aubrey in Aubrey-Lyon Prodns 1976; joined MGM-TV Feb 1980; Sept 1980 became P Rastar Televison.

TV inc: The Other Side of Hell; Love's Savage Fury; City In Fear; Ripley's Believe It or Not!; Sins Of The Father.

LYON, Sue: Act. b. Davenport, IA, Jul 10, 1946. Films inc: Lolita; Seven Women; Night of the Iguana; The Flim Flam Man; Evel Knievel; Crash!; End of the World; Who Stole My Wheels?; Invisible Strangler (made in 1979 as The Astral Factor).

LYONS, Stuart: Prod. b. Manchester, England, Dec 27, 1928. e. Manchester U, BA. Asst dir TV, 1955-56; casting dir Associated British, 1956-60; joined 20th Century-Fox Prodns as casting dir, 1963; apptd dir 20th Century-Fox Prodns Ltd, 1967; M dir 1968; left Fox 1971 on closure European prodn. Joined Hemdale Group as head of prodn, 1972; left Hemdale 1973 to resume prodn.

Films inc: Those Magnificent Men in Their Flying Machines; High Wind in Jamaica; The Blue Max; The Slipper and the Rose; Meetings with Remarkable Men.

MABRY, Moss: Cos Dsgn. b. FL, Jul 5. Desgd more than 75 films inc: Giant; The Manchurian Candidate; What A Way To Go; Morituri; The Cactus Flower; Butterflies Are Free; The Way We Were; King Kong; Casey's Shadow; The One and Only; Sunburn; Continental Divide; Beyond Reason.

MacARTHUR, James: Act. b. Los Angeles, CA, Dec 8, 1937. e. Harvard. S of Helen Hayes and Charles MacArthur. Films inc: The Young Stranger; The Light in the Forest; Kidnapped; Swiss Family Robinson; The Interns; Spencer's Mountain; Angry Breed.

TV inc: Strike a Blow; Hawaii Five-0; Alcatraz--The Whole Shocking Story; The Night the Bridge Fell Down.

MacCORKINDALE, Simon: Act. b. England, Feb. 12, 1953. H of Susan George. Films inc: Death on the Nile; Riddle of the Sands; Quatermass Conclusion; Caboblanco; The Sword And The Sorcerer; Jaws 3-D; Robbers of the Sacred Mountain (Falcons Gold).

TV inc: I Claudius; The Life and Times of Shakespeare; Just Williams; Romeo and Juliet; Within These Walls; Baby; Three Weeks; Jesus of Nazareth; The Manions of America; Manimal; Falcon Crest; Obsessive Love.

Thea inc: The Dark Lady of the Sonnets; Pygmalion; French Without Tears; The Importance of Being Oscar.

MacGRAW, Ali: Act. b. Pound Ridge, NY, Apr 1, 1939. Began career as a model. Films inc: Goodbye Columbus; Love Story; The Getaway; Convoy; Players; Just Tell Me What You Want.

TV inc: The Winds of War; China Rose.

MACHT, Stephen: Act. b. Philadelphia, May 1, 1942. e. Dartmouth; Tufts; U of IN, PhD. Films inc: Ring of Passion; The Choirboys; Nightwing; The Mountain Men; Galaxina; Hakhoref Ha'Acharon (The Last Winter).

TV inc: The Tenth Level; Raid on Entebbe; Amelia Earhart; Big Hawaii; The Immigrants; Enola Gay--The Men, The Mission, The Atomic Bomb; American Dream; Killjoy; Knots Landing; A Caribbean Mystery; Samson and Delilah; Flight 90--Disaster on the Potomac; George Washington; A Contract For Life--The S.A.D.D. Story.

Thea inc: When You Comin' Back, Red Ryder; A Man For All Seasons.

MACKAILL, Dorothy: Act. b. Hull, England, 1903. Began as chorus girl at London Hippodrome; came to U.S., joined Ziegfeld's Midnight Follies; replaced Marilyn Miller in Sally, spotted by Marshall Neilan and brought to Hollywood.

Films inc: The Lotus Eaters; Twenty One; Dancer of Paris; Convoy; Children of the Ritz; Once a Sinner; Lady Be Good; Kept Husbands; No Man of Her Own; Bulldog Drummond at Bay; The Man Who Came Back.

MacKENZIE, Giselle: Singer. b. Winnipeg, Canada, Jan 10, 1927. With CBC 1946-1950; to U.S. 1951.

TV inc: Bob Crosby Show; Mario Lanza; Your Hit Parade; Giselle MacKenzie Show; Kraft Theatre; General Electric Theatre; Studio One.

MACKENZIE, John: Dir. b. Edinburgh, Scotland. e. Edinburgh U. TV inc: Voices in the Park; Profile of a Gentleman; Rain; Bangelstein Boys; Just Another Saturday; Double Dare; The Wild West Show; Passage to England; The Elephant's Graveyard; Talking Blue; Just A Boy's Game; Sense of Freedom.

Films inc: Unman, Wittering and Zigo; One Brief Summer; Made; The Long Good Friday; Beyond the Limit; The Innocent.

MACKIE, Bob: Dsgn. Films inc: Lady Sings the Blues; Funny Lady; Goin' Coconuts; The Villain; All The Marbles; Pennies From Heaven; Staying Alive.

TV inc: Eunice; Baryshnikov In Hollywood; Burnett "Discovers" Domingo; Mama's Family (Emmy-concept-1984).

MacLAINE, Shirley: Act. (nee Beaty)b. Richmond, VA, Apr 24, 1934. S of Warren Beatty. On Bway in chorus of Me and Juliet; understudied Carol Haney in Pajama Game; took over starring role on fourth night when Haney fractured ankle. Signed by Hal Wallis; made screen debut in The Trouble With Harry, 1955.

Films inc: Artists and Models; Around the World in 80 Days; The

Matchmaker; Some Came Running; Can-Can; The Apartment; My Geisha; The Children's Hour; Two for the Seasaw; Irma La Douce; What A Way To Go; John Goldfarb; Please Come Home; Sweet Charity; Two Mules for Sister Sara; Desperate Characters; The Possession of Joel Delaney; The Turning Point; Being There; Loving Couples; A Change of Seasons; Terms of Endearment *(Oscar*-1983); Cannonball Run II.

TV inc: Shirley's World; If They Could See Me Now; *(Emmy*-1976); Shirley Mac Laine at the Lido; Shirley Mac Laine-Every Little Movement; Gypsy In My Soul; Baryshnikov in Hollywood; Shirley MacLaine--Illusions; Shirley MacLaine; AFI Salute To Gene Kelly.

World tour with one-woman show. Prod, co-dir of doc on China, The Other Half of the Sky; April 1984, Shirley MacLaine On Broadway (One-Woman Show).

MacLEOD, Gavin: Act. b. Feb 28, 1931. Films inc: I Want To Live; Compulsion; Operation Petticoat; McHale's Navy; The Sand Pebbles; Deathwatch; The Party; Kelly's Heroes.

TV inc: Hogan's Heroes; Mary Tyler Moore Show; The Love Boat; Captains and the Kings; Alan King's Third Annual Final Warning; Murder Can Hurt You; Scruples; "I Love T.V." Test (host); Dean Martin's Celebrity Roast.

MacMAHON, Aline: Act. b. McKeesport, PA, May 3, 1899. Screen debut 1931 Five Star Final.

Films inc: The Mouthpiece; Life Begins; Once In A Lifetime; Gold Diggers of 1933; Heroes For Sale; Babbitt; Kind Lady; Ah, Wilderness; When You're In Love; Back Door to Heaven; The Lady Is Willing; Dragon Seed; Guest In the House; The Search; The Flame and the Arrow; The Eddie Cantor Story; The Man from Laramie; All the Way Home.

Bway inc: The Dover Road; Artists and Models; Beyond the Horizon; Once in a Lifetime; Eve of St. Mark; Galileo; Cyrano De Bergerac; The Crucible; Trelawny of the Wells.

MacMURRAY, Fred: Act. b. Kankakee, IL, Aug 30, 1908. Sang, played with band. Also performed in vaudeville, niteries. On screen since 1935.

Films inc: The Gilded Lily; The Trail of the Lonesome Pine; Maid of Salem; Cafe Society; Dive Bomber; Above Suspicion; Double Indemnity; Captain Eddie; The Egg and I; The Caine Mutiny; The Apartment; The Absent Minded Professor; The Happiest Millionaire; Charley and the Angel; The Shaggy Dog; Kisses For My President; Son of Flubber; The Swarm; George Stevens--A Filmmaker's Journey (Doc-int).

TV inc: My Three Sons.

MACNAUGHTON, Robert: Act. b. Dec 19, 1966. TV inc: Angel City; The Electric Grandmother; Big Bend Country; Hear Me Cry.

Films inc: E.T. The ExtraTerrestrial; I Am The Cheese.

Thea inc: The Diviners; Henry V.

MacNEE, Patrick: Act. b. London, 1922. Films inc: The Life and Death of Colonel Blimp; Hamlet; Flesh and Blood; Three Cases of Murder; Les Girls; Incense for the Damned; The Sea Wolves; The Howling; The Creature Wasn't Nice; Young Doctors In Love; Hot Touch; Sweet Sixteen; Spinal Tap; A View To A Kill.

TV inc: Mr Jericho; The Avengers; The New Avengers; The Billion Dollar Threat; Stunt Seven; Comedy of Horrors; Rehearsal For Murder; Gavilan; Return of the Man from U.N.C.L.E.; For the Term of His Natural Life; Automan; Empire.

MacNEIL, Robert: TV newsman. b. Montreal, Canada, Jan. 9, 1931. e. Dalhousie U; Carleton U. Worked for CBS before moving to England for Reuters; 1960 joined NBC News as London corr; 1963, Washington bureau; 1964, co-anchor Scherer-MacNeil Report; 1967 joined BBC Panorama news pgm; 1968 joined Public Broadcasting Laboratory.

TV inc: The Big Ear; The Right to Bear Arms; The Whole World is Watching; America 73; Senate Watergate Hearings *(Emmy*-1974); The MacNeil-Lehrer Report; Goodbye America; Mountbatten; Edward the King; Artur Rubenstein at 90; A Conversation With Miss Lillian.

MacNICOL, Peter: Act. b. TX, 1957. In rep with Guthrie Theatre. Bway inc: Crimes of the Heart.

Films inc: Dragonslayer; Sophie's Choice.

MacRAE, Gordon: Act. b. E Orange, NJ, Mar 12, 1921. Performed in

stock, radio, TV. On screen from 1948.

Films inc: Look for the Silver Lining; The Daughter of Rosie O'-Grady; Tea for Two; West Point Story; On Moonlight Bay; By the Light of the Silvery Moon; The Desert Song; Oklahoma!; Carousel; The Best Things in Life Are Free.

TV inc: 100 Years of Golden Hits; Bob Hope's All-Star Celebration Opening the Gerald R. Ford Museum.

MacRAE, Meredith: Act. b. Houston, TX, 1945. D of Gordon MacRae. Film debut age seven as extra, By The Light Of The Silvery Moon.

Films inc: Beach Party; Bikini Beach; Footsteps in the Snow; Norwood; Chinese Caper; Grand Jury; Earthbound; I'm Going to be Famous; My Friends Need Killing (made in 1976); The Census Taker.

TV inc: My Three Sons; The Young Marrieds; Petticoat Junction.

MacRAE, Sheila (nee Stephens): Act. b. London, Sep 24. TV inc: Jackie Gleason Show; Sheila MacRae Show; The Secret War of Jackie's Girls; Goldie and the Boxer Go to Hollywood; Search For Tomorrow.

Thea inc: O.K. (off-Bway).

MACY, Bill (William Macy Garber): Act. b. Revere, MA, May 18, 1922. e. NYU. Films inc: The Late Show; The Jerk; Serial; My Favorite Year; Movers & Shakers.

TV inc: Maude; Moviola (The Scarlett O'Hara War); The Day The Bubble Burst.

Bway inc: The Threepenny Opera; The Balcony; America Hurrah; The Cannibals; Oh, Calcutta!; And Miss Reardon Drinks a Little; The Roast.

MADDEN, John: TV Sports. b. Austin, MN, Apr. 10, 1936. e. Cal Poly, BA, MA. Coached Oakland Raiders pro football team for 10 years before becoming CBS Sports broadcaster. Analyst on CBS telecasts of NFL games *(Emmys*-1982, 1983); CBS Sports Saturday/Sunday.

MADIGAN, Amy: Act. b. Chicago, IL, 1957. e. Chicago Conservatory of Music; studied with Lee Strasberg. Thea inc: Prairie Avenue; In the Boom Boom Room.

TV inc: Crazy Times; Victims; Ambush Murders; Travis McGee; The Day After; Eureka Stockade; The Laundromat (PC).

Films inc: Love Child; My Love Letters; Streets of Fire; Places In The Heart; Alamo Bay.

MADISON, Guy (Robert Moseley): Act. b. Bakersfield, CA, Jan 19, 1922. Films inc: Since You Went Away; Till the End of Time; Honeymoon; Texas; Drums in the Deep South; Hilda Crane; Adventures of Tortuga; Duel at Rio Bravo; Shatterhand.

TV inc: The Rebels.

MAGEE, James E.: Wri. b. Chicago, IL. e. Loyola U, Chicago. Creator & Pres International Producers Center, Grand Bahama; Pres Media Finance Corp; vp Cinemerica Satellite Network.

TV inc: Jerry Lester Show; GE Theatre; Schiltz Playhouse; Zane Grey Theatre; Four Star Playhouse; Jackie Gleason Show; Bob Newhart Show; Tonight Show.

MAGIDSON, Herb: Comp. b. Braddock, PA, Jan 7, 1906. e. U of Pittsburgh. Film inc: The Great Ziegfeld; Life of the Party; Music in Manhattan; Sing Your Way Home.

Songs inc: The Continental *(Oscar*-1934); Music, Maestro, Please; Gone With the Wind; Enjoy Yourself (It's Later Than You Think); Say A Prayer For The Boys Over There; The Masquerade Is Over; Roses In December; I'll Buy That Dream; A Pink Cocktail For A Blue Lady.

MAGUIRE, Charles H.: Exec. b. NYC. e. Fordham U. Started as asst dir, later unit mgr, prodn mgr. VP Athena Enterprises Corp, 1954-1978; exec prodn conslutnt & prod, WB, 1967-1970; exec prod Dogwood Prodns 1978-1979; named vp & exec prodn mgr features div Par 1980. Films inc: (asso prod) America, America; The Sand Pebbles; Bye Bye Braverman; The Arrangement; Fuzz; The Friends of Eddie Coyle; The Parallax View; Shampoo; Audrey Rose. (prod) I Love You Alice B Toklas. (Exec prod) Heaven Can Wait.

MAHARIS, George: Act. b. Sep 1, 1928. Films inc: Exodus; Sylvia; Quick Before It Melts; The Satan Bug; Covenant With Death; The Happening; The Desperadoes; The Sword And The Sorcerer.

TV inc: Route 66; The Most Deadly Game; Rich Man, Poor Man.

MAHIN, John Lee: Wri. b. Evanston, IL, 1902. Films inc: Scarface; Captains Courages; Naughty Marietta; Treasure Island; Too Hot to Handle; Dr Jekyll and Mr Hyde; Red Dust; Boom Town; Tortilla Flat; Down to the Sea in Ships; Quo Vadis; Johnny Eager; Elephant Walk; Mogambo; Heaven Knows Mr Allison; Bad Seed; The Horse Soldiers (& prod); The Spiral Road; Moment to Moment.

(Died April 18, 1984).

MAHONEY, Jock (Jacques O'Mahoney): Act. b. Chicago, Feb 7, 1919. e. U of IA. Films inc: The Doolins of Oklahoma; A Day of Fury; Away All Boats; I've Lived Before; A Time to Love and a Time to Die; Tarzan the Magnificent; Tarzan Goes to India; Tarzan's Three Challenges; The Walls of Hell; The End.

TV inc: The Range Rider; Yancey Derringer.

MAIBAUM, Richard: Wri-Prod. b. NYC, May 26, 1909. e. NYU; U of IA, BA, MA. Films inc: They Gave Him a Gun; I Wanted Wings; Ten Gentlemen From West Point; O.S.S. (& prod); The Great Gatsby; The Big Clock; Ransom; Cockleshell Heroes; The Day They Robbed the Bank of England; Battle at Bloody Beach; Dr. No; From Russia With Love; Goldfinger; Thunderball; Chitty, Chitty, Bang, Bang; On Her Majesty's Secret Service; Diamonds Are Forever; The Man with the Golden Gun; The Spy Who Loved Me; For Your Eyes Only; Octopussy (wri); A View To A Kill (wri).

Plays inc: The Tree; Birthright; Sweet Mystery of Life; See My Lawyer.

TV inc: Fearful Decision; S*H*E.

MAIN, David: Prod-Dir-Wri. b. Essex, England, 1929. Films inc: Sunday in the Country (sp); It Seemed Like a Good Idea at the Time (sp); Find the Lady (sp & prod); Double Negative (prod).

TV inc: (dir) Moment of Truth; Quentin Durgens M.P.; Famous Jury Trials.

MAJORS, Lee: Act. (nee Yeary):b. Wyandotte, MI, Apr 23, 1939. Films inc: Strait-Jacket; Will Penny; The Liberation of Lord Byron Jones; The Norsemen; Naked Sun; Killer Fish; Agency; Steel (& exec prod); The Last Chase.

TV inc: The Big Valley; The Man from Shiloh; The Ballad of Andy Crocker; Owen Marshall, Counselor-at-Law; The Six-Million Dollar Man; The Bionic Woman; Weekend of Terry; The Gary Francis Powers Story; High Noon Part II--The Return of Will Kane; The Fall Guy (& co-prod); Starflight--The Plane That Couldn't Land; America's Heroes--The Athlete Chronicles (host); The Cowboy and the Ballerina (& exec prod).

MAKAROVA, Natalia: Dancer. b. Leningrad, Russia, Nov 21, 1940. With Leningrad Kirov Ballet; toured to Britain, U.S.; Defected 1970, joined American Ballet Theatre; danced with Nureyev. Roles inc: Giselle; Swan Lake; Les Sylphides; Sleeping Beauty.

Bway inc: On Your Toes (& London) (Tony-1983). TV inc: The President's Command Performance.

MAKAVEJEV, Dusan: Dir. b. Yugoslavia, Oct 13, 1932. e. Belgrade U. Made several shorts, dox for Zagreb Studios before feature debut. Films inc: Man Is Not A Bird; Love Affair (An Affair of The Heart); Innocence Unprotected; WR; Mysteries of the Organism; Sweet Movie; Montenegro (Pigs and Pearls); The Coca-Cola Kid.

MAKEBA, Miriam: Singer. b. Johannesburg, S Africa, Mar 4, 1932. Brought to the US by Harry Belafonte, 1959, to appear with his group. Then made recordings, appeared on radio, TV. Films inc: Amok (act & music) (Grammy-Folk Recording-1965).

MAKO (Mako Iwamatsu): Act. b. Dec. 10, 1933.Films inc: The Ugly Dachshund; The Sand Pebbles; The Private Navy of Sgt O'Farrell; The Hawaiians; Tora! Tora! Tora!; The Killer Elite; Prisoners; The Big Brawl; Under the Rainbow; An Eye For An Eye; The Bushido Blade; Conan The Barbarian; Testament; Conan the Destroyer.

TV inc: When Hell Was in Session; The Last Ninja; Girls of the White Orchid; Hawaiian Heat.

Bway inc: Pacific Overtures.

MALDEN, Karl (Mladen Sekulovich): Act. b. Gary, IN, Mar 22, 1914. Screen debut 1940 They Knew What they Wanted.

Films inc: Boomerang; The Gunfighter; A Streetcar Name Desire (Oscar-supp-1951); Ruby Gentry; Desperate Hours; The Hanging Tree; On the Waterfront; Bombers B-52; Fear Strikes Out; Time Limit (dir only); One Eyed Jacks; How the West Was Won; Patton; Meteor; Beyond The Poseidon Adventure; The Sting II; Twilight Time.

Bway: Golden Boy; Key Largo; All My Sons; Meteor; A Streetcar Named Desire; Desperate Hours.

TV inc: The Streets of San Francisco; Skag; Word of Honor; Miracle On Ice; With Intent To Kill; Fatal Vision; Kennedy Center Honors 1984.

MALICK, Terrence: Dir-Wri. b. IL, Nov 30, 1944. e. Harvard U; Oxford U. Films inc: Deadhead Miles (wri); Badlands; Days of Heaven.

MALKOVICH, John: Act. b. IL., 1955. Co-founder of Steppenwolf Theatre Company. Thea inc: Of Mice And Men; The Glass Menagerie; Say Goodnight Gracie; Fifth of July; Curse Of the Starving Class; True West; Balm In Gilead (dir); Death Of A Salesman (Bway); Arms And The Man (dir)(Bway).

Films inc: Places In The Heart; The Killing Fields.

TV inc: True West; Say Goodnight Gracie.

MALLE, Louis: Dir. b. Thumeries, France, Oct 30, 1932. Started as cin. Co-dir Oscar-winning doc, The Silent World. Doc inc: Humain, Trop Humain; Vive Le Tour; Phantom India; Calcutta; Place de la Republique.

Films inc: Elevator to the Gallows; The Lovers; Zazie dans le Metro; Vie Privee; Viva Maria; The Fire Within; The Thief; Le Souffle au Coeur; Lacombe, Lucien; Black Moon; Pretty Baby (& prod-sp); Atlantic City, USA; My Dinner With Andre; Before the Nickelodeon--The Early Cinema of Edwin S Porter (voice); Crackers; Der Waag Naar Bresson (The Way to Bresson) (Doc-int); Alamo Bay (& prod).

MALLORY, Victoria: Act. b. Fort Lee, VA, Sep 20, 1948. e. AMDA. Bway inc: West Side Story (rev); Carnival (rev); Follies; A Little Night Music.

TV inc: After Hours--Singin', Swingin' and All That Jazz; The Emperor's New Clothes; Aladdin; The Young and the Restless.

MALMUTH, Bruce: Dir. b. Brooklyn, NY, Feb 4, 1937. e. Brooklyn Coll, B.A.; Columbia; USC. Film inc: Nighthawks; The Man Who Wasn't There (& act). TV inc: Heartbreak Winner.

MALONE, Dorothy: Act. b. Chicago, IL, Jan 30, 1930. Screen debut 1946, The Big Sleep.

Films inc: Young at Heart; Battle Cry; Written on the Wind (Oscar-supp-1956); Man of a Thousand Faces; The Last Voyage; Warlock; Fate Is the Hunter; Winter Kills; Good Luck Miss Wyckoff; The Day Time Ended.

TV inc: Dr. Kildare; The Untouchables; The Greatest Show on Earth; Peyton Place; Condominium; The Being; He's Not Your Son; Peyton Place--The Next Generation.

MALTBY, Richard E.: Comp-Cond-Mus. b. Chicago, Jun 26, 1914. e. Northwestern U. Cond of own orch, 1945; recording artist. Works inc: Requiem for John F Kennedy.

MALTBY, Richard Jr: Dir-Wri-Lyr. b. Oct 1937. e. Yale, BA. Thea inc: (Dir) Glass Menagerie; Long Day's Journey Into Night; staged Geraldine Fitzgerald tour of Street Songs; Daarlin' Juno; Starting Here, Starting Now; Ain't Misbehavin' (conceived & dir) (Tony-dir-1978); Baby (lyr & dir);3 Guys Naked From The Waist Down (prod); Hang On To The Good Times (conceived & dir).

MALTZ, Albert: Wri. b. NYC, Oct 28, 1908. e. Columbia Coll, AB. Films inc: This Gun for Hire; Destination Tokyo; Pride of the Marines; Cloak and Dagger; Naked City; (career interrupted when he served year in jail for refusing to testify before Un-American Activities Committee 1950, subsequently on blacklist for years); Two Mules for Sister Sara.

Special Oscar for writing The House I Live In, (Doc) 1945. Also wrote Oscar-winning Moscow Strikes Back (Doc).

(Died April 26, 1985)

MAMET, David: Plywri. b. Chicago, IL. e. Goddard College. H. of Lindsay Crouse. Co-founder Dinglefest Theatre Company; associate artistic dir Goodman Theatre, Chicago. Plays inc; Lakefront; The Woods; A Life in the Theatre; Water Engine; American Buffalo; Sexual Perversity in Chicago; Duck Variations; The Long Canoe; Edmond; Glengarry Glen Ross *(Pulitzer*-1984); The Spanish Prisoner; The Shawl.
Films inc: The Postman Always Rings Twice; The Verdict.

MAMOULIAN, Rouben: Dir. b. Russia, Oct 8, 1897. e. Lycee Montaigne, Paris; Moscow U (law). Stage dir since 1918. Came to US in 1923. Prod dir, Eastman Theatre, Rochester, NY, 1923-26. After that dir operas, operettas, musicals.
Films inc: Applause; City Streets; Dr. Jekyll and Mr. Hyde; Song of Songs; Queen Christine; Gay Desperado; Becky Sharp; Golden Boy; Mark of Zorro; Blood and Sand; Summer Holiday; Silk Stockings; Never Steal Anything Small (co-author); George Stevens--A Filmmaker's Journey (doc-int).
Bway inc: Porgy; Marco's Millions; Wings Over Europe; Sadie Thompson; Farewell to Arms; Porgy and Bess; Oklahoma!; Carousel; St. Louis Woman; Lost in the Stars; Arms and the Girl.

MANCHESTER, Melissa: Singer. b. Bronx, NY, Feb 15, 1951. e. Performing Arts High School. Singer with Bette Midler before going solo.
Recordings inc: Home to Myself; Bright Eyes; Melissa; Better Days and Happy Endings; Help is on the Way; You Should Hear How She Talks About You *(Grammy*-pop vocal-1982).
Bway inc: Dancin'.
TV inc: I'll Be Home for Christmas; Bob Hope's Spring Fling Of Glamour and Comedy; I Love Liberty; A Concert of the World.
Films inc: The Last Starfighter (sngwri).

MANCINI, Henry: Comp-Arr-Cond. b. Cleveland, OH, Apr 16, 1924. Film scores inc: Breakfast at Tiffany's *(Oscars*-score and song-Moon River-1962); Days of Wine and Roses *(Oscar*-song-1963); Hatari; The Pink Panther; Charade; Two for the Road; Darling Lili; Sunflower; Alex and the Gypsy; W.C. Fields and Me; The Pink Panther Strikes Again; Silver Streak; House Calls; Revenge of the Pink Panther; Who Is Killing The Great Chefs of Europe; Nightwing; The Prisoner of Zenda; A Change of Seasons; Back Roads; S.O.B; Condorman; Mommie Dearest; Victor/Victoria *(Oscar*-1982); Trail of the Pink Panther; Second Thoughts; Curse of the Pink Panther; Better Late Than Never; The Man Who Loved Women; Harry & Son; Angela; That's Dancing!; Lifeforce.
TV inc: The Shadow Box; Live From Studio 8H--100 Years of America's Popular Music; Ripley's Believe It or Not; Pink At First Sight; 100 Years of Golden Hits. Remington Steele; Newhart; The Thorn Birds; Arthur Hailey's "Hotel"; Olympic Gala (perf).
Bway inc: A Woman of Independent Means.
Guest cond with the leading symphony orchestras in the US and around the world. *(Grammys*-(20)-record of the year-1961, 1963; song of the year-1961, 1963; album of the year-1958; arrangement-1958, 1960, 1961; inst arr-1962, 1964, 1969, 1970; orch-1960, 1961; Jazz group-1960; soundtrack-1961; background arr-1963; inst composition-1964; inst perf-1964; contemporary inst perf-1970).

MANCUSO, Frank: Exec. b. Buffalo, NY, Jul 25, 1933. Started in exhib; film buyer Basil Circuit; 1962 booker Buffalo branch Par; 1964 branch sales rep; 1967 branch mgr; 1970, vp-gen sls mgr Par Canada; 1972, P Par Canada; 1976 Par Western Div mgr, hq in LA; 1977, gen sls mgr, NY, later vp dom dist Par; 1979, mktg & dist vp; Jan 1983 P of entire Par motion picture division; Sept. 1984, Chmn & CEO.

MANCUSO, Frank, Jr.: Prod. b. Buffalo, NY, Oct. 9, 1958. e. Upsala College. Worked in booking and legal depts of Par before serving as location asst on Urban Cowboy. Films inc: Friday the 13th, Part II (asso prod); Off the Wall; Friday the 13th Part III; The Man Who Wasn't There; Friday the 13th--The Final Chapter; Friday The 13th--A New Beginning.

MANDAN, Robert: Act. b. Clever, MO, Feb 2. e. Pomona Coll; NYU. TV inc: Search for Tomorrow; One Day at a Time; Caribe; Soap; You Can't Take it With You; Goldie and the Boxer Go to Hollywood; Return

of the Rebels; Private Benjamin; In Love With An Older Woman; For Members Only; The Outlaws; Three's A Crowd.
Bway inc: There's a Girl in My Soup; Applause.
Films inc: The Best Little Whorehouse in Texas; Zapped!.

MANDEL, John Alfred (Johnny): Comp-Arr-Cond. b. NYC, Nov 23, 1935. Trumpeter, trombonist with numerous orchs.
Film scores inc: You're Never Too Young; I Want to Live; The Americanization of Emily; The Sandpiper; Harper; The Russians Are Coming, the Russians Are Coming; An American Dream; Deadly Hero; Agatha; The Baltimore Bullet; Caddyshack; Deathtrap; Soup For One; Lookin' To Get Out; The Verdict.
Songs inc: Emily; The Shadow of your Smile *(Oscar*-1965); A Time for Love.
TV inc: Markham; GE Theatre; Too Close For Comfort; Evita Peron; AfterMASH.
Bway inc: Peg (orchs).
(Grammys-(3)-song & soundtrack album-1965; inst arr-1981).

MANDELKER, Philip: Exec Prod. b. NYC, May 18, 1938. e. Northwestern U. Dir daytime pgmg CBS, 1971; dir primetime dvlpt ABC, 1972; exec prod Warner Bros TV, 1973-79; exec prod, Time-Life Films, Inc, 1979.
TV inc: The New Land; The Dark Side of Innocence; Sidekicks; The Possessed; The Fitzpatricks; Champions--A Love Story; The Dukes of Hazzard; Sex and the Single Parent; Cruisin'; Amber Waves; The Women's Room; Blinded By the Light; Freedom; Dream House (& wri); Mae West; Dreams Don't Die; Tucker's Witch; Having It All; High School U.S.A.; Girls of the White Orchid; The Parade.
(Died March 26, 1984).

MANDELL, Abe: Exec. b. Oct 4, 1922. e. U of Cincinnati, BA. Worked as act. briefly before WW2; after serving in Army in Southwest Pacific, formed indie film distribution company in Far East in 1947; retd to US 1957, joined Ziv TV in network sls; joined Independent Television Corp. (now ITC Entertainment Inc.,) 1958 as dir Foreign ops; 1960, vp foreign ops; later vp wldwde sls; 1962 exec vp; 1965, P; became P of US ops July 1982 following takeover of Company, also named to exec board of mgt. of Associated Communications Corp; resd, June 1983.

MANDRELL, Barbara: Act. b. Houston, TX, Dec 25, 1948. Recording artist; niteries. *(Grammy*-Inspirational-1982).
TV inc: Merry Christmas From the Grand Ole Opry House; The Concrete Cowboys; Elvis Remembered-Nashville to Hollywood; Bob Hope's Birthday Party; John Schneider--Back Home; Barbara Mandrell and the Mandrell Sisters; All-Star Salute To Mother's Day; Good Evening, Captain; An Evening with the Statler Bros.--A Salute to the Good Times; Bob Hope's Stand Up and Cheer for the National Football League's 60th Year; Country Comes Alive; Country Gold; Conway Twitty on the Mississippi; Happy Birthday, Bob; Louise Mandrell--Diamonds, Gold & Platinum; The Mac Davis Special--The Music of Christmas; Ringling Bros. and Barnum & Bailey Circus (emcee); On Stage America; Burning Rage.

MANGANO, Silvana: Act. b. Rome, April 23. 1930. W of Dino De Laurentiis. Films inc: Bitter Rice; Ulysses; The Sea Wall; Gold of Naples; Tempest; Five Branded Women; Barabbas; Theorem; The Decameron; Death in Venice; Oedipus Rex; Ludwig; The Great War; Anna; Mamo; Witches; Dune.

MANGIONE, Chuck: Comp-Mus. b. Rochester, NY, Nov 29, 1940. Formed jazz quartet; toured Europe. Recording artist. Film scores inc: The Children of Sanchez. TV theme music for: The Dorothy Hamill Special; ABC Super Stars; ABC Wide World of Sports; NBC Tomorrow Show; World Championship Tennis; London and Davis In New York.
(Grammys-(2)-inst comp-1976; pop inst perf-1978).

MANILOW, Barry: Act-Sngwri. b. Brooklyn, Jun 17, 1946. e. NY Coll of Music; Juilliard. Started with CBS TV in mailroom, became night flm ed, arranged new musical theme for The Late Show; left CBS to do nitery tour with Jeanie Lucas; mus dir Callback, WCBS-TV; mus dir Ed Sullivan Prodns; mus dir off-Bway prodn The Drunkard; wrote & sang commercials for radio, tv; mus dir for Bette Midler; went solo as recording artist, perf; two-week stand at Uris Theatre, NY *(Special*

Tony-1977); (Grammy-male vocal-1979).

TV inc: Barry Manilow Specials (Emmy-variety show-1977); Laugh Trax; Live--And In Person.

Films inc: Tribute (mus). TV inc: Goldie And Kids--Listen To Us.

Songs inc: Sweet Life; I Am Your Child; Sweetwater Jones; Could It Be Magic?

Albums inc: This One's For You; Barry Manilow Live; Even Now; Greatest Hits; One Voice.

MANKIEWICZ, Don: Wri. b. Berlin, Jan 20, 1922. e. Columbia U, BA. S of late Herman J Mankiewicz. Films inc: Trial; House of Numbers; I Want to Live.

TV inc: On Trial; One Step Beyond; Profiles in Courage; Ironside; Sarge; Lanigans Rabbi; Father Brown, Detective; I Want To Live; Murder Ink.

MANKIEWICZ, Frank: Wri-Exec. b. NYC, May 16, 1924. e. UCLA, AB; Columbia, MS; Berkeley, LLB. S of late Herman Mankiewicz. Syndicated columnist, TV commentator. P National Public Radio 1977; resd May 1983.

MANKIEWICZ, Joseph L.: Prod-Wri-Dir. b. Wilkes-Barre, PA, Feb 11, 1909. e. Columbia U. B of late Herman J Mankiewicz. Films inc: (wri) Skippy; Million Dollar Legs; Forsaking All Others; (wri-dir) Dragonwyck; Somewhere in the Night; The Late George Apley; The Ghost and Mrs Muir; A Letter for Three Wives (Oscars-dir & sp-1949); House of Strangers (dir only); No Way Out; All About Eve (Oscars-dir & sp-1950); People Will Talk; Julius Caesar; Five Fingers; The Barefoot Contessa; Guys and Dolls; The Quiet American (& prod); Suddenly Last Summer (dir only); Cleopatra; The Honey Pot; There Was a Crooked Man; Sleuth (dir only). (As prod) Fury; The Bride Wore Red; Three Comrades; Huckleberry Finn; Strange Cargo; The Philadelphia Story; Woman of the Year; The Keys to the Kingdom; George Stevens--A Filmmaker's Journey (doc-int).

MANKIEWICZ, Tom: Wri-Prod-Dir. b. Los Angeles, Jun 1, 1942. e. Exeter Acad; Yale. S of Joseph Mankiewicz. Films inc: (wri) The Sweet Ride; Diamonds Are Forever; Live and Let Die; The Man With The Golden Gun; The Eagle Has Landed; Mother, Jugs & Speed (and co-prod); Ladyhawke; served as creative consultant Superman, the Movie; Superman II.

TV inc: Hart to Hart (dir-wri); Gavilan (crea).

MANKOWITZ, Wolf: Wri. b. London, 1924. Films inc: A Kid for Two Farthings; Expresso Bongo; Waltz of the Toreadors; The Day the Earth Caught Fire; Where the Spies Are; Casino Royale; Dr Faustus; The 25th Hour; Bloomfield; The Hireling; Almonds and Raisins (doc).

TV inc: Make Me an Offer; It Should Happen to a Dog; Conflict; The Killing Stones; The Model Marriage; The Battersea Miracle; Dickens of London.

MANN, Abby: Wri. b. Philadelphia, 1927. e. NYU. Films inc: Judgment at Nuremberg (Oscar-1961); Ship of Fools; A Child Is Waiting; The Detective; War And Love.

TV inc: The Marcus-Nelson Murders (& exec prod) (Emmy-wri-1973); Medical Story (& exec prod); King (& co-prod-dir); This Man Stands Alone; Skag (& exec prod); The Atlanta Child Murders (& exec prod).

MANN, Daniel: Dir. b. NYC, Aug 8, 1912. Films inc: Come Back Little Sheba; About Mrs Leslie; I'll Cry Tomorrow; The Teahouse of the August Moon; Hot Spell; The Last Angry Man; Butterfield 8; Ada; Who's Got the Action?; Who's Been Sleeping in My Bed?; Our Man Flint; For Love of Ivy; Willard; The Revengers; Maurie; Interval; Lost in the Stars.

Bway inc: Come Back Little Sheba; Rose Tattoo; A Streetcar Named Desire; Paint Your Wagon.

Playing For Time; The Day the Loving Stopped.

MANN, Delbert: Dir. b. Lawrence, KS, Jan 30, 1920. e. Vanderbilt U; Yale U; School of Drama. Films inc: Marty (Oscar-1955); Bachelor Party; Desire Under the Elms; Separate Tables; The Dark at the Top of the Stairs; Lover Come Back; That Touch of Mink; A Gathering of Eagles; Quick Before It Melts; Mister Buddwing; The Pink Jungle; Kidnapped; The Birch Interval; Night Crossing; Krull (exec prod); Bronte;

TV inc: TV Playhouse; Producer's Showcase; Omnibus; Playhouse 90; Lights Out; Masterpiece Theatre; Ford Startime; Heidi; David Copperfield; Jane Eyre; The Man Without A Country; A Girl Named Sooner; Torn Between Two Lovers; All Quiet on the Western Front; To Find My Son; All the Way Home; Insight/God's Guerrillas; The Member of the Wedding; The Gift of Love--A Christmas Story; Love Leads The Way; A Death In California.

Bway inc: A Quiet Place; Speaking of Murder; Zelda; Wuthering Heights.

MANN, Johnny (John R): Comp-Cond-Prod. b. Baltimore, Aug 30, 1928. e. Baltimore City Coll; Peabody Cons. Choral dir NBC; arr and cond for various artists inc: Danny Kaye, George Gobel, Julie London; cond The Johnny Mann Singers (Grammys-(2)-chorus-1961, 1967).

Film title song: Hang Up Your Stockin'.

MANN, Larry D.: Act. b. Toronto, Dec 18, 1922. e. Oxford, BA. Films inc: The Singing Nun; The Russians Are Coming, The Russians Are Coming; The Appaloosa; In the Heat of the Night; The Wicked Dreams of Paula Schultz; Oklahoma Crude; Black Eye; The Sting; Pony Express Rider; The Octagon.

TV inc: Columbo; Quincy; Hogan's Heroes; It Takes a Thief; Donovan's Kid; Dennis the Menace--Mayday For Mother (voice).

MANN, Michael: Wri. TV inc: Starsky and Hutch; Police Story; Gibbsville; Bronk; Vega$ (& crea); The Jericho Mile (& dir) (Emmy-wri-1979); Swan Song; Miami Vice (exec prod).

Films inc: (doc) Juanpari; Insurrection; 17 Days Down the Line. (Features) Thief (& exec prod-dir); The Keep (& dir).

MANN, Stanley: Wri. b. Aug 8, 1928. e. McGill U. Films inc: The Mouse That Roared; The Mark; High Wind in Jamaica; The Collector; Naked Runner; Circle of Iron; Damien - Omen II; Meteor; Eye of the Needle; Firestarter. Conan the Destroyer.

TV inc: Draw! (Pc).

MANN, Ted: Exec. b. Wishek, ND, Apr 15, 1916. e. U of MN. Acquired first theatre 1935, St Paul: expanded into other states, 1968, entered film prodn 1973, took over National General Theatres (266 in 27 states).

Films inc: Extreme Close-Up (exec prod); The Illustrated Man (co-prod); Buster and Billie (exec prod); Lifeguard (exec prod); Brubaker (exec prod).

MANN, Theodore (nee Goldman): Prod-Dir. b. Brooklyn, NY, May 13, 1924. e. Columbia U; NYU; Brooklyn Law School. Co-founder Circle in the Square. Bway inc: Summer and Smoke; The Grass Harp; American Gothic; The Iceman Cometh; The Quare Fellow; And Things That Go Bump in the Night; A Moon for the Misbegotten; The Waltz of the Toreadors; Hot L Baltimore; An American Millionaire; Scapino; The Royal Hunt of the Sun; The Zulu and the Zayda; Past Tense; The Caine Mutiny Court Martial (artistic dir); Awake and Sing; Design For Living (artistic dir); The Loves Of Anatol (artistic dir).

MANNE, Shelley: Mus-Comp. b. NYC, Jun 11, 1920. Drummer with various bands inc Bobby Byrne; Bob Astor; Joe Marsala; Raymond Scott; Stan Kenton; Jazz at the Philharmonic; Woody Hermann.

Films inc: (act) I Want To Live; Five Pennies; The Gene Krupa Story. (Scores) Proper Time; The Trial of the Catonsville Nine; Trader Horn.

TV inc: (score) Daktari!

(Died Sept. 26, 1984)

MANNERS, Sam (Savino Maneri): Prod. b. Cleveland, OH, Mar 29, 1921. e. UCLA, BA. TV inc: Before and After; Hot Rod; Dummy; Pearl; Sparrow; Guyana Tragedy-The Story of Jim Jones; The Pride of Jesse Hallam; Divorce Wars--A Love Story; Hardcase.

Films inc: Dead Man's Chest; Mischief.

MANOFF, Dinah: Act. D of Lee Grant. Films inc: Possessed; Grease; Ordinary People; I Ought to Be in Pictures.

TV inc: Like Mother, Like Me; The Great Cherub; Night Drive; Raid on Entebbe; Sweepstakes; Soap; For Ladies Only; A Matter of Sex; Celebrity; Flight 90--Disaster on the Potomac.

Bway inc: I Ought To Be In Pictures (Tony-supp-1980); Leader Of The Pack.

MANSON, Arthur: Exec. b. NYC, Feb 21, 1928. e. CCNY. Prod pub rep, Stanley Kramer Corp, Samuel Goldwyn Prodns, 1950-52; regional ad-pub dir, Stanley Warner Cinerama Corp, 1953-58; worldwide ad-pub dir, 1958-61; adv Mgr, Col, 1961-62; national ad-pub dir, Dino De Laurentiis, 1962-64; exec asst to vp, adv and pub, Fox, 1964-67; worldwide ad-pub VP, Cinerama, Inc, Cinerama Releasing Corp, 1967-74; exec VP, sls mktg, BCP, Feature Film Div of Cox Broadcasting Corp, 1974-75; worldwide ad-pub VP WB, 1976-77; P, Cinemax Marketing and Distributing Corp, 1977.

MANSON, Eddy Lawrence: Comp-Arr. b. NYC, May 9, 1925. e. Juilliard. Harmonica soloist, Town Hall; Carnegie Hall; also on TV and on Russian tour with Ed Sullivan show.
    Film background scores inc: The Little Fugitive; Lovers and Lollipops; Johnny Jupiter; Day of the Painter; The River Nile; Polaris Submarine; The Woman Inside; Tiger Town.
    TV inc: American Spectacle; DuPont, Kraft, Armstrong series.
    Songs and instrumentals: Paisano; Boy on a Carousel; New Gray Mare; Fandango; The Lovers; Cornball Rag; Night Beat; Joey's Theme; Day of the Painter; Theme for Strings.

MANTEE, Paul (nee Marianetti): Act. b. San Francisco, Jan 9, 1936. e. U of CA, BA. Films inc: Robinson Crusoe on Mars; Blood on the Arrow; An American Dream; A Man Called Dagger; They Shoot Horses Don't They?; Day of the Animals; The Greatest; The Manitou; Wolf Lake; The Great Santini.
    TV inc: Fugitive Family; Alcatraz--The Whole Shocking Story; Death Ray 2000.

MANTEGNA, Joe: Act. b. Chicago, Nov. 13, 1947. e. Goodman School of Drama. Thea inc: Hair (natl co.); Godspell (natl co.); A Life In The Theatre; The Disappearance of the Jews; Glengarry Glen Ross (Tony-featured-1984)
    TV inc: Bleacher Bums (& wri); Open All Night; The Outlaws; Now We're Cookin'; Comedy Zone; Bigshots In America.

MANTLEY, John: Exec Prod. b. Toronto, Canada, Apr 25, 1920. e. U of Toronto; Pasadena Playhouse MTA. Started as actor, became live TV prod-dir in early days of TV. Exec prod Gunsmoke 11 years.
    TV inc: Wild Wild West; Dirty Sally; How the West Was Won. Author of more than 50 teleplays and two novels, "27th Day" and "Snow Birch," both made into films.

MANTOOTH, Randolph: Act. b. Sacramento, CA, Sep 19, 1945. e. AADA. TV inc: Marcus Welby, MD; Emergency; The Seekers; Insight/ The Sixth Day.

MANULIS, Martin: Prod. b. NYC, May 30, 1915. e. Columbia U, BA. M, dir, Westport Country Playhouse, 1945-50; staff prod, dir CBS-TV, 1951-58; prod, 20th Century-Fox-TV. P. Martin Manulis Prodns, Ltd.
    Films inc: Days of Wine and Roses; The Out-of-Towners; Luv; Duffy.
    TV inc: Suspense; Studio One; Climax; Best of Broadway; Playhouse 90; The Day Christ Died; The Fighter (exec prod); Chiefs (exec prod); Space.
    Thea inc: Private Lives; Made in Heaven; The Philadelphia Story; Laura; The Men We Marry; The Hasty Heart; The Show Off.

MANZ, Linda: Act. b. NYC, Aug 20, 1961. Films inc: Days of Heaven; King of the Gypsies; Boardwalk; Out of the Blue; The Wanderers;
    TV inc: The Orphan Train.

MANZA, Ralph: Act. b. San Francisco, Dec 1, 1921. e. Berkeley (premed). On Bway in Oh Men, Oh Women, then toured with show, winding up in Hollywood. Films inc: The Wild Party; Dear Heart; Kisses For My President; The Hunters; The Enemy Below; What Did You Do In the War, Daddy?; That Touch of Mink; Blazing Saddles; The Shootist; Love At First Bite; The Cat From Outer Space; Herbie Goes to Monte Carlo; The Apple Dumpling Gang; Fatso; Little Miss Marker.
    TV inc: The D.A's Man; General Hospital; Climax; Matinee Theatre; Banacek; Forever Fernwood; Barney Miller; Mama Malone.

MARA, Adele: Act. b. Dearborn, MI, Apr 28, 1923. Singer, dancer with Xavier Cugat. Films inc: Shut My Big Mouth; Blondie Goes to College; Alias Boston Blackie; Passkey to Danger; Traffic in Crime;

Exposed; Blackmail; Sands of Iwo Jima; Count the Hours; Wake of the Red Witch; Back from Eternity.

MARAIS, Jean (Jean Villain): Act. b. Cherbourg, France, 1913. Films inc: Histoires de ma Vie; L'Eternel Retour; La Belle et la Bete; Les Parents Terrible; Orphee; Le Paria; Peau d'Ane.

MARCANTEL, Chris: Act. b. NY, Jun 7, 1958. e. AADA. Thea inc: Geraniums; Fugue In a Nursery; Missing Persons.
    Films inc: The Warriors; Hair.
    TV inc: Search for Tomorrow; The Guiding Light; As the World Turns; Nurse; Another World; And Baby Comes Home.

MARCEAU, Marcel: Act. b. Strasbourg, France, Mar 22, 1923. Gives concerts as mime.
    Films inc: Barbarella; Shanks; Silent Movie. TV inc: numerous guest shots. (Emmy-specialty act-1955).

MARCH, Donald: Exec. b. NYC, Jul 26, 1942. e. Fordham U, BA. West Coast story ed RSO Films 1974; dir limited series ABC-TV, 1976; vp in chg telefilm CBS 1977; p feature film div Filmways March 1979; returned to CBS Oct. 1979 as vp theatrical films; April 1981, P CBS Theatrical Films Div; ousted June 1981; sr vp HBO Premiere Films, Jan. 1984.

MARCH, Elspeth: Act. b. London, England. Thea inc: The Writing on the Wall; Autumn; Playboy of the Western World; Lady Precious Stream; Duet for Two Hands; The Turn of the Screw; Peace in Our Time; The King of Friday's Men; The Darling Buds of May; Arms and the Man; On the Town; The Wings of the Dove; A Public Mischief; Abelard and Heloise; Parents Day; Snap; Anastasia; The Last of Mrs Cheyney; Underground.
    Films inc: Mr Emmanuel; The Rise and Rise of Michael Rimmer; Promise at Dawn; Goodbye, Mr. Chips; The Magician of Lublin.

MARCHAND, Nancy: Act. b. Buffalo, NY, Jun 19, 1928. Films inc: The Rise and Rise of Michael Rimmer; Promise at Dawn; Goodbye Mr Chips; Ladybug, Ladybug; Me, Natalie; Tell Me That You Love Me, Junie Moon; The Bostonians.
    TV inc: Little Women; Beacon Hill Look Homeward Angel; After the Fall; A Touch of the Poet; Lou Grant (Emmys-supp-1978, 1980, 1981, 1982); Some Kind of Miracle; Willa; Once Upon a Family; The Golden Moment-An Olympic Love Story; Killjoy; Grandpa, Will You Run With Me?; Sparkling Cyanide.
    Bway inc: The Playboy of the Western World; On the Town; The Eccentricities of a Nightingale; The Duel; Parents' Day; Death on Demand; Morning's at Seven; Awake and Sing; The Octette Bridge Club.

MARCOVICCI, Andrea: Act-Singer. b. NYC, Nov 18, 1948. TV inc: The Ascent of Mt. Fuji; Cry Rape ; Some Kind of Miracle; A Vacation in Hell; Packin' It In; Spraggue; Velvet; Berrenger's.
    Films inc: The Front; The Concorde-Airport 79; The Hand; Kings and Desperate Men; Spacehunter--Adventures in the Forbidden Zone.
    Bway inc: Hamlet.

MARCUS, Louis: Prod-Dir-Wri. b. Cork, Ireland, 1936. e. National U of Ireland. Prod & dir for Louis Marcus Documentary Film Prod of Dublin and Louis Marcus Films Ltd of London. Has made more than 30 documentaries.
    Films inc: Woes of Golf; Children at Work; Conquest of Light.

MARGO (Maria Marguerita Guadalupe Boldao y Castilla): Act. b. Mexico City, May 10, 1918. W of Eddie Albert. Performed as dancer with Xavier Cugat. Films inc: Winterset; Lost Horizon; Crime without Passion; Viva Zapata; I'll Cry Tomorrow; From Hell to Texas.

MARGOLIN, Janet: Act. b. NYC, 1943. Films inc: David and Lisa; Bus Riley's Back in Town; The Greatest Story Ever Told; The Saboteur; Nevada Smith; Enter Laughing; Buona Sera Mrs Campbell; Take the Money and Run; Annie Hall; The Last Embrace.
    TV inc: The Triangle Factory Fire Scandal; The Plutonium Incident.

MARGOLIN, Stuart: Act. b. Davenport, IA, Jan 31. TV inc: Love American Style; My World and Welcome to It; Occasional Wife; The Rockford Files (Emmys-supp-1979, 1980); Suddenly, Love (dir); A Shining Season (dir); Bret Maverick; The Long Summer of George

Adams (dir & mus); Mr. Smith; A Killer in the Family; The Glitter Dome (PC)(& prod-dir-mus).

Films inc: Texas Wheelers (dir); Kelly's Heroes; The Gamblers; Limbo; Death Wish; Days of Heaven; S.O.B; Class; Running Hot.

MARGULIES, Stan: Prod. b. NYC, Dec 14, 1920. e. NYU, BS. Publicist RKO; CBS-Radio; 20th Century-Fox; Walt Disney. Bryna Films, 1955; became vp, Bryna 1958; prod aide Spartacus, 1968; vp Wolper Pictures; July 1984 signed exclusive deal with ABC Circle Films.

Films inc: Forty Pounds of Trouble; Those Magnificent Men in their Flying Machines; Don't Just Stand There; The Pink Jungle; If It's Tuesday, This Must Be Belgium; I Love My Wife; Willy Wonka and the Chocolate Factory; One Is A Lonely Number; Visions of Eight.

TV inc: The 500LB Jerk; She Lives; The Morning After; Unwed Father; Men of the Dragon; The Honorable Sam Houston; I Will Fight No More Forever; Collision Course; Roots (Emmy-prod-1977); Roots-The Next Generation (Emmy-1979); Moviola; Murder Is Easy; The Thorn Birds; A Caribbean Mystery; A Killer in the Family (exec prod); Sparkling Cyanide; The Mystic Warrior (exec prod).

MARIELLE, Jean-Pierre: Act. b. Dijon, France, Apr. 12, 1932. Films inc: Tous peuvent me tuer; La brune que voila; Pierrot la tendresse; Le mouton; Faites sauter la banque; Peau de banane (Banana Peel); Echappement libre; Relaxe-toi, Cherie; Week-end a Zuydcoote; La Bonne occase; Cent briques et des tuiles; Monnaie de singe; Tendre voyou; L'homme a la Buick; 48 heures d'amour; L'amour c'est gai, l'amour c'est triste; Les femmes; Le pistonne; Les caprices de Marie; Quatro mosche di velluto grigio; Sans mobile apparent; Sex-shop; L'affaire Crazy Capo; La valise; Que la fete commence (Let Joy Reign Supreme); La Traque; Calmos; On aura tout vu (We've Seen Everything); Cours apres-moi que je t'attrape (Run After Me Until I Catch You); Sturmtruppen (Stormtroopers); L'imprecateur (The Accuser); Plus ca va, moins ca va (The More It Goes, The Less It Goes); Comme la lune (As the Moon); Un moment d'egarement (In A Wild Moment); L'enterloupe (The Swindle); Asphalt; Petrole, Petrole; Coup de torchon (Pop. 1280); L'indiscretion; Signes exterieurs de richesse (Outer Signs of Wealth).

MARIN, Richard (Cheech): Act-Wri. b. Los Angeles, Jul 13, 1946. Teamed with Tommy Chong in improvisational group; spotted by Lou Adler at Hollywood's Troubadour club; began comedy recordings (Grammy-1973).

Films inc: Cheech and Chong's Up in Smoke; Cheech and Chong's Next Movie; Cheech and Chong's Nice Dreams; Things Are Tough All Over; It Came From Hollywood; Cheech and Chong's Still Smoking; Yellowbeard (act); Cheech and Chong's The Corsican Brothers (& wri).

TV Inc; It Only Hurts When You Laugh.

MARKHAM, Monte: Act. b. Manatee, FL, Jun 21, 1938. e. U of GA. Films inc: One Is a Lonely Number; Hour of the Gun; Guns of the Magnificent Seven; Airport '77; Midway; Off The Wall; Separate Ways.

TV inc: The Second Hundred Years; Mr. Deeds Goes to Town; The New Perry Mason; Visions; The Astronaut; Death Takes a Holiday; Hustling; The Littlest Hobo; The Ghosts of Buxley Hall; Drop-Out Father; Hotline; BreakAway (host); Rituals; Finder Of Lost Loves.

Bway inc: Same Time Next Year; Irene.

MARKLE, Fletcher: Wri-Dir-Prod. b. Winnipeg, Canada, Mar 27, 1921. With Canadian Broadcasting Co and BBC, London, 1942-46; prod-dir Studio One series, CBS, 1947-48; wri, edtr, narr of prize-winning documentary short, V-1, Story of the Robot Bomb, 1944.

Films inc: Jigsaw; Night Into Morning; The Man With a Cloak; The Incredible Journey.

TV inc: Life With Father; Front Row Center; Mystery Theatre; Panic; No Warning; M Squad; Buckskin; Rendezvous; Tales of the Vikings; Hong Kong; Father of the Bride; The Play's the Thing; The Olympics.

MARKOVA, Alicia, Dame (Lillian Alicia Marks): Ballerina. b. London, Dec 1, 1910. Studied under Astafieva. Taken into Russian Ballet 1924 by Serge Diaghilev (Song of the Nightingale created for her); first prima ballerina of the Vic-Sadlers Wells (Now Royal) Ballet, 1933-1935; with Anton Dolin formed Markova-Dolin Ballet 1935,

toured United Kingdom until 1938; Ballet Russe de Monte Carlo 1938-1941; Ballet Theatre 1941-1944; reactivated Markova-Dolin ballet 1944-45; formed Festival Ballet 1950 with Dolin; guest artist principal ballets.

MARKS, Alfred, OBE: Act. b. London, 1921. Films inc: Desert Mice; There Was a Crooked Man; Weekend with Lulu; Frightened City; She'll Have to Go; Scream and Scream Again; Our Miss Fred; Valentino; Sleeps Six.

TV inc: Blanding's Castle; Hobson's Choice; Paris 1900; The Memorandum; Alfred Marks Time.

Thea inc: Can Can; Pleasures and Palaces; Dead Silence; Don't Just Lie There, Say Something; The Entertainer; The Sunshine Boys; Bus Stop; Rolls Hyphen Royce; Underground.

MARKS, Arthur: Prod-Dir. b. Los Angeles, Aug 2, 1927. e. USC. Films inc: Togetherness; Bonnie Kids; Roommates; Detroit 9000; A Woman for All Men; Class of '74; Bucktown; Friday Foster; J D's Revenge; Monkey Hustle.

TV inc: (prod-dir) Perry Mason. (dir) I Spy; Mannix; Starsky and Hutch.

MARKS, Richard: Film Edtr. b. NYC, Nov 10, 1943. Films inc: Little Big Man; Bang The Drum Slowly; Lies My Father Told Me; Serpico; Godfather Part II; The Last Tycoon; Apocalypse Now; The Hand; Pennies From Heaven; Max Dugan Returns; Terms of Endearment; The Adventures Of Buckaroo Banzai--Across the 8th Dimension; St. Elmo's Fire.

MARLAND, Douglas: Wri-act. b. West Sand Lake, NY. e. AADA. Former actor. Films inc: (act) The Great Impostor; The Pleasure of His Company; Toward the Light.

TV inc: (act) Brighter Day; The Doctors; As the World Turns. (Wri) Another World (Emmy-1975). General Hospital; Guiding Light (Emmys-1981, 1982); Loving (& co-crea).

MARLEY, John: Act. b. 1919. Bway inc: Enemy of the People; Gramercy Ghost; Sing Me No Lullaby; The Strong Are Lonely; Skipper Next to God; The Investigation.

On screen from 1952. Films inc: My Six Convicts; Faces; Cat Ballou; America, America; Love Story; The Godfather; W C Fields and Me; The Car; The Greatest; Hollywood Stuntmen; Hooper; Tribute; Threshold; Mother Lode; Utilities; Robbers of the Sacred Mountain (Falcons Gold); On The Edge.

TV inc: Greatest Heroes of the Bible; Moviola (This Year's Blonde); Word of Honor; The Glitter Dome (PC).

(Died May 22, 1984).

MARLOW, Lucy (nee McAleer): Act. b. Los Angeles, Nov 20, 1932. Films inc; A Star Is Born; Lucky Me; Tight Spot; My Sister Eileen; Queen Bee; Bring Your Smile Along.

MARMELSTEIN, Linda: Prod. b. Washington, DC. TV inc: Over Seven; Wide World of Adventure; Little Vic; Henry Winkler Meets William Shakespeare; The Great Wallendas; The Secret Life of Charles Dickens; The Bloodhound Gang; Jennifer's Journey; New York City Too Far From Tampa Blues; The Late Great Me--The Story of a Teenage Alcoholic (Emmy-1980); Blood and Honor--Youth Under Hitler (Supv prod).

MARON, Mel: Dist. b. NYC, Apr 21, 1931. e. CCNY. P Maron Films Ltd; exec vp Trans America Film Corp; p Cinema Shares Int'l Dist Corp; exec vp United Prodns of America; exec vp World Northal Corp.

MARQUAND, Christian: Act. b. Marseilles, France, Mar 15, 1927. Films inc: Beauty and the Beast; Jenny Lamour; Dirty Hands; Sins of the Borgias; Lady Chatterley's Lover; Love At Night; And God Created Woman; I Spit on Your Grave; The Longest Day; Of Flesh and Blood (dir-wri only); La Bonne Soupe; Behold A Pale Horse; Lord Jim; The Flight of the Phoenix; Candy (dir); The Apprentice Sorcerers; The Other Side of Midnight; Je Vous aime (I Love You).

TV inc: Beggarman, Thief.

MARQUAND, Richard: Dir. b. England. Directed commercials. TV inc: The Search For the Nile; Birth Of the Beatles.

Films inc: The Legacy; Eye Of the Needle; Return Of the Jedi; Until

September.

MARRE, Albert: Dir-Prod. b. NYC, Sep 20, 1925. e. Oberlin Coll; Harvard. Bway inc: The Little Blue Light; Love's Labour's Lost; Misalliance; Kismet; Festival; The Chalk Garden; Shangri-La; Fledermaus; Saint Joan; Good as Gold; South Pacific; Time Remembered; Rape of the Belt; Milk and Honey; Too True to be Good; A Rainy Day in Newark; Never Live Over a Pretzel Factory; Man of La Mancha *(Tony-1966)*; Cry for Us All (& wri); Home Sweet Home; A Meeting by the River.

TV inc: Androcles and the Lion; Craig's Wife.

MARSAC, Maurice: Act. b. La Croix, France, Mar 23, 1920. Films inc: (in US) How to Marry a Millionaire; What a Way to Go; The Art of Love; Dien Bien Phu Story; Pleasure Seekers; Clarence; Caprice; How Do I Love Thee?; The Jerk; Big Red One; European films inc: Sa Petite Folie; King of Kings; Armored Command; La Chapelle Noire; Scent of Mystery; Natika; Come Fly With Me; Lycantropus; Stray Dog.

Thea inc: Saint Joan; The Happy Time; Sabrina Fair.

TV inc: Studio One; Our Miss Brooks; Combat; FBI; It Takes a Thief; Mission Impossible; Legendary Curse of the Hope Diamond; Tony Randall Show; Rockford Files; Ike, the War Years; Jacqueline Bouvier Kennedy; Family Ties; Bare Essence; The Jerk, Too; Robert Kennedy & His Times.

MARSH, Jean: Act. b. England, Jul 1, 1934. As a child dancer appeared in films Tales of Hoffman, Where's Charley. Other films inc: Return To Oz. Thea inc: (London) Bird of Time. (Bway) Much Ado About Nothing; Habeas Corpus; Too True To be Good; Whose Life Is It Anyway?

TV inc: Upstairs, Downstairs (& co-creator) *(Emmy-1975)*; 9 to 5; The Corsican Brothers.

MARSHALL, Alan: Prod. b. London, 1938. Started as film ed. In 1970, teamed with Alan Parker to form Alan Parker Film Company. Films inc: Bugsy Malone; Midnight Express; Fame; Shoot the Moon; Pink Floyd--The Wall; Another Country; Birdy.

TV inc: No Hard Feelings; Our Cissy; Footsteps.

MARSHALL, Armina: Prod-Act-Wri. b. Alfalfa County, OK, 1899. e. UCLA. M of Philip Langner. NY stage debut, 1928, in The Tidings Brought to Mary. Bway inc: Peer Gynt; The Race with the Shadow; Fata Morgana; The Glass Slipper; Merchants of Glory; Right You Are If You Think You Are; Man's Estate; The Pillars of Society; The Bride the Sun Shines On; If This be Treason. Ret from acting in 1935 to write and produce plays with her husband, the late Lawrence Langner, inc: Pursuit of Happiness; Suzanna and the Elders; co-prod Sunrise at Campobello *(Tony*-prod-1958); Absurd Person Singular; Golda.

MARSHALL, E. G.: Act. b. Owatonna, MI, Jun 18, 1910. e. Carlton Coll; U of MN. Films inc: The House on 92nd Street; The Caine Mutiny; Pushover; Twelve Angry Men; The Bachelor Party; Town Without Pity; The Chase; The Bridge at Remagen; The Pursuit of Happiness; Billy Jack Goes To Washington; Interiors; Superman II; Creepshow.

TV inc: The Plot to Kill Stalin; Look Homeward Angel; A Quiet Game of Cards; The Defenders *(Emmys*-1962 & 1963); The Bold Ones; The Poppy is Also a Flower; Collision Course; Gold!; The Lazarus Syndrome; Vampire; Disaster on the Coastline; National Geographic Special (host); Mysteries of the Mind (host); Superliners-Twilight of an Era (host); Etosha--Place of Dry Water (host); Gorilla (host); The Phoenix; The Sharks (host); Eqypt--Quest for Eternity (host); Polar Bear Alert (host); The Thames (host); Eleanor, First Lady of the World; Born of Fire (host); The President's Command Performance (host); Kennedy; Thank You Mr. President--The Press Conferences of JFK (host); Saigon--Year of the Cat; John Steinbeck's The Winter of Our Discontent; Television and the Presidency; Egypt--Quest For Eternity (host).

Bway inc: The Skin of Our Teeth; The Survivors; The Crucible; Red Roses for Me; The Little Foxes; The Imaginary Invalid; Old Movies; John Gabriel Borkman; She Stoops To Conquer (Off-Bway).

MARSHALL, Garry: Prod-Dir-Wri. b. NYC, Nov 13, 1934. e. Northwestern U, BS. Worked as copy boy, later reporter NY Daily News while writing comedy material for Phil Foster, Joey Bishop; partnered with Jerry Belson for almost ten years.

TV inc: (wri) Jack Paar Show; Joey Bishop Show; Danny Thomas Show; Lucy; Dick Van Dyke Show; I Spy; Hey, Landlord (& crea); The Odd Couple (& exec prod). (Crea-exec prod) The Little People; Happy Days; Laverne & Shirley; Mork and Mindy; Angie; Sitcom--The Adventures of Garry Marshall; Beane's of Boston; Who's Watching the Kids; Evil Roy Slade (& wri); Show Business (host); The Way They Were (prod); Joanie Loves Chachi (exec prod); The New Odd Couple (exec prod); Herndon (exec prod-crea); Television--Our Life And Times (int).

Films inc: How Sweet It Is (wri-prod); The Grasshopper (wri-prod); Young Doctors In Love (exec prod-dir); The Flamingo Kid (wri-dir); Lost In America (act).

MARSHALL, Penny: Act. b. NYC, Oct 15, 1942. Sis of Garry Marshall. TV inc: Happy Days; Let's Switch; Paul Sands' Friends and Lovers; More Than Friends; Barry Manilow Special; Laverne & Shirley; Working Stiffs (dir); Lily For President?; Love Thy Neighbor; Comedy Zone; Challenge Of A Lifetime.

Films inc: How Sweet It Is; 1941; Movers & Shakers.

Thea inc: Eden Court.

MARSHALL, Peter (Pierre La Cock): Act. b. Huntington, WV, Mar 30. Films inc: The Rookies; Swingin' Along; Ensign Pulver; The Cavern; Americathon.

TV inc: The Hollywood Squares *(Emmys*-host-1974, 1975, 1980, 1981; Host of Year-1974); Peter Marshall Salutes The Big Band Era (& exec prod); A Gift of Music.

MARTA, Lynne: Act. b. Philadelphia, PA, Oct. 30, 1946. TV inc: Numerous segs; Love American Style; A Country Christmas; Homeward Bound.

Films inc: Blood Beach.

MARTI, Jill: Prod. (nee Rehmar)b. Chicago, Oct 22, 1950. e. U WI, BS; U PA, MS. Wri-co-host, later prod Cleveland Amory Show, WPVI-TV; free lance photojournalist Viet Nam, Europe, Asia; wri-prod WCAU-TV; supv exec prod WCVB-TV. TV inc: No Cover, No Minimum (pay tv); The Shadow Box; Candida (cable).

MARTIN, Allan: Exec. b. Auckland, NZ, May 2, 1926. Dir gen SPTV; P Prods & Dirs Guild of Australia.

MARTIN, Andrea: Wri-act. b. Portland, Me, Jan. 15. e. Sorbonne; Emerson College. Thea inc: Godspell (Toronto); Second City Revue; Sorrows of Stephen; Hard Sell; She Loves Me.

Films inc: Foxy Lady; Soup for One.

TV inc: The Hart and Lorne Terrific Hour (Canada); SCTV Network 90 *(Emmys*-wri-1982, 1983).

MARTIN, Charles E.: Wri-Dir-Prod. b. Newark, NJ, 1916. e. NYU; NJ Law School. Films inc: My Dear Secretary; No Leave No Love; Death of a Scoundrel; If He Hollers Let Him Go; Remember Vivian Valentine; Seduction American Style; How to Seduce a Woman; Hotshot; The Cop Who Played God; One Man Jury.

TV inc: Tallulah Bankhead Show; Gertrude Lawrence Show; Philip Morris Playhouse.

MARTIN, David Lloyd: Thea Mgr. b. Sydney. Australia, Apr 30, 1934. Tivoli Circuit Australia 1954; chmn, joint m dir, 1961-66; chmn & m dir Sydney Opera House, 1966-72; deputy GM, 1973.

MARTIN, Dean (Dino Crocetti): Act. b. Steubenville, OH, Jun 7, 1917. Joined Jerry Lewis, 1946, in Atlantic City. The duo played niteries, theatres before making screen debut in My Friend Irma. They appeared together until 1956. For joint credits see Jerry Lewis. From 1957 Martin appeared in: Ten Thousand Bedrooms; Some Come Running; Rio Bravo; Toys in the Attic; The Sons of Katie Elder; Airport; Showdown; Mr. Ricco; The Cannonball Run; Bonjour Monsieur Lewis (doc); Cannonball Run II.

TV inc: Dean Martin Show; Celebrity Roasts; Dean Martin's Christmas in California; Dean Martin Christmas Special; Ladies and Gentlemen--Bob Newhart, Part II; Dean Martin's Christmas At Sea World; Dean Martin At the Wild Animal Park;Dom DeLuise And Friends; Dean Martins's Celebrity Roast; Dom DeLuise and Friends--Part II; On Stage, America; All Star Party For Lucille Ball; Half Nelson.

MARTIN, Dick: Act. b. Detroit, 1922. Half of the Rowan-Martin comedy team. Films inc: Once Upon a Horse; The Glass Bottom Boat; The Maltese Bippy; Carbon Copy.

TV inc: Laugh-In (Emmy-1969); Ladies and Gentlemen--Bob Newhart, Part II; Take One; The First All-American Ultra Quiz; There Goes The Neighborhood (dir).

MARTIN, Elliot: Prod. b. Denver, CO, Feb 25, 1924. e. U of Denver. Bway inc: A Moon for the Misbegotten; Henry IV; Of Mice and Men; When You Comin' Back, Red Ryder? (off-Bway); More Stately Mansions; Dinner at Eight (all-star revival); A Touch of the Poet; Clothes For A Summer Hotel; Kingdoms; The Wake of Jamey Foster; American Buffalo (rev); Glengarry Glen Ross; Woza Albert (off-Bway); Harrigan 'n Hart.

MARTIN, Ernest H.: Prod. b. Pittsburgh, PA, Aug 28, 1919. e. UCLA, AB. Bway inc: Where's Charley; Guys and Dolls; Can-Can; The Boy Friend; Silk Stockings; How to Succeed in Business Without Really Trying (Tony-1962); Skyscraper; Walking Happy; The Goodbye People; The Act (all in asso with Cy Feuer).

Films inc: Cabaret; Piaf. M-dir LA and San Francisco Civic Light Opera Assn, 1975.

MARTIN, Freddy: Orch Leader. b. Cleveland, OH, Dec 5, 1906. Formed own orchestra 1931. Performed in St. Regis; Waldorf; Astor; Pennsylvania; Commodore Hotels, NY; St. Francis Hotel, SF; Los Angeles Cocanut Grove from 1940-70; made coast-to-coast tours, inc Carnegie Hall.

(Died Sept. 30, 1983)

MARTIN, Henry H. (Hi): Exec. b. Holcomb, MS, Mar 22, 1912. Joined Universal as accessory mgr in 1935. Moved on to booker, salesman, branch mgr, div mgr. Named gen sls mgr in 1957, became vo 1959. Succeeded Milton R. Rackmil as president Universal Pictures on Jan 1, 1973. Ret 1978; 1981 Pres, Cinema Associates Corp.

MARTIN, Jared: Act. b. NYC, Dec. 21, 1941. e. Columbia; Sarah Lawrence. Thea inc: NY Shakespeare Festival; Tom Paine.

TV inc: Fantastic Voyage; How the West Was Won; Dallas; The Big Easy.

Films inc: Arthur's Private Room; Murder a la Mod; The Second Coming of Suzanne; The Lonely Lady; The Californians (doc-narr).

MARTIN, Mary: Act. b. Wetherford, TX, Dec 1, 1914. On screen from 1939 in The Great Victor Herbert; Rhythm on the River; Love Thy Neighbor; New York Town; Kiss the Boys Goodbye; Birth of the Blues; Star Spangled Rhythm; True To Life; Happy Go Lucky; Night and Day; Main Street To Broadway.

Bway inc; (Special Tony-1948) Lute Song; Leave It to Me; One Touch of Venus; South Pacific; Annie Get Your Gun; Kind Sir; Peter Pan (Tony-1955); Jennie; The Sound of Music (Tony-1960); I Do I Do; Do You Turn Somersaults?.

TV inc: Peter Pan (Emmy-1955); Valentine; Bob Hope's All Star Birthday Party at West Point; Over Easy (host); The 39th Annual Tony Awards.

MARTIN, Millicent: Act. b. Romford, England, Jun 8, 1934. Thea inc: (London) Expresso Bongo; The Crooked Mile; The Dancing Heiress; The Lord Chamberlain Regrets; State of Emergency; Our Man Crichton; Peter Pan; The Beggar's Opera; Absurd Person Singular; Side by Side By Sondheim. (Bway) The Boy Friend; Side by Side by Sondheim; King of Hearts.

TV inc: That Was The Week That Was; Mainly Millicent; Orphans, Waifs and Wards; The 39th Annual Tony Awards.

MARTIN, Nan: Act. Films inc: The Buster Keaton Story; For the Love of Ivy; Goodbye Columbus; Toys in the Attic; The Other Side of the Mountain; The Other Side of the Mountain, Part 2.

TV inc; A Circle of Children.

Bway inc: A Story for a Sunday Evening; The Constant Wife; J.B.; The Great God Brown; The Merchant of Venice; Hamlet; A Sign of Affection; Come Live With Me; The Taming of the Shrew; Summer Brave.

MARTIN, Pamela Sue: Act. b. Westport, CT, Jan 5, 1953. Model, TV commercials. Films inc: To Find a Man; The Poseidon Adventure; Buster and Billie; Our Time; The Lady In Red; Torchlight (& wri-asso prod).

TV inc; The Hemingway Play; The Gun and the Pulpit; The Girls from Huntington House; Angel on My Shoulder; Nancy Drew Mysteries; Dynasty.

MARTIN, Peter G.: Exec. b. Sydney, Australia, Sep 12, 1940. Commissioner (full time), Australian Film Commission.

MARTIN, Quinn: Prod. b. Los Angeles, May 22, 1927. e. Berkeley. Formed Quinn Martin Prods which subsequently sold to Taft Broadcasting. TV inc: The Untouchables; The Fugitive; The FBI; The New Breed; Cannon; Banyon; Barnaby Jones; Dan August; Manhunter; Most Wanted; Streets of San Francisco; 12 O'Clock High.

MARTIN, Steve: Act. b. Waco, TX, 1945. e. Long Beach State Coll; UCLA. Writer for various TV shows inc: The Smothers Brothers Comedy Hour; Sonny and Cher. TV inc: (act) Steve Martin--A Wild and Crazy Guy; Comedy Is Not Pretty; All Commercials; Steve Allen Comedy Hour; Steve Martin's Best Show Ever (& wri); Twilight Theatre (& co-exec prod); Domestic Life (exec prod-crea); The Jerk, Too (exec prod); The New Show; Johnny Carson Presents The Tonight Show Comedians; Martin Mull Presents The History Of White People In America--Part 1 (feevee); AFI Salute To Gene Kelly.

Films inc: The Kids Are Alright; The Muppet Movie; The Jerk (& wri); Pennies From Heaven; Dead Men Don't Wear Plaid; The Lonely Guy; All of Me; Movers & Shakers.

Albums inc: Let's Get Small (Grammy-1977); A Wild and Crazy Guy (Grammy-1978).

MARTIN, Tony: Act. b. Oakland, CA, Dec 25, 1913. H of Cyd Charisse. Performed with bands; played niteries. Screen debut 1936, Pigskin Parade. Films inc: Sing, Baby, Sing; Follow the Fleet; You Can't Have Everything; Sally, Irene and Mary; Ziegfeld Girl; Two Tickets to Broadway; Hit the Deck; Dear Mr. Wonderful.

MARTINDALE, Wink: Bcast Personality. b. Jackson, TN, Dec 4. e. Memphis State Coll. Game show host; LA disc jockey. TV game shows inc: Words and Music; How's Your Mother-in-Law?; What's the Song?; Everbody's Talking; Can You Top This?; Gambit; The New Tic Tac Dough; Las Vegas Gambit.

MARTINSON, Leslie H.: Dir. b. Boston. Films inc: Hot-Rod Girl; Hot-Rod Rumble; Lad: A Dog; Black Gold; FBI Code 98; PT-109; For Those Who Think Young; Batman; Fathom; The Challengers; Millions May Die; Mrs Pollifax-Spy; Escape from Angola; Cruise Missile.

TV inc: Big Shamus, Little Shamus; The Kid With the Broken Halo; Private Benjamin; The Kid With The 200 I.Q.; Small & Frye; The Fantastic World of D.C. Collins.

MARTON, Andrew: Dir-Prod. b. Budapest, Hungary, Jan 26, 1904. To Hollywood with Ernst Lubitsch, 1923. Directed chariot race in Ben Hur; amphibious landings in The Longest Day; battle scenes in 55 Days at Peking. Films inc: (as dir) The Thin Red Line; Crack in the World; Green Fire; The Devil Makes Three; Into The Night (act only).

TV inc: Man and the Challenge; Daktari; Cowboy in Africa; The Sea Hunt.

MARVIN, Lee: Act. b. NYC, Feb 19, 1924. Films inc: You're in the Navy Now; Duel at Silver Creek; Eight Iron Men; The Wild One; Gorilla at Large; The Caine Mutiny; Bad Day at Black Rock; Violent Saturday; Not as a Stranger; Pete Kelly's Blues; Attack; Raintree County; The Man Who Shot Liberty Valance; Donovan's Reef; The Killers; Attack!; Cat Ballou (Oscar-1965); Ship of Fools; The Professionals; The Dirty Dozen; Point Blank; Paint Your Wagon; The Iceman Cometh; Emperor of the North; Shout at the Devil; The Great Scout and Cathouse Thursday; Avalanche; The Big Red One; Death Hunt; Gorky Park; Canicule (Dog Day).

TV inc: M Squad; Lawbreaker; Bob Hope Laughs with the Movie Awards; The Hilarious Unrehearsed Antics Of The Stars; The Dirty Dozen--The Next Mission.

MARX, Samuel: Wri-Prod. b. NYC, Jan 26, 1902. e. Columbia U. Started as story ed MGM, later prod at MGM, Goldwyn, Col, U.

Films inc: Lassie Come Home; This Man's Navy; My Brother Talks to Horses; The Beginning or the End; A Lady Without A Passport; Grounds for Marriage; Kiss of Fire; Ain't Misbehavin'; Waterloo; Rome; The Ravine.

June 1980, special story assignment for MGM.

MASINA, Giulietta: Act. b. Bologna, Italy, Feb 22, 1921. e. U of Rome. W of Federico Fellini. School teacher before becoming act. On radio, Rome stage; met Fellini when he asked her to audition for radio soap opera. Films inc: Without Pity; The White Sheik; Lights of Variety; La Strada; Il Bidone; The Nights of Cabiria; Europa; Fortunella; Juliet of the Spirits.

MASLANSKY, Harris J.: Exec. b. NYC, May 25, 1944. e. NYU Law School, LLM. Sr. VP Col, NY; 1980 P Motion Picture Division Time-Life Films; 1982, into indie prodn. Bway inc: Beyond Therapy.

MASLANSKY, Paul: Prod. b. NYC, Nov 23, 1933. e. Washington & Lee U, NYU Law School. Films inc: Jason and the Argonauts; The Long Ships; The Running Man; Castle of the Living Dead; The Blood Beast; The Red Tent; Deathline; Gun in the Pulpit; Hard Times; Race with the Devil; The Black Bird; Damnation Alley; Circle of Iron; When You Comin' Home, Red Ryder?; Hot Stuff; The Villain; Scavenger Hunt; Love Child; The Salamander; Police Academy; Police Academy 2--Their First Assignment; Return To Oz.

TV inc: King.

MASON, James: Act. b. Huddersfield, England, May 15, 1909. e. Marlborough Coll. On screen from 1935. More than 120 films inc: Late Extra; I Met a Murderer; The Night Has Eyes; The Man in Grey; The Seventh Veil; The Wicked Lady; Odd Man Out; Pandora and the Flying Dutchman; The Desert Fox; Five Fingers; The Prisoner of Zenda; Julius Caesar; 20,000 Leagues Under the Sea; A Star is Born; Journey to the Center of the Earth; Lolita; The Pumpkin Eater; The Blue Max; Georgy Girl; The Deadly Affair; Harrowhouse; Inside Out; Cross of Iron; Heaven Can Wait; The Boys from Brazil; Murder by Decree; The Passage; Sidney Sheldon's Bloodline; The Water Babies; Ffolkes; Evil Under the Sun; A Dangerous Summer; The Verdict; Yellowbeard; Alexandre; The Shooting Party; Dr. Fischer Of Geneva.

TV inc: The Pioneers (narr); The Search For Alexander The Great (narr); Ivanhoe; The Unknown Chaplin (narr); The Popes and Their Art--The Vatican Collections (host); George Washington; A.D.

Bway inc: The Faith Healer.

(Died July 27, 1984).

MASON, Marsha: Act. b. St Louis, MO, Apr 3, 1942. e. Webster Coll, BA. Films inc: Blume in Love; Cinderella Liberty; Audrey Rose; The Goodbye Girl; The Cheap Detective; Promises in the Dark; Chapter Two; Only When I Laugh; Max Dugan Returns.

TV inc: The Love of Life; Cyrano de Bergerac; Lois Gibbs and the Love Canal; Surviving.

Bway inc: Happy Birthday, Wanda June; The Good Doctor; Cactus Flower; Whatever Happened to Lori Jean Lloyd?; Old Times (off-Bway).

MASON, Marshall W.: Dir. b. Amarillo, TX, Feb 24, 1940. e. Northwestern U, BS; Actors Studio. Off-Bway inc: Little Eyolf; Home Free!; Hot L Baltimore; The Sea Horse; Battle of Angels; The Mound Builders; Knock Knock; Serenading Laurie; 5th of July; Talley's Folly; Full Hookup. Bway inc: Knock Knock; Gemini; Murder at the Howard Johnson's; Talley's Folly; 5th of July; Passion.

TV Inc: 5th of July.

MASON, Pamela: Act-Wri. b. Westgate, England, Mar 10, 1918. Stage debut, 1936, The Luck of the Devil. Films inc: I Met a Murderer; They Were Sisters; The Upturned Glass; Pandora and the Flying Dutchman; Lady Possessed.

TV inc: Pamela Mason Show; My Wicked, Wicked Ways.

MASON, Paul: Wri-Prod. b. Chicago, IL, Jun 21, 1936. e. Northwestern U. Films inc: Angel Baby; Action in the North Atlantic; To Die In Paris; King Kong Vs Godzilla; California Kid.

TV inc: Chrysler Theatre; Eleventh Hour; Laredo; Tammy; Ironsides; It Takes a Thief; McMillan and Wife; SFX; Chico and the Man; Welcome Back, Kotter; The Wolper Specials; CHiPS (exec prod-wri); joined Danny Thomas and Ronald Jacobs as partner in Danny

Thomas Prodns; Manimal (exec prod).

MASON, Tom: Act. b. Brooklyn, NY, Mar 1. Bway inc: Kid Champion. Films inc: King of the Gypsies; Apocalypse Now.

TV inc: Feasting With Panthers; Brother to Dragons; Walking Through Fire; Grandpa Goes to Washington; Nero Wolfe; Alien Force; Freebie and the Bean; Return of The Man From U.N.C.L.E.; Two Marriages; George Washington; Kicks.

MASSARI, Lea: Act. b. France. Films inc: L'avventura; From a Roman Balcony; Colossus of Rhodes; Made In Italy; Murmur of the Heart; Impossible Object; Escape to Nowhere; Christ Stopped at Eboli; Le Divorcement; Sarah; Le Septieme Cible (The Seventh Target); Segreti Segreti (Secrets Secrets).

MASSEY, Anna: Act. b. Sussex, England, Aug 11, 1937. D of the late Raymond Massey. Films inc: Peeping Tom; Bunny Lake is Missing; The Looking Glass War; David Copperfield; Frenzy; A Little Romance; Sweet William; Five Days One Summer; Another Country; Sakharov; The Little Drummer Girl; Sacred Hearts; The Chain.

Thea inc: (London) The Reluctant Debutante; Slag; Spoiled; Flipside; The Doctor's Dilemma; School for Scandal; Close of Play; The Seagull; The Importance of Being Earnest.

TV inc: A Doll House; Remember the Germans; Wicked Woman; The Corn is Green; I Remember Nelson; The Potting Shed (cable); Anna Karenina.

MASSEY, Daniel: Act. b. London, Oct 10, 1933. S of the late Raymond Massey. Films inc: Girls At Sea; Girls in Arms; Upstairs and Downstairs; Mary, Queen of Scots; Fragment of Fear; Star!; The Jokers; The Incredible Sarah; Bad Timing; Victory.

Thea inc: (London) The Happiest Millionaire; Living for Pleasure; School for Scandal; The Rivals; Barefoot in the Park; She Loves Me; The Importance of Being Ernest; Bloomsbury; The Gay Lord Quex; Heloise and Abelard; Man and Superman; The Hypochondriac; The Mayor of Zalamea.

TV inc: Venus Observed; On Approval; War and Peace; Vikings.

MASSEY, Raymond: Act. b. Toronto, Aug 30, 1896. On stage from 1922 in England and U.S. On screen from 1931. Films inc: The Scarlet Pimpernel; The Prisoner of Zenda; Reap the Wild Wind; Action in the North Atlantic; Lincoln in Illinois; Arsenic and Old Lace; Stairway to Heaven; Mourning Becomes Electra; The Fountainhead; East of Eden; The Naked and the Dead; The Great Impostor; How the West Was Won; Mackenna's Gold.

Bway inc: Ethan Frome; Abe Lincoln in Illinois; Pygmalion; John Brown's Body.

(Died July 29, 1983)

MASTERSON, Peter: Act. b. Houston, TX, Jun 1, 1934. e. Rice U. Thea inc: Marathon 33; Blues for Mr. Charlie; Trail of Lee Harvey Oswald; Great White Hope; That Championship Season; Poison Tree. Co-wri, co-dir Best Little Whorehouse In Texas.

Films Inc: Ambush Bay; Counterpoint; In the Heat of the Night; Exorcist; Von Richtofen and Brown; Man on a Swing; Stepford Wives; The Best Little Whorehouse In Texas (wri).

TV inc: Pueblo; Delta County; A Question of Guilt; City in Fear (exec prod).

MASTRANTONIO, Mary Elizabeth: Act. b. Oak Park, IL. e. U of IL. Bway inc: West Side Story (rev); Copperfield; Oh, Brother; Amadeus; The Human Comedy (Off-Bway); Henry V (Off Bway).

Films inc: Scarface.

MASTROIANNI, Marcello: Act. b. Fontane Liri, Italy, Sep 28, 1924. On screen from 1947. Films inc: Three Girls from Rome; The Miller's Beautiful Wife; Fever to Live; The Ladykillers of Rome; Love a La Carte; La Dolce Vita; Divorce Italian Style; La Notte; A Very Private Affair; Where the Hot Wind Blows; The Organizer; Yesterday, Today and Tomorrow; Marriage Italian Style; Casanova '70; Kiss the Other Sheik; The Poppy Is Also a Flower; A Place for Lovers; Sunflower; Jealousy Italian Style; The Priest's Wife; The Grande Bouffe; Massacre in Rome; Down the Ancient Stairs; The Sunday Woman; The Divine Creature; Goodnight Ladies and Gentlemen; A Special Day; We All Loved Each So Much; Revenge; Wifemistress; Bye Bye Monkey; Cosi Come Sei; L'ingorgo; The Terrace; Todo Modo; City of Women;

Fantasma D'Amore (Ghost of Love); La Pelle (The Skin); La Nuit de Varennes (The Night of Varennes); Oltre la Porta (Beyond the Door); Gabriela; Storia di Piera; Le General de l'Armee Morte (The General of the Dead Army); Enrico IV (Henry IV); Le Due Vite de Mattia Pascal (The Two Lives Of Mattia Pascal).

MASUR, Richard: Act. b. NYC. e. Yale School of Drama. Bway inc: The Changing Room.
Films inc: Semi-Tough; Hanover Street; Scavenger Hunt; Heaven's Gate; Who'll Stop The Rain; I'm Dancing as Fast as I Can; The Thing; Timerider; Risky Business; Under Fire; Nightmares; The Mean Season.
TV inc: One Day at a Time; Rhoda; Betrayal; Mr. Horn; John Steinbeck's East of Eden; Fallen Angel; Money on the Side; An Invasion of Privacy; The Demon Murder Case; John Steinbeck's The Winter of Our Discontent; Empire; Flight 90--Disaster on the Potomac; The Bounder; The Burning Bed; Obsessed With A Married Woman.

MATALON, Vivian: Dir. b. Manchester, England, Oct 11, 1929. e. Munro Coll, Jamaica. Thea inc: (London as act) The Caine Mutiny Court Martial; A Hatful of Rain; The Iceman Cometh. (Dir) The Admiration of Life; Season of Goodwill; The Chinese Prime Minister; The Glass Menagerie; Suite in Three Keys; First Day of a New Season; Two Cities; I Never Sang for My Father; The Gingerbread Lady.
Bway inc: (dir) After the Rain; Noel Coward in Two Keys; PS Your Cat is Dead; Brigadoon (rev); Mornings at Seven (rev) (& London) (Tony-1980); The American Clock; The Corn Is Green (rev); The Tap Dance Kid.
TV inc: For Ladies Only; Private Contentment.

MATHESON, Richard: Wri. Films inc: The Incredible Shrinking Man; Somewhere In Time; Twilight Zone--The Movie; Jaws 3-D.
TV inc: Twilight Zone; Night Gallery; The Night Stalker; Duel; The Martian Chronicles.

MATHESON, Tim: Act. b. LA, Dec 31, 1949. Films inc: Divorce American Style; Yours, Mine and Ours; How to Commit Marriage; Magnum Force; Almost Summer; National Lampoon's Animal House; Dreamer; The Apple Dumpling Gang Rides Again; 1941; A Little Sex; To Be or Not to Be; The House of God; Up the Creek; Impulse; Fletch.
TV inc: The Quest; Lock, Stock and Barrel; Hitched; Remember When; The Runaway Barge; The Last Day; What Ever Happened to the Class of '65?; Bus Stop (cable); Tucker's Witch; Listen To Your Heart; The Best Legs In the 8th Grade; Obsessed With A Married Woman.

MATHEWS, Carole: Act. b. Montgomery, IL, Sep 13. Started as nightclub, radio entertainer. To Hollywood 1944. Films inc: Massacre River; The Great Gatsby; Meet Me at the Fair; Shark River; Requirement for a Redhead; Look in Any Window; Thirteen Men; Tender Is the Night; End of the Road.

MATHIS, Johnny: Singer. b. San Francisco, Sep 30, 1935. Recording artist. Performs in niteries; tours U S, abroad. Films inc: Lizzie; Wild in the Wind (sang title song); A Certain Smile. TV inc: Olympic Gala; Music Of Your Life.

MATHIS, Sherry: Act-Sing. b. Memphis, TN., Feb. 2. e. Memphis State U; Studied with Stella Adler. W of Jerry Lanning. Bway inc: A Little Night Music; Music Is; Truckload; Camelot. Other thea inc: Parto; Gone With the Wind; Brigadoon.
Films inc: W.W. and the Dixie Dancekings.
TV inc: Search for Tomorrow (since 1978).

MATTHAU, Walter: Act. (nee Matuschanskayasky):b. NYC, Oct 1, 1923. On screen from 1955 in The Kentuckian. Other films inc: A Face in the Crowd; Lonely Are the Brave; Charade; Fail Safe; The Odd Couple; The Fortune Cookie (Oscar-supp-1966); Hello, Dolly!; Cactus Flower; Kotch; The Front Page; Earthquake; The Bad News Bears; The Sunshine Boys; House Calls; California Suite; Casey's Shadow; Little Miss Marker (& exec prod); Portrait of a 60% Perfect Man (doc); Hopscotch; First Monday In October; Buddy Buddy; I Ought To Be In Pictures; The Survivors; Movers & Shakers.
Bway inc: Anne of the Thousand Days; Will Success Spoil Rock Hunter; A Shot in the Dark (Tony-supp-1962); The Odd Couple (Tony-1965).
TV inc: Tallahasee 7000; Entertainment Tonight; Hollywood, The

Gift of Laughter; The Gentleman Tramp.

MATTSON, Robin: Act. b. Los Angeles, Jun 1, 1956. TV inc: Flipper; Gentle Ben; Island of the Lost; The Guiding Light; Battles (pilot); James at 15; Mirror Mirror; Hot Rod; Are You In the House Alone; Countdown to Super Bowl; Doctors Private Lives; General Hospital.
Films inc: Namu, The Killer Whale; Return to Macon County.

MATURE, Victor: Act. b. Louisville, KY, Jan 29, 1916. Early training in Pasadena Theatre, Playbox Theatre. On Broadway in Lady in the Dark. On screen from 1939 in The Housekeeper's Daughter; One Million B.C.; Captain Caution; I Wake Up Screaming; My Darling Clementine; Kiss of Death; Samson and Delilah; Androcles and the Lion; The Robe; The Big Circus; The Tartars; Every Little Crook and Nanny; Firepower.
TV inc: Samson and Delilah.

MATZ, Peter: Comp-Cond. b. Pittsburgh, PA, Nov 6, 1928. e. UCLA. TV inc: (mus dir) My Name is Barbra (Emmy-1965); The Sound of Burt Bacharach (Emmy-1970); The Carol Burnett Show 1971-1978 (Emmy-1973); First You Cry; White Mama; The Big Show; Fun and Games; Omnibus; Good Time Harry; Damien...The Leper Priest; From Raquel With Love (mus dir); The Mouseketeer Reunion (cond); Doug Henning's World of Magic; Musical Comedy Tonight II; The Killing of Randy Webster; Crazy Times; Sixty Years of Seduction (mus-dir); The Steeler and The Pittsburgh Kid; Doug Henning's World of Magic (1982); Eunice (mus-dir); I Love Liberty (mus-dir); Baryshnikov In Hollywood (mus-dir); It's Not Easy Being Me, The Rodney Dangerfield Show (mus-dir). Shirley MacLaine-Illusions (mus dir); Drop-Out Father; Take Your Best Shot; George Burns & Other Sex Symbols (mus-dir); Doug Henning's Magic On Broadway (mus dir); Mama's Family; Amanda's; Ace Crawford, Private Eye; Sheena Easton--Act One (mus dir); Casablanca; George Burns Celebrates 80 Years in Show Business (mus dir); Live--and In Person (mus); Burnett 'Discovers' Domingo (mus dir); Rodney Dangerfield Exposed (mus dir).
Films inc: Funny Lady (arr-cond); Private Eyes (mus); Lust In The Dust (mus).
Recordings (arr) for Barbra Streisand (Grammy-1964); Tony Bennett; Chicago.

MAULDIN, Bill: Cartoonist. b. Santa Fe, NM, 1922. Winner of two Pulitzer Awards for his cartoons. Appeared on screen in films: Teresa; The Red Badge of Courage; Up Front.

MAXWELL, Lois: Act. That Hagen Girl; The Big Punch; The Decision of Christopher Blake; The Dark Past; The Crime Doctor's Diary; Scotland Yard Inspector; Satellite in the Sky; Lolita; The Haunting; Dr No; From Russia With Love; Goldfinger; Thunderball; The Man With the Golden Gun; You Only Live Twice; Diamonds Are Forever; The Spy Who Loved Me; Lost and Found; Moonraker; For Your Eyes Only; Octopussy; A View To A Kill.
TV inc: Claim To Fame.

MAXWELL, Ronald: Dir. b. Tripoli, Libya. e. NYU. TV inc: Theatre In America; Sea Marks; Verna--Uso Girl. Films inc: Little Darlings; The Night The Lights Went Out In Georgia; Kidco.

MAY, Billy: Comp-Arr-Cond. b. Pittsburgh, Nov 10, 1916. Arr & cond for many leading vocalists, 1950-60; comp & cond for TV shows inc: Naked City; Batman; Green Hornet; Mod Squad; Emergency; CHiPS; Return of the Beverly Hillbillies; The 25th Man.
Bway inc: Peg (orchs)
(Grammys-best orch-1958; best arr-1959).

MAY, Elaine: Act-Wri. b. Philadelphia, Apr 21, 1932. Comedy team with Mike Nichols. Films inc: Luv; Enter Laughing; A New Leaf (& dir, sp); Such Good Friends (sp); The Heartbreak Kid; Mikey and Nicky (dir, sp); California Suite; Heaven Can Wait (sp).
(Grammy-comedy perf-1961).

MAYBERRY, Russ: Dir. Films inc: The Jesus Trip; Unidentified Flying Oddballs.
TV inc: The Monkees; Love on a Rooftop; Fer De Lance; Who Killed the Centerfold Model; The Million Dollar Dixie Deliverance; The Snatching of Little Freddie; The Young Runaways; Arnie; Probe; Baa Baa Black Sheep; The Rebels; The $5.20 an Hour Dream; Marriage Is

Alive and Well; Reunion; A Matter of Life and Death; Sidney Shorr; The Fall Guy; Side By Side--The True Story of the Osmond Family; The Circle Family; Rooster; Manimal; Challenge Of A Lifetime; Goldie & The Bears.

MAYER, Roger L.: Exec. b. NYC, Apr 21, 1926. e. Yale U, BA; Yale Law School, LLB, JD. Atty for Columbia Pictures, 1952-57; then corporate exec from 1957-61; joined MGM as both VP-operations & asst sec; VP-administration, exec VP-MGM laboratories; Feb. 1983, P MGM Labs.

MAYES, Wendell: Wri. b. Hayti, MO, Jul 21, 1919. Films inc: Spirit of St. Louis; The Way to the Gold; The Hanging Tree; The Enemy Below; The Hunters; Anatomy of a Murder; Advise & Consent; In Harm's Way; Von Ryan's Express; Hotel; Poseidon Adventure; The Revengers; The Stalking Moon; The Bank Shot; Death Wish; Love and Bullets, Charlie; Go Tell the Spartans; Love and Bullets; Monsignor.
TV inc: Savage: In the Orient.

MAYFIELD, Curtis: Mus-Comp-Singer. b. Chicago, IL, Jun 3, 1942. With group Impression 1958-1970 before going solo. Albums inc: Curtis; Curtis Live; Roots; Back to the World; Sweet Exorcist; America Today; Never Say You Can't Survive; Do It.
Films inc: (scores) Superfly; Short Eyes; A Piece of the Action.

MAYO, Virginia (nee Jones): Act. b. St. Louis, MO, Nov 30, 1920. Performed on stage in stock, niteries. Screen debut in 1944. Films inc: Up in Arms; Jack London; Seven Days Ashore; The Princess and the Pirate; Wonder Man; The Kid From Brooklyn; The Best Years of Our Lives; The Secret Life of Walter Mitty; Out of the Blue; Smart Girls Don't Talk; A Song Is Born; Flaxy Martin; Colorado Territory; The Girl From Jones Beach; White Heat; Red Light; Always Leave Them Laughing; Backfire; The Flame and the Arrow; West Point Story; Along The Great Divide; Captain Horatio Hornblower; Painting the Clouds with Sunshine; Starlift; She's Working Her Way Through College; The Iron Mistress; She's Back On Broadway; South Sea Woman; King Richard and the Crusaders; The Silver Chalice; Pearl of the South Pacific; The Proud Ones; The Big Land; Congo Crossing; The Tall Stranger; The Story of Mankind; Fort Dobbs; Jet Over the Atlantic; Young Fury; Castle of Evil; Won Ton Ton the Dog Who Saved Hollywood; French Quarter.
TV inc: Police Story; Bob Hope's Road to Hollywood; Santa Barbara.

MAYRON, Melanie: Act. b. Philadelphia, PA, Oct 20, 1952. e. AADA. Films inc: Car Wash; Gable and Lombard; Harry and Tonto; Girlfriends; The Great Smoky Roadblock; Heartbeeps; Missing.
TV inc: Hustling; Playing For Time; The Best Little Girl In The World; Will There Really Be A Morning?; Wallenberg--A Hero's Story.
Thea inc: Godspell (tour); The Goodbye People (Bway).

MAZURKI, Mike: Act. b. Tarnopal, Austria, Dec 25, 1909. e. Manhattan Coll, NY, BA. Toured US, Canada, as heavyweight wrestler. Screen debut 1941 Shanghai Gesture. Films inc: I Walk Alone; Unconquered; Nightmare Alley; Come to the Stable; Rope of Sand; Samson and Delilah; Ten Tall Men; My Favorite Spy; The Egyptian; New York Confidential; Some Like It Hot; A Pocketful of Miracles; Requiem for a Heavyweight; Challenge to be Free; Agnes; The Magic of Lassie; Gas Pump Girls; The Man with Bogart's Face;
TV inc: The Adventures of Huckleberry Finn (Classics Illustrated); Revenge of the Gray Gang.

MAZURSKY, Paul: Prod-Dir-Wri. b. NYC, Apr 25, 1930. Films inc: I Love You Alice B Toklas (co-sp); Bob and Carol and Ted and Alice. (co-sp, dir); Alex in Wonderland (co-sp, dir); Blume in Love (sp-dir); Harry and Tonto; Next Stop Greenwich Village; An Unmarried Woman (& act); A Man, A Woman, And A Bank (act); Willie & Phil; History of the World--Part I (act); Tempest; Moscow on the Hudson; Into The Night (act).

McANALLY, Ray: Act. b. Buncrana, Donegal, Ireland, Mar 30, 1926. e. St Eunan's Coll; St Patrick's Coll. Appeared in over 150 plays with the Abbey Theatre Company, 1947-63. On London stage 1964 in Who's Afraid of Virginia Woolf?. Thea inc: Lorna and Ted; The Devil's Disciple; The Devil's Own People; Living Quarters; Translations; Kolbe (Dublin) (Dir); The Midnight Door; The Unexpected Death of Jimmy

Blizzard.
Films inc: She Didn't Say No!; Shake Hands With the Devil; The Naked Edge; Billy Budd; The Outsider; Angel; Cal.
TV inc: Leap in the Dark; The Little Father; Court Martial; The Death of Adolf Hitler.

McARDLE, Andrea: Act. b. Philadelphia, Nov 5, 1963. Thea inc: Annie.
TV inc: Search for Tomorrow; Rainbow; Come On Saturday; Doug Henning's Magic On Broadway.

McCALLION, James: Act. b. Glasgow, Scotland, Sep 27, 1918. Films inc: Boy Slaves; Code of the Streets; Gantry the Great; Hero for a Day; Tribute to a Bad Man; Vera Cruz; North by Northwest; How Do I Love Thee. TV inc: National Velvet.

McCALLISTER, Lon: Act (ret). b. Los Angeles, Apr 17, 1923. Started as an extra, 1935. Films inc: Stage Door Canteen; Home In Indiana; Winged Victory; The Red House; Thunder in the Valley; Scudda Hoo, Scudda Hay; The Big Cat; The Story of Seabiscuit; The Boy from Indiana; A Yank in Korea; Montana Territory; Combat Squad (last film, 1953).

McCALLUM, David: Act. b. Scotland, Sep 19, 1933. Films inc: Prelude to Fame; The Secret Place; Violent Playground; The Long, the Short and the Tall; Billy Budd; Freud; The Great Escape; The Greatest Story Ever Told; Around the World Under the Sea; Three Bites of the Apple; Sol Madrid; Mosquito Squadron; Frankenstein, The True Story; Dogs; The Watcher in the Woods; Terminal Choice.
TV inc: The Man from U.N.C.L.E.; Colditz; The Invisible Man; Return of the Man from U.N.C.L.E.

McCALLUM, John: Prod-Dir-Act. b. Brisbane, Australia, Mar 14, 1918. In repertory theatres 1937-39; Man dir J C Williamson Theatres, Aus, 1959-66; Chmn, exec dir John McCallum Prods, 1976; prod TV series: Skippy; Barrier Reef; Boney.

McCAMBRIDGE, Mercedes: Act. b. Joliet, IL, Mar 17, 1918. e. Mundelein Coll, BA. Performed on radio, stage. Films inc: All The King's Men *(Oscar*-Supp-1950); Giant; Lightning Strikes Twice; Johnny Guitar; A Farewell to Arms; Suddenly Last Summer; The Exorcist (voice of Satan on soundtrack); Thieves; Concorde-Airport '79; Echoes.
Bway inc: Hope for the Best; A Place of Our Own; Woman Bites Dog.

McCANN, Elizabeth I.: Prod. b. NYC. e. Manhattanville Coll, BA; Columbia U, MA; Fordham U, LLD. Worked with Maurice Evans Productions, Saint Subber, Martin Tahsi, Harold Prince before becoming M-Dir of the Nederlander Organization 1975; prod My Fat Friend with James Nederlander; 1976, formed McCann and Nugent Prodns with Nelle Nugent. Bway inc: Dracula *(Tony*-revival-1978); Night and Day; The Elephant Man *(Tony*-1979); Morning's At Seven *(Tony*-revival-1980); Piaf; Rose; Amadeus *(Tony*-1981); The Life and Adventures of Nicholas Nickleby *(Tony*-1982); Mass Appeal; The Dresser; Good; All's Well That Ends Well; Total Abandon; The Glass Menagerie; Cyrano de Bergerac; Much Ado About Nothing; Leader Of The Pack. Other thea inc: Pilobolus Dance Theatre; 1982 Joffrey Ballet Benefit Gala.
TV inc: The Elephant Man; Morning's At Seven (cable); Piaf (Cable).

McCARTHY, Frank: Prod. b. Richmond, VA, Jun 8, 1912. e. VMI; U of VA. In WW II was Asst Secy later Secy of War Dept General Staff, Secy to Chief of Staff Gen. Marshall. Joined MPAA, 1946, serving as asst to vp, later European mgr. Joined Darryl F. Zanuck as a 20th Century-Fox exec prod, 1948.
Films inc: Decision Before Dawn; Sailor of the King; A Guide for the Married Man; Patton *(Oscar*-best pic-1970); MacArthur.

McCARTHY, Kevin: Act. b. Seattle, WA, Feb 15, 1914. Bway debut in Abe Lincoln in Illinois. Other Bway inc: Flight To the West; Truckline Cafe; Joan Of Lorraine; The Survivors; Anna Christie; Alone Together. Screen debut 1951 Death of a Salesman. Films inc: Drive a Crooked Road; Stranger on Horseback; The Misfits; A Gathering of Eagles; Mirage; A Time for Heroes; Buffalo Bill and the Indians; Invasion of the Body Snatchers; Piranha; Hero At Large; The Howling; My Tutor; Montgomery Clift; Twilight Zone--The Movie.

TV inc: Flamingo Road; Portrait of An Escort; Rosie--The Rosemary Clooney Story; The Making of a Male Model; Bay City Blues; Invitation To Hell; Deadly Intentions.

McCARTHY, Nobu (nee Atsumi): Act. b. Ottawa, Canada, Nov 13, 1940. e. LACC. Films inc: The Hunters; Geisha Boy; Five Gates to Hell; Wake Me When It's Over; Two Loves; Walk Like a Dragon.

TV inc: Lost Flight; Farewell to Manzanar; The Man On The Beach.

McCARTNEY, Paul: Singer-Mus. b. Liverpool, England, Feb 25, 1943. Member of The Beatles (see group listing). Individual film credits inc: Live and Let Die (title song); Oh Heavenly Dog (songs); Rock Show; Beyond the Limit (theme); Give My Regards To Broad Street (wri-act-mus).

TV inc: Fridays. Formed group Wings for p.a. and recordings.

(Grammys-(5)-(in addition to group awards). Song of Year, 1966; Contemporary vocal solo, 1966; Soundtrack, 1970; Arrangement-vocalists, 1971; Pop vocal group, 1974).

McCASHIN, Constance (nee Broman): Act. b. Chicago, Jun 18, 1947. e. Manhattanville Coll. Worked with off-Bway group; in tv prodn WPIX, NY. TV inc: Contest winner on $25,000 Pyramid; Daddy, I Don't Like It Like This; A Special Kind of Love; First Ladies Diaries--Edith Bolling Wilson; The Two Worlds of Jennie Logan; Are You A Missing Heir?; Married--The First Year; Knots Landing; Love Thy Neighbor; Obsessive Love.

McCAUGHEY, William L.: Snd. b. Kansas City, MO, Dec 21, 1929. Films inc: Logans Run; Audrey Rose; Norman Is that You?; Piece of the Action; King Kong; Deer Hunter (Oscar-1978); California Suite; Voices; The Runner Stumbles; The Champ; Fast Break; Voices; The Villian.

McCLANAHAN, Rue: Act. b. Healdton, OK, Feb 21. e. Tulsa U. TV inc: Maude; Who's Happy Now; Move Over, Mrs Markham; Apple Pie; Rainbow; Mother and Me; Topper; The Great American Traffic Jam; Word of Honor; And they Lived Happily Ever After; The Day the Bubble Burst; Mama's Family; Masquerade.

Bway inc: The Secret Life of Walter Mitty; Jimmy Shine; California Suite.

McCLORY, Sean: Act. b. Dublin, Ireland, Mar 8, 1924. e. U of Galway. With Abbey Theatre. Came to U S 1946. Films inc: Dick Tracy vs The Claw; Beyond Glory; Storm Warning; What Price Glory; The Quiet Man; Ring of Fear; The Long Grey Line; Botany Bay; Moonfleet; Day of the Wolves; Follow Me Boys; The Gnomobile; Well of the Saints; Roller Boogie.

Thea inc: Shining Hour; Juno and the Paycock; Anna Christie; The Lady's Not for Burning; Billy Budd; Dial M for Murder; Shadows of a Gunman; Saint Joan.

TV inc: Captains and the Kings; Once an Eagle; Kate McShane; Battlestar Galactica.

McCLURE, Doug: Act. b. Glendale, CA., May 11, 1935. Films inc: Because They're Young; The Unforgiven; Shenandoah; Beau Geste; The King's Pirate; Nobody's Perfect; The Land that Time Forgot; At the Earth's Core; Warlords of Atlantis; Humanoids From the Deep; The House Where Evil Dwells; Cannonball Run II.

TV inc: Checkmate; Overland Trail; The Virginian; Shirts/Skins; Search; The Judge and Jake Wyler; The Rebels; Nightside; Automan; Cover Up; Half Nelson.

Bway inc: The Roast.

McCLURE, Marc: Act. b. San Mateo, CA, Mar 31, 1957. Films inc: Freaky Friday; Coming Home; Superman; I Wanna Hold Your Hand; Supergirl; Back To The Future.

TV inc: The Cop and the Kid; numerous segs.

McCOOK, John: Act-Singer-Cond. b. Ventura, CA, Jun 20, 1945. In stock, touring shows; cond for various headline acts in Las Vegas. Bway inc: West Side Story (rev).

TV inc: The Young and the Restless; From Janice and John and Mary and Michael...With Love; Singin', Swingin', and All That Jazz; Mitzi--What's Hot, What's Not; The Rainbow Girl; Codename Foxfire;

Robert Kennedy & His Times.

McCORD, Kent: Act. b. Los Angeles, Sep 26, 1942. Began acting career on Ozzie and Harriet Show. TV inc: The Virginian; Jigsaw; Dragnet; Adam 12.

Films inc: The Young Warriors; Airplane II--The Sequel.

McCORMACK, Patricia: Act. b. Aug 21, 1945. Made Bway debut at age 6 (billed as Patty McCormack). Bway inc: Touchstone; The Bad Seed. Films inc: The Bad Seed; The Day They Gave Babies Away; Huckleberry Finn; Kathy-O; Explosive Generation; The Young Runaways.

TV inc: I Remember Mama; The Miracle Worker; Shower of Stars; Peck's Bad Girl; The New Breed; The Best of Everything; Friends; As The World Turns; The Ropers; Night Partners; Invitation To Hell.

McCORMICK, Pat (Arley D. McCormick): Wri-Act. b. Jul 17, 1934. Comedy writer for Phyllis Diller, Jonathan Winters, Henny Youngman. TV inc: (wri) Jack Paar Show; Don Rickles Show; Tonight Show; We Dare You (act); Rooster; Gun Shy; The Jerk, Too; The Cracker Brothers.

Films inc: (act) Buffalo Bill and the Indians; If You Don't Stop It You'll Go Blind; Smokey and the Bandit; A Wedding; Hot Stuff; Scavenger Hunt; Smokey and The Bandit II; History of the World--Part I; Under the Rainbow (& wri); Smokey & the Bandit Part 3; Bombs away.

McCOWEN, Alec: Act. b. Tunbridge Wells, England, May 26, 1925. e. RADA. In repertory 1943-45. Thea inc: (London) Ivanhoe; The Mask and the Face; Tishoo; The Portage to San Cristobal of A.H; Kipling. (Bway) Antony and Cleopatra; The Holy Terrors; Escapade; The Matchmaker; The Caine Mutiny Court Martial; No Laughing Matter; The Elder Statesman; After the Rain; Hadrian the Seventh.

Films inc: The Cruel Sea; Time Without Pity; A Midsummer Night's Dream; The Loneliness of the Long Distance Runner; The Agony and the Ecstasy; The Devil's Own; The Hawaiians; Frenzy; Travels With My Aunt; Stevie; Hanover Street; Never Say Never Again; Forever Young; The Young Visiters.

TV inc: Plays For Pleasure.

McCREA, Joel: Act. b. Los Angeles, Nov 5, 1905. H of Frances Dee. On screen from 1923. Films inc: Penrod and Sam; The Jazz Age; So This Is College; Dynamite; Lightnin'; Once A Sinner; The Lost Squadron; Bird Of Paradise; The Silver Cord; Private Worlds; Barbary Coast; Dead End; Union Pacific; Foreign Correspondent; Sullivan's Travels; The Great Man's Lady; The More The Merrier; Ramrod; Four Faces West; Stars in my Crown; Buffalo Bill; The Oklahoman; Fort Massacre; Ride The High Country; Mustang Country; George Stevens--A Filmmaker's Journey (doc-int).

McDERMOT, Galt: Comp. Plays inc: Hair; Isabel's A Jezebel; Two Gentlemen of Verona; A Gun Play; Sticks and Bones; Dude; The Human Comedy.

McDOUGALL, Gordon: Dir. b. Inverness, Scotland, May 4, 1941. e. Cambridge. Started in repertoire, then artistic dir of the Traverse, Edinburgh, 1966-68. Later dir The Vicar of Soho; The Dark River; Twelfth Night; The Country Wife; in 1974 became artistic dir of the Oxford Playhouse Company; prodns inc: The Government Inspector; As You Like It; Happy End; Uncle Vanya; Fitting for Ladies; For Heaven's Sake Don't Walk Around With Nothing On.

McDOWALL, Roddy: Act. b. London, Sep 17, 1928. On screen in England from 1936 in Murder in the Family. Films in U.S. inc: How Green Was My Valley; Confirm or Deny; The Pied Piper; My Friend Flicka; Lassie Comes Home; Keys of the Kingdom; Midnight Lace; Cleopatra; Inside Daisy Clover; Planet of the Apes (and its sequels); The Poseidon Adventure; Funny Lady; The Cat From Outer Space; Laserblast; Rabbit Test; Circle of Iron; Nutcracker Fantasy; Scavenger Hunt; Charlie Chan and the Curse of the Dragon Queen; Evil Under the Sun; Class of 1984.

Bway inc: Misalliance; Escapade; The Doctor's Dilemma; No Time for Sergeants; Compulsion; A Handful of Fire; Look After Lulu; The Fighting Cock (Tony-supp-1960); Camelot.

TV inc: Not Without Honor (Emmy-1961); The Thief of Baghdad; The Immigrants; The Martian Chronicles; The Memory of Eva Ryker;

The Return of the King (voice); The Million Dollar Face; Twilight Theatre (host); Mae West; Natalie--A Tribute To A Very Special Lady (host); This Girl For Hire; The Zany Adventures of Robin Hood; London and Davis In New York; Hollywood Wives.

McDOWELL, Malcolm: Act. b. Leeds, England, Jun 1943. H of Mary Steenburgen. Films inc: If...; Figures in a Landscape; The Raging Moon; A Clockwork Orange; O Lucky Man!; Royal Flash; Aces High; Voyage of the Damned; The Passage; Time After Time; Caligula; Cat People; Britannia Hospital; Blue Thunder; Cross Creek; Get Crazy; The Compleat Beatles (doc) (narr).
TV inc: She Fell Among Thieves; Gulag; Arthur The King.
Thea inc: In Celebration (Off-Bway).

McELWAINE, Guy: Exec. B. Culver City, CA, Jun 29, 1936. Started in pub dept MGM, 1954; 1959 joined Rogers & Cowan; 1964, launched own pub relations firm; 1969 joined CMA; VP in chg Wldwde Motion Picture activities; 1975 to WB as Sr exec vp in chg wldwde motion picture prodn; 1977 to ICM (new corp name of CMA) as P Film Mktng; 1981, P & CEO Rastar Films; July, 1982 P, Columbia Pictures; Oct. 1983, P & CEO; June, 1984, chmn.

McEVEETY, Bernard: Dir. B of Vincent McEveety. Films inc: Napoleon and Samantha; One Little Indian; The Bears and I.
TV inc: Bonanza; Gunsmoke; Combat; Cimarron Strip (& prod); Man Undercover; Donovan's Kid; Young Maverick; Roughnecks.

McEVEETY, Vincent: Dir. TV inc: Gunsmoke; High Flying Spy; The Buffalo Soldiers; Buck Rogers; McClain's Law; Skyward Christmas.
Films inc: The $1,000,000 Duck; The Biscuit Eater; Charley and the Angel; Superdad; The Strongest Man in the World; Treasure of Matecumbe; Herbie Goes to Monte Carlo; The Apple Dumpling Gang Rides Again; Herbie Goes Bananas; Amy.

McGAVIN, Darren: Act. b. Spokane, WA, May 7, 1922. Bway inc: Death of a Salesman; My Three Angels; The Rainmaker; Dinner at Eight (revival).
Films inc: A Song to Remember; Counter Attack; Summertime; The Man with the Golden Arm; Beau James; Ride the High Wind; Mrs. Polifax, Spy; Run, Stranger, Run (dir); American Reunion (dir); No Deposit, No Return; Airport '77; Hot Lead and Cold Feet; Hangar 18; A Christmas Story; The Natural; Turk 182.
TV inc: Mike Hammer; The Outsider; Riverboat; The Night Stalker; Tribes; Something Evil; Say Goodbye Maggie Cole; Cyborg; Crime of the Century-The Brink's Robbery; Ike; Love For Rent; The Martian Chronicles; Waikiki; Small & Frye; The Return of Marcus Welby, M.D.; The Baron and the Kid; My Wicked, Wicked Ways.

McGILL, Everett: Act. b. Miami Beach, FL, 1945. e. RADA. Bway inc: Equus; A Texas Trilogy; Dracula (rev).
Films inc: Yanks; Union City; Brubaker; Quest for Fire; Dune.

McGOOHAN, Patrick: Act. b. NYC, Mar 19, 1928. Films inc: Passage Home; Zarak; High Tide at Noon; Hell Drivers; The Gypsy and the Gentleman; Two Living One Dead; The Quare Fellow; Life for Ruth; Dr Syn; Ice Station Zebra; Mary Queen of Scots; Catch My Soul (dir); The Genius; Silver Streak; Brass Target; Escape From Alcatraz; Scanners; Kings and Desperate Men; Trespasses; Baby.
TV inc: Danger Man (Secret Agent); The Prisoner; Columbo (Emmy-supp-1975); Three Sovereigns For Sarah; Jamaica Inn.
Bway inc: Pack Of Lies.

McGOVERN, Elizabeth: Act. b. Evanston, IL. e. Juilliard, ACT. Thea inc: Dwarfman; Everyman; Skin Of Our Teeth; To Be Young, Gifted And Black; My Sister In This House; The Visit.
Films inc: Ordinary People; Ragtime; Lovesick; Racing With the Moon; Once Upon A Time In America.

McGUIRE, Biff (William J): Act. b. New Haven, CT, Oct 25, 1926. e. MA State; Shrivenham U, Eng. Bway inc: Make Mine Manhattan; South Pacific; The Moon Is Blue; The Time of Your Life; A View From the Bridge; Greatest Man Alive; Happy Town; Beg Borrow or Steal; Beggar on Horseback; Trial of the Catonsville Nine; That Championship Season.
Films inc: Serpico; The Last Word.
TV inc: Act of Violence; Rex Stout's Nero Wolfe.

McGUIRE, Dorothy: Act. b. Omaha, NE, Jun 14, 1919. Films inc: Claudia; A Tree Grows in Brooklyn; The Spiral Staircase; Claudia and David; Gentlemen's Agreement; Mister 880; Three Coins in a Fountain; Friendly Persuasion; Old Yeller; The Remarkable Mr Pennypacker; The Earth Is Mine; Dark at the Top of the Stairs; Swiss Family Robinson; Flight of the Doves; Summer Magic; The Greatest Story Ever Told; Jonathan Livingston Seagull (voice only).
TV inc: She Waits; The Runaways; Rich Man, Poor Man; The Outlander; Little Women; The Incredible Journey of Dr Meg Laurel; Ghost Dancing; The Young and The Restless.
Bway inc: A Kiss for Cinderella; Our Town; Kind Lady; Medicine Show; Claudia; Summer and Smoke; Legend of Lovers; Winesburg, Ohio; The Night of the Iguana.

McINTIRE, John: Act. b. Spokane, WA, Jun 27, 1907. H of Jeanette Nolan. Films inc: Asphalt Jungle; Saddle Tramp; Winchester 73; A Lion Is In the Streets; Apache; Phenix City Story; The Lawless Breed; The Tin Star; Psycho; Summer and Smoke; Rough Night in Jericho; Two Rode Together; Challenge To Be Free; Herbie Rides Again; Rooster Cogburn; The Rescuers (voice); The Fox and The Hound; Honkytonk Man; Cloak And Dagger.
TV inc: Naked City; Wagon Train; The Virginian; The Jordan Chance; Mrs. R's Daughter; Shirley; Goliath Awaits; All the Way Home; Lone Star; The Cowboy and the Ballerina.

McKAY, Bruce: Exec. b. Helena, MT. e. Gettsburg Coll; Syracuse U. Joined NBC TV in 1973. Appointed vp, Variety Programs, NBC Entertainment in April, 1979.

McKAY, Jim (nee McManus): TV Sportscaster. b. Philadelphia, Sep 24, 1921. e. Loyola Coll, Baltimore. Reporter, Baltimore Sunpapers, joined Sunpapers' WMAR-TV 1974 as wri-prod-dri; 1950 CBS as variety show host, sports commentator; 1961, host ABC Wide World of Sports (Emmys-1968, 1971, 1974, 1975, 1976, 1980); also (Emmy-1973 for coverage of Munich Olympic Tragedy; 1982, sports personality); commentator all Olympiads since 1960; Indianapolis 500; Kentucky Derby; Masters & PGA Golf Championships.

McKAY, Scott: Act. (Carl Gore):b. Pleasantville, IA, May 28, 1922. e. U of CO. Films inc: Duel in the Sun; Kiss and Tell; A Guest in the House; Thirty Seconds Over Tokyo; The Front; The Bell Jar.
TV inc: Love of Life; Edge of Night; Search for Tomorrow; Keeping On.
Bway inc: Good Hunting; Three Sisters; Letters to Lucerne; The Eve of St. Mark; Dark Eyes; The Moon is Down; Requiem for a Nun; Pillar to Post; Another Part of the Forest; The Night Before Christmas; The American Way; Sabrina Fair; Dream Girl; Born Yesterday; Bell, Book and Candle; The Little Foxes; The Live Wire; Once for the Asking.

McKEAN, Michael: Act-Mus-Sngwri. b. NYC, Oct 17. e. NYU; Carnegie Tech. Teamed with David L. Lander in comedy group The Credibility Gap, toured US for four years. TV inc: More Than Friends; American Bandstand; Laverne & Shirley; The Bounder.
Films inc: 1941; Young Doctors In Love; Spinal Tap (& sp); D.A.R.Y.L.

McKECHNIE, Donna: Act-Dancer-Singer. b. Detroit, MI, 1940. Bway inc: How to Succeed in Business Without Really Trying; The Education of H*Y*M*A*N K*A*P*L*A*N; Promises, Promises; Company; On the Town; Sondheim--A Musical Tribute (& chor); Music, Music, Music; A Chorus Line (Tony-1976).
TV inc: Twirl; McGruder & Loud.

McKELLEN, Ian: Act. b. Burnley, England, May 25, 1939. e. Cambridge. Thea inc: (London) A Scent of Flowers; Much Ado About Nothing; Armstrong's Last Goodnight; Trelawny of the Wells; A Lily in Little India; Their Very Own; Golden City; O'Flaherty, VC; The Man of Destiny; The White Liars; Black Comedy; Dr. Faustus; The Marquis of Keith; King John; The Clandestine Marriage (dir); Ashes; Too True to Be Good; Romeo and Juliet; Cowardice. (Bway) The Promise; Amadeus (Tony-1981); Ian McKellen Acting Shakespeare.
Films inc: Alfred The Great; The Promise; A Touch of Love; Priest of Love; The Keep.
TV inc: David Copperfield; Ross; Hedda Gabler; Ian McKellen Act-

ing Shakespeare; Hamlet (cable); The Scarlet Pimpernel.

McKENNA, Siobhan: Act. b. Belfast, N Ireland, May 24, 1923. e. Natl U of Ireland. Appeared in Galway Theatre, Abbey Theatre Dublin before London stage bow 1947, The White Steed. Thea inc: (London) Berkeley Square; Ghosts; Heloise; Joan of Arc; Playboy of the Western World; Play With A Tiger; The Cavern; On a Foggy Day; Best of Friends; Memoir. (Bway) The Chalk Garden; Saint Joan; The Rope Dancers; A Meeting by the River.
Films inc: Hungry Hill; Daughter of Darkness; The Lost People; The Adventurers; King of Kings; Of Human Bondage; Dr Zhivago; Here Are Ladies (filmed in 1971).
TV inc: The Letter; Cradle Song; What Every Woman Knows; The Last Days of Pompeii.

McKENNA, T P (Thomas Patrick McKenna): Act. b. County Cavan, Eire, Sep 7, 1929. e. Abbey Theatre School. With the Abbey Theatre for eight years before going to London. Thea inc: Stephen D; Julius Caesar; Too True to be Good; Recall the Years (opening prodn of new Abbey); Breakdown; The Contractor; Exiles; The Balcony; Sleuth; The Devil's Disciple; Nightshade; The Seagull.
Films inc: Ulysses; The Charge of the Light Brigade; Anne of the Thousand Days; Straw Dogs; It's Not The Size That Counts; The Outsider; Portrait of the Artist as a Young Man.
TV inc: The Rivals; The Duchess of Malfi; The Changeling; Levkas Man; The Manions of America; The Year of the French; The Scarlet and the Black; The World of James Joyce; To The Lighthouse.

McKENNA, Virginia: Act. b. London, England, Jun 7, 1931. Thea inc: (London) A Penny for a Song; The Winter's Tale; The River Line; The Bad Samaritan; I Capture the Castle; various Shakespearean roles with Old Vic; The Devils; The Beggar's Opera; The Beheading; A Little Night Music; The King and I. A Personal Affair.
Films inc: The Second Mrs. Tanqueray; Father's Doing Fine; The Cruel Sea; Simba; The Ship That Died of Shame; A Town Like Alice; The Smallest Show on Earth; The Barretts of Wimpole Street; Carve Her Name With Pride; The Wreck of the Mary Deare; Born Free; Ring of Bright Water; An Elephant Called Slowly; Waterloo; Swallows and Amazons; The Chosen; The Link.
TV inc: The First Olympics--Athens 1896.

McKEON, Douglas: Act. b. NJ., June 10, 1966. TV inc: Edge Of Night; Tell Me My Name: Daddy I Don't Like It This; Centennial; Big Shamus, Little Shamus; The Comeback Kid; An Innocent Love; Desperate Lives.
Films inc: Uncle Joe Shannon; On Golden Pond; Night Crossing.
Thea inc: Dandelion Wine; Truckload.

McKEON, Nancy: Act. b. Westbury, NY., April 4, 1966. TV inc: A Question of Love; Please Don't Hit Me, Mom; Stone; The Facts Of Life; Miss Switch To the Rescue; Candid Kids; Poison Ivy.

McKEON, Philip: Act. b. Westbury, NY, Nov 11, 1964. Films inc: Up the Sandbox; Once Is Not Enough; American Moments.
TV inc: Sweepstakes; Alice; Kids Are People Too; Leadfoot; The Bet.
Bway inc: Medea and Jason.

McKERN, Leo (Reginald McKern): Act. b. Sydney, NSW, Australia, Mar 16, 1920. Thea inc: Love's Labour's Lost; She Stoops to Conquer; Hamlet; The Merry Wives of Windsor; Timon of Athens; Toad of Toad Hall; The Queen and the Rebels; The Good Sailor; Cat on a Hot Tin Roof; A Man for All Seasons; Peer Gynt; The Alchemist; Coriolanus; The Housekeeper; Number One.
Films inc: A Man for All Seasons; Help! Ryan's Daughter; The Adventures of Sherlock Holmes' Smarter Brother; Omen; Candleshoe; The Blue Lagoon; The Voyage of Bounty's Child (doc-narr); Ladyhawke; The Chain.
TV inc: The House on Garibaldi Street; Rumpole of the Bailey; Laurence Olivier Presents King Lear; Reilly, Ace of Spies; Rumpole Returns!; Murder With Mirrors.

McKINSEY, Beverlee: Act. b. McAlester, OK, Aug 9. Began on children's show The Make-Believe Playhouse on PBS. Bway inc: Man and Boy; Who's Afraid of Virginia Woolf?; Barefoot in the Park.
TV inc: Another World; Texas; The Demon Murder Case.

McKUEN, Rod: Comp-Act-Poet. b. Oakland, CA, Apr 29, 1933. Concert, nitery perf; record prod for Frank Sinatra, Kingston Trio, Petula Clark, others. Film scores inc: Joanna; The Prime of Miss Jean Brodie; Me, Natalie; A Boy Named Charlie Brown; Come to Your Senses; Wildflowers; Lisa, Bright and Dark; The Borrowers; Emily; The Unknown War.
Songs inc: Jean; Love's Been Good To Me; Listen to the Warm; Olly Olly Oxen Free; The Lovers; Joanna; I'll Catch the Sun; The Ever Constant Sea; April People; Forever Young Forever Free; The Winds of Change; If You Go Away; Seasons in the Sun; I'm Not Afraid.
(Grammy-spoken word-1968).

McLAGLEN, Andrew V.: Dir. b. London, Jul 28, 1920. Began career as Asst Dir, 1944. Films inc: Man in the Vault; Gun the Man Down; The Abductors; Freckles; The Little Shepherd of Kingdom Come; McLintock!; Shenandoah; The Rare Breed; Seven Men from Now; The Way West; The Ballad of Josie; Monekys, Go Home; The Devil's Brigade; Bandolero; The Undefeated; Fool's Parade; Something Big; One More Train to Rob; Cahill, United States Marshall; Mitchell; Breakthrough; The Last Hard Men; Ffolkes; The Sea Wolves; Sahara.
TV inc: Gunsmoke; Have Gun-Will Travel; Perry Mason; Rawhide; The Lineup; The Lieutenant; The Shadow Riders; The Blue and The Gray; Travis McGee; The Dirty Dozen--The Next Mission.

McLAREN, Norman: Dir. b. England, 1914. Specializes in animated shorts. Films inc: Allegro; Dots and Loops; Boogie Doodle; Hoppity Pop; Fiddle-de-fee; Begone Dull Care; Around is Around; Neighbours; Blinkety Blank; Rhythmetic; A Chairy Tale; Blackbird; Parallels; Pas de Deux; Mosaic.

McLAUGHLIN, Emily: Act. b. White Plains, NY, Dec 1, 1928. e. Middlebury Coll, BA. Theatre inc: The Frogs of Spring; The Lovers.
TV inc: Studio One; Kraft Theatre; Young Dr. Malone; General Hospital (since April 1963).

McLENDON, Gordon Barton: Broadcast Exec-Prod. b. Paris, TX, Jun 8, 1921. e. Yale U; Harvard Law School. Established Liberty Broadcasting System with Baseball's Game of the Day and football Game of the Week. Known as The Old Scotchman since days of sports broadcasting. Owned and operated numerous radio and tv stations. Films inc: The Giant Gila Monster; The Killer Shrews; My Dog Buddy; Victory (exec prod).

McLERIE, Allyn Ann: Act. b. Grand'Mere, Quebec, Canada, Dec 1, 1926. Films inc: Words and Music; Where's Charley; Desert Song; Battle Cry; The Reivers; They Shoot Horses Don't They; Cowboys; The Way We Were; Cinderella Liberty; All the President's Men.
TV inc: Music for a Summer Night; Shadow of a Gunman; A Tree Grows in Brooklyn; Born Innocent; Death Scream; Sister Terri; Return Engagement; And Baby Makes Six; A Shining Season; Beulah Land; To Find My Son; Fantasies; Rascals and Robbers--The Secret Adventures of Tom Sawyer and Huck Finn; Living Proof--The Hank Williams Story; The Thorn Birds; After George; Two Kinds of Love; Fraud Squad.
Bway inc: One Touch of Venus; On the Town; Finian's Rainbow; Time Limit; West Side Story; South Pacific; My Fair Lady; The Beast in Me; The Mind with the Dirty Man; The Night of the Iguana.

McLIAM, John (John Joseph Williams): Act. b. Alberta, Canada, Jan 24, 1918. e. St Mary's Coll, BA. Films inc: RPM; Halls of Anger; The Reivers; Cool Hand Luke; My Fair Lady; In Cold Blood; Lucky Lady; The Iceman Cometh; The Missouri Breaks; First Blood.
Bway inc: Barefoot in Athens; Tiger at the Gates; Desire Under the Elms; St Joan; One More River.
TV inc: The Five Of Me; Mistress of Paradise; Bret Maverick; The Ambush Murders; Two Marriages; A Death In California.

McMAHON, Ed: Act. b. Detroit, Mar 6, 1923. e. Boston Coll. Films inc: The Incident; Fun with Dick and Jane; Butterfly.
TV inc: Who Do You Trust; The Tonight Show (since 1962); Fortune Phone; The Missing Links; The Kid From Left Field; The Golden Moment-An Olympic Love Story; The Great American Traffic Jam; The Star Maker; All-Star Salute To Mother's Day (host); It's the Real Thing--Television's Greatest Commercials IV (host); TV'S Bloopers and Practical Jokes (exec prod); Return To Iwo Jima (host).

McMAHON, Jenna: Wri. TV inc: Carol Burnett Show *(Emmys*-1974, 1975, 1978); Carol Burnett and Co; Facts of Life (& crea); The Grass Is Always Greener Over the Septic Tank; Flo (& crea); Eunice; Mama's Family (prod).

McMAHON, John J.: Exec. b. Chicago, IL., 1932. e. Northwestern U, BA. Began on staff WGN-TV, Chicago; 1952 Ziv-UA TV Prodns; 1958, vp-gm WXYZ-TV, Detroit; 1968, vp-gm WABC-TV, LA; joined NBC 1972 as vp pgms, West Coast; 1974, vp pgm ops; 1978 sr vp pgms & talent; 1979, P Rastar TV.
TV inc: (exec prod) The Star Maker; Why Us?; Fire On the Mountain; Johnny Goes Home; Johnny Carson's Greatest Practical Jokes; Passions; Johnny Carson Presents The Tonight Show Comedians.

McMILLAN, Kenneth: Act. b. Brooklyn, NY, Jul 2, 1932. e. High School of Performing Arts; studied with Uta Hagen, Irene Dailey. Bway inc: The Borstal Boy; Kid Champion; Streamers; American Buffalo.
Films inc: Serpico; The Taking of Pelham 1-2-3; The Stepford Wives; Oliver's Story; Bloodbrothers; Head Over Heels; Hide In Plain Sight; Carny; Little Miss Marker; Eye Witness; True Confessions; Borderline; Ragtime; Heartbeeps; Partners; Blue Skies Again; Reckless; The Pope of Greenwich Village; Dune; Protocol; Cat's Eye.
TV inc: Love of Life; Ryan's Hope; Johnny We Hardly Knew Ye; Search for Tomorrow; Rhoda; Salem's Lot; Caring; A Death In Canaan; King: In The Custody of Strangers; Packin' It In; Dixie--Changing Habits; Murder One--Dancer 0; Suzanne Pleshette is Maggie Briggs; Concrete Beat.

McNAIR, Barbara: Singer-Act. b. Racine, WI, Mar 4, 1934. Bway inc: The Body Beautiful; No Strings.
Films inc: Spencer's Mountain; Stiletto; Change of Habit; Venus in Furs; They Call Me Mr. Tibbs.
TV inc: The Barbara McNair Show; Glitter.

McNALLY, Stephen (Horace McNally): Act. b. NYC, Jul 29. e. Fordham, U, LLB. Practiced law for two years before becoming act. Films inc: The Man From Down Under; The Harvey Girls; Johnny Belinda; Rogue's Regiment; Winchester 73; Wyoming Mail; No Way Out; Air Cadet; Apache Drums; Raging Tide; The Lady Pays Off; Devil's Canyon; Make Haste to Live; A Bullet is Waiting; The Man from Bitter Ridge; Panic in the Streets; Tribute to a Bad Man; Once You Kiss a Stranger; Requiem for a Gunfighter. TV inc: Target--The Corruptors.

McNALLY, Terrence: Wri. b. St Petersburg, FL, Nov 3, 1939. e. Columbia U, BA. Plays inc: And Things That Go Bump in the Night; Sweet Eros; Witness; Where Has Tommy Flowers Gone; Bad Habits; The Ritz; Broadway, Broadway; The Rink.
TV inc: Mama Malone (prod-wri-crea).

McNEILL, Don: Radio-TV Pers. b. Gelena, IL, Dec 23, 1907. e. Marquette U. Started on radio with WISN, Milwaukee 1928, also worked in Louisville and San Francisco before returning to Chicago to start Breakfast Club on ABC 1933; pgm spanned 36 years of radio, later tv; has made numerous guest appearances, specials for PBS.

McNICHOL, James Vincent (Jimmy): Act. b. Los Angeles, Jul 2, 1961. TV inc: Sunshine; The Fitzpatricks; Champions-A Love Story; The Carpenters-A Christmas Portrait; California Fever; Blinded By the Light; First The Egg.
Films inc: Smokey Bites the Dust; Night Warning.

McNICHOL, Kristy: Act. b. Los Angeles, Sep 9, 1963. Films inc: Black Sunday; The End; Little Darlings; The Night The Lights Went Out In Georgia; Only When I Laugh; White Dog; The Pirate Movie; Just The Way You Are.
TV inc: Fawn Story; Me and Dad's New Wife; The Pinballs; Family *(Emmy*-supp-1977, 1979). Summer of My German Soldier; The Carpenters-A Christmas Portrait; My Old Man; Blinded By the Light; I Love Liberty.

McPHILLIPS, Hugh: Act-Dir. b. Suffern, NY, Mar 31, 1920. e. Fordham U; Neighborhood Playhouse. Joined NBC staff 1951, working as stage mgr., asso dir, staff dir, occasional act; 1968, dir-asso producting dir The Doctors. Since 1975 freelance dir-act. TV inc: The Open Mind (dir); The Doctors (dir); Days of Our Lives (act) *(Emmy-*

cameo-1980).

McQUAID, John: Exec. b. Brewarrina, NSW, Australia, Oct 16, 1932. Commissioner, Australian Film Commission. Member Australian Film Institute; member National Film Theatre of Australia.

McQUEEN, Butterfly: Act. b. Tampa, FL, 1911. Films inc: Gone With the Wind; Cabin in the Sky; Flame of the Barbary Coast; Mildred Pierce; Duel in the Sun; The Phynx; Amazing Grace.
TV inc: The Seven Wishes of a Rich Kid *(Emmy*-1980); The Seven Wishes of Joanna Peabody; Movie Blockbusters! The 15 Greatest Hits of all Time.

McRANEY, Gerald: Act. b. Collins, MS., Aug. 19, 1948. Studied with Jeff Corey. TV inc: Where the Ladies Go; Love Story; The Law; The Trial of Chaplain Jenson; Women in White; The Jordan Chance; How the West Was Won; Roots II; Simon & Simon; Memories Never Die; City Killer.
Films inc: Keep Off My Grass; Night of Bloody Horror; The Neverending Story.

McSHANE, Ian: Act. b. Blackburn, England, Sep 29, 1942. e. RADA. Thea inc: (London) The House of Fred Ginger; How Are You, Johnnie; Easter Man; The Glass Menagerie; The Promise. (Bway) The Promise.
Films inc: The Wild and the Willing; The Pleasure Girls; The Battle of Britain; If It's Tuesday, This Must Be Belgium; Pussycat, Pussycat, I Love You; Tam Lin; Villain; The Last of Sheila; Ransom; Journey Into Fear; The Fifth Musketeer; Yesterday's Hero; Cheaper To Keep Her; Exposed; Ordeal By Innocence; Too Scared To S cream.
TV inc: A Sound From the Sea; You Can't Win; Wuthering Heights; The Pirate; Disraeli--Portrait of a Romantic; The Letter; Marco Polo; Bare Essence; Grace Kelly; Evergreen; A.D.

McWILLIAMS, Caroline: Act. b. Seattle, WA, Apr 4, 1945. e. Carnegie Institute of Tech. Bway inc: The Rothschilds; Cat On a Hot Tin Roof.
TV inc: Guiding Light; Barney Miller; Soap; Benson; Alien Force; Amusement Park; The Day The Bubble Burst; The Day the Bubble Burst; The Gift of Life; Cass Mallory; Shattered Vows.

MEADOWS, Audrey: Act. b. Wu Chang, China, Feb 8, 1924. Sis of Jayne Meadows. Films inc: That Touch of Mink; Take Her She's Mine; Rosie.
TV inc: The Honeymooners *(Emmy*-supp-1954); Lily--Sold Out; Too Close For Comfort.
Bway inc: Top Banana.

MEADOWS, Jayne: Act. b. Wu Chang, China, 1926. W of Steve Allen. Films inc: Undercurrent; Dark Delusion; Lady in the Lake; Song of the Thin Man; Luck of the Irish; Enchantment; David and Bathsheba; College Confidential; Da Capo.
TV inc: Danger; Robert Montgomery Presents; I've Got A Secret; What's My Line; Laugh-Back; Sex and the Married Woman; Ten Speed and Brownshoe; The Gossip Columnist; A Funny Thing Happened On the Way to the White House (cable); Aloha Paradise; Meeting of the Minds; Rise and Shine; I've Had It Up To Here; Miss All-American Beauty; It's Not Easy; The Ratings Game (PC).

MEARA, Anne: Act. b. NYC, Sep 20, 1929. W of Jerry Stiller. Films inc: Lovers and Other Strangers; The Out-Of-Towners; Nasty Habits; The Boys From Brazil; Fame; In Our Hands (doc).
TV inc: Kate McShane; Take Five; Archie Bunker's Place; The Other Woman (& wri).
Thea inc: A Month in the Country; Maedchen in Uniform; Ulysses in Nighttown; Spookhouse; member Joseph Papp's Shakespeare Co; toured in a comedy act with husband Jerry Stiller.

MEDAVOY, Mike: Exec. b. Shanghai, China, Jan 21, 1941. e. UCLA. Came to US in 1957. Started in mail room at U; became a casting dir; joined GAC, CMA where he was a vp in the motion picture dept. In 1971 joined IFA as vp; involved in packaging The Sting; Young Frankenstein; Jaws before joining UA May 1974 as sr vp in charge of West Coast prod. Resigned 1978, joined other former UA execs in forming Orion Pictures Co of which he is exec vp.

MEDFORD, Don: Dir. TV inc: Kraft Theatre; US Steel Hour; Climax;

General Electric Theatre; Dr Kildare; Alfred Hitchcock Presents; The Fugitive; The Man From UNCLE; 12 O'Clock High; The FBI; Baretta; Police Story; Kaz; Coach of the Year; Sizzle; Hell Town.

Films inc: The Hunting Party; The Organization.

MEDINA, Patricia: Act. b. England, Jul 19, 1921. W of Joseph Cotten. Films inc: Double or Quit; Secret Journey; Kiss The Bride Goodbye: They Met in the Dark; Hotel Reserve; Waltz Time; The Secret Heart; The Three Musketeers; The Fighting O'Flynn; Lady in the Iron Mask; Siren of Baghdad; Lady and the Bandit; Moss Rose; Foxes of Harrow The Black Knight; Pirates of Tripoli; Count Your Blessings; The Killing of Sister George; Stranger at My Door.

MEDOFF, Mark: Plywri. b. Mt Carmel, IL, Mar 18, 1940. e. U of Miami (FL), BA; Stanford, MA. Plays inc: When You Comin' Back, Red Ryder?; The Wager; The Kramer; The Halloween Bandit; The Conversion of Aaron Weiss; Firekeeper; The Last Chance Saloon; Children of A Lesser God (Tony-1980); The Hands Of Its Enemy.

Films inc: When You Comin' Back, Red Ryder?

MEEKER, Ralph (nee Rathgeber): Act. b. Minneapolis, MI, Nov 21, 1920. e. Northwestern U. Films inc: Teresa; Four in a Jeep; The Naked Spur; Jeopardy; Code Two; Kiss Me Deadly; Desert Sands; Paths of Glory; Ada; The Dirty Dozen; The St Valentine's Day Massacre; Gentle Giant; The Detective; The Anderson Tapes; The Happiness Cage; The Food of the Gods; The Alpha Incident; Winter Kills; Without Warning.

TV inc: Lost Flight.

Bway inc: Doughgirls; Strange Fruit; Cyrano de Bergerac; Mr Roberts; A Streetcar Named Desire; Picnic.

MEHTA, Zubin: Cond. b. Bombay, India, Apr 29, 1936. e. State Academy of Music, Vienna. Mus dir Montreal Symphony, 1961-67; Los Angeles Philharmonic 1967-1978; New York Philharmonic 1978; guest conductor Salzburg Festival; Berlin Philharmonic; Metropolitan Opera; Vienna Philharmonic; La Scala; Philadelphia Orch; L'Orchestre de Paris; Israel Philharmonic (since 1969).

TV inc: Zubin and the I.P.O. (Emmy-1983).

(Grammy-Inst Soloist with Orch-1982).

MEKKA, Eddie: Act. b. Worcester, MA, Jun 14, 1952. Bway inc: Jumper; The Magic Show; The Lieutenant.

TV inc: Laverne and Shirley; Eubie Blake--A Century of Music.

MELATO, Mariangela: Act. b. Milan, Italy, 1938. Films inc: Nada; The Seduction of Mimi; Dear Michael; Love and Anarchy; Swept Away; To Forget Venice; Flash Gordon; The Beach House; Help Me Dream; So Fine; Il buon Soldato (The Good Soldier); Domani si balla (Tomorrow we Dance); Segreti Segreti (Secrets Secrets).

MELCHIOR, Ib Jorgen: Wri-Dir-Prod. b. Copenhagen, Denmark, Sep 17, 1917. e. Stenhus Coll; U of Copenhagen. S of the late Lauritz Melchior. Films inc: (wri) Live Fast, Die Young; When Hell Broke Loose; The Angry Red Planet (& dir); Robinson Crusoe on Mars; Reptilicus; Journey to the Seventh Planet; The Time Travelers (& dir); Ambush Bay; Planet of the Vampires; Death Race 200; The Gingerbread Man (& prod).

TV inc: (wri) Men Into Space; The Outer Limits; (dir) The Perry Como Show; The Eddie Arnold Show; The March of Medicine.

MELLE, Gil: Comp-Cond. b. Jersey City, NJ, Dec 31, 1935. Films inc: The Ultimate Warrior; Starship Invasion; Secret Life of Plants; Embryo; You'll Like My Mother; The Savage Is Loose; The Sentinel; The Andromeda Strain; Borderline.

TV inc: Perilous Voyage; Legend In Granite; Killdozer; Hitchhiker; If Tomorrow Comes; The President's Plane Is Missing; A Cry for Help; Frankenstein-The True Story; That Certain Summer; My Sweet Charlie; Starship Invasions; Colombo; Night Gallery; The Night Stalker; Executive Suite; The Curse of King Tut's Tomb; Rape and Marriage--The Rideout Case; The Intruder Within; World War III; Through Naked Eyes; Jealousy; Hollywood's Most Sensational Mysteries; Best Kept Secrets; Flight 90--Disaster on the Potomac; Sweet Revenge; Fatal Vision; When Dreams Come True; Starcrossed.

MELNICK, Dan: Exec. b. NYC, Apr 21, 1934. Joined CBS TV 1954 as staff prod, later exec prod; vp chg prgmg ABC-TV; 1964 partner

in Talent Associates; 1972 VP chg wldwde prodn MGM; 1974 sr vp; 1976 left to go into indie prodn; 1977 prodn head Col; 1978 P Columbia Pictures Industry film ops; 1979 retd to indie prodn.

TV inc: Ages of Man (Emmy-prod-1966).

Films inc: (exec prod) That's Entertainment 2; All That Jazz; Altered States; First Family; Making Love; Unfaithfully Yours; Footloose.

MELVILLE, Sam: Act. b. Utah, Aug 20, 1940. e. Brigham Young U; U of UT. Films inc: Hour of the Gun; The Thomas Crown Affair; Big Wednesday.

TV inc: Terror in the Sky; Lust; City by Night; Roughnecks.

MELVIN, Allan: Act. b. Kansas City, MO, Feb 18. Started on radio, shows inc: Lorenzo Jones; Pepper Young's Family. TV inc: The Phil Silvers Show; Andy Griffith Show; Gomer Pyle; All in the Family (later Archie Bunker's Place) since 1972; Yogi Bear's All-Star Comedy Christmas Caper (voice).

MEMMOLI, George: Act. b. NYC, Aug 3, 1938. Former member of Ace Trucking Company (group). Films inc; Mean Streets; Rocky; New York, New York; Phantom of the Paradise; Lunch Wagon.

TV inc: Hello, Larry.

(Died May 20, 1985.)

MENDELSON, Lee: Prod-Dir-Wri. b. San Francisco, Mar 24, 1933. e. Stanford U. TV inc: A Man Named Mays; Travels With Charley; Hot Dog; It Couldn't Be Done; Wild Places; The Fabulous Funnies (& dir-wri); exec prod all Charlie Brown features and specials inc A Charlie Brown Christmas (Emmy-1966); John Steinbeck's America and the Americans (Emmy-1968); You're A Good Sport, Charlie Brown (Emmy-1976); Happy Anniversary Charlie Brown (Emmy-1976); Happy Birthday Charlie Brown; You're The Greatest Charlie Brown; She's A Good Skate Charlie Brown; The Fantastic Funnies; Life Is A Circus Charlie Brown (Emmy-1981); It's Magic Charlie Brown; You Asked For It (exec prod); Someday You'll Find Her, Charlie Brown; No Man's Valley; A Charlie Brown Celebration; Here Comes Garfield; Is This Goodbye, Charlie Brown?; The Sunday Funnies; It's An Adventure, Charlie Brown; Movie Blockbusters! The 15 Greatest Hits of all Time; What Have We Learned, Charlie Brown?; Garfield on the Town (Emmy-prod-1984); It's Flashbeagle, Charlie Brown; John Ritter, Mr. T and Jacqueline Bisset--Going Back Home; Snoopy's Getting Married Charlie Brown; The Romance Of Betty Boop.

Films inc: Bon Voyage Charlie Brown (And Don't Come Back).

MENDES, Sergio: Mus. b. Nitero, Brazil, Feb 11, 1941. Formed Brasil 65; later with Tijuana Brass; Brasil 77. Albums inc: Vintage 74; So Nice; Paris Tropical; Sergio Mendes.

MENGERS, Sue: Agent. b. NYC. Joined MCA NY 1961 as receptionist, later secy. Became agent 1963 with small agency, joined Creative Management Associates 1965; tsfd to Hwd; remained as exec with International Creative Management when CMA merged with Marvin Josephson.

MENON, Vijaya Bhaskar: Exec. b. Trivandrum, India, May 29, 1934. e. St. Stephens Coll, BA; U of Delhi, MA; U of Oxford. Chmn & chief exec Capitol Records, Inc.; dir EMI Ltd, London; P & CEO Capitol Industries-EMI, Inc.

MENOTTI, Gian Carlo: Comp. b. Caddegliano, Italy, Jul 7, 1911. Operas: Amelia Goes to the Ball; The Telephone; The Medium; The Consul (Pulitzer Prize-1950); The Saint of Bleecker Street (Pulitzer Prize-1955); Vanessa (Pulitzer Prize-1958); The Last Savage. Ballets: Sebastian; The Unicorn, the Gorgon and the Manticore; Errand into the Maze.

(Kennedy Center Honoree-1984)

MENUHIN, Yehudi: Violinist. b. NYC, Apr 22, 1916. Began playing at age 4; soloist with San Francisco Orchestra at 7; recital at Manhattan Opera House at 8; debut Carnegie Hall at 10 with NY Symphony; soloist with Berlin Symphony at 12; toured Europe and U.S. at 15; debut as cond American Symphony 1966. (Grammys-chamber mus-1967; class album of year-1977).

MENZEL, Jiri: Dir. b. Czechoslovakia, 1938. Films inc: Closely Watched Trains (& act-co-sp); Capricious Summer (& act-co-sp); Crime At the Nightclub; Seclusion Near a Forest; The Apple Game (act); Those Wonderful Men With a Crank (& act-co-sp); Postriziny (Short Cut); Szivzur (Heartaches) (act); Upir z Feratu (Ferat Vampire); Felhojatek (Passing Fancy) (act); Buldoci a Tresne (Bulldogs and Cherries) (act); Slavnosti Snezenek (Snowdrop Celebration).

MENZIES, Heather: Act. b. Toronto, Dec 3, 1949. Screen debut, 1965 Sound of Music. Films inc: Hawaii; Sssssssss; Piranha.
TV inc: The Farmer's Daughter; Tail Gunner Joe; Logan's Run.

MERCER, Marian: Act-Singer. b. Akron, OH, Nov 26, 1935. e. U MI, BMus. In stock and on tour before Bway debut Greenwillow (understudy) 1960. Bway inc: Fiorello!; Little Mary Sunshine; New Faces of 1962; Your Own Thing; Promises, Promises (Tony-supp-1969); A Place for Polly.
TV inc: Dean Martin Show; Bosoms and Neglect; The Cracker Factory; It's A Living; Ladies And Gentlemen--Bob Newhart, Part II; Life of the Party--The Story of BeAtrice; 9 to 5; Dom DeLuise and Friends--Part II; Booker.
Films inc: Oh, God! Book II.

MERCHANT, Ismail: Prod. Films inc: The Creation of Woman (short); The Householder; Shakespeare Wallah; The Guru; Bombay Talkie; Savages; The Wild Party; Hullabaloo Over Georgie and Bonnie's Pictures; Mahatma and the Wild Boy (short) (& dir); Roseland; The Europeans; Jane Austen In Manhattan; Heat and Dust; The Courtesans of Bombay (& dir-wri); The Bostonians.
TV inc: Noon Wine.

MERCOURI, Melina: Act. b. Athens, Greece, Apr 18, 1915. Appeared on stage in Athens, Paris. Thea inc: Medea. Screen debut in Stella. Films inc: Never On Sunday; He Who Must Die; The Gypsy and the Gentleman; The Victors; Never on Sunday; Where the Hot Wind Blows; Phaedra; Topkapi; 10:30 pm Summer; A Man Could Get Killed; Gaily, Gaily; Once Is Not Enough; Nasty Habits; Promise At Dawn; Keine Zufallige Geschichte (Not By Coincidence) (doc).

MEREDITH, Burgess: Act-Dir. b. Cleveland, OH, Nov 16, 1908. e. Amherst Coll. On stage from 1929. Bway inc: The Barretts of Wimpole Street; Little Old Boy; She Loves Me Not; The Star Wagon; Winterset; High Tor; The Remarkable Mr Pennypacker; Teahouse of the August Moon; Ulysses in Nighttown (dir); God and Kate Murphy (dir); A Thurber Carnival (Tony-special-1960); An Evening with Burgess Meredith; Blues for Mr Charlie (dir); The Latent Homosexual (dir); Love Remembered (dir). Films inc: Winterset; Idiot's Delight; Of Mice and Men; That Uncertain Feeling; Tom, Dick and Harry; The Story of G.I. Joe; Miracles Can Happen; The Diary of a Chambermaid; Magnificent Doll; Mine Own Executioner; The Man of the Eiffel Tower; Joe Butterfly; Advise and Consent; The Cardinal; In Harm's Way; A Big Hand for the Little Lady; Madame X; Batman; Hurry Sundown; Mackenna's Gold; There Was a Crooked Man; Such Good Friends; Golden Needles; The Day of the Locust; The Hindenberg; Rocky; The Sentinel; Shenanigans; Foul Play; The Manitou; Magic; Rocky 2; When Time Ran Out; Final Assignment; The Last Chase: Clash of the Titans; True Confessions; Rocky III.
TV inc: Search; U.F.O.'s; Johnny We Hardly Knew Ye; Tail Gunner Joe (Emmy-supp-1977); SST-Earth Flight; The Last Hurrah; How the West Was Won; The Return of Capt Nemo; Kate Bliss; Puff the Magic Dragon in the Land of the Living Lies (voice); Those Amazing Animals (host); Gloria; Wet Gold.

MEREDITH, Don: Sports Commentator-Act. b. Mt Vernon, TX, Apr 10, 1938. Former pro-football star. TV inc: Monday Night Football (Emmy-1971); Undercover With the KKK; The Night the City Screamed; Terror Among Us; Legends of the West--Truth and Tall Tales; Omnibus.

MERIWETHER, Lee: Act. b. Los Angeles, May 27, 1935. Miss America, 1955. Films inc: 4-D Man; Batman; Namu, the Killer Whale; The Legend of Lylah Clare; The Courtship of Eddie's Father; Angel in My Pocket; The Undefeated.
TV inc: The Clear Horizon; The Young Marrieds; Time Tunnel; Shirts/Skins; The New Andy Griffith Show; Barnaby Jones; Dean Martin's Xmas in California; True Grit; Tourist.

MERKEL, Una: Act. b. Covington, KY, Dec 10, 1903. On screen since 1921 in more than 100 films inc: Eyes of the World; Abraham Lincoln; Command Performance; The White Robe; Love's Old Sweet Song; Daddy Long Legs; Private Lives; Reunion in Vienna; Bombshell; Emergency Wedding; My Blue Heaven; Rich, Young and Pretty, Golden Girl; The Maltese Falcon; Day of Reckoning; Merry Widow; Born to Dance; Riffraff; Saratoga; Test Pilot; On Borrowed Time; Road to Zanzibar; Millionaire for Christy; With A Song in My Heart; The Kentuckian; Twin Beds; This is the Army; It's A Joke Son; The Bride Goes Wild; I Love Melvin; Bundle of Joy; The Mating Game; Summer and Smoke; Summer Magic; A Tiger Walks; Spin-out.
Bway inc: Two By Two; Poor Nut; Pigs; Gossipy Sex; Coquette; Salt Water; The Ponder Heart (Tony-supp-1956); Take Me Along.

MERLIN, Joanna: Act. Bway inc: Becket; Fiddler on the Roof; The Survivor; Solomon's Child.
Films inc: Fame; All That Jazz; Soup for One; Love Child; Baby It's You.
TV inc: Starstruck; The Last Tenant; Another World; Jacobo Timerman, Prisoner Without a Name, Cell Without a Number.

MERLIS, George: Prod. e. U of PA; Columbia. Began as sports editor Rome (Italy) Daily American; with NY World-Telegram-Sun, World-Journal-Tribune, Daily News before joining ABC pub relations dept; 1973 ABC Evening News; ABC Weekend News; 1975 Good Morning America; 1978, sr. prod; 1979 exec prod; April, 1983 exec prod Entertainment Tonight; fired Jan. 1984.

MERMAN, Ethel (nee Zimmerman): Act. b. NYC, Jan 16, 1909. Started in niteries, vaudeville. On stage in: Girl Crazy; George White's Scandals; Stars in Your Eyes; Du Barry Was A Lady; Panama Hattie; Annie Get Your Gun; Call Me Madam (Tony-1951); Happy Hunting; Hello Dolly! (Special Tony-1972). Screen debut 1930 Follow the Leader.
Films inc: The Big Broadcast of 1932; Kid Millions; Strike Me Pink; Alexander's Ragtime Band; Call Me Madam; There's No Business Like Show Business; It's a Mad, Mad, Mad, Mad World.
TV inc: 100 Years of Golden Hits; Love Boat (spec); Texaco Star Theatre--Opening Night.
(Grammy-cast album-1959).
(Died Feb. 15, 1984).

MERRICK, David (ne Margulies): Prod. b. Hong Kong, 1911. Bway inc: Fanny; The Matchmaker; Look Back in Anger; Romanoff and Juliet; The Entertainer; The World of Suzie Wong; Epitaph For George Dillon; La Plume de Ma Tante; Destry Rides Again; Gypsy; A Taste of Honey; Do Re Mi; Becket (Tony-1961; also special award)Irma La Douce; Carnival; Sunday in New York; Subways Are for Sleeping; I Can Get it For You Wholesale; Ross; Carnival; Stop the World, I Want to Get Off; Tchin Tchin; Oliver!; Rattle of a Simple Man; Luther; One Flew Over the Cuckoo's Nest; Hello, Dolly (Tony-1964); The Milk Train Doesn't Stop Here Anymore; Oh, What a Lovely War!; I Was Dancing; The Roar of the Greasepaint-The Smell of the Crowd; Hot September; Inadmissible Evidence; The Cactus Flower; Marat/Sade; Philadelphia, Here I Come; How Now, Dow Jones; Don't Drink the Water; I Do! I Do!; Keep It In the Family; Rosencrantz and Guildenstern Are Dead; The Seven Descents of Myrtle; Rockefeller and the Red Indians; Play It Again, Sam; Promises, Promises; Child's Play; The Philanthropist; Vivat! Vivat Regina; Sugar; Mack and Mabel; The Misanthrope; Dreyfus in Rehearsal; Very Good Eddie; Travesties; (Special Tony-1968); 42nd Street (Tony-1981); I Won't Dance.
Films inc: The Great Gatsby; Semi-Tough; Rough Cut.

MERRILL, Bob: Comp. b. Atlantic City, NJ, May 17, 1920. e. Temple U. Started as nightclub singer, comedian. Bway scores inc: New Girl in Town; Take Me Along; Carnival; Funny Girl; Henry, Sweet Henry; Take Me Along.
Film scores inc: The Wonderful World of the Brothers Grimm. Songs inc: How Much is that Doggie in the Window; My Truly, Truly Fair; If I Knew You Were Comin' I'd've Baked a Cake; Take Me Along; Love Makes the World Go Round; I Am Woman; Don't Rain on My Parade.
(Grammy-show score-1964).

MERRILL, Dina (Nedinia Hutton): Act. b. NYC, Dec 9, 1925. e. George Washington U; AADA. W of Cliff Robertson. Films inc: Desk

Set; Catch Me If You Can; The Sundowners; The Courtship of Eddie's Father; The Pleasure Seekers; I'll Take Sweden; Running Wild; The Greatest; A Wedding; Just Tell Me What You Want.
Bway inc: My Sister Eileen; Major Barbara; Misalliance; Angel Street; On Your Toes.
TV inc: The Tenth Month; Hot Pursuit.

MERRILL, Gary: Act. b. Hartford, CT, 1914. e. Bowdoin Coll; Trinity Coll. Films inc: Winged Victory; Slattery's Hurricane; Twelve O'Clock High; All About Eve; Decision Before Dawn; Phone Call From a Stranger; Blueprint for Murder; Bermuda Affair; The Pleasure of His Company; The Woman Who Wouldn't Die; Around the World Under the Sea; Destination Inner Space; The Power; Huckleberry Finn; Thieves. TV inc: The Mask; Justice; Dr Kildare; The Seekers.
Bway inc: Born Yesterday; At War With the Army; Morning's at Seven (rev).

MERRILL, Kieth W.: Dir-Wri-Prod. b. May 22, 1940. e. Brigham Young U, BA. Films inc: Matter of Winning; The Great American Cowboy (Oscar-doc-1973); Indian; Three Warriors; Take Down; Windwalker; Harry's War.
TV inc: Kenny Rogers and the Cowboys; Mr Kreuger's Christmas; The Stranger At Jefferson High (wri); Louis L'Amour's The Cherokee Trail.

MERRILL, Robert: Baritone. b. Brooklyn, NY, Jun 4, 1919. Winner Metropolitan Opera Audition of the Air 1945; made opera debut 1945; with NBC 1946; opened Met Opera Season 1950; guest artist Covent Garden; with Toscanini for latter's final opera and recording sessions; with 1973 appearance became first American singer to do 500 performances at Metropolitan Opera.
Bway inc: Fiddler on the Roof.

MERZBACH, Susan K: Exec. b. Amherst, MA, Apr 20, 1946. e. Bucknell. 1972, story analyst MGM; 1978 story ed; 1978 exec story ed Col; 1980 vp crea aff Fox; Jan. 1983, resd to become vp of Jaffe-Lansing Productions

METCALFE, Burt: Prod-Dir. b. Saskatchewan, Canada, Mar 19, 1935. e. UCLA, BA. TV inc: M*A*S*H, asso prod, 1971-75; co-prod, '76; prod, (& dir) '77-'82; Little House on the Prairie; AfterMASH (exec prod & dir).

METRANO, Art: Act-Wri. b. Brooklyn, NY, Sep 22. e. College of the Pacific, BA. Studied with Stella Adler. TV inc: Lohman & Barkley; The Tonight Show; Superbowl Saturday Nite; The Chicago Teddy Bears; Movin' On; Baretta; Barney Miller; Benson; A Cry for Love; Rise and Shine; No Man's Valley (voice) Joanie Loves Chachi; Matt Houston.
Films inc: They Shoot Horses Don't They?; The Choirboys; They Only Kill Their Masters; All-American Boy; Seven; Cheaper To Keep Her; Going Ape; History of the World--Part I; Breathless; Teachers; Police Academy 2--Their First Assignment.
Thea inc: The Hairy Ape; Of Mice and Men; Tea and Sympathy; The Death and Life of Jesse James.

METZGER, Radley: Prod-Dir. b. 1930. Worked as asst dir; distributor of Swedish film I, A Woman before making own product. Films inc: Passionate Sunday; The Dirty Girls; The Alley Cats; Carmen Baby; Theresa and Isabelle; Camille 2000; Little Mother; Naked Came the Stranger; The Image; The Opening of Misty Beethoven; The Cat and the Canary; The Princess and the Call Girl.

MEYER, Irwin: Prod. b. Brooklyn, Jul 21, 1935. e. NYU, BS. P Pound Ridge Prodns Ltd; involved in financing numerous companies and film projects. Films inc: Hollywood on Trial (doc) (Exec prod).
Bway inc: Going Up; Night of the Tribades; Break a Leg; Home Again; Annie (Tony-1977); Working.
TV inc: In Love With An Older Woman (exec prod).

MEYER, Nicholas: Wri-Dir. b. NYC. Films inc: The Seven-Per-Cent Solution (sp); Time After Time; Star Trek II--The Wrath of Khan (dir).
TV inc: Judge Dee; The Night That Panicked America; The Day After (dir).

MEYER, Russ: Prod-Dir. b. Oakland, CA, Mar 21, 1922. Films inc: The Immoral Mr Teas; Fanny Hill; Finders Keepers, Lovers Weepers;

Lorna; Motorpsycho; Faster Pussycat; Kill, Kill; Goodmorning and Goodbye; Vixen; Beyond the Valley of the Dolls; The Seven Minutes; Blacksnake; Supervixens; Up!; Beneath the Valley of the Ultravixens.

MEYERS, Robert: Exec. b. Mt Vernon, NY, Oct 3, 1934. e. NYU, BS. Joined Columbia 1956 as trainee, U.S. Distribution, moved to Intl Dept 1960; 1965 M-Dir Columbia, Brussels; 1967, European sls supv; 1969, vp foreign sls National General Pictures; 1974, founder-owner JAD Films Int'l; 1977, P Lorimar Distribution Int'l; 1981, P & COO Filmways Pictures, Inc.; left Filmways following takeover by Orion; co-founder, P American Film Marketing Association; Sept. 1984, formed Taliafilm II Ltd., with Jack Schwarzman, becoming exec vp of new firm.

MICHAEL, Ralph (nee Shotter): Act. b. London, Sep 26, 1907. Thea debut 1930 with Henry Baynton rep company; joined Old Vic company 1931; appeared with several rep companies 1932-36. Thea inc: The Amazing Dr. Clitterhouse; The Man Who Meant Well; Comedienne; Charlie's Aunt; Men in Shadow; Private Lives; Love Goes to Press (& Bway); Peace In Our Time; Medea; The Heiress; The Seventh Veil; A Shred of Evidence; Guilty Party; A Sense of Detachment; Dandy Dick.
Films inc: John Halifax, Gentleman; The Hasty Heart; Doctor in the House; Grand Prix; Khartoum; San Demetrio, London; The Assassination Bureau.
TV inc: The Cocktail Party; Sapper; Somerset Maugham; Kessler; A Tale of Two Cities; The Borgias; The Quest; Romance On The Orient Express.

MICHAELS, Joel B.: Prod. b. Buffalo, NY., Oct 24, 1938. Studied acting with Stella Adler. Films inc: The Peace Killers; Your Three Minutes Are Up (prodn supv); Student Teachers (prodn supv); The Prisoners (asso prod); Lepke (asso prod); The Four Deces (asso prod); Bittersweet Love; The Silent Partner; The Changeling; Tribute; The Amateur; Losin' It (exec prod); The Philadelphia Experiment.

MICHAELS, Lorne: Wri-Prod. b. Toronto, Canada, Nov 17. TV inc: Lily (Emmy-wri-1974); Laugh-In; Lily Tomlin (Emmy-1976-wri); Flip Wilson Special (& prod); NBC's Saturday Night Live (Emmys-prod-wri-1976; wri-1977; wri-1978); The Paul Simon Special (Emmy-wri-1978); NBC's Saturday Night Live (prod); Steve Martin's Best Show Ever; The Coneheads (exec prod); The New Show (prod-wri).
Films inc: Gilda Live (prod-wri); Nothing Lasts Forever (prod); Bigshots In America.

MICHAELS, Richard: Dir. b. Feb. 15, 1936. TV inc: Ellery Queen; Love American Style; The Odd Couple; Delvecchio; Bewitched; Charlie Cobb; My Husband Is Missing; Having Babies II; Leave Yesterday Behind; Once Upon A Family; And Your Name Is Jonah; Scared Straight! Another Story; Homeward Bound; Berlin Tunnel 21; The Children Nobody Wanted; One Cooks, The Other Doesn't; Sadat; Jessie; Silence Of The Heart; The Heart Of a Champion--The Ray Mancini Story.
Films inc: Blue Skies Again.

MICHAUD, Henri (Ricky): Exec. b. Ismailia, Egypt, Sep 24, 1912. Joined WB Paris 1934; To Par Int'l 1944; when Par and U formed Cinema International Corp 1970, became co-chmn with Arthur Abeles, also P Par Int'l; 1977, formed, with Abeles, A-M Film Consultants Ltd.

MICHEL, Werner: Exec. b. Germany, Mar 5, 1910. e. U of Berlin; U of Paris. Radio wri prior to WW 2; dir Voice of America Bcast Div 1942-1946; with CBS as prod-dir, pgm dir 1946-1950; dir tv dept Kenyon & Eckhart ad agcy 1950; prod Dumont TV net 1952; prod Benton & Bowles agcy, Proctor & Gamble, NW Ayer before joining ABC-TV Hollywood 1975 as pgm exec; 1976 dir dramatic pgms; 1977 sr vp crea aff MGM-TV; 1979 exec vp Wrather Entertainment Intl; 1980 sr vp pgms MGM-TV; Dec 1981, sr vp crea aff; July, 1982, Sr vp in chg current pgmng; resd Oct 1982; Dec, 1982, named VP & COO TV div Guber-Peters Co.; June 1984, Senior VP Kenyon & Eckhardt.

MICHELET, Michel: Comp. b. Kiev, Russia, Jun 27, 1899. e. Graduate of three conservatories: Leipzig (Germany), St. Petersburg (Russia), Lev (Russia). Scored 108 movies in Paris, Italy, Germany,

Spain, US. To US, 1941.

Films inc: Diary of a Chambermaid; Anastasia; The Journey; The Man on the Eiffel Tower; Lured; Outpost in Morocco; Music for Millions; Impact; Voice in the Wind; The Challenge-A Tribute to Modern Art (documentary, narrated by Orson Welles).

Compositions inc: Memories; Hommage to Bach; Concert Songs and Arias; Hanelle.

MICHELL, Keith: Act. b. Adelaide, Australia, Dec 1, 1928. e. Adelaide U. Thea inc: (London) And So to Bed; Troilus and Cressida; Romeo and Juliet; The Lady's Not for Burning; Antony and Cleopatra; Irma La Douce; The Art of Seduction; Abelard and Heloise; Man of La Mancha; On The 20th Century. (Bway) Irma La Douce; The Rehearsal; Man of La Mancha; Hamlet; Dear Love; Tonight We Improvise; Cyrano de Bergerac; The Apple Cart; The Crucifer of Blood; La Cage aux Folles.

Films inc: Hell Fire Club; All Night Long; Seven Seas to Calais.

TV inc: Pygmalion; The Mayerling Affair; Traveller Without Luggage; Tiger at the Gates; Catherine Howard *(Emmy*-1972); Ring Around the Moon; The Six Wives of Henry VIII; The Tenth Month; The Day Christ Died; The Treasure of Alpheus T. Winterborn; Grendel, Grendel, Grendel (voice).

MICHENER, James A.: Wri. b. NYC, Feb 3, 1907. Works filmed inc: South Pacific; Return to Paradise; The Bridges of Toko Ri; Sayonara; Hawaii.

Works done on TV inc: Space. Other TV inc: Centennial (narr).

MIDDLETON, Ray: Act. b. Chicago, IL, Feb 8, 1907. e. Juilliard School of Music. Bway inc: Roberta; Annie Get Your Gun; South Pacific; Man of La Mancha.

Films inc: Knickerbocker Holiday; American Jubilee; Lady for a Night; I Dream of Jeannie; Sweethearts on Parade; Road to Denver; 1776.

TV inc: Border Pals.

(Died April 10, 1984).

MIDGLEY, Leslie: Exec. b. Salt Lake City, Jan 18, 1915. H of Betty Furness. TV inc: prod Eyewitness, CBS 1959-1963; prod CBS Evening New with Walter Cronkite 1967-1972; has produced hundreds of documentaries and special report broadcasts including four one-hour reports on Robert Kennedy assassination 1967; The Senate and the Watergate Affair *(Emmy*-exec prod-1974); Showdown In Iran *(Emmy*-1979); resigned CBS News after 24 years to join NBC News as vp special pgms Oct 1979.

MIDGLEY, Robin: Dir. b. Torquay, England, Nov 10, 1934. e. King's Coll; Cambridge. Dir debut The Seagull; London dir debut Kill Two Birds (1961); Bway debut Those That Play The Clowns 1967.

Thea inc: Victor; Picnic on the Battlefield; The Pedagogue (all for Royal Shakespeare Co); Oedipus The King; Right You Are If You Think So; The Professor; Let's Get a Divorce; Rafferty's Chant; Young Churchill; How the Other Half Loves; Lloyd George Knew My Father; Six of One; Cause Celebre; Oliver! (rev); My Fair Lady (rev); Sextet.

TV inc: Royal Shakespeare Co prodn of The Wars of the Roses; The Mayfly and the Frog.

MIDLER, Bette: Act. b. Honolulu, Dec 1, 1945. Recording artist; niteries; TV guest shots. Films inc: The Divine Mr J; The Rose; Divine Madness (doc); Jinxed! Bway inc: Fiddler on the Roof; Bette! Divine Madness (& dir). *(Special Tony*-1974).

TV inc: Ol' Red Hair is Back *(Emmy*-1978); Belafonte Sings; Bette Midler--Art or Bust. *(Grammys*-new artist-1973; pop vocal-1980).

MIFUNE, Toshiro: Act. b. Tsing-tao, China, Apr 1, 1920. Film debut in 1946 These Foolish Times. Films inc: Rashomon; Scandal; The Seven Samurai; Throne of Blood; Rickshaw Man; Red Beard; Midway; Love and Faith; Shag (& prod); Winter Kills; Oginsaga; 1941; Inchon; The Challenge;The Bushido Blade. TV inc: Shogun.

MIGDEN, Chester L.: Exec. b. Brooklyn.b. NYC, May 21, 1921. e. CCNY, BA; Columbia U, LLB. National exec secy, Screen Actors Guild; vp, California Labor Federation; p, Film and Television Coordinating Committee; vp, Associated Actors and Artists of America; vp, International Federation of Actors (FIA); vp, Hollywood Film Council; Nov

1981, resd to become exec dir of Association of Talent Agents.

MIGHTY CLOUDS OF JOY: Gospel Singers. Group inc: Johnny Martin, Joe Ligon, Elmo Franklin, Richard Wallace, Paul Beasley. Films inc: Gospel.

(Grammys-Soul Gospel Performance, traditional-1979, 1980).

MIKHALKOV-KONCHALOVSKY, Andrei: Dir. b. Russia, Aug 20, 1937. Films inc: A Boy and a Pigeon (short) (& sp); The First Teacher; Asya's Happiness; A Nest of the Gentry (& co-sp); Uncle Vanya (& sp); A Lover's Romance; Siberiade; Maria's Lovers (& sp).

MILES, Bernard, Sir: Act. b. Hillingdon, England, Sep 27, 1907. Films inc: Channel Crossing; Quiet Wedding; In Which We Serve; (& sp-co-dir); Great Expectations; Never Let Me Go; The Man Who Know Too Much; Moby Dick; The Smallest Show on Earth; Tom Thumb; Sapphire; Heavens Above; Run Wild Run Free; The Specialist.

TV inc: Treasure Island; Why Didn't They Ask Evans?

Thea inc: Various Shakespearean roles with Old Vic Company; Lock Up Your Daughters; John Gabriel Borkman; All in Good Time; Schweyk in the Second World War; Treasure Island; The Great Society; On the Rocks; Tawny Pipit.

MILES, Christopher: Dir. b. England, 1939. Films inc: Up Jumped a Swagman; The Virgin and the Gypsy; Time for Loving; The Maids; That Lucky Touch; Priest of Love (& prod).

MILES, Sarah: Act. b. England, Dec 31, 1941. e. RADA. Films inc: Term of Trial; The Ceremony; Those Magnificent Men in Their Flying Machines; Blow Up; Ryan's Daughter; Lady Caroline Lamb; The Hireling; The Man Who Loved Cat Dancing; The Sailor Who Fell with Grace from the Sea; The Big Sleep; Priest of Love; Venom; Ordeal By Innocence; Steaming.

TV inc: Great Expectations; Dynasty.

Thea inc: Vivat! Vivat Regina!

MILES, Sylvia: Act. b. 1932. Films inc: Midnight Cowboy; Heat; Farewell My Lovely; 92 in the Shade; The Great Scout and Cathouse Thursday; The Sentinel; The Funhouse; Evil Under The Sun.

MILES, Vera: Act. b. Boise City, OK, Aug 23, 1930. Screen debut 1952, For Men Only. Films inc: The Wild Country; Psycho; Hellfighters; It Takes All Kinds; Gentle Giant; The Man Who Shot Liberty Valance; Kona Coast; Run for the Roses; Psycho II; BrainWaves; The Initiation; Into The Night.

TV inc: Climax; Ford Theatre; Pepsi Cola Playhouse; And I Alone Survived; Rougnecks; Our Family Business; Rona Jaffe's Mazes & Monsters; Travis McGee; Helen Keller--The Miracle Continues; International Airport.

MILFORD, John: Act. b. Johnstown, NY, Sep 7, 1929. e. Union Coll. Films inc: Marty.

TV inc: Wyatt Earp; The Lieutenant; The Legend of Jesse James; The Bold Ones; Enos; Policewoman Centerfold.

MILFORD, Penelope: Act. b. St Louis, MO. Films inc: Maidstone; Man on a Swing; Valentino; Coming Home; Take This Job and Shove It; Endless Love; The Golden Seal; The Link.

Bway inc: Lenny; Shenandoah. TV inc: Seizure-The Story of Kathy Morris; The Oldest Living Graduate; Rosie--The Rosemary Clooney Story; The Burning Bed.

MILIAN, Tomas: Act. b. Italy, Mar 3, 1938. Films inc: The Fine Night; The Dolphins; A Day of Lions; The Casaroli Gang; Time of Indifference; The Money; Bounty Killer; Run, Man, Run; Face to Face; The Cannibals; Conjugal Love; The Chosen Victims; A Man With Tough Skin; The J and S Gang; Criminal Story of the West; The Last Movie; Antimafia Squad; Luna; Winter Kills; Almost Human; Crime at Porta Romana; Identificazione D'Una Donna (Identification of A Woman); Monsignor; Rambo Sfida la Citta (Syndicate Sadists); Delitto Al Blue Gay (Crime At the Blue Gay).

TV inc: The Day Christ Died.

MILIUS, John: Wri-Dir. b. St Louis, MO, Apr 11, 1944. e. LA City Coll; USC. Films inc: Deadhead Miles (act); (sp) Devil's 8; Evel Knievel; Dirty Harry; Jeremiah Johnson; The Life and Times of Judge

Roy Bean; Magnum Force; Dillinger (& dir); The Wind and the Lion (& dir); Big Wednesday (& dir); Apocalypse Now; Used Cars (exec prod); Conan The Barbarian; Uncommon Valor (prod); Red Dawn.

MILKIS, Edward K.: Prod. b. Los Angeles, Jul 16, 1931. e. USC. Started as asst edtr ABC-TV 1952; Disney 1954; MGM 1957; edtr MGM 1960-65; asso prod Star Trek 1966-1969; exec in chg post prodn Par 1969-1972; formed Miller-Milkis Prodns 1972; Miller-Milkis-Boyett, 1979.

TV inc: (exec prod) Happy Days; Laverne and Shirley; Petrocelli; Angie; Out of the Blue; Goodtime Girls; Bosom Buddies (& crea); Foul Play (supv prod); Feel the Heat.

Films inc: (co-prod); Silver Streak; Foul Play; The Best Little Whorehouse In Texas.

MILLAND, Ray (Reginald Truscott-Jones): Act. b. Neath, Wales, Jan 3, 1908. On screen, England, from 1929, in US, from 1931. Films inc: Ambassador Bill; We're Not Dressing; Charlie Chan in London; Jungle Princess; Ebb Tide; Men with Wings; Beau Geste; The Major and the Minor; Lady in the Dark; Kitty; I Wanted Wings; The Lost Weekend (Oscar-1945); Reap the Wild Wind; The Major and the Minor; Golden Earrings; Big Clock; Bugles in the Afternoon; The Thief; Dial M for Murder; Hostile Witness; Love Story; Frogs; The House in Nightmare Park; Escape to Witch Mountain; Swiss Conspiracy; The Last Tycoon; Slaves; Blackout; Oliver's Story; Battlestar Galactica; Survival Run.

TV inc: Rich Man, Poor Man; Seventh Avenue; Testimony of Two Men; The Darker Side of Terror; The Dream Merchants; Our Family Business; The Royal Romance of Charles and Diana; Starflight--The Plane That Couldn't Land; Cave-In!

MILLAR, Stuart: Dir. b. NYC, 1929. e. Stanford; Sorbonne, Paris. Wrote, directed documentary films for US State Dept; to Hollywood as asso to William Wyler. Films inc: The Young Stranger; Stage Struck; The Birdman of Alcatraz; The Best Man; Paper Lion; Little Big Man; When Legends Die; Rooster Cogburn; Shoot the Moon (exec prod).

MILLER, Ann (Lucille Ann Collier): Act. b. Houston, TX, Apr 12, 1923. In vaudeville. Screen debut New Faces of 1937. Films inc: Life of the Party; Stage Door; Room Service; You Can't Take it with You; Eadie Was a Lady; Easter Parade; On the Town; Lovely to Look At; Kiss Me Kate; Deep in My Heart; Hit the Deck; The Opposite Sex; The Great American Pastime.

Bway inc: George White's Scandals; Mame; Sugar Babies.

TV inc: Entertainer of the Year Awards; Love Boat (spec).

MILLER, Arthur: Wri. b. NYC, Oct 17, 1915. e. U of MI, BA. Plays inc: All My Sons; (Special Tony-1947) Death of a Salesman; (Pulitzer Prize & Tony-1949); The Crucible (Tony-1953); A View from the Bridge; After the Fall; Incident at Vichy; The Price; Up for Paradise (& dir-act) Situation Normal; The American Clock.

Film: The Misfits.

TV inc: Death of a Salesman (Emmy-1976); Fame; Playing For Time (Emmy-1981).

(Kennedy Center Honoree-1984).

MILLER, Barry: Act. b. Feb 8, 1958. Studied with Michael V Gazzo. TV inc: Joe and Sons; Szysznyk; Bill Cosby Show.

Films inc: Voices; Fame; The Chosen.

Bway inc: Biloxi Blues (Tony-featured-1985).

MILLER, Burton: Cos dsgn. b. Pittsburgh, PA, Jan 17, 1928. e. Carnegie Tech; Parsons School of Design. Films inc: Counterpoint; Sugarland Express; Earthquake; The Front Page; Roller Coaster; Swashbucker; When You Comin' Back, Red Ryder?; The Omen II; Airport '77; House Calls; The Concorde--Airport '79; The Nude Bomb; The Sting II.

TV inc: Chrysler Theatre; Run For Your Life; It Takes A Thief; Switch; The $6 Million Man; The Immigrants, The Gossip Columnist; Condominium.

MILLER, Cheryl: Act. b. Sherman Oaks, CA, Feb 4, 1943. Appeared in over 100 films as child. Recent films inc: The Monkey's Uncle; Clarence the Cross-Eyed Lion; The Initiation; The Man from Clover Grove; Doctor Death; Goldie and the Boxer Go to Hollywood.

MILLER, David: Dir. b. Paterson, NJ, Nov 28, 1909. Films inc: Billy the Kid; Sunday Punch; Flying Tigers; Love Happy; Top o' the Morning; Saturday's Hero; Sudden Fear; Twist of Fate; The Opposite Sex; Happy Anniversary; Midnight Lace; Back Street; Lonely are the Brave; Captain Newman, M.D.; Hammerhead; Hail, Hero; Executive Action; Bittersweet Love.

TV inc: The Best Place To Be; Love for Rent; Goldie and the Boxer; Goldie and the Boxer Go To Hollywood.

MILLER, Dick: Act. b. NYC, Dec 25, 1928. e. CCNY; Columbia U. Films inc: Not of This Earth; Thunder over Hawaii; Rock All Night; Sorority Girl; The Terror; War of the Satellites; The Long Ride Home; St Valentine Day Massacre; Capone; Cannonball; New York, New York; Corvette Summer; I Wanna Hold Your Hand; Piranha; Starhops; The Lady in Red; Rock 'n' Roll High School (sp) TNT Jackson; Which Way to the Front; Four Rode Out; Gremlins.

MILLER, Dr. George: Dir-Wri. b. Brisbane, Australia, 1945. Films inc: Violence in the Cinema Part One (short) (& wri); Frieze--An Underground Film (doc) (edtr only); Devil in Evening Dress (doc) (& wri); Mad Max (& wri); Chain Reaction (asso prod only); Mad Max 2 (Road Warrior); Twilight Zone--The Movie; Mad Max Beyond Thunderdrome.

TV inc: Five Mile Creek; The Cowra Breakout.

MILLER, George: Dir. b. Australia. TV inc: Cash and Company; Against the Wind; The Last Outlaw; The Dismissal; All The Rivers Run; Bodyline (& wri).

Films inc: In Search of Anna (asst dir); The Man From Snowy River; The Aviator.

MILLER, Harvey: Wri. b. NYC, Jun 15, 1935. e. Emerson Coll, BS. Began as comedy wri for Dick Gregory; Alan King; Shecky Greene. TV inc: The Odd Couple (&-dir). Films inc: Private Benjamin; Student Bodies; Jekyll and Hyde--Together Again; Cannonball Run II (wri).

MILLER, J. Philip: Dir b. Barberton, OH, Jul 10, 1937. e. Haverford Coll, AB; Harvard Grad School of Ed, EdM. Started as prodn coord Candid Camera; later unit mgr various NBC shows. TV inc: Mugsy Series; Figuring All The Angles; A Piece of Cake; Go-Show (Emmy-prod-1976); Christmastime With Mr. Rogers; The Bloodhound Gang; 3-2-1 Contact.

MILLER, Jason: Wri-Act. b. NYC, Apr 22, 1939. e. U of Scranton; Catholic U. Made stage debut as actor, 1969, Pequod. As plywri: That Championship Season (Tony & Pulitzer Prize-1973).

Films inc: The Exorcist (act); The Nickel Ride (act); A Home of Our Own (act); Fitzgerald in Hollywood (act); A Love Story (sp); The Ninth Configuration (act); Monsignor (act). That Championship Season (dir-wri); Toy Soldiers (act).

TV inc: Vampire (act); Reward (wri); The Henderson Monster (act); Marilyn--The Untold Story; The Best Little Girl In The World (act); A Touch Of Scandal (act).

MILLER, Jonathan: Prod-Dir-Wri. b. London, Jul 21, 1934. e. Cambridge. Thea inc: (London) Out of the Blue (act); Beyond the Fringe (act & co-wri). (Dir) Under Plain Cover; King Lear; The Merchant of Venice; Danton's Death; School for Scandal; The Marriage of Figaro; Three Sisters.

TV inc: What's Going on Now (dir); Alice in Wonderland (dir); Whistle and I'll Come To You (dir); The Merchant of Venice (exec prod); Anthony and Cleopatra (prod-dir); All's Well That Ends Well (prod); Othello (exec prod); Timon of Athens (exec prod-dir); A Midsummer Night's Dream (prod); Troilus and Cressida (prod-dir); King Lear (dir); King Henry VI (exec prod); The Beggar's Opera.

MILLER, JP: Wri. b. San Antonio, TX, Dec 18, 1919. e. Rice U. Films inc: The Rabbit Trap; Days of Wine and Roses; The Young Savages; Behold a Pale Horse; The People Next Door.

TV inc: Hide and Seek; Old Tasslefoot; The Pardon-me Boy; The People Next Door (Emmy-1969); Days of Wine and Roses; The Lindbergh Kidnapping Case; Helter Skelter; Gauguin the Savage.

MILLER, Linda G.: Act. b. Sep. 16, 1942. e. Catholic U. D of Jackie Gleason. Bway inc: The Black Picture Show. Films inc: One Summer Love; An Unmarried Woman; The Night of the Juggler.

TV inc: A Little Bit Different; Shakespeare on Love; Seizure-The Story of Kathy Morris; The Mississippi.

MILLER, Marvin (nee Mueller): Act. b. St Louis, MO, Jul 18, 1913. Films inc: Johnny Angel; Intrigue; Off Limits; Peking Express; The Naked Ape; Where Does It Hurt; I Wonder Who's Killing Her Now; Prime Time.

TV inc: The Millionaire; The FBI (narr); Burrud Nature Specials (narr); Evita Peron. Radio: Marvin Miller, Storyteller.

(Died Feb. 8, 1985)

MILLER, Mitch: Mus-Cond. b. Rochester, NY, Jul 4, 1911. e. Eastman School of Music, BA. Oboist with Rochester Philharmonic 1931-1933; Metropolitan Museum of Art concerts 1934; oboe soloist CBS Symphony 1935-1947; also with Saidenburg Little Symphony, Budapest String Quartet; A&R dir Mercury Records 1947-1950; head pop records div Columbia Records 1950-1961; guest cond major symphonies.

TV inc: Sing Along With Mitch.

MILLER, Robert Ellis: Dir. b. NYC, Jul 18, 1932. e. Harvard U. Films inc: Any Wednesday; Sweet November; The Heart Is a Lonely Hunter; The Buttercup Chain; Big Truck and Poor Claire; The Girl from Petrovka; The Baltimore Bullet; Reuben, Reuben.

TV inc: The Voice of Charlie Pont; And James Was a Very Small Snail; Ishi, The Last of His Tribe; Madame X; Her Life As a Man.

MILLER, Roger: Singer-Sngwri. b. Fort Worth, TX, Jan 3, 1936. TV inc: Larry Gatlin and the Gatlin Bros. Band; The Glen Campbell Music Show; Janie Fricke--You Ought To Be In Pictures.

Bway inc: Big River *(Tony-mus & lyr-1985)*

Songs inc: Chug-A-Lug; Dang Me *(Grammys-*(4)-C&W single-C&W vocal-C&W song-new C&W artist-1964); King of the Road *(Grammys-*(5)-contemporary (R&R) single-contemporary voc-C&W single-C&W voc-C&W song-1965); In the Summertime; England Swings; You Can't Rollerskate in a Buffalo Herd; Hey Little Star.

Albums inc: Dang Me/Chug-a-Lug *(Grammy-*C&W album-1964); Return of Roger Miller *(Grammy-*C&W album-1965); Roger Miller's Golden Hits; Roger Miller--Off The Wall.

MILLER, Ronald W.: Prod. b. Los Angeles, Apr 17, 1933. e. USC. Asso prod. TV series Walt Disney Presents; asso or co-prod 37 one-hour episodes Disney TV; exec prod. Walt Disney's Wonderful World of Color; 1980, P & COO Walt Disney Prodns; CEO Feb 1983 on retirement of Card Walker; resd. Sept. 1984.

Films inc: Bon Voyage; Summer Magic; Son of Flubber; Moon Pilot; The Monkey's Uncle; That Darn Cat; Lt. Robin Crusoe, U.S.N.; Monkeys, Go Home!; Never a Dull Moment; The Boatniks; Wild Country; Now You See Him, Now You Don't; Snowball Express; The Castaway Cowboy; No Deposit, No Return; Gus; Freaky Friday; Herbie Goes to Monte Carlo; The Rescuers; Pete's Dragon; Candleshoe; The Littlest Horse Thieves; The Cat From Outer Space; Hot Lead and Cold Feet; Return From Witch Mountain; The North Avenue Irregulars; The Apple Dumpling Gang Rides Again; Unidentified Flying Oddballs; The Black Hole; Midnight Madness; The Kids Who Knew Too Much; The Watcher in the Woods; The Last Flight of Noah's Ark; Herbie Goes Bananas; The Devil and Max Devlin (exec prod); The Fox and the Hound (exec prod); Condorman (exec prod); Night Crossing (exec prod); Tron (exec prod); Tex (exec prod); Never Cry Wolf (exec prod).

TV inc: Donovan's Kid; The Omega Connection; The Sky Trap; The Secret of Lost Valley.

MILLER, Sidney: Act-Mus-Comp-Dir. b. Shenandoah, PA, Oct 22, 1916. In films as child act, later in vaude, on radio; became dir on Saturday Night Show for NBC; wrote spec material and staged acts for Eddie Albert; George Gobel; Totie Fields; Milton Berle; Red Buttons, others; teamed with Donald O'Connor in nitery act for 9 years.

TV inc: (Dir) Get Smart; Bewitched; Please Don't Eat the Daisies; Broadside; McHale's Navy; Disneyland Anniversary; Celebrity Playhouse; Mouseketeers; Honey West; Tightrope; Saturday Night Revue; What's Happening; Toni Tennille Talk Show (wri); Lucy Moves to NBC (act); No Soap, Radio (act); The Joke Book (voice); Clue You In (voice).

Films inc: (Scores) Chip Off the Old Block; Babes on Swingstreet; Patrick the Great; On Stage, Everybody; Are You With It? (Dir) Get Yourself a College Girl; Secret Bride; Star 80.

MILLER, Steve: Mus. b. Dallas. Started the Ardells with Boz Scaggs; later with Barry Goldberg in Goldberg-Miller Blues Band.

Recordings inc: Children of the Future; Sailor; Brave New World; Your Saving Grace; Number Five; Rock Love; Recall The Beginning; Fly Like an Eagle; Book of Dreams; Steve Miller Band's Greatest Hits 1974-1978.

MILLER, Walter C.: Dir. TV inc: George M; Jack Lemmon in 'S Wonderful, 'S Marvelous, 'S Gershwin *(Emmy-*1972); You're A Good Man Charlie Brown; The Borrowers; Can I Save My Children; Doug Henning's World of Magic; Johnny Cash Christmas; Fourth annual Daytime Emmy Awards; 32d Annual Emmy Awards; All Commercials; George Burns In Nashville?; Osmond Family Christmas Show (& prodwri); 111th edition Ringling Bros. Barnum & Bailey Circus (& prod); 100 Years of Golden Hits; George Burns Early, Early, Early Christmas Special; The Mac Davis Special--Christmas Is A Song; It's Not Easy Being Me--The Rodney Dangerfield Show; Sinatra--Concert for the Americas (cable); George Burns and Other Sex Symbols (& prod); Doug Henning's Magic on Broadway (& prod); Second Annual NBC Family Christmas; Movie Blockbusters! The 15 Greatest Hits of all Time (& prod); Country Comes Home; George Burns Celebrates 80 Years in Show Business (& prod); The Rodney Dangerfield Special--I Can't Take It No More; The Mac Davis Special-- The Music of Christmas; Stevie Wonder Comes Home (feevee); George Burns' How To Live To Be 100 Or More; Rodney Dangerfield Exposed.

MILLIGAN, Spike (Terence Alan Milligan): Act-Wri-Comp. b. India, Apr 16, 1918. Founding member of BBC radio series The Goon Show. Author of several comedy books. Plays inc: The Bed Sitting Room; Oblomov. Thea inc: Treasure Island (& co-dir); The Bed Sitting Room; Oblomov; For One Week Only.

Films inc: The Running, Jumping and Standing Still Film; Watch Your Stern; The Bed Sitting Room; The Magic Christian; The Magnificent Seven Deadly Sins; The Cherry Picker; Digby, The Biggest Dog in the World; Alice's Adventures in Wonderland; The Three Musketeers; The Four Musketeers; The Hound of the Baskervilles; The Life of Brian; History of the World--Part I; Ghost in the Noonday Sun (made in 1973).

TV inc: Muses With Milligan; The Beachcomber; The Q 5; Curry and Chips; The Marty Feldman Comedy Machine; Oh, In Colour; A Milligan For All Seasons; The Royal London Gala For Bob Hope's Happy Birthday Homecoming

MILLS BROTHERS: Singing Act. On radio, in niteries for more than a half century. There are only two now. Originals were Harry (Died Jun 28, 1982), Don, Herb and John Jr, (died in 1968). Began as children on small Ohio radio station in 1925.

Films inc: The Big Broadcast of 1932; Broadway Gondolier; He's My Guy; Reveille With Beverly; Chatterbox.

TV inc: 100 years of Golden Hits.

Recorded more than 1,300 songs inc: Tiger Rag (their first); Dinah; Goodbye Blues (their theme); Paper Doll (their greatest success, 6 million copies); I'll Be Around; You Always Hurt the One You Love.

MILLS, Donna: Act. b. Chicago, IL, Dec 11, 1944 TV inc: The Secret Storm; Love Is a Many Splendored Thing; The Good Life; Waikiki; Doctor's Private Lives; Superdome; The Hunted Lady; Woman on the Run; Fire; Curse of the Black Widow; Hanging By a Thread; Knots Landing; Insight/Mr. and Mrs. Bliss; Bare Essence; I Love Men (emcee); He's Not Your Son; Bob Hope Lampoons Television 1985; Rape! (host).

Films inc: The Incident; Play Misty for Me.

MILLS, Hayley: Act. b. London, Apr 18, 1946. D of John Mills. Screen debut 1959, Tiger Bay. Films inc: Pollyana *(Special Oscar-*1960); The Parent Trap; Whistle Down the Wind; In Search of the Castaways; Summer Magic; The Chalk Garden; The Trouble with Angels; The Family Way; A Matter of Innocence; Take a Girl Like You; Silhouettes; What Changed Charley Farthing; The Diamond Hunters.

TV inc: Disney Animation---The Illusion of Life (host); The Flame Trees of Thika.

MILLS, John, Sir: Act. b. Suffolk, England, Feb. 22, 1908. Began as chorus boy in The Five O'Clock revue; later joined The Quaints repertory group which toured Far East. Other thea inc: Charley's Aunt; The

1931 Revue; Cavalcade; Words and Music; Jill Darling; Red Night; She Stoops to Conquer; Of Mice and Men; Men in Shadow; Duet for Two Hands; The Uninvited Guest; Ross (Bway); Good Companions; Great Expectations; Separate Tables.

Films inc: The Midshipmaid; The Ghost Camera; The River Wolves; The Lash; Doctor's Orders; Those Were the Days; Blind Justice; Royal Cavalcade; Brown on Resolution; Charing Cross; First Offense; Tudor Rose; The Green Cockatoo; Goodbye Mr. Chips; All Hands; Old Bill and Son; The Young Mr. Pitt; The Big Blockade; In Which We Serve; We Dive At Dawn; This Happy Breed; Waterloo Road; The Way to the Stars; Great Expectations; So Well Remembered; The October Man; Scott of the Antarctic; The History of Mr. Polly (& prod); The Rocking Horse Winner (& prod); The Long Memory; Hobson's Choice; The Colditz Story; End of the Affair; Above Us the Waves; Escapade; War and Peace; It's Great to be Young; Around the World in 80 Days; Town on Trial; The Circle; Ice Cold in Alex; I was Monty's Double; Tiger Bay; Summer of the Seventeenth Doll; Swiss Family Robinson; Tunes of Glory; The Singer Not the Song; The Desert Hawk; The Chalk Garden; King Rat; Operation Crossbow; The Wrong Box; Africa--Texas Style; Gypsy Girl (dir only); Chuka; Run Wild, Run Free; Oh! What A Lovely War; Lady Hamilton; Ryan's Daughter (Oscar-supp-1970) Dulcima; Young Winston; Lady Caroline Lamb; Oklahoma Crude; The Human Factor; The Big Sleep; The Making of a Lady; 39 Steps (remake); Zulu Dawn; Quatermass Conclusion; Gandhi; Sahara.

TV inc: The Letter; The Interrogator; Dundee and the Culhane; The Adventures of Little Lord Fauntleroy; A Woman Of Substance.

MILLS, Juliet: Act. b. London, Nov 21, 1941. D of John Mills. Stage debut age 14, Alice Through the Looking Glass. On screen as an infant, 1942.

Films inc: So Well Remembered; The History of Mr. Polly; No, My Darling Daughter; Twice Around the Daffodils; Nurse on Wheels; Carry On, Jack; The Rare Breed; Wings of Fire; Oh! What a Lovely War; The Challengers; Avanti!; Riata; Beyond the Door; The Second Power; The Last Melodrama; Le Guepiot.

TV inc: Mrs. Miniver; The Morning After; QB VII (Emmy-supp-1975); Man of the World; The Cracker Factory.

MILLS, Dr. Peter B.: Prod-Exec. b. Chicago, May 11, 1936. e. Harvard U. Films inc: The Farmer (exec prod); ofcr of numerous record cos. Medical examiner, DeKalb County, GA.

MILLS, Steve: Exec. b. Russell, KS, Apr 19. e. U of KS, BA; OH State U, MA. On staff WBNS-TV, Columbus, OH, 1951-53 as prod-dir; 1953-1960, staff prod-dir OKCMO-TV, Kansas City, MO, also freelance dir major league baseball; 1960 joined ABC; in various prodn & exec capacities until 1968 when named VP in chg West Coast; 1973, exec prod in chg motion pix for tv, CBS-TV; 1976, VP prime time prodn; 1979, VP Movies for TV; April, 1982, VP Movies & Mini-series CBS Entertainment.

MILNER, Martin: Act. b. Detroit, Dec 26, 1927. e. USC. Films inc: Life with Father; Our Very Own; I Want You; Pete Kelly's Blues; The Sweet Smell of Success; Marjorie Morningstar; Thirteen Ghosts; Sullivan's County; Valley of the Dolls.

TV inc: The Trouble with Father; The Life of Riley; Route 66; Adam 12; The Last Convertible; The Seekers; The Ordeal of Bill Carney; Prime Times.

MIMIEUX, Yvette: Act. b. Los Angeles, Jan 8, 1942. Screen debut 1960 Platinum High School. Films inc: The Time Machine; Light in the Piazza; The Wonderful World of the Brothers Grimm; Diamond Head; Toys in the Attic; The Mercenaries; Skyjacked; The Neptune Factor; Journey Into Fear; Jackson County Jail; The Black Hole; Mystique.

TV inc: Tyger Tyger; Most Deadly Game; Death Takes a Holiday; Black Noon; Disaster on the Coastline; Forbidden Love; Night Partners; Obsessive Love (& co-prod); Berrenger's.

Bway inc: I Am a Camera; The Owl And The Pussycat.

MINER, Jan: Act. b. Boston, MA, Oct 15, 1917. Studied with Lee Strasberg. In rep, stock. Bway inc: Obbligato; Viva Madison Avenue; The Decameron; Cricket; The Milk Train Doesn't Stop Here Anymore; The Freaking Out of Stephanie Blake; Othello; Butterflies Are Free; The Women; Saturday, Sunday, Monday; The Heiress; Heartbreak House.

Films inc: Lenny.

TV inc: Pottsville; Willy and Phil.

MING CHO LEE: Dsgn. See LEE, Ming Cho

MINNELLI, Liza: Act. b. Los Angeles, Mar 12, 1946. D of the late Judy Garland and Vincente Minnelli. Films inc: Charlie Bubbles; Tell Me That You Love Me, Junie Moon; The Sterile Cuckoo; Cabaret (Oscar-1972); A Matter of Time; Lucky Lady; New York, New York; Arthur; The Muppets Take Manhattan; That's Dancing!

Bway inc: Flora. The Red Menace (Tony-1965); (Special Tony-1974); The Act (Tony-1978); The Rink.

TV inc: Liza With a Z (Emmy-1973); Goldie and Liza Together; Baryshnikov On Broadway; Entertainer of the Year Awards; The President's Command Performance.

MINNELLI, Vincente: Dir. b. Chicago, Feb 28, 1910. As child toured circuses, carnivals with Minnelli Bros. Served as Art Dir for Radio City Music Hall during 30s. Designed sets, costumes for editions of Ziegfeld Follies and Earl Carroll Vanities. Signed by MGM. 1st directorial film 1943, Cabin in the Sky. Films inc: Brigadoon; An American in Paris; The Cobweb; Kismet; Lust for Life; Designing Woman; The Reluctant Debutante; Gigi (Oscar-1958); Some Came Running; Home from the Hill; Bells Are Ringing; The Four Horsemen of the Apocalypse; Two Weeks in Another Town; The Courtship of Eddie's Father; Goodbye Charlie; The Sandpiper; On a Clear Day You Can See Forever; A Matter of Time.

MINOW, Newton: Exec. b. Milwaukee, WI, Jan 17, 1926. e. Northwestern U, BA, JD. Chmn FCC 1961-1963; chmn Board of Govs PBS, 1979.

MINSKY, Howard G.: Prod. Agency exec Wm Morris; p Cinema Consultants. Prod Love Story.

MINTER, Mary Miles: Act. b. 1902. One of the top stars of the silent screen, made approximately 50 films between 1912 and 1923 when she retired. Films inc: The Nurse; Emma of Stork's Nest; Barbara Frietchie; Dimples; Lovely Mary; The Gentle Intruder; Melissa of the Hills; Her Country's Call; The Mate of Sally Ann; A Bit of Jade; The Ghost of Rosy Taylor; A Bachelor's Wife; Anne of Green Gables; Nurse Marjorie; Jenny Be Good; The Little Clown; Moonlight and Honeysuckle; Tillie; The Heart Specialist; South of Suva; The Trail of the Lonesome Pine; The Cowboy and the Lady.

(Died Aug. 4, 1984)

MINTZ, Robert: Prod. b. Los Angeles, Jul 7, 1929. e. UCLA, BA F. TV inc: (wri) Room 222; Outer Limits; Batman, David Cassidy-Man Under Cover. (co-prod) Feather and Father Gang; Tabitha. (Prod) The French Atlantic Affair.

MIOU-MIOU: Act. b. Paris, Feb 22, 1950. Films inc: La Cavale; Themroc; Quelques Messieurs trop Tranquilles; Les Granges Brulees; Elle court, elle court la banlieue; The Mad Adventures of Rabbi Jacob; Going Places; Tendre Dracula; Pas de Probleme; La Marche Triomphante; F Comme Fairbanks; Love and Cool Water; We've Seen Everything; The Bottom Line; Dites-lui que je l'aime; Les Routes du Sud; La Femme Flic; Jonah, Who Will Be 25 in the Year 2000; La Derobade; Au Revoir...a Lundi; L'Ingorgo; Est-ce Bien Raissonable? (Is This Really Reasonable?); La Gueule du Loup (The Jaws of the Wolf); Josepha; Guy de Maupassant; Coup De Foudre; Attention, une femme peut en cacher une autre (Warning, One Woman May Be Hiding Another); Canicule (Dog Day); Le Vol du Sphinx (The Flight Of the Sphinx).

MIRANDA, Isa (Ines Sampietro): Act. b. Milan, Italy Jul 5, 1917. Films inc: Darkness; Everybody's Lady; Red Passport; Hotel Imperial; Adventure in Diamonds; La Ronde; Seven Deadly Sins; Rasputin; We Women; Summertime; The Yellow Rolls Royce; The Great Train Robbery; The Shoes of the Fisherman.

MIRISCH, Marvin E.: Exec. b. NYC, Mar 19, 1918. e. CCNY, BA. Print dept, contract dept, asst booker, NY Exchange, head booker, Grand National Pictures, Inc, 1936-40; GM vending concession operation 800 theatres, Midwest Theatres Candy Co, Inc, 1941-52;

corporate ofcr in chge, ind prod negotiations, Allied Artists Pictures, 1953-57; Formed Mirisch Prodns 1957 with brother Walter, serving as ChmnB, CEO in chg of all business affairs, admin & financing, distr liaison; P, Mirisch Films. Films inc; Dracula; (prod); Romantic Comedy (exec prod).

MIRISCH, Walter: Prod. b. NYC, Nov 8, 1921. e. U WI, BA; Harvard Grad. School. Partnered with brother, Marvin, in The Mirisch Corp, formed 1957.

Films inc: The Magnificent Seven; Two for the Seasaw; Toys in the Attic; Hawaii; In the Heat of the Night; Midway; Gray Lady Down; Same Time Next Year; Dracula; The Prisoner of Zenda; Romantic Comedy.

(Irving Thalberg Award 1977; Jean Hersholt Award 1982).

MIRO, Pilar: Dir. b. Spain, 1940. Films inc: The Cuenca Crime; La Peticion (The Betrothal); Sabado de Gloria; Gary Cooper que esta en los cielos (Gary Cooper, Who Art in Heaven) (& wri); Hablamos esta noche (Let's Talk Tonight).

Appointed Dir-Gen of Cinematography by the Spanish Govt, Dec 1982.

MIRREN, Helen: Act. b. England, 1946. Thea inc: (London) Various Shakespearean roles; The Silver Tassie; Bartholomew Fair; Enemies; The Man of Mode; Miss Julie; The Balcony; Teeth 'n' Smiles; The Sea Gull; The Bed Before Yesterday; Faith Healer; The Roaring Girl.

Films inc: Age of Consent; Savage Messiah; O! Lucky Man; Hamlet; Caligula; The Long Good Friday; The Fiendish Plot of Dr. Fu Manchu; Excalibur; Cal; 2010.

TV inc: Miss Julie; The Applecart; The Little Minister; Mrs Reinhardt; A Midsummer Night's Dream; Cymbeline.

MISCHER, Don (Donald L. Mischer): Dir. b. San Antonio, TX, Mar 5, 1941. e. U of TX, BA, MA. TV inc: Great American Dream Machine (& prod) *(Emmy-1972)*; Making Television Dance with Twyla Tharp; Goldie Hawn Special; Kennedy Center Honors; John Denver and the Ladies; The Third Barry Manilow Special; Goldie and Liza Together (& prod); The Barbara Walters Specials; The Donna Summer Special; Cheryl Ladd Special--Souvenirs; Omnibus; The Kennedy Center Honors, 1980 *(Emmy-1981)*; The Best of Times (& prod); Donahue and Kids *(Emmy-1981)*; Cheryl Ladd--Scenes From A Special (& prod); Baryshnikov in Hollywood (& prod); Ain't Misbehavin'; Shirley MacLaine--Illusions (& prod); Kennedy Center Honors 1982; Love, Sex...& Marriage? (prod) Motown 25; Yesterday, Today, Forever (& prod) *(Emmy-prod-1983)*; Happy Birthday Bob; Small World; Lynda Carter Body and Soul (& prod); Jump; Kennedy Center Honors 1984; Shirley MacLaine (& prod); Motown Returns To The Apollo (& prod); AFI Salute To Gene Kelly.

MISSEL, Renee: Prod. b. Montreal, Canada. e. UCLA; McGill U. Freelance photojournalist; prodn asst New World Pictures; post prodn supv Tomorrow Entertainment; story ed Kings Road Prodns. Films inc: Main Event; Resurrection.

TV inc: The Great American Dream Machine.

MR. T. (Lawrence Tero): Act. b. Chicago, IL., May 21, 1952. Professional bodyguard before act. Films inc: Rocky III; Penitentiary; D.C. Cab.

TV inc: The A-Team; Mr. T (ani); Bob Hope's Wicky-Wacky Special From Waikiki; John Ritter, Mr. T and Jacqueline Bisset--Going Back Home; The Secret World Of the Very Young; The Toughest Man In the World; S.O.S.--Secrets of Surviving; Mr. T. and Emmanuel Lewis in A Christmas Carol; Bob Hope Lampoons Television 1985.

MITCHELL, Cameron: Act. b. Dallastown, PA, Nov 4, 1918. Films inc: They Were Expendable; Cass Timberlane; High Barbaree; Command Decision; Homecoming; Some Like It Hot; Slaves; Viva Knievel; Haunts; The Swarm; The Toolbox Murders; Supersonic Man; Silent Scream; Without Warning; Screamers; Kill Squad; Raw Force; My Favorite Year; Killpoint; Prince Jack; Mission Kill; Night Train To Terror; The Link.

TV inc: High Chaparral; Andersonville Trial; Swiss Family Robinson; Ohms; Wild Times; The Bastard; Turnover Smith; Kenny Rogers as the Gambler--The Adventure Continues.

Bway inc: The Taming of the Shrew; The November People.

MITCHELL, David: Set Dsgn. Bway inc: Medea; Macbeth; Volpone; Hamlet; The Increased Difficulty of Concentration (& cos); Grin and Bare It; Postcards; Steambath; Trelawny of the "Wells"; Colette; How the Other Half Loves; The Basic Training of Pavlo Hummel; The Incomparable Max; The Cherry Orchard; Barbary Shore; In the Boom Boom Room; Enter a Free Man; Annie *(Tony-1977)*; Working; Barnum *(Tony-1980)*; Bring Back Birdie; Brighton Beach Momoirs; Private Lives; Dance A Little Closer; La Cage Aux Folles; Harrigan 'n Hart; Biloxi Blues; The Odd Couple.

MITCHELL, Keith: Act. b. Palm Springs, CA, Jan 13, 1970. Grandson of Jackie Coogan. Started in commercials. TV inc: The Waltons; a Question of Love; Battered; Animal Talk; Norma Rae; Tales of the Apple Dumpling Gang; Gun Shy; All Summer In A Day.

Films inc: The Fox and the Hound.

MITCHELL, Wayne: Cin-Dir. b. Detroit, Apr 5, 1926. e. USC. TV inc: Holiday USA; Confidential File; Viet Nam.

Films inc: Attack of the Jungle Women; Gangster Story; Surf Monster; Philippine Adventure.

MITCHELL, Yvonne: Act-Wri. b. London, 1925. Thea inc: The Cradle Song; The Seagull; Twelfth Night; Jassy; A Month in the Country; The Flies; The Merchant of Venice; The Taming of the Shrew; Less Than Kind (dir); The Wall; The Oresteia; Ivanov; Horizontal Hold; Out of Order; Children of the Wolf; Electra; Bloomsbury; The Same Sky (wri). Films inc: The Queen of Spades; Turn the Key Softly; The Divided Heart; Woman in a Dressing Gown; Tiger Bay; Sapphire; The Trials of Oscar Wilde; Genghis Khan; The Corpse; The Great Waltz; The Incredible Sarah; Widow's Nest.

MITCHUM, Chris: Act. b. Los Angeles, Oct 16, 1943. e. U AZ, AB. S of Robert Mitchum. Films inc: Bigfoot; Suppose They Gave A War and No One Came; Cactus in the Snow; Chisum; Rio Lobo; Summertime Killer; To Love, Perhaps to Die; Rico; Costa Nostra Asia; Hell's Heroes; The Agency; Dynamite Sun; The Last Hard Man; One Man Jury; Sting Ray; Dangerous Passage; Tusk; The Day Time Ended; Ritoru Chanpion (My Champion).

TV inc: Dundee and the Culhane; Danny Thomas Hour; A Time for Love; Flight to Holocaust; A Rumor of War.

MITCHUM, Robert: Act. b. Bridgeport, CT, Aug 6, 1917. On screen from 1943. Films inc: Hopalong Cassidy Series; Gung Ho!; The Story of G.I. Joe; Undercurrent; Till the End of Time; Crossfire; Rachel and the Stranger; Red Pony; Blood on the Moon; Macao; Racket; She Couldn't Say No; River of No Return; Track of the Cat; Night of the Hunter; Heaven Knows, Mr. Allison; Not As a Stranger; The Sundowners; Cape Fear; The Longest Day; Two for the Season; Secret Ceremony; Ryan's Daughter; Farewell My Lovely; Friends of Eddie Coyle; Midway; The Last Tycoon; Amsterdam Kill; The Big Sleep; Breakthrough; Nightkill; Agency; That Championship Season; The Ambassador; Maria's Lovers.

TV inc: One Shoe Makes It Murder; It Only Hurts When You Laugh; The Winds of War; "I Love T.V." Test; A Killer in the Family; The Hearst & Davies Affair; Reunion At Fairborough.

MITGANG, Herbert: Wri. b. NYC, Jan 20, 1920. e. St. John's Law School. With NY Times as copy edtr; reviewer; supv ed Sunday drama section.

Plays inc: Mr. Lincoln.
TV inc: Mr. Lincoln.

MIZRAHI, Moshe: Dir-wri. b. Egypt, 1931. Asst dir for decade before debut as dir. Films inc: Le client de la morte saison (The Customer of the Off-Season); Stances a Sophie (Sophie's Way); Ani Ohev Otach Rosa (I Love You, Rosa); The House on Chelouche St.; Daughters Daughters; La Vie devant soi (Madame Rosa); Chere Inconnu (I Sent A Letter To My Love); War And Love.

MOBLEY, Mary Ann: Act. b. Biloxi, MS, Feb 17, 1939. Former Miss America, 1959. Films inc: Girl Happy; Get Yourself a College Girl; Young Dillinger; Harum Scarum; Three on a Couch; For Singles Only; Istanbul Express.

Bway inc: Nowhere to Go but Up.

TV inc: The Lie; Third Annual Circus of the Stars; The Secret of Lost Valley; The World of Entertainment (guest host).

MOCKY, Jean Pierre (nee Mokijewski): Act-Dir. b. Nice, France, Jul 6, 1929. Films inc: (Act) Vive la Liberte; Orpheus; I Vinti; Gli Sbandati; La Tete Contre les Murs. (Dir) The Chasers; Un Couple; Snobs; Les Vierges; Thank Heaven for Small Favors; La Bourse et la Vie; Les Compagnons de la Marguerite; Solo (& act); The Albatross; Chut; L'Ibis Rouge; Le Roi des Bricoleurs; Le Temoin; Litan (& Prod-act); Y'at-il un Francis dans La Salle? (Is There a Frenchman in the House?) (& wri); A Mort l'Arbitre (Kill the Referee) (& wri).

MODINE, Matthew: Act. Studied with Stella Adler. Films inc: Baby, It's You; Streamers; Hotel New Hampshire; VisionQuest; Mrs. Soffel; Birdy.

MOFFAT, Donald: Act-Dir. b. Plymouth, England, Dec 26, 1930. e. RADA. London stage debut 1954, Macbeth. Films inc: (Act) Pursuit of the Graf Spee; Rachel, Rachel; The Great Northfield Minnesota Raid; Showdown; The Trial of the Catonsville Nine; Earthquake; The Terminal Man; Winter Kills; Promises in the Dark; On The Nickel; Health; Popeye; The Land of No Return; Ritoro Chanpion (My Champion); The Thing; The White Lions; The Right Stuff; Alamo Bay.

Bway inc: Under Milk Wood; A Passage to India; The Affair; Much Ado About Nothing; The Tumbler; The Hostage; The Wild Duck; Right You Are (If You Think You Are); Forget-Me-Not Lane; Cock-A-Doodle Dandy (dir); Father's Day (dir); Play Memory (act).

TV inc: The Snoop Sisters; The New Land; The Word; The Gift of Love; Logan's Run; Mrs. R's Daughter; The Long Days of Summer; Jacqueline Bouvier Kennedy; Denmark Vesey's Rebellion; Who Will Love My Children?; License to Kill.

MOFFITT, John C.: Dir. TV inc: Andy Williams Show; Perry Como Show; New Year's Rockin' Eve; Good Vibrations from Central Park; 4 AM Music Awards; 28th annual Emmy Awards (Emmy-1977); Lily Tomlin's 4th Special; Van Dyke and Company; Dick Clark's Live Wednesday; Circus Festival of Monte Carlo (& prod); Ringling Bros. Circus Highlights (& prod); Low Moan Spectacular (& prod); Helen Reddy Special; 31st annual Emmy Awards (& prod); Fridays (& prod).

MOGULL, Artie: Exec. b. NYC, Mar 26, 1927. e. Columbia U, BA. Partner, Tetragrammaton Records, 1966-68; vp Capitol 1970; vp MCA (1972-74); ownr, Signpost Records, 1974; United Artists Records, 1976-77; bought UA Records 1978, co-ownr & co-chmn with Jerry Rubinstein of UA Records.

MOHLA, J.G.: Prod. b. India, Nov 26, 1909. e. U of Lahore. Films inc: Insaan; Ehsaan; Senapati; Adarsh; Yogeshwar Krishna.

MOHYEDDIN, Zia: Act. b. Lyallpur, Pakistan, Jun 20, 1933. e. Punjab U; RADA. Thea inc: A Passage to India; The Alchemist; Volpone; The Guide; The Merchant of Venice; On the Rocks.

Films inc: Lawrence of Arabia; Sammy Going South; The Sailor From Gibraltar; Ashanti.

TV inc: Death of a Princess; Staying On; The Jewel In The Crown.

MOISEIWITSCH, Tanya, CBE: Dsgn. b. London, England, Dec 3, 1914. Thea inc: More than 50 prodns at Abbey Theatre Dublin. (London) The Golden Cuckoo; Uncle Vanya; The Critic; Cyrano de Bergerac; The Time of Your Life; The Beggar's Opera (Sadlers Wells); The Cherry Orchard; A Month in the Country; Passing Day; Figure of Fun; Othello (Royal Shakespeare prodn); The Deep Blue Sea; Two Gentlemen of Verona; Wrong Side of the Park; Ondine; The Alchemist; Volpone; Phaedra Brittanica; in US des several prodns for Tyrone Guthrie Theatre, Minneapolis; The Misanthrope (Bway).

TV inc; Laurence Olivier Presents King Lear.

MOKAE, Zakes: Act. b. Johannesburg, South Africa, Aug 5, 1935. e. RADA; American Film Institute. Thea inc: (London) The Dumbwaiter; The Tempest; Brother Jero (& dir); Macbeth; Othello; The Blood Knot; Boesman and Lena (& dir). (Bway) Last Days of British Honduras; Boesman and Lena; The Cherry Orchard; A Lesson From Aloes; Master Harold...and the Boys (Tony-featured-1982).

Films inc: Darling; The Comedians; The Island.

TV inc: Market in Honey Lane; Suffer the Little Children; Galloping Major; The Blood Knot; Raid On Entebbe; One In A Million-the Ron LeFlore story; A Caribbean Mystery.

MOLINARO, Al: Act. b. Kenosha, WI, Jun 24, 1919. Started as guitarist in four-piece combo; became local tv producer in LA, before act.

TV inc: Get Smart; The Odd Couple; Happy Days; Anson and Lorrie; The Ugily Family; The Great American Traffic Jam; Joanie Loves Chachi.

MOLINARO, Edouard: Dir-Wri. b. Bordeaux, France, May 13, 1928. Started out making short documentaries. Films inc: Back to the Wall; Des Femmes Disparaissent; A Mistress for the Summer; The Passion of Slow Fire; A Touch Of Treason; The Seven Deadly Sins; Arsene Lupin against Arsene Lupin; The Warm Blooded Spy; Male Hunt; Quand Passent Les Faisans; Peau D'Espion; Oscar; Hibernatus; Mon Oncle Benjamin; Les Aveux Les Plus Doux; Le Gang des Otages; The Pain in the Ass; L'Ironie du sort; The Pink Telephone; Dracula, Father & Son; L'Homme Presse; La Cage Aux Folles; Sunday Lovers; La Cage Aux Folles II; Pour 100 Briques, T'as Plus Rien Maintenant (For 100 Grand You Get Nothing Now); Just The Way You Are (dir); La Tete Dans le Sac (Led By The Nose) (wri only); Palace (dir only); L'Amour en Douce (Love On The Quiet).

MONASH, Paul: Prod-Wri. b. NYC, Jun 14, 1917. e. U of WI, BA; Columbia U, MA. Started as TV script wri. Authored two-part teleplay which launched The Untouchables.

Films inc: Butch Cassidy and the Sundance Kid (exec prod); Slaughter House Five (prod); The Friends of Eddie Coyle (prod & sp); Front Page (prod); Carrie (prod).

TV inc: The Lonely Wizard (wri) (Emmy-1957); Cain's Hundred (prod); Peyton Place (prod); Judd for the Defense (prod); All Quiet on the Western Front (wri); Salem's Lot (wri); The Day The Loving Stopped (exec prod); Child Bride at Short Creek; V (The Series) (wri).

MONICELLI, Mario: Dir. b. Rome, May 15, 1915. Films inc: Big Deal on Madonna Street; The Great War; Tears of Joy; Boccaccio; The Organizer; Casanova; Girl With a Pistol; Amici Mie; Viva Italia!; Travels With Anita; Lovers and Liars (& wri); Il Marchese del Grillo (& wri); Amici, Miei, Atto 2 (All My Friends 2) (& wri); Bertoldo, Bertoldini E Cacasenna (& wri); Le Due Vite di Mattia Pascal (The Two Lives Of Mattia Pascal) (& wri).

MONKEES, The: Peter Tork (nee Torkelson); Mike Nesmith; Micky Dolenz; Davy Jones. Films inc: Head.

TV inc: The Monkees.

MONKHOUSE, Bob: Act. b. Beckenham, Kent, England, Jun 1, 1928. e. Dulwich Coll. Started with BBC 1949 on Works Wonders radio show; first tv series 1953 Monkhouse, Fast & Loose.

TV inc: Bob Monkhouse Comedy Hour; The Golden Shot (8 yrs); What's My Line (Brit vers); Celebrity Squares (Brit vers: since 1974); Candid Camera (Brit vers) I'm Bob, He's Dickie; Mad Movies; Family Fortunes.

Films inc: Carry On Sergeant; Dentist in the Chair; Weekend with Lulu; She'll Have to Go; The Bliss of Mrs. Blossom.

Thea inc: Start Time with Bob; Aladdin; Boy from Syracuse; Come Blow Your Horn;

MONROE, Bill (William Blanc Monroe Jr.): Exec prod-TV personality. b. New Orleans, LA., Jul. 17, 1920. e. Tulane. Reporter for United Press; WNOE, New Orleans; associate editor New Orleans Item; 1955, news director WDSU-TV; joined NBC 1961 as Washington bureau chief; 1968, Washington editor Today show; 1975 succeeded Lawrence E. Spivak on Meet the Press.

MONTAGNE, Edward J.: Prod-Dir. b. NYC. e. Loyola Coll; Notre Dame. Films inc: McHale's Navy Joins the Air Force; The Ghost and Mr Chicken; The Reluctant Astronaut; Shakiest Gun in the West; P J; Travelling Saleslady; Angel in my Pocket; How to Frame a Fig; They Went Thataway & Thataway.

TV inc:Man Against Crime; You'll Never Get Rich; McHale's Navy; Hurricane; Terror on the 40th Floor; Francis Gary Powers; Million Dollar Rip Off; Spider Man; Crash; Quincy; Delta House; High Noon Part II--The Return of Will Kane; The Munster's Revenge (exec prod).

MONTALBAN, Ricardo: Act. b. Mexico City, Nov 25, 1920. Attended school in US before returning to Mexico to make 13 Spanish-language films. US screen debut, 1947, Fiesta. Films inc: The Kissing Bandit; Border Incident; My Man and I; Sombrero; Latin Lovers; A Life in the Balance; Sayonara; The Money Trap; Madame X; Sol Madrid; The Singing Nun; Blue; Sweet Charity; The Train Robbers; Return to the Planet of the Apes; Star Trek II--The Wrath of Khan; Cannonball Run II.

TV inc: Desperate Mission; Captains Courageous; Fantasy Island; How the West Was Won Part 2 *(Emmy*-1978); The Magic of David Cooperfield VI (host); International OTI Song Festival (host); On Top All Over The World; Kraft All-Star Salute To Ford's Theatre.

Bway inc: Her Cardboard Lover; The King and I; Don Juan In Hell.

MONTANA, Montie (Owen Harlan Mickel): Act. b. Wolf Point, MT, 1910. On screen from 1930 in many Tom Mix and Buck Jones westerns. Films inc: Circle of Death; Riders of the Deadline; Down Dakota Way; Arizona Bushwhackers.

MONTAND, Yves (Yvo Livi): Act. b. Monsumano, Italy, Oct 13, 1921. H of Simone Signoret. Singer niteries, music halls. On screen since 1946 in: Star Without Light; Where the Hot Wind Blows; My Geisha; The Sleeping Car Murder; Is Paris Burning?; Grand Prix; Live For Life; Z; On a Clear Day You Can See Forever; The Confession; State of Siege; Gates of the Night; The Wages of Fear; Witches of Salem; Let's Make Love; Vincent, Francois, Paul and the Others; Lovers Like Us; The Menace; Police Python 357; The Big Operator; Les Routes De Sud; Claire De Femme; I Comme Icarus; Le Choix des Armes (Choice of Weapons); Tout Feu, Tout Flamme (All Fired Up); Garcon!

MONTEVECCHI, Liliane: Act. Films inc: The Glass Slipper; Moonfleet; Meet Me in Las Vegas; The Sad Sack; The Young Lions; King Creole; Me and the Colonel.

Bway inc: Nine *(Tony*-featured-1982).

MONTGOMERY, Belinda: Act. b. Winnipeg, Manitoba, Canada, Jul 23. Films inc: The Other Side of the Mountain; The Other Side of the Mountain, Part II; Blackout; Stone Cold Dead; Silent Madness.

TV inc: The Man from Atlantis; Murder in the Music City; Marciano; Turnover Smith; Trouble In High Timber Country; Concrete Cowboys; Uncommon Valor.

MONTGOMERY, Elizabeth: Act. b. Los Angeles, Apr 15, 1933. D of the late Robert Montgomery. Films inc: The Court Martial of Billy Mitchell; Johnny Cool; Who's Been Sleeping in My Bed?

TV inc: Bewitched; The Awakening Land; Jennifer-A Woman's Story; Act of Violence; The Legend of Lizzie Borden. Belle Starr; When The Circus Came to Town; The Rules of Marriage; Missing Pieces; Second Sight--A Love Story.

MONTGOMERY, Ralph: Act. b. OH, Jul 4, 1911. Films inc: Willy Dynamite; How to Frame a Figg; Which Way to the Front; The Day the President's Plane Was Missing; Terminal Man; Watermelon Man; Soylent Green; Hello Dolly; Hustle; Which Way Is Up.

TV inc: Sam Houston; Woman of the Year; Helter Skelter; Ziegfeld, the Man and His Woman.

MONTY, Gloria (nee Montemuro): Dir. b. Weehauken, NJ, 1921. TV inc: Secret Storm; Bright Promise; General Hospital (& prod) *(Emmys*-prod-1981, 1984); Confessions of a Married Man (exec prod); The Hamptons (exec prod).

MONTY PYTHON'S FLYING CIRCUS: Group of British comedians who performed for BBC during the 60's and 70's. Now seen in the US. Regular cast inc: Eric Chapman. John Cleese, Terry Gilliam, Eric Idle, Terry Jones and Michael Palin.

MOODY, Ron (nee Moodnick): Act. b. London, Jan 8, 1924. e. London U. Thea inc: (London) Intimacy at Eight; For Amusement Only; For Adults Only; Candide; Oliver! (& wri-comp); Joey; Peter Pan; The Clandestine Marriage; Saturnalia (& dir-wri-comp); Move Along Sideways. (Bway) Candide; Oliver!.

Films inc: Davy; Summer Holiday; Mouse on the Moon; Ladies Who Do; Murder Most Foul; The Sandwich Man; Oliver!; David Copperfield; Twelve Chairs; Flight of the Doves; Dominique; Legend of the Werewolf; Unidentified Flying Oddballs; Wrong Is Right; Where Is Parsifal?

TV inc: I Want to Go Home; Who's a Good Boy, Then; The Word; Benji's Very Own Christmas; Dial "M" For Murder; Tales of the Gold Monkey (pilot).

MOONJEAN, Hank: Prod. b. Evanston, IL., Jan. 19, 1935. e. Dartmouth; USC, MA. Began as asst dir at MGM working on Cat On a Hot Tin Roof; Raintree County; Lust for Life; Sweet Bird of Youth; Mutiny on the Bounty (remake). Other films inc: (asso prod) The Great Gatsby; WUSA; Spinout. (Prod) The Fortune (exec prod); The End (exec prod); Hooper; Smokey and the Bandit II; The Incredible Shrinking Woman; Paternity; Sharky's Machine; Stroker Ace.

TV inc: Beauty and the Beast (released theatrically internationally).

MOORATOFF, George Walter: Exec. b. Shanghai, China, Sep 14, 1933. M dir Par Pictures (Australia) P/L.

MOORE, Clayton: Act. b. 1908. Best known for TV role: The Lone Ranger. Films inc: Kit Carson; Black Dakotas; The Cowboy and the Indians; Along the Oregon Trail; Night Stage to Galveston; Montana Territory; Down Laredo Way.

MOORE, Colleen: Act. b. Port Huron, MI., Aug. 19, 1900. On screen from 1917 to 1934. Films inc: Bad Boy; An Old Fashioned Young Man; Hands Up!; The Savage; A Hoosier Romance; Little Orphant Annie; The Busher; Wilderness Trail; Man in the Moonlight; Common Property; The Devil's Claim; So Long Letty; When Dawn Came; Dinty; The Sky Pilot; The Lotus Eater; His Nibs; Broken Hearts of Broadway; Come On Over; The Wallflower; Affinities; Forsaking All Others; Broken Chains; The Ninety and Nine; Look Your Best; Slippy McGee; The Nth Commandment; April Showers; Through the Dark; Flaming Youth; Painted People; The Perfect Flapper; Flirting With Love; So Big; Sally; The Desert Flower; We Moderns; Irene; Ella Cinders; It Must Be Love; Twinkletoes; Orchids and Ermine; Naughty But Nice; Her Wild Oat; Happiness Ahead; Oh Kay!; Lilac Time; Synthetic Sin; Why Be Good?; Smiling Irish Eyes; Footlights and Fools; The Power and the Glory; Success at any Price; Social Register; The Scarlet Letter.

MOORE, Constance: Act. b. Sioux City, IA, Jan 18, 1920. On screen since 1938. Films inc: A Letter of Introduction; The Crime of Dr. Hallet; You Can't Cheat an Honest Man; Charlie McCarthy, Detective; Framed; I Wanted Wings; Take a Letter, Darling; Earl Carroll's Sketch Book; Hit Parade of 1947.

Bway inc: The Boys From Syracuse; By Jupiter.

MOORE, Demi b. 1963. TV inc: Act. General Hospital; Bedrooms (cable). Films inc: Choices; Young Doctors In Love; Blame It On Rio; No Small Affair; St. Elmo's Fire.

MOORE, Dickie: Act. b. Los Angeles, Sep 12, 1925. First screen appearance 1926 at 11 mos old in The Beloved Rogue. Films inc: Oliver Twist; Peter Ibbetson; Dangerous Years; Out of the Past; Eight Iron Men; Member of the Wedding.

MOORE, Dudley: Act-Comp. b. London, Apr 19, 1935. e. Oxford. Thea inc: Beyond the Fringe; Play It Again, Sam; Serjeant Musgrave's Dance (comp music); The Caucasian Chalk Circle (comp music); Good Evening *(Grammy*-spoken word-1974); *(Special Tony Awards*-1969 & 1974).

Film inc: (Act) The Wrong Box; Bedazzled; Thirty Is a Dangerous Age; Cynthia; The Bed-Sitting Room; Alice in Wonderland; Foul Play; The Hound of the Baskervilles; 10; Wholly Moses!; Derek and Clive Get The Horn (& mus); Arthur; Six Weeks (& mus); Lovesick; Romantic Comedy; Unfaithfully Yours; Best Defense; Micki & Maude.

TV inc: The Muppets Go To The Movies.

MOORE, Garry (Thomas Garrison Morfit): Act. b. Baltimore, MD, Jan 31, 1915. On radio as announcer, sports commentator, comedian, writer. Teamed with Jimmy Durante on radio to 1947. MC Take It or Leave It; Breakfast in Hollywood.

TV inc: Garry Moore Show; I've Got a Secret; To Tell the Truth; The TV Academy Hall Of Fame.

MOORE, Juanita: Act. b. 1922. Films inc: Lydia Bailey; Witness to Murder; Ransome; The Girl Can't Help It; Imitation of Life; Walk on the Wild Side; The Singing Nun; Rosie; Fox Style; Paternity.

TV inc: The Notorious Jumping Frog of Calaveras County.

MOORE, Kevan: Exec. b. Bradford, England, Dec 29, 1937. Pgm controller, South Pacific Television, New Zealand.

MOORE, Mary Tyler: Act. b. NYC, Dec 29, 1936. Films inc: X15; Thoroughly Modern Millie; What's So Bad About Feeling Good?; Don't Just Stand There; Change of Habit; Ordinary People; Six Weeks.

TV inc: Richard Diamond; Steve Canyon; The Dick Van Dyke Show (Emmys-1964 & 1966); The Mary Tyler Moore Show (Emmys-1973, 1974, 1976 and actress of year-1974). Run a Crooked Mile; How To Survive The 70's and Maybe Even Bump Into Happiness; First You Cry; The Mary Tyler Moore Hour; I Love Liberty; Heartsounds; Finnegan Begin Again; Night Of 100 Stars II.

Bway inc: Whose Life Is It Anyway (Special Tony-1980).

MOORE, Melba: Singer-Act. b. NYC, Oct 29, 1945. Rec artist; niteries. Bway inc: Hair; Purlie (Tony-supp-1970); Timbuktu; Inacent Black.

Films inc: Pigeons; Cotton Comes to Harlem; Hair.

TV inc: The Melba Moore-Clifton Davis Show; The Beatrice Arthur Special; Flamingo Road; Kennedy Center Tonight--Broadway to Washington!; Ellis Island; Charlotte Forten's Mission--Experiment In Freedom; Night Of 100 Stars II; How To Be A Man.

MOORE, Richard: Cin-Dir. b. Jacksonville, IL, Oct 4, 1925. e. Westminster Coll; USC. Films inc: (as cin) The Wild Angels; Wild in the Streets; The Scalphunters; Winning; The Rievers; WUSA; Myra Breckinridge; Sometimes a Great Notion; The Life and Times of Judge Roy Bean; The Stonekillers; Annie. (As dir) The Circle of Iron.

MOORE, Robert: Act-Dir. b. Detroit, Aug 17, 1927. e. Catholic U of America. First appeared on stage under name of Brennan Moore, 1948, in Jenny Kissed Me. Bway inc: (dir) The Boys in the Band; Promises, Promises; Last of the Red Hot Lovers; The Gingerbread Lady; Lorelei; My Fat Friend; Deathtrap; They're Playing Our Song; Woman of the Year.

Films inc: (act) Tell Me That You Love Me, Junie Moon; (dir) Murder by Death; The Cheap Detective; Chapter Two.

TV inc: Fit For A King (dir).

(Died May 10, 1984).

MOORE, Roger: Act. b. London, Oct 14, 1927. e. RADA. Films inc: Last Time I Saw Paris; Interrupted Melody; King's Thief; Rachel Cade; Caesar and Cleopatra; Trottie True; Live and Let Die; Gold; The Man With the Golden Gun; The Lucky Touch; Street People; Shout at the Devil; Sherlock Holmes in New York; The Spy Who Loved Me; The Wild Geese; Escape to Athena; Ffolkes; The Sea Wolves; Sunday Lovers; The Cannonball Run; For Your Eyes Only; Octopussy; The Naked Face; A View To A Kill.

TV inc: Maverick; The Persuaders; The Saint; Ivanhoe; On Top All Over The World.

MOORE, Terry (Helen Koford): Act. b. Los Angeles, Jan 1, 1929. Photographer's model as a child; on radio; Pasadena Playhouse. On screen under four different names. As child in: The Howards of Virginia (as Helen Koford); My Gal Sal; Gaslight; Son of Lassie; Sweet and Low Down (as Judy Ford); The Devil on Wheels (as Jan Ford); The Return of October (The first as Terry Moore). Other films inc: Mighty Joe Young; The Barefoot Mailman; Man on a Tightrope; Beneath the 12-Mile Reef; King of the Khyber Rifles; Daddy Long Legs; Peyton Place; A Private Affair; Waco; A Man Called Dagger; Hellhole.

TV inc: I Love Men.

MOORE, Thomas W.: Prod-Exec. Former adv mgr, entered tv as account exec CBS-TV film sales; 1965 Gen sls mgr CBS-TV film sales; 1958, vp chg pgmg & talent; 1962 P ABC-TV net; 1968, bd chmn Ticketron; 1971 P Tomorrow Entertainment.

TV inc: (exec prod) The Body Human (Emmy-1978); I Know Why The Caged Bird Sings; The Body Human--The Sexes; Lifeline (Emmy-1979); Roll of Thunder, Hear My Cry; The Body Human--The Magic Sense (Emmy-1980); White Mama; The Body Human--The Body Beautiful; Damien...The Leper Priest; The Body Human--The Sexes II; Gnomes; The Body Human--The Facts For Boys; Faeries; The Body Human--The Bionic Breakthrough (Emmy-1981); The Body Human--The Living Code; Kudzu; The Body Human--The Journey Within; Attack On Fear (exec prod).

MORAHAN, Christopher: Dir. b. London, Jul 9, 1929. Thea inc: Little Murders; This Story of Yours; The Caretaker; State of Revolution; Brand.

Films inc: Diamonds for Breakfast; All Neat in Black Stockings; Fruits of Enlightment; Sisterly Feelings; Man and Superman.

TV inc: Talking to a Stranger; Uncle Vanya; The Gorge; The Jewel In The Crown (& prod).

MORAN, Erin: Act. b. Burbank, CA, Oct 18, 1961. Films inc: How Sweet It Is; 80 Steps to Jonah; Watermelon Man; Galaxy of Terror.

TV inc: Stanley vs. the System; Daktari; Don Rickles Show; Mirror, Mirror; Lisa, Bright and Dark; Happy Days; Greatest Heroes of the Bible; Sweepstakes; Twirl; Joanie Loves Chachi.

MORAN, Lois: Act. b. Pittsburgh, PA, 1907. Raised and educated in France where she entered films with a French firm while dancing in the ballet of the Paris Grand Opera Company. Returned to the US to star in Stella Dallas. Films inc: Just Suppose; The Road To Mandalay; The Music Master; Sharp Shooters; Prince of Sinners; Behind That Curtain; Love Hungry; The River Pirate; The Dancers; Transatlantic; The Spider; The Men in Her Life; West of Broadway.

Bway inc: Of Thee I Sing,

TV inc: Waterfront.

MOREAU, Jeanne: Act. b. Paris, Jan 23, 1928. Films inc: The She Wolves; The Lovers; Les Liaisons Dangereuses; La Notte; Jules et Jim; Eva; The Trial; The Victors; Diary of a Chambermaid; The Yellow Rolls-Royce; The Train; Mata Hari; Viva Maria; Chimes at Midnight; Sailor from Gibraltar; The Bride Wore Black; Great Catherine; Monte Walsh; Alex in Wonderland; Louise; Mr Klein; The Last Tycoon; Lumiere (& dir-sp); L'Adolescente (dir-sp); Joana Francesca (Jeanne the Frenchwoman); Plein Sud (Heading South); Mille Milliards de Dollars (A Thousand Billion Dollars); The Wizard of Babylon (doc); Querelle; La truite (The Trout); Lillian Gish (doc) (prod-dir-int); Jean-Louis Barrault--A Man Of The Theater (doc-int).

TV inc: Parade of Stars.

MORECAMBE, Eric (John Eric Bartholomew, OBE): Comedian. b. England, May 14, 1926. Teamed with Ernie Wise beginning 1941. On radio, tv with Morecambe and Wise Shows. Films inc: The Intelligence Man; That Riviera Touch; The Magnificent Two.

(Died May 29, 1984).

MORENO, Rita (Rosa Dolores Alvario): Act. b. Humacao, Puerto Rico, Dec 11, 1931. Films inc: Toast of New Orleans; Pagan Love Song; Singin' in the Rain; Garden of Evil; The Vagabond King; Seven Cities of Gold; Untamed; The Yellow Tomahawk; The King and I; West Side Story (Oscar-supp-1961); The Night of the Following Day; Popi; Carnal Knowledge; The Ritz; Happy Birthday, Gemini; The Four Seasons.

Bway inc: Skydrift; The Sign in Sidney Brustein's Window; Gantry; Last of the Red Hot Lovers; Detective Story; The National Health; The Ritz (Tony-supp-1975); She Loves Me; Wally's Cafe; The Odd Couple.

TV inc: The Muppet Show (Emmy-1977); Rockford Files (Emmy-1978); Anatomy of a Seduction; Evita Peron; Orphans, Waifs and Wards; 9 To 5; Working; Portrait of a Showgirl; Natalie--A Tribute To A Very Special Lady; The 39th Annual Tony Awards.

(Grammy-childrens rec-1972).

MORGAN, Christopher: Prod. b. Los Angeles, Aug 31, 1942. e. U OR; Sorbonne; UCLA, BA. S of Harry Morgan. TV inc: Police Story; Medical Story; The Quest; Hunter; Quincy; Colorado C.I.; Portrait of a Rebel--Margaret Sanger; Beulah Land; Riker (supv prod); Today's FBI; The Neighborhood; The Mississippi (co-supv prod); A Good Sport.

MORGAN, Dennis (nee Stanley Morner): Act. b. Prentice, WI, Dec 10, 1910. e. Carroll Coll. Films inc: Suzy; The Great Ziegfeld; Kitty Foyle; Captains of the Clouds; Thank Your Lucky Stars; Two Guys from Texas; My Wild Irish Rose; Painting the Clouds with Sunshine; The Gun that Won the West; Uranium Boom; Rogues' Gallery.

TV inc: Beacon Street.

MORGAN, Harry (also billed as Henry Morgan)(nee Bratsburg): Act. b. Detroit, Apr 10, 1915. Screen debut, 1942, The Omaha Trail. Films inc: To the Shores of Tripoli; Crash Dive; Wing and a Prayer; A

Bell for Adano; State Fair; Dragonwyck; All My Sons; The Saxon Charm; Madame Bovary; High Noon; What Price Glory?; Not as a Stranger; The Teahouse of the August Moon; Inherit the Wind; How the West Was Won; John Goldfarb, Please Come Home; The Flim Flam Man; Charlie and the Angel; Support Your Local Sheriff; Viva Max; Snowball Express; The Apple Dumpling Gang; The Barefoot Executive; The Shootist; The Cat From Outer Space; The Apple Dumpling Gang Rides Again.

TV inc: December Bride; Pete and Gladys; The Richard Boone Show; Oh, Those Bells; Dragnet; The D.A.; Hec Ramsey; M*A*S*H (Emmy-supp-1980); Backstairs at the White House; The Wild Wild West Revisited; The Bastard; Better Late Than Never; Scout's Honor; More Wild Wild West; Rivkin--Bounty Hunter; AfterMASH; Sparkling Cyanide.

MORGAN, Jaye P.: Singer. b. Mancos, CO, Dec 3, 1931. With Frank De Vol Orch 1950-53 then solo. Recordings inc: That's All I Want From You; Life Is Just a Bowl of Cherries; The Longest Walk.

Films inc: The Gong Show Movie; Loose Shoes; Night Patrol.

MORGAN, Michele (Simone Roussel): Act. b. Paris, Feb 29, 1920. First Amer film 1942, Joan of Paris. Films inc: Higher and Higher; Passage to Marseilles; The Fallen Idol; The Seven Deadly Sins; The Mirror Has Two Faces; Landru; Lost Command; Benjamin; Cat and Mouse.

MORIARTY, Michael: Act. b. Detroit, Apr 5, 1941. e. Dartmouth; London Academy of Mus and Dramatic Art. Films inc: Glory Boy; Hickey & Boggs; Bang the Drum Slowly; The Last Detail; Report to the Commissioner; The Dog Soldiers; Shoot It Black Shoot It Blue!; Reborn; Too Far To Go; The Winged Serpent; Pale Rider; The Link.

TV inc: The Glass Menagerie (Emmys-supp and supp act of year-1974); Girls of Summer; The Deadliest Season; Holocaust (Emmy-1978); The Winds of Kitty Hawk; Too Far To Go; The Sound of Murder (cable).

Bway inc: Find Your Way Home (Tony-1974); Richard III; G R Point; The Caine Mutiny Court Martial.

MORIN, Alberto (Salvador R Lopez): Act-Dial Coach. b. Puerto Rico, Nov 26, 1902. Films inc: Wings of the Navy; Gone with the Wind; The Desert Song; House of Strangers; The Gunfighter; Tripoli; Lydia Bailey; Rio Grande; My Sister Eileen; Will Success Spoil Rock Hunter?; Two Mules for Sister Sara; The Cheyenne Social Club; Chisum; The Mephisto Waltz.

TV inc: The Wild, Wild West Revisited.

MORISON, Patricia: Act. b. NYC, 1915. Films inc: Persons in Hiding; I'm from Missouri; Untamed; One Night in Lisbon; A Night in New Orleans; Beyond the Blue Horizon; Are Husbands Necessary; Silver Skates; Hitler's Madman; The Fallen Sparrow; The Song of Bernadette; Lady on a Train; Dressed to Kill; Queen of the Amazons; Tarzan and the Huntress; Son of the Thin Man; Walls of Jericho; The Return of Wildfire; Sofia; Song without End.

MORITA, Noriyuki 'Pat': Act. b. CA., 1930. Interned during WW II. After war worked at several jobs before becoming comedian, working niteries, TV commercials. TV inc: For The Love Of It; Crash Island; Happy Days; Mr. T. and Tina.

Films inc: Thoroughly Modern Millie; Midway; When Time Ran Out; Savannah Smiles; Jimmy the Kid; The Karate Kid.

MORITZ, Milton I.: Exec. b. Pittsburgh, PA, Apr 27, 1933. Owned and operated theatres in in LA from 1953-55; U.S. Navy 1955-1957; joined AIP 1957 as asst gen sls mgr; 1958 nat'l pub-ad dir; 1967, vp & bd member; 1975, sr vp; 1980 resigned to form own mdsng & cnsltng firm; 1981, with Murray Weissman, formed Moritz-Weissman Co.

MORLEY, Karen (Mildred Linton): Act. b. Ottumwa, IA., Dec. 12, 1905. e. Pasadena Playhouse. W of the late Lloyd Gough. Career halted after she was named in testimomy before the House Committee on Un-American Activities. Films inc: Inspiration; Daybreak; The Sin of Madelon Claudet; The Cuban Love Song; Mata Hari; Arsene Lupin; Scarface; Man About Town; The Washington Masquerade; The Mask of Fu Manchu; Flesh; Gabriel Over the White House; Dinner at Eight; The Crime Doctor; Our Daily Bread; Wednesday's Child; Black

Fury; The Littlest Rebel; Devil's Squadron; Beloved Enemy; Outcast; The Last Train from Madrid; On Such a Night; Kentucky; Pride and Prejudice; Jealousy; Framed; The 13th Hour; M.

TV inc: Banyon.

MORLEY, Robert: Act-Wri. b. Wiltshire, England, May 26, 1908. e. RADA. Films inc: Marie Antoinette; Major Barbara; The Young Mr Pitt; African Queen; Edward My Son; Melba; Gilbert and Sullivan; Beat the Devil; Around the World in 80 Days; The Doctor's Dilemma; The Journey; Oscar Wilde; Nine Hours to Rama; Murder at the Gallop; Those Magnificent Men in their Flying Machines; Topkapi; The Alphabet Murders; Genghis Khan; A Study in Terror; Hotel Paradiso; Way, Way, Out; The Trygon Factor; When Eight Bells Toll, Theatre of Blood; Song of Norway; The Blue Bird; Hugo the Hippo (voice only); Who Is Killing The Great Chefs of Europe; The Human Factor; Scavenger Hunt; Oh Heavenly Dog; Loophole; The Great Muppet Caper; High Road to China; Second Time Lucky.

Thea inc: Pygmalion; Edward My Son (co-author & act).

TV inc: Call My Bluff; The Deadly Game (cable).

MORODER, Giorgio: Composer-Record producer. b. Ortisei, Italy, Apr. 26, 1940. Produced several Donna Summer albums and various soundtrack albums. Film scores inc: Midnight Express (Oscar-1978); Foxes; American Gigolo; Cat People; Flashdance (Oscar-song-1983) (Grammy-score-1983); Superman III; Scarface; D.C. Cab; The Neverending Story.

MOROSS, Jerome: Comp. b. NYC, Aug 1, 1913. e. NYU, BS; Juilliard. Film scores inc: Hans Christian Andersen; The Big Country; Seven Wonders of the World; The Cardinal; The War Lord. TV inc: Wagon Train; Lancer; Gunsmoke; Have Gun Will Travel.

Thea inc: Parade; Ballet Ballads; The Golden Apple; Gentlemen, Be Seated.

Songs inc: You Ain't So Hot; I've Got Me; Yellow Flower; Lazy Afternoon; My Rebel Heart; Stay With Me.

(Died July 25, 1983).

MORRICONE, Ennio: Comp-Arr. b. Rome, 1928. Films inc: A Fistful of Dollars; El Greco; Fists in the Pocket; The Good, the Bad, and the Ugly; The Big Gundown; Matchless; Theorem; Once Upon a Time in the West; Investigation of a Citizen; Fraulein Doktor; Cat O'Nine Tails; The Decameron; The Burglars; The Black Belly of the Tarantula; Bluebeard; The Serpent; Down the Ancient Stairs; Divine Creature; Desert of the Tartars; Exorcist II-The Heretic; La Grande Bourgeoise; 1900; Orca; Sunday Woman; Days of Heaven; Leone; The Tempter; La Cage Aux Folles; Sidney Sheldon's Bloodline; La Banquiere (The Woman Banker); Uomini e no (Men or Not Men); La Cage Aux Folles II; White, Red and Verdone Green; The True Story of Camille; La Tragedia di un Uomo Ridicolo (Tragedy of a Ridiculous Man); Butterfly; So Fine; Le Professionel; Espion Leve-Toi (Rise Up, Spy); The Thing; White Dog; Treasure of the Four Crowns; Le Ruffian; Nana; Order of Death; La Chiave (The Key); Le Marginal (The Outsider); Sahara; Les voleurs de la nuit (Thieves After Dark); Once Upon A Time In America; Don't Kill God; The Link.

TV inc: Marco Polo; The Scarlet and the Black.

MORRIS, Garrett: Act. b. New Orleans, Feb 1, 1937. Singer, arr with Harry Belafonte Folk Singers.

Bway inc: Hallelujah Baby; I'm Solomon; Porgy and Bess; Showboat; Ain't Supposed To Die A Natural Death; Great White Hope; What The Winesellers Buy.

Films inc: The Angel Levine; Where's Papa?; The Anderson Tapes; Car Wash; Cooley High; The Census Taker.

TV inc: NBC Saturday Night Live; E.T. & Friends--Magical Movie Visitors; At Your Service.

MORRIS, Greg: Act. b. Cleveland, OH, Sep 27, 1934. e. OH State U; U of IA. Films inc: The New Interns; The Lively Set; The Sword of Ali Baba; S.T.A.B.

TV inc: Mission Impossible; Vega$; The Jesse Owens Story.

MORRIS, Howard: Dir-Act. b. NYC, Sep 4, 1919. e. NYU. Films inc: Boys Night Out; Who's Minding the Mint?; With Six You Get Egg Roll; Don't Drink the Water; High Anxiety; Goin' Coconuts; History of the World--Part I;

TV inc: Your Show of Shows; Caesar's Hour; The Munster's Re-

venge; Bunnicula The Vampire Rabbit (voice); Portrait of a Showgirl.
 Bway inc: Hamlet; Call Me Mister; John Loves Mary; Gentlemen Prefer Blondes.

MORRIS, John: Comp. b. Elizabeth, NJ, Oct 18, 1926. e. Juilliard; U WA. TV inc: The Adams Chronicles; The Scarlet Letter; The Tap Dance Kid; Doctor Franken; Splendor In The Grass; The Electric Grandmother; Ghost Dancing.
 Films inc: The Producers; The 12 Chairs; Blazing Saddles; Young Frankenstein; Silent Movie; High Anxiety; Sherlock Holmes' Smarter Brother; The Last Remake of Beau Geste; The In-Laws; The Bank Shot; The Elephant Man; In God We Trust; History of the World Part I; Table For Five; Yellowbeard; To Be or Not to Be; The Woman In Red; Johnny Dangerously.
 Bway inc: Bye Bye Birdie; Bells are Ringing; Mack and Mabel.

MORRIS, John Jackson: Wri-Dir-Prod. b. Sydney, Australia, Nov 11, 1933. Head of Prod, South Australian Film Corp; dir, South Australian Film Corp, 1976. Deputy Chmn, Australian Film and TV School.

MORRIS, Judy: Act. b. Toowoomba, Queensland, Australia. e. Australian National Institute of Dramatic Art. Thea inc: Rollicking Frolics; Catch Me a Girl; Some of My Best Friends Aren't; Abelard and Heloise.
 Films inc: Libido; Three to Go; Checkmate; Between the Wars; Scoobie Malone; Trespassers; The Picture Show Man; In Search of Anna; Maybe This Time; Strata; Journeys; Phar Lap; Razorback; Niel Lynne.

MORRIS, Oswald: Cin. b. London, 1915. Films inc: Green for Danger; Moulin Rouge; Beat the Devil; Beau Brummell; Moby Dick; A Farewell to Arms; Heaven Knows, Mr. Allison; The Key; Look Back in Anger; Our Man in Havana; The Entertainer; Lolita; Of Human Bondage; The Pumpkin Eater; The Hill; The Spy Who Came in From the Cold; Stop the World I Want to Get Off; The Taming of the Shrew; Oliver; Goodbye Mr Chips; Scrooge; Fiddler on the Roof (*Oscar*-1971); Lady Caroline Lamb; The Mackintosh Man; The Odessa File; The Man Who Would be King; The Seven Per Cent Solution; Equus; The Wiz; The Great Muppet Caper; The Dark Crystal.

MORRISON, Hobe: Wri-Critic. b. Germantown, PA, Mar 24, 1904. 1943, drama ed Philadelphia Record; joined Variety 1937; drama ed-critic.
 (*Tony*-honorary-1980).

MORRISON, Robert L.: Cin. TV inc: Hawaii Five-O (series); QB VII; The Million Dollar Face; The Violation of Sarah McDavid; Jacqueline Susann's Valley of the Dolls; The Day the Bubble Burst; I, Desire; Malibu; Blood Feud.
 (Died Aug. 3, 1983).

MORRISSEY, Paul: Dir. b. NYC, 1939. e. Fordham U. Started as prodn asst to Andy Warhol. Films inc: Taylor Mead Dances; Civilization And Its Discontents; Flesh (& wri-cin); Lonesome Cowboy (exec prod-cin-edtr); Trash; Blue Movie (exec prod); Andy Warhol's Women; Heat; L'Amour (exec prod-co-dir-wri); Andy Warhol's Frankenstein (& wri); Andy Warhol's Dracula (Blood For Dracula)(& wri); Madame Wang's (& wri); The Hound Of the Baskervilles; Forty Deuce (& wri); Mixed Blood (& wri).

MORROW, Jeff: Act. b. NYC, Jan 13, 1917. e. Pratt Institute. Films inc: The Robe; Tangier; Siege at Red River; Tanganyika; Sign of the Pagan; Captain Lightfoot; The Giant Claw; The Story of Ruth; Harbour Lights. Bway inc: Romeo and Juliet; St Joan; January Thaw; Billy Budd; Three Wishes for Jamie; The Suspects.
 TV inc: Iron Horse.

MORROW, Karen: Act-Singer. b. Des Moines, IA, Dec 15. e. Clarke Coll. Thea inc: (Bway) I Had a Ball; A Joyful Noise; I'm Solomon; The Grass Harp; The Selling of the President; Oklahoma!; Most Happy Fella; Brigadoon; Carnival; teamed with Nancy Dussault for Town Hall concert appearances. (Off-Bway) Sing Muse; The Boys From Syracuse.
 TV inc: The Jim Nabors Show; The Boy in the Plastic Bubble; Tabitha; Friends; Song by Song; Ladies Man; A Gift of Music; Singin

(Love Songs) (& crea) (cable); I Was A Mail Order Bride.

MORROW, Richard T.: Exec. b. Glendale, CA, 1926. e. UCLA, BA; USC, LLB. Became a vp at Walt Disney Productions in 1964. Elected to the Board of Directors in Dec, 1971; trustee of the Disney Foundation.

MORSE, Barry: Act. b. England 1919. Films inc: The Goose Steps Out; When We Are Married; There's A Future In It; Late At Night; No Trace; Kings of the Sun; Justine; Asylum; Love at First Sight; Power Play; The Shape of Things To Come; Klondike Fever; The Changeling; The Hounds...of Notre Dame; Cries In The Night; Murder By Phone.
 TV inc: The Fugitive; The Zoo Gang; The Adventurer; Space 1999; The Martian Chronicles; The Deptford Trilogy; A Tale of Two Cities; The Winds of War; The Rothko Conspiracy; The Innocents Abroad; Strange But True; Sadat; Master of the Game; A Woman Of Substance; Reunion At Fairborough.

MORSE, Hollingsworth: Dir. b. Los Angeles, 1910. Has directed approximately 2,000 tv shows. Films inc: Pufnstuf; Daughters of Satan.
 TV inc: The Lone Ranger; The Mark of Zorro; The Grey Ghost; Riverboat; Laramie; No Time for Sergeants; Adam 12; Man from Shiloh; Emergency; Marcus Welby; Dukes of Hazzard; National Lampoon Delta House; Crash Island; Secret of Isis; Ark II; The Oregon Trail.

MORSE, Robert: Act. b. Newton, MA, May 18, 1931. Films inc: The Matchmaker; Honeymoon Hotel; Quick Before it Melts; The Loved One; Oh Dad, Poor Dad; How to Succeed in Business Without Really Trying; Where Were You When the Lights Went Out?; The Boatniks.
 TV inc: That's Life; The Stingiest Man In Town; Jack Frost (voice); Kennedy Center Tonight--Broadway to Washington; Masquerade; The Calendar Girl Murders.
 Bway inc: Darling; Take Me Along; How to Succeed in Business Without Really Trying (*Tony*-1962); Sugar; Damn Yankees; So Long 174th St.

MORTON, Bruce: TV newsman. b. Norwalk, CT. e. Harvard. With various broadcasting organizations before joining CBS as Washington Bureau reporter 1964; 1966 named Washington correspondent; 1974 Washington correspondent CBS Morning News; 1975 Washington anchorman. TV inc: Reports from Lt. Calley Trial (*Emmy*-1971); Watergate--The White House Transcripts (*Emmy*-1974); Coverage of American Unemployment.

MOSES, Charles Alexander (Chuck): Pub exec. b. Chicago, IL, Mar 1, 1923. e. Northwestern U. Began pub career with Howard Mayer Associates, Chicago; prod radio shows for Chicago dept store chain; 1951, prod Radio Free Europe; 1952, European ad-pub dir UA; 1955, ad-pub dir Bel-Air Productions; 1959, pub exec Screen Gems, Warner Bros, Mirisch; 1962, pub-ad-dir Sinatra Enterprises; 1964, pub-ad dir Aldrich & Associates; 1966, exec in chg pub-ad dept U; 1969, formed Charles A Moses Co.

MOSES, Charles, Sir: Exec. b. Lancashire, England, Jan 21, 1900. e. Royal Military Coll, Sandhurst. GM, Australian Broadcasting Comm, 1935-65; secy-gen Asian Broadcasting Union, 1965-77.

MOSES, Gilbert III: Dir. b. Cleveland, OH, Aug 20, 1942. e. Oberlin Coll. Thea inc: LeRoi Jones' Slaveship; Bloodknot; Rigoletto; Mother Courage; No Place to be Somebody; Charlie Was Here and Now He's Gone; Aint Supposed to Die a Natural Death; The Duplex; Don't Let It Go to Your Head; The Taking of Miss Janie; 1600 Pennsylania Avenue.
 Films inc: Willie Dynamite (& comp); The Fish That Saved Pittsburgh.
 TV inc: Hang Tight, Willy Bill.

MOSS, Arnold: Act-Dir. b. NYC, Jan 28, 1910. e. CCNY, BA; Columbia U, MA, NYU, PHD. Films inc: Temptation; The Black Book; Kim; Viva Zapata; Casanova's Big Night; The Twenty-Seventh Day; The Fool Killer; Gambit; Caper of the Golden Bulls.

MOSS, Irwin: Exec. Started with Dancer-Fitzgerald-Sample ad agcy pgm dept; joined CBS-TV as dir bus aff, later dir bus aff Cinema Center Films; joined ICM agency as sr vp bus aff, creating & packaging pgms; to NBC Entertainment as sr vp entertainment acquisitions;

Aug 1980 named P Marble Arch Television; company phased out, July 1982; became sr vp Paramount Motion Picture div in chg of bus, legal aff Nov 1982; Aug. 1984, exec VP D.L. Taffner Ltd.

MOST, Donny: Act. b. NYC, Aug 8, 1953. Films inc: American Dream; Leo and Loree.
TV inc: Huckleberry Finn; Mel and Susan Together; The Donna Fargo Show; With This Ring; The $1,000 Bill; Happy Days.

MOSTEL, Josh: Act. b. NYC, Dec. 21, 1957. e. Brandeis U. S of the late Zero Mostel. Performed with Metropolitan Opera while still in grade school. Thea inc: (Off Bway) The Proposition; Straws in the Wind; More Than You Deserve. (Bway) Unlikely Heroes; A Texas Trilogy; An American Millionaire.
Films inc: Going Home; Jesus Christ Superstar; The King of Marvin Gardens; Harry and Tonto; Dead Ringer; All The Sad Young Men; Sophie's Choice; Star 80; The Brother From Another Planet; Windy City; Almost You.
TV inc: Seventh Avenue; Off Campus; Hereafter; Delta House; At Ease; The Boy Who Loved Trolls.

MOUNT, Thom: Exec. b. May 26, 1948. e. Bard Coll; CA Institute of the Arts, MFA. Started in industry as asso prod Selznick/Glickman Prod; 1976 asst to U exec vp Ned Tanen; 1977, vp supv feature films; 1978 exec vp in chg prodn; Jan. 1983 P Wldwide Motion Picture prodn for Universal Motion Picture Group; Nov. 1983 relieved of duties by Frank Price when latter became P of MCA Motion Picture Group.

MOUSSA, Ibrahim: Prod. b. Alexandria, Egypt, Sep 30, 1946. Talent agent before turning prod in 1979. Films inc: La Cicala (The Cricket); Gabriela.

MOXEY, John Llewellyn: Dir. TV inc: Mission Impossible; Mannix; Hawaii 5-0; Judd for the Defense; Charlie's Angels (pilot); San Francisco International (pilot); Intimate Strangers; The President's Mistress; Foster and Laurie; The Night Stalker; Father Brown, Detective; The Power Within; Ebony, Ivory and Jade; The Solitary Man; The Children of An Lac; The Mating Season; No Place To Hide; The Violation of Sarah McDavid; (& co-prod) Killjoy; I, Desire; The Cradle Will Fall; Through Naked Eyes; Legmen; When Dreams Come True.
Films inc: Horror Hotel; Circus of Fear; Foxhole in Cairo.

MOYERS, Bill: TV Newsman. b. Hugo, OK, Jun 5, 1934. e. U TX, BJ; Southwestern Baptist Theological Sem. Asst to Sen Lyndon B Johnson 1959-1960, 1961-63; asso dir Peace Corps 1961-63; spec asst to Pres Johnson 1963-1967 also press sec 1965-1967.
TV inc: A Question of Impeachment (Emmy-1964); Henry Steele Commager (Emmy-1974); Essay on Watergate (Emmy-1974) (all aired on PBS show Bill Moyers Journal); (ATAS Broadcast Journalism Award-1978); edtr & chf corr CBS Reports shows inc: Battle For South Africa (Emmy-wri-1979); Bittersweet Memories--A Viet Nam Reunion; Our Friends, The Germans; A Walk Through The 20th Century With Bill Moyers--The Democrat and the Dictator (crea) (cable); Our Times with Bill Moyers (Emmy-wri-1980); Judge; A Conversation with Zbigniew Brzezinski; Clark Gifford on Presidents and Power (Emmy-int-1981); George Steiner on Literature, Language and Culture (Emmy-int-1981); Our Friends The Germans; People Like Us; Title V; The Trouble with Temik; A Portrait of Maya Angelou; Marshall, Texas (Emmy-wri-1984); Crossroads.

MUDD, Roger: TV News. b. Washington, DC, Feb 9, 1928. e. Washington & Lee U, AB; U NC, MA. Reporter Richmond News-Leader 1953; news dir WRNL 1954; WTOP, Washington 1956; joined CBS News 1961 as Congressional corr; 1977 Nat'l Aff Corr; 1978, corr CBS Reports; 1980 joined NBC as Chief Washington Corr; 1982 co-anchor NBC Nightly News; dropped as co-anchor, Sept. 1983.
TV inc: The Selling of the Pentagon; The Shooting of Gov. Wallace (Emmy-1973); The Agnew Resignation (Emmy-1974); Watergate--The White House Transcripts (Emmy-1974); The Senate and the Watergate Affair (Emmy-1974); Teddy (Emmy-int-1980); The Presidency and the Nation; Christmas In Washington; Reagan At Midterm; Meet The Press.

MUHL, Edward E.: Exec. b. Richmond, IN, Feb 17, 1907. GM Universal, 1948-53 vp chg prod, 1953-68; consultant, 1969-72. Ret:

1982 consultant to Cinema Group.

MUIR, Esther: Act. b. NY, 1895. Thea inc: Greenwich Village Follies; Earl Carroll's Vanities; Queen High; Honeymoon Lane; My Girl Friday; Baby Blue.
Films inc: My Girl Friday; A Dangerous Affair; So This is Africa; The Bowery; Wine, Women and Song; Public Stenographer; A Day at the Races; Gilded Lily; I'll Take Romance; City Girl; Romance in the Dark; Battle of Broadway; The Girl and the Gambler; The Gay Deception; The Law West of Tombstone; Misbehaving Husbands; Stolen Paradise; X Marks the Spot.

MULDAUR, Diana: Act. b. NYC, Aug 19, 1943. e. Sweet Briar Coll, BA. Films inc: The Swimmer; Number One; The Lawyer; The Other; One More Train to Rob; McQ; The Chosen Survivors; Beyond Reason.
TV inc: McCloud; Ordeal; The Word; A Cry For Justice; The Miracle Worker; The Return of Frank Cannon; Fitz and Bones; Too Good To Be True; The TV Academy Hall Of Fame 1985.
Bway inc: Seidman and Son; Poor Bitos; A Very Rich Woman.

MULGREW, Kate: Act. b. Dubuque, IA, Apr 29, 1955. e. NYU. TV inc: Ryan's Hope; The Word; Jennifer: A Woman's Story; Kate Columbo; A Time For Miracles; The Manions of America.
Thea inc: Othello; Three Sisters; The Plow and the Stars; Orpheus Descending.
Films inc: A Stranger Is Watching.

MULHARE, Edward: Act. b. Ireland, Apr 8, 1923. Films inc: Hill Twenty-Four Doesn't Answer; Signpost to Murder; Von Ryan's Express; Our Man Flint; Eyes of the Devil; Caprice; Megaforce.
TV inc: The Ghost and Mrs Muir; Gidget Grows Up; Knight Rider.

MULHOLLAND, Robert E.: Exec. b. 1934. e. Northwestern U, BA, MA. Joined NBC Chicago 1962 as newswriter, became field prod for Huntley-Brinkley report; 1964 to London as European prod NBC News; 1967, Washington prod Huntley-Brinkley; 1967, news dir West Coast; 1972, exec prod NBC Nightly News; 1973, vp NBC News; 1974, exec vp NBC News; 1977 P NBC TV network; Jul 1981, P & COO NBc; resd March 1984.

MULL, Martin: Act-Wri. b. Chicago, IL, Aug 18, 1943. Humorist, hired by Warner Records to develop hit singles, wrote A Girl Named Johnny Cash; recorded for Capricorn, ABC Records, Electra-Asylum Records.
Films inc: FM; Serial; My Bodyguard; Take This Job and Shove It; Mr. Mom; Growing Pains.
TV inc: Mary Hartman, Mary Hartman; Fernwood 2 Night; America 2 Night; guest host Tonight Show; Johnny Cash Spring Special; Chevy Chase National Humor Test; Big City Comedy; Tom and Dick Smothers Brothers Special; Twilight Theatre; Grandpa, Will You Run With Me?; Domestic Life (& crea); California Girls; Lots Of Luck; Michael Nesmith In Television Parts; Martin Mull Presents The History Of White People In America--Part 1(& exec prod)(feevee).

MULLAVEY, Greg: Act. b. Buffalo, NY, Sep 10, 1939. e. Hobart. H of Meredith MacRae. Bway inc: Romantic Comedy.
TV inc: Mary Hartman, Mary Hartman; Centennial; Children of Divorce; Number 69; Crash Island; This is Kate Bennett; She's With Me; Insight/Every Ninety Seconds; Insight/The Fiddler; The Fourth Wise Man.
Films inc: Raid on Rommel; The Hindenburg; The Love Machine; I'm Going To Be Famous; I Dismember Mama; My Friends Need Killing (made in 1976); The Census Taker.

MULLER, Romeo: Wri-Prod. b. NYC, Aug 7, 1928. TV inc: Love Me to Pieces; Rudolph the Red Nosed Reindeer; Little Drummer Boy; Santa Claus is Comin' to Town; Frosty the Snowman; Here Comes Peter Cottontail; Marco; Rudolph's Shiny New Year; Frosty's Winter Wonderland; Puff the Magic Dragon (& prod); The Little Rascals Christmas (& prod); The Hobbit; Jack Frost; Strawberry Shortcake; Puff the Magic Dragon in the Land of Living Lies (& prod); The Return of the King; Thanksgiving in the Land of Oz (& prod); Pinocchio's Christmas; The Leprechaun's Christmas Gold.

MULLIGAN, Richard: Act. b. NYC, Nov 13, 1932. Films inc: The Mixed Up Files of Mrs. Basil E. Frankweiler; Irish Whiskey Rebellion;

One Potato, Two Potato; The Group; The Big Bus; Little Big Man; Scavenger Hunt; S.O.B.; Trail of the Pink Panther; Meatballs Part II; Teachers; Micki & Maude.

Thea inc: All the Way Home; Never Too Late; Nobody Loves an Albatross; Thieves; Special Occasions.

TV inc: Having Babies; The Hero; The Diana Rigg Show; Soap *(Emmy-1980)*; Malibu; Reggie; Jealousy.

MULLIGAN, Robert: Dir. b. NYC, Aug 23, 1925. e. Fordham U. Films inc: Fear Strikes Out; The Rat Race; The Great Impostor; Come September; The Spiral Road; To Kill a Mockingbird; Summer of '42; Love with a Proper Stranger; Inside Daisy Clover; Up the Down Staircase; The Stalking Moon; The Pursuit of Happiness; Baby, The Rain Must Fall; The Nickel Ride; The Other; Bloodbrothers; Same Time Next Year; Kiss Me Goodbye (& prod).

TV inc: Philco-Goodyear Playhouse; Alcoa-Goodyear Playhouse; The Moon and Sixpence *(Emmy-1960)*; Billy Budd; Ah, Wilderness; The Human Comedy, What Every Woman Knows; The Member of the Wedding; The Catered Affair; A Tale of Two Cities.

Bway inc: Comes a Day.

MUNDY, Meg: Act. b. London. Brief career as concert singer before act. Bway inc: Ten Million Ghosts; Hooray For What, The Fabulous Invalid; Three To Make Ready; How I Wonder; The Respectful Prostitute; Detective Story; Love's Labours Lost; Love Me Little; Philadelphia Story; You Can't Take It With You.

Films inc: Oliver's Story; The Bell Jar; Ordinary People.

TV inc: Playhouse 90; Omnibus; Breaking Up; The Doctors.

MUNSEL, Patrice: Soprano. b. 1925. Made Metropolitan Opera debut at age 17. Opera, concert appearances.

Bway inc: A Musical Jubilee.

Films inc: Melba

MURPHY, Ben: Act. b. Jonesboro, AR, Mar 6, 1942. e. U IL, BA; Pasadena Playhouse. TV inc: The Name of the Game; Alias Smith and Jones; Griff; Gemini Man; The Chisholms; Wild Bill Hickock; Heatwave; The Secret War of Jackie's Girls; Unit 4; Uncommon Valor; The Winds of War; The Cradle Will Fall; Lottery!; Berrenger's; Gidget's Summer Reunion. Films inc: Sidecar Racer; Time Walker.

MURPHY, Eddie: Act. b. Hempstead, NY, April 3, 1961. Standup comic. TV inc: Saturday Night Live (& wri); 1983 Emmy Show (host); The Joe Piscopo Special (cable).

Films inc: 48 Hours; Trading Places; Best Defense; Beverly Hills Cop.

(Grammy-comedy-1983).

MURPHY, George: Act. b. New Haven, CT, Jul 4, 1902. e. Yale U. Vaude, nitery dancer, stage debut in 1927 Good News; Of Thee I Sing; Roberta. Screen debut 1934 Kid Millions, 1934. Films inc: Broadway Melody of 1938; A Letter of Introduction; Two Girls on Broadway; A Guy, A Girl and A Gob; Tom, Dick and Harry; For Me and My Gal; This Is the Army; Bataan; Cynthia; Battleground; It's a Big Country; Walk East on Beacon. *(Special Oscar-1950.)* U S Senator (Cal) 1964-1971.

MURPHY, Michael: Act. Films inc: That Cold Day in the Park; Brewster McCloud; McCabe and Mrs. Miller; What's Up, Doc?; Phase IV; Nashville; The Front; The Class of Miss McMichael; An Unmarried Woman; Manhattan; Dead Kids; Talk To Me; Cloak and Dagger.

TV inc: The Autobiography of Miss Jane Pittman; The Rules of Marriage; Two Marriages; Countdown to Looking Glass (cable).

MURPHY, Richard: Wri-Dir. b. Boston, 1912. e. Williams Coll. Films inc: Boomerang; Deep Waters; Cry of the City; Panic in the Streets; Les Miserables; The Desert Rats; Broken Lance; The Wackiest Ship in the Army; Compulsion; The Last Angry Man; The Kidnapping of the President (wri).

TV inc: Our Man Higgins; The Felony Squad (creator).

MURRAY, Anne: Singer. b. Springhill, Nova Scotia, Jun 20, 1945. e. U of New Brunswick. Recording artist.

Albums inc: Let's Keep It That Way; Greatest Hits.

(Grammys (4)-country vocal-1974, 1980; pop vocal-1979, 1983).

TV inc: The Johnny Cash Christmas; Perry Como's Christmas in New Mexico; A Special Anne Murray Christmas; Country Comes Home; Anka; Anne Murray's Caribbean Cruise; A Special Eddie Rabbitt; Anne Murray's Winter Carnival--From Quebec; Anne Murray--The Sounds Of London; Night Of 100 Stars II.

MURRAY, Bill: Wri-Act. b. Evanston, IL, Sep 21, 1950. With Second City group; wrote and performed in National Lampoon Show off-Bway and National Lampoon Radio Hour.

TV inc: All You Need is Cash; Saturday Night Live *(Emmy-wri-1977)*; Late Night With David Letterman; Twilight Theatre; It's Not Easy Being Me--The Rodney Dangerfield Show; Second City--25 Years In Revue.

Films inc: Next Stop, Greenwich Village; Coming Attractions; Meatballs; Mr Mike's Mondo Video; Where the Buffalo Roam; Caddyshack; Stripes; Loose Shoes; Tootsie; Ghostbusters; Nothing Lasts Forever; The Razor's Edge (& wri).

MURRAY, Don: Act-Dir-Wri. b. Los Angeles, Jul 31, 1929. Films inc: Bus Stop; Bachelor Party; A Hatful of Rain; The Hoodlum Priest; Shake Hands With The Devil; Advise and Consent; The Cross and the Switchblade;; Conquest of the Planet of the Apes; The Plainsman; Escape from East Berlin; The Borgia Stick; Deadly Hero; Damien--Omen II; Endless Love; I Am the Cheese.

Bway inc: Insect Comedy; The Rose Tattoo; The Skin of Our Teeth; The Hot Corner; The Norman Conquest.

TV inc: Rainbow; Knots Landing; If Things Were Different; The Boy Who Drank Too Much; Confessions of a Lady Cop; Fugitive Family; Return of the Rebels; Thursday's Child; Branagan & Mapes; Quarterback Princess; License to Kill; A Touch Of Scandal.

MURRAY, Jan: Act. b. NYC, 1917. Performed in niteries, vaudeville, Bway, radio. TV inc: (MC) Songs for Sale, Sing It Again; Jan Murray Time; Treasure Hunt. (Act) The Dream Merchants.

Films inc: Who Killed Teddy Bear?; The Busy Body; Thunder Alley; A Man Called Dagger; History of the World--Part I; Fear City.

MURRAY, John B.: Prod-Dir-Wri. b. Australia. Films inc: 2000 Weeks (asso prod); The Naked Bunyip (prod-dir); Libido (co-exec prod); A Personal History of the Australian Surf (exec prod); We of the Never Never (co-exec prod); Lonely Hearts (prod).

MURRAY, Ken (Don Court): Act. b. NYC, 1903. On NY stage as MC; Hollywood stage in Ken Murray's Blackouts, 1942-9. Screen debut 1929 in Half-Marriage. Films inc: Leathernecking; A Night at Earl Carroll's; Juke Box Jenny; The Man Who Shot Liberty Valance; Son of Flubber; The Power; Ken Murray's Shooting Stars. *(Oscar Special-1947).*

TV inc: Ken Murray Show; Hollywood Without Makeup.

MUSANTE, Tony: Act. b. Bridgeport, CT, Jun 30, 1936. e. Oberlin Coll. Films inc: Once A Thief; The Incident; The Detective; A Professional Gun; The Love Circle; The Bird with the Crystal Plumage; The Last Run; Anonymous Venetian; The Pope of Greenwich Village.

TV inc: Toma; Breaking Up Is Hard To Do; The Thirteenth Day-The Story of Ruth; Weekend; Rearview Mirror; MacGruder & Loud.

Bway inc: 27 Wagons Full of Cotton; Memory of Two Mondays; Lady From Dubuque.

MUSBURGER, Brent: Sportscaster. b. Portland, OR, May 26, 1940. Started as sports director WBBM radio; later shitted to WBBM-TV; news anchor KNXT; Joined CBS sports 1975. Hosts The NFL Today; CBS Sports Saturday; CBS Sports Sunday (& man ed); and SportsTime.

Films inc: The Main Event; Rocky 2.

MUSSER, Tharon: Light dsgn. b. Roanoke, VA, Jan 8, 1925. e. Yale School of Drama, MFA. Light dsgn for Provincetown Playhouse; Jose Limon tour; Stratford (CT) Shakespeare. Bway inc: The Rivalry; The Great God Brown; Only in America; Five Finger Exercise; Giants, Sons of Giants; The Crucible; All in Good Time; Flora, The Red Menace; The Lion in Winter; House of Flowers; Applause; The Boy Friend; Follies *(Tony-1972)*; The Trial of the Catonsville Nine; The Prisoner of Second Avenue; The Creation of the World and Other Business; The Sunshine Boys; A Little Night Music; Sondheim--a Musical Tribute; The Wiz; Same Time Next Year; A Chorus Line *(Tony-1976)*; Pacific

Overtures; The Act; Ballroom; They're Playing Our Song; Whose Life Is It Anyway?; Fools; The Moony Shapiro Song Book; Special Occasions; Dreamgirls *(Tony*-1982); Merlin; Brighton Beach Memoirs; Private Lives; The Real Thing; Open Admissions; The Odd Couple; Biloxi Blues.

MUTI, Ornella (Francesca Romana Rivelli): Act. b. Rome, 1955. Films inc: La Moglie Piu Bella; Breakup; Viva Italia; A Man Alone in Revolt; Primo Amore; Bishop's Bedroom; Nest of Vipers; Flash Gordon; Taming of the Scoundrel; Tales of Ordinary Madness; Innamorato Pazzo (Madly In Love); Love & Money; La Vita e Bella (Life Is Wonderful); Un Amour de Swann (Swann in Love); Il Futuro E' Donna (The Future Is Woman).

MYERS, Harold: Journalist. b. London, Jul 10, 1912. Started as reporter with the Daily Film Renter, London, 1933; resigned in 1946; edtr, Cine-Technician, 1946-48; joined Variety 1948 as London Bureau Chief; named first European mgr in 1957; later named senior international correspondent on world-wide assignments.

MYERS, Peter S.: Exec. b. Toronto, May 13, 1920. e. U of Toronto. Salesman Warners, 1946; Toronto br mgr Eagle Lion, 1947; Toronto br mgr 20th Century-Fox, 1948; Canadian div mgr, 1951; Canadian GM, 1955; gen sls mgr in charge of dom. distribution 1968; named vp, 1969; sr vp Fox Entertainment Inc, 1980.

NAAR, Joseph T: Prod. b. San Diego, CA, Apr 25, 1925. e. UCLA, BA. TV inc: GE Theatre; Schlitz Playhouse; Checkmate; Starsky and Hutch; Strike Force.
Films inc: All American Boy; Blacula. Sept. 1982, exec VP Blake Edwards Entertainment.

NABORS, Jim: Act. b. Sylacauga, AL, Jun 12, 1932. TV inc: Andy Griffith Show; Gomer Pyle, USMC; The Jim Nabors Show; Aloha Paradise; All-Star Salute to Mother's Day; Jim Nabors Christmas In Hawaii; An All-Star Party For Carol Burnett.
Films inc: The Best Little Whorehouse In Texas; Stroker Ace; Cannonball Run II.

NADEL, Arthur H.: Wri-Prod-Dir. b. NYC, Apr 25. Films inc: Clambake; Lola; Underground; No Trumpets, No Drum; The Secret Of The Sword (prod).
TV inc: The Rifleman; The Plainsman; Arrest and Trial; The Virginian; Daniel Boone; Cowboy in Africa; Bonanza; Banyon; Welcome Home; The Chase; Crime Without Passion.

NADER, George: Act. b. Los Angeles, Oct 19, 1921. e. Occidental Coll. Films inc: Monsoon; Six Bridges to Cross; Lady Godiva; Away All Boats; Four Girls in Town; Joe Butterfly; The Human Duplicators; The Million Eyes of Sumuru.

NAGY, Ivan: Wri-Dir. b. Budapest, Hungary, Jan 23, 1938. e. UCLA, MFA. Films inc: Deadly Hero; Five Minutes of Freedom.
TV inc: Midnight Lace; A Gun in the House; Once Upon a Spy; Captain America II; Mind Over Murder; Midnight Lace; Jane Doe; A Touch Of Scandal; Playing With Fire.

NAGY, Ivan: Dancer-Chor. b. Debrecen, Hungary, Apr 28, 1943. e. Budapest State Opera House School. With Budapest Opera House Ballet; 1965 won silver medal at Int'l Ballet Competition, Bulgaria; joined Nat'l Ballet of Washington as guest artist; 1968 joined NYC Ballet, 1969 principal dancer; 1970 became premier dancer; has danced with may leading ballerinas inc Dame Margot Fonteyn; Makarova; Cynthia Gregory.

NAISMITH, Laurence (nee Johnson): Act. b. Surrey, England, Dec 14, 1908. Thea debut 1927 in chorus of Oh, Kay!; in rep, managed own rep company. Thea inc: (London) Rocket to the Moon; Larger Than Life; Colombe; The Apple Cart; The Burning Glass; The Lark; Summer Song; Candide; School for Scandal. (Bway) School for Scandal; Here's Love; A Time for Singing; Billy.
Films inc: High Treason; Trouble in the Air; A Piece of Cake; The Beggar's Opera; Mogambo; The Black Knight; Richard III; The Man Who Never Was; Lust for Life; The Barretts of Wimpole Street; Boy on a Dolphin; A Night to Remember; Tempest; I Accuse; Solomon and Sheba; Sink the Bismarck; The World of Suzie Wong; Greyfriars

Bobby; The Singer Not the Song; Jason and the Argonauts; Cleopatra; The Three Lives of Thomasina; Deadlier Than the Male; Camelot; Fitzwilly; The Long Duel; The Amazing Mr. Blunden; Young Winston.
TV inc: I Remember Nelson.

NAKADAI, Tatsuya: Act. b. Tokyo, 1932. Films inc: Seven Samurai; Black River; The Human Condition; Enjo; Odd Obsession; Sanjuro; Yojimbo; High and Low; Harakiri; Kwaidan; Rebellion; I Am A Cat; Queen Bee; Bird of Fire; Kagemusha; Onimasa; Ran.

NAMATH, Joe: Act. b. Beaver Falls, PA, May 31, 1943. e. U of AL. Former pro football star. Films inc: Norwood; C C & Co; The Last Rebel; Avalanche Express.
TV inc: The Waverly Wonders; Marriage Is Alive and Well; All American Pie; Bonnie and the Franklins; Texaco Star Theatre--Opening Night; Night Of 100 Stars II.

NANKIN, Michael: Wri-Dir. b. Los Angeles, Dec 26, 1955. e. UCLA, BFA. Films inc: Gravity (short); Junior High School (short); Midnight Madness.

NAPIER, Alan: Act. b. Birmingham, England, Jan 7, 1903. Films inc: The Uninvited; In a Monastery Garden; Loyalties; For Valour; The Four Just Men; The Invisible Man Returns; Ministry of Fear; Lost Angel; Forever Amber; Julius Caesar; The Court Jester; Journey to the Center of the Earth; Marnie.
TV inc: Batman; Centennial; The Contest Kid Strikes Again.
Thea inc: 10 yrs leading roles London inc Old Vic; Lady in Waiting.

NAPIER, John: Dsgn. b. London, Mar 1, 1944. e. Hornsey College of Art; Central School of Art and Crafts. Thea inc: A Penny for the Song; Fortune and Men's Eyes; The Ruling Class; The Fun War; Isabel's a Jezebel; Mister; The Lovers of Viorne; Lear; The Devils; Equus; The Party; Knuckle; several plays for Royal Shakespeare Company; co-designed permanent set at Stratford. Other shows inc Hedda Gabler; The Life and Adventures of Nicholas Nickleby (& Bway) *(Tony-scenic design*-1982); Cats (& Bway); *(Tony*-costume-1983); Starlight Express.

NARDINO, Gary: Exec. b. Garfield, NJ, Aug 26, 1935. e. Seton Hall U, BS. Joined ICM agency, became Sr VP; moved to William Morris as VP in chg NY TV Dept; became P Paramount Television Prodns 1977; resd July 1983 to produce. Films inc: Star Trek III--The Search For Spock (exec prod). TV inc: Brothers (PC) (exec prod); At Your Service (exec prod); Joanna (exec prod).

NARIZZANO, Silvio: Dir. b. Montreal, Feb 8, 1928. e. U of Bishop's, BA. Films inc: Die, Die, My Darling: Georgy Girl; Blue; Loot; Redneck; The Sky Is Falling; Why Shoot the Teacher?; The Class of Miss MacMichael; Choices.
TV inc: Death of a Salesman; War and Peace; The Little Farm; Staying On.

NASATIR, Marcia: Prod. b. NYC, May 18, 1925. Ed Dell Publishing, Bantam Books; ed, The Ladies Home Journal; East Coast story ed National General Pictures; vp in charge of Motion Picture Dev, UA; vp in charge of Motion Picture Dev, Orion Pictures; Oct 1981, exec vp in chg prodn Carson Films; Sept. 1982, P.; June 1983, sr vp prodn Fox; resd. Nov. 1984 to form Nasatir Prodns.Films inc: The Big Chill (exec prod).

NASH, N. Richard (nee Nusbaum): Wri. b. Philadelphia, Jun 8, 1913. e. U of PA. Plays inc: The Young and Fair; See the Jaguar; The Rainmaker; Girls of Summer; Handful of Fire; Echoes.
Films inc: Nora Prentiss; Welcome Stranger; Porgy and Bess; The Rainmaker.
TV inc: The Parade.

NAT, Marie-Jose: Act. b. Corsica, 1940. Films inc: Crime et Chatiment; Club de Femmes; Secret Professional; Rue des Prairies; Safari Diamant; Le Paria; Elise ou La Vraie Vie; Une Mere, Une Fille (Anna); La Disobbidienza (Disobedience); Litan.
Thea inc: Desire.

NATWICK, Mildred: Act. b. Baltimore, MD, Jun 19, 1908. e. Bryn Mawr. Films inc: The Long Voyage Home; The Enchanted Cottage;

The Late George Apley; Three Godfathers; The Kissing Bandit; She Wore a Yellow Ribbon; Cheaper by the Dozen; The Quiet Man; The Trouble with Harry; The Court Jester; Tammy and the Bachelor; Barefoot in the Park; If It's Tuesday This Must be Belgium; The Maltese Bippy; Daisy Miller; At Long Last Love; Kiss Me Goodbye.

TV inc: Do Not Fold, Spindle or Mutilate; The Snoop Sisters (Emmy-1974); The Easter Promise; Little Women; You Can't Take It With You; Maid In America.

Bway inc: End of Summer; Love from a Stranger; Candida; Missouri Legend; Blithe Spirit; Waltz of the Toreadors; Critic's Choice; Barefoot in the Park; Our Town.

NAUGHTON, Bill: Wri. b. Ballyhaunis, Ireland, Jun 12, 1910. Plays inc: All In Good Time; Alfie; Spring and Port Wine; He Was Gone When They Got There; June Evening; Keep It In the Family; Lighthearted Intercourse.

Films inc: Alfie.

NAUGHTON, David: Act-Singer. b. Hartford, CT, Feb 13, 1951. e. U PA, BA; LAMDA. Numerous commercials inc all Dr Pepper mus commercials since 1978. TV Inc: Making It; I, Desire; At Ease; Getting Physical.

Films inc: Midnight Madness; An American Werewolf In London; Separate Ways; Hot Dog--The Movie; Not For Publication.

Bway inc: Hamlet; Da.

NAUMOV, Vladimir: Dir. b. Russia, Dec 6, 1927. e. Moscow Film Institute. Always co-directs with Alexander Alov. For credits, See ALOV.

NAZARRO, Ray: Dir. b. Boston. e. Boston Coll. Films inc: The Tougher They Come; Counterspy; Palomino; Bullfighter and Lady (co-sp); Cripple Creek; Bandits of Corsica; Top Gun; Apache Territory; The Night Is Fatal; Arrivederci Cowboy.

TV inc: Mickey Spillane; State Trooper; Fury.

NEAGLE, Anna, Dame (Marjorie Robertson): Act. b. Forest Gate, England, Oct 20, 1904. On screen since 1929 in Mary Was Love (as Marjorie Robertson). Films inc: Bitter Sweet; Victoria the Great; Nurse Edith Cavell; Irene; No, No, Nanette; Forever and a Day; The Yellow Canary; Odette; The Man Who Wouldn't Talk; The Lady is a Square.

Thea inc: (London) This Year of Grace; Wake Up and Dream; As You Like It; Peter Pan; Charlie Girl; No, No, Nanette; Maggie; My Fair Lady.

TV inc: The Spice of Life; What's My Line; The Elstree Story; A Letter From The General; Shadow of the Sun.

NEAL, Patricia: Act. b. Packard, KY, Jan 20, 1926. In summer stock. Bway debut in Another Part of the Forest (Tony-supp-1947). Also in Children's Hour. Screen debut 1948, John Loves Mary.

Films inc: The Fountainhead; The Day the Earth Stood Still; A Face in the Crowd; Breakfast at Tiffany's; Hud (Oscar-1963); In Harm's Way; The Subject Was Roses (first film after recovering from a stroke); Happy Mother's Day...Love, George; Baxter; Widow's Nest; The Passage; Ghost Story.

TV inc: All Quiet On The Western Front; The Way They Were; Glitter; Love Leads The Way; Shattered Vows.

NEAME, Ronald: Dir-Prod. b. London, Apr 23, 1911. Started as asst cam 1929, Blackmail, first British sound film. Films inc: (as cin) Drake of England; The Gaunt Stranger; The Crimes of Stephen Hawke; Major Barbara; In Which We Serve; Blithe Spirit; Brief Encounter; Great Expectations.

(dir) Take My Life; The Golden Salamander; The Card (& prod); The Million Pound Note; The Man Who Never Was; Windom's Way; The Horse's Mouth; Tunes of Glory; The Chalk Garden; Mister Moses; A Man Could Get Killed; Gambit; The Prime of Miss Jean Brodie; The Poseidon Adventure; The Odessa File; Meteor; Hopscotch; First Monday in October.

TV inc: The Knowledge (prod).

NEDERLANDER, James: Prod-Thea Ownr. b. Detroit, Mar 31, 1922. e. Detroit Inst Tech; U of ND. P Nederlander Theatre Cos. Formed Nederlander-Weintraub Group, Sept. 1984, with Jerry Weintraub. Bway inc: (prod or co-prod) On a Clear Day You Can See Forever; The Ninety-Day Mistress; Applause; Not Now, Darling; Abelard and Heloise; Seesaw; Annie; My Fat Friend; Otherwise Engaged; Night and Day; Oklahoma! (rev); Betrayal; West Side Story (rev); Peter Pan; Whose Life Is It Anyway; Frankenstein; Broadway Follies; Woman of the Year; Can-Can (rev); Lena Horne--The Lady and Her Music; Fiddler On the Roof (rev); The Supporting Cast; The Life and Adventures of Nicholas Nickleby (Tony-1982); The Dresser; Little Johnny Jones; (Tony-1982); Ghosts; A Doll's Life; Merlin; Show Boat; Teaneck Tanzi, The Venus Flytrap; Dance A Little Closer; La Cage Aux Folles (Tony-1983); Noises Off; Oliver!; Cyrano de Bergerac; Much Ado About Nothing; Strange Interlude; Grind; Aren't We All.

NEEDELMAN, Julius: Dist. b. NYC, Jul 1, 1918. e. USC, BA; U of Denver, MBA. VP Tower Film Corp, 1968-72; p Tower Film Corp. 1972-present.

NEEDHAM, Hal: Dir. b. Memphis, TN, Mar 6, 1931. From 1956-76, stuntman, stunt coordinator, second unit dir. Films inc: (dir) Smokey and the Bandit; Hooper; Foul Play; Hooper; The Villain; Smokey and the Bandit II; The Cannonball Run; Megaforce (& sp); Stroker Ace (& sp); Cannonball Run II (& sp).

TV inc: Death Car on the Freeway; Hal Needham's Wild World of Stunts; Stunts; The Stockers.

NEELEY, Ted: Act. b. Ranger, TX, 1943. Formed rock group while in college. Performed in clubs, Las Vegas, LA.

Films inc: Jesus Christ Superstar; The Last Picture Show; A Perfect Couple (& mus); Hard Country; Blame It On The Night (vocals).

TV inc: Of Mice and Men.

NEFF, Hildegarde. (See KNEF, Hildegarde).

NEGRI, Pola: Act. b. Poland, 1897. On screen in US from 1922 in: The Red Reacock; Bella Donna; Passion; Forbidden Paradise; East of Suez; A Woman of the World; Loves of an Actress; The Woman from Moscow; Forbidden Paradise; Madame Bovary; Hi Didle Diddle; The Moonspinners.

NEGULESCO, Jean: Dir. b. Rumania, Feb 29, 1900. Films inc: Kiss and Make Up; The Mask of Dimitrios; The Conspirators; Three Strangers; Humoresque; Roadhouse; Johnny Belinda; Under My Skin; Three Came Home; The Mudlark; Phone Call from a Stranger; Titanic; How to Marry a Millionaire; Three Coins in the Fountain; Woman's World; Daddy Longlegs; The Rains of Ranchipur; Boy on a Dolphin; Count Your Blesings; The Best of Everything; Jessica; The Pleasure Seekers; The Invincible Six; Hello and Goodbye.

NEILL, Sam: Act. b. New Zealand, 1948. e. U of Canterbury (NZ). With repertory company before joining New Zealand National Film Unit, acting & directing docs and shorts. Films inc: Landfall; Ashes; Sleeping Dogs; The Journalist; My Brilliant Career; Just Out Of Reach; Attack Force Z; The Final Conflict; Possession; From a Far Country--Pope John Paul II; Enigma; The Country Girls; Le Sang des Autres (The Blood of Others); Robbery Under Arms.

TV inc: The Sullivans; Young Ramsay; Lucinda Brayford; Ivanhoe; Reilly, Ace of Spies.

NELL, Nathalie: Act. b. France, Oct. 1950. Films inc: Les Risques du Metier; L'Amour Viole (The Rape of Love); Tout es Nous; Suversion; Mourir d'Aimer (To Die of Love); Adolphe ou l'age Tendre; Echoes; Man, Woman and Child; Qu-est-ce qui fait courir David (What Makes David Run?); Malamore; Notre Histoire (Our Story).

NELLIGAN, Kate: Act. b. London, Mar 16, 1951. Thea inc: Barefoot in the Park; Misalliance; A Streetcar Named Desire; The Playboy of the Western World; Private Lives; Knuckle; Heartbreak House; Plenty; A Moon For the Misbegotten; Virginia.

Films inc: The Count of Monte Cristo; The Romantic Englishwoman; Dracula; Mr Patman; Eye of the Needle; Without A Trace.

TV inc: The Onedin Line; The Lady of the Camelias; Therese Raquin; Bethune; Victims; Forgive Our Foolish Ways.

NELSON, Barry (Robert Neilson): Act. b. Oakland, CA, Apr 16, 1920. Screen debut, 1941, Johnny Eager. Films inc: Shadow of the Thin Man; Dr. Kildare's Victory; Stand By for Action; Eyes in the Night; A Yank on the Burma Road; The Human Comedy; Bataan; A Guy Name Joe; Undercover Maisie; Tenth Avenue Angel; The Man

With My Face; Forty Guns; Mary, Mary; The Only Game in Town; Airport; Pete 'n Tillie; The Shining.

Bway inc: Light Up the Sky; Rat Race; The Moon Is Blue; Mary, Mary; Cactus Flower; Every Thing in the Garden; Seascape; The Norman Conquests; The Act.

TV inc: The Hunter; My Favorite Husband; Washington: Behind Closed Doors; Greatest Heroes of the Bible.

NELSON, Craig T.: Act. b. Apr. 4, 1946. Films inc: And Justice for All; Rage: The Formula; Where the Buffalo Roam; Private Benjamin; Stir Crazy; Poltergeist; Man, Woman and Child; All the Right Moves; The sterman Weekend; Silkwood; The Killing Fields.

TV inc: Diary of a Teenage Hitchhiker; Murder in Texas; Inmates--A Love Story; Chicago Story; Rage; Private Benjamin; Paper Dolls; Toast of Manhattan; Call To Glory..

Thea inc: The Fantastiks; Taming of the Shrew; Who'll Save the Ploughboy; Hello, Dolly; The Misanthrope; Everyman; Friends.

NELSON, David: Act. b. NYC, Oct 24, 1936. e. USC. S of Harriet Hilliard and the late Ozzie Nelson. Films inc: Here Come the Nelsons; Peyton Place; The Remarkable Mr. Pennypacker; Day of the Outlaw; The Big Circus; 30; The Sinners; Cheech and Chong's Up in Smoke; Last Plane Out (prod-dir); A Rare Breed (dir).

TV inc: Adventures of Ozzie and Harriet; Annual Circus of the Stars; The Rock 'n' Roll Show; High School U.S.A.

NELSON, Ed: Act. b. Dec 21, 1928. Films inc: Attack of the Crab Monsters; New Orleans Uncensored; Hell on Devil's Island; Invasion of the Saucer Men; Street of Darkness; The Young Captives; Soldier in the Rain; Judgment at Nuremberg; Elmer Gantry; The Man From Galveston; Time to Run; Airport '75; That's The Way of the World; The Silent Force; Midway; For the Love of Benji.

TV inc: Peyton Place; Doctor's Private Lives (High Rollers); Anatomy of a Seduction; The Girl, The Gold Watch and Everything; The Return of Frank Cannon; Enola Gay--The Men, The Mission, The Atomic Bomb; Born To Be Sold; Help Wanted--Male; Capitol; Peyton Place--The Next Generation.

NELSON, Gene (Eugene Leander Berg): Act-Dir. b. Seattle, WA, Mar 24, 1920. Began dancing and singing while in high school; joined Sonja Henie and toured in her ice shows, 1940-41; during WW II played in Irving Berlin's GI prodn of This Is The Army.

Films inc: I Wonder Who's Kissing Her Now; Apartment for Peggy; Gentlemen's Agreement; The Daughter of Rosie O'Grady; Tea for Two; Lullaby of Broadway; She's Working Her Way Through College; Three Sailors and a Girl; The West Point Story; Oklahoma!; Atomic Man; So This Is Paris; (dir) Wake Me When the War Is Over; The Cool One; Harum Scarum; Your Cheatin' Heart.

TV inc: (dir) McNaughton's Daughter; The Invisible Man; Starsky and Hutch; Christy Love; New Land; Diana Rigg Show; Barnaby Jones; Cannon; Rookies; The Letters; Salvage; Murder in Coweta County (supv prod); The Baron and the Kid (& supv prod).

Bway inc: (act) Lend An Ear; Music, Music; Good News; Hit the Deck; Oklahoma!; Pal Joey.

NELSON, Harriet (nee Hilliard): Act. b. Des Moines, IA, Jul 18, 1914. Singer with late husband Ozzie Nelson's band, later appeared in dramatic and musical roles with him. On radio shows: Believe It Or Not; Seeing Stars; Adventures of Ozzie & Harriet. On Screen in Here Come the Nelsons.

TV inc: Adventures of Ozzie & Harriet; Death Car On The Freeway; A Christmas For Boomer; The First Time; The Kid With The 200 I.Q.; High School USA.

Thea inc: Marriage-Go-Round; Impossible Years; State Fair.

NELSON, Haywood: Act. b. NYC, Mar 25, 1960. Films inc: Mixed Company. Thea inc: Thieves. TV inc: As the World Turns; What's Happening!.

NELSON, James (nee Falkinburg): Prod. b. Los Angeles, Sep 25, 1932. e. USC. Worked as editor, supv sound fx ed some 140 feature films. Films inc: Star Wars (asso prod); China Syndrome (asso prod); Borderline (prod).

NELSON, Ralph: Dir. b. NYC, Aug 12, 1916. Started as act on Bway in Cyrano De Bergerac, 1934; Bway inc: Romeo and Juliet; Taming of the Shrew; Hamlet; There Shall Be No Night. (Dir) Here's Mama; The Trouble Makers; Man In the Dog Suit; (prod) Look to the Lilies; (wri) Mail Call; The Wind Is Ninety.

From 1948 to 1960 dir more than 1,000 tv shows inc: Playhouse 90; Studio One; Philco Playhouse; Dupont Show of the Month; Requiem For a Heavyweight (Emmy-1956); Doyle Against The House; The Old Vic Hamlet; Man In the Funny Suit; Rodgers & Hammerstein's Cinderella; Cole Porter's Aladdin; This Happy Breed; Lady of the House; You Can't Go Home Again; Christmas Lilies of the Field (& exec prod).

Films inc: Requiem For a Heavyweight (& act); Lilies of the Field (& prod-act); Soldier in the Rain (& act); Fate is the Hunter; Father Goose; Duel at Diablo (& prod-act); Charly (& prod); Counterpoint (& act); Soldier Blue (& act); Flight of the Doves (& prod-wri); The Wrath of God (& prod-wri); The Wilby Conspiracy; Embryo (& act); A Hero Ain't Nothin' But a Sandwich.

NELSON, Rick: Act. b. Teaneck, NJ, May 8, 1940. S of Ozzie and Harriet Nelson. Recorded for Decca Records. Films inc: Here Come the Nelsons; Wackiest Ship in the Army; Rio Bravo; A Story of Three Loves; Love and Kisses.

TV inc: Adventures of Ozzie and Harriet; A Tale Of Four Wishes; High School USA; Fathers And Sons.

NELSON, Willie: Comp-Singer. b. Abbott, TX, Apr 30, 1933. Began writing songs in the 60's, started performing in 1970.

Songs inc: Family Bible; Funny How Time Slips Away; On the Road Again.

Films inc: Electric Horseman; Honeysuckle Rose; Thief; Barbarosa; Hells Angels Forever; Songwriter (act & songs); Streetwise (exec prod); 1918 (sang songs).

TV inc: Coming Out of the Ice; The Glen Campbell Music Show; Willie Nelson & Family (& prod) (cable); Johnny Cash--Christmas On The Road.

Albums inc: Stardust; Willie Nelson & Family Live; (Grammys-(5)-country vocal male-1975, 1978, 1982; country vocal group-1978; country song-1980).

NERO, Franco: Act. b. Italy, 1942. Films inc: The Tramplers; The Bible; Camelot; The Day of the Owl; A Quiet Place in the Country; Tristana; The Virgin and the Gypsy; The Battle of Neretva; Pope Joan; The Monk; Victory March; Force 10 from Navarone; Roses of Danzig; Mimi; The Man With Bogart's Face; Banovic Strahinja (The Falcon); Enter the Ninja; Kamikaze; The Wizard of Babylon (doc); Querelle; Mexico In Flames; Grog; The Salamander; Red Bells - I've Seen the Birth of the New World; Wagner; The Day Of The Cobra.

TV inc: The Last Days of Pompeii.

NESMITH, Mike: Act-Prod-Sngwri. b. Houston, TX., Dec. 30, 1942. Member of the group the Monkees, records and tv. Films inc: Head (act); Timerider (exec prod-wri-mus); Repo Man (exec prod).

TV inc: Michael Nesmith In Television Parts (host & exec prod).

NETHERTON, Tom: Act. b. Munich, Germany, Jan 11. Singer with Lawrence Welk Show; recording artist, niteries.

NETTER, Douglas: Exec. b. Seattle, WA, May 23, 1921. e. Holy Cross, BS. After WW2 joined PRC (later merged with Eagle Lion) in sales dept; 1947-55 gen sls mgr Altec; 1955-58, vp & gm Todd-AO; 1958, Samuel Goldwyn Prodns; 1964 formed own firm as prods rep; 1969 vp MGM; 1970-73 exec vp; 1974 into ind prodn.

Films inc: Mr Ricco.

TV inc: The Buffalo Soldiers; Wild Times; Roughnecks; Louis L'Amour's The Cherokee Trail.

NETTLETON, Lois: Act. b. Oak Park, IL, circa 1929. Films inc: Period of Adjustment; Come Fly with Me; Mail Order Bride; The Good Guys and the Bad Guys; Dirty Dingus Magee; Sidelong Glances of a Pigeon Kicker; The Honkers; Echoes of a Summer; Deadly Blessing; Butterfly; The Best Little Whorehouse In Texas.

Thea inc: The Biggest Thief in Town; Darkness at Noon; God and Kate Murphy; Silent Night, Lonely Night; The Wayward Stork; The Hemingway Hero; The Only Game in Town; Strangers.

TV inc: The Brighter Day; Portrait of Emily Dickinson; Duet for Two Hands; The Hidden River; Centennial; Tourist; Insight/A Gun For Mandy (Emmy-1983); Insight/So Little Time.

NEUCHATEAU, Corinne: Act. b. Staten Island, NY, Jul 20, 1952. Thea inc: Golda; The Three Sisters; A View from the Bridge; The Story Teller; In the Beginning; Skipping.
TV inc: Love of Life.
Films inc: The Last Tycoon (VO).

NEUFELD, Mace: Prod-Comp-Dir. b. NYC, Jul 13, 1928. e. Yale U, BA; NYU Law School. Films inc: The Omen (exec prod); The Frisco Kid (prod); The Funhouse (exec prod); The Aviator (prod).
TV inc: (exec prod) Angel On My Shoulder; John Steinbeck's East of Eden; American Dream; A Death In California.
Bway inc: The Flying Karamazov Brothers (prod).

NEUFELD, Sigmund Jr b. Los Angeles, May 12, 1931. TV inc: Dir. Lassie; Kojak; Invisible Man; Doctors Hospital; Serpico; Baretta; Switch; Project UFO; Incredible Hulk; Buck Rogers in the 25th Century; Me and Mr Stenner; Here's Boomer; Simon and Simon; Partners In Crime.

NEUMAN, E. Jack: Wri-Prod. b. Toledo, OH, Feb 27, 1921. e. U of MO, BJ; UCLA, LLD. Films inc: Viva Vasquez; Seven Cakes for Christmas; Man From Tomorrow; The Outlanders; Heat Wave; Most Dangerous Game; The Venetian Affair (& prod); Company of Killers (& prod); The Berlin Affair (& prod); The Cable Car Murder (& prod); Snow Job (& prod); Occurrence On A Dark Street (& prod); Police Story (& prod); The Blue Knight (& prod).
TV (prod-wri) Dr Kildare; Sam Benedict; Mr Novak; A Man Called Shenandoah; Night Games; Kate McShane; Law and Order; Inside the Third Reich.

NEWAY, Patricia: Act. b. NYC, Sep 30, 1919. e. Notre Dame Coll for Women. Bway inc: The Consul; Sound of Music (Tony-supp-1960); Morning Sun; The King and I; Salome.
TV inc: The Dialogue of the Carmelites; Golden Child; The Consul; Marie Golovin; Macbeth; Wozzeck.

NEWELL, Mike: Dir. TV inc: The Man in the Iron Mask; The Gift of Friendship (cable); Blood Feud.
Films inc: The Awakening; Bad Blood; Dance With A Stranger.

NEWHART, Bob: Act. b. Oak Park, IL, Sep 5, 1929. Performed in niteries before cutting talk album; weekly TV variety show, 1961. Films inc: Hell Is for Heroes; Hot Millions; Catch-22; On a Clear Day You Can See Forever; Cold Turkey; Little Miss Marker; First Family.
TV inc: The Bob Newhart Show; Thursday's Game; Packy; Marathon; Ladies and Gentlemen--Bob Newhart Part II; The Visitation Mystery; Newhart.
(Grammys-(3)-new artist-comedy-artist of year-1960).

NEWLAND, John: Act-Dir-Prod. b. Cincinnati, OH, Nov 23, 1917. Films inc: Bulldog Drummond; That Night; The Violators; The Spy with My Face; Hush-a-Bye Murder.
TV inc: Robert Montgomery Show (& dir); My Lover, My Son; One Step Beyond (host & dir); The Next Step Beyond; The Suicide's Wife; Angel City (prod); The Five Of Me (exec prod); The Execution (exec prod); Arch Of Triumph (prod).

NEWLEY, Anthony: Act. b. Hackney, England, Sept. 24, 1931. On screen from 1946 in: Adventures of Dusty Bates; Little Ballerina; Oliver Twist; The Weak and the Wicked; Fire Down Below; How to Murder a Rich Uncle; Killers of Kilimanjaro; The Small World of Sammy Lee; Willi Wonka and the Chocolate Factory; Doctor Doolittle; Sweet November; Mr. Quilp.
TV inc: Sammy; Sunday Night at the Palladium; The Strange World of Gurney Slade; Saturday Spectaculars; Hollywood Squares; The Tonight Show; Animal Talk; Linda In Wonderland; Malibu (song); Blade In Hong Kong.
Bway inc: Stop the World--I Want To Get Off; Roar of the Greasepaint; Good Old Bad Old Days. (London) The Traveling Music show (mus & lyr).
(Grammy-song of year-1962).

NEWMAN, Barry: Act. b. Boston, MA, Nov 7, 1938. e. Brandeis U. Films inc: Pretty Boy Floyd; The Lawyer; Vanishing Point; The Salzburg Connection; Fear is the Key; City on Fire; Amy.
TV inc: Petrocelli; Sex and the Married Woman; King Crab; Fanta-

sies; Having It All; Second Sight--A Love Story; Fatal Vision.

NEWMAN, David: Wri. b. NYC, Feb 4, 1937. e. U MI. Films inc: (all in collab with Robert Benton) Bonnie and Clyde; There was a Crooked Man; Floreana; What's Up Doc; Money's Tight; Bad Company; Superman; Superman II; Jinxed!; Superman III; Sheena.
Plays inc: It's A Bird, It's a Plane, It's Superman; Oh! Calcutta (one Sketch).

NEWMAN, Edwin: TV Newsman. b. NYC, 1919. Joined NBC News in London, 1952; served as bureau chief London, Rome, Paris. Based in NY since 1961. Serves as newscaster, anchors specials.
TV inc: Reading, Writing and Reefer; The American Family; An Endangered Species; No More Vietnams...But; Just Plain Folks--The Billionaire Hunts; Pleasure Drugs--The Great American High; Lily For President?; Ambassadors of Hope; Crime and Insanity; Kids, Drugs and Alcohol (Emmy-moderator-1983); Marvelous Machines--Expendable People; The Bishops and the Bomb (moderator); Earthlings; National Science Test 1984.

NEWMAN, Joseph M.: Dir. b. Logan, UT, Aug 7, 1909. Dir short subjects 1938. Films inc: Jungle Patrol; 711 Ocean Drive; The Outcasts of Poker Flats; Pony Soldier; The Human Jungle; Dangerous Crossing; Kiss of Fire; This Island Earth; Flight to Hong Kong (prod); Gunfight at Dodge City; The Big Circus; Tarzan the Ape Man; King of the Roaring Twenties; A Thunder of Drums; The George Raft Story.
TV inc: The Twilight Story.

NEWMAN, Laraine: Act. b. Los Angeles, Mar 2. Films inc: American Hotwax; Wholly Moses!; Perfect.
TV inc: NBC's Saturday Night Live; Steve Martin's Best Show Ever; E.T. & Friends--Magical Movie Vistors; Prime Times; The Coneheads (voice); Her Life As a Man; This Wife For Hire.
Bway inc: Fifth of July.

NEWMAN, Lionel: Comp-Cond. b. Los Angeles. B the late Alfred Newman. Began career age 16 as lead pianist Earl Carroll's Vanities, wrote first song, Dust in your Eyes, which was featured in Vanities; 1943 joined brother who was head of Fox music dept; became head of dept when Alfred died 1970; 1977 named vp Fox; May 1982, Sr VP Music.
Films inc: The Cowboy and the Lady; Street With No Name; Cheaper By the Dozen; I'll Get By; There's No Business Like Show Business; The Best Things In Life Are Free; Mardi Gras; Move Over Darling; Do Not Disturb; The Pleasure Seekers; Hello, Dolly! (Oscar-scoring-1969); Salzburg Connection.
TV inc: Daniel Boone; Adventures in Paradise; Hong Kong; Dobie Gillis.
Songs inc: Kiss; Never; Adventures in Paradise; Again.

NEWMAN, Nanette: Act. b. Northampton, England, 1934. Films inc: Personal Affair; House of Mystery; Faces in the Dark; The League of Gentlemen: Twice Around the Daffodils; The L-Shaped Room; The Wrong Arm of the Law; Of Human Bondage; Seance on a Wet Afternoon; The Wrong Box; The Whisperers; Deadfall; The Madwoman of Chaillot; Captain Nemo and the Underwater City; Long Ago Tomorrow; The Stepford Wives; The Love Ban; Man at the Top; International Velvet; Restless Natives.

NEWMAN, Paul: Act-Dir. b. Cleveland, OH, Jan 26, 1925. H of Joanne Woodward. Started in summer stock, Woodstock (IL) Players. Bway inc: Picnic. Screen debut in The Silver Chalice.
Films inc: (act) Somebody Up There Likes Me; Helen Morgan Story; Until They Sail; The Long Hot Summer; The Left Handed Gun; Cat on a Hot Tin Roof; Rally Round The Flag Boys; The Young Philadelphians; Exodus; The Hustler; Paris Blues; Hud; Sweet Bird Of Youth; The Prize; The Outrage; What A Way To Go; Lady L; Harper; Hombre; Cool Hand Luke; Secret War of Harry Frigg; Winning; Butch Cassidy and the Sundance Kid; Sometimes A Great Notion (& dir); Pocket Money; Life and Times of Judge Roy Bean; The Mackintosh Man; The Sting; The Towering Inferno; Slap Shot; The Drowning Pool; Buffalo Bill and the Indians; Quintet; Angel Dust (doc-narr); When Time Ran Out; Fort Apache, The Bronx; Absence of Malice; The Verdict. (Dir) The Effect of Gamma Rays on Man-in-the-Moon Marigolds; Rachel, Rachel; Harry & Son (& prod-act-sp).
TV inc: The Shadow Box (dir); Get High On Yourself; Entertain-

ment Tonight; Natalie--A Tribute To A Very Special Lady.

NEWMAN, Phyllis: Act-Singer. b. Jersey City, NJ, Mar 19, 1935. e. Columbia U. W of Adolph Green. Bway inc: Wish You Were Here; I Feel Wonderful; Bells Are Ringing; First Impressions; Moonbirds; Subways Are for Sleeping *(Tony-*supp-1962); The Apple Tree; On the Town; The Madwoman of Central Park West (one woman show).

Films inc: Picnic; Let's Rock; To Find a Man.

NEWMAN, Randy: Act. b. Los Angeles, Nov 28, 1943. Films inc: Ragtime; The Natural. Songs inc: Mama Told Me Not To Come; I Think It's Going to Rain Today; Short People.

Thea inc: Maybe I'm Doing It Wrong (mus & lyr).

NEWMAN, Stanley: Exec. b. NYC, Jul 24, 1935. e. Columbia Coll, BA. VP, MCA, Inc; VP U TV; VP U Pictures.

NEWMAN, Susan Kendall: Act. b. NYC, Feb 21, 1953. D of Paul Newman. Bway inc: We Interrupt This Program.

Films inc: The Wedding; I Wanna Hold Your Hand.

TV inc: The Shadow Box (prod); Candida (prod) (cable); July 1983, vp crea aff Anthony B Unger Co.

NEWMAN, Walter: Wri. Films inc: Ace in the Hole; Underwater; The Man With the Golden Arm; The True Story of Jesse James; Crime and Punishment USA; The Interns; Cat Ballou; Bloodbrothers; The Champ.

NEWMAR, Julie: Act. b. Hollywood, Aug 16, 1935. Screen debut, 1954, Seven Brides for Seven Brothers. Films inc: Li'l Abner; The Rookie; Marriage-Go-Round; For Love or Money; MacKenna's Gold; Hysterical; Streetwalkin'; Evils Of The Night.

TV inc: My Living Doll; Monster Squad; Batman; Omnibus; Route 66; High School USA.

Bway inc: Marriage Go 'Round *(Tony-*supp-1959); Dames at Sea; Ziegfeld Follies.

NEWTON, Connie: Act. b. Anaheim, CA, Dec 5, 1962. TV inc: The New Mickey Mouse Club Show; Jimmy Osmond Special; Eight is Enough.

NEWTON, Wayne: Act. b. Roanoke, VA, Apr 3, 1942. Recording artist. Appears in niteries. Purchased Aladdin Hotel, Las Vegas, 1980. Films inc: 80 Steps to Jonah. TV inc: The Wayne Newton Special--Coast to Coast.

NEWTON-JOHN, Olivia: Singer-Act. b. Cambridge, England, Sep 26, 1948. Singer in Australia before coming to U S in 1965. Films inc: Grease; Xanadu; Two of a Kind.

TV inc: Olivia Newton-John--Let's Get Physical; Countdown '81--A Solid Gold Special; The Merriest of the Merry--Bob Hope's Christmas Show--A Bagful of Comedy; Standing Room Only--Olivia Newton-John in Concert (pay TV); Olympic Gala; AFI Salute To Gene Kelly.

Recordings inc: If Not For You; Let Me Be There *(Grammy-*country voc-1973); I Honestly Love You *(Grammys-*record of year & pop voc-1974); You're The One That I Want; Hopelessly Devoted To You; Summer Nights; Totally Hot.

*(Grammy-*Video of the Year-1982).

NEY, Richard: Act. b. NYC 1917. Bway inc: Life With Father. Films inc: Mrs. Miniver; The War Against Mrs. Hadley; The Late George Apley; Ivy; Joan of Arc; The Fan; The Secret of St. Ives; Lovable Cheat; Babes in Baghdad; Midnight Lace; Premature Burial. Ret from films 1962 for new career as financial cnsltnt.

NICHOLLS, Allan: Act-Wri-Comp. b. Montreal, Canada. Worked with rock groups. Bway inc: Hair; Jesus Christ Superstar; Sgt Pepper's Lonely Hearts Club Band.

Films inc: (act) Nashville (& songs); Buffalo Bill and the Indians; Welcome to L A; A Wedding; Slap Shot; A Perfect Couple (& songs); Quintet (asso prod); Health; Popeye; Dead Ringer (wri-dir).

TV inc: I Am A Hotel (dir).

NICHOLS, Charles August: Dir. b. Milford, UT, Sep 15, 1910. Ani and live action dir Walt Disney Prodns, 1935-61; sr ani dir Hanna-Barbera Prodns, 1961; vp, exec - ani feature films, Hanna-Barbera.

Dir Oscar winning cartoon Toot, Whistle, Plunk and Boom, 1954. Other films inc: Last of the Curlews; Charlotte's Web; Bunnicula The Vampire Rabbit.

TV inc: Scruffy; Miss Switch to the Rescue; A Chipmunk Reunion.

NICHOLS, Mike (Michael Igor Peschkowsky): Dir. b. Berlin, Nov 6, 1931. Stage, nitery performer. Films inc: Who's Afraid of Virginia Woolf?; The Graduate *(Oscar-*1967); Catch 22; Carnal Knowledge; The Day of the Dolphin; The Fortune; Gilda Live. Silkwood (& prod).

Bway inc: Barefoot in the Park *(Tony-*1964); The Knack; LUV *(Tony-*1965); The Odd Couple *(Tony-*1965); Apple Tree; The Little Foxes; Plaza Suite *(Tony-*1968); Uncle Vanya; Prisoner of Second Ave *(Tony-*1972); Annie *(Tony-*exec prod-1977); Billy Bishop Goes To War (prod); Lunch Hour; Grownups (prod); Fools; The Real Thing *(Tony-*dir-1984); Hurlyburly (off-Bway); Whoopi Goldberg (& prodn supv).

TV inc: (act) The Red Mill; Journey to the Day; An Evening With Mike Nichols and Elaine May; Family (exec prod); The 39th Annual Tony Awards.

*(Grammy-*Comedy-1961).

NICHOLS, Peter: Wri. b. England, Jul 31, 1927. Plays inc: The Hooded Terror; A Day in the Death of Joe Egg; The National Health; Forget-Me-Not Lane; Chez Nous; The Freeway; Harding's Luck; Jungle Jamboree; Passion Play; Poppy (& lyr).

Films inc: Georgy Girl; Joe Egg; National Health.

NICHOLSON, Jack: Act-Prod. b. Neptune, NJ, Apr 22, 1936. Films inc: (act) Easy Rider; Five Easy Pieces; Ride the Whirlwind (wri-prod); Drive, He Said (wri-dir-prod); Carnal Knowledge; The Last Detail; Chinatown; Tommy; The Shooting (prod); Head (wri-prod); One Flew Over the Cuckoo's Nest *(Oscar-*1975); The Missouri Breaks; The Last Tycoon; Goin' South (& dir); The Shining; The Postman Always Rings Twice; Reds; The Border; Terms of Endearment *(Oscar-*supp-1983); Prizzi's Honor.

NICHTERN, Claire: Prod. b. NYC. Joined Phoenix Theatre 1955 as casting dir; 1959, prodn coord; 1960 asst to GM Playwrights Company before becoming prod. Bway inc: The Banker's Daughter; The Typist and the Tiger; Luv *(Tony-*1965); Jimmy Shine; The Trial Of A. Lincoln; I Got A Song; House of Blue Leaves; Absent Friends; Cold Storage; Crimes of the Heart; Beyond Therapy; Foxfire.

NICKS, Stevie: Singer-Sngwri. b. Los Angeles, May 26, 1948. With Lindsay Buckingham; Fleetwood Mac before solo. Songs inc: Rhiannon. Recordings inc: Whenever I Call You Friend. Films inc: Heavy Metal (songs).

NICOL, Alex: Act-Dir. b. Ossining, NY, Jan 20, 1916. e. UCLA. Films inc: The Sleeping City; Because of You; Law and Order; The Man from Laramie; Under Ten Flags; Three Came Back (& prod-dir); The Savage Guns; Ride and Kill; Bloody Mama; Point of Terror (dir only); The Night God Screamed; King Kong. TV inc: (dir) The Westerners; The Wackiest Ship in the Army; Jesse James; Daniel Boone; Wild, Wild West; Tarzan; Escape. Thea inc: (dir) The Best Man; Cat on a Hot Tin Roof; River in a High Place; La Ronde.

NIELSEN, Leslie: Act. b. Regina, Sask, Can, Feb 11, 1922. Summer stock, TV. Screen debut, 1956, Vagabond King. Films inc: Forbidden Planet; Ransom!; The Opposite Sex; Hot Summer Night; Tammy and the Bachelor; Night Train to Paris; Harlow; Dark Intruder; Beau Geste; Gunfight in Abilene; The Reluctant Astronaut; Counterpoint; Rosie; Dayton's Devil; How to Commit Marriage; Change of Mind; The Resurrection of Zachary Wheeler; The Poseidon Adventure; Viva Knievel!; The Amsterdam Kill; City On Fire; Airplane; Prom Night; The Creature Wasn't Nice; Wrong Is Right; Creepshow; The Homefront.

TV inc: Studio One; Kraft Playhouse; Robert Montgomery Presents; Suspense; Danger; Man Behind the Badge; Death of a Salesman; The New Breed; Swamp Fox; Peyton Place; Ben Casey; The Loner; Institute For Revenge; Backstairs At The White House; OHMS; National Geographic Society Special (narr); Police Squad; All Hands On Deck For Bob Hope's All-Star Birthday Party At Annapolis; The Night the Bridge Fell Down; Prime Times (host); Cave-In!; Shaping Up; Reckless Disregard.

NILES, Fred A.: Exec. b. Milwaukee, WI, Sep 12, 1918. e. U of WI,

BA. Former radio commentator; organized film div of Kling Enterprises, 1948. Since 1955, founder-pres of Fred A Niles Communications Centers.

NIMOY, Leonard: Act. b. Boston, Mar 26, 1931. Screen debut 1951 Queen For A Day. Films inc: Deathwatch; The Balcony; Francis Goes To West Point; Kid Monk Baroni; Invasion of the Body Snatchers; Star Trek-The Movie; Star Trek II--The Wrath of Khan; Stark Trek III--The Search For Spock (& dir).
  TV inc: Bonanza; Dr Kildare; Gunsmoke; Dragnet; Star Trek; Mission Impossible; Seizure-The Story of Kathy Morris. Thea inc: My Fair Lady; Sherlock Holmes; Twelfth Night; Caligula; Fourposter; A Woman Called Golda; Marco Polo; The Sun Also Rises.

NIMS, Ernest J.: Exec. b. Des Moines, IA, Nov 15, 1908. e. U of IA. Started in cutting dept Fox Films, 1930; joined Universal Pictures 1946; post prod exec, 1949-58; asso prod CBS-TV, 1958-61; pre prod exec Universal, 1962-64; vp & pre prod exec, 1965-75. Retired.

NITZSCHE, Jack: Comp. b. Chicago, IL, 1937. H of Buffy Sainte-Marie. Films inc: Performance; One Flew Over the Cuckoo's Nest; The Exorcist; Blue Collar; Hardcore; Greaser's Palace; When You Comin' Back Red Ryder; Cruisin; Cutter and Bone; Personal Best; Cannery Row; An Officer and A Gentleman (Oscar-song-1982); Without A Trace; Breathless; Windy City; The Razor's Edge; Starman.

NIVEN, David: Act. b. Kirriemuir, Scotland, Mar 1, 1910. Films inc: Thank You Jeeves; Dodsworth; The Charge of the Light Brigade; The Prisoner of Zenda; Three Blind Mice; Wuthering Heights; Raffles; Stairway to Heaven; The Bishop's Wife; Around the World in 80 Days; Oh Men! Oh Women!; Bonjour Tristesse; Separate Tables (Oscar-1958); The Guns of Navarone; The Pink Panther; The Impossible Years; The Kremlin Letter; The Paper Tiger; No Deposit, No Return; Murder by Death; Death On The Nile; Escape To Athena; Rough Cut; The Sea Wolves; Trail of the Pink Panther; Better Late Than Never.
  TV inc: A Man Called Intrepid; AFI Salute To Fred Astaire.
  (Died July 29, 1983).

NIVEN, David Jr: Exec. b. London, Dec 15, 1942. Joined William Morris Agency, 1963; next five yrs worked for agency's European offices in Rome, Madrid, London; in 1968 joined Columbia UK office as prodn exec; 1972, named UK m-dir Paramount; 1976, became indep prod, forming partnership with Jack Wiener;
  Films inc: The Eagle Has Landed; Escape To Athena; Monsignor; Better Late Than Never; Kidco; That's Dancing!
  TV inc: The Night They Saved Christmas (Exec prod-wri).

NIVEN, Kip: Act. b. Kansas City, MO, May 27, 1945. Films inc: In Cold Blood; Magnum Force; Newman's Law; Earthquake; Airport '75; The Hindenburg; New Year's Evil.
  TV inc: A Fire In the Sky; Shadow of Fear; The Sky Trap; Blind Ambition; A Matter of Life and Death; Comedy of Horrors; Goliath Awaits; A Wedding On Walton's Mountain; Mother's Day On Walton's Mountain; Wings.

NIXON, Agnes (nee Eckhardt): Wri-Prod. b. Nashville, TN, Dec. 10, 1927. e. Northwestern U. TV inc: (wri) Studio One; Robert Montgomery Presents; Armstrong Circle Theatre; Hallmark Hall of Fame; Cameo Theatre; Guiding Light; Another World; Search For Tomorrow (& crea-prod); As The World Turns; One Life to Live (& crea-prod); All My Children (& crea-prod); The Manions of America (& crea-prod); Loving (& crea-prod)
  (NATAS Trustees Award 1981).

NIXON, Graeme Lewis: Sls Exec. b. Gillingham, Kent, England, Jan 13, 1936. e. Auckland U Coll. GM, TV Int'l Ent Ltd, UK 1962-67; European controller MCA records & U Pictures, UK 1967; 70: group controller Cinema Int'l Corp, Holland 1970-74; Far East and Australia sls supv CIC TV, Australia 1976.

NIXON, Marni: Act. b. 1929. Singer, who "ghost-sang" for many stars inc: Margaret O'Brien in Big City; Deborah Kerr in The King and I; Natalie Wood in West Side Story; Audrey Hepburn in My Fair Lady. Appeared in The Sound of Music, 1965.

NIZER, Louis: Atty. b. London, Feb 6, 1902. e. Columbia Coll, BA; Columbia U, LLB. Exec secy NY Film Board of Trade since 1928. Atty for many personalities in films; stage; opera; counsel to mp cos, prods, film, stage, radio execs. Author: Analysis of Standard Exhibition Contract; Analysis of Motion Picture Code.

NOBLE, James: Act. b. Dallas, TX, Mar 5, 1922. e. SMU. TV inc: As The World Turns; The Doctors; Circle of Children, Part II; The Split; Equal and Orderly Justice; The Summer of My German Soldier; Benson; Baby Comes Home; This is Kate Bennett; The Woman Who Willed A Miracle.
  Films inc: What's So Bad About Feeling Good?; The Sporting Club; 1776; Being There; 10; The Nude Bomb; Who?
  Bway inc: Come of Age; A Far Country; Johnny No Trump; 1776; The Runner Stumbles.

NOEL, Magali: Act. (nee Guiffrai):b. Turkey 1932. Films inc: Rififi; The Grand Maneuver; Paris Does Strange Things; Passionate Summer; No Escape; The Road to Shame; La Dolce Vita; D'Artagnan's Secret; Toto and Cleopatra; Z; Fellini's Satyricon; Tropic of Cancer; The Man Who Had Power Over Women; Amarcord; Ou-est-ce Qui Fait Courir David (What Makes David Run?); La Mort de Mario Ricci (The Death of Mario Ricci); Les Annees 80 (Golden 80s); Vertiges.

NOIRET, Philippe: Act. b. France, 1931. With Theatre National Populaire, worked as nitery entertainer before film debut in Agnes Varda's short.La Pointe Court.
  Films inc: Zazie; Ravissante; The Billionaire; Crime Does Not Pay; Therese Desqueyroux; None But the Lonely Spy; Death, Where Is Thy Victory; Les Copains; Lady L; La Vie de Chateau; Tender Scoundrel; Night of the Generals; Woman Times Seven; The Assassination Bureau; Mr Freedom; Justine; Topaz; Clerambard; Give Her the Moon; A Room in Paris; Murphy's War; The French Conspiracy; The Serpent; La Grande Bouffe; Custer; Let Joy Reign Supreme; The Old Gun; The Judge and the Assassin; A Woman at Her Window; Desert of the Tartars; Dear Inspector; Due Pezzi di Pane; Who Is Killing the Great Chefs of Europe; Death Watch; Rue du Pied-de-grue; Une Semaine de Vacances; Pile Ou Face (Heads or Tails); Three Brothers; Il Faut Tuer Birgitt Haas (Kill Birgitt Haas); Coup de Torchon (Pop. 1280); L'Etoile Du Nord (The North Star); Amici, Miei, Atto 2 (All My Friends 2); L'Africain; L'Ami De Vincent (A Friend of Vincent); Le Grand Carnaval (The Big Carnival); Fort Saganne; Les Ripoux; Souvenirs, Souvenirs (Memories, Memories); L'Ete Prochain (Next Summer).
  TV inc: Aurora.

NOLAN, Jeanette: Act. b. Los Angeles, Dec 30, 1911. With Dick Powell in radio series, Hollywood Hotel. Also played other roles on radio. On screen from 1948.
  Films inc: Words and Music; Macbeth; No Sad Songs for Me; The Big Heat; Tribute to a Bad Man; April Love; The Great Impostor; Two Rode Together; The Man Who Shot Liberty Valance; My Blood Runs Cold; The Reluctant Astronaut; Did You Hear the One about the Traveling Saleslady; Avalanche; The Manitou; The Fox and the Hound; Cloak and Dagger.
  TV inc: Hotel de Paree; Better Late Than Never; The Hustler of Muscle Beach; Goliath Awaits; All The Way Home; The Wild Women of Chastity Gulch.

NOLAN, Kathleen: Act. b. St Louis, Sep 27, 1933. Career began on a Mississippi show boat which traveled between Cincinnati and New Orleans. Elected 1st woman pres Screen Actors Guild, 1975; reelected 1977.
  Films inc: The Desperadoes Are in Town; No Time to be Young; Benjie Gault; Limbo; Amy.
  TV inc: The Real McCoys; Playhouse 90; Jamie; Broadside; Name of the Game; The Immigrants; Jacqueline Susann's Valley of the Dolls 1981.

NOLAN, Lloyd: Act. b. San Francisco, Aug 11, 1902. Joined Pasadena Playhouse 1927. Worked as stage hand, Cape Cod. On screen from 1934. Films inc: Stolen Harmony; Guadalcanal Diary; Bataan; Circumstantial Evidence; Captain Eddie; The House on 92nd Street; Lady in the Lake; Wild Harvest; Two Smart People; Street with No Name; Easy Living; Bad Boy; The Lemon Drop Kid; Island in the Sky; Crazylegs; Santiago; Abandon Ship; A Hatful of Rain; Peyton Place; Susan Slade; Circus World; Sergeant Ryker; Airport; Earthquake; Prince Jack.

Thea inc: The Front Page; Reunion in Vienna; One Sunday Afternoon; Caine Mutiny Court Martial.

TV inc: The Caine Mutiny Court Martial (Emmy-1955); Martin Kane Private Eye; Julia; Valentine; Adams House; It Came Upon A Midnight Clear.

NOLAN, Patrick J.: Wri. b. Bronx, NY, Jan 2, 1933. e. Villanova, BA; Detroit U, MA; Bryn Mawr, Phd. TV inc: Hourglass Movement; The Jericho Mile (Emmy-1979).

NOLTE, Nick: Act. b. Omaha, NE, Feb. 8, 1934. Appeared in repertory. Films inc: The Deep; Dog Soldiers; Who'll Stop the Rain; North Dallas Forty; Heart Beat; Cannery Row; 48 Hours; Under Fire; The Ultimate Solution of Grace Quigley; Teachers.

TV inc: Winter Kill; Rich Man, Poor Man.

NOONE, Peter: Singer-Mus. b. Nov 5, 1947. Original Herman of Herman's Hermits; ret for some years, returned with group The Tremblers.

NORGARD, John Davey: Exec. b. Adelaide, Australia, Feb 3, 1914. Chmn, Australian Broadcasting Commission.

NORMAN, Marsha: Plywri. b. Louisville, KY., Sep. 21, 1947. e. Agnes Scott College, BA; U of Louisville, MAT. Plays inc: Getting Out; Third and Oak--The Laundromat/The Pool Hall; Circus Valentine; The Holdup; 'Night, Mother (Pulitzer Prize-1983); Traveler In The Dark.

TV inc: It's the Willingness; Skag; The Laundromat.

NORRIS, Christopher: Act. b. NYC, Oct 7, 1953. Bway inc: The Sound of Music; The Secret Life of Walter Mitty; The Playroom.

TV inc: Mr and Mrs Bo Jo Jones; Lady of the House; Great American Beauty Contest; Suddenly Love; Trapper John; The Great American Traffic Jam.

Films inc: Summer of '42; Airport 75; Mortadella; Eat My Dust.

Bway inc: The Sound Of Music; Roar Like A Dove; The Secret Life Of Walter Mitty; The Playroom.

NORRIS, Chuck (Carlos Ray): Act. b. Ryan, OK, 1942. Studied karate in Army, became World Middleweight Karate champion. Films inc: Breaker Breaker; Good Guys Wear Black; A Game of Death; A Force of One; The Octagon; An Eye for an Eye; Slaughter in San Francisco; Silent Rage; Forced Vengeance; Lone Wolf McQuade; Missing In Action; Missing In Action 2--The Beginning; Code Of Silence.

NORTH, Alex: Comp. b. Chester, PA, Dec 4, 1910. e. Curtis Institute; Juilliard; Moscow Conservatory. Film scores inc: Death of a Salesman; Viva Zapata!; A Streetcar Named Desire; Member of the Wedding; Desiree; I'll Cry Tomorrow; The Rose Tattoo; The Rainmaker; Unchained; The Bad Seed; The Long Hot Summer; The Sound and The Fury; Spartacus; The Misfits; Cleopatra; The Agony and the Ecstasy; Who's Afraid of Virginia Woolf?; The Devil's Brigade; The Shoes of the Fisherman; Lost in the Stars; Shanks; Bite the Bullet; Passover Plot; Somebody Killed Her Husband; Carny; Dragonslayer; Under the Volcano; Prizzi's Honor.

TV inc: Playhouse 90; Nero Wolfe; I'm a Lawyer; F.D. Roosevelt Series; Silent Night; The Man and the City; Rich Man, Poor Man (Emmy-1976); Sister, Sister.

Bway inc: Death of a Saleman; Innocents; Coriolanus; Richard III; 'Tis of Thee; Queen of Sheba; The Great Campaign; Death of a Salesman (rev).

NORTH, Edmund H.: Wri. b. NYC, Mar 12, 1911. e. Stanford. Films inc: One Night of Love; I Dream Too Much; Dishonored Lady; Flamingo Road; Young Man With A Horn; Day The Earth Stood Still; Outcasts of Poker Flat; Destry; Cowboy; Sink the Bismarck; H M S Defiant; Patton (Oscar-1970); Meteor.

NORTH, Sheree: Act. b. Los Angeles, Jan 17, 1933. Films inc: Excuse My Dust; How to be Very Popular; The Best Things in Life are Free; The Way to the Gold; No Down Payment; Mardi Gras; Madigan; The Gypsy Moths; Charley Varick; Breakout; The Shootist; Only Once In A Lifetime; Rabbit Test.

TV inc: Eddie; Breaking Point; A Real American Hero; Amateur Night At The Dixie Bar & Grill; Women In White; Portrait of a Stripper;

A Christmas For Boomer; Marilyn--The Untold Story; I'm A Big Girl Now; Legs; Bay City Blues; Scorned and Swindled.

Bway inc: Hazel Flagg; I Can Get It for You Wholesale.

NORTON, B.W.L. Wri-Dir. (William Lloyd Norton)b. CA, Aug 13, 1943. S of William Norton Films inc: Cisco Pike (& dir); Outlaw Blues; Convoy; More American Graffiti (& dir); Losin' It.

TV inc: Gargoyles.

NORTON, William (Liam Oneachtain): Wri. b. Ogden, UT., Sept. 24, 1925. Films inc: The Scalphunters; Sam Whiskey; The McKenzie Break; Hunting Party; Gator; White Lighting; Big Bad Mama; Dirty Tricks; Night of the Juggler; I Dismember Mama.

TV inc: September Gun.

NORVET, Robert W: Exec. b. Forest City, IA, Aug 17, 1922. e. Grinnell Coll, BA. Bus M, MGM-TV, 1952-60; dir, film prod operations, CBS-TV; GM, CBS Studio Center; VP, CBS Studio Center; VP, Prodn facilities, CTN Hollywood.

NORVO, Red: Mus. b. Beardstown, IL, Mar 31, 1908. First to play jazz on xylophone, vibraharp. Began as sideman with Paul Ash orch; with Victor Young as staff musican NBC; sideman Paul Whiteman Band; married Mildred Bailey, formed own orch which backed her for nitery, recording dates; later with Benny Goodman; Woody Herman. Films inc: Talmadge Farlow (doc).

NOSSECK, Noel: Prod-Dir. Started as edtr David Wolper Prodns; formed own doc film, later into features. Films inc: Best Friends; Las Vegas Lady; Youngblood; Dreamer; King of the Mountain.

TV inc: Return of the Rebels; The First Time; Night Partners; Summer Fantasies.

NOURI, Michael: Act. b. Washington, DC. e. Emerson Coll. Thea inc: Nefertiti; Forty Carats (Bway); Coconut Beach; The Crucible.

TV inc: Search For Tomorrow; Somerset; Beacon Hill; With Love; Contract on Cherry Street; Cliffhangers; The Last Convertible; The Gangster Chronicles; Bay City Blues; Spraggue.

Films inc: Goodbye Columbus; Flashdance.

NOVAK, Kim (Marilyn Novak): Act. b. Chicago, Feb 13, 1933. Began as model. Screen debut, 1953, The French Line. Films inc: Pushover; Phfft; Five Against the House; Picnic; Man with the Golden Arm; The Eddie Duchin Story; Jeanne Eagles; Pal Joey; Middle of the Night; Bell, Book and Candle; Vertigo; Pepe; Strangers When We Meet; The Notorious Landlady; Boys' Night Out; Of Human Bondage; Kiss Me, Stupid; The Amorous Adventures of Moll Flanders; The Legend of Lylah Clare; The Great Bank Robbery; Tales That Witness Madness; The White Buffalo; Just A Gigolo; The Mirror Crack'd.

TV inc: Third Girl from the Left; Malibu; Alfred Hitchcock Presents.

NOVELLO, Don (Father Guido Sarducci): Act-Wri. b. Ashtabula, OH. Ad agency copywriter, began writing comedy material, emerged as stand-up comic; created character of Father Guido Sarducci, performs under that name but writes as Novello. TV inc: Smothers Brothers Show; Saturday Night Live; SCTV Network (& prod); Blondes Vs. Brunettes.

Bway inc: Gilda Radner--Live from New York.

Films inc: Gilda Live.

NOYCE, Philip: Dir. b. Australia. Films inc: Castor and Pollux (doc); God Knows Why, But It Works (Doc) (& wri); Backroads (& prod-wri); Newsfront (& wri); Heatwave (& wri); Another Saturday Night (short) (prod).

TV inc: 3 Vietnamese Stories.

NUGENT, Nelle: Prod. b. Jersey City, NJ, 1939. e. Skidmore, BS. Stage mgr various Bway & off-Bway shows; prodn supv for Theatre Now, Inc; asso M-dir Nederlander Org before forming partnership, 1976, with Elizabeth I. McCann. Bway inc: Dracula; The Elephant Man (Tony-1979); Night and Day; Morning's At Seven (Tony-revival-1980); Piaf; Home; Rose; Amadeus (Tony-1981); The Life and Adventures of Nicholas Nickleby (Tony-1982); Mass Appeal; The Dresser; Pilobolus Dance Theatre; Good; All's Well That Ends Well; Total Abandon; The Glass Menagerie; Cyrano de Bergerac; Much Ado

About Nothing; Leader Of The Pack.

TV inc: The Elephant Man; Morning's At Seven (cable); Piaf (cable); Pilobolus Dance Theatre (cable).

NUGENT, Ted: Sngwri-Singer. b. Detroit, MI, Dec 13, 1948. Started group Amboy Dukes, name later changed to Ted Nugent and the Amboy Dukes, finally Ted Nugent. Albums inc: Journey to the Center of the Mind; Migration; Survival of the Fittest; Tooth, Fang and Claw; Ted Nugent; Free for All; Cat Scratch Fever; Double Live Gonzo; Weekend Warriors; Scream Dream.

NUNN, Trevor: Dir. b. Ipswich, Suffolk, England, Jan 14, 1940. e. Downing Coll Cambridge. Thea inc; (London) The Thwarting of Baron Bolligrew; Henry IV; Tango; The Revenger's Tragedy; The Taming of the Shrew; King Lear; Much Ado About Nothing; The Winter's Tale; Henry VIII; Hamlet; The Romans; Macbeth; Hedda Gabler; Antony and Cleopatra; The Comedy of Errors; Once In a Lifetime; The Life and Adventures of Nicholas Nickleby (also Bway) (Tony-1982); Juno and the Paycock; Cats (also Bway) (Tony-1983); All's Well That Ends Well; Starlight Express.

NUREYEV, Rudolf: Act. b. Russia, Mar 17, 1938. Attended Leningrad Ballet School. Joined Kirov Ballet Company as soloist. While performing in Paris in 1961, asked for and was granted political asylum. Joined Marquis de Cuevan Ballet Company. Films inc: An Evening With the Royal Ballet; Swan Lake; Romeo and Juliet; The Sleeping Beauty; Don Quixote; Valentino; Exposed. TV inc: Julie Andrew's Invitation to the Dance with Rudolf Nureyev.

NUYEN, France: Act. b. Marseilles, Jul 31, 1939. Began career as an artists' model. Films inc: South Pacific; In Love and War; The Last Time I Saw Archie; Diamond Head; A Girl Named Tamiko; Man in the Middle; Dimension 5; One More Train to Rob.

TV inc: Jealousy.

NYBY, Christian: Dir. b. Los Angeles, Sep 1, 1913. Films inc: The Thing; Hell on Devil's Island; Six-Gun Law; Young Fury; Operation CIA; First to Fight.

NYBY, Christian II: Dir-Wri. b. Glendale, CA, Jun 1, 1941. e. USC, BA. TV inc: Emergency; Ironside; Adam 12; Six Million Dollar Man; Rockford Files; Sword of Justice; Swiss Family Robinson; CHiPs; The Hardy Boys; Battlestar Galactica; B J and the Bear; The Devlin Connection; Riptide; Double Dare.

NYKVIST, Sven: Cin. b. Sweden, 1922. Films inc: Sawdust and Tinsel; Karin Mansdotter; The Virgin Spring; Winter Light; The Silence; Loving Couples; Persona; Hour of the Wolf; The Last Run; One Day in the Life of Ivan Denisovitch; Cries and Whispers (Oscar-1973); Black Moon; The Tenant (& act); Serpent's Egg; Pretty Baby; Autumn Sonata; Starting Over; Hurricane;. Marmalad Upporet (The Marmalade Revolution); From the Life of the Marionettes; Willie & Phil; The Postman Always Rings Twice; Cannery Row; Fanny and Alexander (Oscar-1983); Star 80; La Tragedie de Carmen; Un Amour de Swann (Swann in Love).

NYPE, Russell: Act. b. Zion, IL, Apr 26, 1924. e. Lake Forest Coll, BA. Bway inc: Regina; Great To Be Alive; Call Me Madam (Tony-supp-1951); Wake Up, Darling; Carousel; Goldilocks (Tony-supp-1959); Brigadoon; My Fair Lady; The Girl in the Freudian Slip; Hello, Dolly! Tallulah (off-Bway).

TV inc: The Milton Berle Show; Ed Sullivan Show; One Touch of Venus.

Films inc: Can't Stop the Music.

OAK RIDGE BOYS: Country Music Group. Members: William Lee Golden; Richard Sterban; Joe Bonsall; Duane Allen. TV inc: A Country Christmas; Country Comes Home; Entertainer of the Year Awards; Loretta Lynn--The Lady, The Legend; Country Comes Home ('82); Johnny Cash--Cowboy Heroes; Country Comes Alive; Country Comes Home ('83).

(Grammys-(5)-gospel perf-1970, 1974, 1976, 1977; country duo-1981).

OAKLAND, Simon: Act. b. NYC, 1922. Films inc: The Brothers Karamazov; I Want to Live; Psycho; West Side Story; Wall of Noise;

The Satan Bug; The Plainsman; The Sand Pebbles; Tony Rome; Chubasco; On a Clear Day You Can See Forever; Chato's Land; Happy Mother's Day...Love, George.

TV inc: Man Undercover.

Bway inc: The Shadow Box.

(Died Aug. 29, 1983).

OBOLER, Arch: Prod-Dir-Wri. b. Chicago, Dec. 7, 1909. Started as wri on radio; created series Lights Out. Films inc: Escape (sp); Bewitched; The Arnelo Affair; Five; The Twonky; Bwana Devil (in 3-D); The Bubble.

O'BRIAN, Hugh (Hugh J Krampe): Act. b. Rochester, NY, Apr 19, 1930. Films inc: Young Lovers; Vengeance Valley; Sally and St. Anne; Meet Me at the Fair; Saskatchewan; Broken Lance; There's No Business Like Show Business; Come Fly With Me; Strategy of Terror; Killer Force; The Shootist; Game of Death.

TV inc: Wyatt Earp; Dial M for Murder; A Punt, A Pass and A Prayer; Murder on Flight 502; Greatest Heroes of the Bible; The Seekers; Bush Doctor.

Bway credits inc: Destry Rides Again; First Love; Guys and Dolls.

O'BRIEN, David: Act. b. Chicago, IL, Oct 1. e. Stanford, BA; LAMDA on Fulbright Scholarship. Bway inc: A Passage to India; The Resistable Rise of Arturo Ui; A Time for Singing.

TV inc: The Secret Storm; Search for Tomorrow; Our Private World; The Doctors (since 1967); First Ladies Diaries--Rachel Jackson.

O'BRIEN, Edmond: Act-Dir. b. NYC, Sep 10, 1915. Films inc: The Hunchback of Notre Dame; Parachute Battalion; The Killers; The Web; A Double Life; Another Part of the Forest; An Act of Murder; White Heat; Between Midnight and Dawn; Two of a Kind; Julius Caesar; The Hitch Hiker; Man in the Dark; The Bigamist; The Barefoot Contessa (Oscar-supp-1954); Shield for Murder; 1984; The Third Voice; Mantrap (prod-dir); The Great Imposter; The Man Who Shot Liberty Valance; Birdman of Alcatraz; Seven Days in May; Sylvia; Fantastic Voyage; The Viscount; The Wild Bunch; The Love God; Jigsaw; 99 44/100ths% Dead.

TV inc: Johnny Midnight; Wyatt Earp; 333 Montgomery Street; Flesh and Blood; Sam Benedict.

(Died May 9, 1985)

O'BRIEN, Jack: Dir. b. Saginaw, MI, Jun 18, 1939. e. U of MI, AB, MA. APA staff dir, 1964-1969; San Diego Shakespeare Festival, 1969-1977; Houston Grand Opera, 1976-1979. Bway inc: Cock-A-Doodle-Dandy; The Time of Your Life (rev); Porgy and Bess (rev).

O'BRIEN, Margaret: Act. b. Los Angeles, Jan 15, 1937. Screen debut age 4, Babes in Arms. (Honorary Oscar-1944). Films inc: Journey for Margaret; Lost Angel; Thousands Cheer; Jane Eyre; The Canterville Ghost; Meet Me in St. Louis; Three Wise Fools; Tenth Avenue Angel; Secret Garden; Little Women; Her First Romance; Anabelle Lee; Diabolic Wedding; Amy.

O'BRIEN, Pat: Act. b. Milwaukee, WI, Nov 11, 1899. Started career as a chorus boy on Bway, 1919. Screen debut 1931, The Front Page. Films inc: Oil For The Lamps Of China; Knute Rockne; Ceiling Zero; Angels With Dirty Faces; Having A Wonderful Crime; The Fighting 69th; The Iron Major; The Last Hurrah; Fighting Father Dunne; The Boy With Green Hair; Some Like It Hot; The Phynx; The End; Ragtime.

TV inc: The Other Woman (2 Emmys-actor in daytime special & daytime actor of year-1974); Scout's Honor; Life's Most Embarrassing Moments.

(Died Oct. 15, 1983).

O'BRIEN, Virginia: Singer-Act. b. Los Angeles, April 18, 1919. Originated "deadpan" singing technique in stage revue Meet the People.

Films inc: Hullabaloo; The Big Store; Ship Ahoy; Lady Be Good; Ringside Maisie; Thousands Cheer; Meet the People; DuBarry Was A Lady; Two Girls and a Sailor; The Harvey Girls; Ziegfeld Follies; Till The Clouds Roll By; Ziegfeld Follies; Merton of the Movies; Frances In The Navy.

O'CONNELL, Helen: Singer. b. Lima, OH, 1920. Singer with name bands, recording artist.

TV inc: Co-host Miss USA Beauty Pageant; Miss Universe Beauty Pageant; numerous guest appearances; segs.

O'CONNOR, Carroll: Act. b. NYC, Sep 2, 1925. e. University Coll, Dublin; U of MT. With Dublin Gate Theatre before NY. Bway inc: Ulysses in Nighttown; Playboy of the Western World; The Big Knife; Brothers (& dir); Home Front.

Films inc: Fever in the Blood; By Love Possessed; Lonely Are the Brave; Cleopatra; In Harm's Way; What Did You Do in the War Daddy?; Hawaii; Not With My Wife You Don't; Waterhole No. 3; The Devil's Brigade; For Love of Ivy; Kelly's Heroes; Doctors' Wives; Law and Disorder.

TV inc: US Steel Hour; Armstrong Circle Theatre; Kraft Theatre; All In The Family *(Emmys-1972-1977-1978-1979)*; The Last Hurrah (& wri); Bender (exec prod); Archie Bunker's Place.

Writer: Ladies of Hanover Tower (play); Little Anjie Always; The Great Robinson (screenplays).

O'CONNOR, Donald: Act. b. Chicago, Aug 28, 1925. In vaudeville before screen debut 1938, Sing You Sinners. Films inc: Men With Wings; Million Dollar Legs; Beau Geste; On Your Toes; What's Cookin'?; The Merry Monahans; Singin' in the Rain; No Business Like Show Business; The Buster Keaton Story; Cry Me Happy; That Funny Feeling; That's Entertainment; The Big Fix; Ragtime.

TV inc: The Donald O'Connor Show *(Emmy-1953)*; Lucy Moves To NBC; A Gift of Music; Texaco Star Theatre--Opening Night; Kennedy Center Honors 1982; Alice in Wonderland; Night Of 100 Stars II; AFI Salute To Gene Kelly.

Bway inc: Bring Back Birdie; Show Boat.

O'CONNOR, Robert: Exec. b. Philadelphia, PA., May 18, 1951. e. Hamilton College, BA. Dir pgm dvlpt Paramount TV; vp TV prodn Miller-Milkis-Boyett; vp comedy dvlpt CBS Entertainment; Sept. 1984, P film prodn Guber-Peters Co.

O'DAY, Anita: Singer. b. Chicago, IL, Dec 18, 1919. Singer with Gene Krupa, Stan Kenton. Recordings inc: Let Me Off Uptown; And Her Tears Flowed Like Wine. Albums inc: Anita Swings Cole Porter; Anita Sings; The Lady is a Tramp; Anita Sings the Winners.

ODELL, David: Wri. b. 1947. e. Harvard. Films inc: Cry Uncle; Dealing; The Muppet Movie; The Dark Crystal.

TV inc: Between Time and Timbuktoo; The Muppet Show *(Emmy-1981)*.

ODETTA (Odetta Holmes): Act. b. Birmingham, AL, Dec 31, 1930. Folk music recording artist; recitals inc: Town Hall; Carnegie Hall. Films inc: Cinerama Holiday.

TV inc: TV Tonight.

OGIER, Bulle: Act. Films inc: Les idoles; L'amour feu; Pierre et Paul; 48 Hours of Love; Piege; Paulina s'en va; M comme Mathieu; Out One; Les stances a Sophie; Rendezvous at Bray; The Salamander; The Valley; The Discreet Charm of the Bourgeoisie; Meet Some of My Best Friends; Bel Ordure; Projection Privee; Celine and Julie Go Boating; La Paloma; Mariage; Un divorce heureux; Maitresse; Flocons d'or; A Short Memory; Never Again Always; Serail; Les Aventures de Holly and Wood; Navire Night; The Third Generation; Seuls (Loners); Le Pont du Nord (North Bridge) (& wri); Les Tricheurs (The Cheaters).

Thea inc: Terre Entrangere (Undiscovered Country).

O'HARA, Gerry: Dir. b. Boston-Lincs, England, 1924. Film inc: That Kind of Girl; Game for Three Lovers; Pleasure Girls (& sp); Maroc 7; Love in Amsterdam; All the Right Noises (& sp); The Bitch; Fanny Hill.

TV inc: The Avengers; Man in a Suitcase; Journey into the Unknown.

O'HARA, Maureen (nee FitzSimons): Act. b. Dublin, Aug 17, 1920. e. Abbey School of Acting. On Screen from 1938. Films inc: Kicking the Moon Around; Jamaica Inn; The Hunchback of Notre Dame; A Bill of Divorcement; How Green Was My Valley; To the Shores of Tripoli; Ten Gentlemen from West Point; The Black Swan; The Fallen Sparrow; Buffalo Bill; The Spanish Main; Do You Love Me?; Miracle on 34th Street; The Foxes of Harrow; The Homestretch; Sitting Pretty; Sentimental Journey; Sinbad the Sailor; Father Was a Fullback;

Comanche Territory; Tripoli; Bagdad; Rio Grande; At Sword's Point; Flame of Araby; The Quiet Man; Against All Flags; The Redhead from Wyoming; Fire Over Africa; Lady Godiva; The Long Gray Line; Wings of Eagles; The Deadly Companions; Our Man in Havana; Dr. Hobbs Takes a Vacation; McLintock!; Spencer's Mountain; The Parent Trap; The Rare Breed; The Battle of Villa Fiorita; How Do I Love Thee?; Big Jake; The Red Pony.

O'HEANEY, Caitlin: Act. b. Whitefish Bay, WI, Aug 16, 1953. e. Juilliard. Thea inc: Hothouse; Yentl; Gogol; Voice of the Turtle; Scenes and Revelations.

TV inc: Apple Pie; Mark Twain's America; The Seeding of Sarah Burns; One Life to Live; Tales of the Gold Monkey.

Films inc: He Knows You're Alone.

O'HERLIHY, Dan (Daniel Peter O'Herlihy): Act. b. Wexford, Ireland, May 1, 1919. e. National U of Ireland. With Abbey Theatre, Dublin. Films inc: Odd Man Out; At Swords Point; Actors and Sin; Adventures of Robinson Crusoe; Black Shield of Falworth; Bengal Brigade; Purple Mask; The Virgin Queen; That Woman Opposite; City After Midnight; Failsafe; Home Before Dark; 100 Rifles; The Tamarind Seed; MacArthur; Halloween III--Season of the Witch; The Last Starfighter.

Thea inc: The Ivy Green; Red Roses For Me.

TV inc: A Man Called Sloan; Hunter's Moon; Mark Twain--Beneath the Laughter; Death Ray 2000; Two By Forsyth.

O'HERLIHY, Michael: Dir. b. Dublin, Ireland, Apr 1, 1928. e. Castleknock Coll, Dublin. TV inc: Maverick; 77 Sunset Strip; Hawaiian Eye; Surfside 6; Mr. Novak; Richard Boone Theatre; Profiles in Courage; Rawhide; Gunsmoke; Fighting Prince of Donegal; The One and Only Family Band; Smith; Willie and the Yank; The Loner; Hawaii Five-O (42 episodes); Deadly Harvest; Young Pioneers I; Young Pioneers II; Kiss Me, Kill Me; Peter Lundy and the Medicine Hat Stallion; The Magnificent Hustle; The Dublin Incident (& prod); Backstairs at the White House; The Flame Is Love; Dallas Cowboy Cheerleaders II; Detour to Terror; The Great Cash Giveaway; Cry of the Innocent; Desperate Voyage; A Time For Miracles; Nero Wolfe; The Million Dollar Face; I Married Wyatt Earp; O'Malley; Two By Forsyth.

OHLMEYER, Don: Prod. e. Notre Dame. Joined ABC Sports 1967 as prod-dir all leading sports events; 1977 to NBC as exec prod sports; July 1982, with Jerry Weintraub formed Intercontinental Broadcasting Systems but will remain with NBC.

TV inc: NFL Monday Football *(Emmy-1976)*; Monday Night Baseball; Wide World of Sports *(Emmy-1976)*; Superstars; 1968, 1972, 1976 Summer Olympics; 1976 Winter Games (Emmy); Battle of The Network Stars; US against the World; Super Bowl Saturday Night; The Golden Moment--An Olympic Love Story; Olympic Trials; Games People Play; Super Bowl XV; College Basketball; NFL '80 Super Sunday Countdown; The Arlberg Kandahar Downhill from St. Anton *(Emmy-1981)*; Friday Night Fights *(Emmy-1981)*; Special Bulletin (exec prod) *(Emmy-1983)*; America's Heroes--The Athlete Chronicles (exec prod-wri); Hollywood's Most Sensational Mysteries (exec prod); People Are Funny (exec prod); Olympic Gala (exec prod).

OISTRAKH, David: Violinist. b. Odessa, Russia, 1908. e. Odessa Conservatory. Made professional debut age 12; toured USSR several times, later made world tours as guest soloist major symphonies. Recs inc: Brahms Double Concerto *(Grammy*-class inst solo-1970); Shostakovich Violin Concerto No. 1 *(Grammy*-class inst solo with orch-1974).

O'KEEFE, Michael: Act. e. AADA. Thea inc: The Killdeer; Streamers; Fifth of July; Mass Appeal.

Films inc; Grey Lady Down; The Great Santini; Caddyshack; Split Image; Nate and Hayes; Finders Keepers; The Slugger's Wife.

TV inc: Rumors of War; Harvest Home.

OKUN, Milt: Act. b. NYC, Dec 23, 1923. e. CCNY; Oberlin Conservatory of Mus. Folk Mus recording artist; mus dir for various groups.

OLBRYCHSKI, Daniel: Act. b. Poland 1945. Films inc: Wounded in the Forest; Ashes; The Boxer; Jovita; Everything For Sale; The Leap; Colonel Wolodyjowski; Family Life; The Deluge; Dagny; Panny Z Wilka (The Young Ladies of Wilno); The Tin Drum; Kung-Fu; Rycerz (The Knight); Wizia Lokalna 1901 (Inspection of the Scene of a Crime

1901); Fall of Italy; Les unes et les autres (The Ins and the Outs); Rosa; La Truite (The Trout); Eine Liebe in Deutschland (A Love In Germany); Lieber Karl (Dear Karl); La Diagonale du Fou (Dangerous Moves); Der Bulle und Das Madchen (The Cop And The Girl).
Thea inc: Autant en emporte le vent (Gone With the Wind).

OLIANSKY, Joel: Wri-Dir. b. NYC, Oct 11, 1935. e. Yale, MFA. TV inc: The Senator (Emmy-1971); Kojak; Quincy; The Law; Masada (wri); Alfred Hitchcock Presents.
Films inc: The Competition.

OLIM, Dorothy: Prod-Manager. b. Oct 14, 1934. Thea inc: (prod) I Must Be Talking to My Friends; Pimpernel!; The Golden Apple; The Lion in Love; A Worm in Horseradish. (asso prod): The Fantasticks.

OLIVER, Gordon: Prod-Act. b. Los Angeles, Apr 27, 1910. On screen from 1936 in Draegerman Courage. Films inc: Fugitive in the Sky; The Go Getter; War Lords; Since You Went Away; The Spiral Staircase; Born to be Bad; Station West; Las Vegas Story.
TV inc: (prod) Peter Gunn series; Mr. Lucky; Profiles in Courage; It Takes a Thief.

OLIVER, Susan (Charlotte Gercke): Act. b. NYC, Feb 13, 1937. e. Swarthmore Coll. Films inc: Green-Eyed Blonde; The Gene Krupa Story; Looking for Love; The Disorderly Orderly; Your Cheating Heart; A Man Called Gannon; Change of Mind; Widow's Nest; Hardly Working.
TV inc: Peyton Place; Tomorrow's Child; M*A*S*H (dir); International Airport.

OLIVIER, Lawrence, Lord: Act. b. Dorking, England, May 22, 1907. On stage London, NY since 1925; Knighted 1947; Peerage created, 1970. Films inc: As You Like It; Romeo and Juliet; Fire Over England; Wuthering Heights; Rebecca; Henry V (& dir) Hamlet (& prod-dir) (Oscar-act-1948); Term of Trial; Prince and the Showgirl; Devil's Disciple; Three Sisters; Sleuth; Nicholas & Alexandra; The Ruling Class; Lady Caroline Lamb; Marathon Man; A Bridge Too Far; The Betsy; The Boys From Brazil; A Little Romance; Dracula; The Jazz Singer; Inchon; Clash of the Titans; Wagner; The Bounty; The Jigsaw Man.
(Honorary Oscars-1948, 1978).
TV inc: The Moon and Sixpence (Emmy-1960); The Power and the Glory; Uncle Vanya; Long Day's Journey into Night (Emmy-1973); Love Among the Ruins (Emmy-1975); Brideshead Revisited (Emmy-supp-1982); Laurence Olivier Presents King Lear (Emmy-1984); A Voyage Round My Father; Laurence Olivier and Jackie Gleason as Mr. Halpern and Mr. Johnson (cable); The Gentleman Tramp; The Last Days of Pompeii.
Thea inc: Antony & Cleopatra; Venus Observed; Sleeping Prince; The Entertainer; Becket; Othello; The Crucible; Long Day's Journey into Night; Amphitryon 38 (dir); Saturday, Sunday, Monday; Eden End (dir); Filumena (dir).

OLIVO, Frank: Dir. b. NYC, Nov 18, 1941. e. Queens Coll, NY. TV inc: Eyewitness News Conference; A.M. New York. (Docs): NYPD; Paul Robeson - The Man; City in Crisis; Harlem; Black Out; Underground Railroad; Tribute to Paul Robeson; Israel Today; Littlest Junkie; Teenage Alcoholics; Dr Luther King; Sidney Poitier; Harry Belafonte; Count Basie; Lionel Hampton; Jazz Today.

OLMOS, Edward James: Act. Started as rock singer with group Eddie James and the Pacific Ocean before act. Bway inc: Zoot Suit. Films inc: El Alambrista; Wolfen; Zoot Suit; Blade Runner.
TV inc: Evening in Byzantium; 300 Miles for Stephanie; Seguin; Y.E.S. inc; The Ballad of Gregorio Cortez; Miami Vice.

O'LOUGHLIN, Gerald S.: Act. b. NYC, Dec 23, 1921. e. U of Rochester. Bway inc: Streetcar Named Desire; Shadow of a Gunman; The Dark at the Top of the Stairs; A Touch of the Poet; A Cook for Mr. General; One Flew Over the Cuckoo's Nest; Calculated Risk.
Films inc: Lovers and Lollypops; Cop Hater; Hatful of Rain; Ensign Pulver; A Fine Madness; In Cold Blood; The Valachi Papers; Desperate Characters; The Organization; Twilight's Last Gleaming.
TV inc: For the People; Going My Way; The Rookies; Women in White; Blind Ambition; Detour to Terror; Pleasure Palace; A Matter Of Life and Death; McClain's Law; The Blue and The Gray; Automan;

London and Davis In New York; Brothers-in-Law.

OLSEN, Merlin: Act. b. Logan, UT, Sep 15, 1940. e. UT State, BS, MS. Former pro football star. Films inc: Mitchell; Something Big; One More Train to Rob; The Undefeated.
TV inc: Little House on the Prairie; The Golden Moment-An Olympic Love Story; Bob Hope's All-Star Comedy Look At the New Season; Father Murphy; The Juggler of Notre Dame; Time Bomb; Fathers And Sons.

OLSON, James: Act. b. Evanston, IL, Oct 8, 1930. Bway inc: The Young and the Beautiful; Romulus; The Chinese Prime Minister; Breakfast at Tiffany's.
Films inc: Moon Zero Two; Rachel, Rachel; The Andromeda Strain; The Groundstar Conspiracy; The Mafu Cage; Ragtime; Amityville II--The Possession.
TV inc: Greatest Heroes of the Bible; Moviola; Cave-In!; The Parade.

OLSON, Nancy: Act. b. Milwaukee, WI, July 14, 1928. e. U of WI, UCLA. Films inc: Canadian Pacific; Union Station; Sunset Boulevard; Submarine Command; Force of Arms; So Big; Battle Cry; Pollyanna; The Absent Minded Professor; Son of Flubber; Smith!; Snowball Express; Airport 1975; Making Love.
TV inc: Paper Dolls.

OLSSON, Nigel: Act-Sngwri. b. Wallasey, England, Feb 10, 1949. Recording artist. Played drums behind Elton John, Rod Stewart, Linda Ronstadt before writing and recording own songs.

O'MALLEY, Kevin: Exec. b. Springfield, MA, 1947. e. Boston Coll. Joined CBS Sports 1973 as dir Pgm Dvlpt; dir Pgm Plnng; 1977, VP Communications; 1979, VP Pgm Plnng & Dvlpt; Sept. 1981, exec prod NCAA Basketball & Football.

ONDRA, Anny (nee Ondrakova): Act. b. Poland, May 15, 1903. Made several films in Czechoslovakia and Germany before moving to London. Films inc: God's Clay; Chorus Girls; Blackmail; The Manxman; Glorious Youth; Das Madel aus USA; Die Fledermaus; Kiki; A Night in Paradise; Knockout; Donogoo Tonka; Schonn muss man sein; Die Zuercher Verlorung.

ONDRICEK, Miroslav: Cin. b. Czechoslovakia. Films inc: Audition; Loves of a Blonde; The Fireman's Ball; the White Bus; Intimate Lighting; If; Taking Off; Slaughterhouse 5; O Lucky Man; Hair; The World According to Garp; Ragtime; Silkwood; Amadeus; Heaven Help Us.

O'NEAL, Patrick: Act. b. Ocala, FL, Sep 26, 1927. Films inc: The Mad Magician; From the Terrace; The Cardinal; In Harm's Way; King Rat; A Fine Madness; Alvarez Kelly; Assignment to Kill; Castle Keep; The Kremlin Letters; Corky; The Way We Were; The Stepford Wives.
TV inc: Dick and the Duchess; The Deadliest Season; Kaz; Make Me An Offer; True Position (dir); Fantasies; Emerald Point N.A.S.; Spragque.
Thea inc: Oh Men, Oh Women; Laurette; A Far Country; Stalag 17; The Night of the Iguana.

O'NEAL, Ron: Act. b. Utica, NY, Sep 1, 1937. Began as member of Karamu Theatre, Cleveland; then off-Bway in American Pastorale; The Mummer's Play; No Place to Be Somebody.
Films inc: Move; The Organization; Super Fly; Super Fly TNT (& dir); The Master Gunfighter; When a Stranger Calls; The Final Countdown; St. Helens; Red Dawn.
TV inc: Freedom Road; Brave New World; Guyana Tragedy--The Story of Jim Jones; The Sophisticated Gents; Bring 'Em Back Alive; Two Of Hearts (cable); Playing With Fire.

O'NEAL, Ryan (Patrick Ryan O'Neal): Act. b. Los Angeles, Apr 20, 1941. Films inc: The Big Bounce; The Games; Love Story; Wild Rovers; What's Up, Doc?; Paper Moon; The Thief Who Came to Dinner; Barry Lyndon; Nickelodeon; A Bridge Too Far; The Driver; Oliver's Story; The Main Event; Green Ice; So Fine; Partners; Irreconcilable Differences.
TV inc: Peyton Place; Dobie Gillis; The Untouchables; Bachelor Father; My Three Sons; Under the Yum Yum Tree; Love Hate Love.

O'NEAL, Tatum: Act. b. Los Angeles, Nov 5, 1963. D of Ryan O'Neal. Debuted on screen age 9, Paper Moon (Oscar-supp-1973). Films inc: The Bad News Bears; Nickelodeon; International Velvet; Little Darlings; Circle Of Two; Certain Fury.

O'NEILL, Jennifer: Act. b. Rio de Janeiro, Feb 20, 1948. Model. Films inc: Rio Lobo; Summer of '42; Such Good Friends; The Carey Treatment; The Reincarnation of Peter Proud; The Flower in the Mouth; The Intruder; Caravans; The Innocent; The Psychic; A Force Of One; Steel; Scanners.
TV inc: The Other Victim; Bare Essence; Cover Up; A.D.

ONO, Yoko: Wri-Mus. b. Tokyo, Feb 18, 1933. e. Sarah Lawrence Coll. W of the late John Lennon. Best known as an artist until her marriage to Lennon with whom she later wrote and performed. Made several short films inc: Bottoms; The Ballad of John and Yoko; Smile; Two Virgins; Legs; Fly; Rape--Part II.
Albums inc: Two Virgins; Unfinished Music No. 2; Wedding Album; Live Peace in Toronto; Fly; Double Fantasy (Grammy-1981).

ONTKEAN, Michael: Act. b. Jan 24, 1946. Films inc: Slap Shot; Voices; Willie & Phil; Making Love; Le Sang des Autres (The Blood of Others); Just The Way You Are.
TV inc: The Rookies; Summer; Kids Don't Tell.

OOSTHOEK, Eric: Dir-Prod. b. Bilthoven, Holland, Sep 13, 1948. From 1970-77, with political and educational theatre, Holland; now TV director, Dutch Television.

OPATOSHU, David: Act. b. NYC, Jan 30, 1918. Films inc: The Naked City; Thieves Highway; The Brothers Karamazov; Exodus; Guns of Darkness; Torn Curtain; The Defector; Enter Laughing; The Fixer; Death of a Gunfighter; Romance of a Horse Thief; Who'll Stop The Rain; Americathon; Beyond Evil; Forced Vengeance; Almonds and Raisins (doc).
Thea inc: Me and Molly; Once More with Feeling; Silk Stockings; The Wall; Bravo Giovanni.
TV inc: Masada; Flash Gordon--The Greatest Adventure of All (voice).

OPHULS, Marcel Dir. b. Frankfurt, Germany, 1927. S of the late Max Ophuls. Began as asst. to Julian Duvivier, Anatole Litvak, Max Ophuls. First dir assignment was segment of L'Amour a Vingt Ans (Love At Twenty). Films inc: Peau de Banane (Banana Peel) (& wri); Feu de Volante; Le Chagrin et la Pitie (The Sorrow And The Pity) (& wri); A Sense Of Loss (& wri); The Memory Of Justice (& wri).

OPPENHEIMER, Alan: Act. b. NYC, Apr 23. e. Carnegie Institute of Technology. Films inc: Star!; The Hindenburg; Freaky Friday; Little Big Man; The Secret Of The Sword.
TV inc: Washington - Behind Closed Doors; Helter Skelter; Tail Gunner Joe; To Kill A Cop; Dinky Hocker; Six Million Dollar Man; Bionic Woman; Blind Ambition; Eischied; Smurfs (voice); Divorce Wars--A Love Story; The Smurf Springtime Special (voice); The Smurf's Christmas Special (voice); The Smurfic Games (voice); My Wicked, Wicked Ways; The Execution. Smurfily Ever After (voice).
Thea inc: The Devils; The Latent Heterosexual.

OPPENHEIMER, Jess: Wri-Prod-Dir. b. San Francisco, Nov 11, 1913. Wri: (Radio) Packard Hour, Fred Astaire, 1936-38; Rudy Vallee, 1940-41; Fanny Brice Baby Snooks Show, 1942-47 (also dir & prod).
TV inc: Head wri, prod, dir Lucille Ball My Favorite Husband, 1948-51; I Love Lucy (prod & wri) 1951-56; exec prod General Motors Fiftieth Anniversary Show, 1956; exec prod, creator, Angel, 1960-61; exec prod, creator, Glynis Johns Show; 1963-64; prod, dir, wri, Bob Hope Chrysler Theatre; prod, wri, dir Get Smart; exec prod, creator, wri, Debbie Reynolds Show; prod Danny Kaye Show with Lucille Ball.

ORBACH, Jerry: Act. b. NYC, Oct 20, 1935. e. U of IL, Northwestern U. Thea inc: Threepenny Opera; The Fantasticks; Carnival; The Cradle Will Rock; Guys and Dolls; Carousel; Annie Get Your Gun; The Natural Look; Scuba Duba; Promises, Promises (Tony-1969); The Rose Tattoo; The Trouble with People...and Other Things; Chicago; 42d Street.

Films inc: Please Come Home; The Sentinel; Prince of the City; Brewster's Millions.
TV inc: The Nurses; The Way They Were; An Invasion of Privacy; The Special Magic of Herself the Elf (voice); The Streets; Night Of 100 Stars II.

ORBISON, Roy: Act-Comp. b. Wink, TX, Apr 23, 1936. C&W recording artist. Films inc: Fastest Guitar Alive; Roadie.
(Grammy-country group vocal-1980).

OREAR, Richard H.: Exec. b. Kansas City, MO, Jun 11, 1911. e. Findlay Engineering Coll. In exhibition since 1931 in all phases; publicist-purchasing agent for Hughes-Franklin, which carried over to newly formed Commonwealth Theatres; 1947 elected to board of Commonwealth; 1955 exec vp; 1959 bd chmn.

ORGOLINI, Arnold: Prod. b. Los Angeles, Oct 16, 1936. e. USC, BS, MBA. Films inc: Cactus; Embryo; Meteor; Smorgasbord. TV inc: Callie and Son (exec prod); A Small Killing; Starflight--The Plane That Couldn't Land; Two Kinds of Love.

ORLANDO, Tony (Michael Orlando Cassivitis): Singer. b. NYC, Apr 3, 1944. Record promoter for April/Blackwood Records; formed group Dawn with Thelma Hopkins and Joyce Vincent Wilson, 1970 before solo.
TV inc: Tony Orlando and Dawn; Three Hundred Miles For Stephanie (exec prod); Entertainer of the Year Awards; Bob Hope's All-Star Celebration Opening the Gerald R. Ford Museum; Lynda Carter-Street Life; Rosie--The Rosemary Clooney Story; Louise Mandrell-Diamonds, Gold & Platinum; Salute to Lady Liberty.
Recordings inc: Halfway to Paradise; Knock Three Times; Tie a Yellow Ribbon Round the Old Oak Tree. Albums inc: Greatest Hits; Before Dawn; The World of Tony Orlando and Dawn; Tony Orlando.

ORMANDY, Eugene: Cond. b. Budapest, Hungary, Nov 18, 1899. Child prodigy at 3; at 5 1/2, youngest pupil ever admitted to Royal State Academy of Music, received BA at 14 1/2. Toured Hungary as child prodigy. To US 1921, subbed for Toscanini as cond Philadelphia Orchestra; cond Minneapolis Symphony 1931-1936; Philadelphia Orchestra 1936; guest conductor major world orchestras.
(Grammy-class performance choral-1967).
TV inc: The Kennedy Center Honors 1982 (honoree).
(Died March 12, 1985)

ORNITZ, Arthur J.: Cin-Dir. b. NYC, Nov 28, 1916. e. UCLA. S of Sam Ornitz. Films inc: (Cin) The Goddess; Requiem for a Heavyweight; The World of Henry Orient; A Thousand Clowns; Serpico; Death Wish; Next Stop Greenwich Village; An Unmarried Woman; The Chosen; Tattoo; Hanky Panky; Heart Of The Garden.
TV inc: Make A Wish (dir); Playing for Time; The Royal Romance of Charles and Diana; Jacobo Timerman--Prisoner Without A Name, Cell Without A Number; First Affair.

ORR, Mary: Act-Wri. b. NYC, Dec 21, 1918. e. Briarcliff; Syracuse U. Bway debut 1938, Bachelor Born. Bway inc: Of Mice and Men; Jupiter Laughs; Jeannie; Without Love; Wallflower; Dark Hammock; Sherlock Holmes; The Desperate Hours.
Films inc: Pigeons.
TV inc: Suspect.
Plays inc: Wall Flower; Dark Hammock; Round Trip; The Platinum Set; Be Your Age. Short story Wisdom of Eve was basis of film All About Eve.

ORR, William T.: Exec. b. NYC, Sep 27, 1917. Started in niteries, Bway. Joined WB 1947 as exec, talent dept; later named asst to Steve Trilling, exec asst to Jack Warner; VP in charge of prod both features and TV, 1961-62; asst to P, exec prod, TV div, 1963-65; formed Wm T Orr Co, 1966, for prodn of film and TV.
Films inc: My Love Come Back; Thieves Fall Out; Navy Blues; The Mortal Storm; The Big Street; Unholy Partners; Wicked, Wicked.

ORTOLANI, Riziero (Riz): Comp. b. Pesaro, Italy, Mar 25, 1931. e. Giaocchino Rossini Conservatory. Films inc: Mondo Cane; The Yellow Rolls Royce; The Seventh Dawn; Woman Times Seven; Buona Sera Mrs. Campbell; The Mackenzie Break; Say Hello to Yesterday; The Valachi Papers; Madrom; Drama Borghese; The Fifth Musketeer;

From Hell to Victory; Fantasma D'Amore (Ghost of Love); Valentina; Madhouse; Giuseppe Fava Siciliano Como Me; Uno Scandalo Perbene (A Proper Scandal).

Songs inc: More (Grammy-instrumental theme-1963); Forget Domani; Till Love Touches Your Life.

OSBORN, Paul: Wri. b. Evansville, IN, Sep 4, 1901. e. U MI, AB, MA; Yale Dramatic Workshop. Plays inc: The Vinegar Tree; Oliver Oliver; On Borrowed Time; Morning's At Seven; The Innocent Voyage; A Bell for Adano; The World of Suzie Wong; Maiden Voyage; Hot September; Contessa.

Films inc: The Yearling: Mme. Curie; The Young in Heart; East of Eden; Homecoming; Portrait of Jennie; Sayonara; South Pacific; Wild River; John Brown's Body.

OSBORNE, John: Wri-Act. b. London, Dec 12, 1929. e. Belmont Coll. Plays inc; Look Back in Anger; Epitaph for George Dillon; The Entertainer; The World of Paul Stickey; Luther (Tony-1964); Inadmissible Evidence; Watch It Come Down.

Films inc: Look Back in Anger; The Entertainer; Tom Jones (Oscar-1963).

TV inc: The Right Prospectus; Very Like A Whale; A Subject of Scandal and Concern; Almost a Vision; The Gift of Friendship (cable).

OSCARSSON, Per: Act. b. Stockholm, Sweden, 1927. Films inc: The Street; Meeting Life; Defiance; Barabbas; Karin Mansdotter; Wild Birds; The Summer Night Is Sweet; The Doll; Adam and Eve; Hunger; Doktor Glas; A Dandy in Aspic; The Last Valley; The Night Visitor; Honeycomb; The New Land; The Blockhouse; Dream City; Dagny; Victor Frankenstein; The Brothers Lionheart; Secrets; Montenegro (Pigs and Pearls); Ronja Rovardotter (Ronya--The Robber's Daughter); DaCapo.

OSGOOD, Charles: TV news. b. NYC, Jan 8, 1933. e. Fordham, BS. Pgm dir, WGMS, Washington; GM WHCT, Hartford; joined ABC 1964 as general assignment reporter; 1967, morning anchor WCBS (radio) NYC; 1971, CBS-TV as corr; 1981, anchor Sunday night news; also anchors Newsbreak and The Osgood File on CBS Radio net. TV inc: Walter Cronkite's Universe (corr).

O'SHEA, John: Prod-Dir. b. New Plymouth, New Zealand, 1920. e. Victoria U; U of New Zealand. Films inc: Broken Barrier; Runaway; Don't Let It Get You; Leave All Fair.

O'SHEA, Milo: Act. b. Ireland, 1926. With the Abbey Players, Dublin before screen. Films inc: Carry On Cabby; Never Put It In Writing; Ulysses; Romeo and Juliet; Barbarella; The Adding Machine; The Angel Levine; Paddy; Sacco and Vanzetti; Loot; Digby, The Biggest Dog in the World; Arabian Adventure; It's Not the Size That Counts; The Verdict; The Purple Rose Of Cairo.

Bway inc: Staircase; Dear World; Mrs. Warren's Profession; The Comedians; A Touch of the Poet; My Fair Lady (rev); Mass Appeal. Other thea inc: Corpse! (London)

TV inc: Two By Forsyth; Ellis Island.

O'SHEA, Tessie: Act. b. England, Mar 13, 1918. Films inc: The Shiralee; The Russians Are Coming, The Russians Are Coming; The Best House in London; Bedknobs and Broomsticks.

Bway inc: The Girl Who Came to Supper (Tony-supp-1964); Something's Afoot; Broadway Follies.

TV inc: The Word.

OSHIMA, Nagisa: Dir-Wri. b. Kyoto, Japan, Mar 31, 1932. e. U of Kyoto. Joined Shochiku Co Ltd, as asst dir; debut as dir 1959, A Town of Love and Hope. Films inc: Cruel Story of Youth; The Sun's Burial; The Catch; The Revolutionary; A Child's First Adventure; The Pleasures of the Flesh; Violence at Noon; Ban on Ninja; Death by Hanging; He Died After the War; The Ceremony; Dear Summer Sister; In the Realm of the Senses; Phantom Love; Empire of Passion; Merry Christmas, Mr. Lawrence; Seishun Zankoku Monogatari (Cruel Story Of Youth).

OSMOND, Cliff: Act. (nee Ebrahim).b. Feb 26, 1937. Films inc: Irma La Douce; Kiss Me Stupid; The Fortune Cookie; Three Guns for Texas; The Devil's Eight; The Front Page; Shark's Treasure; The Mouse and His Child (voice only); The Apple Dumpling Gang Rides Again; The

North Avenue Irregulars; Hangar 18.

TV inc: Beggarman, Thief; California Gold Rush; Incident At Crestridge.

OSMOND, Donny: Act. b. Ogden, UT, Dec 9, 1957. The fifth member of the Osmond Family to become a professional singer. First appeared on The Andy Williams Show at age 4.

TV inc: The Donny & Marie Show; The Gift of Love; Donnie and Marie Christmas Special; The Osmond Family Christmas Show; The Osmond Family Holiday Special; The Wild Women of Chastity Gulch; Christmas In Washington; Night Of 100 Stars II.

Films inc: Goin' Coconuts.

Bway inc: Little Johnny Jones.

OSMOND, Marie: Act. b. Ogden, UT, Oct 13, 1959. Began career at age 7 while touring with her brothers. When she joined the group the act was changed from the Osmond Brothers to the Osmonds.

TV inc: Donny & Marie Show; The Gift Of Love; The Donnie and Marie Christmas Special; The Osmond Family Christmas Show; Bob Hope 30th Anniversary Special; Doug Henning's World of Magic; Bob Hope's All-Star Birthday Party At West Point; The Osmond Family Holiday Special; The Suzanne Somers Special; Bob Hope's Women I Love--Beautiful and Funny; Side by Side--The True Story of the Osmond Family; Rooster; I Married Wyatt Earp; Bob Hope's Salute to NASA--25 Years of Reaching for the Stars; Here's Television Entertainment (host); Salute to Lady Liberty; Christmas In Washington; Disneyland's 30th Anniversary Celebration.

Films inc: Goin' Coconuts; Hugo The Hippo.

O'STEEN, Sam: Dir-Edtr. b. Nov 6, 1923. Films inc: (Edtr) Kisses for My President; Robin and the 7 Hoods; Youngblood Hawke; Marriage on the Rocks; None But the Brave; Who's Afraid of Virginia Woolf; Cool Hand Luke; The Graduate; Rosemary's Baby; The Sterile Cuckoo (supv ed); Catch-22; Carnal Knowledge; Portnoy's Complaint; Day of the Dolphin; Chinatown; Straight Time; Sparkle (dir); Hurricane; Silkwood.

TV inc: (dir) A Brand New Life; I Love You, Goodbye; Queen of the Stardust Ballroom; High Risk; Look What's Happened to Rosemary's Baby; The Best Little Girl In The World; Kids Don't Talk.and the 7 Hoods; Youngblood Hawke; Marriage on the Rocks; None

OSTERMAN, Lester: Thea prod. b. NYC, Dec 31, 1914. e. U of VA. Member of NY Stock exchange 1945-59; began theatrical career as prod Mr. Wonderful, 1956, has prod or co-prod Candide; High Spirits; Fade Out Fade In; Hadrian VII; Butley; The Rothschilds; Sizwe Banzi Is Dead; The Island; A Moon for the Misbegotten; The Shadow Box (Tony-1977); Da (Tony-1978); Crucifer of Blood; Watch on the Rhine (rev); The Lady From Dubuque; A Life.

TV inc: The Littlest Angel; Raggedy Ann.

OSTERWALD, Bibi: Act. b. New Brunswick, NJ, Feb 3, 1920. e. Catholic U. Films inc: Parris; The World of Henry Orient; Tiger Makes Out; Bank Shot; The Great Smokey Road Block.

TV inc: Captain Billy's Mississippi Music Hall; Our Town; Where the Heart Is; Beulah Land; The Wonderful World Of Philip Malley; A Tale of Four Wishes; Happy Endings.

Bway inc: Sing Out Sweet Land; Gentlemen Prefer Blondes; Three to Make Ready; Bus Stop; Golden Apple; Hello Dolly.

OSTROW, Stuart: Prod. b. NYC, Feb 8, 1932. Bway inc: We Take the Town; Here's Love; The Apple Tree, 1776; Scratch; Pippin; Stages; The Moony Shapiro Songbook.

O'SULLIVAN, Maureen: Act. b. Voyle, Ireland, May 17, 1911. M of Mia Farrow. On screen from 1930. Films inc: Song O' My Heart; MGM Tarzan series; The Barretts of Wimpole Street; The Thin Man; Anna Karenina; A Day at the Races; Cardinal Richelieu; David Copperfield; A Yank at Oxford; The Big Clock; As I Desire; The Steel Cage; Never Too Late; Too Scared To Scream.

Thea inc: The Front Page; No Sex Please, We're British; Morning's At Seven (rev).

OSWALD, Gerd: Dir. b. Berlin, Jun 9, 1919. Films inc: A Kiss Before Dying; Brass Legend; Crime of Passion; Fury at Showdown; Valerie; Paris Holiday; Screaming Mimi; The Day the Rains Came (sp, prod); The Longest Day (sequence); Scarlet Eye; Agent for Harm; 80 Steps to Jonah (sp, prod); Bunny O'Hare; To the Bitter End.

TV inc: Ford Theatre; GE Hour; Playhouse 90; Perry Mason; Rawhide; Outer Limits; Star Trek; Shane; Gentle Ben; Bonanza; It Takes a Thief; Nichols.

OSWIN, James Henry Martin: Exec. b. Lismore, Australia, Aug 5, 1923. e. Scots Coll. Station mgr ATN Channel 7 Sydney, 1955-57; gm 1957-72; dir M7 Records 1971-72; m dir 7 Network 1972-73; secy Australian Govt Dept of the Media 1973-75; Australian ambassador, Permanent Delegate to UNESCO, Paris 1975-76; vice chmn Australian Broadcasting Tribunal.

O'TOOLE, Annette (nee Toole): Act. b. Houston, TX, Apr 1, 1952. Films inc: Smile; One on One; King of the Gypsies; Foolin' Around; Cat People; 48 Hours; Superman III.

TV inc: The Entertainer; The War Between the Tates; Ladies In Waiting; Class of '65; Love for Rent; Stand By Your Man; The Secret World Of The Very Young; The Best Legs in the 8th Grade (PC); Bridge To Terabithia; Alfred Hitchcock Presents.

O'TOOLE, Peter: Act. b. Ireland, Aug 2, 1932. e. RADA. Early career with Bristol Old Vic. Thea inc: (London) The Long, The Short and the Tall; Macbeth; Dead Eyed Dicks (Dublin); Man and Superman; Pygmalion.

Screen debut 1959, Kidnapped. Films inc: The Day They Robbed the Bank of England; Lawrence of Arabia; Becket; The Lion in Winter; Goodby Mr. Chips; The Ruling Class; What's New Pussycat?; Lord Jim; How to Steal a Million; Murphy's War; Man of La Mancha; Rosebud; Man Friday; Power Play; Foxtrot; Zulu Dawn; Caligula; The Stunt Man; My Favorite Year; Supergirl.

TV inc: Rogue Male; Masada; Strumpet City (cable); Svengali; The World of James Joyce; Kim.

OURY, Gerard: Act-Dir-Wri. b. Paris, Apr 29, 1919. e. Nat'l Conservatory Dramatic Art. On Stage in Paris at Comedie Francaise, also in Geneva.

Films inc: (act) Antoine and Antoinette; La Belle que voila; Le Passe-Muraille; Le Nuit est mon Royaume; The Rose and the Sword; Sea Devils; The Heart of the Matter; Father Brown; La Fille du Fleuve; La Meiullure Part; The House of Secrets; Le Septieme Ciel; The Mirror has Two Faces; The Journey; The Prize. (Dir): La main chaude (& wri); La Menace; Crime Does Not Pay (& wri); The Sucker (& wri); Don't Look Now (& wri); The Brain (& wri); Delusions of Grandeur (& wri); The Mad Adventures of Rabbi Jacob (& wri); La Carapate; Le Coup du Parapluie (& wri); L'As des As (Ace of Aces) (& wri); La Vengeance du Serpent a Plumes (The Vengeance of the Plumed Serpent (& wri).

OWEN, Alun: Wri. b. Liverpool, England, Nov 24, 1925. Plays inc: a Little Winter Love; Maggie May; Progress in the Park; The Rough and Ready Lot; There'll Be Some Changes Made; Fashion of Your Time; The Male of the Species.

Films inc: The Criminal; A Hard Day's Night.

TV inc: No Trams to Lime Street; After the Funeral; Lena, Oh My Lena; The Ruffians; The Ways of Love; You Can't Win 'Em All; The Stag; Park People; Giants and Ogres; Just the Job; Forget Me Not.

OWENS, Bonnie: Act-Sngwri. b. Blanchard, OK, Oct 1, 1933. W of Buck Owens. C&W recording artist. Teamed with Merle Haggard.

OWENS, Buck: Act. b. Sherman, TX, Aug 12, 1929. Country mus artist. TV inc: Hee Haw; Dean Martin's Christmas At Sea World.

Films inc: Murder Can Hurt You.

Songs inc: Crying Time; Together Again.

OWENS, Gary: Act-TV pers. b. Mitchell, SD, May 10, 1936. e. Wesleyan U. Disc jockey, KMPC Hollywood; KPRZ Hollywood. TV inc: Laugh-In; host of Letters to Laugh-In; The Hudson Brothers; The Green Hornet; Gong Show (orig host); No Soap, Radio; Gary Owen's All Nonsense News Network Special (& wri); Break Away.

Cartoons inc: (voice) Roger Ramjet; Space Ghost; The Blue Falcon; Perils of Penelope Pitstop!

Films inc: Hysterical.

OWENSBY, Earl: Prod-Act. b. North Carolina, 1936. Has own studio in Shelbyville, NC. Films inc: Challenge; Dark Sunday; Buckstone

County Prison; Frank Challenge--Manhunter; Death Driver; Wolfman; Seabo; Day of Judgment; Living Legend; Lady Grey.

OZ, Frank: Act. (nee Oznowicz):b. Hereford, England, May 25, 1944. VP, Henson Associates. TV inc: Sesame Street; The Muppet Show (Emmys-1974, 1976, 1978); Big Bird in China; various variety shows.

Films inc: The Blues Brothers; The Empire Strikes Back; The Muppet Movie; The Great Muppet Caper (& prod); American Werewolf in London; The Dark Crystal (& dir); Return of the Jedi; The Muppets Take Manhattan (& dir-wri).

OZAWA, Seiji: Cond. b. Shenyang, China, Sep 1, 1935. e. Toho School of Music. Studied with Herbert von Karajan, Leonard Bernstein. Asst cond NY Philharmonic 1961-1962; dir Ravinia Festival, 1964-1969; cond Toronto Symphony 1965-1969; mus dir San Francisco Symphony 1970-76; mus dir Berkshire Music Festival Tanglewood 1970-1973; mus dir Boston Symphony. TV inc: Central Park In The Dark/A Hero's Life (Emmy-mus dir-1976).

PAAR, Jack: TV Pers. b. Canton, OH, 1918. Host NBC's Tonight show, 1957; in 1958 network changed title to The Jack Paar Show. Switched to weekly variety show in 1962. In 1973, signed with ABC and for a time did a one-week-a-month show; Other TV inc: Take One.

PACINO, Al: Act. b. NYC, Apr 25, 1940. Thea inc: The Indian Wants the Bronx; Does a Tiger Wear a Necktie? (Tony-supp-1969); The Connection; Hello Out There; Tiger at the Gates; The Basic Training of Pavlo Hummel (Tony-1977); Richard III; American Buffalo (rev) (also London).

Films inc: Panic in Needle Park; The Godfather; Scarecrow; Serpico; The Godfather Part II; Dog Day Afternoon; Bobby Deerfield; And Justice For All; Cruising; Author! Author!; Scarface.

PACKER, Kerry Francis Bullmore: Exec. b. Sydney, Australia, Dec 17, 1937. Chmn, Australian Consolidated Press Ltd & Publishing and Broadcasting Ltd; dir, General Television Ltd.

PADNICK, Glenn: Exec-wri. b. Brooklyn, NY., Sept. 8, 1947. e. Harvard, AB; Harvard Law, JD. Joined Embassy TV 1977 as vp legal affairs; sr. vp current programs; March, 1984, exec vp comedy programs; June, 1984, P Embassy TV. TV inc: (wri) Diff'rent Strokes; Facts Of Life; Silver Spoons; Hello, Larry

PADOVANI, Lea: Act. b. Italy, 1920. L'Innocente Casimiro; Il Diavolo bianco; Give Us This Day; Three Steps North; Rome 11 O'Clock; Don Lorenzo; The Anatomy of Love; Gran Varieta; An Eye for an Eye; Montparnasse 19; The Naked Maja; The Princess of Cleves; The Reluctant Saint; Germinal; Amore all 'Italiana; Candy; Ciao Gulliver; Ehrengard.

PAGE, Anthony: Dir. b. Bangalore, India, Sep 21, 1935. e. Oxford. Films inc: Inadmissible Evidence; Alpha Beta; I Never Promised You A Rose Garden; Absolution; The Lady Vanishes.

Thea inc: Inadmissible Evidence; Evidence; A Cuckoo in the Nest; Waiting for Godot; A Patriot for Me; Diary of a Madman; Look Back in Anger; Uncle Vanya; The Rules of the Game; Absolution; Cowardice.

TV inc: Pueblo; The Missiles of October; Collision Course; F. Scott Fitzgerald in Hollywood; Stephen D; The Parachute; The Hotel in Amsterdam; F.D.R. - The Last Year; The Patricia Neal Story; Bill; Johnny Belinda; Grace Kelly; Bill--On His Own; Forbidden.

PAGE, Genevieve: Act. b. France, 1931. Films inc: Fanfan La Tulippe; The Silken Affair; Michael Strogoff; Song Without End; El Cid; Paris Blues; Grand Prix; Youngblood Hawke; Belle De Jour; Decline and Fall; Private Life of Sherlock Holmes; Buffet Froid (Cold Cuts); Mortelle Randonee (Deadly Circuit).

PAGE, Geraldine: Act. b. Kirkville, MO., Nov. 22, 1924. W of Rip Torn. Bway debut 1945, Seven Mirrors. On Screen from 1953. Films inc: Hondo; Summer And Smoke; Sweet Bird Of Youth; Toys In The Attic; Dear Heart; The Happiest Millionaire; You're A Big Boy Now; Trilogy; What Ever Happened To Aunt Alice; The Beguiled; J.W. Cooper; Pete ∎N' Tillie; The Day Of The Locust; Nasty Habits; Interiors; Harry's War; Honky Tonk Freeway; I'm Dancing As Fast As I Can.

Thea inc: Mid-Summer; The Immoralist; Summer And Smoke

(rev); The Rainmaker; Separate Tables; Sweet Bird Of Youth; Strange Interlude; Absurd Person Singular; The Three Sisters; Angela; Black Comedy; Clothes For A Summer Hotel; Mixed Couples; Agnes Of God.

TV inc: A Christmas Memory *(Emmy-1967)*; The Thanksgiving Visitor *(Emmy-1969)*; Barefoot In Athens; The Name Of The Game; The Blue And The Gray.

PAGE, LaWanda: Act. b. Cleveland, OH, Oct 19, 1920. Started as dancer in niteries. TV inc: The Sanford Arms; B.A.D. Cats; Good Evening, Captain. Films inc: Mausoleum.

PAGE, Patti (Clara Ann Flower): Act. b. Claremore, OK, Nov 8, 1927. Staff performer, radio sta KTUL, Tulsa. Appeared on CBS radio; Patti Page Show; TV film series, The Big Record. Other TV: Here's Television Entertainment (host); In the Swing; Music Of Your Life.

Films inc: Elmer Gantry; Dondi; Boys Night Out.

PAGET, Debra (Debralee Griffin): Act. b. Denver, CO, Aug 19, 1933. Films inc: Cry of the City; House of Strangers; Broken Arrow; Les Miserables; Prince Valiant; Love Me Tender; From the Earth to the Moon; Tales of Terror; The Haunted Palace.

PAGETT, Nicola (nee Scott): Act. b. Cairo, Egypt, Jun 15, 1945. e. RADA. Thea inc: A Boston Story; Widowers' Houses; The Misanthrope; A Voyage Round My Father; The Ride Across Lake Constance; Ghosts; The Seagull; A Family and a Fortune; Gaslight; Yahoo; Taking Steps; Old Times.

Films inc: Anne of the Thousand Days; There's a Girl in My Soup; Operation Daybreak; Oliver's Story; Privates On Parade.

TV inc: Upstairs Downstairs; The Timeless Land; A Woman Of Substance.

PAIGE, Janis (Donna Mae Jaden): Act. b. Tacoma, WA, Sep 16, 1923. Sang with Tacoma Opera Co. Screen debut 1944, Hollywood Canteen. Films inc: Of Human Bondage; The Time, the Place and the Girl; Her Kind of Man; Silk Stockings; Please Don't Eat the Daisies; Bachelor in Paradise; The Caretakers; Follow the Boys; Welcome to Hard Times.

TV inc: Columbo; Mannix; Hec Ramsey; Valentine Magic On Love Island; Angel On My Shoulder; Bret Maverick; Bob Hope's Road to Hollywood; The Other Woman; Baby Makes Five; No Man's Land.

Thea inc: The Pajama Game; Remains to be Seen; Alone Together (Bway).

PAKULA, Alan: Prod-Dir. b. NYC, Apr 7, 1928. e. Yale, BA. Joined MGM 1950, prod apprentice; prod asst Para 1951; prod Para 1955; own prod co, Pakula-Mulligan Prod. Films inc: (prod) Fear Strikes Out; To Kill a Mockingbird; Love With the Proper Stranger; Baby the Rain Must Fall; Inside Daisy Clover; Up the Down Staircase; The Stalking Moon; (dir) The Sterile Cuckoo; Klute; Love and Pain and the Whole Damned Thing; The Parallax View; All the President's Men; Comes A Horseman; Starting Over; Rollover; Sophie's Choice (& sp); George Stevens--A Filmmaker's Journey (doc-int).

Thea inc: There Must Be a Pony; Blood and Thunder; Comes a Day; Laurette.

PALANCE, Holly: Act. b. Los Angeles, Aug 5, 1950. e. Webber-Douglas Acad of Dramatic Art, London. D of Jack Palance. Worked with rep groups in England before London debut in Happy End. Other thea inc: A Streetcar Named Desire; Period of Adjustment; Romantic Comedy (Bway).

Films inc: The Omen; The Comeback.

TV inc: Dickens of London; Play for Today; Cynthia; Leather Stocking Tales; Ripley's Believe It Or Not; The Thorn Birds.

PALANCE, Jack: Act. b. Lattimer, PA, Feb 18, 1920. On screen from 1950. Films inc: Star of Tomorrow; Flight to Tangier; Man in the Attic; Sign of the Pagan; Sudden Fear; Shane; Silver Chalice; Kiss of Fire; The Big Knife; I Died a Thousand Times; Attack!; Lonely Man; House of Numbers; Ten Seconds to Hell; Warriors Five; Barabbas; Contempt; Torture Garden; Kill a Dragon; They Came to Rob Las Vegas; The Desperadoes; Che; The Mercenary; Justine; Legion of the Damned; A Bullet for Rommel; The McMasters; Monte Walsh; Companeros; The Horsemen; The Professionals; Oklahoma Crude; Craze; The Four Deuces; The Diamond Mercenaries; The Shape of Things to Come; Without Warning; Hawk The Slayer; Alone In the Dark; George

Stevens--A Filmmaker's Journey.

TV inc: Requiem For A Heavyweight *(Emmy-1956)*; Dr. Jekyll and Mr. Hyde; Dracula; Bronk; The Last Ride of the Dalton Gang; The Golden Moment-An Olympic Love Story; Ripley's Believe It Or Not (host).

Thea inc: The Big Two; Temporary Island; The Vigil; A Streetcar Named Desire; Darkness at Noon.

PALEY, William S.: Exec. b. Chicago, Sep 28, 1901. e. U of PA. Pres. Columbia Broadcasting System 1928; chairman of board, 1946-April 1983 when he became cnslt while remaining as chmn of exec comm of board of directors. During WW II, on leave to supervise OWI radio in Mediterranean area. Chief of radio of Psychological Warfare Division, SHAFE, 1944-45. Dep Chief Info Control Div of USGCC 1945. Colonel, AUS Deputy Chief Psychological Warfare Div, SHAFE, 1945.

(First Annual ATAS Governor's Award, 1978); (Television Academy Hall Of Fame 1984)

PALIN, Michael: Act-Wri. b. Sheffield, Yorkshire, England, May 5, 1943. e. Oxford. Member of Monty Python Flying Circus. Thea inc: Hang Down Your Head and Die; Aladdin; Monty Python's First Farewell Tour; Monty Python Live at Drury Lane; Monty Python Live at City Center (NY); Secret Policeman's Ball.

Films inc: And Now For Something Completely Different; Monty Python and the Holy Grail; Jabberwocky; Life of Brian; Time Bandits; Missionary (& prod); Monty Python's The Meaning of Life (& mus); A Private Function; Brazil.

TV inc: Now; The Frost Report; The Late Show; A Series of Birds; Twice A Fortnight; Do Not Adjust Your Set; Marty Feldman Comedy Machine; How To Irritate People; The Complete and Utter History of Britain; Pythons in Deutschland; Secrets; Three Men In A Boat; Tomkinson's Schooldays; Ripping Yarns.

PALMER, Betsy (Patricia Hrunek): Act. b. East Chicago, IN, Nov 1, 1929. e. IN U; De Pauw U. Thea inc: The Grand Prize; Affair of Honor; Roar Like a Dove; Cactus Flower; A Doll's House.

Films inc: The Long Gray Line; The Tin Star; The Last Angry Man; Mister Roberts; Friday The 13th; Friday the 13th Part 2.

TV inc: Studio One; US Steel Hour; Climax; Kraft Theatre; Number 96; Isabel's Choice.

PALMER, Lilli: Act. b. Austria, May 24, 1914. On screen in England from 1934. Films in US from 1946 inc: Cloak and Dagger; My Girl Tisa; Body and Soul; No Minor Vices; The Fourposter; But Not For Me; The Pleasure of His Company; The Counterfeit Traitor; Maedchen in Uniform; Sebastian; Murders in the Rue Morgue; The House That Screamed; The Boys From Brazil.

Thea inc: Bell, Book and Candle; Suite in 3 Keys; Venus Observed; Love of Four Colonels; Feine Gesellschaft Beschraentke Haftung (Society Limited).

TV inc: Lilli Palmer Presents; Sarah In America (Kennedy Center Tonight).

PALTROW, Bruce: Prod-Dir-Wri. b. NYC, Nov. 26, 1943. e. Tulane U, BFA. H of Blythe Danner. Thea inc: (prod) Someone's Comin' Hungry; Whispers in the Wind.

TV inc: Shirts and Skins; You're Gonna Love It Here; Big City Boys; The White Shadow (crea-dir); St. Elsewhere (exec prod-dir).

Films inc: A Little Sex (co-prod & dir).

PALUZZI, Luciana: Act. b. Italy, 1939. Films inc: Three Coins in the Fountain; Tank Force; Man In A Cocked Hat; Return to Peyton Place; Muscel Beach Party; Sea Fury; Thunderball; The Venetian Affair; Chuka; 99 Women; The Green Slime; Black Gunn; War Goddess; The Klansman; The Greek Tycoon.

TV inc: Five Fingers.

PAM, Jerry: Pub-Prod. b. London, England, Oct 17, 1926. e. Cambridge, London U. To US 1953 after career as freelance writer. Reporter-critic Hollywood Reporter, Beverly Hills Citizen, Valley Times. Entered pub field 1959, Pam and Joseph; Jerry Pam & Associates; Guttman & Pam Ltd. Films inc: Highpoint (exec prod).

PAN, Hermes: Chor. Films inc: Roberta; Damsel in Distress *(Oscar-1938)*; Top Hat; Old Man Rhythm; Follow the Fleet; Swing Time;

Shall We Dance; Let's Dance; Three Little Words; Texas Carnival; Lovely to Look At; Kiss Me Kate; Student Prince; Hit the Deck; Jupiter's Darling; Meet Me In Las Vegas; Porgy and Bess; Can-Can; Flower Drum Song; Cleopatra; My Fair Lady; Finian's Rainbow; Darling Lili; Lost Horizon; Aiutami A Sognare (Help Me Dream); George Stevens--A Filmmaker's Journey (doc-int).

TV inc: Frances Langford Show; Sounds of America; Astaire Time; An Evening with Fred Astaire (Emmy-chor-1959); AFI Salute to Fred Astaire (guest).

PANAMA, Norman: Wri-Prod-Dir. b. Chicago, Apr 21, 1914. e. U of Chicago. Films inc: My Favorite Blonde; Happy Go Lucky; Star Spangled Rhythm; And the Angels Sing; The Road to Utopia; Duffy's Tavern; Monsieur Beaucaire; The Return of October; Mr Blanding Builds His Dream House; The Reformer and the Redhead; Strictly Dishonorable; Callaway Went Thataway; Knock on Wood; White Christmas; The Court Jester; That Certain Feeling; Li'l Abner; The Facts of Life; The Road to Hong Kong; Strange Bedfellows; Not With My Wife, You Don't!; How to Commit Marriage.

TV inc: Coffee, Tea, or Me; Li'l Abner.

Plays inc: A Talent For Murder.

PANFILOV, Gleb: Wri-Dir. b. Russia, Dec 21, 1934. H of Inna Churikova. Films inc: Join Our Ranks (doc); Nina Melovizinova (short); Killed At War (short); The Case of Kurt Clausewitz (short); No Ford in the Fire; The Beginning; I Wish to Speak; Valentina, Valentina; Tema; Vassa.

PAPAS, Irene: Act. b. Corinth, Greece, 1926. Films inc: The Man from Cairo; Tribute to a Bad Man; Attila the Hun; Antigone; The Guns of Navarone; Electra; The Moon-Spinners; Zorba the Greek; The Brotherhood; A Dream of Kings; Anne of the Thousand Days; The Trojan Women; Moses; Mohammed, Messenger of God; Iphigenia; Christ Stopped At Eboli; Sidney Sheldon's Bloodline; Lion of the Desert; La Ballade De Mamlouk; Erendira; Il Disertore (The Deserter); Into The Night.

Thea inc: The Idiot; Journey's End; Inherit the Wind; Iphigenia in Aulis.

PAPATHANASSIOU, Vangelis: (See VANGELIS)

PAPAZIAN, Robert A.: Prod. b. Boston, MA. e. USC, CSU Los Angeles. Started as page at KNXT, Los Angeles; 1969, exec in chg prodn ABC Circle Films; later with Metromedia; Taft Broadcasting.

TV inc: Murder by Natural Causes; Topper; The Seeding of Sarah Burns; The Great Cash Giveaway Getaway; The Yeagers; Trouble in High Timber Country; Crisis at Central High; Stand By Your Man; The Two Lives of Carol Letner; Intimate Agony; Prototype; The Day After; Why Me?; Sweet Revenge; For Love Or Money; A Reason To Live; Guilty Conscience; The Heart Of A Champion--The Ray Mancini Story; The Rape Of Richard Beck.

PAPP, Joseph (nee Papirofsky): Prod-Dir. b. NYC, Jun 22, 1921. Worked with Actors Lab in Hollywood; 1953 founded Shakespeare Workshop which became basis of NY Shakespeare Festival; prod & dir complete Shakespearean repertory; founded Public Theatre. Prod inc: Hair; Ergo; The Memorandum (& dir); Huui, Huui (& dir); The Expressway; Romania; That's The Old Country; Invitation to a Beheading; No Place to be Somebody; Sambo; The Wonderful Years; Play on the Times; X Has No Value; Subject to Fits; Slag; Here Are Ladies; Sticks and Bones (Tony-1972); musical version of Two Gentlemen of Verona (Tony-1972); The Black Terror; The Wedding of Iphigenia; Iphigenia in Concert; That Championship Season (Tony-1973); The Hunter; The Corner; Boom Boom Room; The Au Pair Man; More Than You Deserve; What the Wine Sellers Buy; The Kildeer; Where Do We Go From Here; Mert and Phil (& dir); Last Days of British Honduras; Black Picture Show; Little Black Sheep; A Chorus Line (Tony-1976); Streamers; The Leaf People; For Colored Girls Who Considered Suicide; Sticks and Bones; Jesse and the Bandit Queen; Runaways; The Water Engine; Pirates of Penzance (Tony-1981); Tracers; Tom and Viv; Coming Of Age in Soho; Virginia.

(Tony-special-1958).

TV inc: Alice at the Palace.

Films inc: The Pirates of Penzance.

PARIS, Jerry: Prod-Dir-Act. b. San Francisco, Jul 25, 1925. e. NYU;

UCLA. On stage in Medea; revival of Anna Christie; toured in Front Page. Films inc: (act) Marty; The Wild One; The Caine Mutiny; The Naked and the Dead; D Day--The Sixth of June; Good Morning, Miss Dove; Cyrano De Bergerac. (Dir) The Grasshopper; Viva Max; How Sweet It Is; Don't Raise the Bridge; Star-Spangled Girl; Leo and Loree (& act); Police Academy 2--Their First Assignment.

TV inc: (dir) That Girl; The Partridge Family; The Dick Van Dyke Show (Emmy-1964); Love, American Style; Odd Couple; The Feminist and the Fuzz; Evil Roy Slade; How to Break Up a Happy Divorce; Happy Days; Beane's of Boston; Make Me An Offer.

PARKER, Alan: Dir. b. London, Feb 14, 1944. Films inc: Bugsy Malone (& sp); Midnight Express; Fame; Shoot the Moon; Pink Floyd--The Wall; Birdy.

TV inc: The Evacuees; No Hard Feelings (& wri); Our Cissy (& wri); Footsteps (& wri).

PARKER, Eleanor: Act. b. Cedarville, OH, Jun 26, 1922. In summer stock Martha's Vineyard; at Pasadena Playhouse. On screen from 1941 in They Died With Their Boots On; Mission to Moscow; Of Human Bondage; Caged; Detective Story; Valentino; Scaramouche; Above and Beyond; Interrupted Melody; The Man with the Golden Arm; A Hole in the Head; Return to Peyton Place; The Sound of Music; Warning Shot; The Tiger and the Pussycat; Eye of the Cat; Sunburn.

TV inc: Bracken's World; Vanished; The Bastard; She's Dressed To Kill; Once Upon A Spy; Madame X.

PARKER, Fess: Act. b. Ft Worth, TX, Aug 16, 1925. e. U of TX. Thea inc: 1951, nat'l co Mr. Roberts. Films inc: Untamed Frontier; No Room for the Groom; Springfield Rifle; Thunder Over the Plains; Island in the Sky; Them; Battle Cry; Davy Crockett, King of the Wild Frontier; The Great Locomotive Chase; Westward Ho the Wagons; Old Yeller; The Light in the Forest; The Hangman; The Jayhawkers; Hell Is for Heroes; Smoky.

TV inc: Mr. Smith Goes to Washington; Daniel Boone; Jonathan Winters; Phyllis Diller; Joey Bishop; Dean Martin; Red Skelton; Glen Campbell.

PARKER, Jameson: Act. b. Baltimore, MD, Nov 18, 1947. e. Beloit Coll. Worked with stock groups, in commercials. Films inc: The Bell Jar; A Small Circle of Friends; White Dog;

TV inc: Somerset; One Life to Live; Women at West Point; Anatomy of a Seduction; The Promise of Love; Callie and Son; Simon and Simon; A Caribbean Mystery.

PARKER, Jean (Lois Stephanie Zelinska): Act. b. Butte, MT, 1915. On screen from 1932. Films inc: Rasputin and the Empress; Little Women; Two Alone; Caravan; Princess O'Hara; Penitentiary; Beyond Tomorrow; Torpedo Boat; Alaska Highway; Minesweeper; The Navy Way; One Body Too Many; The Gunfighter; Toughest Man in Arizona; Those Redheads from Seattle; Black Tuesday; The Parson and the Outlaw; Apache Uprising.

Thea inc: Dream Girl; Born Yesterday; Burlesque.

PARKER, Sarah Jessica: Act. b. Nelsonville, OH., March 25, 1965. With Cincinnati Ballet Company as child. Bway inc: The Innocents; Annie. Danced in Les Sylphides at Metropolitan Opera with Baryshnikov.

TV inc: Do Me A Favor, Don't Vote For My Mom; My Body, My Child; The Kennedy Center Honors--Broadway to Washington; Square Pegs; Going For The Gold--The Bill Johnson Story.

Films inc: Rich Kids; Firstborn; Girls Just Want To Have Fun.

PARKER, Suzy (Cecelia Parker): Act. b. San Antonio, TX, Oct 28, 1932. Former model. Films inc: Kiss Them for Me; Ten North Frederick; The Best of Everything; Circle of Deception; The Interns; Chamber of Horrors.

PARKER, Tom: Prod-Dist. b. New Haven, CT, Dec 20, 1913. Films inc: Initiation; Somebody Help Me; Amazing Love Secret; Frustrations; Love Clinic; Country Girl; Streets of Paris; Reunion; Antique Shop; Wacky Wagon Train.

PARKINS, Barbara: Act. b. Vancouver, Canada, May 22, 1942. Films inc: Valley of the Dolls; Bear Island; The Kremlin Letter; Puppet On A

Chain; The Mephisto Waltz; Bear Island; Breakfast In Paris.

TV inc: Peyton Place; Captains And The Kings; Young Joe, The Forgotten Kennedy; Ziegfeld--The Man And His Women; The Critical List; The Manions of America; Uncommon Valor; To Catch A King; The Calendar Girl Murders; Peyton Place--The Next Generation.

PARKS, Bert: TV MC. b. Atlanta, GA, Dec. 30, 1914. Network announcer for Eddie Cantor Show; TV inc: MC for Xavier Cugat's Show; Miss America Pageant; Break the Bank; Stop the Music; Fast Lane Blues; Replaced As MC Miss America Jan 1980.

Films inc: That's the Way of the World.

PARKS, Gordon: Wri-Dir. Fort Scott, KS, Nov 30, 1912. Films inc: The Learning Tree; Shaft; Shaft's Big Score (& mus); Supercops (dir); Leadbelly (dir).

TV inc: Solomon Northrup's Odyssey (dir-mus).

PARKS, Hildy: Act-wri-prod. b. Washington, DC., March 12, 1926. e. Mary Washington College, BA. W. of Alexander Cohen. Bway inc: (act) Bathsheba; Summer and Smoke; Magnolia Alley; To Dorothy A Son; Be Your Age; The Tunnel Of Love. (London): Mister Roberts. (Prodn Asso): Baker Street; The Devils; Ivanov; A Time For Singing; White Lies; Little Murders; Home; Prettybelle; Fun City; 6 Rms Riv Vu; Ulysses In Nighttown; Who's Who In Hell; We Interrupt This Program. (Asso prod): The Unknown Soldier And His Wife; Halfway Up The Tree; Dear World. (Prod): I Remember Mama; A Day In Hollywood, A Night In the Ukraine; 84 Charing Cross Road; Edmund Kean; La Tragedie de Carmen; Play Memory. Also prod The Unknown Soldier And His Wife in London.

Films inc: (act) The Night Holds Terror; Seven Days In May; Fail-Safe; The Group.

TV inc: On The Air; Tony Awards (wri since inception, wri-prod since 1977)(Emmy-prod-1980); Parade Of Stars; Night Of 100 Stars (Emmy-prod-1982); The Best Of Everything; Night Of 100 Stars II; Placido Domingo Steppin' Out With The Ladies.

PARKS, Michael: Act. b. Corona, CA, 1938. Films inc: Wild Seed; Bus Riley's Back in Town; The Bible; The Idol; The Happening; The Last Hard Men; Sidewinder One; The Evictors; ffolkes; Hard Country; Savannah Smiles; French Quarter Undercover; King Of The City.

TV inc: Can Ellen Be Saved; Bronson; Rainbow; Fast Friends; Reward; Turnover Smith; Dial "M" For Murder.

PARRISH, Robert: Dir-Prod. b. Columbus, GA, Jan 4, 1916. Films inc: Body and Soul (Oscar-ed-1947). (Dir). Cry Danger; The Mob; My Pal Gus; The San Francisco Story; The Purple Plain; Lucy Gallant; Fire Down Below; Saddle the Wind; In the French Style; Up from the Beach; The Bobo; Duffy; Journey to the Far Side of the Sun; A Town Called Bastard; The Marseilles Contract; Mississippi Blues (doc) (& prod).

PARSONS, Estelle: Act. b. Marblehead, MA, Nov 20, 1927. e. CT Coll for Women, BA. Joined NBC-TV's Today Show as prodn asst, then wri, feature prod, commentator. Films inc: Ladybug, Ladybug; Bonnie and Clyde (Oscar-supp-1967); Rachel, Rachel; Don't Drink the Water; I Never Sang for My Father; The Watermelon Man; I Walk the Line; Two People; For Pete's Sake.

Thea inc: Happy Hunting; Next Time I'll Sing to You; Suburban Tragedy; Ready When You Are, C.B.; The Seven Descents of Myrtle; And Miss Reardon Drinks a Little; Mert and Phil; The Norman Conquests; Ladies at the Alamo; Miss Margarida's Way; A Way of Life; Pirates of Penzance; A Sense of Humor.

TV inc: The Gambling Heart; The Nurses; The Verdict Is Yours; Faith for Today; A Memory of Two Mondays; The UFO Incident; Guests of the Nation; The Gentleman Bandit; Come Along With Me.

PARSONS, Lindsley Sr: Prod-Exec. b. Tacoma, WA, Sep 12, 1915. With Monogram, Allied Artists, Warner Bros. Columbia, 20th Century-Fox since early 40s. Films inc: Big Timber; Call of the Klondike; Sierra Passage; Yukon; Manhunt; Yellow Fin; Northwest Territory; Desert Pursuit; Jack Slade; Cry Vengeance; Finger Man; Return of Jack Slade; The Intruder; Cruel Tower; Dragon Wells Massacre; Portland Expose; Oregon Passage; Wolf Larsen; Crash Boat; The Purple Gang; Good Times; The Big Cube; Bravo Hennessey; Coasts of War.

TV inc: Gray Ghost.

PARTON, Dolly: Singer-Sngwri. b. Sevierville, TN, Jan 19, 1946. Recording artist, has own diskery, White Diamond Records. Records inc: Here You Come Again (Grammy-country vocal-1979); 9 To 5 (Grammys-country vocal & country song-1981).

TV inc: A Christmas Special With Love, Mac Davis; Barbara Mandrell and the Mandrell Sisters; Lily--Sold Out; Entertainer of the Year Awards; Live--and in Person; Kenny & Dolly--A Christmas To Remember.

Films inc: Nine To Five (act); The Best Little Whorehouse In Texas (act & add'l songs); Rhinestone (& mus).

PASETTA, Marty: Prod-Dir. b. Jun 16, 1932. e. U of Santa Clara. TV inc: A Gift of Song; Salute to Israel; Gene Kelly Special; Elvis in Hawaii; Oscar, Emmy and Grammy Award Shows; A Country Christmas, 1979; Debbie Boone--The Same Old Brand New Me; The Monte Carlo Show (exec prod); A Country Christmas, 1980; AFI Salute to Fred Astaire (dir); A Country Christmas 1981; AFI Salute to Frank Capra (dir); Texaco Star Theatre--Opening Night; AFI Salute to John Huston (dir); "I Love T.V." Test (exec prod-dir); A Concert of the World (dir); Live--and in Person; John Schneider's Christmas Holiday; Burnett 'Discovers' Domingo; 56th Oscar Show; AFI Salute to Lillian Gish; Disneyland's 30th Anniversary Celebration.

PASTERNAK, Joe: Prod. b. Hungary, Sep 19, 1901. 2nd asst dir Paramount, 1923; asst dir Universal, 1926; then prod mgr Berlin; made pictures in Vienna and Budapest; returned to Hollywood, 1937; asso prod then prod. Films inc: Three Smart Girl; Mad About Music;s; 100 Men and a Girl; First Love; Destry Rides Again; That Certain Age; Three Smart Girls Grow Up; Spring Parade; The Flame of New Orleans; It Started With Eve; Seven Sweethearts; Presenting Lily Mars; Thousands Cheer; Song of Russia; Two Girls And A Sailor; Music For Million; Thrill of a Romance; Anchors Aweigh; Two Sisters From Boston; Holiday in Mexico; The Unfinished Dance; This Time For Keep; Three Daring Daughters; On An Island With You; A Date With Judy; Luxury Liner; The Kissing Bandit; In the Good Old Summertime; That Midnight Kiss; Summer Stuck; The Great Caruso; Rich Young and Pretty; The Merry Widow; The Student Prince; Hit the Deck; Love Me Or Leave Me; Meet Me In Las Vegas; Ten Thousand Bedrooms; This Could Be the Night; Please Don't Eat the Daisies; Where The Boys Are; The Horizontal Lieutenant; Jumbo; The Courtship of Eddie's Father; A Ticklish Affair; Girl Happy; Made In Paris; Spinout; The Sweet Ride.

PATAKI, Michael: Act. b. Jan 16, 1938. e. USC. Films inc: The Return of Count Yorga; Airport '77; Love At First Bite; Dracula's Dog; The Onion Field; The Glove; Sweet Sixteen.

TV inc: Samurai; The Survival of Dana; Marciano; Phyl & Mikhy; High Noon Part II--The Return of Will Kane; Wendy Hooper, U.S. Army; Insight/God's Guerrillas; In Love With An Older Woman; Cowboy; The Cowboy and the Ballerina.

PATE, Michael: Act-wri-prod. b. Sydney, Australia, 1920. Began as act in Australia in Forty Thousand Horsemen; The Rugged O'Riordans. In Hollywood, The Strange Door; Five Fingers; The Black Castle; Julius Caesar; Houdini; Hondo; All the Brothers Were Valiant; Secret of the Incas; King Richard and the Crusades; The Silver Chalice; A Lawless Street; The Court Jester; A Killer Is Loose; The Revolt of Mamie Stover; Something of Value; Green Mansions; Sergeants 3; PT-109; McLintock!; Advance to the Rear; Major Dundee; The Singing Nun; Return of the Gunfighter. Retd to Australia to make Little Jungle Boy; Mad Dog Morgan; The Mango Tree (prod-wri only); Tim (prod-dir-wri); Duet For Four; The Return of Captain Invincible; The Wild Duck; The Camel Boy (voice).

PATERSON, Neil: Wri. b. Scotland, Dec 31, 1915. e. Edinburgh U. Films inc: Man on a Tight Rope; The Little Kidnappers; High Tide at Noon; Room at the Top (Oscar-1959); The Spiral Road; Mister Moses.

PATINKIN, Mandy: Act. b. Chicago, Nov 30, 1952. e. U KS; Juilliard. Films inc: Night of the Juggler; The Big Fix; The Last Embrace; French Postcards; Ragtime; Daniel; Yentl.

Bway inc: The Shadow Box; Evita (Tony-supp-1980); Sunday in the Park with George.

TV inc: That Thing on ABC; Charleston.

PATRICK, John (nee Goggin): Wri. b. Louisville, KY, May 17, 1905. e. Holy Cross Coll, Columbia U. Films inc: Educating Father; 36 Hours To Live; Time Out for Romance; International Settlement; The President's Lady; Three Coins in a Fountain; Love is a Many Splendored Thing; The Teahouse of the August Moon; High Society; Les Girls; Some Came Running; The World of Suzie Wong; Gigot; The Main Attraction (& prod); Shoes of the Fisherman. Plays inc: Hell Freezes Over; The Hasty Heart; The Teahouse of the August Moon *(Pulitzer Prize & Tony*-1954); Good as Gold; Everybody's Girl; Scandal Point; A Barrelful of Pennies; Love Is a Time of Day; Opal Is a Diamond; Macbeth Did It; A Bad Year for Tomatoes; Noah's Animals; Enigma (& dir).

PATTERSON, Lorna: Act. b. Whittier, CA, Jul 1, 1957. e. Rio Hondo Coll. Trained at LA Civic Light Opera's Musical Theater workshop. TV inc: Working Stiffs; The Goodtime Girls; Sidney Shorr; Osmond Family Holiday Special; The Book of Lists (co-host); Private Benjamin; The Imposter; The Flying Doctors.
Films inc: Airplane!.

PAUL, M.B. (ne Bloomfield): Cin-Dir. b. Montreal, Sep 30, 1909. e. St. Paul U. Newsreel, publicity, picture service, 1925-30; Part. Seymour Studious, 1930-33; Film test biz own studio, Hollywood, 1933-35. Oscar 1949, for the first successful large-area seamless translucent backgrounds. Designed, patented, Scenoramic process, 1965. Sceno 360 surround system development. Sidney Sheldon's Bloodline.

PAULEY, Jane: TV Newscaster. b. Indianapolis, IN, Oct 31, 1950. e. IN U, BA. W of Garry Trudeau. Reporter WISH-TV, Indianapolis, 1972; anchor WMAQ-TV, Chicago, 1975; joined NBC Today show, Oct. 1976 after Barbara Walters left show. TV inc: Women, Work And Babies...Can America Cope? (& wri).

PAULSEN, Albert: Act. b. Guayaquil, Ecuador, Dec 13, 1929. Bway inc: Night Circus; Three Sisters; Only Game in Town.
Films inc: The Manchurian Candidate; Gunn; Che!; The Amazing Mrs Pollifax; The Laughing Policeman; The Next Man; Eyewitness.
TV inc: A Day in the Life of Ivan Denisovich *(Emmy*-1964); Side Show; The African Queen. Ryan's Four.

PAULSEN, Pat: Comedian. Featured on Smothers Brothers Comedy Show *(Emmy*-special-1968). TV inc: Pat Paulsen Show; You Had To Be There; The Palace; Tom and Dick Smothers Brothers Special I.
Films inc: Ellie; Night patrol.

PAVAN, Marisa (nee Pierangeli): Act. b. Cagliari, Sardinia, Jun 19, 1932. Sis of Pier Angeli. In US from 1950. Films inc: What Price Glory?; Down Three Dark Streets; The Rose Tattoo; The Man in the Grey Flannel Suit; The Midnight Story; Solomon and Sheba; John Paul Jones; Stella Emigranti (Wandering Stars).

PAVAROTTI, Luciano: Lyric Tenor. b. Modena, Italy, Oct 20, 1935. Former teacher and insurance salesman; operatic debut 1961 in La Boheme.
Operas inc: Lucia de Lammermoor; Rigoletto; Daughter of the Regiment; guest artist at La Scala; Vienna Staatsopera; Metropolitan Opera; San Francisco Opera; Paris Opera; Chicago Opera.
Recordings inc: Hits from Lincoln Center *(Grammy*-class voc-1978); O Sole Mio *(Grammy*-class voc-1979); Live from Lincoln Center *(Grammy*-class voc-1981).
TV inc: La Gioconda *(Emmy*-1980); Entertainer of the Year Awards; Pavarotti and Friends; Pavarotti in Philadelphia--La Boheme *(Emmy*-1983).
Films inc: Yes, Giorgio.

PAVLIK, John Michael: Exec. b. Melrose, IA, Dec 3, 1939. e. U of MN, BA. Joined Association of Motion Picture and Television Prod, 1968, as asst dir of PR; then dir of PR, 1972; vp 1978-79; resigned to become exec administrator Academy of Motion Picture Arts and Sciences, 1979; April 1982 named exec dir Motion Picture & Television Fund.

PAXTON, John: Wri. b. Kansas City, MO, Mar 21, 1911. e. U of MO. Films inc: Murder My Sweet; Cornered; So Well Remembered; Crossfire; Crack-up; Rope of Sand; Fourteen Hours; The Cobweb; How to

Murder a Rich Uncle; On the Beach; Kotch.
(Died Jan. 5, 1985)

PAYCHECK, Johnny: Act-Sngwri. b. OH, May 31, 1941. Country mus recording artist. Started as a sngwri; later sang background for recording artists, then solo. TV inc: The Hawk.
Thea inc: There Must Be a Pony; Blood and Thunder; Comes a Day; Films inc: Hells Angels Forever.

PAYNE, John: Act. b. Roanoke, VA, May 23, 1912. On screen from 1936 in Dodsworth. Films inc: Wings of the Navy; To the Shores of Tripoli; Indianapolis Speedway; The Great Profile; Tin Pan Alley; The Great American Broadcast; Moon Over Miami; Footlight Serenade; Iceland; Springtime In The Rockies; Hello, Frisco, Hello; Sentimental Journey; The Razor's Edge; Miracle On 34th Street; The Saxon Charm; The Edge and the Hawk; The Vanquished; Hold Back the Night; Hidden Fear; They Ran For Their Lives; The Savage Wild.
TV inc: Gunsmoke; Columbo.
Thea inc: Good News.

PEARL, Minnie (Sarah Ophelia Cannon): Singer-Act. b. Centerville, TN, Oct 25, 1912. With Grand Ole Opry since 1940. TV inc: Grand Ole Opry; Jubilee USA; HeeHaw; A Country Christmas, 1979; George Burns In Nashville?; A Country Christmas, 1980; Country Comes Home; Johnny Cash and the Country Girls; A Country Christmas, 1981; The Christmas Legend of Nashville; On Stage, America.
Albums inc: Minnie Pearl; Minnie Pearl at the Party; Answer to Giddyup and Go.

PECK, Gregory: Act. b. La Jolla, CA, Apr 5, 1916. On screen from 1944 in Days of Glory. Films inc: The Keys of the Kingdom; The Yearling; Gentleman's Agreement; Paradine Case; Twelve O'Clock High; The Valley of Decision; Spellbound; Duel in the Sun; The Macomber Affair; The Paradine Case; The Gunfighter; David and Bathsheba; Captain Horatio Hornblower; The Snows of Kilimajaro; Roman Holiday; The Man in the Gray Flannel Suit; Moby Dick; The Big Country (& co-prod); Pork Chop Hill; On The Beach; Beloved Infidel; The Guns of Navarone; To Kill A Mockingbird *(Oscar*-1962); Captain Newman, MD; How the West Was Won; Arabesque; Mackenna's Gold; The Chairman; Marooned; The Stalking Moon; I Walk the Line; Billy Two Hats; The Omen; MacArthur; The Boys From Brazil; The Sea Wolves. (Prod) Trial of the Catonsville Nine; The Dove.
(Jean Hersolt Humanitarian Award-1967).
TV inc: A Holiday Tribute to Radio City Music Hall; The Blue and the Gray; The Scarlet and the Black; Olympic Gala.

PECKINPAH, Sam: Dir. b. Fresno, CA, Feb 21, 1925. e. USC, MA. Produced, directed shows for the Huntington Park Theatre near LA. Wrote for TV series Gunsmoke. Continued in TV as prod, dir, wri on such series as Broken Arrow; Tales of Wells Fargo; The Westerner; The Rifleman; Route 66; The Dick Powell Theatre.
Films inc: Deadly Companions; Ride the High Country; Major Dundee; The Wild Bunch; The Ballad of Cable Hogue; Straw Dogs; The Getaway; Pat Garrett and Billy The Kid; Bring Me The Head of Alfredo Garcia; The Killer Elite; Cross of Iron; Convoy; Il Visitatore (The Visitor); The Osterman Weekend.
(Died Dec. 28, 1984)

PEERCE, Jan (Jacob Pincus Perelmuth): Tenor. b. NYC, 1904. F of Larry Peerce. Originally a violinist, playing with pickup bands, worked Borscht belt; hired by Roxy Rothafel as singer at Radio City Music Hall; appeared on Roxy Sunday radio shows; starred at NY Paramount; started "tabloid" versions of opera at Music Hall, remaining there 10 seasons and appearing on Music Hall of Air; started concert career 1937; debuted Metropolitan Opera House 1941. Bway inc: Fiddler on the Roof.
(Died Dec. 15, 1984)

PEERCE, Larry: Wri-Dir. b. NYC. S of the late Jan Peerce. Films inc: One Potato, Two Potato; The Incident; Goodbye Columbus; The Sporting Club; A Separate Peace; Ash Wednesday; The Other Side of the Mountain; Two Minute Warning; The Other Side of the Mountain Part II; The Bell Jar; Why Would I Lie?; Love Child.
TV inc: I Take These Men; Love Lives On.

PELIKAN, Lisa: Act. b. Berkeley, CA. Studied at Juilliard. Thea inc:

Dynamo; Spring Awakening; Elephant in the House.

TV inc: The Country Girl; The Blue Hotel; Beacon Hill; Valley Forge; Perfect Gentlemen; True Grit; I Want to Keep My Baby; The Best of Families; James at 15; The Last Convertible; Studs Lonigan; The Women's Room; A Bunny's Tale.

Films inc: Julia; Jennifer; Labrynth; The House of God; Swing Shift; Ghoulies.

PENDERGRASS, Teddy: Mus-Singer. b. Philadelphia, Mar 26, 1950. Drummer with various groups, became lead singer with reorganized Blue Notes 1970; solo 1977. Albums inc: Teddy Pendergrass; Life Is A Song Worth Singing; Teddy; TP.

Films inc: Soup For One; Choose Me.

PENDLETON, Austin: Act. b. Warren, OH, Mar 27, 1940. e. Yale U. Thea inc: Oh Dad, Poor Dad, Mama's Hung You in the Closet and I'm Feelin' So Sad; Fiddler on the Roof; Hail Scrawdyke!; The Little Foxes; The Last Sweet Days of Isaac; American Glands; An American Millionaire; The Runner Stumbles; Say Goodnight Gracie (dir); John Gabriel Borkman (dir); The Little Foxes (rev) (dir) (also London); Doubles.

Films inc: What's Up Doc?; Every Little Crook and Nanny; The Thief Who Came to Dinner; The Front Page; The Great Smokey Roadblock; Starting Over; The Muppet Movie; Simon; First Family; Talk To Me.

TV inc: Alice in Wonderland; Masquerade.

PENE Du BOIS, Raoul: Dsgn. b. NYC, Nov 29, 1914. First des in NY were costumes for Life Begins at 8:40, 1934. Bway inc: Jumbo; The Ziegfeld Follies; Du Barry Was a Lady; Panama Hattie; Carmen Jones; Heaven on Earth; Lend an Ear; Call Me Madam; Wonderful Town (*Tony*-sets-1953); Plain and Fancy; Bells Are Ringing; The Student Gypsy; Maurice Chevalier; P.S. I Love You; Rain; Irene; No, No, Nanette (*Tony*-costumes-1971); Gypsy; Dr. Jazz; Sugar Babies. Also des for The Ballet Russe de Monte Carlo.

Films inc: Louisiana Purchase; Lady in the Dark; Dixie.

(Died Jan. 1, 1985)

PENN, Arthur: Dir. b. Philadelphia, Sep 27, 1922. e. Black Mountain Coll, Ashville, NC; Universities of Perugia and Florence, Italy. Began stage career as actor, Neighborhood Playhouse, Philadelphia, 1940. Dir first Bway prodn, Two for the Seesaw, 1958, Thea inc: The Miracle Worker (*Tony*-1960); Toys in the Attic; An Evening with Mike Nichols and Elaine May; Golden Boy; Wait Until Dark; The Sly Fox; Monday After the Miracle.

Films inc: The Left-Handed Gun; The Miracle Worker; Mickey One (& prod); Bonnie and Clyde; Alice's Restaurant; Little Big Man; Visions of Eight; Night Moves; The Missouri Breaks; Four Friends (& prod).

TV inc: Man on a Mountain; The Miracle Worker.

PENN, Bill: Act-Prod-Dir. b. Reading, PA, Jun 15, 1931. e. Franklin and Marshall Coll, UCLA. Bway debut 1953, The Fifth Season. Toured in Stalag 17. Since 1958, dir, prod. Thea inc: The Potting Shed; Fugue for Three Marys; The Women at the Tomb; Susannah and the Elders; The Bible Salesman; Tobacco Road; Medium Rare; The Miracle; Double Entry; Bartleby; Put It In Writing; Three Cheers for the Tired Businessman; That Thing at the Cherry Lane; By Hex.

PENN, Christopher B of Sean Penn. Films inc: Act. Rumble Fish; All The Right Moves; Footloose; The Wild Life; Pale Rider.

PENN, Sean: Act. b. Santa Monica, CA 1960. B of Christopher Penn. Bway inc: Heartland; Slab Boys.

TV inc: Hellinger's Law; The Killing of Randy Webster.

Films inc: Taps; Fast Times at Ridgemont High; Bad Boys; Crackers; Racing With the Moon; The Falcon And The Snowman.

PENNY, Joe: Act. b. London, England. Studied with Lee Strasberg. TV inc: The Nancy Drew Mysteries; Samurai; The Gangster Chronicles; Flamingo Road; Delta County; Death Moon; The Gossip Columnist; Savage--In the Orient; Riptide.

Films inc: Our Winning Season; S.O.B.; Happy Birthday.

PEPPARD, George: Act-Prod-Dir. b. Detroit, Oct 1, 1928. e. Carnegie Mellon Institute, BFA. Early experience on stage. Screen debut

1957, The Strange One. Films inc: Pork Chop Hill; Home from the Hill; Breakfast at Tiffany's; How the West Was Won; The Victors; The Carpetbaggers; The Blue Max; Tobruk; Rough Night In Jericho; What's So Bad About Feeling Good?; Pendulum; The Executioner; Cannon for Cordoba; One More Train to Rob; The Groundstar Conspiracy; Newman's Law; Damnation Alley; Five Days from Home; From Hell to Victory (& prod-dir); Battle Beyond the Stars; Race to the Yankee Zephyr; Target Eagle.

TV inc: The Bravos; One of Our Own; Guilty or Innocent; The Sam Sheppard Murder Case; Banacek; Doctors Hospital; Torn Between Two Lovers; Twilight Theatre; The A-Team; Hollywood Stars' Screen Tests (host).

PEPPER, Buddy (Jack R. Starkey): Sngwri-sing-act. b. LaGrange, KY, April 21, 1922. Radio debut age 5 as pianist-singer-actor; won Major Bowes Sngwri-Singer-Mus-Act. Portrait in Black; Sorry; Oldham County Line. Amateur Hour Contest at 13; in vaude before films; subsequently conductor-arranger for top singing acts inc Judy Garland, Marlene Dietrich, Lisa Kirk, Margaret Whiting, Jane Russell, Gordon MacRae.

Films inc: (Act) Golden Hoofs; Small Town Deb; The Reluctant Dragon; Seventeen; Men of Boys Town. (Sngwri)Top Man; This Is the Life; Rhythm of the Islands; Follow the Boys; The Hucksters; The Winning Team; Pillow Talk; Portrait in Black.

Songs inc: Vaya Con Dios; The Champion Strut; Don't Tell Me; Pillow Talk;

PERENCHIO, Jerry (Andrew Jerrold Perenchio): Exec. b. Fresno, CA, Dec 20, 1930. e. UCLA. Started as agent; 1958 vp MCA; 1962 vp GAC; 1964 formed Chartwell Artists; 1973 bd chmn Tandem Productions/TAT Communications; also pres ON TV; Nov 1981, with Norman Lear, bought Avco-Embassy, changed name to Embassy Communications; April 1983, P & CEO Embassy Pictures.

PERKINS, Anthony: Act. b. NYC, Apr 14, 1932. e. Columbia U; Rollins Coll. S of late Osgood Perkins. Screen debut, 1953, The Actress. Films inc: Friendly Persuasion; The Lonely Man; Fear Strikes Out; The Tin Star; This Bitter Earth; Desire Under the Elms; The Matchmaker; Green Mansions; On the Beach; Tall Story; Psycho; Goodbye Again; Phaedra; The Trial; The Fool Killer; Is Paris Burning?; The Champagne Murders; Pretty Poison; Catch-22; Someone Behind the Door; Ten Days' Wonder; WUSA; Play It As It Lays; Lovin' Molly; Murder on the Orient Express; Mahogany; Remember My Name; Winter Kills; Tree Vrouwen; The Black Hole; ffolkes; Double Negative; Psycho II; Crimes of Passion.

Thea inc: Greenwillow; Look Homeward Angel; Steambath (& dir); Equus; Romantic Comedy.

TV inc: Kraft Theatre; Studio One; US Steel Hour; Armstrong Theatre; First You Cry; Les Miserables; For The Term of his Natural Life; The Sins of Dorian Gray; The Glory Boys.

PERKINS, Jack: TV newscaster b. Cleveland, OH. e. Western Reserve U, BA. Started at WGAR, Cleveland while still in college; later, news dir WEWS-TV, Cleveland; joined NBC 1961 as global corr; 1965, Hong Kong Bureau; 1967 to NBC West Coast Bureau; 1983-April 1984, anchor KNBC; June 1984, commentator KNBC. TV inc: Prime Time Saturday; NBC Magazine with David Brinkley; Heart Transplant (*Emmy*-corr-1980); Teen Models (*Emmy*-corr-1981); Solar Eclipse--A Darkness at Noon; The Perkins Pieces; Prison Benefits; Getting Straight.

PERKINS, Millie: Act. b. 1939. Films inc: The Diary of Anne Frank; Wild in the Country; Ensign Pulver; Wild in the Streets; Cockfighter; Lady Cocoa; The Witch Who Came From The Sea; Table for Five; George Stevens--A Filmmaker's Journey (doc-int).

TV inc: The Trouble With Grandpa; The Haunting Passion; License to Kill; Anatomy of an Illness; Shattered Vows; A.D.

PERLMAN, Itzhak: Concert violinist. b. Tel Aviv, Aug 31, 1945. e. Juilliard. Guest soloist with Indianapolis Symphony; NY Philharmonic; National Symphony; Philadelphia Orchestra; Baltimore Symphony; Cleveland Orchestra; Buffalo Symphony; major festivals.

(*Grammys*-(10)-class inst-1977, 1980, 1981; class inst with orch (3)-1977, 1980, 1982; class album of year-1978; chamber mus perf-1978, 1980, 1981).

TV inc: John Denver--Music and the Mountains; Live From Lincoln

Center-An Evening With Itzhak Perlman and the N.Y. Philharmonic; Kennedy Center Honors 1984; The TV Academy Hall Of Fame 1985.

PERLMAN, Rhea: Act. b. Brooklyn, March 31. E. Hunter College. W. of Danny DeVito. TV inc: Mary Jane Harper Cried Last Night; I Want To Keep My Baby; Intimate Strangers; Having Babies II; Taxi; Drop Out Father; Cheers *(Emmy-supp-1984)*; The Ratings Game (cable).
   Films inc: Love Child.

PERLMUTTER, David M.: Prod. b. Toronto, Sep 22, 1934. e. U of Toronto. P, Quadrant Films Ltd. Films inc: The Neptune Factor; Dead of Night; Blue Blood; Sunday in the Country; It Seemed Like a Good Idea at the Time; Love at First Sight; Find the Lady; Blood and Guts; Nothing Personal; Double Negative.

PERRINE, Valerie: Act. b. Galveston, TX, Sep 3, 1943. Performed as showgirl in Las Vegas. Screen debut, 1972, Slaughterhouse Five. Films inc: The Last American Hero; Lenny; W.C. Fields and Me; Mr. Billion; Superman; The Electric Horseman; Magician of Lublin; Can't Stop The Music; Superman II; Agency; The Border; Water.
   TV inc: Marion Rose White; It's Not Easy Bein' Me--The Rodney Dangerfield Show; Malibu; When Your Lover Leaves.

PERRY, Barbara: Act. Films inc: Period of Adjustment; From the Terrace; I Was a Male War Bride; The Mirage; Maybe I'll be Home in the Spring; Thief; Opening Night.
   TV inc: Family Affair; Andy Griffith Show; Side By Side; I Take These Men.
   Thea inc: Rumple; Happy as Larry; Swan Song; If the Shoe Fits; Passionate Ladies (& wri).

PERRY, Frank: Dir. b. 1930. Films inc: David and Lisa; Ladybug, Ladybug; The Swimmer; Trilogy; Last Summer; Diary of a Mad Housewife; Doc; Play It as it Lays; Man on a Swing; Rancho de Luxe; Mommie Dearest; Monsignor.
   Thea inc: Ladies at the Alamo (dir).
   TV inc: Skag; The Dummy; JFK--A One Man Show.

PERRY, John Bennett: Act. b. Williamstown, MA, Jan 4, 1941. e. St Lawrence U. Lead singer with Serendipity Singers before act. Thea inc: (tours) Irma La Douce; Annie Get Your Gun; Hello, Dolly!; Leonard Bernstein's Mass.
   Films inc: Midway; Lipstick; The Legend of the Lone Ranger; Only When I Laugh.
   TV inc: EveryDay (host); 240-Robert; Singin (Love Songs) (cable); Tales of the Apple Dumpling Gang; Money on the Side; I Married Wyatt Earp.

PERSKY, Bill: Wri-Dir. b. New Haven, CT, 1931. e. Syracuse. Ad writer, teamed with Sam Denoff (1953), writing nitery acts, then tv; partnership lasted 21 years.
   TV inc: Steve Allen Show; Andy Williams Show; Dick Van Dyke Show (& prod) *(Emmys-wri-1964, 1966)*; Sid Caesar-Imogene Coca-Carl Reiner-Howard Morris Special *(Emmy-1967)*; McHale's Navy; Dick Van Dyke and the Other Woman (& prod); The First Nine Months Are the Hardest (crea-prod); Pure Goldie (& prod); Confessions of Dick Van Dyke (prod); The Funny Side (crea-exec prod); Don Rickles Show (crea-exec prod); Lotsa Luck (crea-exec prod); That Girl (crea-exec prod); Bill Cosby Special; The Man Who Came To Dinner. Since splitting with Denoff, dir Big City Boys; Joe and Valerie; How to Survive the 70's and Maybe Even Bump Into Happiness; The Single Life; My Wife Next Door; Love at First Sight; Comedy of Horrors; Rise and Shine; Just Wait Till Your Mother Gets Home; Johnny Garage (& title song); Sutters Bay; Trackdown--Finding the Goodbar Killer; Found Money; Kate & Allie (& prod) *(Emmy-dir-1984)*; Not in Front of the Kids (dir); Who's The Boss? (dir); Spencer (dir).
   Films inc: Water (wri).

PERSKY, Lester: Prod. b. NYC, Jul 6, 1927. e. Brooklyn Coll. Former ad agcy owner. Formed Persky-Bright organization which financed indie films, company then became Persky-Bright Prodns.
   Films inc: Fortune and Men's Eyes; Equus; Hair; Yanks.
   TV inc: Almost Heaven.

PERSOFF, Nehemiah: Act. b. Israel, Aug 14, 1920. e. Hebrew Tech Inst. Films inc: On the Waterfront; The Harder They Fall; The Angry Age; Never Steal Anything Small; Al Capone; Some Like It Hot; The Big Show; The Hook; Fate is the Hunter; The Greatest Story Ever Told; Panic in the City; Red Sky at Morning; Psychic Killer; In Search of Historic Jesus; O'Hara's Wife; Yentl.
   Thea inc: Only in America; Galileo; Richard III; Peter Pan; Peer Gynt; Tiger at the Gates.
   TV inc: The Word; Greatest Heroes of the Bible; A Cry For Justice; The Rebels; The French Atlantic Affair; The Thirteenth Day-The Story of Esther; B.A.D. Cats; F.D.R-The Last Year; The Henderson Monster; Turnover Smith; Condominium; Sadat.

PERTWEE, Michael: Wri. b. London, Apr 24, 1916. Plays inc: Death on the Table; The Paragon; It's Different for Men; She's Done It Again; Don't Just Lie There, Say Something; A Bit Between the Teeth; Birds of Paradise; Six of One; Ace in a Hole.
   Films inc: Silent Dust; The Interrupted Journey; Daughter in Paradise; The Naked Truth; The Mouse on the Moon; Ladies Who Do; A Funny Thing Happened on the Way to the Forum; Finders Keepers; The Magnificent Two; Salt and Pepper; One More Time; Digby the Biggest Dog in the World.
   TV inc: The Paragon; Chain Male; Strictly Personal; The Firghtened Man; Never a Cross Word; Men of Affairs.

PESCI, Joe: Act. b. Newark, NJ., Feb. 9, 1943. On radio as child performer. Films inc: The Death Collector; Raging Bull; I'm Dancing As Fast As I Can; Dear Mr. Wonderful; Eureka; Easy Money; Once Upon A Time In America; Tutti Dentro (Put 'Em All In Jail).
   TV inc: Half Nelson.

PESCOW, Donna: Act. b. NYC, Mar 24, 1954. Films inc: Saturday Night Fever. TV inc: Angie; Advice to the Lovelorn; The Day the Bubble Burst; Policewoman Centerfold; Obsessed With A Married Woman.

PETER, PAUL, AND MARY: Trio. Members are Peter Yarrow, Noel Paul Stookey and Mary Travers; Films inc: In Our Hands (doc). Recs inc: If I Had a Hammer *(Grammys-group & folk-1962)*; Blowin' In the Wind *(Grammys-group & folk-1963)*; Peter Paul and Mommy *(Grammy-children-1969)*; Puff the Magic Dragon; Reunion.

PETERS, Bernadette: Act. b. NYC, Feb 28, 1944. Professional debut at age 5 on TV's Horn and Hardart Children's Hour. Also on Juvenile Jury, Name That Tune. Legit deubt NY City Center production The Most Happy Fella. At age 13 toured in Gypsy, playing Baby June. Other thea inc: Sunday in the Park with George.
   Films inc: Ace Eli and Rodger of the Skies; W.C. Fields & Me; Vigilante Force; The Silent Movie; The Jerk; Tulips; Pennies From Heaven; Heartbeeps; Annie.
   TV inc: All's Fair; They Said It With Music; Sha Na Na; The Tim Conway Special; A Mac Davis Special Christmas Odyssey; The Martian Chronicles; The Starmakers; Lonely Man; House of Numbers; Ten Seconds to Hell; Warriors Five; Party at Annapolis; Texaco Star Theatre--Opening Night; George Burns & Other Sex Symbols; Rich, Thin & Beautiful (host); Night Of 100 Stars II.

PETERS, Brock: Act. b. NYC, Jul 2, 1927. Films inc: Carmen Jones; Porgy and Bess; To Kill a Mockingbird; Major Dundee; The Pawnbroker; The Incident; P.J.; Daring Game; Ace High; The McMasters; Black Girl; Soylent Green; Framed; Lost in the Stars; Two-Minute Warning; Joe Louis--For All Time (doc-narr).
   Thea inc: King of the Dark Chamber; Othello; The Great White Hope; Lost in the Stars; Framed.
   TV inc: It Takes a Thief; Judd for the Defense; Felony Squad; Gunsmoke; Mannix; Mod Squad; Welcome Home, Johnny Bristol; The Incredible Journey of Doctor Meg Laurel; Mark Twain's America--Abe Lincoln, Freedom Fighter; Adventures of Huckleberry Finn; Denmark Vesey's Rebellion; A Caribbean Mystery.

PETERS, Jean: Act. b. Canton, OH, Oct 15, 1926. Gave up career 1957 to marry Howard Hughes. Div 1971. On screen from 1947. Films inc: The Captain from Castile; Deep Waters; It Happens Every Spring; Anne of the Indies; Wait Till the Sun Shines, Nellie; Take Care of My Little Girl; As Young as You Feel; Viva Zapata; Lure of the Wilderness; O'Henry's Full House; Niagara; Pickup on South Street; Blueprint for Murder; Vicki; Three Coins in the Fountain; Apache; Broken Lance; A Man Called Peter.

TV inc: Winesburg, Ohio; Peter and Paul.

PETERS, Jon: Prod. b. Van Nuys, CA, 1947. Started local hair-styling business, built it into multi-million dollar corporation before turning prod with Jon Peters Organization; 1980 joined with Peter Guber, Neil Bogart to form new entity, The Boardwalk Co; Partnership dissolved June, 1981.

Films inc: A Star Is Born; The Eyes of Laura Mars; The Main Event; Die Laughing; Caddyshack; An American Werewolf In London (exec prod); Six Weeks; Flashdance (exec prod); D.C. Cab (exec prod); Vision Quest.

TV inc: Parole (act); Television and the Presidency (exec prod); Double Platinum (exec prod); Dreams (exec prod); The Toughest Man In the World (exec prod).

PETERS, Roberta: Opera Singer-Act. b. NYC, May 4, 1930. Soloist with Metropolitan Opera since 1951; with Royal Opera-Covent Garden; Salzburg Festival; Vienna State Opera; Munich Opera; Berlin Opera; Kirov Opera (Leningrad); Bolshoi Opera; frequent guest tv appearances.

PETERSDORF, Rudy: Exec. b. Germany, Jan 24, 1930. e. UC Berkeley, LLB. 1955 with Capitol Records legal dept; 1957, vp bus aff Desilu Prodns; 1963 vp bus aff U; 1978, vp bus aff WB; 1980 P Australian Film Office; April 1981 became vp bus aff Filmways.

PETERSEN, Wolfgang: Dir. b. Emden, Germany, March 14, 1941. e. Berlin Film & Television Academy. Began career as stage dir Ernst Deutsch Theatre, Hamburg. Began dir for German TV in 1970. TV inc: Ich Werde Dich Toten Wolf (I Will Kill You Wolf); Anna And Toto; Strandgut (Debris); Nachtfrost (Night Frost); Jagdrevier (Hunting Ground); Smog; Kurzschluss (Short Circuit); Reifezeugnis (For Your Love Only); Van der Valk And The Rich; Einer von uns Beiden (One Of Us Two); Aufs Kreuz gelegt (Pinned Down); Stadt im Tal (City In The Valley); Stellenweiss Glatteis (Beware Of Slippery Ice); Hans In Luck; Wir Gegen die Bank (We're Going To The Bank); Planuebung (Mock Exercise).

Films inc: Schwarz Und Weiss wie Tage Und Naecht (Black And White Like Days And Nights); Die Konsequenz (The Consequence)(& wri); Das Boot (The Boat)(& wri); The Neverending Story (& wri).

PETERSON, Arthur: Act. b. Mandan, ND, Nov 18, 1912. e. U of MN. Began on radio in hundreds of dramas inc original Guiding Light. Films inc: Call Northside 777.

TV inc: That's O'Toole (& crea); Soap.

PETERSON, Oscar: Mus. b. Montreal, Canada, Aug 15, 1925. With Johnny Holmes Orch in Canada; with Jazz at the Philharmonic; toured U.S. & Europe; established own trio with Ray Brown, Irving Ashby.

(Grammys-(4)-jazz group-1974; jazz soloist 1977, 1978, 1979).

PETHERBRIDGE, Edward: Act. b. Yorkshire, England, Aug 3, 1936. With various rep groups, provincial tours before London debut. Thea inc: Midsummer Night's Dream; All In Good Time; with the National Theatre Company 1964-1970 in Rosencrantz and Guildenstern are Dead; The Soldier's Tale; The Misanthrope; Lulu; Morality; John Bull's Other Island; Swan Song; founder member of the Actors Company; Phantom of the Opera; Tartuffe; The Bacchae (& dir); Do You Love Me (& dir); The Importance of Being Earnest; Game of Kings; Is There Honey Still for Tea?; Crucifer of Blood; Nicholas Nickleby; The Suicide; Strange Interlude (Bway).

TV inc: The Soldier's Tale; After Magritte; A True Patriot; Schubert; Pyramid of Fire; The Life And Adventures of Nicholas Nickelby; King Lear; Pericles, Prince of Tyre.

PETIT, Pascale (Anne-Marie Petit): Act. b. Paris, Feb 27, 1938. Films inc: The Witches of Salem; The Cheaters; Women Are Weak; Girls for the Summer; Demons at Midnight; Cross of the Living; The Last Mercenary; Four Times That Night; A Strange Love Affair.

PETIT, Roland: Chor. b. Paris, Jan 13, 1924. e. Paris Opera Ballet School. H of Rene Jeanmaire. Premier Danseur Paris Opera 1940-41; founder Les Vendredis de la Danse; Les Ballets de Champs Elysees; Les Ballets de Paris; Les Ballets de Marseille; dir Paris Opera

Ballet 1970; Chor revival of Can-Can on Bway 1981.

Chor works inc: Le Rossignol et la Rose; Le Demoiselles de la nuit; Le Loup; Cyrano de Bergerac; Carmen; Hans Christian Anderson; Folies Bergere; Paradise Lost; Pelleas et Melisande.

PETITCLERC, Denne Bart: Wri. b. Montesano, WA, May 15, 1929. Former newspaper reporter. TV inc: Bonanza; High Chaparral; Shane; Along Came Bronson; The Cowboy and the Ballerina.

Films inc: Red Sun; Islands in the Stream.

PETRIE, Ann (Margaret Ann Petrie): Wri-Prod-Dir. b. Windsor, Ont, Canada, May 15, 1939. e. U of Guanajuato, Mexico, MA. TV inc: (field prod) People, Places, Things; That's Incredible; Those Amazing Animals; The Future--What's Next. (Wri-Prod-Dir) The World of Mother Teresa.

PETRIE, Daniel: Dir. b. Glace Bay, Nova Scotia, Nov 26, 1920. e. St. Francis Xavier U, BA; Columbia U, MA. Films inc: The Bramble Bush; A Raisin in the Sun; Stolen Hours; The Idol; The Spy with a Cold Nose; Buster and Billie; Lifeguard; The Betsy; Resurrection; Fort Apache, The Bronx; Six Pack; Bay Boy (& sp); Into The Night (act).

TV inc: Eleanor and Franklin (Emmy-1976); Sybil; Eleanor and Franklin-The White House Years (Emmy-1977); Harry Truman-Plain Speaking; The Dollmaker.

PETTET, Joanna: Act. b. Nov 16, 1944. Films inc: The Group; Night of the Generals; Robbery; Blue; The Evil; Othello (Black Commando).

TV inc: The Weekend Nun; Captains and the Kings; The Return of Frank Cannon; Knots Landing.

PETTIT, Tom: Newsman-Exec. b. Cincinnati, OH. e. U Northern IA, BA; U of MN, MA. Began as reporter WOI-TV, Cedar Rapids, IA; joined NBC 1959 as reporter WRCV, Philadelphia; to NBC LA Bureau 1962; 1968, West Coast correspondent Public Broadcast Laboratory of National Educational Television; 1969 retd to NBC; with NBC News Washington, 1975; 1982, exec vp NBC News.

TV inc: CBW--The Secrets of Secrecy (Emmy-1969); Some Footnotes to 25 Nuclear Years (Emmy-1970); Between Two Rivers; The Business of Blood; America's Nerve Gas Arsenal (Emmy-1974).

PEVNEY, Joseph: Dir. b. NYC 1920. Former vaudevillian-actor. Films inc: (Act) Nocturne, Outside the Wall; Street With No Name; Body and Soul; Thieves Highway. (Dir) Shakedown; Air Cadet; Iron Man; The Lady From Texas; Meet Danny Wilson; Flesh and Fury; Desert Legion; It Happens Every Thursday; Yankee Pasha; Three Ring Circus; Six Bridges to Cross; Foxfire; Away All Boats; Tammy and the Bachelor; The Midnight Man; Man of a Thousand Faces; Twilight for the Gods; Torpedo Run; Cash McCall; The Plunderers (& prod); The Crowded Sky; Portrait of a Mobster; Night of the Grizzly.

TV inc: My Darling Daughters Anniversary; Who Is the Black Dahlia?; Mysterious Island of Beautiful Women; A Contract For Life--The S.A.D.D. Story.

PEYSER, John J.: Wri-Prod-Dir. b. NYC, Aug 10, 1916. e. Colgate U, BA. Films inc: Spain; The Open Door; Kashmiri Run; Four Rode Out; Massacre Harbor.

TV inc: Hawaii 5-O; Mannix; Movin' On; Swiss Family Robinson; Bronk; Combat; The Untouchables; Honeymoon With A Stranger; Rat Patrol; Stunt Seven.

PFEIFFER, Jane C.: Exec. b. Sep 29, 1932. Named Bd chmn NBC and a member of the RCA board Oct 4, 1978; Relieved of duties Jul 9, 1980 by Fred Silverman.

PFEIFFER, Michelle: Act. b. CA., 1962. Films inc: Falling in Love Again; Hollywood Knights; Charlie Chan and the Curse of the Dragon Queen; Grease II; Scarface; Into The Night; Ladyhawke.

TV inc: Delta House; B.A.D. Cats; Callie and Son; The Children That Nobody Wanted; Splendor in the Grass; One Too Many.

PFLUG, Jo Ann: Act. Films inc: M*A*S*H; Catlow; Where Does It Hurt? TV inc: Shakespeare Loves Rembrandt; The Day The Women Got Even; The Fall Guy; Rituals.

PHILIPS, Lee: Dir. b. Brooklyn. Started as act. TV inc: (Act) Marty; 12 Angry Men; Ellery Queen. (Dir) Dick Van Dyke Show; Andy Griffith

Show; The Waltons; Red Badge of Courage; Sweet Hostage; The War Between the Tates; Louis Armstrong--Chicago Style; James A Michener's Dynasty; The Comedy Company; Hard Hat and Legs; A Special Kind of Love; Valentine (co-wri); Crazy Times; A Wedding On Walton's Mountain; Mae West; Inspector Perez; Lottery!; Happy; Samson and Delilah; Space.

Films inc: (Act) Peyton Place; The Hunters. (Dir) On the Right Track.

PHILLIPS, Julia: Prod. b. NYC. e. Mt. Holyoke College. Films inc: Steelyard Blues; The Sting *(Oscar-1973)*; Taxi Driver; The Big Bus; Close Encounters Of The Third Kind.

PHILLIPS, MacKenzie: Act. b. Richmond, VA, Nov 10, 1959. Screen debut, 1973, American Graffiti. Films inc: The Converstation; Rafferty and the Gold Dust Twins; More American Graffiti; Love Child.

TV inc: Go Ask Alice; One Day At A Time; Miles To Go Before I Sleep; Eleanor and Franklin; Moviola (The Silent Lovers).

PHILLIPS, Michael: Prod. b. NYC, Jun 29, 1943. e. Dartmouth Coll, AB; NYU Law School, JD. Films inc: Steelyard Blues; The Sting *(Oscar-1973)*; Taxi Driver; The Big Bus (exec prod); Close Encounters of the Third Kind; Heartbeeps; Cannery Row; The Flamingo Kid.

PHILLIPS, Robert: Act. b. Chicago, Apr 10. e. IN U. Films inc: The Silencers; The Dirty Dozen; Hour of the Gun; MacKenna's Gold; Telefon; Killing of a Chinese Bookie.

PHILLIPS, Wendy: Act. b. NYC, Jan 2, 1952. e. UC Berkeley. Films inc: Fraternity Row. TV inc: Executive Suite; Capra.

PICCOLI, Michel: Act. b. Paris, Dec 27, 1925. Films inc: French Cancan; The Witches of Salem; Le Bal des Espiona; Le Mepris; Diary of a Chambermaid; De L'Amour; Lady L; La Curee; The Young Girls of Rochefort; Un Homme de Trop; Belle de Jour; Diabolik; La Chamade; Dillinger Est Mort; Topaz; L'Invasion; The Last Woman; Leonor; Mado; The Accuser; Le Mors Aux Dents (The Bit Between The Teeth); The Little Girl In Blue Velvet; The Price of Survival; Le Sucre; Le Divorcement; Todo Modo; Salto Nel Vuoto (Leap Into The Void); Atlantic City, USA; La Fille Prodigue (The Prodigal Daughter); Espion Leve-Toi (Rise Up, Spy); Une Etrange Affaire (A Strange Affair); Passion; La Passante du Sans Souci (The Passer-by of the Sans Souci Cafe); Gli ochi, La Bocca (The Eyes, The Mouth); Oltre la Porta (Beyond the Door); Que les gros salaires levent le doigt!!! (Will the High Salaried Workers Please Raise Their Hands); Une Chambre En Ville (A Room in Town); La prix du danger (The Prize of Peril); Le General de l'Armee Morte (The General of the Dead Army) (& prod-wri); Success Is The Best Revenge; Viva La Vie! (Long Live Life!); Peril en la Demeure (Danger In The House); La Diagonale du Fou (Dangerous Moves); Partier Revenir (Departure, Return); Adieu, Bonaparte.

Thea inc: Terre Entrangere (Undiscovered Country).

PICERNI, Paul: Act. b. NYC, Dec 1, 1922. e. Loyola U. Films inc: Breakthrough; I Was a Communist for the FBI; Mara Maru; Desert Song; House of Wax; Omar Khayyam; Strangers When We Meet; The Scalphunters; The Land Raiders; Airport; Kotch; Capricorn One; Beyond the Poseidon Adventure.

TV inc: The Untouchables; Marciano; Alcatraz--The Whole Shocking Story.

PICKENS, Slim (Louis Bert Lindley. Jr): Act. b. Kingsberg, CA, Jun 29, 1919. Rodeo performer 1931-36. On screen from 1940. Films inc: Rocky Mountain; The Boy From Oklahoma; The Outcast; Santa Fe Passage; Last Command; When Gangland Strikes; Stranger at My Door; The Great Locomotive Chase; One-Eyed Jacks; Dr. Strangelove; The Honkers; Pat Garrett and Billy the Kid; Blazing Saddles; Rancho Deluxe; White Line Fever; Mr. Billion; The White Buffalo; The Swarm; Beyond The Poseidon Adventure; Spirit of the Wind; 1941; Tom Horn; Honeysuckle Rose; The Howling; Pink Motel.

TV inc: Bonanza; Mannix; Ironside; Name of the Game; Gunsmoke; Alias Smith and Jones; The Devil and Miss Sarah; Undercover with the KKK; Swan Song; Jake's Way; Charlie and the Great Balloon Chase; The Nashville Grab; The Nashville Palace; Filthy Rich; Sawyer & Finn.

(Died Dec. 8, 1983).

PICKER, David V.: Exec. b. NYC, May 14, 1931. e. Dartmouth, BA. S of Eugene Picker. United Artists, 1956-73; P, 1969-73; P. Paramount, 1976-77; vp Lorimar Prodns. 1979-1981; ind. prod. Films inc: Juggernaut; Lenny; Smile; Royal Flash; Oliver's Story; The One and Only; Sidney Sheldon's Bloodline; The Jerk; Dead Men Don't Wear Plaid; Beat Street; The Goodbye People.

PICKER, Eugene D.: Exec. b. NYC, Nov 17, 1903. e. NYU School of Business. F of David V Picker. Entered film bus with father operating theatres Bronx, NY; joined Loew's, NY 1920; vp Loews Theatres 1954; exec vp 1958; p 1959; to UA as vp 1961; Trans-Lux Corp. Exec vp Jan 1967; p & CEO Sep 1967; formed EDP Fllms 1974.

PICKETT, Cindy: Act. b. Norman, OK., April 18. e. U TX; U of Houston. TV inc: The Guiding Light; Mickey Spillane's Margin For Murder; Ivory Ape; Louis L'Amour's The Cherokee Trail; Cry For The Strangers; Cocaine and Blue Eyes; Family In Blue; Call To Glory.

Films inc: Night Games; Mystique; Hysterical.

PICKMAN, Jerome (Jerry): Exec. b. NYC, Aug. 24, 1916. e. St. John's U, BA; St. Lawrence U, LL B. Originally a reporter on NY newspapers, he turned to adv-pub after WW 2, joining 20th-Fox; 1947, Eagle-Lion; 1949, Paramount; 1951, VP & dir ad-pub Paramount; 1962, VP & dom gen sls mgr; 1963, exec Columbia Pictures; 1967, P Continental Films div of Walter Reade; 1970, P Levitt-Pickman Film Corp; 1979, sr. VP dom dist Lorimar Prodns.

PICON, Molly: Act. b. NYC, Feb 28, 1898. Appeared in vaudeville, Yiddish repertory. On screen from 1937. Films inc: Yiddle and his Fiddle (Poland); Mamale (Poland); Come Blow Your Horn; Fiddler on the Roof; For Pete's Sake; The Cannonball Run.

Bway inc: A Majority of One; Milk and Honey; Dear Me, the Sky Is Falling; Madame Mousse; How to Be a Jewish Mother; Paris Is Out; The Front Page; How Do you Live with Love?; Something Old, Something New.

TV inc: Grandma Didn't Wave Back.

PIDGEON, Walter: Act. b. East St John, NB, Can, Sep 23, 1897. In vaudeville with Elsie Janis prior to appearing on Broadway in You Never Can Tell, 1925. On screen from 1925. Films inc: The Gorilla; Turn Back the Hours; Saratoga; My Dear Miss Aldrich; The Girl of the West; Shopworn Angel; Nick Carter, Master Detective; Man Hunt; How Green Was My Valley; Madame Curie; Mrs. Parkington; Weekend At the Waldorf; Holiday In Mexico; Cass Timberlane; If Winter Come; Command Decision; Soldiers Three, The Bad and the Beautiful; That Forsythe Woman; Mrs. Miniver; Executive Suite; Men of the Fighting Lady; Hit the Deck; Forbidden Planet; Voyage to the Bottom of the Sea; Advise and Consent; Funny Girl; Skyjacked; The Neptune Factor; Harry in Your Pocket; Two Minute Warning.

Thea inc: Take Her She's Mine; Dinner at Eight; The Happiest Millionaire; Take Me Along.

TV inc: Swiss Family Robinson; Meet Me in St. Louis; The Vanishing 400.

(Died Sept. 25, 1984)

PIERCE, Frederick S.: Exec. b. NYC, Apr 8, 1933. e. CCNY. Joined ABC, 1956 as research analyst. Named dir of Sales Planning and Sales Development, 1962; elected vp, 1964; national dir of sales for ABC-TV, 1964-68; vp in charge of planning and asst to the p of ABC-TV until 1972; named p of ABC-TV, 1974; also exec vp ABC Inc, 1979; named P & COO Jan 1983.

PIERSON, Frank: Dir-Wri. b. NYC, May 12, 1925. Films inc: Cat Ballou (co-sp); Cool Hand Luke (sp); The Anderson Tapes (sp); The Looking Glass War (sp & dir); Dog Day Afternoon *(Oscar-sp-1975)*; A Star is Born (sp & dir); King of the Gypsies (sp & dir).

TV inc: Nichols (prod); Haywire (wri).

PIGOTT-SMITH, Tim: Act. b. England, 1946. With Bristol Old Vic, Royal Shakespeare Company. Thea inc: As You Like It; Major Barbara; School For Scandal; Traps; Cymbeline; Sherlock Holmes (& Bway); Titus Andronicus; Antony and Cleopatra; The Benefactors.

TV inc: The Lost Boys; In Hiding; 'Tis Pity She's A Whore; Henry IV Part I; The Day Christ Died; Measure For Measure; The Hunchback of Notre Dame; Fame Is the Spur; Glittering Prizes; Winston Churchill--The Wilderness Years; The Jewel In the Crown.

Films Inc: Man In a Fog; Escape To Victory; Richard's Things; Clash Of the Titans; Joseph Andrews.

PILBROW, Richard: Prod. b. Beckenham, Kent, England, Apr 28, 1933. Former lighting des. Thea inc: (Prod) A Funny Thing Happened on the Way to the Forum; She Loves Me; A Scent of Flowers; Fiddler on the Roof; Cabaret; The Beggar's Opera; She Stoops to Conquer; Edward II; Richard II; Erb; Catch My Soul; Company; I and Albert; The Good Companions; A Little Night Music. (Light) Windy City; Singin' In the Rain.
Films inc: Swallows and Amazons.
TV inc: All You Need Is Love — The Story of Popular Music.

PILSON, Neal H.: Exec. b. 1940. e. Hamilton Coll, AB; Yale Law School, LLB. In private practice, later with Metromedia, then William Morris before joining CBS, 1976, as dir sports business Aff; VP Bus Aff; VP Bus Aff & Admn; Aug 1980, VP & dir Sports Bus Aff; Feb 1981, sr vp Planng & Admn CBS Broadcast Group; Nov 1981, P CBS Sports; Sept. 1983 also exec VP Sports and radio.

PINE, Phillip: Act. b. Hanford, CA, 1925. e. UC Berkeley. Films inc: The Lost Missile; Murder by Contract; Price of Fear; Men in War; Glass Houses.
TV inc: Playhouse 90; Studio One; Stone; The Gift; Enola Gay--The Men, The Mission, The Atomic Bomb.
Thea inc: A Stone for Danny Fisher; The Immoralist; See the Jaguar; One Bright Day.

PINE, Robert: Act. b. Scarsdale, NY, Jul 10, 1941. e. OH Wesleyan U. Films inc: Gunpoint; Young Warriors; Out of Sight; Munster, Go Home; Faceless Man; Journey to Shiloh; Day of the Locust; The Graduate; One Little Indian; The Bears and I; The Apple Dumpling Gang Rides Again.
TV inc: Brotherhood of the Bell; Incident on a Dark Street; Young Prosecutors; CHiPs; Enola Gay--The Men, The Mission, The Atomic Bomb; Insight/Matchpoint.

PINSENT, Gordon: Act. b. Newfoundland, Canada, 1933. Films inc: The Thomas Crown Affair; Colossus--The Forbin Project; The Rowdyman (& wri); Who Has Seen The Wind?; Klondike Fever; Silence of the North; Gordon Pinsent and the Life and Times of Edwin Alonzo Boyd; The Devil At Your Heels (doc) (narr).
TV inc: (Canada) Quentin Durgens MP; A Gift to Last; People Talking Back (host); His Mother. (US) The Suicide's Wife; Escape From Iran--The Canadian Caper; A Case of Libel; Sam Hughes's War (Some Honorable Gentlemen).

PINTER, Harold: Dir-Wri-Act. b. London, Oct 10, 1930. Started as actor; then wri, dir. Plays inc: The Birthday Party (& dir); The Caretaker; The Homecoming; Landscape; Silence; Old Times; No Man's Land; The Hot House (& dir).
Thea inc: (dir) The Man in the Glass Booth; Exiles; Butley; Otherwise Engaged; Blithe Spirit; The Rear Column; Close of Play; Quartermaine's Terms.
Films inc: (wri) The Servant; The Pumpkin Eater; The Quiller Memorandum; Accident; The Go-Between; Butley (dir only); The Last Tycoon; The French Lieutenant's Woman; Betrayal.
TV inc: A Night Out; Night School; The Lover; Tea Party; The Basement.

PINTOFF, Ernest: Dir-Wri-Prod. b. Dec 15, 1931. Dir Oscar winning short, The Critic (1963). Films inc: Who Killed Mary Whats'ername; Blade; Harvey Middleman; Fireman; Dynamite Chicken; Jaguar Lives; Lunch Wagon; St. Helens.
TV inc: Hawaii Five-O; Kojak; Bionic Woman; The Six Million Dollar Man; James at Sixteen; Movin' On; Feather and Father; Young Dan'l Boone; The White Shadow; The Wild Wild East; This is Marshall McLuhan; This Is Sholem Aleichem; This is Al Capp; Human Feelings; Zack and the Magic Factory.

PIROSH, Robert: Wri. b. Baltimore, MD, Apr 1, 1910. Films inc: The Winning Ticket; A Day at the Races; I Married a Witch; Rings on Her Fingers; Up in Arms; Battleground *(Oscar-1949)*; Go For Broke (& dir); Washington Story (& dir); Valley of the Kings (& dir); Spring Reunion (& dir); Hell is for Heroes; A Gathering of Eagles; What's So Bad About Feeling Good? TV inc: (wri-prod pilots) Laramie; Combat.

PISIER, Marie-France: Act. b. Dalat, Indo-China, 1944. Films inc: Love at Twenty; Les Saintes Nitouches; Les Amoureux du France; La Mort D'Un Tuer; Les Yeaux Cernes; The Vampire of Dusseldorf; Trans-Europe Express; Stolen Kisses; L'Ecume Des Jours; Nous N'Irons Plus Au Bois; Journal of a Suicide; Feminin, Feminin; Celine and Julie Go Boating; French Provincial; The Phantom of Liberte; Cousin Cousine; Serail; Barocco; Le Corps De Mon Ennemi; The Other Side of Midnight; Les Apprentis Sourciers; The Bronte Sisters; French Postcards; Love on the Run; La Banquiere (The Woman Banker); Chanel Solitaire; Der Zauberberg (The Magic Mountain); L'As des As (Ace of Aces); Hot Touch; Le Prix du danger (The Prize of Peril); Der Stille Ocean (The Silent Ocean); L'Ami de Vincent (A Friend of Vincent).
TV inc: The French Atlantic Affair; Scruples.

PITCHFORD, Dean: Wri-act. b. Honolulu, HI., July 29, 1954. e. Yale. Studied with San Francisco Ballet. Thea inc: (Act) Godspell; Pippin; Umbrellas Of Cherbourg. Contributed songs to Up In One.
TV inc: (Act) Search For Tomorrow; All My Children.
Films inc: Fame *(Oscar-lyrics-1980)*; Footloose (wri-lyr).
Songs inc: Fame; I Sing The Body Electric; You Should Hear How She Talks About You; Don't Fight It; Don't Come Cryin' To Me; Solid Gold.

PITLIK, Noam: Dir. b. Philadelphia, PA, Nov 4, 1932. e. Temple U, BA; NYU, MA. Films inc: (act) The Graduate; The Fortune Cookie; The Hallelujah Trail; Front Page.
TV inc: (dir) The Dick Van Dyke Show; The Practice; Barney Miller (& prod) *(Emmy-*dir-1979); I'm A Big Girl Now; The Ordeal of Bill Carney; 9 to 5 (& prod); One More Try; Taxi; Now We're Cookin'; Branagan & Mapes; Over Here, Mr. President (cable); Henry Hamilton, Graduate Ghost; Off The Rack.

PLACE, Mary Kay: Act-Sing-Wri. b. Sep 23, 1947. TV inc: (wri) The Mary Tyler Moore Show; Phyllis; M*A*S*H; (act) Mary Hartman, Mary Hartman *(Emmy-*supp-1977); Fernwood Forever; Act of Love; Mom's On Strike; For Love Or Money; Martin Mull Presents The History Of White People In America--Part 1 (fevee).
Films inc: (act) Bound for Glory; New York, New York; More American Graffiti; Starting Over; Private Benjamin; Modern Problems; Waltz Across Texas; The Big Chill.

PLATO, Dana: Act. b. Maywood, CA, Nov 7, 1964. Films inc: The Heretic; Beyond the Bermuda Triangle; California Suite.
TV inc: Diff'rent Strokes; He's My Baby Now; Kraft Salutes Walt Disney World's 10th Anniversary; Twilight Theatre; High School U.S.A.

PLEASENCE, Angela: Act. b. Chapeltown, Yorkshire, England. e. RADA. D of Donald Pleasence. Thea inc: A Midsummer Night's Dream; The Ha-Ha; The Three Sisters; The Tempest; The Plough and the Stars; You Were So Sweet When You Were Little; The Entertainer; Round House; The Journey; The Bitter Tears of Petra von Kant; The Hothouse.
Films inc: Here We Go Round the Mulberry Bush; Hitler - The Last Ten Days; Symptoms; The Godsend.
TV inc: The Six Wives of Henry VIII; Breath; The Wood Demon; Les Miserables; A Christmas Carol.

PLEASENCE, Donald: Act. b. Worksop, England, Oct 5, 1919. Thea inc: (London) Twelfth Night; The Brothers Karamazov; Hobson's Choice; Ebb Tide (& wri); The Impresario from Smyrna; The Rules of the Game; The Lark; Misalliance; The Caretaker; The Man in the Glass Booth; Reflections. (Bway) Caesar and Cleopatra; Antony and Cleopatra; The Caretaker; Poor Bitos; The Man in the Glass Booth; Wise Child.
Films inc: Tale of Two Cities; The Shakedown; Spare The Rod; The Caretaker; The Great Escape; The Greatest Story Ever Told; The Hallelujah Trail; Fantastic Voyage; Cul-de-Sac; You Only Live Twice; Arthur, Arthur; THX 1138; Soldier Blue; Jerusalem File; Innocent Bystanders; Death Line; The Black Windmill; Journey Into Fear; Escape to Witch Mountain; Hearts of the West; The Last Tycoon; The Passover Plot; The Eagle Has Landed; Oh, God!; Fear; The Uncanny; Telefon; Halloween; Sgt. Pepper's Lonely Hearts Club Band; The Order and Security of the World; Power Play; Jaguar Lives; Night Creature; Dracula; Good Luck, Miss Wyckoff; The Monster Club; Escape From New York; Halloween II; Alone In the Dark; Race to the Yankee Ze-

phyr; The Devonsville Terror; The Ambassador; A Breed Apart; Where Is Parsifal?; Terror In the Aisles; Phenomena; Frankenstein's Great-Aunt Tillie; Warrior Of The Lost World; El Tesoro del Amazones (The Treasure Of The Amazon).

TV inc: Fate and Mr. Browne; The Silk Purse; A House of His Own; The Traitor; The Millionairess; The Bastard; All Quiet on the Western Front; The French Atlantic Affair; Blade On The Feather; Computercide; Witness For the Prosecution; Master of the Game; The Barchester Chronicles; The Corsican Brothers; Arch Of Triumph.

PLESHETTE, John: Act. b. NYC, Jul 27, 1942. e. Brown U; Carnegie-Mellon; studied with Stella Adler and Sanford Meisner. Bway inc: The Zulu and the Zayda; Jimmy Shine; Love's Labour's Lost; Measure for Measure; Richard III. Other thea inc MacBird!; Green Julia; It's Called the Sugar Plum; Says I, Says He.

Films inc: The End of the Road; Won Ton Ton--The Dog That Saved Hollywood; Slap Shot; Rocky II; Micki & Maude.

TV inc: The Trial of Lee Harvey Oswald; The Users; Seventh Avenue; Once Upon a Marriage; Knots Landing; The Kid With The Broken Halo; Burning Rage; MacGruder & Loud; Stormin' Home; Malice In Wonderland.

PLESHETTE, Suzanne: Act. b. NYC, Jan 31, 1937. e. Syracuse U. Screen debut, 1958, The Geisha Boy. Films inc: Rome Adventure; The Birds; 40 Pounds of Trouble; Wall of Noise; A Rage to Live; Youngblood Hawke; A Distant Trumpet; The Ugly Dachshund; Bull-whip Griffin; Fate Is The Hunter; Mr. Buddwing; Nevada Smith; Blue-beard's Ghost; The Power; If It's Tuesday This Must Be Belgium; Suppose They Gave a War and Nobody Came; Support Your Local Gunfighter; The Shaggy D.A.; Hot Stuff; Target Harry; Oh, God! Book II.

Bway inc: Compulsion; The Cold Wind and the Warm; The Golden Fleecing; The Miracle Worker; Two for the Seesaw; Special Occasions.

TV inc: The Bob Newhart Show; Wings of Fire; Along Came a Spider; Hunters Are for Killing; River of Gold; In Broad Daylight; Flesh and Blood; If Things Were Different; The Star Maker; Fantasies; Help Wanted--Male; Dixie--Changing Habits; One Cooks, The Other Doesn't; Suzanne Pleshette is Maggie Briggs (& crea); For Love Or Money; Kojak--The Belarus Files.

PLESKOW, Eric: Exec. b. Vienna, Apr 24, 1924. Started in 1948 as asst GM, Motion Picture Export Assoc, Germany; 1950-51, continental rep, Sol Lesser Prodns; joined UA in 1951 as Far East sls mgr; 1952, named mgr, S Africa; 1953-58, mgr, Germany; 1958-59, exec asst, to continental mgr; 1959-60, asst continental mgr; 1960-62, continental mgr; 1962, in charge of foreign dist; 1973, exec VP & COO; 1973, P, & CEO; resigned 1978, formed Orion Pictures Co, P, CEO.

PLITT, Henry G.: Exhibition exec. b. NYC, Nov. 26, 1918. e. Syracuse U., BA; St. Lawrence U Law School. Joined United Paramount Theatres 1946 as district mgr; 1949, div mgr Paramount-Richards circuit; 1951, vp; 1955, P of circuit; 1959, P ABC Films Inc; 1966, P ABC Great States Inc; 1971, vp ABC Theatre Holdings; 1974, bought Northern Theatre Circuit from ABC, forming Plitt Theatres; 1978, bought remainder of ABC Theatres.

PLOWRIGHT, Joan: Act. b. Brigg, England, Oct 18, 1929. W of Laurence Olivier. Performed in repertory; member of Old Vic Co during tour of S. Africa, 1952.

Thea inc: (London) Saint Joan; Uncle Vanya; Hobson's Choice; The Master Builder; The Three Sisters; Tartuffe; Love's Labour's Lost. (Co-Dir) An Evasion of Women; The Travails of Sancho Panza. (Dir) Rites; Enjoy. (Bway) The Chairs; The Lesson; A Taste of Honey (Tony-1961); Eden End; The Sea Gull; The Bed Before Yesterday; Filumena.

Films inc: Moby Dick; The Entertainer; Three Sisters; Equus; Britannia Hospital; Brimstone and Treacle; Wagner.

TV inc: Odd Man In; The Secret Agent; The School for Scandal; The Diary of Anne Frank.

PLUMMER, Amanda: Act. b. Mar 23, 1957. D of Tammy Grimes and Christopher Plummer. Bway inc: A Taste of Honey; Agnes of God (Tony-featured-1982); The Glass Menagerie.

Films inc: Cattle Annie and Little Britches; The World According to Garp; Daniel; The Hotel New Hampshire.

TV inc: The Unforgiveable Secret; The Dollmaker.

PLUMMER, Christopher: Act. b. Toronto, Dec 13, 1929. Professional debut with Canadian Repertory Theatre, Ottawa. Broadway debut 1954 The Constant Wife. Films inc: Across the Everglades; Stage Struck; The Sound of Music; Triple Cross; Lock Up Your Daughters; The Man Who Would Be King; The Return of the Pink Panther; The Disappearance; Assassination In Sarajevo; The Assignment; International Velvet; Murder by Decree; Starcrash; Hanover Street; Highpoint; The Silent Partner; Arthur Miller on Home Ground; Somewhere In Time; Eyewitness; Being Different (doc) (narr); The Amateur; Dreamscape; Ordeal By Innocence; Jatszani Kell (Lily In Love).

Bway inc: Starcross Story; Home is the Hero; The Dark is Light Enough; Night of the Auk; J.B.; The Lark; Hamlet; Macbeth; Cyrano de Bergerac (Tony-1974); Othello (1982 rev).

TV inc: The Moneychangers (Emmy- 1977); Desperate Voyage; The Olympics (narr); The Shadow Box; When The Circus Came To Town; Dial "M" For Murder; Little Gloria--Happy At Last; The Scarlet and the Black; The Thorn Birds; Parade of Stars; Movie Blockbusters! The 15 Greatest Hits of all Time (mc); Prototype; Raymond Massey--Actor of the Century; The Velveteen Rabbit.

PODESTA, Rossana: Act. b. Libya, Jun 20, 1934. Films inc: Luxury Girls; Cops and Robbers; Ulysses; Raw Wind in Eden; The Slave of Rome; Sodom and Gemorrah; Helen of Troy; The Golden Arrow; Seven Golden Men; Man of the Year; Sunday Lovers; Hercules.

POITIER, Sidney: Act-Dir. b. Miami, Feb 20, 1924. Formed First Artists Prod Co Ltd, 1969, with Paul Newman and Barbra Streisand. On screen since 1949. Films inc: No Way Out; Cry the Beloved Country; Red Ball Express; Go Man Go; The Blackboard Jungle; Good-Bye My Lady; Edge of the City; Something of Value; The Defiant Ones; Porgy and Bess; All the Young Men; Devil at Four O'Clock; A Raisin in the Sun; The Long Ships; Paris Blues; Pressure Point; Lilies of the Field (Oscar-1963); The Long Ships; The Greatest Story Ever Told; The Bedford Incident; Slender Thread; A Patch of Blue; Duel at Diablo; To Sir With Love; In the Heat of the Night; Guess Who's Coming to Dinner; The Lost Man; They Call Me Mr. Tibbs; Brother John; For Love of Ivy; Buck and the Preacher. (Dir-act) A Warm December; Uptown Saturday Night; The Wilby Conspiracy; Let's Do It Again; A Piece of the Action. (Dir) Stir Crazy; Hanky Panky.

Thea inc: Lysistrata; Anna Lucasta; Freight; Fast Forward.

TV inc: Paul Robeson--Tribute To An Artist (narr); Stanley Kramer On Film; On Top All Over The World.

POLAN, Lou: Act. b. Ukraine, Russia, Jun 15, 1904. To US as youth. Early training Neighborhood Playhouse; NY School of the Theatre. Bway debut, 1922, in walk-on part. First speaking role 1922. The Bootlegger; toured in vaudeville.

Thea inc: The Gentleman from Athens; Desire Under the Elms; Coriolanus; Saint Joan; Seidman and Son; Hamlet; The Tenth Man; The Creation of the World and Other Business.

Films inc: Fourteen Hours; You Never Can Tell; Murder, Inc; The Seven Ups.

POLAND, Albert: Thea GM-Prod. b. Syracuse, NY., Apr. 30, 1941. e. American Theatre Wing. General press rep American Conservatory Theatre. Thea inc: (GM) The Dirtiest Show in Town; And They Put Handcuffs on Flowers; Let My People Come; Tommy Tune Atop the Village Gate; A Life in the Theatre; The Neon Woman; Are You Now or Have Your Ever Been; The Price; Das Lusitania Songspiel; An Evening with W.S. Gilbert; The Buddy System; Marry Me A Little; Entertaining Mr. Sloane; Tomfoolery; Little Shop of Horrors. (Prod) The Fantasticks; Now is the Time for All Good Men; Futz (asso prod); Peace; The Unseen Hand/Forensic and the Navigators; Acrobats/Line; The Bar That Never Closes; Dear Nobody; Modigliani.

POLANSKI, Roman: Dir-Wri-Act. b. Paris, Aug 18, 1933. e. Polish National Film Academy. Originally and actor in several Polish films, entered dirs school of Polish Academy where he made several shorts inc Two Men and a Wardrobe, Le Gros et le Maigre; Mannals. Films inc: Knife in the Water; Repulsion; Cul de Sac; The Fearless Vampire Killers or Pardon Me But Your Teeth Are in My Neck; Rosemary's Baby; Macbeth; What?; A Day At The Beach; The Tenant (& act); Chinatown. Arrested in 1978 in Hollywood on sex charges involving a minor, he jumped bail while awaiting sentence and returned to France. Resumed career in France with Tess (dir-wri).

POLIKOFF, Gerald: Dir. Staff dir NBC News. TV inc: No More Vietnams, but; We're Moving Up--The Hispanic Migration; American Fashion--Rags to Riches; Gambling.

POLITO, Gene: Cin. b. NYC, Sep 13, 1918. e. USC. Films inc: Downhill Racer; Prime Cut; Five on the Black Hand Side; Futurewold; Westworld; Trackdown; That's Entertainment; Bad News Bears Go To Japan; Cheech and Chong's Up in Smoke.
TV inc: A Time for Love; Sam Hill; Judge Dee; Delaney; The Man Who Could Talk to Kids; All Together Now; My Sweet Charlie; Death Scream; Life Goes To War; Profiles in Courage; Lost in Space.

POLL, Martin: Prod. b. NYC, Nov 24, 1924. Films inc: Love Is a Ball; Sylvia; The Lion in Winter; The Appointment; The Magic Garden of Stanley Sweetheart; The Man Who Loved Cat Dancing; Night Watch; Love and Death; The Sailor Who Fell From Grace With The Sea; Somebody Killed Her Husband; Nighthawks; Gimme An ⫶F' (exec prod).
TV inc: Stunt Seven; Arthur The King.

POLLACK, Sydney: Dir. b. South Bend, IN, Jul 1, 1934. Films inc: The Slender Thread; This Property is Condemned; The Scalphunters; Castle Keep; They Shoot Horses, Don't They?; Jeremiah Johnson; The Way We Were; The Yakuza; Three Days of the Condor; Bobby Deerfield; The Electric Horseman; Honeysuckle Rose; Absence of Malice (& prod); Tootsie (& prod-act); Songwriter (prod); Sanford Meisner--The Theater's Best Kept Secret (exec prod).
TV inc: A Cardinal Act of Mercy; Something About Lee Willey; Two is the Number; The Game (Emmy-1966).

POLLARD, Michael J. (ne Pollack): Act. b. May 30, 1939. Films inc: Adventures of a Young Man; Summer Magic; The Russians Are Coming, The Russians Are Coming; The Stripper; Bonnie and Clyde; Hannibal Brooks; Little Fauss and Big Halsy; Dirty Little Billy; Sunday in the Country; Between the Lines; Melvin and Howard; Heated Vengeance.

POLONSKY, Abraham: Dir-Wri. b. NYC, Dec 5, 1910. e. CCNY, BA; Columbia Law School. Golden Earrings; I Can Get It for You Wholesale; Body and Soul; Force of Evil; career interrupted by blacklist after refusal to testify before House Committee on UnAmerican Activities; Madigan; Tell Them Willie Boy is Here (& dir); Romance of a Horse Thief (dir); Avalanche Express (wri); Monsignor.

PONTECORVO, Gillo: Dir. b. Italy, Nov 19, 1919. Films inc: Kapo; The Battle of Algiers; Burn; Ogro; Tunnel.

PONTI, Carlo: Prod. b. Milan, Italy, Dec 11, 1913. e. U of Milan. H of Sophia Loren. Films inc: Little Old World; A Dog's Life; The Knight Has Arrived; Musolino; The Outlaw; Romanticism; Sensuality; The White Slave; Toto in Color; The Three Corsairs; Ulysses; The Woman of the River; An American of Rome; Attila; War and Peace; La Strada (Oscar-Foreign film-1956); The Black Orchid; Heller In Pink Tights; Two Women; Lola; Cleo From 5 to 7; Boccaccio '70; The Last Lover; The Great Spy Mission; Happily Ever After; The Girl and the General; The Condemned of Altona; Yesterday, Today and Tomorrow; Marriage Italian Style; Dr Zhivago; Blowup; Zabriskie Point; Sunflower; Best House in London; Lady Liberty; White Sister; What?; Andy Warhol's Frankenstein; The Passenger; The Cassandra Crossing; A Special Day; The Naked Sun; Permette Signora Che ami vostra figlia (Claretta and Ben).

PORTER, Don: Act. b. Miami, OK, Sep 24, 1912. Films inc: Top Sergeant; Night Monster; The Curse of the Allenbys; Ocean Drive; Because You're Mine; The Racket; Our Miss Brooks; Bachelor In Paradise; Youngblood Hawke; The Candidate; Forty Carats; White Line Fever.
TV inc: Private Secretary; Our Miss Brooks; The Ann Sothern Show; Murder or Mercy; The President's Mistress; Happy Birthday Charlie Brown; The Legend of Lizzie Borden; Battles-The Murder That Wouldn't Die; The Last Song; All Together Now.

PORTER, Eric: Act. b. London, Apr 8, 1928. Films inc: The Heroes of Telemark; Kaleidoscope; The Lost Continent; Hands of the Ripper;

Antony and Cleopatra; Nichols and Alexandra; The Day of the Jackal; The Belstone Fox; Callan; Hennessy.
TV inc: The Forsyte Saga; Hamlet; Little Lord Fauntleroy; Churchill and the Generals; Why Didn't They Ask Evans?; Winston-Churchill--The Wilderness Years; The Jewel In The Crown.

PORTER, Nyree Dawn: Act. b. New Zealand, 1940. Films inc: Two Left Feet; The Cracksman; Jane Eyre; The House That Dripped Blood; From Beyond the Grave.
TV inc: The Forsyte Saga; The Protectors; The Martian Chronicles.
Thea inc: Murder In Mind.

PORTMAN, Richard: Snd. b. Los Angeles, Apr 2, 1934. Films inc: Kotch; The Candidate; Paper Moon; Day of the Dolphin; Young Frankenstein; Godfather; Nashville; Funny Lady; The End; The Deer Hunter (Oscar-1978); A Perfect Couple; Quintet; Rich Kids.
TV inc: Dynasty; Eleanor and Franklin--The White House Years.

POST, Ted: Prod-Dir. b. NYC, Mar 31, 1918. Films inc: Hang 'Em High; The Legend of Tom Dooley; Beneath the Planet of the Apes; The Harrad Experiment; Magnum Force; Go Tell The Spartans; Good Guys Wear Black; Whiffs; Nightkill.
TV inc: Studio One; Ford Theatre; Playhouse of Stars; Fred Astaire Show; Gunsmoke; Rawhide; Twilight Zone; Wagon Train; Combat; Peyton Place; Defenders; Route 66; Baretta; Columbo; Diary of a Teenage Hitchhiker; The Girls in the Office; Beyond Westworld; Cagney and Lacey; Insight/Duttons Choice; Clay Feet.
Thea inc: The Happy Dollar; Claudia; The Eve of St. Mark; Watch on the Rhine; The Male Animal; Counsellor-at-Law; The Philadelphia Story; Yes, My Darling Daughter; Room Service; Home of the Brave; The Front Page; Three Men on a Horse; The Fatal Weakness; Made in Heaven; George Washington Slept Here; Anna Lucasta; The Dark Tower; Burlesque.

POSTON, Tom: Act. b. Columbus, OH, Oct 17, 1927. Films inc: The City that Never Sleeps; Zotz!; Soldier in the Rain; The Old Dark House; Cold Turkey; The Happy Hooker; Rabbit Test; Up The Academy; Carbon Copy.
TV inc: Macbeth; The Tempest; Steve Allen Show (Emmy-supp-1959); On the Rocks; We've Got Each Other; To Tell The Truth; Fame; Beane's of Boston; Mork and Mindy; The Girl, The Gold Watch and Dynamite; Newhart.

POWELL, Anthony: Dsgn. b. Chortlon-Cum-Hardy, England, Jun 2, 1935. e. Central School of Art and Design. Thea inc: Women, Beware Women; The Rivals; School for Scandal; Fish Out of Water; Comedy of Errors; Private Lives; Ring Round the Moon.
Films inc: Royal Hunt of the Sun; Joe Egg; A Town Called Bastard; Nicholas and Alexandra (advsr); Travels With My Aunt (Oscar-cos-1972); Papillon; That Lucky Touch; Buffalo Bill and the Indians; Sorcerer; Death on the Nile (Oscar-cos-1978); Tess (Oscar-cos-1980); Priest of Love; Evil Under the Sun; Indiana Jones and the Temple of Doom.

POWELL, Charles M.: Exec. b. NYC, Feb 17, 1934. e. NYU, BS. Col Natl pub-exp mgr 1959. Natl Pub Coord Par, 1963-64; WNBC Radio/TV, adv Promo Mgr, 1965; ad-pub-dir M J Frankovich, 1969-71; joined MGM as ad-pub-expl dir 1972; named div vp & corp vp, 1974; Columbia Pictures vp, ad-pub-expl 1975; Universal Pictures vp ad-pub-prom 1976; formed ind pub-marketing firm with Buddy Young, Jan 1980.

POWELL, Jane (Suzanne Burce): Act. b. Portland, OR, Apr 1, 1929. On screen from 1944 in Song of the Open Road. Films inc: Holiday in Mexico; Three Daring Daughters; A Date With Judy; Luxury Liner; Two Weeks with Love; Royal Wedding; Rich, Young and Pretty; Small Town Girl; Three Sailors and A Girl; Seven Brides for Seven Brothers; Athena; Deep In My Heart; Hit the Deck; The Girl Most Likely; The Female Animal; Enchanted Island.
Thea inc: Irene; I Do! I Do!

POWELL, Michael: Wri-Prod-Dir. b. Canterbury, Kent, England, Sep 30, 1905. Teamed for 15 years with Emeric Pressburger in a series of prodns. Films inc: Caste (wri); Park Lane (wri); Hotel Splendide (wri); Night of the Party (wri); Lazy Bones (wri); The Man Behind the Mask (wri); The Edge of the World; The Spy in Black; The Lion Has

Wings; The Thief of Baghdad; 49th Parallel; One Of Our Aircraft Is Missing; The Life and Death of Col Blimp; The Silver Fleet; A Canterbury Tale; I Know Where I'm Going; A Matter of Life and Death; Black Narcissus; The Red Shoes; The Small Back Room; The Elusive Pimpernel; The Tales of Hoffman; The Battle of the River Plate; Ill Met By Moonlight; Honeymoon; Age of Consent; The Boy Who Turned Yellow; Pavlova (English version).

POWELL, Norman: Prod. b. Los Angeles, 1934. e. Cornell U, BA. S of Joan Blondell and Dick Powell. Dir movies-for-tv, CBS Entertainment; Aug. 1983, named VP. TV inc: (Prod) Flatbush; Salvage I; More Than Friends; Rafferty; Washington Behind Closed Doors.

POWELL, Randolph: Act. b. Iowa City, IA, Apr 14, 1950. e. U Denver. TV inc: Babe; Eleanor and Franklin--The White House Years; Logan's Run; Doctors' Private Lives; The Concrete Cowboys; Dallas; Brothers-in-Law.

POWELL, Robert: Act. b. Lancashire, England, Jun. 1, 1944. Thea inc: Ladies from the Sea; Pirates; Glasstown; Travesties; Private Dick.
Films inc: Mahler; Tommy; Four Feathers; The 39 Steps; Beyond Good and Evil; Jigsaw Man; The Survivor; Imperativ; The Jigsaw Man.
TV inc: Jesus of Nazareth; Doomwatch; Jude the Obscure; Lookin for Clancy; The Hunchback of Notre Dame.

POWELL, William: Act. b. Pittsburgh, PA, Jul 29, 1892. Started on Broadway, to Hollywood 1922. Films inc: Sherlock Holmes; When Knighthood Was in Flower; Under the Red Robe; Dangerous Money; Too Many Kisses; Desert Gold; Aloma of the South Seas; Beau Geste; The Great Gatsby; The Last Command; Beau Sabreur; Partners in Crime; The Canary Murder Case; The Benson Murder Case; For the Defense; Man of the World; One Way Passage; The Kennel Murder Case; Manhattan Melodrama; The Key; The Great Ziegfeld; Libeled Lady; My Man Godfrey; The Thin Man; After the Thin Man; The Last of Mrs. Cheyney; The Emperor's Candlesticks; Another Thin Man; Shadow of the Thin Man; Crossroads; The Thin Man Goes Home; Ziegfeld Follies; The Hoodlum Saint; Life With Father; Song of the Thin Man; The Senator Was Indiscreet; Mr. Peabody and the Mermaid; Take One False Step; Dancing in the Dark; It's A Big Country; Treasure of Lost Canyon; The Girl Who Had Everything; How To Marry a Millionaire; Mister Roberts.
(Died March 5, 1984).

POWERS, Dave (David Price Powers): Dir. b. Los Angeles, Dec 2, 1932. Began as prodn asst CBS 1953; stage mgr 1957; asso dir 1964; dir since 1968.
TV inc: Carol Burnett Show *(Emmys*-1974, 1975, 1977, 1978); John Ritter, Being of Sound Mind and Body; Three's Company; Three's A Crowd.

POWERS, Mala: Act. b. San Francisco, Dec 20, 1931. Films inc: Outrage; Edge of Doom; Cyrano De Bergerac; Rose of Cimarron; City Beneath The Sea; Rage at Dawn; Bengazi; Tammy and the Bachelor; Daddy's Gone A-Hunting; Six Tickets to Hell.
TV inc: Hazel; The Man and the City; SWAT.
Thea inc: Absence of a Cello; The Rivalry; Night of the Iguana; Hogan's Goat; Critic's Choice; Sabrina Fair; Roman Candle; King of Hearts.

POWERS, Stefanie: Act. b. Hollywood, Nov 2, 1942. On screen from 1961. Films inc: Among the Thorns; Experiment in Terror; The Interns; If a Man Answers; McLintock!; Tammy Tell Me True; Die! Die! My Darling; Stagecoach; Love Has Many Faces; Warning Shot; The Love Bug Rides Again; Crescendo; Escape to Athena; Invisible Strangler (made in 1979 as The Astral Factor).
TV inc: The Girl from UNCLE; The Interns; Fanatic; A Death In Canaan; Feather and Father; Washington--Behind Closed Doors; Hart to Hart; Family Secrets (& prod); Mistral's Daughter; Hollywood Wives; Placido Domingo Steppin' Out With The Ladies; Deceptions; The 39th Annual Tony Awards.

PRECHT, Robert H.: Prod. b. Douglas, AZ, May 12, 1930. e. UCLA; UC Berkeley, BA. CBS-TV 1956-60, assoc prod; 1960-71, prod Ed Sullivan Show; since, 1971 ind, prod network specials inc: Lily Tomlin; Carroll O'Connor; Andy Williams; Grammy Awards; 50th Anniversary of Grand Ole Opry; The Crystal Gayle Special; Crystal; Enter-

tainer of the Year Awards; An NBC Family Christmas; The Best of Sullivan; Second Annual NBC Family Christmas; Screen Actors Guild 50th Anniversary Celebration.

PREMINGER, Otto: Dir-Prod. b. Vienna, Dec. 5, 1906. e. U of Vienna, LLD. At 17, actor with Max Reinhardt troupe; to U.S., 1935 where he worked as act-dir-prod on Bway; on faculty Yale Drama School. To Hollywood 1936. Films inc: (Dir) Margin for Error (& act); Royal Scandal; Forever Amber; Laura; In the Meantime Darling; Fallen Angel; Stalag 17 (act only); River of No Return; The Court-Martial of Billy Mitchell; Porgy and Bess; (Prod-dir) Centennial Summer; Daisy Kenyon; Whirlpool; Where the Sidewalk Ends; The Thirteenth Letter; Angel Face; The Moon Is Blue; Carmen Jones; The Man With Golden Arm; Saint Joan; Bonjour Tristesse; Anatomy of a Murder; Exodus; Advise and Consent; The Cardinal; In Harm's Way; Bunny Lake Is Missing; Hurry Sundown; Skidoo!; Tell Me That You Love Me, Junie Moon; Such Good Friends; Rosebud; The Human Factor.
Bway inc: Margin For Error; The Moon Is Blue; Critic's Choice; Full Circle.

PRENTISS, Paula (nee Ragusa): Act. b. San Antonio, TX, Mar 4, 1939. e. Northwestern U, BA. W of Richard Benjamin. On screen from 1961 in Where the Boys Are. Films inc: Bachelor in Paradise; The Horizontal Lieutenant; Follow the Boys; Man's Favorite Sport; The World of Henry Orient; In Harm's Way; What's New Pussycat?; Catch 22; Last of the Red Hot Lovers; The Parallax View; The Stepford Wives; The Black Marble; Saturday the 14th; Buddy Buddy.
TV inc: He & She; Friendships, Secrets and Lies; The Top of the Hill; The Way They Were; Packin' It In; M.A.D.D.--Mothers Against Drunk Drivers.
Thea inc: As You Like It; Arf!; The Norman Conquests.

PRESLE, Micheline (nee Chassagne): Act. b. Paris, Aug 22, 1922. Films inc: Jeunes Filles en Detress; La Nuit Fantastique; Boule de Suif; Le Diable au Corps; Under My Skin; The Adventures of Captain Fabian; Villa Borghese; The She Wolves; Blind Date; The Prize; King of Hearts; Peau d'Ane; Nea; We Forget Everything; Je Te Tiens, Tu Me Tiens par la Barbichette; Your Turn, My Turn; Rien Ne Va Plus; Demons du Midi; Tout Depend Des Filles (It All Depends on Girls); En Haut des Marches (At the Top of the Stairs); Les voleurs de la nuit (Thieves After Dark); Le Chien (The Dog); Les Sang des Autres (The Blood of Others); Les Fausses Confidences (The False Confidences).
Thea inc: Colinette; Am Stram Gram; La Main Passe; Lili Lamont.

PRESNELL, Harve: Singer-Act. b. Modesto, CA, Sep 14, 1933. Films inc: The Unsinkable Molly Brown; The Glory Guys; When the Boys Meet the Girls; Paint Your Wagon.
Bway inc: Annie.

PRESSBURGER, Emeric: Wri. b. Hungary, 1902. Teamed with Michael Powell for 15 years. For joint credits see Michael Powell. Solo films inc: The Invaders *(Oscar*-1942-orig story); Twice Upon a Time (& prod-dir); Miracle in Soho (& prod); Behold a Pale Horse; Operation Crossbow; They're a Weird Mob; The Boy Who Turned Yellow.

PRESSMAN, David: Dir. b. Tiflis, Russia, Oct 10, 1913. e. Columbia; NY Neighborhood Playhouse. Started as act on Bway in Brooklyn, USA; Eve of St. Mark; Dream Girl; began dir at Toronto Theatre of Action.
Bway inc: The Disenchanted; Roman Candle; A Cook for Mr. General; Summertree.
TV inc: Actors Studio Theatre; T-Men in Action; Westinghouse Summer Theatre; The Nurses; Another World; One Life To Live (since 1970) *(Emmys*-1976, 1977, 1982, 1984).

PRESSMAN, Edward R.: Prod. b. NYC. e. Stanford U. Films inc: Girl (short); Out Of It; The Revolutionary; Dealing; Lost Bag Blues; Sisters; Badlands; Phantom of the Paradise; Paradise Alley; Old Boyfriends; Heart Beat; Despair; You Better Watch Out; The Hand; Conan The Barbarian (exec prod); The Pirates of Penzance (exec prod); Conan the Destroyer; Crimewave (& act).

PRESSMAN, Lawrence: Act. b. Cynthiana, KY, Jul 10, 1939. e. KY Northwestern U, BA. Bway inc: Man in the Glass Booth (& London); Never Live Over a Pretzel Factory; Play It Again Sam.
TV inc: Rich Man, Poor Man; A Bedtime Story; Blind Ambition; The

Gathering, Part 2; Ladies Man; Insight/Mr. and Mrs. Bliss; Darkroom; Rehearsal For Murder; Cry For the Strangers; The Winds of War; The Red-Light Sting; Getting Even--Victims Fight Back (HBO) (narr); The Three Wishes Of Billy Grier; Victims For Victims--The Theresa Saldana Story; For Love Or Money; Street Hawk.

Films inc: Man in the Glass Booth; The Crazy World of Julius Vrooder; Helstrom Chronicles; Shaft; Making It; Nine To Five; Some Kind of Hero.

PRESSMAN, Michael: Dir. b. NYC, Jul 1, 1950. e. CA Inst of the Arts. Films inc: The Great Texas Dynamite Chase; The Bad News Bears in Breaking Training; Boulevard Nights; Those Lips, Those Eyes; Some Kind of Hero; Doctor Detroit.

TV inc: Like Mom, Like Me; The Imposter; And The Children Shall Lead; On Our Way; Private Sessions.

PRESTON, Robert (nee Meservey): Act. b. Newton Highlands, MA, Jun 8, 1918. e. Pasadena Playhouse. Screen debut, 1938, King of Alcatraz. Films inc: Illegal Traffic; Disbarred; Union Pacific; Beau Geste; Typhoon; Moon Over Burma; Northwest Mounted Police; The Macomber Affair; Wild Harvest; Tulsa; Whispering Smith; The Sundowners; When I Grow Up; Cloudburst; Face to Face; The Last Frontier; Dark at the Top of the Stairs; The Music Man; Junior Bonner; Child's Play; Mame; Semi-Tough; S.O.B.; Victor/Victoria; The Last Starfighter.

Thea inc: 20th Century; The Male Animal; His and Hers; The Tender Trap; Janus; The Hidden River; The Music Man (Tony-1958); Too True to be Good; Nobody Loves an Albatross; The Lion in Winter; I Do! I Do! (Tony-1967); Mack and Mabel.

TV inc: Playhouse 90; Omnibus; The Bells of St. Mary's; Dupont Show of the Month; The Chisholms; Rehearsal For Murder; September Gun; Finnegan Begin Again.

PREVIN, Andre: Comp-Cond. b. Berlin, Apr 6, 1929. Conductor, London Symphony Orchestra; guest cond of major symphony orchestras, US, Europe; mus dir Pittsburgh Symphony; May 1984 named mus dir L.A. Philharmonic effective Oct. 1986. Films inc: Three Little Words; Cause for Alarm; It's Always Fair Weather; Bad Day at Black Rock; Invitation to the Dance; Catered Affair; Designing Woman; Silk Stockings; Gigi (Oscar-1958); Porgy and Bess (Oscar-co-score-1959); Subterraneans; The Bells Are Ringing; Pepe; Elmer Gantry; Four Horsemen of the Apocalypse; One Two Three; Thoroughly Modern Millie; Valley of the Dolls; Paint Your Wagon; The Music Lover; Jesus Christ, Superstar; Every Good Boy Deserves Favor.

Thea inc: Rough Crossing (songs). (Grammys-(7)-soundtrack-1958, 1959; orch perf-1959; jazz perf-1960, 1961; choral perf, classical, 1973, 1976).

PREVIN, Dory (nee Langan): Sngwri-Singer. b. Rahway, NJ, Oct 22, 1930. Lyricist for Andre Previn, also collab with Harold Arlen, Johnny Green; Jimmy Van Heusen; John Williams.

Songs inc: You're Gonna Hear From Me; A Faraway Part of Town; Second Chance; Valley of the Dolls; Come Saturday Morning; With My Daddy in the Attic; Esther's First Communion; Third Girl from the Left; We'll Win This World; (Emmy-1983); Home Here.

PREVIN, Steve: Exec. b. NYC, Oct 21, 1925. Film edtr 1943-50, UI & MGM; to Europe, 1950-60, dir TV series; Foreign Intrigue; Sherlock Holmes; Captain Gallant; The Vikings (for Disney); Almost Angels; Waltz King; Escapade in Florence; 1966-69, Paramount, London, prodn exec; 1969-72, Commonwealth United, London, prodn exec; 1973, Paramount, prodn exec; 1974 AIP, VP in charge of European prodn.

PRICE, Frank: Exec. b. Decatur, IL, 1930. e. MI State. Joined CBS-TV NY 1951 as story ed; to Hollywood as story ed Screen Gems; story ed NBC; joined U-TV as asso prod-wri; 1971, Sr vp U-TV; 1973, exec vp; 1974 P U-TV & VP MCA; 1978 resd to become P Columbia Pictures Prodns; 1979 P Columbia Pictures; April 1981 named Chmn and P of Studio; July 1982, Chmn & CEO when Guy McElwaine became P of studio; Oct. 1983, resd; Nov. 1983, Chmn MCA Motion Picture Group & VP MCA Inc.

TV inc: (exec prod) The Virginian; Ironside; It Takes A Thief; The Doomsday Flight; Kojak; $6 Million Man; Bionic Woman; Rockford Files; Quincy; Rich Man, Poor Man; 79 Park Ave; Captains and the Kings.

PRICE, Leontyne: Opera Singer. b. Laurel, MS, Feb 10, 1927. e. Central State College OH, BA. Played Bess in State Dept European tour of Porgy and Bess; guest soloist with major orchs around world; NBC-TV 1955-1958, other starring appearances 1960, 1962, 1964; guest soloist Vienna Staadtopera; Berlin Opera; Rome Opera; Paris Opera; Covent Garden; Salzburg Festival; Metropolitan Opera where now resident member.

(Grammys-(12)-class voc solo-1960, 1963, 1964, 1965, 1966, 1967, 1969, 1971, 1973, 1974, 1980, 1982).

TV inc: The Kennedy Center Honors, 1980; Live From Lincoln Center--Leontyne Price, Zubin Mehta and the NY Philharmonic (Emmy-1983); In Performance At The White House--An Evening Of Spirituals and Gospel Music (Emmy-1984); Noel.

PRICE, Lorin E.: Prod. b. NYC, Apr 1, 1921. e. Yale, BA. Bway inc: The Moon Besieged; The Natural Look; George M; Seesaw; No Hard Feelings.

Films inc: Night of the Zombies (& act).

PRICE, Paul B.: Act. b. Carteret, NJ, Oct 7, 1933. e. U of AL, BS. TV inc: Sesame Street; Naked City; Get Smart; The Hero; Hey, Landlord; Busting Loose.

Thea inc: A Cook for Mr General; Let Me Hear You Smile; Bad Habits; The Ritz.

Films inc: Butch and Sundance-The Early Days.

PRICE, Ray: Singer-Sngwri. b. Perryville, TX, Jan 12, 1926. C&W recording artist. Started on radio; became regular on the Grand Ole Opry. TV inc: Texas & Tennessee--A Musical Affair. (Grammy-C&W vocal-1970).

PRICE, Roger: Wri-Act. b. Charleston, VW, Mar 6, 1922. e. U MI; American Academy of Art; studied in Max Reinhardt School, LA. Worked niteries, TV. Bway inc: Tickets Please. TV inc: Whatever Turns You On; For The Love of It.

Films inc: Pete's Dragon; The Cat From Outer Space; Just You and Me, Kid.

PRICE, Stanley: Wri. b. London, Dec 8, 1931. e. Cambridge U, MA. Films inc: Arabesque; Gold; The Devil Within Her; Shout at the Devil; The Last Pentathlon.

Plays inc: Come Live with Me; Horizontal Hold; The Two of Me; The Starving Rich; Why Me?

PRICE, Vincent: Act. b. St Louis, MO, May 27, 1911. e. Yale U; U of London; Nuremberg U. On screen from 1938 in Service de Luxe. Films inc: The Tower of London; The Private Lives of Elizabeth and Essex; The Invisible Man Returns; The Song of Bernadette; Laura; The Keys of the Kingdom; Leave Her to Heaven; Dragonwyck; The Three Musketeers; Rogues' Regiment; The Web; Up in Central Park; House of Wax; The Mad Magician; The Ten Commandments; The Raven; The Last Man on Earth; Scream and Scream Again; The Devil's Triangle; Dr. Phibes; Dr. Phibes Rises Again; Madman; It's Not The Size That Counts; Scavenger Hunt; The Monster Club; The House of Long Shadows; Bloodbath at the House of Death.

TV inc: Time Express; John Ritter, Being of Sound Mind and Body; Dr. Jekyll and Mr. Hyde; A Father Brown Story (host); Out of Control; Reilly--Ace of Spies (host); Rumpole Returns!; Praying Mantis.

Bway inc: Diversions and Delights.

PRIDE, Charley: Singer. b. Sledge, MS, Mar 8, 1938. C&W recording artist. (Grammys-(3)-sacred perf, gospel perf-1971; C&W-1972). TV inc: A Country Christmas 1981; Country Comes Home; A Tribute to Martin Luther King Jr.--A Celebration Of Life. Films inc: Ellie.

PRIESTLEY, J.B.: Wri. b. Bradford, England, Sep 13, 1894. e. Cambridge, MA, LLD, DLitt. Plays inc: The Roundabout; People at Sea; When We Are Married; They Came to a City; An Inspector Calls; The Linden Tree; Dragon's Mouth; Mr Kettle and Mrs Moon; The Golden Entry; A Severed Head; Eden End.

Films inc: The Foreman Went to France; Britain at Bay; Priestley's Postscripts; Battle for Music; They Came to a City; Last Holiday; The Insepctor Calls.

TV inc: Lost City (& act); You Know What People Are (& act).

(Died Aug. 14, 1984)

PRIMUS, Barry: Act. b. NYC, Feb 16, 1938. Lincoln Center Repertory Company; improvisational theatre, St. Louis; Bway inc: Teibele and Her Demon; off-Bway, Huui, Huui; The Changeling.

Films inc: The Brotherhood; Been Down So Long It Looks Like Up to Me; Gravy Train; Avalanche; Night Games; Heartland; Absence of Malice.

TV inc: Portrait of a Showgirl; Paper Dolls; The Shooting; I Want to Live; Over Here, Mr. President (cable); Heart of Steel; Brotherly Love.

PRINCE, Harold S.: Prod-Dir. b. NYC, Jan 30, 1928. e. U of PA, AB. Worked as stage mgr for George Abbott, later coproduced and/or dir the following: The Pajama Game (Tony-1954); Damn Yankees (Tony-1955); New Girl in Town; West Side Story; Fiorello (Tony and Pulitzer Prize-1959); Tenderloin; A Call on Kuprin; They Might Be Giants (London); Take Her She's Mine; A Funny Thing Happened on the Way to the Forum (Tony-1962); She Loves Me (London); Fiddler on the Roof (Tony-1964); Poot Bitos; Flora The Red Menace; Superman; Cabaret (Tony-1966); Zorba; Company (Tonys-musical & dir-1970); Follies (Tony-dir-1972); A Little Night Music (Tony-1973); Love For Love; Candide (Tony-dir-1974); Pacific Overtures; Side by Side by Sondheim; Some of My Best Friends; On the Twentieth Century; Sweeney Todd (Tony-dir-1978); Evita (Tony-dir-1980); Merrily We Roll Along; A Doll's Life (dir); Play Memory (dir); End of the World (dir); Diamonds (off-Bway)(dir); Grind.

Films inc: The Pajama Game (co-prod); Damn Yankees (co-prod); Something For Everyone (dir); A Little Night Music (dir).

TV inc: Willie Stark (Great Performances) (dir).

PRINCE, William: Act. b. Nichols, NY, Jan 26, 1913. On screen from 1943. Films inc: Destination Tokyo; Cinderella Jones; The Very Thought of You; Roughly Speaking; Objective Burma; Pillow to Post; Lust for Gold; Cyrano de Bergerac; Secret of Treasure Mountain; Macabre; Sacco and Vanzetti; The Heartbreak Kid; The Stepford Wives; Rollercoaster; The Cat From Outer Space; The Promise; Bronco Billy; Love & Money; The Soldier; Kiss Me Goodbye; Movers & Shakers.

Thea inc: Guest in the House; Across the Board on Tomorrow Morning; The Eve of St. Mark; John Loves Mary; As You Like It; I Am a Camera; Forward the Heart; Affair of Honor; Third Best Sport; The Highest Tree; Venus at Large; Strange Interlude; The Ballad of the Sad Cafe; Mercy Street; The Man Who Had Three Arms; Heartbreak House.

TV inc: The Jericho Mile; City in Fear; Gideon's Trumpet; A Matter of Life and Death; Moonlight; Found Money; George Washington; Concealed Enemies; Goldie & The Bears.

PRINCIPAL, Victoria: Act. b. Fukuoka, Japan, Jan 30, 1950. Films inc: The Life and Times of Judge Roy Bean; The Naked Ape; Earthquake; I Will, I Will. . .For Now; Vigilante Force.

TV inc: The Night They Stole Miss Beautiful; Dallas; Pleasure Palace; Delaney; Command Performance--The Stars Salute the President; Sixty Years of Seduction (host); Not Just Another Affair; On Top All Over The World.

PRINE, Andrew: Act. b. Jennings, FL, Feb 14, 1936. e. U of Miami. Films inc: Advance to the Rear; Company of Cowards; Generation; The Devil's Brigade; Chisum; Grizzly; The Evil; Amityville II--The Possession; They're Playing With Fire.

TV inc: Tail Gunner Joe; Last of the Mohicans; Law of the Land; The Road West; Wide Country; W.E.B.--The Girl Who Saved Our America; Mark Twain's America-Abe Lincoln-Freedom Fighter; Callie and Son; A Small Killing; Mind Over Murder; V; V--The Final Battle; And The Children Shall Lead.

Thea inc: Look Homeward, Angel; A Distant Bell.

PRINZ, Le Roy: Prod-Dir-Chor. b. St Joseph, MO, Jul 14, 1895. Ran away from home at 15, joined French Foreign Legion, served with French aerial corps; remained Paris after WW1 as chor, Folies Bergere. To Hwd 1931 as chor for Cecil B DeMille.

Films inc: Sign of the Cross; The Bing Crosby-Bob Hope Road Films; Yankee Doodle Dandy; Desert Song; This Is The Army; Night and Day; The Ten Commandments; Helen Morgan Story; Sayonara; South Pacific. Dir Oscar-winning short A Boy and His Dog; prod-dir films for U.S. Navy; commercial films.

Prod-dir stage revue Red, White and Blue for the American Legion.

(Died Sept. 15, 1983).

PRITCHETT, James: Act. b. Lenoir, NC, Oct 27, 1922. e. U of NC, AB, JD; U of Chicago, BS. Bway inc: Two for the Seesaw; Lord Pengo; Sail Away; Selling of the President.

TV inc: Hotel Cosmopolitan; The Secret Storm; As the World Turns; The Doctors (since 1963) (Emmy-1978).

PROCHNOW, Jurgen: Act. b. Berlin, June 10, 1941. Films inc: Zoff; Hans im Gluck; Einer von uns Beiden (One or the Other); Das Jagdrevier; Die Konsequenz (The Consequence); Operation Ganymed; Die Ferrohung das Franz Blum; Die Verlorene Ehre der Katharina Blum; Das Boot (The Boat); Comeback; Krieg und Frieden (War and Peace); The Keep; Love Is Forever; Dune; Der Bulle und Das Madchen (The Cop And The Girl).

TV inc: Harbor At the River Rhine; Forbidden.

PROSKY, Robert: Act. b. 1930. Has spent most of his career as a member of the Arena Stage, Washington DC. Bway inc: Moonchildren; Glengarry Glen Ross.

Films inc: Thief; Hanky Panky; Monsignor; Lords of Disipline; Christine; The Keep; The Natural.

TV inc: The Adams Chronicles; Beacon Hill; The Ordeal Of Bill Carney; Hill Street Blues.

PROVINE, Dorothy: Act. b. Deadwood, SD, Jan 20, 1937. e. U of WA. On screen from 1958 in The Bonnie Parker Story. Films inc: The Thirty Foot Bride of Candy Rock; It's a Mad, Mad, Mad, Mad World; Good Neighbor Sam; That Darn Cat; The Great Race; One Spy Too Many; Who's Minding the Mint?; Never a Dull Moment.

TV inc: The Alaskan; The Roaring 20's.

PROWSE, Juliet: Act. b. Bombay, Sep 25, 1936. On screen from 1960. Films inc: Gentlemen Marry Brunettes; Can-Can; G.I. Blues; The Second Time Around; The Right Approach; Who Killed Teddy Bear?; Dingaka; Run for Your Wife; Spree.

Thea inc: I Do! I Do!

TV inc: Glitter; Night Of 100 Stars II; Placido Domingo Steppin' Out With The Ladies; The 39th Annual Tony Awards.

PRYCE, Jonathan: Act. b. North Wales, 1947. e. RADA. Thea inc: (London) Comedians; joined Royal Shakespeare Co appearing in the Taming of the Shrew; Measure for Measure; Antony and Cleopatra; Hamlet. Bway inc: Comedians (Tony-1977).

TV inc: Comedians; Playthings; Daft as a Brush; Partisans; For Tea on Sunday; Glad Day; Timon of Athens; Murder Is Easy; Praying Mantis.

Films inc: Voyage of the Damned; Breaking Glass; Loophole; Praying Mantis; The Ploughman's Lunch; Something Wicked This Way Comes; Brazil.

PRYOR, Nicholas: Act. Bway inc: That Championship Season; Thieves; The Boys in the Band.

Films inc: The Fish That Saved Pittsburgh; The Gumball Rally; Well in the USA; Washington Behind Closed Doors; Gideon's Trumpet; The $5.20 an Hour Dream; The Plutonium Incident; Reunion; The Last Song; John Steinbeck's East of Eden; Homeroom; Revenge of the Gray Gang; A Few Days In Weasel Creek; The Kid From Nowhere; The Big Easy; Blood Feud; Insight/Dutton's Choice; Amazons; Second Sight--A Love Story; Crazy Like A Fox.

PRYOR, Richard: Act. b. Peoria, IL, Dec 1, 1940. Worked as standup comic in niteries, TV. Wrote scripts for Lily Tomlin, Flip Wilson; co-sp of film, Blazing Saddles; recorded several albums.

Films inc: (perf) Lady Sings the Blues; Bingo Long and the Travelin' All Stars; Silver Streak; Greased Lightning; Blue Collar; California Suite; The Wiz; Richard Pryor Live in Concert; The Muppet Movie; Wholly Moses; In God We Trust; Stir Crazy; Bustin' Loose (& prod); Richard Pryor Live On Sunset Strip (& wri-prod); Some Kind of Hero; The Toy; Superman III; Richard Pryor Here and Now (& wri-dir); Brewster's Millions.

TV inc: Lily (Emmy-wri-1974); Hollywood--The Gift of Laughter; The Best of Sullivan; Motown 25--Yesterday, Today, Forever (host); Pryor's Place.

(Grammys-(5) comedy recording-1974, 1975, 1976, 1981, 1982).

PRYOR, Thomas M.: Newspaperman. b. NYC, May 22, 1912. Joined NY Times, 1929; mp dept 1931 as reporter, edtr, asst film critic; Hollywood bureau chief, NY Times, 1951-59. Editor Daily Variety, since 1959.

PULVER, Liselotte (Lilo): Act. b. Switzerland, 1929. Films inc: Four Days Leave; Heidelberger Romanze; Der Letzte Sommer; The Adventures of Arsene Lupin; The Confessions of Felix Krull; The Spessart Inn; A Time To To Love and a Time to Die; One Two Three; Where the Truth Lies; La Religieuse (The Nun); Le Jardinier d'Argenteuil; Pistol Jenny; Brot Und Steine.

PUNCH-McGREGOR, Angela: Act. b. Sydney, Australia, Jan 21, 1953. e. Natl Institute of Dramatic Arts. Worked with Old Tote Theatre, Tasmanian Theatre Company, Nimrod Theatre in Australia. Thea inc: Playboy of the Western World; Collaborators; Kennedy's Children; Case for the Defense; Mother Courage; Romeo and Juliet; The Bride of Gospel Place.
TV inc: La Boheme; Alvin Purple; Kiss and Ride a Ferry; The Timeless Land.
Films inc: The Chant of Jimmie Blacksmith; Newsfront; The Island; The Survivor; The Best of Friends; We of the Never Never; Double Deal; Annie's Coming Out.

PURCELL, Lee: Act. b. NC, Jun 15, 1949. Films inc: Adam at 6 A.M.; Stand Up and Be Counted; Dirty Little Billy; Necromancy; Mr. Majestyk; Almost Summer; Big Wednesday; Stir Crazy; Homework; Eddie Macon's Run; Valley Girl.
TV inc: Death Works Overtime; The Amazing Mr. Hughes; Summer of Fear; Murder in Music City. Kenny Rogers as the Gambler; My Wife Next Door; The Secret War of Jackie's Girls; The Girl, The Gold Watch and Dynamite; Killing at Hell's Gate; My Wicked, Wicked Ways.

PURCELL, Noel: Act. b. Dublin, Dec 23, 1900. e. Irish Christian Brothers. Started as child actor, appeared with Abbey Players; also worked in vaude as comedian.
Films inc: Odd Man Out; The Blue Lagoon; Captain Boycott; Island Rescue; Crimson Pirate; Shake Hands With the Devil; Pickwick Papers; Doctor in the House; Moby Dick; Doctor at Sea; Lust for Life; Lord Jim; Arriverderci, Baby; Sinful Davy.
(Died March 3, 1985)

PURCELL, Sarah: Act. b. Richmond, IN., Oct. 8, 1948. e. UC San Diego; U of Hamburg, Germany. Started as weather girl, movie host, asst pgm dir KFMB-TV (San Diego); 1975, co-host AM Los Angeles, KABC-TV; other tv inc: The Better Sex (co-host); Sunday Funday (host); Sandlot Superstars (co-host); Guide for a Married Woman; Terror Among Us; Real People (host); Shape of Things; Emergency Room; Ballad of Gregori.
Films inc: Billy Jack Goes to Washington.

PURDOM, Edmund: Act. b. Welwyn Garden City, England, Dec 19, 1924. Thea inc: (London) The Way Things Go; Malade Imaginaire; Caesar and Cleopatra; Antony and Cleopatra.
Films inc: Titanic; The Student Prince; The Egyptian; The Prodigal; The Kings Thief; The Cossacks; Nights of Rasputin; The Comedy Man; The Beauty Jungle; The Yellow Rolls Royce; The Man in the Golden Mask; The Black Corsair; Evil Fingers; L'Altra Donna; Ator; Pieces; Don't Open Till Christmas (& dir); After The Fall Of New York.
TV inc: Sophia Loren--Her Own Story; The Scarlet and the Black; The Winds of War.

PURL, Linda: Act. b. Greenwich, CT, Sep 2, 1955. Moved to Japan at age 2. Appeared in Japanese theatre, TV. To US in 1971. Films inc: Jory; W C Fields & Me; Crazy Mama; Leo and Loree; The High Country; Visiting Hours.
TV inc: The Secret Storm; Happy Days; Eleanor and Franklin; Beacon Hill; Little Ladies of the Night; Testimony of Two Men; A Last Cry for Help; Women at West Point; The Young Pioneers; A Very Special Love; Like Normal People; The Flame Is Love; The Night the City Screamed; The Adventures of Nellie Bly; The Manions of America; Money On The Side; Happy Days; I Do, I Don't; The Changing Family (host); The Last Days of Pompeii.

PUTTNAM, David: Prod. b. London, 1941. Films inc: Melody; The Pied Piper; That'll Be the Day; Mahler; Bugsy Malone; The Duellists; Midnight Express; Foxes; Chariots of Fire *(Oscar*-1981); Experience Preferred But Not Essential (exec prod); Local Hero; Red Monarch (exec prod); Kipperbang (exec prod); Cal; Secrets (exec prod); Forever Young (exec prod); The Killing Fields; Winter Flight (exec prod); The Frog Prince; Mr. Love (exec prod).
TV inc: The Making of a Local Hero--with a Little Help from his Friends; Those Glory Glory Days.

PUZO, Mario: Wri. b. NYC, Oct 15, 1920. Films inc: The Godfather *(Oscar*-1972); The Godfather Part II *(Oscar*-1974); Earthquake; Superman; Superman II; A Time to Die (story); The Cotton Club (& story).

PYLE, Denver: Act. b. Bethune, CO, May 11, 1920. Films inc: The Man from Colorado; To Hell and Back; Shenandoah; Bonnie and Clyde; Five Card Stud; Something Big; Cahill; Escape to Witch Mountain; The Adventures of Frontier Fremont; Welcome to LA; Return from Witch Mountain.
TV inc: The Doris Day Show; The Life and Times of Grizzly Adams; The Dukes of Hazzard.

QUAID, Dennis: Act. b. Houston, TX, Apr 9, 1953. e. U of Houston. Films inc: Crazy Mama; 9/30/55; Our Winning Season; Seniors; Breaking Away; Gorp; The Long Riders; All Night Long; Caveman; The Night the Lights Went Out In Georgia; Tough Enough; Jaws 3-D; The Right Stuff.
TV inc: Bill; Johnny Belinda; Bill--On His Own.
Thea inc: True West.

QUAID, Randy: Act. b. 1950. Films inc: The Last Picture Show; What's Up Doc?; The Last Detail; Lolly Madonna XXX; Paper Moon; The Apprenticeship of Duddy Kravitz; Breakout; The Missouri Breaks; Bound for Glory; Three Warriors; The Choirboys; Midnight Express; Foxes; The Long Riders; Heartbeeps; National Lampoon's Vacation; Dreamscape; The Wild Life; The Slugger's Wife.
TV inc: The Last Ride of the Dalton Gang; Guyana Tragedy-The Story of Jim Jones; Of Mice and Men; Inside The Third Reich; Cowboy; A Streetcar Named Desire.
Thea inc: True West; The Golem.

QUALEN, John (nee Oleson): Act. b. Vancouver, BC, Dec 8, 1899. Films inc: Arrowsmith; Counsellor-At-Law; The Farmer Takes A Wife; The Three Musketeers; The Country Doctor; Black Fury; Seventh Heaven; The Grapes of Wrath; Four Wives; All That Money Can Buy; Tortilla Flat; Casablanca; The Fugitive; The Big Steal; Hans Christian Andersen; The High and the Mighty; The Big Land; Anatomy of a Murder; Two Rode Together; The Man Who Shot Liberty Valance; The Prize; The Seven Faces of Dr Lao; Cheyenne Autumn; The Sons of Katie Elder; A Patch of Blue; A Big Hand for the Little Lady; Firecreek; Hail Hero; Frazer The Sensuous Lion; Criss Cross.
TV inc: Mr Ed; Hazel; Partridge Family.

QUAYLE, Anna: Act. b. Birmingham, England, Oct 6, 1937. e. RADA. Thea inc: Do You Mind?; Look Who's Here!; Stop the World - I Want to Get Off; *(Tony*-supp-1963); Homage to T S Eliot; Full Circle; Out of Bounds; Pal Joey; Kings and Clowns; The Case of the Oily Levantine.
Films inc: Drop Dead Darling; Smashing Time; Chitty Chitty Bang Bang; Up the Chastity Belt.
TV inc: S O S Titanic; Brideshead Revisited.

QUAYLE, Anthony, CBE: Act. b. Ainsdale, Lancashire, England, Sep 7, 1913. e. RADA. Stage debut London 1931, Robin Hood. Thea inc: (London) various Shakespearean roles with Old Vic Co; Anna Christie; Pride and Prejudice; The Silent Knight; Trelawney of the Wells; The Rivals; Crime and Punishment (dir); director of Shakespeare Memorial Theatre 1948-1956; A View from the Bridge; Look After Lulu; Incident at Vichy; Sleuth; Harvey (dir); Hobson's Choice; A Coat of Varnish (& dir); The Rules of the Game (dir); The Clandestine Marriage; After The Ball Is Over. (Bway) The Country Wife; Tamburlaine The Great; The Firstborn (& dir); Galileo; Halfway Up the Tree; Sleuth; Do You Turn Somersaults?
Films inc: Hamlet; Battle of the River Plate; The Wrong Man; No Time for Tears; The Man Who Would Not Talk; Ice Cold in Alex; The Nelson Affair; Guns of Navarone; Lawrence of Arabia; Barefoot in

Athens; Fall of the Roman Empire; MacKenna's Gold; Anne of the Thousand Days; The Tamarind Seed; The Eagle Has Landed; The Chosen; Murder By Decree.

TV inc: QB VII (Emmy-supp-1975); Henry IV; Masada; Dial "M" For Murder; The Manions of America; Lace; The Last Days of Pompeii; The Key To Rebecca.

QUEEN: Group. Members are Freddie Mercury; John Deacon; Brian May, Roger Taylor. Formed in Britain in 1971. Innovators of effects, costumes for rock tours of Us, Japan. Albums inc: Queen; Sheer Heart Attack; A Night at the Opera; A Day At The Races; News of the World; We Are The Champions; Jazz; The Game.

Films inc: Flash Gordon (score).

TV inc: Teenage Suicide--Don't Try It! (score); Saturday Night Live.

QUENNESSEN, Valerie: Act. b. Paris. e. Conservatoire Nationale d'Arts Dramatiques. Thea inc: Bajazet; Phedre; Chers Oiseaux.

Films inc: Le Plein de Super (Fill 'er up with Super); Le Petit Marcel; La Tortue sur le dos (As a Turtle on its Back); French Postcards; Conan, the Barbarian; Summer Lovers.

QUESTED, John: Dir-Prod. Started as asst dir, later prodn mgr for Col, France; WB, Spain; UA, Ireland. Films inc: A Lion in Winter (asso prod); All The Right Noises (prod); Philadelphia, Here I Come; The Brute; Leopard in the Snow (prod); The Stud (prod); The Passage (prod); Sunburn (exec prod); Loophole (dir); Here Are Ladies.

QUIGLEY, Martin Jr: Edit-Wri-Publ. b. Chicago, IL, Nov 24, 1917. e. Georgetown U, AB; Columbia U, Ed.D. S of founder of Motion Picture Herald, Motion Picture Daily.

Special edit rep, later asso edtr, edtr Quigley Publications. Author Magic Shadows (on origins of film business); New Screen Techniques; co-author Films in America.

QUILLAN, Eddie: Act. b. Philadelphia, PA, Mar 31, 1907. In vaude as child with family act.

Films inc: Up and At 'Em; Night Work; Big Money; A Little Bit of Everything; The Big Shot; Mutiny on the Bounty; Young Mr. Lincoln; Grapes of Wrath; Margie; This is the Life; A Guy Could Change; Flying Blind; Sideshow; Brigadoon; Promises! Promises!; Move Over Darling; The Ghost and Mr. Chicken; Angel In My Pocket; How to Frame a Figg.

TV inc: White Mama; The Great Cash Giveaway Getaway; For The Love Of It; Highway To Heaven.

QUILLEY, Denis: Act. b. London, Dec 26, 1927. Thea inc: Lady From the Sea; King John; Richard III; The Lady's Not For Burning; Wild Thyme; Irma La Douce (& Bway); The Boys From Syracuse; High Spirits; Long Day's Journey Into Night; The Front Page; Macbeth; School for Scandal; The Crucible.

Films inc: Life at the Top; Anne of the Thousand Days; Murder on the Orient Express; Evil Under the Sun; Privates on Parade; Memed, My Hawk; King David.

TV inc: The Father; Murder in the Cathedral; Contrabandits; Your're On Your Own; Masada; A.D.

QUINE, Richard: Dir. b. Detroit, MI, Nov 12, 1920. Former act on Bway in Very Warm For May; My Sister Eileen. Films inc: (act) The World Changes; Babes on Broadway; My Sister Eileen; For Me and My Gal. (Dir) The Sunny Side of the Street; Drive a Crooked Road; My Sister Eileen; The Solid Gold Cadillac; Operation Mad Ball; Bell, Book and Candle; The World of Suzie Wong; The Notorious Landlady; Paris When It Sizzles; How to Murder Your Wife; Oh Dad, Poor Dad, Mama's Hung You in the Closet and I'm Feelin' So Sad; Hotel; A Talent for Loving; The Moonshine War; W.; Prisoner of Zenda.

QUINLAN, Kathleen: Act. b. Pasadena, CA, Nov 19, 1954. Films inc: American Graffiti; Lifeguard; Airport '77; I Never Promised You a Rose Garden; The Promise; The Runner Stumbles; Sunday Lovers; Hanky Panky; Independence Day; Hakhoref Ha' Acharon (The Last Winter); Twilight Zone--The Movie; Blackout.

TV inc: She's In The Army Now; When She Says No.

QUINN, Aileen: Act. b. Yardley, PA, 1971. Bway inc: Annie. Film inc: Annie. TV inc: Andy Williams' New England Christmas.

QUINN, Anthony: Act. b. Chihuahua, Mexico, Apr 21, 1916. Films inc: The Plainsman; The Buccaneer; Union Pacific; They Died With Their Boots On; The Ox-bow Incident; Guadalcanal Diary; Buffalo Bill; China Sky; Back to Bataan; Black Gold; Tycoon; The Brave Bulls; Against All Flags; East of Sumatra; Ulysses; Viva Zapata (Oscar-supp-1952); La Strada; Attila the Hun; Hunchback of Notre Dame; Lust For Life (Oscar-supp-1956); The Guns of Navarone; Barabbas; Requiem for a Heavyweight; Zorba the Greek; The Don Is Dead; Mohammed, Messenger of God; The Shoes of the Fisherman; The Destructors; Caravans; The Children of Sanchez; The Greek Tycoon; The Inheritance; The Passage; Lion of The Desert; High Risk; Mystique (exec prod); Valentina; The Salamander.

TV inc: Schlitz Playhouse; The Vise; Man and the City; Jesus of Nazareth; Ready When You Are, Mr. De Mille; Salute to Lady Liberty.

Bway inc: Zorba.

QUINN, Bill: Act. b. NYC, May 6 1912. Bway debut at age 2 in Daddies. Other Bway inc: The Blue Bird; That Smith Boy; They All Want Something; Winterset. On radio in several series inc Just Plain Bill; Mrs. Wiggs of the Cabbage Patch; Front Page Farrell.

Films inc: The Last Hurrah; The Mountain Road; Cry for Happy; Advise and Consent.

TV inc: The Rifleman; The Mary Tyler Moore Show; McMillan and Wife; All in the Family; Archie Bunker's Place; Dark Mirror; Velvet. subtotal? (Y/N):

QUINTERO, Jose: Dir. b. Panama City, Panama, Oct 15, 1924. e. USC. Thea inc: Long Day's Journey Into Night (Tony-co-prod-1957); Pousse Cafe; More Stately Mansions; The Seven Descents of Myrtle; Gandhi; A Moon for the Misbegotten (Tony-1973); The Skin of Our Teeth; Anna Christie; A Touch of the Poet; Clothes For A Summer Hotel.

Opera inc: Pagliacci; Cavalleria Rusticana.

Films inc: The Roman Spring of Mrs Stone.

TV inc: Medea; Our Town.

RABAL, Francisco: Act. b. Aguilas, Spain, Mar 8, 1925. Legitimate theatre, Madrid. Films inc: The Eclipse; Nazaran; Viridiana; Belle du Jour; Desert of the Tartars; Sorcerer; Stay As You Are; Corleone; Reborn; La Colmena (The Bee-Hive); Treasure of the Four Crowns; Truhanes (Rogues); City of the Walking Dead; Epilogo; Los Santos Inocentes (The Holy Innocents); Los Zancos (The Stilts); Un Delitto (A Crime); Padre Nuestro (Our Father).

TV inc: Los desastres de la Guerra (Guerilla).

RABB, Ellis: Act-Dir-Prod-Wri. b. Memphis, TN, Jun 20, 1930. e. U of AZ; Carnegie Institute of Technology, BFA; Yale U. Made stage debut 1952, King John. NY debut 1956, A Midsummer Night's Dream; founded and became artistic dir of the Association of Producing Artists, 1960; also dir for the Old Globe Theatre; The Kansas City Center of the Performing Arts; Dallas Civic Opera. Bway inc: (dir) The School for Scandal; The Tavern; The Seagull; The Grass Harp; Sleuth; Veronica's Room; Who's Who In Hell; Edward II; Caesar and Cleopatra (rev); The Royal Family (Tony-1976); In A Life in the Theatre (act); The Man Who Came To Dinner (rev); The Philadelphia Story (rev); You Can't Take It With You (rev); The Loves Of Anatol (& adapt).

TV inc: The Royal Family; The Dain Curse (act).

RABBITT, Eddie (Edward Thomas Rabbitt): Singer-Sngwri. b. Brooklyn, Nov 27, 1941. Songs inc: Kentucky Rain; Pure Love; Forgive and Forget; Rocky Mountain Music; Drinkin' My Baby Off My Mind; Two Dollars in the Jukebox.

TV inc: The Eddie Rabbitt Show; Crystal; Music City News' Top Country Hits of the Year; Anson 'N' Lorrie; Johnny Cash--A Merry Memphis Christmas; Anne Murray's Caribbean Cruise; A Special Eddie Rabbitt; Bob Hope Goes to College; Lynda Carter Body and Soul.

RABE, David William: Plywri. b. Dubuque, IA, Mar 10, 1940. Plays inc: The Basic Training of Pavlo Hummel; Stickes and Bones; The Orphan; In the Boom Boom Room; Streamers; Hurlyburly.

Films inc: I'm Dancing As Fast As I Can (exec prod-wri); Streamers.

RACHMIL, Lewis J.: Exec. b. NYC, Jul 3, 1908. e. NYU; Yale School of Fine Arts. Started as art dir Par (Long Island Studios) 1930; to Hollywood as art dir, asst prod.

Films inc: Parson of Panamint; Tombstone; Hopalong Cassidy Series; Bunco Squad; Crackdown; Hunt The Man Down; Roadblock; Androcles and the Lion (co-prod); Whiphand; Gun Fury; Human Desire; They Rode West; Violent Men; Tight Spot; The Brothers Rico; Gidget; Reprisal; Kings of the Sun; 633 Squadron; 1977 vp & exec prodn mgr MGM; resd Sept. 1981, joined Daniel Melnick's Indie Prod Co. Films inc: Footloose (prod); Protocol (asso prod).
(Died Feb. 19, 1984).

RADEMAKERS, Fons (Alphonse M Rademakers): Prod-Dir. b. Roosendaal, Netherlands, Sep 5, 1920. Films inc: Village on the River; That Joyous Eve; The Knife; The Spitting Image; The Dance of the Heron; Because of the Cats; Max Havelaar; Mijn Vriend; Mysteries (act); Friday (act).

RADIN, Paul B.: Prod. b. NYC, Sep 15, 1913. e. NYU. Assoc prod: The Journey; Once More with Feeling; Surprise Package. Prod: Born Free; Living Free; Phase IV; The Blue Bird.
TV inc: Born Free; Kate; The Incredible Journey of Doctor Meg Laurel; The Two Worlds of Jenny Logan; The Ordeal of Dr. Mudd; The Wild and the Free; Jane Doe; The Haunting Passion.

RADNER, Gilda: Act. b. Detroit, MI, Jun 28. TV inc: The Muppet Show; All You Need is Cash; Saturday Night Live *(Emmy*-supp-1978).
Films inc: Mr. Mike's Mondo Video; Gilda Live; First Family; Hanky Panky; It Came From Hollywood; The Woman In Red; Movers & Shakers.
Bway inc: Lunch Hour.

RADNITZ, Robert B.: Prod. b. Great Neck, NY, Aug 9, 1924. e. U of VA. Reader for Bway dir Harold Clurman. Wrote doc scripts for RKO-Pathe; worked as stage mgr; produced (Bway and London) The Young and the Beautiful. First feature film, A Dog of Flanders, 1960.
Films inc: Misty; Island of the Blue Dolphins; My Side of the Mountain; Little Ark; Sounder; Birch Interval; Sounder II; A Hero Ain't Nothin' But A Sandwich; Cross Creek.
TV inc: Mary White.

RAE, Charlotte (nee Lubotsky): Act. b. Milwaukee, WI, Apr 22, 1926. e. Northwestern U, BS. Bway inc: Romeo and Juliet; Li'l Abner; Pickwick; Morning, Noon and Night.
Films inc: Rabbit Test; Hair.
TV inc: Sesame Street; Car 54 Where Are You?; Hot L Baltimore; Queen of the Stardust Ballroom; The Triangle Factory Fire Scandal; Beane's of Boston; Diff'rent Strokes; Facts of Life; Emily Dickinson; The Way They Were; An NBC Family Christmas; Kennedy Center Tonight--Broadway to Washington.

RAFELSON, Bob: Prod-Dir-Wri. b. NYC, 1935. Films inc: Head (co-sp); Five Easy Pieces (co-prod-dir); The King of Marvin Gardens (prod-dir); Stay Hungry (co-prod, co-sp, dir); The Postman Always Rings Twice (prod-dir); Always (act).
TV inc: The Monkees *(Emmy*-prod-1967).

RAFFIN, Deborah: Act. b. Los Angeles, March 13, 1953. Former model. Films inc: 40 Carats; The Dove; God Told Me To; The Sentinel; Once Is Not Enough; Maniac; Touched By Love.
TV inc: Willa; The Last Convertible; Mind Over Murder; Haywire; For The Love Of It; Foul Play; Killing At Hell's Gate; For Lovers Only; Running Out; Threesome; On Top All Over The World; Lace II.

RAFKIN, Alan: Dir-Prod. b. NYC, Jul 23, 1938. e. Syracuse U (BS). TV inc: Mary Tyler Moore Show; Laverne and Shirley; M*A*S*H; One Day At A Time (& exec prod) *(Emmy*-dir-1982); Harry's Battles; We Got It Made; Charles In Charge; Sam.

RAGAWAY, Martin: Wri-Prod. b. Jan 29, 1928. e. NYU. TV inc: Peter Donald; Milton Berle; Abbott & Costello, Phil Baker; Bob Hope; I Love Lucy, Phil Silvers; Red Skelton *(Emmy*-wri-1961); Dick Van Dyke Show; Mary Tyler Moore Show; The Courtship of Eddie's Father; Entertainer of the Year Awards (wri). Films inc: Ma and Pa Kettle Go to New York; The Milkman.

RAGIN, John S.: Act. b. Newark, NJ, May 5, 1929. e. Carnegie Tech. Films inc: Earthquake; The Parallax View; Marooned; Doctor's Wives; Bob and Carol & Ted and Alice; I Love You, Alice B Toklas.

TV inc: Sons and Daughters; Quincy.

RAGLAND, Robert Oliver: Comp-Arr-Cond. b. Chicago, Jul 3, 1931. e. Northwestern U, BS; Amer Cons, BA, MA. Comp, arr, pianist for orchs inc Tommy & Jimmy Dorsey; Ralph Marterie; Dick Contino; Woody Herman. Film scores inc: Grizzly; Sharks Treasure; Seven Alone; The Saga of Jimmy D; The Kill Machine; Return to Macon County; Where's Willie?; Only Once in a Lifetime; The Babysitter; Weekend with the Babysitter; Jaguar Lives; The Glove; The Winged Serpent; 10 to Midnight; Lovely But Deadly; A Time to Die; Evils Of The Night.
TV inc: Reflections (Girl on the Edge of Town).

RAILSBACK, Steve: Act. b. Dallas, TX. Studied with Lee Strasberg. Thea inc: Bluebird; Orpheus Descending; This Property Condemned; One Sunday Afternoon; The Cherry Orchard; The Skin of Our Teeth.
Films inc: The Visitors; Angela; The Stunt Man; Turkey Shoot; The Golden Seal; Deadly Games; Torchlight; Lifeforce.
TV inc: Helter Skelter; From Here To Eternity.

RAINER, Luise: Act. b. Vienna, 1910. On stage in Austria 1930; to Hollywood 1934. Films inc: Ecstasy; Escapade; The Great Ziegfeld *(Oscar*-1936); The Good Earth *(Oscar*-1937); The Emperor's Candlesticks; The Big City; The Toy Wife; The Great Waltz; Dramatic School; Hostages.

RAINES, Cristina: Act. b. Manila, Philippines, Feb 28, 1953. Films inc: Hex; The Stone Killer; Nashville; Russian Roulette; The Sentinel; The Duellists; Silver Dream Racer; Touched By Love; Nightmares; Real Life.
TV inc: Doctors Hospital; Sunshine; Loose Change; The Tenth Month; Centennial; The Child Stealer; Flamingo Road; The Nashville Grab; The Return of Marcus Welby, M.D.; Generation.

RAINES, Ella: Act. b. Snowquainde Falls, WA, Aug 6, 1921. On screen from 1943 in Corvette K-225; Hail the Conquering Hero; Tall in the Saddle; White Tie and Tails; Time Out Of Mind; The Web; Brute Force; The Senator Was Indiscreet; Impact; Ride the Man Down; Man in the Road.
TV inc: Janet Dean, R.N.

RAINS, Robert H.: Exec. b. NYC, Aug 12, 1921. e. NYU. Started as PA with International Pictures, 1946; dir of radio activities; asst casting dir, 1952; radio-TV activities, 1955; exec in chg of TV press dept, Universal City, 1961; Universal vp, 1966; ret Apr 21, 1978.

RAITT, Bonnie: Singer. b. Burbank, CA, Nov 8, 1949. D of John Raitt. Recording artist; concerts.
Films inc: No Nukes.

RAITT, John: Act. b. Santa Ana, Jan 29, 1917. Bway from 1945 in Carousel; Magdalena; Three Wishes For Jamie; Carnival in Flanders; The Pajama Game; A Joyful Noise; A Musical Jubilee.
Films from 1940 inc: Flight Command; Billy The Kid; Ziegfeld Girl; The Pajama Game.
TV inc: Buick Circus Hour; Chevy Show; Annie Get Your Gun; America Sing; Grammy Hall of Fame; Kennedy Center Tonight--Broadway To Washington!

RAIZMAN, Yuly: Dir. b. Moscow, Dec. 15, 1903. e. Moscow U. Started as literary conslt Mezhrabpom-Rus Studios, served as asst dir, also act, on Chess Fever. Films inc: The Bear's Wedding (asst dir); The Trial of the Three Millions (asst dir); The Forty-First (asst dir); The Ring (Duty and Love) (co-dir); Forced Labor; The Earth Thirsts; The Tale About Umar Khaptsoko; The Pilots; The Last Night (co-dir, co-sp); Virgin Soil Upturned; Mashenka; A Propos of the Truce with Finland (doc); Moscow Sky; Berlin (doc); The Westward-Bound Train; Rainis; The Knight of the Gold Star; A Lesson in Life; The Communist; What If It Is Love?; Your Contemporary; A Courtesy Call; A Strange Woman (& co-sp); Private Life; Vremia Jelanii (Wishing Time).

RAKSIN, David: Comp-Cond-Arr. b. Philadelphia, Aug 4, 1912. Films scores inc: Modern Times; Laura; The Bad and the Beautiful; Forever Amber; The Secret Life of Walter Mitty; Suddenly; Separate Tables; Force of Evil; The Magnificent Yankees; Al Capone; Sylvia; A Big Hand for the Little Lady. Songs inc: Laura; Forever Amber; The Bad and the Beautiful; A Song After Sundown. TV themes inc: Ben Casey; The Breaking Point.

RALSTON, Esther: Act. b. Bar Harbor, ME, Sep 27, 1902. Starred on radio series Portia Faces Life for two years. In over 150 films from 1917 to 1942. Vaudeville headliner. Films inc: The Phantom Fortune (serial); Peter Pan; A Kiss for Cinderella; Lucky Devil; Old Ironsides; Figures Don't Lie; The Sawdust Paradise; The Prodigal; Sadie McKee; Hollywood Boulevard; Tin Pan Alley.

RALSTON, Vera (nee Hruba): Act. b. Prague, 1919. Widow of Herbert J Yates. Ice skating champion in Europe. Appeared in ice shows in U.S. Screen debut, 1941, Ice Capades (as Vera Hruba); The Lady and the Monster; Lake Placid; Murder in the Music Hall (billed Vera Hruba Ralston); and, after 1946 billed Vera Ralston, The Plainsman and the Lady; The Flame; Wyoming; I, Jane Doe; The Wild Blue Yonder; Hoodlum Empire; Fair Wind to Java; Timberjack; Accused of Murder; The Man Who Died Twice.

RAMBALDI, Carlos: Dsgn-Sculptor. b. Ferrara, Italy, Sep 16, 1925. e. Academy of Fine Arts, Bologna. Creator of special effects for screen, stage, TV. Films inc: King Kong (Oscar-special-1976); The White Buffalo; Barabbas; Frankenstein; Dracula; Last Woman; Alien (Oscar-visual effects-1979); E.T. The ExtraTerrestrial (Oscar-visual effects-1982).

RAMBO, Dack: Act. b. Delano, CA, Nov 13, 1941. TV inc: The New Loretta Young Show; Never Too Young; The Guns of Will Sonnett; Dirty Sally; River of Gold; Hit Lady; Sword of Justice; Waikiki; All My Children; No Man's Land; Paper Dolls.
Films inc: Wild Flowers; Deadly Honeymoon.

RAMIN, Sid: Comp-Cond. b. Boston, Jan 22, 1924. e. Boston U; Columbia U. Bway inc: West Side Story; Gypsy; A Funny Thing Happened On the Way to the Forum; Wildcat; I Can Get It For You Wholesale; The Girls Against the Boys; Kwamina.
TV inc: (Mus dir) Patty Duke Show; Milton Berle Show; Candid Camera. (Comp) All My Children (Emmy-1983).
Films inc: West Side Story (Oscar-1961).
Songs inc: Simon Says; Where There's a Man; Ecstasy Waltz; Come Alive (Pepsi Cola Commercial).
(Grammy-soundtrack-1961).

RAMPLING, Charlotte: Act. b. Stumer, England, Feb 5, 1946. Films inc: The Knack; Rotten to the Core; Georgy Girl; Ski Bum; Corky; Tis a Pity She's A Whore; Asylum; The Night Porter; Zardoz; Farewell My Lovely; Foxtrot; Orca; The Purple Taxi; Target-Harry; Stardust Memories; The Verdict; Viva la Vie! (Long Life Life!).
TV inc: The Six Wives of Henry VIII; The Strangers; Infidelities.

RANDALL, Tony: Act. b. Tulsa, OK, Feb. 26, 1920. e. Northwestern U. On screen from 1957 in Oh Men! Oh Women!. Films inc: Will Success Spoil Rock Hunter?; The Mating Game; Pillow Talk; Boy's Night Out; The Seven Faces of Dr. Lao; Send Me No Flowers; The Alphabet Murders; Everything You Always Wanted to Know About Sex; The King of Comedy.
TV inc: One Man's Family; Mr. Peepers; Playhouse 90; The Odd Couple (Emmy-1975); The Tony Randall Show; Sleep From A to Zzzz (host); Sidney Shorr; Love, Sidney; Doug Henning's Magic On Broadway; Off Sides; Hitler's SS--Portrait In Evil; The 39th Annual Tony Awards.
Bway inc: Circle of Chalk; The Corn is Green; Antony & Cleopatra; Caesar and Cleopatra; Oh, Men! Oh, Women!; The Barretts of Wimpole Street; Inherit the Wind; Oh Captain.

RANDELL, Ron: Act. b. New South Wales, Australia, Oct 8, 1923. e. St Mary's Coll, Sydney. Bway inc: The Browning Version; Harlequinade; The World of Suzie Wong. (London) Candide; Sweet Peril; The Fifth Season; Sabrina Fair; Mary, Mary; The Button; The Passionate Husband; Mrs Warren's Profession; Bent.
Films inc: Pacific Adventure; I Am a Camera; King of Kings; Exposed.

RANSOHOFF, Martin: Exec. b. New Orleans, LA, 1927. e. Colgate U. With Young & Rubicam, 1948-49. Wri, dir, Gravel Films, 1951;

formed Filmways, 1952, later formed Filmways TV Prod, Filmways, Inc, Filmways of Calif. Resigned as bd chmn. Filmways 1972 to start new independent co. Films inc: The Loved One; The Cincinnati Kid; Ten Rillington Place; King Lear; Topkapi; Ice Station Zebra; Catch 22; Save the Tiger; The White Dawn; Silver Streak; Nightwing; The Wanderers; A Change of Seasons; American Pop; Hanky Panky; Class.
TV inc: Mister Ed; The Beverly Hillbillies; Petticoat Junction; The Addams Family.

RAPF, Matthew: Prod. b. NYC, Oct 22, 1920. Films inc: Adventures of Gallant Bess; Desperate Search; Big Leaguer; Half a Hero. TV inc: Loretta Young Show; Frontier; The Great Gildersleeve; The Web; Two Faces West; Ben Casey; Slattery's People; The Young Lawyers; Terror in the Sky; On the Land; Marcus-Nelson Murders; Kojack; Doctor's Private Lives; Eischeid; The Oklahoma City Dolls.

RAPHAEL, Frederic: Wri. b. Chicago, 1931. e. Cambridge. Films inc: Nothing But the Best; Darling (Oscar-1965); Two for the Road; Far from the Madding Crowd; A Severed Head; Daisy Miller; The Glittering Prices; Rogue Male; Roses, Roses; Richard's Things; Sleeps Six.
TV inc: School Play.

RAPHAELSON, Samson: Wri. b. NYC, Mar 30, 1896. e. U of IL. Plays inc: The Jazz Singer; Young Love; The Wooden Slipper; Accent on Youth; White Man; Skylark; Jason; The Perfect Marriage.
Films inc: The Magnificent Lie; The Smiling Lieutenant; Trouble In Paradise; Broken Lullaby; One Hour With You; Angel; Shop Around the Corner; Suspicion; Heaven Can Wait; Green Dolphin Street; That Lady in Ermine; A Prince In Disguise; Main Street to Broadway.
(Died July 16, 1983).

RAPHEL, David: Exec. b. Boulogne-sur-Seine, France, Jan 9, 1925. 1950 asst sls mgr Fox France; 1951 asst mgr Italy; 1954 mgr Holland; 1957 asst European mgr; 1959 European mgr for TV; 1961 Continental mgr; 1964 vp chg intl sls (NY); 1973 P Fox Int'l; 1975 sr vp wldwde mktg features; 1976 ousted from Fox, joined International Creative Management heading new unit to rep indie prods; 1979 p ICM Film Marketing; 1980 founded Cambridge Film Group Ltd. Film inc: The Secret Diary of Sigmund Freud (exec prod).

RAPPAPORT, Michelle: Prod. b. NY, Mar 15, 1952. e. Simmons Coll. Films inc: Old Boyfriends (co-prod); TV inc: Paper Dolls; Something About Amelia (Emmy-Prod-1984).

RAPPER, Irving: Dir. b. London, England, 1900. e. NYU. Films inc: Shining Victory; One Foot in Heaven; The Gay Sisters; Adventures of Mark Twain; Rhapsody in Blue; The Corn is Green; Deception; Now, Voyager; Voice of the Turtle; Anna Lucasta; Glass Menagerie; Bad for Each Other; The Brave One; Marjorie Morningstar; The Miracle; Joseph and His Brethren; The Christine Jorgensen Story; Born Again.

RASKER, Frans: Prod. b. Amsterdam, Jul 12, 1945. Prod mgr, Scorpio Films; then independent prod, 1976. Films inc: Blind Spot; Pastorale 1943. Shorts: (Dir) Wintertime Love; Hairdressers; De Weg Naar Bresson (The Way to Bresson) (doc); De Prooi (The Prey).

RASKIN, Carolyn: Prod. b. IA, Aug 22. e. U of IA. TV inc: Rowan & Martin's Laugh In (Emmys-1968 & 1969); Arte Johnson Pilot; Frank Sinatra Special; Wacky World Special; Hellzapoppin; Up With People; John Ford Tribute; Helen Reddy Summer Series; The Shape of Things; One More Time; Travelin' On; Funny World of Sports; Dinah! (Emmys-1975 & 1976); Jim Nabors Show; All Star Salute to Women's Sports; Us Against the World; Beverly and Friends; Big City Comedy; Laugh Trax (& dir); Bob Hope's Road to Hollywood; The Rock Palace (exec prod); Bob Hope's Wicky-Wacky Special from Waikiki.

RASKY, Harry: Prod-Dir-Wri. b. Toronto, May 9, 1928. e. U of Toronto, BA. Films inc: (doc) Homage to Chagall; The Colours of Love; Arthur Miller on Home Ground; Being Different; The Spies Who Never Were.
TV inc: The 49th State; Perspective on Greatness; Meet the Professor; Cuba and Castro; The African Revolution; A Child is to Love; The Lion and the Cross; This Proud Land; Hall of Kings (Emmy-doc-1967); The Legend of Silent Night; Tennessee Williams' South; The Wit and World of George Bernard Shaw; The Song of Leonard

Cohen; Stratasphere (cable); Raymond Massey--Actor of the Century.

RASULALA, Thalmus (Jack Crowder): Act. b. 1939. Films inc: Cool Breeze; Blacula; Willie Dynamite; Mr Ricco; Bucktown; Fun with Dick and Jane; The Last Hard Men; The Bermuda Triangle.

TV inc: The Sophisticated Gents; For Us, the Living; The Jerk, Too; Booker.

RATHER, Dan: TV Newsman. b. Wharton, TX, 1931. Member of the CBS staff since 1962. Served as White House Correspondent anchorman, CBS Evening News. (Emmys-(6)-Coverage of The Watergate Affair, 1973; shooting of Gov Wallace, 1973; Agnew resignation-1974; Watergate, The White House transcripts-1974; The Senate and the Watergate Affair-1974; 60 Minutes-1980). Named co-edtr 60 Minutes, Oct 1975; Succeeded Walter Cronkite on latter's retirement as CBS Anchorman, March 9, 1981; TV inc: A Conversation With the President; Eye On the Media--Business and the Press (anchor).

RAVETCH, Irving: Wri-Dir-Prod. b. 1915. H of Harriet Frank. Films inc: The Long Hot Summer; The Sound and the Fury; Home from the Hill; The Dark at the Top of the Stairs; Hud; Hombre; The Reivers (& prod); Conrack; Norma Rae.

RAWLINS, Lester (nee Rosenberg): Act. b. Sharon, PA, Sep 24, 1924. e. Carnegie-Mellon, BFA. Charter founder member of Arena Stage, Washington. In repertory, stock and off Bway inc: The Quare Fellow; Camino Real; Nightride; Hedda Gabler; Benito Cereno. Bway inc: Othello; Henry IV; Macbeth; Romeo and Juliet; The Lovers; Hamlet; A Man for All Seasons; The Golden Age; The Child Buyer; The Reckoning; Da (Tony-supp-1978).

Films inc: Mr Congressman; Diary of a Mad Housewife; They Might Be Giants.

TV inc: Salome; The Life of Samuel Johnson; Secret Storm; Edge of Night; The Nurses.

RAWLS, Eugenia: Act. b. Macon, GA, Sep 11, 1916. e. U of NC. Bway inc: Member of Clare Tree Major's childrens theatre; The Children's Hour; Pride and Prejudice; Strange Fruit; The Little Foxes; Fanny Kemble (one woman show); Just the Immediate Family; The Daughter of the Regiment (Boston Opera Co).

TV inc: Hedda Gabler; The Great Sebastians; The Doctors; The Nurses.

RAWLS, Lou: Singer. b. Chicago, IL, Dec 1, 1936. Started as member of Pilgrim Travelers, gospel group; solo in 1962; recordings (Grammys-R&B vocal-1961, 1971, 1977).

Films inc: Angel, Angel Down We Go; Believe in Me.

TV inc: Soul; Lou Rawls and the Golddiggers; Uptown--A Tribute to the Apollo Theatre; The Fall Guy; Here Comes Garfield (voice); The President's Command Performance; Garfield on the Town (vocals); Black Gold Awards (exec prod & co-host); The Secret World Of The Very Young; E.R. (sings theme); Garfield In the Rough (voice); Motown Returns To The Apollo.

RAY, Aldo (Aldo DaRe): Act. b. Pen Argyl, PA, Sep 5, 1926. Screen debut, 1951, Saturday's Hero. Films inc: The Marrying Kind; Pat and Mike; Miss Sadie Thompson; Battle Cry; The Naked and the Dead; God's Little Acre; What Did You Do in the War, Daddy?; Welcome to Hard Times; The Violent Ones; The Green Berets; Inside Out; Seven Alone; Psychic Killer; Haunts; Sweet Savage; Human Experiments; The Glove; The Secret of NIMH (voice); Boxoffice; Bog; Evils Of The Night; Flesh And Bullets.

TV inc: Women in White.

RAY, Johnnie: Singer. b. Dallas, OR, 1927. Performs in niteries. Known for his rendition of song, Cry. On screen 1954, There's No Business Like Show Business.

RAY, Satyajit: Dir. b. India, May 2, 1921. Films inc: Pather Panchali; The Unvanquished; The Music Room; The World of Apu; The Goddess; The Adventures of Goopy and Bagha; The Adversary; Distant Thunder; The Middle Man; The Chess Player; The Elephant God (& wri-mus); The Kingdom of Diamonds (& wri-mus); Phatikchand (Phatik and the Juggler) (& wri-mus); Ghare Baire (The Home and the World (& wri-mus).

RAYBOULD, Harry: Act-Prod-Dir. b. Jun 16, 1932. Films inc: The Amazing Colossal Man; Girl in the Woods; The Wizard of Bagdad; The Scorpio Letters; The Young Goodman Brown; Genesis II.

TV inc: Playhouse 90; Twilight Zone; Ozzie and Harriet; Lost in Space; Meeting of the Minds.

RAYBURN, Gene: TV Pers. b. Christopher, IL, Dec 22, 1917. Started as radio announcer. Rayburn and Finch Show, WNEW, NY, 1945-52; Gene Rayburn Show, NBC radio; TV variety shows; game shows. TV inc: Tonight; Helluva Town; Amateur's Guide to Love; The Match Game.

Bway inc: Bye Bye Birdie; Come Blow Your Horn.

RAYE, Martha (Margaret Theresa Yvonne Reed): Act. b. Butte, MT, Aug 27, 1916. In vaudeville, 1919-29, with parents. Bway debut 1934, Calling All Stars. Bway inc: Earl Carroll's Sketchbook; Hold on to Your Hats; Annie Get Your Gun; The Solid Gold Cadillac; Personal Appearance; Separate Rooms; Call Me Madam; Everybody Loves Opal; Hello Dolly!.

First appeared on screen 1934 in short subjects. Films inc: Rhythm on the Range; The Big Broadcast of 1937; Waikiki Wedding; Mountain Music; Double or Nothing; Artists and Models; College Swing; Give Me a Sailor; $1,000 a Touchdown; The Boys from Syracuse; Navy Blues; Keep 'Em Flying; Hellzapoppin; Pin-Up Girl; Four Jills in a Jeep; Monsieur Verdoux; Jumbo; The Phynx; Puf n Stuf; Concorde-Airport '79.

TV inc: All Star Revue; The Martha Raye Show; Carol Burnett Show; Skinflint; The Gossip Columnist; Bob Hope 30th Anniversary Special; Pippin (cable); Bob Hope's Road to Hollywood.

With USO during WW II, toured South Viet Nam annually as both nurse and entertainer during Viet Nam conflict.

(Jean Hersholt Humanitarian Award 1968).

RAYMOND, Gene (Raymond Guion): Act. b. NYC, Aug 13, 1908. H of late Jeanette MacDonald. Films inc: Personal Maid; Zoo In Budapest; Smilin' Through; Red Dust; If I Had a Million; Flying Down To Rio; The House on 56th Street; Seven Keys to Baldpate; The Woman in Red; The Life of the Party; The Locket; Hit the Deck; I'd Rather Be Rich; The Best Man.

TV inc: Climax; Playhouse 90; Uncle; Girl from Uncle; Laredo; Ironsides; Julia; Judd; McNaughton's Daughter.

Bway inc: The Potters; Cradle Snatchers; Young Sinners; Shadow of My Enemy; The Best Man (nat'l co).

RAYVID, Jay: Exec prod. b. NYC, Feb 28, 1932. e. U Miami, BA. Exec dir PBS Children's & Family Consortium. Sr VP & Exec Prod Metropolitan Pittsburgh Public Broadcasting Inc (WQED). TV inc: (Prod) The Place; Ofoeti; The 39th Witness; A Mother Janek. (Exec Prod) Once Upon A Classic series inc David Copperfield; Heidi; The Prince and the Pauper; Man From Nowhere; Robin Hood; John Halifax-Gentleman; Lorna Doone; The Secret Garden; The Boy With Two Heads; Leatherstocking Tales (Emmy-1980); The Legend of King Arthur; A Tale of Two Cities (Emmy-1981); also exec prod Previn and the Pittsburgh; The People's Business.

READ, John, Sir: Exec. b. Brighton, England, 1918. Joined EMI Jan, 1965; apptd to board in Dec; in 1966 became dep man dir (UK); in 1967 apptd jnt man dir; exec dir Associated British Picture Corp (now EMI film and Theatre Corp); apptd chf exec and group man dir in 1969; appt chmn EMI in 1974.

READ, Timothy Philip: Prod. b. Hamilton, Bermuda, Jul 26, 1941. Head of prodn, Film Australia. Films inc: Stirring; When Will the Birds Return?; Do I Have to Kill My Child? N S W Chmn Film Edtrs Guild of Australia; vice chmn Australian Film Council; VP Producers & Directors Guild of Australia; dir Australian Film Institute.

REAGAN, Ronald: Act. b. Tampico, IL, Feb 6, 1911. Governor of California, 1968-1975; Elected President of United States, 1980. Screen debut, 1937, Love Is On the Air. Films inc: Cowboy From Brooklyn; Boy Meets Girl; Brother Rat; Dark Victory; Knute Rockne-All American; Kings Row; Desperate Journey; This Is The Army; The Killers; That Hagen Girl; Stallion Road; The Voice of the Turtle; John Loves Mary; Girl From Jones Beach; The Hasty Heart; Storm Warning; She's Working Her Way Through College; Law and Order; Hellcats of the Navy; The Killers.

TV inc: Death Valley Days (host); GE Theatre (host).

REASONER, Harry: TV Newsman. b. Dakota, IA, Apr 17, 1923. e. Stanford U; U of MN. Began as reporter, Minneapolis Times, 1941-43. US Army, WW II. Drama critic Minneapolis Times 1946-48; radio newswriter, 1950-51; writer U.S. Information Agency, Manila, 1951-54; news-dir, KEYD-TV (now KMSP-TV), Minneapolis 1954. Joined CBS News, NY, 1956; joined ABC News 1970 *(Emmy*-outstanding news broadcast-1974); returned to CBS, Aug 1978; co-editor 60 Minutes.

TV inc: What About Ronald Reagan *(Emmy*-1968); 60 Minutes; American Dream, American Nightmare; Boys and Girls Together; The Trouble With Women; Gay Power-Gay Politics; The Defense of the United States--Nuclear Nightmare *(Emmy*-corr-1981); Candle in the Dark; Welcome to Palermo *(Emmy*-corr-1982); The Best Movie Ever Made (Casablanca).

REDACK, Jay: Wri-Prod. b. Los Angeles, Nov 13, 1936. e. Occidental Coll. Has written more than 40 TV comedies; prod-wri The Hollywood Squares since 1963 *(Emmys*-prod-1975, 1976, 1979, 1980; wri 1974); The Real Trivial Pursuit.

Films inc: (Wri) Rabbit Test.

REDDY, Helen: Act. b. Melbourne, Australia, Oct 25, 1941. Night club and recording artist. Came to US at age 15. Films inc: Airport 1975; Pete's Dragon.

TV inc: Midnight Special; Tonight Show; American Music Awards Show; American Song Festival.

(Grammy-pop vocal-1972).

REDEKER, Quinn: Act. b. Woodstock, IL, May 2, 1936. Films inc: The Candidate; Airport; The Andromeda Strain; Rollercoaster; The Electric Horseman; The Deer Hunter (story); Coast to Coast; Ordinary People.

TV inc: The Young and the Restless; Days of Our Lives.

REDFORD, Robert: Act. b. Santa Monica, CA, Aug 18, 1937. e. AADA. Films inc: Warhunt; Barefoot in the Park; The Chase; Butch Cassidy and the Sundance Kid; Downhill Racer; The Candidate; The Way We Were; The Sting; The Great Gatsby; Three Days of the Condor; All The President's Men; A Bridge Too Far; The Electric Horseman; Brubaker; Ordinary People (dir) *(Oscar*-dir-1980); The Natural.

Bway inc: Tall Story; Sunday in New York; Barefoot in the Park.

TV inc: In the Presence of Mine Enemies; Moment of Fear; The Iceman Cometh; Black Monday; Natalie--A Tribute To A Very Special Lady; Following the Tundra Wolf (narr); Everest North Wall (narr).

REDGRAVE, Corin: Act. b. London, Jul 16, 1939. e. Cambridge. S of Sir Michael Redgrave. Thea inc: England Stage Company; A Midsummer Night's Dream; Twelfth Night; Chips With Everything (& Bway); The Right Honourable Gentleman; Lady Windermere's Fan; Abelard and Heloise; Julius Caesar; Anthony and Cleopatra; The Comedy of Errors.

Films inc: A Man For All Seasons; The Deadly Affair; Charge of the Light Brigade; The Magus; Oh, What A Lovely War!; When Eight Bells Toll; Von Richtofen and Brown; Serail; Excalibur; Eureka.

REDGRAVE, Lynn: Act. b. London, Mar 8, 1943. D of Sir Michael Redgrave. Films inc: Tom Jones; Georgy Girl; Girl with the Green Eyes; A Celebration of Life. Film inc: Ellie. The Virgin Soldier; Every Little Crook and Nanny; Everything You Always Wanted to Know About Sex; Don't Turn the Other Cheek; The Happy Hooker; The Big Bus; Sunday Lovers.

TV inc: Pretty Polly; The Power and the Glory; The End of the Tunnel; What's Wrong With Humpty Dumpty?; Pygmalion; Turn of the Screw; Daft As A Brush; Not For Women Only; Centennial; Sooner or Later; Beggarman, Thief; Gauguin the Savage; The Seduction of Miss Leona; To Tell the Truth (panelist); House Calls; Linda In Wonderland; An NBC Family Christmas; Shape of Things; ;Teachers Only; Rehearsal For Murder; The Shooting; The Faint-Hearted Feminist; The Weight Watchers Magazine (Show Cable); The Bad Seed; The 39th Annual Tony Awards.

Thea inc: (London) Various Shakespearean roles; Saint Joan; The Recruiting Officer; Hay Fever; The Two Of Us; Born Yesterday. (Bway): Black Comedy; My Fat Friend; Mrs. Warren's Profession; Saint Joan; Aren't We All.

REDGRAVE, Michael, Sir: Act. b. Bristol, England, Mar 20, 1908. F of Vanessa and Lynn Redgrave. Screen debut, 1938, The Lady Vanishes. Films inc: The Browning Version; The Importance of Being Earnest; The Dam Busters; The Quiet American; Mourning Becomes Electra; Shake Hands With The Devil; The Wreck of the Mary Deare; The Innocents; Young Cassidy; The Hill; The Heroes of Telemark; The Battle of Britain; Goodbye, Mr. Chips; Oh What A Lovely War; The Go-Between; Nicholas and Alexandra.

Thea inc: (London) Various Shakespearean roles: Beggar's Opera; Jacobowsky and the Colonel; Tiger at the Gates; The Sleeping Prince; A Touch of the Sun; The Complaisant Lover; Voyage Round My Father; Hobson's Choice; The Master Builder; Close of Play. (Bway) Macbeth; Tiger At The Gates; The Sleeping Prince.

Plays inc: The Seventh Man; Circus Boy; Amoureuse (A Woman in Love); The Aspern Papers.

(Died March 21, 1985)

REDGRAVE, Vanessa: Act. b. London, Jan 30, 1937. D of Sir Michael Redgrave. Films inc: Morgan; A Suitable Case for Treatment; A Man for All Seasons; Blow-up; Red and Blue; Camelot; Charge of the Light Brigade; The Loves of Isadora; Oh! What a Lovely War; The Seagull; The Devils; The Trojan Women; Mary, Queen of Scots; Murder on the Orient Express; Out of Season; Seven-per-cent Solution; Julia *(Oscar*-supp-1977); Agatha; Yanks; Bear Island; Wagner; The Bostonians; Wetherby; Steaming.

Thea inc: (London) A Touch of the Sun; Major Barbara; Cato Street; The Threepenny Opera; Twelfth Night; As You Like It; The Taming of the Shrew; Cymbeline; The Sea Gull; The Prime of Miss Jean Brodie; Anthony & Cleopatra; Design for Living; Macbeth; The Aspern Papers. (Bway) Lady from the Sea.

TV inc: A Farewell to Arms; Katherine Mansfield; As You Like It; Playing For Time *(Emmy*-1981); My Body, My Child; Three Sovereigns For Sarah.

REDMAN, Joyce: Act. b. Ireland, 1918. e. RADA. Films inc: Tom Jones; Othello. Thea inc: (London) Affairs of State; The Merry Wives of Windsor; The Long Echo; The Party; The Rape of the Belt; The Dutch Courtesan; The Crucible; Dear Antoine; The Undiscovered Country; The Fruits of Enlightenment; The Clandestine Marriage.

TV inc: Les Miserables; The Seven Dials Mystery.

REDMOND, Liam Act. b. Limerick, Ireland, Jul 27, 1913. e. National U. Started as an Abbey Player, appearing in over 50 plays at the Abbey Theatre. Thea inc: (London) The White Steed; Happy as Larry; The Playboy of the Western World; The Anatomist; The King of Friday's Men; The Devil Came From Dublin; It's the Geography That Counts; The Doctor's Dilemma; On the Rocks; Murder In Mind.(Bway) The White Steed; The Wayward Saint.

TV inc:The Loves of Cass Maguire; Loot.

Films inc: I See a Dark Stranger; Captain Boycott; High Treason; The Gentle Gunman; The Divided Heart; The Boy and the Bridge; The Ghost and Mr Chicken; Tobruk; The Twenty-Fifth Hour; The Last Safari.

REDMOND, Moira: Act. b. England. London stage debut 1957 in Titus Andronicus. Thea inc: Verdict; Detour After Dark; The Winter's Tale; Horizontal Hold; The Trojan Women; Journey of the Fifth Horse; Early Morning; The Watched Pot; The Widowing of Mrs Holroyd; The Three Arrows; Night Watch; The National Health; Hearthbreak House; Habeas Corpus; Murder In Mind.

Films inc: Doctor in Love; Nightmare; Jigsaw; The Limbo Line.

TV inc: Melissa.

REDSTONE, Sumner M.: Exec. b. Boston, MA, May 27, 1923. e. Harvard, BA, LLB. Legal career inc spec asst to US Atty-gen; 1961, exec vp New England Drive In Theatres; 1967, P New England Theatre Corp.

REED, Alan Jr: Act. b. NYC, May 10, 1936. e. UCLA, BA. Films inc: Rock, Pretty Baby; Peyton Place; Going Steady; The New Interns.

REED, Donna (nee Mullenger): Act. b. Denison, IA, Jan 27, 1921. Screen debut, 1941, The Get-Away. Films inc: The Human Comedy; The Courtship of Andy Hardy; Calling Dr. Gillespie; Thousands Cheer; See Here, Private Hargrove; The Picture of Dorian Gray; They Were Expendable; Green Dolphin Street; Saturday's Hero; From Here To

Eternity *(Oscar*-supp-1953); The Last Time I Saw Paris; The Benny Goodman Story; Ransom; Backlash; Pepe.

TV inc: The Donna Reed Show; The Best Place to Be; AFI Salute to Frank Capra; Deadly Lesson; Dallas.

REED, Dr. Donald: Wri-Prod. b. New Orleans, LA, Nov 22, 1935. e. USC. Founder-president Academy of Science Fiction; The Dracula Society.

REED, Jerry: Sngwri-Singer-Act. b. Mar 20, 1937. Started as backup guitarist for Nashville recording sessions; later teamed with Chet Atkins on album Me and Jerry *(Grammy*-country inst-1970); solo album When You're Hot You're Hot *(Grammy*-country vocal-1971).

Songs inc: Amos Moses; Guitar Man; U.S. Male; That's All You Gotta Do; Remembering; A Thing Called Love; Eastbound and Down.

Films inc: W.W. and the Dixie Dancekings; Gator; Smokey and the Bandit (& mus); High-Ballin' (& mus); Hot Stuff (& mus); Smokey and the Bandit II; The Survivors; Smokey & the Bandit Part 3.

TV inc: Nashville 99; The Concrete Cowboys; Lynda Carter--Celebration; The Nashville Palace; A Country Christmas; Dean Martin At The Wild Animal Park; Texas & Tennessee--A Musical Affair. Jerry Reed and Special Friends; The Great American Sing-A-Long; Louise Mandrell--Diamonds, Gold & Platinum.

REED, Oliver: Act. b. Wimbledon, England, Feb 13, 1938. Films inc: Oliver!; The Prince and the Pauper; Tommy; Great Scout and Cathouse Thursday; Burnt Offerings; Sell Out; The Three Musketeers; The Four Musketeers; The Big Sleep; Crossed Swords; Maniac; The Brood; The Class of Miss MacMichael; Dr. Heckyl and Mr. Hype; Lion of the Desert; Condorman; Venom; The Sting II; Fanny Hill; Al mas a la al Kubra; (Clash of Loyalties); Two of a Kind; Spasms.

TV inc: Richard III; It's Dark Outside; Masquerade; Christopher Columbus.

REED, Pamela: Act. b. Tacoma, WA., 1953. e. U of Wa. Thea inc: Best Little Whorehouse in Texas; Curse Of The Starving Class; Getting Out; Seduced; Fools.

Films inc: The Long Riders; Melvin and Howard; Eyewitness; Young Doctors In Love; The Right Stuff; The Goodbye People.

TV inc: Mugsy; The Andros Targets; Spencer's Pilots; Inmates--A Love Story; Until She Talks; I Want to Live; Heart of Steel; Scandal Sheet..

REED, Rex: Critic. b. Fort Worth, TX., Oct. 2, 1940. e. LSU., BA. Freelance writer; later critic for Cosmpolitan, Status, Womens Wear Daily, Holiday, NY Daily News. Appeared as act in films Myra Breckenridge; Inchon. TV inc: Inside America.

REED, Robert (John Robert Rietz): Act. b. Highland Park, IL, Oct 19, 1932. e. Northwestern U. Films inc: Hurry Sundown; Star!; The Maltese Bippy.

TV inc: The Defenders; Mannix; The Brady Bunch; Love's Savage Fury; Mandrake; The Seekers; Scruples; Nurse; Casino; The Brady Brides; The Way They Were; Death of A Centerfold-- The Dorothy Stratten Story; International Airport.

Bway inc: Barefoot in the Park; Avanti.

REED, Susan: Singer. b. Columbia, SC, 1927. Folk Song recording artist. Appeared in niteries, NY's Town Hall, concert halls throughout US, TV, radio; plays Irish harp, zither.

REES, Roger: Act. b. Wales May 5, 1944. Joined Royal Shakespeare Company in 1967. Thea inc: Julius Caesar; Merry Wives of Windosr; Twelfth Night; A Winter's Tale; The Plebeians; Rehearse the Uprising; Major Barbara; London Assurance (& Bway); Paradise; Moving Clocks Go Slow; Factory Birds; The Way of the World; Nicholas Nickleby (& Bway) *(Tony*-1982); The Real Thing.

Films inc: Star 80.

TV inc: A Bouquet of Barbed Wire; Comedy of Errors; Macbeth; The Voysey Inheritance; The Life and Adventures of Nicholas Nickleby; Saigon--Year of the Cat; A Christmas Carol.

REESE, Della (Deloreese Patricia Early): Singer. b. Detroit, MI, Jul 6, 1932. Recording artist; niteries. Films inc: Let's Rock; Psychic Killer.

TV inc: Della; Sanford and Son; Chico and the Man; God In The Dock; With Ossie and Ruby; Love Boat (spec).

REEVE, Christopher: Act. b. NYC, Sep 25, 1952. e. Cornell, BA. Films inc: Gray Lady Down; Superman, I, II & III; Somewhere In Time; Death Trap; Monsignor; The Bostonians; The Aviator.

Bway inc: The Irregular Verb To Love; A Matter of Gravity; The Fifth of July. (London) The Aspern Papers.

TV inc: Love of Life; Latch Key Kids (narr); I Love Liberty; Olympic Gala; Anna Karenina; Night Of 100 Stars II.

REEVES, Steve: Act. b. Glasgow, MT, Jan 21, 1926. Mr. America of 1947. Films inc: Athena; Hercules; Goliath and the Barbarian; The Giant of Marathon; Hercules Unchained; The Last Days of Pompeii; The Thief of Bagdad; The Trojan Horse; Duel of the Titans; The Slave; The Pirate Prince; The Long Ride From Hell.

REGEHR, Duncan: Act. b. Canada. TV inc: Goliath Awaits; The Blue And The Gray; Wizards and Warriors; The Last Days Of Pompeii; My Wicked, Wicked Ways--The Legend of Errol Flynn.

REGGIANI, Serge: Act. b. France, 1922. Films inc: Les Portes de la Nuit; Manon; Le Ronde; Secret People; Casque d'or; The Wicked Go To Hell; Les Miserables; Paris Blues; The Leopard; The 25th Hour; Les Aventuriers; Day of the Owl; The Good and the Bad; Cat and Mouse; The Terrace; The Imprint of Giants; Fantastica.

REHME, Robert G.: Exec. b. Cincinnati, OH, May 5, 1935. Pres B & R Theatres, 1975; vp April Fools Films, Inc, 1976; vp New World Pictures, 1977; Pres Avco Embassy Pictures, Jan 1980; June 1981 became P of dist & mktg Universal; Dec 1982, P Universal Theatrical Motion Picture Group; resd, Dec. 1983; Jan. 1984, co-chmn CEO New World Pictures. Films inc: (exec prod); An Eye For An Eye; Vice Squad.

REICHENBACH, Francois: Documentarist-Cin. b. Paris, Jul. 3, 1922. Songwriter for Edith Piaf, other French entertainers before making dox. Films inc: New York Ballade; Visages des Paris; Impressions de New York; Le Grand Sud; Au Pays du Porgy et Bess; Les Marines; Carnaval a la Nouvelle Orleans; Retour a New York; L'Amerique Lunaire; Le Paris de Mannequins; Artifices; Anges Gardiens; East African Safari; Aurora; Impressions de Paris; The Winner; Treize Jours en France; Mexico, Mexico; Arthur Rubinstein; Arthur Rubinstein--Love of Life; The Indiscreet; Medicine Ball Caravan; Yehudi Menuhin; La Raison du plus fou; F for Fake; Don't You Hear the Dogs Bark?; Sex O'Clock U.S.A.; Another Way to Love; Pele; Houston, Texas; Forty Deuce (cin); Francois Reichenbach's Japan.

REID, Beryl: Act. b. Hereford, England, Jun 17, 1920. Started in radio. London stage debut, 1951, in the revue After the Show. Thea inc: (London) Rockin' the Town; The Killing of Sister George; Spring Awakening; Campiello; Counting the Ways; Born in the Gardens. The Killing of Sister George *(Tony*-1967).

Films inc: The Belles of St Trinian's; The Extra Day; Star!; Inspector Clouseau; The Assassination Bureau; The Killing of Sister George; The Beast in the Cellar; Psychomania; Father Dear Father; No Sex Please, We're British; Joseph Andrews; Carry On Emmanuelle.

REID, John A.: Exec. b. Sydney, Australia, Mar 24, 1932. GM, chief exec, G U O Film Dist, PTY Ltd. Formerly M-dir, UA (Aust); Films Inc: Carry Me Back (dir).

REID, Kate: Act. b. London, Nov 4, 1930. Performed in stock in Canada, Bermuda. Joined The Stratford Shakespeare Festival in Canada, remained for seven seasons playing a variety of major roles. Films inc: This Property Is Condemned; The Side Glances of a Pigeon Kicker; The Andromeda Strain; A Delicate Balance; Equus; Highpoint; Death Ship; Double Negative; Plague; Circle of Two; Atlantic City, USA; Le Sang de Autres (The Blood of Others); Heaven Help Us.

Bway inc: Dylan; Slapstick Tragedy; Cat On A Hot Tin Roof; The Freedom of the City; Bosoms and Neglect; Death of a Salesman.

TV inc: Nellie McClung; Crossbar; Robbers, Rooftops and Witches; Gavilan.

REID, Tim: Act. b. Norfolk, VA, Dec 19, 1944. e. Norfolk State Coll. Originally standup comic Chicago niteries.

Films inc: Mother, Jugs and Speed; Uptown Saturday Night; The Union.

TV inc: The Marilyn McCoo and Billy Davis Jr Show; The Frankie

Avalon Summer Show; That's My Mama; What's Happening; Fernwood 2Night; You Can't Take It With You; WKRP in Cincinnati; Simon & Simon.

REILLY, Charles Nelson: Act. b. NYC, Jan 13, 1931. e. U of CT. Bway inc: Best Foot Forward; The Saintliness of Margery Kempe; Lend an Ear; The Billy Barnes Revue; The Inspector General; How to Succeed in Business Without Really Trying (Tony-supp-1962); Hello, Dolly; God's Favorite; The Belle of Amherst (dir); Charlotte; Break A Leg (dir).
Films inc: A Face in the Crowd; Two Tickets to Paris; The Tiger Makes Out; Cannonball Run II.
TV inc: The Broadway of Lerner and Loewe; The Ghost and Mrs Muir; The Dean Martin Show; Baryshnikov In Hollywood; Texaco Star Theatre--Opening Night.

REINER, Carl: Act-Wri-Dir. b. NYC, Mar 20, 1922. Films inc: (act) Happy Anniversary; The Gazebo; Gidget Goes Hawaiian; It's a Mad, Mad, Mad, Mad World; The Art of Love (& sp); The Russians Are Coming; A Guide for the Married Man; The Comic (sp-dir); Where's Poppa? (dir only); Oh, God (dir only); The End; The One And Only; (dir only); The Jerk (& dir); Dead Men Don't Wear Plaid (& dir); All of Me (dir).
TV inc: Caesar's Hour (Emmy Awards-supp-1956, 1957); Dick Van Dyke Show (Emmys-wri-1962, 1963, 1964; Prod 1965, 1966); Sid Caesar, Imogene Coca Special (Emmy-wri-1967); Comedy Is Not Pretty; 30 Years of TV Comedy's Greatest Hits (co-host); Skokie; Walt Disney--One Man's Dream (prod); High Hopes--The Capra Years; Twilight Theatre; Johnny Carson's Greatest Practical Jokes; All Star Party For Lucille Ball; Kennedy Center Honors 1984; TV Academy Hall Of Fame 1985; AFI Salute To Gene Kelly.
Bway inc: (act) Call Me Mister; Inside USA; Alive and Kicking; The Roast (dir).
Recordings inc: (with Mel Brooks) The 2000 Year Old Man; The 2001 Year Old Man; The 2013 Year Old Man.

REINER, Rob: Act. b. NYC, Mar 6, 1945. S of Carl Reiner. Apprentice, Bucks County Playhouse, New Hope, PA. Wrote for The Summer Brothers Smothers Show; The Smothers Brothers Comedy Hour. Films inc: Fire Sale; Enter Laughing; Hall of Anger; Where's Poppa; Spinal Tap (& Dir-wri-mus-lyr); The Sure Thing (dir).
TV inc: All In The Family; (Emmys-supp-1974, 1978); The Partridge Family; That Girl; Gomer Pyle-USMC; Headmaster; Million Dollar Infield (& prod-wri).
Bway inc: The Roast.

REINKING, Ann: Act. b. Nov 10, 1949. Bway inc: Cabaret; Pippin; Chicago; Over Here; Goodtime Charlie; A Chorus Line; Dancin'; Ann Reinking--Music Moves Me (Off-Bway).
TV inc: Julie Andrews' Invitation to the Dance With Rudolf Nureyev; Kennedy Center Tonight-- Broadway to Washington!; Doug Henning's Magic On Broadway.
Films inc: Movie Movie; All That Jazz; Annie; Micki & Maude.

REISBERG, Richard S.: Exec. b. NYC, May 24, 1941. e. MI State U; Fordham Law School. Started in broadcast dept. J. Walter Thompson; with all three nets in various capacities before joining Viacom as vp Bus Aff; later Sr vp Pgmg & Prodn; 1980, P. Viacom Prodns; Jan. 1982, P UA TV Prodns.; June 1982, P MGM/UA TV Prodns.; resd, June 1984.

REISCH, Walter: Wri-Dir. b. Vienna, Austria, May 23, 1903. European screenplays inc: Two Hearts in 3/4 Time; The Song Is Ended; Men Are Not Gods. US screenplays: The Great Waltz; Ninotchka; Gaslight; Comrade X; Journey to the Center of the Earth; The Girl on the Red Velvet Swing; The Mating Season; Titanic (Oscar-story and sp-1953); Niagara.
(Died March 28, 1983).

REISFELD, Bert: Comp. b. Vienna, Dec 12, 1906. e. Conservatory of Music, Vienna. Comp. films scores, Berlin, Paris. To US, 1938. Songs inc: Call Me Darling; You Rhyme with Everything that's Beautiful; The Three Bells; California Concerto for Piano.

REISNER, Allen: Dir. b. NYC. Films inc: The Day They Gave Babies Away; St. Louis Blues; All Mine to Give.

TV inc: The Untouchables; Mary Jane Harper Cried Last Night; The Captains and the Kings; Your Money or Your Wife; To Die in Paris; The Cliff; Climax; Hawaii 5-0; Kojak; Streets of San Francisco; Gunsmoke; The Love Tapes.

REISZ, Karel: Dir. b. Czechoslovakia, 1926. Wrote Technique of Film Editing for British Film Academy. Worked with British Film Institute and National Film Library. Films inc: Momma Don't Allow; Every Day Except Christmas; We Are the Lambeth Boys; Saturday Night and Sunday Morning; This Sporting Life; Night Must Fall; Morgan; Isadora; The Gambler; Who'll Stop the Rain; The French Lieutenant's Woman.
TV inc: On the Road.

REITMAN, Ivan: Prod. b. Czechoslovakia, Oct 26, 1946. e. McMaster U. Films inc: Foxy Lady; Cannibal Girls; Shivers; Death Weekend; Blackout; Animal House; Meatballs (& dir); Stripes (& dir); Heavy Metal; Spacehunter--Adventures in the Forbidden Zone (exec prod); Ghostbusters.
Bway inc: The Magic Show; The National Lampoon Show; Merlin.
TV inc: The Delta House.

RELPH, Michael: Prod-Dir. b. England, 1915. Films inc: The Captive Heart; Frieda; Saraband for Dead Lovers; The Blue Lamp; The Rainbow Jacket; Davy; Rockets Galore; Sapphire; The League of Gentlemen; Victim; Life for Ruth; The Mind Benders; Woman of Straw; Masquerade; The Assassination Bureau; The Man Who Haunted Himself; Scum (exec prod).

RELYEA, Robert: Prod. b. Santa Monica, CA, May 3, 1930. e. UCLA, BA. VP, Melvin Simon Prod, Inc.; Aug. 1983 joined Keith Barish Prodns as exec vp prodn. Films inc: Bullitt; The Reivers; Le Mans; Adam at Six A.M.; Day of the Dolphin; Seven (act); Blame it on Rio (asso prod).

REMBUSCH, Trueman T.: Exhb. b. Shelbyville, IN, Jul 27, 1909. S of Frank Rembusch. Pioneer exhib and inventor of Glass Mirror Screen; left Notre Dame to install snd eqpt in his father's circuit; became mgr 1932; on bd dir Allied Theatre Owners of Ind IN., 1932-39; P 1945-1951; named by Allied as one of triumvirate heading COMPO 1952; chmn joint comm on toll tv 1954; currently P Syndicate Theatres Inc.

REMICK, Lee: Act. b. Boston, Dec 14, 1935. Began in summer stock. Toured in Jenny Kissed Me; The Seven Year Itch. Bway stage debut at 16 in Be Your Age. Screen debut, 1957, A Face in the Crowd.
Films inc: The Long Hot Summer; Anatomy of a Murder; Experiment in Terror; The Days of Wine and Roses; The Detective; A Delicate Balance; The Omen; Telefon; The Medusa Touch; The Europeans; Tribute; Montgomery Clift.
TV inc: The Blue Knight; Jennie; QB VII; Torn Between Two Lovers; Ike; Haywire; The Women's Room; The Ambassadors; The Letter; The Gift of Love--A Christmas Story; A Good Sport; Mistral's Daughter; Rearview Mirror.
Thea inc: (London) Bus Stop.

REMSEN, Bert: Act. b. Glen Cove, NY, Feb 25, 1925. e. Ithaca Coll. Films inc: Pork Chop Hill; Kid Galahad; Moon Pilot; Brewster McCloud; Thieves Like Us; Baby Blue Marine; McCabe and Mrs. Miller; Sweet Hostage; Nashville; The Awakening Land; California Split; Tarantulas; A Wedding; Buffalo Bill and the Indians; The Rose; Uncle Joe Shannon; Carny; Borderline; Second Hand Hearts; Joni; Inside Moves; Lookin' to Get Out; The Sting II; Independence Day; Code Of Silence.
TV inc: Love for Rent; Victims; The Phoenix; M.A.D.D.--Mothers Against Drunk Drivers; Policewoman Centerfold; Hobson's Choice; Burning Rage; I Married A Centerfold; Generation; Barbara Mandrell--Something Special; Space.

RESNAIS, Alain: Dir. b. Vannes, France, Jun 3, 1922. Made several shorts, beginning 1948; inc: Van Gogh, Gauguin; Guernica; Statues Also Die; Toute la Memoire du Monde.
Films inc: Hiroshima Mon Amour; Last Year at Marienbad; Muriel; The War Is Over; Je n'Aime, Je t'Aime; Stavisky; Providence; My Uncle in America; La vie est un Roman (Life Is a Novel); L'Amour A'Mort

(Love Unto Death).

RESNICK, Patricia: Wri. b. Miami, FL, 1953. e. USC, BA. AFI Intern grant to work with Robert Altman on Buffalo Bill and the Indians; The Late Show; Three Women; Wrote sketches for Lily Tomlin's Appearing Nitely on Bway.

Films inc: A Wedding (& act); Quintet; Nine to Five.

TV inc: Ladies in Waiting.

REVERE, Anne: Act. b. NYC, Jun 25, 1907. On screen from 1940. Films inc: Double Door; One Crowded Night; The Howards of Virginia; Men of Boys Town; Star Spangled Rhythm; The Song of Bernadette; Dragonwyck; National Velvet (Oscar-supp-1945); Body and Soul; Forever Amber; Gentleman's Agreement; A Place in the Sun; The Great Missouri Raid; Tell Me That You Love Me, Junie Moon; Birch Interval.

Bway inc: The Great Barrington; The Lady With A Lamp; Wild Waves; Double Door; The Children's Hour; Three Sisters; Toys in the Attic (Tony-supp-1960).

REVIER, Dorothy: Act. b. San Francisco, Apr 18, 1904. Films inc: The Wild Party; Rose of Paris; Just a Woman; Poker Faces; Red Dance; Drop Kick; Beware of Blondes; The Siren; The Iron Mask; The Donovan Affair; Father and Son; Burlesque; The Black Camel; Unknown Blonde; The Lady in Scarlet; Light Fingers; The Cowboy and the Kid. Ret 1936.

REVILL, Clive: Act. (nee Selsby):b. Wellington, New Zealand, Apr 18, 1930. e. Rongotai Coll; Victoria U. Films inc: Bunny Lake is Missing; Modesty Blaise; A Fine Madness; The Double Man; Fathom; Nobody Runs Forever; A Severed Head; Avanti; The Legend of Hell House; The Black Windmill; One of Our Dinosaurs Is Missing; Galileo; The Empire Strikes Back; Zorro, the Gay Blade; Ghost in the Noonday Sun (made in 1973).

TV inc: Chicken Soup With Barley; Volpone; Bam, Pow, Zapp; Candida; A Bit of Vision; The Piano Player; Licking Hitler; Centennial; She's Dressed to Kill; Moviola (The Scarlett O'Hara War); The Diary of Anne Frank; Death Ray 2000; Wizards and Warriors; 13 Thirteenth Avenue; Samson and Delilah; George Washington; The Hoboken Chicken Emergency.

Thea inc: (London) Irma La Douce; The Mikado; Oliver!; Marat/Sade.

Bway inc: Irma La Douce; Oliver; Sherry; The Incomparable Max; Sherlock Holmes; Lolita.

REY, Alejandro: Act-Dir. b. Buenos Aires, Argentina, Feb 8, 1930. Films inc: Solomon and Sheba; The Battle of Bloody Beach; Blindfold; Synanon; Mr. Majestyk; Breakout; The Swarm; Sunburn; Cuba; The Ninth Configuration; Moscow on the Hudson.

TV inc: Stunts Unlimited; Cassie & Co; Grace Kelly; Rita Hayworth-The Love Goddess.

REY, Fernando: Act. b. Spain, Sep 20, 1915. Films inc: Welcome Mr Marshall; The Adventurers; The French Connection; The Discreet Charm of the Bourgeoisie; French Connection II; A Matter of Time; Desert of the Tartars; Elisa My Love; The Second Power; The Assignment; La Grande Bourgeoisie; That Obscure Object of Desire; The Last Romantic Lover; Memoirs of Leticia Valli; Quintet; L'ingorgo; The Cuenca Crime; Caboblanco; The True Story of Camille; Tracalo,Pero (Swallow It, Doc); Cercasi Geso (Looking for Jesus); Monsignor; La Sala de las Munecas (Bearn); The Hit; Una Strana Passione (Nicole ou ﻟL'Enfant Trouve')(A Strange Passion); Padre Nuestro (Our Father); Rustler's Rhapsody.

TV inc: A.D.

REYNOLDS, Burt: Act. b. Waycross, GA, Feb 11, 1936. e. FL State U. Bway debut, revival of Mister Roberts. Worked as film stunt man. Films inc: Armored Command; Angel Baby; Operation CIA; Navajo Joe; Shark; 100 Rifles; Fade-In; Skullduggery; Everything You Always Wanted To Know About Sex; Fuzz; Silent Movie; Deliverance; Shamus; White Lightning; The Man Who Loved Cat Dancing; The Longest Yard; WW & The Dixie Dancekings; At Long Last Love; Hustle; Lucky Lady; Gator; Nickleodeon; Smokey and the Bandit; Semi-Tough; The End; Hooper; Starting Over; Rough Cut; Smokey and the Bandit II; The Cannonball Run; Paternity; Sharky's Machine (& dir); The Best Little Whorehouse In Texas; Best Friends; Stroker Ace;

Smokey & the Bandit Part 3; The Man Who Loved Women; Cannonball Run II; City Heat; Stick (& dir).

TV inc: Gunsmoke; Riverboat; Hawk; Dan August; Entertainment Tonight; All Star Party Fort Burt Reynolds High Hopes--The Capra Years; Hollywood--The Gift of Laughter; Jerry Reed and Special Friends; Dom DeLuise and Friends; The 1/2 hour Comedy Hour; All Star Party For Lucille Ball.

REYNOLDS, Debbie: Act. b. El Paso, TX, Apr 1, 1932. Screen debut, 1948, June Bride. Films inc: The Daughter of Rosie O'Grady; Three Little Words; Singing in the Rain; Susan Slept Here; Tender Trap; Catered Affair; Bundle of Joy; Tammy and the Bachelor; The Mating Game; It Started With a Kiss; The Gazebo; How The West Was Won; Goodbye Charlie; The Unsinkable Molly Brown; The Singing Nun; What's The Matter With Helen; That's Entertainment.

Bway inc: Irene; Annie Get Your Gun; Woman of the Year.

TV inc: The Debbie Reynolds Show; Aloha Paradise; All-Star Salute To Mother's Day; Barbara Mandrell and The Mandrell Sisters; Kennedy Center Tonight--Broadway to Washington!; The American Film Institute Salute To Gene Kelly; The Royal London Gala For Bob Hope's Happy Birthday Homecoming; AFI Salute To Gene Kelly.

REYNOLDS, Frank: TV Newscaster. b. East Chicago, IN, Nov 29, 1923. e. IN U; Wabash Coll. Reporter with WJOB, Hammond IN, 1947; WBKB-TV, Chicago, 1950; WBBM, Chicago 1951; ABC corr Chicago 1963; Washington corr 1965; anchor World News Tonight, 1978. TV inc: Post Election Special Edition Nightline (Emmy-1980). (Died July 20, 1983.)

REYNOLDS, Gene: Prod-Dir-Act. b. Cleveland, OH, Apr 4, 1925. Began as child radio actor, Detroit; on screen from 1934 in Our Gang comedies and Babes in Toyland. Films inc: In Old California; Sins of Man; Captains Courageous; Thank You, Jeeves; Madame X; Heidi; In Old Chicago; Boys Town; Love Finds Andy Hardy; They Shall Have Music; Edison the Man; The Mortal Storm; 99 River Street; The Country Girl; The Bridges of Toko-Ri; Diane.

TV inc: (as dir-prod) Room 222 (Emmy-prod-1970); M*A*S*H (Emmy-prod-1974; dir-1975, 1976); in 1976, became exec prod of M*A*S*H; The Ghost and Mrs Muir (prod & dir); Anna and the King (exec prod of pilot); Roll Out! (co-prod-dir); Karen (exec prod); Hogan's Heroes; My Little Margie; My Three Sons; Father of the Bride; The Andy Griffith Show; Lou Grant (Emmys-exec prod-1979, 1980); In Defense of Kids; The Duck Factory; Bliss.

REYNOLDS, William H.: Film Ed. e. Princeton U, BA. Films inc: The Day the Earth Stood Still; Three Coins in the Fountain; Desiree; Daddy Longlegs; Love Is A Many Splendored Thing; Carousel; Bus Stop; South Pacific; Compulsion; Beloved Infidel; Fanny; Tender Is The Night; The Sound of Music; (Oscar-1965); The Sand Pebbles; Star; Hello, Dolly; The Godfather; The Sting (Oscar-1973); The Great Waldo Pepper; The Seven Percent Solution; The Turning Point; Old Boyfriends; A Little Romance; Nijinsky; Heaven's Gate; Author! Author!; The Little Drummer Girl.

RHINE, Larry: Wri. b. San Francisco. TV inc: Duffy's Tavern (& radio); Brady Bunch; Mr. Ed; Red Skelton Show; Lucy; Bob Hope Show; All in the Family; Nuts and Bolts (prod).

RHOADES, Barbara: Act. b. Poughkeepsie, NY, 1948. Bway inc: Funny Girl.

Films inc: Don't Just Stand There; Shakiest Gun in the West; The Choir Boys.

TV inc: Conspiracy of Terror; The Day The Women Got Even; The Goodbye Girl; Serial; Side Show.

RHODES, Cynthia: Act-dancer. b. Nashville, TN., Nov. 21. 1956. TV inc: Opryland USA; Music Hall America.

Films inc: Xanadu; One From the Heart; Flashdance; Staying Alive; Runaway.

RHODES, Mike (Michael Ray Rhodes): Prod-Dir. b. Estherville, IA, Jul 11, 1945. e. Yale, BA; Pacific School of Religion, M Div; USC, MFA (film). Films inc: The Bus Is Coming (Cin); Bloomin' Human (series of 16 shorts).

TV inc: Capital Cities Family Theatre; Insight/This Side of Eden; This One For Dad; Chicken; Insight/Holy Moses; Insight/Checkmate;

Princess (dir); God In The Dock; 17 Going Nowhere; The Long Road Home; The Soup Man; Who Loves Amy Tonight; Reflections (Girl on the Edge of Town); Insight/Resurrection (prod); Insight/Thea (dir); Insight/Goodbye (prod); Insight/Cargoes (prod); Insight/Mr. and Mrs. Bliss; Insight/The Needle's Eye; A Step Too Slow; Insight/Missing Persons Bureau; Insight/Decision To Love; To Climb A Mountain; Insight/Rendezvous; Insight/The Sixth Day; The Trouble With Grandpa; Insight/God's Guerrillas; High Powder; The Shooting; Insight/Little Miseries (prod); Insight/When Heroes Fall; Insight/ Teddy; The Juggler of Notre Dame *(Emmy-Prod-1983); Insight/For Love Or Money (prod); Insight/White Star Garage (prod); Leadfoot; Hang Tight, Willy Bill; Insight/A Gun For Mandy (prod); Insight/So Little Time (prod); Insight/Leave Me Alone, God; Insight/Every Ninety Seconds (& act). Insight/The Fiddler; Insight/Matchpoint; Insight/ The Day Everything Went Wrong; Insight/The Clearing House (prod); Insight/Dutton's Choice (prod); Clay Feet (prod); Insight/The Hit Man (prod); Insight/Butterfly; Insight/The Game Room.*
(*Emmys*-series prod-1981, 1982, 1984).

RHUE, Madlyn (Madeline Roche): Act. b. Washington, DC, 1934. Films inc: Operation Petticoat; Escape from Zahrain; It's a Mad, Mad, Mad, Mad World; He Rides Tall; Stand Up and Be Counted.
TV inc: Bracken's World; Executive Suite; The Best Place To Be; Goldie and the Boxer; Fantasies; Days of Our Lives.
Bway inc: Two for the Seesaw; The Best Laid Plans.

RHYS-DAVIES, John: Act. b. England. Films inc: Sphinx; Misdeal; Raiders Of the Lost Ark; Victor/Victoria; Sahara.
TV inc: Henry VIII; Shogun; I, Claudius; The Naked Civil Servant; The Sweeney; The Merchant of Venice; Peter and Paul; Ivanhoe; Reilly, Ace Of Spies; Kim; Sadat; The Nairobi Affair.

RIBMAN, Ronald: Plywri. b. NYC, May 28, 1932. e. U Pittsburgh, BA, MA, PhD. Former English prof. Plays inc: Harry, Noon and Night; Journey of the Fifth Horse; The Ceremony of Innocence; Passing Through from Exotic Places; Fingernails Blue as Flowers; A Break in the Skin; The Poison Tree; The Angel Levine.
TV inc: The Final War of Olly Winter.

RICE, Tim: Lyr. b. Amersham, Bucks, England, Nov 10, 1944. Thea inc: The Amazing Technicolour Dreamcoat; Jesus Christ Superstar; Evita *(Tonys-book & lyr-1980).*
Films inc: Gumshoe; The Odessa File; Octopussy.
TV inc: Musical Triangles; Disco.
(*Grammy*-cast album-1980).

RICH, Buddy (Bernard Rich): Mus. b. Brooklyn, NY, Jun 30, 1917. In vaude as child with family act (Wilson & Rich); on Bway in Pinwheel at 4; toured Australia at 6. With various bands inc Joe Marsala; Bunny Berigan; Artie Shaw; Tommy Dorsey; Benny Carter before forming own band to tour with Jazz at the Philharmonic; later with Harry James.
Albums inc: Bird and Diz; Jazz on the Air; Jam Session; Jazz Scene; Stick It; Roar of 74; A Different Drummer; Take It Away.
TV inc: Sinatra--Concert For the Americas.

RICH, Charlie: Singer-Comp. b. Forrest City, AR, Dec 14, 1932. e. U of AR. Country mus recording artist. *(Grammy*-country voc-1973).

RICH, David Lowell: Dir. b. NYC, Aug 31, 1920. Began career in NY in live TV; worked on Studio One; Big Town; The Big Story; Playhouse 90. In 1957 moved to Hollywood; dir Naked City; Route 66; Arrest and Trial; The Sex Symbol; The Defection of Simas Kudirka *(Emmy*-1978); Little Women; Nurse; Enola Gay--The Men, The Mission, The Atomic Bomb; Thursday's Child; The Fighter; I Want to Live; The Sky's the Limit (& prod); His Mistress; Scandal Sheet; The Hearst & Davies Affair.
Films inc: Senior Prom; Hey Boy, Hey Girl; Have Rocket Will Travel; Madame X; The Plainsman; Rosie; A Lovely Way to Die; Eye of the Cat; Concorde-Airport '79; Chu Chu and the Philly Flash.

RICH, Irene (nee Luther): Act. b. Buffalo, NY, Oct 13, 1897. On radio, Dear John, several years. Films inc: Stella Maris; Beau Brummel; So This Is Paris; Craig's Wife; Lady Windermere's Fan; Shanghai Rose; That Certain Age; The Lady in Question; This Time for Keeps; Angel and the Badman; Fort Apache; New Orleans; Joan of Arc.

Bway inc: Seven Keys To Baldpate; As The Girls Go.

RICH, John: Prod-Dir. b. Rockaway Beach, NY, Jul 6, 1925. e. U of MI, MA. Films inc: Boeing-Boeing; The New Interns; Wives and Lovers; Roustabout; Easy Come, Easy Go.
TV inc: The Dick Van Dyke Show *(Emmy*-dir-1963); All in the Family *(Emmy*-dir-1972; prod-1973); Newhart; Condo; Amanda's.

RICH, Lee: Exec prod. b. Cleveland, OH. Adv exec, resd as sr tv vp Benton & Bowles to become P Mirisch-Rich TV 1965; Prod Rat Patrol; The Good Life; resd 1967 to join Leo Burnett Agency; resd 1969 to form Lorimar Productions.
TV inc: (exec prod) Helter Skelter; The Waltons *(Emmy*-exec prod-1973); Sybil; Eric; Green Eyes; The Blue Knight; The Long Journey Back; Kaz; Eight Is Enough; Dallas; Some Kind of Miracle; Mr. Horn; Studs Lonigan; A Man Called Intrepid; Big Shamus, Little Shamus; Young Love, First Love; Mary and Joseph--A Story of Faith; Knots Landing; Skag; Flamingo Road; Reward; Willow B--Women in Prison; Joshua's World; A Perfect Match; Secret of Midland Heights; A Matter of Life and Death; Our Family Business (supv prod); Killjoy; Kings Crossing; A Wedding On Walton's Mountain; Mother's Day On Walton's Mountain; This Is Kate Bennett; In Security (cable); Two Of A Kind; A Day For Thanks On Walton's Mountain; One Cooks, The Other Doesn't.
Films inc: (exec prod) The Man; Who Is Killing the Great Chefs of Europe?; Marriage is Alive and Well; The Big Red One.

RICHARD, Cliff: Act-Singer. b. India, Oct 14, 1940.
Films inc: Serious Charge; Expresso Bongo; The Young Ones; Summer Holiday; Wonderful Life; Finders Keepers; Two A Penny; His Land; Take Me High.
TV inc: Cliff Richard Show; Sunday Night at the London Palladium; Oh, Boy.

RICHARD, Pierre: Act. b. France, Aug 16, 1934. Films inc: (Act) Alexandre le Bienheureux; La Coqueluche; The Tall Blond Man with One Black Shoe; La Raison du plus fou; Juliette and Juliette; Un nuage entre les dents; Return of the Tall Blond Man; La Course à l'echalote; The Bottom Line; We've Seen Everything; The Castaways of Turtle Island; The Toy; The Wild Goose Chase; Le Coup du Parapluie (The Umbrella Coup); La Chevre (The Goat); Un chien dans un jeu de Quilles (A Dog in a Game of Nine-pins) (& Prod); Les Comperes (The Co-Fathers); Le Jumeau (The Twin).(Dir) Le Distrait (& wri-act); Les Malheurs d'Alfred (& wri-act); Je Ne Sais Rien, Mais Je Dirais Tout (& wri-act); C'est Pas Moi, C'est Lui (It's Not Me, It's Him) (wri-act); The Daydreamer (& wri-act); I'm Timid But I'm Treating It (& co-sp-act); Tranches de Vie (Slices Of Life).

RICHARDS, Beah: Act-Plywri. b. Vicksburg, MS. e. Dillard U. Bway inc: The Miracle Worker; Purlie Victorious; A Raisin in the Sun; Macbeth.
Films inc: Take a Giant Step; The Miracle Worker; Guess Who's Coming To Dinner?; Heat of the Night; Hurry Sundown; Great White Hope; Mahogany.
TV inc: One Angry Man; A Dream for Christmas; Just An Old Sweet Song; Kinfolk; A Black Woman Speaks; Roots II--The Second Generation; A Christmas Without Snow; The Sophisticated Gents; Banjo The Woodpile Cat (voice); Too Good to be True; Fade Out-- The Erosion of Black Images in the Media (int); And The Children Shall Lead; Generation.

RICHARDS, Dick: Dir. b. 1936. Films inc: The Culpepper Cattle Co.; Farewell My Lovely; Rafferty and the Gold Dust Twins; March or Die (& prod-wri); Death Valley; Tootsie (prod); Man, Woman and Child.

RICHARDS, Kim: Act. b. Long Island, NY, Sep 19, 1964. Films inc: Escape to Witch Mountain; No Deposit, No Return; Anderson's Alamo; Special Delivery; Kotch; The Car; Return from Witch Mountain; Meatballs Part II; Tuff Turf.
TV inc: Nanny and the Professor; Here We Go Again; Raid on Entebbe; Ben Franklin in Paris; Portrait of Dorian Gray; The Horrible Honchos; Angel's Nest; Death Trap; James at 15; Why Us?

RICHARDS, Martin: Prod. b. March 11, 1932. H of Mary Lea Johnson. Off-Bway inc: Dylan; March Of The Falsettos; Mayor. Bway inc: The Norman Conquests; Chicago; On The Twentieth Century;

Sweeney Todd (Tony-1979); Crimes of The Heart; A Doll's Life; La Cage Aux Folles (Tony-1984); Grind.

Films inc: The Shining; The Boys From Brazil; Fort Apache, The Bronx.

RICHARDSON, Don: Dir. b. NYC, Apr 30, 1918. e. AADA. TV inc: I Remember Mama: The Elgin Hour: The 13 Clocks; The Defenders; Mission Impossible; Bonanza; Get Smart; The Virginian; High Chaparral; Arnie; The Lancers; One Day at a Time.

RICHARDSON, Ian: Act. b. Edinburgh, Scotland, Apr 7, 1934. e. Glasgow Coll Dramatic Art. With Birmingham Repertory; Royal Shakespeare Company. Thea inc: (London) The Duchess of Malfi; Much Ado About Nothing; The Taming of the Shrew; Comedy of Errors; The Representative; The Miracles; King Lear; Marat/Sade; The Jew of Malta; The Merry Wives of Windsor; The Revenger's Tragedy; Coriolanus; Measure for Measure; The Tempest; Trelawney of the Wells; Love's Labour's Lost; Richard III. (Bway) The Comedy of Errors; Marat/Sade; My Fair Lady; Lolita.

Films inc: The Darwin Adventure; Man of La Mancha; The Sign of the Four; The Hound of the Baskervilles; Brazil.

TV inc: Churchill and the Generals; Private Schulz; The Master of Ballantrae; Mistral's Daughter.

RICHARDSON, Sir Ralph: Act. b. Cheltenham, Gloucestershire, England, Dec 19, 1902. Stage debut 1921 The Merchant of Venice; recent thea inc: Separate Tables; The Sleeping Prince; The Waltz of the Toreadors; Flowering Cherry; The School for Scandal; Six Characters in Search of an Author; What the Butler Saw; Home; No Man's Land; The Kingfisher; The Cherry Orchard; Alice's Boys; The Fruits of Enlightenment; Early Days; The Understanding.

Screen debut, 1933, The Ghoul. Films inc: The Return of Bulldog Drummond; Things to Come; The Man Who Could Work Miracles; The Citadel; Four Feathers; The Avengers; Anna Karenina; The Heiress; The Fallen Idol; An Outcast of the Islands; Breaking the Sound Barrier; The Holly and the Ivy; Richard III; Oscar Wilde; Our Man in Havana; Exodus; Long Day's Journey Into Night; Doctor Zhivago; Khartoum; The Midas Run; The Battle of Britain; Oh! What a Lovely War; Eagle in a Cage; Lady Caroline Lamb; Tales From the Crypt; A Doll's House; OLucky Man; Rollerball; Watership Down; (voice); Dragonslayer; Time Bandits; Wagner; Greystoke--The Legend of Tarzan, Lord of the Apes; Give My Regards To Broad Street.

TV inc: Hedda Gabler; Twelfth Night; Blandings Castle; Early Days (cable); Witness For The Prosecution.

(Died Oct. 10, 1983).

RICHARDSON, Tony: Dir-Prod-Wri. b. Shipley, England, Jun 5, 1928. e. Oxford. Films inc: Look Back in Anger; The Entertainer; Sanctuary; A Taste of Honey; The Loneliness of the Long Distance Runner; Tom Jones (Oscar-1963); The Loved One; Red and Blue; The Charge of the Light Brigade; Laughter in the Dark; Hamlet; Ned Kelly; A Delicate Balance; Dead Cert; Joseph Andrews (& wri); The Border; The Hotel New Hampshire.

RICHIE, Lionel Sing-sngwri-prod. b. Tuskegee, AL., June 20, 1949. e. Tuskegee Inst. Joined grup The Commodores (originally called The Mystics) which played weekend, summer dates before playing as opening act for Jackson Five's 1971 European tour; signed with Motown Records; 1980, went solo as singer-composer, continued to produce records for Commodores. Songs inc:Easy; Sail On; Still; Three Times A Lady; Brick House; Lady; Hello; Truly; All Night Long; Penny Lover; Can't Slow Down; Hello; Endless Love; Lady You Bring Me Up.

(Grammys (3)Pop Vocal 1983; album of year & prod of year, 1984)

RICHMAN, Peter Mark: Act. b. Philadelphia, April 16, 1927. e. Philadelphia Coll of Pharmacy and Science, BS. Films inc: Friendly Persuasion; The Black Orchid; The Dark Intruder; Agent for H.A.R.M.; For Singles Only.

TV inc: Cain's Hundred; Longstreet; Blind Ambition; Greatest Heroes of the Bible; Dynasty; Dempsey; Santa Barbara; City Killer.

Bway inc: End as a Man; Masquerade; The Zoo Story; Detective Story; Rose Tattoo.

RICHMOND, Bill: Wri-Prod. b. Central City, KY, Dec 19, 1921. e. U of IL. Films inc: The Ladies Man; The Errand Boy; The Nutty Professor; The Patsy; The Family Jewels; The Big Mouth; Smorgasbord.

TV inc: The Jerry Lewis Show; Diahann Carrol Show; The Singers; Laugh In; The Carol Burnett Show (Emmys-wri-1974, 1975 & 1978); Tim Conway Special; Welcome Back Kotter (prod); Three's Company (prod); The Tim Conway Show; Wizards and Warriors; The Jerry Lewis Show (1984).

RICHMOND, Ted: Prod. b. Norfolk, VA, Jun 10, 1912. e. MIT. Films inc: So Dark the Night; The Milkman; Smuggler's Island; The Strange Door; Desert Legion; Francis Joins the WACS; Forbidden; Count Three and Pray; Nightfall; Abandon Ship; Solomon and Sheba; Bachelor in Paradise; Advance to the Rear; Return of the Seven; Villa Rides; Red Sun; Papillon; The Fifth Musketeer.

RICHTER, Richard: Prod. Began as reporter on Newsday; NY World Telegram Sun before joining CBS 1959 as wri-news editor; 1960 won CBS Fellowship for advanced study at Columbia U; 1963-1967 with Peace Corps; joined ABC 1969 as prod Evening News; 1976 senior prod ABC Evening News; 1978 senior prod ABC News Doc unit.

TV inc: The American Army--a Shocking State of Readiness; Youth Terror--The View from Behind the Gun; Youth Terror--Is There an Answer?; Asbestos--The Way to a Dusty Death; Arson! Fire For Hire!; The Police Tapes; Terror in the Promised Land; Politics of Torture; The Killing Ground; The Shooting of a Big Man--Anatomy of a Criminal Case; Infinite Horizons--Space After Apollo; This Shattered Land; Lights, Camera. . .Politics; The Apocalypse Game; The Shattered Bridge; A Matter of Survival; Invasion; Soldiers of the Twilight; Near Armageddon--The Spread of Nuclear Weapons In The Middle East; Hooray For Hollywood; Rain of Terror; Japan--Myths Behind the Miracles; Fortress Israel; The Oil Game; Vietnam Requiem; Mexico--Times of Crisis; Swords, Plowshares and Politics; Asbestos--The Way To Dusty Death; Adapt or Die; The Money Masters; The American Inquisition; Alias A. John Blake; Water-- A Clear and Present Danger; The Cocaine Cartel; JFK; To Save Our Schools, To Save Our Children; The Supreme Court Of The United States; The Fire Unleashed.

RICHTER, W.D.: Wri. e. USC film School. Films inc: Slither; Peeper; Nickelodeon; Invasion of the Body Snatchers; Dracula; Brubaker; All Night Long; Hard Feelings; The Adventures Of Buckaroo Banzai--Across the 8th Dimension (prod-dir).

RICKERT, John F.: Exec. b. Kansas City, MO, Oct 29, 1924. e. USC, BS. In film industry since 1950. P, CineWorld Corp.

RICKLES, Don: Act. b. NYC, May 8, 1926. e. AADA. Films inc: Run Silent, Run Deep; The Rabbit Trap; The Rat Race; Enter Laughing; Where It's At; Kelly's Heroes.

TV inc: The Don Rickles Show; CPO Sharkey; For The Love of It; Ladies And Gentlemen--Bob Newhart Part II; Foul-Ups, Bleeps and Blunders (host); Dean Martin's Celebrity Roast.

RIDDLE, Nelson: Comp-Cond. b. Hackensack, NJ, 1921. Film scores inc: A Kiss Before Dying; St Louis Blues; Ocean's Eleven; Lolita; L'il Abner; Can Can; Robin and the Seven Hoods; Marriage on the Rocks; El Dorado; Paint Your Wagon; The Great Gatsby (Oscar-1974); Fugitive Girls (perf); Guyana-Cult of the Damned; Cagney and Lacey;

TV inc: The Carpenters-Music, Music, Music; Mickey Spillane's Margin For Murder; All Star Party for Burt Reynolds; Help Wanted--Male; AFI Salute to Frank Capra; All-Star Party for Frank Sinatra; All Star Party For Lucille Ball.

(Grammys-composition-1958; arr accomp vocal-1983).

RIEFENSTAHL, Leni: Dir. b. Berlin, 1902. Former dancer who made Nazi propaganda films for Hitler. Films inc: Peaks of Destiny (act only); The Blue Light (& act); Triumph of the Will; Olympische Spiele 1936; Tiefland (& act); SOS Iceberg (act); Stuerme Uber Dem Mount Blanc (act); Der Weisse Rauch (act).

RIGG, Diana: Act. b. Doncaster, Yorks, England, Jul 20, 1938. e. RADA. London stage debut, 1961, Ondine. Thea inc: (London) The Devils; Becket; The Physicists; Jumpers; Macbeth; Pygmalion; Phaedra Britannica; Abelard and Heloise; The Guardsman; Heartbreak House. (Bway) King Lear; Abelard and Heloise.

Films inc: Assassination Bureau; On Her Majesty's Secret Service;

Julius Caesar; The Hospital; Theatre of Blood; A Little Night Music; The Great Muppet Caper; Evil Under the Sun.

TV inc: The Avengers; Comedy of Errors; The Diana Rigg Show; In This House of Brede; The New Avengers; Witness For The Prosecution; Laurence Olivier Presents King Lear; Bleak House.

RILEY, Jeanie C. (nee Stephenson): Singer-Sngwri. b. Stamford, TX, Oct 19, 1945. Songs inc: Harper Valley PTA (Grammy-country voc-1968). TV inc: Country Comes Home.

RINGWALD, Molly: Act. b. Sacramento, CA., Feb. 16, 1968. Thea inc: The Glass Harp; Annie.

TV inc: Facts of Life; Packin It In; P.K. and the Kid; Surviving.

Films inc: Tempest; Spacehunter --Adventures in the Forbidden Zone; Sixteen Candles; The Breakfast Club.

RINTELS, David W.: Wri-Prod. b. Boston, MA. e. Harvard. Joined NBC 1961 as researcher, began freelance writing. TV inc: The Defenders; Run for Your Life; Slattery's People; The Invaders; The Young Lawyers; A Continual Roar of Musketry (The Senator); Clarence Darrow (Emmy-1975); Fear on Trial (Emmy-1976); The Oldest Living Graduate (exec prod); Gideon's Trumpet (& prod); All the Way Home (exec prod); The Member of the Wedding (exec prod); Choices of the Heart (prod); Mr. Roberts (exec prod).

Films inc: Scorpio (wri). subtotal? (Y/N):

RIOMFALVY, Paul H.: Prod. b. Budapest, Hungary, Dec 24, 1924. To Australia, 1949. Prod over 60 plays, musicals and revues, inc: A Cup of Tea; Is Australia Really Necessary?; Beyond the Fringe; Canterbury Tales; Private Lives; The Boyfriend; Anything Goes; A Severed Head; Godspell; The Private Ear and Public Eye. Chmn, Interim Film Commission; chmn, New South Wales Film Corp; chmn, Australian Film Office Inc.

RISI, Dino: Dir. b. Italy. Films inc: The Sign of Venus; Poveri ma Belli; Il Sorpasso; Scent of Woman (& wri); Viva Italia!; I'm Photogenic; Sunday Lovers; Fantasma D'Amore (Ghost of Love); Le Bon Roi Dagobert (Good King Dagobert) (& wri); Scemo di Guerra (Madman At War) (& wri).

TV inc: E La Vita Continua (And Life Goes On) (& wri).

RISSNER, Danton: Exec. b. Brooklyn, Mar 27, 1940. Started as agent with Ashley Famous, later International Famous; joined WB 1969, vp chg European Prodn; 1972 UA vp chg European prodn; 1974, vp chg East Coast & European prodn; 1978 sr vp in chg West Coast prodn; resigned Sept 1978 to enter ind prodn; July 1980 named vp Motion Pictures, Marble Arch Prodns; July, 1981, exec vp 20th Fox Prodns; Jan. 1984 sr vp UA prodn div of MGM/UA.

Films inc: Up the Academy.

RITCHIE, Clint: Act. b. Grafton, ND, Aug 9. Films inc: The St. Valentine's Day Massacre; Bandolero; Patton; A Force of One.

TV inc: Wild Wild West; Centennial; Thunder; One Life to Live.

RITCHIE, Michael: Dir. b. Waukesha, WI, 1938. e. Harvard U. TV inc: asso prod, later dir on Ford Foundation's Omnibus TV series; The Man From U.N.C.L.E.; Dr. Kildare; Run For Your Life.

Films inc: Downhill Racer; Prime Cut; The Candidate; Smile; The Bad News Bears; Semi-Tough; The Bad News Bears Go to Japan (prod); An Almost Perfect Affair (& sp); The Island; Divine Madness (& prod); The Survivors; Fletch.

RITT, Martin: Dir. b. NYC, Mar 2, 1919. Films inc: Edge of the City; No Down Payment; The Long Hot Summer; The Sound and the Fury; Paris Blues; Hemmingway's Adventures of a Young Man; Hud; The Outrage; The Spy Who Came in from the Cold; Hombre; The Brotherhood; The Molly Maguires; The Great White Hope; Sounder; Pete 'n Tillie; Conrack; The Front; Casey's Shadow; Norma Rae; End of the Game (act); Hollywood on Trial (act); Back Roads; Cross Creek; The Slugger's Wife (act).

TV inc: Danger.

Bway inc: (act) Golden Boy. (Dir) The Man; Set My People Free; A View From the Bridge.

RITTENBERG, Saul N.: Atty. b. Chicago, Aug 4, 1912. e. UCLA, BA; Northwestern Law School, JD. Partner Loeb and Loeb law firm. Asst

sec MGM 1956-70; Board Trustees, Directors Guild Pension & Health and Welfare Plans, 1960-70; Director, Association of Motion Picture and TV Producers, 1956-70.

RITTER, John: Act. b. Burbank, CA, Sep 17, 1948. e. USC, BA. S of the late Tex Ritter. TV inc: The Waltons; Three's Company (Emmy-1984); Leave Yesterday Behind; Completely Off The Wall; That Thing on ABC; The Comback Kid; Echoes of the 60's (host); John Ritter, Being of Sound Mind and Body; Pray TV; Insight/Little Miseries; The Fantastic Miss Piggy Show; In Love With An Older Woman; Life's Most Embarrassing Moments (host); Sunset Limousine; John Ritter, Mr. T and Jacqueline Bissett--Going Back Home; Love Thy Neighbor; The Secret World Of The Very Young (host); Three's A Crowd; Donald Duck's 50th Birthday; All Star Party For Lucille Ball; TV Academy Hall of Fame 1985; Letting Go.

Films inc: The Barefoot Executive; The Other; The Stone Killer; Nickelodeon; Breakfast in Bed; Americathon; Hero at Large; They All Laughed.

RITZ BROTHERS (nee Joachim): Comedians. Al (1901-65), Jim (1903-), and Harry (1906-). Zany nitery comedians. Films inc: Sing, Baby, Sing; One in a Million; On the Avenue; You Can't Have Everything; The Goldwyn Follies; Straight, Place and Show; The Three Musketeers; The Gorilla; Argentine Nights; Behind the Eight Ball; Hi Ya chum; Never a Dull Moment; Won Ton Ton the Dog That Saved Hollywood; Blazing Stewardesses; Real Life.

RIVA, Emmanuelle: Act. b. Chenimenil, France, 1932. Films inc: Hiroshima Mon Amour; Hungry for Love; Kapo; Leon Morin Priest; Climats; Therese Desqueyroux; Soledad; L'Homme de Desir; La Modification; Y'at-il Un Francois Dans La Salle? (Is There A Frenchman In the House?); Gli ochi, la Bocca (The Eyes, The Mouth); L'Exil (The Exile); Un Homme a ma Taille (A Man of my Measure); Liberta la Nuite (Liberty at Night); Un Delitto (A Crime).

RIVERA, Chita (Concita del Rivero): Act. b. Washington, DC, Jan 23, 1933. Bway debut 1952, Call Me Madam. On stage in: Guys and Dolls; Can-Can; Seventh Heaven; Mr. Wonderful; West Side Story; Bye Bye Birdie; Bajour; The Three Penny Opera; Flower Drum Song; Zorba; Sweet Charity; Born Yesterday; Jacques Brel Is Alive and Well and Living in Paris; Sondheim: A Musical Tribute; Kiss Me Kate; Ivanhoe; Father's Day; Chicago; Bring Back Birdie; Merlin; The Rink (Tony-1984).

Films inc: Sweet Charity.

TV inc: The New Dick Van Dyke Show; Kennedy Center Tonight--Broadway to Washington!; Pippin (cable); Toller Cranston's Strawberry Ice; TV Academy Hall Of Fame 1985; The 39th Annual Tony Awards.

RIVERA, Geraldo: TV newsman. b. NYC, Jul 4, 1943. e. U AZ, BS. TV inc: Reporter WABC-TV, 1968; Goodnight America (host) 1974; corr Good Morning America, 1976; corr ABC News & 20/20 since 1977; Other TV inc: Willowbrook-- 10 Years After; Orbis (Distant Visions); Great Arctic Adventure; Arson For Profit (Emmy-corr-1980); Formula For Disaster (Emmy-corr-1981); Eye On the Media--Business and the Press.

RIVERS, Joan: Act-Wri-Dir. b. NYC, June 8, 1933. Mostly TV, niteries. As of July, 1983, sole guest host for Johnny Carson; 1983 Emmy (host); Live--and in Person; Johnny Carson Presents The Tonight Show Comedians.

Films inc: (Act) The Swimmer; Rabbit Test (& dir-wri); Uncle Scam; The Muppets Take Manhattan.

RIVETTE, Jacques: Dir. b. Rouen, France, 1928. Films inc: Le Coup de Berger; Paris Nous Appartient; La Religieuse (& sp); L'Amour Fou (& sp); Out One: Spectre; Celine and Julie Go Boating; Le Pont du Nord (North Bridge) (& wri); L'Amour Par Terre (Love On The Ground) (& wri).

RIVKIN, Allen: Wri-Edtr. b. Hayward, WI, Nov 20, 1903. e. U of MN, BA. Films inc: 70,000 Witnesses; Madison Square Garden; Headline Shooter; Picture Snatcher; Meet the Baron; Dancing Lady; Cheating Cheaters; Your Uncle Dudley; Half Angel; Love Under Fire; Straight, Place and Show; Let Us Live; Typhoon; Joe Smith, American; The Kid Glove Killer; Till the End of Time; The Thrill of Brazil; Dead Reckoning; The Farmer's Daughter; My Dream is Yours; Grounds for Marriage; Battle Circus; Timberjack; Prisoner of War; The Eternal Sea; Big Operator.

TV inc: M-Squad; Small Explosion; Troubleshooters; Beginning of the End; Billion Dollar Swindle; Saints and Sinners.

RIX, Brian: Act. b. Yorkshire, England, 1924. Films inc: Reluctant Heroes; What Every Woman Wants; Up to His Neck; Dry Rot; The Night We Dropped a Clanger; And the Same to You; Nothing Barred; Don't Just Lie There, Say Something!

Thea inc: A Bit Between the Teeth (& prod); Jack the Ripper (prod); Beatlemania.

ROACH, Hal E.: Prod. b. Elmira, NY., Jan. 14, 1892. Originally in trucking business. Entered films with Universal as stock cowboy. Teamed with Harold Lloyd to produce first film which they sold for $850. Opened Roach Studios at Edendale, later moved to Hollywood, then to Culver City where Hal Roach Studio was built in 1919. For many years concentrated on comedy shorts inc: Lonesome Luke series; Our Gang comedies; made several early Laurel & Hardy shorts. Shorts inc: The Music Box *(Oscar-short-1931)*; Bored of Education *(Oscar-short-1936)*. Features inc: Fraternally Yours; Way Out West; Topper; Of Mice and Men; The Three Musketeers; One Million B.C.; Turnabout; Topper Returns; George Stevens--A Filmmaker's Journey (doc-int).

TV inc: The Last Movie Mogul (int).

ROBARDS, Jason: Act. b. Chicago, Jul 26, 1922. e. AADA. Stage debut at the Children's World Theatre 1947, as the rear end of The Cow in Jack and the Beanstalk. Bway credits inc: The Iceman Cometh; Long Day's Journey Into Night; The Disenchanted *(Tony-1959)*; Toys in the Attic; After the Fall; Hughie; We Bombed in New Haven; A Moon for the Misbegotten; A Touch of the Poet; You Can't Take It With You.

Screen debut 1958, The Journey. Films inc: By Love Possessed; Tender Is the Night; Long Day's Journey Into Night; A Thousand Clowns; A Big Hand for the Little Lady; Any Wednesday; The St. Valentine's Day Massacre; The Night They Raided Minsky's; The Loves of Isadora; The Ballard of Cable Hogue; Johnnie Got His Gun; The War Between Men and Women; Pat Garrett and Billy the Kid; Play It As It Lays; A Boy and His Dog; Mr. Sycamore; All the President's Men *(Oscar-supp-1976)*; Julia *(Oscar-supp-1977)*; Comes a Horseman; Hurricane; Raise The Titanic; Melvin and Howard; Caboblanco; The Legend of the Lone Ranger; Max Dugan Returns; Something Wicked This Way Comes; The World of Tomorrow (doc) (narr); Sakharov.

TV inc: The Iceman Cometh; The Doll's House; For Whom the Bell Tolls; The Easter Promise; A Christmas to Remember; Haywire; For the Last Year; Houseman Directs Lear for the Acting Company (cable tv-host); Polar Bear Alert(Narr); The Last Round-Up of the Elephants (narr); The Day After; The Atlanta Child Murders.

ROBB, Jillian Claire: Prod. b. London. Films inc: Skippy the Bush Kangaroo; They're a Weird Mob; Wake in Fright; Contra Bandits; Careful, He Might Hear You. Marketing and dist m for the South Australian Film Corp; chief exec, Victorian Film Corp.

ROBBE-GRILLET, Alain: Wri-Dir. b. Brest, France, Aug 18, 1922. Films inc: Last Year at Marienbad; L'Imortelle (sp & dir); Trans Europ Express (sp & dir); L'Homme qui ment; L'Eden et Apres; Glissements progressifs du plaisir; Le Jeu avec le feu; Piege a Fourrure; La Belle Captive (The Beautiful Prisoner).

ROBBIE, Seymour Mitchell: Dir. TV inc: Omnibus; Jackie Gleason Show; The Man from U.N.C.L.E.; F. Troop; Mr. Roberts; Lost in Space; Name of the Game; It Takes a Thief; Mannix; Mission-Impossible; Cannon; Mod Squad; Streets of San Francisco; Kojak; Moving On; The New Adventures of Wonder Woman.

Films inc: C.C. & Company; Marco.

ROBBINS, Jerome (nee Rabinowitz): Dancer-Chor. b. NYC, Oct 11, 1918. Bway inc: Fancy Free; Billion Dollar Baby; High Button Shoes; Look Ma, I'm Dancin' (& dir); Miss Liberty (& dir); Call Me Madam (& dir); The King & I; Peter Pan (& dir); Bells Are Ringing (& dir); West Side Story (& dir); *(Tony-chor-1958)*; Gypsy (& dir); Oh Dad, Poor Dad, Mama's Hung You In The Closet and I'm Feeling So Sad (dir

only); Fiddler on the Roof *(Tonys-(2)-dir & chor-1966)*; also chor for many ballet cos inc: Ballet Russe; The Royal Danish Ballet; New York City Ballet; and his own co, Ballet USA.

Films inc: The King and I; West Side Story *(Oscar-co-dir-1961)*; *(Honorary Oscar 1961 "for his brilliant achievements in the art of choreography on film.")*

TV inc: Peter Pan, 1956 & 1960 *(Emmy-1956)*.

Ballets inc: Interplay; Facsimile; Age of Anxiety; The Cage; Dances At A Gathering; The Watermill; Dybbuk Variations.

ROBBINS, Matthew: Wri-Dir. e. USC. Writes in collab with Hal Barwood. Films inc: The Sugarland Express; The Bingo Long Traveling All-Stars and Motor Kings; Corvette Summer (& dir); Dragonslayer (& dir).

ROBERT, Yves: Act-Dir-Prod. b. Saumur, France, Jun 19, 1920. H of Daniele Delorme. Films inc: (act) Les Dieux de dimanche; Trois telegrammes; La Rose rouge; Deux sous de violette; Suivez cet homme; Nina; La Francaise et l'amour; La Brune que voila; Cleo de 5 a7; Le Voyou; La distrait; Chere Louise; The Judge and the Assassin; Vive la Sociale!; Garcon! (Dir) Les Hommes ne pensent qu'a ca; Signe Arsene Lupin; The War of the Buttons; Bebert et l'omnibus; Les Copains; Monnaie de singe; Very Happy Alexander; Clerambard; The Tall Blond Man With One Black Shoe; Salut l'artiste; The Return of the Tall Blond; Pardon mon affaire; We Will All Meet in Paradise; Courage, Fuyons; A Bad Son; Un Etrange Voyage (On the Track); La Fille Prodigue (The Prodigal Daughter); Qu'est-ci Qui Fait Courir David? (What Makes David Run?).

ROBERTS, Ben (ne Eisenberg): Wri-Prod. b. NYC, Mar 23, 1916. e. NYU. Films inc: White Heat; Goodbye My Fancy; Captain Horatio Hornblower; Come Fill the Cup; White Witch Doctor; Green Fire; Serenade; Midnight Lace; Portrait in Black; Man of a Thousand Faces; The Legend of the Lone Ranger.

TV inc: The Rogues; Charlie's Angels; Mannix; Time Express; Nero Wolfe.

(Died May 12, 1984).

ROBERTS, Doris: Act. b. St Louis, MO, Nov 4, 1930. e. NYU. Bway inc: The Death of Bessie Smith; Desk Set; The Office; The Natural Look; Last of the Red Hot Lovers; The Secret Affairs of Mildred Wild; Cheaters.

Films inc: Something Wild; A New Leaf; No Way to Treat a Lady; The Honeymoon Killers; A Lovely Way to Die; Little Murders; Such Good Friends; The Taking of Pelham 1,2,3; Heartbreak Kid; Hester Street; Once In Paris; Good Luck Miss Wyckoff; The Rose; Rabbit Test.

TV inc: Ruby and Oswald; The Storyteller; Look Homeward, Angel; The Neil Simon Comedy Hour; Mary Hartman, Mary Hartman; Soap; Jennifer--A Woman's Story;Angie; The Diary of Anne Frank; In Trouble; Maggie; Another Woman's Child; St. Elsewhere *(Emmy-supp-1983)*; Remington Steele; California Girls.

ROBERTS, Eric: Act. b. Biloxi, MS, Apr 18, 1956. e. RADA, AADA. Thea inc: Rebel Women; A Streetcar Named Desire; Mass Appeal.

TV inc: Another World; Paul's Case; Miss Lonelyhearts.

Films inc: King of the Gypsies; Raggedy Man; Star 80; The Pope of Greenwich Village; The Coca-Cola Kid.

ROBERTS, James M.: Exec. b. Canada, 1923. Exec dir Academy of Motion Picture Arts and Sciences.

ROBERTS, Pernell: Act. b. May 18, 1930. Films inc: Desire Under the Elms; The Sheepman; Ride Lonesome; The Errand Boy; Four Rode Out; The Magic of Lassie.

TV inc: Bonanza; The Silent Gun; Centennial; The Immigrants; The Night Rider; Hot Rod; Trapper John M.D.; High Noon Part II--The Return of Will Kane; Incident At Crestridge.

Bway inc: Tonight in Samarkand; The Lovers; A Clearing in the Woods.

ROBERTS, Tanya: Act. b. Bronx, NY, Oct 15. Studied with Herbert Berghof; Lee Strasberg. TV inc: Pleasure Cove; Zuma Beach; Vega$; Charlie's Angels; Mickey Spillane's "Murder Me, Murder You".

Films inc: The Beastmaster; I Paladini--Storia D'Amori (Hearts in Armor); Forced Entry; Sheena; A View To A Kill.

ROBERTS, Tony: Act. b. NYC, Oct 22, 1939. e. Northwestern U, BS. Films inc: Million Dollar Duck; The Star Spangled Girl; Play it Again, Sam; Serpico; The Taking of Pelham, One, Two, Three; Lovers Like Us; Annie Hall; Just Tell Me What You Want; Stardust Memories; A Midsummer Night's Sex Comedy; Amityville 3-D; Key Exchange.

Bway inc: Play It Again, Sam; How Now, Dow Jones; Promises, Promises; Barefoot in the Park; The Last Analysis; Absurd Person Singular; Sugar; Doubles.

TV inc: Messiah on Mott Street; The Lindbergh Kidnapping Case; Rosetti and Ryan; The Girls in the Office; If Things Were Different; The Way They Were; A Question of Honor; Packin' It In; The Four Seasons; The Lucie Arnaz Show; The 39th Annual Tony Awards.

ROBERTSON, Cliff: Act. b. La Jolla, CA, Sep 9, 1925. Screen debut 1956, Picnic. Films inc: Autumn Leaves; The Naked and the Dead; Battle of the Coral Sea; Gidget; The Interns; My Six Loves; PT-109; The Honey Pot; The Devil's Brigade; Charly (Oscar-1968); Too Late the Hero; Three Days of the Condor; Midway; Shoot; Class; Brainstorm; Star 80; Dominique (made in 1977); Shaker Run.

TV inc: The Man Without a Country; The Game (Emmy-1966); Overboard; Washington Behind Closed Doors. Two Of A Kind; Falcon Crest; The Key To Rebecca;

Bway inc: The Wisteria Tree; Mr. Roberts; Late Love; The Lady and the Tiger; Orpheus Descending.

ROBERTSON, Dale: Act. b. Oklahoma City, OK, Jul 14, 1923. Films inc: Fighting Man of the Plains; Caribou Trail; Two Flags West; Return of the Texan; Outcasts of Poker Flats; The Farmer Takes a Wife; The Gambler from Natchez; Blood on the Arrow; The Walking Major.

TV inc: Wells Fargo; The Iron Horse; Death Valley Days; Kansas City Massacre; The Last Ride of the Dalton Gang; Dynasty; Big John.

ROBERTSON, Hugh Aston: Prod-Dir-Film edtr. b. NYC, May 28, 1932. e. CCNY; New Institute for Motion Pictures and Television; Sorbonne. Films inc: (edtr) The Miracle Worker; Run Away; Andy; Harvey Middleman, Fireman; Midnight Cowboy; Shaft. (Dir) featurettes: April Fools; Tick-tick-Tick; Kelly's Heroes; Shaft. Features: Melinda; Bim; The Haunting of Avril.

TV inc: Marathon; Dream on Monkey Mountain; And Beautiful II; Great American Dream Show Machine; Love American Style; Roll-Out; Caribbean Roots.

ROBIN, Leo: Lyr. b. Pittsburgh, Apr 6, 1900. e. U of Pittsburgh Law School; Carnegie Tech Drama School. Films scores inc: Innocents in Paris; Little Miss Marker; Big Broadcast of 1935, '37 & '38 (Oscar-best song-Thanks for the Memories-1938); Paris Honeymoon; Gulliver's Travels; My Gal Sal; The Time, the Place and the Girl; Meet Me After the Show; Latin Lovers; Hit the Deck; My Sister Eileen.

Bway inc: Girl in Pink Tights; Hit the Deck; Greenwich Village Follies; Judy; Bubbling Over.

Songs inc: Hallelujah; Love in Bloom; June in January; Louise; Prisoner of Love; So in Love; Beyond the Blue Horizon; My Ideal; For Every Man There's a Woman.

(Died Dec. 29, 1984)

ROBINSON, Amy: Act-Prod. b. Trenton, NJ., Apr. 13, 1948. e. Sarah Lawrence. Films inc: Sisters (act); Mean Streets (act); Head Over Heels (prod); Baby, It's You (prod).

ROBINSON, Chris: Act. b. Nov 5, 1938. Films inc: Birdman of Alcatraz; The Hawaiians; 13 West Street; Because They're Young; Young Savages; Darker than Amber; Amy; Savannah Smiles.

TV inc: 12 O'Clock High; Deep Lab; Alvin Karpis, F B I; Busters; Cabot Connection; The Wilds of 10,000 Islands; Travis Logan, D A; Men From Shiloh; The Intruder; The Dream Merchants; General Hospital.

ROBINSON, Earl: Comp-Cond-Act. b. Seattle, WA, Jul 2, 1910. e. U of WA. Began as folk singer in the 40's. Films scores inc: California; A Walk in the Sun;

Cantatas inc: Ballard for Americans; Battle Hymn; The Lonesome Train; The Town Crier. The Romance of Rosy Ridge; Man from Texas; The Roosevelt Story; also Army films. Ballet: Bouquet for Molly.

Songs inc: Joe Hill; Abe Lincoln; The House I Live In (Special Oscar-1945); Free and Equal Blues; Molly O'.

ROBINSON, Jay: Act. b. 1930. Films inc: The Robe; Demetrius and the Gladiator; The Virgin Queen; My Man Godfrey; Bunny O'Hare; Shampoo; Nightmare Honeymoon; Born Again; The Man With Bogart's Face; Partners.

TV inc: Memories Never Die.

ROBINSON, Madeleine (nee Svoboda): Act. b. France, 1916. Films inc: Soldiers Without Uniforms; Douce;Une Si Jolie Petite Plage; Dieu a Besoin des Hommes; Le Garcon Sauvage; The She Wolves; A Double Tour; The Trial; A Trap For Cinderella; A New World; Le Petit Matin; A Simple Story; Body to Heart; J'ai espouse une Ombre (I Married A Dead Man); Hors-la-Loi (Outlaws).

ROBINSON, Max: TV news. b. Richmond, VA, May 1, 1939. e. Indiana U. Joined WTOP-TV, Washington as newsman, 1965, became anchor 1969; joined ABC 1978 as anchor World News Tonight. TV inc: Three Mile Island--A Nuclear Nightmare; Inflation--The End of the American Dream; Recession--Bitter Medicine for Inflation; Post Election Special Edition ABC News Nightline (Emmy-corr-1980); The Bunny Raasch Special; Incident At Crestridge; The Executioner's Song.

ROBINSON, Roger: Act. b. Seattle, WA, May 2, 1940. Films inc: Believe In Me; Willie Dynamite; Newman's Law; Silver Bears; It's My Turn.

Bway inc: Does a Tiger Wear a Necktie?; Amen Corner.

TV inc: Kojak; Only the Pretty Girls Die.

ROBINSON, Smokey: Singer-Comp. b. Detroit, MI, Feb 19, 1940. Formed Smokey Robinson and the Miracles 1957; co-founder Tamla Records 1959.

Recordings inc: (with Miracles) Sweet Harmony; Virgin Man; Agony and the Ecstasy; Quiet Storm; Open; There Will Come A Day. (Solo) Smokey; Smokey's Family Robinson; Deep In My Soul.

TV inc: Countdown '81--A Solid Gold Special; Motown 25--Yesterday, Today, Forever (host); Motown Returns To The Apollo.

ROBSON, Flora, Dame: Act. b. South Shields, England, Mar 28, 1902. e. RADA. On screen from 1931. Films inc: Dance Pretty Lady; Catherine the Great; Fire Over England; Wuthering Heights; We Are Not Alone; The Sea Hawk; Saratoga Trunk; Bahama Passage; Caesar and Cleopatra; Black Narcissus; 55 Days in Peking; Those Magnificent Men in Their Flying Machines; Fragment of Fear; The Beast in the Cellar; The Beloved; Dominique (made in 1977).

Thea inc: Black Chiffon; The Importance of Being Ernest; Ring Around the Moon.

TV inc: The Corn is Green; A Message for Margaret; The Untouchables; David Copperfield; Heidi; A Man Called Intrepid; Les Miserables; Gauguin the Savage; A Tale of Two Cities.

(Died July 7, 1984).

ROCCO, Alex: Act. b. Cambridge, MA, Feb 29, 1936. Films inc: The Godfather; Slither; Freebie and the Bean; Three the Hard Way; Rafferty and the Gold Dust Twins; Voices; The Stuntman; House Calls; Rabbit Test; Herbie Goes Bananas; Nobody's Perfekt; The Entity; Cannonball Run II; Stick; Gotcha.

TV inc: Three for the Road; Lily--Sold Out; The First Time; High Performance; The Best Of Times.

ROCHE, Eugene: Act. b. Boston. e. Emerson Coll. Films inc: The Happening; Cotton Comes to Harlem; Slaughterhouse Five; Newman's Law; Mr. Ricco; The Late Show; Corvette Summer; Foul Play; Voices; Oh, God! You Devil;

TV inc: The Murderers; Winter Kill; Crawl Space; People Like Us; Crime Club; Possessed; Ghost of Flight 401; You Can't Take It With You; Soap; Corner Bar; Love for Rent; Good Time Harry; Rape and Marriage--The Rideout Case; Two The Hard Way; Farrell For the People; The Juggler of Notre Dame; Cocaine and Blue Eyes; Life's Most Embarrassing Moments; Johnny Blue; Airwolf; Off Sides.

Bway inc: Blood Sweat and Stanley Poole; Great Day in the Morning; Time for the Barracudas; All In Good Time; In the White House; Mother Courage; The Price.

ROCHEFORT, Jean: Act. b. Paris, 1930. Films inc: Une balle dans le canon; 20,000 lieues sur la terre; Cartouche; The Man in the Iron Mask; Symphony for a Massacre; Les Pieds nickeles; Angelique, Mariquise of the Angels; Up to his Ears; Angelique et le Roy;The Devil by the Tail; Le temps de mourir; Celeste; The Tall Blond Man with One Black Shoe; The Inheritor; Bel Ordure; The Clockmaker; The Phantom of Liberty; Let Joy Reign Supreme; Dirty Hands; Till Marriage Do Us Part; Les Magiciens; Pardon Mon Affaire; Femmes Fatales; We Will All Meet in Paradise; Who is Killing the Great Chefs of Europe?; French Postcards; Les Gradissou; Courage Fuyons; Chere Inconnu; Un Etrange Voyage (On The Track); Odio Le Blonde (I Hate Blondes); Il faut Tuer Birgitt Haas (Kill Birgitt Haas); Le Grand Frere (The Big Brother); Un Dimanche de flics (A Cop's Sunday); L'Ami de Vincent (A Friend of Vincent); Frankenstein 90; Reveillon Chez Bob (New Year's Eve At Bob's); Sortuz Ege Fekete Bivalyert (Volley For A Black Buffalo).

ROCHIN, Aaron: Sound. b. Los Angeles, Jun 25, 1935. Films inc: The Dirty Dozen; Point Blank; Candy; Alfred the Great; Castle Keep; Shaft; Soylent Green; That's Entertainment, Part I; That's Entertainment, Part II; The Wind and the Lion; King Kong; Telefon; Audrey Rose; Coma; Corvette Summer; Voices; The Champ; Grease; The Deer Hunter *(Oscar-1978)*; The Villain.

RODDAM, Franc: Dir. b. El Paso, TX, Aug 19, 1921. Former airline pilot and LAPD sergeant.
TV inc: Star Trek (crea-prod); Questor; The Lieutenant; Genesis 2; Spectre.
Films inc: Pretty Maids All In A Row; Star Trek--The Motion Picture; Star Trek III--The Search For Spock (exec cnslt).

RODDENBERRY, Gene: Wri-Prod. b. El Paso, TX, Aug 19, 1921. Former airline pilot and LAPD sergeant. TV inc: Star Trek (crea-prod); Questor; The Lieutenant; Genesis 2.
Films inc: Pretty Maids All In A Row (wri-prod); Star Trek—The Motion Picture; Star Trek III—The Search For Spock (exec prod).

RODGERS, Anton: Act. b. England, Jan 10, 1933. e. LAMDA. Thea inc: Carmen; The Boy Friend; The Crooked Mile; And Another Thing; Pickwick (& Bway); The Owl and the Pussycat; Mixed Doubles (devised-dir only); An Enemy of the People; The Fantasticks (dir only); The Threepenny Opera; The Picture of Dorian Gray; Gaslight; Are You Now Or Have You Ever Been?; Flashpoint (dir); Songbook; Windy City.
Films inc: Rotten to the Core; The Man Who Haunted Himself; Scrooge; The Day of the Jackal.
TV inc: Ukridge; The Elusive Pimpernel; The Flaxborough Chronicles; Lillie; Disraeli; Rumpole of the Bailey; Murder With Mirrors.

RODGERS, James Charles (Jimmy): Act. b. Camas, WA, 1933. Recording artist. Films inc: The Little Shepherd From Kingdom Come; Back Door to Hell.

RODGERS, Mary: Comp-Wri. b. NYC, Jan 11, 1931. D of the late Richard Rodgers. Plays inc: Once Upon A Mattress; Hot Spot; The Mad Show; Davy Jones Locker (Baird Marionettes); Pinocchio.
Films inc: Freaky Friday; The Devil and Max Devlin.

RODRIGUES, Percy: Act. b. Canada, 1924. Films inc: The Sweet Ride; The Plainsman; The Heart is a Lonely Hunter; Come Back Charleston Blue; Hugo the Hippo (voice); BrainWaves; Invisible Strangler (made in 1979 as The Astral Factor).
TV inc: Peyton Place; Sanford and Son; Silent Force; Executive Suite; Genesis II; The Lives of Jenny Dolan; Last Survivor; The Night Rider; Angel Dusted; The Fall Guy; This Girl For Hire; The Atlanta Child Murders.
Bway inc: Blues for Mr. Charlie.

RODWAY, Norman: Act. b. Dublin, Feb 7, 1929. e. Trinity Coll, Dublin. Appeared in various Dublin prodns for several years before making London debut in Cock-A-Doodle Dandy. Other thea inc: Stephen D; The Poker Session; joined Royal Shakespeare Co 1966; Henry The Fourth; Twelfth Night; The Revenger's Tragedy; Romeo and Juliet; Much Ado About Nothing; Silence; Richard the Third; A Midsummer Night's Dream; The Patrick Pearse Motel; London Assurance; Butley; Love's Labour's Lost; Wild Oats; Children of the Sun; Shadow of a Gunman; Juno and the Paycock; Love Girl & The Innocent.
Films inc: The Quare Fellow; This Other Eden; A Question of Suspense; Four in the Morning; Chimes at Midnight; The Penthouse; I'll Never Forget What's 'is Name; Who Dares Wins.
TV inc: To See How Far It Is; An Imaginative Woman; Bay Blues; Out; Danton's Death; The Beaux Stratagem; Best of Friends; Timon of Athens; The Critic; King Lear; Reilly, Ace of Spies; Pericles, Prince of Tyre.

ROE, David: Exec. b. Perth, Australia, Dec 1949. Prodn, mktg consultant, New South Wales Film Corp; exec consultant, Australian Film Institute . Films inc: The Coca-Cola Kid.

ROEG, Nicholas: Dir. b. London, 1928. Started as cin. Films inc: Far From the Madding Crowd; Fahrenheit 451; Judith; A Funny Thing Happened on the Way to the Forum; Petulia. (Dir) Walkabout; Don't Look Now; Performance; The Fan Club; The Man Who Fell to Earth; Bad Timing; Eureka.

ROEMHELD, Heinz: Cond-Comp. b. Milwaukee, WI, May 1, 1901. e. WI Coll of Music. Film scores inc: Ruby Gentry; Valentino; The Moonlighter; Strawberry Blonde; Yankee Doodle Dandy *(Oscar*-1942).
(Died Feb. 11, 1985)

ROEVES, Maurice: Act-Wri-Dir. b. Sunderland, England, Mar 19, 1937. e. Royal Academy of Drama & Music, Glasgow. Thea inc: Macbeth; Romeo and Juliet; Tunes of Glory; Carnegie.
Films inc: Ulysses; Oh, What A Lovely War!; A Day At the Beach; Victory; Who Dares Wins.
TV inc: Danger UXB; The Gambler; The Journal of Brigitt Hitler; Inside the Third Reich.

ROGELL, Albert S.: Dir. b. Oklahoma City, OK, Aug 21, 1901. e. WA State Coll. Began as cin, later title wri for silents; film edtr. Prod more than 2000 films.
Films inc: Mamba; Shepherd of the Hills; Riders of Death Valley; Argentine Nights; The Black Cat; Tight Shoes; In Old Oklahoma; Heaven Only Knows; Magnificent Rogue; Earl Carroll's Sketchbook; Northwest Stampede; The Admiral Was A Lady; Shadow of Fear.

ROGERS, Anne: Act. b. Liverpool, England, Jul 29, 1933. Theatre inc: My Fair Lady; Zenda; She Loves Me; Walking Happy; I Do! I Do!; A Shot in the Dark; No, No, Nanette; The Turning Point; Camelot.
TV inc: Birds on the Wing; Song of Songs; Sparkling Cyanide.

ROGERS, Charles (Buddy): Act. b. Olathe, KS, Aug 13, 1904. H of late Mary Pickford. On screen from 1926 in Fascinating Youth. Films inc: Wings; My Best Girl; Abie's Irish Rose; Half Way to Heaven; Young Eagles; Best of Enemies; Sing for Your Supper; The Mexican Spitfire; An Innocent Affair; The Parson and the Outlaw.

ROGERS, Fred: Prod-Wri-TV pers. b. Latrobe, PA, Mar 20, 1928. e. Rollins Coll, B Mus; Pittsburgh Theological Seminary, M Div. Joined NBC-TV 1951 as asst prod The Voice of Firestone; NBC Television Opera Theatre; later supv Lucky Strike Hit Parade; joined WQED, Pittsburgh, 1953 to set up pgm sched. TV inc: Children's Corner; Misterogers; Mister Rogers Neighborhood; Mister Rogers Goes to School *(Emmy*-1980); Old Friends. . .New Friends.

ROGERS, Ginger (Virginia Katherine McMath): Act. b. Independence, MO, Jul 16, 1911. On screen from 1930. Films inc: Young Man of Manhattan; The Sap from Syracuse; Follow the Leader; Honor Among Lovers; The Tenderfoot; You Said A Mouthful; Flying Down to Rio; 42nd Street; Gold Diggers of 1933; Professional Sweetheart; Sitting Pretty; The Gay Divorcee; Roberta; Top Hat; Follow the Fleet; Swingtime; Shall We Dance; Carefree; Bachelor Mother; The Story of Vernon and Irene Castle; Stage Door; Kitty Foyle *(Oscar*-1940); Tom, Dick and Harry; Roxie Hart; The Major and the Minor; Once Upon A Honeymoon; I'll Be Seeing You; Weekend at the Waldorf; It Had to Be You; Barkleys of Broadway; Monkey Business; Perfect Strangers; Black Widow; On, Men, Oh Women; The First Traveling Saleslady; True Confession, Harlow; George Stevens--A Filmmaker's Journey (doc-int); Night Of 100 Stars II.
Bway inc: Hello, Dolly; Coco; Auntie Mame.
TV inc: All-Star Salute To Mother's Day.

ROGERS, Henry C.: Pub exec. b. Irvington, NJ, Apr 19, 1914. e. U of PA. Studio publicist; formed own company; 1949 launched Rogers & Cowan inc with Warren Cowan; 1969 became bd chmn of firm.

ROGERS, Kenny: Singer-Songwri. b. Crockett, TX, Aug 21, 1938. C & W singer. Films inc: Six Pack.
TV inc: Kenny Rogers and the America Cowboy; A Christmas Special With Love from Mac Davis; Lynda Carter's Special; Kenny Rogers as the Gambler; Coward of the County; Sheena Easton--Act One;

Grandpa, Will You Run With Me?; Personal and Confidential; Live--and in Person; Kenny Rogers as the Gambler--The Adventure Continues; Salute to Lady Liberty; Donald Duck's 50th Birthday; Kenny & Dolly--A Christmas to Remember; Night Of 100 Stars II; On Top All Over The World.

Albums inc: Ten Years of Gold; The Gambler; Kenny; Gideon; Greatest Hits.

(Grammys-Country Vocal-1977, 1980).

ROGERS, Roy (Leonard Slye): Act. b. Cincinnati, OH, Nov 5, 1911. Started as radio singer. On screen from 1935. Films inc: The Old Corral; Under Western Stars; Frontier Pony Express; Robin Hood of the Pecos; Silver Spurs; My Pal Trigger; Heart of the Rockies; Son of Paleface; Mackintosh and T.J.

TV inc: Numerous shows with wife, Dale Evans; An Evening With The Statler Bros.--A Salute To the Good Times; Country Comes Home; Kenny Rogers as the Gambler--The Adventure Continues.

ROGERS, Suzanne: Act. Started as Rockette at Radio City Music Hall. Bway inc: 110 in the Shade; Funny Girl; Hallelujah Baby; Coco; Follies.

TV inc: Days of Our Lives *(Emmy-support-*1979).

ROGERS, Wayne: Act. b. Birmingham, AL, Apr 7, 1933. e. Princeton U, BA. Films inc: Odds Against Tomorrow; The Glory Guys; Chamber of Horrors; Cool Hand Luke; Astro Zombies; WUSA; Pocket Money; Once in Paris; Hot Touch.

TV inc: Edge of Night; Stagecoach West; M*A*S*H; City of Angels; Attack on Terror; Mitzi Zings Into Spring; It Happened One Christmas; Making Babies II; House Calls; The Top of the Hill; Chiefs; He's Fired, She's Hired; The Lady From Yesterday.

ROGERS, Will Jr: Act. b. NYC, Oct 20, 1912. e. Stanford U. On screen from 1949 in Look for the Silver Lining. Films inc: The Story of Will Rogers; The Eddie Cantor Story; The Boy from Oklahoma; Wild Heritage. Toured West with solo stage show: My Father's Humor.

ROGOSIN, Joel: Prod-Wri. b. Boston, Oct 30, 1932. e. Stanford U, AB. TV inc: Hawaiian Eye; Surfside 6; 77 Sunset Strip; The Bold Ones; Destry; Ironside; The Virginian; Longstreet; Ghost Story; Circle of Fear; Jerry Lewis Labor Day Telethon (1972-73); The Blue Knight; The Gift; The Gathering, Part II; Magnum P.I. (supv prod); Welcome to Paradise (prod).

ROHMER, Eric (Jean Maurice Scherer): Dir-Wri. b. France, Apr 4, 1920. Films inc: Le Signe du Lion; La Collectioneuse; My Night at Maude's; Claire's Knee; Chloe in the Afternoon; The Marquise of O. . .; Perceval; Plays and Proverbs; The Aviator's Wife; Le Beau Mariage (A Perfect Marriage); Pauline a la plage (Pauline at the Seaside). Les Nuits de la plein Lune (Full Moon In Paris).

TV inc: Don Quixote; Edgar Poe; Pascal; Louis Lumiere.

ROIZMAN, Owen: Cin. b. Brooklyn, NY., Sep. 22, 1936. Films inc: Stop; The French Connection; The Gang That Couldn't Shoot Straight; Play It Again Sam; The Heartbreak Kid; The Exorcist; The Taking of Pelham 1-2-3; Three Days of the Condor; The Return of a Man Called Horse; Network; Straight Time; Sgt. Pepper's Lonely Hearts Club Band; The Electric Horseman; True Confessions; The Black Marble; Absence of Malice; Taps; Tootsie; Vision Quest.

ROKER, Rennie: Act. b. NYC, Sep 6. e. Inter-American U, Puerto Rico. Worked as record promoter, later exec with Liberty Records, UA Records while acting in little theatres. Films inc: Skidoo; Brothers.

TV inc: Gomer Pyle, USMC; My Friend Tony; Nobody's Perfect.

ROKER, Roxie: Act. b. Miami, FL, Aug 28, 1929. e. Howard U, BA; postgrad work at Skakespeare Institute, England on Hattie M. Strong Fellowship. Bway inc: Rosalee Pritchet; The River Niger.

TV inc: Roots; Billy--Portrait of a Street Kid; The Jeffersons; Take My Word For It; The Making of a Male Model.

ROLAND, Gilbert (Luis Antonio Damasco De Alonso): Act. b. Juarez, Mexico, Dec 11, 1905. On screen from the 20s. Films inc: Camille; The Last Train from Madrid; The Sea Hawk; Captain Kidd; The Bullfighter and the Lady; My Six Convicts; The Big Circus; Run Wild;

Islands in the Stream; Caboblanco; Barbarosa.

ROLAND, Rita: Film edtr. Films inc: A Patch of Blue; Justine; To Find A Man; Where Were You When the Lights Went Out?; Penelope; The Betsy; Fort Apache, the Bronx; Six Pack; The New Kids.

TV inc: The Lindbergh Kidnaping Case; Sybil; Eleanor and Franklin *(Emmy*-1977); The Dollmaker.

ROLFE, Sam: Wri-Prod. Started as radio wri on Suspense; Hollywood Star Playhouse; Richard Diamond; Sam Spade. Films inc: Naked Spur; Target Zero; The McConnell Story; Bombers B-52.

TV inc: Playhouse 90 (wri); Climax (wri); Fireside Theatre (wri); Have Gun--Will Travel; Hotel de Paree; Man from U.N.C.L.E.; Girl From U.N.C.L.E.; Dundee and the Culhane; The Manhunter; The Delphi Bureau; Delvecchio; Rossetti & Ryan; Kaz; Big Shamus-Little Shamus; Killjoy.

ROLLE, Esther: Act. b. Pompano Beach, FL, Nov 8. One of the original members of the Negro Ensemble Co. Films inc: Cleopatra Jones; I Know Why the Caged Bird Sings.

Bway inc: The Amen Corner; Blues for Mister Charlie; Don't Play Us Cheap; Macbeth; Horowitz and Mrs. Washington.

TV inc: One Life to Live; Maude; Good Times; Summer of My German Soldier *(Emmy*-supp-1979); Momma the Detective.

THE ROLLING STONES: Group. Originally formed 1962. Members are Mick Jagger; Keith Richards, Ron Wood, Bill Wyman, Charlie Watts. Films inc: Gimme Shelter; No Nukes; Sound of the City--London 1964-73; Time Is On Our Side; Hero (music).

Albums inc: Rolling Stones I; Rolling Stones II; Rolling Stones Now; Out Of Our Heads; Aftermath; Between the Buttons; Their Satanic Majesties Request; Beggar's Banquet; Let It Bleed; Sticky Fingers; Exile on Main Street; Black and Blue; Some Girls; Emotional Rescue.

ROLLINS, Howard E. Jr: Act. b. Baltimore, MD. 1952. e. Towson State College. TV inc: The Edge of Night; Eliza--Our Story; King; Roots, the Next Generation; My Old Man; The Neighborhood; Thornwall; The Member of the Wedding; For Us, The Living; A Doctor's Story; The House Of Dies Dear (WonderWorks); He's Fired, She's Hired; Wildside.

Films inc: Ragtime; Chytilova vs. Forman; The House of God; A Soldier's Story.

Thea inc: Traps; Streamers; The Mighty Gents; Medal of Honor Rag; G.R. Point (Bway).

ROMAIN, Yvonne: Act. b. France, 1938. Films inc: The Baby and the Battleship; Seven Thunders; Corridors of Blood; Chamber of Horrors; Curse of the Werewolf; Devil Doll; The Swinger; Double Trouble; The Last of Sheila.

ROMAN, Joseph: Act. b. S Philadelphia, May 23. Films inc: St. Ives; The White Buffalo; Love and Bullets.

TV inc: Quincy.

Bway inc: Mr. Roberts; Twilight Walk; Child of the Morning.

ROMAN, Ruth: Act. b. Boston, MA, Dec 23, 1923. On screen from 1943 in Stage Door Canteen. Films inc: Since You Went Away; Gilda; The Big Clock; Champion; The Window; Beyond the Forest; Three Secrets; Dallas; Strangers on a Train; Mara Maru; Blowing Wild; Down Three Dark Streets; The Far Country; Bottom of the Bottle; Bitter Victory; Look in any Window; Love Has Many Faces; The Killing Kind; A Knife for the Ladies; Dead of Night; Want a Ride, Little Girl? Echoes.

TV inc: Medical Center; Cannon; Marcus Welby; The Long Hot Summer; Go Ask Alice; Willow B--Women In Prison.

ROME, Sydne: Act. b. Akron, OH, 1947. Studied At Pasadena Playhouse. Films inc: Some Girls Do; Vivi o Preferibilmente Morti; La Ragazza di Latta; Un Doppio a Meta; What?; Merry-Go-Round; Creezy; That Lucky Touch; Folies Bourgeoises (The Twist); Stop Calling Me Baby; Speed Fever; Just a Gigolo; Looping; Red Bells--I've Seen the Birth of the New World.

ROMERO, Cesar: Act. b. NYC, Feb 15, 1907. On screen from 1934. More than 100 films inc: Metropolitan; Wee Willie Winkie; Cisco Kid (series); The Gay Caballero; The Thin Man; Clive of India; The Devil Is a Woman; Diamond Jim; Weekend in Havana; Tales of Manhattan;

The Captain from Castile; Vera Cruz; Villa; Ocean's 11; Donovan's Reef; Marriage on the Rocks; Batman; The Spectre of Edgar Allen Poe; Crooks and Coronets; The Midas Run; The Strongest Man in the World; Carioca Tiger; Target-Harry; Lust In The Dust; Flesh And Bullets.

TV inc: Batman; The Rainbow Girl; Berrenger's.

ROMERO, George: Dir. b. 1939. Films inc: Night of the Living Dead; The Crazies; Hungry Wives; Dawn of the Dead; Knightriders (& wriedtr); Creepshow.

TV inc: Tales From the Dark Side (exec prod-wri).

RONET, Maurice: Act. b. France, Apr 13, 1927. Films inc: Rendezvous de Juillet; He Who Must Die; Lift to the Scaffold; Carve Her Name with Pride; Plein Soleil; La Ronde; Three Weeks in Manhattan; Lost Command; La Scandale; The Road to Corinth; How Sweet It Is; The Marseilles Contract; Sidney Sheldon's Bloodline; Sphinx; Beau-Pere (Stepfather); La Balance (The Nark); Surprise Party.

(Died March 14, 1983).

RONSTADT, Linda: Singer. b. Tucson, AZ, Jul 15, 1946. Recording artist. Toured niteries, colleges with own band. Recordings inc: I Can't Help It If I'm Still In Love With You (Grammy-country voc-1975); Hasten Down The Wind (Grammy-pop vocal-1976); Greatest Hits; Simple Dreams; Living In The U.S.A.; Mad Love.

TV inc: The Unbroken Circle--A Tribute to Mother Maybelle Carter; The Women's Room (song); Live--and in Person.

Thea inc: Pirates of Penzance (Bway); La Boheme (Off-Bway).

Films inc: Pirates of Penzance.

ROONEY, Andy (Andrew Aitken Rooney): Wri-Dir-Act. b. Albany, NY, Jan 14, 1920. e. Colgate U. Began as wri for Arthur Godfrey; Garry Moore; Sam Levenson; Victor Borge; Perry Como; Harry Reasoner. Later prod-dir-perf in doc essays inc: Black History-Lost, Strayed or Stolen (Emmy-wri-1969); An Essay on War; An Essay on Churches; In Praise of New York City--The Colleges; Mr Rooney Goes to Washington; The Great American Dream Machine; Mr. Rooney Goes To Dinner; Mr. Rooney Goes To Work; 60 Minutes (Emmys-1981, 1982); Andy Rooney Takes Off.

ROONEY, Mickey (Joe Yule): Act. b. NYC, Sep 23, 1920. In vaudeville during infancy with parents. From age 5 to 12 created screen version of newspaper comic character Mickey McGuire in series of shorts; took name of Mickey Rooney, returned to vaudeville; resumed screen career 1934. (Special Oscar-1938) "for setting a high standard of ability and achievement" as a juvenile actor. Films inc: Fast Companions; My Pal, the King; Chained; The Devil Is a Sissy; A Family Affair (and 15 other Andy Hardy films); Boys Town; Stablemates; Babes in Arms; Young Tom Edison; A Yank at Eton; Girl Crazy; The Human Comedy; National Velvet; Killer McCoy; Summer Holiday; Quicksand; Off Limits; Drive a Crooked Road; The Bridges of Toko-Ri; The Bold and the Brave; The Last Mile; King of the Roaring 20's; Breakfast at Tiffany's; It's a Mad, Mad, Mad, Mad World; The Secret Invasion; The Extraordinary Seaman; The Comic; The Cockeyed Cowboys of Calico County; Skidoo; Pulp; Richard; B.J. Presents; That's Entertainment; The Domino Principle; Pete's Dragon; The Magic of Lassie; The Black Stallion; Arabian Adventure; The Fox and The Hound; La traverse de la Pacific (Odyssey of the Pacific); The Care Bears Movie.

(Honorary Oscar-1983).

TV inc: Playhouse 90; Pinocchio; The Dick Powell Theater; The Mickey Rooney Show; Name of the Game; Evil Roy Slade; Night Gallery; Donovan's Kid; Rudolph and Frosty's Christmas in July (voice); From Raquel With Love; My Kidnapper, My Love; Misunderstood Monsters (voice); Leave 'Em Laughing; Bob Hope's All-Star Birthday Party at West Point; Entertainer of the Year Awards; Bill (Emmy-1982); One of the Boys; Senior Trip; Stanley Kramer On Film; O'-Malley; Bill--On His Own; Bob Hope's Who Makes the World Laugh--Part II; It Came Upon A Midnight Clear.

Bway inc: Sugar Babies.

ROONEY, Pat: Prod-Wri. b. NE. e. Marquette U; UCLA. Started in vaudeville, niteries. Formed Pat Rooney Prodns, 1962. Films inc: Dime With a Halo: Danger Pass; Caged; Law of the Lawless; Requiem for a Gunfighter; Bounty Killer; Young Once; Fools; Christmas Couple; Black Eye; Deadmans Curve.

ROOS, Fred: Prod. b. Santa Monica, CA, May 23, 1934. e. UCLA, BA. Started as a casting dir. Films inc: The Conversation; The Godfather Part 2 (Oscar-1974); Apocalypse Now; The Black Stallion; One From the Heart; The Escape Artist (exec prod); Hammett; The Outsiders; The Black Stallion Returns; Rumble Fish; The Cotton Club (co-prod).

ROOT, Wells: Wri. b. Buffalo, NY, Mar 21, 1900. e. Yale, BA. Films inc: I Cover the Waterfront; Tiger Shark; The Prisoner of Zenda; The Magnificent Obsession; Texas Across the River. TV inc: Ford Theatre; TV inc Ford Theatre; G.E. Theatre; Fireside Theatre; Cheyenne; Four Star Theatre; The Rogues; Maverick.

Author: Writing the Script.

RORKE, Hayden: Act. b. NYC, Oct 24, 1910. e. Villanova Coll; AADA. Toured with Walter Hampden Repertory: Cyrano; Hamlet; Macbeth; Richelieu. Films inc: Pillow Talk; Spencer's Mountain; The Law and the Lady; An American in Paris; Midnight Lace; The Nightwalker.

TV inc: I Love Lucy; The Jack Benny Show; Dr. Kildare; Cannon; The Legend of Lizzie Borden; The Money Changers; etc.

Bway inc: Three Men on a Horse; The Philadelphia Story; Personal Appearance; The Iceman Cometh; Dream Girl.

ROSE, Alex (Alexandra): Prod. b. 1946. e. U of WI, BS. In dist, 1970 with Medford Films; asst sls mgr New World Pictures; teamed with Tamara Assayev to prod Drive-In; I Wanna Hold Your Hand; Big Wednesday; Norma Rae. Partnership dissolved Nov. 1983.

TV inc: Norma Rae.

ROSE, David: Comp-Cond. b. London, Jun 24, 1910. e. Chicago Coll of Music. To US 1914. Pianist in dance orchs inc: Ted Fiorito; formed 1st orch. 1936; staff arr radio; 1938, music dir Mutual Network, Hollywood. While in USAAR, WW II, comp & dir music for Winged Victory. Music Dir MGM.

Films inc: The Princess and the Pirate; Rich, Young and Pretty; The Clown; Operation Petticoat; Please Don't Eat the Daisies; Jupiter's Darling; Port Afrique; Sam's Son.

TV inc: Red Skelton Show; An Evening with Fred Astaire (Emmy-1959); Bonanza (Emmy-1971); Suddenly Love; Little House on the Prairie (Emmys-1979, 1982); Father Murphy; Dear Mr. President; Look Back to Yesterday; Little House--The Last Farewell; Highway To Heaven; Bless All The Dear Children.

Songs inc: Holiday for Strings; Our Waltz; Manhattan Square Dance; Never Too Late.

ROSE, George: Act. b. Bicester, England, Feb 19, 1920. With Old Vic Company 1944-1948. Thea inc: (London) The Government Inspector; People Like Us; A Penny for a Song; The Square Ring; The Apple Cart; My Three Angels; The Chalk Garden; Living for Pleasure; The Visit; A Man for All Seasons. (Bway) The Government Inspector; Much Ado About Nothing; A Man For All Seasons; Hamlet; Slow Dance on the Killing Ground; Royal Hunt of the Sun; Walking Happy; Loot; Coco; Wise Child; Sleuth; My Fat Friend; My Fair Lady (rev) (Tony-1976); Pirates of Penzance; Dance A Little Closer; Beethoven's Tenth; Aren't We All.

Films inc: Pickwick Papers; Grand National Night; The Sea Shall Not Have Them; The Night My Number Came Up; Brothers In Law; A Night To Remember; Jack the Ripper; The Flesh and the Fiends; Hawaii; A New Leaf; No Love for Johnnie; From the Mixed-Up Files of Mrs. Basil E Frankweiler; The Pirates of Penzance.

ROSE, Jack: Prod. b. Chicago, Jul 4, 1939. Films inc: Moonshine; Forever My Love; Sniper; Starhops; Other Roads; The Warrior.

ROSE, Jack: Wri. b. Warsaw, Poland, Nov 4, 1911. e. OH U, BA. Films inc: (mostly in collab with Mel Shavelson) Ladies Man; Sorrowful Jones; The Great Lover; Pale Face; The Road to Rio; Daughter of Rosie O'Grady; Always Leave Them Laughing; On Moonlight Bay; I'll See You in My Dreams; April in Paris; The Seven Little Foys; Houseboat; The Five Pennies; Beau James; It Started in Naples; Double Trouble; Papa's Delicate Condition; Who's Got the Action; Who's Been Sleeping in My Bed?; A Touch of Class; The Duchess and the Dirtwater Fox; Lost and Found; The Great Muppet Caper.

ROSE, Peter N.C.H.: Mktg Exec. b. Rawalpindi, India, Aug 1, 1947. Merchandising m, Hoyts Theatres Ltd; mktg m, South Australian Film Corp.

ROSE, Philip (nee Rosenberg): Prod. b. NYC, Jul 4, 1921. Bway inc: A Raisin in the Sun; Semi-Detached; Purlie Victorious; Bravo, Giovanni; Nobody Loves an Albatross; Cafe Crown; The Owl and the Pussycat; Nathan Weinstein; Mystic, Connecticut; The Ninety-Day Mistress; Does a Tiger Wear a Necktie?; Purlie; Shenandoah *(Tony-*co-author-1975); Angel; Comin' Uptown (& book); Amen Corner (wri).

ROSE, Reginald: Wri-Prod. b. NYC, Dec 10, 1920. Films inc: Crime in the Streets; The Man in the Net; Man of the West; Twelve Angry Men; Baxter; Somebody Killed Her Husband; The Wild Geese; The Sea Wolves; Whose Life Is It Anyway?; Who Dares Win; Wild Geese II.
TV inc: The Remarkable Incident at Carson Corners; Thunder on Sycamore Street; A Quiet Game of Cards; The Cruel Day; The Sacco-Vanzetti Story; Twelve Angry Men *(Emmy*-1954); The Defenders *(2 Emmys-*1962 & 1963); Tragedy in a Temporary Town; Black Monday; Dear Friends; Studs Lonigan; The Rules of Marriage.

ROSE, William: Wri. b. Jefferson City, MO, 1918. Films inc: Once a Jolly Swagman; The Gift Horse; Genevieve; The Maggie; The Lady Killers; The Smallest Show on Earth; It's a Mad, Mad, Mad, Mad World; The Russians Are Coming; The Flim Flam Man; Guess Who's Coming to Dinner *(Oscar-*1967); The Secret of Santa Vittoria.

ROSE MARIE (nee Mazzetta): Act. b. NYC, Aug 15. Child actress as Baby Rose Marie. Films Inc: Cheaper To Keep Her; Lunch Wagon.
TV inc: Dick Van Dyke Show; Robert Cummings Show; Doris Day Show; regular on Hollywood Squares.
Bway inc: Top Banana.

ROSEMONT, Norman: Prod. b. NYC, Dec 12, 1924. TV inc: Brigadoon; Carousel; Kiss Me Kate; Kismet; Stiletto; The Man Without a Country; Miracle on 34th Street; A Tree Grows in Brooklyn; The Red Badge of Courage; The Count of Monte Cristo; The Man in the Iron Mask; The Mad Mad Mad Mad World of the Super Bowl; Captains Courageous; The Court Martial of George Armstrong Custer; The Four Feathers; Les Miserables; All Quiet on the Western Front; Pleasure Palace; Little Lord Fauntleroy; A Tale of Two Cities; Big Bend Country; The Hunchback of Notre Dame; Ivanhoe; The Adventures of Little Lord Fauntleroy; Witness For the Prosecution; Master of the Game; Camille.

ROSEN, Larry (Lawrence Richard Rosen): Wri-Prod. b. Newark, NJ., Feb. 8, 1936. e. U of MI., BA. Started as staff prod dir WKBN-TV Youngstown, OH; 1961, asso prod Mike Douglas Show; 1965, prod; 1967 joined Col/Screen Gems as prod; 1976 formed Larry Larry Prodns with Larry Tucker. TV inc: Spencer's Pilot (crea-prod); Andros Targets (exec prod); Pals; Mr. Merlin (& crea); Jennifer Slept Here (& crea).

ROSEN, Robert Lewis: Prod. b. NYC, Oct 7, 1935. e. Lehigh U, BSC. Films inc: Prophecy; Going Ape; The Challenge; Courage (& dir); Porky's Revenge.
TV inc: Puff The Magic Dragon; The Little Rascals Christmas Special; Seiko World Tennis Tournament; The World of Strawberry Shortcake; Puff The Magic Dragon in the Land of Living Lies; NCAA Japan Bowl; Thanksgiving in the Land of Oz.

ROSENBERG, Frank P.: Prod-Wri. b. NYC, Nov 22, 1913. Joined Columbia Pictures, NY, as office boy, 1929. Promoted to publicist, became national dir adv, publicity, exploitation, 1944. Resigned 1947 to enter prodn. Films inc: Man Eater of Kumaon; Where the Sidewalk Ends; Secret of Convict Lake; Return of the Texan; The Farmer Takes a Wife; King of the Khyber Rifles; Miracle in the Rain; The Girl He Left Behind; One-Eyed Jacks; Critic's Choice; Madigan; The Steagle; The Reincarnation of Peter Proud; Gray Lady Down (adapt only).
TV inc: Exec prod and prod for Schultz Playhouse programs during 1957-58; exec prod Arrest and Trial, 1963-64; exec prod Kraft Suspense Theatre, 1964-65.

ROSENBERG, Mark: Exec. b. 1948. e. U WI. Ed University Review; ad exec, Seiniger & Associates; agent with ICM, Adams, Ray & Rosenberg; joined WB 1975 as vp prodn; 1980 sr vp prodn; July 1983, P theatrical prodn.

ROSENBERG, Meta: Prod-Former Agent. TV inc: The Rockford Files *(Emmy-*exec prod-1978); Off the Minnesota Strip; Bret Maverick; The Long Summer of George Adams.

ROSENBERG, Rick: Prod. b. Los Angeles. e. UCLA. Asst film edtr, later asst to prod Jerry Bresler. Films inc: The Reivers (asso prod); Adam At 6 A.M.; Hide in Plain Sight. TV inc: Suddenly Single; The Glass House; A Brand New Life; The Autobiography of Miss Jane Pittman *(Emmy-*1974); I Love You. . .Goodbye; Queen of the Starlight Ballroom; A Death in Canaan; Strangers--The Story of a Mother and Daughter; Wishman; Robert Kennedy & His Times; Kids Don't Tell (exec prod).

ROSENBERG, Stuart: Dir-Prod. b. NYC, 1928. e. NYU. Films inc: Murder Inc; Question 7; Cool Hand Luke; April Fools; Move; W U S A; Pocket Money; The Laughing Policeman; The Drowning Pool; Voyage of the Damned; The Amityville Horror; Love and Bullets; Brubaker; The Pope of Greenwich Village.
TV inc: The Untouchables; Naked City; The Defenders *(Emmy-*dir-1953); Espionage; Run for Your Life.

ROSENBLUM, Ralph: Dir-Edtr. b. NYC., Oct. 13, 1925. Films inc: (edtr) Long Day's Journey Into Night; The Pawnbroker; A Thousand Clowns; The Group; The Producers; Goodbye Columbus; Take the Money and Run; Bananas; Bad Company; The Night They Raided Minsky's; Sleeper; Love and Death; Annie Hall; Interiors; The Grey Fox (edtrl cnslt); Marvin and Tige (crea cnslt).
TV inc: (Dir) The Greatest Man in the World; The Man that Corrupted Hadleyburg; Any Friend of Nicholas Nickleby is a Friend of Mine; Summer Solstice; Amy and Angel. (Edtrl cnslt) Playing For Time; Prisoner Without a Name, Cell Without a Number.

ROSENFELT, Frank E.: Exec. b. Peabody, MA, Nov 15, 1921. e. Cornell U, BS, LLB. Served as atty for RKO before joining MGM in 1955. Named VP, gen. counsel 1969; pres. in 1973. Also CEO, 1974; April 1982 in reorganization became Chmn & CEO of MGM Film Co., & vice chmn & COO of MGM/UA Entertainment Co.; Sept 1982, chmn & CEO.

ROSENFIELD, James H.: Exec. b. Boston, MA. e. Dartmouth. Worked as radio announcer while in college; account exec NBC-TV Participating Program Sales; ad mgr Polaroid Corp; 1966, account exec CBS Network sales; 1969, dir Eastern Sales; 1972, VP Eastern Sales; Feb 1977, VP-Nat'l Sls Mgr; Oct 1977, P CBS TV Network; Nov 1981, Exec VP CBS/Broadcast Group, responsible for CBS TV Network, CBS Entertainment, CBS Sports; Sept. 1983, Sr exec VP.

ROSENFIELD, Jonas Jr: Exec. b. Dallas, TX, Jun 29, 1915. e. U of Miami, BA. VP, worldwide adv., publicity & promo Italian Films Export, 1950-55; same post at Columbia Pictures, 1960-63; same with 20th Century-Fox, 1963-77. Formed own marketing consultant company, 1977; Sr vp worldwide mktg Melvin Simon Prodns 1978; May 1981, exec vp wldwde ad-pub-promo, Filmways; Feb 1982, left Filmways and resumed own indie company when Orion took over Filmways; Sept. 1983, exec dir American Film Marketing Assn; June, 1985 became P.

ROSENMAN, Howard: Prod. b. Brooklyn, NY. Worked as asst to Sir Michael Benthall on Bway prodns; became prod Benton & Bowles agcy; with ABC TV; RSO Prodns before becoming indie prod. TV inc: Virginia Hill; The Bees.
Films inc: The Main Event; Resurrection.

ROSENMAN, Leonard: Comp. b. NYC, Sep 7, 1924. Film scores inc: East of Eden; Cobweb; Rebel Without a Cause; Edge of the City; The Savage Eye; The Chapman Report; Fantastic Voyage; Hellfighters; Beneath the Planet of the Apes; Barry Lyndon *(Oscar-*1975); Bound For Glory *(Oscar-*1976) The Car; September 30,l955; Promises In the Dark; Prophecy; Hide in Plain Sight; The Jazz Singer; Making Love; Miss Lonely Hearts; Cross Creek; Heart of the Stag; Sylvia.
TV inc: Sybil *(Emmy-*1977); Friendly Fire *(Emmy-*1979); City in Fear; Murder In Texas; The Wall; Miss Lonelyhearts; Celebrity; The Return of Marcus Welby, M.D.; Heartsounds; First Steps.

ROSENTHAL, Rick: Dir. b. NYC 1950. e. Harvard; AFI. Filmmaker-in-residence with NH Television Network. TV inc: The Incredible Hulk (wri); Fire on the Mountain (co-prod); Secrets of Midland Heights (prod-dir); Darkroom; Code Of Vengeance.

Films inc: Moonface (AFI short); Halloween II; Bad Boys; American Dreamer.

ROSHKIND, Michael: Exec. b. NYC, Oct 4, 1921. e. Northwestern U, BS. Joined NBC 1941 as news ed; 1942 dir news & spec events ABC; 1948, exec vp Weintraub Adv agcy; 1950, exec vp AA Schechter Public Relations; 1960, partner Strauss Public Relations; 1966, vp & COO Motown; resd 1980 to form own company; Feb 1983 retd to Motown as cnslt.

ROSI, Francesco: Dir-Wri. b. Naples, Italy, Nov 15, 1922. Worked as assistant to Luchino Visconti, Michelangelo Antonioni before directorial debut. Films inc: The Challenge; I Magliari; Salvatore Giuliano; La Mani Sulla Citta (Hands Over the City); Il Momento della Verita (Moment of Truth); More Than A Miracle; Uomini Contro; Il Caso Mattei (The Mattei Affair); Lucky Luciano; Il Contesto (dir only); Cadaveri Eccelenti (Illustrious Corpses); Christ Stopped At Eboli; Tre Fratelli (Three Brothers); Carmen.

ROSS, Diana: Singer-Act. b. Detroit, MI, Mar 26, 1944. Member of Supremes as teenager. Over period of 10 years the trio had 15 consecutive hit records. Went solo in 1969, appearing in niteries, TV. Screen debut 1973, Lady Sings the Blues. Films inc: Mahogany; The Wiz. (Special Tony-1977).

TV inc: Diana (& exec prod-wri); Motown 25--Yesterday, Today, Forever; Motown Returns To The Apollo.

ROSS, Frank: Prod. b. Boston, Aug 12, 1904. e. Exeter; Princeton. Films inc: Of Mice and Men; The Devil and Miss Jones; The More the Merrier (sp only); The Robe; The Rains of Ranchipur; Kings Go Forth; Mister Moses; Where It's At.

ROSS, Herbert: Dir. b. NYC, May 13, 1927. H of Nora Kaye. Bway inc: (chor) On a Clear Day You Can See Forever; A Tree Grows in Brooklyn; House of Flowers; I Can Get It For You Wholesale; Anyone Can Whistle. (Dir): Chapter Two; I Ought To Be In Pictures. Later became resident choreographer for American Ballet Theatre, staging Caprichos; The Maids.

Film debut as choreographer/musical sequence dir. Inside Daisy Clover, 1966. Also Dr. Dolittle; Funny Girl. Films Dir: Goodbye Mr. Chips; The Owl and the Pussycat; T.R. Baskin; Play It Again, Sam; The Last of Sheila; Funny Lady; The Sunshine Boys; The Seven Per Cent Solution; The Turning Point; The Goodbye Girl; California Suite; Nijinsky; Pennies From Heaven (& prod); I Ought To Be In Pictures (& prod); Max Dugan Returns (& prod); Footloose; Protocol.

TV inc: The Bell Telephone Hour; Fred Astaire Special.

ROSS, Katharine: Act. b. Los Angeles, Jan 29, 1943. Screen debut, 1965, Shenandoah. Films inc: Mister Buddwing; The Singing Nun; Games; The Graduate; The Ski Bums; A Nice Girl Like Me; Bullitt; Hellfighters; Butch Cassidy and the Sundance Kid; Tell Them Willie Boy Is Here; Fools; They Only Kill Their Masters; The Stepford Wives; Voyage of the Damned; The Betsy; The Swarm; The Legacy; The Final Countdown; Wrong Is Right.

TV inc: Sam Benedict; Doctors at Work; The Longest Hundred Miles; Ben Casey; The Bob Hope-Chrysler Theatre; The Virginian; Wagon Train; The Road West; Rodeo Girl; Murder In Texas; Marion Rose White; The Shadow Riders; Travis McGee; Secrets of a Mother and Daughter.

ROSS, Marion: Act. b. Albert Lea, MN, Oct 25, 1928. e. San Diego State Coll. Films inc: Forever Female; The Glenn Miller Story; Sabrina; The Proud and the Profane; Operation Petticoat; Teacher's Pet; Lust for Life; Colossus; The Forbin Project; Airport; Honkey; Grand Theft Auto.

TV inc: Life with Father; Paradise Bay; Happy Days; Pearl; Skyward; Midnight Offerings; Who Loves Amy Tonight; True Life Stories; Joanie Loves Chachi; Sins Of The Father; Martin Mull Presents The History Of White People In America--Part 1 (feevee).

Bway inc: Edwin Booth.

ROSSEN, Carol: Act. b. Aug. 12, 1937. W of Hal Holbrook. D of late Robert Rossen. Films inc: The Arrangement; The Stepford Wives; The Fury.

TV inc: Greatest Heroes of the Bible; Portrait of a Rebel--Margaret Sanger; A Question of Honor; Happy Endings.

ROSSI DRAGO, Eleanora (Palmira Omiccioli): Act. b. Italy, Sep. 23, 1925. Films inc: I Pirati di Capri; Verginita; Three Forbidden Stories; La Tratta delle Bianche; Sensualita; Hell Raiders of the Deep; La Fiammata; Daughters of Destiny; L'Affaire Maurizius; Napoleon; The Girl Friends; The Awakening; Kean; The Facts of Murder; Violent Summer; David and Goliath; Under Ten Flags; Sword of the Conqueror; Love at 20; Hypnosis; Love and Marriage; Uncle Tom's Cabin; The Bible--in the Beginning; Camille 2000; Dorian Gray.

ROSSIF, Frederic: Dir. b. Yugoslavia, Aug 14, 1922. Worked for Cinematheque Francaise. Films inc: The Witnesses; To Die in Madrid; The Animals; A Wall in Jerusalem; Why America?; Aussi loin que l'amour; La Fete Sauvage (The Savage Party); Sauvage et Beau (Wild And Beautiful).

ROSSON, Hal: Cin. b. 1895. Started in silent films. Films inc: Manhandled; Gentlemen Prefer Blondes; Tarzan of the Apes; The Scarlet Pimpernel; The Ghost Goes West; The Garden of Allah (Honorary Oscar-1936); The Wizard of Oz; Johnny Eager; The Hucksters; On the Town; The Red Badge of Courage; Singin' in the Rain; The Bad Seed; No Time for Sergeants; El Dorado.

ROSTEN, Irwin: Wri-Prod. b. NYC, Sep 10, 1924. Started as newsman with Dumont Network; 1954 wri-prod news, pub aff KNXT, LA; 1960 news dir KTLA; 1963 wri-prod Wolper Prodns; 1967-1972 chief of doc dept MGM; then indie.

TV inc: Grizzly!; The Incredible Machine; The Volga; The Legacy of LSB Leakey; Gold!; Mysteries of the Mind (Emmy-prod-wri-1980); Trial by Wilderness; Hollywood--The Dream Factory; Kifaru--The Black Rhinocerous; The Thames (& dir).

ROSTROPOVICH, Mstislav: Cellist. b. Baku, USSR, Aug. 12, 1927. Moscow concert debut, 1935; concert with Moscow Philharmonic, 1946; started teaching Moscow Conservatory, 1953; Carnegie Hall debut 1956; left Russia 1975 to live and work in West, appearing with all leading orchs in addition to solo concerts. TV inc: Rostropovich at the White House; The Kennedy Center Honors --A Celebration of the Performing Arts.

Recs inc: Beethoven Sonatas for Piano & Cello; Dvorak Concerto in B Minor for Cello; Brahms Double Concerto (Concerto in A Minor for Violin & Cello) (with David Oistrakh) (Grammy- class inst - 1970) ; Beethoven Triple Concerto (Concerto in C Major for Violin , Piano & Cello); Strauss Sonata in F for Cello and Piano; Don Quixote; Concert of the Century (Grammy-Album of Year - 1977); Rachmaninoff Sonata for Cello and Piano in G Minor; Schumann Concerto for Cello and Orchestra in A Minor; Schubert Quintet in C Major for Strings; Dvorak Concerto for Cello in B Minor & Saint Saens Concerto for Cello No. 1 in A Minor; Shostakovich Lady Macbeth of Mtsensk; Brahms Double Concerto (with Itzhak Perlman (Grammy-class inst-1980).

ROTH, Ann: Cos dsgn. Bway inc: Maybe Tuesday; Make a Million; The Cool World; Face of a Hero; Purlie Victorious; This Side of Paradise; A Portrait of the Artist as a Young Man; Children From Their Games; A Case of Libel; In the Summer House; Slow Dance On a Killing Ground; I Had a Ball; The Odd Couple; Star Spangled Girl; The Deer Park; Play It Again Sam; Tiny Alice; Father's Day; Fun City; 6 Rms Riv Vu; Enemies; Seesaw; The Royal Family; The Crucifer of Blood; They're Playing Our Song; Lunch Hour; The Misanthrope; Open Admissions; Design For Living; Hurlyburly (off Bway); Biloxi Blues; Arms And The Man; The Odd Couple.

Films inc: Up the Down Staircase; Pretty Poison; Midnight Cowboy; The Owl and the Pussycat; Klute; They Might Be Giants; The Pursuit of Happiness; Law and Disorder; The Valachi Papers; The Goodbye Girl; California Suite; Coming Home; Nunzio; Hair; Promises in the Dark; Nine to Five; Honky Tonk Freeway; Only When I Laugh; Silkwood; Places In The Heart; The Slugger's Wife.

ROTH, Richard: Prod. b. Chicago, Sep 16, 1940. e. Stanford U Law School. Films inc: Summer of '42; Our Time; The Adventures of Sherlock Holmes' Smarter Brother; Julia; Outland; Feb 1982, Prodn VP CBS Theatrical Films.

ROTHMAN, Mo: Exec. b. Montreal, Jan 14, 1919. Worldwide rep for Edward Small, 1950; int'l sls dept UA, 1952; sls mgr, Continent, Near East, 1955; Cont'l mgr 1957; VP int'l ops, 1960; Exec VP Col Pict Int'l, 1960; VP world distrib 1966; distrib, Chaplin Pictures, 1971. Films inc: ffolkes (exec prod).

ROTHSCHILD, Eileen: Prod Coord. b. NYC, Mar 3, 1947. e. Brooklyn Coll. Bway inc: Jesus Christ Superstar. Films inc (Prod exec): Tommy; Survive.

ROTHSTEIN, Freyda (nee Simon): Prod. b. NYC, Jul 25, 1939. e. Carnegie-Mellon U; NYU; Columbia. Half of Frey & Martin, folk song duo; field researcher for Library of Congress, made 200 field recordings in KY, TN. Thea inc: Take a Giant Step, Anna Christie; Ghosts.

TV inc: Search for Tomorrow (asso prod); Where the Heart Is (asso prod); Love of Life (prod); dir daytime dvlpmt for Par TV, prod Women in Chains; joined Talent Associates, asso prod, Johnny We Hardly Knew Ye; On Our Own; Who'll Save the Children; exec prod, The Unknown; VP Network Dvlpmt Time-Life Films, co-prod, Sex and the Single Parent; Supv Prod, Between the Lines; Exec Prod, The Family Man; Mom, The Wolfman and Me; Father Figure; Crisis at Central High; formed indie Freyda Rothstein Prodns, exec prod Dial "M" For Murder; The Princess and the Cabbie; Emerald Point N.A.S. (prod); Aug. 1984, Sr Vp Crea Aff & exec prod Peregrine Producers Group. Films inc: Blackout (exec prod).

ROTHSTEIN, Roger M.: Prod. b. Altoona, PA, Aug 31, 1935. e. Ithaca Coll. Served as prodn mgr Panic in Needle Park; The Effect of Gamma Rays on Man-In-The-Moon Marigolds. Films inc: (asso prod) Turning Point; Serpico; Hero At Large; The Goodbye Girl. (Exec Prod) Chapter Two; It Seems Like Old Times; I Ought To Be In Pictures;, (Co-prod) Only When I Laugh; Max Dugan Returns (exec prod); Two of a Kind.

ROTUNNO, Giuseppe: Cin. b. Italy. Films inc: Scandal in Sorrento; Anna of Brooklyn; White Nights; The Naked Maja; The Angel Wore Red; Rocco and His Brothers; The Best of Enemies; The Leopard; Yesterday, Today and Tomorrow; Anzio; The Secret of Santa Vittoria; Fellini's Satyricon; Sunflower; Carnal Knowledge; Man of La Mancha; Amarcord; Divine Creature; The End of the World In Our Usual Bed in a Night Full of Rain; Orchestra Rehearsal; All That Jazz; City of Women; Popeye; Five Days One Summer; E la nave va (And the Ship Sails On); American Dreamer; Non Ci Resta Che Piangere (Nothing Left To Do But Cry).

TV inc: The Scarlet and the Black.

ROUNDTREE, Richard: Act. b. New Rochelle, NY, Jul 9, 1937. e. Southern IL U. Films inc: Shaft; Shaft's Big Score; Shaft in Africa; Charley One-Eye; Earthquake; Man Friday; Diamonds; Escape to Athena; Inchon; An Eye For An Eye; The Winged Serpent; One Down, Two To Go; Young Warriors; The Big Score; Killpoint; City Heat.

TV inc: Shaft; Firehouse; Roots; Masquerade; The Baron and the Kid; A.D.

ROUSE, Russel: Dir-Wri. b. NYC, 1916. Films inc: D O A; The Well; The Thief; New York Confidential; The Fastest Gun Alive; Pillow Talk (Oscar-1959); Thunder in the Sun; A House is Not a Home; The Oscar; Caper of the Golden Bull.

ROUTLEDGE, Patricia: Act. b. Birkenhead, Cheshire, England, Feb 17, 1929. e. U of Liverpool. Thea inc: (London) The Duenna; Zuleika; The Love Doctor; Follow That Girl; Little Mary Sunshine; How's the World Treating You?; Darling of the Day; The Country Wife; The Magistrate; First Impressions; And A Nightgale Sang; Noises Off; When the Wind Blows. (Bway) Darling of the Day (Tony-1968);- 1600 Pennsylvania Ave; On Approval.

TV inc: Sense and Sensibility; Tartuffe; David Copperfield; The Beggar's Opera.

ROWAN, Dan: Act. b. Beggs, OK, 1922. Performed in niteries with Dick Martin. On TV in Rowan & Martin's Laugh-In, NBC, 1967-73 (Emmys-1968 & 1969); The First All-American Ultra Quiz.

Films inc: Once Upon a Horse; The Maltese Bippy.

ROWLAND, Jada: Act. b. NYC, Feb 23. Thea inc: That Lady; Mrs. McThing; The Remarkable Mr. Pennypacker; Sunday Breakfast; The

Cold Wind and the Warm; A Season in the Sun; The House of Bernarda Alba.

TV inc: The Secret Storm (20 years); As the World Turns; The Doctors.

ROWLAND, Roy Dir. b. NYC, Dec. 31, 1909.e. USC. Started as script clerk; dir shorts at MGM before features. Films inc: A Stranger In Town; Lost Angel; Our Vines Have Tender Grapes; Boys Ranch; The Romance Of Rosy Ridge; Tenth Avenue Angel; Killer McCoy; Scene Of The Crime; The Outriders; Two Weeks With Love; Excuse My Dust; Bugles In The Afternoon; The 5000 Fingers of Dr. T.; Affair With A Stranger; The Moonlighter; Rogue Cop; Witness To Murder; Many Rivers To Cross; Hit The Deck; These Wilder Years; Meet Me In Las Vegas; Gun Glory; The Seven Hills of Rome; The Girl Hunters; Gun Fighters of Casa Grande; They Called Him Gringo; The Sea Pirate; Land Raiders.

ROWLANDS, Gena: Act. b. Cambria, WI, Jun 19, 1936. e. U of WI; AADA. W of John Cassavetes. Bdwy debut as understudy and then succeeded to role of the Girl in The Seven Year Itch. Screen debut, 1958, The High Cost of Living. Films inc: Lonely Are the Brave; The Spiral Road; A Child is Waiting; Tony Rome; Faces; Minnie and Moskowitz; A Woman Under the Influence; Two Minute Warning; Gloria; Tempest; Love Streams; "I'm Almost Not Crazy. . ."John Cassavetes--The Man And His Work (doc-int).

TV inc: The Philco Playhouse; Studio One; Alfred Hitchcock Presents; Dr. Kildare; Bonanza; The Kraft Mystery Theatre; Strangers--The Story of a Mother and Daughter; Thursday's Child.

Bway inc: The Middle of the Night.

ROYER, Robb: Comp-Wri. b. Los Angeles, Dec 6, 1942. Songs for films inc: (w. Fred Karlin) Cover Me Babe; Lovers and Other Strangers (Co-Oscar-song-1970); California Dreaming.

TV inc: Awakening Land; Roll of Thunder.

ROZSA, Miklos: Comp. b. Budapest, Apr 18, 1907. e. Leipsig Cons. Film scores inc: The Four Feathers; The Thief of Badgad; Lady Hamilton; Sundown; Lydia; Jungle Book; Five Graves to Cairo; Double Indemnity; The Lost Weekend; Spellbound (Oscar-1945); The Killers; Brute Force; A Double Life (Oscar-1947); Adam's Rib; The Asphalt Jungle; Quo Vadis; Ivanhoe; Julius Caesar; Lust for Life; Ben Hur (Oscar-1950); King of Kings; El Cid; Sodom and Gomorrah; The VIPs; The Power; The Green Berets; Providence; Fedora; Last Embrace; Time After Time; Eye of the Needle; Dead Men Don't Wear Plaid.

RUBAN, Al: Prod. b. NYC, Nov 4, 1934. Films inc: Faces; Husbands; Minnie and Moskowitz; Opening Night (& cin); The Big Fix (act); Jetlag (cin); Love Streams (& cin).

RUBIN, Benny: Act. b. Boston, 1899. On screen from 1929. Films inc: Naughty Baby; Marianne; George White's Scandals of 1935; Here Comes Mr. Jordan; Yankee Pasha; Meet Me in Los Vegas; A Hole in the Head; A Pocketful of Miracles; The Patsy; That Funny Feeling; Thoroughly Modern Millie; Airport; Won Ton Ton, the Dog Who Saved Hollywood; Coma.

RUBIN, Mann: Wri. b. NYC, Dec 11, 1926. e. NYU. TV inc: Philco Playhouse; Studio One; Climax; Playhouse 90; Armstrong Circle Theatre; Mod Squad; The Rookies; Mannix; Barnaby Jones; Quincy; See the Man Run.

Films inc: The Best of Everything; Brainstorm; An American Dream; Warning Shot; Once You Kiss a Stranger; The First Deadly Sin.

RUBIN, Stanley: Wri-Prod. b. NYC, Oct 8, 1917. e. UCLA. Films inc: The Narrow Margin; My Pal Gus; Destination Gobi; River of No Return; Destry; Promise Her Anything; The President's Analyst; The Take.

TV inc: Channing; The Ghost and Mrs. Muir; Bracken's World; The Man and the City; Executive Suite; Babe; And Your Name Is Jonah; Escape From Iran--The Canadian Caper (exec prod); Don't Look Back.

RUBINEK, Saul: Act. b. Fohrenwold, Germany, Jul. 2, 1948. Born in DP camp, moved to Canada as infant, began acting at eight with little theatre groups, on radio. Films inc: Slow Gun; Highpoint; Death Ship; Agency; Ticket to Heaven; By Design; Soup for One; Young Doctors in

Love; The Terry Fox Story; Against All Odds.

TV inc: Concealed Enemies; Clown White.

RUBINSTEIN, John: Act-Comp. b. Dec 8, 1946. S of the late Artur Rubinstein. Films inc: (Act) Zachariah; Journey to Shiloh; Getting Straight; The Wild Pack; The Car; The Boys From Brazil; In Search of Historic Jesus; Daniel. (Score) Paddy; The Candidate; Jeremiah Johnson; Kid Blue.

TV inc: (Act) A Howling in the Woods; All Together Now; God Bless the Children; Something Evil; Jack and the Princess; Family (& theme song); The Gift of the Magi; She's Dressed to Kill; Make Me An Offer; Amber Waves; Moviola (The Silent Lovers).; Killjoy; Skokie; Johnny Belinda (mus); I Take These Men; M.A.D.D.--Mothers Against Drunk Drivers; Secrets of a Mother and Daughter (mus); Choices of the Heart (mus); The Dollmaker (mus); City Killer (mus); Crazy Like A Fox .

Bway inc: Pippin; On a Clear Day You Can See Forever; Metamorphoses; Children of a Lesser God (Tony-1980); Fools (& music); The Caine Mutiny Court Martial;

RUBY, Harry: Comp-Lyr. b. NYC, Jan 27, 1895. Pianist, song plugger; also played vaudeville, cafes. Bway inc: Helen of Troy, New York; The Ramblers; Lucky; The Five O'Clock Girl; Animal Crackers; Top Speed.

Films inc: Check and Double Check; The Cuckoos; Horsefeathers; The Kid from Spain; Look for the Silver Lining; Bright Lights; Duck Soup.

Songs inc: Daddy Long Legs; A Kiss to Build A Dream On; Who's Sorry Now?; I Wanna Be Loved by You; Watching the Clouds Roll By; Three Little Words.

RUDD, Hughes: TV newsman. b. Wichita, KS, Sep 14, 1921. With Kansas City Star, Minneapolis Tribune before joining CBS 1959 as corr; 1965 chf Moscow Bureau; 1966, Bonn Bureau; 1974 anchorman Morning News; 1979 to ABC-TV as spec corr. TV inc: St. Paul's Bells (Emmy-1981).

RUDDY, Albert: Prod. b. Montreal, Mar 28, 1934. e. USC, BS. Films inc: The Wild Seed; Little Fauss and Big Halsey; Making It; The Godfather (Oscar-1972); The Longest Yard; Coonskin; Matilda; Death Hunt (exec prod); The Cannonball Run; Megaforce (& sp); Lassiter; Cannonball Run II (& sp).

TV inc: The Macahans; The Stockers.

RUDIN, Scott Exec. b. NYC. Feb. 14, 1958. Started as prodn asst on Bway for producers Kermit Bloomgarden, Robert Whitehead, Emanuel Azenberg, later casting director. Joined 20th Fox, Jan. 1984 as prod; Dec. 1984, exec vp prodn. Films inc: I'm Dancing As Fast As I Can (exec prod) (Oscar-doc-1983; Emmy-children's-1984); Reckless; Mrs. Soffel.

TV inc: Little Gloria, Happy At Last (exec prod).

RUDOLPH, Alan: Dir. b. Los Angeles, 1943. Member Directors Guild's Assistant Directors Training program. Worked as asst to Robert Altman. Films inc: Buffalo Bill and the Indians (co-wri); Welcome to LA; Remember My Name; Roadie; Endangered Species; Choose Me (& wri); Songwriter.

RUEHMANN, Heinz: Act. b. Germany, 1902. Films inc: Drei von der Tankstelle; Man Braucht Kein Geld; If We Were All Angels; Captain From Kopenick; It Happened in Broad Daylight; The Judge and the Sinner; Ship of Fools; The Chinese Miracle; Scrounged Meals; On A Silver Platter.

RUGOLO, Pete: Comp. b. Sicily, Dec 25, 1915. e. St Francis State Coll. To US 1919. Pianist; arranger for orchs. Films inc: The Strip; Skirts Ahoy; Glory Alley; Latin Lovers; Easy to Love; Jack the Ripper; Chu Chu and the Philly Flash.

TV inc: Run for Your Life; The Fugitive; The Challengers (Emmy-1970); The Bold Ones (Emmy-1972); Alias Smith & Jones; The Virginian; Jig Saw John; Carter Country; Family; The Home Front; Revenge of the Gray Gang; For Lovers Only.

RULE, Elton H.: Exec. b. Stockton, CA, Jun 13, 1917. e. Sacramento Coll. VP and gen mgr, KABC-TV, LA, 1961-68; pres, ABC TV Network, 1968-70; pres ABC (broadcast division), 1970-72; P & CEO

ABC, Inc, 1972-1983; named bd vice chmn Jan 1983; resd effective Dec. 31, 1983; June 1984 formed Rule/Starger Prods with Martin Starger.

(ATAS Governors Award 1981).

RULE, Janice: Act. b. Cincinnati, OH, Aug 15, 1931. Films inc: Starlift; Holiday for Sinners; Rogue's March; Woman's Devotion; Gun for a Coward; Subterraneans; Invitation to a Gunfighter; The Chase; Welcome to Hard Times; The Ambushers; Kid Blue; Three Women; Missing; Rainy Day Friends.

Bway inc: Picnic; The Flowering Peach; Princess in a Carefree Tree; Night Circus; Happiest Girl in the World; The Homecoming.

RUSH, Barbara: Act. b. Denver, CO, Jan 4, 1930. On screen from 1951. Films inc: The First Legion; Molly; When Worlds Collide; It Came From Outer Space; Magnificent Obsession; Bigger than Life; Oh Men! Oh Women!; No Down Payment; The Young Philadelphians; Bramble Bush; Strangers When We Meet; Come Blow Your Horn; Robin and the 7 Hoods; Hombre; Airport; Superdad; Can't Stop the Music; Summer Lovers.

TV inc: Death Car on the Freeway; The Seekers; Flamingo Road; The Night the Bridge Fell Down; At Your Service.

Bway inc: A Woman of Independent Means.

RUSH, Herman: TV Exec. b. Philadelphia, Jun 20, 1929. e. Temple U. 1957-60 P Flamingo Telefilms Inc; 1960-71 P TV division of Creative Mgt Asso; 1971-77 P Herman Rush Asso Inc; 1977-78 chmn bd Rush-Flaherty Agency Inc; 1979 P Marble Arch TV; 1980 P Col TV; June, 1984, P new Col TV group.

TV inc: Touch of Grace; Love Thy Neighbor; DHO; Death Stalk; Celebration-The American Spirit.

RUSH, Richard: Prod-Dir-Wri. b. NYC. e. UCLA. Films inc: Too Soon to Love; Of Love and Desire (dir-sp); A Man Called Dagger (dir); The Fickle Finger of Fate (dir); Thunder Alley (dir); Hells's Angels on Wheels (dir); Psych-Out (dir-wri); Savage Seven (dir); Getting Straight (dir-prod); Freebie and the Bean (dir-prod); The Stunt Man (dir-prod).

RUSSEL, Del: Act. b. Pasadena, CA, Sep 27, 1952. Films inc: Tammy Tell Me True; Cleopatra. TV inc: Men into Space; Arnie.

RUSSELL, Harold: Act. b. MA, 1914. Handless ex-paratrooper. Acted in one film, The Best Years of Our Lives (Oscars-(2)-supp & honorary-1946).

RUSSELL, Jane: Act. b. Bemidji, MN, Jun 21, 1921. Films inc: The Outlaw; The Paleface; Son of Paleface; Maccao; Montana Belle; His Kind of Woman; The Las Vegas Story; Gentlemen Prefer Blondes; Underwater; Gentlemen Marry Brunettes; Foxfire; Hot Blood; The Tall Men; The Revolt of Mamie Stover; The Fuzzy Pink Nightgown; Waco; Darker than Amber.

TV inc: Bob Hope's Road to Hollywood.

RUSSELL, John: Act. b. Los Angeles, Jan 3, 1921. e. U of CA. Films inc: Frameup; Story of Molly X; Slattery's Hurricane; Yellow Sky; Sitting Pretty; Forever Amber; Bell for Adano; Barefoot Mailman; Hoodlum Empire; Fair Wind to Java; Jubilee Trail; Last Command; Rio Bravo; Yellowstone Kelly; Fort Utah; The Outlaw Josie Wales; Pale Rider.

TV inc: Lawman; Soldiers of Fortune; Jason and the Star Command; How the West Was Fun.

RUSSELL, Ken: Dir. b. Southampton, England, 1927. Early career as dancer, actor, still photog, doc prod for BBC. Feature films inc: French Dressing; Billion Dollar Brain; Women in Love; The Music Lovers; The Devils; The Boy Friend; Mahler; Tommy; Lisztomania; Valentino; Altered States; Crimes of Passion.

TV inc: Ralph Vaughan Williams.

RUSSELL, Kurt: Act. b. Mar 17, 1951. Films inc: It Happened At the World's Fair; The Absent- Minded Professor; Follow Me Boys; The Horse in the Gray Flannel Suit; Charley and the Angel; Superdad; Used Cars; Escape From New York; The Fox and the Hound; The Thing; Silkwood; Swing Shift; The Mean Season.

TV inc: Elvis; Miracle in Caulfield, U.S.A.; The Deadly Tower; Amber Waves.

RUSSELL, Mark (nee Ruslander): Comedian. b. Buffalo, NY, Aug 23, 1932. Stand-up comic. TV inc: The Mark and Inga Show (Cleveland); Real People. Recs inc: Mark Russell's Wild, Weird, Wired World of Watergate.

RUSSELL, Nipsey: Act. b. Atlanta, GA, Oct 13, 1925. Performs on TV, nightclubs, stage, summer stock appearance in The Odd Couple; Cabin in the Sky. Bway credits inc: Tambourines to Glory.
 Films inc: The Wiz; Dream One (Nemo).
 TV inc: Fame; Uptown-A Tribute to the Apollo Theatre; A Funny Thing Happened On the Way to the White House (cable tv); Motown Returns To The Apollo.

RUSSELL, Theresa: Act. b. Burbank, CA. Films inc: The Last Tycoon; Straight Time; Bad Timing; The Razor's Edge; Insignificance.
 TV inc: Blind Ambition.

RUSSELL, Willy: Wri. Plays inc: John, Paul, George, Ringo..and Bert; Educating Rita; Blood Brothers (& mus-lyr).
 Films inc: Educating Rita; Mr. Love (mus).

RUTHERFORD, Ann: Act. b. Toronto, 1920. On screen from 1935. Appeared in 17 Andy Hardy pictures. Other films inc: Gone With The Wind; Pride and Prejudice; Whistling in the Dark; Bermuda Mystery; Bedside Manner; Murder in the Music Hall; The Secret Life of Walter Mitty; Adventures of Don Juan; Operation Haylift; They Only Kill Their Masters.

RUTTENBERG, Joseph H.: Cin. b. Russia, Jul 4, 1889. Films inc: Over the Hill; Fury; The Great Waltz (Oscar-1938); Broadway Melody; Waterloo Bridge; The Philadelphia Story; Comrade X; Dr. Jekyll and Mr. Hyde; Mrs. Miniver (Oscar-1942); Madame Curie; Adventure; Gaslight; BF's Daughter; The Forsythe Saga; The Great Caruso; Kind Lady; Prisoner of Zenda; Julius Caesar; The Last Time I Saw Paris; The Swan; Somebody Up There Likes Me (Oscar-1956); Until They Sail; Gigi (Oscar-1958); The Reluctant Debutante; Butterfield 8; Who's Been Sleeping in My Bed?; Sylvia; Harlow; Love Has Many Faces; The Oscar; Speedway.
 (Died May 1, 1983).

RYAN, Mitchell: Act. b. Cincinnati, OH, Jan 11, 1934. Started on stage with Barter Theatre, Abingdon, VA; then off-Bway, Bway. Films inc: Monte Walsh; The Hunting Party; The Old Man's Place; High Plains Drifter; Magnum Force; Electroglide in Blue; Friends of Eddie Coyle; Labrynth.
 TV inc: Bonanza; High Chaparral; O'Hara, US Treasury Agent; Cannon; Chase; Executive Suite; Flesh and Blood; The Chisholms; Angel City; The Five of Me; Death of A Centerfold--The Dorothy Stratten Story; Of Mice and Men; Uncommon Valor; High Performance; Medea; Kenny Rogers as the Gambler--The Adventure Continues; Robert Kennedy & His Times; Fatal Vision.
 Bway inc: Medea (rev).

RYAN, Natasha: Act. b. Los Angeles, May 14, 1970. TV inc: Days of Our Lives (since 1974); Sybil; Mary Jane Harper Cried Last Night; Good Against Evil; Sex and the Single Parent; Honor Thy Father; The Pirate; Ladies' Man.
 Films inc: Fatso; Kingdom of the Spiders; Boulevard Nights; The Amityville Horror; The Day Time Ended; The Entity.

RYAN, Peggy: Act. b. Long Beach, CA, Aug 28, 1924. Films inc: Top of the Town; Give Out Sisters; Top Man; The Merry Monahans; Bowery to Broadway; That's the Spirit; On Stage Everybody; All Ashore.
 TV inc: Hawaii Five-O; Pleasure Palace.

RYDELL, Mark: Dir. b. Mar 23, 1934. e. Juilliard School of Music. Films inc: The Fox; The Reivers; The Cowboys (& prod); Cinderella Liberty (& prod); Harry and Walter Go to New York; The Rose; On Golden Pond; The River.

RYDER, Alfred (Alfred Jacob Corn): Act-Dir. b. NYC, Jan 5, 1919. H of Kim Stanley. As child actor played Sammy in radio show The Rise of the Goldbergs, 1930-33. Bway inc: (as Alfred Corn) East of Broadway; Another Love; Come What May. (As Ryder) Our Town;

Medicine Show; Winged Victory; The Tower Beyond Tragedy; One More River; A Far Country (dir); Rhinocerous; Hey You; Light Man! (& dir); Windows (dir); The Exercise (dir).
 Films inc: Winged Victory; T-Men; Story on Page One; Invitation to a Gunfighter; Hotel; The Stone Killer; Who Fears the Devil. TV inc: Lago; Tiberius; Mark Antony; John Wilkes Booth; I Rise in Flames, Cried the Phoenix; The Lady of Larkspur Lotion; Bogie.

RYDER, Jeff: Exec. b. 1954. e. Rider Coll. Started in mailroom, ABC; later prodn asst, researcher; 1977 casting director several CBS-TV shows; 1978, mgr of Casting, NBC; 1979, director of casting; 1980, director of Miniseries and Novels for Television, West Coast; March, 1981 vp Daytime Programs East Coast, NBC Entertainment.

RYDER, Loren: Exec. b. Pasadena, CA, Mar 9, 1900. e. UC Berkeley, BA. Research engr Telephone Co, 1924-25; radio importer Sherman-Clay Co, 1926-28; snd dir. Paramount Pictures, 1929-45; chief engr Paramount, 1945-48; President Ryder Sound Services, 1948-76; gen mgr Nagra Magnetic Recorders, Inc, NYC, 1967-78. (Oscars-1938, 1941, 1945, 1949, 1950, 1953, 1955 for technical and scientific achievement).
 (Died May 28, 1985)

RYDGE, Norman, Sir, CBE: Exec. b. Sydney, Australia, Oct 18, 1900. Chmn Carlton Hotel Ltd; Carlton Investments Ltd; Amalgamated Holdings Ltd; Manly Hotels Pty, Ltd; Greater J D Williams Amusement Co Ltd; Hon Pres & Chmn Greater Union Organisation Pty.

RYERSON, Ann: Act. b. Fond du Lac, WI, Aug 15, 1949. With Chicago's Second City improv group for three years. Films inc; A Wedding; A Perfect Couple; Health; Caddyshack.
 TV inc: Flatbed Annie and Sweetipie, Lady Truckers; Getting Married; Private Benjamin.

RYSKIND, Morrie: Wri. b. 1895. Films inc: Animal Crackers; Palmy Days; A Night at the Opera; My Man Godfrey; Stage Door; Room Service; Man About Town; Penny Serenade; Where Do We Go from Here?; Heartbeat.
 Bway inc: Of Thee I Sing (Pulitzer Prize-1932); Animal Crackers; Louisiana Purchase.

SACCHI, Robert: Act. b. 1941. Thea inc: Play It Again, Sam (Bway); Bogey's Back (One-man show on tour).
 Films inc: The Man With Bogart's Face.

SACKHEIM, William B.: Wri-Prod. b. Gloversville, NY, Oct 31, 1921. e. UCLA. Sr vp, Rastar Films; joined U-TV, Jan. 1981 as creative consultant. Films inc: Smart Girls Don't Talk; One Last Fling; Yank in Korea; Paula; Reunion in Reno; Border River; Tanganyika; Chicago Syndicate; Art of Love; The In-Laws; The Competition; First Blood; The Survivors (prod); No Small Affair (prod).
 TV inc: Alcoa-Goodyear Presents (Emmy-1959); Gidget; The Neon Ceiling; A Clear and Present Danger; The Impatient Heart; The Harness; The Law (Emmy-1975).

SADDLER, Donald: Chor. b. Van Nuys, CA., Jan. 24, 1920. Started as a dancer in Hollywood Bowl prodns; later with Ballet Theatre; appeared in High Button Shoes; Dance Me A Song; Bless You All. Bway inc: (chor) Blue Mountain Ballads for Markova & Dolin; Wonderful Town (Tony-1953); John Murray Anderson's Almanac; Shangri-La; Milk and Honey; No No Nanette (Tony-1971); Berlin to Broadway; Much Ado About Nothing; Gala Tribute to Josh Logan; The Robber Bridegroom; The Grand Tour; Happy New Year; On Your Toes; The Loves Of Anatol (mus staging).
 Films inc: By the Light of the Silvery Moon; Young at Heart; Main Attraction.

SAFER, Morley: TV Newsman. b. Toronto, 1931. e. U of Western Ontario. CBS Saigon Bureau Chief 1965; London Bureau Chief, 1967-70. Co-edtr 60 Minutes since 1970. TV inc: Morley Safer's Red China Diary; Coverage of Nigerian-Biafran War; The Ordeal of Anatoly Kuznetsov; The Second Battle of Britian; Heart Attack; Marixa; Pops (Emmy-1979); Teddy Kolleck's Jerusalem (Emmy-1979); Anne Lindbergh; Walking Small in Pitkin County; The Cowboy, The Craftsman and the Ballerina; Let We Forget; Air Force Surgeon (Emmy-corr-1982); It Didn't Have To Happen (Emmy-corr-1982); Don't Touch That Dial; Eye On the Media--Private Lives, Public Press; Anatomy Of A Libel Case--Business vs. the Media.

SAFRAN, Henri: Dir-Prod. b. Paris, Oct 7, 1932. TV inc: The Trouble Shooters; Softly Softly; Somerset Maugham; The Inheritors; Elephant Boy; Storm Boy; Listen to the Lion; The Wild Duck (wri-dir); Bush Christmas (dir); Relatives (prod).

SAGAN, Carl Edward: Astronomer-TV Pers. b. NYC, Nov 9, 1934. e. U Chicago, BS, MS, PhD, ScD. Created Murmurs of Earth recording for Voyager space probe. TV inc: Cosmos (wri-host).

SAGANSKY, Jeff Exec. b. 1953. Joined CBS 1976 in Broadcast Finance; 1977, to NBC as associate in pgm dvlpt; 1977, mgr. film pgms; 1978, dir dramatic dvlpt; 1978, vp dvlpt David Gerber Co.; 1981 retd to NBC as series dvlpt vp; 1983, senior vp series pgmmg; Jan. 1985, resd to become P of prodn, Tri-Star Pictures.

SAGAR, Ramanand: Dir. b. India, Dec 29, 1917. e. U of Lahore. Films inc: Mehman (The Guest); The Message; Aarzoo; The Eyes; The Song; Lalkar; Hamrahi; Charas.

SAGE, Liz: Wri. b. South Bend, IN, Nov 23, 1953. e. LA City Coll. TV inc: The Carol Burnett Show (Emmy-1978); Welcome Back Kotter (exec story conslt); Dorothy (exec story cnslt); The Rodney Dangerfield Special--I Can't Take It No More; Punky Brewster (prod); Rodney Dangerfield Exposed.

SAGER, Carole Bayer: Lyr. b. Mar 8, 1946. Films inc: The Spy Who Loved Me; Nobody Does It Better; Paradise Alley; Ice Castles; Starting Over.
    TV inc: Aloha Paradise.
    Bway inc: They're Playing Our Song.
    Songs inc: Through the Eyes of Love; I'd Rather Leave While I'm In Love; Come In From The Rain; Break It To Me Gently; I Don't Wanna Go; Best That You Can Do (Arthur's Theme) (Oscar-1981).

SAHL, Mort: Act. b. Montreal, 1927. TV, niteries. Films inc: In Love and War; All the Young Men; Don't Make Waves; Doctor You've Got to be Kidding; Nothing Lasts Forever.
    TV inc: Inside The Third Reich.

SAINT, Eva Marie: Act. b. Newark, NJ, Jul 4, 1924. Screen debut, On the Waterfront (Oscar-1954), Films inc: That Certain Feeling; Raintree County; A Hatful of Rain; North by Northwest; Exodus; All Fall Down; Grand Prix; The Stalking Moon; Loving; Cancel My Reservation.
    TV inc: One Man's Family; Philco Playhouse; Kraft Theatre; Omnibus; Producers Showcase; How the West Was Won; A Christmas to Remember; When Hell Was in Session; The Curse of King Tut's Tomb; The Best Little Girl In The World; Splendor In the Grass; Malibu; Jane Doe; Love Leads The Way; Fatal Vision.
    Bway inc: Trip to Bountiful; First Monday In October.

SAINTE-MARIE, Buffy: Singer-Sngwri. b. Canada (or Sebago Lake, ME), Feb 20, 1941. W of Jack Nitzsche. Folk singer; toured US, Canada concert halls; recordings inc the controversial The Universal Soldier, 1963. Films inc: An Officer and a Gentleman (Oscar-song-1982)
    TV inc: Perry Como's Christmas In New Mexico.

ST. JACQUES, Raymond (James Johnson): Act-Dir. b. 1930. Films inc: (Act) Black Like Me; Mister Moses; Mister Buddwing; The Comedians; The Green Berets; If He Hollers Let Him Go; Uptight; Change of Mind; Cotton Comes to Harlem; The Book of Numbers (& prod-dir); Lost in the Stars; Cuba Crossing; The Evil That Men Do.
    Thea inc: The Blacks; Night Life; The Cool World; Seventh Heaven.
    TV inc: The 416th; Insight/Cargoes; The Sophisticated Gents; Murder. She Wrote.

SAINT JAMES, Susan (nee Miller): Act. b. LA, Aug 14, 1946. e. CT Coll for Women. Films inc: What's So Bad About Feeling Good?; Jigsaw; P J; Where Angels Go...Trouble Follows; Outlaw Blues; Love At First Bite; How to Beat the High Cost of Living; Carbon Copy; Don't Cry It's Only Thunder.

TV inc: The Name of the Game (Emmy-supp-1969); McMillan & Wife; Magic Carpet; The Girls in the Office; Sex and the Single Parent; S.O.S. Titanic; How to Beat the High Cost of Living; The Kid From Nowhere; I Take These Men; After George; Kate & Allie.

ST. JOHN, Jill (nee Oppenheim): Act. b. Los Angeles, Aug 10, 1940. On radio series One Man's Family. Tv debut 1948, A Christmas Carol. Film debut 1957 Summer Love. Films inc: The Remarkable Mr. Pennypacker; Holiday for Lovers; The Roman Spring of Mrs. Stone; Tender Is the Night; Come Blow Your Horn; Who's Been Sleeping In My Bed?; Honeymoon Hotel; The Oscar; Banning; Tony Rome; Diamonds Are Forever; The Concrete Jungle; The Act.
    TV inc: Fame is the Name of the Game; Dupont Theatre; How I Spent My Summer Vacation; Fireside Theatre; Brenda Starr; Bob Hope's Spring Fling of Glamour and Comedy; Rooster; Bob Hopes's Road to Hollywood.

ST. JOHNS, Adela Rogers: Wri. b. Los Angeles, May 20, 1894. Newspaperwoman, first female sportswriter. Author of books, articles on Hollywood. Films inc: A Free Soul; Single Standard. TV inc: Hollywood's Most Sensational Mysteries.

ST. JOHNS, Richard Rogers: Prod-Exec. b. Los Angeles, Jan 30, 1929. e. Stanford U, BA; Stanford Law School, JD. S of Adela Rogers St. Johns and Richard Hyland. On graduation joined O'Melveny & Myers, specializing in entertainment law; 1963 became partner; 1968 sr. vp Filmways, Inc.; 1969 P, CEO Filmways; 1972 formed ind packaging firm; 1975 formed Guinness Film Group; April 1982 partnered with Eric Bercovici in Bercovici-St. Johns Prodns.
    Films inc: (prod or exec prod) Circle of Iron; Nightwing; The Wanderers; The Mountain Men; Matilda; The Final Countdown; A Change of Seasons; American Pop; Dead and Buried; Venom; Fire And Ice.
    TV inc: McClain's Law (supv prod); Cowboy.

SAINT-SUBBER, Arnold: Prod. b. Washington, DC, Feb 18, 1918. Started as assistant stage mgr for John Murray Anderson shows inc Billy Rose's Aquacade (NY Worlds Fair 1939); Ringling Brothers Circus; Ziegfeld Follies. Bway prodns inc: Kiss Me Kate (Tony-1949); Out of This World; The Grass Harp; My Three Angels; House of Flowers; The Square Root of Wonderful; The Dark at the Top of the Stairs; A Loss of Roses; The Tenth Man; Look, We've Come Through; Harold; Barefoot in the Park; The Odd Couple; The Star Spangled Girl; Dr. Cook's Garden; The Little Foxes; There's A Girl In My Soup; Plaza Suite; Carry Me Back to Morningside Heights; Weekend; House of Flowers; Last of the Red Hot Lovers; The Gingerbread Lady; The Prisoner of Second Avenue; Gigi; K-2.

SAITO, Bill: Act. b. Oklahoma City, Dec 22, 1936. e. UCLA, BS. Films inc: Sand Pebbles; Too Late the Hero; The Wrecking Crew; Yakuza; Sidewinder One; Rollercoaster.
    TV inc: The Wackiest Ship in the Army; That Girl; Get Smart; Hawaii Five-O; Six Million Dollar Man; The Hardy Boys.

SAKS, Gene: Dir-Act. b. NYC, Nov 8, 1921. e. Cornell U. H of Bea Arthur. Films inc: (Dir) Barefoot in the Park; The Odd Couple; Last of the Red Hot Lovers; Mame; Cactus Flower; (act) A Thousand Clowns; Prisoner of Second Avenue; The One and Only; Lovesick; The Goodbye People.
    Bway inc: (dir) Enter Laughing; Nobody Loves an Albatross; Generation; Half a Sixpence; Mame (act); A Mother's Kisses; Sheep On The Runway; How The Other Half Loves; Same Time Next Year; I Love My Wife (Tony-dir-1977); The Supporting Cast; Special Occasions; Brighton Beach Memoirs (Tony-dir-1983); Biloxi Blues (Tony-1985); The Odd Couple. (Act): Middle Of The Night; Howie; The Tenth Man; Love and Libel; A Shot In the Dark; A Thousand Clowns; The Goodbye People; The Prisoner Of Second Avenue.
    TV inc: Love, Sex...& Marriage?

SALANT, Richard S.: Exec. b. NYC, Apr 14, 1914. e. Harvard, LLB. Originally an attorney, joined CBS in 1952 as vp, general exec. Named head of CBS News 1961, first non-journalist ever named to such a network post. P CBS News 1961-1964; special asst to CBS prexy 1964-1966; resumed P CBS News 1966, remained there until forced out by network's mandatory retirement policy at 65. Two weeks later became V ChmnB NBC with overall responsibility for NBC News; Aug 1981 became "general advisor" to NBC management on long range planning.

SALE, Richard: Wri-Prod-Dir. b. NYC, Dec 17, 1911. Pres Voyager Films Inc; VP Libra Productions, Inc Films inc: Find the Witness; Shadows Over Shanghai; Strange Cargo; Rendezvous with Annie; Mother Is a Freshman; Mr. Belvedere Goes to College; Father Was a Fullback; Driftwood; I'll Get By; A Ticket to Tomahawk; When Willie Comes Marching Home; Meet Me After the Show; My Wife's Best Friend; Let's Make It Legal; The Girl Next Door; A Woman's World; French Line; Let's Do It Again; Lady at Midnight; Suddenly; Fire Over Africa; Half-Angel; Gentlemen Marry Brunettes; Abandon Ship; The Oscar; The White Buffalo.

TV inc: Yancy Derringer Series (wri-prod-dir); High Chapparal; Wackiest Ship in the Army; Bewitched; Please Don't Eat the Daisies; Everywhere a Chick-Chick; Legend of Custer; The FBI.

SALES, Soupy (Milton Hines): Act. b. Franklinton, NC, Jan 8, 1926. TV inc: Soupy Sales Show; What's My Line; To Tell the Truth.

Films inc: The Two Little Bears; Birds Do It.

SALINGER, Pierre: TV news. b. San Francisco, CA, Jun 14, 1925. e. U San Francisco, BS. Reporter, later night city edtr San Francisco Chronicle; 1955 West Coast edtr Colliers; 1956 Contributing edtr; 1959 press sec to Sen John F Kennedy, became Kennedy's presidential press sec; press sec Pres Lyndon B Johnson until March 1964; 1965 vp National General Corp; 1968 P Fox Overseas Theatres Corp; 1976 roving corr ABC Olympics coverage; 1977 contributing corr for ABC News, based in Paris.

TV inc: On Borrowed Time (host & wri); Alias A. John Blake; On Top All Over The World.

SALKIND, Alexander: Prod. Films inc: Three Musketeers; Light at The Edge of the World; The Prince and the Pauper; Superman (Oscar-special achievement-1978); Superman III.

SALKIND, Ilya: Exec-Prod. b. Mexico City, 1948. S of Alexander Salkind. Films inc: Crossed Swords; Superman; Superman II; Superman III; Supergirl.

SALKOWITZ, Sy: Exec. b. Philadelphia, Apr 21, 1926. e. Yale U, BA. TV inc: Sr wri Ironside series; same position for Police Story. Joined Fox TV, July 1974, as vp dev; then vp primetime pgm; p FOX TV, July 1976-March 1979; April 1982, P Viacom Prodns; resd May 1984.

SALLAN, Bruce Jay Exec. b. Los Angeles, Nov. 8, 1953. e. UC Santa Cruz, BA; UCLA, MBA. Joined Jozak Co., 1975 as dir dvlpt; 1977, vp crea aff Cypress Point Prodns; 1981, Paramount TV; 1984, vp motion pictures for tv ABC. TV inc: Having Babies I, II and III (asso prod); Ski Lift To Death (prod); With This Ring (prod); Act Of Love (prod); Steeltown (exec prod); Berlin Tunnel 21 (exec prod).

SALMI, Albert: Act. b. 1928. Films inc: The Brothers Karamazov; The Unforgiven; Wild River; The Ambushers; The Deserter; Lawman; The Take; Black Oak Conspiracy; Empire of the Ants; Moonshine County Express; Viva Knievel!; Love and Bullets; Cuba Crossing; Cloud Dancer; Brubaker; Caddyshack; Steel; Dragonslayer; St. Helens; Love Child; Hard to Hold; Superstition.

TV inc: Greatest Heroes of the Bible; Undercover with the KKK; The Great Cash Giveaway Getaway; Portrait of a Rebel--Margaret Sanger; Thou Shalt Not Kill; Ace Crawford, Private Eye; Best Kept Secrets; Fatal Vision.

SALT, Jennifer: Act. b. Los Angeles, Sep 14. e. Sarah Lawrence Coll. D of Waldo Salt. Films inc: Midnight Cowboy; Sisters; Hi, Mom!; The Revolutionary; Brewster McCloud; Play it Again, Sam; It's My Turn.

TV inc: Family; The Great Niagara; Gargoyles; Soap; Terror Among Us; Old Friends.

Bway inc: Father's Day; Water Color.

SALT, Waldo: Wri. b. Chicago, Oct 18, 1914. e. Stamford U, AB. Films inc: The Shopworn Angel; The Wildman of Borneo; Tonight We Raid Calais; Mr Winkle Goes to War; Rachel and the Stranger; The Flame and the Arrow; M (addl dialog); career interrupted when he refused to testify before the House Committee on Un-American Activities; Taras Bulba; Flight from Ashiya; Wild and Wonderful; Mid-

night Cowboy (Oscar-1969); The Gang That Couldn't Shoot Straight; Serpico; The Day of the Locust; Coming Home (Oscar-1978).

SALTER, Hans J.: Comp-Mus dir. b. Vienna, Jan 14, 1896. e. U of Vienna. Films inc: Beau Geste; Bedtime Story; Autumn Leaves; Don't Trust Your Husband; The Oklahoman; Hold Back the Night; The Spoilers; Ghost of Frankenstein; It Started with Eve; The Amazing Mrs. Halliday; Christmas Holiday; Can't Help Singing; The Merry Monahans; This Love of Ours; Love from a Stranger; Phantom Lady.

TV inc: Maya; Wagon Train; Laramie; The Law and Mr. Jones; Dick Powell; Lost in Space.

SALTMAN, Sheldon A.: Prod. b. Newton, MA, Aug 17, 1930. e. U of MA, BA; Boston U, SPRC; Boston Coll, LLD. Pub-promo dir for all Star Baseball; World Series; promo dir WBZ-TV; promo dir WJW-TV; vp pub-ad-promo MCA-TV; formed Barnaby Records; vp-gm 20th Fox Telecommunications; vp-gm 20th Fox Sports; resd Dec 1980 to form own firm.

TV inc: Challenge of the Sexes (co-crea); Celebrity Superstars; Pro Fan; Fights of the 70's.

SALTZMAN, Harry: Prod. b. St John, NB, Oct, 1915. Films inc: The Iron Petticoat; Look Back in Anger; The Entertainer; Saturday Night, Sunday Morning; Call Me Bwana; Dr No; From Russia with Love; Goldfinger; The Ipcress File; Thunderball; Funeral in Berlin; You Only Live Twice; The Billion Dollar Brain; Play Dirty; Battle of Britain; On Her Majesty's Secret Service; The Man with the Golden Gun; Nijinsky.

TV inc: Robert Montgomery Show; Capt Gallant of the Foreign Legion.

Bway inc: A Little Family Business.

SALTZMAN, Philip: Exec-Prod-Wri. b. Mexico, Sep 19, 1928. e. UCLA, BA, MA. TV inc: (wri) Rifleman; Fugitive; Dr. Kildare; Perry Mason. (Asso prod) Twelve O'Clock High. (Prod) Felony Squad; The FBI; Barnaby Jones; Alvin Karpis; Brinks; The Great Robbery; Attack on Terror; Crossfire (& prod). (Exec prod) Barnaby Jones; Escapade; Paradise Connection; A Man Called Sloan; The Aliens Are Coming; Freebie and the Bean; Death Ray 2000; Unit 4; Bare Essence.

Films inc: (wri) The Swiss Conspiracy.

SALVATORI, Renato: Act. b. Forte dei Marmi, Italy, Mar 20, 1934. Films inc: The Girls on the Spanish Steps; Big Deal on Madonna Street; Rocco and His Brothers; Two Women; Smog; The Organizer; One Out of Three; The Harem; Queimada, Z; State of Siege; The Burglars; Suspicion; The Lighthouse at the End of the World; Todo Modo; Flic Story; The Gypsy; Armageddon; Ernesto; Luna; Oggetti Smariti (Lost and Found); Asso (Ace).

SAMOILOVA, Tatyana: Act. b. Russia, May 4, 1934. e. Shchukin Drama School. Films inc: The Mexican; The Cranes Are Flying; An Unposted Letter; Leon Garros is Looking for His Friend; They Headed For the East; Anna Karenina; Long Journey Into a Short Day; The Ocean; No Return.

SAMPSON, Will: Act. b. Okmulgee, OK, 1935. Screen debut, 1975, One Flew Over the Cuckoo's Nest. Films inc: Buffalo Bill and The Indians or Sitting Bull's History Lesson; The Outlaw Josey Wales; The White Buffalo; Fishhawk; Insignificance.

TV inc: Alcatraz--The Whole Shocking Story; Born To The Wind (Night Eyes); The Mystic Warrior.

SAMUELSON, David Wylie: Exec. b. London, Eng, Jul 6, 1924. S of Pioneer prod G B Samuelson. Cin for British Movietone News 1941-1960 inc svs as RAF photographer; freelance cin; joined family firm, Samuelson Service Ltd.

(Oscar-Engineering-1980).

SAMUELSON, Sydney, CBE: Exec. b. London, Dec 7, 1925. Entered film ind age 14 as projection asst; became cin & dir of documentaries after World War II; founded Samuelson Film Service 1955; currently Chmn & CEO.

SAND, Paul (nee Sanchez): Act. b. Los Angeles, Mar 5, 1944. Films inc: Viva Max!; The Hot Rock; The Second Coming of Suzanne; The Main Event; Wholly Moses!; Can't Stop The Music.

TV inc: Brothers Grimm; Friends and Lovers; The Legend of Sleepy Hollow; St. Elsewhere.

Bway inc: Star Spangled Girl; Second City; Festival of Two Worlds; Story Theatre (Tony-supp-1971).

SANDA, Dominique (nee Varaigne): Act. b. Paris, 1948. Films inc: A Gentle Woman; The Conformist; The Garden of the Finzi-Continis; Without Apparent Motive; The Impossible Object; Steppenwolf; The Inheritance; Bertolucci's 1900; Damnation Alley; Le Voyage en Douce; Caboblanco; Les Ailes de la Colombe (Wings of the Dove); L'indiscretion (The Indiscretion); Une Chambre En Ville (A Room in Town); Hong von phu (Dust of Empire); De Weg Naar Bresson (The Way to Bresson) (doc).

SANDBERG, Anders: Prod-Dist Exec. b. Denmark, May 7, 1945. Happy Film, Copenhagen.

SANDBERG, Henrik W.: Prod-Dist Exec. b. Denmark, May 15, 1919. Merry Film Prodns, Copenhagen.

SANDERS, Denis: Prod-Dir-Wri. b. NYC, Jan 21, 1929. e. UCLA, MA. Films inc: A Time Out of War (Oscar-ss-1954); The Naked and the Dead; Crime and Punishment; Shock Treatment; War Hunt; One Man's Way; Elvis, That's the Way it Was; Czechoslovakia, 1968 (Oscar-doc-1969); Soul to Soul; Invasion of the Bee Girls.

TV inc: The Day Lincoln was Shot; Alcoa Premiere; Route 66; Defenders; Naked City; Mannix; Trial; City and County of Denver vs Laureen Watson; American West of John Ford; In Search of...; Computers Are People Too.

Docs & edu films inc: West Point; Adlai Stevenson; Subject: Narcotics; Me, An Alcoholic?; A Declaration; The Right to Eat; Arbitration: The Truth of the Matter.

SANDERS, Marlene: TV news. b. Cleveland, OH, Jan 10, 1931. e. OH State U. Wri-prod WNEW-TV 1955; pgm dir Westinghouse, NY, 1960; retd to WNEW 1962 as asst dir news & pub aff; 1964 corr ABC-TV; 1971, doc prod; 1976 VP TV Doc ABC News; 1978, corr-prod CBS Doc; corr CBS Reports.

TV inc: The Right To Die; Up-Date--Since Gary Gilmore; Promise Now, Pay Later; Taiwan Dilemma; Going, Going, Gone; Whatever Happened to Civil Defense; How Much for the Handicapped?; What Shall We Do About Mother? (Emmys-wri & corr-1980); What's Good For General Motors...; A Time To Die.

SANDERS, Richard: Act. b. Harrisburg, PA, Aug 28, 1940. e. Carnegie Tech, BFA. Dir at State Theatre, Paraiba, Brazil, while with Peace Corps. Bway inc: Raisin.

TV inc: Ruby and Oswald; Alexander; Good Against Evil; Victory at Entebbe; They've Killed President Lincoln; Surrender at Appomattox; Stop Thief; WKRP in Cincinnati; The Joke's On Mr. Little; Spencer.

SANDERS, Terry Barrett: Prod-Dir-Wri. b. NYC, Dec 20, 1931. e. UCLA. Freelance doc film maker; co-prod-cin A Time Out of War (Oscar-ss-1954); The Naked and the Dead (sp); Portrait of Zubin Mehta (prod-dir).

TV inc: The Day Lincoln Was Shot (wri); Hollywood and the Stars (prod-dir); The Legend of Marilyn Monroe; National Geographic specials; Screenwriters--Word Into Image (Prod-dir); The Kids From Fame (dir).

SANDLER, Barry: Wri. b. Buffalo, NY, 1947. e. UCLA, MFA. Films inc: Kansas City Bomber; The Duchess and the Dirtwater Fox; Gable and Lombard; The Mirror Crack'd; Making Love; Crimes of Passion (& prod).

SANDRICH, Jay: Dir. b. Los Angeles, Feb 24, 1932. e. UCLA. TV inc: He and She; Mary Tyler Moore Show (Emmy-1971, 1973); Soap; Phyllis (pilot); Tony Randall Show (pilot); Bob Newhart Show (pilot); Benson (pilot); Insight/This Side of Eden; Packy; Insight/Checkmate; Fog; Love, Sidney; Insight/Little Miseries; Adams House; It Takes Two; Insight/The Day Everything Went Wrong; (Emmy-1984); Earthlings; Side By Side; The Cosby Show; Off The Rack; Staff Of 'Life'.

Films inc: Seems Like Old Times.

SANDS, Tommy: Act. b. Chicago, Aug 27, 1937. Films inc: Sing Boy Sing; Mardi Gras; Love in a Goldfish Bowl; Babes in Toyland; The

Longest Day; None But the Brave.

SANDY, Gary: Act. b. Dayton, OH, Dec 25, 1945. e. AADA. Films inc: Some of My Best Friends Are; Hail to the Chief; Last of the Cowboys.

TV inc: As The World Turns; Somerset; The Secret Storm; Melvin Purvis--The Kansas City Masscare; The Shell Game; All That Glitters; WKRP in Cincinnati; The Nashville Grab; For Lovers Only; How To Be A Man.

SANFORD, Donald S.: Wri. b. Mar 17, 1920. Films inc: Thousand Plane Raid; Mosquito Squadron; Submarine X One; Midway; The Ravagers.

SANFORD, Isabel: Act. b. NYC, Aug 29, 1917. Films inc: Guess Who's Coming to Dinner; Pendulum; Stand Up and Be Counted; The New Centurions; Love at First Bite. TV inc: The Carol Burnett Show; The Great Man's Whiskers; The Jeffersons (Emmy-1981); The Sensational, Shocking Wonderful Wacky 70's.

Bway inc: The Amen Corner.

SANGSTER, Jimmy: Wri-Prod-Dir. b. England, Dec 2, 1927. Films inc: The Trollenberg Terror; The Curse of Frankenstein; Dracula; The Mummy; Jack the Ripper; Brides of Dracula; Taste of Fear (& prod); Maniac (& prod); Hysteria (& prod); The Nanny (& prod); Deadlier than the Male; The Anniversary (& prod); Horror of Frankenstein (& prod-dir); Lust for a Vampire (& dir); Fear in the Night (& prod-dir); Phobia (wri).

TV inc: Motive for Murder; The Assassins; I Can Destroy the Sun; Murder in Music City; The Billion Dollar Threat (wri); Ebony, Ivory & Jade; The Concrete Cowboys (wri); Once Upon A Spy (wri); No Place To Hide (wri); Ripley's Believe It or Not ! (dir); The Toughest Man In The World (wri).

SANTON, Penny (Pierina della Santina): Act. b. NYC, Sep 2, 1916. Films inc: Interrupted Melody; Full of Life; Dino; West Side Story; Cry Tough; Love With the Proper Stranger; Captain Newman, M.D.; Don't Just Stand There; Funny Girl; Kotch; Rhinestone.

TV inc: Moonlight; When Your Lover Leaves.

SANTOS, Joe: Act. b. NYC, Jun 9. Films inc: Panic in Needle Park; The Gang that Couldn't Shoot Straight; Shamus; Zandy's Bride; Blue Thunder; Fear City.

TV inc: The Blue Knight; The Rockford Files; Man Undercover; Power; Me and Maxx; The Hustler of Muscle Beach; a.k.a. Pablo; Cover Up; The Ratings Game (PC).

SAPERSTEIN, Henry G.: Prod. b. Chicago, IL, Jun 2, 1918. e. U Chicago; IL Inst of Tech. TV inc; All-Star Golf; Championship Bowling; Ding Dong School; Mr. Magoo Cartoons; Gerald McBoing-Boing Cartoons; The T.N.T. Show; Turn On, Tune In, Drop Out; Tschaikovsky Competition in Moscow.

Films inc: Gay Purr-ee; What's Up Tiger Lily; T-A-M-I; Swan Lake; Hell in the Pacific; War of the Gargantuas; Invasion of the Astro Monsters.

SAPHIER, Peter: Exec. b. Aug. 5, 1940. e. Antioch College. S of the late James L. Saphier. Prodn VP Universal Pictures, 1972-1981; P, Martin Bregman Prodns; Dec. 1983, sr vp motion picture activities Taft Entertainment Co. Films inc: Eddie Macon's Run (exec prod); Scarface (co-prod). TV inc: The Four Seasons.

SARAFIAN, Richard: Dir. b. NYC, Apr 28, 1932. Films inc: Andy; Run Wild, Run Free; Fragment of Fear; Vanishing Point; Man in the Wilderness; The Man Who Loved Cat Dancing; Lolly Madonna XXX; Sunburn; The Bear; Songwriter (act).

TV inc: Bronco; Maverick; Hawaiian Eye; Roaring 20's; 77 Sunset Strip; Bonanza; Ben Casey; Twilight Zone; Disaster on the Coastline; The Golden Moment-An Olympic Love Story; The Gangster Chronicles; Splendor In the Grass; Shannon; Wildside.

SARANDON, Chris: Act. b. July 24, 1942. Films inc: Dog Day Afternoon; Lipstick; The Sentinel; Cuba; Atlantic City, USA; The Osterman Weekend; Protocol.

TV inc: You Can't Go Home Again; The Day Christ Died; A Tale of Two Cities; Broken Promise; Bliss.

Bway inc: Censored Scenes From King Kong. Off-Bway inc: The

Voice Of The Turtle.

SARANDON, Susan (nee Tomaling): Act. b. NYC, 1946. Films inc: Joe; The Great Waldo Pepper; The Front Page; The Rocky Horror Show; Dragonfly; The Other Side of Midnight; Pretty Baby; Checkered Flag or Crash; The Great Smoky Road Block; King of the Gypsies; Atlantic City; Something Short of Paradise; Loving Couples; Tempest; The Hunger; The Buddy System; In Our·Hands (doc); Eo E II Duce (Mussolini And I).

    TV inc: Who Am I This Time?; A.D.

    Thea inc: A Couple of White Chicks Sittin' Around Talking; Extremities.

SARDE, Philippe: Comp. b. Paris, 1945. e. Paris Conservatory. Films inc: The Things of Life; Max and the Junk Dealers; Caesar and Rosalie; Vincent, Francois, Paul and Others; Mado; Liza; Bye-Bye Monkey; Barocco; Le Juge et L'Assassin; Le Crabe-Tambour; A Simple Story; Le Mors Aux Dents (The Bit Between The Teeth); Chere Inconnu (I Sent a Letter to My Love); Le Guignolo; Un Mauvais Fils (A Bad Son); Tess; Beau-Pere (Step-Father); Le Choix Des Armes (Choice of Weapons); Kill Birgitt Haas; Ghost Story; Quest for Fire; Coup de Torchon (Pop 1280); A Strange Affair; Mille Milliards de Dollars (A Thousand Billion Dollars); L'Honneur D'un Capitaine (A Captain's Honor); Que Les Gros Salaires Levent Le Doigt!! (Will The High Salaried Workers Please Raise Their Hands); Lovesick. J'ai espouse une Ombre (I Married A Dead Man); Stella; L'Ami de Vincent (A Friend of Vincent); Garcon!; Premiers Desirs (First Desires); Fort Saganne; La Pirate; Joyeuses Paques (Happy Easter); Ca N'Arrive Qu'a Moi (It Only Happens To Me); Signe Charlotte (Signed Charlotte); L∎Ete Prochain (Next Summer); Le Cowboy; Rendezvous; Joshua Then And Now; Hors-la-loi (Outlaws).

SARGENT, Alvin: Wri. Films inc: The Stalking Moon; Gambit; The Sterile Cuckoo; The Effect of Gamma Rays on Man-in-the-Moon Marigolds; Love and Pain and the Whole Damn Thing; Paper Moon; Julia *(Oscar-1977)*; Bobby Deerfield; Straight Time; The Electric Horseman; Ordinary People *(Oscar-1980)*.

SARGENT, Herb: Wri. TV inc: Annie--The Women in the Life of A Man *(Emmy-1970)*; Jack Lemmon Special; Burt Bacharach Specials; Lily (& prod) *(Emmys-prod-wri-1974)*; Alan King Specials; George Siegel Show; Funny Girl to Funny Lady; Saturday Night Live *(Emmys-1976-1977)*; Inaugural Eve Gala Performance; The New Is the News (& prod).

SARGENT, Joseph Daniel (Giuseppe Danielle Sorgente): Dir. b. Jersey City, NJ, Jul 25, 1925. Films inc: The Man; White Lightning; The Taking of Pelham 1-2-3; MacArthur; Golden Girl; Coast to Coast; Nightmares.

    TV inc: Tribes; Maybe I'll Come Home in the Spring; The Marcus-Nelson Murders *(Emmy-1973)*; Sunshine; Hustling; Friendly Persuasion; The Night That Panicked America; Amber Waves; Freedom; The Manions of America; Tomorrow's Child; Choices of the Heart (& prod); Terrible Joe Moran; Space.

SARRAZIN, Michael: Act. b. Quebec, Canada, May 22, 1940. Began career at 17 on CBC-TV. Screen debut, 1967, Gunfight in Abilene. Films inc: The Flim-Flam Man; The Sweet Ride; Journey to Shiloh; A Man Called Gannon; Eye of the Cat; In Search of Gregory; They Shoot Horses, Don't They?; The Pursuit of Happiness; Sometimes a Great Notion; Believe In Me; The Groundstar Conspiracy; The Reincarnation of Peter Proud; The Loves and Times of Scaramouche; The Gumball Rally; Caravans; Double Negative; The Seduction; Fighting Back; Matushka (Viadukt); Joshua Then And Now.

    TV inc: Chrysler Theatre; The Virginian; The Doomsday Flight; Beulah Land.

SARSON, Christopher: Prod-Dir-Wri. TV inc: Elizabeth R *(Emmys-exec prod series & new series-1972)*; Zoom *(Emmys-prod-1973, 1974)*; An Evening With Alan Jay Lerner (supv prod) (cable); Tonight Scandinavia (prod).

SATLOF, Ron: Dir. TV inc: Benny and Barney; From Here to Eternity; Barnaby Jones; Salvage; Dukes of Hazzard; Capra; Quincy; Hawaii 5-0; Class of 65 (& prod); Get Christie Love (& prod); Spiderman (& prod); McCloud; From Here to Eternity--The War Years; Battles--The

Murder that Wouldn't Die; Waikiki; Flamingo Road; Bush Doctor; The Powers of Matthew Star; Hunter.

SAUNDERS, Peter: Prod. b. London, Nov 23, 1911. Thea inc: (London) Fly Away Peter; The Perfect Woman; Breach of Marriage; My Mother Said; The Mousetrap; Witness for the Prosecution; Spider's Web; The Bride and the Bachelor; Subway in the Sky; The Trial of Mary Dugan; A Day in the Life Of...; And Suddenly It's Spring; Alfie; On a Foggy Day; Cockie; Double Edge; The Reluctant Peer; The Jockey Club Stakes; A Murder Is Announced; Cards On the Table.

SAURA, Carlos: Dir. b. Huesca, Spain, Jan 4, 1932. Films inc: Sunday Afternoon; Riffraff; Lament for a Bandit; The Hunt; Peppermint Frappe; Stress is Three, Three; The Honeycomb; The Garden of Delights; Ana and the Wolves; Cousin Angelica; Dear Ravens; Cria Cuervos; Elsa, Vida Mia; Mom's 100 Years Old (& wri); Blindfolded Eyes; Hurry, Hurry; Blood Wedding (& wri); Dulces Horas (Sweet Hours) (& wri); Antonieta (& wri); Carmen (& wri-chor); Los Zancos (The Stilts) (& wri).

SAUTER, Van Gordon: Exec. b. Middletown, OH, Sep 14, 1935. e. Ohio U, BA; U of MO Journalism, MA. Worked as reporter, Chicago Daily News, Vietnam correspondent Detroit Free Press before joining CBS 1968 as chief corr, man ed WBBM-AM, Chicago; 1970, exec producer special events CBS Radio; 1972, news director WBBM-TV, Chicago; 1975, chief Paris Bureau CBS; 1976, VP Pgm Practices CBS-TV Net; 1977, VP-GM KNXT, LA; July 1980, P CBS Sports; Nov 1981, deputy P CBS News; named P March 1982; Sept. 1983, exec VP in chg of News and Owned-Stations division.

SAUTET, Claude: Dir. b. Paris, Feb 23, 1924. e. Ecole des Arts Decoratifs. Dir 1st film 1951, a short, Nous n'irons plus au bois. Films inc: The Big Risk; Guns for the Dictator; The Things of Life; Max et les Ferrailleurs; Cesar and Rosalie; Vincent, Francois, Paul et les Autres; Mado; A Simple Story; A Bad Son (& wri); Garcon!

SAVAGE, John: Act. b. Old Bethpage, NY, Aug 25. Films inc: Bad Company; The Killing Kind; Steelyard Blues; No Deposit, No Return; The Deer Hunter; Hair; The Onion Field; Inside Moves; Cattle Annie and Little Britches; The Amateur; Maria's Lovers; Brady's Escape; The Little Sister.

    Bway inc: Fiddler on the Roof; Ari; Dance on a Country Grave; American Buffalo.

    TV inc: All The Kind Strangers; Cade's County; Eric (& wrote theme song); Gibbsville; Omni--The New Frontier (prod); Coming Out of the Ice; Nairobi Affair.

SAVALAS, George: Act. b. NYC, Dec 5. B of Telly Savalas. Films inc: Kelly's Heroes; The Greatest Story Ever Told; The Silent Thread; RPM; Johnny Cool; Genghis Khan; The Outfit; Good Neighbor Sam.

    TV inc: Kojak; Kojak--The Belarus File.

SAVALAS, Telly (Aristotle Savalas): Act. b. Garden City, NY, Jan 21, 1924. e. Columbia U, BS. Joined Information Services, State Dept; made exec dir. Then named sr. dir of news, special events for ABC where created Your Voice of America series. Acting career began with debut in Bring Home a Baby on Armstrong Circle Theatre TV. Films inc: Birdman of Alcatraz; Young Savages; Cape Fear; The Man from the Diner's Club; Battle of the Bulge; The Greatest Story Ever Told; Beau Geste; The Dirty Dozen; Crooks and Coronets; Kelly's Heroes; On Her Majesty's Secret Service; Killer Force; Lisa and the Devil; Capricorn One; Beyond the Poseidon Adventure; Escape to Athena; The Muppet Movie; Fakeout; Cannonball Run II; Beyond Reason (& wri-dir).

    TV inc: Mongo's Back in Town; Visions; The Marcus-Nelson Murders *(Emmy-1974)*; The French-Atlantic Affair; Alcatraz--The Whole Shocking Story; Hellinger's Law; My Palikari; America's Heroes--The Athlete Chronicles; Dom DeLuise and Friends--Part II; The Cartier Affair; Kojak--The Belarus File.

SAWYER, Diane: TV News. b. Glasgow, KY, 1945. e. Wellesley, BA. Joined WLKY-TV, Louisville, 1966 as reporter; 1970, joined Pres Nixon's administration staff as asst to deputy press sec, later administrative asst to press sec, staff asst to Pres; worked with Nixon transition office, later as full-time asst on Nixon memoirs; 1978, joined CBS Washington Bureau; Feb. 1980, corr; Aug. 1980 state dept corr; 1981 co-anchor Morning With Charles Kuralt; co-anchor CBS Morning News; Aug. 1984, 60 Minutes.

SAXON, John (Carmine Orrico): Act. b. NYC, Aug 5, 1936. Films inc: Running Wild; Rock Pretty Baby; The Reluctant Debutante; Cry Tough; The Big Fisherman; Portrait in Black; The Unforgiven; War Hunt; Mr. Hobbs Takes a Vacation; The Cardinal; The Appaloosa; Winchester 73; For Singles Only; Death of a Gunfighter; Black Christmas; Mitchell; The Swiss Conspiracy; The Bees; The Electric Horseman; Fast Company; Beyond Evil; Battle Beyond The Stars; The Glove; Blood Beach; Wrong Is Right; Cannibals in the Streets; Desire; The Big Score; Prisoners of the Lost Universe; A Nightmare On Elm Street.

TV inc: The Bold Ones; Raid on Entebbe; Moonshine County Express; Shalimar; Killer Bees; The Glove; Greatest Heroes of the Bible; The Immigrants; Golden Gate; Rooster; Savage - In the Orient; Hardcastle and McCormick; Solomon Northrup's Odyssey; Brothers-in-Law.

SAYER, Leo: Singer-Sngwri. b. Brighton, England, May 21, 1948. Vocalist; recording artist. (Grammy-R&B Song-1977).

TV inc: Lynda Carter's Special. Films inc: The Missing Link (songs).

SAYLES, John: Wri-Dir. b. Schenectady, NY., Sep. 28, 1950. e. Williams College. Films inc: Piranha (wri); Battle Beyond the Stars (wri); Lady in Red (wri); Return of the Secaucus Seven; Alligator (wri); The Howling (wri); The Challenge (wri); Lianna; Baby, It's You; The Brother From Another Planet (& edtr-act); Hard Choices (act).

TV inc: A Perfect Match; Enormous Changes at the Last Minute.

Plays inc: Turnbuckle.

SCAGGS, Boz (nee William Royce Scaggs): Mus-Sngwri. b. OH, Jun 8, 1944. With Steve Miller band; formed own R&B group, The Wigs; rejoined Miller, then solo.

Recordings inc: Boz Scaggs; Moments; Boz Scaggs and Band; My Time; Slow Down; Silk Degrees; Down Two, Then Left.

(Grammy-R&B song-1976).

SCAIFE, Ted: Cin. b. England, 1912. Films inc: Bonnie Prince Charlie; An Inspector Calls; Sea Wife; Night of the Demon; Khaartoum; The Dirty Dozen; Play Dirty; Sinful Davey; Forbush and the Penguins; Hannie Caulder; Catlow.

SCALI, John: TV news. b. Canton, OH, Apr 27, 1918. e. Boston U, BSJ. Reporter Boston Herald; Boston Bureau United Press; Washington Bureau Associated Press; war corr, AP; postwar traveling corr until 1961 when joined ABC as State Dept & diplomatic corr; in 1963 backstage role as negotiator credited with helping avert possible war during Cuban missile crisis; 1971 apptd special consultant foreign aff and communications by Pres. Nixon; 1973 became permanent US rep to UN; 1975 retd to ABC as senior corr.

SCARDINO, Don: Act. b. Canada. Bway inc: Godspell; Angel; The Unknown Soldier and His Wife: King of Hearts; Johnny No Trump; The Sorrows of Stephen; As You Like It; I'm Getting My Act Together; Boy Meets Girl; Hang On To The Good Times (Off-Bway).

Films inc: The People Next Door; Homer; Squirm; Cruising; He Knows You're Alone.

TV inc: Guiding Light.

SCARPELLI, Glenn: Act. b. Staten Island, NY, Jul 6, 1968. Bway inc: Golda; Richard III; Peter Pan; Pippin.

TV inc: Fisherman's Wharf (pilot); Jumpstreet (pilot); Rivkin-Bounty Hunter; One Day At A Time; Jennifer Slept Here.

SCARWID, Diana: Act. b. Savannah, GA. e. AADA; Pace U. TV inc: Gibbsville; Forever; Battered; Kingston Confidential; Desperate Lives; Thou Shalt Not Kill; A Bunny's Tale.

Films inc: Pretty Baby; Honeysuckle Rose; Inside Moves; Mommie Dearest; Strange Invaders; Rumble Fish; Silkwood.

SCHAEFER, George: Dir-Prod. b. Wallingford, CT, Dec 16, 1920. e. Lafayette Coll; Yale Drama School. Films inc: Once Upon a Scoundrel; Generation; Doctors' Wives; Pendulum; Right of Way.

TV inc: Hamlet; One Touch of Venus; Alice in Wonderland; The

Devil's Disciple; The Corn Is Green; The Good Fairy; Born Yesterday; Man and Superman; The Little Foxes; Green Pastures; On Borrowed Time; Little Moon of Alban (Emmy-dir-1959); Dial M for Murder; Victoria Regina; Macbeth (Emmy-dir-1961); Harvey; Gift of the Magi; Johnny Belinda; The Magnificent Yankee (Emmy-prod-1965); Kiss Me Kate; Green Pastures; Elizabeth the Queen (Emmy-prod-1968); The Cradle Song; A Doll's House; Pygmalion; F Scott Fitzgerald; Sandburg's Lincoln; Truman at Potsdam; The Last of Mrs Lincoln; Amelia; Our Town; A War of Children (Emmy-prod-1973); First You Cry; Sad Figure Laughing; Who Will Save Our Children; Enemy of the People; Blind Ambition; Mayflower-The Pilgrim's Adventure; Barry Manilow-One Voice; The Bunker; People vs Jean Harris; A Piano For Mrs. Cimino; The Deadly Game (cable); The Best Christmas Pageant Ever; Children In the Crossfire. March 1982 formed Schaefer-Karpf Prodns with Merrill H. Karpf.

Bway inc: Darling, Darling, Darling; The Linden Tree; Man and Superman; She Stoops to Conquer; The Corn is Green; The Heiress; Idiot's Delight; The Male Animal; Tovarich; The Teahouse of the August Moon (Tony-co-prod-1954); To Broadway with Love; Write Me a Murder; Mixed Couples. Other thea inc: Lyndon.

SCHAFER, Natalie: Act. b. Rumson, NJ, Nov 5. Widow of Louis Calhern. On screen from 1944. Films inc: Marriage Is a Private Affair; Keep Your Powder Dry; Dishonored Lady; Secret Beyond the Door; Time of Your Life; Snake Pit; Oh Men, Oh Women; Anastasia; Bernardine; Back Street; Susan Slade; Forty Carats; Day of the Locust.

Bway inc: Lady in the Dark; Doughgirls; A Joy Forever; Susan and God; Romanoff & Juliet; The Highest Tree.

TV inc: Kraft Theatre; Philco Playhouse; Topper; Gilligan's Island; Three's Company; Doctor's Private Lives; The Harlem Globetrotters on Gilligan's Island.

SCHAFFEL, Robert: Prod. b. Washington, DC., Mar. 2, 1944. Partnered with Jon Voight in Voight-Schaffel Prods. Films inc: Gordon's War; Sunnyside; Lookin' To Get Out; Table for Five.

SCHAFFNER, Franklin: Dir. b. Tokyo, Japan, May 30, 1920. e. Franklin Marshall Coll, BA. Films inc: The Stripper; The Double Man; The Best Man; Planet of the Apes; Patton (Oscar-1970); Nicholas and Alexandra; Papillon; Islands in the Stream; The Boys From Brazil; Sphinx (& exec prod); Yes, Giorgio. TV inc: Person to Person; Studio One; Playhouse 90; Kaiser Aluminum Hour (& prod); DuPont Show of the Week (& prod); Twelve Angry Men (Emmy-1954); Caine Mutiny Court Martial (Emmys-dir-wri-1955); The Defenders (Emmy-1962).

SCHALLERT, William: Perf. b. Los Angeles, Jul 6, 1922. e. UCLA; Fulbright Fellowship, England. Films inc: The Man from Planet X; Flat Top; The Red Badge of Courage; Riot in Cell Block 11; Written on the Wind; Friendly Persuasion; Cry Terror; Pillow Talk; In the Heat of the Night; Colossus; Will Penny; The Computer Wore Tennis Shoes; The Strongest Man in the World; Charley Varrick; Hangar 18; Twilight Zone--The Movie; Teachers.

TV inc: Dobie Gillis; Nancy Drew Mysteries; Little Women; Ike; The Stableboy's Christmas; Blind Ambition; Grace Kelly; Through Naked Eyes; Amazons; Gidget's Summer Reunion.

SCHARF, Walter: Comp-Cond-Arr. b. NYC, Aug 1. Accomp to Kate Smith; accomp, arr, Rudy Vallee; mus dir, Phil Harris-Alice Faye radio show. Films inc: Mercy Island; Hit Parade; The Fighting Seabees; Dakota; The Saxon Charm; Brazil; Hans Christian Anderson; Living It Up; Hollywood or Bust; A Pocketful of Miracles; Where Love Has Gone; Pendulum; The Cheyenne Social Club; Willy Wonka and the Chocolate Factory; Funny Girl; Ben; Final Chapter-Walking Tall; Gasp; This Is Elvis; Twilight Time.

TV inc: The Tragedy of the Red Salmon (Emmy-1971); Beneath the Frozen World (Emmy-1974); From Here to Eternity-The War Years; The Long Days of Summer; Midnight Offerings.

SCHATZBERG, Jerry: Dir. Former fashion photog. Films inc: Panic in Needle Park; Puzzle of a Downfall Child; Scarecrow; Dandy, The All American Girl; Sweet Revenge (& prod); The Seduction of Joe Tynan; Honeysuckle Rose; Misunderstood; No Small Affair.

SCHEERER, Robert: Dir. b. Santa Barbara, CA. Originally act-singer-dancer. Bway inc: (Act) Lend An Ear; Top Banana; The Boy Friend; Films inc: (Dir) Adam at Six A.M.; The World's Greatest Athlete;

How to Beat The High Cost of Living.

TV inc: (Dir) Dick Van Dyke Show (Emmy-1964); Mary Tyler Moore Show; Barbra Streisand Special; Frank Sinatra Special; Perry Como Special; AFI Tribute to John Ford; AFI Tribute to Bette Davis; Andy Williams Show; Supershow; Superbowl Special; Number 96; The Future--What's Next?; You Asked For It; How To Eat Like A Child (Project Peacock) (& chor); Fame; Live From Lincoln Center--An Evening with Danny Kaye and the N.Y. Philharmonic.

SCHEIDER, Roy: Act. b. Orange, NJ, Nov 10, 1932. e. Franklin Marshall Coll. Films inc: Loving; Paper Lion; Klute; The French Connection; The Outside Man; The Seven Ups; Jaws; Sorcerer; Jaws II; Last Embrace; All That Jazz; Still of the Night; Blue Thunder; In Our Hands (doc); 2010; Mishima.

TV inc: Hallmark Hall of Fame; Studio One; Jacobo Timerman--Prisoner Without a Name, Cell Without a Number; Tiger Town (cable).

Bway inc: Betrayal.

SCHELL, Maria: Act. b. Vienna, 1926. Sis of Maximilian Schell. Films inc: The Angel with the Trumpet; The Magic Box; So Little Time; The Heart of the Matter; The Last Bridge; White Nights; Gervaise; The Brothers Karamazov; Cimarron; The Mark; Women; The Odessa File; Folies Bourgeoises (The Twist); Superman; Just a Gigolo; Die Erste Polka; La Passante du Sans Souci (The Passer-by of the Sans Souci Cafe); 1919.

TV inc: Christmas Lilies of the Field; The Martian Chronicles; Inside The Third Reich; Samson and Delilah.

Bway inc: Poor Murderer.

SCHELL, Maximilian: Act-Prod-Dir. b. Vienna, Dec 8, 1930. Stage debut at age 11, Zurich. Films inc: (act) The Young Lions; Judgment at Nuremberg (Oscar-1961); Reluctant Saint; The Condemned of Altona; Return from the Ashes; The Deadly Affair; Counterpoint; Five Finger Exercise; Topkapi; Krakatoa; Simon Bolivar; The Castle (& prod); First Love (& dir); The Odessa File; The Pedestrian; Man in the Glass Booth; The Assassination at Sarajevo; End of the Game (prod-dir); Cross of Iron; A Bridge Too Far; Julia; Avalanche Express; Players; The Black Hole; Tales From the Vienna Woods; Amo non Amo; The Chosen; Marlene (doc) (dir-wri); Morgen in Alabama (A German Lawyer).

TV inc: Judgment at Nuremberg; The Fifth Column; Turn the Key Deftly; The Diary of Anne Frank.

Bway inc: A Patriot for Me; Tales from the Vienna Woods (dir).

SCHELL, Ronnie: Comedian-Act. b. Richmond, CA, Dec 23. e. San Francisco State Coll. Started as nitery comic. TV inc: Gomer Pyle, USMC; Good Morning, World; The Jim Nabors Hour; The Impostor; Honeymoon Suite; The Shape of Things; Hellzapoppin Special; 2d annual CBS Super Comedy Bowl; Friends and Nabors Special; California Fever; The Jokebook (voice); Gary Owens' All Nonsense News Network Special; Henry Hamilton, Graduate Ghost.

Films inc: The Cat From Outer Space; The Shaggy D.A.; Gus; The Strongest Man in the World; Love at First Bite; How to Beat the High Cost of Living.

SCHENKEL, Chris: Sportscaster. b. Bippus, IN, 1924. e. Purdue U. Covers a variety of sporting events for ABC's Wide World of Sports. Reporter on Professional Bowlers Tour since 1962. Films inc: Dreamer.

SCHEPISI, Fred: Prod-Dir-Wri. b. Melbourne, Australia, Dec 26, 1939. Films inc: The Devil's Playground; The Chant of Jimmie Blacksmith; Barbarosa (dir only); Iceman (dir only).

SCHERICK, Edgar J.: Prod. b. NYC. e. Harvard, BA. Conceived and developed Wide World of Sports for ABC-TV through his company, Sports Programs, Inc. In June 1963, named vp in charge of programming for ABC-TV. Left ABC Jan 1, 1967 to form Palomar Pictures Int'l. Films inc: For Love of Ivy; The Birthday Party; Ring of Bright Water; Take the Money and Run; They Shoot Horses, Don't They?; The Killing of Sister George; Sleuth; The Heartbreak Kid; Law and Disorder; The Stepford Wives; The Taking of Pelham One, Two, Three; I Never Promised You a Rose Garden; The American Success Company; Shoot the Moon; I'm Dancing As Fast As I Can; White Dog (exec prod); Reckless; Mrs. Soffel.

TV inc: A Circle of Children (exec prod); Raid on Entebbe (exec prod); Mother and Daughter-The Loving War (exec prod); The Seduction of Miss Leona; Revenge of the Stepford Wives; Thou Shalt Not Kill (exec prod); Born to the Wind (Night Eyes) (exec prod); Little Gloria--Happy At Last (exec prod); He Makes Me Feel Like Dancin' (Emmy-exec prod-1984); Evergreen (exec prod).

SCHICK, Elliot: Prod. b. NYC, Dec 24, 1924. e. Brooklyn Coll, BA. Films inc; Sugar Hill; Return to Macon County; Futureworld; The Island of Dr Moreau; Deerhunter (exec in charge of prodn); The Earthling.

TV inc: Private Benjamin.

SCHICKEL, Richard: Wri-Prod-Dir-Critic. b. Milwaukee, WI, Feb 10, 1933. e. U WI. Film critic Life Magazine 1965-1972; Time, 1973 to present. Author of several books on film industry inc: The Disney Version; Second Sight Notes on Some Movies; His Picture in the Papers; The Men Who Made the Movies; The Platinum Years; The Fairbanks Album.

TV inc: The Movie Crazy Years (wri); Hollywood--You Must Remember This (wri-prod); The Men Who Made the Movies; Life Goes to the Movies (wri-prod); Into the Morning--Willa Cather's America; The Making of Star Wars; Funny Business; The Horror Show; SPFX--The Empire Strikes Back; James Cagney, That Yankee Doodle Dandy; High Hopes--The Capra Years (wri).

SCHIEFFER, Bob: Newscaster. b. Austin, TX. e. TCU, BA. With CBS News since 1969. Member of the Emmy Award-winning team that reported the war in Indochina for CBS, 1972. named anchorman of the Saturday edition of the CBS Evening News, 1976. TV inc: The Air War (Emmy-1972); Watergate-The White House Transcripts (Emmy-1974); Eye On the Media--Private Lives, Public Press.

SCHIFRIN, Lalo: Comp-Cond. b. Buenos Aires, 1932. e. Paris Conservatoire of Music. Films inc: Rhino; Once a Thief; Cincinnati Kid; Cool Hand Luke; Bullitt; The Fox; The Brotherhood; Dirty Harry; Enter the Dragon; Magnum Force; The Four Musketeers; Voyage of the Damned; The Eagle Has Landed; Rollercoaster; Telefon; Nunzio; The Cat From Outer Space; The Manitou; Return From Witch Mountain; Boulevard Nights; The Amityville Horror; The Concorde-Airport '79; Love and Bullets; Serial; When Time Ran Out; The Nude Bomb; Brubaker; The Big Brawl; The Competition; Loophole; Caveman; La Pelle (The Skin); Los Viernes de la Eternida (The Fridays of Eternity); Buddy Buddy; The Seduction; A Stranger is Watching; Fast-Walking; Amityville II--The Possession; The Sting II; Doctor Detroit; Sudden Impact; Tank; Robbers of the Sacred Mountain (Falcons Gold); The Mean Season; The New Kids.

TV inc: T.H.E. Cat; Mission Impossible; Rise and Fall of the Third Reich; Mannix; The Making of the President, 1964; Medical Center; The World of Jacques Cousteau; The Young Lawyers; Starsky & Hutch; Bronk; Most Wanted; The Chicago Story; Victims; Starflight--The Plane That Couldn't Land; Rita Hayworth--The Love Goddess; Princess Daisy; Spraggue; Glitter; Hollywood Wives; Private Sessions; A.D.

(Grammys-Jazz comp-1964, 1965; Inst Theme-1967; Orig TV score-1957).

SCHILLER, Bob: Wri-Prod. b. San Francisco, Nov 8, 1918. e. UCLA, BA. Wrote for radio 1946-49; Ozzie & Harriet; Mel Blanc; Jimmy Durante; Abbott & Costello; Duffy's Tavern. TV inc (writes with Bob Weiskopf): Ed Wynn; Danny Thomas; I Love Lucy; Phyllis Diller; Carol Burnett; Flip Wilson Show (Emmy-1971); Maude (& prod.); All's Fair (& prod., creator); All in the Family (& script cnslt); Side By Side (Emmy-wri-1978); Walter (exec prod-wri).

SCHILLER, Lawrence: Prod. b. NYC, Dec 28, 1936. Originally still photog. TV inc: The Winds of Kitty Hawk; Hey, I'm Alive (& dir); The Trial of Lee Harvey Oswald; A Place For Noah; Marilyn--The Untold Story (& dir); The Patricia Neal Story; Child Bride at Short Creek; The Executioner's Song (& dir); Her Life as a Man (exec prod).

SCHILLER, Tom: Wri. TV inc: Staff Saturday Night Live (Emmys-1976, 1977). Films inc: Nothing Lasts Forever (& dir).

SCHINE, G. David: Prod. b. Gloversville, NY, Sep 11, 1927. e. Harvard U, BA. P & GM Schine Hotels. Films inc: The French Connection (exec prod); That's Action (prod-dir-wri).

SCHISGAL, Murray: Wri. b. NYC, Nov 25, 1926. e. Brooklyn Law School, LLB. Plays inc: The Typists and the Tiger; Ducks and Lovers; Knit One, Purl Two; Jimmy Shine; The Chinese & Doctor Fish; An American Millionaire; All Over Town; Twice Around the Park.

TV inc: The Love Song of Barney Kempinski; Natasha Kovolina Pipshinsky.

Film inc: The Tiger Makes Out; Tootsie.

SCHLATTER, George: Prod-Dir-Wri. b. Dec 31, 1932. e. George Pepperdine Coll. TV inc: Laugh-In (Emmys-(2)-series & program-1968); Shirley MacLaine Specials; Great American Laugh-Off; Just For Laughs; Laugh-In Specials; Goldie Hawn Special; Goldie And Liza Together; Speak Up, America!; Real Kids; The Best of Times; Look At Us (exec prod); Real People (exec prod); Shape of Things (exec prod & wri); Magic Or Miracle (exec Prod-wri); Salute to Lady Liberty (exec prod); S.O.S.--Secrets Of Surviving (exec prod-wri).

SCHLESINGER, John Richard: Dir. b. London, Feb 16, 1926. e. Oxford. Films inc: A Kind of Loving; Billy Liar; Darling Far From the Madding Crowd; Midnight Cowboy (Oscar-1969); Sunday, Bloody Sunday; The Day of the Locust; Marathon Man; Yanks; Honky Tonk Freeway; Privileged (consltg dir).

Thea inc: No Why; Timon of Athens; Days in the Trees; I and Albert; Heartbreak House; Julius Caesar.

TV inc: Separate Tables (cable); An Englishman Abroad.

SCHLOENDORFF, Volker: Dir. b. Wiesbaden, Germany, March 31, 1939. e. IDHEC. Films inc: Young Torless; Der Rebell; Degree of Murder; Baal; The Sudden Fortune of the Poor People of Kombach; The Moral of Ruth; Summer Lightning; The Coup de Grace; The Tin Drum (Oscar-Foreign Film-1979); Rece do Gory (Hands Up!) (act); Die Faelschung (Circle of Deceit) (& wri); Krieg und Frieden (War and Peace); Un amour de Swann (Swann in Love) (& wri).

SCHLOSSER, Herbert S.: Exec. b. Atlantic City, NJ. e. Princeton U; Yale U. Atty, Calif Nat'l Prodns (subsid NBC); VP, GM, 1960; dir talent & program admin, NBC TV, 1961; vp talent & pgm admin, 1962; VP pgms, west coast, 1966-72; exec vp, NBC-TV, 1972; p, NBC-TV, 1973; P & COO, 1974-76; P & CEO, 1977.

SCHMIDT, Harvey: Comp. b. Dallas, TX, Sep 12, 1929. e. U of TX, BFA. Plays inc: Kaleidoscope; Shoestring '57; Four Below; Demi-Dozen; The Fantasticks; 110 in the Shade; I Do! I Do!; Celebration; Colette (incidental mus); Texas Fourth (ballet); Philemon; Portfolio Revue; The Bone Room; Collette Collage.

Films inc: A Texas Romance 1909; Bad Company.

TV inc: New York Scrapbook; The Fantasticks; Philemon; I Do! I Do!

SCHNABEL, Stefan: Act. b. Berlin, Feb 2, 1912. e. Bonn U. Bway 1937, Julius Caesar. Plays inc: Shoemaker's Holiday; Glamour Preferred; Everyman; Land of Fame; The Cherry Orchard; Around the World in 80 Days; Faust; The Love of Four Colonels; Plain and Fancy; Small War on Murray Hill; In the Matter of J Robert Oppenheimer; Older People; Enemies; Rosmersholm; Little Black Sheep; Passion of Dracula; Teibele and Her Dream.

Films inc: Journey Into Fear; The Iron Curtain; Diplomatic Courier; The Great Houdini; The Twenty-Seventh Day; The Ugly American; The Counterfeit Traitor; Two Weeks in Another Town; Rampage; Firefox.

TV inc: The Guiding Light.

SCHNEER, Charles: Prod. b. Norfolk, VA, May 5, 1920. e. Columbia Coll. Films inc: The Seventh Voyage of Sinbad; The Three Worlds of Gulliver; 20 Million Miles to Earth; Good Day For A Hanging; I Aim at the Stars; Mysterious Island; Jason and the Argonauts; The First Men in the Moon; You Must be Joking; Landraiders; Half a Sixpence; The Executioner; Sinbad's Golden Voyage; Sinbad and the Eye of the Tiger; Clash of the Titans.

SCHNEIDER, Alan: Dir. b. Kharkov, Russia, Dec 12, 1917. e. U WI, BA; Cornell U, MA; Johns Hopkins U. Dir plays at Catholic University Theatre, Washington, prior to Bway; dir drama division Juillard.

Bway inc: Storm Operation (act only); A Long Way From Home; The Remarkable Mr. Pennypacker; All Summer Long; Anastasia; To-

night in Samarkand; Miss Lonelyhearts; Endgame; The American Dream; The Ballad of the Sad Cafe; Who's Afraid of Virginia Woolf? (Tony-1963); Happy Days; A Delicate Balance; You Know I Can't Hear You When the Water's Running; The Birthday Party; I Never Sang for My Father; Krapp's Last Tape; The Sign in Sidney Brustein's Window; Zalmen, or the Madness of God; The Lady from Dubuque; Other Places (off-Bway).

Films inc: Samuel Beckett's Film.

TV inc: Pullman Car Hiawatha; Oedipus the King; The Life of Samuel Johnson; Waiting for Godot; The Years Between.

(Died May 3, 1984).

SCHNEIDER, John: Act-Singer. b. Mt Kisco, NY, Apr 8, 1954. Started as fashion model; worked summer stock, off-Bway.

Films inc: Smokey and the Bandit; Eddie Macon's Run.

TV inc: The Million Dollar Dixie Delivery; The Dukes of Hazzard; John Schneider--Back Home. Barbara Mandrell and the Mandrell Sisters; Dream House; A Country Christmas; Kraft Salutes Walt Disney World's 10th Anniversary; Texaco Star Theatre--Opening Night; George Burns & Other Sex Symbols; Christmas In Washington; Happy Endings; Janie Fricke-- You Ought to be in Pictures; The Raccoons and the Lost Star (voice and original song material); John Schneider's Christmas Holiday (& exec prod); Gus Brown & Midnight Brewster.

SCHNEIDER, Maria: Act. b. Paris, Mar. 27, 1952. D of Daniel Gelin. Films inc: The Love Mates; La Vieille Fille; Helle; Last Tango in Paris; Merry-go-Round; The Passenger; Baby Sitter; Caligula; Io Sono Mia (I Belong To Me); Een vrouw als Eva (A Woman Like Eve); Sizona Mira u Parizu (Season of Peace in Paris); Cercasi Gesu (Looking for Jesus); Balles Perdues (Stray Bullets).

SCHOEDSACK, Ernest B.: Dir-cin. b. Council Bluffs, IA., June 8, 1893. Started as cameraman for Mack Sennett; combat cameraman during WW I; partnered with Merian C. Cooper from 1920 through mid 30's. Films inc: Grass (doc); Chang (doc); The Four Feathers (& co-prod); Range (doc)(prod); The Most Dangerous Game; King Kong; Son Of Kong; Blind Adventure; The Last Days Of Pompeii; Trouble In Morocco; Outlaws Of The Orient; Dr. Cyclops; Mighty Joe Young; This Is Cinerama (prolog).

SCHOENDOERFFER, Pierre: Wri-Dir. b. France, May 5, 1928. Originally war correspondent-photographer, captured at Dien Bien Phu; after release continued photo coverage, made first film, La passe du diable. Other films inc: (Doc), Than le pecheur; Attention Helicopters; Sept jours en mer, (Features) Ramuntcho; Pecheurs d'islande; The 317th Platoon; Objectif 500 Millions; The Anderson Section (Oscar-Feature doc-1967); Le Crabe Tambour; L'honneur d'un Capitaine (A Captain's Honor).

SCHOENFELD, Joe: Exec. b. NYC, Jun 2, 1907. Reporter in NY before joining Variety, 1932; resd 1943 to join William Morris Agency on coast as exec; 1950 became edtr Daily Variety; 1959 retd to William Morris; resd 1974 to open consltnt office; 1978 joined Ted Mann Prodns as prodn exec.

SCHOONMAKER, Thelma: Film edtr. b. Algiers, Jan. 3, 1940. e. Cornell, BA. Films inc: Woodstock; Raging Bull (Oscar-1980); King of Comedy.

SCHORR, Daniel L.: TV newsman. b. NYC, Aug 31, 1916. e. CCNY, BSS. With various news services and newspapers before joining CBS in 1953 on special assignment; 1955 reopened CBS Bureau, Moscow; 1958-1960 on roving assignment; 1960-1966 chief German Bureau; 1966-1976, chief of Washington Bureau; 1979 Public Radio and TV; 1980 Cable News Network.

TV inc: The Watergate Affair (Emmy-1973); Watergate--The White House Transcripts (Emmy-1974); The Senate and the Watergate Affair (Emmy-1974).

SCHRADER, Paul: Wri. b. Grand Rapids, MI, Jul 22, 1946. e. Calvin Coll, BA; UCLA, MA. Films inc: The Yakuza; Taxi Driver; Obsession; Rolling Thunder; Blue Collar (& dir); Hardcore (& dir); Old Boyfriends (& exec prod); American Gigolo (& dir); Raging Bull; Cat People; De Weg Naar Bresson (The Way to Bresson) (doc) (int); Mishima (& dir).

SCHRAGER, Sheldon: Prod-Exec. b. Los Angeles, Apr 30, 1938. e. UCLA. Exec prod Orion; 1979 VP & Prodn Mgr Columbia Pictures Productions; Oct 1981, sr VP. Film inc: (Asso Prod) Dog Soldiers; Breakout; Day of the Locust; Harry and Walter Go To New York. (Co-prod) Mr. Billion; Who'll Stop the Rain. (Exec prod) Promises in the Dark.

SCHREGER, Charles: Exec. b. NYC, Oct 12, 1952. e. Brandeis U, BA; Northwestern, MA. Freelance writer in Chicago before joining Variety staff 1976; moved to Daily Variety, Hollywood, 1978; L.A. Times, 1979; joined Columbia Pictures 1981 as executive trainee; July, 1981, VP of film acquisitions; Aug 1981 given charge of new art circuit unit; Feb 1982, P of Triumph Films, Col subsid, while continuing as VP Acquisitions for parent company; Aug. 1984, stepped down as P of Triumph; Dec. 1984, left company; March, 1985, special projects VP Samuel Goldwyn Co & exec asst. to Samuel Goldwyn Jr.

SCHREIBER, Avery: Act. b. Chicago, IL, Apr 9, 1935. With Second City troupe; teamed with Jack Burns in comedy act; then solo. Bway inc: How To Be a Jewish Mother (dir); Ovid's Metamorphoses; Dreyfus in Rehearsal; Can-Can (rev).
TV inc: My Mother The Car; Burns and Schreiber Comedy Hour; Sammy Davis & Friends; Ben Vereen Summer Show; Harlem Globetrotter's Popcorn Machine; Second City Comedy Show (host); Flatbed Annie and Sweetipie--Lady Truckers; All Commercials; More Wild Wild West; Misunderstood Monsters (voice).
Films inc: Swashbuckler; The Last Remake of Beau Geste; Scavenger Hunt; Concorde--Airport '79; Silent Scream; Galaxina; Loose Shoes; Jimmy The Kid.

SCHREIBMAN, Myrl A.: Prod-Dir. b. OH, Apr 17, 1945. e. UCLA, MFA; USC, PhD. TV inc: It Takes a Thief; 7th Annual Sci-Fi Awards; The Girl, The Gold Watch and Everything (prod); 1980/81 Emmy Awards Show (prod).
Films inc: Parts, The Clonus Horror (prod); Angel of H.E.A.T.

SCHRODER, Ricky: Act. b. Staten Island, NY, Apr 13, 1970. Began modeling at four months; did scores of commercials before film debut in The Champ. Films inc: The Last Flight of Noah's Ark; The Earthling.
TV inc: Little Lord Fauntleroy; Doug Henning's World of Magic. Kraft Salutes Walt Disney World's 10th Anniversary; Silver Spoons; Something So Right; Two Kinds of Love; S.O.S.--Secrets Of Surviving; A Reason To Live; Missing--Have You Seen This Person?

SCHROEDER, Barbet: Prod-dir. b. Teheran, Iran, Aug. 26, 1941. e. Lycee Francais; Sorbonne. Originally a photographer, later a critic for Cahiers du Cinema; worked as asst. to Jean-Luc Godard on Les Carabiniers (The Riflemen). Films inc: (prod) La Boulangere de Monceau; La Carriere de Suzanne; Paris Vu Par (Paris As Seen By..); Mediterranee; La Collectioneuse (The Collector); Tu Imagines Robinson; Ma Nuit Chez Maud (My Night At Maud's); Le Genou de Claire (Claire's Knee); L'Amour L'Apres Midi; Out One; La Maman et la Putain (The Mother And The Whore); Celine et Julie Vont en Bateau (Celine and Julie Go Boating); La Paloma; Flacons d'Or; La Marquise d'O; Roulette Chinois (Chinese Roulette); L'Ami Americain (The American Friend); Le Passe-Montage; Les Rites de la Mort; Perceval le Gallois; Le Pont du Nord (North Bridge); Improper Conduct. (Dir) More; Sing-Sing (doc); Le Cochon Aux Patates Douces (doc); Maquillages (doc); Le Repas Rituel (doc); La Valle; General Idi Amin Dada (doc); Maitresse; Koko, Le Gorille qui Parle (Koko, The Talking Gorilla); Tricheurs (Cheaters).
TV inc: Charles Bukowski.

SCHUCK, John: Act. b. Boston, Feb 4. e. Denison, BA. Films inc: M*A*S*H; Brewster McCloud; McCabe and Mrs Miller; Thieves Like Us; Butch and Sundance-The Early Days; Just You and Me Kid; Earthbound; Finders Keepers.
TV inc: McMillan and Wife; Holmes and YoYo; The Halloween That Almost Wasn't; Turnabout; Orphans, Waifs and Wards.
Bway inc: Annie.

SCHUENZEL, Dr Rolf G.: Prod-Dist. b. Dresden, Germany, Dec 24, 1934. e. U of WI, EE, PhD. Founded Profilm, 1967; Viva-Film, 1972; Look Filmverleih, 1978; all in Munich. Film distributor with 5 offices in Germany.

SCHULBERG, Budd Wilson: Wri. b. NYC, Mar 27, 1914. e. Dartmouth Coll. S of the late Ad and B P Schulberg. Publicist, Paramount Pictures, 1931. Screenwriter from 1932. Films inc: A Star Is Born (add dial); Little Orphan Annie; Winter Carnival; Weekend for Three; City Without Men; On the Waterfront (Oscar-Story, sp-1954); A Face In The Crowd; Wind Across The Everglades; Joe Louis--For All Time (& prod).
Bway inc: The Disenchanted; What Makes Sammy Run?
TV inc: The Angry Voice of Watts (Emmy-special-1966); A Question of Honor.

SCHULMAN, Arnold: Wri. b. Philadelphia, Aug 11, 1925. e. U of NC; American Theatre Wing; Actor's Studio. Films inc: Wild in the Wind; A Hole in the Head; Love with the Proper Stranger; The Night They Raided Minsky's; Goodbye, Columbus; Funny Lady; Players (& prod).

SCHULTZ, Michael A.: Dir. b. Milwaukee, WI, Nov 10, 1938. e. U of WI; Marquette U. Thea inc: Song of the Lusitanian Bogey; Kongi's Harvest; God Is A (Guess What?); Does a Tiger Wear a Necktie?; Every Night When the Sun Goes Down; What the Winesellers Buy.
Films inc: To Be Young, Gifted and Black; Sgt Pepper's Lonely Hearts Club Band; Scavenger Hunt; Carbon Copy; The Last Dragon.
TV inc: To Be Young, Gifted and Black; Ceremonies In Dark Old Men; Benny's Place; For Us, The Living; The Jerk, Too; Fade Out--The Erosion of Black Images in the Media (doc-int).

SCHULZ, Charles Monroe: Cartoonist-Wri. b. Minneapolis, MN, Nov 26, 1922. Created comic strip Peanuts in 1950; strip has been the basis for books, plays, films, tv.
Films inc: Bon Voyage, Charlie Brown and Don't Come Back.
TV inc: A Charlie Brown Christmas (Emmy-wri-1966); A Charlie Brown Thanksgiving (Emmy-wri-1974); Happy Birthday, Charlie Brown; You're the Greatest, Charlie Brown; She's a Good Skate, Charlie Brown; The Fantastic Funnies; Life Is A Circus, Charlie Brown; The Big Stuffed Dog; It's Magic, Charlie Brown; Someday You'll Find Her, Charlie Brown; A Charlie Brown Celebration; Is This Goodbye, Charlie Brown?; It's An Adventure, Charlie Brown; What Have We Learned, Charlie Brown?; Snoopy's Getting Married, Charlie Brown.

SCHULZ-KEIL, Wieland: Wri-prod. b. Muschenheim, Germany, May 22, 1945. Founder-dir of NY Center for Visual History. Films inc: The New Deal For Artists (doc); Shamans Of the Blind Country (doc-prod only); Kojak & Co. (doc); Jackpot (doc-prod only); Jetlag (doc-prod only); Our Nazi (doc-prod only). Features inc: Under the Volcano (prod).

SCHUMACHER, Joel: Wri. b. NYC, 1942. Before turning to screenplays, held jobs as art dir, costume designer. Created designs for The Last of Sheila; Blume in Love; Sleeper. Film scripts inc: Car Wash; Sparkle; The Wiz.
TV inc: Virginia Hill; Amateur Night at the Dixie Bar & Grill; Now, We're Cookin' (& exec prod); Codename Foxfire (exec prod).
Films inc: The Incredible Shrinking Woman (dir); D.C. Cab (& dir); St. Elmo's Fire (& dir).

SCHWARTZ, Al (Albert A. Schwartz): Wri-prod. b. Passaic, NJ., Nov. 29, 1910. e. Fordham U; Brooklyn Law School. Originally an atty. TV inc: (Prod) Kate Smith Show; Frank Fontaine Show; Stan Freberg Show. (Wri) Eddie Cantor; Bob Hope; Jimmy Durante; Alan Young; Milton Berle; Red Skelton (Emmy-wri-1961); Jackie Gleason; Frank Sinatra; Max Liebman Specials; Petticoat Junction; Green Acres; The Brady Bunch; created Dotto Game Show.

SCHWARTZ, Al (Allen Schwartz) Prod-dir. b. Chicago, Jan. 3, 1932. e. U of WI. Started at WKOW-TV, Madison, WI.; with CBS-TV 1957-1963, then freelance. TV inc: International Hour-American Jazz; Ghost Of Mr. Kicks; The Unwed Mother; Repertory Workshop; Women In Prison; The World Of Andrew Wyeth; The Opera Makers; What's It All About, World; The Many Moods Of Ravinia; A Child's Garden Of Pollution; Cinderella; The Canterville Ghost; The Real World Of Make Believe; Jacques Cousteau's People Of The Sea; Far Out Space Nuts; Wonderbug; Academy Of Country Music Awards; Dick Clark's Grand Old Days; Welcome Back Kotter; The Sensational 70's; Men Who Rate A '10'; Whatever Became Of..; TV's Censored

Bloopers; Dick Clark's Live Wednesday; Night Of Stars And Future Stars; Inside America; TV's Bloopers and Practical Jokes.

SCHWARTZ, Arthur: Comp. b. NYC, Nov 25, 1900. e. NYC, AB, JD; Columbia U, MA. Bway inc: The Little Show; Princes Charming; the Second Little Show; Three's A Crowd; The Band Wagon; Flying Colors; Revenge With Music; At Home Abroad; Virginia; Stars in Your Eyes; American Jubilee; Park Avenue; Inside U.S.A. (& prod); A Tree Grows in Brooklyn; The Gay Life; Jennie; That's Entertainment; Nicholas Nickleby.

Films inc: Under Your Spell; That Girl from Paris; Navy Blues; Thank Your Lucky Stars; The Time, the Place and the Girl; Excuse My Dust; Dangerous When Wet; The Band Wagon; You're Never Too Young; Cover Girl (prod); Night and Day (prod).

Songs inc: Dancing in the Dark; I See Your Face Before Me; You and the Night and the Music; That's Entertainment; I Guess I'll Have to Change My Plans; Something To Remember You By; I Love Louisa; They're Either Too Young or Too Old.

(Died Sept. 4, 1984)

SCHWARTZ, Sol A.: Exec. b. NYC. Started as asst mgr RKO Theatres 1922, subsequently mgr several houses before becoming western zone mgr 1942; became GM RKO out-of-town theatres 1944; VP, RKO 1947; P & GM, 1951; VP Columbia Pictures 1961; VP 20th-Fox 1968.

(Died March 16, 1985)

SCHWARTZ, Stephen: Comp-Lyr. b. NYC, Mar 6, 1948. e. Carnegie-Mellon U, BFA; Juilliard. Bway inc: Butterflies Are Free (title song); Godspell; Mass; Working; Pippin; The Magic Show; Straws in the Wind; The Baker's Wife.

Films inc: Godspell.

TV inc: Working.

(Grammys-comp & prod-1971).

SCHWARTZMAN, Jack: Exec. b. NYC, Jul 22, 1932. e. UCLA, BS; UCLA Law School, LLB. Film atty, joined Lorimar Prodns 1978 as exec vp; 1980 into indie prodn; Sept. 1984, formed Taliafilm II Ltd. with Robert Meyers and became P. Films inc: Being There (exec prod); Never Say Never Again; I Am the Cheese.

SCHWARY, Ronald L.: Prod. b. OR., May 23, 1944. e. USC. Films inc: California Suite (asso prod); Casey's Shadow (asst dir); The Electric Horseman; Ordinary People (Oscar-1980); Absence of Malice; Time is On Our Side; A Soldier's Story.

SCHWARZENEGGER, Arnold: Act. b. Graz, Austria, Jul 30, 1947. Former Mr Universe. Films inc: Stay Hungry; Pumping Iron (doc); The Villain; Conan the Barbarian; Conan the Destroyer; The Terminator.

TV inc: The Jayne Mansfield Story.

SCHYGULLA, Hanna: Act. b. Kattowitz, Germany, Dec 25, 1943. Worked with Rainer Werner Fassbinder in Munich's Action-Theater; one of the founders of the 'anti-teater' group. Films inc: Love Is Colder Than Death; Katzelmacher; Gods of the Plague; The Bridegroom, The Comedienne and the Pimp; Hunting Scenes From Bavaria; Baal; Rio Das Mortes; Whity; Niklashauser Fahrt; Beware of a Holy Whore; Pioneers in Ingolstadt; Mathias Kneissl; The Merchant of Four Seasons; Jacob Von Gunten; The Bitter Tears of Petra Von Kant; The House By the Sea; Jail Bait; The Wrong Move; Effi Briest; The Third Generation; The Clown; The Marriage of Maria Braun; Berlin Alexanderplatz; Lili Marleen; Die Faelschung (Circle of (Deceit); La Nuit de Varennes (The Night of Varennes); Passion; Antonieta; Heller Wahn (A Labor of Love); Storia di Piera; Eine Liebe in Deutschland (A Love in Germany); Il Futuro E'Donna (The Future Is Woman).

SCOFIELD, Paul: Act. b. Hurstpierpoint, England, Jan 21, 1922. Films inc: That Lady; Carve Her Name with Pride; The Train; A Man for All Seasons (Oscar-1966); King Lear; Bartleby; Scorpio; A Delicate Balance; 1919.

Bway inc: A Man for All Seasons (Tony-1962); King Lear.

London Thea inc: Desire Under the Elms; numerous Shakespearean roles; Pericles (& prod); A Question of Fact; Time Remembered; The Power and the Glory; Expresso Bongo; A Man for All Seasons; The Government Inspector; Staircase; Hotel in Amsterdam; Dimetos; The Madras House; Amadeus; Don Quixote.

TV inc: Male of the Species (Emmy-1969); The Curse of King Tut's Tomb (narr); The Ambassadors; The Potting Shed (cable); Anna Karenina.

SCOLA, Ettore: Dir-wri. b. Italy, 1931. Films inc: Two Nights With Cleopatra (sp only); Lo Scapolo (sp only); Love and Larceny (sp only); Ghosts of Rome (sp only); The Easy Life (sp only); Wayward Love (sp only); Let's Talk About Women; High Infidelity (sp only); Il Gaucho (sp only); Made in Italy (sp only); The Devil in Love; Anyone Can Play (sp only); Il Profeta; Il Commissario Pepe; A Drama of Jealousy; Rocco Papaleo; We All Loved Each Other So Much; A Special Day; Viva Italia; La Terraza (The Terrace); Passione d'amour (Passion of Love); La Nuit de Varennes (The Night of Varennes); Le Bal.

SCORSESE, Martin: Wri-Dir. b. NYC, 1942. While attending NYU produced two award winning film shorts, What's A Girl Like You Doing in A Place Like This?; It's Not Just You, Murray.

Films inc: Woodstock (supv ed); Who's That Knocking At My Door; Mean Streets; Boxcar Bertha; Alice Doesn't Live Here Anymore; Taxi Driver; New York, New York; Raging Bull; Bonjour Monsieur Lewis (doc); Pavlova (act).

SCOTT, Brenda (nee Smith): Act. b. Cincinnati, OH, Mar 15, 1943. Films inc: Johnny Tiger; Journey to Shiloh; This Savage Land; Simon, King of the Witches.

TV inc: Window on Main Street; The Road West; Donovan's Kid.

SCOTT, Debralee: Act. b. Elizabeth, NJ, Apr 2, 1953 Films inc: American Graffiti; The Candidate; Dirty Harry; Superdad; Our Time; Crazy World of Julius Vrooder; Reincarnation of Peter Proud; Just Tell Me That You Love Me.

TV inc: Lisa, Bright and Dark; Summer Without Boys; Senior Year; Earthquake; Sons and Daughters; Welcome Back Kotter; Mary Hartman, Mary Hartman; Forever Fernwood; Angie.

SCOTT, Eric: Act. b. Los Angeles, Oct 20, 1958. TV inc: Norman Rockwell's America; The Clowns; The Waltons; Mother's Day On Walton's Mountain.

SCOTT, George C.: Act. b. Wise, VA, Oct 18, 1927. On screen from 1959. Films inc: The Hanging Tree; Anatomy of A Murder; The Hustler; The Power and the Glory; The List of Adrian Messenger; Dr. Strangelove; The Bible; The Flim Flam Man; Patton (Oscar-1970, refused to accept); They Might Be Giants; Hospital; New Centurions; Oklahoma Crude; The Day of the Dolphin; The Hindenburg; Islands in the Stream; Crossed Swords; Movie Movie; Hard Core; Arthur Miller on Home Grounds; The Changeling; The Formula; Taps; Firestarter; The Indomitable Teddy Roosevelt.

Bway inc: Comes a Day; The Andersonville Trial; The Little Foxes; Plaza Suite; Uncle Vanya; Death of a Salesman (& dir); Sly Fox; Tricks of the Trade; Present Laughter (& dir); Design For Living (dir).

TV inc: The Crucible; Jane Eyre; The Price (Emmy-1971); Fear on Trial; Beauty and the Beast; Dear Liar (host); Bob Hope's All-Star Birthday Party at West Point; Oliver Twist; Happy Birthday Bob; China Rose; World's Greatest Mysteries; A Christmas Carol.

SCOTT, Gordon (nee Werschkul): Act. b. Portland, OR, Aug 3, 1927. e. OR U. Screen debut, Tarzan's Hidden Jungle, 1955. Films inc: Tarzan and the Lost Safari; Tarzan's Greatest Adventure; The Tramplers; Arm of Fire.

SCOTT, J.C. (Judith Cheryl Scott): Exec b. Los Angeles, Feb. 21, 1953. e. UCLA, BA. Dir crea aff Edward S. Feldman Co.; 1983, vp crea aff Marvin Worth Prodns.; 1983, exec asst to P Walt Disney Pictures; 1984, vp film prodn Disney. Films inc: The Sender (asso prod).

TV inc: Not In Front Of The Children (asso prod).

SCOTT, Janette: Act. b. Morecambe, England, Dec 14, 1938. Films inc: Went the Day Well?; No Place for Jennifer; No Highway; The Magic Box; As Long as They're Happy; Now and Forever; The Good Companions; The Devil's Disciple; The Old Dark House; The Beauty Jungle; Crack in the World.

SCOTT, Lizabeth: Act. b. Scranton, PA, 1922. On screen from 1945. Films inc: The Strange Love of Martha Ivers; Dead Reckoning;

I Walk Alone; Desert Fury; Pitfall; Too Late for Tears; Paid in Full; Bad for Each Other; Quantrill's Raiders; Pulp.

SCOTT, Margaretta: Act. b. London, Feb 13, 1912. Films inc: Dirty Work; Things to Come; Quiet Wedding; Sabotage at Sea; Fanny by Gaslight; The Man from Morocco Idol of Paris; Where's Charley?; Town on Trial; The Last Man to Hang; A Woman Possessed; An Honourable Murder; Crescendo; Percy.

Thea inc: Confrontation; Country Wife; Alien Corn; Oedipus Rex; A Woman of No Importance; Equus.

SCOTT, Martha: Act. b. Jamesport, MO, Sep 22, 1916. Began in summer stock, radio. Screen debut, 1940, Our Town. Films inc: The Howards of Virginia; One Foot in Heaven; So Well Remembered; Strange Bargain; The Desperate Hours; The Ten Commandments; Sayonara; Ben-Hur; Airport 1975; First Monday In October.

TV inc: The Bob Newhart Show; Route 66; The Nurses; The Word; Charleston; Married--The First Year; Beulah Land; Father Figure; Secret of Midland Heights; Summer Girl; Adam.

Bway inc: Soldier's Wife; Voice of the Turtle; The Male Animal; The Remarkable Mr. Pennypacker; The Skin of Our Teeth.

SCOTT, Randolph: Act. b. Orange Co, VA, Jan 23, 1903. e. U of NC On screen from 1929. Films inc: Far Call; Island of Lost Souls; To The Shores of Tripoli; Bombardier; The Spoilers; Captain Kidd; My Favorite Wife; Badman's Territory; Virginia City; Belle Starr; Pittsburgh; Albuquerque; Colt '45; Man in the Saddle; The Bounty Hunter; Decision at Sundown; Comanche Station; Ride the High Country.

SCOTT, Ridley: Dir. b. England. Films inc: The Duellists; Alien; Blade Runner.

SCOTTI, Vito: Act. b. San Francisco, Jan 26, 1918. Films inc: Where the Boys Are; The Explosive Generation; Two Weeks in Another Town; Captain Newman, M.D.; Rio Conchos; The Pleasure Seekers; Von Ryan's Express; What Did You Do in the War, Daddy?; The Caper of the Golden Bulls; The Secret War of Harry Frigg; How Sweet It Is; Head; Cactus Flower; The McCullochs; Chu Chu and the Philly Flash.

TV inc: Playhouse 90; Climax; To Rome With Love; The Flying Nun; Barefoot in the Park; The Bionic Woman; Colombo; The Ghosts of Buxley Hall; The Haunting of Harrington House; Blood Feud.

SCOTTO, Renata: Soprano. b. Savona, Italy, Feb 1936. Won nat'l competition for young artists, debuted 1953 Milan's Teatro Nuovo; 1954 La Scala debut; guest artist Buenos Aires; Moscow; Tokyo; Covent Garden; 1966 Metropolitan opera debut; 1976 became first soprano in Met history to sing all three heroines in Puccini's trilogy, Il Trittico.

TV inc: La Boheme; Renata Scotto, Prima Donna; La Gioconda (Emmy-1980).

SCOURBY, Alexander: Act. b. NYC, Nov 13, 1913. e. U of WV. Films inc: Affair in Trinidad; The Big Heat; The Silver Chalice; Giant; Seven Thieves; The Big Fisherman; Confessions of a Counterspy; The Final Solution (doc) (narr).

TV inc: (narr) The World of Maurice Chevalier; The World of Jacqueline Kennedy; The World of Bob Hope; The World of Sophia Loren; The World of Benny Goodman; The Death of the Hired Man; Project 20; The Superliners-Twilight of an Era; The Body Human, The Body Beautiful; The Body Human--The Sexes II; Etosha--Place of Dry Water; The Body Human--The Bionic Breakthrough (narr); The Sharks (narr); Strange True Stories; Australia's Animal Mysteries (narr); The Body Human--The Living Code (narr); Among the Wild Chimpanzees (narr); The Body Human--The Journey Within (narr); Olympic Gala.

Bway inc: Hamlet; The Deputy of Paris; Crime and Punishment; Detective Story; Darkness at Noon; Saint Joan; An Inspector Calls.

(Died Feb. 23, 1985)

SCRUGGS, Earl: Singer-Mus. b. Cleveland County, NC, Jan 6, 1924. With partner Lester Flatt became the undisputed kings of Bluegrass music during the 50s and 60s. With their Foggy Mountain Boys, Flatt & Scruggs were regular cast members of the Grand Ole Opry until they split up in early 1969. Team won (Grammy-1968).

TV inc: Return of the Beverly Hillbillies. (See also FLATT, Lester).

SCULLY, Vin: Sportscaster. b. NYC, Nov 29, 1927. e. Fordham U. Joined CBS sports 1975. Hosts The Challenge of the Sexes. Has been associated with the Dodgers baseball club since 1950. Still handles Dodger broadcasts along with CBS sports assignments; Elected to Baseball Hall of Fame 1982; Dec 1982 signed with NBC to handle baseball and host golf tournaments while remaining with Dodgers. TV inc: Kennedy Center Honors 1984.

SEAL, Elizabeth: Act. b. Genoa, Italy, Aug 28, 1933. e. Royal Academy of Dancing

Thea inc: (London) The Pajama Game; Camino Real; Irma La Douce; Cat Among the Pigeons; The Recruiting Officer; Cabaret; Fajeon Reviewed; Salad Days. Bway inc: Irma La Douce (Tony-1961); The Corn Is Green.

Films inc: Town on Trial; Cone of Silence; Vampire Circus.

TV inc: Trelawney of the Wells; Philby, Burgess and MacLean.

SEALS AND CROFTS: (See CROFTS, Dash and SEALS, James).

SEALS, James: Mus-Singer. b. Sidney, TX. With The Champs, The Dawnbreakers before teaming with Dash Crofts. Albums inc: Seals and Crofts I and II; Year of Sunday; Summer Breeze; Diamond Girl; Unborn Child; I'll Play for You; Greatest Hits; Get Closer; Sudan Village; Takin' It Easy.

SEARS, Sally: Prod. b. NYC, Nov 13, 1937. P, Primavera Productions, Ltd 1962-63, special Asst The Washington Ballet; 1965, Co-Dir Manhattan Festival Ballet. VP, Continental Concert Service; advisory board, Performance Theatre Center & School, Ltd

Thea inc: (prod) Please Don't Cry and Say No (off-Bdwy) Nellie Toole & Co. (off-Bdwy); Summer Brave; The Royal Family; Tickles by Tucholsky; The Night of the Tribades; An Almost Perfect Person; Dancing In The End Zone.

SEDAKA, Neil: Singer-Sngwri. b. Mar 13, 1939. e. Juilliard. Songs inc: Stupid Cupid; Calendar Girl; Oh, Carol; Stairway to Heaven; Happy Birthday, Sweet 16; Laughter in the Rain; Bad Blood; Love Will Keep Us Together; Lonely Night; Breaking Up Is Hard To Do.

Albums inc: Sedaka's Back; Hungry Years; Stepping Out; All You Need Is Music.

SEEGER, Pete: Singer-Comp. b. NYC, May 3, 1919. Developed into an authority on folk music. Founded the Almanac Singers, 1940; later was one of the founders of The Weavers; indicted 1955 after refusing to testify before House Un-American Activities Committee; charges dismissed in 1962. Gave concerts throughout the world on American Folk Music and its origins.

Songs inc: Where Have All the Flowers Gone; If I Had a Hammer; Kisses Sweeter Than Wine.

TV inc: Smothers Brothers Comedy Hour; Rainbow Quest (educational).

Films inc: The Weavers--Wasn't That A Time; Seeing Red; In Our Hands (doc).

SEGAL, Erich: Wri. b. Brooklyn, NY, Jun 16, 1937. e. Harvard. Films inc: Yellow Submarine; The Games; Love Story; RPM; Oliver's Story; A Change Of Seasons; Man, Woman and Child.

TV inc: The Ancient Games (wri-narr); Mourning Becomes Electra (narr); 1972, 1976, 1980 Olympic Games (Commentator).

SEGAL, George: Act. b. Great Neck, NY, Feb 13, 1934. e. Columbia U, BA. On screen from 1961. Films inc: The Young Doctors; The Longest Day; Act One; The New Interns; Invitation to a Gunfighter; Ship of Fools; King Rat; The Lost Command; Who's Afraid of Virginia Woolf?; The Quiller Memorandum; The St. Valentine's Day Massacre; Bye Bye Braverman; No Way to Treat a Lady; The Southern Star; The Bridge at Remagen; The Girl Who Couldn't Say No; Loving; The Owl and the Pussycat; Where's Poppa?; Born to Win; The Hot Rock; A Touch of Class; Blume in Love; The Terminal Man; California Split; The Black Bird; Russian Roulette; The Dutchess and the Dirtwater Fox; Fun with Dick and Jane; Rollercoaster; Who is Killing the Great Chefs of Europe?; Lost and Found; Last Married Couple in America; Carbon Copy; The Cold Room; Stick; Killing 'Em Softly.

TV inc: Death of a Salesman; Of Mice and Men; The Desperate Hours; TV's Censored Bloopers; The Deadly Game (cable); Trackdown--Finding the Goodbar Killer; The Zany Adventures of

Robin Hood; Kennedy Center Honors 1984; Not My Kid.

Bway inc: The Iceman Cometh (revival); Antony and Cleopatra; Leave It to Jane; The Premise; Rattle of a Simple Man; The Knack; Doubles.

SEGAL, Jonathan: Act. b. NYC, Jul 8, 1953. TV inc: The Lie; Quincy; The Paper Chase; Brave New World; Miracle On Ice.

Films inc: Lemon Popsicle 3; Sapiches (Private Popsicle); Megilah '83.

SEGAL, Vivienne: Act. b. Philadelphia, PA, 1897. Bway inc: The Blue Paradise; My Lady's Glove; Miss 1917; Oh! Lady, Lady!; The Little Whopper; The Yankee Princess; Ziegfeld Follies; Florida Girl; Castles In The Air; The Desert Song; The Chocolate Soldier; The Three Musketeers; Maria's Lovers; Brady's Escape; Music in the Air; I Married An Angel; Pal Joey; A Connecticut Yankee; Forever Is Now.

On screen from 1930. Films inc: Song of the West; Bride of the Regiment; Golden Dawn; Viennese Nights; The Cat and the Fiddle.

SEGELSTEIN, Irwin: Exec. b. NYC. e. CCNY. With Benton & Bowles Advertising agency for 18 years before joining CBS in 1965. Left CBS-TV in 1973 to become pres, CBS Records Division; joined NBC in 1976 as exec vp, programs; appointed exec vp, Broadcasting, NBC, Jun 9, 1978; Pres June 1980; Aug 1981, named board vice chmn.

SEGOVIA, Andres: Guitarist. b. Linares, Spain, Feb 18, 1894. Debut, Granada 1909; has toured world extensively; made NY debut 1928 at Town Hall.

(Grammy-Classical Inst-1959).

SEIDELMAN, Arthur Allen: Wri-Dir-Prod. b. NYC. e. Whittier Coll, BA; UCLA, MA. Films inc: Children of Rage (wri-dir); Echoes (dir).

TV inc: (dir) Ceremony of Innocence; Which Mother Is Mine (Emmy-1979) A Special Gift; Schoolboy Father; I Think I'm Having a Baby; A Matter of Time; She Drinks A Little (Emmy-1982); Macbeth; Family; I Love Liberty (& wri); Actors On Acting (host).

Thea inc: The Awakening of Spring; Hamp; Inherit the Wind; Billy; The World Of My America; Ceremony of Innocence; The Justice Box; The Four Seasons; Vieux Carre.

SEIZER, Bob: Wri-Prod. b. Des Moines, IA, May 13, 1931. TV inc: Challenge Golf; Big Three Golf; Winter Olympic Games, 1972; Challenge of the Sexes; Three on Three Basketball; Walter Alston-The Quiet Man; World Team Tennis; Memories of Elvis; Rock 'N Roll Sports Classic.

SELDEN, Albert W.: Prod-Comp. b. NYC, Oct 20, 1922. e. Yale U. Bway inc: Small Wonder (comp): Grey-Eyed People; A Month of Sundays (comp); His and Hers; Waiting for Gilliam; Body Beautiful; The Amazing Adele (prod-comp-lyr); Hallelujah Baby (Tony-1968); Girls Against the Boys; Man of La Mancha (Tony-1972); What Do You Really Know About Your Husband; Portrait of a Queen; Come Summer; The Lincoln Mask; Irene; Comin' Uptown.

SELDES, Marian: Act. b. NYC, Aug 23, 1928. Bway inc: Medea; Crime and Punishment; That Lady; Come of Age; The High Ground; Ondine; The Chalk Garden; The Wall; A Gift of Time; The Milk Train Doesn't Stop Here Anymore; A Delicate Balance (Tony-1967); Father's Day; Equus; The Merchant; Deathtrap.

Films inc: Mr Lincoln; The Big Fisherman; The Greatest Story Ever Told; Fingers.

TV inc: Macbeth. Radio: Mystery Theatre.

SELF, William: Exec. b. Dayton, OH, Jun 21, 1921. e. U of Chicago, BS. TV inc: (Prod) Schlitz Playhouse of Stars, CBS 1952-56; Frank Sinatra Show, 1957-58; exec. prod. CBS TV Network, 1959; exec. prod. 20th Century-Fox-TV, 1960-61; VP in charge of prod., 20th Century-Fox-TV, 1961-69; pres., 20th Century-Fox-TV, 1969-74; Frankovich-Self Prods, 1975; VP, programs, CBS-TV, 1976-77; VP, motion pictures and Mini-series CBS Entertainment Division, 1978; March 1982, P CBS Theatrical Films; Dec. 1984, became indie prod when CBS killed off Theatrical Films division.

SELLARS, Elizabeth: Act. b. Glasgow, Scotland, May 6, 1923. Films inc: Floodtide; Madeleine; Cloudburst; The Gentle Gunman; The Bare-

foot Contessa; Three Cases of Murder; The Shiralee; The Day They Robbed the Bank of England; The Chalk Garden; The Mummy's Shroud; The Hireling.

Thea (London) The Remarkable Mr Pennypacker; South Sea Bubble; Tea & Sympathy; The Sound of Murder.

TV inc: Too Late for the Mashed Potato; The Happy Ones; R 3; A Voyage Round My Father.

SELLECCA, Connie: Act. b. Bronx, NY., May 25, 1955. Former model. TV inc: The Bermuda Depths; Flying High; She's Dressed to Kill; Captain America; Beyond Westworld; The Greatest American Hero; Arthur Hailey's Hotel; International Airport.

SELLECK, Tom: Act. b. Detroit, MI, Jan 29, 1945 e. USC. Films inc: Myra Breckenridge; Seven Minutes; Daughter of Satan; Coma; Midway; High Road to China; Lassiter; Runaway.

TV inc: Bracken's World; Countdown at the Superbowl; The Sacketts; Gypsy Warriors; Boston and Kilbride;The Rockford Files; The Concrete Cowboys; Magnum, P.I.(Emmy-1984); Jim Nabors' Christmas In Hawaii; Divorce Wars--A Love Story; The Shadow Riders; Happy Birthday, Bob; Bob Hope's Wicky-Wacky Special From Waikiki; TV Academy Hall Of Game.

SELLERS, Arlene: Prod. b. Sep 7, 1921. e. UC Berkeley, BA, LLB, JD. Films inc: Silver Bears; Cross of Iron; End of the Game; The Lady Vanishes; The Seven-Per-Cent Solution; House Calls; Cuba; Blue Skies Again; Scandalous; Swing Shift (exec prod); Irreconcilable Differences.

SELLIER, Charles E. Jr: Prod. Films inc: The Adventures of Frontier Fremont (& wri); In Search of Noah's Ark (& wri); The Lincoln Conspiracy (& wri); Beyond and Back; The Bermuda Triangle; In Search of Historic Jesus; Hangar 18; The Boogens; Silent Night, Deadly Night (dir).

TV inc: The Deerslayer; Greatest Heroes of the Bible; The Life and Times of Grizzly Adams; Mark Twain's America--Tom Edison, Lightning Slinger; Mark Twain's America--Abe Lincoln, Freedom Fighter; The Legend of Sleepy Hollow; The Adventures of Nellie Bly; Adventures of Huckleberry Finn; California Gold Rush; The Nashville Grab; The Capture of Grizzly Adams; The Fall of the House of Usher.

SELTZER, Leo: Prod-Dir-Wri. b. Montreal, Mar 13, 1913. e. U of MA, BA. Prod & dir docs, informational, theatrical, TV films for various private and governmental orgs. Films inc: Day in Malaysia; Summit; Sinews of Freedom; Traditional Chinese Opera.

SELTZER, Walter: Prod. b. Philadelphia, Nov 7, 1914. e. U of PA. Pub for WB Theatres, Philadelphia; Fox West Coast Theatres; to Hollywood with MGM 1936-39. Col 1940-41; USMC 1941-44. Pub dir, Hal Wallis, 1945-54; vp in chg adv & pub; Hecht-Lancaster 1954-55; partner Glass-Seltzer PR firm; & Glass-Seltzer Prodns; vp & exec prod Pennebaker Prodns. Films inc: The Boss (asso prod); One-Eyed Jacks; Shake Hands With the Devil; Paris Blues; The Naked Edge; Man in the Middle; Wild Seed; War Lord; Beau Geste; Will Penny; Number One; Darker Than Amber; The Omega Man; Skyjacked; Soylent Green; The Cay; The Last Hard Men.

SELZNICK, Daniel: Prod. b. LA.,CA., May 18, 1936. e. Harvard, BA; studied with Stella Adler and Lee Strasberg. S. of the late David O. Selznick and Irene Mayer Selznick. Worked as stage mgr. Films inc: Targets (asso prod).

TV inc: (co-prod) Night Of Terror; Blood Feud.

SELZNICK, Irene Mayer: Prod. b. NYC, Apr 2, 1910. D of the late Louis B Mayer; ex-wife late David O Selznick. Exec with Selznick Int'l 1936-40; Vanguard Films, 1941-49. Formed own company, NY, 1949.

Bway inc: Streetcar Named Desire; Bell, Book and Candle; Flight Into Egypt; The Chalk Garden; The Complaisant Lover. (London): The Last Joke.

SEMEL, Terry: Exec. b. NYC, Feb 24, 1943. e. CCNY, MBA. Originally a CPA, joined WB 1966 working NY, Cleveland, LA; 1971, domestic sls mgr CBS Cinema Center Films; 1973, vp-gen sls mgr Buena Vista; 1975 retd to WB as vp-gen sls mgr; 1978, exec vp, COO; Jan 1980 became P in swap of duties with Frank Wells.

SEMPLE, Lorenzo Jr: Wri. Films inc: Pretty Poison; Marriage of a Young Stockbroker; The Drowning Pool; Three Days of the Condor; King Kong; Hurricane; Flash Gordon; Never Say Never Again; Sheena.
TV inc: Rearview Mirror.
Plays inc: Golden Fleecing.

SENENSKY, Ralph: Dir. b. Mason City, IA, May 1, 1923. e. Northwestern U. TV inc: Dr. Kildare; Twilight Zone; Route 66; Naked City; Arrest and Trial; The Fugitive; Twelve O'Clock High; Star Trek; Mission Impossible; Ironside; Mannix; The Name of the Game; The Courtship of Eddie's Father; Dan August; Night Gallery; The Rookies; Barnaby Jones; The Waltons; The New Adventures of Heidi; Insight/ Unfinished Business; Big Bend Country; Casablanca.

SERKIN, Peter: Concert pianist. b. NYC, Jul 24, 1947. e. Curtis Inst of Music. S of Rudolf Serkin. Recitals major cities; guest soloist with NY Philharmonic; Cleveland Symphony; London Symphony.
(Grammy-New class artist-1965).

SERKIN, Rudolf: Concert pianist. b. Eger, Bohemia, Mar 28, 1903. Child prodigy at 4, guest artist with Vienna Symphony at 12. Began concert career Europe 1920; US debut 1933 Coolidge Festival, Washington; with Toscanini 1936. Guest artist major world orchestras in series of annual tours.
TV inc: America Entertains Vice Premier Teng Hsiao-Ping.

SERNA, Pepe: Act. b. Corpus Christi, TX, Jul 21, 1944. Films inc: Red Sky at Morning; Shootout; Hangup; Car Wash; Honeysuckle Rose; Inside Moves; Vice Squad; Heartbreaker; Scarface; The Adventures of Buckaroo Banzai--Across the 8th Dimension; Fandango.
TV inc: The Deadly Tower; City in Fear; Three Hundred Miles For Stephanie; Seguin; The Ballad of Gregorio Cortez; The 25th Man; White Water Rebels; Los Alvarez; Sadat; Best Kept Secrets.

SERRAULT, Michel: Act. b. France. Films inc: L'Argent des Autres; Get Out Your Handkerchiefs; The Associate; La Cage Aux Folles; La Gueule de l'autre; Heads or Tails; La Cage Aux Folles II; Malevil; Garde A Vue (The Grilling); Les Fantomes Du Chapelier (The Hatter's Ghosts); Nestor Burma, Detective de Choc (Nestor Burma, Shock Detective); Les Quarantiemes Rugissants (The Roaring Forties); Deux heures moint le quart avant Jesus Christ (A Quarter to Two Before Jesus Christ); Mortelle Randonee (Deadly Circuit); Le Bon Plaisir; A mort l'Arbitre (Kill the Referee); Le Bon Roi Dagobert (Good King Dagobert); Les Rois du Gag (The Gag Kings); Liberte, Egalite, Choucroute (Liberty, Equality, Sauerkraut).

SEVAREID, Eric: News Commentator. b. Velva, ND, Nov 26, 1912. e. U of MN. Started career as reporter Minneapolis Journal, Paris Herald Tribune, United Press. Joined CBS radio news staff in Paris at outbreak of WW II. Later natl correspondent with CBS. Ret. from network 1977. TV inc: LBJ--The Man and the President (Emmy-1973); Flashback (The Great Plague) (host); Christmas in Washington; Enterprise (narr); Countdown to Looking Glass (cable).
Films inc: The Right Stuff.
(ATAS Broadcast Journalism Award 1977).

SEVAREID, Michael: Exec. b. Paris, Apr 25, 1940. e. Middlebury Coll, BA. S of Eric Sevareid. Actor 1960-1971. Films inc: The Shoot Horses, Don't They?; Airport; They Call Me Mr. Tibbs; Raid on Rommel.
TV inc: numerous segs as actor. Exec prod, CBS-TV, 1970-79. Named VP prodn, MGM, Sept 1979; Happy Endings (supv prod).

SEVEN, Johnny (John Anthony Fetto): Act-Prod-Dir. b. NYC, Feb 23, 1930. Films inc: Never Steal Anything Small; Sweet Smell of Success; The Last Mile; Guns of the Timberlane; The Apartment; Johnny Gunman; The Greatest Story Ever Told; Navajo Run (prod. & dir.); What Did You Do in the War, Daddy?; Gunfight in Abilene; The Destructors; The Love God.
TV inc: Ironside; Switch; CHiPs; Rockford Files; Police Woman; The New Terror (doc., prod. & dir.).
Bway inc: The Story Teller; Rose Tattoo.

SEVERINSEN, Carl H. (Doc): Comp-Cond. b. Arlington, OR, Jul 7, 1927. Trumpeter in orchs inc Ted Fiorito; Benny Goodman; Charlie Barnet; Tommy Dorsey; Vaughn Monroe.

TV inc: Tonight Show (cond); Uptown-A Tribute to the Apollo Theatre.

SEVERN, Maida: Act. b. Aug 6, 1902. Films inc: Loving You; Marjorie Morningstar; Imitation of Life; Bells Are Ringing; Back Street; Mr. Hobbs Takes a Vacation; Story of Ruth; Dear Brigitte; Airport 1975; Young Frankenstein; Wonder Woman.
TV inc: General Hospital; Divorce Court; Ellery Queen.

SEYLER, Athene, CBE: Act. b. London, May 31, 1889. e. Bedford Coll. Stage debut 1909 in The Truants. Thea (London) The Dover Road; The Corn Is Green; The Cherry Orchard; Watch on the Rhine; The Last of Mrs Cheyney; Lady Windermere's Fan; Harvey; Who Is Sylvia; First Person Singular; Bell, Book and Candle; The Iron Duchess; Breath of Spring; The Gentleman Dancing Master; The Dark Stranger; The Reluctant Peer; Too True to be Good; Arsenic And Old Lace.
Films inc: This Freedom; The Perfect Lady; The Citadel; Quiet Wedding; Dear Octopus; Nicholas Nickleby; Queen of Spades; Young Wives' Tale; Pickwick Papers; Yield to the Night; Campbell's Kingdom; The Inn of the Sixth Happiness; Make Mine Mink; Nurse on Wheels.

SEYMOUR, Anne (nee Eckert): Act. b. NYC, Sep 11, 1909. On radio, about 5000 network programs inc: Grand Hotel; Story of Mary Marlin.
Bway inc: School for Scandal; Sunrise at Campobello; Ring Around the Moon.
Films inc: All the King's Men; The Whistle at Eaton Falls; Man on Fire; Pollyanna; Desire Under the Elms; Gift of Love; Home from the Hill; Misty; Good Neighbor Sam; Mirage; How To Succeed In Business Without Really Trying; Fitzwilly; Stay Away, Joe; Hearts of the West; Triumphs of a Man Called Horse; Gemini Affair--A Diary.
TV inc: Empire; I Never Said Goodbye; The Last Survivors; General Hospital; Sandburg's Lincoln; James at 15; Studs Lonigan; The Miracle Worker; Angel on My Shoulder; Charlie and the Great Balloon Chase; Good Evening, Captain; Tough Girl; Life of the Party-- The Story of BeAtrice; Chiller.

SEYMOUR, Jane (Joyce Frankenberg): Act. b. England, Feb 15, 1951. With London Festival Ballet at age 13 before act. Films inc: Live and Let Die; Sinbad and the Eye of the Tiger; Battlestar Galactica; Oh, Heavenly Dog; Somewhere In Time; Lassiter.
TV inc: Captains and the Kings; Four Feathers; The Dallas Cowboy Cheerleaders; John Steinbeck's East of Eden; The Scarlet Pimpernel; The Haunting Passion; Dark Mirror; The Sun Also Rises; Obsessed With A Married Woman; Jamaica Inn.
Bway inc: Amadeus.

SEYRIG, Delphine: Act. b. Beirut, 1932. Formal dramatic training in Paris, later Actors Studio NY. Films inc: Pull My Daisy; Last Year in Marienbad; Muriel; La Musica; Accident; Mr. Freedom; Stolen Kisses; Daughters of Darkness; Milky Way; Peau d'Ane; The Discreet Charm of the Bourgeoisie; The Day of the Jackal; The Black Windmill; Aloise; Doll's House; Dear Michael; Le Dernier Cri; India Song; Faces of Love; Utkozben; Chere Inconnue; Le Chemin Perdu (The Lost Way); Documenteur--An Emotion Picture (voice); Freak Orlando; Jeanne Dielman, 23 Quai du Commerce, 1080 Bruxelles; Dorian Gray in Spiegel der Boulevardpresse (The Image of Dorian Gray in the Yellow Press).
Thea inc: The Lover; The Seagull; Old Times; The Garden of Delight; The Bitter Tears of Petra Von Kant.
TV inc: The Ambassadors.

SHACKELFORD, Ted: Act. b. Oklahoma City, OK, Jun 23, 1946. e. U Denver. TV inc: Another World; The Defection of Simas Kudirka; The Jordan Chance; Knots Landing; Terror Among Us; I Love Men; Summer Fantasies.

SHAFFER, Anthony: Wri. b. Liverpool, England, May 15, 1926. e. Cambridge. B of Peter Shaffer. Films inc: Forbush and the Penguins; Frenzy; Sleuth; The Wicker Man; Death on the Nile; Absolution; Evil Under the Sun.
Plays inc: The Savage Parade; Sleuth (Tony-1971); The Case of Oily Levantine (on Bway as Whodunnit).
TV inc: Pig in the Middle.

SHAFFER, Louise: Act. b. New Haven, CT, Jul 5. e. CT Coll for Women; Yale Drama School. Bway inc: First One Asleep, Whistle; We Have Always Lived In The Castle; Keep It In The Family; The Women.
TV inc: Autumn Garden; All That Glitters; Search For Tomorrow; Where The Heart Is; Edge of Night; Ryan's Hope *(Emmy*-Supp-1983); Search For Tomorrow (retd).

SHAFFER, Paul: Comp-Wri-Act. b. Thunder Bay, Ont, Canada. Played with Canadian jazz group; became mus dir Toronto company of Godspell.
Bway inc: The Magic Show (cond); Godspell (cond); Gilda Radner--Live from NY (wri-act).
Films inc: Gilda Live (wri-act).
TV inc: Saturday Night Live (wri); A Year at the Top (act).

SHAFFER, Peter: Wri. b. Liverpool, England, May 15, 1926. e. Cambridge. B of Anthony Shaffer. Plays inc: Five Finger Exercise; The Private Ear and the Public Eye; The Merry Roosters Panto; The Royal Hunt of the Sun; Black Comedy; The Battle of Shrivings; Equus *(Tony*-1975); Amadeus *(Tony*-1981).
Films inc: The Lord of the Flies; Equus; Amadeus *(Oscar-screenplay-1984)*
TV inc: The Salt Land; Balance of Terror.

SHAGAN, Steve: Wri. b. NYC, Oct 25, 1927. Films inc: Save the Tiger (& prod); Hustler; Voyage of the Damned; Nightwing; The Formula (& prod).
TV inc: River of Mystery (& prod); Spanish Portrait (& prod); Sole Survivor (& prod); A Step Out of Line (& prod); The House on Garibaldi Street (& exec prod).

SHAH, Krishna: Wri-Dir. b. May 10, 1938. Films inc: Rivals; River Niger; Shalimar; Cinema Cinema; American Drive-In (& prod).
TV inc: Ironside; Six Million Dollar Man; Love American Style; Man from U.N.C.L.E.; The Flying Nun; Maya.

SHAKESPEARE, Frank: Exec. b. NYC, Apr 9, 1925. e. Holy Cross, BS. Started with WCBS-TV, NY became vp-gm then moved to CBS net as sr vp; P CBS-TV Services; resd 1969 to become dir US Information Agency; 1973, exec vp Westinghouse; 1975 P, RKO General.

SHALIT, Gene: TV pers. b. NYC, 1932. e. U of IL. With NBC Radio Network. In Jan., 1973 became regular film critic NBC-TV Today Show.
TV inc: Mystery! (host).

SHANGE, Ntozake (Paulette L Williams): Act-Wri-Dir. b. Trenton, NJ, Oct 18, 1948. e. Barnard, BA; USC, MA. Plays inc: For Colored Girls Who Have Considered Suicide/ When the Rainbow is Enuf; Where the Mississippi Meets the Amazon; The Mighty Gents (& dir).
TV inc: (wri) An Evening With Diana Ross.
Films inc: Poetry in Motion (Doc).

SHAPIRO, Arnold: Prod-Exec. b. Los Angeles, Feb 1, 1941. e. UCLA, BA. VP for tv TAT Communications Co. Began as doc wri, prod. TV inc: (Prod-wri) Medix series; The Feminine Mistake; The Science Fiction Film Awards (prod); Scared Straight (& dir) *(Emmy*-1979); Gene Autry--An American Hero; The Real Rookies; Scared Straight--Another Story; Return To Iwo Jima.
Films inc: Scared Straight *(Oscar*-doc-1978).

SHAPIRO, Dan: Wri. b. NYC, Jan 3, 1910. Wrote TV, night club material for Milton Berle; Bob Hope; Jackie Gleason; Eddie Cantor; Joe E. Lewis. Bway inc: Artists and Models; Follow the Girls; Peep Show; Ankles Aweigh. Songs: I Wanna Get Married; The Next Time Around; You Are Romance.

SHAPIRO, Irvin: Exec. e. George Washington U. P Films Around the World, Inc; P Filmworld Export Corp. Films inc: Crimewave (exec prod).

SHAPIRO, Ken: Prod. b. NJ, 1943. e. Bard Coll. Films inc: The Groove Tube; Modern Problems (dir-wri). TV inc: TV's Censored Bloopers (wri); TV'S Bloopers and Practical Jokes (wri).

SHAPIRO, Robert W.: Exec. b. Brooklyn, Mar 1, 1938. e. USC.

Started with William Morris Agency 1960; vp & m-dir William Morris (UK) Ltd. 1968-74; vp in charge intl mp dept 1974-77; formed Robert W Shapiro Prodns; named exec vp in charge worldwide prodn WB May 1977; Nov 1980, P WB prodn; resd. July 1983.

SHAPIRO, Stanley: Wri-Prod. b. NYC, Jul 16, 1925. Wrote for Fred Allen's radio show; also wrote for Burns & Allen, TV. Screenwriting debut, 1958, The Perfect Furlough. Films inc: Pillow Talk *(Oscar-co-sp-1959)*; Operation Petticoat; Come September; Lover Come Back; That Touch of Mink; Bedtime Story (& prod); How to Save a Marriage (prod only); For Pete's Sake; Seniors; Carbon Copy.

SHARAFF, Irene: Cos Dsgn. b. 1910. Films inc: B.F.'s Daughter; An American in Paris *(Oscar*-1951); Brigadoon; A Star Is Born; Guys and Dolls; The King and I *(Oscar*-1956); Porgy and Bess; Can Can; Flower Drum Song; West Side Story *(Oscar*-1961); Cleopatra *(Oscar*-1963); Who's Afraid of Virginia - Woolf? *(Oscar*-1966); Call Me Madam; Taming of the Shrew; Hello, Dolly!; The Other Side of Midnight; Mommie Dearest.
Bway inc: The King and I *(Tony*-1952); The Flower Drum Song; The Girl Who Came To Supper; Sweet Charity.

SHARIF, Omar (Michel Shahoub): Act. b. Alexandria, Egypt, Apr 10, 1932. On screen from 1953 in The Blazing Sun (Egyptian). Films inc: Lawrence of Arabia; Genghis Khan; The Fall of the Roman Empire; The Yellow Rolls-Royce; Behold a Pale Horse; Doctor Zhivago; Night of the Generals; More Than a Miracle; MacKenna's Gold; Che!; Funny Girl; The Appointment; Mayerling; The Horsemen; The Burglars; The Tamarind Seed; The Mysterious Island of Captain Nemo; Juggernaut; Funny Lady; Crime and Passion; The Baltimore Bullet; Ashanti; Oh Heavenly Dog; Green Ice; Ayoub (Patience); Top Secret.
TV inc: S*H*E*; Pleasure Palace; The Far Pavilions (PC).

SHARKEY, Ray: Act. Films inc: Stunts; Paradise Alley; Who'll Stop the Rain; Willie & Phil; The Idolmaker; Love & Money; Some Kind of Hero; duBEAT-e-o; Body Rock; Hellhole.
TV inc: The Ordeal of Bill Carney.

SHARP, Phil: Wri. b. Chicago, Feb 6, 1919. e. U of Chicago. Radio: Duffy's Tavern; Alan Young Show; December Bride; Life with Luigi; The Aldrich Family.
TV inc: Ed Wynn Show; Danny Thomas; Saturday Night Revue; Joan Davis Show (pilot); Sid Caesar Hour; The Phil Silvers Show *(Emmy*-1957); Bob Newhart Show; Andy Williams Show; Doris Day Show; Hogan's Heroes; Maude; All in the Family.

SHATNER, William: Act. b. Montreal, Mar 22, 1931. e. McGill U. Toured Canada in various stock, repertory companies. Bway debut, 1956, Tamburlaine the Great. Bway inc: The Merry Wives of Windsor; Henry V; The World of Suzie Wong; A Shot in the Dark; Remote Asylum.
Films inc: The Brothers Karamazov; Judgment at Nuremberg; The Explosive Generation; The Intruder; The Outrage; Big Hot Mama; Dead of Night; The Devil's Rain; Kingdom of the Spiders; Star Trek-The Motion Picture; The Kidnapping of the President; The Land of No Return; Visiting Hours; Star Trek II--The Wrath of Khan; Airplane II--The Sequel; Star Trek III--The Search For Spock.
TV inc: Star Trek; The Statesman; The Bastard; Disaster on the Coastline; The Baby Sitter; T.J. Hooker; Fridays; The Magic Planet (narr); Prime Times; "I Love T.V." Test; Secrets Of a Married Man.

SHAVELSON, Melville: Wri-Dir-Prod. b. NYC, Apr 1, 1917. e. Cornell U, AB. Started as radio writer: We the People; Bicycle Party; Bob Hope Show; then screen writer, prod., WB.
Films inc: The Princess and the Pirate; Always Leave Them Laughing; Room for One More; The Seven Little Foys (& dir.); Beau James (& dir.); Houseboat (& dir.); The Five Pennies (& dir.); The Pigeon that Took Rome (& dir. & prod.); A New Kind of Love (& dir., prod.); Cast a Giant Shadow (& dir. & prod.); The War Between Men and Woman (co-sp & dir.); Mixed Company.
TV inc: Creator of Emmy-winning series: Make Room for Daddy; My World and Welcome to It; The Legend of Valentino; The Great Houdini; Ike; True Life Stories (dir-wri); The Other Woman (dir); Deceptions (dir-wri).

SHAVER, Helen: Act. b. St. Thomas, Ont, Canada, Feb 24, 1951. e.

U of Alberta. Films inc: Christina; High-Ballin'; Starship Invasions; In Praise of Older Women; Who Has Seen the Wind; The Amityville Horror; The Dogs of War; Gas; Harry Tracy, Desperado; The Osterman Weekend; Best Defense.

TV inc: United States; Jessica Novak; Between Two Brothers; Countdown To Looking Glass (cable).

SHAW, Artie: Orch Ldr. b. NYC, May 23, 1910. Started as clarinetist with various orchestras. Organized own orchestra in 1936. Films inc: Dancing Co-Ed; Second Chorus; Bix (doc); Artie Shaw--Time Is All You've Got (doc).

TV inc: The Long Night of Lady Day.

SHAW, Harold: Dist-Exhb. b. Singapore, Apr 1, 1939. S of Sir Run Run Shaw. Dir Shaw Organization Group of Companies.

SHAW, Irwin: Wri. b. NYC, Feb 2, 1913. Films inc: Talk of the Town; I Want You; Fire Down Below; The Young Lions; Tip on a Dead Jockey.

Plays inc: Bury the Dead; Siege; Quiet City; The Gentle People; Retreat to Pleasure; The Assassin; The Survivors.

(Died May 16, 1984).

SHAW, Lachlan Charles: Exec. b. Forbes, Australia, Nov 15, 1932. Dir, Creative Dev Branch, Australian Film Commission. Former dir Current Affairs, Australian Broadcasting Commission & dir, Film, Radio & Television Board, Australian Council.

SHAW, Lou: Wri-Prod. b. St Paul, MN, Apr 29, 1926. TV inc: Nancy Drew; McCloud; Quincy (pilot); Pleasure Cove (Pilot); Beyond Westworld (Wri-prod of pilot & exec prod of series);Fitz and Bones (exec prod); The Fall Guy; Half Nelson.

SHAW, Rose Tobias: Casting Dir. b. Germany. Films inc: Equus; A Little Night Music; The Greek Tycoon; The Seven Per Cent Solution; The Last Remake of Beau Geste; Baby.

TV inc: The Word; The Corn Is Green; A Man Called Intrepid; Lady Oscar; Brass Target.

SHAW, Tan Sri Dr. Runme: Prod-Dist-Exhb. b. Shanghai, Oct 24, 1901. B of Sir Run Run Shaw. Chmn Shaw Organization; Chmn Shaw Foundation.

(Died March 3, 1985)

SHAW, Sir Run Run. Prod-Dist. b. Shanghai, Oct 14, 1907. B of Tan Sri Dr. Runme Shaw. P, Shaw Organization since 1962. Chmn Shaw Brothers (Hong Kong) Ltd; Chm Television Broadcasts Ltd; Chmn Federation of Motion Film Producers of Hong Kong. Recent films inc: Teenage Dreamers; The Pure and the Evil; Horror Planet; Ghosts Galore; Twinkle, Twinkle, Little Star; On the Wrong Track; Hong Kong Playboys; Prince Charming; Love In a Fallen City; Behind the Yellow Line.

SHAW, Sebastian: Act-wri. b. England, May 29, 1905. e. RADA. Stage debut age 9 in The Cockyolly Bird; with various repertory groups before London debut 1925 in The Sign of the Sun. Thea inc: Come With Me; The Comic Artist; The Constant Nymph; The Age of Unreason; Rope (& Bway); Everyman; The Outsider; Carpet Slippers; Measure for Measure; Melo (Bway); Full Fathom Five; Romeo and Juliet; Sunshine Sisters; A Kiss for Cinderella; Goodness, How Sad; His Excellency; His House in Order; Hunter's Moon; Take A Life; The Poison Tree; A Patriot for Me; joined Royal Shakespeare Company; Heartbreak House; Cymbeline; The Portage To San Cristobal of A.H.

Plays inc: Take A Life; The Cliff Walk.

Films inc: Caste; Taxi to Paradise; Four Masked Men; Brewster's Millions; Men Are Not Gods; Murder on Diamond Row; The Flying Squad; East of Piccadilly; Journey Together; Glass Mountain; Scotch on the Rocks; A Midsummer Nights Dream; Return of the Jedi; The Weather in the Streets.

SHAW, Vee King: Dist-Exhb. b. Singapore, Jun 25, 1944. S of Tan Sri Dr. Runme Shaw. Dir Shaw Organization Group of Companies; Dir Cinecolor Laboratory Thailand.

SHAWLEE, Joan: Act. b. Forest Hills, NY, Mar 5, 1929. Films inc: House of Horrors; Inside Job; Buck Privates Come Home; Prehistoric Women; The Marrying Kind; A Star Is Born; Conquest of Space; A

Farewell to Arms; Some Like It Hot; The Apartment; Critic's Choice; Irma La Douce; Tony Rome; Live A Little, Love A Little; One More Train To Rob; Willard; Flash and Firecat; Buddy Buddy.

TV inc: Child Bride at Short Creek.

SHAWN, Dick (Richard Schulefand): Act. b. Buffalo, NY, Dec 1, 1928. e. U of Miami. Films inc: The Opposite Sex; It's A Mad, Mad, Mad, Mad World; The Wizard of Bagdad; Wake Me When It's Over; What Did You do in the War, Daddy; Penelope; Way Way Out; The Producers; The Happy Ending; Love at First Bite; Young Warriors; Angel; The Secret Diary of Sigmund Freud.

Bway inc: For Heaven's Sake, Mother!; The Egg; A Funny Thing Happened on the Way to the Forum; Peterpat; Fade Out--Fade In; I'm Solomon; A Musical Jubilee.

TV inc: Fast Friends; Mr and Mrs Dracula; Legmen; Hail To The Chief.

SHAWN, Wallace: Plywri-act. b. NYC., Nov. 12, 1943. e. Harvard, Oxford. Studied with Herbert Berghof. Taught English in India on a Fulbright. Plays inc: Our Late Night; The Mandrake (translation); A Thought In Three Parts; Marie and Bruce; The Hotel Play; My Dinner With Andre; Ode To Napoleon Bonaparte.

Thea inc: (Act) The Mandrake; The Master and Margarite; Chinchilla; The First Time; Ode To Napoleon Bonaparte.

Films inc: (act) Manhattan; Starting Over; Simon; Cheaper To Keep Her; A Little Sex; Atlantic City; All That Jazz; My Dinner With Andre (& co-wri); Lovesick; The First Time; Strange Invaders; Deal Of the Century; Saigon--Year Of the Cat.Crackers; The Hotel New Hampshire; Heaven Help Us.

SHEA, Jack: Dir. b. NYC, Aug 1, 1928. e. Fordham U, BA. TV inc: Insight; Hawaii 5-0; Calucci's Dep't (pilot); Glen Campbell Goodtime Hour; Sanford & Son; We'll Get By; The Waltons; The Jeffersons; Checking In; Pen 'n' Inc; Wendy Hooper, U.S. Army; Kangaroos In the Kitchen; Mr. Success; Punky Brewster.

SHEA, John: Act. b. 1949. e. Bates U. BA; Yale Drama School, MFA. Thea inc: Yentl (Bway); Master and Margarite; Long Day's Journey Into Night; Romeo and Juliet; The Sorrows of Stephen; American Days (Bway); End Of the World (Bway).

Films inc: Hussy; Missing; In Our Hands (doc); Windy City.

TV inc: The Nativity; The Last Convertible; Family Reunion; Kennedy; Hitler's SS--Portrait In Evil.

SHEARER, Moira: Ballerina. b. Scotland, 1926. Joined Sadler's Wells (The Royal Ballet now) at age 16. Screen debut, 1948, The Red Shoes.

Films inc: Tales of Hoffman; The Story of Three Loves; The Man Who Loved Redheads; Peeping Tom; Black Tights.

Thea inc: Man and Wife.

SHEARER, Norma: Act. b. Montreal, 1904. On screen from 1920. Films inc: The Stealers; The Divorcee (Oscar-1929/30); Their Own Desire; A Free Soul; The Barretts of Wimpole Street; Romeo and Juliet; Marie Antoinette; The Student Prince; The Actress; The Trial of Mary Dugan; Private Lives; Smilin' Through; Strange Interlude; Riptide; Idiot's Delight; Her Cardboard Lover (last film made in 1942).

(Died Jun 12, 1983).

SHEARING, George: Mus-Comp. b. London, England, Aug 13, 1919. Blind since birth. Studied class mus but moved to jazz while in his teens. Began playing piano in pub, later with Frank Wier Quartet; Claude Bampton All-Blind Band; became arr for various bands inc Ted Heath; nitery, recording star in US since 1941 appearing all top clubs, Carnegie Hall; appeared with major symphonies. Composer Lullaby of Birdland.

Recordings inc: September in The Rain; Cherokee; I'll Remember April. Albums inc: The Best of George Shearing; Light, Airy and Swinging; The Way We Are; As Requested.

SHEEDY, Ally: Act. b. NYC, 1963. Danced with American Ballet Theatre as child. TV inc: Homeroom; Splendor in the Grass; The Day The Loving Stopped; The Violation of Sarah McDavid; The Best Little Girl in the World; Hill Street Blues.

Films inc: Bad Boys; WarGames; Oxford Blues; The Breakfast Club; Twice In A Lifetime; St. Elmo's Fire.

SHEEN, Martin (Ramon Estevez): Act. b. Dayton, OH, Aug 3, 1940. On screen from 1967. Films inc: The Incident; The Subject Was Roses; Catch 22; No Drums, No Bugles; Badlands; The Little Girl Who Lives Down the Lane; The Cassandra Crossing; Apocalypse Now; The Eagle's Wing; The Final Countdown; Loophole; Gandhi; That Championship Season; Enigma; Man, Woman and Child; The Dead Zone; Firestarter; In The Name Of The People.

TV inc: That Certain Summer; Letters for Three Lovers; The Execution of Private Slovik; The Missiles of October; Sweet Hostage; Third Annual Circus of the Stars; Blind Ambition; The Long Road Home (Emmy-1981); I Love Liberty; In the Custody of Strangers; Kennedy; Choices of the Heart; When Silence Kills (host); Actors On Acting; Jack London's California; The Guardian (cable); The Atlanta Child Murders; Consenting Adult; The Fourth Wise Man; Spaceflight (narr).

Bway inc: The Subject Was Roses.

SHEINBERG, Jonathan Jay: exec. b. NYC, Dec. 30, 1957. e. Franklin College, Lugano, Switzerland. S of Lorraine Gary and Sidney J. Sheinberg. Joined Columbia Pictures 1979 in publicity dept; 1983, crea aff dir Lorimar Prodns; Dec. 1984, crea aff dir 20th Fox Prodns.

SHEINBERG, Sid (Sidney J Sheinberg): Exec. b. Corpus Christi, TX, Jan 14, 1935. e. Columbia Coll; Columbia Law School. H of Lorraine Gary. Joined legal dept Revue Prodns (prodn arm of MCA before divorcement of agency operation) 1959; vp in chg prodn U-TV, 1968; P U-TV & exec VP MCA Inc, 1970; P & COO of MCA Inc, June 1973.

SHELDON, James (ne Schleifer): Dir. b. NYC, Nov 12. e. U of NC, AB. TV inc: Armstrong Circle Theatre; Studio One; Robert Montgomery Presents; Mr Peppers; Twilight Zone; Naked City; The Virginian; My World and Welcome to It; Love, American Style; Room 222; Insight; Sanford and Son; Rich Man, Poor Man; Love Boat; Family; The Gossip Columnist; Nurse; Seven Brides For Seven Brothers.

SHELDON, Sidney: Wri. b. Feb 11, 1917. Films inc: The Bachelor and the Bobbysoxer (Oscar-1947); Dream Wife (& dir); You're Never Too Young; Pardners; The Buster Keaton Story (& prod-dir); Jumbo; The Other Side of Midnight (sp).

Bway inc: Redhead (Tony-1959).

TV inc: Rage of Angels (exec prod).

SHELLEY, Carole: Act. b. London, Aug 16, 1939. e. RADA. London stage debut 1955 in Simon and Laura. Thea inc: (London) The Art of Living; New Cranks; Boeing Boeing; Mary, Mary. (Bway) The Odd Couple; The Astrakhan Coat; Loot; Sweet Potato; Little Murders; Absurd Person Singular; The Norman Conquests; Elephant Man (Tony-1979); The Misanthrope; Noises Off.

Films inc: Little Nell; The Man from Morocco; It's Great to be Young; Give Us This Day; The Odd Couple; The Boston Strangler; Robin Hood and the Aristocrats (voice).

TV inc: The Odd Couple.

SHENAR, Paul: Act. b. Milwaukee, WI., Feb. 12, 1936. e. U of WI., BS. TV inc: The Execution of Private Slovik; The Night That Panicked America; Cyrano de Bergerac; Suddenly Love; Ziegfeld--The Man and his Women; Beulah Land; Three Eyes; Paper Dolls.

Films inc: Deadly Force; Scarface.

SHENGELAYA, Eldar: Dir. b. Russia, Jan. 26, 1933. S of the late Nikolai Shengelaya. Films inc: Legend About an Icy Heart; A Snowy Fairytale (co-dir); The White Caravan (co-dir,co-sp); Mikela; An Extraordinary Exhibition; The Eccentrics; Samanishvili's Step-Mother (& co-sp); Gouloubye Gory (The Blue Mountains) (& wri).

SHENGELAYA, Georgy: Wri-dir. b. Moscow, Oct. 15, 1937. B of Eldar Shengelaya. Originally an act in Our Courtyard; Otar's Widow; A Story of a Girl. Films inc: Prosmani; Alaverdoba; Melodies of the Veri Suburb; Our Daily Water.

SHENSON, Walter: Prod. b. San Francisco, CA. e. Stanford. Started in trailer dept, Col, later in pub dept; to London 1955 as pub supv European prodn before becoming prod.

Films inc: The Mouse That Roared; A Matter of WHO; The Mouse on the Moon; A Hard Day's Night; Help!; 30 is a Dangerous Age; Don't Raise the Bridge, Lower the Water; A Talent for Loving; Welcome to The Club; The Chicken Chronicles; Reuben, Reuben.

SHEPARD, Sam: Wri-Act. (Samuel Shepard Rogers). b. Fort Sheridan, IL, Nov 5, 1943. Plays inc: Cowboys; Rock Garden (a short play later included in the revue Oh! Calcutta!); La Turista; Forensic and the Navigators; Melodrama Play; Tooth of Crime; Operation Sidewinder; 4-H Club; The Unseen Hand; Mad Dog Blues; Shaved Splits; Curse of the Starving Class; Buried Child (Pulitzer Prize-1979); True West.

Films inc: (Act) Days of Heaven; Renaldo and Clara; Resurrection; Raggedy Man; Frances; The Right Stuff; Paris, Texas (wri); Country.

SHEPHARD, Harvey: Exec. b. NYC, 1937. e. CCNY. Started with Lennen & Newell ad agcy; joined CBS 1967 as mgr Audience Measurement; 1969, mgr audience measurement-tv network research; 1973, dir pgm projects; 1975, vp pgm planning; March 1977, vp-pgms, NY; Oct 1977, vp-pgms, NY, CBS Entertainment; 1978, vp-pgm administration; 1980, vp pgms; Nov 1982, sr vp pgms.

SHEPHERD, Cybill: Act. b. Memphis, TN, Feb 18, 1950. Former model. Films inc: The Last Picture Show; Daisy Miller; Taxi Driver; Special Delivery; The Silver Bears; The Lady Vanishes.

TV inc: The Yellow Rose; Masquerade; Secrets Of a Married Man; Moonlighting; Seduced.

SHEPHERD, Jean: Wri-act. b. Chicago, Jul. 26, 1929. As act, has played Carnegie Hall with one-man comedy show, has appeared at hundreds of colleges and universities inc 19 consecutive annual dates at Princeton. Other thea inc: New Faces of 1964. Asylum.

TV inc: Jean Shepherd's America; The Great American Fourth of July and Other Disasters; Shepherd's Pie; The Star-Crossed Romance Of Josephine Cosnowski.

Films inc: A Christmas Story (wri only).

SHEPHERD, Richard: Exec. b. Kansas City, MO, Jun 4, 1927. e. Stanford U. Began career 1948 at MCA; 1956 Head of Talent, Col; 1962 joined CMA talent agency, serving as exec VP; to WB 1972-1974 as exec. VP, prod; 1974-76; ind prod; 1976 named MGM sr. VP & worldwide head of prod; resigned May 1980 to return to ind prodn.

Films inc: Twelve Angry Men; The Hanging Tree; The Fugitive Kind; Breakfast at Tiffany's; Robin and Marion; Alex and the Gypsy; The Hunger.

SHER, Jack: Wri-Prod-Dir. b. Minneapolis, MN, 1913. Films inc: My Favorite Spy; Off Limits; Shane; Kathy 'O; The Wild and the Innocent; The Three Worlds of Gulliver; Paris Blues; Critic's Choice; Move Over, Darling; George Stevens--A Filmmaker's Journey (doc-int).

Plays inc: The Perfect Setup.

TV inc: The Kid from Left Field.

SHERA, Mark (ne Shapiro): Act. b. Bayonne, NJ, Jul 10, 1949. e. Boston U, BFA. TV inc: Nicky's World; S.W.A.T.; Barnaby Jones; Adams House; His Mistress.

Bway inc: Godspell.

SHERDEMAN, Ted (AKA John Elton): Wri-Prod-Dir. b. Lincoln, NE, Jun 21, 1909. Films inc: Lust for Gold; Breakthrough; Scandal Sheet; Retreat Hell!; The Winning Team; The Eddie Cantor Story; The McConnell Story; From Hell to Eternity; Away All Boats; Toy Tiger; Maracaibu; St. Louis Blues; Dog of Flanders; Misty; The Big Show; Island of the Blue Dolphins; And Now Miguel; My Side of the Mountain; Latitude Zero; Nocturne for Nero; The Day the Band Played.

TV inc: Wagon Train; Californians; Astronaut; Hazel; Men Into Space; My Favorite Martian; Bewitched; Family Affair; The Monroes; Flying Nun.

SHERIDAN, Dinah: Act. b. Hampstead, London, England, Sep 17, 1920. Thea inc: Let's All Go Down to the Strand; A Boston Story; The Gentle Hook; The Pleasure of His Company; In the Red; A Murder Is Announced; Present Laughter.

Films inc: Irish and Proud of It; Where No Vultures Fly; Sound Barrier; Genevieve; The Railway Children; The Mirror Crack'd.

SHERIN, Edwin: Dir-Act. b. Harrisburg, PA, Jan 15, 1930. e. Brown U. Thea inc: (act) Romeo and Juliet; As You Like It; A Desert Incident.

(Dir) Joan of Lorraine; Mister Roberts; The Wall; The Inspector General; The Iceman Cometh; The Lonesome Train; The Great White Hope; Look at Any Man; Hallelujah!; Nourish the Beast; Find Your Way Home; Of Mice and Men; Eccentricities of a Nightingale; Rex; First Monday in October; Goodbye, Fidel.

Films inc: Valdez Is Coming; My Old Man's Place.

TV inc: Deirdre of the Sorrows; King Lear; An American Christmas.

SHERMAN, George: Prod-Dir. b. NYC, 1908. Films inc: Sword in the Desert; Target Unknown; Against All Flags; The Lone Hand; Dawn At Socorro; Johnny Dark; Count Three And Pray; Comanche; Reprisal; Panic Button; Joacquin Murieta; Smokey; Big Jake; For The Love of Mike.

TV inc: Little Mo; Daniel Boone; Sam.

SHERMAN, Harry R.: Prod. b. Los Angeles, Sep 21, 1927. e. UCLA. Worked For Directors Guild America; toured world as prodn mgr Wonderful World of Golf; exec in chg prodn for Talent Associates.

TV inc: Eleanor and Franklin (Emmy-1976); Eleanor and Franklin--The White House Years (Emmy-1977); The Gathering (Emmy-1978); Studs Lonigan; This Man Stands Alone; She's In The Army Now; The Wall; The Rules of Marriage; Sentimental Journey; Victims For Victims--The Theresa Saldana Story; The Dirty Dozen--The Next Mission.

SHERMAN, Hiram: Act. b. Boston, MA, Feb 11, 1908. e. U of IL. Bway inc: Horse Eats Hat; The Cradle Will Rock; The Shoemaker's Holiday; Sing Out the News; Mum's The Word; The Alchemist; Brigadoon; Two's Company (Tony-supp-1953); Goodbye Again; Measure for Measure; The Merry Widow; The Killer; Troilus and Cressida; Mary, Mary; How Now Dow Jones (Tony-supp-1968); Anne of Green Gables.

Films inc: One Third of a Nation; The Solid Cadillacs; Mary, Mary; O Dad, Poor Dad, Mama's Hung You in the Closet and I'm Fellin' So Sad.

SHERMAN, Richard M.: Comp-Lyr. b. NYC, Jun 12, 1928. e. Bard Coll, BA. Films (collab. with brother, Robert) Parent Trap; Bon Voyage; In Search of the Castaways; Moon Pilot; Sword in the Stone; Summer Magic; Mary Poppins (2 Oscars-1964-best score & best song, Chim Chim Cher-ee); The One and Only Genuine Original Family Band; Bedknobs and Broomsticks; Huckleberry Finn (& sp); The Slipper and the Rose; The Magic of Lassie.

Bway inc: Victory Canteen; Over Here!

TV inc: Wonderful World of Color; Bell Telephone Hour.

Songs inc: It's a Small World; You're Sixteen; Let's Get Together; A Spoonful of Sugar. (Grammy-Film Score-1964).

SHERMAN, Robert B.: Comp-Lyr. b. NYC, Dec 19, 1925. e. Bard Coll, BA. All work in collab, with brother. See Richard M. Sherman.

SHERMAN, Robert M.: Prod-Exec. S of late Edward Sherman. Started as agent with MCA; later publ; ret to agency biz with CMA, serving as vp film div in London; became prod 1972; named prodn vp Fox 1974; 1977 joined MGM as vp; 1978 joined newly-formed Orion Pictures as sr vp prod; Jan 1982, resd to become ind prod for Orion. Films inc: (Prod) Scarecrow. Night Moves; Missouri Breaks; Convoy; Blockbusters; Oh, God! You Devil.

SHERMAN, Vincent (Abram Orovitz): Dir. b. Vienna, GA, Jul 16, 1906. e. Oglethorpe U, AB; Atlanta Law School, LLB. Actor, writer then dir. Films inc: Return of Dr. X; Saturdays Children; Man Who Talked Too Much; Underground; All Thru the Night; The Hard Way; Old Acquaintance; In Our Time; Mr. Skeffington; Pillow to Post; Janie Gets Married; Unfaithful; Nora Prentiss; Adventures of Don Juan; The Hasty Heart; Harriet Craig; Goodbye, My Fancy; Affair in Trinidad; The Young Philadelphians; The Naked Earth; The Second Time Around; The Young Rebel.

TV inc: Medical Center; The Waltons; Baretta; Executive Suite; Doctors Hospital; The Last Hurrah; Hagen; Bogie; The Dream Merchants; Trouble in High Timber Country; High Hopes--The Capra Years.

SHERRIN, Ned: Prod-Dir-Plywri. b. Low Ham, Somerset, England, Feb 18, 1931. e. Oxford; Gray's Inn. Former barrister who turned to

playwriting; became performer, later BBC prod.

Thea inc: (wri) No Bed For Bacon; Cindy-Ella or I Gotta Shoe; The Spoils; Nicholas Nickleby; Sing a Rude Song; Fish Out of Water; Come Spy With Me (dir); Side By Side With Sondheim (dir-act); Beecham; The Mitford Girls.

Films inc: (prod) The Virgin Soldier; Every Home Should Have One; Girl Stroke Boy; Up Pompeii; Rentadick; Up the Chastity Belt; The Alf Garnett Saga.

TV inc: That Was The Week That Was; Not So Much A Program; Benbow Was His Name; We Interrupt This Week; The Great Inimitable Mr. Dickens.

SHERWOOD, Madeleine Thornton: Act-Dir. b. Montreal, Canada, Nov 13, 1922. Bway inc: The Crucible; Cat on a Hot Tin Roof; Sweet Bird of Youth; Invitation to a March; All Over; Inadmissible Evidence; Do I Hear a Waltz; Hey, You, Light, Man!

Films inc: Baby Doll; Cat on a Hot Tin Roof; Sweet Bird of Youth; The 91st Day; Hurry Sundown; Pendulum; Wicked, Wicked.

TV inc: The Flying Nun; Rich Man, Poor Man.

SHIELDS AND YARNELL (Robert Shields and Lorene Yarnell): Mime Duo. Started as street mimes in San Francisco; won first place in Ted Mack amateur contest, signed for Las Vegas show Doo Dah Daze; worked niteries, concerts. TV inc: Toys on the Town (& wri); Dean Martin Christmas Special 1975; Mac Davis Show; Sonny and Cher Show; American Moments; Bob Hope on the Road to China; The Wild Wild West Revisited; Doug Henning's World of Magic; An Evening at the Improv; A Christmas Fantasy; Generation (Yarnell alone); Clown White (Yarnell alone).

Films inc: The Conversation.

Bway inc: Broadway Follies.

SHIELDS, Brooke: Act. b. NYC, May 31, 1965. Films inc: Alice, Sweet Alice; King of the Gypsies; Pretty Baby; Just You and Me, Kid; Wanda Nevada; Tilt; The Blue Lagoon; Endless Love; Sahara; The Muppets Take Manhattan.

TV inc: The Prince of Central Park; After the Fall; The Bob Hope 30th Anniversary Special; Bob Hope's Spring Fling of Glamour and Comedy; All-Star Salute To Mother's Day; Bob Hope's All-Star Birthday Party at West Point; Christmas, A Time of Cheer and A Time for Hope; All Hands on Deck For Bob Hope's All-Star Birthday Party At Annapolis; Bob Hope's USO Christmas in Beirut; Salute to Lady Liberty; Olympic Gala; Wet Gold; It's Ho-Ho Hope's 35th Jolly Christmas Hour; The Royal London Gala For Bob Hope's Happy Birthday Homecoming.

SHIGETA, James: Act. b. HI, 1933. Films inc: The Crimson Kimona; Cry for Happy; Walk Like a Dragon; Bridge to the Sun; Flower Drum Song; Paradise Hawaiian Style; Nobody's Perfect; Lost Horizon; Midway; Enola Gay--The Men, The Mission, The Atomic Bomb.

TV inc: Samurai; Tomorrow's Child; The Renegades.

SHIMKIN, Arthur: Exec. b. NYC, Oct 8, 1922. e. Columbia, BA. Started with Simon & Schuster; 1951-55, exclusive publ of Disney Books and Records; later, dir of all CBS Children's Book and Record Publications: 1973-76, p Children's Records of America Inc; 1977 p, Sesame Street Records; merged co with Children's Television Workshop.

SHIRE, David: Comp. b. Buffalo, NY, Jul 3, 1937. e. Yale, BA. Films inc: Two People; Conversation; The Taking of Pelham 1-2-3; Farewell, My Lovely; The Hindenburg; All the President's Men; Saturday Night Fever; Straight Time; Old Boyfriends; Norma Rae (Oscar-song-1979); Fast Break; The Promise; Only When I Laugh; Paternity; Max Dugan Returns; Oh, God! You Devil; Return To Oz.

TV inc: Tell Me Where It Hurts; Raid on Entebbe; The Defection of Simas Kudirka; Norma Rae; Darkroom; Do You Remember Love.

Bway inc: Sap of Life; Graham Crackers; Unknown Soldier and His Wife; How Do You Do, I Love You; Love Match; Baby.

Recordings inc: Saturday Night Fever (Grammys-Artist & Prod-1978).

SHIRE, Talia: Act. b. Long Island, NY, Apr 25, 1946. Sis of Francis Ford Coppola. Films inc: The Dunwich Horror (as Talia Coppola); Gas-s-s; The Christian Licorice Store; The Outside Man; The Godfather; The Godfather, Part II; Rocky; Rocky II; Old Boyfriends; Prophecy;

Windows; Rocky III.
TV inc: Rich Man, Poor Man; Kill Me If You Can.

SHIRLEY, Anne (Dawn Evelyeen Paris): Act. b. NYC, 1918. On screen from 1934. Films inc: Steamboat Round the Bend; Make Way for a Lady; Law of the Underworld; Mother Carey's Chickens; A Man to Remember; Stella Dallas; West Point Widow; All That Money Can Buy; Bombardier; The Powers Girl; The Man from Frisco; Music in Manhattan.

SHOBERG, Richard: Act. b. Grand Rapids, MI, Mar 1. e. Albion Coll. TV inc: Somerset; Edge of Night; The Silence; All My Children.

SHOEMAKER, Ann: Act. b. NYC, Jan 10, 1891. Bway inc: The Noose; The Ladder; We All Do; The Novice and the Duke; The Rich Full Life; The Bad Seed; The Importance of Being Earnest; Half-a-Sixpence.
Films inc: A Dog of Flanders; Alice Adams; Stella Dallas; Babes in Arms; Conflict; A Woman's Secret; Sunrise at Campobello; The Fortune Cookie.
TV inc: Omnibus; Roberta.

SHORE, Dinah (Frances Rose Shore): Singer-TV Pers. b. Winchester, TN, Mar 1, 1917. e. Vanderbilt, BA. Began as singer on WSM, Nashville while attending college. Radio and thea appearances in NYC led to first recordings with Xavier Cugat. Radio inc: Chamber Music Society of Lower Basin Street; Ben Bernie; Eddie Cantor; into TV 1951 with Chevy Show.
TV inc: Dinah Shore Show (Emmy-singer, 1954, 1955, 1957, 1959; personality 1956); Dinah Shore Specials; Dinah's Place (Emmys-1973, 1974); Dinah! (Emmy-1976); Death Car on the Freeway; Pat Boone and Family Christmas Special; Christmas In Washington; Parade of Stars; Here's Television Entertainment (host); Night Of 100 Stars II; The TV Academy Hall Of Fame.
Films inc: Thank Your Lucky Stars; Up In Arms; Belle of the Yukon; Follow the Boys; Make Mine Music; Till the Clouds Roll By; Fun and Fancy Free; Aaron Slick from Punkin Crick.

SHORT, Bobby: Singer-Mus. b. Danville, IL, Sep 15, 1924. Performs in concert, niteries. At Cafe Carlyle, NYC, since 1968.
TV inc: Hardhat & Legs; Paper Dolls.

SHOSTAK, Murray: Prod. b. Montreal, Canada, 1936. e. McGill U., BC. In private accountancy practice handling many film industryites; 1968 set up Potterton Productions; 1977, P of Universal Productions Canada.
Films inc: (co-prod) The Selfish Giant (ani); Child Under A Leaf. (Exec prod) Tiki Tiki; The Apprentice; The Rainbow Boys. (Prod) Silence of the North; Death Hunt; Maria Chapdelaine; Paroles et Musiques (Words and Music).
TV inc: Pinter People.

SHOWALTER, Max (formerly known as Casey Adams): Act. b. Caldwell, KS, Jun 2, 1917. Films inc: Always Leave Them Laughing; With a Song in My Heart; Bus Stop; The Naked and the Dead; Elmer Gantry; Bon Voyage; Fate Is the Hunter; The Moonshine War; The Anderson Tapes; Sgt. Pepper's Lonely Hearts Club Band; 10; Sixteen Candles.
Bway inc: Knights of Song; Very Warm for May; My Sister Eileen; Showboat; John Loves Mary; Make Mine Manhattan; Lend An Ear; Harrigan 'n Hart (mus).
TV inc: The Stockard Channing Show.

SHRINER, Kin: Act. b. NYC, Dec 6, 1953. e. UCLA. S of the late Herb Shriner. TV inc: The Young and The Restless; Rich Man Poor Man Book Two; General Hospital; Texas; Once An Eagle; MacNamara's Band; retd to General Hospital; Rituals; Obsessive Love.
Films inc: Macarthur; Young Doctors in Love.

SHROYER, Sonny: Act. b. Valdosta, GA, Aug 28. e. U GA. Films inc: Payday; Like a Crow on a June Bug; The Longest Yard; Smokey and the Bandit; Greased Lighting; The Devil and Max Devlin.
TV inc: The Million Dollar Dixie Deliverance; Freedom Road; The Summer of My German Soldier; King; The Lincoln Conspiracy; The Dukes of Hazzard; Enos.

SHRYACK, Dennis: Wri. b. Duluth, MI, Aug 25, 1936. e. U of MN. Films inc: The Good Guys and the Bad Guys; Rise Up in Anger; The Car; The Gauntlet; Murder By Phone; Flashpoint; Code Of Silence; Pale Rider.

SHULER, Lauren: Prod. b. Cleveland, OH, Jun 23, 1949. e. Boston U. Dir creative affairs, Motown Prodns; asso prod, Thank God It's Friday; Mr. Mom; St. Elmo's Fire.
TV inc: Amateur Night at the Dixie Bar and Grill.

SHULL, Richard B.: Act. b. Evanston, IL., Feb. 24, 1929. e. IA State, BA. Bway inc: Minnie's Boys; Goodtime Charley; Fools; Oh, Brother,
Films inc: The Anderson Tapes; B.S. I Love You; Such Good Friends; Slither; Hail To the Chief; The Black Bird; Hearts Of the West; SSSSSSSS; Wholly Moses; Heartbeeps; Spring Break; Lovesick; Unfaithfully Yours; Splash.
TV inc: Holmes & Yoyo; Good Times; Lou Grant; The Ropers; Will There Really Be A Morning; Sutter's Bay.

SHULMAN, Max: Wri. b. St Paul, MN, Mar 14, 1919. e. U of MN, BA. Films inc: Always Leave Them Laughing; Confidentially Connie; Affairs of Dobie Gillis; Half a Hero.
Bway inc: Barefoot Boy with Cheek; The Tender Trap; House Calls.
TV inc: The Many Loves of Dobie Gillis; House Calls; Help Wanted--Male.

SHYER, Charles: Wri. b. Los Angeles, Oct 11, 1941. e. UCLA. Worked as film AD, prodn mgr before writing career. TV inc: Lily Tomlin; The Odd Couple.
Films inc: Smokey and the Bandit; Goin' South; House Calls; Private Benjamin (& prod); Irreconcilable Differences.

SHYRE, Paul: Plywri-Prod-Dir-Act. b. NYC, Mar 8, 1929. e. U FL; AADA. Plays: USA; Pictures in the Hallway; I Knock at the Door; Drums Under the Windows; The Child Buyer; An Unpleasant Evening; Will Rogers USA; Blasts and Bravos--an Evening with H.L. Mencken; Hizzoner The Mayor.
Bway inc: I Knock at the Door (prod-dir-act); USA (dir); A Fair Game for Lovers; Blasts and Bravos (dir-act); Will Rogers' USA (dir); Absurd Person Singular (act).
TV inc: Carl Sandburg--Echoes and Silences (wri).
(Tony-Special-1957).

SIDARIS, Andy: Prod-Dir. b. Chicago, Feb 20, 1932. e. Southern Methodist U, BA. Films inc (dir): Stacey; The Racing Scene; M*A*S*H (football sequence); Seven.
TV inc (dir): The Racers/Mario Andretti/Joe Leonard/Al Unser; ABC's Championshop Auto Racing; ABC's NCAA Game of the Week; 1968 Summer Olympics (Emmy-1969); Wide World of Sports; The Racers/Craig and Lee Breedlove; XII Winter Olympics (Emmy-1976).

SIDARIS, Arlene T. (nee Smilowitz): Prod-Wri. b. NYC, Apr 21. W of Andy Sidaris. TV inc: Hardy Boys/Nancy Drew Mysteries (prod-wri); Missiles of October (asst prod); Glen Campbell Variety Hour (asst prod); Obsessed With A Married Woman (prod-story).

SIDNEY, George: Dir-Prod. b. NYC, Oct 4, 1916. Shorts dir, MGM, 1932. Pres Hanna-Barbera Prodns, 1961-66. Films inc: Free and Easy; Pacific Redezvous; Pilot No. 5; Thousands Cheer; Bathing Beauty; Anchors Aweigh; The Harvey Girls; Cass Timberlane; The Three Musketeers; Red Danube; Annie Get Your Gun; Holiday in Mexico; Showboat; Scaramouche; Young Bess; Kiss Me Kate; Jupiter's Darling; The Eddy Duchin Story; Jeanne Eagles; Pal Joey; Pepe; Bye Bye Birdie; Viva Las Vegas; Who Has Seen The Wind?; The Swinger; Half a Sixpence.

SIDNEY, Sylvia: Act. b. NYC, Aug 8, 1910. e. Theatre Guild School. On stage, then screen debut in Through Different Eyes, 1929. Films inc: City Streets; An American Tragedy; The Miracle Man; If I Had a Million; The Trail of the Lonesome Pine; Fury; You Only Live Once; Dead End; The Searching Wind; Les Miserables; Violent Saturday; Behind the High Wall; Summer Wishes, Winter Dreams; God Told Me To; Damien-Omen II; Hammett; Order of Death.
TV inc: Do Not Fold, Spindle or Mutilate; Death at Love House; Raid on Entebbe; The Gossip Columnist; FDR-The Last Year; The

Shadow Box; A Small Killing; Come Along With Me; Having It All; Finnegan Begin Again.

Bway inc: Crossroads; To Quito and Back; The Gentle People; The Fourposter; Enter Laughing.

SIEBERT, Charles: Act. b. Kenosha, WI, Mar 9, 1938. e. Marquette U. Studied at LAMDA, later taught there.

TV inc: Search for Tomorrow; As the World Turns; Another World; Husbands, Wives and Lovers; One Day at a Time; The Blue Knight; The Miracle Worker; The Seeding of Sarah Burns; Willow B: Women in Prison; Trapper John; A Cry For Love.

Films inc: Deadly Hero; Blue Sunshine; The Other Side of Midnight; All Night Long.

Bway inc: Jimmy Shine.

SIEGEL, Andrew M. (Andy): Exec. b. Los Angeles, Nov 18, 1941. e. UCLA, BA. S of the late Sol E Siegel. Started as asst dir, telefilms; 1971, movie of the week dir ABC-TV; 1973, dir comedy dvlpmnt; 1976, VP Comedy dvlpmnt CBS-TV; 1980, VP comedy MTM Enterprises; 1982, VP crea aff UA TV; Sept, 1982, sr vp crea aff MGM/UA TV.

SIEGEL, Don: Dir. b. Chicago, IL, Oct 26, 1912. Joined Warner Bros. as asst. film librarian, 1934. Became asst. cutter. Organized montage dept. Started dir shorts inc Oscar winning Hitler Lives and Star in the Night.

Features inc: The Verdict; Annapolis Story; Big Steal; No Time for Flowers; China Venture; Private Hell 36; Riot in Cell Block 11; Madigan; Coogan's Bluff; Two Mules for Sister Sara; Dirty Harry; The Shootist (& act); Telefon (& act); Invasion of the Body Snatchers (act); Escape From Alcatraz (prod-dir); Rough Cut; Jinxed!; Into The Night (act).

SIEGEL, Larry: Wri. b. NYC, Oct 29, 1925. e. U of IL, AB. TV inc: Bob Newhart Show; That Was the Week That Was; Laugh-In; The Carol Burnett Show (Emmys-1971, 1973, 1978).

SIEGLER, Scott Merrill: Exec. b. Cleveland, OH, Feb 15, 1948. e. Union Coll, BA. Prod numerous docs for PBS, NBC. April 1980 named vp dramatic dvlpmnt CBS; July 1982, sr vp crea aff WB TV.

Films inc: The Manitou (asst prod); Cloud Dancer (asst prod).

SIGNORET, Simone (nee Kaminker): Act. b. Weisbaden, Germany, Mar 21, 1921. W of Yves Montand. On screen from 1938. Films inc: The Living Corpse; Bolero; Macadam; Dedee; The Cheat; La Ronde; Diabolique; Room at the Top (Oscar-1958); Witches of Salem; The Sleeping Car Murders; Term of Trial; Is Paris Burning?; The Deadly Affair; Games; The Sea Gull; Ship of Fools; The Confession; Police Python 357; Madame Rosa; Chere Inconnu; L'Adolescente; Chere Inconnu; L'Etoile Du Nord (The North Star); Guy de Maupassant; Des "Terroristes" a la Retraite ("Terrorists" in Retirement) (doc) (narr).

TV inc: A Small Rebellion (Emmy-1966).

SIKKING, James B.: Act. b. Los Angeles, Mar 5. e. UCLA, BA. Thea inc: Damn Yankees; Waltz of the Toreadors; Plaza Suite.

Films inc: The Magnificent Seven; Von Ryan's Express; The New Centurions; The Electric Horseman; Capricorn One; Outland; The Star Chamber; Up the Creek; Star Trek III--The Search For Spock; Morons From Outer Space.

TV inc: Turnabout; General Hospital; Hill Street Blues; The Jesse Owens Story; First Steps.

SILLIPHANT, Stirling: Wri-Prod. b. Detroit, Jan 16, 1918. e. USC, BA. Films inc: The Joe Louis Story (sp); Five Against the House (sp, co-prod); Nightfall (sp); Damn Citizen (sp); The Slender Thread (sp); In the Heat of the Night (Oscar-sp-1967); Shaft (prod); Shaft in Africa (sp); The New Centurions (sp); The Poseidon Adventure (sp); The Towering Inferno (sp); The Killer Elite (sp); The Enforcer (sp); Telefon (sp); Circle of Iron; When Time Ran Out (sp).

TV inc: The Naked City; Route 66; Pearl (exec prod-wri); Salem's Lot (exec prod); Fly Away Home (prod-wri); Golden Gate (wri); Hardcase (wri); Travis McGee (wri); Welcome to Paradise (exec prod-wri); Fade Out--The Erosion of Black Images in the Media (int).

SILLS, Beverly (Belle Silverman): Soprano. b. NYC, May 25, 1929. e. Professional Childrens School. On radio at age 3; won Major Bowes Amateur contest at age 6; as child made film shorts with Willie Howard; appeared in musicomedys on road; starred in radio show Our Gal Sunday; debut with NYC Opera 1955; LaScala 1969; Metropolitan Opera 1975; retired 1980 to become dir NYC Opera.

TV inc: NY Philharmonic Young People's Concerts; A Conversation with Beverly Sills; Profile in Music (Emmy-1975); In Performance at Wolf Trap; Dean Martin Christmas Special 1980; John Denver--Music and the Mountains; An All-Star Party For Carol Burnett; TV Academy Hall Of Fame.

(Grammy-Class voc-1976).

SILVA, Henry: Act. b. Puerto Rico, 1928. Films inc: Viva Zapata; Crowded Paradise; A Hatful of Rain; The Bravados; Green Mansions; Cinderfella; The Manchurian Candidate; Johnny Cool; The Return of Mr Moto; The Reward; The Plainsman; The Hills Ran Red; Never a Dull Moment; Five Savage Men; Shoot; Buck Rogers In The 25th Century; Love and Bullets; Thirst; Virus; Almost Human; Alligator; Sharky's Machine; Wrong Is Right; Megaforce; Chained Heat; Le Marginal (The Outsider); Cannonball Run II; Lust In The Dust; Escape From The Bronx; Code Of Silence.

TV inc: Numerous segs; Happy.

SILVER, Franelle: Wri. b. Toronto, Canada, Sep 12, 1952. TV inc: Excuse My French; David Steinberg Show; Custard Pie; The Carol Burnett Show (Emmy-1978); Donny & Marie; Three's Company; The Kristy & Jimmy McNichol Special; The Tim Conway Special.

SILVER, Joan Micklin: Dir-Wri. b. Omaha, NE, May 24, 1935. e. Sarah Lawrence Coll. Films inc: Limbo (sp); Hester Street (sp & dir); Bernice Bobs Her Hair (sp & dir); Between the Lines (dir only); On the Yard (prod); Head Over Heels (sp & dir).

Thea inc: Maybe I'm Doing It Wrong; Album.

SILVER, Joe: Act. b. Chicago, Sep 28, 1922. Films inc: Diary of a Bachelor; Move; They Came from Within; The Apprenticeship of Duddy Kravitz; Rabid; Rhinoceros; You Light Up My Life; Boardwalk; Deathtrap.

Bway inc: Tobacco Road; Doughgirls; Nature's Way; Heads or Tails; You Know I Can't Hear You When the Water's Running; Lenny; The World of Sholom Aleichem.

TV inc: Illusions.

SILVER, Raphael D.: Prod-Dir. H of Joan Micklin Silver. Films inc: Hester Street (prod); Between the Lines (prod); On the Yard (dir).

Thea inc: Maybe I'm Doing It Wrong.

SILVER, Ron: Act. b. NYC, Jul 2, 1946. e. St. Johns U, U of Valencia in Spain. Films inc: Tunnelvision; Welcome to LA; Silent Rage; The Entity; Best Friends; Lovesick; Silkwood; The Goodbye People; Garbo Talks; Oh, God! You Devil.

TV inc: Rhoda; Betrayal; The Stockard Channing Show; Word of Honor; Baker's Dozen.

SILVERMAN, Fred: Exec. b. NYC, 1938. e. OH State U. Started at CBS at age 25 as dir of daytime programs; later served as VP, programs, at CBS-TV for five years; 1975 P, ABC Entertainment; To NBC 1978 as P, & CEO; ousted June 30, 1981; Oct 1982 formed Intermedia Entertainment Co with George Reeves. TV inc (Exec Prod): Farrell For the People; Thicke of the Night; We've Got It Made; Great Day; Big John.

SILVERMAN, Ron: Prod. b. Los Angeles, Jun 13, 1933. e. UCLA, U of AZ. Daily Variety staff, 1957-61; then asst to Mark Robson; later vp Daystar Prodns; vp Ted Mann Prodns.

Films inc: Buster and Billie; Lifeguard; Brubaker; Krull.

TV inc: Stoney Burke; O.K. Crackerby.

SILVERMAN, Syd: Publ-Edtr. b. NYC, Jan 23, 1932. e. Princeton U. S of Sidne Silverman, grandson of Sime Silverman. Publisher, exec ed Variety; P, Daily Variety.

SILVERS, Phil: Act. b. NYC, May 11, 1912. In vaudeville as boy tenor, later comedian in burlesque, then on Bway. Screen debut, 1940, The Hit Parade. Films inc: You're In the Army Now; Diamond Horseshoe; Something for the Boys; Lady Be Good; Roxie Hart; My Gal Sal; Cover Girl; Top Banana; 40 Pounds of Trouble; It's a Mad,

Mad, Mad, Mad World; A Guide for the Married Man; The Strongest Man in the World; The Chicken Chronicles; Won Ton Ton; The Cheap Detective; The Happy Hooker Goes to Washington; There Goes The Bride.

TV inc: The Phil Silvers Show (Sgt. Bilko) *(Emmy-1955; also Best Comedian-1955)*; Goldie and the Boxer.

Bway inc: Yokel Boy; High Button Shoes; Top Banana *(Tony-1952)*; Do Re Mi; How the Other Half Loves; A Funny Thing Happened on the Way to the Forum (rev.) *(Tony-1972)*.

SILVERSTEIN, Elliot: Dir. b. Boston, MA, 1927. e. Boston Coll, BS; Yale, MFA. Films inc: Belle Sommers; Cat Ballou; The Happening; A Man Called Horse; Deadly Honeymoon; The Car.

TV inc: The Firm.

SIMMONS, Jean: Act. b. London, Jan 31, 1929. Screen debut, 1944, Give Us the Moon. Films inc: Hamlet; Caesar and Cleopatra; The Way to the Stars; Great Expectations; Hungry Hill; Black Narcissus; The Woman in the Hall; Blue Lagoon; Hamlet; Adam and Evalyn; Trio; So Long at the Fair; Cage of Gold; The Clouded Yellow; Androcles and the Lion (US film debut); Angel Face; Young Bess; Affair with a Stranger; The Robe; Kiss the Boys Goodbye; The Actress; The Egyptian; Desiree; Footsteps in the Fog; Guys and Dolls; Hilda Crane; This Could Be the Night; Until They Sail; The Big Country; Home Before Dark; Elmer Gantry; Spartacus; The Grass Is Greener; All the Way Home; Life At the Top; Divorce American Style; Mister Buddwing; Rough Night in Jericho; The Happy Ending; Say Hello to Yesterday; Dominique (made in 1977).

TV inc: Beggarman, Thief; The Easter Promise; The Dain Curse; The Home Front; Golden Gate; Jacqueline Susann's Valley of the Dolls 1981; A Small Killing; The Thorn Birds; *(Emmy-Supp-1983)*.

SIMMONS, Matty: Prod. b. Oct 3, 1926. Bd Chmn Nat'l Lampoon Inc. Prod Nat'l Lampoon Radio Hour; Nat'l Lampoon Lemmings; Nat'l Lampoon Show. Films inc: That's Not Funny, That's Sick!; Nat'l Lampoon's Animal House; National Lampoon's Vacation; National Lampoon Goes to the Movies.

TV inc: Delta House; National Lampoon's Hot Flashes.

SIMMONS, Richard Alan: Wri. TV inc: Trials of O'Brien; The Price of Tomatoes *(Emmy-1961)*; Doyle Against the House; Wichita Town; Adventures in Paradise; Columbo (prod); Mrs. Columbo; The Gangster Chronicles.

Films inc: Woman on the Beach; Bengal Brigade; Tanganyika; Looters; The Private War of Major Benson; King and Four Queens; Tarawa Beachhead; Istanbul; The Trap; Juggernaut; The Island of Dr. Moreau; The Sentinel.

SIMON & GARFUNKEL: See SIMON, Paul & GARFUNKEL, Art.

SIMON, Carly: Singer-Comp. b. Jun 25. Studied with Pete Seeger. Films inc: No Nukes; In Our Hands (doc).

Albums inc: Carly Simon *(Grammy-New Artist-1971)*; Playing Possum; The Best of Carly Simon; Another Passenger; The Boys in the Trees.

SIMON, Danny: Wri-Dir. b. NYC, Dec 18, 1920. Wrote in collab with brother, Neil, from 1947-56.

TV inc: Kraft Music Hall; What's Happening (dir); Blondes vs. Brunettes (wri).

Thea inc: Sunshine Boys (dir London prod).

SIMON, Melvin: Exec. b. NYC. e. CCNY. After WW2 service worked as salesman for shopping center development company; formed own firm, developed more than 80 centers; became interested in film industry, formed Mel Simon Productions to function as production firm to attract independent filmakers; Chmn Simon/Reeves/Landsburg Prodns, Nov. 1981 to Aug, 1983 when company dissolved.

Films (as exec prod) Dominique; When a Stranger Calls; The Runner Stumbles; Scavenger Hunt; Cloud Dancer; The Stunt Man; My Bodyguard; Zorro, The Gay Blade; Chu Chu and the Philly Flash; Porky's; Porky's II--The Next Day; Uforia; Wolf Lake; Porky's Revenge.

SIMON, Neil: Plywri. b. NYC, Jul 4, 1927. Wrote comedy for radio with brother, Danny. supplied sketches, other material for Phil Silvers Arrow Show for TV, 1948; wrote material for Tallulah Bankhead Show; contributed sketches to Broadway show Catch a Star; New Faces of 1956. Wrote first full-length Broadway show, Come Blow Your Horn, 1961; also wrote for Garry Moore Show; The Sid Caesar Show; Jackie Gleason; Red Buttons.

Plays: Barefoot in the Park; The Odd Couple *(Tony-1965)*; Sweet Charity; The Star Spangled Girl; Plaza Suite; Promises, Promises; Last of the Red Hot Lovers; The Prisoner of Second Ave; The Sunshine Boys; God's Favorite; The Gingerbread Lady; Chapter Two; California Suite; I Ought to Be in Pictures; They're Playing Our Song; Fools; Brighton Beach Memoirs; Biloxi Blues *(Tony-1985)* *(Tony-special-1975)*.

Films inc: After the Fox; Barefoot in the Park; The Odd Couple; Sweet Charity; The Out-of-Towners; Last of the Red Hot Lovers; The Prisoner of Second Avenue; Plaza Suite; The Sunshine Boys; Murder by Death; The Goodbye Girl; The Cheap Detective; Chapter Two; Seems Like Old Times; Only When I Laugh (& prod); I Ought To Be In Pictures (& prod); Max Dugan Returns (& prod); The Slugger's Wife.

SIMON, Paul: Singer-Comp. b. Newark, NJ, Nov 8, 1942. Sngwri half of the Simon and Garfunkel (Art) duo. The vocal and instrumental duo split in 1970 to embark on separate careers. Prior to breaking up they appeared in concerts inc Carnegie Hall.

Films inc: The Graduate (songs); Annie Hall (act); One-Trick Pony (wri-act-comp).

TV inc: The Paul Simon Special *(Emmy-wri-1978)*.

(Grammys-(9)-Song of Year-1970; Record of Year-1968, 1970; Album of Year-1970, 1975; Arr Accomp Vocalist-1970; Contemporary Song-1970; Pop Voc-1975; Film Score-1968).

SIMONE, Simone: Act. b. Marseilles, France, Apr 23, 1914. On screen from 1931 in France. Films in U.S. inc: Girls' Dormitory; Seventh Heaven; Love and Hisses; Ladies in Love; Josette; The Human Beast; All That Money Can Buy; The Cat People; Tahiti Honey; Johnny Doesn't Live Here Anymore; Mademoiselle Fifi; Curse of the Cat People; La Ronde; Pit of Loneliness; House of Pleasure; Double Destiny; The Extra Day.

SIMONS, Susan A.: Exec. b. Lincoln, NE., Nov. 12. e. CA. State Northridge. Started as prodn asst with Ralph Edwards Prodns. working various game shows; joined Heatter-Quigley as prodn asst; later prodn asst on Bob Hope Specials before joining NBC as mgr Compliances and Practices; dir daytime pgmg; May, 1983, vp Daytime for Columbia Pictures TV; Sept, 1984 added dvlpt of first-run syndication to her duties.

SIMPSON, Donald C.: Exec. b. Anchorage, AK, Oct 29,1945. e. U of OR, BA, MA. 1969 With Jack Woodell Agency as acct exec handling WB; 1971 joined WB as ad-mktg exec; 1975 to Par as prodn exec; 1977 prodn vp; 1978 top prodn vp; 1980 SR vp chg wldwde prodn; April 1981, Prodn Pres for motion picture div; June 1982 resd to enter indie Prodn. Films inc: (Prod) Flashdance; Thief Of Hearts; Beverly Hills Cop.

SIMPSON, O.J. (Orenthal James Simpson): Act. b. San Francisco, CA, Jul 1947. e. USC. Star collegiate and professional football player; Heisman Trophy Winner 1968; Films inc: The Towering Inferno; The Klansman; Killer Force; Cassandra Crossing; Capricorn 1; Firepower; Hambone and Hillie.

TV inc: A Killing Affair; Roots; Goldie and the Boxer (& exec prod); Detour to Terror (& exec prod); The Golden Moment-An Olympic Love Story; Goldie and the Boxer Go To Hollywood (& exec prod); Bob Hope's Stand Up and Cheer For the National Football League's 60th Year; High Five (exec prod); Cocaine and Blue Eyes (& exec prod); America's Heroes--The Athlete Chronicles.

SINATRA, Frank: Perf. b. Hoboken, NJ, Dec 12, 1915. Singer on radio; joined Harry James orch., later Tommy Dorsey. Appeared as band vocalist in films Las Vegas Nights; Ship Ahoy; Reveille with Beverly. Debut as act 1943, Higher and Higher. Films inc: Step Lively; Anchors Aweigh; Words and Music; It Happened in Brooklyn; Miracle of the Bells; The Kissing Bandit; Take Me Out to the Ball Game; On the Town; Double Dynamite; Meet Danny Wilson; From Here to Eternity *(Oscar-supp-1953)*; Suddenly; The Man With the Golden Arm; Young at Heart; Not as a Stranger; Johnny Concho; High Society; The Pride and the Passion; The Joker Is Wild; Pal Joey; Kings Go Forth; Some Came Running; A Hole in the Head; Never So Few;

Can Can; Ocean's 11; Pepe; The Devil at Four O'Clock; Sergeants 3 (& prod); The Road to Hong Kong; The Manchurian Candidate; The List of Adrian Messenger; Come Blow Your Horn; Four For Texas; Robin and the Seven Hoods; None But the Brave (dir); Von Ryan's Express; Marriage On the Rocks; The Oscar; Cast A Giant Shadow; Assault on a Queen; The Naked Runner; Tony Rome; The Detective; Lady in Cement; Dirty Dingus Magee; That's Entertainment (narr); The First Deadly Sin (& exec prod); Cannonball Run II.

TV inc: Frank Sinatra-A Man and His Music *(Emmy*-1966); The Frank Sinatra Show; Contract on Cherry Street; Sinatra-The First 40 Years; Sinatra, The Man and His Music; Natalie--A Tribute To A Very Special Lady; Sinatra--Concert for the Americas (cable); Salute to Lady Liberty; All Star Party For Lucille Ball.

(Grammys-(7)-Album of the Year-1959, 1965, 1966; Vocal-1959, 1965, 1966; Record of the Year-1966).

(Oscar-special-1945). *(Jean Hersholt Humanitarian Award-1970).*

SINATRA, Frank, Jr: Singer-Act. b. Jersey City, NJ, Jan 10, 1944. Performs in niteries. Films inc: A Man Called Adam. TV inc: Confessions of a Lady Cop.

SINATRA, Nancy, Jr: Act. b. Jersey City, NJ, Jun 8, 1940. D of Frank Sinatra, Sr. On screen from 1964. Films inc: For Those Who Think Young; Marriage on the Rocks; Get Yourself a College Girl; Last of the Secret Agents?; The Ghost in the Invisible Bikini; The Wild Angels; Speedway.

SINCLAIR, Madge: Act. b. Kingston, Jamaica, Apr 28, 1938. e. Shortwood Teacher Training Coll, Jamaica. School teacher for six years. Films inc: Leadbelly; I Will, I Will...for Now; Conrack; Convoy; Uncle Joe Shannon.

TV inc: The Mad Messiah; Jimmy B and Andre; I Know Why the Caged Bird Sings; Roots; The Autobiography of Miss Jane Pitman; Trapper John; Victims; Three Eyes; Backwards--The Riddle of Dyslexia.

SINDEN, Donald: Act. b. Plymouth, England, 1923. In repertory; joined Shakespeare Memorial Theatre, then Old Vic Company. Thea inc: London Assurance; Haebeas Corpus; Shut Your Eyes and Think of England; Present Laughter; Two Into One.

Films inc: The Cruel Sea; Mogambo; Doctor in the House; Simba; Eyewitness; Doctor at Large; Decline and Fall; The National Health; The Captain's Table; Your Money or Your Wife; The Siege of Sidney Street; The Day of the Jackal; The Island at the Top of the World; That Lucky Touch.

TV inc: All's Well That Ends Well.

SINGER, Carla: Exec. b. Winnipeg, Canada, Mar 4, 1945. e. Brandeis U, BA; Hebrew University, MA. Started 1970 as asst dir CTV Network, Toronto; 1972, dir City-TV, Toronto; 1973, dir-wri BBC-TV, London; 1976, exec prod Westinghouse TV; prod PM Magazine, Everyday; Dir dvlpmt & crea Hour Magazine; Jun 1980, dir dramatic dvlpmt CBS-TV; 1983, VP.

SINGER, Marc: Act. b. Vancouver, B.C., Canada. e. U of Washington, BFA. TV inc: The Taming of the Shrew; 79 Park Avenue; Roots--The Second Generation; Things in Their Season; Something for Joey; Journey From Darkness; The Two Worlds of Jenny Logan; The Contender; For Ladies Only; Paper Dolls; V; V (The Series).

Films inc: If You Could See What I Hear; The Beastmaster.

SINGER, Robert: Prod. b. Nyack, NY. e. NYU, BS. TV inc: Lacy and the Mississippi Queen; Dog and Cat series; Night Stalker; 7 Wide World of Entertainment Specials; The Children Nobody Wanted; Three Eyes; Sadat; V--The Final Battle (exec prod); V (The Series)-(exec prod).

Films inc: Independence Day; Cujo.

SINGLETON, Penny (Dorothy McNulty): Act. b. Philadelphia, PA, Sep 15, 1908. On screen from 1930 as Dorothy McNulty in: Love in the Rough; Good News; After the Thin Man; as Penny Singleton from 1938 in Swing Your Lady; Men Are Such Fools; Boy Meets Girl; The Chump; The Mad Miss Manton; Blondie (series of 28); Go West Young Lady; Footlight Glamor; Young Widow; The Best Man.

Bway inc: No, No, Nanette; Follow Through; Hey Nonny Nonny.

SIPES, Donald: Exec. b. 1928. e. OH U, BA; Harvard, LLB. Joined NBC legal staff, NY, 1957; 1961 with Frank Cooper Agency; 1963, VP Bus Aff & Planning, CBS; 1974, sr exec VP ICM; 1975, VP Universal TV; 1976, sr vp; 1977, sr vp U TV & corp VP MCA; 1978, P U TV; 1981, P & COO MGM; with MGM purchase of UA 1982 also became sr vp MGM/UA Entertainment Co; Feb 1983, chmn & CEO United Artists Corp; resd Aug, 1983; Nov. 1983, P. Lorimar Distribution Group.

SJOMAN, Vilgot: Dir. b. Sweden, 1924. Films inc: 491; I Am Curious Blue; I Am Curious Yellow; Blushing Charlie; Linus (& wri); Jag Rodnar (I'm Blushing) (& prod-wri); The Karlsson Brothers; Till Sex Do Us Part; The Garage; Tabu.

SKALA, Lilia: Act. b. Vienna. Films inc: Call Me Madam; Lilies of the Field; Ship of Fools; Caprice; Charly; Deadly Hero; Roseland; Heartland; Flashdance; Testament.

TV inc: Search for Tomorrow; Guiding Light; Secret Storm; Valiant Lady; Eleanor and Franklin; Sooner or Later.

Bway inc: Letters to Lucerne; With a Silk Thread; Call Me Madam; Diary of Anne Frank; Zelda; Forty Carats; Medea and Jason; The Survivor.

SKELTON, Red (Richard): Act. b. Vincennes, IN, July 18, 1913. Joined medicine show at age 10. Later in showboat, stock, minstrel shows, vaudeville, burlesque, circus. On radio from 1936, TV from 1950. Screen debut, 1939, Having Wonderful Time.

Films inc: Flight Command; Lady be Good; Dr. Kildare's Wedding Day; Ship Ahoy; Maisie Gets Her Man; Panama Hattie; DuBarry Was A Lady; Whistling in the Dark; Bathing Beauty; Ziegfeld Follies; Merton of the Movies; Neptune's Daughter; The Fuller Brush Man; Three Little Words; A Southern Yankee; The Clown; Public Pigeon No. 1; Those Magnificent Men in Their Flying Machines.

TV inc: The Red Skelton Show *(Emmy*-Comedian-1952; wri-1961); Red Skelton--A Royal Command Performance.

SKERRITT, Tom: Act. b. Detroit, MI, Aug 25, 1933. Films inc: War Hunt; M*A*S*H; Fuzz; Turning Point; Ice Castles; Alien; Savage Harvest; Silence of the North; Fighting Back; A Dangerous Summer; The Dead Zone.

TV inc: Ryan's Four; The Calendar Girl Murders; The Last Day; A Touch Of Scandal.

SKIRBALL, Jack H.: Prod. b. Homestead, PA, Jun 23, 1896. e. Western Res U, BA; Hebrew Union Coll, LLD. Gen. Mgr charge Prod. Educational Films, NY, 1939-39; Ind. film producer, Hollywood, 1933-46; Pres, Skirball-Manning Prods, 1946-54;

Films inc: The Howards of Virginia (asso prod); Half a Sinner; Miracle on Main Street; The Lady from Cheyenne; This Woman Is Mine; Saboteur; Shadow of a Doubt; It's in the Bag; Guest Wife; So Goes My Love; The Secret Fury; Payment on Demand; A Matter of Time.

SKOLIMOWSKI, Jerzy: Dir. b. Poland, 1938. Films inc: Identification Marks--None; Walkover; The Barrier; The Departure; Hands Up; Dialogue; The Adventures of Gerard; Deep End; King, Queen, Knave; The Shout; Die Faelschung (Circle of Deceit) (act); Moonlighting (& wri-prod); Success Is the Best Revenge.

SKOLSKY, Sidney: Columnist-Prod. b. NYC, May 2, 1905. e. NYU. Bway press agent before becoming columnist for NY Sun, later NY Daily News; NY Mirror; United Feature Syndicate. Films inc: The Daring Young Man (wri); The Jolson Story (prod); The Eddie Cantor Story (prod).

TV inc: Hollywood--The Golden Era (prod).

(Died May 3, 1983).

SKOURAS, Plato A.: Prod. b. NYC, Mar 7, 1930. e. Yale, BA. S of late Spyros P Skouras. In theatre mgt 1952-54 with Skouras Theatres; joined Fox 1954 in story dept, later prodn asst; wrote narr for (short) Gods of the Road.

Films inc: Apache Warrior; Under Fire; Sierra Baron; Villa!; Frances of Assisi.

SLADE, Bernard (B.S. Newbound): Wri. b. Canada, May 2, 1930. Films inc: Stand Up and Be Counted; Same Time, Next Year; Tribute.

Plays inc: Simon Says Get Married; A Very Close Family; Same Time, Next Year; Tribute; Romantic Comedy; Special Occasions; Fatal Attraction.

TV inc: Bewitched; Love on a Rooftop; The Flying Nun; The Partridge Family; Mr Deeds Goes to Town; The Bobby Sherman Show; The Girl with Something Extra; Everything Money Can't Buy.

SLATE, Jeremy: Act. Films inc: Wives and Lovers; I'll Take Sweden; The Sons of Katie Elder; Devil's Brigade. TV inc: Mr. Horn.

SLAVIN, George F.: Wri. b. Newark, NJ, Mar 2, 1918. e. Bucknell U, Yale U. Films inc: Intrigue; The Nevadan; Mystery Submarine; Peggy; Red Mountain; City of Bad Men; Weekend with Father; Thunder Bay; Rocket Man; Smoke Signal; Uranium Boom; Desert Sands; The Halliday Brand; Son of Robin Hood.

SLESAR, Henry: Wri. b. Brooklyn, NY, Jun 12, 1927. TV inc: Man From U.N.C.L.E.; Name of the Game; Batman; Here Come the Brides; Alfred Hitchcock Presents; Executive Suite (pilot); Two On a Guillotine; Murders in the Rue Morgue; The Edge of Night (since 1968) (Emmy-1974); Alfred Hitchcock Presents.

SLEZAK, Erika: Act. b. Los Angeles, Aug 5, 1946. D of the late Walter Slezak. Member of the Milwaukee Repertory Co. TV inc: One Life to Live (Emmy-1984).

SLEZAK, Walter: Act. b. Vienna, Austria, May 3, 1902. Hollywood debut 1942, Once Upon a Honeymoon.

Films inc: This Land Is Mine; Cornered; The Fallen Sparrow; Lifeboat; The Pirate; The Princess and the Pirate; The Yellow Cab Man; Salome; Riffraff; Sinbad the Sailor; Call Me Madam; The Miracle; The Gazebo; Come September; Emil and the Detectives; The Wonderful World of the Brothers Grimm; Dr. Coppelius; Black Beauty; The Mysterious House of Dr. C.

Bway inc: Meet My Sister; Music in the Air; Ode to Liberty; May Wine; I Married an Angel; My Three Angels; Fanny (Tony-1955); The Gazebo.

Opera inc: La Perichole; The Gypsy Baron; Die Fledermaus.
(Died Apr 21, 1983).

SLICK, Grace: Singer. b. Chicago, IL, Oct 30, 1939. e. U of Miami. With Great Society; Jefferson Airplane; Jefferson Starship before solo.

SLOAN, Michael: Prod-Wri. b. NYC, Oct 14, 1946. e. Arts Educational Trust, England. S of Paula Stone and the late Mike Sloan. Films inc: Hunted; Assassin; Moments. TV inc: Colombo (wri); Switch (wri); McCoy (wri); Harry-O (wri); McCloud; Quincy; Hardy Boys Mysteries; Nancy Drew Mysteries; Evening in Byzantium; Sword of Justice; B J and the Bear (wri-exec prod); Return of the Man from U.N.C.L.E. (wri-exec prod); The Master (exec prod-crea-wri).

Plays inc: Underground.

SLOCOMBE, Douglas: Cin. b. London, Feb. 10, 1913. Films inc: Dead Of the Night; The Captive Heart; Hue and Cry; It Always Rains On Sunday; Saraband; Kind Hearts and Coronets; Cage Of Gold; The Lavender Hill Mob; The Man In the White Suit; Mandy; The Titfield Thunderbolt; Ludwig II; Lease On Life; The Smallest Show on Earth; The Mark; The L-Shaped Room; Freud; The Servant; A High Wind In Jamaica; The Blue Max; Promise Her Anything; Vampire Killers; Boom; The Lion In Winter; The Italian Job; The Buttercup Chain; The Music Lovers; Murphy's War; Travels With My Aunt; Jesus Christ Superstar; The Great Gatsby; Rollerball; Hedda; The Sailor Who Fell From Grace With the Sea; Nasty Habits; Julia; Close Encounters Of the Third Kind; Caravans; Lost and Found; The Lady Vanishes; Raiders Of the Lost Ark; The Pirates of Penzance; Water.

TV inc: Love Among the Ruins.

SMALL, William J.: News exec. b. Chicago, IL, Sep 20, 1926. e. U of Chicago, MA. News dir WLS Chicago, 1951; News dir WHAS AM-TV, Louisville, 1956; news dir & Washington bureau chief CBS 1962; sr vp CBS News 1974; VP CBS Inc., 1978; Pres NBC News, 1979; resd Mar 1982; Sept 1982 P & COO United Press Int'l.

SMIGHT, Jack: Dir. b. Minneapolis, MN, Mar 9, 1926. e. U of MN, BA. Began as disc jockey; into tv as Dir One Man's Family 1953. TV inc: Eddie (Emmy-1959); Banacek; Columbo; Roll of Thunder, Hear My Cry; Remembrance of Love.

Film dir debut, I'd Rather Be Rich. Films inc: The Third Day; Harper; Kaleidoscope; The Secret War of Harry Frigg; No Way to Treat a Lady; Strategy of Terror; The Illustrated Man; The Traveling Executioner; Rabbit Run; Dr. Frankenstein; Frankenstein--The True Story; Airport 1975; Midway; Damnation Alley; Fast Break; Loving Couples.

SMITH, Alexis: Act. b. Penticton, Canada, Jun 8, 1921. Films inc: Dive Bomber; Gentleman Jim; The Animal Kingdom; The Constant Nymph; Night and Day; Of Human Bondage; Any Number Can Play; Split Second; The Sleeping Tiger; The Young Philadelphians; Once Is Not Enough; The Little Girl

TV inc: Kennedy Center Tonight--Broadway to Washington!; A Death In California.

SMITH, Charles Martin: Act. b. Van Nuys, CA., Oct. 30, 1953. Films inc: The Culpepper Cattle Company; Fuzz; American Graffiti; More American Graffiti; Pat Garrett and Billy The Kid; The Buddy Holly Story; Never Cry Wolf (& wri); Starman.

TV inc: Gabe and Walker.

SMITH, Connie: Singer. b. Elkhart, IN, Aug 14, 1941. C&W recording artist. Regular with the Grand Ole Opry.

Films inc: Road to Nashville; Las Vegas Hillbillies; Second Fiddle to a Steel Guitar.

SMITH, Ethel: Organist. b. Pittsburgh, PA, 1921. Theatre, nitery performer. Films inc: Bathing Beauty; George White's Scandals; Twice Blessed; Easy to Wed; Cuban Pete; Melody Time; C'mon, Let's Live a Little; Pigeons.

SMITH, Gary: Prod. b. NYC, Jan 7, 1935. e. Carnegie-Mellon U. Former art dir. TV inc: Kraft Music Hall (Emmy-Art Dir-1962); (as prod) Herb Alpert and the Tijuana Brass; Judy Garland Show; Singer Presents Burt Bacharach (Emmy-1971); James Paul McCartney; Wings; Steve and Eydie - Our Love Is Here To Stay; Barbra Streisand and other Musical Instruments; Merry Christmas, Fred...from the Crosbys; Ann-Margret Smith; Peter Pan; America Salutes Richard Rodgers; Neil Diamond Special; Mac Davis Christmas Special; Ben Vereen...His Roots; Elvis in Concert; Steve and Eydie - From This Moment On; Bette Midler - Ole Red Hair Is Back (Emmy-1978); Rockette - A Holiday Tribute to the Radio City Music Hall; Shirley MacLaine at the Lido; Steve and Eydie Celebrate Irving Berlin (Emmy-1979); An American Christmas Carol; Baryshnikov on Broadway (Emmy-1980); The Cheryl Ladd Special; Merry Christmas From Grand Ole Opry House; Kraft Salutes Disneyland's 25th Anniversary; Ann-Margret---Hollywood Movie Girls; Shirley MacLaine-Every Little Movement (& dir); Uptown-A Tribute to the Apollo Theatre; Linda In Wonderland; Larry Gatlin and the Gatlin Bros. Band; A Special Anne Murray Christmas; Walt Disney--One Man's Dream; Kraft Salutes Walt Disney World's 10th Anniversary; Pavarotti and Friends; Goldie And Kids--Listen To Us; EPCOT Center--The Opening Celebration; Christmas In Washington 1982; Anne Murray's Caribbean Cruise; Sheena Easton--Act One; Live--and in Person; Romeo and Juliet on Ice; Here's Television Entertainment; The Television Academy Hall of Fame; Anne Murray's Winter Carnival--From Quebec; On Stage America; Screen Acotrs Guild 50th Anniversary Celebration (exec prod); Christmas In Washington 1984; Anne Murray--The Sounds Of London; The TV Academy Hall Of Fame 1985.

SMITH, Howard K.: News Commentator. b. Ferriday, LA, May 12, 1914. e. Tulane U, Heidelberg U, Oxford U, Rhodes Scholarship. United Press, London, 1939; UP, Copenhagen; UP, Berlin. Joined CBS News, Berlin corr., 1941; covered Nuremberg trials, 1946; returned to US, moderator, commentator or reporter. Joined ABC News, Jan. 1962, anchorman and commentator. TV inc: The Population Explosion (Emmy-wri-1960); Is Congress Out of Date?; V; V (The Series).

Films inc: The Best Little Whorehouse in Texas.

SMITH, Jaclyn: Act. b. Houston, TX, Oct 26, 1947. Films inc: Bootleggers; Adventurers; Deja Vu.

TV inc: Charlie's Angels; Escape From Bogen County; Nightkill; Jacqueline Bouvier Kennedy; Rage of Angels; George Washington;

Sentimental Journey; The Night They Saved Christmas; Florence Nightingale.

SMITH, Jacqueline: Exec. b. Phila, May 24, 1933. e. Antioch Coll. Wrote and prod more than 100 children's shows for KPIX-TV, San Francisco; in 1963 appointed exec prod, daytime programs, CBS-TV; dir of special projects, Warner Bros; vp, daytime programs, ABC Entertainment since 1977.

SMITH, Kate: Singer. b. Greenville, VA, May 1, 1909. Performed on Broadway in musicals, Honeymoon Lane; Hit the Deck; Flying High. Joined the late Ted Collins for radio programs 1931. Later on NBC-TV in own show.
  Films inc: Hello, Everybody!; This Is the Army.

SMITH, Keely: Singer. b. Norfolk, VA, 1935. Performs in niteries. On screen in: Senior Prom; Thunder Road; Hey Boy! Hey Girl! (Grammy-vocal group-1958).

SMITH, Kent: Act. b. NYC, Mar 19, 1907. Films inc: Cat People; Hitler's Children; This Land Is Mine; The Spiral Staircase; Nora Prentiss; The Fountainhead; The Damned Don't Cry; Comanche; Strangers When We Meet; Moon Pilot; A Distant Trumpet; The Trouble With Angels; Death of a Gunfighter; Pete 'n Tillie; Cops and Robbers.
  TV inc: Peyton Place; Outer Limits; Profiles in Courage.
  Bway inc: Measure for Measure; Sweet Love Remembered; The Best Man; Ah, Wilderness.
  (Died April 23, 1985)

SMITH, Maggie: Act. b. Ilford, England, Dec 28, 1934. On screen from 1957. Films inc: Nowhere to Go; The V.I.P.s; Young Cassidy; Othello; The Honey Pot; Hot Millions; The Prime of Miss Jean Brodie (Oscar-1969); Oh What a Lovely War; Love and Pain; Travels With My Aunt; Murder by Death; California Suite (Oscar-supp-1978); Death on the Nile; Quartet; Clash of the Titans; Evil Under The Sun; The Missionary; Better Late Than Never; A Private Function; Jatszani Kell (Lily In Love).
  Thea inc: Twelfth Night; Share My Lettuce; The Double Dealer; As You Like It; Richard II; The Merry Wives of Windsor; The Private Ear; The Public Eye; Mary, Mary; The Three Sisters; Snap; Private Lives; Virginia.
  TV inc: Much Ado About Nothing; Man and Superman; On Approval; Home and Beauty.

SMITH, Malcolm Neil: Prod. b. London, Jun 6, 1941. Joined Film Australia, 1966. Freelance filmmaker, mainly on documentary films, 1971-72; edited feature film Shirleen Thompson Versus the Aliens; exec prod South Australian Film Corp, responsible for edu pgms and doc, 1973-77.

SMITH, Oliver: Dsgn. b. Wawpawn, WI, Feb 13, 1918. e. PA State U, BA. Bway inc: Rosalinda; The New Moon; On the Town (& co-prod); Billion Dollar Baby (& co-prod); No Exit (& co-prod); Beggar's Holiday; Brigadoon; High Button Shoes; Topaze; Look Ma, I'm Dancin'!; Me and Molly; Gentlemen Prefer Blondes (& co-prod); Paint Your Wagon; Pal Joey; Carnival in Flanders; On Your Toes; Mr. Wonderful; My Fair Lady (Tony-1957); Auntie Mame; Candide; Visit to a Small Planet (& co-prod); West Side Story (Tony-1958); Destry Rides Again; The Sound of Music (Tony-1960); Five Finger Exercise; Camelot (Tony-1961); Becket (Tony-1961); Barefoot in the Park; Hello, Dolly! (Tony-1964); Baker Street (Tony & Special Tony-1965); How Now Dow Jones; Plaza Suite; Last of the Red Hot Lovers; Gigi; Endgame; Mixed Couples; A Talent For Murder; The Golden Age.
  Films inc: Band Wagon; Oklahoma!; Guys and Dolls; Porgy and Bess.
  TV inc: Barefoot In The Park (cable).
  Also des Ballets for American Ballet Theatre and Opera for The Met.

SMITH, Paul J.: Comp-Cond. b. Calumet, MI, Oct 30, 1906. e. UCLA, BA, Juilliard. Films inc: Snow White and the Seven Dwarfs; Pinocchio (Oscar-1940); Saludos Amigos; Victory Through Air Power; Three Caballeros; Song of the South; Cinderella; Perri; 20,000 Leagues Under the Sea; The Parent Trap.
  (Died Jan. 25, 1985)

SMITH, Roger: Act. b. South Gate, CA, Dec 18, 1932. e. U of AZ. H of Ann-Margret. With Meglin Kiddies while in grade school. Films inc: No Time To Be Young; Crash Landing; Operation Madball; Man of a Thousand Faces; Never Steal Anything Small; Auntie Mame; Rogues Gallery. TV inc: (Act) 77 Sunset Strip; Mister Roberts. (Prod) Ann-Margret Olsson; Ann-Margret Smith; Ann-Margret--Rhinestone Cowgirl.

SMITH, William: Act. b. Columbia, MO, Mar 24, 1932. e. Syracuse U, BA; UCLA, MA. Films inc: Darker Than Amber; C.C. and Company; The Losers; Run, Angel, Run; Blood and Guts; Seven; Fast Company; No Knife; Twilight's Last Gleaming; The Frisco Kid; Any Which Way You Can; Red Dawn.
  TV inc: Zero-1; Rich Man, Poor Man (1 & 2); Hawaii 5-O; Tales of the Apple Dumpling Gang; The Jerk, Too; Wildside.

SMITHERS, Jan: Act. b. North Hollywood, CA, Jul 3, 1949. Films inc: Where the Lilies Bloom; Our Winning Season.
  TV inc: WKRP in Cincinnati; The Love Tapes; Legmen.

SMOTHERS, Dick: Act. b. NYC, Nov 20, 1939. Part of comedy team with brother Tom. TV inc: The Smothers Brothers Comedy Hour; Tom and Dick Smothers Brothers Special I (& exec prod); Fitz and Bones; The Secret World Of The Very Young.

SMOTHERS, Tom: Act. b. NYC, Feb 2, 1937. Appeared with brother Dick on The Smothers Brothers Comedy Hour; Tom and Dick Smothers Brothers Special I (& exec prod).
  Films inc: Get to Know Your Rabbit; Silver Bears; The Kids Are Alright; Serial; There Goes The Bride.
  TV inc: The Bear Who Slept Through Christmas (voice); Take One; Fitz and Bones; The Secret World Of The Very Young.

SNODGRESS, Carrie: Act. b. Park Ridge, IL, Oct 27, 1946. e. Northern IL U. Bway inc: All the Way Home; Oh What a Lovely War; Caesar and Cleopatra; Tartuffe.
  Films inc: Rabbit Run; Diary of a Mad Housewife; Fast Friends; The Fury; Homework; Trick Or Treats; A Night in Heaven; Nadia; Pale Rider; Rainy Day Friends.
  TV inc: The Forty-Eight Hour Mile; Silent Night, Lonely Night; The Whole World Is Watching; The Solitary Man; Andrea's Story--A Hitchhiking Tragedy; A Reason To Live.

SNOW, Hank: Singer. b. Liverpool, Nova Scotia, Canada, May 9, 1914. C&W recording artist. Joined the Grand Ole Opry 1950. Originally known as Hank, the Singing Ranger.

SNYDER, Tom: TV pers. b. Milwaukee, WI, May 12, 1936. Newscaster-anchorman WSAV, Savannah, GA.; KTLA, LA; KYW-TV, Philadelphia; KNBC-TV, LA before starting Tomorrow Show 1973. (Emmy-host-1974); departed Tomorrow Show 1981; Sept 1982, anchorman WABC-TV. Other TV inc: The Legionaires Disease; The National Disaster Survival Test; The National Love, Sex and Marriage Test.

SNYDER, William L.: Prod. b. Baltimore, MD, Feb 14, 1920. e. Johns Hopkins U, BA. Cartoons inc: Tom and Jerry; Popeye; Krazy Kat; Munro (Oscar-1960). Short subjects: Self Defense for Cowards; The Game; How to Avoid Friendship; Nudnik. Cartoon features: Alice in Paris; I Am a Woman II; The Daughter.

SOADY, William: Exec. b. Oct 7, 1943. Joined Universal 1970 as Toronto br mgr; later Canadian sls mgr; Jan 1981, VP-GSM Universal Pictures (based in NY); Aug 1981, moved sales op to studio; Nov 1982, exec vp & GSM; Dec. 1983, P of new distribution division.

SOBIESKI, Carol: Wri. (nee O'Brien):b. Chicago, Mar 16, 1939. e. Smith Coll, BA, Trinity Coll. TV inc: Mr Novak; Peyton Place; Neon Ceiling; Dial Hot Line; A Little Game; Reflections of Murder; Sunshine, Sunshine; Amelia; Harry Truman: Plain Speaking; Where the Ladies Go; The Women's Room; Two Marriages.
  Films inc: Casey's Shadow; Honeysuckle Rose; Annie; The Toy; Sylvester.

SOFAER, Abraham: Act. b. Rangoon, Burma, Oct 1, 1896. London stage debut 1925 in Gloriana. Thea inc: (London) Scotch Mist; Black

Velvet; The Man in Dress Clothes; Before Midnight; The Matriarch; Twelfth Night; Hamlet; Street Scene; The Mask and the Face; Victoria Regina; The Witch; The Flies; Skipper Next to God; A Doll's House.

Bway inc: The Matriarch; Victoria Regina; In the Matter of J Robert Oppenheimer.

Films inc: His Majesty O'Keefe; Elephant Walk; The Naked Jungle; Out of the Clouds; Bhowani Junction; Sinbad; King of Kings; Head.

SOGARD, Philip Wayne: Dir. b. Oakland, CA, Apr 6, 1933. e. UC Berkeley. TV inc General Hospital (since 1975) (Emmys-1981, 1982).

SOKOLOW, Diane (nee Schwartz): Exec. b. NYC. e. Temple, BS. W of Mel Sokolow. VP east coast ops Lorimar Prodns 1975; vp east coast prodn WB 1977; resd 1980, formed Sokolow Company with husband to make films for WB release; resumed as VP East Coast prodn WB, March 1982; resd. Oct. 1, 1984; became vp Motown Prodns. Oct. 29, 1984, heading NY office.

SOKOLOW, Mel: Exec. b. NYC, Jan 2, 1934. VP Warner Books 1971; exec vp Casablanca Filmworks 1977; Pres Mel Sokolow & Associates 1977; formed Sokolow Company with wife 1980 to make films for WB release. TV inc: Thin Ice (exec prod).

SOLNICKI, Victor: Exec prod. b. Paris, Jan 12, 1938. Entered film biz as atty; VP Filmplan Int'l. Films inc: The Brood; Hog Wild; Scanners; Dirty Tricks; Gas; Visiting Hours; Videodrome; Covergirl.

SOLO, Robert H.: Prod. b. Waterbury, CT, Dec 4, 1932. e. U of CT, BA. VP Foreign Prodn WB 1971-1974; exec VP prodn WB 1974-1975. Ind prodn 1976. Films inc: Scrooge; The Devils; Invasion of the Body Snatchers; The Awakening; I, The Jury; Bad Boys.

SOLOW, Herbert: Prod-Dir-Wri. b. NYC, Dec 14, 1930. e. Dartmouth. With William Morris Agency as packager; dir pgms NBC; dir daytime pgmg NBC; dir daytime pgmg CBS; vp tv pgmg Par; vp prodn Desilu Studios; tv prodn head MGM, later vp motion picture and tv prodn; P Solow Prodn Co; formed Sherwood Prodns. Films inc: Brimstone and Treacle (prod); Get Crazy (exec prod).

TV inc: Killdozer; Heatwave.

SOLOW, Sidney Paul: Exec. b. Jersey City, NJ, Sep 15, 1910. e. NYU, BS. Chief chemist, Consolidated Film Industries, 1932-36; plant supt, 1937-42; gen mgr, 1942; pres, 1954; chmn, exec committee Consolidated Film Industries. (Oscar-tech-1964).

(Died Jan. 2, 1985)

SOLT, Andrew: Prod-Wri-Dir. b. London, Dec 13, 1947. e. UCLA, BA. Films inc: The Explorers; The Roy Campanella Story; Pioneer Woman; Where Have All the People Gone?; The Cousteau Odyssey Specials; Heroes of Rock 'N Roll; This Is Elvis; It Came From Hollywood (exec prod-dir); E.T. & Friends--Magical Movie Visitors.

TV inc: Prime Times (exec prod); Donald Duck's 50th Birthday; America Censored (prod-dir).

SOLTI, Georg, Sir: Cond. b. Budapest, Hungary, Oct 21, 1912. Mus asst Budapest Opera House 1930-1939; pianist, Switzerland 1939-1945; Gen mus dir Munich State Opera, 1946-1952; Frankfurt City Opera 1952-1960; mus dir Royal Opera House Covent Garden 1961-1971; cond Chicago Symphony 1969-1972; Orchestre de Paris 1972-1975; guest cond London Philharmonic; NY Philharmonic; Vienna Philharmonic; London Symphony; Los Angeles Philharmonic; Salzburgh Festival; Edinburgh Festival; Ravinia Festival; Vienna Staadtsopera; Concertgebouw, Amsterdam.

Films inc: Wagner (mus dir).

(Grammys-22)-Opera Rec-1962, 1966, 1974, 1983; Class Perf Orch-1972, 1974, 1976, 1979, 1981, 1983; Choral Perf-1972, 1977, 1978, 1979, 1982, 1983; Class Album of Year-1972, 1974, 1975, 1979, 1981, 1983).

SOMERS, Suzanne (nee Mahoney): Act. b. San Bruno, CA, Oct 16, 1946. Films inc: Daddy's Gone A-Hunting; American Graffiti; Bullitt; Magnum Force; Yesterday's Hero; Nothing Personal.

TV inc: Three's Company; Zuma Beach; Paul Anka In Monte Carlo; The Princess and the Lumberjack; Ants; High Rollers (Host); It Happened at Lake Wood Manor; Jack and the Princess; John Ritter, Being

of Sound Mind and Body; The Suzanne Somers Special; Super Stars and Classic Cars; Hollywood Wives; Goodbye, Charlie.

SOMMARS, Julie: Act. b. Fremont, NE, Apr 15. Named dir dvlpt Montanus Prodns 1980. TV inc: Harry O; The Rockford Files; Three for the Road; The Governor and J J: The Harness; Shirley; Centennial; Sex and the Single Parent; Cave-In!; Emergency Room.

SOMMER, Elke: Act. b. Berlin, Nov 5, 1940. Screen debut in Germany, 1958. Films inc: Don't Bother to Knock; The Money Trap; Love the Italian Way; The Venetian Affair; Deadlier Than the Male; The Corrupt Ones; They Came to Rob Las Vegas; The Wrecking Crew; Zeppelin; Ten Little Indians; The Net; Lisa and the Devil; On a Dead Man's Chest; It's Not the Size That Counts; The Swiss Conspiracy; The Prisoner of Zenda; The Net; The Double McGuffin; Exit Sunset Boulevard; Der Mann Im Pyjama (The Man In Pyjamas); Invisible Strangler (made in 1979 as The Astral Factor); Jatszani Kell (Lily In Love).

TV inc: Stunt Seven; The Top of the Hill; Inside The Third Reich.

SONDERGAARD, Gale: Act. b. Litchfield, MN, Feb 15, 1900. Films inc: Anthony Adverse (Oscar-supp-1936); Maid of Salem; The Life of Emile Zola; Juarez; The Cat and the Canary; The Mark of Zorro; The Letter; A Night to Remember; Sherlock Holmes and the Spider Woman; The Invisible Man's Revenge; Anna and the King of Siam; The Time of Their Lives; The Return of a Man Called Horse; Pleasantville; Echoes.

Bway inc: The Crucible; A Family and a Fortune; Goodbye, Fidel.

TV inc: Medical Center; The Cat Creature; Centennial.

SONDHEIM, Stephen: Comp-Wri. b. NYC, Mar 22, 1930. e. Williams Coll. Bway inc: West Side Story; Gypsy; A Funny Thing Happened on the Way to the Forum; Anyone Can Whistle; Do I Hear a Waltz?; Company (Tony-score & lyrics-1971); Follies (Tony-score & lyrics-1972); A Little Night Music (Tony-score-1973); Candide; Pacific Overtures; Sweeney Todd (Tony-score & lyrics-1979); Merrily We Roll Along; Sunday in the Park with George (Pulitzer prize-1985).

TV inc: Topper (wri); Sweeney Todd (cable).

Films inc: The Last of Sheila (sp); Stavisky (score); A Little Night Music; Reds.

(Grammys-(4)-cast albums-1970, 1973, 1980; Song of Year-1975).

SONTAG, David: Prod-Wri. b. NYC, Aug 17, 1934. e. NC State, BS. From 1955 served in various capacities with NBC, CBS and ABC. TV inc: A Christmas Memory; The Love Song of Barney Kempinsky; Shindig; The Las Vegas Show; In Concert; My Father's House; R I P; The Beaks of Eagles; Billy Liar; Phantom of the Open Hearth; Courthouse; The Texans; Mother, Juggs & Speed; Hunter's Moon; Trapper John, MD; sr vp, crea affairs, Fox TV since 1976.

SORDI, Alberto: Act. b. Rome, Jun 15, 1919. Films inc: La Principessa Tarakanova; La Signorina; His Young Wife; The White Sheik; A Day in Court; Two Nights With Cleopatra; Le Rouge et Noir; An American in Rome; Nero's Weekend; Hell in the City; And Suddenly It's Murder; Mafioso; Those Magnificent Men in Their Flying Machines; Made In Italy; An Italian in America; Le Coppie; Contestazione Generale; Polvere di Stelle (& dir-wri); Viva Italia; Le Temoin; Dove vai in Vacanza?; L'Ingorgo; The Hypochondriac; Io e Caterina (& dir-wri); Il Marchese Del Grillo (& wri); Io So Che Tu Sai Che Io So (I Know That You Know That I Know (& wri); In Viaggio Con Papa (My Trip With Papa) (& dir-wri); Il Tassinaro (The Cabbie) (& dir-wri); Tutti Dentro (Put 'Em All In Jail) (& dir-wri); Bertoldo, Bertoldino E Cacasenno.

SOREL, Louise: Act. b. Los Angeles, Aug 6. e. Neighborhood Playhouse, NY. Bway inc: Take Her, She's Mine; Lorenzo; Philadelphia, Here I Come!; The Dragon; The Sign in Sidney Brustein's Window; The Lion in Winter; Man and Boy.

Films inc: The Party's Over; Plaza Suite; P S I Love You; Every Little Crook and Nanny; Where the Boys Are '84.

TV inc: Cliffhangers; The Survivors; Don Rickles Show; When Every Day Was The Fourth of July; The Girl Who Came Gift-Wrapped; Mr Deeds Goes to Town; Ladies Man; Rona Jaffe's Mazes & Monsters; Insight/Leave Me Alone, God; Sunset Limousine; Santa Barbara.

SORVINO, Paul: Act. b. NYC, 1939. Films inc: Where's Poppa?; The Gambler; A Touch of Class; Day of the Dolphin; Made for Each Other; I Will, I Will, For Now; Oh, God!; Slow Dancing in The Big City; Bloodbrothers; The Brink's Job; Shoot It Black, Shoot It Blue!; Lost and Found; Cruising; Reds; Melanie; I, The Jury; That Championship Season; Off the Wall; Turk 182.

TV inc: Bert D'Angelo, Superstar; We'll Get By; Seventh Avenue; Tell Me Where It Hurts; Dummy; A Friend In Deed; Today's FBI (pilot); A Question of Honor; The 113th Edition Ringling Bros; and Barnum & Bailey Circus; Chiefs; My Mother's Secret Life; With Intent To Kill; Chiller; Surviving.

Bway inc: Bajour; An American Millionaire; The Mating Dance; Skyscraper; King Lear.

SOSNIK, Harry: Comp-Cond. b. Chicago, IL, Jul 13, 1906. Quit engineering studies at age 17 to enroll in American Conservatory of Music; pioneer radio mus adv & arr with CBS Chicago; mus dir Decca Records 1937-1944; in Hollywood as film comp-cond and cond-arr-comp for network radio shows; vp chg music ABC-TV 1967-1976, scores inc Producers Showcase, Philco Playhouse.

Songs inc: You Stole My Heart; Lazy Rhapsody; Gayety; Out of the Night; Who Are We To Say; I'd Like to Fall In Love Again; Night Time in Rio.

SOTHERN, Ann (Harriet Lake): Act. b. Valley City, ND, Jan 23, 1909. On screen from 1929. Films inc: Let's Fall in Love; Kid Millions; The Girl Friend; Don't Gamble with Love; Trade Winds; Maisie (series of nine); Dulcy; Panama Hattie; Cry Havoc; April Showers; A Letter to Three Wives; The Judge Steps Out; Blue Gardenia; Chubasco; The Killing Kind; Golden Needles; Crazy Mama; The Manitou; The Little Dragons.

TV inc: Private Secretary; The Ann Sothern Show; Captains and the Kings.

SOUL, David (ne Solberg): Act. b. Chicago, Aug 28, 1943. Films inc: Johnny Got His Gun; Magnum Force; Dog Pound Shuffle.

TV inc: Starsky and Hutch; Salem's Lot; A Country Christmas; Swan Song (& prod); Homeward Bound; Rage; The Manions of America; World War III; Casablanca; The Yellow Rose; Through Naked Eyes; On Top All Over The World; The Key To Rebecca.

SOULE, Olan: Act. b. La Harpe, IL, Feb 28, 1909. Started on radio 1933; then TV. Films inc: Cuban Fireball; Call Me Madam; Dragnet; Prince of Players; Queen Bee; Daddy Long Legs; Girl Happy; The Destructors; The Seven Minutes; The Towering Inferno.

TV inc: Code Red; The 25th Man; The Jerk, Too.

SOUTENDIJK, Renee: Act. b. Holland, 1957. e. Dutch Academy of Dramatic Arts. Films inc: Spetters; Het Meisje Met Het Rode Haar (The Girl With Red Hair); Van De Koele Meren des Doods (The Cool Lakes of Death); De Vierde Man (The Fourth Man); An Bloem; The Cold Room; Abwarts (Out of Order); De Ijssalon (The Ice-Cream Parlor).

TV inc: Inside the Third Reich.

SPAAK, Catherine: Act. b. Belgium, 1945. Films inc: La Trou; The Easy Life; Of Wayward Love; The Little Nuns; The Empty Canvas; Circle of Love; Weekend at Dunkirk; Made In Italy; The Man With the Balloons; Libertine; Take A Hard Ride; Cat O' Nine Tails; The Precarious Bank Teller; Io E Caterina (Catherine and I); Claretta.

SPACEK, Sissy (Mary Elizabeth Spacek): Act. b. Quitman, TX, Dec 25, 1950. Photographer's model. Films inc: Prime Cut; Ginger in the Morning; Badlands; Carrie; Welcome to L.A. Three Women; Coal Miner's Daughter (Oscar-1980); Raggedy Man; Missing; The River.

TV inc: The Girls of Huntington House; Verna--USO Girl; The Migrants; Katherine; Loretta Lynn--The Lady, The Legend.

SPANO, Joe: Act. b. San Francisco, CA., July 7, 1946. e. UC Berkeley, BA. Worked with improv groups the Wing and the Committee in San Francisco, with Berkeley Repertory Theatre. Films inc: American Graffiti; The Incredible Shrinking Woman; The Enforcer; Northern Lights; Fighting Back; Terminal Choice.

TV inc: Hill Street Blues.

SPANO, Vincent: Act. b. NYC, Oct. 18, 1962. Professional debut age 14 in Long Wharf prodn The Shadow Box, later tsfd to Bway. Other thea inc: A Barbershop in Pittsburgh.

Films inc: The Double McGuffin; Over the Edge; The Black Stallion Returns; Baby, It's You; Rumble Fish; Alphabet City; Maria's Lovers.

TV inc: Search for Tomorrow; The Gentleman Bandit; Senior Trip.

SPARKS, Randy: Act-Comp-Prod. b. Leavenworth, KS, Jul 29, 1933. e. UC Berkeley. Toured college campusus, recorded folk mus during the 50s. In 1961, formed his own folk group, the New Christy Minstrels. In 1962 Sparks retired from performing to concentrate on group's business affairs. In 1964, he sold the group to the management firm of Greif-Harris for $2.5 million. After leaving the Minstrels, Sparks founded the Back Porch Majority and the New Society.

Films inc: Advance to the Rear (score); The Singing Nun (score & lyr).

SPARKS, Robert F.: Cin. b. Hollywood, CA, Jan 9, 1930. Films inc: The Hard Ride; Starbird and Sweet William.

TV inc: Lassie; Wonderful World of Disney; Death Stalk; The Honorable Sam Houston; Shazam; Isis; Ark II; The Return of Jimmy Valentine; My Dear Uncle Sherlock; CHiPs; The Circle Family; Double Dare.

SPARV, Camilla: Act. b. Stockholm, 1943. Started as a fashion model. Films inc: The Trouble With Angels; Murderers' Row; Dead Heat on a Merry-Go-Round; Assignment K; The High Commissioner; Downhill Racer; Greek Tycoon; Winter Kills; Caboblanco.

TV inc: Jacqueline Susann's Valley of the Dolls 1981; Massarati and the Brain; Automan.

SPELLING, Aaron: Exec. b. Dallas, Apr 22, 1928. e. Sorbonne; SMU, BA. Act-wri before producing TV series Johnny Ringo, which he created; prod. on Zane Grey Theatre and The Dick Powell Show; partner for 3 years with Danny Thomas in Thomas-Spelling Prods; had own prod co, filming 57 MOW films; joined forces with Leonard Goldberg to form Spelling/Goldberg Prods, 1972-76; pres. Aaron Spelling Prods, Inc, 1977.

TV inc: Mod Squad; The Rookies; Starsky and Hutch; Family; The Beach Bums; The Love Boat; Charlie's Angels; Beach Patrol; Return of the Mod Squad; Love's Savage Fury; The Power Within; Hart to Hart; The French Atlantic Affair; B.A.D. Cats; Waikiki; Murder Can Hurt You; Casino; Aloha Paradise; The Best Little Girl In the World; Dynasty; Strike Force; Sizzle; T.J. Hooker; Massarati and the Brain; Scared Silly; Matt Houston; The Wild Women of Chastity Gulch; Don't Go To Sleep; At Ease; Shooting Stars; Venice Medical; Arthur Hailey's "Hotel"; The Making of a Male Model; Dean Martin's Celebrity Roast; Dark Mirror; Velvet; Glitter; Finder Of Lost Loves; Mr. Mom (crea cnslt); MacGruder & Loud; Hollywood Wives; International Airport.

Films inc: Mr. Mom.

SPELMAN, Sharon: Act. b. Los Angeles, May 1. e. U of IA, BA. TV inc: Search for Tomorrow; Friends and Lovers; The Cop and the Kid; Deadly Game; The Girl in the Empty Grave; Angie; Number 96. Terror Among Us; The Big Stuffed Dog; Twirl; Second Edition.

SPENCER, Dorothy: Film edtr. b. Covington, KY, Feb 2, 1909. Has edited 74 films inc: Stagecoach; To Be Or Not To Be; Lifeboat; A Tree Grows In Brooklyn; My Darling Clementine; The Snake Pit; Down To the Sea In Ships; Decision Before Dawn; Man in the Gray Flannel Suit; A Hatful of Rain; The Young Lions; The Journey; From The Terrace; Cleopatra; Von Ryan's Express; Lost Command; Valley of the Dolls; Earthquake; Concorde--Airport '79.

SPENGLER, Pierre: Prod. b. Paris, 1947. Films inc: Satan's Brew (act); Chinese Roulette; The Prince and the Pauper; Superman; Superman II; Superman III.

SPERLING, Milton: Wri-Prod. b. NYC, Jul 6, 1912. e. CCNY. Films inc: (as wri): Sing Baby Sing; Happy Landing; Thin Ice; I'll Give a Million; Here I Am a Stranger; The Story of Alexander Graham Bell; The Great Profile; Four Sons; (prod): Sun Valley Serenade; Rings on Her Fingers; I Wake Up Screaming; To the Shores of Tripoli; Hello, Frisco, Hello; Crash Dive; Cloak and Dagger; Pursued; My Girl Tisa; Three Secrets; Distant Drums; The Court Martial of Billy Mitchell (& sp); Marjorie Morningstar; The Enforcer; Top Secret Affair; The Bramble Bush; The Battle of the Bulge (& sp); Capt. Apache.

TV inc: Brave New World; The Dream Merchants; Deadly Intentions (supv prod).

SPEWACK, Bella: Wri. b. Hungary, 1899. W of late Sam Spewack. Wrote mostly in collab with husband. Films inc: Clear All Wires; Boy Meets Girl; Cat and the Fiddle; Rendezvous; The Nuisance; Three Loves of Nancy; My Favorite Wife; When Ladies Meet; Weekend at the Waldorf; Move Over Darling; We're No Angels.

TV inc: Mr Broadway; Kiss Me Kate; My Three Angels; The Enchanted Nutcracker.

Plays inc: Solitaire Man; Poppa; Clear All Wires; Spring Song; Boy Meets Girl; Leave It to Me; Kiss Me Kate (Tony-1949); My Three Angels; Festival.

SPHEERIS, Penelope: Dir. b. 1945. e. UCLA Film School. TV inc: Saturday Night Live (prod). Films inc: Real Life (prod); The Decline of Western Civilization (doc); Suburbia; The Boys Next Door.

SPIEGEL, Sam: Prod. b. Poland, Nov 11, 1903. e. U of Vienna. Films inc: Tales of Manhattan; The Stranger; We Were Strangers; The Prowler; When I Grow Up; The African Queen; Melba; On the Waterfront (Oscar-1954); The Strange One; The Bridge on the River Kwai (Oscar-1957); Suddenly Last Summer; Lawrence of Arabia (Oscar-1962); The Chase; The Night of the Generals; The Happening; The Swimmer; Nicholas and Alexander; The Last Tycoon; Betrayal. (Irving Thalberg Award-1963).

SPIELBERG, David: Act. b. Weslaco, TX, Mar 6, 1939. Films inc: The Effect of Gamma Rays on Man-in-the-Moon Marigolds; The Trial of the Catonsville Nine; Choirboys; Newman's Law; Law and Disorder; Hustle; Real Life; Winter Kills; Christine; War And Love.

TV inc: The Rosenberg Trial; American Girls; Bob & Carol & Ted & Alice; The Practice; The Lindbergh Kidnapping Case; King; Wheels; In the Matter of Karen Quinlan; Air Force vs Matlovitch; From Here to Eternity; One Day at a Time; Henderson Monster; Act of Love; The Best Little Girl In the World; Jessica Novak; Insight/Decision To Love; Maid In America; Games Mother Never Taught You; Policewoman Centerfold; Hear Me Cry; Obsessed With A Married Woman; Space.

Bway inc: Trial of the Catonsville Nine; Black Angel; Thieves; Macbird; After the Fall.

SPIELBERG, Steven: Dir. b. Cincinnati, OH, Dec 18, 1947. e. CA State Coll. Made home movies as child. First professional work, Amblin', a 20-minute short, impressed Universal enough to sign him to contract. Wrote story for Ace Eli and Rodger of the Skies. Films inc: The Sugarland Express; Jaws; Close Encounters of a Third Kind (dir. & sp); I Wanna Hold Your Hand; 1941; The Blues Brothers (act); Used Cars (exec prod); Raiders of the Lost Ark; Continental Divide (exec prod);Poltergeist (Exec prod-wri); E.T. The ExtraTerrestrial (& prod); Twilight Zone...The Movie (& prod); Indiana Jones and the Temple of Doom; Gremlins (exec prod); Room 666 (doc-int); The Goonies (exec prod-story); Back To The Future (exec prod).

TV inc: Night Gallery; Something Evil; The Name of the Game; The Psychiatrist; Marcus Welby, M.D.; Duel.

SPIGELGASS, Leonard: Wri. b. NYC, Nov 26, 1908. e. NYU. Started as reader and story ed., 1930. Films inc: Princess O'Hara; Letter of Introduction; The Boys from Syracuse; Tight Shoes; Butch Minds the Baby; All Through the Night; The Perfect Marriage; So Evil, My Love; I Was a Male War Bride; Mystery Street; Because Your Mine; Athena; Deep In My Heart; Silk Stockings; 10,000 Bedrooms; Pepe; A Majority of One; Gypsy.

TV inc: Eloise; The Helen Morgan Story.

Plays inc: A Majority of One; Dear Me, the Sky is Falling; A Remedy for Winter; The Wrong Way Light Bulb; Look to the Lillies; Mack and Mabel.

(Died Feb. 15, 1985)

SPIKINGS, Barry: Prod. b. Boston, England, Nov 23, 1939. Chmn Elstree Studios; Chmn & CEO EMI Film & Theatre Corp June 1979 to Jan. 1983. Films inc: Conduct Unbecoming; The Man Who Fell to Earth; Convoy; The Deer Hunter (Oscar-1978).

SPINETTI, Victor: Act. b. Monmouthshire, England, Sep 2, 1933. e. Coll of Music and Drama, Cardiff. Thea inc (London): Expresso Bongo; Candide; Make Me An Offer; Oh, What A Lovely War!; Merry Roosters pantomime (matinees); The Odd Couple; In His Own Write (& co-adapt, dir); Cat Among the Pigeons; Windy City. (Dir) Shirley Abicair's Evening; Off The Peg (& devised); Let's Get Laid; Deja Revue; Come Into My Bed; The Biograph Girl.

(Bway) Oh, What A Lovely War! (Tony-supp-1965); La Grosse Valise; The Philanthropist.

Films inc: Hard Day's Night; The Wild Affair; Help!; The Taming of the Shrew; Hieronymous Merkin; Under Milkwood; The Return of the Pink Panther.

TV inc: Infidelities; Mistral's Daughter.

SPINNER, Anthony: Prod. b. NYC, Apr 4, 1930. e. Hofstra U, BA. VP pgm dvlpt 20th Fox TV May 1979; crea aff vp June 1980; Sep 1980 Sr prodn vp Playboy Prodns. TV inc: Dakotas; Invaders; Man from U.N.C.L.E.; Dan August; Mod Squad; Search; F.B.I.; Cannon; Caribe; Baretta; Roger and Harry; Return of the Saint; Supertrain; The Last Ninja.

SPIRES, John B.: Exec. b. NYC. Worked as asst thea mgr, in Par lab prior to WW 2; 1946, European rep RKO; 1947, asst foreign mgr United World Films; 1949 in chg 16m foreign ops U; 1950, asst to GM, U-I; 1955. European GM, U-I; 1958, GM foreign film sales MCA-TV; 1961, dir TV sls Europe, MGM-TV; 1964, dir Int'l TV sls MGM-TV; 1973, vp MGM-TV; 1978, sr vp MGM-TV; 1980, formed Phoenix Int'l Associates.

SPIVACK, Murray: Sound Eng. b. NYC, Sep 6, 1903. e. CCNY. Films inc: King Kong; Around the World in 80 Days; West Side Story; My Fair Lady; The Sound of Music; Sand Pebbles; South Pacific; Tora! Tora! Tora!; Hello, Dolly! (Oscar-1969); Patton.

SPIVAK, Lawrence: TV Pers. b. NYC, 1900. e. Harvard. Prod, panel member, TV inc Meet the Press; A Day For History-The Supreme Court and the Pentagon Papers (Emmy-exec prod-1972).

SPOTTISWOODE, Roger: Dir. b. England. Started as film edtr on tv commercials, documentaries. Films inc: (edtr) Straw Dogs; The Getaway; Pat Garrett and Billy the Kid; Hard Times; The Gambler; Who'll Stop the Rain (asso prod); Baby (exec prod). Films as dir inc: Terror Train; The Pursuit of D.B. Cooper; Under Fire.

TV inc: The Renegades.

SPRADLIN, G.D.: Act. Films inc: Will Penny; Zabriskie Point; Tora! Tora! Toral; Number One; Monte Walsh; Hell's Angels; The Hunting Party; The Only Way Home (& prod-dir); The Godfather--Part 2; Apocalypse Now; North Dallas Forty; Wrong Is Right; The Lords of Discipline; Tank.

TV inc: The Jayne Mansfield Story; The Greatest American Hero; Call To Glory; Robert Kennedy & His Times.

SPRINGFIELD, Rick: Act-Singer-Sngwri. b. Australia, Aug 23, 1949. TV inc: General Hospital; An Evening at the Improv; Countdown '81--a Solid Gold Special.

Films inc: Battlestar Galactica; Hard to Hold (act & add'l music). Songs inc: Jessie's Girl. (Grammy-Rock Voc-1981).

SPRINGSTEEN, Bruce: Mus-Sngwri. b. Freehold, NJ, Sep 23, 1949. With various local groups around NJ; formed E Street Band for concert, recording dates. Songs inc: It's Hard to be A Saint in the City; Blinded by the Light; Born to Run.

Albums inc: Greetings from Asbury Park; The Wild, The Innocent and the E Street Shuffle; Born to Run; Darkness on the Edge of Town. Recs inc: Dancing In The Dark (Grammy-rock vocal-1984)

Films inc: No Nukes; Kvish Lelo Motza (Dead End Street).

STACK, Robert: Act. b. Los Angeles, Jan 13, 1919. On screen from 1939. Films inc: First Love; The Mortal Storm; To Be or Not To Be; A Date with Judy; The Bullfighter and the Lady; The High and the Mighty; Written on the Wind; The Tarnished Angels; John Paul Jones; The Last Voyage; The Caretakers; Is Paris Burning?; The Corrupt Ones; Story of a Woman; A Second Wind; 1941; Airplane; Uncommon Valor.

TV inc: The Untouchables (Emmy-1960); Name of the Game; Most Wanted; Undercover With the KKK (narr); Strike Force; George Washington; Hollywood Wivws; The TV Academy Hall Of Fame.

STACY, James (Maurice W Elias): Act. b. Los Angeles, Dec 23, 1936. TV inc: Gunsmoke; Sayonara; Ozzie & Harriet; Lancer; My Kidnapper, My Love (& prod).
Films inc: Something Wicked This Way Comes.

STADLEN, Lewis J.: Act. b. NYC, Mar 7, 1947. Films inc: Parades; Savages; Portnoy's Complaint; Serpico; Between the Lines; Harvest Home; Soup For One; To Be or Not to Be; Windy City.
Bway inc: Minnie's Boys; The Time of Your Life; Play it Again Sam; The Sunshine Boys; An Evening with Groucho Marx; Candide; The Odd Couple.
TV inc: George M; Feeling Good; Judge Horton and the Scottsboro Boys; Hot L Baltimore; One Day At A Time.

STAFFORD, Jim: TV Pers-Singer. b. Eloise, FL, Jan 16. With rock groups, guitarist for Grand Ole Opry before going solo; opening act for Muddy Waters, Freda Payne, others. Albums inc: Jim Stafford; Not Just Another Pretty Foot.
TV inc: The Jim Stafford Show; Those Amazing Animals (host); Music City News' Top Country Hits of the Year (host); Louise Mandrell...Diamonds, Gold & Platinum; Michael Nesmith In Television Parts.

STAFFORD, Jo: Singer. b. Coalinga, CA, 1918. W of Paul Weston. Started with Stafford Sisters singing act, then joined Pied Pipers singing group with Tommy Dorsey; featured soloist with Dorsey before going single 1943, began recording for Capitol, did comedy singing character Cinderella Q Stump on Red Ingles recording Timtayshun; later with Paul Weston created Jonathan and Darlene Edwards recordings (Grammy-comedy-1960).
Radio inc: The Chesterfield Supper Club. TV inc: The Jo Stafford Show.
Recordings inc: (With Pied Pipers) I'll Never Smile Again; There Are Such Things; Street of Dreams. (Solo) Tumbling Tumbleweeds; Shrimp Boats; You Belong to Me; Jambalaya.

STAHL, Lesley: TV newscaster. b. Lynn, MA, Dec 16, 1941. e. Wheaton. Began as wri-researcher for NBC 1968 election unit; 1969, researcher Huntley-Brinkley report from London; 1970, prod-reporter WHDH, Boston; 1972, Washington corr CBS; 1977 co-anchor CBS Morning News. Other TV inc: Eye On the Media-- Business and the Press.

STALLONE, Frank: Act-sing-songwri. b. Philadelphia, PA. b. of Sylvester Stallone. Worked with pickup bands; formed group Valentine before concentrating on act-songwri. Films inc: Rocky; Paradise Alley; Rocky II; Staying Alive.
TV inc: Take it to the Streets; Hotline.
Songs inc: A Case of You; Street Scat; Two Kinds of Love.

STALLONE, Sylvester: Act. b. NYC, Jul 6, 1946. Films inc: The Lords of Flatbush; Capone; Death Race 2000; Farewell My Lovely; Cannonball; Rocky (& sp); F.I.S.T. (& sp); Paradise Alley (& dir-sp); Rocky II (& dir-sp); Nighthawks; Victory; Rocky III (& dir-sp); First Blood (& wri); Staying Alive (prod-dir-wri); Rhinestone (& wri); Rambo--First Blood Part II (& wri); The Heart Of A Champion--The Ray Mancini Story (exec prod).

STAMP, Terence: Act. b. Stepney, England, Jul 22, 1939. Films inc: Billy Budd; Term of Trial; The Collector; The Thief of Baghdad; Modesty Blaise; Far From the Maddening Crowd; Poor Cow; Blue; Theorem; The Mind of Mr. Soames; Divine Creature; Meetings with Remarkable Men; Amo Non Amo; Superman; Superman II; Monster Island; Morte in Vaticano (Death In the Vatican); The Hill; The Company of Wolves.

STAMPLEY, Joe: Act. b. Jun 6, 1943. Singer; recording artist.

STANDER, Lionel: Act. b. NYC, Jan 11, 1908. On screen from 1935. Films inc: The Scoundrel; We're in the Money; Mr. Deeds Goes to Town; The Music Goes Round; The Milky Way; Soak the Rich; A Star Is Born; Guadalcanal Diary; Spectre of the Rose; Call Northside 777; St. Bennie the Dip; The Black Hand; The Gang That Couldn't Shoot Straight; Pulp; The Loved One; The Black Bird; The Cassandra Crossing; New York, New York; The Sensual Man; 1941; The Squeeze.

TV inc: Hart to Hart.

STANFILL, Dennis: Exec. b. Centerville, TN, Apr 1, 1927. e. Annapolis, Oxford U, MA. Entered film industry 1969 as exec vp, finance, Fox & member of Fox board & exec committee; named p, Fox in March, 1971; named chmn, CEO, Sept. 1971; resd June 30, 1981 after policy dispute with new owner Marvin Davis; Jan 1982, Bd Chmn KCET; P Clarendon Capital Corp., investment fund.

STANG, Arnold: Act. b. Chelsea, MA, Sep 28, 1925. Performed on radio, TV, Broadway. Films inc: Seven Days' Leave; So This Is New York; Two Gals and a Guy; The Man with the Golden Arm; Dondi; The Wonderful World of the Brothers Grimm; It's a Mad, Mad, Mad, Mad World; Skidoo!; Hello Down There; The Gang That Couldn't Shoot Straight.
TV inc: Milton Berle; Danny Thomas; Perry Como; Ed Sullivan; Red Skelton; Bob Hope; Danny Kaye; Jackie Gleason; Feeling Good; Chico & the Man; Supersaws & Catfish; The Robert Klein Show; Funtastic World of Hanna-Barbera Arena Show (voice); No Man's Valley (voice).

STANLEY, Kim (Patricia Reid): Act. b. Tularosa, NM, Feb 11, 1921. e. TX State U, U of NM. Films inc: The Goddess; Seance on a Wet Afternoon; Frances; The Right Stuff.
Bway inc: Yes is for a Very Young Man; Montserrat; Seance on a Wet Afternoon; The Chase; The Great Dreamer; Bus Stop; A Clearing in the Woods; Natural Affection; Picnic.
TV inc: Clash by Night; The Travelling Lady; A Cardinal Act of Mercy (Emmy-1963); You Are There; Cat On A Hot Tin Roof (cable).

STANTON, Dr. Frank Nicholas Exec. b. Muskegon, MI, Mar 20, 1908. e. OH Wesleyan, BA; OH State U, PHD. Entered broadcasting in 1934 with CBS, became research dir 1938; named vp, gm CBS 1945; became pres 1946 when William S Paley resigned; vice chmn and chief operating officer 1971-1973 when he retired under company's mandatory policy at age 65; invented first automatic recording device designed to measure radio listening; made two short (silent) films, Some Physiological Reactions to Emotional Stimuli (1932) and Factors in Visual Depth Perception (1936).
(Special Emmy Awards-1960, 1972); (NATAS Directorate Award-1981).

STANTON, Harry Dean: Act. b. KY, Jul 14, 1926. e. Pasadena Playhouse. Films inc: The Proud Rebel; The Adventures of Huckleberry Finn; Pat Garret and Billy the Kid; Rancho Deluxe; Cool Hand Luke; Dillinger; Missouri Breaks; Straight Time; Renaldo and Clara; Wise Blood; Alien; The Rose; Private Benjamin; Escape From New York; One From the Heart; Young Doctors In Love; Christine; Repo Man; Paris, Texas; Uforia; Red Dawn; The Bear; The Care Bears Movie.
TV inc: I Want to Live.

STANWYCK, Barbara (Ruby Stevens): Act. b. NYC, Jul 6, 1907. On screen from 1929. Films inc: The Locked Door; Ladies of Leisure; Ten Cents a Dance; So Big; Shopworn; The Bitter Tea of General Yen; A Message to Garcia; Stella Dallas; Union Pacific; Golden Boy; Meet John Doe; Two Mrs. Carrolls; Ball of Fire; Double Indemnity; Sorry, Wrong Number; The Mad Miss Manton; B.F.'s Daughter; Titanic; Executive Suite; The Maverick Queen; Walk on the Wild Side; The Night Walker.
(Oscar-Honorary-1981).
TV inc: The Barbara Stanwyck Show (Emmy-1961); The Big Valley (Emmy-1966); The Thorn Birds (Emmy-1983).

STAPLETON, Damien: Union Exec. b. Australia, Oct 8, 1946. e. Harvard U. Trade Union Secy, Australian Theatrical and Amusement Employees Assn.

STAPLETON, Jean: Act. b. NYC, Jan 19, 1923. Bway inc: In The Summer House; Damn Yankees; Juno; Bells Are Ringing; Rhinoceros; Funny Girl.
Films inc: Damn Yankees; Bells Are Ringing; Something Wild; Up the Down Staircase; Cold Turkey; Klute; The Buddy System.
TV inc: All in the Family (Emmys-1971, 1972, 1978); Cher; Sammy & Co; The Carol Burnett Show; Aunt Mary; Angel Dusted; Good Evening, Captain; Isabel's Choice; Eleanor, First Lady of the World; The Kennedy Center Honors 1982; A Matter of Sex.

STAPLETON, Maureen: Act. b. Troy, NY, Jun 21, 1925. Films inc: Lonely Hearts; The Fugitive Kind; A View from the Bridge; Bye Bye Birdie; Trilogy; Airport; Plaza Suite; Interiors; Lost and Found; The Runner Stumbles; Arthur Miller on Home Ground; On The Right Track; The Fan; Reds *(Oscar*-supp-1981); Montgomery Clift; Johnny Dangerously; Cocoon.

TV inc: For Whom the Bell Tolls; All the King's Men; Among the Paths to Eden *(Emmy*-1968); Queen of the Stardust Ballroom; Cat on a Hot Tin Roof; Letters From Frank; The Gathering Part 2; The Electric Grandmother; Little Gloria--Happy At Last; Alice in Wonderland; Family Secrets; Sentimental Journey; Night Of 100 Stars II; Private Sessions.

Bway inc: The Playboy of the Western World; The Rose Tattoo *(Tony*-1951); The Crucible; Richard III; The Seagull; Toys in the Attic; Plaza Suite; Norman Is That You?; The Gingerbread Lady *(Tony*-1971); The Glass Menagerie; The Little Foxes.

STARGER, Martin: Exec Prod. b. NYC, May 8, 1932. e. CCNY, BS. P ABC Entertainment, 1972-75; p & CEO Marble Arch Prodns; into indie prodn after company taken over by Robert Holmes a'Court; June 1984 formed Rule/Starger Prodns with Elton Rule. Films inc: Nashville; The Domino Principle (prod); Movie Movie; The Muppet Movie; Saturn 3; Borderline; From the Life of the Marionettes; Raise the Titanic; Hard Country; The Legend of the Lone Ranger; The Great Muppet Caper; The Elephant Man; Barbarosa; The Last Unicorn (ani); Sophie's Choice; Mask (prod).

Bway inc: (Prod) The Sly Fox; Merrily We Roll Along.

TV inc: (prod) Jennifer; Friendly Fire *(Emmy*-1979); All Quiet on the Western Front; Rodeo Girl; Legends of the West--Truth and Tall Tales; The Two of Us; Omnibus; Harry's Battles; Red Flag-The Ultimate Game; Elephant Man; The Return of Marcus Welby, M.D.; Consenting Adult (exec prod).

STARK, Ray: Prod. b. circa 1914. e. Rutgers U. Started as literary agent; joined Famous Artists Agency, where he represented Marilyn Monroe, Lana Turner, Ava Gardner, William Holden, Kirk Douglas and Richard Burton. Resd in 1957 to form indy prodn co which became Seven Arts Prodns; formed Raystar Prodns in 1966.

Films inc: The World of Suzie Wong; Oh Dad, Poor Dad; The Night of the Iguana; This Property is Condemned; Funny Girl; Reflections in a Golden Eye; The Way We Were; Funny Lady; The Owl and the Pussycat; Fat City; Summer Wishes, Winter Dreams; For Pete's Sake; The Sunshine Boys; The Goodbye Girl; The Cheap Detective; California Suite; The Electric Horseman; Chapter Two; Seems Like Old Times; Annie; The Slugger's Wife.

(Irving Thalberg Award-1979).

Bway inc: Funny Girl.

STARK, Wilbur: Prod-Dir. b. Brooklyn, NY, Aug 10, 1922. e. Columbia U. Produced more than 1,500 live tv shows inc Rocky King; Modern Romances; Colonel Humphrey Flack; Brothers Brannagan; Newstand Theatre; Crime With Father; The Lady Is A Cop.

Films inc: (Prod) Vampire Circus; My Lover, My Son; The Thing.

STARR, Ringo (Richard Starkey): Singer-Mus-Sngwri. b. Liverpool, England, Jul 7, 1940. Member of The Beatles (see group listing).

Individual film credits inc: (act) The Last Waltz; Sextette; The Kids Are Alright; Caveman; Give My Regards To Broad Street.

TV inc: Princess Daisy;D.C. Beach Party--A Musical Celebration (cable).

(Grammys-(2)-(in addition to group awards) Film soundtrack, 1970; Album of the Year, 1972).

STARRETT, Jack: Dir-Wri-Act. b. Refugio, TX, Nov 2, 1936. e. U of the South. Films inc: Run Angel Run; The Losers; Cleopatra Jones; The Gravy Train; Race with the Devil; A Small Town in Texas.

TV inc: Mr. Horn; The Survival of Dana; Wildside.

STATLER BROTHERS: C&W group. Members are Harold Reid, Lew Dewitt, Don Reid, Phil Balsley. TV inc: Country Comes Home; An Evening With The Statler Bros--A Salute to the Great Times; Country Comes Alive (hosts); Jerry Reed and Special Friends.

(Grammys-(3)-Contemp Rock n' Roll group & New C&W artist-1965; country voc group-1972).

STEEL, Anthony: Act. b. London, May 21, 1920. e. Cambridge. Films inc: Saraband for Dead Lovers; Marry Me; The Wooden Horse; Laughter in Paradise; The Malta Story; Albert RN; The Sea Shall Not Have Them; Storm over the Nile; The Black Tent; Checkpoint; A Question of Adultery; Harry Black; Honeymoon; The Switch; Hell is Empty; Anzio; Massacre in Rome; The World Is Full of Married Men; The Mirror Crack'd; The Monster Club.

STEELE, Barbara: Act. b. England, 1938. Films inc: Bachelor of Hearts; The Devil's Mask; The Pit and the Pendulum; 8 1/2; The Ghost; Danse Macabre; Revenge of the Blood Beast; The Crimson Cult; Caged Heat; I Never Promised You A Rose Garden; Pretty Baby; Piranha; La Cle sur La Porte.

TV inc: The Winds of War.

STEELE, Tommy (nee Hicks): Act. b. London, Dec 17, 1936. Thea inc: Cinderella; She Stoops to Conquer; Half-a-Sixpence; The Servant of Two Masters; Dick Whittington; Meet Me in London; Hans Anderson; An Evening With Tommy Steele; Singin' In the Rain (& dir).

Films inc: Kill Me Tomorrow; The Tommy Steele Story; The Duke Wore Jeans; Tommy the Toreador; Light Up the Sky; It's All Happening; The Happiest Millionaire; Half A Sixpence; Finian's Rainbow; Where's Jack?

TV inc: Off the Record; The Tommy Steele Spectaculars; Twelfth Night; Tommy Steele In Search Of Charlie Chaplin; Quincy's Quest.

STEENBURGEN, Mary: Act. b. Newport, AR., 1953. Films inc: Goin' South; Rabbit Test; Time After Time; Melvin and Howard *(Oscar*-supp-1980); Ragtime; A Midsummer Night's Sex Comedy; Cross Creek; Romantic Comedy.

STEIGER, Rod: Act. b. Westhampton, NY, Apr 14, 1925. Films inc: Teresa; On The Waterfront; Oklahoma!; The Court Martial of Billy Mitchell; The Harder They Fall; Back From Eternity; Run of the Arrow; Across the Bridge; Cry Terror; Al Capone; Seven Thieves; The Mark; Reprieve; 13 West Street; The Longest Day; The Pawnbroker; The Loved One; Dr. Zhivago; In the Heat of the Night *(Oscar*-1967); The Girl and the General; No Way to Treat a Lady; And There Came a Man; The Illustrated Man; Three Into Two Won't Go; Waterloo; Duck! You Sucker; Happy Birthday, Wanda June; The Lolly-Madonna War; Lucky Luciano; Hennessy; W.C. Fields and Me; F.I.S.T; Dirty Hands; Breakthrough; The Amityville Horror; Love and Bullets; Klondike Fever; The Lucky Star; Lion of the Desert; Cattle Annie and Little Britches; The Chosen; Der Zauberberg (The Magic Mountain); The Naked Face; Wolf Lake (The Honor Guard).

TV inc: Marty; You Are There; The Lonely Wizard; Jesus of Nazareth; Cook and Peary-- The Race to the Pole; The Glory Boys; Hollywood Wives; Evergreen.

STEIN, James R.: Wri. b. Chicago, Jan 9, 1950. e. USC, BA. TV inc: The New Bill Cosby Show; Lily *(Emmy*-1974); The John Denver Special; Phyllis Diller's 102nd Birthday Party; The Smothers Brothers Show; The Captain & Tennille; Fernwood 2 Night; Dick Clark's Good Ol' Days; Peeping Times; The Carol Burnett Show *(Emmy*-1978); The Helen Reddy Special; Steve Allen Comedy Hour; Private Benjamin (prod); Double Trouble (crea-wir-supv prod); The Cracker Brothers.

STEIN, Joseph: Wri. b. NYC, May 30, 1912. e. CCNY, Columbia U. Bway inc: Inside USA; Plain and Fancy; Mr Wonderful; The Body Beautiful; Take Me Along; Fiddler on the Roof *(Tony*-1965); Zorba; We Bombed in New Haven (co-prod); So Long, 174th St.

Films inc: Enter Laughing; Fiddler on the Roof.

TV inc: NBC Comedy Hour; Your Show of Shows; The Sid Caesar Show.

STEIN, Ronald: Comp-Cond. b. St Louis, MO, Apr 12, 1930. e. WA U, AB; Yale U Music School, USC. Pres US Educational Films; Music Dir Los Angeles Music Theatre Co. Films inc: Apache Woman; Gunslinger; Thunder Over Hawaii; Invasion of the Saucer Men; Sorority Girl; Jet Attack; Suicide Battalion; The Littlest Hobo; Legend of Tom Dooley; Dinosaurus!; The Bashful Elephant; Lost Battalion; Of Love and Desire; The Young and the Brave; Boy On Horseback; The Bounty Killer; Requiem for a Gunfighter; Blood Bath; Portrait In Terror; Curse of the Swamp Creatures; Psych-Out; The Rain People; Getting Straight; Prisoners; Frankenstein's Great-Aunt Tillie.

TV inc: Julius Caesar; Galileo Galilei; Nefertiti; Hernan Cortes; Socrates; Dateline Yesterday.

STEINBERG, David: Act-wri-dir. b. Winnipeg, Canada, Aug. 9, 1942. e. U of Chicago; Hebrew Theological College. Started as member of Second City troupe, starring in London and Bway prodns. Bway inc: Little Murders; Carry Me Back to Morningside Heights.

TV inc: Music Scene (crea-wri-co-host); Tonight Show (guest host); David Steinberg Summer Show; Second City--25 Years In Revue.

Films inc: The End (act); Something Short of Paradise (crea-act); Paternity (dir); Going Berserk (dir-co-wri).

STEINBERG, Herb: Exec. b. NYC, Jul 3, 1921. e. CCNY. In U.S. Army during WW II; joined Paramount Pictures, NY, 1947, as publicity mgr; later national exploitation dir. To LA 1956 as studio publicity and adv dir, Para Joined MCA Inc, 1963: was one of planning team of Studio Tour program: currently VP of MCA Recreation Services, in charge of marketing and promotion.

STEINBERGER, Bert: Exec. b. Brooklyn, Jul 11, 1938. Pgm exec ABC entertainment.

STEINER, Fred: Comp-Cond. b. NYC, Feb 24, 1923. e. Oberlin Conservatory of Music, BM, USC. Films inc: First to Fight; Hercules; The Man from Del Rio; St. Valentine's Day Massacre; Time Limit; The Sea Gypsies.

TV inc: Andy Griffith; Danny Thomas; Gunsmoke; Have Gun Will Travel; Hogan's Heroes; Rawhide; The Bullwinkle Show; Hawaii Five-O; Blood Feud.

Songs: Perry Mason Theme; Navy Log March.

STELLING, Jos: Dir-Prod. b. Utrecht, The Netherlands, Jul 16, 1945. Films inc: Mariken Van Nieumeghen; Elckerlijc; Rembrandt Fecit 1669; De Pretenders; De Illusionist.

STEN, Anna (Anjuschka Stenski Sujakevitch): Act. b. Russia, 1908. Films inc: Storm over Asia; Trapeze; The Brothers Karamazov; Tempest; Nana; We Live Again; The Wedding Night; A Woman Alone; Two Who Dared; Exile Express; The Man I Married; So Ends Our Night; They Came to Blow Up America; Chetniks; Let's Live a Little; Soldier of Fortune; The Nun and the Sergeant. Bway inc: Threepenny Opera.

STENO (Stefano Vanzina): Dir-wri. b. Rome, Jan 19, 1915. e. Centro Sperimentale di Cinematografica, Rome. Films inc: (With Mario Monicelli) Al Diavolo la Celebrita; Toto cerca casa; Cops and Robbers; Toto e i Re di Roma; Le Infedeli; Toto e le Donne. (Solo) Toto a colori; Cinema d'Altra tempi; A Day in Court; An American in Rome; Sins of Casanova; Piccola Posta; Nero's Mistress; Susanna tutta Panna; Toto nella Luna; Toto Eva e il Pennello Proibito; Letto a Tre Piazze; Psycosissimo; La Ragazza di Mille Mesi; Toto Diabolicus; Copacabana Palace; I Due Colonnelli; Toto Contro I Quatro; I Gemelli di Texas; Rose Rosse per Angelica; Superdiabolici; La Feldmarescialla; Cose di Cosa Nostra; Flatfoot; Tre Tigri contro Tre Tigri; Flatfoot on the Nile; Amori Miei; Dr Jekyll Jr.

STEPHEN, Susan: Act. b. London, Jul 16, 1931. e. RADA. Films inc: His Excellency; Stolen Face; Treasure Hunt; Father's Doing Fine; The Red Beret; Private Man; For Better, For Worse, as Long as They're Happy; Value for Money; Barretts of Wimpole Street; Carry on Nurse.

TV inc: Little Women; No Hero; Pillars of Midnight.

STEPHENS, James: Act. b. Mount Kisco, NY, May 18, 1951. TV inc: How the West Was Won; The Paper Chase; True Grit; Only the Pretty Girls Die; The Death of Ocean View Park. Films inc: First Monday in October.

STEPHENS, Laraine: Act. b. Oakland, CA. TV inc: Bracken's World; Eischeid; Dallas Cowboys Cheerleaders; Powers; Women in White; Scruples.

Films inc: None But the Brave.

STEPHENS, Robert: Act. b. Bristol, England, Jul 14, 1931. Thea inc: (London) The Crucible; The Good Woman of Setzuan; The Country Wife; The Apollo de Bellac; Yes--And After; The Waters of Babylon; The Entertainer; Epitaph for George Dillon; Look After Lulu; The Wrong Side of the Park; Saint Joan; The Recruiting Officer; Royal Hunt of the Sun; Armstrong's Last Goodnight; Trelawny of the Wells; The Beaux Stratagem; Apropos of Falling Sleet (& dir); Murderer;

(Bway) Epitaph for George Dillon; Sherlock Holmes.

Films inc: Circle of Deception; Pirates of Tortuga; A Taste of Honey; The Inspector; Cleopatra; Morgan; Romeo and Juliet; The Prime of Miss Jean Brodie; The Private Life of Sherlock Holmes; Travels With My Aunt; The Duellists; The Shout; Les Jeux de la Comtesse Dolingen de Gratz (The Games of the Countess Dolingen of Gratz).

TV inc: The Year of the French; The Box Of Delights.

STEPHENSON, Pamela: Act. b. New Zealand. e. Australian National Institute of Dramatic Arts. Thea inc: Richard II; The Threepenny Opera; Pirates of Penzance.

Films inc: History of the World, Part I; Doctors and Nurses; The Secret Policeman's Other Ball; Superman III; The Comeback; Finders Keepers; Bloodbath at the House of Death.

TV inc: Not the Nine O'Clock News (3 yrs).

STERLING, Jan (nee Adriance): Act. b. NYC, Apr 3, 1923. Films inc: Johnny Belinda; Appointment with Danger; Mating Season; Union Station; Caged; Rhubarb; Flesh and Fury; Pony Express; The Vanquished; The High and the Mighty; Women's Prison; Man with the Gun; 1984; The Harder they Fall; Love is a Goldfish Bowl; The Incident; The Minx; First Monday In October.

Bway inc: Bachelor Born; Panama Hattie; John Loves Mary; Front Page; Over 21; Born Yesterday; The November People.

TV inc: Backstairs at the White House; My Kidnapper, My Love; Dangerous Company.

STERLING, Robert (William Sterling Hart): Act. b. Newcastle, PA, Nov 13, 1917. e. U of Pittsburgh. Films inc: Only Angels Have Wings; I'll Wait for You; Somewhere I'll Find You; The Secret Heart; Bunco Squad; Thunder in the Dust; Column South; Return to Peyton Place; Voyage to the Bottom of the Sea.

TV inc: Topper; Ichabod and Me; Beggarman, Thief; Masquerade.

STERN, Isaac: Violinist. b. Russia, Jul 21, 1920. e. San Francisco Consvervatory. Debut with the San Francisco Symphony. Has performed in concert, as guest soloist with leading orchs. Film soundtracks inc: Humoresque; Fiddler on the Roof. Appeared in films Tonight We Sing; Journey to Jerusalem; From Mao to Mozart--Isaac Stern In China.

(Grammys-(6)-Class solo-1961, 1962, 1964, 1981; chamber mus perf-1970; class album of year-1977).

(Kennedy Center Honoree-1984).

STERN, Leonard B.: Wri-Prod. b. Dec 23, 1923. TV inc: The Honeymooners; The Bilko Show (Emmy-wri-1956); Get Smart (Emmy-wri-1967). (Exec prod): The Governor and JJ; Diana; Faraday & Company; The Snoop Sisters; MacMillan and Wife; Holmes and Yo Yo; Lannigan's Rabbi; Rosetti and Ryan; Operation Petticoat; Windows, Doors & Keyholes.

Films inc: Just You and Me Kid; The Nude Bomb.

STERN, Sandor: Wri-Dir. b. Timmins, Ont, Canada, Jul 13, 1936. e. U of Toronto. TV inc: The Bold Ones; Ironside; Longstreet; All in the Family; Say Goodbye Maggie Cole; Mod Squad (prod); The Strange and Deadly Occurrence (prod & wri); Where Have All the People Gone; Red Alert; Killer on Board; True Grit: A Further Adventure; The Seeding of Sarah Burns; Mysterious Island of Beautiful Women; To Find My Son; Muggable Mary--Street Cop; Memories Never Die; Cutter to Houston; Passions; Secret Weapons.

Films inc: Fast Break (sp); The Amityville Horror (sp).

STERN, Steven H.: Dir-Wri. b. Ontario, Canada, Nov 1, 1937. e. Ryerson Institute of Technology. Films inc: B.S. I Love You; Harrod Summer; Running; The Devil and Max Devlin.

TV inc: Ghost of Flight 401: Getting Married; Anatomy of a Seduction; A Boy and a Girl; Fast Friends; Young Love, First Love; Portrait of an Escort; Miracle On Ice; Jessica Novak; A Small Killing; The Ambush Murders; Portrait of a Showgirl; Not Just Another Affair; Forbidden Love; Rona Jaffe's Mazes & Monster; Baby Sister; Still the Beaver; An Uncommon Love; Getting Physical; Draw! (PC); Obsessive Love; The Undergrads (feevee)(Prod-dir).

STERN, Stewart: Wri. b. NYC, Mar 22, 1922. e. U of IA. Films inc: Teresa; Rebel Without a Cause; The Rack; The James Dean Story;

The Outsider; The Ugly American; Rachel, Rachel; The Last Movie; Summer Wishes - Winter Dreams; Benjy.

TV inc: Crip; And Crown Thy Good; Thunder of Silence; Heart of Darkness; Sybil (Emmy-1977); A Christmas to Remember.

STERNHAGEN, Frances: Act. b. Washington, DC, Jan 13, 1930. e. Vassar, BA. Films inc: Up the Down Staircase; The Tiger Makes Out; The Hospital; Two People; Fedora; Starting Over; Outland; Independence Day; Romantic Comedy.

TV inc: Love of Life; Doctors; Enemies; Mother and Daughter-The Loving War; Prototype; Under One Roof.

Bway inc: The Skin of Our Teeth; The Carefree Tree; The Country Wife; The Chalk Garden; Great Day in the Morning; Cock-a-Doodle Dandy; Great Day in the Morning; The Right Honorable Gentleman; The Playboy of the Western World; The Sign in Sidney Brustein's Window; Enemies; The Good Doctor (Tony-1974); Equus; Angel; On Golden Pond; Peter Pan; The Father; Grownups; Home Front. (London): The War at Home.

STEVENS, Andrew: Act. b. Memphis, TN, Jun 10 1955. S of Stella Stevens. Films inc: Shampoo; Vigilante Force; Massacre at Central High; Las Vegas Lady; The Boys of Company C; Day of the Animals; The Fury; Death Hunt; The Seduction; 10 to Midnight.

TV inc: The Last Survivors; Secrets; Once an Eagle; The Bastard; The Oregon Trail; The Rebels; Women at West Point; Topper (& exec prod); Beggarman, Thief; Miracle On Ice; Code Red; Forbidden Love; Emerald Point, N.A.S.; Hollywood Wives.

STEVENS, Cat (Stephan Demetri Georgiou): Mus-Singer. b. London, Jul 21, 1948. Recording artist. Bway inc: Dancin. Films inc: Sound of the City--London 1964-73.

STEVENS, Connie (Concetta Rosalie Ann Ingolia): Act. b. Brooklyn, Aug 8, 1938. Films inc: Eighteen and Anxious; Young and Dangerous; Drag Strip Riot; Rock-A-Bye Baby; Susan Slade; Palm Springs Weekend; Cruise-A-Go-Go; The Grissom Gang; Last Generation; Grease 2.

TV inc: Hawaiian Eye; Wendy and Me; Sex Symbol; Love's Savage Fury; Scruples; Murder Can Hurt You; Aloha Paradise; Side Show; Harry's Battles; Detective In The House.

Bway inc: Star Spangled Girl.

STEVENS, Craig (Gail Shekles): Act. b. Liberty, MO, July 8, 1918. H of Alexis Smith. Films inc: Affectionately Yours; Dive Bomber; The Doughgirls; Since You Went Away; The Lady Takes a Sailor; Roughly Speaking; Humoresque; Night Unto Night; Where the Sidewalk Ends; Phone Call From A Stranger; The French Line; Abbott and Costello Meets Dr Jekyll and Mr Hyde; The Mighty; The Deadly Mantis; Gunn; The Limbo Line; The Cabot Connection; S.O.B.

TV inc: Peter Gunn; Man of the World; Mr Broadway; The Snoop Sisters; Rich Man, Poor Man; The Home Front; Happy Days.

STEVENS, George, Jr: Prod. b. Los Angeles, Apr 3, 1932. e. Occidental Coll, BA. Started in films as asst to his father on A Place in the Sun; Shane; 1962 named head motion picture div U.S. Information Agency; 1967 helped found, was first dir American Film Institute; 1980 became co-chmn AFI.

Films inc: (Asso prod) The Greatest Story Ever Told; The Diary of Anne Frank (& dir location sequences). (Prod) John F. Kennedy--Years of Lightning, Days of Drums; America at the Movies; George Stevens--A Filmmaker's Journey (doc)(& wri-dir).

TV inc: (prod) The Stars Salute America's Greatest Movies; AFI Salute to James Cagney (Emmy-prod-1975); AFI Salute to Orson Welles; AFI Salute to John Ford; AFI Salute to Henry Fonda; The Kennedy Center Honors--A Celebration of the Performing Arts, 1979, 1980 (& wri), 1982, 1983 (Emmy-prod),1984 (& wri); AFI Salute to Fred Astaire (& wri); AFI Salute to John Huston (& wri); AFI Salute To Gene Kelly (& wri). (Dir) Peter Gunn; Alfred Hitchcock Presents; AFI Salute to Frank Capra (& wri); Christmas In Washington (& wri); AFI Salute to Lillian Gish (& wri).

STEVENS, Jeremy: Wri. TV inc: The Electric Company (Emmy-1973); Mac Davis Specials; Diahann Carroll Show; Fernwood 2night; Richard Pryor Show; What's Happening; America 2night; Barbara Mandrell Show; Steve Allen Comedy Hour; Thicke of the Night (supv prod).

STEVENS, K.T. (Gloria Wood): Act. b. Los Angeles, 1919. e. USC. D of late Sam Wood. Films inc: Peck's Bad Boy; The Great Man's Lady; Kitty Foyle; Nine Girls; Address Unknown; Harriet Craig; Vice Squad; Tumbleweed; Missile to the Moon; Bob & Carol & Ted & Alice; Pets; They're Playing With Fire.

TV inc: The Young and the Restless.

STEVENS, Leslie: Wri-Prod-Dir. b. Washington, DC, Feb 3, 1924. e. Yale Drama School. Films inc: The Left-Handed Gun; Private Property (& prod-dir); The Marriage-Go-Round; Hero's Island (& prod-dir); Buck Rogers in the 25th Century (wri); Sheena (story).

TV inc: Stony Burke (crea, prod-dir); The Outer Limits; It Takes a Thief; McCloud; Men from Shiloh; Name of the Game.

Thea inc: Champagne Complex; The Lovers; The Marriage-Go-Round; The Pink Jungle.

STEVENS, Mark (Richard Stevens): Act. b. Cleveland, OH, Dec 13, 1916. On stage and radio in Canada before Hollywood. Early films as Stephen Richards inc Two Faced Woman; Passage to Marseilles; The Doughgirls; Objective Burma; Pride of the Marines.

Films (as Stevens) Within These Walls; From This Day Forward; The Dark Corner; God Is My Co-Pilot; I Wonder Who's Kissing Her Now; Reunion in Reno; Mutiny; The Big Frame; The Street With No Name; The Snake Pit; Jack Slade; Torpedo Alley; Cry Vengeance (& prod-dir); Timetable (& prod-dir); September Storm; Fate is the Hunter; Sunscorched.

TV inc: Martin Kane; Big Town.

STEVENS, Morton: Comp-Cond. (Ne Suckno) b. Newark, NJ, Jan 30, 1929. e. Juilliard. Arr-cond for Sammy Davis Jr in concerts, niteries before turning to scoring. TV inc: 87th Precinct; Wild and Wonderful; Wheels; A Thousand Pardons, You're Dead (Emmy-1970); Hawaii 5-0 (Emmy-1974); Policewoman; Apple's Way; Backstairs at the White House; Lucy Moves to NBC; Detour to Terror; Fugitive Family; The Million Dollar Face; Masada; The Manions of America; Memories Never Die; Cocaine and Blue Eyes; Savage: In the Orient.

Films inc: Hardly Working; Smorgasbord; Slapstick of Another Kind.

STEVENS, Rise: Mezzo-Soprano. b. NYC, 1913. Gave up singing career in 1964, to serve as co-general manager of the Metropolitan Opera National Company for two years. Later a voice coach and tutor. Films inc: The Chocolate Soldier; Going My Way; Carnegie Hall.

STEVENS, Roger L.: Prod. b. Detroit, Mar 12, 1910. e. U of MI. Bway inc: Twelfth Night; The Cellar and the Well; Peter Pan; Peer Gynt; The Fourposter; Barefoot in Athens; Tea and Sympathy; The Remarkable Mr Pennypacker; Sabrina Fair; Ondine; Bus Stop; Cat on a Hot Tin Roof; Tiger at the Gates; Separate Tables; A Clearing in the Woods; The Waltz of the Toreadors; Orpheus Descending; A Hole in the Head; West Side Story; Nude with Violin; The Pleasure of His Company; Five Finger Excercise; Under the Yum Yum Tree; The Caretaker; A Man for All Seasons; (Tony-1962); Sheep on the Runway; Conduct Unbecoming; Lost in the Stars; Leonard Bernstein's Mass; Jumpers; A Matter of Gravity; 1600 Pennsylvania Avenue; Betrayed; Bedroom Farce; Lunch Hour; The West Side Waltz; On Your Toes; Death of a Salesman (rev.) (Tony-1984).

(Tony-Special-1971).

STEVENS, Ronnie: Act. b. London, England, Sep 2, 1925. Thea inc: Ad Lib; High Spirits; Intimacy at 8:30; For Amusement Only; The Lily White Boys; The Billy Barnes Revue; Rose Marie; The Lord Chamberlain Regrets; Round Leicester Square; The Man of Mode; Twelfth Night; The Bird Watcher; Two Gentlemen of Verona; The Merchant of Venice; Much Ado About Nothing; Ruling The Roost; Royal Hunt of the Sun; The Caretaker; Joseph and the Amazing Technicolor Coat; The Owl and the Pussycat; The Tempest; Sgt. Musgrave's Dance; Habeas Corpus; Hard Times; Dry Rot.

Films inc: I'm Alright Jack; A Home of Your Own; Goodbye Mr. Chips.

STEVENS, Stella: Act. b. Hot Coffee, MS, Oct 1, 1938. M of Andrew Stevens. Began as model. On screen from 1959. Films inc: Say One for Me; Li'l Abner; Too Late Blues; The Courtship of Eddie's Father; Synanon; Sol Madrid; The Poseidon Adventure; Slaughter; Las Vegas Lady; Nickelodeon; The Manitou; Wacko; Chained Heat.

TV inc: Ben Casey; The Jordan Chance; The French Atlantic Affair; Friendships, Secrets and Lies; Make Me An Offer; Flamingo Road; Children of Divorce; Twirl; Women of San Quentin; Amazons; No Man's Land.

STEVENSON, Douglas C.: Act. b. Minneapolis, MN, Jul 18, 1955. e. AADA. Thea inc: Company; Picnic; Summer of the Seventeenth Doll; Eurydice; Look Homeward Angel; Dinner At Eight.

TV inc: The Doctors; One Life to Live; Search for Tomorrow.

STEVENSON, Margot: Act. b. NYC, Feb 8, 1914. Bway inc Firebird; The Barretts of Wimpole Street; Stage Door; You Can't Take It With You; The Male Animal; The Rugged Path; Sweet Peril; The Seven Year Itch; The Happiest Millionaire; The Sea Gull; Hostile Witness; End of Summer; The Royal Family.

Films inc: Smashing the Money Ring; Castle on the Hudson; Valley of the Dolls; The Brotherhood; Rabbit Run.

STEVENSON, McLean: Act. b. Normal, IL, Nov 14, 1929. e. Northwestern U. TV inc: That Was the Week That Was (& wri); The Smothers Brothers Comedy Hour (wri); The Doris Day Show; The Tim Conway Comedy Hour; M*A*S*H*; Shirts/Skins; In The Beginning; Hello, Larry; Alan King's Thanksgiving Special--What Do We Have To Be Thankful For; The Way They Were; The Astronauts; Condo.

STEVENSON, Parker: Act. b. Philadelphia, PA, Jun 4, 1952. Films inc: A Separate Peace; Our Time; Lifeguard; Stroker Ace.

TV inc: Hardy Boys Mysteries; House Possessed; The Mike Douglas Show (co-host); Shooting Stars; Falcon Crest.

STEVENSON, Robert: Dir. b. London, 1905. e. Cambridge U. Films inc: King Solomon's Mines; Tom Brown's Schooldays; Back Street; Jane Eyre; To the Ends of the Earth; The Las Vegas Story; Old Yeller; Kidnapped; The Absent Minded Professor; Son of Flubber; Mary Poppins; That Darn Cat; Blackbeard's Ghost; The Love Bug; Bedknobs and Broomsticks; Herbie Rides Again; One of Our Dinosaurs is Missing; The Shaggy DA.

STEWART, Alexandra: Act. b. Canada, June 10, 1939. Films inc: Exodus; Le Feu Follet; Dragees au Poivre; The Bride Wore Black; The Man Who Had Power Over Women; The Marseilles Contract; Zeppelin; Day for Night; Because of the Cats; Black Moon; The Little Girl In Blue Velvet; In Praise of Older Women; Le Soleil en Face (Face to the Sun); Phobia; Final Assignment; Agency; Help Me Dream; The Last Chase; Madame Claude 2 (Intimate Moments); Sans Soleil (Sunless); Femmes (Women); Le Bon Plaisir; Le Sang des Autres (The Blood of Others).

TV inc: Separation; Mistral's Daughter.

STEWART, Catherine Mary: Act. b. Edmonton, Alta., Canada. Studied dance and drama at London Studio Center. With rock ballet group. Films inc: The Apple; Powderhead; Nighhawks; The Last Starfighter; Mischief.

TV inc: Days Of Our Lives; A Killer In The Family; With Intent To Kill; Night Of The Comet; Hollywood Wives.

STEWART, Don: Act-Singer. b. Staten Island, NY, Nov 14, 1935. e. Hastings Coll. Sang with American Choral Society; Schola Cantorum; Radio City Chorus. Thea inc: The Fantasticks; Jo; Babes in the Woods. TV inc: Guiding Light (since 1968).

STEWART, Elaine: Act. b. Montclair, NJ, May 31, 1929. Films inc: Sailor Beware; The Bad and the Beautiful; Young Bess; Brigadoon; The Tattered Dress; The Adventures of Hajji Baba; The Rise and the Fall of Legs Diamond; The Most Dangerous Man Alive.

STEWART, Jackie (John Young Stewart): TV Sports Commentator. b. England, Jun 11, 1939. Former World Champion Driver, holds record of 27 Grand Prix victories. TV inc: 1976 Winter Olympics; The American Sportsman; ABC auto race telecasts.

STEWART, James: Act. b. Indiana, PA, May 20, 1908. On screen from 1935. Films inc: Murder Man; Rose Marie; Wife vs. Secretary; Next Time We Love; Born to Dance; Seventh Heaven; You Can't Take it With You; Mr. Smith Goes to Washington; The Philadephia Story (Oscar-1940); It's a Wonderful World; Destry Rides Again; The Shop

Around the Corner; It's a Wonderful Life; Magic Town; Call Northside 777; Rope; You Gotta Stay Happy; The Stratton Story; Malaya; Winchester '73; Broken Arrow; Harvey; The Jackpot; No Highway in the Sky; The Greatest Show on Earth; Carbine Williams; Bend of the River; Thunder Bay; The Glenn Miller Story; Far Country; The Rear Window; Strategic Air Command; The Man from Laramie; The Man Who Knew Too Much; The Spirit of St. Louis; Night Passage; Vertigo; Bell, Book and Candle; The FBI Story; Two Rode Together; The Man Who Shot Liberty Valance; Mr. Hobbs Takes a Vacation; How the West Was Won; Take Her, She's Mine; Dear Brigette; Shenandoah; The Rare Breed; The Flight of the Phoenix; Fire Creek; Bandolero; The Cheyenne Social Club; Fool's Parade; That's Entertainment!; The Shootist; Airport '77; The Big Sleep; The Magic of Lassie; Afurika Monogatari (A Tale of Africa); Right of Way.

(Honorary Oscar-1984).

Bway inc: Spring in Autumn; All Good Americans; Yellow Jack; Journey at Night; Harvey.

TV inc: Jimmy Stewart Show; Hawkins on Murder; Take One; AFI Salute to Frank Capra; An All-Star Party For Carol Burnett; All-Star Party For Lucille Ball; On Top All Over The World; AFI Salute To Gene Kelly.

STEWART, Michael (nee Rubin): Plywri. b. NYC, Aug 1, 1929. e. Yale, MFA. Contributed material to Sid Caesar hour.

Plays inc: Shoestring Revue; Shoestring '57; Bye Bye Birdie (Tony-1961); Hello, Dolly! (Tony-1964); Those That Play the Clowns; George M!; Mack and Mabel; Barnum; 42d Street; Bring Back Birdie; Harrigan 'n Hart.

STEWART, Paul (nee Sternberg): Act-Dir. b. NYC, Mar 13, 1908. Appeared on approximately 5,000 radio shows between 1933 and 1944; also prod Mercury Theatre of the Air and dir daytime serials.

Bway inc: Subway Express; Wine of Choice; Native Son; Mr. Roberts.

Films inc: Citizen Kane; Johnny Eager; Mr. Lucky; Champion; The Window; 12 O'Clock High; Edge of Doom; Deadline U.S.A.; the Bad and The Beautiful; The Juggler; A Child is Waiting; The Greatest Story Ever Told; In Cold Blood; Jigsaw; How To Commit Marriage; The Day of the Locust; Bite the Bullet; W.C. Fields and Me; F For Fake; Opening Night; Revenge of the Pink Panther; Nobody's Perfekt; Tempest.

TV inc: (Dir) The Defenders; Twilight Zone; Peter Gunn; Checkmate; M-Squad; Hawaiian Eye. (Act) The Nativity; The Dain Curse; Power; Emergency Room; Seduced.

STEWART, Rod: Mus-Singer. b. London, Jan 10, 1945. With Jeff Beck Group 1965-1968; Faces 1968-1970 before solo.

Albums inc: Rod Stewart; Gasoline Alley; Every Picture Tells A Story; Never A Dull Moment; A Night on the Town; Atlantic Crossing; Smiles; Foot Loose and Fancy Free; Blondes Have More Fun; Do Ya Think I'm Sexy; Rod Stewart's Greatest Hits.

Films inc: Sound of the City--London 1964-73; New York Nights (songs).

TV inc: Saturday Night Live; Double Platinum; Motown Returns To The Apollo.

STEWART, Trish: Act. b. Hot Springs, AR, Jun 14. Films inc: Time Travelers; Mansion of the Doomed People.

TV inc:The Young and the Restless; Salvage; Breaking Up Is Hard To Do; Wild Times.

STICKNEY, Dorothy: Act. b. Dickinson, ND, Jun 21, 1900. Widow of Howard Lindsay. Bway inc: The Squall; March Hares; The Front Page; The County Chairman; The Small Hours; Kind Sir; A Lovely Light; Pippin.

Films inc: Working Girls; The Little Minister; What a Life; The Remarkable Mr Pennypacker; I Never Sang for My Father.

TV inc: Arsenic and Old Lace; Cinderella; A Lovely Light.

STIERS, David Ogden: Act. b. Peoria, IL, Oct 31, 1942. Films inc: Drive, He Said; THX 1138; Oh, God!; The Cheap Detective; Magic; Harry's War.

TV inc: The Mary Tyler Moore Show; Doc; A Circle of Children; M*A*S*H; Breaking Up Is Hard To Do; The Oldest Living Graduate; Damien. . .The Leper Priest; Me and Mr Stenner; The Day the Bubble Burst; The Innocents Abroad; Anatomy of an Illness; The First Olympics--Athens 1896; The Bad Seed.

Bway inc: The Magic Show; Ulysses in Nighttown; The Three Sisters; The Beggar's Opera; Measure for Measure.

STIGWOOD, Robert C.: Prod. b. Adelaide, Australia, 1934. Talent agent London 1962; became ind record prod; co-m dir NEMS Enterprises, which controlled Beatles, Jan 1967; formed Robert Stigwood Organization Nov 1967; prod in London: Hair; Oh! Calcutta!; Pippin; Sweeney Todd; acquired British tv shows Till Death Do Us Part and Steptoe and Son, sold U.S. rights to Norman Lear to provide basis for All in the Family and Sanford and Son.
Bway inc: Jesus Christ Superstar; Joseph and the Amazing Technicolor Dreamcoat; John, Paul, George, Ringo. . .and Bert; Happy End; Evita *(Tony-1980)*.
Films inc: Jesus Christ Superstar; Tommy; Saturday Night Fever; Grease; Sergeant Pepper's Lonely Hearts Club Band; Moment by Moment; Times Square; The Fan; Gallipoli; Grease 2; Staying Alive.
TV inc: Beacon Hill; The Prime of Miss Jean Brodie.

STILLER, Jerry: Act. b. NYC, Jun 8, 1929. e. Syracuse U, BS. H of Anne Meara. Films inc: The Taking of Pelham 1-2-3; The Ritz; Nasty Habits; In Our Hands (doc).
TV inc: Joe and Sons; Madame X; Orphans, Waifs and Wards; The Other Woman.
Bway inc: Member Joseph Papp's Shakespeare Co; The Ritz; Unexpected Guests; Passione; Hurlyburly (off-Bway); toured in comedy act with wife.

STING (Gordon Matthew Summer): mus-act. b. Newcastle-Upon-Tyne, England, 1931. e. Warwick U. Originally a schoolteacher; helped form rock group The Police. Films inc: Quadrophenia; Radio On; Brimstone and Treacle; Dune.
TV inc: Artemis.

STITT, Milan: Wri. b. Detroit, MI, Feb 9, 1941. e. U of MI, BA; Yale, MFA. Bway inc: The Runner Stumbles.
Films inc: The Runner Stumbles.
TV inc: Between the Lions (& host-moderator); Ephraim McDowell's Kentucky Ride (pilot for Tales of Medical Life series); The Gentleman Bandit.

STIX, John: Dir. b. St Louis, MO, Nov 14, 1920. e. Yale U, MFA. Bway inc: Mary Rose; Take A Giant Step; The Wisteria Trees; What Every Woman Knows; Too Late The Phalarope; The Price (revival).
Film inc: The Great St Louis Bank Robbery.
TV inc: Omnibus (10 segs); Family Business.

STOCKWELL, Dean: Act. b. Los Angeles, Mar 5, 1936. Former child star. On screen from 1945. Films inc: Anchors Aweigh; Home Sweet Homicide; The Romance of Rosy Ridge; Song of the Thin Man; Gentleman's Agreement; The Boy with Green Hair; Down to the Sea in Ships; Stars in My Crown; Kim; Gun for a Coward; Compulsion; Sons and Lovers; Long Day's Journey Into Night; Psych-Out; The Dunwich Horrors; Win Place or Steal; The Pacific Connection; Wrong Is Right; Human Highway (& dir-wri); Alsino y el Condor (Alsino and the Condor); Paris, Texas; Dune.
TV inc: Greatest Heroes of the Bible; Born To Be Sold.

STODDARD, Brandon: Exec. b. Cannan, NY, Mar 31, 1937. e. Yale U, Columbia Law School. With BBD&O before joining Grey Advertising; joined ABC 1970; named vp daytime programs for ABC entertainment, 1972; vp children's programs, 1973; named vp motion pictures for TV, 1974; in 1976 named vp dramatic programs and motion pictures for TV; in 1979 appointed P of new ABC motion picture unit.

STODDARD, Haila: Thea Prod-Act. b. Great Falls, MT, Nov 14, 1913. e. USC. Bway inc: (Act): Merrily We Roll Along; Tobacco Road; Yes, My Darling Daughter; The Moon Vine; Rip Van Winkle; Joan of Lorraine; The Voice of the Turtle; Her Cardboard Lover; Glad Tidings; Lunatics and Lovers; Who's Afraid of Virginia Woolf?; Dark Corners. (Prod) A Thurber Carnival; Sail Away; The Affair and The Hollow Crown; The Birthday Party; The Last Sweet Days of Isaac; The Lemon Sky; The Survival of St Joan; Lady Audley's Secret; Love.
TV inc: Secret Storm (act); adapted Men, Women and Less Alarming Creatures From Thurber's works for tv series.

STOLL, George E.: Mus Dir. b. Minneapolis, MN, May 7, 1905. Film scores inc: Broadway Melody of 1938; Babes in Arms; Strike Up the Band; Ziegfeld Girl; For me and My Gal; Cabin in the Sky; Meet Me in St Louis; Anchors Aweigh *(Oscar-1945)* The Kissing Bandit; Love Me or Leave Me; Meet Me in Las Vegas; Jumbo; The Courtship of Eddie's Father; Viva Las Vegas; Girl Happy; Made In Paris.
(Died Jan. 18, 1985)

STOLLER, Morris: Exec. b. NYC, Nov 22, 1915. e. CCNY, BBA; NYU, CPA; Brooklyn Law School, LLB. Joined William Morris Agency, NY in 1937; shifted to Coast office 1947; named vp, later exec-vp & treas; Dec 1980 named bd chmn.

STOLOFF, Victor: Prod-Wri-Dir. b. Mar 17, 1913. e. French Law U. Films inc: Why?: Intimacy; Of Love and Desire.
TV inc: Israel Is Real; Hawaii 5-0; High Adventure with Lowell Thomas; Volcano; Sinner; Desert Boy; Little Isles of Freedom; Woman of Iran; Ballet Gayane.

STOLTZ, Eric Act. b. American Samoa. e. USC. Worked with an American rep company in Scotland in Tobacco Road; You're A Good Man, Charlie Brown; Working.
Films inc: Fast Times At Ridgemont High; Next Of Kin; The Wild Life; Mask; The New Kids.
TV inc: Paper Dolls; A Killer In The Family; St. Elsewhere; Things Are Looking Up.

STONE, Andrew L.: Prod-Dir. b. Oakland, CA, Jul 16, 1902. Films inc: Hi Diddle Diddle; Sensations of 1945; Bedside Manner; Highway 301; Confidence Girl; Steel Trap; Blueprint for Murder; Bachelor's Daughter; Fun on a Weekend; Night Holds Terror; Julie; Cry Terror; The Decks Ran Red; The Last Voyage; Ring of Fire; Password Is Courage; Never Put It In Writing; Secret of My Success; Song of Norway; The Great Waltz.

STONE, Cliffie: Mus-Exec. b. Burbank, CA, Mar 1, 1917. C&W disc jockey 1935; formed own band; 1946 Capital Records consultant on folk artists. Radio inc: Hollywood Barn Dance. TV inc: Hometown Jamboree.

STONE, Ezra (nee Feinstone): Prod-Dir-Wri-Act. b. New Bedford, MA, Dec 2, 1917. e. AADA. Child Actor on radio; crea Henry Aldrich role. Bway inc: (Act) Parade; Ah, Wilderness; Oh, Evening Star; Three Men on a Horse; Brother Rat; What a Life (origin of Aldrich character); Pal Joey; Best Foot Forward; Boys From Syracuse. (Dir) See My Lawyer; Reunion in New York; This Is The Army; January Thaw; Me and Molly; At War With the Army; The Man That Corrupted Hadleyburg; Count Your Blessings; The Blue Danube; The Pink Elephant.
Films inc: Those Were The Days; This Is The Army; Tammy and The Millionare (dir).
TV inc: (Act) The Aldrich Family; Danny Thomas Show; Life With Father; The Hathaways; The Eternal Light; Actor; The 40 Million (& prod-dir); The Munster's Revenge. (Dir) I Married Joan; Bachelor Father; The Munsters; Petticoat Junction; Lost in Space; The Flying Nun; Please Don't Eat the Dasies; My Living Doll.
Dir more than 150 docs, staged 45 conventions for IBM.

STONE, Harold J.: Act. b. 1911. e. NYU, Buffalo Medical School. Bway inc: The World We Make; Mr. and Mrs. North; Apology; Counter Attack; One Touch of Venus; Stalag 17.
Films inc: The Harder They Fall; The Wrong Man; The Garment Jungle; These Thousand Hills; Spartacus; The Chapman Report; The Greatest Story Ever Told; The St. Valentine's Day Massacre; The McCullochs; Mitchell; Hardly Working.
TV inc: The Untouchables.

STONE, Oliver (William Oliver Stone): Wri. b. NYC, Sep 15, 1946. e. NYU, BFA. Films inc: Seizure (& dir); Midnight Express *(Oscar-1978)*; The Hand.

STONE, Peter: Wri. b. Los Angeles, Feb 27, 1930. e. Yale U, MA. Films inc: Charade; Father Goose *(Oscar-co-sp-1964)*; Mirage; Arabesque; The Secret War of Harry Frigg; Sweet Charity; Skin Game; 1776; Taking of Pelham 1-2-3; Silver Bears; Who Is Killing The Great Chefs of Europe?; Why Would I Lie?.
Plays inc: Kean; Skyscraper; 1776 *(Tony-1969)*; Sugar; Two by

Two; Full Circle; Woman of the Year *(Tony*-book-1980); My One and Only.
TV inc: The Defenders; Espionage; Adam's Rib; Asphalt Jungle; Happy Endings; Androcles.

STONE, Virginia Lively: Prod-Dir. b. Miami Beach, FL, May 3, 1931. Films inc: Blueprint for Murder; Steel Trap; The Night Holds Terror; Julie; Cry Terror; The Decks Ran Red; The Last Voyage; Ring of Fire; The Password is Courage; Song of Norway; Jamaica Reef; Evil in the Deep; Daddy's Girl.

STOPPARD, Tom: Wri. b. Czechoslovakia, Jul 3, 1937. Former journalist. Plays inc: Rosencrantz and Guildenstern Are Dead *(Tony*-1968); Enter a Free Man; The Real Inspector Hound; If You're Glad I'll Be Frank; After Magritte, Where Are They Now?; Jumpers; Travesties; Dirty Linen and New Found Land; Night and Day; Every Good Boy Deserves Favor (& dir); On the Razzle; The Real Thing *(Tony*-1984); Rough Crossing.
Films inc: Despair; The Human Factor; Brazil.

STORCH, Arthur: Act-Dir. b. NYC, Jun 29, 1925. e. Brooklyn Coll, New School for Social Research. NY stage debut, 1953, in End as a Man.
Bway inc: Time Limit!; Girls of Summer; The Long Dream. (Dir) Two By Saroyan; Three By Three; The Typists; The Tiger; The Owl and the Pussycat; The Impossible Years; Under the Weather; Golden Rainbow; 42 Seconds from Broadway; Twice Around the Park.
Films inc: The Strange One; The Mugger; The Girl of the Night.
TV inc: (dir) Harry Belafonte Special; 100 Years of Laughter; George Washington Crossing the Delaware.

STORCH, Larry: Act. b. NYC, 1925. Nitery comedian and impressionist before Bway appearance in Who Was That Lady I Saw You With. Repeated role in film version. Other films inc: The Prince Who Was a Thief; Who Was That Lady?; 40 Pounds of Trouble; Captain Newman, MD; Sex and the Single Girl; That Funny Feeling; Bus Riley's Back in Town; The Great Bank Robbery; The Happy Hooker Goes to Washington; Without Warning; Fake-out; Sweet Sixteen.
TV inc: The Larry Storch Show; My World and Welcome To It; F Troop; Better Late Than Never; Jack Frost (voice); The Great American Traffic Jam; Adventures of Huckleberry Finn; Musical Comedy Tonight II.
Bway inc: Porgy and Bess.

STORM, Gale (Josephine Cottle): Act. b. Bloomington, TX., April 5, 1922. Won 'Gateway To Hollywood' contest in High School. Films inc: Tom Brown's Schooldays; Jesse James At Bay; Foreign Agent; Rhythm Parade; Campus Rhythm; Where Are Your Children?; Revenge Of The Zombies; Forever Yours; Sunbonnet Sue; It Happened On Fifth Avenue; Stampede; Curtain Call At Cactus Creek; The Underworld Story; Between Midnight And Dawn; Al Jennings Of Oklahoma; Woman Of The North Country.
TV inc: My Little Margie; Oh, Susannah; The Gale Storm Show.

STRACHAN, Alan: Dir. b. Dundee, Scotland, Sep 3, 1946. e. Oxford. Thea inc: (London) OK for Sound; The Watched Pot; John Bull's Other Island; Children; Confusions; Yahoo; Present Laughter; Design For Living.

STRADLING, Harry, Jr: Cin. b. NYC, Jan 7, 1925. Films inc: Welcome to Hard Times; support Your Local Sheriff; Something Big; Fool's Parade; 1776; The Way We Were; Bite the Bullet; Airport 77; Midway; The Big Bus; Born Again; Convoy; Go Tell the Spartans; Prophecy; S.O.B.; The Pursuit of D.B. Cooper; Buddy Buddy; O'Hara's Wife; Micki & Maude.
TV inc: George Washington.

STRAIGHT, Beatrice: Act. b. Old Westbury, NY, Aug 2, 1918. Bway debut, 1935, Bitter Oleander. On screen from 1952.
Films inc: Phone Calls From a Stranger; Patterns; The Silken Affair; The Nun's Story; Network *(Oscar*-supp-1976); The Promise; Sidney Sheldon's Bloodline; The Formula; Endless Love; Poltergeist; Two of a Kind.
Bway inc: Eastward in Eden; Macbeth; The Heiress; Heartbreak House; The Crucible *(Tony*-supp-1953); Sing Me No Lullaby; The River Line; Phedre; Everything in the Garden.

TV inc: Beacon Hill; Mission Impossible; Felony Squad; Matt Lincoln; The Dain Curse; King's Crossing; Chiller; Robert Kennedy & His Times.

STRANGIS, Greg: Wri-Prod. b. Los Angeles, Jan 5, 1951. e. UCLA. TV inc: Love American Style (story ed); Eight is Enough (story ed, later prod); Rainbow (exec prod); Better Late Than Never (wri-exec prod); Shirley (wr;i-exec prod); The Great American Traffic Jam (exec prod); Bulba--Our Man in Okalatown (exec prod); Rivkin--Bounty Hunter; Not Just Another Affair (prod); Off Sides (exec prod); I Gave At The Office (exec prod).

STRANGIS, Sam: Prod. b. Tacoma, WA, Jun 19, 1929. e. Loyola U. Pgm prodn vp Par TV 1974-1976; P & exec prod Ten/Four Prodns. TV inc: Nikie; $6 Million Man; The Great American Traffic Jam; Not Just Another Affair; Off Sides (exec prod); I Gave At The Office (exec prod); He's Not Your Son (prod); Stark (supv prod).

STRASBERG, Susan: Act. b. NYC, May 22,1938. D of the late Lee Strasberg. Performed off-Broadway. On Broadway in The Diary of Anne Frank.
Films inc: The Cobweb; Picnic; Stage Struck; Scream of Fear; Hemingway's Adventures of a Young Man; Chubasco; The Name of the Game Is Kill; The Brotherhood; Rollercoaster; The Manitou; In Praise of Older Women; Acting--Lee Strasberg and the Actors Studio (doc); The Returning; Sweet Sixteen.
TV inc: The Marriage; The Duchess and the Smugs; Catch a Falling Star; The Immigrants; Beggarman, Thief; Rona Jaffe's Mazes & Monsters.

STRASSER, Robin: Act. b. NYC, May 7, 1945. e. Yale Drama School. Bway inc: Shadow Box; Chapter II. TV inc: Another World; All My Children; This Child is Mine; The Bones Came Together; Murder--Impossible; One Life to Live (Emmy-1982).

STRASSMAN, Marcia: Act. b. NYC, Apr 28, 1948. Debut age 15 in off-Bway prodn Best Foot Forward; appeared stock, off-Bway. TV inc: M*A*S*H; Welcome Back Kotter; Brave New World; Nightengales; Once Upon A Family; Good Time Harry; E.R.
Films inc: Soup for One; The Aviator.

STRATTON, David: Exec. b. Trowbridge, England, Sep 10, 1939. e. Bradfield Coll, Oxford. Film festival dir. Founded Newbury Film Society, England, Dir, Sydney Film Festival, from 1966. Programme advisor to London, LA, Chicago Film Festivals.

STRAUB, Jean-Marie: Dir. b. Metz, France, 1933. Films inc: Machorka Muff; Nicht Versohnt; The Chronicle of Anna-Magdalena Bach; Othon; History Lessons; Moses and Aaron.

STRAUSS, Helen M.: Exec-Wri. b. NY. e. Columbia U. Assoc story ed, Paramount; NY rep for Walter Wanger; literary agent; vp WB 7 Arts; vp U-MCA; in chg motion pictures, Readers Digest.
Films inc: Mr Quilp; Incredible Sarah. Autobiography: A Talent for Luck.

STRAUSS, Peter: Act. b. Croton-on-Hudson, NY, Feb 20, 1947. Screen debut, 1969, Hail, Hero!. Thea inc: Dance Next Door; The Dirty Man; Einstein and the Polar Bear.
Films inc: Soldier Blue; The Trial of the Catonsville Nine; The Last Tycoon; The Secret of NIMH (voice); Spacehunter--Adventures in the Forbidden Zone.
TV inc: The Man Without a Country; Attack on Terror; Rich Man, Poor Man; The Forgotten Kennedy; The Jericho Mile *(Emmy*-1979); Angel On My Shoulder; A Whale For the Killing (& co-prod); Masada; The Village at the Border; Heart of Steel (& exec prod).

STRAUSS, Theodore: Wri. TV inc: Four Days in November; The Legend of Marilyn Monroe; They've Killed President Lincoln *(Emmy*-1971); The Rise and Fall of the Third Reich; Appointment With Destiny; I Will Fight No More Forever; America at the Movies; America Salutes Richard Rodgers--The Sound of His Music *(Emmy*-1977); National Geographic Series; Cousteau Odysseys; Clipperton--The Island Time Forgot (& narr); Jacques Cousteau-- Cries From the Deep (and narr); Born of Fire; America Remembers John F. Kennedy; Cousteau/Amazon--Journey to a Thousand Rivers.

Films inc: The Indomitable Teddy Roosevelt (doc).

STREEP, Meryl: Act. b. Bernardsville, NJ, Apr 22, 1949. e. Vassar, Yale Drama School, MFA. Films inc: Julia; The Deer Hunter; Manhattan; The Seduction of Joe Tynan; Kramer vs Kramer (Oscar-supp-1979); The French Lieutenant's Woman; Still of the Night; Sophie's Choice (Oscar-1982); Silkwood; In Our Hands (doc); Falling In Love.

TV inc: The Deadliest Season; Holocaust (Emmy-1978); Alice at the Palace.

Bway inc: Trelawny of the Wells; 27 Wagons Full of Cotton; Memory of Two Mondays; Secret Service; The Cherry Orchard; Happy End.

STREISAND, Barbra: Act. b. NYC, Apr 24, 1942. Bway inc: I Can Get It for You Wholesale; Funny Girl.

Films inc: Funny Girl (Oscar-1968); Hello Dolly; On a Clear Day You Can See Forever; The Owl and the Pussycat; What's Up Doc?; The Way We Were; Funny Lady; A Star Is Born; Main Event; All Night Long; Yentl (& prod-dir-wri).

TV inc: My Name Is Barbra (Emmy-1965); Color Me Barbra; Belle of 14th Street; A Happening in Central Park.

Albums inc: A Star Is Born; Superman; Songbird; Barbra Streisand's Greatest Hits, Vol II; Wet; Guilty. (Grammys-(7)-Vocal Perf 1963, 1964, 1965, 1977; Album of Year 1963; Song of Year-1977; Vocal duo-1980).

STRICK, Joseph: Dir. b. Braddock, PA, Jul 6, 1923. e. UCLA. Films inc: Muscle Beach; The Savage Eye; The Balcony; Ulysses; Tropic of Cancer; Interviews with My Lai Veterans; (Oscar-Doc-1970); Road Movie; A Portrait of the Artist as a Young Man; The Space Works; Never Cry Wolf.

STRICKLAND, Gail: Act. b. Birmingham, AL, May 18. e. FL State U. Studied with Sanford Meisner. Bway inc: Status Quo Vadis; I Won't Dance. TV inc: Letters From Frank; The Gathering; The President's Mistress; Ski Lift to Death; King Crab; Rape and Marriage--The Rideout Case; A Matter of Life and Death; Jack London--A Personal Perspective; My Body, My Child; Eleanor, First Lady of The World; Amy and the Angel; Life of the Party--The Story of BeAtrice; Starflight--The Plane That Couldn't Land; Night Court.

Films inc: The Drowning Pool; Bittersweet Love; Bound for Glory; One on One; The Dog Soldiers; Who'll Stop the Rain; Norma Rae; Oxford Blues; Protocol.

STRITCH, Elaine: Act. b. Detroit, MI, 1926. On screen from 1956. Films inc: The Scarlet Hour; Three Violent People; A Farewell to Arms; The Perfect Furlough; Kiss Her Goodbye; Who Killed Teddy Bear?; Pigeons; Providence.

TV inc: Two's Company; Kennedy Center Tonight--Broadway to Washington!

STROCK, Herbert L.: Prod-Wri-Dir. b. Boston, Jan 13, 1918. e. USC, BA. Films inc: Storm Over Tibet; Magnetic Monster; Riders to the Stars; The Glass Wall; Gog; Battle Taxi; Donovan's Brain; Rider on a Dead Horse; Devil's Messenger; Brother on the Run; One Hour of Hell; Witches' Brew (dir addl sequences).

TV inc: Highway Patrol; Harbor Command; Men of Annapolis; I Led Three Lives; The Veil; Dragnet; 77 Sunset Strip; Maverick; Cheyenne; Bronco; Sugarfoot; Bonanza; The Small Miracle; Hans Brinker; What Will We Say to a Hungry World (Telethon); The Search for Survival.

STROLLER, Louis A.: Prod. b. Brooklyn, NY., Apr. 3, 1942. e. Nicholas College, BBA. Started as unit mgr The Producers; 1977 joined Martin Bregman Prodns; May 1984, vice chmn. Films inc: (asst dir) Charly; Take the Money and Run; Lovers and Other Strangers; They Might be Giants; Man on the Swing; 92 in the Shade. (Prodn mgr) Mortadella; Sisters; Sweet Revenge; The Eyes of Laura Mars. Other films inc: Badlands (asso prod); Carrie (asso prod); Telefon (asso prod); The Seduction of Joe Tynan (exec prod); Four Seasons (exec prod); Simon (exec prod); Venom (Sr. exec prod); Eddie Macon's Run (prod); Scarface (exec prod).

STROMBERG, Gary: Prod. b. Los Angeles, May 14, 1942. Films inc: Car Wash; The Fish that Saved Pittsburgh.

STROSS, Raymond: Prod. b. Leeds, England, May 22, 1916. e. Oxford. H of Anne Heywood. Films inc: As Long as They're Happy; An Alligator Named Daisy; The Flesh is Weak; A Question of Adultery; The Angry Hills; A Terrible Beauty; The Mark; The Very Edge; The Leather Boys; Ninety Degrees in the Shade; The Fox; The Midas Run; I Want What I Want; The Woman Who Rode Away; Good Luck Miss Wyckoff.

STROUD, Don: Act. b. 1937. Films inc: Madigan; Games; What's So Bad about Feeling Good; Coogan's Bluff; Bloody Mama; Explosion; Von Richtofen and Brown; Tick Tick Tick; Joe Kidd; Scalawag; The Killer Inside Me; The Choirboys; The House by the Lake; The Buddy Holly Story; The Amityville Horror; The Night the Lights Went Out In Georgia; Search and Destroy; Sweet Sixteen.

TV inc: Supertrain; God In The Dock; Mickey Spillane's "Murder Me, Murder You"; I Want to Live; More Than Murder; Mickey Spillane; Gidget's Summer Reunion.

STRUDWICK, Shepperd: Act. b. Hillsboro, NC, Sep 22, 1907. e. U of NC, BA. Bway inc: Yellow Jacket; Both Your Houses; Biography (tour); Let Freedom Ring; End of Summer; As You Like It; The Three Sisters; Christopher Blake; Affairs of State; Ladies of the Corridor; Night Circus; Only in America; Who's Afraid of Virginia Woolf? (matinees & tour); Last Days of Lincoln; Galileo; In the Matter of J. Robert Oppenheimer; The Desert Song; The Eccentricities of a Nightingale.

Films inc: (from 1941-1947 billed as John Shepperd) Congo Maisie; Fast Company; Flight Command; Remember The Day; Joan of Arc; Enchantment; The Red Pony; All the King's Men; A Place in the Sun; Eddie Duchin Story; Autumn Leaves; Psychomania; The Daring Game; The Sad Sack; Cops and Robbers.

TV inc: Julius Caesar; Love of Life; Kent State.

(Died Jan. 16, 1983).

STRUTHERS, Sally: Act. b. Portland, OR, 1948. Films inc: The Phynx; Charlotte; Five Easy Pieces; The Getaway.

TV inc: The Summer Brothers Smothers Show; The Tim Conway Comedy Hour; The Great Houdinis; Aloha Means Goodbye; Hey, I'm Alive; All in the Family (Emmys-supp-1972 & 1979); Gloria; The Changing Family (host); The Secret World Of The Very Young.

Bway inc: Wally's Cafe; The Odd Couple.

STUART, Malcolm: Prod-Exec. Started 1950 as agent, MCA; 1955 formed own literary agency with Ingo Preminger; sold to GAC 1962, he remained with GAC until 1965 when entered indpt prodn; became agent with IFA (now ICM); 1972 vp chg dvlpmt Metromedia Producers Corp; 1974 vp dvlpmt Charles Fries Prodns; 1976 vp crea aff; 1980 vp chg vidpix, miniseries Lorimar Prodns. TV inc: (exec prod) Delaney; Call of the Wild; The Home Front; The Children of An Lac; A Cry For Love; High Noon, Part II--The Return of Will Kane; Mistress of Paradise; Washington Mistress; Two of A Kind; Johnny Belinda; One Cooks, the Other Doesn't; John Steinbeck's the Winter of our Discontent; Why Me?; A Death In California (exec prod).

STUART, Mary: Act. b. Miami, FL., Jul. 4, 1929. Films inc: No Leave, No Love; This Time for Keeps; The Hucksters; Dark Delusion; Good News; Adventures of Don Juan; The Big Punch; The Girl from Jones Beach; Thunderhoof; Caribou Trail; Father Makes Good.

TV inc: Search for Tomorrow (since 1951--orginal cast member); After Hours; From Janice, John, Mary and Michael, with Love.

STUART, Maxine (nee Shlivek): Act. b. Elberon, NJ, June 28. e. AADA. Films inc: Days of Wine and Roses; Dear Heart; Winning; Prisoner of Second Avenue; Fun With Dick & Jane; Coast to Coast.

Thea inc: Tunnel of Love; At War with the Army; A Goose for the Gander; Sun-Up to Sundown; Cry Havoc.

TV inc: Kill Me If You Can; Executive Suite; Doctor's Hospital; Revenge of the Gray Gang; Fit for A King; The Rousters; Carpool; Two Marriages; Hail To The Chief.

STUART, Mel: Dir. b. Sep 2, 1928. Films inc: The White Lions; If It's Tuesday, This Must Be Belgium; Willie Wonka and the Chocolate Factory; One Is A Lonely Number; I Love My Wife; Wattstax; The White Lions.

TV inc: China, The Roots of Madness (Emmy-prod-1967); The Making of the President, 1960, 1964, 1968 (Emmy-prod-1970); Rise and Fall of the Third Reich; Life Goes to the Movies; The Triangle Factory Fire Scandal; The Chisholms; Sophia Loren--Her Own Story; The Future--What's Next? (prod); Bill; Ripley's Believe It Or Not! (& Supv prod).

STUART, William Victor: Exec. b. Glendale, CA, Dec 29, 1946. e. College of Switzerland, Emerson Coll. Trainee Mgr, Fox, Amsterdam, 1973-75; asst European sls Mgr, inc Near and Far East. Fox, 1975-77; M-dir, Fox, Madrid and supervisor of Portugal, 1977-78; M dir, UA (A/Asia), 1978; VP MGM-UA & exec asst to dist & mktg pres; July 1982, VP & exec dir UA classics.

STULBERG, Gordon: Exec. b. Toronto, Canada, Dec 17, 1923. e. U of Toronto, BA; Cornell, LLD. With Law firm of Pacht, Ross, Warne and Bernhard specializing in film law; Joined Col as exec asst to vp 1956; vp & chief admn officer 1960; P Cinema Center Films 1967; P 20th Century-Fox 1971; returned to law practice 1975; named P Polygram Pictures (former Casablanca Records and Filmworks), March 18,1980.

STUMPF, Richard J.: Snd eng. b. Glendale, CA, Oct 15, 1926. e. UC Berkeley, BS. With NBC in tv eng dept; 1959 proj coord for Project Mercury (first man-in space program); 1961 to RCA where he created first digitally controlled automatic sound mixdown system; 1968 to U; 1973 head of Sound & Electronics Dept; principal co-inventor Sensurround (Oscar-scientific-1974); (Oscar-Technical Achievement for Engineering of a 24-frame color video system-1981).

STURGES, John: Dir. b. Oak Park, IL, Jan 3, 1911. Films inc: The Man Who Dared; Shadowed; Keeper of the Bees; The Best Man Wins; The Sign of the Ram; The Magnificent Yankee; Kind Lady; Right Cross; The People Against O'Hara; The Girl in White; Jeopardy; Escape from Fort Bravo; Bad Day At Black Rock; Underwater; Gunfight at the OK Corral; The Law and Jake Wade; Never So Few; The Magnificent Seven; By Love Possessed; Sergeants Three; The Great Escape; The Old Man and the Sea; The Satan Bug; The Hallelujah Trail; The Hour of the Gun; Ice Station Zebra; Marooned; Joe Kidd; McQ; The Eagle Has Landed.

STYNE, Jule (nee Stein): Comp-Prod. b. London, Dec 31, 1905. e. Northwestern U, Chicago Musical Coll. Child prodigy as a pianist, appearing with Chicago Symphony at age 8.
Bway inc: (scores) High Button Shoes; Gentlemen Prefer Blondes; In Any Language; Hazel Flagg; Peter Pan; Say Darling; Bells Are Ringing; Gypsy; Do Re Mi; Subways Are For Sleeping; Funny Girl; Fade Out-Fade In; Hallelujah Baby (Tony-1967); Darling of the Day; Sugar; Peter Pan. (Prod) Make A Wish; Pal Joey; Will Success Spoil Rock Hunter; Mr. Wonderful; Teibele and Her Demon.
Films inc: Sailors on Leave; Follow the Boys; The Kid From Brooklyn; The West Point Story; Anchors Aweigh; Tars and Spars; Three Coins in the Fountain (Oscar-1954-title song); My Sister Eileen.
TV inc: Ruggles of Red Gap; Mr. Magoo's Christmas Carol; The Dangerous Christmas of Red Riding Hood. ..or Oh Wolf, Poor Wolf. (Prod) Anything Goes; Panama Hattie; The Best of Broadway; The Eddie Fisher Show.
Songs inc: I've Heard That Song Before; I'll Walk Alone; I Fall in Love Too Easily; It's Magic; Let it Snow. (Grammy-cast album-1964).

SUBOTSKY, Milton: Wri-Prod. b. NYC, Sep 27, 1921. Films inc: Rock, Rock, Rock; The Last Mile; Laugh Parade; The World of Abbott and Costello; City of the Dead; Dr Terror's House of Horrors; The Skull; The Deadly Bees; Dr. Who and the Daleks; The Psychopath; Daleks Invasion Earth; 2150 AD; Torture Garden; The House That Dripped Blood; Tales from the Crypt; Asylum; Madhouse; The Land that Time Forgot; The Mind of Mr. Soames; Scream and Scream Again; At the Earth's Core; The Uncanny; Dominique; The Monster Club (prod); Cat's Eye (co-prod).
TV inc: The Martian Chronicles.

SUGAR, Joseph M.: Exec. b. NYC, Jun 4, 1916. e. NYU. In contract dept Republic 1938. After military service World War II, joined Producers Releasing Corp as asst contract mgr, later mgr; following merger with Eagle Lion became exec asst to distribution vp; 1953 UA NY exchange; 1959 sales vp Magna Theatres Corp; joined 20th Fox 1962 as road show mgr, became vp domestic dist following year; 1967 exec vp Warner-Seven Arts; 1968 P Cinerama Releasing

Corp; 1975 P Gamma III Distributing Co; from 1976-78 operated own firm; 1978 joined AIP as exec vp worldwide sls, P AIP Distributing Co; when AIP merged with Filmways, became exec vp parent company; assumed newly created post as exec vp; resd Aug 1981; formed Youngstein-Sugar Associates with Max E Youngstein; June 1983, exec vp for sales Embassy Pictures.

SUGARMAN, Burt: Prod. b. Los Angeles. e. USC. TV inc: The Midnight Special; Celebrity Sweepstakes; Bob Dylan Special.

SUKMAN, Harry: Comp-Cond-Pianist. b. Chicago, Dec 2, 1912. Film scores inc: Song without End (Oscar-1960); Fanny; The Singing Nun; The Naked Runner; A Thunder of Drums; Welcome to Hard Times; A Bullet for Joey; Screaming Eagles; If He Hollers, Let Him Go; Riders to the Stars; Gog; Battle Taxi; Verboten.
TV inc: Dr. Kildare; Eleventh Hour; High Chaparral; Bonanza; Gentle Ben; The Family Kovak; The Monroes.
Songs: You Are There; My Consolation; I Love Your Gypsy Heart; The Gentle Ben Theme.
(Died Dec. 2, 1984)

SULLIVAN, Barry (Patrick Barry): Act. b. NYC, Aug 29, 1912. Summer stock, NY stage. On screen from 1942. Films inc: We Refuse to Die; High Explosives; Lady in the Dark; Rainbow Island; And Now Tomorrow; Suspense; The Gangster; Any Number Can Play; The Great Gatsby; A Life of Her Own; Payment on Demand; Bad and the Beautiful; Jeopardy; Strategic Air Command; Julie; Light in the Piazza; A Gathering of Eagles; My Blood Runs Cold; An American Dream; Tell Them Willie Boy Is Here; Earthquake; Take a Hard Ride; The Human Factor; Oh, God!; Caravan.
Bway inc: The Man Who Came to Dinner; Brother Rat; Idiot's Delight; The Land Is Bright; The Caine Mutiny Court Martial.
TV inc: Cool Million; Sixth Sense; The Immigrants; Backstairs at the White House; The Bastard; The Secret of Lost Valley; Casino.

SULLIVAN, Susan: Act. bb. NYC, Nov 18, 1944. e. AADA; Hofstra. Thea inc: The Beauty Part; She Stoops to Conquer; Jimmy Shine (Bway).
TV inc: A World Apart; Another World; Rich Man-Poor Man Book II; Having Babies; Julie Farr, M.D.; Marriage Is Alive and Well; Panic on Page One; Breaking Up Is Hard To Do; The Comedy Company; The Ordeal of Dr. Mudd; It's A Living; Falcon Crest; Cave-In!. Guys and Dolls;

SULLIVAN, Tom: Mus-act. b. West Roxbury, MA., Mar. 27, 1947. e. Harvard, BA. Film "If You Could See What I Hear" based on his college career. Films inc: Black Sunday; Airport '77.
TV inc: Special corr Good Morning, America; Search for Tomorrow.

SULTZMAN, Phillip: Exec prod-Wri. b. Mexico, Sep 19, 1928. e. UCLA, BA, MA. TV inc: (wri) Rifleman; Fugitive; Dr Kildare; Perry Mason. (Asso prod) Twelve O'Clock High. (Prod) Felony Squad; The FBI; Barnaby Jones; Alvin Karpis; Brinks--The Great Robbery; Attack on Terror.

SUMMER, Donna: Singer-Act. b. Boston, MA, Dec 31, 1948. Appeared in German prodns of Hair; Godspell; The Me Nobody Knows; Vienna folkopera prodns of Showboat; Porgy & Bess.
Albums inc: Love To Love You, Baby; A Love Trilogy; The Four Seasons of Love; I Remember Yesterday; Once Upon a Time; Live & More; Thank God It's Friday; Hot Stuff; Bad Girls; Greatest Hits on the Radio, Vol 1 & 2.
(Grammys-(3)-R&B vocal 1978; rock vocal 1979; inspirational 1983).
Films inc: The Deep (mus); Thank God It's Friday (act).
TV inc: The Donna Summer Special; A Special Eddie Rabbitt; 56th Oscar Show (1984); Donald Duck's 50th Birthday; Disneyland's 30th Anniversary Celebration.

SUMMER, Gordon Matthew: mus-act. See STING.

SUMMERALL, Pat: Sportscaster. b. 1932. e. U of AR. Former pro football player. Covers various sports for CBS; host of CBS Sports Spectacular.

SUMMERFIELD, Eleanor: Act. b. London, Mar 7, 1921. Films inc: London Belongs to Me; Scrooge; It's Great to be Young; Dentist in the Chair; The Running Man; The Yellow Hat; Private Eye; Some Will, Some Won't.

TV inc: The Two Charles; The Rather Reassuring Show; You're Lovely in Black; Murder at the Panto; Husband of the Year; Madly in Love.

SUMNER, Gabe: Exec. b. NYC, Apr 20, 1929. e. NYU BA. Joined Par pub dept 1950; ass't pub dir Schine Theatre Circuit 1951-53; Par 1953-55; ind agcy 1955-1960; to UA 1960; named sr vp, prodn head 1977; Orion Pictures Co 1979 as sr vp sales-ad-pub; P of CBS Theatrical Films Dist Co., Oct. 1981 to April 1983.

SURTEES, Bruce: Cin. b. Los Angeles. S of Robert Surtees. Films inc: Play Misty for Me; Dirty Harry; The Great Northfield Minnesota Raid; The Beguiled; High Plains Drifter; Blume In Love; Joe Kidd; Lenny; Leadbelly; Sparkle; Three Warriors; Big Wednesday; Movie Movie; Dreamer; Escape From Alcatraz; Inchon; Firefox; White Dog; Ladies and Gentlemen The Fabulous Stains; Honkytonk Man; Bad Boys; Risky Business; Sudden Impact; Tightrope; Beverly Hills Cop; Pale Rider.

SURTEES, Robert: Cin. b. Covington, KY, Aug 9, 1906. Films inc: Thirty Seconds Over Tokyo; Act of Violence; Intruder in the Dust; King Solomon's Mines (Oscar-1950); Quo Vadis; The Bad and the Beautiful (Oscar-1952); Trial; Oklahoma!; Raintree County; Ben Hur (Oscar-1959); The Collector; The Satan Bug; Doctor Dolittle; The Graduate; Sweet Charity; Summer of '42; The Last Picture Show; Oklahoma Crude; The Sting; The Great Waldo Pepper; The Hindenberg; A Star is Born; The Turning Point; Bloodbrothers; Same Time Next Year.

(Died Jan. 5, 1985)

SUSSKIND, David: Prod-TV pers. b. NYC, Dec 1920. Films inc: Edge of the City; A Raisin in the Sun; Requiem for a Heavyweight; All the Way Home; Lovers and Other Strangers; Loving Couples; Fort Apache, The Bronx.

TV inc: Ages of Man (Emmy-1966); Blind Ambition; Transplant; Eleanor and Franklin (Emmy-Exec Prod-1976); Eleanor and Franklin-The White House Years (Emmy-Exec Prod-1977); Sex and the Single Parent; The Family Man; The Plutonium Incident; Father Figure; Mom, The Wolfman and Me; The Bunker; Crisis at Central High; Mr. Lincoln; Dear Liar; Casey Stengel; The Wall; Ian McKellen Acting Shakespeare; Lovers and Other Strangers; Rita Hayworth--The Love Goddess; JFK--A One Man Show (exec prod).

Thea inc: Mister Lincoln (Bway); Dear Anyone (London); Tallulah (off Bway).

SUTHERLAND, Donald: Act. e. U of Toronto, BA. Films inc: The Castle of the Living Dead; Die, Die My Darling; The Bedford Incident; Oedipus Rex; M*A*S*H; Kelly's Heroes; Johnny Get Your Gun; Klute; Steelyard Blues; The Day of the Locust; The Disappearance; Blood Relatives; The Invasion of the Body Snatchers; The Eagle Has Landed; Fellini's Casanova; The Great Train Robbery; Nat'l Lampoons Animal House; Murder By Decree; A Man, A Woman and a Bank; Bear Island; Nothing Personal; Ordinary People; Eye of the Needle; Gas; Threshold; A War Story; Max Dugan Returns; Crackers; Ordeal By Innocence; Heaven Help Us.

TV (British): Marching to the Sea; The Death of Bessie Smith; Hamlet at Elsinore; (U.S.) The Game And Its Glory--Baseball's Hall of Fame (host); Heart of Gold (narr); John Steinbeck's The Winter of our Discontent.

Thea inc: On a Clear Day You Can See Canterbury; The Shewing Up of Blanco Posnet; The Spoon River Anthology; Lolita.

SUTHERLAND, Joan: Coloratura Soprano. b. Sydney, Australia, Apr 7, 1926. Concert and oratorio artist. Opera debut Covent Gardens 1952 in the Magic Flute; guest appearances La Scala; Metropolitan Opera; Lyric Opera of Chicago; Melbourne Opera; Carnegie Hall; Films inc: Carmen. TV inc: Die Fledermaus (Australian).

(Grammys-Class vocal-1961, 1981).

SUZMAN, Janet: Act. b. Johannesburg, S Africa, Feb 9, 1939. e. Kingsmead Coll, U of Witwatersrand. Joined the Royal Shakespeare Company 1962. London stage debut in The Comedy of Errors. Thea

inc: The Greeks; Cowardice.

Films inc: A Day in the Death of Joe Egg; Nicholas and Alexandra; The Black Windmill; Nijinsky; Priest Of Love; The Draughtsman's Contract; E la nave va (And the Ship Sails On).

TV inc: The Three Sisters; Hedda Gabler; The House on Garibaldi Street; The Zany Adventures of Robin Hood.

SVENSON, Bo: Perf. b. Sweden, Feb 13, 1941. Films inc: Maurie; The Great Waldo Pepper; Walking Tall, Part II; Breaking Point; Special Delivery; Walking Tall--Final Chapter; Jim Buck; The Inglorious Bastards; Our Man in Mecca; Son of the Sheik; Night Flight; North Dallas Forty; Virus; Night Warning.

TV inc: Walking Tall; I Do, I Don't; Jealousy.

SWACKHAMER, E.W.: Dir. Films inc: Man and Boy. TV inc: In Name Only; Gidget Gets Married; Death Sentence; Death at Love House; Once An Eagle; Night Terror; Spider Man; The Dain Curse; The Winds of Kitty Hawk; Vampire; The Death of Ocean View Park; 10 Speed and Brown Shoe; Reward; The Oklahoma City Dolls; Foul Play; Tales of the Apple Dumpling Gang; Bring 'Em Back Alive; Cocaine and Blue Eyes; Malibu; The Rousters; Carpool; The Sheriff and the Astronaut.

SWADOS, Elizabeth: Wri-Dir-Comp. b. Feb 5, 1951. e. Bennington Coll. Wrote music for the Andre Serban trilogy at La Mama (The Trojan Woman, Electra, Medea); The Cherry Orchard; Agamemnon; Nightclub Cantata (& dir); Ghost Sonata; Step By Step; Sky Dance. Other thea inc: Runaways (& chor); Wonderland in Concert; Dispatches; Haggadah; The Girl with the Incredible Feeling (wri-act); Doonesbury (comp); Rap Master Ronnie (comp).

TV inc: (comp) The Girls in Their Summer Dresses and other Stories by Irwin Shaw; Alice at the Palace; King of America; The Killing Floor; What Do Children Think Of When They Think of the Bomb? (& dir).

Films inc: (comp) Four Friends; Too Far To Go.

SWAIM, Bob: Wri-dir. b. Evanston, IL., 1944. Films inc: (Shorts) Le Journal de M Bonnafous; Self Portrait of a Pornographer; Vive les Jacques. (Features) La Nuit de Saint-Germain-des-Pres; La Balance (The Nark).

SWANSON, Glen: Dir. TV inc: Sports Challenge; Movie Game; The Way It Was; Grease-Pay; Dinah's Place; Make Me Laugh; Dinah Salutes Broadway (Emmy-1975); Dinah Salutes Tony Orlando and Dawn on their Fifth Birthday (Emmy-1976); Dinah!; Hour Magazine (Emmy-1983).

SWANSON, Gloria: Act. b. Chicago, Mar 27, 1899. On screen from 1913 in The Romance of an American Duchess. Appeared in many silent films inc Mack Sennett comedies. In 1926 became producer-star as an owner-member of United Artists.

Films inc: Don't Change Your Husband; For Better, For Worse; Male and Female; Zara; Manhandled; Wages of Virtue; The Love of Sunya; Sadie Thompson; The Trespasser; What a Widow; Indiscreet; Tonight or Never; Music in the Air; Father Takes a Wife; Sunset Boulevard; 3 for Bedroom C; Nero's Mistress; Airport 1975; Queen Kelly (Unfinished Erich Von Stroheim film made in 1929).

Bway inc: Twentieth Century; Nina; Butterflies Are Free.

TV inc: Killer Bees; Ready When You Are, Mr. De Mille.

(Died April 4, 1983).

SWAYZE, John Cameron: Broadcaster. b. Wichita, KS, Apr 4, 1906. Reporter and editor Kansas City, MO, Journal-Post; news dept. KMBC, Kansas City; head of News, NBC western network, Hollywood; NBC radio news, NYC; TV, 1948-52. TV inc: News Caravan; Who Said That; Watch the World; Sightseeing with the Swayzes; Circle Theatre; To Tell the Truth.

SWAYZE, Patrick: Act. b. Houston, TX., Aug. 18. Started as dancer, appearing in Disney On Parade, on tour. Bway inc: Goodtime Charley; Grease.

Films inc: Skatetown, U.S.A.; The Outsiders; Uncommon Valor; Red Dawn; Grandview, U.S.A. (& chor).

TV inc: The New Season; Pigs vs. Freaks; The Comeback Kid; The Return Of the Rebels; The Renegades.

SWEET, Blanche: Act. b. Chicago, Il, Jun 18, 1896. Silent screen star, made her debut in 1909 in The Rocky Road.

Films inc: Was He a Coward?; A Country Cupid; The Eternal Mother; The Making of a Man; The Painted Lady; The Lesser Evil; Broken Ways; Judith of Bethulia; The Battle of Elderberry Gulch; The Storm; Quincy Adams Sawyer; Tess of the D'Urbervilles; Anna Christie; The Sporting Venus; Bluebeard's Seven Wives; Diplomacy; The Silver Horde; The Five Pennies; Before the Nickelodeon--The Early Cinema of Edwin S Porter (doc) (narr).

SWEET, Dolph: Act. b. NYC, Jul 18, 1920. Bway inc: Rhinoceros; Streamers; The Penny Wars; Billy; The Sign in Sidney Brustein's Window.

Films inc: You're A Big Boy Now; The New Centurions; Which Way Is Up?; Heaven Can Wait; Reds.

TV inc: Another World; When the Whistle Blows; Jacqueline Bouvier Kennedy; The Two Lives of Carol Letner; Gimme a Break.

(Died May 8, 1985)

SWENSON, Inga: Act. b. Omaha, NE, Dec 29, 1934. e. Northwestern U. Bway inc: Twelfth Night; New Faces of 1956; The First Gentleman; 110 Degrees in the Shade; Baker Street.

Films inc: The Miracle Worker; Advise and Consent; The Betsy; Wind River.

TV inc: Playhouse 90; U S Steel Hour; Soap; Androcles and the Lion; Testimony of Two Men; Benson.

SWERLING, Jo: Wri. b. Russia, Apr 8, 1897. Newspaper and mag wr; auth vaudeville sketches; co-author plays, The Kibitzer; Guys and Dolls (Tony-1951).

Films inc: The Kibitzer; The Pride of the Yankees; Guys and Dolls; Platinum Blonde; Washington Merry-Go-Round; Dirigible; No Greater Glory; Pennies from Heaven; Made for Each Other; Confirm or Deny; Blood and Sand; The Lady Takes a Chance; Crash Dive; Lifeboat; Leave Her to Heaven; Thunder in the East.

TV: The Lord Don't Play Favorites.

SWERLING, Jo, Jr: Prod. b. Los Angeles, Jun 18, 1931. e. UCLA. Joined Revue Prodns 1957 as prodn coord; became asso prod, later prod Kraft Suspense Theatre. TV inc: (Prod) Run For Your Life; The Bold Ones; Drive Hard, Drive Fast; The Lonely Profession; The Whole World is Watching; The Sound of Anger; How to Steal an Airplane; Cool Million; Toma; The Story of Pretty Boy Floyd; This is the West That Was; Baretta; Captains and the Kings; The 3,000 Mile Chase; Aspen; The Jordan Chance; Pirate's Key. (Exec Prod) Target Risk; City of Angels; Hazard's People; The Invasion of Johnson County; The Last Convertible (& dir). The Rockford Files (asso exec prod of pilot, supv prod series); Lobo (supv prod); The Quest; Hardcastle and McCormick (supv prod); The Rousters (exec prod); Riptide (supv prod); Hunter (supv prod); The A Team (supv prod).

SWIFT, Lela: Dir. TV inc: Studio One; Dupont Show of the Week; Norman Corwin Presents; Years Without Harvest; A Gift of Terror (Emmy-1973); Purex Specials for Women; Ryan's Hope (Emmys-1977, 1979, 1980).

SWIFT, Susan: Act. b. Houston, TX, Jul 21, 1964. Films inc: Audrey Rose; Harper Valley PTA.

SWINK, Robert E.: Film Ed-Dir. b. Rocky Ford, CO, Jun 3, 1918. Films inc: Detective Story; Carrie; Roman Holiday; Desperate Hours; Friendly Persuasion; The Diary of Anne Frank; The Children's Hour; The Best Man; How to Steal a Million; Flim Flam Man; Funny Girl; The Cowboys; Skyjacked; Papillon; Three the Hard Way; Rooster Cogburn; Midway; Islands in the Stream; Gray Lady Down; The Boys From Brazil; The In-Laws; Sphinx.

SWIT, Loretta: Act. b. Passaic, NJ, Nov 4, 1937. Films inc: Deadhead Miles; Stand Up and be Counted; Freebie and the Bean; Race with the Devil; S.O.B.

TV inc: M*A*S*H (Emmys-supp-1980,1982); The Last Day; Shirts/Skins; Coffeeville; Mirror, Mirror; Friendships, Secrets and Lies; The Love Tapes; Bob Hope All-Star Comedy Christmas Special; Cagney and Lacey (pilot); The Kid From Nowhere; Texaco Star Theatre--Opening Night; Games Mother Never Taught You; First Affair; Animals Are the Funniest People (host); The Best Christmas Pageant Ever; The Execution; The Real Trivial Pursuit; Sam.

Bway inc: Same Time, Next Year.

SWOFFORD, Ken: Act. b. DuQuoin, IL, Jul 25. Films inc: Captain Newman, M.D.

TV inc: Rich Man, Poor Man II; Ellery Queen; Switch; Capra; Sultan and the Rock Star; All God's Children; M.A.D.D.--Mothers Against Drunk Driving; I Want to Live; Fame; The Rousters; Kenny Rogers as the Gambler--The Adventure Continues.

SWOPE, Mel: Prod-Dir. TV inc: (Dir) Tennessee Ernie Ford Show; Partridge Family; Land of Tinkerdee (Muppets pilot); Everything Money Can't Buy (& prod). (Prod) California Fever; Man Undercover; Paradise Cove; Police Story; The Girl With Something Extra (pilot); The Night The City Screamed; Walking Tall; Fame (prod); The Kids From Fame (exec prod); Miami Vice (prod).

SYBERBERG, Hans-Jurgen: Dir-Cin. b. E Germany, Dec 8, 1935. Worked with Brecht and the Berliner Ensemble as cin. Films inc: Fritz Kortner Rehearses Schiller's "Kabale und Liebe" (doc); Romy--Anatomy of a Face (doc); Kortner Speaks Monologs for a Record (doc); Count Pocci (doc); Scarabea--How Much Earth Does Man Need?; Sex Business Made in Passin (doc); San Domingo; After My Last Move (doc); Ludwig--Requiem for a Virgin King; Theodor Hiernies--Or How To Become the Cook of the Court; Karl May; Winifried Wagner and the story of the "Haus Wahnfried" (doc); Our Hitler--A Film From Germany; Parsifal.

SYLBERT, Anthea: Exec. b. NYC, Oct 6, 1939. e. Barnard Coll, Parsons School of Design. Started as costume desgn; 1977 vp special projects WB; 1978 vp prodn; 1980, vp prodn UA; Oct 1982 resd.

Films inc: (cos dsgn) Rosemary's Baby; A New Leaf; Carnal Knowledge; The Heartbreak Kid; Chinatown; Shampoo; The Fortune; Julia; F.I.S.T. (part). (Prod): Protocol.

Bway Inc: (cos dsgn) The Real Thing.

SYLBERT, Paul: Dsgn-Dir. Films inc: (Dsgn) The Steagle (& wri-dir); The Drowning Pool; One Flew Over the Cuckoo's Nest; Hardcore; Heaven Can Wait (Oscar-1978); Kramer vs. Kramer; Resurrection; Blow Out; Without A Trace; Gorky Park; The Pope of Greenwich Village; Firstborn.

TV inc: (Dsgn) Studio One; Suspense; Ed Sullivan Show. (Dir) The Defenders; The Nurses.

Has also dsgn for NY City Opera Company.

SYLBERT, Richard: Art Dir. b. NYC, Apr 16, 1928. e. Temple U. VP prod. Paramount Pictures Corp, 1975-76. Films inc: Baby Doll; Splendor in the Grass; Walk on the Wild Side; The Manchurian Candidate; How to Murder Your Wife; The Pawnbroker; Who's Afraid of Virginia Woolf (Oscar-1966); Rosemary's Baby; Catch 22; Carnal Knowledge; Chinatown; Shampoo; The Fortune; Players; Frances; Breathless; The Cotton Club.

TV inc: Cheers; Partners.

SYMS, Sylvia: Act. b. London, Dec 3, 1934. Films inc: My Teenage Daughter; No Time for Tears; Birthday Present; Ice Cold in Alex; The Devil's Disciple; Moonraker; Ferry to Hong Kong; Expresso Bongo; The World of Suzie Wong; Flame in the Streets; The Quare Fellow; The World Ten Times Over; East of Sudan; The Eliminator; Operation Crossbow; Hostile Witness; The Marauders; Run Wild, Run Free; The Tamarind Seed; Give Us This Day.

TV inc: The Human Jungle; Bat Out of Hell; Depart in Terror; Friends and Romans; The Root of All Evil; My Good Woman; Love and Marriage; There Goes the Bride.

SZABO, Istvan: Dir. b, Hungary, 1938. e. Budapest Academy of Film Art. Films inc: Concert, Variations on a Theme (short); You (Short); Age of Illusions; Father; A Film About Love; Firemen's Street; Tales of Budapest; The Hungarians; The Green Bird; Mephisto; Oberst Redl (Colonel Redl) (& wri).

SZWARC, Jeannot: Dir. b. Paris, Nov 21, 1939. Films inc: Extreme Close-up; Bug; Jaws 2; Somewhere In Time; Enigma; Supergirl.

TV inc: Ironside; To Catch A Thief; Kojak; Columbo; Night Gallery; Crime Club; True Life Stories.

TABORI, George: Wri. b. Budapest, Hungary, May 24, 1914. Plays inc: Flight Into Egypt: The Emperor's Clothes; Brouhaha; Brecht on Brecht; Demonstration, and Man and Dog (one-acters); The Cannibals; Pinkville.

Films inc: Young Lovers; I Confess; The Journey; No Exit; Secret Ceremony; Parades.

TABORI, Kristofer: Act. b. Aug 4, 1955. S of Viveca Lindfors and Don Siegel. H of Judy Geeson. Films inc: Weddings and Babies; Making It; Journey Through Rosebud; Girlfriends.

TV inc: QB VII; A Memory of Two Mondays; The Glass House; The Lady's Not for Burning; Mad About the Boy; The Greatest Heroes of the Bible; Brave New World; The Chicago Story; Small & Frye.

Bway inc: A Cry of Players; Habeas Corpus.

TACCHELLA, Jean-Charles: Dir. b. France, 1926. Films inc: Les derniers hivers (short); Un belle journee (short); Voyage to the Grand Tartarie; Cousin Cousine; Le Pays bleu (The Blue Country); Croque la Vie (A Bite of Living).

TAHSE, Martin: Prod. TV inc: Exec prod ABC Afternoon Specials (Emmy-Very Good Friends-1980); (Emmy-A Matter of Time-1981); She Drinks A Little. Tough Girl; Daddy, I'm Their Mama Now; Andrea's Story--A Hitchhiking Tragedy; The Hoboken Chicken Emergency; First The Egg.

TAIT, Don: Wri. Films inc: The Castaway Cowboy; The Apple Dumpling Gang; Treasure of the Matecumbe; The Shaggy D A; The North Avenue Irregulars; The Apple Dumpling Gang Rides Again; Unidentified Flying Oddballs; Herbie Goes Bananas (& co-prod).

TV inc: The Green Hornet; The Iron Horse; The Outcasts; The Virginian; Here Come the Brides; The Bold Ones.

TAKA, Miiko: Act. Films inc: Cry for Happy; Hell to Eternity; A Girl Called Tamiko; Operation Bottleneck; A Global Affair; The Art of Love; Walk, Don't Run; Lost Horizon; Paper Tiger; The Big Fix.

TV inc: Shogun.

TAKEI, George: Act. Films inc: Ice Palace; Red Line 7000; Walk Don't Run; The Green Berets; Which Way to the Front; Star Trek--The Motion Picture; Star Trek II--The Wrath of Khan; Star Trek III--The Search for Spock.

TV inc: Star Trek.

TALANKIN, Igor: Wri-dir. b. Russia, Oct 3, 1927. e. State Institute of Theatrical Art; Glazunov School of Music and Drama; Advanced Directors Course, Mosfilm Studios. Films inc: Kuzmich; Seryozha; Introduction; Stars By Day; Tschaikovsky; The Choice of a Goal (dir only); Father Serge.

TALBOT, Lyle (Lysle Henderson): Act. b. Pittsburgh, PA, Feb 8, 1904. Screen debut, 1932, Love Is a Racket.

Films inc: Up in Arms; One Body Too Many; Vicious Circle; Sky Dragon; The Jackpot; Oil for the Lamps of China; 20,000 Years in Sing Sing; The Life of Jimmy Dolan; White Lightning; The Great Man; Sunrise at Campobello; Adventures of Batman and Robin; Glen or Glenda.

TV inc: The Case of Dashiell Hammett (doc)(voice).

TALBOT, Nita (Anita Sokol): Act. b. NYC, Aug 8, 1930. Films inc: Bundle of Joy; I Married a Woman; Once Upon a Horse; Who's Got the Action?; A Very Special Favor; That Funny Feeling; Girl Happy; The Cool Ones; Buck and the Preacher; The Manchu Eagle; The Sweet Creek County War; Night Shift; The Concrete Jungle; Chained Heat; Frightmare; Fraternity Vacation; Movers & Shakers.

TV inc: Stage Door; Here We Go Again; The Movie Murderer.

Thea inc: Never Say Never; The Fifth Season; Uncle Willie; Zelda; Insight/Mr. and Mrs. Bliss; The Other Woman; Insight/Dutton's Choice; You Are The Jury.

TALLAS, Gregory: Prod-Dir-Edtr. b. Athens, Greece, Jan 25, 1915. e. Princeton. Films inc: (edtr) Shanghai Gesture; Three Russian Girls; Summer Storm; The Southerner; Whistle Stop; Night in Casablanca; Without Honor; Flight to Nowhere; Captain Apache. (Dir) Siren of Atlantis; Red Rock Outlaw; Prehistoric Women; Barefoot Battalion; Bed of Grass; Forbidden Love; Bikini Paradise; S-007; Espionage in Tangiers; Love is Out; Cataclysm.

TV inc: (dir) Ford Theatre; Rheingold Theatre; You Be The Jury.

TALLCHIEF, Maria: Dancer. b. Fairfax, OK, 1925. Generally regarded as the first great American prima ballerina. With the Ballet Russe de Monte Carlo; New York City Ballet; guest prima ballerina American Ballet Theatre; last danced professionally in 1965; founder, artistic dir Lyric Opera Ballet, Chicago; in 1980 group renamed Chicago City Ballet while retaining ties to Lyric Opera. Films inc: Million Dollar Mermaid.

TAMBLYN, Russ: Act. b. Los Angeles, Dec 30, 1934. Films inc: Father of the Bride; Father's Little Dividend; Seven Brides for Seven Brothers; Hit the Deck; Don't Go Near the Water; Peyton Place; Tom Thumb; Cimarron; West Side Story; The Wonderful World of the Brothers Grimm; The Haunting; Son of a Gunfighter; Blood of Frankenstein; The Last Movie; Win, Place or Steal; Human Highway (& wri)

TAMBOR, Jeffrey: Act. b. San Francisco, CA, Jul 8. e. San Francisco State, BA; Wayne State, MA. Worked with Seattle Repertory; Old Globe Theatre, San Diego; Louisville Actors Theatre. Bway inc: Sly Fox; Measure for Measure.

Films inc: And Justice for All; Saturday the 14th; 9 to 5; Mr. Mom; The Man Who Wasn't There; No Small Affair.

TV inc: The Ropers; Alcatraz--The Whole Shocking Story; The Star Maker; Pals; The Zertigo Diamond Caper; Take Your Best Shot; Cocaine--One Man's Seduction; Sadat; The Three Wishes Of Billy Grier; Robert Kennedy & His Times.

TANAKA, Tomoyuki: Prod. b. Osaka, Japan, 1910. P of Toho Pictures, Inc. Has prod more than 200 films since joining Toho 1944. Films inc: Godzilla; The Rickshaw Man; The Bad Sleep Well; Yojimbo; Sanjuro; High and Low; Red Beard; The Emperor and the General; The Submersion of Japan; Mount Hakkoda; Kagemusha; Rengo Kantai (The Great Fleet); Sasame Yuki (The Makioka Sisters) (exec prod); Ohan.

TANDY, Jessica: Act. b. London, England, Jun 7, 1909. W of Hume Cronyn. Thea inc: (London) The Rumour; Theatre of Life; Water; The Unknown Warrior; Autumn Crocus; Juarez and Maximilian; Children In Uniform; Lady Audley's Secret; various Shakespearean roles. (Bway) The Matriarch; The Last Enemy; Time and the Conways; The White Steed; Geneva; Jupiter Laughs; A Streetcar Named Desire (Tony-1948); The Little Blue Light; Hilda Crane; The Fourposter; Madame Will You Walk; The Man in the Dog Suit; Five Finger Exercise; The Physicists; A Delicate Balance; All Over; Noel Coward in Two Keys; The Many Faces of Love; The Gin Game (Tony-1978); Rose; Foxfire (Tony-1983); The Glass Menagerie; Salonika (off-Bway).

Films inc: The Indiscretions of Eve; The Green Years; Forever Amber; The Seventh Cross; Dragonwyck; Valley of Decision; September Affair; The Four Poster; The Desert Fox; Butley; A Light in the Forest; The Birds; Honky Tonk Freeway; The World According to Garp; Still of the Night; Best Friends; The Bostonians; Cocoon.

TANEN, Ned: Exec. b. Los Angeles. e. UCLA. Joined MCA, Inc, 1954; app'd VP, 1968. Bought Uni Records, since absorbed by MCA Records. Became active in film prod, 1972. In 1976 named P Universal Theatrical Motion Pictures; Dec 1982, resd to become ind prod; Oct. 1984, P Motion Picture Group, Paramount. Films inc: Sixteen Candles (exec prod); The Breakfast Club (prod); St. Elmo's Fire (exec prod).

TANNENBAUM, Tom: Exec. Started as asst in MGM casting dept; with Famous Artists as agent, co-head tv dept; exec asst to Ray Stark at Seven Arts; vp David Wolper Prodns; sr vp Paramount TV; sr VP U-TV; Nov 1978, exec vp Columbia Pictures TV; May 1980 P MGM-TV; resd June 1982 to become P for TV of Centerpoint Prodns; Aug. 1984, resd. to become P Viacom Prodns.

TAPLIN, Jonathan L.: Prod. b. Cleveland, OH, Jul 18, 1947. e. Princeton U, BA. Concert mgr for Judy Collins; The Band; The Concert for Bangladesh; bought Robert Altman's Lion's Gate Film facilities, July 1981, became P of Lion's Gate, Dec 1981; resd Nov. 1983. for indie prodn; April 1985, joined Merrill Lynch Investment Bankers as VP mergers and acquisitions.

Films inc: Mean Streets; The Last Waltz; Carny; Under Fire;

Grandview, U.S.A. (exec prod); Baby.

TARADASH, Daniel: Wri-Dir. b. Louisville, KY, Jan 29, 1913. e. Harvard Coll, AB; Harvard Law School, LLB. Films inc: Golden Boy ; A Little Bit of Heaven ; Knock On Any Door ; Don't Bother to Knock; Rancho Notorious; From Here To Eternity (Oscar-1953); Picnic; Desiree; Storm Center (& dir); Bell Book and Candle; Hawaii; Castle Keep; Doctor's Wives; The Other Side of Midnight. Plays: American adaptation, Red Gloves; There Was a Little Girl.

TV inc: Bogie.

TARKENTON, Fran: TV pers. b. Richmond, VA, Feb 3, 1940. e. U of GA. Former pro football QB with Vikings 1961-1967, 1972-1979; Giants 1967-1972. TV inc: Monday Night Football; That's Incredible (host).

TARKOVSKY, Andrei: Dir. b. Russia, Apr 4, 1932. e. Moscow Film Institute. Films inc: The Roller and the Violin (short) (& sp); Ivan's Childhood; Andrei Rublev (& co-sp); Solaris (& co-sp); The Mirror (& co-sp); Stalker (& co-sp, sets); Nostalghia; De Weg Naar Bresson (The Way to Bresson) (doc-int); Andrei Tarkovsky (doc-wri).

TARLOFF, Frank: Wri. Films inc: Father Goose (Oscar-1964); The Secret War of Harry Frigg; Once You Kiss A Stranger.

TV inc: Shirley MacLaine Show (crea); The Jeffersons; A Guide for the Married Woman.

TARNOFF, John B.: Exec. b. NYC, Mar 3, 1952. e. Amherst Coll, BA. With Billy Jack Enterprises, 1974: literary agent, Bart-Levy Assoc, 1975-77; head of tv dept, Kohner-Levy Assoc; vp motion picture devlpmnt, MGM, 1979; sr vp in chg prodn & devlpmt Dec. 1980; Jan 1983, exec vp Kings Road Prodns; Jan. 1985, joined Orion as prodn. vp.

TARTIKOFF, Brandon: Exec. b. NY, Jan 13, 1949. e. Yale U, BA. Joined ABC-TV in 1976 as m, dramatic development; moved to NBC Entertainment in Sep 1977, as dir, comedy programs; apptd vp, programs, West Coast NBC Entertainment, July 1978; P NBC Entertainment, July 1980; Guest-hosted Saturday Night Live, Oct 11, 1983.

TATUM, Donn B.: Exec. b. Los Angeles, Jan 9, 1913. e. Stanford, Oxford. Chmn Bd & CEO of Walt Disney Productions. With company since 1956 when he left ABC to become Disney's prodn business mgr.

TAVEL, Ronald: Wri. b. NYC, May 1941. e. U of WY. Plays inc: Tarzan of the Flicks; Screen Test; The Life of Juanita Castro; Shower; The Life of Lady Godiva; Gorilla Queen; Boy on the Straight-Back Chair; How Jacqueline Kennedy Became Queen of Greece.

TAVERNIER, Bertrand: Wri-Dir. b. Lyons, France, Apr 25, 1941. Originally a film publicist, he studied techniques of prods with whom he worked; debuted as dir with one of five episodes in Les Baisers; later contributed episode to La Chance et L'Amour.

Films inc: (wri) Coplan Ouvre le feu a Mexico; Capitaine Singrid. (Wri-dir) The Clockmaker of Saint Paul; Let Joy Reign Supreme; The Judge and the Assassin; Spoiled Children; Deathwatch (& co-prod); Une Semaine De Vacances; Coup de Torchon (Pop 1280); La Trace; Un Dimanche a la Campagne (A Sunday in the Country); Mississippi Blues (doc).

TAVIANI, Paolo: Wri-dir. b. Italy, 1931. B of Vittorio Taviani with whom he works. Films inc: A Man for the Burning; I Fuorilegge del Matrimonio; Under the Sign of Scorpio; San Michele aveva un Gallo; Allonsanfan; Padre Padrone (Father Master); Il Prato (The Meadow); La Notre di San Lorenzo (Night of the Shooting Stars); Kaos (Chaos).

TAVIANI, Vittorio: Wri-dir. b. Italy, 1929. For credits, see TAVIANI, Paolo.

TAYBACK, Vic: Act. b. NYC., Jan. 6 Films inc: Bullitt; Papillon; The Gambler; Report to the Commissioner; The Big Bus; The Shaggy D A; Alice Doesn't Live Here Anymore; The Choirboys; Special Delivery; The Cheap Detective.

TV inc: MacKenzie's Raiders; Honor Thy Father; Getting Married;

Rage; Alice; Moviola (This Year's Blonde); Portrait of A Stripper; The Great American Traffic Jam; The Night the City Screamed; Through the Magic Pyramid; Shape of Things; Mysterious Two; Small World (host); The Jesse Owens Story; The New Man; Finder Of Lost Loves.

Thea inc: The Diary of Anne Frank; Death of a Salesman; Stalag 17.

TAYLOR, Don: Act-Dir. b. Freeport, PA, Dec 13, 1920. Films inc: (act) Naked City; For the Love of Mary; Ambush; Father of the Bride; Submarine Command; The Blue Veil; Stalag 17; Men of Sherwood Forest; I'll Cry Tomorrow. (Dir) The Savage Guns; Ride the Wild Surf; Jack of Diamonds; Five Man Army; Escape from the Planet of the Apes; Tom Sawyer; Echoes of a Summer; The Great Scout and Cathouse Thursday; The Island of Dr Moreau; Damien-Omen II; The Final Countdown.

TV inc: (dir) The Gift; The Promise of Love; Broken Promise (& prod); Red Flag-The Ultimate Game; Drop-Out Father; Listen To Your Heart (& prod); September Gun; He's Not Your Son; My Wicked, Wicked Ways (& wri); Secret Weapons; Going For The Gold--The Bill Johnson Story.

TAYLOR, Elizabeth: Act. b. London, Feb 27, 1932. Danced before Princess Elizabeth & Princess Margaret at age 3. Came to US at outbreak WW II. Screen debut, 1943, Lassie Come Home.

Films inc: National Velvet; Life With Father; Cynthia; Courage of Lassie; Little Women; The White Cliffs of Dover; Jane Eyre; Father of the Bride; Father's Little Dividend; A Place in the Sun; Ivanhoe; The Girl Who Had Everything; Elephant Walk; Beau Brummell; The Last Time I Saw Paris; Giant; Raintree Country; Cat on a Hot Tin Roof; Suddenly, Last Summer; Butterfield 8 (Oscar-1960); Cleopatra; The V.I.P.'s; The Night of the Iguana; Who's Afraid of Virginia Woolf? (Oscar-1966); The Taming of the Shrew; The Sandpiper; Doctor Faustus; Reflections in a Golden Eye; The Comedians; The Only Game in Town; X, Y, and Zee; Hammersmith Is Out; Night Watch; Ash Wednesday; That's Entertainment!; The Driver's Seat; The Blue Bird; A Little Night Music; The Mirror Crack'd; Genocide (doc-narr); George Stevens--A Filmmaker's Journey (doc-int).

Bway inc: The Little Foxes (rev) (& London); Private Lives (& prod); The Corn Is Green (prod).

TV inc: General Hospital; Bob Hope's Stand Up and Cheer for the National Football League's 60th Year; Between Friends (cable); Hotel.

TAYLOR, James: Comp-Mus. b. Boston, MA, Mar 12, 1948. Albums inc: Sweet Baby James; Mud Slide Slim and the Blue Horizon; One Man Dog; Walking Man; Gorilla; In the Pocket; J.T.; James Taylor's Greatest Hits; Flag. Singles inc: You've Got a Friend (Grammy-pop male voc-1971); Handy Man (Grammy-pop male vocal-1977).

TV inc: Working (& act).

TAYLOR, Jud: Dir. b. Feb 25, 1940. TV inc: Hawkins; Winter Kill; Sara; Future Cop; Return to Earth; Tail Gunner Joe; Mary White; Circle of Children II; Lovey; The Last Tenant; Flesh and Blood; Act of Love; Incident At Crestridge (& exec prod); A Question of Honor; The Big Easy; Packin' It In; License to Kill.

June 1983 became P of prodn Columbia Pictures; resd Dec. 1983.

TAYLOR, Kent (Louis Weiss): Act. b. Nashua, IA, May 11, 1907. On screen from 1931. Films inc: Road to Reno; The Devil and the Deep; Blonde Venus; Death Takes a Holiday; Mrs. Wiggs of the Cabbage Patch; David Harum; Ramona; Mississippi Gambler; Roger Touhy-Gangster; Payment on Demand; Brides of Blood; Girls for Rent.

TAYLOR, Noel: Cos Dsgn. b. Youngstown, OH, Jan 17, 1917. Bway inc: Alice in Wonderland; Twentieth Century; Stalag 17; One Bright Day; Dial M for Murder; Teahouse of the August Moon; Ladies of the Corridor; In the Summer House; Festival; No Time for Sergeants; Time Limit; Auntie Mame; The Body Beautiful; Tall Story; Write Me a Murder; Night of the Iguana; Desire Under the Elms; One Flew Over the Cuckoo's Nest; What Makes Sammy Run?; The White Devil; We Have Always Lived in the Castle; We Bombed in New Haven; A Funny Thing Happened on the Way to the Forum; The Last of Mrs Lincoln; The Norman Conquests; Mixed Couples.

Films inc: Rhinoceros.

TV inc: The Hallmark Hall of Fame; NBC Opera; Dupont Show of the Week; Turn of the Screw; Bus Stop (cable).

TAYLOR, Renee: Act-Plywri. b. Mar 19, 1945. W of Joseph Bologna. (Writes in collaboration with husband). Bway inc: Luv (act); Agatha Sue I Love You (act); Lovers and Other Strangers; It Had To Be You.

Films inc: The Last of the Red Hot Lovers; The Errand Boys; The Detective; The Producers; The New Leaf; Lovers and Other Strangers (& wri); Made for Each Other (& wri); Lovesick.

TV inc: (wri) Acts of Love and Other Comedies (*Emmy*-1973); Paradise; Calucci's Department (created); The American Dream Machine; Drink, Drank, Drunk; A Cry For Love; Love, Sex. . .& Marriage?; Lovers and Other Strangers (& prod); Lottery! (act); St. Elsewhere (act).

TAYLOR, Rod: Act. b. Sydney, Australia, Jan 11, 1929. e. Fine Arts Coll. Originally an artist. Screen debut, 1955, Long John Silver. Films inc: The Virgin Queen; Giant; Separate Tables; Step Down to Terror; The V.I.P.s; The Birds; Young Cassidy; A Gathering of Eagles; 36 Hours; The Glass Bottom Boat; Hotel; Chuka; The Train Robbers; Blondy; Trader Horn; On a Dead Man's Chest; Hell River; A Time to Die; On the Run.

TV inc: Cry of the Innocent; Hellinger's Law; Jacqueline Bouvier Kennedy; Charles and Diana--A Royal Love Story; Masquerade; Half Nelson.

TAYLOR, Ron: Cin-Prod. b. Sydney, Australia, Mar 8, 1934. Underwater photography for Blue Water White Death; live shark footage for Jaws; Jaws II; Orca. Films inc: Sharks (prod); Sharks, The Death Machine (cin); The Silent One.

TAYLOR, Ronnie: Cin. b. England. Started in Camera dept Gainsborough Studios, worked on many films with Freddie Francis before becoming dir of photography. Films inc: Savage Harvest; High Road to China; Gandhi (*Oscar*-1982); The Hound of the Baskervilles; Champions; Splitz.

TV inc: Master of the Game; Nairobi Affair.

TAYLOR, Samuel A.: Plywri. b. Chicago, Jun 13, 1912. Plays inc: The Happy Time; Sabrina Fair; The Pleasure of His Company; First Love; No Strings; Beekman Place: Avanti; A Touch of Spring; Legend; Perfect Pitch; Gracious Living.

Films inc: Sabrina.

TAYLOR-YOUNG, Leigh: Act. b. Washington, DC, Jan. 25, 1944. Films inc: I Love You Alice B. Toklas; The Big Bounce; The Adventurers; The Buttercup Chain; The Horsemen; The Gang That Couldn't Shoot Straight; Soylent Green; Can't Stop the Music; Looker; Secret Admirer.

TV inc: Peyton Place; Marathon; The Devlin Connection; The Hamptons.

TEAGUE, Lewis: Dir. b. 1941. e. NYU. Films inc: Dirty O'Neil (co-dir); Lady in Red (& edtr); Alligator; Fighting Back; Cujo; Cat's Eye.

TV inc: Alfred Hitchcock Presents; Daredevils.

TEASDALE, Verree: Act. b. Spokane, WA, Mar 15, 1906. Films inc: Syncopation; The Sap from Syracuse; Luxury Liner; Roman Scandals; Madame Du Barry; A Midsummer Night Dream; The Milky Way; Topper Takes a Trip; I Take This Woman; Love Thy Neighbor; Come Live With Me.

TEBALDI, Renata: Lyric soprano. b. Pesaro, Italy, Jan 2, 1922. Debut La Scala, 1946; sang with opera companies in Naples, Rome, Venice, Bologna, Turin before US debut 1950 with San Francisco Opera Company; Metropolitan Opera debut 1955. Best known roles in Aida; Othello; La Boheme; Madame Butterfly; Tosca.

(*Grammy*-Class vocal-1958).

TEBET, David W.: Exec. b. Dec 27, 1920. Sr VP, NBC-TV 22 years; joined Marble Arch Prods as talent consultant March 1979.

TECHINE, Andre: Wri-Dir. b. France, 1943. Critic for Cahiers de Cinema. Teacher at IDHEC. Films inc: Pauline s'en va; French Provincial; Barocco; The Bronte Sisters; Hotel des Ameriques (Hotel of the Americas); Rendezvous.

TEDROW, Irene: Act. b. Denver, Aug 3, 1907. e. Carnegie Tech, BA. Radio-Corliss Archer, 11 years.

Films inc: They Won't Forget; Cheers for Mrs. Bishop; Journey Into Fear; The Moon and Sixpence; They Won't Believe Me; A Lion in the Streets; Not as a Stranger; The Ten Commandments; Never So Few; Please Don't Eat the Daisies; The Parent Trap; The Greatest Story Ever Told; The Cincinnati Kid; The Comic; Getting Straight; Midnight Madness.

TV inc: Father of the Bride; Dennis The Menace; Eleanor and Franklin; Special Olympics; Quincy; James at 16; Mary Tyler Moore; Little House on the Prairie; Never Say Never; The Two Worlds of Jenny Logan; Isabel's Choice; The Last Ninja; Welcome Home, Jellybean; Family Secrets.

Thea inc: Look Homeward Angel; Skin of Our Teeth; Camino Real; Our Town; Children of the Wind; Hot L Baltimore.

TEICHMAN, Howard: Plywri. b. Chicago, Nov. 22, 1916. e. U of WI, BA. Joined Orson Welles' Mercury Theatre of the Air, 1938 as stage mgr; 1940, prod.; with OWI during war; VP Shubert Organization 1962-1972. Plays inc: The Solid Gold Cadillac; Miss Lonelyhearts; The Girls in 509; Julia, Jake and Uncle Joe; A Rainy Day in Newark.

TEITEL, Carol (nee Carolyn Kahn): Act. b. Brooklyn, NY., Aug. 1, 1929. e. American Theatre Wing (scholarship); studied with Leo Bulgakov, Lee Strasberg. Founding member of ACT. Thea inc: The Power of Darkness; Theatre As You Like It; Billy the Kid; The Way of the World; The Anatomist (Bway); Nude With Violin; Under Milkwood; The Alchemist; Merchant of Venice; Pullman Car Hiawatha; An Evening With Ring Lardner; Juana La Loca; Marat/Sade (Bway); The Bench; A Flea in Her Ear; Long Day's Journey Into Night Mary Stuart; Juno and the Paycock; Six Characters in Search of an Author; All Over Town (Bway); The World of Sholem Aleichem; The Entertainer; Every Good Boy Deserves Favour (Bway); Big and Little; Faces of Love (one-woman show); The Flight of the Earls.

TV inc: Little Moon of Alban; A Country Scandal; Misalliance; Under Milkwood; Edge of Night; The Guiding Light; The Verdict is Yours; Figures in the Sand; Six Faces of Love; Woman of Valor; Interrogation in Budapest; My Old Man; Lovers and Other Strangers.

TEITELBAUM, Pedro: Exec. b. Brazil, Nov 21, 1922. Started 1939 with Col; 1943, WB; 1948 Latin-American supv Republic; 1957 became prod-dist-exhb in Brazil; 1968, area supv UA; 1973 vp Intl sls; 1975, vp intl sls & dist; 1977 sr exec vp CIC; July 1977, P CIC; 1980 P Filmcrest International Corp; resd Oct 1981.

TEMPLE, Shirley: Act. b. Santa Monica, CA, Apr 23, 1927. On screen at age 3 in short films. Feature debut 1932 Red Haired Alibi. After film career entered public life, served as U.S. Ambassador to Ghana 1974-76.

Films inc: To the Last Man; Out All Night; Carolina; Mandalay; Stand Up and Cheer; Now I'll Tell; Change of Heart; Little Miss Marker; Baby Take a Bow; Now and Forever; Bright Eyes; The Little Colonel; Our Little Girl; Curly Top; The Littlest Rebel; Captain January; Poor Little Rich Girl; Dimples; Stowaway; Wee Willie Winkie; Heidi; Rebecca of Sunnybrook Farm; Little Miss Broadway; Just Around the Corner; The Little Princess; Susannah of the Mounties; The Blue Bird; Young People; Kathleen; Miss Annie Rooney; Since You Went Away; I'll Be Seeing You; Kiss and Tell; Honeymoon; The Bachelor and the Bobby Soxer; That Hagen Girl; Fort Apache; Mr. Belvedere Goes to College; Adventure in Baltimore; A Kiss for Corliss; The Story of Seabiscuit.

TV inc: Shirley Temple Storybook.

(*Oscar*-honorary-1934).

TENNANT, Victoria: Act. b. London, Sep. 30, 1953. e. Central School of Speech and Drama. d. of ballerina Irene Baronova, talent agent Cecil Tennant. Films inc: The Ragman's Daughter; The Speckled Band; The Killing; Strangers Kiss; Horror Planet (Inseminoid); All of Me.

TV inc: La Guerre des Insectes; The Winds of War; Dempsey; Chiefs.

TENNILLE, Toni: Singer-Mus. b. Montgomery, AL. May 8, 1943. Co-wrote rock-ecology musical Mother Earth for which Daryl Dragon was hired as pianist between tours of Beach Boys group with which he worked. Tennille joined group briefly before she and Dragon married and teamed as Captain and Tennille.

(Grammy-record of the year-1975).

TV inc: The Captain and Tennille; The Toni Tennille Show; A Gift of Music; The Great American Sing-A-Long; Music Of Your Life (host).

TER-ARUTUNIAN, Rouben: Dsgn. b. Tiflis, USSR, Jul 24, 1920. e. Friedrich Wilhelm U, U of Vienna, Ecole des Beaux Arts. First des in US were for TV, 1951; since then has designed scenery and costumes for American Shakespeare Festival; NYC Opera; NYC Ballet & most ballet and dance companies in US and Europe.

Bway inc: New Girl in Town; Who Was That Lady I Saw You With?; Redhead (Tony-1959) The Milk Train Doesn't Stop Here Anymore; The Lady From Dubuque; Goodbye, Fidel.

TV inc: The Would-Be Gentleman; Ariadne auf Naxon; The Magic Flute; Antigone; The Taming of the Shrew; The Flood; Twelfth Night (Emmy-1957).

TERRY, Alice (nee Taafe): Act. b. Vincennes, IN, Jul 24, 1901. W of Rex Ingram. On screen from 1916 in Not My Sister. Film inc: The Four Horsemen of the Apocalypse; The Prisoner of Zenda; Mare Nostrum; The Garden of Allah; The Three Passions.

TERRY, Megan: Plywri. b. Seattle, WA, Jul 22, 1932. e. U of WA, U of Alberta, Yale. Plays inc: Ex-Miss Copper Queen on a Set of Pills; The Magic Realist; People vs. Ranchman; The Gloaming; O My Darling; Calm Down; Keep Tightly Closed In a Cool, Dry Place; Viet Rock; Comings and Goings; Jack-Jack; The Key Is on the Bottom; The Tommy Allen Show; One More Little Drinkie; Approaching Simone; Choosing a Spot on the Floor; Grooving; Fado; Madwoman With Carrot; Nightwalk; Hothouse; Attempted Rescue on Avenue B; The Mother Jones and Mollie Bailey Family Circus.

TERRY, Phillip: Act. b. San Francisco, Mar 7, 1909. e. Stanford U, RADA. Films inc: Navy Blue and Gold; Mannequin; Balalaika; The Parson of Panamint; Wake Island; The Lost Weekend; Seven Keys to Baldpate; The Leech Woman; The Navy vs the Night Monsters.

TERRY-THOMAS (Thomas Terry Hoar-Stevens): Act. b. London, Jul 14, 1911. Professional debut London nitery as impressionist. In British films since 1948. Hollywood debut 1961.

Films inc: Private's Progress; The Naked Truth; Carleton Browne of the FO; I'm All Right, Jack; School for Scoundrels; The Wonderful World of the Brothers Grimm; It's a Mad Mad Mad Mad World; Those Magnificent Men in Their Flying Machines; How to Murder Your Wife; Kiss the Girls and Make Them Die; The Perils of Pauline; Where Were You When the Lights Went Out?; 2000 Years Later; The Abominable Dr. Phibes; Vault of Horror; Spanish Fly; The Last Remake of Beau Geste; Hound of the Baskervilles.

TESHIGAHARA, Hiroshi: Dir. b. Tokyo, Japan, 1927. Films inc: (Doc) Hokusai; Sofu Teshigahara; Jose Torres; Otoshi Ana. (Features) Woman in the Dunes; The Face of Another; Bakuso; The Man Without A Map; Summer Soldiers.

TESICH, Steve: Wri. b. Titovo Uzice, Yugoslavia, 1941. e. IN U, BA; Columbia, MA. Plays inc: The Carpenters; Baba Goya; Lake of the Woods; Gorky; A Passing Game; Division Street.

Films inc: Breaking Away; Eyewitness; Four Friends; The World According to Garp.

TV inc: Nourish the Beast (version of Baba Goya); Breaking Away; Division Street.

TETZLAFF, Ted: Dir. b. Los Angeles, Jun 3, 1903. Films inc: (cin) Enchanted Cottage; Notorious; (dir) World Premiere; Riffraff; Fighting Father Dunne; Johnny Allegro; Dangerous Profession; Gambling House; White Tower; Under the Gun; Treasure of Lost Canyon; Terror on a Train; Son of Sinbad.

TEWES, Lauren: Act. b. Trafford, PA, Oct 26. TV inc: Love Boat; The Dallas Cowboys Cheerleaders.

Films inc: Eyes of A Stranger.

TEWKESBURY, Joan: Wri-Chor-Dir. b. Redlands, CA, 1937. Films inc: Thieves Like Us (co-sp); Nashville (sp); Old Boyfriends (dir); A Night in Heaven (wri).

TV inc: The Tenth Month; The Acorn People.

THACHER, Russell: Prod-Wri. b. Hackensack, NJ, May 29. e. Bucknell U, AB. Exec story edtr MGM, 1963-72. Films inc: (Prod) Travels with My Aunt; Soylent Green; The Last Hard Men.

TV inc: The Cay (& wri).

THARP, Twyla: Dancer-Chor. b. Portland, IN, Jul 1, 1941. e. Barnard; American Ballet Theatre School. With Paul Taylor Dance Co., 1963; joined Joffrey Ballet, American Ballet Theatre 1965; chor Tank Dive; Re-Moves; Forevermore; Generation; Eight Jelly Rolls; The Raggedy Dances; As Time Goes By; Push Comes to Shove; Mud; Baker's Dozen.

Films inc: (Chor) Hair; Ragtime; Amadeus (& opera staging).

THAU, Benjamin: Exec. b. Dec 15. Started with Keith vaude booking office; head booker Orpheum Circuit; when Keith and Orpheum Circuits merged in 1927, resd to become booker for Loew's Inc; 1932 casting dir MGM; 1940 named asst to Louis B Mayer; 1944, vp Loew's Inc; 1956 became administrative head MGM Studios. Ret.

(Died July 5, 1983.)

THAXTER, Phyllis: Act. b. Portland, ME, Nov 20, 1921. Films inc: 30 Seconds Over Tokyo; Weekend at the Waldorf; Bewitched; Tenth Avenue Angel; Blood on the Moon; Come Fill the Cup; Springfield Rifle; Women's Prison; The World of Henry Orient.

TV inc: Wagon Train; The Fugitive; Three Sovereigns For Sarah.

Thea inc: What a Life; There Shall Be No Night; Claudia; Take Her She's Mine.

THEODORAKIS, Mikis: Comp. b. Greece, 1925. Films inc: Eva; Night Ambush; Shadow of the Cat; Phaedra; Five Miles to Midnight; Zorba the Greek; The Day the Fish Came Out; The Trojan Women; State of Siege; Serpico; Iphigenia.

THINNES, Roy: Act. b. Chicago, 1938. Films inc: Journey to the Far Side of the Sun; Charlie One-Eye; Airport 75; The Hindenberg.

TV inc: The Long Hot Summer; The Invaders; The Psychiatrist; The Horror at 37,000 Feet; The Norliss Tapes; Return Of The Mod Squad; From Here To Eternity-The War Years; Stone; Freedom; Scruples; Sizzle; One Life To Live.

THOMAS, B.J.: Singer. b. Houston, TX, Aug. 7, 1942. (Grammys(5)-inspirational perf-1977, 1978, 1979, 1980, 1981).

THOMAS, Betty: Act. b. St Louis, MO, Jul 27, 1948. e. Ohio State U. Taught school for short time then with Chicago's Second City improv group. TV inc: The Fun Factory; Nashville Grab; Hill Street Blues; When Your Lover Leaves; Child Abuse--The Day After (host-narr); Yearbook--Class Of 1967.

Films inc: Tunnelvision; Jackson County Jail; Used Cars; Loose Shoes; Chesty Anderson--U.S. Navy.

THOMAS, Bill: Cos Dsgn. b. Chicago, Oct 13, 1921. e. USC, AB. Films inc: High Time; Beloved Infidel; By Love Possessed; Babes in Toyland; Spartacus (Oscar-1960); Seven Thieves; Bon Voyage; Toys in the Attic; Inside Daisy Clover; The Happiest Millionaire; The Hawaiians; The Children of Sanchez.

THOMAS, Danny (Amos Jacobs): Act. b. Deerfield, MI, Jan 6, 1914. Performed in niteries, radio, TV. Films inc: Unfinished Dance; Big City; Call Me Mister; I'll See You in My Dreams; The Jazz Singer.

TV inc: (act) Make Room For Daddy, (Emmy-1954); Make Room for Grandaddy; The Practice; I'm A Big Girl Now. (Exec prod) The Return Of The Mod Squad; Samurai; The Unbroken Circle-A Tribute to Mother Maybelle Carter; The Bob Hope 30th Anniversary Special; Bob Hope's All-Star Celebration Opening the Gerald R. Ford Museum; Louise Mandrell--Diamonds, Gold & Platinum; The Cracker Brothers.

THOMAS, Henry: Act. b. 1972. Films inc: The Raggedy Man; E.T. The Extra Terrestrial; Misunderstood; Cloak And Dagger.

TV inc: The Pittsburgh Steeler and the Cincinnati Kid.

THOMAS, Mark (Ernest Tumolillo): Act. b. Brooklyn, NY, Jun 19, 1941. e. St John's U. Films inc: St Ives; 9/30/55; Rollercoaster; Final Countdown.

TV inc: General Hospital; Panic on the 522; Black Market Baby; The Night the City Screamed; Evita Peron; Palms.

THOMAS, Marlo: Act. b. Detroit, MI, Nov 21, 1938. e. USC. D of Danny Thomas. Thea inc: Barefoot in the Park (London); Thieves.
TV inc: That Girl; Free To Be--You And Me (Emmys-as prod & star-1974); The Body Human--Facts for Girls (Emmy-1981); Love, Sex. . .& Marriage? (& exec prod); The Lost Honor of Kathryn Beck (& exec prod); Consenting Adult.
Films inc: The Knack--and How To Get It; Jenny; Thieves.

THOMAS, Richard: Act. b. NYC, Jun 13, 1951. TV inc: The Waltons (Emmy-1973); No Other Love; All Quiet on the Western Front; To Find My Son; Berlin Tunnel 21; Barefoot In The Park (cable); Pavarotti and Friends; Johnny Belinda; Living Proof. The Hank Williams Jr Story (& exec prod); Fifth of July; Hobson's Choice; The Master of Ballantrae.
Films inc: Winning; Last Summer; The Todd Killings; Red Sky At Morning; You'll Like My Mother; September 30, 1955; Battle Beyond The Stars.
Thea inc: Sunrise At Campobello; Merton of the Movies; St. Joan; Everthing in the Garden; Whose Life Is It Anyway (tour).

THOME, Karin: Wri-Dir-Prod-Act. b. Tubingen, W Germany, Sep 16, 1943. e. Leicester Coll of Art, England. Films inc: Emigration (sp, dir, prod); The Joint (sp, dir, prod); Crash Theo (sp, dir, prod, act); Blinker (prod, act); The Pretty Things (sp, dir, prod); Supergirl (co-prod); Amerika (sp, dir, act); Willi and the Chinese Cat (sp, prod, dir).

THOMERSON, Tim: Act. Films inc: Car Wash; Which Way Is Up; A Wedding; Carny; Fade to Black; Take This Job and Shove It; St. Helens; Jekyll and Hyde--Together Again; Some Kind of Hero; Metalstorm--The Destruction of Jared-Syn; Uncommon Valor; Rhinestone; Future Cop.
TV inc: Shadow in the Streets; Hustling; Quark; The Associates; Golden Gate; Bare Essence; The Two of Us; Gun Shy; His Mistress.

THOMOPOULOS, Anthony D.: Exec. b. Mt Vernon, NY, Feb 7, 1938. e. Georgetown U. Started at NBC, 1959. Dir Foreign Sales RCA SelectaVision, 1964; named vp, 1965; to ABC as vp, prime-time programs, 1973; vp, prime time TV Creative Operations, 1974; p of ABC Entertainment, 1978; June 1983, P ABC Broadcast Group.

THOMPSON, Ernest: Wri. b. 1950. Former act in TV series West Side Medical. Plays inc: On Golden Pond; West Side Waltz; A Sense of Humor.
Films inc: On Golden Pond (Oscar-1981).

THOMPSON, Hank: Singer-Sngwri. b. Waco, TX, Sep 3, 1925. C&W recording artist. Formed his own band, the Brazos Valley Boys, 1946.

THOMPSON, J. Lee: Dir. b. England, 1914. Films inc: An Alligator Named Daisy; Tiger Bay; Northwest Frontier; I Aim at the Stars; The Guns of Navarone; Cape Fear; Taras Bulba; Kings of the Sun; What a Way to Go; John Goldfarb Please Come Home; Eye of the Devil; MacKenna's Gold; Before Winter Comes; The Chairman; Conquest of the Planet of the Apes; Huckleberry Finn; The Reincarnation of Peter Proud; The White Buffalo; The Greek Tycoon; The Passage; Cabo-blanco; Happy Birthday To Me; 10 to Midnight; The Ambassador; The Evil That Men Do.
TV inc: Code Red.

THOMPSON, Jack: Act. b. Sydney, Australia, Aug 31, 1940. e. Queensland U. Films inc: Outback; Libido; Sunday Too Far Away; Scobie Malone; Caddie; Mad Dog; Because He's My Friend; Jock Peterson; Breaker Morant; The Earthling; The Club; The Man From Snowy River; Bad Blood; Flesh & Blood.
TV inc: A Woman Called Golda; The Letter; Waterfront.

THOMPSON, Robert C.: Prod. b. Palmyra, NY, May 31, 1937. e. Ithaca Coll, BS. Joined U 1961 in talent dept, later heading dept; 1968 head talent & creative affairs Cinema Center Films; 1972 formed Thompson-Paul Prodns. TV inc: (prod) Paper Chase (& dir); Lanigan's Rabbi; The Mark of Zorro; Bud and Lou (& dir); Tough Girl; First The Egg (dir); Love Lives On.

THOMPSON, Robert E.: Wri. Films inc: They Shoot Horses Don't They? TV inc: Sherlock Holmes; Jigsaw (crea); Footsteps; Children of

God; A Case of Rape; Niagara; DA's Investigator (pilot); The Francis Gary Powers Story; Childhood of Lee Harvey Oswald; Brave New World; The $5.20 an Hour Dream.

THOMPSON, Sada: Act. b. Des Moines, IA, Sep 27, 1929. e. Carnegie Tech. Films inc: You are Not Alone; The Pursuit of Happiness; Desperate Characters.
Bway inc: Under Milkwood; The Effect of Gamma Rays on Man-in-the-Moon Marigolds; Morning Becomes Electra; Twigs (Tony-1972); The Cherry Orchard; Saturday, Sunday, Monday. (London) The Little Foxes.
TV inc: Sandburg's Lincoln; The Entertainer; Our Town; Family (Emmy-1978); Marco Polo; Princess Daisy.

THOMSON, Virgil: Comp. b. Kansas City, MO, Nov 25, 1896. e. Harvard, AB. Film scores inc: The Plough That Broke the Plains; The River; Louisiana Story (Pulitzer Prize-1949); The Goddess.
Thea inc: Four Saints in Three Acts; Negro Macbeth; Filling Station; The Mother of Us All; Lord Byron; Measure for Measure; Parson Weems and the Cherry Tree.
TV inc: Virgil Thomson--Composer; The Day After (music from The River).

THORNTON, Sigrid: Act. b. Brisbane, Australia. TV inc: Matlock; Case for the Defence; Young Ramsay; Father Dear Father; Skyways; Cop Shop; Outbreak of Love; 1915; All the Rivers Run; The Boy in the Bush.
Films inc: The Getting of Wisdom; F.J. Holden; Snapshot; Duet for Four; The Man From Snowy River; Street Hero; Niel Lynne.

THORPE, Jerry: Dir. b. 1930. Films inc: The Venetian Affair; The Day of the Evil Gun (& prod).
TV inc: Kung Fu (Emmy-1973); A Question of Love; Fast Lane Blues; The Lazarus Syndrome; All God's Children (& prod); The Devlin Connection (exec prod); Happy Endings (& exec prod); Dirty Work.

THORPE, Richard: Dir. b. Hutchinson, KS, Feb 24, 1896. Act, wri, flm ed, studio exec before becoming a dir. Now retired.
Films inc: Double Wedding; The Crowd Roars; Earl of Chicago; Huckleberry Finn; White Cargo; Two Girls and a Sailor; Malaya; Three Little Words; The Great Caruso; It's a Big Country; Ivanhoe; Carbine Williams; The Prisoner of Zenda; All the Brothers Were Valiant; Knights of the Round Table; Student Prince; Athena; The Prodigal; The Tartars; The Honeymoon Machine; The Horizontal Lieutenant; Follow the Boys; The Truth About Spring; That Funny Feeling; The Scorpio Letters; Last Challenge.

THORPE-BATES, Peggy: Act. b. London, Aug 11, 1914. e. RADA. With Shakespeare Memorial Theatre, with repertory groups. Thea inc: The Country Wife; The Young Elizabeth; Sacrifice to the Wind; All in the Family; A Public Mischief; The Thunderbolt; Dead Silence; toured South Africa in Crown Matrimonial; tours and recitals around Britain.
TV inc: Sanctuary, Rumpole of Bailey; Rumpole Returns!

THRELKELD, Richard: TV newsman. b. Cedar Rapids, IA, Nov 20, 1937. e. Ripon College, BA; Northwestern U, BSJ; Columbia School Int'l Affairs. Wri-prod WHAS-TV, Louisville, KY.; newsman WMT-AM-TV, Cedar Rapids; joined CBS News 1966; corr Viet Nam; 1970, San Francisco bureau chief; April 1977, Rome bureau; Nov 1977, co-anchor CBS Morning News. TV inc: The Defense of the United States--The War Machine (Emmy-corr-1981).

THULIN, Ingrid: Act. b. Solleftea, Sweden, Jan 27, 1929. Films inc: Where the Wind Blows; Foreign Intrigue; Wild Strawberries; So Close to Life; The Face; The Four Horsemen of the Apocalypse; Winter Light; The Silence; Return from the Ashes; The War Is Over; Night Games; The Damned; The Rite; Cries and Whispers; Moses; The Cassandra Crossing; Madame Kitty; The Voyage Into The Whirlpool Has Begun; Brusten Himmel (Broken Sky) (wri-dir); Efter Repetition (After the Rehearsal).
Thea inc: Of Love Remembered.
TV inc: Il Corsaro (The Corsair).

TIDYMAN, Ernest: Wri. b. Cleveland, Jan 1, 1928. Started as newspaperman; turned to writing fiction at age 42.

Films inc: The French Connection (Oscar-Sp-1971); Shaft; Shaft's Big Score; High Plains Drifter; Report to the Commissioner; A Force of One; Street People; Last Plane Out.

TV inc: To Kill a Cop; Dummy (& dir); Power; Guyana Tragedy - The Story of Jim Jones; Alcatraz--The Whole Shocking Story (& co-prod); Velvet; Stark; Brotherly Love.

(Died July 15, 1984).

TIERNEY, Gene: Act. b. NYC, Nov 20, 1920. On screen from 1940 in The Return of Frank James. Films inc: Tobacco Road; Belle Starr; Son of Fury; Heaven Can Wait; Laura; A Bell for Adano; Leave Her to Heaven; Dragonwyck; The Razor's Edge; The Ghost and Mrs. Muir; Whirlpool; Close to My Heart; Never Let Me Go; The Egyptian; The Black Widow; Left Hand of God; Advise and Consent; The Pleasure Seekers.

TV inc: Daughter of the Mind; Scruples.

TIERNEY, Lawrence: Act. b. NYC, Mar 15, 1919. Films inc: The Ghost Ship; Dillinger; Step by Step; San Quentin; The Devil Thumbs a Ride; Shakedown; The Hoodlum; A Child is Waiting; Custer of the West; Such Good Friends; Andy Warhol's Bad; Midnight; Prizzi's Honor.

TV inc: Terrible Joe Moran.

TIFFIN, Pamela: Act. b. Oklahoma City, OK, Oct 13, 1942. On screen from 1961 in Summer and Smoke. Films inc: One, Two, Three; State Fair; Come Fly With Me; For Those Who Think Young; The Pleasure Seekers; Harper; The Protagonists; Paranoid; Kiss the Other Sheik; Viva Max;

Thea inc: Dinner at Eight.

TIKHONOV, Vyacheslav: Act. b. Feb 8, 1928. e. Moscow Film Institute. Films inc: The Young Guard; Peace Time; Maximka; It Must Not Be Forgotten; Stars on the Wings; The Heart Beats Anew; It Happened in Penkovo; An Extraordinary Event; Midshipman Panin; Two Lives; Seven Winds; An Optimistic Tragedy; War and Peace; We'll Get By Till Monday; The Man From the Other Side; Front Without Flanks; They Fought for Their Country; White Bim with Black Ear.

TV inc: Seventeen Moments of Spring.

TILLER, Nadja: Act. b. Austria, March 16, 1929. Films inc: Eroica; The Life and Loves of Mozart; Rosemary, Portrait of a Sinner; The World in My Pocket; And So to Bed; The Upper Hand; The Making of a Lady.

TILLIS, Mel: Mus-Singer-Sngwri. b. Aug 8, 1932. Films inc: The Villain; Smokey and the Bandit II; The Cannonball Run. TV Inc: Dean Martin's Christmas in California; Skinflint; Dean Martin Christmas Special 1980; The Stockers; Country Comes Home ('82); Country Gold; Louise Mandrell--Diamonds, Gold & Platinum.

TILLMAN, Floyd: Singer-Sngwri. b. Ryan, OK, Dec 8, 1914. C&W recording artist. Played guitar, mandolin, banjo with various groups.

TILLSTROM, Burr: Act. b. Chicago, Oct 13, 1917. e. U of Chicago. Traveled with puppet, marionette, stock shows. Created puppet troupe headed by Kukla and Ollie; TV: started Kukla, Fran and Ollie Show 1947 (Emmy-1971); That Was The Week That Was (Emmy-1967-spec); Happy Birthday, Beulah Witch.

TILLY, Meg: Act. b. CA. Films inc: Tex; One Dark Night; Psycho II; The Big Chill; Impulse.

TV inc: The Trouble With Grandpa.

TILTON, Charlene: Act. b. San Diego, CA, Dec 1, 1958. Films inc: Freaky Friday; Big Wednesday; Sweater Girl; The New Centurions.

TV inc: Go Ask Alice; Dallas; Diary of a Teen-age Hitchhiker; The Fall of the House of Usher.

TINKER, Grant: Exec. b. Stamford, CT, Jan 11, 1926. e. Dartmouth Coll. Joined NBC radio program dept in 1949; with McCann-Erickson ad agency, TV dept, 1954; in 1958, joined Benton & Bowles, TV dept; from 1961-65 with NBC, vp programs, West Coast; vp in chg of programming, NY, 1966-1967; joined Universal TV as vp, 1968-1969; Fox vp, 1969-1970; p MTM Enterprises, Inc, 1970;

became chmn & CEO NBC July 1, 1981.

TIPTON, George Aliceson: Comp. b. Huntington Park, CA, Jan 23, 1932. Films inc: Phantom of the Paradise; Badlands; Skidoo; Griffin and Phoenix; Hit Lady; Nights at O'Rear's.

TV inc: The Courtship of Eddie 's Father; The Gift; Soap; Benson; The Yeagers; Trouble in High Timber Country; It's A Living; I'm a Big Girl Now; Side By Side-- The True Story of the Osmond Family; It Takes Two; The Demon Murder Case; Just Married; Gidget's Summer Reunion.

TISCH, Laurence A.: Exec. b. Brooklyn, NY, Mar 5, 1923. e. NYU, Harvard Law School. Chmn, CEO Loew's Corp.

TISCH, Preston Robert: Exec. b. Brooklyn, NY, Apr 29, 1926. e. Bucknell, U of MI. Chmn Exec Comm Loew's Theatres, Chmn & CEO, Loew's Hotels.

TISCH, Steve: Prod. b. Lakewood, NJ, 1949. e. Tufts U. S of Preston Tisch. Films inc: Outlaw Blues; Almost Summer; Coast to Coast; Homeward Bound; Risky Business; Deal of the Century.

TV inc: No Other Love; Prime Suspect; Something So Right (exec prod); The Calendar Girl Murders (exec prod); Call To Glory (exec prod); The Burning Bed (exec prod); Silence Of The Heart (exec prod).

TOBIAS, Harry: Sngwri-Music publisher. b. NYC, Sep 11, 1895. To Hollywood, 1929; wrote for films. Chief collaborators: Chas. Tobias, Henry Tobias (brothers). Songs: Sweet and Lovely; Miss You; It's a Lonesome Old Town; Sail Along, Silv'ry Moon; No Regrets; At Your Command; I'm Sorry Dear; The Daughter of Peggy O'Neill; When It's Harvest Time; Somebody Loves Me; The Broken Record; Girl of My Dreams; I Want You to Want Me; Oh, Bella Mia; May I Have the Next Dream With You; If I Knew Then What I Know Now; Moonlight Brings Memories; In God We Trust; Star of Hope.

TOBIN, Genevieve: Act. b. NYC. Nov. 29, 1901. Stage debut at age 11 in children's performance of Disraeli; A Polish Wedding. Bway inc: Oh, Look; Palmy Days; Little Old New York; Polly Preferred; King Lear; Dear Sir; The Youngest; Treat 'Em Rough; This Woman Business; Murray Hill; Trial Of Mary Duggan (London); Fifty Million Frenchmen.

Films inc: No Mother To Guide Her; A Lady Surrenders; Free Love; Seed; Up For Murder; The Gay Diplomat; One Hour With You; Hollywood Speaks; Perfect Understanding; Pleasure Cruise; The Wrecker; Goodbye Again; I Loved A Woman; Easy To Love; Dark Hazard; The Ninth Guest; Success At Any Price; Kiss And Make Up; Uncertain Lady; The Woman In Red; The Goose And The Gander; Here's To Romance; The Case Of The Lucky Legs; Broadway Hostess; The Petrified Forest; Snowed Under; The Great Gambini; Dramatic School; Zaza; No Time For Comedy; Queen Of Crime.

TOBIN, Michele: Act. b. Chi, Jan 25, 1961. Films inc: Yours, Mine and Ours; The One and Only, Genuine, Original Family Band; The Happy Ending; Eighty Steps to Jonah; Freaky Friday. TV inc: Imagination; The Fitzpatricks.

TODD, Ann: Act. b. England, 1909. On screen from 1931. Films inc: Keepers of Youth; The Ghost Train; Ships With Wings; The Seventh Veil; Daybreak; So Evil My Love; Madeleine; Breaking the Sound Barrier; Taste of Fear; Son of Captain Blood; Beware of the Brethren; The Human Factor.

Thea inc: When Ladies Meet; Man in Half-Moon Street; Peter Pan.

TV inc: The Vortex; The Door; The Snows of Kilimanjaro; The Last Target. Produces travelogues.

TODD, J. Hunter: Film Festival Exec. b. New Orleans, Aug 9, 1938. e. U of VA, William & Mary Coll. Atlanta Intl Film Fest, 1968-74; Virgin Islands Intl Film Fest, 1975-77; Miami Intl Film Fest, 1978; Houston Intl Film Fest, 1979; resd Jan. 1984. Prod doc films, shorts.

TODD, Richard: Act. b. Dublin, Jan 11, 1919. In repertory, 1937. On screen from 1948. Films inc: For Them That Trespass; Stage Fright; Lightning Strikes Twice; The Story of Robin Hood; The Assassin; A Man Called Peter; The Hasty Heart; The Virgin Queen; D-Day, the Sixth of June; The Longest Day; The Love-Ins; Dorian Gray; Asylum; The Sky Is Falling; The Big Sleep; The House of Long Shadows.

Thea inc: An Ideal Husband; Roar Like a Dove; The Marquise; Sleuth; Thunder By Numbers;

TODMAN, Howard: Exec. b. NYC, Nov 24, 1920. e. Hamilton Coll. Dir. business affairs, Goodson-Todman Productions; treas. Goodson-Todman Associates, Inc; VP & treas, Goodson-Todman Enterprises, Ltd; treas, Peak Prods, Inc.

TOEPLITZ, Jerzy: Film Historian. b. Kharkov, USSR, Nov 24, 1909. e. U of Warsaw. 1945, secy gen Polish Film; 1948, dir, Foreign Dept Polish Film; dir, Polish Film School, Lodz; 1949-72, Head of Film Dept, Inst of Art, Polish Academy of Science; 1972-73, visiting professor, La Trobe U, Melbourne; 1973, foundation dir, The Australian Film and Television School, Sydney.

TOGNAZZI, Ugo: Act. b. Italy, March 23, 1922. Films inc: His Woman; The Fascist; Queen Bee; The Magnificent Cuckold; An American Wife; A Question of Honor; Barbarella; Blowout; Duck in Orange Sauce; Goodnight Ladies and Gentlemen; Bishop's Bedroom; Viva Italia!; La Cage Aux Folles; L'Ingorgo; Dove Va in Vacanza?: First Love; The Terrace; Casotto; Sunday Lovers; La Cage Aux Folles II; La Tragedia di un Uomo Ridicolo (Tragedy of a Ridiculous Man); Amici, Miei, Atto 2 (All My Friends 2); Permette Signora che ami vostra figlia (Claretta and Ben); Scherzo Del Destino In Agguato Dietro L'Angolo Come Un Brigante Di Strada (A Joke of Destiny Lying in Wait Around the Corner Like A Robber); Le Bon Roi Dagobert (Good King Dagobert); Bertoldo, Bertoldino E Cacasenno.

TOKOFSKY, Jerry: Prod. b. NYC, Apr 14, 1936. e. NYU, BS. Exec VP prodn Columbia 1963-70. Into ind prodn 1970. Films inc: Where's Poppa; Born to Win; Fear City (co-prod).

TOLAN, Michael: Act. b. Detroit, MI, Nov 27, 1925. e. Wayne U, BA. Founder-member & asso dir The American Place. Bway inc: Will Success Spoil Rock Hunter?; A Hatful of Rain; The Genius and the Goddess; Romanoff and Juliet; A Majority of One; A Far Country; Unlikely Heroes.

Films inc: The Enforcer; The Greatest Story Ever Told; The Lost Man; John and Mary; Five on the Black Hand Side (prod); All That Jazz; Four Friends (exec prod); Talk To Me.

TV inc: The Bold Ones; Loose Change; The Best of Families; Valley Forge; The Adams Chronicles (narr); The Mountbatten Story (narr); Solomon Northrup's Odyssey.

TOLKIN, Mel: Wri. b. Russia, Aug 3, 1913. TV inc: Your Show of Shows; Caesar's Hour; The Sid Caesar, Imogene Coca, Carl Reiner, Howard Morris Special (Emmy-1967); Danny Kaye Show; Bob Hope; All in the Family (co-story edtr); Nuts and Bolts.

TOLKSDORF, Gittana (Formerly known as Birgitta Tolksdorf): Act. b. Osnabruck, W Germany, Dec 9, 1947. In stock and repertory. Thea inc: The Secretary Bird.

TV inc: Love of Life.

TOMLIN, Lily: Act. b. Detroit, MI, 1939. Performed in cafes and niteries. In December, 1969, first appeared on Laugh-In, TV series. Films inc: Nashville; The Late Show; Moment By Moment; Nine To Five; The Incredible Shrinking Woman; All of Me.

TV inc: Lily; The Lily Tomlin Show (Emmys-wri & star-1974); The Paul Simon Special (Emmy-wri-1978); Lily--Sold Out (& exec prod) (Emmys-prod & star-1981); The Muppets Go To The Movies; Lily For President?; Live--and In Person.

Thea inc: Appearing Nightly (dir-wri-act). (Tony-Special-1977). (Grammy-Comedy-1971).

TOMLIN, Pinky: Comp-Singer. b. Eureka Springs, AR, Sep 9, 1907. e. U of OK. While in college organized own dance band, played quitar and sang. Wrote song Object of My Affections which led to professional career.

Films inc: Times Square Lady; King Solomon of Broadway; Paddy O'Day; Don't Get Personal; Down in Arkansas; Here Comes Elmer.

TOMLINSON, David: Act. b. Henley-on-Thames, England, May 7, 1917 Thea inc: (London) The Little Hut; All for Mary; Dear Delin-

quent; The Ring of Truth; Boeing Boeing; Mother's Boy (& dir); A Friend Indeed; The Impossible Years; The Turning Point (& dir).

Films inc: Quiet Wedding; Journey Together; The Way to the Stars; Master of Bankdam; Pimpernel Smith; Miranda; Sleeping Car to Trieste; The Chiltern Hundreds; Hotel Sahara; Three Men in a Boat; Up the Creek; Follow That Horse; Tom Jones; Mary Poppins; The Truth About Spring; The Liquidator; The Love Bug; Bedknobs and Broomsticks; From Hong Kong with Love: The Waterbabies; The Fiendish Plot of Dr. Fu Manchu; Wombling Free; Dominique (made in 1977).

TOMPKINS, Angel: Act. b. Albany, CA, Dec 20, 1943. Began as a model before TV appearances in Dragnet; The Wild, Wild West; Hang Your Hat On The Wind.

Films inc: I Love My Wife; Kansas City Prime; How To Seduce A Woman; The Don Is Dead; The Bees.

TOMS, Carl, OBE: Dsgn. b. England, May 29, 1927. e. Royal Coll of Art, Old Vic School. First head of dsgn for Young Vic; dsgd operas and ballets for Sadlers Wells, Covent Garden. Thea inc: (London) The Apollo de Bellac; Beth; Something to Hide; The Complaisant Lover; The Merry Wives of Windsor; New Cranks; Camille; Write Me a Murder; A Time To Laugh; Who'll Save the Plowboy?; A Singular Man; The Burglar; Fallen Angels; The Magistrate; Sleuth; Vivat! Vivat Regina!; The Beheading; Sherlock Holmes; The Waltz of the Toreadors; Travesties; Windy City; The Real Thing; The Aspern Papers; Rough Crossing. (Bway) Sleuth; Sherlock Holmes (Tony-1975); Travesties.

TOOMEY, Regis: Act. b. Pittsburgh, PA, Aug 13, 1902. e. U of Pittsburgh, Carnegie Inst of Technology (drama). On NY and London stage. Screen debut, Alibi, 1929. Films inc: Spellbound; The Big Sleep; Magic Town; The Bishop's Wife; The Boy With Green Hair; Mighty Joe Young; Cry Danger; Union Pacific; Come to the Stable; Northwest Passage; The High and the Mighty; Guys and Dolls; Warlock; Man's Favorite Sport?; Gunn; Change of Habit; The Carey Treatment; C.H.O.M.P.S.

TV inc: December Bride; Hey Mulligan; Dodsworth; Richard Diamond; Burke's Law; Petticoat Junction.

TOONE, Geoffrey: Act. b. Dublin, Ireland, Nov 15, 1910. e. Christ's Coll, Cambridge. Student at Old Vic, played various Shakespearean roles; appeared in repertory. Thea inc: (London) A Man's House; Dodsworth; Watch on the Rhine; The End of Summer; Quality Street; Lady Windermere's Fan; The Little Hut; Auntie Mame; The Rivals; Hedda Gabler; Conduct Unbecoming.

Films inc: Sword of Honor; The King and I; Zero Hour; The Entertainer; Once More With Feeling.

TV inc: The Scarlet Pimpernel.

TOPOL (Chaim Topol): Act. b. Israel, 1935. Films inc: Cast a Giant Shadow; Sallah; Before Winter Comes; Fiddler on the Roof; Follow Me; Galileo; Flash Gordon; For Your Eyes Only.

Thea inc: Fiddler on the Roof.

TV inc: The House on Garibaldi Street; The Winds of War.

TOPPER, Burt: Wri-Dir-Prod. b. NYC, Jul 31, 1928. Films inc: Hell Squad; Tank Command; Diary of a High School Bride; War Is Hell; The Strangler; Sex and the Teenager; Thunder Alley; Devils Angels; Fireball 500; Wild in the Streets; Devils Eight; The Hard Ride.

TV inc: Taggart; First Woman in Space.

TORME, Mel: Singer. b. Chicago, IL, Sep 13, 1925. Started in vaudeville, radio. On screen from 1943. Films inc: Higher and Higher; Pardon My Rhythm; Let's Go Steady; Good News; Words and Music; Girls' Town; Walk Like a Dragon; A Man Called Adam; The Land of No Return; Artie Sha w--Time Is All You've Got (doc-int).

TV inc: Pray TV; Jazz Alive; Night Of 100 Stars II.

(Grammys-jazz vocal-1982, 1983).

TORN, Rip: Act. b. Temple, TX, Feb 6, 1931. e. TX A & M, U of TX. Films inc: Time Limit; The Cincinnati Kid; Beach Red; Sol Madrid; Tropic of Cancer; Maidstone; Payday; Crazy Joe; The Man Who Fell To Earth; Nasty Habits; Coma; The Seduction of Joe Tynan; Heartland; One-Trick Pony; First Family; A Stranger Is Watching; The Beastmaster; Jinxed!; Airplane II--The Sequel; Cross Creek; Misunderstood; Flashpoint; Songwriter; City Heat.

TV inc: Betrayal; Blind Ambition; Steel Cowboy; A Shining Season; Sophia Loren--Her Own Story; Rape and Marriage--The Rideout Case; The Blue and the Gray; When She Says No; Cat On A Hot Tin Roof (cable); The Execution. The Atlanta Child Murders.

Bway inc: Cat On A Hot Tin Roof; Sweet Bird of Youth; Daughter of Silence; Strange Interlude; Blues for Mr. Charlie; The Cuban Thing; Dance of Death; Mixed Couples.

TORS, Ivan: Wri-Prod-Dir. b. Budapest, Hungary, Jun 12, 1916. e. U of Budapest, Fordham U. In Hollywood from 1941. Films inc: Song of Love (sp); The Forsyte Saga (sp); Storm Over Tibet (sp & prod); The Magnetic Monster (sp & prod); Gog (sp & prod); Return to the Stars (prod); Battle Taxi (prod); Flipper (prod); Rhino (prod & dir); Zebra in the Kitchen (sp); Escape from Angola (exec prod); Galyon File (exec prod).

TV inc: (as prod) The Man and the Challenge; Sea Hunt; Daktari; Gentle Ben; Flipper; Primus.

(Died June 4, 1983).

TOSI, Mario: Cin. Films inc: Some Call It Loving; Buster and Billie; Hearts of the West; The Killing Kind; Report to the Commissioner; Carrie; MacArthur; The Betsy; The Main Event; The Stunt Man; Coast to Coast; Whose Life Is It Anyway?; Six Pack.

TOTTEN, Robert: Dir-Wri-Act. b. Los Angeles, Feb 5, 1937. Films inc: The Quick and the Dead (sp & dir); The Wild Country (dir).

TV inc: Gunsmoke (dir-wri-act); The Red Pony (wri-dir); The Sacketts (dir).

TOTTER, Audrey: Act. b. Joliet, IL, 1919. Films inc: Main Street After Dark; Her Highness and the Bellboy; The Postman Always Rings Twice; Lady in the Lake; The Saxon Charm; A Bullet for Joey; The Carpetbaggers; Chubasco; The Apple Dumpling Gang Rides Again.

TV inc: Medical Center; Our Man Higgins; Nativity; The Great Cash Giveaway Getaway; City Killer.

TOWERS, Constance: Act. b. Whitefish, MT, May 20, 1933. e. Juilliard School of Music. Thea inc: Anya; Show Boat; Carousel; The Sound of Music; Dumas & Son; The King and I; I Do! I Do!; The Desperate Hours.

Films inc: Horse Soldiers; Sergeant Rutledge; Fate Is the Hunter; Shock Corridor; Naked Kiss; The Spy; Sylvester.

TV inc: Love Is a Many Splendored Thing; Once in Her Life; Capitol.

TOWERS, Harry Alan: Exec Prod. b. London, 1920. Films inc: Victim Five (& sp); Mozambique (& sp); The Face of Fu Manchu; Ten Little Indians; Our Man in Marrakesh (Bang, Bang, You're Dead); The Brides of Fu Manchu; Rocket to the Moon; Treasure Island; Call of the Wild; Count Dracula; The Shape of Things to Come; Fanny Hill; Black Venus (& wri); 'Frank' And I (& wri); Christina (& wri).

TOWNE, Robert: Wri. Films inc: Villa Rides; The Tomb of Ligeia; The Last Detail; Chinatown *(Oscar-1974)*; Shampoo (co-sp); The Yakuza (co-sp); Personal Best (& prod-dir).

TOWNES, Harry: Act. b. Huntsville, AL, Sep 18, 1914. Films inc: Operation Manhunt; The Brothers Karamazov; The Screaming Mimi; Cry Tough; Sanctuary; The Bedford Incident; Fitzwilly; Heaven with a Gun; In Enemy Country; Strategy of Terror.

Thea inc: Tobacco Road; Mr. Sycamore; Twelfth Night; Finian's Rainbow; Gramercy Ghost; In the Matter of J. Robert Oppenheimer.

TV inc: The Immigrants; Casino; Falcon Crest.

TOWNSEND, Claire: Exec. b. NYC, Feb 20, 1952. e. Princeton, BA. Worked with Ralph Nader, authored book Old Age; The Last Segregation. Entered film ind as reader, researcher for Martin Ransohoff; West Coast story edtr Frank Yablans Presentations; 1976 West Coast Story edtr Fox; Feb 1978, crea aff vp; Oct 1978 vp-prodn UA; Jan 1980 returned to Fox as prodn VP; resd Jan 1982 to enter indie prodn.

TOWNSEND, Leo: Wri. b. Faribault, MN, May 11, 1908. e. MN U. Films inc: It Started with Eve; The Amazing Mrs Holliday; Chip off the Old Block; Night and Day; The Black Hand; Port of New York; Southside 1-1000; A Life in the Balance; White Feather; Running Wild;

Fraulein; Bikini Beach; How to Stuff a Wild Bikini; Fireball 500; I'd Rather be Rich.

TV inc: Beulah; Wagon Train; Dinah Shore Chevy Show; Maverick; Roaring Twenties; Destry; Bachelor Father; The Eve Arden Show; Shirley Temple Show; Death Valley Days; Patty Duke Show; The Munsters; Batman; Andy Griffith Show; Bewitched.

TOWNSHEND, Peter: Mus-Comp. b. London, England, May 19, 1945. Member The Who. Films inc: Tommy (mus-lyr); The Kids Are Alright (act).

TOYE, Wendy: Dancer-Dir-Chor-Act. b. London, May 1, 1917. Appeared as dancer at Royal Albert Hall at age 4; prod ballet at Palladium at age 10; at 13 joined Ninette de Valois' Old Vic-Sadlers Wells Ballet Co.

Thea inc: (dancer) The Golden Toy; toured with Anton Dolin, later with Dolin and Alicia Markova; Aladdin; Camargo Society Ballet. (Chor) Mother Earth; The Legend of the Willow Pattern; all George Black prodns between 1937-1945; Gay Rosalinda; Concerto for Dancers; Robert and Elizabeth. (Act) Toad of Toad Hall; Hiawatha; The Miracle; Tulip Time; Love and How To Cure It; Simple Simon; Annie Get Your Gun. (Dir) Tough at the Top; And So To Bed; Second Threshold; Wild Thyme; Lady at the Wheel; Fledermaus; As You Like It; A Majority of One; Orpheus in the Underworld; The Great Waltz; The Soldier's Tale; Show Boat; Colette; This Thing Called Love; Singin' In the Rain (asso prod).

Films inc: (Dir) The Stranger Left No Card (short); On the 12th Day (short); Three Cases of Murder; All For Mary; True as a Turtle; We Joined the Navy; The King's Breakfast;

TV inc: (Dir) Esme Divided; Cliff in Scotland; Girls Wanted; Chelsea at Nine; Orpheus in the Underworld; Girls, Girls, Girls; Istanbul; A Goodly Manor for a Song.

TRAKTMAN, Peggy Simon: Wri-Dir-Prod. b. NYC, Jul 19, 1932. e. Columbia School of Dramatic Arts, BFA. Wri-dir Maximillion Prodns, 1962-78. Dir Village Green Summer Prodns.

TRAMONT, Jean-Claude: Dir. b. Brussels, Belgium, May 5, 1934. e. IDHEC. H of Sue Mengers. Films inc: Le Point De Mire (Focal Point); All Night Long.

TRAPNELL, Coles (Valentine C Trapnell): Wri-Prod-Story ed. b. NYC, Aug 2, 1910. e. VMI, NYU. Story ed 1945, Within These Walls. TV inc: Prod 1954-58, Four Star TV; Maverick (prod-wri); Lawman (prod); 12 O'Clock High (wri). Exec story consl, Universal, 1967-77. Author: Teleplay: An Introduction to Television Writing.

TRAUBE, Shepard: Prod-Dir. b. Malden, MA, Feb 27, 1907. Plays inc: No More Frontier; A Thousand Summers; The Sophisticats; Angel Street; Winter Soldiers; Patriots; Bell, Book and Candle; The Girl in Pink Tights; Goodbye Again; Holiday for Lovers; The Tunnel of Love; Venus at Large; Memo; Undercover Man; Children of the Wind.

Films inc: Goose Step; Street of Memories; The Bride Wore Crutches.

(Died July 23, 1983).

TRAUNER, Alexander: Art Dir. b. France, 1906. Films inc: Les Enfants du Paradis; Les Portes de la Nuit; Maneges; Othello; Love in the Afternoon; The Nun's Story; The Apartment *(Oscar-1960)*; One, Two, Three; Irma La Douce; The Night of the Generals; A Flea in Her Ear; Mr Klein; The First Time; Fedora; The Fiendish Plot of Dr. Fu Manchu; Matushka (Viadukt); Tchao Pantin (So Long, Stooge); Vive les Femmes (Long Live Women!); Subway.

TRAVALENA, Fred: Act. b. NYC, Oct 6, 1942. Singer-impressionist in niteries.

TV inc: The Funny World of Fred and Bunni; Shooting Stars. Films inc: The Buddy Holly Story.

TRAVANTI, Daniel J.: Act. b. Kenosha, WI, Mar 7, 1940. e. U WI, BA; Yale School of Drama. Thea inc: Twigs; Othello. Films inc: St. Ives. TV inc: numerous segs; Hill Street Blues *(Emmys-1981, 1982)*; Parade of Stars; A Case of Libel; Adam; Aurora.

TRAVERS, Bill: Act. b. England, 1922. Films inc: The Square Ring; Geordie; Bhowani Junction; The Barretts of Wimpole Street; The

Smallest Show on Earth; The Seventh Sin; The Bridal Path; Gordo; Two Living, One Dead; Born Free; Duel at Diablo; A Midsummer Night's Dream; Ring of Bright Water; The Belstone Fox.

TV inc: Jane Goodall and the World of Animal Behavior (Emmy-1973); The First Olympics--Athens 1896.

TRAVILLA (William Travilla): Cos dsgn. b. Avalon, CA, Mar 22, 1925. Films inc: Adventures of Don Juan (Oscar-1949); Viva Zapata; Gentlemen Prefer Blondes; Don't Bother To Knock; How to Marry a Millionaire; The Stripper; River of No Return; Seven Year Itch; Bus Stop.

TV inc: Moviola (Emmy-1980); Evita Peron; The Thorn Birds.

TRAVIS, Merle: Singer-Sngwri. b. Rosewood, KY, Nov 29, 1917. Folk singer, C&W recording artist; performed with Grand Ole Opry; wrote such classics as Sixteen Tons; Dark As a Dungeon; So Round, So Firm, So Fully Packed. (Grammy-Country Inst-1974).

(Died Oct. 20, 1983).

TRAVIS, Richard (William Justice): Act. b. Carlsbad, NM, Apr 17, 1913. Films inc: The Man Who Came to Dinner; The Big Shot; Buses Roar; Jewels of Brandenberg; Alaska Patrol; Skyliner; Operation Haylift; Mask of the Dragon; Fingerprints Don't Lie; City of Shadows.

TV inc: Treasury Men in Action; Pride of the Family; The Falcon; Missile to the Moon.

TRAVOLTA, John: Act. b. Englewood, NJ, Feb 18, 1954. Stage debut in Who Will Save the Plowboy?. On Broadway in Grease; Over Here.

Films inc: Carrie; Saturday Night Fever; Grease; Moment By Moment; Urban Cowboy; Blow Out; Staying Alive; Two of a Kind; Perfect.

TV inc: Emergency; Owen Marshall; The Rookies; Medical Center; Welcome Back, Kotter; The Boy in the Plastic Bubble.

TRBOVICH, Thomas E. (Tom): Dir. TV inc: United Cerebral Palsy Telethon; Ontario 500; Long Beach Grand Prix; Orange Bowl; Fun Factory; Phyllis Diller Special; Andy Kaufman Special; Vic Damone Show; Manhattan Transfer; This Is Burlesque; Hot Hero Sandwich; Sugartime; Archie Special; Sirota's Court; Bette Midler Live; 34th Golden Globe Awards; 29th Emmy Awards; Waylon, Starring Waylon Jennings; The Mousketeer Reunion; I'll Be Home for Christmas; Laverne & Shirley; Joanie Loves Chachi; Lily for President?; Grandpa, Will You Run With Me? Baby Makes Five; The 1/2 Hour Comedy Hour; National Lampoon's Hot Flashes; D.C. Beach Party--A Musical Celebration (PC).

TREAS, Terri: Act. b. Kansas City, KS., Jul. 19, 1959. Studied at Joffrey Ballet school. Bway inc: Pal Joey; Pippin; One Night Stand; Working; Dancing; My Fair Lady (rev).

Films inc: All That Jazz; So Fine; Annie; The Best Little Whorehouse in Texas.

TV inc: Seven Brides for Seven Brothers.

TREBEK, Alex: Act. b. Sudbury, Ontario, Canada, Jul 22, 1940. TV inc: High Rollers; The $128,000 Question; The New High Rollers.

TREBITSCH, Gyula: Prod. b. Budapest, Hungary, Nov 3, 1914. Films inc: The Captain of Kopenick. Pres, Trebitsch Productions Int.

TREMAYNE, Les: Act. b. London, Apr 16, 1913. Films inc: The Racket; The Blue Veil; It Grows on Trees; War of the Worlds; A Man Called Peter; The Perfect Furlough; North by Northwest; The Gallant Hours; The Story of Ruth; The Fortune Cookie; Daffy Duck's Movie--Fantastic Island (voice); Starchaser--The Legend Of Orin.

Thea inc: Woman in My House; Errand of Mercy; One Man's Family; Heads or Tails; Detective Story.

TV inc: Perry Mason; Adventures of Ellery Queen; Raggedy Ann & Andy in the Pumpkin Who Couldn't Smile.

TREVOR, Claire: Act. b. NYC, 1909. e. AADA. On screen from 1933. Films inc: Life in the Raw; Stagecoach; Allegheny Uprising; Murder, My Sweet; Johnny Angel; Crack-Up; Key Largo (Oscar-supp-1948); Hoodlum Empire; The High and the Mighty; Dead End; The Babe Ruth Story; Lucy Gallant; Marjorie Morningstar; Two Weeks in Another Town; The Stripper; How to Murder Your Wife; Capetown Affair; Kiss Me Goodbye.

TV inc: Dodsworth (Emmy-1956).

TRIKONIS, Gus: Dir. b. NYC. Started in chorus West Side Story Bway. Later act before turning dir. Films inc: Moonshine County Express; Nashville Girl; The Evil; Touched By Love; Take This Job and Shove It.

TV inc: The Darker Side of Terror; The Last Convertible; She's Dressed to Kill; Flamingo Road; Elvis and the Beauty Queen; Twirl; Miss All-American Beauty; Dempsey; First Affair; Malice In Wonderland.

TRINDER, Tommy: Act. b. London, Mar 24, 1909. Thea inc: Tune In; In Town Tonight; Band Wagon; Top of the World; Gangway; Best Bib and Tucker; Happy and Glorious; Here, There and Everywhere; Cinderella; Puss in Boots; several command performances.

Films inc: Almost a Honeymoon; Laugh It Off; Sailors Three; The Foreman Went to France; Champagne Charlie; Fiddlers Three; Bitter Springs; You Lucky People.

TV inc: Master of Ceremonies; Sunday Night at the London Palladium; My Wildest Dream; The Trinder Box.

TRINTIGNANT, Jean-Louis: Act. b. Pont-Saint-Esprit, France, Dec 11, 1930. Films inc: Race for Life; And God Created Woman; Austerlitz; Chateau en Suede; Mata Hari; Angelique; A Man and a Woman; Trans-Europe Express; The Sleeping Car Murders; Is Paris Burning?; The Libertine; Les Biches; Z; Ma Nuit Chez Maud; The American; The Conformist; The Crook; Without Apparent Motive; The Outside Man; The French Conspiracy; Simon the Swiss; Aggression; Sunday Woman; The Honeymoon Trip; Desert of the Tartars; Les Violins du Bal; Faces of Love; Melancholy Baby; Les Argent de Autres; La Terrazza; La Banquiere; I Love You; Passione D'Amore (Passion of Love); Un Assassin Qui Passe (A Passing Killer); Malevil; Eaux Profondes (Deep Water); Une Affaire D'Hommes (A Man's Affair); Le Grande Pardon (The Big Pardon); Colpire al cudre (Strike At the Heart); Vivement Dimanche (Let It Be Sunday); La Crime (Coverup); Under Fire; Le Bon Plaisir; Femmes de Personne (Nobody's Women); Viva la Vie! (Long Live Life!).

TRINTIGNANT, Nadine (nee Marquand): Dir-wri. b. Nice, France, Nov 11, 1934. W of Jean Louis Trintignant. Films inc: Mon amour, mon amour; Le voleur de crimes; It Only Happens to Others; Defense de savoir; Le Voyage de Noces (The Honeymoon Trip); Premier Voyage (First Voyage); L'Ete Prochain (Next Summer).

TROELL, Jan: Wri-Dir. b. Sweden, July 23, 1931. Films inc: Stay in the Marshland; Here is Your Life; Eeny, Meeny, Miny, Mo; The Emigrants; The New Land; Zandy's Bride; Hurricane; Ingenioer Andrees Luftfaerd (The Flight of the Eagle (& cin-ed).

TROUP, Bobby: Act. b. Harrisburg, PA, Oct 13, 1918. e. U of PA. H of Julie London. Comp, singer, recording artist. Films inc: Bop Girl; The Five Pennies; The High Cost of Loving; The Gene Krupa Story; First to Fight; Number One; M*A*S*H.

TV inc: Emergency; The Rebels; The 25th Man.

TROUT, Robert: Radio-TV News. b. Wake County, NC., Oct. 15, 1909. Started with WJSV in 1928, station moved to Washington 1932 changing letters to WTOP; Perennial radio introducer of Pres. Franklin D. Roosevelt, credited with coining the phrase "fireside chats" to describe presidential talks; 1935 to WABC, which was then the CBS NY flagship; covered coronation of George VI in 1937, became European news chief 1941; with NBC 1948-1950 then retd to CBS; joined ABC 1974 as special corr both radio tv.

TRUDEAU, Garry: Wri. b. NYC, 1948. e. Yale and Yale School of Art & Architecture. H of Jane Pauley. Crea cartoon strip Doonesbury. TV inc: A Doonesbury Special; Bway inc: Doonesbury (Book & lyrics); Rap Master Ronnie (lyrics).

TRUEMAN, Paula: Act. b. NYC, Apr 25, 1907. e. Neighborhood Playhouse. Debut as teenage dancer in Michael Fokine's The Thunderbird; appeared in six editions of Grand Street Follies from 1924 to 1929. Bway inc: Lovers and Enemies; If; Love Nest; Maya; Sweet and Low; Ladies of Creation; Midsummer Night's Dream; Merchant of Venice; A Woman in Panic; You Can't Take It With You; George Washington Slept Here; Kiss and Tell; For Love or Money; Gentlemen Prefer Blondes; Wake Up, Darling; A Family Affair; Wonderful Town; The

Sunday Man; The Long Christmas Dinner; Sherry!; Postcards; Dr Fish.

Films inc: Crime and Punishment; One Foot in Heaven; Paint Your Wagon; The Anderson Tapes; On A Clear Day You Can See Forever; Homebodies; The Outlaw Josey Wales; Annie Hall; The Ultimate Solution of Grace Quigley; Mrs. Soffel.

TV inc: Better Late Than Never; Breaking Away; The Electric Grandmother; O'Malley; Murder Ink.

TRUFFAUT, Francois: Dir-Wri. b. Paris, Feb 6, 1932. Worked as journalist, becoming France's most controversial film critic. Directorial debut 1957 with Les Mistons, a short subject.

Films inc: The Four Hundred Blows; Shoot the Piano Player; Soft Skin; The Bride Wore Black; Stolen Kisses; Mississippi Mermaid; The Wild Child; Bed and Board; Two English Girls; Such a Gorgeous Kid Like Me; Day for Night; The Story Of Adele H; Small Change; The Man Who Loved Women; The Green Room; Love on the Run; Close Encounters of the Third Kind (act); The Last Metro; La Femme D'a Cote (The Woman Next Door); Vivement Dimanche (Let It Be Sunday).

(Died Oct. 21, 1984)

TRUMBULL, Douglas: Dir-Wri-Cin. Crea sfx for Silent Running; 2001, A Space Odyssey; The Andromeda Strain; Close Encounters of the Third Kind; Blade Runner (spec photo effects supv); Brainstorm (Prod-dir).

TRYON, Tom: Act-Wri. b. Hartford, CT, Jan 14, 1926. e. Yale U. Films inc: The Scarlet Hour; Three Violent People; I Married a Monster from Outer Space; Moon Pilot; Marines Let's Go; The Cardinal; In Harm's Way; The Glory Guys; The Horsemen.

Thea inc: Wish You Were Here; Cyrano de Bergerac; Richard III.

Books inc: The Other; Crowned Heads.

TUBB, Ernest: Singer-Comp. b. Crisp, TX, Feb 9, 1914. Country mus recording artist. Became a regular on Grand Ole Opry. Elected to Country Music Hall of Fame, 1965. Films inc: Fighting Buckaroo; Ridin' West; Jamboree; Hollywood Barn Dance. TV inc: Loretta Lynn--The Lady, The Legend; Texas & Tennessee--A Musical Affair; An All-Star Tribute To Ernest Tubb--An American Original. Appeared at Carnegie Hall.

(Died Sept. 6, 1984)

TUCCI, Maria: Act. b. Florence, Italy, Jun 19, 1941. e. Actors Studio. Bway inc: The Jackhammer; The Milk Train Doesn't Stop Here Anymore; The Deputy; The Rose Tattoo; The Cuban Thing; The Little Foxes; School For Wives; A Lesson From Aloes; Kingdoms; Requiem For A Heavyweight.

Films inc: Daniel; Enormous Changes at the Last Minute.

TV inc: Concealed Enemies.

TUCHNER, Michael: Dir. b. England. Films inc: Villain; Fear Is The Key; Mr Quilp; Likely Lads; Trenchcoat.

TV inc: The One and Only Phyllis Dixie; Summer of My German Solider; Haywire; The Hunchback of Notre Dame; Parole; Adam; Generation; Not My Kid.

TUCKER, Forrest: Act. b. Plainfield, IN, Feb 12, 1919. Screen debut, 1940, The Westerner. Films inc: New Wine; Canal Zone; Keeper of the Flame; Renegades; The Yearling; Hellfire; Sands of Iwo Jima; Bugles in the Afternoon; Trouble in the Glen; Auntie Mame; The Night They Raided Minsky's; Chisum; Cancel My Reservation; The Wild McCullochs; Final Chapter--Walking Tall; A Rare Breed.

TV inc: F Troop; Crunch and Des; A Real American Hero; The Rebels; Music Man; Fair Game for Lovers; Pottsville; Adventures of Huckleberry Finn; Blood Feud.

TUCKER, Larry: Wri-Prod. b. Philadelphia, PA., Jun. 23, 1933. e. Los Angeles City College. TV inc: (wri) The Danny Kaye Show; The Monkees (& co-crea); 1976;, joined with Larry Rosen in Larry Larry Prodns; Ethel is an Elephant; Pals (& prod) Mr. Merlin (co-crea, exec prod); Jennifer Slept Here (co-crea, exec-prod).

Films inc: Bob and Carol & Ted and Alice (wri-prod); Alex in Wonderland (wri-prod).

TUCKER, Melville: Prod. b. NYC, Mar 4, 1916. e. Princeton. Started in mailroom at Consolidated Labs, NY, became asst purchasing agent; to Hollywood as edtr Republic, later AD; after war service

became prod; 1956 to 1970, prodn exec-vp U. Films inc: The Missourians; Thunder in God's Country; The Rodeo King and the Senorita; Utah Wagon Train; Drums Across the River; Black Shield of Falworth; A Warm December; Uptown Saturday Night; Let's Do It Again; A Piece of the Action; Stir Crazy; Hanky Panky; Fast Forward.

TUCKER, Tanya: Singer-Act. b. Seminole, TX, Oct 10, 1958. Films inc: Jeremiah Johnson; Hard Country.

TV inc: Amateur Night at the Dixie Bar and Grill; The Rebels; Georgia Peaches; A Country Christmas; Bob Hope 30th Anniversary Special; Country Comes Home; Music City News' Top Country Hits of the Year; Opryland--Night of Stars and Future Stars; Entertainer of the Year Awards; The Nashville Palace (host); Texas & Tennessee-- A Musical Affair; The Hawk; Pump Boys & Dinettes On Television.

Albums inc: Delta Dawn; What's Your Mama's Name; Greatest Hits; Here's Some Love; Tanya Tucker; Lovin' and Learnin'; Ridin' Rainbows.

TUMARIN, Boris (nee Tumarinson): Act-Dir. b. Riga, Latvia, Apr 4, 1910. e. Academy of Arts Berlin. Came to the US in 1939. Thea inc: The Emperor's New Clothes; Winter Soldiers; A Checkov Carnival; Paths of Glory; He Who Gets Slapped; Venus at Large; Whisper into My Good Ear; The Tenth Man; The Three Sisters (dir).

TV inc: The Great Sebastian; Ninotchka; The Eternal Light.

TUNBERG, Karl: Wri. b. Spokane, WA, 1908. Films inc: My Lucky Star; Down Argentine Way; Tall, Dark and Handsome; You Gotta Stay Happy; The Scarlet Coat; Ben Hur; Libel; Taras Bulba; Harlow; Where Were You When the Lights Went Out.

TUNE, Tommy: Act-Chor-Dir. b. Feb 28, 1939. e. U TX. Bway inc: (Act) The Boy Friend; Hello, Dolly!; Seesaw (Tony-supp-1974). (Dir) The Club; The Best Little Whorehouse in Texas; A Day in Hollywood, A Night in The Ukraine; Cloud 9; Nine (Tony-Dir-1982); My One and Only (Tonys-act & chor-1983).

TUNICK, Eugene: Exec. b. Cincinnati, OH, Oct 21, 1920. e. U of Cincinnati. Started as shipping clerk with RKO Cincinnati. On return from military service became booker; Office mgr 1946; Salesman 1948; sales mgr 1949; sales mgr Eagle Lion 1949-51; branch mgr Indianapolis 1951-52; Lippert branch mgr, franchise holder 1951-53; branch mgr UA, Philadelphia 1957; district mgr 1961; Eastern and Canadian division mgr 1968; joined National General Pictures as vp-gen sales mgr 1970, became exec vp following year; exec vp National Amusements 1975; western vp General Cinema 1977; joined American International as vp special projects 1978, became VP gen sales mgr after merger with Filmways; May 1981, exec vp in chg dom dist.

(Died March 16, 1984).

TUNICK, Jonathan: Comp-Cond-Arr. Bway inc: (arr) A Little Night Music; Company; Follies; Pacific Overtures; A Chorus Line; Ballroom; Sweeney Todd; Merrily We Roll Along; Alice In Wonderland (mus adapt & supv); Dance A Little Closer (orchs); Baby (orchs).

Films inc: A Little Night Music (Oscar-adapt-1977); Fort Apache, The Bronx; Endless Love; I Am the Cheese.

TV inc: (comp) Swan Song; Blinded by the Light; Night of 100 Stars (arr) (Emmy-1982); Alice In Wonderland (score); Live From Lincoln Center Marilyn Horne's Great American Songbook (mus dir); Concealed Enemies (score); Brotherly Love (score).

TURKEL, Ann: Act. W of Richard Harris. Films inc: Paper Lion; 99 44/100ths % Dead; The Cassandra Crossing; Ravagers; Humanoids From the Deep; The Shining.

TV inc: Greatest Heroes of the Bible; Death Ray 2000; Massarati and the Brain; Modesty Blaise.

TURMAN, Lawrence: Prod. b. Los Angeles, 1926. e. UCLA. Started as agent, 1960, partnered with Stuart Miller on The Young Doctors; I Could Go On Singing; Stolen Hours; The Best Man. Solo Prod: The Flim-Flam Man; The Graduate; Pretty Poison; The Great White Hope; Marriage of a Young Stockbroker. Partnered with David Foster on The Drowning Pool; Heroes; Walk Proud; Tribute; Caveman; The Thing; Second Thoughts (& dir); Mass Appeal.

TV inc: Between Two Brothers (exec prod); The Gift of Love (exec prod).

TURNBULL, Dale: Exh exec. b. Melbourne, Australia, Nov 19, 1927. GM Hoyts Theatres Ltd & GM Fox Film Corp, Australia; m dir Hoyts Theatres Ltd; p The Old Tote Theatre Co.

TURNER, Ike: Mus-Singer. b. Clarksdale, MS, 1934. Formed Ike Turner Kings of Rhythm; Ike and Tina Turner Revue. Concerts, world tours. Recordings inc: Proud Mary (Grammy-R&B voc group-1971).
    Films inc: Gimme Shelter; Soul to Soul; Sound of the City--London 1964-73.

TURNER, Kathleen: Act. b. Springfield, MO., 1954. Films inc: Body Heat; The Man With Two Brains; Romancing the Stone; A Breed Apart; Crimes of Passion; Prizzi's Honor.
    TV inc: The Doctors.
    Thea inc: Gemini (Bway); A Midsummer Night's Dream; The Toyer.

TURNER, Lana: Act. b. Wallace, ID, Feb 8, 1920. On screen from 1937 in They Won't Forget. Films inc: The Great Garrick; The Adventures of Marco Polo; Love Finds Andy Hardy; Rich Man, Poor Girl; Dancing Coed; Ziegfeld Girl; Dr. Jekyll and Mr. Hyde; Honky Tonk; Johnny Eager; Somewhere I'll Find You; Marriage Is a Private Affair; Weekend at the Waldorf; The Postman Always Rings Twice; Green Dolphin Street; Cass Timberlane; A Life of Her Own; The Merry Widow; The Sea Chase; Diane; Peyton Place; Imitation of Life; Portrait in Black; Bachelor in Paradise; By Love Possessed; Who's Got the Action?; Madame X; The Big Cube; Persecution; Bittersweet Love; Witches' Brew.
    TV inc: The Survivors; Entertainment Tonight.
    Thea inc: Forty Carats; Legendary Ladies; The Pleasure of His Company.

TURNER, Ted (Robert Edward Turner 3rd): Exec. b. Cincinnati, OH, Nov 19, 1938. e. Brown U. Owner WTBS (Atlanta, Ga, tv "superstation"); owner-founder of of Cable News Network. Also owns Atlanta Braves baseball team; Atlanta Hawks basketball team.

TURNER, Tina (Annie Mae Bullock): Sing-Act. b. Brownsville, TX, Nov 26, 1939. Formerly married to Ike Turner and appeared with him in Ike Turner King of Rhythm; Ike and Tina Turner Revue. Recs inc: Proud Mary (Grammy-R&B voc group-1971); What's Love Got To Do With It (Grammys-Record of Year-Song of Year-Pop Vocal-1984); Better Be Good To Me (Grammy-Rock vocal-1984)
    Films inc: Gimme Shelter; Soul to Soul; Tommy; Sound of the City--London 1964-73; Mad Max Beyond Thunderdrome.
    TV inc: Tina Turner--Private Dancer (PC).

TURTELTAUB, Saul: Wri-Prod. b. Teaneck, NJ, May 5, 1932. e. Columbia Coll, BA; Columbia Law School, JD. TV inc: (Wri) Shari Lewis Show; Candid Camera; That Was the Week That Was; The Les Crane Show; The Steve Lawrence Show; The Jackie Gleason Show; The Pat Boone Show; The Carol Burnett Show. (Prod) That Girl; The New Dick Van Dyke Show; A Touch of Grace; Love American Style; Sanford and Son; What's Happening; Carter Country; One In A Million; One of the Boys; Double Trouble (exec prod-wri); E.R. (wri-prod).

TUSHINGHAM, Rita: Act. b. Liverpool, England, Mar 14, 1942. Films inc: A Taste of Honey; The Leather Boys; The Girl with Green Eyes; The Knack; Dr Zhivago; The Trap; Smashing Time; Diamonds for Breakfast; The Guru; The Bed-Sitting Room; Straight On Till Morning; The Human Factor; Spaghetti House.
    Thea inc: The Giveaway; Lorna and Ted; Mistress of Novices; The Undiscovered Country; Mysteries.

TUTIN, Dorothy: Act. b. London, Apr 8, 1930. e. RADA. Thea inc: The Thistle and the Rose; As You Like It; Captain Carvallo; The Provoked Wife; The Merry Wives of Windsor; Thor With Angels; The Living Room; Othello; The Cherry Orchard; The Hollow Crown; The Beggar's Opera; Old Times; What Every Woman Knows; A Month in the Country; Anthony and Cleopatra; Reflections; The Provok'd Wife; Other Places.
    Films inc: The Importance of Being Earnest; The Beggar's Opera; A Tale of Two Cities; Cromwell; Savage Messiah; The Shooting Party.
    TV inc: Six Wives of Henry VIII; South Riding; Willow Cabins; Life After Death; Laurence Olivier Presents King Lear; Murder With Mirrors.

TUTTLE, Lurene: Act. b. Pleasant Lake, IN, Aug 29, 1907. e. USC. On stage, radio. Films inc Heaven Only Knows; Mr. Blandings Builds His Dream House; Goodbye, My Fancy; Don't Bother to Knock; Niagara; The Affairs of Dobie Gillis; The Glass Slipper; Sweet Smell of Success; Psycho; Critic's Choice; The Fortune Cookie; The Ghost and Mr. Chicken; The Horse in the Gray Flannel Suit; Walking Tall; Walking Tall, Part II; Nutcracker Fantasy; The Manitou; Parts-The Clonus Horror; Testament.
    Radio inc: Sam Spade; Hollywood Hotel.
    TV inc: Life With Father; Julia; White Mama; For The Love Of It; Thanksgiving In the Land of Oz (voice); Adventures of Huckleberry Finn; Return of the Beverly Hillbillies; Shooting Stars; It Came Upon A Midnight Clear.

TWIGGY (Leslie Hornby): Act. b. London, Sep 19, 1949. Former model. Films inc: The Boy Friend; The Blues Brothers; There Goes The Bride. TV inc: A Gift of Music (host).
    Bway inc: My One and Only.

TWITTY, Conway: Singer-Sngwri. b. Friarspoint, MS, Sep 1, 1933. Rock 'n' roll singer 1965 to 1969 then switched to C&W. Songs inc: It's Only Make Believe; Hello Darlin'.
    TV inc: Music City News' Top Country Hits of the Year; Loretta Lynn--The Lady, The Legend; An Evening With The Statler Bros--A Salute to the Good Times; Country Comes Alive; Loretta Lynn in Big Apple Country; Conway Twitty on the Mississippi; Janie Fricke--You Ought to Be in Pictures.
    (Grammy-C&W group-1971).

TYNE, George (Martin Yarus): Act-Dir. b. Philadelphia, Feb 6, 1917. Films inc: (act) A Walk in the Sun; Objective Burma; Call Northside 777; Sands of Iwo Jima; Decision before Dawn; Not With My Wife You Don't; Don't Make Waves; Willie Boy; Marlowe; Skin Game; Ricco; The Boston Strangler; Guide for a Married Man; Fun and Games.
    TV inc: (dir) Good Morning World; Governor and JJ; The Odd Couple; Love American Style; Sanford and Son; The Brady Bunch; Mary Tyler Moore Show; The Ghost and Mrs Muir; M*A*S*H; Miss Winslow and Son (pilot); Friends; Love Boat; Fighting Nightingales (pilot); The 416th; Fun and Games.
    Thea inc: (act) Romanoff and Juliet; Three Penny Opera; Hotel Paradiso; Too Late the Phalarope.

TYRRELL, Susan: Act. b. San Francisco, 1946. Films inc: The Steagle; Fat City; Catch My Soul; The Killer Inside Me; Islands in the Stream; I Never Promised You A Rose Garden; Andy Warhol's Bad; Another Man, Another Chance; September 30, 1955; Forbidden Zone; Subway Riders; Tales of Ordinary Madness; Loose Shoes; Fast-Walking; Liar's Moon; Fire and Ice; Night Warning; Angel; The Killers; Avenging Angel; Flesh & Blood.
    TV inc: Lady of the House; Willow B-Women In Prison; Midnight Lace; Open All Night; Jealousy; MacGruder & Loud.
    Thea inc: Father's Day.

TYSON, Cicely: Act. b. NYC, Dec 19, 1933. Films inc: A Man Called Adam; The Comedians; The Heart Is a Lonely Hunter; Sounder; The River Niger; The Blue Bird; A Hero Ain't Nothin' But a Sandwich; The Concorde-Airport '79; Bustin' Loose.
    TV inc: The Autobiography of Miss Jane Pittman (Emmys-1974 & actress of year); Roots; East Side, West Side; A Woman Called Moses; King; The Marva Collins Story; Benny's Place; The Body Human--Becoming A Woman (host); A Tribute to Martin Luther King Jr--A Celebration of Life; Playing With Fire.
    Bway inc: The Corn Is Green.

UGGAMS, Leslie: Singer-Act. b. NYC, May 25, 1943. e. Professional Children's School, Juilliard. Began singing career at age 5; TV debut, age 7, Johnny Oleson's TV kids.
    Bway inc: Hallelujah Baby (Tony-1968); Blues In the Night.
    Radio: Peter Lind Hayes-Mary Healy Show; Milton Berle; Arthur Godfrey; Star Time.
    TV inc: Milton Berle Show; Name That Tune; Sing Along With Mitch; Backstairs at the White House; A Gift of Music; Sizzle; Book of Lists (co-host); Fantasy (Emmy-Host-1983); I Love Men; Night Of 100 Stars II; Placido Domingo Steppin' Out With The Ladies; The 39th Annual Tony Awards.

ULLMANN, Liv: Act. b. Tokyo, Dec 16,1939. Films inc: Short is the Summer; Persona; Hour of the Wolf; Ann-Magrit; Cold Sweat; The Night Visitors; A Passion; Pope Joan; Cries and Whispers; The Emigrants; Face To Face; A Bridge Too Far; Autumn Sonata; Leonor; Richard's Things. Love (Dir-wri); The Wild Duck; Bay Boy.

Bway inc: I Remember Mama; Anna Christie; Ghosts. London inc: Old Times.

TV inc: Lady From The Sea (cable); Jacobo Timerman: Prisoner Without A Name, Cell Without A Number; Jenny.

UMEKI, Miyoshi: Act. b. Japan, 1929. Films inc: Sayonara (Oscar-supp-1957); Cry for Happy; Flower Drum Song; The Horizontal Lieutenant; A Girl Named Tamiko.

UNGER, Anthony B.: Prod. b. NYC, Oct 19, 1940. e. Duke U, USC. Films inc: The Desperate Ones (asso prod); The Madwoman of Chaillot; The Battle of Neretva; The Magic Christian; Julius Caesar; The Devil's Widow; Don't Look Now; Force 10 From Navarone; The Unseen; Silent Rage.

UNGER, Daniel: Prod. b. Tel Aviv, Apr 6, 1948. Films inc: Puppet on a Chain; Pope Joan.

UNGER, Kurt: Prod. b. Berlin, Jan 10, 1922. Dir RoadShow Prodns, Ltd London. Films inc: Judith; Best House in London; Puppet on a Chain; Pope Joan.

UNGER, Stephen A.: Exec. b. NYC, May 31, 1946. e. Syracuse U, BA; NYU Film School. S of the late Oliver Unger. vp Intl Sls, U; 1980, sr vp Filmways Pictures Inc; Dec 1980, VP foreign sls CBS Theatrical Films. TV inc: (co-prod) Verna--USO Girl.

URICH, Robert: Act. b. Toronto, OH, Dec 19. e. FL State U, BA. Films inc: Magnum Force; Endangered Species; The Ice Pirates; Turk 182.

TV inc: Bob and Carol and Ted and Alice; S.W.A.T.; Soap; Tabitha; Vega$; Merry Christmas From the Grand Ole Opry House; A Christmas Special With Love-Mac Davis; The Starmakers; Fighting Back; Bob Hope 30th Anniversary Special; Sixty Years of Seduction (host); Bob Hope's All-Star Birthday Party at West Point; Killing at Hell's Gate; Take Your Best Shot; Gavilan; Princess Daisy; The Rodney Dangerfield Special--I Can't Take it No More; Invitation to Hell; Mistral's Daughter; His Mistress; Scandal Sheet.

USTINOV, Peter: Act-Wri-Dir. b. London, Apr 16, 1921. On Brit. stage from 1937. Screen debut 1940, Mein Kampf. Films inc: (act) Quo Vadis; Hotel Sahara; Beau Brummell; We're No Angels; An Angel Flew Over Brooklyn; Spartacus (Oscar-supp-1960); The Sundowners; Romanoff and Juliet (& wri-prod-dir); Billy Budd (& dir-prod); Topkapi (Oscar-supp-1964); John Goldfarb, Please Come Home; Lady L. (prod-dir); Blackbeard's Ghost; The Comedians; Hot Millions (& sp); Viva Max; Hammersmith Is Out (& dir); Big Truck; Poor Clare; One of Our Dinosaurs Is Missing; Logan's Run; Treasure of Matecumbe; The Purple Taxi; Last Remake of Beau Geste; Death on the Nile; The Mouse and His Child; Nous Maigrirons Ensemble; Ashanti; Charlie Chan and the Curse of the Dragon Queen; The Great Muppet Caper; Grendel Grendel Grendel (voice); Evil Under the Sun; Memed, My Hawk.

TV inc: The Life of Samuel Johnson (Emmy-1958); Barefoot in Athens (Emmy-1967); A Storm in Summer (Emmy-1970); Omnibus; Babar the Elephant; Hallmark Hall of Fame; The Thief of Bagdad; The Seven Dials Mystery; Omni--The New Frontier (host); James Clavell's The Children's Story (host); Strumpet City (cable); The Life and Adventures of Nicholas Nickleby (host).

Plays inc: Romanoff and Juliet; Photo Finish; The Love Of Four Colonels; Halfway Up the Tree; The Unknown Soldier and His Wife; Who's Who in Hell; Overheard; The Marriage (adapt); Beethoven's Tenth.

(Grammy-childrens-1959).

UTLEY, Garrick: TV news. b. Chicago, IL., Nov. 19, 1939. e. Carleton College, BA. Joined NBC News 1963, stationed in Brussels; 1964, Saigon bureau; 1966, anchored Vietnam Weekly review; 1967, European corr; later anchor weekend editions NBC Nightly News, First Tuesday; 1973 to London bureau; 1980, principal reporter NBC Magazine with David Brinkley. TV inc: Inside AWACS (Emmy-corr-1981); Rockets for Sale (Emmy-corr-1981).

VACCARO, Brenda: Act. b. NYC, Nov 18, 1939. Bway inc: Everybody Loves Opal; The Affair; Cactus Flower; toured in Tunnel of Love.

Films inc: Midnight Cowboy; I Love My Wife; Summertree; Going Home; Once Is Not Enough; Airport '77; House by the Lake; Capricorn One; Fast Charlie the Moonbeam Rider; The First Deadly Sin; Zorro, the Gay Blade; Supergirl; Water.

TV inc: The FBI; The Name of the Game; The Helen Reddy Show; The Pride of Jesse Hallam; The Star Maker; A Long Way Home; Paper Dolls; Deceptions.

VADIM, Roger: (R V Plemiannikov): Dir. b. Paris, Jan. 26,1928. Films inc: Futures Vedettes; And God Created Woman (& wri); Heaven Fell That Night (& wri); Les Liaisons Dangereuses (& wri); Blood and Roses; Warrior's Rest; Vice and Virtue (& Prod-wri); La Ronde; Nutty Naughty Chateau; The Game Is Over; Histoires Extraordinaires; Barbarella; Pretty Maids All in a Row; Ms Don Juan (& wri); Night Games; Charlotte; A Faithful Woman (& wri); Hot Touch; Into The Night (act).

VALDEZ, Luis: Plywri-Act. b. Delano, CA, Jun 26, 1940. e. San Jose State Coll. Founder of El Teatro Campesino, drama group of farmworkers union. Plays inc: The Shrunken Head of Pancho Villa; Zoot Suit.

Films inc: Which Way Is Up (act); Zoot Suit (& dir).

TV inc: Los Vendidos.

VALE, Eugene: Wri. b. Zurich, Apr 11, 1916. Films inc: A Global Affair; Francis of Assisi; The Second Face; The Bridge of San Luis Rey.

TV inc: Four Star Playhouse; Fireside Theatre; Schlitz Playhouse; Crusader; Lux Video Theatre; Danger; Chevron Theatre; Waterfront; Christophers; Cavalcade of America; Hallmark Hall of Fame.

Plays inc: Devils Galore; The Buffoon; Of Shadows Cast by Men.

Author: Technique of Screenplay Writing; Some State of Affairs; The Children's Crusade.

VALENTE, Renee: Prod. Started as sec with David Susskind, later becoming story ed, asso prod; 1963 to Col in casting; 1964 to Screen Gems as prod; 1973 talent vp; 1976, vp telepix & longform; resd 1977 to enter indie prodn.

TV inc: (exec prod) Contract on Cherry Street; Kill Me If You Can; The Last Hurrah. Blind Ambition; Swan Song; Masquerade; Love Thy Neighbor.

Films inc: Loving Couples.

VALENTI, Jack J.: Exec. b. Houston, TX, Sep 5, 1921. e. U of Houston, BA; Harvard, MBA. Air Force pilot, WW II. Special asst and advisor to p Lyndon B Johnson, 1963-66; p, MPAA; elected p, AMPTP, June, 1966.

VALENTINE, Karen: Act. b. Sebastopol, CA, May 25, 1947. Films inc: Forever Young, Forever Free; Hot Lead and Cold Feet; The North Avenue Irregulars.

TV inc: Room 222 (Emmy-supp-1970); Karen; My Friend Tony; Hollywood Squares; Laugh-In; The Bold Ones; Sonny and Cher; Gidget Grows Up; Daughters of Joshua Cabe; The Girl Who Came Gift Wrapped; Murder at the World Series; Having Babies; America 2100; Only the Pretty Girls Die; Muggable Mary--Street Cop; Goodbye Doesn't Mean Forever; Adams House; Money On the Side; Skeezer; Illusions; Jane Doe; A Girl's Life; Children In the Crossfire; He's Fired, She's Hired.

Thea inc: Stop the World, I Want to Get Off;The Moon Is Blue; Born Yesterday; Bus Stop.

VALLEE, Rudy (Hubert Prior Vallee): Singer-Mus-Act. b. Island Point, VT, Jul 28, 1901. e. U of ME, Yale U. Org. own band, Connecticut Yankees. Later featured on radio, various NY musicals. On screen from 1929. Films inc: The Vagabond Lover; George White's Scandals; The Palm Beach Story; I Remember Mama; The Helen Morgan Story; Live a Little, Love a Little; The Phynx.

VALLI, Alida (nee von Altenburger): Act. b. Pola, Italy, May 31, 1921. Films inc: Vita Ricomincia; Giovanna; The Paradine Case; Miracle of the Bells; The Third Man; Walk Softly Stranger; White Tower; Lovers of Toledo; Stranger's Hand; The Castilian; Ophelia; Spider's Stratagem; The Cassandra Crossing; Suspiria; 1900; The Tempter; Luna; Ce Cher Victor; The Bailiff of Griefensee; That House in the Outskirts; Sezona Mira U Parizu (Season of Peace In Paris); La

Caduta Degli Angeli Ribelli (The Fall of the Rebellious Angels); Segreti Segreti (Secrets Secrets).

VALLONE, Raf: Act. b. Turin, Italy, 1916. Films inc: Bitter Rice; Vendetta; Anna; Therese Raquin; The Beach; The Sign of Venus; El Cid; A View from the Bridge; Phaedra; The Cardinal; Harlow; Beyond the Mountains; Nevada Smith; The Italian Job; Cannon for Cordoba; The Kremlin Letter; A Gunfight; Rosebud; The Human Factor; The Other Side of Midnight; The Greek Tycoon; An Almost Perfect Affair; Arthur Miller on Home Ground; Return to Marseilles; Lion of the Desert; Sezona Mira U Parizu (Season of Peace In Paris); A Time to Die.

TV inc: Fame (Hallmark Hall of Fame); Honor Thy Father; Catholics; The Scarlet and the Black; Christopher Columbus; Goya.

Van ACKEREN, Robert: Prod-dir-wri. b. Berlin, Dec. 22, 1946. Films inc: Einer weiss mehr; Sept. 19; Wham; Sticky Fingers; Der Magische Moment; NouNou; Eve; Die endlose Reise; Fur immer und ewig; Blondie's No. 1; Kuss mich, Fremder (Kiss Me, Stranger); Harlis; Der letzte schrei (The Last Cry); Belcanto; Das andere Lacheln (The Other Smile); Die Reinheit des Herzens (The Purity of Heart); Deutschland privat (Germany Private); Die flambierte Frau (A Woman in Flames); Die Tigerin (The Tigress).

Van ARK, Joan: Act. b. NYC, Jun 16. e. Yale U. Films inc: The Frogs.

TV inc: Temperatures Rising; We've Got Each Other; Knott's Landing; A Testimony of Two Men; The Last Dinosaur; Big Rose; Red Flag-The Ultimate Game; Glitter; Bob Hope's Comedy Salute To The Soaps.

Thea inc: Barefoot in the Park; School for Wives; Cyrano de Bergerac; Ring Around the Moon; Chemin de Fer; As You Like It.

VANCE, Leigh: Wri-Prod. b. Harrogate, England, Mar 18, 1922. e. Shrewsbury Coll. Films inc: The Flesh Is Weak; Heart of a Child; The Shakedown; The Frightened City; It's All Happening; Dr Crippen; Walk Like a Man; Cross Plot; The Black Windmill.

TV inc: Mannix; Mission Impossible; The Avengers; Cannon; Caribe; Bronk; Baretta; Switch; The Phoenix.

Van CLEEF, Lee: Act. b. Somerville, NJ, Jan 9, 1925. Films inc: High Noon; Arena; Yellow Tomahawk; A Man Alone; Joe Dakota; Guns, Girls and Gangsters; The Man Who Shot Liberty Valance; For a Few Dollars More; Day of Anger; The Good, the Bad and the Ugly; Death Rides a Horse; Sabata; Barquero; El Condor; Captain Apache; Bad Man's River; The Magnificent Seven Ride; Take a Hard Ride; The Squeeze; The Octagon; Escape From New York.

TV inc; The Master.

VANDERBES, Romano R.: Exec. b. Amsterdam, The Netherlands, Jan 16, 1938. e. U of Amsterdam, Yale U, UCLA. P, wri-dir-prod Pace Productions, Inc, 1961-68; P-American-European Films, Inc, New York, Paris, Madrid; P, IFM Releasing Corps, NY. Films inc: New York Nights (prod-wri).

Van De VEN, Monique: Act. b. Holland, Jul 28, 1952. e. Acad Dramatic Arts. W of Jan DeBont. Films inc: Turkish Delight; Lost Monday; Dakota; Syl, the Beachcomber; Anita; Keetje Tippel; Doctor Vlimmen; Farewell Doctor; A Woman Like Eve; Separation; Uit Elkaar (Splitting Up); Ademloos (Breathless); Brandende Liefde (Burning Love); De Schorpioen (The Scorpion).

TV inc: Dixie--Changing Habits.

Van DEVERE, Trish: Act. b. Tenafly, NJ, 1943. W of George C Scott. Films inc: Where's Poppa? The Last Run; One Is a Lonely Number; The Day of the Dolphin; The Savage is Loose; Fifty-Two Pickup; Movie Movie; The Changeling; The Hearse.

TV inc: Mayflower-The Pilgrim Adventure; All God's Children; Haunted.

Thea inc: Sly Fox; Tricks of the Trade.

Van DOREN, Mamie (Joan Lucille Olander): Act. b. Rowena, SD, Feb 6, 1933. Prof. debut as singer with Ted Fio Rita orch. Appeared in stock. Films inc: Forbidden; All American; Yankee Pasha; The Girl in Black Stockings; Teacher's Pet; Untamed Youth; Sex Kittens Go To College; Girls Town; Running Wild; High School Confidential; Born Reckless; The Beat Generation; Four Nuts in Search of a Bolt; You've Got to be Smart; Arizona Kid.

Van DREELEN, John (Jacques Van Dreelen Gimberg): Act. b. Amsterdam, Netherlands, May 5, 1922. Debut with Royal Theatre, The Hague; on stage in Europe before coming to US. Bway inc: Daphne Laureola; The Sound of Music; The Deputy; Private Lives; Marriage-Go-Round; Write Me a Murder.

Films inc: A Time To Live, A Time To Die; Monte Carlo Baby; Von Ryan's Express; Madame X; Dirty Business; Topaz; Flying Fontaines; Too Hot To Handle; The Formula.

TV inc: The Great Wallendas; The Clone Master; The Word; The Ultimate Impostor; Swan Song; Evita Peron.

VANDROSS, Luther: Singer-Sngwri. b. NYC, Apr 20, 1951. Sang back-up vocals on LP's by Ringo Starr; Carly Simon; David Bowie; Bette Midler; Cat Stevens; Roberta Flack; Martha Reeves. Songs inc: Brand New Day; Fascination.

Van DYKE, Dick: Act. b. West Plains, MO, Dec 13, 1925. Films inc: Bye Bye Birdie; What a Way to Go!; Mary Poppins; The Art of Love; Chitty Chitty Bang Bang; Some Kind of Nut; The Comic; Cold Turkey; The Runner Stumbles.

Thea inc: The Girls Against the Boys; Bye Bye Birdie (Tony-1961); The Music Man (rev).

TV inc: The Merry Mute Show; The Music Shop; The Dick Van Dyke Show (Emmys-1964,1965,1966); Dick Van Dyke & Company (Emmy-1977); Carol Burnett Show; How to Survive the 70's and Maybe Even Bump into Happiness; 30 Years of TV Comedy's Greatest Hits (co-host); Highlights of Ringling Brothers and Barnum & Bailey Circus-111th Edition (host); Harry's Battles; True Life Stories; How To Eat Like A Child (Project Peacock); Drop-Out Father; Found Money; The Wrong Way Kid (Emmy-1984); Donald Duck's 50th Birthday (host); Night Of 100 Stars II; Breakfast With Les & Bess; The 39th Annual Tony Awards.

Van DYKE, Jerry: Act. b. Danville, IL, Jul 27, 1931. TV inc: My Mother the Car; The Judy Garland Show; Accidental Family; Headmaster.

VANE, Edwin T.: Exec. b. NYC, Apr 29, 1927. e. Fordham, BA; NYU, MBA. Joined ABC 1964 as dir daytime pgm East Coast; 1966 VP chg daytime pgm; 1969, primetime prodn ABC Entertainment; 1972 VP & net pgm dir; 1979, VP net pgm aff; 1979 P & CEO Group W Productions.

Van FLEET, Jo: Act. b. Oakland, CA, Dec 30,1919. Films inc: East of Eden (Oscar-supp-1955); The Rose Tattoo; I'll Cry Tomorrow; The King and Four Queens; Gunfight at the O.K. Corral; Wild River; Cool Hand Luke; I Love You Alice B. Toklas!; 80 Steps to Jonah; The Gang That Couldn't Shoot Straight; The Tenant.

Thea inc: Winter's Tale; The Whole World Over; King Lear; Flight into Egypt; Camino Real; Trip to Bountiful (Tony-1954); Look Homeward Angel; The Glass Menagerie.

TV inc: Power.

VANGELIS (Vangelis Papathanassiou): Comp-Cond. b. Greece. Formed band Formynx in Greece; later launched Aphrodite's Child in Paris. TV inc: Apocalypse des Animaux; Cosmos.

Films inc: Chariots of Fire (Oscar-1981); Missing; Blade Runner; The Bounty; Wonders of Life (doc); Sauvage et Beau (Wild And Beautiful).

Van HEUSEN, James (Edward Chester Babcock): Comp-Pianist. b. Syracuse, NY, Jan 26, 1913. Films inc: Love Thy Neighbor; Road to Zanzibar; Road to Morocco; Dixie; Going My Way; And the Angels Sing; Road to Utopia; Road to Rio; A Connecticut Yankee in King Arthur's Court; Road to Bali; Road to Hong Kong; Bells of St Mary's; Little Boy Lost.

Songs inc: All This and Heaven Too; Moonlight Becomes You; Suddenly It's Spring; Swinging on Star (Oscar-1944); Love and Marriage (Emmy-1955); All the Way (Oscar-1957); Come Fly with Me; High Hopes (Oscar-1959); The Second Time Around; Call Me Irresponsible (Oscar-1963); My Kind of Town.

Film title songs inc: The Tender Trap; Indiscreet; Pocketful of Miracles; Come Blow Your Horn.

Thea inc: Swingin' the Dream; Nellie Bly; Carnival in Flanders; Skyscraper.

Van NIE, Rene: Prod-Dir-Wri. b. Amsterdam, Netherlands, Oct 1, 1939. Films inc: Anna, Child of the Daffodils; Silent Love; The Deadly Sin.

VANOCUR, Sander: TV News Pers. b. Cleveland, OH. e. Northwestern U, BA. Started as journalist in London. Joined NBC, 1957; hosted First Tuesday Series; resigned 1971, to become correspondent of the National Public Affairs Center for PBS; June 1977 joined ABC News as vp, special reporting units.

VANOFF, Boris: Prod. b. Buffalo, NY, Dec 7, 1939. Cameraman, ABC-TV; talent coordinator; prodn m. TV inc: King Family; Milton Berle Show. Record prod, Nico records; M & L Records; Sunburst Records; Capitol records. Pres Boris Music Inc.

VANOFF, Nick: Prod. b. Greece, Oct 25, 1929. e. McCune School of Music and Art, Salt Lake City. Began career with Charles Weidman Dance Theatre; brief career as dancer on tv, Bway; now owner, with Saul Pick, Sunset-Gower Studios. Films inc: White Dog (exec prod).

TV inc: Perry Como Show (asso prod); Steve Allen Tonight Show; Perry Como Kraft Music Hall; The Milton Berle Show; The King Family; Hollywood Palace; The Julie Andrews Hour (Emmy-1973); The Don Knotts Show; Hee Haw; Swing Out, Sweet Land; Perry Como Christmas Show; The Sonny and Cher Show; The Kennedy Center Honors, 1979, 1980, 1982, 1983 (Emmy-prod), 1984; The Big Show; On Stage, America.

Van PALLANDT, Nina: Singer-Act. b. Copenhagen, Denmark, Jul 15, 1932. e. USC, Sorbonne. Films inc: The Long Goodbye; Assault on Agathon; Quintet; A Wedding; American Gigolo; Cutter and Bone; The Sword and the Sorcerer; Jungle Warriors.

Van PATTEN, Dick: Act. b. NYC, Dec 9, 1928. Bway debut age 7 as Melvyn Douglas' son in Tapestry and Gray; 27 other Bway plays inc: On Borrowed Time; The American Way; The Skin of Our Teeth; Kiss and Tell; The Wind is 90; O Mistress Mine; Mr. Roberts; The Male Animal; Have I Got a Girl for You; Thieves.

Films inc: Charly; Zachariah; Joe Kidd; Snowball Express; Dirty Little Billy; Westworld; Soylent Green; Super Dad; Strongest Man in the World; Gus; Shaggy D.A.; Treasure of the Matecumbe; High Anxiety; Nutcracker Fantasy.

TV inc: I Remember Mama (8 years); The Dick Van Dyke Show; The Partners; Arnie; When Things Were Rotten; Eight is Enough; Diary of a Teen-Age Hitchhiker; Alan King's Thanksgiving Special--What Do We Have to be Thankful For?; Take One; Whatever Became Of . . .? (host); High Powder; Fit For A King; Andy Williams' Early New England Christmas; Insight/The Day Everything Went Wrong; The Hoboken Chicken Emergency.

Van PATTEN, Joyce: Act. b. Queens, NY, Mar 9, 1934. Films inc: The Goddess; I Love You Alice B Toklas; Something Big; Thumb Tripping; Mikey and Nicky; The Falcon And The Snowman; St. Elmo's Fire.

TV inc: The Bravos; Shadow of Fear; Mary Tyler Moore Hour; A Christmas for Boomer; The Martian Chronicles; Bulba--Our Man In Okala Town; Eleanor, First Lady of the World; Bus Stop (cable); Another Woman's Child; The Demon Murder Case; In Defense of Kids; Crazy Like A Fox; Malice In Wonderland.

Bway inc: Same Time Next Year; I Ought to be in Pictures; The Supporting Cast; Brighton Beach Memoirs.

Van PEEBLES, Melvin: Dir-Wri-Comp. Films inc: The Story of a Three-Day Pass; Watermelon Man; Sweet Sweetback's Baadasssss Song.

Plays inc: Aint Supposed to Die a Natural Death; Don't Play Us Cheap; Reggae; Waltz of the Stork.

TV inc: Just an Old Sweet Song; The Sophisticated Gents .

Van VALKENBURGH, Deborah: Act. b. NY 1953. In off-Bway plays, understudied in Hair. Films inc: The Warriors; King of the Mountain; Streets of Fire.

TV inc: Too Close for Comfort; A Bunny's Tale.

Van VLEET, Richard: Act. b. Denver, CO, Jan 19. e. Western State Coll, AADA. Films inc: Airport; Ben. TV inc: All My Children.

VARDA, Agnes: Wri-Dir. b. 1928. Began as still photog for Theatre National Populaire. Launched herself as a filmmaker with La Pointe Courte, regarded as a forerunner of the French new wave. Other films inc: O Saisons, O Chateaux (short); L'Opera Mouffe (short); Du Cote de la Cote (short); Cleo de 5 a 7; Salut Les Cubains (short); Le Bonheur; Les Creatures; Uncle Yanco (short) (& prod); Black Panthers (short) (& prod); Lions Love (& prod); Last Tango in Paris (dialog credit only); Daguerreotypes (& prod); One Sings, The Other Doesn't; Lady Oscar (prod only); Murs, Murs (Walls, Walls); Documenteur: An Emotion Picture.

VARSI, Diane: Act. b. San Francisco, 1938. Films inc: Peyton Place; Ten North Frederick; From Hell to Texas; Compulsion; Sweet Love, Bitter; Wild in the Streets; Killers Three; Bloody Mama; Johnny Got His Gun; I Never Promised You a Rose Garden.

VAUGHAN, Sarah: Singer. b. Newark, NJ, Mar 27, 1924. Recording artist; sang with bands, niteries.

TV inc: Uptown-A Tribute to the Apollo Theatre; Live From Studio 8H--100 Years of America's Popular Music; Rhapsody and Song--A Tribute to George Gershwin (Emmy-1981); Olympic Gala; Night Of 100 Stars II; Motown Returns To The Apollo.

(Grammy-Jazz vocal-1982).

VAUGHN, Robert: Act. b. NYC, 1932. Films inc: Hell's Crossroads; No Time to be Young; Unwed Mother; Good Day for a Hanging; The Young Philadelphians; The City Jungle; The Magnificent Seven; The Big Show; The Caretakers; To Trap a Spy; The Spy with My Face; One Spy Too Many; The Venetian Affair; How to Steal the World; Bullitt; The Bridge at Remagen; The Mind of Mr. Soames; If It's Tuesday, This Must Be Belgium. Julius Caesar; The Statue; The Clay Pigeon; The Towering Inferno; Brass Target; Starship Invasions; Good Luck Miss Wyckoff; Virus; Cuba Crossing; Battle Beyond the Stars; Hangar 18; S.O.B.; Superman III.

TV inc: The Man From U.N.C.L.E.; Washington--Behind Closed Doors (Emmy-1978); One of Our Spies Is Missing (Brit. TV); The Spy in the Green Hat (Brit. TV); Greatest Heroes of the Bible; Centennial; The Rebels; Mirror, Mirror; Dr. Franken; The Gossip Columnist; City in Fear; Fantasies; The Day the Bubble Burst; A Question of Honor; Inside The Third Reich; The Blue and The Gray; Intimate Agony; Silent Reach; Return of the Man from U.N.C.L.E.; The Last Bastion; Evergreen; Private Sessions; International Airport.

VEITCH, John: Exec. b. NYC, Jun 22, 1920. Under contract to David O Selznick as actor, switched to asst dir

Films inc: The Greatest Story Ever Told; Ship of Fools; Major Dundee; Horse Soldiers (prodn mgr); Magnificent Seven (Prodn mgr); Some Like It Hot (prodn mgr). 1961 exec asst prodn mgr Col; 1963 exec prodn mgr; 1966 vp-exec prodn mgr; 1977 exec vp-exec prodn mgr; 1979 P Col Pictures Productions; March 1983 resd to become ind prod.

VELDE, James R.: Exec. b. Bloomington, IL, Nov 1, 1913. e. IL Wesleyan U. Started as night shipper, PAR, 1934; then city salesman; office mgr and branch mgr for Selznick, Eagle Lion Classics and to UA in 1951 as West Coast dist mgr; gen sales mgr in 1956; vp in 1958; dir UA in 1968; sr vp 1972; retired 1977; joined Rastar as sr vp in charge of distribution in May, 1979.

VELLA, Lawrence Kay: Exec. b. Auckland, New Zealand, Aug 26, 1932. GM Kerridge Odeon; member NZ Film Trade Industry Bd.

VENTURA, Lino: Act. b. Parma, Italy, Jul 14, 1919. Films inc: Touchez Pas au Grisbi; Marie Octobre; Crooks in Clover; Les Aventuries; The Valachi Papers; Wild Horses; La Bonne Annee; A Butterfly on the Shoulder; The Medusa Touch; Sunday Lovers; Garde A Vue (The Grilling); Espion Leve-Toi (Rise Up, Spy); Les Miserables; Le Ruffian; Cento Giorni A Palermo (100 Days in Palermo); Le Septieme Cible (The Seventh Target).

VENUTA, Benay: Act. b. San Francisco, 1912. Films inc: Trail of 98; Kiki; Repeat Performance; Jane Doe; Annie Get Your Gun; Call Me Mister; Richochet Romance; The Fuzzy Pink Nightgown.

Thea inc: Dear Me, The Sky Is Falling; A Quarter for the Ladies Room; Nanus.

VENZA, Jac: Prod-Exec. b. Dec 23, 1926. e. Goodman Theatre

Chicago Art Institute. Started as dsgn; later exec producer N.E.T.; head of drama N.E.T.

TV inc: 24 Hours in the Life of a Woman (Emmy-art dir-1961); Five Ballets of the Five Senses (Emmy-prod-1968); N.E.T. Playhouse (Emmy-exec prod-1971); The Adams Chronicles (Emmys-exec prod-1976, 1977); Classical Dance in America--City Centre Joffrey Ballet (Emmy-exec prod); The Martha Graham Dance Company (Emmy-exec prod-1977); Billy The Kid--The American Ballet Theatre; American Ballet Theatre (Emmy-exec prod-1977); Artur Rubinstein at 90; Balanchine--Dance in America (I, II, III, IV) (Emmy-exec prod-1979); Fred Astaire--Change Partners and Dance With Me (Emmy-exec prod-1980); Big Blonde; The Taming of the Shrew; The Merchant of Venice; The Girls In Their Summer Dresses and Other Stories by Irwin Shaw (Great Performances); The Shady Hill Kidnapping; For Colored Girls Who Have Considered Suicide/When The Rainbow Is Enuf; Carl Sandburg--Echoes and Silences; Private Contentment; Brideshead Revisited; King Lear; The File on Jill Hatch; Fifth of July; Alice in Wonderland.

VERDON, Gwen: Act. b. Los Angeles, 1926. On screen from 1951. Films inc: On the Riviera; David and Bathsheba; Mississippi Gambler; Meet Me After the Show; The Farmer Takes a Wife; Damn Yankees; The Cotton Club; Cocoon (& special music and dance coordinator).

Bway inc: Can Can (Tony-1954); Damn Yankees (Tony-1956); New Girl in Town (Tony-1958); Redhead (Tony-1959); Chicago.

TV inc: Strippers (host) (cable); Legs; Parade of Stars; The Jerk, Too; Night Of 100 Stars II.

VERDUGO, Elena: Act. b. Hollywood, 1926. Films inc: Belle Starr; The Moon and Sixpence; Rainbow Island; House of Frankenstein; Little Giant; Song of Scheherazade; The Lost Volcano; Cyrano De Bergerac; The Thief of Damascus; Knights of the Round Table; How Sweet It Is!; Angel In My Pocket.

TV inc: Meet Millie; Marcus Welby, M.D.; The Return of Marcus Welby, M.D.

VEREEN, Ben: Singer-Act-Dancer. b. Miami, FL, Oct 10,1946. Films inc: Gas-sss; Funny Lady; All That Jazz; Sabine; The Zoo Gang.

TV inc: Roots; Ben Vereen--His Roots; Ten Speed and Brown Shoe; Uptown-A Tribute to the Apollo Theatre; Opryland--Night of Stars and Future Stars; The World of Entertainment; Pippin (cable); Christmas In Washington; The President's Command Performance; Here's Television Entertainment (host); Webster; Lynda Carter Body and Soul; Salute to Lady Liberty; The Jesse Owens Story; The Secret World Of The Very Young; Ellis Island; A.D.; Ringling Bros. and Barnum & Bailey Circus; The 39th Annual Tony Awards.

Bway inc: Sweet Charity; No Place to be Somebody; Jesus Christ Superstar; Pippin (Tony-1973); Grind.

VERHOEVEN, Michael: Dir-Prod-Wri. b. Berlin, Jul 13, 1938. Films inc: Dance of Death; Sonja Gets Rid of Reality; Killing Them Softly; On Silver Platter; Sunday's Children; Die Weisse Rose (The White Rose).

VERHOEVEN, Paul: Dir. b. Holland, 1938. Films inc: (shorts) Een Hagedis Teveel; Let's Have A Party; Het Korps Mariniers; A. Mussert; The Wrestler. (Features) Wat Zien Ik; Turkish Delight; Keetje Tippel; Soldier of Orange; Spetters; Die Vierde Man (The Fourth Man); Flesh & Blood (& wri).

TV inc: Floris.

VERNEUIL, Henri: Dir. b. Turkey, Oct 15, 1920. Films inc: La Table Aux Creves; Forbidden Fruit; Public Enemy Number One; The Sheep Has 5 Legs (sp); Paris Palace Hotel; The Cow and I; Weekend at Dunkirk; The Big Snatch; Guns for Sebastian; The Burglars; The Sicilian Clan; The Serpent; The Night Caller; Le Corps de Mon Ennemi; I Comme Icarus (& sp-prod); Mille Milliards de Dollars (A Thousand Billion Dollars) (& sp-prod); Les Morfalous (The Vultures) (& sp).

VERNON, Anne (Edith Vignaud): Act. b. Paris, Jan 24, 1925. Films inc: Le Mannequin Assassine; Warning to Wantons; Shakedown; Edward and Caroline; The Love Lottery; Time Bomb; The Umbrellas of Cherbourg.

VERNON, John: Act. b. Canada, 1932. e. Banff School of Fine Arts, RADA. TV inc: Wojeck; Three Sisters; Uncle Vanya; Wild Duck; Mary Jane Harper Cried Last Night; The Sacketts; The Blue and the Gray; Coast of Dreams; Hail To The Chief.

Films inc: 1984 (voice); Point Blank; Justine; Topaz; Tell Them Willie Boy Is Here; One More Train to Rob; Dirty Harry; Charlie Varrick; The Black Windmill; Fear is the Key; Cat and Mouse; Brannigan; The Outlaw Josey Wales; Angela; A Special Day; National Lampoon's Animal House; Fantastica; Crunch; Herbie Goes Bananas; The Kinky Coaches and the Pom-Pom Pussycats; Airplane II--The Sequel; Curtains (& dir); Chained Heat; Savage Streets; Jungle Warriors; Fraternity Vacation.

VERONA, Stephen F.: Prod-Dir-wri. b. IL., Sept. 11, 1940. Started as dir of commercials. Films inc: The Rehearsal (short); The Lords of Flatbush; Pipe Dreams; Boardwalk (dir-wri).

TV inc: Class of 1966 (prodn dsgn-ani dir); Different Strokes; The Music People; Double Exposure; Flatbush Avenue; Sesame Street; Take A Giant Step.

VERSINI, Marie: Act. b. Paris, Oct 8, 1939. Films inc: Tale of Two Cities; Le Chien de Pique; Paris Blues; The Young Racers; Is Paris Burning; Liebesnachte in der Taiga.

TV inc: Il ne Faut Jurer de Rien; Britannicus; Cinq Mars; Inferno; La Foire; Les Pieds.

Thea inc: Tessa; Romeo and Juliet; Les Rustres.

VERSTAPPEN, Wim: Dir-Wri-Prod. b. Holland, Apr 5, 1937. e. Dutch Film Academy. Films inc: Joszef Katus; Confessions of Loving Couples; Drop Out; Blue Movie; VD; Dakota; Alicia; Learning from Las Vegas; Pastorale; Rubia's Jungle; Frank and Eva; Living Apart Together; My Nights with Susan; Olga, Julie, Bill and Sandra; Zwarte Ruiter (Black Rider); Grijpstra & De Gier (Outsider In Amsterdam).

VERTUE, Beryl: Prod. b. Mitcham, Surrey, England, Apr 8, 1931. Worldwide head of TV for Robert Stigwood Organisation.

Films inc: The Spy With a Cold Nose; Tommy; Till Death Us Do Part; Pompeii; Up the Chastity Belt.

TV inc: Beacon Hill; Almost Anything Goes; The Entertainer; Dominick Ayres; All Star Anything Goes; The Prime of Miss Jean Brodie (exec prod); Charleston; Steptoe & Son; The Plank; Parole.

VETTER, Richard: Exec. b. San Diego, CA, Feb 24, 1928. e. Pepperdine Coll, BA; San Diego State Coll, MA; UCLA, PhD. VP United Artists Theatres. Oscar (Class III) for development of Todd-AO 35 widescreen system, 1973.

Films inc: (tech dir) The Bible; Patton; Macbeth; Junior Bonner; The Getaway; Logan's Run.

VICAS, George A: Prod-Dir-Wri. b. Berlin, May 12, 1926. e. Harvard, AB; Columbia, MA. TV inc: Berlin--The End of the Line; Money and the Next President; The Great Holiday Massacre; The Trials of Charles de Gaulle; Germany--Fathers and Sons; Britain--The Changing Guard; The Kremlin; The French Revolution; The Middle Ages; The Spanish Armada; The Reformation; An Austrian Affair; Leningrad; The French Army; Siberia--A Day In Irkutsk; The Soviets in Space; The Aviation Revolution; The Pope and the Vatican; A Young American in Paris; Paris--A Story of High Fashion; The Whale Hunters of Fayal; Artur Rubinstein (Emmy-prod-1970); The Last of the Vikings; The Methadone Connection.

VICAS, Victor: Prod-Dir-Wri. b. Moscow, Mar 25, 1918. Films inc: No Way Back; Double Destiny; Master Over Life and Death; Back To Kandara; The Wayward Bus; Count Five and Die; Les Disparus; La Donna Dell'Altro; Zwei Unter Millionen; The Third Front; The Camp Followers; The Middle Ages; The Bonapartes; The Hapsburgs; Tolstoy; The Indians; The Bourbons; The Romanoffs; The Hohenzollerns; The Sons of the Queen of Sheba; A Young American in Paris; Passport to Prague; Color Me German; The Crusades; The French Revolution; Charlemagne; The Making of a Dictator; L'Attentat de la rue St Nicaise; Johan-Sebastian Bach; Rallye; Le Calvaire d'un Jeune Homme Impeccable; Portrait d'une Femme sans Pieds.

TV inc: Aux Frontieres du Possible; Les Brigades du Tigre; Rainer; Mission To Israel.

VICTOR, David: Prod-Wri. b. Odessa, Russia. e. Columbia U. NYC Newspaperman, began wri scripts for radio. VP Arena Prodns 1966; TV vp Filmways 1967 before joining U as prod.

TV inc: Junior Miss (wri); Date With Judy (wri); Gunsmoke (wri);

Restless Gun (wri); The Rebel (& asso prod); The Man From Uncle (prod); Memories Never Die (exec prod); Ryan's Four (exec prod).

VICTOR, James: Act. b. Dominican Republic, Jul. 27, 1939. Films inc: Girls Incorporated; Shadows; Too Late Blues; A Global Affair; Girl in Gold Boots; The President's Analyst; Little Fauss and Big Halsey; Faces; Fuzz; Rolling Thunder; Boulevard Nights; Defiance; Borderline; Losin' It.

TV inc: Viva Valdez; A Man Named John; Devil Dog; The Streets of L.A.; Twin Detectives; Mixed Nuts; I Desire; Falcon Crest; Condo.

VIDAL, Gore: Wri. b. West Point, NY, Oct 3, 1925. Plays inc: A Visit to a Small Planet; The Best Man; Romulus; Weekend; An Evening with Richard Nixon and . . . Films inc: The Catered Affair; I Accuse; The Scapegoat; Suddenly Last Summer.

TV inc: Omnibus; Studio One; Philco Playhouse.

VIGODA, Abe: Act. b. NYC, Feb 24, 1921. e. NY School of Dramatic Arts, American Theatre Wing. Films inc: The Godfather; The Godfather, Part II; The Cheap Detective.

Thea inc: NY Shakespeare Festival; Inquest; The Man in the Glass Booth; Tough to Get Help.

TV inc: Barney Miller; Fish; Death Car on the Freeway; The Great American Traffic Jam; The Big Stuffed Dog.

VILLECHAIZE, Herve: Act. b. Paris, Apr 23, 1943. Films inc: Guitar; Hollywood Blvd No 2; Hot Tomorrow; Man with the Golden Gun; Crazy Joe; The Gang That Couldn't Shoot Straight; Seizure; The One and Only; Forbidden Zone.

TV inc: Fantasy Island; Louise Mandrell--Diamonds, Gold & Platinum; National Snoop; I Love Men.

Theatre inc: Elizabeth the First; Gloria Esperenza.

VILLIERS, James: Act. b. London, Sept. 29, 1933. e. RADA. Thea inc: with Old Vic Company in Julius Caesar; Troilus and Cressida; Richard III (& Bway); Tomorrow--With Pictures; Write Me A Murder; The Burglar; The Happy Apple; Private Lives; Henry IV; The Little Hut; The Doctor's Dilemma; The Ghost Train; Look Back In Anger; The White Devil; The Last Of Mrs. Cheyney.

Films inc: Children Of the Damned; Nothing But the Best; King and Country; Ever Eve; Half A Sixpence; Otley; The Damned; The Ruling Class; Joseph Andrews; Saint Jack; Under the Volcano.

TV inc: The Scarlet Pimpernel.

VINCENT, Jan-Michael: Act. b. Denver, CO, Jul 15, 1944. Films inc: The Undefeated; Going Home; The Mechanic; The World's Greatest Athlete; Buster and Billie; Bite the Bullet; White Line Fever; Baby Blue Marine; Vigilante Force; Shadow of the Hawk; Damnation Alley; Big Wednesday; Hooper; Defiance; Hard Country; Last Plane Out.

TV inc: Tribes; Sandcastles; The Catcher; The Survivors; The Banana Splits; The Winds of War; Airwolf.

VINNICOF, Cecil: Exh. b. Los Angeles, Jun 24, 1914. e. USC, LLB. P, Vinnicof Theatre Circuit (California).

VINSON, Helen: Act. b. Beaumont, TX, 1907. On screen from 1932. Films inc: Jewel Robbery; Two Against the World; I Am a Fugitive from a Chain Gang; The Power and the Glory; Broadway Bill; Private Worlds; In Name Only; Are These Our Parents; The Thin Man Goes Home (last film, 1945).

VINTON, Bobby: Singer. b. Canonsburg, PA, Apr 16, 1935. e. Duquesne U. Recording artist. Films inc: Big Jake; Train Robbers.

TV inc: The Gossip Columnist.

VISCUSO, Sal: Act. b. Brooklyn, NY, Oct 5. e. U of CA Davis, BA; NYU, MFA. Films inc: The Taking of Pelham 1-2-3; Max Dugan Returns.

TV inc: Mary Hartman, Mary Hartman; The Montefuscos; Fantasies; Princess Daisy; This Wife For Hire.

VITALE, Milly: Act. b. Rome, Jul 16, 1930. Films inc: Difficult Years; The Juggler; Rasputin; The Seven Little Foys; War and Peace; The Flesh is Weak; A Breath of Scandal; Catherine of Russia.

VITTI, Monica (Monica Luisa Ceciarelli): Act. b. Italy, Nov. 3, 1931.

Films inc: L'avventura; La Notte; L'Eclipse; Dragees du Poivre; The Nutty Naughty Chateau; The Red Desert; Modesty Blaise; The Chastity Belt; Girl With a Pistol; The Pacifist; Duck in Orange Sauce; An Almost Perfect Affair; The Mystery of Oberwald; Il Tango Della Gelosia (Jealousy Tango); Io So Che Tu Sai Che Io So (I Know That You Know That I Know); Flirt (& wri); Letti Selvaggi (Tigers In Lipstick).

TV inc: My Passion.

VLADY, Marina (Marina de Poliakoff-Baidaroff): Act. b. Clichey-la-Garenne, France, 1938. Films inc: Orage d'Ete; Avant le Deluge; The Wicked Go to Hell; Crime and Punishment; Toi le Venin; La Steppa; Climats; Enough Rope; Dragees au Poivre; Queen Bee; Chimes at Midnight; Sapho; The Two of Them; Women; The Hypochondriac; L'oeil du Maitre; Les Jeux de la Comtesse Dolingen de Gratz (The Games of the Countess Dolingen of Gratz).

TV inc: The Thief of Baghdad.

VOELPEL, Fred: Dsgn. b. Sep 23, 1927. e. Yale, MFA. Thea inc: Fallout; From A to Z; The Alligators; Rosemary; Young Abe Lincoln; Hang Down Your Head and Die; Tiger at the Gates; Spitting Image; Oh! Calcutta!; Blueprints; No Strings; The Critic; The Effect of Gamma Rays on Man-in the-Moon Marigolds; Her Ten Stout-Hearted Men; And Miss Reardon Drinks a Little; Small Craft Warnings; Hurry, Hurry; The Little Theatre of the Deaf; Smith; The Beauty Part; Dybbuk; Priscilla; Very Good Eddie; Bring Back Birdie; Einstein and the Polar Bear.

VOGEL, Jesse: Wri-Prod. b. NYC, Oct 24, 1925. e. CCNY, Paris Conservatory of Music. Films inc: Carmen, Baby (sp); Therese & Isabelle (sp); Who's Harriet? (prod); My Pleasure Is My Business (prod).

VOGEL, Virgil W.: Dir-Prod. b. Peoria, IL. Films inc: The Mole People; Land Unknown; Ma and Pa Kettle; Animal People; Sword of Ali Baba.

TV inc: Cannon; Barnaby Jones; Super Cop; Bonanza; Big Valley; Wagon Train; Police Story; Law of the Land; Centennial; Power; Portrait of a Rebel-Margaret Sanger; Beulah Land; Unit 4; Today's FBI; Street Hawk.

VOIGHT, Jon: Act. b. Yonkers, NY, Dec 29, 1938. Films inc: The Hour of the Gun; Fearless Frank; Out of It; Midnight Cowboy; The Revolutionary; The All American Boy; Catch 22; Deliverance; Conrack; The Odessa File; Coming Home (Oscar-1978); The Champ; Lookin' To Get Out (& wri); Table For Five.

TV inc: The Dwarf; Cimarron Strip; Centennial.

Thea inc: The Sound of Music; A View From the Bridge; Romeo and Juliet; That Summer, That Fall.

VOLONTE, Gian-Maria: Act. b. Italy, 1933. Films inc: Girl With A Suitcase; Four Days of Naples; A Fistful of Dollars; For a Few Dollars More; We Still Kill the Old Way; East Wind; Investigation of a Citizen Above Suspicion; Sacco & Vanzetti; Lucky Luciano; Christ Stopped At Eboli; Ogro; Todo Modo; The True Story of Camille; La Mort de Mario Ricci (The Death of Mario Ricci).

TV inc: The Charterhouse of Parma (cable).

Von FURSTENBERG, Betsy: Act. b. Neiheim Heusen, Germany, Aug 16, 1933. Thea inc: Second Threshold; Dear Barbarians; The Petrified Forest; The Secret Man; Oh, Men! Oh, Women!; The Chalk Garden; What Every Woman Knows; Wonderful Town; Mary, Mary; The Paisley Convertible; The Gingerbread Lady; Absurd Person Singular.

Films inc: Women Without Names.

TV inc: The Fifth Column.

Von KARAJAN, Herbert: Cond. b. Salzburg, Austria, Apr 5, 1908. e. Vienna Coll of Music. Cond debut 1929, Ulm, Germany; cond Ulm Opera, 1929-1934; gen dir Aachen Opera 1935; debut with Vienna Staadstopera 1937; artistic dir Berlin State Opera 1938; founder London Philharmonic 1948; permanent cond since 1950. (Grammys-(3)-opera recording-1964, 1969; classical orch-1978).

VONNEGUT, Kurt, Jr: Wri. b. Indianapolis, IN, Nov 11, 1922. Author of several novels. Plays inc: Happy Birthday, Wanda June.

TV inc: Between Time and Timbuktu; Breakfast of Champions; Life On the Mississippi (host).

Von SYDOW, Max: Act. b. Lund, Sweden, Apr 10, 1929. Films inc: Miss Julie; The Seventh Seal; Wild Strawberries; The Face; The Virgin Spring; Through a Glass Darkly; The Mistress; The Greatest Story Ever Told; The Reward; Hawaii; The Quiller Memorandum; Hour of the Wolf; The Shame; The Kremlin Letter; The Touch; The Emigrants; The Exorcist; Foxtrot; Three Days of the Condor; Desert of the Tartars; Exorcist II-The Heretic; March or Die; Brass Target; Hurricane; Deathwatch; Flash Gordon; She Dances Alone; Victory; Conan The Barbarian; Ingenioer Andrees Luftfaerd (The Flight of the Eagle); Strange Brew; Le Cercle des Passions (Circle of Passions); Never Say Never Again; Dreamscape; Target Eagle; George Stevens--A Filmmaker's Journey (doc-int).

Bway inc: Duet For One.

TV inc: Samson and Delilah; Kojak--The Belarus File; The Last Place On Earth; Christopher Columbus.

von ZERNECK, Frank: Prod. b. NYC. Nov. 3, 1940. e. NY High School of the Performing Arts; Hofstra College (BA). TV inc: The Desperate Miles; 21 Hours at Munich; Delta County, U.S.A.; Escape From Bogen County; Sharon--Portrait Of A Mistress; Getting Married; Katie--Portrait Of A Centerfold; Flatbed Annie & Sweetipie--Lady Truckers; Anatomy Of A Seduction; Portrait Of A Stripper; Disaster On The Coastliner; Portrait Of An Escort; Texas Rangers (exec prod); The Babysitter; Miracle On Ice; Return Of The Rebels; Lois Gibbs And The Love Canal; In The Custody Of Strangers; Forbidden Love (exec prod); Answers (cable); The First Time; Baby Sister; Night Partners; Policewoman Centerfold: Obsessive Love; Invitation To Hell; Summer Fantasy; I Married A Centerfold; Romance On The Orient Express; On Our Way (exec prod).

Thea inc: Me and Bessie (tour); I Have A Dream (tour & Bway); A Sense Of Humor.

VREELAND, Byron: Exec. b. Bozeman, MT, Jun 1, 1900. e. MT State Coll. Carpenter MGM Studios, 1917; grip Hal Roach studios, 1921; head grip, 1927; studio supt, 1937; studio mgr, 1946-62; coord, TV series, Fugitive. Retired 1968.

WAGER, Michael (Mendy Weisgal): Act-Dir-Prod. b. NYC, Apr 25, 1929. e. Harvard, AB, MA. Bway inc: A Streetcar Named Desire; Small Hours; Bernardine; The Merchant of Venice; Misalliance; Six Characters in Search of an Author; Saint Joan; Firstborn; Noontide; Brecht on Brecht; The Three Sisters; Where's Daddy (prod); Sunset; Cuban Thing; Trelawney of the Wells; The Interview; Visions of Kerouack; The Dream; Songs at Twilight.

Films inc: Hill 24 Does Not Answer; Exodus; King of Kings; Jane Austen In Manhattan.

WAGGONER, Lyle: Act. b. Kansas City, KS, Apr 13. TV inc: The Carol Burnett Show; host of game show, It's Your Bet; Sonny and Cher Show; Once Upon a Mattress; The Love Boat II; The New Adventures of Wonder Woman; The Gossip Columnist; The Ugily Family; The Great American Traffic Jam; Bulba--Our Man In Okalatown; Two the Hard Way.

Films inc: Love Me Deadly; Journey to the Center of Time; Catalina Caper; Surf II.

WAGNER, Jane: Wri-Dir. b. Morristown, TN, Feb 2, 1935. Bway inc: Appearing Nitely. TV inc: Lily (Emmy-Wri-1974); Lily Tomlin (Emmy-Wri-1976) J.T.; Earthwatch; People; Lily--Sold Out (exec prod) (Emmy-1981); Lily For President? (wri-exec prod).

Films inc: Moment by Moment; The Incredible Shrinking Woman (exec prod-wri).

WAGNER, Lindsay: Act. b. Los Angeles, Jun 22, 1949. Sang with rock group. Screen debut, 1973, Two People. Films inc: Paper Chase; Second Wind; Nighthawks; High Risk; Martin's Day.

TV inc: The F.B.I.; Owen Marshall; Counselor at Law; Night Gallery; The Bold Ones; Marcus Welby, M.D.; The Rockford Files; The Six Million Dollar Man; The Bionic Woman (Emmy-1977); The Incredible Journey of Dr Meg Laurel; The Two Worlds of Jennie Logan; Scruples; Callie and Son; Memories Never Die; I Want to Live; Princess Daisy; Two Kinds of Love; Jessie; Passions.

WAGNER, Robert: Act. b. Detroit, MI, Feb 10, 1930. Films inc: The Happy Years; Halls of Montezuma; With a Song in My Heart; What Price Glory; Titanic; Prince Valiant; Broken Lance; White Feather; The Mountain; A Kiss Before Dying; The Hunters; Say One For Me; All The Fine Young Cannibals; The Longest Day; The War Lover; The Condemned of Altona; The Pink Panther; Harper; Banning; Don't Just Stand There; Winning; The Towering Inferno; Midway; Concorde--Airport 79; Curse of the Pink Panther; I Am the Cheese.

TV inc: It Takes a Thief; Cat on a Hot Tin Roof; Colditz; Death at Lovehouse; Pearl; Switch; Hart to Hart; The Warm Blooded Sea--Mammals of the Deep (narr); Ernie Kovacs--Television's Original Genius (cable); To Catch A King; Olympic Gala (host); S.O.S.--Secrets of Surviving.

WAGNER, Robin: Dsgn. b. San Francisco, Aug 31, 1933. Thea inc: And the Wind Blows; The Prodigal; Between Two Thieves; A Worm in Horseradish; A View from the Bridge; An Evening's Frost; The Condemned of Altona; The Trial of Lee Harvey Oswald; Hair; Lovers and Other Strangers; The Cuban Thing; The Great White Hope; Promises, Promises; The Watering Place; The Engagement Baby; Jesus Christ Superstar; Seesaw; Full Circle; Mack and Mabel; Sergeant Pepper's Lonely Hearts Club Band on the Road; A Chorus Line; On the 20th Century (Tony-1978); 42d Street; Dreamgirls.

Films inc: Glory Boy.

WAGONER, Porter: Singer. b. West Plains, MO, Aug 12, 1930. C&W recording artist; regular member of the Grand Ole Opry; on radio, TV with own show. (Grammys-(with Blackwood Bros.)-Sacred Recording-1966; Gospel Perf-1967, 1969).

WAGSTAFF, Stuart: Act-Prod. b. Salisbury, England, Feb 13, 1925. Repertory in England, then Australia. Host TV shows Channel 7 Sydney.

TV inc: Blankety Blanks; Showcase. Formed Stuart Wagstaff Enterprises Ltd, Sydney.

WAHL, Ken: Act. b. Chicago, 1953. Films inc: The Wanderers; Fort Apache, The Bronx; The Soldier: Race to the Yankee Zephyr; Running Scared; Jinxed; Purple Hearts.

TV inc: The Dirty Dozen--The Next Mission; Double Dare.

WAIN, Bea: Singer-Bcst pers. b. NYC. W of Andre Baruch. Featured singer with Larry Clinton Band; radio-tv inc: Your Hit Parade; Your All-Time Hit Parade; The Bea and Andre Show; recordings, concerts.

WAINWRIGHT, James: Act. b. Danville, IL, Mar 5, 1938. TV inc: Daniel Boone; Jigsaw; The President's Plane is Missing; Man On the Move; Killdozer; A Woman Called Moses; Freedom Riders; Beyond Westworld.

Films inc: Joe Kidd; Hooper; Mean Dog Blues; Battletruck; The Survivors.

WAISSMAN, Kenneth: Prod. b. NYC, Jan 24, 1943. e. U of MD, NYU. Bway inc: Grease; Over Here!; And Miss Reardon Drinks a Little; Agnes of God; The Octette Bridge CLub.

WAITE, Ralph: Act. b. White Plains, NY, Jun 22, 1928. e. Bucknell U, BA; Yale U, divinity degree. Films inc: A Lovely Way to Die; Five Easy Pieces; Lawman; The Grissom Gang; Dime Box; Sporting Club; On The Nickel (prod-dir-wri).

TV inc: The Waltons; Red Alert; Roots; OHMS; Angel City; The Gentleman Bandit; A Wedding on Walton's Mountain; Mother's Day On Walton's Mountain; A Day For Thanks On Walton's Mountain; The Mississippi (& supv prod); A Good Sport; Growing Pains.

Thea inc: Hogan's Goat; Watering Place; The Trial of Lee Harvey Oswald; Blues for Mister Charlie; The Father.

WAITE, Ric: Cin. TV inc: Captains and the Kings (Emmy-1977); Tail Gunner Joe; Huey P. Long; Revenge of the Stepford Wives; Baby Comes Home.

Films inc: The Other Side of the Mountain II; The Long Riders; On the Nickel; The Border; Tex; 48 Hours; Class; Footloose; Red Dawn; Brewster's Millions.

WAJDA, Andrzej: Prod-Dir. b. Suwalki, Poland, Mar 6, 1926. e. Polish Film School. Films inc: Generation; Dunikowski; Kanal; Ashes and Diamonds; Lot A; The Innocent Charmers; Samson; Love at Tventies; Siberian Lady Macbeth; Ashes; Gates of Paradise; Roly Poly; Hunting Flies; Landscape after Battle; The Birch Wood; Pilate and Others; The

Wedding; Land of Promise; The Man of Marble; Invitation to the Interior; Without Anaesthesia; Young Ladies from Wilno; Drygent (The Orchestra Conductor); Czlowiek Z Zelaza (Man of Iron); Danton (Dirwri); Wajda's Danton (doc); Eine Liebe in Deutschland (A Love in Germany) (dir-wri).

TV inc: Interview with Ballmayer; Another Wife; Macbeth; November Night.

WALBERG, Garry: Act. b. Buffalo, NY, Jun 19. TV inc: The Odd Couple; Quincy; Rage.

WALCH, Reiner: Prod. b. Berlin, May 30, 1932. e. Berlin U. Films inc: The Second Spring; Fort Travis.

WALD, Malvin: Wri-Prod. b. NYC, Aug 8. e. Brooklyn Coll, BA; Woodland U, JD. Films inc: The Naked City; Behind Locked Doors; The Dark Past; Ten Gentlemen from West Point; The Powers Girl; Two in a Taxi; Undercover Man; Outrage; Battle Taxi; Man on Fire; Al Capone; Venus in Furs; In Search of Historic Jesus.

TV inc: (wri) Hollywood; The Golden Years; The Rafer Johnson Story; D-Day; Project: Man in Space; Climax; Shirley Temple Storybook; Peter Gunn; Perry Mason; Dobie Gillis; Combat; Daktari; The Legend of Sleepy Hollow. (Asso prod) Primus; California Tomorrow. (Prod): Mod Squad; Untamed World; Around the World of Mike Todd; The Billie Jean King Show; Mark Twain's America-Abe Lincoln, Freedom Fighter.

WALD, Richard C.: Exec. b. NYC, 1931. e. Columbia Coll, BA; Columbia U, MA; Clare Coll, Cambridge (England) BA. Corr for NY Herald-Tribune while in college, joined paper after college, serving as religion edtr, political reporter, foreign corr in London and Bonn, asso edtr, managing edtr; 1967, exec vp Whitney Communications; 1968 vp news NBC; 1973, P NBC News; 1977, asst to bd chmn Times-Mirror Co; 1978, sr vp ABC News.

WALDEN, Robert (nee Wolkowitz): Act. b. NYC, Sep 25, 1943. e. CCNY. Films inc: Hospital; Bloody Mary; Pigeons; New York, New York; Capricorn One; Rage; Audrey Rose; All The President's Men.

TV inc: Shirts/Skins; The Great Ice Rip-Off; Larry; The Marcus-Nelson Murders; Lou Grant; Enola Gay--The Men, The Mission, The Atomic Bomb; Brothers (PC).

WALDLEITNER, Luggi: Prod. b. Kirchseeon, Germany, Dec. 1, 1913. Began as asst cameraman Leni Reifenstahl Film Co (Olympia Film); later asst dir, asst prod mgr, founded Gloria Film Distribution Company; 1952 launched Roxy-Film. Films inc: Die Barrings; Regina Amstetten; El Hakim; Das Madchen Rosemarie; Bumerang; Elf Jahre und ein Tag; Ich Habe Sie gut Gekannt; Frau Cheney's Ende; Venus im Pelz; Sieben Tage Frist; Liebe ist nur ein wort; Alle Menschen werden bruder; Einer von uns beiden; Das Netz; Der Sternsteinhof; Kurzschluss; Die Glaserne Zelle; Lili Marleen.

WALKEN, Christopher: Act. b. NYC, Mar 31, 1944. e. Hofstra U. Films inc: The Anderson Tapes; The Happiness Cage; Next Stop Greenwich Village; Roseland; The Sentinel; Annie Hall; The Deer Hunter (Oscar-supp-1978); Last Embrace; Heaven's Gate; The Dogs of War; Pennies From Heaven; Brainstorm; The Dead Zone; A View To A Kill.

Thea inc: JB; High Spirits; Baker Street; West Side Story (road tour); The Lion In Winter; Kid Champion; The Rose Tattoo (rev); The Unknown Soldier and his Wife; Sweet Bird of Youth; Hurlyburly (off-Bway).

TV inc: Who Am I This Time?; Night Of 100 Stars II.

WALKER, Cardon E. (Card): Exec. b. Rexburg, ID, Jan 5, 1916. e. UCLA, BA. Joined the Disney organization as a traffic boy, 1938. Subsequently unit manager on short subjects, eventually handled budget control for short subjects. After service in WW II, returned to Disney, receiving a number of promotions until in December, 1971, he was elected P, COO; Jun 1980, P & CEO; ret Feb. 1983.

WALKER, Clint: Act. b. Hartford, IL, May 30, 1927. First film job as extra in The Ten Commandments.

Films inc: Fort Dobbs; Yellowstone Kelly; None But The Brave; The Great Bank Robbery; The Dirty Dozen; More Dead Than Alive; Pancho Villa; The White Buffalo; Bakers Hawk; Hysterical.

TV inc: Cheyenne.

WALKER, Jimmie: Act. b. NYC, Jun 25. Films inc: Let's Do It Again; The Greatest Thing That Almost Happened; Rabbit Test; Concorde-Airport '79.

TV inc: Good Times; B.A.D. Cats; Murder Can Hurt You; At Ease.

WALKER, Nancy: Act. b. Philadelphia, PA, May 10, 1921. D of the Vaudeville team Barto and Mann. Singer, comedienne. Films inc: Girl Crazy; Stand Up And Be Counted; Murder By Death; Can't Stop The Music (dir).

Thea inc: Best Foot Forward; Look Ma, I'm Dancing; Pal Joey; Wonderful Town; The Cherry Orchard; A Funny Thing Happened On The Way to the Forum.

TV inc: The Danny Kaye Show; Family Affair; The Mary Tyler Moore Show; Rhoda; MacMillan and Wife; The Nancy Walker Show; Blansky's Beauties.

WALKER, Zena: Act. b. Birmingham, England, Mar. 7, 1934. e. RADA. Thea inc: The Tempest; Romeo and Juliet; A Midsummer Night's Dream; South; with old Vic 1955-56, appearing in Henry V; The Devil's Disciple; 'Tis Pity She's A Whore; Man and Superman; The Fighting Cock; A Day in the Death of Joe Egg (& Bway) (Tony-Supp-1968); The Waltz of the Toreadors; Away From It All; The Case in Question; Separate Tables; Close of Play.

Films inc: Tammy Going South; The Reckoning; Cromwell; Banner in the Sky; The Dresser.

TV inc: Baby Blues; From the West; An Act of Betrayal; Country Matters; Four Beauties; Man at the Top; Telford's Change; Abide With Me; Albert and Victoria; That Crazy Woman; Sun Trap; Dead Earnest; Number 10.

WALLACE, Irving (ne Wallechinsky): Wri. b. Chicago, Mar 19, 1916. e. Williams Inst., Berkeley. Best-selling author, many of whose books have been filmed. Sp inc: The West Point Story; Meet Me at the Fair; Desert Legion; Gun Fury; Split Second; The Burning Hills; Bombers B-25.

WALLACE, Jean (nee Wallasek): Act. b. Chicago, Oct 12, 1923. W of Cornel Wilde. Films inc: You Can't Ration Love; Jigsaw; The Good Humor Man; Song of India; Sudden Fear; The Big Combo; Maracaibo; Lancelot and Guinevere; Beach Red; No Blade of Grass.

WALLACE, Mike: TV Commentator. b. Brookline, MA, May 9, 1918. e. U of MI. Night Beat, WABD, NY; The Mike Wallace Interview, ABC; newspaper col, NY Post, 1957-58; News Beat, WNTA-TV, 1959-61; correspondent, CBS News, 1963. TV inc: Mike Wallace at Large; coedtr, 60 Minutes (Emmys-1971, 1972, 1973, 1979, 1980(2), 1981, 1982); The Selling of Colonel Herbert (Emmy-1973). The Mike Wallace Profiles; The Uncounted Enemy--A Vietnam Deception; Eye On the Media-- Business and the Press; The TV Academy Hall Of Fame 1985.

WALLACH, Eli: Act. b. NYC, Dec 7, 1915. e. U of TX; CCNY; Neighborhood Playhouse. Studied with Lee Strasberg. H of Anne Jackson. Bway inc: Yellowjack; Antony and Cleopatra; Mister Roberts; The Rose Tattoo (Tony-supp-1951); Camino Real; Teahouse of the August Moon; Major Barbara; The Cold Wind and the Warm; Rhinocerous; Luv; Saturday, Sunday and Monday; Every Good Boy Deserves Favor; Twice Around the Park.

Films inc: Baby Doll; The Misfits; The Magnificent Seven; How the West Was Won; Nasty Habits; The Domino Principle; The Sentinel; Movie, Movie; Girlfriends; Circle of Iron; Firepower; Winter Kills; The Hunter; The Salamander; Sam's Son.

TV inc: The Poppy Is Also A Flower (Emmy-1967); The Pirates; Fugitive Family; The Pride of Jesse Hallam; Skokie; The Wall; The Executioner's Song; Anatomy of an Illness; Kennedy Center Honors 1984; Christopher Columbus.

WALLERSTEIN, Herb: Dir-Exec. b. Brooklyn, Nov 28, 1925. TV inc: I Dream of Jeanie; Farmer's Daughter, The Iron Horse; Here Come the Brides; Wild Wild West; Star Trek; Mission Impossible; Temperatures Rising; Brady Bunch; Petrocelli; Happy Days; Paper Moon; Partridge Family; New Perry Mason; Swiss Family Robinson; Barbary Coast; Snowbeast; Tabitha; Mulligan Stew; Quincy; Wonder Woman. From 1973 to 1975, VP Prodn Paramount TV; 1978 named VP

Prodn Mgt 20th-Fox Prodns; resd. Jan. 1, 1985.

WALLIS, Hal B.: Prod. b. Chicago, Sep 14, 1898. H of Martha Hyer. Started as thea mgr in LA; pub dept WB before becoming prod. Has made approximately 300 films.

Films inc: Little Caesar; Five Star Final; Dawn Patrol; Midsummer Night's Dream; Story of Louis Pasteur; Anthony Adverse; King's Row; Sergeant York; Yankee Doodle Dandy; Now, Voyager; Casablanca; Saratoga Trunk; Strange Love of Martha Ivers; Sorry, Wrong Number; My Friend Irma; The Stooge; Sailor Beware; Come Back, Little Sheba; Rose Tattoo; The Rainmaker; Gunfight at the OK Corral; Visit to a Small Planet; Summer and Smoke; Becket; The Sons of Katie Elder; Boeing-Boeing; True Grit; Norwood; Anne of the Thousand Days; Red Sky at Morning; Shoot Out; Mary Queen of Scots; Bequest to the Nation; The Don Is Dead; Rooster Cogburn.

(Irving Thalberg Award 1938 and 1943.

WALSH, David M.: Cin. b. Cumberland, MD. Films inc: Monte Walsh; I Walk the Line; Everything You Always Wanted to Know About Sex and Were Afraid to Ask; The Laughing Policeman; The Other Side of the Mountain; W.C. Fields; Murder by Death; The Sunshine Boys; Rollercoaster; The Goodbye Girl; Foul Play; House Calls; California Suite; The In-Laws; Private Benjamin; Seems Like Old Times; Only When I Laugh; Making Love; I Ought To Be In Pictures; Max Dugan Returns; Romantic Comedy; Unfaithfully Yours; Country; Teachers; Johnny Dangerously.

TV inc: Queen of the Stardust Ballroom *(Emmy-1975).*

WALSH, M. Emmet: Act. Films inc: Midnight Cowboy; Stiletto; Alice's Restaurant; End of the Road; The Traveling Executioner; Little Big Man; Cold Turkey; Loving; Escape From the Planet of the Apes; They Might Be Giants; The Fish That Saved Pittsburgh; The Jerk; Straight Time; Back Roads; Cannery Row; Reds; Fast-Walking; The Escape Artist; Blade Runner; Silkwood; Scandalous; Blood Simple; Courage; The Pope of Greenwich Village; Missing In Action.

TV inc: High Noon Part II--The Return of Will Kane; Hellinger's Law; The Woman Who Willed A Miracle; Night Partners; You Are the Jury; The Outlaws.

WALSTON, Ray: Act. b. New Orleans, LA, Nov 2, 1917. Films inc: Kiss Them for Me; South Pacific; Damn Yankees; The Apartment; Tall Story; Convicts Four; Wives and Lovers; Who's Minding the Store?; Kiss Me, Stupid!; Caprice; Paint Your Wagon; Viva Max!; The Sting; Silver Streak; The Happy Hooker Goes to Washington; Popeye; Galaxy of Terror; Fast Times At Ridgemont High; O'Hara's Wife; Private School; Johnny Dangerously.

TV inc: Suspense; The State of the Union; Uncle Harry; There Shall Be No Night; My Favorite Martian; Institute for Revenge; The Kid With the Broken Halo; The Fall of the House of Usher; This Girl for Hire; The Jerk, Too; For Love Or Money; Otherworld.

Bway inc: The Front Page; Summer and Smoke; South Pacific (tour); Me and Juliet; House of Flowers; Damn Yankees *(Tony-1956);* Who Was That Lady I Saw You With?

WALTER, Jessica: Act. b. NYC, Jan 31, 1940. Films inc: Lilith; The Group; Grand Prix; Bye Bye Braverman; Number One; Play Misty for Me; Goldengirl; Going Ape!; Spring Fever; The Flamingo Kid.

TV inc: Amy Prentiss *(Emmy-1975);* Vampire; She's Dressed to Kill; Miracle On Ice; Trapper John, M.D.; Scruples; Thursday's Child; Bare Essence; The Return of Marcus Welby, M.D.; T.L.C; The Execution.

Thea inc: Advise and Consent; Photo Finish; Night Life; A Severed Head.

WALTERS, Barbara: TV pers. b. Boston, MA, Sep 25, 1931. e. Sarah Lawrence Coll. Started in TV after graduation. Joined Today Show in 1961 as writer, occasionally on-camera; 1963 full-time on camera. In April, 1974, named permanent co-host *(Emmy-1975).* In 1976 joined ABC-TV as first female anchor on a network newscast and highest-paid news personality in TV with a five-year contract guaranteeing $1 million a year. TV inc: Post Election Special Edition Nightline *(Emmy-1980);* The Barbara Walters Specials *(Emmy-1982);* Eye On the Media--Private Lives, Public Press; Olympic Gala; Night Of 100 Stars II.

WALTERS, Julie: Act. b. Birmingham, England. e. Manchester Poly-

technic. Thea inc: Educating Rita.

TV inc: Talent; Nearly a Happy Ending; Wood and Walters; Family Man.

Films inc: Educating Rita; Unfair Exchanges; She'll Be Wearing Pink Pajamas.

WALTON, Kip: Dir. TV inc: Perry Como Special; Diana Ross Special; Johnny Mathis Christmas Hour; In Session with Sarah Vaughn; In Session with Seals and Crofts; In Session with Aretha Franklin; Touch of Gold; Split Second; Coliseum Concert; Jackson Five Special; Miss America Teenager Pageant; Almost Anything Goes; Paul Williams Special; Hot City; Teddy Pendergrass at the Greek; Hope for President; Bob Hope's 30th Anniversary Special; Bob Hope's All-Star Comedy Look at the New Season; Christmas, A Time of Cheer and A Time For Hope; Bob Hope's Women I Love--Beautiful and Funny; Sound Festival; Perry Como's Christmas In Paris; Bob Hope's Road to Hollywood; Music Of Your Life.

WALTON, Tony: Dsgn. b. Walton-on-Thames, Surrey, England, Oct 24, 1934. e. Radley Coll. Thea inc: Fool's Paradise; The Pleasure of His Company; The Ginger Man; Pieces of Eight; Most Happy Fella; Once There Was a Russian; A Funny Thing Happened on the Way to the Forum; Caligula; Golden Boy; The Apple Tree; Pippin *(Tony-1973);* The Good Doctor; Uncle Vanya; Bette Midler's Clams on the Half Shell Revue; Chicago; Streamers; Sophisticated Ladies; Woman of the Year; The Real Thing; Hurlyburly (off Bway); Whoopi Goldberg (visual cnslt); Leader Of The Pack.

Films inc: Mary Poppins; Farenheit 451; The Seagull; The Boy Friend; Murder on the Orient Express; The Wiz; All That Jazz *(Oscar-art dir-1979);* Star 80 (visual cnslt); The Goodbye People.

WALTON, William, Sir: Comp. b. England, 1902. Films inc: Escape Me Never; As You Like It; A Stolen Life; Major Barbara; The Foreman Went To France; Next of Kin; The First of Few; Henry V; Hamlet; Richard III; Battle of Britain; Three Sisters.

(Died March 3, 1983).

WAMBAUGH, Joseph: Wri. b. East Pittsburgh, PA, Jan 22, 1937. e. CA State Coll, BA. LA policeman from 1960-1974. Created Police Story TV series.

Films inc: The Onion Field; The Black Marble.

WANAMAKER, Sam: Act-Prod-Dir. b. Chicago, Jun 14, 1919. e. Drake U. Films inc: My Girl Tisa; Give Us This Day; The Concrete Jungle; Taras Bulba; The Man in the Middle; Those Magnificent Men in Their Flying Machines; The Spy Who Came in from the Cold; Warning Shot; The Day the Fish Came Out; The Executioner (dir); Catlow (dir); The Sell Out; Billy Jack Goes to Washington; Voyage of the Damned; Sinbad and the Eye of the Tiger (dir); Death on the Nile; From Hell to Victory; Private Benjamin; The Competition; Irreconcilable Differences; The Aviator.

TV inc: Mousey; Espionage; Outer Limits; The Holocaust (& dir); Dark Side of Love; Man Undercover; Hart to Hart; Jimmy Breslin's Neighborhood; My Kidnapper, My Love (dir); The Killing of Randy Webster (dir); Our Family Business; I Was A Mail Order Bride; Winston Churchill--The Wilderness Years; The Ghost Writer; Heartsounds; Berrenger's; Deceptions.

Thea inc: This, Too, Shall Pass; Joan of Lorraine; A Hatful of Rain (& dir); Ding Dong Bell (dir); A Case of Libel (dir).

WANNBERG, Kenneth: Mus ed-Comp. b. Inglewood, CA, Jun 28, 1930. Films inc: (mus edtr) Hello, Dolly!; Patton; Tora Tora Tora; At Long Last Love; French Connection I & II; The Last Waltz; Star Wars; Close Encounters of the Third Kind. (Comp): Four Deuces; Lepke; Bitter Sweet Love; Tribute; The Amateur; Losin' It; Of Unknown Origin; Blame it on Rio.

TV inc: (comp) Silent Partner; Remember My Name; Draw! (PC).

WARD, David S.: Wri. b. Oct 24, 1945. e. Pomona Coll, UCLA. Films inc: Steelyard Blues; The Sting *(Oscar-1973);* Cannery Row (& dir); The Sting II.

WARD, Douglas Turner: Act-Wri-Dir. b. Burnside, LA, May 5, 1930. e. Wilberforce U, U of MI. Thea inc: (act) The Iceman Cometh; Lost in the Stars; A Raisin in the Sun; Pullman Car Hiawatha; One Flew Over the Cuckoo's Nest; Coriolanus; Happy Ending; Day of Absence. (Wri-prod) Brotherhood; Happy Ending; Day of Absence.

Films inc: Man and Boy.

TV inc: The First Breeze of Summer; Ceremonies In Dark Old Men; Go Tell It On The Mountain (act).

WARD, Fred: Act. b. 1943. Studied under Alice Spivak at HB Studio. Thea inc: In a Coma; Angel City; The Glass Menagerie; One Flew Over the Cuckoo's Nest.

Films inc: No Available Witness; The Power of the Cosimo; Cartesia; Tilt; Escape From Alcatraz; Southern Comfort; Timerider; The Right Stuff; Silkwood; Uncommon Valor; Swing Shift; Uforia; Secret Admirer.

TV inc: Noon Wine.

WARD, Rachel: Act. b. England. W of Bryan Brown. Former model. Films inc: Night School; Three Blind Mice; Sharky's Machine; Dead Men Don't Wear Plaid; Against All Odds; The Final Terror.

TV inc: The Thorn Birds.

WARD, Simon: Act. b. Beckenham, England, Oct 19, 1941. Films inc: Frankenstein Must be Destroyed; Start Counting; Young Winston; Hitler-The Last 10 Days; The Three Musketeers; The Four Musketeers; The Battleflag; Deadly Strangers; All Creatures Great and Small; Aces High; Dominique; Zulu Dawn; La Sabina; The Monster Club; L'Etincelle (Tug of Love); Supergirl; Leave All Fair.

TV inc: Spoiled; Chips with Everything; All Creatures Great and Small; Dracula; The Last Giraffe; The Corsican Brothers.

Thea inc: Hamlet; The Rear Column.

WARDEN, Jack: Act. b. Newark, NJ, 1925. Films inc: From Here to Eternity; Twelve Angry Men; Run Silent, Run Deep; Mirage; Shampoo; All The President's Men; The White Buffalo; Heaven Can Wait; Death on the Nile; Dreamer; Beyond the Poseidon Adventure; The Champ; And Justice for All; Being There; Used Cars; The Great Muppet Caper; Chu Chu and the Philly Flash; Carbon Copy; So Fine; The Verdict; Crackers; The Aviator.

TV inc: The Wackiest Ship in the Army; N.Y.P.D.; Brian's Song (Emmy-1972); Bad News Bears; Topper; A Private Battle; Hobson's Choice; Helen Keller-- The Miracle Continues; Robert Kennedy & His Times; Crazy Like A Fox; A.D.

Bway inc: Stages.

WARDROPE, Alan J.: Exec. b. Australia, Aug 8, 1912. Ad-pub M, Par, 1958-67; CBS (Cinema Center Films). Dir, Australia, New Zealand, Far East, 1968-72; CIC Int'l Sls, London & Singapore, 1972-75; Australian Film Commission. mktg,

WARHOL, Andy: Dir-Prod. b. Pittsburgh, PA, 1928. Films inc: Sleep; Blow Job; Harlot; The Chelsea Girls; Blue Movie; Trash (prod only); Flesh (prod only); Bad; L'Amour; C S Blues; The Look (act).

TV inc: (act) Saturday Night Live; Donald Duck's 50th Birthday.

WARING, Fred: Mus. b. Tyrone, PA, Jun 9, 1900. Inventor of Waring Blender. Launched his band, The Pennsylvanians, in the early thirties, still does concert, recording dates. Began on radio in 1935. Sponsors music education through Waring Music Workshop and Shawnee Press music pubbery. Films inc: Variety Show.

(Died July 29, 1984).

WARNER, David: Act. b. Manchester, England, Jul 29, 1941. e. RADA. London stage debut, 1962, A Midsummer Night's Dream. Thea inc: Afore Night Come; The Tempest; The Wars of the Roses; The Government Inspector; Twelfth Night; I, Claudius.

Films inc: Tom Jones; Morgan; Work Is a Four Letter Word; The Bofors Gun; The Ballad of Cable Hogue; Straw Dogs; A Doll's House; Tales from the Crypt; Providence; Cross of Iron; The Omen; Silver Bears; The 39 Steps (remake); Time After Time; Concorde-Airport '79; Nightwing; The Island; Time Bandits; Tron; The Company of Wolves.

TV inc: War of the Roses; The Blue Hotel; Holocaust; SOS Titanic; Masada (Emmy-supp-1981); Marco Polo; A Christmas Carol; Hitler's SS--Portrait In Evil; Love's Labour's Lost.

WARREN, Charles Marquis: Wri-Dir-Prod. b. Baltimore, MD, Dec 16, 1917. e. Baltimore City Coll. Films inc: Only the Valiant (wri); Little Big Horn (wri-prod-dir); Hellgate (wri-prod-dir); Springfield Rifle

(wri); Pony Express (wri); Arrowhead (wri-dir); Flight to Tangier (wri-dir); Seven Angry Men (wri-dir); Tension at Table Rock (dir); Black Whip (prod-dir); Trooper Hawk (wri-dir); Charro! (wri-prod-dir); Down to the Sea (wri-prod-dir); Hunter (wri).

TV inc: Gunsmoke; Rawhide; Gunslinger; The Virginian; Iron Horse.

WARREN, Gene: SFX Prod-Dir. b. Denver, CO, Aug 12, 1916. e. LA Art Center School. Films inc: The Monster From the Green Hell; Jack the Giant Killer; The Lost Balloon; Atlantis, the Lost Continent; Around the World Under the Sea; Tom Thumb; The Time Machine (Oscar-1960); Wonderful World of the Brothers Grimm; The Seven Faces of Dr. Lao; The Power; My Name is John; Black Sunday; Avalanche.

TV inc: Twilight Zone; Outer Limits; Star Trek; Man from Atlantis.

WARREN, Jennifer: Act. b. NYC., Aug. 12. e. U WI. Thea inc: Scuba Duba; 6 Rms Riv Vu; P.S. Your Cat Is Dead; Big River.

Films inc: Night Moves; Another Man, Another Chance; Slap Shot; Ice Castles; Night Shadows (Mutant).

TV inc: First You Cry; Steel Cowboy; Champions, A Love Story; Angel City; The Intruder Within; Freedom; Paper Dolls; Confessions of a Married Man; Amazons; Celebrity; Double Dare.

WARREN, Lesley Ann: Act. b. Aug. 16, 1946. Films inc: The Happiest Millionaire; The One and Only Genuine Family Band; Race to the Yankee Zephyr; Victor/Victoria; A Night in Heaven; Choose Me; Songwriter.

TV inc: Cinderella; Mission Impossible; Betrayal; Pearl; Portrait of a Stripper; Beulah Land; 79 Park Avenue; Portrait of a Showgirl; A Special Eddie Rabbitt; Evergreen.

Bway inc: 110 In the Shade; Drat the Cat; Metamorphosis; Three Penny Opera. (London) Gone With the Wind.

WARREN, Madeline: Exec. b. Greenport, NY, Sep 10, 1949. e. NYU, BA, MA. Worked as story edtr before becoming dir dvlpmt The Fields Co; vp prodn-dvlpt Begelman-Fields Co; Jan 1980 to MGM as prodn exec; Dec 1980, vp prodn MGM.

WARREN, Michael: Act. b. South Bend, IN, Mar. 5, 1946. e. UCLA. Films inc: Drive, He Said; Cleopatra Jones; Butterflies Are Free; Norman. . .Is That You?; Fast Break.

TV inc: Days of Our Lives; Sierra; Paris; Hill Street Blues; Just a Little More Love; A Tribute to Martin Luther King Jr.--A Celebration of Life.

WARRICK, Ruth: Act. b. St Louis, MO, Jun 29, 1915. On screen from 1941. Films inc: Citizen Kane; The Corsican Brothers; Journey Into Fear; China Sky; The Iron Major; Perilous Holiday; Daisy Kenyon; The Great Dan Patch; Three Husbands; Ride Beyond Vengeance; The Great Bank Robbery; The Returning.

TV inc: Peyton Place; As The World Turns; Father of the Bride; All My Children; Sometimes I Don't Love My Mother; Peyton Place--The Next Generation.

Thea inc: Pal Joey; Take Me Along; Conditions of Agreement; Irene.

WARTLIEB, Jack: Exec. b. Chicago, IL, Feb 7, 1930. e. Columbia Coll, BA. TV prodn mgr on CBS remotes; prodn mgr David Frost Show; Merv Griffin Show; Norman Corwin Presents; vp chg prod Westinghouse in chg of Mike Douglas Show; Peter Marshall Show; Every Day; May 1980 prodn-ops vp Golden West Broadcasters.

WARWICK, Dionne: Singer. b. East Orange, NJ, Dec 12, 1941. Albums inc: Here Where There Is Love; Golden Hits; Valley of the Dolls; A Decade of Gold; I'll Never Fall In Love Again (Grammy-contemporary voc-1970); Dionne.

Singles inc: I Say A Little Prayer; Do You Know the Way to San Jose? (Grammy-contemporary voc -1968); Then Came You; I'll Never Love This Way Again (Grammy-pop vocal-1979); Deja Vu (Grammy-R&B vocal-1979)

TV inc: Dionne Warwick Special: History of Jazz; Solid Gold (co-host); Barry Manilow--One Voice; Crystal; Entertainer of the Year Awards; A Gift of Music (host); Debby Boone's One Step Closer; Bob Hope Goes to College; Here's Television Entertainment (host); All-Star Party for Frank Sinatra; Anne Murray's Winter Carnival--From

Quebec; Kennedy Center Honors 1984; Women In Song.

WASHAM, Wisner McCamey: Wri. b. Mooresville, NC, Sep 8, 1931. e. U NC, BA; LAMBDA. Stage mgr various Bway prodns 1967 through 1971; since 1971, head wri (TV) All My Children.

WASHBOURNE, Mona: Act. b. Birmingham, England, Nov 27, 1903. Theatre inc: Mourning Becomes Electra; Blithe Spirit; The Winslow Boy; Honour and Obey; The Foolish Gentlewoman; The Mortimer Touch; Mornings at Seven; Nude With Violin; Billy Liar; Semi Detached; The Anniversary; Misalliance; Home; Getting On.
   Films inc: The Winslow Boy; The Good Companions; Billy Liar; Night Must Fall; My Fair Lady; The Collector; Quilp; The Bluebird; Stevie.
   TV inc: A Hundred Years Old; Dear Petitioner; Homecoming; Brideshead Revisited; Charles and Diana--A Royal Love Story.

WASHINGTON, Denzel: Act. b. Mount Vernon, NY., Dec. 28. e. Fordham U, BA; ACT. Thea inc: When the Chickens Come Home To Roost; Coriolanus; Spell # 7; The Mighty Gents; Ceremonies in Dark Old Men; A Soldier's Play.
   TV inc: Wilma; Flesh and Blood; St. Elsewhere; License to Kill.
   Films inc: Carbon Copy; A Soldier's Story.

WASILEWSKI, Vincent T.: Exec. b. Athens, IL, Dec 17, 1922. e. U of IL, BA, JD. 1949 joined legal staff National Ass'n Broadcasters; 1953, chief counsel; 1955 Mgr Govt relations; 1960 VP Govt Aff; 1961, exec VP; 1965, Pres; Ret Oct 1982.

WASS, Ted: Act. b. Lakewood, OH, Oct 27. TV inc: Family; Handle with Care; Loves Me, Loves Me Not; Daughters; Soap; The Triangle Factory Fire Scandal; I Was A Mail Order Bride; Baby Sister; Sins Of The Father.
   Films inc: Curse of the Pink Panther; Sheena; Oh, God! You Devil.

WASSERMAN, Dale: Wri. b. Rhinelander, WI, Nov 2, 1917. Started as theatrical lighting dsgn, later a dir and prod. Became wri during era of live tv.
   TV inc: Elisha and the Long Knives; Collision; The Man That Corrupted Hadleyburg; The Citadel; Long After Summer; The Fog; Brotherhood of the Bell; The Blue Angels; The Power and the Glory; Stranger; I, Don Quixote; The Lincoln Murder Case; Eichmann--Engineer of Death; The Luck of Roaring Camp; Circle of Death; The Fool Killer.
   Plays inc: 998; Livin' The Life; Beggar's Holiday (prod); Man of La Mancha; Pencil of God; One Flew Over the Cuckoo's Nest.
   Films inc: The Power and the Glory; Quick Before It Melts; Mister Buddwing; Doctor, You've Got to Be Kidding; A Walk With Love and Death (& asso prod); Man of La Mancha.

WASSERMAN, Lew R.: Exec. b. Cleveland, OH, Mar 15, 1913. Joined MCA on Dec. 12, 1936, and 10 years later to the day was named President of the Corporation. Currently Chairman of the Board, CEO.
   (Jean Hersholt Humanitarian Award, 1973).

WASSON, Craig: Act-Mus. b. Eugene, OR, Mar 15, 1954. Thea inc: Godspell (tour); Fire in the Mind House; All God's Chillun Got Wings; Death of a Salesman (& incidental mus); The Glass Menagerie.
   TV inc: (Act) Phyllis (& mus); Rafferty; Baa Baa Black Sheep; Skag; Serpico; Thornwell; The Innocents Abroad; Why Me?
   Films inc: (Act) Past is Prologue to the Future (doc) (mus); The Boys in Company C (& mus); Go Tell The Spartans; The Outsider; Carny; Schizoid; Nights At O'Rear's; Ghost Story; Second Thoughts; Four Friends; Body Double.

WATERHOUSE, Keith: Wri. b. Leeds, England, Feb 6, 1929. Plays inc: Billy Liar; Celebration; England, Our England; All Things Bright and Beautiful; Come Laughing Home; Say Who You Are; Children's Day; Who's Who; Saturday, Sunday, Monday (adapt); Filomena (adapt).
   Films inc: Whistle Down the Wind; A Kind of Loving; Billy Liar; Man in the Middle; Pretty Polly; Lock Up Your Daughters; The Valiant.
   TV inc: Charters & Caldicott.

WATERS, Muddy (nee McKinley Morganfield): Mus-Singer. b. Rolling Fork, MS, Apr 4, 1915. Discovered in 1941 by musicologist Alan Lomax who first recorded him; moved to Chicago 1943, joining other Delta musicians who were creating the Chicago Blues style.
   (Grammys-(7)-Ethnic or traditional-1971, 1972, 1975, 1977, 1978, 1979,1980).
   (Died April 30, 1983)

WATERSTON, Sam: Act. b. Cambridge, MA, Nov 15, 1940. Films inc: Fitzwilly; Generation Three; Who Killed Mary Wat's 'ername?; Savages; A Time for Giving; A Delicate Balance; The Great Gatsby; Rancho de Luxe; Capricorn One; Interiors; Sweet Revenge; The Eagles Wing; Sweet William; Hopscotch; Heaven's Gate; The Killing Fields.
   TV inc: Friendly Fire; Oppenheimer; Q.E.D; Games Mother Never Taught You; In Defense of Kids; Dempsey; The Boy Who Loved Trolls; Finnegan Begin Again; Love Lives On.
   Thea inc: Hamlet; Much Ado About Nothing; Lunch Hour.

WATFORD, Gwen: Act. b. London, Sep 10, 1927. Thea inc: Dear Octopus; No Room At the Inn; Daddy Long Legs; The Queen and the Rebels; Mary Stuart; Midsummer Night's Dream; When Did You Last See My Mother?; Howard's End; Come Sunday; Parents Day; The Constant Wife; Three Sisters; Marching Song; Hamlet; Singles; Bodies; Present Laughter; The Jeweller's Shop.
   Films inc: Cleopatra; Never Take Sweets From A Stranger; The Very Edge.
   TV inc: Jesus of Nazareth; Till Time Shall End; Eden End; The Winslow Boy; The Twelve Pound Look; Don't Forget to Write; In This House of Brede; The Case of the Middle-Aged Wife.

WATSON, Arthur A.: Exec. b. Brooklyn, May 4, 1930. e. Fordham School of Business, BS. Joined NBC as operations analyst; tsfd to WRCV radio and TV, Philadelphia, as business mgr; Nov. 1961, station mgr WRCV-TV; 1965, GM WRCV radio and tv; Aug 1965, VP & GM WKYC-TV when NBC acquired station in swap of WRCV operations with Westinghouse; 1969, P NBC Radio Division; 1970, exec VP & GM WNBC-TV, net's O&O station in NYC; April, 1976, exec VP NBC Television Stations Division; Jan. 1979, exec VP NBC TV Network; July 1979, P NBC Sports.

WATSON, Douglass (Larkin Douglass Watson III): Act. b. Jackson, GA, Feb 24, 1921. e. U NC, BA; studied with Maria Ouspenskaya. Bway inc: Anthony and Cleopatra; Command Decision; Leading Lady; The Happiest Year; The Wisteria Trees; Romeo and Juliet; Desire Under the Elms; The Brass Ring; Cyrano de Bergerac; The Confidential Clerk; The Young and Beautiful; The Little Glass Clock; The Chinese Prime Minister; Marat/Sade; The Prime of Miss Jean Brodie; The Pirates of Penzance; Much Ado About Nothing.
   Films inc: Julius Caesar; Sayonara; The Trial of the Catonsville Nine; Ulzana's Raid.
   TV inc: Man and Superman; Abe Lincoln in Illinois; The Taming of the Shrew; Much Ado About Nothing; Moment of Truth; Another World *(Emmys-1979,1980)*

WATSON, Mills: Act. b. Oakland, CA, Jul 10, 1940. e. RADA. Films inc: The Midnight Man; Dracula's Castle; Charlie and the Angel; Cheech and Chong's Up in Smoke; Cujo; Heated Vengeance.
   TV inc: The Migrants; Amy Prentiss; The Misadventures of Sheriff Lobo; I'll Be Home For Christmas; Lobo; Half Nelson.

WAYNE, David (Wayne McKeekan): Act. b. Travers City, MI, Jun 30, 1916. Bway inc: Park Avenue; Finian's Rainbow *(Tony-Supp-1947)*; Mister Roberts; Teahouse of the August Moon *(Tony-1954)*; Say Darling; Incident At Vichy; The Happy Time.
   Films inc: Portrait of Jennie; Adams Rib; The Reformer and the Redhead; My Blue Heaven; Stella; M; Up Front; As Young as You Feel; With a Song in My Heart; Wait 'Til the Sun Shines, Nellie; Down Among the Sheltering Palms; We're Not Married; Tonight We Sing; How to Marry a Millionaire; Hell and High Water; The Tender Trap; The Last Angry Man; The Big Gamble; The Andromeda Strain; The African Elephant (narr); Huckleberry Finn; The Front Page; The Apple Dumpling Gang; The Prize Fighter; Finders Keepers.
   TV inc: Arsenic and Old Lace; The World of Disney; Matt Lincoln; The Name of the Game; The Good Life; Cade's Country; Streets of San Francisco; The FBI Versus Alvin Karpis; The Gift of Love; The Statesman (Benjamin Franklin); The Girls in the Office; Ellery Queen; House Calls; Matt Houston.

WAYNE, Jerry (Jerome Marvin Krauth): Prod-Wri. b. Buffalo, NY, Jul 24, 1926. e. U of Buffalo, OH State Dental. Began as singer; recording artist. On stage in Guys and Dolls; Pajama Game; Silk Stockings.
    Plays inc: (prod-wri) Two Cities (London); King's Mare (London).

WAYNE, Michael: Exec. b. Los Angeles, Nov 23, 1934. e. Loyola U, BBA. S of late John Wayne. Worked as asst dir, became P Batjac Prodns (Wayne indie). Films inc: China Doll; Escort West; The Alamo; McClintock; Cast A Giant Shadow; The Green Berets; Chisum; Big Jake; The Train Robbers; Cahill, US Marshall; McQ; Brannigan; Alley Cat (act).

WAYNE, Patrick: Act. b. Los Angeles, Jul 15, 1939. S of late John Wayne. Screen debut at age 11, Rio Grande. Films inc: The Searchers; The Alamo; The Comancheros; McLintock!; The Bears and I; Mustang Country; Sinbad and the Eye of the Tiger; The People That Time Forgot; Rustler's Rhapsody.
    TV inc: Shirley; The Rounders; Flight To Holocaust; Yesterday's Child; The Last Hurrah; The Monte Carlo Show (host).

WAYNE, Sid: Lyr-Comp. b. NYC, Jan 26, 1923. Entertainer in niteries; wrote songs for Bway musicals inc: Ziegfeld Follies; Thirteen Daughters.
    TV inc: Victor Borge; Peter Lind Hayes & Mary Healy.
    Films inc: G.I. Blues; From Hell to Borneo; Cleopatra; Only Once in a Lifetime.
    Songs inc: It's Impossible; I'm Gonna Knock On Your Door; Two Different Worlds; I Need Your Love Tonight; Mangos; Winner Take All; 99 Years in the Penitentiary; My Love For You; First Anniversary. Also songs for 30 Elvis Presley films.

WEATHERSTONE, Roger Seddon: Exec-TV prod. b. Gunning NSW, Australia, May 29, 1943. M Mobbs Lane Prodns for ATW, 1976-77; gm Vidio Tape Corp, Sydney.

WEAVER, Dennis: Act. b. Joplin, MO, Jun 4, 1924. e. U of OK. TV inc: Gunsmoke (Emmy-supp-1959); Kentucky Jones; Duel; Gentle Ben; McCloud; Intimate Strangers; Ishi; Pearl; The Islander; The Ordeal of Patty Hearst; A Cry for Justice; Stone; Amber Waves; The Ordeal of Dr. Mudd; Country Gold--The First Fifty Years; The Day The Loving Stopped; Don't Go To Sleep; Cocaine--One Man's Seduction; Emerald Point, N.A.S.; Going For The Gold--The Bill Johnson Story.
    Films inc: Dragnet; The Bridges at Toko-Ri; Ten Wanted Men; Seven Angry Men.

WEAVER, Fritz: Act. b. Pittsburgh, PA, Jan 19, 1926. e. U of Chicago, BA. Thea inc; Chalk Garden; Protective Custody; Miss Lonely Hearts; Loreno; All American; Shot in the Dark; Absurd Person Singular; Baker Street; Child's Play (Tony-1970); The Price.
    Films inc: Demon Seed; Marathon Man; Black Sunday; The Day of the Dolphin; The Guns of August; The Big Fix; Jaws Of Satan (King Cobra); Creepshow.
    TV inc: The Legend of Lizzie Borden; Holocaust; The Martian Chronicles; Children of Divorce; Nightkill; Momma the Detective; Maid In America; Alice in Wonderland; The Hearst & Davies Affair; A Death In California.

WEAVER, Gordon R.: Exec b. Farmerville, LA, Nov 21, 1937. Joined MGM pub dept NY, later handled pub for MGM Europe; 1968, exec asst to wldwde pub vp, Cinema Center Films; 1970, dir pub-promotion National General Pictures; 1971, natl pub dir Paramount; 1974, vp in chg pub & asst to chmn-CEO; 1975, vp wldwde mktg Paramount Motion Picture Division; 1977, vp corporate communications Paramount Pictures Corp; 1978, sr vp mktg for motion picture division; 1981, sr vp wldwde mktg; June 1983, P Wldwde Mktg; Studio announced he was aked to resign following preliminary investigation of relationship with suppliers; Oct/ 1984, named to head new entertainment and mktg division of Y&R ad agency.

WEAVER, Marjorie: Act. b. Grossville, TN, Mar 2, 1913. On screen from 1936. Films inc: China Clipper; This Is My Affair; Second Honeymoon; The Cisco Kid and the Lady; You Can't Ration Love; Fashion Model; We're Not Married.

WEAVER, Sigourney: Act. b. Los Angeles, Oct 8, 1949. e. Stanford; Yale School of Drama. D of Sylvester J (Pat) Weaver. Thea inc: The Constant Wife; The Nature and Purpose of the Universe; Gemini; Marco Polo Sings a Solo; Das Lusitania Songspiel; Hurlyburly (Off-Bway).
    Films inc: Alien; Eyewitness; The Year of Living Dangerously; Deal of the Century; Ghostbusters. TV inc: The Best of Families; Somerset; The Sorrows of Gin.

WEAVER, Sylvester J. (Pat): Exec. b. Los Angeles, Dec 21, 1908. e. Dartmouth Coll. Young & Rubicam adv agency, 1935-38; American Tobacco Co, adv mgr, 1938-47; VP Y&R, 1947-49. Joined NBC as VP charge of TV, 1949; appt'd VP chg. NBC Radio & TV networks, 1952; vice chmn bd, NBC, 1953; p NBC, Dec, 1953; bd chmn, Dec, 1955; resigned 1956, formed own broadcast company and then became advertising exec with McCann-Erickson. From 1963-66 he headed Subscription Television Inc. Returned to advertising field as cnsltnt to the Wells, Rich, Greene agency.
    (Emmy-Trustees Award-1968)(TV Academy Hall of Fame 1985)

WEBBER, Robert: Act. b. Santa Ana, CA, Oct 14, 1924. Films inc: Highway 301; Twelve Angry Men; The Stripper; Hysteria; The Sandpiper; The Third Day; No Tears for a Killer; Harper; Dead Heat on a Merry-Go-Round; The Silencers; The Dirty Dozen; Dollars; Bring Me the Head of Alfredo Garcia; Midway; The Choirboys; Pacific Challenge (& narr); Madame Claude; L'Imprecateur; Casey's Shadow; Revenge of the Pink Panther; 10; Courage, Fuyons; All Stars; Private Benjamin; Sunday Lovers; S.O.B.; Wrong Is Right; Who Dares Wins; Wild Geese II.
    TV inc: The Two Lives of Carol Letner; Not Just Another Affair; Don't Go To Sleep; Starflight--The Plane That Couldn't Land; Getting Physical; No Man's Land; Cover Up; Half Nelson.

WEBSTER, Nicholas: Dir. b. Spokane, WA, Jul 24. e. LA City Coll. TV inc: Apple's Way; Mannix; Bracken's World; Get Smart; Bonanza; Johnny Cash Ridin' the Rails; The Great American Train Story; Appointment with Destiny; Showdown at OK Corral; Last Days of John Dillinger; Long Childhood of Timmie; Walk in My Shoes; Violent World of Sam Huff; Purlie Victorious; Escape (& co-prod).

WEBSTER, Paul Francis: Sngwri. b. NYC, Dec 20, 1907. e. Cornell U, NYU. To Hollywood 1935; under contract to 20th Century-Fox to write for Shirley Temple; then freelance. Films inc: Minstrel Man; Hit the Ice; Calamity Jane; Rose Marie; The Merry Widow; Tender Is the Night; Marjorie Morningstar; Student Prince; The Great Caruso; 55 Days at Peking; April Love.
    Thea inc: Casino de Paree; Jump for Joy; Windy City; Christine.
    Songs inc: Masquerade; Two Cigarettes in the Dark; How Green Was My Valley; Rainbow on the River; The Lamplighter's Serenade; I Got It Bad and That Ain't Good; The Loveliest Night of the Year; Merry Widow Waltz; Tender Is The Night; Secret Love (Oscar-1953); Love Is A Many-Splendored Thing (Oscar-1955); The Twelfth of Never; There's Never Been Anyone Else But You; Giant; Anastasia; Friendly Persuasion; The Shadow of Your Smile (Oscar-1965); Somewhere My Love.
    TV title songs: Maverick; Sugarfoot.
    (Died Mar 22, 1984).

WECHTER, David: Wri-Dir. b. Los Angeles, Jun 27, 1956. e. USC, BA. S of Julius Wechter. Films inc: Gravity (short); Junior High School (short); Midnight Madness.

WECHTER, Julius: Band ldr-Comp. b. Chicago, May 10, 1935. Played vibes with Martin Denny; comp and played with Herb Alpert and the Tia Juana Brass, 1962; then leader of the Baja Marimba Band.
    Film scores inc: Midnight Madness.
    Songs inc: Spanish Flea; Brasilia.

WEDEMEYER, Herman: Act. b. Hilo, HI, May 20, 1924. e. St. Mary's Coll. TV inc: Hawaii Five-O.

WEDGEWORTH, Ann: Act. b. Abilene, TX, Jan 21. e. SMU. Bway inc: Thieves; Make a Million; Blues for Mr. Charlie; The Last Analysis; Chapter Two (Tony-supp-1978).
    TV inc: The Edge of Night; Another World; Somerset; All That Glitters; The War Between the Tates; Three's Company; Elvis and the Beauty Queen; Killjoy; Filthy Rich; Right To Kill?

Films inc: Handle With Care; Thieves; Bang the Drum Slowly; Scarecrow; Law and Disorder; Dragon Fly; The Birch Interval; No Small Affair.

WEIDMAN, Jerome: Wri. b. NYC, Apr 4, 1913. e. CCNY, NYU Law School. Plays inc: Fiorello! *(Pulitzer Prize & Tony*-1959); Tenderloin; I Can Get It For You Wholesale; Cool Off!; Pousse-Cafe; Ivory Tower; The Mother Lover.
Films inc: The Damned Don't Cry; House of Strangers; I Can Get It For You Wholesale.
TV inc: The Reporter (series).

WEILEY, John Francis: Wri-Dir-Prod. b. Grafton NSW, Australia, Jan 28, 1942. e. Sydney U. Films inc: Journey Among Women; Third Person Plural; Dimboola. The Coolangatta Gold (prod).
TV inc: Autopsy on a Dream; Tomorrow's World; The Controllers; Sob Sisters; Horizon; The Total War Machine.

WEILL, Claudia: Dir. b. NYC, 1947. e. Radcliffe. Worked as prodn asst on doc Revolution; later made doc shorts inc This is the Home of Mrs. Levant Grahame; Roaches' Serenade. Films inc: Girlfriends; It's My Turn.
TV inc: Joyce at 34; Sesame Street; The Other Half of the Sky--a China Memoir; The Great Love Experiment.

WEINBERGER, Ed. (Edwin B. Weinberger): Wri. TV inc: The Bill Cosby Specials; The Dean Martin Show; Hey, Hey It's Fat Albert; Mary Tyler Moore Show (& prod) *(Emmys*-prod-1975, 1976, 1977; Wri-1975, 1977); Phyllis; Doc; Betty White Show; Cindy; Taxi (& prod-crea) *(Emmys*-exec prod-1979, 1980, 1981); The Associates (& prod-crea); Mr. Smith (exec prod-dir); Brothers (PC); The Cosby Show (& co-crea).

WEINBLATT, Mike: Exec. e. Syracuse U. Joined NBC in 1957. Serving in various capacities, he has been exec vp and gm of the NBC TV Network Aug, 1977; P of NBC Entertainment Sep 6, 1978; P NBC Enterprises Div Jan 15, 1980; resigned May 29, 1980 to become P of Showtime; Sept. 1983, P & CEO of merged Showtime/The Movie Channel; resd. July 31, 1984, became P Multimedia Entertainment.

WEINGARTEN, Lawrence: Exec. b. Chicago, IL. Started as publicist for Thomas Ince; became prod 1920. Films inc: Buster Keaton films; Marie Dressler-Polly Moran series; Broadway Melody; A Day at the Races; Libeled Lady; I Love You Again; When Ladies Meet; Escape; Adam's Rib; Invitation; Pat and Mike; The Actress; Tender Trap; I'll Cry Tomorrow; Don't Go Near The Water; Cat On a Hot Tin Roof; The Gazebo; Period of Adjustment; Unsinkable Molly Brown.
(Irving Thalberg Award-1973).

WEINSTEIN, Hannah: Prod. b. NYC. e. NYU, BA. M of Paula Weinstein. Films inc: Escapade; Claudine; Greased Lightnin'; Stir Crazy.
TV inc: Robin Hood; Buccaneers; Sword of Freedom; Scotland Yard.
(Died Mar 9, 1984).

WEINSTEIN, Henry T.: Exec prod. b. NYC, Jul 12, 1924. e. CCNY, Carnegie Tech. Worked with various rep groups, stock companies; 1970, exec in chg prodn American Film Theatre; 1975, became ind prod.; Jan. 1985, exec vp Cannon Films. Films inc: Tender Is The Night; Joy in the Morning; Cervantes; Madwoman of Chaillot; The Battle of Neretva; A Delicate Balance; The Homecoming; The Iceman Cometh; Lost in the Stars; Butley; Luther; Rhinoceros; Galileo; The Man In the Glass Booth; In Celebration.

WEINSTEIN, Paula: Exec. b. Nov 19, 1945. e. Columbia U. Started as publicist; then film ed; agent William Morris; vp prod, Warner Bros; studio exec, sr vp worldwide prodn, Fox; prodn vp The Ladd Co, 1980; Nov 1981, P of new picture division of UA; Oct 1982, announced by studio as having resigned, she filed with American Arbitration Association to resolve her status; March 1983 to Columbia as prod and prodn cnslt.

WEINSTOCK, Lew: TV prod-Dir. b. Los Angeles, Jun 2, 1945. Prodn dir for numerous concerts, festivals and fairs.
TV inc: The Grant Griffin Special; Total Environment Concert Special; In Concert/California Jam; California Jam II; Canada Jam.

Films inc: Symphony in Glass; That Tender Touch (prodn cnsltnt).

WEINTRAUB, Fred: Prod. b. NYC, Apr 27, 1928. e. U of PA. Formed Weintraub-Heller Productions, 1974. Films inc: Enter the Dragon; Rage; Black Belt Jones; The Ultimate Warrior; Dirty Knights Work; Checkered Flag or Crash; The Pack; Outlaw Blues; The Promise (& sp); Die Laughing; The Big Brawl; Tom Horn; Force Five; High Road to China; Gymkata; Out Of Control.

WEINTRAUB, Jerry: Prod-Mgr-Promoter. (Jerome Charles):b. NYC, Sep 26, 1937. Personal mgr talent inc Beachboys; John Davidson; John Denver; Neil Diamond; Bob Dylan; Waylon Jennings; Wayne Newton; 1982, formed Intercontinental Broadcasting Systems with Don Ohlmeyer, also formed Jerry Weintraub-Armand Hammer Prodns; Sept. 1984, bought into Nederlander legit organization and formed the Nederlander-Weintraub Group.
TV inc: John Denver's Rocky Mountain Christmas *(Emmy*-1974); An Evening With Main Event; Good Night America; The Higher We Fly; Blue Jeans; The Wayne Newton Special--Coast to Coast; Rocky Mountain Holiday with John Denver and the Muppets; Poor Richard; Olympic Gala (exec prod); The Cowboy and the Ballerina (exec prod).
Films inc: Nashville; Oh, God!; Sept. 30, 1955; All Night Long; Cruising; Diner; The Karate Kid.

WEINTRAUB, Sy: Exec. b. NYC, 1923. e. U of MO. Formed Flamingo Films, tv synd firm, 1949, created Superman and Grand Ole Opry tv series; bought Sol Lesser's rights to Tarzan films 1958, creating Banner Films which prod several new Tarzan adventures; 1965 purchased Panavision, later acquired Nassour Studios; 1967 sold Banner Prodns to National General Corp, becoming P National General's tv arm; 1978 became chmn Columbia Pictures Entertainment; 1979 became chmn exec committee of Columbia Pictures Industries and member of three-man office of chief exec. Films inc: (Exec Prod) The Sign of the Four; The Hound of the Baskervilles.

WEIR, Bob: Mus. b. Oct 16, 1947. Founder-member of The Grateful Dead. Occasionally records with other musicians. Albums inc: Ace; Heaven Help The Fool.
(See The Grateful Dead for group credits).

WEIR, Peter: Dir. b. Sydney, Australia, Aug 8, 1944. Films inc: Homesdale; The Cars that Ate Paris; Picnic at Hanging Rock; The Last Wave (& sp); The Plumber (& sp); Gallipoli (& orig story); The Year of Living Dangerously (& sp); Witness.

WEIS, Don: Dir. b. Milwaukee, WI, May 13, 1922. e. USC. Films inc: (dial dir) Body & Soul; Home of the Brave; Champion; The Men. (Dir): Letter from a Soldier; sequence in It's a Big Country; Bannerline; Just This Once; You for Me; I Love Melvin; Remains to be Seen; A Slight Case of Larceny; Half a Hero; Affairs of Dobie Gillis; Adventures of Hajji Baba; Ride the High Iron; Catch Me If You Can; The Gene Krupa Story; Critic's Choice; Looking for Love; The King's Pirate.
TV inc: Dear Phoebe; The Longest Hundred Miles; It Takes a Thief; Ironside; M*A*S*H; Happy Days; Planet of the Apes; Bronk; Petrocelli; The Magician; Mannix; Night Stalker; Barbary Coast; The Courtship of Eddie's Father; Starsky & Hutch; Andros Targets; Kingston Confidential; Hawaii Five-0; The Millionaire; The Munster's Revenge; Quick and Quiet.

WEISBORD, Sam: Exec. b. NYC, Sep 21, 1911. Joined William Morris Agency 1929; moved to West Coast office 1945; named sr exec vp 1965; became pres 1975.

WEISKOPF, Bob: Wri. Writes with Bob Schiller. TV inc: I Love Lucy; Red Skelton Show *(Emmy*-1971); Flip Wilson Show; Maude; All's Fair (crea); All in the Family *(Emmy*-1978); Archie Bunker's Place; Living in Paradise (pilot); Side By Side (& prod); Walter (& exec prod).

WEISMAN, Ben: Comp-Arr. b. Providence, RI, Nov 16, 1921. e. Juilliard School of Music. Films inc: Jailhouse Rock; It Happened at the World's Fair; The Trouble with Girls; G.I. Blues; Blue Hawaii; Roustabout; Frankie and Johnnie; Wild in the Country; Change of Habit; Tickle Me; The Young Americans; Wild Honey.
TV inc: Dick Tracy; Joey Bishop.
Songs inc: The Night Has a Thousand Eyes; Lonely Boy Blue; Got a Lot of Livin' to Do; Pocketful of Rainbows; Summer Kisses, Winter

Tears; Frankie and Johnnie; When I Am With You.

WEISMAN, Michael: Exec prod. e. Queens College. Started with NBC 1971 as page, moved to sports department year later; 1974, asso prod; 1977, Prod; 1977, coord prod; Feb. 1983, exec prod. TV inc: World Series (1978,1980,1982) (Emmy-live Sports Special-1983); Major League Championship Games (1977, 1979, 1981); Orange Bowl (1978 thru 1983); Super Bowl XIII (Emmy-1979); AFC/NFL Football; Sportsworld; NCAA Basketball; Wimbledon '83 (Emmy-Sports Special-1983).

WEISSBOURD, Burt: Prod. b. 1950. e. Yale; Northwestern U. Films inc: Raggedy Man; Ghost Story.

WEISSMULLER, Johnny: Act. b. Chicago, IL, Jun 2, 1904. e. Chicago U. Champion swimmer. Screen debut in Tarzan, the Ape Man, 1932. Played Tarzan in 12 films. Other pictures inc: Jungle Jim; Swamp Fire; The Lost Tribe; Pygmy Island; Captive Girl; Savage Mutiny; Cannibal Attack; Jungle Man-Eater; The Phynx.
(Died Jan 20, 1984).

WEITMAN, Robert M.: Exec. b. NYC, Aug 18, 1905. e. Cornell U, BS. M, Paramount Theatres, Greater NY, 1933-35; M dir NY Para, 1935-53, instituted big-name personality and big-band policy; VP-programming and talent, ABC-TV when United Paramount Theatres merged with ABC, 1953-56; VP-program development, CBS-TV, 1956; VP, TV prodn, MGM, 1960; VP-all prodn, feature and TV for MGM; elected to MGM bd. of directors, 1963-68; VP, Motion Picture Prodn, Columbia Pictures, 1968-70; appointed 1st VP in charge of all prodn, 1969; 1970 ret to Ind Prodn.
Films inc: The Anderson Tapes; Shamus.
TV inc: Shamus; A Matter of Wife. . .and Death.

WEITZ, Bruce: Act. b. Norwalk, CT, May 27, 1943. e. Carnegie Tech, BA, MFA. Studied at Long Wharf Theatre and the Tyrone Guthrie Theatre. In rep at Arena Stage, Washington, D.C. Bway inc: Norman, Is That You?; The Basic Training of Pavlo Hummel; Death of a Salesman.
TV inc: Hill Street Blues (Emmy-Supp-1984); Every Stray Dog and Kid; Death of a Centerfold; Catalina C-Lab; A Reason To Live.

WEITZMAN, Bernard: Exec. b. Springfield, MA. e. Southwestern U School of Law, U of Alabama, USC. Dir of business affairs, CBS-TV, 1948-54; Desilu Productions, vp & board member, 1954-67; MCA, VP, 1961-72; pres, Cinemobile Systems/Taft Broadcasting, 1972-74; vp, MGM, 1974-77; Lorimar Productions, exec vp since 1977.

WEITZNER, David A.: Exec. b. NYC, Nov 13, 1938. e. MI State U. Entered film industry 1960 in Columbia adv dept. Subsequently with Donahue & Coe Agency, Loew's Theatres, Embassy Pictures in adv dept; dir adv-expl Palomar Pictures; Ad-Pub-Expl vp ABC Pictures Corp; vp entertainment & leisure div Grey Advertising; vp worldwide adv 20th Fox, Feb 1977; Exec vp ad-pub-expl Universal Jan 1980; Nov 1982, VP Embassy Communications and exec VP Embassy Pictures; March 1985, P 20th Fox Marketing Div.

WELCH, Ken: Wri-Lyr-Comp. b. Kansas City, MO, Feb 4, 1926. e. Carnegie-Mellon. H of Mitzie Welch. Spec material wri, teamed with Mitzie Cottle (later Welch) writing spec material for Carol Burnett, others; worked niteries as team.
TV inc: The Garry Moore Show; Julie and Carol at Carnegie Hall; Carol and Company; Carol Plus Two; The Entertainers; Kraft Music Hall; Burt Bacharach specials; Petula Clark special; Julie and Carol at Lincoln Center; Barbra Streisand and other Musical Instruments (Emmy-mus-dir-1974; also musician of year); Duke Ellington Special; Bing Crosby and Friends; Olivia Newton-John Special; Sills and Burnett at the Met; Carol Burnett Show (Emmy-song-1976); Ben Vereen--His Roots (Emmy-song-1978); Hope for President (& prod); Linda in Wonderland (& prod) (Emmy-song-1981); Walt Disney--One Man's Dream (prod); Bonnie and the Franklins (prod-chor); Life of the Party--The Story of BeAtrice (exec prod); Burnett "Discovers" Domingo (wri); Disneyland's 30th Anniversary Celebration (wri).
Films inc: Movers & Shakers (mus).

WELCH, Mitzie (Marilyn Cottle): Wri-Lyr-Comp. b. McDonald, PA, Jul

25. e. Carnegie-Mellon. W of Ken Welch. Singer at Pittsburgh Playhouse; vocalist with Benny Goodman at Waldorf-Astoria, NY; teamed with Welch writing spec material for Carol Burnett, others; worked niteries as team. Bway inc: (act) Student Gypsy; Fade Out, Fade In; Do I Hear A Waltz; Second City.
TV inc: The Garry Moore Show; Julie and Carol at Carnegie Hall; Carol and Company; Carol Plus Two; The Entertainers; Kraft Music Hall; Burt Bacharach Specials; Petula Clark Specials; Julie and Carol at Lincoln Center; Barbra Streisand and Other Musical Instruments (Emmy-mus-dir-1974; also musician of year); Duke Ellington Special; Bing Crosby and Friends; Olivia Newton-John Special; Sills and Burnett at the Met; Carol Burnett Show (Emmy-song-1976); Ben Vereen--His Roots (Emmy-song-1978); Hope for President (& prod) Linda in Wonderland (& prod) (Emmy-song-1981); Bonnie and the Franklins (& prod-chor). Walt Disney--One Man's Dream; Life of the Party--The Story of BeAtrice (exec prod-wri); Burnett 'Discovers' Domingo (wri); Disneyland's 30th Anniversary Celebration (wri).
Films inc: Movers & Shakers (mus).

WELCH, Raquel (nee Tejada): Act. b. Chicago, IL, 1942. Fashion and photographic model. Co-Hostess, Hollywood Palace. Screen debut in Roustabout, 1964. Films inc: A House Is Not a Home; Fantastic Voyage; Our Man Flint; One Million Years B.C.; Lady in Cement; 100 Rifles; Myra Breckinridge; Kansas City Bomber; The Wild Party; Mother, Jugs and Speed; Crossed Swords.
TV inc: From Raquel With Love (& wri); The Legend of Walks Far Woman.
Bway inc: Woman of the Year.

WELCH, Robert L.: Prod-Wri. b. Chicago, IL, Nov 23, 1910. e. Northwestern, U of IL. In stock with Hedgerow Theatre, Pasadena Playhouse. In radio as wri-prod Kate Smith Show, Fred Allen Show; Jack Benny Show; Henry Aldrich Shows; US Armed Forces Radio Shows during WW 2.
Films inc: Variety Girl; Paleface; Sorrowful Jones; Top O' The Morning; Fancy Pants; Mr. Music; The Lemon Drop Kid; Son of Paleface.

WELD, Tuesday (nee Susan Weld): Act. b. NYC, Aug 27, 1943. On screen from 1956. Films inc: Rock, Rock, Rock; Rally Round the Flag, Boys!; The Five Pennies; The Private Lives of Adam and Eve; Return to Peyton Place; Wild in the Country; Bachelor Flat; Soldier in the Rain; The Cincinnati Kid; Lord Love A Duck; Pretty Poison; I Walk the Line; A Safe Place; Play It As It Lays; Looking for Mr. Goodbar; Dog Soldiers; Who'll Stop the Rain; Serial; Thief; Author! Author!; Once Upon A Time In America.
TV inc: The Many Loves of Dobie Gillis; Dupont Show of the Month; The Greatest Show on Earth; Mr. Broadway; Fugitive; The Crucible; Cimarron Strip; Mother and Daughter-The Loving War; Madame X; The Rainmaker (cable); John Steinbecks's the Winter of Our Discontent; Scorned and Swindled.

WELDON, Duncan: Prod. b. England, Mar. 19, 1941. Thea inc: (London) When We Are Married; The Chalk Garden; Big Bad Mouse; Bunny; Grease; The King and I; The Case in Question; Hedda Gabler; Dad's Army; On Approval; 13 Rue de l'Amour; A Bedful of Foreigners; Three Sisters; The Seagull; Fringe Benefits; The Circle; Separate Tables; Good Woman of Setzuan; Rosmersholm; The Apple Cart; Laburnum Grove; Waters of the Moon; Kings and Clowns; Traveling Music Show; Look After Lulu; The Millionairess; The Crucifer of Blood; The Last of Mrs. Cheney (act); Overheard; Murder in Mind; Hobson's Choice; Heartbreak House; Call Me Madam; Beethoven's Tenth; The Aspern Papers; Strippers.
Bway inc: Dead Easy; Brief Lives; Aren't We All?
Films inc: Hedda Gabler.

WELDON, Joan: Act. b. San Francisco, CA, Aug 5, 1933. e. SF Conservatory of Music, UC Berkeley, SF City Coll. With SF and LA Civic Light Opera Companies.
Films inc: The System; So This Is Love; The Stranger Wore A Gun; The Command; Riding Shotgun; Them; Deep In My Heart.

WELK, Lawrence: Orch Ldr. b. Strasburg, ND, Mar 11, 1903. Played hotels, ballrooms. 1951 started weekly TV show from Aragon Ballroom, Pacific Ocean Park, CA. Champagne Music Makers, ABC-TV, July, 1955; The Lawrence Welk Show, ABC; signed lifetime contract,

Hollywood Palladium, July 1961; Syndicated network show started 1971.

WELLAND, Colin: Act-Wri. b. England, Jul 4, 1934. Films inc: (Act) Kes; Villain; Straw Dogs; Sweeney. (Wri) Yanks; Chariots of Fire *(Oscar*-1981); Farmers Arms.

TV inc: (Act) Roll On Four O'Clock; Kisses at 50; Leeds United; Your Man From Six Counties.

Plays inc: Say Goodnight to Grandma; Roll On 4 O'Clock.

WELLER, Mary Louise: Act. b. East Hampton, NY. Films inc: Serpico; Deception; The Evil; The Bell Jar; Animal House; Red Tide; Forced Vengeance; Blood Tide.

WELLER, Michael: Plywri. b. NYC, Sept 24, 1942. e. Brandeis U, BA; Manchester U. Plays inc: How Ho-Ho Rose and Fell; Open Space; Moonchildren; More Than You Deserve; Twenty-Three Years Later; Fishing Split (one-act); Loose Ends; Dwarfman; The Ballad of Soapy Smith.

Films inc: Hair; Ragtime.

WELLER, Peter: Act. b. Stevens Point, WI., 1947. e. AADA. Studied with Uta Hagen. Bway inc: Sticks And Bones (& London); Streamers; The Woods; Summer Brave. Off-Bway inc: The Woolgatherers; Serenading Louie.

Films inc: Butch And Sundance--The Early Days; Of Unknown Origin; Shoot The Man; Just Tell Me What You Want; Adventures Of Buckaroo Banzai--Across The 8th Dimension; Firstborn.

WELLES, Orson: Prod-Dir-Wri-Act. b. Kenosha, WI, May 6, 1915. Started in radio: March of Time; The Shadow; War of the Worlds; Campbell Playhouse, co-prod: Julius Caesar; Doctor Faustus; Macbeth; Heartbreak House.

Films inc: (act) Citizen Kane (also prod, dir & co-sp) *(Oscar*-co-sp-1941); Magnificent Ambersons (sp & dir only); Journey into Fear; Jane Eyre; Follow the Boys; Tomorrow Is Forever; The Stranger (& dir); The Lady from Shanghai (& dir); Macbeth (& dir); Prince of Foxes; The Third Man; Othello (& dir); Trouble in the Glen; Napoleon; Moby Dick; Touch of Evil (& dir); The Long Hot Summer; David and Goliath; Compulsion; The Mongols; Lafayette; The Trial (& dir); Is Paris Burning?; A Man for All Seasons; I'll Never Forget Whatshisname; Casino Royale; Start the Revolution Without Me; The Kremlin Letter; Catch 22; Necromancy; Treasure Island; Ten Days Wonder; The Other Side of the Mountain; The Late, Great Planet Earth; The Muppet Movie; The Shah of Iran (doc-narr); The Secret of Nikola Tesla; The Man Who Saw Tomorrow (narr); History of the World--Part I; Butterfly; Genocide (narr); In Our Hands (doc); Slapstick of Another Kind; Almonds and Raisins (doc-narr); Where Is Parsifal? Orson Welles at the Cinematheque (doc-int).

(Special Oscar-1970-for "superlative artistry and versatility in the creation of motion pictures.")

TV inc: The Man Who Came to Dinner; Shogun (narr); The One Thousand Dozen (Tales of the Klondike) (narr); Magic With the Stars (host); Baryshnikov In Hollywood (narr); Natalie--A Tribute To A Very Special Lady; Dom De Luise and Friends; King Penguin--Stranded Beyond the Falklands (narr); Don DeLuise and Friends--Part II; Scene Of the Crime (narr); Snowstorm In The Jungle (Cousteau/Amazon)- (narr).

(Grammys-spoken word-1976, 1979, 1981).

WELLMAN, William, Jr.: Act. b. Los Angeles, Jan 20, 1937. e. Duke U, UCLA. Films inc: Darby's Rangers; Sayonara; The Horse Soldiers; Pork Chop Hill; Dondi; How the West Was Won; The Errand Boy; Rebel in the Ring; The Disorderly Orderly; A Swinging Summer; Winter A-Go-Go; The Happiest Millionaire; Which Way to the Front; The World Within; Billy Jack Goes to Washington; MacArthur; Private Files of J. Edgar Hoover.

TV inc: U.F.O.; Fire in the Sky; Midway; The Eleanor and Lou Gehrig Story; Logan's Run; Hunter; The Blue and The Gray; Space.

WELLS, Frank G.: Exec. b. Mar 4, 1932. e. Pomona Coll, Rhodes Scholar at Oxford (Jurisprudence, Stanford Law School. Joined Hollywood law firm of Gang, Tyre & Brown; became partner three years later; 1969, vp WestCoast, WB; 1972, P; 1975 became chmn, CEO when Ted Ashley stepped out; reverted to presidency year later with Ashley's return; Nov 1980, co-chmn & CEO; Jan 1981 became

Vice Chmn in swap of positions with Terry Semel; Sept. 1984, resd. to become P & CEO of Disney Prodns. with Michael Eisner.

WELLS, George: Wri. b. 1909. Films inc: Take Me Out to the Ball Game; Three Little Words; Everything I Have is Yours (& prod); Jupiter's Darling (prod); Designing Woman *(Oscar*-sp-1957); Ask Any Girl; The Honeymoon Machine; The Horizontal Lieutenant; Penelope; The Impossible Years.

WELLS, Kitty (Muriel Deason): Singer-Sngwri. b. Nashville, TN, Aug 20, 1919. Country mus recording artist. Performed with Grand Ole Opry.

WENDERS, Wim: Dir. b. Dusseldorf, Germany, 1945. Films inc: Summer in the City; Di Angst Des Tomanns Beim Elfmeter; The Scarlet Letter; Aus Der Familie Der Panzerechsen; Falsche Bewegung; Alice in the Cities; The Goalie's Anxiety at the Penalty Kick; Kings of the Road; In the Course of Time; The American Friend; Long Shot (act); Radio On; Lightning Over Water (Nick's Movie) (& act); Hammett; Der Stand der dinge (The State of Things) (& wri); Paris, Texas; Room 666 (doc) (& wri); Tokyo-Ga; King Kongs Faust (King Kong's Fist).

TV inc: The Case of Dashiell Hammett (doc-int).

WENDKOS, Paul: Dir. b. 1922. Films inc: The Burglar; Tarawa Beachhead; Gidget; Face of a Fugitive; Because They're Young; Angel Baby; Gidget Goes to Rome; Miles to Terror; Guns of the Magnificent Seven; Cannon for Cordova; The Mephisto Waltz; Special Delivery.

TV inc: Haunts of the Very Rich; Honor Thy Father; Betrayal; The Legend of Lizzie Borden; A Woman Called Moses; The Ordeal of Patty Hearst; Act of Violence; The Ordeal of Doctor Mudd; A Cry For Love; The Five of Me; Golden Gate; Farrell For the People; Cocaine--One Man's Seduction; Intimate Agony; Big John; Celebrity; Scorned and Swindled; The Bad Seed; The Execution.

WERBLIN, David (Sonny): Exec. b. Brooklyn, Mar 17, 1910. Joined MCA in 1932 as band mgr, later agent; P MCA-TV 1951, regarded as father of package sold Jets 1968 formed (with Johnny Carson) Raritan Enterprises with real estate, showbiz holdings and prod, for a period, the Tonight Show starring Carson; returned to sports 1971 as Chairman NJ Sports and Exposition Authority; resigned Dec, 1977, became P, CEO of Madison Square Garden; Jan 1983, bd chmn.

WERNER, Oskar: Act-Dir-Prod. b. Vienna, Nov 13, 1922. Began as apprentice with Burgtheater, Vienna, later with Josefstadt Theater, Volkstheater; formed own theatre company 1959; dir at Salzburg Festival. Films inc: Angel With the Trumpet; Eroica; A Wonder of Our Days; Decision Before Dawn; The Last Act; Lola Montes; One Named Judas (& dir); Jules and Jim; Ship of Fools; The Spy Who Came in from The Cold; Fahrenheit 451; Interlude; Shoes of the Fisherman; Voyage of the Damned.

(Died Oct. 23, 1984)

WERNER, Peter: Prod. b. NYC, Jan 17, 1947. e. Dartmouth Coll, BA. Films inc: In the Region of Ice *(Oscar*-ss-1976); Don't Cry, It's Only Thunder (dir).

TV inc: Battered; Barnburning; Learning in Focus; Aunt Mary (dir); Hard Knox (dir); I Married A Centerfold (dir); Women In Song (dir); Sins Of The Father (dir).

WERNER, Theo M.: Prod-Dir. b. Munich, May 15, 1926. M-dir Neue Regina Film.

WERRIS, Snag: Wri-Act. b. NYC, Nov 19, 1915. e. CCNY. In vaudeville, burlesque; then started writing material for comedians, inc: Bert Wheeler, Bert Lahr, Alan Young, Vilma & Buddy Ebsen, Phil Silvers. In radio wrote for: Dinah Shore, Frank Sinatra, Bing Crosby, Colonel Stoopnagle, Ben Bernie, Rudy Vallee, Abbott & Costello. In TV for: Fred Allen, Ritz Bros., Ben Blue, Judy Canova, Perry Como, Martin & Lewis, Ken Murray, Jack Carter, Jerry Lester, Eddie Albert, Ed Wynn, Jackie Gleason.

WERTMULLER, Lina: Dir. b. Rome, Aug 14, 1928. Worked as an Asst Dir in legitimate theatre; wrote plays and musicals. Dir first feature film, 1963, The Lizards. Films inc: This Time Lets's Talk About

Men; Rita the Mosquito; The Seduction of Mimi; Love and Anarchy; All Screwed Up; Swept Away; Seven Beauties (& sp); The End of the World in Our Usual Bed in a Nightful of Rain (& sp); Revenge (& sp); Scherzo Del Destino Agguato Dietro L'Angolo Come un Brigante di Strada (A Joke of Destiny Lying in Wait around the Corner Like a Robber (& sp).

WESKER, Arnold: Plywri. b. London, England, May 24, 1932. Plays inc: Chicken Soup With Barley; Roots; The Kitchen; I'm Talking About Jerusalem; Chips With Everything; Their Very Own and Golden City; The Four Seasons; The Friends; The Old Ones; The Merchant.
 TV inc: Menace.
 Films inc: The Kitchen.

WESNES, Hans: Prod-Dist. b. Berlin, Apr 12, 1950. Chmn of Lux-meta Filmveleih Dist Co. Films inc: Youth's Blues; Belcanto.

WEST, Adam (William Anderson): Act. b. 1929. Films inc: The Young Philadelphians; Robinson Crusoe on Mars; Mara of the Wilderness; Batman; The Girl Who Knew Too Much; Marriage of a Young Stockbroker; The Specialist; Partisans; Hell River; Hooper; One Dark Night; Young Lady Chatterley II; Hell Riders.
 TV inc: The Detectives; Batman; For the Love of It; I Take These Men.

WEST, Dottie: Singer-Sngwri. b. McMinnville, TN, Oct 11, 1932. e. TN Technological U. Country mus recording artist. Performed on Grand Ole Opry. Films inc: Second Fiddle to a Steel Guitar; There's a Still on the Hill.
 TV inc: Larry Gatlin and the Gatlin Bros. Band; A Country Christmas; Bob Hope's Stars Over Texas; The Christmas Legend of Nashville 1982, 1983; The Raccoons and the Lost Star (voice & song material); (Grammy-C&W voc-1964).

WEST, Timothy: Act. b. Yorkshire, England, Oct 20, 1934. Originally a recording engineer; in rep; joined Royal Shakespeare Company 1964; Dec 1979 apptd artistic controller Old Vic. Thea inc: Caught Napping; The Life of Galileo; various Shakespearean roles with RSC; Marat/Sade; The Government Inspector; Abelard and Heloise; Henry IV; Jumpers; Homecoming (dir); Great English Eccentrics; Beacham; Undisputed Monarch of the English Stage (& dir); Master Class; The War at Home; Big In Brazil.
 Films inc: The Deadly Affair; Nicholas and Alexandra; The Looking Glass War; Hedda; Agatha; The Last Bastion.
 TV inc: Joy; Horatio Bottomley; Edward VII; Hard Times; Henry VIII; Crime and Punishment; Churchill and the Generals; Masada; Murder Is Easy; Oliver Twist; Florence Nightingale.

WESTCOTT, Helen (Myrthas Helen Hickman): Act. b. Los Angeles, 1929. Former child actress. Films inc: A Midsummer Night's Dream; The New Adventures of Don Juan; The Gunfighter; With a Song in My Heart; The Charge at Feather River; Hot Blood; The Last Hurrah; I Love My Wife.

WESTIN, Av (Avram Robert Westin): TV News exec. b. NYC, Jul 29, 1929. e. NYU, BA; Columbia U, MA. Started 1950 as wri, CBS News; 1951, reporter CBS; 1953 news edtr CBS; 1955, dir; 1958, prod-dir; 1961 CBS news prod in Europe; 1965 exec prod CBS News; 1967 exec prod-dir Columbia Broadcast Lab; 1968 dir Public Broadcast Lab; 1969, exec prod ABC news; 1973vp news docs; 1977 vp news; 1979 vp pgm dvlpt, exec prod World News Tonight.
 TV inc: The Ruble War; The Arab Tide; Jordan--Key to the Middle East; Moonshot; Where They Stand--Part 2; Hawaii--The 50th State; The Population Explosion (Emmy-wri-1960); Hungary--Five Years Later; Germany--Red Spy Target; Pres. Nixon's China Trip (Emmy-exec prod-1972); Heros and Heroin; The National Citizen Test; We Will Freeze in the Dark; The Pope and His Vatican; One On One.

WESTON, Jack: Act. b. 1915. Films inc: Stage Struck; Please Don't Eat the Daisies; All in a Night's Work; The Honeymoon Machine; The Incredible Mr Limpet; Mirage; The Cincinnati Kid; The Thomas Crown Affair; The April Fools; Cactus Flower; A New Leaf; Fuzz; Marco; Gator; The Ritz; Cuba; Can't Stop the Music; The Four Seasons; High Road to China.
 TV inc: Rod Browning of the Rocket Rangers; The Four Seasons; numerous segs.

Bway inc: Season in the Sun; South Pacific; Crazy October; The Ritz; California Suite; Cheaters; Break A Leg; The Floating Light Bulb.

WESTON, Jay: Prod. b. NYC, Mar 9, 1929. e. NYU, BA. Former publicist. In 1967, prod exec, Palomar-ABC Pictures; p Jay Weston Productions Inc.
 Films inc: For Love of Ivy; Lady Sings the Blues; W.C. Fields and Me; Night of the Juggler; Chu Chu and the Philly Flash; Buddy Buddy.
 Thea inc: Does a Tiger Wear a Necktie? (co-prod.).

WESTON, Paul (ne Wetstein): Mus-Comp. b. Springfield, MA, Mar 12, 1912. e. Dartmouth, BA; Columbia. H of Jo Stafford. Arr for Rudy Vallee; Tommy Dorsey; Bob Crosby; arr-cond for top girl singers inc Connee Boswell, Lee Wiley; Ella Fitzgerald; Doris Day; Dinah Shore; Kate Smith; Sarah Vaughan; Jo Stafford; A&R dir Capitol Records when it was organized 1943; A&R dir Columbia 1950; retd to Capitol 1958; regarded as creator of mood music albums; later, with Stafford, created Jonathan and Darlene Edwards recordings (Grammy-comedy-1960).
 TV inc: The Chevy Show; The Danny Kaye Show; Jim Nabors Show.
 Comps inc: I Should Care; Day By Day; Shrimp Boats; Mr. Postman; No Other Love; Autumn in Rome; Cresent City Suite; Mass for Three Voices; Memories of Ireland.

WEXLER, Haskell: Cin. b. Chicago, 1926. e. U CA. Started as doc cinematographer. Films inc: The Living City (doc); The Savage Eye (doc); T for Tumbleweed (doc); Stakeout on Dope Street (doc); Studs Lonigan; Five Bold Women; Angel Baby; Hoodlum Priest; A Face in the Rain; America, America; The Best Man; The Loved One (& co-prod); Who's Afraid of Virginia Woolf? (Oscar-1966); In the Heat of the Night; Medium Cool (& dir); The Thomas Crown Affair; Brazil--A Report on Torture (doc); Trial of the Catonsville Nine; Interviews With Mai Lai Veterans (doc); Interview--Chile's President Allende (doc); Introduction to the Enemy (doc); American Graffiti; Underground; One Flew Over the Cuckoo's Nest; Coming Home; Bound for Glory (Oscar-1976); Days of Heaven; Second Hand Hearts; Lookin' to Get Out; Bus II (prod); The Man Who Loved Women; Latino (dir-wri).

WEXLER, Norman: Wri. b. New Bedford, MA. Aug. 16, 1926. Films inc: Joe; Serpico; Mandingo; Drum; Saturday Night Fever; Staying Alive.

WEXLER, Peter: Dsgn. b. NYC, Oct 31, 1936. e. U of MI, Yale U. NY debut as dsgn decor, costumes, light of the NY Shakespeare Festival prodn of Antony and Cleopatra, 1959. Thea inc: The Big Knife; Brecht on Brecht; The Curate's Play; Portrait of the Artist as a Young Man; The Taming of the Shrew; Abe Lincoln in Illinois; On a Clear Day You Can See Forever (tour); The Happy Time; Uncle Vanya; The Trial of the Catonsville Nine; The Trial of A Lincoln; The Web and the Rock.
 Films inc: Andy; Watch the Birdie; The Trial of the Catonsville Nine.

WEXLER, Yale: Prod-Act. b. Chicago, Feb 6, 1930. e. Carnegie Tech, BFA. B of Haskell Wexler. Thea inc: Tea and Sympathy; The Best House in Naples; Once Over Lightly (coprod); A Sound of Hunting. TV inc: You Are There; Stakeout; Time Limt.

WHEATLEY, Glenn: Mus publ. b. Nambour, Australia, Jan 23, 1948. Dir Tumbleweed Mus Pty Ltd & Antipodes Mus P/L; The Little River Band.

WHEDON, Peggy (Margaret Brunssen): TV prod. b. NYC. e. U Rochester, BA; Hunter Coll. Prod ABC Issues and Answers since 1960.

WHEELER, Hugh: Wri. b. London, 1912. e. London U. Plays inc: Big Fish, Little Fish; Look, We'e Come Through; We Have Always Lived in the Castle; A Little Night Music (Tony-book-1973); Candide (Tony-book-1974); Love for Love; Sweeney Todd (Tony-book-1979).
 Films inc: Something for Everyone; Travels with My Aunt; Cabaret; Nijinsky.
 TV inc: The Snoop Sisters; Sweeney Todd (cable).

WHELCHEL, Lisa: Act. b. Fort Worth, TX, May 29, 1963. Professional debut as Mousketeer on New Mickey Mouse Club. TV inc: The

Healer; The Facts of Life; Twirl; The Wild Women of Chastity Gulch. Films inc: The Magician of Lublin; The Double McGuffin.

WHERRETT, Richard: Thea Dir. b. Sydney, Australia, Dec 10, 1940. e. U of Sydney, BA. Dir: Lincoln Theatre Royal; Manchester Library Theatre; ADA; LAMDA, 1968-70; asso dir: Old Tote Theatre, 1970-72; co-artistic dir Nimrod Theatre, 1974-78. Thea inc: The Cobra; A Jubilee (Shorts At The Wharf II).

WHITAKER, Jack: Sportscaster. b. Philadelphia, May 18, 1924. Started in radio 1947. In 1961 took over as host of CBS Sports Spectacular. Also host announcer on horse-racing programs and golf tournaments. (Emmy-Sports personality-1978).

WHITE, Betty: Act. b. Oak Park, IL, Jan 17, 1924. W of the late Allen Ludden. Began on radio in Blondie; The Great Gildersleeve; This is Your FBI. Moved into TV with live local show, LA.
　　TV inc: Life With Elisabeth (Emmy-female personality-1953); Tonight Show; Mary Tyler Moore Show (Emmys-supp-1975, 1976); The Pet Set; annual Rose Parade; Macy's Thanksgiving Parade; The Betty White Show; The Best Place to Be; The Gossip Columnist; Stephanie. Bob Hope's Stand Up and Cheer For the National Football League's 60th Year; Eunice; Shape of Things; Just Men (Emmy-Host-1983); Mama's Family.

WHITE, Joan: Act-Prod-Dir. b. ALexandria, Egypt, Dec 3, 1909. e. RADA. London stage debut, 1931, in Betrayal. Thea inc: The Black Eye: The Luck of the Devil; Junior Miss; Ten Shilling Doll; The Romantic Young Lady; A London Actress; The Happiest Days of Your Life; The Cocktail Party; The School for Scandal; Love's Labours Lost.
　　TV inc: The Citadel; Vanity Fair; The Invincible Mr Disraeli.

WHITE, Jules J.: Prod-Dir. b. Budapest, Hungary, Sep 17, 1900. Started as child actor, then edtr, cin. Prod-dir-cowri of more than 700 shorts while under contract MGM 1922-1933; Columbia 1933-1959. Prod approx 200 Three Stooges shorts and two-reel series starring Billie Burke; Buster Keaton; Harry Langdon; Bert Wheeler; Leon Errol; Chester Conklin; Pete Smith; co-dir Keaton feature Sidewalks of New York; dir Three Stooges feature Stop Look and Laugh.
　　TV inc: Oh, Those Bells (co-prod).
　　(Died April 30, 1985).

WHITE, Lawrence R. (Larry): Prod. b. 1926. e. Syracuse, U. Started with Dumont TV in 1948 as prod-dir; 1951 Benton & Bowles dir pgmg; 1959 vp daytime pgmg CBS-TV; 1963 dir pgm dvlpt; 1965 vp daytime pgms NBC-TV; 1969 vp pgms east coast; 1972 vp pgms; 1972 into ind prodn for Col Pictures-TV; 1976 vp Col Pictures-TV; 1978, Pres; 1980 resd to return to ind prod; TV inc: (exec prod) Goliath Awaits; The Blue and the Gray; The Master of Ballantrae; The First Olympics--Athens 1896.

WHITE, Maurice: Singer-Mus. b. Chicago, Dec 19, 1941. Founder, lead voc, percussionist Earth, Wind and Fire. See group listing.
　　(Grammy-(in addition to group awards)-arr accomp voc-1978).

WHITE, Michael Simon: Prod. b. Scotland, Jan 16, 1936. e. Sorbonne. Thea inc: The Connection; The Secret of the World; The Scatterin'; Jungle of the Cities; The Voices of Shem; Cambridge Circus; Saint's Day; Saturday Night and Sunday Morning; Hogan's Goat; Sleuth (Tony-1971); A Doll's House; The Championship Season; Too True to be Good; The Chairman; Carte Blanche; Annie; Censored Scenes from King Kong; Pass The Butler; Good; Pirates of Penzance; The Understanding; Top People.
　　Films inc: Moviemakers; Monty Python and the Holy Grail; The Rocky Horror Picture Show; Polyester; Shock Treatment; Urgh! A Music War (doc); Stranger's Kiss (exec prod).

WHITE, Miles: Cos Dsgn. b. Oakland, CA, Jul 27, 1914. Thea inc: Right This Way; Best Foot Forward; The Pirate; Ziegfeld Follies; Oklahoma!; Bloomer Girl: Carousel; The Duchess of Malfi; High Button Shoes; Gentlemen Prefer Blondes; Bless You All (Tony-1951); Pal Joey; Hazel Flagg (Tony-1953); The Girl in Pink Tights; Strip for Action; Oh Captain; Bye, Bye Birdie; The Unsinkable Molly Brown; Song of Norway; A Quarter for the Ladies Room; Sleeping Beauty (American Ballet Theatre).

Films inc: Up in Arms; The Kid from Brooklyn; The Greatest Show on Earth; There's No Business Like Show Business; Around the World in 80 Days.

WHITE, Onna: Chor. b. Nova Scotia, Canada. Films inc: The Music Man; Bye Bye Birdie; Oliver (Special Oscar-1968); 1776; The Great Waltz; Mame; Pete's Dragon.
　　Bway inc: Carmen Jones; The Music Man; Take Me Along; Irma La Douce; Gantry; Girls; Gigi; Goodtime Charley; I Love My Wife; Working.

WHITE, Peter: Act. e. Northwestern U, Yale Drama School. Bway inc: The Boys in the Band; P.S. Your Cat is Dead. Films inc: The Boys in the Band. TV inc: Another World; Secret Storm; The Nurses; Love Is A Many Splendored Thing; All My Children.

WHITE, Theodore H.: Wri. b. Boston, MA, May 6, 1915. e. Harvard, AB. China Bureau Time Mag 1939-1945; edtr New Republic Magazine; author of books The Making of the President.
　　TV inc: The Making of the President 1960 (Emmy-1964); China-The Roots of Madness (Emmy-1977); America In Search of Itself; Television and the Presidency (& commentator).

WHITEHEAD, Robert: Prod. b. Montreal, Mar 3, 1916. e. Trinity Coll. Thea inc: Medea; Crime and Punishment; Desire Under the Elms; Mrs McThing; Golden Boy; Four Saints in Three Acts; The Time of the Cuckoo; The Remarkable Mr Pennypacker; The Confidential Clerk; Bus Stop; Separate Tables; The Waltz of the Toreadors; A Hole in the Head; Orpheus Descending; The Visit; A Touch of the Poet; A Man for All Seasons (Tony-1962); The Changeling; The Prime of Miss Jean Brodie; Sheep on the Runway; The Creation of the World and Other Business; A Matter of Gravity; 1600 Pennsylvania Avenue; Bedroom Farce; Betrayal; Lunch Hour; The West Side Waltz; Medea (dir); Death of a Salesman (Tony-1984).
　　TV inc: The Skin of Our Teeth.

WHITELAW, Arthur: Prod. Thea inc: Best Foot Forward; Cabin in the Sky; A Woman and the Blues; You're a Good Man, Charlie Brown; Butterflies Are Free; Minnie's Boys; 70, Girls, 70; Children! Children!; Thoughts; Snoopy!!! (& dir); Blockheads (& dir-wri).

WHITELAW, Billie: Act. b. Coventry, England, Jun 6, 1932. London debut, 1956, Hotel Paradiso. On screen from 1955 in No Love for Johnnie; Mr. Topaze; Hell Is a City; Payroll; Charlie Bubbles; The Adding Machine; Twisted Nerve; Start the Revolution; Without Me; Leo the Last; Eagle in a Cage; Gumshoe; Frenzy; Nightwatch; The Omen; Leopard in the Snow; The Water Babies; An Unsuitable Job For A Woman; The Dark Crystal (voice); Slayground The Chain.
　　Thea inc: Progress to the Park; A Touch of the Poet; Othello; Trelawney of the Wells; After Haggerty; Not I; Alphabetical Order; Footfalls; The Greeks; Happy Days; Passion Play.
　　TV inc: No Trains to Lime Street; Lady of the Camelias; Resurrection; The Pity of it All; You and Me; A World of Time; Dr. Jekyll and Mr. Hyde; Poet Game; Wessex Tales; The Fifty Pound Note; Private Schultz; Camille; Jamaica Inn.

WHITLOCK, Albert: Special effects. b. London, 1915. Started in British film industry, 1929. Painted signs, scenery, ran errands. One of 1st assignments at age 19 was painting all the signs for Alfred Hitchcock's The 39 Steps. Came to US in 1954. Worked for Walt Disney Studios; designed the titles for 20,000 Leagues Under the Sea. Left Disney 1961 to freelance.
　　Films inc: The Birds; Marnie; Ship of Fools; Torn Curtain; Tobruk; Diamonds Are Forever; Frenzy; Earthquake (Oscar-1974); The Hindenburg (Oscar-1975); Bound for Glory; Airport '77; The Car; MacArthur; The Last Remake of Beau Geste; High Anxiety; The Thing; Greystoke--The Legend of Tarzan, Lord of the Apes; Dune.

WHITMAN, Stuart: Act. b. San Francisco, Feb 1, 1936. Films inc: When Worlds Collide; The Day the Earth Stood Still; China Doll; Johnny Trouble; Hell Bound; No Sleep 'Till Dawn; Ten North Frederick; Three Thousand Hills; The Deck Ran Red; The Sound and the Fury; The Story of Ruth; Murder, Inc.; Francis of Assisi; The Fiercest Heart; The Mark; The Comancheros; Reprieve; The Day and the Hour; Signpost to Murder; Rio Conchos; Last Escape; Last Generation; Night of the Lepus; Crazy Mama; Call Him Shatter; Las Vegas Lady;

Strange Shadows in an Empty Room; The White Buffalo; Maniac; Woman From the Torrid Land; Run for the Roses; Guyana-Cult of the Damned; Cuba Crossing; The Monster Club; Butterfly; Demonoid; The Delta Fox; Deadly Intruder; El Tesoro del Amazones (The Treasure Of The Amazon).

TV inc: The Crowd Pleaser; Highway Patrol; Dr. Christian; Hangman's Noose; Women in White; The Last Convertible; The Seekers; Condominium.

WHITMORE, James: Act. b. White Plains, NY, Oct 1, 1921. e. Yale U. Bway debut 1947 Command Decision. On screen from 1949. Films inc: The Undercover Man; The Asphalt Jungle; Kiss Me, Kate; Across the Wide Missouri; Battle Cry; The McConnell Story; Oklahoma; Planet of the Apes; Madigan; Give 'Em Hell, Harry; The Split; The Harrad Experiment; Bully; The First Deadly Sin; Mark Twain.

TV inc: The Law and Mr. Jones; Give 'Em Hell, Harry; The Word; The Golden Honeymoon; Mark, I Love You; Rage; Parade of Stars; Celebrity.

Thea inc: Give 'Em Hell, Harry; Will Rogers, USA; Almost an Eagle; Kraft All-Star Salute To Ford's Theatre.

(Special Tony-1948*).*

WHITTINGHILL, Dick: Act. b. Helena, MT, Mar 5, 1913. e. U of MT. Founded the Pied Pipers, singing group featured with Tommy Dorsey Band, in 1936. Spent more than 25 years as deejay with radio KMPC, Los Angeles. Appeared in more than 59 films, also in numerous TV segs. Retired from KMPC in 1979; 1982, KPRZ.

WIARD, William: Dir. TV inc: Scott Free; Ski Lift to Death; The Girl, The Gold Watch and Everything; Key Tortuga; The Seal; Fantasies; Help Wanted--Male; Deadly Lesson; Kicks.

Film inc: Tom Horn.

WICKES, Mary (Mary Isabelle Wickenhauser): Act. b. St Louis, Jun 13. e. WA U, BA. Films inc: The Man Who Came to Dinner; Now Voyager; My Kingdom for a Cook; Higher and Higher; Anna Lucasta; The Petty Girl; On Moonlight Bay; The Story of Will Rogers; By the Light of the Silvery Moon; White Christmas; Good Morning, Miss Dove; Don't Go Near the Water; The Music Man; Fate Is the Hunter; How to Murder Your Wife; The Trouble with Angela; Where Angels Go, Trouble Follows; Snowball Express; Touched By Love.

TV inc: Doc; Dennis the Menace; Mary Poppins; Make Room for Daddy; Julia; The Halls of Ivy; Annette; Willa; First The Egg.

Thea inc: The Farmer Takes a Wife; Stage Door; The Cat and the Canary; The Constant Nymph; The Good Fairy; You Can't Take It With You; The Man Who Came to Dinner; Wonderful Town; The Great Sebastian; Oklahoma! (rev).

WICKI, Bernhard: Act-Dir. b. St Polten, Switzerland, Oct 18, 1919. e. Academy of Fine Arts, Vienna. Films inc: (act) The Last Bridge; Kinder, Mutter und ein General; Jackboot Mutiny; The Face of the Cat; La Notte; Despair; (dir) The Bridge; The Miracle of Malachias; The Longest Day; The Visit; Morituri; The False Weight; The Career of Mr Karpf; The Left Handed Woman; The Conquest of the Citadel; Domino; Fruehlingssinfonie (Spring Symphony) (act); Eine Liebe in Deutschland (A Love in Germany) (act); Paris, Texas (act); Bereg (River Bank) (act); Die Grunstein-Variante (Grunstein's Clever Move) (dir-wri); La Diagonale du Fou (Dangerous Moves) (act).

TV inc: The Mysterious Stranger (act).

WIDENER, Don: Wri-Prod. b. Holdenville, OK, Mar 13, 1930. e. Compton Coll. TV inc: Slow Guillotine (doc); A Sea of Trouble (doc); Timetable for Disaster (doc); Power and the People (doc); Plutonium; Element of Risk.

WIDERBERG, Bo: Dir-Wri. b. Sweden, 1930. Films inc: Raven's End; Karleck; Thirty Times Your Money; Elvira Madigan; Adalen 31; The Ballad of Joe Hill; The Man on the Roof; Victoria; Mannen Fran Mallorca (The Man From Mallorca) (& edtr).

WIDMARK, Richard: Act. b. Sunrise, MI, Dec 26, 1914. e. Lake Forest U. Started on radio. Bway debut Kiss and Tell. Screen debut, 1947, Kiss of Death.

Films inc: Street With No Name; Slattery's Hurricane; Yellow Sky; Halls of Montezuma; Panic in the Streets; Destination Gobi; Warlock; The Long Ships; Madigan; The Alamo; How the West Was Won;

Broken Lance; Judgement at Nuremberg; Death of a Gunfighter; Murder on the Orient Express; To The Devil A Daughter; The Sellout; Twilight's Last Gleaming; The Domino Principle; Roller Coaster; Coma; The Swarm; Bear Island; Hanky Panky; Who Dares Wins; National Lampoon Goes to the Movies; Against All Odds; Blackout.

TV inc: The Last Day; Madigan; Mr. Horn; All God's Children; A Whale for the Killing.

WIENER, Jack: Prod. b. Paris, Jun 8, 1926. Started as U.S. field publicist with MGM; 1956 to Paris as continental pub mgr Col; 1966 vp Col Int'l; 1968 continental prodn exec; 1970 vp Col Pictures Corp; 1970 became ind prod. Films inc: Vampire; The Eagle Has Landed; Escape To Athena; Green Ice.

WIESEN, Bernard: Prod-Dir. b. NYC, Oct 6, 1922. e. CCNY, BBA. Films inc: (asst dir) The King and I; The Left Hand of God; The Rains of Ranchipur; To Catch a Thief; The Trouble with Harry; (prod & dir); Fear No More. TV inc: Executive Suite; The Jimmy Stewart Show; Julia; Valentine's Day; Three on an Island; Cap'n Ahab; Sally and Sam. Plays inc: (co-prod) Tribute to the Lunts; First Monday in October. (Dir): Under the Yum Yum Tree; Toys in the Attic; Trojan Woman; Once Upon a Christmas.

WIEST, Dianne: Act. b. Kansas City, MO. Worked with American Shakespeare Company; Long Wharf Theatre; Arena Stage Theatre; Joseph Papp's Public Theatre. Thea inc: The Art of Dining; Other Places. Bway inc: Othello; Frankenstein; Beyond Therapy.

Films inc: It's My Turn; I'm Dancin as Fast As I Can; Independence Day; Footloose; Falling In Love; The Purple Rose Of Cairo.

TV inc: Zalman or the Madness of God; Out of Our Father's House; The Wall; The Face of Rage.

WIGAN, Gareth: Exec. b. London, England, Dec 2, 1931. e. Oxford. Agent, MCA London, 1957; 1960 with John Redway & Asso; 1961 co-founder, agent Gregson & Wigan Ltd; 1968, co-founder, agent London International; 1970 became ind prod; 1975, VP Crea Aff Fox; 1976, VP Prodn; 1979 left Fox with Alan Ladd Jr to become VP The Ladd Company; resd Nov 1, 1983. Films inc: Unman Wittering & Zigo; Running Scared; Divorce His, Divorce Hers; Ghost in the Noonday Sun (made in 1973).

WILBUR, Richard: Lyr-Poet. b. NYC, Mar 1, 1921. e. Amherst Coll, Harvard U. Wrote lyrics for Leonard Bernstein's operetta Candide. Thea inc: translations of most of Moliere's plays. Books of poetry inc: Things of This World *(Pulitzer Prize*-1956) TV inc: Tartuffe.

WILCOX, Larry: Act. b. San Diego, CA, Aug 8. TV inc: Lassie; Police Story; Death Stalk; Sorority Kill; CHiPs; The Raid on Coffeyville; The Last Ride of the Dalton Gang; The Love Tapes; Death of A Centerfold-The Dorothy Stratten Story (Exec prod); Deadly Lesson; The Dirty Dozen--The Next Mission.

WILCOXON, Henry: Act-Prod. b. British West Indies, Sep 8, 1905. On London stage from 1925. Films inc: The Perfect Lady; The Flying Squad; Cleopatra; The Crusades; The Last of the Mohicans; Mrs Miniver; Samson and Delilah; Scaramouche; The Greatest Show on Earth; The Ten Commandments (& coprod); The Buccaneer (& prod); The Private Navy of Sergeant O'Farrell; Man in the Wilderness; Against a Crooked Sky; Pony Express Rider; F.I.S.T.; The Man with Bogart's Face; Caddyshack; Sweet Sixteen.

TV inc: When Every Day was the 4th of July; Married; The Two Worlds of Jennie Logan.

(Died Mar 6, 1984).

WILD, Jack: Act. b. England, 1952. Films inc: Oliver!; Pufnstuf; Melody; Flight of the Doves; The Pied Piper; The Fourteen.

TV inc: Pufnstuf; Our Mutual Friend; The Government Inspector.

WILDE, Cornel: Act-Prod-Dir-Wri. b. NYC, Oct 13, 1915. e. CCNY, Columbia Coll of Physicians. Films inc: Lady with Red Hair; High Sierra; The Perfect Snob; Wintertime; A Song to Remember; A Thousand and One Nights; The Bandit of Sherwood Forest; The Homestretch; Centennial Summer; Forever Amber; Two Flags West; The Greatest Show on Earth; Walls of Jericho; Woman's World; Storm Fear (& prod-dir); The Devil's Hairpin (& prod-dir-co-wri); The Naked Prey (& prod-dir); Beach Red (& prod-dir, co-wri sp); No Blade of

Grass (prod-dir-sp); Shark's Treasure (& prod-dir-sp); The Norsemen; The Fifth Musketeer; Flesh And Bullets.
TV inc: Gargoyles.

WILDER, Billy: Prod-Dir-Wri. b. Austria, Jun 22, 1906. Worked as reporter, Vienna, Berlin; then turned to screen writing. To Hollywood, 1934. Films inc: Bluebeard's Eighth Wife; Ninotchka; Arise My Love; Hold Back the Dawn; Ball of Fire; The Major and the Minor; Five Graves to Cairo; Double Indemnity; The Emperor Waltz; A Foreign Affair; Lost Weekend (2 Oscars-sp & dir-1945); Sunset Boulevard (Oscar-story and sp-1950); The Big Carnival; Stalag 17; Sabrina; Love in the Afternoon; Some Like It Hot; The Apartment (3 Oscars-sp-dir-prod-1960); One, Two, Three; Irma La Douce; Seven Year Itch; Spirit of St. Louis; Witness for the Prosecution; The Fortune Cookie; The Private Lives of Sherlock Holmes; Avanti; The Front Page; Fedora; Portrait of a 60% Perfect Man (doc on Wilder); Buddy Buddy.

WILDER, Clinton: Prod. b. Irvine, PA, Jul 7, 1920. e. Princeton U, BA. Stage mgr for Arthur Laurents' Heartsong 1947; A Streetcar Named Desire; since then prod or co-prod following plays: Regina; The Tender Trap; Six Characters in Search of an Author; A Visit to a Small Planet; The World of Suzie Wong; The American Dream; Bartleby; The Death of Bessie Smith; Gallows Humor; Happy Days; Who's Afraid of Virginia Woolf? (Tony-1963); The American Dream; The Zoo Story; The Giant's Dance; Hunting the Jingo Bird; The Long Christmas Dinner; The Butter and Egg Man; Match Play; A Party for Divorce; A Delicate Balance; The Party on Greenwich Avenue; Johnny No Trump; How Much, How Much?; The Enclave; Seascape.

WILDER, Gene (Jerry Silberman): Act. b. Milwaukee, Jun 11, 1933. e. U of IA. Thea inc: One Flew Over the Cuckoo's Nest; The Complaisant Lover; The White House; Luv; Mother Courage.
Films inc: Bonnie and Clyde; The Producers; Start the Revolution Without Me; Quackser Fortune Has an Uncle in the Bronx; Willie Wonka and the Chocolate Factory; Everything You Always Wanted to Know About Sex; Blazing Saddles; Rhinoceros; Young Frankenstein; The Little Prince; Adventures of Sherlock Holmes Smarter Brother (& sp, dir); Silver Streak; The World's Greatest Lover (& sp, dir); The Frisco Kid; Stir Crazy; Sunday Lovers; Hanky Panky; The Woman In Red (& wri-dir).
TV in: Baryshnikov In Hollywood.

WILDER, John (Keith Magaurn): Prod. b. Tacoma, WA, 1936. e. UCLA. Child actor on radio; story ed Branded; wrote 134 episodes Peyton Place before becoming prod. TV inc: Paris 7-000; Streets of San Francisco; Most Wanted; Law of the Land; The City (& wri); Quinn Martin's Tales of the Unexpected; Centennial; The Devlin Connection (crea); The Yellow Rose (exec prod-wri).

WILDER, Yvonne: Act. b. NYC, Sep 20. e. RADA. Films inc: West Side Story; Silent Movie; High Anxiety; Bloodbrothers; Seems Like Old Times.
TV inc: Operation Petticoat; Honeyboy; Condo; The Return of Marcus Welby, M.D.
Thea inc: The Princess and the Pea; The Body Beautiful; West Side Story.

WILHITE, Thomas L.: Exec. b. Keswick, IA, Sep 18, 1952. e. IA State, BA. Started with Walt Disney Prodns in publicity dept; June 1980, named VP crea dvlpmt; Sept 1981, VP film & TV prodn; resd, Nov. 1983; Jan. 1985, formed Hyperion Entertainment.

WILKOF, Lee: Act. b. Canton, OH, Jun 25. e. Temple U, U of Cincinnati. TV inc: W.E.B.; The Girl Who Saved Our America.
Thea inc: Diary of a Scoundrel; The Last Straw; The Dybbuk.

WILLENS, Rita Jacobs: Exec. b. Chicago, Jun 13, 1927. Co-founder WFMT, Chicago; prod Gamut Productions; Shows inc: Gamut-The Great Ideas of Man; Follies of 1952; Raisins with Almonds.

WILLIAM, David (nee Williams): Act-Dir. b. London, Jun 24, 1926. e. Oxford. Thea inc: Hamlet; King John; A Man for All Seasons; Peer Gynt; Naked (dir); Queen B (dir); The Canker and the Rose (dir); Saint's Day (dir); Studies of the Nude (dir); What the Butler Saw (dir); The Way of the World (dir); Robin Red Breast; Sentenced to Life (dir).

TV inc: An Age of Kings; The Cruel Neccessity; Troubleshooters.

WILLIAMS, Andy: Act. b. Wall Lake, IA, 1930. Recording artist. Niteries. Films inc: Something in the Wind (as part of the singing Williams Brothers); I'd Rather Be Rich.
TV inc: Tonight Show (3 years); Andy Williams In Music from Shubert Alley; The Andy Williams Show (Emmy-1966); The Andy Williams Christmas Show; The Andy Williams Special; Grammy Hall of Fame; 100 Years of Golden Hits; Johnny Cash--Christmas In Scotland; Christmas A Time of Cheer and A Time For Hope; Andy Williams' Early New England Christmas (& exec prod).

WILLIAMS, Anson: Act. b. Los Angeles, Sep 25. In summer stock; later in niteries as singer. Films inc: Money Tree; Heed the Call.
TV inc: Anson Williams at Sea World; The Paul Lynde Show; Happy Days; Greatest Heroes of the Bible; Skyward (prod); All-Star Salute to Mother's Day; Lisa, Bright and Dark; Bridget Loves Bernie; Anson 'N' Lorrie; Skyward Christmas (exec prod); Little Shots (exec prod); I Married A Centerfold.

WILLIAMS, Bill (Herman Katt): Act. b. Brooklyn, 1916. e. Pratt Institute. H of Barbara Hale; F of William Katt. In vaude, stock before Hollywood. Films inc: Murder in the Blue Room; Thirty Seconds Over Tokyo; Deadline at Dawn; Till The End of Time; The Clay Pigeon; The Stratton Story; Son of Paleface; Apache Ambush; The Halliday Brand; Legion of the Doomed; Oklahoma Territory; The Scarface Mob; The Hallelujah Trail; Buckskin; Rio Lobo; The Giant Spider Invasion.

WILLIAMS, Billy: Cin. b. England, 1929. Films inc: Just Like A Woman; Billion Dollar Brain; The Magus; Women In Love; Two Gentlemen Sharing; Tam Lin; Sunday Bloody Sunday; X, Y and Z; Pope Joan; Kid Blue; Night Watch; The Exorcist (co-cin); The Wind and the Lion; Voyage of the Damned; Eagle's Wing; The Silent Partner; Saturn 3; On Golden Pond; Gandhi (Oscar-1982); The Survivors; Ordeal By Innocence.

WILLIAMS, Billy Dee: Act. b. NYC, Apr 6, 1937. Acting debut age 7, The Firebrand. Adult Broadway debut, The Cool World. Films inc: The Last Angry Man; Lady Sings the Blues; Mahogany; The Bingo Long Traveling All-Stars; Scott Joplin; The Empire Strikes Back; Nighthawks; Return of the Jedi; Marvin and Tige; Fear City. F0029
TV inc: Brian's Song; The Glass House; Mission Impossible; Mod Squad; Christmas Lilies of the Field; The Hostage Tower; Children of Divorce; Eubie Blake--A Century of Music (mc); Shooting Stars; Chiefs; A Tribute to Martin Luther King Jr.--A Celebration of Life; Time Bomb; Dynasty; Double Dare; On Top All Over The World.
Thea inc: A Taste of Honey; Hallelujah, Baby.

WILLIAMS, Cara (Bernice Kamiat): Act. b. NYC, 1925. e. Hollywood Professional School. Film inc: The Happy Land; Don Juan Quilligan; Boomerang; Something for the Boys; Meet Me In Las Vegas; Sitting Pretty; Never Steal Anything Small; The Girl Next Door; The Defiant Ones; The Man From the Diner's Club; The White Buffalo; Doctor's Wives.
TV inc: Pete and Gladys; The Cara Williams Shows; In Security (cable).

WILLIAMS, Cindy: Act. b. Van Nuys, CA, Aug 22, 1948. Beware the Blob; Drive, He Said; American Graffiti; Travels with My Aunt; The Conversation; More American Graffiti; The Creature Wasn't Nice; Uforia.
TV inc: Room 222; Nanny and the Professor; Suddenly, Love; Donny and Marie Christmas Special; All-Star Salute to Mother's Day; When Dreams Come True; Joanna.

WILLIAMS, Clarence III: Act. b. NYC, Aug 21, 1939. Thea inc: The Long Dream; Walk in Darkness; Sarah and the Sax; Slow Dance on the Killing Ground; The Great Indoors; The Party on Greenwich Avenue; King John; Suspenders; Night and Day.
TV inc: Mod Squad; Return of the Mod Squad; The House of Dies Drear.
Films inc: Purple Rain.

WILLIAMS, Clifford: Dir. b. Wales, Dec 30, 1926. Originally act; founder Mime Theatre Company. London thea (as dir) inc: Yerma; Radio Rescue; Quartet for Five; The Marriage of Mr. Mississippi; A

Moon for the Misbegotten; joined Royal Shakespeare Company 1961, appointed asso dir 1963; Afore Night Come; Comedy of Errors; The Tempest; The Representative; The Merchant of Venice; Our Man Crichton; The Flying Dutchman; The Meteor; Sleuth (& Bway); Major Barbara; The Taming of the Shrew; Murderer; Mouth Organ (& co-devised); Too True to Be Good; Carte Blanche; Wild Oats; Stevie; The Passion of Dracula; Three Penny Opera; Born in the Gardens; Overheard; The Love Girl and the Innocent; Pack of Lies; Aren't We All.

WILLIAMS, Darnell: Act. b. London, England, Mar. 3. e. Los Angeles City College. Thea inc: The Care and Feeding of Lenny Drover; Toyland; Helen; Reach for the Sky; Your Arms Too Short to Box With God.

TV inc: Rich Man, Poor Man; Sammy & Company; The White Shadow; All My Children (Emmy-supp-1983).

WILLIAMS, Elmo: Film Edtr-Prod. b. Oklahoma City, OK, Apr 30, 1914. Worked as film edtr British & Dominion Studios; RKO. VP wldwde prodn Fox 1971; P Ibex films 1974; 1981, P, Gaylord Prodns.

Films inc: High Noon (Oscar-edit-1952); The Tall Texan (& dir); The Cowboy (& prod-dir); 20,000 Leagues Under The Sea; Apache Kid (dir); The Vikings; The Big Gamble. (Asso prod) The Longest Day. (Prod) Tora! Tora! Tora!; Sidewinder One; Caravans. (Exec prod) Those Magnificent Men in Their Flying Machines; The Blue Max; Zorba the Greek; Man, Woman and Child.

Thea inc (London) Marilyn!

WILLIAMS, Emlyn: Wri-Dir-Act. b. Mostyn, Flintshire, Wales, Nov 26, 1905. e. Oxford. On stage since 1927. Thea inc: (act) And So to Bed; The Pocket-Money Husband; Glamour; Night Must Fall; He Was Born Gay; Bleak House; A Boy Growing Up; The Deputy; A Month In the Country; Emlyn Williams, As Charles Dickens (& dir). Plays inc: Full Moon; The Late Christopher Bean; Vessels Departing; The Corn Is Green; The Wind of Heaven; Spring 1600; Trespass; Accolade; Beth; Dylan Thomas Growing Up. Dir many of his own plays.

Films inc: (act) The Case of the Frightened Lady; Men of Tomorrow; Friday the Thirteenth; Sally Bishop; Broken Blossoms; The Citadel;The Stars Look Down; Major Barbara; Hatter's Castle; The Last Days of Dolwyn (& sp-dir); Three Husbands; Ivanhoe; The Deep Blue Sea; I Accuse; Beyond This Place; The L-Shaped Room; Eye of the Devil; The Walking Stick; David Copperfield.

TV inc: The Deadly Game (cable).

WILLIAMS, Esther: Act. b. Los Angeles, Aug 8, 1923. e. USC. Professional swimmer, appeared in Aquacade, SF World's Fair; professional model before act. Screen debut 1942 Andy Hardy Steps Out. Films inc: A Guy Named Joe; Bathing Beauty; The Thrill of A Romance; This Time for Keeps; Ziegfeld Follies; Easy to Wed; Fiesta; Hoodlum Saint; On an Island With You; Neptune's Daughter; Pagan Love Song; Duchess of Idaho; Texas Carnival; Skirts, Ahoy!; Million Dollar Mermaid; Dangerous When Wet; Easy to Love; Jupiter's Darling; The Big Show.

TV inc: Olympic Gala.

WILLIAMS, JoBeth: Act. b. Houston, TX, 1953. e. Brown U. Thea inc: Moonchildren; The Daughters In Law; A Couple White Chicks Sittin' Around Talkin'; Lydie Breeze.

Films inc: Kramer vs; Kramer; Stir Crazy; The Dogs of War; Poltergeist; Endangered Species. The Big Chill; Teachers; American Dreamers.

TV inc: Somerset; Guiding Light; Fun and Games; Feasting With Panthers; Jabberwocky; The Big Black Pill; Joe Dancer; Adam; The Day After; Kids Don't Tell.

WILLIAMS, John: Act. b. Chalfont St Giles, Bucks, England, Apr 15, 1903. e. Lansing Coll. Films inc: Next of Kin; A Woman's Vengeance; Dial M for Murder; Sabrina Fair; To Catch a Thief; The Solid Gold Cadillac; Island in the Sun; Witness for the Prosecution; Visit to a Small Planet; The Secret War of Harry Frigg; A Flea in Her Ear; Coming Home; Hot Lead and Cold Feet; The Swarm.

TV inc: The Hound of the Baskervilles.

Thea inc: Numerous perf dating back to 1916; recent perfs inc: The Velvet Glove; Venus Observed; Dial M for Murder (Tony-supp-1953); The Dark Is Light Enough; The Chinese Prime Minster;

Hay Fever.

(Died May 5, 1983).

WILLIAMS, John T.: Comp. b. NYC, Feb 8, 1932. e. UCLA, Juilliard. Succeeded late Arthur Fiedler as conductor of Boston Pops, Jan 1980, resd June 1984, but retd two months later.Film scores inc: I Passed for White; Diamond Head; Gidget Goes to Rome; John Goldfarb Please Come Home; The Rare Breed; The Plainsman; Not With My Wife You Don't; A Guide for the Married Man; Valley of the Dolls; Goodbye Mr Chips; The Reivers; Fiddler on the Roof (Oscar-1971); Images; The Poseidon Adventure; The Paper Chase; The Sugarland Express; Earthquake; The Towering Inferno; Jaws (Oscar-1975); Family Plot; Midway; Black Sunday; Star Wars (Oscar-1977); Close Encounters of the Third Kind; The Fury; Jaws II; Meteor; Quintet; Superman; Dracula; 1941; The Empire Strikes Back; Raiders of the Lost Ark; E.T. The ExtraTerrestrial (Oscar-1982); Yes, Giorgio; Monsignor; Return of the Jedi; Indiana Jones and the Temple of Doom; The River.

TV inc: Once Upon a Savage Night; Sergeant Ryker; Heidi (Emmy-1969); Jane Eyre (Emmy-1972); Great Movie Stunts-Raiders of the Lost Ark; Heartbeeps; Movie Blockbusters! The 15 Greatest Hits of All Time; he 23d Olympiad; Kennedy Center Honors 1984.

(Grammys-(13)-original score film-1975, 1977, 1979; 1980, 1981, 1982; arrangement on Inst-1982). soundtrack album-1978; 1980; pop inst perf-1977; inst comp-1977, 1978, 1979).

WILLIAMS, Lenny: Act-Sngwri. b. Little Rock, AR, 1945. Recording artist.

WILLIAMS, Mason: Comp-Mus-Wri. b. Abilene, TX, 1938. TV inc: (wri) Smothers Brothers Show (Emmy-1968); Andy Williams Show; Petula Clark Show; Glen Campbell Show; Pat Paulsen Show; Tom and Dick Smothers Brothers Special I; Adam (act).

Comp: Classical Gas (Grammys-inst theme, contemp inst perf-1968). Recs inc: Mason Williams Phonograph Record; Ear Show; Music; Hand Made; Share Pickers; Fresh Fish.

WILLIAMS, Michael George: Prod. b. London, Sep 8, 1938. Member Queensland Film Corp; consultant, Australian Film TV School. Films inc: Final Cut.

WILLIAMS, Patrick: Comp. b. Bonne Terre, MO, Apr 23, 1939. e. Duke U, BA. Films inc: The One and Only; Casey's Shadow; The Cheap Detective; Cuba; Breaking Away; Butch and Sundance--The Early Years; Hero At Large; Used Cars; Wholly Moses; It's My Turn; Charlie Chan and the Curse of the Dragon Queen; Some Kind of Hero; The Toy; Marvin And Tige; Two Of A Kind; The Buddy System; All Of Me; Best Defense; The Slugger's Wife.

TV inc: Bob Newhart Show; Streets of San Francisco; The Mary Tyler Moore Show; Lou Grant (Emmy-1980); The Two Of Us; Stephanie; The Miracle of Kathy Miller; The Princess and the Cabbie (Emmy-1982); Maggie; Tomorrow's Child; Family In Blue; The Devlin Connection; The Fighter; A Girl's Life; Mr. Smith; Empire; Walter; Fathers And Sons; Seduced.

WILLIAMS, Paul Lyr-comp-act. b. Omaha, NE., Sept. 19, 1940. Began as set painter and stunt parachutist. Played bit and character parts in commercials. Seen briefly in The Chase and The Loved One. Became songwri, collaborating briefly with Biff Ross and later with Roger Nichols.

Songs inc: You're So Nice To Be Around; We've Only Just Begun; Rainy Days and Monday; Just An Old Fashioned Love Song; Evergreen (Oscar-1976; Grammy-1976).

Films inc: Cinderella Liberty (score); Phantom of the Paradise (score & act); Bugsy Malone (score); A Star Is Born (score); Smokey and the Bandit (act); One on One (score); The Cheap Detective (act); The End (score); Grease (title song); Agatha (score); The Muppet Movie (act); Stone Cold Dead (act); Smokey and the Bandit II (act); Smokey and the Bandit Part 3 (act).

TV inc: The Wild Wild West Revisited (act); Emmet Otter's Jug-Band Christmas (mus-lyr); The Fall Guy (act); We Dare You (act); Rooster (act-wri); It Takes Two (song); A Concert of the World (host); The Night They Saved Christmas (act & songs).

Thea inc: (London) Bugsy Malone.

WILLIAMS, Robin: Act. b. Chicago, IL, Jul 21. Performed in niteries.

TV inc: Laugh In; The Great American Laugh Off; Ninety Minutes Live; The Alan Hamel Show; Mork & Mindy; The Billy Crystal Comedy Hour; I Love Liberty; E.T. & Friends--Magical Movie Visitors.

Films inc: The Last Laugh; Popeye; The World According to Garp; The Survivors; Moscow on the Hudson. (Grammy-comedy rec-1979).

WILLIAMS, Roger: Pianist. b. Omaha, NE, 1926. e. Drake U, ID State Coll. Public debut on TV's Arthur Godfrey Talent Scout and Chance of a Lifetime. Other TV appearances inc: Ed Sullivan; Hollywood Palace; Kraft Summer Series; Celanese Special. Tours in addition to US: Australia; Japan; Mexico; South Africa. Recording artist. Guest artist several films.

WILLIAMS, Simon: Act. b. London, England. Thea inc: (London) A Friend Indeed; The Last of Mrs. Cheyney; Underground (dir).

Films inc: The Fiendish Plot of Dr. Fu Manchu.

TV inc: His, Hers and Theirs; Upstairs, Downstairs; Return of the Man From U.N.C.L.E.

WILLIAMS, Tennessee (Thomas Lanier Williams): Plywri. b. Columbus, MI, Mar 26, 1914. e. U of MO, 1931-33; WA U, St. Louis, 1936-37; U of IA, AB, 1938. Plays inc: Battle of Angels; The Glass Menagerie; You Touched Me; Streetcar Named Desire (Pulitzer Prize-1948); Cat On a Hot Tin Roof (Pulitzer Prize-1955); Camino Real; Summer and Smoke; Rose Tattoo (Tony-1951); Orpheus Descending; Sweet Bird of Youth; Period of Adjustment; Small Craft Warnings; Red Devil Battery Sign; Vieux Carre.

Films inc: The Glass Menagerie; Streetcar Named Desire; Baby Doll; Rose Tattoo; Night of the Iguana.

TV inc: The Kennedy Center Honors: A Celebration of the Performing Arts.

(Died Feb. 25, 1983).

WILLIAMS, Tex: Act-Sngwri. b. Ramsey, Fayette County, IL, Aug 23, 1917. C&W recording artist. Formed band, The Western Caravan, in 1946; toured US, appeared with Grand Ole Opry; various TV shows.

WILLIAMS, Tony: Dir-Prod. b. New Zealand, May 31, 1942. e. Victoria U. TV inc: Freedom; Deciding; Rally; Getting Together; Lost in the Garden of the World; Solo (co-prod, co-wri).

WILLIAMS, Treat: Act. Bway inc: Over Here!; Grease; Danny Zuko; The Pirates of Penzance.

Films inc: The Ritz; The Eagle Has Landed; Hair; Why Would I Lie?; Prince of the City; The Pursuit of D.B. Cooper; Once Upon A Time In America; Flashpoint.

TV inc: James Cagney--That Yankee Doodle Dandy (Narr); Dempsey; A Streetcar Named Desire; Some Men Need Help.

WILLIAMSON, David: Wri. b. Melbourne, Australia, Feb 24, 1942. e. Melbourne U; Monash U. Plays inc: The Removalists; Don's Party; Juggler's Three; What If You Died Tomorrow; The Department; A Handful of Friends; Traveling North; Celluloid Heroes; Sons Of Cain (& dir).

Films inc: Stork; Petersen; Eliza Fraser; The Removalists; Don's Party; The Club; Gallipoli; Duet For Four; The Year of Living Dangerously; Phar Lap.

TV inc: The Department; The Last Bastion (& co-prod).

WILLIAMSON, Fred: Act. b. Gary, IN, Mar 5, 1938. Films inc: M*A*S*H; The Legend of Nigger Charley; Hammer; Black Caesar; Crazy Joe; That Man Bolt; Boss Nigger; Darktown; The Inglorious Bastards; Take a Hard Ride; No Way Back (& prod-dir-wri); Death Journey (& prod-dir); Fist of Fear, Touch of Death; One Down, Two To Go (& prod-dir); Vigilante; Blind Rage; 1990 The Bronx Warriors; The Last Fight (& wri-dir); The Big Score (& dir); I Nuovi Barbari (Warriors of the Wasteland); Vivre Pour Survivre (White Fire); Warrior Of The Lost World.

TV inc: Julia; Police Story; Monday Night Football; Half Nelson.

WILLIAMSON, Nicol: Act. b. Hamilton, Scotland, Sep 14, 1938. Joined Dundee Repertory Theatre, 1960. London debut, 1961, That's Us. On screen from 1964. Films inc: Six-Sided Triangle; The Bofors Gun; Laughter in the Dark; The Reckoning; The Jerusalem File; The Wilby Conspiracy; Robin and Marian; The Seven-Per-Cent Solution; The Cheap Detective; The Human Factor; Excalibur; Venom;

I'm Dancing As Fast As I Can; Sakharov; Return To Oz.

TV inc: Of Mice and Men; Arturo Ul; I Know What I Meant; Terrible Jim Fitch; The Word; Macbeth; Christopher Columbus.

Thea inc: Awakening; Kelly's Eye; The Ginger Man; Inadmissable Evidence; A Cuckoo In the Nest; Waiting For Godot; The Diary of a Madman; Uncle Vanya; Coriolanus; Macbeth; Twelfth Night; Rex; Macbeth (& dir).

WILLINGHAM, Calder: Wri. b. Atlanta, GA, Dec 23, 1922. e. The Citadel, U VA. Plays inc: End As A Man.

Films inc: End As A Man; Paths of Glory; The Vikings; One-Eyed Jacks; Little Big Man; The Graduate; Thieves Like Us.

WILLIS, Bob: Singer-Sngwri. b. Hall County, TX, Mar 6, 1905. C&W recording artist. Elected to Country Music Hall of Fame, 1968. Formed the Texas' Playboys, which grew from a small unit to 25 musicians. In addition to radio shows band also was featured in several movies.

WILLIS, Gordon: Cin. Films inc: End of the Road; Loving; The Landlord; Little Murders; Bad Company; Klute; Up the Sandbox; The Paper Chase; The Godfather; The Parallax View; The Godfather Part 2; All The President's Men; Sept. 30, 1955; Annie Hall; Comes a Horseman; Interiors; Manhattan; Windows (& dir); Stardust Memories; Pennies From Heaven; Zelig; The Purple Rose Of Cairo; Perfect.

TV inc: The Lost Honor of Kathryn Beck.

WILLIS, Larry: Mus. b. NYC, Dec 20, 1942. See Blood, Sweat & Tears.

WILLIS, Ted, Lord: Films inc: Holiday Camp; The Blue Lamp; It's Great to Be Young; Woman in a Dressing Gown; No Trees in the Street; Bitter Harvest.

Plays inc: Buster; No Trees in the Street; The Lady Purrs; The Blue Lamp; The Magnificent Moodies; Kid Kenyon Rides Again; Doctor in the House; Hot Summer Night; God Bless the Guvnor; Brothers-in-Law; The Eyes of Youth; Doctor at Sea; Woman in a Dressing Gown; A Slow Roll of Drums; A Murder of Crows; Queenie; A Fine Day for Murder; Dead on Saturday.

TV inc: Dixon of Dock Green; Mrs. Thursday; Crimes of Passion; Hunter's Walk; The Young and the Guilty; Strictly for Sparrows; Four Seasons of Rosie Carr; Look in any Window.

Life peerage created 1963.

WILLMAN, Noel: Dir-Act. b. Londonderry, Northern Ireland, Aug 4, 1918. Thea inc: (act) Adventure Story, Accolade, The Prisoner, Legend of Lovers, Isle of Children, The Devil's Disciple (& dir); Saint Joan. (Dir); The White Carnation; Someone Waiting; A Man For All Seasons (Tony-1961); The Lion In Winter; A Matter of Gravity; The West Side Waltz.

Films inc: (act) The Cone of Silence; Dr Zhivago;

TV inc: The Green Bay Tree; Strange Interlude; The Crucible.

WILLS, Mary: Cos Dsgn. b. Prescott, AZ, Jul 4, 1919. e. U AZ; U NM, BA; Yale Drama School, MFA. Desgd more than 60 films inc: Song of the South; Enchantment: Roseanna McCoy; My Foolish Heart; Edge of Doom; Hans Christian Anderson; Prince of Players; The Virgin Queen; Carousel; The Rains of Ranchipur; Love Me Tender; Between Heaven and Hell; Teenage Rebel; Jesse James; Hatful of Rain; The Wayward Bus; 10 North Frederick; No Down Payment; Bernardine; Sing, Boy, Sing; Fraulein; The Remarkable Mr. Pennypacker; A Certain Smile; The Diary of Anne Frank; Cape Fear; The Wonderful World of the Brothers Grimm (Oscar-1963); Camelot; Funny Girl; The Passover Plot.

TV inc: Playhouse 90; Closed Set; Barbara Stanwyck Show. Bway inc: Quick Change. Also cost for Shipstad's and Johnson's Ice Follies, 1962-1967.

WILLSON, Meredith: Comp-Lyr-Cond. b. Mason City, IA, May 18, 1902. e. Damrosch Inst. Solo flutist with John Philip Sousa Band; NY Philharmonic, mus dir western division ABC Network.

Bway inc: Music Man (Tonys-(3) musical, book, score-1958); Unsinkable Molly Brown; Here's Love.

Films scores inc: The Great Dictator; The Little Foxes.

Songs inc: You and I; May the Good Lord Bless and Keep You; 76 Trombones.

*(Grammy-*cast album-1958).
(Died June 15, 1984).

WILSON, Daniel: Prod. b. Chicago, 1931. Started with ad agency writing, prod-dir commercials.

TV inc: Discovery; The Great Wallendas; Rookie of the Year *(Emmy-*1974); The Amazing Cosmic Awareness of Duffy Moon; The Barbara Walters Specials; Me and Dad's New Wife; Hewitt's Just Different *(Emmy-*1978); Mom and Dad Can't Hear Me; Henry Winkler Meets William Shakespeare: The Secret of Charles Dickens; New York City Too Far From Tampa Blues; The Terrible Secret; The Horrible Honchos; Little Vic; P.J. and the President's Son; The Quinns; Blind Sunday; The Sophisticated Gents; The Late Great Me--Story of a Teenage Alcoholic *(Emmy-*1980); The House at 12 Rose St; Here's Boomer; Charlie and the Great Balloon Chase; The Sophisticated Gents; Blood and Honor--Youth Under Hitler.

WILSON, Dave: Dir. TV inc: The Bob and Ray Special; The Paul Simon Special; NBC Saturday Night Live *(Emmy-*1976); Steve Martin's Best Show Ever; The News is the News; Saturday Night Live.

WILSON, Elizabeth: Act. b. Grand Rapids, MI, Apr 4, 1925. NY stage debut, 1953, Picnic. Bway inc: The Desk Set; The Tunnel of Love; Yes is for a Very Young Man; Little Murders; Sheep on the Runway; Dark of the Moon; Sticks and Bones *(Tony-*supp-1972); The Secret Affairs of Mildred Wild; Uncle Vanya; Morning's at Seven (rev); You Can't Take It With You (rev); Salonika (off-Bway).

Films inc: Little Murders; Day of the Dolphin; Man on the Swing; Nine To Five; The Ultimate Solution of Grace Quigley.

TV inc: Doc; Million Dollar Infield.

WILSON, Flip (Clerow Wilson): Act. b. Jersey City, NJ, 1933. Performed in niteries. TV inc: The Flip Wilson Show *(Emmy-*1971); Uptown-A Tribute to the Apollo Theatre; Take One; The Suzanne Somers Special; Happy Birthday, Bob; People Are Funny (host).

Films inc: Uptown Saturday Night; Skatetown USA; The Fish That Saved Pittsburgh.

WILSON, Irv: Exec. b. NYC. Sales and pgmg exec with WGN-TV, Chicago and ABC-TV, NY; agent with CMA; 1971, Pgmg VP Viacom; joined U as prod; formed Rush-Wilson Productions with Herman Rush; to 20th-Fox TV as head of drama dvlpt; 1978, VP Pgm Dvlpt Charles Fries Prodns; Jul 1979, VP Special Pgms NBC; 1980, VP Motion Pictures for TV, NBC Entertainment; Sept, 1980, Sr. VP Programs, East Coast.

TV inc: (exec prod) The Missiles of October; Honeyboy.

WILSON, Lanford: Plywri. b. Lebanon, MO, Apr 13, 1937. e. U of Chicago. Plays inc: So Long at the Fair; Home Free !; No Trespassing; Sand Castle; The Madness of Lady Bright; Ludlow Fair; Balm in Gilead; This is the Rill Speaking; Sex Is Between Two People; Wandering; The Gingham Dog; Lemon Sky; Serenading Louie; The Family Continues; Hot L Baltimore; Talley's Folly *(Pulitzer Prize-*1980) The Fifth of July.

TV inc: This is the Rill Speaking; The Sandcastle; Stoop; The Migrants.

WILSON, Nancy: Singer. b. Chillicothe, OH, Feb 20, 1931. Worked small clubs in the Columbus area, then joined Rusty Bryant band. Began recording for Capitol in 1960. Films inc: The Big Score.

*(Grammy-*R&B recording-1964).

WILSON, Richard: Prod-Dir-Wri. b. McKeesport, PA, Dec 25, 1915. e. Denver U. Started as radio act, joined Orson Welles' Mercury Theatre group, asso with all Mercury films through 1951.

Films inc: Lady From Shanghai; Macbeth; Ma and Pa Kettle on Vacation; Redhead from Wyoming; Ma and Pa Kettle at Home; Golden Blade; Man With a Gun; Ma and Pa Kettle in the Ozarks; The Big Boodle; Raw Wind in Eden; Al Capone; Pay or Die; Invitation to a Gunfighter; Three in an Attic.

WILSON, Theodore: Act. b. NYC, Dec 10, 1943. e. Florida A&M. Worked with Negro Ensemble Company, Arena Stage before Hollywood.

Films inc: The River Niger; Come Back, Charleston Blue; The Greatest.

TV inc: The Partridge Family; The Waltons; Roll Out; That's My Mama; The Sanford Arms; Irene; The Ambush Murders; Malice In Wonderland.

WINANT, Ethel (nee Wald): Exec. b. Worcester, MA, Aug 5, 1925. e. Yuba Coll; UC Berkeley, BA; Pasadena Playhouse; Whittier Coll, MTA. Casting exec on Bway; with Talent Associates; Playhouse 90; 1954, CBS casting dir West Coast; 1963, CBS VP Talent & Casting; 1975, VP pgm dvlpt & talent Childrens Television Workshop; 1978, VP talent, NBC; 1980, VP Mini-series, Novels for TV, NBC; 1981, VP crea affairs, Metromedia.

TV inc: General Electric Theatre (asso prod); The Great Adventure (prod); The Best of Families (prod).

WINCELBERG, Shimon: Wri. b. Kiel, Germany, Sep 26, 1924. e. Providence Coll. Short stories: New Yorker; Harper's Bazaar; Punch.

TV inc: Naked City; Have Gun Will Travel; Gunsmoke; Mannix; Star Trek; Police Woman.

WINCHELL, Paul: Ventriloquist. b. NYC, 1924. At 13 won first prize on Major Bowes Radio Amateur Hour. Films inc: Stop! Look! and Laugh!; Which Way to the Front?; The Fox and The Hound.

TV inc: Paul Winchell-Jerry Mahoney Show; Smurfs (voice); The Smurf Springtime Special (voice); The Smurfs' Christmas Special (voice); The Smurfic Games (voice); Smurfily Ever After (voice); TV Academy Hall Of Fame 1985.

WINDOM, William: Act. b. NYC, 1923. Films inc: To Kill a Mockingbird; Cattle King; One Man's Way; The Americanization of Emily; The Detective; The Gypsy Moths; The Man; Echoes of a Summer; Last Plane Out; Separate Ways; Grandview, U.S.A.

TV inc: My World and Welcome To It *(Emmy-*1970); Blind Ambition; Thurber; Portrait of a Rebel: Margaret Sanger; Landon, Landon and Landon. Leave 'Em Laughing; Side Show; 100 Years of Golden Hits; Quick and Quiet; Denmark Vesey's Rebellion; Desperate Lives; The Rules of Marriage; The Tom Swift & Linda Craig Mystery Hour; Why Me? Off Sides; Velvet; Dirty Work.

Thea inc: Thurber.

WINDSOR, Marie (Emily Marie Bertelsen): Act. b. Marysvale, UT, Dec 11, 1921. Films inc: Abbott & Costello Meet the Mummy; Force of Evil; Outpost in Morocco; The Beautiful Blonds from Bashful Bend; The Fighting Kentuckian; Dakota Lil; Hellfire; The Showdown; Frenchie; Little Big Horn; Two Dollar Bettor; Support Your Local Sheriff; Japanese War Bride; The Sniper; The City That Never Sleeps; Hell's Half Acre; The Bounty Hunter; No Man's Woman; The Parson & the Outlaw; The Killing; Stars in the Backyard; Island Women; Hurricane Island; Mail Order Bride; One More Train to Rob; Cahill, US Marshal; Hearts of the West; Freaky Friday; Lovely But Deadly. TV inc: Alias Smith and Jones; Hec Ramsey; Man Hunter; Barnaby Jones; Police Story; Salem's Lot.

WINFIELD, Paul: Act. b. 1941. Films inc: The Lost Man; RPM; Brother John; Sounder; Gordon's War; Conrack; Hustle; Damnation Alley; The Greatest; A Hero Ain't Nothin' But a Sandwich; Twilight's Last Gleaming; Carbon Copy; Star Trek II--The Wrath of Khan; White Dog; On the Run; Mike's Murder. Go Tell It on the Mountain; The Terminator.

TV inc: King; Backstairs at the White House; Angel City; Key Tortuga; The Sophisticated Gents; Dreams Don't Die; Sister, Sister; The Blue and The Gray; For Us, The Living.

WINGER, Debra: Act. b. Columbus, OH, May 16, 1955. Films inc: Thank God It's Friday; Urban Cowboy; French Postcards; Cannery Row; An Officer and a Gentleman; Terms of Endearment; Mike's Murder.

TV inc: Wonder Woman.

WINITSKY, Alex: Prod. b. NYC, Dec 27, 1924. e. NYU, BS, LLB, JD. Films inc: The Seven-Per-Cent Solution; Cross of Iron; End of the Game; House Calls; Silver Bears; The Lady Vanishes; Breakthrough; Cuba; Blue Skies Again; Scandalous; Swing Shift (exec prod); Irreconcilable Differences.

WINKLER, Henry: Act. b. NYC, Oct 30, 1946. e. Emerson Coll, Yale School of Drama. Yale Repertory Co; in radio; TV commercials.

Films inc: The Lords of Flatbush; Crazy Joe; Nickelodeon; Heroes; The One and Only; Night Shift; The Sure Thing (exec prod).

TV inc: The Great American Dream Machine; Masquerade; The Mary Tyler Moore Show; Rhoda; Happy Days; Laverne & Shirley; Katherine; Run, Don't Walk (exec prod); Gabe & Walker (exec prod); Joanie Loves Chachi; Starflight--The Plane That Couldn't Land (exec prod); Ryan's Four (exec prod); When Your Lover Leaves (exec prod); Donald Duck's 50th Birthday; Scandal Sheet (exec prod).

WINKLER, Irwin: Prod. b. NYC. e. NYU, BS. Films inc: Double Trouble; Point Blank; The Split; They Shoot Horses Don't They?; The Strawberry Statement; Believe in Me; The Gang That Couldn't Shoot Straight; The New Centurions; Up the Sandbox; The Mechanic; Busting; SPY's; The Gambler; Breakout; Rocky (Oscar-1976); Nickelodeon; New York, New York; Valentino; Comes A Horseman; Uncle Joe Shannon; Rocky II; Raging Bull; True Confessions; Rocky III; Author! Author!; The Right Stuff.

WINNER, Michael Robert: Prod-Dir-Wri. b. London, Oct 30, 1935. e. Cambridge U. Wrote, prod & dir docs and short films, 1955-61. Feature film inc: Man with a Gun; Shoot to Kill; Play It Cool; The Cool Mikado; The Girl Getters; You Must Be Joking; I'll Never Forget What'slsname; Hannibal Brooks; The Games; Lawman; The Nightcomers; Chato's Land; The Mechanic; Scorpio; The Stone Killer; Death Wish; Won Ton Ton, the Dog Who Saved Hollywood; The Sentinel; The Big Sleep; Firepower; Death Wish II; The Wicked Lady; Scream For Help.

WINTER, Edward: Act. b. Ventura, CA. e. U of OR. Bway inc: Cabaret; Promises, Promises; The Birthday Party; Night Watch.

TV inc: Somerset; Karen; Adam's Rib; Eleanor and Franklin; Project UFO; M*A*S*H; The Second Time Around; The Big Black Pill; Fly Away Home; The Adventures of Pollyana; Family In Blue; The 25th Man; The First Time; Empire; The Lost Honor of Kathryn Beck.

Films inc: A Change of Seasons; Porky's II--The Next Day; The Buddy System.

WINTER, Vincent: Act. b. England, 1947. Started as child actor. Films inc: The Kidnappers (Special Oscar-1954); The Dark Avenger; Time Lock; Beyond This Place; Gorgo; Greyfriars Bobby; Almost Angels; The Three Lives of Thomasina; The Horse Without a Head.

WINTERS, David (nee Weizer): Dir-Chor-Prod. b. London, Apr 5, 1939. TV inc: Dr Jekyll and Mr Hyde; The London Bridge Special; Raquel Welch Special; Once Upon a Wheel; 2 Ann-Margret Specials; The Monkees; Lucy in London; Moving with Nancy; The Big Show.

Thea inc: Of Love Remembered.

Films inc: A Star is Born (chor); The Last Horror Film (prod-dir-wri-act); Mission Kill (prod-dir).

WINTERS, Jerry: Prod-Dir. b. Waterbury, CT, Aug 18, 1917. e. Antioch Coll. Films inc: (shorts) Herman Melville's Moby Dick; Central Park; Speak to Me Child; Renoir. Specialist in preparing foreign films for US import inc Seventh Continent; The Loves of Liszt; The Lost Talisman; A Look At Liv.

WINTERS, Jonathan: Act. b. Dayton, OH, Nov 11, 1925. Deejay, Dayton, Columbus stations; niteries. On screen from 1963. Films inc: It's a Mad, Mad, Mad, Mad World; The Loved Ones; Penelope; The Russians Are Coming, The Russians Are Coming; Eight on the Lam; Oh Dad, Poor Dad, Mama's Hung You in the Closet and I'm Feeling So Sad; Viva Max!; The Fish That Saved Pittsburgh.

TV inc: Jonathan Winters Show, NBC; More Wild Wild West; Hope For President; Take One; Suzanne Somers--and 10,000 GI's!; Texaco Star Theatre Presents Bob Hope in "Who Makes The World Laugh".

WINTERS, Marian: Act-Wri. b. NYC, Apr 19, 1924. e. Brooklyn Coll. Thea inc: The Dream Girl; I Am A Camera (Tony-supp-1952); Sing Me No Lullaby; The Dark Is Light Enough; Medea; The Cherry Orchard; Nobody Loves An Albatross; Mating Dance; King John. Plays inc: Animal Keepers; A is for All; All Saint's Day; All Is Bright.

WINTERS, Roland: Act. b. Boston, MA, Nov 22, 1904. In stock cos, radio around Boston, later on West Coast before entering films. Films inc: 13 Rue Madeleine; Return of October; series of Charlie Chan films for Monogram; West Point Story; Follow the Sun; Inside Straight; She's Working Her Way Through College; Jet Pilot; So Big.

TV inc: You Can't Go Home Again.

WINTERS, Shelley (Shirley Schrift): Act. b. St Louis, MO, Aug 19, 1922. Started in vaude. Screen debut 1944. Films inc: Nine Girls; Sailor's Holiday; Larceny; Take One False Step; Johnny Stool Pigeon; My Man and I; Executive Suite; Saskatchewan; Playgirl; Night of the Hunter; The Big Knife; The Great Gatsby; South Sea Sinner; Winchester '73; A Place in the Sun; I Am a Camera; The Treasure of Pancho Villa; I Died a Thousand Times; Cash on Delivery; The Diary of Anne Frank (Oscar-supp-1959); The Young Savages; Lolita; The Chapman Report; A House Is Not a Home; A Patch of Blue (Oscar-supp-1966); Alfie; Enter Laughing; The Scalphunters; Wild in the Streets; Buena Sera Mrs. Campbell; Bloody Mama; What's the Matter With Helen?; The Poseidon Adventure; Cleopatra Jones; Something to Hide; Blume in Love; Diamonds; Next Stop Greenwich Village; The Tenant; An Average Man; Tentacles; City on Fire; Magician of Lublin; The Visitor; Looping; S.O.B; My Mother, My Daughter; Fanny Hill; Over the Brooklyn Bridge; Ellie; George Stevens--A Filmmaker's Journey (doc-int); Witchfire (& asso prod); Deja Vu.

Bway inc: A Hatful of Rain; Girls of Summer; Minnie's Boys; The Effect of Gamma Rays on Man-In-The-Moon-Marigolds (rev).

TV inc: Sorry, Wrong Number; The Woman; Wagon Train; Two Is the Number (Emmy-1964); A Death of Innocence; The Adventures of Nick Carter; Elvis; The French Atlantic Affair; Rudolph & Frosty's Christmas in July (voice); Dom DeLuise and Friends--Part II.

WINWOOD, Estelle (nee Goodwin): Act. b. England, Jan 24, 1883. e. Lyric Stage Academy. On stage at age 15 with Manchester rep group, appeared in more than 150 plays inc (London) The Younger Generation; Mrs. Skeffington; When Knights Were Bold; The Cage; Trelawny of the Wells; The Love Game; See Naples and Die; Hotel Universe; Gigi. (Bway) A Successful Calamity; Why Marry? Too Many Husbands; The Red Poppy; Fallen Angels; Scarlet Sister Mary; Eden End; On the Rocks; When We Are Married; Ten Little Indians; The Madwoman of Chaillot; Lute Song.

Films inc: The House of Trent; Quality Street; The Glass Slipper; The Swan; 23 Paces to Baker Street; This Happy Feeling; Alive and Kicking; The Misfits; Darby O'Gill and the Little People; The Notorious Landlady; Dead Ringer; Camelot; Games; The Producers; Jenny; Murder By Death.

TV inc: Blithe Spirit; Great Expectations; Miss Miller.

(Died Jun 20, 1984).

WISBERG, Aubrey: Wri-Prod. b. London, Oct 20, 1909. e. Columbia U. Films inc: (sp only) Submarine Raider; Escape in the Fog; Just Before Dawn; Power of the Whistler; After Midnight; So Dark the Night; The Wreck of the Hesperus; Treasure of Monte Cristo; The Big Fix; Son of Sinbad; At Sword's Point; They Came to Blow Up America. Bomber's Moon; The Lady in the Iron Mask; The Horn Blows at Midnight; The Snow Devils; Casanova's Big Night; Mission: Mars. (sp & prod): The Man from Planet X; Captive Women; Sword of Venus; Port Sinister; The Neanderthal Man; Capt. John Smith & Pocahontas; Return to Treasure Island; Capt. Kidd & the Slave Girl; Problem Girls; Murder is My Beat; The Women of Pitcairn Island; Hercules in New York.

WISDOM, Norman: Act. b. London, Feb 4, 1920. Films inc: Trouble in Store; One Good Turn; Up in the World; Just My Luck; The Square Peg; Follow a Star; There Was a Crooked Man; A Stitch in Time; The Early Bird; The Sandwich Man; The Night They Raided Minsky's; What's Good for the Goose.

Thea inc: Walking Happy; Not Now Darling; A World of Wisdom.

WISE, Alfie: Act. b. Altoona, PA. Nov. 17. Films inc: The Longest Yard; Hustle; Midway; Swashbuckler; Smokey and the Bandit; The End; Hooper; Choirboys; Hot Stuff; Starting Over; Cannonball Run.

TV ic: Sandy Duncan Show; Uncle Croc's Block; Mary Hartman Mary Hartman; Call Her Mom; Death Car on The Freeway; Come Blow Your Horn (cable).

WISE, Ernie (Ernest Wiseman, OBE): Comedian. b. England, Nov 27, 1925. Teamed with Eric Morecambe since 1941. On radio, tv with Morecambe and Wise Shows. Films inc: The Intelligence Man; That Riviera Touch; The Magnificent Two.

WISE, Herbert (ne Weisz): Dir. b. Vienna, Aug 31, 1924. Thea inc: While The Sun Shines; So What About Love; I Want To Marry a Goldwyn Girl.

TV inc: Vienna 1900--Games With Love and Death; I Claudius; Skokie; Pope John Paul II; Reunion At Fairborough.

WISE, Robert E.: Dir-Prod. b. Winchester, IN, Sep 10, 1914. Started in cutting dept RKO, 1933; film ed, 1939; edited Citizen Kane; dir; 1943; ind prod 1959; partner Filmakers Group, The Tripar Group.

Films inc: (dir) Curse of the Cat People; Mademoiselle Fifi; The Set-Up; Two Flags West; The Day the Earth Stood Still; The Desert Rats; Executive Suite; Helen of Troy; Somebody Up There Likes Me; Run Silent; Run Deep; I Want to Live! (Prod-dir) Odds Against Tomorrow; West Side Story (2 Oscars-dir & prod-1961); Two for the Seesaw; The Haunting; The Sound of Music (2 Oscars-dir & prod-1965); The Sand Pebbles; Star!; The Andromeda Strain; Two People; The Hindenburg Audrey Rose; Star Trek-The Movie.

(Irving Thalberg Award-1966).

WISEMAN, Frederick: Prod-Dir. b. Boston, MA, Jan 1, 1930. e. Williams Coll, BA; Yale Law School; U of Paris. Taught law for two years. Founded Zipporah Films to enter film ind as prod of doc The Cool World. Since then has pro & dir. Films inc: Titicut Follies; High School; Manoeuvre; The Store.

TV inc: Law and Order (Emmy-1969); Hospital (Emmys-prod & dir-1970); Basic Training; Essene; Model.

WISEMAN, Joseph: Act. b. Montreal, May 15, 1918. Films inc: Detective Story; Viva Zapata; Les Miserables; The Prodigal; The Garment Jungle; The Unforgiven; Dr No; The Night They Raided Minsky's; Bye, Bye, Braverman; Stiletto; The Valachi Papers; The Apprenticeship of Duddy Kravitz; Homage of Chagall (narr); The Betsy; Buck Rogers in the 25th Century; Jaguar Lives.

Thea inc: King Lear; Golden Boy; The Diary of Anne Frank; Uncle Vanya; The Last Analysis; Enemies; The Golem.

TV inc: Masada; Rage of Angels; The Ghost Writer.

WITHERS, Googie (Georgette Lizette Withers): Act. b. Karachi, India, Mar 12, 1917. Stage debut, 1929, The Windmill Man. Thea inc: Hand in Glove; The Deep Blue Sea; Janus; The Complaisant Lover; Woman in a Dressing Gown; Exit the King; Beekman Place; Getting Married; The Cherry Orchard; An Ideal Husband; The Circle.

Films inc: Girl in the Crowd; Accused; Strange Boarders; The Lady Vanishes; One of Our Aircraft Is Missing; On Approval; It Always Rains on Sunday; Miranda; White Corridors; Derby Day; Devil on Horseback; Port of Escape; The Nickel Queen.

WITHERS, Jane: Act. b. Atlanta, GA, April 12, 1926. On screen as a child from 1933. Films inc: Bright Eyes; Ginger; North Star; Johnny Doughboy; My Best Girl; Dangerous Partners; Affairs of Geraldine; Giant; The Right Approach; Captain Newman, M.D.

TV inc: All Together Now (First appearance after 12 years as Comet Cleanser's TV character Josephine the Plumber); Zack and the Magic Factory.

WITT, Paul Junger: Prod-Dir. b. NYC, Mar 20, 1943. e. U of VA, BA. Asso prod-dir Screen Gems, 1965; prod-dir 1967; prod Spelling-Goldberg 1972; P-exec prod Danny Thomas Prodns 1973; founder exec prod Witt/Thomas Prodns 1975.

TV inc: The Rookies; Brian's Song (Emmy-prod-1972); Griffin and Phoenix; Trouble In High Timber Country; The Yeagers (exec prod); It's A Living; I'm A Big Girl Now; It Takes Two; Condo (prod); Hail To The Chief (exec prod); Just Married (exec prod).

Films inc: Firstborn (prod).

WITTOP, Freddy (nee Koning): Cos dsgn. b. Bussum, Holland, Jul 26. Originally a dancer, toured with Argentinita as Frederico Rey; Bway inc: Heartbreak House; Carnival; Subways Are for Sleeping; Toured US & Europe with own dance co from 1951-1958. Hello, Dolly! (Tony-1964); To Broadway With Love; Bajour; The Roar of the Greasepaint-The Smell of the Crowd; Pleasures and Palaces; On a Clear Day You Can See Forever; I Do! I Do!; The Happy Time; George M!; Dear World; A Patriot for Me; Lovely Ladies, Kind Gentlemen; The Three Musketeers.

WIZAN, Joe: Prod. b. Los Angeles, Jan 7, 1935. e. UCLA. P CBS

Theatrical Films June 1981 to April 1982; Jan 1983, P 20th Century-Fox Prodns; ousted, July 1984. Films inc: Jeremiah Johnson; Junior Bonner; Prime Cut; 99 44/100% Dead; The Last American Hero; Audrey Rose; Voices; And Justice for All; Two of a Kind; Unfaithfully Yours.

TV inc: The Two Worlds of Jennie Logan; Dark Night of the Scarecrow (exec prod).

WOLF, Emanuel: Exec. b. NYC, May 27, 1927. e. Syracuse U, BA, MA. Named director Allied Artists Pictures Corp 1963. Became Pres & bd chmn 1968.

WOLF, Fred: Prod-Dir-Ani. b. Brooklyn, NY, Mar 27, 1933. Pres Murakami-Wolf-Swenson Films. Films inc: The Bird; The Box (Oscar-cartoon-1967); The Mouse and His Child.

TV inc: The Point; Carlton Your Doorman; Puff The Magic Dragon in the Land of the Living Lies; Thanksgiving in the Land of Oz.

WOLF, Harry L.: Cin. b. San Francisco, Jun 20, 1912. TV inc: Hennessy; Beverly Hillbillies; Sunshine; Devil and Miss Sarah; Get Smart; What's a Nice Girl Like You; Hound of the Baskervilles; Little Mo; Columbo (Emmy-1974); Baretta (Emmy-1975); Brave New World; The Munster's Revenge; The 25th Man.

WOLF, Herbert: Prod. b. NYC, Jul 11, 1917. e. NYU. Radio, TV prod, Wolf Presentations, Inc. TV inc: Masquerade Party; Break the Bank; Hold That Note; Keep Talking; Window Shopping.

WOLF, Richard A.: Prod-Wri. b. NYC, Dec 20, 1946. e. U of PA. Films inc: Skateboard (sp, prod); Gas (wri).

WOLFE, Digby: Wri-Prod-Dir. b. England, Jun 4, 1932. e. Thurlestone Coll. TV inc: (Eng) Chelsea At Nine; I've Got A Secret; Wolfe at the Door; Saturday Spectacular; (U.S.): Laugh-In (Emmy-wri-1968); The Doris Day Special; The Tennessee Ernie Ford Special; Diana Ross; Opryland USA; John Denver & Friend; The Cher Series; The New Bill Cosby Variety Series; Lampoon; Li'l Abner; The Goldie Hawn Special; The Flip Wilson Special; The Wayne Newton Special; The Tammy Awards Show; Real People; Oz 81 (prod).

WOLFE, Robert L.: Film Edtr. b. Los Angeles, Jul 5, 1928. Films inc: The Wild Bunch; Straw Dogs; The Getaway; The Wind and the Lion; Terminal Man; Junior Bonner; Pat Garrett and Billy the Kid; The Deep; All The President's Men; Big Wednesday; The Rose; The Hunter.

WOLFF, Lother: Prod-Dir. b. Bromberg, Germany, 1909. Asst prod, The March of Time; VP & prod, Louis de Rochemont Assoc. Films inc: Lost Boundaries; Martin Luther; Windjammer; Question Seven; Fortress of Peace.

WOLFMAN JACK (Bob Smith): Act. b. NYC, Jan 21. Films inc: The Seven Minutes; American Graffiti; More American Graffiti; Motel Hell.

TV inc: The Midnight Special; Stanley the Ugly Duckling (voice).

WOLMAN, Dan: Wri-dir-prod. b. Oct. 28, 1941. e. Film Institute CCNY; NYU, BA. Films inc: The Living (doc); Habit (doc); The Race (doc); The Samaritans (doc); The National Poet (doc); The Dreamer; Flock; My Michael; Hide and Seek; Nana (dir only); Baby Love (dir only); Soldier Of the Night; Up Your Anchor (wri-dir).

TV inc: The Story of Bashe; Gimpel the Fool.

WOLPER, David L.: Exec. b. NYC, Jan 11, 1928. e. Drake U, USC. In 1949, partnered in Flamingo Films, a TV dist co; merged with Associated Artists 1951 and became known as Motion Pictures for Television, Inc; formed Wolper Productions, Inc, 1958. Docs inc: Race for Space; Hollywood-The Golden Years; Hollywood-The Fabulous Era; Project--Man In Space; Biography of a Rookie; The Rafer Johnson Story; D-Day; The Making of the President, 1960; 39 half-hour programs titled The Story Of. . .; Escape to Freedom; The Legend of Marilyn Monroe; Berlin: Kaiser to Khrushchev; The Battle of Britain; Trial at Nuremberg; Korea: The 38th Parallel; Four Days in November; The Teenage Revolution; Pro Football: Mayhem On a Sunday Afternoon; National Geographic Society Specials; The World of Animals; The Undersea World of Jacques-Yves Cousteau.

Feature films inc: I Love My Wife; The Devil's Brigade; It It's Tuesday, This Must Be Belgium; The Bridge At Remagen; The Confessions of Nat Turner; Couples; King, Queen, Knave; Blessed McGill; The Great Cowboy Race; Willy Wonka and the Chocolate Factory; Visions of Eight; Birds Do It, Bees Do It; The Man Who Saw Tomorrow; This Is Elvis.

TV inc: Get Christie Love!; Chico and the Man; Sandburg's Lincoln; Welcome Back, Kotter. (Exec Prod) Roots *(Emmy-*1977); Roots - The Next Generations *(Emmy-*1979); Moviola; Murder Is Easy; Hollywood--The Gift of Laughter; The Thorn Birds; Casablanca; Small World; The Mystic Warrior; produced opening and closing ceremonies 23d Olympiad (Summer 1984) *(Emmy-special-1984)*; His Mistress (exec prod).

(Jean Hersholt Humanitarian Award-1984)

WOLSK, Eugene V.: Prod. b. NYC, Aug 16, 1928. e. Allegheny Coll, BA; Yale U Drama School, NYU. Bway inc: The Father; Chaparral; The Lion in Winter; Mark Twain Tonight!; The Investigation; Something Different; Aint Supposed to Die a Natural Death; The Sunshine Boys; The Good Doctor; Scapino; Miss Moffat; God's Favorite; Charlotte; Fiddler On the Roof (rev); Steaming.

TV inc: The Investigation.

WOLSKY, Albert: Cos Dsgn. b. Paris, France, Nov 24, 1930. Films inc: The Heart Is a Lonely Hunter; Where's Poppa?; Harry and Tonto; Lenny; Beauty and the Beast; An Unmarried Woman; The Turning Point; Grease; Manhattan; All That Jazz *(Oscar-*1979); The Jazz Singer; All Night Long; Paternity; Tempest; Still of the Night; Sophie's Choice; Star 80; To Be or Not to Be; Moscow on the Hudson.

Thea inc: Tricks of the Trade (Bway); Ann Reinking--Music Moves Me (Off-Bway).

WONDER, Stevie: Singer-Mus-Sngwri-Rec prod. (nee Steveland Morris):b. Saginaw, MI, May 13, 1950. Blind since birth. A natural mus, began writing, recording songs as a child; first gold album, Fingertips, at age 13 (billed as Little Stevie Wonder). Writes own material, produces own records.

Songs inc: Purple Raindrops; Someday at Christmas; I'm Wondering; Every Time I See You I Go Wild; Shoo Be Doo Be Doo Da Day; My Girl; For Once in My Life; My Cherie Amour; Yester Me Yester You, Yester Day; Never Had A Dream Come True; Superstition *(Grammys-*R&B song & R&B voc-1973); You Are The Sunshine of My Life *(Grammy-*pop vocal-1973); Boogie on a Reggae Woman *(Grammy-*R&B voc-1974); Living For the City *(Grammy-*R&B song-1974); You Haven't Done Nothin'; High Ground; I Wish *(Grammy-*R&B voc-1976).

Albums inc: 12-year-old Genius; Tribute To Uncle Ray; Jazz Soul; With A Song in My Heart; Uptight; Down to Earth; I Was Made to Love Her; Stevie Wonder's Greatest Hits; Music on My Mind; Innervisions *(Grammys-*artist & prod-1973); Fullfillingness First Finale *(Grammys-*artist-prod-pop voc-1974); Songs in the Key of Life *(Grammys-*artist, pop vocal, prod also prod of year-1976).

Films inc: Bikini Beach; Muscle Beach Party; CS Blues; The Woman In Red *(Oscar-song-1984)*.

TV inc: Fridays; Eubie Blake--A Century of Music; A Tribute to Martin Luther King Jr.--A Celebration of Life; Stevie Wonder Comes Home (feevee); Motown Returns To The Apollo.

WOOD, John: Act. b. Derbyshire, England. e. Jesus Coll, Oxford. Thea inc: (London) various Shakespearean roles with Old Vic; Camino Real; The Making of Moo; Brouhaha; The Fantasticks; Exiles; Enemies; The Man of Mode; Collaborators; A Lesson in Blood and Roses; Sherlock Holmes; Travesties; The Devil's Disciple; Ivanov; The Provok'd Wife. (Bway) Rosencrantz and Guildenstern Are Dead; Deathtrap; Sherlock Holmes; Travesties *(Tony-*1976); Amadeus.

Films inc: Nicholas and Alexandra; Slaughterhouse Five; Somebody Killed Her Husband; WarGames; The Purple Rose Of Cairo; Ladyhawke.

TV inc: The Last Bastion; The Jewel In The Crown.

WOOD, Peter: Dir. b. Colyton, Devon, England, Oct 8, 1927. e. Cambridge. Resident dir Arts Theatre, London, 1956. Thea inc: No Laughing Matter; The Iceman Cometh; The Birthday Party; Who's Your Father?; Five Finger Excercise; The Winter's Tale; The Devil; Hamlet; The Private Ear and the Public Eye; The Master Builder; Poor Richard; Love for Love; Design for Living; Jumpers; Travesties; Night and Day; The Provok'd Wife; On the Razzle; Windy City; The Real

Thing; The Rivals; Rough Crossing.

Films inc: In Search of Gregory.

TV inc: Song for Songs; Long Day's Journey Into Night; Dear Love.

WOOD, Robert D.: Exec. b. Boise, ID, Apr 17, 1925. e. USC, BS. Joined KNX (CBS Radio) as slsmn; 1951 account exec KTTV-TV; 1952 account exec KNXT (CBS TV); 1954 account exec CBS TV natl sales dept, NY; 1955 gen sls mgr KNXT; 1960 vp-gm KNXT; 1966 exec vp CBS tv stations div; 1967 P; 1969 P CBS-TV; 1976 resd to enter ind prodn; 1980 P Metromedia Producers Corp; resd May, 1983.

TV inc: The Cheap Show; Maneaters Are Loose!; Gauguin the Savage; No Place To Hide; The Million Dollar Face.

WOODARD, Alfre: Act. b. 1953. e. Boston U., BA. Thea inc: Me and Bessie (Bway & tour); Horatio; A Christmas Carol; Bugs, Guns; Leander Stillwell; For Colored Girls Who Have Considered Suicide/When the Rainbow is Enuf.

TV inc: Palmerstown USA; The Class of '65; Ambush Murders; Sophisticated Gents; Freedom Road; For Colored Girls Who Have Considered Suicide/When The Rainbow is Enuf; Trial of the Moke; The Good Witch of Laurel Canyon (Tucker's Witch); The Killing Ground; Sweet Revenge; Hill Street Blues *(Emmy-Supp-1984)*; Sara.

Films inc: Health; Remember My Name; Cross Creek; Go Tell It On the Mountain.

WOODARD, Charlaine: Act. Bway inc: Ain't Misbehavin'. Films inc: Hair; Taxi. TV inc: Ain't Misbehavin'.

WOODFIELD, William R.: Wri-Prod. b. San Francisco, Jan 21, 1928. e. U of CA, BA. TV inc: (wri) Sea Hunt: Voyage to the Bottom of the Sea; Time Tunnel; (wri-prod): Mission Impossible; San Francisco International Airport; Shaft; Earth II; Satan's Triangle.

WOODS, James: Act. b. RI. Bway inc: Borstal Boy; Conduct Unbecoming; Saved; The Trial of the Catonsville Nine; Green Julia; Finishing Touches.

Films inc: Visitors; The Way We Were; Alex and the Gypsy; The Onion Field; The Black Marble; Split Image; Fast-Walking; Videodrome; Against All Odds; Once Upon A Time In America; Cat's Eye; Joshua Then And Now.

TV inc: All the Way Home; The Disappearance of Aimee; Raid on Entebbe; And Your Name is Jonah; Billion Dollar Bubble; Holocaust.

WOODWARD, Charles: Prod. b. Niagara Falls, NY, Oct 14, 1923. e. U of PA, BS. Thea inc: Johnny No-Trump; The Boys in the Band; The Front Page; What the Butler Saw; The Last of Mrs. Lincoln; All Over; Drat!; The Grass Harp; Noel Coward in Two Keys; Seascape; P.S. Your Cat Is Dead!; Sweeney Todd *(Tony-*1979); Home Front.

WOODWARD, Edward: Act. b. Surrey, England, Jun 1, 1930. e. RADA. Thea inc: (London) Where There's A Will; A Girl Called Jo; Doctor in the House; The Queen and the Welshman; with Shakespeare Memorial Theatre, 1958 playing various roles and appearing with the company during Russia n tour; The Art Of Living; The Little Doctor; Scapa; Rattle of a Simple Man; The High Bid; Two Cities; Cyrano; The Wolf; The Male of the Species; On Approval. (Bway) Rattle Of a Simple Man; The Best Laid Plans.

Films inc: Becket; Young Winston; Sitting Target; The Wicker Man; Breaker Morant; Who Dares Wins; Comeback; Champions; King David.

TV inc: Callan; Major Barbara; A Dream Divided; Edward Woodward Specials; Winston Churchill-The Wilderness Years; Love Is Forever; A Christmas Carol; Arthur The King.

WOODWARD, Joanne: Act. b. Thomasville, GA, Feb 27, 1930. e. LA State U, Neighborhood Playhouse, Actor's Studio, NY. W of Paul Newman. On screen from 1955 in Count Three and Pray. Films inc: A Kiss Before Dying; The Three Faces of Eve *(Oscar-*1957); No Down Payment; The Long Hot Summer; Rally Round the Flag Boys; The Sound and the Fury; From The Terrace; The Fugitive Kind; Paris Blues; The Stripper; A New Kind of Love; Signpost to Murder; A Big Hand for the Little Lady; Rachel, Rachel; Winning; WUSA; The Effect of Gamma Rays on Man-in-the-Moon Marigolds; Summer Wishes, Winter Dreams; The Drowning Pool; The End; Angel Dust (doc-narr); Harry & Son.

Thea inc: Picnic; Candida.

TV inc: Robert Montgomery Presents; US Steel Hour; G.E. Theatre; Studio One; Four Star Playhouse; Playhouse 90; Hallmark Hall of Fame; Sybil; See How She Runs *(Emmy*-1978); A Christmas To Remember; The Streets of L. A.; Fred Astaire-Putting On His Top Hat (narr); Fred Astaire-Change Partners and Dance (narr); The Shadow Box; Crisis At Central High; Come Along With Me (wri-dir); Candida (cable); Impact '83--Hunger in the Promised Land (host); Passions; Do You Remember Love.

WOOLERY, Chuck: Act. b. Ashland, KY, Aug 22. Films inc: Treasure of Jamaica Reef.

TV inc: The Jimmy Dean Show; Your Hit Parade; Wheel of Fortune (host); Scrabble (host).

WOOLEY, Sheb: Singer-Sngwri. b. Erick, OK, Apr 10, 1921. C&W recording artist. Films inc: Rocky Mountain; The Boy From Oklahoma; High Noon; Giant; Little Big Horn.

TV inc: Rawhide; The Dollmaker.

WOOLF, John b. England, 1913. Films inc: Exec. Pandora and the Flying Dutchman; The African Queen; Moulin Rouge; Beat the Devil; Carrington V.C.; I Am a Camera; Sailor Beware; Three Men in a Boat; The L-Shaped Room; Life at the Top; Oliver! *(Oscar*-1968); The Day of the Jackal; The Odessa File.

WOPAT, Tom: Act. b. Lodi, WI., Sep. 9. Thea inc: A Bistro Car on the NCR; The Robber Bridegroom; I Love My Wife (Bway); Oklahoma!

TV inc: One Life to Live; The Dukes of Hazzard; A Country Christmas; The Great American Sing-along; Burning Rage; The 39th Annual Tony Awards.

WORLEY, JoAnne: Act. b. Lowell, IN, 1942. Films inc: Moon Pilot; Nutcracker Fantasy.

TV inc: Laugh-In; Love American Style; The Gift of the Magi; Through the Magic Pyramid; Gary Owens' All Nonsense News Network Special.

WOROB, Malcolm: Dir-Prod. b. Newark, NJ, Oct 17, 1944. e. Rochester Institute of Technology. Films inc: The Sister-In-Law; Panic Rock.

WORTH, Irene: Act. b. NE, Jun 23, 1916. e. UCLA. Films inc: One Night with You; Secret People; Orders to Kill; Seven Seas to Calais; King Lear; Nicholas and Alexandra; Rich Kids; Eyewitness; Deathtrap; Fast Forward.

Thea inc: Tiny Alice *(Tony*-1965); A Song at Twilight; Come into the Garden; Heartbreak House; Sweet Bird of Youth *(Tony*-1976); The Lady From Dubuque; John Gabriel Borkman; The Golden Age.

TV inc: Stella in the Lake; The Lady from the Sea; The Duchess of Malfi; Prince Orestes; Happy Days; Separate Tables (cable); Coriolanus; Forbidden.

WORTH, Marvin: Prod. b. Brooklyn, NY. Originally jazz promoter and mgr before becoming wri of special material for Alan King; Buddy Hackett; Joey Bishop. TV inc: Steve Allen Show; Jackie Gleason Show; Milton Berle Show; Colgate Comedy Hour; Judy Garland; Where's Poppa.

Films inc: (wri) Boys Night Out; Three on a Couch; Promise Her Anything. (Prod) Where's Poppa? Lenny: Fire Sale; The Rose; Up the Academy; Soup For One; Unfaithfully Yours; Rhinestone; Falling In Love.

WRATHER, Jack: Prod. b. Amarillo, TX, May 24, 1918. H of Bonita Granville. Co-ownr, KFMB-TV, San Diego; KERO-TV, Bakersfield, CA; Muzak Corp; Lone Ranger, Inc, Lassie Programs, Inc; ownr, Disneyland Hotel; P, Wrather Corp; dir, TelePromTer.

Films inc: The Guilty; High Tide; Perilous Waters; Strike It Rich; Guilty of Treason; Lone Ranger; The Lone Ranger and the Lost City of Gold; The Magic of Lassie.

TV inc: Lassie; Sgt Preston of the Yukon; Lone Ranger.

(Died Nov. 12, 1984)

WRAY, Fay: Act. b. Alberta, Canada, Sep 10, 1907. On screen from 1928. Films inc: The Legion of the Condemned; The Four Feathers; Dirigible; Doctor X; The Countess of Monte Cristo; Viva Villa!; King Kong; Alias Bulldog Drummond; Adam Had Four Sons; The Cobweb; Summer Love.

TV inc: Gideon's Trumpet.

WRIGHT, Amy: Act. b. Chicago, IL. e. Beloit Coll. Started teaching career before act. Bway inc: Hamlet; Fifth of July; Noises Off.

Films inc: Not A Pretty Picture (doc); Girlfriends; The Deer Hunter; The Amityville Horror; Breaking Away; Wise Blood; Inside Moves.

TV inc: A Fine Romance.

WRIGHT, Norman H.: Wri-Dir-Prod. b. Redlands, CA, Jan 8, 1910. e. USC. Field prod for Wonderful World of Disney. TV inc: Pancho the Fastest Paw in the West; Cristobalito the Calypso Colt; Chandar, Black Leopard of Ceylon; Deacon the High Noon Dog (& wri-dir); Saving of Sam the Pelican (wri); Golden Dog (wri); Grizzly (wri).

Films inc: Fantasia (story dir); Bambi (sequence dir).

WRIGHT, Samuel E.: Act. b. Camden, SC, Nov 20, 1948. e. SC State, C W Post Coll. Bway inc: Jesus Christ Superstar; Two Gentlemen of Verona; Over Here; Pippin; The Tap Dance Kid. Other thea inc: Downriver (Off-Bway); Georgie Porgie (Off-Bway); Mushroom (Off-Bway); Two Gentlemen of Verona (London).

TV inc: Ed Sullivan's Broadway; Patchwork Family; Positively Black; Ball Four; Enos.

WRIGHT, Teresa: Act. b. NYC, Oct 27, 1919. On screen from 1940. Films inc: The Little Foxes; Mrs. Miniver *(Oscar*-supp-1942); The Pride of the Yankees; Casanova Brown; The Best Years of Our Lives; The Steel Trap; Track of the Cat; The Search for Bridie Murphy; The Restless Years; Hail Hero!; The Happy Ending; Somewhere In Time.

Thea inc: Death of a Salesman; Ah Wilderness!; I Never Sang for My Father; The Master Builder; Morning's At Seven (rev) (& London).

TV inc: The Margaret Bourke-White Story; The Miracle Worker; The Golden Honeymoon; Bill--On His Own.

WRYE, Donald: Dir. TV inc: The Man Who Could Talk To Kids; Death Be Not Proud (& prod-wri); It Happened One Christmas; Fire On the Mountain; Divorce Wars--A Love Story (& prod-wri); The Face of Rage (& wri); Heart of Steel; Right To Kill? (exec prod).

Films inc: Ice Castles (& wri).

WYATT, Jane: Act. b. NYC, Aug 10, 1913. On screen from 1934. Films inc: One More River; Great Expectations; Lost Horizon; None but the Lonely Heart; Boomerang; Gentleman's Agreement; Pitfall; Never Too Late; Treasure of Matecumbe.

Thea inc: The Autumn Garden; The Bishop Misbehaves; Conquest; The Mad Hopes.

TV inc: Father Knows Best *(Emmys*-1957, 1959, 1960); The Virginian; Wagon Train; My Luke and I; Amelia Earhart; The Nativity; The Millionaire; Missing Children--A Mother's Story.

WYENN, Than: Act. b. NYC, May 2, 1919. Films inc: Pete Kelly's Blues; Beginning of the End; The Invisible Boy; Imitation of Life; The Boy and the Pirates; Thunderbolt; Black Sunday; The Other Side of Midnight.

TV inc: Six Million Dollar Man; Switch; Barnaby Jones; The Lou Grant Show; Quincy; Victory at Entebbe; Power; Unit 4; The Two Lives of Carol Letner.

WYLER, Gretchen (nee Wienecke): Act. b. Bartlesville, OK, Feb 16, 1932. Thea inc: Where's Charley; Silk Stockings; Damn Yankees; Sweet Charity (London); Sly Fox.

TV inc: Step This Way; Somerset; On Our Own; Portrait of an Escort; When the Circus Came To Town; The Adventures of Pollyana; For Members Only.

Films inc: Devil's Brigade.

WYMAN, Jane (Sarah Jane Fulks): Act. b. St Joseph, MO, Jan 4, 1914. Radio singer using name Sarah Durrell. On screen from 1935. Films inc: My Man Godfrey; The Crowd Roars; Crime By Night; Lost Weekend; One More Tomorrow; The Yearling; Johnny Belinda *(Oscar*-1948); Here Comes the Groom; Blue Veil; The Story of Will Rogers; So Big; Magnificent Obsession; Lucy Gallant; All that Heaven Allows; Miracle in the Rain; Holiday for Lovers; How to Commit Marriage; Bon Voyage.

TV inc:; Fireside Theatre (host); Jame Wyman Theatre; The Incredible Journey of Doctor Meg Laurel; Falcon Crest.

WYMORE, Patrice: Act. b. Miltonville, KS., Dec. 17, 1926. Bway inc: Mexican Hayride; Up In Central Park; Hold It; All For Love. Films inc: Tea for Two; Rocky Mountain; I'll See You In My Dreams; The Man Behind the Gun, She's Back on Broadway; Oceans Eleven; Chamber of Horrors.

WYNETTE, Tammy (Virginia Wynette Pugh): Act. b. Red Bay, MS, May 5, 1942. C&W recording artist.
(*Grammys*-country voc-1967, 1969).
TV inc: Country Comes Home; Music City News' Top Country Hits of the Year; Conway Twitty on the Mississippi; Olympic Gala; Women In Song.

WYNGARDE, Peter: Act. b. Marseilles, France. Thea inc: (London) With Bristol Old Vic in various Shakespearean roles and dir Long Day's Journey Into Night; The Good Woman of Setzuan; Duel of Angels; The Duel; The King and I; Present laughter (& dir); Anastasia (& dir); Underground. (Bway) Duel of Angels.
Films inc: The Siege of Sidney Street; Night of the Eagle; Flash Gordon.
TV inc: Department S; Jason King.

WYNN, Keenan: Act. b. NYC, Jul 27, 1916. S of late Ed Wynn. On screen from 1942. Films inc: See Here, Private Hargrove; Marriage Is a Private Affair; Without Love; The Clock; Easy to Wed; The Hucksters; Neptune's Daughter; Annie Get Your Gun; Kiss Me Kate; The Great Man; Don't Go Near the Water; The Great Race; Welcome to Hard Times; Finian's Rainbow; The Devil's Rain; Nashville; The Killer Inside Me; The Shaggy D.A.; Coach; Laserblast; Piranha; The Dark; Sunburn; Parts - The Clonus Horror; Just Tell Me What You Want; The Glove; The Last Unicorn (voice); Best Friends; Hysterical; Wavelength; Prime Risk.
TV inc: Dallas; The Bastard; The Billion Dollar Threat; Mom, The Wolfman and Me; The Capture of Grizzly Adams; Insight/The Sixth Day; Highway Honeys; Return of the Man from U.N.C.L.E.; Quincy; Call To Glory; Code Of Vengeance.

WYNN, Tracy Keenan: Wri. b. Los Angeles, Feb 28, 1945. e. Switzerland, UCLA. S of Keenan Wynn. Films inc: The Longest Yard; The Deep.
TV inc: The Glass House; Tribes *(Emmy*-1971); The Autobiography of Miss Jane Pittman *(Emmy*-1974); The Drowning Pool; Quest.

WYNTER, Dana (Dagmar Wynter): Act. b. London, Jun 8, 1930. Launched career on TV, Robert Montgomery Presents series.
Films inc: The View from Pompey's Head; Invasion of the Body Snatchers; D-Day; The Sixth of June; Something of Value; Fraulein; Shake Hands with the Devil; In Love and War; Sink the Bismark!; The List of Adrian Messenger; If He Hollers, Let Him Go; Airport.
TV inc: My Three Sons; Twelve O'Clock High; The Rogues; Wild, Wild West; Companions in Nightmare; Any Second Now; Owen Marshall; The Man Who Never Was; Backstairs At The White House; M-Station Hawaii; Dana Wynter In Ireland; Aloha Paradise; The Royal Romance of Charles and Diana.

YABLANS, Frank: Prod. b. NYC, Aug 27, 1935. Started as WB booker, 1957; eastern sls mgr, 1967; sls mgr, 1967; sls vp, 1968; vp, gen sls mgr, Par, 1969; vp, dist, 1970; exec vp, 1971; named p, 1971. In 1975 became independent prod, (Frank Yablans Presentations Inc); Feb. 1983, vice chmn & COO of MGM/UA Entertainment; Jan. 1985, P & CEO MGM Films, retaining vice chmnshp MGM/UA; ousted, March 1985; May, 1985 teamed with PSO Delphi to form Northstar Entertainment Co.
Films inc: Silver Streak; The Other Side of Midnight; The Fury; North Dallas Forty (& wri); Mommie Dearest (& wri); Monsignor; The Star Chamber; Kidco.

YABLANS, Irwin: Exec-Prod. b. NYC, Jul 25, 1934. P, Irwin Yablans Co. Film salesman before joining Paramount 1962 as Los Angeles Mgr; western sales Mgr 1964; into ind prodn; Sept 1982, exec VP Lorimar Prodns; April 1985, chmn Orion Pictures Dist. Corp.
Films inc: Badge 373 The Education of Sonny Carson; Halloween; Roller Boogie; Fade To Black; Hell Night; Halloween II; The Seduction;

Parasite; Halloween III--Season of the Witch (exec prod); Tank; Scream For Help (exec prod).

YANNE, Jean (nee Gouille): Act. b. Brittany, Jul 18, 1933. Films inc: La Vie a L'Envers; L'Amour a la Chaine; La Saint Contre; Bang Bang; Weekend; Erotissimo; Le Boucher; Le Saut de L'Ange; The Accuser; State Reason; Je Te Tiens, Tu Me Tiens par la Barbichette; Asphalt; Une journee en Taxi (Day In A Taxi); Deux heures moint le quatre avant Jesus Christ (A Quarter To Two Before Jesus Christ) (& wri-dir-mus); Hannah K; Pappy Fait de la Resistance (Gramps is in the Resistance); Liberte, Egalite, Choucroute (Liber ty, Equality, Sauerkraut) (& wri-dir-mus); La Telephone Sonne Toujous Deux Fois (The Telephone Always Rings Twice).
TV inc: Les Grands Enfants.

YARROW, Peter: Comp-Singer. b. NYC, May 31, 1938. e. Cornell U. Member, Peter, Paul and Mary Trio. Songs inc: Puff, The Magic Dragon; A-Soulin'.
TV inc: Puff The Magic Dragon in the Land of Living Lies (& prod).
Films inc: The Willmar 8 (mus); Citizen: The Political Life of Allard K. Lowenstein (doc).

YATES, Cassie: Act. b. Macon, GA, Mar 2, 1951. Studied at Lee Strasberg Theatre. TV inc: Rich Man, Poor Man; The Seeding of Sarah Burns; Who'll Save the Children; Having Babies II; Nobody's Perfekt; Father Figure; Mark, I Love You; Norma Rae (pilot); Of Mice and Men; The Gift of Life; Listen to Your Heart; A Caribbean Mystery; Love Thy Neighbor; Detective In The House.
Films inc: Rolling Thunder; The Evil; Convoy; F.I.S.T.; FM; St. Helen's; The Osterman Weekend; Unfaithfully Yours.

YATES, Peter: Dir. b. England, 1929. Films inc: Summer Holiday; One Way Pendulum; Robbery; Bullitt; John and Mary; Murphy's War; The Hot Rock; The Friends of Eddie Coyle; For Pete's Sake; Mother Jugs and Speed; The Deep; Breaking Away (& prod); Eyewitness (& prod); Krull; The Dresser (& prod).
TV inc: The Saint; Danger Man; Breaking Away (exec prod).

YATES, William Robert: Prod-Exec. b. Glendale, CA, 1930. e. U IL, BA; Columbia, LLD. 1955, publicist KNXT; 1959, story ed Studio One, Camera Three; 1961, Dir Pgm Dvlpmnt ABC-TV; 1963 retd to KNXT as dir Repertoire Workshp; 1967 dir pgm dvlpmnt Selmur Prodns; 1970 to Disney writing Wonderful World of Disney; 1973, exec story cnsltnt Streets of San Francisco; 1975 prod; 1978 vp crea aff Quinn Martin Prodns, prod Tales of the Unexpected; The Runaways; 1979 vp tv prodn Disney.
TV inc: Lefty; Disney Animation--The Illusion of Life; Tales of the Apple Dumpling Gang; Beyond Witch Mountain; Herbie, The Love Bug; The Adventures of Pollyanna; Gun Shy; Zorro and Son.
Films inc: Amy (exec prod).

YAWITZ, Paul: Wri. b. St Louis, MO, Feb 5, 1905. Publicist; Bway columnist, NY Mirror. Films inc: She Has What It Takes; They Knew What They Wanted; The Affairs of Annabelle; Go Chase Yourself; The Chance of a Lifetime; The Racket Man; Breakfast for Two; A Close Call for Boston Blackie; Walk Softly; Models, Inc.; The Black Scorpion.
(Died June 10, 1983).

YELLEN, Linda: Prod. b. Queens, NY. e. Barnard, BA; Columbia, PhD. TV inc: Mayflower--The Pilgrims's Adventure; Hard Hat and Legs; Playing for Time *(Emmy-Drama Special*-1981); The Royal Romance of Charles and Diana (& wri); Jacobo Timerman; Prisoner Without A Name, Cell Without A Number (& dir-wri).
Films inc: Looking Up (& dir).

YORDAN, Philip: Wri. b. Chicago, 1913. e. U of IL, BA; Kent Coll Law, LLD. Films inc: Syncopation; Dillinger; House of Strangers; Detective Story; Johnny Guitar; El Cid; Broken Lance *(Oscar*-1954); 55 Days at Peking; The Fall of the Roman Empire; (& prod): The Harder They Fall; Men in War; God's Little Acre; Day of the Outlaw; Studs Lonigan; The Day of the Triffids; The Thin Red Line; The Battle of the Bulge; Captain Apache; Night Train To Terror.

YORK, Michael: Act. b. Fulmer, England, Mar 27, 1942. e. Oxford U. With Dundee Repertory Theatre. Thea inc: Any Just Cause; Hamlet; Outcry. On screen from 1967. Films inc: The Taming of the Shrew;

The Strange Affair; Romeo and Juliet; The Guru; Zepplin; Cabaret; Lost Horizon; The Three Musketeers; The Four Musketeers; Murder on the Orient Express; Conduct Unbecoming; Logan's Run; Seven Nights in Japan; The Last Remake of Beau Geste; The Island of Dr. Moreau; Fedora; Riddle of the Sands; Final Assignment; The White Lions; Au nom de tous Miens (For Those I Loved); The Weather in the Streets; Success Is the Best Revenge.

TV inc: The Forsyte Saga; Revel in the Grave; Great Expectations; Jesus of Nazareth; A Man Called Intrepid; Misunderstood Monsters (voice); Twilight Theatre; The Master of Ballantrae; Space.

YORK, Susannah: Act. b. London, Jan 9, 1942. TV inc: The Crucible; The Rebel and the Soldier; The First Gentleman; The Richest Man in the World; The Golden Gate Murders; A Christmas Carol.

Films inc: Tunes of Glory; There Was a Crooked Man; Freud; Tom Jones; Loss of Innocence; A Man for All Seasons; Lock Up Your Daughters; The Killing of Sister George; They Shoot Horses, Don't They?; Images; Conduct Unbecoming; Heaven Save Us From Our Friends; Sky Riders; The Shout; Mrs Eliza Fraser; Superman; The Silent Partner; The Awakening; Falling In Love Again (& wri); Superman II; Loophole; Montgomery Clift; Yellowbeard; Nelly's Version.

Thea inc: A Cheap Bunch of Flowers; Wings of the Dove; A Singular Man; Man and Superman.

YORKIN, Alan (Bud): Prod-Dir-Wri. b. Washington, PA, Feb 22, 1926. e. Carnegie Tech. Started in tv on NBC engineering staff; became asso dir Colgate Comedy Hour; partnered with Norman Lear in Tandem Productions; with Saul Turtletaub and Bernie Orenstein in Toy Productions.

TV inc: (dir) Martin & Lewis Show; Dinah Shore Show; The Tony Martin Show; Ernie Ford Show; George Gobel Show; An Evening With Fred Astaire (Emmys-dir-wri-1959); Another Evening With Fred Astaire; Jack Benny Specials (Emmy-1960); We Love You Madly; Duke Ellington Special; All in the Family; Sanford and Son; Good Times; Maude; Carter Country.

Films inc: Come Blow Your Horn; Never Too Late; Divorce American Stye; Inspector Clouseau; Start the Revolution Without Me (& prod); Cold Turkey (exec prod); The Thief Who Came to Dinner (& prod); Deal of the Century (prod).

YOUNG, Alan: Act. b. Northumberland, England, Nov 19, 1919. Films inc: Margie; Chicken Every Sunday; Mr Belvedere Goes to College; Aaron Slick from Punkin Crick; Androcles and the Lion; Gentlemen Marry Brunettes; Tom Thumb; Time Machine; Bakers Hawk; The Cat from Outer Space.

TV inc: The Alan Young Show (Emmy-1950); Mister Ed; The Gift of the Magi; Scruffy (voice); The Puppy Saves the Circus (voice); Bunnicula, The Vampire Rabbit (voice); Smurfily Ever After (voice).

Thea inc: Finian's Rainbow; Damn Yankees; Best Little Whorehouse In Texas; The Girl In the Freudian Slip (Bway).

YOUNG, Buddy: PR exec. b. NYC, Jun 15, 1935. e. CCNY. Joined UA publicity dept, 1952; asst pub mgr, 1963; west coast dir of adv, pub; in 1975 dir worldwide of adv, pub, exp col; 1976 named MGM adv, pub coordinator MGM; 1977: VP ad, pub, promo, U; formed ind pub marketing firm with Charles Powell, Jan 1980.

YOUNG, Burt: Act. b. NYC April 30, 1940. Films inc: Carnival of Blood (& sp); Born To Win; The Gang That Couldn't Shoot Straight; Cinderella Liberty; The Gambler; The Killer Elite; Chinatown; Harry and Walter Go to New York; Rocky; The Choirboys; Twilight's Last Gleaming; Convoy; Uncle Joe Shannon (& sp); Rocky II; Blood Beach; All the Marbles; Rocky III; Amityville II--The Possession; Lookin' To Get Out; Over the Brooklyn Bridge; Once Upon A Time In America; The Pope of Greenwich Village.

TV inc: The Great Niagara; Hustling; The Deadly Game; M*A*S*H; Murder Can Hurt You.

YOUNG, Dalene: Wri. TV inc: Dawn--Portrait of a Runaway; Christmas Coal Mine Disaster; Dead Man's Curve; Can You Hear the Laughter--The Story of Freddie Prinze; Plutonium, Inc; Marilyn--The Untold Story; Will There Really Be A Morning?; Why Me? (& exec prod).

Films inc: Little Darlings; Cross Creek.

YOUNG, Faron: Singer-Sngwri. b. Shreveport, LA, Feb 25, 1932.

Country music recording artist; regular on Grand Ole Opry. Films inc: Country Music Holiday; Daniel Boone; Hidden Guns.

TV inc: Country Comes Home; Jerry Reed and Special Friends.

YOUNG, Frederick (Freddie): Cin. b. England, 1902.

Films inc: Bitter Sweet; Nell Gwyn; When Knights Were Bold; Goodbye Mr Chips; The Young Mr Pitt; Edward My Son; Treasure Island; Ivanhoe; Lust for Life; Invitation to the Dance; Island in the Sun; Lawrence of Arabia (Oscar-1962); Lord Jim; Doctor Zhivago (Oscar-1965); The Deadly Affair; You Only Live Twice; The Battle of Britain; Ryan's Daughter (Oscar-1970); Nicholas and Alexandra; The Tamarind Seed; Permission to Kill; Stevie; Sidney Sheldon's Bloodline; Rough Cut; Richard's Things; Sword of the Valiant.

TV inc: Ike.

YOUNG, Loretta (Gretchen Young): Act. b. Salt Lake City, UT, Jan 6, 1913. On screen from 1928. Films inc: Laugh, Clown, Laugh; Man's Castle; The House of Rothschild; Bulldog Drummond Strikes Back; Clive of India; The Farmer's Daughter (Oscar-1947); Suez; Kentucky; Bedtime Story; The Bishop's Wife; Come to the Stable; Half Angel; Because of You; It Happens Every Thursday.

TV inc: A Letter to Loretta, 1953; The Loretta Young Show, 1954-60 (Emmys-1954, 1956, 1959); The New Loretta Young Show, 1962.

YOUNG, Neil: Mus-Sngwri. b. Toronto, Canada, Nov 12, 1945. Formed Buffalo Springfield with Stephen Sills; went solo 1968 then rejoined Crosby, Stills & Nash. Films inc: Journey Through the Past (wri-dir-act); Rust Never Sleeps (wri-dir-act); Where the Buffalo Roam (score); Human Highway (mus & act).

Albums inc: Everybody Knows This Is Nowhere; After the Goldrush; Harvest; Journey Through the Past (soundtrack); Time Fades Away; On the Beach; Tonight's The Night; Zuma; American Stars 'n' Bars; Rust Never Sleeps.

YOUNG, Robert: Act. b. Chicago, IL, Feb 22, 1907. On screen from 1931. Films inc: Lullaby; The Black Camel; The Sin of Madelon Claudet; Strange Interlude; Tugboat Annie; The House of Rothschild; Stowaway; Married Before Breakfast; The Bride Wore Red; Northwest Passage; Western Union; H M Pulham, Esq; Joe Smith, American; Claudia; The Searching Wind; The Half Breed; Secret of the Incas.

TV inc: Father Knows Best (Emmys-1956, 1957); Marcus Welby, MD (Emmy-1970); Little Women; The Return of Marcus Welby, M.D.

YOUNG, Robert M.: Dir. b. NYC, Nov 22, 1924. e. Harvard U.

Films inc: Nothing But A Man; Short Eyes; Rich Kids; The World Is Full of Married Men; One-Trick Pony; The Inferno (doc)(& prod-wri-cin-edtr).

TV inc: Sit-In; Angola--Journey To A War; Anatomy Of a Hospital; Eskimo-Fight for Life (Emmy-1971); The Ballad of Gregorio Cortez.

Thea inc: Gaslight.

YOUNG, Roger: Dir. b. Champaign, IL, May 13, 1942. e. U IL, MS. TV inc: Lou Grant (Emmy-1980); Magnum P.I. (Pilot); Bitter Harvest; An Innocent Love; Dreams Don't Die; Hardcastle and McCormick; Legmen; Gulag; Eye To Eye.

Films inc: Lassiter.

YOUNG, Sean: Act. b. Louisville, KY., Nov. 20, 1959. Films inc: Jane Austen in Manhattan; Stripes; Blade Runner; Young Doctors in Love; Dune; Baby; Under The Biltmore Clock.

YOUNG, Terence: Dir. b. Shanghai, China, Jun 20, 1915. e. Cambridge U.

Films inc: Corridor of Mirrors; They Were Not Divided; The Tall Headlines; The Red Beret; Zarak; Too Hot to Handle; Doctor No; From Russia With Love; The Amorous Adventures; Thunderball; The Poppy is Also a Flower; Wait Until Dark; Mayerling; The Christmas Tree; Grand Slam; Cold Sweat; Red Sun; The Valachi Papers; War Goddess; The Klansman; Jackpot; Sidney Sheldon's Bloodline; Inchon; The Jigsaw Man; Where Is Parsifal? (exec prod).

YOUNG, Tony: Act. b. 1932. Films inc: He Rides Tall; Taggart; Charroi; Chrome and Hot Leather; A Man Called Sledge; The Outfit; Policewomen; Act of Vengeance.

TV inc: Gunslinger.

YOUNGERMAN, Joseph C.: Exec. b. Chicago, May 1, 1906. Started as prop man, Par, 1926; second asst dir 1928; first asst unit prodn mgr, second unit dir, 1930; dir US Signal Corps under Darryl F Zanuck, 1940-45; asst to VP, Par Pictures, 1945-50; National exec sec, Directors Guild of America, 1950-78; Board of Trustees, Motion Picture Television Fund. Smokey and the Bandit Part 3 (act).

YOUNGMAN, Henny: Comedian-Act. b. Liverpool, England, 1906. Films inc: A WAVE, A WAC and a Marine; Nashville Rebel; Won Ton Ton, the Dog Who Saved Hollywood; The Silent Movie; History of the World--Part I; The Comeback Trail; National Lampoon Goes to the Movies.
TV inc: The 1/2 Hour Comedy Hour; Night Of 100 Stars II.

YOUNGSTEIN, Max E.: Exec. b. NYC, Mar 21, 1913. e. Fordham Law School, LLB; Brooklyn Law School, LLM. 1942-43, dir ad-pub-expl, Fox; 1945, VP & GM, Stanley Kramer Prodns; 1946, dir ad-pub-expl. Eagle-Lion; 1949, dir ad-pub-expl, member exec comm Par Pictures; 1950, vp & dir Paramount Film Distrib Corp; 1955, vp & member of board UA; 1957-62, founder, p, UA Records, UA Music; 1962, exec vp Cinerama, Inc; 1962, independent prod, p, Max Youngstein Enterprises; 1972, vp, Todd-A O Corp; 1973, P, Taylor-Laughlin Distributing Co; sr VP, Billy Jack Prodns & National Student Film Corp; VP Billy Jack Records and Publishing, 1974-75; 1975-78 cnsltnt to various ind prodn firms, studios; gen film cnsltnt to Reader's Digest; co-exec prod-Diahann Carrol TV specials; 1980, Chmn, CEO Taft International Enterprises; resd June 1981 to reactivate indie company; March, 1982 formed MYM Entertainment Corp; Nov 1982 with Joe Sugar formed Youngstein-Sugar Associates.
Films inc: (Prod) Best of Cinerama; Man in the Middle; Fail Safe; The Money Trap; Young Billy Young; co-prod. The Dangerous Days of Kiowa Jones; Welcome to Hard Times.

YULIN, Harris: Act. Films inc: Doc; The Midnight Man; Night Moves; Steel; Scarface.
TV inc: The Thirteenth Day--The Story of Esther; When Every Day Was The Fourth of July; Last Ride of the Dalton Gang; Robert Kennedy & His Times.
Bway inc: Watch on the Rhine (rev); A Lesson From Aloes.

YUTKEVICH, Sergei: Dir-Wri. b. Russia, Dec 28, 1904. Set designer before becoming dir. Films inc: (Silent) Radio Now!; Lace; The Black Sail (Dir). (Sound) Mountains of Gold; The Counter-Plan (Co-dir & Sp); Miners (dir); The Man With A Rifle (dir); New Adventures of Schweik (dir); Othello; The Bathhouse (Ani); Lenin in Poland; A Plot for a Short Story (dir); Mayakovsky Laughs. (Doc) Ankara--Heart of Turkey (dir); Liberated France; Young Years of Our Country; Yves Montand Sings; Meeting With France; Lenin U Parize (Lenin In Paris). (Died April 23, 1985).

ZADAN, Craig: Prod-Dir-Wri. b. Miami, FL, Apr 15, 1949. e. Hofstra. Dir spec proj for Joseph Papp's Shakespeare Festival; co-prod Sondheim-A Musical Tribute; crea vp Casablanca Filmworks (later Polygram); 1980, vp crea aff UA; fired, March 1981; Films inc: Footloose (prod).

ZADORA, Pia: Singer-Act. b. NY, 1955. e. High School of Professional Arts. On Bway in Henry, Sweet Henry, in niteries as singer; appeared many talk, variety shows. Films inc: Butterfly; Fakeout; The Lonely Lady.
TV inc: Pajama Tops (cable).

ZAENTZ, Saul: Prod. b. Passaic, NJ.
Films inc: One Flew Over the Cuckoo's Nest (Oscar-1975); Three Warriors; The Lord of the Rings; Amadeus (Oscar-1984)

ZAL, Roxana: Act. b. 1969. Films inc: Table for Five; Testament.
TV inc: Something About Amelia (Emmy-Supp-1984).

ZAMPA, Luigi: Dir. b. Rome, 1905. Films inc: American on Vacation; To Live in Peace; Difficult Years; Angelina; The White Line; City on Trail; Two Gentlemen in a Carriage; His Last 12 Hours; We Women; Woman of Rome; Art of Getting Along; Girl in Australia; Letti Selvaggi (Tigers In Lipstick).

ZANUCK, Richard Darryl: Exec. b. Los Angeles, Dec 13, 1934. e.
Stanford U. S of the late Darryl Zanuck. Story dept 20th Century-Fox, 1954; NY pub dept, 1955; asst to prod, Island in the Sun, 1957; vp, Darryl F Zanuck Prod, 1958; prod, Compulsion, 1959; Sanctuary, 1961; The Chapman Report, 1962; asst to prod, The Longest Day, 1962; president's prod rep, 20th Century-Fox Studio 1963; vp charge of prod 20th Fox; p, 20th Fox TV; exec vp charge prod, 20th Fox, 1967; P, 1969; joined WB, Mar 1971, as sr exec vp; resigned July 1972, to form (with David Brown) Zanuck/Brown Prodns.
Films inc: Sssssss; The Sugarland Express; Willie Dynamite; The Sting (Oscar-1973); The Black Windmill; The Girl from Petrovka; Jaws; MacArthur; Jaws 2; The Island; Neighbors; The Verdict; Cocoon.

ZANUSSI, Krzysztof: Dir. b. Warsaw, Poland, Jul 17, 1939. Films inc: Death of a Provincial (short); Face to Face (short); The Structure of Crystals; Family Life; Behind the Wall; Illumination; The Catamount Killing; A Woman's Decision; Barwy Orchronne (Camouflage); Spirala (Spiral); Kontrakt; Constans (Constancy); Die Unerreichbare (The Unapproachable); Imperativ; Blaubart (Bluebeard).
TV inc: From A Far Country.

ZAPATA, Carmen: Act. b. NYC, July 15, 1927. Films inc: (Sol Madrid) Hail Hero; I Will, I Will. . .For Now; Rabbit Test; How To Beat the High Cost of Living; There Goes the Bride.
TV inc: Man in the City; New Dick Van Dyke Show; Storefront Lawyer; Viva Valdez; Hagen; One Last Ride; Homeward Bound; Children of Divorce; Moments To Be Remembered (& prod); Not Just Another Affair; The Tom Swift & Linda Craig Mystery Hour; Impact '83--East of the L.A. River; Hear Me Cry.
Bway inc: Oklahoma!; Bloomer Girl; Carnival; Bye Bye Birdie; No Strings; Stop the World I Want to Get Off.

ZAPPA, Frank: Comp. b. Baltimore, MD, Dec 21, 1940. Film scores inc: Freak Out; 200 Motels; Burnt Weenie Sandwich; A Token of His Extreme; Baby Snakes (Musical Doc) (& prod-dir-ed-act); Sheik Yerbouti.

ZARKHI, Alexander: Wri-Dir. b. Russia, Feb 18, 1908. Began as a writer, collaborating with Iosif Heifits while both were students at Leningrad Film Factory; after two films, The Moon on Your Left and Fiery Transport, they began directing in tandem and turned out a dozen films inc: Wind In the Face; Midday; My Homeland; Those Were the Days!; The Baltic Deputy; Member of the Government; His Name is Sukhe-Bator; Precious Grains; The Lights of Baku. Solo dir inc: Height; People on The Bridge; My Younger Brother (& co-sp); Anna Karenina (& co-sp); Cities and Times (& co-sp). Story About an Unknown Actor (& co-sp); 26 Days in the Life of Dostoyevsky.

ZASLOW, Michael: Act. b. Inglewood, CA, Nov 1, 1942. e. UCLA.
Films inc: You Light Up My Life; Meteor; There's a Girl in My Soup.
TV inc: Love is a Many Splendored Thing; Search for Tomorrow; Guiding Light; Star Trek; Unit 4; King's Crossing.
Thea inc: Fiddler on the Roof; Cat on a Hot Tin Roof (rev); Boccaccio.

ZASTUPNEVICH, Paul: Cos Dsgn. b. Homestead, PA, Dec 24, 1931. e. Duquesne, B Ed; U of Pittsburgh, M Ed; Pasadena Playhouse, MA; Louise Salinger School Dress Design. Films inc: The Big Circus; The Lost World; Voyage to the Bottom of the Sea; Five Weeks In a Balloon; The Poseidon Adventure; The Towering Inferno; The Swarm; Beyond the Poseidon Adventure; When Time Ran Out.
TV inc: Voyage to the Bottom of the Sea; Swiss Family Robinson; Lost In Space; The Time Tunnel; Land of the Giants; City Beneath the Sea; Flood; Fire; Adventures of the Queen; The Return of Captain Nemo; Hanging By a Thread; The Memory of Eva Ryker.

ZAVATTINI, Cesare: Wri. b. Italy, 1902.
Films inc: Shoeshine; Bicycle Thieves; Miracle in Milan; First Communion; Umberto D; Gold of Naples; The Roof; Two Women; Marriage Italian Style; A Brief Vacation; The Children of Sanchez; Ligabue; La Veritaaa (The Truuuuth).

ZEFFIRELLI, Franco: Dir. b. Italy, Feb 12, 1923.
Films inc: The Taming of the Shrew; Romeo and Juliet; Brother Sun, Sister Moon; The Champ; Endless Love; La Traviata (& wri-dsgn).

Thea inc: Saturday, Sunday and Monday; Filumena (& prod). (Tony-special-1962).

ZEITMAN, Jerome M.: Prod. Started as agent in band dept MCA, later tv packaging vp; when MCA agency dissolved, moved to William Morris; became prod when he became partner on Playboy Prodms. Films inc: Damnation Alley; Just You and Me Kid; How to Beat the High Cost of Living.
TV inc: My Old Man; Devil Dog/Hound of Hell; I Love Her Anyway; The Day The Loving Stopped (exec prod).

ZEMAN, Jackie (formerly billed as Zeman-Kaufman): Act. b. Englewood, NJ, Mar 6. e. NYU on dance scholarship. Dancer and model before turning to act. Films inc: The Groove Tube; The Day The Music Stopped; Young Doctors In Love; National Lampoon's Class Reunion.
TV inc: One Life to Live; General Hospital.

ZEMECKIS, Robert: Wri-Dir. b. Chicago, 1952. e. USC.
Films inc: I Wanna Hold Your Hand; 1941; Used Cars; Romancing the Stone (dir); Back To The Future.
TV inc: The Nightstalker.

ZERBE, Anthony: Act.
Films inc: Will Penny; The Liberation of L B Jones; Cotton Comes to Harlem; Farewell My Lovely; Rooster Cogburn; Who'll Stop The Rain; The First Deadly Sin; The Dead Zone.
TV inc: Harry O (Emmy-supp-1976); The Statesman (Benjamin Franklin); Centennial; Attica; The Seduction of Miss Leona; Rascals and Robbers--The Secret Adventures of Tom Sawyer and Huck Finn; A Question of Honor; Return of the Man from U.N.C.L.E.; George Washington; A.D.
Bway inc: The Little Foxes (rev); Solomon's Child.

ZETTERLING, Mai: Act-Dir. b. Sweden, May 24, 1925. Screen debut in Sweden in Frenzy.
Films inc: Torment; Frieda; Quartet (The Facts of Life episode); The Bad Lord Byron; Hell Is Sold Out; Desperate Moment; Knock on Wood; A Prize of Gold; Abandon Ship; The Truth About Women; Only Two Can Play; Night Is My Future; The Bay of St Michel. In 1965-66 wrote, dir Loving Couples; Night Games; 1968; Dr Glas; The Girls; Love (wri-dir); Scrubbers (wri-dir). Since 1969 dir doc for BBC and in Sweden.

ZIDI, Claude: Dir. b. Paris, Jul 25, 1934. Originally cin. Films inc: Les Bidasses En Folie; Les Fous du Stade; Le Grand Bazaar; La Moutarde Me Monte Au Nez!; Les Bidasses s'en vont en Gue; La Course a L'Echalote; L'Aile ou la Cuisse; L'Animal; La Zizanie; Bete Mais Discipline (Dumb But Disciplined); La Boite a bac; Les Sous-doues (The Under-gifted) (& prod-wri); Inspecteur La Bavure (Inspector Blunder) (& wri); Banzai (& wri); Les Ripoux (& wri); Les Rois du Gag (The Gag Kings) (& prod-wri).

ZIEFF, Howard: Dir. b. Los Angeles, 1943. While in Navy enrolled in Photographic School, made film, A Day in the Life of a Cadet; after service became tv newsreel cin; directorial debut Slither. Films inc: Hearts of the West; House Calls; The Main Event; Private Benjamin; Unfaithfully Yours.

ZIMBALIST, Efrem, Jr: Act. b. NYC, Nov 30, 1923.
Bway debut 1946, The Rugged Path. On screen from 1949.
Films inc: House of Strangers; Bombers B-52; Band of Angels; Too Much, Too Soon; Home Before Dark; By Love Possessed; The Chapman Report; Wait Until Dark; Airport 1975; Harlow.
TV inc: Maverick; 77 Sunset Strip; The FBI; The Black Dahlia; Terror Out Of The Sky; The Best Place To Be; The Gathering, Part II; A Family of Winners; Scruples; Insight/Checkmate; Beyond Witch Mountain; Family In Blue; Charley's Aunt (cable); Baby Sister; Shooting Stars; Insight/The Hit Man; You Are the Jury (host); Kennedy Center Honors 1984.

ZIMBALIST, Stephanie: Act. b. Encino, CA, Oct 8, 1956. D of Efrem Zimbalist, Jr. Films inc: Lassie, My Lassie; The Magic of Lassie; The Awakening.
TV inc: Forever; The Gathering; In the Matter of Karen Ann Quinlan; Yesterday's Child; The Best Place To Be; Long Journey Back; The Triangle Factory Fire Scandal; The Golden Moment-An Olympic Love

Story; The Baby Sitter; Elvis and the Beauty Queen; Tomorrow's Child; Remington Steele.

ZIMMER, Kim: Act. b. Grand Rapids, MI, Feb 2, 1955. Studied at ACT. Thea inc: Accent on Youth; The Big Knife; Godspell; Night at the Fights.
Films inc: Body Heat.
TV inc: One Life to Live; The Doctors.

ZINBERG, Michael: Exec. b. San Antonio, TX. e. U of TX. With Mary Tyler Moore Productions for eight years as a wri-dir-prod. Joined NBC in June 1979 as vp, comedy development, West Coast, NBC Entertainment; resd Oct 1980 to ret to prodn.
TV inc: (Prod) Bob Newhart Show; Mary Tyler Moore Show; Tony Randall Show; Rhoda; Homeroom (dir); 9 to 5 (dir); A Girl's Life (exec prod-dir); The Yellow Rose (exec prod); Walter; Fathers And Sons (exec prod-dir-story).

ZINDEL, Paul: Plywri. b. Staten Island, NY, May 15, 1936. e. Wagner Coll. Plays inc: The Effect of Gamma Rays on Man-In-The-Moon Marigolds (Pulitzer Prize-1971); And Miss Reardon Drinks A Little; The Secret Affairs of Mildred Wild; Ladies at the Alamo.
TV inc: Let Me Hear You Whisper.
Films inc: Maria's Lovers.

ZINNEMANN, Fred: Dir. b. Vienna, Austria, Apr 29, 1907. e. Vienna U. Studied photographic technique, lighting & mechanics (Paris); cam 1 yr (Berlin). Came to US 1929; extra in All Quiet on the Western Front, 1930; asst to dir Berthold Viertel; asst to Robert Flaherty, 1931; dir Mexican doc The Wave; short subjects dir, MGM, winning Oscar, 1938, That Mothers Might Live. Feature dir, 1941.
Films inc: The Seventh Cross; The Search; The Men; Teresa; High Noon; Benjy (short for LA Orthopedic Hospital, for which Oscar best doc short, 1951); Member of the Wedding; From Here to Eternity (Oscar-1953); Oklahoma; A Hatful of Rain; The Nun's Story; The Sundowners; Behold a Pale Horse; A Man for All Seasons (& prod) (2 Oscars-dir & picture-1966); Day of the Jackal; Julia; Rece do Gory (Hands Up!) (act); Five Days One Summer (& prod); George Stevens--A Filmmaker's Journey (doc-int).

ZINNEMANN, Tim: Prod. b. LA.,CA., e. Columbia U. S. of Fred Zinnemann. Started as asst. editor on films in Rome; later asst. editor on U.S. films inc: THe Pink Panther; Bullitt; The Great White Hope; Carnal Knowledge; The Day Of the Locust; worked as prodn mgr on Day Of The Dolphin; Farewell My Lovely; King Of Marvin Gardens; Cinderella Liberty. Films inc: The Cowboys (asso prod); Smile (asso prod); Straight Time; A Small Circle of Friends; The Long Riders; Tex; Fandango; Impulse.
TV inc: The Jericho Mile.

ZINNER, Peter: Flm ed. b. Vienna, Austria, Jul 24, 1919.
Films inc: The Professionals; Changes; Darling Lili; Peter Gunn; In Cold Blood; The Red Tent; Godfather; Valdez' Horses; Crazy Joe; Godfather II; Mahogany; A Star is Born; Fox Trot; The Deer Hunter (Oscar-1978); Foolin' Around; Tintorera; An Officer and A Gentleman; The Salamander (dir); War And Love.
TV inc: The Winds of War.

ZIPPRODT, Patricia: Cos dsgn. b. Evanston, IL Feb 25, 1925. Bway inc: The Potting Shed; Visit To a Small Planet; The Virtuous Island; The Apollo of Bellac; Miss Lonelyhearts; The Rope Dancers; The Crucible; Back to Methuselah; The Night Circus; Our Town; Camino Real; Period of Adjustment; The Blacks; Sunday in New York; Oh Dad, Poor Dad, Mama's Hung You In the Closet and I'm Feeling So Sad; Step On a Crack; The Dragon; She Loves Me; Fiddler on the Roof (Tony-1965); Anya; Pousse-Cafe; Cabaret; The Little Foxes; Plaza Suite; Zorba; Georgy; Pippin; Dear Nobody; Mack and Mabel; Fools; Kingdoms; Alice in Wonderland; Whodunnit; Brighton Beach Memoirs; The Glass Menagerie; Sunday in the Park with George; Accidental Death of an Anarchist.
Films inc: The Graduate; Last of the Mobile Hotshots.
TV inc: Alice in Wonderland.

ZMED, Adrian: Act. b. Chicago, IL., March 14, 1954. e. Goodman School of Drama. Bway inc: Grease. Films inc: Grease II.
TV inc: Flatbush; Goodtime Girls; Angie; T.J. Hooker; Glitter.

ZORINA, Vera (Brigitta Hartwig): Dancer-Act. b. Berlin, Germany, 1917. On screen from 1938.

Films inc: The Goldwyn Follies; On Your Toes; I Was an Adventuress; Louisiana Purchase; Follow the Boys; Lover Come Back.

ZSIGMOND, Vilmos: Cin. b. Czeged, Hungary, Jun 16, 1930. e. U of Film and Theatre Art, Budapest.

Films inc: Hired Hand; Red Sky at Morning; McCabe and Mrs Miller; Deliverance; Images; The Long Goodbye; Scarecrow; Sugarland Express; Cinderella Liberty; The Girl from Petrovka; Obsession; Close Encounters of the Third Kind (Oscar-1977); The Deer Hunter; The Last Waltz; Sweet Revenge; Winter Kills; The Rose; Heaven's Gate; Blow Out; Jinxed!; Table For Five; No Small Affair; The River.

TV inc: Flesh and Blood.

ZUGSMITH, Albert: Prod. b. Atlantic City, NJ, Apr 24, 1910. e. U of VA. Newspaper exec before turning to pictures.

Films inc: Invasion USA; Top Banana; Written on the Wind; Man in the Shadow; Red Sundown; Star in the Dust; The Incredible Shrinking Man; The Girl in the Kremlin; Touch of Evil; Captive Women; Sword of Venus; High School Confidential; Slaughter on Tenth Avenue; The Beat Generation; Private Lives of Adam and Eve; Dondi; Fanny Hill; The Rapist!.

ZUKERMAN, Pinchas: Violinist. b. Tel Aviv, Jul 16, 1948. e. Juilliard. Has appeared with Mostly Mozart Festival; English Chamber Orchestra; Los Angeles Philharmonic; Boston Symphony; Philadelphia Orhestra; toured with Isaac Stern and NY Philharmonic; member of trio with Daniel Barenboim and Jacqueline du Pre. Recs inc: Vivaldi's Four Seasons; Duets for Two Violins; Bolling Suite for Violin and Jazz Piano; Berg Chamber Concerto for piano and violin; Bartok Concerto for Violin and Orchestra; Music for Two Violins (Grammy-chamber music-1980); Berg Concerto for Violin & Orchestra and Concerto in D-Major for Violin and Orchestra (Grammy-inst soloist with orch-1980); Brahms Double Concerto (Grammy-inst soloist with orch-1980); Virtuoso Violin; Isaac Stern's 50th Anniversary Celebration (Grammy-inst soloist with orch-1981); Bartok; Duos for Violins; Oboe Quartets.

ZUKOR, Eugene J.: Exec (ret). b. Chicago, Oct 25, 1897. S of late Adolph Zukor. With Par from 1916, pub and adv dept to asst treas, member of Par board of dir.

ZWICK, Joel Dir. b. Brooklyn, Jan 11, 1942. e. Brooklyn Coll, BA, MA. Thea inc: Shenandoah; Cold Storage; Merry Go Round; Dance With Me (Bway).

TV inc: Laverne and Shirley; Mork and Mindy; Angie (pilot); It's A Living; Bosom Buddies (pilot); Struck By Lightning (pilot); America 2100; Goodtime Girls; Hot W.A.C.S (& exec prod); Little Darlings; Joanie Loves Chachi; Star of the Family (pilot); The New Odd Couple (& supv prod); Webster; Brothers (PC) (supv prod).